THE LUKAN PASSION NARRATIVE
THE MARKAN MATERIAL IN LUKE 22,54 – 23,25

NEW TESTAMENT TOOLS
AND STUDIES

EDITED BY

BRUCE M. METZGER, Ph.D., D.D., L.H.D., D. Theol., D. Litt.

Professor of New Testament Language and Literature, Emeritus
Princeton Theological Seminary
and
Corresponding Fellow of the British Academy

AND

BART D. EHRMAN, Ph.D.

Bowman and Gordon Gray Professor
Department of Religious Studies
University of North Carolina at Chapel Hill

VOLUME XXX

THE LUKAN PASSION NARRATIVE
THE MARKAN MATERIAL
IN LUKE 22,54 – 23,25

A Historical Survey: 1891-1997

BY

JAY M. HARRINGTON

BRILL
LEIDEN · BOSTON · KÖLN
2000

This book is printed on acid-free paper.

Die Deutsche Bibliothek – CIP-Einheitsaufnahme

Harrington, Jay M.:
The Luke passion narrative : the Markan material in Luke 22,54- 23,25 /
a historical survey : 1891-1997 / by Jay M. Harrington. – Leiden ; Boston ;
Köln: Brill, 2000
　　(New Testament tools and studies ; Vol. 30)
　　ISBN 90–04–11590–0

Library of Congress Cataloging-in-Publication Data

Library of Congress Cataloging-in-Publication Data is also available

ISSN　0077-8842
ISBN　90 04 11590 0

PRINTED IN THE NETHERLANDS

CONTENTS

PART II
LATE 1960'S TO THE PRESENT

PART III
THE CONUNDRUM OF THE HEROD PERICOPE:
SOURCE-CRITICAL THEORIES AND AN EXEGESIS

PART IV
BIBLIOGRAPHY, APPENDICES, INDEXES

PREFACE

This book originated in a doctoral dissertation which was successfully defended at the Katholieke Universiteit Leuven in Belgium in June, 1998. It was prepared under the guidance of Professor Frans Neirynck. To him I express my deep gratitude for his astute direction, useful critiques and wise and patient counsel. I also wish to thank Professor Donald Senior, who had supervised my previous Synoptic research, and who suggested I consider the Lukan passion narrative as the subject of my doctoral research. He followed the progress of my work with interest and enthusiasm.

I also express my deep appreciation to the editorial board of *New Testament Tools and Studies* for accepting this study into the series.

I gratefully acknowledge the technical assistance provided me by Rita Merlevede-Corstjens in preparing the manuscript for publication.

St. Paul, MN   Jay M. HARRINGTON
                                                                      January, 2000

INTRODUCTION

Observing that "l'évangile de Marc n'est pas abandonné en Lc., XXII, 14 (ou 15), mais [...] continue de guider l'évangéliste jusqu'en XXIV,12", F. Neirynck suggested a direction for subsequent studies: "Je le sais, je ne puis me contenter d'exprimer cette opinion: elle est contestée et doit donc devenir un programme d'études ultérieures"[1]. The passion narrative has been and continues to be one of the most studied sections of the Gospel of Luke[2]. The problem is that many differences exist between the Lukan account and the passion in Mk, encompassing at times the absence of some material and the addition of other material as well as the difference in the order of various accounts. Our purpose is to reexamine the use of the Markan material in Lk. In recent years the discussion has once more focused on the question of Luke's sources as part of ongoing source-critical and redaction-critical research. The issue of Luke's use of a special source (or sources) for his passion narrative has again generated much scholarly debate[3]. Consequently, some believe that the discussion has arrived at an impasse[4]. Led by proponents of the new literary criticism, a number of exegetes now prescind from source-critical investigation, and even from any supposition concerning sources.

Scholars remain divided as regards the origin of the passion narrative. Several solutions have been suggested. Some argue that Mk is Luke's primary source and the differences can be ascribed to redactional activity. Others suggest that non-Markan materials, written sources or oral tradition(s), have been inserted. Finally, some posit a continuous non-Markan passion story, as a secondary source besides Mark, or even Luke's primary source in chapters 22-23. In most cases, the issue is not whether Luke employed Mk, but rather to what degree. Is the Markan Gospel the primary source, or is it used only secondarily, providing various

---

1. F. NEIRYNCK, *La matière marcienne dans l'évangile de Luc*, in ID. (ed.), *L'évangile de Luc*, 1973, 157-201, p. 199 (= ²1989, 67-111, p. 109 = *Evangelica*, 1982, 37-82, p. 79). See also F. UNTERGASSMAIR, *Kreuzweg und Kreuzigung Jesu*, 1980, p. 112.

2. Unlike the passion narrative in the Gospel of Matthew which was presented by D.P. Senior in 1972 "a somewhat neglected area of Matthaean exegesis" (cf. *The Passion Narrative according to Matthew*, Preface).

3. Note the numerous dissertations treating aspects of the Lukan passion narrative including G. Schneider (1968), D.R. Catchpole (1968), F.G. Untergassmair (1977), A. Büchele (1978), M. Soards (1984), J.B. Green (1985), and W. Reinbold (1992-93). Cf. F. VAN SEGBROECK, *The Gospel of Luke. A Cumulative Bibliography 1973-1988* (BETL, 88; CoBRA, 2), Leuven - Brussels, 1989; index, p. 220 (Passion Narrative) and 236-238 (Lk 22-23). See F. NEIRYNCK, *Literary Criticism: Old and New*, in C. FOCANT (ed.), *The Synoptic Gospels. Source Criticism and the New Literary Criticism* (BETL, 110), Leuven, 1993, p. 11-38, esp. p. 20-27.

4. Consider the remark by E.E. Ellis reflecting on the general situation: "In the present state of affairs source criticism appears either to have come full circle or to have reached something of an impasse" (*Gospel Criticism*, in P. STUHLMACHER [ed.], *Das Evangelium und die Evangelien* [WUNT, 2/28], Tübingen, 1983, 27-84, p. 38 = *The Gospel and the Gospels*, tr. J. VRIEND, Grand Rapids, MI, 1991, 26-52, p. 36).

insertions to supplement and embellish Luke's non-Markan special source? For scholars who advocate the use of non-Markan material, Luke's special material, often referred to as L, is differently configured as collections of assorted materials or as a nearly complete Gospel. A combination of L+Q was proposed as the special source by adherents of the Proto-Lk hypothesis.

Although the Lukan passion narrative has been the focus of much analysis, no adequate history has sketched the contours of the debate. Our goal is not only to present a recent history, but to trace the discussion to its beginnings. We have generally followed a combination of a chronological and systematic order alternating between proponents and opponents of the theory of a special source or sources. It has also been our intention to report dependence of scholars upon one another.

The survey, covering roughly the period from the 1880's to 1997, is divided into two major sections. The first details the development from P. Feine through the 1960's. The second period begins with the work of G. Schneider and continues up through 1997. In the treatment of each scholar's position, insofar as it is possible, we review their underlying Synoptic theory, their source theory as applied to the passion in general, then the trial of Pilate, and finally any contributions regarding the trial before Herod. Three appendices are provided: 1) Special LQ vocabulary and constructions according to J. Weiss, 2) Lukan priority theories, and 3) the Gospel of Peter and its relation to the Herod pericope.

More specifically, we propose to examine the Markan material in a particular section of the Lukan passion narrative: the trials in Lk 22,54–23,25, par. Mk 14,52–15,20. The sheer amount of bibliography devoted to the Lukan account of the passion necessitated some limits. By focusing on the pericopes of Peter's denial (22,54-62), the mockery (22,63-65), the Sanhedrin trial (22,66-71), the trial before Pilate (23,1-5.17-25) and before Herod (23,6-16), we are able to study the evangelist's redactional technique in a significant portion of the Markan material, the phenomenon of differences in the relative order, notable minor agreements (22,62.64), and a section without direct parallel in Mk (23,6-16). The final section of the dissertation is devoted to my interpretation of Lk 23,6-16.

There exist a few histories of the special source hypothesis in its various forms. Allen Freeman Page (1968) supplied a review of the main participants in the debate on the source question hypothesis in the Lukan passion narrative, i.e. concerning Proto-Lk and supposed non-Lukan material as contrasted with Lukan redaction of Mk[5]. It was followed by a posthumously published work of Vincent Taylor (1972) which offered a comprehensive overview[6]. Martin Rese (1984) provided a brief but useful survey of the source question for Lk[7]. He further

___

5. *Proto-Luke Reconsidered: A Study of the Literary Method and Theology in the Gospel of Luke*, Diss. Duke, Durham, NC, 1968 (dir. D.M. SMITH), esp. p. 2-35.

6. *The Passion Narrative of St Luke. A Critical and Historical Investigation* (ed. O.E. EVANS) (SNTS MS, 19), Cambridge, 1972, p. 3-24. Cf. p. vii-ix. See also his *Behind the Third Gospel. A Study of the Proto-Luke Hypothesis*, Oxford, 1926, p. 2-27.

7. *Das Lukas-Evangelium. Ein Forschungsbericht*, in *ANRW* II.25.3 (1984), p. 2275-2280;

commented, "von den Lösungsversuchen im 19. und zu Beginn des 20. Jhdt. weiss man freilich erstaunlich wenig"[8]. As he keenly observed, the passion narrative was so central to Taylor's understanding of the Proto-Lk theory that this hypothesis stands or falls on this section of the Gospel. Taylor used the passion narrative, the weakest point of Streeter's argument, as the central element of his own[9]. Indicative of current interest are the essay by F.G. Untergassmair (1996), who briefly mentioned German contributions commencing in the 1950's[10] and M.-É. Boismard's contribution on the search for Proto-Lk (1997) which referred to P. Feine, B. Weiss, and frequently to V. Taylor[11].

2284-2288. Note his dissertation, *Die "Stunde" Jesu in Jerusalem (Lukas 22,1-53). Eine Untersuchung zur literarischen und theologischen Eigenart des lukanischen Passionsberichts*, unpublished Habil., Münster, 1971.

8. *Das Lukas-Evangelium*, p. 2284.

9. *Ibid.*, p. 2286.

10. *Zur Problematik* (1996), 273-292. See also F. MORELL BALADRÓN (1996) who reviewed major figures in the history of the debate on Lk 22–23 from B.H. Streeter to R.E. Brown (*El Relato de la Pasión según San Lucas. De Streeter a Brown: 70 años de investigación de la composición de Lc 22-23 [1ᵃ Parte]*, in *EstBib* 54 [1996] 79-114; *[2ᵃ Parte]*, 225-260). This is significant for two reasons. It appears that little attention has been given to this matter in Spanish journals and books. Secondly, the author highlighted many of the important studies. In a note he briefly treated attempts prior to Streeter, including FEINE (1891) and B. WEISS (1908), among others (p. 79-[80], n. 3).

11. *En quête du Proto-Luc* (EB 37), Paris, 1997. Regarding Feine and Weiss, see p. 335. Taylor was a frequent interlocutor, especially in the chapter dealing with the passion narrative, e.g. p. 106-130. In our survey, studies of complementary scholars are included in a smaller font. Note: in our text "Luke" refers to the evangelist and "Lk" to the gospel.

Part I

SURVEY OF THE RESEARCH 1885-1960'S

CHAPTER ONE

THE FIRST PROPONENTS OF A SPECIAL PROTO-LUKAN SOURCE

PAUL FEINE THROUGH BURTON SCOTT EASTON

Paul Feine (1891) and Johannes Weiss (1892)

In order to trace the development of how scholars conceived of the passion narrative in a Proto-Lukan source, we first turn our attention to Paul FEINE[1], whose theory set in motion a series of investigations. Feine anticipated his study of the special source in Lk (1891) with several articles in which he examined the Synoptic question fully (1885-1888)[2]. In the course of his analysis he referred to and described what he termed the "C" source. Drawing upon the source theory of R.A. Lipsius[3] of Jena, he maintained that Matthew made use of a narrative source (A) and the *Redenquelle* (B), while Mark employed only A, and that Luke depended on Mk, in addition to A and C, which is a reworked form of B and constituted "wohl ein vollständiges Evangelium"[4].

These Synoptic studies were followed by an analysis of the sources in Acts (1890)[5]. In line with H.J. Holtzmann and B. Weiss, Feine argued that in the first twelve chapters of Acts Luke employed an old and valuable written source. The source detailed the growth and history of the early Jerusalem community which the author knew intimately[6]. Although according to Feine the author made occasional mistakes, by and large the information was reliable[7]. Feine was convinced that the

---

1. Paul Feine (1859-1933), Privatdozent in Göttingen (1893), prof. in Vienna (1896), Breslau (1907), Halle (1910). Feine obtained a doctorate in classical philology in Jena (1883) after which he taught in a gymnasium in Göttingen. During this time he attended the university and published his article on Acts (1890) and his book on Lk (1891), receiving a licentiate in theology at Göttingen in 1893 for a study on the authenticity of the Letter of James.

2. P. FEINE, *Ueber das gegenseitige Verhältnis der Texte der Bergpredigt bei Matthäus und bei Lukas*, in *JPTh* 11 (1885) 1-85; *Zur synoptischen Frage*, in *JPTh* 12 (1886) 462-528; [*II*]: 13 (1887) 39-102; [*III*]: 14 (1888) 275-313, 388-422; [*IV*]: 14 (1888) 504-549. Feine treated, in essence, Mk 1,29–4,34 and the parallel Synoptic texts. The final article was dedicated to a study of parables.

3. On Lipsius, see n. 9 below.

4. *Zur synoptischen Frage*, in *JPTh* 12 (1886), p. 463: "Die Quelle *C*, die Lukas neben dem Urmarkus und dem kanonischen Markus benutzt hat, ist eine in den ebjonitischen Kreisen Palästinas etwa ums Jahr 80 entstandene Ueberarbeitung von *B*. Den Grundstock derselben bilden also ebenfalls Redestoffe. Aber mit diesen ist so reicher Erzählungsstoff verarbeitet worden, dass diese Quelle wohl ein vollständiges Evangelium gebildet hat, mit Kindheits- und Passionsgeschichte. Gemäss ihrer Entstehung unter den Ebjoniten betonte *C* in scharfer Weise den Gegensatz zwischen arm und reich, d.h. gerecht und ungerecht" (cf. *Ueber das gegenseitige Verhältnis*, p. 2).

5. *Die alte Quelle in der ersten Hälfte der Apostelgeschichte*, in *JPTh* 16 (1890) 84-133. See esp. p. 85.

6. *Ibid.*, p. 117.

7. *Ibid.*, p. 118. For example, while some scholars believed that the number of 120 disciples

source had been composed in Jerusalem, but was tentative about its date. He also expressed reservation in offering an opinion about the date of composition, since he had not as yet examined the relationship of this source to Lk, which he suspected had been influenced by it[8].

In the following year, Feine resumed and expanded his thesis to include the Gospel in *Eine vorkanonische Überlieferung des Lukas* (1891)[9]. It was obvious that he had been laboring for a number of years with his theory which he explained more fully in this book[10]. Prompted by the reference to various sources in Luke's prologue, he summed up his position, incorporating the results of his article on Acts: "Ich meine nun nicht, hier alle judenchristlichen Partieen des Evangeliums und der Apostelgeschichte herausgehoben zu haben. Sondern ich habe eine nach meiner Ansicht zusammengehörige aus judenchristlicher Vermittelung stammende Überlieferung zusammengestellt"[11]. Though Feine accepted that B. Weiss had shown the dependence of Lk on Mk[12], he also remarked that he was reacting to B. Weiss and his works on Mk by suggesting an additional *Quellenschrift* for Lk.

The book first treated the special source in Lk, then in Acts. For the matters pertaining to the Gospel, Feine initially discussed the relationship among its sources. This was followed by an exposition of the narrative material from the special source and then of the parable and speech material also from Luke's unique tradition. In his treatment of the nature of the special written source in Lk, he touched on matters which he believed supported his assertion that L and Q were already combined, the order of the material, its connections with the Letter of James, the special vocabulary and the time and place of its composition. The main written sources for the first twelve chapters of Acts were analyzed next, followed by a discussion of the historical value of the special source. The final chapter argued that the written sources of the Gospel and Acts belonged to the same tradition.

---

had a mythical significance, Feine maintained that this accurately reflected the situation. The account of Stephen was also regarded, in all probability, as based upon authentic information (p. 101, 105-106, 122-124).

8. *Ibid.*, p. 133: "Ein abschliessendes Urtheil über die Zeit der Abfassung kann aber hier nicht gegeben werden, da die Untersuchung sich jetzt nur auf die Apostelgeschichte beschränkt hat und die Frage, in welchen Theilen des dritten Evangeliums dieselbe Quelle auch verwendet zu sein scheint, nicht behandelt worden ist".

9. *Eine vorkanonische Überlieferung des Lukas in Evangelium und Apostelgeschichte. Eine Untersuchung*, Gotha, 1891. He acknowledged the suggestion and assistance of one of his teachers, Professor R.A. Lipsius in Jena, whose work on similar materials led him also to posit a Jewish-Christian *Quellenschrift* for Luke (p. v), but no reference was given to any work of Lipsius. Feine also mentioned him in the articles of 1885 (p. 1) and 1886 (p. 463).

10. Cf. above, n. 2, 9.

11. *Ibid.*, p. iv.

12. *Ibid.*, p. 4: "Der Nachweis der Abhängigkeit des dritten vom zweiten Evangelisten ist geführt worden von B. Weiss in seinem Markusevangelium".

Although Feine conceded that Luke adopted the greater part of the contents and followed the order of, and made changes on, Mk[13], he nevertheless argued that Lk contained a great amount of material which clearly indicated "jüdische Anschauungs-, Denk- und Sprachweise"[14]. It appeared to him that the canonical author obtained much in Lk-Acts from a Jewish-Christian tradition, containing "einen hebräischartigen Ton" and, on the basis of similarities existing between certain parts of Lk and Acts, he concluded that Luke probably used a continuous, pre-canonical source and he attempted to reconstruct such a source[15].

In addition to Mk, Luke was believed to have used the synoptic *Grundschrift* (hereafter, GS)[16], the *Redenquelle*, and "eigentümliche Stoffe"[17]. It was this latter material which was drawn from Jewish-Christian tradition in the form of a written source, already available to the evangelist in combination with the *Redenquelle* (L+Q)[18]. Thus, Luke based his work not upon the eyewitness testimony, but rather upon a written tradition from those who, from the beginning, were eyewitnesses and ministers of the Gospel. He was judicious in his use of his predecessors' works, but only insofar as it was necessary to support his own viewpoint[19]. Because he stressed the value of the chronological order, considerable changes of the previous accounts would be expected[20]. Since

---

13. *Ibid.* In his opinion, Luke's changes frequently signal "eine Zurechtstellung" of the Markan story.

14. *Ibid.*, p. [III].

15. *Ibid.*, p. IV. The final section of the foreword mentioned the publication of Friedrich Spitta's work on Acts: F. SPITTA, *Die Apostelgeschichte* (1891). Though it contained conclusions similar to Feine's earlier study, it appeared too late to be included. Feine welcomed the book as an "ausgezeichnete Untersuchung" in which Spitta attempted to explain the circumstances of the origin of the Book of Acts (p. V-VI).

16. FEINE, *Eine vorkanonische Überlieferung*, p. 4. Cf. p. 5: "...eine Quellenschrift mit überwiegendem Erzählungsstoff ..., welche von allen drei Synoptikern benutzt worden ist"; "...der dritte Evangelist, wenngleich er in der Hauptsache nach Markus erzählt, (ist) daneben, weil er auch den Bericht der synoptischen Quelle eingesehen hat und einsieht, durch denselben beeinflusst worden" (p. 7).

17. *Ibid.*, p. 10-12: "Ausserdem hat nun das dritte Evangelium noch eine grosse Zahl von Stoffen als Sondereigentum, zum Teil Erzählungsstoffe, zum Teil Gleichnisse und Redestoffe, auch kürzere Notizen und Sprüche, deren Herleitung aus einer der eben angeführten Quellenschriften zweifelhaft oder unwahrscheinlich ist. Meine Ansicht geht dahin, *dass der weitaus grösste Teil dieser dem Lukas eigentümlichen Stoffe ihm aus judenchristlicher Überlieferung bekannt war, und dass es eine schriftliche Vorlage gewesen ist*, aus Grund deren er diese Stoffe in sein Evangelium aufgenommen hat" [emphasis added].

18. *Ibid.*, p. 124-125.

19. *Ibid.*, p. 2. Though Luke informed us many (πολλοί) had undertaken to compile a narrative of the events (1,1), Feine suggested that the number was not necessarily great, nor must it be believed that Luke used them all. Rather, he used a few which best corresponded to his claims (p. 4).

20. *Ibid.* The changes, according to Feine, resulted from Luke's effort to provide historically precise data, rather than reflecting his theological interests or concerns or circumstances of his own times. Thus, the reliability of Luke's account was underscored: "Dann hofft er, dass seine

Theophilus was a heathen proselyte, and the Lukan account addressed the concerns ("berechnet auf") of such a person, Feine asserted this explained why there was a quantity of material which did not agree, or agreed only in part, with the Jewish material[21].

Feine believed Luke obtained from the Church in Jerusalem around the year 67 AD the special information which he incorporated into his Gospel[22]. Evidence supporting this view, according to Feine, was additional material not found in either Mt or Mk[23], differences in the details of the Lukan account and in the ordering of the material common to all three Synoptics[24]. Such a conclusion was warranted for two reasons: the source contained valuable historical information and its form was also Jewish-Christian[25]. He therefore maintained that such a source enhanced considerably our historical knowledge of the person and ministry of Jesus[26].

How did Luke make use of his sources? Alternating between Mk and the synoptic GS and other sources, Luke added details and notices which he borrowed

genauen und eingehenden Studien auch die Zuverlässigkeit seiner Berichte gewährleisten werden".

21. *Ibid.*

22. *Ibid.*, p. 11-12. Cf. p. 150, 153-154, 236. This source was concerned not only with the history of the early community, but with the primitive apostolic preaching (p. 159). Frederic GODET excluded Luke's use of the present forms of Mt or Mk as possible sources (*Commentaire sur l'évangile de saint Luc*, Neuchâtel, 1871, ²1872 = *A Commentary on the Gospel of St. Luke*, tr. from the second French ed., by E. SHALDERS and M. CUSIN, Edinburgh, ³1894, p. 552. Godet maintained that Luke made use of: 1) oral tradition, 2) detached writings, 3) Gospels that were more complete, though now lost, and 4) "l'un ou l'autre de nos évangiles encore existants" (Vol. 1, 1871, p. LI-LV, esp. p. LV). Luke worked mainly with written Aramaic documents and was unfamiliar with the Matthean Logia or the Markan narratives of Peter (ET, p. 566). While Godet acknowledged that some parts of the Gospel reflecting an Aramaic basis stemmed from the Judeo-Christian Church, he argued that the account of the passion derived either from Luke himself or from one of the Greek Gospel sources Luke was using (ET, p. 554). His position was predicated on the presence of classical terminology, such as προϋπῆρχον (23,12).

23. FEINE, *Eine vorkanonische Überlieferung*, p. 61.

24. *Ibid.* He also weighed the possibility that the position of Peter's denial different from Mk may be due to a literary decision by Luke or, as H.J. Holtzmann (*Die synoptischen Evangelien*, 1863, p. 240) assumed, pointed to a tradition with which Luke had come into contact, seeming to suggest that the first interpretation did not exclude the second (p. 67).

25. FEINE, *Eine vorkanonische Überlieferung*, p. 61-62.

26. *Ibid.*, p. 12: "Auf der andern Seite haben wir nach meiner Auffassung in der besonderen Überlieferung des Lukas einen sehr wertvollen Besitz, der unsere geschichtliche Kenntnis des Lebens und Wirkens Jesu recht erheblich erweitert". The concluding sentence of the section on the relation of the sources is especially significant: "Dem gegenüber glaube ich zeigen zu können, dass auch die heutige Form der in Frage stehenden Stücke durch genaue Kenntnis jüdischen Volkslebens, jüdischer Sitten und Bräuche, jüdischer Denk- und Anschauungsweise, der geographischen Verhältnisse Palästinas, hebräischartiger Ausdrücke und Wendungen und ähnliches deutliche Spuren dafür aufweist, dass nicht ein Mann wie der Heidenchrist Lukas, der seine Kenntnis über alles dies nur Studien verdankt, diese Stücke aufgezeichnet haben wird, sondern dass sie innerhalb der judenchristlichen Gemeinden aufbewahrt und erstmalig niedergeschrieben worden sind".

from Mk[27], and included material from the GS that was not contained in the older form of the Markan *Grundlage*[28]. Luke's method involved sometimes referring to the one or the other and at other times considering both together[29]. J. Weiss criticized Feine's view that Luke would have oscillated between two very similar sources as suffering from a "psychologische Unmöglichkeit"[30]. Feine countered by claiming that Weiss was "zu subjectiv", being mistaken about Luke's literary method. Feine maintained that Luke, faced with two such similar sources, simply exercised his prerogative to use the shorter version of the same event. Indeed, Luke did not adopt all the sources available to him. What is more, he often omitted and shortened materials[31].

Feine called attention to what he considered the peculiar views of A. Resch on the relationship of the sources of the Synoptic Gospels, which also highlighted some of Feine's differences with B. Weiss[32]. Resch concurred with B. Weiss that Mt and Lk were composed chiefly from Mk and a special pre-canonical *Evangelienschrift* containing speeches of Jesus, which Mark had also used. Resch deviated from B. Weiss, however, in asserting that Mark made a more extensive use of the pre-canonical writing. Not only did this source have all the "Herrenreden" which Mark reproduced, it contained a passion narrative in brief outlines worded in Hebrew[33]. Resch assigned more of the narrative material to the *Urevangelium* than Weiss had done, but to Feine even B. Weiss's own argument was not conclusive[34].

The contents of Luke's special source suggested by Feine were the following verses in the present order of Lk[35]: chapters 1 and 2; 3,10-14.23-34 or 38; 4,14-

27. *Ibid.*, p. 4; cf. p. 131.
28. *Ibid.*, p. 7-8, n. 1. "Sein Evangelium bietet auch in sonstigen Abschnitten ausreichend viele Belege dafür, wie der Evangelist, auch wenn er im grossen und ganzen nach einer bestimmten Überlieferung erzählt, daneben doch auch einen anderen Bericht kannte und benutzte, z.B. in der Synagogenscene zu Nazareth (4,16-30), in der Erzählung von Petri Fischzug (5,1-11), von der Salbung durch die Sünderin (7,36-50) u.s.w. und namentlich in der Leidensgeschichte".
29. *Ibid.*, p. 8.
30. J. WEISS, *Die Parabelrede bei Markus*, in *TSK* 64 (1891) 289-321, esp. p. 290; see also p. 295: "Die Ansicht Feines, wonach das ὁ ἔχων ὦτα aus A, das ἀκούειν aus Markus stammen soll, ist ebenso wenig psychologisch vorstellbar...". Weiss was here referring to Feine's earlier article, *Zur synoptischen Frage. III. Fortsetzung*, in *JPTh* 14 (1888) 388-422, p. 397, which treated the parable of the sower.
31. FEINE, *Eine vorkanonische Überlieferung*, p. 8: "Es kommt dem Lukas nicht darauf an, alles dasjenige an Stoff in sein Evangelium aufzunehmen, was ihm überhaupt bekannt gewesen ist. Er hat mannigfach ausgelassen und gekürzt".
32. A. RESCH, *Agrapha. Ausserkanonische Evangelienfragmente* (TU, 5/4), Leipzig, 1889.
33. FEINE, *Eine vorkanonische Überlieferung*, p. 9, n. 1.
34. *Ibid.*, p. 10, n. 1: "Resch verpflanzt in das Urevangelium noch mehr Erzählungsstoff als Weiss thut, und doch ist schon die Begründung von B. Weiss für ein solches Verfahren wenig beweiskräftig".
35. Feine proposed that the order of the source itself was as follows (the asterisk signifies Lukan material which has been combined with Markan; pericopes in parentheses indicate placement which is doubtful or cannot be determined): 1-2; 3,23-34 or 38; (3,1-17); (4,16-30*);

30; 5,1-11; 6,20-49; 7,1-10.11-17.36-50; 8,1-3; 9,51-56; 10,1-12.17-20.25-37.38-42; 11,5-8.27-28.37-52; 12,13-21.22-34.34-48.49.50.54-56; 13,1-9.10-17.22-30; 14,1-6.12-14.16-24.28-33; 15,4-10; 16,1-13.19-31; 17,11-19.20-37; 18,1-8.9-14; 19,1-10.11-27; 21,12-15; and in the passion narrative, 21,37f.; 22,14-23.29.30.31-34.35-38.39-46.47-53.54-62.63-71;   23,1-12.13-25.26-49.50-56;   24,1-12.13-35.36-49.50-53. No detailed information was provided, however, about the passion narrative within his discussion of the order of the source material. He said only that in that section of the Gospel Luke had combined his special written source with Mk and the synoptic narrative source[36]. Feine indicated further his hesitancy in reconstructing the source in the passion narrative: "Wir können aus dem heutigen Text des Lukas nicht mehr mit Wahrscheinlichkeit auf die Form und den Umfang der Darstellung der Leidensgeschichte schliessen, welche die Quellenschrift gehabt hat"[37]. But the Jerusalem origin of the special traditions in the passion narrative was confirmed[38].

In his commentary on the passion narrative Feine defended a written source[39]. This portion of the Gospel extended from 21,37 through 24,53. In the material dealing with the trial of Jesus, Feine claimed that Luke "weiss also nichts" of a pre-trial on the same night as the arrest. Further, the Sanhedrin pronounced no formal judgment against Jesus. The special Jewish-Christian written source accounted for such variations[40]. Feine analyzed the sources in 22,54–23,25 and asserted that the denial of Peter (22,54-62) was based upon Mk or the GS. The mistreatment of Jesus and the Sanhedrin trial (22,63-65.66-71) derived from Mk and the GS, though it was possible that the special Jewish-Christian tradition was responsible for the Messiah question in 22,67. The sentencing of Jesus to death (23,18-25) was obtained from Mk, except for the detail that the people had been in agreement with the religious leadership from the beginning (23,18), which was due to the special tradition[41]. Luke had not taken up the mockery of Jesus which was described in the other Synoptics (Mt 27,27-31 / Mk 15,16-20).

(5,1-11*); 6,20-49; 7,1-10 + 8,1-3 [6,20-8,3 is according to Feine a continuous section]; 7,11-17* + 7,36-50*; 9,51-18,14 [within this section Feine listed: 9,51-56; 10,17-20.25-37*.38-42; 9,57-62; 11,1-13.14-37; (11,37-54); 12; 13; 13,28-30; 14,7-24; 15; 16; beginning of 17; (17,11-19) (17,20-37); 18,1-8; (18,9-14)]; 19,1-10.11-27.39-44*.

36. *Ibid.*, p. 131. Feine did not list particular verses or pericopes from the passion narrative at this point in his discussion, but his book contained a commentary on the whole Gospel from which these verses from that part of Lk have been taken.

37. *Ibid.*, p. 146.

38. *Ibid.*, p. 154.

39. *Ibid.*, p. 61-75.

40. *Ibid.*, p. 68-69. Cf. p. 68: "Dann erst, am anderen Morgen, kam nach Lukas der hohe Rat zusammen. Lukas weiss also nichts von einer Vorverhandlung gleich am Abend der Gefangennahme".

41. *Ibid.*, p. 70: "Eine Abweichung von Markus ist in seinem Bericht durch seine besondere Überlieferung insofern bedingt, als das Volk von vornherein mit den Obersten im Einverständnis ist, daher nicht erst überredet zu werden braucht und V. 18 gleich den Ruf erhebt, Jesum zu töten und Barrabas freizugeben".

In Feine's view, the account of the trial before Pilate and Herod (23,1-12) was based upon a special Jewish-Christian tradition, with the exception of v. 3 which was borrowed from Mk 15,2[42]. The account of 23,13-16, without parallel in the other Gospels, probably stemmed from a special written tradition[43]. In an examination of the vocabulary, Feine noted that in the NT, the term ἐσθής occurred only in Lk 23,11; 24,4; Acts 1,10; 10,30; 12,21; and in Jas 2,2.3[44]. The word λαμπρός occurred in the Synoptics only at Lk 23,11 and Acts 10,30. In both instances it was combined with ἐσθής. Beyond that, the term was found in Jas and Rev. In addition to two occurrences in 2 Cor (3,7.13), the word ἀτενίζειν was found only in the Lukan corpus (4,20; 22,56; Acts 1,10; 3,4.12; 6,15; 7,55; 10,4; 11,6; 13,9; 14,9; 23,1). The term could have stemmed from the special source and could have been used independently by Luke[45].

The source in the first half of Acts (1–12) was a continuation of the source in Lk[46]. Dominating the Jewish-Christian source was the view that although non-

---

42. *Ibid.*, p. 69-70. Feine recalled that Holtzmann, *Die Synoptiker* (Hand-Commentar), p. 288, believed that 23,6-12 was based on older material (p. 69).

43. FEINE, *Eine vorkanonische Überlieferung*, p. 69. Whereas Holtzmann maintained that "hat Lukas eine eigentümliche und genaue Tradition über den Hergang" recounted in 23,1-16, Feine tempered this view by claiming that it was only probable that Luke followed a written tradition. Cf. HOLTZMANN, *Die Synoptiker*, 1889, p. 288: "Ein dem Lc eigenthümlicher Abschnitt, zu dessen Ausführung jedoch ältere Stoff benutzt sind"; [2]1892, p. 289; [3]1901, p. 417, with reference to J. Weiss and Feine. See also HOLTZMANN, *Die synoptischen Evangelien*, 1863, p. 241: "Eingeschoben aus der Tradition". Cf. below.

44. FEINE, *Eine vorkanonische Überlieferung*, p. 251.

45. *Ibid.*, p. 252.

46. *Ibid.*, p. 156-212. His results should be compared with those in *Die alte Quelle* (page references within brackets). 1,3-12: p. 160 [p. 87]. These derived from a set, probably written tradition. 1,12-26: p. 163 [p. 88-89]. This section contained clear traces of a special written source. Certain elements appeared to be later insertions. For the story of the choice of a replacement for Judas, Feine was more direct in his assertion of the special source in his earlier article. 2,1-42: p. 167-168 [p. 91]. This passage derived from an older report. 2,43-47: p. 171, 172 [p. 93]. Feine claimed it was hard to determine whether this stemmed from the older *Quellenvorlage*, though there is much to recommend such a view. In his earlier article Feine claimed that the section was not taken from the source in this form, but aspects from it were incorporated by the author. 3,1-4,31: p. 173 [p. 93]. The essential elements were drawn from the source. He maintained the same in his earlier article. 4,32-5,16: p. 180 [p. 96]. The stories reflected how matters had been handled in the early community. In his 1890 article he pointed out that this section was continuous. 5,17-42 p. 181 [p. 98-99]. It appeared to Feine that this section was comprised of various reports having connection with Acts 4,1ff. and Acts 12 which Luke reworked. But at the base of this section was a report from the special Jewish-Christian source. 6,1-7: p. 184 [p. 99]. This material rested on a set tradition, but different from the Jewish-Christian source Feine has been attempting to isolate. 6,8—8,3: p. 186 [p. 109]. Feine argued "mit grosser Wahrscheinlichkeit" that this presentation was literarily dependent on present-day reports found in "irgendwelcher Quellenvorlage". The same position was argued in the article [p. 101]. But the special source contained the story of Stephen, only in a different place (*Eine vorkanonische Überlieferung*, p. 194). Feine noted both in the article and in the book that similarities existed between the death of Stephen and the death of Jesus. In the book Feine added

Israelites should not be excluded from salvation, Jesus came as Messiah for the people of Israel[47]. The influence of B. Weiss upon Feine's study of the source question for Acts did not go unnoticed. W. Heitmüller described Feine's investigation as "eine Wiederaufnahme und wertvolle Weiterführung" of Weiss's examination[48]. Feine was praised for using Weiss's methodology in treating the literary-critical problems, but he was criticized for employing historicity as a criterion. Further, Heitmüller believed that Feine had overestimated the historical value of the Jerusalem source[49].

that similarities existed in the "Verurteilung" as well. 8,4-24: p. 196 [p. 109]. Partly from the special source, but another part was foreign to it. 9,31-43: p. 200. Certain elements corresponded to the Jewish-Christian source. 10,1–11,18: p. 200 [p. 111-114]. By and large this section was drawn from the special source. 11,19-23: p. 208 [p. 114]. Connections between this section and Acts 8,1.4 led Feine to conclude that this section also rested on the special source. Cf. the article where Feine qualified his position by stating that it was "wahrscheinlich" that it was derived from the ancient source. 12,1-24: p. 209 [Die alte Quelle, p. 115]. These Peter stories, as the earlier ones, pointed to dependence upon the special source. In the previous article Feine passed over the material dealing with Peter to concentrate on the material dealing with Herod. In the book Feine wrote that the story of Herod's death was framed by material taken from other sources. Although in his earlier article he argued that the death of Herod story stemmed from the ancient source, his view on the framing nature of the material from the other sources represents a development in Feine's thinking.

While we have listed the sections in Acts where Feine recognized a source, W. HEITMÜLLER, Die Quellenfrage in der Apostelgeschichte (1886-1898) I, in TR 2 (1899) p. 56, offered a detailed analysis of the elements. (Those marked with an asterisk were reworked by the redactor or did not completely belong to the source). These included: 1,4.5.8*.9-12.13-17.20-26; 2,1-4a.12.13.14*-42 (43-47); 3,1-8a.11-26; 4,4.7b-14.18.(21).22.(23).24-31.33.36.37;5,1-11.12-16.24-35.37-42;6,(8).9-11.15;7,22until38.35-43.51-56.59.60;8,1b.2.4-9.11-13;9,31-43;10,1-27.29b-33.36-42a.44-48; 11,3-17.19-33; 12,1-24. Verses which reflected the hand of the canonical author were: 1,1-3.6.7.18.19; 2,4b.5.6b-11; 3,8b-10; 4,1-3.5-7a.15-17.19.20; 5,17-23.36; 6,7; 8,10.14-24; 10,28.29a.34.35.42b;11,1.18.24.

47. FEINE, Eine vorkanonische Überlieferung, p. 239.

48. HEITMÜLLER, Die Quellenfrage, p. 55. Cf. B. WEISS, Einleitung, 1886, p. 569-586; ²1889, p. 570-586; see also ³1897. Heitmüller also referred to Weiss's Die Apostelgeschichte. Textkritische Untersuchungen und Textherstellung (TU 9/3,4), Leipzig, 1893.

49. HEITMÜLLER, Die Quellenfrage, p. 58-59. In another assessment Llewellyn John Montfort BEBB (1901) appeared to endorse Feine's proposition, calling his effort "the most elaborate attempt to reproduce the special source used by St. Luke" (Gospel of Luke, in J. HASTINGS and J.A. SELBIE [eds.], A Dictionary of the Bible, Vol. 3, New York, p. 167). Evidence of the special source in Acts 1–12 and some similarities with the Johannine Gospel, according to Bebb, suggested acceptance of Feine's theory (p. 168). He was of the opinion that Luke had used, in addition to Mk and Q, oral tradition and a special written source. He adopted the view that Luke used a special written source in Chapters 1, 2 and in the material following 9,51, but he was not so clear about the passion narrative (Ibid.). He rejected the idea that the special source was Ebionite in nature. A close examination of the language of Lk revealed that the evangelist was quite familiar with Septuagintal vocabulary (p. 169-170). But the Hebraisms, such as εἶπεν δέ and ἐν ἐκείνῃ τῇ ἡμέρᾳ rendered little help in discerning sources (p. 167, 170). Bebb was persuaded that oral tradition could account for some of the additional material, as in the case of the Herod episode (23,4-12).

As can be seen from a cursory review of his later works, Feine remained interested in the topic of Luke's special source. He still maintained in his *Theologie des Neuen Testaments* (1910) that the Lk "am wahrscheinlichsten" contained a gospel tradition emanating from a poor Palestinian Jewish-Christian circle, which he increasingly described as Ebionite[50]. That Feine had not definitively decided the question was evident in his *Einleitung in das Neue Testament* (1913):

> Seine zahlreichen Sonderüberlieferungen stammen [...] wahrscheinlich zum grossen Teil auch aus einer Quellenschrift. Dass diese Sonderüberlieferung in einer Rezension mit der Redenquelle bereits zusammengearbeitet ihm vorgelegen habe, ist möglich. Aber auch diese Frage muss wohl offen bleiben. Die Abweichungen des *Lk*. von den anderen beiden Synoptikern in der Leidensgeschichte gehen wohl auch auf eine schriftliche Grundlage zurück[51].

In *Die Religion des Neuen Testaments* (1921) he argued that Mk contained the most reliable tradition extending from the appearance of John the Baptist until the resurrection[52]. Further, that tradition provided the basis for Lk regarding the activity of Jesus. The main sources for Luke were the Markan tradition and Q. Feine shifted to the view that some changes were due to the evangelists, though without denying that differences may also stem from other traditions or from the still many surviving witnesses[53].

The idea of an *Urmarkus* was rejected by appealing to B. Weiss (*Das Marcusevangelium*) and Hawkins (*Horae Synopticae*, 1899). Bebb used the [8]1892 edition of J. Weiss's commentary on Lk (p. 173). Likewise, he dismissed the theory of Simons and Holtzmann that Luke had used Mt (p. 166; no bibliographical references to Simons or Holtzmann appeared on this page or at the end of the article under "Literature", p. 173).

Bebb, following the lead of Lightfoot, argued that the transposition of material concerning Peter's denials was due to Luke, heightening the dramatic force, though in other cases, differences in order were due to the special source (p. 172; cf. p. 167). Other transpositions occurred as Luke tied together events "separate in time and place". What was of greatest importance was his conviction that the order Luke followed in the Gospel was that of Mk. The influence of Hawkins was seen in the work of Bebb who considered the MAs to have most likely resulted from oral tradition, though scribal efforts to harmonize the accounts was not to be excluded (p. 166). As noted in the introduction, our study of the trial enables us to study two significant MAs.

50. *Theologie des Neuen Testaments*, Leipzig, 1910, ²1912 (⁵1931, ⁸1950), p. 684. Page references are to the second edition, unless otherwise noted. Cf. p. 109, n. 1, 688-689. In the fifth edition he conceded that some of the themes common to popular philosophy were also present. Nevertheless, he maintained his long held position that the special material derived from the Jewish-Christian community and reflected connections with the Letter of James (⁵1931, p. 423).

51. *Einleitung in das Neue Testament*, Leipzig, 1913, p. 119. Commenting on the special material in Lk he indicated: "... ferner in der Leidensgeschichte eine Anzahl von ihm eigentümlichen Überlieferungen" (p. 112). Surprisingly, Feine did not mention J. Weiss in regard to this idea of a special source.

52. *Die Religion des Neuen Testaments*, Leipzig, 1921, p. 4-5.

53. *Ibid.*

Feine wrote in reaction to source critics, such as H.J. Holtzmann, who ascribed a large share of the special material to the evangelist, to affirm the historical value of the special material. Early in his book *Eine vorkanonische Überlieferung des Lukas* he announced his position that he believed that the source derived from oral tradition, preserved and first committed to writing by the early Jewish-Christian community rather than the evangelist[54]. Some confusion about Feine's idea whether the special source was written or oral may be due to Feine himself. Later in his discussion of the time of composition of the special source he wrote:

> Aber eine Zusammenstellung von Reden und Worten des Herrn, wie die Logienschrift in der Hauptsache nur gedacht werden kann, dürfen wir wahrscheinlich nicht als eine Schrift betrachten, die nach ihrer erstmaligen Aufzeichnung ihrem Inhalt nach abgeschlossen gewesen wäre. Vielmehr wird sich an diese Stoffe allmählich noch manches andere angefügt haben; die Redenquelle hatte schon eine Entwicklung hinter sich, als sie in den Evangelien verarbeitet worden ist. Unsere Quellenschrift des Lukas ist ja auch nicht anderes, als eine weitere Ausgestaltung dieser ältesten Redenquelle[55].

Referring to Feine's book as "une étude sérieuse", A. Loisy wrote favorably of it, though noting he exaggerated in assigning all the material proper to Lk to this one source[56]. Nevertheless, Loisy found another of Feine's conclusions "assez bizarre": Feine contended that this document was the same as was found at the base of the primitive document and the compilation of discourse which were employed in the writing of Mt[57]. Loisy ended on a positive note with the belief that Feine's contribution, though hypothetical, provided a useful means for understanding Luke's literary composition[58].

In 1892, Johannes Weiss penned a very favorable review of Feine's work, though not without some dissent[59]. Beginning with the more positive elements,

54. *Eine vorkanonische Überlieferung*, p. 12.

55. *Ibid.*, p. 151.

56. A. LOISY, *Chronique*, in *L'enseignement biblique* 2 (mars-avril, 1893) 29-32, p. 30: "Le critique allemand exagère sans doute en rapportant à une source unique tous les éléments du troisième Évangile qui ne se rencontrent pas dans les deux premiers. Mais il est difficile de ne pas reconnaître à son hypothèse, considérée dans l'ensemble, une assez grande probabilité".

57. *Ibid.*, p. 32.

58. *Ibid.*: "Il va sans dire que tout cela est hypothétique; mais ce ne sont pas des hypothèses en l'air. [...] Cette hypothèse [...] arrivera difficilement à une formule satisfaisante, parce que les moyens de contrôle font absolument défaut et que les retouches littéraires que saint Luc a fait subir à ses documents, s'il en avait, ne permettent pas de les reconnaître aisément".

59. J. WEISS, in *TLZ* 11 (1892) 273-276. J.H. MOULTON also wrote positively of Feine's "able and careful" study, even while noting "there is of course a great deal of subjectivity in all this, and most readers will find plenty to quarrel with in the details" (*CritR* 2 [1892] 368-375, p. 368). His evaluation was that this work "certainly deserves our respectful consideration" (p. 369). Still, Moulton was not convinced that there was a need for such a *Quellenschrift* since oral exchange between Luke and the Jerusalem community could likewise have provided the special material (p. 374).

Weiss believed that Feine's study helped to oppose the view that Luke's special material was the result of the evangelist's creative impulse[60]. Feine was also complimented for pointing out numerous connections between LQ and the Letter of James[61]. That Luke possessed LQ in Greek form and that it stemmed from Palestine or Judea plus the probability that the material was originally Hebrew or Aramaic was seconded by Weiss. In his opinion, Feine was also correct in assuming that Luke significantly reworked the vocabulary of his sources. The shortcomings of Feine's book included the fact that he presented assertions with great certainty without providing the proof[62]. What is more, Feine had not given sufficient attention to the LQ material in the passion narrative[63]. Finally, Weiss contended that the vocabulary Feine had isolated as coming from the source was too limited and could be expanded[64].

Also in 1892, Johannes WEISS published a revision of the Meyer commentary on Lk[65]. In the *Vorwort*, he announced: "Anstatt, wie in der 7. Aufl. geschehen,

---

60. J. WEISS, *TLZ*, p. 273.

61. To further enhance his position that Luke's special material derived from a Jewish-Christian source, Feine paralleled material from the Letter of James and the Gospel: Jas 1,9f.; 2,5f; 4,9f.; 5,1-3.5 / Lk 1,46-48.52.53; 6,20.21.24.25; 12,21; 16,19.25. Another comparision was made between Jas 4,13-15 and Lk 12,16-21. Regarding care of the poor similarities were found in Jas 2,15f.; 3,17 and Lk 3,11; 12,33; 16,9. Both Jas 5,17 and Lk 4,25 agreed against the account in 1 Kgs 17,1; 18,1 concerning the length of the drought. Further agreement was found in Jas 5,20 and the Lukan material about seeking and finding that which was lost. Jas 3,1 called to mind Lk 12,48. Additional examples were Jas 4,17 / Lk 12,47 and Jas 1,17 / Lk 11,13. Cf. FEINE, *Eine vorkanonische Überlieferung*, p. 132-133.

At many points throughout his own commentary (1892, see below) J. Weiss also noted special relations of Lk with the Letter of James: p. 388, 390, 443, 461, 464, n. 1, 470, 486, 497, 499, 506, 509, 518, 525, 530, 534, 541, 548, 561, 562, 564, 566, 572, 598, 607, 609, and 623 (cf. below n. 79).

62. *TLZ*, p. 273.

63. *Ibid.*, p. 274: "Noch lange nicht genug beachtet sind die von F. in der Leidensgeschichte gesammelten Stoffe aus LQ. Diese dominiren so stark und die Abweichung von Mc. ist so gross, dass man annehmen möchte LQ sei hier für Luc. die Hauptquelle gewesen: Namentlich die starken Auslassungen aus dem Marcusfaden sprechen hierfür. Ausserdem wäre noch die Frage zu erwägen, ob nicht auch in Stücken, die Luc. aus Mc. entlehnt, ein nebenhergehender Einfluss der LQ auzuerkennen sei, wie mir dies z.B. bei der Verklärungsgeschichte wahrscheinlich ist".

64. *Ibid.*, p. 276.

65. J. WEISS, in B. WEISS and J. WEISS, *Die Evangelien des Markus und Lukas* (KEK 1/2), Göttingen, [8]1892, p. III-IV: "Vorwort zur 8. Auflage"; p. 271-666: "Evangelium des Lukas". This revision of his father's commentary on Lk (in the Meyer series, [7]1885) reflected an adoption of Feine's theory with certain modifications. See the introduction, § 2: "Entstehung des Evangeliums", p. 274-281 (esp. 279-281, on Feine). Weiss's work was more influential than Feine's monograph because it appeared as a commentary in the classic Meyer series. See Appendix I, "Special LQ Vocabulary and Constructions according to J. Weiss" (891-915), where the notes of J. Weiss are collected in a threefold catalogue: first a short list of references in the Markan sections; then, a much longer list of references in the LQ sections; and third, the same references in an alphabetical arrangement of words and phrases with annotation in the margin of

neben der Markusquelle für Lukas noch die 'apostolische Quelle', die Logia des Matthäus (Q) und eine Special-Lukasquelle (L) *nebeneinander* anzunehmen, bin ich durch die Schrift von Feine [1891] überzeugt worden, dass Lukas diese beiden Ueberlieferungen schon in eine Schrift zusammengearbeitet (LQ) benutzt hat". Weiss believed that this theory would have consequences for the interpretation of various texts[66].

Weiss noted that the assumption that Luke used Mk as his chief source enjoyed the widest consensus, but adherents had to admit this theory was not without its difficulties. While Lk contained almost all of Mk and essentially followed it there was still the unclarified matter of the two interpolations (6,20–8,4; 9,46–18,15)[67]. A further unsolved challenge to Holtzmann's[68] and B. Weiss's assertion of Lukan dependence upon Mk was the great omission (Mk 6,45–8,26)[69]. Moreover, according to J. Weiss, there were numerous places where Lk in agreement with Mt had a more original text than Mk[70].

Continuing in the line of B. Weiss he also rejected Simons's hypothesis of Luke's secondary dependence upon Mt. He quoted Simons, claiming that he himself presented the evidence to reject the theory: "'eine Einwirkung des Mt auf die Komposition des Lk im Grossen haben wir nicht wahrgenommen'. Das allein scheint mir entscheidend gegen die ganze Hypothese zu sein"[71]. In arguing against Simons Weiss maintained that we have Q because of the theory of Markan priority.

A second effort to explain the agreements of Lk and Mt in conjunction with Markan priority was profferred by B. Weiss. Such a source, composed by the apostle Matthew, contained pieces of narrative. Luke and Matthew had, in addition to their use of Mk, known and reproduced this text directly thus providing a more original version in places where Mk had done so only secondarily. J. Weiss described as problematic B. Weiss's position on the Mt-Lk agreements against Mk arguing that Mk was not "ein ursprüngliches Werk", but had incorporated "eine ältere Quelle"[72]. But this view suffered from two difficulties. First was the assumption that this source common to Mt and Lk contained narrative in addition to discourse, but no passion narrative[73]. Meyer and a supposed majority of unnamed critics criticized this idea[74]. Secondly, B. Weiss did not view it as

---

B.S. Easton's classification of the L vocabulary according to B. Weiss.

66. *Vorwort*, p. III.

67. *Lukas*, p. 275. Cf. B. WEISS, *Lehrbuch der Einleitung in das Neue Testament*, Berlin, [2]1889, p. 538, and *Das Marcusevangelium und seine synoptische Parallelen*, Berlin, 1872.

68. See the discussion of Holtzmann's position below.

69. *Lukas*, p. 275. See p. 433.

70. J. WEISS, *Lukas*, 275-277, p. 275: "Denn es giebt eine ausserordentlich grosse Zahl von Stellen, in welchen nicht Lk den secundären Text bietet, sondern zweifellos Mk, während Lk und zwar *in Uebereinstimmung mit Mt* ursprünglicher lautet" (the so-called "minor agreements").

71. *Ibid.*, p. 276, n. 1.

72. *Lukas*, p. 277. Cf. [7]1885, p. 251-255.

73. *Ibid.*, p. 277.

74. *Ibid.*: "eine Annahme, die schon bei Meyer, aber auch heute noch bei den Meisten auf

necessary that Mark "in solche Perikopen" over against Mt and Lk used the "apostolische Quelle". J. Weiss is unable to make the exception B. Weiss did. J. Weiss, in agreement with A. Resch, assumed Mark's use of such a source to a much wider extent[75]. He therefore accepted the possibility of *Urmarkus* which, in his opinion, avoided the two difficulties.

J. Weiss stated his conviction about the secondary nature of our Markan text which was composed from various traditions[76]. In an attempt to avoid the two pitfalls of B. Weiss's position, J. Weiss adopted an Urmarkus hypothesis. He rejected Holtzmann's articulation of *Urmarkus* in favor of Weizsäcker's insistence that the Mt-Lk agreements against Mk were due to the dependence of Mt and Lk upon "eine ältere und einfachere Form" of Mk[77]. Luke thus used a document basically the same as our Mk in structure but lacking some of the material. This document Weiss designated "A"[78]. He further recalled that Feine advocated "eine etwas andere Form der Urmkhypothese". What distinguished it from Weizsäcker's formulation was that Luke possessed both *Urmarkus* and canonical Mk and Luke's compositional method was to oscillate between the two[79].

In addition, Weiss stated the material common to Mt and Lk was not merely oral, but was already available to the evangelists in written form, the Q source. While Luke was more faithful to the order, Matthew had retained "wohl sehr oft" the original vocabulary. This gave rise to the question whether the changes in Lk stemmed from the evangelist or from Q in a form different from that possessed by Mt.

Concentrating next on the special Lukan material, he asserted that this information cannot merely be explained as deriving from oral tradition because linguistically and materially it had a pronounced character and it was distinct from Luke's Gentile-Christian standpoint[80]. His conceptualization of this theory afterall

---

starken Widerspruch gestossen ist".

75. *Ibid.*, p. 278; cf. A. RESCH, *Agrapha* (TU 5/4) 1889, p. 26.

76. *Vorwort*, p. iii.

77. *Ibid.*, p. 278. See C. WEIZSÄCKER, *Untersuchung über die evangelische Geschichte*, Leipzig - Tübingen, 1864. Beyschlag was credited with a view similar; cf. W. BEYSCHLAG, *Zu den vorstehenden Aussatz von D. B. Weiss: Zu Evangelienfrage*, in *StKr* 3 (1883) 594-602.

78. J. WEISS, *Lukas*, p. 278: "Somit würde das Urtheil lauten: Eine Hauptquelle des Lk, welche er als geschichtlichen Faden und Skelett seiner Darstellung zu Grunde legte, war eine Schrift, welche im Wesentlichen dem Aufbau nach mit unserem Mk übereinstimmte, aber noch nicht in allen Stücken unseren heutigen Mktext hatte). Sigle: A".

79. *Ibid.*, n. 1, referring to Feine's articles in *JPTh* 12, 14, 15. (He must have intended Vol. 16 since no article by Feine is found in Vol. 15).

80. J. WEISS, *Lukas*, p. 279. The argument centered on the combination of L and Q prior to its reception by Luke. While Feine argued that L derived from oral tradition, Weiss preferred to view it as written, though he conceded that such a distinction could not be answered "mit Sicherheit" (p. 280, n. 1). Cf. p. (398-)399, n. 2: "Dann wäre allerdings wahrscheinlich, dass L nicht bloss eine mündliche Tradition (Feine), sondern eine bereits schriftlich fixirte Ueberlieferung war".

stemmed from Weizsäcker[81]. Observing that certain "Pauline pieces"[82] suggested to scholars a particular Jewish-Christian source[83], Weiss credited Feine with establishing "die greifbarste Gestalt" of such a source in the line of Weizsäcker. Weiss agreed that L and Q were joined prior to the evangelist[84]. He argued that Luke employed a revision of the *Logiaquelle* Q, which was reshaped according to its spirit and was expanded by material from L[85].

While he enthusiastically embraced Feine's idea of a special source, Weiss nonetheless differed on several points. He asserted, for example, that the number of pre-canonical gospels could not have been small (cf. Lk 1,1 πολλοί)[86] while Feine argued that the number was not necessarily great, nor was it necessary to believe that Luke employed all such earlier sources. Weiss thought that the "Pauline" anti-Pharisaic sections detected by Feine and others extended back to Jesus himself[87]. The conception of the special source by J. Weiss was practically that of Feine. However, the latter accepted *Urmarkus* and Mk, but for Weiss there was only *Urmarkus*. Further, while Feine argued that L stemmed from oral tradition Weiss favored an already fixed written form before it was combined with

81. See below. Weiss acknowledged that his theory was in the line of C. Weizsäcker: "Ich hoffe nun, das gerade meine Erklärung für diese Hypothese, die übrigens von Weizsäcker stammt, ein Gewicht in die Wegschale werfen wird" (p. III). In the commentary he observed that Feine, too, built upon Weizsäcker's conjecture: "Es ist nun aber schon von Wzs., dann von Feine zur Wahrscheinlichkeit gebracht, dass diese dem Lk eigenthümliche Ueberlieferung (L) dem Evangelien bereits in Vereindung mit Stoffen aus der Redenquelle (Q) vorlag" (p. 280; also 279).

82. E.g. the parables of the Prodigal Son (15,11-32) and the Pharisee and the Tax Collector (18,9-14); cf. *Lukas*, p. 279.

83. Weiss rehearsed various scholars' positions which termed Luke's special source "Ebionite" (Strauss and Keim), the gospel of the poor (Volkmar), of a southern Palestinian origin (Köstlin, a position which Weiss regarded "wohl mit Recht"), or directly from the Jerusalem community (Feine, *Eine vorkanonische Überlieferung*) (*Lukas*, p. 279). See already Feine in 1885: the "Ebionite" source C (*Ueber das gegenseitige Verhältniss*, p. 2). Weiss believed that the Ebionitism of the Gospel stemmed from LQ (*Lukas*, p. 283).

84. J. WEISS, *Lukas*, p. 280. Cf. p. 643, n. [3], Luke received his source Q in the form of LQ. See also p. 398, n. 2. Cf. J. WEISS, *Die Parabelrede*, p. 289-321, esp. p. 294: "Dies würde dann nicht Q sein, sondern die Spezialquelle des Lukas (L-Q). Möglicherweise ist dies ja allerdings nur eine umgearbeitete und vermehrte Gestalt von Q (Feine: C.)". Cf. F. NEIRYNCK, *The Symbol Q (=Q)*, in *Evangelica*, 1982, p. 687: "Weiss referred to Feine when he first mentioned LQ in 1891".

85. J. WEISS, *Lukas*, p. 279-280. Cf. p. III.

86. J. WEISS, *Lukas*, p. 274. Cf. FEINE, *Eine vorkanonische Überlieferung*, p. 3-4. Weiss also assumed that evidence of the use of written sources was proved by comparison with the other Synoptics (*Lukas*, p. 275).

Note the numerous references to Feine in the commentary: 373, n. 2; 274, n. 2; 378, n. 1; 382, n. 1; 386, n. 3; 401, 1; 420, n. 2; (432-)433, n. 1; 446, n. 3; 449, n. 2; 464, n. 2.

87. J. WEISS, *Lukas*, p. 279; see also p. 282. Cf. FEINE, *Eine vorkanonische Überlieferung*, p. 12. See Feine's discussion of the parables of the Prodigal Son (15,11-32) and the Pharisee and the Tax Collector (18,9-14) (p. 96-101, 102-104).

Q, but conceded that the problem could not be answered with certainty[88]. He was also prompted to offer his own reconstruction because Feine had not defined the form and extent of the passion narrative in the source[89]. Although disposed toward Feine's theory, he nonetheless cautioned that one must examine in each case whether there was evidence of Feine's special source[90]. Like Feine, Weiss saw the solution to the puzzle of the source question in the Gospel as involving the separation of sources in Acts. Yet Weiss was not as resolute as Feine inasmuch as "die Quellenscheidung hier noch keine genügend festen Resultate ergeben hat"[91]. Very important for our purpose was Weiss's estimate that a great deal of special stories in the passion narrative probably stemmed from LQ[92].

As Weiss began his discussion of Lk 22 he summarized his views on the sources of passion narrative[93]. Weiss argued on the basis of omissions and much evidence of greater originality that LQ even served as "die Hauptquelle"[94]. For example, inasmuch as there was a variation between Lk and the other Synoptics in the timing of Peter's denial and the Sanhedrin trial on the following morning, the detail that Peter had arrived at the house of the high priest was not related, and the words of the denial were found in a different order[95], Weiss surmised that 22,54-71 was more basic and thus independent of A. Although the night, filled as it was in Lk 22 by the accounts of Peter's denial and the mistreatment by the guards, could be a literary transformation by Luke, which allowing time for the Sanhedrin to be summoned to pass after Jesus' arrest, Weiss discounted this view since the action of the Sanhedrin was already mentioned in v. 52[96]. He demurred at B. Weiss's suggestion that vv. 58-59 "gegen v. 57" represented an intensification, and saw these verses as a weakening instead. What was more, v. 60 would be an enormous weakening in contrast to Mk (A), a redactional shift of which Luke could not be capable. It was possible that A transferred the trial in the night. But it was also possible that Luke's report, independent from Mk and Mt in

88. *Ibid.*, p. 280, n. 1.

89. Feine was possibly reticent to offer a reconstruction due to the fluidity of the oral tradition.

90. *Ibid.*, p. 280-281. He claimed that Feine sought to prove as "sehr wahrscheinlich" that the LQ source continued in the first part of Acts.

91. *Ibid.*, p. 281. Cf. p. 291, in a discussion of Lk 1-2: "eine Scheidung der Zuthaten des Lk von dem Bestande von LQ ist bisher kaum ernstlich versucht worden". Writing about some of the characteristics of the author of LQ: "Vielleicht schon der zwar judenchristliche, aber doch universalistiche Verf. von LQ" (p. 350; see also p. 386[-387], n. 3).

92. *Ibid.*, p. 281: "eine grosse Zahl von Nachrichten besonderer Art in der Leidensgeschichte".

93. *Ibid.*, p. 613-614.

94. *Ibid.*, p. 614.

95. *Ibid.*, p. 635. Not only were the events differently ordered, but the words of denial in the Lukan account varied from the other two Synoptics.

96. *Ibid.*, p. 633.

the remaining details, contained the more original account[97]. Weiss insisted that the account was independent of A in the particulars.

Dissenting from B. Weiss's position that oral tradition, accounted for the Mt-Lk agreement detailing the more emphatic portrayal of Peter's remorse (v. 62), J. Weiss argued that it could be explained either as a Lukan reminiscence from Mt or as a result of a revision of A (*Urmarkus* in Mt and Lk) by Mark, but then suggested the possibility that the phrase was a later insertion in Lk[98]. For the MA in 22,64 Weiss commented that the solution rested in a choice between the hypothesis of Simons or the *Urmarkus* hypothesis if Luke was here following A[99].

Concerning the mockery of Jesus (22,63-65), J. Weiss considered it to be not only independent of A but more original[100]. The difference in order from the account in A was noted[101]. Luke's use of the LQ source also appeared evident, according to Weiss, because of differences in vocabulary[102]. Commenting on 23,24-25 about the absence of φραγελλώσας from A and the mistreatment by the soldiers, he offered the following explanation:

> Die Misshandlung durch die Soldaten soll doch wohl die Ausführung des φραγελλώσας sein. Das ist aber nur verständlich, wenn A jenes Stück aus einem anderen Bericht hier eingesetzt hat. Ueberhaupt hat man den Eindruck, dass Mk 14,65 und 15,16-20a nichts als 2 Parallelberichte sind, welche A an zwei Stellen seines Compilationswerkes eingefügt hat. Hier läge dann ein Beweis, dass A mehrere Quellen zusammengearbeitet habe. Lk hat sich hier an den Faden der einen, sagen wir Q, gehalten, der ihm in der Gestalt von LQ dargeboten war[103].

The independence from *Urmarkus* (A) was especially clear in the account of the Sanhedrin trial (22,66-71). Weiss seemed compelled to adopt this view given the

---

97. According to the account contained in A the trial before Caiaphas terminated in the early morning. Also it probably occurred in the house of the high priest since the door of the Temple mount was closed at night. Lk 22,66, on the other hand, inadequately reported that that it took place in the συνέδριον as the place where the Sanhedrin met. Earlier it was indicated that Weiss favored LQ as the main source in the passion narrative because of omissions and traces of more originality (supra, n. 94; *Lukas*, p. 614). Omissions in 22,54-71 involved the testimony of the witnesses about the Temple and reference to Peter's arrival at the house of the high priest. The report found in A was more complete: "Ferner ist der Bericht des Lk darin rudimentär, dass nicht gesagt wird, Petrus sei bis zum Hause des Hohenpriesters gelangt. Dies alles hat der Bericht von A ergänzt: ἠκολούθ. ἕως τ. αὐλῆς τ. ἀρχιερέως ... μετὰ τ. ὑπηρετῶν. Also A. ist reflectirter, pragmatischer".

98. *Ibid.*, p. 635(-636), n. 2.

99. *Ibid.*, p. 636, n. 1.

100. *Ibid.*, p. 636. Weiss concurred with Schleiermacher who earlier argued for the originality of the Lukan account based on the reference to the guards as οἱ συνέχοντες. No bibliographical information concerning Schleiermacher was provided.

101. In A the mockery and mistreatment was reported after the Sanhedrin trial.

102. *Ibid.* LQ terms included οἱ συνέχοντες [19,43 LQ], ἐνέπαιζον (14,29. 23,11.36 LQ, 18,32?), δέρειν (12,47f. 20,10f. LQ. Act 5,40; 16,37; 22,19) and βλασφημεῖν (23,29 [sic] 23,39).

103. *Ibid.*, p. 643, n. 3.

omissions in the account, including the non-mention of the Temple and the promise of the return of the Son of Man[104]. A further distinction attesting to the originality of Lk was that it lacked the condemnation for blasphemy treating only the Messiah claim and not the "mehr metaphysisch gedachte Gottheit Jesu" as in A. The Lukan report of the Sanhedrin trial was independent from Mk/Mt in the following respects: the lack of reference to the witness trial and only this account treats the Jewish-Christian Messiah question. Insofar as there was no judgment resulting from the blasphemy, and since Luke did not treat the divinity of Jesus as *Urmarkus* (A) had, Weiss concluded that Luke's account was more original than the other two Synoptics[105]. It was pointed out that Lk 22,69 and Acts 2,36 both regard the exaltation of Christ as the point at which Jesus was made both Lord and Messiah[106].

In the account of Pilate and Herod (23,1-12), J. Weiss (1892) wrote that only v. 3 bore some relationship to A (*Urmarkus*). He claimed the rest of the material was entirely unique to Luke which stemmed from LQ, noting the similarity with Acts 4,27[107]. Concerning the charges brought against Jesus (23,2), Weiss viewed the third one as the most important and maintained that the political accusations were raised against Christians in Luke's own time[108]. The silence of Jesus in

---

104. *Ibid.*, p. 637. Weiss argued that it was inconceivable that Luke would have omitted this reference to the promise of the return if A had been available to him. The Jewish-Christian notions of δόξα and δύναμις were genuine terms which had fallen away in the A account. This paved the way for the messianic confession (v. 70) (p. 638). According to the Jewish-Christian source (Acts 2,36) Christ became Lord and Messiah at the resurrection (p. 637).

105. *Ibid*, p. 638. See also p. 636. In addition Weiss argued that it was unlikely that Luke would omit the witness trial concerning the words about the Temple since as a Paulinist it would have been of keen interest to him (p. 633). On the other hand, Lukan redaction would also take into consideration what was useful, interesting and understandable to those who read the work. The phrases ἀπὸ τοῦ νῦν 22,69 (1,48; 5,10; 12,52; 22,18 LQ; Acts 18,6) and ἀπὸ τ. στόματο (22,71) (1,64.70; 4,22; 6,45; 11,45; 19,22 LQ; 21,15?) were seen as special vocabulary (p. 637, 638).

106. *Ibid.*, p. 637.

107. *Ibid.*, p. 638. The charges reflected those raised against Christians in Luke's own time (p. 639). Weiss distinguished additional LQ vocabulary (23,1) (πλῆθος, 1,10; 2,13; 5,6; 19,37; 23,27 LQ; 6,17; 8,37 Lk, and often in Acts). Despite maintaining that these verses (1-12) came from LQ, Weiss nevertheless invited the reader to compare Mk 15,5f. with vv. 8f. and Mk 15,3f. with v. 10. Once more, Weiss listed vocabulary which he considered indicative of LQ. In v. 12 was found the phrase ἐν αὐτῇ τ. ἡμέρᾳ (LQ in 24,13) and φίλοι (15 occurrences from LQ in Lk). Vocabulary common to Lk - Acts included: βραχύ, 22,58f. and Acts 5,34 (p. 635), ἐπεφώνουν, 23,21 and Acts 12,22; 22,24 (p. 643). Other similarities include ἀρξάμενος ἀπὸ τῆς Γαλιλαίας (23,5 - Acts 10,37), ἀναπέμπω (23,7 - Acts 25,21), ἐξ ἱκανῶν χρόνων (23,8 - Acts 27,9), εὐτόνως (23,10 - Acts 18,28), ἐξουθενήσας (23,11 - Acts 4,11; also Lk 18,9 LQ), στρατεύμασιν (23,11 - Acts 23,10.27) and ἐσθῆτα λαμπράν (23,11 - Acts 10,30; see also James 2,2 and Acts 1,10; 12,21).

108. *Ibid.*, p. 638-639. Weiss did not consider the phrase "Christ a king" to be original and proposed that either βασιλέα or χριστόν was added as an explanatory gloss or Luke employed χριστόν as a proper name or adjective (p. 639, n. 1).

response to Herod's question (23,9) can be well explained by the manner ("Art") of the question and allowed Herod's purpose to be made known[109]. Still, Weiss called attention to Markan similarity by inviting comparison with Mk 15,5[110]. He attributed the observation in v. 10 possibly to Luke though he compared the verse to Mk 15,3f.[111]. J. Weiss recognized connections between Lk and Acts in the following verses:

Luke	Acts
23,6	10,37
23,7	25,21
23,8	27,9
23,10	18,28
23,11	4,11; 23,10.27; 10,30; 1,10; 12,21
23,14	3,26; 4,9; 12,19; 24,8; 28,18; 19,40
23,15	26,31
23,18	21,36; 22,22
23,19	15,2; 19,40; 23,7.10; 24,5
23,20	21,40; 22,2
23,21	12,22; 22,24
23,22	3,13

In contrast to B. Weiss, J. Weiss saw no Markan influence in the composition of the Herod story. He merely invited comparison between Lk 23,8ff. and Mk 15,5 and between Lk 23,10 and Mk 15,3f.[112].

Yet, 23,13-25 was likened to Mk 15,6-15 though altered in presentation[113]. Lk 23,20 was somewhat like Mk 15,9 while the question in 23,22 was exactly as

---

109. *Ibid.*, p. 640: "Das Schweigen Jesu ist wohl aus der Art der Fragen, welche die leichtfertige Absicht der Herodes erkennen liessen, zu erklären. Vgl. Mk 15,5".

110. *Ibid.*, p. 640. Cf. B. WEISS, ⁷1885, p. 623: "erinnert aber an Mark. 15,5". A difficulty arose here with J. Weiss's position since none of the questions asked by Herod are recounted. The narrative related only that Herod questioned Jesus. One cannot deduce "der Art der Fragen" unless one was thinking of Pilate's questions or Markan influence. Though B. Weiss had held that the absence of an answer on Jesus' part stemmed from the nature of the question, nonetheless B. Weiss argued more strongly for Markan influence. "Dies ist wohl aus der Beschaffenheit der Fragen und aus der durchshaueten Absicht des Herodes zu erklären, erinnert aber an Mark. 15,5" (⁶1878, p. 579). J. Weiss also invited comparison of the vehement accusations of the Jewish religious leaders (v. 10) with Mk 15,3f.

111. J. WEISS, ⁸1892, p. 640. So B. WEISS, ⁷1885, p. 623. Later, with a greater degree of certainty, J. Weiss asserted that v. 10 was an insertion of Luke into LQ (⁸1892, p. 641).

112. *Ibid.*, p. 642. See also Acts 26,31: οὐδὲν θανάτου ἢ δεσμῶν ἄξιόν τι πράσσει ὁ ἄνθρωπος οὗτος. Contrast the absence of any chastisement (23,16; cf. 23,22), merely a suggestion in Lk, as opposed to Mk 15,15.

113. *Ibid.*, p. 641. This idea was quoted from the seventh edition. cf. p. 643, n. 3. Changes included the absence of φραγελλώσας from A and the mistreatment by the soldiers. In an accompanying note Weiss explained that the abuse by the soldiers still constituted the carrying out of φραγελλώσας (Mk 15,15), but it was only understandable if A had inserted some detail here from another report. Weiss considered Mk 14,65 and Mk 15,16-20a to be parallel accounts.

found in Mk 15,14[114]. The account of vv. 13-16 was considered "ganz selbständig". The result of Herod's trial was that Jesus had done nothing worthy of death (23,15). Once more the absence of certain details prompted Weiss to assume that Luke's was the simpler version[115]. Whoever argued that Luke had still not known the present Gospel of Mark, can see "sachlich" agreement in 23,18 between LQ and Deutero-Markus (i.e. canonical Mk) in Mk 15,7f.[116]. Lk 23,20 was somewhat like Mk 15,9[117]. Shortly thereafter Weiss observed that the question of 23,22 was exactly as it was found in Mk 15,14 (τί γὰρ κακὸν ἐποίησεν)[118].

In a note, Weiss recalled that Meyer previously detected the mark of originality in the story of Jesus being sent by Pilate to Herod[119], though he added: "ein Grund zur Erdichtung ist nicht zu erkennen"[120]. Weiss objected to Holtzmann's suggestion that the story derived from older material, including the idea that ἐσθὴς λαμπρά (23,11) was a substitution for πορφύραν in Mk 15,17[121].

In defense of his position, J. Weiss observed that Lk and Acts were shown to share not only a common vocabulary, which most often occurred within the first twelve chapters of Acts, but also similar theology and an allusion to the Lukan account of the trials before Pilate and Herod in Acts.

From our survey, it is evident that J. Weiss was far less willing than Feine to admit Markan influence in this section of the passion narrative. *Urmarkus* (A) appeared more motivated and advanced than the Lukan account[122]. In contrast, the Lukan report was simpler and less artificially composed than A, and, to Weiss, this suggested a more original account. Lukan independence from *Urmarkus* (A)

---

114. *Ibid.*, p. 643.

115. *Ibid.*, p. 642. The absent details were that the release of a prisoner was the custom of Pilate and there was a choice between Jesus and Barabbas, details which were found in A. "Ein pragmatischer Schriftsteller" would not have omitted this information prior to v. 18, since the episode with Barabbas was totally unprepared for.

116. *Ibid.*, p. 642-643. Weiss was able in some cases to differentiate between Q (7,32) vocabulary and that of LQ (13,12) as in the case of προσφωνέω (23,20).

117. *Ibid.*, p. 643. Cf. B. WEISS, ⁷1885, p. 626, where there was no mention of Mk in relation to 23,20.

118. *Ibid.*, p. 643. Missing from Luke's account was the term φραγελλώσας (A) and the mistreatment by the soldiers. Weiss did not regard Mk 14,65 and Mk 15,16-20 as two parallel accounts but as evidence that A incorporated numerous sources. In contrast, "Lk hat sich hier an den Faden einen, sagen wir Q, gehalten, der ihm in der Gestalt von LQ dargeboten war" (n. 3). But Feine noted that Luke's redactional technique included omitting as well as shortening his source material (1891, p. 8, n. 1). Cf. B. WEISS, ⁷1885, p. 626, who noted that the only similarity between 23,22 and Mk 15,14 was the term γάρ.

119. *Ibid.*, p. 641, n. 1; cf. H.A.W. MEYER, *Kritisches exegetisches Handbuch über die Evangelien des Markus und Lukas* (KEK, 1/2), Göttingen, ³1855, p. 493; ⁵1867, p. 586.

120. J. WEISS, ⁸1892, p. 641, n. 1.

121. *Ibid.*: "Insonderheit ist es völlig aus der Luft gegriffen, wenn Htzm. sie aus älteren Stoffen entstanden sein lässt". Weiss provided no bibliographical information for Holtzmann.

122. J. WEISS, *Lukas*, p. 642: "viel motivirter und fortgeschrittener". See Weiss's vocabulary list in Appendix I, p. 902-915.

was garnered from difference in word order, as in the words of Peter's denial, choice of vocabulary, and in the varying sequence of events. More often than not, Weiss claimed the presence of LQ, where material found in A was missing in Lk[123]. The several elements, however, where Weiss pointed out striking similarities with Markan material should not be overlooked[124]. The resemblences between Lk and Acts were manifested in variety of ways including a common vocabulary, especially in Acts 1–12, similar theology and a reference in Acts to the Lukan account of the trials before Pilate and Herod[125].

J. Weiss defended the use of the special source in another work published in 1892[126]. In *Die drei älteren Evangelien* (1906) he maintained that although Luke followed Mk, he likewise omitted a significant amount of Markan material[127]. In its place he inserted materials reflecting the special tradition, as well as changed many other details from Mk. All this convinced J. Weiss that in addition to Mk, Luke possessed other traditions from which he drew and to which he gave preference particularly in the passion narrative[128]. He continued to support the probability that Luke's special source was a revision of the Reden-Quelle[129].

The contributions of P. Feine and J. Weiss were significant, but the theory of a special source would require further refinement. Feine and Weiss laid an influential foundation upon which other scholars would build.

The scholarship of Feine and J. Weiss drew attention to the question of Luke's literary style and redactional capability. In the passion narrative inclusion of

123. *Ibid*. In addition to the omissions already noted, the flogging (Mk 15,15), which in A followed the permission for crucifixion, was missing at that point in Lk (23,25) (p. 642).

124. The words of Jesus (22,61) up to the inserted word σήμερον agreed more exactly with Mk 14,72 than with Lk 22,34 (p. 635); The silence of Jesus in response to Pilate's question (p. 640; Lk 23,9 diff. Mk 15,5) and the vigorous and numerous charges by the religious leadership (23,10; cf. Mk 15,3f) were similar to Lk 23,20 and perhaps equaled Mk 15,9, though Weiss was unsure. Also, the question τί γὰρ κακὸν ἐποίησεν (23,22) was entirely the same as Mk 15,14 (p. 643). Finally, Weiss conceded that 23,3 bore a close resemblance to Mk.

125. *Ibid*., p. 280-281. "In der Erklärung ist versucht worden, ein Bild von dem einheitlichen Sprachcharakter dieser aus LQ abzuleitenden Stücke zu geben" (p. 281). Cf. p. (386-)387, n. 3. Verbal links between Lk and Acts subsequently highlighted by J. Weiss consisted in ἀποστρέφοντα (23,14 - Acts 3,26) and ἀνακρίνας (23,14 - Acts 4,9; 12,19; 24,8; 28,18) (p. 641).

126. J. WEISS, *Die Predigt Jesu vom Reiche Gottes*, Göttingen, 1892 (= *Jesus' Proclamation of the Kingdom of God*, tr. R.H. HIERS and D.L. HOLLAND, Philadelphia, PA, p. 60; [2]1900, Göttingen; [3]1964, ed. F. HAHN). The contents of LQ consisted of narratives, parables and sayings. Weiss seemed more hesitant in the second edition when he noted that LQ was less clearly recognizable than the other Lukan sources, Mk and Q ([2]1900, p. 38, in F. HAHN [ed.], [3]1964).

127. J. WEISS, *Die drei älteren Evangelien* (SNT), Göttingen, 1906, p. 469. Omitted were the anointing at Bethany (Mk 14,3-9), the first part of the trial, and the mockery by the soldiers (Mk 15,16-20a). Cf. *Lukas*, [8]1892.

128. *Die drei älteren Evangelien*, p. 469.

129. *Ibid*., [2]1907, p. 37: "Man pflegt sie auf eine Sonder-Quelle des Lukas zurückzuführen, deren Ursprung dunkel ist, die aber wahrscheinlich nichts anderes war, als eine erweiterte und umgearbeitete Form der Reden-Quelle".

material unique to Lk and differences in timing of events, their order, the
surprising omissions, numerous traces of originality in Lk over against Mk and
special vocabulary signaled a separate source (LQ), and in Weiss's opinion, it
served as "die Hauptquelle"[130]. Though they held differing opinions on the
significance of the omissions and the question of Lukan dependence upon Mk for
the account Peter's denials, they were allied in an effort to prove Luke's use of a
special source.

Bernhard Weiss

Before considering how Bernhard WEISS[131] reacted to the commentary by J.
Weiss, it is necessary to examine how the elder Weiss understood the relation of
Mk and Lk prior to that publication in 1892. As early as 1861 and continuing in
1864, 1865, 1872 and in the commentary on Lk ([6]1878, [7]1885)[132], Weiss asserted
that Mk was older than the other Synoptics. "Für den Unbefangenen glaube ich den
Beweis erbracht zu haben, dass unter unseren drei Evangelien Marcus das älteste
ist, dass er aber in vielen Partieen auf einer älteren schriftlichen Darstellung ruht,
die in den beiden anderen, namentlich in unserm Matthäus, oft noch ursprünglicher
erhalten ist"[133]. He maintained that more original material was found in speeches
and narratives of Mt[134].

130. *Ibid.*, p. 613-614; see also p. 281, though Weiss did not specify the special material in
the passion narrative. The differences in timing concerned the Lukan account of the Sanhedrin
trial in the morning as opposed to the nocturnal trial recounted in Mt/Mk (p. 633). The denial and
the mistreatment were said to have filled out the night. As to differences in order, the words of
the denial were arranged differently from those found in Mt/Mk (p. 635) and the mistreatment
occurred before the Sanhedrin trial (p. 636) were mentioned. References to omissions were more
numerous. These included the omission of: mention that Peter arrived at the house of the high
priest (p. 634), the investigation regarding the words about the Temple (p. 636), the prophecy
of the second coming of the Son of Man (p. 637), the condemnation because of blasphemy (p.
638), and the φραγελλώσις from A and the mistreatment by the soldiers (p. 643).
    131. Bernhard Weiss (1827-1916), Privatdozent (1852), assoc. prof. of NT in Königsberg
(1857), later prof. in Kiel (1863) and finally in Berlin (1876).
    132. *Zur Entstehungsgeschichte der drei synoptischen Evangelien*, in *TSK* 1 (1861) 29-100;
*Die Redestücke des apostolischen Matthäus. Mit besonderer Berücksichtigung von "Dr.
Holtzmann, Die synoptischen Evangelien"*, in *JDT* 9 (1864) 49-140; *Die Erzahlungsstücke des
apostolischen Matthäus*, in *JDT* 10 (1865), 319-376; *Das Marcusevangelium und seine
synoptischen Parallelen*, Berlin, 1872; *Die Evangelien des Markus und Lukas*, Göttingen, [6]1878,
[7]1885.
    133. *Marcusevangelium*, p. VII. Weiss credited H.J. Holtzmann (1863) with providing proof
of the secondary character of the two later Synoptics, their independence from one another and
their use of Q (p. 18).
    134. *Ibid.*, p. 14: "... dass in einer Reihe von Rede- und Erzählungsstücken unser Matthäus
dem Marcus gegenüber einen ursprünglicheren Text zeigt ...". See already p. 11: "Die
Ueberlieferung, aus welcher die Reihenfolge unserer Evangelien stammt, setzt also zunächst nur
voraus, dass jene älteste Apostelschrift älter ist als unser Marcusevangelium und dass dieses

In his most important work, *Das Marcusevangelium und seine synoptischen Parallelen* (1872), B. Weiss argued that for the detail that Jesus was led to the high priest with Peter following (Lk 22,54.55) Luke borrowed συλλαβόντες from Mk 14,48 and in the process of expanding the narrative with Jesus' entrance into the high priest's house, made it more explicit than it was in Mk[135]. Because Luke combined this material with the Peter's denials, the Sanhedrin trial followed (22,66). Luke's description of the servants sitting around and lighting a fire was an attempt to explain Mark's account more precisely. Luke borrowed the Markan expression πρὸς τὸ φῶς (Lk 22,56 / Mk 14,54).

For the story of Peter's denials (22,56-62 / Mk 14,66-72)[136] Weiss noticed Luke's immediate connection of the denial to the initial mention of Peter's lingering at the high priest's house (Mk 14,54) with reference to his sitting near the fire (from Mk 14,55) at 22,56, allowing the maid to identify Peter. Luke simplified the term for the maid (παιδίσκη τις) and employed ἀτενίζειν which he frequently used. The second question was addressed directly to Peter (22,58) as in Mk 14,67.70. The words καὶ σὺ ἐξ αὐτῶν (22,58) were based upon Mk 14,67(καὶ σύ).69(ἐξ αὐτῶν). By not adopting the Markan change of venue to the gateway, by indicating the passage of time, and by the use of vague references for the second and third challengers of Peter's association with Jesus, Luke intensified the denials.

Luke's use of Mk was further evidenced in Peter's response in which he heightened the final denial (22,60) by using Peter's answer from Mk 14,68. The agreement of Jesus' words about the denial (22,60 / Mk 14,72) also attested that Luke employed Mk[137]. Weiss recognized other echoes of Mk in ἄνθρωπε (22,58 / Mk 14,71 ἄνθρωπον) and the substitution of ὅ (22,60) for τί (Mk 14,68). Furthermore, Lukan redaction was responsible for the omission of ἐκ δευτέρου (Mk 14,72 / 22,61) because it was not included in Luke's version of the denial prediction (Mk 14,30 / 22,34).

Hints of another source, however, were suggested by the first and third statements of identification about Peter (22,56.59). Because of this difference and because the phrase σὺν αὐτῷ was unconnected, Weiss contended that another description was assumed in which Jesus had been named[138]. Finally, he attributed the MA in 22,62 / Mt 26,75 to the customary way Peter's conversion was described in the tradition[139].

The material from Lk 22,63-65 was set in parallel with Mk 14,65. Weiss called attention to Luke's revision of the material ("ganz freie Umgestaltung") by

---

wirklich auf schriftlichen Aufzeichnungen eines Augenzeugen mit beruht ...".

    135. *Ibid.*, p. 471. For material pertinent to Lk 22,54–23,25 see p. 469-493 (esp. p. 471, 476, 481, 482-483, 486, 491, 493).
    136. *Ibid.*, p. 481.
    137. *Ibid.*, p. 482, 483.
    138. *Ibid.*, p. 481.
    139. *Ibid.*, p. 483.

transposing the account of the mockery. The MA in 22,64 / Mt 26,68 was also ascribed to the tradition[140].

Luke revised the Sanhedrin trial (22,66-71) much more freely than Matthew[141]. Recollections of Mk were found in Jesus' avoidance of an answer (Mk 14,60.61) as well as the words drawn from the high priest to which had been added ἀπὸ τοῦ στόματος αὐτοῦ. In contrast, no judgment was pronounced. Other changes included omitting the testimony of the witnesses in order to proceed more immediately to the messiah question, dividing the question in Mk 14,61, placing ἐκ δεξιῶν before τῆς δυνάμεως with which τοῦ θεοῦ (22,69) was combined, and adding the phrase υἱὸς τοῦ θεοῦ (22,70). On account of the phrase ἀπὸ τοῦ νῦν Luke rightly omitted reference to the parousia.

Weiss credited Luke with situating the Sanhedrin trial at the break of day, allowing for the immediate transition to Pilate (23,1-4 / Mk 15,1-5)[142]. The evangelist attempted to extrapolate on the accusations made by the hierarchy and to formulate more charges (Mk 15,3). Further, 23,9.10 recalled Mk 15,3.4. In Weiss's opinion 23,11 was an obvious reminiscence from Mk 15,16-20[143].

An Attempted Rescue ("Ein Rettungsversuch"), as he entitled 23,16-25, contained many (unspecified) verbal reminiscences from Mk and Luke borrowed Mark's description of Barabbas[144]. The term στάσις (23,19 / Mk 15,7) was specifically referred to and βληθεὶς ἐν τῇ φυλακῇ (23,19) paraphrased δεδεμένος (Mk 15,7). A further Markan connection was κακόν (23,22 / Mk 15,14).

In order to appreciate B. Weiss's stance in 1901 we must consider how it evolved from his ideas in 1878. An important shift in his position occurred between the sixth edition of the Lukan commentary and the ninth edition concerning the use of a special source in the passion narrative. Initially he reached no conclusion: "Ob dieselbe [written source peculiar to Luke] grade südpalästinensischen Ursprungs (Köstlin, Holtzm., Mangold), ob sich auf sie alle dem Luk. eigenen Stoffe, insbesondere alle Abweichungen von Mark. in der Leidensgeschichte, zurückführen lassen, muss dahingestellt bleiben"[145]. He later amended his position due to Feine:

> Nun hat aber nach dem Vorgange von Weizsäcker und C. Wittichen [1881] Feine [1891] den Beweis erbracht, dass jene Stücke nach ihrem schriftstellerischen Charakter nicht nur unter sich, sondern auch mit Abschnitten in der ersten Hälfte der Apostelgeschichte, die ohne Frage eine Bearbeitung älterer Ueberlieferung zeigen, so auffallend übereinstimmen, dass sie aus einer einheitlichen Quelle stammen müssen. ... dass sie südpalästinensischen Ursprungs ist (Koestl., Hltzm., Mng., Aufl. 8), folgt aus wiederholten Berufungen auf in Judaea gesammelte

---

140. *Ibid.*, p. 477.
141. *Ibid.*, p. 476.
142. *Ibid.*, p. 486.
143. *Ibid.*, p. 493.
144. *Ibid.*, p. 491.
145. *Lukas*, ⁶1878, p. 239.

Ueberlieferungen; und dass sie jünger als Q, aus der Art, wie sichtlich an vielen
Stellen die Zerstörung Jerusalems bereits vorausgesetzt wird[146].

But since in the 1878 edition he had not yet been swayed by Feine, how did this
affect his interpretation? Because the sixth edition is a revision of Meyer's
commentary Weiss reacted to his propositions. In introductory remarks to the
denials, mockery and Sanhedrin trial (22,54-71) Weiss observed the difference in
order, asserting "Dies kann ohne Zweifel lediglich schriftstellerische Umgestaltung
sein" of Mark's presentation[147]. Luke's redactional reflection prompted him to
allow some time to pass, which he filled in with the mockery, so that the Sanhedrin
could assemble. Meyer, on the other hand, claimed a special tradition for the
mistreatment (22,63-65) as far as it harmonized with Jn[148].

Meyer wrongly assumed that Annas was the acting high priest and in so doing
posited another agreement with Jn to which Weiss objected that Lk contained
nothing about a trial before Annas (cf. Jn 18,19-24). Luke clearly redacted Mk for
the denials by retaining Markan expressions (e.g. πρὸς τὸ φῶς 22,56 / Mk 14,54)
but also by making some elements more explicit (the maid was clearly able to
recognize Peter by the light of the fire), by changing to third person from second
(22,59 dif. Mk 14,67.70) and by exact verbal agreements with Mk (Lk 22,61 until
the word σήμερον / Mk 14,72)[149].

Weiss rejected Meyer's assertion of a special source for the mockery: "V. 63-
65 beruht schwerlich auf besondrer Ueberlierferung (Meyer)"[150]. The change of
the mockers (Mk 14,65) emerged from the situation that Jesus was still in the
house waiting for the Sanhedrin.

Weiss observed how in Mark's version the Sanhedrin trial took place
immediately after Jesus was brought into the house of the high priest (Mk 14,55-
64). But because 1) there was no mention of witnesses, 2) of other details unique
to his account and 3) the change in time which occasioned a different order for the
mockery, Luke could have been following his own source (Lk 22,66-71)[151].
Weiss offered no comparisons with Mk, but noted the use of πρεσβυτέριον (22,66
- Acts 22,5).

In the section on Pilate and Herod (23,1-12) only 23,3 showed a literary
agreement with Mk 15,2 and the introduction of Herod pointed to a special Lukan
source[152]. Referring to the charge that Jesus stirred up (ἀνασείει) the people
(23,5) Weiss recalled the term in Mk 15,11. Undecided whether some details were

146. [9]1901, p. 259.
147. [6]1878, p. 573.
148. *Ibid.*; cf. H.A.W. MEYER, *Evangelien des Markus und Lukas*, Göttingen, [5]1867, p. 579:
"Luk. folgt einer ganz verschiedenen Ueberlieferung, verschieden hinsichtlich der Zeit, des Ortes
und der verspottenden Personen".
149. B. WEISS, [6]1878, p. 574-575.
150. *Ibid.*, p. 575.
151. *Ibid.*, p. 575-576.
152. *Ibid.*, p. 577.

due to Luke or his source, Weiss highlighted the report which assumed that Jesus was effective in Jerusalem, though these events were not recounted.

Weiss attributed the MA (22,62) to oral tradition which described the event more emphatically[153]. The source of the other MA (22,64) was not identified. He commented simply that it was an explanation of the bare Markan προφήτευσον.

In the account of sentencing Jesus to the cross (23,13-25) Weiss maintained that the material was like Mk 15,6-15 but almost entirely changed in presentation[154]. He contrasted the proposed chastisement (23,16) with Mk where the scourging took place after the crucifixion was authorized (Mk 15,15). In commenting on 23,18, he emphasized the lack of the people's initiative, the religious leaders stirring up the people and the allusion to the usual Passover amnesty all of which pointed to the use of a source[155]. It was in 23,18-25 that Weiss recognized the most connections with vocabulary in Acts[156]: αἶρε (23,18 - Acts 21,36; 22,22), προσεφώνησε (23,20 - Acts 21,40) both already cited by Meyer[157], and ἐπεφώνουν (23,21 - Acts 12,22; 22,24).

Meyer believed that the story of the sending of Jesus to Herod reflected originality and credited it to Luke's research, comparing it to Acts 4,27, while Weiss posited either Luke's investigation or his source[158]. He suggested that 23,9 recalled Mk 15,5 and noted the use of εὐτόνως (23,10; Acts 18,28), inviting comparison with Mk 15,3.4[159].

To rehearse briefly his views in the sixth edition, Weiss concluded that the transposition of the denials, mockery and Sanhedrin trial was the result of Lukan redaction. While he rejected the suggestion of a special source for the mockery (22,63-65), he considered it possible for the Sanhedrin trial (22,66-71). The reference to Herod and the sentencing of Jesus (23,18-25) pointed to a source other than Mk.

We turn next to the ninth edition of *Die Evangelien des Markus und Lukas*[160]. As regards Lk, even though it reproduced almost all of Mk and followed its order, Weiss did not consider this the primary proof of Lukan dependence upon Mk[161].

153. *Ibid.*, p. 575.
154. *Ibid.*, p. 580.
155. *Ibid.*, p. 581.
156. *Ibid.*, p. 581-582.
157. MEYER, ⁵1867, p. 587.
158. B. WEISS, ⁶1878, p. 580; cf. MEYER, ⁵1867, p. 586.
159. B. WEISS, ⁶1878, p. 579.
160. B. WEISS, *Die Evangelien des Markus und Lukas*, Göttingen, ⁹1901. It is important to note that this ninth edition was a complete revision of the eighth edition by J. WEISS (1892). B. Weiss wrote that the 8th edition had become an entirely new book (p. III). The elder Weiss criticized his son for having more deeply examined critical questions than was in keeping with the purpose of the Meyer commentary series: a commentary was not considered the proper genre for a response to such a detailed analysis of the vocabulary (p. 259, n. 1).
161. ⁹1901, p. 253-254. Weiss contended that while it cannot be proved from παρέδοσαν (1,2) neither can it be refuted that the traditions referred to in the Prologue already existed in

What was most convincing was that Lk appeared to be a revision of Mk, "stilistische, reflektirende und erläuternde Bearbeitung"[162]. Luke did not use Mt as a source[163], but was dependent upon "die apostolische Quelle" already in Greek translation. Weiss believed that Luke retained the more original order and form of Q[164]. Material peculiar to Lk was drawn from what was thought to be a unified source of unknown origin, designated "L". Here was the main point vis-à-vis J. Weiss: Luke (!) combined Q and L in a harmonizing fashion just as he joined the parallel traditions of Mk and L[165].

Obviously inspired by the detailed research of J. Weiss, B. Weiss drew attention to the striking freedom with which Luke treated Mark's passion story. Embracing the conclusion of J. Weiss, B. Weiss came to accept the passion narrative in Lk as having been composed with the help of another source[166]. In his view only isolated Markan reminiscences were inserted and in general the account differed materially and formally from Mk. There were completely unmotivated omissions of Markan material. Thus he concluded Luke undoubtedly ("zweifellos") followed another source. As to whether Luke used *Urmarkus* as J. Weiss supposed would become clear in his analysis of Lk.

Regarding the L source, Weiss admitted that not much was known of its origin. Although it was Jewish-Christian, the language characteristics were not so unique as to permit distinguishing it from Q or Mk. References to Judea indicated southern Palestinian roots. Finally, it was more recent than Q because the destruction of Jerusalem was assumed at many places[167]. Determining the extent of the source and the degree to which Luke borrowed from it remained the most difficult problem. Weiss believed that L was a written source and that sometimes

written form prior to Luke; even less can it be made clear from his vocabulary that he used one or more of his sources. Weiss reacted to Godet (*Lukas*, 1872), G.L. Hahn (Vol. 1, 1892) and Nösgen (1897) who rejected the theory of written sources and literary interdependence of the Synoptics. He stated that the majority position was that Luke used Mk as his main source.

162. *Ibid.*, p. 254, from B. WEISS, *Einleitung* (1886, ²1889), p. 538, and noted by J. Weiss (cf. ⁸1892, p. 275).

163. *Lukas*, ⁹1901, p. 255. Weiss asserted that since C.H. WEISSE, *Die evangelische Geschichte kritisch und philosophisch bearbeitet*, Leipzig, 1838, the majority position was that Luke did not know Mt. A reason for rejecting Luke's use of Mt was that Lk contained none of the verbal peculiarities characteristic of Mt.

164. ⁹1901, p. 255; cf. ⁶1878, p. 238: "Ebendaselbst ist auch nachgewiesen, wie Luk. in jenen beiden Einschaltungen (6,20–8,8. 9,51–18,14) vorzugsweise die Stoffe der apostolischen Quelle, grossentheils in ihrer ursprünglichen Ordnung und vielfach in ursprünglicher Gestalt, in den aus Mark. entlehnten Rahmen seiner Erzählung eingeschaltet hat".

165. B. WEISS, *Lukas*, ⁹1901, p. 260.

166. *Ibid.*, p. 254: "Lk 19 und 22-24 ... Lk (folgt) hier zweifellos einer andern Ueberlieferung". See also p. 258: on sayings material (diff. Mt): "genau derselbe Fall ..., wie bei seinem Verhältniss zu Mk in der Leidensgeschichte". See further p. 259: "(ist) sie südpalästinensischen Ursprungs".

167. B. WEISS, *Lukas*, p. 259. Because of references to the destruction of Jerusalem (19,42f.; 21,24), Lk was clearly composed after that event, but the dating of the Gospel, in Weiss's opinion, cannot extend beyond 80 AD (p. 263).

Luke preferred it to Mk while at other times he joined the two accounts. Agreeing, in principle, that Luke knew and used a unique, unified source designated as L, B. Weiss proposed that Luke derived some material from oral tradition and in other cases combined the two documents[168].

B. Weiss thought πολλοί (1,1) meant Luke had two, perhaps three sources at most, among which would be counted his special L source[169]. He expressed agreement with Feine, who, in his opinion, supplied proof that some material from Lk and some sections in the first half of Acts derived from a unified source which constituted a revision of older traditions. Further, he affirmed that J. Weiss was likewise correct in assuming that Luke drew on a unified special source, a conclusion based on J. Weiss's careful study of the vocabulary[170].

However, in contrast to J. Weiss, B. Weiss insisted that although the vocabulary was Jewish-Christian, it could not be distinguished from Q or Mk. The most perplexing problem, according to B. Weiss, was to what extent Luke borrowed from the special source[171]. He also disagreed with the solutions offered by Feine and J. Weiss because they did not solve the chief problem of the numerous verbal agreements between the Matthean and Lukan Q material on the one hand, and the frequent differences in their form and content on the other. Instead the proposed solutions simply pushed them back to a pre-canonical source. B. Weiss preferred the solution that L did not contain a revision of Q, but comprised parallel traditions as well as speech material derived from oral tradition. In his view, Luke combined Q and L in the same fashion as he had Mk and L. Such an interweaving of Q with L overcomes these obstacles in his view.

How did this theory apply to the passion? Specifically with regard to the denials, mockery and Sanhedrin trial (22,54-71) Weiss explained this section as "wieder Mk 14,53-72 gegenüber in mehrfacher Beziehung ganz eigenthümlich"[172]. Here he reversed his 1878 position, and the issue of order resurfaced when he claimed that the reference to Jesus having to wait until the Sanhedrin could assemble resulted not from Luke's reflection on Mk, but from one of the not infrequent

---

168. *Ibid.*, p. 260. Reference to nr. 2 = p. 254. Weiss noted that, although Schleiermacher's thesis (1817) that Lk was a compilation of individual written documents had long since been refuted, many still subscribed to the view that the special material was drawn from a variety of written sources (p. 258). Cf. F. SCHLEIERMACHER, *Über die Schriften des Lukas.*

169. B. WEISS, ⁹1901, p. 259; see also p. 264, n. 1.

170. *Ibid.*, p. 259: "Mit vollem Rechte ist daher J. Weiss (8. Aufl.) von der Annahme einer solchen einheitlichen dem Lk eigenthümlichen Quelle (Sigle: L.) ausgegangen und hat sie durch überaus sorgfältige sprachliche Nachweisungen im Einzelnen zu begründen versucht". Like J. Weiss, B. Weiss rejected Simons's solution (p. 254). Note the incorrect date (1890) assigned to Simons (p. 256).

171. *Ibid.*, p. 260.

172. *Ibid.*, p. 652.

reminiscences of the Johannine tradition (Jn 18,13) found in L[173]. Though he accepted Markan influence for neither συλλαβόντες (22,54 - Acts 1,16; cf. Mk 14,48) - a shift from his 1872 position - nor καὶ γὰρ Γαλιλαῖός ἐστιν (22,59 / Mk 14,70)[174], he recognized Markan influence in numerous other instances: μακρόθεν (22,54 / Mk 14,54)[175]; πρὸς τὸ φῶς (22,56) was definitely from Mk 14,54[176]; ἰδοῦσα αὐτόν (22,56 / Mk 14,67)[177]; οὐκ οἶδα ὃ λέγεις (22,60 / Mk 14,68); the cock crow (22,60 / Mk 14,72)[178]; ὑπεμνήσθη (22,61) was certainly a recollection of ἀνεμνήσθη (Mk 14,72); and ὡς εἶπεν αὐτῷ ὅτι (22,61) corresponded with Mk 14,72 and was redactionally joined with τοῦ λόγου (v.l.) τοῦ κυρίου[179]. Weiss commented further on the Lukan relationship to Mk: "Das wird aber unzweifelhaft dadurch, dass das Warnungswort Jesu bis auf das hinzugefügt σήμερον ganz mit Mk V. 72 stimmt im Unterschiede von V. 34, und bestätigt damit, dass auch der Hahnenschrei V. 60 aus Mk herstammt"[180]. Though other scholars sought to identify 22,66 with Mk 15,1, B. Weiss maintained this effort failed, in part, since the account lacked a definitive judgment[181].

J. Weiss apparently influenced B. Weiss in identifying ὁ κύριος as frequently occurring in L[182] and in the use of στραφείς citing three of the instances J. Weiss assigned to LQ[183]. But he objected that it was not clear how J. Weiss could claim that the Lukan report of the denials was "reflektirter und pragmatischer"[184]. An indication of a connection of this story in Luke's special source with Jn was that the report of the denials happened immediately in the house of Annas[185]. B. Weiss continued to argue that the denials reflected an

---

173. *Ibid.*; cf. [6]1878, p. 573.

174. *Ibid.*, p. 652, 654. He maintained this need not be a reminiscence of Mk, but easily could have been composed in the tradition. See *Marcusevangelium*, p. 471, 481.

175. Also Lk 18,13.

176. *Ibid.*, p. 653.

177. *Ibid.* Whereas Mark had ἰδοῦσα τὸν Πέτρον ... ἐμβλέψασα αὐτῷ, Luke employed ἀτενίσασα αὐτῷ (as in 4,20 and often in Acts). Weiss was less sure about τις located near παιδίσκη which could have originated from Mk or might have stemmed from the original story (L).

178. *Ibid.*, p. 655. n. 1. B. Weiss registered his rejection of J. Weiss's view that Mk represented "eine künstlichere Steigerung unseres Bericht" (cf. [8]1892, p. 635). The L account was completely different from Mk except for reminiscences in 22,54.60f.

179. B. WEISS, [9]1901, p. 654. The ὁ κύριος (v. 61) was an echo of the source in Weiss's opinion. Again, J. Weiss had not addressed the similarity with Mk.

180. *Ibid.* While he maintained his position that 22,61 originated in Mk 14,42, he more carefully contrasted the wording of 22,34 in [6]1878, p. 575.

181. [9]1901, p. 656.

182. [9]1901, p. 654; [8]1892, p. 635.

183. *Ibid.*; cf. [6]1878, p. 574-575.

184. [9]1901, p. 652; cf. [8]1892, p. 634.

185. *Ibid.*, p. 652. Another sign of the Lk-Jn relationship was the οὐκ εἰμί (22,58) which recalled Jn 18,17.25 (p. 654).

intensification[186]. The omission of Peter's cursing and swearing (ἀναθεματίζειν καὶ ὀμνύναι) was yet another indication to Weiss that Luke was not following Mk.

Weiss began his discussion of the mockery (22,63-65) by referring to the different order of the account found in Luke's special source. Even though B. Weiss did not treat αὐτόν in 22,63 directly, he referred to earlier occurrences, indicating that an original text was altered by an insertion. "Dass aber hier ein ursprünglicher Text durch Einschaltung geändert ist, zeigt das auf das αὐτόν V. 54 zurückweisende σὺν αὐτῷ (vgl. V. 14), was doch zu ungeschickt wäre, wenn, der es schrieb, eben vorher ein auf ὁ Πέτρος V. 55 bezügliches αὐτόν geschrieben hätte"[187]. The αὐτόν (22,64) indicated, according to Weiss, that Mark's account was not available to him[188]. Arguing that 22,63-65 was not possibly a revision of Mk 14,65, Weiss contended "da kein Bearbeiter das einfache περικαλύπτειν αὐτοῦ τὸ πρόσωπον in das unklare περικαλύψαντες αὐτόν verwandeln konnte"[189]. He observed that the mockery did not proceed to the spitting as found in Mk. B. Weiss also repudiated J. Weiss's suggestion that the Lukan account was more original[190]. But for the rest he agreed with J. Weiss that the changes could not be attributed to redaction ("schriftstellerische Reflexion").

The account of the Sanhedrin trial (22,66-71) ought to be the same as what was recounted in Mk 14,53-64. Since nothing was said about the location, Weiss surmised this was a reminiscence of the tradition in Jn 18,24. Because the high priest played no role in the Lukan account, Weiss regarded this as evidence that Luke had not reflected upon Mk 14,61[191]. Consequently, Luke completely passed over the Markan witness trial (Mk 14,55-61) and out of the whole trial only the answer of Jesus to the official about the Messiah question was given prominence. Whereas J. Weiss concluded on the basis of the phrase τί ἔτι ἔχομεν μαρτυρίας χρείαν (v. 71) that a trial with witnesses had taken place in another assembly[192], B. Weiss maintained that this phrase definitely, and the expression ἐγώ εἰμι (v. 70) perhaps, were indications of Markan reminiscences[193]. B. Weiss disagreed with J. Weiss who contended that this verse proved there was a trial with witnesses which occurred in another meeting, probably with Annas[194]. But he agreed with J. Weiss that the division of the claim to be the Son of God from the future

186. *Ibid.*, p. 654; ⁶1878, p. 574.

187. *Ibid.*, p. 653.

188. *Ibid.*, p. 655-656.

189. *Ibid.*, p. 223. Cf. B. WEISS, *Die Quellen der synoptischen Überlieferung*, 1908, p. 156.

190. *Lukas*, ⁹1901, p. 656, n. 1: "Dass die Darstellung, welche die Misshandlung auf die Knechte allein überträgt, die ursprüngliche sei (Aufl. 8), ist schon dadurch ausgeschlossen, dass diese ja auch bei Mk an ihr betheiligt sind".

191. *Ibid.*, p. 657. Weiss observed that a Gentile writer such as Luke might not be privy to many of the details of Jewish law or how certain officials functioned within their respective system.

192. J. WEISS, ⁸1892, p. 638, n. 1.

193. B. WEISS, ⁹1901, p. 658.

194. *Ibid.*; cf. ⁸1892, p. 638, n. 1.

Messiah "...(ist) für die judenchristliche Quelle des Lk (L) sehr
charakteristisch"[195]. However, it did not follow that Mark's was a later
reconstruction, only that Mk and L were completely independent of one another.
     B. Weiss explained both MAs as resting upon oral tradition. He attributed the
agreement in 22,62 / Mt 26,75 to the customary way the event was described in
the tradition using an OT expression[196]. He dismissed the proposal that τίς ἐστιν
ὁ παίσας σε; derived from Mt 26,68 because it lacked περικαλύψαντες. He
rebuffed J. Weiss's solution that the phrase τίς ἐστιν ὁ παίσας σε (22,64) was
later omitted from *Urmarkus*[197].
     Turning to Lk 23, B. Weiss proposed the possibility that the source contained
only a general reference to Pilate hearing the charges which Luke expanded
through his use of Mk, harmonizing his sources[198]. In support of this view,
Weiss remarked that while Lk 23,3 verbally resembled Mk 15,2, 23,1 lacked any
reminiscences of Mk 15,1[199], and vv. 1-2 did not show the slightest connection
with Mk 15,1. Yet he observed κατηγορεῖν αὐτοῦ (23,2) "wie Mk 15,3". B.
Weiss countered the position of J. Weiss who contended that the charge that Jesus
forbade people to pay their taxes arose at the time of Luke[200]. Weiss highlighted
the similarity of ἀνασείει (23,5) with Mk 15,11.
     B. Weiss's assessment of the sentencing to the cross (23,13-25) likewise
changed. Whereas he earlier stated this section was "sachlich gleich Mark. 15,6-
15, aber in der Darstellung fast ganz abweichend"[201], in the later edition he
maintained that it was "parallel" with the Markan section, "aber nach Inhalt und

---

195. B. WEISS, ⁹1901, p. 658-659, n. 1; J. WEISS, ⁸1892, p. 637-638.
196. B. WEISS, ⁹1901, p. 654 (22,62) and 656 (22,64). In B. WEISS, *Das Matthäus-evangelium und seine Lucas-Parallelen*, Halle, 1876, p. 560, he basically repeated his position of 1872 for the MA in 22,62 / Mt 26,75. He passed over in silence the other MA as a textual problem (cf. p. 559). See also B. WEISS, *Das Matthäus-Evangelium* (KEK), Göttingen, ¹⁰1910. No mention was made at 26,68 of the MA, but Weiss invited comparison with Num 22,28 and Is 14,29 (p. 471). Nor did he refer to the MA at 26,75. He indicated that ἐξελθὼν ἔξω was drawn from Mk 14,68 and he compared πικρῶς with Is 22,4; 33,7 (p. 473). See also his *Handbuch über das Evangelium Matthäus*, Göttingen, ⁷1883, p. 528, in which he attributed the phrase in Mt 26,68 to a later tradition, but definitely excluded the possibility that Luke borrowed from Mt. He did not treat Lk 22,61 / Mt 26,75 as a MA (⁷1883, p. 529-530; ¹⁰1910, p. 473).
197. B. WEISS, ⁹1901, p. 656. n. 1. He continued: "Im Uebrigen wird gerade hier recht klar, wie jede schriftstellerische Berührung zwischen der Quelle des Lk und Mk fehlt, da ihre Abweichungen von ihm unmöglich auf schriftstellerische Reflexion zurückgeführt werden können". Cf. J. WEISS, ⁸1892, p. 635-636, n. 2.
198. B. WEISS, ⁹1901, p. 659-660.
199. *Ibid.*, p. 659: "Dass Jesus sich unumwunden zu seinem Königthum bekannt haben soll, fällt hier um so mehr auf, als die Hierarchen eben noch alle politischen Konsequenzen deselben gezogen haben". The similarity between 23,3 and Mk 15,2 can be "nur eine der harmonisirenden Reminiscenzen des Lk aus Mk". Weiss suggested that this was mentioned generally in the source, noting a reminiscence of the Johannine tradition in Jn 18,36ff. On 23,3 as a Markan insertion see also p. 662.
200. *Ibid.*, p. 659; cf. J. WEISS, ⁸1892, p. 639.
201. B. WEISS, ⁶1878, p. 580.

Form fast ganz eigenthümlich, daher sicher der Grundlage nach aus L"[202]. It was entirely clear that the account of the trial in the other story was presented differently than the Markan version. Yet the αὐτούς (23,14) exhibited similarity with Mk 10,13[203]. B. Weiss rejected J. Weiss's suggestion that πρὸς ἡμᾶς (v. 15) constituted the plural of majesty[204]. Whereas previously B. Weiss simply noted that the scourging was absent in Lk 23,25 diff. Mk 15,15[205], in the ninth edition Weiss conceded that Luke probably had in mind the scourging in Mk 15,15 when he penned παιδεύσας (23,16)[206]. In Weiss's opinion there was also a reminiscence of the Johannine tradition in Pilate's use of the scourging (Jn 19,1) which in Lk remained only a suggestion[207]. As in the cases of 23,3.10, Weiss viewed the words αἶρε τοῦτον (23,18) and ὅστις (23,19) as reminiscences from Mk, in this case Mk 15,7[208]. The dual points that Barabbas was imprisoned and that he was being offered freedom were also highlighted in the Markan account[209]. Because there had been neither previous mention in the Lukan account of the passover amnesty custom nor of Barabbas, the sudden demand for his release, without the least consideration from Pilate, was "ganz undenkbar"[210]. The question τί γὰρ κακὸν ἐποίησεν οὗτος (23,22) was a reminiscence of Mk 15,14[211]. Finally, 23,25 was a reminiscence of Mk 15,15 in light of other additions made in 23,18ff.[212]. Mk also supplied the "charakteristische" term παρέδωκεν. The θελήματι harkened back to 22,42 and clarified that 23,25 was a commentary taken from Mk. The ἠτοῦντο was a Markan reminiscence (Mk 15,6).

Though in the sixth edition Weiss assigned the introduction of Herod to Luke's special source, in the ninth edition he stated this was certain ("gewiss"), adding that it was the origin of the entire passion narrative[213]. Weiss, nonetheless, found certain similarities with Mk: καὶ αὐτόν (23,7 - Mk 15,43)[214]; the silence of Jesus (23,9 - reminiscent of Mk 14,61; 15,5)[215]; εἱστήκεισαν (23,10 - Mk 9,1)[216]; εὐτόνως (23,10 - Mk 15,3, a Markan reminiscence inserted by Luke, already noted

---

202. *Ibid.*, ⁹1901, p. 662.
203. *Ibid.* προσηνέγκατέ μοι (23,14) was similar to Mk 10,13 *v.l.*
204. *Ibid.*, p. 663; cf. J. WEISS, ⁸1892, p. 642.
205. B. WEISS, ⁶1878, p. 581.
206. *Ibid.*, ⁹1901, p. 663; cf. B. WEISS, ⁶1878, p. 581. He disputed J. Weiss's argument for 23,16 that the *Urmarkus* report "ist ... viel motivirter und fortgeschrittener als der einfache des Lk" (⁸1892, p. 642; cf. B. WEISS, ⁹1901, p. [663]-664, n. 1).
207. *Ibid.*, p. 663.
208. *Ibid.*, ⁹1901, p. 664.
209. *Ibid.* Cf. B. WEISS, ⁶1878, p. 581.
210. B. WEISS, ⁹1901, p. 664.
211. *Ibid.* In ⁶1878, only γάρ was indicated as similar to Mk 15,14 (p. 582).
212. B. WEISS, ⁹1901, p. 665.
213. *Ibid.*, p. 660; ⁶1878, p. 577.
214. Cf. ⁶1878, p. 578.
215. Partially already in ⁶1878, p. 579.
216. Cf. ⁶1878, p. 579.

by J. Weiss)[217]. B. Weiss also highlighted connections of the Herod pericope with other parts of the Gospel: ἐπιγνούς (23,7 - 7,37)[218], ἐξουσίας (23,7 - 4,6)[219], ἐξ ἱκανῶν χρόνων (23,8 cf. 8,29 πολλοῖς γὰρ χρόνοις)[220], ὑπ' αὐτοῦ γινόμενον (23,8 - 13,17)[221], οἱ ἀρχιερεῖς καὶ οἱ γραμματεῖς (23,10 - 22,2)[222], ἐξουθενήσας (23,11 - 18,9)[223], φίλοι (23,12 - 16,9)[224] and ἐν αὐτῇ τῇ ἡμέρᾳ (23,12 - 13,31[225], the verse dealing with Herod's desire to kill Jesus). He demonstrated verbal relationships with Acts which are listed below.

Further, Weiss attempted to isolate the vocabulary of L: ἐξουσία (20,20; 22,53; 23,7), ἐπιγνούς ὅτι (1,22; 7,37; 23,7), ἐξουθενεῖν (18,9; 23,11), ἐμπαίξας (14,29; 22,63; 23,11.36). However, in examining this collection closely, we observed that ἐξουσία occurred in both the LXX and Mk. Its use in 20,20, in all probability an editorial comment introduced by Luke, set the stage for the charges in 23,2 in much the same way that 9,9 prepared for Jesus' trial before Herod. The term ἡγεμόνων is found at Mk 13,9 / Lk 21,12, and occurred a total of seventeen times in the Synoptic Gospels[226], in addition to thirteen instances in Acts, and in the LXX. The word ἐξουθενεῖν, also a Septuagintal term, appeared in Mk 9,1[227]. The same is true of ἐμπαίξας, occurring both in the LXX and Mk (Mk 10,34 / Lk 18,32; Mk 15,20 / cf. Lk 23,11; Mk 15,31 / cf. Lk 23,36). This last example used the term of the soldiers rather than of the high priests. But Luke earlier employed ἐκμυκτηρίζω (16,14) of the Pharisees. The term also occurred in LXX Ps 21,8a (= NAB 22,8; NRSV 22,7). Although the word στρατεύματα (23,11) is unique, στρατιῶται is found in other places in the Gospel (7,8; 23,36).

Overall, in the ninth edition, B. Weiss was much more alert not only to the similar occurrences of words in other parts of Lk but in Acts as well[228]. For the denials, mockery and Sanhedrin trial these included: συλλαβόντες (22,54; Acts 1,16; 12,3), εἰσήγαγον εἰς (22,54; Acts 21,28f.), ἀτενίσασα αὐτῷ (22,56; 4,20; often

217. [9]1901, p. 661; J. WEISS, [8]1892, p. 640. Already in [6]1878, B. Weiss compared 23,10 with Mk 15,3.4 (p. 579) but his later assertion was more explicit.
218. Cf. [6]1878, p. 578.
219. Cf. [6]1878, p. 578.
220. Cf. [6]1878, p. 579.
221. Cf. [6]1878, p. 579.
222. Cf. [6]1878, p. 579.
223. Cf. [6]1878, p. 579.
224. Cf. [6]1878, p. 579.
225. Cf. [6]1878, p. 579.
226. NTV, p. 251. Weiss listed the term in 7,37. J. JEREMIAS, Die Sprache, 1980, p. 168, considered it to be Lukan redaction. Note the parallels: Mk 2,8 / Lk 5,22; Mk 5,30 / Lk 8,46, where Luke transformed the Markan statement into direct speech (Mk 6,33 / Lk 9,11).
227. Although some mss contained ἐξουδενωθῇ, the significance was still the same.
228. It was apparent from a comparison of the ninth edition ([9]1901) with the sixth ([6]1878, p. 574, 576, 578, 579, 580, 581, 582), that the vocabulary common to Lk and Acts became an increasingly significant element of B. Weiss's study.

in Acts), βραχύ (22,58; Acts 5,34), διϊσχυρίζετο (22,59; Acts 12,15), βλασφημοῦντες (22,65; Acts 13,45), λέγειν εἰς (22,65; Acts 2,25), συνήχθη (22,66; Acts 4,5), μαρτυρίας (22,71; Acts 22,18). Weiss also noted the similarity of thought between 22,70 and Acts 2,36[229].

In Lk 23, he highlighted the following connections: κατηγορεῖν αὐτοῦ (23,2; Acts 25,5), κωλύοντα with the infinitive (23,2; Acts 16,6), αἴτιον (23,4; Acts 19,40), mention of Galilee (23,5; Acts 5,37; 10,37), ἀνέπεμψεν (23,7; Acts 25,21), ἐσθῆτα λαμπράν (23,11; Acts 10,30), προϋπῆρχον (23,12; Acts 8,9), ἀνακρίνας (22,14; Acts 24,8), ἄξιον (23,15; Acts 25,11), αἶρε τοῦτον (23,18; Acts 21,36; 22,22), προσεφώνησεν αὐτοῖς (23,20; Acts 22,2). It should be noted that Weiss differentiated between the use of ἄρχοντες in Acts 3,17 where it referred to the priests from its use in 23,13[230].

Links between this section of the Gospel and (generally) earlier portions did not escape his attention: ἐὰν εἴπω (22,67; cf. 20,5f.), ἀπὸ τοῦ νῦν (22,69; 22,18), αὐτοὶ ἠκούσαμεν ἀπὸ τοῦ στόματος αὐτοῦ (22,71; cf. 1,70; 11,54; 19,22), ἀναστάν (23,1; 4,29), ἅπαν τὸ πλῆθος (23,1; cf. 1,10; 19,37), ἐπί with acc. (23,1; 21,12), ἤγαγον (23,1; 22,54), τὸ ἔθνος ἡμῶν (23,2; 7,5), χριστός (23,2; 2,11), ὄχλους (23,4; 14,25), καθ᾽ ὅλης (23,5; cf. 4,14), συγκαλεσάμενος (23,13; 9,1), τὸν ἄνθρωπον τοῦτον (23,14; cf. 23,4), ὡς (23,14; 16,1), τὸν λαόν (23,14; 23,5; also 23,13), ἐγώ (23,14.15), ἐνώπιον (23,14; 8,47), ἀνέπεμψεν (23,15 referred back to 23,11), ἀπολύσω (23,16; 22,68 v.l.), ἀνέκραγον (23,18; 8,28), ὅστις (23,19; 7,37), φυλακῇ (23,19; 3,20), θέλων (23,20; 23,8), "die Wiederholte Unschuldserklärung" (23,22; 23.4.14), ἐπέκειντο (23,23; 5,1), φωναῖς μεγάλαις (23,23; 4,33), θελήματι (23,25; 22,42).

While B. Weiss's general position remained constant, the later commentary reflected his efforts to highlight similarities within the Gospel and Acts, and in some cases, with Mk. He also delineated the Herod passage as 23,6-12, which he had not done in the sixth edition.

J. Weiss reviewed the ninth edition of the commentary observing that B. Weiss refuted the *Urmarkus* theory "Punkt für Punkt". B. Weiss concurred with J. Weiss that Luke used a non-Markan source in the passion narrative (L)[231], but refused the latter's suggestion that Luke employed a combined version of L and Q. Instead B. Weiss assumed that each of those sources contained parallels of much of the speech and story material which Luke then blended together in a harmonizing fashion[232]. Despite the differences, J. Weiss recommended the book: "So ist

---

229. B. WEISS, ⁹1901, p. 658.
230. *Ibid.*, p. 662.
231. J. WEISS, *Synoptische Fragen*, in *TR* 6 (1903) 199-211 (esp. p. 200-201). Cf. B. WEISS, *Lukas*, ⁹1901, p. 259.
232. J. WEISS, *Synoptische Fragen*, p. 201.

dieser Kommentar ein neues Buch geworden, das kein Lukasexeget ohne Schaden unberücksichtigt lassen darf"[233].

One critic outside the continent, H.A.A. Kennedy, observed B. Weiss's running dialogue with the eighth edition "largely in the way of criticism"[234]. Somewhat surprisingly, J. Weiss was described as an adherent of Weizsäcker's theory, with no mention of Feine. B. Weiss's recourse to "the ever-convenient factor of oral tradition" to explain some of the Mt-Lk agreements seems not to have been convincing in this case. More to the reviewer's liking was the demonstration that what J. Weiss had assumed to be additions were "in style and conception" Markan materials. Attention was drawn to the fact that B. Weiss adopted J. Weiss's view of a special Lukan source and to how very different were their conceptions of how Lk was composed. While the reviewer was obviously impressed by only some of Weiss's solutions, he had a great respect for the German exegete[235].

Detailed attention to the sources of Lk became the focus of two later studies by B. Weiss[236]. In *Die Quellen des Lukasevangeliums* (1907)[237] he analyzed Lk

233. *Ibid.*

234. *ExpT* 13 (1901-02) 544-545, p. 544: "Indeed, their theories as to the composition of the Gospels are so divergent that the older scholar feels it necessary to go much more elaborately into critical questions than has been his custom, of set purpose, in former revisions of Meyer. Hence we have a full though concise introduction to Luke".

235. *Ibid.*, p. 545: "Whether we agree with the suggested solutions of the various problems or not, the Introduction is valuable as presenting us with the mature conclusions of a most careful and judicious scholar in a department of criticism to which he has devoted the energies of a long and strenuous life".

236. B. WEISS, *Die Quellen des Lukasevangeliums*, 1907 (esp. p. 220-228); *Die Quellen der synoptischen Überlieferung* (TU 32/5), 1908 (esp. p. 97-198, 235-253). The 1907 study contained five chapters which treated 1) Lk and Mk, 2) Lk and the Matthean source, 3) Lk and the Matthean source in Markan parallels, 4) the Lukan source, and 5) the composition of Lk. For the second work, Weiss attempted to construct "den Text der Matthäus- und Lukasquelle" (*Vorwort*, p. III) (p. 97-198 for Luke) followed by a discussion of 1) the material and order of the special source, 2) its character and 3) vocabulary (p. 169-198). A final section within "Die jüngeren Evangelien" was devoted to Lk (p. 235-253).

237. Feine offered this comment in his *Einleitung*: "In der Schrift über die Quellen des *Lkev*. 1907 baut WEISS seine Hypothese betreffend das *Lkev*. dahin aus, dass er das ganze Sondergut des *Lk*. aus einer einheitlichen judenchristlichen Quellenschrift herleitet" (1913, p. 115).

In an essay treating the state of the question of the Synoptic problem, Henry Latimer Jackson made use of this work by Weiss, though this was only one among many. In writing of resemblances among the Synoptics Jackson observed: "the 'drama of the Passion' unfolds itself in striking concert" (*The Present State of the Synoptic Problem*, in H.B. SWETE [ed.], *Essays on Some Biblical Questions of the Day by Members of the University of Cambridge*, London, 1909, 421-460, p. 428). In his discussion of Markan priority he called also attention to Lukan priority in stating that "voices are faintly heard on behalf of Luke (cf. Spitta on Noack and Mandel)" (p. 437; cf. SPITTA, *Streitfragen*). He maintained, however, that "there is widespread agreement that our Second Gospel is 'not excerpt but ingredient' (Wellhausen) of the other two Synoptics" (JACKSON, p. 438). He listed four books by Wellhausen in his bibliography but did not specify to which he was referring in this case (cf. p. 460).

with characteristic precision and care and attempted to show that in 22,54–23,25 the evangelist blended two distinct, but sometimes harmonious accounts. For the story of Peter's denials (22,55-62) Luke borrowed from Mk 14,54 to expand 22,54b. The first denial was taken from Mk 14,66f.[238]. Weiss noted the unique phrase πρὸς τὸ φῶς appeared in both the Markan and Lukan accounts[239]. On the other hand, Luke would certainly not have used the general phrase σὺν αὐτῷ (22,56) to replace μετὰ τοῦ Ναζαρηνοῦ (Mk 14,67)[240]. The reference in 22,56 that Peter had been "with him" reflected the havoc played by the Markan insertion[241]. The phrase οὐκ οἶδα ὃ λέγεις was a reminiscence from Mk 14,70.68. Luke's method of harmonizing the two accounts became especially clear at the end of the account of Peter's denial where Luke combined material from Mk 14,72 and the δίς from Mk 14,30.

The account of the abuse of Jesus (22,63-65) also stemmed from L to fill out the time between the arrest of Jesus and the trial. This decision was based on the observation that in the Markan version the religious leaders mistreated Jesus and later the servants took a turn. In the L account other blasphemies were directed to Jesus. Therefore, although 22,64 reminded one of Mk 14,65, Weiss dismissed the latter as a source, considering it only a parallel tradition[242].

In a discussion of the sources of Mt and Lk, Jackson claimed that "the priority of Mark is an established result" and the "prevailing opinion is that a main source of the later Evangelists is the Mark Gospel" (p. 444). Regarding Luke's treatment of Mk Jackson argued he freely redacted it, which included seven transpositions. He further stipulated, "[Luke] too is prompt with emendation and alteration, not in comparatively trivial details only, but often in respect of graver matters. Thus in the story of the Passion there are numerous and conspicuous variations from the Marcan record. Something is expunged and something substituted ... In the case of both Gospels [Mt and Lk] matter drawn from other sources will have been interwoven with the borrowings from Mark" (p. 447).

As for sources beyond Mk and Q Jackson surmised: "Two extreme hypotheses are instanced. According to the one the matter peculiar to Matthew and Luke is attributed to a written source, an ancient and lost Gospel; the other attributes it to the free invention of the Evangelists. As thus stated, neither can be entertained; the theory of an Ur-evangelium will find but few supporters; an evangelist capable of inventing all the parables, narrative, incidents, in question might equally well have been inventor of Christianity itself (Wernle). When narrowed down and modified it may be conceded, however, that elements of truth are contained in them. To begin, something will unquestionably be due to the Evangelists themselves; ... In the second place, there may well be a question, not indeed of an Ur-evangelium, but of written sources" (p. 452). Adopting the position of Wernle, Jackson subscribed to the view that Luke employed other written sources and handled them with as much freedom as he had Mk and Q and in accord with Nicolardot, we do not know the full extent of Luke's sources (p. 453). He also recognized that, "some resort to oral tradition is generally admitted", which in the case of Luke may have been information supplied by Philip and his daughters as Harnack proposed.

238. B. WEISS, *Die Quellen des Lukasevangeliums*, 1907, p. 220.

239. *Ibid.*, p. 220-221.

240. *Ibid.*, p. 221.

241. *Ibid.*

242. *Ibid.*, p. 222-223. Weiss rejected this possible relationship because of difference in time,

In reaction to J. Weiss (⁸1892), B. Weiss continued to argue that the phrase τίς ἐστιν ὁ παίσας σε; stemmed from the oral tradition, and may have already stood in the L source, though such a contention could not be proven²⁴³. For the MA in 22,62 the solution of an omission by a later redactor of *Urmarkus* was rejected. Weiss detected some similarity with Is 22,4 but opted to resolve the matter of both MAs by recourse to oral tradition²⁴⁴.

Weiss insisted that the Markan and Lukan versions of the Sanhedrin trial (22,66-71) were entirely different because the version in Lk occurred at daybreak, Jesus was led to the high priest's house (22,54) and then to "their council" (22,66), as opposed to being led to the high priest (Mk 14,53), and on account of the omission of the witness's testimony which permitted an immediate transition to the question of Messiahship. The Lukan account must be based upon a Jewish-Christian source rather than be the redaction of Mk by a Gentile. Nevertheless, Weiss drew our attention to a few common elements between Mk and Lk. The trial occurred before the second cock crow and τῆς δυνάμεως (22,69) possibly reflected Markan influence from Mk 14,62²⁴⁵. Luke added ὅτι ἐγώ εἰμι (v. 70) from Mk 14,62 as well as τί ἔτι ἔχομεν μαρτυρίας χρείαν (v. 71) from Mk 14,63.

Moving next to Pilate's trial, all of 23,3 was exactly as found in Mk 15,2 and 23,4 was expanded from Mk 15,2. Weiss found it even more incomprehensible than in the case of Mk that Pilate should declare Jesus innocent on the basis of his response in 23,3 but it was colored by the evangelist's presupposition as a believer. A resonance of Mk 15,3f. was found in 23,9b.10 and Luke incorrectly assumed that the trial with Herod must have transpired like the trial before Pilate.

Weiss claimed that the section leading to the crucifixion (23,18-25) was drawn from the special source, to which was added details from Mk. The Passover amnesty was not related in the source nor was there reference to the religious leadership stirring up the people to oppose Pilate's recommendation. Deduction led Weiss to the view that 23,18 was an addition to the source. Information about Barabbas in 23,19 stemmed from Mk 15,7 just as Mk 15,13f. was taken up in 23,22. The phrases τί γὰρ ἐποίησεν and οὐδὲν αἴτιον θανάτου εὗρον ἐν αὐτῷ (23,22) were borrowed from Mk 15,14. The ὃν ἠτοῦντο (23,25) derived from Mk 15,6.

The L account provided the detail that the religious leaders twice rejected Pilate's suggestion (23,18.23), so the Markan information about the scourging (Mk 15,15) and mistreatment in the praetorium (Mk 15,16-20) was not related. Once more, Weiss paid attention to similarities with Acts which were detected for αἶρε

---

location and persons involved. Cf. H.A.W. MEYER, *Lukas*, ⁵1867, p. 579, who opted for a special source in the mockery because of "verschieden hinsichtlich der Zeit, des Ortes und der verspottenden Personen".

243. *Ibid.*, p. 222. Cf. *Die Quellen der synoptischen Überlieferung* (1908), p. 156. In Weiss's opinion, verse 22,64 showed that the oral tradition was already fixed in written form.

244. *Die Quellen des Lukasevangeliums*, p. 222, 223.

245. *Ibid.*, p. 223.

τοῦτον (23,20; cf. Acts 21,36; 22,22) and ἐπεφώνουν (23,21; cf. Acts 12,22; 21,34; 22,24).

In *Die Quellen der synoptischen Überlieferung* (1908), a subsequent discussion of Luke's sources, Weiss attributed the account of Jesus' arrest (22,54.55) to L, but reserved deciding whether the term συλλαβόντες (Acts 1,16; Jn 18,12) was used in that rendition[246]. Luke added ὁ δὲ Πέτρος ἠκολούθει μακρόθεν from Mk 14,54. The flight of the disciples was not recounted by L and mention that Peter was sitting in the midst of the servants was enough to imply that he had followed Jesus.

Mk supplied the first denial (Lk 22,56.57 / Mk 14,66ff.) as well as the phrase πρὸς τὸ φῶς (Mk 14,54). The response to the accusation in 22,57 clearly harkened back to the αὐτόν (22,54) and referred to Jesus. Although Luke wanted to make the first Markan denial more specific, he wished to avoid the answer of the maid in Mk.

Weiss rejected the suggestion that a literary motif could explain the interval of about an hour (22,59), and thus ascribed it to a written tradition from a good source. The insistence that Peter was a companion of Jesus could very well have come from Mk 14,70, which Weiss held was absent from the L account. Certain vocabulary (στραφείς, ὁ κύριος, αὐτός 22,56.57.59) testified to L[247]. Evidence

---

246. B. WEISS, *Die Quellen der synoptischen Überlieferung*, 1908, p. 154.

247. *Ibid.*, p. 156. In the *Vorwort* to his book, Georg Hermann MÜLLER (1908) acknowledged the recent publication of B. Weiss's, *Die Quellen der synoptischen Überlieferung*, but conceded that his own views were not altered by it. While asserting that Mk served as a source for Lk, Müller nonetheless adhered to the view that Luke employed a special continuous source in the passion narrative (*Zur Synopse. Untersuchung über die Arbeitsweise des Lk und Mt und ihre Quellen, namentlich die Spruchquelle, im anschluss an eine Synopse Mk-Lk-Mt*, Göttingen, 1908, p. 6, 18, 19). The section 22,54–23,1 was compared with Mk 14,53–15,5 and 23,18-25 with Mk 15,16-20. He also referred to Feine (1891) and B. Weiss (*Lukas*, ⁹1901). Müller offered reasons for his conviction: "Dass hier eine besondere, vielleicht ursprünglich (durch andere Stücke) zusammenhängende Quelle anzunehmen ist ergibt sich nicht nur daraus, dass überhaupt Sondernachrichten neben Mk vorliegen. Viel mehr Beweis ist, dass gerade in den sich mit Mk enger berührenden Teilen völlig unmotivierte Auslassungen, Änderungen, Umordnungen vorkommen" (p. 18).

Material he ascribed to that source included: 19,36-44; 22,15-32.35-38? 39-53? 54-23,5.6-16 ? 18-25.27-31.39-43.46a.48-49a(p. 18); the manner in which the verses were printed can cause some confusion, though it appeared that Müller intended to call into question 22,35-38.39-53 and 23,6-16. More particularly, material in 22,54–23,25 derived from Mk alone included 22,55-61 (= Mk 14,66-72), and 63-65 (= Mk 14,65). That which was a combination of Mk and the special source was 22,54.66-71; 23,1.3-5.18-19.20-23.24-25.Special Lukan material alone was found in 23,2.6-12.13-16. Text interpolations were responsible for 22,62 and 23,17 (p. 58-59). For Müller it was a question only of whether the Markan material had been inserted into the special source or vice versa (p. 19). He further conjectured: "Die Sonderquelle zur Leidensgeschichte ist vielleicht der letzte Teil der Wanderberichte gewesen, man kann es für sehr wahrscheinlich halten, dass diese ebenfalls mit dem Ende der Wanderungen (in Jerusalem) schlossen" (p. 21).

that the evangelist harmonized his sources was found in the Markan insertions of the cock crow (Mk 14,72) and reference to the quotes of Jesus which are close to Mk in form. Weiss rejected, as before, the possibility that 22,61 was introduced by a redactor of *Urmarkus* and continued arguing that the MA in 22,62 / Mt 26,75 originated in oral tradition.

For the mockery (22,63-65) Weiss considered the source to be an independent parallel tradition rather than a redaction of Mk. His decision was predicated on the different people reported holding Jesus, the variation in timing and observations regarding the vocabulary[248]. The MA (22,64 / Mt 26,68) was due to oral tradition, but its presence in Mt indicated that it was in fixed written form.

"Eine völlig selbständige Parallelüberlieferung" was also responsible for the Sanhedrin trial (22,66-71)[249]. Nevertheless, a few additions were taken from Mk: ἀρχιερεῖς τε καὶ γραμματεῖς (22,66 / Mk 14,53), τῆς δυνάμεως (22,69 / Mk 14,62), τί ἔτι ἔχομεν μαρτυρίας χρείαν (22,71 / Mk 14,63). However, the disagreements suggested a special source: the time of the trial, the lack of testimony from witnesses, that the Sanhedrin conducted the proceedings rather than the high priest, the trial began immediately with the Messiah question, and Jesus

---

Herbert McLACHLAN (1920) viewed the question of Luke's sources, especially the L source advanced by B. Weiss, as an open question though Harnack withheld judgment on the matter and Sanday was "critical" of it (*St. Luke. The Man and His Work*, Manchester - London - New York, 1920, p. 19). However, McLachlan recognized the problematic nature of Weiss's solution. Not only would the proof of two hypothetical sources be difficult, but Luke was portrayed as an author and editor for the Gospel differently than for Acts. "All the materials in the gospel belong to these three sources, and, in a large measure, the differences from Q^Mt. in Q^Lk. (so called) are ascribed to the third evangelist's use of (L). This solution of the problem raises difficulties of its own. Granted the theory of 'Q' and (L), then, as Harnack urges, 'exact proofs as to the analysis are impossible in the case of two unknowns.' What is more, the character of Luke that emerges in Weiss's discussions is hardly that of the editor, translator, and author who appears in Acts" (p. 55-56). It was clear that while Luke made use of Mk, he also employed other sources as indicated by the additions. McLachlan likewise left open the nature of the sources, though he recalled that various proposals had been put forward, including Philip the Evangelist, his daughters, as well as Joanna, and for matters pertaining to the Herods, Manaen served as the informant (p. 96; see also p. 27, 218). Although he regarded the special Lukan material as having value whose "unique worth is unquestioned", McLachlan also acknowledged that it is difficult to distinguish between "the editor and his source or sources" (p. 95). Regarding Mk, Luke followed the Markan order in a fashion that was basically chronological. McLachlan referred the reader to Hawkins for various explanations of Lukan omissions of Markan material (p. 17; see HAWKINS, *Three Limitations* [1911] p. 68-74). The use of ἤρξαντο (23,2) was thought to reflect Lukan editorial influence in a section containing a Markan parallel (McLACHLAN, p. 61). H.J. Cadbury was highly critical of the work which he regarded as flawed and "only an expansion" of McLachlan's earlier book, *St. Luke. Evangelist and Historian*, London, 1912 (*JR* 1 [1921] 328-329).

248. B. WEISS, *Die Quellen der synoptischen Überlieferung*, p. 156. Although ἐμπαίζειν was found in a Markan passion prediction (10,34), the term κολαφίζειν was omitted, and Mk did not contain δέρειν or βλασφημεῖν.

249. *Ibid.*, p. 157.

responded differently than in Mk. Weiss reasoned that only a Jewish-Christian source would have declared Jesus already as chosen of God using the term Son of God.

One gets the impression that Weiss regarded Luke as haphazardly blending his sources for 23,1-5, though only 23,3 stemmed from Mk (Mk 15,2). Yet, Weiss admitted that Mk 15,8 influenced Luke with the information that the people were somehow involved in Pilate's trial. Luke was responsible for the insertion of καθ' ὅλης τῆς 'Ιουδαίας (23,5) because L contained no reference to the effectiveness of Jesus in Judea[250].

In Weiss's analysis of the sentencing to the cross (Lk 23,13-23), L contained the detail that Pilate first called the religious leadership together, thus excluding the possibility that they attended the trial of Herod. Weiss acknowledged that 23,18ff. were an insertion from Mk[251]. He asserted that it was "sehr möglich" that Pilate repeated his own suggestion in light of an objection, though nothing more can be said about that. Lk 23,21 was taken from Mk 15,13 while 23,22a was drawn verbatim from Mk 15,14a. Mk 15,15 was also suspected of having influenced Lk 23,25 (Pilate's flexibility concerning the crucifixion), with the addition of ὃν ᾐτοῦντο taken from Mk 15,6.

Weiss continued his practice of pointing out connections between Lk and Acts. These included: συλλαβόντες (22,54; Acts 1,16)[252], καθ' ὅλης τῆς 'Ιουδαίας (4,14; 23,5; Acts 9,31; 10,37)[253], αἶρε τοῦτον (23,18; Acts 21,36; 22,22) and ἐπεφώνουν (23,21; Acts 12,22; 21,34; 22,24)[254].

B. Weiss consistently argued that the Herod story stemmed from the special L source[255]. While he designated the pericope as 23,6-12 in 1901 and 1908, he defined it as 23,5-13 in 1907[256]. In his commentary he noted verbal and material similarities between Lk and Mk: καὶ αὐτόν (23,7; Mk 15,43), the silence of Jesus

---

250. *Ibid.*, p. 158.
251. *Ibid.*, p. 160.
252. *Ibid.*, p. 154. In the ninth edition of the commentary (⁹1901), p. 652, Weiss also noted an additional instance of συλλαβεῖν in the arrest of Peter (Acts 12,3).
253. *Ibid.*, p. 158.
254. *Ibid.*, p. 160.
255. *Lukas*, ⁹1901, p. 660; *Die Quellen des Lukasevangeliums*, 1907, p. 225. He added further: "Selbstverständlich kann auch L wenig davon gewusst haben, was eigentlich zwischen Herodes und Jesu vorgegangen war; die Quelle meint nur zu wissen, dass der Tetrarch ihn in einem spöttischen Königsaufputz zu Pilatus zurückgeschickt habe, um sein Urteil zu motivieren, dass man es nicht mit einem Hochverräter, sondern mit einem Narren zu tun habe (23,11)"; *Die Quellen der synoptischen Überlieferung*, 1908, p. 159, n. 29.
256. *Lukas*, ⁹1901, p. 660; *Die Quellen des Lukasevangeliums*, 1907, p. 225; *Die Quellen der synoptischen Überlieferung*, 1908, p. 159, n. 29. The subsequent pericope was described in ⁹1901 as 23,13-25 (p. 662) and in 1908 as 23,13-23 (p. 159). There was no explicit mention of the extent of the passage in 1907. Although in the sixth ed. of the commentary vv. 1-12 were treated together, in the ninth ed. they were divided into two sections: vv. 1-5 and 6-12 (cf. ⁶1878, p. 578, and ⁹1901, p. 660).

(23,9; Mk 14,61 before the high priest; Mk 15,5 before Pilate)²⁵⁷, and εἰστήκεισαν (23,10; Mk 9,1). Since nothing was said about the chief priests and scribes accompanying Jesus to Herod Weiss declared that the reference to them in 23,10 was certainly an indication that Luke inserted material from Mk 15,3, an observation J. Weiss had already made in the eighth edition²⁵⁸. Similarities between Lk and Acts included ἀνέπεμψεν (23,7; Acts 25,21), περιβαλών (23,11; Acts 12,8), ἐσθῆτα λαμπράν (23,11; Acts 10,30), προϋπῆρχον (23,12; Acts 8,9)²⁵⁹. Attention was also given to vocabulary and related details found in the earlier parts of Lk: ἐπιγνούς (23,7 - 7,37), ἐξουσίας (23,7 - 4,6), ἐξ ἱκανῶν χρόνων (23,8 - cf. 8,29), Herod's wish to see Jesus because he had heard much about him (23,8 - 9,9), γινόμενον ὑπ' αὐτοῦ (23,8 - 13,17), οἱ ἀρχιερεῖς καὶ οἱ γραμματεῖς (23,10 - cf. 22,2), ἐξουθενήσας (23,11 - 18,9), φίλοι (23,12 - 16,9), ἐν αὐτῇ ἡμέρᾳ (23,12 - 13,31).

For the section 23,13-16 B. Weiss also examined these verbal and material similarities in the commentary. Concerning resemblance with Mk: προσηνέγκατέ μοι (23,14; Mk 10,13). Links between Lk and Acts consisted of ἄρχοντες (23,14; Acts 3,7), ἀνακρίνας (23,14; Acts 24,8), and ἄξιον θανάτου (23,15; Acts 25,11). Material found in earlier portions of Lk: συγκαλεσάμενος (23,13 - 9,1), τὸν λαόν (23,13 - 23,5), τῷ ἀνθρώπῳ τούτῳ (23,14 - cf. 23,4), ὢν (23,14 - 16,1), ἀποστρέφοντα (23,14 - cf. 23,5 ἀνασείει), ἐνώπιον (23,14 - 8,47), and ἀνέπεμψεν (23,15 - 23,11).

In his work of 1907 he observed, as he had done in the commentary, that 9,9 prepared for 23,8²⁶⁰. He further made the point in 1907 of emphasizing that the detail in 23,12 must have come from circles having a good knowledge of the relationship between Pilate and Herod, a position he repeated in 1908²⁶¹. In the commentary he maintained it was certainly conceivable that the detail of the silence of Jesus stemmed from Mk. In addition, the mention of the presence of the chief priests and scribes (23,10) recalled Mk 14,61 and Mk 15,5²⁶². In his 1907 study he referred to this as "ein Nachklang von Mk. 15,3f." adding in 1908 that it was

257. *Lukas*, ⁹1901, p. 661. In ⁹1901, Weiss more definitively favored Markan influence when contrasted with his earlier position in ⁶1878: "Dies ist wohl aus der Beschaffenheit der Fragen und aus der durchschaueten Absicht des Herodes zu erklären, erinnert aber an Mark. 15,5" (p. 579).

258. ⁹1901, p. 661, with the parenthetical remark "vgl. schon Aufl.8" (⁸1892, p. 641). Although Weiss seemed earlier to have detected the possible influence of Mk 15,3.4 by the mention of the attendance of the Jewish religious leaders in 23,10 (⁶1878, p. 579), he was considerably more assertive in the ninth ed. in assigning influence of 23,10 to Mk 15,3 in much the same way as 23,3 was influenced by Mk 15,2.

259. No mention was made in ⁶1878, p. 579, of ἐσθῆτα λαμπράν in Acts 10,30 and προϋπῆρχον in Acts 8,9 as there was in ⁹1901, p. 661.

260. *Die Quellen des Lukasevangeliums*, p. 225. See ⁹1901, p. 661.

261. *Die Quellen des Lukasevangeliums*, p. 225. *Die Quellen der synoptischen Überlieferung*, p. 159, n. 29.

262. ⁹1901, p. 661.

"ein blosser Nachklang von Mk. 15,3f."[263]. What generally distinguished the 1908 study from the two earlier ones was his attention to what he perceived to be L vocabulary in other parts of Lk[264].

What is clear from a comparison of the three works is that his commentary, where he highlighted verbal connections with Mk, Acts and earlier portions of Lk, contained more detailed analysis than the later works. The studies of 1907 and 1908 were briefer in their treatment of the Herod pericope, offered very little attention to Markan material and did not refer to Acts.

William SANDAY indicated his openness when he mentioned in his 1893 Bampton Lectures Feine's theory (1891) that Lk-Acts made use of "one and the same document" as a source[265]. In 1907 he noted his agreement with the conclusions of B. Weiss's 1907 study[266]. The next year he signaled his agreement with the theory of Feine and J. Weiss and B. Weiss[267]. His main reason was that

263. *Die Quellen des Lukasevangeliums*, p. 225. *Die Quellen der synoptischen Überlieferung*, p. 159, n. 29.

264. *Die Quellen der synoptischen Überlieferung*, p. 159, n. 29. Examples included ἐξουσία (23,7; 20,20; 22,53), a term used differently by Luke, ἐπιγνοὺς ὅτι (23,7; 1,22; 7,37; cf. 24,16.31), ἐξουθενεῖν (23,11; 18,9), ἐσθῆτα (23,11; 24,4), and ἐμπαίξας (23,11; 14,29; 22,63; 23,36). Weiss observed further that στρατεύματα (23,11) stood for στρατιῶται in other parts of Lk (7,8; 23,36).

265. *Inspiration. Eight Lectures on the Early History and Origin of the Doctrine of Biblical Inspiration* (Bampton Lectures, 1893), London - New York, 1893, 1901, p. 318-319: "All that applies to the third Gospel of course applies also to the Acts. Both works are certainly by the same author; they are addressed to the same person; they maintain the same general character; and if we are to accept one of the theories most recently put forward they make use not only of similar documents but of one and the same document, of which there are large traces in the earlier treatise, but which also extends a long way into the later". Feine (1891) was mentioned on p. 319, n. 2.

266. *The Life of Christ in Recent Research*, Oxford, 1907, p. 173-174: "Only in the last few weeks a monograph has reached me by the veteran Dr. Bernhard Weiss himself on the Sources of the Gospel of St. Luke (*Die Quellen des Lukasevangeliums* [...], 1907). The views expressed in this are already pretty well known: they are most interesting where they relate to the peculiar matter of the Gospel. In regard to this I am more inclined to agree with Dr. B. Weiss than with his colleague Prof. Harnack".

267. *The Bearing of Criticism upon the Gospel History*, in *ExpT* 20 (1908-09) 103-114, p. 112: "Many interesting questions arise as to the special matter of St. Luke, which are still *sub judice*. The most important is whether we are to speak of 'source' or 'sources,' and how far this new information on which St. Luke relies was oral or in writing. I have a strong suspicion myself, which is shared by more than one good writer, such as Feine, who was the first to go into the subject, and both Bernhard and Johannes Weiss, that St. Luke made use of a single writing which not only embraced most of the peculiar matter of his Gospel, but also supplied him with a substantial portion of his material for the Acts". Already in 1900 Sanday had signaled his support of Feine: "The theory of the use by St. Luke of a 'special source,' which, where it was available, he preferred to all other sources, I believe to be one of the most hopeful and helpful of recent contributions to the Synoptic Problem. In Germany it is associated more especially with Prof. Feine. In England the idea was take up and developed, quite independently of Feine, by Mr. C. Badcock of Lincoln College, who I trust may some day publish the fruit of his studies" (*A

44   CHAPTER ONE

there were "certain common qualities that run through at least all of the peculiar matter of the Gospel".

Nearly a decade after his death, the theological faculty of the University of Berlin organized a celebration in honor of what would have been B. Weiss's one hundredth birthday at which Adolf Deissmann noted that one of Weiss's special interests had been source criticism[268]. Indeed it was remarkable that Weiss wrote his works of 1907 and 1908 when he was in his eighties. A. von Harnack assessed these two works as "die gründlichste und geschlossenste Kritik der Synoptiker [...], die wir überhaupt besitzen". Deissmann described these source-critical studies as "die Summa seiner Lebensarbeit". He not only showered praise but sided with Weiss's position: "Die von Bernhard Weiss hier richtig gezeigten Linien, die vielen seitdem den rechten Weg bedeutet haben, scheinen mir in diesem Falle besonders diejenigen zu sein, die auf die Priorität des Markusevangeliums, auf seine Benutzung durch Matthäus und Lukas, sowie auf die hinter Matthäus und Lukas stehenden Sonderquellen hinweisen, namentlich auf die den Beiden gemeinsame Redequelle"[269].

What general comparison can be made of B. Weiss's position with that espoused by J. Weiss? Both looked to Acts, though sometimes J. Weiss less so, as corroborating evidence[270]. Furthermore, B. Weiss often emphasized connections to earlier portions of the Gospel which J. Weiss overlooked. B. Weiss was much less optimistic about the possibility of isolating a special vocabulary. Despite their differences arising from the form of the special source and which version of Mk Luke adopted, they were united in the conviction that Luke employed an independent, non-Markan source in the passion narrative. B. Weiss exerted extensive influence through his "accurate scholarship, cautious judgment, minute attention to details"[271].

Could not the common vocabulary[272] of Acts and Lk and the virtual "indistinguishability" of a special word list suggest common redaction rather than a separate source? These considerations would seem to lend support to the view that Luke, as a skillful redactor, had carefully woven early elements into later

Plea for the Logia, in ExpT 11 [1899-1900] 471-473, p. 473, n. 1).

268. A. DEISSMANN, D. Bernhard Weiss, in Theologische Blätter 6 (1927) cols. 241-251, col. 246.

269. Ibid., col. 247.

270. J. Weiss, [8]1892, did not mention Acts 1,12 or 12,3 in his discussion of συλλαβόντες (22,54). While treating the phrase καθ᾽ ὅλης τῆς Ἰουδαίας (23,5) he recalled Acts 10,37, but neglected 9,31.

271. H.A.A. KENNEDY, ExpT 13 (1901-02), p. 544. J.S. RIGGS, Introduction, in B. WEISS, A Commentary on the New Testament. Vol. 1. Matthew - Mark, tr. G. SCHODDE and E. WILSON, London - New York, 1906, p. ix, wrote this tribute: "There is no department of New Testament study which Dr. Weiss has not made debtor to him. It is safe to say that no man has in his day exerted a wider influence toward a sound, careful, fruitful study of the Scriptures than he".

272. On vocabulary: Lukas, [9]1901, p. 259, n. 1.

accounts in order to prepare for them and employed vocabulary in Acts which could serve as an echo of the Gospel.

Although inspired and convinced by the work of B. Weiss that almost all of Lk was based upon three written sources, Burton Scott EASTON (1910) was also dissatisfied and sought to rearrange Weiss's evidence to show that the style of the third source (L) differed significantly from that of Luke[273]. But as he continued, the differences between Easton and Weiss became even more numerous. Their word lists varied, though Easton used Weiss's list as the basis of his own. Weiss relied partially on linguistic proof for the existence of L, Easton almost entirely. Easton complained that Weiss possibly included too much in L[274]. Easton queried whether the limits of L can be determined with any exactitude. If they could be, "linguistic considerations" alone were insufficient.

He attributed 22,54-65.66-71; 23,1-2.13-25 to passages from L that reflected influence from other sources[275]. He contended the proportion of L vocabulary was diluted by that of other sources. The material of 23,4-12, on the other hand, was not suspected of having been influenced by Mk or Q[276]. Words from L appeared in this passage less than "one characteristic word or phrase in every two phrases"[277]. Relying on the linguistic data, Easton concluded there was "very strong evidence for the substantial unity of L as a source"[278].

Luke was seen as little more than an editor[279]. Certain linguistic characteristics were regarded as the weightiest evidence supporting the special Lukan source[280]. Because the author of Lk was obviously a Gentile who directed

273. B.S. EASTON, *Linguistic Evidence for the Lucan Source L*, in *JBL* 29 (1910) 139-180. Easton's specific criticisms of B. Weiss's endeavors were threefold: 1) the evidence was awkwardly arranged; 2) the table (*Die Quellen der synoptischen Überlieferung*, 1908, p. 197-198) was incomplete; 3) the figures were inaccurate (p. 141).

274. EASTON, *Linguistic Evidence*, p. 144: "To judge from the tests I have made, Weiss has certainly included in his reconstruction of L all that properly belongs to it, with the exception, perhaps, of the Transfiguration narrative. On the other hand, it is possible that he has included a little too much; but these questions as to the precise extent of L must be left open for the present".

275. *Ibid.*, p. 169.

276. *Ibid.*, p. 168. Easton included 23,4-12 among passages "where admixture from Mc. or Q is not suspected". But then he was quick to add: "In almost all of the above cases, a reminiscence or a short quotation from Mc. is probable" (p. 169). Strangely, there was no reference to 23,3 in any of the following categories, whether thought to be from L or from Mk (cf. 1910, p. 168-169; *The Special Source of the Third Gospel*, in *JBL* 30 [1911] 78-103, esp. p. 78-79). This is significant, especially in light of the following statement: "After this point [22,7-13] Lc.'s resemblances to Mc. rarely extend closely for even a verse at a time, and are often mere linguistic touches" (1911, p. 79).

277. *Ibid.*, p. 169.

278. *Ibid.*, p. 170.

279. EASTON, *Linguistic Evidence*, p. 139-140.

280. *Ibid.*, p. 141. Cf. p. 139 where Easton qualified his stance with "probably".

his work to Gentile readership, that material which treated Jewish matters in a very knowledgeable way very probably stemmed from Jewish origin[281]. In explaining the rationale and procedure of his study, Easton eliminated words taken over from Mk. "When, for instance, a word from Mc. is taken over into Lc. in connection with the rest of the Marcan passage, no conclusion for Lc.'s fondness or otherwise for that word may be drawn, and it should be barred out of such lists as the present"[282]. Easton focused on Markan material, revised by Luke, and not dependent upon parallel accounts, paying particular attention to avoidance or alteration of usual Markan wording as well as additions of words or phrases to the narrative of Mk[283]. Easton criticized both V.H. Stanton and F. Nicolardot for not understanding Weiss's position[284].

A continuation of Easton's article appeared one year later in which he contended that after 22,13 any similarities between Lk and Mk were simply "linguistic touches" and generally do not exceed one verse[285]. Although Easton refrained from determining the "precise limits" of the source, nevertheless he delineated the contents and order of the L source[286]. He made clear that in his estimation, L was a redaction of a written source and not Luke's composition of

281. *Ibid.*, p. 140. But we would ask, is it not possible that because Antioch was such a crossroads of culture and language that Luke was adept in both languages?

282. *Ibid.*, p. 142. But such a methodology will necessarily skew the results by neglecting a significant amount of material. Earlier Easton himself stated: "Consequently, it is incumbent on the student of the Synoptic Problem to subject the other matter in Lc. to a close examination with a view to determining how much else may possibly belong to a source rather than to Lc.'s free composition" (p. 140).

283. *Ibid.*, p. 142-143.

284. *Ibid.*, p. 141, n. 1. Cf. V.H. STANTON, *Gospels* (1909), p. 224, and F. NICOLARDOT, *Les procédés* (1908), p. 182. Easton stated that Stanton "misstates Weiss' position". Stanton wrote: "Now, with Harnack, I believe, what some critics appear to deny, that it should be possible to distinguish between passages which the author of the third Gospel and the Acts has wholly composed himself and those in which he has simply revised the language of a document written in a very different style from his own". In a note Stanton referred to Weiss saying: "E.g. as to passages in the Gospel, B. Weiss, *Die Quellen d. Lukas Evs.* p. 195 ff. See also below, p. 256, n. 1" (*Gospels*, p. 224, n. 2). Easton also asserted that "Nicolardot ... in a very obvious reference to Weiss ... appears also to miss Weiss' point". Nicolardot was discussing the raising of the widow's son at Nain (7,11-18).

285. EASTON, *Special Source*, in *JBL* 30 (1911), p. 79. Excluding 1) material obviously drawn from Mk, 2) material based upon Mk, though differing from it and agreeing with Mt, 3) material based upon Mk but differing from both Mk and Mt, 4) material where Luke and Mt agree against Mk, 5) Lukan material parallel with Mt but not easily explained by "mutual editing of a common source", and 6) material unique to Luke but probably based upon Q, Easton concluded: "Then, it is the present contention that substantially all the remaining matter was taken by Lc. from a single written source" (p. 82). Cf. p. 92-93, where Easton wrote of a number of inconsistencies in 23,4-18.

286. *Ibid.*, p. 95-96. Cf. p. 83: "Naturally, no attempt is made to assert a dogmatic conclusion as to its precise limits". Easton agrees with Weiss's arrangement of the L material (p. 100).

oral traditions[287]. Easton would also reject the view of those, such as W.C. Allen, who promoted the idea of an extensive use of oral tradition. Omission of material concerning the conversion of Gentiles as well as confusion in matters geographical after 9,50, pointed, in Easton's view, to Luke's use of "a rather extended written source"[288]. A certain awkwardness resulted from the inclusion of Markan reminiscences in sections from L. Whereas Wernle argued that divergences from Mk were explained by Luke's redactional freedom, Easton surmised it was due rather to the use of other sources[289]. Easton summed up his research by saying that "L was composed by a strict Jewish-Christian, and written for the benefit of other Jewish-Christians and in order to convert Jews to Jewish Christianity"[290].

Such differences between L and Mk notwithstanding, Easton noted that: "The contents of this source [...] shows a remarkable correspondence with the general contents of Mc."[291]. Lukan redaction consisted in the blending of Mk and L. Based on a comparison with Luke's use of Mk, Easton reasoned that Luke had probably not reproduced all of the L document.

In an article devoted to the trial of Jesus, Easton (1915) singled out W. BRANDT'S *Die evangelische Geschichte* (1893) as "the first thoroughly critical treatment of the trial of Jesus that was supported by adequate historical knowledge"[292]. J. Weiss and F. Spitta were highlighted as upholding the Lukan account as more historical than Mk[293]. H.J. Holtzmann and B. Weiss were cited for having made "important contributions to the more conservative side of the debate"[294]. Easton's purpose in this article was to "undertake a summary and analysis of the arguments of these writers", as well as a few others, even as he offered "a fresh investigation" of the trial[295]. While he subscribed to the theory of Markan priority he maintained that the relationship of Lk to Mk "is not quite so simple" as that of the relation of Mt to Mk[296].

Initially, he focused on the differences between the Lukan and Markan accounts. Recalling the various arguments put forth by Brandt, Holtzmann,

287. *Ibid.*, p. 90.

288. *Ibid.*

289. *Ibid.*, p. 94; cf. WERNLE, *Die synoptische Frage*, p. 107.

290. EASTON, *Special Source*, p. 102-103. If such was the case, why would Luke have included it in his Gospel which was destined for Gentiles?

291. *Ibid.*, p. 99.

292. B.S. EASTON, *The Trial of Jesus*, in *AJT* 19 (1915) 430-452, esp. p. 447-451.

293. J. WEISS, *Das älteste Evangelium*, 1903. His conclusions were elaborated in *Schriften des neuen Testaments*, 1906, ²1907. See also SPITTA, *Die synoptische Grundschrift*, 1912.

294. EASTON, *Trial*, p. 430. See HOLTZMANN, *Das messianische Bewusstein Jesu* (1907), and *Handcommentar zum Neuen Testament* 1, ³1901. Among the contributions of B. Weiss were *Die Quellen des Lukasevangeliums*, 1907; *Die Quellen der synoptischen Überlieferung*, 1908; and the commentaries in the Meyer series including the ⁹1901 edition of the commentary on Mk and Lk.

295. EASTON, *Trial*, p. 431.

296. *Ibid.* Indeed, in his opinion, "Luke's narrative is so different from Mark's" (p. 447).

Wellhausen and Loisy that Luke's account of the trial was a revision of Mark's, Easton concluded, "These arguments are not very convincing"[297]. He dismissed the view that the omission of the words about the Temple (cf. Mk 14,58 diff Lk 22,66-71) in the Gospel could be accounted for by their use in Acts 6,13-14, a position which he termed "perverse". His observations led him to what he believed to be "the only natural conclusion [...] that Luke is here based, not directly on Mark at all, but on some other source", a conclusion also reached by B. Weiss, J. Weiss and Spitta[298]. The material in 22,70-71 was derived from Mk. The special source was responsible for 22,66b-69 "or an account of the trial reduced to its barest essentials"[299]. Yet in his summary, Easton seemed to restrict the special material even further: "Luke's account rests partly on material drawn from Mark, partly on a separate tradition. This last was very brief but has preserved Jesus' words more accurately than have Mark or Matthew"[300].

In the material which followed in Lk 23 Easton suggested that "separate tradition may have played a part here"[301]. 23,13-25 was said to continue "much as does Mark's, with a still greater insistence on Pilate's unwillingness to pass judgment"[302].

The account of Jesus before Herod (23,5-10) also indicated that Luke employed a separate tradition, material which had been prepared for "as far back as Luke 9:9". In this episode Herod "does nothing except return Pilate's courtesy (vss. 11-12)"[303].

In his commentary on Lk (1926), Easton held that Luke followed a non-Markan source after Mk 12 which was nonetheless embellished by material from Mk[304]. Such a position notwithstanding, he acknowledged that it was difficult to determine in Chapters 22–23 "whether some passages are really based on Mk or not"[305]. Easton followed B. Weiss and Streeter in assigning the passion narrative to a third

---

297. *Ibid.*, p. 448.

298. *Ibid.*, p. 449. The three authors were not in agreement on the historical value of the Lukan version. B. Weiss contended it was inferior to Mk while J. Weiss and Spitta were of the opposing point of view.

299. *Ibid.*, p. 450.

300. *Ibid.*, p. 451.

301. *Ibid.*, p. 450. B. Weiss's view that 23,3 stemmed from Mk was rehearsed.

302. *Ibid.*, p. 450-451.

303. *Ibid.*, p. 450.

304. B.S. EASTON, *The Gospel According to St. Luke*, New York - Edinburgh, 1926, p. xvi, xxiv. Easton contended that 24,36-49 belonged to a source other than Mk or L. That which was taken from Mk in the latter part of the Gospel included Mk 13,1-7.28-31; 14,12-16 (p. xv). Easton acknowledged his debt to both Weiss's and noted that the literary-critical insights of J. Weiss "have failed of acceptance". Yet the first hint of Easton's reserve was found on p. ix. "But a very important qualification of the discussion arises when St. Luke's source was simply St. Mark".

305. *Ibid.*, p. xxv.

written source, designated as L[306]. Luke used the non-Markan sources much more freely than he used Mk[307]. Although Easton called attention to the lists of vocabulary characteristic of Luke compiled by Hawkins and Cadbury, he faulted them for assigning as Lukan a good deal which really belonged to L[308].

Although Easton conceded that much of the account of Peter's denial was based upon Mk, he nevertheless argued that Luke was here following a continuous, non-Markan source[309]. He based this decision on the differing order, Luke's non-Markan version of the mockery, the unlikelihood that the special source would have omitted this story, and the presence of special "L" vocabulary[310]. Easton gave a great deal of attention to what he termed "Luke-Matthew contacts", which generally were improvements of Mark's faulty Greek[311]. With unfortunate ambiguity, Easton merely stated that 22,62 resulted from textual interpolation, but did not indicate point of origin[312]. The other MA, termed "noteworthy", was an equally possible result of any of the three feasible explanations, though he seemed to favor oral tradition or primitive textual influence[313]. Easton did not dedicate much space to the question of order. In his critical notes on the denial of Peter, he called attention to the change of position of this pericope as well as that of the mockery, which suggested a source other than Mk[314].

The mockery stemmed from a non-Markan source due to the difference of timing as well as those responsible for the mistreatment. The vocabulary of L was represented by ἐμπαίζειν[315]. The trial, likewise originated from the special source, though it contained Markan reminiscences[316]. Easton implied that L was aware of two Sanhedrin trials, but passed over the first as "unimportant". The Markan version was seen as a revision of the one provided by L. Jewish thought was more accurately reproduced by L and the continuity flowed between this pericope and what has preceded and what followed. Since in 23,1-5 only v. 3 was shared in common between Lk and Mk, Easton reasoned that this section rested upon L[317]. Although Easton was convinced that L must have reported the

---

306. *Ibid.*, p. xxiii.
307. *Ibid.*, p. xxx.
308. *Ibid.*, p. xxxi.
309. *Ibid.*, p. 334.
310. *Ibid.* The special words were κύριος and στραφείς.
311. *Ibid.*, p. xvii. Cf. p. xxi-xxii. Easton did not assign much importance to most of these contacts. Possible explanations were: 1) corresponding, independent editing or 2) "'primitive' textual influence of Luke on Mt (or *vice versa*)", though one must be cautious about this explanation. A final possibility was that the Markan text was corrupted following use by Luke and Matthew.
312. *Ibid.*, p. 334.
313. *Ibid.*, p. 336.
314. *Ibid.*, p. 334.
315. *Ibid.*, p. 336.
316. *Ibid.*, p. 339.
317. In his effort to establish that L was the basis for the account, Easton gave little attention in his articles and commentary to the nearly identical question of Pilate in 23,3 / Mk 15,2. In the

sentencing of Jesus, nevertheless, he admited that much of 23,18-25 was based upon Mk. Mk contributed vv. 18-19.20 (probably).21, v. 19 being a paraphrase of Mk. Mk 15,14 supplied part of 23,14 with the rest based upon 23,16. Mk also was the basis for v. 25 which was expanded by Luke. Only vv. 23 and 24 seemed to rest upon L[318].

Easton conceded a heavy influence from the LXX, but argued that this coloring was twice as much in L as in the other portions of Gospel or Acts[319]. His evaluation of the historical value of L was much more in accord with Streeter than with Taylor, but in the passion narrative, its value was highly esteemed[320]. Easton construed L to be a Greek document which may have been authored by Philip the Evangelist as Harnack proposed[321]. The evangelist Luke, in Easton's opinion, sometimes did damage to the simple writing known as L (e.g. 7,36-50).

Easton listed Luke's characteristics of his redaction of Mk[322]. In highlighting the removal of notes of time, general fidelity when reproducing Jesus' words, but less with narrative or surrounding setting, Easton contended that the most significant changes took place where Mk and another source had been combined. Luke's omissions included repetitions by Mark as well as "merely picturesque details"[323]. Easton distinguished sources primarily on the basis of vocabulary: Markan, Lukan and L. It was remarkable, then, that he paid no attention to the work of Perry[324].

Easton (1910) asserted that the material of 23,4-12 was not suspected of influence by Mk or Q[325]. But then he was quick to add: "In almost all of the above cases, a reminiscence or a short quotation from Mc. is probable"[326]. Based

first installment of the article (1910) 23,3 was not included in any of Easton's categories. The section 23,4-12 was classified among "words found in L passages where admixture from Mc. or Q is not suspected". Further, low verbal correspondence in 23,1-2 (.50) and 23,13-25 (.00) prompted Easton to include these verses among "words found in L passages where there is evidence of admixture from other sources" (*Linguistic Evidence*, 1910, p. 168-169). In the continuation of the article, he clearly affirmed that Mk was the source of 23,3: "Why 23,4 follows from 23,3 is anything but clear; but 23,3 is Marcan (Mc. 15,2). Probably something like 'Pilate examined him' stood in its place in L, but the narrative is clearer even if the verse be cancelled entirely and nothing substituted" (*Special Source*, 1911, p. 92). He again drew attention to the similarity, but less emphatically, in the commentary. "Outside of v. 3 Lk and Mk are quite different" (*Gospel*, 1926, p. 341).

318. *Ibid.*, p. 345-346.
319. *Ibid.*, p. xxvii, n. 1.
320. *Ibid.*, p. xxviii.
321. *Ibid.*
322. *Ibid.*, p. xvii.
323. *Ibid.*
324. That Easton was aware of Perry's work was evident from the bibliographical reference to Perry at the end of the introduction (p. xxxvii).
325. B.S. EASTON, *Linguistic Evidence*, p. 168. He included 23,4-12 among passages "where admixture from Mc. or Q is not suspected".
326. *Ibid.*, p. 169.

on the linguistic analysis that words from L appeared in this passage less than "one characteristic word or phrase in every two phrases"[327], Easton concluded there was "very strong evidence for the substantial unity of L as a source"[328].

His position remained the same in his commentary (1926). The Herod pericope also derived from L and emphasized the special Jerusalem tradition. Easton refuted Wellhausen's claim that the story was invented, contending that "Christ's acquittal would have been made much less unambiguous and undignified"[329]. Similarly, Easton rejected Loisy's solution that the story served to reduce the Roman responsibility for the death of Jesus. Herod would not have been assigned culpability for Christ's death unless he had taken part in it. Easton admitted the peculiarity of the striking similarity between the mockery by Herod's soldiers and the mockery in Mk 15,17-19, saying that a transfer such as this "would have been extremely easy". Also peculiar to L is 23,13-16, which continued what had preceded. Verse 23,14 was a reminiscence of Mk 15,11.

J.M. Creed was highly critical of Easton's commentary[330]. The negative evaluations ranged from Easton's use of a confusing set of abbreviations to "arguments and conclusions [which] do not inspire confidence". Not only that, but the exegesis of the passages was "frequently unconvincing". Creed panned the work in its entirety.

T.S. Duncan, more complimentary than Creed, had some reservations about Easton's approach[331]. Accepting the fact that assigning various elements to particular sources was always to some extent a subjective exercise, the task was especially difficult in the case of Lk. Duncan offered a critique about the use of vocabulary as a criterion in distinguishing sources. "In this connection, it may be well to observe that the vocabulary test cannot be considered final. Unless it can be shown that in given passages an author could easily have used a different vocabulary than he did to express the same idea, not much argument can be drawn from word lists"[332].

A.T. Robertson, in a positive vein, suggested that Easton's commentary would supplement, though by no means replace, the work of Plummer[333]. Robertson countered Easton's estimation of the number of sources saying: "In simple truth, we do not know how many sources he had". E.F. Scott took note of the similarity between Easton and Streeter, especially since Easton was nearing completion of his commentary when Streeter's work was published. Nevertheless, Scott lamented the

---

327. *Ibid.*
328. *Ibid.*, p. 170.
329. EASTON, *Gospel*, p. 343.
330. *JTS* 28 (1926-27) 420-421.
331. *BS* 83 (1926) 366-368.
332. *Ibid.*, p. 367.
333. *RExp* 24 (1927) 85.

fact that Easton had not provided a more complete investigation of the sources and editorial techniques employed by Luke[334].

To briefly summarize, though united in the conviction that Luke employed a special source in the passion narrative, there were numerous issues on which Feine, J. Weiss and B. Weiss, and Easton disagreed. As regards the particular form of Mk, Feine and J. Weiss agreed that Luke used *Urmarkus*, though Feine insisted this was in addition to Mk. B. Weiss, on the other hand, rejected *Urmarkus*. J. Weiss criticized Feine for his view of the method utilized by the evangelist, contesting that Luke would not have alternated between sources. On the question of origin of the special source, Feine ascribed it to Jerusalem while B. Weiss was less sure where it had originated. There was also a dispute whether the source was Ebionite or not.

Further, J. Weiss claimed Feine had not sufficiently considered the LQ material in the passion narrative and limited the special vocabulary too much. B. Weiss was less enthusiastic about the possibility of isolating a special vocabulary. Easton, relying almost entirely on linguistic proof, disputed some of the vocabulary B. Weiss attributed to the special source. Finally, each of the scholars had their own view of the form of the special source. For Feine it was oral, for J. Weiss it was written, and for B. Weiss it was written, though it included oral material. Easton sided with B. Weiss that the source would have been written. As to the form in which Luke received the special source, J. Weiss insisted L and Q were already combined while B. Weiss argued they were separate and combined by Luke himself.

---

334. *JR* 6 (1926) 426. In a different but related matter, J.F. Bethune-Baker saw the strength of Easton's other study, entitled *The Gospel before the Gospels*, in his review of the history of Gospel research for the preceding twenty years, particularly in the field of form criticism, in *JTS* 30 (1928-29) 99.

CHAPTER TWO

IN DEFENSE OF MARKAN PRIORITY
I. HEINRICH JULIUS HOLTZMANN THROUGH FIRMIN NICOLARDOT

The theories of Feine, J. Weiss and B. Weiss attracted the attention of scholars who maintained the Markan basis of the Lukan passion narrative. In this chapter we examine the reaction to those who defended a special source and the contrasting view, that Luke redacted Mk.

Heinrich Julius HOLTZMANN, in *Die synoptischen Evangelien* (1863)[1], originally maintained that Lk was dependent upon Λ (Urmatthäus) and A (Urmarkus) as his two main sources[2]. As for the sources peculiar to Luke, some were oral and some were written, and were evident especially in the passion narrative[3]. In composing his Gospel Luke basically followed A which he altered with insertions and omissions. He described the insertions as coarse grain ingredients, particularly in the passion narrative, which accordingly modified the Markan account[4]. Activity within Galilee was ascribed to A, that outside Galilee to Λ. Luke followed the order of whatever source he was using[5]. Holtzmann was convinced that in Lk 22–24 the evangelist drew on other sources because these chapters differed so much from A[6].

---

1. H.J. HOLTZMANN, *Die synoptischen Evangelien, ihr Ursprung und geschichtlicher Charakter*, Leipzig, 1863. The book contained the following chapters: 1) Das Problem und seine geschichtliche Entwickelung, 2) Composition des Markus. - Quelle A (Urmarkus), 3) Composition des Matthäus und Lukas. Quelle Λ (Urmatthäus), 4) Proben and 5) Die synoptischen Evangelien als Geschichtsquellen. H.J. Holtzmann (1832-1910), Privatdozent (1858), Associate Prof., Heidelberg (1861), Prof. (1865), Strassburg (1874-1904).

2. *Ibid.*, p. 126-157, where *Urmarkus* and *Urmatthäus* were described as "die zweite Hauptquelle".

3. *Ibid.*, p. 166: "Dass nämlich unter den ganz eigenthümlichen Quellen des Lucas – seien es mündliche, seien es schiftliche – meist solche seien, denen wir das südliche Palästina als Heimathsort anzuweisen haben, hat zuerst Köstlin ausgesprochen und in seiner Weise erwiesen. Dahin gehören Stellen, [...], vor Allen aber die zahlreichen selbstständigen Relationen, womit Lucas den Gang der Leidensgeschichte unterbricht, nicht minder auch die Veränderungen, die er daselbst in A anbringt". Cf. K.R. KÖSTLIN, *Die Ursprung und die Composition der synoptischen Evangelien*, Stuttgart, 1853, p. 217f., 230f.

4. *Die synoptischen Evangelien*, p. 167-168. The special materials were also identified as "südpalestinensische Traditionen" (p. 168). Within 22,54–23,25 only 23,2-5.6-12.13-16 was designated as unique to Lk (p. 161). See also p. 157: "Aber auch, nachdem wir das Gemeinsame aller drei Synoptiker auf A, das der beiden Seitenreferenten auf Λ zurückgeführt haben ...". On πολλοί see p. 244-245.

5. *Ibid.*, p. 210.

6. *Ibid.*; so also p. 104: "Ebenso tritt klar zu Tage, dass Lucas eine Zeit lang sich an A hält, diese Quelle aber zuerst durch die kleine, dann durch die grosse Einschaltung unterbricht. Vorher fügt er blos genealogische und chronologische Notizen ein, nachher bereichert er besonders die Leidengeschichte durch eine grosse Anzahl von Nachtrichten, die ihm durch die mündliche Tradition zugekommen waren, so dass nur einzelne Sätze, wie 22,10-13. 23,3.44.52 in

With regard to 22,54-23,25, he contended that Peter's story (22,54-62) was recounted according to A though it was combined with another tradition[7]. The mockery and trial (22,63-71) were reported in connection with A[8]. The mockery (22,63-65), which was identical to Mk 14,65, followed immediately upon the Markan denial (14,66-72). The Sanhedrin trial was related in a summary and incomplete fashion. Although Urmarkus formed the basis, Luke followed "eine unklare Tradition" in recounting the trial and, influenced by Meyer, Holtzmann claimed that 22,67-68 were catechetically revised[9]. The testimony of the witnesses was omitted as was the incriminating statement of Jesus. Although the ὄψεσθε of Mk 14,62 was omitted in 22,69, still readers were invited to compare Acts 7,56.

In a discussion of the accusations presented to Pilate (23,1-5), a section also attributed to *Urmarkus*[10] Luke was credited with expressly and accurately determining the charges and learning of Pilate's fourfold judgment of Jesus' innocence. He possessed a unique and exact tradition concerning the events in 23,13-16[11]. At 23,18 he resumed his account with A, but in summary fashion[12]. The account of Jesus before Herod (23,6-12) was an insertion from tradition. Luke transferred the silence of Jesus (Mk 15,4.5 = Mt 27,12-14) to 23,9[13].

Luke stylistically revised A, often substituting vocabulary[14]; small clarifying details were added (22,59.61; 23,2.20.23)[15]. Other indications of his literary skill were abbreviation, variations and composing with a certain freedom. But Holtzmann believed Luke was also aware of other sources which he followed not only in the passion narrative, but in other parts of his Gospel.

In *Die Disposition des dritten Evangeliums* (1883) Holtzmann drew, in part, upon the work of Simons[16]. He divided the Gospel into three parts. The first part,

---

vollständiger Abhängigkeit von A geschrieben sind; desshalb hat Reuss sogar erweisen wollen, das von Lucas benutzte Exemplar von A habe keine Leidensgeschichte enthalten – eine Behauptung, die mit einer gleich zu erwähnenden und zu widerlegenden andern auf einer Linie steht". He provided only partial bibliographical information: [E.] REUSS, *Nouvelle revue* 2, p. 55.

   7. *Die synoptischen Evangelien*, p. 239-240.
   8. *Ibid.*, p. 240. Lk 22,63-65 represented a free rendering of the account of Mk 14,65 in *Urmarkus*.
   9. *Ibid.* See MEYER, [5]1867, p. 580.
   10. Here the section 23,1-5 was entitled "Die Klage vor Pilatus" (p. 240), though he previously referred it to as "Verhandlungen vor Pilatus" (23,2-5) (p. 161).
   11. *Ibid.*, p. 241. Indications of the special tradition were the change of place and the meaning of the chastisement (23,16).
   12. *Ibid.* Execution of the chastisement also was omitted, in part, because something similar was recounted in the scene before Herod (23,11).
   13. *Ibid.*, p. 241.
   14. *Ibid.*, p. 326.
   15. *Ibid.*, p. 329.
   16. HOLTZMANN, *Die Disposition des dritten Evangeliums*, in *ZWT* 26 (1883) 257-267. References to Simons (1880), p. 258, 260, 265, 266. See already Holtzmann's remarks about

describing Jesus' activity in Galilee, was mainly recounted according to the "Geschichtsquelle". The second part, relating miracles in Samaria, contained most of the "Spruchsammlung", while the third part, with events happening in Judea, "in der Hauptsache nach der gemeinsamen Quellen berichtet, freilich mit so zahlreichen eigenthümlichen Relationen vermischt, dass Reuss wenigstens die Leidensgeschichte schon aus einer besonderer Quelle hat ableiten wollen"[17]. After confirming Weiss in detecting the relationship between Lk and Jn he continued: "Ich möchte nur die Gelegenheit ergreifen, die Nöthigung zur Annahme einer besonderern 'ebionitischen Quelle' [...], eines Evangelium pauperum [...] u. dgl. bestimmt in Abrede zu stellen und meine Uebereinstimmung mit der Beurtheilung auszusprechen, welche Weiss [...] den betreffenden Partien zu Theil werden lässt"[18].

Holtzmann noted in the third edition of his *Einleitung* ([3]1892) how his position changed from what he previously maintained[19]. The material from the "Spruchsammlung" was occasionally more expanded in Lk than in Mt. It was possible it also contained stories in rough outlines as frames for the words of Jesus. The question concerning additional sources remained open. In addition to using Mk, Luke had at least known, and perhaps even used, Mt. Most of the reasons for distinguishing an *Urmarkus* from Mk had disappeared. Finally, Mt was composed around 70 AD and Lk around 100 AD[20].

Holtzmann treated Feine's theory in his *Einleitung*, in the section on *Die Urevangeliumshypothese*[21]. B. Weiss's delineation of the "apostolische Quelle" distinguished itself from a pure primitive Gospel theory[22], a concept which

Luke's disposition in *Die synoptischen Evangelien*, p. 208-209.

17. HOLTZMANN, *Die Disposition*, p. 265-266.

18. *Ibid.*, p. 266: "Die Gründe finden sich in meinem Vortrage über 'die ersten Christen und die sociale Frage' (Wissenschaftliche Vorträge über religiöse Fragen, V, 1882, S. 20f.). Doch haben wir es hier nicht mit den Quellen, sondern mit der Disposition des dritten Evangeliums zu thun".

19. *Lehrbuch der historisch-kritischen Einleitung in das Neue Testament*, Freiburg, 1885, [2]1886, [3]1892, p. 350. Page references are from the third edition unless otherwise noted.

20. *Ibid.*, p. 350.

21. *Einleitung*, p. 352 (= [2]1886, 359). In the third edition, as he rehearsed the history of the synoptic problem and its various proposed solutions (p. 342-350), Holtzmann offered a brief summary of Feine's position with reference to his articles in *JPTh* 1885, 1886 (Lk = A+C+Mk), 1887, 1888, as well as *Eine vorkanonische Überlieferung* (1891), but provided no evaluation of it, save to point out that it was a combination of the Utilization hypothesis with the *Urevangelium* hypothesis. See additional references to Feine, p. 366, 367.

22. *Einleitung*, p. 353 (= 360): "Noch entschiedener bereits auf dem Uebergang zur Benutzungshypothese begriffen erscheint das Urevglm in Gestalt der sog. apostolischen Quelle von WEISS, deren Signalement auf eine Combination von Ewald's ältester (Philippus-)Quelle ('locker angereihte Erzählungen', 'Erzählungsgruppen') mit jenem Werke einheitlichen Inhalts und Charakters hinausläuft, welches die Anderen 'Spruchsammlung' zu nennen pflegen ('eine Sammlung von grösseren Reden, Gleichnissen, einzelnen Sprüchen und Spruchreihen, denen oft

Holtzmann held as inadequate in favor of Simons[23]. He argued that the tradition upon which Luke based his writing was in good part oral and stemmed from eyewitnesses, though not necessarily exclusively so. In the Prologue, Luke assured a thoroughly new study and examination of the secondary works of his predecessors[24]. The first part of the Gospel (3,1–9,50) basically followed Mk while the latter third of the Gospel, designated as Jewish, contained parallels to Mk 10–16 and Mt 19–28. Because he dated Lk around 100 AD[25], it was argued that Luke possessed the same sources as the other Synoptics in addition to Mt and Mk[26].

Since Lk-Acts shared a common "ganz allgemeine Disposition" as well as common vocabulary, he saw Luke as having assimilated and revised his written and oral traditions[27]. The material in the Gospel sometimes continued in Acts as in the case of 21,15 shaping the apologia of Stephen in Acts 6,10. On the contrary, the contents of Mk 14,58 = Mt 26,61 were transferred into the story of Stephen (Acts 6,11-14), but were left out at Lk 22,66[28]. To B. Weiss and Feine were ascribed the view that for Acts Luke possessed an essentially historical documentary source[29].

jede geschichtliche Einleitung fehlte'). Da dieser Hypothese aber gleich der zuvor besprochenen nur in Verbindung mit der Annahme einer Benutzung des Mc durch Mt, also der Marcushypothese auftritt, beweist auch sie, dass mit der reinen Urevglmstheorie nichts mehr auszurichten ist".

23. *Ibid.*, p. 357 (= 365): "Aber auch seit abermaliger Wiederaufnahme des Mr-Fadens bei Mr 10,13 (= Lc 18,15) ist Kenntnis des Mt-Berichtes auf Schritt und Tritt erweisbar und bei der Leidens- und Auferstehungsgeschichte erfährt jener sogar bemerkliche Bevorzugungen (SIMONS S. 106), so dass jetzt die 'apostolische Quelle' von WEISS, die gerade da versiegt, wo sie befrufen wäre, die erheblichsten Dienste zu leisten, ihre Unbrauchbarkeit und Ueberflüssigkeit am deutlichsten documentirt (Stockmeyer S. 143)". Holtzmann provided only a partial bibliographical citation: STOCKMEYER, *ThZS*, 1884, p. 143-146.

24. *Einleitung*, p. 386 (= 397-398).

25. *Ibid.*, p. 350 (= 384: "um oder nach 100").

26. *Ibid.*, p. 387 (= 398). Luke would not have considered Mt an apostolic work. Holtzmann maintained that "Spuren von Lectüre des Josephus stimmen würden" (p. 374 = 384) in a series of articles treating Luke and Josephus: *Lucas und Josephus*, in ZWT 16 (1873) 85-93; *Noch einmal Lucas und Josephus*, in ZWT 20 (1877) 535-549; *Anzeigen: K.F. Nösgen, Lukas und Josephus*, in ZWT 23 (1880) 121-125. It was claimed that the author of Acts had read Josephus (ZWT 16 [1873] p. 90) and Lk 19,43; 21,24 referred to his description of the destruction of Jerusalem (p. 92). Summarizing the position of his first two articles in the third, Holtzmann wrote: "Ausdrücklich habe ich meine Ansicht dahin formulirt, Lukas habe 'im Josephus sich umgesehen' (1873, S. 89; ausdrücklich habe ich erklärt, diese seine Lectüre habe, als Lukas zur Abfassung seiner beiden Werke schritt, bereits hinter ihm gelegen, und sehr tiefringend und genau sei sie überhaupt nie gewesen (1877, S. 536)".

27. *Einleitung*, p. 391 (= 403).

28. *Ibid.*

29. *Ibid.*, p. 396. On Feine see also p. 404. Cf. B. WEISS, *Einleitung*, [2]1889, p. 570ff., and Feine, *JPTh*, 1890, p. 84f., in addition to *Eine vorkanonische Ueberlieferung*, p. 156f. and 213f.

According to Holtzmann (1886, ³1892), "Die durch Ps 2,2 veranlasste Coordination von Pilatus und Herodes Act 4,27 hat Lc 23,6-12 zum Hintergrund". The Pilate and Herod pericope was identified in his synoptic table as 23,6-16[30]. He pointed out that Lukan redaction involved connecting later parts of the Gospel with earlier ones, such as the reference of 23,8 to 9,9[31].

In the third revised edition of the commentary (³1901) the title of the *Composition des Lc* section was revised to *Schriftstellerischer Charakter und Composition des Lc* and the material expanded[32]. A section on the Two-Source theory was added, following the material on "die Spruchsammlung"[33] as was another on parallel passages[34]. Because of the numerous peculiarities in the latter third of the Gospel he believed there to be a special Lukan source[35]. Luke made the effort to connect later portions of his Gospel with earlier, e.g. 23,8 and 9,9. Reference was made to Feine's contributions in *JPTh* 1885-1888[36]. Luke's thorough revision of Mk, Holtzmann remarked, was not simply stylistic[37]. He maintained it cannot be disputed that Luke used sources beyond that of Mk and Mt and "die Spruchsammlung" (Q), especially in the second (Samaritan) part of the Gospel (9,51-18,14) and in the passion narrative[38]. The term πολλοί (1,1) suggested to the more ancient exegetes heretical and apocryphal gospels[39]. In treating the Two-Source theory Holtzmann noted the work of Feine and J. Weiss and the opposing

30. HOLTZMANN, *Einleitung*, p. 372.

31. *Ibid.*, p. 386 (= 398). Cf. F. BLEEK, *Synoptische Erklärung der drei ersten Evangelien*, (ed. H.J. HOLTZMANN), Leipzig, 1862.

32. *Die Synoptiker – Die Apostelgeschichte* (Hand-Commentar zum Neuen Testament, 1), Tübingen, 1889, (esp. p. 13: *Composition des Lucas*); 284-290, containing Lk 22,54–23,25); ²1892 (= 12-13; 285-291); ³1901 (= 18-20 [*Schriftstellerischer Charakter und Composition des Lc*]; 37-108, esp. p. 101-103: *Die parallelen Abschnitte*, a new section, drawing frequently on Brandt, focused on how the trial was carried out; 301-424, esp. 415-418: *Das Evangelium nach Lucas*).

33. *Ibid.*, ³1901, p. 15-17; cf. 1899, ²1892.

34. *Ibid.*, ³1901, p. 37-108. It was clear that in this section the book by W. BRANDT, *Die evangelische Geschichte* (1893) exercised a great deal of influence. See esp. p. 101-103.

35. HOLTZMANN, *Die Synoptiker*, p. 13 (cf. 18-19). References to ³1901 in parentheses. In relation to Mk: "Dieser 3. Theil setzt übrigens 18,15 mit Mc 10,13 (für 1-12 war Lc 16,18 eingetreten), ein und läuft von 24,10 (= Mc 16,8) an über Mc hinaus bis zum Schlusse (24,53) weiter".

36. *Ibid.*, p. 25 (cf. XVII), where *Eine vorkanonische Ueberlieferung* replaced the journal articles.

37. *Ibid.*, p. 18. Cf. 1889, ²1892, p. 13.

38. *Ibid.*, ³1901, p. 19. Holtzmann came to this judgment because of the presence of the particular character of many of the components in this Gospel.

39. *Ibid.*, p. 26 (= 303).

position adopted by Wernle[40]. But the combination of L and Q was fraught with problems:

> So hat in der oben (S. 17) besprochenen Sonderquelle FN'S Jesu Armenevglm eine Vereinseitigung erfahren (142f 144f), welche auf die Ueberlieferung der armen Christengemeinden Palästinas, speziell Jerusalems zurückweisen soll (81f 89f 110 121 142 154f 233 243f). Aber gerade hier wollen Andere wieder des Lc eigensten Geist recognosciren (H. HTZM, NtTh I, 448-452), und die Scheidung zwischen dem aus der Spruchsammlung übernommenen Material und dem in einer gewissen Verbindung damit stehenden Sondergut des Lc ist mit so grossen Schwierigkeiten verknüpft, dass auch bezüglich dieser Dinge der Exegese noch Zurückhaltung obliegen wird[41].

Much of Luke's redaction revolved around replacement of simpler forms of the older tradition with "reichere Nebenformen"[42]. Particular changes were required because Luke was writing later than Mark. While Luke generally avoided repetition, he occasionally succumbed to it as a result of the overlap in his sources[43]. Lk was sometimes affected by overzealous abbreviation. Holtzmann added that one cannot appeal to the contrary linguistic elements (for example good Greek or Semitic speech) as proof of a special (Jewish?) source, as it simply reflected the influence of the LXX.

In the passion narrative Holtzmann called attention to Luke's redactional change of order in the denial, mockery and Sanhedrin trial (22,56-71) and the great freedom with which he treated the last segment:

> Hier brennt ein Kreisfeuer Lc 55, daran auch Petrus, als ob er hieher gehörte, sich wärmt; denn die Nächte sind in Syrien zur Passazeit oft noch kält. So berichtet nur Mc, hier und v. 67. Den Pleonasmus ἀπὸ μακρόθεν entfernt Lc, indem er an die betreffende Notiz sofort v. 56-62 die ganze Verleugnungs-geschichte anschliesst, um auch dann 63-65 die Verspottung noch vor die

---

40. *Die Synoptiker*, ³1901, p. 17: "Dabei gilt zwar als ausgemacht, dass die Quelle beiden Evglsten schon in der griechischen Uebersetzung bekannt war (FN 10f 149f), nur dass mehrfach behauptet wird, sie müsse dem Lc bereits in erweitertem Rahmen – als Quelle LQ bei J. WS – vorgelegen haben (FN 130f 151, WZS 378f SLT 2 4f 32 37 39, umgekehrt WRL 184f 231-333)". Wernle, cf. below. Cf. FEINE, *Eine vorkanonische Ueberlieferung*, WEIZSÄCKER, *Untersuchungen*, and SOLTAU, *Eine Lücke*.

41. *Die Synoptiker*, p. 20. See *Lehrbuch der neutestamentlichen Theologie*, Vol. 1, Tübingen, 1897, p. 438-463; ²1911, p. 525-530, esp. 528-(529), n. 6, with mention of the special source theories of J. Weiss, Feine (again Wernle's opposition is recalled), B. Weiss and Spitta.

42. *Ibid.*, p. 18. In a discussion of 4,16-30 (Nazareth pericope) and 5,1-11 (the call of Peter) Holtzmann offered insight into his own understanding of Lukan redaction: "Zugleich sind beide Abschnitte bezeichnend für die Liebhaberei des Lc, einfachere Bilder der älteren Ueberlieferung durch reichere Nebenformen zu ersetzen, welche allegorisirende oder typologisirende Weiter-führungen des Gedankens enthalten: dort Uebergang des Evglms von den Juden zu den Heiden, hier apost. Menschenfischerei auf dem weiten Völkermeer".

43. *Ibid.*, p. 19.

Gerichtsscene zu setzen, Letztere endlich 66-71 in ganz freier Umarbeitung zu reproduciren[44].

Concerning Peter's denials (22,56-62), Luke abandoned the usual order to recount the Peter story all at once[45]. Although Holtzmann considered 22,54-62, at the very least, an entirely free revision, the question of Feine's and J. Weiss's proposal of a special source remained open, a view contrasted with Brandt's position: "Die Processgeschichte ist erdichtet; Lukas hat neben dem Marcusevangelium mindestens eine andere Quellenschrift benutzt: vielleicht ist in dieser oder einer andern die Verläugnung des Petrus nach jener Tradition erzählt gewesen"[46]. Holtzmann, and Brandt before him, argued one could doubt neither the historicity of the incident which stemmed from Peter himself, nor that the changes in Mt and Lk resulted from "die Phantasie der Gemeindetradition und die schriftstellerische Reflexion"[47]. Holtzmann observed that in the second denial Luke used ἕτερος (22,58) to refer to the interlocutor, who spoke directly to Peter, while Mk 14,69 referred to the same maid as in the first denial (Mk 14,67). Luke mentioned the passing of about an hour (22,59) "weil diese Auftritte bei ihm die Nacht ausfüllen sollen"[48]. Peter's response (22,60) stemmed from Mk 14,68. The only verbal link with Acts was διϊσχυρίζετο (22,59 – Acts 12,15)[49].

In a brief discussion of the mockery, Holtzmann noted that in accordance with the context, αὐτόν (v. 63) obviously referred to Peter, a consequence of the transposition[50]. The MA 22,62 / Mt 26,75, at least "wept bitterly", was mentioned as being according to Is 22,4[51]. The origin of the MA 22,64 / Mt 26,68 was not explicitly treated[52]. The spitting was omitted. Lk 22,65 was designated "Sondereigenthum"[53].

Commenting on the trial before the Sanhedrin (22,54.55.66-71) Jesus was brought during the night (22,54) to the house of the high priest and the Sanhedrin was summoned[54]. Holtzmann observed that Luke removed the pleonasm ἀπὸ

44. *Ibid.*, p. 284.
45. ³1901, 415-416, 102; cf. 1889, p. 286-287 (= 287-288).
46. ³1901, 415; cf. J. WEISS, ⁸1892, FEINE (1891), p. 67f., and BRANDT, p. 74-75.
47. ³1901, p. 102; cf. BRANDT, p. 29f., 159f. "Als geschichtliches Ereigniss postuliert der Vorfall einen ursprünglichen Bericht entweder aus dem eignen Munde des Petrus, oder von einem Augen- und Ohrenzeugen, dessen Aussage der Jünger dann bestätigt haben muss: ohne dies würde man die Sache nicht geglaubt haben" (p. 159).
48. 1889, p. 286 (= ²1892, 287; ³1901, 415).
49. *Ibid.*
50. ³1901, 416.
51. *Ibid.*, 1889, p. 287 (= ²1892, 287-288); cf. ³1901, 416 and 178). In the third edition Holtzmann did not focus just on the single phrase of the MA. The dependence on Is was also amended.
52. 1889, p. 286 (= ²1892, 287; cf. ³1901, 416, but see p. 178 on Mk 14,65). In the third edition he clearly stated in his comments on Mk 14,65 and Lk 22,64 this was a Mt-Lk agreement against Mk (cf. p. 292 on Mt 26,68).
53. 1889, p. 286 (= ²1892, 287; ³1901, 416).
54. 1889, p. 284-286 (= ²1892, 285-287; cf. ³1901, 415, 101-102). In the third edition the

μακρόθεν (Mk 14,54 / Lk 22,54) uniting all the material concerning Peter thus changing the order permitting the mockery to occur before the trial[55]. Luke employed Mk 15,1 to signal a morning trial according to the Roman custom (Lk 22,66)[56]. Jesus' statement (Mk 14,58) about the Temple not made by human hands was taken up in Acts 7,48 and 17,24[57]. The witness testimony (Mk 14,58) was transferred to the trial of Stephen (Acts 6,13-14) where it served to abrogate Mosaic religion[58]. The influence of Jer 38,15 was claimed for 22,68[59] and v. 69 like Acts 7,55 was a reminder that the future brought accountability for one's deeds[60]. The morning Sanhedrin trial (23,1) had already been anticipated by Luke (22,66)[61]. Within the trial before Pilate (23,2-5) similarities between 23,2 and Acts 24,5 were recognized[62]. Lk 23,3 equaled Mk 15,2 and Mt 27,11. For the rest, Luke changed Mark's account in order to show how the Roman judgment had been adversely influenced by Jewish hatred (vv. 4-5)[63].

trial before the Sanhedrin was referred to as 22,63-23,1 since vv. 54.55 were transferred to the account of Peter's denials (p. 415). Reference was made to Mk 13,2 / Mt 24,2 / Lk 21,6 concerning the foretelling of the destruction of the Temple. That Jesus was condemned on the basis of a misunderstanding was assumed in 23,3 / Mk 15,2 / Mt 27,11 (101).

55. 1889, p. 284 (= [2]1892, 285; cf. [3]1901, 415). On the order of the pericopes ([3]1901) he remarked: "Da hier die Verurtheilung noch nicht erfolgt ist, geschieht die Misshandlung" (416).

56. 1889, p. 284 (= [2]1892, 285; cf. [3]1901, 416). As if the Sanhedrin had not already been assembled (22,52), in contrast to the high priests in Mk and Mt, they gathered together at the break of day. The term πρεσβυτέριον appeared in Lk 22,56 as in Acts 22,5, while συνέδριον referred to the place (ctr. Mk 15,1).

57. 1889, p. 285 (= [2]1892, 285; [3]1901, 177, comment on Mk 14,58; cf. 416).

58. 1889, p. 285 (= [2]1892, 285; [3]1901, 416).

59. 1889, p. 285 (= [2]1892, 286; [3]1901, 416): "Dieses einzige wirkliche Novum des lucanischen Berichtes klingt wie Erinnerung an Jer 38,15". Brandt also referred to Jer. (p. 72-73).

60. 1889, p. 285 (= [2]1892, 286; [3]1901, 416). Omissions, such as no reference to the prospect that the judges of Jesus would see the coming of the Son of Man, were explained by the fact that Luke's was a later Gospel (so P. WERNLE, 1899, p. 14). Holtzmann regarded Mk 14,63 and Mt 26,65 as parallels of 22,71. It was on account of this that Luke reproduced only the leading of Jesus to Pilate (23,1) and not the session already anticipated in 22,66. He therefore concluded that for the changes in the common text of this and the account of Peter's denials Luke shortened them to the point of senselessness (pace Wernle, p. 33f.) or adhered to another tradition which knew nothing of a real trial before the Sanhedrin ([3]1901, 417).

61. 1889, p. 287 (= [2]1892, 288; [3]1901, 417). Holtzmann agreed with Wernle that Luke, by combining the two Synoptic Sanhedrin sessions, essentially simplified the account (415). He once again depended upon Brandt favoring the Lukan presentation at 23,1 over the timing prescribed in the OT: "Sofern aber Act 12,3-4 gegen eine solche, übrigens auch nirgends direct nachweisbare, Praxis spricht [...], müsste man zuletzt seine Zuflucht zu der lucanischen Darstellung nehmen" (102; BRANDT, p. 59, 286).

62. 1889, p. 288 (= [2]1892, 289; [3]1901, 417). Verse 2 contained the political accusations which were similar to Acts 24,5 and known to be false in light of 20,25. The reference to ἀρξάμενος ἀπὸ τῆς Γαλιλαίας (v. 5) called to mind for Pilate the menacing memory of the insurrection of Galileans (Acts 5,37). Holtzmann indicated Brandt's position that the Romans preferred trials right after sunrise (p. 103; BRANDT, p. 198).

63. 1889, p. 288 (= [2]1892, 289; [3]1901, 417).

For the material treating Jesus and Barabbas (23,17-25)[64], Holtzmann noted that v. 17 was found only in the Western MS witnesses[65]. At v. 18 Lk again commenced with an excerpt from Mk 15,9-11[66]. Lk 23,19, standing in possible connection with 13,1, drew upon Mk 15,7, as did the detail about the release of Jesus (23,20 / Mk 15,12 / Mt 27,22). Luke then introduced a short excerpt from Mk 15,9-11 where the plea by the people for Barabbas coincided with the incitement by the priests[67]. Connections between Lk and Acts were discerned: ἐπεφώνουν: 22,21; Acts 12,22; 21,34; 22,24) and earlier portions of this chapter (23,22; 23,4.14; ἐπέκρινεν: 23,24; 5,1. Linguistic evidence was once more given to show how, through the use of vocabulary, Luke connected one section to another[68].

The Pilate and Herod pericope (23,6-16) was defined as a unique story drawn from older material having a parallel in Acts 25,23–26,32[69]. The account in Lk reflected Markan influence by older material. He noted in the third edition that J. Weiss and Feine supported the views that derived from Luke's special source[70]. Lk 23,9 stemmed from Mk 15,4.5 and 23,10 from Mk 15,3. The white clothing (23,11) anticipated the detail in Mk 15,17, which was lacking. The term ἐξουθενεῖν stemmed from the LXX and also exhibited a relationship with Acts (12,21). Changes reflected the tension between Jewish and Roman authorities.

Reviewing Holtzmann's contribution, he originally accepted Proto-Mk, though he later abandoned that view. It can be said he accepted not only heavy Markan influence on Lk, but that the passion account was also shaped by the LXX. In addition, Lk bore a close relationship to Acts based upon shared themes and vocabulary. Luke built on what he had written earlier in the Gospel and thus revealed himself as the master littérateur who so crafted his account that the earlier portions fittingly served as the anticipation of what followed. Nevertheless, Holtzmann did not dispute the possibility of a special source in the passion narrative, especially in the accounts of Peter's denials and Herod's trial, but viewed the suggestion with caution. Finally, although he initially (1863) designated the Herod story as 23,6-12, in his commentary and *Einleitung* ([3]1892) he referred to it as 23,6-16.

---

64. 1889, p. 289-290 (= [2]1892, 290-291; [3]1901, 103, 418). In the third edition Holtzmann stated that the Romans were favored over the Jews in Luke's presentation by means of the repeated declarations of innocence and attempts to save Jesus (p. 103).

65. 1889, p. 289 (= [2]1892, 290; cf. [3]1901, 418), where he commented in the third edition "fällt sie aus" and thus the demand of the Jews (23,18) appeared unmotivated.

66. 1889, p. 290 (= [2]1892, 291; [3]1901, 418).

67. *Ibid*. The term for the people calling (ἐπεφώνουν) for his crucifixion was also found in Acts 12,22; 21,34; 22,24.

68. *Ibid*. A form of ἐπίκειμαι appears in 5,1 where the crowd was pressing to hear Jesus.

69. 1889, p. 288-289 (= [2]1892, 289-290; [3]1901, 417-418). According to Wernle this presupposed an apologetical tendency (WERNLE, 1899, p. 95, 106). Further, Herod sent Jesus back to Pilate, to the higher authority, just as was done in Acts 25,21 (HOLTZMANN, 417).

70. [3]1901, p. 417: "nach J. WS, FN 69 aus der Quelle"; cf. 1889, 288-289; [2]1892, 289.

Because Brandt had so influenced Holtzmann's third edition of the commentary, we will briefly survey his contributions. Inspired by Holtzmann's earlier commentaries on the Gospels and Acts as well as Weizsäcker's *Das apostolische Zeitalter der christlichen Kirche*, Wilhelm BRANDT (1893)[71] asserted that, in addition to Mk, Luke employed at least one other written source[72]. Further, he believed there were good reasons for raising objections against such an explanation. The other large, non-continuous special Lukan source, beginning with Chapter 3, contained chiefly sayings, parables, stories and occasionally introduction to dialogue and instructions[73].

Brandt judged the kernel of the denial story (22,54-62) to be historical[74]. He supported the idea that the MA in 22,62 was an insertion from Mt[75]. An account of the mockery of Jesus by the Jews in Lk was not lacking, but in contrast in Mk and Mt Luke allowed the incident to occur around the same time as Jesus waited in the house[76].

The Lukan account of the Sanhedrin trial (22,66-71) was considered to be a freely redacted and abbreviated form of Mark's account, as he also noted the omission of the reference to false witnesses[77]. He concluded: "die Erzählung des Lukas ist nicht historischer als die der beiden andern Synoptiker"[78]. Brandt offered nothing specific on 23,1-5 and argued that Lk contained nothing original in 23,13-25, maintaining that Luke depended upon Mk in the account of Jesus and Barabbas[79].

71. W. BRANDT, *Die evangelische Geschichte und der Ursprung des Christenthums auf Grund einer Kritik der Berichte über das Leiden und die Auferstehung Jesu*, Leipzig, 1893, p. XII. cf. C. WEIZSÄCKER, *Das apostolische Zeitalter der christlichen Kirche*, Freiburg i.Br., 1886-1889; Tübingen, ²1886; Tübingen - Leipzig, ³1902, p. 399: "Unter die ältesten Erzählungen gehört ohne Zweifel die Leidensgeschichte. Aber sie bildet gleichsam eine Gattung für sich". On Luke's redactional technique: "Der Verfasser des dritten Evangeliums und der Apostelgeschichte hat vielfach in der Weise gearbeitet, dass er mit grosser Freiheit seine Quellen ohne Rücksicht der Zeit nach sachlichen Gesichtspunkten kombiniert, ja geradezu Stücke aus ihrem überlieferten Zusammenhang herausnimmt, um denselben an einem anderen Ort ihre volle demonstrative Bedeutung zu geben" (p. 180; see also p. 207, 400).

72. BRANDT, p. 74.

73. *Ibid*, p. 75. He reacted to the position of E. REUSS, *Geschichte der Heiligen Schriften Neuen Testaments*, Halle, 1842; Braunschweig, ⁵1874, p. 186, who claimed that only Mt was dependent upon Mk while Mk, Lk and Jn contained independent and original reports of Jesus' final destiny.

74. BRANDT, *Die evangelische Geschichte*, p. 34.

75. *Ibid.*, p. 31.

76. *Ibid.*, p. 76. The manner in which he treated this scene was typical of how Luke used other stories. Brandt discussed only Mk 14,65 and Mt 26,67-68 in his treatment of the mockery, not even listing Lk 22,63-65 as a parallel (p. 69-71).

77. *Ibid.*, p. 68, 72. It was clear that Luke knew the information about the witness testimony.

78. *Ibid.*, p. 73.

79. *Ibid.*, p. 85-93, 100.

The proposal that some special historical tradition lies at the basis of the Herod pericope (23,6-12) was rejected by Brandt[80]. It was a combination of storyteller's art and transmitted story, particularly from material derived from the sketch of Jesus before Pilate. The stories were strikingly alike so that the Herod account was seen only as a variant of the story of Jesus before Pilate[81]. So similar were the two stories that they can be interchanged. Luke planned well for the Herod tale as can be seen from 9,7-9 and 13,31-33. Further, the description of Jesus before Herod paralleled that of Paul in Acts 21–26[82]. The puzzling question as to why Pilate transferred Jesus to Herod was resolved, not by appeal to duty, but out of courtesy, though the reason for Herod's trip to Jerusalem was left unresolved. Two further details captured Brandt's attention. First, there was the mockery as recounted in 23,11. Luke ommitted the mockery in Mk 15,16-20 / Mt 27,27-31. Instead, he used the main elements at other places[83]. Secondly, the gorgeous apparel (v. 11) was perhaps intended by Luke to refer to the royal purple. He may simply have wanted to vary the expression[84].

Finally, Brandt surmised that the author of the GP used the four canonical Gospels in the formulation of his own[85]. His composition combined information that "the Jews" crucified Jesus with the Lukan Herod story as well as the Matthean account of the handwashing[86]. It is clear that Brandt was a strong advocate of the view that Luke freely redacted Mk.

Marie-Joseph LAGRANGE (1895-96) reacted strongly against the proto-Mk and LQ theories of J. Weiss while ably defending the view that Luke not only claimed to be, but indeed was an original writer. He was not simply a compiler, though he drew upon written sources[87]. He interpreted the Lukan Prologue as revealing that

---

80. *Ibid.*, p. 117.

81. *Ibid.*, p. 116. See also p. 113.

82. *Ibid.*, p. 115.

83. *Ibid.*, p. 108.

84. *Ibid.*, p. 116-117. Brandt did not regard the vesting of Jesus as part of the mockery, but as an aspect of returning Jesus the prisoner to Pilate.

85. *Ibid.*, p. 543-544.

86. *Ibid.*

87. M.-J. LAGRANGE, *Les sources du troisième Évangile*, in *RB* 4 (1895) 5-22; 5 (1896) 5-38. The article consisted of the first lecture of his course on Lk (1891-95). He noted two previous articles by Semeria and Batiffol in *RB* had been devoted to the question on the origin of the Gospels (1895, p. 6, n. 1). In the inaugural volume Giovanni B. SEMERIA (1892) judged it "très probable" that Mk and Lk were directly and immediately related while an indirect connection existed between Mt and Lk (*La question synoptique*, in *RB* 1, 1892, 520-559, esp. p. 548). But it was the divergences between Lk and Mk which presented the greatest obstacle to firmly establishing a direct relationship between Mk and Lk (p. 549). And although Lk agreed with Mk less than with Mt in the passion narrative, Lk nevertheless resembles the Markan account (p. 529). Semeria envisioned the possibility that what Lk 22,66 described may be what was contained in Mt 27,1 and Mk 15,1 which they have mentioned only in passing while concentrating more attention on the nocturnal judgment (p. 530, n. 1).

Luke knew Mk but not Mt[88]. The position of G.L. Hahn, that the author of Lk
was Silas in the Emmaus story, was contrasted with that of Feine, who advocated
a primitive Jewish-Christian document, to which Lagrange added: "La tradition ne
nous empêche pas de reconnaître dans le troisième évangile une couleur fortement
araméenne; si nous arrivons à la constater, que penser des deux systèmes [Hahn
and Feine] qui cherchent à l'expliquer?"[89]. The source theory of A. Loisy as it
appeared in *L'enseignement biblique* (1893) was also highlighted and criticized for
exaggerating Pauline influence[90]. Loisy had not only written that Feine's proposal
showed "une assez grande probabilité"[91], but he railed against exegetes who
viewed Luke as having freely redacted from dubious traditions.

In the second installment of his article, Lagrange examined various theories
of the literary composition of Lk. The proposal of a primitive Mk, whether
espoused in the Utilization hypothesis or Markus hypothesis, as well as
Schleiermacher's suggestion of fragments, were judged insufficient[92]. P. Schanz,
on the other hand, according to Lagrange, had done justice to Luke by proposing
a combination of catechesis and written sources[93]. Lagrange reserved the most
detailed criticism for J. Weiss[94]. Citing B. Weiss and J. Weiss as typical of
independent criticism, he complimented both men for not only having a grasp of
the field but also knowing the difficulties of each theory[95]. His critique addressed,

---

Commenting on the order, Semeria discerned that there was a "singulière conformité" where
Luke followed Mk in the part of the Gospel preceding the first multiplication of loaves. In
contrast Matthew distanced himself. And while Matthew more closely follows Mk in the section
containing the passion, Luke's divergences were not as great as Matthew's had been in the first
segment (p. 525). Although Lk differed in some aspects of the passion narrative, the three
Synoptics agreed to a great extent on the Gethsemane scene. Other variations were due to Luke's
arranging the material in a more independent manner (p. 529-530). See the analysis of Semeria's
article by LOISY, *Chronique*, in *L'enseignement biblique* 2 (mars-avril, 1893) 1-29.

The other article dealing with the origin of the NT was P. BATIFFOL, *Comment s'est formé le
Nouveau Testament. À propos des Bampton Lectures de 1893*, in *RB* 3 (1894) 375-386, a reaction
to W. SANDAY, *Inspiration. Eight Lectures on the Early History and Origin of the Doctrine of
Biblical Inspiration* (Bampton Lectures, 1893), London, 1893.

88. LAGRANGE, *Les sources*, 1895, p. 21. Mk was numbered among the sources designated
by πολλοί. In his conclusion, Lagrange tempered his view concerning Mt, proposing that it was
possible that Luke used canonical Mt. It was more probable, however, that there were partial
translations of the original Mt or a stereotyped tradition of oral translations (1896, p. 31-32, 37).

89. *Ibid.*, p. 19. Clarifying the tradition to which he referred he stated: "La tradition des
Pères ne connaît ni *logia* de Matthieu, ni proto-Marc, ni proto-Luc, soit hiérosolymitain, soit
ébionite, soit paulinien" (p. 20). Cf. FEINE (1891). Lagrange presumably referred to [G.L.] Hahn
(1892/1894) but erred in the notes (p. 18, 19).

90. LAGRANGE, *Les sources*, p. 19; cf. LOISY, in *L'enseignement biblique* 2 (1893).

91. LAGRANGE, *Les sources*, p. 19; cf. LOISY, p. 30.

92. *Les sources*, in *RB* 5 (1896) 6-7.

93. *Ibid.*, 1896, p. 7-8. He noted that Schanz's writings antedated Feine's hypothesis. Cf. P.
SCHANZ, *Commentar über das Evangelium des heiligen Lucas*, Tübingen, 1883.

94. LAGRANGE, *Les sources*, 1896, p. 8-9.

95. *Ibid.*, p. 8.

in part, their too narrow regard for the literary ability of Luke: "Luc prétend être et est écrivain original". Ultimately, he dismissed the proposal of J. Weiss because: "Indémontrable est le principe de l'emprunt total"[96]. Specific criticisms included the impossibility of distinguishing between Luke and LQ. Further, one cannot say that Luke, a Gentile convert, was responsible for that material which was obviously Judaeo-Christian and Ebionite[97]. What made Weiss's proposal even less likely was that Luke could have composed a work, the language of which was so heavily imbued with Semitisms[98]. Lagrange accused Feine and Weiss of suggesting two differing forms of redaction: one for the Gospel, in which Luke copied sources, and another for Acts, where he composed for his account[99]. Finally, Lagrange rejected Godet's characterization of Luke as a historian as exclusive and exaggerated[100]. The evangelist sought to situate the life of Jesus within history.

Presenting his own position, Lagrange argued that in the triple tradition, Luke's source was Mk[101]. Luke borrowed from Mk, but borrowed freely. He was not able to determine the proportion of oral and written tradition, but alleged Luke combined oral catechesis with the written sources[102]. As a composer Luke was obviously in control of the sources and not subjected to their influence[103].

Changes from Luke's primary source stemmed from his own tendencies and his objective[104]: "Luc a en vue une suite, un dessein particulier, et c'est pour cela qu'il s'écarte de Marc"[105]. Lukan redaction entailed an exact presentation that dismissed emotion in favor of a precision that was both "élégant et délicat"[106]. The deliberate choice not to include certain material from Mk was often made with a view to Luke's Gentile convert readership[107]. Omissions,

---

96. *Ibid.*, p. 9. He expressed the doubt that J. Weiss would assign so much as a chapter to the redactor.

97. *Ibid.*, p. 34. Lagrange argued one cannot clearly define Ebionism. On J. Weiss and LQ see further p. 32-34.

98. *Ibid.* The more Hellenistic parts of the Gospel reflected Luke's imitation of Greek sources. The Semitic elements derived from written Semitic sources or the testimony of witnesses (p. 35).

99. *Ibid.* He noted that the latest contribution to the question regarding sources for Acts attributed a good part of the first chapters to Luke. Cf. J. JÜNGST, *Die Quellen der Apostelgeschichte*, Gotha, 1895.

100. LAGRANGE, *Les sources*, 1896, p. 15.

101. *Ibid.*, p. 13. Lagrange rejected Proto-Mk in favor of a combination of written sources and tradition. He bade farewell to the Proto-Mk theory: "Grâce à Dieu, le Proto-Marc a disparu" (p. 10).

102. *Ibid.*, p. 36.

103. *Ibid.*, p. 19; cf. p. 37.

104. *Ibid.*, p. 24.

105. *Ibid.*, p. 20.

106. *Ibid.*, p. 16.

107. *Ibid.*, p. 16-18. With regard to details about Palestine or other topography, Luke sometimes omitted these while at other times he retained them, providing a word of explanation.

which critics highlighted as indicative of another source, according to Lagrange, pointed directly to the literary process[108]. Other changes, such as presenting the Sanhedrin, as well as the Romans, in a better light, also were credited to Luke's literary program and style[109]: "S'il n'a pu recueillir dans la tradition un autre souvenir, c'est donc lui, qui disposant la matière évangélique conformément à ses tendances et à son but, a donné au récit de la Passion une physionomie particulière. En un mot, il compose avec exactitude, avec un souverain respect de la vérité, mais il compose avec art"[110].

Lagrange, speaking generally about agreements between Mt and Lk, stipulated that they likely resulted from an indirect connection. Oral translation which had been stereotyped through the tradition or incomplete translations of the original Mt could give rise to agreements[111].

He believed Luke was governed by a chronological perspective which was more precise than Mk. Rearrangement of material by Luke was dictated by Luke's conviction that his order reflected more chronological precision or that the resulting order underscored the unfolding of Jesus' ministry[112].

Accordingly, Lagrange opposed Feine's proposal that Luke inserted a block of material, such as a Jerusalem Gospel, into a canonical Gospel[113]. From such a point of view, Luke was seen merely as a compiler and not an author in his own right. While Lagrange agreed that Lk reflected a heavy Semitic style[114], it certainly rarely, if at all, exceeded that of Mk and Mt[115].

In his commentary on Lk (1921), for which he also drew upon Holtzmann's *Die Synoptiker* ([3]1901), Lagrange affirmed that Luke knew and followed Mk, though he acknowledged it will be difficult to establish that fact in the section containing the passion and resurrection (22-24)[116]. Outside the sections specially designated as Markan, Lagrange noted the omission of the following Markan material: the first appearance before the Sanhedrin and the prophecy about the destruction of the Temple (Mk 14,53-65) and the mockery and crowning with thorns (Mk 15,16-20[a]), together with transpositions which Lagrange contended

---

108. *Ibid.*, p. 20.

109. *Ibid.*, p. 18-19.

110. *Ibid.*, p. 19. See *Les sources*, 1895, p. 22: "il [Luc] conserve sa liberté vis-à-vis de ses sources ...".

111. *Ibid.*, 1896, p. 37; cf. p. 31-32. Although he conceded Luke might have used Mt, it was more probable that the similarities can be explained by a stereotyped tradition or partial translations.

112. *Ibid.*, p. 20-21. Variations from the Markan source betrayed "le but et les tendances de l'auteur" (p. 24).

113. *Ibid.*, 1895, p. 19.

114. *Ibid.*

115. *Ibid.*, 1896, p. 35.

116. *Évangile selon saint Luc*, Paris, 1921 (= [8]1948), p. XLVIII. Cf. p. XLIX, LVIII. He admitted being especially indebted to the commentaries of Plummer ([4]1901), Schanz, (1883) in addition to Holtzmann ([3]1901) (p. V).

were in concert with Luke's plan for his Gospel[117]. Luke retained but transposed what he considered the most important of the two Sanhedrin trials and gave indication in 22,71 that he knew them[118]. The mockery remained during the night but took place prior to the Sanhedrin trial.

In response to the claim that the special source had been Ebionite, Lagrange argued that those texts within Lk did not form a special grouping[119]. He used L to designate Luke's own style which in some places had been influenced by written sources. Lagrange assessed the attempt by Feine, B. Weiss, and later J.V. Bartlet to differentiate between Luke, L and LQ as "un échec complet"[120]. What was lacking was criteria to establish written sources[121]. D.R. Wickes, following the example of W. Soltau, attempted to assign to Q a certain number of episodes proper to Lk. But this too resulted in failure since he was not able to establish the existence of two documents, each displaying its own language and literary character in presenting the life and teaching of Jesus[122]. The solution lies in assigning a large part of the special material to oral tradition[123]. Because Luke dedicated a great deal of attention to women, Lagrange believed the information derived from them[124]. The Hebrew constructions can be attributed to a well grounded familiarity with the LXX[125]. Leaving introductory material aside we turn now to the commentary on 22,54–23,25.

Jesus was judged twice: once by the religious leaders and the second time by Pilate. Lagrange insisted that the Lukan order, as in the case of the trial, was more probable since the Jews also had the custom of not judging at night[126]. The

117. *Évangile*, p. LIX.
118. *Ibid.*, p. LIX-LX.
119. *Ibid.*, p. LXXXIX-XC.
120. *Ibid.*, p. XC. Lagrange reprised the position from his article, *Les sources*, 1896, p. 32: "Rien ne nous empêche de conclure que le prétendu rédacteur est vraiment l'auteur et non seulement le copiste du troisième évangile". He apparently confused B. Weiss for J. Weiss when he spoke of "le Commentaire de B. Weiss"; cf. p. IV, ⁸1892! In the Addenda to the commentary, Lagrange declared that in comparing the view of V. Bartlet (1911) with that of Streeter and Taylor, Taylor himself had not been able to distinguish Proto-Lk from Luke on the basis of a distinctive style or doctrine (²1926, p. 623). Cf. Lagrange's review of Taylor's *Behind the Third Gospel* in *RB* 36 (1927) 120-123.
121. LAGRANGE, *Évangile*, p. XCI. Having admitted the difficulty of trying to offer a resumé of the commentary, José M. Bover, highlighted Lagrange's discussion of the synoptic problem and the efforts of Feine and Weiss, quoting this statement of Lagrange (*Bib* 3 [1922] 353-358, p. 355).
122. *Ibid.*, p. XCI. Cf. D.R. WICKES, *Sources* (1912), and W. SOLTAU, *Die Anordnung der Logia in Lukas 15-18*, in *ZNW* 10 (1909) 230-238.
123. LAGRANGE, *Évangile*, p. XCI. Lagrange based this on the Prologue where Luke announced that his information derived from early witnesses.
124. *Ibid.* He opposed Harnack's thesis that the daughters of Philip would have been influential on the grounds that the apostles would have been more qualified and Luke scarcely referred to Philip's daughters.
125. *Ibid.*, p. XCVII.
126. *Ibid.*, p. 567. Contra Holtzmann and Schanz who believed Luke shifted the material in

Markan source of the denials underwent some modification and change of order by Luke to bring together without interruption all the material related to Peter. Although neither Mark nor Luke mentioned the name of the high priest (22,54 / Mk 14,53), Luke mentioned Annas before Caiaphas earlier in the Gospel (3,2[127]) and later in Acts (4,6). According to Holtzmann and Schanz Luke presumably had Annas in mind. The order in v. 55, for example, was characterized as chronological and impersonal, though the verse recounted exactly what was found in Mk 14,54[128].

Luke's desire for some variety prompted the change from the maid servant to the man as the second inquisitor (v. 58). The MA in 22,62 was described as "exactement comme Mt"[129].

The mockery was carried out by the soldiers who arrested Jesus. Luke did not have the mockery by the Roman soldiers[130]. Although Mk 15,16-20 influenced Lk 22,63-65, it was omitted in Lk 23! In this way Luke did not return to the cruelties which Mark ascribed to the Sanhedrin and their servants. Owing to the fact that Luke did not recount the first Sanhedrin session he cannot introduce the Sanhedrin in 22,66. Examining some of the vocabulary, the term συνέχω was described as "extremely rare" and ἐνέπαιζον is the same term as Mk 15,20 and Mt 27,31. Forms of δέροντες were found earlier in Lk at 12,47 and 20,10. It was remarked that τίς ἐστιν ὁ παίσας σε; the MA in 22,64 / Mt 26,68 "paraît bien répondre à l'intention de Mc."[131]. In 22,65 Luke avoided mention of the most painful traits and moderated the excessive suffering.

Lagrange contended the absence of the Markan material from Lk was easily explained. The account of the trial resulted from Luke's efforts at simplification in light of his readers and nothing of any importance was omitted. Lagrange believed that Luke was familiar with Mark's account and merely simplified it, retaining only one trial, though it contained details of the nocturnal trial as well. The omission of the reference to the testimony of witnesses (22,67) was also noted, though 22,71 supposed well what the testimony intended. The lack of reference to the destruction of the Temple was accounted for as something Luke would have had to explain to his Gentile readers. Jesus' response in 22,68 fit perfectly in the situation and resembled Jer 38,15[132]. In relation to 22,69 the response of Jesus in Mk employed two texts (Ps 111 and Dn 7,13) in order to present the idea of the triumph of the Messiah. Luke retained the phrase "sitting at the right hand of God" but substituted ἔσται for ὄψεσθε since the parousia would not be seen by the Sanhedrin[133]. The omission focused less on the exterior glory of Jesus than on

light of the Roman custom.

127. Lagrange mistakenly listed 3,1.
128. *Ibid.*, p. 568.
129. *Ibid.*, p. 570.
130. *Ibid.*
131. *Ibid.*, p. 571.
132. *Ibid.*, p. 572.
133. *Ibid.*, p. 572, 573. He also referred to a previous article: *Mélanges*, in *RB* 111 (1906)

his nearness to God. In 22,71 Luke had not composed rigorously but reproduced faithfully his Markan source.

Although 23,1-49 initially appeared quite different from Mk, Lagrange said this resulted from various additions and omissions by Luke[134]. In certain sections, Luke included everything that Mk had. Among the significant additions were the Herod episode (23,6-12), which Luke discovered in the tradition, and the protest of Pilate (23,13-16) which were due to Luke's "enquête particulière"[135].

In the first trial before Pilate (23,1-5), unlike Mk and Mt, Jesus was not chained. Pilate's question and Jesus' response (23,3) were like in Mk. The term αἴτιον, a term proper to Lk, was repeated in 22,14.22 while the adjectival form was found in Acts 19,40.

The background of 23,17-25 was like that found in Mk[136]. The role "des sanhedrites" was omitted. The term ἐπιφωνέω (23,21) was found only in Lk and Acts. The phrase φωναῖς μεγάλαις was Lukan style (cf. 4,33; 8,28; 17,15; Acts 8,7 and so on, but always in the singular). Luke refrained from mentioning the flagellation and mockery which followed[137].

Lagrange suspected that, though contrary to history, the Herod pericope contained elements which were conceivable[138]. Thus Lagrange believed that Luke had access to reference to the role of Herod in the tradition[139]. It was probable that Herod was in Jerusalem at the time of Passover. Lagrange was sensitive to the dichotomy between the presentation of Herod in 9,7 and 13,31ff.

He contended that the analogy between 23,11 and Mk 15,16ff. was "incontestable". Luke exercised great freedom in not electing to adhere strictly to the various aspects of the Roman procedure[140]. Though Lagrange had not concerned himself with the shared vocabulary of Lk and Acts, he highlighted a few terms: ἀναπέμπω[141] and ἀνακρίνας[142].

The position of Lagrange, that Luke freely redacted Mk, remained constant. In examining Luke's compositional method he evaluated the hypotheses of Feine, J. Weiss and B. Weiss and rejected them, since it was impossible to distinguish

---

561-574 (esp. p. 571-573). He stated: "Cette préoccupation des Juifs connue, rien de plus clair et de plus logique que l'ordre de Luc. [...] Il est difficile d'admettre que Luc, sans autre source que Mc., ait restitué de lui-même un ordre aussi vraisemblable. La vraisemblance est ici une garantie du vrai. Luc suit la tradition la plus exacte; les autres ont bloqué. [...] Si Luc n'a pas conservé le texte primitif, il a du moins prétendu le traduire, il nous transmet fidèlement la manière dont on l'entendait de son temps" (p. 572-573). He erroneously printed 23,60 rather than 22,60 (p. 571).

134. *Évangile*, p. 575.
135. *Ibid.*, p. 575, 578-579.
136. *Ibid.*, p. 581.
137. *Ibid.*, p. 584.
138. *Ibid.*, p. 578 (= [8]1948).
139. *Ibid.*, p. 578-579.
140. *Ibid.*, p. 581.
141. *Ibid.*, p. 579. The word was also found in Acts 25,21 and in Josephus, Bell II, 20,5.
142. *Ibid.* The term occurred in 23,14 and Acts 4,9; 12,19; 24,8; 28,18.

between Luke and the supposed LQ source. Luke omitted Markan material for the purpose of simplification. Additional material could be explained by oral tradition.

Inasmuch as some scholars maintained that Paul had the greatest influence on Luke, Adolf JÜLICHER (1894) argued that the themes of compassion and sympathy in Lk were "nur Steigerungen des auch bei Mc und Mt Mitgeteilten" directed toward Hellenistic readers[143]. Luke was prompted to write his own account because he considered the older Gospels inadequate. Not only was their chronological order faulty, but the predecessors had not recorded the developments precisely.

Jülicher labeled as "sehr mit Unrecht" the attempt to discover within Lk the stamp of Ebionism and signs of Jewish influence. Whatever traces of such themes may be found there were unintentional[144]: "Eine besondere 'ebionitische' Nebenquelle aber für Lc zu postuliren liegt kein Grund vor, weil die ebionitische Färbung von ihm hinzugebracht ist und gerade so stark wie an anonymem Gut an dem aus Mc und der Logienschrift entlehnten haftet"[145]. Jülicher argued that providing a more accurate order, which involved chronologically rearranging individual portions, prompted Luke, in part, to compose his Gospel[146].

As a redactor, Luke was responsible for creating some of the material. Jülicher (1901) maintained Luke himself should probably be credited with introducing Herod into the trial of Jesus (23,6-16)[147]. Jülicher remained somewhat general in contrasting the redactional techniques of Matthew and Luke except to suggest that Matthew employed the oral tradition while Luke seemed to have had recourse more often to written documents. And though Jülicher was critical of Wernle who ascribed to Christian apologia the differences between Mt and Lk in relation to Mk, Jülicher himself appeared to advocate something very similar in arguing that Luke's purpose was to provide a Gospel "which should at

---

143. A. JÜLICHER, *Einleitung in das Neue Testament* (Grundriss der theologischen Wissenschaften 3/1), Tübingen, [1,21894], 3,41901, p. 262; 5,61906, p. 292 (= *An Introduction to the New Testament*, tr. J. PENROSE WARD, London, 1904, 333).

144. *Ibid.*, 1,21894, p. 206; 3,41901, p. 264; 5,61906, p. 295 (= *Introduction*, 336).

145. *Ibid.*, 1,21894, p. 225; 3,41901, p. 286: "Eine besondere 'ebionitische' Nebenquelle aber für Lc zu postuliren liegt kein Grund vor, weil die ebionitische Färbung *zu gleichmässig sein ganzes Evgl. durchzieht* und gerade so stark wie an anonymem Gut an dem aus Mc und der Logienschrift entlehnten haftet"; 5,61906, p. 319 (= *Introduction*, 363).

146. *Ibid.*, 1,21894, p. 202; 3,41901, p. 260: 5,61906, p. 290 (= *Introduction*, 330).

147. *Ibid.*, 3,41901, p. 285: "Er [Luke] ist zu einem Teil Dichter, die Hereinziehung des Herodes in den Process Jesu 23,6-16 könnte er allein zu verantworten haben: Könige und Procuratoren (βασιλεῖς καὶ ἡγεμόνες) sollen Jesu Unschuld bezeugt haben, damit man gegenwärtig die Unschuld der Christen vor den gleichen Instanzen wahrscheinlich machen kann" (= *Introduction*, 362). Cf. 1,21894, p. 224; 5,61906, p. 318: "Er ist zu einem Teile Dichter, die Hereinziehung des Herodes in den Prozess Jesu 23,6-16 *darf man wie die neuen Kreuzesworte einfach auf sein Konto setzen* ..." [revision indicated by italics].

once be complete, and well adapted both to refute unjust accusations from outside and to edify the believers themselves"[148].

Alfred PLUMMER (1896)[149] viewed all three Synoptic authors as having used the early narrative, which served as the primary segment of Mk. Though he appeared somewhat tentative in proposing that Luke may have had a copy of Mk "pretty nearly in the form in which we have it", Plummer considered it certain that Luke associated with Mark in Rome. He also proposed that Luke probably drew information from some of the Apostles and disciples, and the mother of Jesus in addition to Paul[150]. In the final analysis, Plummer argued there was not much difference between oral or written material. "A document cannot have much influence on a writer who already knows its contents by heart"[151]. This similarity notwithstanding, Plummer wrote that for material unique to Luke, some of these sources were oral. But it was likely that most of this material had been written down before it reached Luke's hands[152].

In line with Feine and opposed to Wernle, Plummer evaluated the frequent occurrence of Hebraisms as evident that "a great deal of Luke's material was originally in Aramaic", especially in chapters 1 and 2[153]. But Plummer dismissed the proposal of Ebionite influence, recommending instead that the theme of poverty and riches stemmed from Luke himself, as Holtzmann also had advocated[154].

Taking note of omissions, as others had done, Plummer regarded these as a dimension of Lukan redaction. Luke intentionally omitted material based either on

---

148. *Ibid.*, p. 367; cf. p. 292. See P. WERNLE, *Altchristliche Apologetik im N.T.*, in *ZNW* 1 (1900), p. 42-65. Jülicher described Wernle's contribution as "a clever but somewhat one-sided attempt to explain the differences between Mk and the later Gospels as the results of the needs of Christian Apologetics against Jews and Gentiles respectively".

149. A. PLUMMER, *A Critical and Exegetical Commentary on the Gospel according to S. Luke*, Edinburgh, 1896, ⁴1901. Plummer treated Luke's sources in §3, p. xxiii-xxix. In his preface to ³1900 (p. viii), reprinted in ⁴1901, he noted three studies bearing on Lk which students "cannot afford to neglect": HAWKINS, *Horae*; A. WRIGHT, *The Gospel according to S. Luke in Greek*; and J. HASTINGS, *Jesus Christ*, in *A Dictionary of the Bible*. A comparison of the fourth edition with the ninth edition (⁹1910, New York), showed only two minor additions in the section pertinent to our study. In the later edition on p. 515, and again p. 527, Plummer made brief references to the article of J. Hastings in *A Dictionary of the Bible*.
The omission of certain material, according to Plummer, argued against the view that Luke had a copy of Mk in his possession (p. xxiii). Among the texts cited were Mk 2,27 at Lk 6,5, the whole of Mk 6,45-8,9, and the incident with the Syrophonecian woman (Mk 7,24-30 / Mt 15,21-28).

150. PLUMMER, *S. Luke*, p. xxiii.

151. *Ibid.*

152. *Ibid.*, p. xxiv-xxv. Quoting Schleiermacher, Plummer asserted that the omission of 23,8-12 from Jn was not a serious threat to the genuineness of the passage (SCHLEIERMACHER, *S. Luke*, 1825). Further, Joanna, the wife of Chuza, who was Herod's steward (8,3), would be a likely source of information (cf. 24,10) (PLUMMER, *S. Luke*, p. 522; cf. p. 216).

153. *Ibid.*, p. xxvi. Ctr. WERNLE, *Die synoptische Frage*, p. 25.

154. PLUMMER, *S. Luke*, p. xxv-xxvi. Cf. H.J. HOLTZMANN, *Die Synoptiker*, ³1901, p. 20. In support of his view, Plummer quoted A. JÜLICHER, *Einleitung*, §27, p. 206.

its similarity to something he already recorded or how it would affect his Gentile readers. Other material would be lacking because Luke was ignorant of it[155]. Plummer received the dictum that Luke *avoids duplicates on principle* less enthusiastically. While Luke may have omitted some material because it was like other material he already included, there may have been other redactional reasons at work in the decision for the majority of cases. That the mocking of Pilate's soldiers may have been omitted in favor of the mockery by the soldiers of Herod was cited as one example[156]. "It is quite evident that in appropriating material Luke works it over with his own touches, and sometimes almost works it up afresh; and this is specially true of the narrative portion of the Gospel"[157]. And while the wording of particular sections may be different from Mk and Mt, as in 23,13-25, the substance was nonetheless the same[158].

Plummer made no direct assertion about the Lukan account of Peter's denial apart from saying it was different from Mk and Mt. In the mockery the omissions were invoked in witness that Luke was not using Mt or Mk[159]. Luke's version of the Sanhedrin trial was "quite independent".

Concerning 22,54ff., Plummer held that neither of the examinations were formal. Because they were held at night, no sentence was declared, since it would have been invalid[160]. Luke related only the third "ecclesiastical trial", which had been reported by Mk and Mt as well (Lk 22,66; Mt 27,1; Mk 15,1)[161]. "Lk. assumes that his readers know that Jesus was condemned to death by the Sanhedrin. But it was necessary to have Him condemned by the Roman procurator also, in order that the sentence might be executed, and without delay, by him who possessed μέχρι τοῦ κτείνειν ἐξουσίαν (Jos. B.J. ii.8.I). It is almost certain that at this time the Jews were deprived of the right of inflicting capital punishment. They sometimes did inflict it and risked the consequences, as in the case of S. Stephen: ..."[162].

Plummer wrote that for material unique to Luke, some of these sources were oral and probably one of them relayed the information concerning Herod's court (3,1.19; 8,3; 9,7-9; 13,31; 23,7-12; Acts 13,1). It was possible the material about Herod was authentic, with Joanna being a likely informant, though it was probable,

155. *S. Luke*, p. xxvii.

156. *Ibid.*, p. xxviii.

157. *Ibid.*, p. xxvii. WERNLE, *Die synoptische Frage*, p. 18, also made this observation.

158. *S. Luke*, p. 524.

159. *Ibid.*, p. 517.

160. *Ibid.*, 1896, ⁴1901, ᴿ1908, p. 514. To support his position, Plummer quoted R.H. LIGHTFOOT, *Biblical Essays*, London, 1893, p. 191: "St. Luke adds force to the episode by placing all three denials together. With St. John, however, dramatic propriety is sacrificed to chronological accuracy".

161. PLUMMER, *S. Luke*, p. 514-515. Jn reported only the first trial.

162. *Ibid.*, p. 519.

in Plummer's opinion, that this material was already in written form before Luke received it[163].

Arthur WRIGHT (1898) defended the influence of oral tradition, in part, by suggesting that changes in order and differences in up to forty percent of the vocabulary must be ascribed to it and by noting that the Church Fathers endorsed such a position[164]. He understood the Prologue to mean oral testimony derived from eyewitnesses. As proof he referred to situations in the East (India, China) where missionaries testified to the remarkable memories of the people. Wright asserted that each of the evangelists was a catechist, but that Luke was also an historian[165]. What is more, Wright concurred with J. Armitage Robinson that Luke imitated the language of the LXX in those places where the evangelist had "a free hand" in composing[166].

According to Wright (1900), while Mk served as Luke's primary source, and provided the historical framework for Lk, it too underwent a process of development[167]. Omissions which signaled to B. Weiss and J. Weiss the use of another source, for Wright simply indicated an earlier form of the Gospel of Mark used by Luke[168]. The non-Markan material, reflecting strong oral influence, was attributed to conversations with Palestinian visitors, letters, as well as information from catechists[169]. Oral teaching, fixed in form through catechetical

163. PLUMMER, *S. Luke*, 1896, ⁴1901, p. xxiv-xxv.

164. A. WRIGHT, *Some New Testament Problems*, London, 1898, p. 91 (esp. p. 91-103); cf. p. 101.

165. *Ibid.*, p. 99.

166. *Ibid.*, p. 100. Wright provided no bibliographical reference as to which work of Robinson he was referring.

167. A. WRIGHT, *The Gospel according to S. Luke in Greek. After the Westcott and Hort Text*, London, 1900, p. vii. Cf. p. xii, xxviii. "S. Mk is seen to be S. Lk's principal, if not only, guide in the arrangement of the whole book" (p. xxviii). Wright maintains that Luke was influenced not only by Proto-Mk, but by deutero-Mk as well, though material from the latter was boldly, if sometimes rather carelessly inserted (cf. p. xiv, xxxii). Luke placed deutero-Markan scraps where they conveniently fit, as he has also done with the non-Markan matter (p. xiv). Wright even posits a trito-Mk, though both Luke and Matthew would have been ignorant of it (p. xxxiii). Eventually, yielding to his second thoughts, Wright backtracked a bit: "Of course the divisions into proto-Mk, deutero-Mk, and trito-Mk are to some extent hypothetical and can only claim to be approximately correct in details" (p. xxx). PLUMMER (⁴1901), p. viii, considered Wright's commentary indispensable for the study of Lk.

168. A. WRIGHT, *S. Luke in Greek*, p. xii: "Therefore it is difficult to believe that S. Lk received S. Mk's Gospel at full length as we know it, for he has omitted at least one-third of it, including many sections which would have possessed the highest interest for himself and for his readers". Luke received the oral Proto-Mk which, like Lk, continued to grow and expand due to later additions.

169. *Ibid.* He described his variety of sources as "practically useful and reasonably probable, rather than actually established" (p. viii). Contending that the sources were oral, Wright said that this view had been rejected on the Continent and in America, while the question was still being debated in England (p. ix). Terms found in the preface, i.e. ἀνατάξασθαι, παρέδοσαν and

instruction[170], not only preserved the material but retained the order[171]. The Prologue, in Wright's view, probably indicated that Luke sought to assure the readers of chronological order, though he was not always able to accomplish that. This resulted from the fact that Luke's account was likewise adversely affected by a lack of information[172]. "[Luke] has certainly sometimes, probably often, misplaced events, and that occasionally very seriously"[173].

What Wright labeled as the fifth Markan segment (19,29–24,11) was derived both from Mk and special sources[174]. Non-Markan material was not so significant in the last third of Lk[175]. Luke conflated his sources throughout the Gospel and in the "Midnight Scenes" (22,39-42.45-65). Of a total twenty-five verses, fifteen stemmed from Proto-Mk, three were Lukan and seven derived from Luke's editorial notes[176]. In events transpiring on Good Friday, totaling sixty-one verses, twenty-two were Markan, twenty-seven belonged to Lukan special sources, and twelve were editorial notes[177]. Deutero-Mk contributed some material, often in the form of scraps, including 22,58-60[178].

κατηχήθης, supported the oral hypothesis (p. xiv-xv). Dismissing the view that Mark probably composed in Rome, Luke in Antioch and Matthew in Alexandria, Wright proposed "they all worked in the same spot" (p. xv).

170. *Ibid.*, p. x. An additional reason for the prevalence of oral instruction rather than written documents was fear of persecution (p. x). But this seems an unlikely possibility since the words of Jesus encourage his followers not to shrink in the face of martyrdom (Lk 12,4-9).

171. *Ibid.*, p. xi.

172. *Ibid.*, p. xvi. Luke's order was compromised for two reasons: he was not an eyewitness and the *logia* lacked a preface when Luke acquired them in pieces (p. xvi, xiii).

173. *Ibid.*, p. xxi.

174. *Ibid.*, p. xxix. In an important note, Wright added: "Sections 62-70 (from the prediction of Peter's denial, xxii.34 through xxiv.11) were expanded by additional matter in the deutero-Mk, which S. Mt follows, the subject posssessing exceptional interest and eye-witnesses being numerous" (p. xxxi, n. s).

175. *Ibid.*, p. xix. Wright included the appearance of Jesus before Herod in this material, saying that because of its nature, it cannot be easily misplaced.

176. *Ibid.*, p. xxix. Unfortunately, Wright did not specify which verses belong to what sources. However, it was clear that Mk was the chief source. Wright warned that the editorial notes were historically untrustworthy and usually function as literary connections. (Cf. p. viii; see also p. xxxix where he acknowledged "it is impossible to distinguish them all with certainty".) Wright called attention to such a high percentage of Lukan influence throughout the body of the Gospel as typical of his redaction. Proto-Mk was responsible for 22,54.66[b]-71.63-65; 22,56.59[c]-62; 23,1.3.18-25 (p. xxxi).

177. *Ibid.*

178. *Ibid.*, p. xxxiii. Wright described this and similar scraps as "editorial notes, not really derived from S. Mk though similar in content" (p. xxxii, n.[d]). It was unclear why Wright placed Lukan material dealing with Peter's denial on a par with "Details in the Crucifixion" and suggested it was even remotely similar to material in Mk 15,23.30[b]-32[a].34-36.

Deutero-Mk appeared to be responsible for the second and third denials[179]. Because Luke misplaced such a scrap, he presented the formal Sanhedrin trial in the morning. Luke's account lacked the clarity shown by Mk and Mt in presenting Jesus as having been found guilty of blasphemy[180]. In his revision of the *Synopsis* (²1903) some verses were said to be the result of conflation, not simply editorial notes, but additions from other sources. These included 22.59,60b,66, and 23,2[181]. Whereas in his commentary Wright maintained that nothing in 22,54-23,25 came from deutero-Mk, he now assigned 22,66-71.63-65 to that source[182]. But he also reversed himself by denying to Proto-Mk some verses in Ch 23 which he previously ascribed to it, namely 23,18-21[183].

In Wright's opinion, variations in order were later explained by the editorial process in assuming that prior to publication, both Luke and Matthew used written sources in conjunction with oral instruction which they "copied down ... in its common form"[184]. A later clarification (1908) stipulated that Luke's order was not necessarily "any nearer to the truth"[185].

Wright's *Synopsis* and commentary treated Luke's sources in six divisions[186]. According to the *Synopsis* Mk was the source for 22,54a.54b.55.56.57; 22,59*,60a.60b*-62; 23,2*.3.23-25. Material derived from deutero-Mk included 22,66-71.63-65 (their "dislocation in order" being duly noted). Material which had been conflated, that was "increased by accretions from other sources and not merely by editorial notes", included 22,59.60b.66 and 23,2.22[187]. The last part of the Gospel (19,29-24,11), which constituted the fifth Markan block, now was

---

179. *Ibid.*, p. 199. Wright was not certain whether Luke was conflating new sources with old, or simply drawing upon new sources for the denials. He suggested that τρίς may stem from the oral teaching of John carried over into deutero-Mk.

180. *Ibid.*, p. 201.

181. A. WRIGHT, *A Synopsis of the Gospels in Greek*, London, 1896, ²1903, p. xlvii.

182. *Ibid.* See A. WRIGHT, *S. Luke in Greek*, 1900, p. xxxii-xxxiii.

183. WRIGHT, *Synopsis*, ²1903, p. xlvii. In a category of the anonymous fragments peculiar to Luke designated as historical, Wright now assigned 22,61a; 23,4-19.22b-25 (p. liii). In his commentary, Wright included 22,61a and 23,18-25 as deriving from Proto-Mk (*S. Luke in Greek*, p. xxxi). The saying in 22,67b likewise was now ascribed to anonymous fragments where it previously had been ascribed to Proto-Mk. These changes were reflected in his table which indicated Luke's sources for the fifth Markan portion (xix.29-xxiv.11) so it now read: "I (Mk); III (Pauline); IV (Anonymous Fragments)".

184. WRIGHT, *Synopsis*, ²1903, p. xvii. Oral tradition, continually shaped by catechesis, assured that the order was preserved (*The Gospel According to S. Luke in Greek*, 1900, p. xi). Though Luke intended to present a chronologically accurate account, a lack of information hampered his plans.

185. A. WRIGHT, *The Gospel according to Luke,* in J. HASTINGS and J. SELBIE (eds.), *DCG*, New York, Vol. 2, 1908, 84-91, p. 87.

186. WRIGHT, *Synopsis*, ²1903, p. xi-xiii. The sources were: Mk, the Matthean Logia, Pauline material, anonymous fragments, Mary, the mother of Jesus and her family, and editorial notes. See WRIGHT, *S. Luke in Greek*, 1900, p. xxxii-xxxix, tables VII-XIII.

187. A. WRIGHT, *Synopsis*, p. xlvii.

said to comprise, in addition to Markan material, a Pauline collection and
anonymous fragments[188].

In a still later contribution (1908), Wright's stringent defense of an oral Gospel
of Mk seemed to wane. He now allowed that it may be oral or written[189]. The
wording of the Pauline source (third division) was due more to a "sympathetic
collector" than to Paul, the anonymous fragments were numbered at eighty and
Luke's editorial comments grew in Wright's estimation[190].

While Wright categorized the sending of Jesus to Herod among a classification
of anonymous fragments, it was not listed in his study of the Greek text of Lk in
any of his tables[191]. In his *Synopsis* (1903), Wright reformulated his position on
a number of questions[192]. Concerning the anonymous fragments, which provided
the story of Jesus before Herod, though they appeared to stem from one source,
Wright concluded they derived from a number of authorities, not all of whom were
apostles[193]. Elements not originating from Mk were 23,4-12.13-16. Anonymous
fragments unique to Luke contributed the historical elements of 23,2.4-19[194].
Although Wright sought to combine those anonymous fragments which stemmed
from one source, he believed they came from numerous, obscure authorities. Their
authenticity rested upon ecclesiastical authority.

From the outset in *Horae Synopticae* (1899) John C. HAWKINS made it clear that
he would not be concerned with the issues of the "number and nature" of Luke's
sources[195]. Writing of verses in Lk without parallel to Mt and Mk he listed only

188. *Ibid.*, p. lxvii. Cf. *S. Luke in Greek*, 1900, p. xxix, which spoke of Mk and special
material.
189. WRIGHT, *The Gospel according to Luke*, 1908, p. 85. Wright continued to refine his
positions in this work. Although he did not commit himself to declaring whether Mk existed as
an oral or written Gospel for Luke, he was adamant that Mk not only was used by Luke but
shaped the very work (p. 85). Wright counted 80 Pauline fragments and spoke of the very great
influence of the editorial elements in all the Gospels (p. 89). Luke's own were not only
numerous, but significant.
190. *Ibid.*, p. 87-89. Whereas in the commentary, Wright believed that the Lukan editorial
notes were often no more than connections, he now rated them much more highly and indicated
they were based on sources rather than simply from Luke himself (p. 89; cf. *S. Luke in Greek*,
p. viii).
191. WRIGHT, *The Gospel according to S. Luke in Greek*, 1900, p. xxviii-xxxix, esp. Table
XI, p. xxxvi-xxxix.
192. WRIGHT, *Synopsis*, ²1903.
193. *Ibid.*, p. xxvii, xxviii. This view was similar to that of Wernle.
194. *Ibid.*, p. liii. Wright attributed 23,2 to Luke observing that it "is editorial, expressing
S. Luke's sense of what history demanded" (p. 275).
195. J.C. HAWKINS, *Horae Synopticae. Contributions to the Study of the Synoptic Problem*,
Oxford, 1899, ²1909, p. viii: "... some important departments of the Synoptic Problem - such
as the number and nature of the sources used by St. Luke only - have been passed over, merely
because I could not see that any light would be thrown upon them by such statistics and
observations as I had been able to put together".

23,7-12[196]. Other smaller additions in Lk "which seem to imply the use of a source or sources (probably written)" included 22,61a.65.66a.67.68; 23,2.4-6.14-16.22b.23[197]. In the section on the transpositions of the order of words and phrases, he did not include the change of order in 22,54-71 in his list of Mk-Mt agreements against Lk[198]. This may have been due either to an oversight or he may not have considered it a "principal" case of transposition of order. He called attention, however, to the MAs (22,62 / Mt 26,75 and 22,64 / Mt 26,68)[199]. He judged it "almost impossible" that Matthew and Luke could have "accidentally concurred" in creating these MAs. He opted in favor of "some influence, direct or indirect, of a common source"[200].

While in a later article (1903-04) he affirmed that Luke and Matthew used Mk to provide their basic information and framework, Hawkins suggested that the sometimes significant differences between Lk and its Markan source, can be explained by oral transmission, owing to Luke's previous experience as a missionary preacher and possibly as a catechist[201]. He referred both to Luke's

---

Following a preliminary section devoted to the words and phrases characteristic of Lk (p. 13-23; ²1909, p. 15-25), his main treatment of Lk was divided into linguistic relations between Lk and Acts (p. 140-158; ²1909, p. 174-193) and another part dealing with smaller additions in Lk (p. 158-161; ²1909, p. 194-197).

In a remark in the second edition, almost made in passing, he observed: "I do not think that nearly all of [the linguistic differences] are such as can be caused by differences in the sources used by Luke in the two books [Lk-Acts]; for we know how freely he dealt with Mark, and probably with Q also, in matters of style, and even of vocabulary" (²1909, p. 177, n. 1). See further F. NEIRYNCK, *Hawkins's Additional Notes to His «Horae Synopticae»*, in *ETL* 46 (1970) 78-111 (= ALBO, 5,2, Leiden, 1970), which contained Hawkins's personal notes which were discovered posthumously with a view to a third edition of *Horae Synopticae* (p. 81). Of the references particularly relevant to us are: *P. 19, no. 70*, on the term Jerusalem (p. 85); *P. 25, l. 24*: "On the probability that some at least of the peculiar portions of Luke were grounded upon oral sources and first written by him, see Stanton, *G.H.D.* II, 291-312 *passim*" (p. 86); *P. 36*, ἀπὸ τοῦ νῦν (p. 87); *P. 71, last l.*, concerning Lk XX [= 22].71, Mk 14,63f. and Mt 26,65 (p. 90); *P. 79, l. 9*, on the subject of two transpositions treated by Stanton (p. 91); *P. 112, l. 7*, with reference to PERRY, on *St. Luke's Passion Narrative*, on the MAs in 22,62.64 (p. 93); *P. 113, l. 5*, "*(the relative priority of Mk and Q)*. – In the former view, could Q possibly have omitted all matter relating to the passion, unless the compiler knew that an account of it was already available?" (p. 94). See further p. 105-109, which contain Hawkins's notes *On the Gospel of St. Luke*.

196. HAWKINS, *Horae Synopticae*, 1899, p. 13. Cf. ²1909, p. 15.

197. *Ibid.*, p. 158. Cf. ²1909, p. 194.

198. *Ibid.*, p. 63. Cf. ²1909, p. 79, though he added two other examples beyond the first edition.

199. *Ibid.*, p. 174. Cf. ²1909, p. 211.

200. *Ibid.*, p. 174. Cf. ²1909, p. 210.

201. *St. Luke's Passion-Narrative Considered with Reference to the Synoptic Problem*, in *ExpT* 15 (1903-04) 122-126, 273-276, esp. p. 276. Here Hawkins appeared to concur generally with W.C. Allen.

J.C. HAWKINS, *St. Luke's Passion-Narrative Considered with Reference to the Synoptic Problem*, in W. SANDAY (ed.), *Studies in the Synoptic Problem*, Oxford, 1911, p. 75-94, was a

new information, as well as to his "remarkable freedom" in his use of Mk, a view
very reminiscent of Lagrange and Holtzmann[202]. Hawkins observed that the
evangelist introduced new material to reshape Mk, though such adaptation would
be consistent with its continued oral use[203]. Although Hawkins admitted that
Feine's theory had once held some appeal, he now rejected that theory of an early
gospel because "such a 'three-document hypothesis', as it may be called, does not
give much help towards the interpretation of the phenomena here presented to us.
Luke's additions are (unlike Matthew's) so mixed up with the *Grundschrift*, and
they have caused alterations and modifications of such kinds, that they suggest a
long and gradual conflation in the mind rather than a simple conflation by the
pen"[204]. The evidence pointed rather to the oral use of elements. "It seems then
that more probability would attach to a hypothesis that would represent our author
as having been accustomed to make oral use of the materials which he embodies
in this part of his Gospel"[205]. The effect of this oral influence would especially
have been felt in the passion narrative since it was central to Paul's preaching.
Thus, rather than drawing on his Markan source, Luke instead referred back to the
"memories of his past teaching". Consequently, Luke's background and experience
as a preacher and possibly catechist contributed to the transposition and
modification of materials, particularly in the passion narrative[206].

Hawkins was a strong proponent of Lukan dependence upon Mk. Changes
were due to Luke's redactional ability, but more importantly, to his background as
a companion of Paul and a preacher. Modifications in material as well as in order
result from his oral teaching impinging upon the account rather than in reaction
against Mk. Hawkins not only rejected Feine's theory, but also the views of J.

---

slightly revised reprise in one chapter of the two earlier articles in *ExpT*. He abbreviated the
introductions to both parts for their inclusion in Sanday's collection. Further, he amended the
"(?Logian)" with "Q (or Logia)" in the following sentence: "It may be remarked in passing that
the extreme fewness and slightness of these correspondences seems to show that the (? Logian)
source upon which Matthew and Luke had previously drawn so largely did not extend over the
period of the Passion" (1903-04, p. 124 = 1911, p. 79). Otherwise, the articles stand
substantially unchanged in the book.

202. *Ibid.*, p. 123. Among the additions are 22,61a.67b.68; 23,2.5-12.15, as well as a
smaller addition containing the reference to the morning in 22,66.

203. *Ibid.*, p. 124. Hawkins offered 22,67f. and 23,5-12 as examples of such modification.

204. *Ibid.*, p. 275 (= 90): "the well-known theory of Feine and others". Cf. Sanday. While
"personal idiosyncrasies" and "the special objects of their literary works" can account for the
differing use of Mk by Matthew and Luke, Hawkins was not content with these solutions. The
explanation for the short additions and differences from Mk need not have recourse to a theory
of a non-Markan source. "The point of view before us now is that these small additions do not
often contain any substantially new matter, such as would require the hypothesis of a non-Marcan
source to account for it". The smaller additions to which he referred were enumerated in *Horae
Synopticae*, 1899, p. 158f.

205. *St. Luke's Passion-Narrative*, in *ExpT* 15 (1903-04) 275.

206. *Ibid.*, p. 276 (= 92).

Weiss and F.C. Burkitt who assumed that the Logia source would have included material on the passion[207].

Transpositions were treated in depth as Hawkins called attention to the twelve examples in the Lukan passion narrative as opposed to none in the Matthean account[208]. Noting the difference in order in Lk (denials, mockery, trial) from Mk and Mt (trial, mockery, denials), Hawkins proposed a plausible reason why Luke would have transposed the denials of Peter *before* the examination: Luke united in vv. 55-56 what Mark divided in vv. 54 and 66[209]. Hawkins offered no reason why the mockery should have been recounted before the trial, other than to suggest, as he did for all of the transpositions, that it was due to the fact that the material had been transmitted orally[210]. According to Hawkins's calculations, transpositions occurred in the Lukan passion narrative *"four times as freely"* as in the ministry narratives based upon Mk[211].

Hawkins (1903) held that the special material pertaining to Jesus' "appearance" before Herod, which Hawkins referred to as "Luke's longest insertion", was prompted, not by the needs or influence of preaching, but because of Luke's unique interest in, and possible relationship to, the Herodian court[212].

What was of particular note was the reaction Hawkins's essay in *Oxford Studies in the Synoptic Problem* provoked from William SANDAY. While Sanday concurred that Luke not only used Mk in the section 22,14-24,10 but treated it "with greater freedom than elsewhere", he found fault with Hawkins's more recent

---

207. *Ibid.*, p. 124 (= 79; cf. 129).

208. *Ibid.*, p. 124-125 (= 81-82). Material affected by transpositions in the passion narrative alone are the following: 1) 22,15-23; 2) 22,17 for the short Western text or 22,18-20 for the usual and longer text; 3) 22,21-23; 4) 22,33-34; 5) 22,56-71; 6) 22,63-71; 7) 23,35-38; 8) 23,36; 9) 23,45-46.; 10) 23,50-54; 11) 23,56; 12) 24,10.

209. *Ibid.*, p. 125 (= 82).

210. *Ibid.* Hawkins referred to A. WRIGHT, *Some New Testament Problems*, p. 91, 136f., as well as to his own *Horae Synopticae*, p. 62f., where he wrote: "There is nothing to make copyists and compilers likely to invert, either intentionally or accidentally, the order of the material before them, whatever omissions or abbreviations or adaptions they may make in dealing with those materials". In his second edition (²1909), Hawkins added the reference to Wright's *New Testament Problems*, as well as his *St. Luke*, p. xxii. (p. 78, n. 1). Further, Hawkins made mention of a fuller treatment of the transpositions in the Lukan passion narrative in his "forthcoming" contribution in p. 80, 108, n. 2. Cf. *Additional Notes*, p. 91, referring to *Oxford Studies*: "See pages 81-4 of that volume".

211. HAWKINS, *St. Luke's Passion-Narrative*, p. 275 (= 89).

212. *Ibid.*, p. 122-126, 273-276, esp. p. 276 (= 76-94, 94). Hawkins mentioned 3,1; 8,3; 24,10 and Acts 13,1. Joanna and Manean were thus intimated to be possible sources of information. A. Wright referred to the "Pilate and Herod" account (23,4-19) as an "historical incident" found among the anonymous fragments. These materials were supplied by "many anonymous authors" including "apostles, prophets, evangelists, private Christians, not excluding women". He saw the massacre described in 13,1 as the reason for the animosity between the two rulers and regarded Pilate's sending Jesus to Herod as an attempt at reconciliation. It appeared that the silence of Jesus in Herod's presence was due to Luke (*S. Luke in Greek*, p. viii, 202-203).

proposal that Luke used oral materials derived from his preaching the Pauline
Gospel[213]. Sanday judged Hawkins's explanation of Luke having written down
from memory information he frequently preached, with only occasional reference
to documentation, inadequate[214].

In his *Einleitung*, Theodor ZAHN (1899) traced the history of the synoptic problem,
noting that with an increase of scholarly support for Markan priority, "gewann
H.J. Holtzmann den Mut, im Anschluss an diese Hypothese die Quellen, aus
welchen die synoptischen Evv zusammengearbeitet sein sollten, nach Art und
Umfang genau zu beschreiben, und fast bis aufs Wort wiederherzustellen"[215]. He
also called attention to B. Weiss's attempts to discover Lukan sources[216].

Zahn cast his vote for Lukan dependence upon Mk, even while noting
particular additions as well as divergences[217]. He dismissed the idea that Luke
used Mt as a source, though one could still consider Matthew and Luke as having
drawn upon the same source. Luke used written sources, and in addition to Mk,
another similar writing was suggested[218].

Zahn observed a change in order did not, in and of itself, suggest a separate
source: "In allen 5 Reihen aber [Lk 4,31–6,19; 8,4–9,17; 9,18-50; 18,15-43;
19,29–24,8] ist ausnahmslos die Folge des Mr innegehalten. Dies allein schon
fordert zur Erklärung die Abhängigkeit eines Ev vom andern, zumal die Folge in
vielen Fällen nicht Wiedergabe der wirklichen Aufeinanderfolge ist. Bemerkt dies

213. *Introductory*, p. vii-xxvii, esp. p. xi-xv. "And, as at present advised, I should be
inclined to agree with his earlier views rather than with those which he holds at present" (p. xiii).
It will be recalled that A. Wright, *S. Luke in Greek* (1900) and W.C. Allen (1899-1900) both
advocated greater recourse to the influence of oral tradition.

214. SANDAY, *Introductory*, p. xiii: "But I confess that, at the first blush, the suggestion (for
so Sir John himself describes it, p. 94) does not seem to me to account for the phenomena as we
find them". Sanday noted that many of the Lukan additions constituted historical details which
were *"narrative for narrative's sake"* and not doctrinal as would be found in the Pauline material.
Although Hawkins ascribed the Herod episode to a possible connection with sources within the
Herodian court, Sanday pointed out that this historical information was "for the most part of
secondary importance". Since this was not essentially at variance from the other added historical
details Sanday leaned toward Luke's use of a special source but the "doctrinal teaching of St.
Paul" would not have been the likely source (p. xiv).

215. *Einleitung in das Neue Testament*, Bd. 2, Leipzig, 1899. Section 50: *"Geschichte des
'synoptischen Problems'"*, 182-199, esp. p. 190-191; ³1907 (= *Introduction to the New
Testament*, tr. J.M. TROUT, et al., Edinburgh, 1909, *History of the "Synoptic Problem"*, Vol. 2,
p. 400-427, 415). In a note Zahn commented that in *Die Synoptiker*, ²1892, p. 1-13, Holtzmann
offered "eine bequeme Zusammenstellung" (p. 199, n. 14; see *Introduction*, p. 426, n. 14).

216. ZAHN, *Einleitung*, p. 192, 199, n. 15. See *Introduction*, p. 417-418, 427, n. 15. In the
note he mentioned various writings of B. Weiss, beginning with the *TSK* article (1861) extending
through his *Einleitung* (³1897).

217. ZAHN, *Einleitung*, Bd. 2, 1899. Section 61: *"Die von Lucas benutzten Quellen"*, p. 394-
424; ³1907, 400-431 (= *Introduction*, 1909, *The Sources Used by Luke*, Vol. 3, 94-142). The
pagination in this section generally refers to the 1899 edition unless otherwise noted.

218. *Ibid.*, p. 402. See *Introduction*, p. 109.

der aufmerksame Leser des Mrev schon an diesem, so zeigt Lc ein klares Bewusstsein darum"[219].

Referring to the work of Feine, Zahn declared: "Nach Analogie seiner Benutzung des Mrev ist man auch zu der Annahme berechtigt, dass die grössere Eleganz des Ausdrucks z.B. Lc 6,47-49 = Mt 7,24-27 auf Rechnung des Lc kommt. Viel weiter aber als zu solchen Annahmen wird man mit der Ermittelung der Quellen, welche Lc im Ev ausser Mr benutzt hat, überhaupt nicht kommen"[220]. Zahn seemed to have reserved his strongest censure for J. Weiss, though he did not specifically mention him by name. Efforts to distinguish sources by means of the comparison of speech employed will prove fruitless because Luke stylistically revised his sources so extensively[221].

Zahn noted in his commentary on Lk (1913) the inseparable relationship between the questions of Luke's sources and the whole of the synoptic problem[222]. Further, the relationship of Lk to Acts must not be overlooked[223]. Although Zahn maintained Mark was not a disciple of Jesus, Luke had met Mark at Rome and had not only an exact knowledge of his Gospel, but used it "streckenweise" as his primary source[224]. Luke improved the Markan narrative stylistically, eliminating unnecessary details[225]. Zahn counseled that such similarities as the MAs could stem partly from records of other apostolic disciples[226].

According to Zahn, the Prologue made no reference to written sources, and those which were oral were derived in part, from direct eyewitnesses and disciples of the early witnesses[227]. Some of the latter included those who, following Stephen's death, emigrated to Antioch from Jerusalem and served as teachers in that community (Acts 11,19f.; 13,1) and were eventually responsible for Luke's

---

219. *Ibid.*, p. 399. See *Introduction*, p. 102.

220. *Ibid.*, p. 404. Cf. p. 420, n. 17 (Feine). See *Introduction*, p. 112, 137, n. 17.

221. *Einleitung*, p. 405: "Ein beliebtes Mittel der Quellenscheidung, das der Sprachvergleichung, hat uns Lc selbst beinah gänzlich aus der Hand genommen, indem er, wie sein Verhältnis zu Mr und auch die Vergleichung mit Mt zeigt, seine Vorlagen stilistisch stark umgearbeitet hat". See also p. 400, 418-419, n. 9-12. See further *Introduction*, 1909, p. 114, 104-105, and 135-136, nn. 9-12.

222. ZAHN, *Das Evangelium des Lucas*, Leipzig - Erlangen, [1-2]1913, [3-4]1920, p. 19. §2. *Über die Quellen des Lucas* (19-31).

223. *Ibid.* Zahn mentioned he devoted a great deal of attention to these questions in *Einleitung* 2[3], p. 163-452.

224. *Das Evangelium des Lucas*, p. 23; cf. p. 26. "Das einzige sichere Ergebnis der Vergleichung des Lc mit den vorhandenen Quellen ist, abgesehen von seiner Ausbeutung des Mrev, die Erkenntnis, dass er unser griechisches Mtev nicht benutzt hat".

225. *Ibid.*, p. 23-24.

226. *Ibid.*, p. 27: "Die trotzdem unverkennbaren Übereinstimmungen des Wortlautes zwischen Mt und Lc, welche nicht in der Abhängigkeit des Lc von Mr ihre Erklärung finden, können ... teilweise durch Aufzeichnungen anderer Apostelschüler vermittelt sein".

227. *Ibid.*, p. 20-21; cf. p. 25.

conversion. Zahn joined a chorus of voices in naming Palestine as the area from which numerous sources emanated[228].

As to whether oral information or other written sources could account for the variation of the timing in the Sanhedrin trial, Zahn admitted it was more probable to suggest the latter[229]. In recording the trial at morning, Zahn saw Luke as having made room for the correctly understood story recounted in Jn 18,12-28[230]. Although Luke borrowed a great deal from Mk, Luke's description reflected independence on this point. Such information was obtained not only from the oral information of eyewitnesses, but also probably from written sources. Zahn arrived at this conclusion based on Luke's use of Mk. In a criticism apparently directed to B. Weiss, Zahn judged it "um so unglaublicher" that one would assume that the non-Markan material of Lk was not written down prior to Luke[231].

While Luke, according to the Prologue, sought to present his account in chronological order, Zahn claimed Luke diverged from the general order because the evangelist discovered it was simply not possible[232]. It rendered questionable whether Luke can indeed offer a true and accurate account of the events.

Zahn (1899) maintained that small insertions, such as 23,6-12, do not ultimately disrupt the Markan sequence[233]. The material proper to Luke, which included the account of the trial before Herod, was not the creation of Luke nor did it originate outside Palestine, but information concerning its origin was beyond hope of recovery[234]. This did not prevent Zahn from noting that one of the female companions of Jesus was the wife of one of Herod's servants (Lk 8,3), that a foster brother of the prince was teaching in the community at Antioch (Acts 13,1), and that the person recounting events in the community at Antioch (Acts 11,27f.) also belonged to that community[235]. Like so many others, Zahn proposed Manaen as a source for Herod for Lk 3,1.19; 23,7-12.

Another articulate voice for and staunch supporter of Luke's use of Mk was Paul WERNLE (1899)[236]. Ten years prior to the publication of his book he had the

---

228. *Ibid.*, p. 21.

229. *Ibid.*, p. 25.

230. *Ibid.*

231. *Ibid.*, p. 25-26: "Je sicherer aus der Untersuchung der beiden Bücher des Lc und unbefangener Würdigung der Überlieferung eine vergleichsweise späte Abfassung des 3. Ev und der AG sich ergibt, um so unglaublicher ist die Annahme, dass alle die grossen Stoffe des Lcev, für die bei Mr keine Parallelen sich finden, entweder bis dahin überhaupt noch nicht schriftstellerisch dargestellt worden seien, oder dass Lc alle vorhandenen Aufzeichnungen über diese Gegenstände verächtlich bei Seite geschoben haben sollte".

232. *Ibid.*, p. 24.

233. ZAHN, *Einleitung*, Bd. 2, p. 399.

234. *Ibid.*, Bd. 2, p. 405. See *Introduction*, 1909, p. 113.

235. *Ibid.* See *Introduction*, 1909, p. 114.

236. P. WERNLE, *Die synoptische Frage*, Freiburg, 1899, see p. 45-61. P. Wernle (1872-1939), Privatdozent in NT at Basel (1897), assoc. prof. of Church History and History of Dogma at Basel (1900), prof. (1905). Consider F. Neirynck's evaluation of Wernle's "well-balanced

opportunity to hear the lectures of B. Weiss which fascinated him about the synoptic problem[237]. So indebted was Luke to Mk that Wernle commented: "so darf man von einer Neu-Übersetzung des Mr durch Lc reden"[238]. Comparing the contents, order and texts of both Gospels, Wernle concluded that Luke utilized almost all of Mk as the basis of his own presentation and with few exceptions, Luke retained the Markan order[239]. The greatest difference occurred in the texts where Luke completely revised his source linguistically in accord with his own reflective judgment. Rarely did Luke combine other sources with his primary source[240].

What then of Luke's special material? Though Wernle traced the largest part of Lk back to Mk and the logia collection, there remained a quantity of stories that went back neither to Mk nor to Mt parallels[241]. Wernle earlier referred to these as "die jerusalemischen Geschichten"[242]. He dismissed as "Thorheit" (foolishness) the suggestion that the *Sondergut* stemmed from Luke himself, favoring instead the view that it derived from a written source, an old Gospel which had been lost to us[243]. Unfortunately, a supposed source such as this can neither be refuted nor proven[244]. Those who adhered to the view that the whole *Sondergut* stemmed from this supposed Gospel, as well as those who advocated that the material came from Luke himself, suffer the same mistake however: the hasty generalization which assumed that the *Sondergut* was a homogeneous mass[245].

exposition of the two-document hypothesis", in *The Minor Agreements*, Leuven, 1974, p. 16. See *Evangelica*, 1982, esp. p. 10.

237. *Ibid.*, p. VII.

238. *Die synoptische Frage*, p. 26.

239. *Ibid.*, p. 40. The seven transpositions are: 1) Lk 3,19f. cf. Mk 6,17f.; 2) Lk 4,16-30 cf. Mk 6,1-6a; 3) Lk 5,1-11 cf. Mk 1,16-20; 4) Lk 6,12-16 cf. Mk 3,13-19 and Lk 6,17-19 cf. Mk 3,7-12; 5) Lk 8,4-18 cf. Mk 4,1-25 and Lk 8,19-21 cf. Mk 3, 31-35; 6) 22,15-20 cf. Mk 14,22-25 and Lk 22,21-23 cf. Mk 14,18-21; 7) Lk 22,54-62 cf. Mk 14,53f.66-72 and Lk 22,63-65 cf. Mk 14,65 and Lk 22,66-71 cf. Mk 14,55-64 with 15,1 (p. 7).

240. *Ibid.*

241. *Ibid.*, p. 91-92. In Wernle's view, the *Sondergut* material in the passion narrative includes: 22,28-38 words at the Last Supper; 23,6-12 Jesus before Herod; 23,27-31 words spoken on the way to Golgotha; and 23,39-43 the thieves on the cross (p. 92-93).

242. *Ibid.*, p. 39-40, where he listed only 22,31f.35-38 and included a reference to Herod and Pilate up through v. 16, while here only through v. 12 (p. 92-93).

243. *Ibid.*, p. 93. This is not to say that Luke was not capable of composing and adding details within stories, since Wernle credited Luke with composing the detail in the denial story that Jesus turned and looked at Peter (p. 34).

244. *Ibid.* Wernle adopted what might be called a restrictive endorsement. The hypothesis of a special written source had not been sufficiently nuanced. Any attempt to determine the original order of the stories of the Gospel must be abandoned. The most that could be said was that they were closely related and perhaps belonged together. Likewise, it was not possible to distinguish between the text of the Gospel and the revision by the evangelist because the language and style was peculiar to Luke (p. 93-94). Cf. T. ZAHN, *Einleitung*, 1899, p. 405.

245. *Die synoptische Frage*, p. 94.

At one point, Wernle suggested that "für manche kleinere Episoden, mündliche Tradition (könnte) angenommen werden"[246]. While Luke showed himself a very free editor, he was no creative inventor. Infrequently, in a few paragraphs, the hand of Luke may be perceived in contrast to the hand of the source[247].

In contrast to Mk (14,53-54.66-72), Luke related the denial of Peter in one piece because he combined the two sessions of the Sanhedrin[248]. Luke extended the μετὰ μικρόν of Mk 14,70 to διαστάσης ὡσεὶ ὥρας μιᾶς (22,59) because he needed to fill the time until daybreak with this story (22,66). Luke had surely not read the second cock crow in his Mk. Other modifications included shifting the provocation of the three-part denial to three different people (vv. 56.58.59) and softening the guilt of Peter[249].

Some scholars, drawing attention to the term αὐτόν in 22,63, suggested that the shift to Jesus following Peter's denial was not adequately marked. Wernle admitted that a careless reader could think that the pronoun referred to Peter. But it referred to Jesus. The confusion was owing to the transposition[250].

To the two MAs in 22,62.64, Wernle added a third, ἀπ᾽ ἄρτι / ἀπο τοῦ νῦν (Mt 26,64 / Lk 22,69), which he considered to be independent redactions of Mk by Luke and Matthew[251]. The details of the command to prophesy and Peter's exit in tears were logical conclusions, suggested by the material and arrived at independently[252].

Appropriately because of his merger, Luke omitted the notice of Mk 14,53 concerning the assembly of the Sanhedrin. It followed from that, first of all, that certainly nothing was known about what happened with Jesus in the house of the high priest (22,54). After that, the mockery and mistreatment of Jesus were narrated (22,63f.). Wernle stated Luke translated into Greek the Latinisms in Mk, one case being παιδεύειν (23,16) for φραγελλοῦν (Mk 15,15)[253]. Luke suppressed the appearance of both false witnesses and the words of Jesus about the Temple (Mk 14,57f.). As proof that Luke indeed knew this information, Wernle

---

246. *Ibid.*, p. 93.

247. *Ibid.*, p. 94. However, Wernle offered no examples.

248. *Ibid.*, p. 33-34; also p. 8: "Die letzte grosse Umstellung ist dadurch bedingt, dass Lc zunächst die Petrusgeschichte (Mr 14,54.66ff.) in einem Zug erzählen...".

249. *Ibid.*, p. 34. LAGRANGE, *Les sources* (1896), p. 18-19, also noted that Luke's redaction showed mercy in his presentation of the Sanhedrin and the Romans.

250. *Die synoptische Frage*, p. 8.

251. *Ibid.*, p. 47. A similar substitution took place in the Last Supper account, at least as regards Matthew's redaction of Mk and in the Majority text containing Lk 22,18, which reflected the more customary Lukan usage of ἀπὸ τοῦ νῦν. Both later redactors, offended by the unsightly οὐκέτι οὐ μὴ πίω, supplied οὐ μὴ πίω ἀπ᾽ ἄρτι / ἀπὸ τοῦ νῦν (p. 61). See B. METZGER, *A Textual Commentary*, p. 173-177. On 22,64 as an example of Luke replacing of main sentences with καί by participial and relative sentences, see *Die synoptische Frage*, p. 23.

252. *Die synoptische Frage*, p. 60. The detail about Peter was developed early in the story.

253. *Ibid.*, p. 18.

pointed to its inclusion in Acts 6,14 uttered by Stephen[254]. The reason for the deletion in the Gospel was possibly the lack of clarity in Mk, who labeled the word already as "false" testimony (Mk 14,57). In the haste of abbreviating, Luke unfortunately forgot the primary detail, namely that the death sentence of Jesus was pronounced by the Sanhedrin (Mk 14,64).

According to Wernle, Luke presented only one Sanhedrin trial not merely to simplify, but also because the meaning of the second was unclear to him[255]. Further, the Sanhedrin trial was said to have occurred at daybreak because that seemed more reasonable than in the middle of the night[256].

Luke formulated the charges of the Jews before Pilate (23,2) in light of charges made by the Jews against the Christians of Luke's own time, who claimed they were a threat to the state. In response, the Roman judge thrice declared his conviction of the complete innocence of Jesus (23,4.14.22). Here Luke offered his apologia for Christianity. Luke radically abbreviated his Markan source, leaving out the notice of the custom of freeing one of the prisoners on the feast (Mk 15,6), and deleted the portrayal of the mockery of the king of the Jews (Mk 15,16-20), because Luke already related a mockery (22,63f.). Besides, rather than the Gentiles, he would prefer to portray the Jews in a negative light.

Wernle stressed Luke's great freedom in dealing with his sources[257]. While he exhibited a great deal of liberty in his redaction of Markan stories, he showed more restraint where it concerned the words of the Lord[258]. Feine noted that Luke's redactional technique involved abbreviating and sometimes omitting parts. Where J. Weiss cited the absence of certain material in the Lukan texts as substantiating his view that Luke was following an independent source, Wernle explained the omissions as intentional. Whereas J. Weiss regarded the absence of certain details as indicative of the LQ source, Wernle asserted that in the passion narrative, only the Markan pericopes of the anointing at Bethany (Mk 14,3-9) and the second session of the Sanhedrin (Mk 15,1) were missing from Lk[259], and

---

254. *Ibid.* Cf. J. WEISS, *Lukas*, [8]1892, p. 636-638, who attributed this to a more original source.

255. *Die synoptische Frage*, p. 8.

256. *Ibid.*

257. *Ibid.*, p. 40. Cf. LAGRANGE, *Les sources*, 1896, p. 19, 24.

258. *Die synoptische Frage*, p. 10, 18. Cf. F. NEIRYNCK, *La matière marcienne*, in ID. (ed.), *L'Évangile de Luc*, 1973, 157-201 (esp. p. 182) (= [2]1989, 67-111 = *Evangelica*, 1982, 37-82). In n. 121, Neirynck wrote: "L'auteur s'intéresse plus directement à la différence entre récits et paroles". Cfr *ibid.*: "The dichotomy in Luke's treatment between Markan sayings and narratives is substantiated by the distribution of 'characteristically Lukan words and phrases' in Luke. Since the work of H.J. Holtzmann, *Wernle*, Cadbury, Hawkins, and others, it has been reasonable to assume that these words are a valid indication of Luke's editorial presence (or absence)" [emphasis added].

259. *Die synoptische Frage*, p. 4. Wernle concluded there were a total of 12 pieces of Markan material which were not contained in the Lk two of which in the passion narrative: the anointing at Bethany (Mk 14,3-9) and the second Sanhedrin session (Mk 15,1). Apart from these, Lk contained Mk in its entirety. He divided the parts of Lk having contact with Mk into three

these omissions are easily explainable. The anointing at Bethany was omitted because Luke regarded it as a doublet of the anointing recounted in 7,36-50[260], Luke merged into one the two sessions of the Sanhedrin in Mk 14,53-65 and 15,1. Wernle acknowledged evidence of omission and contracted forms observing that, "Den stärksten Verstoss aber hat er sich in der Verkürzung des Prozesses Jesu geleistet"[261]. However, in Mark's account, the mockery and abuse filled in the gap between the two sessions, before a trial occurred and a judgment was rendered. Because Luke passed over the custom of the release of a prisoner in his account of the trial before Pilate, the demand of the Jews for the release of Barabbas was incomprehensible (23,18)[262]. All this pointed to Luke's attempt to improve Mark's account linguistically. Unfortunately, it also demonstrated the effects such verbal abbreviation could have upon a story[263].

But Luke's revision of Mk was not limited exclusively to omissions and contractions. Lukan redaction also included use of other vocabulary, better style, making connections, new introductions and the anticipation of later notices and transpositions[264].

While noting that the great majority of German researchers held the Two-Source hypothesis, Wernle cited Feine and J. Weiss for giving special attention to the Ebionite source[265]. Because Luke customarily used Hebrew style in his introductory formulae, beginning Markan stories with καὶ ἐγένετο or ἐγένετο δέ, Wernle warned that one cannot draw conclusions about a Hebrew, more especially an Aramaic, source on the basis of this style[266]. Though Wernle concurred that Luke employed special sources, he departed from Feine and Weiss in maintaining,

sections: 3,1-6,19; 8,4-9,50; 18,15-24,10 (p. 4). Concerning the parallel of the sinful woman Lk 7,36-50 / Mk 14,3-9, Wernle noted that the following details were identical in Lk and Mk (p. 38-39): 1) the anointing by a woman; 2) the vessel – alabaster jar; 3) Jesus in the house of a Simon. In Lk the name appeared in 7,40 completely unmotivated; 4) the ending (7,48-50) contained genuine Markan words, obviously not from the anointing story: Mk 2,5 / Lk 5,20 (ἀφίενταί σου αἱ ἁμαρτίαι - ἀφέωνταί σοι αἱ ἁμαρτίαι σου); Mk 2,6f. / Lk 5,21; Mk 5,34 / Lk 8,48. Therefore Luke did not invent the story of the great (female) sinner, but rather, at most, combined with parts of the anointing story in Mk 14. Wernle concluded a separation was possible even on this point, not in vocabulary, but according to the contents. The elements of the anointing, vessel, Simon and the concluding verse stemmed from Mk. All other material ought to be ascribed to the special source of Luke (p. 39).

260. *Ibid.*, p. 6.

261. *Ibid.*, p. 25.

262. *Ibid.* As a further example of the effects of Luke's shortening accounts, Wernle pointed out that Luke related information about the stone which had been rolled away (24,1) without first mentioning that there had been such a stone.

263. *Ibid.*

264. *Ibid.*, p. 26.

265. *Ibid.*, p. IV. Wernle supported the view that traces of Ebionism can indeed be found in Lk. This element was contained in the theme that Jesus came primarily for the Jews, which Luke strongly emphasized, according to Wernle (p. 108).

266. *Ibid.*, p. 25. Cf. FEINE (1891), p. 9, n. 1, where he discussed the position of scholars such as A. Resch, against whom Wernle was arguing.

not only that Mk continued to form the basis of Luke's presentation of the passion narrative, but that the changes in Lk reflected redaction and not a separate, independent source[267]. Further, Wernle rejected J. Weiss's idea that Luke used A (Urmarkus)[268].

Wernle addressed the changes concerning the trial of Jesus as indicative of the difference of the times when the Gospels were written[269]. While admitting Luke had special sources and conceding the possibility of a lost Gospel, he rejected the position of those scholars, such as Feine and J. Weiss, who attempted to define its form and maintained that it was of a homogeneous nature. For many of the smaller episodes he considered oral tradition a possibility[270]. Still in all, Wernle did well in pointing out how many of the changes can be explained as Lukan redaction of Markan material.

One piece of *Sondergut*, the account of Jesus before Herod (23,6-12), according to Wernle, could have been formed by Luke himself out of apologetical interests[271]. Aside from Luke, only the GP, which was based upon Lk, knew this episode[272]. Our lack of knowledge about the process of the trial alone ruled out a solid judgment. Luke's own creation seemed to account for five *Sondergut* pericopes, including the Herod story, and ultimately could stem from the evangelist[273]. Other materials appeared to have been remodeled or expanded by Luke and thus may support Wernle's contention that the *Sondergut* material was not homogeneous. Lukan redaction involved preparing for a later story or event by laying the foundation earlier in the Gospel. An example of such anticipation included the reference in 9,9 to Herod's desire to see Jesus, which prepared for 23,8[274]. Reference to the hostility between Herod and Pilate (23,12) stemmed from Luke rather than the tradition and reflected an apologetical motif symbolizing Gentiles and Jews coming together in their hostilty towards Christians[275].

Willoughby C. Allen (1900), in reaction to *Die synoptische Frage*, offered substantial praise, saying that Wernle "summarized and restated with great clearness and force" the evidence for Lukan and Matthean dependence upon Mk. Allen nonetheless continued to argue for a greater place for oral tradition in

267. *Die synoptische Frage*, p. 88; see also p. 83-84.

268. *Ibid.*, p. 223.

269. *Ibid.*, p. 14. Wernle dated Mk in the 70's (p. 223) and Lk in the 90's (p. 108).

270. *Ibid.*, p. 93.

271. *Ibid.*, p. 95, 106. The passage was earlier identified as 23,6-12, but also designated as 23,6-16 (p. 92; cf. p. 39). He highlighted four chief characteristics of Lk: universalistic/anti-Jewish, which contained authentic traces of Ebionism, the catholicizing, the edifying and the apologetical. The last was seen most clearly in the passion narrative (p. 108).

272. *Ibid.*, p. 95; also p. 251-253, esp. p. 251.

273. *Ibid.* Wernle listed the following pericopes as "Stücke, bei denen die eigene Bildung des Lc überwiegt": 3,10-14; 14,1-6; 17,11-19; 19,41-44; 23,6-12, 24,36-53 (p. 94-95).

274. *Ibid.*, p. 30. This was an observation Holtzmann also made. Cf. HOLTZMANN, *Einleitung*, ³1892, p. 386 (= ²1886, 398). Cf. above.

275. *Die synoptische Frage*, p. 106.

explaining, not the whole synoptic problem, but the material unique to a particular
Gospel as well as that which was common to Lk and Mt[276].

Wernle (1904) left open the possibility that some of the material peculiar to
Lk could have resulted from the creativity of the evangelist, though he would not
have been responsible for all of it[277]. The Prologue suggested that Luke possibly
had access to other written sources, but this was not certain. Wernle thought that
the assumption of Luke's use of "an older source" for the special material
"remains entirely uncertain"[278]. The traditions employed by Luke could have
been oral. Furthermore, he rejected the view that such unique accounts were of an
exceptional historical value[279].

Wernle provided the classic exposition on Markan material in Lk, in part as
a reaction to Feine and J. Weiss. Luke adopted the contents and followed the order
of Mk, "die er mit Bewusstsein verbessert und umgestaltet"[280]. Very seldom did
Luke combine and merge Mk with other sources. While some portions were
ascribed to oral sources, other special material was attributed to apolgetical motifs.
Wernle argued Luke attempted to adjust the tradition to his time.

Other scholars who regarded Mk as the basis of Lk included F.H. WOODS
(1890)[281], Joseph Estlin CARPENTER (1890, [4]1906)[282], James Hardy ROPES

---

276. W.C. ALLEN, *Did St. Matthew and St. Luke use the Logia?*, in *ExpT* 11 (1899-1900)
424.

277. P. WERNLE, *Die Quellen des Lebens Jesu*, Halle, 1904, [2]1905; Tübingen, [2]1906, p. 99
(= *The Sources of our Knowledge of the Life of Jesus*, tr. E. LUMMIS, London, 1907, p. 53-54).

278. *Ibid.*, p. 143 (= p. 76).

279. *Ibid.*, p. 151 (= p. 80): "If Luke really made use of traditions they were not necessarily
written ones, and above all they were not necessarily trustworthy in an historical sense".

280. *Ibid.*, p. 9.

281. F.H. WOODS, *The Origin and Mutual Relation of the Synoptic Gospels*, in S.R. DRIVER,
T.K. CHEYNE, and W. SANDAY (eds.), *Studia Biblica et Ecclesiastica. Essays Chiefly in Biblical
and Patristic Criticism by Members of the University of Oxford*, Vol. 2, Oxford, 1890, 59-104,
p. 94. He concluded "that the common tradition upon which all the three Synoptics were based
is substantially our St. Mark as far as *matter, general form, and order* are concerned". See also
p. 67: "that St. Matthew and St. Luke both made use of a Gospel very nearly agreeing with our
present St. Mark in its subject-matter and the order of its contents". While he "obtained some
valuable insights" from Holtzmann's *Die synoptischen Evangelien* (1863), he was nonetheless
critical of his position on Urmarkus. To the delight of Woods, although it was too late to
incorporate additional material in his essay, Holtzmann emended his position. *Origin*, p. 94-95:
"Unfortunately, it was not till after this essay was in the press that I had an opportunity of seeing
Dr. Holtzmann's new work *Die Synoptiker*, Freiburg, 1889. It is gratifying to find that he has
given up I believe all the opinions which I have ventured to criticise, especially that fundamental
theory of an *Ur-Marcus* larger than our Synoptical Gospel. He now holds that St. Mark itself was
the main source of both St. Matthew and St. Luke. In fact the argument on which he lays the
greatest stress is just what it has been my chief object to point out, the continuity of the Marcan
order traceable in these two Gospels". Even as Woods claimed that Luke used sources in addition
to Mk, he marveled at how intact the Markan material was "in its original form and order" after
incorporation (*Origin*, p. 68). Concerning the order in the last part of the Lk (18,15–24,9a) he

$(1901)^{283}$, Edwin ABBOTT $(1901)^{284}$ and V. ROSE $(1904)^{285}$. Johannes E.

declared: "the relative order of St. Mark is again practically preserved. The rather frequent, but for our present inquiry unimportant, transpositions which occur, especially in chapters xxii. and xxiii, have already been noticed. Several Marcan passages appear to have been omitted, because incidents like them are related elsewhere. This seems to be the principle of almost all the omissions in this section" (p. 74). One of the examples cited was the omission of Mk 15,16-20a because of 23,11. For a critique of Woods's essay, see D.J. NEVILLE, *Arguments from Order in Synoptic Source Criticism. A History and Critique* (New Gospel Studies, 7), Macon, GA, 1994, 60-82.

282. *The First Three Gospels*, London, 1890, ⁴1906, p. 235. In his work, which was highly esteemed by Wernle, he argued it was "highly probable" that Luke used Mk as the basis of his Gospel, although at times he opted not to follow it closely. In Carpenter's view, the form of Mk available to Luke was not necessarily the form which we now possess (p. 238, n. 1). Wernle praised the book: "Moreover, English literature is already in possession of one of the finest and best introductions to the most important chapter of the gospel problem, 'The First Three Gospels,' by J. Estlin Carpenter" (*Sources*, 1907, p. v; cf. infra). The order of pericopes provided one of the clues for Luke's use of Mk. The reference in the Prologue to "many" (1,1) was interpreted as written sources, minimally two, but probably more (CARPENTER, *First*, p. 233; cf. p. 252). Carpenter maintained that the general order was so similar that it was very likely that Luke followed Mk (p. 234). But even where they were divergent it still appeared that Luke has Mk in mind: "The probability that Luke drew some of his material from Mk, is increased by this fact – the general order of Mk reappears in Lk. It is occasionally dislocated ... And where the arrangement of the Second Gospel is disturbed, the Third Gospel still seems to pre-suppose it" (p. 237). With probable reference to the suggestion that the MAs stemmed from Mt, Carpenter rejected the view that Luke used Mt due, in part, to the absence of Matthew's name from the Prologue (p. 251; cf. p. 239).

283. *An Observation on the Style of St. Luke*, in *Harvard Studies in Classical Philology* 12 (1901) 300. Ropes analyzed the Lukan style and concluded that it was marked by "great variety within the similar phrases, by a manifest fondness for change of expression, and by a notable copiousness of vocabulary in the terms used for things and actions often mentioned". These variations of expression, evident both in the Gospel and Acts, rather than being indications of written sources, were characteristics of the unity of Luke's authorship (p. 304). Ropes left open the possibility that in Acts some of the material in the first half of the book might have originally existed in written form. In considering Acts 1–14, Ropes noted that while there are some blocks of "more or less connected narratives", scholars had not yet had the opportunity to determine whether they had been in written form prior to incorporation into Acts (p. 304). Such diversity relieved the otherwise tedious reading of similar oft-repeated turns of phrase.

Concerning the issue of Hebraisms at various places throughout the Gospel, Ropes adhered to the position of G. Dalman that these merely reflected second-hand Septuagintal influence (p. 300). Unfortunately, Ropes did not provide any reference to Dalman's work(s) on this page or in the entire article. In order for a complete analysis of the Semitic influence to occur, such an investigation would require competence both in non-Christian literature as well as Semitic languages (p. 300). Necessary tools for such a comprehensive study would consist in an "ample knowledge of the non-Christian literature of the period, and especially of the rhetorical principles and habits of the most widely read writers. It would also have required sufficient familiarity with Hebrew and Aramaic to determine the true character and weigh the significance of the Semitic element". A study of this caliber, Ropes contended, had not yet appeared.

Further, Ropes called attention to what he considered Luke's propensity to repeat material from the Gospel in Acts. Such an insight could have far-reaching impact if this principle could be shown to be at work, for example, in the trials of Jesus and Paul. "Luke is fond of repeating his material. Thus, Luke 24,44-53 and the use with differences of the same material in Acts 1,1-12" (p. 303). Cf. Lk 22-23 and Acts 24-25.

In a later work Ropes sided with those who viewed Mk as the foundation of Lk (*The Apostolic Age in the Light of Modern Criticism*, New York, 1921, p. 228). A rather large amount of material, mostly sayings and parables, was inserted into it. He rejected the idea that this special material would have been contained in Q, and judged it ultimately impossible to uncover all the stages of this very complicated compositional process (p. 230). He contended that Luke followed the Markan order very closely (p. 228-229). He did interrupt it, however, by the insertion of the two interpolations (6,20–8,3 and 9,51–18,14).

284. *The Corrections of Mark Adopted by Matthew and Luke* (Diatessarica Pt. 2), London, 1901, p. 50. Cf. F. NEIRYNCK, *The Minor Agreements of Matthew and Luke against Mark*, Leuven, 1974, p. 17-20. Abbott believed that Luke and Matthew used a version of Mk identical to the one which we possess (albeit with some corrections), or perhaps even a shorter version. The idea was further entertained that both later Synoptists may have been working from differing editions of Mk. "But if they did, those editions did not agree in including anything of importance that is not found in our Mark".

The MA of 22,62 / Mt 26,75 was noted but not explained (*Corrections*, p. 247). Implicitly, it seemed Abbott attributed it to the harmonization of Lk to Mt.

Owing to a lack of clarity in the original of the other MA (22,64 / Mt 26,68), there was confusion about who was responsible for striking Jesus (p. 225). Proposing that linguistics and history favored the Lukan version as the more probable, presenting the guards as the perpetrators (p. 232). Abbott came to this conclusion based on what he believed was a corruption of the word "guard" (דחא)   to the word "one" or "some" (דחא), Abbott ultimately concluded that "mistranslation in one or other of the Synoptists" was the probable cause of this MA (p. 236-237). Unsure whether the mockery in Lk was a parallel of that in Mk, Abbott conjectured that Luke could have been using the word "mocking" in place of the Markan term "spitting" which Luke elected to omit (p. 229).

285. V. ROSE, *Évangile selon S. Luc*, Paris, 1904, p. V, VI (esp. 215-222). From the beginning, Rose noted that the tradition upon which Lk was composed was later than the testimony contained in the other two Synoptics and that the redaction shows that Lk and Acts were works of the same author. Luke's sources comprised a journal of travels by a disciple of St. Paul. To this had been added other written documents about Jesus and Peter. The original nature of the writing was not preserved, but rather recast by the redactor. Rose further declared that Catholic exegetes adopted the date of composition between 70 and 80 (p. X). He called attention to the charges brought against Jesus by the high priests in the Lukan account. Rose also detected the similarity of development in the Gospel and Acts. The Prologue referred to others in addition to Mt and Mk, though they were not necessarily complete gospels (p. 2). Nevertheless the historicity of Lk was assured by, among other things, the excellent sources which Luke employed. Some information was derived from Joanna (8,3): "Aussi a-t-on émis l'opinion qu'il avait connu cette pieuse suivante du Maître pendant le séjour de trois ans qu'il fit en Palestine quand S. Paul était captif à Césarée" (p. 84).

Although Rose believed there were two trials before the Jews, he conjectured that Luke omitted the nocturnal trial, changing it to a morning one (p. 215). The first was able to be omitted since it could not have been official. Concerning 22,61, it was not very likely that Jesus was in the court nor as some exegete proposed, that Jesus had seen Peter through a window. The Sanhedrin trial, according to Luke's recounting contained the "proper and original details".

Rose claimed that Pilate wishing to unload an awkward case, sent Jesus to Herod who was flattered by the gesture (p. 219). The origin of the story was attributed to Joanna (p. 219-220).

BELSER (1901)[286] and Alexander Balmain BRUCE (1897) were among those who

Rose interpreted the dazzling apparel as serving the irony of the scene in which Jesus was vested in royal robes. Rose saw in 23,13-25 a Lukan apologetic at work "en faveur de Jésus", that Jesus was in no way an insurrectionist set against the Roman law (p. 222).

286. Johannes Belser acknowledged that one cannot deny Lukan dependence upon Mk in the last part of the Gospel (19,19–24,8 = Mk 11,1–16,8) (*Einleitung in das Neue Testament*, Freiburg, 1901, p. 187-191, esp. p. 188). Shortly thereafter he wrote *Geschichte des Leidens und Sterbens, der Auferstehung und Himmelfahrt des Herrn nach den vier Evangelien ausgelegt*, Freiburg, 1903; Freiburg - St. Louis, MO, ²1913 (= *History of the Passion. Death and Glorification of Our Saviour, Jesus Christ*, tr. F.A. MARKS, ed. A. PREUSS, St. Louis, MO – London, 1929, p. ix-x [esp. p. 353-474]). The ET was based upon the first edition (1903) though comparison was also made with the second edition (²1913). Pagination is from the ET. Belser noted that Luke's account of the passion highlighted Jesus' innocence . Although it appeared Luke passed over the nocturnal session of the Sanhedrin, he combined the hearing and sentence (p. 351). Belser maintained that Mark and Luke "followed the example of St. Matthew". Belser regarded the mockery (22,63-65) as the same as recounted in the other Synoptics, but maintained that they had more accurately related the order of events. In an extended note he referred to the change of order, again affirming that Mt and Mk provided the historical order (p. 394-395, n. 1). Belser offered no reason why the order would have been different in the Lukan account.

However, that seemed to contradict what he wrote later in speaking of Peter's denial: "As in other cases, St. Luke makes the transition to the chronologically correct account. He first describes how Jesus was led from Mt. Olivet into the palace of the High Priest, connects this incident directly with the denial by Peter, and then speaks of the official session of the Sanhedrin (XXIII, 54ff.)" (p. 381-382). The difference of timing of the Sanhedrin trial did not pose a problem for Belser who faulted Luke for not recording both sessions. The discussion indicated that the evangelist was conversant with the other Synoptics, a view Belser shared with Brüll (p. 372, n. 1). Belser provided no bibliographical information on Brüll. Yet, Belser credited Luke with the "greater accuracy" in recounting two separate questions (22,67-70). The approach taken by Belser also was one of harmonization of accounts.

It was Luke who reproduced "the actual charge" made against Jesus at Pilate's trial (23,2). Belser attributed the hostility between Pilate and Herod (23,12) to Pilate's permitting imperial portraits to be carried into Jerusalem (p. 412-413). In Belser's opinion the Synoptics did not provide an adequate account of Pilate's trial and thus needed to be supplemented by information from Jn. In 23,13-25 it was Luke who offered "the most detailed account" (p. 439).

Belser (1903) accepted the Herod account as historical and claimed that the objections of Strauss, Baur and Keim "have nearly all been abandoned" (p. 438; see esp. p. 431-438). If a critic stressed the silence of the other evangelists regarding this episode then the same can be said of other material peculiar to Luke. Notice was also taken of the absence of the story from the other Gospels and that it did not affect the flow of events. Matthew omitted it since his Jewish-Christian readers were familiar with Herod's exploits. Mark imitated Matthew. John passed it over since it did not contribute anything to his Gospel (p. 434-435). Belser further rejected the view that there would not have been sufficient time for the Herodian trial to take place. Acts 4,27 seemed to confirm the account, though there were discrepancies between them. Also, the "plain, candid, unpretentious manner of describing the event" was convincing for Belser. So also the facts were confirmed by Philo and Josephus who detailed the rulers' behavior.

Belser contended that Pilate transferred Jesus to Herod not to relieve himself of "the predicament", but to extend a courtesy and achieve a reconciliation (p. 431, 432; see esp. p. 431-438). Belser did not regard the appearance of Jesus before Herod as a legal matter, but simply to satisfy Herod's curiosity and to permit him to ridicule Jesus. Herod repaid the compliment to

believed Luke may have used, or did in fact use, Mt in addition to Mk. Bruce complimented B. Weiss's *Das Marcusevangelium und seine synoptischen Parallelen* (1872) as Feine had done, showing that Mk formed the basis of the other two Synoptics, which was, at Bruce's time the "prevailing opinion"[287]. He clearly affirmed that Mk served as the basis of Luke's account of the passion: "Thereafter our author joins the company of Mark once more, and keeps beside him to the end of the Passion history"[288].

Pilate by returning Jesus to him.

Belser understood the dazzling apparel to be white, such as was worn by Jewish royalty for celebrations (p. 434; cf. p. 437). Nevertheless, it was also understood to present Jesus as a "mock king" (p. 444). He dismissed the views that it was either the *toga candida* of Roman government candidates or a high priestly vestment. Belser equated Herod's ill-treatment of Jesus in concert with the fact that he did not declare Jesus innocent as a condemnation. Later, he called it an acquittal (p. 434). The term ἀναπέμπειν signified that Herod was the competent judge, rejecting the other interpretations that Herod's palace was located higher than Pilate's or that Herod had greater power.

287. A.B. BRUCE, *The Synoptic Gospels* (The Expositor's Greek Testament, 1), London, 1897, ²1907 (esp. p. 3-26, 44-51, 632-638) p. 9. Cf. p. 8. Bruce considered it possible that both Mk and Mt were among the "many" Luke referred to in his Prologue (p. 458).

288. *Ibid.*, p. 45. To explain the additional material, Bruce was enamored of the idea of a third source and possibly even a fourth (p. 44). He referred to the work of J. Weiss and P. Feine who attributed the differences to documents which they believed Luke had employed (p. 48; cf. p. 623). However, Bruce expressed reservations about their hypothesis: "This may be a perfectly legitimate hypothesis for solving certain literary problems connected with this Gospel, and the argument by which Feine seeks to establish it is entitled on its merits to serious consideration. But I hardly think it suffices to account for all the traces of editorial discretion in Luke's Gospel" (p. 48).

Bruce gave the impression he believed Luke was responsible for relating the story of Peter's denial "without interruption". The denials were anti-climatic in Lk as opposed to the parallel accounts (p. 632). The construction of the dative with εἰς was a frequent Lukan expression found likewise in Acts. In response to J. Weiss, Bruce wondered – hypothetically – whether Luke might not have had access to both J. Weiss's L+Q and Mk and still "preferred the milder" Jewish-Christian account. The MA in v. 62 was noted but not explained. In v. 64 Luke was following Mt instead of Mk (p. 633).

There was correspondence between 22,66-71 and the Synoptic parallels, though Luke shortened his version. The omission of the Temple testimony was explained by its "futility". It served to reveal the attitude of the judges. Bruce perceived that J. Weiss had subordinated the view of Jesus as Son to that of Christ and rejected that view as contrary to the Lukan theology (p. 634).

Luke was credited with adding the two other charges brought against Jesus. Bruce further noted that in contrast to Mt and Mk, it was not said that Jesus was led away bound. A "later hand" was responsible for inserting v. 17 into Luke's account from the Synoptic parallels, to complete his "meagre narrative". Luke recast the demand for Barabbas to be "voluntary" on the part of the people; reference to the shouting of the people was found both in the Gospel and in Acts (23,21; Acts 12,22) (p. 638).

Bruce gave fair consideration to the hypotheses of Feine and most especially that of J. Weiss, but concluded that Luke composed his passion narrative under the influence and with the guidance of the Mk. Bruce also pointed out the relations between Luke's two-volume work at various points.

According to Wilhelm SOLTAU (1901), in addition to Mk, Luke used an embellished form of the Logia collection, the sources of Acts and a brief early legend[289]. The Logia collection had been enlarged with material about the Samaritans. This source developed in the following manner: beginning with the Aramaic form of Matthew it was translated into Greek (Λ A), which was then used in Mt. It formed the basis of the enlarged edition Λ B employed by Luke[290].

Taking note of the investigations of Feine and Weiss, Soltau wrote: "Aber alle Versuche dieser Art dürfen als misslungen angesehen werden, wenn man eben zugeben muss, dass eine erweiterte Logiasammlung (Λ B) die zweite Hauptquelle des Lukas gewesen ist"[291]. Soltau contended that when the material of 9,50-18,14 was subtracted from the Logia collection nothing would remain for the supposed historical source, except perhaps 5,1-11; 7,11-17; 23,6-12; 24,14f. which he believed ultimately derived from oral tradition[292]. Envisioning three possible solutions for the Mt-Lk agreements – Lk as source for Mt; Mt as source for Lk; or both later Synoptics used a revision of Mk in which they found the agreements – he opted for the third[293]. In a table detailing the sources for various parts of the Gospels, Soltau assigned 22,39-71; 23,1-5.17-27 to Mk while 23,6-16 was attributed to "Lc"[294].

Soltau detected the similarities between Jesus in Lk and Paul in Acts[295]. The double judgment by Festus and Agrippa (Acts 25,22f.) resembled that of Herod and Pilate. Agrippa's curiosity was likened to Herod's (23,8) just as the declarations of Paul's innocence by Festus and Agrippa (Acts 25,25; 26,31) corresponded to those of Pilate and Herod (23,4.15). Although primarily from the

Bruce contended with Meyer, that Jesus had been sent to the proper tribunal, rather than a higher one, and the presence of Herod in Jerusalem was explained – implicitly – by the Passover feast (esp. p. 636-637). Bruce appeared to accept the historicity of the trial before Herod and argued that the omission of the account from the other Gospels was perhaps due to Jesus' silence and the lack of results from this trial. Bruce at least recognized a Markan parallel in the term ἐξουθενήσας (23,11) in Mk 9,12. So too, the connection with Acts was shown both in the use of the term εὐτόνως (23,10; Acts 18,28) and possibly in 23,12 and Acts 8,9 (p. 637). By not omitting ὄντες after προϋπῆρχον (23,12) as in Acts 8,9 Luke continued to highlight the ill will between Herod and Pilate. Connections with Acts were also seen in v. 14 in common vocabulary (ἀποστρέφοντα, cf. Acts 3,26 and ἀνακρίνας, cf. Acts 24,8).

289. W. SOLTAU, *Unsere Evangelien. Ihre Quellen und ihr Quellenwert vom Standpunkt des Historikers aus betrachtet*, Leipzig, 1901. He rejected the need to posit additional written sources.

290. *Ibid.*, p. 47.

291. *Ibid.*, p. 48-49.

292. *Ibid.*, p. 50, n. 1. Though he considered the possibility that these stories stemmed from additional written records or legends (p. 63-64), he finally concluded they were due to oral tradition.

293. *Ibid.*, p. 72: "Somit kann, wie sonderbar es anfänglich auch erscheinen mag, nur eine besondere Markusbearbeitung, neben Markus selbst, die gemeinsame Quelle der kanonischen Evangelien des Matthäus und des Lukas gewesen sein".

294. *Ibid.*, p. 146. Soltau believed Lk was written around the year 90 AD (p. 142).

295. *Ibid.*, p. 65. He generally defined the scene as 23,6-16 ("Jesus vor Herodes", p. 62, 64, 65, 68; see also p. 146), though he also referred to 23,6-12 as the "Verhör vor Herodes" (p. 50).

oral tradition, the story was crafted with assistance of other elements from his sources, including motifs found in Mk and Acts[296].

Julius WELLHAUSEN (1904) made no reference to a special source used by Luke. Rather, Luke simplified the Markan account by ridding it of some of the superfluous details and repaired the breach in the flow of the Markan narrative[297]. Wellhausen considered the MA in 22,62 as an insertion from Mt[298]. The Markan basis was rearranged by Luke to establish better continuity. Jesus was mistreated by the guards rather than the Sanhedrin. Lk 22,63-65 was the same as Mk 14,65 and Mt 26,67-68. Mk 15,1-5 was listed beside Lk 23,1-5. And although Mk was silent about the charges, Luke presented them in such a way as to impress the Romans (23,2). The sentencing of Jesus (23,13-25) was parallel to Mk 15,6-15, but in Lk, more than in Mk, Pilate was relieved of more burden. Mk 15,8-11, which included that detail about the religious leaders inciting the people, was missing at Lk 23,18. Wellhausen saw the transposition of the material concerning the denial, mockery and trial as joining together factually related material from Mk[299].

Luke added other details, and being a littérateur, built on what has preceded, as is the case of 9,9 preparing for the trial before Herod[300]. The Herod episode (23,6-12) was regarded as an addition of Luke while vv. 10-12 were a later growth.

In his *Einleitung* (1905) his preference for an Aramaic tradition underlying the Gospels became clear[301]. Mt and Lk knew Mk in the same form and the same

---

296. *Ibid.*, p. 66; cf. p. 68. Soltau pointed out that GP extrapolated on the involvement of Herod in Jesus' trial, but he did not discuss the relationship of the two writings (p. 69). See also p. 97. Other pericopes deriving from oral tradition included 5,1-11; 7,11-17 and 24,12-36.

J. Belser (1901) also pointed to Luke's use of oral sources regarding information concerning Herod (*Einleitung*, p. 188). The foster brother of Herod Antipas, a teacher in the Antiochene community, was responsible for information concerning the leader (9,9; 13,21; 23,6-12. Lk 8,3 Cf. Acts 13,1). In Belser's opinion, while one cannot disprove that Luke utilized oral information, still one must examine the material to determine whether it bore "den Stempel echter Überlieferung" (p. 191).

297. *Das Evangelium Lucae*, Berlin, 1904 (esp. p. 128-132) (= *Evangelienkommentare*, [ed. M. HENGEL], Berlin - New York, 1987). Luke's tendency to simplify was evident in that the Markan circumstances surrounding Jesus' claim of messiahship were regarded as unnecessary. In addition, the form of the statement in 22,69 was simplified by Luke (p. 130). Because the account of Peter was disrupted in the Markan context, Luke drew the related material together (p. 129).

298. *Ibid.*, p. 129.

299. *Ibid.*

300. *Ibid.*, p. 131.

301. J. WELLHAUSEN, *Einleitung in die drei ersten Evangelien*, Berlin, 1905, p. 35-36: "Liegt den Evangelien nur die mündliche aramäische Tradition zu grunde? haben die Verfasser diese sofort griechisch niedergeschrieben, wobei sie natürlich des Aramäischen kundig sein mussten und unter dem Einfluss desselben standen? Denken liesse sich das, aber das Wahrscheinliche ist doch, dass das Evangelium, das von Haus aus aramäisch war, zuerst

extent as we now know it[302]. Luke followed his order, and few Markan pericopes are missing in Lk[303]. A number of Markan pieces occur as variants in Lk, usually in other places. These included the Nazareth periope (4,16-30); the call of the first disciples (5,1-11) and the anointing by a sinful woman (7,36-50).

> Diese Varianten haben nun nicht wenig zu bedeuten: die Markustradition zeigt sich in ihnen weit von ihrem ursprünglichen Stande entfernt, sehr verändert und aufgeputzt. Das Urteil, welches sich daraus über Lukas ergibt, bestätigt sich weiter durch die Passionsgeschichte. [...]. In allen diesen Punkten steht die Erzählung bei Lukas auf einer anderen und weit entwickelteren Stufe als bei Matthäus. Dieser kürzt zwar mehr als Lukas, hält sich aber doch im Wesentlichen viel treuer an Markus und renovirt ihn nicht so frei und ausschweissend[304].

The special material appeared to be Hellenistic rather than Palestinian-Jewish[305].

In the view of Wellhausen Lukan redaction simplified and unified Markan material. His perspective that 23,10-11 was a later insertion will influence a number of later scholars.

Firmin NICOLARDOT (1908) surmised that "bien probablement" Luke invented the Herod scene (23,4-13.14-16), which was described as an interview[306]. Only the smallest amount of material in 23,14-16 appeared to reflect a particular tradition, the purpose of which was to exonerate the procurator. The fact that the story did not appear in the other Synoptics argued against its historicity[307]. Nicolardot proposed that the redactor of Lk was inspired to create Herod's interview of Jesus by Paul's trials in Acts 25–26[308]. The redactional process became something of a vicious circle, as Nicolardot explained: "Il faut se garder toutefois d'affirmer que toutes les imitations sont du côté de l'évangile. Le renvoi de Jésus à Hérode aurait-il été inspiré du renvoi de Paul à Agrippa, cela n'empêche pas que certains détails

---

niedergeschrieben wurde. Und dafür sprechen eine Anzahl Misverständnisse und ähnliche Erscheinungen, bei deren Erklärung man nicht ohne Annahme einer schriftlichen aramäischen Vorlage auskommt". This section was revised by Wellhausen in his second edition, though he continued to argue in favor of "die Annahme einer nichtgriechischen Grundlage der Evangelien" ([2]1911, p. 8).

302. *Ibid.*, p. 57 (= [2]1911, 49).

303. *Ibid.*, p. 61, 62 (= 52, 54).

304. *Ibid.*, p. 63-65 (= 55-56).

305. *Ibid.*, p. 71 (= 63).

306. F. NICOLARDOT, *Les procédés de rédaction des trois premiers évangélistes*, Paris, 1908, p. 204. The affair with Herod was elsewhere defined as 23,6-13 (p. 129). He used J. WEISS, *Lukas*, [8]1892. Regrettably, Nicolardot generally passed over in silence other material concerning Peter's denial (but see p. 205), the Sanhedrin trial (though he included a note on 22,69 on p. 121), and Pilate's trial (with the exception of material included in a note, p. 129, n. 4).

307. *Les procédés*, p. 201.

308. *Ibid.*, p. 202.

aient pu être empruntées, inversement, par le rédacteur des Actes, à la page similaire de son récit de la Passion"[309].

Nicolardot contrasted Luke's version with that of Mark in the composition of the Herod story. In contrast to Mk 15,14 Luke carefully recast the story to exonerate Pilate. As an introduction Lk 23,4 was a bit abrupt. Lk 23,5 like 23,2 was similar to Mk 15,3. An additional and even better way of excusing Pilate was through sending Jesus to Herod (23,7)[310]. But here the influence of Festus in Paul's trials in Acts was even more influential.

Lk 23,8, like Mk 6,14-17, reflected Herod's interest in Jesus. Nicolardot did not believe that the relationship of 9,9 with 23,8 excluded "la création du second passage"[311].

The interrogation in 23,9 corresponded with that before Pilate in Mk 15,4.5. Luke omitted some of the Markan verses which referred to Jesus' silence around Mk 15,4 where Pilate questioned Jesus. The mockery by means of vesture (23,11) was a reminiscence of Mk 15,5. What Luke did in redacting the Markan account was to economize the account of Mk 15,16-20[312]. It was the soldiers who were involved in the mockery, though in the Herod scene they were not Pilate's cohort. Finally, Nicolardot, in line with Wernle, conjectured that the purpose of the segment was expressed in 23,12 that the Jews and Gentiles were reconciled in their conspiracy against the Christians[313].

Nicolardot proposed a most satisfactory interpretation. We take exception, however, to his view that "l'idée centrale du morceau" contained in 23,7, was to exonerate Pilate, for in the end Herod sent Jesus back to Pilate who eventually yielded to the demands for the crucifixion of Jesus. But Nicolardot rightly saw the Herod episode as borrowing Markan materials as well as economizing the Markan account to serve Lukan themes.

Scholars such a Holtzmann, Lagrange and Wernle firmly and articulately defended Markan priority. During this early period opposition to the theories of Feine, J. Weiss and B. Weiss surfaced as scholars detected the Lukan hand in the supposed special material. Their approach was criticized for lacking criteria to distinguish between Lk and LQ. Many of the differences between Mk and Lk were accounted for by Luke's redaction of Mk. Several appealed to oral tradition to explain the variations between Mk and Lk. Evidence of the LXX was recognized in the Lukan material. Even the Herod pericope was variously explained as reflecting Markan influence, constituting a variant of the Pilate story, influenced by Acts or simply beyond recovery of its source.

309. *Ibid.*, n. 3.
310. *Ibid.*, p. 203.
311. *Ibid.* Cf. B. Weiss, *Lukas*, p. 225. This referred to *Die Quellen des Lukasevangeliums* (1907).
312. *Les procédés*, p. 203-204. See also p. 212, 213.
313. *Ibid.*, p. 204. Cf. WERNLE, *Die synoptische Frage*, p. 106, where he suggested the episode arose from apologetical motives. Cf. above.

II. V.H. STANTON THROUGH R. BULTMANN

Toward the end of this period we will see the introduction of form criticism. Differences between Lk and Mk could be explained by Luke's redaction of Mk and these changes were thought to reflect Luke's apologetic interests.

Vincent Henry STANTON (1909) proposed that Luke "knew and used an earlier and briefer form of our St. Mark"[314] in addition to Q which had been enlarged by other matter from Palestine[315]. Additions and substitutions of narratives and sayings alike were made in the account of the passion. In a view strongly resembling that of Hawkins, Stanton considered much of the special material in Lk to have been written down by Luke and not borrowed from a document[316]. In other cases, Stanton proposed that rather than thinking that Luke was influenced by a parallel document, as B. Weiss assumed, Luke was simply revising Mk in an independent fashion. Recourse to a special narrative was unnecessary[317]. Stanton obviously sided with Feine against Weiss in arguing that the single source would have been less complete than Weiss envisioned it. Though the most convincing argument in favor of the special source, according to Stanton, may be the Jewish-Christian tone of some of the material, he did not consider that it necessarily implied that the peculiar matter was derived from the same work[318]. Stanton regarded the MA in 22,64 / Mt 26,68 as deriving either from assimilation of texts by copyists or "the influence of some document distinct from both the Marcan and the Logian, or of oral tradition, or habits of oral teaching"[319]. The MA in 22,62 / Mt 26,75 was attributed to assimilation by copyists[320]. Any confusion surrounding the trials was owing to the rather simple disciples who would have relayed information[321]. The

314. V.H. STANTON, *The Gospels as Historical Documents*. Pt. 2. *The Synoptic Gospels*, Cambridge, 1909, p. 220.

315. *Ibid.*, p. 239. The combination of Q with the other material would have taken place in Jerusalem or some other Palestinian city.

316. *Ibid.*, p. 222, 240.

317. *Ibid.*, p. 222. Cf. p. 240: "The evangelist himself has added a few passages, gathered by him probably from oral tradition. In particular the accounts of incidents in the history of the Passion and Appearance of the Risen Christ, peculiar to this Gospel, owe (it would seem) their written form to him. This being so, and as the rest of the narrative of the Passion, though differing a good deal from the Marcan in arrangement, may well have been founded upon it, there is no reason for thinking that another document was used".

318. *Ibid.*, p. 223. In this, Stanton paralleled P. Wernle's view. "This, however, does not shew that they were taken from the same work, though it may shew that the several traditions were transmitted, or that documents containing them were composed, in the same Christian community, or in similar ones".

319. *Ibid.*, p. 219. Cf. p. 207. Stanton joined the ranks of Wernle and Hawkins against the assumption that Luke knew Mt (p. 207, n. 1).

320. *Ibid.*, p. 219.

321. *Ibid.*, p. 200: "And as to points that are not clear in the course of the several trials, it may be remarked generally that the immediate disciples of Jesus must themselves have been dependent upon what they could learn from others for their knowledge of much that passed, and that Mk could only give the account that was current among these simple, uncultured people,

morning trial, in the opinion of Stanton, corresponded to Mk's nocturnal trial: "[Luke] might well, also, consider that the morning trial was the one which most deserved to be described, even if he did not think (as he may have done) that it was an error to suppose that a trial (or examination) took place in the night. But in reality there seems to be no difficulty in conceiving that the account in St. Mk may be substantially correct"[322]. Differences between the Markan and Lukan renditions might be ascribed to those who served as oral sources for the disciples. They may have lacked familiarity with Jewish and Roman legal procedure[323].

Luke made use of an early form of Mk, in addition to material from the oral tradition which Luke himself collected and committed to writing[324]. In sum, Stanton wrote: "This being so, and as the rest of the narrative of the Passion, though differing a good deal from the Marcan in arrangement, may well have been founded upon it, there is no reason for thinking that another document was used"[325]. The transposition involving Peter's denial was made in order to gather together all the material pertaining to Peter[326]. According to Stanton Luke himself was responsible for some of the material in the passion narrative, including the report of Jesus before Herod (23,5-12)[327].

In a review R. Brook disagreed with Stanton that Luke used an earlier Mk and Matthew used a later and expanded version of Mk. Brook, following Hawkins, recognized legitimate reasons why Luke would have elected to omit some of the Markan material[328]. But he was very impressed with the view that both Matthew and Luke used different editions of Q which had been expanded. Such a theory could explain not only the material special to Lk and Mt, but variations in language in sections common to both. In contrast to Stanton, Brook held that some differences in the material peculiar to Matthew and Luke resulted from one adopting the material and the other choosing to omit it. What was more, he saw the later evangelists as themselves contributing more of the additions than Stanton would envision[329].

---

whose ideas may naturally have been affected by their want of familiarity with processes of law, whether Jewish or Roman". Aligned with Harnack against B. Weiss, Stanton maintained that one could differentiate between material Luke composed and that which he simply revised, borrowing from another document (p. 224).

322. *Ibid.*, p. 166.
323. *Ibid.*, p. 200.
324. *Ibid.*, p. 239-240.
325. *Ibid.*, p. 240. See p. 163.
326. *Ibid.*, p. 166.
327. *Ibid.*, p. 239. Stanton also maintained Ch 24 was probably composed by Luke. Stanton later examined the style in the matter peculiar to Luke and noted the similarities between this account in the Gospel and material in Acts as well as some in the Pauline corpus. He asserted the information may have been given to Luke orally (p. 306-307). Luke's redaction may have included deducing a group being addressed by means of the subject matter. Luke's own imagination as well as his source may have provided some details (p. 229).
328. *JTS* 13 (1911-12) 115.
329. *Ibid.*, p. 119.

Maurice GOGUEL (1910) noted important differences between Lk and the other Gospels in the section 22,54-71, especially the variation in order and the reporting of only one Sanhedrin session[330]. He maintained Luke was familiar with the saying about the Temple (Mk 14,58), though it did not appear in Lk[331]. In his *Introduction* (1923) Goguel called attention to the problematic nature and significance of the question of sources in Lk[332]. He noted that it was not always possible to determine the nature and extent of sources[333]. The passion narrative was distinguished by "un caractère et une tendance apologétiques"[334]. Lukan redaction was evident in the changes found in the Sanhedrin trial, the charges (23,2) and the double innocence declaration (23,4-5.13-16). He rejected the idea that the Herod episode (23,6-16) was a Lukan creation[335].

In an article on the trial of Jesus (1932) Goguel took as his starting point the earlier *ZNW* articles of Lietzmann, Dibelius and Büchsel which treated the trial of Jesus. On a methodological note, Goguel chided Lietzmann and Dibelius for isolating the trial, stating that the conflict of the passion in Jerusalem stemmed from a conflict which had already arisen with Jesus in Galilee. Observing the clear redactional nature of the other Evangelists' use of Mk, Goguel penned: "Matthieu, Luc et Jean ont développé le récit de Marc sous l'influence des idées des milieux dans lesquels ils ont vécu"[336]. Goguel sided with Dibelius against Lietzmann

---

330. M. GOGUEL, *Les sources du récit johannique de la Passion*, Paris, 1910, p. 80-81. The differences between the Johannine and Lukan accounts of Jesus before Pilate (Jn 18,28–19,16 / 23,1-25) were also indicated (p. 85). Goguel credited the Johannine redactor with borrowing different parts from the Synoptic tradition, including additions to the primitive account of the Jewish trial (Jn 18,13-14.19-24) and the Roman trial (Jn 18,28–19,26) (p. 106-107). Reference to Mt and Lk which "reproduisent la disposition" of Mk was also asserted (p. 10). In discussing Pilate's trial of Jesus Goguel wrote: "Des trois premiers évangélistes, c'est Luc qui se rapproche le plus du récit johannique. Il paraît représenter un stade intermédiaire entre Marc et Jean" (p. 85-86).

331. *Ibid.*, p. 83-84.

332. M. GOGUEL, *Introduction au Nouveau Testament*, t. 1. *Les évangiles synoptiques*, Paris, 1923, p. 494-495: "La question des sources particulières de Luc pose donc un problème d'une tout particulière importance". His treatment of the principal source theories included LAGRANGE, *Luc*, 1921; F. DIBELIUS, *Die Herkunft der Sonderstücke des Lukasevangeliums*, in *ZNW* 12 (1911) 325-343; HARNACK, *Lukas der Arzt*, (1906); B. WEISS, *Die Quellen* (1907), whose work he contended was analogous to that of Feine; HAWKINS, *Three Limitations*, and *St. Luke's Passion Narrative*; SOLTAU, *Unsere Evangelien*; V.H. STANTON, *Gospels*. Vol. 2; WERNLE, *Die synoptische Frage*.

333. GOGUEL, *Introduction*, p. 510.

334. *Ibid.*, p. 512-513.

335. *Ibid.*, p. 513: "D'autres, au contraire, tel l'épisode de la comparution devant Hérode (23,6-16), peuvent difficilement être des créations de Luc, ce qui n'augmente pas d'ailleurs leur valeur historique. En tout cas, le caractère nettement tendancieux et apologétique de toutes ces additions doit faire penser à une adaptation de plus en plus parfaite du récit de la passion aux besoins de la polémique et de la prédication chrétiennes et non à l'utilisation d'un récit homogène et indépendant".

336. GOGUEL, *À propos du procès de Jésus*, in *ZNW* 31 (1932) 289-301, p. 292.

concerning the homogeneity of the Mk 14,26–15,1 section. Luke was responsible for redacting 22,71 from Mk because the evangelist found the statement too bold. Goguel further disagreed with Lietzmann's suggestion that the trial of Stephen served as the model for the account of the Sanhedrin trial, though Lietzmann correctly emphasized the parallelism between the accounts[337].

As an articulate supporter of Lukan dependence upon Mk, and a staunch critic of Streeter, Goguel (1933) viewed the majority of critics at that time as endorsing the Two-Source theory[338]. Furthermore, he rejected as not being "well founded" the reasoning which suggested that the grouping of the greater (9,51–18,14) and lesser interpolations (6,20–8,3), and what some termed an Ebionite tendency, as support for the view that Luke employed a special source[339]. Concerning the order, Luke went to great lengths in retaining the Markan structure[340]. Goguel had, in his earlier publications, rejected the view of a single special source[341]. He thought instead that Luke, using Mk as his primary source, added material from a variety of sources "organically unrelated to one another and of various origins"[342].

Goguel noted that Streeter's theory garnered "some" support, though mainly from Great Britain[343]. Like many other scholars, Goguel lamented the difficulty in separating out the Markan elements of the passion narrative because all the elements were so intricately combined[344]. According to Goguel, Q was more responsible for material in all three Synoptics than Streeter was willing to admit, and thus Streeter's special source would be responsible for less material and consequently would not be as cogent or quantitatively significant[345].

Goguel enunciated several questions to consider when attempting to solve the source question: 1) whether material was independent, or an "elaboration" of Mk; 2) whether the passages stemmed from a special, unified source; 3) whether through an analysis of the reputed insertions the narrative was cohesive or a

---

337. *Ibid.*, p. 299; cf. GOGUEL, *Jésus et les origines de l'universalisme chrétien*, in *RHPR* 12 (1932) 193-211.

338. GOGUEL, *Luke and Mark: With a Discussion of Streeter's Theory*, in *HTR* 26 (1933) 1-55, p. 1. He also adopted the view of a Proto- and Deutero-Mk, though the second was quite faithful to the original. See the diagram depicting, in a not so clear fashion, the traditions earlier than Mk or Q (p. 53). He dated Proto-Mk at between 70 and 75 AD with Deutero-Mk appearing between 80 and 85 AD (p. 55).

339. *Ibid.*, p. 2. The lack of unity and the presence of elements from Q are evidence against the special source.

340. *Ibid.*, p. 3.

341. *Ibid.*, p. 4, 5, n. 6. Cf. GOGUEL, *Introduction au Nouveau Testament. 1. Les évangiles synoptiques*, Paris, 1923, p. 494ff.; *Jésus et les origines du christianisme* 1, Paris, 1932, p. 468ff.

342. GOGUEL, *Luke and Mark*, p. 4-5.

343. *Ibid.*, p. 5. Yet, later Goguel will emend this assessment to indicate that Streeter's theory won "wide acceptance" in England (p. 39).

344. *Ibid.*, p. 6.

345. *Ibid.*, p. 8.

collection of disjointed stories inserted into the Markan structure. Streeter's methodology was deficient in yet another way: he did not include a comparison with Mt to see whether Luke and Matthew both departed from Mk in the same place, though he allowed for differences arising from the redactional tendencies and styles of both later Synoptic evangelists. Goguel conceded that initially Streeter's theory was impressive[346]. Even if the conclusion could be drawn that Luke obtained his passion narrative from some source other than Mk, that in itself did not prove the Proto-Lk theory[347]. Like Schmidt and Dibelius, Goguel believed it probable that the account of the passion was the first part of the Gospel to be committed to writing. He stated clearly his own position that Lk was primarily constructed upon Mk: "But the better view is that Luke's passion narrative was derived from Mark with the addition of some fragmentary traditions of no great importance"[348].

Goguel was adamant that the changes by Luke over against Mk were the result of deeper reflection and were not from a separate, unified source[349]. Luke related only one session of the Sanhedrin, a result of the unification of the material dealing with Peter's denial[350]. Luke was motivated to make these changes in order to tell the story of Peter in as unified a fashion as possible and to avoid the "improbability of the hastily summoned night session". As a consequence of the transposition involving the Petrine material, the mistreatment by the soldiers occurred before Jesus was declared guilty. But because it happened at the same time as in Mk, and because of the great degree of similarity between the two accounts, Goguel concluded that Luke derived his material from Mk[351].

Regarding the Sanhedrin trial, the omission of witness testimony and reference to the destruction of the Temple were not insurmountable problems for Goguel, who considered Jesus' prophecy recorded in Mk to be authentic, though at a later time it dropped out of the tradition of a timid church[352]. Luke passed over reference to witnesses at the beginning of the pericope to avoid the Temple saying, but was not so cautious in the second part. While it was said there was no further need for witnesses, none had previously been presented. Since both accounts were alike in their arrangement and ready explanations can be brought forward for the changes, these were indications that Luke was relying on Mk once again.

In the reading of Pilate's trial, notice was made that Mk began immediately with the interrogation, but Lk with the charges. Goguel contended that nothing was

---

346. *Ibid.*, p. 26: "The argument for a Proto-Luke drawn by Streeter from Luke's passion narrative is at first reading impressive".

347. *Ibid.*

348. *Ibid.*, p. 26-27; cf. GOGUEL, *Jésus et les origines du christianisme*, Vol. 1, 1932, p. 468ff.

349. *Luke and Mark*, p. 30.

350. *Ibid.*, p. 33. Goguel conjectured Mk contained two sessions of the trial because he was relying on "two separate traditions".

351. *Ibid.*

352. *Ibid.*, p. 33, 34.

missing from Mk, since Pilate had authorized the questioning of Jesus[353]. Though
in Mk Pilate was surprised, his reaction in Luke was that of declaring Jesus'
innocence. The later Synoptics increasingly assigned the responsibility of Jesus'
death to the Jews, while presenting Pilate in a much more favorable light. He only
succumbed to the pressure of the crowd.

Goguel's summary of the section devoted to the passion narrative is worth
repeating:

> The foregoing analysis of Luke's passion narrative leads to a conclusion entirely
> opposed to the theory of a special homogeneous source. Luke's narrative is a
> literary elaboration of that of Mark, supplemented by certain fragmentary
> traditions. It does not support Streeter's hypothesis of a Proto-Luke; indeed it
> presents a weighty objection; for if Luke had had access to an otherwise unknown
> gospel, and had made it his principal source, it is inconceivable that in his story
> of the passion he should not have followed it for the main outlines; and if, on the
> other hand, we have to conclude that Proto-Luke did not include the passion, that
> work was certainly a very singular gospel[354].

In a note, Goguel pointed out Dibelius's justified dissatisfaction with Taylor's
mathematical approach to proving the amount of Lukan dependence upon Mk[355].
But in the end, Goguel complimented Streeter for having demonstrated "that the
problem of the relation between Mark and Luke is more complex than had been
assumed, and that it calls for renewed and more intensive study"[356].

Goguel (1932) rejected the historicity of the trial before Herod for three
reasons: 1) the improbable transfer of authority; 2) it added nothing to the story,
since Pilate's trial resumed as if nothing happened; and 3) the story has no
point[357]:

> This legend is based, no doubt, upon a confused recollection that Herod had been
> hostile to Jesus during the Galilean ministry; it may also have been suggested by
> the idea expressed in Acts iv.27, that all of the powers of this world were arrayed
> against Jesus. Later, if the trial of Jesus took place before the palace of Herod,
> a confusion could have given rise to the idea that Herod played some part in the
> trial[358].

Goguel cited Dibelius and Lietzmann as representative of critics who supported the
view of "the legendary character" of the episode. In an article also published that
year Goguel maintained that the Herod episode portrayed the conspiracy of human

353. *Ibid.*, p. 36, n. 58.
354. *Ibid.*, p. 38.
355. *Ibid.*, p. 39, n. 60. Cf. M. DIBELIUS, *Review: V. TAYLOR, Behind the Third Gospel, 1926*, in *TLZ* 52 (1927) 146-148.
356. *Luke and Mark*, p. 39.
357. *La Vie de Jésus*, 1932 = *The Life of Jesus*, 1945, p. 515, n. 1. See also *Das Leben Jesu*, tr. R. BINSWANGER, Zürich - Leipzig, 1934, p. 479, n. 811.
358. *Ibid.*

powers against the Messiah[359]. It was cited as an example of material borrowed from the ancient tradition though it contradicted the context and general spirit of the narrative[360].

Like Dibelius, Goguel (1933) dismissed the Herod episode (23,6-16) as an historical account. Rather, the scene, like Acts 4,27, was a fulfillment of the prophecy that Jesus was the victim of a conspiracy of the earthly powers. It was more likely that Luke found the legend in circulation than that he created it. In order "to give substance" to the story, Luke drew on Mk 15,16-20, borrowing the elements of the mistreatment by soldiers and the clothing in the garment[361].

Goguel also published in 1932 an essay treating the denial of Peter (22,54b-62 and pars.)[362]. Despite the differences between Lk and Mk he concluded that Luke was dependent solely upon Mk for this episode[363]. His suggested solution for the MA in 22,62 / Mt 26,75 was independent redaction by Matthew and Luke upon Mk[364].

Walter ADENEY (1900) joined his voice with those who saw Mk as Luke's primary authority[365] while Otto PFLEIDERER (1902) gave attention to the means by which

359. GOGUEL, À propos du procès de Jésus, in ZNW 31 (1932) 289-301, p. 292.

360. Ibid.: "Ce fait, néanmoins, n'exclut pas que, sur tel ou tel point de détail, les évangélistes postérieurs aient pu conserver quelque donnée venant de la tradition ancienne et répondant à ce qui s'est réellement passé. C'est une hypothèse qui doit être envisagée chaque fois que, dans l'un ou dans l'autre des récits secondaires, on trouve un détail en contradiction avec son contexte et avec l'esprit général de la narration".

361. Luke and Mark, p. 36-37.

362. Did Peter Deny His Lord? A Conjecture, in HTR 25 (1932) 1-27.

363. Ibid., p. 9: "This analysis, I think, shows that, apart from the question of arrangement, there is no reason for assuming any source for Luke's account other than Mark".

364. Ibid., n. 10: "It may be that the obscurity of Mark's phrase led Matthew and Luke to replace it by 'he wept bitterly'".

365. St. Luke, London, 1900, p. 25-26. Adeney supposed Luke, having selected his material from "all reliable sources" (p. 4), would have employed both oral and written traditions, generally revising these in his own style (p. 24). Earlier writings, as well as oral statements, were reflected in Lk. Adeney rejected the view of A. Wright that Luke was dependent in large part upon an oral version of Mk (p. 25; cf. A. WRIGHT, St. Luke's Gospel in Greek). "If the Gospel was as 'rigid and set in phrase' as some of the classical Greek poems, then there is not much that distinguishes this from a written document and so the documentary theory best explains the interrelation of the Synoptic gospels". Adeney pointed out that Luke reflected more Hebraistic language and style in comparison to the other Gospels and proposed Luke may have been working on a Hebrew or Aramaic original at these points in his Gospel (ADENEY, St. Luke, p. 5-6; cf. PLUMMER, S. Luke, ⁴1901, p. xxiii). A comparison of the Lukan and Markan versions indicated those places where Luke followed his source as well as those others where he departed from it, omitting some material in favor of introducing new (ADENEY, St. Luke, p. 26). "Thus we see that the beginning and the end are not from Mk – neither the infancy narrative, nor the accounts of the resurrection appearances of our Lord. Then having taken up Mk, Luke inserts five blocks of narrative at five places where he breaks off from the second gospel. These divisions are only rough and general. Scraps from Mk appear in the non-Marcan portions, and various smaller

Luke redacted Mk[366]. Willoughby C. ALLEN (1911), in a study of the Aramaic
background of the Gospels, argued that Lk depended upon Greek sources, of which

insertions from other sources occur in the Marcan portions" (p. 27). By omitting the saying about
the Temple as well as the blasphemy in the Sanhedrin trial, Luke simplified the account to obtain
"a clear, consistent narrative" (p. 377). Adeney contended Lk included no account of Caiaphas
interrogating Jesus as in Mt 26,57-68, since this was merely informal anticipation of the
Sanhedrin trial (p. 374). Adeney surmised that where close verbal similarity was concerned,
transfer of the material from one writing to another was "the easiest explanation" (p. 25).

In his new and enlarged edition (1924) Adeney credited the influence of Sanday and the authors
of the essays in *SSP* on the issue of sources (*St. Luke. Introduction. Revised Version with Notes,
Index and Maps* [The New Century Bible], Edinburgh - New York, 1924 [New and Enlarged
Ed.], p. vi-vii). Adeney counted 19,29-24,11 among the materials drawn from Mk (p. 26). He
concluded the introduction with an explanation of symbolic letters related to the various sources
which appeared throughout the commentary (p. 46). These comprised Mk, Q, S (for *Sondergut*)
and I, the infancy narrative. S referred to various sources: "A term employed by J. Weiss, Dr.
Bartlet, and others, for Luke's special sources. His preface to the gospel suggests that they were
numerous and various. They may have been partly documentary and partly oral. Some of the
documents may have been in Greek, some in Aramaic, for there is reason to think that Luke,
though a Gentile, knew the Aramaic language. With the exception of the Infancy narratives, it
is impossible to separate these materials and sort them out in detail". Adeney provided no
bibliographical information on which works of J. Weiss or Bartlet he was referring.

Adeney assigned the following verses in our section of the passion narrative to Mk: 22,54-
65.69b-23,1.3.16-26. Those he claimed stemmed from S included: 22,66-68; 23,2.4-15 (p. 309-
316). Related to this latter group, which also comprised other verses and passages, he explained:
"Several of these brief insertions may be attributed to Luke's general knowledge - e.g. his
reference to historical data; others may have been acquired by word of mouth. The longer
passages seem to point to written authorities" (p. 341). In the commentary the Herod pericope
is designated as 23,8-12 (p. 314). Commenting on 8,3 Adeney proposed that Joanna had possibly
helped convert Manaen to the faith (p. 144), though in his discussion of 23,8-12 he did not
mention either of them as possible sources of information concerning Herod. Although he did not
expressly specify GP, he clearly did not value the apocryphal gospels and assigned to them a date
later than the canonical gospels: "The extant apocryphal gospels are of much later date and of
very inferior quality, abounding in foolish legends" (p. 51).

366. Viewing many of the changes as stemming from Luke, Pfleiderer (1902) regarded the
Lukan transposition of the denial, mockery and trial as permitting Jesus to be present (*Das
Urchristentum: Seine Schriften und Lehren in gesichichtlichem Zusammenhang*, 2 vols., Berlin,
1902 = *Primitive Christianity*, Vol. 2, New York, 1909, p. 183). Luke abbreviated the Markan
account by omitting the reference to the Temple for the same reason Luke reduced the Temple
cleansing: he refrained from presenting his heroes as "bold innovators and reckless opponents of
established usages". Such an apologetic motif was found in the trial where Jesus (and his
movement) were declared to be harmless to the authorities. Luke, unlike Mk, out of respect for
the legal authorities, had Jesus respond promptly to Pilate (p. 183-184. Cf. p. 186, where
Pfleiderer contended Luke's presentation ameliorated the guilt of the lower classes to affix it to
the Jewish upper classes).

Pfleiderer did not deny the basic historicity of the trial account, but the repeated declarations
of Jesus' innocence followed by his condemnation, the handing of Jesus over to Jewish authorities
(though this flew in the face of accepted juridical practice), and the silence of the other evangelists
on this matter did not bode well for a decision of historical reliability (p. 184). Luke's additions
to the narrative thus became suspect.

one was "a Greek Gospel practically identical with our St. Mark"[367]. James MOFFATT (1911, ³1918) contended that Luke followed Mk very closely in the latter part of the Gospel[368]. Walter Fletcher BURNSIDE (1913) held that Luke used Mk "much in the form that we have now" to provide the structure of his own

367. W.C. ALLEN, *The Aramaic Background of the Gospels*, in W. SANDAY (ed.), *SSP*, 1911, 287-312, esp. p. 292-293. Rather than constituting a translation of a Hebrew original, the LXX was believed to have contributed to the language and style. H. Latimer Jackson faulted Allen for not giving sufficient credit to the validity of the Two-Source theory: "there is something to be said for the assertion: 'similarity of language does not always prove identity of source.' In the net result, however, I am left with the feeling that, if the Two-Documents hypothesis be not as yet an established result of criticism, it rests on stronger ground than the essayist will allow" (*Review: W. SANDAY [ed.], SSP, 1911*, in *JTS* 13, 1911-12, 110).

368. J. MOFFATT, *An Introduction to the Literature of the New Testament*, Edinburgh, 1911, ²1912, ³1918. Luke's method in this section involved omission of certain Markan material, the change of order, and important additions (p. 265). Moffatt conjectured that Luke was disaffected by his predecessors' works, and thus resolved to compose a new account (p. 263). But contrary to Farrar who regarded Luke as conveying the actual order of events, Moffatt viewed the chronology as "more graphic than historical" (p. 265). Such changes in sequence were due more to homiletic or catechetical influence than to allegiance to historical order or fact (p. 266). Like Lagrange, Moffatt recognized Luke's freedom in selecting and collating his sources. In addition to Mk and Q, Luke utilized "more or less fragmentary sources, written and oral (the latter obtained, for example at Antioch and Caesarea)". Moffatt declared that "Luke's relation to the Marcan order is of primary significance in an estimate of his work" (p. 264). Although Luke followed the Markan order very closely, he was not averse to reversing that order (p. 265). Cf. p. 266: "All through, whenever he leaves Mk, and even sometimes when he follows him, we have therefore to distinguish between a sequence which is apt enough in an edifying homily or in a catechetical manual, but unlikely to be historical". Further, Moffatt noted the close resemblances of the Lukan passion narrative with Acts 22-24 (p. 264, n. 3). Moffatt showed that in some cases Luke adhered to preference for Attic style: "Luke, true to the Atticist-tradition, prefers ἀπὸ τοῦ νῦν (22,18.69) to ἀπ᾽ ἄρτι (Mt 26,29.64)" (p. 278). Moffatt sided with Wright's interpretation of Luke's special material as opposed to Feine or B. Weiss or J. Weiss (p. 276-277). Like Wernle and Wright, Moffatt highlighted the "heterogeneous character of Luke's *Sondergut*". Moffatt castigated the contribution of the two latter exegetes as "unconvincing" or "too subjective" (p. 277-278). He critiqued B. Weiss in the following way: "In this case, as in that of the cognate analyses, Luke must have assigned high importance to his source, for which he repeatedly leaves even Mk. But the precision with which L is picked out, and materials assigned to it or to Q, carries very little conviction ... The linguistic and inward criteria for determining what belongs especially to L are too subjective in the large majority of cases. A similar criticism applies as forcibly to (c) J. Weiss' analysis of the gospel in three sources: Q, M (Mk), and S (Luke's special source)" (p. 277).

A.T. Robertson was highly critical of Moffatt: "But I do not think the positions taken fairly represent either British, American or German scholarly opinion. The book naturally reflects and expresses the views of Dr. Moffatt, as it should, but the student who follows Dr. Moffatt's lead in this volume is out of touch with the robust judgment of modern scholarship" (*RExp* 9 [1912] 259-260). In Moffatt's analysis, as regards the Herod episode (23,6-12) and other similar narratives, Luke was apparently drawing on two or three traditions interweaving them in such a way that the sources cannot be distinguished (p. 278; also 275). The same was said of whatever written sources Luke used in the passion narrative (p. 266).

work[369]. It was obvious, according to William HOLDSWORTH (1913), that Luke employed Mk and Holdsworth recommended readers to consult the presentations of Stanton and Hawkins[370]. Carl S. PATTON (1915) held that Luke used our Mk

369. *The Gospel According to St. Luke*, Cambridge, 1913, p. xviii. Burnside qualified his perspective of Luke's arrangement of the Markan material by saying that Luke had "for the most part" kept to the Markan order (p. xii). In addition, "one or more collections of the saying of Jesus" were available to both Luke and Matthew. What was more, Luke freely adapted material from his sources (p. xii). K. Lake judged this book as excellent in achieving its purpose. Though it did not constitute original research, it was a clear and concise presentation and offered "the best elementary exposition" on the synoptic question for this type of literary genre (*Review* in *HTR* 8 [1915] 559).

370. *Gospel Origins. A Study in the Synoptic Problem*, New York, 1913, p. 148; cf. p. 152. Changes in vocabulary were attributed variously to Luke's superior grasp of the Greek language, his medical background, and the differences between the copy of Mk which Luke possessed and used compared to the one with which we are familiar (p. 152). It was this last mentioned phenomenon which provided Holdsworth with an explanation in confronting the omissions of certain Markan material from Lk (p. 154-155). He ascribed the majority of the material in 22,38-23,26 to Mk, less 23,6-19. What remained, however, was the sense that the Markan narrative continued to guide the evangelist of the Third Gospel well to the end of his work. Like Plummer and Harnack, Holdsworth saw fit to ascribe to Joanna what he regarded as the Jewish and feminine aspects of Lk. Luke's order had been primarily chronological. Because of his great respect for the sources he employed, Luke exercised greater freedom in dealing with the sayings source which lacked any chronological indications (p. 148). Holdsworth supported the view that for the non-Markan portions of his Gospel Luke employed a single written source, which included details of the passion and resurrection (p. 184). Holdsworth opposed the view of those like A. Wright concerning the influence of oral tradition (p. 147). While agreeing with Stanton that the written source betrayed Jewish elements and stemmed from Palestine, Holdsworth disagreed that Luke incorporated bits of oral tradition into Q (p. 160; cf. p. 169). Holdsworth rejected the idea that Q would have included a passion narrative since it would then have constituted a Gospel in itself (p. 149). He saw in a document such as Q containing a passion narrative the same obstacles which faced *Urmarkus*. The objections were threefold: 1) if such documents would have existed, they would not have disappeared without at least some mention in the writings of the early church; 2) as W. Sanday suggested, the bulk of the coincidences pertain to the later rather than an earlier form of Mk; 3) Schmiedel argued that it was difficult to envision that two such very similar books existed (p. 108; regrettably, Holdsworth did not list Schmiedel in his bibliography, p. 210). Further, Bartlet's theory of "an original apostolic tradition" seemed too formal and more developed than would be expected in the time of Luke (cf. p. 108, 165). What distinguished him from most of the other like-minded scholars was that he attributed authorship to Joanna (p. 170-171; cf. p. 166). In a note, Holdsworth observed that Sanday, in an article entitled, *Jesus Christ*, in J. HASTINGS (ed.), *Dictionary of the Bible*, p. 639, had earlier also come to this same conclusion. As noted above, Burnside also considered Joanna a likely informant of details concerning Herod. The reasoning that led Holdsworth to his decision was that she would have access to information about Herod and the Samaritans through her husband, that she was Jewish by birth and educated, she had been associated with Mary, the mother of Jesus, and that the writings often reflected a feminine interest or empathy. Not to be overlooked was the fact that Luke identified her by name, and the other Synoptics did not. Somewhat mystifying was that, while Holdsworth argued against *Urmarkus*, he followed the lead of A. Wright in supporting the idea of a proto-, deutero- and trito - Mk. However, Holdsworth distinguished himself from

as a source, which provided the historical framework[371]. Spencer CARPENTER (1919) declared his solidarity with those who resolutely affirmed Luke's dependence upon Mk[372].

Wright saying this applied to written documents rather than the oral tradition as Wright maintained (p. 108-109). Harnack and others contended that the daughters of Philip the evangelist contributed the feminine element. Holdsworth dismissed this last conjecture because unlike Joanna they had not been associated with Jesus during his ministry (Acts 8,3; 23,55) (*Gospel Origins*, p. 163).

Holdsworth held the opinion that only 23,6-19 was attributed to the special source (p. 172). But this analysis was a bit deceiving. Upon closer inspection, it was apparent he altered his position. Lukan redaction took the Markan narrative and interwove it with brief passages from the special source (p. 181-182). These short sections included 23,6-16. Holdsworth took issue with Stanton who argued that 23,5-12.14-15 were derived from oral tradition. Because of "a certain unity", Holdsworth maintained they had their origin in a documentary source (p. 184).

371. C.S. PATTON, *Sources of the Synoptic Gospels* (U. of Michigan Humanistic Series, 5), London, 1915, p. 88. See p. 13: "Matthew and Luke have thus taken between them, with trifling exceptions, the entire Gospel of Mark". In his preface Patton expressed his indebtedness to Wernle, as well as Hawkins and the other authors of *SSP* (p. vi). He leaned towards acceptance of the view that Luke had many sources for his single tradition (p. 210-211). With regard to the possibility of a Jerusalem source, Patton retorted: "Nothing can perhaps be said in support of such a hypothesis, except what is suggested in the analysis on those pages and lies upon the surface of the passage" (p. 217-218). He observed that transpositions occurred in verses or brief passages more frequently in the passion narrative of the Gospels than in other sections (p. 13). Luke held fast to the order as found in Mk and departed from it for "assignable reasons". "Matthew and Luke also used a Mark which contained the story of Jesus in the same order given by our present Mark. Tho both of them deviate from this order for assignable reasons, one or the other of them is found following it all the time" (p. 88).

372. S.C. CARPENTER, *Christianity According to S. Luke*, London, 1919, p. 126-128. In his preface, Carpenter stated that the book resulted from lectures he delivered at Cambridge in 1915. They were "rewritten and considerably enlarged". Chapters IX-X, p. 122-148, dealt with the issue of sources. That Luke was dependent upon Mk was especially true of the latter part of Lk. "At xviii.15 [Luke] turns again to Mk x.13, and from that point to the end he follows the Markan outline, though he makes to it a number of important additions" (p. 135). Rejecting the Proto-Mk hypothesis, Carpenter reasoned that what Luke used "was identical, or practically identical with what we now call the Gospel of S. Mark" (p. 127-128). Carpenter also responded to J. Weiss's challenge to explain the great omission (p. 142).

Lukan redaction, like Matthean, consisted in improving Markan style (p. 129). But unlike Matthew who very closely followed Mk, Luke exercised great freedom and likewise added material (p. 145; p. 145-147, were most important for our survey). Luke avoided Mark's use of the historic present and substituted δέ for καί (p. 130). The reference to the freedom with which Luke treated his sources was reminiscent of comments by Lagrange and Wernle. Luke compressed some narrative and omitted other stories. Doublets were the result of borrowing from Mk and Q (p. 125-126; cf. p. 112).

Carpenter agreed with Harnack and Bacon against Burkitt and Bartlet in believing that Q did not contain a passion narrative (p. 137). While Carpenter was open, in principle, to the idea of an independent written account of the passion, it seemed improbable to him and evidence was lacking. Luke continued to use Mk as a source in the passion narrative, but did so with great freedom, as evidenced by the additions. Basically, though, Luke followed the Markan outline.

On June 26, 1912 the PONTIFICAL BIBLICAL COMMISSION (PBC) rendered two decisions concerning different aspects of Lk. The Commission avowed the chronological order of the writing of the Gospels as Aramaic Mt, Mk and finally Lk[373]. In addition, the teaching was affirmed that just as Mark depended upon Peter as a source for his Gospel, so Luke relied upon the preaching of Paul. But the Commission also advanced the opinion that both Mark and Luke had other sources available to them which were "either oral or already written"[374].

Furthermore, the PBC affirmed the historical reliability of Mk and Lk despite the fact that "in both Evangelists lack of order and discrepancy in the succession of facts are not infrequently found ..."[375]. The Commission did not believe that because, in the view of the time, Mk and Lk had been written later, these Gospels had been unduly affected by elements derived from the popular imagination or from the evangelists's own ideas.

The treatment of the synoptic question occasioned a response which gave free reign among scholars for the discussion of a possible solution to the dilemma. Avenues of investigation could include reference to oral or written tradition, as well as mutual dependence[376]. Unfortunately, the Two-Source theory did not fare so well. Exegetes were not permitted to hold this theory, which lacked "any testimony of tradition or ... any historical argument"[377].

Dismissing the view that Luke possessed some travel document, Carpenter adopted the view that a third source, such as an early Palestinian disciple like Philip, informed Luke (p. 144-145). Carpenter took issue with Harnack (*Luke the Physician*, p. 152, 153), that Philip and his daughters could not be considered reliable sources (p. 148). Carpenter, in line with Sanday, countered Hawkins's theory about the added material by declaring that "the Lukan additions here are not particularly 'Pauline'" (*Christianity*, p. 146).

Carpenter noted that the Synoptics "agree, in the selection and order of events, and in a good many of the actual words for pages at a time" (p. 122). He recalled that Hawkins attributed such phenomena as transpositions of order to the impulse of oral tradition (p. 124-125. Reference to *Horae Synopticae*, ²1909, Pt. II, §2, 3).

373. PONTIFICAL BIBLICAL COMMISSION, *De auctore, de tempore compositionis et de historica veritate Evangeliorum sec. Marcum et sec. Lucam, die 26 Junii 1912*; (= *On the Author, Time of Composition and Historical Truths of the Gospels According to St. Mark, and St. Luke*, p. 242-245) and *De quaestione synoptica sive de mutuis relationibus inter tria priora Evangelia, eodem die 26 Junii 1912*; (= *On the Synoptic Question or the Mutual Relations Between the First Three Gospels*, p. 245-246), in J.J. MEGIVERN (ed.), *Bible Interpretation* (Official Catholic Teachings), Wilmington, NC, 1978, p. 244. It was not uncommon for Catholic introductions to the NT to include the decrees of the PBC, such as P. GAECHTER, *Summa Introductionis in Novum Testamentum*, Leipzig, 1938, p. 1*-7*. In regard to these and other early decrees of the PBC, R. BROWN and T.A. COLLINS have lately assessed their value in the following manner: "Many [of the decrees] now have little more than historic interest, being implicitly revoked by later decrees, by DAS [*Divino Afflante Spiritu*], and by Vatican II". (*Church Pronouncements*, in *NJBC*, 1990, p. 1171).

374. *Ibid.*
375. *Ibid.*, p. 245.
376. *Ibid.*, p. 245-246.
377. *Ibid.*, p. 246.

Herbert DANBY (1919), frustrated by the continual application of similar methodology to the Sanhedrin trial, approached the question from a somewhat different vantage point[378]. It was undeniable that Luke built on the Markan basis throughout 22,54–23,1, though Luke treated his source differently in this section of the Gospel than in others which were considered a redaction of Mk[379]. The account in Lk more nearly approximated what actually happened, than that which was found in Mk[380]. The Markan version was suspicious because of the unlikelihood that a midnight trial would have occurred and the degree of difficulty of assembling both witnesses and judges at such a late hour.

The Lukan rendition, on the other hand, was "free from any suspicion of unreality"[381]. It rested, at least partially, on Mk, yet appeared to be an intentional correction based on new and better information. Whereas in Mk Jesus was accused of blasphemy, though subsequently no mention was made of that charge in the trial before Pilate, the Lukan account omitted any reference to it. Luke offered a more favorable view of Pilate in contrast to a comparatively unflattering description of the Jews. Building on Loisy's argument that the Jewish condemnation was intrinsic to the more universalistic apologetic, it was improbable that Luke would have passed over the formal condemnation "unless in the interests of historical accuracy"[382]. Thus, it was probable that Luke captured and related the events as they transpired.

George A. BARTON (1922) complimented the work of R.W. Husband and H. Danby declaring they had "not only written in excellent temper, but by their scientific method, have put the matter in a new perspective"[383].

---

378. H. DANBY, *The Bearing of the Rabbinical Criminal Code on the Jewish Trial Narratives in the Gospels*, in *JTS* 21 (1919) 51-76. See also *The Bearing of the Rabbinical Criminal Code on the Jewish Trial Narratives in the Gospels with a Translation of the Mishnah and Tosefta of the Tractate Sanhedrin*, B.D. Thesis, Oxford, 1919.

379. *Ibid.*, p. 61. Examples included 22,54b / Mk 14,58; 22,61 / Mk 14,67; 22,71 / Mk 14,63b.

380. *Ibid.*, p. 64. Danby earlier warned that his and all other conclusions were at best probabilities (p. 60).

381. *Ibid.*, p. 61.

382. *Ibid.*, p. 63.

383. G.A. BARTON, *On the Trial of Jesus Before the Sanhedrin*, in *JBL* 41 (1922) 205-211. See HUSBAND, *Prosecution*, 1916, and DANBY, *Bearing*, 1920. And while Husband and Danby agreed that Luke's version was probably the more reliable, Barton argued that Lk was not a "better authority than Mark" (p. 206). He continued: "Personally I am much impressed by the arguments of Harnack and Torrey for the early date of Acts, and the Gospels of Luke and Mark. If Acts was written during St. Paul's imprisonment at Rome, Mark, one of the sources of Luke, must have been composed as early as 50 A.D. and perhaps earlier. [...] There is no reason to suppose that it was not the aim of its author to state events as nearly as he could as they happened. As many admit, there is much evidence that a good deal of its material comes from an eye witness of the events described. Its account of the trial is, accordingly, worthy of great respect. It seems to me our best source of information as to Jewish practice for the period which it covers" (p. 206-207). By his estimation, in addition to Mk, which Luke freely redacted, Luke had access to other sources "which were probably not earlier than Mark", though he did not

Erich KLOSTERMANN (1919), a strong proponent of Lukan dependence upon Mk, insisted that Lk reflected conscious changes upon the *Vorlage*[384]. In a discussion of the first main section of Lk (3,1-9,50), he pointed to a very extensive agreement between Lk and Mk in material, order and expression. Affirming that Luke used Mk as his basis, correspondence between Lk 3,1-6 + 8,(1)4 + 9,50 + 18,25-24,11 and Mk 1,1-6,44 + 8,27-16,8 was recognized with the exception of a few changes in the order of pericopes. Differences in the order were the result of Luke's deliberate choices. While Lk was partly intended to improve the work stylistically, this was not the extent of the recasting. There were few changes in the sequence of events and minuscule additions and omissions. Further, Luke introduced other material into the Markan framework.

In contrast, Spitta (1912) contended that Lk and Mk were independent of one another. Klostermann questioned whether the *Sonderüberlieferungen* "so ganz einheitlichen Charakter haben" that scholars such as B. Weiss, Feine and J. Weiss can speak of "eine Sonderquelle (L)"[385]. Appreciating the difficulty of separating material taken from the "Spruchsammlung" which was combined with the Lukan *Sondergut*, Klostermann urged caution quoting Holtzmann:

> Aber gerade hier wollen andere wieder des Lc eigensten Geist rekognoszieren, und die Scheidung zwischen dem aus der Spruchsammlung übernommenen Material und dem in einer gewissen Verbindung damit stehenden Sondergut des Lc ist mit so grossen Schwierigkeiten verknüpft, dass auch bezüglich dieser Dinge der Exegese noch Zurückhaltung obliegen wird[386].

elaborate on their nature or extent.

384. E. KLOSTERMANN, *Das Lukasevangelium* (HNT, 2), Tübingen, 1919, p. 411 [= 48-49]. The pages in brackets refer to the second edition [²1929]. See "Die Hauptquellen des Lc", p. 411-412 [= 48-49].

385. *Ibid.*, p. 412 = [cf. 49].

386. *Ibid.* See H.J. HOLTZMANN, *Die Synoptiker*, 1/1, ³1901, p. 20, and *Neutestamentliche Theologie* I, ²1911, p. 525-530, esp. p. 528-(529), n. 6. Cf. above. The influence of Holtzmann on Klostermann should not be underestimated. In addition, Klostermann cited Jülicher and Bousset. The caution now extended to include Streeter, Taylor and Easton: "Auch nach BHStreeter The Four Gospels 1925, Taylor Behind the Third Gospel 1926 und BSEaston The Gospel acc. to St. Luke 1926 wird diese Zurückhaltung geboten bleiben" [49].

Further, he appended after Holtzmann's quotation "vgl. jetzt auch Feine Einleitung³, 39f. und Lagrange CX f." To quote Feine: "Da sprachlich und zum Teil auch sachlich das ganze besondere Überlieferungsgut des Lk eine gewisse Verwandtschaft zeigt, dies Gut aber mit der Redenquelle in engem Zusammenhang steht – eine Verwandtschaft, welche sich übrigens auch auf die Apg erstreckt –, so liegt die Hypothese nahe, alles eben Genannte auf eine einheitliche Evangelienschrift des Lk zurückzuführen. Ich habe selbst in der S. 12 genannten Untersuchung diese Ansicht vertreten, in verwandter Weise baut B. Weiss diese Hypothese aus. *Doch sehe ich auch die Bedenken, welche ihr entgegenstehen*" (*Einleitung*, Leipzig, ³1923, p. 39; italics mine). It seemed Klostermann transposed the pagination for Lagrange since it appeared he intended p. XC-XCII and not "CX f." as written (p. 49).

In reaction to the work of Feine and B. Weiss, Lagrange repeated what he stated for his article on the sources of Lk: "Rien ne nous empêche de conclure que le prétendu rédacteur est vraiment l'auteur et non seulement le copiste du troisième évangile" (*RB* [1896] 32).

In the section 22,54-71 Klostermann examined two possibilities: Luke abbreviated his Markan *Vorlage*, or he used a second source (J. Weiss)[387]. Unlike Mk and Mt, the material pertaining to Peter was told without interruption. Luke transferred the mockery (22,63-65) to a time later in the night. All of the changes, including the omission of reference to the witnesses concerning Jesus' words about the Temple, led Klostermann to the following conviction: "Mit alledem scheint Lc die Mcgrundlage selbständig so stark bearbeitet und verkürzt (etwa, weil er dem Ende des Buches zueilte, Zahn) zu haben"[388]. An opposing theory offered by J. Weiss following B. Weiss advocated a special non-Markan source which was superior in several areas: 1) the more historically correct description of a morning session of the Sanhedrin; 2) the surprising and evasive answer of Jesus in 22,67.70 in place of Mk 14,62; and 3) avoiding the error of ascribing the power of the death penalty to the Sanhedrin[389]. In an analysis of 22,63-64 Klostermann gave attention to the more significant changes in Lk over against Mk[390]. For the discussion of the Sanhedrin trial, he highlighted similarities with Acts, e.g. in the use of temporal phrases (22,66 / Acts 27,39) or that the omission of the words about the Temple (Mk 14,55-61a) in Lk 22,71 showed some similarity with Acts 6,14[391].

All the responsibility for the condemnation of Jesus in Luke's version of Pilate's trial (23,1-25) fell upon the Jews. Influenced by Wernle[392] and J. Weiss, Klostermann noted the tendency of the author of Lk-Acts to highlight the non-threatening nature of the Christian movement while Christians were being maligned by Jews[393]. He regarded this section as a redaction of Mk. B. Weiss argued that the entire section derived from L (with the exception of insertions or reminiscences from Mk vv. 3.10.22.25)[394]. Klostermann countered by insisting that only 23,6-12 (16) went back to a special tradition of Luke. In the second edition he seemed less sure that there was not some influence of a special source in 23,1-25 as indicated by the shift from declarative statement to questions. Perhaps the argumentation of B. Weiss and others supportive of the special source was increasingly appealing to him.

---

387. KLOSTERMANN, *Lukasevangelium*, p. 585-586 = [218-219].

388. *Ibid.*, p. 585 = [218]. In the second edition Klostermann slightly recast this line into a question: "Hat nun mit alledem ...?". Because of the transposition of Peter's denials, the αὐτόν (v. 63) must refer to Peter, an insight he attributed to Holtzmann (p. 585 = [218]).

389. *Ibid.*, p. 586. Klostermann amended this in the second edition by revising the statement into a question. "Oder hat Lc hier noch einen ursprünglicheren, gelegentlich mit Jo sich berührenden Bericht besessen, zwischen dem und seiner Mcvorlage er als Redaktor einen Ausgleich schuf (so u. a. B. und JWeiss, Bultmann, Loisy)?" [p. 219]. See also p. 589 = [cf. 221], where the absence of the condemnation in Lk was contrasted with Mk and Mt.

390. *Ibid.*, p. 587 = [220].

391. *Ibid.*, p. 588 = [220].

392. *ZNW* 1 (1900) 50.

393. KLOSTERMANN, *Das Lukasevangelium*, p. 589 = [221]. Again, in the second edition, he revised the statement into a question.

394. *Ibid.*, p. 589 = [cf. 221].

The MA in 22,62 was believed to have been drawn from Mt 26,75 and thus Klostermann agreed with Blass, Wellhausen and J. Weiss that it should be omitted[395]. Curiously, though he noted the MA in v. 64, he provided no explanation[396].

Citing Plummer's and Zahn's identification of Joanna as the source of the Herod pericope, and J. Weiss's statement that that there was nothing inherently unhistorical about Herod's role in the trial of Jesus (23,6-12 [16]), which was also recounted in the GP, Klostermann also recalled Holtzmann's suggestion of a parallel in Acts 25,22-26,32 and Feigel's solution that Ps 2 provided the motive for the story[397]. Klostermann seemed not to have excluded these last contributions, but may even have been leaning in their direction. The mockery by Herod's soldiers (23,11) was possibly a substitute for that of the Roman soldiers in Mk 15,16-20[398].

Betraying an obvious indebtedness to M. Dibelius, Karl Ludwig SCHMIDT (1919) declared that in comparison to other passages, the passion narrative served apologetic goals. He determined that, having already been set in a fixed form at an early date, it reflected liturgical and missionary coloration[399]. Although firmly established, certain speeches could have been put into the mouth of Jesus to edify or to serve as apologia[400]. The basic narrative would be of extraordinary

395. *Ibid.*, p. 587 = [cf. 219]. In the second edition, Loisy's name replaced that of Weiss.
396. *Ibid.*, p. 587 = [221].
397. *Ibid.*, p. 589 = [221-222]. It was certainly curious that Klostermann made no mention of M. Dibelius's 1915 article in the first edition. In the second edition he added the name of E. Meyer, Vol. 1, p. 202, n. 1, to the previous list of B. Weiss, Feine and J. Weiss following Feigel. DIBELIUS, *Herodes und Pilatus*, was also said to have supported the idea that the account arose from Ps 2 though Luke was responsible for creating the scene. Bultmann and Loisy attributed it to the insertion of "eine schon vorher entstandene Legende" [222]. Finally, Klostermann's doubts regarding the source of the Herod story were indicated now by his claim that the Herod story could (könnte) be dependent upon a special tradition. The weight of the arguments by Feigel, Meyer and Dibelius seemed to have influenced him.
Klostermann referred to F.K. FEIGEL, *Der Einfluss des Weissagungsbeweises und anderer Motive auf die Leidensgeschichte. Ein Beitrag zur Evangelienkritik*, Tübingen, 1910, p. 42, n. 2: "Schon bei der Herodesepisode könnte man versucht sein, an ein alttestamentliches Motiv zu denken: Act. 4 25ff. wird Ps. 2,1.2 zitiert und auf die Erfüllung dieser Weissagung durch die Herodesepisode hingewiesen". The inclusion of the story was due to the special interests of the tradition. The Gentile Church would have been interested to learn the development of the Church (p. 98). The story of Herod clarified that Pilate did not wish to sentence Jesus and that the responsibility for it stemmed only from the Jews.
398. KLOSTERMANN, *Das Lukasevangelium*, p. 591.
399. K.L. SCHMIDT, *Der Rahmen der Geschichte Jesu*, Berlin, 1919; Darmstadt, 1964, p. 303-309. The passion narrative would have been read as *lectio continua* in the context of liturgy (p. 305). The article, *Herodes und Pilatus* by Dibelius was described as "die instruktive Abhandlung" (p. 308, n. 1).
400. *Der Rahmen*, p. 305-306.

historical worth. Schmidt observed there were few joints and seams in the passion narrative.

Luke's revision of Mk was not as slavish as that of Matthew[401]. The account of Pilate's trial confirmed this[402]. Some passages, such as Peter's denials, were augmented by information from eyewitness reports, whereas for episodes such as the Sanhedrin trial, the evangelist would have needed to use whatever information was available. In those places where lacunae existed, Luke compensated by regrouping material offered by Mk[403].

In addition to edifying or apologetical material, Luke's redaction also attempted to strengthen the context of the passages. Though offering no rationale why Luke would have omitted the account of the mockery by the Roman soldiers (Mk 15,16-20 = Mt 27,27-31), Schmidt deduced that the omission was intentional[404]. These comments notwithstanding, and with the exception of the Herod pericope, Schmidt stood fast in holding that the passion narrative was a continuous report. Though there were indeed gaps in the presentation, this allowed for later insertions.

In contrast to Luke, Mark and Matthew presented the denial after the trial and mistreatment of Jesus which interrupted the context. The transposition reflected Luke's effort to better organize the material[405]. He concluded the section "Wenige Fugen und Nähte in der Leidensgeschichte" with a word about transpositions: "Es liegen Lücken vor, und der Zusammenhang ist nicht immer recht gefestigt, aber Umstellungen der einzelnen Szenen und ein Zurückführen auf verschiedene Traditionsschichten lassen sich im ganzen nicht vornehmen"[406].

Schmidt contended that Luke was able to insert the Herod story because of the loose context surrounding the account of the trial before Pilate. He insisted that the report existed for a long time in a fixed form which was no longer subject to change. The insertion corresponded with the edifying and apologetic goals of the author[407].

---

401. *Ibid.*, p. 307-308. In comparison to Mt Schmidt referred to Luke's "planmässigere Verarbeitung des vom zweiten Evangelisten ihm dargebotenen Stoffes" (p. 308).

402. *Ibid.*, p. 308.

403. *Ibid.*, p. 306. He argued there were a few gaps in the passion narrative (p. 307).

404. *Ibid.*, p. 307. Schmidt referred to the hypothesis of J. Weiss that Luke wished to avoid a doublet while Wellhausen decided that it was not possible to understand Luke's motivation (p. 307, n. 1).

405. *Ibid.*, p. 306-307.

406. *Ibid.*, p. 309.

407. *Ibid.*, p. 307; cf. p. 305-306: "Eine spätere Zeit hätte vielleicht gern aus erbaulichen und apologetischen Zwecken Jesus Worte und Reden einem Hohen Rat, einem Pilatus, einem Herodes gegenüber in den Mund gelegt, aber der Bericht hatte schon längst feste Form angenommen und konnte ohne Schädigung der festgewordenen Gemeindeanschauung nicht mehr angeändert werden".

Rudolph BULTMANN, in his seminal work *Die Geschichte der synoptischen Tradition* (1921) insisted that "It cannot be maintained that the Passion story as we have it in the Synoptic gospels is an organic unity. Even here what is offered us is made up of separate pieces"[408]. At various places Luke used an older tradition in addition to Mk[409]. This was the case for Peter's denial (22,54-62) and for 22,66 of the Sanhedrin trial[410]. Bultmann asserted that it was impossible to distinguish in the denial story how much came from the earlier tradition, from Mk or from Luke himself[411].

The account of the mistreatment (22,63-65) stemmed from Luke's special source (v. 63), Markan influence (v. 64) and Luke's own hand (v. 65)[412]. Bultmann regarded the position of the abuse of Jesus as found in Lk to be the more original[413]. He considered the order reflective of the earlier tradition.

He rejected the idea of a special source for the account of the Sanhedrin trial (22,66-71, except for v. 66), maintaining that this simply reflected Lukan redaction[414]. The phrase τί ἔτι ἔχομεν μαρτυρίας χρείαν was evidence that Luke was familiar with the Markan account. He gave conflicting assessments of the source question for Pilate's trial. Though he earlier suggested that the Lukan account was simply a revision of Mk prompted by the sense that the Jewish leaders would have had to provide more detailed information concerning the charges, he later declared that the account had been so radically revised by Luke that it was no

---

408. R. BULTMANN, *Die Geschichte der synoptischen Tradition*, Göttingen, 1921; ²1931, 282-308 (*Die Passionsgeschichte*), p. 297 (= *The History of the Synoptic Tradition*, tr. J. MARSH, Oxford - New York, 1963 [= ⁵1961], Peabody, MA, 1993, p. 275). Page numbers in parentheses refer to the ET and those accompanied by an asterisk direct the reader to supplementary notes at the end of the book.

409. *Ibid.*, p. (269*).

410. *Ibid.*, p. 163; ²1931, 290 (= *269): "Lk, der hier neben Mk noch ältere Tradition zu benutzen scheint". Bultmann argued that Mk 15,1 may be later than 22,66 (p. 165; ²1931, 294 = 272*). Further the trial did not interrupt the account of Peter's denial (p. 170; ²1931, = 280*). Bultmann and Dibelius concurred that the passion narrative originally consisted of "a series of isolated units" (*Supplement, Revised*, 1962, p. 440; cf. *Ergänzungsheft*, 1958, p. 24). See *Ergänzungsheft*, ⁴1971, p. 97-98, and 102.

411. *Ibid.*, p. 163; ²1931, p. 290 (= 269).

412. *Ibid.*, p. 164; ²1931, 293 (= *271): "Es wird schon Bestandteil eines älteren Berichts gewesen sein, da Lk es offenbar nach anderer Quelle bringt". Bultmann did not consider Mk 14,65 or Lk 22,63 and Mk 15,16-20a as doublets (p. 167 = 276). See *Ergänzungsheft*, ⁴1971, p. 99.

413. *Ibid.*, p. 164; ²1931, 293 (= *271). The Markan arrangement reflected a "besonders unglücklicher Stelle". While he contended that the ill treatment of Jesus was placed in Lk in the morning, he did not explain his rationale (p. 170 = 280).

414. *Ibid.*, p. 164; ²1931, 292 (= *271). He further suggested that a few verses (Mk 14,57-59) may have been missing from Luke's copy of Mk and that apologetic reasons may have accounted for the omission of the reference to the prophecy about the destruction of the temple. Bultmann modified his view, convinced by Finegan, that 22,66 "[ist] eine Konflation aus Mk 14,53b und 15,1" (*Ergänzungsheft*, 1958, p. 41; cf. FINEGAN, *Überlieferung*, 1934, p. 24). See *Ergänzungsheft*, ⁴1971, p. 98-99.

longer possible to determine, not whether Luke had another source, but to what extent the new material was derived from it[415]. Bultmann simply pointed to the extensive literature on the issue of the Sanhedrin's competence. He seemed content to point out the opposing viewpoints on the matter[416].

He did not treat the MA in 22,62. The MA in 22,64 "ist wohl erst ganz sekundäre Konformation nach Mt"[417].

While the Lukan version of the events surrounding the passion can be used to confirm "gewisse kritische Beobachtungen", it cannot be used to reconstruct an older version of the passion narrative[418]. Such comments could be applied to the efforts of Streeter and Taylor. He summarized his position in a discussion of the history of the passion tradition: "Da jedoch hier durch den Vergleich mit Mk keine Nebenquelle ermittelt werden kann, ist es am wahrscheinlichsten, dass Lk ein andere – wohl ältere – Redaktion der Vorlage der Passionsgeschichte des Mk neben Mk benutzte; dafür spricht auch die grosse Verwandtschaft der Verleugnungsgeschichten des Lk und Mk"[419].

Bultmann followed Dibelius's lead in regarding the Herod episode (23,6-16) as a legendary outgrowth of Ps 2,1-2. This story, inserted in the Markan account of Pilate's trial, divided that account into two[420].

A few reactions to various early editions of Bultmann's work are worthy of note. Though Lagrange complained that Bultmann exaggerated the degree to which the evangelists invented material, he charged that Catholic exegetes erred in the other direction, by not sufficiently crediting the evangelists with reworking their memories and the traditions which they received[421]. Easton, writing about the second edition of Bultmann's work, lamented that Bultmann ignored the criticisms leveled by other scholars[422].

Bultmann continued to repudiate the view that Luke employed a special source in addition to Mk[423]. In his *Ergänzungsheft* (1958) he called attention to Taylor's

---

415. *Ibid.*, p. 165; p. 170 (= *272; cf. p. *280).
416. *Ergänzungsheft*, 1958, p. 40 (= *History, Supplement*, 438).
417. *Ibid.*, p. 164; ²1931, 293 (= *271: "is in all probability").
418. *Ibid.*, p. 170 (= 280*).
419. *Ibid.*, p. 171; ²1931, 303 (= 280*).
420. ²1931, 294 = ˙273; cf. p. 276˙).
421. M.-J. LAGRANGE, *Review: R. BULTMANN, 1921*, in *RB* 31 (1922) 291. Cf. p. 292.
422. B.S. EASTON, *Review: R. BULTMANN, ²1931*, in *ATR* 14 (1932) 195.
423. *GST*, p. 170; ²1931, 303: "...beweisen nichts für eine eigene Quelle". Cf. *Ergänzungsheft zur 3. durchgesehenen Auflage*, Göttingen, 1958, p. 42 (= *History, *280); cf. *Supplement, Revised* 1962, p. 440: "The view that Luke had some other source besides Mark available for the passion narrative shows itself untenable, as has been already frequently shown in the supplements to the preceding analyses, especially in connection with Finegan. Cp. also N.A. Dahl, op.cit., p. 20f. (See the later addition in *Ergänzungsheft*, Göttingen, ⁴1971, rev. by G. THEISSEN and P. VIELHAUER, ⁴1971, p. 94-100: *Die Passionsgeschichte*; 101-102: *Die Geschichte der Passionstradition*, p. 102: Tyson, 1959; Rehkopf, 1959; Schneider, 1969). On the other hand, P. Winter produces good arguments for the opposite view in Z.N.T. 50 (1959), p. 14-33, 221-52. His analysis agrees almost exactly with that given above". See also p. 437, where

effort in *Behind the Third Gospel* (1926) to reconstruct Proto-Lk in line with Streeter, although no evaluation of the work was offered[424]. He was, however, critical of the attempts by Hirsch, Helmbold and Vaganay[425].

The evolution of Biblical studies was marked by the beginnings of the application of form criticism to the NT. Scholars viewed Luke as a writer rather than simply a compiler of traditions, motivated by apologetic interests. Changes in order over against Mk were prompted by Luke's desire to unify similar materials.

Bultmann sided with Finegan in declaring that the denial story was based on Mk alone (so *Ergänzungsheft*, [4]1971, p. 98). It is striking that Bultmann did not mention Streeter at this point.

424. *Ergänzungsheft*, 1958, p. 5; [4]1971, 15 (= 1993, p. 381, concerning p. 3 n. 3). In the fourth edition Theissen and Vielhauer added references to Schramm (1966), Schürmann (1957), Schneider (1969) and Rehkopf (1959) as those who supported the proposal of Luke's use of non-Markan material, the last three particularly in the passion narrative.

425. *Ibid.*: "Höchst kompliziert, in ausgesprochenem Gegensatz zur Formgeschichte und wenig überzeugend rekonstruiert Em. Hirsch die Entstehungsgeschichte der synopt. Evgelien (Frühgeschichte des Evangeliums I 1941. [2]1951. II 1941). Noch weniger überzeugend ist die Fortführung der Hirsch'schen Rekonstruktion durch Heinr. Helmbold (Vorsynopt. Evglien 1953). Auch die Quellentheorie von L Vaganay (Le Problème Synoptique 1954) ist nicht überzeugend".

CHAPTER THREE

THE GOLDEN AGE OF SPECIAL SOURCE THEORIES
The Apex of Proto-Luke

As the theory of a special source evolved we begin also to see support from British and American scholars. German researchers remained engaged in the debate. Already in his *Einleitung in die Bibel* (1894, [3]1901) Adolf SCHLATTER held that in Lk 22-24 Luke combined with Mk "einen neuen selbständigen Bericht"[1]. The differences included the displacement of the story of Peter's denial, the postponement of the account of Jesus before the Sanhedrin and the introduction of the pericope of Jesus before Herod.

The relationship of Lk to Mk and Mt was very different. For the most part the Markan material was reproduced accurately and carefully. Some small omissions and slight changes in order were attributed to similar stories Luke drew from other sources[2]. Schlatter maintained that Luke also borrowed material from Mt. In addition to Mk and Mt Luke was thought to possess a third witness to the Jesus story which included the material concerning the infancy, and passion and resurrection narratives[3]. Schlatter insisted that the detail about the women who served Jesus (8,3) was part of a continuous narrative involving the passion[4].

In his commentary on Lk (1908) following his comments on 22,7-13 Schlatter wrote of the increased use of the third witness as opposed to the Markan report in the passion narrative, but did not treat the source question for each individual pericope[5]. He noted the difference in the placement of the denial of Peter and the mockery in respect to the trial before the Sanhedrin[6].

The more detailed source-critical analysis appeared in *Das Evangelium des*

---

1. A. SCHLATTER, *Einleitung in die Bibel*, Stuttgart, 1894, p. 340; [3]1901, p. 357. See also his discussion of the Synoptics, 1894, p. 299-304; [3]1901, p. 315-319. K.H. Rengstorf was a great admirer of Schlatter. Cf. below. Note the recent work by W. NEUER, *Adolf Schlatter. Ein Leben für Theologie und Kirche*, Stuttgart, 1995, esp. 694-699, concerning his 1931 Lukan commentary. For a select list of reviews of that book, see p. 846.

2. *Einleitung*, 1894, p. 341, n. 1; [3]1901, p. 358, n. 1.

3. *Ibid.*, [3]1901, p. 360; cf. 1894, p. 343.

4. *Ibid.*, [3]1901, p. 351: "Dazu wird noch ein Bericht über die Frauen gefügt, welche Jesus in Galiläa dienten, der bereits auf die Passions- und Ostergeschichte vorwärts sieht, und dadurch erkennbar macht, dass diese Stücke einem zusammenhängenden Bericht über Jesu Geschichte angehörten, der ihn von Galiläa nach Jerusalem hinauf begleitet hat". Cf. 1894, p. 322.

5. *Erläuterungen zum Neuen Testament*. Bd. 1. *Die Evangelien und die Apostelgeschichte*, Stuttgart, 1908, p. 577: "Von nun an zieht Lukas die reichen Angaben seines dritten Zeugen über Jesu Abschied von den Seinen heran und lässt den Bericht des Markus in der Leidens- und Ostergeschichte zunehmend zurücktreten, so dass uns die Angaben des andern Erzählers über Jesus Ende wohl nahezu vollständig erhalten sind". See also his *Theologie des Neuen Testaments*, T. 2. Stuttgart, 1910, p. 414, n. 1, regarding 22,61.66-70; 23,1-12.

6. *Ibid.*, p. 586.

Lukas aus seinen Quellen erklärt (1931)[7]. Although Schlatter stated it was not known how many gospels Luke knew, he argued that it must have been three: Mk in the Greek Church, Mt in the Palestinian Church and possibly in Syria a third gospel[8]. Luke incorporated a large portion of Mk and Mt, though Mk formed the "Grundlage" for Lk[9]. Schlatter also compared the Lukan vocabulary with that found in Josephus.

He repeated his assertion that the information about the women (8,3) stemmed from the special Gospel source[10]. He also remarked about a special source in his discussion of Herod's judgment about Jesus (9,7-9)[11].

The material in Lk was divided into three categories: "Die neue Fassung des Markus" among which was included some of the material in 22,54-71; 23,1-25; "Der neue Erzähler" which included 22,58.59.61.66-71; 23,1-25; and "Das Evangelium des Matthäus bei Lukas".

In assessing the sources in 22,54-71 Schlatter observed that 22,54.55 corresponded to Mk 14,53-54 and that 22,56 showed contact with Mk 14,54[12]. Although 22,59.60.61b were similar to Mk 14,70.72 the influence of other Evangelists was stronger than Mk. Lk 22,64 showed connection not only with Mk 14,65, but also with Mt 26,68. Lk 22,69 reflected a weak relationship with Mk 14,62 in the fashion of 22,71 to Mk 14,63.

For the section 23,1-25 Schlatter detected the similarity between 23,3 and Mk 15,2[13]. Part of 23,19 has a connection with Mk 15,7, although there was new information which had been added to the Lukan verse. Regarding the basis of information for Jesus' trial by Pilate (23,1-25), Schlatter wondered whether the source may have only referred to a trial of Pilate with the Jews, so that the reader had to infer that Pilate would wish to interrogate Jesus[14].

In the section of the book about "Der neue Erzähler" Schlatter returned to the source question, which in some ways repeated material he previously discussed[15]. With the events occurring in the house of the high priest the distance from the Markan account became ever greater, according to Schlatter. "Die Passions-

---

7. *Das Evangelium des Lukas aus seinen Quellen erklärt*, Stuttgart, 1931.

8. *Ibid.*, p. 19. See also p. 561.

9. *Ibid.*, p. 33. See U. LUCK, *Kerygma und Tradition in der Hermeneutik Adolf Schlatters* (AFLN-W, 45), Cologne - Opland, 1955, p. 60.

10. *Das Evangelium des Lukas*, p. 267: "Diese Angabe stand nicht in einer Spruchsammlung, sondern in demjenigen Evangelium, das mit der von L. wiedergegebenen Passions- und Ostergeschichte schloss".

11. *Ibid.*, p. 92-93: "Damit wird sichtbar, dass [Luke] jener Passionsbericht gegenwärtig ist, der die Begegnung des Herodes mit Jesus am Tage seiner Kreuzigung erzählte, 13,31; 23,8-11, war es nicht leicht vereinbar, dass sich Herodes mit abergläubischer Angst vor Jesus gefürchtet und in ihm den vom Tod erweckten Täufer vermutet habe, wenn sich auch nicht ermessen liess, in welchem Mass wilde Schwankungen und Widersprüche im Verhalten des Herodes vorkamen".

12. *Ibid.*, p. 140.

13. *Ibid.*, p. 141.

14. *Ibid.*, p. 439-440.

15. *Ibid.*, p. 436-443.

geschichte der Quelle erscheint nahezu lückenlos"[16]. Luke possibly recounted the story of Peter's denial with few changes[17]. Mk 14,53.54 probably influenced 22,54.55 just as Mk 14,70.72 likely exerted influence upon 22,59.60 and Mk 14,72b upon 22,61b. Luke drew on Mt 26,75 to conclude the Markan sentence in 22,62. The source explained much more why the testimony of the witnesses was unnecessary since the Sanhedrin immediately put the Messiah question to Jesus. A distant connection between Jesus' response to the Christ question and Mk 14,62 was acknowledged[18]. Jesus' answer to the question whether he was the Son of God took the same form as Mt 26,64.

Lk 23,3 clearly stemmed from Mk 15,2[19]. Lk 23,14 reported that the trial of Jesus occurred, but Schlatter queried whether the source had recounted it. "Vielleicht sprach sie nur von der Verhandlung des Pilatus mit den Juden, so dass Vers 4 die Fortsetzung von Vers 2 enthält"[20].

Pilate desired to make Herod "dienstbar" and thus sent Jesus to him. Clothing Jesus in a white garment signified in mocking fashion both his innocence and his claim to be the Messiah. But it was the weak Christ who mocked Herod by his silence. Concerning 23,12 Schlatter suggested the narrator knew of the hostile relationship between Pilate and Herod. Pilate simply concurred with Herod's judgment[21].

Paul Fiebig highlighted initially the distinctiveness of the style of Schlatter's Lukan study. Rather than offering a continuous commentary it was divided into three sections: 1) Markan sections in Lk; 2) material which went back to Luke; and 3) parts which Mt and Lk had in common[22]. Commenting on Schlatter's examination of the language of Lk, Fiebig criticized the author for focusing too much on expressions and vocabulary to the neglect of the historical problem of forms[23]. Indeed there were a whole series of historical questions Schlatter did not address, which Bultmann, Dibelius and Klostermann maintained were important for the then contemporary Church[24].

In reviewing the book, L. Vaganay commented on the "forme originale" of the commentary stating that it attracted "beaucoup de sympathie"[25]. Identifying the three principle parts of the Gospel which corresponded "aux trois sources où a puisé l'évangéliste", he concluded: "En somme, les travaux du savant professeur

---

16. *Ibid.*, p. 436.
17. *Ibid.*, p. 436-437.
18. *Ibid.*, p. 438.
19. *Ibid.*, p. 439.
20. *Ibid.*, p. 439-440.
21. *Ibid.*, p. 441.
22. *TLZ* 57 (1932) 293-295, col. 293.
23. *Ibid.*, col. 294: "... aber Sch. stellt alles zu sehr auf Redewendungen und Vokabeln ab und lässt das Problem der Gattungen, des Lukas als eines antiken Historikers, der 'Formgeschichte', das historische Problem am Wege liegen".
24. *Ibid.*, col. 295.
25. *RevSR* 12 (1932) 605-607, p. 605.

de Tübingen méritent l'attention, ils seront consultés avec fruit, mais l'on devra toujours tenir compte du point de vue particulariste de l'auteur"[26].

In *An Introduction to the New Testament* (1900)[27], Benjamin Wisner BACON declared: "We should expect Luke to be able to draw, as he does, with special copiousness from his unique source in the story of the Passion and Resurrection"[28]. He further delineated an Urevangelium, which "only Luke has utilized in its most fully developed form"[29] serving as Luke's "main stock"[30]. A later reference (1909) was made to the special source of Luke which was both independent of Mk and provided a useful comparision with it[31]. According to Bacon, Luke would have regarded the matter of order as a "perplexity"[32].

A brief survey of synoptic studies at the turn of the twentieth century was found in his article *A Turning Point in Synoptic Criticism* (1917)[33]. The turning point occurred in 1899 with the publication of the works by Wernle and Hawkins[34]. Holtzmann's *Die synoptischen Evangelien* was recognized as having established the basis for the "now-accepted two-document theory"[35]. The

26. *Ibid.*, p. 607.

27. B.W. BACON, *An Introduction to the New Testament*, New York - London, 1900 (p. 211-229: *Luke - Acts*).

28. *Ibid.*, p. 220. He interpreted Herod's mockery (23,7-12) as a "contrast between the high and the lowly", the latter being understood as the penitent thief (23,39-43). Later 23,11 was defined as a substitution for Mk 15,16-20a (p. 224, n. 1). In his discussion of Acts he referred to Feine (1891) but mentioned his work only in passing (p. 226, n. 2). For characteristics of literary style, vocabulary and themes which Bacon attributed to the special source, see p. 213(-214), n. 1.

29. *Ibid.*, p. 223. Even Luke was "more faithful than Mark to the proto-gospel" (p. 224).

30. *Ibid.*, p. 224.

31. *The Beginnings of the Gospel Story. A Historico-Critical Inquiry into the Sources and Structure of the Gospel According to Mark, with Expository Notes Upon the Text, for English Readers*, New Haven, CT - London, 1909, p. xxxiv. See also p. xxi, xxxviii.

32. *The Making of the New Testament*, London - New York - Toronto, n.d., p. 27. He added: "The *order* of even such events as secured perpetuation was already hopelessly lost at a time more remote than the writing of our earliest Gospel. This is true not only for Mark, as 'the Elder' frankly confesses, but for Matthew, Luke and everyone else" (p. 139). And still later: "On the other hand Luke, while expressly undertaking to improve in this special respect upon his predecessors, almost never ventures to depart from the order of Mark, and when he does has never the support of Matthew, and usually not that of real probability. In short, incorrect as they knew the order of Mark to be, it was the best that could be had in the days when the evangelists began to go beyond the mere *syntagmas*, and to write 'gospels' as we understand them" (p. 140). On order see further, *Is Mark a Roman Gospel* (HTS, 7), Cambridge, MA, 1919, p. 2, 35. The term καθεξῆς was taken to mean "better chronological order" (*An Introduction*, p. 217).

33. *A Turning Point in Synoptic Criticism*, in *HTR* 1 (1917) 48-69.

34. *Ibid.*, p. 49. He evaluated their contributions in the following way: "We owe much to Wernle and Hawkins for their strict application of scientific method to the identification of the synoptic *Grundschrift*" (p. 53).

35. *Ibid.*, p. 50. On the relation of Mt and Lk, Bacon added: "Holtzmann himself, in earlier

contributions of B. Weiss and J. Weiss did not fare so well[36]. Lk, together with Acts, once again came under scrutiny with the appearance of Harnack's *Luke the Physician* and Hobart's *Medical Language of St. Luke*[37].

Bacon (1918) offered high praise for Torrey's "cogent proof" that Acts 1,2-15,35 constituted a translation from the Aramaic[38]. Carefully avoiding the name Luke, referring instead to "Autor ad Theophilum", Bacon maintained that the author added a Greek version of the Acts of Paul to a larger Aramaic document, which the author valued more highly[39]. Identifying, however, with Bousset, Bacon acknowledged that Luke so reworked his written sources, that it was almost impossible to distinguish them[40].

Bacon also attacked the view that simply because a document was written in one of the Semitic languages implied that it was, de facto, earlier than the Greek. Indeed, quite the opposite was the case[41]. The Gospels were Greek compositions which contained materials translated from Aramaic. On another point, Bacon showed that while Luke made Mk the foundation of his own, he occasionally omitted Markan material from the Gospel only to insert it in Acts[42].

days, was not unwilling to concede to E. Simons reminiscences of Matthew, to account for minor elements of the coincident non-Marcan material. But the great reciprocal omissions and unreconciled contradictions, which must be admitted to exist on any theory of real literary dependence, compelled its limitation to the vague form of a mental echo; the third Evangelist might have heard the reading of Matthew at the Lord's day service and carried away impressions which unconsciously reproduced themselves in his own composition" (p. 53).

36. *Ibid.*, p. 57: "The contention of the elder and younger Weiss for a larger narrative content of Q, and a dependence of all three Evangelists on it, is not so easily met, when this weak point of method and the unsolved problem of the coincident variations of Matthew and Luke are fairly considered". Cf. B. WEISS, *Das Marcusevangelium*, 1872; *Lukas*, ⁹1901; *Die Geschichtlichkeit des Markusevangeliums*, 1905, and J. WEISS, *Das älteste Evangelium*, 1903; *Die Schriften des Neuen Testament*, Vol. 1, ²1907.

37. BACON, *Turning Point*, p. 57. Cf. A. HARNACK, *Lukas der Arzt*, 1906 = *Luke the Physician*, London, 1907 (cf. below), and W.K. HOBART, *The Medical Language of St. Luke: A Proof from Internal Evidence that "The Gospel according to St. Luke" and "The Acts of the Apostles" Were Written by the Same Person, and that Writer was a Medical Man*, Dublin, 1882; Grand Rapids, MI, ᴿ1954.

38. *More Philological Criticism of Acts*, in *AJT* 22 (1918) 4. Cf. C.C. TORREY, *Composition* (1916).

39. BACON, *More Philological Criticism*, p. 12.

40. *Ibid.*, p. 18. Cf. W. BOUSSET, *Der Gebrauch des Kyriostitels als Kriterium für die Quellenscheidung in der ersten Hälfte der Apostelgeschichte*, in *ZNW* 15 (1914) 141-162, p. 142-143.

41. BACON, *More Philological Criticism*, p. 6: "There is a kind of mental inertia which inclines us to take for granted the priority of documents in Semitic languages over those written in Greek ... As a matter of fact, the earliest known Gospels are all Greek (probably because the Palestinian Christians relied longer on oral tradition), where as *all* the Aramaic Gospels of which we have actual record are more or less elaborated translations from Greek originals". Bacon cited the testimony of Epiphanius to substantiate his point (p. 6-7).

42. *Ibid.*, p. 11, n. 1 The charge made against Jesus (Mk 14,58) was not repeated in the

Mk was thought by Bacon (1928) to have basically provided a "true historical outline" of the ministry of Jesus[43]. Fittingly, Matthew and Luke adopted it as the basis of their own works and appropriately they made changes in the Markan account[44]. However, in the passion narrative, Bacon believed Luke presented "an account which is not wholly nor even mainly derived from Mk, and is closely related to the Second Source"[45]. The denial of Peter, unflattering as it was, must have stemmed from Peter himself. Bacon rejected the account of the nocturnal Sanhedrin trial as unhistorical, unlikely as it would be that the religious leaders would gather at an illegal time only to leave and regroup in the early morning. Instead, he contended that the Lukan account mirrored "the later trials of Christians for blasphemy because they declare Jesus to be the Son of God, and await his coming on the clouds"[46].

Bacon offered only general, but nonetheless interesting, comments on Luke's adherence to Markan order, stating that Mk's order was not improved upon significantly by either Matthew or Luke[47]. Other than substituting the theoretical journey to Jerusalem for the theoretical journey in the Gentile areas, Mk's order was relatively unaffected[48].

In an article also published in 1928, Bacon made several references to L[49]. Commenting on Mk 12,28-34 / Lk 10,25-37 he wrote criticizing Streeter: "Luke has made two changes in this Markan anecdote. He has (a) revised the form in a way to express his own neo-legalism, (b) he has added a supplement from L of opposite bearing, that is, one which displays the anti-legalism of the older sources, among which we include Mk., as well as S and L. The inconsistency between L

parallel in Lk, but was inserted in Acts 6,13-14.

43. *The Story of Jesus and the Beginnings of the Church*, London, 1928, p. 127. He continued: "The Evangelists Matthew and Luke were justified in making it fundamental to their own compositions. But the later Evangelists were also justified in their correction of Mark's outline". Having said this, Bacon later stated: "... we cannot accept as historical Mark's depiction of a public gathering of the Sanhedrin at the illegal hour of midnight only to disperse and reassemble at dawn" (p. 246).

44. *Ibid.*, p. 127. See also *La date et l'origine de l'évangile selon Marc*, in *RHPR* 3 (1923) 268-285, p. 268: "'Marc' est universellement reconnu comme la principale source synoptique, et que l'on s'accorde unanimement à admettre qu'il a été utilisé par 'Luc'".

45. *Story*, p. 225. Bacon expressed this regret: "It is a pity that Matthew's close adherence to the Passion story of Mark makes it for the most part impossible to say whence Luke derives the widely divergent material by which he supersedes Mark almost throughout this section. If Luke and Matthew had coincided in their divergences, we should have been able to identify the source with other sections of similar character" (p. 260).

46. *Ibid.*, p. 246.

47. *Ibid.*, p. 173.

48. *Ibid.*

49. *Jesus and the Law*, in *JBL* 47 (1928) 203-231, p. 213: "[Luke's] own independent source (L)"; 214: "Its testimony is all the more important in support of Mark because it comes from L rather than from the third evangelist"; 219: "For the remainder of the Markan section Luke is satisfied to supply material from L".

revised and L unrevised constitutes one of the strongest objections to Streeter's view of the relation, viz., that Luke himself, our third evangelist, is the writer of both, the present Gospel being only an expansion of Luke's own earlier work prepared before he had become acquainted with the Gospel of Mark"[50].

In *Studies in Matthew* (1930) Bacon adopted the designation P^{lk} for material peculiar to Lk^{51}. He offered a brief survey of works on the special Lukan source in his discussion of Matthean omissions[52] during which he admitted that his investigation of Lukan "interpolations" led him to the conviction that Luke used another non-Markan source, generally termed L, in addition to S^{53}. Bartlet's approach did not fare so well[54], but the 1907 work of B. Weiss was praised for

---

50. *Ibid.*, p. 221. Cf. B.H. STREETER, *The Four Gospels* (1924). Cf. below.

51. *Studies in Matthew*, London, 1930, p. viii.

52. *Ibid.*, p. 105-106: "In particular the question of Lk's order in the Q passages has been discussed by the present writer also in a series of articles in the *JBL* (XXXIV-XXXVII, 1915-1917) under the title 'The 'Order' of the Lukan 'Interpolations'." This study led to the conviction that Lk employs in the make-up of these 'interpolations' another non-Markan source besides S, for which the designation L has been commonly employed since the publication in 1891 of P. Feine's *Vorkanonische Ueberlieferung des Lukas in Evangelium und Apostelgeschichte*. Streeter's restatement of the theory of L has brought it recently into new prominence. Now if in addition to S Luke has mingled L factors in his blocks of non-Markan material, whether L was already combined with S or conflated with it by Lk himself, a new factor of great importance will be added to the problem. This will be still further complicated by the question what relation L will have borne, if any, to Mk. No wonder critics find it hard to reach a unanimous verdict if this be so, and Lk's reference to 'many' predecessors in his work of drawing up a narrative (διήγησις) of the things concerning Jesus suggests at least one 'narrative' in addition to Mk and S. Under these circumstances our Studies in Mt must leave discussion of Lk's sources and editorial methods to others. The theory of L is discussed in recent commentaries such as Preuschen's (1912), Loisy's (1920), and B.S. Easton's (1926). It comes more into the foreground in such critical studies as Wellhausen's *Evangelium Lucae* (1904), B. Weiss' *Quellen des Lk-evangeliums* (1908) [sic], and Vincent Taylor's *Behind the Third Gospel, a Study of the Proto-Lk Hypothesis* (1926), not to mention the four [*Beiträge*] of Harnack. Cf. HARNACK, *Lukas der Arzt* (1906), *Sprüche* (1907), *Neue Untersuchungen* (1911). Cf. below.

The series of articles to which he referred, *The 'Order' of the Lukan 'Interpolations'*, was published *JBL* 34 (1915) 166-179: *General Survey*; *II*: 36 (1917) 112-139: *The Smaller Interpolation, Lk. 6:20-8:3*; *III*: 37 (1918) 20-53: *The Longer Interpolation, Lk. 9:51-18:14*). In the first installment he asserted: "We may lay it down with great confidence as a first and important principle that Mark's order is for Luke of great authority" (*JBL* 34, 1915, 167; so also p. 169). Further, p. 175: "The fact remains that Luke ... is clearly attempting like any other historian to put his material in chronological order". Consider *JBL* 36 (1917) 115: "Alterations of Markan order are very rare in Lk., and always have cogent occasion".

53. Cf. BACON, *Studies*, p. viii: "This 'double-tradition' material, as it is still often called, has come to be known as Q (from the German *Quelle* = Source), although it is not itself the source, but only the most easily traceable factor of a lost work which we shall designate S".

54. *Studies*, p. 106. Bartlet was also cited as a supporter of a Proto-Lk theory and Bacon was well aware of the possible confusion arising from the use of the designation S by both scholars, for different elements (p. 106, n. 2; so also p. 505, n. 1). He critiqued Bartlet's conception on the grounds that "the characteristics of this L document are too intensely Jewish to permit it being

a systematic working out of the theory[55]. Bacon opted for an expanded form of
L drawing on S[56]. He remarked that he was a long time supporter of "the theory
of L": "accepted since 1900 by the present writer"; cf. *INT*, p. 214ff.[57].
Streeter's support of the Proto-Lk theory provided it with "great impetus"[58].

Roy A. Harrisville, the author of a Bacon biography, delineated several
sources used by Luke as proposed by Bacon[59]. In addition to Mk, S (the Second
source, based on Q), and Q, Luke also employed L. Bacon differentiated between
two forms of the special source[60]. Luke also incorporated Jewish oral material in
the genealogy and infancy narrative, and oral tradition or redaction in other parts
of the Gospel. Harrisville evaluated Bacon's appreciation of Streeter's contribution
to the synoptic problem in the following way: "Bacon was loathe to credit Streeter
with originating the Proto-Luke hypothesis, since he believed Streeter's arguments
advanced but little the theories earlier developed by Paul Feine in his *Eine
vorkanonische Überlieferung des Lukas in Evangelium und Apostelgeschichte*. He
insisted that Streeter's chief contribution to the hypothesis lay in his identification
of the author of 'L' with Paul's travel-companion. In his *Studies in Matthew*,
Bacon wrote: 'In view of the success attending his advocacy of the Proto-Lk theory
it was natural that Canon Streeter should seek to merit more fully the title of
originator by extending the same hypothesis to Mt'"[61].

ascribed to the Gentile Lk. Hence the dubious expedient of supposing it to have been a 'private'
compilation made for Lk's benefit at Casearea perhaps by 'Philip the evangelist,' which Lk took
over without change of its Semitic style".

55. *Studies*, p. 107: "In B. Weiss' *QL* [*Quellen des Lucas*] will be found the most systematic
argument for S[p] and S[mk], that is, such narrative material in S as has filtered down through Mk and
L and thus escapes recognition by the school of critics who are guided in their view of S by the
method favored by Mt rather than the Lukan".

56. *Ibid.*, p. 108: "Lk has more sense of the value of history. His predecessor L (if we may
forestall demonstration) had already shown similar appreciation by copious expansion of the
biographic content of S, whether with or without influence from Mk. Lk's term for a gospel
writing of this kind, including his own work, is a 'narrative' (διήγησις). Obviously its tendency
will be the opposite from Mt's in the use of S. We may expect in Lk (and even more in L)
expansion on the side of narrative and 'story' parable. Every element S could furnish of the
'doings' will be exploited in this interest, reversing completely the tendency of Mt toward the
gnomic method and ideal, of the rabbis".

57. *Ibid.*, p. 505. See further p. 359. The abbreviation "INT" would appear to refer to
Bacon's *An Introduction*, 1900.

58. *Studies*, p. 505.

59. R.A. HARRISVILLE, *Benjamin Wisner Bacon. Pioneer in American Biblical Criticism*
(BSNA, 2), Missoula, MT, 1976, p. 36-37. See NEIRYNCK, *ETL* 59 (1983) 149.

60. HARRISVILLE, p. 37: "To this source, revised or unrevised, Bacon on occasion credited
the use of 'S', but not in a form identical with that known to Matthew".

61. *Ibid.*, p. 52(-53), n. 65. See the discussion of Bacon's source theory, ch. 4, p. 32-48: *The
Gospel of Jesus*. Cf. BACON, *Studies*, p. 506. One wonders whether Harrisville was too harsh in
his assessment. Consider, for instance, Bacon's reference to "Canon Streeter's able volume *FG*"
(*Studies*, p. 505). As regards "Streeter's chief contribution", Bacon termed it, "the dubious
identification of the author of L with Luke the companion of Paul".

Without making any direct reference to J. Weiss, Francis Crawford BURKITT (1906) in similar fashion accepted an early, independent source which contained the logia combined with an account of the passion, thus making Q a 'Gospel' "like one of our Gospels"[62]. Admitting on the one hand his reluctance to offer a literary reconstruction of lost documents, given their unreliability, Burkitt nonetheless believed "there is ... a considerable element of valuable history in S. Luke's account of our Lord's Passion, wherever he drew his information from"[63]. The final form of Lk "reflects the style and personality of the Evangelist"[64]. Noting the disagreement existing between Mk and Lk concerning the time and order of the events of Peter's denial, the Sanhedrin trial, the beating of Jesus and the mockery, Burkitt confessed he was impressed by the Lukan account. But he was of the opinion that the principal events reflected the "point of view of the chief priests"[65]. The criterion to show that a text was derived from Q was that it was contained in both Lk and Mt. However, since Burkitt already stated his belief that Mt simply reproduced Mk in the passion narrative, he concluded that Luke must have derived his account of the passion from Q[66].

Burkitt offered some remarks concerning Luke's redactional technique. Luke would have treated Q as he had Mk. Finally, the transmission of the Gospel history contrasted material that was remembered and recorded rather than invented by an early Christian[67]. Not only that, "the Evangelists and the sources from which they drew sometimes remembered better than they understood"[68].

A rather significant indication for Burkitt that Luke was not employing Mk in the passion narrative was the change in arrangement found in the sources, given Luke's penchant for not disturbing the order of his sources[69]. The difference in

---

62. F.C. BURKITT, *The Gospel History and Its Transmission*, Edinburgh, 1906, [2]1907 (Preface: "an almost unchanged reprint of the former Edition"), esp. p. 133-142; [3]1911 (Preface: "After consideration it seems to me better not to make any great changes in the text as originally written."). Burkitt was listed by J. FITZMYER, *Luke*, p. 1365, among those who support the view that Luke "used another, independent connected account of the passion in addition to 'Mk'". See M.E. GLASSWELL, *Francis Crawford Burkitt*, in *TRE* 7 (1981) 424-428, esp. p. 426.

63. *The Gospel History*, p. 135-136; cf. [3]1911: "from whatever sources he may have drawn his information".

64. *Ibid.*, [2]1907, p. 136.

65. *Ibid.*, p. 136-137. Luke's account was impressive, in Burkitt's view, when "regarded as a narrative of events".

66. *Ibid.*, p. 134-135. Mark supplied only an occasional detail such as the mention of Simon of Cyrene (Lk 23,26) (p. 134). Burkitt also stated his impression of Matthew's redaction of Mk. "Even in the account of the Last Supper and the Words from the Cross Matthew has nothing to add to what Mark tells us" (p. 133). Cf. also p. 137, 138 (Mk 15,16-20 / Mt 27,27).

67. *Ibid.*, p. 141.

68. *Ibid.*, p. 142.

69. *Ibid.*, p. 134. The argument from order was thus used once more to suggest a source other than Mk. "We have seen that Luke does not, as a rule, disturb the relative order of the sources which he employs, and so the question arises whether this narrative of the Passion may not have been derived from the same source as most of Luke's non-Marcan material, i.e. from

timing can be explained by Jesus' arrest in the middle of the night and so the trial
had to wait until the following morning when the Jewish leaders could be
assembled. Burkitt concluded, in contrast to Mk and even Mt, that Luke's account
was "the more probable"[70].

While acknowledging that many consider Herod's trial to be unhistorical,
Burkitt (1907) argued that it could have happened and would not have taken much
time in the course of the morning. Furthermore, the term χριστὸν βασιλέα Burkitt
judged to be "genuinely Jewish". This led him to conclude that "Luke is using a
valuable source"[71].

W. Sanday praised Burkitt for bringing "a surprising amount of freshness to
old themes"[72]. Sanday affirmed his own belief in a single source for Luke, to
which Luke gave preference over others, and criticized Burkitt for overloading Q
with too much material[73]. Sanday confronted Burkitt for arguing that the MAs
were the result of "accidental coincidence", which was the case only in a small
number of instances. Sanday put stock in the idea that the Markan text used by the
two later Synoptics was different from that from which later copies were made[74].

Q itself".

70. *Ibid.*, p. 138. Is it not possible that Luke also saw the improbability of timing in the
Markan account and sought to rectify it? "We can hardly suppose that the Jewish grandees kept
vigil all night on account of the Galilean Agitator; according to S. Luke they did not do so" (p.
137). In his discussion Burkitt relied on what would seem reasonable or logical in the course of
events, as for example when he explained that once Jesus had been arrested and deserted by his
followers, he would fall victim to the abuse of the Temple police.

71. *Ibid.*, p. 139. There seems to be a real paucity, that for all of the passion narrative,
Burkitt listed only one reference to some "genuinely Jewish" phrase which would support his
claim of an independent source. He also referred to a mention of Herod's trial in GP, suggesting
first that it does not appear to have been derived from the canonical Gospel of Luke, and second,
that it may have been omitted by Mk as inconclusive (p. 138). See [3]1911, p. xi-xv, p. xi-xii: "I
have altered a phrase here and there, and rewritten a paragraph in order to bring Chapter IV.
more definitely into line with the conclusions so eloquently set forth by Dr. Verrall in his *Christ
before Herod*. [...] And while Dr. Schweitzer seems to exclude Herod from one point of view,
Dr. Verrall from another reminds us that 'the 'hostility of Antipas,' 'the designs of Antipas,' 'the
danger from Antipas,' are phrases easily found, as one may say, anywhere except in the
Evangelists.' Perhaps this is a little over-stated, unless we are careful to understand it exclusively
of the personal attitude of the Tetrarch; but it may serve to warn a reconstructor of the Gospel
history against unduly magnifying the political prominence of our Lord and His disciples, or of
the danger in which they stood from the government of Galilee."; 138; Cf. VERRALL, 1909 (=
ID., *Bacchants*, 1910). Cf. below. Burkitt was referring to A. SCHWEITZER, *The Quest for the
Historical Jesus. A Critical Study of Its Progress from Reimarus to Wrede* (tr. W. MONTGOMERY)
London, 1910, p. 362 (= *Von Reimarus zu Wrede. Eine Geschichte der Leben-Jesu-Forschung*,
Tübingen, 1906, p. 361).

72. W. SANDAY, *Professor Burkitt on the Gospel History*, in *ExpT* 18 (1906-07) 249-255, p.
249.

73. *Ibid.*, p. 251.

74. *Ibid.*, p. 250. W. Horbury suggested "subsequent criticism has not lessened the force of
the contention, which Burkitt himself had sponsored for St Luke, that the Passion Narratives
preserve some information not dependent upon St Mark. Yet, with exceptions such as we have

In *The Earliest Sources for the Life of Jesus* (1910, ²1922) Burkitt acknowledged the priority of Mk as the result of the previous century's investigation of the synoptic problem, that Mk served as the basis for Mt and Lk, very nearly in the form which we now possess[75]. While both Luke and Matthew treated Mk with a great deal of literary freedom, their redactional styles differed[76]. Burkitt continued to defend his position that the other source which Luke used throughout his Gospel was Q, though he admitted it was impossible to reconstruct the sources of Lk from the narrative. He described as "especially insecure" theories then popular that Q contained no account of the passion, a view supported by Harnack. Burkitt's conception of Q was not simply of a collection of sayings of Jesus, but of a document which also included stories about Jesus stressing eschatological hope[77]. Burkitt dismissed the argument that Q, like the *Didache*, would not have contained the passion, since the purpose of the Didache was not to recount the Gospel story.

In yet another work, *The Use of Mark in the Gospel According to Luke* (1922), Burkitt investigated how Luke used Mk in an attempt to understand the purpose and compositional technique of Acts, asserting that Acts 1–12 "corresponds to the lost part of Mark that followed Mark xvi.8"[78]. He considered Acts to be the second volume to Lk based upon written or oral sources[79]. What distinguished the two was that in the Gospel comparisons may be made with Mk. For Acts, on the other hand, we can rely only upon the information Luke provided[80]. Although Burkitt maintained that Luke used Mk much in the form we now have it, and that differences between the two Gospels in parallel segments were due, not to new information, but to Luke's literary method, he nonetheless held that the special source possibly provided "a detailed itinerary" or "connected story" about the public ministry of Jesus[81]. Burkitt placed the historical credibility of Luke's

---

noted, proportionate attention seems not to have been given to these sources of information" (*The Passion Narratives and Historical Criticism*, in *TLond* 75 [1972] 58-71, p. 62).

75. *The Earliest Sources for the Life of Jesus*, London, 1910, ²1922, p. 35. Cf. p. 36-37, 40.

76. *Ibid.*, p. 96.

77. *Ibid.*, p. 103-104. The Q version containing the passion would have contributed special material to Lk, particularly Lk 22,15f.,24-32,35-38 (p. 106, n. 1). Their absence from Mt was not a formidable obstacle "because Matthew is not combining Q with Mark, but enriching and illustrating Mark from Q and other sources". Cf. Harnack, *Sprüche* (1907); cf. below n. 110.

78. *The Use of Mark in the Gospel According to Luke*, in F.J. FOAKES JACKSON and K. LAKE (eds.), *The Beginnings of Christianity*, Pt. 1, *The Acts of the Apostles*, Vol. 2, London, 1922, p. 106-120, p. 118. An analysis of Acts would not enable one to "reconstruct the lost narrative of Mark", any more than a study of Lk 19–23 will yield the chronology of Luke's source for the events of Holy Week (p. 118-119).

79. *Ibid.*, p. 106.

80. *Ibid.*, p. 120.

81. *Ibid.*, p. 107: "And I assume that for all the public life of Jesus, with the possible exception of the actual Passion, Luke's other sources gave him nothing like a detailed itinerary or connected story of our Lord's public career".

account of Jesus' visit to Jerusalem on a par with Markan information[82]. However, earlier Burkitt stated that Mk was "the best source we have"[83]. Luke's redaction included referring to Mk for large amounts of material, which he freely reorganized into what he might consider "to be a form essentially more true to the underlying reality"[84]. And while Burkitt confined his comments generally to the material concerning the final visit of Jesus to Jerusalem, it was argued that what may be said of the latter section of the Gospel pertained equally to other portions of the Gospel as well[85].

Luke inserted such material by changing some and omitting others which radically altered the manner in which they originally appeared in Mk. Burkitt noted that in focusing on Jesus' final visit to Jerusalem, despite the fact that Luke added new material, the resulting Lukan text was still shorter than the Markan. Thus, Burkitt concluded Luke abbreviated the source. Such revision occurred because Luke desired to "give a clear and readable account" of the beginnings of Christianity, and of what transpired, "but it did not necessarily include meticulous accuracy of detail"[86]. Burkitt rejected the view that a travel diary was revealed in the material. Further, Luke's method included a great deal of revision, but very little creation of material, because Luke's tendency was to employ his sources completely[87].

Luke, in Burkitt's view, followed the Markan order closely[88]. Where Luke departed from such arrangement, it served the "literary effect"[89]. However, Luke was not transposing Markan material. Rather he opted to employ other sources. Burkitt observed that Luke generally followed the order of his source, whether that was Mk or the sources of his non-Markan material[90]. He noted that at least in one case, Luke certainly made a transposition[91]. In two other articles, Burkitt addressed related issues[92].

82. *Ibid.*, p. 119.
83. *Ibid.*, p. 106-107.
84. *Ibid.*, p. 107.
85. *Ibid.*, p. 116.
86. *Ibid.*, p. 111.
87. *Ibid.*, p. 115; cf. p. 118.
88. *Ibid.*, p. 118.
89. *Ibid.*
90. *The Earliest Sources*, p. 97-98; cf. p. 112.
91. *Ibid.*, p. 100, n. 1: "The only serious transposition of the Marcan matter in these sections is that Mark iii.31-35 ('Who is my Mother or my Brethren?') is placed after the Parables instead of before them".
92. *Vestigia Christi according to Luke*, Appendix B, p. 485-487. Because Luke so thoroughly revised his source materials, they cannot be separated (p. 485). Furthermore, the sources cannot be reconstructed based on Luke's text alone. The other article was *Commentary on the Preface of Luke*, Appendix C, p. 489-510. By means of an analysis of the Prologue to Lk, Burkitt reacted to an interpretation of the term παρέδοσαν, "whereby written sources are excluded. ... The word, therefore, provides no objection to attributing an important written source of the first volume to John Mark (called in Acts xiii.5 ὑπηρέτην) and an important written source of the second volume

Ernest De Witt BURTON (1904) was of the conviction that Lk and Mt were based upon "our Mark, or a document in large part identical with it"[93]. Generally dissimilar minor sources for Luke and Matthew, however, provided "the almost wholly independent additions to Mark's account in the passion and resurrection history"[94]. Although he initially claimed that 23,4-16 was the only peculiar Lukan material in 22,54-23,25, he augmented his view to include 22,66.67 and 23,2[95]. With respect to the phenomenon of order, Burton did not include the differences in 22,54-71 in his section on the Mt/Mk agreements against Lk[96].

On the MAs he wrote: "The agreements of Matt. and Luke against Mark in triple narrative which are scattered through the gospels are an unexplained remainder. ... This unexplained remainder probably owes its origin to causes that belong to the border line between editorial revision and scribal corruption, or else to some slight influence of one of these gospels in its final form on the mind of the writer of the other"[97].

In his 1911 presidential address to the Society of Biblical Literature, Burton announced his endorsement of and identification with the majority view that Luke was dependent upon Mk[98]. Such a view notwithstanding, Burton advocated a multiple-document hypothesis as he considered the two-document hypothesis inadequate[99]. He proposed that there was at least one other source, on a par with Q, in terms of age and historical value. Lk and Mt were regarded as representing at least the third generation of Gospel writings. Concerning Luke's probable literary method, Burton stipulated that Luke generally followed the order of his sources, refrained from offering duplicate material, and unhesitatingly modified the language of his sources with a view either to improving the literary quality or portraying Jesus "more in accordance with the evangelist's ideal of his character

to an αὐτόπτης" (p. 497).

93. *Some Principles of Literary Criticism and their Application to the Synoptic Problem* (The Decennial Publications printed from Vol. V), Chicago, IL, 1904, p. 52 (= 244). See p. 49 (= 241): "The gospel of Mark, substantially as we now possess it".

94. *Ibid.*, p. 53 (= 245). "Each of the two later evangelists pursued a consistent and easily intelligible method in the use of the sources, but each his own method". Luke's minor source was composed of narratives not found in other sources, and additional material for the passion and resurrection accounts. Designated #8, p. 49 (= 241). He suggested that this material "may perhaps not have been reduced to writing" before it was included in Lk.

95. *Ibid.*, p. 16 (= 208) then 48 (= 240). He added a further explanation: "It is a very notable fact that, while Matt. and Luke each have in their Jerusalem period considerable material not found in Mark, they have no such material in common. This fact clearly indicates that the sources additional to Mark from which Matt. and Luke drew were not, as in the John the Baptist period and the Galilean ministry, the same, but quite distinct" (p. 48 = 240).

96. *Ibid.*, p. 18 (= p. 210).

97. *Ibid.*

98. *Some Phases of the Synoptic Problem*, in *JBL* 31 (1912) 95-113. One of Burton's working assumptions was that the form of Mk used by Luke was as we presently have it or nearly so (p. 97). This study did not extend beyond 19,28.

99. *Ibid.*, p. 112.

and teaching"[100].

In an attempt to recover the Lukan Gospel's earlier reputation as an historical authority, Adolf VON HARNACK (1906) maintained that in addition to his certain principal authority, Mk, and Q[101], Luke probably made use of special traditions originating in Jerusalem or Judea from the evangelist Philip and his daughters who were prophetesses, around 55-60 AD (Acts 8; 9,30; 21,9)[102]. Harnack argued that Acts confirmed his conclusion about the sources[103].

As with many of his predecessors, Harnack highlighted the numerous omissions of Markan material. "Had not history itself in its inexorable yet providential progress made evident what a writer about the year 80 AD must relate and what he had to pass over?"[104]. Although Luke adopted three-fourths of the Markan material, his revision of Mk's wording was striking. Conspicuous by its absence was the mention of Mark's name in the Prologue as one of his predecessors. "... Apart from numerous corrections in style and other small points, on the ground of what he considered better information [Luke] has in important details condemned [Mk] as wrong in its order of events, too unspiritual, and imperfect and incorrect"[105]. He added that this can be seen most clearly in the

100. *Ibid.*, p. 98.

101. Adolf von Harnack (1851-1930), Privatdozent (1874), assoc. prof. in Church History at Leipzig (1876), prof. Giessen (1879), in Marburg (1886), in Berlin (1888). *Lukas der Arzt. Der Verfasser des dritten Evangeliums und der Apostelgeschichte*, Leipzig, 1906 (= *Luke the Physician*, Crown Theological Library, NT Studies, 1, tr. J.R. WILKINSON, London, 1907, p. 152). Cf. *Sprüche und Reden Jesu*, Leipzig, 1907 (= *The Sayings of Jesus*, Crown Theological Library, NT Studies, 2, tr. J.R. WILKINSON, London, 1908, p. 181, 223), where he made it very clear, in opposition to Burkitt, that Q contained neither mention nor discourses of the passion. Burkitt remained intransigent after considering Harnack's position: "I have convinced myself that Q is a real 'Gospel' and that it contained a story of the Passion, and I still cling to my prejudices even after reading Dr. Harnack's arguments on the other side" (*The Lost Source of Our Savior's Sayings* [review of Sprüche und Reden Jesu], in *JTS* 8 [1907] 457).

102. *Lukas der Arzt* (= *Luke the Physician*, p. 124-125). Harnack explained these special traditions as those "whose authenticity is almost entirely dubious, and which must, indeed, be described as for the most part legendary" (p. 152). This special source highlighted prophecy and the feminine element of Lk, this last detail having also been observed by Plummer (p. 153-154; cf. *Commentary on St. Luke*, p. xlii). It was probable that this information came to Lk in oral form from Christians who emigrated from Palestine or Judea during or subsequent to the Great War. Harnack suggested that if the material did reach Lk and Jn in written form, then it must have been in Aramaic (*Luke the Physician*, p. 152, n. 4). Inasmuch as Harnack maintained that the special traditions were oral and that it was Luke who committed them to writing, his position corresponded, in this detail at least, more closely to that of B. Weiss. On the question of the dating of these materials unique to Lk, see p. 157-158.

103. *Ibid.*, p. 156-157. Lk used at least three sources. Harnack conceded there may have been more (p. 164-165).

104. *Ibid.*, p. 152. Harnack proposed Ephesus or another location in Asia or Achaia as the place of composition at about 80 AD.

105. *Ibid.*, p. 158. In n. 1 Harnack wrote: "Numerous examples may be adduced from the

accounts of the Passion and the Resurrection: "With regard to the latter, St. Lk, following his special source, has replaced St. Mk's account by later legends which had arisen in Jerusalem, and, in direct opposition to St. Mk, has ascribed the first announcement of the Resurrection to women"[106]. Harnack considered the changes in order of Lk over against Mk to have been a corrective of the earlier Gospel which had been recorded in erroneous order[107]. He was struck by how Luke portrayed the Roman authorities in a much more favorable light, in contrast to the Jews, and while this revealed Luke's bias, it was a bias that corresponded with historical fact[108]. Harnack judged Lk to be an historical rather than theological work[109]. In his analysis of the sayings material (1907) Harnack stated that Q contained no account of the passion[110].

The attempt to date the Synoptic Gospels and Acts prompted Harnack (1911) to speculate that Luke had definitely known an almost identical version of Mk, albeit an earlier one[111]. Luke possessed a source or sources (oral or written) for the first half of Acts[112]. Identifying the new material as coming from second or third hand tradition, Harnack rejected the idea that they were not composed until after the destruction of Jerusalem (or even after 60 AD) and that they were anything but Palestinian in origin. Harnack tentatively expressed the view that the account of Jesus and Herod may be historical, given the evidence that Luke possessed special sources concerning Herod[113]. Luke's redaction was, in the main, a

---

comparison of the two gospels to show that St. Lk criticised the gospel of St. Mk from these points of view. Some of them agree remarkably with those from which the presbyter Jn, as recorded by Papias, has criticised the book. The presbyter admits (1) the incompleteness of St. Mk, and, moreover, (2) its faulty order; but he maintains its exactness, its veracity, and the conscientious effort of the evangelist to give a full reproduction of the information which he had received" (p. 158-159).

106. *Ibid.*, p. 158-159.

107. *Lukas der Arzt* (= 158).

108. *Ibid.*, p. 135.

109. *Ibid.*, p. 165-166.

110. *Sprüche und Reden Jesu. Die Zweite Quelle des Matthäus und Lukas* (Beiträge zur Einleitung in das Neue Testament, 2), Leipzig, 1907, p. 120 (= *The Sayings of Jesus. The Second Source of St. Matthew and St. Luke* [Crown Theological Library, NT Studies, 2], tr. J.R. WILKINSON, London - New York, 1908, p. 170). See also p. 162, n. 1 (= 233[-234], n. 1). However, consider p. 130 (= 185).

111. *Neue Untersuchungen zur Apostelgeschichte und zur Abfassungszeit der synoptischen Evangelien* (Beiträge zur Einleitung in das Neue Testament, 4) Leipzig, 1911, p. 93 (= *Date of the Acts and the Synoptic Gospels* [Crown Theological Library, NT Studies, 4], tr. J.R. WILKINSON, London, 1911, p. 133). Cf. *Lukas der Arzt*, 1906 (= *Luke the Physician*, p. 153), where he added that the Markan version with which Luke would have been familiar would not have been the final version.

112. *Neue Untersuchungen*, p. 18 (= 25). Certain discrepancies in Acts resulted from the use of oral and written information. In an accusation similar to Wernle, Harnack indicated that Luke "ein sorgloser und unachtsame Erzähler im einzelnen gewesen ist, der sich viele grössere und kleinere Unstimmigkeiten hat zuschulden kommen lassen" (p. 21-22 = 30-31).

113. *Ibid.*, p. 110, n. 2 (= 157, n. 2).

stylistic revision of Mk and Q.

Insisting that the special Lukan materials "gehören zu den kostbarsten Überlieferungen über Jesus, die wir besitzen", Franz DIBELIUS (1911) argued against certain aspects of the positions of Feine and B. Weiss[114]. While he concurred with Feine that the special stories of Lk circulated in the original Jewish community and that Luke reproduced them accurately, he disputed Feine's view that they all stemmed from the same source[115]. The grounds for his disagreement were that southern Palestinian Christianity was great at that time and, further, it would be difficult to prove that the material had already been compiled into a continuous source. In addition, he did not find Feine's argumentation convincing. In some cases Dibelius would choose to explain the origin of the special material as coming from oral tradition[116].

As regards the 1907 and 1908 investigations of B. Weiss, which he termed "scharfsinnig", Dibelius acknowledged that the results did not give rise to a certainty of judgment ("eine Sicherheit des Urteils")[117]. Conclusions such as those reached by Weiss concerning individual phrases and words would always be open to dispute. Neither was he entirely persuaded about B. Weiss's views explaining the relationship of various pieces[118]. He considered Weiss's assertion that the special Lukan material comprised a complete story of Jesus more abundant than Mk, to be only a possibility and did not constitute proof[119].

Dibelius was more receptive to the views of A. Harnack[120]. For stories dealing with the Samaritans, as well as possibly other special material in Lk, Philip and his daughters could have been the informants[121]. Still this would not explain the origin of the majority of the information unique to Lk. Luke himself experienced the beginning of the community in Antioch, which had been founded by exiles from Jerusalem[122]. From this Dibelius reasoned that the majority of special material stemmed from oral tradition, from those Christians who followed Stephen from Jerusalem to Antioch. Of his own speculation Dibelius wrote: "Das ist vorläufig blosse Vermutung. Noch fehlt der Beweis ...", though he was convinced he could provide the proof[123].

The common view among scholars at the time Dibelius was writing, he declared, was that Luke knew and used Mk and in particular followed Markan

---

114. *Die Herkunft der Sonderstücke des Lukasevangeliums*, in ZNW 12 (1911) 325-343.
115. *Ibid.*, p. 326. Cf. FEINE (1891).
116. F. DIBELIUS, *Die Herkunft*, p. 326, n. 2.
117. *Ibid.*, p. 326. Cf. B. WEISS (1907) and (1908). Cf. above.
118. DIBELIUS, *Die Herkunft*, p. 326-327.
119. *Ibid.*, p. 327.
120. Cf. A. HARNACK, *Lukas der Arzt*, 1906.
121. F. DIBELIUS, *Die Herkunft*, p. 329. See the comment that it was probable that Philip, a member of the original community, contributed to Lk (p. 329-330).
122. *Ibid.*, p. 337. See also p. 339-340.
123. *Ibid.*, p. 337.

order[124]. He nevertheless maintained that many of the Markan stories in Lk appeared "in einer selbstständigen und nicht schlechteren Form", and this was the case in regard to the passion narrative[125]. He considered contemporary scholarship as weighing the possibilities of either a written Lukan source, or going back to an Urmarkus or an apostolic "Grundschrift". Dibelius judged an error of Gospel criticism of his day as placing so little emphasis on oral tradition and the capacity of memories of people in unliterary times and cultures[126]. Agreements between Lk and Mk were "sehr wahrscheinlich" due to records of older disciples with whom Luke would have had contact in Antioch. What was more, Luke probably had heard Peter. Although Lk was the latest of the Synoptic Gospels, it depended upon the oldest traditions available[127]. Dibelius called attention to Luke's frequent references to Herod[128]. On the basis of the Herod pericope (23,7-12) he proposed that someone in the house of Herod had communicated the information, rather than those who brought charges against Jesus. The evidence, according to Dibelius, pointed to Manaen who belonged to the Christian community in Antioch[129].

Some similarity existed between Harnack's position and that of Johannes JEREMIAS (1930) on the influence of Philip the evangelist. Jeremias believed that oral tradition was responsible for the special material though Luke shaped it. Unfortunately, Jeremias did not give any specifics about what he included in the special material as it affected the passion narrative. He assumed two sources for the Synoptic Gospels, one for sayings and the other containing stories. Two additional sources for Lk, one consisting of the oral tradition and the second stemming from Philip the deacon, were broadly described[130]. Although Lk resembled Mk in the treatment of the narrative material and Mt in reproducing the speech material, Jeremias was not certain that either of the other Synoptics served

124. *Ibid.*, p. 342.

125. *Ibid.*: "vollends in der Leidensgeschichte geht Lukas auf eigenen Bahnen".

126. *Ibid.*, p. 342-343.

127. *Ibid.*, p. 343: "Soviel lässt sich jedenfalls behaupten, dass uns im Lukasevangeliums, dem am spätesten abgefassten unter den synoptischen Evangelien, im grossen und ganzen die älteste Überlieferungsschicht vorliegt – ein Ergebnis, das sich mit dem, was am Anfang über den Charakter der Sonderstücke gesagt wurde, gut zusammenfügt. Bei der Erforschung des Lebens Jesu ist nicht das Markusevangelium, sondern das Lukasevangelium in den Vordergrund zu stellen".

128. *Ibid.*, p. 340, including 3,19-20; 8,3; 9,9; 13,31-33; 23,7-12 Acts 13,1.

129. Although this contention did not constitute proof, it had already been entertained. "Der Schluss, dass [Manaen] dem Lukas die Geschichten von Herodes erzählte, die dieser teils in sein Evangelium aufnahm, teils nur andeutete (3,20), ist zwar nicht zu beweisen, liegt aber doch sehr nahe und ist bereits gezogen worden". Dibelius referred to ZAHN, *Einleitung*, Bd. 2, 1899, p. 405, in this regard.

130. Joh.J. JEREMIAS, *Das Evangelium nach Lukas. Eine urchristliche Erklärung für die Gegenwart*, Chemnitz-Leipzig, 1930 (esp. p. 10-18). Surprisingly, the works of Harnack were missing from Jeremias's bibliography and register of persons. Jeremias dated the composition of Lk at somewhere between 75 and 80 AD. (p. 8).

as sources for Lk[131]. In his earlier Markan commentary he also apparently treated the relation of Mk and Lk. In his Lukan commentary he indicated those Lukan verses which referred back to Mk proposing as parallels Mk 14,53.54.66-72 for the denials (22,54-62); Mk 14,65 for the mockery (22,63-65); Mk 14,55-61 for the Sanhedrin trial (22,66-71); and Mk 15,1-20 for Pilate's trial (23,1-25)[132].

Lk challenged the Two-Source theory, in Jeremias's opinion, because of the additional material. While Luke generally followed the Markan order there were also temporal and geographical indications where he was independent of Mk. Differences can be accounted for by oral traditions which Luke fashioned in his own manner[133]. These would have contained both the words and deeds of Jesus.

Regarding the discrepancy among the Synoptics whether there were one or two trials before the Sanhedrin Jeremias surmised that it was probable that, in the interest of haste, some of the members of the Sanhedrin assembled to prepare for the morning session[134]. Luke followed a distinctive tradition for the Sanhedrin hearing.

In a work published a short time later on the apostolic origin of the Gospels (1932), Jeremias insisted that Luke had a personal relationship with Philip and obtained valuable information from him around Easter in 58 AD[135]. Jeremias advanced the idea that there were three identifications for L. The first (L[1]) referred to the author of the Prologue and the one who revised the old sources. The next version (L[2]) consisted of a translation or revision of a tradition stemming from Philip in Aramaic or possibly Greek. The third (L[3]) contained redactional additions "in Satzprosa mit Stimmumlage"[136]. The influence of Philip on Lk was significant: "Die persönliche Note des Philippus gibt dem Sondergut des Lukas die Überzeugungskraft des religiösen Erlebnisses"[137]. The Lukan *Sondergut* was drawn from five sources: L[2], J, B, C and P[138]. On the Lukan order of the Sanhedrin trial and its similarity to the teaching of James Jeremias wrote: "Endlich ist in der Leidensgeschichte die Stelle Mark. 15,1 hervorzuheben, wo Jakobus von

131. *Ibid.*, p. 10. Consider his remark on the Markan content of Lk: "Lukas ist für einem grösseren Teil seines Evangeliums in den Spuren der dem zweiten Evangelium zu Grunde liegenden Überlieferung ..." (p. 25).

132. *Ibid.*, p. 316. See *Das Evangelium nach Markus. Versuch einer urchristlichen Erklärung für die Gegenwart*, Chemnitz - Leipzig, 1928 (esp. p. 204-217).

133. *Das Evangelium nach Lukas*, p. 10-11.

134. *Ibid.*, p. 246.

135. *Der apostolische Ursprung der vier Evangelien. Mit einer kurzgefassten Einleitung in die neueste Geschichte der Schallanalyse*, Leipzig, 1932, p. 80. He based his work on that of Eduard SIEVERS, *Textaufbau der griechischen Evangelien* (Klanglich untersucht. 41, Bd. d. Abh. d. Sächs. Akad. d. Wiss.), Leipzig, 1931.

136. *Der apostolische Ursprung der vier Evangelien*, p. 162. See also p. 88, concerning L[2].

137. *Ibid.*, p. 87.

138. *Ibid.*, p. 123. The complete explanation of the abbreviations can be found on p. 161-162. J referred to reports from the apostles John and Jude; B signified "Sagverse" drawn from the translation of the Aramaic source of John; C contained "Zeilenprosa" provided by the translator of the Aramaic tradition of James; P was the Petrine report.

der Morgensitzung des Hohenrates am Todestage Jesu redet: Lukas hat demnach 22,66 eine Sitzung am frühen Morgen mit historischem Recht in seine Darstellung aufgenommen, obwohl das Verhör hinter 22,54 seine richtige Stelle hat. Auf den Inhaltsbericht des Verhör vor Kaiphas, den Jakobus gibt, komme ich weiter unten zu sprechen. Mark. 15,29 bricht die Jakobuslehre ab"[139].

In remarking about the Herod story Jeremias (1930) contended that Luke portrayed Jesus as the suffering just one. Though not offering specifics about the source of the story, Jeremias contrasted the lengthy speeches found in the acts of the martyrs with the silence in the Herod story reasoning: "Die urchristliche Überlieferung von dem Leiden des Herrn bewahrt auch darin ihre Ursprünglichkeit und Unberührtheit, dass sie vor der schweigenden Majestät des leidenden Herrn ehrfurchtsvoll halt macht"[140].

Confessing the complexity of the synoptic problem, Alfred LOISY (1907) rejected the idea of proto-gospels[141]. In a review of modern criticism Loisy noted that since 1861 B. Weiss defended a particular form of the Two-Source theory "avec beaucoup de finesse critique"[142]. He alluded to the work of Feine only in a note[143]. Loisy devoted a chapter to the origin and composition of Lk where he claimed Luke knew not only Mk but the sources of Mk and other writings[144]. He offered preliminary observations about 22,54-23,25[145]. Redaction was responsible for the delay of the denials of Peter and the scene was further dramatized by the presence of Jesus. Elements of Luke's morning Sanhedrin trial seem to have been borrowed from the night trial which Mark assumed. But Mark's source probably influenced the recounting of the trial before Pilate (23,1-3.16-25) so that the accusations of the priests preceded the interrogation by Pilate[146]. Luke improved on Mk in the Barabbas episode by introducing a formal declaration of innocence, which provided the necessary incident to explain Jesus' appearance before Herod. Luke rejoined Mk at the Barabbas story paraphrasing details from Mk in multiplying the declarations of innocence and insisting that Pilate ceded to the "véhémentes supplications" of the Jews.

139. *Ibid.*, p. 65.

140. *Das Evangelium*, p. 253.

141. A. LOISY, *Les évangiles synoptiques*, Paris, Vol. 1, 1907; Vol. 2, 1908. Contra proto-gospels, Vol. 1, p. 62. The first volume contains a useful overview of the history of modern criticism. His study of the origin and sources of Lk is found in Vol. 1, p. 144-174. C.G. Montefiore was especially influenced by Loisy's study of the Synoptics. See below, n. 247 and 249.

142. *Ibid.*, p. 71, n. 2. Cf. B. WEISS, *TSK* (1861), *JDT* (1864, 1865), *Das Marcusevangelium* (1872), *Leben Jesu* (1882, ³1888), *Einleitung* (1886, ³1897) and the commentaries in the Meyer series.

143. LOISY, *Les évangiles synoptiques*, p. (71)-72, n. 3. Cf. FEINE, *JPTh* (1885-1888); 1891.

144. LOISY, *Les évangiles synoptiques*, p. 144-174, p. 144.

145. *Ibid.*, p. 161-162.

146. *Ibid.*, p. 162.

In the section containing the translation and commentary on the trial Loisy argued that rather than being considered historically reliable, 22,54-55 was interpreted in the light of faith and the needs of Christian apologetics[147]. In 22,54 Luke combined Mk 14, and 14,53[148]. The mockery (22,63-65) stemmed from Mk and the move to a morning session of the Sanhedrin was based on the Markan material[149]. On the MA in 22,62 he maintained: "La leçon ἐπιβαλών, si autorisée qu'elle soit, ne laisse pas d'être suspecte, et peut-être n'est-elle qu'une très ancienne faute de copiste (cf. Mt. 75. ἐξελθών). Tenir compte néanmoins de ce que cette finale a été substituée à la finale primitive, v. 68b"[150]. He considered 22,62 an import from Mt[151]. He also reckoned with Matthean influence for the MA in 22,65: "L'accord des deux évangélistes en ce point suggère l'ideé d'une influence de Matthieu sur Luc, à moins que l'explication, τίς ἐστιν ὁ παίσας σε, n'ait été ajoutée de très bonne heure dans le troisième Évangile, d'après le premier, ce qui n'a rein d'impossible"[152]. With the story of Barabbas, Luke rejoined Mk[153].

For the Sanhedrin trial (22,66-71) it was evident that Luke was dependent upon Mk[154]. He expressed doubts whether the Sanhedrin still retained the right to render a capital sentence without having obtained Roman approval[155]. They could not render a judgment in criminal cases on the same night as the accused had been interrogated, thus the interrogation and sentencing were separated by a day. Thus, what occurred in double sessions in Mk was, through combination and redaction by Luke, amended simply to one which was indeed equivalent to those described in the other Synoptics[156]. The morning trial before the Sanhedrin was a transposition, adaptation and interpretation of Mk's trial at night[157].

In 23,1 Loisy regarded the phrase τὸ πλῆθος αὐτῶν as a echo of Mk 15,1 (ὅλον τὸ συνέδριον)[158]. He insisted that while Luke was dependent upon Mk for much in his Gospel, at times he referred to a source better than Mk[159]. At 23,2

147. Vol. 2, p. 596.
148. *Ibid.*, p. 592, n. 1.
149. Vol. 1, p. 161; cf. Vol. 2, p. 611.
150. Vol. 2, p. 617, n. 2.
151. Vol. 2, p. 621: "Plusieurs manuscrits de l'ancienne Vulgate omettent la conclusion: 'Et s'en allant dehors, il pleura amèrement', qui pourrait avoir été littéralement importée de Matthieu dans le texte traditionnel de Luc". Cf. p. 619, n. 7.
152. Vol. 2, p. 613, n. 2.
153. Vol. 2, p. 638. Loisy noted that modern critics attacked the Herod passage either as a fictional legend or a Lukan creation.
154. Vol. 2, p. 599; see also Vol. 1, p. 162.
155. Vol. 2, p. 593. In n. 4 Loisy referred to E. Schürer 2³, 208-210, the passage Jer. Sanhedrin 1,1 (fol. 18ᵃ) and 7,2 (fol. 24ᵃ) and J. Weiss, *Das älteste Evangelium*, p. 316.
156. *Les évangiles synoptiques*, Vol. 2, p. 599. Cf. p. 594.
157. Vol. 2, p. 609.
158. Vol. 2, p. 624, n. 2.
159. Vol. 2, p. 634. Loisy made this statement concerning, e.g. Lk 23,2-5. Luke discovered mention of Herod in one of his predecessors' Gospels (Vol. 2, p. 638), but Loisy also suggested

Luke was independent of Mk, but 23,3 was conformed to Mk 15,2[160].

Loisy had high praise for Wernle's *Die synoptische Frage*. He called it "une étude fort bien conduite" which showed that Luke knew Mk and used it as the basis of his own account, profoundly modified the style of his source, interpreted the details, rarely combining it with other documents[161]: "La plupart de ces conclusions semblent fondées. Les plus contestables doivent être celles qui concernent le rapport de Marc avec la tradition de Pierre, son indépendance à l'égard du recueil de discours, l'originalité de sa composition et le degré d'historicité qui lui appartient"[162].

In his commentary on Acts (1920), Loisy mentioned Feine's view (1891), that the special source in Lk continued in Acts, was "dans l'esprit et selon la méthode de B. Weiss"[163]. He criticized Feine's position[164].

Offering a brief critical history of the study of Lk in his Lukan commentary (1924), Loisy focused primarily on German scholars[165]. He regarded Feine's theory as analogous to that of B. Weiss on Luke's special source[166]. Wernle and Hawkins reached, generally speaking, the same conclusions. Loisy took a less favorable view of the opinions of Wellhausen whose ideas were "plus hardies et plus discutables" than those of Wernle. The views of T. Zahn were no less reassuring than those of Harnack. Loisy deemed Spitta's study (1912) a "réaction légitime contre la thèse critique touchant l'originalité de Marc, mais analyse trop exclusivement littéraire et qui n'emporte pas la conviction"[167]. J. Weiss considered the first three evangelists as "auteurs impersonnels" and had posited a Judeo-Christian source[168]. In contrast to Weiss, Bultmann (1921), employed "une méthode sensiblement différente et plus large" which led him to believe that tradition was shaped and developed in the first generation of believers, that was in the first Judeo-Christian community. Loisy himself concluded the survey maintaining that the Gospels were almost totally products of the Christian tradition,

---

that here Luke might have cleverly made corrections of Mk. He rejected the proposal that Luke created the story ("inventeé"), saying that elsewhere Luke used written sources.

160. Vol. 2, p. 634, 633, n. 3.

161. Vol. 1, p. 75; reprised in 1924, p. 18. See above.

162. Vol. 1, p. 76.

163. *Les Actes des Apôtres*, Paris, 1920, p. 34. Cf. FEINE, *Eine vorkanonische Überlieferung*.

164. LOISY, *Les Actes des Apôtres*: "Analyse qui concorde pour le principal avec celle de B. Weiss, et avec celle de Wendt pour la distinction de deux couches dans le discours d'Etienne. Sorof était mieux inspiré en détachant I,3ss. du prologue, en imputant à une rédaction secondaire la majeure partie de ce que Feine attribue à sa source précanonique; c'est un grand abus d'accorder à cette prétendue source une valeur historique de premier ordre quand on y met tant de choses". Cf. M. SOROF, *Die Entstehung der Apostelgeschichte*, Berlin, 1890.

165. *L'Évangile selon Luc*, Paris, 1924, p. 13-24.

166. *Ibid.*, p. 17.

167. *Ibid.*, p. 21.

168. *Ibid.*, p. 22. Streeter (1921) and Stephenson (1923) were mentioned in passing as others who speculated on the particular Lukan source. These were viewed in opposition to Goguel and Wernle who envisioned a plurality of sources.

comprising liturgical literature[169]. The heart of this material, the passion and resurrection narrative, "est étroitement coordonnée aux observances pascales des communautés primitives"[170].

In his treatment of the composition of Lk he again announced his conviction that Luke was certainly dependent upon Mk[171], having employed written documents, "notamment le document fondamental de Marc"[172]. The rearrangement of the story of Peter and his denial following the arrest prior to the Sanhedrin trial restored what Mark annoyingly disturbed by the night session of the Sanhedrin. Luke was credited with slightly stretching out the account of Peter's denials to fill the night and putting Jesus at the scene. On the other hand, details from the nocturnal Sanhedrin trial (Mk 14,60-64) were incorporated into Luke's morning session[173]. Rather than consider the account of the Sanhedrin trial a summary and abbreviation of Mk, Lk and the fundamental source of Mk "ignorait l'impossible et imaginaire séance du sanhédrin"[174]. Luke returned to Mk at the point involving Barabbas[175]. The scene where the Jews demanded the freedom of Barabbas and the death of Jesus was described as "un incident rédactionnel". In this case, the evangelist "ne pouvait pas rendre plus invraisemblable l'incident de Barabbas, il l'a rendu plus obscur"[176]. Other means by which Luke redacted Mk were paraphrase or simplification[177]. Loisy regarded the MA in 22,62 as apparently having been taken from Mt[178].

The Lukan version of the mockery not only retained the Markan scene following the condemnation of Jesus by the Sanhedrin, but 22,63-65 was a replacement for the Markan account of the mistreatment by the Roman soldiers (Mk 15,16-20), owing to the sensitivities of the evangelist[179]. Loisy pointed to similarities between Jesus before the Sanhedrin in Lk and Paul before the Sanhedrin in Acts 14,5-6. Likewise, the motif of Paul's innocence (Acts 26,32)

---

169. *Ibid.*, p. 23-24.

170. *Ibid.*, p. 24.

171. *Ibid.*, p. 47-48: "Car le troisième évangile dépend sûrement de Marc, et le rédacteur pratique souvent à l'égard de Marc une méthode analogue à celle qu'il a suivie dans les Actes à l'égard de la relation de Luc". For the section on the composition of Lk, see p. 44-62. Because his commentary on Acts intervened between his work on the synoptic gospels and this commentary, one notes in the present work frequent statements comparing Lk to Acts.

172. *Ibid.*, p. 74. See also p. 41-42, concerning the contributions of the source of Mk in 22,54-23,25.

173. *Ibid.*, p. 41. Although there was no mention of witnesses in the Lukan account, the author was utilizing a source which contained reference to them, but they were "un développement sans intérêt" for him and thus omitted (p. 540).

174. *Ibid.*, p. 534. See below, n. 183.

175. *Ibid.*, p. 41: "On rejoint Marc pour l'incident de Barabbas, ajouté, à ce qu'il semble, dans la rédaction ...". Cf. above n. 152.

176. *Ibid.*, p. 550.

177. *Ibid.* p. 551. One case of paraphrase was 23,23. Luke simplified Mk in 23,25.

178. *Ibid.*, p. 537. Cf. above, n. 151.

179. *Ibid.*, p. 538.

showed that the accounts were parallel and stemmed from the same hand[180]. Loisy did not regard the Lukan perspective of the judgment as any more true than that of Mk or Mt[181]. On the contrary, because of the insertion of the Herod material, it was even less so.

Loisy later (1936) adopted a form of the special source hypothesis, explaining the passion narrative as having been combined with material from Proto-Mk, Proto-Lk (which included material offered by the author of the Prologue), and later editorial revisions[182]. Though the idea of Urmarkus was falling into disfavor with numerous scholars, Loisy still had recourse to it in explaining the differences between Lk and Mk. The nocturnal session of the Sanhedrin had been omitted, because Luke did not find it in his Proto-Markan source[183]. Though less certain, Loisy posited that Proto-Mk may have been responsible for mentioning the charges of the Sanhedrin before the trial of Pilate. The editor of Lk utilized the Markan account of the Barabbas episode, but additions which had been made to this by the editor involved repeated statements concerning the innocence of Jesus[184]. Luke possessed in his source a conglomeration of stories and sayings which lacked temporal or geographical references. Loisy conjectured that Proto-Lk consisted in a writing addressed to Theophilus, but made little attempt to elaborate on it. The editor was responsible for spreading the denials of Peter over the course of the night and mentioning the detail that Jesus glanced at Peter, bringing about his pangs of conscience.

From canonical Mk, Luke derived not only the report of the mistreatment, but also elements of the nocturnal Sanhedrin trial which Luke transferred to the morning. The fluidity of the tradition became apparent. "Tous ces emprunts prouvent beaucoup moins la fixité que l'indigence de la tradition"[185]. In the end, Luke penned his two-volume work to catechize and to edify[186].

---

180. *Ibid.*, p. 544-545. Loisy maintained that the Gospel account was less successful than the one in Acts. Rather than inventing the version in Acts, the author adapted it to the goals of his work.

181. *Ibid.*, p. 551.

182. *Les origines du Nouveau Testament*, Paris, 1936, esp. p. 179-183 (= *The Origins of the New Testament*, tr. L.P. JACKS, London, 1951, esp. p. 165-169). Loisy's conception of the composition of Lk was that it represented, "Le premier livre à Théophile n'a pas seulement été augmenté des légendes de la naissance, il a été substantiellement remanié et complété, comme l'a été le second livre dans les Actes des Apôtres" (183 = 169-170). Loisy distinguished between two forms of Lk and Acts. The original form was thought to have been written in the "early years of the second century". The date of the canonical form was set at "a little before 140" (p. 170).

183. *Ibid.*, p. 179. See above, n. 174.

184. *Ibid.*, p. 180 (= 167).

185. *Ibid.*, p. 180 (= 166).

186. *Ibid.*, p. 207 (= 192). James Branton's claim, in a review of the ET, that Loisy's book was "most stimulating" seemed inconsistent with the criticisms he made against Loisy. Asserting that Loisy's approach was outdated, that "many sweeping conclusions are dogmatically stated with little evidence of support", and that Loisy had generally ignored the works of other scholars, Branton's analysis pointed up the diminished value of the book (*JBR* 19 [1951] 157).

Loisy (1907) claimed the nucleus of the Herod story (23,4-15) probably stemmed from tradition and the related response of Jesus (13,32) stemmed from a primitive source[187]. However, its meaning was completely lost in the redaction of the evangelist[188]. He continued to insist (1908) that the trial before Herod came from Luke's highly esteemed source, which contained an apologia for Christianity in regard to Roman authority[189]. He dismissed Wellhausen's contention that 23,10-11 were a gloss arguing that these verses were required by the context between 23,9 and 2,13[190]. Noting that modern critics debated the source of the pericope in a lively fashion, he acknowledged those who believed that Luke either received "une fiction légendaire" or created it himself, rejecting this latter option as "invraisemblable" since Luke was dependent upon written sources[191]. While it was agreed that Luke prepared for the intervention of Herod ahead of time, Loisy did not believe that Luke was responsible for the meeting of Jesus and Herod but had found reference to it in one or another document. The idea that the story was found in the source of Mark was rejected, but Loisy described the source as "une source analogue à l'Évangile de Pierre, à moins que ce ne fût une ancienne rédaction de cet Évangile, et parallèle à Marc et à Matthieu"[192]. He also dismissed the theories of Holtzmann, B. Weiss, J. Weiss and Feine that Luke had taken "une donnée traditionnelle" and embellished it with details drawn from Mk as an idea "ne s'appuie sur aucun indice véritablement

187. Vol. 1, p. 156; see also p. 920: "... la source où Luc a trouvé qu'Hérode avait joué un rôle dans la passion du Sauveur". Note futher Vol. 2, p. 634, where he spoke of the tradition or the source containing the Herod pericope.

188. *Ibid.*, p. 169.

189. Vol. 2, 1908, p. 635-636. He rejected the idea that Luke invented the story, noting that everywhere else Luke was dependent upon written sources. Rather, Luke found mention of Herod made in one of the Gospels he referred to and the apologetical interest accounts for Herod's reaction to Jesus' preaching ministry (p. 638-640). See also Vol. 1, p. 162, where Loisy insisted that Herod had been substituted for the condemnation.

The insertion of the episode was not a smooth one. According to Loisy: "Ainsi Luc rejoint le récit de Marc, à l'égard duquel cette histoire d'Hérode se présente comme une intercalation artificielle. L'incohérence de la rédaction, à l'endroit où Pilate mande les sanhédristes, qui cependant auraient dû retourner avec Jésus chez les procurateur, tient à l'effort que Luc doit faire, après avoir donné en raccourci le jugement du Christ par Hérode, pour rejoindre le récit de Marc touchant Barabbas" (Vol. 2, p. 631).

190. *Ibid.*, p. (637)-638, n. 5; cf. Wellhausen (1904), p. 132.

191. Vol. 2, p. 638. Strauss, Brandt and Wernle were listed as the critics. In a reproach seemingly directed to Holtzmann, Loisy stated: "Le rapport que l'on trouve entre Lc. 6-16, et Act. XXV,23-XXVI,32, ne touche pas au fond, et le récit des Actes n'a exercé qu'une influence assez légère sur la mise en scène de Lc. 6-16" (p. 638, n. 3; but cf. *L'Évangile selon Luc*, 1924, p. 544).

192. Vol. 2, p. 639-640. Mention was also made that in the GP it was Herod who gave the orders to Jesus' executioners (p. 637, n. 2; see also *L'évangile de Luc*, p. 546). Regarding the friendship between Herod and Pilate (23,12), Loisy pointed out that in the GP Herod called Pilate "brother" (Vol. 2, p. 637, n. 3). Cf. WERNLE, *Die synoptische Frage*, 1899, p. 95, who maintained that the Herod episode found in the GP rested upon Lk.

probant"[193].

A shift from Loisy's 1907-08 position took place when in *L'Évangile selon Luc* (1924) he claimed that the Herod episode (23,4-15) was "fiction pure" which resulted from apologetical interests and was viewed as the fulfillment of prophecy (Acts 4,25-28)[194]. At this time he more readily accepted Markan influence, at least in certain elements. He now saw Mk as the source of the motif of Jesus' silence (23,9 / Mk 15,4-5)[195]. In Loisy's later work (1936), his posited that redaction introduced the story (23,4-16) which was perhaps then borrowed by another gospel, current at the time Luke composed his, such as GP[196].

Loisy's position from 1907-1908 is marked more by consistency than by change. For the commentary he drew from his earlier study on the Synpoptics, sometimes verbatim. While in the earlier work he argued that there was probably an historical core for the Herod pericope, he modified his position in 1924 contending that it was pure fiction.

In a lengthy article, Arthur W. VERRALL (1909) praised Loisy's "two elaborate and interesting volumes on the Synoptic Gospels", which prompted his study of the Herod pericope. He recalled the criticism which Loisy referred to, that the Herod episode was "a legendary fiction accepted, or even invented by Luke"[197], recommending instead that Luke probably had access to information from the servants in the Herodian court[198]. Though the text from Ps 2,1-2 may have influenced the Gospel narrative somewhat, it was not very influential[199]. Whereas Loisy implied that much that was said of Pilate was transferred to Herod, Verrall contended that Herod was merely being asked to indicate how he saw the charges of the Jewish religious leadership[200]. Luke assumed that Herod really had no opinion of the Christian movement[201]. In contrast to Mk and Mt, Luke

---

193. *Les évangiles synoptiques*, p. 640.

194. *L'Évangile selon Luc*, 1924, p. 41. He continued: "beaucoup en attribuent l'invention à l'évangéliste lui-même; mais peut-être celui-ci n'a-t-il fait qu'exploiter un récit de la passion où la responsabilité de la mort du Christ était hardiment transportée de Pilate à Herode, comme dans l'évangile apocryphe de Pierre". Strangely, no mention was made of Dibelius (1915).

195. *Ibid.*, p. 546.

196. *Les origines*, p. 180 (= 167).

197. A.W. VERRALL, *Christ before Herod*, in *JTS* 10 (1908-09) 321-353, p. 321 (= *Bacchants of Euripides and Other Essays*, London, 1910, 335-390, p. 336; cf. Loisy, Vol. 2, p. 638). Curiously, Verrall defined the pericope as 23,1-16, though Herod is not introduced until 23,6. He made the strange confession at the beginning of the article that he had "no special competence in the subject" (p. 321 = 335). Yet, the article is significant since it continues to be cited in the literature, e.g. by G. Schneider (1977), L.T. Johnson (1991), R.E. Brown (1994) and S. Légasse (1995).

198. *Ibid.*, p. 334 (= 355). Verrall suggested there were possibly two, a secretary and a page (p. 334 = 356).

199. *Ibid.*, p. 322 (= 337).

200. *Ibid.*, p. 351 (= 382).

201. *Ibid.*, p. 327, 335 (= 344, 357).

reproduced material that was generally favorable to Herod[202].

Already in 1907 Friedrich SPITTA signaled his support of Luke's dependence upon a Synoptic GS:

> "Leider ist in Bezug darauf von massgebender Seite das Urteil gefällt worden, ich hätte die seit 100 Jahren fast nur noch von Noack und Mandel vertretene Reihenfolge Lukas, Markus, Matthäus aufgegriffen. Das ist unrichtig. Wenn ich behaupte, Lukas habe neben seiner Abhängigkeit von Markus und Matthäus, bezw. von verwandten Schriftwerken, auch die jenen zu Grunde liegende synoptische Grundschrift selbständig und nicht selten in weniger alterierter Form benutzt und Matthäus habe einen älteren als den kanonischen Markustext vor sich gehabt, so lässt sich das nicht mit der Reihenfolge Lukas, Markus, Matthäus charakterisieren. In jener Linie bewegen sich doch auch andere Forscher, und die Erkenntnis, dass Lukas viel öfter, als man früher anzunehmen pflegte, das Ursprüngliche erhalten habe, spricht sich in der neueren Literatur mit immer grösserer Entschiedenheit aus. Wenn ich, in der Beurteilung des Umfangs und der Treue der Benutzung der synoptischen Grundschrift bei Lukas sehr weit gehe, so habe ich dafür überall meine Gründe angegeben"[203].

Spitta (1912), reacting against the "Grundirrtum" of Markan priority, sought to establish an Aramaic original which resulted in our Gospels as translations[204].

---

202. *Ibid.*, p. 328-329 (= 347-348). In contrast to Mk and Mt in the scenes of the robing, Verrall wrote: "There is simply no analogy at all. Circumstances, actors, things said and done, the meaning of them, – all are different; and it is not even conceivable that the story in Luke should be an equivalent or compensation for the other" (p. 345 = 373). Verrall saw the account of Herod as honoring Jesus rather than mocking him (p. 343 = 370).

203. F. SPITTA, *Streifragen der Geschichte Jesu*, Göttingen, 1907, p. 4.

204. *Die synoptische Grundschrift in ihrer Überlieferung durch das Lukasevangelium*, Leipzig, 1912, p. XI. Spitta rebutted the position of E. Wendling that Mk served as the source for Mt and Luke. He considered Wendling's position typical of those who support Markan priority. E. WENDLING, *Urmarkus*, Tübingen, 1905; *Die Entstehung des Markus Evangeliums*, Tübingen, 1908 (SPITTA, p. V).

Only a few years earlier Caspar René GREGORY (1909) counted among Luke's sources the following: the primitive Gospel (*Urschrift*), Mk and some third written source or sources, and the oral tradition, though to a smaller degree than was available to Mt (*Einleitung in das Neue Testament*, Leipzig, 1909, p. 767). Luke's technique consisted in weaving the various sources together into a unified whole, while retaining as much as possible from his source.

Similar to Spitta, Frederic William FARRAR (1884, 1891) argued that where the style is of a lower quality and there are numerous Hebraisms, Luke "is following some Aramaic document in which the oral tradition had been reduced to writing" (*The Gospel according to St. Luke* [Cambridge Greek Testament for Schools and Colleges], Cambridge, 1891, p. 28, n. 2 = *The Gospel according to St. Luke* [The Cambridge Bible for Schools and Colleges], 1884, p. xxxvii, n. 2 [pages in brackets]). The text was popular, used in schools and frequently reprinted. But unlike Spitta, Farrar absolutely rejected Lukan dependence upon Mk (p. 9 = [xvi]. See also 1891, p. 42 = [83]). Though each of the Gospels followed a common outline Farrar rejected any interdependence among the Synoptics, insisting instead that they were "four separate, and mainly if not absolutely, independent Gospels" (p. 7 = [xiv]). As proof, Farrar pointed "to the minute

Encouraged by the recent development which advanced the judgment that the Lukan tradition, rather than the Markan or Matthean, formed the basis of a presentation of the life of Jesus, Spitta delved into what he considered an otherwise neglected area of NT studies[205]. Though the Prologue (1,1-4) indicated that Luke presented none of the oldest sources[206], his intent was to offer a complete and exact account of the early Christian community which emphasized historical reliability rather than edification or an artificial unity[207]. Spitta dated the composition of the GS not later than the beginning of the fortieth year, when even more Apostles would have been alive than when Mk was composed[208].

Luke's redactional method involved joining other materials to the GS. In addition to two larger compact sources, the Infancy Narrative (Luke 1-2) and the Logia of Jesus (9,57-18,14)[209], there were a number of small sources, some of

---

and inexplicable differences which incessantly occur even amid general similarity" (p. 9 = [xvi]). Mt was regarded as the first, with Mk and Lk following shortly thereafter (p. 9 = [xv]). Peter's denials were cited as a "valuable proof of independence [of the Gospels]" because, although they differed from one another, they were not opposed to each other (p. 335 = [379]). Though it was difficult to assess the extent of influence exerted by written accounts or oral teaching, the Prologue indicated apostles and original disciples were the sources of oral tradition (p. 43 = [84]).

Farrar, attempting to harmonize the differences between the four Gospels, suggested the trial of Jesus occurred in three phases and ascribed equal importance to each trial (p. 334 = [378]). Phase 1, the trial before Annas (Jn 18,12-18); Phase 2, before Caiaphas (Lk 22,54; Mt 26,59-78; Mk 14,55-65); Phase 3, before the entire Sanhedrin at dawn (Lk 22,66; Mt 27,1; Mk 15,1). The Sanhedrin trial served only as a preliminary inquiry because it was held at night and "left the final decision only formal" (p. 334 = [378]).

Farrar regarded the order of Lk the "most artistic and historical" (p. 16 = [xxii]). He asserted that Luke's version was the most historical of the Synoptics and, while the order was chiefly chronological, rendered the "actual sequence of events" (p. 31 = [xl]). He wrote next to nothing about the source question for Lk, though in referring to Herod's trial, he proposed that Luke had access to "special information about Herod's court" (p. 341 = [384]).

205. SPITTA, *Grundschrift*, p. VI.

206. *Ibid.*, p. VIII: "Dass das Lukasevangelium keine der ältesten Quellen darstellt, sagt es selbst im Prolog 1,1-4 so deutlich ...".

207. SPITTA, *Grundschrift*, p. 464: "Nicht das war der Zweck seines Werkes, die verschiedenen Stoffe zu einer künstlerischen Einheit zusammenzuschmelzen, sondern durch sorgfältige Benutzung der besten Berichte eine möglichst zuverlässige Darstellung der Geschichte der ersten Jahrzente des Christentums zu geben".

208. *Ibid.*, p. 476. More precisely: "Mithin wird die Abfassung der GS spätestens in den Anfang der vierziger Jahre fallen, also früher als alle uns erhaltenen Paulusbriefe und so nahe der Lebensgeschichte Jesu, dass eine genaue Erinnerung an die Ereignisse derselben bei denen, die sie miterlebt haben, garantiert ist, wenigstens soweit als es möglich ist, wenn nicht unmittelbar nach denselben Aufzeichnungen gemacht worden sind" (p. 478).

209. *Ibid*, p. 461. Because Luke organically joined the Logia with the synoptic GS, unlike Mk and especially Mt, he had not interrupted the content of the Logia. Likewise individual pericopes were organically joined to the GS and thus can be easily differentiated (p. 466). Spitta referred to Luke's method of inserting these individual pericopes and cited Jesus' trial before Herod as one example (p. 468; note the typographical error reads "22,6-12" and should, of

which were independent pericopes[210], while others were additions to the pericopes of the GS[211]. Additions to the GS from Mk-Mt went back to an older form of Mk which formed the basis of Mt and canonical Mk[212]. Spitta further maintained that this older Mk (Mrk[1]) was not to be identified with the synoptic GS, but represented an intermediate stage. It went back to a still older writing, Gr[m], which like Gr[1], were forms of the GS, offering two different translations of the Aramaic original[213]. The Lukan version descending directly from the Aramaic original, influenced only slightly by Proto-Mk, retained the more original order.

On the other hand, Mk was presented as a substantial expansion of the GS. Excluding the smaller additions, Spitta listed thirty-two pericopes[214]. In his view,

course, read "23,6-12"). Luke employed a similar method for smaller insertions, such as Jesus' circuitous affirmation (22,70), even in the midst of his refusal to answer (p. 469).

210. *Ibid.*, p. 462. Among the sixteen smaller, independent pericopes which Spitta maintained were added to the GS were the following which have some relation to the passion narrative: the preparation of the passover meal (22,7-13) and three other pericopes were taken over from the Mk-Mt tradition; the great female sinner (7,36-50), the dispute regarding the rank of the disciples at the Lord's Supper (22,24-27), and the prayer of Jesus in Gethsemane (22,41-46), plus four others, have in the other Gospels more or less clearly imprinted parallels. The pericopes Jesus before Herod (23,6-12) and the thieves on the crosses (23,39-43), and two others, actually have no parallels in any manner in the Gospel literature. While one could possibly agree with the assessment of the Herod pericope, the conclusion that there are no parallels for the account of the thieves on the crosses is questionable.

211. *Ibid.*, p. 463. It was inconclusive, according to Spitta, whether Mk or Mt had been the source for a greater number of additions. But where they were responsible for the additions, they ultimately derived from Proto-Mk (Mk[1]), which was distinguished from the Markan Greek translation of the GS and the Aramaic original.

212. *Ibid.* Spitta also conceded that for a considerable number of additions it cannot be decided whether Mk or Mt had been the source, e.g. 22,70.

213. *Ibid.*, p. 499. Consult the useful diagrams both here and on p. 464. These graphic presentations of Spitta's position do not indicate any relationship between Gr[m] (referred to as "eine ältere Schrift" and Gr[1] ["die aus Lukas gewonnene Grundschrift"]). The diagram on p. 499 presented the earliest stage of development, the Aramaic original. Carl Weizsäcker (1864, [2]1901) adopted the Two-Source theory and maintained that Luke had access to many sources, but was reluctant to determine their form or content (*Untersuchungen über die evangelische Geschichte ihre Quellen und den Gang ihrer Entwicklung*, Tübingen - Leipzig, 1864, [2]1901, p. 7: "Man geht zu weit, wenn man meint, die schriftliche Aufzeichnung sei hier als das Werk einer zweiten Periode der ursprünglichen Ueberlieferung als einer bloss mündlichen entgegengesetzt. In welcher Form diese Ueberlieferung gegeben hat, darüber ist Nichts gesagt". That the Synoptic evangelists based their accounts upon a common GS became very clear to Weizsäcker in the passion narrative (*Untersuchung*, p. 60). While Mark confined himself to the GS, it was obvious that Luke employed numerous traditions which he judiciously used to correct the flow of the account. In abandoning the Synoptic text and preferring his own special sources, Luke offered a "genauerer pragmatischer Erzählung" (p. 62). As a case in point, Luke supplanted his version of the mockery for that of the Roman soldiers as a correction. Weizsäcker proposed that Luke used special sources which often provided him with "eine eigenthümliche Darstellung", among which he counted the Herod scene (23,6-15) (p. 62-63).

214. SPITTA, *Grundschrift*, p. 478-479. In the Markan passion narrative the following were

Mark's addition of more than thirty pericopes at varying places must have changed the GS more radically than the sixteen additional pericopes in Lk[215]. Besides the additions by Mark, the abbreviations had no small effect upon the GS. Rather than regarding the Lukan material as expansions of Mk, as those who argued for Markan priority would maintain, Spitta viewed Mk as an abbreviation of parts of the GS found in Lk[216]. From all this, Spitta concluded that the earliest Synoptic Gospel was Luke's[217]. Spitta contended the establishment of the GS from the Lukan tradition meant a radical change for Mk insofar as the traditional assessment had viewed Mk as *Grundlage* for both other Synoptics[218].

Spitta gave very little credit to Luke's abilities as an author (and redactor) since he claimed that what was literarily remarkable in both of Luke's works was due to the form of the writings which he used, rather than Luke's own efforts[219]. An author of this manner, Spitta argued, left much unsettled by the editing of the different sources to form a literary unity. Consequently, materials can be easily distinguished which Luke only loosely placed beside one another[220].

Dismissing all the similarities in detail in the denial of Peter, mockery of Jesus, and the gathering of the Sanhedrin (22,54-71), Spitta focused instead on the difference in the Lukan arrangement of the material over against Mk-Mt, conceding one could easily, though mistakenly, conclude that Luke joined another source to the synoptic GS[221]. Difference in arrangement of the entire section governed the decision whether the synoptic GS was to be recognized in the account of Jesus before the Sanhedrin[222]. Disharmony occurred in Lk as compared to the GS, due to later insertions from Mk and Mt[223]. Spitta deduced that the GS

---

additional: the anointing in Bethany (14,3-9); the preparation of the passover meal (14,12-16); the prophecy about the scattering of the disciples (14,26-28); Gethsemane (14,32-42); the mockery of the king of the Jews (15,16-20). Some of the additional pericopes stand also in Luke within the great interpolation of the book of Logia: the speech about humility, zealous service (Mk 10,41-45 / Luke 22,24-27).

215. *Ibid.*, p. 479-480. Spitta did not include additions from the book of Logia in his calculations of Lukan insertions.

216. *Ibid.*, p. 481: "An erster Stelle sind die Verkürzungen der Grundschrift ins Auge zu fassen".

217. *Ibid.*, p. 498.

218. *Ibid.*, p. 478.

219. *Ibid.*, p. 464.

220. *Ibid.*, p. 469-470.

221. *Ibid.*, p. 394-395: "...dass es begreiflich ist, wie man annehmen konnte, ersterer habe mit der synoptischen GS eine andere verbunden. Die bisher untersuchten Perikopen der Leidensgeschichte haben das entgegengesesste Resultat gehabt. Es wird sich zeigen, dass es auch in diesem Abschnitt nicht anders steht". A rather significant typographical error appears on p. 395, where an entire line seems to be missing.

222. *Ibid.*, p. 395.

223. *Ibid.*, p. 399: "Die so oft erwiesene Unstimmigkeit des Lukastextes, in dem neben der rein erhaltenen GS unvermittelt spätere Einschaltungen aus Markus-Matthäus stehen, zeigt sich auch hier, sofern auf die Antwort Jesu V.67-69 die Synedristen in V.70 erwidern ... V.70 ist nichts anderes als Herübernahme von Mark. V.61f.; Matth.V. 63f.".

existed in Lk 23,2.3.13.14.18-24 into which only a total of five words in vv. 13 and 14 had been inserted[224].

Spitta often noted the change of function of a particular pericope and such was the case with the trial. Rather than portraying the trial as the vehicle for passing a death sentence upon Jesus, the Lukan account described a conspiracy in which the Sanhedrin twisted the facts to present Jesus as having claimed to be Christ, a king[225]. Previously, Spitta noted that the second session of the Sanhedrin hearing in Mk and Mt was completely lacking in content[226]. But for the nocturnal session, Mark and Matthew refer in many ways to the trial which Luke recorded as occurring in the morning[227]. The whole of the difference of the legal proceedings between Lk on the one hand, and Mk and Mt on the other, was predicated on the presentation of Jesus, that the divine sonship proclaimed in Mk and Mt had taken on a physical dimension in Lk[228].

Spitta concluded his investigation by saying that of the three canonical Gospels the third could readily be the most recent, if one supposed its author inserted the supplements into the GS from the Mk-Mt tradition which he borrowed from canonical Mk[229]. But Spitta considered that as now having been proven improbable[230]. Because it was not known how long a time lay between Mrk[1] and its use, not merely by Mrk[2]-Mt, but also by Luke, Spitta entertained the possibility that Lk represented the earliest Synoptic writing[231]. From all this he deduced that Lk and Mk went back to two Greek forms of the GS (Gr^m, Gr^l), which presented differing translations of an Aramaic original. How much one influenced the other in the course of time or how much of its original linguistic hue it lost from manuscript to manuscript can hardly be determined exactly[232].

Although Spitta would concede that some of the material found in Luke 22,54–23,25 was borrowed from Mk, (more specifically Mrk[1])[233], there was a

224. *Ibid.*, p. 414.
225. *Ibid.*, p. 396. Concerning the power of the Sanhedrin to render the death sentence, Spitta wrote: "Dass jener, geschichtlich betrachtet, völlig unhaltbar ist, da die Juden das Recht der Todestrafe unter römischem Regiment nicht besassen (vgl. Joh.18,31), dass aber die spätere Geschichtsdarstellung die ganze Schuld der Beurteilung Jesu den Juden zuzuschieben (vgl. Matth. 27,24; Petrusevangelium), bedarf keiner weiteren Ausführung" (p. 400).
226. *Ibid.*, p. 395.
227. *Ibid.*, p. 396. Cf. p. 400: "Aus alledem ergibt sich, dass schon rein literarkritisch betrachtet der Bericht über die Synedriumsitzung bei Markus-Matthäus der bei Lukas unterlegen ist".
228. *Ibid.*, p. 398.
229. *Ibid.*, p. 498.
230. *Ibid.*, p. 463f.
231. *Ibid.*, p. 498.
232. *Ibid.*, p. 499. See the diagram on this page.
233. This would include aspects of the Sanhedrin trial (22,66-71), πρὸς ἡμᾶς (23,15) and 23,17, although Luke's redactional method reflected a manner in which material had been forcibly inserted in a disturbing manner.

good deal more that was derived from the synoptic GS[234]. Still other material, such as the trial before Herod (23,6-12) was assigned to Luke's supply of independent pericopes. Finally, some material was defined as additions from the hand of Luke himself or a final redactor[235]. Spitta thus considered Lk not only to represent a Greek translation of the Aramaic GS which he supplemented by materials from a variety of sources, but also to be the earliest of the Synoptic Gospels.

Spitta advocated the view that Lk was the earlier and direct descendant of the Synoptic GS and that the parallel in Mt 26,64 betrayed dependence upon Lk 22,69 based on the similarity of the phrases ἀπὸ τοῦ νῦν (22,69) and ἀπ᾿ ἄρτι (Mt v. 64). The counterpart in Mk must have been deleted in the last recension of that Gospel as destructive of the sense[236].

Spitta contended that because Lk descended directly from the Aramaic original, and because it was only slightly influenced by Proto-Mk, it retained the original order. The GS contained a few transpositions of the pericopes which had been modified as a result of abbreviation. The story of the denial of Peter (Lk 22,56-62) stood before the mockery of Jesus by the servants of the high priest and the trial of the Sanhedrin and in Mk both followed it (Mk 14,66-72)[237]. This order suggested that the design of the life picture of Jesus in the GS had been recast[238]. Thus, Spitta deduced that Luke reproduced the original order from the GS while Mark made transpositional changes.

According to Spitta, the trial before Herod (23,6-12) was assigned to Luke's supply of independent pericopes[239]. He was of the opinion that the Herod story

234. *Ibid.*, p. 414. Among the GS material would be the statement that Peter went out and wept bitterly (22,62, with Mk 14,72 being due to the final redaction of Mk), the mockery (vv. 63-65) and elements of the trial before Pilate (23,2.3.13.14.18-24). Spitta's position on the trial of Pilate seemed to reflect a modification, at least in part, of an earlier statement when he indicated that 23,2-5 presented the text of the GS (p. 407).

235. *Ibid.*, p. 409: "Dass V.4f. ganz aus der Hand des Lukas stammt, ist leicht nachzuweisen. V.4 ist unverständlich". Spitta continues: "Übrigens ergibt sich aus ὡς ἀποστρέφοντα τὸν λαόν, dass καὶ τὸν λαόν in V.13 späterer Zusatz ist, von derselben Hand, die in V.4 τοὺς ἀρχιερεῖς καὶ τοὺς ὄχλους geschrieben" (p. 410). Material derived from Luke himself or a later redactor's hand included 23,14 ἐνώπιον ὑμῶν and 23,15 (p. 410).

A final general observation may be offered that Spitta provided valuable insights into the use of the LXX in showing OT parallels to the material, which, in our opinion, often could have served as sources.

236. *Ibid.*, p. 399.

237. *Ibid.*, p. 480-481. Spitta also noted that the information about the betrayer (Luke 22,21f.) followed in Lk upon the words about the Lord's Supper and its completion in the kingdom of God; in Mk 14,18-21 it stood entirely at the beginning of the meal time.

238. *Ibid.*, p. 481; cf. p. 395, where Spitta discussed the variations between the Gospels in the section containing the Peter story and the account of the trial. "Ob man darin ein Stück der synoptischen Grundschrift erkennen kann, davon wird die Beurteilung der Differenz in der Anordnung des ganzen Abschnittes abhängen".

239. *Ibid.*, p. 462. He added that there were no parallels to this pericope in the rest of the Gospel literature.

fit better with the Markan and Matthean accounts than with Lk, and thus its absence from those accounts was highlighted all the more[240]. The omission ("Wegfall") of the pericope was easily explained since Mk and Mt contained details of a similar mockery (Mk 15,16-20 / Mt 27,27-31). Rather than being dependent upon these, Lk 23,11 seemed to be a reflection of Jn 19,1-7. Spitta argued that the Herod episode did not belong to the GS because it was absent from Mk and Mt[241]. It was clear that Spitta had a low opinion of Luke's literary abilities, as for example claiming that 23,4.5 stemmed from Luke's own hand, with the proof being that v. 4 was incomprehensible. Spitta astutely pointed out the connections between 23,13 and 23,3 as well as 23,14 and 23,2[242]. This technique, connecting earlier elements with later ones, however, had often been shown to be characteristic of Lukan redaction.

Spitta focused a great deal of attention on additions to the pericope. The phrase ἐνώπιον ὑμῶν was thought to be an addition by the "letzte Hand". Given the fact that ἐνώπιον did not occur in either Mk or Mt, that it occurred twenty-two times in Lk and a further thirteen times in Acts, and since the term occurred very frequently in the LXX, it would seem to reflect Lukan redaction.

This "later hand" was also claimed to be responsible for καὶ τὸν λαόν (23,13) as well as τοὺς ἀρχιερεῖς καὶ τοὺς ὄχλους[243]. Spitta observed that the people did not play a hostile role in the other Synoptics. Rather, it would appear once again that these phrases reflected Lukan redaction in light of increasing hostilities between the Jewish and Christian communities, as evidenced by the expulsion of Christians from the synagogues.

The whole of v. 15 was considered to be an addition, made necessary by the insertion of the Herod pericope. The phrase πρὸς ἡμᾶς was not a plural of majesty, since previously Pilate always spoke in the singular[244]. It referred to Pilate and the Sanhedrin. Spitta concluded that this derived from the GS, since it was different from the accounts given by Mark and Matthew. It would appear, however, in our opinion, that the term could well betray Lukan redaction.

The interrogation in Mk 15,1-5 gave no indication that the "chief priests, with the scribes and elders, and the whole council" departed from the scene once they delivered Jesus to Pilate. Further, the chief priests were acknowledged as being present (Mk 15,3) for Pilate's questioning (Mk 15,2). Once again Mk did not indicate that the chief priests departed the scene. Rather, they were joined by the crowds (Mk 15,8: καὶ ἀναβὰς ὁ ὄχλος) and the chief priests incited the crowds to riot (Mk 15,11). Luke was quite correct in making explicit what Mark left only

---

240. *Ibid.*, p. 408. Lk 23,8 conflicted with the image of Herod as portrayed in 9,7-9 and 13,31-33. More in line with Herod as presented in 23,8ff. were the accounts in Mk 6,14-16 and Mt 14,1.2.

241. *Ibid.*, p. 409.

242. *Ibid.*, p. 409-410.

243. *Ibid.*, p. 410.

244. *Ibid.* It seemed that here Spitta was taking issue with the interpretation of J. WEISS, *Lukas*, ⁸1892, p. 642.

vague.

Finally, Spitta commented that the repetition of the words of Pilate in 23,16.22 was "dieselbe Methode" as found in the reiteration of Jesus' words in the garden of Gethsemane (22,40.46)[245]. Pilate's triple insistence on the innocence of Jesus, coupled with Pilate's expressed desire not to inflict any punishment more severe than the scourging, boded well with Luke's pro-Roman apologetics and need not be explained away by the carelessness of the evangelist resulting from awkward insertions. Luke, with Mk 14,38 in mind, instructed the disciples in the Gethsemane scene to do as he did, and not simply to sit and wait as instructed in Mk. Addressing the prayer to the Father (22,42) linked the petition of being delivered from temptation with Jesus' teaching the prayer to his disciples (11,4) as well as his teaching the disciples on this point (8,13). Jesus did not suffer the passion alone, but in the company of those who persevered with him through his trials (22,28). Connecting subsequent portions of the Gospel with earlier ones was characteristic of Luke's method, as Holtzmann and Wernle pointed out[246].

---

245. SPITTA, *Grundschrift*, p. 468. Note the typographical error in Spitta's reference to the Herod pericope (22,6-12 [sic]).

246. James Iverach wrote correctly of Spitta's contribution. "But after reading Spitta's work, we have just to say that in our view he has not solved the problem, but has simply added another complexity to this the most complex problem set to the New Testament critic at the present time" (*ExpT* 24 [1912-1913] p. 162).

Gustav Lippert praised Spitta's simple and clear study (*Pilatus als Richter. Eine Untersuchung über seine richterliche Verantwortlichkeit an der Hand der den Evangelien entnommenen amtlichen Aufzeichnung des Verfahrens gegen Jesus*, Vienna, 1923, p. 10). See *Beilage* 1 for Lippert's chart comparing Spitta and Weiss's version of L in 23,1-24 and *Beilage* 2 portraying the Markan and L accounts of Pilate's trial. In another work published the same year as Spitta's, Karl Kastner adhered to the view that Luke was familiar with the story material of both Mk and Mt (*Jesus vor Pilatus. Ein Beitrag zur Leidensgeschichte des Herrn*, Münster, 1912, p. 148). In addition to these sources, he believed Luke had access to at least one other source, but was unable to decide whether it was oral or written (p. 149). To explain some of the discrepancies between the various accounts, Kastner asserted that neither Mk nor Mt present a precise rendition of the events, thus allowing for other events to occur between the scourging and the final judgment. Arguing that the most significant argument against the authenticity of the Herod episode (23,5-15) was its absence from the other Gospels, he saw the story as confirming Pilate's evaluation that Jesus was non-threatening (p. 150; cf. p. 76). Arguing that 23,16 could follow immediately upon 23,4, Kastner cited this as a reason why 23,1-25 was not a free composition of Luke or a fictitious account (p. 149). Although somewhat indecisive, Kastner concluded that the story probably emanated from an oral source, but he did not exclude the possibility that it stemmed from a report referred to in the Prologue by "many" (p. 70). Lippert complimented Kastner's work for containing "sehr reichhaltigen Quellenangaben" (*Pilatus*, p. 7, n. 4). In his opinion, the Markan and L accounts were quite similar and he attributed this to the idea that the authors of both Mk and L were familiar with early accounts of Pilate's trial derived from the oldest Christian community. Lippert trusted the reliability of Lk, since it was based upon eyewitness testimony.

Claude G. MONTEFIORE (1909)[247] critiqued B. Weiss's work as a "thorough investigation" and an "extremely complicated" theory, conjecturing "it is very doubtful whether his conclusions as a whole would stand the test of time"[248]. One specific criticism was that he had perhaps assigned too much to one source[249]. Loisy, in Montefiore's opinion, had not permitted sufficient possibility for other sources which Luke may have used[250]. Though he took notice of Loisy's theory that in the passion Luke used the source of Mk, he offered no evaluation of it as he had done in other cases.

Contrasting Streeter's *The Four Gospels* and Loisy's *L'Évangile selon Luc*, Montefiore ([2]1927) commented they "show us scholarly conservatism on the one hand, and learned skepticism on the other"[251]. Montefiore, in discussing the trial, further demurred from Loisy's view that Luke had no other source than Mk[252]. Montefiore regarded Loisy as having reduced the historical content in Mk and Lk to a minimum[253]. A mediated position between the two scholars would likely hold the key to the solution in his estimation.

But it was for Streeter and Loisy that Montefiore saved his strongest censure, seeing the solution lying somewhere between the extreme positions of these two scholars. Montefiore, himself a Jew, sought to reclaim Jesus for Judaism. He

---

247. *The Synoptic Gospels*, Vol. 2, New York, 1909: *Luke*, 783-1099; Vol. 1, p. lxi-lxii: § 26: "B. Weiss and Loisy on the sources of Luke"; [2]1927 "revised and partly rewritten", p. 360-646; Vol. 1, p. lxxxvi-xciii: § 21. "The Gospel of Luke"; p. xciii-xcvii: § 22. "Streeter and Loisy on Luke". The second edition was reprinted (1968) in the series *Library of Biblical Studies* (ed. H. ORLINSKY), to which L.H. Silberman contributed a prolegomenon and was inserted before Montefiore's Preface (p. 1-18). The Preface to the second edition contained the following: "The first edition of this Commentary was published in 1909, and it has been out of print for many years. The second edition has been carefully revised and considerably changed" (p. vii). Of the scholars who influenced his thought, Montefiore wrote: "In my first edition I quoted most often from Loisy, Wellhausen and Johannes Weiss. In this new edition I still frequently quote from these distinguished scholars (two of whom have now passed away), but I also frequently quote from others whose books and articles have been published since 1908 or 1909. I would especially wish to mention the names of Streeter, Burkitt, and Lake among English scholars, and of Bultmann from Germany. Canon Streeter's *Four Gospels*, on the one side, and Bultmann's *Geschichte der synoptischen Tradition*, upon the other, seem to me the two most important and valuable works upon the gospels which have appeared in the last seventeen years" (p. x).

248. *The Synoptic Gospels*, 1909, Vol. 1, p. lxi, lxii. Cf. [2]1927, p. xciii-xcvii. Montefiore did not refer in these passages from the 1909 edition to which work(s) of B. Weiss he was referring. But in the preface he cited *Quellen*, 1907 and 1908 (p. ix).

249. Vol. 1, 1909, p. lxi. In the second edition, the material on B. Weiss was replaced by material on Streeter in contrast to Loisy ([2]1927, p. xciii-xcvii).

250. Vol. 1, 1909, p. lxii. Whereas in the first edition Loisy's *Les évangiles synoptiques* (1907) was the subject of his analysis, in the second edition, to this work has been added *L'évangile selon Marc* (1912) and *L'évangile selon Luc* (1924) (cf. p. xcv: "*L'évangile de Luc*").

251. *The Synoptic Gospels*, Vol. 1, [2]1927, p. xcv. Loisy, cf. above, p. 135; Streeter, cf. below, p. 181.

252. Vol. 2, 1909, p. 1072; cf. [2]1927, p. 616.

253. Vol. 1, [2]1927, p. xcvi; cf. Vol. 1, 1909, p. lxii.

evaluated Streeter's Proto-Lk as "a very odd sort of 'Gospel': it is, indeed, 'a half-way house,' and a very queer one. One wonders if it really ever did exist. There seems also some reason to doubt whether Luke did not finally use more 'sources' than Streeter's hypothesis would allow, i.e. Mark, Q, and his own early 'notes' (L)"[254]. Montefiore was convinced neither that the passion narrative would derive from that source which contained such accounts as the widow of Nain or the call of Peter, nor that it stemmed from one source. "Criticism will have, I suspect, a good deal to say about Streeter's hypothesis"[255].

Montefiore contended that where Luke strayed from Mark's order "he seems to go wrong"[256]. Montefiore regarded Luke as a compiler, and his sources, rather than being derived from eye-witnesses, are others like himself who "gathered, whether directly or indirectly, what the contemporaries of Jesus had said"[257]. The number and forms of the sources were beyond recovery, but Mk and Q were considered two of the most important written sources employed by Luke[258].

Examining the phenomenon of order in 22,54-71 he stated that Luke was responsible for the change in order where Peter's denial was moved ahead of the Sanhedrin trial[259]. For 22,54.55 Luke adopted either another tradition or he himself was responsible for the changes over against Mk[260]. Peter's denial (22,56-62) was ascribed either to "a special source (B. Weiss) or to the use of Mark's source (Loisy)"[261].

The mockery (vv. 63-65) was a combination of "touches" from Mk and Mt. Luke was responsible for placing the incident here[262]. Subsequently in the second edition, though drawing no firm conclusion himself, Montefiore raised three possibilities for the lack of clarity in this perciope: 1) that Luke erred in redacting his Markan source; 2) that Luke combined two sources; 3) that the confusion stemmed from L or Proto-Lk. But the third explanation would not suffice because Streeter assigned vv. 54-62 to Mk[263].

---

254. Vol. 1, ²1927, p. xciv.

255. Vol. 1, ²1927, p. xcv.

256. Vol. 2, 1909, p. 845: "As a matter of fact he mainly follows Mark, and when he deviates from Mark, he seems to go wrong. But right order to the Evangelist may have meant a right logical order, or one in which each event and saying is given its suitable place". In the second edition he added that Luke's deviations from Mk's order reflected literary form, rather than signifying chronological order (Vol. 2, ²1927, p. 362).

257. Vol. 2, 1909, p. 845; Vol. 2, ²1927, p. 361, where he also added: "It is not likely that Luke can have known many, if any, persons who had seen much of Jesus himself".

258. Vol. 1, 1909, p. lx; Vol. 1, ²1927, p. lxxxvi.

259. *Ibid.*

260. Vol. 2, 1909, p. 1068; ²1927, p. 611.

261. Vol. 2, 1909, p. 1069; ²1927, p. 612, where he omitted the references to Weiss and Loisy.

262. Vol. 2, 1909, p. 1069; (= ²1927, p. 613).

263. Vol. 2, ²1927, p. 613. Cf. STREETER, *The Four Gospels*, p. 222.

The use of a source for the Sanhedrin trial (22,66-71) was highly probable[264]. Noting that some scholars believed that 22,67.68 stemmed from "some more authentic tradition", Montefiore recalled Brandt's solution as the more probable, that Luke redacted Jer 38,15 LXX[265]. He later clarified that for the trial "it is probable that [Luke] used besides Mark a separate source"[266]. Montefiore proposed that Luke made use of Mk's source which did not contain the nocturnal session of the Sanhedrin[267]. Because Luke's account mentioned only one "trial" (v. 66) and since the Lukan account did not recount that the Sanhedrin were permitted "to pass any formal verdict", Montefiore held that this was more historic. The assembly of the Sanhedrin was not considered a genuine trial[268].

Concerning the guilt of the Jews and Pilate as described in 23,1-5, Montefiore wrote: "Though [Luke's] account may depend upon another source as well as upon Mark, what he gives us shows that the source cannot be too much relied on for accuracy"[269]. The position of B. Weiss that v. 3 was an insertion from Mk was mentioned[270].

At 23,18 Luke inserted the Markan account of the Barabbas incident[271]. Luke's decision to pass over the mockery by the Roman soldiers was possibly motivated by his choice to use elements of it in the Herod pericope and to improve the portrayal of the Romans[272].

Though Montefiore stated Luke most probably did not know Mt[273], he allowed that the MA in 22,62 was probably inserted from Mt 26,75, acknowledging that the insertion was "an excellent one"[274]. After rehearsing

---

264. Vol. 2, 1909, p. 1070-1071: "Does his version rest upon a separate, or at all events, an additional, source? This seems highly probable whether that source be L or no". Though not of "a greater historic value than the traditions which are embedded in Mark", it was used in combination with Mk (Vol. 2, ²1927, p. 614).

Montefiore rejected Bertram's suggestion that the special source omitted the mention of the Temple in the course of the trial (Vol. 2, ²1927, p. 612). Though in the first edition he referred to the omission of the statement about the destruction of the Temple, this was indicated as part of B. Weiss's argumentation in support of his theory (Vol. 2, 1909, p. 1070). It was suppressed because the primitive Christian community, still tightly bound to the cult of the Temple, was offended by the reference.

265. Vol. 2, 1909, p. 1071; cf. Vol. 2, ²1927, p. 614-615: "In Luke, Jesus refuses to say whether he is the Messiah or not. His reply seems characteristic, and perhaps it not only rests upon a separate tradition, but is authentic". He now rejected Brandt's solution, claiming that it "seems rather strained" (p. 615). Brandt, cf. above.

266. Vol. 2, ²1927, p. 614.

267. Ibid., p. 612.

268. Ibid., p. 614-616.

269. Vol. 2, ²1927, p. 617; cf. Vol. 2, 1909, p. 1073.

270. Vol. 2, 1909, p. 1073-1074; cf. Vol. 2, ²1927, p. 618, where specific mention of B. Weiss was omitted.

271. Vol. 2, 1909, p. 1077 (= ²1927, p. 622).

272. Ibid.

273. Vol. 2, ²1927, p. xci, 361; cf. Vol. 2, 1909, p. 845.

274. Ibid., Vol. 2, 1909, p. 1069 (= ²1927, p. 612).

three proposed solutions for the MA in 22,64, no preference was indicated[275]. In the second edition Montefiore followed Streeter in asserting that all three were incorrect. He argued instead that the phrase did not occur in the original Matthean text so that there were two different accounts[276].

Montefiore reasoned that the Herod episode (23,6-16) was drawn from another source[277]. He also offered an evaluation of Verrall's assessment of the Herod episode as historical[278]. Calling M. Dibelius's article on Pilate and Herod "worth reading", Montefiore ([2]1927) subscribed to the view that either the special source or Luke intimated Herod's responsibility in the trial[279].

A.E. Brooke penned an extremely favorable review of Montefiore's second edition on the Synoptic Gospels[280]. "The new edition is as useful and serviceable a guide to the criticism of recent years as the first was to the available literature down to the year 1909. The impartial judgement of Liberal Judaism on recent Gospel criticism makes his two volumes one of the best approaches to the study of the Synoptic Gospels"[281].

James Vernon BARTLET (1911) was persuaded that Luke possessed one special unified source that could account for all non-Markan material[282]. This special source (S) consisted of Q (in oral form until Luke wrote it down) in combination with L which he designated as (S+QL)[283]. This written source, which Luke

---

275. Vol. 2, 1909, p. 1070. The solutions were: 1) oral tradition (B. Weiss), 2) Matthean influence, and 3) Luke assimilated to Mt at an early date.

276. Vol. 2, [2]1927, p. 615. Cf. STREETER, FG, p. 322.

277. MONTEFIORE, Synoptic Gospels, Vol. 2, 1909, p. 1074-1075; [2]1927, 1968, p. 619.

278. Vol. 2, 1909, p. 1075-1076; [2]1927, 1968, p. 620: "Dr. Verrall wrote a most ingenious and subtle article in the Journal of Theological Studies, April, 1909 (p. 321-352), in which he essayed to prove that the entire scene with Herod is strictly historical, if properly understood and properly translated. But that right understanding of Dr. Verrall's, especially of verse 11, is hardly likely to win the permanent approval of scholars". However, Montefiore was skeptical that Herod desired to see Jesus. "This scene [23,6-16] is only found in Luke, and its historical character is dubious. Moreover, the incident has been prepared for by Luke in ix.9, and partly depends upon Herod's desire to see Jesus, which, itself, is unlikely" (p. 619). On Verrall, cf. above.

279. Ibid., Vol. 2, [2]1927, p. 619: "Acts iv.24-29 shows that Psalm ii.1,2 had brought about the belief that Pilate and Herod must have been the kings and rulers about whom the Psalm speaks". He also recommended BERTRAM, Die Leidensgeschichte Jesu, 1922, p. 65, and BULTMANN, Die Geschichte, 1921, p. 165. Cf. 1909, p. 1075.

280. JTS 29 (1927-28) 47-48.

281. Ibid., p. 48.

282. J.V. BARTLET, The Sources of St. Luke's Gospel, in W. SANDAY (ed.), SSP, Oxford, 1911, p. 313-363. Although Bartlet held fast to this idea of a single source, he also yielded to the view that various usage, such as ἐγένετο, may point to "the influence of one or more Jewish-Christian sources" (p. 320).

283. Ibid., p. 314. See also p. 358-360. Luke probably had originally penned S for use in his ministry "as an evangelist or catechist of the oral Gospel", although someone else may have committed the material to writing for Luke (p. 350-351). Bartlet cast a vote in favor of Feine's theory that the special source provided material for the early chapters of Acts as well as the

favored over Mk, also contained news about the passion and was distinguished not only by its style and ideas but also by its contents[284]. The order was determined and the details provided by "a single authoritative informant" whom Bartlet identified as Philip, an "associate of apostles and other personal disciples of Jesus in Jerusalem"[285]. In contrast to Wernle and Hawkins, Bartlet characterized the material as very homogeneous. Such a proposition, he declared, eliminated the need for explaining changes in Lk over against Mk and Q and facilitated understanding otherwise baffling deviations, especially from Mk.

Bartlet stipulated that the order of the passion material in Q was already situated in various contexts without recourse to Markan material[286]. Such arrangement, reflecting the "real historical order", emanated from Philip who served as Luke's special informant[287]. But Luke lightly edited S, mostly out of concern for an "ordered sequence"[288]. Whereas the information available to converts or inquirers in the region where Luke was writing was partial and uncoordinated, Luke sought "to supply one that could appeal to the Greek sense of rational order and development, as belonging to genuine history"[289].

Bartlet, like Allen in the same volume, regarded the Hebraisms as a result of the influence of the LXX: "[Luke] consciously writes his Gospel on the lines of the Greek Bible"[290]. Bartlet further likened his position to that of V.H. Stanton who argued that Luke utilized an expanded Palestinian Q but differed on the point at which Q was written down and the spartan passages containing details about the passion added by Luke[291].

Gospel [p. 353; cf. p. 362, conclusion (c)]. "In other words, we can best conceive S as *the tradition collected in a single Judaeo-Christian mind*, embodying the common Apostolic tradition (Q) along with other elements peculiar to its own personal information, and as probably written down by Luke himself more or less in the language of this 'minister of the word', as he responded to Luke's special inquiries (Lk i.2f). Thus S was a peculiar form of written memoirs elicited by our Third Evangelist *ad hoc*, not immediately for the literary purpose to which he finally put it, but rather as a permanent record of the most authentic tradition to which it had been his lot to obtain access, for use in his own work as an evangelist or catechist of the oral Gospel" (p. 350-351).

284. *Ibid.*, p. 315; cf. p. 333: "But if Q contained any part of the Passion story, it must have contained it all in outline, seeing that it hangs together. This is borne out by positive evidence elsewhere". See also p. 335.

285. *Ibid.*, p. 352. Cf. Acts 6,1-6. Bartlet suggested further that Philip obtains additional information through John the Apostle. Bartlet credited Philip as the source of the detail that Peter and John were the two disciples whom Jesus sent to prepare the Passover (Lk 22,8) as well as the information that John had been sent to inspect Philip's work in Samaria (Acts 8,14f.). Later in the article, Bartlet qualified Philip as "one who had been perhaps in part an eyewitness, but at any rate an early associate of eyewitnesses" (p. 356).

286. *Ibid.*, p. 335.

287. *Ibid.*, p. 336.

288. *Ibid.*, p. 354.

289. *Ibid.*, p. 355-356.

290. *Ibid.*, p. 317.

291. *Ibid.*, p. 358-359; cf. p. 335: "All this points to Q as in some form including the

H. Latimer Jackson was critical of Bartlet, expressing doubt and irritation: doubt that the proposal would stand up under close scrutiny by other scholars, and irritation at the manner in which Bartlet employed the symbol Q[292]. Latimer Jackson was not convinced by Bartlet that the Prologue did not refer to written source documents.

Charles Cutler TORREY (1912) advocated the view that Luke made use of Aramaic originals as sources for his Gospel as he called attention to a "favorite theory in recent years that the compiler of the Third Gospel deliberately imitated the language of the Greek Old Testament, in order to give his narrative the flavor of the sacred books"[293]. Regrettably, he did not identify those scholars whose view he disputed. He dismissed this belief because, in his opinion, this method "falls far short of accounting for the facts. No theory of imitation is tenable; unconscious imitation could not possibly produce anything like what we have, and the deliberate effort could serve no end worthy of an author who was writing seriously and with high purpose"[294].

Though the Gospel was originally compiled in Greek, "most of its sources were at least ultimately Semitic, and there is good reason to believe that a very considerable and important part of the material actually lay before the compiler (Luke) in the form of Aramaic and Hebrew documents"[295]. The majority of this material, in Torrey's estimation, would have been published only shortly before Luke compiled his Gospel[296].

Torrey acknowledged that both Mk and Q were Luke's main sources[297]. He

Passion story, so full of sayings bearing on Jesus the Messiah and His Mission. When, however, we add the striking diversity of Luke's order both in chapter xxii and in the whole Passion story, it is most probable that his Q matter had already taken its place in the contexts in which it actually occurs in his pages, i.e. without reference to the Marcan narrative".

292. H.L. JACKSON, *Review: W. SANDAY (ed.), SSP, 1911*, in *JTS* 13 (1911-12) 112. Cf. above, n. 54, regarding Bacon's critique of Bartlet.

293. *The Translations Made from the Original Aramaic Gospels*, in D.G. LYON and G.F. MOORE (eds.), *Studies in the History of Religions Presented to Crawford Howell Toy*, New York, 1912, 269-317, p. 286.

294. *Ibid.*, p. 288.

295. *Ibid.*; cf. p. 289: "But among the 'many gospels' and briefer compositions which formed the earliest group of writings dealing with the Prophet of Nazareth and his teachings it is altogether likely that some few would have been written in Hebrew".

296. *Ibid.*, p. 290.

297. *Ibid.*, p. 296. Consider the following comment on the superior value of Lk: "It seems plain that Luke took it for granted that Mark and Matthew would continue in circulation side by side with his own Gospel. If he had not believed this, he would certainly not have omitted so much of Mark's material. He criticised what lay before him, to the best of his ability, aiming to cancel variant accounts of the same occurrence, to omit disturbing elements, to improve the arrangement of the matter, and to revise and expand where such revision seemed to be needed. Then, with the addition of all the new material which he had collected, he built up a Gospel which must have seemed to him far superior to the others" (p. 307).

had great confidence in Luke's ability to uncover original Semitic sources[298]. The evangelist possessed not only a Greek version of Mk, but also an Aramaic. These were supplemented by material drawn from some of the "many" gospels referred to in 1,1[299]. Luke also had access to Mt. Whereas Matthew had greatly changed the Markan order, such was not the case with Luke[300]. Luke's redaction included expanding, embellishing and omitting material, thus employing and changing his sources with great freedom.

As to the material peculiar to Lk, Torrey argued that this was translation of Semitic originals[301]. In selecting and compiling material Luke would have valued Semitic documents more highly than Greek. With regard to Greek recensions, "translation-Greek would be given the preference, other things being equal"[302]. The determination of what precisely stemmed from the evangelist was sometimes difficult in cases where Luke employed Mk or Q in the double tradition[303]. Torrey judged that the method Luke apparently was using in the first two chapters of the Gospel extended throughout the entire work[304].

Torrey continued to promote his theory in subsequent studies. In an investigation of the date and composition of Acts (1916) he reiterated his belief that Luke made use of "*Palestinian sources* in their original Semitic form"[305]. Later

---

298. *Ibid.*, p. 297: "An evangelist who really took his task seriously, who knew that there were many accounts of Jesus and wished to compile the best possible one, who thought it worth his while to look for the most authentic material, could not fail at least to become aware of the existence of these original documents. Luke was such an evangelist, and was also one who (as we now know) did actually collect and translate Semitic sources".

299. *Ibid.*, p. 297-298.

300. *Ibid.*, p. 302.

301. *Ibid.*, p. 306: "In Luke's Gospel, it is certainly the case that at least considerable portions of the new material are translations from Semitic originals. Through how many hands they may have passed, we do not know. Where the form of words is plainly Luke's own, it may be the case either that he himself is translating, or that he is revising a rendering made by some one else. If in any instance it happens that the marks of his own hand are abundant while at the same time the rendering is so close as to be noticeably awkward, the presumption strongly favors the conclusion that he himself was the translator". See further, p. 317: "In general, the evidence is striking that where Luke goes his own way he is usually closely following written documents, mostly Aramaic".

302. *Ibid.*, p. 306-307.

303. *Ibid.*, p. 308.

304. *Ibid.*, p. 309: "Luke is translating: there is no other theory equally plausible. He has done throughout his whole Gospel what we found him doing in the first two chapters. It was his purpose to base all his work on 'authentic' original documents. He searched out the native (i.e. Semitic) material and translated the greater part of it himself. In his renderings of the new material he seems usually to have followed the original quite closely, though he may have used to some extent translations made by others who are unknown to us".

305. C.C. TORREY, *The Composition and Date of Acts* (HTS, 1), Cambridge, 1916, p. 68: "Now the all-important feature of Luke's own labors in compiling his Gospel history (see my *Translations made from the Original Aramaic Gospels*, p. 288-297) was the searching out and employing of 'authentic' documents, that is, of *Palestinian sources* in their original Semitic form.

(1919), responding to criticism which had been leveled against his 1916 study, he again emphasized Luke's role as mainly a translator[306]. Luke, then, was a translator and compiler who neither added nor adapted anything of real significance. Torrey also made a clarification of his 1912 essay. "I should modify now some things which I said in my *Translations Made from the Original Aramaic Gospels*. I was not then so sure as I am now that Luke used only Semitic sources in compiling his Gospel"[307]. Torrey believed that his early dating of the Gospel prevented many from accepting his theory[308]. The Gospel was still dated at 60 AD as he had originally proposed in his 1912 essay, and Acts was assigned a date of 50 AD and Acts II 64 AD. As for work still to be done, Torrey announced, "the language of the Synoptic Gospels has not yet been adequately examined from the Semitic side. Wellhausen and Dalman have gone but a short distance leaving the main work still to be done"[309]. Finally, the importance of Luke's own language and style was underscored as signalling either translation or free composition[310].

The collection of such material could only be made in Palestine, and would necessarily occupy considerable time. It is certainly a striking coincidence, that a few years before the date which has seemed most probable for the composition of Acts, Luke should have made an extended stay in Palestine. It is a conjecture which is more than merely plausible, that during the two years (24, 27) of Paul's imprisonment at Caesarea Luke was collecting, examining, and translating the materials for his Gospel. We may then venture the conclusion, that the Third Gospel was written before the year 61, probably in the year 60". On Torrey's view of Luke as a compiler who was a competent translator of documents from Hebrew and Aramaic, see also p. 5.

306. *Fact and Fancy in Theories Concerning Acts*, in *AJT* 23 (1919) 61-86; 189-212, p. 62-63: "Professor Foakes Jackson, in an interesting review of my *Composition and Date of Acts*, put his finger on one of these points. He says on page 352: 'That Luke translated this [the Aramaic document of I Acts] with meticulous accuracy, adding nothing of importance of his own and adapting nothing to prove those points which he desired to establish, is, *judging by his use of Mark and Q*, to me at least incredible.' But when the evidence of translation in the Gospels has been mustered (and it has never yet been examined with sufficient care) it will be seen that the activities such as Professor Jackson has in mind nearly all pass out of Luke's hands into those of the author of an Aramaic Third Gospel. Luke's own work there is almost solely that of translator, and its characteristic features are precisely those which appear in his rendering of I Acts". Cf. F.J. FOAKES JACKSON, *Professor C.C. Torrey on the Acts*, in *HTR* 10 (1917) 352-361.

307. TORREY, *Fact*, p. 210, n. 2.

308. *Ibid.*, p. 192-193: "The *one* weighty consideration which will seem to many to forbid accepting my conclusion is the generally accepted view of the origin and date of the Synoptic Gospels. This is no difficulty for me, for I have long been convinced, apart from any investigation of Acts, that these Gospels are of much earlier date than has been supposed, and that they are all three close renderings, without any considerable change, from Semitic originals".

309. *Ibid.*, p. 194, n. 1. See a similar statement in *Fact*, 1919, p. 63.

310. *Ibid.*, p. 210: "It is also the rule in the oriental profane literature, of whatever sort or language. *Wherever*, in the Gospel or Acts, Luke's own vocabulary and style appear, Luke is either translating or composing freely. And if in the Gospel, for instance, Luke's own characteristic forms of speech are seen to be mingled with unmistakable material from Mark or Matthew, the explanation, barring the possibility of later harmonizing hands, is that his own rendering was colored by sight or memory of the other Gospels. Language and style have always been, and will always continue to be, among the very best of criteria. A man may easily change

Torrey (1936) conceived of Lk as being a collection of Semitic documents gathered during Luke's imprisonment at Caesarea (Acts 24,27), at which time Luke organized and then translated them into Greek[311]. Luke had access to the Greek version of both Mt and Mk[312]. Torrey rejected Wellhausen's supposition that Luke employed later Greek documents, while presupposing "an Aramaic Urmarkus". Instead, Torrey believed Luke used of a written Aramaic *Grundlage* "in every part of the Gospel". Thus, Lk exhibited traits of being a translation[313].

Henry J. CADBURY (1920) had reacted negatively to C.C. Torrey's proposal that Luke "translated written Semitic sources"[314]. What was more, a chief complaint was that those who reviewed the work had not examined Torrey's evidence. Luke's use of Mk and Q suggested that Luke employed only "one or at most two sources at a time", rather than the simultaneous use of many sources[315]. What Torrey regarded as translations of Semitic originals, Cadbury considered to be "due to the extensive influence of the LXX"[316]. His well summarized position effectively dismissed Torrey's contention: "According to the alternative hypothesis here commended, Luke took over his material from sources which so far as they were written in Greek, he recast all his material in his own style, but varied the style to suit the situation, and in particular in the case of lyric passages, dialogue, and public addresses he put into the lips of Jews something of the Semitic idiom which was known to him from the Greek Old Testament"[317].

Edgar J. GOODSPEED (1937) vigorously opposed the notion that an Aramaic original lay behind the Gospels, a position he viewed as espousing "erratic views", citing numerous methodological deficiencies[318]. He included Torrey and Streeter

his opinions, or his chief interests, from time to time; his language and literary habits are not so readily altered or concealed". Cf. *Translations*, 1912, p. 306, where Torrey maintained Luke's vocabulary indicated either the evangelist's translation either of the original or of someone else's version. At that time there seemed to be no consideration of the possibility that Luke could freely compose as he now suggested.

311. C.C. TORREY, *Our Translated Gospels. Some of the Evidence*, London, [1936], p. ix.

312. *Ibid.*, p. lii.

313. *Ibid.*, p. lix. Cf. WELLHAUSEN, *Das Evangelium Lucae*, p. 11, also his *Einleitung*, p. 79. Cf. above.

314. *Luke - Translator or Author?*, in *AJT* 24 (1920) 436-455. Cf. TORREY, *Facts and Fancy*, as well as his earlier works: *Translations*, 1912, and *The Composition and Date of Acts*, 1916.

315. *Luke - Translator or Author?*, p. 442.

316. *Ibid.*, p. 452.

317. *Ibid.*, p. 455.

318. *New Chapters in New Testament Study*, New York, 1937, p. 156-157. Of special interest is chapter 6, *The Original Language of the New Testament*, p. 127-168. Goodspeed observed that this position recurs in NT study from time to time and referred the reader to D.W. RIDDLE, *The Aramaic Gospels and the Synoptic Problem*, in *JBL* 54 (1935) 121-138, esp. 127, for a historical review of this idea (p. 143-144). Goodspeed made no reference to Feine or Spitta.

among those who belonged to the "Aramaic school of Gospel origins"³¹⁹.
Goodspeed remained undaunted and steadfast in defense of the view that the
Gospels were originally composed in Greek³²⁰. One of the most serious defects
of those who supported the idea of Aramaic originals, was that the translator drew
from a thesaurus of various Semitic roots and forms which sometimes antedated
the text by hundreds of years³²¹. More than that, proponents of such originals
failed to provide a list "of Aramaic works created in Palestine in the first half of
the first century. There is no record of any written composition in Aramaic at that
time"³²².

W.F. HOWARD (1929) referred to Torrey's "brilliant work [1916]" on the
composition of Acts³²³. In his treatment of Semitisms in the New Testament he
provided insights on some elements of Lukan composition. Based on the research
of Kieckers, he noted that the verb more frequently occurred in the initial or end
position in Lk while Mk showed a propensity for placing it in the middle³²⁴.
Howard commented on the us of the imperfect of εἰμί with the present participle,
as is found in 23,8: "The most important results from an analysis of these data are
Mt's almost complete avoidance of this locution when following Mark's narrative,
Luke's rejection of it in every instance where a Marcan parallel allows comparison,
and yet the freedom with which it occurs in the Lucan writings"³²⁵. A redundant
use of the participle, ἀναστάς or ἐγερθείς followed by a verb of motion (23,1)
suggested a "Semitic flavor"³²⁶. The redundant auxiliary verb as a characteristic
of Hebrew and Aramaic was also cited in 23,2³²⁷. On the use of the future for
the imperative he cited ἔσται (23,11 so Mk 9,35)³²⁸. A final example was the
dative of agent following a passive participle, which Howard considered to be
"perfectly good Greek"³²⁹.

319. *Ibid.*, p. 141, 158.
320. *Ibid.*, p. 164.
321. *Ibid.*
322. *Ibid.*, p. 165.
323. J.H. MOULTON and W.F. HOWARD, *A Grammar of the New Testament*. Vol. 2.
Accidence and Word-Formation with an Appendix on Semitisms in the New Testament, Edinburgh,
p. vi. Howard supplied the appendix, *Semitisms in the New Testament*, p. 411-485.
324. *Semitisms*, p. 417-418. Cf. E. KIECKERS, *Die Stellung des Verbs im Griechischen und
in den verwandten Sprachen* (Untersuchungen zur indogermanischer Sprach- und Kulturwissenschaft, 2), Strassburg, 1911.
325. *Ibid.*, p. 452. He continued: "It is so often introduced by Luke when absent from the
Marcan source that one hesitates to suggest its frequency in cc. 1,2, in 'Proto-Luke,' and in Ac
1–12 as evidence of fidelity to Aramaic originals". (Lagrange *S. Luc.* p. cv, observes that most
of the examples in the Gospel accord with Greek usage).
326. *Ibid.*, p. 453. See also his reference to ἀρξάμενος (23,5) when treating participles (p.
454).
327. *Ibid.*, p. 455.
328. *Ibid.*, p. 458; cf. LAGRANGE, *S. Matthieu*, p. xcv.
329. *Ibid.*, p. 459: "The one NT example is 23,15 ἐστὶν πεπραγμένον αὐτῷ. It is not easy

Later Howard (1939) was non-committal regarding Torrey's theory that an Aramaic source lay behind Acts 1-15. However, he stipulated that occasionally in the later chapters, the language was reminiscent of the LXX[330].

Walther HAUPT (1913) wondered whether Spitta was correct concerning the Lukan passion narrative[331]. He was of the opinion that Luke favored the L version of the passion narrative over Mk, so much so, that in this section of the Gospel Luke "sich hier nur noch lediglich an G und L hält"[332]. Haupt conceived of Luke as a historian (as opposed to Matthew the theologian) who carefully preserved and relayed the contents of his sources[333]. But Luke had not simply reproduced that material. Rather, he himself was responsible for redacting his three sources (Mk, Q and L) with his own thoughts which cast on the materials an Ebionite hue[334].

The material in 23,4-19 appeared to admit of no Markan material[335]. Even 23,3 was attributed to the synoptic GS report, rather than Mk. Although Haupt acknowledged that Lk 23,10 would seem to have derived from Mk 15,3, he instead argued that it more probably stemmed from L[336]. B. Weiss proposed that 23,10 was a Markan reminiscence inserted by Luke[337]. Luke was credited with 23,8-10

to see why Lk should have preserved the Roman procurator's statement in Aramaised Greek. But the numerous examples of the dat. of the agent after a perfect passive given by K-G i. 422 show that it was perfectly good Greek". Cf. R. KÜHNER, *Ausführliche Grammatik der griechischen Sprache*, 4 vols., Third edition by F. BLASS and B. GERTH, Hannover - Leipzig, 1890-1904.

330. W.F. HOWARD, *The Language of the New Testament*, in T.W. MANSON (ed.), *A Companion to the Bible*, Edinburgh - New York, p. 24-25: "But 'nests of Hebraism' (as they have been called) can be found throughout the Gospel [of Luke], and to a much smaller degree Aramaic or Hebrew influence can be traced throughout Acts. Prof. C.C. Torrey would even contend that an Aramaic source lies behind chapters 1-15. Whether this be so or not, from time to time in later chapters phrases recall the language of the LXX". No bibliographical information about Torrey was given.

331. W. HAUPT, *Worte Jesu und Gemeindeüberlieferung. Eine Untersuchung zur Quellengeschichte der Synopse*, Leipzig, 1913, p. 4: "Kann es richtig sein, dass Spitta in der Passionsgeschichte mit Vorliebe grade den lucanischen Sonderbericht in die 'synoptische Grundschrift' versesst, wahrend er von allen drei Synoptikern übereinstimmend gebrachte Berichte aus der gemeinsamen Grundschrift ausschliesst". See Haupt's diagram which contrasted Spitta's theory with his own (p. 6) and where he stated that while he believed Matthew and Luke were dependent upon canonical Mk, they also had recourse to the *Grundschrift*, which had served as a source for Mk.

332. *Ibid.*, p. 230. He defined G as "die Sonderquelle des Mc" (p. 255).

333. *Ibid.*, p. 231; cf. p. 229, 233.

334. *Ibid.*, p. 235: "Es ist also nicht so, dass die ebionitischen Stellen nur in den Q Text hineinredigiert wären, sondern sie finden sich auch in L ja auch in solchen Stellen, die Lc direkt dem Mc Text entnommen hat. Da es nun weuig [sic] wahrscheinlich ist, dass zufällig alle drei Quellen, die Lc gebrauchte, ebionitisch überarbeitet waren, so bleibt nur die Annahme, dass Lc selbst es war, der wo immer sich eine Gelegenheit ihm bot, seine eigenen Gedanken über die Stellung zum irdischen Gut in die Quellen eintrug".

335. *Ibid.*, p. 254.

336. *Ibid.*, p. 142.

337. *Ibid.* Cf. B. WEISS, ⁹1901, p. 661.

(or possibly L).13-15 while L was responsible for 23,11-12.16-19[338].

Presented summarily according to their sources, we find verses attributed to G included 22,54-64.69-71; 23,3.20-23a; those attributed to Luke were 22,65.66-88[sic]68; 23,13-15; those derived from L comprised 23,2.4-7.11-12.16-19.23b-25; those ascribed to G and Lk only 23,1; and 23,8-10 stemmed from either Luke or L[339].

Although Richard HUSBAND (1916) was not directly concerned with the source question in his study of the trial of Jesus, some of his insights were nonetheless quite significant[340]. He argued that Luke's account reflected the accurate course of events as they transpired[341]. Only one Sanhedrin trial occurred, and this on the morning after the arrest. Thus, the Sanhedrin gathered entirely in keeping with the dictate of the law, for a hearing which was only preliminary and not a formal trial[342]. Following the establishment of Judea as a Roman province, the Jewish courts lost the right of jurisdiction in cases of criminal law[343].

Husband maintained that Luke's account reflected "the original form of the story" concerning the events beginning with the arrest of Jesus through the morning session of the Sanhedrin[344]. He regarded the Markan account of Peter's denial to have been an interpolation into the text.

Commenting that the "argument for the genuineness of the [Herod] episode is based merely upon probability", Husband was quick to point out the striking similarity between how Herod and Pilate treated Jesus. The account of Herod stemmed from that of Pilate and was due to confusion in the tradition surrounding who actually had condemned Jesus[345]. One critic praised the work highly as useful and for having considered a wealth of information[346]. P. Parker noted as late as 1962 that Husband's was "probably the most widely used study in English"[347].

Alfred Morris PERRY (1920), following the lead of his mentor, E.D. Burton,

338. HAUPT, *Worte Jesu*, p. 260.
339. *Ibid.*, p. 259-260.
340. R.W. HUSBAND, *The Prosecution of Jesus*, Princeton, NJ, 1916, p. 4.
341. *Ibid.*, p. 205. Unlike many scholarly works of the early twentieth century, Husband provided a useful and rather extensive bibliography of works on the trial of Jesus, from the Roman, Jewish and Christian perspectives. In his preface he confided his methodology and his position. "I soon became convinced that the approach to the study of the trial of Jesus should be made through Roman, and not, as is commonly done, through the Hebrew criminal law. So, naturally, I would reject the current opinion that Jesus was formally tried by the Sanhedrin for an alleged offense against the Hebrew criminal code" (p. iii).
342. *Ibid.*, p. 281.
343. *Ibid.*, p. 280.
344. *Ibid.*, p. 205-206.
345. *Ibid.*, p. 266.
346. ANONYMOUS, in *BS* 74 (1917) 169.
347. P. PARKER, *Trial of Jesus*, in *IDB* 4, p. 697-698, p. 698.

promoted the idea that Luke used two written sources in the passion narrative, one
of which was a Markan Gospel, much like our own[348]. The second written
source, also much like Mk, Perry designated as the "Jerusalem source" since it
detailed events which took place in that city during the final days of Jesus' life[349].
Whatever Markan material appeared in the Lukan passion narrative occurred
simply as insertions[350]. Because both the J document and Mk treated the same
material, overlap was to be expected[351]. Outside the passion narrative, in addition
to the Markan-like Gospel, Luke employed two other sources which were common
to Mt: one containing details about Jesus' ministry in Galilee and the other used
for the Perean section[352]. But these three segments, Galilean (G), Perean (P), and
Jerusalem (J), with the addition of the infancy narratives, did not constitute a
unified source. "It is not possible, then, to connect the Jerusalem document with
any of the other sources of the Third Gospel"[353]. The authorship of the Jerusalem
document, a short Gospel itself, Perry hesitantly assigned to a Jewish Christian
whom he identified as Cleopas in the Emmaus account (24,18)[354]. The document
reflected the situation in Jerusalem at 45 AD and stemmed from that period[355].
Though it was a Greek document, it probably was a translation from the
Aramaic[356]. In choosing between two sources, Luke opted to follow this special

---

348. A.M. PERRY, *The Sources of Luke's Passion-Narrative* (Historical and Linguistic Studies
in Literature Related to the NT, Second Series - Vol. 4, Pt. 2), Chicago, 1920. Diss. Chicago
[n.d.] (dir. E.D. BURTON) p. 6; cf. p. 21.

349. *Ibid.*, p. 30. Perry attempted a reconstruction of the document in Appendix 3, p. 116-
126, and briefly set out the contents of the source at the end Chapter 3 (p. 54) and again at the
end of Chapter 5 (p. 89). Differences should be noted when comparing these two lists. The latter
list enumerated the special source as containing v. 61ab where the earlier list contained only v.
61a. Lk 23,3 was dropped from the later list, presumably yielding to the certainty of Markan
influence. Whereas the list at the conclusion of Chapter 3 contained 23,4-16.18-21.22b-24, the
subsequent list was 23,4-22a.22c-25. This is significant when one recalls that Perry admitted that
vv. 18-19.25a could have stemmed from Mk and seemingly the rest of v. 25 as well (p. 46). If
this is the case, then Perry must further concede either that the J document contained Markan
material or the Markan passion narrative was based upon the Jerusalem document.

350. *Ibid.*, p. 55: "But it must be observed ... that in the latter portion of the Passion-
narrative the groundwork of the narrative is non-Markan and the Markan materials appear in short
interpolations, in which the evangelist would be much more likely to copy the language accurately
than in the reproduction of longer paragraphs". Later, Perry asserted that while Mk and the J
document exhibited extensive similarities, and even though the history "is essentially the same"
as that contained in the final Markan chapters, "there was no close literary relationship" between
Mk and J (p. 101; cf. p. 21).

351. *Ibid.*, p. 29.

352. *Ibid.*, p. 13. Another study directed by Burton in an attempt to establish his solution for
the synoptic problem was D.R. WICKES, *The Sources of Luke's Perean Section* (Historical and
Linguistic Studies, Second Series - Vol. 2, Pt. 2), Chicago, 1912. Cf. PERRY, p. 13, n. 2.

353. PERRY, *Sources*, p. 101.

354. *Ibid.*, p. 91.

355. *Ibid.*, p. 98.

356. *Ibid.*, p. 86, 106.

source rather than Mk because of his interest in history, though he made it his aim to edify his readers. The author gave great attention to proper chronological order[357]. Where Luke was forced to choose between these two concerns, he favored historical reliability.

Luke's redaction technique had previously been to include blocks of Markan material and so he simply continued that practice, albeit with a different source[358]. He remained faithful to the original order primarily out of a historical interest. Rather than conflating source materials, he chose between them. However, Perry seemed to reverse himself when he later stated that Luke "sometimes preserves 'doublets' of the words of Jesus, often closely similar in language, and more frequently presents 'veiled doublets' by preserving the non-Markan version of a story or saying which appears also in Mark"[359]. Perry concurred with Wernle that Luke used great freedom in relating "details of the narrative" but was more conservative when treating the words of Jesus[360]. Some revision was made with a view to improving the language of the sources[361].

Reasons Perry offered to explain why Luke was not dependent upon Mk in the passion account were the variation in order of sections, dissimilarity of language and the addition of new material[362]. Evidence in support of a special source included a unified quality of the material, the use of specially characteristic words and rare synonyms, distinctive style, rhetoric, syntax and language, the last reflecting a stronger Semitic influence than Mk. Finally, the thought and perspective differed from that offered at other points in Lk[363].

Three categories delineated sources for the various materials in the passion narrative. Class I were those materials which were peculiar to Lk. Class II contained those in which there was minimal agreement with Mk. Class III referred to those betraying "fairly close" Markan agreement[364]. This independent source which evinced a sure and certain arrangement included, for our section of the passion narrative, the following verses: 22,*54a*,55-60a,*61a*,62,63-65, *66a*,67-68,70; 23,1-2(3),4-16,18-21,*22b*-24[365]. Italicized verses indicate material where "considerable editorial re-working may have taken place as they now stand"[366]. Analyzing more closely Perry's assessment of the individual pericopes, we found first in the arrest of Jesus and subsequent denial by Peter (22,54-62) that while v. 54a "may be drawn from the Markan document"[367] and v. 54b "agrees closely

---

357. *Ibid.*, p. 5.
358. *Ibid.*, p. 6; cf. p. 12, 19.
359. *Ibid.*, p. 20.
360. *Ibid.*, p. 7-8, 20.
361. *Ibid.*; cf. p. 20, #5.
362. *Ibid.*, p. 105.
363. *Ibid.*, p. 105-106.
364. *Ibid.*, p. 31.
365. *Ibid.*, p. 54.
366. *Ibid.*, p. 54, n. 3.
367. *Ibid.*, p. 43.

with Mk"³⁶⁸, Perry nevertheless decided that v. 54ab was probably from the Jerusalem document³⁶⁹! The mockery (22,63-65) was attributed wholely to "J". Within the Sanhedrin trial (22,66-71), vv. 69, 71 were Markan interpolations and v. 66b was "probably" from Mk, while v. 70 agreed slightly with Mk (Class II)³⁷⁰. Because v. 66a contained a reference to "the priests of the people", Perry suggested this may have served as the introduction to the Jerusalem source. Originally Perry declared vv. 67b-68 to be peculiar to Lk, though in his conclusion he ascribed all of v. 67 to the special source³⁷¹.

Moving now to the events described in Lk 23, v. 3 reflected fairly close agreement with Mk. Verses 1.2 showed slight agreement with Mk. However, the remaining verses, though they contained details parallel with material from Mk, were assigned to the Jerusalem narrative³⁷². In the pericope where Jesus was condemned by Pilate (23,18-25), v. 22b was recognized as a Markan interpolation and vv. 18-19,25a "might easily be supplied from Mk". Finally, v. 25 may be Markan because of likeness of thought, order of expressions and language³⁷³. These elements notwithstanding, Perry attributed the entire pericope to the Jerusalem source, except for τί γὰρ κακὸν ἐποίησεν (23,22b)³⁷⁴.

Perry held that the MAs can be explained as accidents rather than based upon any literary relationship, though Mt 26,75 and 68b showed strong agreement with J (Lk 22,62.64b)³⁷⁵. In addition, Perry listed agreements in non-Markan single words or brief phrases of Mt with 22,67.70³⁷⁶.

368. *Ibid.*, p. 44.
369. *Ibid.*, p. 43-44.
370. *Ibid.*, p. 45.
371. *Ibid.*; cf. p. 54.
372. *Ibid.*, p. 45-46.
373. *Ibid.*, p. 46.
374. *Ibid.* His concluding statement did not take into consideration all the elements he attributed to his Markan source. "This entire section, therefore, with the exception of one phrase, v.22b, may be ascribed to J". Perry also made passing reference to his 1920 study in a later article (*Jesus in Jerusalem. A Note on Chronology*, in *JBL* 43 [1924] p. 19): "Now the importance of this last group of testimony depends upon a theory which I have advanced elsewhere, that in the latter part of chapter 19, in chapter 21, and in most of chapters 22-24, the evangelist drew primarily upon a source independent of Mark and at least the equal of the Second Gospel in historical value. It is noteworthy that of the chronological hints just cited, all but the second stand in close proximity to, and apparently in definite connection with, these non-Markan materials, and therefore ought not to be dismissed as purely editorial expansions of Mark by Luke". He continued, "... to sum up: each of the three great sources for this period of Jesus' ministry – Mark, the source of the Great Interpolation in Luke, and Luke's special passion source – bears testimony, both in its narrative, and in words of Jesus which it records, to a more or less extended period of teaching by Jesus in Jerusalem".
375. *Sources*, p. 102. Cf. Appendix I, VII: A and B, p. 108.
376. *Ibid.*, p. 108. The agreements consisted of εἶπον ἡμῖν (v. 67) and τοῦ θεοῦ (v. 70). In a yet later work, Perry contended that most of the MAs were inconsequential (*The Growth of the Gospels*, Nashville, TN, 1951, p. 63). Though not treating our two specifically, a great number concurred simply by accident. Some few were due to textual corruption, while "many ...

The total vocabulary of the J materials was determined in the dissertation to be 582 words[377]. Eliminating more than one third which are "fairly common in the New Testament", greatly reduces the field. Among the more distinctive aspects of the Jerusalem document, according to Perry, was a unique vocabulary numbering 251 words. When Perry's total list was compared to a concordance of the LXX, 53 significant words did not occur, while another 65 words were not included either because they were insignificant and generally did not appear in concordance lists (καί, ἐκ, γάρ), or because the particular form as listed by Perry was not found in the concordance[378]. These exclusions notwithstanding, there was still a total of 464 words or almost 80% of the supposed J vocabulary which are found in the LXX and consequently what was suspected to be the Jerusalem document may very well reflect Septuagintal influence. Of the 36 words Perry designated as "especially characteristic of J"[379], only six did not occur in the Septuagint[380]. Four of these occurred in Josephus, in addition to Greek authors. One of the terms, σταυρόω (23,21.23.33), appeared in classical Greek literature (Polybius), Scripture (Esther 7,9; 8,12), and Jewish Hellenistic writings (Josephus).

The literary style of the J materials was characterized by precise as well as descriptive details[381], repetition of like phrases[382], the arrangement of events in groups of threes[383], and an accurate and believable description of persons and

---

disappear in light of other textual readings". In this last explanation he followed the suggestion of Streeter. But Perry rejected Proto-Mk as a way of explaining the differences, arguing that Luke used a form of Mk virtually as we have it.

377. *Sources*, p. 56. Cf. Appendix II, p. 110-115. This list should be compared with those of B. Weiss and Easton.

378. G. MORRISH, *A Concordance of the Septuagint*, London, 1887; Grand Rapids, MI, R1980. One of the difficulties with Perry's list of 251 words was that he did not designate the words to which he is referring.

379. PERRY, *Sources*, Appendix II, p. 110.

380. Each of the thirty-six words was compared with *HR*. One discovers that most of these terms occurred in the LXX. The following is worth noting: "In the Greek world to which the early Christian writings belong there were not only gentile literary men, but Jewish authors as well; this fact militates against the unity of later Greek literature at a point that is important for its understanding. We are incomparably better informed concerning the language of Hellenistic Judaism than we are about its gentile counterpart ... It is all too easy to yield to the inclination to assume that Jewish influence is present, when, in reality, a typical Greek sentiment may be expressed in a Jewish Greek source" (Introduction, *BAGD*, 1975, p. xxi-xxii).

381. *Sources*, p. 62-63. The indefinite reference of "a little later" (22,58), Peter sitting by the fire (22,56), the Lord glancing at Peter (22,61) and Pilate and Herod becoming friends (23,12) were some of the characteristics assigned to J.

382. *Ibid.*, p. 63. Perry cited the interrogation of Jesus (22,67.70) and the portrayal of Barabbas (23,19.25) in support of his view.

383. *Ibid.*, p. 64. Examples were the three denials of Peter (22,55-60) and Pilate's threefold defense of Jesus (23,14-16.20.22). But Perry conceded that the Evangelist may have been responsible for the triple condemnation of Jesus (23,24-25).

their dialogue[384]. Concerning syntax, while periphrastic construction was rare in the Lukan writings, it was even more so in J. Here Perry cited 23,19 as an example. The use of pronouns expressing the dative of agent used in conjunction with passive verbs was "somewhat frequent, proportionately". J exhibited a predilection for terms meaning past, present and future. Finally, the article was used extensively in a variety of situations[385].

Perry viewed Luke as keeping strictly to the order of his source, the sole exception being when he regarded the order as faulty[386]. In examining Luke's attention to Markan order, however, Perry noted that Luke presented three sections out of thirty-eight in an order different from Mk, and thus showed that Luke can and did transpose Markan source material[387]. He further observed that as Luke was editing, he also transposed details within narratives[388]. Such evidence can explain changes in the order of words and pericopes. Nonetheless, Perry later concluded that Luke was not responsible for any variation in the sequence of events[389]. Declaring that in the passion narrative "transpositions are numerous and important"[390], Perry counted four significant changes of order and seven smaller ones which must be explained by means other than Luke's literary method, i.e. the Jerusalem document[391].

Perry argued that the J document shone through the Lukan passion narrative and reflected Jewish perspectives even where it did not really seem to[392]. The relative exoneration of Pilate (23,4.14.22), when contrasted with the guilt and responsibility cast upon the Jewish authorities, was just such a case. It should not be overlooked, however, that earlier Perry noted that the hostility on the part of the Jewish leaders was not assumed to be "peculiar to J"[393].

Perry maintained that such a document would have been preserved in the midst of the persecution directed by Herod Agrippa I in order that the dispersed community, bereft of leaders, could preserve cherished traditions[394]. It served the purpose of describing the death and resurrection of Jesus from apologetic and

---

384. *Ibid*. While the charges made against Jesus dealt with Jewish issues in the presence of the Sanhedrin (22,66.70), they were reformulated before Pilate to stress their political content (23,2.5).

385. *Ibid*., p. 65-66.

386. *Ibid*., p. 5.

387. *Ibid*., p. 6. All three instances (3,19-20; 6,12-16; 8,19-21) preceded Lk 19,1.

388. *Ibid*., p. 17.

389. *Ibid*., p. 24.

390. *Ibid*.

391. *Ibid*., p. 24-25. Cf. Appendix I, V: B, p. 107.

392. *Ibid*., p. 90.

393. *Ibid*. Cf. p. 74, n. 1: "This notion [of the hostility of the Jewish authorities], however, appears in the editorial section of Luke's Passion-narrative (20:1,19,20,26; 22:2,5,52,66) and in the Markan version as well. It cannot, therefore, be supposed peculiar to J". Quite correct, for it appears that it could well derive from Mk and/or from Luke's redaction in light of the circumstances affecting the community for whom he is writing.

394. *Ibid*., p. 98.

parenetic vantage points, with the main focus being Jesus as the Messiah[395].
Perry dismissed Feine's suggestion of Pauline influence noting that there was
"none of the Pauline interest in [Jesus] as savior from sin"[396].

Although Perry agreed with Burkitt's basic contention that Luke employed a
non-Markan source for his passion narrative[397], he nonetheless rejected Burkitt's
view that it was embedded in the Q material, aligning himself with Stanton and
Weizsäcker in arguing that Luke would not have intricately interwoven materials
from a variety of sources[398]. And yet, that is the impression one is left with at
the conclusion of Perry's study. He regarded the J document as a single, but
unified, independent source for the account of the passion of Jesus, unrelated to
any of the other sources employed by Luke.

One matter not adequately addressed by Perry was that even though Matthew
shared two special sources (G and P) in common with Luke, why Matthew either
1) did not have access to the J document, or 2) why he did not opt to use it like
Luke. Perry was of the opinion that Luke discarded Mk in favor of another
document, itself very much like Mk, because it reflected the more historically
accurate description of the events which transpired in the course of the passion.
Perry opposed the view that the Lukan passion narrative was a correction of the
Markan. And yet in discussing the relation of the special source to Mk, he wrote:

> In spite of these diversities, however, it should be noted that there are extensive
> resemblances. The historicity related in the Jerusalem document is essentially the
> same as that in the closing chapters of Mk; the majority of the events are the same
> (including even events as little necessary to the course of the narrative as the
> prayer in the garden, Peter's denial, and the mocking of Jesus), and they are
> narrated in essentially the same order, although there are transpositions as great
> as the necessary sequence of events will permit. The explanation of the
> agreements, however, cannot be literary, but will be found rather in the
> supposition that both go back to the common apostolic tradition, if not to the very
> events which they describe[399].

395. *Ibid.*, p. 95. Cf. p. 72, 90.

396. *Ibid.*, p. 90.

397. *Ibid.*, p. 2; cf. BURKITT, *Gospel History*, p. 134.

398. *Sources*, p. 11. Cf. V.H. Stanton (1909), p. 227f., and C. Weizsäcker (1864), p. 205f.
Perry seemed to contradict himself noting that, in the Apocalyptic Discourse, Luke in fact
conflated the J document with Markan materials "formed by the interweaving of two documents".
The question may then be asked, if Luke was capable of doing it in one portion of the Gospel,
would he not likely utilize similar redactional techniques in other parts as well (p. 85)? The whole
distinction must rest upon whether the interweaving Luke was supposed to have undertaken is
elaborate or simple. Ten years after the publication of the dissertation Perry published an article
in which he investigated an aspect of Streeter's theory agreeing substantially with Streeter's
finding for that portion of Lk. "With this we conclude the review of Canon Streeter's second
'block of Q;' and the detailed analysis goes to support his conclusion that the materials lay before
the evangelist (even when composing Proto-Luke) as a continuous document ..." (PERRY, *A
Judaeo-Christian Source in Luke*, in *JBL* 49 [1930] 181-194, p. 187).

399. PERRY, *The Sources*, p. 101-102.

As a result of his study, Perry (1920) concluded that verses 23,1.2 showed slight agreement with Mk. The remaining verses, though they contained details parallel with material from Mk, were assigned to the Jerusalem narrative[400].

At the same time as the appearance of Perry's dissertation, Alfred WAUTIER D'AYGALLIERS (1920) published a book treating the sources in Luke's passion narrative[401]. After an impressive bibliography, he offered an introduction followed by a discussion of eight theories which he believed were typical of the approaches to the question of Luke's sources. Next he provided a literary analysis of 19,28–21,38 which he called "récit du ministère à Jerusalem", then of the passion (22–23) followed by an appendix treating the chronology of the events. He focused primarily on the Lukan passion (19,28–23,49), though he noted that other Lukan source-critical studies did not. The final chapter contained his understanding of Luke's use of sources.

The first of the eight theories to which Wautier D'Aygalliers gave attention was that of Theodor Vogel. In the line of Reuss, Vogel advocated Luke's use of

---

400. *Ibid.*, p. 45-46. Burkitt, unpersuaded by Perry's attempt to establish a coherent and consistent narrative, gave the work a cavalier examination, adding "if Mr. Perry's thesis gains a following it will be time to examine it in detail" (*JTS* 22, 1920-21, 69). Burkitt faulted the study for not considering the early Jerusalem document in relation to any documents which might have been used in the early chapters of Acts (p. 70).

Burkitt's negative assessment was directly opposed to that of a review found in *Bibliotheca Sacra* which judged Perry's conclusion "to be fairly well proved" (ANONYMOUS, in *BS* 77 [1920] 239). The benefit of Perry's study was to underscore the theory that the Gospels relied not simply on oral tradition, but also written documents near the time of the events. E.J. GOODSPEED (1937) was convinced by the work of Perry. The special passion source was believed to have contributed, among other passages, 23,5-10.12-15 (*An Introduction to the New Testament*, Chicago, IL, p. 206).

401. *Les sources de récit de la passion chez Luc*, Alençon, 1920 (esp. p. 158-210, 255, 259-262, 268-269). The title page indicated that he held a licentiate in theology. He listed Wernle's *Die synoptische Frage* and Hawkins's *Horae Synopticae* as indispensable tools for the study (p. 3-4). See T. VOGEL, *Zur Charakteristik des Lukas nach Sprache und Stil*, Leipzig, 1897, ²1899. See also R. REUSS, *La Bible*. 1. *Histoire évangelique. Synopse des trois premiers évangiles*, Paris, 1876, who contended that Luke's special material was derived from the oral Aramaic tradition.

Wautier d'Aygalliers also posited three forms of Mk as Wright had done. The fact that Wright earlier set upon the idea of three forms of Mk is not necessarily to assume that Wright had influenced Wautier d'Aygalliers, though the latter listed two books by Wright including *Some New Testament Problems* (1898) and *The Composition of the Four Gospels* (1899).

In an earlier French work, P. GIRODON (1903) asserted that Luke used the text of Mk as we have it (*Commentaire critique et moral sur l'évangile selon saint Luc*, Paris, 1903, p. 18, 19). There was, in addition, oral tradition (p. 18, 19; cf. p. 105), which underlay Mk, the Logia, an Infancy document, a history of Jesus' final sojourn to Jerusalem which may have been oral or written, plus an account of the passion and resurrection. Girodon followed Godet in dividing the account of the passion into three sections: 22,1-46; 22,47-23,46; 23,46-56 (p. 480). As compared with Mk 14,62 and Mt 26,64, Luke offered a clarified form of Jesus' response (p. 510).

Aramaic sources which had been translated into Greek[402]. Wautier D'Aygalliers argued that the majority of critics, and especially Zahn, rejected this perspective. A second typical source theory was that of Godet and Harnack who credited the special material to Mnason (Acts 21,16) and above all Philip the deacon (Acts 21,8-14). It constituted a collection of written memoirs and portrayed a particular local tradition. A third type, represented by F. Blass, sought to promote the idea that the evangelist edited two forms of the Gospel just as he had for Acts. The first edition was composed during Paul's imprisonment in Caesarea and the second at Rome. Blass also supported the idea of a primitive Aramaic writing. Wautier D'Aygalliers stipulated that the two stage compositional process was more likely for Acts than for the Gospel. Resch, Marshall and Hoffmann followed Eichhorn's hypothesis concerning a single Hebrew or Aramaic document[403]. In a similar vein, but approaching the question from a different methodology, was E.A. Abbott who ascribed the Lukan passion account to a special Judaeo-Christian source[404]. A fifth typical hypothesis, working from the Two-Source theory, attempted to demonstrate what stemmed from tradition and what from the redactors. Unfortunately, according to Wautier D'Aygalliers, the results were often subjective and at variance from one another. He contrasted Harnack, Wernle, O. Holtzmann, Hawkins, Wellhausen, Wendt and J. Weiss who did not believe that the passion narrative had any connection to Q ("la source des Discours") on the one hand, with Feine, Soltau, B. Weiss and Spitta who believed that the passion tradition contained some of the words of Jesus[405]. A mediating position to this latter view was adopted by Pfleiderer and Burton who proposed that Luke combined elements of the Jerusalem passion tradition with Q. This position had been further developed by J.V. Bartlet.

A sixth type of approach to sources was characterized by Spitta whose work was described as a "remarquable volume". Luke's use of Mk or a Proto-Mk had been the accepted position to this point. Wautier D'Aygalliers was obviously impressed by Spitta's study since he remarked that he often returned to it in the course of his own research.

B. Weiss reflected a seventh model in which he, as well as Feine, argued in favor of a single source which was responsible for the details particular to Lk. The final typical theory was that of W. Soltau whose "vues originales" were published in various works, and reprised in *Unsere Evangelien, ihre Quellen und ihr Quellenwert*[406]. Soltau put forward the idea that there were two versions of Q,

402. WAUTIER D'AYGALLIERS, *Les sources*, p. 4.

403. *Ibid.*, p. 7. See A. RESCH, *Agrapha*, 1889; *Aussercanonische Paralleltexte zu den Evangelien*, 1897. The first was not listed in his bibliography and the dates of the second title here do not correspond with the dates he listed earlier (p. XVIII). MARSHALL in *Expositor* (1891-93). R.-A. HOFFMANN, *Das Marcusevangelium und seine Quelle*, Königsberg, 1904.

404. *Les sources*, p. 8-9.

405. *Ibid.*, p. 9-10.

406. *Ibid.*, p. 14. See W. SOLTAU, *Unsere Evangelien, ihre Quellen und ihr Quellenwert*, Leipzig, 1901. Other works where he discussed the source theory included *Eine Lücke der*

one which had been used by Matthew (Λ A) and another by Luke (Λ B). Luke's version contained 22,28-32.35-38 and 23,6-16. Although Soltau believed that Luke based his account of the passion upon that of Mk, it had been embellished by a very reliable oral tradition which supplied 19,39-44; 22,17-20.51; 23,27ff.34.39-43.46. Soltau concluded that the theory of one particular source was "absolument injustifiée". It demonstrated instead that Luke exercised great freedom in arranging the Markan material.

Luke's redaction, according to Wautier D'Aygalliers, was considerably complex ("fort complexe"), involving "la réduction des particularités des diverses sources utilisées, la transposition d'épisodes dans des cadres étrangers, l'introduction de fragments nouveaux"[407]. His approach in the passion was described as "un travail de collation et de combinaison autrement compliqué"[408].

The denial of Peter (22,56-62 / Mk 14,66-72) also demonstrated the priority of the Lukan account, as indicated by the order of the denial following upon the arrest. Wautier D'Aygalliers took issue with J. Weiss's idea that the denial stemmed from a source common to Jn since this suggestion did not explain "la rupture de contact avec la tradition johannique dans la suite du récit"[409]. Wautier D'Aygalliers maintained the view that the MA in 22,62 as attributed to a revisor on the basis of the Matthean text was "fort improbable"[410]. Instead, the text of Mk had been modified and Luke and Matthew both used the earlier uncorrected Markan version. Wautier D'Aygalliers's viewpoint was summed up well in the following statement: "Nous croyons pouvoir conclure que Luc a connu le récit primitif qui est à l'origine du récit de Marc, et qu'il en a gardé l'enchaînement"[411]. But Luke was also familiar with the developments Mark made upon the primitive account. While keeping the order found in the primitive account, Luke employed Mk making further corrections out of concern for literary order[412].

In the discussion of the section of the Sanhedrin trial (22,54-55.63-71) Wautier D'Aygalliers noted the differences in order in Lk as compared to the other Synoptics. He also stated that the mistreatment (22,63-65) was found in a more probable order in Lk. Apparently Luke was following an earlier source[413]. Markan influence was detected only in 22,70-71. The absence of the nocturnal session was probably due to its absence from the source[414].

Evangelienforschung, Leipzig, 1899, and *Die Entstehung des ersten Evangeliums*, in *ZNW* 1-2 (1900) 219-248. Wautier D'Aygalliers commented that Soltau's views in these two latter works approximated those of E. Simons (1880).

407. *Les sources*, p. XXVI.
408. *Ibid.*, p. 20. See his table of comparison of the various Synoptic pericopes (p. 101).
409. *Ibid.*, p. 185.
410. *Ibid.*, p. 189.
411. *Ibid.*
412. *Ibid.*, p. 255.
413. *Ibid.*
414. *Ibid.*, p. 260.

Concerning Jesus' words about the Temple, Wautier D'Aygalliers insisted it was difficult to determine whether Jesus said them, but they existed in the primitive tradition and Luke was aware of them as evidenced by their appearance in his account of the martyrdom of Stephen (Acts 6,14)[415]. They did not, however, appear in Luke's source. The other Gospel accounts reflected three stages of development. The details recounted in the Lukan trial were transferred to the nighttime. Wautier D'Aygalliers was convinced that Mk influenced how the trial was recounted, but it was an earlier version of Mk containing an apologetical tendency[416].

The Lukan account of the mocking and beating of Jesus (22,63-65) was regarded as more primitive than that found in the other Synoptics and as was derived from oral tradition though it would be difficult to prove that. Having the members of the Sanhedrin in Mk and Mt serve as the perpetrators was "inconstestablement tendancieux". The originality of the Lukan version was based on the likelihood that this was how events transpired and also on the basis of the "indépendance de tout motif testamentaire"[417]. Wautier D'Aygalliers attributed the MA in v. 64 to oral tradition[418].

The historicity of the blasphemy discourse was treated as "très contestable". Wautier D'Aygalliers concluded that the Markan version did not represent a homogeneous account. The single trial was more primitive while the duplication as found in Mk resulted from the desire to make the Jews responsible, in part, for the death of Jesus.

No eyewitness provided the tradition with information of Jesus' trial before Pilate (23,1-5), which was also described as the Roman trial. Nevertheless, Wautier D'Aygalliers asserted that 23,1-5 represented the primitive text[419]. Mark was believed to have known a source common to Lk which would explain the similarity of Lk 23,3 and Mk 15,2. Apologetics were also at work in 23,1-5. The most important accusation, reflecting the historical situation, was preserved in 23,2. The current apologetic was visible in 23,4 and 23,5 served as a redactional transition.

Wautier D'Aygalliers believed that the Barabbas story was clearly historically improbable. It was pointed out that it was necessary to engage in the historical questions when treating the matter of sources. Wautier D'Aygalliers supported Goguel's view that Pilate did not regard Jesus as a political threat[420]. Mk 15,7 was the inspiration for 23,19. As in the case of many other scholars, v. 17 was seen as a gloss. Because of the verbal similarities between 23,19-22 and Mk 15,7.12-14, Wautier D'Aygalliers rejected the theory of a special Lukan source,

415. *Ibid.*, p. 162-163.
416. *Ibid.*, p. 168.
417. *Ibid.*, p. 169.
418. On the MAs see also p. 246-247.
419. See p. 255, where Wautier D'Aygalliers did not list 23,1-16 in his discussion of Luke's use of Mk though he later ascribed 23,1-3 to Mk[1] (p. 269).
420. *Ibid.*, p. 204. See M. GOGUEL, *Juifs et Romains*, Paris, 1910, p. 15.

noting that even B. Weiss who favored the theory of assigning elements to L in this case recognized these elements as Markan[421]. Mk 15,14 served as the basis for 23,22b. In 23,24.25 Luke was believed to have "dévie nettement" from the Markan parallel. 23,24 was the conclusion of the primitive account[422]. It was apparent that Luke criss-crossed two traditions. The omission of the mockery by the soldiers resulted either from an attempt to spare the Romans or to prepare for the analogous scene found in the Herod episode[423].

Wautier D'Aygalliers was convinced that Luke made use of many sources more than Mk and with much greater freedom and was credited with occasionally transposing material. Luke was considered both an artist and a historian[424]. Luke as well Matthew used a form of Mk different from that preserved in extant manuscripts. Mk was not seen as a homogeneous composition, but rather the result of various redactional stages. Wautier D'Aygalliers proposed at least two forms prior to canonical Mk, all of which he designated as Mk 1, Mk 2 and Mk 3[425]. He hesitated suggesting which form Luke knew. In a view somewhat similar to Soltau, Wautier D'Aygalliers held that Luke employed a second form of the Logia. As for sources Luke used ancient traditions, information parallel to that of Mk and independent material. These traditions had been occasionally superimposed on the more recent accounts including the trial of Jesus. Luke's methodology included combining, collating and redactional improvement of the sources[426]. Wautier D'Aygalliers credited the evangelist with creating some of the material himself, including conclusions of episodes.

Apologetics also helped to amend the early accounts, favoring the Romans and casting the Jewish religious leaders in a disparaging light. Wautier D'Aygalliers concluded that the primitive tradition was fragmentary because in some cases Luke alone possessed particular information. Wautier D'Aygalliers further rejected the suggestions that Lk was Ebionite or Pauline[427].

Wautier D'Aygalliers defined the Herod story as 23,6-16[428]. He rehearsed the numerous suggestions for the origin of the story including the idea that Luke composed the episode. Brandt suggested that the popularity of Herod the Great improved as a result of a comparison with his descendant[429]. Loisy insisted that the story was a doubling of the Markan account where Herod had been substituted for a judgment. Nicolardot and J. Weiss viewed the episode as a redactional and

---

421. *Les sources*, p. 207, n. 2. See also p. 255.
422. *Ibid.*, p. 255.
423. See also p. 266-267.
424. See his comments on this view which have been taken up in recent times by various scholars (p. 264).
425. *Ibid.*, p. 247: "Il faut admettre au moins deux formes antérieures à la forme actuelle". See further p. 249, n. 1.
426. *Ibid.*, p. 248-249. Note his comments on redactional motifs (p. 250).
427. *Ibid.*, p. 265.
428. *Ibid.*, p. 194 (esp. p. 194-202, 261-262).
429. *Ibid.*, p. 194. Cf. W. Brandt (1893), p. 112. See above.

apologetic piece, the purpose of which was to unburden the Romans. Soltau was of the opinion that the story derived from Luke's edition of the Logia (Λ B). Additional motifs had been borrowed from the other Synoptics. B. Weiss favored the idea that the account stemmed from L. Renan envisioned Luke placing two written documents end to end, one containing the Pilate story and the other the Herod pericope portraying them as responsible parties in the death of Jesus[430]. Feine supposed that Luke employed a particular tradition combining it with material drawn from Mk. Streeter and Wright settled on the idea that there was an historical kernel which gave rise to "un développement apocryphe". The source of the information was Manaen (Acts 13,1) or Joanna (Lk 8,3; 24,10).

For Wautier d'Aygalliers one of the most convincing arguments against the idea of a source was the analogous account in Acts 25,14-27 of Paul being sent to Agrippa[431]. Although he was open to the idea that the Gospel account had influenced the one in Acts, he viewed Nicolardot's suggestion of the inverse as being "beaucoup moins probable". Wautier d'Aygalliers concurred with B. Weiss that if there was an historical element in the story it was v. 12. The verses 13-16, containing a redactional note, were an introduction to the Barabbas story which followed. Verse 15 was clearly an addition. Wautier d'Aygalliers rejected J. Weiss's contention that Pilate's phrase in v. 15 was a plural of majesty. Rather, it referred to Pilate in collaboration with the Sanhedrin[432].

Wautier d'Aygalliers reasoned that the Herod episode stemmed from a tradition probably originating in Jerusalem. This tradition was also found in Acts 4,27-28. However, this did not exclude the possibility that Joanna or Manaen were the source of this tradition[433]. In its original form, the information was probably brief. Wautier d'Aygalliers suggested that Herod account appeared in a cycle of tradition which contained no information about the participation of the Sanhedrin in the passion of Jesus. In 23,9b-10 Wautier d'Aygalliers was reminded of Mk 15,3ff. Evidence of the redactor's hand was recognized in 23,13-16 which introduced the Barabbas story.

It was Wautier d'Aygalliers's conviction that Luke had materials from Mk for the Herod episode connecting it with the story which followed. He rejected the suggestion that 23,6-16 was "un développement personnel au rédacteur"[434]. The insertion of the Herod story stemmed from the evangelist's desire to spare the Roman authorities[435]. Lk allowed the reader to recover the original order and detail with the least amount of difficulty.

A useful table was provided at the end of the book to help distinguish his

---

430. *Les sources*, p. 196. See E. RENAN, *Vie de Jésus*, Paris, [n.d.], 1863; Berlin, ⁷1863; New York, ᴿ1974, p. 422. Note Wautier D'Aygalliers's later comment (p. 255).
431. *Les sources*, p. 197.
432. *Ibid.*, p. 201.
433. *Ibid.*
434. *Ibid.*, p. 262.
435. *Ibid.*, p. 267.

perception of the various sources[436]. Verses attributed to M^1 were 23,1-3; M^2 provided 22,54-55.56-60.61b-62.66-69; 23,24; M^3 was responsible for 22,70-71; 23,9-10.18-23.25. Particular sources (P), either stemming from oral tradition or through written documents yielded 22,63-65; 23,4-5a.6-8.11-12. Redaction (R), Luke's revision of received material or that which he himself composed was found in 22,61a; 23,5b.13-16. A final source (S) was not credited with adding any material in this section[437].

Frederick GRANT compared the work of Wautier d'Aygalliers with that of Perry, describing the former as "an equally elaborate investigation"[438]. But the works were nonetheless different because Wautier d'Aygalliers "contents himself with distinguishing non-Marcan source material and redactional additions, confessing in the end that no closer approximation to the state of Lk.'s traditions is possible" rather than positing a single, written non-Markan source[439].

Grant took issue with Wautier d'Aygalliers's disclaimer against subjectivism arguing that it "is simply unavoidable in historical research" and further noted that the French author engaged in it as was apparent in several conclusions[440].

But neither the findings of Perry nor of Wautier d'Aygalliers were convincing to Grant who viewed much of the *Sondergut* as "purely editorial"[441]. In addition, Grant believed it was possible that Luke had access to traditions which were not used by the other Synoptics. In some sense, though, if forced to choose between Perry or Wautier d'Aygalliers, Grant favored Wautier d'Aygalliers's more cautious approach, believing it was not possible to define very precisely the content of the particular traditions[442].

Perry continued to devote some attention to the question of a special source

436. *Ibid.*, p. 268-269.

437. *Ibid.* See p. 248: "Mais ces remarques valent surtout pour la partie du troisième évangile antérieure au récit de la passion, lequel ne fait appel aux *logia* que dans une mesure très restreinte (S)". "But these remarks apply particularly for the part of the Third Gospel before the account of the passion, which only refers to the Logia in a very limited way [S]".

438. *ATR* 5 (1922) 137.

439. *Ibid.*

440. *Ibid.*

441. *Ibid.*, p. 138: "A glance at this table will suggest, what a detailed examination of the text will confirm, that a very large part of Lk.'s *Sondergut* is purely editorial; and that the selection from this of what are supposed to be the vestiges of a written non-Marcan source is a highly speculative business; and that the case is not much much advanced by either of the hypotheses tablulated".

442. *Ibid.*: "And when we come to the Passion, which was doubtless the very earliest subject of primitive Christian tradition ..., it is not unlikely that Lk. knew and used, because he had collected and as far as possible verified, traditions not incorporated in the other synoptics. It is when the attempt is made to define more closely this tradition, to differentiate it from the rest, prove its homogeneity and assign it to a particular document or documents, that we get into difficulties – difficulties which are either insoluble or which each student must solve for himself without guarantee of final certainty and general acceptance".

throughout his career. In 1928 he lamented that Burton had never given a full explanation of his source theory, though he highlighted similarities between Burton and Streeter[443]. Perry's purpose was to show that the Proto-Lk material was used in blocks. He argued, contrary to Burton, that it was possible that Mk had been interpolated into the early source[444]. As to the time and place of origin, the source stemmed from a poor community which may have been in Galilee because there was nothing within the source to indicate that it was associated with Jerusalem. Dating of the primitive source was conjectured following "the first conversions of Samaritans and Gentiles but earlier than Galatians"[445].

More than thirty years after the appearance of his dissertation Perry (1951) still conceded, concerning special sources, that beyond Mk and Q, "there is not sufficient evidence in the Gospels to describe these sources as adequately as the other two"[446]. In light of what has preceded in our study, one must question the truthfulness of Perry's following assertion: "It is generally recognized that in his narrative of the Passion (Luke 22:14–24:53; also 19:37-44; 21:10-38) Luke's relation to Mark is quite altered"[447]. The argument of variation in order served as Perry's chief support as he once again asserted Luke's use of a separate, independent and written source. Reflecting the influence of Hawkins in alluding to "at least twelve" transpositions, Perry himself opened the way to see the transpositions as a redactional technique of Luke when he wrote that the changes in order occurred "wherever the course of events permits"[448]. Nonetheless, some significant additions and a lower verbal agreement (betraying Taylor's mathematical influence?) plus the argument from order, all convinced Perry that Luke employed a written source different from Mk.

Because form criticism developed simultaneously with Perry's original contribution to the study of the Lukan passion narrative, he took the opportunity to draw support from this school of thought. Arguing that the assorted versions of the primitive passion story were in basic agreement, while varying on certain details, Perry reasoned that on account of this, Luke could have easily preferred his independent source to the Markan because of the passion[449].

---

443. *Proto-Luke and the "Chicago Theory" of the Synoptic Problem*, in *JBL* 47 (1928) 91-116, p. 91. The "fullest treatment" of Burton's theory is found in his writings in The Decennial Publications of the U. Chicago, Vol. 5 (1904). He was referring to *Some Principles of Literary Criticism and their Application to the Synoptic Problem*.

444. *Proto-Luke*, p. 105.

445. *Ibid.*, p. 116.

446. *The Growth of the Gospels*, p. 62. See the material on the Lukan passion narrative (p. 65). The high degree of speculation involved in supporting the Proto-Lk hypothesis was summed up well by Perry himself: "The original form of this source we may only guess" (p. 65). So elusive is this source that it cannot be determined whether Luke employed a continuous written source which included a passion narrative, or an assortment of documents (p. 66).

447. *Ibid.*, p. 65. Perry was using V.H. STANTON (1909), p. 54-60, as his authority.

448. *Growth*, p. 65.

449. *Ibid.*

Although allowing for the possibility that Luke might have drawn on oral sources, Perry found the idea that the sources were both numerous and documentary in nature more appealing. He nodded in the direction of Burkitt that it was "not unlikely" that, because of the presence of L material in Q passages, "some of L was actually part of the Q document but was omitted by Matthew"[450].

Though noting that scholars were "widely divided" on Streeter's Proto-Lk theory, Perry still maintained that there was "much to commend it"[451]. One cannot help but notice that the enthusiasm waned somewhat, when in his conclusion he mentioned only that "there is some reason" to endorse Streeter's concept[452]. Perry categorically rejected Torrey's view of the Gospels having been originally composed in Aramaic, and cited the rejection of Torrey as the consensus of the majority of scholars[453].

A final comment must be made regarding one of Perry's conclusions in a later essay (1951). He wrote: "In the liberal direction the pregospel tradition can no longer be regarded as a static deposit, directly delivered by Peter or another, but as a living testimony organic to the experience of the Church"[454]. Had Perry also been able to apply that dictum to the growth of the Gospels as a whole, he might have been able to view the changes in the Lukan passion narrative in another light: not as the repetition of a static deposit, but as living testimony influenced by and adapted to the Church's experience.

Others during this period who advocated Luke's use of a special source or sources included George CARY (1900)[455], Johannes Maurinus Simon BALJON (1908)[456],

450. *Ibid.*, p. 66.
451. *Ibid.*
452. *Ibid.*, p. 67. It is quite puzzling that for all of Perry's interest in Luke he omitted any conjecture about the place of origin for L, though he treated that issue for Mk, Q, M and even the Johannine material (p. 73).
453. *Ibid.*, p. 67, 68.
454. *Ibid.*, p. 72.
455. *The Synoptic Gospels*, New York, 1900, esp. p. xxvii-xxxiii. Citing results of then current scholarship, Cary sided with those who espoused the view that Luke had drawn heavily from Mk, or Proto-Mk at the very least. This material was augmented from other sources, including Ebionite, which were particularly evident in the initial segment of the Gospel. Regarding the material which was unique to Lk, it was no longer possible to determine from which sources he derived them (p. xxvii). This position was similar to that of T. ZAHN; cf. *Einleitung*, 1899, p. 405.
456. J.M.S. BALJON, *Commentaar of het Evangelie van Lukas*, Utrecht, 1908, p. 2 (esp. p. 533-550). Baljon concluded that it cannot be deduced how many sources Luke used (πολλοί, v. 1), but asserted that Mk was certainly among them. He was attentive to the changes made upon Mk by Luke. Luke principally followed Mk in the passion narrative, but Baljon believed that Luke had his own special source (p. 499). The Markan accounts of Peter's denial and Jesus' trial were redaction of Luke (p. 534). Baljon figured the account of Peter's denials in Mk to be more original.

Eugène MANGENOT (1908), who originally argued against Feine, but later adopted the view of a special source[457], Johan MADER (1911)[458], Willoughby C. ALLEN

With regard to the MA in v. 62 he admitted he did not know why it was missing in some of the old Latin versions (p. 536-537). He simply referred to the opinion that some scholars considered it an insertion from Mt.

Baljon clearly affirmed that Luke followed Mk for the mockery but did not address the MA in 22,64. For the Sanhedrin trial, he regarded the material as basically the same as found in the other Synoptics. But Luke was following his own special source, which however, was not more credible than Mk (p. 537-538). Although the testimony of the witnesses did not appear, Baljon argued that either Luke or his source was aware of it. The mockery of Mk 15,16-20 was passed over by Luke so that there was no doublet.

Baljon was uncertain how Luke obtained the Herod story, though Joanna was considered a strong candidate as Luke's source (p. 545). He regarded 23,10 as an insertion of Mk 15,3 by Luke. Lk 23,19 agreed with Mk 15,7 but with an addition. He also made several comparisons with the GP (p. 545, 546, 550).

457. *Luc (Évangile de saint)*, in *DB* 4, Paris, 1908, p. 397. He summed up the contemporary state of scholarship with regard to Lukan sources as comprising written canonical or extracanonical documents in addition to oral tradition. He countered Feine's proposition by saying that said portions did not constitute an original composition based upon spirit or style. The Jewish-Christian tendency, as well as the alleged special vocabulary which Feine claimed to have discovered, was found throughout the Gospel. Omissions and other changes relative to Mk, Mangenot attributed to Luke's freedom in employing his sources (p. 398). According to Mangenot, transpositions of Markan material resulted from Luke's license in the use of his sources: "Les omissions, les modifications, et les transpositions de saint Luc relativement à saint Marc, s'expliquent par la liberté d'allure que le troisième évangéliste a gardé, en utilisant ses sources" (p. 398).

But his position on sources changed. In his study of the Synoptic Gospels (1911), Mangenot clearly asserted that it was "très vraisemblable" that in addition to Mk and the Logia, Luke made use of a special written source of probable Palestinian origin which was older than Mk (E. MANGENOT, *Les évangiles synoptiques. Conférences apologétiques faites à l'Institut catholique de Paris*, Paris, 1911, p. 63). In this work, he referred frequently to LOISY, *Les évangiles synoptiques*, 1907-1908. In support of this view he cited Feine, V.H. Stanton, and J. Weiss (*Ibid.*, n. 3). He commented on Weiss: "M. J. Weiss lui-même admet cette source particulière, quoiqu'il pense qu'elle n'était vraisemblablement qu'une forme plus développée et remaniée des *Logia*; elle contenait peut-être l'histoire de l'enfance provenant de la tradition judéo-chrétienne et palestinienne". B. Weiss (1907, 1908) was credited with having "reconstitué le texte et déterminé les caractères" (*Les évangiles synoptiques*, p. 63-64). In the midst of the ongoing debate, Mangenot surmised: "Il restera prouvé que saint Luc, qui n'a pas été un témoin oculaire des faits, a été, au moins, un collecteur diligent de renseignements traditionnels et qu'il a puisé à des sources anciennes et de bonne marque" (*Les évangiles synoptiques*, p. 64). In the section dealing with the trial before Caiaphas and Pilate, see his comments on the Lukan account (p. 302-322, esp. p. 304, 314).

458. J. MADER, *Die heiligen vier Evangelien und die Apostelgeschichte*, Einsiedeln, 1911, p. xxix. Mader recommended the idea that sections of Lk and the first half of Acts, where they contained Hebraisms, stemmed from corresponding written copies (either written in Aramaic or translated into Greek by those who had been born Jews), though according to Mader, Luke would have been equally adept in the use of Aramaic or Hebrew. Neither Luke's goal of historical reliability nor his improvement of the style of his sources could disguise the Jewish hue. Mader's view on this point was strongly reminiscent of Feine (1891). In Mader's view the Synoptic

(1913)[459] and George MILLIGAN (1913)[460].

Gospels were composed independently of one another, which assumed the shared source of the oral Gospel (p. xxxiv). Mader still retained the Catholic principle current at that time which favored Matthean priority. Luke's sources, as indicated in the Prologue, included written documents, in addition to oral testimony (p. 267). Among the oral sources would be contemporaries of Jesus, especially James, son of Alphaeus, Mark and probably Peter (who most likely provided the story about the denial (p. 391ff. cf. [p. XXVIII]). Luke possessed written sources for both the Gospel and Acts containing information which he had not gleaned either from experience or from Paul. Regarding Luke's relationship to Paul, Mader insisted it was not of the same type as that between Mark and Peter, though "the Third Gospel can certainly be called Pauline, because [Luke] has written it in the sense and spirit of Paul" (p. XXVI). In the passion narrative, though Mk and Mt recounted parallel stories, Luke's was modified by additions and omissions. And though Lk generally parallels Mk, a few transpositions and large insertions were noted (p. XXXI-XXXII). Luke's rendition was at variance sometimes because of his concern for the historical order, and occasionally because he was expanding the framework and desired to fill it out. Omissions which attracted the scrutiny of J. Weiss, were attributed to Luke's desire to present people in a more favorable light or because other details would simply be assumed (p. 394-396). Like LAGRANGE, Les sources, 1896, p. 18-19, Mader suggested Luke passed over the reference to the high priest inciting the people as an act of mercy. Further, Luke omitted the scourging because it was expected as prescribed Roman custom. Luke's new account was not prompted by dissatisfaction with earlier attempts, but the desire to provide a veritable copy of the original vocabulary contained in the then known New Testament writings (p. V). Mader noted the parallel accounts of the passion narrative in the three Synoptics, adding that Luke's contained a few conspicuous transpositions (p. XXXI-XXXII). He observed further that sometimes when Luke was unsure of the tradition, he inserted information without any temporal indication, in a more suitable context, such as Luke had done in the "Reisebericht" (p. XXXIV). Mader insisted that Luke passed over the official trial of Jesus in favor of the account of Peter's denial. Verse 66, in Mader's estimation, proved that the trial before Caiaphus had taken place, but that for the legal session the Sanhedrin assembled according to the prescribed time and place (p. 392). The form of the question (v. 67) also presupposed the nocturnal trial. The Sanhedrin did not have the power to return a death sentence, thus their recourse to Pilate (p. 393; cf. Appendix 7, p. 761-762). Admitting that oral tradition was insufficient to explain verbal agreements, Mader posited the idea that none of the written sources Luke utilized was a complete Gospel, and some had been written partly in Aramaic and partly in Greek (p. XXXVI). Luke 9,25 / Mk 8,36 / Mt 16,26 were cited as different translations of the same Aramaic original. Similarity of Greek patterns could also explain such phenomena.

459. W.C. ALLEN and L.W. GRENSTED, Introduction to the Books of the New Testament, Edinburgh, 1913, p. 39-40. Allen authored the sections on the Synoptic Gospels and Acts (Preface). He viewed Mk as a source for Lk, though in some places Luke omitted or abbreviated Mk, or in other cases Lk contained alternative narrative. Allen seemed favorable to the idea of a special written source: "The fact that Luke substitutes sometimes for a narrative found in Mk, another similar narrative, suggests that he may have had a special written source for these which he valued highly. If so, it will be possible that much of the matter peculiar to him came from this source" (p. 47). He included material concerning Herod (13,31-33; 23,4-12) as possibly stemming from a such a source (p. 47). See also p. 46, where in addition to 23,4-12 he mentioned 23,2 as among the material peculiar to Lk.

460. The New Testament Documents. Their Origin and Early History, London, 1913. This book was a compilation of a series of Croall lectures Milligan presented in Edinburgh at the end of 1911. Our particular interest is in Lecture 4, The Literary Character of the New Testament

The methods of J. Weiss and B. Weiss were variously critiqued for not giving sufficient attention to the MAs and for assigning too much to a single source. The idea of a special source attracted the attention and support of British and American scholars. In some cases, such as A.M. Perry, attempts were made to isolate the vocabulary of the supposed special source as J. Weiss had done, a methodology which had already been criticized by B. Weiss. Some scholars appealed to oral tradition to help account for the differences between Mk and Lk. Others noted the use of Markan material, which had been omitted from Lk, later in Acts. Whether Luke employed Septuagintal language continued to be debated and Philip the evangelist was repeatedly singled out as the likely source of the special material.

BURNETT HILLMAN STREETER THROUGH HEINZ SCHÜRMANN

The period which includes the British scholars B.H. Streeter and V. Taylor and the German scholars H. Schürmann, J. Jeremias and F. Rehkopf may be considered the Golden Age of the Proto-Lk hypothesis.

Notice should first be taken of the work of Eric Reid BUCKLEY (1912) since B.H. Streeter admitted that he might have been influenced by it[461]. His

---

Writings - The Gospels and Acts, p. 129-168 (esp. p. 138-139, 149-153). In Milligan's opinion Luke made use of a revised edition of Mk, a copy of Q (which had been translated into Greek from Aramaic), and a special Lukan source. The three documents were the primary, though by no means exclusive, sources for Luke. He would also have had access to other narratives and oral tradition, being still in flux at this period. Mk was altered because of the "literary freedom of the day" (p. 140-141). But Mk supplied the framework into which the other material was incorporated. Lukan redaction of Mk included replacing colloquialisms with more cultured language, while the revision of Q consisted in improving the material stylistically. Changes often occurred in various passages simply to heighten the literary quality. The style gave evidence that Luke was responsible for the Gospel as well as Acts (p. 149). The two chief sources for Acts included an Aramaic one in which Peter played a central role and a travel diary which provided the we-section material (p. 162-164).

Milligan, though dissenting on certain details, agreed with Sanday's evaluation of Streeter's study, claiming it represented a revolutionary breakthrough in portraying the developmental stages of the Gospel (p. 141; cf. SANDAY, *SSP*, p. xvi; STREETER, *SSP*, p. 209ff.). Milligan characterized the work as "such an interesting study" (MILLIGAN, *New Testament*, p. 139-140). The special source was very probably a written document, originating in Palestine, collected and put into writing by Luke himself (p. 138). Philip the Evangelist was possibly the source of this information (cf. p. 163, for Milligan's description of "a Jewish-Christian document" as one of the sources for Acts). While he acknowledged Burkitt's view that a part of Q may have contained an account of the passion, Milligan showed partiality to Hawkins's position that Luke reflected Pauline influence in representing aspects of the passion story (p. 152). Milligan wrote that Hawkins's proposal garnered a favorable reception "in various quarters" (p. 152, n. 2; cf. J.H. MOULTON, *The Gospel According to Paul*, in *The Expositor*, Eighth Series, 2 [1911] 16-28).

461. E.R. BUCKLEY, *An Introduction to the Synoptic Problem*, London, 1912. B.H. STREETER, *The Four Gospels*, 1930, p. ix, n. 1: "It may well be that an unconscious recollection of his theory contributed something to the direction of the investigations I then [i.e. 'several years

Introduction was intended as a *status quaestionis* with critique where appropriate. Buckley drew heavily on Hawkins's *Horae Synopticae* as well as the *Synopsis of the Gospels in Greek* by A. Wright[462]. In light of the solution which he proposed, the absence of the names of Feine and Weiss is particularly striking. He rejected the view that Luke was an eyewitness and tentatively dated the Gospel "not earlier than 95 A.D."[463]. The author endorsed the two-document theory, but did not limit these to the only written sources available to the evangelists. Comparing the material common to Mk and Lk, Buckley wrote that the Markan material "is not evenly distributed throughout S. Luke's Gospel, but is found chiefly, if not wholly, in Chapters iii.-ix. and xviii.-xxiv."[464], though later declaring that no Lukan parallels existed for Mk 14,53-64; 15,1.3-5.10-12.16-20a[465]. The additional materials in Lk were a decisive factor in Buckley's judgment that Luke employed "a second narrative other than the common source". For the differences in 22,61 it seemed that Mk more accurately reflected the common Greek source[466].

In addition to Mk, Buckley envisioned a second source as a self-contained gospel which was designated as "T" for *tertium*, Luke's third source and comprised Q material and the material peculiar to Luke[467]. Omissions, additions, changes in order, variations in style and constructions not characteristic of Luke, as well as the reference to πολλοί (1,1) were cited as evidence of this other source. Five changes in order were highlighted, the position of the account of the Sanhedrin trial among them. Responding to the criticism that such a view of the combination of sources portrayed the evangelist as simply a compiler, Buckley retorted that such would be the case for any thesis concerning Luke's adoption and combination of various sources. Buckley was sympathetic to the view that Luke authored "T", though a significant counter-argument was that the unemphatic καὶ αὐτός and ἐγένετο + a finite verb, were not characteristic of Acts.

---

later' and after a 're-reading of one of Sir John Hawkins' Essays'] began; had the recollection been conscious, I should have been proud to acknowledge my debt to such an acute and original student of the subject".

462. *Introduction*, p. vii.
463. *Ibid.*, p. 286.
464. *Ibid.*, p. 56.
465. *Ibid.*, p. 59.
466. *Ibid.* p. 74.
467. *Ibid.*, p. 179. Matthew and Luke did not use the same version of Q. Buckley distinguished between two forms of Q on the ground that it was unlikely that a single Q document would have contained both the parables of the pounds and the talents, as well as the parables of the wedding of the king's son and the great feast (p. 180). This did not exclude the possibility that Luke may have used two different forms of Q (p. 206). Matthew's form of Q was referred to as MQ (p. 249). Like Wernle, Buckley observed that Matthew and Luke exercised greater freedom in editing the narrative material than the logia.
    Buckley appeared to qualify his assertion about "T" when subsequently he wrote it was "practically a Gospel" (p. 188) though later insisted again that "T" was "a second complete gospel" (p. 206). He further speculated that the Q material was "already combined in T with other matter, some of which was akin to S. Mark." (p. 203).

Buckley appeared to leave open the possibility of a proto-Markan Gospel. "T", representing the Jerusalem tradition, was the primary source and provided the structure of Lk, with Markan material supplementing it[468]. The accounts of Pilate's trial (23,13-25 / Mk 15,6-15) were compared in an effort to show that their differences cannot be accounted for by Luke's principal use of Mk. Without taking Lk 1-2 into consideration, Buckley conjectured that "T" comprised the following elements from Lk: 3,1.2.10-15.18.23-28; 4,1-30; 5,1-11.12-16 ("partly", though not specified).20-49; 7,1-17.36-50; 8,1-3; 9,10.11(?).28-36 ("partly", not specified)9,51-56.61.62; 10,1-42; 11,1-8.21.22.27.28.33-54; 13,1-18,14 ("except possibly a few scattered verses") 19,1-28.39.44; 22,15-46.66-71; 23,1-25.27-31.39-43.46.56; 24[469].

Lk developed in two stages. In the first, an extensive sayings source, which had been grouped together, was integrated into narrative material. The second stage occurred when Mk and "T" were fused[470]. While the evidence for a primitive Aramaic Gospel was "inconclusive", Buckley left open the possibility of such a document with the following stipulation about the extent of its influence: "As far as we are able to judge, the written sources, which lie immediately behind our canonical Gospels, were all Greek, so that Aramaic documents, if such ever existed, have had little direct effect on the composition of the Gospels"[471].

Burnett Hillman STREETER'S fundamental contribution to a solution of the synoptic problem, later to be expanded, appeared in his article in *HJ* (1921)[472]. It was here that he first set forth his proposal that Proto-Luke (Q+L) was Luke's primary authority for 22,14ff., which was embellished only slightly by occasional details from Mk[473]. This was predicated, in part, on Hawkins's view that there were

---

468. *Ibid.*, p. 181. Buckley divided the Gospel into four sections: 1-2; 3,1-9,50; 9,51-18,14; 18,15 to the end. Mk was not used in the first or third portions. Writing of the final section of the Gospel he proposed: "... especially in the account of the passion, the traces of the use of S. Mark often consist only of the use of Marcan phrases and turns of expression in the midst of what may well be an independent narrative of the same event" (p. 182).

469. *Ibid.*, p. 204.

470. *Ibid.*, p. 252.

471. *Ibid.*, p. 270.

472. B.H. STREETER, *Fresh Light on the Synoptic Problem*, in *HJ* 20 (1921-22) 103-112. In 1920 Streeter contributed an essay on the synoptic problem without reference to Proto-Lk (*The Synoptic Problem*, in A.S. PEAKE and A.J. GRIEVE [eds.], *A Commentary on the Bible*, London, 1920, p. 672-680). While he affirmed Luke's dependence on Mk he also noted some exceptions: "The following passages of Mk. do not appear in Lk. in the same context as in Mk., but what may be regarded as different versions of the same incident or saying, occur in a different context". Among these passages (total, fifty verses) he counted Mk 15,16-20, cf. Lk 23,11 (p. 673). Though Luke generally followed Markan order, he observed: "But in his account of the Passion he seems to follow wholly or in part a tradition or document which related certain details in a slightly different order" (p. 673 = *FG*, p. 202; cf. *SSP*, p. 76-84 [Hawkins]; see also p. 677). As for passages unique to Lk in our section of the passion he included 22,61a.68.70; 23,2.4-12.13-19 (cf. Mk 15,6-9) (p. 680).

473. *Fresh Light*, p. 105. Such a contention notwithstanding, Streeter still argued that this

some sections of Lk that evinced a "disuse of Mk". This other authority, which
Luke valued more than Mk, was of such a unified nature that it constituted a
complete Gospel, providing the framework for the narrative.

As for the question of authorship, Streeter suggested that "the author of Proto-
Luke may well be St Luke himself and our present gospel may be his much later
and enlarged edition"[474]. His reasoning was based on the "tendency" which is
found in Lk-Acts and Proto-Lk[475]. Yet, he also seemed to distance himself from
this position: "Whether or not the compiler of Proto-Luke was St Luke
himself..."[476].

Streeter claimed that Luke omitted Markan material on the basis of space
limitation, particularly when it was "of inferior interest"[477]. Streeter was not
blind to the difficulty of distinguishing sources which his theory posed, especially
in the latter part of the Gospel. Nevertheless, he asserted that the following
probably belonged to the special source: 3,1–4,30; 6,20–8,3; 9,51–18,14; 19.1-27;
24,13 through the end. In addition, there were elements of 22,14 to 24,52 which
Streeter seemed sure would also be attributed to Proto-Lk. In contrast, the most
that Streeter would assign to Mk in 22,54–23,25 would be 22,54-65.69.71;
23,3.18-19.25[478]. The two principles he laid down for determining Markan
influence were verbal similarity and the ability to excise certain Markan elements
without disturbing the context.

Luke was credited with combining Q with other written and oral sources,
prefixing the infancy narrative, including Markan extracts and "possibly making
certain minor alterations and additions". Despite Streeter's intense dislike of
viewing Luke as a compiler, it was the impression that remained. Luke was viewed

hypothesis "in no way conflicts with the generally accepted 'two-document hypothesis' which
asserts that Matthew and Luke are ultimately dependent on Mk and Q, meaning by Q a single
written source"(p. 105-106). He also maintained that Q, in its original form, did not contain an
account of the passion (p. 106).

474. *Ibid.*, p. 106. See further p. 110 (= *FG*, p. 218, without the emphasis; cf. p. 200): "My
suggestion is that the author of Proto-Luke – by which I mean the person who combined together
in one document the materials derived from Q and those derived from other sources, oral or
written – was no other than St Luke, the companion of St Paul, and that he compiled it during
the two years he spent in Cæsarea while the Apostle was in prison. And I suggest that the same
St. Luke some twenty years afterwards *expanded his own early work* by prefixing the stories of
the Infancy, by inserting extracts from St Mark, and possibly making certain minor alterations
and additions". Luke would have employed the same method in composing Acts.

475. By "tendency" he means the selection of materials and "emphasis and proportion ... is
exactly the same" (p. 110 = *FG*, p. 219).

476. *Ibid.*, p. 112 (= *FG*, p. 221). See also p. 110: "The suggestion I propose to make as
to its *authorship* does not, from the nature of the case, admit of verification in the same way".
Cf. *FG*, p. 218: "But the suggestion I make as to its authorship is one which, from the nature of
the case, does not admit either of verification or refutation to anything like the same extent".

477. *Ibid.*; cf. p. 111.

478. *Ibid.*, p. 109, n. 1. He added a disclaimer that a substantial amount of these "are partly
derived from another source".

as author of both the Gospel and Acts because of the presence of certain "tendencies" involving choice of material and similarity of presentation.

Vincent TAYLOR (1921) reacting to Streeter's article in *HJ*, termed it "a theory which calls for serious consideration" and focused his attention on the passion narrative[479]. Streeter's position was viewed as a development of propositions by Feine, J. Weiss, V.H. Stanton and J.V. Bartlet. Even at this early point much of Taylor's argument rested on counting words. Verses or verse parts which, in his opinion, clearly indicated Lukan dependence upon Mk were: 22,18.22.46b. 47?.52.53a.54b-62; 23,3.22b.26.34b.38.44f.49.50-53; 24,10a[480]. Taylor did not include the Sanhedrin trial on the grounds that "no phrase seems sufficiently distinctive to show dependence", though the verbal correspondence was "fairly high". The timing of the trial and the arrangement of the pericope suggested it did not rely on Mk. Because the low rate of Markan terms and their distribution were also contributing factors, Taylor credited the changes in order to what he termed "the Markan additions". K. LAKE (1922) also believed that the theory was correct[481].

T. STEPHENSON (1922), also responding to Streeter's article in *HJ*, affirmed Streeter's findings with the exception of his insistence on "the secondary character of Mark"[482]. Mk and Q were primary sources for Luke and he treated them in the same manner. Differences in order may be due to Luke himself. On the question of whether Q+L constituted a complete Gospel, Stephenson responded negatively. He also stated that such a document was "rather amorphous, chronologically"[483]. He claimed there was little difference whether Q+L had

---

479. V. TAYLOR, *Proto-Luke*, in *ExpT* 33 (1921-22) 250-252.

480. *Ibid.*, p. 251.

481. K. LAKE, *The Problem of Christian Origins*, in *HTR* 15 (1922) 97-114, esp. p. 97, where Lake specifically listed Streeter's 1921 article. See also p. 111: "[Streeter's] arguments ... seem to me to be as convincing as any hypothesis of the kind can be". Surprisingly, Lake devoted very little attention to the theory when he wrote *An Introduction to the New Testament*, London, 1938. As regards general sources besides Mk and Q Lake believed "Matthew and Luke each have much material not found elsewhere" (p. 14). He nuanced Streeter's position by suggesting, "Once more the best discussion of the subject is in Streeter's *Four Gospels*, p. 242 ff., even if his 'four document' theory be emended by writing 'source' for 'document'" (p. 38, n. 15). Lake viewed Lk as a correction of Mk (p. 42, 43, 45, 46). Although he raised the possibility that Luke obtained information from "local oral tradition (Luke i.1-4)" (p. 43), which included the women mentioned in 8,3 and particularly Joanna, as Sanday proposed (p. 46), on the basis of the generally close parallelism between Lk and Mk in 18,15–24,12, including the same sequence of events, Lake adopted the view that Luke was redacting Mk. He maintained this view despite the fact that "the language of Mark is noticeably revised" (p. 44). It was this verbal difference which caused scholars to postulate other sources. Lake specified the addition of the Herod story (p. 45), explaining its presence as Luke's presentation of the Jews instead of the Romans as responsible for hostility toward the Christians. This stance was also evident in Acts (p. 46-47).

482. T. STEPHENSON, *Fresh Light on the Synoptic Problem*, in *JTS* 33 (1922) 250-255, p. 250.

483. *Ibid.*, p. 254.

been inserted into Mk or vice versa. But it could not be the case that Q+Mk had been inserted into L. In Stephenson's opinion, the determination of Mk as providing the structure of Lk would not "in the least invalidate the other arguments" put forward by Streeter.

Arthur HEADLAM (1923) did not believe that Streeter's "ingenious theory" as formulated in *HJ* article was correct on the grounds that "there is not sufficient evidence to justify us in assuming two editions", though he agreed that Luke "probably collected much material and planned his work before he came in contact with St. Mark's Gospel, which he would not do until he reached Rome"[484]. The characteristics which distinguished Streeter's theory from others were twofold: "it recognizes the unity of style which runs through the two works [Lk-Acts], a recognition which we do not always find among advocates of partition theories, and that it accounts fairly well both for the facts which imply an early and those which imply a late date"[485]. Streeter wrote he had "no particular objection to this modification" of "two stages in its composition"[486].

In his second edition (1927), while retaining his earlier critique, Headlam complimented Streeter's theory for rightly stressing that Luke used "early and independent sources"[487]. In his Preface Headlam concurred with the general view of four (source) documents as Streeter explained them in *The Four Gospels* and which he himself had suggested in 1923[488]. Apart from that, Headlam's statement about the value of Luke's special source still stood: "If Dr. Streeter's conjectures have anything in them (and they help, as we have seen, to solve certain problems), St. Luke came across his special source a considerable time before he came across St. Mark, very probably, in fact, before St. Mark was written. It is, therefore, not only earlier in date, but perhaps in some ways more original"[489].

---

484. A.C. HEADLAM, *The Life and Teaching of Jesus the Christ*, London, 1923, p. 21, n. 1.

485. *Ibid*, p. 21.

486. *FG*, p. 202.

487. *Life*, [2]1927, p. 21, n. 1. Headlam slightly revised his comments on Streeter's article in light of the publication of Streeter's book: "... since then [the theory] has been worked out more fully in his work on 'The Four Gospels'. I do not think that in its complete form it has obtained general assent, as there is not sufficient evidence to justify us in assuming two editions; but it brings out the importance of recognizing the existence in St. Luke's Gospel of independent and early sources". His revision deleted the following sentence from the note following the semicolon: "but it has, I believe, this amount of truth - St. Luke had probably collected much material and planned his work before he came into contact with St. Mark's Gospel, which he would not do until he reached Rome" (1923, p. 21, n. 1).

488. *Ibid.*, [2]1927, p. vii: "For the 'two-document theory' [Streeter] substitutes a 'four-document theory'. In fact, he puts forth with greater learning, with more detailed argument and weightier authority, the conclusion which I had ventured to suggest". Headlam then quoted from his first edition: "We have really, at least, four independent sources. We have St. Mark, *The Discourses*, St. Luke's special source, and St. Matthew's source or sources" (1923, [2]1927, p. 36-37).

489. *Ibid.*, 1923, [2]1927, p. 36.

Luke's general method of using Markan material was to insert it in "three considerable sections", the last of which was 18,15 to the end of the Gospel[490]. Drawing on information from several sources, both oral and written, Luke did not seem to have had another "consecutive history" in addition to Mk. If he had, Luke continued to prefer Mk. Stressing the conjectural nature of any view on the third source, Headlam maintained it was probable that Luke used a third source which was written, and possibly supplemented this by accounts from the oral tradition which Luke himself gathered[491].

Headlam, praising highly the work done at Oxford which Sanday had inspired, repeated Harnack's laudatory estimation of Hawkins[492]. Headlam upheld the "almost univerally agreed" belief that Mk "or a record virtually identical with it" served as the basis for the other Synoptics[493]. Siding with Hawkins against Stanton, Headlam denied that the great omission was due to Urmarkus. Omissions of Markan material by Luke were generally prompted to avoid duplication of similar material and to economize on space. Headlam complained that Luke rearranged Mk's chronological order, though "perhaps" not always with the best results[494].

It was Streeter, in what many consider the classic exposition of his ground-breaking proposal of the four-document theory (1924), who solidly set the Proto-Lk hypothesis before the English speaking world[495]. Attributing authorship of Proto-Lk to Luke, who was also the author of the Third Gospel, Streeter followed the lead of B. Weiss in asserting that Luke himself may have joined Q and L together into one document[496]. Further, Streeter assigned this document to roughly the

490. *Ibid.*, p. 22. The other two sections were 4,31–6,19 and 8,1–9,51.

491. *Ibid.*, 1923, p. 23-24. Cf. p. 21. Note his comment: "But there is still much information which does not come from either of these sources [Mk and Q]. Whence was it derived? Now, as regards this, we have no documentary assistance. Any conclusion must be purely conjectural. It is interesting, therefore, to notice how many writers first reconstruct their sources according to their own imaginations, and then argue from them as if they really existed" (p. 23).

492. *Ibid.*, 1923, ²1927, p. 5-6.

493. *Ibid.*, p. 6.

494. *Ibid.*, p. 21-22. See p. 11. He also called attention to Burkitt's "interesting remarks on St. Luke's use of Mark", some of them also dealing with Luke's chronology, in the article, *Use of Mark* (1922) (HEADLAM, *Life*, 1923, ²1927, p. 25, n. 1). Cf. above.

495. B.H. STREETER, *The Four Gospels*, London, 1924. Ch. VIII: Proto-Luke (199-222). The book expanded arguments presented in his earlier article in *HJ* (1921-22). Later on he attempted to interest the German scholarly community with *Die Ur-Lukas Hypothese*, in *TSK* 102, 1930, 332-340. M.S. Hostetler indicated this article was simply a translation of the preface of the fourth impression of *FG* (1930). Cf. below, n. 569 (*The Place of B.H. Streeter in the Study of the Synoptic Problem*, 1952, p. 16). Nevertheless, what is striking is that in *The Primitive Church Studied with Special Reference to the Origins of the Christian Ministry*, London - New York, 1929, which he considered to be "in some respects, a sequel" to *FG*, there was no reference at all to Proto-Lk (p. ix).

496. STREETER, *FG*, p. 200. Strangely, there was not one reference to Weiss in *FG*!

same time as Mk, but later than Q[497]. Like others before him who had argued for the existence of a special source, Streeter pointed to differences in substance, wording and order to justify his position[498]. Thus, in the section 22,14–24,12 Streeter argued that Luke made primary use of a single source, independent of Mk, though parallel with it. Both were of "approximately equal" historical value[499]. He maintained that while one can delete various additions from the Matthean account without doing serious harm to the flow of the narrative, the same cannot be done with the Lukan narrative without inflicting grave damage[500]. Streeter sought to draw on parallel evidence of Luke's method by relying on the work of Hawkins to conclude that Luke did not use Mk in the central section of Lk[501]. Streeter credited Perry with "the most elaborate attempt" to reconstruct such a source[502].

The influence of Hawkins upon Streeter was again evident when the latter referred to twelve transpositions of Markan material in Lk[503]. Proto-Lk provided the framework. Streeter raised the ante, however, when the issue of order was drawn into the discussion. "My point is, firstly, that the frequency of [Luke's] preference, and especially the fact that it extends to matters of order, is explicable only if the non-Marcan materials formed a complete Gospel so considerable as to seem worthy not only of being compared with, but even of being preferred to, Mark"[504]. Order was seen as one of the foundational supports which undergird the Proto-Lk hypothesis[505].

What was perhaps unique in Streeter's study was that Proto-Lk was not held to be eminently historically superior to Mark's account. Rather, in some material, e.g. Peter's denial, the information was not as reliable as in Mk. On the other hand, the special source was better than Mk since it included the episode of the trial before Herod (23,6-12)[506]. Luke did not have the original Q, but a document composed of Q+L[507]. The result was a type of Gospel only slightly larger than

---

497. *Ibid.*; cf. p. 222.

498. *Ibid.*, p. 202, 207.

499. *Ibid.*, p. 222.

500. *Ibid.*, p. 202. Streeter wrote that Hawkins's evidence (*SSP*) led him to such results, though Hawkins was reluctant to reach such a conclusion.

501. *Ibid.* p. 203-205. See HAWKINS, *Three Limitations*. Pt. 1. *The Disuse of the Marcan Source in St. Luke IX.51-XVIII,14*, in *SSP*, 35-41 (= *ExpT* 14 [1902-03] 21-23).

502. *FG*, p. 202-203. He noted that Feine earlier offered a proposal "which implied something of the sort" (p. 203, n. 1). Cf. p. 217, n. 1, where Streeter referred to Perry's dissertation on source analysis of the Lukan passion narrative as "the most thorough attempt". Cf. above.

503. *Ibid.*, p. 211. Cf. HAWKINS, *St. Luke's Passion-Narrative*, in *ExpT* 15 (1903-04) 124-125 (= *SSP*, 78-84).

504. *FG*, p. 212; also p. 202, 207. Cf. F. NEIRYNCK, *The Argument from Order*, in *ETL* 49 (1973) 784-815 (esp. p. 787-788) = *Evangelica*, 1982, 737-768 (esp. p. 740-741).

505. *FG*, p. 216.

506. *Ibid.*, p. 222.

507. *Ibid.*, p. 208. Streeter rejected the view of BURKITT, *Gospel History*, ²1907, p. 134-135,

Mk, to which Q would have contributed "about one-third of its total contents"[508].

Streeter contended it was extremely difficult to determine which of the verses following 22,14 derived from Mk[509]. Those which probably stemmed from Mk were 22,52-61.71; 23,3.22.25f. Lk 22,69 was among those verses which could be from Mk or could reflect Proto-Lk likened to a parallel in Mk. All the rest was to be ascribed to Proto-Lk[510]. Streeter added his voice to the majority in regarding 22,62 as "an assimilation to Matthew"[511]; its absence from Old Latin manuscripts prompted his adoption of this view.

Streeter described the MA of 22,64 / Mt 26,67-68 as "the most remarkable of all the minor agreements", adding that this case "illustrates in a peculiarly interesting way the extent to which the problem we are considering belongs to the sphere, not of documentary, but of textual criticism"[512]. He was influenced in his proposed text-critical solution by his view of a special source in the passion narrative[513]. Streeter argued that the veiling with the blindfold and the phrase τίς ἐστιν ὁ παίσας σε; were original to Lk but were both omitted in Mt and Mk. He explained that "from Luke the first has got into the Alexandrian (but not into the earliest Antiochene and Western) text of Mark; the second has got into all the texts of Matthew"[514]. In the second case all lines of transmission were corrupted with Mt being assimilated to the parallel in Lk.

Lukan redactional method was different from the Matthean and simpler, insofar as Luke was seen as alternating blocks of Markan and non-Markan material. This observation, combined with the view that the beginning and the end of Lk consisted of non-Markan material, plus the degree of difficulty involved in determining whether material in the passion narrative onwards stemmed from Mk

that Q would have contained an account of the passion. Although L would have been a written document by the time it reached the author of Lk, it "probably ultimately derived from more than one source" (p. 167). Cf. above. In this, Streeter sounded similar to WERNLE, *Die synoptische Frage*, 1899, that there would have been a variety of sources: "Das sogenannte Sondergut wird falsch beurteilt, wenn es als gleichartige Masse betrachtet wird" (p. 94).

508. *FG*, p. 208.

509. *Ibid.*, p. 209, 222. A comparion of the material which Hawkins assigned to Mk (p. 216) and that which Streeter did (p. 222) showed that Streeter was much less inclined to see Markan influence at work in the Lukan passion narrative.

510. *Ibid.* Note that these vv. were somewhat different than those indicated in his article in *HJ*. See above. Cf. the diagram detailing a survey of the Markan insertions in the passion narrative proposed by Streeter in F. NEIRYNCK, *La matière marcienne dans Luc*, 1973, 196-197; ²1989, 106-107 (= *Evangelica*, 76-77).

511. *FG*, p. 222, n. 1.

512. *FG*, p. 325-329, p. 325.

513. Ibid., p. 327: "Further, the view argued in Chapter VIII, that Luke had an account of the Passion which was quite independent of, and in certain ways very different from, that of Mark, affects our judgement on this issue".

514. *Ibid.* Cf. the analysis of F. NEIRYNCK, Τίς ἐστιν ὁ παίσας σε, in *ETL* 63 (1987) 5-47 (= *Evangelica II*, pp. 95-138).

or a non-Markan source, inspired Streeter to pursue this avenue of research[515]. As further proof that Q and L were already combined, he cited among other examples, Luke's omission of the Markan account of the anointing at Bethany in favor of the anointing by the sinful woman (7,36-50)[516]. The use of ὁ κύριος also was put forward in defense of the gospel-like source[517]. This appellation was used in place of the name "Jesus". Taking note of fifteen occurrences, though never in material *clearly* derived from Mk, seven examples were drawn from L material, four from Q material with an additional two instances stemming from L or Q. Finally, in 22,61, ὁ κύριος occurred twice; the first appeared in L material, while the second may stem from Mk[518]. It is this last example that did not fit the mold of Streeter's hypothesis that the title did not occur when Luke copied Mk. Streeter explained this exception by assimilation of Mk's "Jesus" notice that the ancient literary practice not refer with different names to the same person in a given context. Streeter believed that Luke was responsible for combining Q and L[519]. The Proto-Lk document, Luke's primary source, was occasionally embellished by material inserted from Mk[520]. The omission of Markan materials which had previously so attracted the supporters of the special source was explained by the hypothesis of Proto-Lk[521].

Streeter called attention to the "tendency" that appears to be shared by the author of Lk and Acts with the author of Proto-Lk[522]. If the perspective was so similar, the need for a separate document waned.

He also acknowledged that the statistics about linguistic usage "were not sufficiently striking to be worth quoting as evidence"[523]. Streeter also conceded

---

515. *Ibid.*, p. 208-209.

516. *Ibid.*, p. 210.

517. *Ibid.*, p. 212-213.

518. *Ibid.*, p. 213, on 22,61a.b. Instances from L were 7,13; 10,39.41; 13,15; 18,6; 19,8; 22,31. Those from Q were 7,19; 10,1; 11,39; 12,42. Coming from either L or Q were 17,5.6.

519. *Ibid.*, p. 200, where he stated: "Luke himself may have been the person who originally combined Q and L, and then, at some subsequent date, produced an enlarged edition of his earlier work". Cf. p. 211 (= *HJ*, p. 108), where Streeter supposed that "Q+L lay before the author of the Third Gospel as a single document". He continued: "Later on, probably not till after the death of Paul, a copy of Q came his way, and on the basis of this and his own notes he composed Proto-Luke as a Gospel for the use of the Church in the place where he was then living. Still later a copy of Mark came his way, and he then produced the second and enlarged edition of his Gospel that has come down to us" (p. 219). The comprehensiveness of Proto-Lk was indicated by such phrases as "a kind of 'Gospel'" (p. 208), "practically a Gospel" (p. 217), "a complete Gospel" (p. 221). The language was very reminiscent of BUCKLEY, *An Introduction*, 1912, p. 188, 206.

520. *FG*, p. 167. Cf. p. 202, 208. "To Luke the non-Marcan source is the more primary authority. To it he prefixes chaps. i. and ii. as an introduction, and into the framework which it provides he fits materials derived from Mark" (p. 208).

521. *Ibid.*, p. 214.

522. *Ibid.*, p. 219.

523. *Ibid.*, p. 214, n. 1.

that his source analysis of "[Lk] 22,14 to the end" was "in points of detail highly speculative"[524]. Descriptions of the same events in the two sources "would be determined as much by the necessary vocabulary of the subject matter as by the taste of a writer". The criteria by which material in the Passion was ascribed to Mk rather than to Proto-Lk were twofold: close verbal similarity and the ability to "detach" such verses without disturbing the sense of the context[525]. The "remarkable variations in order" between Mk and Lk suggested that Luke was employing a separate source.

Although he stated that the relation of Luke to Mk in 22,14 through 24,12, was different than in other sections of Lk, further on he qualified his position, arguing that Mk served as Luke's main source from 23,33 to 24,10a[526]. Streeter did not reject the modification of his hypothesis offered by Headlam that rather than two editions of the Gospel, there were two stages in the compositional process[527]. Streeter proposed that L preserved the traditions of the Church in Caesarea[528].

Streeter's essay on the trial before Herod in *SSP* (1911) focused attention on his agreement with Wright in arguing for the historicity of the account in opposition to Loisy[529]. Streeter dismissed the contrary view for two reasons: there appeared to be no apologetic reason for the account and it accorded with the historical situation[530]. Confronted by the insurmountable opposition of Judaism, there was an increased tendency to blame the Jews and excuse the Romans. Responding to the question why the episode would have been lacking in Mk, Streeter suggested that Mark may have been unaware of it[531]. In his *HJ* article Streeter regarded the replacement of non-Markan stories, such as the mockery by Herodian soldiers rather than those of Pilate and a morning trial in contrast to a nocturnal, as supporting his argument that Luke preferred the Proto-Lk source[532]. Streeter's position became even stronger in *The Four Gospels*. The special source was considered better than Mk since it included the episode of the trial before

524. *Ibid.*, p. 216.

525. *Ibid.*; cf. *HJ*, p. 109.

526. *FG*, p. 201-202, 209; cf. p. 217. Cf. below Taylor, n. 605, 643.

527. *Ibid.*, p. 221. Cf. A.C. HEADLAM, *The Life and Teaching of Jesus Christ*, London, 1923, p. 20f., offered his critique in response to Streeter's earlier contribution in *HJ*.

528. *FG*, p. 223.

529. STREETER, *On the Trial of Our Lord before Herod: A Suggestion*, in W. SANDAY (ed.), *Studies in the Synoptic Problem*, Oxford, 1911, p. 229-231. In a note, Streeter declared that he reached this conclusion independently of A. Wright, who much earlier put forth such a view in *St. Luke's Gospel in Greek*, London, 1900, p. 203. Streeter's position also concurred with that of A.H. Verrall, though Streeter made no reference to him. Cf. Verrall (1909).

530. *On the Trial*, p. 229.

531. *Ibid.*, p. 231. Because the apostles dispersed, they would have recounted the condemnation emanating from Pilate's trial, while Herod's trial would have gone unreported since no condemnation resulted.

532. *Fresh Light*, p. 108.

Herod (23,6-12)[533].

Without being committed to one side of the Proto-Lk debate or the other, one reviewer of *The Four Gospels* commented that Streeter "makes out an excellent case for a very interesting theory"[534]. Jackson Case, who seconded Streeter's efforts to assign the various traditions to particular geographical locations, asserted that the study fell short, being limited to textual and literary criticism while ignoring social aspects of the historical experience of the early Christians[535].

Despite a laudatory overall reaction to Streeter's work James Moffatt took issue with the Proto-Lk theory[536]. Expressing some doubt as to whether it would pass muster among the critics, two main criticisms were leveled against it. First, the hypothesis rested on "romantic speculation", which built on yet further speculation, such as how Streeter can profess to know where Luke stayed in an attempt to explain the Samaritan material in the Gospel[537]. Secondly, the theory did not fulfill its promise that what was arrived at in the end was "a better historical tradition"[538]. In the final analysis, when compared with the views of Spitta and B. Weiss, Moffatt did not believe that Streeter's view of Luke was better than theirs[539]. Moffatt assessed the majority opinion concerning sources up to the time of Streeter that Luke was dependent upon Mk and Q, with the addition of "some special sources"[540].

F.C. Burkitt, noting the progress Streeter made in refining his theory, commented that it was "certainly better than the first sketch", a reference to the introduction of the Proto-Lk hypothesis in *HJ* (1921)[541]. Burkitt was "in very near agreement with Streeter" that "the majority of these [minor] agreements do not require any explanation at all (Streeter, p. 295)"[542]. Correctors would just naturally decide upon the same word. Burkitt considered the MAs the "main issue" in the synoptic problem[543]. E.F. Scott was lavish in his praise of Streeter's work, especially where it concerned the treatment of the Synoptic Gospels[544]. However, some of the arguments for Proto-Lk were characterized as "precarious", without stipulating which ones he had in mind[545].

533. *FG*, p. 222.
534. ANONYMOUS, in *ExpT* 36 (1924-25) 387.
535. *JR* 5 (1925) 430.
536. *HJ* 23 (1925) 562-564.
537. *Ibid.*, p. 562.
538. *Ibid.*, p. 563: "The various special sources posited for Matthew and Luke are not inferior necessarily to those demanded by this theory".
539. *Ibid.*
540. *Ibid.*, p. 562.
541. *JTS* 26 (1924-25) 278-294, p. 279.
542. *Ibid.*, p. 292.
543. *Ibid.*, p. 292.
544. *The Yale Review* 15 (1925) p. 609.
545. *Ibid.*, p. 610.

E.G. Selwyn described the theory as "the most interesting product of recent literary criticism"[546]. He noted that Streeter exceeded Taylor in claims regarding the completeness of the special source. But he expressed reservation about Taylor's contention that Luke being the author of Proto-Lk would not have edited heavily, a claim he was reluctant to accept in light of Luke's redaction of Mk. He pointed out that Burkitt and Lake already endorsed the theory.

Joseph W. HUNKIN (1927) appeared to straddle the fence between supporting Luke's use of Mk and adoption of Streeter's Proto-Lk hypothesis[547]. Although Hunkin proported to accept Streeter's theory with some modification, the refinement was so extreme as to make one wonder whether Hunkin had not dismantled the hypothesis altogether. Complete agreement between Hunkin and Streeter was limited to the Lukan authorship of Proto-Lk and the belief that Q and L once formed a document because these materials were generally found in combination[548]. Beyond that, Hunkin had taken issue with almost every aspect of the Proto-Lukan hypothesis. For example, while Streeter maintained that this special source formed the framework for the Gospel in 3,1-4,30, Hunkin contended that though Luke employed elements from Proto-Lk at this early point in the Gospel, the framework was provided by Mk[549]. While Streeter attempted to reconstruct the limits of Proto-Lk, Hunkin argued that such a herculaean task would be "very difficult, if not impossible"[550]. Further, Hunkin was not convinced that all the material unique to Lk came from Proto-Lk, suggesting that the *Sondergut* might have been contained in notes appended to it[551].

Arguing that Streeter was on "more doubtful ground" in attempting to use the passion narrative to support his theory, Hunkin took aim at Taylor's interpretation particularly with regard to the argument from order. Dismissing one of the examples of transposition cited by Taylor (23,36 / Mk 15,16-20) "as hardly a case in point", Hunkin continued his examination concluding that six of the eleven cases raised by Taylor did not reflect significant change from the Markan text. They were simply the result of Luke's attempt to make stylistic improvements or to smoothen the flow of the narrative[552]. The amount of change in any given

---

546. E.G. SELWYN, *Editorial, The Earliest Gospel?*, in *TLond* 14 (1927) 121.

547. *The Composition of the Third Gospel, with Special Reference to Canon Streeter's Theory of Proto-Luke*, in *JTS* 28 (1926-27) 250-262 (esp. p. 255-258). He was using the 1926 reprint.

548. *Ibid.*, p. 250, 254.

549. *Ibid.*, p. 252. Cf. STREETER, *FG*, 1926, p. 214. Hunkin, even borrowing from Taylor, wrote: "The simplest hypothesis is that St. Luke deliberately corrects the Markan narrative. As Dr Taylor himself admits, he had it in mind, 'very much in mind'. I would add that it seems to provide the general outline, the framework, of the whole story" (*Composition*, p. 256).

550. *Composition*, p. 254.

551. *Ibid.*, p. 254, 258, 259.

552. *Ibid.*, p. 256: "Of these eleven, six represent differences not in the order of the events themselves, but simply in the order in which they are mentioned by the evangelist. There is no sign that St Luke regarded the denial of St. Peter or the rending of the Temple Veil or the Preparation of Spices and Ointments as having occurred at points of time differing from those to which they are referred by Mark". Hunkin conceded that the other five cases describing events

passage taken over from Mk varied to the degree in which Luke wished to add to it or improve upon it. Furthermore, Hunkin did not find Taylor's argument that Luke inserted Markan material convincing: "It is significant that the fourteen passages which Dr. Taylor calls 'Markan insertions' occur in Luke, with only one exception, precisely in the same relative order in which they stand in Mark". As regards the order of the mockery and night session of the Sanhedrin, Hunkin gave equal weight to the possibility that Luke was either following a separate tradition or making needed corrections of the Markan source[553]. Finally, Hunkin distanced himself from Taylor's long held opinion that L was to be ascribed to a particularly early period. Hunkin was of the mind that the original elements of L can be determined only partially, and then with difficulty[554].

Taylor wasted no time in responding to Hunkin's article. He highlighted their agreement on the existence of the document consisting of Q+L as well as their basic agreement of its contents as outlined by Streeter. But two very significant differences separated the two scholars, namely how they envisioned the form of the special source as well as whether Mk constituted the framework of the Lk[555]. Hunkin conceived the elements of the passion narrative unique to Luke as contained in the detached notes and not in the Q+L document. Further, while Hunkin envisioned the document as a "loose construction of discourse", Taylor countered that it "possessed relative fixity of structure"[556].

Once again, Taylor underscored the relative merit of the methodology which examined the amount of verbal correspondence between Mk and Lk, while he dismissed any claim on the part of opponents to have a majority, suggesting rather that they may be using a faulty methodology. He contested Hunkin's charges with regard to the historical value of Proto-Lk and defended himself, recalling among other earlier material, a quote from *Behind the Third Gospel*. "It would be absurd to suggest that the comparison leads to any wholesale depreciation of Mark as a historical authority", since its position in this respect is 'much too well assured'. But Taylor qualified this statement by eliminating the passion narrative from this

---

which occurred the night before the crucifixion were taken from a tradition other than Mk. Cf. TAYLOR, *Behind*, p. 73.

553. *Ibid.*, p. 258: "There follows in xxii 63-71 the story of the mocking and the trial before the Council taken perhaps from a tradition which St. Luke prefers to the Markan". In n. 1, Hunkin added: "It is conceivable that St Luke is himself simply correcting the Markan account, knowing that the Sanhedrin did not meet by night, and perceiving that the mocking and buffeting (Mk. xiv 65) must be that of the temple police, and not of the chief priests and elders themselves".

554. *Ibid.*, p. 262.

555. *Is the Proto-Luke Hypothesis Sound?*, in *JTS* 29 (1927-28) 148. Apparently unknowingly Taylor specified each as the most significant difference between the two scholars' positions. Taylor began: "There are however, important differences, of which the chief is the inclusion of the Lukan elements in the Passion narrative in the Evangelist's detached notes (L¹) rather than in Q+L". But a little later he continued: "The main point of difference is the question of the framework of the Third Gospel" (p. 148).

556. *Ibid.*, p. 153.

part of the discussion[557]. Their debate became almost humorous when one considers both are trying to determine the extent of a hypothetical document which lies beyond the scope of scientific verification.

In the midst of accolades for a stimulating work, Joseph Huby was nonetheless highly critical of the Proto-Lk theory[558]. Aside from the fact that Streeter's hypothesis was very complicated and consisted in the pure conjecture of a two stage process, Huby believed it was "trop détachée des données de l'ancienne tradition", though he did not explain what he meant by the phrase. While Streeter had effectively pointed out some of the weaknesses of the Two-Source theory, still he attempted to solve the dilemma with almost exclusively external criteria. Huby predicted that the Proto-Lk hypothesis would not survive as long as Proto-Mk had.

Streeter briefly revisited the topic of Luke's special sources in a 1926 article[559]. As for the passion narrative he maintained: "Luke also seems to have had an account of the Passion story, from the Last Supper onwards, independent of that found in Mark"[560]. Without mentioning the passion or indeed what he considered to be the contents of the special material Streeter claimed that the majority of the material unique to Luke may have stemmed from Philip the evangelist and his daughters[561].

Streeter (1934) gave a great deal of attention to his Proto-Lk theory, to the "wide acceptance among English scholars" as well as to some of the negative reaction it had received, in an essay M.S. Hostetler described as Streeter's "final contribution to Synoptic studies"[562]. Streeter also noted the mixed reaction which Taylor's work had drawn and seemed to distance himself from him[563].

Streeter responded to Creed's criticism that what appeared to be an amorphous collection of material once the Markan material had been removed, "so far from being a valid objection, is exactly what we should expect *at that date*"[564]. He

557. *Ibid.*, p. 154, 155. See TAYLOR, *Behind*, p. 245.

558. *RSR* 17 (1927) 167.

559. *Sources of the Gospels*, in E.F. SCOTT and B.S. EASTON (eds.), *An Outline of Christianity. The Story of Our Civilization*, Vol. 1, New York, 1926, 349-359.

560. *Ibid.*, p. 353.

561. *Ibid.*, p. 354.

562. B.H. STREETER, *Modern Criticism and the Synoptic Gospels*, in *The Modern Churchman* 24 (1934) 435-451, p. 437. Cf. the excellent study of M.S. HOSTETLER, *The Place of B.H. Streeter*, p. 16, who also observed that this was the published version of a paper "read at the 1934 Conference of Modern Churchmen at Birmingham". See below, n. 569.

563. *Ibid.* "In certain ways [Taylor] has fortified the arguments for [the Proto-Lk theory]; though, to the mind of some critics, he has weakened the case in its larger issues by over-elaboration of points of detail. At any rate, it is my own statement of it, not his, that I am prepared to defend". Creed highlighted the difference between Streeter and Taylor: "In this year's Conference number of *The Modern Churchman* (October, 1934), Canon Streeter has reaffirmed his adherence to the theory, though it is to be noted that his interpretation as here given shows him to be unwilling to adopt the more radical form of the doctrine espoused by Dr. Vincent Taylor" (*Some, ExpT* 46 [1934-35] 101-107, p. 103).

564. *Ibid.*, p. 438. Cf. CREED, *Gospel*, p. lviii, n. 1. See below.

elaborated on the nature of the hypothetical document: "Proto-Luke, which is Q expanded in a biographical direction, is a movement in the direction of supplying that demand, but, doubtless for lack of suitable material, its author was unable to go the whole way"[565]. Concerning the critique of Creed that the framework was Markan, Streeter countered: "If by 'framework' is meant biographical outline, this of course is true of all that intervenes between the sermon at Nazareth, with which Luke opens the public ministry, and the Last Supper. Proto-Luke contains so little narrative that, if Luke wanted to produce anything like a biography, he was obliged to take the narrative outline from Mark"[566].

As to the conundrum of the differences in order Streeter pointed to Hawkins's observation that there were "no less than twelve times" in which the Lukan order differed from Mk and this was "easily explicable if he was following the order of a parallel source which he was conflating with Mark"[567]. Rather than diminishing his belief in the value of the hypothesis, Streeter confessed that "for these and other reasons the lapse of time has enhanced my belief that the Proto-Luke theory, in some form or other, is on the right lines"[568].

Marion S. HOSTETLER (1952), in a detailed study of Streeter's role in the study of the synoptic problem, praised the work of the English scholar, but also cited weaknesses of his approach[569]. Hostetler disagreed that Luke's apparent preference for non-Markan material necessarily bolstered the Proto-Lk theory[570]. He further rejected the argument about Proto-Lukan style[571]. A repeated critique was that Streeter had ignored his predecessors' work[572]. In addition, Hostetler charged that Streeter assigned too much to documentary sources and did not give sufficient credit to the evangelist's redaction[573]. Further, Hostetler believed that

---

565. STREETER, *Modern Criticism*, p. 438.

566. *Ibid.*, p. 439.

567. *Ibid.*

568. *Ibid.*, p. 441.

569. M.S. HOSTETLER, *The Place of B.H. Streeter in the Study of the Synoptic Problem*, Diss. Hartford Seminary Foundation, Hartford, CT, 1952 (dir. G. JOHNSTON). See in particular Chapter 5 in which he discussed the reception of the Proto-Lk theory, dividing the categories into those who accepted, those who were non-committal, and those who ignored or rejected the hypothesis (p. 146-184).

570. *Ibid.*, p. 124.

571. *Ibid.*, p. 131.

572. *Ibid.*, p. 145, 172, 184, 199, 200. "Streeter exaggerated the originality of his conjecture, both by ignoring previous German work in the field and by forgetting to mention the very similar theory propounded earlier by E.R. Buckley " (p. 200). But see above, n. 1. In *HJ* Streeter remarked: "The disentanglement of the elements derived from Mark and from Proto-Luke from xxii.14 onwards has exercised the ingenuity of several scholars who have tried to verify different forms of the hypothesis of a non-Marcan Passion story. In points of detail it is necessarily highly speculative" (*Fresh*, p. 109; cf. above, n. 59; see also *FG*, p. 209).

573. HOSTETLER, *Place*, p. 199: "In the light of more recent Synoptic studies it seems probable that Streeter attributed too large a proportion of the words in Matthew and Luke to documentary sources and made too little allowance for editorial freedom and for the writers'

the Lukan structure was more due to Mk than Streeter was "prepared to admit". Finally, the supposition was that Q and L were joined prior to Luke "does not seem to be susceptible of conclusive proof"[574].

Stephen NEILL (1964, [2]1988), in an assessment of Streeter's contribution, remarked about the lack of support for the Proto-Lk theory, pointing out the extensive influence in Britain of Creed's judgment in matters exegetical[575]. Neill nevertheless suggested that the hesitation on the part of German scholars to investigate it more fully was possibly "premature"[576]. His hope for a revivification of the debate was evident: "In handling such a complex question it is rarely possible to reach more than reasonable probability; scholarship may yet come round to the view that reasonable probability is exactly what Streeter had been successful in establishing"[577].

What Neill considered so remarkable for Streeter's readers was that despite his liberal theological stance, he accepted the Gospels "as generally reliable historical documents". Neill ended with a fitting testimony to the enduring value of *The Four Gospels*: "No book has quite taken the place of Streeter's; any serious student of the Gospel is bound to consult it, though at many points he may feel free to dissent from its conclusions"[578].

The publication of Streeter's *The Four Gospels* provided V. TAYLOR (1925) with another opportunity to promote the theory[579]. He lamented that Streeter had not developed the theory much beyond the *HJ* article, except to propose a later date and discuss the relevance for the synoptic problem. In addition to those scholars mentioned in his previous article (1921) who adhered to a special source theory, Taylor added B. Weiss, Burkitt and Perry. One of the merits of the theory was that it demonstrated the place of women in the development of the Gospel.

Taylor, being particularly inspired by the work of Streeter, fashioned a defense and proposed a further development of the Proto-Lk hypothesis in *Behind the Third*

knowledge of the Christian tradition as it was customarily used in preaching and worship".

574. *Ibid.*, p. 200.

575. S. NEILL and T. WRIGHT, *The Interpretation of the New Testament 1861-1986* [1st ed.: S. Neill, 1861-1961, 1964, London - New York, p. 124; Oxford - New York, [2]1988, p. 134: "But Professor J.M. Creed, who was at the time working on his *Commentary on St. Luke's Gospel* (published in 1930), felt that there was little to be said for the theory, and dismissed it almost contemptuously in a footnote. Creed's authority in such matters was great". Neill added in n. 1: "Creed was an excellent classical scholar, a slow, patient, meticulous worker, unwilling, in the good Cambridge tradition, to print anything until he was sure that he had considered the whole of the available evidence. He had come deeply under the influence of the 'religio-historical' school in Germany ... as is evident from his *Commentary on Luke's Gospel*. His death in 1940 at the early age of fifty was a grave loss to English New Testament scholarship".

576. NEILL and WRIGHT, *Interpretation*, p. 134.

577. *Ibid.*

578. *Ibid.*, p. 135.

579. TAYLOR, *The Value of the Proto-Luke Hypothesis*, in *ExpT* 36 (1924-25) 476-477. Cf. above, n. 495.

Gospel (1926)[580]. He began with a survey of source-critical studies on Lk done by Feine, B. Weiss and J. Weiss, F.C. Burkitt, V.H. Stanton, J.C. Hawkins, J.V. Bartlet, W. Sanday, A.M. Perry and B.H. Streeter[581]. As early as 1883 B. Weiss was said to have promoted the idea that in addition to Mk, Luke used "another comprehensive delineation of the whole life of Jesus", even though all the special Lukan material could not be attributed to this source[582]. Despite this early effort, Taylor credited Feine with "the first complete statement of a special documentary source, other than Mk. and Q"[583]. He disputed B. Weiss's construction of the special source claiming that Weiss ascribed to the special source material "where it is more reasonable to think that St. Luke's debt was to Mk"[584]. Three objections presented against Feine and the two Weiss's by Moffatt and Stanton were, according to Taylor, "insuperable"[585]. The criticisms involved: 1) "'The linguistic and inward criteria ... are too subjective in the large majority of cases'"[586]; 2) "sections are included in the special source which are more naturally explained as the work of St. Luke himself"[587]; and 3) "the reconstructed source lacks unity and completeness"[588].

Next he treated Burkitt who, while following his own unique line of argument, fit into the development of source-critical studies of Lk. This theory which was "widely rejected" and for good reason, failed to explain why Matthew would have ignored the passion narrative in Q[589]. Burkitt had made the historically valuable Lukan passion narrative the foundation of his case, which, though his argument failed to convince, served as the basis upon which other scholars, particularly Bartlet and Streeter, would build. "The contention that St. Luke's Passion narrative rests upon an early and valuable source, which is independent of St. Mark's Gospel, has very great force and is the permanent contribution of Burkitt's argument"[590].

Stanton "laid all New Testament scholars under his debt by his judicial discussion of all problems relating to the criticism of the Gospels"[591]. Nevertheless, Taylor critiqued him for reducing the role Luke played in the

580. *Behind the Third Gospel*, Oxford, 1926.

581. *Ibid.*, p. 2-27.

582. *Ibid.*, p. 2. Cf. B. WEISS, *Life of Christ*, Vol. 1, 1883, p. 80 (= *Das Leben Jesu*, Berlin, 1882). Weiss's theory continued to develop through 1908 with *Die Quellen der synoptischen Überlieferung*. Taylor relied on Moffatt's summary of the contents according to Feine (TAYLOR, *Behind*, p. 3, n. 2; cf. MOFFATT, *Introduction*, [3]1918, p. 276).

583. *Behind*, p. 2-3.

584. *Ibid.*, p. 3. This material included 18,31-34, parts of Ch 20 and 22,1-6.

585. *Ibid.*, p. 3-4.

586. *Ibid.*, p. 4. Cf. MOFFATT, *Introduction*, [3]1918, p. 277.

587. *Behind*, p. 4, drawing on V.H. STANTON (1909), p. 222.

588. *Behind*, p. 4.

589. *Ibid.*, p. 5. Cf. BURKITT (1906).

590. TAYLOR, *Behind*, p. 7.

591. *Ibid.*, p. 8. Cf. V.H. STANTON (1909).

composition of an expanded Logia source[592].

Taylor pointed out that Hawkins was a staunch advocate of the Two-Document theory and did not support the idea of "a special Lukan source or enlarged Logian document"[593]. Hawkins's proposal of Luke's use of a travel-document, which, however, would be adopted and expanded by others was yet another stage in the development.

Bartlet was praised for his work which "raises fresh issues and supplies full and detailed material for their discussion", even as it agrees with various positions of Stanton[594]. Taylor highlighted four objections to Bartlet's position[595].

Sanday's comment that several proponents of the special source theory, namely Feine, J. Weiss, V.H. Stanton and Bartlet, included Q material within the special source was noted. "... Dr. Sanday was disposed to regard favourably the hypothesis of a special source containing material collected by St. Luke, provided the fusion of this material with Q can be viewed as the work of the Evangelist"[596].

Taylor characterized Perry's 1920 dissertation as "an invaluable contribution" building upon the work of E.D. Burton and C.C. Torrey, as well as drawing upon Hawkins, Burkitt, and V.H. Stanton[597]. The weaknesses of Perry's study were "perhaps a tendency to overprecision and an undue emphasis upon phenomena, linguistic and otherwise, which are thought to establish a distinction between the author of J and the Third Evangelist"[598]. He also observed, "nor are the 'thought and viewpoint' of J irreconcilable with the Evangelist's authorship"[599]. In addition, Taylor took issue with Perry's early dating of the J document and the assignment of authorship of such a source to someone other than Luke. Rather than presenting Luke as an author in his own right, Taylor argued that Perry's conception presented him as a compiler[600]. Despite these criticisms, he credited Perry's dissertation with being one of the "strongest foundations" for Streeter's articulation of the Proto-Lk hypothesis[601].

Beginning with Streeter's 1921 article in *HJ*, Taylor claimed that one of the distinguishing marks between Perry and Streeter was that the latter "lays

592. TAYLOR, *Behind*, p. 9.

593. *Ibid.*, p. 10. Cf. HAWKINS, *The Disuse of the Markan Source in St. Luke ix.51-xviii.14*, in W. SANDAY (ed.), *SSP*, 1911, p. 29-59 (= *ExpT* 14 [1902-03] 18-23, 90-93, 137-140).

594. TAYLOR, *Behind*, p. 15.

595. *Ibid.*, p. 16-18.

596. *Ibid.*, p. 20. Cf. SANDAY, *Introductory*, in *SSP*, p. xix-xxiii.

597. TAYLOR, *Behind*, p. 20. Taylor extolled Perry for his "remarkably thorough examination" declaring the work was a "permanent contribution" to the source analysis discussion (p. 21). Cf. above.

598. *Ibid.*, p. 21. Taylor's critique of Perry's overprecision seems similar to Streeter's evaluation of Taylor's "over-elaboration of points of detail". See n. 563.

599. *Ibid.*

600. *Ibid.*, p. 22.

601. *Ibid.*

comparatively little stress upon linguistic evidence in its bearing on the authorship
of the non-Markan material"[602]. While Streeter would agree with Feine, B.
Weiss and J. Weiss that a special Lukan source constituted part of Lk, he would
differ in not promoting a "mere string of fragments"[603]. Streeter demonstrated
similarity of thought with Feine, Stanton and Bartlet in arguing that the Lukan
material had been combined with Q material. Streeter's form of the theory
addressed the objections made against Bartlet's, though unlike Bartlet, he held to
the Two-Document hypothesis. "The frank recognition of Canon Streeter's debt to
earlier workers in no ways dims the brilliance and originality of his theory. On the
contrary, it is the more satisfactory to find that it stands in a path the earlier stages
of which have been well and wisely trodden. Indeed, the entire course of the
development we have been tracing shows that, in spite of apparent confusion, there
is real progress in Synoptic Criticism"[604]. Despite such a laudatory remark,
Taylor was quick to point out where he differed with Streeter on an important
aspect of the research. "It is probable, however, that [Streeter] makes too great a
concession in the opinion that from xxiii.33 to xxiv.10a 'Luke reverses his
ordinary procedure and makes Mark his main source (p. 217)'"[605].

Taylor regarded the theory as he expounded it as something of a hybrid, a
culmination of various contributions. Mk was simply a secondary source in the
composition of the Lukan passion narrative, offering only occasional supplementary
material[606]. Superseding it was an independent source, consisting of an expanded
version of Q to which an account of the passion was appended, composed by the
evangelist Luke during the period 60-65 AD, initially at Caesarea[607]. Its historical
value was assured since it rested upon reliable information provided by women
such as the daughters of Philip the Evangelist and Joanna. The passion narrative
held pride of place and provided a necessary foundation for the entire hypothesis
of an extensive written source. But if Taylor's assertions concerning this portion
of the Gospel should collapse, it would bring into question all the other pericopes
he claims were associated with it[608]. Taylor proposed a continuous non-Marcan

602. *Ibid.*, p. 24.
603. *Ibid.*, p. 26.
604. *Ibid.*, p. 27.
605. *Ibid.* Cf. above, n. 478; below, n. 643.
606. Note the extent of Markan material in the passion and resurrection narratives was almost
inconsequential: "If we are right in thinking that for this account of the Passion and Resurrection
St. Luke has followed an independent written source, *drawing merely a few extracts from Mk.*,
this conclusion must of necessity react upon the problem as a whole" (*Behind*, p. 134) [emphasis
added]. Cf. F. NEIRYNCK, *The Argument from Order*, in *ETL* 49 (1973) 806-807 = *Evangelica*,
1982, 759-760: "Both British scholars [Streeter and Taylor] accepted an important number of
Marcan 'insertions' in the Lucan Passion narrative".
607. *Behind*, p. 185.
608. *Ibid.*, p. 201: "The problem is very far from being one of merely subjective criticism,
since throughout speculation is controlled by objective facts of a documentary kind. These facts
are most clearly seen in the Passion and Resurrection narrative in Lk. xxii.14-xxiv., because we
can compare this section with the parallel story in Mk. xiv.-xvi.8".

documentary source evident in Lk 3,13–4,30; 5,1-11; 6,12–8,3; 9,51-18,14; 19,1-28.37-44.47-48 and 22,14 through Chapter 24 (excluding the insertions from Mk)[609].

Peter's denial was attributed entirely to Mk with the exception of v. 62 which can be explained by oral tradition[610]. Taylor contended that the Proto-Lk source did not contain an account of the denial[611]. The mocking of Jesus (22,63-65), the trial before the priests (22,66-71) and the trials before Pilate and Herod (23,1-25) were all regarded as deriving from the non-Markan tradition[612]. Verse 22,69, which at first glance may seem to depend upon Mk, Taylor alleged, resulted from the flow of the account itself[613]. The same may be said of 22,71, since there was no direct reference to blasphemy as in Mk[614]. Only 23,3 can be ascribed to Mk[615]. Taylor considered all of 23,1-25 as a literary unit wherein the Herod episode hung together without any assistance from Markan material.

The omission of a great deal of Markan material, both within and without the passion narrative "raises a question of great difficulty for all who hold that Mk. is St. Luke's primary source"[616]. Taylor argued that Markan material was omitted in general for three reasons: 1) some was unsuited for Luke's purpose, 2) still other material was already included in Luke's expanded version of Q, and 3) Luke preferred "parallel or similar passages in Proto-Luke" to what was available in Mk[617]. All of these reasons, in one way or another, showed that Taylor opted for the view that the Markan material was omitted because Luke had access to and chose to employ another source[618].

Differences in order, according to Taylor, sometimes were simply the consequence, an unintended by-product, of the insertion of Markan material into the continuous non-Markan source[619]. He brought to the fore the issue of order stating that "the question of *order* is of very great importance"[620]. And although oral tradition could account for some variation in the organization of the material, he distinguished it from that found in written sources. If one assumed, as Hawkins

---

609. *Ibid.*, p. 180; cf. p. 246-247.
610. *Ibid.*, p. 49.
611. Such an absence would be unlikely, if, as Taylor argued, Luke were well aware of Mk. The predictions of Peter's failure would have been left unfinished.
612. *Behind*, p. 49-54.
613. *Ibid.*, p. 51.
614. *Ibid.*
615. *Ibid.*, p. 52.
616. *Ibid.*, p. 143.
617. *Ibid.*, p. 189-191. The absence of reference in Lk to blasphemy, rather than indicating it had been intentionally deleted by Luke, reflected use of an independent source (cf. p. 51).
618. *Ibid.*, p. 188-193.
619. *Behind*, p. 50. Such a conclusion was implied by Taylor as he suggested that Markan material was abruptly inserted between 22,54a and 22,63. Cf. p. 48. Taylor gave attention to references to Luke's order as found in earlier scholars such as Burkitt (p. 5-6, where he reiterated the axiom that generally Luke does not alter the order of his sources), and Bartlet (p. 15).
620. *Ibid.*, p. 30.

had, that Mk was Luke's primary source, then Taylor was satisfied with the explanation of the variations in order resulting from oral transmission[621]. "But the fixity of oral tradition can never be quite the same thing as that of a document"[622]. Because Luke followed Mk's order whenever he used Mk, Taylor concluded that any diversion from that must be explained by some other means. However, Taylor noted one instance in which Luke clearly changed Mk's order (8,19-21 / Mk 3,31-35)[623]. So the explanation of Markan insertions best accounted for the inversion of order when one assumed, as Taylor has done, that Luke's principal source was not Mk, but rather some other unified written document[624]. Proto-Lk, and not Mk, was Luke's principal source in the compilation of the Third Gospel[625].

Vocabulary was another criterion used in source analysis. Taylor statistically analyzed common words and their distribution in both Gospels. Further, he attended to unusual words or phrases such as πρὸς τὸ φῶς (Lk 22,56 / Mk 14,53, which apparently helped Taylor reach the conviction that the denial of Peter was Markan material). Further, he studied the "stylistic improvements and editorial modification". Taylor made the following observation that necessitated a shift in his own methodology: "Linguistic arguments at present appear to command less sympathy than they received a decade ago"[626]. He concluded, however, in the matter of the Semitisms, that they simply reflected Septuagintal influence and pointed only to the evangelist and not to some source which St. Luke used, as Bartlet maintained[627].

Because Taylor contended that the account of Peter's denial was a later Markan insertion, whereas 22,54a was originally followed immediately by 22,63 in the non-Markan source, the term Ἰησοῦν was unnecessary and the pronoun αὐτόν needed no further clarification as some of the English translations would seem to indicate[628]. The repetition of the term "him" was "surely intentional"[629]. Thus, Taylor highlighted a stylistic characteristic of his proposed unified source.

To support the view that the Proto-Lk hypothesis was consistent with the evangelist's methods in the Gospel as well as Acts, Taylor argued that they both

---

621. *Ibid.*, p. 72.

622. *Ibid.*, p. 30.

623. *Ibid.*, p. 195 = Streeter, in *Peake's Commentary*, p. 673 (cf. above, n. 472). This number has been minimalized by Taylor who recognized non-Markan parallels in passages other scholars would attribute to Lukan redaction of Markan material, e.g. 4,16-30. Cf. NEIRYNCK, *The Argument from Order*, in *ETL* 49 (1973) 797-798, n. 38 (= *Evangelica*, p. 750-751, n. 38).

624. TAYLOR, *Behind*, p. 71-72. However, he was quick to affirm that Luke indeed knew the Markan order (p. 73).

625. *Ibid.*, p. 182.

626. *Ibid.*, p. 203.

627. *Ibid.*, p. 206-207. Cf. BARTLET (1911), p. 316-322, 334, 337, 350.

628. *Ibid.*, p. 50.

629. *Ibid.*

contained a similar geographical arrangement[630]. There were a further five features they shared in common which helped to explain the literary method adopted by the evangelist[631]. Both the "We-Sections" of Acts and Proto-Lk exhibited material which was expanded by the author's "own personal experience or by other informants"[632]. Taylor referred to Harnack's suggestion that the informants were Philip the Evangelist and his daughters[633] and also proposed that some of the early portion of Acts (3-4,35) constituted a "continuation of the Markan narrative"[634].

Taylor advanced several reasons why Proto-Lk should be considered a unified and documentary source. In support of the source's intrinsic unity Taylor cited: 1) the continuity between several non-Markan narratives in Lk 22-24; 2) cross references and connections between individual narratives; 3) a consistent portrayal of Christ throughout the work. Proto-Lk was a written document because 1) the Markan materials appeared clearly as insertions; 2) there were variations in order; 3) from a comparison with other parts of the Gospel, it was obvious that Luke was well aware of the Markan order[635].

Perhaps inadvertently, Taylor himself set upon an aspect of Lukan redaction which could explain the arrangement of Peter's denial as something other than a Markan insertion into non-Markan material: "... we shall see that for the most part St. Luke found homogeneous blocks of Markan material ready for use in the Second Gospel. In some cases, however, he appears to have broken up a Markan section so as to obtain two portions, one or both of which has a unity of its own"[636]. By this same redactional technique might not Luke have separated the Sanhedrin trial and mockery, simultaneously reversing their order to arrive at the arrangement as we now find it in Lk? Taylor did not address the MA in 22,62 but seemed to adopt the view that Mt 26,68 was interpolated from Lk[637].

---

630. *Ibid.*, p. 199.

631. *Ibid.*, p. 200. The five common aspects, which also explained the form, were revealed in the following: "Both are travel documents, and both are rich in miracle stories. Each contains a story of raising from the dead and a farewell address. Each has a city as its goal".

632. *Ibid.* BURKITT, *Use of Mark*, 1922, p. 115, rejected the idea that a travel diary was manifested through the material.

633. *Behind*, p. 200, n. 4. Joanna was named as a likely informant of many stories, among them the account of the trial before Herod, and especially those accounts involving women (p. 248). She could have provided the daughters of Philip with the information. They in turn informed Luke. Reasons supporting such a view were that the four daughters would be in a special position to have access to such information because their father was "pre-eminently the Evangelist of Samaria", Acts 21,8f. implies direct contact with the four daughters (p. 211-212), and since the narratives are both simple and vague, it seems to Taylor that they "rest upon early and good tradition" (p. 251, n. 1).

634. *Ibid.*, n. 5.

635. *Ibid.*, p. 68-75. Cf. NEIRYNCK, *La matière marcienne*, p. 198, n. 171 (= *Evangelica*, p. 78, n. 171).

636. *Behind*, p. 129.

637. *Ibid.*, p. 50, n. 1: "The independence of St. Luke's narrative is still more manifest if

Taylor argued that because Luke referred to a trial during the day and Mark
wrote of a trial by night, this was sufficient reason to reject the view that Mk
served as Luke's source[638]. Granting that a preliminary examination may have
occurred on the same night as the arrest, Taylor asserted that Proto-Lk was
probably to be preferred to Mk[639]. Mk's version "is the more misleading", and
following Burkitt Taylor contended it was unlikely that the Sanhedrin would have
kept a nocturnal vigil for Jesus[640].

Although Taylor was indebted to Streeter for many of his views, he
nevertheless differed from his precursor on a number of points. Taylor advocated
a later date of 60-65 AD rather than 60 AD. It was apparent that Taylor laid greater
stress on verbal statistics than Streeter. Taylor saw his version of the hypothesis
as being closer to the traditional Two-Source theory than the four sources proposed
by Streeter[641]. In that regard Taylor viewed Proto-Lk as a safe haven from any
developments like revisions to Q or special sources such as M and L[642]. But what
was perhaps most significant for our study was that Streeter was far more willing
to accept Markan influence in the passion narrative than Taylor. Thus, Taylor
chastised Streeter for having conceded too much in assigning 23,33–24,10a to Mk
as the source[643]. Finally, Taylor's enthusiasm at the possiblity of discovering a
third source of incomparable historical value was more pronounced than
Streeter's[644].

Without a doubt, one of the greatest services that Taylor provided was his
systematic treatment of the history and development of the special source theory
in Lk from Feine (1891) to Streeter (1924)[645]. Thus, Taylor sought to garner

the question 'Who is he that struck thee?' is an interpolation in Mt from Luke".

638. *Ibid.*, p. 241.

639. *Ibid.*, p. 240.

640. *Ibid.*, p. 241, n. 1. Cf. BURKITT (1906), p. 137. Cf. above.

641. *Ibid.*, p. vi.

642. *Ibid*: "I am not inclined to regret this, for it is important to insist that the Proto-Luke
Theory is not really dependent upon any views we form of Q or other early documents such as
M and L".

643. *Ibid.*, p. 27. Cf. p. 217: "Canon Streeter rightly points out that the reconstruction of QL
from xxii,14 is 'in points of detail highly speculative'. It is probable, however, that he makes too
great a concession in the opinion that from xxiii.33 to xxiv.10a 'Luke reverses his ordinary
procedure and makes Mark his main source'". Cf. above, n. 60.

644. *Ibid.*, p. 246: "The real conclusion is the solid worth of Proto-Luke ... it is a first-rate
authority for all that relates to the Passion and Resurrection. Here, indeed, it is everywhere
comparable to Mk. as a competent witness and where the two disagree it is Proto-Luke as a rule
which preserves the better tradition". Cf. STREETER, *The Four Gospels*, 1924, p. 222: "The
essential point is that Proto-Luke is independent of Mark. Where the two are parallel it would
seem that Proto-Luke is sometimes inferior (e.g. in the details of the Call of Peter), sometimes
superior (e.g. the addition of an account of the trial before Herod). Neither Mark nor Proto-Luke
is infallible; but as historical authorities they should probably be regarded as on the whole of
approximately equal value". It will be remembered that Taylor maintained Proto-Lk did not
contain an account of Peter's denial which stemmed entirely from Mk (*Behind*, p. 49, 67-68).

645. *Behind*, p. 2-27.

evidence from differences in order, vocabulary and timing of events, omissions of Markan material and similarity to other accounts in Acts to support his hypothesis that Luke used both Proto-Lk and Mk, though he gave pride of place to the first source in the passion narrative. Taylor recognized, at least in some points, that the argument could be reversed to suggest that non-Markan sections had been interjected into Markan material[646]. Whatever deficiencies existed in the theory proposed by Bartlet were remedied by Streeter. Likewise, Taylor filled in the gaps left by Streeter assuring that the Proto-Lk hypothesis would remain one with which scholars would have to contend.

Taylor's initial reference in *Behind the Third Gospel* (1926) to the trial before Herod recalled Burkitt's insistence that the mockery by Herod's soldiers was superior to the account of the mockery of the Roman soldiers in Mk 15,16-20[647]. The omission of this Markan account from Lk was adequately explained by Luke's "conscious preference for this source"[648]. Taylor considered all of 23,1-25 as a literary unit wherein the Herod episode hung together without any assistance from Markan material[649]. Taylor originally contended that it was "quite possible" that 23,3 was adopted from oral tradition, but then concluded that Luke based this one verse on Mk[650].

Reception of Behind the Third Gospel

G.S. Duncan (1926) remarked: "Proto-Luke is no longer a hypothesis: it is an established fact. And the unearthing of it means the discovery, not merely of a new Gospel source, but also (we are surely justified in saying) of what is our earliest Gospel"[651].

W.K.L. Clarke valued Taylor's contribution as a book "of first class importance" concerning Luke's sources[652]. Clarke offered a brief but useful historical overview of the special-source question after which he raised no less than

---

646. *Ibid.*, p. 187: "There is force in this argument so long as we limit ourselves to the Q element in the non-Markan sections".

647. *Behind*, p. 7.

648. *Ibid.*, p. 54.

649. *Ibid.* See further his comment, p. 241.

650. *Ibid.*, p. 52-53; cf. p. 54.

651. *Review: V. TAYLOR, Behind, 1926*, in *The Review of the Churches* 3 (1926) 438-439, p. 439. Taylor recalled this acclaim in his last work on Proto-Lk (*The Passion Narrative*, 1972, p. 9).

652. CLARKE, *Review: V. TAYLOR, Behind the Third Gospel, 1926*, in *TLond* 13 (1926) 46-49, p. 46 (= *New Testament Problems*, London, 1929, p. 66-70, p. 66). In his dedicatory epistle to *New Testament Problems*, he wrote about his ability in reviewing other peoples' works: "For many years now I have read more that 1,000 books a year, printed and in manuscript. This leaves me no time for sustained effort. But it does teach me the knack of tearing the hearts out of a book in a short time. So in the following pages you will find a good many summaries of recent books" (p. vi).

nine objections to the Proto-Lk theory, many of them quite substantial. What makes this review so important is that, in spite of these objections, he heartily welcomed Taylor's theory and accepted "the position in the main". With prophetic insight, Clarke predicted that the theory would be better received in Britain than in France or Germany[653]. He took issue with Taylor's contention that "Proto-Luke ... is a scientific hypothesis which is, to a considerable extent, capable of verification". Rather, it was only "a scholar's hypothesis"[654]. The sources of the Lukan passion narrative were not as old as Taylor believed[655]. Further, Clarke accused Taylor of multiplying sources beyond what was necessary for having excluded the infancy narrative and the eschatalogical discourses from Proto-Lk. While the "editorial touches" on the Markan material in Lk reflected "a later stage of the tradition", it was puzzling to consider that Luke would have so drastically revised Mk if he had access to reliable sources of an earlier period. Whereas Taylor (and Streeter before him) claimed that Proto-Lk represented a complete gospel by itself, Clarke observed that it was no wonder that Luke hesitated publishing it, because of its disproportionate make-up. What was more, Clarke effectively and astutely pointed out that Taylor was excessive in his attempt to eliminate Markan influence, as for example in the baptism story[656]. Clarke decried as "arbitrary" Taylor's effort on the one hand, to credit some differences to Luke's free redaction of Mk, while on the other hand attributing still other differences "to a non-Markan (and parallel) source". But what was for Clarke the most formidable objection was that whereas Luke, supposedly having gathered material around 60 AD could not obtain information about the Galilaean ministry of Jesus, Mark almost a decade later, was able to procure such details.

Such herculean objections from a friend of the hypothesis, nonetheless, would all but dismantle it entirely. Arguing that the personal notes comprising the copy of Proto-Lk would not have survived the shipwreck (Acts 27,26), Clarke responded that Luke "had to rewrite them from memory and that this accounts in a measure for the freedom of his editing"[657].

In the final analysis, Clarke judged the proper solution depended upon documentary sources which were amplified by a "considerable use of oral tradition" in addition to the creative redaction of the evangelist[658]. Thus, the writing of Clarke represented a serious challenge to Taylor's position in exposing the inherent weaknesses of the theory.

Taylor responded to each of the nine queries raised by Clarke. Taylor was,

653. *Ibid.*, p. 47 (= 67).

654. *Ibid.* (= 68).

655. *Ibid.* One wishes that Clarke had clarified his statement: "The excellence of Luke's Passion-narrative is a sheet anchor of the theory, but we may well imagine sources of this part of the Gospel-story which did not extend backwards". What would been the nature and extent of these sources in Clarke's opinion?

656. *Ibid.*, p. 48 (= 68-69).

657. *Ibid.*, p. 49 (= 70). Cf. FITZMYER, *Luke*, p. 91.

658. CLARKE, *Review*, p. 49 (= 70).

quite naturally, drawn to Clarke's welcoming assessment that a theory like Proto-Lk was "bound to dominate English speaking Synoptic criticism in the near future". The first objection was a matter of semantics according to Taylor, but the second was much more to the matter at hand. Taylor wrote: "I should hesitate to describe the excellence of St. Luke's Passion-narrative as 'a sheet anchor' of the theory, though the point is one of very great importance"[659]. The apparent alternating nature of the Markan and non-Markan blocks, the secondary nature of the former and the seeming continuity of the latter were far more significant for Taylor. In addressing the fourth objection, Taylor maintained that Luke had not so drastically revised Mk, but that omissions of the Markan material should be assessed in light of Luke's need to reduce such material in favor of the other source. In the fifth case, Taylor reaffirmed that the Proto-Lk hypothesis could stand independent of whatever form Q may take. In the sixth objection, Taylor tempered Streeter's designation of Proto-Lk as a "complete Gospel" by noting that this was introduced as a reaction to Headlam's intervention and that the special source was not circulated precisely because it was incomplete. Clarke had critiqued Taylor saying that he arbitrarily shifted between assigning free editing in some cases to Luke's revision of Mk, but in other cases, to Luke's recasting of the special source[660]. In defense of his position, Taylor relied on a statistical argument and a reference to variations in order. The final bone of contention surrounded the value of Mk in light of the early dating of Proto-Lk, the main difference being that Mark relied on a more complete information about the Galilean ministry, bolstered by his memory of Petrine preaching while Luke had only oral Galilean tradition, in addition to whatever was derived from Proto-Lk.

A.T. Robertson disagreed with Taylor, as he would later with Easton, over the question of sources[661]. "The truth is probably Luke had access to many documents of which we know nothing. He read them all with skill and discernment, as he explains in Luke 1:1-4. I doubt if it can be shown that he had only three". Despite citing the attempt on the part of Taylor to demonstrate that the special material formed a unity as the "least convincing part of the argument at present", H.G. Wood nevertheless believed that the theory was highly probable[662].

Martin Dibelius complimented Taylor's work, filled as it was with good observations[663]. But he termed Taylor's mathematical approach a "sehr

659. V. TAYLOR, *The Proto-Luke Hypothesis. A Reply to Dr. W.K. Lowther Clarke's Queries*, in *TLond* 14 (1927) 73.

660. *Ibid.*, p. 75.

661. *RExp* 23 (1926) 496. Cf. *Review: B.S. EASTON, The Gospel according to St. Luke, 1926*, in *RExp* 24 (1927) 85.

662. *The Friend* 66 (1926) 671-672, p. 672: "But in my judgment, Canon Streeter and Dr. Taylor have made out a very strong case for the proto-Luke hypothesis. [...] This theory is certainly attractive, and I should say that a high degree of probability attaches to it".

663. *TLZ* 52 (1927) 146-148.

bedenkliche Methode"[664]. He suggested that OT influence and the storytelling technique of Luke must first be considered before positing a hypothetical source. Taylor had not given sufficient attention to oral tradition and "die selbständige Arbeit des Lukas". Dibelius did not find Taylor's presentation convincing, e.g. since the continuity of the supposed source was not proven. He nonetheless welcomed the work and saw it as necessary, but called for another study which would examine the literary character of the author of Lk to illuminate the relation of tradition and composition.

In *The First Draft of St. Luke's Gospel* (1927), Taylor was concerned only to provide "a *provisional* form" of Proto-Lk, rather than explaining or defending it[665]. Luke was identified as the compiler around 65 AD. A Q source formed the basis of the special source. Mk only supplemented certain information and did not constitute the structure of Lk. The L material was defined as "matter peculiar to the Third Gospel, either oral or documentary in origin"[666]. The value of the material was indirectly underscored in Taylor's stating that after Q Proto-Lk was the "earliest form of the Gospel".

Assessing British contributions to scholarly debate Taylor (1928) gave pride of place to those of Streeter, especially as they concerned the four-document theory and Proto-Lk. Taylor indicated that British scholarship had benefitted from American counterparts, particularly B.W. Bacon, E. de Witt Burton, C.C. Torrey, G.F. Moore, H.J. Cadbury, S. Jackson Case, and A.M. Perry. Taylor took pains to separate the Proto-Lk hypothesis from that of the four-document theory[667]. In fact, Proto-Lk "is not tied down to any theory of the composition and nature of Q". He proffered seven reasons in support of the special source, including the idea that it, not Mk, provided the basic framework of Lk. He also recognized that the matter of the authorship of Proto-Lk would become the subject of debate. The British reaction was described as offering "a large measure of sympathy and support" as Taylor listed the "general agreement" of F.C. Burkitt, A.S. Peake, A.H. McNeile, H.G. Wood, J.V. Bartlet, W.K.L. Clarke, H.T. Andrews, W.F. Howard, G.S. Duncan as well as other unnamed sympathizers[668]. Taylor viewed his proposal as related to the earlier work of Feine, B. Weiss, J. Weiss, Burkitt, V.H. Stanton, Hawkins, Bartlet, Sanday and Perry. He noted that the assertion that the Lukan passion narrative rested on a non-Markan account had come under attack and considered it important. In calling attention to the article by Hunkin, Taylor again relied on statistical methodology to discuss his case. One significant difference between Hunkin and Taylor was Hunkin's insistence that the framework

---

664. *Ibid.*, p. 147.

665. *The First Draft of St. Luke's Gospel*, in *TLond* 14 (1927) 131-164. He recognized the futility of trying to recover the original form of Proto-Lk, describing such efforts as "speculative in the extreme" (p. 132-133).

666. *Ibid.*, p. 133.

667. *The Synoptic Gospels and Some Recent British Criticism*, in *JR* 8 (1928) 225-246, p. 235.

668. *Ibid.*, p. 238, n. 42. Once again, Taylor failed to provide bibliographical information.

was Markan. Taylor seemed willing to back away from his own position, but still held that whatever decision was rendered on this aspect of the argument affected the value of Proto-Lk, though he still insisted that the structure derived from it rather than Mk[669]. While Taylor continually emphasized the historical value of the special source, as he did in this article, he conceded that it was a good but only secondary work. It was not dependent upon eyewitnesses[670].

In *The Gospels. A Short Introduction* (1930) Taylor devoted a chapter to the Proto-Lk theory and named Feine, B. Weiss, J. Weiss, Burkitt, V.H. Stanton, Hawkins, Bartlet, Sanday and Perry as supporters[671]. Taylor rejected the necessity of presuming that L was a written source. Instead, he preferred to use it to indicate the Caesarean oral tradition, a shift from his position in his article, *The First Draft of Luke's Gospel*. In a seeming concession to those like Hunkin advocating Lukan dependence upon Mk, Taylor now appeared more inclined to accept the view that Mk provided the structure for the passion narrative of Lk. He identified the Markan insertions in that section of Lk as 22,19a.22.34.46b (?).50b.52-53a.54b-61;23,3.26.34b (?).38.44-45.50-54; 24,10(?), to which he added in the ninth edition that 22,39.47.66(?).69.71; 23,33; 24,1-3 had possibly been influenced by Mk[672]. While he adhered to the view that Proto-Lk rested upon the testimony of female disciples of Jesus, he muted the force of his assertion[673].

The passion narrative was Taylor's first argument in support of Proto-Lk with reference made to alternating blocks of Markan and non-Markan material, differences in order, and a further observation that the Markan order was evident in the Markan material in Lk. Taylor insisted that the Markan material did not form a "continuous whole", an argument that had already been put forward in opposition to Proto-Lk. On the contrary, for Taylor, the non-Markan material exhibited a certain continuity. The absence of Markan details from Lk was due to Luke's having followed a parallel account in Proto-Lk or intentional omissions deemed unnecessary by Luke for his purposes.

Taylor continued to suggest Luke himself as the author of the special source, composed between 60 and 65 AD, after his departure for Rome from Caesarea. The value of Proto-Lk would stem from 1) the idea that it would be an authority on a

---

669. *Ibid.*, p. 242: "The point might be thought to be one of subordinate importance, and in a sense it is, but on the other hand, the opinion we form on this question must affect the value we put upon Q+L, and determine our right to speak of this document as Proto-Luke".

670. *Ibid.*, p. 246. Cf. p. 239.

671. *The Gospels. A Short Introduction*, London, 1930, [8]1956, [9]1960, p. 37, n. 1. In the eighth ed. he referred readers to other works including his own *Formation of the Gospel Tradition*, Appendix A; F.C. GRANT, *Growth*, 1933; and F.B. CLOGG, *An Introduction*, 1937, 191-196, 241. In the ninth ed. works by Jeremias, Schürmann and Rehkopf were suggested.

672. *The Gospels*, p. 41.

673. *Ibid.*, [8]1956, p. 43, n. 2. Cf. [9]1960, p. 43. In the eighth ed., Taylor claimed that "Proto-Lk is pre-eminently the Gospel of Women" who made the "first attempt" to transmit the story of Jesus. This note was dropped in the ninth ed.

CHAPTER THREE

par with Mk, 2) the Johannine traditions rested on early traditions because of agreement with Proto-Lk, 3) its ideas from the early Gospel tradition similar to those found in Paul, and 4) the portrayal of Jesus reflected an "early stage of the Gospel".

Taylor did not back down in the face of his critics, including J.M. Creed[674]. Taylor asserted that 22,71 could very well have stemmed from an independent account of the Sanhedrin trial and that 23,3 was "detachable", though it enriched and clarified the concept of kingship and Pilate's declaration of innocence. The differing order resulted from the special source as well as from the manner in which the Markan material has been introduced into the narrative. Taylor argued that Hawkins's position that the differences were the result of a "conflation by the pen" will not stand. Finally, although Creed argued in favor of the view that Luke rewrote the Markan denial scene, a position amenable to Taylor, the amount of Markan words was not so high in other parts of the passion account. He summarized his point of view: "This hypothesis is suggested because, whereas the Markan element is relatively small, its clearest examples are (a) detachable, (b) capable of being regarded as enrichments, (c) present practically in the same succession as in Mark, in spite of twelve differences of order in Luke when compared with Mark"[675].

Despite Taylor's efforts to the contrary, C. Stewart PETRIE (1943-44) was still not convinced by his argumentation[676]. Petrie's "real criticism" was that Taylor made too much of the Markan and non-Markan blocks, "especially of the latter". Taylor's argument was shown to be lacking in another respect: "Dr. Taylor's statement turns upon himself. If it were shown that Mark were supplementary in the Passion Narratives, there is no presumption that it is so elsewhere: just as the use of Mark in the Galilean section allows no presumption of its use elsewhere. The non-use of Mark in the Central section vitiates either assumption"[677].

The question of order was also central for Petrie. There was evidence of "basic Marcan order" even in those places where there were differences between Lk and Mk. Petrie would have pursued this line of argumentation had it not been for "Dr. Taylor's later admission of 'the *fact* that Luke follows the Markan sequence so closely'"[678]. The extent of Markan material combined with the closeness to Markan order provided the basis for Petrie's rejection of Proto-Lk. Although Petrie admired the work involved in developing and defending Proto-Lk, he rejected the hypothesis. Nor was he necessarily convinced that Mk was "'the main source' for the whole of Luke", though he did not elaborate on this final

674. *Professor J.M. Creed and the Proto-Luke Hypothesis*, in *ExpT* 46 (1934-35) 236-238. See also *Passion Narrative*, p. 12-15. Cf. below.

675. *Ibid.*, p. 237-238.

676. C.S. PETRIE, *The Proto-Luke Hypothesis: Observations on Dr. Vincent Taylor's Rejoinder*, in *ExpT* 55 (1943-44) 52-53.

677. *Ibid.*, p. 52.

678. *Ibid.*

point[679].

For an essay about the life and ministry of Jesus (1951), Taylor supported the idea that Luke relied on the Markan account as well as the special passion account from L[680]. In his Markan commentary (1952), Taylor briefly alluded to the special Lukan passion source citing Perry, Streeter, Bultmann and himself in favor of the idea, and only Creed as opposed[681]. Avoiding any detailed description, he simply stated there was "good reason" for postulating such a view. That statement was unaltered in the second edition (1966), but Taylor added a brief note on two recent articles by Ivor Buse who claimed that Luke drew material from an independent passion source prior to using Mk. Taylor also referred to Rehkopf's *Die lukanische Sonderquelle* (1959)[682].

In *The Names of Jesus* (1953) Taylor argued that, of the seven Son of Man sayings probably contained in the L source, 22,69 was described as eschatological[683]. The verse was regarded as different from Mk because in Lk there was only mention of the Son of Man sitting at the right hand of God. Yet, in Taylor's discussion of the title Christ, for which he listed six instances in Lk (22,67; 23,2.35.39; 24,26.46), he declared that they "resemble those in Mk."[684].

In a discussion of the Sanhedrin trial in *Jesus and His Sacrifice* (1955) Taylor commented: "The relation of the saying in the Lukan account of the trial before the Priests (xxii.66-71) to Mk. xiv.55-64 is difficult to determine"[685]. Though he acknowledged that most scholars favored Lukan dependence upon Mk, he

---

679. *Ibid.*, p. 53: "For the industry expended on Proto-Luke I have a sincere admiration, but this does not bind me to accept the hypothesis. When its claims are called in question, especially (I must insist) against the demonstrable Mark, the onus of proof surely is on those who contend for Proto-Luke. There is no necessary call for the re-establishment of Mark as 'the main source' for the whole of Luke. For that is not the only alternative to Proto-Luke. Indeed, the claim that there is only one 'main source' may have no support from the facts".

680. *The Life and Ministry of Jesus*, in *IB* 7, 1951, 114-144, esp. p. 114, n. 1 and 137 (= *The Life and Ministry of Jesus*, rev. and enlarged, London, 1954).

681. V. TAYLOR, *The Gospel According to St. Mark. The Greek Text with Introduction, Notes and Indexes*, London, 1952, ᴿ1963, ²1966, p. 526. He also referred the reader to the article of A. BARR, *The Use and Disposal of the Marcan Source in Luke's Passion Narrative*, in *ExpT* 55 (1943-44) 227-231.

682. *The Gospel According to St. Mark*, ²1966, p. 671. The articles were: I. BUSE, *St. John and the Marcan Passion Narrative*, in *NTS* 4 (1957-58) 215-219; *St. John and the Passion Narratives of St. Matthew and St. Luke*, in *NTS* 7 (1960-61) 65-76. The reader should be cautioned that the 1981 reprinting of the second ed. of Taylor's Markan commentary (Grand Rapids, MI, ᴿ1981) does not contain the section "Recent Markan Studies", p. 667-671, which provided this information about Buse and Rehkopf. Nor does the index appear to be updated. The more complete information can be found in V. TAYLOR, *The Gospel of Mark*, London, ²1966, ᴿ1977.

683. TAYLOR, *The Names of Jesus*, London, 1953, ᴿ1962, p. 29. The book contained the first series of the Speaker's Lecture at Oxford, 1951-52.

684. *Ibid.*, p. 19.

685. *Jesus and His Sacrifice, A Study of the Passion Sayings in the Gospels*, London, 1955, p. 196.

nevertheless held his own ground. He described the L source as "less than two-thirds the size of Mark".

Taylor was prompted to write again (1955) in light of the "hesitation" of scholars to use the hypothesis[686]. Though critics assailed it, the theory survived, in Taylor's opinion, because they did not treat the entire theory. He listed the major opponents as well as quoted several scholars' opinion of the theory[687]. In reference to Creed's oft quoted dismissal of the theory in a footnote, Taylor maintained that Streeter successfully refuted it[688]. Hunkin's modification of Streeter's theory was not convincing since it did not adequately take the omissions into consideration. Petrie's attack was faulted for focusing too narrowly on 3,1–9,50. In response to Kilpatrick, Taylor found it unlikely that Luke would have substituted "innocent man" for "Son of God"[689]. He called for further study of A. Barr's suggestion that the verbal correspondence was low at points in brief narratives where non-Markan material was connected to the Markan. Rather than being dissuaded, Taylor welcomed the criticisms as a chance to review the hypothesis. As for matters pertaining to the passion narrative, while the theory would need to be honed in details, it had withstood the criticisms. He admitted the possibility that Mk had been employed in 23,18-25. Further on the relation of Proto-Lk to Mk Taylor wrote: "No serious damage is done to the hypothesis by the admission that, in expanding Proto-Luke, Luke on occasion gave priority to Mark"[690]. It was an appeal for cooperation from both sides of the debate, but especially for constructive criticism from the opposition.

Writing about the books which had most significantly affected him, Taylor (1959) listed Streeter's *The Four Gospels* and credited it with his lifelong interest in the subject. He acknowedged a debt to Perry and Hawkins for the matter of the

---

686. *Important Hypotheses Reconsidered. 1. The Proto-Luke Hypothesis*, in *ExpT* 67 (1955-56) 12-16 (= *Passion Narrative*, p. 15-17; see below).

687. *Ibid.*, p. 12-13. The critics included: J.M. Creed (1930, p. lviii n., lxiv, 86, 140, 262), J.W. Hunkin (*JTS* 28, 1927, see above), C.S. Petrie (*ExpT* 54, 1942-43), A. Barr (*ExpT* 55, 1943-44), G.D. Kilpatrick (*JTS* 43, 1941-42), S. McL. Gilmour (*JBL* 67, 1948, but also his commentary in *IB*). Taylor's response to the arguments of these scholars provided the bulk of the article. Negative assessments had also been rendered by R.H. Lightfoot (*ExpT* 53, 1941-42) p. 51; *History*, p. 164), E.C. Hoskyns and N.F. Davey (*Riddle*, p. 16f.), A. Richardson (*Gospels*, p. 18f.) and A. Farrer (*Study*, 1951, p. 210). Others who rejected the idea were W. Bussmann (*Synoptischen Studien*), L. Vaganay (*Le problème synoptique*) and M. Goguel (*HTR* 26, 1933; cf. A.H. McNeile, *Introduction*, rev. C.S.C. Williams, p. 61). Among the supporters Taylor counted Streeter (1924) W.F. Howard (*The London Quarterly and Holborn Review*, 1952, p. 11; cf. TAYLOR, *Passion Narrative*, p. 15), R. Bultmann (*GST*, p. 284, 290, 292f., 302f.), J. Jeremias (*Eucharistic*, p. 69f.), F.C. Grant (*Growth*, p. 9, 170), B.W. Bacon (*Studies*, p. 505), B.S. Easton (1926).

688. *Important*, p. 13. Cf. STREETER, *Preface* to *The Four Gospels*, 1930, p. xiiif. Cf. below Creed.

689. *Important*, p. 15; cf. KILPATRICK, *JTS* 43 (1942) 34-36 (= *Principles*, 313-318), and *JTS* 1 (1950) 56-60 (= *Principles*, 245-249).

690. *Important*, p. 16.

passion narrative and explained that W. Bussman and J. Jeremias also helped him. Taylor's conviction remained strong: "... I do not think that the criticisms which have been brought against this hypothesis are likely to prevail"[691].

Taylor took the opportunity to reiterate his views in favor of Proto-Lk in *IDB* (1962), although he admitted that Luke's use of Mk was indisputable and the consensus was that Mk provided the framework for Lk[692]. Mk was a principal source, though clearly not the primary one. Despite objections to the hypothesis, because Taylor regarded the special source as having been "widely accepted" and its existence probable, he assumed that Proto-Lk constituted a stage in the Gospel's development. But it was the theory's detractors who demanded too much of the hypothesis. "In general, one must say that the hypothesis has suffered from attempts to determine too precisely the contents of Proto-Luke, especially in the passion narrative"[693]. Imprecision, then, favored the special source hypothesis. In a companion article on the synoptic problem, Donald T. ROWLINGSON noted that while the Proto-Lk theory appealed to some, a still greater number rejected it in favor of other explanations[694]. Reaction was particularly strong against the view that this supposed source provided the framework[695].

Offering a retrospective a few years after Taylor's death (1970), C.L. MITTON declared: "Dr. Taylor sensed the importance of this brilliant suggestion ..."[696]. The testimony continued: "He remained convinced, to the very end of his life, that this theory explained better than any other the literary facts he found in Luke's Gospel". Mitton listed Dodd, T.W. Manson, Jeremias, Grant and Fuller as supporters, in addition to Rehkopf and Schürmann[697]. Mitton drew attention to what he termed the reluctance of opponents to address the argument in detail, characterizing W.G. Kümmel's evaluation in his *Introduction* (1966, p. 92-95) as being the "fullest statement" opposing the theory. G.B. Caird, in turn, was seen as refuting Kümmel's attack drawing from the storehouse old as well as new arguments. But Mitton, despite his obvious appreciation of the theory and admiration for Taylor concluded: "If the Proto-Luke hypothesis ever wins its way into scholarly orthodoxy, it will be due to Streeter's flash of insight and Vincent

---

691. *Milestones in Books*, in *ExpT* 70 (1959) 231-233, p. 232 (= *New Testament Essays*, London, 1970, 31-35 p. 33).

692. *Gospel of Luke* in *IDB* 3, 1962, p. 184.

693. *Ibid.*, p. 185.

694. *Synoptic Problem*, in *IDB* 4, 1962, p. 495. Supporters included Taylor, Manson and Parker. Alternate explanations were provided by Perry, Grant, Cadbury, Hunkin, Montefiore, Goguel, and Creed.

695. *Ibid.* Rowlingson also stated there was a majority of scholars who rejected Burkitt's proposal that Q contained a passion narrative (p. 494).

696. *Vincent Taylor: New Testament Scholar*, in TAYLOR, *New Testament Essays*, 1970, p. 10. In the same volume O.E. Evans provided a useful bibliography of Taylor's published works covering the period 1919-1964 (p. 141-146).

697. *Ibid.*, p. 11. Mitton did not specify, but it was probably F.C. Grant to whom he was referring.

Taylor's patient and detailed demonstration of its validity - what Dr. Taylor himself called his 'substantial verification' of it"[698].

In *The Passion Narrative of St Luke* (1972) edited posthumously by a former student, Owen E. Evans, Taylor revived his long held thesis prompted by four factors: the vocabulary studies of Schürmann and Rehkopf, and to a lesser degree of Jeremias; the fact that *Behind the Third Gospel* was out of print; because he had reviewed both sides of the debate and was convinced more than ever of the correctness of the position; his desire to see confirmed the historical reliability of a source on a par with Mk[699]. The book was divided into three parts. The first part, his introduction, contained a survey of the main figures of the debate, as well as a discussion of various methodological approaches, including the statistical approach which he pursued in this work. Taylor also offered the most comprehensive historical survey of the Proto-Lk hypothesis available at that time. The second part presented a detailed examination of Lk 22–24. In the final section he set forth his conclusions, reconstructing the (English) text of that portion of the Gospel, and assessing the historical and theological value of the special Lukan passion narrative.

In the preface he recalled that the Proto-Lk hypothesis had been welcomed initially "with very considerable favor" but attributed its demise to Creed, Hunkin and R.H. Lightfoot[700]. Other developments within the field of biblical criticism, namely the shift away from literary criticism to form criticism and biblical theology, were also contributing factors. Taylor distinguished his present study from his earlier one (1926) by means of a "greater use of linguistic arguments". Taylor limited his study to the passion narrative, yet claimed that if his case were proven there, it was proven for the entire Gospel (which is not true). He was

---

698. *Ibid.*, p. 12.

699. V. TAYLOR, *The Passion Narrative of St Luke. A Critical and Historical Investigation* (SNTS MS, 19), ed. O.E. EVANS, Cambridge, 1972. See p. 41. Taylor continued working on the book "from early 1962 to late 1965" (editorial note, p. xi). It seems that he viewed his book as an invitation addressed only to British scholars, thinking perhaps that the idea would receive a more favorable hearing just as it had in the early days of the theory (p. viii).

Evans noted that even as the work was being published, the study by Schramm appeared "which to some extent confirms Dr Taylor's views concerning Luke's method of using his sources" (p. 37). It was also observed that the results of E. BAMMEL (ed.), *The Trial of Jesus* and G. SCHNEIDER, *Verleugnung* were not included in Taylor's second section. Though Schneider rejected Proto-Lk, their views were similar that Luke used a continuous narrative in addition to Mk. Evans made his comments based not on his reading of Schneider's work, but on a recension by C.F.D. Moule (*Review* in *JTS* 22 [1971] 194-197).

700. *The Passion Narrative*, p. vii. Cf. p. 11. R.H. Lightfoot's criticisms were contained in *Form Criticism and Gospel Study*, in *ExpT* 53 (1941-42) 51-54, esp. p. 51 (= *The Gospel Message of St Mark*, Oxford, 1950, 98-105, esp. p. 99). Evans added in an editorial note (27-30) that W.G. Kümmel and E.E. Ellis also rejected the Proto-Lk hypothesis. Evans denied Kümmel's claim that Taylor eventually admitted that Mk formed the framework for the Gospel (p. 28). But Evans was mistaken. Taylor's article, *Methods of Gospel Criticism*, in *ExpT* 71 (1959-60) 68-72, constitutes a portion of *The Passion Narrative*, p. 30-37, "with some modifications".

correct in assuming that any advance in this section of the Gospel, which Streeter viewed as the weakest link, would bolster the validity of the theory. The later work then was much the same as *Behind the Third Gospel* with only a few modifications: Luke was responsible for combining L+Q.

In the historical portion of the study, he dedicated only several lines to the views of Feine, B. Weiss and J. Weiss[701]. Burkitt's view that Luke used a form of Q containing an account of the passion was rightly criticized since it did not explain why Matthew would have ignored it.

Taylor responded to the criticism that the theory was more popular in Great Britain than in Germany or America, by indicating that Germany was veering toward acceptance. Taylor lamented the fact that some of the opponents dismissed the theory without presenting their arguments.

In his evaluation of Rehkopf's vocabluary list of pre-Lukan terms, Taylor rejected a combined sum of nine words and phrases from the proposed total of 82 and twice warned against employing the list "in a mechanical manner"[702]. He regarded it as a corrective of Hawkins's list. Evans added an update on Schürmann's analysis of Rehkopf's list, in which Schürmann concluded, as B. Weiss had much earlier, that it was not possible to determine Proto-Lk "by means of linguistic and stylistic criteria". It was not clear what effect these results would have had on Taylor's estimation of the list.

Taylor recognized that statistics alone were insufficient to prove the special source, but when combined with literary and style criticism, could be considered nearly certain. He favored this method though this method too was subjective as the other methods were[703]. He rightly observed that apologetic and doctrinal motives helped shape the account as did the fulfillment of Scripture[704].

Taylor regarded 22,54a as the end of the arrest account rather than the beginning of the story of Peter's denials. Words common to Lk and Mk were συλλαβόντες, εἰσήγαγον, τοῦ ἀρχιερέως, differed in form, though Taylor did not discuss the verse part in the commentary which followed.

For the account of Peter's denials (22,54b-61) there was Markan vocabluary in each of the verses, constituting nearly half the total so that Taylor reasoned: "The conclusion to be drawn is that Mark is Luke's source and perhaps his only written source". The differences between the two Gospels "can be adequately explained" as drawing on and developing Markan material, though they were probably due to oral tradition[705]. Nevertheless Taylor did not entirely dismiss the

701. It should be noted that in referring to the position of J. Weiss, Taylor used *Die Schriften des Neuen Testaments* (1906) rather than his commentary of 1892.

702. TAYLOR, *The Passion Narrative*, p. 20, 27. See also p. 30.

703. *Ibid.*, p. 37: "It is subjective, but attains increasing objectivity the more its conclusions are widely adopted by competent scholars, although rarely if ever to the exclusion of alternative explanations".

704. *Ibid.*, p. 37.

705. *Ibid.*, p. 77. Taylor enumerated the differences: lighting a fire (22,55); the passage of time (22,59); various accusers (22,58.59); no reference to Peter going to the gateway (Mk 14,68),

possibility of another source which could have been responsible for v. 61. Lukan redaction unified the Petrine material over against Mk and was recognized in some of the vocabulary[706].

The mockery (22,63-65) was the evangelist's revision of the account taken from the special source. Taylor deduced on the basis of a low percentage of agreement in vocabulary[707], difference in pericope order and variation in the characters. Taylor followed Streeter's interpretation of the MA in 22,64, original to the Lukan account, but he did not explain its appearance in Mt.

The decision regarding the Sanhedrin trial (22,66-71) was a most difficult one. Agreeing with Easton that although the story contained Markan reminiscences, it was not a redaction of Mk, Taylor believed that the special source, aware of the morning setting of the trial, lacked specific information about it except that the Messiah question had been pivotal. Vocabulary, in this case, was not helpful in reaching a conclusion. It was here that his case for the special source appeared the weakest. Taylor failed to indicate clearly from whence the account originated.

Taylor was certain that 23,1-5 stemmed from the non-Markan source, except for the Markan insertion in v. 3. He was less sure about 23,18-25 which seemed to him to come from the special source, with the exception of v. 25 which was a Lukan composition[708]. It seemed to Taylor that Luke resumed the special source in 23,23-24, a view which coincided with B. Weiss who believed that Luke resumed his use of "L" in v. 23. Vocabulary common to both Mk and Lk were signaled in 23,1.3-4.18-25[709]. Once again a low percentage of verbal agreement was cited as a major factor in the decision. Taylor noted common vocabulary between Lk-Acts in the term αἶρε (23,18; Acts 21,36; 22,22). Though redaction of Mk or the special source could have accounted for this section, Taylor decided that the special source was "the more probable" solution based on agreements between Lk and Jn.

The Lukan passion narrative was based on a non-Markan source or sources with the exception of 22,1-13.54b-61; 23,50-54 and certain other Markan insertions, additions and editorial compositions[710]. In a more detailed enumeration of Markan elements he listed: 22,1-13.22.34.46b.50b.52b-53a.54b-61;

---

to the cursing or to the double cock crow (Mk 14,71.72) or καὶ ἐπιβαλὼν ἔκλαιεν (Mk 14,72).

706. *Ibid.*, p. 78. Characteristic Lukan terms were: ἄγω, a συν-compound (συνκαθίζειν), τις, ἀτενίζειν, σύν, ἕτερος, ὡσεί, παραχρῆμα and στραφείς. Words occurring only in Lk-Acts included: διϊσχυρίζεσθαι and διΐστημι. Taylor also indicated vocabulary from Rehkopf's list of pre-Lukan terminology: three vocatives (γύναι and ἄνθρωπε - twice), ὁ κύριος (twice), εἶπεν with the dative, μακρόθεν and στραφείς.

707. *Ibid.*, p. 79. Markan vocabulary was seen in vv. 63.64: καὶ, αὐτῷ, καὶ περικαλύψ-, λέγ-, προφήτευσον. Typical Lukan terms were: ἀνήρ, συνέχειν, and ἕτερος. It was customary for Luke to use participles, and in contrast to Mark's use of the aorist, to employ the imperfect.

708. *Ibid.*, p. 89.

709. *Ibid.*, p. 85-86. Characteristic Lukan words were: ἀναστάς, ἅπαν τὸ πλῆθος, ἄγω, τοῦτον, ἐρωτάω, πρός and λαός.

710. *Ibid.*, p. 119.

23,3.26.34b.38.44f.49.50-54; 24,10a. A few other verses seemed to indicate Markan influence: 22,47.69.71; 24,1-3. By the end of his examination, Taylor changed his mind on several verses including 22,69. He now rejected it "as possibly Markan or partially assimilated to the Markan parallel"[711].

Although the account within the passion narrative from the arrest to the centurion's confession originally circulated independently, Taylor declared that the non-Markan passion and resurrection comprised a continuous narrative prior to Lk for three reasons: it constituted a story in itself; it formed a narrative unity replete with cross-references and connections; it presented a consistent portrayal of Jesus. Based on the manner in which he conceived that Mk was used Taylor conjectured that this special source was a document. He cited Feine, Hawkins and Sanday in support of this view. This viewpoint was further substantiated, in his opinion, because it appeared that the Markan material had been inserted, and thus was secondary. In addition, there were differences in order. He rejected Hawkins's suggestion that they resulted from oral transmission since it was unlikely that the evangelist had forgotten the order. Instead he simply adopted the order of the non-Markan source, with variations resulting from the Markan insertions. But Taylor did not explain how Mark would have arrived at a different order from that given in the special source. Despite this new order, Taylor contended that Luke was well aware of the Markan order. Because of its apparent historical reliability, stemming from people very familiar with the tradition, the special material of the passion and resurrection comprised only a part of a larger (Proto-Lk) document.

Taylor modified his earlier position of *Behind the Third Gospel*. Relying on Rehkopf's findings, he stated that the vocabulary of the special source was distinct from that of Lk-Acts and thus Luke did not compile the special source[712]. Although he still considered it probable that it was composed around 60-65 AD, and that Luke obtained it during his visit to Caesarea (Acts 21,8), he now believed that the unknown author of the special source was associated with Philip the evangelist and his daughters.

Several sections were cited where the Lukan passion was thought to be historically superior. One was the unlikelihood that the religious leaders participated in the mockery (22,63-65). What was more, the response of Jesus to the question about messiahship (v. 67) could not have been a "Christian formation" and from that Taylor claimed that it was much more similar to what Jesus had really said. Luke's account was also more believable because of the morning timing of the Sanhedrin trial. The politicization of the charges persuaded Taylor that they rested on a more reliable source. Though Taylor acknowledged that Luke revised his sources, he was convinced that it was possible to distinguish their original form from what they had become in his hands[713].

Taylor concluded "that [23,]6-16 was composed by Luke himself out of

711. *Ibid.*, n. 1.
712. *Ibid.*, p. 125-126.
713. *Ibid.*, p. 140.

tradition contained in the non-Markan source"[714]. While both Mark and Luke used οἱ γραμματεῖς, Taylor downplayed any Markan influence because Luke used the term in 22,66. What was more he rejected Easton's suggestion that the story stemmed from the L special source unless Luke had authored it, a view Taylor considered highly unlikely[715]. He believed that though the author was unknown, he was associated with Philip the evangelist and his four daughters[716].

The matter of historicity was problematic, in part, because there was no previous reference to any dispute between the two leaders. But Taylor admitted that Streeter may have been right in assuming that it arose from the murder of the Galileans described in 13,1-5. Other elements favored the historicity. Luke appeared to have had special access to information about Herod (8,3). The point of view in Ps 2, fulfilled in Acts 4,25f. as well as the motif of the silence of the Servant of God, appeared to be consistent with 23,12. Taylor did not raise the discussion about Dibelius. Taylor continued to defend the special-source theory throughout his scholarly life.

Reviews of Taylor's "The Passion Narrative of St. Luke"

Ernst Best (1972) judged that Taylor's case had been reinforced by the contributions of Schürmann and Rehkopf[717]. Unlike many of the other reviewers, Best was convinced that Luke had drawn on other material in the passion, but stopped short of agreeing that it was a continuous source. However, in concert with the others, Best criticized Taylor's methodology. The starting point, assuming that Luke employed either Mk or another source, ignored other possibilities. The cumulative effect was, "All this combines to vitiate Taylor's attempt to construct *the* non-Markan pre-Lukan Passion narrative and nullifies his claim to see in it better history than in Mark"[718]. Yet Best issued a challenge to redaction critics not only to state their position, but to show how the changes coincided with Luke's redaction of Mk.

George Caird entitled his positive review, "The Return of Proto-Luke" and insisted "that the Proto-Luke theory has been abused, attacked, or ignored, but never answered"[719]. Creed and Gilmour were accused of bypassing the theory and attacking "an Aunt Sally of their own making". Caird believed that the theory had been strengthened by the work of other scholars. He was most impressed by Taylor's presentation on the matter of order, in which Taylor showed where Luke

714. *Ibid.*, p. 89. Taylor rejected Creed's assessment that 23,10-11 should be excised (p. 87, n. 5).
715. *Ibid.*, p. 87. See also p. 125ff. In addition, Taylor dismissed the view that the story derived from a source since only two words cited by Rehkopf occurred in the pericope (p. 87).
716. *Ibid.*, p. 125-126.
717. *ScotJT* 25 (1972) 474-475.
718. *Ibid.*, p. 475.
719. *ExpT* 83 (1972-73) 379.

followed the Markan order and agreed with the assessment that differences in order were due to Markan insertions, without giving consideration to any other possibilty.

Hendrikus Boers (1973) joined voices with those who were unconvinced by Taylor's argumentation and "speculative" conclusions, particularly where it concerned a single continuous narrative source[720]. Although Boers conceded that Luke used non-Markan material, he denied the degree that Taylor postulated.

Christian Ceroke was attentive to a shift that occurred in Taylor's thinking from his doctoral dissertation (published as *Behind the Third Gospel*), wherein he earlier denied that Mk formed the outline for Lk[721]. The benefits derived from the work included redirecting attention to the relation of Mk and Lk and the matter of the L material.

Morton Enslin did not "share Taylor's optimism regarding the certainty – or even the likelihood – of the existence of Proto-Luke", and also stated his distrust of sources L, M and Q[722]. Taylor's shortcoming was his refusal to consider Luke as a redactor in a broader sense of the term: "It appears to me that the basic reason leading to the contention that Luke 'preferred a different source for his narrative of the passion than he found in Mark' is unwillingness to see Luke unhesitatingly altering, even contradicting, Mark when by doing so he felt he could improve his story". Differences were attributed to sources, rather than to evangelists out of regard for the sacred nature of the biblical word. But Enslin concluded with a prediction worth quoting: "Luke will come to be seen as an extraordinarily able and versatile author who had no slightest scruples against altering earlier accounts in the better whole which he was sure he was writing; the growing arcana of written sources which exerted so momentous but also so momentary an influence will become conspicuously fewer, and while still tolerated will be styled and regarded 'hypothetical,' as they most surely are"[723].

C.F. Evans expressed admiration for Taylor's willingness to reexamine his earlier work and seemed to issue a challenge in declaring that Taylor's arguments in *Behind the Third Gospel* had never been comprehensively answered[724]. He noted the difficulty of discerning tradition and redaction citing Rehkopf's and Schürmann's differing conclusions on the prediction of betrayal (22,21-23). Taylor was justified to insist that linguistic arguments alone were insufficient, but Evans disagreed with Taylor, who like Jeremias, believed that differences in order signified another source. An additional difficulty was determining whether the Markan material was primary, especially when there was a smaller amount of it. A final difficulty, addressed by form criticism, was attempting to decide if the oral

---

720. *Interpr* 27 (1973) 114.
721. *CBQ* 35 (1973) 558: "Although this study does not confirm the Proto-Luke hypothesis as T. developed it in 1926 (when he denied that the Marcan outline was a principal frame of reference for Lk) ...".
722. *Religion in Life* 42 (1973) 276.
723. *Ibid.*
724. *TLond* 76 (1973) 35-36.

stage was not responsible to a great extent for written verbal agreements. Though one senses that Evans saw various weaknesses in the work, for him it set a standard: "Nevertheless, the most important thing about this book is not whether the reader agrees or disagrees with it, but that he has set out here with care and clarity the evidence and arguments on which agreement or disagreement are to be based"[725].

Lloyd Gaston pointed out that while Taylor referred to Schürmann and Rehkopf, he passed over the work of Sahlin[726]. Gaston also highlighted development in Taylor's thought by ascribing more material to Lukan editorial writing than was the case in 1926. Consequently, Luke could not have been the author, as Enslin also noted. Despite these developments, those who were unimpressed by Taylor's arguments in 1926 will not change their position as a result of the present work. The question was still open, but one detects in Gaston's statement a question whether the exact nature of a special source can ever be determined[727].

A.R.C. Leaney, who debated Taylor in earlier forums, was unimpressed by the theory. Not only had Leaney examined it in his commentary, but in an unpublished Oxford B.D. thesis[728]. Referring to the centrality of the passion narrative for the theory, Leaney rightly observed: "If protagonists of Proto-Luke cannot persuade us on this ground they have lost the battle"[729]. Taylor's perspective was determined, in part, by his perception that Luke was a historian rather than a theologian, which for Leaney skewed the result of the vocabulary study. He further contended that Taylor's conclusion that Proto-Lk was a document rested "on flimsy grounds". Taylor seemed to have it both ways. The order of the special source was different from Mk, though Luke was quite aware of the Markan order. While the work was useful, it remained unconvincing for Leaney who asserted that the theory was one which can be "all too easily resisted"[730].

John Drury focused on the central concern for Taylor in relentlessly pursuing the theory, that of historical reliability[731]. But regarding Taylor's methodology, Drury wrote: "Statistical criticism is at the same time the most precise of

---

725. *Ibid.*, p. 36.

726. *JBL* 93 (1973) 455-456.

727. *Ibid.*, p. 455: "Compelling demonstrating of the thesis of a special Lucan source still lies in the future *if at all;*" [emphasis added].

728. *ATR* 55 (1973) 511-513. The thesis was unavailable to me. He incorporated sections of this work entitled *The Sources of the Gospel according to St. Luke* (1952), in his Lukan commentary. "I had grappled in great detail with all the relevant areas of the two gospels in an Oxford B.D. thesis which was never published and which Taylor never saw; in my *Commentary on the Gospel according to St. Luke* some of these arguments, especially in the Little Apocalypse and Passion Narrative sections, are used in the actual commentary" (*ATR*, p. 511).

729. *Ibid.*, p. 512.

730. *Ibid.*, p. 513.

731. *JTS* 24 (1973) 541-543.

disciplines and the hardest to use and assess"[732]. Even a single Markan sentence could have inspired Luke to compose at greater length. The isolation of a few sentences, though high in Markan content, can have the effect of blunting the overall influence when separated from the general context. Taylor, according to Drury, had not sufficiently considered this. One's presuppositions have an influence on the results of one's studies and such was the case with Taylor. Part three of Taylor's work which Leaney and Luz criticized, also came under attack by Drury, but this time as being "too short" to come to any adequate solution. The theory was alive, but Taylor had not triumphed over Creed. Taylor's shortcomings were his almost exclusive reliance on the statistical criticism while, as Best had also claimed, not taking into consideration Luke's literary capability.

Gerhard Schneider noted that Taylor renewed his theory in part due to the research of Schürmann and Rehkopf, which had also pointed out the inadequacy of the statistical approach that had been in use[733]. Material drawn from Mk included: 22,1-13.22.34.46b.50b.52b-53a.54b-61; 23,3.26.34b.38.44-45.49.50-54; 24,10a. Probable Markan influence was recognized at 22,47.69.71; 24,1-3. Taylor also indicated 23,25 as a Markan element, though he remained undecided about 22,19a. In an earlier article in *ExpT*, Taylor considered 22,39.66; 23,33 as possibly Markan. The difficulty was that he relied on Rehkopf's list of Proto-Lukan vocabulary, which Schneider described as "problematisch". He further termed Taylor's reliance on the statistical method "unsinnig". Schneider faulted Taylor's reasoning for positing a non-Markan source simply on the basis of the lack of Markan vocabulary. Schneider asserted his belief that Mk 15 formed the basis for Lk 23. Regarding differences in order, he penned: "Der Einwand, dass Lukas hier – gegen seine Gewohnheit – Mk-Perikopen umgestellt haben müsste, geht darum ins Leere, weil die 'Umstellungen' nicht auf Perikopenebene erfolgen, sondern minderen Ranges sind"[734]. Because little of Taylor's overall conclusions had changed since 1926, Schneider judged that the book would do little to revive the theory.

Ulrich Luz (1974) complimented Taylor for the care with which he treated his topic and judged the second part of the book to be the most important[735]. While noting the primary methodology resting on statistics of vocabulary and an analysis of the style criticism, Luz pointed out that Taylor only "sehr züruckhaltend" offered theological arguments, the most problematic area since he never explained or substantiated his case. Though Taylor did not press much beyond Hawkins's analysis of Luke's preferred terms, his inclusion of details from Rehkopf and Schürmann was carefully nuanced. Luz was not as optimistic as Taylor that a

---

732. *Ibid.*, p. 542.

733. *TRev* 69 (1973) 285: "Die Arbeiten von H. Schürmann und F. Rehkopf zu Lk 22 gaben T. nicht nur den Mut zu erneuten Darstellung seiner früheren These, sie trugen auch dazu bei, die bisher angewandte statistische Methode als unzureichend zu erkennen".

734. *Ibid.*, p. 286.

735. *TZ* 30 (1974) 239-240. Luz described the Proto-Lukan theory as "ein Lieblingskind der englischen Forschung" (p. 239).

reconstruction of the special source was possible. Whereas Streeter recognized the difficulties inherent in the passion narrative for the hypothesis, Taylor made it the capstone of his own theory. Luz wrote: "Und noch problematischer ist das Postulat eines Protolukas aufgrund der Passionsquelle"[736]. Nevertheless, Luz believed that Taylor had convincingly pressed his case. Quite often, in the various reviews, the word used to describe Taylor's work was "clarity". Despite that, it seems that his argumentation was not sufficient to convince the reviewers.

As early as 1924 Thomas Walter MANSON believed that chronologically Lk followed Mk but preceded Mt[737]. Lk and Mt used two different forms of Q, Luke's being the more primitive of the Aramaic versions. But Mk was only a secondary source from which Luke selectively drew additional material[738]. Manson affirmed Streeter's theory: "It seems to me that Streeter was right in his main contention that the document Proto-Lk was a definite stage in the composition of our Luke and that the next step was the incorporation of extracts from Mark into Proto-Lk rather than the expansion of Mark by the insertion of Proto-Lukan material"[739]. Manson distinguished two types of Gospel literature, that which was intended internally for the community (Q and Mk definitely, Mt and Jn probably) and the second which was destined for publication in order to instruct outsiders (Lk), though this does not necessarily apply to Proto-Lk.

Manson's reconstruction of the development of Proto-Lk began with Luke's obtaining a copy of Q in Greek from Antioch to which he added material he had gathered, especially at Caesarea. At Rome he added Markan material in line with his decision to present his work to non-believers. Dating the publication of Lk-Acts 64-70 AD or a little later, the process of composing Lk-Acts could have been as early as the year 39 or as late as 55 AD Like others who supported the special source, Manson was of the conviction that Luke faithfully reported from his sources and followed their order.

In contrast to Feine's understanding of Luke's method of using sources, Manson believed that Luke used only one source at a time and generally did not blend two versions of the same account. Although Manson believed that the various layers could be easily distinguished, it was not the case in the passion

---

736. *Ibid.*, p. 240.

737. *The Life of Jesus: A Survey of the Available Material. (3) The Work of St. Luke*, in *BJRL* 28 (1944) 382-403, p. 382 (= ID., *The Work of St. Luke*, in M. BLACK [ed.], *Studies in the Gospels and Epistles*, Philadelphia, PA, 1962, p. 46-67, p. 46). The article was the published form of part of a series of lectures delivered at the John Rylands Library in 1944. In the preface to the book, M. Black asserted these "contained some of Manson's finest scholarly work" (p. iii). The essay from which this quotation was taken was written in 1944 (cf. NEILL and WRIGHT, *Interpretation*, ²1988, p. 134, n. 2).

738. *Work*, p. 382 (= 46): "Matthew produces a new, enlarged, and enriched edition of Mark, while Luke uses Mark as a quarry from which to extract such materials as he chooses to incorporate in a new work of his own".

739. *Ibid.*, p. 390 (= 54).

narrative[740].

Luke's apologetic interest was evident in the account of the passion which served to disassociate the Christian community from the Jewish community of his time. The Herod trial and the insistence of the people calling for Jesus' death at Pilate's trial were part of this thematic[741]. Noted, too, was the continuation of the hostility in Acts.

The order of the disparate accounts which Luke gathered over time presented a major problem for the evangelist. It would appear that the order was due to the evangelist as many of the early witnesses were dead. Further research would require traveling to secure more information, but Luke was in a hurry to compose his work[742]. In 1939 Manson reaffirmed his endorsement of Proto-Lk, claiming it was probable that the combining of Q and L was the first stage of composition, comprising "a document about the size of Mark"[743].

Despite his own view in support of the Proto-Lk, Manson (1938) still regarded the question as open[744]. But he considered the L material to have stemmed from oral tradition which Luke added to Q[745].

Matthew BLACK (1959), in the FS for Manson, unconvinced that Luke would dare to "correct" Mk, claimed that the Lukan passion narrative was primarily based on a non-Markan tradition, into which Markan materials had been inserted[746]. Crediting Hawkins with establishing the kernel of the hypothesis, and Perry with enunciating three aspects of his theory, Black noted that the idea "attracted increasing attention"[747]. Arguing against Knox that Mk 15,1 was an echo of Luke's earlier tradition, rather than 22,66 being a redaction of Mk 15,1, Black viewed Luke's account as fuller, though he noted that the morning Sanhedrin session in Lk contained the same question found in Mk's nocturnal version[748]. Black concurred with Dahl that not all of the MAs resulted from the efforts of scribes to harmonize the accounts[749].

Black had written of Mark's "telescoping" technique, which Black then

---

740. *Ibid.*, p. 393 (= 57).

741. *Ibid.*, p. 396 (= 60). Manson assigned 23,6-12.18-23 to L (p. 61, n. 7, 8).

742. *Ibid.*, p. 399 (= 63).

743. T.W. MANSON (ed.), *A Companion to the Bible*, Edinburgh - New York, 1939, p. 116. Manson authored Ch 5: *The New Testament and Other Christian Writings of the New Testament Period* (p. 97-129).

744. T.W. MANSON, *The Sayings of Jesus*, in *MMJ*, p. 318.

745. *Ibid.*, p. 320.

746. M. BLACK, *The Arrest and Trial of Jesus and the Date of the Last Supper*, in A.J.B. HIGGINS (ed.), *New Testament Essays*, Manchester, 1959, p. 23. The particular focus of the present article was to show how this special source was apparent in the Lukan version of the arrest and trial (p. 21).

747. *Ibid.*, p. 21.

748. *Ibid.*, p. 22.

749. *Ibid.*, p. 22-23. Cf. N.A. DAHL, *Die Passionsgeschichte bei Matthäus*, in *NTS* 2 (1955-56) 17-32.

claimed Luke used in 23,13-16[750]. The special material of the Herod episode
(23,5-12), Black regarded as historical and offered three reasons for the transfer
of Jesus from Pilate to Herod: 1) Jesus was from Herod's jurisdiction, 2) Pilate
had found no guilt in him, and 3) the Roman governor was unwilling to give in to
Jewish pressure[751]. One of the most substantial arguments against the historicity
of the Herod episode was its absence from Mk. Black suggested that Mk had once
again telescoped events and this particular story fell out. The historicity was
emphasized because of Luke's recourse to a special independent source.

    Archibald M. HUNTER (1945) wrote more favorably of Proto-Lk in the third
edition of *Introducing the New Testament* than in the original, maintaining that this
perspective was much more convincing than that Mk provided the framework for
Lk[752]. According to Hunter, Luke did not freely edit the portions of Mk which
he adopted. Yet contributions by William Ramsey and A.N. Sherwin-White
convinced Hunter that "on the matter of geography, politics, law and
administration Luke was exceedingly accurate"[753]. But, in our opinion, this does
not necessitate a single, independent source. In a later work (1975), Hunter seemed
to continue to advocate the Proto-Lk theory, though he did not devote much
attention to the question[754].

    Hunter (1950) asserted that "many good scholars" held the view that Luke
made use of a special passion source[755]. He argued that Luke's account of the
trial of Jesus was seemingly superior to that of Mk at certain points[756]. Luke
correctly related the Sanhedrin trial, which was more the case of "grand jury

---

750. BLACK, *Arrest*, p. 25. On one of the occasions the Jews came to Pilate but on the other
Pilate approached them. Cf. T.W. MANSON, *The Cleansing of the Temple*, in *BJRL* 33 (1951)
271-282.

751. *Ibid.*, p. 23-24. Douglas MOO (1983) asserted that Luke viewed the Herod scene as
corresponding to Ps 2, though not arising from it. Rather, he believed with his teacher M. Black,
that there was some historical foundation relating Herod to the death of Jesus (*The Old Testament
in the Gospel Passion Narratives*, Diss. U. St. Andrews, 1979 [dir. M. BLACK], Sheffield, 1983,
p. 349). See his references to Black, Hoehner, Rengstorf, Benoit and Schneider (p. 349, n. 3.
Moo was referring to M. BLACK, *Arrest*, p. 24). Moo recalled the position of Hooker who
rejected the idea that the silence motif (Mk 14,61 / Mt 26,63; Lk 23,9) stemmed from Is 53,7,
assigning it rather to "an authentic feature of Jesus' behavior during the judicial proceedings" (p.
148-149).

752. *Introducing the New Testament*, Philadelphia, PA, ³1972, p. 50 (cf. 1945, p. 41). Hunter
conceived of L as oral tradition which Luke collected and ultimately put down in writing (p. 32).
Hunter commended the summary of the theory in G.B. CAIRD, *St. Luke*, 1963, p. 23-26, as "an
excellent brief statement".

753. HUNTER, *Introducing*, p. 51.

754. *The New Testament for Today*, Atlanta, GA, 1975, p. 23-24.

755. *The Work and Words of Jesus*, London, 1950 (esp. p. 17, 118-120, 122, 169-192), p.
122. Hunter believed that L dated 57-59 AD and was originally oral tradition from the Caesarea
area (p. 17, 169).

756. *Ibid.*, p. 118-119. However, he later indicated that the Lukan account of the trial (22,66-
71) was based upon the Markan material (p. 187).

proceedings" as happening in the early morning. In an appendix Hunter offered his proposed text of L[757]. He defined the passion and resurrection narratives as 22,14–ch. 24. Eliminating verses from 22,54–23,25 "which seem to be based on Mark" we are left with 22,63.65; 23,1-2.4-16. Verse 17 was not recorded at all. Conversely, material derived from Mk was quite extensive: 22,54-62.64.66-71; 23,3.18-25.

Shortly thereafter Hunter (1951) described Streeter's *Four Gospels* as the finest book on form criticism (sic)[758]. He credited Perry with establishing a useful foundation for Streeter's theory and praised Perry who "ably argued" that Luke employed an independent passion narrative[759]. Though there were some impressive arguments on the side of Proto-Lk, "echoes of Mark at all the high points of the narrative" were recognized[760]. According to Hunter, the jury was still out. While the theory was still considered hypothetical twenty five years after its introduction, nevertheless Hunter argued it had only been criticized, not disproven. The definitive evaluation was still awaited[761].

Arguing that "the question of Luke's sources is complicated by Streeter's theory", R. HEARD (1950) seemed open to the possiblity of that solution, though he also observed that "many critics" argue in favor of Mk as the basis of Luke's passion narrative[762]. E.W. BAUMAN (1961) observed that while Proto-Luke could explain some problems in Lk, it was not widely accepted[763].

Roland KOH (1953) wrote out of the conviction that the special material in Lk was historical, believing that the Proto-Lukan hypothesis helped to corroborate such a view[764]. He adopted the view of J. Alexander Findlay that Acts was written prior to 64 AD[765], advancing the suggestion that the special source was

757. *Ibid.*, p. 169-192 (esp. p. 187-188).

758. *Interpreting the New Testament 1900-1950*, Philadelphia, PA, 1951, p. 40. In his presentation, Hunter pointed out that Streeter considered L to be a written source, while Taylor and T.W. Manson viewed it as oral (p. 43).

759. *Ibid.*, p. 41, n. 1. Hunter further observed that E. De Witt Burton had also espoused a four-document theory, though it "never won wide recognition" (p. 43, n. 1).

760. *Ibid.*, p. 42.

761. *Ibid.*, p. 43.

762. R. HEARD, *An Introduction to the New Testament*, London - New York, 1950, p. 48, 75-77.

763. E.W. BAUMAN, *An Introduction to the New Testament*, Philadelphia, PA, 1961, p. 125.

764. *The Writings of St. Luke. Brief Notes on the Material Peculiar to the Writings of St. Luke and on the Possibility of the Acts of the Apostles being Composed Before the Third Gospel*, Hong Kong, 1953, p. 5. Quite understandably, he depended heavily upon STREETER, *Four Gospels*, and TAYLOR, *The Gospels*; *The Formation*; *First Draft*; *Behind*; The *Gospel*; *The Gospel According to St. Mark*. Kümmel included Koh's name among the Proto-Lk supporters (*Einleitung*, [17]1973, p. 101, n. 13 = *Introduction*, 1975, p. 131, n. 13).

765. *Ibid.*, p. 6. See also p. 28-29, n. 1. The source of this view was found in J.A. FINDLAY, *The Acts of the Apostles*, p. 54. Regrettably, Koh did not supply the date or place of publication for the various books he used. Given that the latest event mentioned in Acts was Paul's living and preaching in Rome, that was after 58-60 AD, and the fall of Jerusalem was the latest event

composed around 50 AD and "originally circulated in the Decapolitan"[766].

Koh followed Streeter's lead in assigning composition of the special source, meaning the writing down of the contents of L and the combination of Q and L, to Luke[767]. In comparing parallel accounts of the passion, the evangelist generally preferred the special source over Mk. In a significant departure from Streeter's theory, he professed that the different sources such as L and M did not reflect various local churches[768]. He also differed with Streeter over the origin of L. While not debating the probability that Luke obtained L at Caesarea or that Philip the evangelist and his daughters may have been the ultimate source of it, he insisted that L reflected a tradition stemming from the Decapolis based upon "special interests, traits, and features, and the peculiarities of style and vocabulary"[769]. Prompted by A.M. Hunter, he asserted that L, composed in 50 AD contained a form of the passion account[770].

Koh assigned the Herod pericope (23,6-16) to L[771]. Although he did not address the historicity of the story, he noted, or at least implied at several points, that Jesus took routes to avoid entering the territory of Herod, though an encounter with Herod's soldiers might be possible in certain areas[772]. Lk 13,31-33 provided the basis for understanding why Herod would have wanted to arrest Jesus. However, Koh made no reference to the Herodian trial of Jesus in these contexts. Koh did not entertain any substantive arguments of those opposed to Proto-Lk,

---

detailed in the Gospel (21,20-24), Koh reasoned that the Gospel was written after Acts. What was significant here was that Koh believed Luke redacted Mk in light of contemporary events (p. 30-31). Acts 1,1 was understood by Koh to refer not to the Gospel but to Proto-Lk. He dated the various elements as follows: Proto-Lk (58-60 AD); Acts (63 AD); Mk (65-70 AD); the fall of Jerusalem (70 AD); the composition of Lk (71-75 AD) (p. 34).

766. KOH, *Writings*, p. 71. Aligning himself with J. Hawkins and A. Wright that Luke too was a catechist, it was probable that Luke also recognized the need for a treatise which would be useful in teaching.

767. Cf. above, n. 496.

768. *Ibid.*, p. 49. Cf. STREETER, *Fresh Light*, p. 112; *FG*, p. 223, 230-235.

769. KOH, *Writings*, p. 58. See also p. 71: "The specialties of L, such as the peculiar teaching of Jesus, peculiar words used in the stories, and their historical, social and geographical settings and references, fit better into the life and conditions of the Decapolis, than into any other place known to have been associated with and visited by Jesus during His Ministry". Koh further identified L as "largely a written source", though he conceded that Luke may occasionally employ material from oral tradition (p. 71). On the identification of Luke as author of Proto-Lk, see p. 23-24, 25, 29, 34. In this Koh agreed with Streeter and Taylor. Cf. above.

770. *Ibid.*, p. 71. See A.M. HUNTER, *The Work and Words of Jesus*, Philadelphia, PA, 1950, [Revised, 1973], p. 169-192.

771. KOH, *Writings*, p. 60. He relied on W. MANSON, *Gospel of Luke*, p. xviii; MCNEILE, *Introduction*, p. 68f.; V. TAYLOR, *The Gospels*, p. 36f.; *MMJ*, p. 319, for his understanding of the makeup of L (p. 58, n. 3). Koh failed to indicate T.W. Manson was the author of this last reference taken from his article, *The Sayings of Jesus*. As Koh listed it, it could give the impression that Taylor was the author.

772. KOH, *Writings*, p. 76, 77, 79-80, 84, 85, 87-88, 89, 91.

though he was quite aware of the various supporters[773].

Heinz SCHÜRMANN (1953, 1955, 1957) expressed his distrust of the various articulations of the Two-Source theory, the idea of a Synoptic GS, Proto-Lk and Lukan dependence on Mt[774]. The German form-critical studies had not been convincing and the British theories proposed statistical results but lacked exacting studies of the parts. Schürmann's detailed three-part examination included literary and form-critical observations. His verbal and stylistic investigation led him to conclude that 22,15-18 represented the Lukan redaction of a pre-Lukan, non-Markan tradition. Although it had been lightly redacted by Luke, it contained an account of the "Paschamahlbericht" which was literarily independent of Mk 14,25. The original introduction was reproduced in a secondary fashion in Mk 14,12-18a, of which Lk 22,7-14 was a parallel. Though Schürmann reasoned it was probable that there was a literary relationship between the two, he left open the possibility that a non-Markan source had been used in addition. He posited a pre-Lukan special form of the passion narrative which included 22,15-18.19-20.24-27.28-30.31-32.35-38[775].

In the second part of his study, he surmised that 22,15-18.19-20a probably comprised a pre-Lukan component of a written *Vorlage*, against the assumption that it had been transmitted orally, specifically in liturgy[776]. His conviction was that 22,19b-20 is part of the original text. He compared the Lukan text with 1 Cor 11,24b-25a and Mk 14,23-24 concluding that Lk was literarily independent of both of these other accounts and, in a few cases, even more original than the Pauline version. The section 22,19-20 had been worked into, and was part of, a written source which Luke employed[777].

In the *Vorwort* to the third part of his study, Schürmann affirmed his belief in the probable existence of a continuous pre-Lukan special form of the passion

773. In addition to Streeter and Taylor, these included Easton, Manson and Redlich.

774. *Der Paschamahlbericht Lk 22, (7-14)15-18. Teil I. Einer quellenkritischen Untersuchung des lukanischen Abendmahlsberichtes Lk 22,7-38* (NTAbh, 19/5), Münster, 1953, p. VII; *Der Einsetzungsbericht Lk 22,19-20. II.* (NTAbh, 20/4), Münster, 1955; *Jesu Abschiedsrede Lk 22,21-38. III.* (NTAbh, 20/5), Münster, 1957, ²1977.

H. SCHÜRMANN, *Protolukanische Spracheigentümlichtkeiten?*, in *BZ* 5 (1961) 266-286 = *Traditionsgeschichtliche Untersuchungen* (= *TrU*), 1968, 209-227.

Schürmann listed the following as proponents of the view that the Lukan *Sondergut* had been combined with Q (referred to as the Mt/Lk-Tradition): C. WEIZSÄCKER, *Das apostolische Zeitalter* (Tübingen, ³1902) 205ff; A. TITIUS, *Das Verhältnis der Herrenworte im Marcusevangelium zu den Logia des Matthäus* (Göttingen, 1897) 6f.; Feine, 124ff.; Perry, 9; STREETER, *FG*, 186ff.; TAYLOR, *Behind*, Patton 193ff. Others considered the special material to be an expansion of Q: E. Hirsch, F.C. Burkitt, Klostermann (*Die Dublettenvermeidungen im Lukasevangelium. Ein Beitrag zur Verdeutlichung des lukanischen Redaktionsverfahrens*, in *ZKT* 75 [1953] 338-345, p. 342, n. 34).

775. SCHÜRMANN, *Der Paschamahlbericht*, 1953, p. 123.

776. *Der Einsetzungsbericht*, p. 142-144. See also p. 150.

777. *Ibid.*, p. 133.

narrative[778]. His study suggested to him that 22,15-20a.24-32.35-38 was a continuous written non-Markan *Vorlage* and was possibly part of a non-Markan version of the passion narrative. Other parts, namely 22,21-23.33-34, were Markan insertions[779]. It was clear to Schürmann that Luke used another source in composing his Gospel and that in the description of the Last Supper, the evangelist gave preference to it rather than to Mk.

Aside from the results of his investigation, Schürmann believed there were other reasons for positing a special source for the passion narrative. These included the addition of special pericopes (23,6-16.27-31.39-43) and minor narrative details (22,43.51.61f.; 23,2.55f.; 24,10-11) which he denied would have been freely composed by Luke[780]. Attention was called to the non-Markan material in the Lukan passion narrative as proposed in differing ways by Streeter, Taylor, Hawkins and Hunkin. Schürmann felt that the discussion of a pre-Lukan, non-Markan form of the passion narrative must be kept separate from the Proto-Lk or Synoptic GS theories because it could have been transmitted outside the context of one of the Gospels. What was still lacking was a verbal and stylistic analysis of the entire passion narrative. Schürmann's distrust of the statistical approach was evident more than once[781].

In the appendix to a second edition (1977) he observed that M. Rese arrived at a very different conclusion for the sources of 22,21-38[782]. He took issue with Rese's apodictically worded conclusions and pleaded for an openness to possible pre-Lukan traditions. Schürmann pointed out as before, the difficulties arising from a lack of "exakte sprachliche Untersuchungen" which made it difficult to determine to what extent Luke redacted the special material[783]. Schürmann admitted that because of his further study on Lk he could agree with Rese that in the passion narrative and particularly in 22,1-53, one could recognize the "'selbständige Arbeit' des Lukas"[784]. This development prompted Schürmann to shift from asserting the probability of a pre-Lukan, non-Markan passion source to reckoning only with its possibility[785].

---

778. *Jesu Abschiedsrede*, 1957, p. VII; [2]1977, p. V. But cf. below, n. 785.

779. *Ibid.*, p. 35.

780. *Ibid.*, p. 140, n. 476: "Wenn sie aber aus der T hat, dann sicher nur aus der einer Passionsgeschichte".

781. *Ibid.*, p. (140-)141, n. 476. See also *Der Paschamahlbericht*, p. VII.

782. *Jesu Abschiedsrede*, [2]1977, p. 161-170. M. RESE, *Die "Stunde" Jesu in Jerusalem (Lukas 22,1-53). Eine Untersuchung zur literarischen und theologischen Eigenart des lukanischen Passionsberichts*, unpublished theol. Habil. Münster, 1971. He concluded that Luke had no other materials in addition to Mk and Q.

783. SCHÜRMANN, *Jesu Abschiedsrede Lk 22,21-38*, [2]1977, p. 165-166. But Schürmann enumerated the existing studies of Rehkopf, Neirynck, Schramm, Schneider, and G. Lohfink.

784. *Ibid.*, p. 168.

785. *Ibid.*: "So wurde ich schon lange nicht mehr den Satz des vorstehenden Vorwortes (S. V, vgl. auch S. 139) schreiben: 'In gleichem Masse wie unsere Untersuchungen in Lk 22,15-18.19-20a.24-26.27.28-30.31-32.35-38 nicht nur einzelne vorlukanische Sondertraditionen, sondern auch ein dem Lukas schon überliefertes zusammenhängendes Quellenstück wahrscheinlich

Schürmann (1954) noted the great variety with which scholars conceived of the Lukan *Sondergut*, but observed that the extent to which it had already been unified prior to Luke could not be determined[786]. In a later article (1961), as we have seen, Schürmann examined Rehkopf's vocabulary[787].

In his 1969 commentary Schürmann subscribed to the view that Luke made use of Mk, Q and at least one collection and possibly more, of his special material[788]. Included among this special matter was a unique rendition of the Lord's supper (22,15-38) and possibly the passion as well as the infancy narratives. Schürmann conceived the order to which Luke referred in the Prologue as both chronological and the orderly arrangement within a story ("das Ordnungsmoment einer Erzählung")[789]. And it was Mk's arrangement that Luke followed, almost without exception[790].

Reception of Schürmann's Studies

Jeremias knew of no other example of such a painstaking verbal analysis of the Lukan text[791]. He contrasted the care with which Schürmann treated his investigations in the matter of the verbal statistics with his "Hypothesenfreudigkeit" in dealing with the literary-critical matters[792].

Jeremias acclaimed the study a very important work[793]. Concerning Part 2 he questioned Schürmann's conclusion that Luke had a whole series of secondary details[794]. Jeremias saw the main value of this study in the investigations of Lukan "Sprachgebrauch" rather than in the tradition and source-critical conclusions[795].

Paul Winter, though disagreeing on details, endorsed Luke's use of a special

---

gemacht haben, in eben diesem Masse ist zugleich damit auch die Existenz einer vorlukanischen Sonderform der Passionsgeschichte wahrscheinlich geworden, und der Verdacht auf eine noch umfassendere Sondervorlage erhebt sich'". Other than this change in position, the second edition was basically the same as the first with a few corrections, an updating of the bibliography for the period 1957-1975, and the addition of an appendix on the redaction-critical method (p. 161-170).

786. *Die Dublettenvermeidungen*, in *ZKT* 76 (1954) 90, n. 64 (= *TrU*, p. 286, n. 64).

787. *Protolukanische Spracheigentümlichtkeiten?*, in *BZ* 5 (1961) 266-286 (= *TrU*, 209-227). See below.

788. *Das Lukasevangelium*. Vol. 1. *Kap.1,1-9,50* (HTKNT, 5), Freiburg, 1969, p. 6, n. 31. Schürmann believed that Mark was among Luke's predecessor's named in 1,1 (p. 12-13).

789. *Ibid.*, p. 12.

790. *Ibid.*, p. 13: "Hier liegt der Grund, warum er mit fast ängstlicher Sorgfalt ohne jede Umstellung dem Aufriss des Mk folgte. Dass Luk Mk kennenlernte, gab ihm wohl erst den Mut, den zerstreuten Einzelstoff – wie geschehen – in 'geordneter Reihenfolge' zusammenzuordnen".

791. *TZ* (Basel) 10 (1954) 141.

792. *Ibid.*, p. 142.

793. *TZ* (Basel) 15 (1959) 64-66, p. 64.

794. *Ibid.*, p. 65.

795. *Ibid.*, p. 66.

source, vindicated by Schürmann's study[796]. One area of disagreement, however, was Schürmann's tendency to view all the Semitisms as reflecting Septuagintal influence[797]. Winter described the work as "*the most thorough and most detailed style-critical investigation, in any language of the sources that went into the Lucan description of the Last Supper*"[798]. Winter and Moule agreed in calling for additional studies in like manner to examine particularly the passion narrative[799].

Taylor saw the work of Schürmann, as well as Rehkopf, as reviving attention for the Lukan passion narrative and the Proto-Lk hypothesis "which had been prematurely docketed"[800]. Form criticism which had long held sway in the field of biblical criticism, now gave way to literary and critical studies. The period 1950-51 was described by Taylor as the period in which the Proto-Lk hypothesis "reached its nadir". Its value, as Taylor had oft repeated, would be providing an ancient authority of comparable value to Mk.

Following Jeremias, Taylor maintained that the variations in order in Lk indicated that Luke was following an independent source. Taylor's purpose in the article, given the depth and breadth of Schürmann's investigation, was only to examine some of his conclusions concerning 22,14-18.19-20.

It has been noted that Joachim JEREMIAS introduced the hypothesis in Germany while his student, Friedrich Rehkopf, attempted to establish the linguistic foundation of the theory[801]. The Markan blocks were thought to have been interpolated into the proto-Lukan Gospel (*Ur-Lukas*)[802]. Unlike Taylor, Jeremias

796. *NTS* 2 (1955-56) 207. Also *NTS* 4 (1957-58) 226.
797. *Ibid.*, p. 208.
798. *Ibid.*
799. *Ibid.* Cf. C.F.D. MOULE, *JTS* 9 (1958) 361.
800. TAYLOR, *Theologians of Our Time. Heinz Schürmann*, in *ExpT* 74 (1962-63) 77.
801. See NEIRYNCK, *La matière marcienne*, p. 159 (= ²1989, p. 69). See also references to Rehkopf and Jeremias in Neirynck's review of SCHNEIDER, *Verleugnung*, in *ETL* 48 (1972) 571.
802. *Abendmahlsworte*, ³1960, p. 91f. Jeremias previously held there were five rather than four blocks of Markan material which Luke inserted into his special source. Cf. J. JEREMIAS, *Die Gleichnisse Jesu*, Göttingen, ³1954, p. 131, n. 2, where he listed the blocks as: 1) Mk 1,21-39; 2) Mk 1,40-3,19; 3) Mk 4,1-25; 3,31-35; 4,35-6,44; 8,27-9,40; 4) Mk 10,13-52; 5) 11,1-14,16. Luke was said to have employed this compositional technique in Acts (Cf. JEREMIAS, *Untersuchungen zum Quellenproblem der Apostelgeschichte*, in *ZNW* 36 [1937] 205-221, esp. p. 219: "Unser Ergebnis, dass der Verfasser der Apostelgeschichte eine ihm vorliegende Quelle derart verarbeitet hat, dass er sie an vier Stellen durch Erzählungseinschübe erweitert hat, – ausser ihnen sind zum mindesten Teile der Reden als Einschübe zu betrachten – wird durch die Feststellung bestätigt, dass er im dritten Evangelium bei der Bearbeitung des Markus dieselbe Technik angewendet hat. Während das Matthäus-Evangelium in der Reihenfolge stark vom Markus-Evangelium abweicht, hat das Lukasevangelium die Reihenfolge des Markus streng gewahrt (die einzigen wesentlichen Umstellungen bis zur Passionsgeschichte sind Lukas 6,17-19 und 8,19-21) und sich darauf beschränkt, den neuen Stoff in Form von kürzeren und längeren Einschüben hinzuzufügen"). Cf. *Gleichnisse*, 1947, p. 95; ⁴1956, p. 151, n. 1; ⁵1958 ("unveränderte Auflage"); ⁶1962 ("neu bearbeitete Auflage"), p. 182, n. 1.

never offered a full scale study of the special source in the passion narrative. In the second edition of *Die Abendmahlsworte Jesu* (²1949) he stated his position on Luke's use of a special source[803]. In the third edition (1960 = ET 1966) he clearly affirmed his stance that 22,14–23,53 stemmed from a special Lukan source[804]. The phrase concerning Luke's treatment of the phenomenon of order for which Jeremias had become famous was found in the second German edition of *Die Abendmahlsworte Jesu* (²1949), when he referred to Luke as "ein Feind von Umstellungen"[805].

Prompted by an inaccurate translation of the now famous and oft repeated statement of Jeremias on transpositions (in *The Eucharistic Words of Jesus*), H.F.D. Sparks contended that Luke's writings were characterized by changes in order in varying amounts of material[806]. The fact of the changes could not be disputed, though Luke's motivation for such variation, whether intentional or accidental, could not be determined[807]. Regrettably, Sparks did not include the later sections of the passion narrative in his study since it appeared that Jeremias excluded these portions of the Gospel. But Sparks argued that the method which Luke followed in other parts of the Gospel would have likely been the same method in the passion narrative[808]. The evidence put forth by Jeremias, according to Sparks, rather than confirming the former's position, argued against it. And while Sparks's working principle did not prove how Luke proceeded, it raised such a methodology to the realm of possibility.

Jeremias responded, lamenting the rather free translation of the term "Reihenfolge der Perikopen"[809]. He labeled Sparks's division of the changes into

803. *Die Abendmahlsworte Jesu*, Göttingen, 1935, ²1949, ³1960, ⁴1967 = *The Eucharistic Words of Jesus*, tr. A. EHRHARDT (from the second German ed.), New York, 1955; tr. N. PERRIN, London, 1966 (from the third German ed. with the author's revisions to July, 1964; Philadelphia, PA, 1977). For the reference to the special source see, *Die Abendmahlsworte Jesu*, Göttingen, ²1949, p. 56 (= ET, 1955, p. 69).

804. *Die Abendmahlsworte Jesu*, ³1960 (= ET, tr. N. PERRIN, London, 1966, p. 98). In addition see *Die Abendmahlsworte Jesu*, ⁴1967, p. 93: "Wir haben also Lk.22,14ff. einen selbständigen Passionsbericht neben Markus/Matthäus und Johannes vor uns – eine für unsere Untersuchung wichtige Feststellung, die sich bei der Analyse von Lk.22,15ff bestätigen wird". Note also his discussion, p. 92, 93, n. 2.

805. *Die Abendmahlsworte Jesu*, ²1949, p. 56, n. 3; ⁴1967, p. 93, n. 2 (= ET, 1955, p. [69]-70, n. 3: "was opposed to rearrangement"); 1966, p. 99, n. 1.

806. *St. Luke's Transpositions*, in *NTS* 3 (1956-57) 219-223. Cf. JEREMIAS, *The Eucharistic Words of Jesus*, p. 116. Sparks delineated four types of transpositions: 1) sentences containing changes in order of words or phrases; 2) sections containing variations in order of words, phrases or subject matter; 3) the change of words, phrases, or subject matter from one section to another; 4) the movement of entire sections or the material of those sections to other locations (p. 220; 222-223).

807. SPARKS, *St. Luke's Transpositions*, p. 222-223.

808. *Ibid.*, p. 223. Sparks's discussion of Lk 5,1-11 deriving from Mk 1,16-20 was very similar to the argument that could be advanced for Lk 23,3 deriving from Mk 15,2, which would show that Mk was the basis of the passage describing Pilate's trial (p. 222, n. 3).

809. JEREMIAS, *Perikopen-Umstellungen bei Lukas?*, in *NTS* 4 (1957-58) 115. The translator

four categories as a "misunderstanding". And though Jeremias concurred with Sparks concerning the first three, he considered the fourth, transpositions of whole sections or material from entire sections, as doubtful[810]. Six transpositions were found in Ch. 22 and two of these Jeremias considered as having been proven by Rehkopf to have stemmed from Luke's special tradition[811]. Thus, for Jeremias, beginning at 22,14 Luke employed his special tradition which accounted for the changes in order.

Later in the investigation of the synoptic problem and the Son of Man saying (22,69) in his *Theologie* (1971, ²1973) Jeremias treated the special source and the question of order[812]. There were only a few instances in 22,14-24,53 where Jeremias believed that there was a possibility of Markan influence[813]. The special non-Markan material in Lk was considered to be: 1,1-4,30; 5,1-11; 6,20-8,3; 9,51-18,14; 19,1-28.39-44; 22,14-24,53. The Markan blocks of material were found in 4,31-44 (Mk 1,21-39); 5,12-6,19 (Mk 1,40-3,19); 8,4-9,50 (Mk 4,1-25; 3,31-35; 4,35-6,44; 8,27-9,40); 18,15-43 (Mk 10,13-52); 19,29-38 (Mk 11,1-10); 19,45-22,13 (Mk 11,15-14,16)[814]. Writing of the special source Jeremias asserted: "Es ist eine Erkenntnis von grosser Tragweite, dass der lukanische Passionsbericht ab 22,14 auf die lukanische Sonderquelle zurückgeht, also eine selbständige Überlieferung gegenüber der markinischer darstellt"[815]. Conceding that Lukan redaction involved a radical revision of Markan style, the omission of doublets and the occasional transpositions of "a few words or a clause", Jeremias rejected the view that Luke refashioned the Markan order[816]. While Burkitt and Wade admitted that Luke transposed the Markan material at 8,19-21 (Mk 3,31-35) Jeremias spoke of it only as a deviation which resulted from Luke's addition of this Markan pericope[817].

In a comparison of the Son of Man saying in Mk 14,62 and Lk 22,69, Jeremias regarded the latter as "schlichter" ("simpler"). Whereas Mk 14,62 "von dem urchristlichen christologischen Schema Erhöhung-Parusie beeinflusst (ist)"

---

rendered the phrase "arrangement of the material" rather than "order of the sections". Cf. NEIRYNCK, *The Argument from Order and St. Luke's Transpositions*, in *ETL* 49 (1973) 805 (= *Evangelica*, 1982, p. 758).

810. *Perikopen-Umstellungen*, p. 115-116.

811. *Ibid.*, p. 117, 119. The six transpositions were 22,1-3.24-27.33f.56-62.63-65.66-71. Those confirmed by Rehkopf's dissertation, which Jeremias directed, were 22,21-23 and 22,47-53.

812. *Neutestamentliche Theologie* 1. *Die Verkundigung Jesu*, Gütersloh, 1971 (esp. p. 48-49, 259-261), ²1973 = *New Testament Theology. The Proclamation of Jesus*, tr. J. BOWDEN, New York, 1971 (esp. p. 40-41, 272-274) [page references within brackets].

813. *Ibid.*, p. 48 (= 40).

814. *Ibid.*, p. 48-49 (= 40-41).

815. *Ibid.*, p. 260 (= 273).

816. *Ibid.*, p. 48 (= 40).

817. *Ibid.* Cf. BURKITT, *Earliest Sources*, ²1922, p. 100, n. 1, and WADE, *Documents*, 1934, p. 261. The addition by Luke was made necessary because he omitted Mk 3,20-35.

such was not the case with 22,69[818]. Acts 7,56 attested that the formula found in 22,69 was an early one. Following Bammel, Jeremias held that the passages in Lk and Acts stemmed from independent traditions, though they were similar in content[819]. The Lukan account, consistent with Dan 7,13f. and Ethiopian Enoch 70f. treated only a single event, while Mk 14,62 portrayed the events in two-part fashion: "*sessio ad dexteram* zu Ostern und Parusie am Ende der Tage"[820].

Intent on distinguishing Lukan from non-Lukan vocabulary rather than in reconstructing the pre-Lukan sources, Jeremias in *Die Sprache des Lukasevangeliums* (1980), repeated his delineation of the blocks of non-Markan material as recorded in *Neutestamentliche Theologie*[821]. The debate surrounding the question of sources in the passion narrative was characterized as "offen und umstritten"[822]. He passed over any mention of the MA in 22,62, but for 22,64 contended that because the MA was also found in Mt 26,68 it had not been composed by Luke[823]. Jeremias ascribed the majority of the elements in the section 23,6-16 to redaction[824].

Though Friedrich REHKOPF (1959) examined Lk 22,21-23.47-55 and did not directly treat the pericopes with which we are concerned, his was an important study arguing for Luke's use of a special source in an attempt to isolate a special vocabulary[825]. He was prompted to investigate because of the frequent variations

818. *Theologie* p. 260 (= 273).

819. *Ibid.* See. E. BAMMEL, *Erwägungen zur Eschatologie Jesu*, in *StEv* 3 (TU, 88), Berlin, 1964, p. 24.

820. *Theologie*, p. 261 (= 274).

821. *Die Sprache des Lukasevangeliums. Redaktion und Tradition im Nicht-Markusstoff des dritten Evangeliums* (KEK), Göttingen, 1980, p. 7, n. 4. For his treatment of 22,54–23,25, see p. 296-303.

822. *Ibid.*, p. 7. The reference bears quoting in full: "Offen und umstritten ist dabei vor allem, ob die lukanische Passionsgeschichte (Lk 22,14ff.) mit ihren Berührungen mit Markus, aber auch mit ihren erheblichen Abweichungen von ihm vor allem in der Stoffanordnung, auf einen wesentlich anderen Umgang des Lukas mit dem vorgegebenen Markusstoff als im übrigen Evangelium zurückzuführen ist oder aber auf eine andere Erzählfolge in einer lukanischen Sonderüberlieferung. Da auch derjenige, der die Markusüberlieferung in der lukanischen Passionsgeschichte für dominierend hält, zumindest mit zusätzlichem Einfluss von non-markinischer Tradition rechnen muss, ist es auf jeden Fall gerechtfertigt, dass die lukanische Passionsgeschichte im Unterschied zu den anerkannten Markusblöcken hier mit behandelt wird. Da es andererseits wahrscheinlich ist, dass die Markusvorlage die Gestaltung der lukanischen Passionsgeschichte zumindest beeinflusst hat, ist bei Verweisen auf die lukanische Markusbearbeitung auch die Passionsgeschichte behutsam mit herangezogen worden" (*Theologie*, 47-49).

823. *Ibid.*, p. 298.

824. *Ibid.*, p. 301-303. Words ascribed to tradition include: ἐν Ἱεροσολύμοις (23,7), λίαν (23,8), ἀπεκρίνατο (23,9), ἐμπαίξας (23,11), πρὸς αὐτούς (23,12), προσηνέγκατε (23,14), and ἀλλ᾿ οὐδέ (23,15).

825. F. REHKOPF, *Die lukanische Sonderquelle. Ihr Umfang und Sprachgebrauch* (WUNT, 5), Tübingen, 1959. Diss. Göttingen, 1956 (dir. J. JEREMIAS).

in order, the new material and the infrequent verbal agreement[826].

Discussing the problem of the order of the material he referred to Feine, Taylor and Perry who attributed the differences to a special source while Hawkins believed the differences in order were due to "memoriter narration"[827]. On the other hand, Grobel, in a study of the twelve transpositions cited by Hawkins, Wernle, Finegan, Hirsch and Haugg explained changes in order by Luke's redactional method[828]. Feine, B. Weiss, Hawkins, Streeter, Perry and Schlatter were mentioned as proponents of a special source to explain the Lukan special material, while only Finegan was named for the opposing point of view[829].

Rehkopf concluded that the prediction of the betrayal (22,21-23) was older than and independent of Mk and the arrest (22,47-53). It was partly derived from an older special report which was enhanced with Markan material[830]. He surmised that the possible answer to the source question in the Lukan passion narrative was that Luke employed a special report as his main source which he supplemented with Mk[831]. In contrast to Perry, Rehkopf isolated only seventy-eight words. The same criticism lodged against Perry may be made against his German successor. The words were often too common to admit of a specialized vocabulary of the passion[832]. Other words, such as σατανᾶς, are also found in Mt and Mk[833].

Taylor noted that Rehkopf's conception of the Proto-Lk hypothesis was similar to that of Streeter. The section entitled "Pre-Lukan Speech Usage in the Gospel of Luke" was deemed "invaluable"[834]. Likening this to the previous work of Hawkins and Cadbury, Taylor contended that words are "characteristic of Luke's *sources* rather than his distinctive usage, and that Rehkopf has provided us with a

---

826. *Ibid.*, p. 1-2. The changes in order referred to were the following sections: 22,54-62 (after 22,63-65); 22,63-65 (22,71/23,1); the following whole verses: 22,66 (before 23,1); 22,70 (67); 23,2 (3/4); 23, 19 (17*v.l.*/18). New material was found in whole verses: 22,65; 22,(67b-)68; in half verses: 22,61b; 22,67b; 23,2b; 23,22b; word agreement which amounted only as high as 40% was found in the following whole verses: 22,61.69.71; 23,3 and in a half verse, 23,22a (p. 2, nn. 1ab, 3 ,4).

827. *Ibid.*, p. 2-3. Feine (1891), p. 61; Hawkins (1910), p. 81f., 84, 99; Taylor (1926), 73, 177; Perry, p. 90f.

828. Ibid., p. 3. Grobel (1937), p. 101, 104; Wernle (1899) p. 8; cf. p. 33; Finegan (1934), p. 9; Hirsch II (1941), p. 255; and D. Haugg, *Judas Iskarioth in den neutestamentlichen Berichten*, Freiburg, 1930, p. 138.

829. *Die lukanische Sonderquelle*, p. 4. Rehkopf provided no bibliographical information here for the advocates of the special source. Cf. the general bibliography (p. 101-104). On the idea that Feine was the first proponent that Q and L were combined and Markan materials were inserted to it, see p. 89, n. 1. There he also mentioned that while Bartlet subscribed to the idea in 1911, the hypothesis had become known through the work of Streeter.

830. *Ibid.*, p. 83.

831. *Ibid.*, p. 84.

832. *Ibid.*, p. 105-106. Common words included αὐτός, γάρ, εἰς.

833. *Ibid.*, p. 106.

834. TAYLOR, *Theologians of Our Time. Friedrich Rehkopf*, in *ExpT* 74 (1962-63), p. 262. Cf. p. 266, n. 1.

new and valuable tool in source-criticism". (Taylor noted that L signified something different for Rehkopf than it did for British scholars: while the latter would understand this to mean Luke's special source, Rehkopf saw it as including parts of Proto-Lk including the birth narratives)[835].

Taylor issued a call to British and American scholars to take up the investigation set in motion by the work of the German scholars Jeremias, Rehkopf and Schürmann. Taylor believed that these studies helped to clarify, on a linguistic basis, the differences between tradition and redaction. But one must question Taylor's statement that "the value of the Markan account is not in question ..."[836]. As a conclusion Taylor observed that Rehkopf and Streeter shared a general agreement in proposing that the special source comprised about two thirds of the material to the Gospel, including 22,14-24,53.

Taylor noted that in the case of καὶ αὐτὸς αὐτοί, Rehkopf sided with W. Michaelis against Hawkins in listing seven unemphatic cases[837]. Another issue raised by Taylor was Rehkopf's interpretation of the term ὁ κύριος. While Taylor agreed that the use of the term could be editorial, it was not necessarily the case that Luke was that editor, as Hawkins suggested. The vocative form, in particular, "must" have stemmed from the person responsible for combining Q with L prior to interjecting the Markan material[838]. It is well to note that Taylor, though enthused about the work and the list, approached it with a great deal of caution: "It is obvious from what has been said already that Rehkopf's list must not be used in a mechanical manner. It is a key, but not a master-key, for use in Synoptic research. This is indeed how Rehkopf himself actually uses it"[839]. The list should be utilized in conjunction with that of Hawkins. These caveats notwithstanding, Taylor believed that source criticism was now better prepared for the task at hand.

In a typically thorough sifting through of the vocabulary for which Schürmann had been highly praised, significant differences between his findings and those of Rehkopf surfaced (1961)[840]. We review here only select vocabulary found in the passion narrative.

---

835. *Ibid.*, p. 262, n. 6. Cf. TAYLOR, *Rehkopf's List of Words and Phrases Illustrative of Pre-Lukan Speech Usage*, in *JTS* 15 (1964) 60. Much of Taylor's article on Rehkopf's pre-Lukan vocabulary was reminiscent of his article on Rehkopf the theologian in *ExpT*.

836. *Theologians*, p. 266. Cf. *Passion Narrative*, p. 1-22.

837. *Rehkopf's List*, p. 60. Cf. *Theologians*.

838. *Rehkopf's List*, p. 61.

839. *Ibid.*, p. 62 (= *The Passion*, p. 27).

840. H. SCHÜRMANN, *Protolukanische Spracheigentümlichkeiten? Zu Fr. Rehkopf, Die lukanisches Sonderquelle. Ihr Umfang und Sprachgebrauch*, in *BZ* 5 (1961) 266-286 (= *TrU*, 209-227).

Rehkopf's Pre-Lukan Vocabulary	Schürmann's Evaluation
ὁ κύριος	Less probable[841]
ἤγγιζεν δέ (22,47 diff. Mk)	Rejected[842]
ἀπὸ τοῦ νῦν	Less probable[843]
ἵνα μὴ ἐκλίπη	Rejected at 23,45 (diff. Mk 15,38)[844]
κατὰ τὸ ἔθος (22,39 diff. Mk)	Rejected[845].
στραφείς	Less probable[846]
φίλοι	Rejected[847]
κλαίετε	Less probable[848]
φοβῇ σὺ τὸν θεόν	Rejected Proto-Lukan origin[849]
καὶ αὐτοί	Less probable[850]

Our survey of Schürmann's analysis of Rehkopf's vocabulary revealed there were some terms shared in common with those of J. Weiss. Schürmann's investigation of Rehkopf's vocabulary, however, resulted in declaring twenty-nine cases doubtfully Proto-Lukan or thirty-seven per cent of the total. Despite the difference of judgment in more than one-third of the instances, Schürmann remained

---

841. p. 282-283. See also p. 274 = reprint in *TrU*, 1968, 224-225. Cf. REHKOPF, *Die lukanische Sonderquelle*, p. 58-59, 95. "Der luk R wird man die auffallend vielen Stellen in S und in Q-Abschnitten nicht gern alle zur Last legen wollen, wenn Luk so sonst nicht schreibt (auch in Apg nicht) ausser 19,31 par Mk und (in Wiederholung von V. 31) in 19,34 Sv diff Mk. ferner in Sv diff Mk noch Lk 24,3 P und 22,61a P (und in Abhängigkeit davon 22,61b diff Mk) an 2 Stellen, wo die luk Sonderform der P auf die Mk-Wiedergabe einwirken könnte".

842. p. 272 = *TrU*, p. 214-215 (REHKOPF, p. 41, 44-46, 93). Insufficient material available for comparison.

843. p. 279 = *TrU*, p. 221 (REHKOPF, p. 92). Rather it appeared to be the work of Lukan redaction.

844. p. 272 = *TrU*, p. 215 (REHKOPF, p. 93). Insufficient material available for comparison.

845. p. 272 = *TrU*, p. 215 (REHKOPF, p. 95).

846. SCHÜRMANN, p. 284. See p. 272 = *TrU*, p. 226 (REHKOPF, p. 97).

847. p. 275, 276 = *TrU*, p. 219, 218 (REHKOPF, p. 97). "7,34 par Mt, darum vielleicht auch 7,6; 12,4 Sv diff Mt und 15,6 diff Mt"; Identified as original manner of speech such as found in Q.

848. p. 282 = *TrU*, p. 224. See also p. 274, n. 41 = *TrU*, 216, n. 41 (REHKOPF, p. 95). Part of his reasoning was that Luke adopted the term three times from Mk and thus the work of a redactor must also be taken into consideration. He was further persuaded because the term also occurred in Acts. Schürmann viewed the occurrence of terms in Acts as leaving open the possibilty of Lukan redaction.

849. p. 277, n. 50 = *TrU*, p. 219, n. 50 (REHKOPF, p. 97). "Obj: God; 12,5 1x par, 2x diff. Mt" stating: "Dass die hier ausgeklammerten Fälle zurecht in Frage gestellt werden, geht auch daraus hervor, dass gleichzeitig von den (jeweils vermerkten) anderen Regeln her Bedenken gegen protoluk Ursprung kommen können; diese Bedenken haben um so mehr Gewicht, als bei den zur Untersuchung stehenden Gemeinsamkeiten fast immer der eine der Vergleichspartner (luk S und Q) nur in ganz wenigen Fällen mit dem anderen übereingeht". He also dismissed Rehkopf's view because the provable use of the term in Q also argued against it.

850. p. 271, 281 = *TrU*, p. 213, 223 (REHKOPF, p. 94). The principle governing Schürmann's judgment was that a Proto-Lukan composition of S + Q cannot be proven if the vocabulary stood only in S or only in Q.

undaunted. Though some would see this as having the effect of further weakening support for the special source, Schürmann did not believe this to be the case[851]. He remained convinced that there was a special Lukan form of the passion narrative, which at the same time did not prove the Proto-Lk hypothesis[852]. The advantages of Schürmann's methodological approach over against Rehkopf rested with the clear set of criteria upon which a judgment may be made. Further, Schürmann recognized that some of the vocabulary may have stemmed from Q or Luke's redaction, the latter may also be indicated by the presence of various terms in Acts. The overall effect was that closer inspection of the vocabulary can yield far different results than Rehkopf and others originally suspected.

O.E. Evans remarked that, "it does appear that Dr. Taylor had seen" Schürmann's critique of Rehkopf, which he described as "a most detailed and searching analysis"[853]. He added: "It is impossible to estimate how far Dr Taylor's confidence in the value of Rehkopf's list would have been shaken had he been able to weigh carefully these arguments of Schürmann. One suspects that he would have repeated, even more emphatically, his proviso that 'Rehkopf's list must not be used in a mechanical manner', that it is 'a key, but not a master-key for use in Synoptic research', and that in assessing the evidence it supplies there must also be taken into account various other considerations"[854].

J.C. HARTWICK (1937-38) called attention to the hypothesis without endorsing it. He merely said that if the theory was sound, it would "increase the historical reliability of the Gospel record of happenings, tracing them to two sources instead of one"[855]. Other scholars who supported the Proto-Lk theory included Frank Bertram CLOGG (1937)[856], D.M. McINTYRE (1929)[857], F.F. BRUCE

---

851. SCHÜRMANN, p. 285 (= *TrU*, p. 227).

852. *Ibid.*, p. 272 (= *TrU*, p. 214).

853. TAYLOR, *Passion Narrative*, 29-30, p. 29.

854. *Ibid.*, p. 30.

855. J.C. HARTWICK, *Burnett Hillman Streeter (1875-1937)*, in *ExpT* 49 (1937-38) 249-254, p. 251.

856. F.B. CLOGG, *An Introduction to the New Testament* (London Theological Library), London, 1937, ³1948, ᴿ1959 (esp. p. 191-196, 241). He rejected the view that Q contained an account of the passion and referred to the origin of the Proto-Lk theory by Streeter, but filled out the arguments by Taylor, relying on *Behind*. He believed that the theory was "widely accepted" though without listing supporters or country of origin. Creed was cited as the only dissenter, but it was obvious that Clogg supported the theory as articulated by Taylor, though with some degree of caution.

857. D.M. McINTYRE, *The Building of the Third Gospel*, in *EvQ* 1 (1929) 130-146, p. 132. Aware of the movement of some unspecified German scholars to propose three sources and Streeter's contention that there were four in reaction to the Two-Document theory, McIntyre maintained that "it is universally conceded that the apostolic testimony underlies our canonical Gospels". It was also his opinion that "Zahn and Stanton may have underestimated it". The Synoptic Gospels originated for the purpose of instructing catechumens. The first stage of composition occurred when these lessons were committed to writing. He cited Barlett, Taylor and

$(1943)^{858}$, J. Alexander FINDLAY $(1937)^{859}$, S.A. CARTLEDGE $(1938)^{860}$,

Sanday in support of this view: "In the same direction Dr. Bartlett offers a hint which meets the approval of Dr. Vincent Taylor and of Dr. Sanday: 'It seems to me a valuable suggestion that 'S was a peculiar form of written memoirs elicited by our Third Evangelist *ad hoc*, not immediately for the literary purpose to which he finally put it, but rather as a permanent record of the most authentic tradition to which it had been his lot to obtain access, for use in his own work as an evangelist or catechist of the oral Gospel'" (p. 137; cf. SSP, p. xx, xxi, 351; TAYLOR, *Behind*, p. 15, 19). The Jesus tradition consisted of documentary sources, as well as a great deal of oral material.

The general consensus among scholars of this period was that "it is generally held that Luke was indebted to Mark – either to the Gospel as we have it, or in a form slightly different" (McINTYRE, *Building*, p. 140. This was the view of WELLHAUSEN, *Einleitung*, p. 57; RAMSAY, *Luke the Physician*, p. 39; HAWKINS, *SSP*, p. 29). At this point, McIntyre called attention to the "interesting suggestion" of Streeter concerning Proto-Lk, which Taylor also has taken up. McIntyre also mentioned Headlam's modification of Streeter's theory, to which Streeter was receptive (McINTYRE, *Building*, p. 140, n. 2). Luke, in evaluating what he had already written, would compare his information with that found in Mk. He would then either correct it or substitute the Markan material for his own.

In treating material peculiar to Lk, McIntyre referred to 22,14–24,12. Basing this section on the apostolic tradition, Luke recounted some of the special material, such as the Herod pericope, "in his own words" (p. 145, quoting V.H. STANTON, *Gospels*, Vol. 2, p. 239).

In 1944, F.F. Bruce edited a brief essay by McIntyre who continued to favor Proto-Lk, a theory he called an "interesting" and "valuable suggestion" (D.M. McINTYRE, *Some Notes on the Gospels*, ed. F.F. BRUCE, London, 1944, p. 24). McIntyre drew on his earlier article. See, for example, p. 33, which was taken verbatim from the previous article with only slight alteration: "The third section (Luke xxii. 14 - xxiv. 12) draws freely from the apostolic tradition, perhaps not at all from Q; it is, however, largely derived from sources laid to the hand of the evangelist. There is literary evidence that many of the particulars to Luke in his Passion and Resurrection history were communicated to him, and by him committed to writing" (Cf. *Building*, p. 145). As before he observed how Streeter had accepted Headlam's modification (*Some Notes*, p. 24, n. 40).

858. F.F. BRUCE, *Are the New Testament Documents Reliable?*, London - Grand Rapids, MI, 1943, ⁴1954, p. 48: "This summary of the way in which the Third Gospel may have been built up is based on Biblical evidence and it accords very well with the internal evidence, based on literary criticism, as presented by B.H. Streeter in The Four Gospels (1924) and by Dr. Vincent Taylor in Behind the Third Gospel (1926)".

859. J.A. FINDLAY, *The Gospel according to St. Luke. A Commentary*, London, 1937, p. 10, fell in line with the Streeter proposal that "this first draft of the Gospel was a combination of Q with traditions which were the outcome of Luke's own researches. ... Afterwards Luke took this Gospel to pieces, and in certain places at which there were gaps in his narrative, inserted material taken from Mark". See further p. 29-30: "If the suggestions made as to the way in which the Gospel and the Acts were put together are accepted, it is clear that we must distinguish between the time and place at which the original 'Proto-Luke' (Q+L) was composed, and the time and place at which the Gospel, as we possess it, was published. The time of the composition of 'Proto-Luke' we may call A.D. 59, its place Caesarea; the publication of the whole Gospel we may assign to the years between A.D. 70 and 80, but we cannot localise it". He also adopted Taylor's view from *Behind the Third Gospel* (1926) and stipulated that while 22,1-13 "is perhaps Marcan – I am not sure of this – but from that point onwards we have only scattered fragments of Mark" (FINDLAY, *Gospel*, p. 13).

Johannes DE ZWAAN (1941/1942)[861], Thomas HENSHAW (1952)[862], Alan Hugh

The account of Peter's denial was, in Findlay's opinion, independent of Mk (p. 230). No
explicit reference was made to the source(s) of 22,63-65.66-71. He observed that Stephen quoted
Mk 14,62 in Acts 7,56, though it was omitted in Lk (p. 231). While Mk indicated the Son of
Man would be sitting, the account in Acts stated that Jesus was standing (Mk 14,62 / Acts 7,56).
There was no reference to the supposed source for 23,1-5.18-25 though Findlay noted the
similarity of phrasing in 23,25 with Acts 3,14 (p. 236). The MA in 22,62 was "perhaps an
interpolation from Matt. xxvi.75", though no mention was made of the MA in v. 64 (p. 230).
    Regarding sources for the Herod material Findlay proposed Joanna and Manaen: "Joanna,
'wife' (or 'widow') 'of Chuza, Herod's steward' (Luke viii.3) and 'Manaen, companion of Herod
the tetrarch' (Acts xiii.1) bespeak connexions with Herod's court" (p. 13; see also p. 100, the
comment on 8,3). Findlay referred to GP, though without discussing the issue of sources or
relationship (p. 236, n. 1). The motivation for the transfer was Pilate's desire to rid himself of
an "embarassing Galilean" (p. 236). In what appeared to be the implication that Luke was
responsible for some redaction of Markan material at this point Findlay stated: "Luke is glad to
discharge the Roman soldiers (Mark xv.16) of responsibility for the outrageous treatment of the
Prisoner; in his narrative first the priests, then Herod's entourage, mock him" (p. 236). It seemed
that Findlay recognized similarities with the Markan story of the robe (Mk 15,17) when he stated
that Luke's reason for omitting it was to avoid suggesting Pilate was promoting insurrection
against the Emperor.
    860. S.A. CARTLEDGE, A Conservative Introduction to the New Testament, Grand Rapids,
MI, 1938, p. 63. Though Streeter offered "some rather convincing proof", Cartledge
optimistically ventured that the theory "has not won general acceptance as yet".
    861. Inleiding tot het Nieuwe Testament, Haarlem, 3 vols.: 1. Evangeliën en Handelingen,
1941, esp. Vol. 1, p. 99-104 (= ²1948, p. 98-104); 2. Brieven van Paulus en Hebreeën, 1941;
3. Algemeene Zendbrieven, Openbaring, Text en Canon, 1942 (esp. p. 21 (= ²1948, p. 22), ²1948
(Tweede herziene druk). He defined the passion narrative as 22,39-23,56 (Vol. 1, p. 94 = Vol.
1, ²1948, p. 92). In an examination of the index of biblical references (Vol. 1, p. 224-237, esp.
p. 230 = ²1948, p. 225-238) it is striking that De Zwaan passed over a significant portion of the
Lukan passion material including 22,33-23,5.13-26.
    In Vol. 3, p. 21 (= Vol. 3, ²1948, p. 22) De Zwaan called attention to the similarities of
Proto-Lk with the Letter of James as Feine had done. "Opvallend is daarbij de verwantschap met
Proto-Lucas, maar de stof, die Lucas te Caesarea verzameld had, verdween nadien niet uit de
mondelinge circulatie!". The sentence was revised in the second edition to read: "Opvallend is
daarbij de verwantschap met Proto-Lucas, doch men bedenke, dat de stof, die Lukas te Caesarea
verzameld had, nadien niet uit de mondelinge circulatie verdween! Ook anderen konden daarvan
kennis nemen" (Vol. 3, ²1948, p. 22).
    For Proto-Lk De Zwaan referred to Feine (1891), E. de Witt Burton (1904); G. [sic] Vernon
Bartlett [sic] (1911); C.S. Patton (1915); F. Spitta (1912), V. Taylor (1926); First Draft (1929);
Streeter, FG (1926); F.C. Grant (1933); K. Grobel, (1933). DE ZWAAN, Vol. 1, p. 110-111 (=
Vol. 1, ²1948, p. 109) adopted the Proto-Lukan theory that Luke inserted Markan material into
"een reeds bestaand verhaal" (DE ZWAAN, Inleiding, Vol. 1, p. 99 = Vol. 1, ²1948, p. 98). De
Zwaan contended that one could only assign with certitude thirty verses in the Lukan passion
narrative as deriving from Mk (Vol. 1, p. 98; cf. Vol. 1, ²1948, p. 98. See also Vol. 1, p. 103
= Vol. 1, ²1948, p. 102): "Tenslotte, heeft Lucas van dat evangelieverhaal méér dan de helft,
òf - indien hij n.l. met Marcus' lijdensgeschiedenis wèl gerekend zou hebben - iets minder dan
de helft ongebruikt gelaten". Thus, by removing the Markan insertions, a coherent account
remained. The material in the passion account which was unique to Luke or in a unique form
included 22,14-20.24-38; 23,6-12.24.25.27-32.43; 24,13-53. Proto-Lk emphasized concern for

MCNEILE (1953)[863] and James PRICE (1953)[864].

women and the poor.

Luke deviated twelve times from the Markan order. In three instances he provided information at variance from Mk: the mockery by Herod (not by Pilate), the morning trial and the appearance in Jerusalem rather than Galilee (Vol. 1, p. 102 = Vol. 1, [2]1948, p. 100-101).

De Zwaan believed that the Herod story (23,6-12) comprised part of Proto-Lk (Vol. 1, p. 101 = Vol. 1, [2]1948, p. 100). He referred to the pericope as "Pilatus en Herodes".

862. *New Testament Literature in the Light of Modern Scholarship*, London, 1952, p. 131 (esp. p. 87, 89-91, 188-189); [2]1957 (the second ed. was not available to us). He supported Streeter's proposal of a Proto-Lk which he termed "the most probable hypothesis". He used the 1930 repr. of Streeter's *The Four Gospels*. Henshaw held that Luke employed four sources: Mk, which he described at one point as "the 'Foundation Gospel' of 'Matthew' and 'Luke'" (p. 88), Q, L (9,51-18,14 and the non-Markan portions of 22,14 through ch. 24), and the Birth and Infancy Narratives (p. 131). To his mind the advantages of such a theory were many. First, it eliminated the need for resorting to a solution involving a defective copy of Mk (Cf. p. 188 where Henshaw, *New Testament*, in referring to Mk, wrote of the "missing end of that Gospel"). Further, the date (3,1), which appeared to have been the opening of a work, the genealogy and the large interpolation (9,51-18,14) were accounted for by the theory (p. 90-91). Luke's methodology, involving an "orderly progress", was the same in the Gospel and in Acts. Luke had done a better job than Matthew of preserving the Markan order (p. 132; see also p. 91).

The passion narrative was chiefly derived from L and Henshaw rejected out of hand the idea that Q may have contained an account of the passion. He adopted the view that the non-Markan material formed a continuous whole. In contrast "the Marcan sections are self-contained and supplementary" (p. 90). See further p. 74: "Luke's version [of the passion narrative] appears to be a slightly different version with some facts from 'Mark' added ... The slight divergences between 'Mark' and 'Luke' must have taken place while the narrative was still being taught orally; but either version or both versions must have been written before they were used by the two Evangelists". On the question of whether Q contained an account of the passion, Henshaw seemed a little less assured later when he wrote: "Since it is practically certain that the document Q contained no narratives of the Passion and the post-Resurrection appearances ..." (p. 133).

Henshaw's concept of the evangelists as authors was that they did not simply copy the material as they received it, but were "historians who were free to select the material which best suited the purpose which they had in view" (p. 87). However, Luke was credited with having collected the L material of the Gospel and the "We" sections of Acts. Henshaw suggested that Joanna or the other women named in 8,3 may have been responsible for the special material in the Lukan passion narrative (p. 133). In addition, in line with Harnack, though without naming him, Henshaw also proposed Philip the evangelist and his four daughters as well as Manaen (Acts 13,1). Luke's sources for the special information were thus oral and their testimony obtained while Paul was imprisoned in Caesarea.

The two-volume Lukan work was sent to Theophilus following Luke's departure from Rome and the death of Paul (p. 188). While this cannot be construed as indication of when the majority of Acts was written, it can suggest the earliest date of the composition of the special source involving the addition of Mk to Proto-Lk, according to Henshaw. Luke first sent the Gospel to Theophilus, followed later by Acts, somewhere between 75 and 85 AD (p. 189).

Henshaw proposed Joanna as the source for the material about Herod's court, including 23,7-12 and that scholars "usually assigned" the information to her (p. 132-133). In addition to the Herod pericope, Henshaw believed that Joanna would have contributed information to 3,1-19; 8,3; 9,7-9; 13,31. The episode was referred to as "the arraignment before Herod".

863. A.H. MCNEILE, *An Introduction to the Study of the New Testament*, Oxford, 1927;

²1953 (rev. C.S.C. WILLIAMS), p. 25. He was sympathetic to Streeter's Proto-Lk hypothesis. Though not entirely convinced by it, he admitted that it was extremely difficult to distinguish the Markan from the non-Markan material in 22,14 to the end of the Gospel. Cf. p. 88, where he offered Streeter's assessment of the material in the passion narrative taken from Proto-Lk and that derived from Mk. Like Streeter, McNeile acknowledged that the attempt to distinguish the component parts of L "must remain largely tentative" (p. 90). If Proto-Lk existed, it consisted of material drawn mainly from L and Q and was "combined before Luke discovered Mark" (p. 62). McNeile added that there was a good chance Proto-Lk lacked a passion narrative, and rejected outright Burkitt's idea that Q contained one (cf. p. 87. See BURKITT, *Gospel History*, ²1907, p. 134-135). While Luke included most of the Markan material, Mk was seen as responsible only for the account of Peter's denial in the passion narrative (MCNEILE, *An Introduction*, ²1953, p. 63; cf. p. 25). A more exact delineation of sources, following Streeter, was given as follows: 22,52-62.71; 23,3.22.25f. from Mk and 22,69 was either possibly from Mk or from Proto-Lk "partially assimilated to the Marcan parallel" (p. 88). McNeile, following Burkitt's lead, suggested that λέγοντες and τίς ἐστιν ὁ παίσας σε (22,64 / Mt 26,68) were possibly taken from Lk and inserted into Mt for the purpose of harmonization (p. 66). McNeile contended this was the probable explanation for other MAs, but did not specify them. Overall he discounted their importance saying, "they do not amount to very much". In the majority of instances, Luke and Matthew independently improved the Markan style. He rejected Spitta's proposal of an Aramaic original pointing to the lack of Aramaisms in the Gospel (p. 44). Though McNeile was attracted to Torrey's theory about a single, continuous source in Acts 1-15, he favored more the idea that Luke took translations of shorter Aramaic narratives, arranging them so that the Gentiles were seen in a propitious light (p. 103; cf. p. 44). He treated the MAs in his Matthean commentary. Regarding Mt 26,68 / Lk 22,65: "τίς ἐστιν ὁ παίσας σε; (Mt., Lk.) is absent from Mk., who perhaps understood the insult differently; [...] Mt. agrees with Lk., but the last clause may have been added later from Lk." (*The Gospel According to St. Matthew. The Greek Text with Introduction, Notes, and Indices*, London - Melbourne - Toronto - New York, 1965, p. 403-404). Concerning Mt 26,75 / Lk 22,61: "In Lk. the clause is identical, and is substituted for Mk.'s difficult ἐπιβαλὼν ἔκλαιεν ... In Lk., however, it is omitted, perhaps rightly, in all O.L. MSS" (p. 406).

864. *The Gospel According to Luke*, in *Interpr* 7 (1953) 195-212, p. 201. Price maintained that those who argued that Mk formed the basis of Lk regarded the special Lukan material as "largely derived from oral tradition", and he cited Gilmour and R. Heard as examples (cf. S. MCL. GILMOUR, *Gospel*, p. 10-16, R. HEARD, *Introduction*, 1950, p. 79f.). Conversely, proponents of a special source theory were divided into two camps. The first, which included Streeter, Taylor and F.C. Grant, argued that Lk was a "revised and enlarged edition of an earlier work" (PRICE, *Gospel*, p. 201; STREETER, *FG*, p. 199-222; TAYLOR, *Behind*; F.C. GRANT, *Growth*). The second, exemplified by Perry, was said to have "derived from a series of short written accounts" (PRICE, *Gospel*, p. 201; cf. PERRY, *Sources*). Except for Mk, Price was hesitant about accepting the results of Lukan source criticism, particularly in the case of the material unique to Lk. "The interpreter of Luke who would seek 'assured results' of criticism in this matter of the sources employed by Luke and his use of them should consider well the comments of Cadbury in his important study, *The Making of Luke-Acts*. The attempt to establish written Greek sources, beyond Mark's Gospel, remains largely a matter of speculation. Many of the inferences drawn from such source reconstructions are insecure foundations for the judgments they are alleged to support. Especially subjective are 'conclusions' concerning 'Special Luke'" (PRICE, *Gospel*, p. 201-202).

Subsequently (1961) Price noted that the Proto-Lk theory held some appeal but echoed Gilmour's critique that the framework was indeed Markan and that several of the passages

We have traced the development, modifications and reception of a special Proto-Lukan theory as we examined the contributions of major figures in Britain and Germany. While Streeter did not refer to or acknowledge the work of his predecessor's, Taylor provided us with one of the most extensive reviews of the history of the special source question. Streeter and Taylor differed on a number of

reflected Lukan redaction of Mk from oral tradition (*Interpreting the New Testament*, New York, 1961, p. 214 = ²1971, p. 224; cf. *The New Testament. Its History and Theology*, New York, 1987 [rev. ed. of *Interpreting*], p. 130: "Several passages, crucial to a proto-Luke theory, probably represent the Evangelist's editing and enrichment of Mark from oral and written sources"). Not only that, if some of the more doubtful passages were eliminated, all that would be left would be "an amorphous collection of traditional materials" (1961, p. 214 = ²1971, p. 224 = *The New Testament*, 1987, p. 131).

Price, swayed by the presentations of Perry and Taylor, was favorably disposed to the idea that Lk displayed probable proof that there had existed "pre-canonical documents" which consisted of an account of the passion (p. 169 = ²1971, p. 179; cf. 1987, p. 103-108). While sundry accounts came together in certain major geographical "centers" (reminiscent of Streeter's suggestion), religious leaders traveling between various early Christian communities would have exercised control to prevent any "fanciful developments" in the passion story (p. 168 = ²1971, p. 178). Those accounts known or believed to have been associated with one of "the Twelve" would supercede the more local versions. Though the low verbal percentage of agreement between Mk and Lk was suggestive, the transpositions were for Price the "most significant of all" (p. 169 = ²1971, p. 179). He summarized: "This evidence has led many to conclude that Luke had access to a Passion Narrative in addition to the one he found in Mark. It is possible that his 'source' consisted in a cycle of oral tradition, but it is more probable that Luke had before him an alternate document" (p. 169 = ²1971, p. 179). Yet not without some hesitation did Price make this assertion. Later, acknowledging that in 22,14–23,56 Lk was "roughly parallel to Mark", Price placed several Lukan elements and passages of our section of the passion narrative in parentheses, denoting they may not have derived from L: "*Passages in parentheses may not belong to L; some may have been drawn from Q" (p. 207, n. * = ²1971, p. 217). These included the mockery (22,63-65, supplied rather by Mk 14,65), the Sanhedrin trial (22,67-71, a variation instead of Mk 14,55-65), Jesus being delivered to Pilate (23,1 or simply Mk 15,1b), and Pilate's question (23,3, which may be a borrowing of Mk 15,2) (p. 209 = ²1971, p. 220). Those definitely attributed to L were the charges involving treason (23,2), Pilate's insistence on the innocence of Jesus (23,4-5), Jesus' trial before Herod (23,6-12), and Pilate's declaration that Jesus did nothing warranting death (23,13-16). Mk, on the other hand, provided the denials of Peter (22,54-62 / Mk 14,53-54.66-72), elements of the night trial (Mk 14,55-65), the freeing of Barabbas and the execution of Jesus (23,[17]-22a / Mk 15,6-14), and Pilate's sentence (23,24-25 / Mk 15,15). The significance of one's conclusion on this issue is far reaching for it touches, not only the issue of the origin of Lk, but "its historical value" (p. 211 = ²1971, p. 221).

Price's overall assessment of the Proto-Lk theory was that while it offered an attractive explanation for certain elements, it garnered only minority support. Because a great many scholars saw the framework of Mk behind Lk, and because some of the passages can be readily explained as Lukan redaction of Mk from oral traditions, Price echoed Creed's foreboding prediction of the demise of the special source into "an amorphous collection" once these have been eliminated (p. 214 = ²1971, p. 224; see J.M. CREED, *The Gospel according to St. Luke*, p. lviii, n. 1). Speaking of the "heterogeneous character" of L (1961, p. 208 = ²1971, p. 218), Price submitted that it may have originated in Caesarea, and following Harnack, noted that Philip the evangelist and his daughters lived there (1961, p. 211 = ²1971, p. 221-222).

points including the extent of Markan influence, the date of the special source and its supposed historical value.

At this time there was a strong emphasis on the attempt to discern the vocabulary of the special source. Despite concerted efforts and what scholars generally welcomed as the most detailed analyses, H. Schürmann eventually concluded that a continuous special Lukan source was no longer considered to be probable, but merely possible. These studies, particularly those which attempted to distinguish pre-Lukan from Lukan usage, provided the foundation for a renewed interest and heightened impetus for further research.

CHAPTER FOUR

CRITIQUE OF PROTO-LUKE
J.M. Creed through S.McL. Gilmour

Streeter's and Taylor's special source theory came under attack from German and American critics, but it was the remarkably brief critique by one of Britain's leading NT scholars which convinced many scholars to reject the Proto-Lk hypothesis.

John Martin Creed (1930) was a strong advocate of Lukan dependence upon Mk and a forceful and influential critic of the Proto-Lk theory[1]. His famous footnote (lviii n. 1), which had devastating effects for the special source hypothesis, bears repeating:

> Streeter, on the other hand, suggests that the non-Marcan sections of the Gospel – 'Proto-Luke' – should be regarded as the fundamental document, into which the Marcan material has been 'interpolated' at a later stage. I dissent from this suggestion, primarily because, whereas Mark appears to give a clue to the disposition of 'Proto-Luke' in the existing Gospel, the subtraction of Marcan material leaves an amorphous collection of narrative and discourse the greater part of which is thrown without intelligible reason into the unsuitable form of a 'travel document' (ix.52-xviii.). Moreover, signs of the use of Mark are clear both in the account of John's mission (iii. 3 and prob. also iii.16) and above all in the Passion narratives. In the latter not only are there complete sections which are unmistakably taken from Mark (e.g. xxii.7-13,54-61), but Marcan phrases appear in the middle of sections which in other respects differ considerably from Mark (see e.g. xxii.19a,22,47,52,71; xxiii.3). These signs of Mark are intelligible if the Lucan narrative is a recasting and expansion of the Marcan text. If, however, Luke had already written or found a full and independent non-Marcan narrative, it seems unlikely that afterwards he would have interpolated occasional sentences and verses from Mark [...]. It appears to me, therefore, that Mark must be regarded as a determining factor in the construction of the existing book from the outset. This, however, is not necessarily inconsistent with the hypothesis that Q and some of the Luke's peculiar material may have been already combined, and may have lain before Luke as a single document.

---

1. J.M. Creed, *The Gospel according to St. Luke*, London, 1930, p. lviii. Acknowledgement was made of his having been influenced by, though critical of Bultmann, K.L. Schmidt and especially J. Wellhausen. This was followed by a reference to his indebtedness to the commentaries of Klostermann, J. Weiss, Loisy and Montefiore, in addition to Streeter's *The Four Gospels* and Hawkins's *Horae Synopticae* (p. vii). Both Luke and Matthew used the same version of Mk, though they were well aware of the shortcomings of their source. In a comment on his methodology, Creed remarked: "The Marcan sections of the Gospel have been more briefly treated than the rest; I have as a rule not done much more in these parts of the Gospel than call attention to Luke's treatment of the Marcan source" (*Preface*, p. vii-viii). Creed rejected the idea of Proto-Mk, insisting that Matthew and Luke worked with a form of Mk essentially the same as our own (p. lx).

Taylor was conscious of the extent of the influence of Creed's dismissal of the hypothesis in the famous note: "Appeal is constantly made to this footnote"[2].

When Creed rehearsed in the Introduction the history of Lk and its interpretation, he highlighted the question of the "origin and value of the material peculiar to" Lk[3]. He cited works of B. Weiss, Feine, Streeter and Taylor, observing the similarity between the hypothesis of Feine and the two British scholars[4].

As regards the whole body of the special material, Creed maintained in his section on the composition and sources of Lk, it was "perhaps improbable" that a single source contributed "this heterogeneous body of material"[5]. In this regard his position was similar to that of Wernle. Luke reproduced the material from the special sources with little revision. As regards the origin of the material peculiar to Lk, Creed agreed with the majority that it stemmed from Palestinian sources, and as with Streeter, that it was formed in Caesarea. He also asserted that much of it was originally written in Greek and reflected a strong Septuagintal influence[6].

According to Creed, Lukan redaction of Mk in general was prompted by a number of reasons[7]. Luke was possibly constrained to limit his material by the length of the scrolls he used. He avoided doublets and omitted material when the meaning was obscure. When the Markan material was offensive to the evangelist or the Gentile readers or not relevant to their needs, the material was dropped. Finally, if Markan verses contributed little or nothing to the course of the story, Luke omitted them. In addition to a "drastic revision of the language" Luke often shortened material out of sensitivity toward those involved in the events or toward those for whom his work was intended. However, as others noted, the words of Jesus were usually retained without change.

---

2. *Important*, p. 13; so also *Passion Narrative*, p. 12-13: "Creed's main criticisms are put foward in an important footnote in his commentary on Luke. It may be doubted if any footnote in works on Synoptic criticism has exerted so much influence. Many critics have based their rejection of the Proto-Luke hypothesis on this footnote".

3. *Ibid.*, p. xxv-lv, p. l.

4. *Ibid.* B. Weiss (1907); Feine (1891), Streeter (1924, 1921), Taylor (1926). He also mentioned Spitta (1912). He concluded: "These hypotheses, so far as they concern the relation of Matthew and Luke to a supposed *Grundschrift* prior to Mark, have failed to establish themselves".

5. *Ibid.*, p. lvi-lxx, p. lxvii.

6. *Ibid.*, p. lxx. It was also claimed that "a certain measure of literary creation may be plausibly ascribed to the evangelist himself", though Creed also affirmed that in addition to Mk and Q Luke had access to "literary material" (p. lxvi).

7. *Luke*, p. lx-lxiv. He was especially focused on the problem of the great omission (Mk 6,45–7,37; 8,1-26). J. Weiss challenged scholars who supported Lukan redaction of Mk to justify this extensive lacuna. In explaining the rationale of the redaction of Mk by Matthew and Luke Creed claimed: "It may be presumed that each was influenced by the same popular sensitiveness to certain inadequacies of the Marcan Gospel and the same desire to consolidate the tradition in a definitive form" (p. lvii; see also p. lv).

Luke followed the plan and generally the order of Mk, though in the passion
and resurrection narratives he more freely redacted that material than in other
sections of the Gospel[8]. The differences between Lk and Mk, including the
transpositions, "lend the chief support to the theories of Feine, Streeter, and others
that Luke has here followed some other continuous source which, in the main, he
has preferred to Mark. It is argued in the special introductions and notes on these
chapters that it is, on the whole, easier to assume that here too Mark has provided
the foundation of the story. The additional matter in general seems to be
secondary. The rearrangements are more extensive, but not essentially different
from what is found elsewhere".

Expanding this further in his special introduction to the Last Supper (22,7-38),
Creed stated:

> "It has been held by some critics (Perry, Streeter, Taylor) that the divergences
> from Mark here and in the rest of the Passion narrative are to be explained from
> a special source which Luke has mainly followed in preference to Mark. It is
> maintained in the notes that the Lucan text does not, on the whole, support the
> hypothesis of a second continuous narrative source. Luke has himself freely
> rewritten, re-arranged, and enlarged St. Mark. He may sometimes preserve
> independent traditions, but the continuous thread of his narrative appears to be
> based upon Mark"[9].

All the pericopes in 22,54-23,25 drew upon Mk, with the exception of the Herod
episode, which Luke redacted with great freedom, reorganizing the material and
expanding what Mk originally offered[10]. In Creed's opinion, Luke's differences
from Mk in Lk 22,54-71 revolved around five aspects[11]: 1) the two Sanhedrin

---

8. *Ibid.*, p. lxiii: "In his account of the Passion and Resurrection Luke has treated the Marcan
source with greater freedom than elsewhere". Markan influence was particularly evident in,
though not limited to, 22,66.71; 23,3.22.

9. *Ibid.*, p. 262.

10. *Ibid.* Creed relied on HAWKINS, in *SSP*, p. 90 (= *ExpT* 15, p. 275, to which in *SSP* he
added a second reference to Sanday, who was supportive of Feine), to refute Feine and others:
"The well-known theory of Feine and others that Luke had before him some kind of record, or
early Gospel, which he used as a third source, in addition to, and frequently in preference to,
Mark and the *Logia*, at once suggests itself. And I used to think that the strongest arguments in
favour of that theory were to be found in his Passion-narrative. But the closer investigation, of
which I have been here summarising the results, has impressed upon me that such a 'three-
document hypothesis,' as it may be called, does not give much help towards the interpretation of
the phenomena here presented to us. *Luke's additions are (unlike Matthew's) so mixed up with
the Grundschrift, and they have caused alterations and modifications of such kinds, that they
suggest a long and gradual conflation in the mind rather than a simple conflation by the pen.'*
(Italics mine.)" (p. lxiv, n. 1). Cf. above, SANDAY, *Plea*, p. 473, n. 1; and *Bearing*, p. 112.

11. *Luke*, p. 276. He conceded that in the accounts of Peter's denials and the Sanhedrin trial
(22,54-71), "Luke may be drawing upon a special source in addition to Mark, or possibly upon
special traditions orally transmitted". Such a view notwithstanding he continued: "But it may be
that his modifications are to be ascribed to intelligent criticism of Mark on the part of himself or
his circle, and to motives - literary and religious - such as we can trace elsewhere".

trials (Mk 14,53; 15,1) were merged into one[12]; 2) Jesus' threat to destroy the Temple was omitted (as also in the corresponding parallel to Mk 15,29); 3) Luke did not relate that the Sanhedrin condemned Jesus to death[13]; 4) Peter's denials were transposed to precede the trial; 5) the mockery was transposed and the attendants were made responsible for the abuse[14]. Creed was of the opinion that while Luke generally followed the Markan order, he "has no scruple in transposing", which was particularly evident in the passion and resurrection narratives[15]. Such rearrangement of material was prompted by Luke's historical criticism of the events[16]. He considered ὁ κύριος (22,61) as "Lukan usage"[17].

In 23,1-25 Luke employed Mk as his "fundamental source" which provided 23,3.18, details of Pilate's repeated efforts to release Jesus and Pilate's final acquiescence to Jewish demands[18]. Further, Luke offered additional material which included specific charges against Jesus, Pilate's triple assertion of Jesus' innocence and the Herod pericope[19]. In his discussion of 23,1-25 Creed drew connections to material in Acts[20].

Concerning the MAs, Creed stipulated that v. 62 had probably been assimilated to Mt[21]. The simplest explanation for the MA in v. 64 was that the words originally occurred in Mk, but dropped out of some manuscripts[22]. In opposition to Bultmann he denied that Lk had been assimilated to Mt in this case because the context of v. 63 (the blindfolding) "almost demands the question"[23]. Attention was also paid to the agreement of ἀπὸ τοῦ νῦν where it was noted that

---

12. *Ibid.* Creed suggested that the Markan reference to two trials stemmed from a combining of sources instead of "distinct tradition".

13. *Ibid.* He contended further it was "improbable" that the Sanhedrin "had jurisdiction to try a prisoner on a capital charge", suggesting it was likely that Mk contained a popular rather than historically accurate account of the trial. See R.W. Husband (1916), H. Danby (cf. above), and I. ABRAHAMS, *Studies in Pharisaism and the Gospels*, Cambridge, 1924, p. 129f. (p. 275).

14. *Luke*, p. 276.

15. *Ibid.*, p. lxii, lxiii. Luke, generally speaking, retained the original order of both Q and Mk (p. lxv). He pointed out that the cleansing of the Temple was transposed to immediately after the arrival of Jesus in Jerusalem (p. 276). Creed understood the term καθεξῆς (1,3) to probably mean "chronological and historical" (p. xi).

16. *Ibid.*, p. lxiv. See p. lxv, where Creed observed that Luke grouped materials "which have some point of contact".

17. *Ibid.*, p. 277.

18. *Ibid.*, p. 279. The Markan narrative was nonetheless simultaneously "both amplified and obscured" by Luke's redaction.

19. *Ibid.*, p. 280.

20. *Ibid.*, p. 280-281. A parallel between the Gospel with Acts involved Herod and Pilate (Lk 23,5-12 / Acts 4,25-26). Shared vocabulary appeared in Lk 23,1 / Acts 23,7, just as in Lk 23,7 / Acts 25,21.

21. *Ibid.*, p. 277.

22. *Ibid.*, p. 277-278.

23. *Ibid.*, p. 278. See BULTMANN, *GST* (1921), p. 164.

this was characteristic of Luke just as ἀπ᾽ ἄρτι was of Matthew[24]. Lk was an enduring testimony to the education and skill of the writer.

Noting that the story about Herod was unique to Luke and that vv. 13-16 provided a transition to the Barabbas scene, Creed observed that the account also appeared in GP[25]. Admitting the source was unknown, Acts 4,25f. was proposed as a clue to its origin. He then rehearsed the view of Dibelius that Herod and Pilate came to be associated in the early Christian community by its interpretation of Ps 2. If the story was derived from tradition, several problems arose. These included the fact that it did not appear in Mk, the unlikelihood of Jesus' transfer, and the inconsistency between 23,10 and 23,15 concerning whether or not the chief priests and scribes accompanied Jesus to Herod[26]. Although he appeared to support the translation of ἀνέπεμψεν as "to send up to a higher authority" in accord with Acts 25,21, he provided no rationale for such an interpretation. Further, Wellhausen's supposition that 23,10-11 were not original was, in his view, unjustified and Verrall's explanation of 23,11 was termed "too subtle", though he credited him with "a very ingenious interpretation of the scene"[27]. Siding with Loisy, Creed understood the phrase ἐσθῆτα λαμπράν (23,11) as avoiding a reference to the imperial purple. Observing that the mockery by the Roman soldiers (Mk 15,16-20) was omitted at the corresponding place in the Lk, he suggested that Luke transferred the mockery to Herod's men[28]. The return of Jesus to Pilate by Herod was taken as an acquittal.

H.J. Cadbury was impressed by Creed's position on the disputed matter of sources[29]. Though he faulted Creed for a seeming ignorance of Torrey's work, as well as that of the compatriot, W.F. Howard, nevertheless Cadbury concluded that Creed's assessment of the language issues was "quite sound"[30]. Easton attacked Creed for holding to the Two-Source theory in the area of literary criticism and suggested that Creed did not go far enough in his analysis of L, chastising him for not referring to the work of other commentators in their effort to explain it[31]. He further criticized Creed who "overloaded with mere statistical

---

24. *Luke*, p. 278-279.

25. *Ibid.*, p. 280. The Herod story was defined as 23,5-12 (p. lxvii). He adopted the view that GP was acquainted with all the canonical Gospels (p. xxvi, referring readers to C.H. Turner, 1913). Lk was "probably" the source for the trial before Herod in the apochryphal gospel (p. xxvi).

26. *Ibid.*, p. 280.

27. *Ibid.*, p. 282.

28. *Ibid.*, p. 280: "Luke was perhaps glad to transfer the outrage from the soldiery of Rome to the soldiery of the local tetrarch". He also noted that there was a further mockery of Jesus on the cross by soldiers at 23,36. In light of the previous omission this would be in line with Luke's penchant for avoiding doublets (p. lxi). Cf. GELDENHUYS, 1951, who responded to each of Creed's three objections. Cf. below.

29. *JR* 11 (1931) 284.

30. *Ibid.*, p. 284-285.

31. *ATR* 13 (1931) 88.

matter of a rather obvious kind" Luke's parallels with Mk, except in the case of the last four chapters. There Creed's defect concerned treating the material in only a general manner[32]. According to Easton, Creed's forte was in the area of historical criticism.

The particular value of Creed's commentary, according to Edwyn Hoskyns, lay in its review of the history of interpretation of Lk, but especially in its refutation of Streeter's Proto-Lukan theory[33]. Both Balmforth and Manson would have likely benefited from referring to it had it been available. Creed, by underscoring Markan framework of Lk, did not exclude the possibility that some of the special Lukan material may have already been combined with Q by the time it reached Luke. Nor was the importance of the special Lukan material, which Creed held derived from Palestinian sources, in any way diminished. But Hoskyns was most critical of Creed for failing to apply his criticism of Streeter's theory in working out his commentary. "It is difficult to discover precisely what Professor Creed really thinks about Lucan editing, since the relevant passage in the introduction (p. lvi-lxiv) does not cover what is demanded in the commentary. Since so much of the commentary is concerned directly or indirectly with the Proto-Luke hypothesis, it would have been convenient to have had the evidence against it gathered together in a detached note. The footnote on p. lviii hardly represents the importance of the issue for English scholars, nor does it give any indication of how much the commentary is concerned with this particular problem"[34]. None of these criticisms devalued Creed's commentary in the eyes of Hoskyns whose final assessment was that Creed "has given us a commentary which is of very great critical importance"[35].

So convincing were the arguments presented by Creed in his commentary, that HOSKYNS (1931, [3]1947) deduced that Streeter's theory was "untenable", but left open the idea that further development might possibly render the theory useful[36]. It was quite clear that, according to Hoskyns, Luke revised Mk[37]. Hoskyns categorically rejected Taylor's view that the non-Markan sections were more historically reliable[38]. He also took issue with Hawkins's proposal that the special

32. *Ibid.*, p. 89.

33. *TLond* 22 (1931) 352-354.

34. *Ibid.*, p. 353.

35. *Ibid.*, p. 354.

36. E. HOSKYNS and N. DAVEY, *The Riddle of the New Testament*, London, 1931, [3]1947, p. 14. "We regard Luke's editing of Mark to be still a prime fact in New Testament criticism, and we have judged that Professor Creed in his recent commentary upon St. Luke's Gospel has made Dr. Streeter's Proto-Luke theory untenable, at least in the form in which he stated it in Chapter VIII of his book on the Four Gospels". It was clear that Hoskyns nonetheless adopted Streeter's four categories of material, or "strata of tradition" (cf. p. 78-79).

37. *Ibid.*, p. 76. Luke's redaction of Mk was warranted to clarify the text, improve the style, refute slanderous accusations of the Jews, and mollify the depiction of the apostles.

38. *Ibid.*, p. 196. One wonders whether Hoskyns may have had the Herod episode in mind when he penned this.

material derived from Paul, arguing that the Lukan perspective did not especially reflect Pauline influence[39].

Josef SCHMID (1930) treated the work of Eduard Simons extensively[40]. Giving a great deal of attention to the MA in 22,64, Schmid reasoned that, based on significant differences in vocabulary, Luke possessed the more original form which had been taken from another source[41]. This, in turn, had been inserted into Mt[42].

Noting numerous differences in the Synoptic accounts of Peter's denial, Schmid concluded that Luke presented this story in a continuous fashion. While the MA in 22,62 in some way could have resulted from the attempt of both later evangelists to improve and clarify the Markan language, Schmid decided that the verse in Lk had probably been a very ancient interpolation taken from the Matthean parallel[43].

Schmid stated in his Lukan commentary (1940, [4]1960) he believed that the author of Lk-Acts was a co-worker of Paul[44]. He delineated the passion as

---

39. *Ibid.*, p. 195.

40. J. SCHMID, *Matthäus und Lukas. Eine Untersuchung des Verhältnisses ihrer Evangelien* (BSt 23/2-4), Freiburg, 1930. Cf. F. NEIRYNCK, *Minor Agreements Matthew-Luke in the Transfiguration Story*, in P. HOFFMANN, N. BROX, and W. PESCH (eds.), *Orientierung an Jesus. Zur Theologie der Synoptiker. Für Josef Schmid*, Freiburg, 1973, 253-266 (= *Evangelica*, 797). Eduard SIMONS (1880) posited the view that Luke knew and used Mt in addition to Mk and Q (*Hat der dritte Evangelist den kanonischen Matthäus benutzt?*, Bonn, 1880). Mt served as a *Nebenquelle* for Lk which in Simons's opinion explained better than other proposed solutions such as "common source, oral tradition, accidental editorial coincidence", the similarity between Lk and Mt, as well as their differences from Mk (F. NEIRYNCK, *The Minor Agreements of Matthew and Luke against Mark*, p. 15, 16. See SIMONS, *Hat*, p. 107, 108). It offered "the first specific study of the minor agreements" (F. NEIRYNCK, *The Minor Agreements of Matthew and Luke against Mark*, p. 15. See also T.A. FRIEDRICHSEN, *The Matthew-Luke Agreements Against Mark*, Vol. 1, p. 179, n. 249; Vol. 2, p. 312). The influence of Mt was both limited in degree and interspersed rather than continuous (SIMONS, *Hat*, p. 105: "Eine Einwirkung des Mt. auf die Komposition des Lc. im Grossen ... haben wir nicht wahrgenommen ... Zum Theil; denn wir haben gesehn, dass die Matthäischen Einwirkungen keine ununterbrochene Kette darstellen"). It was in the passion and resurrection narratives that the Lukan dependence upon Mt was clearest. Matthean influence was further evidenced by examining Luke's redaction of Mk, which included "stilistischen oder lexikalischen Nüancirungen, in Auslassungen oder kleinen Zuthaten" (p. 107). Luke memorized much of Mt and freely redacted it (p. 108).

Rejecting the influence of an Urmarkus, Simons maintained Matthew transformed Mk's ἐπιβαλών into a term that was strong and comprehensible, which Luke then borrowed. Similarly, Matthew sought to supplement the Markan προφήτευσον with the MA in Mt 26,68 (p. 98). Once again, Luke adopted Matthew's phrase. A further proof seemed to be that Luke, in imitation of Mt, supplied λέγοντες in place of Mk's καὶ λέγουσι.

41. SCHMID, *Matthäus und Lukas*, p. 159. The Lukan version did not contain any text-critical problems or difficulties with the content.

42. *Ibid.*, p. 158.

43. *Ibid.*, p. 160.

44. J. SCHMID, *Das Evangelium nach Lukas* (RNT, 3), Regensburg, 1940, [2]1951, p. 7. In the fourth edition Schmid described Paul's companion as "zeitweilig" ([4]1960, p. 6). One of

22,1–23,56 and insisted that Luke based the structure of his own work upon that of Mk[45]. In general Luke adopted the Markan order though he transposed some material, among which was counted 22,66-71[46]. Schmid argued that Luke followed the Markan order on the whole, but even in places where Luke was borrowing material from Mk, it was clear that the changes in order were the result of Luke the historian or skilled writer, rather than other sources[47]. Such was the case in the transposition of the account of Peter's denial. The change enabled Luke "ein fortlaufender und klarer Bericht zu geben", thus repairing the breach found in the Markan account[48]. Luke reordered the Markan material in order to render a clearer presentation, though not with a particularly strong chronological perspective. In his second edition he added that much more radical changes in order, over against Mk, were seen in the passion narrative[49].

Although Luke borrowed much from Mk he did not include all of it. A notable omission was Mk 6,17-29 for which Luke supplied 3,19f. Drawing upon other sources in addition to Mk, Luke inserted certain material including 23,6-16, the placement of which was determined by the contents[50]. Material from Mk was omitted or passed over for several reasons. The matter created difficulties for Luke's readers[51]. Luke wanted to avoid doublets and in some instances opted to use material from other sources in a different context[52]. Other changes were prompted by Luke's softening of the Markan presentation, even in the case of Peter's denials and their prediction[53]. But Schmid denied Luke had a better

Luke's undisputed sources was the preaching of Paul and Schmid emphasized that the majority of Luke's sources would have been written (1940, p. 19-20; [2]1951, p. 20; [4]1960, p. 22, adding: "aber dies doch nur in einem eng begrenzten Ausmass"). Schmid called Lagrange's commentary "der beste katholische Kommentar" (1940, p. 23; [2]1951, p. 24; [4]1960, p. 27).

45. *Ibid.*, 1940, [2]1951, p. 10; [4]1960, p. 8, 9. See also 1940, [2]1951, p. 11; [4]1960, p. 10, where he also insisted Luke inserted materials drawn from other sources into the Markan framework.

46. See also the comment on chronological order, 1940, p. 16; [2]1951, p. 17; [4]1960, p. 18, with additional information.

47. *Ibid.*, [2]1951, p. 256; [4]1960, p. 317-318. Note also 1940, [2]1951, p. 10; [4]1960, p. 9.

48. *Ibid.*, [2]1951, p. 255; [4]1960, p. 316, 317. See also [4]1960, p. 9, 317-318. Cf. 1940, p. 241. Schmid contended the most strongly emphasized change was the transfer of the trial to the morning ([2]1951, p. 255; [4]1960, p. 316. See further 1940, p. 240, [2]1951, p. 276; [4]1960, p. 339-340).

49. *Ibid.*, [2]1951, p. 12; [4]1960, p. 11. He directed the reader to his introduction to the passion story ([2]1951, p. 254-257; [4]1960, p. 315-319).

50. *Ibid.*, 1940, [2]1951, p. 11; [4]1960, p. 10.

51. *Ibid.*, 1940, [2]1951, p. 10; [4]1960, p. 9. This explained why some of the Palestinian color was obscured (1940, p. 17; [2]1951, p. 18; [4]1960, p. 19).

52. *Ibid.*, 1940, [2]1951, p. 10-11; [4]1960, p. 9-10.

53. *Ibid.*, [2]1951, p. 256; [4]1960, p. 318.

chronological flow of events than Mk, nor was such his intention[54]. At times he
departed from chronological order on account of his sources.

Concerning the *Sondergut*, rather than a unified source, this material stemmed
from a variety of sources, including oral tradition[55]. Although Luke drew his
material from various sources, Schmid maintained that the work reflected Luke's
own spirit and literary art[56].

Commenting on Luke's literary style, Schmid maintained Luke was familiar
not only with the style of the LXX, but consciously imitated it. In relating the
"heilige Geschichte", he bestowed upon his Gospel an OT flavor[57]. Schmid
further observed that the evangelist used a considerable number of Septuagintal
expressions which gave Lk "eine atl Färbung"[58]. Schmid also called attention to
Luke's substitution of "tetrarch" for "king" in referring to Herod. Luke's
preference for the words "entire" or "all" was evident[59]. He passed over some
of the colorful details found in Mk such as in 22,55.56. He also softened certain
details or scenes as in the case of 22,60 and portrayed Jesus as savior of sinners
in 22,61[60] just as he improved the portrayal of the Romans, namely Pilate and his
soldiers, in the account of the trial (cf. 23,13-25)[61]. Schmid did not treat the MAs
in 22,62.64.

His expanded introduction to the passion narrative in the second edition
allowed Schmid to add some insights. Though Luke made extensive use of Mk as
the basis for his own Gospel, it was not simply a stylistic improvement. Lukan
redaction in the passion narrative comprised: 1) a greater number of omissions[62],
2) a series of additions of varying lengths, 3) repetition by another arrangement of

---

54. *Ibid.*, 1940, p. 11; [2]1951, p. 11-12; [4]1960, p. 10-11. Luke was attempting to follow Mk's
geographical plan, but difficulties were created for this by Luke's connecting various sources
(1940, [2]1951, p. 13; [4]1960, p. 12-13).

55. *Ibid.*, 1940, [2]1951, [4]1960, p. 13.

56. *Ibid.*, 1940, p. 13; [2]1951, p. 14; [4]1960, p. 13: "Obgleich nach dem Gesagten das Lukas-
Evangelium eine aus verschiedenen Quellen geschöpfte Schrift ist, so ist es doch anderseits ein
Werk aus einem Guss, dem der Verfasser den Stempel seines Geistes, seiner schriftstellerischen
Kunst und religiösen Individualität deutlich sichtbar aufgedrückt hat".

57. *Ibid.*, 1940, [2]1951, [4]1960. p. 15. In the fourth edition he referred to the "evangelische
Geschichte".

58. *Ibid.*

59. *Ibid.*, 1940, p. 15; [2]1951, p. 16; [4]1960, p. 16. In the second edition he added 22,67-71
to his list of passages where the terms occurred.

60. *Ibid.*, 1940, p. 18; [2]1951, p. 19; [4]1960, p. 20, 21.

61. *Ibid.*, [2]1951, p. 256; [4]1960, p. 318. This reflected a portion of his revised and expanded
introduction to the passion account in the second edition.

62. *Ibid.*, [2]1951, p. 254; [4]1960, p. 315; cf. 1940, p. 229. Luke passed over the reference to
the Temple since it had no meaning for him or his readers ([4]1960, cf. 340; cf. 1940, p. 243;
[2]1951, p. 274), just as he chose not to include the account of the mockery by the Roman soldiers
(Mk 15,16-20a) perhaps because he had a parallel story (22,63-65) and wished to improve the
portrayal of the Romans ([2]1951, p. 277; [4]1960, p. 344; cf. 1940, p. 245).

the material, and 4) a theological tendency unique to Luke[63]. Certain details in the passion were seen as an extension of Jesus' teaching on love of enemy including 22,61a and 23,6-16.

Schmid's concluding observations about Lukan changes to the Markan order are worth noting: "Man sieht beim Rückblick auf diese zahlreichen Änderungen der Markus-Ordnung klar die Hand des 'Historikers' Lukas am Werke, dem daranliegt, die Einzelheiten miteinander zu verknüpfen und dadurch zu erläutern und sie in eine übersichtliche Ordnung zu bringen. Eben darum darf man in diesen Umstellungen nicht Verbesserungen der Markus-Darstellung auf Grund anderer Quellen, genauerer geschichtlicher Information sehen, durch die unser Wissen über den genauen Verlauf der Passion vermehrt würde"[64].

In treating the denial of Peter Schmid noted that the location of the account, in contrast to the other Synoptics, allowed for the telling of the story without interruption[65]. Luke also sought to soften the account by omitting the swearing by Peter. He also highlighted the addition in 22,61a. The description of the trial (22,66-71) was sharply abbreviated from Mk[66].

The mockery (22,63-65) showed that the events transpired over a longer period of time[67]. In contrast to Mk, this particular account was also softened since the references to the spitting and slapping were omitted.

Schmid rejected as "nicht wahrscheinlich" the suggestion that Luke employed a tradition independent of Mk for 22,66-71[68]. In the second edition he repeated the observation that the testimony of the false witnesses (Mk 14,56-61a) was passed over by Luke. The vocabulary was different from Mk at many points. As for the detail about "sitting at the right hand of God" Schmid invited readers to compare Acts 7,55. Luke clarified Mk by adding "of God" to "power".

In 23,1-5 Luke enlarged the brief Markan account with a few details in which he strengthened the innocence of Jesus in contrast to Mk[69]. Schmid judged the third of the three charges to be the most important. He very clearly indicated that Luke was following Mk for the account of the trial of Jesus by Pilate. This section contrasted the charges of the Jews with the declaration of innocence by the Roman judge[70].

As the procurator brought the trial to an end (23,13-25), Pilate, together with Herod, discerned that the charges against Jesus were unfounded. Lk matched Mk

---

63. *Ibid.*, ²1951, p. 254; ⁴1960, p. 315; cf. 1940, p. 229.

64. *Ibid.*, ²1951, p. 256; ⁴1960, p. 317-318.

65. *Ibid.*, 1940, p. 241; ²1951, p. 272; ⁴1960, p. 338.

66. *Ibid.*, 1940,p. 243; ²1951, p. 274; ⁴1960, p. 340.

67. *Ibid.*, 1940, p. 241: "Die sofort anschliesende (V. 63-65) Misshandlung Jesu durch die ihn bewachenden Diener zeigt, dass dies längere Zeit hindurch der Fall war" (cf. ²1951, p. 273, where Schmid deleted "sofort"; so ⁴1960, p. 338).

68. *Ibid.*, 1940, p. 242; ²1951, p. 274; ⁴1960, p. 340, where he added "ja ausgeschlossen" after "wahrscheinlich".

69. *Ibid.*, 1940, p. 244; ²1951, p. 275; cf. ⁴1960, p. 342.

70. *Ibid.*, 1940, p. 244; ²1951, p. 276; ⁴1960, p. 342.

again at 23,17.18-25. Verse 17 was regarded as an insertion from either Mt or Mk. That Luke passed over Mk 15,16-20 was again noted and Schmid contended this was done in light of 22,63-65 and 23,11, which possibly exonerated the Romans[71]. The Lukan account, in contrast to Mk, once more stressed the opposition of Pilate to the judgment against Jesus and the hatred of him by the Jews. Schmid thought Luke passed over the formal death sentence at the Sanhedrin trial because the judgment of the Romans was much more critical for the fate of Jesus[72]. He added in the fourth edition that what was more, Pilate's formal judgment was spoken of less in Lk than in Mk and Mt[73].

Although in previous places Schmid (1940, [4]1960) referred to the Herod pericope as 23,6-16, in the translation and explanation section he designated it as only 23,6-12[74]. This story had no meaning for the destiny of Jesus nor did it have any set theological perspective. Nevertheless, he judged this account to be a piece of a genuine tradition[75]. It was not clear why Pilate would have sent Jesus to Herod. Schmid took note of previous references to Herod in the Gospel (3,1; 9,9; 13,31). He did not accept the meeting of Jesus and Herod as a genuine trial. The apparel was thought possibly to be white and was a mockery of Jesus as king.

The similarities between this scene and the Markan mockery (Mk 15,16-20a) were evident[76]. Luke omitted this Markan material because he already referred to a mockery in 22,63-65 and, adding in the second edition, because he wished to portray the Romans more favorably[77]. The friendship between Pilate and Herod (23,12) could have resulted from Herod feeling flattered by Pilate's courtesy[78].

Martin DIBELIUS (1933) contended there was a continuous, pre-Markan passion narrative that arose from early Christian preaching, in the context of mission or liturgy[79]. While there were differences among the various evangelists, still in the

---

71. *Ibid.*, 1940, p. 246, 247 (*"vielleicht* auch deshalb, um die Römer möglichst zu entlasten"); cf. [2]1951, p. 278; [4]1960, p. 345 (*"wohl* auch deshalb, um die Römer möglichst zu entlasten") [emphasis added].

72. *Ibid.*, 1940, p. 243; [2]1951, p. 275; [4]1960, p. 341.

73. *Ibid.*, [4]1960, p. 345; cf. 1940, p. 247; [2]1951, p. 278.

74. *Ibid.*, 1940, p. 245; [2]1951, p. 276; [4]1960, p. 343. Cf. 1940, p. 11, 13; [2]1951, p. 11, 14, 254; [4]1960, p. 10, 13, 316.

75. *Ibid.*, 1940, p. 245; [2]1951, p. 276; [4]1960, p. 343.

76. *Ibid.*, 1940, p. 245; [2]1951, p. 277; [4]1960, p. 344.

77. *Ibid.*, [2]1951, p. 277; [4]1960, p. 344; cf. 1940, p. 245.

78. *Ibid.*, 1940, p. 246; [2]1951, p. 277; [4]1960, p. 344.

79. M. DIBELIUS, *From Tradition to Gospel*, New York, 1965, tr. from the rev. Second ed. of *Die Formgeschichte des Evangeliums*, Tübingen, [2]1933, p. 23. The work first appeared in German in 1919. The passion story merited a separate chapter, p. 178-217; (= p. 178-218 in the German edition, [2]1933). In the 1936 ET the following editorial note appeared: "The present translation represents a notable advance upon the latest German edition, as it incorporates many additions contributed especially by the author" (p. VII). Despite the thesis that the passion narrative was a continuous work, Dibelius allowed that the account of Peter's denial could have existed independently of the rest of the story (p. 180). "We may assume that even the earliest

latter section of the Gospels there was remarkable agreement in that which was essential[80]. This pointed to the fact that the passion narrative, at the time of the Synoptics, "had duly and uniformly reached its definite form"[81]. In general, Dibelius took a minimalist view of the evangelists as authors. They were, in his estimation, simply collectors and editors[82]. However, Luke merited the title "author" because of his maverick presentation[83]. There was a striking dissimilarity in Luke's manner of authorship between his two works. In the Gospel Luke collected and edited materials, while in Acts Luke was an author in his own right.

The redaction undertaken by the Synoptic authors involved passing on and revising material by choosing, limiting and refashioning the material. Other factors which influenced the final form were the desire to edify, early Christian theology, and apologetics[84]. Changes resulted, Dibelius insisted, from the growth of the tradition in the Church, rather than from Luke's literary style[85]. Luke, in particular, fashioned his account by attending to technical details in the trial. Because he sought to present Jesus as the suffering Savior who, in the face of evil, became "a model of innocent suffering", the resulting narrative took shape as a martyrdom[86]. Consequently, one may not ultimately discern a source.

Dibelius distrusted even the historicity of the Markan presentation of the trial, suggesting that the early Christians would not have been privy to such information as would clarify and settle the issue[87]. Dibelius did not consider the Markan account to be historical[88]. But Luke was attentive to the technical detail that the

---

record told events from the Passion which only had significance because they were known to be announced by Scripture. Then everything shameful and dishonouring done to Jesus – arrest, mishandling, dividing of garments, contemptuous treatment, was legitimatized in the Passion story, for it happened according to God's will. Hence these O.T. relations with the Passion story did not arise from exegetical zeal, but from an understanding of the story of salvation. The Passion had its home, not in teaching and uplifting the individual, but in carrying the message to the church, i.e. the sermon" (p. 185).

80. DIBELIUS, *From Tradition*, p. 22, 179.
81. *Ibid.*, p. 23.
82. *Ibid.*, p. 3.
83. *Ibid.*, p. 203.
84. *Ibid.*, p. 23.
85. *Ibid.*, p. 199-200.
86. *Ibid.*, p. 201. Dibelius contended this was a literary rather than a theological standpoint (p. 300). Similarity on the issue of martyrdom with G. BERTRAM, *Die Leidensgeschichte Jesu und der Christuskult*, p. 55, was to be noted.
87. DIBELIUS, *From Tradition*, p. 192. Nor was the purpose of the Gospel narratives, in the first place, to offer a historical presentation. "The first understanding afforded by the standpoint of Formgeschichte is that there never was a 'purely' historical witness to Jesus. Whatever was told of Jesus' words and deeds was always a testimony of faith as formulated for preaching and exhortation in order to convert unbelievers and confirm the faithful. What founded Christianity was not knowledge about a historical process, but the confidence that the content of the story was salvation: the decisive beginning of the end" (p. 295).
88. *Ibid.*, p. 295-296: "We showed in Chapter VII that the earliest Passion story, as far as

Sanhedrin was permitted to gather only in the morning[89]. Although the earlier presentation of the passion story was concerned with soteriology, the subsequent version by Luke focused on the human elements and psychological aspects[90]. "It was narrated in the Church from the standpoint that it shared the fate of Peter"[91]. The gradual evolution of the early Christian literature later benefited from accretions which provided context, offered interpretation and the explicit announcement of a particular point of view[92]. Dibelius, like Bertram, saw the early Christian community as having played a decisive role in shaping the Christian message, particularly the passion narrative. In response to the need for an explanation of the shameful events of the passion and to resolve the matter of responsibility, the evangelists crafted their narratives around the core of the story.

Dibelius countered Streeter's line of thinking only indirectly[93]. Oddly there was no mention of the Four-Document theory. Instead, Dibelius chose to reaffirm the Two-Source theory and opted to explain other differences from Mk in the later Synoptics as due to the influence of oral tradition, the transmission of some smaller units of special source material and scribal harmonization[94]. Additional redaction in Lk was owing to information drawn from "the current tradition", or Luke's own "phantasy" by which he added the touching and edifying elements, such as Jesus' glance at Peter (22,61)[95]. The legends of martyrs also had a formative influence upon the composition of this section of the Gospel.

Dibelius, in defending the Two-Source theory, argued Lukan dependence upon Mk was evinced by the order[96]. Infrequent changes and omissions did not detract from this view and he contended that Luke's order was the same as Mk's in the section 18,15–24,11. The Two-Source theory, however, cannot explain away "all details of synoptic interrelationship"[97].

Luke's redaction of his two primary sources involved "using more refined and educated modes of expression"[98]. Various historical connections were established by means of insertions, such as the charges leveled against Jesus in 23,2. What

---

it can be recognized in Mark, does not mean to present events in the historical sense. Although in a few places it depends upon the information of eyewitnesses, it does not purpose to narrate and prove the sequence of events, nor to stir and exhort people by the description of the Passion".

89. *Ibid.*, p. 200.

90. *Ibid.*, p. 203.

91. *Ibid.*, p. 214-215.

92. *Ibid.*, p. 287-288.

93. DIBELIUS, *Geschichte der urchristlichen Literatur*, 2 vols., Berlin - Leipzig, 1926; Munich, R1975 (= *A Fresh Approach to the New Testament and Early Christian Literature*, London, 1936). Pagination refers to the ET. That Dibelius was aware of Streeter's work was obvious from the inclusion of the latter's work, *FG*, in the bibliography (p. 274).

94. DIBELIUS, *Fresh*, p. 56.

95. *Ibid.*, p. 63.

96. *Ibid.*, p. 54.

97. *Ibid.*, p. 56.

98. *Ibid.*, p. 62.

was more, according to Dibelius, Luke refined his sources in such a way as to clarify and put the finishing touches on the narratives.

Dibelius maintained that proof of Luke's dependence upon Mk was to be found in the order followed in Lk, which also included Lk 18,15-24,11[99]. The few changes in the order and omissions were understandable.

Dibelius (1947), basing his reasoning on the lack of philological criterion, rejected Feine's view that there was a unified source underlying Acts 1-12[100]. Though Luke had access to a unified, written source for Paul's journeys, which provided a basis for chapters 13-21, for the remainder Luke strung together "current stories", arranging them and drawing out their meaning through accompanying speeches[101].

In what would become a very influential essay, Dibelius (1915) contended Luke did not possess a "konkrete Überlieferung" detailing the trial before Herod[102]. Dibelius made still another contribution to the debate arguing: "So schuf Lukas die Szene aus ein paar übernommenen Zügen, ohne Legenden zu benutzen oder zu erdichten. Der Fall ist symptomatisch: der Weissagungsbeweis beeinflusst die kultische Sprache, diese produziert Tatsachen, die, solange die Überlieferung noch im Fluss ist, sogar noch in ein Evangelium Aufnahme finden"[103].

The most radical changes to Mark's account by Luke included: 1) portraying Pilate as a supporter of Jesus' innocence, 2) that Pilate permitted Jesus to be handed over to the Jews, and 3) incorporation of the Herod scene[104]. The lack of concrete details did not prevent Luke from supplying them from motifs in Ps 2 which played an important role in the early Church. These were then incorporated into the passion narrative.

Dibelius seemed to offer a mediating solution to the dilemma created by A. Loisy on one side, and F.C. Burkitt and A.W. Verrall on the other. Dibelius rebuffed J. Weiss for overestimating Dibelius's opinion concerning the importance

---

99. *Ibid.*, p. 54.

100. DIBELIUS, *Die Apostelgeschichte als Geschichtsquelle*, in *Forschungen und Fortschritte* 21/23 Jahrgang 67-69, Berlin, 1947, 91-95 (= *The Acts of the Apostles as an Historical Source*, in ID., *Studies in the Acts of the Apostles*, ed. H. GREEVEN, tr. M. LING, London, 1956, p. 105). The article was republished as chapter six in the present collection of essays.

101. *Ibid.*, p. 107.

102. DIBELIUS, *Herodes und Pilatus*, in ZNW 16 (1915) 122 (= *Botschaft und Geschichte. Gesammelte Aufsätze*, Vol. 1, Tübingen, 1953, p. 288): "Lukas besass also keine konkrete Überlieferung von den Vorgängen bei Herodes".

103. *Ibid.*, p. 126 (= *BG*, p. 292). Dibelius's study was prompted by a slight shift in methodology to consider this section of the Gospel not only from a historical, but also literary, point of view. He reacted to "den alten Theologenfehler" which assumed that Mk was the more original and thus most historically valuable account (p. 116 = 282).

104. *Ibid.*, p. 120 (= 286). The first two emendations flowed from and pointed to the tendency and character of Luke's redaction which involved decreasing the blame directed toward Pilate and increasing it toward the Jews.

of the judgment of Jesus for the leaders of Jerusalem[105]. Further, the existence of such a tradition, though endorsed by Weiss, was unprovable in the view of Dibelius[106]. In *Die Formgeschichte des Evangeliums*, he repeated the thesis of his earlier article, that the Herod scene was an interpolation, the result of reading the friendship between Pilate and Herod into Ps 2,1f[107].

Kendrick GROBEL (1937) authored an important and well reasoned study of several German, British and American source-critical analyses published between 1913 and 1933[108]. In addition to presenting the various theses, he offered some insightful critiques. He was obviously influenced by Dibelius and the school of Form Criticism. Grobel noted the similarity between that perspective and Haupt's study in which the collective memory of the final days of Jesus in Jerusalem formed the core of the Gospel[109]. While Grobel took issue with Haupt's early dating of the various elements, and contended further they were disputable, he concurred that the "Wortüberlieferung" grew gradually and with the participation of the community[110]. E. Meyer was criticized for the division of sources into a Petrine source and a Dodeka-source, a view Grobel asserted cannot be sustained. What was more, Meyer overestimated Luke, though Grobel did not treat this point in-depth[111]. Some of the strongest censure was directed against W. Bussmann, who turned his back on the commonly accepted source-critical analysis of the Synoptics[112]. The Markan parallels in Lk were really based upon Urmarkus. Even the material where Luke differed was considered change based upon Urmarkus. Mk as we know it was the last of the three Synoptics to be composed. Larfeld interpreted Q differently than was commonly done. What he had written about the style of the different Synoptists, detailed and careful as it was, was long ago done by Hawkins, better and more completely[113]. Grobel stated emphatically that Mk and Q were the sources of Mt and Lk and challenged Haupt, Bussmann and Larfeld to honestly admit that they rejected the Two-Source theory[114].

Grobel observed that the British and the Americans had taken up research on the Synoptics in recent decades. Feine had and continued to have an influence on

105. *Ibid.*, p. 114, n. 2 (= 280, n. 4). Cf. J. WEISS, *Das älteste Evangelium*, p. 322f.

106. DIBELIUS, *Herodes und Pilatus*, p. 114, n. 2 (= 280, n. 4).

107. DIBELIUS, *From Tradition*, p. 199.

108. K. GROBEL, *Formgeschichte und synoptische Quellenanalyse* (FRLANT, 53), Göttingen, 1937. Following an introduction to form criticism and a comparison of Dibelius and Bultmann, Grobel analyzed German source critics W. Haupt, O. Procksch, E. Meyer, W. Bussmann, W. Larfeld and A. Schlatter. British and Americans considered were E.D. Burton, J.V. Bartlet, C.S. Patton, A.M. Perry, B.H. Streeter, V. Taylor (2 works) and F.C. Grant.

109. *Ibid.*, p. 32. Cf. W. HAUPT, *Worte Jesu und Gemeindeüberlieferung*, Leipzig, 1913.

110. GROBEL, *Formgeschichte*, p. 32-34.

111. *Ibid.*, p. 51. Cf. MEYER, *Ursprung*. Bd. 1. *Die Evangelien*, Stuttgart, 1921.

112. GROBEL, *Formgeschichte*, p. 51-57.

113. *Ibid.*, p. 61.

114. *Ibid.*, p. 65.

the main current of the British, though Streeter undergirded the largest part of British investigation[115]. Burton's proposal, which had posited Luke's use of different sources placing one after another, belied a close connection with Streeter in claiming that everything derived from Q occurring before 9,51 had already been combined with a Gospel prior to coming to Luke[116]. Also displaying close similarity with Streeter was J. Vernon Bartlet, who, though he had assumed the priority of Mk, believed that all the rest of the material in Lk came from a second source. In this view, Luke's authorship was reduced to that of a compiler[117].

The Two-Source theory lies at the basis of the view of C.S. Patton. Matthew and Luke had a Q document, partly alike and partly different[118]. Grobel endorsed the view that material common to Lk and Mt was to be ascribed to Q. But he rejected Patton's attempt to assign large blocks of special material in Lk and Mt to Q, arguing that this false assumption undermined the rest of Patton's work[119]. In the end very little can be said absolutely about the special material.

The first three principles postulated by Perry revolved on Lukan transpositions as indicative of a special Lukan source, and possibly only these have any argumentative force[120]. The sixth principle begged the question and Perry rejected the validity of thirteen pages of his own methodology.

Grobel noticed three of Perry's principles rested on an argument from order which Feine had inspired as a characteristic of a special source. Streeter had been quick to draw conclusions from Hawkins's in depth study while Taylor investigated them much more comprehensively than his precursor[121]. Though Grobel would allow that some order possibly had been established prior to Luke, his own investigation revealed that Luke simply imposed his own historicizing transpositions on the Markan order[122]. Grobel faulted Perry, Streeter, E. Meyer and Taylor for not having examined Luke's historicizing method well enough[123]. Had this been done, they would have concluded, like Dibelius, "that the assumption of a special source for Luke's Passion Narrative is not only not necessary, but rather is improbable"[124].

115. *Ibid.*, p. 67-68. Streeter did not receive as great a reception in America as he had at home.

116. *Ibid.*, p. 77. Cf. E.D. BURTON, *Some Principles of Literary Criticism and their Application to the Synoptic Problem*, Chicago, IL, 1904; *Some Phases of the Synoptic Problem*, in *JBL* 21 (1911) 95-113; and with E.J. GOODSPEED, *A Harmony of the Synoptic Gospels*, Chicago, IL, 1917.

117. GROBEL, *Formgeschichte*, p. 79. Cf. BARTLET, *Sources*, p. 315-363.

118. GROBEL, *Formgeschichte*, p. 79-80. Cf. PATTON, *Sources*. The view that Matthew and Luke shared Q pieces in common was subscribed to by Wellhausen, Hawkins, Weiss, and Wernle.

119. GROBEL, *Formgeschichte*, p. 82.

120. *Ibid.*, p. 83-84.

121. *Ibid.*

122. *Ibid.*, p. 95; cf. p. 104.

123. *Ibid.*, p. 104.

124. *Ibid.*, p. 119.

Grobel was skeptical because of Streeter's too neat separation of components, especially where there was such similarity between the elements. While Streeter placed primary emphasis on the argument from order, Grobel argued that the sequence found in Lk did not support Streeter's contention that Proto-Lk formed the backbone of the Gospel. Nonetheless, he conceded that some "Reihenfolge" may have existed prior to Luke. Grobel further dismissed Streeter's claim of the unity of the Proto-Lukan material[125]. The claim of the sizable amount of non-Markan material was dismissed out of hand as being unimportant. Finally, while Streeter maintained that the term ὁ κύριος stemmed from the special source, Grobel asserted it was neither typical of Proto-Lk nor was it especially characteristic of redactional additions[126]. Despite these criticisms, Grobel praised Streeter's study of the text as valuable and useful for an understanding of Luke.

Grobel insisted that Taylor's study failed because of a false method, part of which rested on faulty logic that claimed since Proto-Lk must have been presented with a passion narrative, therefore it had one. While Grobel did not deny that there were special traditions present in that section of the Gospel, generally they were unknown to us. One cannot conclude a special continuous source simply from the presence of these special traditions.

Frederick GRANT was an enthusiastic supporter of the Proto-Lk hypothesis[127]. But Grant's proposal was to be distinguished from that of Streeter and Taylor since he denied that the special source contained a passion narrative. Neither did it have a "Vorgeschichte" and thus it did not constitute a complete Gospel as Streeter imagined. Grant, like Taylor, considered Lk as the most valuable from an historical perspective.

Grobel came down decidedly on the side of the Two-Source theory, maintaining that Luke probably had no continuous, independent source. Instead, he employed individual pieces of tradition[128].

Grant noted that Grobel had carefully and effectively disproved E. Meyer's conception involving two sources underlying Mk, namely the 'disciples' source and the 'Twelve' source[129]. Further, Grobel distanced himself from Streeter's theory without referring to either Creed or Easton. Such omissions were striking inasmuch as Grobel's central argument rejected the "unity and homogeneity of L"[130]. In contrast, Grobel advocated the view that the material ascribed to L was due to

---

125. *Ibid.*, p. 93. Grobel also pointed out a glaring error in Streeter's calculation of the number of verses between 3,1 and 22,14 (p. 93, n. 2).

126. *Ibid.*, p. 95.

127. GROBEL, *Formgeschichte*, p. 116. For a reaction, see F.C. GRANT in *ATR* 19 (1937) 214-216. In addition, see F.C. GRANT, *The Growth of the Gospels*, Cincinnati, OH, 1933.

128. GROBEL, *Formgeschichte*, p. 118. He also entertained two other possibilities for the composition of Lk: the process begins with Mk, Q and then L was added. The third alternative to Streeter's hypothesis was that Q was only later combined with Mk and L.

129. F.C. GRANT, *Review*, in *ATR* 19 (1937) 215.

130. *Ibid.*

Luke and his editorial activity and did not derive from a special source. According to Grant, Grobel rightly dismissed the source designated by Burton as "Perean".

Hans LIETZMANN (1931), in a ground breaking article, contended that Mk was the primary source for the other three canonical Gospels[131]. Though it seemed Luke was in possession of other sources, numerous critics were deceived. He had no source other than Mk which he treated with greater redactional freedom than Mt. Lietzmann believed Luke and Matthew shared a copy of Mk which contained the MA of 22,64 / Mt 26,68, though it was now lacking in our text of the Mk[132]. While the account of Jesus' passion rested upon a historical basis, the Markan report was fashioned by the theology of the community, influenced both by the liturgy and the OT[133]. Lietzmann argued the change in order for the denial and mockery stemmed from Luke's discretion and not from a better witness[134].

Lietzmann was of the opinion that during the reign of Pontius Pilate, the Sanhedrin was able to pass the death sentence in cases violating Jewish religious law and cases of blasphemy[135]. He responded to criticism from F. Büchsel who charged that the Jews possessed juridical competence, but had to submit their judgment to the procurator for approval[136].

For the second Markan mockery (Mk 15,16-20), Lietzmann equated the events which occurred in Herod's palace (23,11)[137]. Endorsing Dibelius's point of view, he regarded the Herod episode as lacking any historical basis, arising instead from Ps 2,2.

Lietzmann's disciple, Jack FINEGAN (1934) called attention to the commonly recognized view of dependence of the later Synoptics upon Mk[138]. He rejected the suggestion that Luke had some other historical source in addition to Mk[139]. Luke did not have access to any new information, with the exception of a few legendary pieces which were available at that time[140]. The differences simply

---

131. H. LIETZMANN, *Der Prozess Jesu*, in *Kleine Schriften II, Studien zum Neuen Testament*, ed. K. ALAND, Berlin, 1958, p. 251, reprinted from *Sitzungsberichte der Preussischen Akademie der Wissenschaften, phil.-hist. Klass.* 14 (1931) 313-322, Berlin, 1934.

132. LIETZMANN, *Der Prozess Jesu*, p. 257, n. 1 (= *Sitzungsberichte*).

133. *Ibid.*, p. 260, 263.

134. LIETZMANN, *Der Prozess Jesu*, p. 251-252. He cited other examples of Lukan transpositions: 22,15-18 / Mk 14,25; 8,29 / Mk 5,14-15; 4,5-12 / Mt 4,5-10 (p. 252).

135. *Ibid.*, p. 260.

136. *Ibid.*, p. 269. In the article, Lietzmann once more declared his belief that the Sanhedrin trial lacked historicity (p. 275). Cf. F. BÜCHSEL, *Die Blutgerichtsbarkeit des Synedrions*, in ZNW 30 (1931) 202-210.

137. LIETZMANN, *Der Prozess Jesu*, 1934 (= *Kleine Schriften II*, 1958, p. 252).

138. J. FINEGAN, *Die Überlieferung der Leidens- und Auferstehungsgeschichte Jesu*, Giessen, 1934, p. 1.

139. *Ibid.*, p. 35. Finegan was equally unimpressed by the presentation of G. LIPPERT, *Pilatus* (1923), who tried to draw connections between Mk and a GS of Luke (p. 27, n. 1).

140. FINEGAN, *Die Überlieferung*, p. 35. Cf. p. 23.

resulted from Luke's free rearrangement and adaption of Mk. The bulk of the material was Markan, while a few details were the creative work of the evangelist himself[141]. Finegan championed the view that Luke, and not another historical source, was responsible for the change in order[142].

Luke brought together Mk's divided story of the denial (vv. 54-62) and sought to present Peter in a better light. In doing this, Finegan reacted against Bultmann's view that the change in order was due to an older tradition[143]. The detail of Jesus' glance toward Peter and the use of the term κύριος were ascribed to Luke. Finegan followed Streeter's lead suggesting that the MA in 22,64 was the result of "individual alteration"[144]. The MA in v. 62, however, probably derived from Mt[145]. The mention of the morning trial was the result of a conflation of Mk 14,53b and 15,1. This change was required because of the historical impossiblity that the Sanhedrin would gather in the dead of night. On account of this, the mistreatment was shifted to its position following the denial, but preceding the morning trial. Because Luke intended to focus on the Christ question, the reference to the statement of the destruction of the Temple was passed over. While other scholars criticized Luke's handling of the return to the Barabbas story in Mk, Finegan praised Luke's adroit interweaving of the accounts. The result was a narrative which showed that the desire of the Jews was fulfilled in the plotting and carrying out of the death of Jesus.

Finegan appraised the motif of silence in Pilate's presence (Mk 15,4ff.) as reappearing in Herod's trial (23,9)[146]. He advanced the view that the Herod trial, which Luke created, was simply an imitation of Pilate's trial, though shorter and less effective[147]. The influence of Dibelius was obvious. Finegan was further convinced that the story developed from Ps 2 and that the mockery (23,11) was a double of the Markan account (Mk 15,16-20)[148].

George Dunbar KILPATRICK (1952) opposed Lietzmann's view that Mark's account of the Sanhedrin trial was an unhistorical, Christian fiction, as he attempted to demonstrate that such an assembly was historically plausible. But he concurred that Luke freely redacted Mk[149].

---

141. *Ibid.*, p. 23. Luke was credited with the following storytelling elements: περιαψάντων δὲ πῦρ (v. 55), μετὰ βραχύ (v. 58), and διαστάσης (v. 59).

142. *Ibid.*, p. 23-24.

143. *Ibid.*, n. 2. Cf. BULTMANN, *Die Geschichte*, ²1931, p. 290.

144. FINEGAN, *Die Überlieferung*, p. 21, n. 2.

145. *Ibid.*, p. 24: "V.62 stammt wahrscheinlich aus Mt und ist nach latt zu streichen". Cf. STREETER, *FG*, 1924, p. 323.

146. FINEGAN, *Die Überlieferung*, p. 27.

147. *Ibid.*, p. 28.

148. *Ibid.* Cf. p. 36.

149. G.D. KILPATRICK, *The Trial of Jesus* (Sixth Lecture of Dr. Williams's Library), Oxford, 1953, p. 16. See p. 6-7. Cf. LIETZMANN, *Der Prozess Jesu*, 1931, p. 313-322. While the Markan account of the Sanhedrin trial may not be accurate in every detail, it rested upon an historical core

Kilpatrick remained unconvinced by Lietzmann's evidence that the Sanhedrin retained the power to carry out capital punishment in the time of Jesus[150]. Rather, he favored the information derived from Jn and the Palestinian Talmud which indicated that someone such as Jesus would have initially been subjected to inquiry by the local authorities and only later examined by the prefect[151].

In a previous article (1942) Kilpatrick argued that Luke changed the Markan υἱὸς θεοῦ at Mk 15,39 to δίκαιος 23,47 which continued the theme developed through chapter 23[152]. It was the evangelist rather than the Proto-Lukan source who was responsible for the change. Such an explanation would account for the reference to the charges in 23,2.5 "in a section otherwise from Mark". Luke 23,18-25 was the Lukan revision of Mk 15,6-15 and 23,13-16.41 would stem from the evangelist himself. Kilpatrick concluded: "If this be so it follows that much that is assigned to Proto-Luke belongs to the evangelist and, more important, all trace of a continuous Passion narrative other than that of Mark as a source for Luke vanishes. With its disappearance there must disappear as well the theory of Proto-Luke itself"[153].

Richard P.C. HANSON (1942) reacted that "so sweeping a claim deserves closer inspection"[154]. He argued that neither Kilpatrick's Septuagintal examples, nor those drawn from the NT, would support the translation. Kilpatrick was faulted for not examining other uses of the term in Lk. One might have expected the term in 11,51 / Mt 23,35, but since it did not occur, either Luke did not copy it from Q or it was a Matthean term. Hanson found it hard to believe that while in 23,41 the evangelist used the term as an adverb meaning "justly" that he would repeat it as an adjective meaning "innocent" only six verses later[155]. Hanson agreed

(p. 16). In n. at the conclusion of the text of the lecture, Kilpatrick referred to the article by J. JEREMIAS, *Zur Geschichtlichkeit des Verhörs Jesu vor dem Hohen Rat*, in ZNW 43 (1952) 145-150, whose support he welcomed in rejecting Lietzmann's view.

150. KILPATRICK, *Trial*, p. 16-19. He rejected Lietzmann's six examples on the grounds they were either irrelevant or that it was unclear whether they would apply in the case of Jesus (p. 19).

151. *Ibid.*, p. 20. The author noted the difficulties of attempting to uncover the historicity of the trial for two reasons: "We do not know the nature of the Roman regulations under which Judaea was governed at this stage. We do not know the details of Jewish law affecting capital cases at this period".

152. KILPATRICK, *A Theme of the Lucan Passion Story and Luke xxiii. 47*, in JTS 63 (1942) 36 (= J.K. ELLIOTT [ed.], *The Principles and Practice of New Testament Textual Criticism. Collected Essays of G.D. Kilpatrick* [BETL, 96], Leuven, 1990, p. 329). In a note Elliott observed how influential this article had been.

153. *Ibid.*

154. R.P.C. HANSON, *Does δίκαιος in Luke XXIII.47 explode the Proto-Luke hypothesis?*, in *Hermathena* 60 (1942) 74. Hanson described Kilpatrick's claim as "simply absurd" (p. 77). In addition, see R.P.C. HANSON, *Further Evidence for Indications of the Johannine Chronology of the Passion to be Found in the Synoptic Evangelists*, in ExpT 53 (1941-42) 178, where he asserted that 22,14-38, and indeed the whole Lukan account of the passion, was probably due to the special non-Markan source.

155. HANSON, *Does δίκαιος*, p. 76.

against Taylor (*Behind the Third Gospel*) that the term was a Lukan change of Mk but insisted the change was "in accordance" with the non-Markan source. Also rejected was Kilpatrick's view that 23,13-16.18-25 was a revision of Mk 15,6-15. Hanson, citing Taylor, pointed to the low percentage of verbal correspondence. Hanson viewed 23,13-25 as "one inseparable passage". Verses 8-12 also constituted a part which cannot be omitted without creating a dislocation of material. Hanson insisted that the special source theory hinged on the entire passion narrative rather than on particular sections within it[156].

Kilpatrick in a later contribution (1970) speculated that Streeter used Mk as a model to piece together his Proto-Lk[157]. But as Streeter conceded that part of his Proto-Lk (3,1-4,30) was derived from Mk, so it would also be found to be the case in the latter part of the Gospel, which would result in the breakdown of the theory. In his earlier article which treated 23,7 Kilpatrick followed the lead of Creed announcing that Mk was the source for the Lukan passion. The differences were dictated by Luke's intention to highlight the theme of Jesus' innocence and to present all the characters supporting the innocence of Jesus except the religious leadership. Kilpatrick confessed that neither his nor Creed's arguments destroyed a modified form of the hypothesis by which it could be maintained that Luke possessed the Q and L material already in blocks for the material in Lk 3-20. Kilpatrick proposed that there were four stages in the development of the evangelist's literary style and this accounted for differences in vocabulary. The stages were: "(i) Luke, the non-Marcan strata. (ii) The Marcan strata: perhaps Lk. i-ii. and xxi-xxiv. belong here. (iii) Acts i-xv. (iv) Acts xv-xxviii"[158]. He concluded from a study of the term λαός which was usually found in the Markan material, that the evangelist's disposition toward the Gentiles was generally the same throughout all the stages and that the second stage even more emphasized "Israel as the people of God's salvation"[159].

Taking note of the appearance of Streeter's book on the four Gospels and the form-critical movement in Germany, Maurice JONES (1934) appraised the Proto-Lk theory as having garnered a good deal of support[160]. Classifying the theory as

---

156. *Ibid.*, p. 78: "On more general principles, Mr. Kilpatrick does not seem to realize that the theory of a continuous non-Marcan source for Luke's Passion-Narrative does not rest only on his account of the Trial before Pilate or some of the details of the Crucifixion, but on the whole appearance of Luke xxii.1-xxiv.1".

157. KILPATRICK, *The Gentiles and the Strata of Luke*, in O. BÖCHER and K. HAACKER (eds.), *Verborum Veritas*, FS G. STÄHLIN, Wuppertal, 1970, 83 (= J.K. ELLIOTT [ed.], *Principles*, 313).

158. *Ibid.*, p. 86 (= 316).

159. *Ibid.*, p. 87, 88 (p. 318).

160. M. JONES, *The New Testament in the Twentieth Century*, London, 1914, ²1924, ³1934, p. v. In the preface to the third ed., Jones referred to Streeter as "our greatest authority" on the synoptic problem (p. xiii). The relative success of Streeter's efforts was explained as follows: "... it was only natural that scholars interested in the subject should continue the quest and search for evidence which would enable them to extend the 'Two-Document Hypothesis,' and this is what Dr. Streeter has been attempting to do, and, in the opinion of many who are qualified to pass

"the more important and more interesting and at the same time, perhaps the more debatable" of Streeter's suggestions, Taylor was characterized as one of the theory's "most capable" proponents[161].

Opposition to the theory, in Jones's estimation was substantial. "There are many scholars who readily admit that the research which produced the 'Four-Document Hypothesis' has been of immense value to Synoptic Criticism, but are not prepared to accept it entirely as it stands"[162].

Robert Henry LIGHTFOOT (1934), a maverick amongst the English who generally subscribed to the view of a special source, resolutely rejected the idea in favor of Lukan redaction of the Markan passion[163].

judgement, has actually accomplished" (p. xiv). Jones's main contribution may be said to summarize the British study of the synoptic problem, of which he was immensely proud (cf. p. 190). See his *The Four Gospels. Their Literary and Their Special Characteristics*, London, 1921.

161. JONES, *New Testament*, p. xvii.

162. *Ibid.*, p. xx. Taylor did not agree with Hoskyns and Davey who argued that the theory exceeded the bounds of its evidence. But Jones was quick to point out that the chief opponents were Creed and Hunkin, noting that Creed rejected the theory primarily because of the difficulty of believing that the passion narrative was composed using only extracts from Mk. In closing the Preface Jones, careful to safeguard the usefulness of Streeter's contribution, also admitted that "the 'Four-Document Hypothesis' may not be capable of substantiation in all its details and Proto-Luke may have no existence outside Dr. Streeter's fertile imagination" (p. xxi).

Jones maintained that the consensus rejected the contention that there was an Aramaic or Hebrew Gospel at the basis of the Synoptic Gospels (p. 193-194). Markan priority was clearly affirmed (p. 194). The use of Mk by the other two Synoptics "seems proved beyond dispute". He reviewed the discussion of whether Q contained a passion narrative, but seemed content simply to rehearse the conclusions of the various authors in *SSP*. He appeared impressed by Hawkins's suggestion that the Lukan passion narrative reflected Pauline influence, calling the idea "very suggestive" (p. 216). He also noted Sanday's objections to the idea. A similar compliment was paid to Holdsworth, who though independent of Sanday, put forward the view that in addition to Mk and Q, there was a special Lukan source which contained elements of the passion (p. 222). Cf. p. 191: "A most excellent summary of the whole question will be found in Holdsworth's *Gospel Origins*, a most suggestive book". Concerning Luke's special source, Jones noted further that Feine had earlier suggested that Luke had combined Mk with another document, a theory endorsed and followed "in its main aspects" by Stanton and Bartlet (JONES, *New Testament*, p. 220).

163. R.H. LIGHTFOOT, *History and Interpretation in the Gospels* (Bampton Lectures 1934), New York, 1935, p. 164. In England, the hypothesis of the special source "is usually assumed". "This theory is, I believe, misleading and unnecessary, if once we have understood [Luke's] method and his purpose" (p. 164; cf. p. 178-179, where Lightfoot suggested the variations from Mk can be attributed to Luke's "peculiar sympathies and purpose"). Luke's changes generally reflected the interests of the church in the development of the passion narrative which resulted in Jesus being presented as a martyr and a portrayal of increased hostility from Jesus' enemies (p. 164; cf. p. 181). Further evolution might be accounted for if Luke had considered Mark's version, especially in detailing events in Jerusalem, "unduly cramped" (p. 165). In addition, Luke composed a coherent account of the passion where Mk failed in this task (p. 167). Lightfoot was undecided as to whether what was recounted in 22,66-71 was indeed a trial: "At the end of the trial, if such it was, and after sentence is passed on the ground of blasphemy, we read of the

Morton Scott ENSLIN (1938) believed that an overemphasis on the new
additions in the passion narrative erroneously led people to posit the special source
in that section of Lk[164]. On the contrary, there was very little in the way of non-
Markan additions. Further, an exaggerated sense of the number of the "many"
Lukan predecessors indicated in the Prologue (1,1), especially by the Chicago
school, deceptively prevented scholars from focusing on the fact that Lk resulted
from "almost complete dependence" upon Mk[165].

rough handling of the prisoner" (p. 168). But without doubt his conviction was that Luke based
his account on Mk and did not have recourse to a second, independent and unified source. What
was more, Luke composed his Gospel with sentiment, removing all elements of tragedy which
so characterized the Markan account (p. 171). The Third Evangelist smoothed over the Markan
foundation where difficulties existed or where the Markan account was too abrupt (p. 169 cf. p.
170). Luke "hellenized" Mk e.g. at 22,69 where he added τοῦ θεοῦ to δυνάμεως (p. 180).
Following Creed, Lightfoot viewed the Hebraic coloring of Lk as deriving from the LXX (p.
168).

Luke's concern for the order, according to Lightfoot, was obvious in the arrangement of events
subsequent to Jesus' arrest (p. 168). The motivation for the change was to bring the material
pertaining to Peter and his denials into a single section (p. 169). Referring the reader to
Hawkins's work, Lightfoot observed that Luke's transpositions were not confined to the passion
narrative (p. (171-)172, n. 1). The list of Lukan changes in order of Markan and Matthean
material included: Lk 4,5-12 / Mt 4,8-10; Lk 6,12-19 / Mk 3,7-19a; Lk 8,23a.b / Mk 4,37.38a
(cf. Mt 8,24-26); Lk 8,28.29a.b / Mk 5,3b-8; Lk 8,51 / Mk 5,37.38a; Lk 8,55b.56 / Mk
5,42.43; Lk 11,31.32 / Mt 12,41.42; Lk 17,1.2 / Mt 18,6.7.

Lightfoot expressed the following lament concerning methodology. "Insufficient attention seems
to have been paid at present to these small differences between the evangelists, for when
considered in the mass, they are of importance, and throw much light upon the special interests
and purposes of the writers" (p. 165, n. 1). Redaction criticism will later address Lightfoot's
concern. Rather than signaling a special source, the redaction over against Mk testified to Luke's
skill as a literary artist: "But the more closely we study the matter, always with reference to our
earliest gospel, the less reason have we to postulate for St. Luke a special source, superior
historically to St. Mark. That this is so often done is a fine testimony to St. Luke's literary skill"
(p. 170). Lightfoot equated Luke's ἀπὸ τοῦ νῦν (22,69) with Matthew's ἀπ' ἄρτι (Mt 26,64),
indicating that both phrases reflected each evangelist's preferred expression, observing that Luke
and Matthew used these in the same two instances (p. 180). In addition to this case, Luke used
his preferred term at 22,18 while Matthew employed his at 26,29.

164. M.S. ENSLIN, *Christian Beginnings*, New York, 1938, p. 406. Although Enslin did not
entirely exclude the possibility of such a special source, it was remote at best. He called the
hypothesis "highly questionable".

165. *Ibid.*, p. 406-407. It was noted that while the *Urmarkus* theory continued to resurface
from time to time, it had been abandoned "by the great majority of students" (p. 430). Although
Enslin conceded Luke had access to "special sources of information", their nature and extent were
not known.

Enslin conceived of the order described by Luke in the Prologue as not inferring chronological
order, but "continuously" or "in a logically unbroken sequence". "Similarly his desire to show
'continuously' the successive great stages of the Christian movement led him drastically to rewrite
Mk's account of the Passion ..." (p. 409-410). Generally, Luke followed the Markan order.
Variations, where they existed, can be accounted by Luke's shortening Mk's account or making
stylistic improvements (p. 407).

Norval GELDENHUYS (1951) was convinced that Luke used Mk extensively[166]. As regards the Proto-Lk hypothesis, the South African exegete remarked: "The 'Proto-Lk' theory has been powerfully and attractively argued, especially by Taylor, but it falls a little short of proof, and has not won the approval of many scholars outside these islands"[167].

Enslin criticized scholars at the University of Chicago (ostensibly Burton and Perry) for multiplying sources while at the same time castigating them for their reluctance to assign changes in the Gospel to the evangelist. Prophetically anticipating the onset of redaction criticism, Enslin predicted that scholars would later credit Luke with greater responsibility in revising Mk (p. 434). "This M source has not secured many champions, and has little to commend it, but several competent scholars are agreed that Luke did make use of a connected source which at times, as in the Passion narrative, he preferred to Mk. But, after all, the whole matter of L depends on the question as to the extent to which Lucan differences can be explained as the work of Luke himself. It appears to me that the sole value of L is that it gives relief to puzzled interpreters of Luke who cannot bring themselves to allow Luke to make (or make up) history, but find it necessary to postulate another source for him to draw upon. Accordingly, it appears to me that the present fondness for multiple sources – scholars in the University of Chicago have discovered many such – is simply but one more consequence of the mistaken emphasis upon editors. The researches of these scholars have been of profound value – not so much for their results but for the incidental light they have thrown on the larger problem – but it would appear to me probable that in the coming years both Matthew and Luke will be obliged to accept responsibility for forsaking Mk when they each thought they could pen better stories". While there was much in Enslin's work to commend it, one must seriously question his viewpoint that Luke's special material was "a possible adaptation of Mt" (p. 434-435). This contention had obvious ramifications for Enslin's view of the MAs. In such a vein Floyd Filson took exception to Enslin's view of Q. Filson, speaking for a great many scholars, voiced his strong opposition. "Few would agree with M.S. Enslin, who in *Christian Beginnings* (1938) denies that Q ever existed and suggests instead that Lk.'s author used Mt. There is a very wide consensus of critical opinion that only the assumption of such a document as Q will explain the agreements" (F.V. FILSON, *Origins of the Gospels*, New York, 1938, p. 133). Characterizing the then current position of scholars on the origin of MAs by Mark's having employed the source of Q while Matthew and Luke favored the Q form instead of Mk, Enslin opted for the view that Luke used Mt (ENSLIN, *Christian Beginnings*, p. 433). While the Prologue did not require one to assume that Mt was one of the "many" (1,1), Enslin insisted "it is not unlikely" (p. 433). The argument he put forward in support of his position, however, seemed rather to militate against it. "Accordingly, it appears to me that a frank recognition of the fact that both of these writers [Matthew and Luke] were authors in the truest sense of the word – both authors who lived in the first century, not the twentieth – deprives the argument that each must have worked independent of the other, because of their omissions and substitutions, of most of its force, and enables us to see the matter of their so-called agreements in a different light" (p. 432).

166. N. GELDENHUYS, *Commentary on the Gospel of Luke* (NIC NT), Grand Rapids, MI, 1951, p. 25. In addition, Luke had personal contact with Mark in Rome. Geldenhuys took the position that Lk reflected Paul's preaching in the same way that Mk was said to represent the preaching of Peter.

167. *Ibid.*, p. 27. In n. 1, Geldenhuys drew attention to Feine as originating the suggestion of Luke having combined Q with the special material before adding material from Mk. Geldenhuys also mentioned the work of J. KNOX, *Marcion and the New Testament*, Chicago, 1942, who posited an entirely different type of "Proto-Lk" in which the Gospel and the Acts were

Samuel MacLean GILMOUR (1948) initially counted 22,63-65.66-71; 23,1-2.4-
25 among the material belonging to a special tradition[168], though he argued
against Streeter and Taylor that QL constituted a complete Gospel and that it
formed the structure upon which Luke composed his own Gospel[169]. Gilmour

composed about the same time to refute the heresies of Marcion (p. 27-28). This tack was
rejected on the grounds that the canonical Lk-Acts was definitely a first century work. With the
exception of Great Britain, the majority of scholars adhere to the position that Mk was Luke's
chief source to which was added material from Q and other sources (p. 28, n. 1). Geldenhuys
himself argued that in addition to Mk and Q, Luke was able to avail himself of numerous
"firsthand sources of information, written as well as oral" (p. 28). Although earlier some scholars
argued Luke was influenced by an Ebionite source, Plummer in his commentary and J. ORR,
Neglected Factors in the Study of the Early Progress of Christianity, London, 1899, p. 103-107,
successfuly refuted this proposal. Another point which distinguished Geldenhuys from Streeter
was that he viewed Luke as much more dependent upon oral sources (GELDENHUYS,
Commentary, p. 24, n. 1).
  Geldenhuys enumerated five different trials variously reported by the four evangelists (p. 586).
He concluded, therefore, that each of the evangelists only recounted some of the whole. Luke
condensed the appearances before the Jewish religious leaders. At 22,63 Geldenhuys recalled the
statement of Zahn that Luke was racing to the conclusion and was further constrained by the
length of the papyrus (p. 588, n. 1; cf. ZAHN, *Introduction*, 1909, in loc.). Commenting on the
similarity between the various trials, Geldenhuys invoked the authority of Plummer that such
similarity was to be expected since the same inquiries would be expected to be made by various
parties. At 23,3 Geldenhuys observed Luke omitted a great deal with a view of adding emphasis
to those details which remained (GELDENHUYS, *Commentary*, p. 596).
  Geldenhuys strongly advocated the historicity of the Herod episode and argued against Creed
who held it to be an invention. The account stemmed from "first-hand sources" (p. 598).
Although he referred to Warschauer, he did not provide any further bibliographical information
(p. 326). Whereas Creed maintained that, if historical, Mk would have mentioned it, Geldenhuys
responded that it must not be assumed that Mk recorded everything that transpired, even the most
significant events. While Creed considered it unlikely that Pilate would have shipped a political
prisoner off to Herod, Geldenhuys, following Warschauer, asserted that Herod would have been
the competent authority and would have been complimented by Pilate's gesture of good will. The
final argument advanced by Creed was based upon internal inconsistencies, that while 23,10
implied the religious leaders accompanied the crowd visiting Herod, 23,15 gave the impression
that they stayed behind with Pilate. Geldenhuys responded that that particular interpretation "is
an arbitrary way of explaining verse 15".
  168. S. McL. GILMOUR, *A Critical Re-Examination of Proto-Luke*, in *JBL* 67 (1948) 143-
152, p. 148. Gilmour attributed only the following to a special tradition, rejecting the idea of a
continuous report. Rather, Luke composed the majority of what follows based on oral tradition:
22,14-18.21.23 (Mk was apparent in 22,19a and 22,22 = Mk 14,22 and Mk 14,21a); 22,25-27
(which "overlaps" with Mk 10,42-45); 22,28-30 (overlapping with Mt's special tradition 19,28);
22,31-33 (22,34 stemmed from Mk 14,30); 22,36-38; 22,63-65; 22,66-71; 23,1-2.4-25 (23,3 was
inserted from Mk 15,2); 23,38b-31; 23,39-43; 23,46b; 24,13-35; 24,36-46. Gilmour made an
exception for the account of the Last Supper, saying that it could have been based on written
sources, since it "is not unreasonable to assume" that it was circulated independently. Even in
four of the cases Gilmour cited, Markan influence was still detected. The denial of Jesus by Peter
(22,54b-62) was affirmed as dependent upon Mk (p. 152).
  169. *Ibid.*, p. 143. Gilmour treated the question of whether QL was a complete Gospel on

faulted Taylor in particular for not adequately crediting Luke either for his own editorial material or for Markan influence, which Taylor mistook for an independent source. Acknowledging that "the source analysis of Lk 22,14-24,50 is notoriously difficult"[170], Gilmour surmised that Luke used Mk in the passion narrative embellishing the account with "a few L pericopes" and composing the special material on the basis of oral tradition[171].

Gilmour (1952) argued that even as Luke made Mk the basis of his own Gospel, in the passion narrative he revised that material from his own Gospel and enriched it "with material of his own composition"[172]. In contast to his earlier article, Gilmour now assigned even less material to "a special literary tradition". Those verses which were previously attributed to a special source, but now were ascribed to Mk included 22,14.33.63-65.66-71; 23,1-2.4-25.39-43; 24,22-24.44-46[173]. Luke's special tradition was defined as "a number of cognate literary sources that can loosely be called L"[174]. Gilmour rejected the Proto-Lk hypothesis of Streeter and Taylor primarily for two reasons. First, he dismissed the hypothesis on the grounds that the non-Markan blocks did not form a Gospel unto themselves, because some of the stories, such as the call of the disciples (5,1-11) were simply Markan variants[175]. Gilmour was critical of Taylor for not taking sufficient stock of the Markan material and for regarding as material from the special source that which was due to Luke's editorial work or influence from Mk[176]. The second reason for rejecting Proto-Lk was that Mk, rather than this supposed source, provided the basic framework of Lk. According to Gilmour, there was simply no evidence that Luke was relying on any continuous source other

p. 143-149, and the issue of the framework of Lk on p. 149-152.

170. *Ibid.*, p. 147.

171. *Ibid.*, p. 149. He defined L in the following way: "... a number of cognate literary collections that can loosely be called L" (p. 148-149). His conviction that Luke revised Mk was strong: "It is clear that Luke was able to draw on a variety of tradition with which to amplify and recast Mark's account of the passion and of the discovery of the empty tomb, just as he had been able to do in connection with the opening scenes of Jesus' ministry, but his basic dependence on Mark's account is equally clear. We possess in Mark, Luke's basic source in 22,14-24,50 just as in 3,1-4,30, and the hypothesis that Proto-Luke constituted the framework of the Third Gospel, while not necesssarily a 'snare and a delusion,' falls short of demonstration and should be abandoned as a brilliant but not convincing vagary of criticism" (p. 152).

172. S. MᶜL. GILMOUR, *The Gospel according to St. Luke* (IB 8), New York, 1952, 3-434, p. 16. This must be contrasted with Gilmour's assertion that the bulk of the special material in the passion and resurrection narratives was most likely derived from oral sources with which Luke was familiar (p. 14). Gilmour reprised his 1948 article on p. 16-18.

173. *Ibid.*, p. 17. Cf. S. MᶜL. GILMOUR, *A Critical Re-Examination*, p. 148.

174. GILMOUR, *Gospel*, p. 17. This explanation of L was exactly that found in his earlier essay, *A Critical Re-Examination*, p. 148-149.

175. *Gospel*, p. 16. But it was clear from a later diagram that Gilmour assigned the call of the disciples, as well as the story of the anointing (7,36-39.44-50) to L, when it might more appropriately be ascribed to creative Lukan redaction of Markan stories.

176. *Ibid.*, p. 17.

than Mk for the passion. Luke employed Mk with great freedom and joined to it material from other sources.

Another significant phenomenon used in defense of the special source was the numerous omissions of Markan material from Lk. Some of the material was jettisoned because it was irrelevant or incomprehensible to Luke or his readers. The tendency to present the disciples in a better light accounted for other changes. Although Gilmour cannot offer an explanation of the omission of 6,45-7,37, he rejected the possibility that Luke was using a defective copy of Mk or an Urmarkus. The material of Mk 8,1-26 originally separate from the rest of the "great omission" contained parallels to the material. Finally, Gilmour again raised the possibility that Luke was restricted in his choice of materials by the length of the papyri he used[177].

Highlighting the basic unity of Lk-Acts, Gilmour called attention to Luke's style in parallels between Paul and Jesus[178]. And while the language could reflect an imitation of the LXX, in the Infancy Narratives and the first half of Acts, he proposed that the former may be translations of early Christian hymns while the latter constituted the expansion of early Christian sermons.

Peter's denials based on Mk, while containing a historical core, also were enriched by elements described as "literary elaborations"[179]. Although Gilmour credited Luke with transposing the denials before the trial, he offered no reason for the change. With regard to the various people who asked Peter about his relationship with Jesus, Gilmour contended these were merely "minor variations from Mk". Gilmour mentioned the change of position of the mockery over against Mk, but said little more.

Luke freely redacted and abbreviated Mk for the Sanhedrin trial. Gilmour favored the view that what was recounted in 22,66-71 was a preliminary hearing, the purpose of which was to formulate a charge to present to Pilate[180]. Gilmour also entertained the idea that this account "is an anti-Semitic doublet of the trial before Pilate"[181]. Verses 67-70 were based on Mk, though Luke divided Mk's interrogation.

In the section 23,1-25, Gilmour advised that the hypothesis must be taken into consideration, but that it lacked force. Verse 23,3 was clear proof Luke was still relying on Mk. The theme of the Jewish responsibility for Jesus' death was consistent with a Lukan tendency and was thus ascribed to Luke[182]. The return of Jesus to Pilate and the sentencing (23,17-25) was a free redaction of Markan material, including 23,19 which stemmed from Mk 15,7. Gilmour summarized his position at one point in this way: "In the passion and resurrection narratives [Luke]

177. *Ibid.*, p. 19.
178. *Ibid.*, p. 4; cf. p. 6.
179. *Ibid.*, p. 392.
180. *Ibid.*, p. 395.
181. *Ibid.*
182. *Ibid.*, p. 397.

used a few L passages to supplement Mark but depended in the main on oral tradition and on his own dramatic and literary genius to achieve the recasting of the narrative that he desired"[183].

McL. Gilmour originally claimed the Herod story derived from a special tradition[184]. He rejected the view, however, that the special material formed any part of a "continuous account", opting in favor of the judgment of a Lukan composition based upon oral tradition[185]. He referred to the episode alternately as "the Hearing Before Herod" as well as "the trial before Herod"[186]. In a later work (1952) he argued that although it was a historical possibility that Herod was in Jerusalem for the feast of Passover, the timeframe in Mk would hardly have allowed for the trial. The influence of Dibelius was seen once more as the meeting of Pilate and Herod was viewed as having been predicted in Ps 2,2 (cf. Acts 4,27-28). This episode, too, was consistent with the tendency to blame the Jews and exonerate the Romans. The mockery by Herod and his coterie was a substitution for the Markan version (Mk 15,16-20) previously omitted[187].

Arguing against the Two-Source theory – and Proto-Lk – was Christopher BUTLER[188]. The shift in his position was intriguing since he previously held the view of Markan priority[189]. It had been noted that his "more radical defense of Matthean priority [...] is at the origin of an anti-Streeter reaction in British and American Gospel Studies"[190]. In the tradition of Augustine he maintained Mark was dependent upon Mt. He further posited there was no need for the Q hypothesis. In reference to a special source for Lk he wrote: "Adherents of Proto-Luke might suggest that Mark derived [the parable of the mustard seed] *via* Matthew from that conjectural parent of Luke, but this possibility will also be excluded if the indications of Luke's dependence on Matthew are allowed to carry weight (for which it will be sufficient here to refer to the rest of this study in general)"[191]. He concluded Luke derived the material from Mt. He also later suggested that in some cases Luke may have had an oral Aramaic source[192]. He correctly observed that Markan influence could be recognized in Lukan material which had been ascribed to Proto-Lk[193].

183. *Ibid.*, p. 17. See GILMOUR, *A Critical Re-Examination*, p. 149.

184. GILMOUR, *A Critical Re-Examination*, p. 148.

185. *Ibid.*

186. *Ibid.* Cf. p. 152.

187. GILMOUR, *Gospel*, p. 399.

188. B.C. BUTLER, *The Originality of St Matthew. A Critique of the Two-Document Hypothesis*, Cambridge, 1951. See already *St. Luke's Debt to St. Matthew*, in *HTR* 32 (1939) 237-308, much of which was incorporated into the book. It was primarily concerned with Mt instead of Q. In the article he acknowledged his debt to Chapman (p. 238).

189. *Originality*, p. 70, n. 2.

190. F. NEIRYNCK, *Synoptic Problem*, in *NJBC*, 1990, p. 594.

191. BUTLER, *St. Luke's Debt*, p. 251-252.

192. *Ibid.*, p. 268. See also p. 299-300, and esp. p. 307-308.

193. *Ibid.*, p. 277: "In general, it may be pointed out again that since Luke used Mark the

In *The Originality of St Matthew* he declared that the Two-Document theory "was regarded in many scholarly circles as no longer requiring proof, criticism or defence"[194]. He was encouraged by the contention of J.H. Ropes that Lukan dependence upon Mt for Q passages "'has never been shown to be impossible'"[195]. He summarized his investigation in the following manner: "In preceding chapters an attempt has been made to show that Mark's discourses depend on a source indistinguishable from Matthew, and that a similar dependence can be discovered in many sections of Mark that are not purely discourse"[196]. He also sharply criticized the *Urmarkus* hypothesis[197]. He continued to believe that Luke had access to some special sources: "St. Luke has taken Mark as his source for the Markan tradition, and just as he hardly ever inserts fragments of Mark into his non-Marcan blocks, so he will not interpolate into his Marcan contexts either verses from Matthew or material from his special sources"[198].

Additional scholars who posited that Luke employed Mk included Joseph KNABENBAUER (1926)[199], Louis SOUBIGOU (1933)[200], John CHAPMAN

---

dependence of Matthew on Luke is excluded by the overlapping Mark-'Q' passages (where it would involve posterity of Mark to Luke) – unless indeed we hypothesize a proto-Luke used by Matthew before it was combined with Marcan material to form the present Luke. But there is Marcan influence in the non-Marcan ('proto-Luke') parts of Luke, and the hypothesis thus becomes complicated and unattractive".

194. *Originality*, p. v. The Index of New Testament Passages indicated that he did not treat any Lukan passage beyond 22,49.

195. *Ibid*. Though Butler did not give the references, they were to J.H. ROPES, *The Synoptic Gospels*, p. 37, 93.

196. BUTLER, *Originality*, p. 157.

197. *Ibid.*, p. 171: "It would seem that the priority of Ur-Markus was first propounded as a direct retort to the absurd theory that Mark depends on both Matthew and Luke. Ur-Markus was later discovered to be as illusory a conjecture as we have tried to show its partner Q (Weisse's *Logian* source), to be ...".

198. *Ibid.*, p. 23.

199. *Commentarius in quatuor S. Evangelica Domini Nostri Jesu Christi*. Vol. 3. *Evangelium secundum Lucam*, Paris, 1896, ²1905 (Editio altera emendata, Reimpressa), 1926, p. 15, announced his utter disdain for source criticism: "Sunt qui in unaquaque narratione inquirunt ex quonam fonte Lucas hauserit vel quos fontes inter se coniunxerit et putare videntur se stupendum quid reperisse, si tandem statuunt haec esse ex 'fonte particulari' ex 'fonte apostolico', vel libere secundum Marcum, vel ex eodem fonte ex quo priscus Matthaeus auctus sit ad nostrum Matthaei librum, vel ex eodem cum Matthaeo fonte additis quibusdam ex alio fonte etc. Ingenue fateor me noluisse ingredi in eiusmodi inquisitiones subtiles quarum existus et plane incertus est et pro arbitrio alius ab aliis statuitur". Such an abhorrence notwithstanding, Knabenbauer argued that Luke had knowledge of Mk and followed its order (p. 13). Although some had earlier explained differences by means of Urmarkus, he stated this view had been "impune omittitur" (p. 13). In a survey of various scholarly positions, Knabenbauer called attention to the work of B. Weiss, endorsed by many critics, that Mk was Luke's primary source. Incorporation into Lk of nearly the entire Gospel of Mark, and the Markan order, supported this view (p. 15). Knabenbauer referred to B. WEISS, *Lukas*, ⁹1901, p. 253f. In addition, Knabenbauer divided Lk into four parts:

(1937)[201] and Max MEINERTZ (1933)[202]. M. KIDDLE (1935) authored a

1,5-4,13; 4,14-9,50; 9,51-19,28; 19,28-24,53 (*Lucam*, p. 21). Knabenbauer remained a staunch supporter of the view that Luke was a companion of Paul and received much information from a sojourn in Jerusalem. It was at that time that Luke had access to various details about the life and ministry of Jesus in Aramaic, or in Aramaic-influenced Greek (p. 12). Referring to recent authors who had written of the place of various proposed sources, including those in the southern part of Palestine, those from the Ebionites or a book of older history which had been conflated with Lk, Knabenbauer took no stand, saying only that people were free to defend or reject such views as they wished (p. 12). Still, it appeared that Knabenbauer favored the Ebionite source: "Quod demum aliqui quasi ex fonte quodam ebionitico haustum in libro Lucae notare non dubitabant, id omne plane iis congruit quae a Paulo quoque continuo commendantur" (1896, p. 18-19; [2]1905, p. 20-21).

Knabenbauer considered indefensible the view Luke transferred to the following day the trial which occurred at night. Such an opinion was further denied because the second trial was clearly recounted as having taken place in the early morning. Luke was correct, which was clearly affirmed by Mt 27,1. Thus, there was no reason to doubt the Lukan narration (p. 603-604). Because of Luke's close association with Paul, Luke obtained information about Peter's denials. The sentiment expressed in the recounting of this event likely stemmed from Paul's recounting the episode as mercifully as possible (p. 605). Knabenbauer affirmed Cornely concerning the manner in which Luke narrated the passion of Jesus which involved highlighting the wickedness of the people in contrast to the innocence of Jesus. Such was done, in part, by the speeches of Herod and Pilate (p. 612, quoting from R. CORNELY, *Historica et Critica Introductio in U.T. Libros Sacros*, Vol. 3. *Introductio Specialis in Singulos Novi Testamenti Libros*, Paris, 1897 [editio altera emendata] [Reimpressa, 1925], p. 167).

In treating the three charges against Jesus, Knabenbauer followed Jansenius who maintained that the subsequent charge always confirmed and verified the preceding one, reinforcing the severity of the crime (KNABENBAUER, *Lucam*, p. 613). As opposed to the version found in the other Synoptics (cf. Mt 27,15; Mk 15,8), Luke related the paschal amnesty more to the point: he emphasized the perversity of the crowd and the weakness of Pilate in allowing himself to be defeated in his every effort to free Jesus (p. 617).

200. *Sous le charme de L'évangile selon saint Luc*, Paris, 1933, p. 10-11. Following the traditional Catholic line, Soubigou accepted the priority of Mt, which was followed by Mk and finally Lk. Luke relied for a large part upon Mk, even for its structure (p. 21). For information unique to Lk, Soubigou subscribed to the view of Lagrange in suggesting Joanna, Manaen, Philip the deacon, John the apostle, the disciples from Emmaus and the women of Galilee as oral sources (p. 22). Paul also exercised influence on Luke's choice of materials.

Soubigou considered Luke's reference to order in the Prologue (1,3) to mean literary order, which formed the background of the strict chronology (p. 23). The reduction of two similar Sanhedrin trials to one, Soubigou ascribed to carelessness on the part of Luke (p. 526).

In the opinion of Soubigou, the story of Herod was seen as a parallel to that of Pilate as both declare Jesus innocent, just as Jesus who was maliciously and wrongly condemned of sedition was contrasted with Barabbas. Soubigou also noted that Herod was mentioned in each of the great sections of Lk (p. 532). Cf. p. 157-158, where Soubigou noted, among other things, that the mention of Herod at 3,19-20 was primarily "un procédé littéraire" (p. 157). The mockery was transformed in order to spare the Roman authorities. Soubigou followed Lagrange who indicated Joanna (8,2) and Manaen (Acts 13,1) as other sources of information for the evangelist (p. 22; cf. LAGRANGE, *Évangile selon Saint Luc*, p. XCI, XCII).

201. *Matthew, Mark and Luke. A Study in the Order and Interrelation of the Synoptic Gospels* (ed. J.M.T. BARTON), London, 1937, p. 99: "I believe it is possible to show that St. Luke did

not meet with the Greek Mt. until his Gospel was already roughly written and complete, out of Mk. and his own collections: he then added in a great quantity of Mt., in short bits, and finally cut out a large quantity of doublets or quasi-doublets, to shorten the whole" (cf. p. v.). By such a compositional hypothesis, Chapman eliminated the need for Q. His main criticisms of documentary theories of sources in general (among which was counted the Two-Document hypothesis) and of Proto-Lk in particular, was that there was no evidence of their existence and contemporary authors were silent on the matter (p. xx). These disagreements notwithstanding, Chapman affirmed the possibility of the documentary theory and that such a view was in conformity with Catholic teaching on inspiration and inerrancy.

The material that Luke added to Mk in the passion narrative was derived from Luke's private sources which he himself collected (p. 153; cf. p. 172-173). Chapman asserted Luke seemed to have some written sources in addition to notes he made (p. 177). Chapman assigned the following to these private sources: 22,61(partial).67b.68; 23,4.5. Luke consciously imitated the LXX in refashioning Mk, which involved a shift from a conversational style to one that was decidedly more historical. Omissions of Markan material were readily explained with a view to the Gentile readership, whom Luke wished to edify, but also out of concern for the length of his work (p. 174-175).

Chapman's theory fell flat when he came to consider the issue of order. While he rightly observed Luke took great pains to observe the Markan order, Chapman claimed where there was a diversion from that order, "it always appears that he has taken it from Mt., not from Mk." (p. 110). Chapman understood order to mean chronology: "This confirms very strongly by its detail that the general impression recorded above that Lk. had a very great respect for Mk., preserved his order (chronology), and made him the backbone and framework of his own book, and refused to interfere with his text" (p. 147). But such was obviously not the case for the denial, mockery and trial scenes since Matthew very clearly followed Mark's order. However, Chapman reversed himself when later he credited Luke with the transposition of the mockery (22,63-65) for the sake of clarity, all the while "preserving the likeness to Mk" (p. 125). The explanation would also appear to pertain to Peter's denials (22,56-62) in light of the table on p. 113.

Chapman acknowledged that Luke added a great deal of material to Mk. Strangely, 23,6-16 is not mentioned where one might expect it in his list of Luke's additions to the passion, though it was previously highlighted among incidents which Luke added (p. 172-173; cf. p. 144). Following Sanday and others, Joanna is once more singled out as a possible source of this special information for Herod's trial, but Chapman went a step further in suggesting that she was perhaps the mother of Manaen (Acts 13,1) (p. 173. Cf. *SSP*: SANDAY, *Introductory*, p. xiv; HAWKINS, *St. Luke's Use*, p. 94; STREETER, *On the Trial*, p. 229-231).

202. *Einleitung in das Neue Testament*, Paderborn, 1933, p. 219. See also his *Das Lukasevangelium*, in *Biblische Zeitfragen* 3³,2, Münster, 1912, p. 1-46. He affirmed with certainty that Mk provided the foundation for Lk which had adopted most of its contents. Lk was composed using both oral and written sources, the latter providing those accounts which were unique to Luke, though it was not possible to determine whether such were due to a continuous source or numerous individual sources (*Einleitung*, p. 219-220). Equally impossible and elusive was a satisfactory solution to the synoptic problem (p. 236-237; cf. p. 234). Meinertz viewed the relation of Lk to Mt as the most problematic aspect of the synoptic question (p. 220). He rejected out of hand the idea that Matthew used Lk (p. 234). Meinertz referred to a portion of the MA in 22,62 / Mt 26,75, but made no suggestion as to how it might have come to be.

In a certain sense, Streeter's problematic proposal could be regarded as a simplification of a solution that was increasingly "immer komplizierter und subjektiver werdenden Feststellung" (p. 230). Meinertz observed that Bussmann repudiated Streeter's theory, suggesting not less than eight individual sources.

fascinating article expounding the view that Luke had to drastically rewrite the Markan passion, since as it stood it "would have been wholly unsuitable" for Luke's needs[203]. W.S. REILLY (1939) was of the opinion that Luke used Mk, in addition to other oral and written sources[204]. Paul GAECHTER (1938)[205], Karl

In reaction to the form critics whose results Meinertz considered radical, he rejected the conception that the framework of the Gospels was the subsequent creation of the respective evangelists, calling such a view an "Übertreibung": "Dazu haften diese viel zu stark an ihren mündlichen und schriftlichen Quellen und behandeln das eigentlich Biographische im Leben Jesu viel zu nebensächlich" (p. 237). Nevertheless, he admitted that the account of the life of Jesus stemmed from the community tradition, but a tradition that was carefully preserved and already fixed at an early date, assuring its reliability (p. 238).

203. *The Passion Narrative in St Luke's Gospel*, in *JTS* 36 (1935) 269. Unable to decide whether the Gentile mission or the desire to minimize the tragedy of the passion was "the strongest of all influences" for Luke, Kiddle offered a number of contributing factors which helped to shape the final form of the Lukan passion as a revision of Mk: "Secondly, since St Luke desired to promote peace, to placate the Judaizers, to convert the Jewish authorities, and to prove that the Church was essentially a quiet, law-abiding society, it seems obvious that these motives must have influenced his account of the Passion, even more than it did in the early Ministry, since the death of Jesus was the root cause of the whole conflict". Only a few pages apart, Kiddle designated the Gentile mission (p. 270), and Luke's desire to downplay the tragedy of the Passion (p. 273), as the most influential perspective that directs Luke's redaction.

This refashioning of tragedy into success was evident in the account of the prediction of Peter's denials. "The prophecy of St Peter's denial has also been transformed from a tragedy to a confident assertion of the ultimate victory that was to be his (xxii 32 Luke only) – an excellent example of Luke's constant tendency to record past failures in the light of subsequent success" (p. 274). Kiddle suggested that Mk may have been Luke's only source, describing such a view as "a hypothesis which can be reasonably upheld" (p. 270). And it was clear to Kiddle, that the perspective of the passion contained in the Gospel was the same as in Acts, irrespective of whether one advocated Lukan redaction or a special independent source.

Kiddle latched on to Creed's argument in his commentary that substracting the Markan material from the Lukan passion would leave only "an amorphous mass of material", an argument which Kiddle maintained "has not yet been refuted" (p. 274, n. 1). He offered an insightful perspective, with which we would identify, since he captured the essence of Lukan redaction as we understand it. The only criticism to be made was that he passed over from the arrest to the death of Jesus, and thus, some of the most difficult parts of the passion.

204. *Saint Luke*, in *CBQ* 1 (1939) 314-324, p. 324: "The most definite thing that can be said about the time when the Third Gospel appeared is that it was written after St. Mark's Gospel. St. Mark was one of the sources of St. Luke. St. Luke made excellent use of this and of other written sources; but as has been pointed out his relations with St. Paul, St. James, St. Philip and with many other well informed witnesses furnished him with much precious material that had not yet been written. For much that is in Acts he was an eye-witness".

205. *Summa Introductionis in Novum Testamentum*, Leipzig, 1938, p. 88. Gaechter equated Lk 22,1-24,53 with Mk 14,1-16,8 and claimed that, minor differences between Lk and Mk aside, Luke generally followed the Markan order. Later, however, Gaechter also wrote that Luke generally followed the order of his sources in arranging his material (p. 91). While Gaechter did not treat the changes in the passion narrative directly, he pointed to an occasion where there was a variation in order. It concerned the healing of the blind man (18,35-43 and pars.). In Mk and Mt the event occurred as Jesus was departing Jericho, while in Lk Jesus healed the man as he

SCHÄFER   (1938)[206],   Martin   ALBERTZ   (1947)[207],   Adalbert   METZINGER

entered the city. The unconvincing explanation offered was: "probabiliter caecus Jesum appropinquantem iam rogaverat" (p. 90). But Gaechter's remarks might well apply to Luke's compositional technique in treating Peter's denials: "Hinc inde auctor Lc historiam ita textuit, ut eventum ad finem usque perduceret, antequam alium eventum narraret, qui priore eventu in ordine rerum nondum expleto iam locum habuerat". This could aptly describe what Luke was attempting to do in drawing together all the material which pertained to Peter, rather than allowing it to be interrupted as in Mk. The only remark made of particular sources dealt with pericopes concerning women, unique to Luke, which probably stemmed from the testimony of women (p. 97).

206. *Grundriss der Einleitung in das Neue Testament*, Bonn, 1938, [2]1952, p. 63. Schäfer maintained that the same order and frequent extensive agreement of vocabulary were indications of Luke's literary dependence upon Mk. Incorporating two large Markan blocks of material (3,1-9,50 and 18,15-24,11) into his Gospel, Luke revised his Markan *Vorlage* from a linguistic point of view. Lk is, in Schäfer's opinion, a true representative of the tradition. Changes were made to improve the form, to clarify and to join individual stories to one another (p. 64). Holding that the Two-Source theory went far to explain many phenomena, but fell short of resolving all of them, the solution seemed to lie in combining various elements of the different theories (p. 73). Schäfer preferred the form-critical study by Albertz to the excessively skeptical analysis of Bertram (p. 74-75; cf. M. ALBERTZ, *Die synoptischen Streitgespräche*, and G. BERTRAM, *Die Leidensgeschichte Jesu*).

207. *Die Entstehung der Botschaft und die Entstehung des Evangeliums*, in ID., *Botschaft des Neuen Testamentes*, Vol. 1/1, Zürich, 1947, p. 209. He believed that Luke basically followed Mk except in a few cases such as the Nazareth pericope (4,16-30), where he preferred the tradition of the relatives of Jesus. Mk and Q were the most important sources, while Mk formed the thread through the entire work (p. 204). Quite surprisingly, when Albertz offered a detailed table of the various sources used throughout Lk, the section extending from 22,44 to the end of chapter 23, however, was missing (p. 206-207)! He isolated three traditions: that of the women (F), of relatives (V), and the Hellenistic tradition (H). He assigned the Nazareth pericope to the tradition of the relatives, and the anointing (7,36-51) to the tradition of the women (F). He denied that Luke was familiar with any Greek writings of any early apostles (p. 204). Certain exceptions being that Mk rested upon the recollections of Peter and Q went back to Mt.

Although recognizing that Luke ordinarily held to the Markan order, Albertz also noted that Luke sometimes diverged from it for reasons that were special, but not always clear to us (p. 209). Many of Luke's redactional changes were improvements on his Markan, Q and Semitic sources, which reflected his modeling on the LXX (p. 207). But the changes which resulted from his stylistic improvements sometimes also recast the substance of his sources: "So sehr die Quellen stilistisch bearbeitet sind, so sehr hütet sich Lk., sie inhaltlich zu verändern" (p. 208). Despite this comment, Albertz later made the claim, echoing the sentiments of Wernle, that Mk and Q were capable of being retrieved in their new form as Lk: "Das Lukasevangelium nimmt die Vorarbeiten von Q und Markus so auf, dass sie beide durch die neue Evangelienform ersetzt werden sollen" (p. 275). Albertz was of the opinion that Chuza and Joanna were possibly the sources behind the Herod story (23,6-12) (p. 205). Thus, it appeared the story was an account dependent upon tradition and redaction.

(1948)[208], Karl Herman SCHELKLE (1949)[209], H.F.D. SPARKS (1952)[210] and

208. H. HÖPFL, B. GUT, and A. METZINGER (eds.), *Introductio Specialis in Novum Testamentum*, Rome, [5]1948, p. 116. In revising the NT introduction of Hildebrand Höpfl and Benno Gut, Metzinger asserted that Luke followed the Markan order, adopted some of the material and the manner of recounting it. Though Luke omitted some material, the reason for which was not quite so obvious, he more than compensated by adding other material of varying lengths (for example 23,6-12). It was most probable that Luke employed written sources, though he also thoroughly scrutinized oral sources, especially at Jerusalem, but in Antioch and Caesarea as well (p. 121-122).

Because tradition made no mention of it, and because canonical Mk reflected a unity of style and composition, Metzinger rejected Proto-Mk on historical and literary grounds (p. 164). Calling Proto-Lk one of the better known source theories, it was noted that the hypothesis was much disputed (p. 169, n. 2). Metzinger listed the supporters of Proto-Lk as R.H. Crompton, W.K.L. Carke [*sic*], and F.F. Bishop. L. Cerfaux merited a "etiam aliquomodo". W. Bussmann, J.M. Creed and C.S. Petrie formed the opposition. The more likely solution to the synoptic problem, in Metzinger's opinion, involved a combination of oral catechesis with mutual dependence: "Ita catechesi orali non solum uniformitas evangeliorum in magnis lineis, sed multae etiam discrepantiae, additamenta scil., omissiones, transpositiones, locutiones differentes, explicantur" (p. 188). But this did not exclude the use of other oral and written sources. The relation between Mk and Lk was, according to Metzinger, very great, but did not result in Luke's slavish dependence upon Mk: "Relatio inter Mc et Lc claret admissa permagna, licet non servili dependentia Lucae a Mc" (p. 189). The puzzling use of the subjunctive "claret" rendered this statement difficult to translate, though it would seem that he intended here to indicate that the relation between the two Gospels "would become clear"). Chuza and Susanna were possible sources of information for the account of Jesus before Herod (23,8-12), as was Manaen (p. 122). Regarding the parts proper to the evangelists, they were seen as deriving from particular sources, both oral and written (p. 189).

209. *Die Passion in der Verkündigung des Neuen Testaments*, Heidelberg, 1949, p. 89. He seemed to have been highly influenced by Bertram. This would seem to be the case in the discussion of the proof from prophecy sayings. The Gospels were not for the most part the work of "einer schriftstellerischen Einzelpersönlichkeit", but reflected the community tradition which came down to the evangelist. But it was also clear Schelkle believed Luke made redactional changes over against Mk. While Luke recounted only one mockery, it was apparent to Schelkle that Luke had both Markan accounts in mind, a view suggested by the use of the term ἐνέπαιζον (22,63) from Mk 15,20 (p. 43). Also, in place of Mk's more technical term, φραγελλώσας (Mk 15,15) Luke substituted παιδεύσας (Lk 23,16) maybe to soften the portrayal or in an effort to push it into the background (p. 45).

Aloys Dirksen complained that throughout his study Schelkle had not clearly offered his own position (*Review*, in *CBQ* 14 [1952] 406; cf. p. 408). Dirksen pointed out that Schelkle adhered to a modified form of Markan priority (see SCHELKLE, p. 1, n. 1, and p. 66, 284). Furthermore, Schelkle had gone "too far" in asserting that the details of the spitting and beating in the passion were not historical events, but were inspired by Is 50,6 (DIRKSEN, p. 408; cf. SCHELKLE, *Die Passion Jesu*, p. 86). However, these did not prevent Dirksen from recommending the work.

In another work Schelkle (1963, [3]1966) was of the opinion that Luke obviously used Mk as his fundamental source and followed it (*Das Neue Testament. Seine literarische und theologische Geschichte*, Kevelaer, p. 50). But Schelkle also entertained the possibility that Luke had, in addition to Mk, another complete passion narrative (p. 74). Such a position notwithstanding, Schelkle contended that Luke could have inserted a great deal of *Sondergut* into the passion narrative). Nevertheless, he proposed that in the sections 3,1-9,50 and 18,15-24,12 Luke took

Reginald GINNS (1953) also treated Luke's use of Mk[211].

over Mk and followed it verbally (p. 72-73). Though exegesis repeatedly attempted to more
precisely determine Luke's various sources, it was not successful in doing so.
    210. *The Formation of the New Testament*, London, 1952, p. 111. Mk, Q and Luke writing
up "the results of his own enquiries" were proposed by Sparks as the explanation of Luke's
sources referred to in the Prologue. Any other documentary sources were "questionable". He also
took notice of Luke's use of Mk. In contrast to Mt, Luke employed Mk in a much more free
manner. This entailed more omissions, more re-arrangements as well as more minor alterations.
    211. *The Gospel of Jesus Christ according to St. Luke*, in *CCHS*, 1953, p. 936. Cf. p. 967.
Even though Ginns argued Luke was dependent upon Mk for substance and the order of events,
generally reproducing "all that Mk contains", in the passion narrative Ginns ascribed material
from 23,1ff. to sources peculiar to Luke. He generally followed Mk, but not slavishly. Ginns
admitted Luke preferred the Markan order "where the Synoptists march together", but was open
to transpositions where it was demanded by his purpose (p. 936). It was proposed that in addition
to a number of written versions of the life of Christ, Luke had access to numerous informants,
not the least of which would be the women designated in 8,3 (p. 936).
    In the denial of Peter and the Sanhedrin trial of Jesus (vv. 54-71) Ginns noted the basic
similarity with the other Gospels except for the "changes of order, omissions and additions" (p.
967). Christian MAURER (1953) attributed the change in order involving Peter's denial to the
evangelist "weil er den Sinn nicht ganze verstanden hat" (*Knecht Gottes und Sohn Gottes im
Passionsbericht des Markusevangeliums*, in *ZTK* 50 [1953] 17; see also p. 27). According to
Ginns, Luke offered only one Sanhedrin assembly, the second one contained in Mk and Mt, in
an effort to simplify and out of a desire to delete that which was not in keeping with his main
purpose (GINNS, *Gospel*, p. 967). The matter of the judgment was left to the inference of the
reader, although it may be credited to Luke's intention to be historically accurate, since the
Sanhedrin had no jurisdiction to impose capital punishment. Beginning at 23,1-5 Ginns insisted
that Luke drew on sources unique to himself (p. 936; cf. p. 967). The unique tradition, according
to C.C. MARTINDALE (1957), as in the view of Ginns, appeared at 23,1ff. and continued until
the death of Jesus (*The Gospel According to St. Luke. With an Introduction and Commentary*
[Stonyhurst Scripture Manuals], Westminster, MD, 1957, p. 185).
    Whereas omissions were critical for some scholars in deciding in favor of a special source for
Lk, Ginns held this was characteristic of Lukan style. Luke omitted Markan material for a number
of reasons: 1) certain details were not germane to the purpose of the Gospel, 2) details
disparaging toward Jesus or those closely associated with him, as well as many references to
human emotion, were deleted, 3) those elements which would create obstacles for the non-Jewish
reader (GINNS, *Gospel*, p. 967). Ginns cited the practice of "demanding the release of a prisoner
at the Pasch" as one example. Luke's redaction often aimed at simplifying his source material.
In a statement strongly reminiscent of the position of Narborough, Ginns advanced the idea that
Luke omitted the more extensive passages which might prevent him from adding to the Markan
and Matthean narrative, material which was unique to himself (p. 937; cf. NARBOROUGH, *The
Synoptic Problem*, p. 41). Like Ropes's analysis of Lukan style, Ginns too observed that Luke
disliked repetition (GINNS, *Gospel*, p. 936). Ginns attempted to introduce some element of doubt
into the belief that Luke's political apologetic sought to present the Roman leaders in a more
positive light by calling attention to the presentation of "the callousness of Pilate" in 23,16.22 (p.
967). On its own, that may have been somewhat convincing, but given the alternative, Pilate must
be seen in a much more favorable light than his Jewish counterparts.
    Ginns suggested that the women designated in 8,3 were among Luke's oral sources (p. 936).
The pericope 23,6-16 resembled an attempt to discredit Jesus' "alleged claim to royalty" which
occurred in Pilate's hall, though Luke elected to omit that account.

The idea of a special source continued to attract the attention of German scholars, especially Bultmann and Dibelius, who rejected the idea. During this period form criticism was applied to the study of the Gospels. Dibelius made a profound impact on this history of research through his contribution on the Herod pericope and by maintaining that Jesus was portrayed as a martyr in the Lukan passion narrative. Creed, in a brief but compelling dismissal of the Proto-Lk theory, led opposition to the idea on the British side.

CHAPTER FIVE

A SPECIAL PROTO-LUKAN SOURCE REVISITED

EDUARD MEYER THROUGH E. EARLE ELLIS

The issue of whether the community helped to shape the Gospel accounts will be discussed during these years. Cadbury will undertake an analysis of Luke's literary style. Benoit devoted a series of articles and later a book to the passion narrative. Finally, Harlow wrote a book focusing entirely on Herod, a work that still receives periodic treatment in contemporary research.

Eduard MEYER (1921) regarded Luke and Matthew as having adopted the Markan account of the passion, as for example, in the story of the high priests, with the exception of some changes and expansions[1]. Still, Meyer believed that Luke used at least one other special source, a second narrative account, in addition to Mk and Q, which possibly contained genuine material[2].

Meyer credited Peter himself with reporting the experience of the denial[3]. News about the trial would have been disseminated by members of the Christian community at Jerusalem, though Meyer did not exclude as sources those who took part in the proceedings, such as members of the Sanhedrin[4]. He gave a good deal of attention to the women named in 24,10, including Joanna. Since she was named by some as a possible source of the special information, we are warranted in reviewing what he said. Luke was entirely correct at 8,3 in stating that the women cared for Jesus from their means[5]. Although Luke omitted their names at 23,49.55, they appeared at 24,10 where Joanna's name was substituted for Salome[6]. Meyer contended that "Diese Namen sind gewiss alle historisch"[7]. The women were responsible for reporting information about the crucifixion and the events which transpired at the cross[8]. He gave the distinct impression that Luke was responsible for many of the more drastic changes encountered in the Lukan passion narrative[9]. Evidence that Luke knew Mk's version of the trial was displaced to the account of Stephen in Acts 6,13f.

1. *Ursprung und Anfänge des Christentums*, Vol. 1, Stuttgart, 1921 (esp. p. 183-203), p. 197.

2. *Ibid.*, p. 223.

3. *Ibid*, p. 184.

4. *Ibid.*, p. 187.

5. *Ibid.*, p. 184, n. 2.

6. *Ibid.*, p. 185, n. 1. Cf. Mk 16,1 which contained the names Mary Magdalene, Mary the mother of James and Salome. Mt 28,1 omitted the name Salome and so spoke only of Mary Magdalene and "the other Mary".

7. *Ibid.*

8. *Ibid.*, p. 186.

9. *Ibid.*, p. 189-190. These included the meeting of the Sanhedrin at morning, Peter's denial occuring at night, the mistreatment of Jesus by servants/bondsmen ("Knechte"), that Jesus appeared as Messiah, the deletion of reference to the false witnesses. The question whether Jesus was the Messiah was avoided, as it had been in Mk.

While noting further differences between the Lukan and Markan accounts, Meyer pointed out that the freeing of Barabbas occupied the same place in Lk as in Mk[10].

According to Meyer (1924), Luke introduced the story of the trial before Herod (23,6-12) from another source[11]. While the information concerning the relationship of Pilate and Herod was "gewiss geschichtlich", the reconciliation resulting from the sending of Jesus was "wohl secundäre Legende"[12]. As Mark reported events of the Pilate trial, there would not have been enough time for such an exchange to have taken place. Obviously influenced by Dibelius, Meyer noted that Luke referred to his account in the prayer of the Christian community in Acts 4,27, the events which Luke regarded as the fulfillment of Ps 2,2[13]. The Herod episode formed part of a second narrative source, in addition to Luke's other sources of Mk and Q. "In einzelnen Fällen mag es vielleicht noch authentische Überlieferungen bewahrt haben"[14]. Meyer displayed great reserve in proposing that this source contained "Jugendgeschichten" such as that of Herod and the additions to the passion[15]. Although Luke thoroughly reworked his various sources imposing his own style upon them, Meyer was nonetheless of the conviction that an educated philological analysis would likely yield substantial results[16].

Adopting the theory that Luke possessed a special source, Georg BERTRAM (1922) nevertheless distanced himself from the view that it was of greater historical value than those traditions available to Mk and Mt[17]. He was much more open to accepting the influence of the community in shaping an evangelist's recounting of the story of Jesus[18]. In Bertram's opinion, the source should not be considered more historical than the traditions behind Mk or Mt. Nevertheless, he conceded the difficulty in distinguishing the various layers of the tradition as they evolved through the missionary effort and those which derived from the inner community proclamation[19].

10. *Ibid.*, p. 196, n. 1.

11. *Ibid.*, Vol. 1, 1921; 1924, ᴿ1962, p. 201; cf. n. 3. Meyer took issue with Wellhausen's view that because vv. 10-12 were absent from some Syriac recensions this proved they were additions. He held rather, that they were "ausgleichende Harmonistik".

12. *Ibid.*, p. 201-202.

13. *Ibid.*, p. 202, n. 1.

14. *Ibid.*, p. 223.

15. *Ibid.*, p. 223-224.

16. *Ibid.*, p. 223, n. 2.

17. *Die Leidensgeschichte Jesu und der Christuskult*, Göttingen, 1922, p. 56-57: "Hier zeigt sich allerdings, dass die Sonderquelle des Lc im ganzen keinen grösseren geschichtlichen Wert beanspruchen darf als die Überlieferungen, die Mc und Mt zur Verfügung standen, dass sie vielmehr teils falsch historisiert, teils ein legendenhaftes Gepräge trägt". In a note, Bertram referred to the study of Perry, *Sources*. Further, Bultmann suggested that Luke may have used an older redaction of the *Vorlage* of Mk in addition to Mk. As a further proof that Luke possessed an older source, Bertram pointed to the anti-Temple saying of Jesus in Stephen's trial (Acts 6,14) (p. 57).

18. *Ibid.*, p. 65.

19. *Ibid.*, p. 2.

Luke reflected a tradition that was more catechetical in nature, which was particularly evident in the speeches of Jesus[20]. The differences among the Gospels were the result of various literary and practical goals of the evangelists. While the material of the Synoptic Gospels, in Bertram's opinion, were basically the same, "wichtig für uns ist namentlich die Frage, wie jeder Evangelist den vor ihm liegenden Stoff behandelt, wer der mündlichen Tradition und ihren Motiven am nächsten steht, oder wer an ihnen deutet und bessert"[21].

For the denial of Peter, Bertram was tentative in ascribing the story to Luke's source, saying only that Luke may have followed his source at this point[22]. Luke's hand was recognized in the denial of the Peter episode as attempting to intensify the account in order to make it touching. However, by introducing Jesus into the story at this point, Bertram claimed that Luke overloaded the story[23]. He argued that the mockery of Jesus formed a parallel to the scourging[24] and maintained that there was no sure tradition concerning the trial before Pilate[25].

Luke's apologetic tendencies perhaps pushed the most important factor in the historical trial of Jesus, the Barabbas motif, into the background which reflected the secondary character of Luke's source[26]. Luke then assimilated his account to Mk and Mt by inserting it into the Barabbas account[27]. Bertram further denied that this material could stem from witnesses who saw or heard the trial because the reports were much too common and not very concrete[28]. While Matthew and Mark kept the Barabbas scene in its original, independent character, the Lukan source using the innocence motif, created a unified Pilate scene[29].

Particularly intriguing in Bertram's view was that what was referred to as the Sanhedrin trial, was not a trial at all[30]. Rather, it was a semblance of a trial in which an especially energetic clique of leaders of the people who were antagonistic toward Jesus gathered to formulate the charges which would then be presented to Pilate[31]. Bertram argued that Luke preserved the unofficial character of the trial, but then formed it according to his own calculations[32]. Bertram was of the opinion that Luke

---

20. *Ibid.*, p. 1. Bertram acknowledged the influence here of HARNACK, *Sprüche und Reden Jesus*, 1907, p. 120f.

21. BERTRAM, *Die Leidensgeschichte Jesu*, p. 3.

22. *Ibid.*, p. 61.

23. *Ibid.*, p. 62.

24. *Ibid.*, p. 72.

25. *Ibid.*, p. 62. Later, Bertram will assert that we do not know how Jesus stood before his judges (p. 71). He briefly noted that the interests in the trial of Jesus were shared by acts of the martyrs found in Christian, Jewish and Gentile circles (p. 55).

26. *Ibid.*, p. 62.

27. *Ibid.*

28. *Ibid.*, p. 66.

29. *Ibid.*, p. 67. There would be nothing in what Bertram said to exclude the possibility that Luke himself created such a unity since he was obviously a skilled littérateur.

30. *Ibid.*, p. 61.

31. *Ibid.*

32. *Ibid.*

shifted the trial to the morning, and in redacting the material, the cultic consciousness determined by the community presentation helped to shape the account of the trial[33].

The Synoptics were simply reproducing the tradition of the people[34]. Bertram maintained that the passion narrative was the cult story of Christianity[35]. Further, from the beginning it constituted a unified kerygma[36]. The liturgical community recognized their Lord once more in the Jewish Scriptures[37]. Nonetheless, when they became independent from the Jewish community, and felt that a life of Jesus should be written, the lacuna, of which the worshipping community had previously been unaware, became evident. Therefore, in order to create a continuous presentation of the life of Jesus, they had to combine, approximate and arrange material in a lively fashion[38].

In his conclusion, Bertram referred to the Synoptics as a later historicizing concoction which appeared to be an historical presentation[39]. So it was an act of self preservation as the Church determined for itself the four Gospels, not because they reproduced an accurate account of the life and ministry of Jesus, rather because they stemmed from the cult and were preserved in the cult[40].

Bertram raised the question whether a report existed at the basis of Luke's presentation in which the Herod pericope was missing and the point of the three declarations of innocence was highlighted[41]. Bertram concluded that the Herod story was only subsequently inserted into Luke's source[42]. The story of Herod furthered the apologetic goal of Luke and was contrasted with GP wherein Herod, together with the Jews, must bear the responsibility for the whole trial[43].

Bultmann criticized the work claiming Bertram "has a too imprecise concept of cult, and fails to distinguish the different motifs adequately"[44]. These weaknesses aside Bultmann referred often to Bertram's study[45].

The position of Leonhard FENDT (1937) seemed very similar to that of Bertram with the common view that the primitive communities had a great influence on the composition of the Synoptic Gospels: "Drückt man das technisch richtig aus, so muss

---

33. *Ibid.*, p. 56.
34. *Ibid.*, p. 71.
35. *Ibid.*, p. 96.
36. *Ibid.*, p. 101.
37. *Ibid.*
38. *Ibid.*
39. *Ibid.*, p. 102.
40. *Ibid.* Cf. M.-J. LAGRANGE, *Review: G. BERTRAM, Die Leidensgeschichte Jesu, 1922*, in *RB* 32 (1923) 442-445.
41. BERTRAM, *Die Leidensgeschichte Jesu*, p. 65.
42. *Ibid.* One senses in Bertram's writing the influence of Dibelius. In a note, Bertram called attention to the article of DIBELIUS, *Herodes und Pilatus*, in *ZNW* 16 (1915) 118f.
43. BERTRAM, *Die Leidensgeschichte Jesu*, p. 62.
44. BULTMANN, *History*, p. 280, n. 1 = *GST*, [2]1931, [3]1957, p. 303, n. 1.
45. *Ibid.*, p. 263, n. 4 (cf. *GST*, 1921, p. 159), p. 264, n. 3 (cf. *GST*, p. 160), p. 265, n. 4 (cf. *GST*, p. 160), p. 269, n. 1 (cf. *GST*, p. 163), p. 270, n. 3 (cf. *GST*, p. 163-164), p. 272, n. 3 (cf. *GST*, p. 164), p. 280, n. 1 (cf. *GST*, p. 171).

man sagen: Den Stoff des Evangeliums hat nicht Markus oder Matthäus oder auch Lukas gemacht, sondern die Gemeinde Jesu selbst, die erste, zweite, dritte Gemeinde, die palästinensische, die hellenistische Gemeinde, je nachdem"[46]. Each of the Synoptic Evangelists arranged the material from what was available to them from the community tradition, resulting in the "bessere Fassung" as well as the "bessere Verständnis"[47]. In addition, Luke had access to two written Gospels, Mk and Mt. Viewing a better order as his valuable contribution, the Third Evangelist nevertheless remained faithful to the order found in the community tradition. Following Bultmann Fendt maintained that Luke may even have had access to two further written collections, one being the sayings source and the other a special source[48]. Lk was an historically reliable Gospel insofar as it drew on tradition stemming from the various early communities (the primitive community of Jesus, followed by the Palestinian and Hellenistic communities) and became the locus for their encounter.

The issue of order was also very important to Fendt who observed that though Luke frequently related correctly the Markan order, there was also a certain independence about his account. Omissions were easily understandable in light of Luke's various contributions. His compositional technique was to collect and arrange various accumulations of anecdotes, pericopes and individual pieces.

Fendt referred to the section 22,54-23,25 as the "Prozess Jesu"[49]. He noted the change in the order of the denials as compared with the other Synoptics. Though the Sanhedrin trial (22,66-70) cannot be held to be historical, nonetheless it correctly described the motives and the entire perception ("der ganzen Geisteslage") of the Sanhedrin membership[50]. The section 23,4-25 testified to the acceptance of Luke and the community of his time that Jesus was considered innocent by the Romans.

Henry Joel CADBURY (1927), noting that Lk contained the most special material of the any of the Synoptic Gospels, examined Luke's literary methods in order to discover his sources[51]. The process of composition, Cadbury deduced, was a complicated one[52]. It was clear Luke employed Mk, very nearly in the same form

---

46. *Der Christus der Gemeinde. Eine Einführung in das Evangelium nach Lukas*, Berlin, 1937, ²1937 (second, unchanged ed.), p. 14. He dialogued, in part, with Lietzmann.

47. *Ibid.*, p. 14-15.

48. *Ibid.*, p. 15. Cf. R. BULTMANN, *Die Geschichte der synoptischen Tradition*, ²1931, p. 392.

49. FENDT, *Der Christus*, p. 232.

50. *Ibid.*, p. 233-234.

51. H.J. CADBURY, *The Making of Luke-Acts*, London, 1927, ²1958, ᴿ1961, p. 7. Cf. p. 2. Cadbury was not insensitive to the deficiencies posed by reprinting a book that had not first undergone a thorough rewriting. What was more, the bibliographical entries were scant and none really extended beyond 1925. Observe his remark in the preface to the book as published in 1958: "With the correction of a dozen misprints and a few other items this edition is photographically reprinted from the first" (p. ix).

52. CADBURY, *Making*, p. 32. Cf. p. 110. Seventy-five percent of Lk-Acts was "without identified sources".

as we have it now. The second written source was Q[53]. No other sources can be regarded as probable as these two definite sources[54]. Luke generally followed the Markan order, though there were a few unspecified exceptions[55]. Luke's literary method in his treatment of Mk and Q can give us insight into Luke's treatment of other sources[56]. But Cadbury was of the opinion it was evident Luke used other parallel material in the passion narrative in such a degree that Luke "appears to be combining Mark with other information, or substituting another narrative for that of Mark altogether"[57]. But only a short time later Cadbury asserted that even where Luke departed from Mk was not necessarily proof Luke was employing another source[58]. Like others before him, Cadbury observed that Luke refined the narratives more drastically than the sayings of Jesus[59].

Because Luke clearly used two written sources, Mk and Q, scholars were inspired to look for other written sources behind Lk. The "safest conjecture" was that, for the most part, Luke employed written sources which were composed in Greek. Cadbury remained open to the possibility that some of the written sources may have been Aramaic. Finally, oral sources were not to be excluded from Luke's thesaurus[60].

Cadbury thought the order of the passion narrative to be chronological[61]. As earlier noted, he observed that Luke generally followed the Markan order[62]. Such

53. *Ibid.*, p. 65; cf. p. 365. Cadbury repeated the observation that Luke, in faithfully reproducing Mk, did not significantly alter the narrative or words of Jesus, though the latter were sometimes rephrased. Cadbury called attention to the June, 1912 statement of the PBC which condemned the Two-Document theory (p. 65-66, n. 1).

54. *Ibid.*, p. 70.

55. *Ibid.*, p. 365.

56. *Ibid.*, p. 75.

57. *Ibid.*, p. 95. Cadbury based this conclusion on transpositions and on the radical departures from the Markan depiction of events. In opposition to Dibelius, Cadbury maintained it was difficult to determine whether the passion narrative had its origin in the liturgy or resulted from the heavy emphasis on Jesus' death and resurrection (p. 56).

58. *Ibid.*, p. 96: "But even when Luke varies considerably from Mark he is often nevertheless using him – merely paraphrasing more freely or elaborating out of his own imagination rather than abandoning Mark for some parallel account". Cadbury's ambivalence became clear a little later when he credited the differences in Lk to "Luke's own ideas" or "some other source" (p. 97). Cadbury was impressed with Mk and maintained that Luke could do little to improve it (p. 237).

59. *Ibid.*, p. 109.

60. *Ibid.*, p. 75; cf. p. 30-31. Cadbury also suggested that πολλοί (1,1) may simply be rhetoric (p. 29). While he was open, in principle, to the idea of Aramaic sources, he stated this view, which Feine proposed and which had been recently revived, though appealing, was "quite in excess of its own inherent probability" (p. 70). Part of the difficulty of reaching any solid conclusion rests on the judgment of those qualified in both Semitics and Greek. But later he remarked: "Neither the tradition of the church nor the inherent possibilities of the case really prove or even make probable the theory of Semitic originals for the works of Luke and for the other gospels" (p. 72).

61. *Ibid.*, p. 56.

62. *Ibid.*, p. 365.

mimicry was often for the sake of convenience[63]. The description in the Prologue indicated that Luke intended to offer "a narrative orderly and continuous in itself" and that the events would be related successively[64]. It must not be forgotten that the differences in order were ascribed either to a separate source or "to Luke's own ideas"[65]. Without specifically mentioning the denial, mockery and trial, Cadbury asserted that inversions in a section or a sentence were logically motivated[66].

The individual pericopes were not treated per se by Cadbury. Though the origin of the Sanhedrin trial (22,66-71) cannot be known for certain, Cadbury argued that Luke's version of Jesus' response which was parallel to Mk, was consistent with Luke's theology[67].

Concerning the relation of the Gospel to Acts, Cadbury emphasized that both must be studied together because they formed a "single continuous work"[68]. Under the banner of the apologia for Christianity in the face of Rome, Cadbury noted the similarities between the charges brought against Paul and those against Jesus: Jewish and Roman authorities concurred in the judgment of "not guilty", the language was similar and the charge was couched in political guise[69]. The move to improve the portrayal of the Romans, while at the same time accusing the Jews of initiating the opposition, though it may stem from the hatred of the Christians for the Jews, was due also to this apologetic[70]. Luke's ultimate purpose, as expressed in his preface, was most probably to rectify misconceptions about Christianity, rather than to "confirm the historical basis of Theophilus's religious faith"[71].

Some omissions, according to Cadbury, can be accounted for by their absence in sources employed by Luke. But since Cadbury affirmed Luke's use of Mk in a form essentially like our own, this cannot explain the differences with which we are concerned. Other omissions deleted "unessential details"[72]. Though Bertram, Dibelius and Loisy sought to determine what influence the Christian community had upon the Scriptures, Cadbury remained somewhat reserved[73]. Nonetheless, he observed that the Scriptures were not protected from such influence. Luke's source material "was told of Christians, by Christians, for Christians"[74]. Concerning the issue of the Semitisms, it was "unmistakable" that Luke was influenced by the LXX and sought to imitate it[75]. The changes in order and omissions of Markan material

63. *Ibid.*, p. 96.
64. *Ibid.*, p. 345.
65. *Ibid.*, p. 97.
66. *Ibid.*, p. 96.
67. *Ibid.*, p. 295.
68. *Ibid.*, p. 8-9.
69. *Ibid.*, p. 310.
70. *Ibid.*, p. 311.
71. *Ibid.*, p. 315; cf. p. 336.
72. *Ibid.*, p. 34.
73. *Ibid.*, p. 40-41.
74. *Ibid.*, p. 38.
75. *Ibid.*, p. 122; cf. p. 74, 222, 242.

were variously ascribed to Luke himself or to a different source[76]. Luke further omitted Markan material which he decided was insignificant or untrue[77]. He "does not profess to know more than Mark about the time or place of his anecdotes, but rather less"[78].

Cadbury sounded very much like Wernle when he wrote that Luke was to be faulted for occasionally not thinking through the narrative[79]. Cadbury, like Wernle, cautioned against assuming that a single written source was homogeneous[80]. In striking contrast to Perry as well as Burton, B. Weiss, Easton, and Streeter, Cadbury maintained it was very difficult to determine from whence Luke's vocabulary came, especially when Luke imposed his own style on the source[81]. But while he conceded the hypothesis put forward by Burton, Perry and Wickes may be possible, "the phenomena prove nothing more than ultimate common derivation and do not preclude intermediate redactorial stages or a plurality of common sources"[82]. Their explanation was far too simple whereas Cadbury envisioned a much more complex compositional process. Though Cadbury echoed Streeter's thought that source analysis was "highly speculative" and the evidence "thoroughly ambiguous", he directed attacks against Streeter and Taylor[83]. Cadbury was most critical of the two scholars for assigning authorship of Proto-Lk to Luke himself[84]. Streeter was further criticized for maintaining that early on the Gospels and their variations enjoyed "a kind of ecclesiastical authority" in a particular geographical region[85]. Cadbury's assessment of Luke's historical reliability tended more toward Streeter than to Taylor[86]. Despite these differences of opinion, Cadbury seemed drawn to

---

76. *Ibid.*, p. 97. The change of venue for the resurrection appearances from Mark's positioning in Galilee to Jerusalem in Lk Cadbury seemed to attribute to Luke (p. 248). But he also held that all the changes not attributed to sources were not necessarily intentional. Some were unconscious changes by Luke (p. 301).

77. *Ibid.*, p. 365.

78. *Ibid.* This seemed to argue against the value of a parallel, independent, non-Markan source.

79. *Ibid.*, p. 334. Wernle accused Luke of carelessly shortening some narratives (*Die synoptische Frage*, p. 25).

80. CADBURY, *Making*, p. 69. Cf. WERNLE, *Die synoptische Frage*, p. 94.

81. CADBURY, *Making*, p. 16. See also p. 104, n. 3. He also wrote: "Sometimes, for example, theories of written sources rely on the evidence of vocabulary. Certain passages, it is argued, reveal a special style unlike Luke's and therefore can be attributed to a written source. But where Luke paraphrases Mark no such alien style betrays his process. There are no peculiarities of Mark's vocabulary that conspicuously distinguish the passages derived from him" (p. 67). The battle lines are drawn when one compares the following statements of Easton and Cadbury. Referring to the evidence of Hawkins's *Horae Synopticae* and Cadbury's *The Style and Literary Method of Luke*, Easton asserted "they include as 'Lukan' much that really belongs to L" (*Luke*, 1926, p. xxxi). At about the same time Cadbury wrote: "Much that critics assign to the tendency of Luke's source may be due to Luke alone" (*Making*, p. 69).

82. CADBURY, *Making*, p. 104.

83. *Ibid.*, p. 69.

84. *Ibid.*, p. 106, n. 4. The proposal was dismissed as "convenient but unlikely".

85. *Ibid.*, p. 331, n. 15.

86. *Ibid.*, p. 367; cf. p. 346: "Luke is neither more credulous nor more scientific than might

the idea of Proto-Lk which would account for differences in material and order[87]. Though Cadbury favored this view, he asserted that the unity of this supposed document cannot be demonstrated.

Although Cadbury tipped his hat in favor of the Proto-Lk theory, it cannot be denied that he perhaps ascribed more to Luke himself than other supporters of the hypothesis. Cadbury also noted that some changes were consistent with Luke's apologetic purpose, the defense of Christianity. He challenged the contention that the vocabulary of the special source can be distinguished from other sources Luke employed, including Mk, and thus would appear to base his decision ultimately upon the argument from order. Still, Cadbury allowed that Luke revised his evangelistic sources based "on his own more recent and intimate experience"[88].

Cadbury discussed Luke's fascination with the Herodian dynasty and inferred that "a Greek evangelist might know them better than he knew their subjects", but gave no further indication of how he might have been acquainted with them[89].

Reviews of the original edition were numerous. Creed was severe in his treatment of Cadbury, complaining the latter "hardly fulfills his promise of giving a 'realistic picture' of the making of Luke-Acts"[90]. In addition, Creed railed against Cadbury for lacking a "general theory of the transmission of the Gospel tradition"[91]. Finally Creed was highly critical of Cadbury's approach to the source question, which in his mind created rather than alleviated confusion, since Cadbury wrote that the sources "were largely written, and written in Greek, is the safest conjecture – though only a conjecture" (p. 75). Creed believed that all scholars would agree that Luke was based upon written Greek sources[92].

Cadbury did not fare much better in the opinion of J. Huby who characterized the work as carried out in "detached skepticism" wherein Cadbury examined, but later dismissed, numerous conjectures[93]. Much more favorable was the appraisal of E.F. Scott who agreed with Cadbury "that Lucan criticism has been too much dominated by preconceived theories". Because of Cadbury's more independent approach he "confines his attention to the facts, which are seen on examination to fit in with none of the theories"[94]. As a result, Cadbury perceived Luke, not as having simplistically manipulated the sources, but as being a creative editor who revised the material according to his personal style and in concert with his interpretation of history.

be expected of one in his circumstances".
87. *Ibid.*, p. 108-110. The theory of Streeter, initially tested by Easton in his commentary and later by Taylor, according to Cadbury, received favorable reviews (p. 109, n. 6).
88. *Ibid.*, p. 347.
89. *Ibid.*, p. 241.
90. *JTS* 29 (1927-28) 433-434.
91. *Ibid.*, p. 434.
92. *Ibid.* Cf. CADBURY, *Making*, p. 75.
93. *RSR* 19 (1929) 188.
94. *JR* 8 (1928) 286-287.

A.T. Robertson, though not always persuaded by Cadbury's arguments, nonetheless paid the compliment that Cadbury had put forward "pleasing and plausible theories" about sources[95]. But Robertson's overall evaluation of the work was negative, because Cadbury had not resolved the most important issues affecting Luke's two-volume work[96].

Among the advocates of additional oral sources for Luke were Albert VALENSIN and Joseph HUBY (1927)[97], while Alphonse TRICOT maintained that Luke's personal information could have been either oral or written[98]. Still others, such as Jacques-

---

95. *RExp* 25 (1928) 105.

96. *Ibid.*, p. 106.

97. *Évangile selon saint Luc* (Verbum Salutis, 3), Paris, [1-11]1927, p. IX. They claimed Luke took advantage of the sojourn in Jerusalem in 57-59 AD to "parfaire sa documentation sur la vie du Christ". Among the witnesses with whom he would have conferred were James, and the elders of Jerusalem, the holy women and early disciples, like Mnason the Cypriot, the deacon Philip and his prophetess daughters (p. X). At Rome he would have encountered Mark, at which time most probably Luke would have definitively redacted the book of Acts. Though somewhat tentative in their assessment, Valensin and Huby submitted that Mk appeared to have been a source for Luke: "... lui-même paraît bien s'être servi, comme d'une source autorisée, de l'évangile de Marc, son compagnon à Rome" (p. 3). In addition, Luke collected "les échos" of the Palestinian catechesis which had been incorporated into the Aramaic Gospel of Mt, which had given rise to additional more or less fragmentary documents (p. 3). The authors attempted to reconcile the differences of the various accounts of Peter's denial in their companion work, *Commentaire de saint Matthieu* (26,69-75) (cf. p. 399, n. 1). Luke was already well aware of large pieces of this which had previously been translated in Greek.

In the opinion of Valensin and Huby, Luke was familiar with the night session of the Sanhedrin but opted not to report it (*Évangile selon saint Luc*, p. 402). Instead everything was reported in the morning assembly. The authors regarded the night session as lacking the legal form of a solemn judgment (p. 402). Thus Luke recounted only the morning session in which the "confession" of Jesus was renewed, leading to his condemnation.

Huby (1960) expressed slight reservation in declaring that it appeared that Luke used Mk as a source (*L'évangile de Luc*, in A. ROBERT and A. TRICOT [eds.], *Initiation biblique*, Paris - Tournai - Rome - New York, ³1954 ["refondue"] = *The Gospel according to Saint Luke* in *Guide to the Bible* [eds. E.P. ARBEZ and M.R.P. McGUIRE], Vol. 1, London, ²1960, p. 404). In addition, there were fragments of documents containing reminiscences of Palestinian catechesis. Further Luke knew numerous segments which had already been translated into Greek. But the written sources were amplified by testimony from living witnesses such as Paul and people in Palestine, Jerusalem and Caesarea. Because Luke adopted a chronological approach he made changes in the Markan order. It was clear that at 18,15 (Mk 10,13) Luke resumed his use of Mk which continued to the resurrection of Christ. A few changes in order and a few additions not found in Mk were noted (p. 406).

98. A. TRICOT, *La question synoptique*, in ROBERT and TRICOT (eds.), *Initiation biblique*, ³1954 ("refondue") (= *The Synoptic Question*, in *Guide to the Bible* [eds. E.P. ARBEZ and M.R.P. McGUIRE], Vol. 1, ²1960, p. 579, #5). This article on the synoptic question in the same volume as Huby's later contribution. He asserted that Lukan dependence upon Mk was indisputable and dismissed the idea of a Proto-Gospel as not adequately explaining the differences between the Synoptic Gospels.

Marie Vosté (1937), promoted the idea that in addition to Mk Luke had access to oral sources[99].

Supporters of the Proto-Lk theory included Reginald H. Crompton (1928)[100],

---

99. *De Passione et Morte Iesu Christi* (STBNT, 3), Rome, 1937, p. 194. In 22,66 and earlier Luke intimated a prior nocturnal session by these last mentioned events. Luke rightly was silent about the illegal gathering, which did not result in anything definitive (p. 116). Vosté claimed that though the Sanhedrin had the power to incarcerate and flagellate for infraction of the Jewish law, they were not able to carry out capital punishment (p. 133-134).

Vosté accepted the Herod episode (23,6-12) as historical, because of the proximity of the residences of Herod and Pilate and because Joanna could have publicized the encounter (p. 158).

See also J.-M. Vosté, *De Synopticorum mutua relatione et dependentia*, Rome, 1928. Vosté's schema (p. 66) showed that in addition to a literary dependence upon Mk, Luke also benefitted from a variety of sources including the catechesis of Paul, the witness of Mary and other sources proper to Luke, as well as a collection of sermons which derived from a Greek version of Mt. Vosté's general conclusion was that he subscribed to the priority of Aramaic Mt and the authenticity of Greek Mt, though the patristic explanation was subject to change and adaptation (p. 67).

Vosté noted Luke's omission of the nocturnal session of the Sanhedrin. Luke then appropriately recorded the denials of Peter after Jesus had been arrested and led to the house of the high priest. He viewed it as improbable that there was an immediate relation between Mk and Lk in the passion narrative, though the order of both was often the same: "Neque immediata relatio inter Marcum et Lucam probabilis videtur quoad ministerium Baptistae et sequentia (III-IV,30), neque quoad passionem et resurrectionem (XXII-XXIV)" (p. 58).

100. *The Synoptic Problem and a New Solution*, Edinburgh, 1928. He was yet another advocate of a Proto-Lk theory. He noted that scholars such as Streeter and Bartlet relegated Mk to a secondary place in the composition of Lk. Regrettably, he did not find it necessary to rehearse the criticisms against such views. However, he asserted that the multiplication of sources by Streeter reduced the probability of that theory to almost nil. Crompton's proposition combined the idea of a Synoptic GS with an intermediate Proto-Lukan stage prior to the final composition of Lk (p. 11-12). He believed that this early source could be recovered from Lk: "... it is almost an inevitable conclusion that the source of all of the Gospels is embedded in [Luke's] Gospel" (p. 10).

The Pre-Synoptic Gospel began in Alexandria where Proto-Lk also originated. The latter resulted from conflict with the Palestinian segment of the Church that had been founded by John the Baptist. The Alexandrians considered the Palestinian Christians to be backsliding into Judaism by their attempt to integrate it into Christianity (p. 76; see also p. 81, 83). As for the date of the Pre-Synoptic Gospel, Crompton suggested only that it "may be years earlier than any other New Testament document" (p. 12). There was a hint of gnosticism in Crompton's characterization of this source. It did not take up historical material, and chronology and geography were irrelevant. Its purpose was religious instruction.

The first edition of Lk contained a reorganization of the Pre-Synoptic Gospel. "But the order in our Luke is interfered with, broken just sufficiently to show that it is not perfectly done, to suggest that it is not quite original" (p. 11; see also p. 54). Crompton wrote that Luke's order reflected an intentional disarrangement of the material and proposed that the Gospel can profitably be read in a "vertical direction" meaning according to the seven stages in the sixteen series as reconstructed in Appendix E (p. 62). He described his understanding of the formation of the Synoptic Gospels: "Matthew is not, like Luke, dependent upon the Pre-Synoptic Gospel. His Gospel rests upon proto-Luke, the re-arrangement of the Pre-Synoptic Gospel which he has taken the liberty of still further re-arranging, largely for an anti-Jewish purpose, some decades after proto-Luke was written. Our

Frederick NARBOROUGH (1928)[101], Charles GORE (1928)[102], E.F. SCOTT (1932),

Gospel of Luke is a revision of proto-Luke, after Matthew was written, which incorporates a good deal of Matthew's anti-Jewish material. Mark is still later, but of Eastern, not Western, origin" and he dated the Gospels, essentially as they now exist, prior to the end of the first century (p. 64). What scholars termed Mk and Q were, in Crompton's opinion, only "two complementary portions of the one Gospel" (p. 9; see also p. 24-25).

In a very complicated and artificially contrived system, Crompton proposed that there were seven stages with an additional sixteen series divided into a symbolic portion and a didactic portion Crompton defined his stages as follows: 1) "of a mystical and even potential character, causing wonder but not understanding by the catechumen" (p. 77); 2) "the beginning of instruction. It contained a simple and elementary statement of the didactic idea" (p. 78); 3) the stages "show the relation of Mosaism to the particular idea of each series" (p. 79); 4) "shows how this section of the Church is not adopting the right attitude" (p. 79); 5) "to show up and condemn" Judaism (p. 79); 6) "Now the conflict is with the power of Darkness, Satan himself, who is very much in the ascendant" (p. 80); 7) "is the triumph of the good, and the complete revelation" (p. 80). For an explanation of the series numbered 1-16, see p. 60-61. Stage five reflected a condemnation of Judaism and the seventh stage was the victory of good (p. 79, 80). Within the passion narrative the fifth stage included 22,54-62 (series 15 which focused on the correct motivation for Christian discipleship) and 22,63-69 (series 8 which was concerned with the "complete victory over evil by Resurrection and Ascension") (p. 79, 80). Peter's denial was referred to on p. 123. See p. 102 for a discussion of 22,68b.69. Stage seven included 22,70-71 (series 1 which highlighted the proclamation of Jesus who will be revealed as the Son of God), 23,1-12 (series 2 concentrated on Jesus who was sent to proclaim "the New Gospel") and 23,13-25 (series 4 which portrayed Jesus seemingly succumbing though he showed his power over evil) (Appendix E). See also Crompton's comments on p. 54.

None of the reviewers saw much value in the work. Perhaps the most positive thing said was that it was "welcome", though inconclusive (A.T. ROBERTSON, in *RExp* 26 [1929] 228). Manfred Manrodt believed that the difficulties inherent in Crompton's theory were apparent in comparing "any two groups of narratives" (*BS* 86 [1929] 350). Another reviewer contended that Crompton's negative critique of the value of Streeter's theory of multiple sources, namely, that additional sources reduce the probability of such a theory "in an almost geometrical progression", could equally be said of Crompton's theory (*ExpT* 40 [1928-29] 258). A.T. Robertson understood Crompton not as multiplying sources but as limiting them, a process he categorized as "artificial simplification" (*RExp* 26 [1929] 228). W.K. Lowther Clarke regarded the book as "quite worthless", calling it "a fantastic theory" (*TLond* 19 [1929] 60).

101. F.D.V. NARBOROUGH, *The Synoptic Problem*, in C. GORE, H.L. GOUDGE, and A. GUILLAUME (eds.), *NCHS*, London - New York, 1928, 33-42, p. 39. This entire work represented the collaborative effort of Anglican scholars, primarily from England. In his essay Narborough rejected Burkitt's contention that Q contained an account of the passion, basing his view on the premise that Matthew would not have ignored the Q source at such an important juncture. Instead, Narborough subscribed entirely to Streeter's Proto-Lk theory, that for the passion narrative (22,14ff.), Luke employed two sources, adding only a "few Markan touches" to this special source. Further enhancing the correctness of this hypothesis, according to Narborough, was the evidence of 1) "a fairly continuous and lengthy narrative" among the non-Markan sections, 2) Luke's preference for parallel accounts to Markan material, as for example in the case of the anointing (7,36ff.), 3) the omission of Mk 6,45-8,26 (p. 41), since Luke was "obliged by the limited length of the papyrus-roll to add from Mark only what was entirely unrepresented by anything in that material", and 4) the use of the appellation "the Lord" in the non-Markan material rather than the name "Jesus". Narborough was sharply critical of Luke's

though he was cautious in what could be said about it[103], Eric F.F. BISHOP (1933-34)[104], George Woosung WADE (1934)[105], C.H. DODD (1935)[106], Henry D.A.

compositional technique, accusing the evangelist of an "apparent lack of intelligence".

102. *The Gospel According to St. Luke*, in C. GORE et al. (eds.), *NCHS*, 1928, p. 208. Gore, the former Anglican Bishop of Oxford, maintained that though Luke depended on Mk for the passion narrative, it was equally clear that he relied on another source. Like Narborough, Gore, who was strongly influenced by Taylor, held the Proto-Lk theory explained the composition of Lk (p. 209). In addition to Mk, Q and Proto-Lk, Lk reflected "the influence of current Hellenistic style and the influence of the Greek bible" (p. 208).

According to Gore, Luke "edited freely", but in such a way as not to distort the sense of the material. Gore had nothing specific to say about sources for the denial of Peter, but argued that Luke was independent of Mk and Mt in the Sanhedrin trial (p. 237). While Luke provided an independent account in 23,18-25, he offered "the same impression as Mark" concerning Pilate's acquiescence to the demands of the Jewish leaders and the crowd. But the Markan account was clearer in presenting the demand of the multitude for Barabbas's release while the chief priests insisted on the conviction of Jesus. Gore concluded by downplaying the differences in the various accounts, stressing instead the basic unity of presentation of the four Gospels in the passion narrative.

103. *The Literature of the New Testament*, New York - London, 1932. Although he maintained it could be affirmed "with certainty" that such a document existed, not much more could be said about it. "Of the two-fifths which is peculiar to Luke, a large portion is homogeneous in character, and there is good ground for supposing that Luke had access to a third document, comparable in extent and value to Mk and Q. This view is now so generally held that it is customary to speak of 'L' or 'Luke's special source'. The chief interest in Lucan criticism centers on this third source. We have seen that, according to one recent theory, Luke has built his Gospel, not on Mark, but on this unknown document; but all that can be affirmed with any certainty is that such a document existed, and that Luke drew on it for much of his most precious information" (p. 83-84). In addition to three main sources, Luke had others, "briefer and less important" (p. 84).

104. *Local Colour in Proto-Luke*, in *ExpT* 45 (1933-34) 151-156, p. 151. Bishop followed Taylor in asserting that the special material was on equal historical footing with Mk and Q. He relied on TAYLOR, *First Draft* and *Behind*. He theorized that one could detect more of the Palestinian background in the special material than in Mk, as Streeter suggested. He further argued that though Lk generally showed a disinterest in matters geographical, he implied that where it did occur, this betrayed the Proto-Lukan source. The reference in 23,5 was cited as an example (p. 156).

105. *The Documents of the New Testament*, London, 1934, p. 259. He supported the Proto-Lk hypothesis, though not without some qualification. He noted that the question of the omission of a great deal of Markan material was linked to the issue of material peculiar to Lk. Wade was sympathetic to the idea that the material was omitted because of the length of the papyri, but cool to the view that Luke supplanted it with material derived from oral traditions. However, for the section 19,28-24,11 Wade maintained this was material "mainly from *Mk.*" and this represents a major departure from Streeter's conception of the hypothesis (Cf. STREETER, *The Four Gospels*, 1924, p. 222). Wade differed from Streeter in other ways, as when he proposed the period somewhere between 61 and 70 AD as the time of the composition of Proto-Lk. Later, around 80 AD, it was incorporated into the Gospel. He closed ranks again with Streeter in assuming that Proto-Lk, rather than Mk, formed the structural basis of Lk. It was this hypothetical document, in Wade's opinion, which best explained the omission of Mk 6,45-8,26. He likewise adopted the view that the use of the term "the Lord" stemmed from Proto-Lk (WADE, *Documents*, p. 263).

MAJOR (1938)[107] and Bernard P.W. STATHER HUNT (1951)[108]. Others, such as

An attempt was made to ascribe verses to their respective sources (Mk, Q and L), though Wade cautioned that such divisions "are in some places uncertain"(p. 264). The task which Wade undertook was described by Streeter as "very problematical" (*FG*, 1924, p. 222).

Wade attributed the following verses and verse parts to Mk: 22,54-57.59-64.66-67(partial v. 67).69.71; 23,1.3.18-25(partial v. 22). L was responsible for 22,58.65.67(partial v. 67)-68.70; 23,2.4-16.22(partial v. 22) (WADE, *Documents*, p. 316-318). It was obvious in comparing the lists that Mk was clearly predominant. Wade observed that Luke generally followed the Markan order but noted an exception (p. 261). The Lukan account of the call of Peter, James and John was recounted in an order different from Mk. It will be remembered that Burkitt saw Luke's insertion of Mk 3,31-35 as a transposition (cf. p. 107, n. 91 above).

106. *The Parables of the Kingdom*, London, 1935; 1936 (Revised ed.), p. 40; London - Glasgow - New York, 1961 (Revised ed.), p. 25-26: "As for the remaining portions of the First and Third Gospels, they come from sources of which we can say little. If the once widely accepted theory of B.H. Streeter is right, we have to allow for four relatively primitive sources, those represented by Mark, 'Q' and the peculiar portions of Matthew and Luke respectively. But although we may suspect that the two latter were possibly as old as Mark or 'Q', we can never know whether a given passage in Matthew or Luke was drawn directly from the early sources, or whether it represents a later development. We know from their treatment of Mark that the other synoptists used their sources with some freedom. Nor, if it be true (as I think it probably is) that behind the Third Gospel lies a 'proto-Luke' which might be as early as Mark, are we entitled to give the same weight to this hypothetical document as we give to the Second Gospel; because (a) we do not know what amount of revision 'proto-Luke' underwent in being incorporated in the Third Gospel, and (b) the peculiarly Lucan material, on its merits, seems in places almost demonstrably secondary to Mark, even though in some places it may be thought to have preserved a more primitive tradition".

107. *Incidents in the Life of Jesus*, in ID., T.W. MANSON, and C.J. WRIGHT (eds.), *MMJ*, New York, 1938, p. 254. Major was swayed by the Proto-Lk theory for its ability to explain various phenomena, including the unusual distribution of the Markan and non-Markan blocks of material. But there were two issues that merited our closer attention. While maintaining that Luke's special material had "high historic value", Major nonetheless put his faith in the reliabilty of the Markan version when it came to the question of order of events. "The facts and sayings which are peculiar to Luke have high historic value, but where his Gospel differs from the Marcan order, Mk. is to be preferred" (p. 258).

Regarding Pilate's sending of Jesus to Herod (23,4-16), Major ascribed this to Luke's "particular source connected with Herod's entourage" (p. 289). Also, despite the fact that Streeter and Taylor would attribute the mockery of Jesus by the Herodian soldiers to the special source, somewhat amazingly Major wrote as if Luke had been editing Mk: "As Lk. relates the mockery of Jesus by Herod and his soldiers, he omits the purple (scarlet) robe and wreath of thorns and the mockery by the Roman soldiers".

108. *Primitive Gospel Sources*, New York, 1951. Unconcerned with attempting to determine what material was drawn from Q or the special L source, Stather Hunt nonetheless inclined generally in favor of Streeter's point of view. "That there were intermediate links between this primitive source and our present Gospels is almost certain, and some of those links may very well have been of the type envisaged by Dr. Streeter and others; so that the theory propounded in this work is not necessarily at various with the findings of those scholars to whose able and elaborate researches we owe so much" (p. 86; cf. p. ix). But Stather Hunt's attitude was certainly not to be construed as strong support. "Sources of the nature of M or L are only intermediate links, so that their existence or non-existence does not affect the main argument" (p. 85), though he

Léonce DE GRANDMAISON (1928) defended the idea of special sources in Luke's passion narrative, though he did not subscribe to Proto-Lk[109]. Floyd FILSON (1938) was opposed to Proto-Lk[110].

castigated Streeter for manipulating the letters Q and L. "In other words, Dr. Streeter admits that somewhere in the background is a source from which both Mark and 'Q' drew certain material; but he brings no evidence that this source was not the original 'Q', nor that the source which Mark did *not* use was not his own Proto-Luke. In other words, the 'decided differences' may be due to L (or to some of Q's growing progeny) and not to Q itself. He lays himself open to the suggestion that he is juggling with letters in order to conceal the breakdown of the original Q hypothesis" (p. 98-99). Without expressly citing Hawkins, Stather Hunt affirmed the possibility that Luke derived information from Paul, including details about Peter, and may have given preference to the Pauline information over Mk (p. 99). But it was Taylor, in *Behind the Third Gospel* who proved most convincingly to Stather Hunt that Luke employed a separate independent source for the passion account. "Vincent Taylor, in *Behind the Third Gospel*, p. 33-75, *appears to prove conclusively that St. Luke utilized an independent Passion Story, into which he inserted 14 passages derived from Mark, in Markan order relative to each other*" (p. 100, n. 1 [emphasis added]). Stather Hunt did not consider Luke as having a multiplicity of sources, simply an "additional source of information". He saw in Acts 2,16-35 a reason to suggest that an account of the passion "as full as that which we find in the Gospels" might have existed (p. 41-42). Other matters drew attention to Stather Hunt's carelessness. R.D. Sawyer, Stather Hunt's source, did not accurately referred to Goguel's position on the passion. One was left with the impression by Stather Hunt that Goguel endorsed the idea that Luke had an account of the passion from a very early Jerusalem source, when in fact Goguel's article in *HTR* made it clear he believed Luke redacted Mk (p. 100; 41-42; cf. GOGUEL, *Luke and Mark*, in *HTR* 26 [1933] 1-55, esp. p. 38: "The foregoing analysis of Luke's passion narrative leads to a conclusion entirely opposed to the theory of a special homogeneous source. Luke's narrative is a literary elaboration of that of Mark, supplemented by certain fragmentary traditions. It does not support Streeter's hypothesis of a Proto-Luke; indeed it presents a weighty objection". Nor was that Stather Hunt's only error. Aside from misstating the pagination for the article by Roland Sawyer to which he referred (in actuality it was p. 91-92), one is given the impression by Stather Hunt that Sawyer was referring to Luke 24,25-27.44-48, when in fact Sawyer referred to 24,13-35. Cf. R.D. SAWYER, *Was Peter the Companion of Cleopas on Easter Afternoon?*, in *ExpT* 61 (1949-50) 91-93!

109. L. DE GRANDMAISON, *Jésus Christ: sa personne, son message, ses épreuves*, Paris, 1928 (esp. p. 91-118) (= *Jesus Christ*, tr. B. WHELAN, New York, 1930). On the consensus that Luke used Mk, see p. 111, n. 2, while concurring with those who held that Luke depended upon Mk and used it as the framework for his own Gospel, noted that Luke's detailed passion narrative suggested other sources. These would at best only be conjecture rather than designated with any certitude. Grandmaison appeared to have had little appreciation of Streeter's theory since the translator drew attention to it when Grandmaison referred to the Two-Source theory as "here and there somewhat battered" (p. 101).

110. *Origins of the Gospels*, New York, 1938. Responding to Feine and others, though without referring to them directly, Filson noted the failure of the hypothesis of a written primitive Gospel and observed: "No form of this theory of a long primitive Gospel has ever been able to win much acceptance", citing complete lack of reference from the Church Fathers (p. 120-121). "Most scholars conclude that while shorter sources no doubt existed, no document complete enough to be called a full Gospel preceded the earliest of our Synoptic Gospels" (p. 123). He identified what he considered to be the two strengths of Streeter's theory: 1) its ability to explain the "elaborate dating" in 3,1ff. and 2) the ability to account for the inclusion of a lesser amount

H. BALMFORTH (1930), another advocate of the Proto-Lk theory, claimed that Luke made use of four sources: Mk, Q, L and a special source containing chapters one and two[111]. Although it was "practically certain" that Luke used Mk, it was "perhaps not the most valued of the writer's documentary sources"[112]. Balmforth regarded Streeter's inestimable contribution to biblical scholarship to be the four document theory and Proto-Lk. His only criticism of Streeter's articulation of the latter was that care should be taken to distinguish between the essential elements of the theory and additional details. He expressed further caution about labeling Proto-Lk "a complete Gospel", preferring terms such as Taylor's "a first draft of a gospel" or Streeter's "a half-way house". He concurred, however, with the views that the author of Proto-Lk was also the author of Lk-Acts and that the initial work should be dated around 64-65 AD as Streeter and Taylor proposed. He further suggested that the Gospel should be dated around 80 AD, but possibly as early as 73 AD, with Acts being composed around 85 AD Balmforth took offense at the characterization of the evangelist as simply a compiler. He was most skeptical of Easton's description of various elements of Proto-Lk which he considered excessive. Easton maintained that "L" was a written source, from around 55-65 AD, composed by a Palestinian Hellenist, who may have been Philip the evangelist, and that it contained distinctive verbal and stylistic qualities[113]. Balmforth's reaction was valuable and worth quoting in full:

> "It is doubtful whether we are justified in claiming as much as this. The assumption of a document is *a priori* probable: S. Luke himself refers to many writers before him, and it is unlikely that Q was the only written collection made; Streeter, again, is probably justified in thinking that each Greek-speaking church

of Markan material in Lk when compared with Mt (p. 129). Filson enumerated the following scholars as among the "intelligent followers" of Streeter's point of view: E.B. Redlich, T.W. Manson, H.D.A. Major and C.J. Wright (p. 131-132), Filson raised three objections to its validity. Like Lowther Clarke, he argued that scholars were unable to prove that the special Lukan material had comprised either a single written source or unified collection of oral tradition (p. 130). Like Huby, Filson further pointed to the rather complex nature of the two stage process, for which there was no corroborating evidence in other extant documents or writings of the early Christian period. Filson's third point was more an analysis than an objection. He concluded that the hypothesis was inadequate since it did not resolve the synoptic question. He summed up the matter: "There is great persuasiveness in Streeter's arguments, but they are not quite convincing. His view is not generally accepted" (p. 134).

Sherman Johnson admitted the similarity of his views with those of Filson: "It is difficult to review a book with which the reviewer finds himself agreeing so largely" (*Review: F. FILSON, Origins of the Gospels, 1938*, in *ATR* 21 [1939] 53). He observed that while Filson affirmed the existence of Q, he did not support the view that Proto-Lk ever assumed the form of a document (p. 54).

111. H. BALMFORTH, *The Gospel According to Saint Luke in the Revised Version with Introduction and Commentary* (The Clarendon Bible), Oxford, 1930, p. 15. The book was obviously a popular resource as it went through subsequent printings in 1933, 1941, 1944, 1946, 1949 and 1958.

112. *Ibid.*, p. 9; cf. p. 7.

113. *Ibid.*, p. 11-12.

would have its own collection. But the attempt to find corroborative evidence from Lk. is doomed to disappointment, when we consider that no surviving peculiarities of Marcan vocabulary or style distinguish those passages of Lk. which are derived from Mk. Mk. we know; Q we can test because *two* extant works use it; but L is unverifiable. Nor can we ever be sure that, even if a document L existed, all the matter peculiar to Lk. is derived from it: some may be obtained orally, some from other documents, as in all probability the birth and infancy narrative was. With this inconclusive result we have perforce to be content. By 'L' we can signify nothing more precise than 'material found only in Lk., which possibly comes from a documentary source'"[114].

Balmforth attributed the denials (22,55-62) to Mk, though allowing that some of the differences stemmed from 'L'. Oral tradition supplied v. 61. The mockery (22,63-65) was regarded as distinct from that recounted in Mk 14,65. Though both accounts "may be equally authentic", the Lukan version had the edge because of the plausibility that the guards mistreated Jesus. The section 22,66–23,25 was entitled "The Trials before the Sanhedrin, Pilate, and Herod". Balmforth adopted a bit of a harmonistic approach in attempting to reconcile the trial accounts in Mk, Lk and Jn. The omission of a night trial in Lk was explained as only an informal hearing, which Luke considered too insignificant to report. In seeking to resolve the question whether the claim to be the Messiah or the Son of God was blasphemy, Balmforth argued that Luke only implied what Mark stated explicitly (Mk 14,63-64). Luke used the term in a "much wider sense" (5,21; 12,10)[115]. Quite remarkably, Balmforth passed over 23,3 in silence.

The abruptness at 23,18 was due to the insertion of a Markan element into the narrative. It was atypical of Luke's otherwise skillfull handling of such material. The evangelist cast Pilate in a positive light as part of the apologia toward Rome.

Balmforth suggested that the Herod story derived from Joanna, but that Herod's trial was not a trial in the strict sense[116]. Concerning the transfer and consultation, Balmforth termed it "a gracious act" and added that the source of the enmity between the two rulers was unknown.

Easton credited Balmforth with a superb familiarity with the "critical literature", though by citing various scholarly positions, exceeded the needs and abilities of his intended readership[117]. Such an impression was just the opposite of the reviewer who maintained that Balmforth achieved his purpose for such a diverse audience[118]. While Balmforth drew upon the works of Streeter and Taylor, it was apparent he was not content simply to repeat their research, but investigated the passages himself.

114. *Ibid.*, p. 12. Balmforth did not explicitly indicate the source of his quote.
115. *Ibid.*, p. 300.
116. *Ibid.*, p. 301; cf. p. 299.
117. *ATR* 13 (1931) 90.
118. *ExpT* 41 (1929-30) 546.

Hoskyns agreed that Balmforth succeeded in writing "the almost perfect commentary" for his target readership[119]. Balmforth was not so successful in nuancing his position where it pertained to Proto-Lk. "On certain occasions Mr. Balmforth has taken a definite side in a critical controversy when he might, with advantage, have left the issue far more uncertain. ... More serious is the general acceptance of Canon Streeter's Proto-Lk hypothesis (p. 10-14), and the consequent loss of an important testing of St. Luke's editorial possibilities"[120]. Hoskyns further took Balmforth to task for explaining the great omission by means of a defective copy of Mk.

Though William MANSON (1930) was able to announce that "it is now established beyond reasonable doubt that one of the sources of Luke was the gospel of Mark", he concluded that it did not form the basis of Luke's passion narrative[121]. Nonetheless, Luke used Mk in that section of his Gospel. For much of the material in the passion and resurrection narratives Luke drew on a third source or a group of sources. According to Manson, Luke followed Mk's order but Manson reasoned that in the Lukan passion narrative he was not following Mk because there were twelve transpositions[122]. Manson contended that various traditions were extent in the early period of the church. Luke's source enjoyed a higher degree of probability than Mark's[123]. The proposal of a special source notwithstanding, Manson attributed the exoneration of Pilate, if not the increased responsibility of the Jews, to an apologetic of Luke[124]. Manson argued that the Sanhedrin did not have the power of capital punishment[125]. Because of the response of Jesus in 22,69 Manson regarded the account as coming from Luke's source. Luke simply preferred this tradition. The Judean source, rather than Luke himself, was credited with the charges in 23,2. Manson maintained that Luke followed Mk in 23,18-22, without relinquishing the influence of the source which cast Pilate in a more favorable light[126]. Luke's redaction of Mk included condensation of narrative as well as improvement by means of language and style. Luke was not wont to offer indications of time or place where they were lacking in Mk[127].

Though the theory that Q and L had previously been combined into a written source enjoyed a certain popularity, Manson decried its characterization of Luke as a compiler. Another view that Luke gathered the L material and combined it

119. *TLond* 22 (1931) 350.
120. *Ibid.*, p. 351.
121. W. MANSON, *The Gospel of Luke* (The Moffatt NT Commentary), London - New York, 1930, p. xiii-xiv; cf. p. xix. Two reasons offered in support of his conclusion were the presence of a great deal of special material and changes in order.
122. *Ibid.*, p. xv; cf. p. xix.
123. *Ibid.*, p. 251.
124. *Ibid.*, p. 255.
125. *Ibid.*, p. 254.
126. *Ibid.*, p. 257.
127. *Ibid.*, p. xv.

with Q was given new life "in an interesting form" by Streeter and Taylor[128]. Manson remained uncommitted, while saying that the special material did indeed stem from "a Judean or Jerusalem source". This was clear because of 1) evidence of familiarity with those from the original circle of Jesus, 2) the theme of poverty and wealth, and 3) its focus on Jerusalem and its environs[129].

Manson subscribed to the view that the Herod episode was "controlled by a definite tradition of fact", the purpose of its inclusion being to emphasize the rejection of Jesus by all the Jews[130]. Easton was much more disposed to the view of Manson who adopted the three document hypothesis than Creed, though Manson "has reached his own conclusions about the extent of L"[131].

Wilhelm BUSSMANN (1931) provided a useful overview and comparison of the extent of the special L source as determined by various scholars in the period extending from 1863 through 1925[132]. Other questions with which he was concerned included whether the tradition was written or oral. Did it represented various perspectives or was it unified? And if it can be shown that Luke relied on one or more written sources, were they revised stylistically or taken over as they were[133]?

Lowther Clarke regarded Bussmann's work as a warning "against accepting current hypotheses too readily"[134]. Bussmann proposed that there first existed "a historical source", designated by the letter G. The author of Lk, using this as the base document, joined other sources to it. Bussmann, according to Lowther Clarke, was too locked into his thinking which required the view that the variations in the tradition giving rise to the Synoptics were due to written sources[135]. Moreover, in the third volume which treated the Synoptics, Bussmann had not taken advantage of the studies of other scholars available to him.

---

128. *Ibid.*, p. xix.

129. *Ibid.*, p. xx. Later Manson declared that Luke, in concert with whatever sources he may have been using, highlighted the aspect of rich/poor (p. xxvi).

130. *Ibid.*, p. 256.

131. *ATR* 13 (1931) 89.

132. W. BUSSMANN, *Synoptischen Studien. 3. Zu den Sonderquellen*, Halle, 1931, p. 89-97. Feine: 22,54-62.63-71;23,1-12.13-25;Hawkins: 23,7-12; Wernle: 23,6-12; J. Weiss: 23,6-9.11-12; B. Weiss: 22,39-24,51;G.H. Müller: 22,54.55-61.63-65.66-71;23,1-5.6-12.13-16.18-19.20-23.24-25 with contents which were connected, referred to the presentation of another source, mostly G.; Spitta: 23,6-12; K.L. Schmidt: a few pieces from the passion narrative, especially 23,6-12; Bultmann argued that occasionally in the passion narrative material was drawn from a source other than Mk or Q; E. Meyer: additions in the passion narrative, as for example 23,6-12; Streeter: 22,61a.68.70; 23,2.4-12.13-19; Larfeld: 22,65.68; 23,2.5.6-12.13-16.

133. *Ibid.*, p. 89.

134. *TLond* 21 (1930) 55.

135. *TLond* 24 (1932) 300: "The Gospels are treated as rigidly literary documents, instead of being the literary representation of the varying types of preaching".

Easton acclaimed Bussmann's first two volumes for the "painstaking" depth of investigation, though the results were "a little too simple"[136]. Easton lamented the fact that Bussmann's first two volumes had "not received the attention it deserves, because scholars are not patient enough to wade through it"[137]. Easton highlighted a defect, influenced by B. Weiss, in which the Gospels were seen as little more than a collection of various sources. The critic then set about attempting to disentangle such a conglomeration[138]. Yet, Lowther Clarke stated that Lk was a prime example of this type of composition and claimed that Matthew and even Mark were much more creative in revising their sources.

Friedrich HAUCK (1934) preferred to leave open the question of sources for the Lukan passion narrative, though for the Herod pericope, as for a few other scenes (Lk 22,31f.35-38; 23,6-12.27-31) he opined that Luke possessed "weitere Überlieferungen"[139]. Yet, Hauck's continuing struggle to determine the solution was evident later when he conceded that the idea that Luke reworked Mk for the Herod scene (23,6-16) was "wohl möglich"[140]. Hauck took notice of the attempts of G.H. Müller and Perry to advocate a complete independent source, as well as efforts of Spitta, Bussmann and Procksch to recommend dependence upon a GS while Lietzmann argued that the changes reflected Luke's literary intervention. Hauck expressed some reservation regarding Lietzmann's perspective: "Das schriftstellerische Können und Gestalten des Lk ist gewiss nicht gering anzuschlagen"[141]. To attribute all changes to Luke's design for literary improvement will not completely convince. Hauck perceived Luke, not as a theologian, but as one who passed along the traditions[142].

Historically speaking, although it offered no essential impulse, Hauck did not abandon the possibility that the episode was due to another tradition, but admitted that the case for Dibelius's view that it arose from Ps 2 was strengthened[143]. The relationship of the two leaders coincided with historical reality according to Philo[144]. Herod's possible presence in Jerusalem for the feast made the story feasible.

On the other hand, the silence of Jesus (23,9) was drawn from Mk 15,4 but Hauck also compared the Servant of God (Is 53,7) and the Mithras liturgy[145]. Dissatisfied with the interpretation that the vesture, a white garment, was not an

---

136. *ATR* 13 (1931) 81.
137. *ATR* 14 (1931) 74.
138. The similarity with the critique of Lowther Clarke on this point is worth noting.
139. F. HAUCK, *Das Evangelium des Lukas*, Leipzig, 1934, p. 6; cf. p. 276, 278.
140. *Ibid.*, p. 276.
141. *Ibid.* See also p. 3, 6.
142. *Ibid.*, p. 10.
143. *Ibid.*, p. 278. Concerning the proposal of the origin in Ps 2 Hauck referred to Feigel, Dibelius, Bultmann and Bertram. Cf. p. 279.
144. *Ibid.*, p. 279.
145. *Ibid.*

indication of Jesus' innocence, Hauck viewed it as another element of the mockery. But he understood the garment on a symbolic level as a sign to Pilate that Jesus was not politically a threat.

The purpose of the scene was to provide an additional witness to the innocence of Jesus[146]. Herod's participation was reinforced and confirmed by Pilate's judgment of guiltlessness. Verses 10-12 were possibly an "alte Ausmalung"[147].

Lucien CERFAUX (1935) observing that Lukan dependence upon Mk was well established, emphasized there were special problems associated with the account of the passion[148]. He referred to Feine, B. Weiss, Wendt, Weizsäcker and Stanton as precursors of Streeter and Taylor. Cerfaux mentioned B.S. Easton and T.W. Manson as adherents and M. Goguel and J.M. Creed as opponents. But the work of Bussmann, Streeter and Schlatter suggested to Cerfaux that Luke employed a non-Markan Gospel account. Cerfaux conceived of the special source as being based on an Aramaic tradition which the apostle Matthew composed[149]. This distinguished his solution from that of Streeter and Taylor, who claimed that Luke arranged the material, but he likened his view to theirs insofar as Lk was based on an early Gospel into which three Markan sections were inserted. The same characteristics which had been used to describe Proto-Lk, Cerfaux assigned to Proto-Mt[150]. Cerfaux (1957) adopted the view that Luke had access to another source which recounted the events of the passion[151].

146. *Ibid.*, p. 278; cf. p. 276.
147. *Ibid.*, p. 279.
148. *À propos des sources du troisième évangile: proto-Luc ou proto-Matthieu*, in *ETL* 12 (1935) 5-27 (= *Recueil Lucien Cerfaux* [BETL, 6-7], Gembloux, 1954, 389-414).
149. *Ibid.*, p. 27 (= 27).
150. *Ibid.*, p. 26 (= 1954, p. 413).
151. *En marge de la Question synoptique*, in J. HEUSCHEN (ed.), *Les formation des Évangiles*, Brugge, 1957, 24-33, p. 31 (= *Recueil Lucien Cerfaux* [BETL, 18], Gembloux, 1962, 99-110, p. 107): "*Lc.* pourrait nous avoir conservé en partie une autre version des événements, qui manifeste plus d'émotion et d'efficience littéraire d'évocation". See also Cerfaux's comment about form criticism (p. 33 = 110). The essays contained in this volume consisted in presentations at the Louvain Bible Days in 1955. In the same volume J. HEUSCHEN noted that the Proto-Lk hypothesis was at that time very strongly attacked. Those opposed included Gilmour, and prior to him, Goguel (1933), Creed (1934) and Cerfaux (1935) (*La Formation des évangiles*, in *La Formation des évangiles*, Brugge, 1957, 11-23, p. 20). He further noted that P. Parker preferred the proto-Lukan theory (p. 21, n. 4. cf. P. PARKER, *The Gospel Before Mark*, Chicago, 1953). J. CAMBIER, who collaborated with Cerfaux in the article on Luke in the *DBS* wrote on the historicity of the Synoptic Gospels and form criticism. In discussing Dibelius's article of 1915, *Herodes und Pilatus*, he observed: "On le voit, la position de Dibelius paraît assez modérée, ici comme dans l'ensemble de ses études sur les récits de la Passion; il essaie de rendre compte de leurs caractéristiques littéraires, de leur genèse et de leur composition" (*Historicité des évangiles synoptique et Formgeschichte*, in *La formation des évangiles* [RB, 2], Brugge, 1957, 195-212, p. 200). See n. 1 regarding Acts 4,25-27. Cambier's conclusion regarding the use of a special source in the Lukan passion was: "Luc doit suivre ici une autre tradition, et la façon dont il la présente ne va pas d'ailleurs sans une certaine confusion, comme les exégètes l'ont fait

Cerfaux (1957) held that "l'hypothèse la meilleure" was the one that Luke possessed a different passion source than the one that served as the basis for Mk and Mt[152]. It probably went back to Aramaic Mt (Mg). This passion source was combined with material from Mk. In addition, Luke had access to information which was unique to him, but Cerfaux did not distinguish where he would assign the Herod pericope.

The position of Cerfaux on the original arrangement of the literary units in the pre-Synoptic tradition was criticized by Léon-Dufour. He quoted the Louvain professor whose view was very reminiscent of Dibelius. "The Passion narrative forms the kernel of a connected account which begins with the first announcement of the Passion at Caesarea Philippi". Cerfaux was faulted for underestimating the role of the evangelists in the composition of their respective Gospels[153].

E. Basil REDLICH (1936), admitting that "the evidence for the priority of Mk is irrefutable and conclusive"[154], nonetheless argued in favor of Proto-Lk[155]. The section 22,14 to the end of the Gospel was regarded as "non-Marcan in main"[156]. Of the thirteen reasons adduced in support of the special source, most were simply a repetition of arguments put forward by Streeter and Taylor. Redlich articulated as one of his arguments that the Markan material was so scarce, that it would not constitute a complete narrative. This argument was likewise raised precisely by the opponents of the hypothesis, that what was designated as the L material was fragmentary and could not stand on its own[157]. This, combined with his next bit

---

remarquer" (p. 209). He cited as an example J.H. BERNARD, *Gospel According to St. John* (ICC), Vol. 2, Edinburgh - New York, 1928, p. 458: "Lk., in short, follows a different tradition from that of Mk. and Mt. in his narrative of the Eucharist".

152. L. CERFAUX and J. CAMBIER, *Luc*, in *DBS* 5, p. 569.

153. X. LÉON-DUFOUR, *The Synoptic Gospels*, New York, 1965, p. 309. In the 1976 edition, Léon-Dufour significantly revised this section of his work. He conceded that though Cerfaux presented a very interesting hypothesis, it slipped into fuzziness and his theory of multiple documentation had not been systematically established (1976, p. 205). He noted further that A. Gaboury made a similar suggestion (*La structure des évangiles synoptiques* [NTSuppl, 22], Leiden, 1970. Diss. PBC, 1962, dir. X. LÉON-DUFOUR). Consult the appraisal of Gaboury's hypothesis by F. NEIRYNCK, *The Gospel of Matthew and Literary Criticism. A Critical Analysis of A. Gaboury's Hypothesis*, in M. DIDIER (ed.), *L'évangile selon Matthieu* (BETL, 29), Gembloux, 1971, 37-69 (= *Evangelica*, p. 691-723).

154. E.B. REDLICH, *The Student's Introduction to the Synoptic Gospels*, London, 1936, p. 39. The book was based primarily upon the research of English scholars (p. viii). This may be said to be one of the weaknesses of the text.

155. *Ibid.*, p. 92: "Streeter's view has gained support from some New Testament scholars, and it is the view adopted in this book. It is reasonable and justifiable" (cf. p. 18). Proto-Lk was dated at about 60 AD (p. 106). Redlich offered his version of the probable text of L (p. 219-244).

156. *Ibid.*, p. 94. Those verses or parts of verses ascribed to Mk were: 22,54-62.71; 23,3.17 ("probably scribal").25. The account of L would have contained: 22,63-65.66-70; 23,1-2.4-24 (p. 99).

157. *Ibid.*, p. 104.

of evidence, did not prove what he purported to demonstrate[158]. What was not clear was why Luke would have preferred the non-Markan version, supported by information from Philip the evangelist and his daughters, as opposed to Mk, the authenticity of which rested upon Peter and Mk[159].

Redlich drew attention to twelve transpositions, showing an obvious indebtedness to Hawkins[160]. Since Redlich subscribed to the Proto-Lk theory, he believed that the changes resulted from the insertion of Markan material[161]. He maintained that both trials were required in order for Jesus to be executed[162]. The first, was a "preliminary inquiry", the second, a formal trial. The trial before Pilate took place because of Jesus' insistence on hearing the evidence of witnesses. There was nothing in the text of the Synoptics to support this. Furthermore, Redlich ascribed the Jewish trial to L. Surprisingly, no mention of Jesus' request was found in Redlich's proposed text of L[163]. It seemed, rather, that he was borrowing from Paul's trial experience (cf. Acts 25,11.16-19) and imposing it upon that of Jesus[164].

Like Harnack, Redlich believed that Philip the evangelist and his daughters were possibly the source of the reliable information about the life of Jesus[165]. In the vein of Streeter and Taylor, Redlich subscribed to the idea that Luke authored both L and Proto-Lk[166]. Contrary to a vast number of scholars, Redlich further suggested that Luke was possibly the author of Q. Even if one were to reject what Redlich believed to be a solid hypothesis, still the four-document theory of Streeter would remain unscathed. The value of Redlich's contribution to the discussion, lies not in its originality, but in its clear and systematic presentation of the arguments in favor of the hypothesis.

While Grant admired Redlich's "very concise text-book" in the line of Streeter, he expressed regret that the author was prone "to push his conclusions a little too rigorously and to claim for them more support than most scholars would be willing

---

158. *Ibid*. Redlich's sixth piece of evidence favoring Proto-Lk was: "The assumption explains Luke's preference for the non-Marcan version as a whole" (p. 104). Aside from being unclear as to whether the "assumption" referred to the whole theory or the evidence listed in no. 5, his argument in no way explained Luke's preference, since Luke would have had the Markan passion narrative before him, as Redlich would readily agree, because he assumed that Luke was conflating his two sources of L and Mk.

159. *Ibid*., p. 96.

160. *Ibid*., p. 102-103. The two pertaining to the section of the passion with which we are concerned were the denials and mockery (nos. 5 and 6).

161. *Ibid*., p. 104, no. 4.

162. *Ibid*., p. 185.

163. *Ibid*., p. 239.

164. *Ibid*. Cf. p. 186. When Redlich related the words of Jesus uttered before the Sanhedrin (22,69) he quoted the Markan text in his "outline of the Life of Christ" (p. 185). However, he earlier attributed this verse to L (p. 99).

165. *Ibid*., p. 108.

166. *Ibid*. This authorship was predicated upon similarities with Acts: 1) an obvious interest in Samaria and Samaritans; 2) emphasis on Gentile Christianity; 3) universal salvation; 4) the prominence of women; 5) universal scope of the Christian missionary efforts.

to grant ..."[167]. A.R. Vidler complained that Redlich was not balanced in his approach, ignoring the opposing position espoused by Creed and other scholars[168].

Redlich continued his defense of the Lukan independent tradition in the passion narrative in his later work (1939) on form criticism[169]. The weight of his argument rested upon the transpositions and the relative completeness of the non-Markan account when the Markan elements were deleted[170]. All this led Redlich to a rather puzzling conclusion in light of his previous endorsement of Markan priority. "Thus we conclude that there are certainly three Passion Narratives in the Gospels and indications of a fourth in Mark"[171].

Karl RENGSTORF (1937), adhering to the view that Luke made use of Mk, adopting its layout ("Aufriss"), made it clear that Lk and Mk were not dependent upon some common source. This was made evident from a comparison of the order of material found in Mt[172]. Luke knew and used Mt[173]. The material special to Lk was spread throughout the entire Gospel[174]. Agreeing with A. Schlatter on several points, Rengstorf subscribed to the view that Luke made use of three sources, Mk, Q and a third source containing special material, in addition to some individual traditions[175].

Pointing to the uniqueness of the Lukan account of the passion Rengstorf insisted that a special tradition contained the joint accounts of the Sanhedrin trial and the denials of Peter[176]. The dissimilarity of the Lukan account became evident when contrasted with Mk and Mt[177]. The connections with Mk in 22,54-

167. *ATR* 18 (1936) 187. But earlier Grant conceded: "It is perhaps inevitable in a text book that the author should be dogmatic rather than tentative ...".

168. *TLond* 32 (1936) 376.

169. *Form Criticism. Its Value and Limitations*, London, 1939, [R]1948, p. 167.

170. *Ibid.* Redlich, as in his earlier work, presented a written narrative of what he supposed the text of L must have contained. The only differences when compared with what he had offered in *The Student's Introduction*, p. 239-240, were that three units unique to Lk (23,6-12.27-31.39-43) were now bracketed, in view of the possibility that they were originally independent units (p. 164).

171. *Ibid.*, p. 176.

172. K. RENGSTORF, *Das Evangelium nach Lukas*, Göttingen, 1937, p. 5; see also p. 10. Cf. [4]1949, p. 7, [12]1967, p. 7, [14]1969, p. 7. Rengstorf referred to the following commentaries: Wellhausen (1904), Zahn (1920), Klostermann ([2]1929), Schlatter (1931), Hauck (1934), in addition to Schlatter, *Erläuterungen* ([4]1928), J. Weiss, *Die drei älteren Evangelien* ([3]1917), Joh. Jeremias (1930) (RENGSTORF, *Lukas*, 1937, p. 9).

173. *Ibid.*, p. 6: "Die folgende Erklärung des Lukas-Evangeliums geht deshalb davon aus, dass sein Verfasser das Matthäus-Evangelium gekannt und benutzt hat". Cf. [4]1949, p. 8, and [12]1967, p. 9.

174. It was in this context that Rengstorf wrote of the "eigenartigen Leidensgeschichte" (p. 7). Commenting on the Prologue he declared: "Mit Sicherheit hat er aber ausser dem Bericht des Markus weitere umfangreiche Überlieferungen benutzt, die sich in den älteren Evangelien nicht finden und uns somit nur bei ihm erhalten sind" (p. 10). Cf. [4]1949, p. 8, and [12]1967, p. 9.

175. *Ibid.*, p. 8. Cf. [4]1949, p. 10, and [12]1967, p. 11.

176. *Ibid.*, p. 236. Cf. [4]1949, p. 245, and [12]1967, p. 256.

177. *Ibid.*, p. 237. Cf. [4]1949, p. 246, and [12]1967, p. 257.

71 were "nur sehr spärlich"[178]. Possible Markan influence was seen in 22,54 (Mk 14,43f.).59ff.(Mk 14,70ff), concluding that Luke had not made great changes to his source. Jesus was portrayed as a prophet in the special tradition of Lk. The detail that the trial took place at daybreak corresponded with rabbinic rules.

The scene of Peter's denial was clearly anchored in the special Lukan tradition[179]. The possible influence of Mk 14,65 in 22,64 as well as the MA in 22,62 / Mt 26,75b were noted[180]. The omission of the witnesses in the trial was not an argument against the historicity of the account in Rengstorf's opinion[181]. He also sided with those who argued that during the time of Jesus the Sanhedrin did not have the power to impose the death penalty[182].

In the account of Jesus before Pilate (23,1-7) Luke also followed his special source[183]. The condemnation of Jesus by Pilate (23,13-25) was so distinctive that this section of Lk was not derived from the other Synoptics[184].

The episode of Jesus before Herod (23,8-12) stemmed from Luke's special tradition[185]. It was noted that already in 9,9 Herod expressed a wish to meet Jesus. The mockery with the splendid garment pointed to the political harmlessness of Jesus, even as he regarded the dazzling apparel as that belonging to a king. Rengstorf responded to Dibelius's suggestion that the story arose from Ps 2, but the suggestion was rejected on the grounds that there was no reason for doubting the existing story[186].

In treating Joanna (8,3) Rengstorf observed that her husband served Herod Antipas. This, combined with the mention of her in the passion narrative and finally in 24,10 was indication that Luke had access to a special tradition[187].

Writing in 1940 of the Sanhedrin trial of Jesus, the famed director of l'École Biblique de Jerusalem, Pierre BENOIT[188] set as his goal a threefold purpose: "pour y retrouver la suite et la nature de faits, en apprécier la valeur historique, enfin en dégager la portée essentielle, c'est-à-dire les vrais motifs qui amenèrent

---

178. *Ibid.*

179. *Ibid.*, p. 239. Cf. [12]1967, p. 258.

180. *Ibid.* Cf. [4]1949, p. 246, and [12]1967, p. 258, to which were added the MA in 22,64 / Mt 26,68.

181. *Ibid.*, p. 240. Cf. [4]1949, p. 248, and [12]1967, p. 258.

182. *Ibid.*, p. 241. So [4]1949, p. 248, and cf. [12]1967, p. 260.

183. *Ibid.*, p. 242. So [4]1949, p. 250, and [12]1967, p. 260. Rengstorf added an excursus: "*Pilatus und seine Rolle in der Passionsgeschichte*" ([4]1949, p. 251-252, and [12]1967, p. 262-263).

184. *Ibid.*, p. 248. See also p. 249. So [4]1949, p. 256, and [12]1967, p. 267.

185. *Ibid.*, p. 245. So [4]1949, p. 250, and [12]1967, p. 263. Note further his discussion of the origin of the Herod pericope, 1937, p. 246. Cf. [4]1949, p. 254, and [12]1967, p. 264-265.

186. *Ibid.*, 1937, p. 246.

187. *Ibid.*, p. 92. Cf. [4]1949, p. 103, and [12]1967, p. 104-105.

188. P. BENOIT, *Le procès de Jésus*, in *Vie Intellectuelle* 2 (1940) 200-213; [*II*] 3 (1940) 371-378; [*III*] 4 (1940) 54-64 (= *Exégèse et Théologie*, Vol. 1, Paris, 1961, 265-289 = *The Trial of Jesus*, in ID., *Jesus and the Gospel*, Vol. 1, Tr. B. WEATHERHEAD, New York, 1973, 123-146).

la condamnation de Jésus, et par suite les vrais responsables"[189]. Observing that all three Synoptics were relating the same Sanhedrin trial, Benoit concluded that Luke's account was probably the historically reliable one, that the trial took place in the morning and that the order recounted in Lk and Jn was correct[190].

Shortly thereafter (1943) Benoit again took up the question of whether there had been one or two Sanhedrin trials and whether they were held in the morning or at night[191]. Admitting the possibility that Luke could have omitted one account of the Sanhedrin trial Benoit detected that Luke's account "ressemble tout à fait" the Markan and Matthean renditions. He repeated his contention that Lk and Jn proved there was only a single Sanhedrin trial, held in the morning[192].

The verses 22,67-71 did indeed depend upon Mk 14,61-64 in Benoit's considered opinion, acknowledging that the omission of the Temple reference was possibly reserved for Acts 6,14[193]. Markan dependence was proven by 22,71a. However, the Lukan order for the mockery and Sanhedrin trial, which was judged superior to that of Mt and Mk, was thought to be due to a special source[194]. It

189. BENOIT, Le procès de Jésus, in Viel 2 (1940) 202 (= ExT, Vol. 1, p. 266 = 124).

190. Ibid., 203, 205 (= ExT, Vol. 1, p. 268, 269 = 125, 127).

191. BENOIT, Jésus devant le sanhédrin, in Angelicum 20 (1943) 143-165 (= ExT, Vol. 1, 290-311 = 147-166). He complimented and recommended the study and bibliography of VOSTÉ, De Passione (1943, p. 143, n. 1 = ExT, p. 290, n. 1 = 147, n. 1).

192. BENOIT, Jésus devant le sanhédrin, in Angelicum 20 (1943) 157 (= ExT, Vol. 1, 303 = 159). As to how Mt and Mk came to have two sessions Benoit remarked: "Ceux-ci [Mt, Mk] parlent de deux séances parce qu'il y eut bien deux séances, mais ils ont substitué à l'interrogatoire nocturne et privé chez Anne le récit de la session matinale et officielle du Sanhédrin, ce qui a entrainé, en eux-mêmes et part rapport aux autres évangiles, toutes les difficultés que nous avons dites" (Jésus devant le sanhédrin, in Angelicum 20 [1943] 160 = ExT, Vol. 1, p. 306 = 162).

193. BENOIT, Jésus devant le sanhédrin, in Angelicum 20 (1943) 149 (= ExT, Vol. 1, p. 295 = 152). Benoit called attention to other Lukan redaction such as the replacement of τοῦ εὐλογητοῦ with τοῦ θεοῦ to make it understandable for his readers. Likewise, ὄψεσθε was changed in favor of ἔσται so as to avoid the possible confusion (Jésus devant le sanhédrin, in Angelicum 20 [1943] 149, n. 3 = ExT, Vol. 1, p. 296, n. 2 = 153, n. 1).

194. BENOIT, Jésus devant le sanhédrin, in Angelicum 20 (1943) 151 (= ExT, Vol. 1, p. 297 = 154). His position is worth quoting in full: "Il n'y a d'ailleurs aucune difficulté à penser que Luc doit ce meilleur arrangement des choses à une tradition originale. Car il paraît établi, par bien d'autres traits, qu'il dispose, spécialement pour la Passion, d'une source personnelle, distincte de Mc., à l'aide de laquelle il le complète et le corrige. Il est donc tout spontané d'attribuer à cette tradition propre l'ordre meilleur par lequel il éclaire les difficultés soulevées par les récits de Mt. et de Mc. L'examen du témoignage de S. Jean va confirmer cette préférence que mérite l'ordre de Luc".

Benoit cited various authors in a note concerning the special passion source, among them Hawkins (1911), Spitta (1912), Danby (1920), Streeter (1924), Schlatter (1931), and Bultmann, Geschichte, ²1931. Taylor, Behind (1926) and Formation (1933) and especially Easton (1926) were highlighted as those who "revendiquent l'originalité de Luc jusque dans sa rédaction". But Benoit preferred to side with Bultmann maintaining that the order was due to the special Lukan tradition, while the narrative was dependent particularly upon Mk (Jésus devant, p. 151, n. 1 = ExT, Vol. 1, p. 297, n. 3 = 154, n. 1).

was more conceivable that Jesus was mocked by guards than by those who had tried him.

Focusing on the mockery (1962) Benoit[195] again ascribed the Lukan account of the mockery to a special source because the actors and their actions were different from those found in Mk. He judged Bultmann's analysis "complexe"[196]. Benoit reiterated his viewpoint that Lk and Jn possessed the better traditions[197]. In addition, the Markan account of the denials of Peter reflected two underlying traditions, one which was close to that of Lk and the other to Jn. The Lukan report represented a version which evolved, though the Markan peculiarities dropped out. Also in the case of the story of the Sanhedrin trial there were two traditions, the better of them "est représentée par Lc"[198].

Benoit termed Streeter's attempt to resolve the MA in 22,64 / Mt 26,68 by dropping the words from Mt as "une solution désespérée"[199]. Accordingly, the more acceptable explanation was to be found in the suggestion of a special passion source available to Luke[200].

In his 1966 study of the passion and resurrection Benoit acknowledged that even though Luke depended upon Mk, he also used of a different tradition which provided new material and a better order[201]. Benoit attributed the change in order both to a separate non-Markan tradition as well as to the fluidity of oral tradition[202]. He gave no indication that he assumed the special source for the account of Peter's denial. Much of the difference had to do with improving Mk's vocabulary. Luke used συλλαβόντες "a more elegant and a more classical" term in place of Mk's κρατοῦσιν. Likewise, the Lukan ἠκολούθει "is so much more expressive" in contrast to Mk's ἠκολούθεν. Though many scholars regarded v. 61 as a storyteller's detail, Benoit considered it historical[203]. For Benoit the MA of v. 62 was best explained by a copyist who changed Lk's text in order to make it

195. BENOIT, *Les outrages à Jésus prophète (Mc xiv 65 par.)*, in W. VAN UNNIK (ed.), *Neotestamentica et Patristica* (NTSuppl, 6), FS O. CULLMANN, Leiden, 1962, 92-110 (= *ExT*, Vol. 3, Paris, 1968, 251-269).

196. *Les outrages*, p. 101, n. 1 (= 260, n. 1). Cf. BULTMANN, *GST*, ³1957, p. 293.

197. BENOIT, *Les outrages*, p. 110 (= 268-269). Benoit noted that the mockery of Herod was found only in 23,11 and the mockery by the Roman soldiers (Mk 15,20) was omitted by Luke (p. 93, n. 3 = 252, n. 3).

198. *Les outrages*, p. 104-105 (= 263).

199. *Les outrages*, p. 100 (= 259). See F. NEIRYNCK, ΤΙΣ ΕΣΤΙΝ Ο ΠΑΙΣΑΣ ΣΕ, 1987, p. 8, n. 22, 9-10, n. 32.

200. BENOIT, *Les outrages*, p. 101 (= 260). On the unlikelihood of Matthew's use of Lk or a source common to both Mt and Lk see p. 106 (= 265). The solution of a source common to both Mt and Lk was adopted, for example, by B. DE SOLAGES, *Synopse grecque des évangiles*, Leiden - Toulouse, 1959, p. 1065 (*Les outrages*, p. 106, n. 3 = 265, n. 2).

201. BENOIT, *Passion et Résurrection du Seigneur*, Paris, 1966, p. 6 (= *The Passion and Resurrection of Jesus Christ*, tr. B. WEATHERHEAD, New York, 1969, p. viii).

202. *Ibid.*, p. 6, 172 (= viii, 151).

203. *Ibid.*, p. 80 (= 66).

agree with Mt's[204]. Benoit did not recommend adopting the view that the phrase of v. 64 originally appeared in Mk. He did not, however, give a clear answer to what he believed was the solution to this conundrum, though he hinted that it might be harmonization by a copyist[205]. He said nothing specific about the source of the mockery account, only that the synoptic narratives disagree[206]. The account of the Sanhedrin trial varied from the other Synoptics. Benoit indicated that the version of Mk and Mt was more fitting for the Jewish perspective[207]. The deletion of the reference to Jesus coming on the clouds of heaven was made lest any think that Jesus promised an imminent Parousia[208]. Luke offered a different outline from Mk in the account of Jesus' trial before Pilate[209]. Benoit noted the similarities between the Gospel and Acts in presenting Paul and Jesus as being found innocent. This constituted part of Luke's apologia for Christianity toward Rome.

Benoit observed that Jews defended the thesis that the religious authorities of Jesus' time had the right to execute anyone found guilty of a capital offense[210]. If the Jews had been responsible, Jesus would have been stoned. But Benoit countered saying that the Romans restricted that power to themselves, a fact assumed in the writings of Josephus.

The gist of this section was that Pilate unwillingly yielded to the demands of the Jews. The differences in the entire passage of Jesus before Pilate nothwithstanding, Benoit observed that the Lukan account related that the people demanded Jesus' death and Barabbas' freedom as in Mk and Mt[211]. One regrets that Benoit did not offer his idea of the nature or extent of the special tradition Luke was supposed to have relied upon in addition to Mk. Neither had Benoit indicated the manner in which the two sources were utilized in the composition of the passion narrative of Lk. Nevertheless, many of his insights were particularly useful in understanding how Luke was able to improve upon the Markan account of the passion.

Benoit (1940) asserted that though the historicity of the Herod story had been fiercely debated, the account was nonetheless historical[212]. That he was not fully convinced of this position was evident from a subsequent line: "Cette hypothèse garde un caractère conjectural, et on ne la propose qu'avec réserve". Doubt seemed also to surround his idea when he referred to the story as "le vague souvenir"[213].

Arguing that Herod was present in Jerusalem at Passover, Benoit claimed that Pilate empowered Herod to try this case as indicated by the word ἀναπέμπειν. The

204. *Ibid.*, p. 80 (= 67).
205. *Ibid.*, p. 102 (= 87).
206. *Ibid.*, p. 103 (= 87-88).
207. *Ibid.*, p. 128 (= 110).
208. *Ibid.*
209. *Ibid.*, p. 163 (= 142).
210. *Ibid.*, p. 130-131 (= 113-114). The cases of Stephen and James were cited as exceptional (p. 131 = 114).
211. *Ibid.*, p. 167 (= 146).
212. P. BENOIT, *Le procès de Jésus*, in *Viel* 2 (1940) 208 (= *ExT*, Vol. 1, p. 272 = p. 129).
213. BENOIT, *Le procès de Jésus*, in *Viel* 2 (1940) 209 (= *ExT*, Vol. 1, p. 272 = 130).

reason Benoit offered for the transfer was as follows: "Pilate, embarrassé et ne dé-couvrant aucun crime positif dans la vie de ce Galiléen qu'il ne connaît pas, aurait délégué son droit d'instruire l'affaire au tetrarque de Galilée qu'il suppose mieux informé"[214].

The splendid clothing was a cast-off robe of Herod's. The absence of the story from the other Gospels was attributed either to ignorance of the matter on the part of the other Evangelists or intentional omission.

Still later Benoit (1966) continued to defend the Herod story as certainly historical[215]. He adopted this view because Luke appeared to have good information about Herod, the earlier part of the Gospel anticipated the later trial, and there were other instances in history to substantiate the probability of such an event. Benoit rejected the proposal of Dibelius on the grounds that the psalm was too vague to give rise to the creation of such a story[216].

Pierson PARKER (1940) argued that the Gospel according to the Hebrews had some connection to the Proto-Lk described by Streeter[217], though Parker apparently did not completely accept the theory as Streeter proposed it[218]. If his hypothesis were correct, Parker supposed it might strengthen Streeter's theory. The Gospel according to the Hebrews was similar to Proto-Lk in that it "seems to have had alternatives to some accounts" in Mk[219]. Parker also conjectured that this apocryphal work "may have a geographical basis in the city of Caesarea" as Streeter suggested for Proto-Lk[220]. In concluding, Parker stated that "the evidence is short of proof"[221]. He again (1953) supported Streeter's Proto-Lk theory in proposing a gospel prior to Mk[222].

In a 1965 essay treating the phrase τὸν πρῶτον λόγον (Acts 1,1) and the date of Acts Parker posited that the phrase referred to a Proto-Lk similar to the one Streeter defined[223]. Acknowledging that C.S.C. Williams had earlier hypothesized

214. BENOIT, *Le procès de Jésus*, in *VieI* 3 (1940) 376 (= *ExT*, Vol. 1, p. 280 = 137).

215. BENOIT, *Passion*, 1966, p. 166 (= 145).

216. *Ibid.*, p. 165-166 (= 144-145).

217. *A Proto-Lukan Basis for the Gospel according to the Hebrews*, in *JBL* 59 (1940) 471-478.

218. *Ibid.*, p. 472: "Without committing oneself to [Streeter's] theory in its entirety, it is convenient to use his term 'Proto-Luke' to designate the non-Markan part of the Third Gospel".

219. *Ibid.*, p. 477.

220. *Ibid.*, p. 478.

221. *Ibid.* He continued: "Yet the presence in this gospel of Lukan qualities and parallels, the absence from it of definitive Matthean or Markan elements, the failure of its own users to ascribe it to Matthew, and its geographical connection with Luke, all point to one conclusion, viz., that the source of the Gospel according to the Hebrews was not our First Gospel, but was most closely related to sources underlying the non-Markan parts of Luke, that is, Proto-Luke".

222. P. PARKER, *The Gospel Before Mark*, Chicago, IL, 1953, p. 161-162; see also p. 4, 36-37. He maintained, however, that it was "not within the scope of this book to discuss the L source or to prove or disprove the existence of a proto-Luke" (p. 162).

223. *The "Former Treatise" and the Date of Acts*, in *JBL* 84 (1965) 52-58, p. 55: "That is to conclude that the document mentioned in Acts 1,1 was not our canonical Luke, but was an earlier

that "former treatise" referred to Lk minus the supposed Markan additions, Parker distinguished himself from that proposition by arguing that Luke had not read Mk before composing Acts[224]. As to the date of Luke's second volume, he suggested a period not later than 62 or 63 AD[225].

In 1981 Parker argued that "the case for a Proto-Luke seems to me to be stronger than ever"[226]. He revisited the view of C.S.C. Williams that the "former treatise" referred to in Acts 1,1 was Proto-Lk[227]. However, he was "somewhat less confident than formerly of the *definitive* value of statistics"[228]. He also called attention to Robert Lindsey's "strongly argued case for the priority of Luke", though he admitted that he was familiar with Lindsey's research only by means of "personal correspondence and conversations, and from two or three articles in the 1969 *Jerusalem Post*"[229]. Although he did not directly address the MAs he mentioned the 1967-68 proposal of H.P. West that Proto-Lk was the source of Matthew's double tradition was "at least as probable" as the existence of Q[230].

Parker repeated the hypothesis of a gospel prior to Mk in 1983, reiterating his view Luke referred to Proto-Lk in Acts 1,1 when he wrote τὸν πρῶτον λόγον[231]. Further, Parker renewed his assertion that it was possible that Luke may have repeatedly revised Proto-Lk before it took final form[232].

Emanuel HIRSCH (1941) supported the idea that Luke employed various sources in addition to Mk and did so in a very careful manner[233]. Based on the differing

---

edition of Luke's gospel. Specifically, *when Luke wrote Acts he had not read Mark*; and the *'former treatise' was a book very like the Proto-Luke that B.H. Streeter identified"*. See also p. 58.

224. *Ibid.*, p. 55-56. Cf. WILLIAMS, *The Date of Luke-Acts*, in *ExpT* 64 (1952-53) 283-284.

225. PARKER, "*Former Treatise*", p. 53, 54, 55.

226. *A Second Look at "The Gospel before Mark"*, in *JBL* 100 (1981) 389-413, p. 392 (= *SBL 1979 Seminar Papers*, P.J. ACHTEMEIER [ed.], Missoula, MT, p. 147-168, p. 149). *The Second Gospel is Secondary* (= 1979, 151-161; 1981, 395-405), in A.J. BELLINZONI (ed.), *Two-Source Hypothesis*, 1985, p. 205-217.

227. *Ibid.*, p. 392 = 1979, p. 149. See WILLIAMS, *Date*, and *The Acts of the Apostles*, New York, 1957, p. 12-13.

228. PARKER, *Second Look*, p. 393 = 1979, p. 149.

229. *Ibid.*, p. 408, 408-409, n. 29 = 1979, p. 164, 167, n. 15.

230. *Ibid.*, p. 410; cf. 1979, p. 166. See H.P. WEST, *A Primitive Version of Luke in the Composition of Matthew*, in *NTS* 14 (1967-68) 75-95. Note the typographical error in Parker, who listed the author's name as W.P. West.

231. P. PARKER, *The Posteriority of Mark*, in W.R. FARMER (ed.), *New Synoptic Studies. The Cambridge Gospel Conference and Beyond*, Macon, GA, 1983, p. 67-142, esp. p. 128-129. At this time he again mentioned Williams's commentary on Acts and added H.G. RUSSELL, *Which Was First, Luke or Acts?*, in *HTR* 48 (1956) 167-174, and a reference to his own study, P. PARKER, *The "Former Treatise"* (PARKER, *Posteriority*, p. 129, n. 101; p. 126, n. 97).

232. PARKER, *Posteriority*, p. 129.

233. *Frühgeschichte des Evangeliums. 2. Die Vorlagen des Lukas und das Sondergut des Matthäus*, Tübingen, 1941, p. 12-13. See also p. 267, 265. Hirsch distinguished three versions of Mk: "Mk I", the first story teller; "Mk II" the corrected version; "Mk" signaled the result of the fusion of both previous editions of Mk. The redactor who made additions and changes was

answers Jesus gave, Hirsch concluded Luke employed a non-Markan source for the Sahnhedrin trial which omitted the nocturnal trial and shifted the Christ question in the morning session. Further, the account of Peter's denial rested upon a non-Markan source. Hirsch divided the passages into "die Verleugnung des Petrus Luk 22,54-65", "Jesus im Synedrium Lk 22,66-23,1" and "Jesus vor Pilatus Luk 23,2-23,25". For the account of the denial, Luke probably drew from Mk I, though it was possible that he borrowed either from "Lu I" and "Lu II" since "Mk II" entirely eliminated the story. The evangelist was responsible for inserting 22,62 and a few words in 22,64. Other additions from Luke included ἀτενίζειν, and possibly ἀτενίσασα αὐτῷ and παραχρῆμα.

The rendition of events with the Sanhedrin transpired in a manner entirely different from that recounted in "Mk I" and "Mk II". Hirsch highlighted differences such as the absence of reference to witnesses or to the Temple words, the centrality of the question about whether Jesus was the Christ and the variation in vocabulary.

The section of Jesus before Pilate (23,2-25) was based partly upon "Mk II" which was inserted into another source[234]. Confirmation of the Markan basis was found in the verbal agreement of 23,3 / Mk 14,2, and the Barabbas story (23,18-22.25). The other material, 23,2.4-16.23.24, derived from a non-Markan account of the special Lukan source "Lu II" which had been embellished by Mk. This group of verses, 23,2.4-16.23.24, stemmed either from levels of "Lu II" or were insertions by Luke from a third source, namely "Lu I"[235].

Concerning the phenomenon of order Hirsch argued that Luke did not retain Markan order where he was following another source[236]. Admitting that the literary development of the Lukan passion account was the most difficult to ascertain Hirsch proposed that the use of non-Markan *Vorlagen* was more extensive in the passion than in the initial stories of Lk. "Mk II" which served as the basis for the account was simultaneously used with other sources. Distinguishing sources was easier in the case of "Mk II" than for other sources: "Natürlich dürfen wir nicht erwarten, die markusfremden Vorlagen des Luk genau so sauber und rund in Luk erhalten zu finden wie Mk II"[237].

The major changes in the Lukan passion account were due either to "Luk II", Luke's special source which was a redaction of an even earlier version which Hirsch designated as "Luk II*" or to the evangelist himself[238].

---

referred to as "R". A source stemming from the Twelve used by Mk II was designated by "Zw". In addition the abbreviation "Lu I" referred to a version of Q; "Lu II" signified the special Lukan source unavailable to Matthew, the earlier form of this being identified as "Lu II*"; "Luk" referred not only to the Gospel but also its author (*Allgemeine Bemerkungen*, Vol. 2, p. 1).

234. *Frühgeschichte des Evangeliums. 2. Die Vorlagen des Lukas*, p. 268.

235. *Ibid.*, p. 269.

236. *Ibid.*, p. 8.

237. *Ibid.*, p. 13.

238. *Ibid.*, p. 250.

Noting that both Luke and Matthew concluded their accounts of the denial by
Peter with the MA in 22,62 / Mt 26,75 Hirsch surmised that this was evidence of
dependence but did not explain the direction[239]. The MA in 22,64 / Mt 26,68
was borrowed by Luke from a source in common with Mt. "Die Ergänzung ist bei
Luk deutlich als Einschlag aus einer mit Matth gemeinsamen Vorlage in den
Zusammenhang einer ganz andern Vorlage erkennbar"[240]. Both MAs were later
identified as stemming from "Lu I"[241].

Hirsch's position showed similarities on the one hand with Wright and Wautier
d'Aygalliers in positing various editions of Mk and, on the other, with Burkitt,
since some of the details were ascribed to Q.

Hirsch defended the position that in 23,2-25 Luke inserted material from Mk
II into another *Vorlage*[242]. Verse 3 and the Barabbas story were drawn from Mk.
For the rest, there was a lack of close formal and material relation to the Markan
account[243]. Verse 10 was considered an addition of Luke to Lu II (Luke's
Sondervorlage). What was more, Luke was responsible for the further depiction
of the charges from καὶ κωλύοντα to διδόναι (23,2). Jesus' innocence of the
political charge of opposing the tribute to Caesar, was further highlighted, because
of Pilate's declaration. Hirsch concluded that the story may have been inserted by
the last pre-Lukan hand[244].

---

239. *Ibid.*, p. 244. See also p. 247.
240. *Ibid.*, p. 244.
241. *Ibid.*, p. 265. Recently, Neirynck called attention to Hirsch's efforts to suggest that the
"Q source contained a passion narrative, on the basis of *Kleinübereinstimmungen* in Mt 26:50 /
Lk 22:48; Mt 26:64 / Lk 22:69; Mt 26:68 / Lk 22:64; Mt 26:75 / Lk 22:62; Mt 28:19 / Lk
24:47" (*The Minor Agreements and Q*, in R.A. PIPER [ed.], *The Gospel Behind the Gospels.
Current Studies in Q* [NTSuppl, 75] Leiden, 1995, 49-72, esp. p. 50-51). See further NEIRYNCK,
The Minor Agreements of Matthew and Luke against Mark, with a Cumulative List (BETL, 37),
Leuven, 1974, p. 175, 178, 179, 182, 195; *The Minor Agreements in a Horizontal-line Synopsis*
(SNTA, 15), Leuven, 1991.
242. HIRSCH, *Frühgeschichte*. II. *Die Vorlagen*, p. 268 (esp. p. 268-270, 423-424). Such a
conclusion was, in Hirsch's opinion, "besonders klar". Of particular importance were the
abbreviations found on p. 1. Lu II referred to the *Sondervorlage* of Lk which Mt did not use. Lu
II* indicated an older layer of this tradition. In preliminary remarks about the passion narrative,
Hirsch asserted that the evangelist took great care to blend the material drawn from Mk with that
stemming from other sources: "Was das Verfahren des Luk im Einzelnen anlangt, so fällt auf, dass
er in der Vermischung des Markus mit den andern Vorlagen sehr vorsichtig gewesen ist" (p. 13).
243. *Ibid.*, p. 269.
244. *Ibid.*, p. 270. "Vor allem aber mag das Zwischenspiel mit Herodes erst von der letzten
vorlukanischen Hand zugefügt sein". He based his decision on the view that from ἐγὼ ἐνώπιον
(23,14) to ἰδού (23,15) was clearly an insertion. But Hirsch offered no criteria why the insertion
necessarily must have come from a pre-Lukan hand and not from the evangelist himself.
Hirsch admitted the difficulty in determining "mit ausreichender Sicherheit" the various levels
of tradition within Lk II (p. 402). It was peculiar that he assigned the Herod story in Lk II (37,1-
9) as stemming from Luk 23,2-12 (p. 423-424). See the apparatus at the bottom of p. 423. "Luk"
was the designation for both the Gospel and the author (p. 1). Lu II, as a whole, had no historical
value. "Geschichtlich ist die Aufteilung auf die Hände von Lu II belanglos. Dem Lu II-Bericht

Inspired in part by Hirsch's *Frühgeschichte des Evangeliums* and E. Meyer's
idea of a Gospel of the Twelve in *Ursprung und Anfänge des Christentums*, Heinrich
HELMBOLD (1953) drew attention to Luke's reference in the Prologue to πολλοί
(1,1) as proof of the existence of pre-synoptic Gospels among which were a Markan
writing and Q. Luke's compositional method was that "er gibt seine Vorlagen
vollständig, sorgfältig und in ihrer literarischen Ordnung wieder"[245]. Nothing was
arbitrarily omitted. Any serious lucunae between Mk and Lk was due to a damaged
copy of the Markan text. Lk and Mt were based on two differing versions of Mk. Mk
L is the older source for Luke. More recent was the Matthean source Mk M. What
Hirsch designated as Mk I Helmbold termed *Grundschrift EV*. A first revision or
correction of that resulted in Mk II for Hirsch and Mk L for Helmbold. A second
revision or redaction constituted Mk R for Hirsch and Mk M for Helmbold.
Canonical Mk was distinguished from Mk M by only the addition of a few glosses
and the unauthentic Gospel ending[246]. Much of the special material for Lk stemmed
from the Gospel of the Twelve ("der Zwölferquelle", XII = Zw).

The development period for the Gospel of the Twelve was in the 60's AD. Mk
L was composed at the time of the Jewish War and Mk M at the end of the
seventieth year. Rome was the place of origin for both Mk L and Mk M where the
EV had probably been brought by Peter[247].

Like Burkitt, Helmbold adhered to the idea that Q was a complete Gospel
containing a passion and Easter narrative[248]. The sources used by Q included the
Grundschrift EV, the Gospel of the Twelve and small pieces designated as
urmatthäische Schrift LG, which Hirsch termed X. The various versions of Q
included the Aramaic Mt Q (= Q*) and the Greek translation Mt M (= Q). This
latter document was the primary source for Mt but was also used by Luke in a
slightly expanded form Mt L (= Lu I). Further there was a Jewish-Christian
Special Gospel Mt N (termed Ma S by Hirsch) which depended directly upon the
Aramaic Mt Q though it contained some variations of translation. The ecclesiastical
tradition from Jerusalem was reflected in the line Mt M – Mt N – Mt. Mt Q was
completed around the year 70 AD, while Mt L (which possibly stemmed from
Antioch) and Mt N were composed within the following decade. Beyond the official
lines there was also the Special Gospel of Cleophas which Luke highly esteemed Kl
II (= Lu II) which stemmed from an Aramaic writing Kl I (= Lu II*).

The pre-Synoptic Gospels arose from a rich oral tradition which contained
primitive material[249]. Helmbold argued that Luke knew of more than three such
sources which became the basis of his own Gospel (Mk L, Mt L, Kl II). The
Gospel of the Twelve had already been completely subsumed into Mk L and Mt

kommt als Ganzem geschichtlicher Wert nicht zu" (p. 270).
    245. *Vorsynoptische Evangelien*, Stuttgart, 1953, p. 9.
    246. *Ibid.*
    247. *Ibid.*, p. 11.
    248. *Ibid.*
    249. *Ibid.*, p. 15.

L. What was more, the Samaritan Gospel according to Nathanael (Nt) which the primitive Johannine Gospel employed, may also have been known to Luke.

As for the order, Luke generally followed that found in Mk which was his preferred source. The Third Evangelist interrupted this only when he employed another source which had an order different from that of Mk. The great omission (Mk 6,48–8,27) was explained by Helmbold as missing from the text of Mk which Luke was using.

In a review of the work, Philipp Vielhauer noted that Helmbold had set himself against the great defenders of Two-Source Theory and operated out of pure literary criticism, ignoring the input of form criticism[250]. Though difficult to read and "kaum verständlich" without some knowledge of Hirsch's analysis, his study had a great value methodologically: "es zeigt, dass der Weg der synoptischen Quellenanalyse mit der Zweiquellentheorie sein Ende erriecht hat"[251]. Martin LEHMANN (1970), although using the literary-critical method of Hirsch, arrived at conclusions different from him[252].

Though Harald SAHLIN (1945) focused primarily on the Lukan Infancy Narrative, his name should be added to the list of those who adhered to the hypothesis of Proto-Lk[253]. Like Feine, he believed that the special source was unified and lay behind Lk, extending from Lk 1,5 through to the end of Acts 15[254]. Although the author of Proto-Lk was unknown to us, he was a convert from Judaism to Christianity. Syria was his probable place of origin and he possibly came from Antioch. Because Proto-Lk was translated into Greek, it was considerably expanded. Luke, the physician and assistant to Paul, was seen as the person who translated and revised Proto-Lk[255]. Sahlin dated the Proto-Lk document at around 50 AD.

Eduard SCHWEIZER (1950) authored an early article dealing with the issue of Lukan sources[256]. While taking note of the lack of Hebraisms in the passion narra-

---

250. *Gnomon* 26 (1954) 460-462.

251. *Ibid.*, p. 462.

252. *Synoptische Quellenanalyse und die Frage nach dem historischen Jesus*, Berlin, 1970, p. 112. In Lehmann's analysis of the account of Peter's denial, the result was that the Lukan version was based upon Mk in basically the same form as we now possess it. Lehmann opposed Hirsch's view of Mk I and II asserting that the existence of Mk I cannot be proved: "Daran ändert sich auch nichts, wenn jemand die eigene Gestaltung des Lukas bei der Verleugnungsgeschichte geringer ansetzen will und deshalb eine Vorlage neben Markus postuliert". The prediction of the denial, which Luke took over from Mk, was positioned in the farewell address of Jesus. See F. NEIRYNCK, *Duplicate Expressions in the Gospel of Mark*, in *ETL* 48 (1972) 150-209, p. 165, n. 64 (= *Evangelica*, 83-142, p. 98, n. 64), who observed that Lehmann provided a "recent critique of Hirsch's exegesis".

253. H. SAHLIN, *Der Messias und das Gottesvolk. Studien zur protolukanischen Theologie*, Uppsala, 1945. He recounted a brief history of the Proto-Lk theory (p. 8, n. 1).

254. *Ibid.*, p. 9.

255. *Ibid.*, p. 10.

256. E. SCHWEIZER, *Eine hebraisierende Sonderquelle des Lukas?*, in *TZ* 6 (1950) 161-185.

tive[257], he claimed that his source theory approximated that of Streeter. The difference was that rather than combining the *Sondergut* with Q as Streeter asserted, Schweizer proposed that Luke joined it to a collection of miracle stories, which was designated as "W"[258].

In his 1982 commentary, Schweizer lamented that determining to what extent Luke drew upon sources other than Mk "ist kaum lösbar"[259]. Similarly, it cannot be determined with any certainty whether Luke used L in the passion narrative[260]. It was more likely, in Schweizer's opinion, that Luke possessed a continuous written source, rather than was dependent upon oral tradition or even a collection of separate written traditions. Those traditions which appeared to be connected included 22,15-17.24-38.39-53.(54-65).66-71; 23,2.4-16.22-23.27-32. 33b.34a.35-37.39-43.46b.(47).48.55-56; 24,10b.-12.13-53. Further, Schweizer suggested Luke may have been drawing on Mk and Q in various segments of the passion narrative, and that within the fluidity of the community's liturgy, Luke felt free to apply his own style to the account. Though not explaining 23,9-11 as deriving from Mk, Schweizer commented that the charges by the chief priests, Jesus' silence and mockery by means of "royal garments" were situated by Mark within Pilate's trial.

When all was said and done, it was at the analysis of 23,4 that Schweizer's true leanings became evident: "Folgt Lukas einer Quelle, die mehr erzählte? Warum ubernähme er sonst nur V. 3 (unverändert!) aus Mk 15,2?"[261].

For the section 22,54-71 Schweizer argued that Luke was "hoch-wahrscheinlich" drawing upon a tradition that contained much original material. One of the strongest indications that Luke was dependent upon a non-Markan source was that he did not borrow the Jewish death sentence from Mk 14,64[262]. Schweizer also referred to the absence of such material as the witnesses, the Temple saying and the silence of Jesus. Later, he pointed to Acts 7,56, though in his discussion of 22,70 he did not raise it, treating rather Acts 13,33 about the resurrection revealing Jesus' exaltation as the Son of God. Schweizer subscribed to the view that the two male servants who interacted with Peter during his denials fulfilled the legal prescription of Dt 19,15.

Yet some Markan elements were found in the account, such as in 22,69. Other details were ascribed to Luke including interpreting the mockery (22,65) as blasphemy. Schweizer highlighted the possible confusion surrounding αὐτόν (22,63) but explained it either as a remnant from the special source or the result of Luke's occasional clumsy editing. The evangelist also was responsible for introducing the

---

257. SCHWEIZER, *Eine hebraisierende Sonderquelle*, p. 164, 170, 173.

258. *Ibid.*, p. 183; cf. p. 182.

259. E. SCHWEIZER, *Das Evangelium nach Lukas übersetzt und erklärt* (NTD, 3), Göttingen, 1982, esp. p. 1-3, 232-234, 235-237), p. 1 (= *The Good News According to Luke*, tr. D.E. GREEN, Atlanta, GA, 1984, esp. p. 2-4, 349-353, 354-356, p. 1): "is an insoluable problem".

260. *Ibid.*, p. 235 (= 354).

261. *Ibid.*, p. 233 (= 351).

262. *Ibid.*, p. 232 (= 349).

lapse of about an hour (22,59) which gave the impression that a deceptive calm had descended. The addition of v. 70 could also be due to the evangelist.

Since the only Markan agreement in 23,1-5 existed in v. 3, Schweizer concluded that Luke was following another source. It was further conjectured that the special tradition upon which the evangelist was drawing understood the Passover amnesty as "ein Einzelfall"[263]. It was also suggested that the charge against Jesus was stated in such a way as to intrigue Pilate. We submit this could have the same effect for Luke's readers. Finally, the blame in the Lukan account did not fall so much on the Romans as on the people, a view confirmed in Acts (Acts 2,23.36; 4,10; 13,28).

Schweizer rejected oral tradition as the solution for the MAs. Instead, he proposed there was a common source with 22,31-34[264]. Schweizer often raised questions about various possible explanations, but did not answer them immediately or directly[265]. Neirynck observed that Schweizer departed from the view of his predecessor in the series, Rengstorf, by rejecting the view that Luke was dependent upon Mt[266]. Schweizer also no longer endorsed the view of a "hebraisierende Sonderquelle" as he had in 1950, which pertained mostly to material on the miracles, though he still adhered to the view of a pre-Lukan redactor who combined the *Sonderquelle* with Q. In contrast to the classical proto-Lukan theory, Schweizer argued that Mk was Luke's principal source.

Schweizer favored the view of a special source for the passion narrative due not only to the omissions and differences in order in contrast to Mk, but what he considered to be non-Lukan language and Johannine parallels[267].

At the time of the publication of his commentary, Schweizer also published an article specifically dealing with Luke's use of sources, wherein he relied to a great extent upon Jeremias[268]. As in the commentary, he noted the similarity of the motifs of the accusations, the silence and the mockery as were found in Mk 15,3ff.17.20. In seeking to reconcile the mockery with the declaration of

---

263. *Ibid.*, p. 235 (= 353). Schweizer referred readers to the introduction of his Markan commentary for the section Mk 15,2-15. E. SCHWEIZER, *Das Evangelium nach Markus übersetzt und erklärt* (NTD, 1), Göttingen, [11(1)]1967; [12(2)]1967; [13(3)]1969; [14(4)]1973; [15(5)]1979; [17(7)]1989 (= *The Good News According to Mark*, tr. D.H. MADVIG, Atlanta, GA - London, 1970).

264. *Lukas*, p. 230 (= 346-347).

265. *Ibid.*, p. 231-232 (= 348).

266. *ETL* 59 (1983) 146-147.

267. *Ibid.*, p. 146. Schweizer elaborated on his position in the article *Zur Frage der Quellenbenutzung durch Lukas*. See below. Neirynck considered the position in this work more conservative than the commentary, yet Schweizer stuck to his view of endorsing the theory of the special source.

268. E. SCHWEIZER, *Zur Frage der Quellenbenutzung durch Lukas*, in ID., *Neues Testament und Christologie im Werden. Aufsätze*, Göttingen, 1982, p. 33-85, p. 33, n. 1. Schweizer dealt with the sources of the passion narrative on p. 54-61. Cf. J. JEREMIAS, *Die Sprache des Lukasevangeliums* (KEK), Göttingen, 1980. He also acknowledged the influence of T. SCHRAMM, *Der Markusstoff bei Lukas* (SNTS MS, 14), Cambridge, 1971 (esp. p. 85-184). For the Herod story, see p. 58-59.

innocence, Schweizer cited K. Müller's study which attempted to explain the dazzling apparel as originally a sign of innocence but Schweizer did not express complete confidence in such a view[269]. He queried whether Luke inserted details about the people (23,4.13.35) into a tradition which incriminated only the authorities. Although Schweizer saw a pre-Lukan tradition behind Acts 4,26f., he was not sure whether this may have also influenced the report about the friendship of Herod and Pilate (v. 12). As can be seen from the material presented, Schweizer tended to raise questions without ever coming to definitive conclusions.

Preliminary observations led Schweizer to suggest that Luke probably made use of a continuous, written source which was reflected in verbal and material uniformity[270]. In concluding, Schweizer conceded while the *Sonderquelle* could not be proven, there were several elements which pointed to it, especially tensions, as in the case of the Herod pericope[271].

While Schweizer believed that un-Lukan style was indicative of sources, he nonetheless pointed to passages where Luke took and redacted Markan accounts (e.g. 8,22-25 / Mk 4,35-41), recasting them in his own particular style[272]. That, in itself, should make Schweizer cautious about making un-Lukan style, isolated from other critical tools, a criteria for determining tradition or redaction. It appeared that Schweizer was looking for pure Markan tradition.

Recently Schweizer (1989) advocated the view that in addition to Mk, Luke employed Q "wohl in einer etwas veränderten Form und vielleicht schon mit seinem Sondergut verbunden" [273]. The special material may have been in some unified form attached to Q and thus Schweizer suggested the possibility of differing strata of Q[274].

Schweizer (1950) did not specifically treat the Herod pericope in an early article dealing with the issue of Lukan sources[275]. Writing his 1982 Lukan commentary, he included 23,4-16 among those special traditions which "belong together and appear to be connected"[276]. Yet he noted not once but twice that the Herod episode was composed of Lukan expressions and "almost no un-Lukan ones", leaving open the question whether it might be based upon oral tradition[277]. Schweizer contemplated the possibility that the reference to the reconciliation

269. SCHWEIZER, *Zur Frage*, p. 59, n. 90. See K. MÜLLER, *Jesus vor Herodes*, p. 135ff.
270. SCHWEIZER, *Zur Frage*, p. 61.
271. *Ibid.*, p. 84, 85.
272. *Ibid.*, p. 33.
273. SCHWEIZER, *Theologische Einleitung in das Neue Testament* (GrNT, 2), Göttingen, 1989, p. 128 (= *A Theological Introduction to the New Testament*, tr. O.C. DEAN, Nashville, TN, 1991, p. 135): "probably in a somewhat modified form and perhaps with his special material already attached".
274. *Ibid.*, p. 130; cf. p. 41 (= 137; cf. 42).
275. SCHWEIZER, *Eine hebraisierende Sonderquelle*.
276. SCHWEIZER, *Das Evangelium nach Lukas*, 1982, p. 236 (= *The Good News According to Luke*, 1984, p. 354).
277. *Ibid.*, p. 236 (= 355). Cf. p. 234 = (351).

between Pilate and Herod may have been inspired by Ps 2,2. The linking of the two leaders "must predate Luke"[278]. Schweizer also subscribed to the view that in finding Jesus innocent, the prescription of Dt 19,15 for two witnesses was fulfilled. In attempting to explain the transfer from Pilate to Herod, Schweizer contended that Pilate honored him and might have been attempting to divest himself of a troublesome case[279]. Recently Schweizer (1989) showed leanings in the direction of historicity for the Herod episode, though not without recognizing some difficulty[280].

Wilfrid KNOX (1953) revived and developed E. Meyer's concept of a Twelve-source, which contained a written summary of Jesus' work and included, among other things, a rather complete account of the passion[281]. Knox posited this special source as having "high historical value", regarding the passion narrative as a sometimes careless conflation of this source, along with what he termed "the Disciples's source". Luke alternated between these two sources and special material or changes from Mk occur where Luke opted to use the Twelve-source rather than Mk, which often closely followed the Disciples's source.

Luke followed Mk in the account of Peter's denial, favoring the threefold denial to the single denial account found in the Twelve-source[282]. Although Luke selected the substance of the denial story from Mk, it was the order from the special source which governed the arrangement[283]. Knox entertained the possibility that 22,61a came either from the Twelve-source or from Luke's redaction of Mk.

Only the notice of the Sanhedrin trial was possibly drawn from the Twelve-source, while the fuller account derived from Mark's other source. Additional changes come from Luke's redaction of Mk or an independent use of Mark's sources[284]. The account of the trial, as found in this special source was longer, and 22,66 perhaps served as the introduction to it. The transition to the next series of events indicated by the phrase ὡς ἐγένετο ἡμέρα (22,64 [sic]), reflected Luke's

---

278. *Ibid.*, p. 234 (= 352).

279. *Ibid.*, p. 234 (= 351).

280. SCHWEIZER, *Theologische Einleitung* (= *A Theological Introduction*, p. 138): "On the night in which Peter denies Jesus, the latter is only arrested, and in the morning only *one* hearing takes place, but later on another one with Herod (23:6-12). It is not impossible that all of that, including the crucifixion of Jesus and his death, took place on the same day, but it is also not easy to imagine".

281. W.L. KNOX, *The Sources of the Synoptic Gospels. 1. The Gospel of Mark*, (ed. H. CHADWICK), Cambridge, 1953, p. 28, 30. Cf. E. MEYER, *Ursprung*, Vol. 1, 1921, p. 121ff. Though Meyer's proposal seemed to be the inspiration for Knox's theory, he confessed that it was quite different from what Meyer initially suggested (p. 3).

282. KNOX, *Sources. 1. The Gospel of Mark*, p. 132-133; See also p. 30. Mark was responsible for combining the Disciples and Twelve sources for the Sanhedrin trial and the denial. He was further credited with breaking up the story of Peter's denial.

283. *Ibid.*, p. 133.

284. *Ibid.*, p. 134.

editing of Mk 15,1, such as he found it in the Twelve-source. Then Luke followed the Markan story of the trial.

Knox argued that only one trial transpired. Mark had simply failed to harmonize his two sources so that the second Markan trial (15,1) was a conflation of sources[285]. The purpose of the first "trial", which may simply have been an inquiry, was to decide how Jesus was to be charged[286]. Lk 22,66 may have been the introduction of the Twelve-source version, though 22,69 definitely and probably 22,70ff. were drawn from Mk. But the bulk of the account of the Sanhedrin trial derived from Mk with changes accounted for by Luke's redaction or maybe his "independent use of Mk's source"[287].

Knox admitted the difficulty of any attempt to separate the two sources which were used for Pilate's trial[288]. The charge (23,2) stemmed from the Twelve-source and Knox concurred with Burkitt that since the term χριστός βασιλεύς had an Aramaic equivalent and since Mark's written sources were also in Aramaic, it was likely that this was genuine[289]. Mark intentionally omitted the charge since his account was not so politically oriented. For the remainder of the trial after the Herod episode, Luke followed the Twelve-source up to 23,20 at which point he returned to Mk[290]. Although Knox initially believed that 23,24-25 probably came from the Twelve-source, he later conceded that they may simply reflect Lukan redaction of Mk[291]. Material which was different from Mk was drawn from one of the sources which Mk generally ignored (e.g. 23,16.22). But even at those points, Luke did not fail to insert Markan elements.

Knox considered Proto-Lk a feasible hypothesis, though it was not clear why such a document would have existed without an account of the passion[292]. He attributed the term στραφείς to Lukan redaction, though at 22,61 he also entertained the possibility that the influence of a non-Markan source could be detected[293].

Knox strongly opposed Dibelius, resolutely defending the view that the Herod episode came from the Twelve-source and was not a creation of the evangelist[294]. Knox responded, point by point, to Creed's objections. The absence of the story from Mk was explained by Mark's minimal interest in the political situation. Creed denied that Pilate would have sent Jesus to be tried by Herod if he had been from his jurisdiction. Knox pointed to the case of Paul before Felix who inquired

285. *Ibid.*, p. 133, 134.
286. *Ibid.*, p. 133.
287. *Ibid.*, p. 133, 134.
288. *Ibid.*, p. 139.
289. *Ibid.*, p. 136; cf. p. 1.
290. *Ibid.*, p. 140. But this special source supplied τρίτον in 23,22.
291. *Ibid.*; cf. p. 142.
292. KNOX, *Sources*. 2. *St. Luke and St. Matthew* (ed. H. CHADWICK), Cambridge, 1957, p. 3, 4.
293. *Ibid.*, p. 87, n. 2.
294. KNOX, *Sources*. Vol. 1. *Mark*, 1953, p. 137. He also admitted that the Herod story could have stemmed from another account or tradition (p. 138).

whence Paul came. The possibility that special powers had been extended to Herod and Pilate's desire to be on better terms with Herod were cited as further reasons for the transfer. Though 23,10 was confusing according to Creed, Knox believed this was a Lukan insertion to emphasize the role the Jewish leaders played in Jesus' death. Finally, Creed likened the mockery by Herod to the one found in Mk 15,15 which Luke omitted. Knox countered there was only one common element, that of the robe. Knox concluded that the Markan account of the mockery was derived from the Disciples's source[295].

Recall that Knox argued that for the remainder of the trial after the Herod episode, Luke followed the Twelve-source up to 23,20 at which point he returned to Mk, though the special source supplied τρίτον (23,22)[296]. Material which was different from Mk was drawn from one of the sources which Mk generally ignored (for example 23,16.22). But even at those points, Luke did not fail to insert Markan elements.

Léon-Dufour dismissed Knox's theory as being more rigid than Taylor's solution, yet like Taylor, far too complicated, a judgment which Knox himself leveled against Taylor[297]. Léon-Dufour concluded with an appeal to consider the role which oral tradition played as extending from the beginning of the Gospel tradition until the point it was set down in writing[298].

Victor Emmanuel HARLOW (1953) authored a biography of Herod Antipas in which he espoused the view that Joanna and Manaean as well as Matthew (or Levi), Herod's tax collector at Capernaum, were sources of information about Herod[299]. Beyond a few references in the NT, Harlow contended that the only real source of information on Herod was Josephus. Harlow imprecisely listed the Gospels as our source for the material dealing with Herod's involvement in Jesus' trial, since the episode is related only in Lk.

---

295. *Ibid.*, p. 139; cf. p. 142.

296. *Ibid.*, p. 140. Knox conceived of this Twelve-source which "as a whole simply gives a general summary of the ministry of Jesus and ends in a Passion story" (p. 18, n. 1). Moreover, "the source has a distinctly uniform character; it is a summary of the methods of Jesus' teaching in the form of a continuous 'biographical' narrative, with a few incidents inserted dealing with his relations with the sons of Zebedee as prominent members of the Twelve" (p. 30-31). The "Twelve" source was to be distinguished from the "Disciples'" source. The latter "follows the ordinary Marcan usage of referring to 'the disciples'" (p. 115).

297. *RSR* 42 (1954) 582.

298. *Ibid.*, p. 584.

299. V.E. HARLOW, *The Destroyer of Jesus. The Story of Herod Antipas Tetrarch of Galilee*, Oklahoma City, OK, 1953, ᴿ1954, p. 151. The 1954 edition was only a second printing, but it contained unspecified revisions. The table of contents contained an error in pagination. Appendix 2, which dealt with the trials of Pilate and Herod, was listed at p. 218. It actually began on p. 229 and extended through p. 242. See also his earlier treatments, *Jesus the Man. An Historical Study*, Oklahoma City, OK, 1924 (esp. p. 242-247), and *Jesus' Jerusalem Expedition*, Oklahoma City, OK, 1936, p. 75-100. Excerpts from both works were reprinted in Appendix 2 of *Destroyer*, p. 230-242.

The whole of his thesis revolved around what he believed to be a mistranslation of ἀλλ᾽ οὐδὲ ῾Ηρῴδης (23,15) which became the basis for the contention that Herod had found Jesus guilty. Harlow believed the correct rendering was "But not so Herod". Harlow realized that his was a minority point of view. In regard to 23,14-16 he wrote: "Every translator, from Wyckliffe to Moffatt and Goodspeed, has approached the speech which Pilate now delivered, with the conviction that Jesus had been acquitted by Herod"[300].

Harlow put forward the unique proposal that Jesus journeyed to Jerusalem to depose the Jewish Jerusalem government and in its place erect a new Messianic regime. This would have involved the apostles and might have given rise to a new Sanhedrin[301]. Herod was, to Harlow's mind, clearly responsible for the death of Jesus. Pilate's involvement was minimal. Indeed, Pilate's culpability was diminished because of Herod's actions. The Sanhedrin formally charged Jesus in the morning session which was in accordance with the law (22,66 / Mt 26,59; Mt 27,1 / Mk 14,55; Mk 15,1)[302]. It was obvious that Harlow was using the Markan order of events and did not allude to the different recounting found in Lk.

Without giving any reference to his authorities, Harlow argued that letters would have been sent when Jesus was transferred from Pilate to Herod and again when he was returned, the first detailing the charges, the second the findings. Harlow attempted a reconstruction of both. Pilate's letter would have related the charges as found in Luke 23,2. Herod's letter contained a guilty verdict advising Pilate to do what was best in his own personal as well as imperial interests.

Three reasons were put forward for the transfer of Jesus. First, Pilate was unwilling to decide on a matter that offended the Herodian power. Secondly, Pilate was reluctant to turn Jesus over to the hateful priests. Finally, it was seen as a courtesy which Herod would later reciprocate[303].

Harlow seemed to view Herod as having power on a par with Pilate. Not only did Harlow repeatedly refer to Herod as a "coordinate Roman official", but reference was also made to Herod's friendship with the Emperor[304]. It was also argued that Herod was only a visitor in Jerusalem not possessing as complete a power as if he had been in his own territory. He was faced with a dilemma about returning Jesus to Pilate. He had two options: he could detain Jesus until he could return to Galilee or send him back to Pilate. Herod opted for the second since it would have been too dangerous to detain Jesus in a crowded city. But Harlow later asserted that if Herod had found Jesus innocent he would have detained him[305].

---

300. *Ibid.*, p. 236. See p. xii-xiii, xiii, n. 4, 237, 239. Cf. *BDF*, p. 233, §448, 6, where it was pointed out that this construction also appeared in Acts 19,2 and 1 Cor 4,3. See also *BAGD*, p. 591, which translated the phrase as "but not even".

301. HARLOW, *Destroyer*, p. viii.

302. *Ibid.*, p. 154-155, n. 4. See also p. 172.

303. *Ibid.*, p. 174. See also p. 234.

304. *Ibid.*, p. 118, where it occurred twice. See also p. 179.

305. *Ibid.*, p. 235. In addition see p. 237.

Harlow seemed to argue against himself when he stated that Herod and Pilate "exchanged jurisdiction over Jesus"[306]. Herod's power would not have been that of a mere visitor: "When Pilate *anepempsen* Jesus to Herod, he surrendered him fully to Herod. He passed out of control and authority of Pilate into the complete authority and control of Herod"[307].

Harlow cited the following as evidence of Herod's guilty verdict: the term for contempt (ἐξουθενήσας), the supposed letter and the garb. He offered varying interpretations for the dazzling apparel: it was the clothing of a king, colored garments for a Messianic claimant and a sign of Jesus' guilt[308]. The term ἐξουθενοῦντας occurred in 18,9. But it was possible that Luke was drawing inspiration from Mk 9,12. There was no explicit reference to any letter. The action of the clothing of Jesus in a purple garment in the Markan account (Mk 15,16-20) was not an indication of guilt, but a mockery of Jesus' purported royal claim. Harlow understood the sending of Jesus back to Pilate as a sign of guilt but 23,15 informs us that Pilate regarded that gesture as a sign of innocence. The evangelist was not adverse to including details when there was opposition to Pilate's plans as in 23,23-25. Why would the evangelist not have included this detail about Pilate giving in to Herod if this were the case? All of these elements suggested by Harlow remain unconvincing, as they are all present in the Markan account where Pilate declared Jesus innocent.

Harlow argued that Herod and his officers were to be included in the term ἄρχοντας (23,13)[309]. If that was the case, one wonders about the necessity for the letters between Herod and Pilate. Why would Herod not give his report orally to Pilate?

In attempting to resolve the differing presentations of Herod in Lk, Harlow suggested that the evangelist had momentarily forgotten the warning in 13,31 when he penned 23,8. Harlow found it implausible that Herod's desire to kill Jesus would have dissipated[310].

Regarding the tensions between Pilate and Herod (23,12) Harlow offered two possible causes. The first was Pilate's soldiers carrying standards bearing an image of the Emperor under cover of night to Castle Antonia in Jerusalem. This would have been grossly disrespectful of the second commandment. The other conflict was the dispute which arose over Pilate's desire to use Temple treasury funds to finance an aqueduct (13,1)[311].

---

306. *Ibid.*, p. 173, n. 23.

307. *Ibid.*, p. 234-235. Harlow observed that the term ἀνέπεμψεν was found in 23,7.11-15 and a form of the term was also used in Acts 25,21 (p. 173, n. 23). The word has the connotation of remanding a prisoner to the custody of a high authority and renouncing one's own authority in the matter (p. 234).

308. *Ibid.*, p. 177, 234.

309. *Ibid.*, p. 179. The words "them", "they", and "their" (23,14-26.33) also referred to the tetrarch and his officials.

310. *Ibid.*, p. 231.

311. *Ibid.*, p. 115-116, 117-118. See also p. 232.

While many scholars have recognized Markan material in 23,3, Harlow regarded this as "evidently an imperfect condensation of the examination or trial of Jesus by Pilate referred to later by Pilate in Verse 14"[312].

Though F.C. Grant sided with Harlow's "convincing interpretation" of the phrase ἀλλ' οὐδὲ Ἡρῴδης (23,15), claiming that the οὖν (23,16) would strengthen the argument even more, he recognized several weaknesses in the reasoning[313]. If Herod believed in Jesus' guilt why did he not give him over to the mob rather than returning Jesus to Pilate? Further, Harlow presupposed a great deal about the relationship between Herod and Pilate. The reconciliation of the two leaders was also puzzling if they came to diametrically opposed judgments. Clearly, in much of his presentation Harlow exceeded what was found in the Scriptures themselves.

Others who embraced a Proto-Lk theory during this period included Walter BUNDY (1955)[314], Robert DEVREESSE (1962)[315], Eduardo Martinez DALMAU (1963)[316]

---

312. *Ibid.*, p. 232.

313. F.C. GRANT, Review in *ATR* 19 (1937) 146.

314. *Jesus and the First Three Gospels*, Cambridge, MA, 1955, p. 39. Bundy threw his support to the Proto-Lk hypothesis, though it appeared at first as though he was a proponent of Lukan redaction. Although he initially discussed Mk as providing the "the general plan and the framework" of Lk, he abandoned this position later, especially in the section on the passion narrative. Concerning the material of chapters 22 and 23, Bundy claimed: "It is obvious, even to the uncritical reader, that Luke is not using Mk as his basic source. If Luke uses Mk at all in this section, it is only incidentally and at only a few particular points" (p. 480). Bundy reasoned to this based on the large amount of additions, the "new and different text" where Luke possessed parallels with Mk, and an order that was different from Mk (p. 480). Yet, Bundy also recognized the disorder found in the Markan account of the Sanhedrin trial (p. 515). However, he contended that the original form of the special material, whether it was contained in a single document by the time it reached Luke or whether he collected the accounts himself at various points throughout his travels, was beyond recovery. Rather than ascribing the differences to Luke's redactional activity, Bundy preferred to credit "the pre-Markan passion story used by Mk" or Taylor's idea of a separated account which was enriched by Markan inserts to form Lk (p. 481). Bundy even went so far as to revive Burkitt's idea that Q contained an account of the passion, and it was this version which Luke may be recounting in his Gospel.

Q or Proto-Lk were said to be responsible for 22,54-23,1, with Feine cited as supporting evidence in the case of 22,63-65 (p. 515; cf. p. 522). According to Bundy, Luke's version "leaves the impression of a preliminary investigation, less that of a formal legal procedure" (p. 523; cf. p. 516). Jesus' appearances before Pilate and Herod (23,2-25) were equally drawn from the non-Markan source, though upon further analysis, this did not accurately reflect Bundy's viewpoint. Verse 3 was regarded as "possibly" stemming from Mk (p. 528). But in at least one case, Bundy seemed to fall back on the idea that Luke may have been redacting Mk when he suggested that Luke's dislike for physical violence was reflected in his omission of the scourging (cf. Mk 15,15 / Mt 27,26) (p. 534).

Bundy argued that 23,2-25 of which "the hearing before Herod (4-12)" was a part, was drawn from the non-Markan source (p. 527). He also defined the passage "Jesus before Herod" as 23,8-12 (p. 529). B. WEISS, *Die Quellen des Lukasevangeliums*, p. 223, and SPITTA, *Grundschrift*, p. 414, were mentioned as supporting a special source in Luke's account of the Roman trial (23,2-

25). He was tentative in assigning 23,5-7 to the non-Markan source, though he posited that the Herod scene "may have been an organic part of Luke's non-Markan version of the death drama" (BUNDY, *Jesus*, p. 529). The detail about the friendship between Pilate and Herod was explained as "probably the invention of pious imagination, for it is not confirmed by any known source" (p. 530). It served to underscore Luke's theme of Jesus' innocence (p. 527, 529-530). Yet, he announced shortly thereafter that the account of Jesus before Herod and Jesus' subsequent return to Pilate was "probably a piece of pure fiction" (p. 530). He also noted that Herod was "made even more responsible for Jesus' death" in GP.

315. *Les évangiles et l'évangile*, Paris, 1962, p. 63, n. 14. He supported the view of a Proto-Lk and a Proto-Mt, even as he spoke of a common source which followed the order as found in Mk. He relied heavily on Catholic scholars such as Benoit and Huby and used Lagrange's commentaries on Mt (^{2}1923) and Lk (^{3}1927) extensively. See also p. 65, with reference to Proto-Mt and Proto-Lk Gospels. Concerning the order of events in the passion Devreesse believed that Lk contained the better version (p. 39, n. 18). He maintained that the sources to which Luke referred in the Prologue included booklets and fragments. Devreesse was also influenced heavily by the views of Lagrange in his Lukan commentary and by Vaganay's book on the synoptic problem (p. 76, n. 1). Six sources were enumerated including: 1) the common source, 2) two versions of doublets, 3) reminiscences of crowds and travels, 4) detached sentences and 5) a Proto-Lk (p. 63-65). See also p. 77, 78. In the final episodes of the Gospel Devreesse attributed 19,33.47-48; 21,1-4; 22,7-13; 23,19.26b.51 to Proto-Lk (p. 80). He declared: "De tant de traits propres à Luc, on conclura naturellement qu'il avait sur la Passion et la Résurrection un document particulier inconnu de deux autres Synoptiques" (p. 81). Among these traits he counted 18,34; 19,1-9.27.28.39-40.41-44; 20,39.40; 21,18.22.23b-24.28.34b-38; 22,15-17.28-29.31-32.35-38.43-44.49.51.65.67b-68; 23,2.4-17.27-32.34a.36a.40-43.45a.54.56; 24,3.7.8.10-11.12.13-35.36.37-43.44-49.50.51.52), and 6) a source particular to Mt and Lk. Luke composed the Gospel before the year 70 AD (p. 86; see also p. 115).

316. *A Study on the Synoptic Gospels. A New Solution to an Old Problem. The Dependence of the Greek Gospels of St. Matthew and St. Luke upon the Gospel of St. Mark*, New York, 1963, (esp. p. 105-112), p. 2. Dalmau held that Luke made substantial use of Aramaic Mt. Dalmau dialogued with reference to the positions of other scholars including Goguel, Deissman, Burkitt, Lachman, Weiss and Ginns. Dalmau's book contained neither bibliography nor footnotes so it was unclear which Weiss he intended. Ginns's commentary was termed "important" (p. 111) and Dalmau seemed to rely most heavily upon it for his own work. It will be remembered that Ginns supported the view of a special source beginning at 23,1, though he did not know Greek Mt. In addition, Luke employed oral tradition and Proto-Lk, at least in the section 9,51-18,14 (On the matter of Proto-Lk see p. 3, 117, where both times Dalmau was referring to the greater interpolation). But it was clear to Dalmau that he used Mk. Both Matthew and Luke attempted to improve the Markan account (p. 13). Dalmau attributed the theory of the priority of Mk to Lachmann and Weiss, the proof for which he himself was responsible (p. 133), though Luke was not considered to have been successful as Matthew in this endeavor (p. 122). As for the dating of the Gospels, Aramaic Mt was set at between 63 AD and 70 AD while Mk was later than 64 AD. "I conclude then by saying that to me Mark is the more original of the three Synoptic Gospels as they now stand" (p. 121). Lk was said only to have been composed after Mk (p. 27). Dalmau called attention to the decision of the PBC that Acts was written after the Gospel.

In comparing Mk and Lk, Dalmau noted the variations in order, though Luke generally followed Markan sequence (p. 106). See Table O for a comparison of the Markan and Lukan passion narratives, p. 105-106. The account of Peter's denials was rendered in a cohesive manner by Luke.

and Andrew Queen MORTON and George Hogarth Carnaby MACGREGOR (1964)[317]. William ARNDT (1956), familiar with the hypothesis and impressed by

In addressing differences between the Gospels generally Dalmau affirmed the inspiration of the Scriptures by which the author may not have been familiar with all the details but did not compose anything that was untrue.

Both Luke and Matthew knew, followed and sought to improve Mk. Without developing the idea in any detail Dalmau seemed sympathetic to the idea of an Ur-Gospel. Dalmau referred to Mark drawing on "oral and written tradition" (p. 117) and that "Mark follows the footsteps of the Aramaic Matthew" (p. 118), devoid of temporal or geographical references, to which Mark had access. The evangelists treated oral tradition with great freedom. Dalmau saw the Herod pericope (23,8-12) as an insertion by which Pilate attempted "to escape the historical responsibility of the death of Christ" by sending Jesus to Herod (p. 109).

317. *The Structure of Luke and Acts*, London, 1964. Appendix A contained the RSV text of Lk where the authors tried to show what material was derived from Proto-Lk as well as from Mk. Morton described the reaction of supporters to Streeter's proposal of the Proto-Lk theory as immediate, but not entirely enthusiastic. The lack of general support was due to the singularity of such a development. The second critique centered around Streeter's view that Lk, as we now have it, was not shaped by "literary considerations". If such were the case, how could it be judged by the standard of literary criticism? Morton suggested that Streeter was unable to conceive of the idea that the Great Omission occurred because of a limitation of space. Streeter's theory was additionally suspect because it ignored Acts. But Morton and MacGregor set out to rescue the floundering hypothesis with Streeter and Taylor as a springboard, by means of a statistical method.

Using as the basis *Novum Testamentum Graece* by A. Souter, Morton suggested that if both Proto-Lk and Mk were of equal length, it was plausible that Luke omitted fifty-two lines of Proto-Lk in lieu of Markan material (p. 28; cf. A. SOUTER, *Novum Testamentum Graece*, Oxford, 1947). In its favor, MacGregor claimed that the Proto-Lk material can be read with some continuity, while the Markan material cannot. Insofar as Luke seemed to prefer Q to Mk where those sources overlapped and he preferred L to Mk, especially in the passion narrative, the authors deduced that Q and L were already combined prior to Luke's reception of Mk. MacGregor, like Taylor, emphasized the significance of the reliability of the Proto-Lukan material. The difficulties present in the passion account were ascribed to a rewriting of primitive Proto-Lk with embellishment of Markan material. MacGregor believed that Morton had confirmed Streeter's hypothesis. But MacGregor and Morton went beyond Streeter, suggesting that there was an equivalent pre-Lukan source for Acts, that was Proto-Acts (or P.A). This supposed source would also have been composed at Caesarea. It would have been enlarged by Source 2. Relying heavily on Harnack's two part Jerusalem source, and Streeter's contention that both the Gospel and Acts were the result of a two stage period of development, they once again departed from Streeter by suggesting that what he considered diaries was a "much more extensive document" (MORTON and MACGREGOR, *Structure*, p. 53). MacGregor authored this chapter of the book. The original material was distinguished from the material garnered in Rome for Acts, in that the latter was not as trustworthy.

Scholarly reaction was minimal and generally negative. J.L. Houlden criticized the work for its brevity and for employing such a method in isolation from others (*JTS* 17 [1966] 140). Cf. p. 142-143: "We shall be interested to see fuller treatment of the consequences of the observations which lie behind this work and a much more thorough-going attempt to set them in the light of other kinds of evidence. Without this, we shall hesitate to accept this approach as possessing an overriding claim among the methods of criticism". The authors's unflagging confidence in the Souter text was also questioned. Houlden further took issue with their approach because of the proximity of some longer paragraphs, which Morton assigned to an extra source. Finally, clarity was occasionally lacking so that "it is hard to know what inferences we are to draw from facts presented" (p. 142).

Streeter's articulation of it, seemed to endorse Lukan redaction of Mk in combination with the use of L[318]. Karl STAAB (1956) favored the idea of a special source in Lk 22-24[319]. Annie JAUBERT (1964-65) adopted the view of a

Cameron Dinwoodie was more sympathetic, calling the proposal "attractive" (*ScotJT* 18 [1965] 212-218). He also lamented: "it is a pity that [Morton] spoils a good case by imagining that the evangelists were compelled to sacrifice their literary ability to the unwillingness of their scribes to adjust the size of their writing, or the number of lines on a page, to the needs of their employers" (p. 214). Not only do some of their arguments suffer from poor logic, but the co-authors sometimes disagreed with one another. Equally unreliable, in Dinwoodie's judgment, was Morton's assumption of the length of NT books. Morton was also taken to task for his demeaning remark about Streeter's background and education.

318. *The Gospel according to St. Luke* (Bible Commentary), St. Louis, MO, 1956, p. 9; cf. p. 13-14. He was impressed by Streeter's hypothesis "developed with remarkable ingenuity and acumen" (p. 10). In regard to the Semitic flavoring of the language, Arndt favored Lagrange's view that it resulted from Luke's familiarity with and use of the LXX (p. 25). He believed that the audience for whom Luke was writing was very familiar with the Greek OT (p. 29). Arndt emphatically rejected the notion that Mk (and Mt) was among the sources referred to by Luke in the Prologue, though he believed it a good possibility that Luke used Mk, which he adoped as a working hypothesis. "Critics are wont to remark that Luke uses his sources with fidelity, introducing but few changes, and these chiefly of a stylistic nature. Such comments presuppose that the sources are known to us. On that score, caution is in place, as our previous discussion has shown. But if we may take for granted that Luke employed Mark, there is an opportunity for examining the former's method" (p. 28). What is more, it formed the foundation of Lk (p. 14). Though Arndt did not address the question of difference in order directly, he acknowledged that one of two phenomena occur in Mt and Lk regarding the Markan order. Either they both follow Mk's arrangement or at least one of them did (p. 14). Luke seldom rejected Mk's order (p. 28).

Relying heavily upon Plummer and Easton, Arndt suggested parallel accounts between Lk and Mk in the context of literary relationships (p. 16). Peter's denial: 22,54-62 / Mk 14,66-72; mistreatment by servants: 22,63-65 / Mk 14,65; Jesus before Pilate: 23,1-5 / Mk 15,1-5; Barabbas: 23,13-19 / Mk 15,6-11; condemnation: 23,20-25 / Mk 15,12-15.). Arndt harmonized the accounts of the four Gospels and argued that Jesus was subjected to three hearings (p. 454). While the nocturnal session sought to collate evidence against Jesus, it was only the third trial which fulfilled the demands of the law. By this time the Jews did not possess the *ius gladii* (p. 458). The great omission did not pose a grave difficulty for Arndt who insisted that Luke included similar accounts in other contexts. For the passion narrative, Arndt said that a widely accepted view was that Luke possessed a special source (p. 20). Other omitted Markan material included the nocturnal hearing (Mk 14,55-65) and the scourging by the Roman soldiers (Mk 15,16-20). But Arndt suggested Luke deleted the first hearing because of the length of the papyri (p. 18). Arndt included the morning session of the Sanhedrin (22,66-71) as well as the Herod episode in the material drawn from L (p. 20). Against those who argued there would not have been sufficient time for Jesus to appear before Herod, he proposed such a trial would only have taken about thirty minutes (p. 462). But Arndt urged caution since the sources of Lk were generally not known to us (p. 28). Concerning the relation to Acts, Arndt took notice of the use of ἀνακρίνω in 23,14 and several verses in Acts (p. 462. Acts 4,9; 12,19; 24,8; 28,18).

Arndt appeared to accept the historicity of the Herod episode in referring to Bultmann as one of the "modern radical critics" who regarded the Herod story as fiction resulting from reflection upon Ps 2,1f. (p. 461).

319. *Das Evangelium nach Markus und Lukas* (Echter Bibel), Würzburg, 1956, p. 6. Staab

continuous special source in the passion narrative which developed into two forms[320]. Other scholars writing on Lk at this time such as Jean-Samuel JAVET

saw the passion narrative as the point where three source trajectories became visible: 1) that which Mt and Mk offered, 2) Luke's tradition, and 3) a Johannine tradition. The sources, in addition to Mk, were no longer able to be recovered (p. 5). There was very little in common between these various sources. Luke took over the largest portion of story material from Mk, with the exception of 6,45–8,26. Nevertheless, Staab claimed that in the final three chapters of the Gospel Luke used a special source (p. 125). He based this decision on the difference in content, order and language forms. Direct references to Mk were reduced to a minimum. The Lukan account of the denial was described as one like the report given by Mt and Mk (p. 132). Staab noted that Luke endeavored to present Peter as gently as possible. We regard that as a redactional tendency on the part of Matthew and Luke since both present the disciples in a much more favorable light than Mark. Staab based his decision for an independent source on the timing: first, that the trial took place in the early morning and that the transfer to Pilate occurred immediately after the Sanhedrin trial (p. 133). Luke had in mind the same scene of the mockery as Mt and Mk. Even the Sanhedrin trial recounted in the other two Synoptics was termed "fast gleichlautend" with that of Lk. Regarding 23,18f. Staab directed readers to compare Mk 15,6-11 while noting that in 23,24f. Luke emphasized more than Mt and Mk that Pilate yielded to the desires of the Jews. Luke was silent about the scourging and the crowning with thorns (p. 136). Though Staab held fast to the hypothesis of a special source, he nonetheless considered some of the variations as due to Luke's redaction. Luke passed over the testimony of the false witnesses (Mt 26,59-62 / Mk 14,55-60) because such detail had no meaning for the trial. However, 22,71 confirmed Luke was familiar with the Markan account and made changes upon it (p. 133). Because Joanna was named in 8,3 Staab concluded she may have been the source of the information for the Herod episode (p. 134). Although Staab decided in favor of a special source, based in part on a change in order, he also recognized that Luke occasionally transposed the Markan order (p. 5; cf. p. 125: "Darum ändert er bisweilen die Mk-Ordnung"). One example was that Jesus' visit to Nazareth was placed at the beginning of his ministry (4,16-30) because the powerful opposition of the whole people is emphasized. This was important because many of the supporters of a special source maintained that the Nazareth pericope was part of that unified whole and not a redaction of the Markan source. Cf. C.J. SCHRECK, *Luke 4,16-30: The Nazareth Pericope in Modern Exegesis: A History of Interpretation.* Diss., KUL, 1990 (dir. F. NEIRYNCK).

320. *Les séances du sanhédrin et les récits de la passion*, in *RHR* 166 (1964) 143-169 (esp. p. 164-169); *RHR* 167 (1965) 1-33. Jaubert argued that Luke, motivated by theological concerns, was "désireux de coordonner et de relier un certain nombre de sources écrites ou orales" (*Les séances*, p. 1-33 and *RHR* 166 [1964] 164). For the Lukan account of the Sanhedrin trial Jaubert proposed Lk was secondary to Mk 14,54-64 and that Luke followed either M, a nocturnal tradition, or a common source. It appeared that Luke used the M tradition in the "suture difficile" between 22,67a and 22,69. Jaubert seemed to have been influenced in her decision about sources by the works of Léon-Dufour, Benoit, Tyson and Taylor (*Les séances*, p. 166, n. 2). See also JAUBERT, *Les séances*, in *RHR* 167 (1965) 16: "Nous avons vu que Luc avait gardé de sa source la mention d'un déplacement de Jésus vers le lieu de session du jugement pour la séance de jour (Lc 22, 66)". Note further her comment on chronology (p. 32). The entire passion constituted a continuous source which evolved into two forms: the more ancient form as found in M (nocturnal) and the J (*Jour*) tradition which reduced the two Sanhedrin gatherings to one (*Les séances*, p. 32 and *RHR* 166 [1964] 167). The J tradition was shaped by catechesis and included elements that were apologetic, doctrinal and liturgical in nature. This evolution of two supposed forms of the continuous source made distinguishing them difficult at times: "Luc a dû naturellement disposer d'autres sources que J pour le récit de la passion, mais nous ne pouvons

(1957)[321] and Helmut GOLLWITZER (1958)[322] expressed the view that the

même assurer qu'il ait connu la tradition M (nocturne), puisque J conservait la même substance; nous ne pouvons dire non plus s'il a eu directement connaissance de la tradition des deux séances de jour (JP)" (*Les séances*, p. 167-168).

In some cases, such as the reference to the Son of Man coming on the clouds of heaven (22,69), Luke redacted his material with a view to his Hellenistic audience (p. 165; see also p. 169). Lukan redaction meant, in part, that Luke "a rationalisé ses sources". It was Luke who was responsible for eliminating that detail and separating the questions because of a more developed christology. In addition to the source of Mk 14,53-54 it appeared to Jaubert that Luke had access to other sources. Simply appealing to Luke's redaction was insufficient to explain the change to a morning session. This M tradition, in Jaubert's estimation, very likely harkened back to the same tradition as M. "Nous avons vu, en effet, que Luc est secondaire par rapport à M. Il nous paraît donc plus vraisemblable de faire remonter la source de Luc à la même tradition que M" (p. 166-167).

Jaubert, though adopting the view of a special source or sources for the Sanhedrin trial in Lk, also posited changes resulting from redaction by the evangelist. She affirmed the historicity of the account concluding that the argument that the influence of anti-Jewish sentiment in NT redaction was without merit to justify the changes in the account. "A l'autre extrême, devant les difficultés d'accepter le déroulement apparent des événements, la majorité des critiques non conservateurs ont renoncé à l'historicité des séances du sanhédrin. Mais il faut alors trouver un motif suffisant pour expliquer la création ou l'amplification de la tradition Mc/Mt" (*Les séances*, in *RHR* 167 [1965] 33).

See also JAUBERT, *Le date de la Cène. Calendrier biblique et liturgie chrétienne* (EB), Paris, 1957, esp. p. 116-133 (= *The Date of the Last Supper*, tr. I. RAFFERTY, New York, 1965, esp. p. 103-117).

321. *L'Évangile de la grâce. Commentaire sur l'Évangile selon saint Luc*, Geneva - Paris, 1957. He depended upon Calvin, whose views, in turn, rested on other commentators. Javet was especially indebted to the Lukan commentaries of Godet (³1888-1889) and Lagrange (1921) (p. 10). He acknowledged that Luke was not the first to compose a life of Jesus, but relied on others (1,1) who based their accounts upon the records of eyewitnesses and ministers of the word. While Javet admitted that a "bon nombre d'historiens" adopted the Two-Source theory, he noted it was difficult to determine the extent to which Luke was familiar with the works of his predecessors.

Javet eschewed addressing the problems involved in comparing the four Gospel accounts of the passion of Jesus, but asserted that Luke was concerned only with reporting what actually happened and did not redact the account to reflect his own theology or shape it to the needs of the community or communities for which he was writing: "L'Evangile se content de nous rapporter les événements. La narration est détaillée, mais elle est d'une extrême sobriété. L'évangeliste dit simplement ce qui s'est passé. Il raconte seulement une histoire. Il n'intervient pas personnellement dans son récit" (p. 243).

Although observing that Luke did not relate the preliminary nocturnal interrogation of Jesus in the palace of the high priest, Javet did not offer a rationale for such an omission (p. 255). The suture at 23,13 indicated that Luke resumed "manifestement le déroulement des événements". The introduction of 23,17 was intended to bring the Lukan account in line with the other Gospels.

Javet made no reference to any possible relation of Joanna (8,3) to the Herodian court or to what role, if any, she may have had in the transmission of information concerning Herod and the trial of Jesus (p. 108-109). He declared further that Herod had appropriately come to Jerusalem for the Passover (23,8-12) (p. 257). The animosity between Herod and Pilate was due, in part, to Pilate's actions of mixing the sacrifices with the blood of Galileans (13,1).

322. *La joie de Dieu*, tr. É. DE ROBERT and J. CARRÈRE, Neuchâtel - Paris, 1958, p. 9.

evangelist was simply attempting to report the information he received. William BARCLAY (1966)[323] did not see the need to postulate a special documentary source for the passion, though he seemed open to the idea of Proto-Lk. Accordingly, Luke simply supplemented the Markan account with other details. Albertus F.J. KLIJN (1965), offering a summary of scholarly positions on Proto-Lk, contended there were problems with several areas of the theory, though he advocated the idea that some traditions in Lk stemmed from a source no longer extant[324].

Gollwitzer failed to include a bibliography but he indicated he relied heavily upon the commentaries of Calvin, J. Chr. von Hofmann and K.H. Rengstorf. He occasionally cited either Luther's translation (p. 80, n. 1, 137, n. 1) or German songs (p. 20, n. 1, 48, n. 1, 253, n. 1). He suggested that Luke did not compose his Gospel as a criticism of those of his predecessors (1,1) who had the advantage of being eyewitnesses. A brief remark on the relation of the evangelists involved frugally reporting the facts (p. 277). Although Gollwitzer compared Lk with the other Synoptics, this was less the case when he treated the trial of Jesus. Surprisingly, Gollwitzer did not treat Peter's denials (22,54-62).

323. *The First Three Gospels*, London - Philadelphia, PA, 1966, p. 129 (= *Introduction to the First Three Gospels. A Revised Edition of The First Three Gospels*, Philadelphia, PA, [2]1975, p. 92). The revised edition contained two new chapters. He argued in favor of Markan priority, insisting that Matthew and Luke improved Mk's "literary style and his theological approach". He maintained, nevertheless, that Luke possessed special sources for the passion and resurrection accounts (p. 147 = 108). He added: "It is not necessary to postulate a new document behind Luke's Passion and Resurrection narrative, for what he has is not so much a new story as a considerable amount of additional detail" (p. 147 = 108). Barclay attempted to explain the composition of Lk by means of the following equation: "Luke = Mk + Q + L + I" (p. 148 = 109). The "I" stood for infancy narratives. See also p. 266 (= 202), where he stated that in final form the composition would be expression by the following equation: "Luke = (Q + L) + Mark + I + R", in which case the "R" represented special material containing resurrection stories). Neglecting for the moment the infancy narrative (Lk 1-2) Barclay claimed that Lk could be divided into thirteen sections, the last of which, containing the passion and resurrection narratives (22,14-24,53, derived from L; p. 262-263 = 199). The remaining "L" passages were: 3,1-4,30; 5,1-11; 6,12-8,3; 9,51-18,14; 19,1-28.37-38. Those attributed to Mk were: 4,31-44; 5,12-6,11; 8,4-9,50; 18,15-43; 19,28-36.49-22,13). But he seemed to be open to the Proto-Lk construction (p. 263-266 = 199-202).

Barclay, though maintaining that Luke had recourse to other "extensive special sources" for the passion and resurrection, argued Luke obtained the information about Herod from early members of the church (p. 149 = 109-110). Barclay defined the passage both as 23,6-16 and 23,6-12 (p. 147 = 107-108; cf. [2]1975, p. 215).

324. A.F.J. KLIJN, *De Wordingsgeschiedenis van het Nieuwe Testament*, Utrecht - Antwerp, 1965 (= *An Introduction to the New Testament*, tr. M. VAN DER VATHORST-SMIT, Leiden, 1967, p. 14). He wrote that the Proto-Lk theory "has found fairly general acceptance", while at the same time noting that it was deficient in several areas. A little later, Klijn reversed himself when he wrote that "very few supporters [of the supposed Proto-Lk] are still to be found" (p. 39). It failed to explain the origin of Mk, the use and contents of Q remained unknown, and it ran counter to the tradition of Papias that an early Mt had been composed in Aramaic. Transpositions, additions (including the Herod episode, 23,6-16) and diversions from Mk raised the issue of a special source for the passion. And though it cannot be definitively claimed, according to Klijn, that Luke used a separate account of the passion, independent of Mk, still he believed it was

While the extent of the influence of the communities on the composition of the Gospels was debated at this time, Cadbury surveyed the Lukan literary style. He concluded it was difficult to explain the source of Lukan vocabulary since Luke recast it according to his own style. Further, while Perry's hypothesis was possible, other explanations could account for the differences in Lk. He was critical of Streeter and Taylor for assigning authorship of Proto-Lk to Luke himself.

Major contributions to the discussion of a special source were offered during this period by Paul Winter. He conceived of a special source differently than Taylor. The idea of a *Grundschrift*, which had its origins in early Christian liturgy, was supported by Trocmé. Other scholars, such as the American Joseph Tyson, over the span of his career, began to eschew the source question in favor of looking at Lk "holistically". The relative merits of a Proto-Lk continued to be debated.

Paul WINTER (1955), although an adherent of the special Lukan source theory, made significant changes from the form presented by Taylor. Winter disputed the latter's view that all the non-Markan material as well as the Q material was grouped into L[325]. He further dissented by claiming that Luke was not the author of the special source[326].

While allowing that the variations in Peter's denial may be due to an editor, Winter nonetheless held that elements of a non-Markan account might also be present[327]. The mockery (vv. 63-65) was definitely not from Mk while the Sanhedrin trial (vv. 66-71) was assigned to the "Sx" material as its source, being a post-Lukan insertion[328]. The material of Ch 23 was a composite from at least three different sources. Stemming from an interpolator are 22,67-71 as well as 23,4.5.18-25. On the other hand, 23,1b-3 was due to L which reflected an ancient account of the trial, though Winter was hardpressed to suggest what other verses it had contained.

certain that the information rested upon traditions from a source no longer available to us. He left the reader with the impression that these traditions had been gathered together in a single source, in which case his position was similar to that of Wernle (p. 39; cf. p. 12, where the passage, "Jesus heard by Herod" was designated as 23,6-12).

325. P. WINTER, *The Treatment of His Sources by the Third Evangelist in Luke XXI-XXIV*, in *ST* 8 (1954) 138-172, p. 139. Winter also took exception to referring to all of the special material as Proto-Lk, preferring instead to call it simply L. He defined L as the special material, suggesting it might have constituted a number of writings, plus Q. In addition to Mk, Luke employed "Sx", which were "non-editorial passages which show a stage in the development of tradition later than the composition of Mk". Like Taylor, Winter believed that L formed a complete Gospel (p. 139, n. 1).

326. *Ibid.*, p. 140; cf. p. 171. Although earlier Winter stated that L and the Gospel stemmed from different authors, based on logic rather than lexical evidence, he later attempted to argue the issue of authorship referring to the manner in which Luke combined the L material with that drawn from Mk. Winter was reluctant to name any particular historical person as the author.

327. *Ibid.*, p. 161.

328. *Ibid.*, p. 162, 163.

When all the component parts were assembled, these various and sundry elements comprised a most peculiar account of the passion, despite Winter's assertion that "most of the non-Markan material in the last four chapters of the Third Gospel formed a coherent account"[329]. The presentation according to L would possibly involve some details of Peter's denial followed by the mockery. Passing over the Sanhedrin trial, Jesus suddenly appeared in the presence of Pilate. The special "non-editorial passages" of Sx portrayed Jesus being exchanged between Pilate and Herod (23,6-16), while the remainder was interpolated. For Winter, the most difficult task facing the exegete was not distinguishing L from Mk, but discerning what stemmed from L and Sx[330].

Taylor disclosed a letter Winter sent in reaction to Taylor's article *The Proto-Luke Hypothesis* (1955), in which Winter held that Taylor did not go far enough in asserting that the theory had not been overturned[331]. While both Winter and Taylor were concerned with the origin of Lk, Winter approached it from a non-Christian point of view. Summarizing Winter's views on the passion narrative, Taylor again appealed for scholars to undertake the work of investigating this section in a more comprehensive and detailed manner than had previously been done in Britain. While there was much to be said in agreement, Taylor wondered whether it was possible to separate the work of the evangelist from that of the author of L. He also appeared to express doubt whether there was post-editorial material in Lk 22-24. Thirdly, it was questionable if L could be differentiated from the special source as well as the non-editorial passages from Mk. Taylor was obvious greatly encouraged: "One thing is clear: the idea that the Lucan Passion Narrative is merely a re-editing of Mark is out of date"[332]. And that enthusiasm was inspired by the conclusions of only one independent scholar.

Eduard LOHSE (1964), on the other hand, affirmed his belief in Markan priority and reacted against Winter's proposal that Luke was in possession of a second source[333]. The third passion prediction was incontrovertible evidence that

---

329. *Ibid.*, p. 170.

330. *Ibid.*, p. 172, n. 1. The material found here was a continuation from p. 171.

331. V. TAYLOR, *Sources of the Lukan Passion Narrative* [P. Winter], in *ExpT* 68 (1956-57) 95. The first portion of the article contained remarks by the editor followed by Taylor's reaction to Winter's article, *Treatment* (1954).

332. TAYLOR, *Sources*, p. 95.

333. E. LOHSE, *Die Geschichte des Leidens und Sterbens Jesu Christi*, Gütersloh, 1964, p. 74 (= *History of the Suffering and Death of Jesus Christ*, tr. M.O. DIETRICH, Philadelphia, PA, 1967, p. 73). Earlier Lohse objected to Winter's position and clearly identified himself as supporting the idea that the Lukan account of the trial of Jesus was dependent upon Mk 14,53-72 (*Der Prozess Jesu Christi*, in G. KRETSCHMAR and B. LOHSE [eds.], *Ecclesia und Res Publica*, FS K.D. SCHMIDT, Göttingen, 1961, 26-27: "Hinsichtlich des Berichtes über den Prozess Jesu kann kein begründeter Zweifel darüber bestehen, dass Lk.22,54-71 allein von Mk.14,53-72 abhängig ist"). See also E. LOHSE, *Lukas als Theologe der Heilsgeschichte*, in *EvTh* 14 (1954) 256-275 (esp. p. 261ff.). Lohse consistently argued against the idea of a special source as championed by Winter as was found also in E. LOHSE, συνέδριον, in *TWNT* 7, p. 868, n. 74 (= *TDNT* 7, 1971, p. 870, n. 74). Lohse rejected the view of a special source and specifically in

Luke was dependent upon Mk[334]. Luke's whole purpose, as opposed to Mk, was to show that the passion was the fulfillment of the message of the prophets[335]. Other indications of Luke's dependence upon Mk were in his abbreviation of various accounts and also in the omission of the two Markan references to the Temple speech, though Luke recounted this later in Acts[336].

Winter (1961, [2]1974), in *On the Trial of Jesus*, maintained that despite the fact that Luke was obviously familiar with Mk, the compositional process of the Lukan passion narrative was quite complicated[337]. Luke did not reproduce the Markan version nor was he careless when he wrote his own, but "in all probability" had access to written source information[338].

Winter believed that the Markan order was nearer to the primitive arrangement[339]. Though that appeared to be the case, in Winter's opinion, Luke possessed the better account of the earlier tradition[340].

Asserting that Lk 22,54-66 (prior to λέγοντες), which included the account of Peter's denial, was historically preferable to the Markan account[341]. While some had argued that 22,66 was a combination of Mk 14,53b and Mk 15,1a, Winter was of the opinion that 22,66 corresponded only to the latter. The event described in 22,66 occurred in a location different from that of 22,54-65[342]. The mockery (22,64-65) betrayed no influence from Mk. This judgment was based

reference to the order of events, arguing instead that Luke had simply abbreviated Mk.

334. LOHSE, *Die Geschichte*, p. 18, 74 (= 11, 72-73).

335. *Ibid.*, p. 74 (= 73).

336. *Ibid.*, p. 84; = ET, p. 84.

337. P. WINTER, *On the Trial of Jesus* (Studia Judaica, 1), Second edition revised and enlarged by T.A. BURKILL and G. VERMES, Berlin, [2]1974, p. 41 = 1961, p. 27-28 [pages in brackets]. Winter's most concise statement was the following: "The extant Passion Narrative of the Third Gospel is of a composite character, consisting of pre-Marcan, Marcan, post-Marcan elements of Lucan editorial modifications, and of post-Lucan insertions. Only the words from καὶ ὡς ἐγένετο ἡμέρα to εἰς τὸ συνέδριον αὐτῶν in Lc 22,66 can be considered as being derived from an old, pre-Marcan, record or tradition" (p. 29, n. 5; = 1961, p. 160, n. 5). Notice should be made of the select list of reviews of the first edition of the book found on p. XXI-XXII of the revised edition. See further P. BENOIT, *Review: P. WINTER, On the Trial of Jesus, 1961*, in *RB* 68 (1961) 593-599 = *Le procès de Jésus selon Paul Winter*, in ID., *ExT*, Vol. 3, Paris, 1965, 243-250. See also the analysis of A. SCHALIT, *Kritische Randbemerkungen zu Paul Winters "On the Trial of Jesus"*, in H. KOSMALA, et. al. (eds)., *ASTI* 2 (1963), 86-102.

338. WINTER, *On the Trial*, [2]1974, p. 41, n. 29. Winter's reaction to the charge of Luke's carelessness recalled Wernle's indictment of Luke. This position was much stronger than the 1961 view that Luke had access to "certain information – possibly a document" (p. 166, n. 29).

339. *Ibid.*, [2]1974, p. 30-31 [= 22].

340. *Ibid.*, p. 31 [= 22]: "It seems that in Lc 22,63-66a the earlier tradition has been best preserved even if in the original order the event recorded in Lc 22,55-62 occupied a place between the events now related in Lc 22,63-65 and Lc 22,66".

341. *Ibid.*, p. 31-32. Since the denial was beyond the scope of his investigation, Winter did not assign it to one of his three source categories (cf. p. 190).

342. *Ibid.*, p. 28 [= 21].

upon the differences in setting, timing and vocabulary, though a similar tradition existed behind both the Markan and Lukan accounts[343].

For the section dealing with Barabbas, any changes over against Mk were simply redaction, since at this point Luke was not in possession of any special material by which he could alter the Markan version[344]. The section 23,16-22 was "obviously editorial"[345]. Those sections which derived from primary tradition were 22,66-23,1 and 23,2-3[346]. Secondary tradition was responsible for references to mockeries in 22,63-65 and and 23,11[347].

Winter followed T.A. Burkill in claiming that even though the Sanhedrin was capable of determining and executing capital punishment, Jesus was nevertheless not condemned to death by the Sanhedrin[348]. The lack of any direct reference to a death sentence passed by the Sanhedrin, Winter claims, was clarified by Acts 13,27-28[349].

343. *Ibid.*, p. 29 [= 21]. Cf. p. 144, n. 1 [= 100 and 202, n. 1]; p. 190, 191; [= 136, 137]. Both were due to an earlier tradition, but their timing was shaped by how this detail was employed by both evangelists.

344. *Ibid.*, p. 132 [= 92]. However, Winter contradicted himself when later he wrote: "Evidently there is some significance in the fact that the Third Evangelist refrained from mentioning a custom, or a habit on Pilate's part, of granting pardon to a prisoner at the Passover festival. This shows that, though he knew the Marcan trial account and made use of it in his own Gospel, the author of Luke was also in possession of other information which induced him to question the trustworthiness of certain items in the Marcan account". Cf. also p. 139 [= 97].

345. *Ibid.*, p. 146 [= 102]. Verses 23,16.22 were not more primitive than Mk 15,16-20. It was a redaction "of the tradition which has been better preserved in the Second Gospel". A specific example of Lukan redaction of Mk was found in 23,19 / Mk 15,7 where Luke rendered Mk's ambiguous wording in a more precise fashion (p. 140 [= 97]).

346. *Ibid.*, p. 190-191 [= 136-137]. Winter defined primary tradition as "scanty information", lacking in "direct first-hand evidence" and formulated according to "cultic, missionary, apologetic and polemical" needs of the early period of Christianity (p. 6-7 [= 6]). Secondary traditions consisted of the combination of primary and secondary elements such as transpositions of original settings, multiplication of themes, shifts in emphasis and the addition of descriptive details (p. 7 [= 6]).

347. *Ibid.*, p. 190, 191 [= 136, 137]. The origins were thus to be distinguished that 22,63-65 stemmed from a "proof from prophecy" while 23,11 derived from a secondary tradition.

348. WINTER, *On the Trial*, ²1974, p. 10-11. This section was significantly revised from the original [p. 15]. See T.A. BURKILL, *The Competence of the Sanhedrin*, in *VC* 10 (1956) 80-96; *The Trial of Jesus*, in *VC* 12 (1958) 1-18. In the second article Burkill pointed to the similarity of Mk 14,55-65 with Acts 6,8ff (p. 11). He concluded: "In other words, the principal features of the nocturnal trial as it is presented in Mk. 14,55-65 corresponds in the main elements in St. Luke's account of the condemnation of Stephen; and this seems to corroborate the view that St. Mark's story is not so much a historical record of a trial which actually took place as a piece of Christian interpretation made in the light of the church's experience of conflict with the Jews and designed to emphasise Jewish responsibility for the outrage of crucifying the Son of God" (p. 13).

349. WINTER, *On the Trial*, p. 41 [= 1961, p. 28]. Yet, though no direct reference was made to a death sentence originating from the Sanhedrin in the trial of Stephen in Acts 6, Winter argued that the "text as it stands warrants the conclusion that Stephen was found guilty by the court". Why would the same not be true of the Gospel account of the trial of Jesus?

The historian Geza Vermes termed Winter's *On the Trial of Jesus* a "magisterial study"[350]. "None of the criticisms formulated against him, including that by D.R. Catchpole in *The Trial of Jesus* [...], have seriously affected any of his main theses"[351].

Turning to the Herod story, according to Winter (1955) "Sx" might have been responsible, post editorially, for contributing 23,6-16[352]. His subsequent view (1961, [2]1974) was that the Herod episode (23,6-10.12) was the product of secondary tradition and editorial modification, either by the Luke or a later redactor. Editorial accretions were found in 23,4.13-16.20-24 as well as 22,67-71[353]. Not only were the evangelist and possibly a post-Lukan redactor responsible for changes, but Winter argued that in 23,13 a copyist could have penned "the rulers and the people" in place of "the rulers of the people"[354].

Winter advocated a position wherein the material of Ch 23 was a composite from at least three different sources. When all the component parts were assembled, these various and sundry elements comprised a most peculiar account of the passion, despite Winter's assertion that "most of the non-Markan material in the last four chapters of the Third Gospel formed a coherent account"[355]. The special "non-editorial passages" of Sx portrayed Jesus being exchanged between Pilate and Herod (23,6-16), while the remainder were interpolated.

The Herod episode (23,6-7.8-12) was judged to be an account supplied either by Luke or a post Lukan editor of the Gospel. Winter considered the account to be based upon a tradition later than that underlying Mk[356]. The mockery in 23,11 derived from secondary tradition[357].

Winter inspired the work of Haim COHN (1967), a rabbi and Justice of the Supreme Court of Israel[358]. Tibor Horvath noted the "many incoherences" in the

---

350. G. VERMES, *Jesus the Jew. A Historian's Reading of the Gospels*, London, 1973; Philadelphia, PA, 1981, p. 36.

351. *Ibid.*, p. 234, n. 159.

352. WINTER, *Treatment*, p. 138-172. In addition to Mk, Luke employed "Sx", which were "non-editorial passages which show a stage in the development of tradition later than the composition of Mk" (p. 139).

353. WINTER, *On the Trial of Jesus*, [2]1974, p. 190-191 [= 136-137]. Though Winter ascribed 22,66-23,1 to the primary tradition, he further qualified the origin 22,67-71, stating that it stemmed from Mt. These verses were radically reformulated, possibly by a post-Lukan redactor. The preface to the second ed. indicated that the revision involved including some notes Winter collected and adding stylistic changes plus additional material, including a bibliography and index. See also the biographical sketch, p. XI-XII.

354. *Ibid.*, [2]1974, p. 141, n. 23 [= 201, n. 23].

355. *Ibid.*, p. 170.

356. WINTER, *On the Trial of Jesus*, 1961, p. 102 and 202, n. 4 [= [2]1974, p. 147, n. 4]. Cf. 1961, p. 137 and 213, n. 1 [= p. 191, n. 1, [2]1974].

357. *Ibid.*, 1961, p. 136, 137 [= [2]1974 p. 190, 191].

358. *The Trial and Death of Jesus*, New York, 1967, [R]1971, p. 331; cf. p. 189). The trial of Jesus attracted the attention not only of exegetes and theologians, but civil lawyers as well. Cohn authored a lengthy, though unconvincing book in an attempt to disprove Jewish complicity in the

hypothesis of Cohn[359]. He also admitted that the problem of the historicity of the

trial of Jesus, refocusing the responsibility upon the Romans. Despite what Luke wrote in the Prologue, Cohn, following Winter, maintained that none of the evangelists had access to direct eyewitness testimony of the events of the arrest, trial and crucifixion (p. xiii). He also cited Winter's attempt to disprove the authenticity of the account of the Sanhedrin trial in Mk (p. 95, n. 2). Cohn stated it was unclear whether the predecessors's works to which Luke referred actually served as sources (p. xviii). He clearly asserted that Matthew used Mk as his model, but made no such clear statement concerning the relation of Mk and Lk (p. 95). "The quest for such traditions has occupied scholars for more than a century now, with the upshot that it appears 'quite certain' that the Gospels were 'preceded by some written accounts, more or less fragmentary, of the Gospel tradition'. Luke testifies (1:1), but, of the manifold settings forth, only those of the four evangelists have been preserved, and we do not know whether the others anteceded them and provided them with source material" (p. xviii). The disinformation disseminated by the evangelist, devoid of technical accuracy or legal fact, was directed more by missionary and theological goals, with the purpose of exonerating Pilate (p. 326-327). The contrast to Sherwin-White was obvious. In composing the Gospels the evangelists ascribed to the Jewish religious leaders of Jesus' time attitudes of the religious leaders from their own times, which Cohn described as the evangelists's "cardinal mistake" (p. xvii).

Cohn considered as calumny against the Jews the charge that the Sanhedrin was responsible for Jesus' death. If they had been responsible, the Jewish leaders would not have resented the accusation as found in Peter's speech in Acts 5,30 (p. 252). But Cohn avoided attempting to distinguish whether this text was tradition or Lukan redaction). According to the law, the Sanhedrin was obliged to fulfill the execution in capital cases (p. 252, n. 17). Cohn rejected the view that the Sanhedrin assembled to try to pass the death sentence upon Jesus, as well as the idea that this served as a preliminary investigation to the trial before the Roman governor (p. 96). Cohn asserted that most modern scholars rejected the idea that a Jewish trial took place before the Sanhedrin during the night (p. 97). We found no reference in Blinzler, as Cohn claimed, that there was "a wall of consensus that no Jewish trial in fact took place" (p. 97, 357, n. 7. Cf. J. BLINZLER, *Der Prozess Jesu*, [3]1960, p. 12). In regard to the competence of the Sanhedrin, Cohn maintained that the Sanhedrin did, in the time of Jesus and even later, "carry out capital sentences" (COHN, *Trial*, p. 96; cf. p. 357, n. 2). The Lukan account clearly reflected the view that a sentence was certainly given (p. 188). The execution of Jesus and the two crucified with him could only have been carried out with the governor's permission.

Cohn rejected Blinzler's suggestion that Joseph of Arimathea could have been a possible source for information about the Sanhedrin, since there was no indication in the Gospel for this (p. xiv). Furthermore, no other Jew or outsider would have gained access to the trial by the Roman governor (p. 145). In treating the omission of the scourging in Lk, Cohn found it unbelievable that the people would have been content to accept such a substitution for capital punishment or even that Pilate would have yielded to the demands of the crowd (p. 195). Cohn echoed Goguel's idea that Luke may have erred, thinking that the scourging referred to was different from the one which accompanied every execution. Cohn denied the historicity of the Barabbas story because of inconsistencies (p. 164). He ultimately attributed this special story to Luke (p. 183). Cohn argued forcefully that in several places in Acts (22,1-21; 23,1-6; 24,10-21; 26,2-27) Luke had many opportunities to implicate the Sanhedrin, but did so only in Paul's speech at Antioch (Acts 13,14ff.) (p. 257-258). Cohn read the biblical text selectively and sought to distinguish 22,71 from Acts 13,27-28 when in fact, both insisted on the culpability of the Jewish people and their leaders (p. 256-257). And while Cohn argued that the portrayals in Acts sometimes varied from those in the Gospel, he nonetheless maintained that Jesus' response (22,69) provided the model for Stephen in Acts (p. 102).

trial of Jesus was "still far from being solved"[360].

E. DĄBROWSKI (1968) accused Winter of absurdity in expunging the trial before Herod from the trial of Jesus[361]. According to Dąbrowski, Finegan rightly laid the blame upon Winter for having followed W. Brandt, J. Wellhausen and M. Dibelius. "These scholars simply excluded the possibility of reconstructing the proceedings of the trial on the basis of the Gospels, which they describe as a theological reflex of events; they saw any interpretation tending to exalt Christ as an – under the circumstances – inevitable amendment of historical evidence"[362]. Thus, it would seem that in this case the Herod scene was accepted as historical.

F.C. Grant noted the similarity between Winter's position and that of Lietzmann, the difference being that Winter "amplified and strengthened" the defense of their viewpoint[363]. Concerned about the extent of power the Sanhedrin possessed power in capital cases Grant wrote: "The conclusion appears to be paradoxical, but really is not: the Sanhedrin possessed full power in capital cases but chose not to exercise it in full (i.e. to the extent of the execution) in the case of Jesus, preferring instead to hand him over to Pilate for trial and, presumably, condemnation. This general thesis is supported by both Dr. Winter and Professor Burkill, and seems quite defensible. But can it be proved? I doubt it"[364]. Grant wrote further that the story of Stephen's trial was "modeled upon the Passion narrative in the Gospels"[365].

In his recent study on the trial of Jesus (1995) Alan WATSON was inspired by Winter's "brilliant *On the Trial of Jesus*", though he was "not entirely persuaded by" it[366]. Firmly convinced that Luke employed Mk, Luke's version was viewed as a reaction against Mk[367]. The Lukan account of the Sanhedrin trial and transfer to Pilate with attendant charges was judged by Watson to be "possible, but very implausible", claiming that neither Lk nor Mt were reliable concerning the "main course of events leading up to the execution of Jesus"[368].

---

359. T. HORVATH, *Why Was Jesus Brought to Pilate*, in *NT* 11 (1969) 174-184.

360. *Ibid.*, p. 181. He noted the divided opinion of scholars (p. 178).

361. E. DĄBROWSKI, *The Trial of Christ in Recent Research*, in *StEv* 4 (Berlin) (1968), p. 23. Most of this article treated the Sanhedrin trial.

362. *Ibid.*, p. 24.

363. F.C. GRANT, *On the Trial of Jesus: A Review Article*, in *JR* 44 (1964) 230-237.

364. *Ibid.*, p. 231.

365. *Ibid.*, p. 234.

366. A. WATSON, *The Trial of Jesus*, Athens, GA - London, 1995, p. ix.

367. *Ibid.*, p. 2, 69, 71. See also p. 70: "The only explanation is that in the community or communities in which Matthew and Luke were written, Mark was the main narrative source of the events leading up to Jesus' arrest, the arrest, trial, and execution, but aspects of Mark's account were the subject of considerable controversy, and various solutions were proffered".

368. *Ibid.*, p. 73. Luke's version of the trials of the Sanhedrin and Pilate was termed "confused" (p. 179). See especially p. 53-76, for a discussion of Luke's account of various aspects of the passion.

Étienne TROCMÉ (1957) believed that the two-volume Lukan work had been composed around 80-85 AD[369]. Taking note of C.S.C. Williams's article proposing that Acts was written around 66-70 AD, after a Proto-Lk though prior to canonical Lk, Trocmé termed the idea "aventureuse et inutilement compliquée"[370]. He was also aware that Feine had been inspired by B. Weiss's theory about an underlying Judaeo-Christian source in the first twelve chapters of Acts[371]. These represented isolated elements which the evangelist arranged in a simple chronological and geographical framework, but probably in an arbitrary fashion. Originating from the churches in Jerusalem, Caesarea and Antioch, Trocmé argued that it would be impossible to regroup them into sources[372]. The theological materials, though apparently composed by Luke, were based upon tradition.

Mk was seen to be Luke's principal source, observing "scrupuleusement" its order, borrowing material from other sources which were then inserted into it[373]. The account of Peter's denials (22,56-62) was seen as corresponding to Mk 14,66-72. The apologetic tendency, which reflected the favorable attitude of the Romans toward the Christians, was displayed in 22,66–23,25 and such was also found in several passages in Acts[374].

Luke was credited with transferring some elements of the Sanhedrin trial to the story of Stephen in Acts. Instead of the false witnesses accusing Jesus at the trial, Luke placed their testimony on the lips of those now accusing Stephen. Trocmé further acknowledged that some materials in Acts are "simples créations de Luc".

While Luke was basically faithful to his principal source, he also took liberty in suppressing certain Markan elements in an effort at greater clarification. These redactional changes included eliminating the nocturnal session of the Sanhedrin, as well as the false witnesses and the sentence of the Sanhedrin and highlighting the political accusations made against Jesus. Three goals helped to guide Luke's redaction: his faithfulness to Mk in essential matters, his attempt to clarify even aspects of the legal process, and his apologetical tendency to exonerate the Romans. This apologia was inspired not only by the anti-Judaism sentiments of the

---

369. É. TROCMÉ, Le "Livre des Actes" et l'histoire, Paris, 1957, p. 72. This was the view of many critics as contained in Goguel's introduction to the NT. Even as recently as 1985, he maintained that the date of the composition of the two-volume Lukan work was "not written before 80 or 85 C.E. ..." (The Jews as Seen by Paul and Luke, in J. NEUSNER and E. FRERICHS [eds.], To See Ourselves as Others See Us: Christians, Jews, "Others" in Late Antiquity, Chico, CA, 1985, p. 147).

370. TROCMÉ, Le "Livre des Actes", p. 72, n. 4. Cf. C.S.C. WILLIAMS, The Date of Luke-Acts, in ExpT 64 (1952-53) 283-284.

371. TROCMÉ, Le "Livre des Actes", p. 6. Trocmé referred to two works of Feine, Die alte Quelle (1890) and Die [sic] vorkanonische Überlieferung (1891) and attributed the basis of the theories to B. WEISS, Lehrbuch der Einleitung in das Neue Testament, Berlin, 1886, p. 569f., and ³1897, p. 532-560.

372. TROCMÉ, Le "Livre des Actes", p. 216-217.

373. Ibid., p. 118-119.

374. Ibid., p. 51. For a similar tendency in Acts see 10,1f.; 13,7f.; cf. 28,7-8; 18,12f.; 19,35f.; 21,31f.; 23,16f.; 25,4-5; 27,42-44; 16,37f.; 22,22f.; 17,5f.; 24,1f.

period but also by the desire to legitimate the Christian religion for Rome[375]. The case of Barabbas was made to seem exceptional (23,18-24) while the blame for the crucifixion was placed squarely on the Jews (23,25-26).

In his study on the development of Mk Trocmé (1963) noted that the theory of a Proto-Lk was frequently defended in Germany prior to 1914 among others by Feine and B. Weiss[376]. But the chief proponents were the British scholars Streeter, Taylor and T.W. Manson. The Americans Easton and F.C. Grant (reserved, though favorable) were also advocates as was the Swedish scholar Sahlin whose view Trocmé termed "assez aventureux". Trocmé, nevertheless, did not find the argument convincing. Lukan redaction of Mk, for example, was seen as an alternative explanation to Proto-Lk. The use of additional traditions, Luke's employment of an independent passion source embellished by borrowing Markan material were also possible solutions, but the one that Trocmé preferred was that Luke based his passion account upon that of an archetype which Mark also used since it most closely conformed to Luke's literary method as Cadbury established in *The Style and Literary Method of Luke* (1920)[377].

Trocmé referred to the theory of A. Wautier d'Aygalliers seen nowhere else in the literature, that use had been made of the Markan passion in three successive recensions to which were added details from other sources[378]. Trocmé rejected this view as well as that of Taylor and Schürmann on the grounds that their views did not fit with Luke's literary method in which the Third Evangelist chose from among various sources available to him. Likewise, neither were Rehkopf's arguments convincing. Trocmé rightly wondered whether in this most important section of the Gospel Luke would abandon the work which formed the basis for the rest of his Gospel. Trocmé proposed a solution that the version of Mk used by Luke contained no account of the passion[379].

Quentin Quesnell faulted the study saying the two chapters dealing with source-critical matters (1 and 4) "laid no solid basis for this attempted redaction-analysis"[380]. Boismard characterized as "une gageure" Trocmé's desire to attribute Mk 1-13 and 14-16 to different authors[381]. Boismard believed that the problem was much more complex and that Mk was the result of several revisions of primitive Mk with a view to harmonizing it with the other Synoptics[382].

---

375. *Ibid.*, p. 101, n. 3.

376. É. TROCMÉ, *La formation de l'Évangile selon Marc* (Études d'histoire et de philosophie religieuses, 57), Paris, 1963, p. 173, n. 13 (esp. p. 173-176) = *The Formation of the Gospel according to Mark*, tr. P. GAUGHAN, Philadelphia, PA, 1975, p. 220-221, n. 3 (esp. p. 220-224) [pages in brackets].

377. *Ibid.*, p. 174-175, n. 16 [= 222, n. 2].

378. *Ibid.*, p. 175, n. 17 [= 223, n. 1]. See WAUTIER D'AYGALLIERS, *Les sources*, 1920.

379. TROCMÉ, *La formation*, p. 176 [= 224].

380. *Bib* 46 (1965) 238.

381. *RB* 72 (1965) 452.

382. *Ibid.*, p. 451-452.

The ET (1975) received a great deal of attention. Cyril Rodd declared that Trocmé "failed to show that the two parts of this gospel are completely distinct"[383]. He also asserted that many of the conclusions, in addition to the approach, were questionable. Dennis Nineham noted, as did J.R. Donahue, that the French original "had received very little notice in English-speaking journals"[384]. While not all would agree with the results, Nineham continued, describing Trocmé as "a writer whose observations and arguments are well worth pondering even by those who have reservations about some of his conclusions". Donahue, in addition to V.K. Robbins and L. Holden, rejected the thesis about Mk 1–13 and 14–16 coming from different authors[385]. Donahue stated that R.H. Lightfoot had earlier convincingly argued against such a position[386]. But some of the sharpest criticism of Trocmé's views on the passion account was advanced by M.E. Glasswell who lamented the fact that it had taken so long for the work to be translated into English. He took exception to Trocmé's theory of a separate passion source:

"But the main difficulty is the extent to which Trocmé leans on a view of Luke's passion-story as an independent version which Luke added to Mark i-xiii. The way Luke has conflated independent traditions with the outline of the Marcan passion-narrative is no different from Luke xxi in relation to Mark xiii, and Trocmé's theory leaves wide open the question of the independent origin of xiv-xvi.8 as another earlier document joined to i-xiii, independent of Luke's narrative, by the ultimate editor of Mark's Gospel. The way Mark's passion narrative is basically the same order of events but without certain traditions in Luke creates a new problem, especially when Trocmé tries to explain Luke xxiv.6 as more original than Mark xvi.7 – a verse admittedly secondary to the Marcan tradition. Mark xvi.7 is seen by Trocmé as the later editor's addition in order to restore the stress of the original ending in xiii, whilst distorting it by localizing the Parousia in Galilee. This presumes a particular interpretation of xvi.7 and builds hypothesis on hypothesis"[387].

Robbins, too, expressed surprise that Trocmé supported such a view[388]. Wansbrough was more than a little perplexed that the translation appeared so many years after the French original since it was not, in his opinion, a seminal work and

383. *ExpT* 87 (1975-76) 248.

384. *TLond* 79 (1976) 173.

385. *Interpr* 31 (1977) 202. See further V.K. ROBBINS, *ATR* 60 (1978) 101. Instead of Lightfoot, Robbins relied on W.H. KELBER (ed.), *The Passion in Mark. Studies on Mark 14–16*, Philadelphia, PA, 1976, to show "there are substantial reasons to believe that many themes introduced in 1–13 reach their conclusion in 14–16". L. HOLDEN, *Modern Churchman* 19 (1976) 173, found some of Trocmé's opinions "unusual", but declared that his was a book not to be ignored, though he had overlooked the "numerous links" between Mk 1–13 and 14–16.

386. *Interpr* 31 (1977) 202. See R.H. LIGHTFOOT, *The Gospel Message of St. Mark*, 1950, p. 48-59.

387. *JTS* 28 (1977) 148.

388. *ATR* 60 (1978) 101: "It would appear that the author still has been influenced too much by the view that one or more Passion narratives existed autonomously before a full Gospel narrative arose. This influence has prevented the author from formulating a 'generic' explanation for the entire Gospel of Mark".

its impact "limited"[389]. Like Glasswell, Wansbrough took exception to Trocmé's position on the passion, writing: "This is really no more than a hypothesis, indeed a guess. To propound it without reasoned rejection of other common and reputable theories (e.g. that Luke relies heavily on a source, known also to John, which he simply considers to be superior) is not the sort of theology which inspires confidence". F.F. Bruce also showed hesitation toward Trocmé's overall theory of the twofold edition of Mk concluding simply *"non liquet"*[390].

While generally favorable, W.R. Edwards argued that Trocmé's study placed "the written gospels so close to Jesus that it seems that the gospels would more likely give a simple historical account of the works and deeds of Jesus"[391]. And that was precisely the point of such a perspective, to highlight the historical reliability of such documents by situating them as near as possible to the events. Lionel Swain welcomed the belated translation and though he did not strictly endorse the view about the passion narrative, he seemed open to it[392]. It was not impossible that the Gospel could have circulated without an account of the passion. But Swain was aware of the divisive effect Trocmé's book could have[393].

Trocmé (1971) did not believe that Lindsey's theory about a very ancient account of the life of Jesus dismantled the priority of Mk[394]. The passion was "bien plus cohérent, bien plus solide et bien plus ancien" than the rest of the material in the four Gospels, which Trocmé acknowledged resulted from the redactional work of the evangelists[395]. Trocmé believed that in the passion narrative Luke used another source that was very different from that employed by Mark[396]. Here, in essence, Trocmé offered his view that the various Gospel accounts of the passion were rooted in the same basic archetype derived from ancient liturgical practice[397]. Though not exact as an historical document, it

389. *ScriptB* 6 (1975) 40.

390. *EvQ* 48 (1976) 118.

391. *PerspRelSt* 4 (1977) 298.

392. *Month* 237 (1976) 248-249.

393. *Ibid.*, p. 249: "This is a book which, like the Gospel, will divide its readers".

394. É. TROCMÉ, *Jésus de Nazareth vu par les témoins de sa vie*, Neuchâtel (Switzerland), 1971, p. 24 (= *Jesus as Seen by his Contemporaries*, tr. R.A. WILSON, London - Philadelphia, PA, 1973, p. 14, 128, n. 2). The section dealing with Lindsey was abbreviated in the ET. The book was based on Speaker's Lectures at Oxford 1965-66. Cf. LINDSEY, *A Modified Two-Document Theory*, in *NT* 6 (1963) 239-263.

395. TROCMÉ, *Jésus de Nazareth*, p. 76 (= 64).

396. *Ibid.*, p. 77 (= 65): "Les divergences beaucoup plus sérieuses qu'il y a entre Marc et Luc tiennent au fait que Luc suit ici une autre source".

397. *Ibid.*, p. 81; = ET, p. 68. Trocmé was inspired to adopt the solution of a liturgically formulated passion account under the influence of two works: P. CARRINGTON, *The Primitive Christian Calendar*, Vol. 1, Cambridge, 1952, p. 75-89 and 204-227, and G. SCHILLE, *Das Leiden des Herrn*, in *ZTK* 52 (1955) 161-205 (TROCMÉ, *Jésus de Nazareth*, p. 79 = ET, p. 67, 129, n. 7 and 8). Carrington (1952) argued that there had been a separate passion narrative in circulation before that of Mk and that the passion narrative was originally separate from Greek Mk (p. 62, 204). This original account extended from the Last Supper on the first evening through the burial

afforded the broad outline of the events as they unfolded. The guarantee of the
authenticity of the facts contained in the accounts of the passion stemmed from
their being based on the archetype which derived from the most ancient Jerusalem
Church. But the community, through its authorized witnesses, also helped to shape
the accounts of the passion which reflect the impact the martyrdom of Jesus had
upon his disciples[398].

Trocmé ascribed to the view that the charges made against Jesus in 23,2 and
Jn 18,29; 19,12 had been drawn from the *titulus* on the cross. The silence of Jesus
during the greater part of his trial too, was an element drawn from the archetype
of the passion. But Trocmé also understood that to be an echo of the Suffering
Servant in Is 53,7. Verse 23,70 was seen as secondary and the role of the Jewish
and Roman authorities was presented in a confusing fashion in the accounts of the
passion, though the emphasis in all of them was focused on Jesus.

As in his 1957 work on Acts, Trocmé drew attention to the absence of the
false witnesses from the Gospel account of Jesus' trial and which has been
transferred to the story of Stephen in Acts 6,13-14[399].

As opposed to his work on the formation of Mk, Trocmé seemed to have
garnered a little more support of his view on the passion narratives in reaction to
the French edition of this later work. G. Schneider referred to Trocmé's position
on the passion narrative, which focused on the circumstances surrounding the
passion as well as the reaction of the disciples to it[400]. Jaubert pointedly noted
that Trocmé's discussion of the so-called biographical narratives was basically the
account of the passion[401]. The major critique as regards the passion stemmed
from Trocmé's apparent oversight that Jaubert, too, argued that the passion texts
were transmitted through the liturgy[402].

on the second evening. The idea that the passion narrative developed "as a ritual for liturgical
purposes" (p. 204) was a view which Carrington asserted was held by numerous, though unnamed,
modern scholars. Carrington believed that Lk was not a liturgical work itself, though its account of
the passion was read on Wednesday of Holy Week (p. 205). Luke derived some materials from
sources earlier than 60 AD and Carrington dated the composition of the two-volume work "as early
as the 60's" (p. 62). He proposed, as Trocmé indicated, the idea that the passion narrative may have
been a *megillah*, a scroll which was designated to be read on special occasions (p. 204-205).

In his Markan commentary (1960) Carrington continued to promote his idea that Mt and Mk "had
been so composed or arranged as to be read through in sequence Sunday by Sunday in accordance
with the Jewish calendar; with the exception of the Passion narrative, which was designed to be read
as a whole at the Feast of the Passover" (*According to Mark. A Running Commentary on the Oldest
Gospel*, London, p. 1; see also p. 8, 346). In an appendix (p. 346-371) he developed his theory "to
meet criticisms, reconsider suggestions, solidify the main lines of the argument, and supply some
background material with regard to the calendar and the textual evidence" (p. 346).

398. TROCMÉ, *Jésus de Nazareth*, p. 84 (= 71).

399. *Ibid.*, p. 130 (= 114). See TROCMÉ, *Le "Livre des Actes"*, 1957, p. 186-187.

400. *BZ* 18 (1974) 110.

401. *RHistRel* 185 (1974) 213.

402. *Ibid.*, p. 214: "Pour les récits de la Passion, il adopte l'hypothèse du document cultuel
et semble ignorer que, nous aussi, nous parlons pour ces textes de transmission liturgique. Dans

The response to the ET was mixed ranging from supportive to cautious and skeptical. Paul Minear evaluated it as a "fascinating and important book which merits wide reading and thorough testing"[403]. For him Trocmé's conception of logia, apothegms and the archetypal passion "constitutes a substantive contribution to Gospel research, enhancing confidence in the reliability of the portrait which results"[404]. Referring to the idea that the passion narrative went back to the liturgy, Nineham commented that this "is an interesting suggestion, though the brevity of the treatment prevents its being much more"[405]. Again, in reference to the passion Nineham wrote: "Perhaps most important of all, [Trocmé's] confidence in distinguishing what belongs to the original, memorized, tradition is sometimes rather astonishing. For instance, he writes apropos some of the meanings the Evangelists found in the passion: 'In this first naïve form, they surely represent the reaction of the first disciples to the tragedy of the cross' (p. 74). Much virtue in your 'surely'!"[406]. The plausibility of his whole thesis was in need of a great deal more argument in Nineham's opinion. Though the work reminded Nineham of Cadbury's study on the Gospels, in contrast, the insights had not been fully carried through.

His study of Jesus of Nazareth was followed in 1983 with Trocmé's, *The Passion as Liturgy*, in which he reprised his idea of an archetypal passion account descending from the liturgical *Sitz im Leben* in which there were three independent accounts[407]. He continued to argue that Luke possessed and worked from a defective copy of Mk which ended at Mk 13,37 and that the Markan passion narrative was separate from Mk 1–13[408]. Also consistent with his 1971 study was

---

ses options, il montre une large information et se tient dans une voie moyenne, loin des hypothèses réductrices pour la personnne de Jésus, réservé par rapport à toute historicisation. On pourrait dire cependant que sa prédilection pour Marc lui donne un angle de vision trop restreint".

403. *Religious Studies* 10 (1974) 359.

404. *Ibid.*, p. 358.

405. *JTS* 25 (1974) 160.

406. *Ibid.*, p. 162.

407. É. TROCMÉ, *The Passion as Liturgy. A Study in the Origin of the Passion Narratives in the Four Gospels*, London, 1983 (esp. p. 27-37: "The Passion Narrative in Luke"). The book was the published form of the Passiontide Lectures presented at Lincoln Theological College, March 31-April 2, 1980. See his comment p. 33: "it is therefore a better hypothesis to assume that the Markan and the Lukan texts are based each on its own tradition, both traditions going back to the same archetype, from which they diverged progressively". See also p. 49, 63. Trocmé offered a list of the narrative elements which he believed constituted the original archetype. Numbers 9-13 were the most pertinent for our discussion (p. 74-75). Later he situated the original passion account as follows: "It seems only natural to assume that a tradition of this kind had its *Sitz im Leben* in the worshipping life of a Christian community which was still influenced by Jewish customs" (p. 80) and centered on a "liturgical commemoration of Christ's death by Christians during the Jewish Passover celebration" (p. 82) dated sometime before 40 AD (p. 85). The historical reliability of the account of the passion would also thus be reinforced. But Trocmé was not unaware that there were discrepancies in relating judicial matters.

408. *Ibid.*, p. 96, n. 15. See p. 12. Trocmé responded to the criticism of Kelber and Donahue, among others, that both Mk 1–13 and 14–16 reflected the redactional work of the

his endorsement of Carrington's idea that the Markan passion stemmed from the *megillah* which was read at the Christian celebration of the Jewish Passover[409]. Inspired by Rehkopf and Taylor Trocmé relied heavily on statistics to make a case for a separate passion account. He conceded that the "vast majority of scholars" considered Mk to be one of Luke's two or three principal sources. Nevertheless, the Markan passion did not influence the Lukan since Luke's edition of Mk did not contain an account of the passion[410].

Since there was only a 30% verbal agreement with Mk for Peter's denials and the trial (22,54-71) and the order and certain details varied from those found in Mk, Trocmé was led to believe that Luke relied on a separate, though not ultimately, independent tradition[411]. The absence of the mockery by the Roman soldiers was rightly seen as due to apologetics in order to show the Romans in a favorable light. It was argued that this pericope would have been found in the original passion narrative[412]. Both Mk and Lk went back to a simpler archetype of the passion. The trial of Pilate (23,1-25) was considered a unit.

These passion accounts were not simply records of facts, but were given a particular order determined by chronology, topography and logic. The archetype drew on a variety of sources later to be composed into a cohesive narrative[413].

---

evangelist basing his disagreement on the lack of scholarly consensus about what precisely constituted Markan style (p. 15). He concluded "no redactional style exists in Mark" (p. 17) but that the differences can be understood by a differing use of christological titles (p. 18). In her 1991 commentary on Mk M. Hooker noted that there had been significant support for the view that the Markan passion was distinct from the remainder of Mk. Without taking a position, she acknowledged that Markan redaction was to be found throughout the entire Gospel and cited J.R. Donahue in support of this latter perspective (*The Gospel According to Saint Mark*, London - Peabody, MA, 1991, p. 325. See J.R. DONAHUE, *From Passion Traditions to Passion Narrative*, in KELBER [ed.], *Passion*, p. 8-16).

In another article published in 1976 Donahue called attention to the question of the relation of Lk to Mk which he termed "problematic" (*Passion Narrative*, in *IDBS*, 1976, 643-645, p. 644). On the issue of order he stated: "Also, while in the body of the gospel Luke carefully follows the Markan order, in the passion narrative there is constant transposition and alteration of this order". He offered no opinion on the source question and summarized by declaring: "While there is no consensus on this subject, a definite Lukan theology does emerge in the passion narrative" (p. 644-645). Part of this theology presented Jesus "as the paradigm of the innocent martyr" (p. 645).

409. TROCMÉ, *The Passion as Liturgy*, p. 81-82.

410. *Ibid.*, p. 37.

411. *Ibid.*, p. 32: "Thus, once again, we are led to assume that the traditions behind the two gospels were independent from each other, but were both derived from a common archetype, and that Luke made no use of the Markan narrative". The Lukan account of Peter's denials lacks the dramatic progression such as is found in Mt, for example. The drama in the Lukan version arises from Jesus' glance at Peter (22,61) (p. 22).

412. See p. 73-74, 75. Trocmé envisioned the possibility that Luke omitted this story in favor of the reference to the soldiers mocking Jesus on the cross (23,36f.).

413. *Ibid.*, p. 54. He continued to maintain, as he had in 1957, that it would be difficult to separate the different elements into the various sources (*The Passion as Liturgy*, p. 54. See TROCMÉ, *Le "Livre des Actes"*, p. 216-217).

The special material of the Lukan passion narrative was accounted for generally by elements some of which were editorial and the remainder being traditional[414].

But his final explanation could be advanced for Lukan redaction of the Markan passion: "First, that long tradition unit must have been built on the same plan as Mark 14-16, apart from minor differences which we noticed as we were going through the narrative. The main divergences occur inside each pericope and have to do with the literary structure, the vocabulary and some details of it. In other words, the skeleton of the two Passion narratives found in the church tradition is the same. The best way to account for that state of things is to assume that both were derived from an archetype which had a firm structure, but remained quite supple as far as the details of the narrative were concerned. That archetype of the Passion narratives existed before the traditions used by Mark and Luke started diverging. This takes us back a long time, well before AD 70 in any case"[415].

Trocmé (1983) was of the opinion that there was very little in 23,1-25 that "coincides" with the Mk[416]. Based on verbal dissimilarities, he concluded that Mk was not the source for Luke in this section. Trocmé advocated the view that in addition to a separate passion account independent of Mk, Luke used "isolated tradition units", of which the Herod story was one[417]. However, Trocmé then proceeded to declare that narrative which Luke purportedly followed "must have built on the same plan as Mark 14-16, apart from minor differences which we noticed as we were going through the narrative"[418]. But Trocmé cannot have it both ways. Either it was completely different[419], or the accounts are remarkably alike[420].

Ignoring verbal similarities as well as likeness of motifs, Trocmé contended that Luke did not know Mk because the Markan text Luke was using was devoid of a passion narrative as well as the appendix[421]. Denying that Luke was dependent upon Mk, Trocmé nonetheless pointed out their similarities which included the same people (Pilate, Jewish religious leaders), an identical situation, and the outcome of a death sentence for Jesus. Once again these were ascribed to the "archetype".

Trocmé further noted that Luke omitted any mention of a mockery as found in the other Gospels, and there was a lack of reference to the suffering of Jesus

---

414. TROCMÉ, *The Passion as Liturgy*, p. 69. He did not specify what he attributed to each.

415. *Ibid.*, p. 36.

416. *Ibid.*, p. 33.

417. *Ibid.*, p. 36.

418. *Ibid.*

419. *Ibid.*: "The differences between [Luke's] narrative in chs. 22-24 and Mark 14-16 are so great that he cannot be said to have opted in favour of Mark's story".

420. *Ibid*: "The main divergences occur inside each pericope and have to do with the literary structure, the vocabulary and some details of it. In other words, the skeleton of the two Passion narratives found in church tradition is the same". Trocmé then suggested they derived from a GS, which he termed an "archetype".

421. *Ibid.*, p. 37.

which served apologetical tendencies to portray Rome in a more positive light[422]. On this last point Trocmé was influenced by Conzelmann.

Though J.L. Houlden considered Trocmé's proposal of the contents of the archetypal passion as "a reasoned statement"[423], Brian McNeil expressed reservations about Trocmé's theory of a common archetype, but did not go into specifics since they "would require more detailed argument for their dispelling than Trocmé" presented in favor of them[424].

Joel Green concluded that Trocmé was not successful in his argument that Luke did not base his passion narrative on that of Mk[425]. Green attacked Trocmé's study of the vocabulary comparison, censuring him for neglecting to credit Luke for what "seems certain" to Green was "a direct literary dependence". This challenge, made also to Taylor earlier, often recurred. Those who argued against Luke's redaction of the Markan passion, often undervalue the evidence. Trocmé was also critiqued by Green for being too certain of the contents of the archetype. Urging greater reserve, Green wrote: "Such reconstructions are at best provisional and should be handled with all due caution". Green further argued against the independent circulation of various elements of the primitive archetype. And while Green differed on many of Trocmé's arguments, he nonetheless endorsed the view that "early Christian worship" provided the *Sitz im Leben* from which a pre-canonical passion narrative arose[426].

Dennis Nineham assessed that though Trocmé might enjoy "more widespread support" of his views on Lk than he had on Mk, "he hardly does justice to the powerful counter-arguments that have been brought forward, for example by J.M. Creed in his magisterial commentary on the Gospel"[427]. In the end, Nineham wondered whether it was possible to ascertain an answer to the quest for the "historical truth behind the Gospels"[428].

Concerning the Herod pericope Trocmé (1957) identified 23,6-16 as one of several isolated passages which Luke inserted into the fundamental Markan schema[429]. The trial before Herod (23,6-12) was justified by Jesus' Galilean heritage[430]. Incorporating elements from the Christian tradition that Pilate participated in the passion and Herod reacted to Jesus' popularity, Luke sought to include these in his account just as Mark did in his own. Lk 23,6-16 and Acts 4,27 were seen in the same light. These elements helped to provide a generally historic

---

422. *Ibid.*, p. 33-34.
423. *ExpT* 94 (1982-83) 278.
424. *HeythJ* 27 (1986) 186-187.
425. *EvQ* 56 (1984) 187.
426. *Ibid.*, p. 188.
427. *TLond* 87 (1984) 226-228.
428. *Ibid.*, p. 228.
429. TROCMÉ, *Le "Livre"*, 1957, p. 119. It should be noted that Trocmé referred to the passage both as 23,6-16 (p. 95, 119) and 23,6-12 (p. 101) without explaining the difference or his rationale.
430. *Ibid.*, p. 101.

framework and identify the work of the evangelist as historical[431]. Though not speaking specifically of the Herod pericope, Trocmé dismissed the idea that the apocryphal gospels could have served as sources for Lk[432]. In his study of the formation of Mk (1963) Trocmé defined the Herod pericope as 23,4-16[433], whereas in his work on Acts he wrote of it both as 23,6-16 and 23,6-12.

Still later Trocmé (1983) continued to define the Herod pericope both as 23,6-12 ("a trial before Herod")[434] as well as 23,6-16 (Herod's trial)[435]. When the story was taken in consort with all of 23,1-25 the verbal agreement with Mk was 12.6% while the percentage increased to 17% when the Herod account was not included in the calculations[436].

Xavier LÉON-DUFOUR (1959) opted for a source "à tout le moins semblable à Mk" besides which Luke utilized "traditions particulières"[437]. Later he argued against himself in attempting to refute Vaganay. "Évoquer à côté de Mc. une autre source à peu près identique, c'est pratiquement renoncer à 'faire le partage entre elle'"[438]. Léon-Dufour offered three reasons for positing the non-Markan source: 1) the sections at the beginning and end of Lk were non-Markan; 2) there was a variation in diction, syntax and style, and 3) shifts in meanings of words occurred between Mk and Lk. Léon-Dufour adopted the proposal of Vaganay that Luke possessed, in addition to Mk, the Greek version of Aramaic Mt, claiming this best explained the similarity of Mt and Lk against Mk[439]. His endorsement must be

431. *Ibid.*, p. 95. Once again Trocmé pointed to important parallels between the Gospel and Acts in regard to Herod. Herod's hostile attitude toward Jesus was seen in 13,31-32 and Acts 4,27 and the trial was described in 23,6-16 and Acts 4,27.

432. *Ibid.*, p. 43: "Un seul fait paraît assuré de toute manière: l'Évangile de Marc figure parmi les prédécesseurs que l'auteur *ad Theophilum* se reconnaissait. Les Évangiles apocryphes sont trop tardifs pour pouvoir entrer en ligne de compte, quoi qu'Origène ait pu en dire".

433. TROCMÉ, *La formation*, 1963, p. 174 (= 222). Like Trocmé, though not necessarily influenced by him, HOOKER defined the trial before Herod pericope both as 23,6-12 and 23,4-16 (*Studying the New Testament*, London, 1979; Minneapolis, MN, 1982, p. 97, 105). She listed other special Lukan material including 22,15-17.31-33.35-38.43-44;23,4-16.27-32.39-43.55-56.

434. TROCMÉ, *The Passion as Liturgy*, p. 33, 37 (where he referred to it as an isolated unit of tradition), 70 ("the questioning of Jesus by Herod").

435. *Ibid.*, p. 63.

436. *Ibid.*, p. 33.

437. X. LÉON-DUFOUR, *Les évangiles synoptiques*, 1959, p. 233 (= *The Synoptic Gospels*, in A. ROBERT and A. FEUILLET [eds.], *Introduction to the New Testament*, tr. P.W. SKEHAN, et al., New York, 1965, p. 225). The section included several chapters important for our study, including *L'évangile selon saint Luc*, 231-257 (= *The Gospel According to Luke*, 223-249; Le fait synoptique, 258-295 = *The Synoptic Problem*, 252-286; and *Aux sources des évangiles*, 296-320; = *The Sources of the Gospels*, 288-310).

438. *Ibid.*, p. 233 (= 272). Cf. VAGANAY, *Le problème synoptique*, p. 313.

439. LÉON-DUFOUR, *Les évangiles synoptiques*, p. 287 (= *The Synoptic Gospels*, 1965, p. 272 = ID. and C. PERROT, *L'annonce de l'Évangile* [Introduction à la Bible. Le Nouveau Testament, 2], Paris, 1976, p. 176-177). Cf. p. 279.

regarded as qualified in the light of later remarks[440]. The French Jesuit exegete's particular approach bore a slight nuance on the matter of Lukan dependence. His conclusion, following the suggestion of Sanday, was that Luke was familiar with Mk and had read it, but put it aside in the composition of his own work[441]. At the very least, there was partial dependence and oral tradition can possibly account for other similarities[442]. For the passion, Léon-Dufour asserted: "... le récit de Passion est substantiellement identique à celui de Mc. avec les insertions habituelles de Lc."[443]. Additional material, such as Manaen's account of the Herod story (23,7-12), was provided through the recollections of individuals and groups.

Léon-Dufour was of the opinion that Luke's plan for his Gospel explained all "les transpositions notables"[444]. The determination of Lukan dependence upon Mk rested on the issue "que son [Lc.] ordonnance est semblable à celle de Mc."[445]. But the question of order cannot be separated from the attendant issues of content and expression.

Lukan redaction sometimes grouped material together, as in the case of Peter's denials (22,54-62), for "dramatic" purposes. Omissions occurred to avoid similar traditions, prevent excessive expansion of the text beyond what the scrolls can hold, or to avoid giving scandal, for example, the family of Jesus believed him to be crazy[446]. Some phenomena which were held to be omissions were, in fact, only transpositions[447].

The passion narrative was seen as a combination of eyewitness reports and literary compositions. The historical value was unquestionable, in part, because their theological significance was inseparable from the question of historical worth[448]. Taking stock of the negative response to the Proto-Lk theory, Léon-Dufour echoed the critique of S. MacLean Gilmour who assessed the hypothesis as a "brillante chimère de la critique"[449]. Luke's variation in Greek style was

440. LÉON-DUFOUR, *Les évangiles synoptiques*, p. 288; *The Synoptic Gospels*, p. 279 (= 1976, p. 177). Léon-Dufour's later edition further criticized Vaganay's attempt at defining precisely the second source which was believed to have been translated into Greek (Sg) and added an additional note on P. Parker, who offered a documentary theory similar to that of Vaganay (p. 177-178).

441. *Les évangiles synoptiques*, p. 283 (= 274 = 1976, p. 169). This proposal, Léon-Dufour contended, was supported by archaeological evidence and avoided the pitfalls of other traditional explanations.

442. *Ibid.*

443. *Ibid.*, p. 280 (= 271).

444. *Les évangiles synoptiques*, p. 279 (= 270 = 1976, p. 164). He did not expressly refer to any transpositions in the passion narrative.

445. *Ibid.*, p. 279 (= 1976, p. 165; cf. p. 164): "L'*ordonnance* des matériaux chez Lc est à peu d'exceptions près identique à celle de Mc".

446. *Ibid.*, p. 269.

447. *Ibid.*

448. *Les évangiles synoptiques*, p. 310 (= p. 300).

449. *Ibid.*, p. 234 (= p. 226). See S. McL. GILMOUR, *A Critical Re-Examination*, in *JBL* 67 (1948) 152.

regarded by Léon-Dufour as a blending of Septuagintal style and Luke's own personal approach with various corrections[450]. Léon-Dufour found this explanation plausible in demonstrating how the Gospel more closely resembled the first rather than the second half of Acts.

In discussing the existence of a primitive account of the passion narrative Léon-Dufour (1960) observed that Feine, Schniewind, Streeter, Taylor, Cerfaux, Schürmann, Jeremias and Rehkopf signaled their support of the idea of a special source for Lk[451]. Spitta was also mentioned for his efforts to resurrect the idea of the GS[452]. The theme of Jesus' innocence had been systematically developed in 23,4-5.13-16.22-23 from the old tradition recorded in Acts 3,13-14 drawn from Is. 53[453].

Concerning the question of Lukan dependence upon Mk, Léon-Dufour distinguished between two camps. The first believed that Lk was based upon Mk and this group included Dibelius, Finegan, Creed and Schmid[454]. Some limited dependence upon Mk to certain pericopes such as the trial before the Sanhedrin (including Lietzmann and Blinzler). Others believed that Luke combined Mk and special sources. He counted Bultmann, Hauck, Rengstorf and Cerfaux among these adherents. The difference in order was also noted[455]. Maintaining that Lk and Mt were independent of each other[456], Léon-Dufour called attention to the MAs in 22,64 / Mt 26,68 and 22,62 / Mt 26,75[457]. The literary analysis confirmed for Léon-Dufour the historical value of some of the material proper to Lk[458].

The insertion of the Herod story (23,6-12) "permet de renforcer le thème de l'innocence par une triple déclaration dans la bouche de Pilate (4,13-16,22)"[459]. The silence of Jesus before Herod (23,9) hardly depicted Jesus as a zealot or revolutionary. Léon-Dufour (1960), under the topic of major problems of historical criticism, referred to the Herod episode which he maintained was basically historical[460]. He considered this a very common scholarly opinion. Later (1965),

---

450. LÉON-DUFOUR, *Les évangiles synoptiques*, p. 233 (= *The Synoptic Gospels*, p. 225 = 1976, p. 113). Note the error in the later work in referring to Gächter as Garchter.

451. X. LÉON-DUFOUR, *Passion (Récits de la)*, in *DBS* 6, 1960, cols. 1419-1492, col. 1424. His later list of strong advocates of a special Lukan source varied only slightly. He added Hawkins and Perry. Rehkopf, following Jeremias, was said to have proven the non-Markan parts of Lk (col. 1447).

452. *Ibid.*, col. 1439.

453. *Ibid.*, col. 1431; see also col. 1443.

454. *Ibid.*, col. 1447.

455. *Ibid.*

456. *Ibid.*, col. 1444.

457. *Ibid.*, col. 1445.

458. *Ibid.*, col. 1476.

459. *Ibid.*, col. 1468.

460. LÉON-DUFOUR, *Passion*, in *DBS* 6, 1960, 1487: "L'épisode est assez communément tenu pour historique dans son fond (même par Bultmann)", citing works by Blinzler as references. Cf. BLINZLER, *Herodes Antipas und Jesus Christus*, 1947; *Herodes und der Tod Jesu*, in *Klerusblatt* 37 (1957) 118-121.

he asserted that additional material, such as Manaen's account of the Herod story (23,7-12), was provided through the recollections of individuals and groups[461].

Frans Neirynck penned a review of *Les Évangiles Synoptiques* in which he keenly observed that, although the book was hailed as updated and completely revised (1976), such was not the case[462]. Rather, it often only reprised the 1959 edition. Though the bibliography had been brought up to date, it did not significantly alter Léon-Dufour's older presentation, even to the point of repeating typographical errors. What was more, the 1976 work often ignored important studies, including Neirynck's study of Gaboury's theory. Léon-Dufour's sympathy for this solution since 1967 was once more apparent, though such a hypothesis appeared to Neirynck "comme la solution du désespoir"[463]. On these grounds, the value of Léon-Dufour's contribution to the discussion on the synoptic problem was greatly diminished.

In conversation with the work of Perry and Danby Joseph B. TYSON (1959) claimed that Luke drew upon two sources for the trial of Jesus (22,66-23,25)[464]. The sources were Mk and L, the latter which Perry designated as J. Mk was responsible for 23,18-25 despite Luke's omission of recalling the custom of the Passover amnesty. Editorial material was found in 23,1.3-5.13-16. Lk 23,3 was cited as definite confirmation that Luke was indeed using Mk at this point in the account. The section 23,13-16 served as a bridge to connect 23,6-12 and 23,18-25. The L source was recognized then in 22,66-71; 23,2.6-12[465]. Luke's use of Mk ranged from less careful than Matthew to utilizing it "with great freedom"[466]. Unfortunately, the combination of the two sources resulted in "a most confused point of view"[467]. The L source "makes good historical and legal sense" to Tyson for three reasons: 1) all legal objections to the idea of a formal trial were resolved by the presentation of a pre-trial hearing; 2) the charges brought against Jesus were presented in a unified fashion and 3) the special source contained the Herod episode and it was reasonable that Herod knew Jesus and had earlier attempted to arrest him[468]. Tyson referred to the order by commenting that in Lk

461. LÉON-DUFOUR, *Les évangiles synoptiques*, p. 234 (= *The Synoptic Gospels*, p. 226).

462. *Review: X. LÉON-DUFOUR, Les Évangiles Synoptiques, 1976*, in *ETL* 55 (1979) 405-409 (= *Evangelica*, 724-728 [728, Note: Le document Q; *Evangelica II*, 1991, 803]).

463. *Ibid.*, p. 407; = 1982, p. 726.

464. J.B. TYSON, *The Lukan Version of the Trial of Jesus*, in *NT* 3 (1959) 251. See PERRY, *Sources*, 1920, and DANBY, *Bearing*, 1920.

465. TYSON, *The Lukan Version*, p. 252. Here he offered a reconstruction of the L source. He considered the material to divide naturally into five sections. Eliminating 23,1.3-5 as editorial additions, these were: 22,66-71; 23,2; 23,6-12; 23,13-16; 23,18-25.

466. *Ibid.*, p. 251. Luke employed Mk "only where necessary".

467. *Ibid.*, p. 257.

468. *Ibid.*, p. 258.

the trial followed the denial of Peter[469]. The phenomenon of order did not figure prominently in Tyson's argumentation.

Tyson rejected Danby's objections to the Lukan trial on the basis that they would apply only if Luke's version were a legal trial. Tyson maintained that it was not[470].

Without direct reference to Burkitt, but in opposition to his point of view, Tyson argued that Q did not serve as a source for this section of the passion narrative[471]. Like Perry and later Taylor, Tyson believed that the account found in the special source was "at many points superior to that of Mark"[472]. The Lukan portrayal cast heavier responsibility upon the Jewish leaders. Tyson took the position that what was recounted in 22,66-71 was not a formal trial but simply a "pre-trial hearing" in which the Sanhedrin evaluated evidence against Jesus in order to decide whether they should present this case to Pilate. To the L source was likewise attributed the two separate questions of whether Jesus was the Christ and the Son of God. The "three-fold charge" contained in 23,2 was regarded as authentic because Luke as well as the Church sought to present the ministry and community of Jesus "as non-political".

In a later work Tyson (1973) alluded to Luke's method of weaving Markan material together with that taken from his special source[473]. In his revision (²1984) Tyson rewrote this section and omitted this reference to the special Lukan source in the trial[474]. Throughout a brief treatment of Lk 22–23 Tyson made no mention of a special source, nor did he comment on Luke's compositional method. He merely indicated a few differences between Lk on the one hand and Mt and Mk on the other[475].

Tyson (1984) prescinded from the source question, which "complicates the task of applying literary perspectives to Luke-Acts", though he conceded certainty in the matter of sources would benefit his literary-critical task[476]. But Tyson

---

469. The differences in order are simply identified in his comparison of the three Synoptic Gospels which he organized by means of parallel columns (p. 249-250).

470. *Ibid.*, p. 253-254. Of a total of 16 objections raised by Danby, 12 did not apply to the Lukan account. Danby himself admitted there was insufficient evidence concerning yet another. The final three pertained only in the case of a formal trial.

471. *Ibid.*, p. 249. See also p. 250, 251.

472. *Ibid.*, p. 251.

473. TYSON, *A Study of Early Christianity*, New York - London, 1973, p. 208: "In the passion narrative, Luke weaves material from Mark with some from his own special source and conveys quite a different impression of Jesus' trial".

474. *The New Testament and Early Christianity*, New York - London, ²1984 ("expanded and reorganized version" of 1973), p. 182, 184. However, he quoted from Streeter regarding the "interweaving of sources" (p. 155).

475. *Ibid.*, p. 184.

476. TYSON, *The Jewish Public in Luke-Acts*, in *NTS* 30 (1984) 575. "In this light it seems advisable to proceed to the study of Luke-Acts, ... but without assuming a particular stance on source questions" (p. 576).

distinguished himself from many other practitioners of the new literary criticism
by also considering other Synoptic parallels.

In *The Death of Jesus in Luke-Acts* (1986), Tyson appealed that the source
question be tabled because of what he perceived to be an impasse, so that attention
might be directed "to face the question of the literary character and genre of these
writings"[477].

In a more recent work (1992) Tyson adopted the reader response method[478].
As such he was not concerned with the question of sources[479]. He defended his
approach by indicating there was benefit to be realized from looking at the Gospel
in an wholistic manner[480]. Tyson was not only intent to show connections
between the Gospel and Acts, as in 23,18-19 and Acts 3,14, but suggested that
earlier narratives in the Gospel were useful in understanding subsequent ones[481].
One example Tyson offered was the parable of the vineyard (20,9-19) which he
suggested was "a reliable guide to the passion narrative in Luke"[482]. Here, Tyson
alluded to a change of order in Lk over against Mt and Mk that Tyson credited to
Luke as a means of preparing for the passion narrative[483]. Finally, in a fashion

477. TYSON, *The Death of Jesus in Luke-Acts*, Columbia, SC, 1986, p. 9.

478. TYSON, *Images of Judaism in Luke-Acts*, Columbia, SC, 1992, p. vii.

479. *Ibid.*, p. 15: "Nor should we, in the case of the Gospel of Luke, draw up an outline in
terms of an alleged source of Luke, be it Mark, or Q, or Matthew. Although comparisons
between Luke and the other two Synoptic Gospels may be of interest and value, the state of our
knowledge about the use of sources by Luke is such that we cannot make defensible and
meaningful observations on the basis of a supposed source theory. The source problems for Acts
are even more serious".

480. *Ibid.*, p. 16: "Even though there are most certainly sources behind both Luke and Acts,
these texts will be treated in their present form, without respect to their supposed sources. The
justification for this procedure has been set forth in a number of articles and monographs and
need not be repeated here. Suffice it to say that recent source-critical studies of the Synoptic
Gospels have questioned the legitimacy of assuming the two-document hypothesis and making use
of it in redaction-critical work. As yet, however, no rival hypothesis has supplanted it. At the
same time, literary-critical studies have shown the utility of approaching a document as a whole
rather than breaking it up into its supposed *Vorlage*. While form-critical and source-critical studies
are certainly valuable, it is also worthwhile to study NT documents in something approximating
their final shape". As has been recently noted, the literary-critical method "appears to be
beneficial for the redactional interpretation of Luke's special material" (F. NEIRYNCK, *Literary
Criticism: Old and New*, in C. FOCANT [ed.], *The Synoptic Gospels*, p. 27).

481. TYSON, *Images*, p. 106.

482. *Ibid.*, p. 86.

483. *Ibid.*, p. 97, n. 13: "Both Matt 21:39 and Mk 12:8 say that the tenants killed the son
and threw him out of the vineyard implying dishonor to the corpse. Luke's order, rejection and
execution, encourages the reader to anticipate a narrative about the official Jewish rejection of
Jesus prior to his execution. As we shall see, Luke 22:66-71 is this anticipated narrative".
Unfortunately, Tyson misread the Gospel texts. Both Mt and Lk agree against Mk in the order.
While Mk 12,8 related that the son was first killed and then cast out of the vineyard, both Mt
21,39 and Lk 20,15 recount that the son was cast out and only then was he killed. Fitzmyer noted
this correctly. "Here both Matthew and Luke reverse the order of actions; the son is driven out
of the vineyard and then killed. They have both undoubtedly done this in light of the passion

similar to Matera and Heil, Tyson spoke of irony in this section of the passion narrative, particularly in 22,70 and 23,3-4[484].

Though his method evolved, he continued to hold that 22,66-71 was not a formal trial and that the responsibility of the Jews for the death of Jesus was skillfully recounted in Lk 22–23[485]. Regarding 23,2 Tyson said that Luke "takes special pains to list specific charges"[486]. It will be remembered that in his 1959 article he espoused the view that this material derived from L[487].

Tyson (1959), though influenced to a certain extent by the view of Perry, offered a perspective that was quite different from his. He asserted that 23,6-12 was a combination of the Markan presentation with that of L[488]. The L source, which Tyson equated with the one designated J by Perry, would have detailed Jesus being delivered to Pilate following a brief early morning examination of the Sanhedrin. The result was a rather confusing narrative. Furthermore, Tyson viewed 23,13-16, which the L source contributed, as editorial material bridging 23,6-12 and 23,18-25[489]. Tyson reacted against the idea that 23,6-12 related to any apologetical goal of Luke, and likewise rejected the view of Dibelius that the story resulted from the influence of Ps 2 since: 1) it was not explicitly mentioned in the trial, and 2) Luke would have clarified this fulfillment of prophecy if such had been his purpose[490].

Although the Herod pericope served "a historical purpose"[491] and made "historical sense"[492], the historicity it presented was one that was consistent with Mk rather than of the J presentation. That according to the Markan portrayal

narrative and the burial of Jesus" (*Luke*, p. 1284-1285. So also F.W. DANKER, *Jesus*, 1972, p. 201, I.H. MARSHALL, *Luke*, 1978, p. 731, G. SCHNEIDER, *Lukas*, ²1984, p. 399, and L.T. JOHNSON, *Luke*, 1991, p. 306).

484. TYSON, *Images*, p. 97, n. 22.

485. *Ibid.*, p. 79. See also p. 106.

486. *Ibid.* p. 79. He also contrasted Mk/Mt with Lk regarding the charges (p. 93).

487. See TYSON, *Lukan Version*, p. 252, 255.

488. TYSON, *Lukan Version*, p. 257. Cf. PERRY, *Sources*, p. 45. Perry declared that 23,4-15 stemmed from the J document. "For the rest of the section, while there are in every verse details paralleled in Mark or in other portions of Luke in different connections, it is inconceivable that the evangelist should suddenly have altered his editorial method (see p. 15-17) to the extent of building up this account out of such scattered hints; and their very transposition to this point (principle I), as well as the originality of the narrative into which they are fitted, is sufficient to prove that we are here dealing with a J narrative" (*Sources*, p. 45-46).

See also J.B. TYSON, *Source Criticism of the Gospel of Luke*, in C.H. TALBERT (ed.), *Perspectives on Luke-Acts* (PerspRelStud SS, 5), Danville, VA, 1978, 24-39, for an analysis of various source theories, including Goulder, Farmer and Lindsey.

489. TYSON, *Lukan Version*, p. 252. Insisting that "Perry's argument is quite convincing", Tyson nonetheless differed in suggesting "there are only two sources for the synoptic account of the trial: Mark and L (or J)" (p. 251).

490. *Ibid.*, p. 256. Note the typographical error referring to Ps 22 instead of Ps 2.

491. *Ibid.*

492. *Ibid.*, p. 257.

Antipas regarded Jesus as an enemy and considered him guilty, "is apparently confirmed in the special source, though Luke himself presents a confused viewpoint"[493]. Tyson made a leap in logic (and practiced eisegesis) when he interpreted the phrase that Herod had long desired to see Jesus (23,8) as meaning that he wanted to arrest him!

But Tyson correctly regarded the Herod episode as a double of the trial before Pilate. Yet, Tyson clung to the belief that it was also historical. Tyson viewed it as a double for two reasons: he saw the mocking and vesting of Jesus in a royal garment as having taken place in the accounts of the other Synoptics. Secondly, in Luke's account this element was missing after the condemnation by Pilate and thus Luke shifted it to this point in his Gospel[494]. Earlier Tyson stated Luke employed Mk "only where necessary"[495]. Yet, one gets the distinct impression that it is the Markan account that has continued to guide the evangelist rather than the L source.

Shortly thereafter (1960), in an article focusing on Jesus and Herod, Tyson observed that Joanna and Manaen served in Herod's court and could have provided Herod with information about Jesus[496]. His observation on the reliability of the Markan account is worth noting: "Mark's outline of the itinerary of Jesus can, in its broadest outlines, be authentic, and at the same time his placing of certain events in the outline can be unhistorical ... We do not and cannot maintain that the itinerary in Mark is exact in the minutest detail"[497]. Tyson noted that in the parallel of Mk 8,15 ("Beware the leaven of the Pharisees and the leaven of Herod"), Luke omitted this reference to Herod (Lk 12,1)[498]. Although Tyson did not treat 23,6-12 in this article, the drift seemed to be suggesting that there was historical substance to the hostility between Herod and Jesus, laying the groundwork for Jesus' trial before Herod[499].

Tyson (1986) wrote of 'bracketing' the source question, a suggestion that many scholars appeared to have embraced: "A more feasible alternative, perhaps the only viable alternative, would seem to be to bracket the source question, as, for the present, unresolved. As a result we would be able to read each synoptic gospel holistically, although not without attention to the similarities and differences among them. Redaction criticism has called attention to the possibility of studies that make use of literary-critical methods. The present situation in source criticism seems to make such studies necessary"[500]. Tyson was not completely convinced

493. *Ibid.*
494. *Ibid.*, p. 256-257.
495. *Ibid.*, p. 251.
496. TYSON, *Jesus and Herod Antipas*, in *JBL* 79 (1960) 240.
497. *Ibid.*, p. 241.
498. *Ibid.*, p. 243.
499. *Ibid.*, p. 245-246: "Several traditions in the Synoptics confirm one another in the rather reluctant admission that Antipas was an enemy of Jesus and from him Jesus was compelled to flee".
500. TYSON, *Death*, p. 9. This did not mean that the question of sources did not interest Tyson. Cf. p. 159-160.

by Büchele's structure which derived from Luke's attempt to present three witnesses for every phase of Jesus' trial, in accord with Dt 19,15[501].

Form-critically the trial before Herod was "similar" to that of the trial before Pilate, though Tyson was also quick to point out differences[502]. But Tyson considered the scene as Luke's interpretation of Ps 2[503]. In a vein similar to Neyrey, Tyson viewed the trial of Jesus as having four parts[504]. Tyson (1992) merely acknowledged that the story was unique to Lk describing Herod as a Jewish ruler who returned a judgment of innocence to Jesus[505].

In his 1960 Duke U. dissertation William WILSON contended that Luke employed a source in the trial account[506]. He argued: "A great many critics, however, are not satisfied with this evaluation of Luke's special material in the passion, and we believe that the work of several of these critics has demonstrated that in the passion narrative Luke is clearly employing a non-Markan source which alone accounts for his differing version of the events. According to this view, it is clear, from Luke's changes in the Markan order, and from Luke's unparalleled treatment of his Markan material in this section, and from Luke's preference for a non-Markan version of several of the passion events, that Luke is not only employing a special non-Markan source, but that he is using it as the basis of his narrative and is merely introducing Markan material into the framework of his other source. We believe this theory to have been conclusively demonstrated and that the establishment of this non-Markan source within the account of Luke is of fundamental importance for any study of the Gospel sources of the trial events themselves"[507]. To this end he relied heavily upon Perry[508].

Wilson rejected the Herod story "as a later and unhistorical addition"[509]. His reasons included the "omission" of the pericope from the other Gospels, the presence of apologetic motives, the relationship of the passage to and fulfillment

501. *Ibid.*, p. 116-117.

502. *Ibid.*, p. 134-135.

503. *Ibid.*, p. 135; cf. p. 162: "The importance of Luke's unique material cannot be overstressed. In comparison with the narratives in Matthew and Mark, Luke's appears to be a carefully crafted account which largely gives expression to the concepts that Jesus was wrongfully charged with certain political crimes and that the Roman judge who presided in his case declared him innocent".

504. *Ibid.*, p. 163.

505. TYSON, *Images*, 1992, p. 79.

506. *The Trial of Jesus: A Judicial, Literary and Historical Study*. Diss. Duke, Durham, NC, 1960 (dir. K.W. CLARK). He referred to the Lukan account of the conspiracy, arrest and trial as 22,1-2.47-71; 23,1-25 (p. 124, n. 1).

507. *Ibid.*, p. 135; see also p. 150. Elsewhere he remarked: "Thus, the precise source from which Luke drew his non-Markan account of the passion may be regarded as uncertain". But Wilson insisted it was a "strong probability" that Luke used such a source (p. 145-146).

508. *Ibid.*, p. 136-139. "...his treatment forms a foundation for all other studies of Luke's non-Markan source" (p. 136). See PERRY, *Sources*.

509. WILSON, *Trial*, p. 203. See his discussion p. 199-203.

of an OT proof-text and significant internal problems. In a book based upon his
dissertation Wilson (1970) continued to maintain Luke's use of a special source in
the passion narrative[510].

Ivor BUSE (1960-61) resorted to the claim that Luke had known a pre-Markan
version of the passion narrative[511]. Such a solution explained not only the
similarities and differences over against Mk in the Barabbas account, but also Lk's
similarities with Jn in that same section. Buse reiterated the criticism leveled
against the Proto-Lk hypothesis by Lowther Clarke, Filson and others that "it falls
short of demonstration", though cautioning that it "cannot be casually

---

510. *The Execution of Jesus. A Judicial, Literary and Historical Investigation*, New York,
1970. Wilson acknowledged that this book originated in his 1960 Duke U. dissertation, *The Trial
of Jesus* (p. x). He held the view that in addition to Mk, which was a primary source, Luke also
had "a special literary tie to Matthew" (p. 53). He endorsed the view of the special source for
the passion in the Jewish and Roman proceedings in concert with Bundy and Winter (p. 61; see
BUNDY, *Jesus*, p. 480; WINTER, *Treatment*, p. 170-171). Luke generally followed Mk and Mt
and Wilson noted that Luke transposed the anointing to an earlier point in the Gospel (7,36-50)
(WILSON, *Execution*, p. 54). In his discussion of the Sanhedrin trial, Wilson penned: "There is
no doubt that in composing his account Luke had Mark's record of the nighttime Sanhedrin before
him, but he substituted an entirely different explanation of the proceedings" (p. 56). For Wilson,
Luke did not revise Mk as much as he rebutted him. Wilson reached his conclusion of Luke's
primary source being a special source based on four criteria: 1) changes in Mk's order; 2)
revisions and additions to the Markan material; 3) non-Markan material in the passion narrative;
4) non-Markan material in the trials before the Sanhedrin and Pilate. Yet, he acknowledged that
all attempts to determine the nature and extent of this special source have "proved fruitless" (p.
61).
    Wilson, in line with Dibelius, advocated the probability that the Herod story (23,6-12) stemmed
from Ps 2,1-2 (p. 137). He argued *contra* Streeter that it was unlikely that the story would have
been forgotten (cf. STREETER, *On the Trial*, p. 231). Though the disciples who fled could not
have provided the details, still there would have been other eyewitnesses.
    Because the story was not found in the other Gospels, Wilson concluded that "the tradition
certainly was not a part of the common early description of the trial" (*Execution*, p. 137). The
Herod account arose because: 1) of the similarity with Ps 2; 2) the likelihood that Herod was
present in Jerusalem for the Passover; and 3) the assumption that because Herod was
concerned with Jesus during his ministry that he also had a part in the trial. Downplaying the
innocence motive, Wilson believed that the inclusion of the episode was due to implicating Jewish
involvement in the trial of Jesus which resulted in a pro Roman apologia.
    Two other considerations were decisive for Wilson (p. 138). The "incongruity" about the
location of Jewish authorities as recorded in 23,10 and 23,15 served as proof that this story was
an awkward insertion. Further, since the account of the mockery before Pilate was omitted by
Luke, he reasoned that the details were shifted to this story. He maintained there was "strong
indication" that Luke borrowed material from the trial before Pilate. He also noted that a tradition
concerning Jesus' trial before Herod was also found in GP which Wilson believed dated "from
the middle of the second century" (p. 78, 138).
    511. I. BUSE, *St. John and the Passion Narratives of St Matthew and St. Luke*, in *NTS* 7
(1960-61) 76.

dismissed"[512]. Markan influence was indicated by Luke's use of Mk 15,2 in 23,3, the inclusion of the Barabbas episode, and the detail that Pilate eventually acquiesced to the pressure of the Jews. Creed's response to Taylor's claim also pertained to Buse's attempted solution[513].

Günter KLEIN (1961) preferred to regard Peter's denial as derived from Luke's special source, though he acknowledged there were numerous traces of Lukan redaction[514]. Drawing upon Rehkopf, Klein believed that the tradition of the denial contained in Lk bypassed the Markan revision of this account[515]. It was beyond question, according to Klein's estimation, that the mockery (22,63-65) had been secondarily inserted into the original context[516]. He ascribed the "Inkonzinnität" of the αὐτόν (v. 63) to "eine vorlukanische Redaktion" rather than to Luke[517].

Walter GRUNDMANN (1961, ²1963) believed that Luke used a special tradition in addition to Mk and Q[518]. Leaning toward support of Streeter, he submitted that the special material was perhaps already joined to Q. Luke followed this special tradition beginning at 22,14[519]. Grundmann simply noted that events following the arrest were arranged differently in Lk than in Mk and obviously attributed this change of order to Luke's use of a special source[520]. The denial of Peter (22,54-62) derived from the special tradition and had been expanded by details from Mk. The proof was in the uniqueness of the account[521]. He asserted that the MA of

---

512. *Ibid.*

513. *Ibid.* Cf. CREED, *The Supposed 'Proto-Luke'*, in *ExpT* 46 (1934-35) 379: "I think the suggestion is highly paradoxical, and, I must add, improbable. It is paradoxical, because a source which is first postulated to explain the extensive *non-Marcan* material in Lk, is then supposed to be a fundamental source of Mk; and it is, in my judgement, improbable, because, while it seems not difficult to conjecture reasons why Luke might have found the rough and sombre narrative of Mk in some respects unsatisfactory and even distasteful, the reverse process is hard to understand". See further CREED, *Some Outstanding New Testament Problems: 2. L and the Structure of the Lucan Gospel*, in *ExpT* 46 (1934-35) 101-107.

514. G. KLEIN, *Die Verleugnung des Petrus*, in *ZTK* 58 (1961) 290, 291 (= *Rekonstruktion und Interpretation*, 1969, p. 54, 55). Cf. p. 298 (= 61) where he claimed that 22,31ff. was a reflection of "a concurrent tradition".

515. *Ibid.*, p. 294, n. 1 (= 58, n. 55).

516. *Ibid.*, p. 295 (= 59).

517. *Ibid.*, p. 291 (= 54).

518. W. GRUNDMANN, *Das Evangelium nach Lukas*, Berlin, 1961, ²1963, p. 17. Luke gave preference to the special tradition rather than Mk, e.g. in the case of the Sanhedrin trial (p. 419). But it was not necessary to speak of special Ebionite tendencies in Lk or in Luke's special tradition (p. 32).

519. *Ibid.*, p. 421.

520. *Ibid.*, p. 415. "Die Übernahme der Spruchüberlieferung bedingt eine Sprengung des Markusrahmens; dies wird unabwendbar durch die dem Lukan eigene Sonderüberlieferung(SLk), die ihm eine grosse Fulle von Stoff zubringt" (p. 11).

521. *Ibid.*, p. 416.

22,62 probably resulted from Luke's early expansion of the original[522]. The phrase in 22,64 stemmed from the special Lukan tradition, and possibly was revised due to influence from Mk[523]. The mockery (22,63-65) was likewise independent from Mk[524]. The reference to the blindfolding was not original to Mk but appeared first in Lk and only later was inserted into Mk 14,65. The Sanhedrin trial (22,66-71) was not based upon Mk[525]. In the special tradition the account basically had the form of vv. 66-68.70.71 into which v. 69, derived from Luke's own hand, had been inserted[526]. Grundmann posed the difficulty of determining whether the Jews could impose capital punishment in terms of the tension between whether Luke possessed reliable information upon which he based his correction of Mk or whether, because the Jews did not have the power to pass a death sentence in his own time, he assumed that the same was true for the time of Jesus. Grundmann concluded saying that Jesus had been handed over to Pilate without judgment[527]. Most of the material in 23,1-25 was taken from the special source[528]. He conceded, nonetheless, that one could view the changes and clarifications as resulting from a redaction of Mk. Because the special Lukan tradition did not relate the trial before Pilate but only assumed it, Luke at this point was forced to rely on Mk, as indicated by the adoption of Mk 15,2. The remaining section of 23,18-25 was a combination of Markan material, special source material and additions from the hand of Luke himself[529]. Verses 18-22 stemmed from Mk while vv. 23.24 belonged to the special tradition. These latter two verses had originally been connected to v. 16. Grundmann argued this was so since both 23,16 and 23,22 concluded in the same way. Finally, Luke formed v. 25 as an ending to the section.

Grundmann was alert to the connections between the Gospel and Acts in regard to the passion of Jesus and of Paul[530]. The basic presentation of the Gospel in 23,25, that Pilate freed a murderer, declared Jesus innocent, but yielded to the demands of the Jews, was confirmed by Acts 3,13-15[531]. The language of

---

522. *Ibid.*, p. 417: "da sie zudem in den altlateinischen Texten sowie in 0171 felht, ist V.62 wahrscheinlich eine sehr frühe Ergänzung der ursprünglich bei Lukas mit V. 61 schliessenden Erzählung".

523. *Ibid.*, p. 417-418.

524. *Ibid.*, p. 417.

525. *Ibid.*, p. 418.

526. *Ibid.*, p. 419.

527. *Ibid.*; cf. p. 420.

528. *Ibid.*, p. 421.

529. *Ibid.*, p. 426. Here Grundmann followed the opinion of HIRSCH, *Frühgeschichte*, Vol. 2, 1941, p. 269.

530. GRUNDMANN, *Lukas*, p. 33. For the relations in general between the two works, consult p. 22-33.

531. *Ibid.*, p. 427.

the LXX became recognizable in stories and speeches[532]. The portrayal of Barabbas in 23,19 was like that of Mk 15,7[533].

In the end, Grundmann declared that the determination of the various sources and traditions remained an open question, as did Frederick C. Grant that the special tradition was a somewhat loose, though seemingly homogeneous collection of materials which Luke brought together from various places[534].

Grundmann (1963) held that most of the material in 23,1-25 was taken from the special source[535]. The Herod episode came, not from Luke as Bultmann suggested, but from the special source and was inserted between Mk 15,5 and 15,6[536]. Though scholars debated the historicity of the account, Grundmann contended that it corresponded to Dt 19,15 and the need for two or three witnesses[537]. The silence of Jesus, mentioned only in 23,11, could be accounted for, not only in presenting Jesus as the servant of God, but also because to the Hellenists, it would be construed as a sign of divinity[538]. Grundmann also pointed out that the milder παιδεύειν (23,16) had been substituted for the Markan φραγελλοῦν (Mk 15,15).

While there were numerous points where the three Synoptics shared an interest in the royalty of Jesus, Augustin GEORGE (1962), highlighted six which were proper to Lk[539]. One of these was at 22,67-70 where Luke introduced two important changes. The first was the separation of the titles which replenished the power of the ancient titles[540]. The second change, indicated by the phrase ἀπὸ τοῦ νῦν showed that Jesus will be enthroned in his royalty. In assessing Luke's plan, George saw the royal texts especially obvious during the sojourn in Jerusalem at the time of the last Passover, which in our pericope was depicted as a confrontation between Jesus and "the princes of the world"[541]. It also served as a rejection of carnal Messianism, that Jesus' kingdom was not of this world, but was of the type announced in Scripture. Luke was trying to add a new meaning to the term "Son of God". George credited the tradition with providing this thematic, though he was quick to clarify that the evangelist had some role in applying it. The method George ascribed to Luke was rather mechanical, such as choosing or organizing

---

532. *Ibid.*, p. 24.
533. *Ibid.*, p. 427.
534. *Ibid.*, p. 17. Cf. F.C. GRANT, *Growth*, p. 62.
535. GRUNDMANN, *Lukas*, ²1963, p. 421.
536. *Ibid.*, p. 423. This would seem to suggest that the framework was Markan rather than that of the special source.
537. *Ibid.*, p. 424.
538. *Ibid.*, p. 425.
539. A. GEORGE, *La royauté de Jésus selon l'évangile de Luc*, in *SEc* 14 (1962) 57.
540. *Ibid.*, p. 62.
541. *Ibid.*, p. 65.

the material[542]. Though he determined that Luke's use of the title "Lord" was significant, George did not treat its appearance in 22,61[543].

In a subsequent article examining Jesus as the Son of God (1965), George noted the term "Son" occurred less in Lk than in the other Synoptics[544]. He argued that the Lukan account in 22,67-71 was "fort originale", and thus reasoned that Luke employed a source different from the other Synoptics[545]. He further suggested the meaning of the title in the Gospels was sometimes difficult to determine. But the Lukan christology clearly surpassed the OT understanding of Son of God. He called attention (1967) to the Proto-Lk theory of Streeter and Taylor, indicating that it had been adopted by a number of British critics[546]. He also conceded the difficulty in determining the material proper to Lk where it differed from Mk and Mt. Impressed by the studies of Schürmann, Rehkopf and Tyson, which he described as "les études les plus poussées", George endorsed the view that Luke was probably using his own sources in the passion narrative[547].

In George's article on the meaning of the death of Jesus according to Luke (1973), he did not explicitly mention the nature and extent of the special sources, but he designated the materials in the passion which were proper to Luke[548]. These included: 22,3.15-18.37.43-45.48; 23,6-12.23.[549]24-25[550].28-31.34.35. 43.46.48.49[551]. Further, 22,69-70 was considered "originale chez de Luc". Several unique elements included: the role of Satan (22,3; cf. 22,53); the presence of the high priests at the arrest (22,52), the Herod story (23,8-12), seven words of Jesus (22,15-18.37.48; 23,28-31.34.43.46); without speaking of the original redaction of the text in 22,19-20.53.69-70, there were Scriptural allusions (22,37.43-45; 23,30.35.46.48.49)[552]. George also noted the relation of the death of Jesus and the martyrdom of Stephen in Acts 6,11-15; 7,55-60. The similarities were: the false witnesses (Acts 6,11.13; not in Lk 22); the Sanhedrin trial (Acts 6,12-15; cf. Lk 22,66); the Temple words (Acts 6,14, not in Lk 22); the vision of

---

542. *Ibid.*, p. 68.

543. *Ibid.*, p. 68-69.

544. GEORGE, *Jésus fils de Dieu dans l'évangile selon saint Luc*, in *RB* 72 (1965) 185-209, p.185 (= *Études*, 1978, p. 215-236).

545. *Ibid.*, p. 198, 199 = *Études*, p. 226, 227.

546. GEORGE, *Tradition et rédaction chez Luc. La construction du troisième Évangile*, in I. DE LA POTTERIE (ed.), *De Jésus aux Évangiles. Tradition et rédaction dans les Évangiles synoptiques* (BETL, 25), Gembloux, 1967, p. 100-129 (= *Études*, p. 15-41).

547. GEORGE, *La construction*, p. 115, n. 49 (= *Études*, p. 28, n. 1): "Luc présente dans cette section [Lk 22–23] la même suite d'épisodes que Mt 26-27 et Mc 14-15, mais il s'écarte plus souvent de leurs récits que dans les sections précédentes et il y ajoute plusieurs éléments nouveaux. On en a conclu qu'il suivait des sources propres, et le fait est probable". See also p. 16, n. 2, where he highlighted the work of Schürmann (1953, 1955, 1957) and Rehkopf (1959).

548. GEORGE, *Le sens de la mort de Jésus pour Luc*, in *RB* 80 (1973) 186-217 (= 185-212).

549. *Ibid.*, p. 190, 202 (= 188-189, 199).

550. *Ibid.*, p. 202 (= 198).

551. *Ibid.*, p. 190-191 (= 189).

552. *Ibid.*, p. 191 (= 189).

the Son of Man (Acts 6,55-56; cf. Lk 22,69), the prayer of Ps 31,6 (Acts 7,59; cf. Lk 23,46); pardon to the murderers (Acts 7,60; Lk 23,34)[553]. George viewed it as probable that the Lukan portrayal of the death of Jesus provided an example of the Christian martyr. The difference between the presentation of the role of Pilate in the Gospel as compared with Acts was attributed to the latter relying on an ancient source[554]. An additional source seemed to be implied by George to account for presenting the Jews as responsible for the death of Jesus[555].

In yet another work published in 1973 George clearly stated his preference for the solution that Luke continued to employ Mk in the passion narrative to which was added various original details[556]. Luke crafted his Gospel using Septuagintal Greek in parts and though varying his style, reproduced the words of Jesus more carefully than other aspects of the tradition. Luke revised his material "d'une manière original". As for the order, Luke's plan was more didactic than chronological. In his discussion of 22,66-23,1 George suggested it was probable that Luke was reworking Mk "pour présenter son intérpretation de l'événement"[557]. The portrayal of the death of Jesus was likened to that of Stephen (Acts 6,13; 7,56-60)[558].

George (1978) asserted that in 23,1-25 Luke followed the same general framework as Mk and Mt adding the Herod scene[559]. The true Messiah king was contrasted with the demi-king of the Jews, an episode which was recalled by Luke in Acts 4,25-28.

Eugen RUCKSTUHL (1963) argued that Luke used an independent non-Markan source as the basis of his passion narrative, but denied any literary interdependence between Mt and Lk[560]. Ruckstuhl attempted a type of harmonization of the

553. *Ibid.*, p. 192 (= 190).
554. *Ibid.*, p. 202 (= 199).
555. *Ibid.*, p. 204 (= 201).
556. GEORGE, *Pour lire l'Évangile selon saint Luc* (CE, 5), Paris, 1973, p. 33 (= *El evangelio según san Lucas* [Cuadernos bíblicos, 3], Estella [Navarra], ⁸1987, p. 33): "Chacun des évangélistes a pourtant ici son originalité par ses données et sa rédaction, et c'est le cas de Luc. Son récit présente tant d'éléments propres, et une pensée si caractéristique, que bon nombre de critiques ont jugé qu'il abandonnait ici le récit de Marc pour suivre une autre source continue tout au long de la Passion. Cette solution est pourtant difficile à fonder solidement. Car, s'il est certain que Luc dispose de nombreux matériaux originaux, il est beaucoup moins sûr que ces éléments soient homogènes et qu'ils proviennent d'une seule source; et it est clair aussi que Luc continue d'utiliser Marc. Quoi qu'il en soit d'ailleurs, Luc a profondément retravaillé ses données et y a introduit une intelligence très personnelle du mystère".
557. *Ibid.*, p. 36 (= 36).
558. *Ibid.*, p. 37 (= 37). Reference was made to J. BLINZLER, *Le procès*, 1962, 169-174 and P. BENOIT, *Passion et résurrection*, p. 109-132.
559. A. GEORGE, *La royauté de Jésus*, in ID., *Études sur l'œuvre de Luc* (SB), Paris, 1978, 257-282, p. 278.
560. E. RUCKSTUHL, *Die Chronologie des Letzten Mahles und des Leidens Jesu* (Biblische Beiträge, 4), Einsiedeln, 1963, p. 40, n. 38 (= *Chronology of the Last Days of Jesus. A Critical*

Gospel accounts, as when he suggested that Jesus' appearance before Herod "was most likely held in the afternoon of the same (second) day"[561]. Ruckstuhl did so without any effort to explain the absence of the scene from the other Gospels.

Later Ruckstuhl (1986) reacted against Soards's position that the Herod story was based, in part, on Mk, because of what he considered to be few similarities in content and language between this mockery and the one recounted in Mk 15,16-20a[562]. Soards was accused of overestimating the evangelist's freedom. Ruckstuhl considered it virtually certain that Herod would have been in Jerusalem for the feast of Passover attending to business as Pilate was doing. But Ruckstuhl's arguments generally tended to insinuate what could have happened in suggesting that a strange turn of events might have led events in a direction different from that intended by Jewish religious leaders. Further, Ruckstuhl regarded the dazzling apparel as a concrete sign to Pilate that Jesus was not guilty of any crime deserving of the sentence of death[563]. What was more, Ruckstuhl rejected the view that there was an apologetic element at work in the story. Finally, the Herod trial would have taken place on Thursday morning since it would have been impossible that the Roman trial would have resumed and concluded[564]. Could it not be that since Luke had so carefully read Mk that the Herod account became an intercalation in the Lukan passion narrative, as has been said of Mark's redactional technique[565]?

Although George CAIRD (1963) clearly favored Lukan dependence upon Mk in many parts of the Gospel[566], he also firmly asserted that Luke used a special source, Proto-Lk. This notwithstanding, he took a dim view of those scholars who regarded Luke as simply a compiler[567]. Caird listed a total of seven reasons in defense of Proto-Lk[568]. Those germane to the passion narrative included the low rate of verbal similarity and numerous changes in order. Further, because the passion narrative in continuous form would have circulated from the early period of the Church, and since L certainly contained a resurrection, Caird assumed that

Study, tr. V.J. DRAPELA, New York, 1965, p. 37, n. 39).

561. RUCKSTUHL, *Die Chronologie*, p. 54-55. Cf. p. 37-38, 47, 53, 122 (= 55. Cf. p. 34, 46, 53, 137-138).

562. RUCKSTUHL, *Chronologie der Leidensgeschichte*, Pt. 2, in A. FUCHS (ed.), *SNTU* 11 (1986), p. 101. Cf. M.L. SOARDS, *Tradition, Composition, and Theology in Luke's Account of Jesus before Herod Antipas*, in *Bib* 66 (1985) 344-364.

563. RUCKSTUHL, *Chronologie der Leidensgeschichte*, Pt. 2, p. 103.

564. *Ibid*. See also p. 106, n. 25. Cf. RUCKSTUHL, *Chronologie der Leidensgeschichte*, Pt. 2, *SNTU* 10 (1985), p. 41.

565. See F. NEIRYNCK, *Mark and His Commentators: Mk 1,1-8,26*, in *ETL* 65 (1989) 381-389 (esp. p. 388-389) (= *Evangelica II*, p. 347-355 [356: Additional Note on the Structure]).

566. G.B. CAIRD, *The Gospel of St Luke* (The Pelican Gospel Commentaries), Harmondsworth - New York, 1963, p. 18.

567. *Ibid.*, p. 25-26; cf. p. 19. Luke gathered the material and committed it to writing.

568. *Ibid.*, p. 24-27. But 22,14-24,53 as well as 3,1-4,30 constituted the "crux of the problem" (p. 23).

a passion narrative would have been joined to it[569]. And though he admitted that the reasons he advanced in support of Streeter's theory did not prove its "soundness", the alternate explanation, Lukan redaction of Mk, was completely lacking[570]. Caird contended that the order of denial, mockery and trial as found in Lk was derived from an independent, non-Markan source, and was "by far the more probable"[571]. Caird considered the question in Mt 22,68 and the mention of the blindfold in Mk 14,65 to have been early harmonizations taken from Luke by scribes[572].

According to Caird, the scholarly results were inconclusive as to whether the Sanhedrin possessed the right to capital punishment[573]. Regardless of the power of the council, their intention was to have the Romans execute Jesus. Caird attributed vv. 18-25 to Luke, rejecting the view that they were a later addition[574]. A smoother account resulted from the deletion of vv. 16.18-20.25.

Caird maintained that the Herod episode (23,6-12) probably stemmed from Joanna or Chuza, as mentioned in 8,3[575]. Dibelius's influence was so strong that Caird, while supporting the likely historicity of the events of this passage, was swayed to accept the influence of Ps 2. Because Jesus was addressed as "thy holy servant" in Acts 4,27, Caird reasoned the silence motif derived from Is 53.

E. Earle ELLIS (1966, ²1974) was unique in claiming that, though the framework was generally ascribed to Mk, no one document formed the basis of Lk. Instead, Luke freely borrowed from a variety of sources[576]. In 22,47–23,56, Luke drew from Mk and L in composing each episode[577]. While Mk formed the structure in some parts of the Gospel, Luke's purposes determined what was most important. Contrary to F.W. Farrar who believed that the order of Lk was chronological, Ellis maintained that Luke pursued a thematic framework[578]. Semitisms, especially in Lk 1–2 and the first twelve chapters of Acts, were ascribed by Ellis to written sources[579].

Ellis was critical of Proto-Lk and concluded that if it existed, it was little more than "a selection of notes and tracts that Luke fitted to his present format"[580].

569. *Ibid.*, p. 26.
570. *Ibid.*, p. 27.
571. *Ibid.*, p. 244.
572. *Ibid.*, p. 245.
573. *Ibid.*
574. *Ibid.*, p. 248. Luke had not as adeptly added his Markan insertions here as he had in earlier parts of the Gospel.
575. *Ibid.*, p. 247.
576. E.E. ELLIS, *The Gospel of Luke* (The Century Bible. New Edition), London, 1966, ²1974; Greenwood, SC, ᴿ1977, p. 27 [pages in brackets].
577. *Ibid.*, p. 26 [= 26].
578. *Ibid.*, p. 7 [= 7]. Ellis observed that Geldenhuys adopted a thematic structure within his commentary. See also p. 31 [= 30].
579. *Ibid.*, p. 3 [= 3]. Note the similarities with Feine's proposal.
580. *Ibid.*, p. 27 [= 26].

Ellis faulted Taylor for having proved only the unity of Lk and not that of the special source. Rehkopf, though he rightly focused on the issue of a pre-Lukan vocabulary, failed to establish the limits of Proto-Lk, owing to an inadequate methodology. As Conzelmann had shown, the non-Markan material assumed both the context and the order of the Gospel as it presently exists[581]. "In conclusion, there are affinities between some passages of the Q and L material which accord with the supposition that the passages came from one pre-Lukan translator or source, but in no case is there sufficient evidence to establish this. In each instance the degree of probability is difficult to assess"[582]. Luke "very likely" obtained information from people involved in the events which he recounted, if he was to be identified as the physician and companion of Paul. Others living and ministering in Jerusalem provided still other information.

Luke divided the material of 19,45–24,53 into three sections each containing six episodes[583]. In the section with which we are concerned, Luke loosely followed the Markan outline, heavily redacted the Markan material where he employed it, and also relied on non-Markan matter. In the denial, the sparce verbal agreement was indicative of another source, while the variation in order was attributed to Luke's redaction of Mk[584]. For Ellis, the change in Markan order was controlled by "Luke's thematic, episodic structure"[585]. Ellis argued that, though Jesus was condemned by the Sanhedrin, they did not possess the power to execute him[586]. Further, the first trial was likely only an informal inquiry, as indicated by 22,66[587]. In 22,63–23,25 Luke followed a separate source, drawing from Mk in a few instances[588].

With Ellis's contribution to the Herod debate, Joanna, once again, was singled out as the possible informant for 23,8-10[589]. Ellis appeared to accept the Herod episode as historical[590]. Both Herod and Pilate testified to the innocence of Jesus and thus fulfilled the prescription of the law as outlined in Dt 19,15. Luke asserted, and it was confirmed in Acts (2,23; 3,14f.), that the Jews precipitated the death of Jesus. At the time of Luke, the Jews continued to raise the charge of sedition against Jesus and the Roman authorities continued to believe them. Thus,

581. *Ibid.*

582. *Ibid.*, p. 29 [= 28].

583. *Ibid.*, p. 228 [= 227]. See also p. 32 [= 32]. The section 19,45–21,38 detailed the "Messiah and the Temple", 22,1–23,25 treated "The Meaning of the Messiah's Death", and 23,26–24,53 was concerned with "The Glorification of Jesus the Messiah".

584. *Ibid.*, p. 259 [= 259].

585. *Ibid*, p. 259 [= 259-260].

586. *Ibid.*, p. 260 [= 261].

587. *Ibid.*, p. 259 [= 259-260].

588. *Ibid.*, p. 260 [= 260-261]. Those elements specifically influenced by Mk were not detailed.

589. *Ibid.*, p. 29 [= 29].

590. *Ibid.*, p. 261 [= 261].

the need for Luke to compose his Gospel became clear[591]. Ellis's position shifted somewhat in 1975 when, influenced by Taylor, he insisted that Luke composed 23,6-12 himself from traditions available to him from his non-Markan source[592].

Even though Ernst HAENCHEN (1966) claimed Luke had taken over the Markan design ("Aufriss"), even more faithfully than Matthew[593], he referred to Streeter's conjecture ("Vermutung") of the special source and adopted that view for some of the variations within Lk[594]. Not only was the story of Peter's denials borrowed from this other source, but also the account of the Sanhedrin trial as well[595]. Owing also to another source were the specific charges preferred against Jesus. This other source likewise contained information about Pilate's declaration of the innocence of Jesus[596]. Haenchen claimed that the question whether there were two sessions or simply one was not as important as many scholars assumed. He offered two possible explanations, though not expressing a preference for either[597]. Haenchen argued that the trial and the sentence only had meaning for the Christian reader, who then learned of the Jewish guilt for Jesus' death[598]. The account of the trial was theologically, rather than historically, based. Haenchen credited Luke however, rather than the source, with recounting the entire story of Peter before the account of the trial[599]. This and other changes occurred because the events of the night could not have transpired in the manner in which Mk recounted them. Other elements, such as Luke's version of Jesus' response to the high priest (22,67) seemed to be secondary, while Haenchen previously argued that this verse harkened back to 20,1-8[600].

591. *Ibid.*

592. ELLIS, *La composition de Luc 9 et les sources de sa christologie*, in J. DUPONT (ed.), *Jésus aux origines de la christologie* (BETL, 40), Gembloux, 1975, ²1989, p. 198, n. 22 (= ID., *The Composition of Luke 9 and the Sources of Christology*, in G.W. HAWTHORNE [ed.], *Current Issues in Biblical and Patristic Interpretation*. FS M.C. TENNEY, Grand Rapids, MI, 1975, p. 125, n. 22). The article was originally presented as a paper to the SBL, Sept. 1-5, 1972. Cf. V. TAYLOR, *Passion*, p. 89.

593. E. HAENCHEN, *Der Weg Jesu. Eine Erklärung des Markus-Evangeliums und der kanonischen Parallelen* (Sammlung Töpelmann, 2/6), Berlin, 1966, p. 34.

594. *Ibid.*, p. 20. Cf. p. 486. "Lukas hat aus einer legendarisch erweiterten Quelle (vermutlich jenem Evangelium, das er in der Leidensgeschichte weithin Mk vorzog) die Züge eingeschoben ..." (p. 495).

595. *Ibid.*, p. 506.

596. *Ibid.*, p. 518.

597. *Ibid.*, p. 508. Equally possible were the proposals that Luke simplified Mk's account or that, as Mark related, Jesus was detained in the house of the high priest until the early morning when the decisive meeting of the Sanhedrin took place. See p. 508, n. 3, for a brief survey of the literature on the question, focusing primarily on the position of P. Winter whose work Haenchen described as "kenntnisreichen und interessanten" (p. 515).

598. *Ibid.*, p. 515.

599. *Ibid.*, p. 505.

600. *Ibid.*, p. 510; cf. p. 506.

Lukan redaction of Mk also accounted for some of the differences among the Synoptic accounts of the passion. Because at the time of Lk the Temple lay in ruins, reference to its destruction was omitted[601]. Little of the material in 23,2-5 has any historical value. Rather, it reflected changes made by Luke. The Barabbas story was not a legend, and served the purpose of incriminating the Jews. So, what changes were made by Luke in view of Mk, were made with a view to the time and circumstances in which the Gospel was written.

Haenchen considered the Herod episode as a legendary expansion[602]. Such elements as the dazzling apparel and the mistreatment by Herod's soldiers had no historical foundation but were placed at the service of Luke's storytelling technique[603].

Wilfrid HARRINGTON (1967) joined his voice with those who voted for Luke's use of Mk as his primary source[604], but employed a special source in the passion[605].

---

601. *Ibid.*, p. 509.

602. *Ibid.*, p. 507-508. The Herod story, drawn from the Lukan *Sondergut*, basically served the purpose and reflected the tendency to demonstrate that Christianity was not a threat to Rome and in attempting to achieve this, exonerated the Romans (p. 518).

603. *Ibid.*, p. 519.

604. *The Gospel according to St. Luke*, Westminster, MD, 1967. Further, it was obvious that Luke followed the order of his source, but Harrington straddled the fence when he contended that though in the passion Luke rearranged the Markan order, the variation was ultimately due to a special source which was related to the Johannine tradition. Harrington earlier suggested that Luke was familiar with the Johannine tradition before it was finally incorporated into Jn. "Luke shows a curious complexity in his approach to his sources. He can, and does, follow the order of Mark very closely, while at the same time he fits it into a new plan" (p. 13).

Some changes resulted from Luke's desire for clarity and because of "literary and religious sensibilities" (p. 10). Verse 22,69 was cited as an example. Harrington, though speaking generally of MAs, concluded they resulted from a common source used by Matthew and Luke (p. 11). Putting the number at thirty-three, it is not clear whether Harrington was referring to vv. 62.64. Transpositions were prompted by a concern for logical order or for a "better literary style". Although Harrington argued that Luke followed Mk's order, though less slavishly in the passion narrative, he ascribed ultimate influence on arrangement of materials to a separate, personal source of Luke which had contact with the Johannine tradition (p. 244). Earlier Harrington noted that several transpositions within the passion narrative were due to Luke (p. 10-11). In a later contribution (1975) Harrington recognized Luke's following of the Markan order, while noting that some variations did exist early in Lk, but more especially in the passion narrative. He was not particularly clear when he wrote: "This fact of numerous transpositions within a common framework should be kept in mind" (*Key to the Bible*. 3. *Record of the Fulfillment. The New Testament*, Canfield, OH, 1975, rev. and updated, p. 22). It should be noted that in his opinion the revision of the book was so drastic that it was "in large measure, a new book" (p. vii).

Harrington observed that the Hebraisms were the result of Luke's conscious effort to imitate Septuagintal style (p. 14). Luke's order was theological rather than chronological (p. 33). Harrington credited a source other than Mk with providing a portion of the account of the trial (22,66-71) (*Gospel*, p. 259). He explained some differences as owing to oral tradition. Verses 67-71 were based on Mk 14,61-64 which had been modified by Luke. Harrington observed that Luke highlighted much more clearly than the other Synoptics the reason why Jesus had been condemned

Winter argued, in contrast to Taylor, that Luke was not the author of Proto-Lk and that L did not contain Q in addition to all the non-Markan material. Trocmé advocated the idea of Luke's use of an archetype, the same which Mark also employed. Though he was critical of the methods of Taylor, Schürmann and Rehkopf, he nonetheless utilized a statistical approach in his own treatment of Lk. Léon-Dufour denied the existence of Proto-Lk, though Caird offered several reasons in support of it. Ellis criticized Taylor for proving only the unity of Lk and faulted Rehkopf's metholology, while praising him for rightly concentrating on an examination of pre-Lukan vocabulary.

(p. 260). Only the Romans had the authority for capital punishment. The omission of the reference to "coming on the clouds" was made so that the readers will not believe that Jesus mistakenly announced his imminent Parousia (p. 260). Because Luke omitted Mk 15,6-11, obviously implying Luke had knowledge of it, he introduced the figure of Barabbas in an abrupt manner. Harrington also subscribed to the view that Luke was attempting to portray the Romans in a positive light, but the Jews in a negative one (p. 263). This accounted for the omission of the mockery by the Roman soldiers (Mk 15,16-20). Pointing out a connection with Acts, Harrington indicated that Paul was always acquitted by the Roman authorities (p. 261; see Acts 16,35-39; 18,12-15; 19,31.35.41; 24,22f; 25,18.25f.31f. Cf. 13,12).

Harrington's updating and revision of a 1966 work gave him the opportunity to adopt Boismard's explanation and solution for the synoptic problem (*Key to the Bible*. Vol. 3. *Record*, 1975, p. 23-24). While not perfect, it "boldly faces up to these difficulties". In Harrington's view, Lk represented the conflation of intermediary Mk with Proto-Lk. Proto-Lk, in turn, was dependent upon intermediary Mt; this explained Lk's agreement with the other Synoptic Gospels (p. 25). Harrington's reasoning was somewhat baffling when he concluded that Luke was the genuine author of the Third Gospel, though the vocabulary of the Proto-Lk and the Lukan redactor were "indistinguishable" (p. 25).

The mockery in the Herod scene was viewed by Harrington (1967) as "strangely like" the ones recounted in Mk 15,16-19 and Mt 27,27-30. He simply presumed the Romans mistreated Jesus on his return to Pilate from Herod (*Gospel*, p. 262). The influence of Dibelius was detected in the reference to Acts 4,25-27 and Ps 2 in 23,12.

605. HARRINGTON, *Gospel*, 1967, p. 8.

CHAPTER SIX

LUKAN REDACTION OF MARK
LÉON VAGANAY THROUGH ANTON DAUER

Significant contributions were made during this period to the view that Luke redacted Mk in the passion narrative, especially by Blinzler and Conzelmann, whose seminal work on redaction criticism has had a lasting effect. Kümmel rejected the Proto-Lk theory and his opposition may have been as influential as Creed's. Talbert, though initially supportive of Markan priority, later in his scholarly career exhibited a shift in his approach to treating the question of sources.

Léon VAGANAY (1954) regarded Mk as the principal source of Luke, whom he deemed an experienced and skillful writer[1]. In Vaganay's delineation of special sources, the line-up curiously resembled Perry, though their conclusions were quite different. He maintained there was a special source for the passion narrative[2]. Vaganay conceded the sources providing the special material to Lk were "très difficiles à découvrir", though he leaned toward the influence of oral tradition[3].

Vaganay demurred at the suggestion that Luke was simply a compiler[4]. Following his own tendencies he shaped his source material. He omitted material to eliminate similar stories and to achieve "un plan plus harmonieux"[5]. Luke corrected Mk, for example, in combining the nocturnal Sanhedrin trial with that of the morning, resulting in a "meilleure économie du récit". The account of the scourging and the crowning with thorns was passed over out of considerateness. Similarly, Luke toned down the mockery (22,63-65)[6]. Among the numerous elements proper to Lk in our section of the passion Vaganay included 22,61a.68; 23,2.4-5.6-16[7]. It was clear to Vaganay that Luke imitated the LXX[8]. Although

---

1. L. VAGANAY, *Le problème synoptique. Une hypothèse de travail*, Tournai, 1954, p. 313. The development of the Gospels was a complex process as the schema on p. 444 indicated. The principal synoptic source was the Aramaic Gospel of Mt (M) which was translated into Greek (Mg). The second synoptic source, composed in Aramaic, would be what was usually designated as Q, though Vaganay used S. This too, was later translated into Greek (Sg). Mark's was the first Gospel and Matthew and Luke both depended upon it. The two later evangelists were mutually independent of one another (p. 444; cf. p. XXIII, 311). See his bibliography on Lk with a brief, but separate section on Proto-Lk (p. XXI-XXII).

2. *Ibid.*, p. XXIII: "Lc P = Source propre à Lc. dans les récits de la Passion et la résurrection". Vaganay listed particular sources, either oral or written, as special sources for the Infancy Narrative, the public ministry, the passion and resurrection accounts in addition to redactional elements (p. 307-311). Since Perry's work was listed in the bibliography, it is clear that Vaganay knew of it (p. XXII).

3. *Ibid.*, p. 308; cf. p. 311.

4. *Ibid.*, p. 313.

5. *Ibid.*, p. 259.

6. *Ibid.*, p. 261. Luke also softened Peter's third denial (22,60 / Mk 14,71).

7. *Ibid.*, p. 308.

some difference still remained in a few of the notes, they appeared to have the same purpose, for example 22,66 / Mk 14,53. Vaganay credited Luke with arranging the material in his own way[9].

The Proto-Lk theory was definitively rejected for the following three reasons: 1) Mk provided the structure for Lk and so the Markan elements were not superficial as Streeter claimed; 2) neither Q nor L possessed a sufficient unity or continuity as individual works; and 3) joined together, they would have created an even more disparate type of gospel[10]. Vaganay referred to the hypothesis as "ce système mort-né" and directed the reader to Goguel's "excellentes remarques" in refuting the theory[11].

Frederick Gast devoted some attention to a critique of Vaganay's theory, observing that most scholars complained that it was "very complex". Though Vaganay attempted to do away with the Two-Source theory, he ended up constructing a similar theory, except for using S in place of Q[12].

A. Robert C. LEANEY (1958) adopted the view that Luke's passion narrative was based upon Mark's, their difference being accounted for by "Luke's editorial additions and changes"[13]. Leaney credited Luke with the transposition in which the account of Peter's denial was transferred before the mockery and trial[14]. Leaney reduced the amount of non-Markan material in the passion narrative to 22,31.36-38.49; 23,27-31, and suggested that 23,6-16 might also be included within this designation[15]. What was unique about Leaney was that despite his view that Luke recast the Markan passion narrative, he still made use of Proto-Lk[16]. Leaney denied that a source other than Mk was responsible for the variation in information concerning the trial. It was simply an attempt to correct the unlikely Markan account[17].

---

8. *Ibid.*, p. 267: "Sans nul doute dans son évangile Luc a cherché à imiter le style des LXX. Conscient d'écrire une Histoire sainte qui continue celle de l'A.T., il a tenu à lui donner, dans la mesure du possible, la même couleur". As an example he cited "Ἰερουσαλήμ, au lieu de la forme grécisée, Ἱεροσόλυμα, conservée seulement quatre fois" (p. 268).

9. *Ibid.*, p. 313. Cf. p. 259, as Vaganay cited various instances where Luke, being concerned for the order, made changes from Mk to achieve "a logical order".

10. *Ibid.*, p. 312-313.

11. *Ibid.*, p. 313. Cf. GOGUEL, *Luke and Mark*.

12. GAST, *Synoptic Problem*, p. 6.

13. A.R.C. LEANEY, *A Commentary on the Gospel according to St. Luke* (BNTC), London, 1958, p. 12: "His careful rewriting is indeed never so apparent as in the Passion Narrative ..." (p. 278).

14. *Ibid.*, p. 275.

15. *Ibid.*, p. 12.

16. *Ibid.*, p. 33. Leaney argued Proto-Lk was still a constitutive element in the composition of Lk, and was, as Streeter and Taylor claimed, authored by Luke himself. Leaney dismissed the view that Proto-Lk was not a "Gospel" because it did not contain an Apocalypse and a passion narrative.

17. *Ibid.*, p. 275.

Lukan redaction of Mk attempted to render the Gospel message more understandable to Gentile readers in Leaney's view[18]. Luke avoided certain Markan terms and substituted others. Some changes were merely cosmetic and literary as in the case of Pilate giving in to the desires of the Jews, whereas the punishment was still inflicted by the Romans[19].

Because the vocabulary found in the trial before Herod was Lukan, Leaney concluded the episode was written by Luke either as a free writing or was based upon oral tradition[20]. But Leaney was more inclined to view the account as a free composition, to give credence to the view of Morgenthaler that Luke was providing dual witness to the innocence required by the Law in Dt[21]. Not only were Pilate and Herod witnesses to this, but by relating it, so too was Luke[22]. The parallel was clear in Acts 25,13ff.[23].

Discussing the "fundamental solution" to the synoptic problem, Leaney (1970) summarized Streeter's Proto-Lk theory. He criticized Taylor arguing he "developed the theory to an extent which most scholars regard as unwarranted, finding in passages which are closely parallel to Mark reason for assigning them to the special source with which Luke now came to be credited"[24].

While not primarily an introduction to the NT, Leaney treated problems associated with the origin of NT documents, including Proto-Lk, in *The New Testament* (1972)[25]. He discussed difficulties presented by the hypothesis. First, if Acts 1,1 was intended to refer to Proto-Lk, why was that not made clear. Secondly, there was no indication that the Gospel, as we know it, was composed after Acts[26].

Josef BLINZLER (1951, [2]1955) adhered to the view that while Luke used Mk for the basis of his Gospel, the account of the trial before Pilate included material from

---

18. *Ibid.*, p. 275-276. Luke substituted the response in v. 67 for the Markan silence in Mk 14,61 which the Gentiles might have considered to be a "lack of effective defence". Further in v. 69 Luke expanded "power" (Mk 14,62) to "power of God" for the benefit of his Gentile readers.

19. *Ibid.*, p. 281.

20. *Ibid.*, p. 280.

21. *Ibid.* Cf. p. 8. See R. MORGENTHALER, *Die lukanische Geschichtschreibung*, 1948. Cf. below.

22. LEANEY, *A Commentary*, p. 8.

23. *Ibid.*, p. 280: "The same motive underlies Acts xxv.13ff. (cf. especially verses 15, 16, 22, and for an echo of Lk xxiii.4-5 see Acts xxv.25; cf. also the words of Agrippa, playing a part in the 'trial' of Paul like that of Herod's in the Passion of the Lord, at Acts xxvi.31)".

24. R. DAVIDSON and A.R.C. LEANEY, *Biblical Criticism* (The Pelican Guide to Modern Theology, 3), Harmondsworth, England - Baltimore - Victoria, Australia, 1970, p. 241. See also p. 239, 240, 243.

25. *The New Testament*, London - Sydney - Auckland - Toronto, 1972, p. 58-60.

26. Leaney used neither references nor footnotes to indicate against whose positions he was arguing.

other sources which all became interwoven[27]. Blinzler regarded attempts to discern the actual events of the trial from Mk or the special Lukan sources as unsuccessful. The evangelists were not so concerned with presenting "a strict chronologically and topographically ordered narrative" but rather a witness to faith in Jesus[28]. The changes in order in this section of the Lukan passion narrative were due to Luke's literary style and his effort to draw together all the material pertaining to the trial of Jesus[29].

As regards sources of particular pericopes, Peter was considered the source of the information about the denials[30]. Joseph of Arimathea passed on details about the Sanhedrin (cf. Lk 23,51) and other converts from among the priests and Pharisees (Acts 6,7; 15,5) likely contributed additional material[31]. Luke inserted an abbreviated form of the mockery, such as was found in Mk, to provide for an uninterrupted account of the trial[32]. Although the account of the Sanhedrin trial in Lk varied from that in Mk, Blinzler did not detect the influence of any special source. Luke was simply modifying some of his Markan source material in order to give greater attention to the special material he obtained concerning Pilate's trial[33]. The arrangement, once again, was due to Luke, who in this case, wished to draw together all the information pertaining to the trial, providing the reader with a version having "the character of a sustained narrative". Luke omitted the Markan detail about the witnesses since it yielded nothing. The independent

27. J. BLINZLER, *The Trial of Jesus*, tr. I. and F. MCHUGH, Westminster, MD, 1959 (= [2]1955), p. 39. Later in the work Blinzler referred to "the separate source in Luke". He further asserted that a majority of scholars ascribed the numerous additions contained in the Lukan account to one or more special written sources (p. 45; see also J. BLINZLER, *Der Prozess Jesu*, Regensburg [3]1960, [p. 50; the pagination to this edition will be in brackets]). See further P. BENOIT, Review: J. BLINZLER, *Der Prozess Jesu*, 1951, in *RB* 60 (1953) 452-453(454) (= *Le procès de Jésus selon J. Blinzler et P. Démann*, in *ExT*, Vol. 1, 312-314).

28. BLINZLER, *Trial*, p. 39.

29. BLINZLER, *Trial*, p. 115 (= 121): "The matter contained in Luke 22:54-71 was not materially fuller than that already offered by Mark. On the other hand, Luke's arrangement of the various parts can be understood if we consider the literary technique of the evangelist". See also p. 111, n. 55, and 116.

Blinzler gave greater attention to the matter of transpositions in the revised third edition by citing several additional references, including works by H.F.D. Sparks, J. Jeremias and J. Schmid, but Blinzler maintained his position that the changes were due to Luke ([p. 121]). Finally, it should be noted that the tendency prior to Blinzler had generally been to suggest that the changes in order when ascribed to Luke, were effected to tie together all the material which treated Peter.

30. *Ibid.*, p. 115-116. The arrangement of this story in Lk was attributed to Luke.

31. *Ibid.*, p. 46-47.

32. *Ibid.*, p. 116; cf. p. 111, n. 55. The ill-treatment of Jesus was "identical with Mk 14:65". The new placement was due to Luke and made better sense, happening after the sentence had been pronounced.

33. *Ibid.* Cf. [p. 121]. He considered Lk 22,66 to be a combination of Mk 14,53b and 15,1a (Cf. p. 147 = 121, 152).

questions whether Jesus was the Messiah and the Son of God could be due to a special tradition, but it was equally possible that this was a redaction of Mk.

Blinzler contended Luke intended only to offer a summary report of the trial[34]. The evangelist chose not to mention the formal death sentence for two reasons. First, the Sanhedrin had not yet succeeded in their objective and second, Luke's readers would have found the two death sentences confusing, that of the Sanhedrin as well as that of Pilate, since they were not conversant with Judean legal proceedings[35]. Blinzler disagreed with both Husband, who denied that the Sanhedrin had the right to act in capital cases and Lietzmann, who argued that the assembly of Jewish leaders possessed the power to carry out capital punishment while echoing the sentiments of U. Holzmeister that the Sanhedrin was subject to the Romans in this period[36]. Observing that the charges raised in the two trials were different, Blinzler concluded that the term παρέδωκεν did not provide sufficient ground upon which to determine if Pilate's decision was a confirmation of that of the Sanhedrin[37]. Doubt surrounded the extent of the Sanhedrin powers in the time of Jesus[38].

Blinzler distinguished between the first proceedings before Pilate, and their resumption, focusing on Barabbas. Although Blinzler argued that Luke employed a special source, he was indecisive as to whether the detailed information about the charges in Lk 23,2 rested upon it, or resulted from a clarification by Luke of Mk[39].

Although Blinzler maintained Luke possessed special information concerning the trial before Pilate, there was little in his treatment of 23,13-25 that would substantiate his claim. On the contrary, the changes seem to all point to Luke's revision of Mk. Luke chose not to mention that the scourging was carried out in order to present Pilate and the Romans in a favorable light[40]. Although the term παρέδωκεν may ultimately derive from the Suffering Servant text in LXX Is

---

34. *Ibid.*, p. 116 (= 122).

35. *Ibid.*, p. 116 (= 121-122). In this view Blinzler rejected the position of Husband, Klausner, Hauck and Rengstorf who argued that the Sanhedrin did not pass a death sentence. Instead, Blinzler sided with J. Schmid and J. Finegan.

36. *Ibid.*, p. 160, 163 (= 166-167, 174). Cf. HUSBAND, *Prosecution*, 1916; LIETZMANN, *Bemerkungen*, in *ZNW* 31 (1932) 78-84; HOLZMEISTER, *Zur Frage der Blutgerichtsbarkeit des Synedriums*, in *Bib* 19 (1938) 43-59; 151-174.

37. BLINZLER, *Trial*, p. 240 (= 252-253).

38. *Ibid.*, p. 290 (= 334): "The only thing that is questionable is whether the death sentence passed by the Sanhedrin was juristically incontestable, that is to say, whether the sanhedrists, in declaring the messianic self-testimony of Jesus to be blasphemy, were giving a judgment in accordance with their convictions and with the criminal law of the time". He had earlier rejected the views that what Pilate had done was to recognize the Sanhedrin sentence or to hand Jesus over to the Jews. He dismissed both of these views as untenable (cf. p. 238-239; see also [p. 251-252]).

39. *Ibid.*, p. 189 (= 201). A subsequent statement seemed to favor the latter choice. "Luke amplifies the meaning of the new charge (23:2)" (p. 241 = 254).

40. *Ibid.*, p. 234 (= 247-248).

53,6.12, we would argue it was also quite feasible that Luke simply read it in Mk[41]. Blinzler seemed to identify with the proposal of Dibelius that the text in Acts conveyed the historical situation, though tempered by the early Christians's desire to see the life of Christ reflected in Ps 2. This portrayal, Blinzler noted, was at odds with that found in the Gospels, since the Sanhedrin was presented as the chief antagonist to Jesus[42]. In the third edition of *Der Prozess Jesu* ([3]1960), which was significantly revised, Blinzler denied the arguments of Feine, Perry, Streeter and Taylor that a special source was evident in 22,47-71 opting rather to view the changes as redaction by Luke of Mk[43].

Blinzler authored an article (1969) affirming Conzelmann's belief that among the new material of the Lukan passion narrative, the most significant changes reflected Lukan redaction[44]. While not excluding the possibility that another source could have existed, it was questionable whether it surpassed that of Mk[45]. The likelihood that the Sanhedrin trial occurred in the morning rather than the night can account for one variation. Other changes, such as certain omissions, were prompted by the particular perspective out of which Luke wrote, such as his views on christology, theology and even pedagogy[46]. Passing over the mockery by the Roman soldiers resulted from apologetics. Blinzler viewed the transpositions as possibly arising from Luke's literary considerations, surpassing the details found in Mk[47]. Luke made additions which stirred the heart, such as 22,61.

Blinzler (1947) surmised that the encounter between Jesus and Herod (23,7-15) did not come about so much as a result of Herod's desire to see Jesus, but was orchestrated by Pilate[48]. The decision to include Herod in the proceedings was Pilate's attempt to offer a hopeful gesture to Herod. Citing the mishandling of the situation recounted in 13,2 as background, Blinzler proposed that Pilate transferred Jesus to Herod for two reasons: to pay a compliment to his opponent and to rid himself of legal dilemma[49]. As regards the silence of Jesus Blinzler viewed it in light of the Suffering Servant of God as found in Is 53,7 but contrasted with Mk

---

41. *Ibid.*, p. 240 (= 253).

42. *Ibid.*, p. 282; cf. [p. 325].

43. BLINZLER, *Der Prozess Jesu*, [p. 121].

44. BLINZLER, *Passionsgeschehen und Passionsbericht des Lukasevangeliums*, in *BK* 24 (1969) 4. Cf. CONZELMANN, *Die Mitte der Zeit*, [2]1957, p. 174 = *Theology*, 1961, p. 200.

45. BLINZLER, *Passionsgeschehen*, p. 3.

46. *Ibid.*, p. 1-2.

47. *Ibid.*, p. 3.

48. BLINZLER, *Herodes Antipas und Jesus Christus* (Bibelwissenschaftliche Reihe, 2), Stuttgart, 1947, p. 20. Though Blinzler initially defined the account "Jesus vor Herodes" as 23,7-15 he later described it as 23,6-12 (p. 6; cf. p. 20). Although Blinzler may be leaning in favor of the historicity of the pericope, his position became more clearly articulated in *Der Prozess Jesu*: "Die Herodesepisode wird nur vom Evangelisten Lukas berichtet. Diese schmale Bezeugung berechtigt aber nicht zur Anzweiflung der Geschichtlichkeit des Vorfalls" ([2]1955, p. 146 = ET, 203).

49. BLINZLER, *Herodes Antipas*, p. 21-22.

15,4. The dazzling garment was seen as an element of the "Spottkönig"[50]. The message communicated by the vesture was that Jesus was not dangerous but laughable. Blinzler referred to Harlow's proposal that the phrase ἀλλ᾽ οὐδὲ Ἡρῴδης (23,15) was often mistranslated. He dismissed the suggestion based on the improbability that there would be a doubling of the adversative particle[51]. Bornhäuser's idea that Herod led Jesus back to Pilate was also rejected as linguistically impossible[52].

Summarizing the various positions on the historicity of the episode, Blinzler highlighted the majority of non-Catholic scholars who maintained that the story was non-historical. Next "die alten Tübinger", who advocated the idea of a legend which stemmed from a tendency to excuse the Romans and to accuse the Jews, was recalled. Blinzler treated Dibelius's position which he termed "haltlos". Blinzler also took issue with O. Holtzmann who supposed it was hardly possible that the other evangelists would have simply forgotten the story if it had been available to them. Blinzler argued that Luke, as opposed to the other evangelists, had a particular interest in Herod and so included the episode[53].

The Herod episode, according to Blinzler (1951, [2]1959), was historical and stemmed from Joanna or Manaen[54]. Blinzler rejected the views that the story reflected either an apologetic or anti-Jewish bias. He also dismissed Dibelius's attempt to show that the episode was a legend linked to Ps 2,1-2. Blinzler curiously admitted that the trial of Jesus before Herod "was devoid of significance for the result of the trial", but argued Luke opted to include this account because Theophilus would certainly have been well versed in juridical matters[55].

In the third edition of *Der Prozess Jesu* (1960) Blinzler added an excursus on the role of Herod[56]. At this time Blinzler utterly rejected the contention of Joseph

50. *Ibid.*, p. 23. He dimissed as "eine unbeweisbare Vermutung" the proposal of Haneberg that the vesture represented the upper garment of a Hasmonean high priest (p. 24; cf. D.B. VON HANEBERG, *Die religiösen Altertümer der Bibel*, Munich, [2]1869, p. 559, 554f. Blinzler incorrectly referred to it as *Die hl. Altertümer der Bibel*. The book was a substantial revision of J.F. ALLIOLI, L.C. GRATZ and D. HANEBERG, *Handbuch der biblischen Alterthumskunde*, Landshut, 1844).

51. BLINZLER, *Herodes Antipas*, p. 24. Cf. HARLOW, *Jesus' Jerusalem Expedition*, 1936, p. 75-100. For Blinzler's more extensive discussion of Harlow's position see *The Trial of Jesus*, p. 200-201. Cf. above.

52. BLINZLER, *Herodes Antipas*, p. 24. Cf. K. BORNHÄUSER, *Die Beteiligung*, 714-718. See BLINZLER, *The Trial of Jesus*, 1959, p. 201-202.

53. BLINZLER, *Herodes Antipas*, p. 25. Cf. O. HOLTZMANN, *Das Neue Testament nach dem Stuttgarter griechischen Text übersetzt und erklärt*. Vol. 1. *Die synoptischen Evangelien. Apostelgeschichte*, Giessen, 1926, p. 327. See further BLINZLER, *The Trial of Jesus*, p. 203, n. 25.

54. *The Trial of Jesus*, p. 203-204 (= *Der Prozess Jesu*, [3]1960, p. 212).

55. *The Trial of Jesus*, p. 204 (= *Der Prozess Jesu*, [3]1960, p. 212). One must view Blinzler's contention with a degree of caution since the title used of Theophilus was also "a form of polite address with no official connotation". Cf. *BAGD*, p. 449, s.v. κράτιστος.

56. BLINZLER, *Der Prozess Jesu*, [3]1960, p. 213-219.

Tyson that Lk 23,6-12 offered a double of Mk 15,2-20 because the passages differed on essential points[57]. In yet a later contribution (1969) Blinzler wrote that though the Herod episode could be accounted for as arising from Ps 2,1-2 or from "sekundäre Bildung", the fact that Pilate tried to pass Jesus off on Herod had a historical basis[58]. The view that Jesus was harmless to the political process coincided with the perspective offered throughout Lk.

Hans CONZELMANN (1952) regarded the trial before the Sanhedrin as stylized dialogue form containing "ein Kompendium der christologischen Terminologie"[59]. The titles Messiah, Son of Man and Son of God were basically identical and reflected Lukan eschatology. The testimony of witnesses was rendered unnecessary and mention of the Temple was eliminated. The statements of Jesus' innocence represented Lukan redaction modelled on Mk and also reflected Luke's apologetics. The sentencing by Pilate was expunged. Instead he simply delivered Jesus to the will of the Jews. Luke had also been careful to eliminate references to the Romans as executioners[60].

In Die Mitte der Zeit (1953, [2]1957) Conzelmann endorsed the view that the bulk of the material in the passion narrative derived from Mk, but did not exclude the possibility of other sources[61]. He was strongly opposed to the Proto-Lk hypothesis. Changes in the Lukan account, such as 22,67-70 were due, not to sources, but to "Luke's Christological terminology"[62]. In reaction against Hirsch, Conzelmann denied that the Lukan ἀπὸ τοῦ νῦν was in any way related to the Matthean ἀπ' ἄρτι because of differing eschatological interpretations[63]. The charge that Jesus was a political messiah in the Gospel as well as Acts, was an accusation that reflected the Lukan apologia toward Rome. Luke was influenced extensively by the LXX[64].

By means of numerous references, it became clear that Conzelmann was opposed to Streeter and Taylor's hypothesis[65]. Though the theory of the special

---

57. Ibid., p. 219. Cf. TYSON, Lukan Version (1959).

58. BLINZLER, Passionsgeschehen, in BK 24 (1969) 2-3.

59. H. CONZELMANN, Zur Lukasanalyse, in ZTK 49 (1952) 16-33, p. 30.

60. Ibid.: "Sämtliche Beziehungen auf die Römer als Vollstrecker sind sorgfältig ausgemerzt (Mk 15,16ff.!)".

61. CONZELMANN, Die Mitte der Zeit. Studien zur Theologie des Lukas, Tübingen, 1953, [2]1957, [3]1960, [4]1962, [5]1964; (= The Theology of St. Luke, tr. G. BUSWELL, New York, 1961 [= [2]1957], p. 140); cf. p. 88. Even if other sources be acknowledged, they were manipulated according to Lukan apologetical goals. The pagination refers to the ET.

62. Ibid., p. 84.

63. Ibid., p. 84, n. 3. Cf. HIRSCH, Frühgeschichte, Vol. 2, p. 243ff.

64. CONZELMANN, Die Mitte der Zeit, p. 173, n. 1.

65. Ibid., p. 22, n. 1. Conzelmann rejected the theory since the genealogy was skillfully adjoined to the Markan context, and not vice versa. The temptation, linked with the passion, gave evidence that Luke was drawing on Q and Mk and Luke carefully constructed the unity from various elements. The unity, therefore, was not inherently due to some continuous source (p. 28, n. 3). He further rejected Streeter's attempt in the Nazareth pericope to determine that S and Q

source should not be ignored, even Taylor undermined his own theory when he proposed that the third block of Markan material was presumed and thus could indicate that Luke used Mk from the start[66].

Reginald H. Fuller, reviewing Conzelmann's contribution of *Die Mitte der Zeit*, pointed out that since he completely rejected the Proto-Lk theory, he was able to assign more creativity to the evangelist[67]. The results of such an approach were twofold: it devalued Lk as a source for the study of the historical Jesus, but enhanced Luke's status "as one of the creative theologians of the New Testament".

In a 1967 article Conzelmann maintained "Es wird vorausgesetzt – ohne dass dies für das Ergebnis essentiell wäre –, dass beide [Mt and Lk] ausser Markus keine durchgehende, zusätzliche Quelle verarbeiten"[68]. Still later, Conzelmann, in collaboration with his former student, Andreas LINDEMANN (1975/⁸1985), continued to reject the Proto-Lk hypothesis contending the theory had "little to commend it"[69]. These authors maintained Proto-Lk would not have been a complete Gospel as it would have lacked a passion account. The Q source as well would not have provided one[70]. The combined special material in the Luke passion would not constitute a complete narrative. The final objection rested on the observation that Luke followed the Markan order. Conzelmann and Lindemann further dismissed Schlatter's idea that the Lukan special material formed a complete Gospel. The material did not seem to have been connected in the early period.

Though he compared Dibelius with Bultmann regarding the origin of the Herod episode, Conzelmann (²1957 = 1961) withheld judgment, permitting only that the story allowed both the Jews and the Romans to find Jesus innocent[71]. The

were joined. Conzelmann cautioned against "drawing conclusions from literary similarities" (p. 29, n. 5). Finally, he refuted Taylor's argument that Luke was following a special source in Ch 23 by pointing to 23,3 as definite proof that Luke was well aware of Mk at that point of the narrative (p. 86).

66. *Ibid.*, p. 55, n. 3.

67. R.H. FULLER, *The New Testament in Current Study*, New York, 1962, p. 87.

68. CONZELMANN, *Historie und Theologie in den synoptischen Passionsberichten*, in F. VIERING (ed.), *Zur Bedeutung des Todes Jesus. Exegetische Beiträge*, Gütersloh, 1967, 37-53, p. 49 (= *History and Theology in the Passion Narratives of the Synoptic Gospels*, in *Interpr* 24 [1970] 178-197, p. 192). The article was translated by C.B. Cousar.

69. CONZELMANN and A. LINDEMANN, *Arbeitsbuch zum Neuen Testament* (UTB, 52), Tübingen, 1975, ⁴1979, ⁸1985 (= *Interpreting the New Testament. An Introduction to the Principles and Methods of N.T. Exegesis*, tr. S.S. SCHATZMANN, Peabody, MA, 1988, p. 231, esp. p. 231-232). They conceded the adherents of the theory were correct in noting that the non-Markan blocks contained material combined from Q and special material. See also CONZELMANN, *Literaturbericht zu den Synoptischen Evangelien*, in *TR* 43 (1978) 325, 327.

70. CONZELMANN and LINDEMANN, *Interpreting*, p. 57-58.

71. CONZELMANN, *The Theology of St. Luke*, p. 86, n. 2. He may favor redaction since he added: "There is a clear connection with the other Herod scenes, which have been considerably edited".

fact that Jesus even appeared before Herod rested on Luke's conception of Palestinian politics. The mistreatment by Herod's soldiers, was nonetheless, a replacement for the earlier Markan story about the mockery by the Roman soldiers which Luke elected not to borrow[72].

John A. BAILEY (1963) argued rightly that John was familiar with Lk and incorporated aspects of it into his own Gospel[73]. Luke used Mk as the basis of his account of Peter's denials[74]. The evangelist was responsible for certain details such as the time interval in 22,59, supplied to lead up to a crescendo[75]. Likewise, the detail of Jesus directing his gaze toward Peter (22,61) was a creation of the evangelist "to enhance the climax". The mockery (22,63-65) probably was based upon Mk[76].

While Luke employed Mk for the scene of the Sanhedrin trial, he departed from the Markan order[77]. Bailey maintained that the Sanhedrin trial was not a formal trial[78]. For a portion of this section (22,67-70) Luke used a written, non-Markan source[79]. Bailey believed that the change of order was due to Luke's plan of simplifying the Markan account, rather than to any special source[80]. But in 22,71 Luke once again redacted Mk to give it a new interpretation, so that it may now be understood to mean, "Why do we need any witnesses at all?".

The account of the trial before Pilate was based upon Mk, which reflected the same two parts[81]. Bailey did not consider it likely that Luke possessed any source other than Mk for the information concerning Pilate's desire to release Jesus. The scourging mentioned in 23,16.22 was unhistorical and rested upon information contained in Mk 15,15-20. The threefold statement of Pilate regarding the innocence of Jesus was also based upon Mk. Finally, for Luke, it was the Jews who carried out the crucifixion. He omitted Mk 15,20b and later did not explicitly declare that the Roman soldiers crucified Jesus[82]. The difference between Lk and Mk Bailey ultimately ascribed to theological or stylistic changes by Luke[83].

Bailey argued that the particularly Lukan material, that is, the charge (23,2) and the Herod episode (23,6-12) derived from Luke's own hand[84]. He rejected

---

72. *Ibid.*, p. 87.

73. J.A. BAILEY, *The Traditions Common to the Gospels of Luke and John* (NTSuppl, 7), Leiden, 1963, p. 115.

74. *Ibid.*, p. 55, n. 1.

75. *Ibid.*

76. *Ibid.*, p. 56, n. 3.

77. *Ibid.*

78. *Ibid.*, p. 59.

79. *Ibid.*, p. 60.

80. *Ibid.*, p. 61, n. 1; cf. p. 56.

81. *Ibid.*, p. 74. Bailey did not clearly delineate the division, though 23,1 and 23,11 each fell into their respective parts. Mk 15,2-5 was said to constitute the first part.

82. *Ibid.*, p. 75.

83. *Ibid.*, p. 77.

84. *Ibid.*, p. 65-66. Bailey qualified his understanding of the charge as coming from a

Taylor's suggestion on the ground that there was no new non-Markan material in the Herod story[85].

Werner Georg KÜMMEL ([14]1964, [17]1973 = ET 1975) was often singled out as having refuted the Proto-Lk theory almost as concisely as Creed had done in his dismissal of the idea in his famous footnote[86]. The theory was one element of two factors that caused scholars to question the Two-Source theory[87]. Grundmann, Rengstorf and Schlatter were listed as supporting the view of an additional narrative source[88], while the names of Klijn (support for a truncated form), Schürmann, Tyson, Rehkopf and Trocmé were enumerated as supporting a special account of the passion[89]. Later Kümmel added the names of George, Schütz, G. Schneider, Schramm and E. Bammel[90]. Those identified as advocates of a Proto-Lk included R.H. Fuller, Henshaw, De Zwaan; Streeter, Taylor, Perry, F.C. Grant; Evans, Jeremias[91]. To this earlier list was added T.W. Manson, Koh, Lohse, Rehkopf, Gaston, Williams, Morton, Marshall and Kilpatrick (1970, for Chs. 3-20)[92]. Jeremias's contribution was subsequently qualified by the statement

"tradition circulating orally in the Christian community" (p. 66, n. 1).

85. *Ibid.*, p. 66, n. 2. His criticism of Taylor was consistent with that of Creed and Finegan (p. 66, n. 3).

86. W.G. KÜMMEL, *Einleitung in das Neue Testament* [[12]1963], [13]1964, Heidelberg, [17]1973 (völlig neu bearbeitete Auflage), XIX-548 (esp. p. 92-120), *Das Lukasevangelium*, [21]1983 (erneute ergänzte Auflage) = *Introduction to the New Testament*, tr. A.J. MATTILL, Jr., Nashville, TN - New York, [[14]1965 rev. ed.]; tr. H.C. KEE, [[17]1973], Nashville, TN, 1975, [5]1984 (esp. p. 122-151, 174), *The Gospel of Luke*. The 17th German ed. (1973 = ET 1975 was used for the basis of our study with comparisons made to the 14th German ed. [1964]). See CREED, *Luke*, p. lviii, n. 1.

87. KÜMMEL, *Einleitung*, [17]1973, p. 22 (= 48-49). See *Einleitung*, [14]1964, p. 20.

88. *Einleitung*, [17]1973, p. 23, n. 9 (= 49, n. 9). See *Einleitung*, [14]1964, p. 20.

89. *Einleitung*, [17]1973, p. 23, n. 10 (= 49, n. 10). Compare *Einleitung*, [14]1964, p. 20. In the later edition Kümmel amended Klijn to reflect his support of a truncated form and the name of Trocmé was also added. See TROCMÉ, *La formation*, 1963, p. 174f. (= *Formation*, 1975, p. 221f).

90. KÜMMEL, *Einleitung*, [17]1973, p. 101, n. 13 (= 131, n. 14). See *Einleitung*, [14]1964, p. 79. Notice that Kümmel's enumeration in the 1964 edition was incorporated into the text and included Taylor, Perry, Grant, De Zwaan, Henshaw, T.W. Manson, Evans, Koh, Lohse, Rehkopf, Gaston and Williams. See further E. BAMMEL, *Das Ende von Q*, in O. BÖCHER (ed.), *Verborum Veritas*. FS G. STAHLIN, Wuppertal, 1970, 39-50, p. 45.

91. KÜMMEL, *Einleitung*, [17]1973, p. 23, n. 11 (= 49, n. 11). See *Einleitung*, [14]1964, p. 20. In the 1964 edition, Kümmel listed Streeter, Taylor, J. Jeremias, Evans, De Zwaan, Perry, Henshaw and Grant while in the 1973 edition he rearranged the order of the names and added Fuller. The groupings seemed to be significant since Kümmel set them off by a semi-colon.

92. *Einleitung*, [17]1973, p. 101, n. 13 (= 131, n. 13). See *Einleitung*, [14]1964, p. 79. In the 1964 edition Kümmel listed Kilpatrick among those who rejected a Proto-Lukan source ([14]1964, p. 79), but in the 1973 edition qualified his statement by listing Kilpatrick among those who believed that Luke expanded his Gospel using the Roman Mk, at least for chs. 3-20 ([17]1973, p. 101, n. 13 = 131, n. 13).

that both he and Winter made a distinction between the author of Lk and Proto-Lk[93]. Scholars tabulated as opponents of a Proto-Lk theory included Ellis, Rigaux, Goguel, Klijn, Michaelis, Kilpatrick (1942), Gilmour, Schürmann, Hastings, O'Neill, Conzelmann, Montefiore, Leaney, Talbert, Schramm, Grobel, Trocmé and Bailey[94]. Those rejecting the theory in particular for the passion narrative included Finegan, Lightfoot, Iber, Bultmann, Vööbus, J. Schreiber, Blinzler and Kee[95]. For Kümmel the matter of the Proto-Lk theory and a special passion source was the same: "In fact, the assumption of a Lukan special source or a Proto-Luke is as questionable as is a special source for the passion narrative", a position he has unwaveringly held since 1964[96].

Luke generally intended to follow the order found in his sources and largely followed the Markan order, with the exception of the passion narrative. Luke employed seventy percent of the Markan material (3,1–6,19; 8,4–9,50; 18,15–24,11)[97]. Luke indeed incorporated Mk, though he did so by "breaking up the Markan structure"[98]. Following Sparks, Kümmel argued that Luke indeed transposed material. As regards the argument that Luke inserted four large blocks of non-Markan material, Kümmel astutely observed that in the cases of the lesser and greater interpolations as with 19,39-44 there was omission of Markan material showing that Mk was Luke's basic source.

Luke was not attempting to provide a better chronological order, but sought to forge a "closer coupling of accounts with each other and by occasional creation of larger connections in the course of the narrative". This was achieved by various

93. *Einleitung*, [17]1973, p. 101, n. 13 (= 131, n. 13). *Einleitung*, [14]1964, p. 79. See Kümmel's bibliography for the works of Winter and Jeremias, [17]1973, p. 93 (= 122-123). See [14]1964, p. 72-73.

94. *Einleitung*, [17]1973, p. 101, n. 16 (= 132, n. 16). See *Einleitung*, [14]1964, p. 79. The 1964 edition contained the names Goguel, Dibelius, Gilmour, Kilpatrick, Michaelis, Grobel, Leaney, Conzelmann, Schürmann, Hastings, O'Neill, Montefiore, Klijn and Beare. To those were added in the 1973 edition Ellis, Rigaux, Talbert, as well as TROCMÉ, *La formation*, 1963, p. 173f., and BAILEY, *Traditions*, 1963, p. 18f. The name of Kilpatrick was qualified with the date of 1942, and the name of Beare was dropped.

95. KÜMMEL, *Einleitung*, [17]1973, p. 101, n. 17 (= 132, n. 17). See *Einleitung*, [14]1964, p. 79. Kümmel listed Iber, Lightfoot, Finegan, Bultmann and Blinzler in 1964. By 1973 he rearranged the names and added Vööbus, J. SCHREIBER, *Die Markuspassion. Wege zur Erforschung der Leidensgeschichte Jesu*, Hamburg, 1969, p. 49f., and H.C. KEE, *Jesus in History*, New York, 1970, p. 183f.

Johannes Schreiber contended that Dibelius rendered all the theories about Luke's special sources completely unnecessary, though it did not exclude the possibility that Luke took up new material occasionally in the passion narrative. However, it was apparent to Schreiber that Luke reinterpreted the Markan material in a new and free manner rather than drawing on preformulated tradition (*Die Markuspassion*, p. 50). In support of his view he listed CONZELMANN, *Die Mitte der Zeit*, 1954, p. 187, and KÜMMEL, *Einleitung*, [12]1963, p. 80f.

96. KÜMMEL, *Einleitung*, [17]1973, p. 101 (= 132). See *Einleitung*, [14]1964, p. 79.

97. *Einleitung*, [17]1973, p. 100 (= 130). See *Einleitung*, [14]1964, p. 78.

98. *Einleitung*, [17]1973, p. 104 (= 134). See *Einleitung*, [14]1964, p. 81.

expressions, among them phrases using καὶ ἐγένετο[99]. It was explicitly remarked
that 22,54–23,49 followed Mk's order in the main.

Kümmel likewise rejected Morgenthaler's view that Luke arranged his material
on the basis of a "principle of duality". He further refuted the position of Feine-
Behm that Lk was characterized as Ebionite, since this was not the case when the
entire Gospel was taken into consideration.

Lukan redaction removed offensive features as found in Mk, highlighted Jesus'
human traits, and used the term ὁ κύριος as in 22,61. Further, Luke was intent on
showing that Jesus was innocent in the view of the Romans which constituted part
of Luke's apologetic toward Rome. But "the decisive motive in Luke's reworking
of Mk, however, is theological"[100]. His purpose was seen as portraying the story
of Jesus as anticipating and preparing for the post-Easter ministry of the disciples.
The revision of Mk for 22,69 resulted from Luke's view of history.

Rehkopf's attempt at identifying pre-Lukan vocabulary was deemed
unsuccessful as shown by Conzelmann and Schürmann. The efforts by Schürmann,
Tyson and Rehkopf to establish a cohesive passion source met with the same result
in Kümmel's opinion[101]. While not totally excluding the possibility that Luke
relied on such a special source, Kümmel more favorably regarded the insertion of
oral tradition or Lukan redaction of Mk as likely solutions[102]. A significant
concession was Taylor's admission that Mk provided the framework of the account
of the passion in Lk. Following his rather brief discussion of the pertinent data
Kümmel concluded: "All this implies that the theories of a Lukan special source
and a 'Proto-Luke' comprising Q + special material are untenable, and that Lk can
scarcely have had a consecutive special tradition for the passion narrative"[103].
The assumptions of adherents of a Proto-Lk or a special passion account were
"undemonstrable". Kümmel again sided with Sparks in determining that Luke's
imitation of the Septuagintal style, rather than some hypothetical Hebraic source,
accounted for the particular phraseology. This was done with a view to Greek
speaking readers.

Arguing against Torrey and Sahlin that Aramaic documents formed the basis
of the first half of Acts, Kümmel discerned that these views were disputed by "the
composite character of Acts 1–15, and especially by the fact that several of the OT

99. *Einleitung*, [17]1973, p. 107 (= 137). See *Einleitung*, [14]1964, p. 84.

100. *Einleitung*, [17]1973, p. 110 (= 141). See *Einleitung*, [14]1964, p. 87.

101. *Einleitung*, [17]1973, p. 103 (= 133). See *Einleitung*, [14]1964, p. 80.

102. *Einleitung*, [17]1973, p. 103 (= 133-134). See *Einleitung*, [14]1964, p. 81. Consider also:
"If, then, Luke did not derive from a consecutive special source the extensive material that goes
beyond Mk and Q, the possibility cannot be excluded that he – as has already been conjectured
for Mk – found assembled in oral or even written form some of the special traditions that he
employed. But that can hardly be demonstrated with certainty" ([14]1964, p. 82; [17]1973, p. 104-105
= 135).

103. *Einleitung*, [17]1973, p. 104 (= 135). See *Einleitung*, [14]1964, p. 82.

quotations were usable for the context only in the LXX wording (e.g. 2:17ff; 15:17), and in this section we find LXX language consistently"[104].

In a later work (1970) Kümmel called attention to Streeter's Proto-Lk theory, stressing Streeter's contention of the purported historical value of the hypothetical source[105]. The assumption of source criticism, that it could "retrace the steps backward from the primitive church's historical picture and faith in Christ to the beginnings of Christianity, and in particular back to the historical Jesus" came to be challenged by form criticism in the works of K.L Schmidt, M. Dibelius and R. Bultmann[106].

One of the more prolific American Lukan scholars is Charles H. TALBERT. There has been a noticeable shift in his approach to dealing with the question of sources. Though initially he declared his support of the Two-Source theory, in later works he abandoned any efforts to refer not only to that approach but to any source theory at all.

Talbert (1966) rejected Proto-Lk in favor of the belief that the changes over against Mk reflected Luke's intention and goals[107]. Talbert's negative reaction to Harald Sahlin was prompted, in part, by the latter's date of the 60's AD for Luke's writings[108]. Talbert formulated his redaction theory, influenced heavily by Dibelius's view of the Lukan passion narrative being constructed as a martyrdom. Such a view was confirmed, according to Talbert, by the descriptions of the deaths of Jesus and Stephen. The purpose of such writing was to establish an apologia for Christians who were suffering death for their faith[109]. Luke's presentation of Jesus as a martyr stemmed from the evangelist and incorporated several changes from Mk, not the least being increasing the political declarations of Jesus' innocence to three as opposed to only one in Mk, as well as adding Herod's testimony that Jesus was not guilty[110].

In an essay discussing Lukan christology (1968) Talbert assumed Luke employed Mk, Q and "certain traditions peculiar to Luke commonly designated L"[111]. He also spoke of how Luke "manipulates his sources"[112]. Examining

---

104. *Einleitung*, [17]1973, p. 141-142 (= 174). See *Einleitung*, [14]1964, p. 114.

105. *Das Neue Testament: Geschichte der Erforschung seiner Probleme*, Freiburg, 1958, 1970, p. 4148-419 (= *The New Testament: The History of the Investigation of Its Problems*, tr. S. MCLEAN GILMOUR and H.C. KEE, Nashville, TN, 1972, p. 327.

106. *Ibid.*, p. 327-338.

107. C. TALBERT, *Luke and the Gnostics*, Nashville, TN, 1966, p. 15. See n. 1. This work represented an aspect of his doctoral dissertation directed by Leander Keck.

108. *Ibid.*

109. *Ibid.*, p. 76.

110. *Ibid.*, p. 73; cf. p. 26-27.

111. *An Anti-Gnostic Tendency in Lucan Christology*, in *NTS* 14 (1968) 259-271, esp. p. 260, n. 5 (= *Die antidoketische Frontstellung der lukanischen Christologie*, in G. BRAUMANN [ed.], *Das Lukas-Evangelium*, Darmstadt, 1974, 354-377).

112. *Ibid.*, p. 262.

Luke as a theologian using the redaction-critical method (1970), Talbert devoted some pages to an analysis of 22,69[113]. He did not dispute Luke's use of Mk as the source for this verse; rather he challenged previous suggestions as to why Luke redacted it.

Talbert co-authored with E.V. McKnight an article (1972) which refuted the Griesbach hypothesis, the traditional formulation, a newer form espoused by W.R. Farmer as well as the Matthean priority theory of B.C. Butler and the Lukan priority hypothesis of R.L. Lindsey[114]. Their study affirmed the validity of Markan priority.

In examining Lukan literary patterns (1974) Talbert acknowledged that the author of Lk-Acts was both a theologian and a "consummate literary artist"[115]. "Luke simply varies his style in terms of the situation he is depicting and the tone that the situation requires"[116]. He drew on Cadbury in highlighting Luke's preferrence for "pairs of words, doubled vocatives ... as well as the wide parallelism between the careers of his heroes, Jesus, Peter, Paul and Stephen"[117]. These "distinctively Lucan tendencies" all served to highlight the parallelism between Jesus and Paul[118]. Such similarities were seen in events in the lives of Jesus and Paul (Lk 22,54 / Acts 21,30; Lk 22,63-65 / Acts 23,2; Lk 22,26[sic][119]; 23,1.8.13 / Acts 23–26). This pattern was also evident in the details of the trials (Lk 23,4.14.22 / Acts 23,9; 25,25; 26,31; Lk 23,6-12 / Acts 25,13–26,32; Lk 23,16.22 / Acts 26,32; Lk 23,18 / Acts 21,36)[120].

The Two-Source theory was assumed and he spoke of various sources including Mk, Q, and the L tradition[121]. In a discussion of the Sanhedrin trial

113. *Redaction Critical Quest for Luke the Theologian*, in *Perspective* 11 (1970) 171-222, esp. p. 186-188.

114. C.H. TALBERT and E.V. MCKNIGHT, *Can the Griesbach Hypothesis Be Falsified?*, in *JBL* 91 (1972) 338-368, esp. p. 338, 367-368, and 368, n. 92.

115. TALBERT, *Literary Patterns. Theological Themes, and the Genre of Luke-Acts* (SBL MS, 20), Missoula, MT, 1974, p. 1.

116. *Ibid.*

117. *Ibid.*, p. 2. See CADBURY, *Making*, 1927, p. 216, 218, 223-225, 231-232. In *Martyrdom in Luke-Acts and the Lukan Social Ethic* (1983), Talbert highlighted the parallelism between Jesus and Stephen whose deaths in Lk-Acts were "portrayed as martyrdom" (p. 99). Though he compared the Lukan material with Graeco-Roman, Jewish and early Christian thinking, he did not compare the portrayal with Mk. He noted that "Jesus is a prophet rejected and killed by God's people (cf. Luke 13:33ff.; Acts 7:52)" (p. 106).

118. TALBERT, *Literary Patterns*, p. 22: "The significance of all the distinctively Lucan tendencies is that each one was necessary in order to have the narrative of Jesus' trial correspond to some similar Pauline situation in Acts. The entire trial sequence in Luke is shaped, therefore, in order to parallel the trial sequence of Paul in Acts".

119. *Ibid.*, p. 17. This error was repeated (p. 22). Since the passage he quoted dealt with the dispute among the disciples as to who is greatest (22,26), it would appear that Talbert intended to refer to the Sanhedrin trial (22,66).

120. TALBERT, *Literary Patterns*, p. 17, 18. On correspondences, see also discipleship, p. 63.

121. *Ibid.*, p. 14, n. 69; also p. 18.

Talbert called attention to Luke's addition of συλλαβόντες to his Markan source (Mk 14,53) in 22,54, noting the similarity with ἐπιλαβόμενοι (Acts 21,30)[122]. For the mockery he asserted "no alteration in Mark 14:65 was necessary for this parallel"[123]. He spoke in terms of "the four trials of Jesus" which Neyrey also did[124]. Talbert, drawing on Winter, entertained the possibility that these trials (22:26[sic]; 23,1; 23,8; 23,13) were due either to Mk or to an independent source[125]. Talbert insisted, however, that the threefold declaration of the innocence of Jesus was "distinctively Lucan", as were Pilate's efforts to release Jesus[126].

Shifting Sands: The Recent Study of the Gospel of Luke (1976) is a seminal article and reflected a turning point in Talbert's own studies. While he continued to defend the view that Jesus' death in Lk-Acts was a martyrdom, he departed from his earlier stand on the Two-Source theory[127]. Stating that there were three significant challenges to Conzelmann's redactional methodology of determining Luke's theology in light of his changes in Mk, he began, based on Schramm's work, to raise the possibility that Luke employed "variant traditions" rather than Mk in certain parallel material[128]. The second challenge, offered by Marshall and Schütz, was that Luke's theology, in some cases, did not vary from the traditions he employed[129]. The third obstacle to Conzelmann's approach was the "significant assault on the 'two-source theory'"[130]. "Although the alternatives proposed have not proved convincing, enough difficulties with Marcan priority have emerged to render its position as an 'assured result' of criticism suspect and to make it a questionable control on redaction-critical work"[131]. This last point of view will undergird his subsequent scholarship.

His commentary *Reading Luke* (1982) adopted a methodological approach common among the proponents of literary criticism that eschews any notion of source theory[132]. Continuing to subscribe to the view that Jesus' death in Lk was

---

122. *Ibid.*, p. 21-22.

123. *Ibid.*, p. 22.

124. *Ibid.* Cf. NEYREY, *Passion*, p. 69 (passim).

125. TALBERT, *Literary Patterns*, p. 22. Cf. WINTER, *Treatment*, 1954, p. 158.

126. *Literary Patterns*, p. 22: "The declaration by Pilate that he will release Jesus (Luke 23:16,22) is Lucan ... The closest thing to it in Mark is found in 15:9 where Pilate asks: 'Do you want me to release for you the King of the Jews?'".

127. *Shifting Sands: The Recent Study of the Gospel of Luke*, in *Interpr* 30 (1976) 381-395 (= J. MAYS [ed.], *Interpreting the Gospels*, Philadelphia, PA, 1981, 231-246).

128. *Ibid.*, p. 392, 393. See further p. 393, nn. 76, 77, for a list of two groups of material Schramm distinguished in the Lk parallel to Mk. Note that Talbert misspelled Schramm's name (p. 392). Cf. SCHRAMM, *Der Markus-Stoff*.

129. TALBERT, *Shifting Sands*, p. 393. Cf. I.H. MARSHALL, *Luke. Historian and Theologian*, p. 19f., 218, and F. SCHÜTZ, *Der leidende Christus*, 1969, p. 19.

130. TALBERT, *Shifting Sands*, p. 393.

131. *Ibid.*

132. *Reading Luke. A Literary and Theological Commentary on the Third Gospel*, New York,

cast as a martyrdom he now adopted the paraenetic perspective wherein the manner of Jesus' death served as a model for his disciples[133]. As in 1974, he continued to speak of the four trials of Jesus[134].

The shift away from source criticism to a study of Luke as a theologian was dated by Talbert (1984) at the time of the Second World War[135]. Here he again addressed the theme of Jesus as prophet and repeated his idea on the correspondence between Lk 9 and Lk 22–24[136].

Talbert (1989), in surveying nearly a half century of studies on Lk-Acts, supported Schramm's methodology and accepted Minear's critique indicating that it was "extremely difficult" to determine Luke's theology from a comparision with Mk[137]. Further, because Markan priority had come under severe attack in recent decades, Talbert questioned the validity of such an approach. "Although these alternatives have not proved convincing, enough difficulties with Marcan priority have merged to render its position as an 'assured result' of criticism suspect and to make it a questionable control on redaction-critical work (Tyson). Employing Mark as a control today is about as compelling as using Colossians and 2 Thessalonians to describe Paul's theology. It may be very legitimate to do so, but so many have problems with the procedure that such an assumption narrows considerably the scholarly circles within which one can converse"[138]. Echoing Bovon, Talbert contended that such a predicament called for a new methodology. Quite rightly Talbert criticized structural analysis and literary criticism for yielding few or insignificant results. More fruitful was the approach which compared Lukan compositional techniques with those of pagan and Jewish authors, yet it too suffered because it did not deal with the entirety of Lk-Acts. Talbert personally favored genre criticism which avoided the question of sources. Despite the various directions that methodology was taking, Talbert believed Lukan scholars viewed Lk-Acts as theology rather than history. While he credited redaction criticism with helping to see Luke as a theologian, the need existed for a methodology which

1982, p. 1-2: "This commentary will not assume the two-source theory, nor any other theory for that matter. Although the movement beyond the study of Lukan alterations of Mark is both necessary and proper, this does not prevent the comparison of Luke's narrative development with that of the other gospels, including Mark, when they run parallel ... In this volume comparisons of Luke with other gospels will be made but without assuming any source theory". He also occasionally made some comparisons with Acts.

133. *Ibid.*, p. 212.

134. *Ibid.*, p. 215-218. See *Literary Patterns*, 1974, p. 22.

135. *Promise and Fulfillment in Lucan Theology*, in ID. (ed.), *Luke-Acts. New Perspectives from the Society of Biblical Literature Seminar*, New York, 1984, 91-103, p. 91.

136. *Ibid.*, p. 99: "It is in this way that some prophetic utterances are used in Luke-Acts (for example, prophecy made by Jesus, when fulfilled legitimates his authority – Luke 9:22 fulfilled in chapters 22-24 ...)".

137. C.H. TALBERT, *Luke-Acts*, in E.J. EPP and G.W. MACRAE (eds.), *The New Testament and its Modern Interpreters*, Philadelphia, PA, 1989, p. 307.

138. *Ibid.*, p. 307-308.

"will not depend on any source theories and that will be able to come to terms with the unity of Lukan thought"[139].

In a recent essay on Lk (1990), Talbert divided Lukan scholarship into two periods. Before 1940 the focus was on source criticism. A shift occurred in the mid-fifties at which time Lk was seen as a theological work[140]. One must take exception to his statement that "the sources of the third Gospel have been a matter of dispute since the mid-sixties"[141]. Without mentioning names, Talbert observed that some scholars chose to simply suspend judgment about source-critical matters "until further evidence is available". He did not regard this as problematic since he believed that one can interpret the Gospel in its present form regardless of a source theory "but the quest for the historical Jesus demands some working hypothesis about sources".

Talbert (1974) considered 23,6-16 as stemming from the L tradition[142]. He showed that "events mentioned in ch. 9 are either referred to or echoed in chs. 22-23, though not often in the same order"[143]. Luke's literary patterns included architectonic schema between the Gospel and Acts and within the Gospel itself. An example of this latter was the relation to Lk 9,7-9 for which Luke drew upon Mk 6,14-16, resulting in a "significant modification of Mark"[144]. Lk 9,7-9 and 23,6-16 both treated Herod's learning of Jesus and desiring to see him (9,9b / 23,8)[145]. The inclusion of the Herod story seemed not to provide a second witness to the innocence of Jesus, but was "in part doubtless due to Luke's desire for this second correspondence". Adopting Winter's view, Talbert held that Luke redacted Mk's threefold trial adding a fourth, in order for Jesus and Paul to both "go through a fourfold trial process"[146]. For Talbert, Luke was constrained to organize the trial in the Gospel as he did. "The significance of all these distinctively Lucan tendencies is that each one was necessary in order to have the narrative of Jesus' trial correspond to some similar Pauline situation in Acts. The entire trial in Luke is shaped, therefore, in order to parallel the trial sequence of Paul in Acts"[147].

While ignoring the source question in his commentary (1982), he continued to espouse the view of four trials. The Herod pericope (23,6-12) could serve three possible functions[148]: 1) to emphasize the innocence of Jesus by providing a

---

139. *Ibid.*, p. 311.

140. TALBERT, *Gospel of Luke*, in W.E. MILLS et al. (eds.), *Mercer Dictionary of the Bible*, Macon, GA, 1990, 529. The section 22,39–23,25 was entitled "A Model for Martyrs" (p. 530).

141. *Ibid.*, p. 531.

142. TALBERT, *Literary Patterns*, 1974, p. 27. He rejected the view that L constituted a "connected narrative" (cf. p. 33, n. 73).

143. *Ibid.*, p. 26. He added: "Except for one or two of these correspondences, to my knowledge, they have so far eluded scholarly detection".

144. *Ibid.*, p. 27.

145. *Ibid.*

146. *Ibid.*, p. 22, n. 37.

147. *Ibid.*, p. 22.

148. *Ibid.*, p. 216-217. In *Literary Patterns*, 1975, p. 27, the pericope was defined as 23,6-

second witness as demanded by Dt 19,15, 2) to fulfill Ps 2,1ff. which was quoted in Acts 4,25-26, and 3) to portray Jews and Gentiles as being reconciled through the death of Jesus[149]. It would appear to Talbert that the central function was to focus on the guiltlessness of Jesus[150].

Robert Horton GUNDRY (1967), in a discussion of 22,69 and parallels (Mt 26,64 / Mk 14,62) rightly recognized that Luke added τοῦ θεοῦ to τῆς δυνάμεως as a clarification for his Gentile readers[151]. In a brief discussion of 22,63f. Gundry followed Bundy and Tyson claiming that Luke was employing a special source in the passion narrative[152].

In his 1982 commentary on Mt Gundry identified himself as a contemporary proponent of the view that Luke both knew and used Mt[153]. As such, he claimed that though Matthew and Luke both used Mk and Q as primary sources, Luke additionally employed Mt as "an overlay" which explained the fact that the Matthean order was rearranged in Lk[154]. The material borrowed from Mt was referred to as "foreign bodies" a nomenclature which Gundry continued to use in his writings in the past decade[155]. In reaction to Neirynck, this process, too, will explain the MA[156].

However, for the MA in 22,64 / Mt 26,68 Gundry rejected Matthean influence in favor of the view that Matthew joined the Markan and pre-Lukan historical traditions. The Lukan setting was a deciding factor for Gundry[157].

Matthean influence was seen or assumed for ὑμεῖς λέγετε (22,70 – but differed in number / Mt 26,64 σὺ εἶπας), ἀπὸ τοῦ νῦν (22,69 / Mt 26,64 ἀπ' ἄρτι), agreement in order of ἐκ ... δυνάμεως, despite a lack of reference to Dan 7,13, λέγοντες (22,63 / Mt 26,68, but a different setting), οὐκ οἶδα (22,57 / Mt 26,70), omission of δίς (22,61 / Mt 26,75), λέγων, ἔφη (23,3 / Mt 27,11).

Matthean influence was possible for εἰπὸν ἡμῖν (22,67 / ἡμῖν εἴπῃς Mt 26,63), ἄνθρωπε, οὐκ εἰμί (22,58 seemed to be a revision / Mt 26,72), ἐξελθών

16.

149. *Ibid.*, p. 217, where he admitted that this theme was "not explicit in the Lukan scheme".

150. *Ibid.*

151. R.H. GUNDRY, *The Use of the Old Testament in St. Matthew's Gospel. With Special Reference to the Messianic Hope* (NTSuppl, 18), Leiden, 1967, p. 60.

152. *Ibid.*, p. 61: "Lk, following as usual in the passion narrative an independent tradition, betrays no reminiscence of Is 50:6". Gundry did not treat the MAs in Mt 26,68.75.

153. GUNDRY, *Matthew. A Commentary on His Literary and Theological Art*, Grand Rapids, MI, 1982 (esp. p. 5, 541-565, 599-640). Particularly noteworthy was his topical index for places in the commentary where he discussed Matthean influence on Luke (p. 650).

154. *Ibid.*, p. 5.

155. *Ibid.* See also GUNDRY, *Matthean Foreign Bodies in Agreements of Luke with Matthew against Mark Evidence that Luke Used Matthew*, in FS NEIRYNCK, 1992, Vol. 2, p. 1467-1495.

156. GUNDRY, *Matthew*, p. 5. See also p. 544: "The frequent agreements between Matthew and Luke against Mark, including two such agreements in v 63, favors Matthean influence rather than independent editing of Mark by Luke".

157. *Ibid.*, p. 547.

(22,62 / Mt 26,75), ἤγαγον (23,1 / Mt 27,2 ἀπήνεγκαν), ὁ δὲ ἀποκριθεὶς αὐτῷ ἔφη (23,3 / a conflation of Mt 27,11 and Mk 15,2).

As regards weaknesses, Gundry did not suggest why Luke would make certain changes over against Mt (pre-Lukan historical tradition perhaps?). While the story of Judas (Mt 27,3-10 and Acts 1,16-20) was seen as a fulfillment of the OT and Matthew was inspired by an account from 2 Sam 17,23, Gundry offered no reason why Luke would have omitted the story at a parallel point in his Gospel and held it until the beginning of Acts. Nor was there any discussion, if Mt was an overlay for Luke, why the stories were so different. Why would Luke have preferred the account found in Acts over the one found in Mt? There did not seem to be any hint of Matthean influence in the Lukan report. At 23,18-19 Luke preserved a non-Markan tradition and Matthew adjusted his account to it (Mt 27,21)[158]. In cases where a word seemed to be a preferred Lukan term, the reverse was not the case that Luke influenced Matthew, but Gundry did not likewise propose that Luke took a Matthean word and employed it more frequently[159]. There was very little M material. Most of that can be explained by Matthew's redaction of Mk and a broader form of Q than scholars normally presuppose. This was further shaped by OT material.

John Meier was not convinced by Gundry's methodology or "theological presuppositions"[160]. Despite Gundry's apologia for not interacting with the wealth of literature[161], Meier found it regrettable[162]. Dennis Sweetland seemed to imply that Gundry was arguing backwards from his conviction that Luke used Mt, so that Gundry assigned a date earlier than 63 AD to accommodate his point of view[163]. Sweetland, like Meier, lamented the lack of debate with other scholarly positions within the commentary. Further, several of Gundry's assertions, including his position that Luke used Mt "demand a response"[164]. Lamar Cope pointed out the significance of Gundry's position on the relation of Lk and Mt: "That position destroys any need for a 'Q' source and undercuts the priority of Mark"[165]. Cope was hopeful that Gundry's commentary would renew theological discussion. Both Cope and David Mealand expressed disappointment that their expectations for the commentary were not realized[166]. As regards Gundry's assertions that Matthew employed traditions which lay at the base of Luke's Infancy Narrative as well as

---

158. *Ibid.*, p. 563.

159. *Ibid.*, p. 565: "Though λαός does not appear in Matthew nearly so often as it does in Luke, Matthew inserts it eight times and includes it in unique material four times, besides two common occurrences".

160. *JBL* 103 (1984) 475. He concluded: "Despite the publisher's claim on the jacket, this volume is neither a full-scale commentary nor a critical work" (p. 477).

161. GUNDRY, *Matthew*, p. 1.

162. *JBL* 103 (1984) 476.

163. *CBQ* 46 (1984) 161.

164. *Ibid.*, p. 162.

165. *ATR* 65 (1983) 218.

166. *JAAR* 52 (1984) 256.

Luke's use of Mt, Mealand responded: "I find these two latter points unduly complex and lacking adequate evidential support"[167]. Yet, in our opinion, Gundry must be complimented for his support of Markan priority and his redaction-critical approach.

Neirynck critiqued Gundry for restricting redactional creativity to Matthew, outside the purview and ability of Luke[168]. Whereas Gundry's conception of Matthew as an evangelist permitted him to compose creatively based on Mk, Luke was seen as slavishly following his sources.

In a recent article (1992), Gundry resumed his argument that Luke used Mt in addition to Mk by focusing once more on MAs[169]. The repeated used of the term "Matthean foreign bodies" made it clear that Gundry continued along the line established in his commentary. He shared with Goulder the conviction that Luke used Mt, but rejected Goulder's perspective that dispensed with Q[170].

Passing over the more notable MAs in 22,62.64, Gundry focused on 22,70[171]. He rightly noted that 22,70 differed from Mt 26,64, which he contended influenced the Lukan verse in several ways: number, tense and position. It would seem better to see this in the light of independent redaction by Luke and Matthew of Mk. Gundry was correct in asserting "Luke has no reason to use σὺ εἶπας", for Luke needed to change Mk since now Jesus was being interrogated by τὸ πρεσβυτέριον τοῦ λαοῦ, ἀρχιερεῖς τε καὶ γραμματεῖς (v. 66). Gundry also detected Mk in Luke's retention of the Markan ἐγώ εἰμι. Gundry maintained that Matthew presented Jesus as "an examplar of refusing to answer under oath"[172]. As Gundry himself pointed out, Luke was more faithful to the Markan presentation so that Jesus was not under oath. This could well reflect Lukan redaction in light of the evangelist's Roman apologetic[173]. The attribution of increasing guilt to the Jews was likely to reflect the *Sitz im Leben* of Luke as well as Matthew. The substitution of τοῦ θεοῦ in both later Synoptics could also reflect independent redaction in light of the evangelists's need for clarification for the Gentile members of the Christian communities for which they wrote[174].

---

167. *Ibid.*, p. 257.

168. *ETL* 63 (1987) 409.

169. *Matthean Foreign Bodies*, p. 1467-1495.

170. *Ibid.*, p. 1468. Cf. M.D. GOULDER, *Midrash and Lection in Matthew* (The Speaker's Lectures in Biblical Studies, 1969-71), London, 1974. Neirynck called attention to the difference between Gundry and Goulder (*Synoptic Problem*, in *NJBC*, p. 595).

171. GUNDRY, *Matthean Foreign Bodies*, p. 1488-1489.

172. *Ibid.*, p. 1488.

173. The matter of oath taking could be a delicate issue. Cf. P.F. ESLER, *Community and Gospel in Luke-Acts. The Social and Political Motivations of Lucan Theology* (SNTS MS, 57), Cambridge, 1987, p. 217: "From the discussion in this chapter, one may conclude that the way Luke has handled the relationship between Rome and Christianity has been motivated and influenced by the pressures upon the Roman members of his community generated by their continuing allegiance to the state they served".

174. GUNDRY, *Matthean Foreign Bodies*, p. 1489.

Another element where the Lukan and Matthean accounts were very similar was in the use of the equivalent phrases ἀπ' ἄρτι (Mt 26,64) and ἀπὸ τοῦ νῦν (22,69). Gundry interpreted the Matthean redaction as "an intellectual seeing of the Son of man's exaltation throughout the interim up to his coming", by which the guilt of the Jewish leaders escalated[175]. Once more, the independent changes should be viewed as independent redaction. Luke, understanding that the prophecy of Jesus as recorded in Mk had not been realized, and in keeping with his theology, refashioned the Markan statement. Gundry observed also that the order for the ἐκ phrase following the καθήμενον(ς) phrase of Mt and Lk conformed to Ps 110,1 prompted by the evangelists's desire "for a smoother word order". Since both Matthew and Luke had as one of their goals to improve the Markan style, recourse need not be had to the use of one by the other to explain this particular phenomenon.

While our disagreements have been made clear, we affirm a number of Gundry's conclusions: the use of Mk as a source for both Mt and Lk (#2); the agreements do not require any assumption of a Proto-Mk or Proto-Lk (#5); oral tradition is not the explanation for this phenomenon (#6)[176].

Albert VANHOYE (1967) determined that the Lukan passion reflected the preoccupations of the historian and writer[177]. It was an account of a disciple who relived the story of his master. The disciple's personal attachment to the master was revealed in the repeated affirmation of innocence and the omission of cruel or offensive details[178]. The order manifested the hand of the historian[179].
The basic schema was the same in all three, but the "l'organisation intérieure" varied among the three[180]. His statement was based not simply on the accounts of the passion, but on the Gospels in their entirety. Specific reference was made

---

175. *Ibid.*

176. *Ibid.*, p. 1493-1494. Gundry also took aim at Burkitt's suggestion that Q had contained an account of the passion denouncing such a view on the grounds that this was "hardly the stuff of Q".

177. *Les récits de la passion chez les Synoptiques*, in *NRT* 89 (1967) 136-163, p. 138 (= *Structure and Theology of the Accounts of the Passion in the Synoptic Gospels*, tr. C.H. GIBLIN [The Bible Today Supplementary Studies, 1], Collegeville, MN, 1967 = *La Passion selon les quatre Évangiles*, Paris, 1981, 11-63, p. 18 = *Struktur und Theologie der Passionsberichte in den synoptischen Evangelien*, in M. LIMBECK [ed.], *Redaktion*, 1981, 226-261, p. 230). The article was translated into German by G. Mayer. Vanhoye referred readers to the article of LÉON-DUFOUR, *Passion*, in *DBS* 6, 1960, 1419-1492, and the book of P. BENOIT, *Passion et Résurrection*, Paris, 1966 (VANHOYE, *Les récits*, 1967, p. 135, n. 1 = *La Passion*, p. 12, n. 1 = *Struktur*, p. 261).

178. VANHOYE, *Les récits*, p. 139, also p. 142 (= *La Passion*, 18, 25 = *Struktur*, 230, 234).

179. *Ibid.*, p. 141 (= *La Passion*, 24 = *Struktur*, 234).

180. *Les récits de la Passion dans les évangiles synoptiques*, in ID., I. DE LA POTTERIE, C. DUQUOC (eds.), *La passion selon les quatre Évangiles* (Lire la Bible, 55), Paris, 1981, p. 19.

to Luke's mentioning the armed resistance before the arrest which provided for a better series of facts[181].

For the transpositions in the denial, mockery and trial, Vanhoye argued this corresponded to Luke's parenetic-personal method of composition[182]. The repentance indicated at 22,62 clearly dermarcated Peter from those who abused him. Vanhoye (1981) treated the MA in v. 62, suggesting that the short form was borrowed from Mt[183]. The omission of the reference to the Temple was explained by Luke's concentration on the identity of Jesus while the theme which shaped 23,2-25 was the innocence of Jesus.

Vanhoye (1967) credited Luke with carefully reporting the transfer of jurisdiction to Herod[184]. The purpose was to provide a chance for false sympathy to be shown to Jesus. Herod's desire to see Jesus arose from curiosity and amusement, without the slightest inclination to. personal responsibility. Vanhoye noted Luke related the mockeries in the Herod episode. "A la fin du procès il s'abstiendra de décrire les cruautés romaines". Arguing that the innocence of Jesus was the "thème principal" in 23,2-25, the Herod pericope provided the proper manner of engagement and attitude for encountering Jesus. Although Vanhoye did not speak directly to the issue of source, it was clear that the story fit well into Luke's apologetic[185].

Samuel Frederick George BRANDON (1968) viewed Luke as relying heavily upon Mk, though in the account of Pilate's trial he used a special source[186]. Brandon was chiefly concerned with Luke's treatment of Mk's account of the trial and the Herod episode. Since Brandon was of the mind that Luke followed Mk in the story of Barabbas (23,13-25)[187], the special source must have been confined to information in 23,1-5. Though on the one hand he stated Luke obviously used Mk, that Lk was a "rationalisation" of Mk, and that none of the later evangelists had additional material which significantly supplemented Mk's account[188], he nonetheless also claimed that Luke had access not only to special information concerning the church at Jerusalem as recounted in Acts, but also seemed to have had material about Pilate's trial[189]. The special source would have offered more

---

181. *Ibid.*, p. 141 (= *La Passion*, 24 = *Struktur*, 234).

182. *Ibid.*, p. 145 (= *La Passion*, 31 = *Struktur*, 239).

183. *La Passion*, p. 32, n. 5. This note, as well as the paragraph to which it is appended, was not in the original and did not appear in the GT. See below for the treatment of Vanhoye on the MAs.

184. *Ibid.*, p. 148 (= *La Passion*, 38 = *Struktur*, 243). The reference to the volume in *NRT* in M. Limbeck to the original French edition was incorrect.

185. *Ibid.*, p. 149 (= *La Passion*, 39 = *Struktur*, 243). Luke's interest in Herod was highlighted by Vanhoye as he listed 6 references in Lk, two in Mk and only one in Mt (p. 148 = *La Passion*, 38 = *Struktur*, 243).

186. S.F.G. BRANDON, *The Trial of Jesus of Nazareth*, New York, 1968, p. 120; cf. p. 116.

187. *Ibid.*, p. 123.

188. *Ibid.*, p. 108, 116.

189. *Ibid.*, p. 117, 120. "In light of these considerations, it would seem feasible, therefore,

detailed information concerning the charges preferred against Jesus, though relating
little about Pilate's rejection of them[190]. But this source was of such a nature that
it did "not seriously challenge Mark's presentation"[191]. Brandon viewed Luke as
aware of Markan order, though the changes the Luke made were sometimes
careless and illogical[192].

Brandon contended that the omissions in and around the Sanhedrin trial can
be easily explained because Luke wished to focus on Pilate's trial for which he had
special information. The omission of Jesus' supposed threat to the Temple was
understandable in light of its appearance in Acts 6,14[193]. Luke's account was
recast according to his own theological point of view as well as in consideration
of the needs of his readers. Luke's Gentile readers were not so concerned about
the details of the Sanhedrin trial, so Luke summarily related information
concerning it. The result was a drastic emendation of the Markan account.
Unfortunately, he did so vaguely and in a "careless inconclusive" manner. Brandon
argued Luke valued the story of Peter's denial and so highlighted it. An indication
that Luke still had Mk's order in mind was the fact that he concluded the account
of Peter's denials with the story of the mistreatment of Jesus[194]. Because of
Luke's reckless, hasty compositional method at this point, the account of the abuse
of Jesus was "badly out of context".

Because Brandon considered Luke's account more complete than that of Mark,
he claimed Luke used a special source. More explicit information about the charges
and meager details about Pilate's dismissal of them undergird Brandon's argument.
It had been left to Luke to devise a way to show that Jesus was not guilty as
charged[195].

Brandon called attention to the pronoun αὐτόν (22,63) referring the reader to
Klostermann[196]. Mark's arrangement of the account seems "more logical" while
Luke's appeared more an "afterthought".

Luke viewed Jesus as a victim of Jewish hatred. In shortening the Sanhedrin
trial and focusing on Pilate's trial, Luke conveyed to his Gentile readers that the
Jews succeeded in crucifying Jesus, while Pilate worked hard to oppose them.

that Luke, who drew on traditions of the Jerusalem Church in the Acts of the Apostles, had
access also to information from that source concerning the trial of Jesus – indeed, perhaps the
same apologia from which Mark so discreetly drew" (p. 120). In the accompanying note, Brandon
took up the puzzling omission of the threat concerning the Temple which was resolved in light
of Acts 6,14. The issue seemed to be whether Luke had direct access to the Jerusalem tradition
(p. 108).

190. *Ibid.*, p. 120.
191. *Ibid.*, p. 116.
192. *Ibid.*, p. 118.
193. *Ibid.*, p. 194, n. 93. Brandon earlier argued that Jesus' statement about the destruction
of the Temple would have been "the chief concern of the Jerusalemite tradition" (p. 108).
194. *Ibid.*, p. 118.
195. *Ibid.*, p. 120.
196. *Ibid.*, p. 118. Cf. KLOSTERMANN, *Lukasevangelium*, ²1929, p. 220.

Brandon mused that the encounter with Herod could have taken place, though it added nothing of substance to the eventual outcome. However, since the purported transgressions occurred within Pilate's jurisdiction, Brandon maintained the improbability of the transfer. The detail about the reconciliation of the two rulers could reflect historical knowledge of the situation, but it was equally likely that this was a Lukan touch to instill a sense of authenticity. It was possible that Luke was privy to information from the Herodian household through Joanna, Chuza and Manaen, but the question was raised once again, why Mark would not have related it since he was intent upon presenting Herod in a disparaging light. Luke's purpose appeared to have been to provide two witnesses to the innocence of Jesus. Nodding to Dibelius, Brandon echoed the idea that the story could have resulted from a prophecy fulfillment of Ps 2,1-2, but the portrayal in the Gospel was at variance with the one in Acts[197]. The omission of the scourging in Lk can be explained by a relatively similar substitution of the mocking by Herod and his cohort[198].

In the opinion of Rudolph PESCH (1969) Luke "höchstwahrscheinlich" worked from a simple martyr account to compose his story of Stephen, to present him as imitating Jesus[199]. Luke transferred the Markan material about the false witnesses in the trial of Jesus to Stephen's trial (Mk 14,58; Acts 6,13f.). This too, was a fulfillment of the prophecy announced at Lk 11,49f. Luke employed this tradition in his message about the expansion of the Christian message[200].

Though Catchpole argued in favor of the special source, Van der Kwaak, Schneider (only vv. 63-65 were independent of Mk) and M. Lehmann have shown such a proposal to be improbable. Indeed, Pesch (1977) considered the entire passion to be a redaction of Mk[201]. The changes, including the transposition of pericopes, of persons involved and the shift to a morning trial were all attributed to Lukan redaction of Mk. As a result Peter became a witness to the mockery. Whereas Schneider argued for a special tradition in vv. 63-65, Pesch demonstrated that some of the vocabulary had been drawn from the omitted Markan mockery[202]. This, in addition to the continuity found in the passages, though transposed to allow for a morning Sanhedrin trial, argued against a special source

---

197. BRANDON, *The Trial*, p. 122. The portrayal of the two rulers in the Gospel provided for their common witness to the innocence of Jesus, while in Acts they opposed Christ "in accordance with divine prophecy".

198. *Ibid.*, p. 124. The Herod episode "provided Luke with a more convenient setting for this account of mocking".

199. R. PESCH, *Der Christ als Nachahmer Christi*, in *BK* 24 (1969) 10.

200. *Ibid.*, p. 11.

201. PESCH, *Das Markusevangelium* (HTKNT, 2,1/2), Bd. 2, Freiburg, 1977, 405-406 (esp. p. 405-410).

202. *Ibid.*, p. 407. These terms included: ἐμπαίζω (from Mk 15,20a. Cf. Mk 10,34 = Lk 18,32; 15,31 with 21,36); δέρω was a preferred Lukan term but found in Mk 12,3.5 (= Lk 20,10f.) and Mk 13,9 and Acts 5,40); συνέχω was likewise a Lukan favorite (4,38; 8,37.45 differently placed from Mk).

for Pesch[203]. He was just as certain that the Sanhedrin trial represented Lukan redaction of the Markan account, confirmed by the absence of witnesses's interrogation ("vernehmung") in the trial scene.

The transitional vv. 13-16 were freely composed by Luke. The final part of our section 23,17-23 was a further revision of Mk influenced by the apologetic toward Rome and the evangelist's tendency to have the Jewish leaders shoulder more of the responsibility[204].

Pesch ignored the MA in v. 62, but opposing Schneider and Benoit showed that the phrase could be Lukan redaction of Mk, conforming the Matthean text to the Lukan[205].

Neirynck complimented and agreed with Pesch's "réserves sagement formulées" on the use of Matthean and Lukan parallels in an attempt to determine tradition and redaction in Mk[206]. Neirynck also called attention to Pesch's treatment of the redaction of the Markan passion by Matthew and Luke and praised Pesch's critique of the hypothesis of the special Lukan source[207].

Rudolf PESCH and Reinhard KRATZ (1980) offered a reaction to the numerous attempts to show that Luke was dependent upon a "Sonderform der Passionsgeschichte" in addition to Mk, their intention being to demonstrate how Luke redacted his Markan *Vorlage*[208]. The transposition of the denial, mockery and trial was attributed to Luke[209]. The change in order allowed Jesus to be guarded until the morning session of the Sanhedrin, permitting him to witness the denial[210]. Following Schneider the denial and mockery can be seen as threatening elements intended to prevent Jesus from speaking openly before the Sanhedrin. This kind of intimidation was found in the accounts of martyrs and thus served a parenetic function[211]. The morning timing of the Sanhedrin trial was seen as analogous to Acts 4,1-7; 5,17-27; 22,30-23,10). The reference to the fire (22,56) was drawn from Mk 14,53.

At v. 54 Luke recorded not only Jesus' arrest but also his being led away (cf. Mk 14,53 and 14,44.46). Lk 22,55 was a revision of Mk 14,54b and 66a. The

203. *Ibid.*, p. 408.

204. *Ibid.*, p. 409.

205. *Ibid.*, p. 408.

206. F. NEIRYNCK, *L'évangile de Marc (I). À propos de R. Pesch, Das Markusevangelium, 1. Teil*, in *ETL* 55 (1979), p. 9, n. 110 (= *Evangelica*, p. 528, n. 110), to which had been added Neirynck's *ETL* recension of Pesch's third edition, *ETL* 56 (1980) 442-445. See also the Additional Note in *Evangelica II*, p. 800.

207. *Ibid.* Cf. PESCH, *Das Markusevangelium* II, 1977, p. 405-406.

208. PESCH and R. KRATZ, *So liest man synoptisch*. Vol. 7. *Passionsgeschichte*, Bd. 2, Frankfurt, 1980, p. 11 (esp. Vol. 7, p. 82-85, 92-94, 97, 101-102, 110-112, 170-173). They drew on the work of G. Schneider, especially *Die Passion Jesu* (1973) and *Das Evangelium nach Lukas* (1977).

209. PESCH and KRATZ, *So liest*, p. 83.

210. *Ibid.*, p. 92.

211. *Ibid.*, p. 93.

membership of the Sanhedrin was drawn from Mk 14,53.55. The witnesses's testimony was dropped here in Lk but reappeared in Acts 6,14 (Mk 14,58), proof for Pesch and Kratz that Luke knew this Markan passage. V. 70 was shaped by LXX Jer 45,15 and echoed Lk 20,2f., which for the authors was clear indication that Luke was redacting Mk. Lk 22,69 was a revision of Mk 14,62). 23,3 = Mk 15,2 and 14,62a. [Pesch and Kratz also indicated where Luke differed from Mk (v. 54 / diff Mk 14,53 "Jesus"; v. 71 / diff Mk 14,63.64)]. Lukan christology was at work here.

The mockery scene was a transformation of the omitted Markan mockery scene (Mk 15,16-20a[212]) and was constructed from vocabulary taken from there as well as Mk 15,27-32. Jesus was the prophet who can prophesy the future as well as what was hidden (22,61; 22,6.21)[213]. Luke inserted v. 65 as a conclusion.

Pesch and Kratz took issue with the synopses which presented Mk 15,1 as equivalent to 22,66. In their opinion, 22,66 referred to Mk 14,53.55[214]. The authors argued Luke formulated the charges against Jesus with a view to Rome[215]. Lk 23,4 was drawn from Mk 15,3. Lk 23,5 was a glance back over the entire Gospel.

The brief section 23,13-16 was redactionally composed material. At 23,18 the authors pointed out the connection with Acts 3,13f. The material dealing with Barabbas went back to Mk 15,7, just as Lk 23,22 depended upon Mk 15,14a. The account was shaped by Luke's apologetical interests of protecting Christians in the Roman empire from the lies of the Jews[216]. Pesch and Kratz considered the MA in v. 62 as a probable insertion from Mt[217].

Rather than a special passion narrative, Pesch and Kratz suggested Luke had access to special passion traditions in his *Sondergut* material and echoed the conclusion of Schneider[218]. They adamantly opposed the special source for three reasons: 1) the omission of Markan material, 2) the non-Markan *Sondergut* material, and 3) the argument from order. Responding to each of these critiques, the authors concluded: "Kein Argument zugunsten einer umfangreichen Sonderquelle neben der Mk-Vorlage hat also beweisende Kraft. Die lk Passionsdarstellung kann als lk Bearbeitung der Mk-Vorlage und einzelner Sondergutstücke erklärt werden"[219].

---

212. *Ibid.*, p. 84. Pesch and Kratz mistakenly identified the mockery of Jesus by the Roman soldiers as Mk 14,16-20a.
213. *Ibid.*, p. 85.
214. *Ibid.*, p. 97.
215. *Ibid.*, p. 102.
216. *Ibid.*, p. 112.
217. *Ibid.*, p. 93.
218. *Ibid.*, p. 170.
219. *Ibid.*, p. 172. Cf. SCHNEIDER, *Das Evangelium nach Lukas*, p. 436.

Pesch (1977) considered the Herod scene to be "historisch wertlose Legende"[220]. He pointed out that even authors like Hoehner who claimed the story was historical, admitted that it served no purpose in the narrative. The tradition found in Acts 4,27f. could have developed from traditions found in Mk 3,6; 6,14-16; 12,13; Lk 13,31[221]. Pesch together with Kratz (1980) argued that 23,13-16 was "eine lk Bildung (vgl. 23,2.4.5.14.15)"[222]. Although it was debated whether 23,6-12 was a Lukan composition, they were insistent that this pericope could not be used to support the theory of a continuous source[223]. Pesch later (1988) maintained that the Lukan version of the passion narrative with its report of the trial was a redaction of the Markan *Vorlage*, which did not reflect a special independent source and probably not even separate special traditions[224].

In his 1968/69 Würzburg dissertation on the Johannine passion narrative, Anton DAUER examined the relationship of Jn's passion to the Synoptics[225]. The order in Jn – transferring Jesus to the high priest, trial, mistreatment – corresponded to the order found in Mt and Mk[226]. Concerning the parts of the Peter story which had parallels to Jn (Lk 22,54 cf. Jn 18,12; Lk 22,58 cf. Jn 18,17.25; Lk 22,55 cf. Jn 18,18; Lk 22,59 cf. Jn 18,26; Lk 22,60 cf. Jn 18,27), he concluded that Luke did not rely on a *Sondertradition*, but had redacted Mk[227]. He observed that Klein's arguments favoring a special source were not convincing, as Linnemann had shown[228]. For the account of Pilate's trial, the report in John's source essentially followed the lead of Lk which was especially clear in Jn 18,28-40[229]. In examining the Lukan parallels to Jn 18,28-19,16a (Lk 23,4 cf. Jn 18,38; Lk 23,18f. cf. Jn 18,40; Lk 23,22b cf. Jn 19,4; Lk 23,21 cf. Jn 19,6; Lk 23,22 cf. Jn 19,6; Lk 23,20 cf. Jn 19,12; Lk 23,2 cf. Jn 19,12; Lk 23,18 cf. Jn 19,15), Dauer again concluded that Luke did not use any special tradition but redacted Mk[230]. In a *Nachtrag* Dauer examined recent works related to the theme including F. HAHN, *Der Prozess Jesu nach dem Johannesevangelium* (1970). One

---

220. PESCH, *Das Markusevangelium*, Bd. 2, p. 409-410.

221. *Ibid.*, p. 410. See also R. Pesch and R. Kratz (1980) who recognized Lk 23,6-12 as Lukan *Sondergut*, but did not treat it or ascribe the nature of its source (*So liest man synoptisch*. Vol. 7. *Passionsgeschichte*, Bd. 2, p. 102).

222. PESCH and KRATZ, *So liest Man*, 1980, p. 172.

223. *Ibid.*

224. PESCH, *Der Prozess Jesu geht weiter*, Freiburg, 1988, p. 27 (= *The Trial of Jesus Continues*, tr. D.G. WAGNER, Allison Park, PA, 1996, p. 17).

225. *Die Passionsgeschichte. Eine traditionsgeschichtliche und theologische Untersuchung zu Joh 18,1-19,30* (SANT, 30), Munich, 1972. Diss. Würzburg, 1968/69 (dir. R. SCHNACKENBURG).

226. *Ibid.*, 91.

227. *Ibid.*, p. 99.

228. *Ibid.*, p. 98. Cf. G. Klein (1961) and E. Linnemann (1966).

229. *Ibid.*, p. 146.

230. *Ibid.*, p. 163. In n. 366, he invited comparison of the conclusions of Dibelius (1915) on Pilate's trial and Schneider (1969) on the use of a special source in Lk 23. See also p. 164, #c1.

of his critiques was that Hahn had not sufficiently examined the striking verbal parallels, especially those which Dauer had shown to be Lukan redaction of Mk[231].

In 1992 he examined the traces of the Synoptic accounts of the Sanhedrin trial in Jn[232]. On the Lk-Jn parallels he concluded that there was in Jn 10,24.25a almost exact verbal agreement with Lk 22,67. There were also great similarities between Jn 10,36 and Lk 22,70[233]. On the basis of the evidence he surmised that the pre-Johannine account of the Sanhedrin trial employed a combination of at least Lk and Mk, if not also Mt[234].

Dauer interacted with the literature of both Schneider and Radl. As to the relation of Luke's account to Mk in 22,54a.66-71 he resolved: "Auch die lk Version dürfte im wesentlichen auf Mk zurückgehen, die Änderungen gegenüber Mk sind wohl durchweg redaktionell. Eine Paralleltradition ist kaum anzunehmen, wenn auch nicht alle Bedenken augeschieden werden können"[235].

Additional scholars who during this period advocated Luke's use of Mk included Alfred WIKENHAUSER (1953)[236], Donald ROWLINGSON (1956)[237], C. MASSON

---

231. *Ibid.*, p. 341; cf. F. HAHN, *Der Prozess Jesu nach dem Johannesevangelium* (EKK NT Vorarbeiten, Heft 2), Neuenkirchen-Vluyn, 1970.

232. *Spuren der (synoptischen) Synedriumsverhandlung im 4. Evangelium. Das Verhältnis zu den Synoptiken*, in A. DENAUX (ed.), *John and the Synoptics* (BETL, 101), Leuven, 1992, 307-339. Note his list of works which treated the relationship between Jn 10,22-39 and Lk 22,66-71 (p. 309-310, n. 10).

233. *Ibid.*, p. 316.

234. *Ibid.*, p. 317.

235. *Ibid.*, p. 336. See his detailed analysis of 22,54a.66-71, p. 320-336. He organized important works according to their source theories: literature pertaining to the discussion of special sources in the Lukan passion narrative, see p. 321-322, n. 66; Lukan redaction of Mk in Lk 22,66-71, see p. 322, n. 67; a Lukan *Sonderquelle*, sometimes in the sense of Proto-Lk, see p. 322-323, n. 68; a combination of Lukan redaction of Mk and a special source or special tradition(s), see p. 323, n. 69. He called attention to RADL, *Sonderüberlieferung* (1988), as "eine der letzten eindringlichen Unterzuchungen zu Lk 22,66-71", which advocated that Luke had essentially redacted Mk (p. 323, n. 72). At various places, Dauer was convinced by the arguments of R. Pesch (p. 332, 336; cf. PESCH, *Das Markusevangelium* (1977).

236. Citing "almost universal agreement" that Luke used Mk, Wikenhauser argued Luke retained Mk's framework inserting other material into it (*Einleitung in das Neue Testament*, Freiburg, 1953, ²1956, ⁴1961 [slightly revised by A. VÖGTLE], ⁵1963, ⁶1973 = *New Testament Introduction*, tr. J. CUNNINGHAM, New York, 1963 (= ²1956 revised and enlarged), p. 210-211. Pagination is according to the ET). Although Schlatter and Rengstorf favored the idea of a complete lost Gospel supplementing Mk as a source, Wikenhauser viewed Luke as having drawn from numerous sources, mostly oral. The LXX formed the model upon which Luke crafted his Hebrew style in the Gospel and first twelve chapters of Acts (p. 214). Wikenhauser echoed the view that Luke changed the sayings of Jesus very little, but revised the narrative portions more heavily (p. 214-215). Directing his attention to the synoptic problem, Wikenhauser asserted that Mk 15,16-20 was not taken up into Lk, nor was there any substitution for it (p. 225). However, Mk formed the foundation of the Lukan passion narrative, a source which Luke treated "with

(1957)[238], Joseph DILLERSBERGER (1958)[239], Martin FRANZMAN (1961)[240],

great freedom" (p. 226). The revision included twelve transpositions, the omission of Markan material (including Mk 15,16-20) and the introduction of new material, most likely from oral sources (p. 226). This additional material included Lk 22,14-23.31-33.36-38.43ff; 23,6-16.27-31.40-43; 24,13-53).

237. *Introduction to New Testament Study*, New York, 1956, p. 71. Rowlingson credited Luke with a striking similarity to Mk, even to the point of employing the Markan framework, though Luke omitted more of the Markan material than Matthew. Rowlingson regarded the Nazareth pericope as having been transposed from its original setting in Mk (p. 72). While he did not entirely exclude the possibility of Proto-Lk, he added "such a theory is not required to explain the characterisitics of [Luke's] writing. The Marcan outline shows through at crucial points". Though Rowlingson had a rather simplistic view of the sources, and an equally simplistic solution to the synoptic problem, his insight that differences and similarities arose based upon each individual evangelist's use of the material was well taken (p. 73). The reference in the index to material concerning Lk appearing on p. 77-80, was an obvious mistake, since those pages treated Jn. The view that the Lukan writings were somehow connected to Paul was dismissed as untenable (p. 208). It will be remembered that Hawkins suggested the Lukan passion narrative resulted from the influence of oral Pauline tradition.

238. *Le reniement de Pierre*, in *RHPR* 37 (1957) 30. Masson viewed the Lukan account of the denial as based upon Mk. He credited Luke with adding moving details to accounts in order to dramatize them (22,61). Luke was following Mk more freely than Matthew in this pericope. Lukan redaction included modification of vocabulary and omission of the Markan reference to Peter's exit (Mk 14,68). Such a reworking of Mk was consistent with Luke's efforts to treat the apostles with respect.

239. *Lukas. Das Evangelium des heiligen Lukas in theologischer und heilgeschichtlicher Schau*, 4 vols., Salzburg, 1939, ³1947 (= *The Gospel of Saint Luke*, tr. from the German, Westminster, MD, 1958. Pagination is from the ET). Although Dillersberger did not clearly and succinctly state his position on the source question, one can piece together some idea from various individual remarks. The Risen Lord informing his mother may have been one source (p. 518). Speaking of the drops of blood in the agony of the garden Dillersberger wrote: "The bright moonlight, their close proximity – described by Luke as 'a stone's cast' – enabled the disciples to see these heavy drops, quite apart from that fact that a later account from Our Lord himself after the Resurrection, perhaps to His mother, may have made other sources available to Luke. Luke, who followed up every matter so carefully, would not have omitted from this account of Our Lord on the Mount of Olives so much that Matthew and Mark had already related, and added this new point in so much detail unless He had had a very reliable source for it". Part of Luke's redaction was to offer a more precise account as when in the third denial, Luke's expression for the timing was more exact than that of Matthew and Mark (p. 521). Luke followed Mk 14,65 for the mockery and the fact of one trial was accounted for by Luke having simply passed over one, but then Dillersberger went on to say that Luke's account of the trial was distinguished from the one related by Mt and Mk (p. 522-523). Cf. p. 525: "After due consideration of all these circumstances, it is difficult to justify serious support for the view that the trial narrated by Luke is the same as that narrated by Mark and Matthew". Yet contrary to what he had been arguing, Dillersberger also stated Luke passed over in silence the first trial mentioned by Matthew and Mark (p. 526).

Dillersberger argued that Pilate alone was vested with the power to enforce the death sentence. Further, the Jewish law dictated the same sentence by two different courts on two different days for the imposition of a death sentence (p. 524). Luke passed over one of the trials and yet presented "a completely fresh one which occurred in the morning" (p. 522-523). On the other

Émile OSTY (1961)[241], Frank W. BEARE (1962)[242], Geoffrey William Hugo

hand, Dillersberger also argued Luke's purpose was "to give a more detailed description of the session casually mentioned by Mark" in 15,1 and that Luke passed over the first trial (p. 526). It was a strange mixture of Luke's use of other sources and Lukan redaction of Mk.

Luke was familiar with the whole of Mark's account and omitted many of the details in order to introduce a quantity of new material (p. 523). Luke also omitted that which he would have considered disrespectful or offensive toward the Lord as in the base of the term "blasphemy". Dillersberger regarded Luke as a careful historian who intended in his apologia to reflect a certain respect for the Roman authorities and to assert that Jesus was not a political threat to the Roman State.

Dillersberger made a feeble and unsuccessful attempt to explain the absence of the Herod pericope from the other Gospels by suggesting that the episode was not recounted by the other evangelists because the silence of Jesus brought the proceedings to a crashing halt (p. 528). Dillersberger mentioned that Joanna and Susanna (8,3) "come from circles far removed from Our Lord" (p. 229-230).

240. *The Word of the Lord Grows*, St. Louis, MO, 1961, p. 199. Franzman regarded Mk as the structural basis for Lk, which was, in the passion narrative, supplemented by numerous additions. Although he did not devote much attention to the question of sources for Lk, he wrote that Luke may have employed written sources both in Aramaic and Greek for Acts, adding, "but as to their nature and extent we can only guess" (p. 209).

Such a lack of tangible evidence has a bearing on Markan priority as well, for though Franzman admitted that there were strong arguments which favored it, one relied ultimately only upon internal evidence: "Unless new evidence is discovered, there will probably always remain a reasonable doubt concerning the priority of Mark" (p. 214). In a sense, Q fared no better since it was "purely hypothetical". And it was the extent of what was hypothetical in the various source theories proposed to solve the synoptic problem that attracted Franzman's attention. "The more elaborate the theories become, the larger the hypothetical element in them becomes. The Two-Source Hypothesis operates with one unknown quantity, Q; the Four-Source Hypothesis (which is really a six-source hypothesis) operates with five unknowns. Where is the evidence by which these conjectures are to be controlled?" (p. 215).

241. *L'Évangile selon saint Luc* (La Sainte Bible traduite en français sous la direction de l'Ecole Biblique de Jérusalem), Paris, [3]1961, p. 8-9. Luke obtained a variety of details from various informants. Among them was the deacon Philip, who supplied the Samaritan episodes for the Gospel. Luke's relationship with other disciples explained points of contact with Jn. Finally, Luke benefited as well from information derived from several women, including Mary Magdalene and Joanna. As regards written sources, Mk was certainly one of Luke's sources (p. 8-9). Osty credited Lagrange with having determined that Luke used the version of Mk which we have today. Like many other scholars, Osty believed Luke treated the other sources in much the same way he used Mk. The changes included omissions, additions and minor alterations, insertions and transpositions (p. 11). Luke omitted those elements which overburdened the narrative such as the first Markan Sanhedrin trial (p. 11). Likewise, scenes of violence, such as Mk 14,65, were rejected. Other elements, like 22,69, were reworked for the sake of clarity, appropriateness or out of compassion for human misery (p. 14). Osty noted Luke added "of God" to "power" as a clarification for his readers (p. 154). The transpositions resulted from a variety of reasons, but reflected a purely literary order (p. 16). Luke's method also included breaking away from the Markan order to pursue a more logical order. Osty ascribed changes in order to Luke's desire to offer a logical, literary order where he departed from the Markan arrangement (p. 16). Luke was generally faithful to Mk in order, the context of the narrative and in a great deal of vocabulary. "Mais c'est surtout dans le récit de la Passion que Luc fait preuve d'indépendance et

d'originalité" (p. 17). Finally, Luke had some of the Greek sources of Mt.

A later contribution by Osty (1973), reprised many of the same positions established in his Lukan commentary. In collaboration with Joseph TRINQUET, he continued espousing the view that Luke was dependent upon Mk very nearly in the form as we know it today, though Osty contended that Luke possibly knew Aramaic or Greek Mt, wholly or partially (*La Bible*. Traduction française sur les textes originaux par Émile OSTY avec la collaboration de Joseph TRINQUET; introductions et notes d'Émile OSTY et de Joseph TRINQUET, [Paris], 1973, p. 2189). Regarding Luke's possible use of Mt see further the note on 1,1 (p. 2201). For the view that Luke was using a form of Mk very similar to that which is in existence today see *L'Évangile selon saint Luc*, p. 9. The conclusion of Lukan dependence was reached by a comparison of the two Gospels which indicated Luke followed Mk's order. Similarity of narrative and detail served also as clues. It was believed that Luke used his other sources, oral and written, in the same way as he used Mk. It was in the passion, which Osty and Trinquet designated as 22,1–23,56, where Luke's independence and originality shone forth, a conviction repeated verbatim from Osty's earlier commentary (*La Bible*, p. 2192; see also p. 2199, and *L'Évangile selon saint Luc*, p. 17).

Osty and Trinquet pointed to four types of changes in Lk over against Mk: 1) omissions, 2) additions and "retouches"; 3) "insinuations", and 4) transpositions. Luke omitted material for aesthetic or literary reasons, because certain material would not have been of interest to his readers and because it was contrary to his plan. Luke omitted Markan doublets which included the trial before the high priest (Mk 14,53-64) (*La Bible*, p. 2190). In addition see the note on 22,66 (p. 2245). Luke omitted material that was harsh as he sought to minimize violent scenes (Mk 14,65). Further omissions were due to religious reverence. Lk 22,69 was an example of "retouches dues au goût de la clarté et à un sentiment affiné des covenances" (p. 2191). Osty and Trinquet cited the transposition of the material of the denial, mockery and trial suggesting that for such rearrangements Luke was motivated by logic or a desire for "belle ordonnance".

In the opinion of Osty (1961, 1973), Luke obtained a variety of details from various oral sources (*L'Évangile selon saint Luc*, ³1961, p. 8-9). Among them were Manaen, who related the trial of Jesus before Herod (23,7-12) (p. 155, n. a. So also *La Bible*, 1973, p. 2189). See further his note on 23,8 (p. 2246).

242. *The Earliest Records of Jesus*, Oxford, 1962, p. 15. Beare contended Luke, like Matthew, was dependent upon Mk, but not to the same degree. Though he conceded the possibility of an independent source for the passion narrative, an analysis of his exposition revealed that the chance was quite remote. He admitted that the change in order and variation in the material of Peter's denial, the mockery and Sanhedrin trial could cause one to question what sources were employed, but it was clear that this section was simply a redaction of Mk: "There is nothing in his version which requires us to suppose that he has had another and more reliable source available; it is all readily enough understood as a reconstruction of Mark, based upon his sense of the historical possibilities" (p. 233). Luke greatly improved upon Mk. Echoing Dibelius, the changes in the passion narrative served to revise the accounts to reflect historical probability. Omissions, such as the night trial and the evidence of witnesses, occurred because, in Luke's mind, it was unlikely that they ever took place. Beare regarded the Lukan version of the one morning trial as the most historically probable (p. 233). Luke offered the basic Markan line, but in different words. Beare ascribed the shift of the mockery to Luke and pointed to the possible confusion as to whether it referred to Peter or Jesus. Though Luke was guilty of this *faux pas*, the change was warranted (p. 232-233).

Adopting the first Markan clause from Mk 15,1, it was clear that Lk 23,1 relied upon it, though it had been adapted. In order to compensate for the abrupt appearance of Pilate's question, Luke presented the charges of the Sanhedrin. This, too, was a transposition. Luke's own hand was responsible for 23,3.4 and his apologetic for Christianity was readily visible in this pericope.

LAMPE (1962)[243], Geoffrey STYLER (1962)[244], J.C. O'NEILL (1974-75)[245],

Beare also drew on the similarities with Paul in Acts.

Once more in 23,17-25 Luke returned to Mk, though here also he made some significant changes. The purpose of the revision was to emphasize the Jewish responsibility for the death of Jesus (p. 235-236). Luke's use of another source was rejected. Beare's assessment of Streeter's theory was that it had not garnered any substantial support and he himself rejected it, though the hypothesis did not receive the attention it deserved because of the shift away from source to form criticism (p. 15).

Entertaining the possibility that the Herod story (23,6-16) stemmed from one of Luke's sources, Beare contended it was more probable that Luke himself was responsible for it and that the story was fictitious. The influence of Dibelius was once again detected. The prayer in Acts 4,25-27 may have given rise to mentioning Herod in the passion narrative (p. 235). The historical improbability was likewise underscored by the fact that there would scarcely have been sufficient time for this event to have taken place.

243. *Luke*, in M. BLACK and H.H. ROWLEY (eds.), *PCB*, London, 1962, p. 820. Lampe generally subscribed to the view that Luke freely redacted Mk. While he did not consider the question of a separate passion source definitively settled, in all likelihood, Luke simply revised Mk drawing additional material from other sources. Much in line with Wernle, Lampe believed that the Lukan special material was quite varied and not a homogeneous collection (p. 820). Some of the material was likely composed by Luke based on his own "oral reminiscences", while other material depended upon "more firmly fixed tradition, written or oral". He rejected Streeter's theory of Proto-Lk primarily because the framework of Lk was Markan but also because he cannot envision Streeter's special source as an independent, self-contained Gospel (p. 820). Omissions, such as the material constituting Mk 6,45-8,26, were made in concert with Luke's theological plan.

Mk was the source for the Lukan account of Peter's denials, with v. 61a being a Lukan detail inspired by Mk (p. 841). Lampe saw the MA in 22,69 (ἀπὸ τοῦ νῦν/ ἀπ' ἄρτι Mt 22,64) to be a clear sign of independence from Mk. He took two differing approaches to the MAs in vv. 62.64. The first was possibly an interpolation from Mt, while the second resulted from independent editing of Mk by Matthew and Luke. Both had inferred the question from the context (p. 841). Other examples of Lukan redaction of Markan material were 23,19 where Luke may be softening the reference to the insurrection for political reasons, and 22,24 which Luke expanded to highlight the guilt of the Jewish leaders (p. 841). In addition, 23,3.22 were Markan while 23,5 was Lukan. Concerning the relationship of the Gospel to Acts, Jesus' attitude toward the Temple (22,67) was recognized in Acts in the account of Stephen's trial.

Lampe contended that those elements where the ambiguity Luke's drawing upon Mk or other sources seemed greatest was where it pertained to the charges preferred against Jesus (23,2) and in Herod's trial: "Luke alone, either by inference from the Marcan narrative as a whole, or from a non-Marcan source, records the actual charge" (p. 841). Regarding the Herod episode, Lampe oscillated between Dibelius's proposal that it was based upon Ps 1,1-2 and the possibility that the story recorded an historical event. From the historical perspective, Herod could have been in Jerusalem at the time. On the other hand, the account may have been based upon Ps 2,1-2 and was also intended to exculpate Pilate. Luke corrected Mk's version of the mockery where the Sanhedrin was involved in the ill treatment of Jesus. Likewise, in 23,11, Herod's men were made to be the perpetrators instead of the Roman soldiers as in Mk.

244. *The Priority of Mark*, Excursus 4, in C.F.D. MOULE, *The Birth of the New Testament*, London, 1962, 223-232, p. 223; San Francisco, CA, ³1982 (completely new and revised), 285-316 = BELLINZONI, A.J. (ed.), *The Two-Source Hypothesis*, 1985, 63-75 (= 1962). Not to be ignored are the views of Styler, particularly on Markan priority, especially as it involved order

and MAs. He observed Streeter offered "the classical statement and defence" in which the Two-Document hypothesis was expanded to four documents, though the idea of the unity of M and L did not recommend itself to some scholars. Styler concluded expressing his conviction that, despite criticisms from Butler and Farmer, support for Markan priority would perdure (STYLER, *Priority*, 1962, p. 232).

A revision of the article appearing in the third edition of Moule's book brought the essay up to date and provided interesting insights (³1982, 285-316). Whereas in the earlier edition, Styler used the 1924 edition of Streeter's *The Four Gospels*, in 1982 he referred to the fourth edition, 1930 (1962, p. 223 = ³1982, 285). A rather significant change was extensive reference to MAs. Noting that the various explanations for such phenomena were coincidence, corruption of the text or assimilation, he said that such instances raised questions about the more simplistic versions of the Two-Document hypothesis (p. 286, n. 2). Styler's conclusion concerning the MAs was worth noting: "These have been called 'minor agreements', although they are of more than minor importance, and have always been a big stumbling-block for advocates of the two-document hypothesis. They do not directly call in question the priority of Mark; but they make it difficult, if not impossible, to be content with the two-document hypothesis in its simplest form" (p. 300). Cf. p. [301]-302, n. 5. Styler called attention to the useful study of Neirynck, 1974, in which the data of the MAs was presented for study and comparison.

Despite arguments against Markan priority from Farrer and Goulder, based on the variations in Markan order in Lk, Styler retorted that plausible explanations can be offered for Luke's rearrangement (p. 303). Cf. A.M. FARRER, *On Dispensing with Q*, in D.E. NINEHAM (ed.), *Studies in the Gospels: Essays in Memory of R.H. Lightfoot*, Oxford, 1955, 55-88, and GOULDER, *Midrash*, 1974, as well as *On Putting Q to the Test*, in *NTS* 24 (1977-78) 218-240. Against the charge that some of the Lukan material seemed to reflect Matthean influence, Styler accepted that may be the case. But it was also possible that Luke was providing "an independent (and possibly more 'original') version" of that which was also found in Mt. Styler affirmed that Mk was Luke's source, despite the changes in order. Regrettably, he excluded the passion narrative since it presented "special problems" (STYLER, *Priority*, ³1983, p. 304, n. 2). Cf. p. 305: "How far Luke is conflating separate sources and how far he is re-working them is a notorious problem; but that his final version is 'secondary' can hardly be denied. The same is true of many smaller touches ... his inclusion of 'scourging' in the third prediction of the Passion, which is inconsistent with his omission of an actual scourging in the Passion narrative itself; ... and his paraphrase of 'The Power' (i.e. the Almighty) as 'the power of God' in xxii. 69". In Styler's opinion Luke may have had one or more other sources, one of which was known to Mark (p. 307).

Also to be considered is Styler's concise summary and sympthetic nod in the direction of Lindsey who posited a primitive Hebrew source and Q behind our Gospels (p. 308; cf. LINDSEY, *Hebrew Translation*). Later, in a suggestion highly reminiscent of Wernle, Styler proposed that some of the Mk-Lk parallels may be accounted for by use of a common lost source (STYLER, *Priority*, ³1982, p. 311, n. 2). Luke employed both of these. Mark, in turn, made use of the Hebrew source and Lk. Finally, Mt drew on Mk and the two primitive sources. While impressed by the theory, Styler judged the examples provided by Lindsey did not prove the argument (p. 309). The MAs resulted from translations of the primitive Hebrew source by Luke and Matthew, which rendered the phrases more faithfully than Mk.

Styler served for thirty-five years as secretary of the Cambridge NT seminar. C.F.D. Moule praised Styler's skill: "Possessed not only of an acute head for administration but of a fastidious scholarship, Geoffrey has been too much of a perfectionist to rush into print; but the quality of his publications is high" (*G.M. Styler and the Cambridge New Testament Seminar*, in W. HORBURY and B. MCNEIL [eds.], *Suffering and Martyrdom in the New Testament*, FS G.M. STYLER, Cambridge, 1981, xi-xxi).

Allan BARR (1963)[246], Robert GRANT (1963)[247], Willi MARXSEN (1963,

245. In a vein somewhat similar to Styler, J.C. O'NEILL (1974-75) posited a common Hebrew source behind the Synoptic Gospels (*The Synoptic Problem*, in *NTS* 21 [1974-75] 273-285; cf. STYLER, *Priority*, ³1982, p. 312). Though envisioned differently than Lindsey's hypothesis, O'Neill's study recommended itself to Styler, not in its entirety, but in suggesting that a Hebrew or Aramaic original provided numerous Gospel sayings, and that there was possibly a "plurality of sources" (STYLER, *Priority*, 1982, p. 313). But in the end there were far too many obstacles which prevented one from adopting his theory. One pertained directly to the passion narrative, where Pilate's words agreed (23,22 / Mk 15,14 / Mt 27,23). Since Hebrew provided "no exact equivalent", the agreement must derive from the Greek tradition (p. 315-316). "The conclusion of this excursus must be that the possibility of a plurality of sources behind the synoptic gospels remains open; but that the dependence of Matthew and Luke on Mark, or on a source which is often indistinguishable from Mark, is proved beyond reasonable doubt" (p. 316).

In an earlier article O'Neill (1968-69) considered the silence as indicative that Jesus was the Messiah (*The Silence of Jesus*, in *NTS* 15 [1968-69] 153-167). "I suggest that most Jews at the time would understand that the Messiah would not be able to claim Messiahship for himself, but must wait for God to enthrone him. If this theory is right, Jesus' silence is part of his messianic role" (p. 165). O'Neill was of the opinion that "our text of Mark has been editorially shortened ... It is unlikely that Matthew and Luke would have independently changed the unequivocal 'I am' into an equivocal σὺ εἶπας (Matt. xxvi. 63 [sic]) or ὑμεῖς λέγετε ὅτι ἐγώ εἰμι (Lk xxii. 70). They could not be trying to make the Jewish leaders out as worse than they were by independently implying that they convicted without a clear assertion from Jesus' mouth, for they probably held that the son of man statement was clear enough in itself" (p. 158). In yet another article, O'Neill (1970) held open the possibility that Luke followed an independent account of the Sanhedrin trial (*The Charge of Blasphemy at Jesus' Trial before the Sanhedrin*, in BAMMEL [ed.], *The Trial of Jesus*, 1970, p. 73).

246. *A Diagram of Synoptic Relationships*, Edinburgh, 1963. The diagram consisted of a large fold out chart and thus had no page references. Barr considered 22,54-62 and 23,3.17-25 to be purely Markan material. The mockery and the Sanhedrin session (22,63-71) were regarded as Markan material mixed with material unique to Luke. But the pink line of his diagram, indicating Markan material in Markan order, did not coincide completely with the indications given by the color coding in Barr's presentation of the sources of Lk. This line linking the columns of Mk and Lk would lead one to believe that the accounts of Jesus before the Sanhedrin, Jesus before Pilate and the condemnation of Jesus were Markan sections in Markan order, though this conflicts with what we have just described above. Barr treated the denials of Peter as Markan material, though out of Markan order. Faithful to the order as found in Mk were the accounts of Jesus before the Sanhedrin, Jesus before Pilate and the condemnation of Jesus. According to Barr, the accounts of Jesus before Pilate and Herod (23,1-16), with the exception of v. 3, were viewed as special Lukan material.

247. *A Historical Introduction to the New Testament*, New York, 1963, p. 5 (Preface). Grant confessed at the beginning of his work that the reader would not find many references to the contemporary literature in the NT field. However, against Grant's approach it may be said that while this type of approach has the value of originality, by referring to the vast field of literature one may possibly avoid some of the pitfalls of previous NT scholars or build upon their solid foundations. Streeter's proposal received only a brief and bland treatment (p. 118). In what was apparently an argument directed against Taylor's contention that Proto-Lk would be more historically reliable than Mk, Grant responded: "... there is usually no ground for absolute faith in one evangelist or one 'source' as against others. In some instances it can be seen that a later evangelist has modified the work of a predecessor; but this fact does not guarantee the

^{3}1964)^{248}, William ROBINSON (1964)^{249}, Arthur Michael RAMSEY (1964)^{250},

predecessor's work" (p. 348). What Grant wrote of this and other source analysis attempts bears repeating: "Almost all analysis of this sort ultimately fails because it neglects the extent to which the evangelists were involved in the transmission of the Christian tradition as well as the extent to which they were free to arrange and rewrite their materials in ways which seemed meaningful to them and to the communities of which they were members" (p. 348).

Luke composed his Gospel in "a Semitizing style full of reminiscences of the Septuagint" (p. 133). Against Torrey and others who supported the view that the Gospels were originally Aramaic documents and who offered "retranslations", Grant argued the majority of these were unconvincing (p. 348). The assumption that Luke was using various sources was unwarranted since Luke was not only a historian but an accomplished writer, whose style varied with the situation he was describing or relating (p. 133-134). Mk was regarded as Luke's principal source, generally following the Markan order and it was Mk 10,13–16,8 which formed the basis for 18,15–24,11 (p. 135, 136). Grant maintained Luke utilized his freedom as an author and historian to change the order of his material "to give an arrangement to his materials which was not necessarily chronological but brought out their meaning as he understood it" (p. 140).

Lukan redaction involved the omission of repetitious wording, elision of references to Jesus' human emotions and the condensing of certain stories. The Great Omission was explained as Luke's conscious intention not to include material which was useless or repetitious. Luke's revision of the Markan passion narrative resulted from his dissatisfaction with Mark's inadequate stress of "non-theological factors" (p. 137). These included listing the charges against Jesus. Grant accepted as historical that Jesus would have had to be questioned by Herod because of his Galilean heritage. Somewhat amusing was Grant's idea that Herod returned Jesus to Pilate because he believed Jesus to be a magician who refused to entertain him (p. 361). And while it was often easy to determine that changes had been made, it was not so simple to understand why. Concerning the exchange of Jesus for Barabbas, Grant held Luke's version as the "more probable", since the action resulted from mob rule rather than a custom (p. 361).

Grant placed great stock in oral tradition and complained that too many scholars ignored its import (p. 117). While proof cannot be offered that Luke indeed did have such sources, either oral or written, the possibility cannot be easily dismissed (p. 138).

248. *Einleitung in das Neue Testament. Eine Einführung in das Neue Testament*, Gütersloh, 1963; ^{3}1964, p. 104 (= *Introduction to the New Testament. An Approach to its Problems*, tr. G. BUSWELL, Philadelphia, PA, 1968, p. 116). Cf. MARXSEN, *Einleitung*, ^{4}1978. Marxsen contended that the theory of an abbreviated Urmarkus was unnecessary. He adhered to the Two-Source theory, and argued that both Mt and Lk reflected theological influence that shaped the models which they employed (*Einleitung*, ^{3}1964, p. 105 = 116-117). His hermeneutic must be recognized: "Das heisst aber, man wird das Mt und das Lk immer vom Mk her (und von Q her) zu exegesieren haben, denn deren Texte bilden den Hintergrund für die späteren Aussagung" (p. 107 = 118). Marxsen denied Burkitt's assumption that Q contained an account of the passion when he wrote that Q lacked narrative material. Therefore, it was possible that the special material was derived either from oral tradition, or may even have been the creation of the evangelists themselves (p. 105-106 = 117).

Regrettably, Marxsen lacked clarity in speaking about sources in the Lukan passion narrative. "In the Passion story (xxii-xxiii) Luke shows great independence in altering his source and decisively shifting the emphasis" (p. 137 = 155). Marxsen took issue with Taylor's hasty assumption that reference in the Prologue necessarily implied that Luke's sources were more historically reliable, because Marxsen argued they were not historical sources (p. 138 = 156). Luke's presentation of the passion demonstrated that he understood what took place as a murder legally carried out by the Jews (p. 140 = 159). Contrary to the majority of scholars, Marxsen

Alois STÖGER (1964/1966)[251], Ernest TINSLEY (1965)[252], William BARCLAY

rejected the idea that 23,3 came from Mk. Rather, Luke was said to be following tradition. Further, 23,4.13-16 was without parallel in Mk and 23,25 was differentiated from Mk, though Marxsen did not say whether these two elements resulted from Lukan redaction (or creation) or the influence of tradition. Also in contrast to the majority of scholars, Marxsen did not subscribe to the view that the guilt of the Jews was increased. Thus, Luke should not be accused of anti-Semitism (p. 141 = 159). Marxsen adopted the view that several of the pericopes in the passion narrative earlier had stood independent of one another. But not so with 23,1-5.13-25, since they can be understood only in the context of the entire passion story (p. 145 = 165).

In his fourth edition (1978), Marxsen emended his earlier position that neither Luke knew or used Mt (or vice versa) (MARXSEN, Einleitung, ⁴1978, p. 125. Cf. Einleitung, ³1964, p. 106 (= 118). Although the claim was made that the fourth edition was a new completely revised work, this did not pertain in the sections with which we are concerned, with the exception of the one difference noted next. His later position was that such an explanation was clever ("gescheitert") but he did not elaborate.

249. Der Weg des Herrn, Hamburg, 1964, p. 52. Robinson, using the work of Conzelmann as a point of reference, argued that Winter had not yet offered convincing argumentation that the non-Markan material in Lk pre-existed in the form of a few documents. Rehkopf did not offer new argumentation. He also lacked proof, being unable to make a distinction between the vocabulary of the non-Markan material and that vocabulary which had been substituted by the Proto-Lukan redactor. To his credit, however, the investigation of the term κύριος may be useful in this regard. Robinson argued that because the perspective found in the journey to Jerusalem was the same as that in the rest of the Gospel and in Acts, it had been independently composed by Luke rather than having been borrowed from Proto-Lk (p. 53).

250. The Narratives of the Passion, in F.L. CROSS (ed.), Studia Evangelica 2/1, TU 87 (1964) 125, 129 (= Contemporary Studies in Theology, 1, London, 1962). Ramsey, the former Archbishop of Canterbury, wrote of the "distinctive literary and didactic emphasis" present in each of the Gospels, but argued on the basis of the additional material and differing narrative flow that Luke was obviously dependent upon written or oral sources in addition to Mk. Ramsey already gave some hint of his position by claiming that Luke omitted the story of the anointing at Bethany. And yet he concurred with Creed that Mk provided the structure for Lk. The Gospel and Acts reveal how great an emphasis Luke placed on the innocence of Jesus. Over against Mk, Luke portrayed the passion as central to the Christian life and something to be imitated as evidenced by the story of Stephen (Acts 7) (p. 130-131). In what may be a more poetic than literary consideration, Ramsey wrote: "The Church which faces that awe will grasp more clearly the compassion and the victory: its power to be Lucan and Johannine will spring from the depth of its Marcan experience" (p. 134).

251. Das Evangelium des Lukas (Geistliche Schriftlesung 3,1/2), 2 vols., Düsseldorf, 1964/1966 (= The Gospel according to St. Luke [New Testament for Spiritual Reading], 2 vols., New York, 1969, Vol. 1, p. 3. Pagination is to the ET). Stöger maintained Luke used Mk. But he also relied on the tradition of eye-witnesses. The evangelist so arranged his account that, more than the others, Lk offered an historical account of the life of Jesus (p. 4-5). Stöger rejected the idea of a separate source, since it cannot be proved and because the changes can be suitably explained by Luke's redaction of Mk (Vol. 2, p. 209). Stöger argued Luke simply presented the events in consecutive sequence, rather than the simultaneity of Jesus' trial and Peter's denial in Mk (p. 209-210). By concentrating on the conclusion of the trial, Luke emphasized that Jesus was Messiah. Jesus was also portrayed as a martyr, as a model for disciples in the way of martyrdom. Two important omissions occurred when in Lk 22,69 ὄψεσθε and καὶ ἐρχόμενον μετὰ νεφελῶν τοῦ οὐρανοῦ were deleted from Mk 14,62. The first resulted because the appearance will only

(1966)[253], Hugh MELINSKY (1966)[254], Donald GUTHRIE (1965)[255], Frederick

take place for some people and its time was delayed. The second omission was occasioned to focus that Christ, now glorified, was empowered by God (p. 213).

The apologetic that placed the blame for Jesus' death on the shoulders of the Jews, was most pronounced in Lk (p. 217). This does not seem to agree with Stöger's later statement: "St. Luke was not interested in investigating and apportioning the blame for Jesus' death" (p. 229). Stöger contended that while the Jews had the privilege of trying capital cases and even passing sentence, only the Roman governor could carry it out (p. 216). Pilate had two options: to accept the findings of the Sanhedrin or to conduct a trial himself. He chose the second. Jesus' trial before Pilate served as an apologia for Christianity in the face of Rome (p. 217-218). Parallels were drawn between Jesus and the difficulties experienced by Paul and Barnabas (Acts 13,50) and the fact that Pilate did not wish to be dragged into purely religious debates (Acts 18,14f.) (p. 220; cf. p. 230).

In an effort to present the Romans in a better light, Luke avoided the term "scourge" and neglected to report whether or not this actually had taken place (p. 226). Conversely, Luke portrayed the Jews as increasingly hostile to Jesus, a depiction which was also found in the account of Stephen in Acts 7,51f. (p. 228). One of the goals of Lk was to show the non-threatening nature of Jesus and his followers. The Romans, then, would do well to ignore the unfounded accusations of the Jews throughout the Roman empire (p. 229).

Stöger (1966) appeared to accept the Herod episode (23,6-12) as historical, the purpose of which was to obtain a second legal opinion and maybe even to pass a sentence, though he referred to Ps 2 and Acts 4,24-30 (*Das Evangelium*, 1966, p. 271-272 = *The Gospel*, 1969, Vol. 2, p. 221-222). Jesus' silence was once again interpreted as the silence of the suffering Servant (Is 53,7), but also following Grundmann, Stöger observed that such a motif denoted divinity for the Greeks (p. 223; cf. W. GRUNDMANN, p. 425).

In a later essay Stöger sided with those who viewed Luke's account as a redaction of Mk, despite new material and the variation in order (STÖGER, *Eigenart und Botschaft der lukanischen Passionsgeschichte*, in BK 24 [1969] 4). Further, the account was shaped under the influence of the martyr report (p. 8).

252. *The Gospel according to Luke* (The Cambridge Bible Commentary. NEB), Cambridge, 1965, p. 21. Tinsley sided with those who argued for Lukan dependence upon Mk, though Luke employed other sources as well. And while he presented Streeter's hypothesis and Farrer's view that Q never existed, Tinsley was content to leave the ultimate decision to the reader (p. 22). Luke's redaction took much greater liberty with Mk in comparison with Matthew's, with the result that Luke presented Jesus as a martyr (p. 187). Tinsley drew parallels between the martyr Jesus in the Gospel and his followers, like Stephen, in Acts.

As Tinsley reported that some scholars questioned the historicity of the Herod episode (23,6-12), he recalled that Luke mentioned Herod and Pilate together in Acts 4,25-28, which was inspired by Ps 2,1-2. Tinsley seemed to lean in the direction that this account was composed by Luke since it exculpated the Romans and the triple declaration of Jesus' innocence was a Lukan device which also served this apologetic goal (p. 198-199).

253. *The First Three Gospels*, Philadelphia, PA, 1966, p. 147. Barclay asserted that Luke had "extensive special sources" which supplied the great amount of new material in the passion narrative. This special material included the charge against Jesus (23,2-5) and the trial before Herod (23,6-12). Though he rejected the view that Luke had a different or separate source for this section of the Gospel, he assigned 22,14-24,53 to L. Cf. p. 263: "It is not necessary to postulate a new document behind Luke's Passion and Resurrection narrative, for what he has is not so much a new story as a considerable amount of additional material". Barclay used the schematic "Mark+Q+L+I" to visualize Luke's compositional method, which he ultimately

rewrote "Luke = (Q+L)+Mark+R" (p. 148, 266; cf. p. 141). "I" signified the infancy and "R" the resurrection narratives. In his exposition of Proto-Lk, he suggested this was the simplest explanation for the form of Lk, though other explanations could also be advanced. Barclay referred to Lukan and Matthean dependence upon Mk with the subsequent addition of Q and their special materials as "the orthodox view" (p. 262). At the very least it seemed that Barclay was intrigued by the Proto-Lk hypothesis.

Barclay (1966, [2]1975), though maintaining that Luke had recourse to other "extensive special sources" for the passion and resurrection, rejected the view that Luke was dependent upon "a new document" ([1966], p. 147 = [2]1975, 108). Instead of comprising a "new story", these sources contributed "a considerable amount of additional detail". Luke obtained this information from early members of the church ([1966], p. 149 = [2]1975, 109-110). Barclay defined the passage both as 23,6-16 and 23,6-12 ([1966], p. 147 = [2]1975, 107-108. Cf. [2]1975, p. 215).

254. *Luke* (The Modern Reader's Guide to the Gospels), London, 1966, p. 10. Melinsky was of the opinion that Mk formed the basis of Lk, but that Luke had access to Q as well as to other sources. Luke shaped his material in a "systematic order" (p. 13). The passion narrative was the first part of the Gospel to take shape as a written document through teaching and worship and formed a continuous whole which the four evangelists then incorporated into their Gospels (p. 95). The differences in the accounts among the four Gospels were accounted for by the speed with which they were formed. Luke was credited with omitting the nocturnal trial (p. 100). Reference was also made to Luke's tendency to present the Roman authorities more favorably (p. 102).

255. *New Testament Introduction. The Gospels and Acts*, London, 1965. Guthrie noted that in general Luke followed the same structure as the other two Synoptics, though he called attention to the conflicting views of Jeremias and Sparks over whether Mk formed the basis in 22,14ff. (p. 91, n. 2. Cf. JEREMIAS, *NTS* 4 [1958] 115-199, and SPARKS, *NTS* 3 [1957] 219-223). The differences in the passion narratives of the Synoptics lie, not in the variation in sequence, since they were relatively alike, but in "detail and wording" (GUTHRIE, *New Testament*, p. 115). In writing of Streeter's four document theory, Guthrie noted that it was the dominant view of British scholars, though form criticism forced a re-evaluation of the emphasis on documentary sources (p. 124). Guthrie recalled H. Montefiore's objection that it was unlikely that L would have been in written form since it would not have survived the shipwreck (Acts 27). Far too complicated was Winter's suggestion of the origin of some of the special material. Guthrie described as "a widely advocated hypothesis" that the special material in Lk was his own "free composition" and concluded that the biblical models shaped the oral tradition (p. 165, 166-167).

Considerable attention was devoted to the Proto-Lk hypothesis by Guthrie (p. 168-176). He complimented Taylor, saying his "admirable presentation of the theory has done much to commend it to many scholars", and Guthrie relied on his treatment to summarize the main arguments of the hypothesis (p. 168). He alerted readers to an admission of Taylor that Proto-Lk "was not, and could not, be published until Luke was able to expand it by drawing upon Mark". This, Guthrie perceptively pointed out, was significant "when assessing the value of the hypothesis" (p. 169).

Though sympathetic to the argument that Luke alternated blocks of Markan and non-Markan material, he refuted Taylor's explanation for the omission of the Markan material, stating that its absence can be explained in ways other than the Proto-Lukan theory (p. 170). In Guthrie's opinion, the dating given in 3,1 presented one of the strongest arguments in its favor. Observing that Morton and Macgregor announced support of the theory based on statistical data, Guthrie responded that such a consideration cannot prove the theory "once the theory has been adopted on other grounds" (p. 171, n. 4; cf. MORTON and MACGREGOR, *Structure*, 1964. Guthrie did not list any particular pages). This was an important factor since many proponents of the special

GAST (1968)[256], Klaus KOCH (1968)[257], Carroll STUHLMUELLER (1968)[258],

hypothesis relied heavily upon mathematical computations.

Approving Creed's characterization of the material as an "amorphous collection", Guthrie challenged the assumption of Proto-Lukan proponents which discounted any form of the Markan material transmitted orally, while holding fast to it solely in the documentary form of Mk (GUTHRIE, *New Testament*, p. 173). But neither did Guthrie offer a wholesale endorsement of Conzelmann's view that Luke freely revised Mk. Rather, having at his disposal Mk, Q and L, Luke could have used the block technique and combined Q with L, yet simultaneously incorporated the Markan material. No intermediate stage need be required (p. 175).

Guthrie called attention to the differing uses of the twelve transpositions by Hawkins and Taylor (p. 173). Whereas Hawkins considered this as part of the process in oral transmission, Taylor viewed these as written insertions imposed on an oral form of the Lukan passion narrative. Guthrie sided with Hawkins.

Guthrie offered a balanced, thoughtful and judicious presentation of the strengths and weaknesses of the Proto-Lukan hypothesis. And though he weighed its various arguments, he found it wanting and thus the changes in the Lukan passion narrative can be adequately explained without recourse to this supposed source. In his own words: "In assessing the *pros* and *cons* of this theory it must be admitted that many of the supporting arguments contain considerable weaknesses when submitted to detailed analysis. Yet in fairness to the advocates of the theory the evidence must also be considered in its cumulative effect. However, although the hypothesis *may* explain certain features in the literary construction of Luke, it cannot be said that these features *demand* the hypothesis" (p. 173). See further Guthrie's insightful analysis of the value of the hypothesis if proven, which was ultimately tied to the dating of Proto-Lk between 60-65 A.D (p. 175-176).

In the fourth edition of his NT introduction (⁴1990), Guthrie took the opportunity to add an additional footnote to his section on Proto-Lk (*New Testament Introduction*, Downers Grove, IL, ⁴1990, p. 208, n. 2). Unfortunately, his assertion was not sufficiently nuanced and one could glean from the material he added that there was increased support of the Proto-Lk hypothesis, or at the very least, that Luke employed a pre-Lukan account of the passion, while a more thorough examination of the scholarly debate would not sustain his position. Only Kümmel was listed as opposing the hypothesis. Most telling of all was that Guthrie's latest entry of scholars favoring Proto-Lk was 1976 (p. 208, n. 2)! Guthrie's authority was J.A.T. ROBINSON, *Redating the New Testament*, London - Philadelphia, PA, 1976, p. 107-117).

The tentativeness of Guthrie's endorsement of the theory, however, was apparent in his additional remarks on the synoptic problem (GUTHRIE, *Further Reflections on the Synoptic Problem* [Appendix D], p. 1029-1045). Aside from a copy of Mk and oral data, much in the form of catechesis obtained during Luke's stay in Caesarea, in addition to didactic and narrative material, Luke was believed to have added the Markan material to his initial draft. But Guthrie was wont to add "if some form of Proto-Luke theory is valid" (p. 1044). He further proposed that it was possible that Luke had access to Mt which he supplemented from oral tradition.

256. *Synoptic Problem*, in *JBC*, pp. 3, 6. Listing the accounts of the morning session of the Sanhedrin and the Herod trial, among others, as unique to Luke, Gast affirmed Lukan dependence upon Mk, though he pleaded for a greater pride of place for oral tradition "Any purely literary solution with no consideration for oral tradition does not present the picture adequately" (p. 6). Markan priority, while "generally accepted" by scholars, did not completely resolve the synoptic problem. Nonetheless, Gast described it as "surely a fine working hypothesis" (p. 5). Gast's assessment of the state of the question was expressed in the following: "The question of whether or not Lk and Mt depend on Mk is greatly discussed. The dependence of Lk on Mk is generally accepted. However, the nature and extent of the dependence is disputed" (p. 5). For a discussion

Glenn BARKER (1969)[259], and two whose positions were not entirely clear, but

of the Proto-Lk theory, Gast referred the reader to R.F. SMITH, *Inspiration and Inerrancy*, in *JBC*, §66:62, p. 510.

257. *Das Buch der Bücher. Die Entstehungsgeschichte der Bibel*, Berlin, 1963 (= *The Book of Books. The Growth of the Bible*, tr. M. KOHL, Philadelphia, PA, 1968, p. 118. Pagination is to the ET). Declaring Luke took over Mk and Q, Koch was not very clear about the additional source material he believed Luke employed, saying only that it could have been oral or written. What was very clear was that Koch rejected Burkitt's suggestion that Q contained an account of the passion (p. 119). He drew attention to Lukan redaction of Mk by pointing out the omission of references to the nearness of God's kingdom as well as "the future judge of the world" (p. 128).

258. Stuhlmueller described Luke's sources as Mk and Q in addition to "various written documents or official traditions, as well as many oral traditions" (*The Gospel according to Luke*, in *JBC*, 1968, 115-164, p. 116, 117). He acknowledged that the "interrelation of the Gospels in the trial scenes" constituted "one of the major problems in the history of the passion" (p. 160). Though somewhat circumspect in his delineation of Luke's sources, Stuhlmueller was also quite direct in refuting the Proto-Lk hypothesis since the Markan material occupied a central place and provided the structure of Lk (p. 118). That was said to be the "main objection" against the theory. Lukan redaction was responsible for the revison of 22,69 while the omitted phrase "seated at the right hand" appeared in Acts. Stuhlmueller left open the matter of whether the Jews had judicial power in capital cases, simply referring readers to Blinzler and Winter (p. 160; cf. BLINZLER, *Trial*, p. 157-163, and WINTER, *On the Trial*, 1961).

Pointing to the divergent views of Dibelius and Bultmann as Conzelmann had done, Stuhlmueller took note of the position that the Herod episode (23,8-12) was due to Lukan theology (STUHLMUELLER, *Gospel*, p. 117, 138; cf. p. 160; DIBELIUS, *ZNW* 16 [1915] 113ff.) and BULTMANN (*HST*, p. 273). He argued: "Luke, however, may have rearranged the chronology and may have disregarded Palestinian geography for the thematic development of his theology; still, he claims to rely upon eyewitnesses and reliable sources" (STUHLMUELLER, *Gospel*, p. 160). Yet, he also called attention to the detail that Luke appeared to possess a special source about Herod and possibly obtained information on Herod from Manaen who, in turn, possibly introduced the evangelist to Joanna (p. 117, 160). See also his comment on 8,3 (p. 138). The passage was defined as 23,8-12.

259. Barker, writing from an evangelical perspective, acknowledged that increasingly scholars were coming to appreciate Luke's theological contributions, a position which reflected the influence of Conzelmann (G.W. BARKER, W. LANE, J.R. MICHAELS, *The New Testament Speaks*, New York, 1969, p. 276). Although the book was a collaborative effort, the preface alerted the reader to the fact that Barker was primarily responsible for Chapter 18 which treated Lk-Acts (p. 13; cf. p. 275-307). While Luke was indebted to Mk for a great deal of the material as well as for the outline, Lukan redaction improved the Markan style (p. 283). Barker affirmed that Luke was capable of transpositions "so that the account runs more smoothly", a technique he claimed, corresponded with the literary practice of the period. Luke had access to both written and oral sources of a superb quality, some of which stemmed from "apostolic personages" (p. 280). In the section treating 19,28-24,53, reference was made only to "traditional materials" (p. 293). Although indication was made to Paul's trials alongside those of Jesus, no mention was made whether the account of Paul's trials influenced those of Jesus or vice versa (p. 293-294).

who seemed to support Lukan redaction of Mk, Helmut FLENDER (1965)[260] and James BLEVINS (1967)[261].

The Proto-Luke hypothesis continued to occasionally find endorsement, e.g. in Edward W. BAUMAN (1960)[262] and H.C. SNAPE (1960)[263]. Other scholars, such

260. *Heil und Geschichte in der Theologie des Lukas*, Munich, 1965. Diss. Theol. Faculty Friedrich-Alexander U. Erlangen-Nürnberg, 1964 (dir. G. FRIEDRICH) (= *St. Luke: Theologian of Redemptive History*, tr. R.H. and I. FULLER, Philadelphia, PA, 1967). The pagination refers to the ET. Flender made few direct statements about Luke's sources, but he gave the impression that Luke rewrote his Markan source in light of the needs of his own time. That Mk was certainly one of the sources was clear by the references to Luke's changes over against Mk (cf. p. 61). "The term πολλοί (1,1) is used to create the impression that a great number of people have been involved in this earthshaking event" (p. 64). Luke also had access to a source for the special material which contained parallelisms of men and women (p. 9-10). Flender called attention to occurrences of the term ὁ κύριος in the special material, in line with Schlatter and Rehkopf (p. 52, n. 2). "Luke does not merely transmit the tradition as it came to him. He is also a theologian, interpreting the Christian message for his own time" (p. 1). Yet all was not creatively recast: "Here, within the canon, is an instance of a writer wrestling with the question of how to expound the Christian message in a new situation. Luke is not original here. In many ways he just carries on what Mark had started. Yet a synoptic comparison will give us a pretty clear view of the gulf between the theology of Mark and that of Luke" (p. 2-3). Flender was obviously strongly influenced by Conzelmann and Dibelius, subscribing to the latter's view that Luke presented Jesus' passion as a martyrdom (p. 17-18; cf. p. 52ff). Flender observed that the MA in 22,69 / Mt 22,64, was to be understood as harmonization by a copyist (p. 101). Luke's usage simply reflected Septuagintal influence.

While not denying the possible historicity of the political Messiah question, many other changes in the Sanhedrin trial can be traced to Luke: "In Lk 22.66ff several typically Lucan statements are collected together" (p. 46; cf p. 44, n. 5). By omitting the statement about the Temple, the trial became a "compendium of Christology" (p. 44). The omission of the phrase "and coming on the clouds of heaven" (Dan 7,13) was explained by Luke's emphasis on the exaltation. Such a shift was necessary to address the problem in Luke's community, to reinforce faltering faith in the final victory of Christ. The omission cannot entirely be accounted for by the delay of the parousia (p. 101-102). Still concerned about the coming of Christ, Luke substituted ἔσται for the Markan ὄψεσθε since God's kingdom will not become visible until the end of time (p. 102). Flender did not indicate his preference between the explanations of the separation of the questions about the Messiah and the Son of God. Luke also changed the interlocutors in 22,67, having already redacted the story about the money tribute (20,19ff.) which set the stage for the charge in 23,2 (p. 62).

261. *The Passion Narrative*, in *RExp* 64 (1967) 513; cf. p. 517. Blevins left his view on the source question in the latter section of Lk somewhat ambiguous. Though he was very clear that Mk 11,1-13,37 formed the basis for Lk 19,28-21,38, he was not so clear for 22,1-23,56. That he often followed Creed, saw a parallel in the depictions of the deaths of Jesus and Stephen as those of martyrs, considered Luke's recasting of the account of Jesus before Pilate to portray the Roman leaders as regarding Jesus as innocent, and understood there to be a lack of reference to a special documentary source, could reasonably lead one to the conclusion that Blevins advocated the view of Lukan redaction over against the special source hypothesis to explain the differences between the two Gospels (p. 513, 519, 520).

262. E. BAUMAN, *The Life and Teaching of Jesus*, Philadelphia, PA, 1960, p. 38, deemed

as Bruce METZGER (1965)[264], W.D. DAVIES (1966)[265], Reginald FULLER (1966)[266], F.J. MCCOOL (1967)[267], R.F. SMITH (1968)[268], and G.H.P.

it probable that Luke used Proto-Lk.

263. In reaction to Streeter, Snape proposed the ideas that Luke was dissatisfied with Mt as lacking "order as a historical document" and with Mk for being "too brief", both of which Luke conflated (H.C. SNAPE, *The Composition of the Lukan Writings: a Re-Assessment*, in *HTR* 53 [1960] 29. Cf. p. 30: "Lummis maintains that the key to Luke's conflation of Mark and Matthew is the word καθεξῆς"). Furthermore, Snape conjectured that in addition to the other two Synoptics, Luke "had local sources which stated sayings in a more original form or at least in a form determined by their own *Sitz im Leben*" (p. 30). Snape impressed by the views of E.W. Lummis, which he believed were largely ignored, bypassed the need for Q, since it had been variously configured by scholars (p. 30; cf. E.W. LUMMIS, *How Luke was Written*, Cambridge, 1915. In a later work, *The Case Against "Q"*, in *HJ* 24 (1925-26) 755-765 (esp. p. 762, 765), Lummis vigorously reacted to the idea of various versions of Q. His solution to the synoptic problem involved Luke's use of Mk and Mt basically in their present forms into which Luke inserted the special material, though Lummis took no position on its origin (p. 765)). The Gospel form contained the following elements: "a birth and infancy narrative, a genealogy, an account of the mission of John Baptist and the temptation" (SNAPE, *Composition*, p. 30). The reason for the similarity of form among the Gospels was explained by utilization. Snape resurrected the view that the special Lukan material reflected the "Ebionite tendency" and thus pointed to the poverty endured by the Palestinian Christians in the period following 70 AD (p. 34).

264. B.M. METZGER, *The New Testament: Its Background, Growth and Content*, Nashville, TN, 1965, p. 84. He leaned toward acceptance of the Proto-Lk theory, despite acknowledging that the majority of scholars were unconvinced by it. He was most impressed by the "elaborate chronological framework at 3:1-2" that fits the beginning of a Gospel.

265. W.D. DAVIES, *Invitation to the New Testament*, New York, 1966, p. 96; see the schema of sources, p. 93. Despite what he considered to be a waning of support for Proto-Lk, Davies nevertheless endorsed it as one of the probable sources of the Synoptic Gospels. Streeter's "picture was so neat that it immediately appealed to scholars and still governs the work of, perhaps, most New Testament scholars. But its validity has lately been questioned. It is premature to sign the death warrant of the four document hypothesis, as Streeter's theory was called, and it is difficult to think that it will ever be wholly discarded". Davies further suggested that NT scholarship was shifting from emphasis on fixed sources to the oral tradition which continued to develop behind the Gospels. Doubts surrounding the theory were a recent phenomenon since the theory was "for a long time convincing" (p. 92). The three reasons advanced for the theory's acceptance were: 1) the meager amount of Markan material, 2) the non-Markan material governed how the Markan material was arranged, and 3) since Q material was combined only with L material, it appeared that they formed a unity prior to their use by the editor of Lk (p. 96).

266. R.H. FULLER, *A Critical Introduction to the New Testament*, London, 1966, p. 79. While noting that Streeter's proposal lacked "general acceptance", Fuller seemed incline to adopt it. Streeter's idea as it pertained to the passion narrative had recently been given a boost by form criticism. Luke's use of a separate and independent source "is the more feasible since form criticism has made the existence of the continuous Passion Narrative in oral tradition exceedingly probable" (p. 80). Observing that the issue of Aramaic sources for Chapters 1–12 in Acts had been much discussed, Fuller sided with H.F.D. Sparks that for the most part what appeared to be translation Greek was simply imitation of the LXX (p. 126; cf. SPARKS, *The Semitisms of Acts*, in *JTS* 1 (1950) 16-28).

267. *Synoptic Problem*, in W.J. MCDONALD (ed.), *NCE* 13, 1967, 890. He endorsed the idea of Proto-Lk, even suggesting that it was growing in popularity. Streeter's concept, when properly

THOMPSON (1972)[269] also saw some value in the theory. H. Philip WEST (1967-68) advocated a modification of Streeter's hypothesis concerning the existence of a primitive version of Lk[270]. L.E. PORTER (1983) considered the Proto-Lk theory interesting but beyond the scope of his essay[271].

Of course, not all subsequent reaction to the Proto-Lk theory has been positive. C.K. BARRETT (1960), apparently arguing against Streeter and Taylor, concluded: "From this it will follow that the occurrence in Luke of alternating blocks of Marcan and of Q+L material cannot bear the weight of argument that has been laid upon it"[272]. He suggested that Luke utilized a variety of traditions to which he alluded in the Prologue.

understood as only a partial, first stage of a Gospel, gains in acceptability. "Whether it will ever be accepted in its entirety or not, the view that Lk's Passion account was based on an independent account, not on Mk, is gaining acceptance".

268. *Inspiration and Inerrancy*, in *JBC*, 1968, 510. Smith, acknowledging that Proto-Lk never enjoyed unamimous acceptance, maintained that the theory was nonetheless somewhat plausible.

269. G.H.P. THOMPSON, *The Gospel According to Luke* (The New Clarendon Bible), Oxford, 1972, p. 19-20. He subscribed to Streeter's view that the non-Markan material joined together to form the structure of Lk. Though without specifying the nature or extent, Thompson asserted that in the section 22,1–23,56 Luke employed "a special source or sources" to which he added sections of Mk 14 and 15 (p. 253; cf. p. 267-268).

270. Drawing on John Knox's study of Marcion, West proposed that there existed a primitive version of Lk, but that what distinguished it from Streeter's Proto-Lk was the addition of Markan content by an editor (H.P. WEST, *A Primitive Version of Luke in the Composition of Matthew*, in *NTS* 14 [1967-68] 75-95. See J. KNOX, *Marcion and the New Testament*, Chicago, IL, 1942). He observed further that "most [scholars] now view Proto-Luke with natural scepticism" (WEST, *Primitive*, p. 75). According to West's theory, this earlier edition of Lk possibly served as a source for Mt. Concerning Lukan redactional methods, West argued that "in some places Luke follows Mark more faithfully than Matthew, and in others the reverse is true" (p. 77). West's hypothesis still allowed for Markan priority (p. 77). He also addressed the question of MAs. "Various attempts to dispense with Q have made major issues of these 'minor agreements'. [...] But these agreements can be explained easily on a Primitive Luke hypothesis: if Matthew had Primitive Luke before him, he would probably follow a fair number of its modifications of Mark". As for a portion of the passion narrative (22,14–23,56), it appears that it resulted from a combination of both Markan and non-Markan traditions (p. 89). The editor of Primitive Luke was responsible for rearranging material "for theological purposes" (p. 89, n. 1.). As for the reason why there is no extant copy of this supposed Primitive Luke West insisted that once canonical Lk was composed there was no further need for its predecessor. His overall conclusion exceeded the limits of his arguments and supporting evidence. See p. 94-95. He concluded: "The existence of Primitive Luke as a source of Marcion, Luke and Matthew cannot be proved, but it seems at least as probable as Q as a source of Matthew and Luke" (p. 95). Cf. p. 76, where he intimated only that "it is at least possible that Matthew drew material from it".

271. *The Gospel of Luke*, in F.F. BRUCE (ed.), *The International Bible Commentary*, Basingstoke - Grand Rapids, MI, 1986 (rev. ed.), 1182-1228, p. 1183.

272. *Luke the Historian in Recent Study* (Facet Book BS, 24), Philadelphia, PA, 1960; ²1968, p. 20; London, 1961.

Although Arthur VÖÖBUS (1968) treated a prior section of the Lukan passion narrative than with which we are concerned, his views are nonetheless noteworthy[273]. He was extremely critical of the method of Streeter, Taylor, Schürmann, Winter and Rehkopf for their "excessive reliance upon vocabulary"[274]. Not only had they ascribed modern methods to ancient writers[275], but their methodology was hampered by a lack of external criteria[276]. Further disapproval took the form of what Vööbus termed the *reductio ad absurdum* for dissecting the texts in atomistic fashion devoid of any concern for the context[277].

He was not opposed, in principle, to the idea of Proto-Lk. On the contrary, he noted that it was "certainly interesting in itself" and indeed can be seen as "very tempting"[278]. But "the arguments put forward in support of this proposal are quite without value"[279]. The attempts to identify this supposed source, whether it be Proto-Lk or Spitta's GS, were simply "guesswork"[280]. For Vööbus, Luke remolded what had been handed on, incorporating materials taken from the tradition, from Mk, and combined them with his own ideas, producing a creative composition[281]. Gilbert BOUWMAN (1968) viewed Proto-Lk as hypothetical as Q[282].

The Proto-Lk theory continued to be opposed by such scholars as Vaganay, Conzelmann and Kümmel. The development of redaction criticism helped scholars to appreciate Luke's role as a theologian in his treatment of Markan material. Kümmel, whose authority loomed large, deemed Rehkopf's study to have been

273. *The Prelude to the Lukan Passion Narrative: Tradition-, Redaction-, Cult-, Motif-Historical and Source-Critical Studies*, Stockholm, 1968.
274. *Ibid.*, p. 12. A further criticism leveled against their approach was that it was "much too dogmatic for historical research".
275. *Ibid.* See also p. 31: "All these speculations are based upon the strange notion that the writers in primitive Christianity handled the tradition in the meticulous fashion of twentieth century scholars".
276. *Ibid.*, p. 13.
277. *Ibid.*, p. 12. A similar criticism will be made against Taylor by M.L. SOARDS, *The Passion according to Luke*, p. 18. Cf. below.
278. VÖÖBUS, *Prelude*, p. 110.
279. *Ibid.* See p. 111. Earlier he wrote: "As a matter of fact, the theory that the diverse pieces and shreds of special tradition in the passion narrative constitute a primitive connected source for Luke into which he occasionally inserted elements from Mark is very dubious. There is no serious a priori or empirical reason to compel us to listen and to accept the dependence of the evangelist upon such a connected special source" (p. 30-31).
280. *Ibid.*, p. 111. Vööbus also included here B. Weiss's concept of Q, Vaganay's solution and the Twelve Source espoused by W.L. Knox.
281. *Ibid.*, p. 136.
282. *De Derde Nachtwake. De wordingsgeschiedenis van het derde evangelie* (Theologische monografieën. Woord en beleving, 2/7), Tielt, n.d. [1968] (= *Das Dritte Evangelium. Einübung in die formgeschichtliche Methode*, Düsseldorf, 1968, p. 81).

unsuccessful as demonstrated by the analyses of Conzelmann and Schürmann. Because of the debate surrounding the Two-Source theory, scholars such as Talbert began to employ other methodologies which neglected the question of sources.

Part II

LATE 1960'S TO THE PRESENT

CHAPTER SEVEN

INTEREST REKINDLED IN A SPECIAL SOURCE
The Dissertations of Gerhard Schneider and David R. Catchpole
and Their Subsequent Contributions

Working independently on the Lukan accounts of the story of Peter, the mockery and the Sanhedrin trial (22,54-71), Gerhard SCHNEIDER[1] and David R. CATCHPOLE[2] arrived at roughly the same conclusions in their 1968 dissertations about Luke's use of a special source. After rehearsing the contributions of Catchpole we will shift our attention to Schneider's seminal work on the trial because he has been a central figure in the study of Lk-Acts. We shall also be alert to how other scholars received them. After a brief exposition of articles by both authors which followed closely upon the completion of their in-depth studies, we will then trace the continuity and change in Schneider's position through the period 1969-1988. Lk 22 will be treated chiefly in the first part of that section while both Lk 22 and 23, including the Herod pericope, will generally be probed following the discussion of the dissertations and the articles. Finally, we will examine the position of W. Radl, a former student and colleague of Schneider's, who, though in the line of Schneider, sometimes reflects a more radical interpretation.

DAVID R. CATCHPOLE AND "THE TRIAL OF JESUS"

Calling attention to "an urgent source-critical problem", namely a detailed analysis of Lk 22,54-71, Catchpole highlighted the previous work done on the Lukan passion narrative by Jeremias, Schürmann and Rehkopf[3]. He hoped his study would show the necessity of a new approach to the "historical problems of Jesus' trial". He introduced his investigation with 1) a survey of rabbinic sources, then 2) a discussion of the charge against Jesus in the Sanhedrin, 3) the problem of the Sanhedrin hearing in Lk[4], 4) the legal setting of the trial of Jesus, and 5) conclusion.

---

1. G. SCHNEIDER, *Verleugnung, Verspottung und Verhör Jesu nach Lukas 22,54-71. Studien zur lukanischen Darstellung der Passion* (SANT, 22), Munich, 1969 (esp. the conclusions, p. 137-139); Habil., Würzburg, 1967/68 (dir. R. SCHNACKENBURG). Although in the dissertation Schneider concentrated on 22,54-71 he offered some observations and conjectures about Lk 23. He strongly supposed that Luke combined Mk with a special passion source in Lk 23 which would have included 23,6-16.27-31.39-43, as well as small non-Markan additions such as 23,2 and 23,55f. (p. 143; see also p. 144). The influence of SCHÜRMANN, *Abschiedsrede*, p. 140, n. 476, was evident.
2. D.R. CATCHPOLE, *The Trial of Jesus. A Study in the Gospels and Jewish Historiography from 1770 to the Present Day* (SPB, 18), Leiden, 1971 (esp. p. 153-220, and the Appendix, p. 272-278). Diss., Cambridge, 1968 (dir. E. BAMMEL).
3. CATCHPOLE, p. XII. He did not specify the particular works to which he was referring.
4. Feine was mentioned three times, always in footnotes (p. 189, n. 1; 212, n. 3; 269, n. 4). "J. and B. Weiss" were mentioned as sources of Montefiore (1909) contemplating "a possible

Peter's Denial in Lk 22,54b-61 (62)[5]

The account of Peter's denial, according to Catchpole, derived from a *Sonderquelle*, though "Luke himself is probably responsible for some features"[6]. Noting that even though Streeter, Taylor, Winter and Schürmann favored "some degree" of independence of the Lukan from the Markan passion, they nonetheless questioned the independence of the Peter story[7]. He was influenced by Rehkopf to regard the Peter story as independent "by reason of its coherence with the pre-Lukan passage Lk 22.33f."[8]. Catchpole examined: 1) common vocabulary, 2) the time scheme, 3) the geographical structure, 4) the challengers and 5) αὐτόν (22,63). Influenced by Lietzmann and Blinzler, Catchpole claimed that the evangelist was responsible for the transpositions of the denial and mockery. This literary technique was not inconsistent with Luke's customary methodology[9]. As to the vocabulary he concluded, "it appears that the verbal parallelism of Lk and Mk in the Denial narrative is not so suggestive of literary dependence as Taylor and others have claimed"[10]. Because of the difference in chronological pattern, he surmised "the use of a non-Markan tradition gains in probability"[11]. Owing to the different settings of the denials Catchpole argued Lk was not dependent upon Mk[12]. The Lukan scheme of those who challenged Peter was different from Mk, thus leading Catchpole to reject Lukan dependence[13]. Recalling that Taylor argued that αὐτόν (22,63) implied that the denials were inserted, Catchpole proposed that in the non-Markan source 22,63 followed immediately on 22,54a, thus there was no confusion as to whom the pronoun referred[14].

separate Lukan tradition" for the Sanhedrin trial (p. 207). This was the only occasion where he referred to J. Weiss whose work was not even included in the Bibliography. B. Weiss fared better, as his 1907 study was cited in the discussion of Peter's denials (p. 161-163, 165, 167) and the trial (p. 196, n. 8, referring to the 1908 work; p. 201, n. 3 and p. 207). Scholars such as Holtzmann and Wernle were not included. Catchpole avoided a discussion of Proto-Lk, briefly referring only to Streeter in favor and Kümmel opposed (p. 182, n. 3).

5. CATCHPOLE, p. 160-174, 272-274.
6. *Ibid.*, p. 174. He cited Spitta (1912), p. 404, and Ruckstuhl (1963), p. 41, as holding similar views (n. 4).
7. *Ibid.*, p. 160, n. 2. Streeter (1924 [1961]), p. 217; Taylor (1926), p. 48f.; Winter (1954; Catchpole misidentified the volume and date), p. 138-172, esp. p. 161f.; Schürmann (1957), p. 34, cf. p. 140.
8. CATCHPOLE, p. 160. Cf. REHKOPF, p. 84.
9. CATCHPOLE, p. 155. See H. LIETZMANN, *Der Prozess Jesu*, 1958, p. 251, and J. BLINZLER, *Der Prozess Jesu*, ⁴1969, p. 171. Catchpole believed that the two examples of Lukan transpositions were 6,17-19 before 6,12-16 and 8,19-21 before 8,4-18 in the Markan source (*Trial*, p. 155, n. 3). He was influenced by JEREMIAS, *Perikopen-Umstellungen* (1957-58).
10. CATCHPOLE, p. 166. Cf. e.g. TAYLOR, *Passion Narrative*, p. 77-78.
11. CATCHPOLE, p. 168.
12. *Ibid.*, p. 172.
13. *Ibid.*, p. 172-174.
14. *Ibid.*, p. 174; TAYLOR, *Behind*, p. 40.

The Mockery of Jesus (22,63-65)[15]

Catchpole sided with Winter, Bussmann, Grundmann and Taylor against Bailey and Blinzler in arguing that Luke used a non-Markan tradition for the mockery (22,63-65), "which is historically the better version"[16]. The primary reason for rejecting Markan influence was the lack of reference to Servant theology which Catchpole argued would have been present if Luke were composing on the basis of Mk 14,65.

Following the lead of Winter, he maintained "that Lk 22.63-65 diverges from Mark 14.65 in setting, timing and vocabulary" and he paid particular attention to the lack of "verbal overlap"[17]. He stated that this was limited to five words: καί, αὐτῷ (v. 63), λέγοντες, προφήτευσον (v. 64), and καί (v. 65), noting that αὐτός and λέγειν reflected differing forms in the Markan account[18]. He dismissed all but προφήτευσον, which will be considered below.

The term ἐμπαίζω occurs five times in Lk: three instances in the passion (22,63; 23,11.36), another was ascribed to L (14,29) and yet another derived from Mk (18,32 / Mk 10,34). He asserted that this was an indication of the *Sonderquelle* in 22,63[19]. His main argument against Markan dependence, however, consisted in surveying how Luke treated the Servant allusion of Is 50,6 LXX in Mk 14,65. He offered four reasons[20]: 1) It was "scarcely likely that Luke would obliterate an O.T. allusion". It ran contrary to his emphasis on fulfillment of the OT in the passion; 2) Luke deviated from "the crucial allusions to Is 50.6" by omitting the reference to spitting and because the scourging was preliminary to release, differently described, and not performed[21]. Normally he retained Servant allusions when he encountered them in Mk; 3) Luke retained and exploited the Servant theme in Mk and tied it closely with the theme of suffering, especially in the Transfiguration account; 4) The absence of this theme in the passion narrative was contrasted with the possible introduction of Servant language in Lk 11,22 where themes such as the Servant, the exodus, the realized presence of the kingdom and discipleship came together as in the Transfiguration account.

15. CATCHPOLE, p. 174-183. SCHNEIDER, *Verleugnung*, p. 96-104.

16. CATCHPOLE, p. 183. BUSSMANN (1931), p. 110; GRUNDMANN (1961), p. 417; TAYLOR (1926), p. 49f.; cf. BAILEY (1963), p. 56; BLINZLER (⁴1969), p. 165.

17. CATCHPOLE, p. 174, 175. P. WINTER, *On the Trial* (SJ 1), Berlin, 1961 [²1974], p. 21. Cf. above. But they will eventually part company since Winter argued that 22,66-71 was a post-Lukan interpolation and Catchpole maintained that the passage represented a separate, more primitive tradition. Catchpole examined v. 63 more extensively than vv. 64-65 (*Trial*, p. 182-183).

18. CATCHPOLE, p. 175. The Markan forms are αὐτοῦ and λέγειν. I corrected the misspelling προφήτευσον.

19. *Ibid.*, p. 179-180.

20. *Ibid.*, p. 180-182. Catchpole alerted us to the fact that his arguments for the *Sonderquelle* underlying 22,63-65 would be "other than literary ones" (p. 180) when he wrote: "Again vocabulary statistics are not compelling, mainly because of the rarity of the words used. But the balance of probability favours a Sonderquelle" (p. 179).

21. *Ibid.*, p. 180-181.

In light of this evidence, Catchpole concluded that Luke was predisposed toward Servant theology. Since an elimination of such material would be atypical of Luke, v. 63 must derive from a non-Markan tradition[22].

Catchpole argued that he had "to leave in abeyance the significance of ἐπηρώτων" in v. 64b[23]. He observed that no reason was offered for the inference that Jesus was a prophet in Mk 14,61f.[24]. On the contrary, the scheme in Lk was more reasonable. "Jesus is first tested, and then directly questioned about messiahship, and it is entirely logical then that the first question in the Sanhedrin hearing should be about this very topic"[25].

Catchpole argued that προφήτευσον (v. 64) did not derive from Mk because it was the sole word connecting the two accounts and the sense varied in the Synoptic presentations[26]. Further, he maintained that it was against Luke's *Tendenz* to introduce "something Jewish and technical", such as the messianic test of sight and smell prescribed in Is 11,3[27]. Had Mk been the source for Luke in the command to prophesy (22,64) he would have been introducing a concept contrary to his usual practice[28]. Thus he concluded: "It is all the more likely that Mk's tradition is a later one in which the original sense has been almost completely lost"[29].

In sum, Catchpole believed that the non-Markan origin of 22,63 was clear. Because the evidence for vv. 64-65 was, in his estimation, obscure or limited, he was more reluctant[30]. Nevertheless, he insisted that 22,63f. "depend on a non-Markan source which is historically the better version"[31].

The Sanhedrin Hearing (22,66-71)

For the account of the Sanhedrin trial (22,66-71), Catchpole dismissed Lietzmann's view that the Lukan version was a redaction of Mk, just as he rejected Winter's position that 22,66-71 was a later interpolation[32]. In reaction against the position of E. Bammel who maintained that Lk 22,69 was an independent tradition, Catchpole asserted that the verse was "best taken as a redaction of Mk 14.62 by Luke, edited and interpolated according to his own design"[33]. In support of this

---

22. *Ibid.*, p. 182.
23. *Ibid.*, p. 182-183.
24. *Ibid.*, p. 176.
25. *Ibid.*, p. 176-177.
26. *Ibid.*, p. 175.
27. *Ibid.*, p. 175-176.
28. *Ibid.*, p. 176.
29. *Ibid.*

30. Catchpole, pointing to "rather a small amount of material upon which to base a decision", stated that his investigation yielded no firm conclusion regarding 22,65 (p. 183).

31. *Ibid.*, p. 183.

32. *Ibid.*, p. 153-155, 184. Cf. LIETZMANN, *Der Prozess Jesu*, p. 251, and WINTER, *On the Trial*.

33. CATCHPOLE, p. 159. BAMMEL, *Erwägungen zur Eschatologie Jesu*, in *TU* 88 (1964) 3-32.

view he offered the following reasons: redactional compression by Luke can account for the fact that v. 69 says less than Mk 14,62[34]. Luke's tendency was in fact disclosed with the choice of ἔσται as opposed to ὄψεσθε which corrected the present affliction of the Son of Man by the immediate exaltation[35].

Lukan redaction was indicated, observed Catchpole, not only by the use of τοῦ θεοῦ, but in the Mk-Lk agreement of τῆς δυνάμεως and καθήμενος. Further, though Rehkopf and Schürmann had "indeed demonstrated the independence and antiquity of the Lukan narrative, Markan details are still believed to have been superimposed upon the account of the Sanhedrin trial"[36]. Surmising that 22,69 may be dependent upon Mk 14,62 he denied the possibility that "this verse takes its context with it"[37]. Its superimposition was confirmed by observing that the δέ of v. 69 was an ineffective connective with the preceding vv. 67b-68[38].

Taking note of what he believed to be increasing support for the view of an independent source for the Lukan version of the Sanhedrin trial, Catchpole concluded: "Here is a narrative which is not only unrelated to Mk in almost all respects, but also historically a better source with widespread agreement with the contemporary setting in matters of law and theology"[39].

Noting that the value of this passage was the most critical for research into the trial of Jesus, Catchpole devoted a sizeable section to its discussion in an attempt to show that the passage was not only historically more reliable than Mk but was also earlier[40]. As he sought to demonstrate independence of Lk 22,66 and Mk 15,1, he acknowledged that at least one phrase may derive from Luke[41].

The phrase ὡς ἐγένετο ἡμέρα, the focus of a great deal of attention, "has often been regarded as the most striking feature of the Lukan narrative"[42]. In examining this phrase, he presented four arguments against an independent tradition and endeavored to refute each of them in turn[43].

Whereas it had been argued that the Sanhedrin session had to be placed in the morning because Luke's narrative had "filled up" the nighttime, Catchpole responded that, due to the absence of the trial, there was less in that period in Lk than was in Mk. Secondly, some suggested that Luke may have been historicizing to eliminate the problem of the Great Council's meeting at night. He countered that

---

34. CATCHPOLE, p. 157. He cited Lk 9,27 = Mk 9,1 as an example.

35. Ibid.

36. Ibid., p. 158. This view was also found in his essay, Answer (1970-71), p. 220: "Luke xxii. 69 and Matt. xxvi. 64 are independent redactions of Mark xiv. 62, the former being an intrusion of material drawn from Mark into a non-Markan context". See below, n. 122.

37. CATCHPOLE, Trial, p. 159.

38. Ibid.

39. Ibid., p. 203.

40. Ibid., p. 183-203.

41. Ibid., p. 189. He studied the time note and concluded that this may be Lukan.

42. Ibid., p. 186. Though he stated "many have felt it rests on better tradition than Mk's nocturnal session" he cited only TAYLOR (1926) and TYSON (1959).

43. Ibid., p. 187-190.

although Luke changed other time notes in Mk, it was obvious the changes were made in accord with his theological purpose[44]. The same cannot be said for 22,66. While leaving open the possibility that the phrase was Lukan, he maintained that Mk was not the underlying source nor was it probable that the time implied in the underlying source was different[45].

Thirdly, it had been argued that Luke omitted the questioning of the witnesses. Thus, only the final portion of the trial, which took place near the morning, was recorded. He responded that this perception was contrary to Luke's understanding. The time note was associated with the entry into the council-chamber and not with the questioning.

Fourthly, A.N. Sherwin-White posited that Luke's account was inferior to Mark's on the basis that, if Luke accurately portrayed the situation, "the Jewish officials would have been late for the early beginning of the procurator's judicial day"[46]. Catchpole's rejoinder was fourfold: 1) no duration was indicated for the Sanhedrin hearing; 2) both Mk and Lk reported morning meetings, though of differing natures; 3) it was unlikely that the Roman official would have retained a normal working routine in light of the turmoil existing in Jerusalem; 4) the fire did not point to the Markan version, but only suggested the period of nighttime.

Centering on three details of Mk 15,1a which were lacking in Mk 14,53b, Catchpole examined the time note, as well as the meaning of the consultation and the council. He referred to his previous findings on the question of the temporal reference in 22,66 but suggested that "dependence would only be assured if *all* the surrounding data showed signs of a Markan origin" [emphasis mine][47].

He also insisted that "the contents of Lk 22.66-71 do not fit the meaning of Mk 15.1"[48]. Luke obviously understood the earlier Markan occurrence of συμβούλιον (Mk 3,6 = Lk 6,11) because of the paraphrasing. Since Lk 22,69 betrayed a redaction of Mk 14,62, and Luke regarded 22,66 as equivalent to Mk 14,53b, there was no need to refer to Mk 15,1[49].

Catchpole's third argument for an independent tradition revolved around the meaning of the phrase ὅλον τὸ συνέδριον, for which he favored council-chamber. Because τὸ πρεσβυτέριον already referred to the assembly, it was unnecessary to repeat it.

Next, συνέδριον had a local sense. εἰς meant "into" rather than "before" and finally, ἀπήγαγον implied a change of place from the house of the high priest. He conditioned his conclusion on the relation of v. 66 to Mk 15,1 with the stipulation

44. *Ibid.*, p. 187-188. His examples were Mk 1,35 = Lk 4,42; Mk 4,35 = Lk 8,22; Lk 9,37 par; Mk 11,12 par.
45. *Ibid.*, p. 189. The possibility of Lukan redaction of Mk was left open because of Lk 19,29 where ὡς was used as a temporal conjunction in light of a similar occurrence at 19,29.
46. *Ibid.*, p. 187. See A.N. SHERWIN-WHITE, *Roman Society*, p. 45.
47. CATCHPOLE, p. 190-191. He did not seem to allow that there may be varying degrees of redaction.
48. *Ibid.*, p. 191.
49. *Ibid.*

that if Mk 14,53a and Lk 22,66 were likewise unrelated, a non-Markan tradition had been preserved[50]. After dismissing the phrase ἀρχιερεῖς ... καὶ γραμματεῖς as ordinary and proposing even ἀπήγαγον could be dispensed with as necessary for the change of venue, he claimed that independence was the result[51].

Catchpole argued that Lk 22,67-68.70 were pre-Lukan and non-Markan for several reasons. Observing that Luke's tendency was to fashion more specific information from general, he steadfastly maintained that it would have been uncharacteristic of Luke to have changed Mark's specific reference to the one high priest to the more general indication of Jewish leadership[52]. Deciding then that the more general reference at Lk 22,66 seemed earlier than Mk 14,53 (= Mt 26,57), this served as an important traditio-historical insight suggesting an independent tradition.

A comparison with the material in Jn suggested to Catchpole that Lk and Jn were dependent upon the same non-Johannine source. Pointing out that Winter argued that John had not used Lk 22,67-71 to construct Jn 10, he enumerated seven differences between the accounts in his attempt to establish independence between Lk and Jn as well as to repudiate the view that Luke was dependent upon Jn or Mk[53].

Other changes, such as the non-committal response of Lk 22,67b.68 from the decisive ἐγώ εἰμι of Mk 14,62, which would be viewed as "inconceivable", did not betray Lukan authorship[54]. What was more, Luke did not normally lengthen Markan dialogues, but did so here if he was using Mk[55].

Citing Lk 4,41 as a redaction of Mk 1,34, as well as recalling Acts 9,20-22, he held that the titles "Son of God" and "Christ" were equivalent in the mind of Luke. Because the response of Jesus to the question of messiahship was so evasive and the titles had been separated, these indicated that Luke was not responsible for the verses and accordingly redaction of Mk was not the solution[56].

All in all, the non-Markan character and the Semitic coloring showed vv. 67-70 to be primitive. The answers of Jesus derived from groups where the equivalence of messiah and Son of God was not yet accepted thus reflecting an earlier stage than Lk[57]. Once again, indications pointed to an independent tradition.

50. *Ibid.*, p. 192-193.
51. *Ibid.*, p. 193.
52. *Ibid.*, p. 193-194.
53. *Ibid.*, p. 195-196. Among these were the observations that we would have expected πρὸς αὐτούς instead of εἶπεν δὲ αὐτοῖς at 22,67 and the parallel structure was not typical of Luke. He concurred with BAILEY (1963), p. 60, that for the trial John and Luke drew upon "the same non-Johannine source".
54. CATCHPOLE, p. 196.
55. *Ibid.*
56. *Ibid.*, p. 198. Like Schneider, he underscored the importance of investigation of sources. "Failure to decide on the exact source-critical situation means that the theologies of Luke and of his sources are not separately exposed" (p. 199; cf. n. 264).
57. *Ibid.*, p. 200.

Catchpole's analysis drew to a close with references to three elements used in the description of the end of the trial (vv. 70-71)[58]. While the use of πάντες may indicate here Lukan redaction, it need not be understood in a strictly mathematical sense[59]. While it was impossible to decide whether this was pre-Lukan or Lukan, "certainly Luke does often use it redactionally and this may be the case here"[60]. Because "v. 71b could stand without v. 71a", it was possible that v. 71a was a Markan insertion. While the Lukan form was consistent with redaction of Mk, it was unclear why Luke would have moved χρείαν to the end of the question. The phrase ἀπὸ τοῦ στόματος probably indicated a special source because it: 1) was unusual, 2) was found in L material, and 3) had a legal "bearing" in each setting[61]. On the important question whether the events of 22,66-71 constituted a trial or a preliminary hearing, Catchpole sided with those who viewed it as a trial[62].

The Minor Agreements (22,62.64)

The MA in 22,62, in Catchpole's view, was a "copyist's insertion"[63]. This agreement does not suggest that Q contained a passion narrative, in opposition to Hirsch[64]. Catchpole did not treat at length the Mt-Lk agreement against Mk τίς ἐστιν ὁ παίσας σε;[65] but declared that v. 64 was part of a layer of tradition older than v. 65 because of the technical procedure which tested a messianic claimant[66].

The Herod Pericope

Catchpole mentioned the Herod story briefly, and only as part of a critique of Winter[67]. He proposed that more material belonged to L than Winter suggested[68].

Catchpole Compares his Work with Schneider's

Because of a later publication date Catchpole was able to offer a "preliminary examination of the points of difference" between the two works in an appendix to his dissertation[69]. He noted "widespread agreement" between his investigation of

---

58. *Ibid.*

59. *Ibid.*, p. 201. Examples noted were Lk 8,45.52; 21,29.

60. *Ibid.*

61. He now reversed himself attributing the phrase to Lukan redaction, as also in 11,54 and 19,22 (*The Quest for Q*, p. 13, n. 29).

62. *Trial*, p. 201-202.

63. *Ibid.*, p. 174: "Allowed by WINTER, *Treatment*, p. 165".

64. CATCHPOLE, p. 174, n. 3. Cf. HIRSCH, *Frühgeschichte*, ²1951, p. 244.

65. CATCHPOLE, p. 175, n. 3. He considered only briefly this issue relative to v. 64 in the main body of his work. He also referred to it indirectly in the appendix which evaluated his differences with Schneider. See below. Neirynck studied the phrase in detail and referred to the confrontation between the two scholars (ΤΙΣ ΕΣΤΙΝ, p. 14-15).

66. CATCHPOLE, p. 183.

67. *Ibid.*, p. 213. Cf. WINTER, *On the Trial*, p. 137, 202, 213.

68. CATCHPOLE, p. 214.

69. CATCHPOLE, p. 272-278, p. 272. Despite the differences, he was nonetheless enthusiastic over his preliminary examination of Schneider's work. "What is certainly significant is the widespread agreement which exists between two entirely independent examinations of the source-

the source-critical problems and that of Schneider, though acknowledging they disagreed over the extent of the special Lukan material[70]. He focused on "the two most important points at issue" which were the origin of the Peter story (22,54-61) and the question whether Jesus was the Son of God (22,70).

While Schneider argued that the account of Peter's denial essentially stemmed from Mk and free Lukan redaction, Catchpole remained "unconvinced of the Markan derivation" of the Peter story[71]. A further difficulty arose with the term ἄνϑπρωπε in the vocative. Schneider stated that Lk 5,20 (Mk 2,5) could have given rise to its use here. Catchpole countered that Luke's change was prepared for by the Markan term τέκνον and that in 5,18 Luke had already altered ἄνϑρωπον ὃς ἦν παραλελυμένος from παραλυτικόν. The occurrence of ἄνϑρωπε in 12,14 offered "no certain support", because it could derive from L or Q[72].

Though he agreed that vv. 54-61 following upon vv. 33-34 fit the Lukan pattern of the prediction-fulfillment theme, he did not concur with Schneider that Luke inserted these passages in order to "shield Peter". Instead, they had the opposite effect. Luke showed no tendency to consistently present the disciples in a better light[73]. With regard to Peter specifically, Lk 5,1-11 and 8,45, which had been redactionally inserted, cast doubt on such a motivation for change from Mk.

In an attempt to spare Peter by replacing the maid with a man, Schneider claimed that the second denial in Lk incorporated material from the third Markan denial. Catchpole doubted this motivation and asserted that there was "no overlap between οἱ παρεστῶτες and ἕτερος"[74]. Luke indicated his understanding that both third denials correspond by his use of καὶ γὰρ Γαλιλαῖός ἐστιν (22,59).

---

critical problems posed by the Lukan account of these events, an agreement which can fairly be claimed as substantially vindicating the conclusions". He was also aware of Schneider's article, *Gab es* (n. 1). See below.

70. CATCHPOLE, p. 272.

71. *Ibid.* Cf. SCHNEIDER, p. 138, #2. He surmised that vv. 55b.c and 60d may be exceptions to this view (p. 134). Catchpole offered five arguments as to why he disagreed with Schneider's assessment of the origin of 22,54-61 (p. 272-274). The first two critiques dealt with whether Lukan redaction tried to improve the image of the disciples. The third criticism took exception to the point of the denial story laying in Peter's knowledge of Jesus. One could perhaps agree with Catchpole. The point, in light of the prediction-fulfillment theme, was rather Jesus' knowledge of Peter, whose faith would be tested. The third argument involved Catchpole, who followed Rehkopf, opting for independent Lukan material rather than Markan influence in 22,57 which was supported by Schneider and Schürmann. Part of the concern rested on the origin of 22,34. The fourth disagreement was based on Luke's reluctance to change to direct speech, though that was the case in 22,58 if the decision in favor of Lukan redaction of Mk were to hold. The fifth matter of dispute involved Schneider's contention that Luke used the third Markan denial in the second Lukan.

72. CATCHPOLE, p. 274.

73. *Ibid.*, p. 273. Catchpole cited the reproach of Jesus to the disciples at the calming of the storm (8,25), the controversy of the disciples forbidding a man who had been casting out demons in Jesus' name (9,49-50), and the episode of the disciples reprimanding those who were bringing their children to Jesus (18,15) as examples of Luke's harsh treatment of the disciples.

74. *Ibid.*

Whereas Schneider argued that Peter's knowledge of Jesus was "the point of interest" in the denials, Catchpole contended that since the interest was lacking in the Markan and Lukan versions of the second denial as well as in the third Lukan denial, this aspect was only of "minor significance"[75]. While conceding that Schürmann and Schneider may have been right in claiming that 22,34 was redacted from Mk 14,30, still Catchpole wondered whether οὐκ οἶδα (Mk 14,71) may not reflect independent Lukan material and perhaps indicated rabbinic ban language[76]. If such were the case, Lk 22,34 would reveal more primitive material than Mk 14,30.

Catchpole compared next the summary form ὁ δὲ πάλιν ἠρνεῖτο (Mk 14,70) with the direct speech found in Lk 22,58. Schneider maintained that this latter usage was a common tendency in the history of the Synoptic tradition[77]. Catchpole argued to the contrary that while the change from summary form to direct speech was common in Mt, the same cannot be said for Lk. Rather, "Luke drops direct speech from Mk and prefers summary form" in support of which Catchpole listed seventeen instances[78]. The peculiarity of the direct speech usage was further underscored for Catchpole by the presence of οὐκ εἰμί in Lk 22,58 and Jn 18,25, which Schneider conceded could not be proven as Lukan redaction[79].

Catchpole's last objection centered around the use of the introductory καί. "Finally, the introductory καί, used once by Mark and twice by John but three times by Luke, shows once again the Lk-Jn relationship is closer than that between Lk and Mk"[80].

In Catchpole's estimation, the controversy surrounding the origin of 22,70 was of much greater import because of the historical implications[81]. He delineated as the "real issues" how central the Markan formulation Son of God title was in the history of tradition and queried whether Schneider's "complex inter-linkings of tradition" could be verified[82].

Catchpole began his rebuttal on 22,70 by arguing that the periphrasis ὁ υἱὸς τοῦ εὐλογητοῦ was indicative not of Mk but rather of "a Semitic stage of the tradition"[83]. On this basis, Mark would have been responsible, at most, for assimilating the two titles. Further, Catchpole did not share Schneider's conviction that there was unanimity of Gospel tradition which regarded messiahship as "the crucial issue". He rejected Schneider's argument of the "pre-Markan Son of God

75. *Ibid.*
76. *Ibid.* The suggestion of rabbinic ban language came from the article by H. MERKEL, *Peter's Curse*, in E. BAMMEL (ed.), *The Trial of Jesus*, London, 1970, p. 69, and built upon Rehkopf's assertion of independent Lukan material.
77. CATCHPOLE, p. 273. Cf. SCHNEIDER, p. 52.
78. CATCHPOLE, p. 273. These included 8,24.29.32.41.42.44; 9,10.13.14.42.46; 18,40bis; 20,7; 21,5; 22,2.
79. *Ibid.*, p. 273-274. Cf. SCHNEIDER, p. 86.
80. CATCHPOLE, p. 274. Cf. SCHNEIDER, p. 89.
81. *Ibid*, p. 274.
82. *Ibid.*, p. 275. He presented a synopsis of Schneider's position.
83. *Ibid.*

involvement" but also in light of Jn 19,7. Appealing to Jn 10,24 Catchpole contended that the controversy extended beyond the question of messiahship to divine sonship, a point which was underscored by Jn 10,33.36[84]. He was of the opinion, as was seen above, that in some aspects Lk was closer to the Johannine tradition than to the Markan[85].

Schneider's position was summarized as maintaining that 22,67-68 was consistent with the material as found in all the Gospels. This derived from a tradition which employed as a model the response in Jer 38,15 and belonged to the non-Markan version source of Lk 20,1-8, that treated the question about Jesus' authority. This tradition was incorporated into Lk 22 because of the "'prophetic' answer ὑμεῖς λέγετε" which likewise had been shaped by Mk 15,2 / Lk 23,3[86].

Concerning the prophetic answer of ὑμεῖς λέγετε, Catchpole asserted that it was reasonable to assume that the phrase was "neither Markan in origin or Lukan in position"[87]. What was more, Luke was certainly not inclined to introduce Semitisms. Oral tradition appeared to have influenced Matthew (σὺ εἶπας 26,64) and a parallel oral tradition may lie behind Lk 22,64 / Mt 26,67, but Catchpole categorically denied "any cross-influence between Lk 22.67b,68 and ὑμεῖς λέγετε in terms of 'prophetic character'" for two reasons: the responses were different in that one was evasive and the other affirmative, and further, none of the statements containing σὺ εἶπας reflected "any prophetic flavour"[88]. He therefore concluded that the early tradition of the trial comprised two non-overlapping answers as well as the double concerns of messiahship and divine sonship[89].

Catchpole treated the difficulty surrounding the relation of Lk 22,67b.68 to the tradition which lies behind 20,1-8, an idea which Schneider had proposed[90]. Common elements consisted of Jesus reducing his opponents to silence and his refusing to answer. Because Catchpole acknowledged that 20,1-8 was dependent upon Mk, he examined the possible relationship of Mk 11,33 to Lk 22,67b.68, but without reference to 20,1-8, claiming "we are here dealing with nothing specifically Lukan"[91]. The connection, if there was one, must exist on one of the following two levels: in a particular layer of the tradition or in events which

---

84. *Ibid.*
85. *Ibid.*, p. 274, with reference to his comment on the introductory καί.
86. *Ibid.* Cf. SCHNEIDER, p. 126.
87. CATCHPOLE, p. 275.
88. *Ibid.* Cf. Jer. 38,15. In n. 3, he referred to his article, *Answer* (1971). See below.
89. *Trial*, p. 275-276.
90. *Trial*, p. 276. See SCHNEIDER, p. 35, n. 71, p. 117, 142-143. Schneider, having passed over the issue of the relation of 22,67-68 to Lk 20,1-8 in his intervening works, returned to it in his 1988 contribution, though only in passing, citing support from R. Pesch (*Markusevangelium*, p. 408). Admitting that the first part of Jesus' response (v. 67c) reflected Johannine formulation (Jn 10,24f.) and thus was probably traditional (*Das Verfahren*, p. 117 = *Jesusüberlieferung*, 282), he was still not convinced that the historicity of the refusal to answer can be regarded as certain for the situation in the Sanhedrin (p. 117-118 = 282-283). Because of the parallel in Jn, this indicated the response was also the theological concern of Luke for the Sanhedrin scene (p. 118 = 283).
91. CATCHPOLE, p. 276.

concern the historical Jesus. Catchpole rejected Schneider's appeal to the Jewish leaders being unable to respond to Jesus (Lk 20,40) as not relevant[92].

An examination of Schneider's discussion on the agreements of Lk and Mt against Mk in Lk 20,1-8 followed. Catchpole directed his attention first to that which clearly reflected typical Lukan redaction. All that remained, in his opinion, was εἰπὸν ἡμῖν (Lk 20,2). Allowing for the possibility that this stemmed from a non-Markan tradition, he qualified this position by stating that there must be other signs attesting to such an origin. If this cannot be confirmed, then Catchpole suggested the occurrence 1) was not important, 2) anticipated Mk 13,4, or 3) was connected by means of a theme to 22,67. If in Luke's mind the incidents of the question of authority and the question about Jesus' identity were related, it meant only that the events had a bearing on one another, "but not that [Luke] had other source material"[93].

The critical examination turned next to those elements which Mt and Lk shared in common. Having isolated fourteen elements, Catchpole concluded that the list "contains none of the decisive elements of the narrative"[94]. The fourteen elements which were considered crucial for the account were those which were held in common between Mk and Lk. He reviewed each of these elements and concluded that there were only four cases where redaction by Luke was questionable. These were εἰπόν, ἡμῖν, καγώ, and πόθεν. Because there was no coherence between them and because the only overlap was εἰπὸν ἡμῖν (22,67 and 20,2), as a result of this investigation, he concluded: "Consequently, it is difficult to be convinced of any traditional link between Lk 20.1-8 and 22.67-68 on the level of pre-Lukan non-Markan strata"[95]. Thus, vv. 67-68.70 should be considered as coming from the *Sonderquelle*.

Catchpole summarized the findings as follows: insofar as two questions and two answers had been combined in 22,67-68.70 he judged that these verses were "pre-Lukan and non-Markan"[96] because: 1) the answers were unrelated and primitive; 2) material taken from the independent Johannine tradition would seem to contradict Schneider's claim that there was unanimity among the Gospel traditions; 3) the reference to divine Sonship reflected the pre-Markan character, and 4) because the whole deviated "from known characteristics of Lukan redaction"[97]. Thus, Catchpole held fast to his conviction that the material of Jesus' response to the Jewish leaders at the Sanhedrin trial derived from special material and extended its area beyond that suggested by Schneider.

92. *Ibid.* The similarity Schneider pointed out with Mt 22,46 which, like Lk 20,40, had been drawn from Mk 12,34, was termed "a less immediate parallel" and therefore dismissed. Cf. SCHNEIDER, p. 118.
93. CATCHPOLE, p. 276-277.
94. *Ibid.*, p. 277.
95. *Ibid.*, p. 278; also p. 200. Cf. SCHNEIDER, *Passion*, 1973, p. 68, n. 31, and *Lukas*, 1977, ²1984, p. 468.
96. CATCHPOLE, p. 278.
97. *Ibid.*

Catchpole broached the subject of the MAs in the appendix. "In fact σὺ εἶπας can be regarded as a witness to the earlier occurrence of ὑμεῖς λέγετε as the answer to the Son of God question, in terms of the influence of oral tradition on Mt (cf. the parallel oral tradition which may have operated behind Lk 22.64 / Mt 26.67[sic])"[98].

Reactions to Catchpole

When in turn Schneider had the opportunity to review Catchpole's work, he summed up his counterpart's position that the three scenes of the mockery, denial and trial before the Sanhedrin were derived from a special Lukan independent tradition of particular historical value over against Mk[99]. Schneider contrasted his own positions maintaining that only the mockery (vv. 63-65) was independent of Mk. He regarded at least vv. 69-71 as Lukan redaction of Mk while the denial scene (vv. 54-61) was taken over entirely from Mk which Luke radically transformed.

Schneider wrote it was natural for two authors to rejoice when, working independently of one another, they arrived at significant agreement. But the joy was tempered by skepticism because, although they had employed similar methodological processes, the resulting conclusions evidenced strong divergence. Schneider held fast to his position that the denial scene was dependent upon Mk, a conviction he felt was vindicated by the study of M. Lehmann[100]. Schneider acknowledged that according to the objections raised by Catchpole, his argumentation concerning the trial scene remained controversial. Schneider wrote further: "Leider hat C. in dieser Analyse die einschlägige Arbeit des Rezensenten ... nicht mehr eingearbeitet. Er geht jedoch in einem Anhang (272-278) auf einige Thesen dieses Buches ein".

Regarding Catchpole's conclusion that "the combination of two questions and two answers in Lk 22.67-68,70 emerged as pre-Lukan and non-Markan", Schneider expressed regret that he had not considered the work of H. van der Kwaak (1969) which evaluated Lukan dependence on Mk in the trial of Jesus[101].

Despite the differences, Schneider viewed Catchpole's study as an important work not to be overlooked. Indicating the need for further studies, the final judgment on the source criticism of the Lukan presentation, however, Schneider would leave others to make[102].

---

98. *Ibid.*, p. 275.

99. *BZ* 16 (1972) 272-274, esp. p. 273. It was at once obvious that Schneider did not offer as detailed a critique as Catchpole.

100. *Ibid.*, p. 273. See M. LEHMANN, *Synoptische Quellenanalyse und die Frage nach dem historischen Jesus* (BZNW, 38), Berlin, 1970 (esp. p. 116-112).

101. *BZ* 16 (1972) 273. Cf. H. VAN DER KWAAK, *Het Proces van Jezus*, Assen, 1969 (esp. p. 132-140). See below.

102. SCHNEIDER, in *BZ* 16 (1972) 274: "In der quellenkritischen Beurteilung der lukanischen Darstellung möchte der Rezensent als Mitbetroffener das letzte Urteil anderen überlassen". Schneider referred to Catchpole's dissertation only briefly in *Passion* (1973) (p. 68, n. 31). In *Lukas* (1977), he made no mention of Catchpole's analysis for the account of Peter's denials and the mockery, but called attention to it for the Sanhedrin trial (p. 467, 468). Schneider recalled Catchpole's work in *Das Verfahren* (1988), not so much to debate the positions, as simply to

Various scholars offered their assessments of Catchpole's study. Writing in the *Freiburger Rundbrief*, E.L. Ehrlich complimented Catchpole for a "sinnvolle Untersuchung" which examined the problem of the trial of Jesus based upon the scientific literature that was essentially concerned with the Jewish recording of the history[103]. The extensive research treated not less than 181 Jewish scholars who commented on the trial of Jesus in one way or another. But conspicuous by their absence were the works of D. Flusser, a lacuna which Ehrlich found hard to understand[104]. Further, other "nicht unwichtige" studies which had not been considered included works by Käsemann, Conzelmann, Haenchen, Flesseman[105], and Lohse. Despite these criticisms, Ehrlich commended the book as containing a wealth of material that required a thorough study.

P. Richardson was lavish in his praise of Catchpole's work[106]. "Well-documented, selective, rigorous, thorough" were some of the words used to describe it. He credited Catchpole with making "a solid contribution to the growing ascription of priority to some of Luke's special features"[107]. What was more, the study reflected a "careful, competent, and methodologically sound examination" not only of the NT but also of pertinent rabbinic material.

The study offered new and significant insights into the passion narrative in Lk and provided a "fresh appreciation" for a generally neglected area of research, that of the Jewish perspective and contributions[108]. The weaknesses stemmed from a not so careful investigation of the Roman legal process, as well as the less direct formulations of Catchpole's own conclusions. Though the study lacked an "overall perspective on the trial", Catchpole offered some answers to vexing problems surrounding the trial of Jesus[109].

In an extensive review, G. Lindeskog, author of *Die Jesusfrage im neuzeitlichen Judentum*, praised Catchpole for the quality of his analysis and systematization, concluding that the work deserved high recognition[110]. The his-

---

acknowledge them and to situate the book in the light of the history of research on the source question (p. 112, 114, 116 = 277, 279, 281). See above. Schneider also made reference to Catchpole's essay, *Problem* (p. 114, n. 18 = 279, n. 14).

103. *Freiburger Rundbrief* 23 (1971) 109-110. "Das wesentliche Anliegen des Verf. ist es, vor allem die jüdische Geschichtsschreibung angesichts dieses Problems zu berücksichtigen".

104. *Ibid.*, p. 110. Ehrlich was referring to a book by D. FLUSSER, *Jesus in Selbstzeugnissen* (1968), which had recently appeared. In contrast to Catchpole, in this book Flusser argued that Jesus was not sentenced to death by the Sanhedrin, a position he held because of the varying statements made by the NT sources concerning the seating of the Sanhedrin.

105. He may have been referring to E. FLESSEMANN VAN LEER, *Die Interpretation der Passionsgeschichte vom AT aus*, in F. VIERING (ed.), *Zur Bedeutung des Todes Jesu*, Gütersloh, 1968, 79-96.

106. *JBL* 91 (1972) 264-266.

107. *Ibid.*, p. 266.

108. *Ibid.* So K. WEISS, in *TLZ* 97 (1972) 444, on attention to a neglected area.

109. RICHARDSON, in *JBL* 91 (1972) 267.

110. *ZRGG* 25 (1973) 189-192. "Wie kein christlicher Autor vor ihm hat Catchpole die jüdischen Untersuchungen zum Problem des Prozesses Jesu mit Scharfsinn und erstaunlicher Genauig-

toricity question of the crucifixion was, according to this reviewer, *the* historical question for both Jews and Christians. The sources, however, were the Gospels which are not historical sources. But because they recount the crucifixion of Jesus "als einem Geschehen an einem bestimmten Platz zu einer bestimmten Zeit", from this standpoint the Gospel tradition must be valued historically[111].

Despite the overall positive evaluation, there were two points where the reviewer disagreed. Lindeskog took issue with Catchpole's view that in the eyes of the leading Jewish theologians Jesus was not a "harmless, normal Jew". Such a view cannot be judged as correct in light of the participation of the Jewish religious leaders in the trial of Jesus.

Secondly, while Catchpole argued that the Lukan passion narrative had decisive meaning for the judgment concerning the tradition history, other questions must still be asked: how close did this tradition come to the historical course of events? Further, what would be the Roman interest in an internal Jewish affair? Although Jesus was regarded as a threat, how was it that the procurator would accuse Jesus of a political role? Despite these drawbacks, Lindeskog credited Catchpole with advancing research on the trial of Jesus in a profound and exemplary manner[112].

In comparison, the review of R. Mayer was less enthusiastic and his assessment mixed. Acknowledging that *The Trial of Jesus* was a thorough literary-critical study and a valuable correction and extension of the work of P. Winter, Mayer suggested that Catchpole devalued his own work by the arrogant way with which he treated and did away with, not only Winter's positions, but those of most of the Jewish teachers[113]. Catchpole's method of going back and forth, as well as a few instances where various positions were interlaced created confusion for Mayer. He indicated his preference for the "unmatched" study of G. Lindeskog who allowed the "contours" of the research personalities to stand out more clearly in bold relief. Despite the fact that Catchpole created a wealth of careful individual observations, Mayer contended that the reader was not supplied with a clear presentation of the statements of Jewish historians concerning Jesus' trial. The impression the reviewer was left with was a certain uneasiness about what he considered "die eindeutig antijüdische Haltung des Verfassers"[114].

---

keit analysiert und systematisiert. Damit hat er auch zugleich einen wertvollen Beitrag zur jüdischen Jesusforschung überhaupt gegeben" (p. 190). See also p. 192: "Das Buch verdient hohe Anerkennung".

111. *Ibid.*, p. 189: "Das Kreuz Jesu ist eine historische Frage, *die* historische Frage des Judentums und des Christentums, und sie muss demnach *historisch* beantwortet werden. Die Quellen sind die Evangelien, von denen behauptet wird, sie seien keine historischen Quellen. Aber sie *erzählen* doch von der Kreuzigung Jesu als einem Geschehen an einem bestimmten Platz zu einer bestimmten Zeit. Eben an diesem Angelpunkt muss die Evangelientradition historisch bewertet werden".

112. *Ibid.*, p. 192.

113. *TZ* 29 (1973) 439-440. "Jedoch entwertet Catchpole diesen seinen Forschungsbeitrag selbst durch die überhebliche Art, mit der er nicht nur Winters wissenschaftliche Leistung, sondern auch die der meisten anderen von ihm behandelten jüdischen Gelehrten abtut" (p. 440).

114. *Ibid.*, p. 440. For a later assessment of Catchpole, see R.A. HORSLEY, *The Death of*

428 CHAPTER SEVEN

Catchpole's Later Articles

In a later article Catchpole (1970) argued that the entire account of the Sanhedrin trial (22,66-71) derived from a pre-Lukan source, with the exception of 22,69, which clearly stemmed from Mk 14,62[115]. And even though a relationship was shown to exist in this one verse, Catchpole denied that such an argument would prove that Luke depended upon Mk for the entire pericope[116]. Mk and Lk offered two independent accounts of the Sanhedrin trial[117]. Catchpole assessed the state of the question on the competence of the Sanhedrin in the following way: "The problem of Jewish capital powers has been treated with wearying frequency and disappointing inconclusiveness"[118]. He sided with Jeremias, Blinzler and Lohse against Burkill and Winter in holding that the Sanhedrin could pass capital punishment, though they could not execute prisoners. The Johannine flavoring in 22,67-68, combined with a Semitic coloration and a more primitive account, plus a preference for the legality as portrayed in Lk, prompted Catchpole to hold that the Lukan version was more primitive than Mk and therefore historically valuable[119].

Catchpole countered Winter who maintained that there was an intentional lack of reference to the death sentence by the Sanhedrin in Acts 13,27-28. Catchpole pointed out that Winter ignored part of the verse[120]. W. Horbury held that Catchpole offered "fresh arguments for the Lucan preservation of an independent account of the Sanhedrin trial"[121].

In his 1971 essay, *The Answer of Jesus to Caiaphas (MATT. XXVI.64)*, he again raised the suggestion that Luke's account of the Sanhedrin trial stemmed from an independent tradition[122]. Admitting that the "analysis of the accounts of

Jesus, in B. CHILTON and C.A. EVANS (eds.), *Studying the Historical Jesus. Evaluation of the State of Current Research*, Leiden, 1994, 394-422, esp. p. 403-404.

115. CATCHPOLE, *The Problem of the Historicity of the Sanhedrin Trial*, in E. BAMMEL (ed.), *The Trial of Jesus* (SBT, SS, 13), Naperville, IL, 1970, p. 64, 65. Catchpole wrote in reaction to H. Lietzmann (*Der Prozess Jesus* [1931], repr. in *Kleine Schriften II: Studien zum Neuen Testament*, Berlin, 1958, 251-263), whose work he termed "epoch-making". While Lietzmann attacked the historicity of the trial, Catchpole defended it. Cf. above.

In a 1993 contribution Catchpole offered the following observation about Luke's compositional style: "Students of Mark and John are familiar with such theologically motivated 'sandwich structures', but these are not a feature of Luke. His inclination is to smooth and refine away interruptions, and certainly not to create them" (*The Quest for Q*, Edinburgh, p. 101). He cited 22,54-71 / Mk 14,53-72 and Lk 23 / Mk 15 as examples (n. 60).

116. *Problem*, p. 64. Contrary to the view of LOHSE, *Die Geschichte*, 1964, p. 75.

117. CATCHPOLE, *Problem*, p. 54.

118. *Ibid.*, p. 59.

119. *Ibid.*, p. 65. The view was reminiscent especially of Taylor. Catchpole denied that Luke was responsible for dividing into two the question to Jesus about being Son of God and Messiah (p. 64-65).

120. *Ibid.*, p. 56.

121. W. HORBURY, *The Passion Narratives and Historical Criticism*, in *TLond* 75 (1972) 61.

122. CATCHPOLE, *The Answer of Jesus to Caiapahs (Matt. xxvi. 64)*, in *NTS* 17 (1970-71) 213. See above, n. 36.

the trial before Pilate in Mark and Luke is extremely complicated", he noted the similarity between Lk 23,3 and Mk 15,2 observing that Luke could have inserted the Markan material into his special source[123]. He then proposed that 23,3 could have been part of L. He also reasoned that Lk 22,69 / Mt 26,64 were "independent redactions of Mark xiv.62, the former being an intrusion of material drawn from Mark into a non-Markan context"[124].

Subsequently Catchpole (1976) argued that the charges against Jesus contained in 23,2 were "almost certainly redactional, stemming from Lukan theology and apologetic"[125]. He continued to promote the idea that Luke employed an alternative tradition as found in 22,63-64.67-68.70(?), dated earlier than Mk, in light of source-, linguistic- and redaction-critical studies[126]. Because of the mention of the location of the συνέδριον and additional references to testimony in 9,22 and Acts 13,27-28, Catchpole asserted that "Luke was probably thinking of a full trial"[127]. A formal trial was explicitly indicated in Mk, while in Lk only implicitly. Of the four arguments presented by Catchpole against the concept of a formal trial, two refer specifically to Lk. It was possible that Luke was drawing upon and expanding inferences found in Mk. Secondly, a Jewish and a Roman trial generally did not "follow consecutively", though exception may be found in the writings of Josephus[128]. Although continuing to argue in favor of a special source for 22,67-68, Catchpole detected the close relationship between these Lukan verses and Mk 11,27-33: "But if the Lukan tradition in 22:67-68 is historical – and it coheres exactly with the approach of Jesus in Mark 11:27-33, while at the same time exhibiting none of the typical tendencies of Christian remodeling – it implies that Jesus was asked about messiahship, but that his answer contained insufficient basis for a charge"[129]. Does that not bring us back to Catchpole's insistence that the charges in 23,2 were clearly redactional? Given the striking similarities of the Lukan verses with a Markan text dealing with the issue of Jesus' authority, which was what the Sanhedrin trial was attempting to clarify, and the view that the charges were redactional should make us cautious about the claim that 22,67-68 derived from some alternative tradition prior to Mk.

123. *Ibid.*, p. 218.
124. *Ibid.*, p. 220. See also p. 226.
125. *Trial of Jesus*, in *IDBS*, 1976, 917-919, p. 918.
126. Catchpole's 1971 study as well as Schneider's *Verleugnung* (1969) were among the works cited in the article's bibliography. Though Catchpole raised the issue whether 22,70 was part of the alternative tradition prior to Mk, later in the article he maintained that it "very probably" belonged to the same strata as 22,67-68 (*IDBS*, p. 919). He also insisted that Mk alone cannot be the basis of determining "traditions and current legal norms".
127. CATCHPOLE, in *IDBS*, p. 918.
128. *Ibid.*, p. 919. Cf. Josephus, War, 6.5.3.
129. *Ibid.*

GERHARD SCHNEIDER: A PRE-EMINENT LUKAN SCHOLAR

Throughout his academic career G. Schneider has been a prolific author in the field of Lk-Acts. His publications include: his seminal work, *Verleugnung* (1969)[130], followed shortly thereafter by three short studies related to his investigation of the trial: *Gab es* (1970), *Jesus* (1970), *Problem* (1972)[131]. A more popular treatment of the passion narrative in the Synoptics appeared in 1973, followed by his important commentary on Lk (1977)[132]. His in-depth article on the political charge against Jesus (Lk 23,2) was published in English (1984) and subsequently in German (1985). He returned in 1988 to an investigation of 22,54–23,25, with special attention to 22,66-71; 23,1-25, especially 23,2.5.6-16, which is significant since he reviews the evolution of his position[133].

"Die Verleugnung, Verspottung und Verhör Jesu nach Lukas 22,54-71"
Schneider structured his *Habilitationschrift* in five chapters: 1) the problems of the Lukan passion narrative; 2) the pre-literary tradition before and beside Mk; 3) a literary analysis of 22,54-62.63-65.66-71, the central part of the dissertation; 4) further observations on the Lukan passion, and 5) the theological statements of the Lukan passion[134]. An excursus on the historical question of the Sanhedrin trial concludes this study.

Surveying the state of the question in light of the older literary criticism Schneider remarked that since the establishment of the two-source theory at the beginning of the twentieth century, difficulties have persisted in the attempts to solve the synoptic problem. Streeter's proto-Lukan theory was acknowledged as still having supporters[135]. A. Schlatter advocated Luke's use of a complete written Gospel as a source for Lk[136] while J. Jeremias defended a modified form

---

130. See above n. 1.

131. Two volumes of *Aufsätze* were published: *Lukas, Theologe der Heilsgeschichte. Aufsätze zum lukanischen Doppelwerk* (BBB 59), Königstein/Ts.-Bonn, 1985, and *Jesusüberlieferung und Christologie. Neutestamentliche Aufsätze 1970-1990*, (NTSuppl 67), Leiden - New York - Copenhagen- Cologne, 1992, in which the three short studies were reprinted. See below, n. 261.

132. He also published a two-volume commentary on Acts (1980-82).

133. An essay on the title "Son of Man" was included in the 1975 FS for A. Vögtle. See below, n. 295. In addition, he served as co-editor of *EWNT* (1980-83). Finally, he has written numerous recensions and articles surveying new literature on Lk-Acts (1990, 1992).

134. Chapter 1 included discussions of the old and new literary criticism, the question of how the events proceded historically, and form and redaction criticism. Chapter 3 preceded a section on the literary problem of the phenomenon of order. Additional attention was given to the relation of Lk and Mk, particularly in the changes in order and smaller changes and in the adoption and omission of Markan material.

135. SCHNEIDER, p. 12. Feine and B. Weiss were identified as precursors (n. 9). Strangely, he referred only to Feine's 1891 book and Weiss's *Die Quellen* (1907). There were merely two references to J. Weiss's Lukan commentary in SNT 1 (⁴1929), one dealing with the MA in 22,62 and the other referring to the Sanhedrin trial (p. 54, 105).

136. SCHNEIDER, p. 12. H. Sahlin's assumptions (*Messias*, 1945) were contrasted with Schlatter, *Lukas*, 1931 (n. 12).

of the Proto-Lk hypothesis, which itself had undergone revision[137]. Those who maintained that Mk served as Luke's source in the passion "mit verschiedenen Variationen behauptet oder vorausgesetzt", were Dibelius, Schmidt, Finegan, Grobel, Schick and Bultmann (since 1958)[138]. Proponents of Proto-Lk included Hawkins, Perry, Streeter, Taylor, Osty, Vaganay, Winter, Tyson, and Buse[139]. Schneider was wary of Taylor's word statistic observations which, while they could prove dependence, could not likewise establish negatively independence.

Turning to the new literary criticism, he concentrated on Schürmann and Rehkopf whose methodology combined literary- and form-critical perspectives with the source-critical search for linguistic peculiarities[140]. Though Rehkopf wanted to prove the existence of a pre-Lukan passion account as the conclusion of a pre-Lukan Gospel, Schneider sided with Schürmann that the question remained open whether the special Lukan traditions constituted a continuous narrative or a variety of traditions. Nevertheless, he was resolute that their research had shown that in the passion Luke had reworked independent traditions and not merely revised Markan parallels. He did not admit that this proved that Q and lk S (L) were already joined to a special Lukan tradition of the passion nor that Luke employed a combination of Q and lk S[141].

As regards Dibelius's view that the Lukan passion was an imitation of an account of Jewish martyrs, Schneider maintained that it was still an open question whether this was due to Luke or to pre-Lukan tradition[142]. He further critiqued the works of authors such as Conzelmann and George who treated Lukan theology warning they "können nicht unterschiedslos den Charakter einer redaktions-

---

137. JEREMIAS, *Abendmahlsworte*, ³1960, p. 91f. Cf. above.

138. SCHNEIDER, p. 13, n. 18. DIBELIUS, *Formgeschichte*, p. 200, 204; SCHMIDT, *Rahmen*, p. 303-308; FINEGAN, *Überlieferung*, p. 35 (and passim); GROBEL, *Formgeschichte*, p. 104; SCHICK, *Formgeschichte*, p. 40; and BULTMANN, *Geschichte* (⁵1961), *Ergänzungsheft* (1958), p. 42.

139. SCHNEIDER, p. 14, n. 19. HAWKINS, *Passion-Narrative* [Schneider's bibliography (p. 227) listed only the 1911 edition of the article]; PERRY, *Sources*, esp. p. 105; STREETER, *Gospels*, p. 202; TAYLOR, *Behind*, p. 33-75; 176f.; OSTY (*Points*); VAGANAY (*Problème*, p. 307-311); WINTER, *Treatment*, esp. p. 170ff.; TYSON, *Lucan Version*; BUSE, *St. John*.

140. SCHNEIDER, p. 14-15. See also the discussion, p. 141-145. It had been noted that Schürmann's efforts to revive the special source theory served as a model for Schneider (F. NEIRYNCK, *ETL* 48 [1972] 570). Part of Schneider's rationale in chosing 22,54-71 was that Schürmann, K.G. Kuhn (*Jesus in Gethsemane*, in *EvTh* 12 [1952-53] 260-285), and Rehkopf already investigated 22,7-38.39-46.47-53 (*Verleugnung*, p. 17-18), and Schürmann called for more analyses of individual pericopes.

141. At one point Schneider hypothesized: "Vielleicht ergibt sich daraus, dass die Redenquelle (Q) doch eine P enthalten hat (die Frage an Jesus auSt berührt sich mit der mt/lk Frage des Teufels in der Versuchungsgeschichte; dazu oben S. 56 Nr. 31) und somit eine Evv-Schrift gewesen ist" (p. 117). Neirynck called attention to this: "et comme l'emploi de εἰ en XXII, 67 peut être rapproché de IV, 3.9, il est suggéré que le récit de la passion faisait partie de Q (p. 117, cfr p. 56). On croit apercevoir pendant un moment l'ombre de E. Hirsch! Mais n'insistons pas et revenons à la thèse principale du livre" (*ETL* 48, 1972, 572).

142. SCHNEIDER, p. 21.

geschichtlichen Untersuchung beanspruchen ... In beiden Fällen müsste das
endgültige Urteil jedoch auf dem festeren Fundament einer traditionsgeschichtlichen
Untersuchung der lk Perikope aufruhen"[143].

Lk 22,54-62 (Verleugnung)

Schneider concluded that the denial story (22,54-61), with the exception of v.
59a.b and 61a, stemmed essentially from Mk[144]. Those verses which did not
derive directly from Mk were the result of free Lukan redaction. Luke made
various changes in order to shield Peter. The order of the scenes was due to Luke
and above all to the non-Markan *Vorlage*[145].

In *Passion* (1973), Schneider continued to adhere to his view that 22,54.-61
was based upon Mk and was an improvement of it linguistically and stylistically.
Not only that, the Lukan version improved the portrayal of Peter and sought to
provide understanding of his behavior[146]. In *Lukas* (1977) Schneider affirmed that
the only source for Peter's denials was Mk 14,(54).66-72[147].

Schneider only noted in *Passion* (1973) that the denial and mockery occurred
before the trial[148]. However, with the publication of *Lukas* it appeared that the
evangelist was as responsible for the order as the special source. The new
arrangement was related to the fact that while the mockery and trial were drawn
from the *Sonderquelle*, Luke had to put the denial ahead of them since the trial
occurred in the morning (22,66a)[149].

Lk 22,63-65 (Verspottung)

Schneider maintained that it was not out of the question that Luke wrote ἐπηρώτων
(22,64) himself as a reminiscence of Mk 14,60.61[150]. Concerning the use of
ἐπερωτάω followed by λέγων (λέγοντες) Schneider penned: "Man kann aus
diesem Befund nicht schliessen, dass diese Konstruktion, deren Substanz ἐπερωτάω
ist, von Luk eigenmächtig verwendet würde"[151].

Although Schneider ascribed v. 63a.b to Luke's adoption of a non-Markan
Vorlage, he did not exclude the possibility that Luke redacted Mk at vv. 63a and
64b.d and that v. 64c was probably taken over from Mk[152]. In his view the

---

143. *Ibid.*, p. 22-23. Cf. CONZELMANN, *Die Mitte*, 1954, and GEORGE, *Jésus*, 1965.
144. *Verleugnung*, p. 138. See his literary-critical analysis, p. 73-96.
145. *Ibid.*, p. 138, #9.
146. SCHNEIDER, *Die Passion Jesu nach den drei älteren Evangelien*, Munich, 1973, p. 80.
See also p. 67.
147. *Das Evangelium nach Lukas* (ÖTNT 3,1/2), Gütersloh - Würzburg, 1977, ²1984, p. 464.
148. *Passion*, p. 80.
149. *Lukas*, p. 464. G. KLEIN, *Verleugnung* and E. HAENCHEN, *Weg Jesu*, were cited as
supporters of a special tradition for the Lukan denials. Catchpole was not mentioned.
150. SCHNEIDER, *Verleugnung*, p. 101.
151. *Ibid.* Schneider listed eight instances in the Gospel (plus one in Acts) where Luke used
a finite form of ἐπερωτάω with λέγων following. Excluding 22,64, two were special Lukan
(3,10.14), four were parallel to Mk (9,18; 18,18; 20,27f.; 21,7) and one differed from Mk
(20,21).
152. SCHNEIDER, *Verleugnung*, p. 99, 100, 103, 138, #3. In a subsequent article he gave us

introductory καί bound the mockery and denial scenes closely together. This καί in Mk 14,65 was more than one of his numerous καί's, a usage which Luke frequently avoided. He may have been inspired in this close connection by Mk 14,65[153].

Günther Klein (1961) regarded the absence of the name "Jesus" as an indication of the original pre-Lukan context in which v. 63 followed immediately upon v. 54a[154]. For Klein who argued that the insertion of the denial was pre-Lukan, Linnemann countered, arguing that it was due to Luke himself[155]. But contrary to both Linnemann and Klein, Schneider posited that, although the discrepancy indeed went back to Lukan redaction, it rested upon the insertion of Markan material (the denial) into a non-Markan context[156].

Regarding ἄρχομαι, there were twenty-six places where this term occurs in Mk with the infinitive: there were sixteen parallels in Lk but only three where ἄρχομαι remained. Schneider reasoned that συνέχω can positively go back to the hand of Luke[157].

Schneider argued that it was not entirely clear why, if Luke retained the reference to spitting in the third passion prediction (18,32), he did not carry over the Markan reference in this verse[158]. He also noted that δέροντες standing near the participle συνέχοντες produced a formal parallel with v. 64a,b. δέροντες can be assumed to be original. But it remained problematic whether Luke wrote this verb himself[159].

Also noting the lack of references to the Servant, Schneider suggested that the Servant of God theology perhaps no longer played a role in the time of Luke. To resolve this dilemma, he proposed that Luke probably followed a tradition which did not consider the mockery scene as a fulfillment of Is 50,6[160].

The Lukan participle καὶ περικαλύψαντες can be regarded as a substitute for Mk and indeed the assumption of Markan dependence was unavoidable (Mk 14,65; Lk 22,64a; Heb 9,4)[161]. While the blindfolding was not necessary for the Markan

---

insight into his understanding of the non-Markan *Vorlage.* "Wer für eine selbständige lukanische Passionsüberlieferung (neben Mk) eintritt, muss das nicht im Sinne der Protolukas-Theorie tun, die unter 'Protolukas' ein selbständiges Evangelium (neben Mk) versteht. Die Frage einer eigenständigen vorlukanischen Passionstradition ist nicht mit der Ablehnung der Protolukas-Hypothese erledigt" (*Das Problem,* 1972, 222-244, p. 235 = 213-235, 226). See below, n. 273.

153. *Verleugnung*, p. 97.

154. *Ibid.* See G. KLEIN, *Die Verleugnung des Petrus. Eine traditionsgeschichtliche Untersuchung,* in *ZTK* 58 (1961) 291, 295 (= *Rekonstruktion*, p. 54, 59). Cf. above.

155. LINNEMANN, *Studien*, p. 97-98.

156. SCHNEIDER, *Verleugnung*, p. 98. Cf. LINNEMANN, *Verleugnung*, p. 27.

157. SCHNEIDER, *Verleugnung*, p. 99. The word was not un-Lukan since it appeared three times in material different from Mk (4,38; 8,37.45) as well as in special Lukan material (12,50; 19,43).

158. *Ibid.*

159. *Ibid.*, p. 100. Two verses with Markan parallels contained the verb (20,10.11) in addition to two verses in Lukan special material (12,47.48).

160. *Ibid.* Cf. SCHNEIDER, *Gab es*, in *NT* 12 (1970) 37 (= 273).

161. SCHNEIDER, *Verleugnung*, p. 100.

sense of "play the prophet for us", the Lukan concept of prophesy would require it[162]. But it was not clear why Luke deleted the Markan κολαφίζειν in favor of δέροντες. For both exegetes, v. 63 was from the non-Markan special tradition, although Schneider did not exclude the prospect of redaction of Mk by Luke, at least in the first part of the verse.

Catchpole and Schneider took different positions concerning the term προφήτευσον (v. 64) and it was this single word that provided the critical grounds for their respective decisions. Schneider argued that because προφήτευσον (v. 64), which had the meaning of prophetic revelation of the hidden, occurred only here in the Synoptics and in the imperative form, this alone was sufficient indication that Luke can be dependent upon Mk[163]. Conceding that the question τίς ἐστιν ὁ παίσας σε; was not obvious in the probable pre-Lukan context, he noted that Luke had an interest in emphasizing Jesus as a prophet. Thus, he could have adopted the Markan challenge and given it a new interpretation according to his sense.

Schneider was not so reserved as Catchpole in offering an opinion on the origin of the final verse of the mockery. Allowing that two elements have a certain correspondence with Mk, he pointed out that ἕτερος was a preferred Lukan term[164]. In Luke's mind, the redaction could have come about in v. 65a as a combination of the Markan mockery with the non-Markan Vorlage. Because the form βλασφημοῦντες was found in the Gospels only here in Lk, with three additional references in Acts (13,45; 18,6; 19,37), the plural of the participle may thus be considered Lukan. For these reasons he opted for a judgment of probable free Lukan redaction for v. 65a.b[165].

Sharing the opinion that v. 63 stemmed from a non-Markan Vorlage, Schneider tempered the certitude with the conjecture that at least for v. 63a, Luke may have redacted Mk[166]. Verse 64 can reflect Markan dependence because of the use of the term προφήτευσον and v. 65 stemmed in all probability from Luke's free redaction. Thus, two certain elements, and perhaps more, were considered by Schneider to be Markan. In contrast to Catchpole, he insisted that the order, which

162. Ibid., p. 101.

163. Ibid., p. 102, though he added: "nicht-mk Vorlage jedoch nicht unmöglich". Cf. SCHNEIDER, Lukas, 1977, ²1984, p. 465: "Auch in der Verspottungsszene ist mit redaktionellen Elementen zu rechnen. Abgesehen von der Schlussbemerkung (V 65), die eine freie Bildung des Evangelisten darstellt, kann man auch bei der Aufforderung "Sag uns, Prophet!" (prophēteuson = rede prophetisch! [zum Erweis deines Anspruches]) an eine Einfügung (als Übernahme aus Mk V 65) in den vorgegebenen Text denken".

164. SCHNEIDER, Verleugnung, p. 103-104. καί corresponded perhaps to the fifth and last καί in Mk 14,65. Further, βλασφημοῦντες could be a reminiscence of Mk 14,64 (p. 103).

165. Ibid., p. 103-104. Cf. SCHNEIDER, Passion, p. 69: "Den Vers 65 indessen hat Lukas von sich aus gebildet". See also Lukas, 1977, p. 465. Cf. n. 69 above.

166. SCHNEIDER, Verleugnung, p. 97. This position was entertained because Luke could have been inspired by Mk in the use of καί in connecting the mockery closely with the trial.

involved the mockery before the trial, was due primarily to the non-Markan source[167].

In 1973 Schneider ascribed the origin of 22,63-64 to a (written) special source with v. 65 having been formed by Luke himself[168]. He further asserted that because of the evidence of Jesus' pre-knowledge Luke took up the Markan challenge to "prophesy"[169]. In the commentary Schneider highlighted Benoit as a supporter of a special source for the mockery, referring to his own dissertation in support of the claim that it was derived from a special source[170]. He continued to regard v. 65 as a formulation of the evangelist[171].

While the *Sonderquelle* was cited as responsible for the order of the pericopes (1973)[172], in *Lukas* (1977) the order was directly related to Luke's drawing on the special source. Luke was constrained to situate the denial and mockery over against the trial. The new sequence was dictated by the fact that Luke's version of the trial took place in the morning[173].

Lk 22,66-71 (Verhör)

Although Schneider argued that the phrase ὡς ἐγένετο ἡμέρα reflected probable Lukan redaction of the Markan *Vorlage* (Mk 15,1), he left open the possibility that Luke reworked a non-Markan (or pre-Markan) tradition[174].

---

167. SCHNEIDER, p. 138, #9.

168. SCHNEIDER, *Passion*, p. 67-68, 69.

169. *Ibid.*, p. 69: "Lukas hat wahrscheinlich die markinische Aufforderung zum 'Prophezeien' aufgegriffen, weil ihm nachweislich auch sonst am Vorauswissen Jesu gelegen war". Cf. also G. SCHNEIDER, *Lukas*, 1977, ²1984, p. 466-467.

170. *Lukas*, p. 464. See *Verleugnung*, p. 137-139, and BENOIT, *Les outrages*.

171. SCHNEIDER, *Lukas*, p. 465.

172. *Passion*, p. 67.

173. *Lukas*, p. 464.

174. *Verleugnung*, p. 106-107. One should also note his concluding comments for v. 66 (p. 112), where he opposed the idea that the time information in v. 66a was connected in the pre-Lukan context with vv. 63-64(65) and v. 66d since the story could have been told without that detail. Luke himself could have added the information and thus there is no need for recourse to a pre-Lukan tradition.

His 1988 contribution removed all ambiguity when he joined R. Pesch in asserting that the information of a morning session was not passed on in a special tradition. "Zusammenfassend kann man mit Pesch sagen: 'Die Morgensitzung des Synedrions in einem vom Haus des Hohenpriesters ... verschiedenen Sitzungslokal ist von Lukas in seiner Mk-Redaktion im Blick auf die Parallelszenen der Apg aufgrund schriftstellerischer historischer Logik konzipiert worden; sie war nicht in einer Sondertradition überliefert'" (*Das Verfahren gegen Jesus in der Sicht des dritten Evangeliums (Lk 22,54 - 23,25). Redaktionskritik und historische Rückfrage*, in K. KERTELGE [ed.], *Der Prozess gegen Jesus. Historische Rückfrage und theologische Deutung* [QD, 112], Freiburg - Basel - Vienna, 1988, p. 117 = *Jesusüberlieferung*, 282). This article, as well as that of W. RADL, *Sonderüberlieferungen bei Lukas? Traditionsgeschichtliche Fragen zu Lk 22,67f; 23,2; und 23,6-12*, in the same volume, p. 131-147, were among the presentations at a meeting of the German language Catholic NT scholars in Graz, Austria in Spring, 1987.

Schneider and Catchpole disagreed further on the relation of 22,66 and Mk 15,1. Catchpole asserted complete independence[175] while Schneider held that v. 66a-c was probably dependent upon Mk[176] and v. 66d reflected the probable redaction of a non-Markan *Vorlage*, although he left open the possibility that Luke could also have redacted Mk at that point[177].

To indicate parallels, Schneider listed Mk 15,1 (Mk 14,53b) and Mt 27,1 (Mt 26,57b). Citing weak agreement with Mk, he observed two striking similarities with Mt[178]. The Matthean parallels consisted of the use of συνάγομαι with the Sanhedrin and the genitive designation τοῦ λαοῦ. συνήχθη was not regarded as a typical addition, but reflected a preferred term of the Matthean passion. This speech usage appeared to also have been available to Luke. Schneider showed that Luke was exposed to the Markan use of συνήχθη (5,21) which he also opted to change.

The τοῦ λαοῦ can also be due to a tradition which Luke commonly drew upon with Matthew. He concluded that v. 66b was due probably to Lukan redaction of the Markan *Vorlage*, in addition to use of a tradition which Mt also offered[179]. In a postscript Schneider stated that Luke may have followed the Markan συμβούλιον ἑτοιμάσαντες with his observation of the coming together of the *presbyterium*. But if Luke had understood the Markan use in this sense, it was not entirely clear why he changed Mark's version. Hence, the possibility existed that Luke followed a non-Markan tradition[180].

Though Catchpole dismissed the phrase ἀρχιερεῖς ... καὶ γραμματεῖς as commonplace, Schneider took a different stance. The particle τε occurred more often in Lk than in the other Synoptics and in all of the Lukan places we have τε καί[181]. Thus its use in 22,66c was a sign of Lukan redaction. For this verse part he opted for probable Lukan redaction, more so of Mk than of a special source[182].

The term ἀπάγω, indicative of legal speech, had a less technical sense in Mk and Lk than in Mt[183]. Verse 66d was best understood as deriving from a non-Markan *Vorlage* because of Luke's preference for ἄγω over ἀπάγω in contrast to Mk/Mt[184]. The phrase εἰς τὸ συνέδριον αὐτῶν appeared to take up the Markan

---

175. CATCHPOLE, p. 192.
176. *Ibid.*, p. 106-107, 108, 109.
177. SCHNEIDER, *Verleugnung*, p. 111, 112.
178. *Ibid.*, p. 107. Lk agreed with Mk only in the preposition συν- and the word stem πρεσβυτ-.
179. *Ibid.*, p. 108.
180. *Ibid.*
181. *Ibid.* Lk had it 9 times, Mt 3, but it never occurred in Mk.
182. *Ibid.*, p. 109.
183. *Ibid.*, p. 109-110.
184. *Ibid.*, p. 110. See p. 61, 63, 64, #2, 74. Schneider investigated the agreements of Lk and Jn which Mk did not offer and pointed to the use of ἤγαγον in Lk 22,54 and Jn 18,13. He also noted several similarities between Lk 22,66 and Jn 18,24 although John did not use

Vorlage. But in contrast to Mk it possibly also referred to the meeting place (*pace* Winter)[185]. Because v. 66d was Luke's only reference to συνέδριον, he could have taken it from Mk. These observations lead him to conclude that there was a great amount of Lukan redaction at this verse part, though it was scarcely possible to determine which *Vorlage* the evangelist used[186].

Because the incongruity remained between v. 66 a-c (probably dependent upon Mk) and v. 66d, (probably Lukan redaction of a non-Markan *Vorlage*, though not entirely excluding Lukan redaction of Mk) the suspicion arose that Luke drew these elements together as they enclosed the trial, mockery and denial[187]. Schneider declared that an opinion of Markan dependence can be based only upon individual linguistic elements and not upon the essential points of the matter which vary a great deal[188]. Once again, Schneider and Catchpole arrived at notably different results. However, we move next to verses upon which there was significant agreement.

While Catchpole insisted that the extent of the Lukan special material should be expanded to include 22,70, Schneider concluded that the trial scene rested partly upon the non-Markan *Vorlage* (essentially vv. 66-68), but that vv. 69-71 depended in their entirety upon Mk[189]. Because two *Vorlagen* had been blended it was scarcely possible at times to separate the sources into individual parts or units[190]. We will examine aspects of his detailed inquiry to understand how he arrived at results at variance with his British counterpart.

Stating that Luke could have reworked the Markan *Vorlage* for λέγοντες (v. 67a), he recalled that Luke often improved Markan Greek through the use of participles. Luke's use of λέγοντες, in particular, was exceptionally well attested[191].

In v. 67b the Lk-Mk agreements were limited to the four words σὺ εἶ ὁ χριστός. Because the phrase was encountered in Mt 16,16 (= Mk 8,29) it can

---

ἀπήγαγον as Luke did. In general, Luke was not reluctant to employ words with the prefix ἀπο-. In his use of καὶ εἰσήγαγον in this context, diff/Mk, Luke avoided the preposition προσ-. J. JEREMIAS, *Die Sprache des Lukasevangeliums*, Göttingen, 1980, p. 296, in observing that 22,54 was redactional, noted that εἰσήγαγον was a term preferred by Luke. He referred also to 2,27. While Luke did not borrow the Markan term ἀπήνεγκαν from Mk 15,1, is it nonetheless possible that he borrowed ἀπήγαγον from Mk 14,53a?

185. SCHNEIDER, *Verleugnung*, p. 110.

186. *Ibid.*, p. 111.

187. *Ibid.* In his addendum he maintained the possibility of Markan dependence existed above all for Mk 15,1.

188. *Ibid.*, p. 112.

189. SCHNEIDER, *Verleugnung*, p. 138, #4. Summarily offering his findings: "Wahrscheinlich beruhen Lk 22,63-64 (65) und 66-68 (69?) auf dieser nicht-mk Quelle. Erst von V. 69 an folgt Luk wahrscheinlich der Mk-Vorlage" (p. 130). Cf. *Passion*, 1973, p. 70, which pointed to the non-Lukan nature of the vocabulary and evidence of pre-Lukan traditions also present in Jn 10,24f.

190. *Verleugnung*, p. 138, #6 and #8.

191. *Ibid.* p. 112.

have its origin in Mk. Further agreements with Mt, as well as with Jn, were also noted[192]. The imperative εἰπόν probably belonged to the non-Markan tradition. The absence of the Markan τοῦ εὐλογητοῦ was simply explained as omitted by Luke and Matthew. He deduced that a non-Markan tradition, containing vocabulary as also found at Jn 10,24c and traces of Mt, was taken over by Luke.

In addition, he posited the possible adoption of a non-Markan *Vorlage* for v. 67c, although he did not exclude redaction of Mk by Luke. Acknowledging that the formulation εἶπεν δὲ αὐτοῖς was attested in the NT only by Luke, which can reflect pre-Lukan ways of speaking[193], Luke himself could have omitted the name "Jesus".

Noting the Johannine character of Jesus' response in v. 67d, that Luke had a noticeable dislike for ἐάν, and that the individual elements appeared to be non-Lukan, he decided in favor of the probable adoption of a non-Markan *Vorlage*. He chose this over an oral tradition besides Mk[194]. Hence, his overall assessment for the entirety of v. 67 was that Luke probably adopted a non-Markan *Vorlage*[195].

Verse 68a contained no Synoptic parallel. It was in this connection that Schneider referred to Lk 20,1-8 (= Mt 21,23-27 par Mk 11,27-33) and declared that the Matthean and Lukan wording betrayed not simply varied Markan material, but an independent tradition besides Mk[196]. This was found partly in the answer of Jesus. Eight instances of MAs of Mt-Lk against Mk explained an independent tradition for Mt and Lk. The judgment on the origin of 22,68a was for the probable adoption of a non-Markan *Vorlage* by Luke[197].

Like Catchpole, Schneider considered the οὐ μή of v. 68b to be non-Lukan[198]. Because Luke had no special preference for the verb ἀποκρίνομαι, it was improbable that Luke composed/placed (*gesetz*) this himself. The evaluation remained unchanged from the first half of the verse: Luke adopted a non-Markan *Vorlage*[199].

---

192. *Ibid.*, p. 113. These include εἰ; εἰπόν (-ης); ἡμῖν.

193. *Ibid.*, p. 114. He referred to three Mt-Lk agreements to support this possibility.

194. *Ibid.*, p. 115.

195. *Ibid.*, p. 116. Schneider left open the possibility of Lukan redaction of Mk for λέγοντες and also, but to a lesser degree, for σὺ εἶ ὁ χριστός and εἶπεν δέ.

196. *Ibid.*, p. 117. Borrowing from Léon-Dufour, *Passion*, 1965, Schneider contended that the answer of Jesus reflected a prophetic manner and further suggested that it stemmed from a relatively old tradition from Palestine (p. 33-34). He referred to this later in the book (p. 164). See also *Passion*, 1973, p. 70. Further, he made a passing reference in a note to the similarity to 20,1-8, where Jesus left his opponents dumbfounded and refused to answer (p. 35, n. 71).

197. SCHNEIDER, *Verleugnung*, p. 117.

198. *Ibid.*, p. 118. See CATCHPOLE, p. 196.

199. SCHNEIDER, *Verleugnung*, p. 138. His dissertation findings on vv. 67-68 were phrased in the following way: "Mit Sicherheit kann der nicht-mk Quelle zugeschrieben werden das Herrenwort der VV. 67d-68b. Wahrscheinlich erzählte sie nach der Gefangennahme die Verbringung Jesu in das Haus des Hohenpriesters (entsprechend dem V. 54a.b), dann die Verspottung (VV. 63-64), darauf (vielleicht noch ohne Terminangabe wie im V. 66a) die Vorführung Jesu im Synedrium und das Verhör (VV. 66-68), anschliessend die Überbringung

Schneider made a case for the probability of a non-Markan tradition in v. 69a since in the wording there were no agreements between Mk and Lk, but there were between Mt and Lk[200]. This was further indicated by the presence of ἔσται[201]. While not dismissing the possibility of Lukan redaction of Mk, probability sided once more with Luke's adoption of a non-Markan *Vorlage*. A strong suspicion existed that there was, in addition to Mk, a special tradition of a dominical saying. This piece of tradition perhaps contained only the saying about the exaltation of Jesus, without being introduced by the word ὄψεσθε[202].

Advancing further, v. 69b showed signs of probable Lukan redaction of the Markan *Vorlage*. Contributing to this assessment were the following particulars: τοῦ θεοῦ can be understood as a Lukan addition, in light of Luke's predilection for ὁ θεός[203]. This addition can certainly be regarded as Lukan redaction because the Markan *Vorlage* had spoken of God's power in a veiled manner. The change in word order could reflect changes from Mk, making appeal to the non-Markan *Vorlage* unnecessary. The Lukan ἔσται reflected the penchant to draw as close as possible to the accompanying participle[204]. If Luke followed and adapted the Markan account it was because the parousia was to be visible to all (Lk 21,27) and Jesus, sitting at the right hand of God, was manifest only to those witnesses who believed (cf. Acts 7,56)[205].

According to Schneider free Lukan redaction can explain v. 70a and its lack of parallels[206]. Since the combination εἶπαν δέ can be considered a Lukan characteristic, so too can δὲ πάντες. While he insisted it was hardly taken over from Mk, this generalizing observation was a Lukan peculiarity, while Catchpole admitted only that in 22,70 it may be[207]. Schneider declared, nonetheless, that

---

Jesu zu Pilatus (23,1f.)".

200. *Verleugnung*, p. 118-119. He concluded that v. 69a was probably due to a non-Markan *Vorlage*, while conceding that Lukan redaction of the Markan *Vorlage* was not impossible (p. 120). The weight of both possibilities seemed to be equally distributed when in 1973 he wrote: "Vers 69 wird nun – vielleicht selbständig, vielleicht aber auch in Abwandlung der Mk-Vorlage – die sessio a dextris des Menschensohnes angekündigt" (*Passion*, p. 70). Next, in his commentary he declared: "VV 69-71 sind hingegen von Mk (VV 62b-64) abhängig" (*Lukas*, 1977, ²1984, p. 468). Finally, again repeating the relationship to Mk, he stated: "Die Aussage Jesu wird in Vers 69 (im Anschluss an Mk 14, 62b) weitergeführt: Der Messias Jesus ist der Menschensohn, der "von nun an zur Rechten der Kraft Gottes sitzen wird". Dass er, "mit den Wolken des Himmels kommen" werde (Mk 14, 62b), übergeht Lukas" (*Das Verfahren*, 1988, p. 115 = 280).

201. *Verleugnung*, p. 119.

202. *Ibid.*, p. 120.

203. *Ibid.*, p. 121. He saw in Kuhn a confirmation of this view. "Luk 22,69 zeigt durch den Zusatz τοῦ θεοῦ, dass ihm (bzw. seinen Lesern) dieser Sprachgebrauch nicht geläufig war" (K.G. KUHN, *Sifre zu Numeri* [Rabbinische Texte 2/2], Stuttgart, 1959, p. 148, n. 10).

204. *Verleugnung*, p. 121.

205. *Ibid.*, p. 122.

206. *Ibid.* He pointed out that the phrase οἱ δὲ πάντες occurred at Mk 14,64.

207. *Ibid.* Cf. CATCHPOLE, p. 201, 193-194.

a consideration of the vocabulary and context of both phrases (εἶπαν δέ, δὲ πάντες) showed them to be Lukan, concluding that free Lukan redaction was probable[208].

The Son of God question according to Mk, in the view of Schneider, was taken up in v. 70 and redactionally attached to the messiah question[209]. The origin of this part of the verse was ascribed to probable free Lukan redaction[210].

Schneider pointed out that v. 70b agreed with Mk 14,61 in the use of the direct question, although it contained some variations. Luke omitted ὁ χριστός and changed τοῦ εὐλογητοῦ to τοῦ θεοῦ, the latter agreeing with Mt 26,63[211]. Catchpole reasoned that the οὖν in v. 70 was used by Luke simply as a connective, in which case it may be original[212]. Schneider contended this indicated Lukan redaction on the basis of statistics[213]. If Luke inserted the οὖν this would support the position that Luke adopted from Mk the Son of God question and redactionally attached the Christ question. He concluded that it was probable that Luke lightly redacted the Markan *Vorlage*[214].

There was no direct parallel for v. 70c although the ὁ δέ of Mk 14,62, he suggested, should be noted. The formulation was explicable by Lukan redaction. The construction ὁ δέ ... ἔφη occurred three times in Lk all of which were Lukan redaction of Mk[215]. In light of this, his judgment was for nearly free Lukan redaction[216].

It will be observed that the ἐγώ εἰμι (v. 70d) agreed with and depended upon Mk[217]. The ὅτι can be ascribed to Lukan redaction. A corresponding construc-

---

208. SCHNEIDER, *Verleugnung*, p. 123.

209. *Ibid.*, p. 124. In a later essay (1970), he maintained that Luke was partly responsible for separating the messiah and divine son titles (*Jesus*, p. 10 = *Lukas, Theologe*, 167). The non-Markan *Vorlage* contained only reference to Jesus as messiah. Shortly thereafter Schneider mused that in all probability, Luke combined the non-Markan tradition with the Markan presentation. The evangelist was also now fully credited with separating the two titles. Far from retaining the primitive, separate tradition, he no longer possessed their original profile. What was more, Schneider maintained that the Son of God appellation surpassed the messiah title (*Passion*, p. 71). It was evident that Luke had read the Markan text, but it was unclear why he should have omitted the testimony of the witnesses, unless of course, he was following a special *Vorlage* (p. 72). Cf. *Das Verfahren*, p. 118 (= 283): "Während bei Markus 'Christus' und 'Sohn des Hochgelobten' nebeneinanderstehen (Mk 14,61), werden diese Titel entsprechend lukanischem Verständnis voneinander getrennt".

210. But in *Verleugnung* he added: "Wenn eine Vorlage in Frage kommt, so sind Mk und eine nicht-mk Tr möglich" (p. 123).

211. *Ibid.*

212. CATCHPOLE, *Trial*, p. 197. He listed eight parallels in support of his position.

213. SCHNEIDER, *Verleugnung*, p. 123. The preponderance of evidence was found in the occurrences in Acts. Occasions in Lk where οὖν occurred in questions following introductory interrogative pronouns numbered six (p. 124).

214. *Ibid.*, p. 124.

215. *Ibid.*, p. 125.

216. *Ibid.*

217. Cf. SCHNEIDER, *Gab es*, p. 36 (= 272), where he stated that the Markan ἐγώ εἰμι was

tion, found at the beginning of a speech by Peter (Acts 15,7), helped to support this finding. Once again, in Schneider's estimation, the characteristics signaled the hand of Luke who probably redacted the Markan *Vorlage*[218].

Consistent with the stance set forth in his dissertation, in 1973 Schneider argued that regarding the Christ question one could also think of the influence of oral tradition[219], a view he seemed to have abandoned in *Lukas*, favoring instead the idea that Luke drew from non-Markan written sources[220]. Observing that vv. 67b.68 had no Markan parallel, he posited that vv. 66-68 probably followed in essence the *Sonderquelle* which already laid at the base of 22,63-65. In his 1988 article, he tempered his view stating that it was possible that Luke drew from a special tradition besides Mk, above all for the beginning of the scene (Lk 22,66-68)[221].

He began his evaluation of v. 71a by noting in v. 71a the similarity of the οἱ δέ in the Synoptic accounts and reasoned that Luke's intention could have been adopted to abbreviate the attached part of the scene[222]. What was more, Luke had not given prominence to the high priest, a fact that was underscored by the change from the singular λέγει to the plural εἶπαν[223]. The presentation of the high priest in a prominent light was based upon the non-Markan *Vorlage*. Nonetheless, it was probable that Luke continued to redact Mk[224].

Even though v. 71b resembled Mk 14,63b very closely it was important to note two variations. Not only did Luke have testimony (μαρτυρίας) instead of witnesses (μαρτύρων), he also changed the Markan word order of χρείαν ἔχομεν. Lukan redaction of Mk was the best explanation according to the German exegete, in light of the use of vocabulary in this verse part[225]. The change of word order was advisable as long as Luke had not reported the statements of the witnesses. Consequently, μαρτυρίας received special emphasis[226]. He considered light Lukan redaction of Mk probable.

---

appended in 22,70 in an indirect manner. In Catchpole's appendix, he took notice of Schneider's position that Mk 14,61-62, a Markan construction, provided the raw material for Lk 22,70. Schneider contended that the Son of God title without additional reference to messiah was unique as it stood "in a human confession and in a question introduced by σὺ εἶ" (*Trial*, p. 274-275; see SCHNEIDER, *Verleugnung*, p. 57, 123, 124).

218. *Verleugnung*, p. 126. Schneider also surmised that the imitation of a non-Markan tradition was possible.

219. SCHNEIDER, *Passion*, 1973, p. 67.

220. *Lukas*, 1977, ²1984, p. 437.

221. *Das Verfahren*, 1988, p. 115-116.

222. *Ibid.*, p. 127.

223. *Ibid.*, p. 127-128. He referred to SCHÜRMANN, *Paschamahlbericht*, p. 88, who observed that Luke replaced 31 of Mk's 72 occurrences of the present λέγει (-ουσιν, φησίν) with εἶπεν (-ον, -αν).

224. SCHNEIDER, *Verleugnung*, p. 128.

225. *Ibid.*

226. *Ibid.*, p. 129.

Turning to v. 71c he conjectured that ἠκούσατε could have been taken from
Mk and redactionally inserted into the words of the Sanhedrin. αὐτοί had already
been shown to be a preferred Lukan term[227]. Luke, on the other hand, was not
especially fond of γάρ. In observing all forms of the verb ἀκούω, the
preponderance of evidence lies with Luke because of its use in Acts[228]. The
solution, in this case, was the acceptance of Luke's possible redaction of Mk,
though the taking over of a non-Markan *Vorlage* was not impossible[229].

Because Luke opted to use ἀπό in v. 71d, rather than the more common ἐκ,
it ought to be assumed that he intentionally employed this form to imitate biblical
speech, though he was evidently familiar with both forms. He took great delight
in a variety of phrasing. Insofar as αὐτοῦ following στόματος was encountered
three times in Lk (twice in special material) and once in Acts, one should
recognize the hand of Luke[230]. Free Lukan redaction was probable. Following
his analysis of 22,54-71, Schneider offered a schematic of the results[231].

The Minor Agreements (22,62.64)

Schneider concluded that Luke had probably taken over a non-Markan *Vorlage*
which was also represented in Mt. Considering the pre-Lukan context, it was
probable that Luke was not originally responsible for placing the question here.
Musing on the various feasible explanations, he acknowledged that Lukan redaction
of Mk, however, was not impossible. In this case, the occurrence in Mt went back
secondarily to Lk[232]. Because of this agreement, it was probable that Luke and
Matthew were dependent upon the same tradition but the question was original in
the Lukan context. Still, it was not inconceivable that Luke wrote τίς ἐστιν
himself[233]. If that were the case, the puzzle was solved with the explanation of
early conformity of Matthew's text to that of Lk.

Conclusion

Following an in-depth investigation of 22,54-71 Schneider concluded that Luke
used a non-Markan source for the mockery and the beginning of the Sanhedrin trial
as his primary source, but inserted the Markan account of Peter's denials and
added some vital information from the Markan version of the trial to round out the

227. *Ibid.*, p. 130.
228. *Ibid.*, p. 131. There were 89 occurrences of the verb in Acts with an additional 65 in
Lk.
229. *Ibid.*
230. *Ibid.*, p. 132. Lk 4,22 *Sondergut*; 11,54 *Sonderverse*, 22,71 and Acts 22,14.
231. *Ibid.*, p. 133 (Lk and Mk) and p. 134 (Lk and the non-Markan *Vorlage*). These
overviews of the individual results of the literary-critical investigation were also published as
"Beilage" to the study.
232. *Ibid.*, p. 103.
233. *Ibid.*

narrative[234]. More specifically, he ascribed the following verses to Mk: 22,54-61.64c(probably).69-71 and possibly a part of 66-67c. However, in 54.55.69-71 non-Markan influence was "nicht unmöglich". A special non-Markan source was responsible for vv. 63-64.66-68, but some Markan influence was not excluded in 63.64.66-67. Lukan redaction was credited with 59a.b.61a(probably).64c.65a.b.70a.71d. Luke redacted all the material in the course of joining the Markan version of the denials with the non-Markan mockery and trial scene. It was probable, in Schneider's estimation, that only vv. 67d-68b remained untouched by Lukan redaction[235].

The order was due primarily to the non-Markan source, but Luke inserted the account of the denials between the non-Markan versions of the arrest and mockery resulting in the present arrangement[236]. The original order of the special source consisted in the material corresponding to 54a.b; 63-64.66(possibly without the temporal reference)-68; 23,1f. Finally, it was the highest probability that the MA in 22,62 was secondary, having been inserted from Mt, while the MA in 22,64 was probably due to Luke and Matthew being dependent upon a similar tradition (to which he added that the question was more original in the Lukan context)[237].

Reactions to Schneider

The overall evaluation in the reviews of Schneider's efforts in *Verleugnung* was extremely positive, though not without disagreement[238]. Reviewers often commented on the thoroughness of the research and how it would advance the study of the passion narrative. While generally convinced J. Galot distanced himself from Schneider's position that the Sanhedrin hearing was only a

---

234. *Ibid.*, p. 139.

235. *Ibid.*, p. 138. Lukan redaction was indicated by a more positive portrayal of Peter, but also by characteristic linguistic and stylistic traits.

236. *Ibid.*, p. 138, #9 and 147-148, ##8, 9, 10, 11.

237. *Ibid.*, p. 139. For 22,64 see p. 102. In a 1995 contribution on Q and the MAs, Neirynck pointed out that Schneider responded to Hirsch's suggestion that Q contained a passion narrative. Schneider proposed haltingly that such a view was possible (*The Minor Agreements and Q*, p. 51; cf. SCHNEIDER, *Verleugnung*, p. 117 [Mk 11,27-33 par.], 56 [22,68a]; 47-60 [Mt-Lk agreements]).

238. J. GALOT, in *Greg* 51 (1970) 771: "L'ensemble de l'ouvrage est de nature à faire progresser l'exégèse de la Passion, en fournissant les éléments d'une meilleure analyse du récit, de son fondement traditionel et de sa part de rédaction. Il stimulera également les efforts d'une plus pénétrante compréhension de la théologie sous-jacente de Luc." The detailed analysis and force of argumentation were convincing. Cf. T. VAN DEN ENDE, in *TT* 10 (1970) 455: "Deze redaktionsgeschichtlichestudie ... bevestigt opnieuw dat Lucas in zijn lijdensverhaal naast Marcus een aparte bron heeft gebruikt". Schneider's contribution to and indelible mark upon Lukan studies was indisputable. "G. Schneider heeft in dit werk een fundamentele bijdrage geleverd aan de redaktionsgeschichtlichte benadering van Lucas, waarbij vanuit een détailstudie tevens de resultaten van de 'totaal-studies' deels worden bevestigd en uitgediept, deels herzien en gerelativeerd".

preliminary investigation in preparation for the trial before Pilate. "On peut se demander si cette interprétation tient suffisamment compte de tous les éléments du récit évangélique, qui paraît retracer un procès juif juridiquement structuré avec une condamnation formelle"[239]. Galot also called attention to Schneider's disagreement with Conzelmann's division and interpretation[240].

In a review appearing in the *JBL*, N. Petersen judged that "the entire book is a useful commentary on Luke's passion narrative and its antecedent history"[241]. Impressed by the argumentation, the reviewer declared that "Schneider has convincingly demonstrated that there is special material in his chosen pericope"[242]. However, he critiqued Schneider for having recourse to a presumed non-Markan source rather than independent traditions[243]. Having voiced this caution, Petersen suggested further study to remedy the situation. "Moreover, the question of Luke's sequence of story units should not be directed to sources without a more careful consideration of Luke's composition"[244].

Citing chapters Two through Four as the most original part of the work, P. Benoit marveled at the extreme detail with which the work was carried out[245]. Conceding that his conclusions were quite plausible, Benoit cited this work as a victory over the tendency among many exegetes to see Mk as the principal source, not only here, but everywhere in the narratives[246]. He critiqued Schneider for considering the non-Markan source as a unique tradition, suggesting, rather, that one should think of several different traditions. At the very least one must contend with two varying traditions: that which Luke would have shared with Matthew and the other with John[247].

C.F.D. Moule, impressed by the great detail and painstaking thoroughness, compared Schneider's "scrutiny" to those of Schürmann and Rehkopf. "But the strength of the thesis is the cumulative nature of its findings; and, all uncertainties

---

239. *Greg* 51 (1970) 771.

240. *Ibid*: "En analysant les thèmes de Luc, l'auteur montre notamment comment pour l'évangéliste la vie et plus spécialement la passion de Jésus est le commencement du temps de l'Église. Dans ce domaine, il marque sa réserve à l'égard de la division proposée par Conzelmann et d'une interprétation psychologique et pragmatique du développement de la vie de Jésus".

241. *JBL* 89 (1970) 496-497.

242. *Ibid*., p. 497.

243. *Ibid*.: "... but his claim that it originated in a continuous passion source rather than in independent traditions is dubiously based on the *presumption* of a non-Markan source. It is only on the basis of this presumption that what was 'possible' as Markan becomes 'possible' as non-Markan".

244. *Ibid*.

245. *RB* 78 (1971) 136. See above.

246. *Ibid*.: "Elles représentent même une victoire sur la tendance de bien des exégètes, – peut-être même de Schneider lui-même avant sa recherche – à faire de Mc ici comme partout dans les recits la source principale".

247. *Ibid*. "Une chose toutefois m'embarrasse: Schneider parle sans cesse de *la* source non-marcienne comme d'une tradition unique. Ne doit-on pas songer plutôt à plusieurs traditions différentes à deux au moins dont l'une serait partagée par Lc avec Mt., et l'autre avec Jn"?

allowed for, a good case seems to emerge for believing, not merely that Lk used non-Markan tradition in the passion-narrative, but, further, that even in passages parallel to Mk, the differences from Mk, are by no means to be explained merely by Lukan editing. Rather, Lk was working with a written, self-contained, continuous narrative in addition to Mk's (p. 137ff., 143f. for summary conclusions), and possibly also using traditions available to Mt and traditions represented in Jn"[248]. Like Galot Moule also highlighted Schneider's conclusion "that the hearing before the Sanhedrin was a preliminary hearing rather than a formal trial leading to a verdict and sentence"[249].

J. Kremer praised Schneider for a remarkable, careful and illuminating study which would be used as a reference work. Although it was not easy reading, those who make the effort will be richly rewarded. He was convinced by Schneider's argumentation that older traditions probably form the basis for the Markan passion[250].

Like Benoit Kremer saw the conclusions of this study as a caution to overestimating Markan influence or limiting such influence to Mk alone. "Dass Lk in seiner Passion so stark von einer nicht-markinischen Vorlage abhängig ist, dürfte auch ein Licht auf andere Themenkreise der Evangelien werfen und vor einer Überschätzung bzw. Verabsolutierung des Mk bzw. der Mk-Vorlagen warnen"[251].

248. *JTS* 22 (1971) 196. Regarding the MAs, Moule observed: "An interesting by-product (in view of the current debates about Streeter) is the observation that the greater number of agreements of Mt and Lk against Mk, in the passage under examination, are to be explained by the independent use of the same methods" (p. 195).

249. *Ibid.*, p. 196.

250. *TPQ* 119 (1971) 176: "Zunächst weist Schneider nach, dass wahrscheinlich schon der markinischen Passion ältere Traditionen zugrunde lagen (26-46)".

251. *Ibid.*, p. 177. Later, Kremer wrote a commentary on Lk in which he maintained that Luke certainly used Mk, borrowing its framework and material (*Lukasevangelium*, Würzburg, 1988, p. 11; see further his comment on 1,1, p. 23). The manner in which Luke employed Mk was to a large extent in block fashion. Since Luke most probably used Q, it was this second source which can account for the many verbal agreements between Lk and Mt (p. 11-12). Insisting that most scholars adhered to the view of a third source containing the special Lukan material, designated "S", he asserted that its extent and character cannot be clearly determined. Because Luke often redacted his sources it is very difficult to prove the evangelist's use of other sources such as Proto-Lk or a special account of the passion (p. 12). Luke recounted the two episodes of Peter's denials and the mockery of Jesus (22,54-65), which were joined chronologically, geographically and thematically, between the arrest and the trial. The account of the mockery by the Roman soldiers was omitted by Luke, though Kremer invited comparison with the derision of Jesus crucified in 23,35f. (p. 222). It was clear that Luke redacted Mk in the denials to provide an uninterrupted account as well as a setting in the presence of Jesus. Kremer called attention to Luke's Markan source in the account of the Sanhedrin trial (22,66-71), remarking that some unnamed exegetes ascribed this section to a special tradition (p. 223). But he also made reference to Luke's presentation as being "in der ältesten Überlieferung fest verankerte" (p. 224).

Kremer affirmed that Luke drew on Mk for 23,1-5: "wohl kaum einer zusätzlichen Sonderquelle" (p. 225). He treated the section as 23,13-16.17.18-22.23-25but it was only in the

X. Jacques hailed the work as "une étude attentive" and complimented Schneider for the prudent manner with which he formulated the conclusions of his detailed analysis and comparison[252]. Similarly, B. Piepiórka signaled the analysis as an exemplary use of the tradition-critical and redaction-critical treatment of the state of the question. This valuable and remarkable contribution to the debate, he observed, was further enhanced by its fluid and thoroughly readable style[253]. W. Grundmann considered the overview of the theological statements of the Lukan passion (Chapter V) as especially valuable[254].

Terming the first four chapters extensive and voluminous, L. Schenke judged the most important conclusion being that the compositional character of Mk 14,53-64 (the hearing) in its current form went back entirely to Mark[255]. Further, he regarded the excursus on the Sanhedrin hearing as instructive and useful. Despite the overall evaluation that the study was an extraordinarily valuable contribution to research on the passion narratives of the Gospels, Schenke concluded: "In der umstrittenen Frage nach der luk. Sonderquelle für die Passionsgeschichte bleiben dem Rezensenten jedoch einige Zweifel"[256].

In his 1972 review F. Neirynck assessed the value of Schneider's dissertation with high praise: "Il formera un complément utile aux travaux de Hawkins, Cadbury, et Schürmann"[257]. Nevertheless, he faulted the study for the hypothesis which extended far beyond the data of his analysis. Affirming that Schneider was

comment on these final three verses that he asserted clearly that Luke borrowed from Mk and redacted it freely in order to emphasize the innocence of Jesus (p. 228). The omission of the Passover amnesty may have been occasioned by Luke not finding any reference to it in other sources.

The origin of the Herod pericope (23,6-12), drawn either from a special tradition or from information known to Luke, was debated. The splendid garment (23,11) was thought to be quasi-royal. Kremer surmised that Luke possibly knew a modified form of the mockery of Jesus by the soldiers (Mk 15,16-20). "Die Historizität dieser Gegenüberstellung – wahrend der Passion oder zu einem früheren Termin – kann daher nicht mit Sicherheit behauptet werden" (p. 226). He cast his vote in favor of the view that the episode underscored the innocence of Jesus. Many questions related to this passage remained open.

For a later treatment of christological titles by Kremer, especially "Son of God" in 22,67-69; 23,2, see *"Dieser ist der Sohn Gottes" (Apg 9,20). Bibeltheologische Erwägungen zur Bedeutung von "Sohn Gottes" im lukanischen Doppelwerk*, in C. BUSSMANN and W. RADL (eds.), *Die Treue Gottes*, 1991, 137-158 (= J. KREMER, *Die Bibel beim Wort genommen. Beiträge zu Exegese und Theologie des Neuen Testaments* [eds. R. KÜHSCHELM and M. STOWASSER], Freiburg - Basel - Vienna, 1995, 59-83).

252. *NRT* 93 (1971) 681, 682.

253. *ZKT* 93 (1971) 226.

254. *TLZ* 96 (1971) 907: "Besonders wertvoll aber ist es, dass der Vf. über die Einzelanalyse der drei Lukasperikopen hinaus einen Gesamtüberblick über die theologischen Aussagen der lukanischen Passion gibt".

255. *TTZ* 80 (1971) 381.

256. *Ibid.*, p. 382.

257. *ETL* 98 (1972) 570-573, p. 573. Schürmann, who served as a model for Schneider's study, attempted to revive the special source hypothesis.

correct in comparing 22,67d-68b and 20,1-8, he noted the similarity of the situation in both instances and argued that the logion was a redactional creation of Luke[258].

A final critique surrounded the fact that while "Le point de vue de Schneider repose finalement sur une appréciation des accords avec Mt. et Jn. d'une part les accords mineurs Mt./Lc. contre Mc., XI,27-33 et d'autre part les ressemblances entre Lc., XX,67-68 et Jn., X,24-25 (cf III, 12; IV, 48)". A little further he added: "On peut regretter que l'auteur n'a pas intégré l'examen des accords mineurs dans l'analyse même du récit"[259]. These criticisms notwithstanding, he concluded: "En général, G. Schneider a bien montré l'influence de Mc. sur Luc., XXII, 54-71"[260].

The Early Development of Schneider's Positions Following the Dissertation

In three articles (1970/1972) which followed shortly after the publication of the dissertation, Schneider continued to devote a great deal of attention to the pericope of Jesus before the Sanhedrin (22,66-71) and the existence of a pre-Synoptic account of the passion[261]. Asserting that the redactional interests or techniques of each of the evangelists can only be determined in light of their sources[262], Schneider noted that the discussion had been intensified by the recent contributions of Schürmann and Rehkopf. He continued to argue that for the Sanhedrin trial (22,66-71) Luke made use of another source[263]. Difference in order, material that

258. *Ibid.*, p. 572: "Après lecture de Lc., XX,1-8, on ne peut que s'étonner sur l'argument de Schneider: l'emploi non-lucanien de ἐάν, πιστεύω, ἐὰν δέ, (ἐρωτάω), ἀποκρίνομαι (p. 115-118, 165). 'Es ist unwahrscheinlich, dass Luk von sich aus das Wort gesetzt habe' (p. 118). Mais il est rare que Luc redige purement 'von sich aus'. Quelques pages plus loin, l'auteur parlera de la 'nouvelle méthode' de Schürmann qui consiste à étudier les réminiscences marciennes en Lc. (p. 129)! Sur οὐ μή, Schneider cite un texte de Schürmann qui date de 1953; il aurait dû signaler comment l'auteur s'est corrigé dans Die Sprache des Christus (1958): Luc peut l'écrire 'von sich aus' (VIII,17; XVIII,30) et encore: 'Auch die Einschübe 21,18; 22,67.68 diff Mk lassen sich nicht leicht als überkommenes Traditionsgut erweisen'" (*TrU*, p. 101, n. 206).

259. NEIRYNCK, in *ETL* 98 (1972) 572.

260. *Ibid.* In a later study, F. Bovon determined that Schneider's dissertation "constitue une solide étude" despite the fact that "elle ne brille peut-être pas par l'originalité": *Luc le théologien. Vingt-cinq ans de recherches (1950-1975)*, Neuchâtel - Paris, 1978, p. 181 (= *Luke the Theologian. Thirty-Three Years of Research (1950-1983)* [PrTMS, 12], tr. K. McKINNEY, Allison Park, PA, 1987, p. 170). Cf. BOVON, *Le récit*, in *BETL* 110, 1993, where he included Schneider's *Verleugnung* in his bibliography, but did not refer to it expressly in the text (p. 422). Compare Neirynck in the same volume: "It may be instructive to study the evolution in the position of a Lukan scholar like G. Schneider" (*Literary*, p. 22). See below.

261. SCHNEIDER, *Gab es eine vorsynoptische Szene "Jesus vor dem Synedrium"?*, in *NT* 12 (1970) 22-39 (= *Jesusüberlieferung*, 258-275); *Jesus vor dem Synedrium*, in *BibLeb* 11 (1970) 1-15 (= *Lukas, Theologe*, 158-172); *Das Problem einer vorkanonischen Passionserzahlung*, in *BZ* 16 (1972) 222-244 (= *Jesusüberlieferung*, 213-235).

262. *Gab es*, p. 22 (= 258); *Jesus*, p. 2 (= *Lukas, Theologe*, p. 159).

263. *Gab es*, p. 35-36 (= 271-272). The article basically served as a summary of his

went beyond what was found in the Markan account, particularly 22,67c.68, and Lukan-Matthean agreements against Mk were cited as convincing evidence. While 22,69-71 rested upon the Markan *Vorlage*, Schneider insisted that 22,66-68 probably stemmed from the non-Markan special source[264]. In attempting to reconstruct the special source, Schneider proposed that following the account of the arrest, it recounted the transfer of Jesus to the high priest (22,54a), the mockery (22,63f.) and the morning Sanhedrin trial containing the question about Jesus being the Messiah (22,66-68). Luke inserted the Markan denial story into this context. This would have accounted for the difference in order over against Mk. The fact that Luke did not include the death sentence (Mk 14,64) was credited to the evangelist's following the non-Markan source at this point. It seemed that the cumulative effect of a number of omissions of Markan material led Schneider to his conclusion[265].

Acknowledging the difficulty of historically reconstructing events, Schneider in the second article listed difference in order first among the numerous variations between Lk and Mk, followed by material which exceeded that found in Mk[266]. After a brief survey of the positions of Ruckstuhl, Winter, Schmid, Bultmann, Schürmann and Rehkopf, he argued that the idea of a special source can be regarded as possible, even probable. Regrettably, the only opposing view cited was found in a brief footnote referring to Kümmel[267]. Refining his earlier position slightly Schneider put forward the view that 22,67b.68 stemmed from a written non-Markan source based on what he considered non-Lukan formulations. Once again he insisted that for the Sanhedrin trial scene, Luke, working from the foundation of a non-Markan source, added Markan material to it[268]. In this non-Markan source vv. 68.69 (though without the statement about the parousia) followed immediately upon the Christ question posed by the Sanhedrin[269]. He appealed to Acts which spoke of the crucifixion of Jesus by the Jews (Acts 2,23.36; 3,13f.; 4,10; 13,27f.) while the Gospel was silent on the matter of Jewish death sentence (22,66-71; 18,31-33 in contrast to Mk)[270].

W.G. KÜMMEL (1980) compared Schneider's treatment in *Gab es* with Catchpole's dissertation, noting they appeared the same year and were completed

---

conclusions from the dissertation.

264. *Ibid.*, p. 36-37 (= 272-273). The special source was lacking information concerning the testimony of witnesses.

265. *Ibid.*, p. 37-38 (= 273-274). These included the absence of the testimony of witnesses (esp. Mk 14,57-59), the concluding remark about the death sentence, allusions to the Servant of Yahweh, the differences in the accounts of the mockery (Lk 22,63f. and Mk 14,60f.) and the open answer of Jesus (Mk 14,62). Contrasts with Mt including the response of Jesus (Lk 22,67f. and Mk 26,64) also contributed to his decision.

266. *Jesus*, p. 5 (= 162).

267. *Ibid.*, p. 6, n. 24 (= 163, n. 24). Cf. KÜMMEL, *Einleitung*, [14]1965, 79-82.

268. SCHNEIDER, *Jesus*, p. 10 (= 167).

269. *Ibid.*, p. 10-11 (= 167-168).

270. *Ibid.*, p. 14 (= *Lukas, Theologe*, p. 171).

independently of one another[271]. Influenced by Pesch, he argued that the proof of a special and historically dependable source in the Lukan trial and passion narrative was not convincing[272].

In an attempt to separate the proposal of a distinct Lukan passion source from the flagging Proto-Lukan theory, Schneider (1972) argued that the rejection of the latter did not imply the defeat of the former[273]. He stated without detailed argument or evidence that 22,19-20a.24-26.28-30.31-32.35-38.63-64.66-68 certainly formed a pre-Lukan, non-Markan unity[274]. In a note he called attention to material in Lk 23 (23,6-16.27-31.39-43) which he seemed also to include[275]. Schürmann's works and Schneider's dissertation provided the basis for the conclusion, while he dismissed Rehkopf's study as unconvincing[276].

Passion (1973) and Lukas (1977)[277]

In his study of the Synoptic passion accounts, *Die Passion Jesu*, Schneider maintained that Luke used the Markan account of Peter's denial, not only improving the language and style, but the portrayal of Peter and eliciting understanding for his behavior[278]. In this pericope Schneider held that Luke changed his Markan *Vorlage* for the purpose of emphasis. Verse 62 was not original to Lk. Schneider offered more of a theological interpretation for the interval of about an hour (22,59) than he had in the dissertation[279]. His position in *Lukas* was that clearly Mk 14,(54)66-72 served as the source for the Lukan account of the denials and that the contrary position of Klein and Haenchen must

---

271. *Jesusforschung seit 1965*. Pt. 6. *Der Prozess und der Kreuzestod Jesu*, in *TR* 45 (1980) 293-337, p. 317 (=ID. [ed.], *Dreissig Jahre Jesusforschung (1950-1980)* [BBB, 60], Königstein/Ts Bonn, 1985, p. 375-419, p. 399). See esp. p. 317-320 (= 399-402), for his discussion of Schneider and Catchpole.

272. *Ibid.*, p. 320 (= 402). Kümmel did not list any titles of Pesch in loc., but see his bibliography (p. 294 = 376).

273. SCHNEIDER, *Das Problem*, p. 235 (= 226). Advocates of the Proto-Lukan theory were listed as the British scholars Streeter and Taylor with similar views advanced by German scholars Schlatter, Jeremias and Rehkopf.

274. *Ibid.*, p. 236 (= 227).

275. *Ibid.*, n. 79 (= n. 79). Once again he referred to SCHÜRMANN, *Abschiedsrede*, p. 140, as he had done in the dissertation (*Verleugnung*, p. 143, n. 20).

276. *Das Problem*, p. 236, n. 79 (= 227, n. 79).

277. In the *Vorwort* to the second edition of *Lukas* he indicated that there were no substantial changes but he supplied "die Literatur-Nachträge" (Vol. 1: p. 254a-c; Vol. 2: p. 510-518). He observed that the question of a special source for the Lukan passion continued to be debated and answered in various ways. Authors of the then newer commentaries, Ernst and Schweizer, were favorably disposed while Fitzmyer remained "betont skeptisch" (p. 11).

278. *Passion*, p. 80. Schneider allowed implicitly for the possibility that the account stemmed from another source when he penned: "Wenn der Evangelist von Markus die Verleugnungs-geschichte übernehmen wollte, musste er sie *vor* dieses Traditionsstück verlegen" (p. 68).

279. *Passion*, p. 82. Cf. *Verleugnung*, p. 86-87.

regarded as disproved[280]. The temporal reference (22,59 / diff. Mk 14,70) was simply identified as one of a number of changes which he regarded as "redaktionelle Eingriffe"[281].

The difference in sequence (denial, mockery, trial) continued to prompt Schneider in *Passion* to adopt the theory of a special source for at least the mockery and trial (22,63-64.66-68)[282]. The Markan account supplied 22,69-71 which was appended to the special source[283]. He seemed cautious about proposing that the source was written, since he set the term off in parentheses. The MAs suggested the influence of oral tradition[284]. There was very little agreement between the Markan and Lukan accounts of the mockery. Verse 65 was formed by Luke, a position he maintained in *Passion* and *Lukas*[285]. The difference in the order of the three pericopes according to *Lukas* was due to the evangelist in light of the special source for the mockery and Sanhedrin trial[286]. Schneider was more insistent in *Lukas* that there were Lukan redactional elements in the mockery than he had been in *Passion*[287].

Schneider restated his position in *Passion* that the material in Lk 22,69-71 was essentially Markan and was subsequently inserted into the piece which was handed down[288]. The use of non-Lukan speech in vv. 66-68 reflected pre-Lukan

280. *Lukas*, p. 464. Cf. G. KLEIN, *Die Verleugnung*, and HAENCHEN, *Der Weg Jesu*, 505f. Those arguing against the special tradition included Linnemann, Schneider, Lehmann and Taylor, *Passion*.

281. *Lukas*, p. 465.

282. *Passion*, p. 67, 68. Cf. *Lukas*, p. 468. In his commentary on the denial and mockery he wrote: "Die Abweichung des dritten Evangelisten hinsichtlich der Reihenfolge der drei Stücke Verleugnung, Verspottung, und Verhör (Mk 14,[53]55-64.65.[54]66-72: Verhör, Verspottung, Verleugnung) geht darauf zurück, dass Lukas für die Verspottungsszene (Benoit) und für das Verhör vor dem Hohen Rat aus einer Sonderquelle schöpfte (Schneider: Verleugnung, 137-139)" (SCHNEIDER, *Lukas*, p. 464).

283. *Passion*, p. 68. But compare p. 70, where Schneider stated that v. 69 was possibly independent or possibly a revision of Mk. For a further specification of 22,67b.68 as stemming from pre-Lukan traditions see p. 70. In 23,70 the evangelist was probably combining non-Markan tradition with Markan presentation (p. 71).

284. *Ibid.*, p. 67.

285. *Ibid.*, p. 69. See also *Lukas*, p. 465.

286. *Lukas*, p. 464.

287. *Ibid.*, p. 465: "Auch in der Verspottungsszene ist mit redaktionellen Elementen zu rechnen". Cf. *Passion*, p. 68: "Der lukanische Bericht hat im Grunde nur eine einzige Übereinstimmung mit dem markinischen (Mk 14,65)".

288. *Passion*, p. 68: "Aus der markinischen Synedriumsperikope stammt wohl im wesentlich 22,69-71; diese Verse sind dann nachtragsweise an das überlieferte Stück angefügt." In his 1977 treatment of the segment of the Sanhedrin trial he offered the simple, unsubstantiated statement that vv. 69-71 were dependent upon Mk 14,62b-64 (*Lukas*, p. 468).

Because Schneider was treating the passion narratives in each of the Synoptic Gospels and since his intent was to present the conclusions of contemporary biblical criticism, this presentation on the Lukan account of the passion was not as detailed as that found in his *Verleugnung* or *Lukas*.

traditions such as were found in the Johannine parallel in Jn 10,24. Reflecting the
ambivalence of his 1969 findings on v. 69, Schneider (1973) entertained both
possibilities of independent tradition and redaction of Mk equally[289]. In *Lukas* he
spoke of the secondary character of v. 69 in contrast to Mk 14,62[290].

Previously he suggested that the phrase ἀπὸ τοῦ νῦν which corresponded to
the Matthean parallel, can be traditional although it ought to be considered as an
addition to the handed on text[291]. It was significant that Luke eliminated the
phrase καὶ ἐρχόμενον μετὰ τῶν νεφελῶν τοῦ οὐρανοῦ probably because of the
connection with ὄψεσθε. Luke adjusted the material in light of the fact that the
Sanhedrin had neither experienced the parousia of Jesus nor could they perceive
Jesus as sitting at the right hand of God[292].

Verse 70 was formerly seen as a combination of the non-Markan tradition and
Mk[293]. In *Lukas* Schneider observed that in Lk the question was divided but other
than writing that vv. 69-71 was dependent upon Mk 14,62b-64, he did not raise the
possibility of differing origins for the two questions[294].

Between *Passion* (1973) and *Lukas* (1977) Schneider reasoned that since the
Stephen story probably did not contain a trial before the Sanhedrin, it was adapted
to the trial of Jesus[295]. Here he was inspired by Conzelmann that the evangelists
were responsible for the Sanhedrin "Rahmen". Schneider argued that Luke
composed the words about the Son of Man in Acts 7,56 and recalled the scene in
22,69, which Schneider pointed out was parallel to Mk 14,62. He further linked
with Conzelmann's conception of the three divisions of time. He designated 22,69
as indicating to Luke the time of the Church. But the idea of the parousia receded
into the background because in Luke's understanding Christians experience their
parousia at death[296]. The Son of Man was raised to receive the martyrs. Under
the influence of Lukan eschatology and exaltation christology, Luke reworked the
Markan   account   to   provide   for   "eine   'Individualisierung'   der
Parusieerwartung"[297].

Continuity and Change in Schneider's Positions

Schneider continued to hold fast to his basic premise that Luke was dependent upon
both Mk and a non-Markan *Vorlage* for his accounts of the mockery and Sanhedrin

---

289. *Passion*, p. 70.
290. *Lukas*, p. 470.
291. *Verleugnung*, p. 119. The phrasing indicated a nuancing, from "probably" to "can be".
This agreement between Lk and Mt made a non-Markan tradition probable.
292. *Passion*, p. 71.
293. *Ibid.*
294. *Lukas*, p. 468, 470.
295. *"Der Menschensohn" in der lukanischen Christologie*, in R. PESCH (ed.), *Jesus und der
Menschensohn*, FS A. VÖGTLE, Freiburg, 1975, 280 (= *Lukas, Theologe*, 111).
296. *Ibid.*, p. 280-281 (= 111-112).
297. *Ibid.*, p. 282 (= 113).

trial, though the account of the denial depended solely upon Mk. In this section we will follow the chronological trajectory in order to ascertain where and in what ways this premise underwent development or remained the same.

In 1973 he concluded that, in essence, the mockery scene (vv. 63-65) belonged to the non-Markan *Vorlage* (vv. 63.64). The closing phrase (v. 65) was attributed to free Lukan redaction and the command to play the prophet (v. 64) probably was due to Mk. At this time he continued to defend the position that Luke was following a special source which differed from the Markan account[298]. In *Lukas* (1977) he no longer qualified his finding for v. 64 with the word "probably"[299]. What became clear in the course of his writings was that vv. 63-65 no longer received the same in depth attention as vv. 66-71 did[300].

Treating vv. 66-68 he originally decided that the dominical saying of vv. 67d-68b could be ascribed "*mit Sicherheit*" to the non-Markan source[301]. His position on this unit underwent continual evolution. In *Passion* he asserted that one could think of an influence of oral tradition, as also in the case of the MAs[302]. Later, but still referring to the findings in the dissertation, he wrote: "*Wahrscheinlich* folgen die VV 66-68 im wesentlichen der Sondervorlage, die schon 22,63-65 zugrunde lag (SCHNEIDER, *Verleugnung*)[303]". A further nuance can be detected in his 1988 article. "*Möglicherweise* hat Lukas neben dem ältesten Evangelium noch eine Sonderüberlieferung ausgeschöpft, vor allem für den Anfang der Szene (Lk 22,66-68)"[304]. While declining to enter into debate with Pesch, he reasserted his dissent from Pesch's position regarding above all vv. 67f. This was followed by a re-focusing of the redaction-critical task. "Ob diese Antwort Jesu auf Überlieferung beruht oder freier lukanischer Redaktion zuzuschreiben ist, wird weniger für die historische Rückfrage als für die Erörterung der theologischen Akzentsetzung des Lukas von Bedeutung sein"[305].

Judging that the end of the trial scene (vv. 69-71) was dependent upon Mk, he originally left open the possibility of non-Markan influence upon these

---

298. *Passion*, p. 69: "Die Divergenz zwischen Lukas und Markus lässt somit das Urteil zu, dass der dritte Evangelist mit seiner Darstellung einer Sonderquelle folgt, die vom Markus-Evangelium verschieden war".

299. *Lukas*, p. 465.

300. Although an entire section was devoted to Jesus before the Sanhedrin (Lk 22,66-71) in his 1988 work, vv. 63-65 received only scant attention (*Das Verfahren*, p. 114-118).

301. *Verleugnung*, p. 138, #10. Cf. also #4.

302. *Passion*, p. 67. Because of the presence of anti-Lukan formulations one is able to hold fast to the hypothesis of a (written) special source. He stated in *Verleugnung* that in the passion the Markan *Vorlage* was simply filled out by elements of oral tradition (p. 137).

303. *Lukas*, p. 468.

304. *Das Verfahren*, p. 116 (= 281). One can also perceive a trend toward an appeal to external authority. In this article Schneider cited the positions of Schweizer and Fitzmyer regarding the matter of the special source for vv. 66-68 just as he mentioned Pesch in his treatment of 22,66 (p. 116, 117 = 281, 282).

305. *Ibid.*, p. 116 (= 281).

verses[306]. While the ambivalence was also reflected in *Passion*[307], his position became more solidified in *Lukas*. "VV 69-71 sind hingegen von Mk (VV 62b-64) abhängig"[308]. He explained his reasoning. The secondary character of v. 69 over against Mk 14,62 was revealed in two changes made by Luke. First, Luke omitted Mark's reference to the parousia and spoke instead of the exaltation of Jesus. Secondly, Ps 110,1 and the simple Son of Man expression were drawn and reduced from Mark's account which included references to Dan 7,13 and Ps 110,1[309]. Finally, in 1988 as he compared the Markan and Lukan accounts, he noted that 22,69 went beyond Mark's version[310].

In his commentary on Acts (1980) Schneider commented on the question of sources for the Gospel, naming only Mk and Q, and characterizing the nature of Lukan redaction, wherein according to the practice of ancient historians, Luke thoroughly reworked his sources[311]. The matter of sources for Acts was even more difficult to unravel. Schneider affirmed that Luke drew from the Markan trial scene (Mk 14,57f.) for Acts 6,13-14, a conclusion based on an almost identical verbal agreement between Mk 14,58 and Acts 6,14b[312].

Schneider regarded the trial of Paul (Acts 25,13-22.23-27; 26,1-32) as a unity precisely on the grounds that Paul was innocent of the charges (25,18.25.31)[313]. He called attention to similarities between the two Lukan works, pointing first to the parallel with the Gospel on the triple declaration of innocence (23,4.14f.22) and the judgment of kings, Herod Antipas in the Gospel, Herod Agrippa II in Acts[314].

306. *Verleugnung*, p. 138, #4 and #8. He decided in favor of probable Lukan redaction of a non-Markan *Vorlage* for v. 69a though he still entertained the possibility of Lukan redaction of the Markan *Vorlage*. In a similar manner, he concluded that Luke probably redacted the Markan *Vorlage* to arrive at v. 69b, but did not exclude the possibility that there was light redactional re-working of a non-Markan source.

307. *Passion*, p. 70: "Vers 69 wird nun – vielleicht selbständig, vielleicht aber auch in Abwandlung der Mk-Vorlage – die sessio a dextris des Menschensohnes angekündigt".

308. *Lukas*, p. 468.

309. *Ibid.*, p. 470.

310. *Das Verfahren*, p. 115 (= 280): "Die Aussage Jesu wird in Vers 69 (im Anschluss an Mk 14,62b) weitergeführt: Der Messias Jesus ist der Menschensohn, der 'von nun an zur Rechten der Kraft Gottes sitzen wird'. Dass er 'mit den Wolken des Himmels kommen' werde (Mk 14,62b), übergeht Lukas".

311. *Die Apostelgeschichte* (HTKNT, 5,1), Freiburg, 1980, p. 83.

312. *Ibid.*, p. 438. Schneider noted differences between the Gospel parallels and the reference in Acts. Luke omitted the positive element that the Temple would be rebuilt in three days, replacing it with the negative statement that Jesus would change the customs handed on by Moses (p. 438-439). A comparision with Stephen's speech in 7,48-53 revealed that Stephen did not believe that God dwelt in the Temple. Further, Stephen desired to be obedient to the law given at Sinai even as he accused the high priest and the Council of disobedience.

313. *Ibid.*, p. 362.

314. *Ibid.*, n. 6. See also p. 370, n. 5, which invited comparison to Lk 23,1-22 with the declaration of innocence of Paul in Acts 23,29; 25,25; 26,1.30-32.

What was remarkable about his research was that, over these past thirty years, it exhibited a clear development regarding Luke's use of sources. Schneider himself detailed this development in *Das Verfahren*[315]:

> In meiner Habilitationsschrift von 1968/69 kam ich – ähnlich wie Heinz Schürmann – zu dem Ergebnis, dass es wahrscheinlich 'eine nicht-mk Sondervorlage' des Lukas gab, die er neben dem ältesten Evangelium bei der Darstellung der Passion verwendete ... In Untersuchungen zur Szene der Gefangennahme Jesu (Lk 22,47-53) und zu Lk 23 kam ich 1973 zu der Auffassung, dass Lukas in seinem Kapitel 23 keine Nicht-Mk-Quelle der Passion benutzte, sondern die Mk-Passion bearbeitete und mit Sonderüberlieferungen auffüllte. Dies gilt – im Gegensatz zu der Arbeit von Friedrich Rehkopf – entsprechend auch für die Inhaftierungsperikope ... Die lukanische Darstellung des *Verhörs Jesu im Synedrium* verdankt ihre Konzentration auf die 'christologische' Frage keiner älteren Quelle. Vielmehr hat Lukas hier die entsprechende Szene des Mk-Evangeliums gekürzt und neugestaltet ... Bei der *Verhandlung vor Pilatus* folgt Lukas ebenfalls der Mk-Vorlage ... Die dreifache (bzw. zweifache) *politische Anklage*, die von den Juden gegen Jesus vorgebracht wird (23,2), beruht ebenfalls nicht auf einer Sonderquelle, sondern ist von Lukas aufgrund des Mk-Stoffes 'rekonstruiert' worden[316].

In the final conclusion of his *Habilitationsschrift*, Schneider penned the statement that the evangelist used the non-Markan source as chief *Vorlage* for Lk 22,54-71, the mockery and the beginning of the trial[317]. While Schneider and Catchpole

---

315. *Das Verfahren*, p. 111-130 (= 276-295).

316. *Ibid.*, p. 112, 113, 128, 129 (= 277, 278, 293, 294). Four years later he also wrote of his progression in the *Vorwort* to *Jesusüberlieferung*, p. viii-ix: "Nicht nur die Botschaft Jesu, sondern auch sein WEG, insonderheit sein WEG ZUM KREUZ, ist für die Evangelien und ihre Jesusdarstellung konstitutiv. Die Passionsberichte am Ende aller vier Evangelien laden wegen ihrer grundlegend gleichen Struktur und ihrer gleichzeitig zu beobachtenden beträchtlichen Differenzen zu synoptischer Betrachtung ein. Dabei stellt sich natürlich die Frage nach einer Urüberlieferung der Jesuspassion, die wohl schon vor dem ältesten Evangelienbericht existiert haben muss. Die Frage nach einer vorsynoptische Leidensgeschichte, der die Studie aus dem Jahr 1972 nachgeht, ist auch heute noch nicht zur Ruhe gekommen, wie der relativ umfangreiche Literatur-Nachtrag zu diesem Thema zeigt. Die Problematik vor-kanonischer Überlieferungen der Passionsgeschichte wird an zwei Perikopen konkret vorgeführt: 'Die Verhaftung Jesu' [1972] und 'Jesus vor dem Synedrium'. Schon in der Szene wo Jesus vor dem Hohen Rat steht und Zeugnis gibt, stellte sich die Frage nach einer lukanischen Sonderüberlieferung der Leidensgeschichte. In dem Aufsatz des Jahres 1970 war ich – unter dem Eindruck meiner Würzburger Habilitationsschrift – eher geneigt, die Existenz einer nicht-markinischen Vorlage des dritten Evangelisten zu postulieren. Als ich mich 1988 noch einmal der Frage stellte, fiel die Antwort eher Negativ aus: in dem Beitrag über das jüdische und das römische Verfahren gegen Jesus". This evolution did not escape the eyes of R.E. Brown: "The journey of Schneider, a major commentator on the Lucan PN, has been particularly interesting" (*Death*, p. 67; see also p. 32: "When Schneider still held the thesis that there was a special preLucan PN ... ").

317. *Verleugnung*, p. 139: "Als Hauptvorlage von Lk 22,54-71 hat der Evangelist die nicht-mk Quelle benutzt (Verspottung und Verhöranfang). Er hat dieser Einheit die Verleugnung vorgeschaltet und wesentliche Teile des mk Verhörs angefügt. In die Verspottungsszene hat er

both subscribed to the idea of a special non-Markan source in a significant portion of 22,54-71, Schneider was, even in the early stages, more open to considering the possibility of Markan influence though he opted in favor of the non-Markan source.

It now has become clear, by means of our chronological review, that while he remained faithful to some positions which were established through the dissertation research, the appeal to a non-Markan source now seems restricted to vv. 67-68 which he referred to in 1988 as a *Sonderüberlieferung* which possibly served as a source in addition to Mk[318]. More and more, Schneider used Markan dependence and/or Markan influence to explain similarities and differences with the Lukan passion narrative in the mockery and Sanhedrin trial[319].

Over the period of more than a quarter of a century Schneider, unlike Catchpole, continued to devote a great deal of scholarly attention to the Lukan passion narrative. Whereas Catchpole rejected the view that Q contained a passion narrative, Schneider haltingly acknowledged that such a view was possible. Both Catchpole and Schneider insisted on the importance of source-critical studies in order to determine the theology of the evangelist[320]. They made use of comparisons with Acts in an attempt to understand Lukan redaction[321]. As Schneider's works are reviewed, one thing becomes clear. While the earlier works, especially the dissertation, gave very detailed reasoning for his opinions, the later works often simply state his positions without offering a defense or entering into debate with his opponents. We now press forward to examine his views on Ch. 23.

The Markan Material in Lk 23,1-25
Introduction

Since Schneider's dissertation and the early articles focused primarily on Lk 22,54-71, or parts thereof, as well as on the existence of a pre-canonical passion account, it was only with the publication of *Passion* (1973) that he gave greater attention to other sections of the Lukan account of the passion as well as the Synoptic passion

---

wahrscheinlich den Versteil 64c aus Mk eingefügt".

318. *Das Verfahren*, p. 116 (= 281).

319. *Ibid.*, p. 128 (= 293). Nowhere was this attitude more clearly evident than in a statement concerning the results of this 1988 article. "Die lukanische Darstellung des Verhörs Jesu im Synedrium verdankt ihre Konzentration auf die 'christologische' Frage keiner älteren Quelle. Vielmehr hat Lukas hier die entsprechende Szene des Mk-Evangeliums gekürzt und neugestaltet".

320. SCHNEIDER, *Gab es*, p. 22 (= 258); *Jesus*, p. 2 (= 159). CATCHPOLE, *Trial*, p. 220.

321. CATCHPOLE, *Trial*, p. 131, did not envision the possibility that Luke transferred the material from Mk 14,58 to Acts. "Does this mean that Luke may, consistently with this view, have omitted material similar to Mk 14.58 from Lk 22.66-71? Almost certainly not, because there are several instances of his retaining material on the Temple even though material diverges from his own attitude. This applies to Lk 13.35, 23.45, Acts 6.13 and 7,48". Schneider more correctly perceived that the appearance of the reference in Acts 6,14 indicated at the very least that Luke had read the Markan account (*Verleugnung*, p. 68; see also p. 80, 130, 131, 201).

narratives in their entirety[322]. Because of their breadth, the subsequent
investigations were understandably not treated in the same depth as was Lk 22,54-
71 in his dissertation.

The purpose of this section is to trace the development of Schneider's position
on tradition and redaction in 23,1-25 from 1973 to the present, comparing his 1988
conclusions with the writings of his former student, Walter Radl[323]. In this first
phase we will chronologically examine the extent to which Schneider assigned
material to the Markan *Vorlage*, to other sources and to redaction. This will enable
us to track the development and continuity or change within his argumentation
which spanned more than two decades. Our initial section presents Schneider's
position as found in *Passion* (1973).

The first detailing of the charge concerns the accusation that Jesus sought to
obstruct the payment of taxes. This portrayed the Jewish leaders as the real
purveyors of sedition. Luke reworked the Markan *Vorlage* of 20,20-26 which
described the cunning that eventually lead to Jesus' being handed over to the
authorities[324].

The charge also specified that Jesus claimed to be "Christ a king" (23,2) and
"geht materiell auf 22,67-70 zurück" which anticipated and prepared for this
verse[325]. Conversely, in Mk, the question whether Jesus was a king appeared
immediately and abruptly. According to Lk Jesus is the Christ in the sense of Son
of God[326]. Luke was correct in thinking that the corresponding charge of the
Sanhedrin (v. 5) must precede the questioning of Pilate about the supposed claim
of Jesus to be the king of the Jews. That is why Luke anticipated Mk 15,3 in 23,2
and concretized the "many" charges against Jesus[327]. Conzelmann's suggestion
that Luke used a pre-Lukan summary for v. 5 was rejected[328]. The catchword
"Galilee" then linked v. 5 to v. 6.

---

322. *Passion* (1973). He wrote this work to respond to what he perceived to be the need for
a composite presentation of the Synoptic passion accounts in light of the number of individual
investigations on specific themes or sections. His double goal was to offer a treatment of the
passion narrative based on the current state of the scholarly discussion and to correct or confirm
still unexplained questions or hypothetical judgments of various authors (p. 5). Catchpole, on the
other hand, has not pressed forward to examine his theory of a special source in Lk 23, with one
minor exception. In his article treating Mt 26,64 and parallels, he ascribed 23,3 and the
surrounding verses to the *Sonderquelle* (*Answer*, p. 218). The work of Rehkopf continued to serve
as a reference for Catchpole (p. 220, n. 6).

323. As noted above, Radl's article, *Sonderüberlieferungen* (1988) was a direct response to
the article of SCHNEIDER, *Das Verfahren* (1988).

324. SCHNEIDER, *Passion*, p. 92.

325. *Ibid.*

326. *Ibid.* Cf. *Lukas*, p. 472.

327. *Passion*, p. 91.

328. *Ibid.*, p. 92. H. CONZELMANN, *Die Mitte*, [4]1962, p. 79, n. 1. Schneider dismissed this
postulated summary as unnecessary when one is familiar with the overall layout of Lk and its
dependence upon Mk. This critique will be repeated in SCHNEIDER, *Political Charge*, 1984, p.
409 (= *Politische Anklage*, p. 179). Cf. below.

With v. 18 Luke resumed the Markan account with the Barabbas scene. Lk 23,18-25, it was observed, was significantly shortened by Luke. Lacking the reference to the custom of Passover amnesty and the offer to free a prisoner, he portrayed the leaders together with the people protesting the intended release of Jesus, calling out in one voice instead for the crucifixion of Jesus[329]. Only in v. 19 did Luke recount something of Barabbas' background which Mark and Matthew had already supplied[330]. Pilate's third declaration of Jesus' innocence (v. 22b.c) can be connected by Luke to Mk 15,14. In contrast to Mk but similar to Mt, Luke hardly presented Pilate as an independent, decisive judge[331]. Nevertheless, Pilate became a witness for Jesus' innocence according to Luke. As with Mark and Matthew, his presentation served less the exoneration of Pilate[332].

The political dimension of the matter was moved into the foreground as Jesus was given over to the will of the Jews (vv. 24f.)[333]. Innocent and non-threatening to Rome, he was handed over by the real insurrectionists[334]. Thus, Luke permitted the reader to think of a Jewish execution ("Vollstrekung") of the crucifixion of Jesus, especially in light of the omission of the mockery by the Roman soldiers (Mk 15,16-20a)[335]. Having concluded our review of Schneider's presentation of Chapter 23 in *Passion*, we now consider the material as found in his Lukan commentary.

Lukas (1977)[336]

The contrast of Luke's redactional style between chapters 22 and 23, in Schneider's view, was summed up best in the phrase: "Die redaktionellen Eingriffe des Evangelisten lassen sich am leichtesten in Kapitel 23 erkennen, wo Lukas die Erzählungs-Abfolge des Mk im ganzen besser bewahrte als in Kapitel 22. Das Sondergut gibt neben der 'Redaktion' der lukanischen Darstellung ihr besonderes theologisches Profil"[337]. As in the preceding section, we will consider Schneider's treatment of Chapter 23 passage by passage.

Lk 23,1-5 was affirmed as basically a revision of Mk 15,1-5[338]. However, Luke passed over Mk at the response of silence by Jesus to the further questioning

329. *Passion*, p. 102, 103.

330. *Ibid.*, p. 102-103. (Mt 27,16; Mk 15,7).

331. *Ibid.*, p. 103.

332. *Ibid.*, p. 104: "Die Darstellung dient also auch hier – wie bei Markus und Matthäus – weniger der Entlastung des Pilatus".

333. *Ibid.*, p. 103.

334. *Ibid.*, p. 104. Luke was writing here of his urgent preoccupation of the political apologetic over against Rome. Cf. *Verleugnung*, p. 193-196.

335. *Passion*, p. 104.

336. *Lukas*, p. 471-480, treated 23,1-25.

337. *Ibid.*, p. 437.

338. *Ibid.*, p. 471. A close reading and comparison of *Lukas* with *Passion* revealed that Schneider repeated, often verbatim, from his earlier work.

as well as at the subsequent astonishment of Pilate (Mk 15,5). Rather, Luke reported a (first) public declaration of Jesus' innocence by Pilate (v. 4) and the renewed accusation against Jesus by the Jewish plaintiffs (v. 5)[339].

Mk 15,3 was anticipated by Luke in v. 2 which concretized the "many" charges against Jesus[340]. Following Grundmann, Schneider maintained that the structure of v. 2 showed that the accusation of stirring up the people was then specified in two points[341]. The facts which would interest Pilate were then emphasized. Materially the statements rested upon previous elements of Lk, namely 19,48; 20,6.19.26; 22,2. Schneider asserted that Luke drew this material from Mk and not from some other source[342]. The contention that Jesus hindered the payment of the imperial tax appeared as slander in light of Lk 20,20-26. The way in which Luke reworked his Markan *Vorlage* revealed the hypocritical questioning of Jesus' opponents, who earlier sought to hand Jesus over to the authority of the governor (20,20). The second concrete charge, that Jesus claimed to be a political Messiah opposing Rome, went back materially to 22,67-70. This charge anticipated the theme of v. 3 and prepared for it. Consequently, Luke developed the concrete charges of the Sanhedrin from Mk.

Because 23,17 was missing from the best manuscripts, Schneider reasoned that it had been imported to the Lukan text from the other Synoptics (Mk 15,6 / Mt 27,15)[343]. In the section 23,18-25 Luke resumed the Markan account relating the Barabbas story. It was especially apparent at 23,22b.c. where Luke connected Pilate's third declaration of Jesus' innocence with Mk 15,14 in asking what evil Jesus had done. In order to heighten the sense of the Jewish responsibility for the crucifixion Luke passed over the mockery by the Roman soldiers (Mk 15,16-20a).

The Political Charge against Jesus (Luke 23:2)[344]

Within the whole of the Lukan passion narrative, Schneider continued to concern himself with aspects of the trial of Jesus before Pilate, and in particular, the accusation against Jesus as it was further specified by Luke. Lk 23,2 was the focus of an article (1984) which investigated the political charge against Jesus. The goal of the study was to determine whether Luke created the detailed charges either because of his belief about how the history should be reconstructed or because of

---

339. *Ibid.*

340. *Ibid.*, p. 471-472, credited CONZELMANN, *Die Mitte*, p. 79, n. 1, with this suggestion of the concretization of the "many" charges.

341. SCHNEIDER, *Lukas*, p. 472. Cf. W. GRUNDMANN, *Lukas*, [1961], ⁶1971, p. 422.

342. SCHNEIDER, *Lukas*, p. 472. Luke was drawing upon Mk 11,18b.32b; 12,12a; 14,2.

343. *Ibid.*, p. 476.

344. *The Political Charge against Jesus (Lk 23:2)*, tr. D. CATCHPOLE, in E. BAMMEL and C.F.D. MOULE (eds.), *Jesus and the Politics of His Day*, Cambridge, 1984, 403-414 (= *Die politische Anklage gegen Jesus (Lk 23,2)*, in ID., *Lukas, Theologe der Heilsgeschichte. Aufsätze zum lukanischen Doppelwerk* [BBB, 59], Königstein/Ts.-Bonn, 1985, 173-183).

his theological viewpoint, or whether Luke was employing a source separate from and perhaps older than Mk[345].

Overall, Lk 23,1-5 was to be regarded as a Lukan composition[346]. Verses 1.2.3 clearly derived from Mk and the charge related to paying the tribute to Caesar stood in formal connection to Lk 20,20-26, a passage which likewise was clearly dependent upon Mk[347]. But if in this matter, 23,2 presupposed redaction of Markan material, then the verse cannot be pre-Lukan.

Schneider reacted against those who maintained that Jesus faced three charges instead of one[348], as well as those who postulated an extra source alongside Mk[349]. Following a review of the narrative in Mk, a consideration of the concrete charges against Jesus, which included a survey of the various scholarly positions[350], and a close reading of the text, he concluded that Mk lies at the source of the concrete charges of the Sanhedrin[351].

Schneider analyzed the vocabulary and style of the verse. Ἤρξαντο δὲ κατηγορεῖν αὐτοῦ λέγοντες. Despite the fact that Mk displayed a preference for the use of ἤρξαντο followed by the infinitive, Luke probably wrote it "von sich aus" in his nine instances[352]. Only Luke offered the infinitive κατηγορεῖν after

---

345. *Ibid.*, p. 404 (= 174-175).

346. *Ibid.*, p. 412-413 (= 182). Schneider referred to 23,1-5 both as a "Bearbeitung der Mk-Vorlage" and as a "lukanische Komposition".

347. *Ibid.*, p. 413 (= 182).

348. *Ibid.*, p. 407-408 (= 177).

349. *Ibid.*, p. 405, n. 4 (= 175, n. 4).

350. *Ibid.*, p. 405-407 = (175-177). Schneider, noting the lack of consensus, stated that the positions concerning tradition and redaction can generally be divided into two camps. One position was represented by J. SCHMID, *Lukas*, ³1955, p. 342, who argued that Luke, writing as a historian, refashioned Mk 15,1-5 in order that the account might be historically more satisfying. "Schmid meint, der "Historiker" Lukas habe in diesem Abschnitt den als historischen Bericht wenig befriedigenden Text Mk 15,1-5 zu einer Darstellung umgestaltet, die geschichtlich eher befriedigen kann" (p. 405 = 175). W. GRUNDMANN, *Das Evangelium nach Lukas*, Berlin, 1961, [Neudruk, 1963], who posited a parallel Lukan source in addition to Mk, exemplified the second camp. Schneider then provided a brief survey of other treatments of the verse. J. BLINZLER, *Der Prozess Jesu*, Regensburg, ²1955, 138 [desgleichen ³1960, 201; ⁴1969, 278] left open the question of sources. P. WINTER, *On the Trial*, 1961, [²1974], p. 136f., assigned Lk 23,2.3 to the oldest (primary) tradition but S.G.F. BRANDON, *Trial*, 1968, p. 119f., ignored the source-critical issue altogether. Schneider, impressed by the study of H. VAN DER KWAAK, *Het Proces*, p. 140-144, was convinced that the author of this study had convincingly argued that "diese Differenzen des dritten Evangeliums aus der Absicht und der Darstellungsweise des Evangelisten erklärt werden können" (p. 407 = 177).

351. SCHNEIDER, *Political Charge*, p. 409 (= 179): "Somit steht fest, dass Lukas die konkreten Anklagen der Synedristen aus Mk erschlossen haben kann. Er brauchte dazu keine neuen Informationen aus einer neuen Quelle. Das gilt auch in bezug auf 23,5. Wer den Aufriss des dritten Evangeliums und dessen Abhängigkeit vom Markusevangelium kennt, braucht für 23,5 kein vorlukanisches Summarium als Vorlage zu postulieren". Cf. *Passion*, p. 92; *Lukas*, p. 472-473.

352. SCHNEIDER, *Political Charge*, p. 409 (= 179). Lk 5,21; 7,49; 11,53; 14,18; 15,24;

ἤρξα(ν)το[353]. He had λέγων (-οντες) following ἤρξα(ν)το with the infinitive five times while it appeared only once in Mt[354]. Lk 5,21 and 19,37f.45f. definitely stemmed from Lukan redaction. Luke favored the term κατηγορέω. Lk 6,7 was undoubtedly due to Luke and contained the infinitive κατηγορεῖν with αὐτοῦ as its subject[355]. As a result of this study, Schneider decided that while Luke derived the content from Mk 15,3, this introductory phrase was formulated by Luke[356].

τοῦτον εὕραμεν διαστρέγοντα τὸ ἔθνος ἡμῶν. Lk 6,7 contained the phrase τοῦτον εὕραμεν. Of the 176 occurrences of εὑρίσκω in the NT, eighty were located in the Lukan work. Obviously the term was a Lukan favorite. τοῦτον also occurred more often in the combined Lukan works than in any of the other Gospels or in the remainder of the NT[357].

διαστρέφω was Lukan (23,2; Acts 13,8.10; 20,30) with two exceptions: Mt 17,17 = Lk 9,41 and Phil 2,15 (γενεᾶς ... διεστραμμένης). The phrase τὸ ἔθνος ἡμῶν was found in the NT only at Lk 7,5 and 23,2. τὸ ἔθνος μου (Acts 24,17; 26,4; 28,19) a comparable phrase, most probably reflected a Lukan mode of expression[358]. On the basis of style, word statistics and Lukan interests Schneider reasoned that for the verse parts extending from τοῦτον εὕραμεν to τὸ ἔθνος ἡμῶν Mk served as the source and Luke shaped the main charge against Jesus[359]. The proposition of a pre-Lukan source, besides Mk, was unnecessary.

καὶ κωλύοντα φόρους Καίσαρι διδόναι καὶ λέγοντα ἑαυτὸν χριστὸν βασιλέα εἶναι. Admitting that the double use of καί was indeed not a Lukan characteristic, nonetheless Luke made use of it as indicated by 5,36b and 22,33[360]. Based on statistical evidence it can be said that κωλύω was a term favored by Luke. Of the twelve combined occurrences in the Lukan double work, three were dependent upon Mk (Lk 18,16 / Mt 19,14 = Mk 10,14; 9,49.50) and three were obviously worked on ("bearbeitet") by the evangelist (6,29; 11,52; 23,2). The remaining instances, all from Acts, can be similarly considered as having been redacted by Luke, at least in part[361].

φόρους διδόναι was reminiscent of Lk 20,22. That Luke placed the verb at the end in these two instances was decisive for Schneider who suggested that the

19,37; 22,23; 23,2; Acts 2,4. Schneider also compared 19:37 with 23,2, each having ἅπαν τὸ πλῆθος in the subject with the following genitive plural.

353. *Ibid*. Lk 23,2; Acts 24,2.

354. *Ibid*., p. 410 (= 179). The singular instance in Mt was 16,22. Luke, however, contained this usage at 5,21; 19,37f.45f.; 23,2; Acts 24,2.

355. *Ibid*. The instances enumerated, in addition to Lk 6,7 were 23,2 and Acts 24,2.

356. *Ibid*.

357. *Ibid*., p. 410 (= 180).

358. *Ibid*.

359. *Ibid*., p. 410-411 (= 180).

360. *Ibid*., p. 411 (= 180). Schneider added that in the Lukan *Sondergut* we find two instances (1,15; 2,46) and six occurences in Acts.

361. *Ibid*.

evangelist was responsible for the formulation in 23,2[362]. Once more, this verse part was due to the hand of Luke[363].

Of the twelve instances of the reflexive ἑαυτόν in Lk, three derived from Mk, four from the sayings source and a further four from the special material (10,29; 15,17; 18,11; 23,2). Only 9,25 was the result of Luke's redaction of Mk. Schneider added that Luke would have extensively remodelled the special material[364]. The situations where ἑαυτόν and εἶναι followed a verb of saying, specifically λέγω, were Acts 5,36; 8,9 and our verse, 23,2. Word statistics showed a Lukan preponderance of the infinitive εἶναι.

The combination of the Christ title and βασιλεύς was found only at Mk 15,32 in the rest of the NT. Luke combined Mk 14,61f. (the messianic confession) with Mk 15,2 (Pilate's question about the kingship of Jesus)[365]. Luke's use of βασιλέα in apposition to "messiah" was clear from Acts 17,7 when compared to Acts 17,3. Similarly, the phrase λέγων βασιλέα εἶναι (23,2) was paralleled by Acts 17,7 (βασιλέα λέγοντες εἶναι) which agreed both in form and content.

While Luke understood the term "king" in a non-political manner, the Jews regarded the "kingship" of Jesus as opposed to the regulations of Caesar[366]. In Schneider's judgment, Luke re-fashioned the Markan account linguistically and stylistically[367]. Without providing the detailed analysis, however, Schneider contended that a similar conclusion can be reached for 23,1.4.5[368]. Familiarity with the scheme of Lk, as well as its dependence on Mk, eliminated the need to suggest, as Conzelmann had done, that the source of 23,5 was a pre-Lukan summary[369].

---

362. *Ibid.*, p. 411 (= 180-181).

363. *Ibid.*, p. 411 (= 181).

364. *Ibid*: "... allerdings wird auch das Sondergut weitgehend vom Evangelisten geformt sein".

365. *Ibid.*, p. 411-412 (= 181). He noted further that Jn 19,12 was not indicative of a special tradition existing between Lk and Jn. Rather John drew on Pilate's question found in Mk.

366. *Ibid.*, p. 412 (= 181).

367. *Ibid.*, p. 412 (= 182).

368. *Ibid.*

369. *Ibid.*, p. 409 (= 179). Schneider reacted once more to the position of CONZELMANN, *Die Mitte*, p. 79, who argued that 23,5 was a summary to indicate that Jesus' ministry included all Judea and Galilee. "23,5: Der Vers ist ein Summar, das zeigt, dass 'ganz Judäa' als Wirkungsfeld Jesu von Anfang an neben Galiläa vorgestellt ist".

In n. 1, Conzelmann wrote: "Samaria ist nicht genannt. Freilich darf man darauf gerade an dieser Stelle kein grosses Gewicht legen. Im Blick auf das Folgende dominiert das politische Element. Zunächst handelt es sich um die Festellung, dass Jesus im Gebiet des Pilatus wie des Herodes aufgetreten ist. Samaria ist daher überflüssig. Von Wert ist die Formel aber weniger wegen ihrer speziellen Verwendung an diesert Stelle als um ihrer selbst willen. Sie ist ein bereits vorlukanisches Summar, wie der Vergleich mit den anderen Stellen zeigt, an denen bei Lukas Galiläa, Galiläer, und das Motiv von der arché auftauchen. Und im vorlukanischen Sinn beschreibt sie allerdings das Wirken Jesu *erschöpfend*".

Schneider regarded the overall purpose of Luke's two-volume work as producing a political apologetic over against the Roman state[370]. Not only did the purpose become clear here, but also in Acts which contained material about the charges against Paul, which were ultimately refuted[371]. Such a revision of Mk was shaped by Luke in the charge against Jesus, therefore, with the purpose of presenting the Jewish perspective of the charge and offering more specific details. While maintaining an interest in the political charge against Jesus (1988), Schneider reconsidered four of the most vexing aspects of the Lukan account of Jesus' passion.

Das Verfahren gegen Jesus in der Sicht des dritten Evangeliums (Lk 22,54-23,25)[372]

Schneider first presented the problematic aspects of the Lukan passion narrative and observed that while Matthew followed Mk extensively in his presentation, Lk contained both adaptations of the Markan material as well as considerable *Sondergut*[373]. In dating Lk around 80 AD, Schneider queried whether the *Sondergut* was based upon reliable information and whether the adaptations differing from Mk derived from true information[374]. Could true and accurate information still be obtained about the trial of Jesus apart from written sources or fixed oral traditions at such a date[375]?

Next, Schneider examined the state of the question by referring to a few selected works which treated the issue of whether Luke possessed a special continuous source in addition to Mk. He mentioned the views of four recent commentators, equally divided among themselves, who held opposing positions on the existence of such a source[376]. Although he himself rejected the proposal of a special source for Chapter 23, and had since 1973, the disagreement among scholars persisted[377].

Eager to solve this dilemma, Schneider selected four parts of the Lukan passion narrative for closer scrunity: Jesus before the Sanhedrin (22,66-71); the

---

370. SCHNEIDER, *Political Charge*, p. 413 (= 183).

371. *Ibid.*, p. 414 (= 183). The information concerning charges against Paul were recounted in Acts 17,7; 24,2-5.10-21; 25,7f.; 26,2-23.

372. SCHNEIDER, *Das Verfahren*, p. 111-130 (= 276-295).

373. *Ibid.*, p. 111 (= p. 276).

374. *Ibid.*

375. *Ibid.*

376. *Ibid.*, p. 113 (= p. 278), where he noted that two recent German commentaries by J. Ernst (1977) and E. Schweizer (1982) accepted the special source, while two English language commentaries, I.H. Marshall (1978) and J. Fitzmyer, (1985) expressed reservation. Cf. *Lukas*, ²1984, "Vorwort zur zweiten Auflage".

377. SCHNEIDER, *Das Verfahren*, p. 113 (= 278). As early as 1973 Schneider concluded that Lk 23 was based upon a reworked Markan passion account which had been filled in with special traditions. Luke employed no non-Markan source.

proceedings before Pilate (23,1-25); the political charge before Pilate (23,2.5) and Jesus before Herod (23,6-16). For each topic he discussed the following aspects: a) the anchoring in the Lukan context; b) the relation to Mk; c) the source question; d) the question of historicity, and e) the theological emphasis of the evangelist. As we have previously examined Schneider's contribution on Jesus before the Sanhedrin (22,66-71), we will concern ourselves only with the the trial before Pilate (23,1-25) and the political charge (23,2.5), excluding the Herod story which will be treated below. We begin with the general survey of the trial before Pilate (23,1-25)[378].

Lk 23,1-25 (A Narrative Unity)

Although Schneider gave special attention to the charge before Pilate (23,2.5) and the Herod scene (23,6-16) out of historical reasons, he affirmed that the whole of 23,1-25 was a unity[379]. Considering this section's anchoring within the Lukan context, he judged in favor of such unity because in 23,1 the Sanhedrin brought Jesus to Pilate and finally in 23,25 Pilate delivered Jesus up to their wishes. This passage stood in connection to the preceding episode of Jesus before the Sanhedrin (22,66-71) by virtue of interpreting the messianic claim of Jesus in terms of a "king". This was accomplished by apposition of the titles "messiah" and "king".

Schneider rightly rejected the suggestion of Jerome Neyrey differentiating four trials in Lk. He maintained instead, that what Neyrey considered to be the last two trials (23,6-12.13-25), were only elements of the trial before Pilate[380]. Aside

---

378. *Ibid.*, p. 119-121 (= 284-286). Following a general overview of 23,1-25, he gave particular attention to 23,2.5 (p. 121-126 = 286-291) and 23,6-16 (p. 126-128 = 291-293). The purpose of the meeting to which Schneider made his presentation was, above all, to consider the possibilities and limits of the historical reconstruction of the condemnation and execution of Jesus (p. 9). Within the scope of this goal, Schneider sought to discover whether the *Sondergut* of Lk was based on reliable tradition and whether the changes over against the arrangement of Mk went back to true/correct ("zutreffende") information. He expressed regret that in recent times the historical inquiry into the events of the passion reported by Luke and the source-critical investigations upon which this inquiry depended, had receded into the background (p. 113-114 = 278-279).

379. *Ibid.*, p. 119 (= 284).

380. *Ibid.* Cf. NEYREY, *Passion*, p. 71-84, where he drew a parallel with the fourfold Pauline trial in Acts (p. 98). MATERA, *Luke 23,1-25*, 1989, p. 551, like Schneider, took issue with the assertion that there were four trials. "Our study proposes that Luke employs Mark's version of the trial of Jesus before the Sanhedrin and Pilate in order to construct *one* trial scene with four panels". While Schneider argued against Neyrey's position, he did not explicitly mention how many trials he posited. Given his reaction to Neyrey, Schneider's position might be one (before Pilate with the Sanhedrin hearing as merely a pre-investigation) or two trials (before the Sanhedrin and before Pilate). In *Das Verfahren*, p. 119, n. 45 (= 284, n. 45) he referred to the suggestion of Conzelmann in *Die Mitte*, ⁴1962, that behind 23,1-25 one could detect *three* authorities among whom the trial of Jesus runs its course: Pilate as the procurator of Judea, Herod as King of the clientele state Galilee and the High Council as "city council of a free city" (the Polis Jerusalem). But even Conzelmann himself seemed not to have been so convinced of such an idea. "Doch

from the Herod scene (23,6-12.[13-16]), which was *Sondergut* material, Luke followed the Markan pattern[381]. The essential differences comprised the concretization of the charges and the presentation of the Jews as slanderers[382]. Luke's redaction more adequately prepared for, and thus gave a more plausible order to, the charge than Mk by mentioning the charge (23,2) before the question of Pilate (23,3 par. Mk 15,2). Luke replaced Pilate's reaction of astonishment to the silence of Jesus (Mk 15,5) with a first declaration of his innocence.

Luke did not refer to the custom of releasing a prisoner for the feast. Rather, he reported that the Jews encouraged the death of Jesus and demanded the release of Barabbas. Thus, he did not recount a practice of Passover amnesty, but an exchange of two prisoners. The emphasis fell upon the encouragement of the crucifixion of Jesus by the Jews[383]. From Schneider's study, it was clear to him that Mk 15,1-15 formed the basis for the Lukan account, exclusive of 23,2 and 23,6-12(13-16). Revisions were possibly due either to Luke's own knowledge or to a historicizing consideration which also pertained to his portrayal of the Barabbas scene. Luke may have expressed doubts about the amnesty custom[384]. The question how close the Lukan presentation came to the legal character of the Roman proceedings against Jesus, which Luke described using judicial terminology, remained "bemerkenswert 'offen'"[385].

versieht Conzelmann selbst eine solche Vermutung mit Fragezeichen".

Previously in *Lukas*, p. 468-469, Schneider referred to the events/proceedings before the Sanhedrin both as a pre-investigation and as a trial. "Historisch lässt sich sichern, dass der Hohe Rat gegen Jesus eine Voruntersuchung gehalten hat, die die Anklage vor Pilatus und damit den römischen 'Prozess' vorbereitete. In dieser Voruntersuchung stand die Frage nach dem Messiasanspruch Jesu im Mittelpunkt". But notice that shortly thereafter he wrote: "Die Verhörszene bildet einen zweifach gestuften Dialog, bei dem die Ratmitglieder die Fragenden sind (VV 66-69.70)". Still further, Schneider will propose the following: "Geht man von der geschichtlich wahrscheinlichen Voraussetzung aus, dass der Hohe Rat gegen Jesu keinen Prozess mit formellen Todesurteil, sondern ein Vorverhör zur einleitung des Verfahrens vor dem römischen Statthalter-Todesurteil nur *bestätigte oder bloss ausführte*. Eine solche Möglichkeit scheidet auch deshalb aus, weil Jesus den römischen Strafjustiz entsprechenden Kreuzestod erlitt (nicht etwa gesteinigt wurde) und aus dem Kreuzestitulus sogar der Kreuzigungsgrund (Jesus als messianischer Prätendent) bekannt ist" (p. 479).

In *Das Verfahren* Schneider referred to 22,66-71 with the designation "Verhör". "Im Verhör legt Jesus ein Selbstzeugnis ab, weshalb weitere Zeugnisse überflüssig erscheinen (22,71). Nach dem Ergebnis des Verhörs zieht der Hohe Rat mit dem Gefangenen zu Pilatus, um ihn dort anzuklagen" (p. 114 = 279).

381. SCHNEIDER, *Das Verfahren*, p. 120 (= 285). Dependence was recognized in the charge and first trial before Pilate (23,1-5 par. Mk 15,1-5); the Barabbas scene (23,18-23 par. Mk 15,6-14); the reference to Jesus being delivered up for the crucifixion (23,24f. par Mk 15,15).

382. *Ibid.* Schneider also noted Luke's use of juridical terminology: ἀνακρίνω (23,14) and ἐπικρίνω (23,24).

383. *Ibid.* Cf. MATERA, *Luke 23,1-25*, e.g. p. 537-538, 548, 550, also recognized the Lukan emphasis on the participation and involvement of the Jews, rulers and people alike.

384. SCHNEIDER, *Das Verfahren*, p. 120-121 (= 285-286).

385. *Ibid.*, p. 121 (= 286).

The theological focal points concerned the initiative of the Jews in conspiring against Jesus and the Romans' role as henchmen for them. Schneider made the point that it was to the Sanhedrin and the people that Pilate finally acquiesced.

"Das Verfahren" on Lk 23,2.5

The political charge before Pilate (Lk 23,2.5) was reviewed next[386]. While the question of the Roman governor to Jesus whether he was the king of the Jews has a Markan parallel (Lk 23,3 / Mk 15,2), the charges brought by the Sanhedrin, which preceded the interrogation by Pilate, reported in 23,2, were *Sondergut*. Following upon the conclusion of the Sanhedrin trial and according to the Markan *Vorlage* 15,2f., Schneider suggested that one should expect that Luke would place the accusation of the claim to be king at the peak. This rearrangement facilitated Pilate's subsequent question[387].

In responding to the matter of sources for 23,2 Schneider maintained, in contrast to his position on Lk 22,66-71 and even 23,6-12 espoused in *Lukas*, that it can be answered "mit grosser Gewissheit"[388]. Luke developed the charges from his Markan *Vorlage* rather than from a tradition or reports. The first charge of "perverting our nation" was probably further specified by the accusations that Jesus advocated the boycott of the imperial tax and claimed to be a king. Conversely, Schneider now also suggested that the messiah-king claim could have given rise to the first two charges[389].

Material for the charge that Jesus was inciting the people was drawn from previous parts of the Gospel, namely Lk 19,48; 20,6.19.26; 22,2 which indicated the people's sympathy for Jesus. But the implication was that the Jewish leadership afforded the real seditionists in 23,18f.21.25. Similarly, the ludicrous and slanderous nature of the charge concerning the tax boycott became understandable in the light of Lk 20,20-26 (Mk 12,13-17).

Historically speaking, Luke certainly discovered the connecting link to the details of the events. Mention of the claim of kingship by Jesus was combined with messiahship in the trial before the Sanhedrin. The rationalization of the death penalty for Jesus was reported later in the chapter in the words of the inscription, "the king of the Jews" (23,38 / Mk 15,26). This reflected a distortion of the true facts; Jesus defined the messiah claim as the heavenly enthronement of the Son of Man and the Son of God (22,69f.)[390]. The Jews defined it in such a way as to present Jesus as anti-Roman and a political threat. The interest of Pilate was aroused because the Sanhedrin interpreted "Christ" by means of the title

---

386. *Ibid.*, p. 121-126 (= 286-291).
387. *Ibid.*, p. 121 (= 286).
388. *Ibid.*
389. *Ibid.*, p. 122 (= 287).
390. *Ibid.*, p. 123 (= 288).

βασιλεύς[391]. In this way, Pilate would be more inclined to take an interest in the case against Jesus.

Schneider rejected the findings of recent investigations which supposed that Luke captured the historical facts. One such study, by August Strobel, maintained that 23,2 reflected a very precise knowledge of the charge and resulting judgment[392]. Further, Strobel's study rested upon the assumption of a *Sonderquelle* which Schneider rejected. Strobel's work served as the basis for additional assertions made by Peter Stuhlmacher in a 1985 published lecture, which, in part, promoted the idea that the Markan passion account deserved much more historical confidence[393]. Stuhlmacher argued that the historical basis for the arrest and sentence of Jesus by the Sanhedrin can be seen against the background of material from Dt 13; 17,12 and 18,20, an idea which he attributed to Strobel[394].

Schneider disagreed with these assertions for two reasons. First, he declared that Strobel still needed to prove his thesis[395]. Secondly, Schneider argued that Mk did not give the impression that Jesus was condemned as a seditionist[396]. He maintained rather that the post-Markan Gospel writings were influenced by the Jewish Jesus polemic around the end of the first century.

In support of his position, Schneider noted Scriptural verses which referred to Jesus being described as a seditionist, Mt 27,63f.; Lk 23,2.5.14; Jn 7,12.47, and recalled the insight of G.N. Stanton who held that in the NT places which referred to the charge of sedition, the hands of the evangelists Matthew, Luke and John can be clearly recognized[397]. The evangelists reflected in their writings the situation of the Christians as it was developing in the decade after the year 70 AD. As the Christians were increasingly viewed as heretics and were being excluded from the synagogues, one sought reasons for the Jewish designation of Jesus as seditionist and false prophet which would ultimately justify the Sanhedrin sentence of death.

---

391. *Ibid.*, p. 122 (= 287).

392. *Ibid.*, p. 123 (= 288). "Nach August Strobel verrät Lk 23,2 'ohne Zweifel ein äusserst präzises Wissen über das jüdische Anklagemoment und das jüdische Urteil'", referring to A. STROBEL, *Die Stunde der Wahrheit. Untersuchungen zum Strafverfahren gegen Jesus* (WUNT, 21), Tübingen, 1980, p. 97, n. 6.

393. SCHNEIDER, *Das Verfahren*, p. 124 (= 289). P. STUHLMACHER, *Warum musste Jesus sterben?*, in *TBei* 16 (1985) 273-285.

394. SCHNEIDER, *Das Verfahren*, p. 124 (= 289). Cf. STUHLMACHER, *Warum*, p. 275, n. 6.

395. SCHNEIDER, *Das Verfahren*, p. 124-125 (= p. 289-290).

396. *Ibid.*, p. 125 (= 290). In his summary, Schneider wrote: "Historisch zutreffend wird der Vorwurf, Jesus habe das Volk 'verführen' wollen, kaum sein" (p. 129 = 294).

397. *Ibid*, p. 125 (= 290). See G.N. STANTON, *Aspects of Early Christian-Jewish Polemic and Apologetic*, in *NTS* 31 (1985) 377-392, p. 380. It is worth noting that immediately preceding this statement of Stanton's was a reference to Schneider's essay, *Political Charge*. Concerning the three accusations against Jesus in Lk 23 he penned: "In all probability, as G. Schneider has recently shown, they come from Luke's redaction of Marcan traditions rather than from pre-Lucan material".

Theologically, the focus of these verses lies with the characterization of the Jews as persistently acting with malice and slander[398]. Jesus was accused of doing what the high priests themselves did (Mk 15,11). Further, Luke wished to highlight the public declaration of Jesus' innocence before the high priests and the assembly of the people by the highest Roman office (23,4).

In a final section, Schneider briefly reviewed the results of his investigation[399]. His concluding sentence brought together the two central themes of redaction criticism and history which he pursued throughout the article and explained the method by which Luke composed his account: "Im ganzen zeigte sich, dass Lukas als 'Historiker' arbeitet, dass er rekonstruiert und plausibel erzählen will. Es wurde jedoch auch deutlich ..., dass er als Historiker aktuelle, vor allem theologische Ziele verfolgt"[400].

Having considered several of Schneider's works pertaining to the Lukan passion narrative, we will sketch an overview of the evolution of his positions from *Lukas* through his article, *Das Verfahren*. What developments may be discerned in Schneider's assessment of the Lukan passion narrative in general, and 23,2.5 in particular, during the period 1977 through 1988? One of the first characteristics to note is that his works have become increasingly focused on the more problematic aspects of the Lukan passion narrative. From studies treating the entire passion account as found in *Passion* and *Lukas*, he has in more recent times concentrated primarily on 23,2.5 and 23,6-16, in addition to 22,66-71.

With regard to 23,2.5 he now entertained the possibility that the charges could be understood in a slightly different manner than he had previously – and consistently – maintained. He continued to advocate that there was only one charge, which was "particularized in two concrete points"[401]. This conclusion was deduced from the grammatical construction. Though he wrote it was probable that the advocating of the tax boycott and Messiah claim were specifications of the first charge of leading the people astray, he now proposed that it could also be understood that leading the people astray and promoting the boycott of the imperial tax were derived from the messiah claim[402].

In his treatment of the charges Schneider made the following observation about their historicity: "That the evangelist has thereby grasped in its essentials the historically true position can be indirectly confirmed from the Jewish tradition

---

398. SCHNEIDER, *Das Verfahren*, p. 126 (= 291).

399. *Ibid.*, p. 128-129 (= 293-294).

400. *Ibid.*, p. 129 (= 294).

401. *Political Charge*, p. 407-408 (= 177). Cf. *Lukas*, p. 471-472.

402. *Das Verfahren*, p. 122 (= 287): "Wahrscheinlich sind die drei erwähnten Punkte so zu verstehen, dass der erste (Volksverführung) durch die beiden folgenden spezifiziert wird (Verweigerung der Kaisersteuer, Messiasanspruch). Man kann indessen auch überlegen, ob Volksaufwiegelung und Aufforderung zum Steuer-Boykott als Vergehen gegen den römischen Kaiser verstanden sind und beide Delikte aus dem messianischen Königsanspruch abgeleitet werden". Cf. *Political Charge*, p. 407-408 (= 175-176); *Lukas*, p. 471-472; *Passion*, p. 91.

about Jesus, a tradition which sees in Jesus one who led the people astray"[403].
He further articulated this statement in his 1988 contribution. "Als das Judentum
die Jesusgläubigen als Häretiker betrachtete und aus dem Synagogenverband
auszuschliessen begann, suchte man die jüdische Position zu begründen, indem man
Jesus als Verführer und Falschpropheten bezeichnete. So glaubte man die im
Synedrium betriebene Todesstrafe rechtfertigen zu können"[404].

The MAs (22,62.64)

Addressing the MA in 22,62 Schneider (1973) stated simply that it did not belong
to Lk[405]. Though for the MAs in *Passion* Schneider appealed generally to the
influence of oral tradition, in discussing the specific MA in Lk 22,64 / Mt 26,68
he raised the possibility that both Matthew and Luke relied on a pre-Markan
tradition[406]. In *Lukas* Schneider affirmed his earlier conclusion that v. 62 was
probably drawn into Lk from Mt and was satisfied with merely calling attention to
v. 64 without offering any explanation[407]. No longer did he make reference to
the similarities of Lk with Mt over against Mk as originating from their common
purpose of presentation as well as the influence of oral tradition as he had done in
Passion[408]. Though in general Schneider's position has remained relatively
constant, there have been some shifts in his views. We now consider his very
detailed treatment of the charges brought against Jesus.

The Herod Pericope (23,6-16)

Taking notice in *Verleugnung* (1969) that Schürmann ascribed 23,6-16 to the
special pre-Lukan passion source[409], Schneider then adopted that view[410]. As

---

403. SCHNEIDER, *Political Charge*, p. 414 (= 183): "Dass der Evangelist damit die
historische Wahrheit im wesentlichen getroffen haben wird, kann indirekt die jüdische
Jesustradition bestätigen, die in Jesus einen Volksaufwiegler sieht".
    404. SCHNEIDER, *Das Verfahren*, p. 125 (= 290).
    405. *Passion*, p. 82.
    406. SCHNEIDER, *Passion*, p. 65. See also p. 67, where the possibility of the influence of oral
tradition was considered for the MAs.
    407. *Lukas*, p. 465, 466. This reflected his conclusion in *Verleugnung*, though at that time
he still entertained the idea that though not probable, it was not impossible that the Lukan verse
could have been the more original. Cf. *Verleugnung*, p. 96, 103.
    408. *Lukas*, p. 465, 466. Cf. *Passion*, p. 143.
    409. SCHNEIDER, *Verleugnung*, p. 22, n. 91. Cf. H. SCHÜRMANN, *Jesu Abschiedsrede*, p.
140, n. 476.
    410. *Verleugnung*, p. 143: "Auch lk Sondergutabschnitte im Kapitel 23 lassen die starke
Vermutung aufkommen, dass Luk neben der Mk-Vorlage eine Sonderquelle der P benutzt habe.
Die folgenden Sonderabschnitte der lk P werden kaum ausserhalb eines Passionszusammenhangs
tradiert worden sein: Lk 23,6-16 (Jesus vor Herodes) ...". Though in n. 19 he called attention
to the article of Dibelius, he invited comparision with SCHMID, *Lukas*, ³1955, ⁴1960, p. 343, and
GRUNDMANN, *Lukas*, ²1961, p. 423.

regards the connection between the Gospel and Acts he stated only: "Ferner wird hier das Zusammenwirken von Herodes und Pilatus gegen Jesus als Ausführung des göttlichen Heilsplanes gewertet (4,25-28). Für den Leser der Apg wird dabei vorausgesetzt, dass er Lk 23,6-16 kennt"[411]. He reiterated his position that the pericope belonged to the special source in his essay on the pre-canonical passion narrative (1972)[412].

Certain shifts in his position can be detected when, in *Passion* (1973), he maintained that Luke inserted a *Sonderüberlieferung* into the Markan account of Pilate's trial, arguing that the story could originally have been independently transmitted[413]. The *Sondergut* narrative of the appearance of Jesus before Herod (23,6-16) served as a bridge, connecting the Markan trial and the subsequent Barabbas scene[414]. As to its historicity he pointed to the "Zuversicht" of Blinzler and Hoehner, but added: "doch darf ein historisches Urteil nicht die traditionsgeschichtliche Beurteilung bestimmen"[415]. Although at this time he suggested only a special tradition, he indicated that Tyson believed that 23,2.6-12 belonged to a special passion source[416]. The rest of the Lukan changes vis-à-vis Mk were not explained by appeal to a special sources. The purpose of the story was to emphasize the innocence of Jesus (23,14-16)[417]. He continued to view v. 2 as containing one charge specified in two ways. In 23,14 Luke wrote based upon previous material in his Gospel (19,48; 20,6.19.26; 22,2) which in turn he borrowed from Mk (Mk 11,18b.32b; 12,12a; 14,2) and not from another source[418]. By interpreting the charge as perverting the people, the Jews, as plaintiffs, won a hearing before Pilate wherein Luke certainly reproduced ("wiedergegeben") the historical course of events[419]. The charge against Jesus

411. SCHNEIDER, *Verleugnung*, p. 214.

412. *Problem*, p. 236 (= 227): "M.E. können mit Sicherheit nur folgende lukanische Einheiten aus Lk 22 als vorlukanisch und nichtmarkinisch gelten", after which he listed 22,19-20a.24-26.28-30.21-32.35-38.63-64.66-68 and added in n. 79: "zu beachten sind auch Lk 23,6-16 (Herodes und Pilatus)", again referring readers to SCHÜRMANN, *Jesu Abschiedsrede*, p. 140.

413. SCHNEIDER, *Passion*, p. 90. See also p. 91. A passing reference to Acts 4,25-27 in the context of a discussion about Dibelius's theory on the origin of the story was the only connection made to Acts for the Herod pericope. However, he stated that the Jewish leaders were the real agitators alluding to 23,18f.25 and Acts 13,50; 14,19; 17,5-8.13; 18,12-17; 21,27f. (p. 92, n. 29). He treated the Herod story on p. 90-94.

414. *Ibid.*, p. 90.

415. *Ibid.*, n. 24.

416. *Ibid.*, p. 91: "Diese Beurteilung des heutigen Textbestandes beruht auf der Annahme, Lukas habe nur für die Herodesgeschichte (VV. 6-16) eine Sonderüberlieferung benutzt, nicht aber für die übrigen Abweichungen gegenüber der Mk-Darstellung". Schneider passed over vv. 7-9 rather superficially, choosing only to paraphrase the action described therein. See also n. 25. Cf. TYSON, *Lucan Version*, p. 252, and *Jesus and Herod Antipas*, in *JBL* 79 (1960) 239-246.

417. This triple declaration of guiltlessness (vv. 4.14f.22) had an "apologetische Funktion" (SCHNEIDER, *Passion*, p. 92-93).

418. *Passion*, p. 91; see *Lukas*, p. 472.

419. *Passion*, p. 91.

must be considered a lie in view of 20,20-26. Herod's desire to see Jesus (23,8) was also compared with earlier Lukan material (9,9). The gorgeous apparel was seen as a mockery and derided Jesus' royal claim. It was somewhat surprising that Luke mentioned the Sanhedrin vehemently bringing charges against Jesus (v. 10), but it served a connecting function[420]. Regarding v. 11, Schneider wondered whether this originally treated a mockery scene[421]. It contained a certain parallelism with the Markan account of the mockery by the Roman soldiers (Mk 15,16-20a) which Luke did not elect to take over. A significant shift occurred that by 1973 he admitted the possibility that the mockery (23,11) was a variant tradition of the Markan mockery by the Roman soldiers[422] which cast the Romans in a better light, therefore serving a political apologetic[423]. Concerning the detail in GP that Jesus was condemned to death by Herod he asserted that such a view was "völlig unbegründet"[424]. Contrary to the Markan account where the crowd approached Pilate on its own initiative, Luke presented the chief priests, rulers and people as going to Pilate in response to his bidding (v. 13)[425]. With the reference to Pilate's wish to release Jesus (23,16), Luke took up Mk 15,9.

Modifications in Schneider's Position (1969-1973)

Though the position of Schneider on the Herod story is to be characterized as unchanged in the years 1969 to 1972, his stance began to evolve in 1973. He gave more detailed attention to the pericope. No longer was the passage thought to be part of a pre-Lukan passion narrative. Some of the material stemmed from Mk.

Lukas (1977)[426]

In referring to the opinion that 23,6-12 was a special tradition brought into the Markan scene, which could have originally been independently transmitted, Schneider continued to observe (1977), nevertheless, there were many objections[427]. He queried whether this story could have had a meaning in and of itself, perhaps as a mockery scene[428]. He acknowledged that v. 9 could possibly

420. *Ibid.*, p. 93.
421. *Ibid.*, p. 90.
422. *Ibid.*, p. 93.
423. *Ibid.*, p. 94.
424. *Ibid.*, n. 32.
425. *Ibid.*, p. 102.
426. *Lukas*, p. 473-475, treated 23,6-12 and p. 476-477, concerned 23,13-16.
427. *Ibid.*, p. 473-474. The statement concerning doubts on the early transmission of the Herod account was quoted verbatim from *Passion*, 1973, p. 90: "Wenn man auch nicht sagen kann [*pace* Dibelius], sie sei aus urkirchlichem Schriftverständnis heraus entwickelt worden", still Schneider was not as convinced as BLINZLER, *Der Prozess Jesu*, ⁴1969, p. 291-293, and HOEHNER, *Herod Antipas*, 1972, p. 227-230, 233-239, of the passage's historicity.
428. SCHNEIDER, *Lukas*, p. 474. This reflected the same position espoused in *Passion*, p. 90.

have been modeled on Mk 15,5 (the silence of Jesus before Pilate) and that the note regarding the friendship of Herod and Pilate (v. 12) could have been Luke's resumption of Mk 3,6[429]. Luke obviously also had in mind Ps 2,1f. (Acts 4,25-28)[430]. Verses 6f. and v. 8b, in addition to v. 10, manifested the redactional connection ("Verklammerung")[431]. Elements of or points of contact with the Markan passion were now beginning to be recognized in this pericope.

Schneider argued that 23,13-16, a *Sondergut* piece containing Pilate's second declaration of Jesus' innocence (v. 14c; cf. v. 4), was a Lukan formation not the least because it formed a transition to the Barabbas scene (vv. 18-25), which was a revision and abridgement of Mk 15,6-15[432]. Because Herod permitted Jesus to be arrayed in dazzling apparel before returning him to Pilate, an action which mocked the kingship claim of Jesus, Schneider now argued that this mockery scene was a certain substitute for the similar scene in Mk 15,16-20a which Luke omitted[433]. He no longer referred to the possibility that the mockery by Herod and his soldiers (vv. 10-12) was a variant tradition of a similar story, having now assigned its formation to Luke[434]. The section vv. 13-16 containing Pilate's judgment of Jesus' innocence (23,14) building upon previous materials, assumed the charges pressed by the Sanhedrin (23,2.5) as well as an element from the Herod story (23,15; cf. 23,11)[435].

Some doubts would be entertained, Schneider mused, from the standpoint of the historian about the Markan presentation that a Roman ruler practiced Passover amnesty[436]. But it could have been possible on the part of the Jews to release a prisoner for the Passover[437].

Modifications in Schneider's Position (1973-1977)

In general, it can be seen from a comparison of the two works, that the position of Schneider is to be characterized more by continuity than by change. From *Passion* (1973) to *Lukas* (1977)[438] he offered some new elements and amended previous ones, which may be summarized as follows. Luke redactionally linked material (23,6f. with 23,5; 23,8b with 9,9; 23,10 with 23,2) and Schneider now

---

429. *Lukas*, p. 474.

430. *Ibid.*, p. 475. Pilate and Herod were instruments of God's plan of salvation.

431. *Ibid.*, p. 474.

432. *Ibid.*, p. 476. Because v. 17 was lacking in the best manuscripts, material from Mk 15,6 and Mt 27,15 was suspected of having infiltrated the Lukan text.

433. *Ibid.*, p. 475. Schneider spoke of "Ersatz" instead of "Parallelität" as he had done in *Passion*, 1973, p. 93.

434. *Lukas*, p. 475. Cf. *Passion*, 1973, p. 93: "Es ist nicht ausgeschlossen, dass es sich um Traditionsvarianten der gleichen Erzählung handelt".

435. *Lukas*, p. 476.

436. *Ibid.* Cf. Mt 27,15 and Jn 18,39.

437. *Ibid.*

438. The article by Verrall was listed in his sectional bibliography of *Lukas* (p. 473).

suggested that the detail of Jesus' silence was possibly borrowed from Mk 15,15.
In *Lukas* he introduced an opinion on v. 12 with the mention of the friendship
between Herod and Pilate that the evangelist obviously had, besides Mk 3,6, Ps
2,1f. (Acts 4,25-28) in mind[439].

Also, in his research for *Lukas* he began to recognize Markan elements in
23,6-12. From an earlier opinion that 23,10-12 reflected a certain parallelism
("Parallelität") with the mockery by the soldiers in Mk, though not excluding that
it may treat tradition variants of a similar story[440], Schneider later suggested that
it was a certain substitute ("ein gewissen Ersatz") for Mk 15,16-20a[441].

The most radical shift during this period came in his assessment of 23,6-16.
While in *Passion*, he seemed to have accepted the judgment with reservation, that
for 23,6-16 Luke used a special tradition[442], he judged as improbable in 1977 that
a story of the approximate extent of vv. 6-12 would have been independently
transmitted[443]. He arrived at this conclusion noting how the passage was
redactionally connected[444].

Refining his position further, he left open the possiblity of "eine historische
Reminiszenz an die Rolle des Herodes Antipas im 'Prozess Jesu'"[445]. What is
more, in *Lukas* he asserted that overall 23,13-16 should be considered "eine
lukanische Bildung" because of its function of leading into the Barabbas scene[446].

Das Verfahren gegen Jesus in der Sicht des dritten Evangeliums
Lk 22,54-23,25[447]
Lk 23,6-16 ("Jesus vor Herodes")[448]

In consideration of the context, Schneider (1988) observed Luke skillfully prepared
for the Herod scene with the addition of a phrase to the charge in 23,5 that Jesus
had been stirring up the people by teaching καὶ ἀρξάμενος ἀπὸ τῆς Γαλιλαίας

439. *Ibid.*, p. 475; see p. 474.
440. *Passion*, p. 93.
441. *Lukas*, p. 475. As noted above, he dropped the suggestion that the verses treated
variations of a tradition containing a similar story.
442. *Passion*, p. 91.
443. *Lukas*, p. 474. He still referred to the pericope as a "Sonderüberlieferung" (p. 473).
444. *Ibid.* While Schneider pointed to the relation of vv. 6f. to 23,5, of v. 8b to 9,9 and v.
10 to 23,2, achieved by redactional activity, he was less sure of the possibility that the silence of
Jesus before Pilate (v. 9) was based upon Mk 15,5 and the allusion to the friendship of Herod and
Pilate (v. 12) was a Lukan resumption of Mk 3,6.
445. *Ibid.*
446. *Ibid.*, p. 476.
447. *Das Verfahren*, p. 111-130 (= 276-295).
448. Schneider, *Das Verfahren*, treated this pericope on p. 126-128, 129 (= 291-293, 294).
Here he listed 23,6-16 as "Jesus vor Herodes" while in *Lukas* 23,6-12 was designated by that title
with vv. 13-16 being included in the section 23,13-25 which he titled "Die Verhandlung vor
Pilatus" (p. 475).

ἕως ὧδε[449]. Once Pilate learned that Jesus fell under the jurisdiction of Herod, he dispatched him to encounter Herod who wished to see a sign from Jesus (23,8). Although the Jews failed to succeed with Herod in their charge against Jesus, Herod, with his soldiers, ridiculed Jesus before sending him back to Pilate. The episode functioned in the overall story as a further testimony to the guiltlessness of Jesus. Both political authorities arrived at the same conclusion.

In *Das Verfahren* Schneider argued more forcefully against the proposition of a source, claiming that the view that Luke possessed a source for the Herod story can hardly be maintained[450]. He was quick to point out possible relations to Mk. Conceding strong Lukan influence in the scene's composition, he suggested that the following three aspects could be dependent upon Mk: the silence of Jesus before Herod (23,9b) could refer to the silence of Jesus before Pilate (Mk 15,4)[451] and the accusing behavior by the chief priests and scribes (23,10) could have been inspired by Mk 15,3. Compared to *Lukas*, where 23,11 was considered a certain substitute for the mockery inflicted by the Roman soldiers, now one ought to suppose most probably ("am ehesten") that the ridicule of Jesus by Herod and the soldiers (23,11) had been transferred from the scene in Mk 15,16-20a[452]. Schneider still held the view that Luke "allenfalls" knew a legendary or anecdotal notice about Herod's participation in the trial[453]. But he proposed it was also possible that Luke shaped the scene from other news about Herod, for example 9,7-9 and 13,31 in conjunction with material from Mk[454].

Responding to the suggestion of P.W. Walaskay, who in drawing attention to the parallelism between Paul's trials in Acts and those of Jesus in the Gospel, proposed that in Lk Jesus encountered an Herodian king because Luke found in his tradition the scene of Paul before Agrippa (Acts 26), Schneider dismissed such a possibility on the ground that it, too, was a free composition of Luke[455].

---

449. *Das Verfahren*, p. 126 (= 291).

450. *Das Verfahren*, p. 127 (= 292). Two reasons were offered in support of this view: "die deutlich redaktionelle Einbettung der Szene (23,5-7.13-16)" and "der wenig zusammenhängende und eher aufzählende Duktus der Szene selbst (23,8f.10.11.12)". He issued a challenge to those who argue to the contrary, saying they must answer the question why Jesus was sent from Pilate to Herod. Ultimately, wrote Schneider, we are unable to answer the question. He referred to Fitzmyer who argued that the scene, after all, "has no significance for the understanding of Jesus' person or fate" (p. 127-128 = 292-293; cf. FITZMYER, *Luke*, p. 1480). The *Sondergut* material 23,6-12.13-16 was referred to as "Jesus vor Herodes Antipas" in various ways (p. 111, n. 2 = 276, n. 2). See also p. 119 (= 284): 23,6-16 and 23,6-12.13-16; p. 120 (= 285): 23,6-12(13-16); p. 121, 127-129 (= 286, 292-294): 23,6-16.

451. SCHNEIDER, *Das Verfahren*, p. 126-127 (= 291-292). Previously, he suggested the possibility that v. 9 was modeled upon Mk 15,5 (*Lukas*, p. 474). See F. NEIRYNCK, *Literary Criticism* (1993), p. 24: "G. Schneider can no longer be cited among those who ascribe to L the episode of the appearance of Jesus before Herod (23,6-12)".

452. *Das Verfahren*, p. 127 (= 292). Cf. *Lukas*, p. 475.

453. *Das Verfahren*, p. 127 (= 292).

454. *Ibid.*, n. 82.

455. *Ibid.*, p. 128. Here Schneider refuted Walaskay by referring to RADL, *Paulus*, p. 197:

His position remained consistent that from a theological perspective, the purpose of 23,6-16 was to name a second prominent witness for the innocence of Jesus[456]. Focusing on 23,12, which mentioned that Herod and Pilate became friends, he interpreted this as implying the peace-keeping reality which was a result of salvation and the passion of Jesus.

Modifications in Schneider's Position (1977-1988)

Perhaps the issue that has shown the greatest development has been Schneider's position concerning the story of Jesus before Herod (23,6-16). In *Passion* he conceded that the account originally could have been passed on independently[457]. Nevertheless, he was not convinced that this adequately responded to all objections[458]. One objection was that this story had no decisive meaning for the course of events in the trial of Jesus[459]. He cautioned, however, "doch darf ein historisches Urteil nicht die traditionsgeschichtliche Beurteilung bestimmen"[460].

Beginning with *Passion* (1973) the account's chief purpose was consistently seen to provide emphasis for the innocence of Jesus[461]. By 1977, still conceding

---

"Dass das hier wiedergegebene Privatgespräch zwischen Festus und Agrippa eine Rekonstruktion darstellt, ist selbstverstandlich. Ebenso sicher aber ist, dass es sich um eine Komposition des Lukas handelt". Radl enumerated Lukan style characteristics of Acts 25,13-22 (p. 198). Still later, Radl addressed the matter whether Luke had knowledge of an encounter between Agrippa and Paul. Because of a series of improbabilities and since Luke's compositional work was reflected from beginning to end in this passage, Radl concurred with H. CONZELMANN, *Die Apostelgeschichte* (HNT, 7), Tübingen, 1963, ²1972, p. 137, that this passage was a "frei entworfene Prunkszene ohne historischen Kern" (*Paulus*, p. 199). The lack of attention previously to parallels in Lk-Acts by Schneider would be all the more surprising since he directed Radl's dissertation which was completed in 1974.

In Schneider's treatment of Acts 25,13-26,32, he called attention to the fact that this passage served as a parallel to the solemn declaration of innocence by Pilate in the trial of Jesus: Lk 23,4.14f.22. He compared the participation of King Herod (23,15) with that of King Agrippa II in Acts 26,31. Furthermore, he decided that three sections, 25,13-22.23-27 and 26,1-32, ought to be considered as a unity. He agreed with the evaluation of Radl that the scene 25,13-22 was a free Lukan composition and deemed Conzelmann's judgment that 25,13-22 was "frei entworfen" as "uberflüssig" (*Die Apostelgeschichte* II [HTKNT, 5/2], Freiburg, 1982, p. 361-362).

456. *Das Verfahren*, p. 128 (= 293). He left open the suggestion of Grundmann, echoed by Fitzmyer, that Luke had in mind a principle from Dt 19,15 which decreed the need for two or three witnesses in matters pertaining to crimes or wrongdoing. Cf. GRUNDMANN, *Lukas*, 1963, p. 424; FITZMYER, p. 1480.

457. *Passion*, p. 90.

458. *Ibid.*

459. *Ibid.* "Die Frage ist, ob diese Erzählung – für sich genommen – einen Sinn hatte". This position was maintained through his 1988 article. "Doch hat diese für den Ablauf des Verfahrens keine besondere Rolle gespielt" (*Das Verfahren*, p. 127; cf. *Lukas*, p. 473-474).

460. *Passion*, p. 90. See *Lukas*, p. 474.

461. *Passion*, p. 91.

that the story could have been originally passed on independently, though questioning its reasonableness as an independent tradition, his position shifted to the point where he rejected the probability that a story of the scope of vv. 6-12 would have been independently transmitted. Instead, the possibility of a historical reminiscence concerning Herod's role in the trial of Jesus was put forward[462]. It was, then, with the appearance of *Lukas*, that Schneider began to see the possible relationship of the Lukan Herod account to Mk[463]. The function of the pericope remained the same however: Herod's testimony highlighted the innocence of Jesus[464].

Schneider's position in *Das Verfahren* (1988) reflected that of 1977, but with additional nuancing. He now argued more forcefully against the proposition of a source. In *Das Verfahren* he wrote that the view that Luke possessed a source for the Herod story can hardly be maintained[465]. Previously, he acknowledged the opinion that an independent tradition could have been circulated, but noted the objections to such a proposal in which he argued against Blinzler and Hoehner. He now offered two arguments against such a special source: 1) the clearly redactional embeddedness of the scene (23,5-7.13-16), and 2) "der wenig zusammenhängende und eher aufzählende Duktus der Szene selbst (23,8f.10.11.12)"[466].

Concerning the origin of the Herod scene (23,6-16), more possible Markan influence was detected as a result of Schneider's 1988 investigation. He now wrestled with the possibility that Jesus' refusal to answer Herod (v. 9b) and Pilate, took up Mk 15,4 whereas in *Lukas* he suggested that v. 9 rested upon Mk 15,5[467]. Further, he subsequently proposed that the vehement accusations by the religious leaders could have been inspired by Mk 15,3[468]. Finally, he did not refer to his earlier idea that v. 12 was a resumption of Mk 3,6[469].

---

462. *Lukas*, p. 474: "Eine selbständig überlieferte Erzählung im ungefähren Umfang der VV 6-12 ist somit unwahrscheinlich, nicht aber eine historische Reminiszenz an die Rolle des Herodes Antipas im 'Prozess Jesu'".

463. *Ibid*. Schneider now discussed not only the redactional elements which reflect Luke's hand, but also possible Markan influence.

464. *Ibid*.

465. *Das Verfahren*, p. 127 (= 292): "Die Auffassung, Lukas habe für die Herodesszene eine Quelle besessen, *wird sich schwerlich behaupten können*". Cf. *Lukas*, p. 474: "Eine selbständig überlieferte Erzählung im ungefähren Umfang der VV 6-12 ist somit *unwahrscheinlich ...*" [emphasis mine].

466. *Das Verfahren*, p. 127, n. 80 (= 292, n. 80). Schneider also believed that the passage had no historical value. "Bei der Frage nach der Historizität der Herodesszene wird man unumwunden einräumen müssen, dass sie im ganzen negativ zu beantworten ist" (p. 127 = 292). The name of Ernst, who was said to be undecided, was added to the debate. See *Lukas*, p. 473-474.

467. SCHNEIDER, *Das Verfahren*, p. 126-127 (= 291-292). Cf. *Lukas*, p. 474, 475.

468. *Das Verfahren*, p. 127 (= 292).

469. *Lukas*, p. 474. Cf. *Das Verfahren*, p. 126, 128 (= 291, 293).

Schneider still yielded to the view that Luke perhaps ("allenfalls") knew a legendary or anecdotal notice about Herod's participation in the trial[470]. But he proposed it was also possible that Luke shaped the scene from other stories about Herod, for example, 9,7-9 and 13,31, in conjunction with material from Mk[471].

Following a lengthy review of Schneider's work, incorporating the changes and continuity of his positions and the reception of his works by other scholars little remains except to briefly summarize. Schneider has made valuable contributions to the study of Lk-Acts through his continued investigation of source-, literary- and redactional-critical aspects of these works. Demonstrating a willingness to re-examine his own positions, he increasingly recognized Markan influence even in passages which he previously assigned to independent, special traditions.

Because the Lukan passion narrative continued to be a central topic of his research for more than twenty-five years, his influence has been extensive. One who benefited directly from collaboration with him is W. Radl. Having traced shifts in Schneider's reasoning from *Lukas* through his detailed investigation of the charges against Jesus up to his 1988 essay, we will now compare Schneider's positions with those of Radl.

THE POSITION OF WALTER RADL (1974-1988)

In his 1974 dissertation directed by G. Schneider, Radl focused on the parallel motifs of Paul and Jesus in Lk-Acts[472]. Those pertaining especially to the Lukan passion narrative (22,54-23,25) included the following.

Lk	Acts (or relationship to Mk)
13,31	12 "die Mordabsicht des Herodes"
20-23	21-26 "das Leiden"
23	27 "der Tod (bei Paulus symbolisch)"
22,54 συλλαβόντες	cf. 21,27 ἐπέβαλον ... τὰς χεῖρας. 30: ἐπιλαβόμενοι. 33: ἐπελάβετο
22,54	cf. Mk
22,63	23,2 "Schläge für die Angeklagten"
22,66-71	cf. 22,30-23,10 "vor dem Hohen Rat"
22,66 συνήχθη	13,44
22,66	cf. 22,30
22,66	cf. 24,21; 25,2
22,66	cf. Mk 14,53.55

470. *Das Verfahren*, p. 127 (= 292).
471. *Ibid.*, n. 82.
472. W. RADL, *Paulus und Jesus im lukanischen Doppelwerk. Untersuchungen zu Parallelmotiven im Lukasevangelium und in der Apostelgeschichte* (EH XXIII/49), Bern - Frankfurt, 1975. Diss. Bochum, 1974 (dir. G. SCHNEIDER).

22,67-70	par. Mk "Das Verhör vor dem Hohen At dreht sich um einen rein religiösen Messiastitel, um Christologie".
22,69; 23,46.34	material parallels with 7,56.59.60 (martyrdom of Stephen)
22,71	diff. Mk 14,64
23,1-5	cf. 24,1-23 [24,1-9]; 25,1-12
23,1	cf. Mk
23,1 ἤγαγον	diff. Mk
23,2-4	cf. 17,7
23,2	material parallel with 21,36; 22,22; similar details: 24,2.5 (agreements in the trials)
23,2	17,2; 25,8
23,2	24,5-8 εὑρόντες ... κινοῦντα
23,2	diff. Mk 15,3
23,2 τοῦτον εὕραμεν	24,5 εὑρόντες ... τοῦτον
23,2	17,7 "Schliesslich bringen sie mit einer eindeutig politischen Verleumdung ..."
23,3f.	diff. Mk
23,3	24,22
23,4	23,29; 24,22; 28,18
23,5	24,5f.; 25,8
23,5 Galilee	5,37; see Lk, 13,31
23,6-16	25,23–26,32 so noted by Zeller
23,6-12	25,13–26,32
23,6-12	4,25-27 "Es kann hier offenbleiben, ob auch Lk 23,6-12 schon eine Schöpfung des Lukas ist, etwa, wie DIBELIUS, Herodes und Pilatus, meint, im Anschluss an die Apg 4,25-27 zitierte und ausgelegte Psalmstelle 2,1f.".
23,6	23,34
23,7	25,13f.
23,7 ἐπιγνούς + ὅτι	19,34
23,7-16	25,13–26,32 so noted by Overbeck
23,8	25,22 the curiosity of Agrippa and Antipas (Lk 9,9d); 26,1-23
23,11	25,23
23,13-25	13,28; 21,36; 22,22ff.; 25,24; 21,27-36
23,13-25	cf. Mk
23,13	13,28
23,14-16	28,18
23,14	25,25; 26,31; 3,13 παραδίδωμι
cf. 23,14	25,7
23,14 κρίνω	4,9; 12,19; 24,8; 28,18; 25,26
23,15	5,14?; 11,24; 26,31
23,15 θέλημα	13,22; 22,14
23,16	26,32
23,18-25	28,18ff.
23,18-23	21,36; 22,22
23,18	21,36; 22,22
23,19	19,40
23,19	par. Mk 15,7
23,20	par. Mk; diff. Mk

23,21	par. Mk
23,22	26,32
23,22	par. Mk
23,22b	par. Mk
23,23a	par. Mk
23,24f.	24,27; 25,9; 24,17 (Overbeck); cf. Mk
23,24	par. Mk; diff. Mk
23,25	19,40; 27,1; 28,17f.
23,25	diff. Mk "und gibt Jesus 'ihrem Willen'"

Radl noted that already in 1854 E. Zeller detected resemblance between 23,2 and Acts 24,2.5; 23,6-16 and Acts 25,23-26,32[473]. Zeller often rejected or accepted texts as parallels based upon verbal likeness which neglected the content and function. Using the former methodology Acts 23,34 and 23,6 would not be seen as parallels[474]. Radl also called attention to the similarities in the trial of Paul in Acts with those of the trial of Jesus in Lk as highlighted by R. Morgenthaler (1949)[475]. In discussing the similarity of the accounts of Paul before Herod Agrippa (Acts 25,31f.) and Jesus' trial before Herod Antipas (23,7) Radl adopted the view that Luke regarded Herod as the king in Ps 2[476]. Acts 4,26 confirmed this. Acknowledging that the mockery by the Roman soldiers (Mk 15,16-20) was absent, Radl nonetheless indicated that this reflected a Lukan tendency and so 23,11 transferred it to Jewish personnel[477]. As shown above, Radl left open the question of the origin of 23,6-12[478].

Radl Compared to Schneider on 23,2 and 22,66-71 (1988)

Reactions to Schneider's article *Das Verfahren* were offered in the same volume in *Der Prozess gegen Jesus* by W. Radl who presented his own assessment of the

---

473. RADL, *Paulus*, p. 47; see also p. 65. E. ZELLER, *Die Apostelgeschichte nach ihrem Inhalt und Ursprung kritisch untersucht*, Stuttgart, 1854, p. 289, focused on the common outcome (23,15; Acts 26,31) of the parallel passages. In 1870 F. OVERBECK recognized the likeness between 23,5 / Acts 24,5f.; 23,2 / Acts 25,8; and 23,7-16 / Acts 25,13-26,32 (*Kurze Erklärung der Apostelgeschichte*, p. 412, 427, 431 = *Kurzgefasstes exegetisches Handbuch zum NT* I,4 W.M.L. DE WETTE, Leipzig, ⁴1870. "Vierte Auflage bearbeitet und stark erweitert von Franz Overbeck") (RADL, p. 48).

474. *Paulus*, p. 61-62.

475. RADL, *Paulus*, p. 52; cf. MORGENTHALER, *Die lukanische Geschichtsschreibung*, Vol. 1, p. 182f. Radl referred to J. BIHLER, *Die Stephanusgeschichte im Zussamenhang der Apostelgeschichte* (MThS, 1/16), Munich, 1963, in his discussion of the similarities between Jesus and Stephen (RADL, p. 40).

476. RADL, *Paulus*, p. 217, n. 1.

477. *Ibid.*, p. 326, n. 4.

478. *Ibid.*, p. 217, n. 2.

tradition-history questions of 22,67f. and 23,2[479]. We begin with a comparison of their views on the political charges against Jesus.

Both Schneider and Radl concurred that the tradition-history issue pertaining to 23,2 was easiest to resolve in comparison to 23,6-12 and 22,66-71[480]. They agreed that there was only one charge, derived from the Markan *Vorlage*, which was specified in two further points[481]. Like Schneider, while noting the parallel constructions, Radl asserted that the three charges can be reduced to one: the common denominator of inciting or alienating the people[482]. This compression/reduction by Luke was also recognized at other points of the trial events[483].

The Markan origin was confirmed by the adoption of the catchword ἀνασείω (23,5) from Mk 15,11[484]. Radl further qualified his position by saying that the individual elements were derived also from purely Lukan *Vorgaben*. Luke himself prepared and planted the charge in the final chapters before the passion account[485]: by the question in 20,20 which contained the redactional addition, ὥστε παραδοῦναι αὐτὸν τῇ ἀρχῇ τῇ ἐξουσίᾳ τοῦ ἡγεμόνος; perhaps by 19,38 which reminded people of the kingly title[486]; and by the accusation of the kingly claim in 22,67-70 which prepared for Pilate's question in 23,3[487].

Both scholars treated 20,20-26 as a point of reference. The charge that Jesus instigated the boycott of the tax, Schneider maintained, was seen as libel in light

---

479. RADL, *Sonderüberlieferungen*, p. 131-147. For a discussion of the Herod pericope (23,6-12) see below.

480. *Ibid.*, p. 131. He treated 23,2 on p. 132-134. Cf. SCHNEIDER, *Das Verfahren*, p. 121-126, p. 121 (= 286-291, p. 286). Radl referred to Schneider's article, *Politische Anklage* (= *Political Charge*), as a prominent, foundational investigation with a clear result (*Sonderüberlieferungen*, p. 132, n. 2).

481. RADL, *Sonderüberlieferungen*, p. 133. SCHNEIDER, *Das Verfahren*, p. 122 (= 287).

482. RADL, *Sonderüberlieferungen*, p. 132. He also cited BÜCHELE, *Der Tod Jesu*, p. 27-28, who held the same position. Cf. SCHNEIDER, *Das Verfahren*, p. 122 (= 287). Radl noted the parallel structures follow upon διαστρέφοντα. Being connected with καί, each began with a participle (κωλύοντα - λέγοντα), ended with an infinitive (διδόναι - εἶναι) and in between stood titles of rulers (Καῖσαρ - βασιλεύς). Given Schneider's suggestion that the first two charges may derive from the third, there may be some disagreement, though he still held that first interpretation was more likely.

483. See RADL, *Das Lukas-Evangelium* (EdF, 261), Darmstadt, 1988, p. 42-45 (esp. p. 44).

484. *Sonderüberlieferungen*, p. 132.

485. *Ibid.* A minor difference appeared in the list of verses upon which the charges rest cited by both scholars. While Schneider compared Lk 19,48 with Mk 11,18b (*Political Charge*, p. 408 = 178), Radl suggested Mk 11,28. Schneider's verse was taken from parallel accounts of the cleansing of the Temple, while Radl's recalled an encounter between Jesus and the chief priests, scribes and elders focusing on his authority ταῦτα ποιεῖς, a phrase which most likely referred to his cleansing the Temple.

486. *Sonderüberlieferungen*, p. 133. Lk 19,38, in turn, will remind the reader of the song in 2,14 which implicitly contrasted the real ruler of the world with the supposed.

487. *Ibid.*

of this passage[488]. Radl noted that 20,20 prepared for the first of the concretizations of the charge[489]. Both agreed that it was the Jewish leaders who were, in fact, the real seditionists[490]. Similarly, Schneider and Radl also concurred that the charge of sedition rested upon material found earlier in Lk: 19,48 (par. Mk 11,28); 20,6.19 (par. Mk 11,32; 12,12); 20,26 (diff. Mk 12,17); 22,2 (diff. Mk 14,2)[491]. Further, Radl agreed with Schneider that the charge in 23,2 prepared for Pilate's question which followed (23,3)[492].

While Schneider made only passing reference to Acts, pointing out that the leadership of the masses was the real source of insurrection among the people[493], similarities and differences between the charge and events in Lk 23 and Acts 17,6f. were highlighted more by Radl[494]. A comparison of these texts showed very clearly, according to Radl, the Lukan view as reflected in the intrigues of the Jews in the Gospel both before and after the episode with Herod (23,5.13) as well as in Acts[495]. In Acts, the Jews have likewise accused the Christian missionaries of rebellion. Thus, the whole combination of the charge in 23,2 appears as Lukan.

Radl saw the charge in 23,2 as having its place in connection with the political apologetic of Luke[496]. At no time in his presentation on 23,2 did Radl address, as Schneider had, the issue of a possible OT influence. In Radl's view, not only was the kingship of Jesus not political, but his disciples were loyal citizens who had no claim to political power[497]. Schneider, too, referred to the non-political nature of the claim of kingship[498]. While he was not directly concerned with the

---

488. SCHNEIDER, *Das Verfahren*, p. 122 (= 287).

489. *Sonderüberlieferungen*, p. 133.

490. *Ibid.*, p. 134. Here Radl referred to Schneider's position in *Passion*, p. 92. Cf. SCHNEIDER, *Lukas*, p. 475: "Doch sie bezeugen auch die Schuldlosigkeit Jesu, und nur die Synedristen erscheinen als böswillige und verleumderische Ankläger". See further *Political Charge*, p. 408 (= 178) and *Das Verfahren*, p. 122, 126 under "e" (= 287, 291).

491. RADL, *Sonderüberlieferungen*, p. 132. Cf. SCHNEIDER, *Das Verfahren*, p. 122 (= 287). Schneider did not list the Markan parallel passages or those different from Mk as Radl had done.

492. RADL, *Sonderüberlieferungen*, p. 133. Cf. SCHNEIDER, *Das Verfahren*, p. 121 (= 286).

493. SCHNEIDER, *Das Verfahren*, p. 122, n. 57 (= 287, n. 57).

494. *Sonderüberlieferungen*, p. 134. See also RADL, *Paulus*. Schneider only made references to Acts in the notes (p. 121, n. 52; 122, n. 57; 123, n. 60 = 286, n. 52; 287, n. 57; 288, n. 60). Cf. also *Passion*, p. 92, n. 29.

495. RADL, *Sonderüberlieferungen*, p. 134. Cf. Acts 13,50; 14,19; 18,12-17. In Acts 17 the charge of disturbing the people, which was raised against Paul and Silas, was concretized as non-observance of the laws of Caesar and affirming the royal/kingly claim for Jesus (p. 133), a position similar to Schneider's (*Political Charge*, p. 412 = 181).

496. *Sonderüberlieferungen*, p. 134. Cf. p. 139-140. See also RADL, *Das Lukas-Evangelium*, p. 125-126, where he addressed the *Sitz im Leben* out of which the accounts with Pilate and Herod grew, stating that Luke already had in mind the situation of the Church.

497. RADL, *Sonderüberlieferungen*, p. 134. Cf. SCHNEIDER, *Das Verfahren*, p. 124 (= 289).

498. SCHNEIDER, *Das Verfahren*, p. 122 (= 287): "Bei dem Messiasanspruch können sich die Ratsmitglieder zwar auf das Bekenntnis Jesu im Synedrium berufen. Indem sie aber 'Messias' durch βασιλεύς erläutern, suggerieren sie vor Pilatus einen politischen Königsanspruch. Der Leser des dritten Evangeliums kann den verleumderischen Charakter der jüdischen Anklage

topic of Luke's political apologetic in his 1988 article, he did comment on it in *The Political Charge*[499].

For Schneider, the charge arose out of Jewish-Christian relations, the Jewish Jesus polemic, during the last third of the first century[500]. Radl did not address this phenomenon, except indirectly by referring to the situation of Christian missionaries as reflected in Acts[501]. He spoke rather of the place that 23,2 occupied in the political apologetic of Luke[502]. We consider now the positions of Schneider and Radl on the Herod pericope.

Radl on 23,6-12: A Reaction to Schneider

Radl wrote *Sonderüberlieferungen* (1988) partially in response to Schneider's article in the same volume[503]. One of the first differences to note is how each scholar divided the pericopes. Although Schneider treated 23,6-16, Radl confined his comments to 23,6-12[504]. He noted that 23,6-12 could give the impression by its extent and singular content that it was an independent legendary, perhaps even historically grounded, special tradition, but such an impression was deceiving[505]. The text was not resolvable ("nicht lösbar") outside the immediate context because it had been so combined with it and entangled within it[506].

Judging that the pericope has been composed from loosely connected building blocks drawn from Mk[507], as well as previous portions of Lk[508], Radl examined selected elements, evaluating the source of the Lukan material, as Schneider had

durchschauen".

499. SCHNEIDER, *Political Charge*, p. 413-414 (= 183).

500. SCHNEIDER, *Das Verfahren*, p. 124-125 (= 289-290).

501. RADL, *Sonderüberlieferungen*, p. 134.

502. *Ibid*.

503. SCHNEIDER, *Das Verfahren*, p. 111-130 (= 276-295). One of the distinguishing marks of Radl's article was that he continually compared the Gospel material with Acts.

504. RADL, *Sonderüberlieferungen*, p. 134. Cf. SCHNEIDER, *Das Verfahren*, p. 126 (= 291).

505. RADL, *Sonderüberlieferungen*, 1988, p. 134-135. Radl treated the scene Jesus before Herod (23,6-12) on p. 134-140.

506. *Ibid.*, p. 135. Radl spoke of "die nahtlose Einbettung der Szene".

507. *Ibid.*: "Was den Text selbst betrifft, so ist er ziemlich lose aus einzelnen Bausteinen zusammengesetzt, und deren 'Fundstellen' lassen sich zum grössten Teil in den vorliegenden Schriften des Lukas bzw. Markus angeben".

508. *Ibid*. For an additional reference to the earlier material in Lk see p. 137. He called attention to the more recent studies on the pericope namely K. Müller, Buck and Soards (1985b). In another work published that same year, following Müller and Soards, he continued to maintain that Luke composed an entire pericope using pre-existing materials and individual verses (*Das Lukas-Evangelium* [EdF, 261], Darmstadt, 1988, p. 33; cf. p. 45). The purpose of the story was to convey the political harmlessness of Jesus (p. 126: "Dass der jüdische König mit dem Fall Jesu befasst wird (23,6-12), dient der Bestätigung des Eindrucks von der politischen Harmlosigkeit Jesu, steht also im Dienst der Wahrheitsfindung, zeigt das Bemühen des römischen Beamten um die Klärung des Sachverhalts (vgl. Apg 22,24.30; 23,28f.; 25,26f.)").

done.[509]. He recognized the word "Galilee" (v. 5) as a catchword, identifying it as a Lukan *topos*, and pointing out where it occurred, both in Lk and Acts[510].

Verses 7 and 8, the appearance of Jesus in Herod's court, were prepared for by various references to Galilee as Herod's territory of jurisdiction (3,1; cf. 13,31) and the term "tetrarch" (3,19; 9,7)[511]. Verse 8, already indirectly anticipated in Lk 9,7-9, reported Herod's desire to meet Jesus[512]. Schneider suggested that the pericope could have been shaped by combining other reports of Herod, such as Lk 9,7-9 and 13,31[513]. Therefore, on this point they were in partial agreement.

They agreed that the material and motifs of Jesus' interrogation and response of silence (v. 9) revealed the Markan *Vorlage*[514]. Both looked to Mk 15,4 as the inspiration of 23,9, though Radl also added Mk 14,60.61[515]. Even the formulation reflected the Markan origin, according to Radl[516]. They considered v. 10 to rest upon Mk 15,3. Because of the abrupt introduction of the chief priests and scribes into the scene, Radl deduced that this reference was taken over from another context. Their being named, as well as their presentation as accusers, were

---

509. *Ibid*. See also RADL, *Das Lukas-Evangelium*, p. 45: "Noch schwieriger zu beurteilen ist der Anteil des Lukas an seinem Sondergut. Seine Redaktion reicht wahrscheinlich von der Überarbeitung und szenischen Rahmung (15,1f.; 16,14), auch wieder mit Hilfe von Fragen (1,34; 3,10.12.14; vgl. Apg 1,6; 8,34; 16,30), bis zur Komposition ganzer Perikopen unter Verwendung vorhandener Bausteine (23,6-12)".

510. RADL, *Sonderüberlieferungen*, p. 135. The material of 23,5f. was stamped with thoughts of the beginning of Jesus' ministry in Galilee. Already prepared for in Lk 1,26; 2,4.39, Luke's programmatic statement, containing two references to Galilee (4,14.31), occurred in 4,14-43. Verse 23,7, which identified Herod as the authority for Galilee, was already announced in 3,1 (cf. 13,31). Cf. SCHNEIDER, *Lukas*, p. 473, and *Passion*, p. 90.

511. RADL, *Sonderüberlieferungen*, p. 135. Other references to Herod included 8,3 and 13,31.

512. *Ibid*., p. 135-136. In addition, see 3,1 and cf. 13,31. Schneider also mentioned this in *Lukas*, p. 474.

513. SCHNEIDER, *Das Verfahren*, p. 127, n. 82 (= 292, n. 82). Although Luke had no source, he possibly could have known a legendary or anecdotal note about Herod's involvement in the trial of Jesus.

514. RADL, *Sonderüberlieferungen*, p. 136. The interrogation theme stemmed from Mk 15,4 and the theme of Jesus' silence originated in Mk 14,60.61 as well as 15,4. Cf. SCHNEIDER, *Das Verfahren*, p. 126-127, where his hesitancy was reflected in his use of terms such as "möglicherweise" and "vielleicht". See also *Lukas*, p. 474, 475. There was no mention of the issue in *Passion* (1973).

515. RADL, *Sonderüberlieferungen*, p. 136. See SCHNEIDER, *Das Verfahren*, p. 126-127 (= 291-292). Whereas Schneider suggested that material in the Herod scene can possibly rest upon the Markan passion, and 23,9b can refer to 15,4, Radl was more forceful, less reticent in assigning certain material to the Markan *Vorlage*. Radl wrote, for example: "Hier (v. 9) hat Lukas offenbar Elemente seiner Markus-Vorlage, die er an ihrem ursprünglichen Ort nicht übernommen hat, als Material für die Gestaltung der Herodesszene benützt. So stammt das Motiv vom "Ausfragen" aus Mk 15,4 und das Schweigenmotiv aus Mk 14.60.61 sowie 15,4f." (*Sonderüberlieferungen*, p. 136).

516. RADL, *Sonderüberlieferungen*, p. 136.

elements taken from the otherwise unused *Vorlage* of the trial before Pilate (Mk 15,3f.)[517].

Radl and Schneider both agreed somewhat hesitantly that Mk 15,16-20a was the source for the material in v. 11[518]. According to Radl, Luke apparently reworked and even changed individual pieces[519]. Though Schneider had not treated the matter of the "dazzling apparel" (ἐσθῆτα λαμπράν) in which Jesus was arrayed (v. 11), choosing rather to refer simply to the mockery by the Roman soldiers, Radl suggested that the clothing revealed ties to the Markan mockery scene, though its function had changed from that prior context. He considered the new raiment as an indication of Jesus' innocence[520]. The appearance of the soldiers and their participation in the mockery of Jesus with Herod was also somewhat abrupt. But the fact of their involvement was reminiscent of Mk 15,16-20a[521].

Verses 11 and 12 presented complexities because of their inherent contradictions[522]. One of the paradoxes of v. 11 was that Herod was described as taunting Jesus thus conflicting with the impression that Herod supported the declaration of his innocence. Radl surmised that the evangelist himself wanted to present Herod as a witness for the guiltlessness of Jesus[523]. In order to reconcile these conflicting dimensions of Herod's attitude, his loathing of Jesus as well as his support for him, Luke seized a means of presentation which enabled him to include both[524].

Asserting that v. 12 had no point of contact with either Lk or Mk, Radl regarded it as comparable with Acts 4,27f., which he acknowledged complicated the problem even more. Radl's position rejected earlier Schneider's suggestion that 23,12 resumed Mk 3,6[525]. It was somewhat contradictory that while Lk 23 and

517. *Ibid*.

518. *Ibid*. See SCHNEIDER, *Das Verfahren*, p. 127 (= 292). Cf. *Lukas*, p. 475, and *Passion*, p. 90.

519. RADL, *Sonderüberlieferungen*, p. 136. Changes included the detail that the soldiers belonged to Herod and not to Pilate and there was no mention of the purple robe as in Mk 15,17.20.

520. *Ibid*. Radl questioned the purpose of the dazzling apparel: "Ob diesem damit Jesus verächtlich gemacht werden soll, ist durchaus fraglich". This responded, in part, to the 1977 position of Schneider, based on Blinzler, that the clothing was intended to make a public mockery of the kingly claim of Jesus (*Lukas*, p. 475; cf. BLINZLER, *Der Prozess*, ⁴1969, p. 290), a position Schneider originally espoused in *Passion*, p. 93.

521. RADL, *Sonderüberlieferungen*, p. 136. Radl maintained though Luke passed over this, he nonetheless reworked individual pieces and altered them in such a way that the soldiers belonged to Herod rather than to Pilate as in the Markan account.

522. *Ibid*., p. 137.

523. *Ibid*.

524. *Ibid*.

525. *Ibid*. Cf. SCHNEIDER, *Lukas*, p. 474. "Vielleicht ist V 9 an Mk 15,5 (Schweigen Jesu vor Pilatus angelehnt und die Schlussnotiz über die Freundschaft von Herodes und Pilatus (V 12) lukanische Wiederaufnahme von Mk 3,6". See also p. 475: "Es ist aber wohl nicht bloss daran

Acts 4 both spoke of a collaboration between the Jews and heathen authorities, in Lk 23 the governing officials appeared for Jesus and in Acts 4 they were against him.

Radl cited the position of Dibelius who maintained that Acts 4,27f. was quite comparable with v. 12[526]. Radl asserted that Luke fashioned this material in Acts not only on the basis of facts, that ultimately Pilate became an accomplice, but also in light of Ps 2,1f., a christologically significant passage which stated that the rulers set themselves against the Lord and his anointed[527]. Luke wrote the Herod account along the same lines as the previous episode with Pilate, influenced by the only distinctive characteristic of the passion narrative, which was that all of them shared in the condemnation of Jesus. Because Luke crafted the attitude of Pilate in his passion account (already indicated in Mk), he was able to portray Herod in a similar vein[528]. What is more, he may have wanted to indicate that what united the two men was their common action for Jesus[529]. Schneider argued, however, that this signified the peace creating reality of salvation and the passion of Jesus[530]. He cautiously expressed the opinion that Luke used news about Herod in composing 23,6-16, but made no reference to the influence of Ps 2 as Radl had done[531].

Radl held that the significance of v. 12 lay in the feature that all had contributed to the condemnation of Jesus[532]. "Die Frage, ob Lukas dabei die historische Information von einem Verhör bei Herodes zur Verfügung stand, ist damit nicht beantwortet. Sie muss man aber verneinen; denn die Tatsache einer solchen Verhandlung hätte die markinische bzw. vormarkinische Passionsgeschichte nicht verschwiegen"[533]. He contended that Luke did not possess "mehr oder bessere historische Information als Markus"[534].

gedacht, dass Herodes die 'Geste' des Statthalters honorierte, sondern der Evangelist hat offenbar (ausser Mk 3,6) Ps 2,1f. im Auge (Apg 4,25-28)".

526. RADL, *Sonderüberlieferungen*, p. 137, n. 20. DIBELIUS, *Herodes und Pilatus*. MATERA, *Luke 23,1-25*, p. 542, n. 21, likewise referred to this article in his treatment.

527. RADL, *Sonderüberlieferungen*, p. 137-138.

528. *Ibid.*, p. 138: "Wenn Lukas nun in seiner Passionsgeschichte die Haltung des Pilatus (wie schon Markus) anders beschreibt, dann kann er ebenso mit Herodes verfahren".

529. *Ibid.* Radl observed that Luke often used the term φίλος, but not always in the sense of a personal friendship. Radl referred in n. 24 to Soards who considered this friendship in a wider sense of "sons of this world" as found, e.g. in Lk 16,8f. (SOARDS, *Tradition, Composition, and Theology in Luke's Account of Jesus before Herod Antipas*, in *Bib* 66 [1985] p. 357).

530. SCHNEIDER, *Das Verfahren*, p. 128 (= 293). Cf. *Lukas*, p. 475, and *Passion*, p. 93.

531. SCHNEIDER, *Das Verfahren*, p. 127, n. 81 (= 292, n. 81). He also drew attention to GP 1,1 and the Syriac Didaskalia 21 as Radl did, but offered no treatment of the internal conflict concerning the presentation of Herod. However, regarding the influence of Ps 2, see *Lukas*, p. 475, and *Passion*, p. 90, n. 23.

532. RADL, *Sonderüberlieferungen*, p. 138.

533. *Ibid.*, p. 138-139.

534. *Ibid.*, p. 147.

Further, Radl took up the debate of the relationship of Acts 25,13–26,32 to Lk 23,6-12(16). Just as Acts 17,6f. was able to shed light upon Lk 23,2, so too can Paul's trial before Festus, Agrippa, and Bernice elucidate the Lukan interests behind the Herod scene. But the account in Acts had been much more freely and broadly composed by Luke and as such offered a political apologetic for the Christian. In both accounts Luke showed the competent representatives of Judaism as a second witness to the innocence and loyalty of those charged[535].

In attempting to establish the purpose of this scene, Radl suggested that it has paranetic, paradigmatic as well as christological meaning[536]. But the prevailing motive for the composition, in his opinion, was to provide an apology for Jesus. Schneider, on the other hand, adopted the position of Fitzmyer who stated that "in the Lucan passion narrative this scene is actually a minor one. It had no significance for the understanding of Jesus' person or fate"[537]. Nonetheless, both Radl and Schneider agreed that the pericope served to present a second prominent witness to the innocence of Jesus[538]. Radl drew attention to the declaration by further accentuating that it was the competent representative of Judaism who rendered this witness.

In his 1988 contribution Schneider denied the historicity of the Herod episode[539]. Radl, quoting K. Müller, who declared that there was no evidence contradicting the position that Lk 23,6-12 was a Lukan composition, further concluded that Luke did not have at his disposal historical information concerning the trial before Herod[540]. Rather, data pointing to Luke's use of the Markan and pre-Markan passion narratives was exhibited[541].

Schneider, notwithstanding, continued to entertain the viewpoint that Luke possibly knew a legendary or anecdotal note which he combined with other reports

535. *Ibid.*, p. 140.

536. *Ibid.*, p. 139. Here, Radl drew upon the works of E. BUCK, *Function*, in W. HAUBECK and M. BACHMANN (eds.), *Wort*, 1980, p. 176, 178. See below. The similarity of this position with that of SCHNEIDER, *Verleugnung*, p. 172, was pointed out. A. BÜCHELE, *Der Tod Jesu*, 1978, p. 33, 64, highlighted the christology as that of the suffering Just One and focused on the silence of Jesus in the face of abuse.

537. SCHNEIDER, *Das Verfahren*, p. 127-128 (= 292-293), from FITZMYER, *Luke*, p. 1480.

538. RADL, *Sonderüberlieferungen*, p. 140. Cf. SCHNEIDER, *Das Verfahren*, p. 128 (= 293).

539. SCHNEIDER, *Das Verfahren*, p. 127 (= 292): "Bei der Frage nach der Historizität der Herodesszene wird man unumwunden einräumen müssen, dass sie im ganzen negativ zu beantworten ist".

540. RADL, *Sonderüberlieferungen*, p. 138-139. "Mag hier [Lk 22,67f] wenigstens die Annahme einer Tradition nicht unmöglich sein, so bietet Lukas jedenfalls an keiner der drei Stellen mehr oder bessere historische Information als Markus. Er schreibt weder als Historiker noch als Jurist, sondern als Theologe" (p. 147). K. MÜLLER, *Jesus*, in G. DAUTZENBERG, H. MERKLEIN and K. MÜLLER (eds.), *Zur Geschichte*, 1979, p. 141. See below.

541. RADL, *Sonderüberlieferungen*, p. 138-139: "Die Frage, ob Lukas dabei die historische Information von einem Verhör bei Herodes zur Verfügung stand, ist damit nicht beantwortet. Sie muss man aber verneinen; denn die Tatsache eine solchen Verhandlung hätte die markinische bzw. vormarkinische Passionsgeschichte nicht verschwiegen".

concerning Herod and Markan texts whose influence Schneider had already discerned. Luke ultimately shaped these materials, in combination with elements previously presented in his own Gospel, into the Herod scene[542].

Radl responded to this proposition, admitting that it was hard to say whether Luke had access to such a legendary note. While Pesch in his Markan commentary suggested as possible evidence the existence of such materials in the GP 1f. and the Syriac Didaskalia 21, in addition to Acts 4,27f., Radl was more inclined to believe that these two examples were dependent upon Lk 23 rather than vice versa[543].

In the respective recent analyses of Schneider and Radl of the Sanhedrin trial (22,66-71), both noted the change in order in the Lukan account[544]. While Schneider now merely maintained that it was possible Luke drew on a special tradition for 22,66-68 in addition to Mk for the scene[545], Radl contended that for 22,67f. the assumption of a tradition was "nicht unmöglich"[546], though he further insisted that if Luke employed a special tradition, he did not offer "mehr oder bessere historische Information als Markus"[547]. Still both scholars were clear that Luke redacted Mk for the account of the Sanhedrin trial instead of relying on a special tradition or special continuous passion source[548].

542. SCHNEIDER, *Das Verfahren*, p. 127 (= 292).

543. RADL, *Sonderüberlieferungen*, p. 135, n. 15. Cf. R. PESCH, *Das Markusevangelium*, 1977, T. 2, p. 409.

544. RADL, *Sonderüberlieferungen*, p. 140-141. He made more explicit reference to it. Cf. SCHNEIDER, *Das Verfahren*, p. 114 (= 279).

545. SCHNEIDER, *Das Verfahren*, p. 116 (= 281). In support he cited his own previous works, *Verleugnung*, p. 137-139, *Jesus*, p. 9f. (= *Lukas, Theologe*, p. 166f.); *Gab es*, p. 35-38 (= 271-274); *Passion*, p. 67-72 as well as LÉGASSE, *Jésus*, 1974, p. 182-189. See below. Schneider recalled the position of Fitzmyer who, arguing generally against the existence of a special Lukan source for the passion narrative, conceded perhaps even vv. 69-71 went back to a special tradition (*Das Verfahren*, p. 116 = 281; see FITZMYER, *Luke*, p. 1458). Schneider suggested that the context derived from the heavenly enthronement of Jesus following his death (*Das Verfahren*, p. 115 = 280).

546. RADL, *Sonderüberlieferungen*, p. 147. See also p. 140, 142. While Radl listed three factors which spoke against Lukan redaction, he was quick to add that they did not prove a special tradition in addition to Mk. These were: Luke normally demonstrated the tendency to abbreviate the dialogue of his *Vorlage*; the change in the Messiah question was atypical for Luke; and the separation of the Son of God title from the Messiah title would seem to contradict their being identified with each other (p. 142). At this point Radl was in dialogue with Catchpole (p. 142-143, nn. 40, 41. Cf. CATCHPOLE, *Historicity*, p. 64, and in a more detailed fashion, *Trial*, p. 197-200). Radl responded that Luke occasionally expanded dialogue and that the other changes can be understood in light of Lukan christology.

547. RADL, *Sonderüberlieferungen*, p. 147.

548. *Ibid.*, p. 140, and SCHNEIDER, *Das Verfahren*, p. 115 (= 280). Till Arend MOHR judged that for 22,54-71 "die Annahme einer lkn. Sonderquelle für die Synedriumsszene ist nicht haltbar", opting instead for an explanation of redaction. The particularly vexing verses of 22,67b.68 rested not on an older tradition, but were redacted by Luke to smooth out the unevenness found in Mk (*Markus- und Johannespassion. Redaktions- und traditionsgeschichtliche*

Conclusion

The independent research of Schneider, who was inspired by the work of Schürmann, and Catchpole, who wrote in reaction to Lietzmann and others, sought to establish the presence of a non-Markan source in a significant portion of the Lukan passion narrative. Though employing similar methodologies they reached differing conclusions. Unlike Catchpole, Schneider continued investigating Lk-Acts throughout his scholarly career and consequently changed his view about the amount of Markan material in the Lukan account of the passion and ultimately rejected the idea of a separate, continuous non-Markan source in that section of the Gospel[549].

Untersuchung der Markinischen und Johanneischen Passionstradition [ATANT, 70], Basel, 1982, p. 271. Diss. Basel, 1980 [dir. H. BALTENSWEILER]). Additionally, Mohr observed that Luke had not reported Mk 15,16-20a. Instead the evangelist chose to offer in 23,11 a milder form of it which excused the Romans. This was achieved, in part, by avoiding references to the spitting and beating (p. 271, n. 99). A. Dauer penned a review of Mohr's work (*TRev* 81 [1985] 18-22).

549. See NEIRYNCK, *Literary Criticism*, p. 22, n. 46.

CHAPTER EIGHT

THE LUKAN PASSION AS A REDACTION OF MARK
THE DISSERTATIONS OF ALLEN F. PAGE AND H. VAN DER KWAAK

At the time Schneider and Catchpole completed their dissertations in an effort to uncover a special source, two other dissertations were also completed which resulted in entirely different conclusions. These scholars were not as prolific or as well known, and unfortunately, their work did not reach as wide an audience. Both set about to examine how Luke redacted the Markan material and criticized the Proto-Lk theory.

   Allen F. PAGE critically examined the Proto-Lk hypothesis in a 1968 Duke University dissertation in which he focused primarily on Taylor, and to a lesser extent, on Streeter[1]. He concluded that Proto-Lk was unnecessary, as changes in Lk vis-à-vis its Markan source could be accounted for by Luke's redactional techniques and goals. "Indeed, the changes which the Third Evangelist has made in Mk can better be accounted for by the view that while using Mk as his *Grundschrift* he has been free to add, delete, and alter his materials in order to bring out his own interests, than by the Proto-Luke hypothesis. The view that Mk provides the *Grundschrift* of the Third Gospel, when combined with an understanding of Luke as author and theologian, accounts for most of the phenomena of the literary structure of the Third Gospel as we now have it. The Proto-Luke hypothesis is unnecessary"[2]. The changes reflected Luke's theological themes, a fulfillment of prophecy motif as well as the political apologetic regarding Rome.

   Dismissing the need to explain variations in order by means of a non-Markan source, following one avenue proposed by Creed, Page adopted the view that Luke presented his readers with an "intelligent criticism of Mark"[3]. Because the noctural session was improbable, Luke attempted to reconstruct events as best he

---

1. A.F. PAGE, *Proto-Luke Reconsidered: A Study of the Literary Method and Theology in the Gospel of Luke*. Diss. Duke, Durham, NC, 1968 (dir. D.M. SMITH). Page alleged Streeter did not contribute much to the testing of the hypothesis (cf. p. 15). Regarding the popularity of the Proto-Lk hypothesis, Page declared: "Although this hypothesis of the literary origin of the Third Gospel has never gained general acceptance, it has been received by some with enthusiasm" (p. iii). He mistakenly dated Streeter's article in the *HJ* at 1920 (p. 15, 280). It was published in 1921.
   2. PAGE, *Proto-Luke*, p. iv-v.
   3. *Ibid.*, p. 139; cf. CREED, *Luke*, p. 277. In justice to those who hold the view of a special source, the entire sentence should be quoted, since Creed also suggested there may be other explanations for the changes. "Luke may be drawing upon a special source in addition to Mark, or possibly upon special traditions orally transmitted. But it may be that his modifications are to be ascribed to intelligent criticism of Mark on the part of himself or his circle, and to motives – literary and religious – such as we can trace elsewhere" (p. 276, not p. 277 as cited by Page).

could and consequently resolved the dilemma by telescoping the dual sessions of the Sanhedrin into one, thus moving the denial to the night as Jesus was being detained[4].

Page ascribed the episode of Peter's denial to Mk[5]. The mockery (22,63-65) was more complex. Taylor suspected that this pericope came from the special source because the mockery was disassociated from the trial. Page countered that might have been necessitated by the shifting the trial to the next morning[6]. He reasoned it did not appear that Luke used Mk directly for this story. Page sidestepped much of the controversy related to these issues by referring readers to another Duke University dissertation[7]. Nevertheless, Page contended Luke sought to blend the two gatherings of the Sanhedrin into one, since it would appear unlikely that the Sanhedrin would gather at night[8].

However, because 1) there was strong verbal agreement in vv. 69.71, 2) v. 70 apparently was a revision of Mk 14,61, 3) the clause εἰ σὺ εἶ ὁ χριστός may be a variant form of the question posed in Mk 14,61, and 4) v. 66 seemed to be a transitional verse required by the shift of the trial to the morning hours, Page rejected Taylor's proposal of the special source for the account of the Sanhedrin trial[9].

Although Page conceded there was a low percentage of words in common between Mk and Lk in 23,1-5, except for v. 3, which Taylor assumed was an addition from Mk, Page asked "why has Luke not used that which originally united them rather than borrowing the connecting link from Mark?"[10]. Insofar as nearly one third of the words in 23,18-25 were shared in common by Lk and Mk and they were well distributed throughout the pericope, and since the argument for the connected special source had not been well substantiated, Page concluded that 23,18-25 probably stemmed from Mk[11].

Most of Page's criticisms were directed against Taylor, who was responsible for the hypothesis's "classic defense"[12]. The framework of Lk was definitely that of Mk, according to Page, and not some other source. Reasons for this position were twofold: most of the episodes shared a Markan parallel. Secondly, material peculiar to Luke offered no framework of its own[13]. Page faulted Taylor for not

---

4. PAGE, *Proto-Luke*, p. 139; cf. p. 121, n. 1.

5. *Ibid.*, p. 121. Page was in complete agreement with Taylor that the account of Peter's denial derived from Mk (cf. TAYLOR, *Behind*, p. 48).

6. PAGE, *Proto-Luke*, p. 122.

7. *Ibid.*, p. 139, n. 2. Cf. W.R. WILSON, *The Trial of Jesus: A Judicial, Literary and Historical Study*. Diss. Duke Durham, NC, 1960 (dir. K.W. CLARK).

8. PAGE, *Proto-Luke*, p. 139.

9. *Ibid.*, p. 123-124.

10. *Ibid.*, p. 126.

11. *Ibid.*, p. 127.

12. For a discussion of the critics and supporters of the Proto-Lk hypothesis from a historical perspective, see p. 15-30.

13. *Ibid.*, p. 144, 230-231, 253.

having proven his claim that the unity of Proto-Lk exceeded that of the material as it presently existed[14]. Closely related to the question of the framework of the Gospel was the matter of order[15]. "The order of the Marcan material indicates no more for Taylor than that Luke has simply gone through the Gospel of Mark in choosing materials to be inserted. The alternative that the reason for Luke's fidelity to the order of Mark is that Mark provides the basic framework for the Third Gospel is just as possible as Taylor's suggestion. The fact that we have seen that there is little evidence of a framework in the Third Gospel other than that provided by Mark, and the idea and motifs embodied therein, makes this alternative decidedly preferable to the Proto-Luke hypothesis"[16]. The reasons for the omission of Markan material, which advocates of the special source pointed to as evidence of its use, can generally be discerned. Page suggested there may have been "limited use of a source common" to both Luke and Matthew to explain the phrase τίς ἐστιν ὁ παίσας σε;[17]. Page will only go so far as to say the mockery did not reflect Luke's "*direct* use of Mark".

Directing attention to methodological concerns, Page castigated Taylor and Streeter for neglecting the overall structure of Lk while focusing too narrowly on smaller units[18]. Charging that form criticism was responsible for the abandonment of the search for sources[19], Page lauded redaction criticism for attention to such detail, saying that source criticism was part and parcel of the new methodology. The lament concerning the reluctance or refusal to engage in source criticism, even and especially by those whose approach was redaction-critical, was one that will be consistently repeated and often ignored[20].

With certain qualifications Page concurred with the two British exegetes on three issues. All three scholars found that various sections, including 22,14–24,53,

---

14. *Ibid.*, p. 244.

15. *Ibid.*, p. 253.

16. *Ibid.*

17. *Ibid.*, p. 122-123.

18. *Ibid.*, p. 145, n. 1; cf. p. vi.

19. *Ibid.*, p. 4: "There has been an increasing tendency to follow the trend which had already begun under the influence of form criticism – namely, the trend to abandon the search for sources to which so much attention was given in earlier decades". Such an observation notwithstanding, Page was obviously indebted to Dibelius for the explanation of the Herod trial resulting from the fulfillment of Ps 2. Nevertheless, for this interpretation Page credited Creed (CREED, *Luke*, p. 280; cf. PAGE, p. 230). Dibelius's influence on Page may even be detected in his viewing Peter as a type for the church. "The change of the time of the prediction of Peter's denial to the setting of the Supper is congruous with Luke's attempt to prefigure the Church in the gathered communion at the Last Supper. In this setting Peter becomes the type of one who is to be tempted, indeed of one who will yield to temptation and yet be reinstated" (PAGE, p. 138). Cf. DIBELIUS, *From Tradition*, p. 214-215: "As a story the denial is full, and it is logically narrated; ... Indeed, the whole composition must be held quite artistic. It has its own importance, for no element points to a soteriological presentation of the Passion, nor even as an element of the oldest report. It was narrated in the Church from the standpoint that it shared in the fate of Peter".

20. PAGE, *Proto-Luke*, p. 5, 6-7.

were composed of non-Markan material[21]. However, Page argued that Taylor and Streeter "greatly" underestimated the amount of Markan material[22]. Secondly, there was consensus that Luke's compositional technique throughout the Gospel had been to alternate between Markan and non-Markan material, closely interweaving them to achieve a literary unity. However, Page submitted that in the passion narrative this type of alternation "occurs at much shorter intervals"[23]. Finally, though Taylor considered Luke an author, Page contended Lk revealed Luke as both an author and a theologian[24].

The trial before Herod (23,6-16), according to Page, reflected "no indication of dependence upon Mark"[25]. Regrettably, Page offered no further explanation of the origin of the Herod pericope[26]. Nevertheless, he not only adopted the view of Dibelius that the episode was used "to fulfill the prophecy of Psalm 2 in both the Passion narrative and Acts", but believed that it "can be explained on the basis of Luke's theological interest"[27].

H. VAN DER KWAAK (1969) treated the Synoptic accounts of the trial beginning with the Sanhedrin trial and, in the case of Lk, through the trial before Herod[28].

---

21. *Ibid.*, p. 142. In his summary Page wrote: "With few exceptions, we agree with Streeter and Taylor that these sections are composed of non-Marcan material". See p. viii, where Page listed the following as sections attributed to Proto-Lk: 3,1-4,30; 5,1-11; 6,12-8,3; 9,51-18,14; 19,1-27; 19,37-44.47-48; 21,18.34-36; 22,14-24,53.

22. *Ibid.*, p. 142; cf. p. vi, 144.

23. *Ibid.*, p. 105-106.

24. *Ibid.*, p. iv-v; cf. p. 4.

25. *Ibid.*, p. 125; cf. p. 140: "Whereas the trial before Herod is the most extensive episode of the Lucan Passion narrative for which Luke is not dependent on Mark, it has no framework of its own".

26. *Ibid.*, p. 230-231.

27. *Ibid.*, p. 230. While not claiming that the Herod pericope was based upon Mk, Page called attention to C. Talbert, who noted that this account was parallel to Mk 9,7-9 (*The Lukan Presentation of Jesus' Ministry in Galilee*, in *RExp* 64 [1967] 485-497, p. 493). Consequently, "there is a Herod episode in each of the stages of Jesus' ministry (Luke 9:7-9; 17:31 f. [sic: read 13:31f.]; and 23:6-16)" (PAGE, p. 230-231). This was consistent with "Luke's fulfillment of prophecy motif" (p. 230).

28. H. VAN DER KWAAK, *Het Proces van Jezus* (VGTB, 42), Assen, 1969. Diss. Leiden. See his conclusions on p. 170-171, as well as his English summary, p. 280-282.

Another, though later Dutch language study of the Lukan passion narrative was Robrecht MICHIELS, *Het Passieverhaal volgens Lucas*, in *Collationes. Vlaams Tijdschrift voor Theologie en Pastoraal* 14 (1984) 191-210. Surprisingly, Michiels made no reference to the study of Van der Kwaak, though he too regarded the Lukan passion as a redaction of Mk. He adopted a "synchronic" reading of the text. Lk 22,1-24,11(12)/ Mk 14,1-16,8 was regarded as the fourth Markan section in Lk (p. 192-193). The theory of a special continuous passion source was considered "overbodig". The differences were accounted by the fact that some of Luke's material had not been incorporated into the Markan account and Luke's theology served to reshape the Markan narrative. Michiels attended to differences under the headings of omissions, additions, and transpositions. The result was a new four-part ("luik") structure: 22,1-6; 22,7-65;

In contrast to Mt, Lk varied greatly from the Markan account[29]. These differences bore Luke's unique imprint and Van der Kwaak concluded that the variations stemmed from Luke rather than some source[30]. He noted the significant divergence of Lk from Mk and attributed the difference to Luke: "het genoemde illustreert al voldoende, dat Lukas' weergave van het proces van Jezus een geheel eigen stempel draagt"[31]. That Luke was clearly dependent upon Mk was evident at 22,67a.69.71; 23,3.22a. Van der Kwaak critiqued the approach of Taylor and others who defended a separate source for the Lukan passion. "Het vraagstuk van de 'Proto-Lukas' kan hier niet aan de orde gesteld worden ..."[32]. A further problematic was that Luke must be assumed to be the author. A principal objection for Van der Kwaak was that the verses originating from Mk took on a particular function. The best methodological approach would be to analyze these changes in the light of Luke's motifs and objectives rather than to ascribe them to a special source[33]. This did not exclude the possibility that Luke employed certain traditions he may have received, but Mk remained his model[34].

22,66–23,25; 23,26-56(-24,11) (p. 195). Luke's redaction consisted in taking over the order, contents and similar themes from Mk, supplementing them with new material and reacting to the Markan account by offering his own theological-christologicaland apologetical character (p. 195; see also p. 208). The transposition of the account of Peter's denial and the mockery (22,56-62.63-65) in conjunction with 22,54-55 allowed Peter to witness the course of events (p. 201).

Michiels was sensitive to exploring the relationship of the Gospel to Acts, as in the case of the Sanhedrin trial (p. 202) and at other points (passim; in particular see p. 208-209). Luke recast the Sanhedrin trial by omitting the Markan reference to the parousia (22,69). The result was "een krachtige Christus- en Zoon-Godsbelijdenis". The Barabbas episode (23,(17)18-25) was slightly abbreviated.

The MA in 22,62 was "tekstkritisch onzeker" (p. 201). No mention was made of the MA in 22,64.

Luke strongly emphasized the absolute innocence of Jesus. Without specific allusion to Dibelius, it would appear that Michiels was influenced by his perspective, claiming the Lukan passion narrative was "een exempelverhaal" (p. 209) and discussing the similarity with story of Stephen in Acts. Consequently, the passion account of Lk was seen as possessing "een sterk parenetisch karakter".

Michiels regarded the Herod story (23,6-12) as "nieuwe historische informatie" and was used in conjunction with 13,31-33 (p. 203). His phrasing was puzzling when he wrote: "Lucas brengt dus nieuwe historische informatie aan die evenwel niet wijst op een eigen Sonderquelle". Nevertheless, 23,13-16 was seen as a Lukan composition emphasizing the innocence of Jesus.

Michiels also dedicated some pages of a book to a study of the Lukan account of the passion: Binnen het jaar. Het lijden en de dood van Jezus (Cahiers voor levensverdieping, 45), Averbode - Apeldoorn, 1983 (esp. p. 92-106).

29. VAN DER KWAAK, Het Proces, p. 127.

30. Ibid., p. 132: "Hier is voldoende om te concluderen dat het aparte karakter van Lukas' weergave van het proces van Jezus een daad van hemzelf is geweest en niet aan een bron moet worden toegescheven".

31. Ibid., p. 127.

32. Ibid., p. 128.

33. Ibid., p. 129.

34. Ibid., p. 129-130.

Not only that, but this relationship was further evidenced by Luke's concentrating on christology and portraying the gathering of the Sanhedrin as a hearing rather than a trial[35]. In the former, Luke focused on Jesus' superiority over his opponents. In the latter, Luke corrected the Markan version. These two main changes over against Mk fit into the Lukan apologetical intention. What was more, Van der Kwaak was convinced that the vocabulary of 22,66-71 was not "on-Lukaans"[36].

Van der Kwaak also noted the close similarities of the trials of Jesus and Paul which betrayed a "speciale interesse" of Luke. The apologetical aim of such material, which concentrated on the relationship to the Roman government, reflected Luke's concerns and thus the account of the trial of Jesus in Lk should be ascribed to Luke himself rather than to a separate source[37].

In Van der Kwaak's opinion, the appearance of Jesus before the Sanhedrin was shaped by Luke in light of his christology and differed still from his Markan *Vorlage* in the fact that it served as only a hearing. In contrast to Mk and Mt, the silence of Jesus in Lk reflected his "superioriteit over zijn tegenstanders"[38]. This section of Lk offered a "christologisch compendium" in light of the various titles used: Son of God, Son of Man and Christ[39]. Luke's interest in the description of the guilt of the Jewish leaders, apparent in the Gospel, was confirmed in Acts. Van der Kwaak understood the *Sitz im Leben* of Lk to be a situation where the Christians were opposed, especially by the Jews. Lk served then to point the way of their discipleship. The emphasis, Van der Kwaak contended, was not simply a polemic or an apologetic, but represented a missionary bias directed towards the Jews themselves.

Luke offered concrete charges in the case of Jesus as opposed to the other Synoptics and provided evidence in Acts that he was familiar with the Roman practice that the accusers must press charges in the presence of the accused[40]. Van der Kwaak also appealed to comparisons with Acts to establish Lukan redactional interests. He held it probable that Luke imported the situation of the Christians to 23,2.5[41]. Van der Kwaak considered the triple declaration of Jesus' innocence as a motif of Luke confirmed in the passion narrative and in Acts[42]. Luke took over the Markan account of the Barabbas story and gave it a negative coloration. The apologetic of the Christians as not dangerous to the political establishment and viewing the destruction of Jerusalem around 70 AD as punishment for the death of Jesus, also helped to shape the account[43].

35. *Ibid.*
36. *Ibid.*, p. 139.
37. *Ibid.*, p. 132.
38. *Ibid.*, p. 134.
39. *Ibid.*, p. 137.
40. *Ibid.*, p. 140.
41. *Ibid.*, p. 142.
42. *Ibid.*, p. 161.
43. *Ibid.*, p. 170-171.

Van der Kwaak claimed Luke was familiar with a tradition which portrayed Herod as having a negative involvement in the trial of Jesus[44]. The scene underscored the innocence of Jesus through the witness of Herod and Pilate. Van der Kwaak considered Acts 4,27 to be a better preservation of the historical situation arising from Ps 2. He noted Joanna and Manaen as people known to Luke. Here Van der Kwaak referred to F.F. Bruce who believed that Luke from Antioch depended upon Manaen for special information concerning Herod Antipas and his family[45]. Assessing Dibelius's view as "zeer invloedrijk" (very influential), Van der Kwaak nevertheless raised several objections to his theory as well as to those of Blinzler[46] and Tyson[47]. Van der Kwaak opposed Dibelius on the grounds that Luke had not treated the matter of "vervulling" (fulfillment) of Ps 2 in 23,6-12. Ps 2 was not explicitly cited. Further, there was no mention in Ps 2 of the friendship which applied to Herod and Pilate. In contrast, all of the elements of Ps 2 found their fulfillment in Acts 4,25-27[48].

Van der Kwaak viewed the Herod scene as typically Lukan, since the vocabulary and style reflected the rest of the Gospel. With the exception of 23,9.11.12, the scene offered little in the way of new material. The account was considered a composite of Luke's work[49]. Verses 23,6.7 built on 23,5. The observation that Herod was interested in Jesus (9,9) was borrowed from Mk. Herod, with Pilate, served as a witness to the innocence of Jesus[50]. The motif of Jesus' silence in 23,6-8.9.10.15 was drawn from Mk[51]. From the use of the term οὐδὲν ἀπεκρίνατο, it was obvious that Luke derived his material from Mk 14,60-61; 15,4. The silence cast Jesus in the light of the Suffering Servant[52]. Verse 23,4 was assuredly dependent upon Mk 15,14[53].

44. *Ibid.*, p. 159. See the English summary of the dissertation, p. 281: "The scene of Jesus before Herod (23:6-12) is discussed in detail by the author. In this scene and elsewhere Luke describes the trial of Jesus as he considered it ought to have been; Jesus should have appeared before the tetrarch of Galilee". M. de Jonge referred readers to Van der Kwaak (p. 144-160) for "the full discussion" of the Herod story (*The Use of* Ο ΧΡΙΣΤΟΣ, 1975, ²1989, p. 185, n. 55).

45. VAN DER KWAAK, *Het Proces*, p. 145, n. 3. Cf. F.F. BRUCE, *Herod Antipas*, (1963-65) 14.

46. VAN DER KWAAK, *Het Proces*, p. 148-149. He wrote: "Het grootste bezwaar tegen zijn aanpak is dat zijn betoog er op is gericht aan te tonen dat het historisch zo gebeurd kan zijn (is) als de evangelisten verhalen" (p. 149). Cf. BLINZLER, *Der Prozess Jesu*, ³1960, p. 205-219.

47. VAN DER KWAAK, *Het Proces*, p. 149-150. Regarding Tyson's view of Herod's role in the trial, Van der Kwaak reacted that "hij kan echter niet zulk een centrale rol gespeeld hebben als Tyson suggereert" (p. 150). Cf. TYSON, *Jesus and Herod Antipas*, in *JBL* 79 (1960) 239-246; *Lukan Version*, in *NT* 3 (1959) 249-258.

48. VAN DER KWAAK, *Het Proces*, p. 147-148.
49. *Ibid.*, p. 151.
50. *Ibid.*, p. 153.
51. *Ibid.*
52. *Ibid.*, p. 153-154.
53. *Ibid.*, p. 161.

Luke wished to describe the trial as it should have occurred ("behoren te verlopen"). Furthermore, Herod was a witness to the innocence of Jesus. Not only were the events according to the plan of God, but the account offered an apologetic that Christians were not a threat to the government. Verses 23,11-12 reflected concrete material which was not constructed out of other materials, such as was the case with 23,6-10[54]. The mockery was omitted because of the apologetic view toward Rome. But Van der Kwaak lamented "het is echter niet aantoonbaar dat [Lukas] de scene in 23:11 heeft gecreëerd naar analogie van Mark. 15:16-20"[55]. For Van der Kwaak the use of the Markan term ἐμπαίζειν did not prove dependence upon Mk. Neither did the motif of the investiture, since Mark and Luke employed different terms[56]. Van der Kwaak considered it "het meest waarschijnlijk" that Luke possessed a report of Jesus' trial before Herod in which he mocked Jesus and vested him in royal clothing. This vesture symbolized not only Jesus' innocence, but his harmlessness[57]. Though situated within the mockery the dazzling apparel has a positive connotation.

Van der Kwaak also pointed out the similarities between the trial of Jesus and Paul's speech before the Council in Acts 3,13-14 as well as the parallels between the trials of Jesus and Paul[58]. Furthermore, the apologetic both in Acts and in the Gospel portrayed the Christians as innocent and presented Jesus' experience of martyrdom as an example to be imitated[59].

Blinzler termed Van der Kwaak's solution for the Herod pericope "eine originelle, wenn auch recht problematische Erklärung"[60]. What was more, Blinzler rejected Van der Kwaak's idea that the "dazzling apparel" (23,11) was white symbolizing innocence. Instead he opted for the interpretation that it was a "dazzling" ("strahlend") garment which signified Jesus' kingship and royal standing[61].

A.F.J. Klijn penned a bland review of the Van der Kwaak's book saying there was nothing "sensational" in the findings, but such a view was in the minority[62]. F.J. Brinkman faulted the study because the starting point had not sufficiently influenced the results[63]. Yet many were enthusiastic about the book, though sometimes not accepting of Van der Kwaak's interpretation.

---

54. *Ibid.*, p. 155.
55. *Ibid.*, p. 156: "There is nothing really demonstrable that [Luke] had created the scene in 23:11 as analogy to Mark. 15:16-20".
56. *Ibid.*, n. 3.
57. *Ibid.*, p. 157.
58. *Ibid.*, p. 162.
59. *Ibid.*, p. 163.
60. *TRev* 66 (1970) 383.
61. *Ibid.*, p. 384.
62. *NedTT* 24 (1969) 61.
63. *VoxT* 40 (1970) 202: "De invloed van het uitgangspunt voor zijn onderzoek op het resultaat ervan en op de visie van de auteur op de Schrift is niet duidelijk genoeg".

Johann Maier expressed the wish that the work would soon appear in other languages[64]. This was never realized and thus, unfortunately, the work did not receive the attention it deserved. Maier pointed out the work differed from Blinzler's attempt at a reconstruction from a legal standpoint. Likewise, it did not follow Winter's approach in examining the question of responsibility[65]. Maier underscored the value of Van der Kwaak's method: "Das Ergebnis der redaktionsgeschichtlichen Forschung, wonach die Evangelisten den ihnen vorliegenden Stoff je und je aus ihrer individuellen Sicht heraus gestaltet haben, ergibt die Möglichkeit zu einer relativistischeren Einschätzung ihrer Aussagen im Rahmen der biblischen Autorität"[66]. Blinzler, also impressed by the work, noted the study was significant because it was the first purely redaction-critical investigation concerning the traditions about the passion narratives "und als solche ohne Zweifel sehr zu begrüssen"[67]. Three motifs, the christology, the polemic against the Jews and the apologetic towards the Romans, helped to shape the Gospel accounts. Blinzler added Acts 9,20.22 to Van der Kwaak's list of places where the titles were found as proof ["Beleg"] for the Lukan identification ["Gleichsetzung"] of the titles Christ and Son of God.

August Strobel gratefully acknowledged the summary in English[68]. Such a comment underscored Maier's hope that the book would become available to a wider readership. Strobel did not take exception to the essential results of Van der Kwaak's study, but he expressed the desire that its results might reach into the consciousness of the church, particularly as they concerned Jewish and Christian relations.

Both Page and Van der Kwaak addressed the Proto-Lk hypothesis in their respective works. Each, working independently, maintained that the theory, especially as it was articulated by Taylor, was unnecessary to explain the Markan material and the variations in order in the Lukan account. Page and Van der Kwaak saw the differences in the Lukan passion narrative as reflecting the theology of Luke.

64. *Bib* 51 (1970) 280.
65. *Ibid.*, p. 281.
66. *Ibid.*, p. 283. Maier offered a glowing review, complimenting the author for his "vorbildlicher Klarheit". The book, in Maier's opinion, was significant not only for historical scholarship, but also for its potential impact in the fields of church history and history of dogma.
67. *TRev* 66 (1970) 382. The typographical errors did not escape the eye of Blinzler. He dutifully recounted on p. 386, those which he found in the work. F.J. BRINKMAN, in *VoxT* 40 (1970) 202, also called attention to these errors, but only generally.
68. *TLZ* 95 (1970) 666. Cf. VAN DER KWAAK, *Het Proces*, p. 280-282.

CHAPTER NINE

SPECIAL SOURCES AND THE SPECIAL MATERIAL
I. Howard Marshall through Darrell L. Bock

A number of Francophone scholars contributed to the view of a special source in this period, most notably Boismard, who proposed a form of Proto-Lk different from that suggested by German scholars. His was a more complex solution to the synoptic problem which appealed to some scholars. Researchers, such as Marshall, called attention to the very limited success of Schürmann and Rehkopf. He pointed to the distinction between a special source separate from Proto-Lk. Hoehner also made a significant contribution to the study of Herod in his Cambridge dissertation. As we will see, this will also be a time when there will be notable shifts in the positions of some who originally held the view of a special source.

I. Howard Marshall (1970) accepted Markan priority as well as Q, though he admitted that it was difficult to make a determination about the special material in Lk[1]. But in the account of the passion Marshall was sympathetic to a special source: "There is also some evidence that an alternative version of some parts of the passive [sic] narrative was available to Luke"[2]. While he admitted that Mk formed the basis for Lk and thus the "full form" of the Proto-Lk theory was disproved, still he accepted "the less ambitious form" that L and Q were joined prior to Luke's reception of it, and that Luke gave preference to it rather than Mk in parallel accounts, though without providing any examples or proof. He also called attention to the "very limited success" of the attempts of Schürmann and Rehkopf to isolate particular elements of a pre-Lukan source[3].

---

1. I.H. Marshall, *Luke: Historian and Theologian*, Exeter, 1970, p. 61 (esp. p. 57-67); [3]1989.

2. *Ibid.*, p. 62. He referred to Schürmann, *Der Paschamahlbericht* (1953); *Der Einsetzungsbericht* (1955); *Jesu Abschiedsrede* (1957); and F. Rehkopf, *Die lukanische Sonderquelle* (1959) in support of this view.

3. Marshall, *Luke: Historian and Theologian*, p. 64. Though he affirmed the Markan basis in this work, in a brief commentary published at the same time he contrasted two options for describing Luke's compositional technique. The first, inserting large blocks of Q and L into the Markan foundation, was thought to be more objectionable than the proto-Lk theory. "The arguments for and against these theories are highly technical, and any theory of composition must remain very hypothetical at the moment, but of the two the proto-Luke theory is perhaps less open to objection" (*Luke*, in D. Guthrie and J.A. Motyer [eds.], *NBC Revised*, London, [3]1970, p. 888). Marshall argued strongly against redaction criticism: "A growing body of radical opinion has stressed the creative ability of Luke and holds that he has manipulated the sources in the interests of his own theology ... Now it must be admitted that Luke has made a thorough stylistic recasting of his sources and has made many changes of a minor character in his narrative, but against this must be set his expressed intention of faithfully recording his story, his great accuracy in portraying the geographical and political background of events, and the way in which he makes very little alteration when reproducing the actual words of Jesus. To say, as some scholars have

With interest one must consider those aspects of Lukan redaction which Marshall highlighted. All sources were stylistically revised by Luke and often the ideas and vocabulary were hellenized. Blocks of material were arranged. Luke followed the order in Mk for the most part, but where he parted from Mk "the reasons are usually fairly obvious"[4]. Luke offered a geography and chronology different from Mk. Luke chose not to adopt much of the Markan theology. In his revision, Luke did not shy away from adding "his own ideas" to Mk. He did not slavishly follow the sources, but allowed himself to change them as he saw fit. But at the same time, Marshall asserted that Luke generally built upon them faithfully. Marshall viewed the use of the Son of Man title in the Stephen speech (Acts 7,56) to recall its use in 22,69.

Marshall reaffirmed his view in his 1978 commentary that Luke depended upon Mk, much in the form as it now exists[5]. Regarding Q he favored the position

---

done, that Luke was not concerned with historical accuracy, is to fly in the face of his own expressed intentions. When these things are borne in mind, the case for Luke's fidelity to his sources is seen to be a strong one" (p. 888). In the fourth edition (⁴1994), Marshall wrote of Mk, Q and L, but made no mention of Proto-Lk (p. 979). The evangelist's method of telescoping was credited with the placement of the denial and mockery before the trial (p. 1016). Lk 23,1-5 was likened to Acts 18,14-15. Though he noted the similarity between 23,11 and Mk 15,16-20, he rejected any further connection observing that one set of troops could have imitated another. Finally, in his discussion of the Herod pericope (23,6-12) Marshall claimed the transfer was effected since Pilate wished to avoid a difficult case, though it was not necessarily an official transfer. He dismissed as unlikely the theory that the passage originated from Acts 4,25-26 (p. 1017). In the same volume, R.T. France observed that "there has [...] not been much enthusiasm for the view that either M or L represents the contents of a single documentary source" (*Reading the Gospels*, p. 900).

4. MARSHALL, *Luke: Historian and Theologian*, p. 65. Here he referred to J. JEREMIAS, *Perikopen-Umstellungen*. Regarding the difference in order of the denial, mockery and trial as found in Lk Marshall remarked in his 1970 commentary on the Gospel: "It is uncertain whether the dialogue reported by Luke really took place at night, or whether Jesus was subjected to a brief re-examination in the morning. This explains why the accounts of Peter's denial and the mockery by the servants occur *before* the (morning) trial in Luke but *after* the (night) trial in Mark" (MARSHALL, *Luke: Historian and Theologian*, 1970, p. 922).

5. I.H. MARSHALL, *The Gospel of Luke. A Commentary on the Greek Text* (NIGCT, 3), Grand Rapids, MI - London, 1978, p. 30 (esp. p. 30-35; 838-861). Cf. p. 32. Note, too, his comments about distinguishing tradition and redaction, p. 32-33.

It does not appear that Spanish-speaking scholars have been very concerned with the debate of the special source versus Lukan redaction. An exception is José Miguel García Pérez (1986) who adopted the hypothesis of the special source in his study of the story of the good thief (23,39-43). He specifically referred to Marshall's commentary in support of his position (*El relato del Buen Ladrón (Lc 23,39-43)*, in *EstBib* 44 [1986] 264-265). García Pérez was of the opinion that current studies favored the special source theory. In addition to Marshall, he cited the following as advocates of the special source theory: Taylor (1972), J. Weiss, *Die drei älteren Evangelien* (1907), B. Weiss (1907), Bartlet (1911), Perry (1920), Streeter (1924), Easton (1926), Winter (1954), Rehkopf (1959), Léon-Dufour (1960), Schramm (1971), Jeremias (1980). Those opposed included J.C. Hawkins (1911), J.W. Hunkin (1927), J.M. Creed, *The Gospel According to St. Luke* (1942 [apparently a reprint]), F. Neirynck (1973) and J. Drury (1976) (GARCÍA PÉREZ, p.

that Matthew and Luke employed different versions of this common source. For the material peculiar to Lk, Marshall supposed it was probable that the evangelist had "drawn from one or two particular cycles of tradition" since the material did not display a homogeneous quality. He was attracted to Schürmann's proposal that some of the special material derived from Q, but rejected the idea from other scholarly circles that Luke created the material to any large extent since the evangelist was generally faithful to his sources[6]. The special material reflected a Palestinian background and Marshall was inclined to see it stemming from more than one Christian community. The date of the composition of the Gospel was placed around 70 AD.

In introducing the section on the passion narrative, Marshall asserted that the story "is essentially the same as that in Mk.", observing that Luke supplied additional material. The variations in order were attributed to Luke highlighting certain themes. Though there was disagreement about the quantity of non-Markan material, Marshall defended its existence.

Despite judging Markan influence in 22,54 from the term συλλαμβάνω (Mk 14,48) and the detail about the high priest's house, Marshall maintained that v. 54 could stem from Mk or the non-Markan source. Schneider had not adequately explained the omission of reference to the guards in v. 55 if this derived from Lukan redaction of Mk. The φῶς in v. 56, however, was seen to parallel the usage in Mk. Marshall offered no explicit judgment on the source of v. 56, but pointed to differences from Mk, especially in the use of a direct accusation against Peter, and the alteration of "the Nazarene". Though the wording in v. 57 was close to Mk 14,71 Marshall claimed that "Lukan redaction seems unlikely"[7]. Moreover, while the use of the term γύναι in Acts argued against a pre-Lukan terminology, the use of the vocative in the special Lukan material favored it. Marshall gave the impression that Luke redacted Mk in v. 58 so that there was a lapse of time rather than Mark's change of location. Luke's revision allowed Peter to stay where he can both see Jesus and be seen by him. The Lukan and Markan accounts were similar in v. 59 in that there was some passage of time before the third exchange, but Marshall could see no justification for the change to the third person. He ended his discussion referring to Catchpole's decision that the phrase καὶ γὰρ Γαλιλαῖός ἐστιν was a Markan insertion within non-Markan material. Luke "softens" Mark's rendering in v. 60. The particular phrasing may stem from a pre-Lukan tradition.

263[-264], n. 1; 264, nn. 2, 3).

Among the special material in Lk, according to García Pérez, was 22,28-30.35-38; 23,8-12.27-32.39-43; 24,13-53. In the following passages, although there were parallels, strikingly differences also exist: 22,14-27.39-46.66-71. The order varied significantly from that found in Mk in these Lukan sections: 22,21-23.17-18.22.31-34.54-62.63-65;23,36-37.45.54.56; 24,10. Based on a study of the Greek in general and the Aramaisms in particular, García Pérez concluded that the special material derived from "una tradición arcaica y palestinense" (GARCÍA PÉREZ, p. 263. See also p. 303-304).

6. MARSHALL, *Luke*, p. 31.

7. *Ibid.*, p. 842.

Marshall defined the phrase ἔτι λαλοῦντος αὐτοῦ as Lukan. The cockcrow also may have derived from a separate tradition. Concerning v. 61, Marshall recalled that Bultmann, Dibelius, Leaney, Klein and Schneider regarded this as a Lukan creation, while only Catchpole was cited as arguing for pre-Lukan status. Though many scholars asserted that στραφείς was pre-Lukan, Marshall judged that it was possibly Lukan. The term ὁ κύριος was often found in the special material, sometimes a result of Lukan redaction, but never in a Markan context. Marshall was reluctant to adopt redaction as the solution for the second part of the verse.

The denial story served several purposes: it was an example of the temptation of the disciples (22,46) as well as of the power of darkness (22,53). Moreover, it highlighted the weakness of Peter and the strength of Jesus and demonstrated the fulfillment of Jesus' prophecy (22,31-34). The structure was the same as in Mk though the details differed. Marshall pointed out that Lukan redaction was the solution preferred by Finegan, Linnemann, Taylor and Schneider, with the last two allowing for the influence of oral tradition. Supporting the hypothesis of a special source were Bultmann, Schlatter, Rengstorf, Grundmann, Klein and Catchpole. Marshall followed closely the position and arguments of Catchpole often comparing them with Schneider, though he "slightly" favored the position of the former[8].

The MA in v. 62 betrayed Matthean language but Marshall did not reach a definitive solution, saying only that omission was indicated by internal evidence while inclusion was supported by external evidence[9]. It was "unlikely" that Mt served as a source for Lk for the MA in v. 64. Rather, Mt depended upon the tradition also found in Lk[10].

No hint of the source of the mockery account was given by the order in which the mockery was found[11]. Marshall based his decision of the special source on the contents and a poor transition from the preceding material. Plummer, Bultmann, Rengstorf (with qualification), Grundmann, Taylor, Schneider and Catchpole favored the appeal to the special source. Strangely, Dibelius was the only scholar listed as opposing this view. His proposal was dismissed due to a lack of reference to Is 50,6 in v. 63. Like Catchpole, Marshall viewed the term αὐτόν as indicative of a combination of two sources. Without signifying his preference, he suggested that either vv. 55-61 (62) or 63-65 may have been inserted into the present context. The term συνέχω was Lukan and Luke's account was more historically accurate in portraying the guards rather than the Sanhedrin as the agents of the mistreatment[12]. He also maintained that the same could be said of the mockery preceding the trial, but did not elaborate. The concluding verse of the mockery (v.

---

8. *Ibid.*, p. 839. Marshall distinguished the two on the grounds that Schneider focused on vocabulary and Catchpole on structure. It was noted that they arrived at different conclusions though they concurred significantly on the origin of much of the non-Markan material.

9. *Ibid.*, p. 845.

10. *Ibid.*, p. 846.

11. *Ibid.*, p. 845. Cf. p. 838, where Marshall asserted that Luke was responsible for the order of the denial, mockery and trial, which was required by the report of the morning session.

12. *Ibid.*, p. 845.

65) was "probably Lucan", a conclusion Marshall arrived at primarly on the basis of the phrase ἕτερα πολλά, which was also found in 3,18; 8,3; Acts 15,35; cf. Acts 2,40.

In his assessment of the Sanhedrin trial (22,66-71) one gets the impression that Marshall viewed this as a combination of Markan material and the non-Markan source. Beginning with more general comments first, Marshall stated that Mark and Luke were recounting the same events "from different points of view"[13]. Lukan redaction could have omitted "inappropriate" details from both sources, though he never discussed why this might have been so. As regards the christology operative within the scene, Marshall sided with Catchpole in rejecting Lukan redaction, on the grounds that it was pre-Lukan. Listed as those who support at least partial dependence upon a special source were Schneider, Catchpole, Taylor, J. Weiss, Schlatter, Rengstorf, Grundmann and Ellis with Creed, Finegan and Blinzler forming the opposition. Winter was also indicated for his unique interpretation of a later interpolation. Marshall was open to the possibility that 22,66 was based upon Mk 15,1. Linnemann had pointed out that the Markan account contained no reference to time. Though the phrase ὡς ἐγένετο ἡμέρα was Lukan, it could have derived either from Mk 15,1 or the special source. It was also possible that Luke conflated the appearance before the high priest with the Sanhedrin trial. The non-Markan source was likely for v. 67 because Luke would not have changed a definite Markan subject into a vague one. Also there were verbal similarities between Lk, Mt and Jn. Marshall explained the separation of the titles by suggesting that Mark conflated them while Luke retained the original division. Marshall opted for Catchpole's argument against Schneider who called attention to the similarity with 20,1-8 and proposed that in addition to Mk, Matthew and Luke employed a non-Markan tradition at this point. The saying of Dan 7,13 was seen "generally" as Lukan redaction of Mk, a view endorsed by Bultmann, Grässer, Conzelmann, Catchpole, Grundmann, Tödt and Higgins while Bammel constituted the minority in arguing for pre-Lukan designation. Marshall presented three arguments in favor of the majority position and three in favor of the minority[14]. He listed Angus John Brockhurst Higgins as supporting the view that 22,69 was Lukan redaction of Mk[15]. Like Ernst, Marshall referred to Heinz

---

13. *Ibid.*, p. 847.

14. *Ibid.*, p. 850. The strength of the majority view was that 1) the saying interrupted vv. 67f. and 70; 2) the Sanhedrin will not see the coming of the Son of Man; and 3) it portrayed the present exaltation of the Son of Man. Without elaborating, Marshall referred to Acts 7,56. The counter argument rested on the perspective that 1) the Son of Man reference was an allusion to the heavenly court of v. 68; 2) the connection to 12,8ff.; and 3) the quasi MA of ἀπὸ τοῦ νῦν/ἀπ᾽ ἄρτι (22,69 / Mt 26,69). Cf. E. GRÄSSER, *Das Problem der Parusieverzögerung in den synoptischen Evangelien und in der Apostelgeschichte*, Berlin, 1957, p. 176, n. 3.

15. A.J.B. HIGGINS, *Jesus and the Son of Man*, London, 1964, p. 96: "Luke 22:69 is an abbreviation of Mark 14:62. The reason for the abbreviation is partly the evangelist's tendency to tone down the parousia idea which he describes in other terms (17: 22ff.; 18: 8b), and partly and perhaps especially the desire not to depict Jesus as telling the unbelieving members of the

Eduard Tödt in the discussion of 22,69[16]. For v. 70 Marshall once again sided
with Catchpole as stemming from the non-Markan source. The final verse of the
Sanhedrin trial account (v. 71) was reminiscent of, though different from, Mk.

Although Marshall initially maintained that 23,1-5 derived from a non-Markan
source which Luke edited, Marshall qualified his statement slightly, saying it was
probable that Luke employed other traditions or a separate, non-Markan source in
addition to Mk[17]. It was undeniable that 23,3 was based upon Mk 15,2. This
section focused attention on the innocence of Jesus. More specifically, concerning
the individual verses, 23,1 could come either from Mk or from the non-Markan
source, but if the former, then the reason for the changes were unclear. Contra
Burkitt, Marshall favored the translation, "Christ, a king" in 23,2. Though the
question (23,4) corresponded to Mk 15,14, Marshall rejected the view that it was
based upon it. The "development of the scene" in 23,5 also corresponded to Mk
with a good part of the phrasing being assigned to Luke, including the Semitic
phrase ἄρχομαι ἀπό.

Marshall discerned a three part division in the following material: 23,13-16;
(17)18-23; 24-25. In this section Luke was believed to have combined the special
source with Mk. Marshall concluded this basing his judgment on Rengstorf and
Grundmann because of the contacts with Jn. Omitting 23,17 due to strong external
evidence also made dependence upon Mk "less likely". In 23,18 Luke was
responsible for the omission of the detail that the religious leadership incited the
crowd. This was an important admission that omissions can be attributed to Luke
by those who supported the hypothesis of the special source. The amnesty custom
stemmed from Mk. As in Mk 15,7 Luke identified Barabbas, though at a later
point in the narrative. Earlier, Marshall detected that 23,20-23 closely resembled

---

sanhedrin that *they* will *see* the day of the Son of man. The Lukan emphasis is here specially
prominent. The stress is on the session of the Son of man at the right hand of God, and since this
session is 'from now on', the exaltation of Jesus is the central thought for Luke".

It is well to note that in a subsequent publication Higgins reversed himself claiming with C.
Colpe, that Mark and Luke were working with independent traditions. Cf. A.J.B. HIGGINS, *The
Son of Man in the Teaching of Jesus*, Cambridge, 1980, p. 10, 70, 78, 79. See also C. COLPE,
ὁ υἱὸς τοῦ ἀνθρώπου, in *TWNT* 8, p. 461 (= *TDNT* 8, 457).

16. H.E. TÖDT, *Der Menschensohn in der synoptischen Überlieferung*, Gütersloh, 1959,
²1963, esp. p. 94-97 (= *The Son of Man in the Synoptic Tradition*, tr. D.M. BARTON, London
- Philadelphia, PA, 1965, esp. p. 101-103). The work was originally Tödt's Heidelberg doctoral
dissertation. He gave the impression that Luke redacted Mk who sought to offer a more direct
statement by using "he will be" in place of "you will see". Luke was aware of the reference to
the coming of the Son of Man on the clouds of heaven (Mk 14,62c) and opted to omit it so that
the focus will be on the sitting at the right hand of God. The redaction was further motivated by
Luke's perception that suffering in earthly existence was distinct from the coming parousia. Luke
further distinguished between the power of the Son of Man and the parousia (p. 96 = 103). Tödt
agreed with Conzelmann that Luke had so rewritten the trial scene (22,66-71) as to provide a
forum for his christology which also served as the climax. The titles Christ, Son of Man, and Son
of God, used successively by the evangelist, served to complement each other.

17. MARSHALL, *Luke*, p. 852.

Mk[18]. In treating the verses individually, he observed that v. 20 corresponded to Mk 15,12, but expressed doubt that Luke was following Mk in 23,21 because of the use of the present imperative σταύρου. In 23,22 Luke employed Markan wording and in v. 23 Lukan editing was obvious. Luke avoided the Markan phrase that Pilate conceded to the crowd's demands as a favor. In v. 25, though the formulation was Lukan, Marshall conjectured that it may be based, to some extent, on the non-Markan source.

Rejecting the view that the Herod episode was inspired by Acts 4,25f. Marshall (1970) argued that Herod, as well as Pilate, was in Jerusalem for the celebration of the Passover. Rather than Pilate seeking to unload a difficult case, Marshall insisted that he was merely seeking a second opinion. The similarity with and possible influence of Mk 15,16-20 upon the mockery of 23,11 was rejected on the grounds that "one set of troops could easily have copied the other's example"[19].

Marshall (1978) treated the Herod episode as historical, but recast and shaped "in the Lucan manner"[20]. Marshall explained the transfer of Jesus to Herod as Pilate's attempt to secure expert advice on Jewish affairs. The silence motif, though present in Mk, was not an "historical invention, based on the prophecy, since, as Hooker, 87-89, has demonstrated, Jesus is consistently presented in all the Gospels as one who 'is prepared to answer an honest question but ignore partisan assertions'"[21]. Marshall rejected Grundmann's suggestion that the silence pointed to the divinity of Jesus. Marshall viewed the vesting of Jesus in the dazzling apparel as part of the mockery. Dismissing Dibelius's view that the reconciliation between the two leaders arose from Ps 2, Marshall reasoned that the event must be historical[22].

Neirynck called attention to the fact that Marshall viewed his work in line with Creed (1930) but differentiated his work by intending to focus on the particularly Lukan perspective in Markan based material[23]. Marshall, in Neirynck's opinion, "too easily" accepted the influence of a non-Markan source for example in chapters 22–23. It could be said that like Gundry, Marshall did not favor a view of Luke as a creative redactor. Marshall had too narrowly limited material judged to have

18. *Ibid.*, p. 858.

19. MARSHALL, *Luke*, in *NBC*, [3]1970, p. 923-924. In *Luke: Historian and Theologian* (1970) Marshall referred only to 23,8 in the Herod pericope stating the "the miracles wrought by Jesus are described in traditional language" (p. 137). But in related material he commented: "Luke has inserted his own ideas into the Marcan material. On occasion he has altered the detail given by Mark. Thus 'Herod the king' (Mark 6:14 et al.) received his proper title of 'tetrarch' (Luke 3:19; 9:7)" (p. 66).

20. MARSHALL, *Luke*, p. 855.

21. *Ibid.*, p. 856. Cf. M.D. HOOKER, *Jesus and the Servant*, London, 1959, p. 89. Regrettably, Marshall referred to two works by Hooker in his bibliography, but did not indicate in this place to which he was referring.

22. MARSHALL, *Luke*, p. 857.

23. *ETL* 56 (1980) 174.

been influenced by Mk. While Marshall demonstrated familiarity with more recent studies of Lukan exegesis, he did not refer to earlier studies.

The pericope of the denials of Peter (22,54-62) was the locus of a debate between Wolfgang DIETRICH (1970) and Dietfried GEWALT (1975). Dietrich, who treated the portrayal of Peter in various pericopes in Lk-Acts, including 22,54-62, followed the lead of G. Klein that the relation of Lk to Mk in this section had not been decisively resolved[24]. At the end of Dietrich's work, he claimed that the denial did not stem from Mk, though he entertained the possibilities that either Luke revised the account (does Dietrich mean Markan?), or that it derived in a set form from Luke's *Sondergut*[25].

Dietfried Gewalt called attention to Dietrich's adverse reaction to redaction-critical methodology and to his own study[26]. He claimed that the focus of Dietrich's study was not the Lukan image of Peter per se, but the "Petrusgestalt" in the Lukan writings. Gewalt argued that Peter whose life cannot be reconstructed on the basis of Lk and Acts was only a "functionselement", a composite of various elements of tradition for the Lukan writings[27]. The tension, as can be seen from this discussion, was that once again the historicity of the Lukan writings was at the center of the debate.

Harold HOEHNER (1970) defended the historicity of the Herod episode and, like Taylor, viewed 23,1-25 as a literary unit[28]. He rejected out of hand the idea that

24. W. DIETRICH, *Das Petrusbild der lukanischen Schriften* (BWANT, 94), Stuttgart, 1972 (esp. p. 116-157, 322-323). Diss. Ev. Theol. Faculty, Wilhelms U. Münster, 1970 (dir. K.H. RENGSTORF). Cf. G. KLEIN, *Verleugnung*, 1961, 285-328 (= *Rekonstruktion*, 49-98).

25. DIETRICH, *Das Petrusbild*, p. 323: "Die Einzelanalyse liess erkennen, dass mit einiger Wahrscheinlichkeit die Berufungsgeschichte, Teile aus dem Bericht von der Berufung der Zwölf und aus der Verklärungsgeschichte sowie die Eingangsverse der Verleugnungsansage (sollte die Verleugnung selbst ein von Lukas redigiertes Produkt sein?) nicht der Markusvorlage entstammen. Es muss daher mit der Möglichkeit gerechnet werden, dass im sogenannten lukanischen 'Sondergut' Petrusteile enthalten waren, die vielleicht schon dort unter einer bestimmten Konzeption standen".

According to Dietrich the denial itself was closer to the Markan version than to the prophecies (22,31-34) (p. 245). Taking note of the transposition, he claimed Luke's reason for the mockery was not immediately apparent. In part, the events of the denial and mockery were separated from the trial (p. 141, 142). But Dietrich suggested that 22,53 indicated the motive for the transferral for the scene on the one hand referring to the denials of Peter and on the other, the mockery. But the context of the pericope indicated that Jesus was referring to Judas and the crowd which accompanied him and not to Peter. That could have explained the order, even if Luke retained the original Markan order. Thus other and more persuasive arguments can be found to explain the transposition of the material. Dietrich did not address the MA in v. 62.

26. D. GEWALT, *Das "Petrusbild" der lukanischen Schriften als Problem einer ganzheitlichen Exegese*, in *LingBib* 34 (1975) 6.

27. *Ibid.*, p. 21. In the English abstract of the article Gewalt employed the term "functional element" (p. 22).

28. H.W. HOEHNER, *Why Did Pilate Hand Jesus over to Antipas?*, in E. BAMMEL (ed.), *The Trial of Jesus*, Naperville, IL, 1970, p. 84. Cf. HOEHNER, *Herod Antipas*, Diss. Cambridge,

the story was created from Markan materials. Jesus' transfer was motivated by three reasons: 1) Jesus was under Herod's territorial jurisdiction, 2) Pilate desired to free himself from an awkward case, and 3) he sought to improve his relationship with Herod[29]. In his published Cambridge dissertation (1972) Hoehner joined forces with those who held that most probably Luke used a non-Markan tradition as the basis of the passion narrative, arriving at this conclusion primarily because of the low degree of verbal similarity[30]. The Herod episode was regarded as a constitutive element of the whole section 23,1-25. While it was most likely that 23,3 was taken over from "the synoptic parallel", Hoehner maintained that it "may have even been in the original Lucan source"[31].

More recently (1992), Hoehner reaffirmed his belief in the historicity of the passage though it was "understandable" why scholars would doubt it on account of its absence from other Gospels[32]. The transfer of Jesus to Herod, warranted by Pilate's desire to remove himself from a difficult situation, made so by the massacre (13,1), "makes historical sense" and would have been of interest to Theophilus, especially since the breach in the relationship of Pilate and Herod had been repaired.

Reception of Hoehner's Theory

Samuel Sandmel praised Hoehner for the balance with which he presented his material. Yet, he disagreed with Hoehner's conservative stance regarding the historicity of Gospel material, particularly the Herod scene. "One sees this especially in his conclusion to the matter of Antipas and Jesus (p. 230): 'There are reasonable grounds, then, for accepting the historicity of this pericope and for believing that Jesus was actually tried by Herod Antipas'"[33]. Jacob Neusner, complimenting Hoehner for what he considered would be a definitive study, lamented Hoehner's disparity in treating sources[34]. Similar to Sandmel, Neusner

---

1968 (dir. E. BAMMEL). Part of Hoehner's criteria for deciding that the whole constituted a single literary unit was that commentators did not uniformly define the extent of the pericope. Hoehner limited the passage to 23,6-12. It should be noted that the reader was directed to Perry's study for an analysis of the characteristic words in the passion narrative (*Why*, p. 84, n. 1). Credence was given to the historicity of the event since it was entirely probable that Herod was in Jerusalem at the time of the Passover (p. 85-86).

29. *Ibid.*, p. 86, 88.

30. HOEHNER, *Herod Antipas*, Cambridge, 1972, p. 225. Hoehner even seemed to go so far as to suggest that the Herod tradition may be based on material derived from Mt. "Therefore, it is reasonable to conclude that Antipas' trial of Jesus is an inseparable part of the Lucan narrative, the whole of which, with few possible exceptions (e.g. 23,3), is based on a non-Marcan (or Matthean) tradition" (p. 227).

31. *Ibid.*, p. 226.

32. HOEHNER, *Herodian Dynasty*, in *DJG*, p. 324; see also HOEHNER, *Pontius Pilate*, in *DJG*, p. 616.

33. *CBQ* 35 (1973) 92.

34. *Interpr* 27 (1973) 106.

observed that Hoehner accepted much in the NT at face value and gave uncritical credence to material drawn from Josephus and rabbinic materials.

S.L. Johnson acknowledged Hoehner's "useful" discussion on the problematic section of 23,8-12[35]. Johnson assigned more blame to Herod and Pilate than Hoehner, although they were in agreement that the NT documents were more reliable than many contemporary scholars were willing to allow[36]. William Horbury took note of Hoehner's "fresh discussion of historical problems", but offered no opinion concerning Hoehner's view on the historicity of the Herod pericope[37].

Eugene LaVerdiere reached a conclusion similar to Neusner. "The validity of historical conclusions concerning Antipas' role in the life of Jesus rested largely on an adequate appraisal of the literary and pre-literary nature of the gospel accounts. Many readers will find that Hoehner did not sufficiently disengage the literary and traditional history of the texts prior to embarking on historical criticism"[38]. This LaVerdiere referred to as "a weakness of perspective".

Fergus Millar, in the most negative of the reactions, introduced his critique of Hoehner's study contending that it should have begun with a "serious discussion of the historicity of Luke. The very elaborate discussions throughout the book which attempt to reconstruct the truth about particular episodes recorded of Herod Antipas are not a substitute for this"[39]. Millar charged that Hoehner's claim that Luke referred to a second source because of the possibility that such a source existed ("a mere hypothesis") was "circular" reasoning[40]. By accepting that Luke was historically correct, Millar argued that Hoehner's proposal led to the conclusion that the other Synoptics were wrong.

Thomas Corbishley commended Hoehner for wrestling "gallantly with the Synoptic Problem"[41]. More than that, he appraised the chief value of the book as showing "that the gospels remain obstinately rooted in the history they imply". He reacted favorably to Hoehner's conclusion that Pilate was forced to compromise because he had fallen into disfavor with his patron Sejanus.

John Wilkinson complimented Hoehner for the "meticulous detail" with which he treated the historical questions[42]. But in highlighting Manaen and Joanna as possible sources of information, Hoehner had on four occasions repeated the same

---

35. *BS* 129 (1972) 256.

36. *Ibid.*: "Much of contemporary gospel criticism exhibits an unwarranted lack of trust in the reliability of the New Testament documents and the teaching they contain. Professor Hoehner, however, at point after point has examined the interpretation of such skeptical criticism and has demonstrated that they are generally poorly founded, sometimes capricious and occasionally simply nit-picking. In reliability the documents are far superior to their critics, to put it mildly".

37. *ExpT* 84 (1972-73) 24.

38. *CBQ* 35 (1973) 158.

39. *JJS* 24 (1973) 93.

40. *Ibid.*, p. 93-94.

41. *HeythJ* 14 (1973) 209.

42. *ATR* 54 (1972) 364.

circumstantial details[43]. Wilkinson also charged that Hoehner's conclusions were banal[44].

Lloyd GASTON (1970) announced his support of the Proto-Lk theory based on references to Jerusalem in special material[45]. Seeing the origins of the theory in the work of Feine upon which B. Weiss elaborated, Gaston argued that Weiss's works threatened the hypothesis by his effort to neatly distinguish Q and L. Perry's work was singled out as the most important work on the theory from the University of Chicago. Gaston expressed regret that too little attention was paid to Easton's list of "L" vocabulary. Taylor was credited with providing the "fullest and best founded form" of the hypothesis to date. Disinterest in the theory in Germany was attributed to the alternative solution offered by Bussmann and, generally, to the shift to form criticism. The advent of redaction criticism addressed "the point most neglected by Streeter and Taylor, the theology and editorial work of Luke"[46]. Gaston was sympathetic to Sahlin's conception of the theory but admited that it required "radical correction". The development of the two-volume Lukan work extended over nearly a century: composition of Proto-Lk (Lk 1,5 – Acts 15,33) in the year 50 AD; a Greek translation of Proto-Lk and Acts was made in 64 AD; Lk, embellished with Markan material and Acts existed in the year 80 AD; the two-volume Lukan work was divided in 140 AD. While not identical, Gaston pointed to scholars such as Bornhaüser, Schlatter and Schweizer who arrived at conclusions similar to Proto-Lk. Bultmann and Dodd were mentioned as those who accepted the probable existence of a Proto-Lukan source in the passion narrative, with Tyson also indicated.

Gaston rightly saw that the classic articulation of the theory did not adequately consider Luke's redactional contribution. Listing the Q+L material as 1,5-4,30; 6,12-8,3; 9,51-18,14; 19,1-48; 21,5-24,49 (with Markan insertions), he reduced the Markan material to 4,31-6,11 (/ Mk 1,21-3,6); 8,4-9,50 (/ Mk 4,1-9,40 less 4,26-34 and 6,45-8,26); 18,15-43 (Mk 10,13-52); 20,1-21,4 (/Mk 11,27-12,44)[47]. For this the Q+L material "reads like a complete gospel". The Markan material did not. He also accepted the differences in order as stemming from the special source or resulting from the insertion of Markan material within it.

Despite a favorable judgment, Gaston did not employ the theory in his work[48]. Part of the difficulty arose from the fact that it was difficult to

43. *Ibid.* Cf. HOEHNER, *Herod Antipas*, p. 120-121, 184, n. 3, 231, 303-306.

44. *ATR* 54 (1972) 365.

45. L. GASTON, *No Stone on Another. Studies in the Significance of the Fall of Jerusalem in the Synoptic Gospels* (NTSuppl, 23), Leiden, 1970 (esp. p. 244-256). Notice should also be taken of GASTON, *Horae Synopticae Electronicae. Word Statistics of the Synoptic Gospels*, Missoula, MT, 1973.

46. *No Stone on Another.*, p. 246.

47. *Ibid.*, p. 251.

48. *Ibid.*, p. 254: "A theory of Proto-Luke cannot today be simply adopted until a great deal

differentiate between initial and later forms of the special material owing to a lack of insufficient "established criteria"[49]. One must question Gaston's assertion that the theory of a special source for the passion "has won more approval than has the Proto-Luke theory generally".

Gaston (1986) supported the view of a special source in the Lukan passion narrative which Luke used in preference to Mk, though he did not describe or identify such a source[50]. Yet, he claimed that not only was it possible to reconstruct it, but it was historically reliable and could be used to determine the situation surrounding the legal proceedings and death of Jesus[51].

The Sanhedrin trial was due to the special source. Other material, however, including 23,13-16.25, was free Lukan composition. It was these verses, rather than the special source information, which shaped this section of the passion account. Writing of the verses composed by Luke, Gaston asserted: "... they are responsible for the present character of the whole passion narrative"[52]. One then wonders why Luke would have used a particular source that had so little effect on the narration of the events. Whereas Gaston agreed with G. Rau that there was "an extreme tension" between the evangelist and the special source, he found the arguments of Catchpole unconvincing[53].

Though Feine believed that anti-Pharisaic material stemmed from Paul and J. Weiss conjectured that it was due to Jesus, Gaston assumed that the negative presentation of the Pharisees in the special material was due to Lukan redaction[54]. The Lukan account was shaped, in part, by Luke's apologetic against contemporary Jews[55]. Like Danker, Gaston rejected the view that the evangelist was writing out of a pro-Roman apologetic. It was the conflict between the synagogue and Luke's community which influenced the narrative. Gaston maintained that the interrogation before Pilate did not constitute a trial, but only a hearing, much as Paul was said to have experienced in Acts. He tempered that view by toying with the idea of the possible influence of Mk in 23,3[56]. Consequently, the "real trial" of Jesus was

---

more work has been done on it. It will not be presupposed in the present work, which can be looked on simply as a study in the Lucan special material. At the same time, it is to be hoped that this study will show enough internal consistency to assist others in working out a more thorough Proto-Luke theory along with the necessary distinction of Luke's own extensive editing".

49. *Ibid.*, p. 255.

50. L. GASTON, *Anti-Judaism and the Passion Narrative in Luke and Acts*, in P. RICHARDSON and D. GRANSKOU (eds.), *Anti-Judasim in Early Christianity*. 1. *Paul and the Gospels*, Waterloo, Ontario, Canada, 1986, p. 144. Gaston was influenced on several points by P. Walaskay. See p. 144, n. 51 and 146, n. 54. Gaston did not treat Peter's denials (22,54b-62) but examined 22,54a.63-23,1.2-5.6-12.13-25. Neither did he pursue the source question, choosing only to examine the passion narrative "in its present form" (p. 144).

51. *Ibid.*, p. 153.

52. *Ibid.*, p. 148.

53. *Ibid.*, n. 60; cf. p. 153, n. 69.

54. *Ibid.*, p. 141-142.

55. *Ibid.*, p. 146.

56. *Ibid.*, p. 147; cf. p. 147, n. 55. Note that Gaston recorded 22,3 when he intended 23,3.

thought to be the one which took place before the people (23,13-25). Another influential Lukan theme was the innocence of Jesus. He was not guilty of any of the charges brought against him. Parallels with Acts suggested that the councils were not judicial bodies and similarity was noted between charges against Jesus and those raised against some Christians in Acts 17,6-7.

Gaston (1970) assigned Lk 23,4-25 to Proto-Lk, but cautioned that such a theory could not "be simply adopted until a great deal more work has been done on it"[57]. More recently (1986) Gaston rejected the view of Dibelius and Bultmann that the Herod story originated from Ps 2 because of the disparity of presentations[58]. Although the possibility existed, as Taylor suggested, that it stemmed from an early tradition, still it betrayed evidence of heavy redaction. Like Fitzmyer, Gaston did not believe that the scene helped to advance the passion narrative. He conjectured that the story was a composite of earlier Lukan material joined to Markan elements. Herod's desire to see Jesus was prompted by 9,9 and 13,31. The silence was inspired by Mk 15,5. The accusations of the religious leaders were drawn from Mk 15,4. The mockery by the soldiers derived from Mk 15,16-20. By not reporting this episode in its place he supplanted the mockery by the Jewish soldiers. The tension between 23,10 where the chief priests accompany Jesus and 23,13 where they have remained behind with Pilate did not pose an insurmountable problem for Gaston[59]. He adopted the view of Walaskay that Luke created this scene (or at least edited it) as a parallel to Paul's experience, a view supported by S. Sandmel as well[60].

Everett HARRISON (1971) observed that though Streeter's Proto-Lk theory "has not been widely adopted" still the four- document approach was quite useful[61]. A much stronger critique was afforded Vaganay, whose theory was dismissed as "complicated" not giving Mk its full due[62]. The theory offered by Pierson Parker also faltered, since it posited an additional source, specifically a Jewish-Christian Gospel prior to Mk, though there was no hard evidence supporting it[63]. Tim SCHRAMM (1971) added his name to those who advocated Luke's use of a special

57. GASTON, *No Stone on Another*, p. 254; cf. p. 255-256. See also p. 329-333, regarding Gaston's views on the Proto-Lukan passion account. For his discussion on Ps 2,1 in Acts 4, see p. 330. For a history of the Proto-Lk theory, see p. 244f.

58. GASTON, *Anti-Judaism*. Vol. 1. *Paul and the Gospels*, 1986, 127-153 (esp. p. 147-148).

59. *Ibid.*, p. 148.

60. *Ibid.*, n. 59. Cf. WALASKAY, *Trial and Death*, p. 88-89. See also S. SANDMEL, *Anti-Semitism in the New Testament*, Philadelphia, PA, 1978, p. 73, 99. The statement regarding Sandmel by Gaston is misleading. To quote from the pages of Sandmel cited by Gaston: "Indeed, Luke portrays Herod's son Antipas and his great-grandson Agrippa II as royal spokesmen respectively for the innocence of first Jesus and then Paul" (p. 73). And again: "As in the Gospel, Herod Antipas had found no crime in Jesus, so Agrippa II in Acts had found none in Paul". This would appear to be the exact opposite of what Walaskay (and Gaston) was arguing.

61. E.F. HARRISON, *Introduction to the New Testament*, Grand Rapids, MI, ²1971, p. 150.

62. *Ibid.*, p. 151.

63. *Ibid.*, p. 152. Cf. P. PARKER, *The Gospel Before Mark*, 1953.

continuous source in the section 22,14ff., with supplemental Markan elements[64]. While 22,1-14 was based upon Mk, at 22,3 Luke introduced a motif from the special source[65]. Changes in order were also cited as evidence of the special source[66]. Gerard SLOYAN (1973) also subscribed to the view that Luke employed a special source for the passion narrative in addition to Mk[67]. Though Leon MORRIS (1974) was not fully convinced of Streeter's Proto-Lk, he certainly was sympathetic to it and adopted it as his working hypothesis[68].

64. T. SCHRAMM, *Der Markus-Stoff bei Lukas. Eine literarische und redaktionsgeschichtliche Untersuchung* (SNTS MS, 14), Cambridge, 1971, p. 50. Diss. Hamburg, 1966 (dir. C.-H. HUNZINGER). In a note Schramm referred to Taylor, Schürmann, Rehkopf and Jeremias (n. 2).

65. *Ibid.*, p. 184.

66. *Ibid.*, p. 50-51.

67. G.S. SLOYAN, *Jesus on Trial. The Development of the Passion Narratives and Their Historical and Ecumenical Implications*, Philadelphia, PA, 1973, p. 89 (esp. p. 89-109). See p. 98-104, for what he considered to be the contents of the special source. The denial scene may depend only upon Mk. The mockery was taken from the special source and preferred Lukan terms gave evidence of the editorial hand of Luke. The variations in timing as well as the order of the Sanhedrin trial convinced Sloyan that Luke at this point was certainly dependent upon the special source. But Sloyan did not exclude the possibility that Markan recollections had been inserted (p. 95). He was certainly in a minority when he referred to the theory of the priority of Luke espoused by Lindsey and Flusser (p. 95, n. 7). Luke inserted Mk 15,2 as his v. 3 but the rest of 23,1-5 came from the source. Either Mk or the source were responsible for 23,18-25, though Sloyan thought it was probably the source. All in all for our section of the passion narrative, he attributed most to the special source: 22,63-65.67.70; 23,2.5.18-25. So all that stemmed from Mk was 22,54-62.69 (probably).71; 23,3. A decisive factor for Sloyan was the "primitive Christology and soteriology" which he found in the sections attributed to the special source (p. 102).

Sloyan considered 23,6-16 to be "peculiarly Luke's composition", since it contained many of his characteristic words (p. 96). Regrettably, Sloyan did not give any indication of the "characteristic words" he had in mind. He observed: "Paul Feine was the first to describe Luke's use of a third source besides Mark and Q, usually noted S on the continent and L by British scholars" (p. 97, n. 8). Therefore, for the Herod scene Luke was not dependent upon a source, a view Sloyan regarded as supported by the view in Acts 4,27.

In a previous and very general treatment of Lk Sloyan (1959) wrote of Luke's use of Mk in addition to sources not available to the authors of the other Synoptics (*The Gospel according to Luke*, in *Worship* 33 [1959] 633-641, esp. p. 634-635 = M.R. RYAN [ed.], *Contemporary New Testament Studies*, Collegeville, MN, 1965, 185-191, esp. p. 186). Luke wrote in an orderly fashion, respecting the order of his sources, including Mk. He was also faithful to the testimony of the eyewitnesses. Lukan redaction included improving Markan phrasing and omitting passages which appeared "too Jewish" (p. 186-187).

68. L. MORRIS, *Luke* (TNTC, 3), Leicester - Grand Rapids, MI, 1974, p. 55-59, p. 57; ²1986; rev. ed. 1988, p. 59-63, esp. p. 61. "It may be saying too much to claim that [Luke] had produced Streeter's Proto-Luke" (1974, p. 59 = p. 63). The revision afforded Morris the opportunity to update his material, particularly in light of the appearance of the commentaries by Marshall and Fitzmyer. He also treated the synoptic problem. Opponents of the Proto-Lk theory, in Morris's opinion, have never adequately explained that Luke combined his special material with Q rather than Mk, and the significant differences in the passion narrative (p. 58 = p. 62). Aside from a rather general statement about Luke's "own source" for what Morris termed the Crucifixion, meaning the passion, Morris remained strictly with the Lukan text and did not

Marie-Émile BOISMARD (1972) postulated a Proto-Lk document which he referred to as Document C abbreviated and refashioned in Lk and used by John[69]. Boismard attempted to explain the Lukan account on the basis of two levels: Proto-Lk and the final Lukan redactor[70]. Luke's principal source in the passion narrative was Document C, whereas for the rest of the Gospel it was intermediate Mk, supplemented only "sporadiquement" by Document C. Matthean influence was acknowledged, but only through the means of intermediate Mt, which served to explain various agreements. Contrary to Rehkopf and others, Boismard argued that it was impossible to distinguish the proto-Lukan vocabulary from that of the final Lukan redactor. Ultimately, Boismard decided that the author of Proto-Lk and the final Lukan redactor were one and the same[71]. Whatever additional sources Luke might have had, Boismard stated that their origin cannot be determined with any precision. Nor did he venture to estimate their number or extent. What was more, for the material particular to Luke, a determination cannot be made as to which level the material was added. It seems better to ascribe the differences to Lukan redaction rather than some intermediate stage of development. While we do not concur with Boismard's suggestion of the various documents involved in the development of the passion narrative, his suggestion that similarities between the passion and transfiguration accounts should be pursued[72].

As to the literary activity of Proto-Lk, what Boismard assigned to that level could equally be ascribed to the evangelist in his redaction of Mk: 1) the text was profoundly changed, 2) Luke added new episodes (Herod, for instance), and 3) certain episodes were transposed, as in the case of the mockeries.

Distinguished from the level of Proto-Lk, were the literary characteristics of the final Lukan redactor. To him was attributed the abbreviation or even

---

compare with the Synoptic parallels or show any relationship with Acts (p. 302 = p. 330). There were no references to the MAs.

Although Morris did not specifically address the source question for the Herod episode, he endorsed the Proto-Lk theory and suggested that after combining oral and written materials Luke supplemented these with material drawn from Mk (p. 59 = p. 63). Morris appeared to accept the Herod episode as historical noting that Herod was probably in Jerusalem for the Passover (p. 321 = p. 350-351). The dazzling apparel, a gesture of mockery meant to suggest that Jesus was a king, was most likely "a cast--off royal robe" (p. 321 = p. 351). The term for dazzling often implied white, but nothing as explicit was stated here.

69. P. BENOIT and M.-É. BOISMARD, Synopse des quatre évangiles en français, Vol. 2, Paris, 1972. The commentary was prepared by Boismard, with the collaboration of A. Lamouille and P. Sandevoir, while Benoit wrote the preface. L. Sabourin observed that Benoit also authored the notes on the Infancy Narrative (The Synoptic Problem: Old and New Approaches, in BTB 3 [1973] 310).

70. BOISMARD, Synopse, Vol. 2, p. 16.

71. Ibid., p. 46: "L'explication la plus probable est donc d'admettre l'unité entre proto-Lc et l'ultime rédaction lucanienne".

72. Ibid., p. 43.

elimination of particular accounts. Earlier Wernle noted that this reflected the style
of the evangelist who added to accounts which he deemed incomplete[73].

More particularly, concerning the Lukan version of the denials of Peter, he
viewed Mk 14,54c as having been taken over by the last Marco-Lukan redactor[74].
Compared with the other Gospels, the Lukan account seemed abbreviated and
Boismard believed there was a lacuna between vv. 54 and 55. Boismard's
conjectured Proto-Lk document contained the mention that Peter entered the high
priest's court with Jesus, as found in the echo of the primitive document in v. 54a.
The evangelist Luke transposed some of the details from Proto-Lk[75]. Markan
influence was also responsible in 22,54 for replacing the name Annas with the
phrase "in the house of the high priest"[76]. The first and third denials, influenced
by Mk-intermediate, were added to the sole denial contained in Document C by the
last redactor of Lk[77]. This final redactor was also responsible for v. 61[78]. The
term "Lord" (22,61) was indicative of the style of the final Lukan redactor, but
was clearly influenced by Mk[79].

The transposition of the mockery by Luke until after the Sanhedrin trial shifted
the abuse of Jesus from the members of the Sanhedrin to the guards[80]. The
Sanhedrin trial was substantially drawn from Proto-Lk[81]. Once more Boismard
judged that the Lukan account was abbreviated. Like Van der Kwaak, Boismard
asserted that the scene focused on issues of Jesus' identity. He further suggested
that Document C was directly dependent upon Document B which served as a
source of Mk[82]. An additional connection was found in the comparison of Lk
22,69, less the words "and coming with the clouds of heaven", and the early form
of Document B. The timing of Jesus' trial before the Sanhedrin was contained in
Proto-Lk, but was also dependent upon Document B[83].

Concerning the historicity of the trial of Jesus, Boismard contended that some
of the objections were unfounded in light of arguments from the literary order.
Boismard agreed that the timing recounted in the Mt/Mk accounts was not very
likely, since it would have been very difficult to assemble members of the
Sanhedrin during the night. Consequently, he concluded that Documents A and B
had the trial in the morning. In treating the mockery, he rightly observed on the
basis of some of Luke's preferred terms, that Luke redacted the account[84]. The

---

73. *Ibid.*, p. 45. Cf. WERNLE, *Die synoptische Frage*, p. 4, 6, 25.
74. *Ibid.*, p. 398.
75. BOISMARD, *Synopse*, p. 399.
76. *Ibid.*
77. *Ibid.*, p. 402.
78. *Ibid.*, p. 403.
79. *Ibid.* Cf. p. 41.
80. *Ibid.*
81. *Ibid.*, p. 406.
82. *Ibid.*
83. *Ibid.*, p. 407.
84. *Ibid.*, p. 408. The favorite Lukan terms were οἱ ἄνδρες and συνέχειν.

change of agents of the mockery was a literary technique employed by Luke. The Lukan version, 22,63b-64, reflected the nearly pure version contained in Document A which the final Lukan redactor added to vv. 63a.65[85]. Boismard suggested a dependence upon intermediate Mt which involved only minor changes. Nevertheless, he argued that the Proto-Lk source contained an account of the mockeries by the Roman soldiers[86].

Describing the ἅπαν τὸ πλῆθος in 23,1 as "de style typiquent lucanien", Boismard held that the text was based upon Proto-Lk, as was the trial before Pilate, upon which Proto-Lk depended in a Matthean form[87]. The block 23,5-16 was considered by Boismard to be an addition to the source which Luke followed[88]. Boismard offered a reconstruction of his supposed source common to both Lk and Jn, which the latter had better preserved[89]. He was more concerned with comparing these two Gospels than with analyzing the relationships between Mk and Lk. Also acknowledged was the redactional technique, ascribed to the final Lukan redaction, of abbreviating accounts. The numerous "lucanisms" of Luke's account were likewise noted, though not enumerated. Both the style and vocabulary distinguished the Lukan (and Johannine) account from those of Matthew and Mark, but these distinguishing elements were confirmed in Acts, particularly in the trial of Paul[90]. Rather than concluding with Boismard that Proto-Lk served as the source, it would be better to attribute the work to Lukan redaction. It was Proto-Lk which was responsible for introducing the charges by the chief priests before Pilate's interrogation of Jesus purely out of logical reasoning. Boismard rejected a special source, but suggested that Proto-Lk was once again dependent upon intermediate Mt. He reached this decision because of two agreements between Mt and Lk where there occurred "le participe 'disant' et le verbe 'déclarer' (ephè) au lieu de 'dire'" (23,2-4) and because the agreements between the two in the mockeries were more significant. Further, the conclusion of Luke's account was different from Mk. We concur with Boismard that the literary relationships were too numerous to be attributed to chance, but it seems reasonable to assume that Luke redacted the Markan account, rather than finding it necessary to explain the contact by recourse to a special source.

Boismard explained the MA (22,62) as having been introduced by a copyist in light of the Matthean parallel[91]. He admitted that on a theoretical level the problem of the MAs may be resolved in multifarious ways[92]. Neirynck had recently made a similar statement: "In theory I can have no objection against some

85. *Ibid.*, p. 409.

86. *Ibid.*, p. 413.

87. *Ibid.*, p. 409, 410. The phrase was also found at 1,10; 8,37; 19,37; Acts 6,5; 15,12 and 25,24. Cf. p. 414.

88. *Ibid.*, p. 412.

89. *Ibid.*, p. 413.

90. *Ibid.*, p. 414.

91. *Ibid.*, p. 403. See also Boismard's *Introduction* which treated the MAs (p. 30-32).

92. *Ibid.*, p. 41-42. Cf. p. 30-32.

influence of oral-tradition variants, some occasional dependence on a revised text
of Mark, or some subsidiary Lukan dependence on Matthew. But a modification
of the Markan hypothesis suggested on the basis of the minor agreements can only
be a minor modification, and it is my impression that no such modification is
needed after serious examination of the Matthean *and Lukan* redactions"[93].

Boismard, relying on a comparison of vocabulary, style and parallels of Jesus'
trials with those of Paul, declared that the Herod scene was indisputably "une
composition entièrement lucanienne" and Boismard attributed it to the final Lukan
redactor[94]. Drawing upon the account of Jesus before Pilate, Luke borrowed two
elements from the Markan/Matthean tradition. The first of these was the
interrogation and the silence of Jesus (23,9-10 / Mk 15,3-5). Boismard noted that
the points of contact rested with Mk. The second element was the account of the
mockery by the soldiers which Luke simplified (23,11 / Mk 15,16-17). If this were
so, then no written source provided the Herod scene.

The "parallèle le plus complet" was found in Paul's trials in Acts 25-26. The
scene of Jesus before Pilate inspired not only the Herod scene but Paul's trials.
This position was directly opposed to that held by Walaskay and later adopted by
Matera. Boismard suggested that this was the case to show that Paul shared in the
passion of Jesus. Mk 13,9 might have further inspired Luke with its reference to
the Christians appearing before governors and kings (where Luke reversed the
order - Lk 21,12).

Boismard rejected the proposal that the account stemmed from Proto-Lk since
it "détruit l'harmonie du récit de la comparution de Jésus devant Pilate"[95].
Furthermore, Boismard dismissed Dibelius's suggestion that the account arose from
Ps 2 for two reasons: the psalm was not explicitly cited in the account and while
the psalm spoke of a conspiracy between the leaders, Herod and Pilate sought to
discover Jesus' innocence and free him.

But Boismard did not entirely reject the possibility that there may be an
historical kernel at the base of the story, citing E. Bickermann who indicated that
there were circumstances where a Roman official sought the advice of high ranking
non-Roman individuals. Oral tradition could have supplied information concerning
the Herod trial, upon which Luke composed his story.

BOISMARD and LAMOUILLE (1990) proposed that the author of Document P
(Petrine traditions) brought together the idea of Herod and "kings of the earth" as
found in Ps 2[96]. They suggested that a tradition existed confirming it by reference
to GP.

---

93. F. NEIRYNCK, *The Minor Agreements and the Two-Source Theory*, in ID., *Evangelica II*,
p. 40-41 (= *Minor Agreements* [GTA, 50], Göttingen, 1993, p. 61-62).
94. BENOIT and BOISMARD, *Synopse*, t. 2, 1972, p. 418, 419.
95. *Ibid.*, p. 419.
96. M.-É. BOISMARD and A. LAMOUILLE, *Les Acts des Deux Apôtres. 1. Introduction -
Textes. 2. Le sense des récits. 3. Analyses littéraires* (EB, 12,13,14), Paris, 1990; Vol. 2, p. 46.
For the material in 4,25-28 which many scholars related to the Herod story see Vol. 3, p. 80-81.

Reception of Boismard's Theory

Walter Wink affirmed Boismard's thesis in its complexity and in reviving source criticism which some had thought no longer useful[97]. But Wink had serious reservations about Boismard's theory of final redactors, a concept Wink found "slippery". Boismard's proposed solution for the MAs were described as "something of an explanatory overkill"[98]. Both Wink and E.P. Sanders concurred that Boismard's theory was best portrayed by means of Boismard's diagram (p. 17) and both endorsed a view that called for a more complex solution to the synoptic question[99]. Wink was enthused by Boismard's treatment of the redaction of passages frequently supported by statistical evidence. While applauding interpretations that were "usually both penetrating and reasonable", Sanders nevertheless faulted the study for rarely citing secondary literature and by not demonstrating the weakness of opposing theories[100]. "The strength of Boismard's hypothesis, to be sure, is that it has the flexibility to accomodate itself to passages best explained on the theory of Matthean or Lucan priority as well as to passages best explained on the theory of Marcan priority"[101]. But Sanders did not endorse it as the correct solution. Moreover, he was reluctant to follow Boismard in asserting that the differences in the Gospels reflect differing sources.

Leopold Sabourin judged the work more negatively. He implied that not only had Boismard erred in assigning to sources what could have been attributed to the evangelists, but that Boismard's literary theory had not always clarified the texts under examination[102]. The hypothesis was not as radical as it may first appear. "Much in this theory is new only in name"[103]. Sabourin took as a test case Boismard's study of Peter's denials, rejecting the conclusions. Boismard claimed that there had only been one denial, but that even the difficulties in the Markan text can be explained by the evangelist's attempt "to give a coherent historical sequence to a strongly attested tradition of three denials"[104]. Aside from the fact that Sabourin believed Boismard manipulated the literary details to fit his theory, he found "no real evidence" for assuming that the traditions originally contained reference to only one denial. In spite of these weaknesses, Sabourin praised the

97. *CBQ* 35 (1973) 225. The evaluation was glowing: "B's. is surely not the last word, but it is a creative, sure-footed, unbiased, and objective one which opens up a whole new way ahead".
98. *Ibid.*, p. 224.
99. E.P. SANDERS, in *JBL* 94 (1975) 129, 130. Cf. W. WINK, in *CBQ* 35 (1973) 223, 225. X. Jacques also viewed a more complex solution as one of the advantages of Boismard's hypothesis in *NRT* 94 (1972) 806.
100. SANDERS, *JBL* 9 (1975) 130.
101. *Ibid.*
102. SABOURIN, *The Synoptic Problem*, p. 310, 311. See above.
103. *Ibid.*, p. 311.
104. *Ibid.*, p. 314.

work as "very informative and often rightly intuitive", which distinguished the particular theological perspective of the synoptic authors[105].

While a favorable review might be expected from a colleague, Jerome Murphy-O'Connor presented a balanced perspective in which he distinguished Boismard's *Synopse* from other works because it was the only synoptic problem theory based on a detailed and complete analysis of all four Gospels[106]. While Murphy-O'Connor found the investigation laudable, he expressed skepticism toward a statistical approach to discerning the style and vocabulary of a particular author[107]. Such a criticism notwithstanding, he argued that the significance of Boismard's work extended beyond an attempted solution to the synoptic problem.

Michel Bouttier pointed out that though Boismard had not given sufficient attention to recent redaction-critical studies, still he provided a useful tool[108]. H.F.D. Sparks critiqued the hypothesis for not being more exact about the nature of the documents, but agreed that there were more documents in circulation than contemporary scholars had heretofore accepted[109]. Though Wink, Sanders and Jacques viewed the complexity as an asset, Sparks considered it "the greatest stumbling-block". But he insightfully offered these words for future studies: "... it is likely that in the future we shall either have to be content with one of the simpler solutions or admit frankly that on the basis of the existing evidence alone the problem is insoluble"[110].

It is not often the case that one of the collaborators of a work offers a review, but such was the case with A. Lamouille[111]. As the strengths of this study he listed the fact that many authors ignored Jn in their search for the solution to the synoptic problem. Not only had Boismard taken this into consideration, but he additionally referred to apocryphal writings and patristic works. A further benefit was Boismard's clear literary analysis. The work was indispensable in the view of Lamouille: "Il nous semble impossible de faire désormais une étude sérieuse sur le problème synoptique sans faire référence à ce livre"[112]. Aside from a Spanish and Swedish review, the majority were French or English.

Concerning the literary relationship of the four canonical Gospels Boismard asserted that Johannine texts resembling Synoptic material shared sources with the Synoptics. Proto-Lk served as John's principal source in the passion narrative[113].

---

105. *Ibid.*, p. 315.
106. *RB* 79 (1973) 431. Murphy-O'Connor summarized his evaluation with the words: "Ce livre est une œuvre remarquable, et son auteur mérite notre gratitude et notre respect" (p. 435).
107. *Ibid.*, p. 433-434.
108. *ETR* 47 (1972) 459.
109. *JTS* 75 (1974) 486.
110. *Ibid.*
111. *RThom* 73 (1973) 273-278.
112. *Ibid.*, p. 278.
113. *Synopse*, Vol. 2, 1972, p. 47 (esp. the Introduction, p. 47-48). For an exposition and critique of Boismard's hypothesis see F. NEIRYNCK, *John and the Synoptics*, in M. DE JONGE (ed.), *L'évangile de Jean*, 1977, ²1987, 73-106 (esp. p. 81-93); *Evangelica I*, 365-398 (399-400:

In Boismard's opinion the same author composed Proto-Lk and the Gospel utilizing a similar style and vocabulary. Neirynck rightly challenged Boismard on this point that since both Proto-Lk and the final Lukan redactor betrayed similar style and vocabulary this did not prove that a proto-Lukan Gospel existed[114]. Neirynck also provided useful distinctions between Boismard's form of Proto-Lk and those of Streeter, Taylor and Jeremias[115].

In refining his position Boismard (1977) accepted John's dependence on the Synoptics, and not simply their sources, at the point of Jn II-B[116]. Document C, stemming from Palestine and originally composed in Aramaic, was divided into five parts. The first four were related to geographical areas of Jesus' ministry, while the fifth was comprised of the passion and resurrection narratives[117]. Jn II-A repeated Document C in the same order[118]. Jn II-B drawing on the text of Jn II-A turned its order around and included material of Document C which Jn II-A omitted. Jn III relied primarily on the text of Jn II-B but inserted material from Jn II-A as well as from Document C in addition to a logia collection which reflected familiarity with Jn II-B[119]. Proto-Lk, though difficult to date, was assigned a date certainly earlier than 70 AD[120].

Boismard took note of the order of the account of Peter's denials suggesting that Jn II-B placed the first denial ahead of the interrogation of Jesus by Annas indicating that the author of Jn II-B was familiar with the Lukan and Markan-Matthean arrangements[121].

Additional Note; *Evangelica II*, 1991, 798-799); *L'évangile de Jean. Examen critique du commentaire de M.-É. Boismard et A. Lamouille*, in *ETL* 53 (1977) 363-478; *Jean et les Synoptiques. Examen critique de l'exégèse de M.-É. Boismard* (BETL, 49), Leuven, 1979, 3-120.

114. NEIRYNCK, *John and the Synoptics*, p. 85 (= *Evangelica*, 377).

115. *Ibid.*, n. 47 (= n. 47). Although Boismard spoke of a Proto-Lk, it was distinct from that proposed by Streeter and Taylor. Boismard's concept relied on a combination of documents A (containing miracle accounts and forming the basis of the Mt/Mk tradition) and Q which formed Intermediary Mt. "The first consequence is that Document Q is not really a common source of which both Matthew and Luke made use independently but a Matthean source known by Luke mainly through Intermediary Matthew" (p. 85 = 377, n. 47). Two differences between the conceptions of Proto-Lk were that, according to Boismard, Luke did not have direct contact with Q, except in limited cases. Secondly, Boismard's version included the Markan blocks in addition to L+Q, a view which Neirynck assessed as a "more important consequence" of the two differences.

116. M.-É. BOISMARD and A. LAMOUILLE, with the collaboration of G. ROCHAIS, *L'évangile de Jean. Commentaire* (Synopse des quatre évangiles en Français, 3), Paris, 1977. See F. NEIRYNCK, *John and the Synoptics*, in ID., *Evangelica*, 1982, p. 399: Additional Note.

117. BOISMARD and LAMOUILLE, *L'évangile de Jean*, p. 16, 25. Document C originated in Palestine from a Christian familiar with the Samaritans around 50 AD (p. 67).

118. *Ibid.*, p. 25, 32. See also p. 31-32.

119. *Ibid.*, p. 48.

120. *Ibid.*, p. 67.

121. *Ibid.*, p. 416.

Boismard's research motivated the work of two other scholars, Jean-Pierre LÉMONON (1981)[122] on the Herod story and Philippe ROLLAND (1984)[123] who opted to modify Boismard's source theory on Lk.

Inspired by the research for his commentary on Acts co-authored by A. Lamouille[124], Boismard explored what he considered to be the stylistic characterics, content and structure of the special Lukan source in *En quête du*

122. *Pilate et le gouvernement de la Judée* (ÉB), Paris, 1981, p. 185. Diss. Lyon, 1979. See also p. 190. Cf. P. BENOIT and M.-É. BOISMARD, *Synopse des quatre Évangiles*, Vol. 2, 1972. Lémonon adopted Boismard's point of view that 23,6-12 was "une construction typiquement lucanienne", based on similarity of expressions between the Gospel and Acts. Lémonon referred to Boismard, p. 418, as well as to Hoehner (*Herod Antipas*, 1972, 224-227), who though defending the historicity, admitted there was a high concentration of Lukan vocabulary and style (p. 185, n. 53). It was the insertion of this material which prompted Luke to radically revamp "le schéma primitif". Building on oral tradition which referred to Herod's involvement in the passion of Jesus, Luke also included the Markan material of Jesus' silence before Pilate (LÉMONON, *Pilate*, p. 179). Although Luke had so composed the story line that "la scène n'a rien d'invraisemblable", there would have been no legal reason for Pilate to transfer Jesus to Herod.

Lémonon stated that Dibelius's explanation was insufficient for a number of reasons, but cited the most damaging: the views portrayed in the Gospel and Acts 4 were inverse. He described Acts 4 as "une interprétation généralisante" (p. 190). Lémonon contended that for this scene Luke made use of an oral tradition that Herod had been involved in the trial of Jesus (p. 190). Verse 23,12 expounded a theological conviction, but Lémonon seemed to suggest that some historical element was hinted (p. 228). Earlier, Lémonon cited two works in discussing the historical background of 23,12. A.T. OLMSTEAD, *Jesus in the Light of History*, New York, 1942, p. 147-149, saw Lk 13,1-2 and the massacre following the protest of the building of the aqueduct as the origin of the enmity between Pilate and Herod. E.M. SMALLWOOD, *The Jews Under Roman Rule*, Leiden, 1976, p. 163, suggested that the massacre of the Galileans was the reason for the hostility (LÉMONON, *Pilate*, p. 134, n. 21). For an opposing viewpoint see H.E.W. TURNER, *The Chronological Framework of the Ministry*, in D.E. NINEHAM (ed.), *Historicity and Chronology in the New Testament* (Theological Collections, 6), London, 1965, p. 73: "Something more than pin pricks natural to the relations between a Roman governor and a neighboring client king seems to be implied. Luke 13.1, whether it refers to Galileans killed in the popular disturbance over the proposed aqueduct or to some otherwise unrecorded incident in the governorship of Pilate, is a less likely explanation of their bad relations. Pilate could hardly be blamed for the fate of Galileans who had become embroiled in a popular disturbance at Jerusalem". Noting the parallel between the trial of Jesus and that of Paul, Lémonon, once more indebted to Boismard, saw this as a kind of imitation by the disciple of the master (*Pilate*, p. 190, n. 78).

123. *Les premiers évangiles. Un nouveau regard sur le problème synoptique* (LD, 116), Paris, 1984 (esp. p. 106, 181-188). Rolland suggested that Mk and Lk were dependent upon a common source. This common source, as used by Luke, was shorter than Mk itself (p. 50-51; cf. p. 148-153). See NEIRYNCK, in *ETL* 60 (1984) 403-404. The "many" in the Prologue (1,1) referred to a number of accounts, presumably written, with which Luke was familiar. In addition, he sought to obtain oral sources (ROLLAND, *Les premiers évangiles*, p. 181). Two of Luke's sources were the Pauline Gospel and the Gospel "des Craignants-Dieu". Rolland considered the Herod story (23,6-12) to have derived from oral sources, with Joanna or Cleophas as possibilities (p. 182).

124. *Les Actes des deux apôtres* (EB 12-14), 3 vols., Paris, 1990.

Proto-Luc (1997)[125]. He divided the work into two major sections: the literary analysis[126] and Proto-Luc[127], devoting a great deal of attention to the passion and resurrection narratives. In his analysis Proto-Luc (= L) included: 22,54a.54b-55.60b-61.63.65.66-70; 23,1-3a.9b.13a.14.16-24[128]. He also distinguished between a Proto-Mk, a much shorter version of "actual" Mk, the latter being systematically harmonized with Mt, "par une main de tradition lucanienne, sinon par Luc lui-même"[129].

Following a list of typical Lukan literary characteristics, Boismard noted that the Lukan tonality was very high in ch 23, though significantly less in ch 22[130]. These elements were found in the trial in 22,56.59.60.66.70; 23,1.2.4.5.7.8. 10.12.14.15[131].

Two principles governed his research on the passion and resurrection. The first, inspired by V. Taylor and F.L. Cribbs[132], sought to recover the elements from L by eliminating the parts which were "quasi" identical with the Markan text[133]. This would also include sections where Lukan redaction was different from the Markan or Matthean parallels to such a degree that "dépendance par rapport à la tradition M/M est pratiquement exclue"[134].

The second principle concerned the contacts between Lk and Jn[135]. Boismard

125. M.-É BOISMARD, *En quête du Proto-Luc* (EB 37), Paris, 1997. See p. 8, where he noted that the method followed in the present work was completely different from that employed in the commentary on Acts. During the same year Boismard also published, *L'évangile de l'enfance (Luc 1-2) selon le proto-Luc* (EB 35), Paris, 1997. See the reviews by Neirynck in *ETL* 73 (1997) 450-452, 453-455.

126. The chapters within this section include: 1) Les caractéristiques stylistiques; 2) La ruine de Jérusalem; 3) Passion et résurrection; 4) Le discours inaugural de Jésus; 5) Début du ministère de Jésus; 6) En route vers Jérusalem; and 7) De Jéricho à Jérusalem. On the trial see especially, p. 106-130.

127. This portion consisted of: 1) Le texte du document L, where the opposing pages contain the Greek text and corresponding French translations inspired by the *Bible de Jérusalem* (cf. p. 11); 2) Structure du document L; and Conclusions.

128. See p. 314-316. For a list of full or partial verses in Lk 22-24 which Boismard assigned to Proto-Lc, see below Neirynck's review.

129. *Ibid.*, p. 10. On the Markan tradition, see further p. 39.

130. *Ibid.*, p. 34. Of the 56 verses in ch 23, Boismard argued there were 41 stylistic characteristics with an average mean of 0.73, compared with 71 verses in ch 22, which he claimed contained only 24 stylistic characteristics, giving an average mean of 0.34.

131. *Ibid.*, p. 31.

132. In his bibliography, Boismard listed the works of Taylor as *Behind* (1926) and *Passion Narrative* (1972). The studies of F.L. Cribbs were: *A Study of the Contacts that Exist between St. Luke and St. John*, in *1973 SBL Seminar Papers*, p. 1-93, and *The Agreements that Exist between John and Acts*, in C.H. TALBERT (ed.), *Perspectives on Luke-Acts*, Danville, VA - Edinburgh, 1978, p. 40-61.

133. BOISMARD, *En quête*, p. 63.

134. *Ibid.*

135. *Ibid.*, p. 64. Here Boismard offered a brief history of works which treated this theme, beginning with B. Weiss (1907). Again drawing on F.L. Cribbs Boismard argued that "Luke was

insisted that the final form of Jn showed familiarity with the Mk/Mt tradition, and, at least in one case, was supplemented by elements borrowed from L[136].

As for the trial, Boismard referred occasionally to Taylor (and Cribbs), but did not always concur with his judgments[137]. Boismard believed that the Mk/Mt tradition was found in the third denial (22,60a).

It is interesting to note how Boismard concluded that 22,71 was an addition by Luke (or the final redactor), under the influence of the Mk/Mt tradition. The phrase ἀπὸ τοῦ στόματος αὐτοῦ was "quasi" identical. This was confirmed by the reference to τί ἔτι ἔχομεν μαρτυρίας χρείαν;, which alluded to the first part of the trial. Luke was aware of the difficulty and thus redacted μαρτύρων to μαρτυρίας. Boismard concluded: "l'emprunt à la tradition M/M reste assez clair"[138].

After comparing the structure of the Lukan and Johannine versions of the trial of Pilate Boismard remarked that the Mk/Mt tradition did not mention Pilate's affirmations of Jesus' innocence nor his intention to free Jesus. In addition, in the latter the Barabbas episode was much more developed[139].

Lk 23,3 has often been cited as clear evidence that Lk employed Mk in this section of his Gospel. Boismard observed that similarities exist with the other Gospels (Mt 15,2 / Mt 27,11 / Jn 18,33b.37). Rather than accepting Markan influence on the Lukan account, Boismard maintained the reverse: the common tradition he saw behind Lk and Jn influenced the Mk/Mt tradition[140].

Boismard also called attention to the phrase τί γὰρ κακὸν ἐποίησεν οὗτος; (23,22) which was expressed in identical terms with Mk 15,14. The redactor's addition of 23,25 paralleled the Mk/Mt tradition[141].

As for the MA in 22,62 Boismard remarked that according to the Two-Source theory, Matthew and Luke each independently corrected Mk to avoid the difficult ἐπιβαλών, a solution which, in his opinion, would be impossible. The "seule solution logique" was that Luke borrowed from the text of the tradition in Mt, which preserved the Mk/Mt tradition[142]. As for the MA in 22,64 / Mt 26,68,

---

influenced by some early form of the developing Johannine tradition in the writing of the Gospel rather than vice versa" (CRIBBS, *Study*, 1973, p. 92, quoted in BOISMARD, *En quête*, p. 64).

136. In the case of the anointing of Jesus by a woman (Jn 12,1-8), he asserted that John modified the account which contained the Mk/Mt tradition, adding details from the account of the tradition which followed the L document.

137. BOISMARD, *En quête*, p. 106, concerning the denials of Peter: "Nos analyses, plus précises que celles de Taylor, vont nous permettre de formuler des conclusions très differentes". Where Boismard parted company with Taylor and Cribbs on particular issues, see e.g. p. 106, 108, n. 1, 109, n. 1, 118, n. 1; cf. p. 116, n. 1 (Cribbs); n. 2 (Taylor); 118, n. 1 (Cribbs).

138. *Ibid.*, p. 120.

139. *Ibid.*, p. 123.

140. *Ibid.*, p. 125.

141. *Ibid.*, p. 129-130.

142. *Ibid.*, p. 113.

either Luke or the redactor added it in order to harmonize the text of the L document with the Mk/Mt tradition[143].

Referring to 23,6-12 as "la comparution de Jésus devant Hérode", he observed that there was an echo of the passage in v. 15[144]. He called attention to Acts 4,25-27 and GP 1,1-2. He reasoned that 23,6-12 was not from the same redactional level as the passage in Acts[145]. The Gospel episode was "certainement plus récent puisqu'il affaiblit le sens de la tradition représentée par l'évangile de Pierre, mieux conservé dans les Actes".

He conjectured that the Herod story was composed by the final redactor and inspired by numerous passages in Lk. The theme of Herod's desire to see Jesus was reprised in Acts 25,22 where Herod Agrippa wanted to see Paul. The "séquence anormale" involving the silence motif in 23,9 following accusations by the high priests was similar to Mt 27,12-14 and Mk 15,2-5. He asserted that the silence of Jesus was transferred by the redactor to the interrogation of Jesus by Herod (23,9)[146].

Lukan style characteristics were reflected in the following words and phrases: ἀκούσας δὲ Πιλᾶτος, ἐπερωτᾶν, always followed by a complement directed to the accusative, ἀναπέμπειν, Ἱεροσόλυμα, ἐν ταῖς ἡμέραις ταύταις (cf. here ἐν ταῖς ἡμέραις ταύταις), ἀπεκρίνατο.

In attempting to offer a reconstruction of L, Boismard acknowledged following the lead of Taylor and Cribbs[147]. He believed that his research established three levels of redaction in Lk as he also surmised for Acts. There was a relationship between L and Acts I, a fundamental level of Acts. Similarly, Lk corresponded to Acts II, and the final redactor of Lk to Acts III. In his opinion the first two levels were confirmed "par une certaine unité de vocabulaire et de style"[148]. In retaining the term Proto-Lk Boismard acknowledged the pioneers in this research B. Weiss and P. Feine[149]. As for the sources of Proto-Lk he admitted this was not an easy problem to solve, though insights from his study on Acts may shed light on this question[150]. He chose to focus in the present study on his proposed reconstruction of the hypothetical Proto-Lk source rather than developing the problem related to its sources[151]. As to the question of authorship of Proto-Lk, Boismard adopted the "position classique, qui, d'ordinaire, n'a pas identifié Luc à l'auteur du document L (ou des matériaux désignés par la lettre L)"[152].

---

143. *Ibid.*, p. 116.
144. *Ibid.*, p. 123; also p. 122.
145. *Ibid.*, p. 124.
146. *Ibid.*, p. 126.
147. *Ibid.*, p. 333.
148. *Ibid.*
149. *Ibid.*, p. 335.
150. *Ibid.*, p. 336.
151. *Ibid.*
152. *Ibid.*, p. 337.

What is important to observe, and what is distinctive from his previously held position, is that Boismard no longer argued that there was a historical core to the Herod episode. It is also interesting to note that despite employing a method he described as entirely different from that which he used in his study of Acts, he was able to arrive at roughly the same results, namely, three levels of redaction.

Neirynck remarked that at several points Boismard argued against his own position, including the question of authorship of Proto-Lk which shifted from *Enfance* to *Proto-Luc*[153]. Though Boismard highlighted the precursory efforts of B. Weiss and P. Feine, Neirynck noted that the pioneering work of J. Weiss appeared to have escaped him[154]. He further observed that the method Boismard employed in *Enfance* was not completely abandoned in *Proto-Luc*. Concerning Boismard's observation on the relatively few "caractéristiques stylistiques lucaniennes" which were found in L Boismard offered a conclusion that was "assez reservée". Tracing the development of Boismard's treatment of Proto-Lk beginning with *Synopsis II* (1972) Neirynck concluded: "Le proto-Luc de 1997 est en effet assez différent de celui de 1972. Pour citer un exemple, les Outrages à Jésus (22,63-65), le texte de proto-Luc en 1972: vv. 63b-64; en 1997: vv. 63.65"[155]. Neirynck rejected Boismard's proposed division of three levels of Lukan redaction.

François BOVON (1974) highlighted source criticism as an important methodological concern in treating the events of the final days of Jesus' life[156]. Focusing on the differences between the Markan and Lukan accounts he noted some scholars' support of the view that Luke had not followed the Markan passion, instead adopting another passion source which was familiar with traditions known to John[157]. Bovon, however, stated it was "plus peut-être vraisemblable toutefois que Luc, suivant son habitude, modifie en l'améliorant le texte de Marc"[158].

---

153. F. NEIRYNCK, *Review of M.-É. Boismard, L'évangile de l'enfance, 1997*, in *ETL* 73 (1997) 450-452. See NEIRYNCK, *Review of M.-É. Boismard, En quête*, p. 453.

154. F. NEIRYNCK, *Review of M.-É. Boismard, En quête du proto-Luc, 1997*, in *ETL* 73 (1997) 453-455, p. 453.

155. *Ibid.*, p. 454.

156. F. BOVON, *Les derniers jours de Jésus. Textes et événements*, Neuchâtel - Paris - Brussels - Montréal, 1974, p. 5: "Notre principale préoccupation a été d'ordre méthodologique. Trop d'ouvrages, même scientifiques, sur le procès de Jésus laissent à désirer sur ce point. C'est pourquoi nous avons porté notre attention sur les sources, le choix d'un point de départ légitime et l'élaboration d'un déroulement vraisemblable des événements".

157. *Ibid.*, p. 19. The differences included the omission in Lk of the nocturnal Sanhedrin session, the absence of any reference to Jesus' words about the Temple (qualified by the observation that it was absent "dans ce contexte"), and the absence of the mockery by Roman soldiers (Mk 15,16-20a). In addition, Luke recorded a morning session of the Sanhedrin about which Mark wrote (Mk 15,1). Further, following a mockery, Luke alone recounted Jesus before Herod (23,6-12) (p. 19-20).

158. *Ibid.*, p. 19. Bovon considered the passion narratives as historical, though Lk and Jn were in some cases considered more historically accurate than Mt and Mk (p. 23; see also p. 49-50). A case in point was the role of the Jews in the condemnation of Jesus. See further p. 15, n. 1.

Tracing twenty-five years of Lukan research (1978)[159] in a section dealing with 22,1–23,56 Bovon treated primarily the Lukan theology of Jesus' death. He devoted, however, a portion of that section to Schneider's dissertation which he deemed "constitue une solide étude [...] Elle ne brille peut-être pas par l'originalité"[160].

Later Bovon (1981), while acknowledging Mk and Q as Luke's sources, was unsure whether Luke was following Mk in Lk 22–23[161]. Aside from these two major sources, Bovon proposed a third: "son 'bien propre' (en divers blocs plutôt qu'en un document suivi), quelques cycles sur la communauté de Jérusalem, les Hellénistes, la conversion et les mission de Paul, des informations isolées, des traces d'itinéraires, etc."[162]. More specifically, it was unclear whether the prophecy of Peter's denial (22,32) and its realization (22,61-62) were to be attributed to Mk or a source proper to Luke, with no consideration given to the possibility of Lukan redaction. The material extending from the trial of Jesus until the end of Acts served the apologetic of demonstrating that the Christian mission was non-threatening to the Romans.

In the first installment of his Lukan commentary (1989) Bovon remarked that Luke used a form of Mk "die von der kanonischen nur wenig abweicht"[163]. Noting the significant differences between the two Gospels in the passion narrative, he acknowledged these could have been the result of Lukan redaction of Mk, but because of Lk – Jn agreements he favored the idea of "eine konkurrierende Erzählung"[164]. Neirynck noted Bovon's heavy emphasis on oral tradition and that

---

159. *Luc le théologien. Vingt-cinq ans de recherches (1950-1975)*, Neuchâtel, 1978, esp. p. 175-181 (= *Luke the Theologian. Thirty-Three Years of Research* [PTMS, 12], tr. K. MCKINNEY, Allison Park, PA, 1987, esp. p. 164-170). Because the French original "quickly sold out", the English translation provided Bovon with the opportunity to update his work. As he explained in the foreword: "The English edition has the advantage of making accessible this state of research which covers the years 1950 to 1975 again. It also has the supplementary advantage of offering the translation of an article which was written later. It brings up to date – in a form a bit different from the book – the studies published concerning Luke between the years 1975 and 1983" (p. xv).

160. *Ibid.*, p. 181 (= 170).

161. *Évangile de Luc et Actes des Apôtres*, in J. AUNEAU et al., *Évangiles synoptiques et Actes des Apôtres* (PBSB NT, 4), Paris, 1981, p. 208, 224. Bovon was influenced particularly by Benoit (1966), M. GOURGUES, *Jésus devant sa passion et sa mort*, in *CE* 30 (1979) 1-64, and *Les psaumes et Jésus, Jésus et les psaumes*, in *CE* 25 (1978) 1-64, and A. Vanhoye (1971). Bovon rejected the view that Luke had "accès direct" to the events but obtained information from eyewitnesses and ministers of the word (*Évangile de Luc et Actes des Apôtres*, p. 255).

162. *Évangile de Luc et Actes des Apôtres*, p. 256.

163. *Das Evangelium nach Lukas. 1. Lk 1,1–9,50*, Zürich - Neukirchen - Vluyn, 1989, p. 20 (= *L'Évangile selon saint Luc [1,1-9,50]*, Geneva, 1991, p. 25). Bovon listed Luke's sources as Mk, Q and S[Lk], arguing in line with Cadbury that the term πολλοί could be a literary technique which did not necessarily refer to Luke's predecessors (p. 34, n. 21 = 36, n. 21). On the question of order Bovon noted that the term (1,3) could suggest "eine chronologisch oder heilsgeschichtlich korrekte Reihenfolge sowie auf eine ausgewogene Komposition" (p. 39 = 41).

164. *Ibid.*, p. 21 (= 26).

even in the first volume of the commentary Bovon indicated his approach to the
source question in the passion narrative (p. 21 = 26), but added: "On se rappellera
cependant la conclusion de M.L. Soards qui, ayant fait le relevé des éléments non
marciens dans Lc 22, devait constater: 'this is not a continuous narrative'"[165].

Bovon (1993) claimed recently that Luke was dependent upon only two sources
in the passion narrative and alternated between the blocks[166]. Bovon found
verification for the hypothesis internally through the philological evidence (which
he did not offer) and externally, contending that the special source had been
employed by one of the authors of a Jewish-Christian Gospel as well as by
Marcion[167].

As a contribution to a gathering of the 1992 Colloquium Biblicum Lovaniense
Bovon delivered a paper on the Lukan passion narrative in which he signaled his
support of the special source theory[168]. Describing the passion account as "un
récit continu" though comprised of distinct episodes, he adopted a literary,
synchronic and narrative approach in the first part of the paper, chosing to address
the source question in the second. In the line of Dibelius and Vanhoye, Bovon
accepted the view that the Lukan presentation fell into the literary genre of the acts
of martyrs.

In examining the state of the source question Bovon treated the relation of Lk
to that of Mk highlighting first the difference in order, the omission of certain

165. *ETL* 67 (1991) 428-429.

166. BOVON, *Le récit lucanien de la passion de Jésus (22-23)*, in C. FOCANT (ed.), *The
Synoptic Gospels. Source Criticism and the New Literary Criticism* (BETL, 110), Leuven, 1993,
393-423. He presented this essay at the Francophone seminar of the Colloquium Biblicum
Louvaniense, August 18-20, 1992.

167. Already in 1901 P.C. SENSE argued "that Luke the Marcionite was the author of the
Marcionite Gospel" (*A Critical and Historical Enquiry into the Origin of the Third Gospel*,
London - Oxford, 1901, p. 406). Canonical Lk was a copy and embellishment of that source (p.
366). Although Sense stated that nothing was known about the compiler and place of publication,
he proposed that "Pantænus, the first Master of the Christian school" at Alexandria had gathered
the material. The date of publication of the canonical Lk was placed at between 168 AD and 177
AD (p. vi, 408, 412). In the section 22,54-62.63-71; 23,1-7.8-12.13-26 the material in the
canonical Gospel was the same as in the Marcionite Gospel with the exception of various
interpolations, substitutions and omissions noted in 22,60.61.63.64; 23,2.7 (p. 266-268, 278).

168. BOVON, *Le récit de la passion de Jésus (Lc 22-23)*. On Bovon's insistence that the
special source was continuous see also p. 420. In an interesting note, Bovon confessed that he was
not "au courant du succès" of the special source hypothesis in France and in French-speaking
countries. He simply referred generally to the works of several French-speaking Catholic scholars
and to the bibliography of Fitzmyer's commentary (p. 409, n. 49). In another article, Bovon
signaled his support more generally of L inspired, in part, by the work of G. Petzke: "Q and L,
the synoptic sayings source and the source of the Lukan special materials, are no longer just
possible, but rather fruitful and productive hypotheses" (*Studies in Luke-Acts*, in *HTR* 85 [1992]
175-196, p. 180 (= *Études lucaniennes*, in *RTP* 125 [1993] 113-135, p. 118): "La Source des
logia (Q) et le bien propre de Luc (S^{Lc}) ne sont plus de fragiles, mais de fécondes hypothèses").
See also his reference to Proto-Lk (p. 193 = 132). Cf. G. PETZKE, *Das Sondergut des
Evangeliums nach Lukas* (Zürcher Werkkommentare zur Bibel), Zürich, 1990.

material such as the references to the false witnesses and the Temple as well as the anointing at Bethany, and additions such as the Herod story (23,8-12)[169].

Bovon envisioned three possible solutions to the Lukan source question; 1) the traditional historical solution which suggested that various traditions, oral and written, gave rise to the differences between Lk and Mk; 2) the redaction historical approach which credited Luke's imagination, convictions and Scriptural references with the variations; and 3) the literary critical explanation which, while holding that Mk was Luke's principal source, blended the form critical with the redaction critical.

Though Bovon did not offer an extensive list of scholars who supported the respective theories, he recounted main figures in the debate covering form criticism[170], redaction criticism[171], a special source[172], recent monographs, some of which evidence a disinterest in the source question[173], and proponents of the new literary criticism[174].

As regards Luke's compositional methods, Bovon believed that Luke would neither have multiplied his sources nor used them at the same time, resulting in Luke's alternating between Mk and the special Lukan source[175]. Bovon defined 22,47-23,5 as parallel to Mk and 23,6-43 as belonging to the special Lukan source. Another characteristic of Luke's writing was that rarely did Luke involve

---

169. BOVON, Le récit, p. 406. On the phenomenon of order and omissions see also p. 413-414. In an article also published in 1981 he called attention to the signs performed by Jesus and the reception they received. "Similarly, with regard to signs: Luke is careful to make note of the refusals of Jesus to perform messianic marvels which could be welcomed with any other attitude than faith. Satan does not manage to tempt him towards efficacious messianism (Luke 4:1-13) and Herod Antipas is left frustrated (Luke 23:6-12). All the signs of Jesus are impossible and ineffective if there is no faith on the part of the beneficiaries, or at least some well-meaning reception" (Le Dieu de Luc, in RSR 69 [1981] 279-300 = The God of Luke, in ID., New Testament Traditions and Apocryphal Narratives [PTMS, 36], Allison Park, PA, 1995, 67-80, p. 70; note that the index [p. 245] erroneously listed the reference to 23,6-12 as occurring on p. 69).

170. Ibid., p. 408. K. Grobel and J. Finegan were mentioned as advocates of the theory that Mk was Luke's only source.

171. Ibid. The names of F. Neirynck, M. Rese, J.A. Fitzmyer, M.L. Soards, F.G. Untergassmair, and D. Senior were rehearsed.

172. Ibid., p. 408-409. P. Feine, B. Weiss, A. Schlatter, J. Jeremias, E. Schweizer, F. Rehkopf, T. Schramm, J.C. Hawkins, A.M. Perry, B.H. Streeter, V. Taylor and J.B. Tyson constituted supporters while R. Bultmann and M. Dibelius were cited as opposing the theory (p. 408, n. 38).

173. Ibid., p. 409-410. A. Büchele, R.J. Karris, J. Neyrey, and M.L. Soards formed this group.

174. Ibid., p. 410. C.H. Talbert, R.C. Tannehill, C. L'Eplattenier, J.-N. Aletti and R. Meynet comprised scholars of the new literary criticism. Bovon earlier indicated that his interest in the literary matters had been stimulated by the work of J.-N. Aletti, among others (p. 393, n. 1). See his praise of Aletti in Studies in Luke-Acts, 1992, p. 196. This text was not found in the French edition Études lucaniennes (1993).

175. BOVON, Le récit, p. 411. See also the schema (p. 415-416).

526 CHAPTER NINE

more than two people in a dialogue, a literary practice also found in the theater and
Roman antiquity[176].

In an attempt to verify his theory, Bovon suggested a process in which the
special material was confirmed by certain grammatical and stylistic indications[177].
Next, the proper material was compared with the canonical Gospel and also ancient
patristic literature.

As to the troubling question of why the special document should have
disappeared, Bovon likened it to that of Q, made obsolete by its inclusion in Mt
and Lk. Luke eclipsed the special source[178]. Bovon remained convinced that a
redactional study of the special source would reveal the literary and theological
themes of Luke.

Bovon (1974) noted the position of some scholars that Pilate had been required
by law to transfer Jesus to Herod[179]. Bovon rejected this view claiming that the
transfer was made out of deference to Herod in relation to the extradition powers
which had been extended to Herod the Great. Indicating that the historicity of the
Herod episode was attested only by Luke, Bovon also entertained the idea that the
account was not genuine, if like Acts 4,27, it was intended to show that the
messianic psalm (Ps 2,2) had been fulfilled. "En ce cas, elle ne serait pas
authentique"[180].

It was apparent that Bovon (1981) was aware of Dibelius's suggestion that Ps
2 inspired 23,6-12[181]. Similarly, he was conversant with the suggestions that the
scene was historical and may have transpired out of deference to Herod who could
have been in Jerusalem for the Passover[182]. Or such a privilege might have
resulted from one originally granted to Herod the Great. Whatever the case,
Roman penal law did not require the transfer of Jesus to Herod.

Subsequently, Bovon (1989) maintained that for chapters 22 and 23 Luke
either radically adapted Mk or followed "eine konkurrierende Erzählung"[183].
With reference to the mention of Joanna in 8,3, Bovon believed it was most
probable that Chuza was "in den privaten Besitztümern der Fürsten"[184]. Further,
since Bovon seemed to follow Hoehner[185], it appeared likely that he would view

176. *Ibid.*, p. 399.
177. *Ibid.*, p. 416.
178. *Ibid.*, p. 420.
179. BOVON, *Les derniers jours de Jésus*, p. 66-67.
180. *Ibid.*, p. 67.
181. BOVON, *Évangile de Luc et Actes des Apôtres*, p. 229.
182. Éduard DELEBECQUE (1976) did not concern himself with the source question, as for
example in not offering any explanation for the term "many" in the Prologue (*Évangile de Luc.
Texte traduit et annoté*, Paris, 1976, p. 2). He indicated, however, that Herod was in Jerusalem
for Passover (p. 142).
183. BOVON, *Das Evangelium nach Lukas*, p. 21 (= 26).
184. *Ibid.*, p. 399-400 (= 390).
185. *Ibid.*, p. 400, n. 26 (= 390, n. 26).

the Herod pericope as deriving from tradition, though we must await the publication of the subsequent volume for any definitive assessment.

Still later, Bovon (1993) adopted the position that Herod was in Jerusalem for the Passover and that Pilate used the opportunity as a loophole, freeing himself from the responsibility[186]. The appearance (*"comparution"*) before Herod was listed alternately as 23,8-12 and 23,6-12[187]. Leaving behind Mk which Luke had been following in 23,1-5 (Mk 15,1-5), Luke turned to his other source where Jesus was portrayed as a king. In a 1993 pastoral commentary on Lk Hugues COUSIN briefly discussed the issue of sources and, influenced by Bovon, adopted the view that Luke employed a special passion source[188].

186. BOVON, *Le récit*, p. 400. See p. 396.

187. *Ibid.*, p. 406; cf. p. 414, 417.

188. *L'Évangile de Luc. Commentaire pastoral*, Paris - Outremont, Quebec, 1993, p. 12-13. Affirming that Luke knew and used Mk and Q, he also noted that Luke derived many accounts and numerous parables from "d'une source qui lui est propre" (p. 12). See further his comment on p. 13: "... je n'ai dressé de comparaison synoptique entre Marc et Luc qu'à titre d'échantillon, notamment dans la Passion. J'ai souhaité lire le premier tome de l'œuvre lucanienne pour lui-même, tel que nous l'offre l'Église – c'est lui qui est Parole de Dieu pour nous, non les reconstructions toujours hypothétiques des sources ou des événements". Introducing the passion narrative (22,1-23,56) Cousin called attention to Markan material absent in Lk as well as material not found in Mk and proper to Lk (22,61a; 23,2.5.4.14.22.6-12.13-16) (p. 285-286). He also observed the difference in the order of episodes between Mk and Lk. Drawing on Bovon Cousin favored the theory that Luke employed a separate passion source which he embellished with Markan material. "'Ou bien Luc a retravaillé Marc plus que de coutume, ou alors il a repris un récit concurrent. Les concordances avec l'évangile de Jean font pencher pour la seconde explication' (F. Bovon). Dans cette dernière hypothèse, Luc, semble-t-il, aura aussi connu le récit de Marc et l'aura utilisé pour enrichir son propre récit" (p. 286). Cousin did not provide a citation for his Bovon source. Presumably it was *L'Évangile selon saint Luc*, t. 1. 1,1 à 9,50, Geneva, 1991 (cf. COUSIN, p. 342).

Although the Herod pericope was defined as 23,6-12 at the beginning of his discussion of the passion account, later he confined it to 23,8-12 (p. 285, 310, 311). Cousin highlighted connections with the story to earlier portions of the Gospel (3,19-20; 9,9; 11,16.29; 21,12) as well as to later material in Acts (23–26). He commented on the relationship of the Gospel and Acts, in a section where he specifically mentioned Acts 4,25-27: "Cela n'empêche pas Luc d'approcher la Passion de Jésus, dans les Actes, sous un autre angle, complémentaire" (p. 314).

In an earlier work, Cousin (1976) dealt with the empty tomb accounts (Mk 16,1-8 and pars.), the narratives of the crucifixion and death of Jesus (Mk 15,20b-41 and pars.) coupled with a general discussion of the events of the passion. His insights on the development of the tradition as it pertained to theological themes are quite useful (*Le prophète assassiné. Histoire des textes évangéliques de la Passion*, Paris, 1976, esp. p. 213-220). In these thematic treaments Cousin followed and expanded on LÉON-DUFOUR, *Passion*, in DBS 6, 1960, 1419-1492. The themes he treated were christology, the fulfillment of Scriptures, the disciples of Jesus, and the Jews and the Romans. While the general sense of the christology was that Jesus who suffered was now risen, Cousin saw a strong affirmation of the innocence of Jesus in Lk (23,4.14.15.16.22) (COUSIN, *Le prophète*, p. 214). That the unfolding of the passion was the result of a divine plan was confirmed in Acts 2,23. Closely related to the christological theme, Jesus was presented as fulfilling God's promise of a prophet who was denied by Peter (22,34) and mocked by guards

Simon LÉGASSE (1974) noted that the source question for the Lukan version of the Sanhedrin trial (22,67-71) was much more complex than that of Mt as he highlighted initially the differences between the Gospel parallels[189]. Like Schneider and Catchpole Légasse advocated the idea of a special source[190]. A great deal of attention was given to 22,66. Concerning the timing of the trial (22,66), although Légasse entertained the idea that the temporal detail may have been transmitted independently, he ultimately rejected it in favor of the view that Luke was dependent upon Mk alone at this point[191]. Luke was not responsible for all the elements of 22,67 some of which did not betray his customary style. To account for this Légasse supposed "une tradition distincte" concerning the messianism of Jesus which was confirmed by verbal contacts with Mt (Mt 26,63 / 22,67)[192]. Nevertheless, Luke did not ignore the Markan account. Légasse accepted that vv. 67b-68 contained non-Markan elements[193]. Though 22,69 was similar to Mk 14,62c, differences existed such as the replacement of the parousia by the celestial exaltation of the Christ, an idea that was repeated in Acts. It was the special source which separated the two titles of Christ and Son of God and which was also inspired by the Markan account[194]. Légasse admitted the

(22,63-64) (p. 215). The tendency concerning the disciples was to excuse them: Luke did not report their flight at Gethsemane and spoke of their sleeping as induced by sorrow (22,45). Cousin seemed to interpret Lk as a model for discipleship after the pattern of martyrs, as can be understood from his comments about Simon of Cyrene and the good thief. The Jews were accused of greater culpability, while the Romans were increasingly excused. The Jews led Jesus to the place of execution (23,25), though the evangelist was careful to distinguish "l'attitude passive du peuple" (p. 217, 218). The discussion of the unbelief of the Jews in God's plan was carried into Acts 28,25-28. Pilate's portrayal was improved by the declarations of innocence.

189. S. LÉGASSE, *Jésus devant le Sanhédrin*, in *RTL* 5 (1974) 170-197. See also p. 192, 196. Légasse referred readers to Schneider's *Verleugnung* for a detailed examination of the account. In the section of the article dealing particularly with the Lukan account Légasse was conversant with the works of Schneider, Catchpole, Winter and Taylor (p. 182-189).

190. *Ibid.*, p. 186: "En réalité, Luc a disposé d'une version particulière de la séance, qu'il a glosée en s'inspirant de Mc".

191. *Ibid.*, p. 194. Légasse also explained: "D'après cet évangile (22,66), l'unique séance se tient à l'heure où Mc réunit le Sanhédrin pour la seconde fois. N'y a-t-il pas là une confirmation de la notice de Mc 15,1a? Oui, pourvu que Lc transmette une donnée indépendante de Mc. Ceci doit être sérieusement examiné, car il ne fait aucun doute que Lc a connu et utilisé le récit marcien de la Passion. Plus précisément, sa propre et unique séance du Sanhédrin n'est qu'une variante de la première séance de Mc dont elle s'inspire en partie" (p. 191-192).

192. *Ibid.*, p. 183. The phrase common to both Mt and Lk was εἰ σὺ εἶ ὁ χριστός.

193. *Ibid.*, p. 185.

194. *Ibid.*, p. 186: "La source distinguait nettement entre Christ et Fils de Dieu. Sous la plume de Luc, cette version subi d'importants changements, de sorte qu'il est difficile de la retrouver dans sa pureté originelle. Parmi ces retouches, la plus importante est l'insertion de la parole sur le Fils de l'homme, à laquelle Luc attribue un rôle déterminant: par l'annonce de sa glorification céleste". The phrase ἀπὸ τοῦ νῦν reflected Lukan redaction, in Légasse's opinion, and was consistent with the theology of the passage (p. 184).

influence of the LXX in some cases, such as the phrase ἀπὸ τοῦ στόματος and was alert to certain verbal similarities between the Gospel and Acts[195].

Declaring "*inutile*" the objection that there would not have been witnesses to relay information about the Sanhedrin trial, Légasse responded that the purpose of the Gospel accounts was to nourish the faith of the Christian communities rather than preserve the memory of the events. He maintained that, in contrast to Taylor, the historical value of such a tradition would not be greater than that of Mark's account[196].

The independent source needed to be supplemented by material drawn from Mk. Luke combined the non-Markan tradition with the Markan account of the Sanhedrin trial contributing elements of his own redaction to form the account. Unfortunately, this literary process rendered recovery of the pristine form of the non-Markan source difficult.

Légasse subsequently published a two-volume study on the trial of Jesus. The first volume (1994) concentrated on the history of the trial while the second (1995) examined the trial as presented in the four Gospels[197]. Two handicaps, evident in the investigations of Winter and Blinzler, attended the study of the trial: the sources would provide only a "un chétif résidu historique" which vary according to the sources used and the hypotheses these sources reflect. The second difficulty was confessional preoccupations[198].

While it was clear that in the passion Matthew did not use a source other than Mk, the situation with Lk is much more difficult to solve, as Légasse noted that a number of scholars detected Luke's use of a special source[199]. Although it was a possibility, "une position définitive sur ce point manquerait de sagesse"[200]. He offered three arguments in opposition to the theory of a continuous source. The incorporation of various traditional elements "erratiques" could explain the account[201]. Secondly, paranetic or christological concerns on the part of Luke also may account for the variations. As an adept writer, Luke would choose materials suitable for his readers. Finally, the order of the Lukan passion generally followed that of Mk. He concluded: "ici Luc a tout aussi bien pu utiliser Marc librement comme il le fait dans le reste de son évangile"[202].

---

195. *Ibid.*, p. 192-193.

196. *Ibid.*, p. 188.

197. S. LÉGASSE, *Le procès de Jésus*. T. 1: *L'Histoire* (LD, 156), Paris, 1994; T. 2: *La Passion dans les quatre évangiles* (LDC, 3), Paris, 1995.

198. *Ibid.*, p. 13. Cf. WINTER, *On the Trial*, 1961, ²1974, and BLINZLER, *Der Prozess Jesu*, 1951, ³1960.

199. LÉGASSE, *Le procès*, t. 1, p. 28-29. For a summary of positions he referred readers to ERNST, *Lukas* (1977), p. 643-644; FITZMYER, *Luke* (1981), 1365-1366; and MATERA, *Passion Narratives* (1986), 152-155, 238-239.

200. LÉGASSE, *Le procès*, t. 1, p. 29.

201. *Ibid.* 23,18-25 was cited as an example and readers were directed to FITZMYER, *Luke*, p. 1487-1488, and RADL, *Sonderüberlieferungen*, p. 131-147.

202. LÉGASSE, *Le procès*, t. 1, p. 29.

The differences between Lk 22,54–23,1 and the other Gospel accounts were highlighted[203]. Concerning the Sanhedrin trial (22,66-71) Légasse commented: "Quant à Luc (22,66-71), qu'il dépende ou non de seul Marc, son récit n'a aucune vraisemblance historique, car ce qu'il décrit n'a rien d'une séance de tribunal et tout concourt ici à instruire le lecteur, par la 'bouche' même de Jésus, des titres et qualités de celui qui subit la Passion"[204]. He also referred to his 1974 article and the hypothesis that Luke employed a non-Markan source in this passage[205]. He now claimed that the use of a special source was very doubtful[206].

Légasse raised the source question for 23,2-6.13-25 stating: "Le reste du récit n'offre pas plus de chances à l'historien que ce qu'on lit parallèlement dans Marc, que Luc dépende sans plus de ce dernier ou qu'il puise à une autre source"[207]. Once more the reader was directed to Fitzmyer for a discussion of 23,1-2.4-5[208].

In the initial volume Légasse treated the historical question whether Jesus appeared before Herod, referring the reader to Fitzmyer for a discussion of the various opinions on the origin and historicity of the pericope (23,6-12)[209]. Légasse indicated that there was nothing improbable that Herod was in Jersualem for the Passover and that it was possible that Pilate wished to take advantage of Herod's advice. He maintained that certain arguments against the historicity of the story, such as that of Dibelius, were not convincing[210]. He viewed Acts 4,25-27 as expressing a view contrary to 23,6-12. He also noted Denaux's argument that material used of John the Baptist in Mk was applied to Jesus in Lk[211]. He further observed the evidence of Lukan composition of the scene, once more drawing upon Fitzmyer, and observed how the scene was not detachable from its context. Detecting the parallels with Paul in Acts he concluded: "Pour toutes ces raisons, il semble bien difficile de recueillir dans la scène en question l'écho d'un fait historique, même en soustrayant la part considérable qui revient ici à Luc, et l'on sera sage en laissant le tétrarque hors du champ des responsbilités de la mort de Jésus"[212].

203. *Ibid.*, p. 69.

204. *Ibid.*, p. 72.

205. *Ibid.*, p. 77. See LÉGASSE, *Jésus*, p. 192-194.

206. LÉGASSE, *Le procès*, t. 1, p. 77: "Sans qu'il soit nécessaire de le confirmer en alléguant Lc 22,66-71, et en envisageant l'emploi, en ce passage, d'une source différente de Marc – recours au demeurant bien douteux –, il est clair que le récit marcien reprend et retouche une composition antérieure, dont la naissance est à situer au stade sémitique des traditions évangéliques".

207. *Ibid.*, p. 95.

208. *Ibid.*, n. 28. Cf. FITZMYER, *Luke*, p. 1472.

209. LÉGASSE, *Le procès*, t. 1, p. 106-108, esp. p. 106, n. 65. Cf. FITZMYER, *Luke*, p. 1478-1479. Légasse also referred to the Herod scene as 23,7-12 (*Le procès*, p. 95) and 23,8-12 (*Le procès*, p. [31]-32, n. 43).

210. LÉGASSE, *Le procès*, t. 1, p. 107.

211. *Ibid.* See DENAUX, *L'hypocrisie*, p. 265-268.

212. LÉGASSE, *Le procès*, t. 1, p. 108.

Concerning the flagellation (Mk 15,15) Légasse called attention to 23,16.[22] where Pilate announced his intention to have Jesus flogged, though without being explicitly said that this action was never carried out[213]. He termed the use of παιδεύειν in 23,16 a euphemism. Légasse first noted the omission of Mk 15,16-20 but drew a connection to "la trace" in 23,11[214]. Later he suggested that Luke freely omitted anything when it offended the dignity of Jesus[215].

In the second volume which offered a commentary on the trial in the four Gospels Légasse defined the passion as 22,1-23,56[216]. He relied on the commentaries of Ernst, Fitzmyer, Bovon and Johnson and the studies of BDR, Hawkins, Jeremias, Schneider, Radl, Standaert, Kodell, Vanhoye, Miller, Walaskay, Matera, Hoehner, Verrall and Corbin[217]. In a brief introduction to the Lukan account he outlined his general source theory for the Gospel which maintained that in addition to Q, Luke employed Mk[218]. He counted three additions of special material to the Markan account in the passion: 23,8-12 (Jesus before Herod), vv. 27-31 (Jesus' words to the women on the way to Calvary), vv. 39-43 (the two criminals crucified with Jesus). He again raised the question of Luke's use of a special source, stating that it was not possible to determine the existence of a continuous source with such certitude as those who argued in favor of it[219]. In part, Luke was capable of composing some details himself.

Légasse began his discussion of the denials of Peter (22,54-62) by calling attention to the difference in order compared with the other Synoptics[220]. The reason was literary, since Luke preferred to treat a person or subject all at once. He termed this "ordre narratif". Légasse was attentive to various Markan vocabulary which occurred in the Lukan account.

213. *Ibid.*, p. 121.
214. *Ibid.*, p. 80. He erroneously listed 22,11. See p. 80-81, for his related comments on 22,63-65.
215. *Ibid.*, p. 123.
216. *Le procès*, t. 2, p. 323. See also his synthesis of the Lukan passion, p. 442-449.
217. See the bibliography on the Lukan section, p. 606-610.
218. *Ibid.*, p. 323, n. 1. He referred the readers to p. 385, 388, 434, that to understand Luke it was necessary to have read Mk.
219. *Ibid.*, p. 324: "Bon nombre d'auteurs envisagent l'emploi d'une 'source de la Passion' dont Luc aurait disposé et à laquelle il emprunterait la matière de ces additions. La thèse est discutée et l'on ne saurait conclure avec quelque certitude, à partir de ces éléments disparates, à l'existence d'un document continu. Encore moins y classera-t-on des détails que Luc était tout à fait capable de produire de lui-même pour le bien de ses lecteurs. Pour donner des exemples, le recours à une source paraît bien inutile quand il s'agit de la guérison de l'oreille du serviteur du grand prête (22,51) ou du regard de Jésus provoquant le repentir de Pierre (22,61-62). On peut en dire autant des accusations politiques portées contre Jésus devant Pilate (23,2.5), de la dernière prière de Jésus (23,46) et d'autres traits qu'éclaire le contexte général de l'évangile, tant du point de vue thématique qu'en ce qui concerne le style et le vocabulaire. Le commentaire qui suit permettra, pensons-nous, de le confirmer". N. 3 pointed the reader back to his discussion of sources in the first volume, p. 28-29.
220. *Ibid.*, p. 336.

Concerning the MA in 22,62 / Mt 26,75c he maintained that the detail in Lk was borrowed from Mt[221]. Following Vanhoye, he showed the connection of this phrase with the theme of prophecy[222]. The MA in 22,64 / Mt 26,68 was treated in the commentary on Mt[223].

The Markan account of the mocking and beating of Jesus was badly composed. Luke offered a parallel account[224]. The use of ἐμπαίζειν "établit un rapport avec les épreuves des prophètes de l'Ancien Testament"[225]. Also noted was the later derision by Herod (23,11). Légasse saw irony in the detail that Jesus was viewed as a false prophet[226]. In 7,16 he had been called a great prophet. Légasse correctly stressed the prophetic element in the passion.

The present treatment of the trial indicated similarities with Acts. Detecting the verbal contacts between 20,1-8 and 22,67-68 with the help of Radl, Légasse concluded: "Ce contact, doublé d'une influence des Septante [...], permet de douter que Luc ait disposé d'une tradition ou d'une source particulière pour composer cette réponse de Jésus"[227]. Luke's eschatology helped to shape this account, though christological interest was central to the account of the Sanhedrin trial[228]. The accusation of blasphemy was omitted by Luke out of regard for the dignity of Jesus[229].

Lk 23,1 reflected a recasting of Mk 15,1, in which Luke attempted to guard the dignity of Jesus as he had done in other parts of his revision of the Markan passion[230]. The term κατηγορεῖν (Mk 15,3) appeared in 23,2a as it had in 6,7; 11,54; and 9 times in Acts[231]. A further indication of Lukan redaction of Mk was found in ἠρώτησεν (23,3 / Mk 15,2a)[232]. The accusation of stirring up the people (23,5) was similar to the action of the high priests in the Markan account (Mk 15,11).

Jesus again appeared before Pilate (23,13-25). There is no proper parallel in the other Gospels for 23,13-16. The term παιδεύσας (23,16) reflected Luke's customary effort to spare Jesus[233]. An echo of Mk 15,9 occurred in 23,18[234]. The end of the section (23,24-25) was a recasting and amplification of Mk

---

221. *Ibid.*, p. 343.
222. See VANHOYE, *L'intérêt*, p. 1546.
223. See LÉGASSE, *Le procès*, t. 2, p. 205.
224. *Ibid.*, p. 345. Here it was also noted that Luke omitted Mk 15,16-20. Readers were directed to p. 374, 444.
225. *Ibid.*, p. 346.
226. *Ibid.*, p. 348.
227. *Ibid.*, p. 354, n. 23. See RADL, *Sonderüberlieferungen*, p. 146-147, for the verbal contacts between 20,1-8 and 22,67-68.
228. LÉGASSE, *Le procès*, t. 2, p. 356, 360.
229. *Ibid.*, p. 359.
230. *Ibid.*, p. 364.
231. *Ibid.*, n. 4.
232. *Ibid.*, p. 367, n. 16.
233. *Ibid.*, p. 383.
234. *Ibid.*, p. 385.

15,15[235]. In this portion Légasse pointed out a number of similarities with Acts, particularly with regard to the trial of Paul[236].

Luke alone recounted "l'entrevue" of Jesus with Herod (23,6-12)[237]. Acts 4,27 "font écho" to this scene in the Gospel[238]. Légasse differed with Corbin on the structure of the passage[239]. For Jesus' absolute silence Luke recalled Mk 14,60-61 and Mk 15,4-5. "Toutefois Luc, qui a omis le thème dans le récit des deux séances, le 'sauve' ici, pour le bien de ses lecteurs"[240]. The resemblance of 23,11 with Mk 15,16-20 was observed, though the Lukan and Markan accounts differed "notablement" with regard to the garment of Jesus[241]. Légasse linked the term gorgeous/brilliant used to describe the apparel with 22,69 where Jesus had spoken of his glory, as well as 24,26 which recalled the prophesy of his suffering which preceded his entrance into glory. He also opposed the view of Verrall that the garment suggested a sign of respect[242]. 23,15 indicated that Pilate and Herod were reconciled.

The difference between Luke' use of Mk as opposed to Matthew's was immediately evident[243]. Luke utilized Mk much more freely, as in the case of substantial recasting of scenes, abbreviations and transposition of material, which was summarily described as "un remaniement systématique de Marc". The Lukan Jesus offered Christians an example to inspire them[244], and Luke so crafted his account of the passion to present it as paranesis and edification[245].

Graham STANTON (1974) maintained not only that the Lukan passion narrative resulted from Luke's preference for non-Markan traditions, but that in the evangelist's own distinctive way of treating the person of Jesus, the differences between tradition and redaction can be discerned[246]. Sympathetic as he was to the

---

235. *Ibid.*, p. 387.

236. *Ibid.*, p. 390. See also LÉGASSE, *L'apologétique à l'égard de Rome dans le procès de Paul, Actes 21,27-26,32*, in RSR 69 (1981) 248-256 (= J. DELORME and J. DUPLACY [eds.], *La parole de la grâce. Études lucaniennes à la mémoire d'A. George*, Paris: Recherches de science religieuse, 1981).

237. He also referred to this scene as "une pièce inédite" (LÉGASSE, *Le procès*, t. 2, p. 363).

238. *Ibid.*, p. 370; see further p. 389.

239. *Ibid.*, p. 370, n. 41; cf. CORBIN, *Jésus*.

240. LÉGASSE, *Le procès*, t. 2, p. 373. He also noted how Luke employed a similar method by reusing the prophesy of Mk 14,62, which Luke omitted in the parallel context, in the account of Stephen (Acts 7,55-56) (n. 55).

241. *Ibid.*, p. 374. On Luke's passing over Mk 15,16-20 in silence see also the remark, p. 444.

242. Cf. VERRALL, *Christ*, p. 344.

243. LÉGASSE, *Le procès*, t. 2, p. 442.

244. *Ibid.*, p. 445.

245. *Ibid.*, p. 448-449. This was similar to the view of BUCK, *Function* (1980), though no reference to his work was made.

246. G.N. STANTON, *Jesus of Nazareth in New Testament Preaching* (SNTS MS, 27), Cambridge, 1974, p. 32.

theory of a special source, he insisted "there are good reasons" for adopting such a view, asserting that "it has yet to be refuted in comparable detail"[247].

247. *Ibid.*, p. 32, n. 2. He rejected Dibelius's conception of the Lukan passion as a martyrdom, due in part, to a lack of parallels in Jewish literature. Further, in opposition to H.W. Surkau, Stanton dismissed the view that Jesus' suffering provided the pattern for the Stephen story in Acts for several reasons (p. 33; cf. H.W. SURKAU, *Martyrien in jüdischer und frühchristlicher Zeit*, Göttingen, 1938, p. 117f.). The differences were more significant than the similarities. References to the Temple were found in Acts and Mk but were missing from Lk. There was no "close parallelism" between the final words of Stephen and Jesus. There was no common vocabulary between Lk 23,34 and Acts 7,6. Stephen did not mimic the words of Jesus (23,46) about his spirit, nor did they serve as Stephen's final cry as it did for Jesus. The concept of modeling a Christian martyr's death on that of Jesus was only a later development. What was more, themes of martyrdom were as frequent in the other Synoptics and Lk lacked the phrase δοῦναι τὴν ψυχήν (Mk 10,45 / Mt 20,28) which was characteristically employed in accounts of the Jewish martyrs.

Mark, in Stanton's opinion, was more interested in exact chronology than Luke. In at least eight instances, Luke either provided no chronological reference or only a general one, though 22,59 was a notable exception. Luke creatively joined non-Markan tradition and the Markan passion together, but in the account of the arrest, it was the special source which highlighted Jesus rather than Judas, as found in Mark's narration (STANTON, *Jesus*, p. 42). Stanton referred to Rehkopf's source analysis for the arrest (p. 42, n. 1). For a differing assessment of Luke's concern for matters chronological see D.L. JONES, *Luke's Unique Interest in Historical Chronology*, in *SBL 1989 Seminar Papers*, p. 378-387. Although the people were different from Jesus, they were nonetheless affected by him. Stanton claimed that distinguishing Jesus from his followers or others in a particular scene was typical of Lukan redaction. However, Stanton proceded to attribute such a characteristic both to the special source (22,48) and to Lukan redaction of Markan material (23,26-27a). But one cannot have it both ways.

Luke was also credited with a "method of indirect characterization" where the disciples and Jesus were contrasted (STANTON, *Jesus*, p. 44). Reference was made to 22,61a "which almost certainly stems from Luke's own hand". The portrayal of Barabbas in contrast to Jesus (23,25) was also the work of Luke using this literary technique. Further, the charges in 23,2.5.14 were the work of Luke and not the special source. It was of considerable importance that Stanton confirmed this Lukan authorship by noting verbal similarities with Acts or other parts of Lk (p. 45, n. 3). Connections with vocabulary in 23,2 were detected in Lk 20,20b.22.26a and Acts 10,37 13,8.10.20; 19,40 24,2. In addition, Lk 23 and Acts 6,11.13; 16,20; 21,28; 24,5-6 were alike since people actively raised charges and the accusations in 23,2 were like those found in Acts 17,6-7. In the end, Luke's unique portrayal of Jesus was due both to the non-Markan source and his Markan material which he combined with refined literary skill.

Birger A. Pierson reacted against Stanton's perception that Luke's contribution was literary rather than theological by stating: "It is doubtful that Stanton's views on this point will be found by many New Testament scholars to be persuasive" (*Interpr* 30 [1976] 330). Trocmé criticized Stanton for ignoring the intention of the evangelists and lamented his lack of references to French language exegetes, which would have resulted in Stanton's delving more deeply into the biblical texts (*TLond* 78 [1975] 556, 557). These criticisms, notwithstanding, Trocmé believed that Stanton was on the right track.

In Stanton's more recent work (1989), he reiterated his tenet that Luke was disinterested in chronology (STANTON, *The Gospels and Jesus*, Oxford, esp. p. 81-101, p. 84). But following Conzelmann he argued that Luke's concept of salvation history involved refashioning Markan chronology into three periods. Transpositions of Markan material by Luke were rare. Stanton's

Hans KLEIN (1976), whose starting point for his investigation was 23,5-16, argued the case that the *Vorlage* of the Johannine passion account as well as the *Vorlage* of the Lukan passion story from the special material stemmed from the same source, which Klein designated as G[248]. Klein noted that J. Schniewind puzzled over the section 23,5-16 finally declaring it "non liquet" (the case is not clear) and G. Schneider ("die Perikope kaum behandelt") believed that Luke combined Mk with the non-Markan special source[249]. Klein first rehearsed three possibilities of origin of the Herod scene: 1) taken from a continuous special or Proto-Lukan report, the latter L. Gaston supported; 2) an account drawn from a non-continuous historical report, circulating prior to Luke, most probably from oral tradition, as espoused by F. Hahn and R. Bultmann; and 3) Luke shaped the report himself, in a manner described by Dibelius[250].

Klein rejected Gaston's arguments which favored a Proto-Lukan source rightly claiming that the parallels in Lk 23 and Acts 23–26 indicated they were written by the same hand[251]. To endorse the view of Bultmann would mean that only vv. 6 and 14a would be ascribed to Luke. Because the scene was pallid and said nothing in addition to what was already stated in Mk about Jesus in relation to Pilate, this proposal was not convincing.

The explanation of Luke's creativity clarified most of the difficulties surrounding the origin of the passage[252]. The detail in 23,12 can be accepted as a historicizing notice. Verses 5f. and 14a were reworked by Luke. It was obvious that 23,8 referred to 9,9. Luke borrowed the most important elements – the silence of Jesus, the charges and the mockery from Mk[253]. The evangelist must have had

assessment of the Proto-Lk hypothesis was that "it has recently fallen out of favour" and that the arguments garnered to support it were "not compelling" (p. 90). His view was that Q and L material were added to the Markan material. The literary technique which emphasized Jesus was attributed to Luke with no mention of any contribution by any special source (p. 99).

248. H. KLEIN, *Die lukanisch-johanneische Passionstradition*, in *ZNW* 67 (1976) 156 (= M. LIMBECK [ed.], *Redaktion und Theologie des Passionsberichtes nach den Synoptikern*, Darmstadt, 1981, 366).

249. *Ibid.*, p. 156 (= 366-367). Cf. J. SCHNIEWIND, *Die Parallelperikopen bei Lukas und Johannes*, Leipzig, 1914; Hildesheim, ²1958; Darmstadt, ³1970, p. 69. SCHNEIDER, *Verleugnung*, p. 144. In Schneider's defense it may be said that he legitimately excluded the Herod story since he was concentrating on 22,54-71.

250. KLEIN, *Die lukanische-johannische Passionstradition*, p. 156-157 (= 367). Cf. GASTON, *No Stone*, p. 333; F. HAHN, *Der Prozess Jesu nach dem Johannesevangelium* (EKK NT Vorarbeiten, Heft 2), Neukirchen-Vluyn, 1970, 23-96, p. 35, n. 17: "Lk 23,7b-12 ist als Sondergut anzusehen. Es handelt sich um eine sekundäre Überlieferung, bei der Mk 6,14-16; 15,2a.5; 15,3 und 15,16-18 das Material geliefert haben. Lukas hat diesen Abschnitt mit 23,5-7a.13-16 verbunden in seine Darstellung des Pilatusverhörs einbezogen"; BULTMANN, *Die Geschichte*, ⁴1961, p. 294.

251. *Ibid.*, p. 157-158 (= 367-369). Here Klein addressed himself to Gaston's contention of a special proto-Lukan source.

252. *Ibid.*, p. 159 (= 369).

253. *Ibid.*, p. 159-160 (= 370).

some information about Herod's participation in the trial, but it did not necessarily originate in a similar report. Rather, as Dibelius suggested, it could have arisen from a christological interpretation of Ps 2. In Acts 4,25ff. the evangelist used a tradition. Luke shaped his account with a view to his apologetic regarding Rome. Both 23,16 and 23,36 indicated that he had knowledge of the mockery by Pilate[254]. The evangelist created the account borrowing materials from the Pilate trial, but also in light of the christological interpretation of Ps 2[255]. In response to claims by G. Rau and L. Gaston, Klein argued that Luke used a source other than Mk for 23,13 and partly for 23,14b. He concluded that G (*Grundschicht*) gave rise to LV (the Lukan *Vorlage* of the passion narrative[256]) and JV (the Johannine *Vorlage* of the passion narrative). Luke then combined Mk with LV. There was near verbal agreement in 23,13.14b.17 with Jn 18,38-19,1[257]. In addition, John further developed JV[258].

Josef ERNST (1977), also one of the more recent supporters of the Lukan special source theory, began by noting in his foreword the necessarily hypothetical nature of the decisions about the source question, specifically mentioning the passion narrative[259]. Affirming that Luke used Mk, Ernst was struck by the variation in order, leading him to adopt the view that Luke employed Proto-Lk which subsequently had been enriched by Markan material citing the variant view of Jeremias concerning alternating Markan blocks with those comprising special material and Q[260]. Ernst sided, however, with those scholars who believed that Mk formed the basis with the additional material being inserted[261]. Three counter-arguments to Streeter's theory were the order of the pericopes, the coherence of the Markan material, and the recent research which pointed to the travel section as a redactional unity rather than a traditional piece. Also, the vocabulary and stylistic studies of Rehkopf and Schweizer had met with great skepticism. Therefore, Ernst argued that the two document theory, including Markan priority, offered the best solution. That being said, he did not exclude the possibility of a unified passion narrative. Although such a theory may be assumed,

254. *Ibid.*, p. 160 (= 370). Cf. also p. 179 (= 389), where Klein argued that material was also drawn from the Pilate scene. This involved changing the purple cloak into the gorgeous apparel and eliminating mention of the crown of thorns.

255. *Ibid.*, p. 160 (= 371).

256. *Ibid.*, p. 156 (= 366).

257. *Ibid.*, p. 177-179 (= 386-389).

258. *Ibid.*, p. 185 (= 395).

259. J. ERNST, *Das Evangelium nach Lukas* (RNT), Regensburg, [5]1977, p. 5. This was a revision of the commentary by J. Schmid.

260. *Ibid.*, p. 24. Unfortunately, he did not indicate to which of Jeremias's six works listed in the bibliography he was referring.

261. *Ibid*: "Das entscheidende Argument für Mk als Leitquelle ist jedoch der weitaus stärkere thematische und sachliche Zusammenhang des lk Mk-Stoffes im Vergleich zu den 'überschiessenden' Abschnitten, die mit grösserer Wahrscheinlichkeit als Einschaltungen anzusprechen sind".

further studies were required to produce certitude[262]. Ernst also held that oral tradition may have played a significant role, though brief written sections or smaller collections also remained possibilities.

Ernst understood πολλοί (1,1) as a true indication that Luke relied on sources and thus it was not a simply a rhetorical convention. The great amount of special material and the "Loslösung" of the Markan order suggested the existence of an independent passion source[263]. Ernst began his treatment of the denials with a note on the change of order and raised the possibility that this was the historically more reliable chain of events. He favored the special source solution because one could hardly imagine Luke compromising the artistic Markan account to allow the confession of Jesus to transpire immediately after the denial. Further, it seemed unlikely that Luke would have changed the night trial into a morning hearing. The Lukan and Johannine traditions were more historically plausible when compared with the Matthean/Markan tradition. The redaction fashioned the account of Jesus before the Sanhedrin in the light of a martyrdom. Word statistics were not much help in deciding the source question at this point. Ernst listed five similarities with the Markan material and six differences. With the exception of vv. 59a.b.61, the Lukan version appeared as a commentary or explanation of the Markan material. Free Lukan redaction accounted for material not derived from Mk.

Concerning the MA in v. 62 Ernst called attention to the judgment of many that it was the result of early addition. In context it seemed required by the story[264].

For the mockery (22,63-65), Ernst followed Bultmann: Luke was borrowing from the special source. Low verbal correspondence, the change in order of pericopes, the difference in timing and perpetrators of the mistreatment all contributed to Ernst's decision[265]. The MA in v. 64 was not explained.

For the Sanhedrin trial, however, neither the word statistics nor the peculiarities of style offered much assistance in resolving the source dilemma. There were more differences than similarities in the content when the Markan and Lukan accounts were compared. On the question whether 22,69 was a redaction of Mk, Ernst suggested that three considerations argued in favor of Lukan redaction: 1) the phrase ἀπὸ τοῦ νῦν reflected salvation history thinking; 2) the Lukan presentation of καθήμενος ἐκ δεξιῶν permitted a revision of the Markan indication of the parousia, and 3) Christianity looked to the Son of Man who now rules (cf. Acts 7,56f.). The sole counter argument put forward was the unabbreviated citation of Dan 7,13 at 21,27[266]. It should be pointed out that 21,27 was dependent upon Mk 13,26. In support of Lukan redaction were the agreements with Mk, but the overall form of the material and its uniqueness in

---

262. *Ibid.*, p. 29-30.
263. *Ibid.*, p. 573.
264. *Ibid.*, p. 615.
265. *Ibid.*, p. 616. Cf. BULTMANN, *Die Geschichte*, p. 293.
266. ERNST, *Lukas*, p. 618.

various parts of the whole spoke for the special source. He finally concluded that
though influenced by Mk (22,69.71), the material derived from a special source
(22,66-68.70).

Ernst entitled the section 23,1-25 "Jesus in der Hand der römischen
Behörden". The foundation of a special source was evinced by the low rate of
verbal agreement with the Markan account and the overall continuity within the
account displayed by the *Sondergut* as well as the smooth transition from the
preceding material[267].

In his commentary for this section of Lk, Ernst frequently cited those who
favored the special source including Hauck, Hirsch, Grundmann, Schneider and
Taylor. Verse 3 was singled out as a tell-tale sign of Markan influence while 23,5
reflected Lukan redaction permitting a smooth transition to the Herod story.

Although vv. 18-25 showed strong connections to Mk, Ernst maintained that
the relationship to Mk 15,6-15 was difficult to assess, concluding that attributing
the entire pericope to the special source was "eine denkbare Alternative"[268]. The
second declaration of innocence, however, reflected Lukan redaction.

Ernst was alert to various connections between the Gospel and Acts in the
following places: 22,66 / Acts 22,5; 22,69 / Acts 7,56; 23,2 / Acts 5,37; 22,18
/ Acts 21,36; 23,25 / Acts 21,11; 28,17; 2,23; 3,18; 13,27; 26,23.

With his sixth edition ([6]1993), his position shifted in his introductory remarks
on literary sources. He no longer posited the possibility of a Proto-Lukan
hypothesis, or the "Blockhypothese" in the line of Jeremias[269]. Instead changes
in order were ascribed to literary view and theological perspective. Thus, the
Markan order was not destroyed. His understanding of πολλοί also underwent
change and he now considered it an open question[270].

Similarly he rethought his views on the source question in the passion
narrative. Whereas earlier he maintained that the presence of special material and
the loosening of the Markan order suggested a special passion source comprised
of three traditions, now he appeared less certain, proposing that these same
elements raise the question of a special source or pieces of tradition of special
origin[271]. In his presentation on the denials of Peter (22,54b-62) the matter of
order continued to be of primary concern, but he now omitted his earlier

267. *Ibid.*, p. 621.
268. *Ibid.*, p. 627.
269. *Lukas*, [6]1993, p. 26: "Den von Mk übernommenen Stoff hat Lk in drei grossen, hier
nur global und undifferenziert vorzustellenden Blöcken tradiert: 3,1-6.19; 8,4-9,50; 18,15-24,10".
Cf. [5]1977, p. 24. The revision was prompted by the publication of a great number of
commentaries and new methodologies which were developed since the fifth edition appeared. Also
he wanted to make the commentary more accessible to those engaged in church ministries
(*Vorwort*, p. 13).
270. [6]1993, p. 46. Cf. [5]1977, p. 47.
271. [6]1993, p. 439. Cf. [5]1977, p. 573. In the latest edition he was more attuned to Lk-Jn
agreements and queried whether there might be two types of passion narratives: Lk-Jn and Mk-
Mt.

conclusion that, "Die besseren Gründe sprechen für eine unabhängige Sonderquelle"[272]. His position on the MA in 22,62 / Mt 26,75 remained the same[273]. For the mockery scene (22,63-65) whereas influenced by Bultmann he previously adhered to the view of a special source, he now declared "dass die Annahme einer Sonderüberlieferung berechtigt erscheint"[274]. No mention was made of the MA in 22,64 / Mt 26,68[275]. He continued to support the view that in the Sanhedrin trial (22,66-71) Luke employed a special source. Although the pericope was influenced by Mk especially in 22,69.71, still with W. Wiefel he argued that 22,66-68.70 reflected the source[276].

Although he recognized the verbal agreement with Mk in 23,3 (/ Mk 15,2) he recently added that 23,1.2.5 grew out from Mk 15,3[277]. Further, he revised his initial comments on this section (23,1-5) omitting the argumentation which favored a special source[278]. He continued to assert that 23,18-25 showed strong contact with Mk but dropped his earlier conclusion that here the relationship to Mk 15,6-15 was hard to determine[279].

Ernst (1977) advocated Luke's use of a separate special source for the passion narrative[280]. He noted the debate whether Luke discovered the story of Herod within the source or he shaped it and then inserted it within the source[281]. While the vocabulary and style would suggest the second possibility, the evidence was not so convincing as to completely eliminate the possibility that it derived from an independent source. In fact, Ernst seemed to favor the view that Luke obtained the story from a special source. Following Rengstorf, Ernst believed that because the story contained typical characteristics of a Jewish messianic mockery, it might have been significant for Luke's special source[282].

272. [5]1977, p. 612. Still the order of vv. 54-62.63-65.66-71 was the primary reason favoring a special Lukan source ([6]1993, p. 467-468).

273. [6]1993, p. 469. So [5]1977, p. 615.

274. [6]1993, p. 470. Cf. [5]1977, p. 616. See BULTMANN, *GST*, p. 293.

275. ERNST, *Lukas*, [6]1993, p. 470; [5]1977, p. 616. The comment was exactly the same in both editions.

276. [6]1993, p. 471 and [5]1977, p. 618. One difference was that in the fifth edition he referred to GRUNDMANN, *Lukas*, [4]1966, p. 419, in support of his contention about vv. 66-68.70. That commentary was replaced in the new edition with W. WIEFEL, *Lukas*, 1988, p. 386 ([6]1993, p. 471). However, both Grundmann and Wiefel also attributed 22,71 to the special source while Ernst saw here, together with 22,69, the strongest Markan reminiscences ([6]1993, p. 471; [5]1977, p. 618).

277. [6]1993, p. 474. Cf. [5]1977, p. 621.

278. *Ibid.* The arguments which favored the special source were low verbal agreement and the order of the *Sondergut* in the wider context.

279. [6]1993, p. 478-479. Cf. [5]1977, p. 627.

280. [5]1977 (esp. p. 29f. and 573).

281. *Ibid.*, p. 624.

282. *Ibid.*, p. 624-625: "K.H. Rengstorf (Lukas, 264) macht darauf aufmerksam, dass die Szenerie vor Herodes die typischen Züge "einer messianischen Verspottung durch Juden" an sich trage. Der Gegensatz zwischen Jesus, dem Mann Gottes, und dem Sünder, der sich völlig an die

Ernst rejected the idea that the story was inspired by the two witnesses required by Dt 19,15, calling it "too hypothetical". The suggestion that the silence of Jesus was indicative of divinity was also deemed "doch fragwürdig" (contra Grundmann and the Mithras liturgy)[283].

The vesting of Jesus in possibly a white garment or analogously to the purple mantle and crown of thorns in Mt 27,28-29, was a response of comedy and ridicule to demonstrate that Jesus was "nur eine Karikatur jenes hohen Amtes"[284]. But Ernst allowed for Dibelius's influence, reporting that the Christian community saw Ps 2 fulfilled in the new found friendship of Pilate and Herod.

Ernst previously observed that the question of the origin of the Herod pericope (23,6-12) was debated reflecting two schools of thought: either Luke discovered the story in his source or he formed it himself and inserted into his source. Neither explanation was convincing[285]. Recently, he referred to Büchele's insight that linguistic and stylistic arguments favored Lukan redaction[286]. He also reckoned with the possibility that it was a variant tradition of Mk 15,16-20a. Despite the fact that it was "durchaus situationsgerecht und historisch glaubwürdig" Ernst was not certain whether the account was historical or not[287].

Following publication of the 1977 edition Neirynck detected Ernst's almost exclusive dependence upon German publications, a drawback that was cited by several other critics[288]. He also seconded Schneider's critique of the view adopted by Ernst in support of a complete continuous passion source supplemented by Markan insertions[289]. In the same line, Agustín del Agua chastised Ernst for not taking a more critical view on this matter. Rather than supporting Schürmann's idea of a special Lukan *Vorlage*, Ernst would have done well to have considered R. Pesch's contribution which spoke of Lukan redaction[290].

The changes in Ernst's position were noticeable and significant. He was less insistent on Luke's overall use of a special source in this section of the passion narrative. Further, he appeared less dependent upon word statistics in making his judgments[291]. While he had been influenced by the work of G. Schneider,

---

Welt ausgeliefert hat, findet in der Begegnung mit Herodes eine besonders deutliche exemplarische Ausprägung. Vielleicht war dieser Gesichtspunkt für die Sonderquelle Lk bzw. für das Ev von besonderer Wichtigkeit".

283. ERNST, *Lukas*, p. 625.

284. *Ibid.*, p. 626.

285. ⁵1977, p. 624.

286. ⁶1993, p. 476. Cf. BÜCHELE, *Der Tod Jesu*, p. 32, n. 55.

287. ERNST, *Lukas*, ⁶1993, p. 476, 478.

288. *ETL* 54 (1978) 192. Schuyler Brown also lamented this limitation: "The use of non-German literature strikes this reviewer as disappointingly restricted" (*JBL* 98, 1979, 151). So also W.S. KURZ in *CBQ* 40 (1978) 631; FITZMYER, in *TS* 40 (1979) 349, pointed out that 90% of the bibliography was German.

289. F. NEIRYNCK, Review, p. 193. Cf. G. SCHNEIDER, *Lukas*, 1977, ²1984, p. 435-437.

290. *EstBib* 36 (1977) 303.

291. ⁵1977, p. 613 (22,54b-62), 616 (22,63-65), 617 (22,66-71).

especially *Verleugnung* in his treatment of Peter's denials[292], his bibliography for the sixth edition was lacking the more recent works such as *The Political Charge Against Jesus* and *Verhor*[293]. Nevertheless, his position on a special source for 22,66-68.70 was similar to that of Schneider[294]. The shift in Ernst's views are important since Schneider referred in the "Vorwort" of the second edition of his commentary to the fact that Ernst advocated a special source[295].

W. Radl reviewed the sixth edition and gave attention to the change in Ernst's position on the theory of a special source[296]. Though Ernst, in his opinion, was unclear in his position on sources for 22,66-71, he clearly distanced himself from the special source in 23,1-5.33-43.44-49[297].

Richard CASSIDY (1978) indicated that generally for the Gospel, the "prevailing" view of scholars was that the sources, including material derived from Mk, were transmitted through various Christian communities before they were assembled and arranged "as a 'source'"[298]. Writing in reaction to Cassidy's tendency to historicize the Lukan account, E. Jane VIA (1983) was particularly strong in her censure of Cassidy for accepting Luke's account as historical rather than seeing possible Lukan redactional motifs at work[299].

292. [5]1977, p. 612, 613 (22,54b-62); 619 (22,66-71).

293. [6]1993, p. 40. Cf. [5]1977, p. 38, 44.

294. Cf. SCHNEIDER, *Verleugnung*, p. 123-126, 133. This was due to the fact that Schneider's position has not varied much since 1969.

295. SCHNEIDER, *Lukas*, [2]1984, "*Vorwort zur zweiten Auflage*".

296. W. RADL, *Review of J. Ernst, Das Evangelium nach Lukas, 1993*, in *TRev* 93 (1997) col. 214.

297. *Ibid.*, col. 214: "Hat er bei der Passionsgeschichte früher für eine lk Sonderquelle plädiert (644), so sprechen ihm inzwischen 'die besseren Gründe für Sonderguteintragungen und lk-red Überarbeitungen der Mk-Passion' (494). Diese Entscheidung hält er allerdings nicht klar genug durch, wenn er zu 22,66-71 meint, dass man hier 'auf die Annahme einer Sonderquelle kaum verzichten kann' (471). Andererseits distanziert er sich von der Theorie einer Sonderquelle besonders deutlich bei der Behandlung von 23,1-5 (474) und 23,33-43.44-49 (484.489)".

298. R.J. CASSIDY, *Jesus, Politics, and Society. A Study of Luke's Gospel*, Maryknoll, NY, 1978, p. 10. The book was based on his 1976 dissertation: *The Social and Political Stance of Jesus in Luke's Gospel*, Graduate Theological Union (dir. E.C. HOBBS). Cassidy suggested an important methodological control: "Luke does not tell us why Jesus refused to cooperate with Herod; accordingly, any interpretation of Jesus' silence has to be based on other passages in Luke or on information derived from other, independent sources" (p. 67 = *Social*, p. 333). While we agree that the interpretation should be based on other Lukan passages, since Luke used Mk it would be essential also to consider those Markan passages referring to the silence of Jesus. Cassidy disputed the interpretations of GRUNDMANN, *Evangelium nach Lukas*, 1971, p. 425 (sign of divinity), J. SCHREIBER, *Das Schweigen Jesu*, in K. WEGENAST (ed.), *Theologie und Unterricht*, Gütersloh, 1969, 79-87 (indication of a martyr) and SCHMID, *Evangelium nach Lukas*, [4]1960, p. 344 (Jesus' silence evoked a response of anger from Herod) concerning the silence of Jesus in the presence of Herod. While he found these explanations inadequate, Cassidy did not propose his own (p. 169, n. 18 = *Social*, p. 361-362, n. 19). In addition, he did not specifically treat the source issue for the Herod pericope.

299. E. Jane VIA, *According to Luke, Who Put Jesus to Death?*, in R.J. CASSIDY and P.J.

Morna HOOKER (1979) appeared tentative in her adoption of the view of a special source in the Lukan passion narrative: "The significant feature of Luke's passion narrative is that for much of the time he seems to be using independent tradition unknown to the other evangelists, even though he continued to make use of Marcan material"[300]. In her recent study of the death of Jesus (1994), Hooker noted the difference in order of the account of Peter's denials in Lk as opposed to Mk and Mt, though the material was similar to that of the other synoptics. In addition she observed various details which were not recounted in Lk[301]. She also declared that "Luke is perhaps aware of the historical problems in Mark's reference to a night session of the Sanhedrin". Without treating the source question, Hooker indicated that Luke's version in 23,17-25 was much clearer than in Mk and Mt. "Thus the way in which Luke tells the story points us to its theological significance: the one who has done no wrong dies in the place of the man who has been justly convicted as worthy of death"[302]. The Herod story (23,6-12) was highlighted as a Lukan addition in which Pilate attempted to "get rid of the problem" by transferring Jesus to Herod. The account was seen as a confirmation of Jesus' innocence[303].

Although August STROBEL (1980) held that Luke deliberately changed the Markan nocturnal Sanhedrin session to morning, Strobel was still open to the

SCHARPER (eds.), *Political Issues in Luke-Acts*, Maryknoll, NY, 1983, p. 124-126. In Via's opinion, because Cassidy assumed that the Herod episode was historical, he then ignored the redaction question and too easily rejected Conzelmann's assessment of the influence of Luke's political and apologetical thrust (p. 125). Rather than viewing the non-cooperation as historical fact, Via suggested that the redactional meaning may be that Luke portrayed Jesus "as one who did not defer to political rulers" (p. 125). In sharp criticism Via argued: "Once more, Luke's interpretation of Jesus may accurately reflect the historical Jesus and his circumstances; but Cassidy's speculation about the understanding of the motives of Herod and Pilate seems to treat Luke's account as factual, without accounting for redactional motifs. Cassidy thereby detracts from the meaning and the emphasis of Luke's perspective, the explanation for which arguably lies in *Luke's Sitz-im-Leben* rather than that of the historical Jesus. Cassidy again neglected the important redactional question: Why would *Luke* emphasize Herod and Pilate's verdict that Jesus was innocent? This question needs to be answered directly and clearly" (p. 126). Via, nonetheless, acknowledged the difficulty of separating tradition from redaction (p. 124-125).

In the same volume as Via's article, Cassidy published an essay in which he only generally stated his position on the source question in the passion: "By drawing upon Mark and other sources available to him, he may have intended to present his readers with a report that would shed new light upon the various events leading up to Jesus' death" (*Luke's Audience, the Chief Priests, and the Motive for Jesus' Death*, p. 146-167, p. 146). He compared and contrasted the Markan and Lukan accounts.

300. *Studying the New Testament*, London, 1979; Minneapolis, MN, 1982, p. 105. Her recommended further readings included the commentaries of Caird, Lampe and Ellis.

301. *Not Ashamed of the Gospel. New Testament Interpretations of the Death of Christ*, Grand Rapids, MI, p. 87.

302. *Ibid.*, p. 88.

303. *Ibid.*, p. 87.

possibility of a special source[304]. Eugen Ruckstuhl (1986) discussed Strobel's general position and objections to it[305]. Though Ruckstuhl had some differences, he agreed that Jesus was (probably) arrested and tried with a view to Dt 13 and 17. He maintained Strobel was right in declaring that 22,54-71 was based upon the Markan *Vorlage* concerning events transpiring after the arrest. Ruckstuhl also argued that Luke had traditions which he considered to be more reliable than Mk. In both cases Luke abbreviated his source material. But Luke's portrayal of the events was, according to Ruckstuhl, "geschichtlich fragwürdig und sachlich unmöglich". He recognized the mockery in the Herod account as a poor substitute for the omitted Markan account of the one committed by the Romans guards.

In his 1980-81 Tübingen dissertation Rainer RIESNER (1981) claimed that the Lukan *Sondergut* "dürfte aus den Kreisen um den 'Herrenbruder' stammen"[306].

---

304. A. STROBEL, *Die Stunde der Wahrheit* (WUNT, 21), Tübingen, 1980, p. 14 (esp. p. 14-18). Luke held back the transitional verse Mk 14,53 in order to recount the denial and then, with dependence upon Mk 15,1 narrated the morning session of the Sanhedrin. In accord with K. Schubert, Strobel acknowledged that the Lukan literary concept was certainly recognizable (STROBEL, *Die Stunde*, p. 15. Cf. K. SCHUBERT, *Kritik der Bibelkritik. Dargestellt an Hand des Markusberichtes vom Verhör Jesu vor dem Synedrium*, in *Wort und Wahrheit* 27 [1972] 421-434, p. 426). The Petrine denial story was thus not interrupted and Luke placed both it and the mockery prior to the break of dawn. But Strobel questioned whether or not the account could have been based upon non-Markan *Vorlage* or traditions (STROBEL, *Die Stunde*, p. 16). He briefly surveyed the case for such a position as espoused by Taylor. Also noted was the conclusion to which Schneider came (and Catchpole independently) that 22,66-68 rested upon a non-Markan *Vorlage*, which in Strobel's opinion, was historically reliable to a high degree (p. 18). As for the origin of this special source, Strobel suggested that it may have previously belonged to a non-Markan account of the passion. While the account of Peter's denial was based "wesentlichen" upon the Markan story, the accounts of the mockery and Sanhedrin hearing certainly stemmed from the non-Markan source. Lk 23,2-5 had been embellished by *Sondergut* and thus the possibility of a special source cannot be excluded (p. 97). A further argument in favor of the special source for Strobel was the "engere Kontext" of 23,6-16 with the preceding section (p. 97, n. 6). Lk 23,15 was identified as *Sondergut* (p. 117). Strobel rejected, however, Schneider's proposed solution for the MA v. 62, but did not offer another in its place. "Wir sehen das Problem der von Lk verarbeitenten Vorlagen (und Quellen, darunter auch Mt) komplezer" (p. 18).

Strobel claimed that 23,2-5 had been enriched by Lukan *Sondergut* material and reformulated in light of the Gentile readers and did not exclude the possibility of a special source (p. 97). Strobel noted his disagreement with Schneider who believed that the charges in 23,2 reprised material from 19,48, 20,6.19.26 and 22,2. Because of the close context of Lk 23,6-16 Strobel favored a special source (p. 97, n. 6). He sided with Blinzler, saying that it was highly questionable that Pilate would have expected Herod to settle the issue about Jesus. Even if Herod had the right to decide such cases in Galilee, he should not invoke it in Jerusalem (p. 111). Strobel observed that A. BAJSIĆ, *Pilatus, Jesus und Barrabas*, in *Bib* 48 (1967) conjectured that Herod had found Jesus guilty, an hypothesis which independently Tyson also endorsed (p. 111, n. 38).

305. RUCKSTUHL, *Chronologie der Leidensgeschichte*, Pt. 2, in *SNTU* 11 (1986) 96-101.

306. R. RIESNER, *Jesus als Lehrer. Eine Untersuchung zum Ursprung der Evangelien-Überlieferung* (WUNT, II/7), Tübingen, 1981, p. 67. Diss. Tübingen, 1980 (dir. O. BETZ).

He rehearsed (1993) his earlier position and demonstrated a great familiarity with
the literature supporting the view of a special Lukan source[307]. Paul-Gerhard
MÜLLER (1984) subscribed to the Two-Source theory and maintained that the
Sondergut material rested on written and oral sources alike[308].

307. RIESNER, *Prägung und Herkunft der lukanischen Sonderüberlieferung*, in *TBei* 24 (1993)
228-248. He seemed far less familiar with the literature of those who favored other explanations.
Indicating that the simplest solution to the source question for the special Lukan material would
be that they were redactional creations ("Bildungen") of Luke, he cited Goulder as an example
of such a minority position (p. 228. Cf. GOULDER, *Midrash and Lection in Matthew*, 1974; *Luke.
A New Paradigm*, 1989). He was equally displeased with the statement of Bovon that in the final
analysis, we do not know the origin of the material unique to Lk. Riesner observed that this
assessment had been "nicht untypisch" during the past twenty years (Cf. BOVON, *Lukas*, 1989,
p. 22: "Wir wissen es letzlich nicht"). He offered several reasons for adopting the special source
theory including the contention that Luke possessed a unique tradition for the passion and
resurrection narratives and that in material common to Mk and Lk, Luke's versions went back
to variants of the tradition.

Riesner identified himself clearly in the line of Feine, J. Weiss, Schlatter and Schweizer that
Luke possessed a special source which extended from the infancy to the resurrection narratives.
He confirmed the view of Streeter and Jeremias that this special tradition rather than Mk formed
the basis for Lk. In a note Riesner remarked how Kümmel's retort to Jeremias's view was "eine
fast kanonisch gewordene Kritik" (RIESNER, *Prägung*, p. 230, n. 13. Cf. KÜMMEL, *Einleitung*,
²¹1983, p. 100-102). Luke simply inserted Markan material into a source which was similar to
Mk. Riesner rejected the view that Luke assembled various disparate pieces into a Proto-Lk.
Rather, the material stemmed from one and the same "Traditionskreis" (RIESNER, *Prägung*, p.
230). He reached this conclusion on linguistic grounds arguing that frequently there was clear
Semitic substratum. Imitation of the LXX can explain only a limited portion. Riesner considered
the special tradition to have existed in documentary rather than oral form. He based this
conclusion on the extent of the material as well as manner in which Luke inserted blocks of
Markan material or material similar to Mk.

Riesner maintained that the particular theological profile of the special tradition reflected the
original Jerusalem community was depicted in the summaries and stories in Acts 1-6, a view
which he believed was further supported by geographical references (p. 239, 240). The clearest
proof to the local origin of the special tradition was the limitation of the resurrection appearances
to Jerusalem and its environs (p. 240). Another piece of supportive evidence that the material
stemmed from circles of conservative Jewish Christians was the attitude toward religious parties.
More specifically as to the source of the information, the origin of the material appeared to be
James. Acknowledging that this was not a completely new suggestion, Riesner rehearsed the
names of several scholars who raised this possibility or adopted such a view (p. 242-243. H.
KLEIN, *Barmherzigkeit gegenüber den Elenden und Geächteten. Studien zur Botschaft des
lukanischen Sonderguts* [BThS 10], Neukirchen -Vluyn, 1987, p. 135; J. STAUDINGER, *Testis
"primarius" Evangelii sec. Lucam*, in *VD* 33 [1955] 65-77.129-142; *Die Bergpredigt*, Vienna,
1957, 248-251; L. LEMME, *Das Jakobsevangelium* [BZSF 13/11-12], Berlin - Lichterfelde, 1920;
T. ZAHN, *Das Evangelium des Lucas* [KNT 3], Leipzig, ³,⁴1920, p. 21). This also helped to
explain why in Acts Luke attempted to connect not only Peter and Paul, but Paul and James as
well (RIESNER, *Prägung*, p. 246). The special tradition would also contain the recollections of
women from the time of Jesus (p. 247). Although Riesner did not necessarily subscribe to the
dating of Lk at 70 AD he believed Luke was able to incorporate this basic source from the Jewish
Christians who fled Jerusalem (p. 245).

308. P.-G. MÜLLER, *Lukas-Evangelium*, Stuttgart, 1984, ²1986, p. 14 (esp. p. 14-21, 23-28,

163-174). Müller counted a significant portion as smaller non-Markan insertions (3,7-14.23-28; 4,1-13; 5,1-11,19,1-27.39-44;22,15-20.24-38; 23,6-16.17-32.34.39-43)even as he dimissed the Proto-Lk theory (p. 16). This, however, did not entirely square with his list of *Sondergut* material in his treatment of the passion narrative. There he listed 22,15-18.24-30.31-32.35-38.43-44;23,6-12.13-16.27-31.39-43.46 (p. 163). Pre-Lukan, non-Markan, unified written traditions were responsible for the mockery and the Sanhedrin trial (22,63-65; 66-68) (p. 164), but he clearly affirmed the overall Lukan redaction of the Markan *Vorlage*. The apparent solution to the dilemma rested in his claim that much of the *Sondergut* could be Q material which Matthew opted not to adopt and that many of the special verses derived from Luke himself. For Müller, the Septuagintal language became the model for Luke's redaction. It was quite feasible that Luke did not use as many sources as he had available. The attempt to determine exactly how many sources Luke knew (cf. Lk 1,1) was "ein müssiges Unterfangen" (p. 24).

While Luke used Mk as the foundation for his account of the passion, he added special material derived from oral and written traditions, and partly changed the order. These variations, plus significant omissions of Markan material, all worked to reflect Luke's "eigenes theologisches Profil".

The change of order for the denial, mockery and Sanhedrin trial was attributed to a special source. The mockery by the Roman soldiers (Mk 15,16-20) was omitted to exonerate the occupying authorities. Müller also pointed out that Luke omitted the Markan elements of the witness trial and the accusation that Jesus intended to destroy the Temple.

While Müller was correct to see 23,1-5 as resulting from significant Lukan redaction of Mk 15,1-5 and that Luke borrowed the element of Pilate's announcement of Jesus' innocence (v. 4), he did not see that Luke had not passed over the reference to silence (Mk 14,5), but made use of it in the Herod pericope (23,9). The changes, in Müller's opinion, improved the portrayal of the Romans and comprised part of Luke's apologia to de-politicize Jesus' life and death.

Luke continued his redaction of Mk in 23,18, though without relating the passion custom of releasing a prisoner (p. 173). The Jews, rather than the Christians, were presented as the enemies of the Roman government. And although Luke's recasting of the Markan account of the trial allowed him the opportunity to correct some of the juridical matters, still that was not the evangelist's main concern. The events as they transpired were part of God's plan of salvation.

Even as Müller (²1986) noted the source of the Herod episode (23,6-12) was debated, he asserted that here Luke employed a special tradition (p. 172). Cf. p. 16, where the section 23,6-16 was defined as a smaller insertion added to the passion material. It was hesitatingly suggested that the purpose of the pericope was to emphasize the innocence of Jesus. In a unique nuance, Müller stated that the Lukan Jesus will dialogue with Rome, but refused to speak with the Jewish king Herod. But then this interpretation would fit better with the Lukan theological viewpoint than with an independent special tradition. Müller accepted this story as Luke's substitution for Mk 15,16-20, which he omitted. The relationship between Herod and Pilate cannot be historically established, which would further seem to support Lukan redaction over against a unique source. The events as they unfolded revealed God's salvific plan for which Müller saw similarities in Acts 4,25-28.

A similar view was advocated by Brian C. McGING (1986) who established his view of the historicity of the Herod story (23,7-12) on the grounds that it "rings true" because it served a diplomatic function (although he did not spell that out) and it corresponded to the image of Pilate as "weak and indecisive" which he believed his other research had shown to be the case (B.C. McGING, *The Governorship of Pontius Pilate: Messiahs and Sources*, in A.D.H. MAYES [ed.], *Proceedings of the Irish Biblical Association* 10 [1986] 55-71, esp. p. 66). He relied, in part, upon Hoehner.

Joel GREEN, in a 1985 Aberdeen dissertation directed by I.H. Marshall, was "virtually certain" that in addition to the Markan passion account, Luke also employed "certain non-Markan source material"[309]. Rather than isolated pericopes, Green maintained that this alternate source was a "developing narrative". In a statement reminiscent of Taylor, Green asserted "... we can reasonably propose that Luke knew a second, unified narrative *like Mark's*"[310]. This account was shaped, not only by the community's celebration of the Lord's Supper, but also by the teaching and preaching ministry of the early church[311]. Despite Green's efforts to the contrary, it appeared that the various pericopes, which served a variety of purposes, were in fact circulating independently of one another, if as Green maintained, they were "welded together" in the context of the eucharist[312]. And while his suggestion "leaves room for the influence of different Christian communities on the developing passion tradition", his analysis rather limited its extent[313]. Biases of Trocmé also shone through at various points. Green left open the possibility of a GS of sorts, an "archetypal passion narrative" as Trocmé termed it[314].

Green's source analysis was as follows: 22,54a (Mk and additional source material); 54b-62 (Mk, pre-Lukan material, and non-Markan parallel tradition); 63-65 (63-64 reflected a pre-Lukan, non-Markan tradition while v. 65 was a Lukan creation); 66-71 (Lukan redaction, pre-Lukan redaction, and additional traditional material); 23,1-5 (v. 1 – Lukan redaction of a source other than Mk probable; v.

In a later article (1991), though somewhat ambivalent, McGing acknowledged that scholarly opinion was divided on the historicity issue, but the author ultimately seemed to presuppose the historicity of the Herod incident (MCGING, *Pontius Pilate and the Sources*, in *CBQ* 53 [1991] 423, 436-437). This view was substantiated for four reasons: 1) the event was plausible; 2) Pilate had "good diplomatic reasons" (though not enumerating these) for wanting to improve his relationship with Herod; 3) Pilate's desire to escape from an annoying case; and 4) the portrayal of Pilate as indecisive, eventually giving in, was consistent with that found in Philo and Josephus. Asserting that 23,7-12 was not "blatantly apologetic", McGing regarded the function of the pericope as underscoring the innocence of Jesus. But on the side of redaction, he noted that in Lk as opposed to the other Gospels, Pilate, who increasingly defended Jesus, was more insistent in his opposition to the Jews.

309. J.B. GREEN, *The Death of Jesus. Tradition and Interpretation in the Passion Narrative* (WUNT, 2/33), Tübingen, 1988, p. 102 (= Ch. 3, p. 142, esp. p. 60-112). Diss. Aberdeen, 1985 (dir. I.H. MARSHALL). Pagination in the typescript began each chapter with p. 1, whereas the published version contained continuous pagination. In the typescript edition Green employed endnotes, but footnotes in the book. I am grateful to the author for making a typescript copy of his dissertation available to me prior to its publication.

310. *Ibid.*, p. 104 (= Ch. 3, p. 145).

311. *Ibid.*, p. 213-214 (= Ch. 7, p. 58-59).

312. *Ibid.*, p. 214 (= Ch. 7, p. 59): "Our proposal envisions a dynamic process wherein the total, integrated life of the Christian community is focused at the anamnesis of the Supper on Christ's death – so that reflection on, and lessons from, the passion of Jesus could be welded together in one continuous narrative".

313. *Ibid.*, p. 214 (= Ch. 7, p. 60).

314. *Ibid.*

3 was possibly Mk; vv. 2.4.5 were non-Markan); vv. 13-25 (the conflation of Lukan redaction of Mk and a non-Markan source plus Lukan creative writing)[315].

Though not always admitting of the possibility or probability of Lukan redaction of Mk, Green often did well in indicating why Luke would have changed certain aspects of the Markan account. For example, his assessment was quite accurate in suggesting that Luke redacted Mk's account of the fire in Peter's denial to focus on the ability of the challengers to identify Peter. No mistake was possible in identifying Peter as a companion of Jesus. This, rather than providing warmth, was the point of recalling the fire[316]. In 22,55 Green called attention to the term ἐν μέσῳ, in a verse which reflected "details unknown to, but not inconsistent with, Mark 14:54c"[317]. For a similar phrase Green should have looked to Mk 14,60 where the high priest "stood up in the midst". Such a turn of phrase could very well be familiar to Luke from Mk, though it may not stand in the exact parallel verse. Green recognized this principle in another case[318]. Green should also be complimented for his attention to parallels between Lk and Acts, data for which he often drew upon other scholars, though he did not always give sufficient weight to their import for Lukan redaction[319].

As with other scholars who advocated a second continuous narrative source, Green placed a great deal of emphasis on linguistic analysis. Similar to others relying on this methodology, he often underestimated or miscalculated the evidence. Just such a case was his treatment of 22,63-65. "In fact, of the 27 words used by Luke in this pericope, only 4 (i.e. 14.8%) are also used in Mark -- and the 4 common words are hardly noteworthy: καί, αὐτός, λέγω, and προφητεύω"[320]. Taylor had already discovered 6 words in common[321]. Neirynck previously corrected Taylor's error, which had been adopted by Ernst and Fitzmyer, noting that even Taylor had miscounted and underestimated the amount of verbal borrowing[322]. Green spoke of words that are "noteworthy" but even he must agree that any word, such as the pronoun "he", must be considered since it can have a significant impact on the interpretation of a passage and may in some cases point to a source-critical issue. This was certainly Green's mindset when he discussed the αὐτόν in 22,63[323].

Further, he did not entertain the possibility that a lack of verbal correspondence could equally signal redaction rather than an additional source.

315. *Ibid.*, p. 61, 66, 68, 76, 79, 86 (= Ch. 3, p. 61, 72, 75, 92, 98-99, 112).
316. *Ibid.*, p. 62, 63 (= Ch. 3, p. 63-64, 65).
317. *Ibid.*, p. 62 (= Ch. 3, p. 62).
318. *Ibid.*, p. 60 (= Ch. 3, p. 60). Green conceded that the term συλλαμβάνω (22,54a) may have been taken from Mk 14,48. This gives the impression Markan terms were frequently used, though simply postponed by Luke.
319. *Ibid.*, p. 65, 76, 77-78 (= Ch. 3, p. 70, 90, 94-96).
320. *Ibid.*, p. 66 (= Ch. 3, p. 72).
321. TAYLOR, *The Passion Narrative*, p. 79.
322. NEIRYNCK, ΤΙΣ ΕΣΤΙΝ, p. 17.
323. GREEN, *Death*, p. 67 (= Ch. 3, p. 73).

Even in cases where the language was very similar, Green refused to part with his preferred solution[324]. Where there was little verbal correspondence, he appealed to what he termed "conceptual correspondence" or "conceptual agreement"[325]. He lamented that such similarity was lacking when Luke did not borrow the Servant of Yahweh references from Mk[326]. But Neirynck had earlier responded to such arguments, indicating the great freedom with which Luke treated scriptural allusions found in Mk[327].

Green was perplexed by the identity of those whose challenges precipitated Peter's denials, contending that a second person different from the first "may be pre-Lukan"[328]. Or more likely, it may be that this reflected Lukan redaction and its concern for authentic witness. Luke's revision may be in line with Dt 19,15 which required two male witnesses, since in the Markan account, the testimony of the maid might not have been accepted[329]. The absence of the second crowing was suggested by Green as indication of another source[330]. Fitzmyer had already shown that the omission of the second crowing "eliminates the problem that the double crowing of the cock causes for plausibility"[331]. Green also noted that Luke did not normally use the term ὁ κύριος in redacting Mk[332]. Cadbury observed the same, though as opposed to Mk, Luke often employed the vocative form[333]. A shift to the substantive would not be difficult. Fitzmyer had shown that the frequent use of the title in narratives was reflective of current usage in Luke's time[334]. Green observed at one point that "Luke's trial narrative is

324. *Ibid.*, p. 75 (= Ch. 3, p. 89): "The language [of v. 71] is very close to Mark's account, and one may readily suggest that here Luke has redacted his Gospel source; of course, the possibility exists that the variation stems from Luke's other source". See Green's discussion of the value of various scholars' lists of linguistic data in notes to p. 25, n. 5 (= Ch. 3, p. 1-2, n. 5).

325. *Ibid.*, p. 71, 74 (= Ch. 3, p. 81, 87).

326. *Ibid.*, p. 66 (= Ch. 3, p. 72). See also p. 71 (= Ch 3, p. 80).

327. NEIRYNCK, ΤΙΣ ΕΣΤΙΝ, p. 26-27.

328. GREEN, *Death*, p. 63 (= Ch. 3, p. 66).

329. Cf. FITZMYER, *Luke*, p. 1460.

330. GREEN, *Death*, p. 64 (= Ch. 3, p. 68).

331. FITZMYER, *Luke*, p. 1459. Cf. p. 1426, where he explained that the point was that Peter will deny Jesus so quickly that the interval between denials would be too brief to allow the cock to crow a second time.

332. GREEN, *Death*, p. 65 (= Ch. 3, p. 69).

333. CADBURY, *Making*, 1927, ²1958, p. 229, n. 26: "The other synoptic Evangelists, however, have habits which Luke does not share, such as their well-known avoidance of 'the Lord' for Jesus in narrative, which F.C. Burkitt calls 'a singular indication of historical feeling on the part of our evangelist' in the matter of nomenclature, and their avoidance (except in connection with Jesus' appointment of missionaries) of 'the apostles' for the twelve disciples. In address to Jesus, Mark uses 'Rabbi,' which Luke avoids, I think not because it was pedantic (Burkitt) but because it was not Greek, while Luke uses freely in address besides 'teacher' and 'master' (see above), the vocative 'Lord,' which Mark limits to the address of the Syro-Phoenician woman".

334. FITZMYER, *Luke*, p. 203. The only occurrence in Mk was 11,3. But influence from this

remarkable for its brevity and lack of details integral to an actual trial" and further concluded that omissions of Markan material reflected a second source[335]. Cadbury likewise detected this stylistic technique, remarking: "Certain scenes in the story are marked by a like effective use of a few details .... Indeed, we can see from comparing Mark that he has often merely retained or even reduced the vigor, the naïve detail, the natural art of his sources ... But even avoiding excess we may acknowledge much artistic quality in parts of his writings"[336].

Agreements between Lk and Jn were often assigned by Green to pre-Lukan, non-Markan tradition[337]. He dismissed the idea that the Synoptics could have served as sources for Jn[338]. Green pointed to the triple declaration of Jesus' innocence as a common agreement between Lk and Jn. Supposing for a moment that the Synoptics served as sources for Jn, how might we account for series of threes in Lukan redaction? Fitzmyer indicated that Jesus was interrogated "by a threefold group of Jewish authorities"[339]. There were three denials, just as in Luke's account there were three challengers, and the statement of Jesus' guiltlessness in triplicate. Three women disciples of Jesus were mentioned by name in 8,3. Three parables grouped around the theme of lost and found were combined in Lk 15. In the Lukan parable of the Great Banquet (14,15-24) three guests who had been invited sent their regrets. In the parable of the Vineyard and the Tenants (20,9-17), the owner sent three servants before sending the son. In the crucifixion scene Jesus together with the two criminals and in the Emmaus story Jesus with two disciples, also formed groups of threes. Might this suggest another aspect of Lukan redaction? Green also took account of the changes in order in Lk as opposed to Mk, but this does not seem to form a central argument in Green's defense of a source other than Mk[340].

point should not be entirely excluded, since the Lord's prayer included the petition to be delivered from the time of trial.

335. GREEN, *Death*, p. 72 (= Ch. 3, p. 82).

336. CADBURY, *Making*, 1927, ²1958, p. 235.

337. GREEN, *Death*, p. 61, 62, 77, 78, 79, 84, 85, 86 (= Ch. 3, p. 61, 63, 94, 96, 98, 105-106, 106, 109, 112).

338. *Ibid.*, p. 103 (= Ch. 3, p. 143).

339. FITZMYER, *Luke*, p. 1459.

340. GREEN, *Death*, p. 61, 77, 79, 82-83 (= Ch. 3, p. 62, 93, 97, 103). More recently he undertook an analysis of the source question in the Lukan passion narrative concentrating on the rending of the Temple veil (*The Demise of the Temple as 'Culture Center' in Luke-Acts: An Exploration of the Rending of the Temple Veil (Luke 23.44-49)*, in *RB* 101 [1994] 495-515). Two developments in thought reflected in his study are especially worth noting. Despite several years of continued research, he was not any closer to identifying the exact nature of this special source. "Our source-critical analysis, although inconclusive in uncovering with any specificity the sort(s) of non-Markan tradition(s) Luke might have known, did underscore the responsibility of the Third Evangelist for staging the death scene" (p. 514). Secondly, he backed away from his original thesis that the special source was unified. In contradistinction to Taylor (*Passion Narrative*) and Jeremias (*Die Sprache*) he now maintained, "we do not assume that, if Luke possessed a non-Markan source for his narrative of Jesus' death, it must have formed an integrated source L with

Green left unresolved any concrete solution to the MA in 22,62, but the proposal of individual redaction by Luke and Matthew of Mk was rejected out of hand[341]. The MA in 22,64 was explained by Green on the basis of "a common source"[342].

Green took up the gauntlet and defended the Herod pericope as stemming from "an alternative continuous narrative tradition", though it betrayed "Luke's redactional hand"[343]. Green responded to those who suggested Luke crafted the episode in its entirety or by using elements drawn from Mk, by reacting to what he considered the "three primary arguments" against the special source for this scene of the Lukan passion. These are: the Lukan style and language of the episode[344]; 2) its purported relation to Acts 4,24-28 as a "fulfillment" of Ps 2,1-2; and 3) Walaskay's contention that the Herod scene was an intentional Jesus-Paul parallel.

Green eliminated the following terms from the stock of Lukan redactional vocabulary: ἀκούω (2x), ἐπερωτάω (2x), ἱκανός (2x), γίνομαι (2x), γραμματεύς and ἀλλήλων. A perusal of a concordance of the LXX indicated that all of these were Septuagintal vocabulary. Those other terms which Green ascribed to Luke may also confidently be attributed to the LXX[345]. Green was reluctant to offer a conclusion concerning ἀναπέμπω[346]. The fact that Luke showed a preference for compounds, plus the fact that four of the five occurrences in the NT were found in Lk-Acts, would seem to favor the view that this term too was due to the hand of Luke[347]. Green correctly noted that the phrase ἐν ταύταις ταῖς ἡμέραις

its own characteristic vocabulary" (p. 496, n. 1; cf. *Death*, p. 104 = Ch. 3, p. 145: "We can reasonably propose that Luke knew a second, unified narrative *like Mark's*").

341. GREEN, *Death*, p. 65 (= Ch. 3, p. 71).

342. *Ibid.*, p. 68 (= Ch. 3, p. 75).

343. GREEN, *Death*, p. 82 (= Ch. 3, p. 102). Cf. p. 81 (esp. p. 80-82) = Ch. 3, p. 101 (esp. p. 99-102).

344. GREEN, *Death*, p. 80-82 (= Ch. 3, p. 99-101). It was to this aspect that Green devoted most of his attention, relying heavily upon Taylor and Büchele.

345. *Ibid.*, p. 80-81 (= Ch. 3, p. 100). The terms were πρός, περί, λόγος. See for example *HR*.

346. GREEN, *Death*, p. 81 (= p. 100-101). The term occurred in Plutarch. Cf. FITZMYER, *Luke*, p. 113: "[Cadbury] gives a concrete, though not complete, demonstration of the studied elegance of Luke's vocabulary. While the Greek of NT writers in general varies considerably from that of writers in the classical period, Luke's writings come closest and are more elegant in diction than most of the others".

An interesting contrast of the definition of ἀναπέμπω may be noted between MOULTON and MILLIGAN, *Vocabulary*, p. 37, where it was defined as "to send up to a higher authority" and H. BALZ, in *EWNT* 1, p. 208 (= *EDNT* 1, p. 87), where it was understood to have two different meanings.

347. GREEN, *Death*, p. 81 (= Ch. 3, p. 101). The only other instance was Phlm 11. Cf. *NTV*, p. 31. MOULTON and MILLIGAN, *Vocabulary*, p. 37, with the meaning of 23,7 and Acts 25,21 sending up to a higher authority, listed several examples from various collections of inscriptions.

was "undoubtedly Lukan"[348]. Where that phrase (or its singular counterpart) existed according to Green, five occurrences were redactions of Markan material (4,2; 5,35; 9,36; 17,31; 21,23) while three were drawn from Q (6,23; 10,12; 21,34) and only one was found in L (2,1).

Dibelius's conviction that Luke created the Herod episode from Ps 2 was dismissed by Green for three reasons: 1) the account of the trial did not contain either a direct or indirect mention of Ps 2; 2) the Gospel and Acts reflected two different renditions: in Acts Herod conspired with Pilate, while in the Gospel Luke's tendency was to put Rome in a better light; 3) Acts presupposed Lk 23,6-12 "for it is doubtful that the psalm could have given rise to this interpretation if Herod had no place in the story of Jesus' death"[349]. This third element was more an assertion than an argument, since Green offered nothing with which to substantiate his claim.

Finally, Green rejected Walaskay's assertion that the story was a Lukan creation and served as a parallel between Jesus and Paul because Jesus stood silent in his trial while Paul waxed eloquent. But this can easily be explained away in proposing that Luke as a skillful author, was careful to present Jesus as the suffering servant and to distinguish him from his disciples. The parallels will under no circumstances be exactly alike and there were obvious reasons for the differences. Green's reason, that it was likely that such a tradition concerning Herod's trial was pre-existent to the Lk, begs the question[350].

Green assumed too, because the episode was well integrated into the adjacent material, that this signaled a separate, independent account. Rather, it could equally be indicative of an adept littérateur who keenly made transitions within his story. This was shown to be the case when Luke connected later elements in the Gospel with earlier ones, such as Herod's desire to see Jesus (9,9; 23,8). If an author can effectively do that with material that is separated by chapters, one would also reasonably expect that it could be done within a single chapter.

Reception of Green's Position

E. Earle Ellis critiqued the study on methodological grounds[351]. He charged Green made an uncritical use of early form-critical presuppositions, incorporating newer developments only as an "afterthought"[352]. Reinhard Feldmeier complimented Green for a good survey of the source question, but faulted him for not always supplying clear distinctions between the Gospels regarding their sources, especially their origin and relationship with one another[353]. Feldmeier

---

348. GREEN, *Death*, p. 80 (= Ch. 3, p. 100).
349. *Ibid.*, p. 102.
350. *Ibid.*
351. *SWJTh* 32 (1989) 60.
352. *Ibid.* Cf. GREEN, *Death*, p. 160, n. 8.
353. *TLZ* 114 (1989) 891.

552 CHAPTER NINE

criticized Green for drawing conclusions, for example in the case of the Markan *Vorlage*, though he had not taken up the meticulous literary-critical and redaction-critical questions. Related to this was Green's use of the phrase about the divine plan of salvation which Feldmeier pointed out occurred only in the Lukan passion and reflected Lukan redaction[354]. Kenneth Grayston had high praise for the central section of Green's work calling it "well-informed, shrewd and lucid"[355]. But Grayston had serious difficulty with Green's treatment of Luke's special source. "Every critic must allow himself several plausible but unsupported conjectures which then make the edifice unstable. Even more precarious is Luke's *Sonderquelle*. Dr Green identifies in the Greek text of Luke 22-23 the probable and possible redaction of Mark and of the *Sonderquelle*, the conflation of Mark and the *Sonderquelle*, and a minute amount of Lukan free creation. But in any case why is it necessary to undertake such critical activity if theological inquiry about the death of Jesus leads to nothing more than a list of some dozen perhaps-unrelated images?"[356]. Frank Matera found the book to be a significant contribution to the debate on the passion, but took issue with it on methodological grounds[357]. While differences between Mk and Lk were explained based on a precanonical passion narrative, that same precanonical source was used to explain differences between Mk and Jn. Matera viewed this as inconsistent insofar as Green claimed that it was the same basic source which underlies Mk, Lk and Jn.

In a later contribution treating the theology of Lk (1995) Green wrote only generally of sources, adding that most scholars favored the view of Luke's use of Mk. He specified the evangelist's "chief contribution as a narrative theologian would be recognized not only in whatever fresh material he was able to include, but also and especially in his ordering and staging of the account"[358]. For his 1997 commentary on Lk Green demonstrated "very little concern for traditional form-critical and redaction-critical issues"[359].

In the first volume of John NOLLAND'S commentary (1989), he stated his belief that Luke was dependent upon Mk, but also used additional material, the unity of which cannot be determined with any certainty[360]. The substitution of Joanna's

354. *Ibid.*, p. 892-893.
355. *JTS* 41 (1990) 183.
356. *Ibid.*, p. 183.
357. *Interpr* 44 (1990) 207.
358. GREEN, *The Theology of the Gospel of Luke*, Cambridge, 1995, p. 20, 21. See the brief comment on the whole of the passion narrative (p. 32).
359. *The Gospel of Luke* (NICNT), Grand Rapids, MI - Cambridge, 1997. As noted by the series editor, G.D. Fee (p. viii). Green observed: "My own introduction to serious study of Luke coincided with this latter shift, marked by the waning of the hegemony of historical study (historical criticism, tradition criticism, redaction criticism, and the rest) and the blooming of the so-called 'newer' approaches (e.g., new literary criticism, narrative criticism, new historicism, and the like)" (p. ix). He referred to the method employed in the commentary as "'discourse analysis' - correlating culture-critical and narratological concerns" (p. 1).
360. J.L. NOLLAND, *Luke 1-9:20* (WBC, 35A), Dallas, TX, 1989, p. xxx-xxxi: "For this

name over against Salome provided by Mk 15,40-41, may have been motivated by "the fact that Christian influence has penetrated to high places"[361].

In the third volume (1993) which covered Lk 18,35–24,53 Nolland acknowledged his support for Luke's use of "a second continuous passion narrative (as distinct from access to isolated items of tradition)" while asserting that "Luke clearly makes use of his Markan source"[362]. Nolland assigned the following verses to Luke's special passion source according to varying degrees of certainty: "clear" 22,15-20.24-30.31-34.35-38.63-64; "very likely" 23,26-32.39-43; "likely" 22,39-46.47-54a.54b-62.66-71; 23,1-5.18-25.33-34; "quite possible" 23,6-12.46-47; "possible" 23,50-56; "unlikely" 23,35-38; "uncertain" 22,21-23; 23,13-16[363].

Nolland argued that the MA in 22,62 "guarantees that Luke (and Matthew) had access to a separate account of the denials of Peter"[364]. From this posited the view that 22,61a was also possibly due to that source and so was any other distinctive feature in Luke's version[365]. The second source also influenced Luke's choice of vocabulary.

---

other material the source discussion proceeds item by item. I have no confidence that we are in any position to identify collections within, or a collection containing all or most of, this additional material. There may indeed be a 'family likeness' reflected in much of this material, but that 'family likeness' comes too close to Lukan interests to be very useful for source separation. Lukan editing, Lukan selection on the basis of congeniality, and genuine source similarity come too close together to be readily separated". E. Franklin, in a review in *JTS*, penned the following: "Nolland does not seem impressed with Proto-Luke though it (unmentioned by name) is allowed as one of the variety of views which are neither affirmed or denied" (*JTS* 42 [1991] 219).

361. NOLLAND, *Luke 1-9:20*, p. 366.

362. NOLLAND, *Luke 18:35-24:53* (WBC 35c), Dallas, TX, 1993, p. 1023. He also favored the idea of a pre-Markan passion source, the extent of which remains in doubt, but this was seen in relation to the idea of the second passion narrative for Luke. For Nolland's treatment of 22,54b–23,25, see p. 1090-1133. In his preface he noted the works of Schürmann and Fitzmyer "have been constant companions" (p. xiv). He also relied upon the works of Marshall, Grundmann, Schlatter, Godet, and Loisy. Nolland further stated that he frequently examined the relationship between the Gospel and Acts. He seems to beg the question on sources when later he wrote: "However, the sheer fact of a second source for so many of the passion pericopes counts in favor of the existence of a second sequential passion source" (p. 1105).

363. *Ibid.*, p. 1023. The following verses were not included in any category: 22,44-45.48-49.65. He believed there were connections between the special Lukan source and the Johannine tradition, but did not believe that these links provided evidence of "literary dependence in one direction or another". Further, he affirmed the historicity of the passion narratives (p. 1024; but cf. p. 1111). It appeared that Nolland changed his opinion on the source of 23,13-16 at least from the time he penned his introduction to the passion narrative till his commentary on the specific verses. Whereas he originally held that the second Lukan source was uncertain for 23,13-16 (p. 1023), he later reversed himself contending that it was "likely" that they stemmed from the special source (p. 1129).

364. *Ibid.*, p. 1092-1093. See his comment on v. 62 (p. 1096).

365. *Ibid.*, p. 1093. He later added: "... though we have another source reflected in Matthew and Luke, so little of it has been preserved that we can know nothing of its ultimate relationship to the Markan stream of tradition" (p. 1094).

Unlike other scholars who supported the view of a second source, Nolland believed that the terms στραφείς and ὁ κύριος "look Lukan"[366]. Although he remarked earlier in the commentary it was likely that the account of Peter's denials stemmed from the second source, in his exegesis of the individual verses it was only in 22,55.58.59 where he specifically, and again somewhat cautiously, mentioned influence from the special passion account. On the other hand, it was remarked that in 22,54b.56.57 and especially in 22,60.61 Luke was evidently redacting Mk.

Nolland called attention to the change in order of the account of the mockery, but argued forcefully that the Lukan version derived from the special source in 22,63-64[367]. He left open the possibility that 22,65 came either from the second source or from Lukan redaction[368]. Like Catchpole and others Nolland maintained that the αὐτόν of 22,63 reflected the use of a source.

By the occurrence of the MA in 22,64 he was inclined to believe that Matthew also may have had access to a second source, though he cited Neirynck's solution of an interpolation into Matthew's Gospel[369].

Nolland began his discussion of the account of the Sanhedrin trial by calling attention to the difference in the order of the denial, mockery and trial, citing Radl as a recent opponent of the special source theory, conceding that Radl was correct in linking 22,67-68 with 20,1-8, though Nolland limited the extent of its influence. He asserted that change in order in Lk frequently indicated the use of a second source. He concluded that 22,71 was "quite likely" a redaction of Mk 14,63b-64a; 22,68 was "likely" a reprisal of 20,1-8[370]; 22,69 could either stem from Mk or the second source[371]; and it was "not likely" that 22,66 depended upon Mk 15,1. The events described in 22,66-71 were seen to be a hearing rather than a formal trial. The attempt to reconstruct the content of the second source in this section highlighted "Jesus' refusal to deny that he is messiah"[372]. The double question (22,67) was regarded as coming from the special source[373]. Though conceding that much in v. 70 "could be Lukan or based on Luke's Markan source", the

---

366. *Ibid.*, p. 1096.

367. *Ibid.*, p. 1098. A second mockery, that which was described in 23,11, was also mentioned.

368. *Ibid.*, p. 1099.

369. *Ibid.*, p. 1098-1099. Cf. NEIRYNCK, *ETL* 63 (1987) 5-47.

370. See also NOLLAND, *Luke 18:35–24:53*, p. 1110.

371. However, in Nolland's comment on the verse, he credited Luke with redacting Mk for the differences contained therein including Luke's probable addition of the phrase "of God". But the second source was not far from Luke as Nolland contended that Luke substituted the phrase ἀπὸ τοῦ νῦν for a temporal reference in the second source (p. 1110).

372. *Ibid.*, p. 1107.

373. *Ibid.*, p. 1109. While a "certain likeness" existed between this verse and Jer 38,14-15, Nolland argued that there was no intentional allusion (p. 1110).

special source was evident to Nolland particularly in Jesus' response[374]. The final verse of the Sanhedrin hearing (22,71) was regarded as Lukan redaction of Mk.

While Mk 15,1-5 was seen as the basis for Lk 23,1-5 due to similarity of sequence and a significant degree of Lukan vocabulary and themes, Nolland believed he detected the influence of "additional tradition" for three reasons: 1) the relatively small amount of common vocabulary, except for 23,3; 2) similarities between Lk and Jn arising not from literary dependence, but from sharing a common tradition; and 3) the surprising omission of παρέδωκαν (23,1) though it frequently occurred in the passion predictions[375]. It would appear that Nolland suggested that 23,5 was a Lukan creation necessitated by the action described in the previous verses and thus not due to the special source[376].

Nolland rejected the view that in 23,18-25 there was a great deal of similarity with the parallel text in Mk 15,6-14[377]. This perception as well as shared vocabulary between Lk and Jn was invoked as evidence of the special source, though he commented "it is difficult to say anything very definite about its precise scope or content"[378]. The account at this point may be a combination of the special source, Mk and Luke's personal contribution of the "threefold nature of the interaction between Pilate and his audience". In 23,18 Lukan vocabulary was probably evident with ἀνέκραγον and possibly in παμπληθεί. Likewise there was probable influence from Mk 15,7 both in content and language in 23,19. Conversely, 23,20 was quite likely formulated by Luke, who was also the source for ἐπεφώνουν in 23,21. Mk 15,14 served as the source for the first clause of Pilate's statement in 23,22 though the second clause was credited to Luke's "Johannine source"[379]. There was a great deal of Lukan vocabulary in 23,23 but both this verse as well as Mk 15,15 indicated that Pilate yielded to the wishes of the crowd. Aside from a partial repetition of 23,19 in 23,25 Nolland ascribed much of this verse to Lukan redaction of Mk 15,15bc while the conclusion of the Lukan verse showed signs of similarity with Jn[380].

Nolland defended the historicity of the Herod pericope and viewed 23,6-12.13-16 as part of the special source[381]. He rejected Müller's suggestion that Luke was responsible for the Herod pericope as well as Soards's view that Luke possessed some tradition relating Herod's involvement in the trial. He further dismissed

374. *Ibid.*, p. 1110.
375. *Ibid.*, p. 1115.
376. *Ibid.*
377. *Ibid.*, p. 1129. V. 17 was rejected as unauthentic on textual grounds (n. a).
378. *Ibid.*
379. *Ibid.*, p. 1132.
380. *Ibid.*
381. *Ibid.*, p. 1121-1122, 1129. Nevertheless, he appeared tentative, initially stating that it was "quite possible" that 23,6-12 formed part of the special source (p. 1023), and later after weighing various source critical solutions concluded: "it seems best to think of it as being part of Luke's second connected passion source", though he came to this decision partly because he cannot envision the story as "freestanding" (p. 1122).

Dibelius's idea that the story evolved from Ps 2,1-2. Originally, Nolland envisioned the transfer as a way Pilate could get out of a difficult situation, but later insisted that "the situation needed to be handled with some delicacy" given its potential for a disruptive outcome, and thus his maneuvering was not simply avoidance[382].

Verse 23,6 provided a "distinctly Lukan linkage with 23,1-5". For 23,7 Nolland offered his own rendition of what the verse may have looked like in Luke's special source. Almost all of 23,8 was Lukan with the exception of λίαν. Nolland asserted it was probably correct to regard 23,9 "as a recasting of Mark 15:4-5" inasmuch as Luke had no room for it in his account of Pilate's trial. The silence of Jesus was seen as a fulfillment of Is 53,7. The next Lukan verse, 23,10 was drawn from Mk 15,3 if the previous verse had been. The sole link with Mk 15,16-20 in 23,11 was the term ἐμπαίζειν, while other vocabulary was attributed to Luke. Nevertheless, Nolland rejected the idea that Luke based this account upon Mk 15,16-20. Nolland distinguished 23,12 from Acts 4,27 by noting that though in the latter Pilate and Herod appeared together, it was not in friendship. The whole story was perceived as a mockery of Jesus that further underscored the innocence of Jesus.

The passage that followed the Herod pericope in 23,13-16 was partly built upon material from 23,1-5, just as v. 15 prepared for 23,22. Nolland regarded 23,13-25 as a unit. Because of the large quantity of Lukan vocabulary, he believed "it is not possible to make any confident judgments about the form and scope of Luke's tradition for this pericope"[383]. The presence of Lukan language was detected in 23,13.14 while 23,15 was ascribed to Luke less for the reason of vocabulary than for the reason that it served to create "a fourfold affirmation by Pilate of Jesus' innocence"[384]. Nolland contended that 23,16 was pre-Lukan because of some similarity with Jn 19,1. This passage was significant in that it provided Pilate's second testimony to the innocence of Jesus. Like Heil and others, Nolland saw irony at work in this pericope[385].

In an essay published in the FS for E.E. Ellis, Peter RICHARDSON (1987) described Streeter's Proto-Lk theory as the "most imaginative part of his conception", though he acknowledged that the idea "has not found much support"[386]. He admitted that Ellis rejected the hypothesis[387]. Richardson's article focused on the question: "is there a setting in the Pauline mission that might account for a 'gospel' such as

382. *Ibid.*, p. 1122.
383. *Ibid.*, p. 1126.
384. *Ibid.*, p. 1127.
385. *Ibid.*, p. 1127, 1128.
386. *Gospel Traditions in the Church in Corinth (with Apologies to B.H. Streeter)*, in G.F. HAWTHORNE and O. BETZ (eds.), *Tradition and Interpretation in the New Testament* (FS E.E. ELLIS), Grand Rapids, MI - Tübingen, 1987, 301-318, p. 301.
387. *Ibid.* Cf. E.E. ELLIS, *The Gospel of Luke*, London, 1966, p. 21-27.

Proto-Luke?"[388]. His theory was that because Paul disliked some aspects of a sayings tradition related to Q, he promoted the composition of what Streeter defined as Proto-Lk[389]. The value of this special source, if it could be proven, was much the same as Taylor envisioned: a gospel prior to and independent of Mk[390]. Richardson conceded that Mk might have provided the structure for Lk. Later in the essay he claimed that "the passion narrative in Proto-Luke is very similar in broad outline to the Markan narrative", but dismissed the resemblance based on the "stereotyped character of the tradition of the passion"[391].

Another similarity between Taylor and Richardson was the view that Proto-Luke and Luke were the same person. While Q did not contain a passion narrative, Proto-Lk rectified this problem, among other things[392]. In contrast to Streeter's conception, Richardson's Proto-Lk contained a "mixture of influences" including "the inheritance from Q, additional oral traditions, his own theological concerns and some of Paul's special interests", which arose from controversies within Corinth[393]. The situation in Corinth was seen as "a kind of middle term between Q and Proto-Luke, being shaped by the one and shaping the other"[394]. Again, like Taylor, Richardson used the passion narrative as a starting point[395]. Consistent with the views of one supporting a Proto-Lukan theory, Richardson asserted: "The trial in Luke is often – I think correctly – seen as almost completely different from and independent of Mark, though it has some Markan insertions"[396]. However, his treatment of the trial reflected only comparisons with Paul, none with Mk. In the discussion which followed he attempted to highlight similarities between 1 Cor and Proto-Lk in the trial. However, none of his comments touch directly on our section of the passion narrative. One statement in particular, based on unsubstantiated assumptions, suffers from faulty logic. "Since the resurrection accounts also do not derive from Mark or Q, Luke's Passion Narrative, less some Markan additions, is attributable to Proto-Luke"[397]. If the resurrection accounts did not stem from Mk or Q, for which Richardson offered no proof, then one need not automatically conclude that they derived from Proto-Lk.

388. RICHARDSON, *Gospel Traditions*, p. 301.

389. *Ibid.*, p. 302.

390. *Ibid.*: "The potential importance of the Proto-Luke hypothesis is that it would present us with an early Gospel, independent of Mark, and with a quite different story-line from that of Q, Mark, or Thomas". Cf. TAYLOR, *Behind*, 1926, p. 28, 246; see also *Passion Narrative*, 1972, p. ix.

391. RICHARDSON, *Gospel Traditions*, p. 306; see also p. 302.

392. *Ibid.*, p. 303. He reiterated that Q did not contain a passion narrative noting that his viewpoint was "widely agreed upon" (p. 304; see further p. 306).

393. *Ibid.*, p. 303.

394. *Ibid.*, p. 304.

395. Cf. TAYLOR, *Behind*, p. 201.

396. RICHARDSON, *Gospel Traditions*, p. 304.

397. *Ibid.*

Richardson maintained that Proto-Lk presented a "revisionist view" of John the Baptist to counteract "a tendency of the redaction of Q to elevate John to a position beside Jesus"[398]. Ascribing the people's curiosity whether John was the Christ (3,15) to Proto-Lk, though noting a similar question was asked of Jesus in Mk 8,27-28 pars., Richardson argued this was significant because the title was not used again in Lk until the trial (22,67). After that "Christ" was used four times: 23,2.39; 24,26.46.

In his study of the christology of Proto-Lk Richardson stated that Q influence was detected in the title "Son of Man". What was strange about this was that the title appeared on the lips of Stephen (Acts 7,56) rather than of Jesus, "but more significantly there is no saying in Proto-Luke to which this can refer"[399]. Richardson further insisted that "Lord" christology was dominant in Proto-Lk. If that were the case, and if the trial stemmed from the special source, then it is all the more surprising that it was the title "Christ" and not "Lord" which was found most frequently in the Lukan trial narrative[400].

In the conclusion of his essay, Richardson remarked: "I have not systematically addressed methodological problems in reconstructing Proto-Luke, or problems in distinguishing Proto-Lukan features from those of the final redaction"[401]. These issues, as we have seen, have been and continue to be major obstacles to this hypothesis. As to the matter of not distinguishing between Proto-Lk and Luke, the criticism Neirynck made of Boismard's theory also applies here[402]. In addition, if as Richardson maintained, "Lord" is the dominant christology of Proto-Lk, why is it lacking from the trial? If Proto-Lk were influenced by Paul, why is the Pauline influence missing here? As for views opposed to Proto-Lk, Richardson left too much unsaid. Indeed, as to Fitzmyer's summation of "arguments against the hypothesis" he simply declared: "Most of the arguments that he uses fall on closer inspection"[403]. Regrettably, Richardson did not highlight which arguments in his opinion fell and which arguments still stand against the Proto-Lk hypothesis.

Richardson recently completed a study of Herod (1996) in which he continued to support a Proto-Lk theory[404]. Suggesting that 8,1-3 and 13,31-33 "may well

---

398. *Ibid.*, p. 306.

399. *Ibid.*, p. 311.

400. *Ibid.*, p. 317-318, which contained an appendix entitled: "Addresses/Titles for Jesus in Proto-Luke".

401. *Ibid.*, p. 313.

402. F. NEIRYNCK, *John and the Synoptics*, in M. DE JONGE (ed.), *L'évangile de Jean*, 1977, p. 85 (= *Evangelica*, 1982, p. 377). Cf. BOISMARD, *Synopse*, Vol. 2, p. 46.

403. RICHARDSON, *Gospel Traditions*, p. 315, n. 4. Cf. FITZMYER, *Luke*, p. 89-91.

404. P. RICHARDSON, *Herod. King of the Jews and Friend of the Romans*, Columbia, SC, 1996, esp. p. 305-314. See p. 309, n. 64: "I here presuppose Proto-Luke, a first edition of Luke before Mark was incorporated into it. At this point in the narrative [13,31-33], Proto-Luke includes the account of John's question to Jesus and his response (7:18-35), the remainder of that chapter, Jesus' travels with Joanna, Mary, and Susanna and the Twelve (8:1-3). It then jumps to

be remnants of an independent tradition about Jesus", he surmised that these pericopes may be indications of connections "with Antipas's household"[405]. The various editions of Proto-Lk, in Richardson's estimation, would help to explain Herod's conflicting reactions to Jesus: one time wanting simply to see him (9,9) and another time attempting to kill him (13,31).

Conceding it is "hard to know what credence to give"[406] to the trial of Herod, Richardson regarded Luke's account of the trial, of which Herod's trial (23,6-16) was a part, to be parallel to Mk but independent of it[407]. He considered it possible that Pilate sent Jesus to Herod, though he was under no obligation to do so and further Herod would not have been competent to try Jesus[408]. As to the enmity between Pilate and Herod (23,12) he concluded it was "not improbable but has by no means been proven"[409]. As to the question whether the trial before Herod could have transpired, Richardson maintained that would not be "an impossible trial", merely "an extremely tight one"[410]. The disparity between Lk and Acts was explained that while Acts 4,27 "supports the claim of a role for Antipas in the trial", Lk 23,15 underscored Herod's guilt[411].

Naymond KEATHLEY (1990) proposed that the way in which the Temple motif was treated in Lk-Acts supported the Proto-Lk theory as developed by Streeter and Taylor and "addresses the chronological sequence of the writing of Luke and Acts as we know them"[412]. Gerd PETZKE (1990) proposed the possibility that someone

9:51, Jesus' decision to go to Jerusalem, the appointment of the seventy, and eventually, as he draws near to Jerusalem, the warning about Antipas".

405. *Ibid.*, p. 308-309. In his 1987 article Richardson mentioned 13,31-33 in the context of a "prophet" christology in his discussion of the christology of Proto-Lk (*Gospel Traditions*, p. 311).

406. RICHARDSON, *Herod*, p. 310-311.

407. *Ibid.*, p. 310, n. 68. He also identified the Herod trial as 23,6-16 in an earlier note (p. 305, n. 45).

408. *Ibid.*, p. 311.

409. *Ibid.*, p. 312.

410. *Ibid.*

411. *Ibid.*, n. 79.

412. N.H. KEATHLEY, *The Temple in Luke and Acts: Implications for the Synoptic Problem and Proto-Luke*, in ID. (ed.), *With Steadfast Purpose. Essays on Acts in Honor of Henry Jackson Flanders, Jr.*, Waco, TX 1990, 77-105, p. 103. He referred to STREETER, *The Four Gospels* (1925); TAYLOR, *Behind* (1926), and *Important Hypotheses* (1955-56). Keathley attributed authorship of Proto-Lk to Luke, who then wrote Acts and at a later stage combined Proto-Lk with the infancy narratives and Mk. In redacting Mk "Luke changed every reference to the temple in Mark, either by deletion or alteration, to reflect his positive view" (*Temple*, p. 105). He summarized: "The emphasis on the temple in Luke and Acts, I conclude, is instructive, not only for the understanding of Lukan theology, but also for the understanding of Lukan composition. The development, arrangement, and editing of these materials are best understood from the perspective of the Proto-Luke hypothesis". Keathley called attention to the fact that there was no Lukan parallel concerning the false witnesses or the accusations about the destruction of the Temple (Mt 26,59-61 / Mk 14,55-59 dif Lk 22,66-71) (p. 90). He also noted the scholarly consensus that Lk was not the first Gospel, highlighting Lindsey as "one notable exception" (p.

prior to Luke joined various traditions together in a so-called "Proto-Lukas" even while observing that the majority of scholars rejected the view that the *Sondergut* constituted a unified source[413]. Another of the contemporary proponents of the Proto-Lk hypothesis was Thomas L. BRODIE[414]. D.L. BOCK (1994) contended

101, n. 65; cf. R.L. LINDSEY, *Modified* [1963]).

413. G. PETZKE, *Das Sondergut des Evangeliums nach Lukas* (ZWB), Zürich, 1990, p. 11, 13. He claimed that the first two verses of the Prologue referred to two different stages of tradition. In the section 22,54–23,25 he treated Jesus before Pilate and Herod (23,(4f.)6-16). Again while noting that the majority of scholars were not convinced that this story represented pre-Lukan *Sondergut*, Petzke maintained that it cannot be excluded that Luke employed a pre-Lukan tradition for this account (p. 184). Arguments against a special source rested on recognition of Lukan interests, particularly the innocence of Jesus and the declarations by Pilate and Herod about release. He recognized that 23,2 served to contradict the charge in 20,25. The political content of the charges was a theme which ran through the trials before Pilate and Herod. Appeal was made to Conzelmann that it cannot be excluded that in 23,5 a pre-Lukan "Sammelbericht" was employed (p. 185-186). Cf. CONZELMANN, *Die Mitte*, ⁵1964, p. 79. The mockery scene in 23,11 was possibly a substitute for the account of the mockery by Pilate's soldiers which Luke did not include (cf. Mk 15,16-20). The friendship between Pilate and Herod (23,12) could be attributed to their similar intention and their mutual respect and consultation. The story was thought to derive from a pre-Lukan tradition with reference made to the tradition found in GP. "Hier wird gelegentlich der Rückgriff aus einer vorlukanischen Überlieferung zugestanden" (PETZKE, *Das Sondergut*, p. 187). In referring to GP 1.2 he stated: "Sicherlich sind beide Belege nachlukanisch, aber sie deuten darauf hin, dass eine Mitwirkung des Herodes bis in Glaubensformeln hinein und in der Ausgestaltung auch motivlich unabhängig von Lukas überliefert wurde" (p. 187-188). While Petzke favored the idea of a pre-Lukan tradition in 23,6-16, the influence of Ps 2 cannot be excluded for in Acts 4,27 Pilate and Herod were combined "unter Verweis auf Ps. 2,1f.". Whereas in the Gospel Pilate and Herod provided the forum for the accusations, in Acts 4,27 they were portrayed as enemies of Jesus.

Reviewing Petzke's work, G. Schneider confirmed his conclusion that the special material did not constitute a continuous source, certainly not in the sense of a Proto-Lk (*Literatur zum lukanischen Doppelwerk*, in *TRev* 88 [1992] 1-18, p. 5). Further, some material in the passion narrative reflected a particularly strong redactional portion of Lk which included Lk 23,6-16. Schneider further observed that the question of the origin and unified nature of the Lukan *Sondergut* was the subject of three studies in a brief two year period (p. 18). In addition to Petzke, he referred to B. HEININGER, *Metaphorik, Erzählstruktur und szenisch-dramatische Gestaltung in den Sondergutgleichnissen bei Lukas* (NTA NF 24), Münster, 1991. Diss. Würzburg (dirs. H.-J. KLAUCK and K. MÜLLER), and B. PITTNER, *Studien zum lukanischen Sondergut. Sprachliche, theologische und formkritische Untersuchungen zu Sonderguttexten in Lk 5-19* (ErfTSt 18), Leipzig, 1991. Diss. 1987-88 (dirs. H. SCHÜRMANN and K.-P. MAERZ).

414. In a presentation at the 1991 SBL meeting he briefly reviewed the history of the theory and outlined his own position (T.L. BRODIE, *A Century of Proto-Luke [1891-1991]: Towards Giving New Life to an Old Theory*, unpublished paper, 1991 SBL Meeting, Kansas City, KS). I am grateful that the author made a copy of his paper available to me. It was not intended as a thorough historical study, but concentrated on the inauguration of the hypothesis by Feine, "the classic formulation" by Perry, Streeter and Taylor, and the "revival" by Sahlin, an effort which "faltered" since the author never got beyond Lk chapter 3 (p. 4). Brodie noted that "variations" of Feine's theory were subsequently articulated by Weiss, Spitta and Burton. Brodie highlighted an important methodological difference between Feine on the one hand and the British and

American schools on the other: "The starting-point now was not the hebraic or semitic quality of some of Luke and Acts but something quite different – the relationship of (A) Luke's gospel to the gospel of Mark, and (B) particularly the relationship of Luke's passion narrative to that of Mark" (p. 5, 6). The general relationship between the two Synoptics focused on the alternation of Markan and non-Markan blocks of material, while the attention to the passion narrative relied upon the arguments that the Lukan account was a complete, self-contained unit when the Markan material was omitted and the order, different from that of Mk, suggested another source. Of the latter two considerations, the second was the more convincing for Brodie.

Owing to a century of "sporadic research" the scholarly community had reached no consensus on the Proto-Lk question. Brodie concluded that the line of research pursued by Feine and Sahlin, investigating the Jewish quality of the material, was, practically speaking, "unworkable". The proper methodology must deal with Luke's treatment of Mk. Nevertheless, Brodie saw his solution as a recollection and vindication of Feine.

Brodie distinguished himself from other Proto-Lukan adherents by proposing a new starting point, that of Luke's use of the LXX. What Feine and Sahlin discerned was, in reality, Luke's probable imitation of the Greek OT. Thus, in the course of his argument Brodie equated Semitic with Septuagintal so that evidence of the LXX may also be indication of Proto-Lk. Building on his own previous research, Brodie claimed that the Septuagintal thread runs through the Lukan corpus, from the infancy narrative into Acts. But Brodie did not apply his theory to the passion narrative which he acknowledged was a centerpiece in the whole hypothesis. He only superficially indicated how such was the case within the first four chapters of Lk (p. 14, n. 5). He referred in a note to his previously published articles on this subject: *A New Temple and A New Law*, in *JSNT* 5 (1979) 21-45; *Luke 7,36-50 as an Internalization of 2 Kings 4,1-37: A Study in Luke's Use of Rhetorical Imitation*, in *Bib* 64 (1983) 457-485; *The Accusing and Stoning of Naboth (1 Kgs 21:8-13) as One Component of the Stephen Text (Acts 6:9-14; 7:58a)*, in *CBQ* 45 (1983) 417-432; *Towards Unraveling the Rhetorical Imitation of Sources in Acts: 2 Kgs 5 as One Component of Acts 8:9-40*, in *Bib* 67 (1986) 41-67; *Towards Unravelling Luke's Use of the Old Testament: Luke 7,11-17 as an Imitation of 1 Kings 17:17-24*, in *NTS* 32 (1986) 247-267; *The Departure for Jerusalem (Luke 9,51-56) as a Rhetorical Imitation of Elijah's Departure for the Jordan (2 Kgs 1,1-2,6)*, in *Bib* 70 (1989) 96-109, esp. p. 109: "To the extent that the OT text accounts for Luke's narrative, the hypothesis of a lost 'L' is less necessary – at least as far as Luke 9,51-56 is concerned. Also less necessary is the hypothesis of a lost Hebrew fragment. As so often with alleged semitisms in Luke-Acts, the data may be accounted for as Septuagintisms. Nor is it necessary to envisage Luke as creating the text freely. If his care in synthesizing 2 Kgs 1,1-2,6 is any guide, he seems to have exercised his creativity with immense discipline and fidelity"; *Luke 9:57-62: A Systematic Adaption of the Divine Challenge of Elijah (1 Kings 19)*, in *SBL 1989 Seminar Papers*, 237-245.). He also advanced the idea that the thread began in Lk 1,5-4,30, was continued at 7,1-8,3 resuming at 9,51, though without stating how far it extended from this point.

The solution, as Brodie saw it, required dispensing with internal analysis in favor of comparison with "an outside text" (*Century*, p. 11). In the final analysis, according to Brodie, "the quest for Proto-Luke is not as elusive as it may once have seemed" (p. 14). In a recent contribution on the sources of Jn (1993), Brodie suggested, "as a tentative working hypothesis", that Jn used 22,66-Ch. 24 continuing through Acts 1,1-15,35 (BRODIE, *The Quest for the Origin of John's Gospel. A Source-Oriented Approach*, New York - Oxford, 1993, p. 169). The other Lukan material employed by John was: 1-2; 3,1-6.10-38; 4,14-30; 7,1-8,3; 9,51-10,20; 16,1-9.19-31; 17,11-18,8; 19,1-10; 22,1-30. See also p. 173-176. He took up this matter in: *Reopening the Quest for Proto-Luke. The Systematic Use of Judges 6-12 in Luke 16:1-18:8*, in *The Journal of Higher Criticism* 2 (1995) 68-101. See further: *Intertextuality and Its Use in Tracing Q and Proto-Luke*, in C.M. TUCKETT (ed.), *Scriptures*, 1997, 469-477.

that in addition to Mk, Luke employed L material in his Gospel claiming it was "likely" the evangelist employed additional sources in Lk 22–23[415]. A.J.

415. Writing a commentary which was based on the Greek text and was intended for scholars and laity alike, D.L. BOCK (1994/1996) asserted that "Luke had access to Mark, special material (L), and traditions (which also are reflected in Matthew, though often with some, even significant divergence)" (*Luke 1:1-9:50* [BECNT, 3], Grand Rapids, MI, 1994, p. 9). He further suggested that it was not excluded "that L and Q might have overlapped". See his excursus, "Sources and Synoptic Relationships" (p. 914-917). There he announced that he avoided "taking a firm position" on Markan priority. "The major problem with Markan priority are the Matthean-Lucan agreements against Mark and the issue of certain Lucan omissions of Mark that, if Luke used Mark, are hard to explain ..." (p. 915). He acknowledged his use of the following Lukan commentaries: Marshall, Fitzmyer, Schürmann, Bovon, Plummer, Luce, Ernst, Klostermann, Grundmann, Nolland, Danker, Tiede and C.A. Evans. The commentary by L.T. Johnson and the second and third installments of Nolland's commentary appeared "after [Bock's] manuscript was substantially completed" (p. xii). The introduction to the two-volume commentary was "an updated and expanded version" of his essay *Luke*, in *DJG* (p. 1). In listing Lukan parallels with Mk, Lk 22,54-71 and Lk 23,1-5.18-25 appeared in parentheses indicating that the "dependence was subject to some doubt" (*Luke 1:1-9:50*, p. 9-10). See also his comments on 22,54–23,25 (p. 25-26). L material, drawing his list from C.F. Evans, included 23,6-16 (p. 11-12). Cf. C.F. EVANS, *Saint Luke*, 1990, 26-27. Bock also included 23,6-16 in the category where "a few texts related to Mark also have material from Q or L" (p. 10). In the Prologue Luke was most likely referring to written sources (BOCK, *Luke 1:1-9:50*, p. 56, n. 11).

In the second volume of his detailed commentary (1996) Bock argued that for 22,54-71 Luke "used additional material" (*Luke 9:51-24:53* [BECNT, 3B], Grand Rapids, MI, 1996, p. 1776) based on the difference in order and sparce verbal agreement with Mk. His discussion of those favoring a special source included Fitzmyer (except 22,54-62), Creed (maybe), Marshall, Grundmann, Ernst, Nolland and Green (p. 1776, n. 1). Soards was presented as advocating a "mixture of tradition, Marcan rewriting, and Lucan rewriting". Only Brown was listed as opposing the hypothesis of a special source (aside from oral material).

Bock simply recalled that Brown appealed to oral tradition to explain the MA in 22,62 (/ Mt 26,75) (p. 1788). Cf. BROWN, *Death*, 1994, p. 607). The MA in 22,64 (/ Mt 26,68) was explained as "Luke's source overlaps with Matthew", a solution very similar to that of Marshall (*Luke 9:51-24:53*, p. 1790; see MARSHALL, *Luke*, 1978, p. 846).

Citing Marshall, Ernst, Grundmann, Nolland and Taylor as supporting the hypothesis of a special source in 23,1-5, Bock also referred to the "little vocabulary overlap" between Lk and Mk with the exception of 23,3. This, plus that fact that Luke did not use παραδίδωμι in 23,1, which was found in the Markan account and was frequent in the Lukan passion predictions, led Bock to conclude that Luke employed "addition traditional material" in this section of the Gospel (BOCK, *Luke 9:51-24:53*, p. 1806-1807. MARSHALL, *Luke*, 1978, p. 852; ERNST, *Lukas*, 1977, p. 621; GRUNDMANN, *Lukas*, 1963, p. 421; NOLLAND, *Luke 18:35–24:53*, 1993, p. 1114-1115; and TAYLOR, *Passion Narrative*, 1972, p. 86-87). Opposing arguments by Fitzmyer, Bultmann, Brown, Schneider and Klostermann were rejected (BOCK, *Luke 9:51-24:53*, p. 1807. FITZMYER, *Luke*, p. 1472; BULTMANN, *History*, 1963, p. 272; BROWN, *Death*, p. 736-738; SCHNEIDER, *Lukas*, 1977, p. 471; KLOSTERMANN, *Das Lukasevangelium*, 1929, p. 221-222). It does not appear that Bock favored the idea of a continuous source in the passion narrative: "Thus, it is likely that Luke had access to additional sources, which he expressed in his own words, especially given the likely presence of sources throughout Luke 22-23" (BOCK, *Luke 9:51-24:53*, p. 1807).

Bock assigned 23,13-16 to an independent source based on Aland's placement in the *Synopsis* (BOCK, *Luke 9:51-24:53*, p. 1823; see K. ALAND, *Synopsis*, [13]1985, §338). He asserted that determining the source for 23,18-25 was "more complex", concluding that Luke's use of an additional source in this section was probable (BOCK, *Luke 9:51-24:53*, p. 1825). Those who favored a mixture of a special source with material similar to that found in Mk 15,6-15, such as Marshall, Rengstorf, Grundmann, Ernst and Nolland, were contrasted with Fitzmyer who argued that here Luke rewrote Mk (p. 1824-1825. MARSHALL, *Luke*, 1978, p. 858; RENGSTORF, *Lukas*, 1968, p. 257; GRUNDMANN, *Lukas*, 1963, p. 426-427; ERNST, *Lukas*, 1977, p., 626-627; and NOLLAND, *Luke 18:35-24:53*, 1993, p. 1129. Cf. FITZMYER, *Luke*, p. 1487-1488).

Bock rehearsed various solutions to the source question on the Herod pericope (23,6-12), favoring the view that Luke used a source, possibly Joanna (8,3) or Manaen (Acts 13,1), or even soldiers who were involved in the mockery (BOCK, *Luke 9:51-24:53*, p. 1816-1817). He admitted, however, that "Lukan style does abound in this unit" (p. 1816).

In a less comprehensive commentary which also appeared in 1994 geared toward pastors, students, Bible teachers and small group leaders, Bock interpreted the Prologue (1,1) as indicating that Luke depended upon mostly written sources. (D.L. BOCK, *Luke* [IVP NTCS, 3], Downers Grove, IL - Leicester, 1994, p. 11). As opposed to his previous, more technical commentary, this was described as "a relevant, more accessible effort". Focusing more particularly on the commentaries of Stein and Johnson, Bock regarded this smaller commentary as drawing "on works that update the earlier commentary" (p. 12). "The ambiguity of the term [διήγησις] means that Luke may be referring to more than the sources biblical scholars mention today when they discuss the Synoptic problem (Mark, Q, L, M or Matthew)" (p. 31). He argued that Lk was composed "sometime in the sixties" (p. 19; so also *Luke 1:1-9:50*, p. 18).

More particularly, as regards the passion narrative, Bock did not enter into a discussion about the sources for 22,54-71, though in a note he declared his support for the historicity of this material. "There is much debate about the historicity of the trials tradition. For the most comprehensive studies, all of which evidence a bit more skepticism than I do about all the historical details of this event, see Blinzler, 1969, Winter, 1961 and Catchpole, 1971" (BOCK, *Luke* [IVP NTCS, 3], p. 359). See further the note on the historicity of 22,66 (p. 362-363). For 23,1-5 he believed that in addition to Mk, Luke was employing "additional information" without suggesting from whence it might have derived: "Luke's version is closest to Mark's, but some of the details suggest that Luke had access to additional information" (p. (364-)365). 23,13-16 was unique to Lk while 23,18-25 constituted, in his opinion, a combination of various source materials: "23:13-25 This account mixes unique Lukan elements with traditional ones. Verses 13-16 are unique to Luke, while verses 18-25 appear to be a mixture of unique material and tradition like that in Mark 15:6-15 and Matthew 27:15-26. Elements unique to Luke include the repeated mention of Jesus' innocence. Such details indicate that Luke likely drew on a special source for his account" (p. 368).

Favoring the historicity of the Herod pericope (23,6-12), Bock did not provide any argumentation, simply referring readers to Sherwin-White and Hoehner (p. 366). Cf. SHERWIN-WHITE, *Roman Society*, 1963, 28-32, and HOEHNER, *Why Did Pilate*, 1970, 84-90. This latter article was not included in Bock's bibliography (p. 402). In his discussion of 8,3 he did not refer to Joanna as a possible source for this episode (p. 144-145; so also *Luke 1:1-9:50*, p. 713-714). Borrowing from LEANEY, *Commentary*, 1958, p. 150, Bock noted that Acts 13,1 indicated that Manaen the foster brother of Herod and a member of his "entourage ... had contact with Christians" (p. 714). Bock was undecided as to whether the gorgeous apparel (23,11) suggested a particular color (BOCK, *Luke*, p. 367). The silence of Jesus was reminiscent of Is 53,7 which was explicitly cited in Acts 8,32. Herod's contempt was seen as a fulfillment of the prophecy in 18,32.

SALDARINI (1997), while noting that the historicity of the Herod accounts in Lk are "disputed", nonetheless maintained that "the report of Herod's concern about Jesus as a potential threat to the civic peace is wholly plausible"[416].

A Synthesis of Evidence for a Special Source

Proposing a special continuous, written source to account for many of the non-Markan portions of the Lukan passion narrative, the scholars we studied suggested the following elements as characteristic of such a special source.

The non-Markan material formed a unity and offered a framework, constituting a whole Gospel.

Differences in order: of passages and even of words.

Change of vocabulary: a distinctive Jewish hue may be discerned and the choice of language was unified extending through chapter 12 of Acts. Jewish concepts such as δόξα, δύναμις also occurred.

Treated only the Messiah question in 22,67.

Certain pronouns, which did not accurately reflect shifts from one person to another, may indicate carelessness in the editing of an insertion of material into various contexts.

Change of persons involved in various events: denial of Peter (Mk: a maid and the bystanders; Lk: a maid, and two individual men); the mockery of Jesus (Mk: some of the Sanhedrin; Lk: the guards).

Certain texts (22,57.60), in comparison to A (Urmarkus), reflected a weakening, rather than an intensification of action in the event, which suggested a separate source.

Unexplained omissions: words concerning the Temple; the promise of a vision of the return of the Son of Man.

A further explanation of certain omissions suggested that Luke was using an earlier, and therefore, less complete version of Mk.

Abruptness in the account: certain verses seemed unprepared for, for example 23,18.

The addition of new material: Herod's trial (23,6-16), provided by one or more individuals associated with Herod's court or others.

Based upon this evidence, various scholars advocated the view that Luke utilized a special written source, attributing it to a variety of persons (unknown and beyond hope of rediscovery; the Jerusalem community; Philip the evangelist and his daughters who were prophetesses and ultimately John the Apostle; Joanna, who

---

accompanied Jesus during his ministry). Differences also existed among these exegetes as to when the source was written. Some saw the special source as having been already written before it reached Luke. Still others contended he was responsible for putting it into writing. But the scholars, whatever their view of authorship, were unanimous in ascribing the place of origin to Palestine. In addition, some scholars viewed the special material as deriving from oral sources such as Manaen.

Several of the authors addressed the question whether Lk had been influenced by Ebionites. While some, even among those who argued for Lukan redaction of Mk, maintained there were genuine traces of Ebionism in Lk, others rejected the view, contending either that such influence was the same as in Mk or that the theme of poverty and riches stemmed from Luke himself. Yet others held that it was not possible to clearly define what was meant by the term.

Luke's compositional method according to some of these scholars, consisted in blending the Markan and special source accounts, harmonizing these two versions. Others steadfastly maintained that Luke gave preference to the special source and sparingly filled in a few gaps with material drawn from Mk. Still others were of the opinion that Lk represented the oldest translation of an Aramaic original, which therefore presented the most historical and authentic account of the life and ministry of Jesus. Most contended, with the exception of Harnack who questioned the value of the material provided by the daughters of Philip the evangelist, that the special source portrayed more accurately than Mk the chronological order of events which comprised the passion of Jesus.

Lukan scholars continued to promote the ideas of a separate special source or a Proto-Lk for the passion narrative. One critique made against the latter was that no methodology had been proposed to distinguish the vocabulary of the Proto-Lk from the evangelist. What is perhaps most significant for our survey is the result that several proponents of a special source in the passion account changed their positions and no longer advocated such a view. These included Legassé, Ernst and Green.

CHAPTER TEN

CONTEMPORARY REDACTION CRITICS' DISPENSING
WITH A SPECIAL SOURCE
RAYMOND E. BROWN THROUGH ROBERT S. STEIN

American contributions to the study of Lk-Acts proliferated, which included
Brown's comprehensive analysis of the passion narratives. In contrast to his earlier
position, he no longer supported the idea of a special source. Fitzmyer offered
what many consider to be the best English language commentary on Lk. While he
rejected the idea of a special source and Proto-Lk, he was open to the perspective
that Luke had access to "L", which may have consisted of oral and written
traditions. Matera also has been a major voice but his view is distinct from that of
Brown and Fitzmyer. Matera argued that Luke used only Mk in the composition
of the passion narrative. Johnson, who has written extensively on Lk-Acts,
employed new literary-critical methods, which reflects current directions of NT
scholarship. Other scholars, namely Müller and Buck, focused on the Herod
pericope, which has been an often debated section of the passion narrative.

While it was apparent to Raymond E. BROWN (1970) that Mk served as a source
for portions of the Lukan passion, he was convinced of a special passion source by
the "thesis ably presented by A.M. Perry"[1]. Brown offered no reasons for his
conclusion. More recently, he reversed himself: "In *Death of the Messiah* I favor
the thesis of those scholars who do not think there is enough evidence to posit a
special preLucan PN"[2].

Brown (1994) recently published a massive two-volume work on the passion
narratives, the fruit of ten years of scholarship[3]. What is perhaps most significant

---

1. R.E. BROWN, *The Gospel According to John (xii-xxi)* (AB 29A), Garden City, NY, 1970,
790-791. He listed B. Weiss, Spitta, Burkitt, Easton, Streeter, Taylor, Jeremias, Benoit and
Winter as advocates of this view.

2. BROWN, *1993 SNTS Seminar Paper*, n. 16. Brown was referring to his book, *The Death
of the Messiah*, which was published in 1994. In a 1986 article he passed over the source
question, promising to treat it in depth in this book, the publication of which he had expected in
1991 (*The Passion according to Luke*, in *Worship* 60 [1986] 2). See below.

3. *The Death of the Messiah from Gethsemane to the Grave: A Commentary on the Passion
Narratives of the Four Gospels* (ABRL), 2 vols., New York, 1994. Early reception of the work
was extremely positive: P. PERKINS, *America* (Feb. 19, 1994) 19-21. She mistakenly listed the
number of total pages. It appears she was working from pre-publication gallies; L.T. JOHNSON,
in *Commonweal* (May 20, 1994) 25-27. For an in-depth analysis, see F. NEIRYNCK, *Gospel Issues
in the Passion Narratives. Critical Note on a New Commentary*, in *ETL* 70 (1994) 406-416. See
also J.M. HARRINGTON, *LouvSt* 21 (1996) 87-90.

Commentaries which Brown deemed significant for his investigation included Fitzmyer,
Grundmann, Marshall, Plummer, Schneider and Schweizer. The structure of Brown's work was:

for our study was the reversal of his position on the issue of the special Lukan passion source. Although he previously supported the hypothesis (1970), he now abandoned it[4]. Also cited were Hawkins and Schneider as two other scholars whose writings reflected the same change[5]. Advocates of a special source theory[6] were contrasted with those who held that Luke redacted Mk possibly drawing on special traditions[7].

Throughout he consistently looked also at Acts comparing and contrasting the material with Lk[8], a focal point being the trials of Stephen[9] and Paul[10] in parallel

---

an introduction which detailed his perspective, followed by a section on issues pertinent to the passion narratives including a discussion of the possible sources of Luke's account. The third part of the introduction contained a general bibliography. (Sectional bibliographies were also provided *in loco*). Next, he divided the passion into four "Acts" (Prayer/arrest; Jewish trial; Roman trial, Crucifixion/burial), some having two "Scenes". Literal translations of the accounts were provided, followed by comment and analysis. Rounding out the work were appendixes and indexes (the bibliographical index was keyed to nearly all the authors of works cited as well as the Gospel Passage Index which included the text of each Gospel printed consecutively in the order of Mk, Mt, Lk and Jn, p. 1583-1608) indicating the principal comments on individual passages (p. viii-x). Of particular importance was Appendix I, p. 1317-1349, which treated the GP.

In the section entitled *General Observations on the Lucan Special Material* he mentioned Feine and J. Weiss but their works (Feine's articles and book 1891 and Weiss's Lukan commentary ⁸1892) were not included in the index or bibliography. Brown mentioned J. Weiss's commentary on Mk in *Schriften*, 1905 (p. 98). See further, p. 67, n. 71. Also missing were Streeter's article (1921), *The Four Gospels* and the name of Wernle and his works.

4. BROWN, *Death*, p. 67. Some hesitation was indicated: "There is no way to solve the source issue with any certitude ...". See the reference to his change of position on the source question for the denial scene, explaining that he "had not studied the issue in detail when, in a passing comment, I favored the opposite stance in BGJ (= *John*) 2.837" (p. 611, n. 43).

5. BROWN, *Death*, p. 67. See also p. 32: "When Schneider still held the thesis that there was a special preLucan PN".

6. *Ibid.*, p. 66, n. 70. These included Bacon, Bammel, Bartlet, Black, Burkitt, Easton, Ernst, Feine, F. Grant, Green, Grundmann, Haenchen, Hawkins, Jeremias, Kuhn, Lagrange, Lescow, Marshall, Perry, Rehkopf, Sanday, Schlatter, Schürmann, Schweizer, Spitta, Streeter, Taylor, B. Weiss, J. Weiss, and Winter.

7. *Ibid.*, p. 67, n. 72. Advocates of Lukan redaction of Mk without a special Lukan passion source included Blinzler, Büchele, Dibelius, Finegan, Fitzmyer, Holtzmann, Lietzmann, Lightfoot, Linnemann, Matera, Schmidt, Schneider, Soards, and Untergassmair.

8. *Ibid.*, p. 432: "In diagnosing Luke's composition, however, we should not forget the comparison between Luke and Acts", as he insisted in his discussion of 22,66. Note also the literal translation of 22,66 was followed immediately by a translation of Acts 6,12-14 (p. 429). See further p. 363, n. 78, 424, n. 33, 504, 505, 519, 521, 527-528, 756.

9. As for example, p. 434: "We note that in Acts 6,13-14 Luke will use much the same stereotyped language to depict the tactics of Stephen's opponents". See also p. 437, 463. In his recent study of christology Brown listed Acts 6,13-14 in place of Lk in Gospel parallels with Mk 14,57-58 / Mt 26,60-61 / Jn 2,19-21 concerning Jesus' prediction of the destruction of the sanctuary. He noted the similarity between Mk and Acts. "Both Mark and Acts suggest that there was an element of falsehood in the Jewish attribution of the statement to Jesus – probably in the way the statement was taken by those who scoffed at Christians, viz., to mean physical

with those of Jesus. On the issue of whether Paul's life may have influenced the account of Jesus, he maintained initially that it is hard to know which way the influence went[11]. However, later Brown affirmed the influence from Paul to Jesus as his own position[12].

Markan priority was regarded as the majority scholarly view. In a general comparison between Mk and Lk, the Lukan presentation was considered to be more positive, in contrast to the "victimization and failure" found in Mk and Mt, and Jesus was portrayed more as a prophet in Lk than in Mk[13]. In speaking of the differences he used the categories of additions[14], omissions, transpositions and substitutions[15]. With regard to omissions in the Gospel, because Luke authored both the Gospel and Acts, he exercised greater freedom in the placement of the material. Additions or expansions of Mk were variously explained as: 1) Lukan creativity; 2) traditions "most often probably oral"; and 3) the evangelist's desire to create parallels between Jesus and Paul. As regards the special Lukan material[16], he was in significant agreement with Soards[17], maintaining there was no special source[18], but differences resulted from Luke's own composition coupled with oral tradition. Luke was variously said to simplify[19], modify and abbreviate[20] the Markan account of the passion[21].

---

destruction by Jesus himself or his rebuilding a material sanctuary like the one destroyed" (*An Introduction to New Testament Christology*, New York - Mahwah, NJ, 1994, p. 51).

10. BROWN, *Death*, p. 738, with reference to RADL, *Paulus*, 211-220.

11. BROWN, *Death*, p. 74-75. In a note he wrote: "It is not impossible that a similar significant detail may have been present in early Christian tradition both about Jesus and about Stephen or Paul; but such a coincidence would hardly explain all the parallels" (p. 75, n. 89). See also p. 401, n. 3. It will be remembered that Matera and others suggested that the influence was in the direction from Paul to Jesus.

12. *Ibid.*, p. 756: "Within Luke-Acts the influence most likely came from Paul's trial to Jesus' trial, rather than vice versa". He drew on S.G. WILSON, *The Jews*, p. 162-164. Examples included 23,2 apparently influenced by Acts 24,5-6; likewise 23,6-7.11b-12 by Acts 25,13ff. (p. 782, n. 40). Consider p. 738: "Luke may have had a source for the trial of Paul; certainly he had popular knowledge of how Roman gubernatorial trials were conducted; and he is following that pattern for both Jesus and Paul".

13. BROWN, *Death*, p. 30, 31.

14. Regarding examples in 22,63-65, "there is no need to posit a special source for such additions" (p. 583).

15. Other ways in which Luke was thought to have changed Mk were to portray sincerity (p. 600), simplification (p. 602), softening harshness (p. 605) to avoid reporting the indignity of Jesus (p. 634) or physical violence (p. 852).

16. *Ibid.*, p. 64-75, which contained a discussion of L (or S).

17. *Ibid.*, p. 75. See SOARDS, *Passion*, p. 116.

18. See also BROWN, *Death*, p. 91, n. 120, and p. 307, n. 8 (concerning the arrest of Jesus in Lk 22,47-53).

19. As in the case of Luke's presentation of only one Sanhedrin trial (p. 423, n. 31).

20. *Ibid.*, p. 431: "Luke has been abbreviating Mark throughout the PN". On omissions see for example p. 989, n. 15.

21. See p. 1325: "In the canonical Gospel PNs, we have an example of Matt working

On the issue of the phenomenon of order he subscribed to the view that Luke transposed Markan material to improve "the logic of the narrative"[22] and the "Markan sequence and plausibility"[23]. Subsequently, he asserted "that Luke depends on the Marcan PN and at times has purposely changed the Marcan order"[24].

Brown defined 22,39–23,56 as the passion narrative, though he granted that the majority of scholars referred to Lk 22–23[25]. He distinguished between a source, understood as a sequential and probably written document, and tradition which was described as isolated items of information[26]. Luke was occasionally faulted for editing that "produced problems that he did not notice"[27]. We turn now to examine 22,54–23,25 to see how Brown applied his theory in practice.

He concluded, as Soards had, that for the denials (22,54b-62) Luke was dependent upon Mk[28]. The mockery (22,63-65) also reflected Lukan dependence upon Mk supplemented with oral tradition "in certain well-remembered phrases"[29]. Several source-critical attempts were roundly criticized. Bultmann was faulted for dissecting the verses to arrive at different sources for each. Benoit, who judged the Lukan account to be the more original, offered a "very complicated theory". Flusser was seen "confusingly mixing the historical and Gospel levels".

---

conservatively and Luke working more freely with the Marcan outline and of each adding material ...". See also p. 555, n. 16.

22. *Ibid.*, p. 64. See also p. 67, 422.

23. *Ibid.*, p. 69. See further p. 74, 488.

24. *Ibid.*, p. 83, n. 106. To which he added: "But one wonders whether the different Lucan placing of Peter's denials (before the Sanhedrin session) and of the Roman mockery (while Jesus is on the cross) was not facilitated by the memory that the placement was not fixed in early tradition".

25. *Ibid.*, p. 39.

26. *Ibid.*, p. 66. He further distinguished between PreGospel oral tradition which he considered certain and preGospel written tradition which was questionable in his mind (p. 68, n. 74).

27. *Ibid.*, p. 71. Examples included "they" in 22,54; αὐτόν in 22,63. So also p. 858: "Luke was unobservant" in some of his changes. At other times, Luke's rearrangement of material gave rise to some confusion (p. 582; see also p. 915, n. 8).

28. *Ibid.*, p. 611. Brown listed Bultmann, Catchpole, Dodd, Grundmann, G. Klein and Rengstorf as proponents of a special source for the denials, with Finegan, Fitzmyer, Linnemann, Schneider and Soards as defending dependence upon Mk, while Taylor, generally a defender of the special source theory, recognized a high proportion of Markan vocabulary scattered throughout (p. 610-611). For brief and general comments on Luke's redaction of the Markan account of the denials see also P. PERKINS, *Peter. Apostle for the Whole Church* (SPNT), Columbia, SC, 1994, p. 18, 31, 86-87.

29. BROWN, *Death*, p. 573. Supporters of a special source in this pericope included Bussmann, Grundmann, Plummer, Streeter, Taylor and Winter. Among the opponents were counted Creed, Finegan, Schneider and Soards (p. 581). Yet Brown admitted his solution was not without two remaining problems: the absence of the echoes of Is 50,6 and the "exact logic of 'prophecy'". Another clue to Lukan redaction was that Luke modified the passion prediction in 18,32-33 and 22,63-65 corresponded to this (p. 582).

The idea of a special source for 22,66 was further rejected in favor of the view that Luke was simplifying Mk, a judgment supported by the research of Légasse[30]. Brown was of the conviction that 22,67-68 stemmed from an independent tradition[31]. With regard to 22,69-71 he believed Luke was employing Markan material and did not have information from any independent tradition[32]. On the question whether what was described in 22,66-71 was a trial or a preliminary hearing, he contended it was the former based on evidence from Lk-Acts that Luke assumed a judgment against Jesus which also had been communicated through apostolic preaching[33].

Lk 23,1-25 was not only seen as an overall unity but judged it to be a significant redaction of Mk[34]. Lk 23,2-5 was considered an Lukan expansion of Mk 15,2-5[35]. Lk 23,17 was a copyist's gloss, while 23,13-16 was a Lukan

---

30. *Ibid.*, p. 431-432. Cf. LÉGASSE, *Jésus*, p. 192-194. Brown concurred with Schneider that Acts 6,14 reflected Luke's redaction of the remarks about the Temple (Mk 14,58) (p. 435, n. 13; see further p. 437, n. 14, p. 557, n. 27 and p. 989, n. 15). Brown contended Luke transferred the Markan trial to the morning (p. 603, n. 24).

31. BROWN, *Death*, p. 528. However, it should be noted that in another work published also in 1994, Brown stated Luke was responsible for the division of the questions and no reference was made to an independent tradition as source (*Introduction*, 1994, p. 77: "Luke, who separates the question of the Messiah from the question about the Son of God, has a very ambiguous answer to the Messiah query ...". In his study of the passion narratives Fitzmyer and Schneider were cited as holding similar views (*Death*, p. 485). See also his comments, p. 424. He arrived at this conclusion based on the lack of evidence for a continuous source as well as the Johannine parallels with Lk 22,67-68 (p. 548, n. 1). Note the similarity with Schneider's position (*Verleugnung*, p. 138; *Das Verfahren*, p. 117-118 = *Jesusüberlieferung*, p. 292-283). On the matter of the Sanhedrin's competence to execute, Brown maintained that it did have the power for certain clear cases of religious offenses, but not in the case of Jesus (p. 371). See Neirynck's response to Schneider that this reflected Lukan redaction (*ETL* 48 [1972] 572).

Matera (*Luke 22*) was critiqued for not having treated 22,67 as carefully as Soards (p. 485, n. 2; cf. SOARDS, *Passion*, p. 103-104). Once again Légasse was credited by Brown with detecting the un-Lukan style of the conditional sentence in 22,67, though the similarity with Jn 10,24-25 was most convincing (p. 486; cf. LÉGASSE, *Jésus*, p. 183).

32. BROWN, *Death*, p. 528. The Sanhedrin decision to put Jesus to death was transferred from 22,71 to Lk 24,20 and Acts 13,27-28. Further, Acts 6-7 recounted that Stephen was killed for witnessing on behalf of Jesus (p. 555, n. 19). In his recent christological study Brown commented on Mk 14,62 adding in a note: "Matt 26:64 and Luke 22:69 (each in its own phrasing) modify the verb in this saying with an adverbial phrase: 'from now on.' Luke omits the reference to the *coming* of the Son of Man, perhaps because the saying seemed to imply an immediate Parousia" (*Introduction*, 1994, p. 53, n. 65).

33. Brown, *Death*, p. 528. See also p. 736, 757, n. 52. Brown included 23,1 in the material pertaining to the Sanhedrin trial "since it is an unbroken part of that session" (p. 633).

34. *Ibid.*, p. 756.

35. *Ibid.*, p. 737. This position was in line with Creed, Dibelius, Fitzmyer, Klostermann and Schneider. However, for the triple declarations of innocence which included 23,4, Brown suggested that Luke may be drawing upon a common, non-Markan tradition with Jn since the threefold declaration was also found in Jn 18,38b; 19,4.6 (p. 742, 756).

composition and 23,18-19 was seen as "a major abbreviation of Mark"[36]. Further, 23,20-22 was a redaction of Mk 15,12-14a though some scholars believed that the duplication of the plea to crucify (23,21) possibly stemmed from a tradition common to Lk and Jn[37]. Lk 23,23 reflected an intensification over Mk 15,14b[38]. Finally, 23,24-25 was a reworking of βουλόμενος τῷ ὄχλῳ τὸ ἱκανὸν ποιῆσαι (Mk 15,15) to clarify the responsibility of the Jews[39].

For the MA 22,62 / Mt 26,75, after acknowledging that one solution was that the text from Mt was interpolated into Lk, Brown appealed to Soards's solution as more plausible that both Luke and Matthew drew on oral tradition[40]. The solution of Neirynck and Senior to explain the MA in 22,64 / Mt 26,68 as copyists' addition in Mt 26,68 was described as unnecessary. He opted once again for independent oral influence from an established game in antiquity[41].

In his discussion of Jesus before Herod (23,6-12)[42] he noted that not only was the surrounding context into which the story had been inserted similar to Mk but the pericope "fits smoothly into the Lucan sequence"[43]. Herod, like Pilate, served as a witness to the innocence of Jesus[44]. He argued that the passage had been

He adopted the view there was one overall charge with two specific examples (p. 738, 741), a view to which Schneider also subscribed: "Wahrscheinlich sind die drei erwähnten Punkte so zu verstehen, dass der erste (Volksverführung) durch die beiden folgenden spezifiziert wird (Verweigerung der Kaisersteuer, Messiasanspruch)" (*Das Verfahren*, p. 122 = *Jesus-überlieferung*, 287). Consider p. 739: "In Acts a similar charge is made against Paul in varying vocabulary".

36. BROWN, *Death*, p. 789. Verse 19 was repeated in 23,25, a verse in which Luke was attempting to make explicit what was only implied in Mk/Mt (p. 850).

37. *Ibid.*, p. 825, 826.

38. *Ibid.*, p. 831.

39. *Ibid.*, p. 856. See also p. 860, where Brown attested that Luke obtained the tradition about the Roman trial from Mk.

40. *Ibid.*, p. 609. See also p. 611, n. 43: "an oral memory of the preGospel tradition".

41. *Ibid.*, p. 45, as well as his general discussion of the MAs (p. 43-45). Brown did not provide any bibliographical information for Neirynck and Senior. He observed that the position of Stein on the MAs also involved the evangelists's use of oral tradition (p. 44, n. 21; see STEIN, *The Matthew-Luke Agreements*, esp. p. 501). Note Brown's specific reference to 22,64 (p. 583, 585).

42. BROWN, *Death*, p. 760-786. Cf. p. 70, where 23,6-16 was termed "a major Lukan addition". Contra Neyrey, this pericope was not a separate trial, since in Lk "clearly Pilate remains the presiding judge" (p. 783, n. 43). In his study of NT christology Brown called attention to the Synoptic tradition wherein Jesus refused to perform any miracle in those situations where he was asked to "show off" simply so that people might admire him. Lk 23,6-9 was listed together with Mt 4,5-7; Mk 8,11-13; Mt 12,38-42; Mk 15,31-32; Mk 6,1-6 as examples of Jesus' reluctance (*Introduction*, 1994, p. 64, n. 83). In Mk 6,1-6, which precedes the Markan account of the death of the Baptist as ordered by Herod (Mk 6,14-29), Jesus was portrayed as a prophet.

43. BROWN, *Death*, p. 760-761. He claimed the pericope could begin either at 23,4 or 23,6 because of the smoothness (p. 761).

44. *Ibid.*, p. 742. So also p. 809: "We saw in §33 that the Herod scene draws on tradition about Herodian opposition to Jesus with a modification to make Herod a reluctant witness of

composed by Luke on the basis of an early tradition[45] which referred to Herod's hostility towards Jesus and was embellished by three additions: 1) Markan material which included the questioning of Jesus, his silence[46] and the mockery[47]; 2) a schema similar to that in Acts 25,13–26,32; and 3) earlier sayings about Herod in Lk especially 13,31-33[48]. Once again he agreed "substantially with Soards"[49]. Insisting that both Joüon and Grundmann presented "very tenuous evidence" for their respective interpretations of the gorgeous apparel, Brown seemed to favor the view that it was a sign of innocence as well as a form of mockery[50].

Jesus' innocence". Pilate requested that Herod perform a preliminary investigation (p. 743, 766). On the difficult question of why Pilate would have transferred Jesus to Herod it was suggested that it "might have been an ingenious diplomatic way to neutralize the tetrarch and prevent further trouble" (p. 767).

Brown argued that in 23,4.14.22 and Jn 18,38b; 19,4.6 the respective evangelists may be drawing on a common, non-Markan tradition. (p. 742, 756). But should this not be seen in the light of the following consideration. "Since we shall see in the Marcan crucifixion narrative several patterns of three, one cannot reject this theory in principle, even though such a consistent pattern as Büchele proposes is very hard to discern" (p. 757). As Brown himself pointed out the patterns of three is found in earlier portions of the Markan passion narrative (n. 51). He later admitted some were genuine (p. 931, n. 32).

Neyrey's fourfold division of the trials was judged as artificial and contrary to Acts 25,17–26,32 and thus rejected (p. 757; cf. NEYREY, Passion, p. 69, 98).

45. At one point Joanna (8,3) and Manaen (Acts 13,1) were mentioned as "possible channels of Luke's information" (BROWN, Death, p. 764, n. 7). Even if Luke was in possession of a special tradition, his motivation may have been to demonstrate resemblance between the lives of Jesus and Paul: "Luke may have had independent tradition supporting his inclusion of Herod Antipas in the Roman trial of Jesus, but his main interest may have been to establish a parallel between this scene aligning the prefect Pilate and Herod as judges of Jesus and the scene in Acts 25-26 aligning the procurator Festus and the Herodian Agrippa II as judges of Paul. Such heavy religious coloring means that the few trial features that are recounted in the Gospels cast little light on the historical motives of those involved" (p. 711).

46. See p. 772. Since it was believed that Luke transferred the reference to Jesus' silence to Herod's trial, the following remark was appropriate: "Is Jesus' silence before Pilate in the Synoptics a historical fact, namely he answered the legitimate question of the governor about his identity as a king but was contemptuously silent about the false charges that the Sanhedrin members urged on Pilate? Or is it a theological motif, e.g. Isa. 53:7: 'He opened not his mouth'? Or is it both historical and theological?" (p. 711, n. 85).

47. Though Luke omitted the Roman mockery (Mk 15,16-20), he nevertheless included a mockery by Roman soldiers in 23,36-37 (p. 782, n. 39; see also p. 583). One should take note of Brown's assertion that "we must take into account Luke's habit of drawing upon the vocabulary of other Marcan passages that he has omitted" (p. 581).

48. Ibid., p. 782. Brown rehearsed three solutions. The first was that Luke had drawn the story from a source, variously configured, the second which Brown adopted, and the third that Luke created the account perhaps either on the basis of Ps 2 or Paul's trial before Agrippa (p. 779).

49. Ibid., p. 782, n. 38. On various disagreements with Walaskay see p. 390, n. 144, p. 783, n. 42 and p. 853, n. 58.

50. Ibid., p. 775-776.

He also tackled the issue of the relation of Lk 23,6-12 to Acts 4,25-28 stating: "While the approaches to Herod's role in Lk 23 and Acts 4 are different, one should not treat them as contradictory [...]. The fact that Justin has both approaches [...] suggests that they were not seen in total conflict"[51]. Along that line, "while they give different pictures of how Jesus was dealt with, [they] agree on cooperation between Pilate and Herod, so that Luke did not waver on that point"[52]. The Gospel account too may be related in such a way as to prepare for Acts 4[53].

Brown's commentary was a significant milestone in the study of the passion narratives. His evident breadth of knowledge and erudition as well as his ability to communicate his research makes this an indispensable tool for scholarly and pastoral investigation. As we have seen throughout our survey, some studies were limited only to the Synoptic accounts, as with Schneider and Matera[54]. Brown, like Senior, also contributed to Johannine passion studies, but unlike Senior, "works through the passion 'horizontally,' studying each episode in all four Gospels simultaneously"[55]. Further, I share Brown's views about the value of some of the new literary studies[56]. His methodological insights, such as being attentive to the Lukan use of Markan vocabulary in passages which Luke omitted, help to strengthen exegesis. He is to be commended not only for his attention to Acts, especially in the parallels with Stephen and Paul, but also for the willingness to reexamine his previous positions, such as Luke's use of a special source. The frequent appeal to oral tradition, however, as an all-purpose solution for special

---

51. *Ibid.*, p. 781, n. 35. See also his earlier comment, p. 71, n. 81, as well as p. 763, 777, 778. On a related matter, an echo of Ps 42,6-7 was found in Mk 14,34 and Jn 12,27. In this regard he wrote: "To recapitulate, I posit that early Christians had a tradition that before he died Jesus struggled in prayer about his fate. I do not know whether they retained or claimed to retain accurate memories of the wording he used; more probably they did not. But they understood his prayer in terms like the hour and the cup, which in the tradition of his sayings he had used to describe his destiny in God's plan. They fleshed out the prayer tradition in light of the psalms and of their own prayers, both of which they associated with Jesus' way of praying" (p. 225-226). To this he appended: "Many have reacted against Dibelius's contention that psalm reflection gave rise to the event described [...]. The fact that Hebrews and Mark/John use different psalms (respectively 116 and 42) suggests that a basic tradition was being developed, not created" (p. 225, n. 17).

52. *Ibid.*, p. 777. See also p. 390, n. 144.

53. *Ibid.*, p. 778. So DARR, *Glorification* [sic], p. 304.

54. Cf. SCHNEIDER, *Die Passion Jesu*, and MATERA, *Passion Narratives*.

55. BROWN, *Death*, p. viii. Some differences may also be accounted for, in part, by their intended audiences. He referred to Senior's study (*Death*, p. 106). Cf. Senior's comment, *The Passion of Jesus in the Gospel of John*, Collegeville, MN - Herefordshire, 1991, p. 9: "Surprisingly, however, few books have been devoted exclusively to John's Passion narrative".

56. BROWN, *Death*, p. 12: "Although I shall stress the narrative aspect, I do not pretend to apply in my study the technicalities of structural and/or literary criticism. I have read literature on the passion from experts in those fields and I am not overly impressed by the results some have achieved. To my embarrassment, at times the jargon of the hermeneutical specialization leaves me behind".

Lukan material as well as for MAs might also be reconsidered. Could not Lukan redaction more adequately explain many of these elements?

Brown's position on the source question in the passion narrative, which also involved a consideration of an argument from order, as elaborated in *An Introduction to the New Testament* (1997) was that Luke drew on Mk and "some special traditions"[57]. Among these he included material related to Herod which he described as "particular items of tradition or information" concerning Herod[58]. The Herod pericope (23,6-12) is both a "continuation of the special Herod material" [9,7-9; 13,31-32; 23,6-12] and an "anticipatory parallel to the trial in Acts 25–26"[59]. He conjectured that such material "probably" stemmed from oral sources such as Manaen (Acts 13,1)[60].

Although Joseph A. FITZMYER (1970) disclaimed any special competence in the area of the synoptic problem, he reaffirmed his belief in Markan priority, while at the same time stating that the problem was "practically insoluable"[61]. He also wrote that some material inserted from the Double Tradition or Luke's special source did not "affect the common order". Even what he termed the "so-called transpositions" in referring to a minimum of five places where Mk and Lk had varying order, were better explained as intentional changes on the part of Luke than of Mark[62].

Fitzmyer referred to Streeter's attempt at a solution for the MAs and recalled the latter's characterization of the MA in 22,64 / Mt 26,28 as "'the most remarkable of the minor agreements'"[63].

In considering the theories of Vaganay and Léon-Dufour, Fitzmyer noted this similarity: "The solutions of L. Vaganay and X. Léon-Dufour have in common a desire to give more place to oral tradition in the formation of the Synoptic Gospels"[64]. He also critiqued Farmer's renewal of the Griesbach hypothesis[65].

57. *An Introduction to the New Testament* (ABRL), New York - London, 1997, p. 255: "We have seen that when Luke follows Mark, he does so with substantial fidelity; but the passion narrative is an exception. Although many scholars posit dependence on a special preLucan passion narrative separate from Mark, a more plausible case can be made for Luke's dependence on Mark combined with some special traditions. Here Luke may simply have done more reordering than elsewhere, perhaps in a desire to make this most important narrative more effective".

58. See p. 267.

59. *Ibid.*, p. 258-259.

60. *Ibid.*, p. 267.

61. J.A. FITZMYER, *The Priority of Mark and the "Q" Source in Luke*, in *Jesus and Man's Hope* (Pittsburgh Festival for the Gospels), Vol. 1, Pittsburgh, PA, 1970, p. 131, 132.

62. *Ibid.*, p. 138.

63. *Ibid.*, p. 144.

64. *Ibid.*, p. 156.

65. *Ibid.*, p. 158-162.

His two-volume Lukan commentary appeared in 1981/1985[66]. Fitzmyer assigned the date of the composition of the Gospel to 80-85 AD, at a place outside Palestine[67]. He identified himself as an adherent of a modified form of the Two-Source theory. "I prefer to speak of the modified Two-Source Theory, a variation on the title used in English, chosen to manifest at once its dependence on the classic Two-Document Hypothesis, but also to allow for a further understanding of 'L' and 'M' as *not necessarily written*"[68]. While this assumption did not exclude the possibility that Luke composed some of the material, Fitzmyer conceded it was impossible to distinguish between "L" and Luke's free composition, though the latter was often indicated by "characteristic Lucan style"[69].

Four reasons were offered for Markan priority: 1) a great deal of common material; 2) the order observed was Markan even at points where there were additions or omissions; 3) identical words within passages; and 4) Mk contained a "more primitive character"[70].

In his discussion of the transpositions, Fitzmyer referred explicitly to the change in order in 22,54-71 for which the evangelist was responsible in order to unify the material dealing with Peter and to present only one Sanhedrin hearing[71].

Fitzmyer reviewed the Proto-Lk hypothesis and provided a partial list of those who favored and opposed it. He offered seven "difficulties" in opposition to it. One particularly applicable for the study of the passion narrative was the unconvincing nature of the attempts to isolate special pre-Lukan vocabulary. Another was recalling H. Montefiore's query whether the text of Proto-Lk could have survived a shipwreck[72].

---

66. FITZMYER, *The Gospel According to Luke*, 2 vols., Garden City, NY, 1981/1985.

67. *Ibid.*, p. 57.

68. *Ibid.*, p. 64. Fitzmyer ascribed 22,63-71(?); 23,6-12.13-16 to "L" (p. 84).

69. *Ibid.*, p. 83. John P. MEIER (1991) viewed the special sources L and M to be "two minor and problematic sources" (*A Marginal Jew. Rethinking the Historical Jesus. Vol. 1. The Roots of the Problem and the Person* [ABRL], New York -London, 1991, p. 44). He referred the reader to FITZMYER, *Luke*, p. 82-91, for a treatment of the special Lukan material (MEIER, *Marginal*, p. 53, n. 19). Any judgment on their historical value was difficult due to a lack of parallels.

70. FITZMYER, *Luke*, p. 66-69.

71. *Ibid.*, 71. Of his position he wrote further: "The arguments against the transpositions have been well analyzed by F. Neirynck, and need not be rehearsed here. I am basically in agreement with his approach both to the transpositions and the Lucan Passion narrative" (p. 72).

72. *Ibid.*, p. 91. See H. MONTEFIORE, *Does 'L' Hold Water?*, in *JTS* 12 (1961) 59-60. Like H.C. KEE, *Jesus in History*, Fitzmyer referred readers to Kümmel's *Introduction*, p. 132-137, for further study. Kee took the view that Luke redacted Mk's passion adding materials from oral and written traditions and refashioned the account in line with his theological concerns (*Jesus in History*, New York, 1970, ²1977, p. 206). No refutation of the special source theory was offered, except by way of reference to Kümmel's rebuttal (KEE, *Jesus*, p. 206, n. 23; see also p. 304. Cf. KÜMMEL, *Introduction*, 1975, p. 131-137). John Meier considered the question of Proto-Lk to be "a special problem" (MEIER, *Marginal*, p. 53, n. 21). He rejected the view of a special source and called for caution in attributing differences to "large amounts of pre-Lucan oral or written

In his commentary, generally regarded as the finest contemporary English language commentary on Lk, Fitzmyer defined the passion narrative as 22,1–23,56a[73]. Following a review of the development of such tradition, he focused on the theological and apologetical motifs present in this section of the Gospel. Among the former were: 1) the dominance of faith in the risen Christ; 2) the accomplishment of God's will; and 3) the tendency to hint at a more-than-human condition of Jesus. Luke's apologetic interests were reflected in: 1) the emergence of declarations of Jesus' innocence; 2) the tendency to exculpate the Roman prefect Pontius Pilate and to inculpate the Jewish leaders[74]; and 3) the tendency to excuse the desertion of the disciples. Fitzmyer regarded the account of Stephen's death (Acts 7,54-8,1) as imitating that of Jesus, part of the hortatory nature of the passion narrative. Fitzmyer regarded the omissions and additions to not be so significant as to challenge the view that Luke based his account on that of Mk[75]. Even the Markan order served to guide Luke in his account.

Fitzmyer observed the number of scholars favoring a special source was about the same as those opposed[76]. Unlike Taylor who considered the low percentage of Markan vocabulary to be indicative of a special source, Fitzmyer judged that Luke more thoroughly revised Mk. His dismissal of the special source theory was based on two criteria: rejection of three reasons advanced in favor of the theory and the strong similarity of order between Mk and the supposed source[77]. The view of the portrayal of the death of Jesus as a martyrdom was adopted as was the perception that Jesus was the example of innocent suffering to be imitated.

The matter of the transposition of the Markan materials in 22,54-71 was also closely related to the question of historicity[78]. Concerning the difference in timing

---

material" in the Lukan passion narrative as Soards and Matera had done (MEIER, p. 420, n. 60. He had in mind SOARDS, *Passion*, and MATERA, *The Death of Jesus*). Many of the differences between Mk and Lk can be assigned to Lukan redaction. Meier directed readers to Fitzmyer for reasons for rejecting Proto-Lk (MEIER, p. [420]-421, n. 60; see FITZMYER, *Luke*, p. 89-91).

73. FITZMYER, *Luke*, p. 1359. He subdivided the Lukan passion narrative into a further twenty units (p. 141-142).

74. *Ibid.* This theme was present in much of Lk 22-23.

75. *Ibid.*, p. 1365. New material was ascribed to L, redacted Markan material or Lukan compositions. Only in the case of 22,28-30 had Q been designated as the source.

76. *Ibid.*, p. 1365-1366. The supporters included: E. Bammel, P. Benoit, M. Black, R.E. Brown, F.C. Burkitt, B.S. Easton, A. George, J. Hawkins, J. Jeremias, A.M. Perry, F. Rehkopf, F. Spitta, B.H. Streeter, V. Taylor, B. Weiss and P. Winter. He counted J. Blinzler, R. Bultmann, J.M. Creed, M. Dibelius, J. Finegan, H.J. Holtzmann, G. Iber, H.C. Kee, H. Lietzmann, R.H. Lightfoot, A. Loisy, and G. Schneider among the opponents and he identified himself with this group.

77. *Ibid.*, p. 1364. The three reasons in support of the source were not completely convincing. These were: a great deal of special, non-Markan material; shared accounts in Lk and Jn; low verbal correspondence with Mk.

78. On the related question of responsibility for the death of Jesus, Fitzmyer sided with those who saw the Roman governor as the person responsible, though the religious leaders participated (p. 1456).

between the Markan and Lukan accounts Fitzmyer said simply that Luke "preserved a better recollection of the time". He held the story of Peter's denials (22,54-62) to be a redaction of Mk (Mk 14,53-54.66-72). Mk was the sole source for 22,54-60.61b. Contrary to B. Weiss's later judgment, Fitzmyer accepted that συλλαβόντες derived from Mk 14,48. Evidence of Lukan redaction was signaled by the use of preferred terms, omissions, and simplification. Luke's account was "more official" than Mark's because of the two male witnesses which recalled Dt 19,15.

The origin of vv. 61a and 62 was not so easily solved. Fitzmyer concluded Luke himself probably composed v. 61a. The MA in v. 62 was perhaps derived from L although Fitzmyer also reckoned with the possibility that Luke wrote it[79].

Fitzmyer straddled the fence when he claimed L was also regarded by the majority of scholars as the source for the mockery (22,63-65), though the scene was inspired by Mk and Luke was responsible for the transposition. His "majority" was made up of those who favored a special source: Taylor, Streeter, Grundmann, Catchpole, Ernst, and Marshall. He seemed to backtrack, too, in basing his decision on the low percentage of verbal agreement. The MA in 22,64 / Mt 26,68 "almost certainly comes from" L[80].

The Sanhedrin trial (22,66-71) stemmed from L though there was evidence of "Lucan rewording" in vv. 66-68.70. But vv. 69 and 71 showed some relation to Mk 14,63b.64, while at least in the first case, it could be due to either Luke or the source. If Luke redacted Mk at v. 69 he did so to downplay some of the apocalyptic flavor. But the ἀπὸ τοῦ νῦν was a Lukan addition. The second case was insoluable whether the omission of the blasphemy and verdict was due to Luke or L. Fitzmyer did not seem completely convinced by his analysis, and so left open the possibility of Lukan redaction of Mk[81]. Fitzmyer rejected out of hand Winter's proposal that the scene was a later addition since it "is sheer speculation and does not merit serious consideration"[82]. Christology was highlighted in this story.

Continuing with Jesus being brought before Pilate (23,1-5), the account was "inspired by Mark 15:1b-5", sharing a similar form, and 23,3 stemmed from Mk 15,2. With the exception of 23,4b, the remainder of the verses reflected thorough Lukan redaction. These verses, then, resulted from a combination of Lukan redaction of Mk, Lukan composition and "L" underlying 23,4b which may also have contributed the triple declaration of innocence. Fitzmyer took issue with Taylor's excessive limitation of Lukan terminology in 23,2.

79. *Ibid.*, p. 1457-1458; cf. p. 1465, n. 62. Earlier he stated that the significance of the MAs "has been exaggerated" (p. 73).

80. *Ibid.*, p. 1465-1466, n. 64; cf. p. 1458.

81. *Ibid.*, p. 1458: "Ascription of vv. 66-71 to 'L' seems to be a better solution than a mere redaction of the Marcan parallel, though one cannot be apodictic about it".

82. *Ibid.*, p. 1459.

Fitzmyer toyed with two possibilities for the origin of the two charges, opting finally for Lukan composition rather than a special source. In a comment reminiscent of M. Black, Fitzmyer insisted this material was a "telescoped version of an interrogation of Jesus by Pilate", though he did not explain why he believed this to be the case.

In the section 23,18-25, Mk once more served as inspiration and Luke resumed the Markan material and order. With the exception of the third declaration of innocence (23,22), Fitzmyer held that the rest was contained in Mk 15,6-15, though it was rewritten and so "it is best ascribed to a Lukan redactional reworking of 'Mk'"[83]. Fitzmyer critiqued Taylor's position of the apparent origin of these verses from a non-Markan source, concluding that it was "not convincing". Elements of Lukan redaction were enumerated[84]. Change was due in part to Luke shortening the story. Here the theme which Fitzmyer previously addressed, the effort to excuse the Romans and accuse the Jews, came to the fore at the same time as it emphasized the triple attestation of innocence. Although Fitzmyer was alert to omissions and additions, he did not always supply what may have been Luke's reason for writing in such a manner[85].

Fitzmyer (1985) began his discussion of the Herod scene (23,6-12) with a review of the suggestion of Dibelius and presented five counter arguments to those which were advanced in support of this view[86]. Fitzmyer contrasted arguments put forward in the discussion of the Herod scene in an attempt to determine whether it was a Lukan creation or an historically based event. He took exception to Dibelius's interpretation that Ps 2 constituted the origin of the story. The transfer was plausible on the grounds that Pilate desired to pass off a problematic case, but it was less clear whether flattery or fear may have prompted Pilate's decision.

Fitzmyer also considered the scholarly position of a piece of the L tradition which was redacted by Luke. "The upshot is that, though one cannot be apodictic about the matter, the evidence does not all point toward Lukan fabrication. The appearance of Jesus before Herod could be just as historical as the Lucan depiction of the morning session of the Sanhedrin interrogation"[87]. Notice was also taken

83. *Ibid.*, p. 1487.

84. *Ibid.*, p. 1488. The list included the following vocabulary and constructions: λέγοντες, τοῦτον, ὅστις, προσεφώνησεν, ἐπεφώνουν, εἶπεν πρός plus the accusative, παιδεύσας, and ἐπέκρινεν. Although he announced that the third declaration of innocence was from "L", he included it also as an element of redaction. This detail recalled 23,4.14-15 and the description of Barabbas (v. 25) rehearsing v. 19, round out the Lukan elements.

85. *Ibid.*, p. 1492. Though he noted there was no reference to the scourging of Jesus (Mk 15,15b), no reason was offered for that omission.

86. *Ibid.*, p. 1478-1479 (esp. p. 1478-1483). In the introduction, he counted 23,6-16 as a minor insertion into the Markan order (p. 67).

87. *Ibid.*, p. 1479. As regards the historicity, Fitzmyer referred the reader to Verrall, Blinzler and Hoehner. In Fitzmyer's analysis of the term πολλοί in the Prologue (p. 291), some of the special information might have been derived from the L source, which consisted of material that was not only written, but oral as well (p. 66-67), though he did not specify the Herod scene.

of those who considered the story deriving from L, supposing that the material was communicated by Joanna or Manaen. But Fitzmyer also pointed out elements of Lukan redaction in certain vocabulary and verbal forms[88]. Regarding the charge that the scene was unhistorical because it was not included in the other Gospels, Fitzmyer contended Mark displayed little interest in Herod and thus could have opted to omit the event as John had done.

Concerning Joüon's interpretation of the dazzling apparel (23,11), Fitzmyer castigated such an interpretation as reading "a Marcan nuance into it"[89]. It served, rather, to make a mockery of the innocence of Jesus. Further, Fitzmyer did not see the silence motif recurring in 23,9. He utterly rejected Derrett's attempt to interpret that scene as a parallel to Daniel before royalty or as an insertion of "Daniel haggadah into the passion narrative"[90].

In contrast to Corbin, Fitzmyer argued the Herod episode was a relatively minor one in the passion narrative, though it served Luke's theological purpose of providing a second witness to Jesus' innocence[91] and emphasized the power of Jesus in reconciling enemies (23,12)[92].

Fitzmyer treated 23,13-16 as a unit separate from 23,6-12, but considered them related and probably deriving from the same source, L. Verses 13-16 reflected a composite of various details from the tradition. But Lukan redaction revealed itself in 23,14.15[93].

Eta LINNEMANN (1970) directed her attention primarily to the Markan passion material, but in some certain cases referred to Lukan parallels, namely the account of Peter's denial and the Temple saying[94]. Linnemann countered the views of Günter Klein who opposed the idea of Lukan dependence upon Mk[95]. In support of his view Klein offered three arguments. First, Luke did not compose a unified account from the Markan components in Mk 14,54.66-72. Though Klein objected that Luke generally observed the Markan order, Linnemann maintained that such a change in order did not necessarily indicate another source. Rather, the changes

---

88. *Ibid.*, p. 1479.

89. *Ibid.*, p. 1482.

90. *Ibid.* Cf. DERRETT, *Daniel and Salvation-History*, in *DownR* 100 (1982) 62-68 (= *StNT*, Vol. 4, 1986, 132-138).

91. FITZMYER, *Luke*, p. 1480. He cited Dt 19,15 and noted Grundmann's position (GRUNDMANN, *Lukas*, p. 424).

92. FITZMYER, *Luke*, p. 1480. Cf. M. CORBIN, *Jésus devant Hérode: Lecture de Luc 23,6-12*, in *Christus* 25 (1978) 190-197, esp. p. 190: "... je propose donc de faire une lecture rigoureuse de *l'épisode central de la Passion de notre Seigneur Jésus Christ selon saint Luc*: la comparution de Jésus devant Hérode (Lc 23,6-12)" [emphasis added].

93. FITZMYER, *Luke*, p. 1483-1484. These elements were εἶπεν πρός, ἐνώπιον (v. 14) and the double καὶ ἰδού (vv. 14, 15).

94. E. LINNEMANN, *Studien zur Passionsgeschichte* (FRLANT, 102), Göttingen, 1970.

95. *Ibid.*, p. 97-101. Cf. G. KLEIN, *Verleugnung*, in *ZThK* 58 (1961) 285-328 (= *Rekonstruktion*, 1969, 49-98).

resulted from apologetic and theological reasons[96]. Secondly, Klein suggested that the clumsy connection of the denial with the mistreatment was indicative of Lukan independence, indeed of a pre-Lukan redaction. Linnemann viewed the connection as due to Luke. Thirdly, because the place of the denials varied in both accounts, Klein inclined to the belief that Lk was independent of Mk[97]. Linnemann retorted that the change did not serve a psychological, but rather a literary purpose in a story where the same person repeated his denial. Both accounts contained literary uniqueness. Even Klein admitted the Lukan version obviously reflected the hand of the evangelist. Linnemann concluded Luke depended on Mk, as evidenced by significant verbal correspondence. Further, the Lukan account possessed the same structure as Mk only with additional details. Linnemann thus stated that a conclusion of literary dependence cannot be avoided[98].

Linnemann considered the transpositions to be the work of Luke. They do not automatically suggest the use of a separate independent source[99]. Changes in order were motivated by Luke's desire to offer the most plausible course of events.

The Temple saying attracted Linnemann's attention in reaction to Finegan who argued that both reference to the false witnesses and the Temple saying in Mk stemmed from Acts 6,11-14[100]. Linnemann defended the view that Acts 6,14 referred to Mk 14,58. The Temple saying simply fell away because of the transposition of the trial pericope[101].

More recently (1992), Linnemann rejected literary dependence denouncing her previous work. Writing of the attempt to solve the synoptic problem using form and redaction criticism, Linnemann, who studied under Bultmann and Ernst Fuchs, disassociated herself from higher criticism, declaring: "I am shocked when I look at the books of my former colleagues, which I used to hold in high esteem, and examine the justification for their position. Instead of proof I find only assertions. Instead of arguments there is merely circular reasoning"[102]. In her opinion, none of the investigations to prove literary dependence had been impartial. Linnemann did not believe that "any conclusive proof" has been shown that Mk was the source of the other two Synoptics. Such an approach "undermines trust in God's word".

---

96. LINNEMANN, *Studien*, p. 98.

97. *Ibid.*, p. 99. Klein observed that, according to Lk, all three of the denials occurred in the αὐλή, while in Mk they occurred in the αὐλή and ἔξω εἰς τὸ προαύλιον (Mk 14,66.68).

98. *Ibid.*, p. 101.

99. *Ibid.*, p. 98.

100. *Ibid.*, p. 117, n. 24. Although Linnemann disagreed with Finegan on this point, they concurred that for the denial story Luke recast the Markan account (p. 100).

101. *Ibid.*, p. 121.

102. LINNEMANN, *Gibt es ein synoptisches Problem?*, Neuhausen, 1992 (= *Is There a Synoptic Problem? Rethinking the Literary Dependence of the First Three Gospels*, tr. R.W. YARBOROUGH, Grand Rapids, MI, 1992, p. 10; note esp. p. 177-191). Consider also her earlier work, *Wissenschaft oder Meinung? Anfragen und Alternativen*, Neuhausen, 1986 (= *Historical Criticism of the Bible: Methodology or Ideology*, tr. R.W. YARBOROUGH, Grand Rapids, MI, 1990). See J. BLAIR, Review in *Grace Theological Journal* 11 (1990) 246-248.

Linnemann described the origin of the Synoptic Gospels by means of a four stage process: 1) tradition, 2) memory, and specifically that of eyewitnesses, formed the basis of all the Gospels and is a forgotten factor, 3) transition from memory to documents, and 4) ancient Christian witness[103]. The debate was situated between evangelicals and scholars of the historical-critical school. In attacking redaction criticism, she asserted: "Historical-critical theology *must* posit different theologies for each Gospel writer. Otherwise it could not account for the discrepancy between the data in the Synoptic Gospels and its theories. Differences among the three Synoptics were inexplicable as mere stylistic improvements. Interpretation that did full justice to Scripture, however, found this approach both unnecessary and inappropriate"[104].

According to Linnemann, scholars who employed higher criticism contended oral tradition did not constitute a stage of Gospel formation. Dealing with the formative stage of the transition from memory to written documents Linnemann placed great weight on "ministers of the word" (Acts 6,4) who transmitted their recollections both in oral and in written form, not simply individually, but as "corporate recollections of many witnesses".

In treating Lk specifically, Linnemann argued it was composed between 64-66 AD in Achaia, as was suggested in ancient Gospel prologues[105]. Linnemann categorically rejected that Mt or Mk or any apocryphal gospels served as sources for Lk. Rather, the term πολλοί indicated oral reports from eyewitnesses who responded to requests for information from converts. Luke himself would have provided such data. Whereas proponents of the Proto-Lk hypothesis regarded the two year sojourn as the time when the supposed document was put into writing, Linnemann saw this as the period when verification was made of the reports of the various eyewitnesses and servants of the word. The positions were quite similar. Like the proponents of the Proto-Lk hypothesis, Linnemann sought to reaffirm the historical value of the Gospel accounts.

In addressing the phenomenon of order in the Synoptics, Linnemann maintained there must be a certain order in the passion and resurrection narratives. However, she painted the order in such broad strokes as to overlook the differences, excluding this section of the Gospels from the discussion[106]. Ignoring, for example, the differences in order between Lk (denial, mockery, trial) and Mk (trial, mockery, denial) she insisted: that there was an "almost seamless

103. LINNEMANN, *Is There*, p. 177.
104. *Ibid.*, p. 178.
105. *Ibid.*, p. 190, n. 16. Mk was written in Rome at the same time as Lk while the Aramaic Gospel of Matthew was set in writing in Judea exactly in the year 63 AD.
106. *Ibid.*, p. 85-91: "Now, surely no one will wish to deny that the order of the passion and resurrection accounts has objective grounds: the cross-examination cannot be reported until after the arrest; the crucifixion cannot be reported until after the sentencing; the resurrection cannot be reported until after the burial. Therefore, to be precise, only the Synoptic agreement in narrative sequences outside the passion and resurrection accounts can be relevant to the question of literary dependence".

similarity in the passion and resurrection accounts, where the order of events is substantially conclusive" of her perspective[107].

Linnemann then employed statistical proof, the results of which must be considered skewed since she excluded the passion and resurrection accounts from her calculations. Differences in order can be explained in three ways: 1) the author did not intend the actual historical sequence, 2) variation in sequence was due to the partial reporting of the Gospels, and 3) repetition of certain pericopes derived from different accounts of the content of Jesus' preaching at various times. Concerning the vocabulary, in a comparision of the pericope of Jesus before Pilate (Mk 15,2-5 and pars.), she counted a total of fifteen words identical in Mk-Lk, whereas there were ninety-one differences[108]. Material unique to Lk in 22,54-23,25 was limited to 23,4-12.13-16[109]. It was obvious Linnemann held redaction in little esteem[110].

Frederick DANKER (1972) noted Luke was largely dependent upon Mk as we now know it, or a source very similar to it, and also upon Q[111]. The evangelist appeared not to have known Mt. Danker also asserted in the revised edition of his commentary that Luke relied on the LXX and particularly the book of Isaiah, in addition to the wisdom tradition[112]. Danker referred to the material unique to Lk ("L") as coming from "a special source". Luke did not slavishly depend on sources but, in keeping with his theological and apologetic concerns, adapted the material[113].

---

107. *Ibid.*, p. 149.

108. *Ibid.*, p. 127.

109. *Ibid.*, p. 79; cf. p. 81.

110. *Ibid.*, p. 37. Mt and Lk were regarded as "secondary witnesses" by higher criticism thus depriving them of any historical value. "At best they were theologically interesting". As regards Luke's redaction of Mk, Linnemann penned: "Only a portion of the differences are explicable; the rest must be attributed to personal theological biases of the Gospel writers".

111. F.W. DANKER, *Jesus and the New Age*, St. Louis, MO, 1972, p. xvii (esp. p. xvii-xix, 228-235); Philadelphia, PA, ²1988, p. 16 (esp. p. 16-17, 359-370). It should be noted that in the revised edition Danker added 19,11-27 and 22,28-30 to his Q source.

C. Kingsley BARRETT (1988) understood that Luke used Mk and envisioned Q as "in all probability a group of sources, some written, some oral, some possessed by Matthew and Luke in virtually identical forms and some in widely different forms" (*Luke/Acts*, in D.A. CARSON and H.G.M. WILLIAMSON [eds.], *It is Written: Scripture Citing Scripture*. FS B. LINDARS, Cambridge, 1988, 231-244, esp. p. 231). Barrett also considered it likely that Luke used sources in composing Acts. Methodologically, source criticism should be applied first to the Gospel since we have the other Synoptics with which to compare it, and then Acts should be analyzed.

112. DANKER, *Jesus*, ²1988, p. 16. Cf. 1972, p. xviii. This concern for and attention to the wisdom element was what distinguished Danker's commentary from others.

113. *Ibid.*, p. xviii (= ²1988, 17). Danker noted that a version of the story of the anointing was located at 7,36-50 (cf. Mk 14,3-9). The new location was prompted so as not to breach the relationship between the religious leaders and Satan. Further, the story of the anointing was more appropriate to a section where Luke was concerned about the treatment of the poor (p. 218 = 341-342).

It was clear no special source was presumed for the denials of Peter. Luke was redacting Mk with more of a dramatic flair[114]. Regarding transpositions, Danker believed they were to be expected as indicated in Luke's Prologue reference to "an orderly account" (1,4). The re-ordering of the denial was intended to contrast Jesus' confession with Peter's denial[115]. In the revised edition (²1988) Danker linked Peter's speeches in Acts with his recollection contained in v. 61. Danker did not mention or explain the MAs in 22,62.64.

The mockery, which Luke constructed with the help of earlier material (18,32), helped to show in light of Peter's experience that Jesus was a prophet[116]. The reference to the coming of the Son of Man was shaped not so much by the common apocalypticism, as by a view to "divine vindication", which corresponded to earlier elements (9,22.44; 18,31). Danker keenly observed that the omission of the Markan account of the false witnesses was transferred to the Stephen scene in Acts (Acts 6,14; 7,44-50)[117]. He contended that it was not particularly boastful to identify oneself as a child of God (for example Ex 4,22; Dt 14,1). The separation of the titles in v. 67 (diff. Mk 14,61) was warranted and focused even more intensely Jesus' full identity[118].

Luke believed it "more probable" that the Sanhedrin trial occurred during that day rather than at night. The evangelist recast the Markan account of the Sanhedrin trial, careful to indicate that those who were hostile to God will not "see" the coming of the Son of Man[119]. "Divine intervention" rather than "end-time demonstration" governed Luke's composition at this point.

For the section 23,1-25, Luke relied not only on Mk, but on "a source that linked Herod and Pilate"[120]. In 23,1-5 Luke changed Markan vocabulary[121], and recast the interrogation of Jesus by Pilate to center more intently on this dialogue. The omission of the Markan statement that the chief priests presented many charges (Mk 15,3) allowed Luke to focus attention upon the interrogation by Pilate. Mk 15,10 was seen as inspiring 23,5 with the detail that the people were inflamed by Jesus' teaching and the understanding that the religious authorities were less in control (see also Acts 4,17; 5,28; 17,6). Acts 10,37-38 offered a corrective or rebuttal to the accusers[122]. In the revised edition Danker added the following insight into Lukan redaction: "One of Luke's ploys in the Passion

---

114. *Ibid.*, p. 229 (= 359). In the later edition Danker was more attuned to similarities with Acts, including Paul's experience and Peter's speeches.

115. *Ibid.*, p. 228 (= 358).

116. *Ibid.*, p. 230; cf. ²1988, p. 360.

117. *Ibid.*, p. 231 (= 362).

118. *Ibid.*, ²1988, p. 361; cf. 1972, p. 230.

119. *Ibid.*, 1972, p. 230. The connection was made to Stephen in Acts 7,56.

120. *Ibid.*

121. *Ibid.*, p. 231 (= 363). The Lukan ἤγαγον (23,1) replaced the Markan παρέδωκαν (15,1).

122. *Ibid.*, ²1988, p. 365. This observation was added with the revised ed. of the commentary.

account is to edit information that comes from Jesus' adversaries, but in such a way that their essential misunderstanding is exhibited"[123].

In 23,18-25 the Lukan account forced attention on the responsibility of the people of Jerusalem by omitting the Markan phrase βουλόμενος τῷ ὄχλῳ τὸ ἱκανὸν ποιῆσαι (Mk 15,15), while toning down the harshness of Mk's presentation of Pilate as a political coward[124]. The omission of Markan material detailing events prior to the demand for Barabbas heightened the difference between Jesus' innocence and the anti-Roman sentiments of those who are opposed to him. Lk 23,20 was compared with Acts 3,13. Danker saw in the detail of Jesus being delivered up to "their will" what he described as "the inverted echo of 22,42"[125].

Consistently throughout Danker showed that Luke redacted Mk. Not only was Danker concerned for the omissions of Markan materials, offering convincing explanations, but he was also attuned to the contrasts presented by Luke's rewriting. The LXX background, particularly noting Isaian influence, was also highlighted.

Danker believed that in the section 23,1-25 Luke not only employed the Mk, but also possessed a special source that tied Herod and Pilate[126]. Alluding to Dibelius's contribution, Danker considered 23,6-7 as a preparation for Acts 4,25-26 and also regarded Pilate and Herod as fulfilling the role of dual witnesses as required by Jewish law (Dt 19,15)[127]. While acknowledging Grundmann's suggestion that Jesus' silence may point to his divinity, Danker believed it may have been indicative of Lukan redaction involving a wisdom motif[128].

Donald P. SENIOR (1972) was of the opinion that just as Matthew altered the Markan account of the passion by stylistic and theological alterations, so this was also the case with Luke[129]. That view continued and became explicit in his more popular treatment (1989) of the Lukan passion narrative[130]. "While the suggestion that Luke had a special source for his Passion story is a seductive one, my own

---

123. *Ibid.*, ²1988, p. 364-365.

124. *Ibid.*, p. 235 (= 369-370). In the revised ed., Danker expanded the section dealing with 23,24-25. He took issue with those who viewed this section as having been redacted in light of Luke's pro-Roman apologetic. Luke's primary concern was "the beneficence of God" rather than the goal of exoneration of Rome. "Customary attempts to charge Luke with a pro-Roman bias must therefore be interpreted as a purchase at the expense of justice to Luke's perception of political realities. Moreover, they prejudice a fair assessment of Luke's attitude toward Jews and they are fatal to a profounder appreciation of Luke's literary texture" (²1988, p. 370).

125. *Ibid.*, ²1988, p. 369; cf. 1972, p. 235.

126. *Ibid.*, p. 231 (= 362).

127. *Ibid.*, p. 232 (= 362).

128. *Ibid.*, p. 233 (= 362). Cf. GRUNDMANN, *Lukas*, ²1963, p. 425.

129. D.P. SENIOR, *The Passion Narrative according to Matthew*, Leuven, 1975, p. 41, n. 1.

130. SENIOR, *The Passion of Jesus in the Gospel of Luke*, Wilmington, DE, 1989 (esp. p. 93-119).

opinion is that the special character of Luke's Passion narrative is due to his creative reinterpretation of Mark's account"[131].

The reason for the change in the Markan order of the Sanhedrin trial, denial, and mockery by Luke, according to Senior, was to join "the Peter episode more tightly with the *previous* scenes about the need for prayer in the face of test", which highlighted two aspects of the test for Jesus: Peter's denials and the mockery[132]. On a related matter, Senior acknowledged the difficulty of settling the question of the historicity of the morning trial in Lk. He observed that it did not necessarily follow that the changes introduced by Luke stemmed from consideration of the historical probability that the trial did in fact occur during the morning[133]. Senior rightly saw the change of the fire in Mk from serving to warm Peter, to providing light for recognition in the Lukan account. Senior called attention to the role of the two male witnesses (Dt 19,15), but offered no opinion on the matter. The detail of Jesus gazing at Peter which evoked the tears of repentance, was credited to Luke[134]. The scene of the denials, offering important instruction on Christian discipleship, contrasted the weakness of the disciples's faith and the strength of Jesus' love for them.

The mockery, by reason of its new location, was "more closely connected with the previous string of events"[135]. The episodes proved Jesus was indeed a prophet and fulfilled earlier predictions of Jesus about rejection and denial (4,24;18,32) which also awaited those disciples who follow Jesus faithfully (6,22-23; 11,47-51; 13,33-35; 20,9-18).

The Sanhedrin scene allowed Luke to continue and intensify the theme of rejection. Addressing the omission of reference to the Temple, Senior contended this was due to Luke's positive attitude toward the Temple, as well as allowing the scene to focus on Jesus' identity and the rejection by the Sanhedrin. In highlighting the identity of Jesus, the questioning centered on Jesus as Christ and as Son of Man, the latter title being used in the Gospel to refer to his rejection (6,22; 7,34; 9,22.26.44.58; 18,31-33), but also his exaltation (12,8.10) and future return (12,40; 17,22.23.26.30; 18,8; 21,27)[136]. The title Son of God conveyed the intimate relationship of Jesus with God. Even as the weakness of Peter was contrasted with the courage of Jesus, the scene recalled the prophecy of Jesus that they would encounter difficulty (21,12-13). Like Van der Kwaak, Senior showed how the changes from Mk could well stem from Luke's christological standpoint[137].

131. *Ibid.*, p. 10. See also n. 8.
132. *Ibid.*, p. 94.
133. *Ibid.*, p. 94-95, n. 3: "Even if it could be established that a night trial was illegal and improbable historically, it is not certain the Luke's presentation differs from Mark's because of sensitivity to this historical issue".
134. *Ibid.*, p. 97.
135. *Ibid.*, p. 98.
136. *Ibid.*, p. 102, n. 5.
137. See VAN DER KWAAK, *Het Proces*, p. 132-137, 170.

While Neyrey and others contended there were four trials in the section 22,66–23,25, Senior observed that in 23,1-25 there were simply three episodes[138]. The theme of the rejection by the leaders tied the first part of this section (23,1-5) with earlier events. The differences between the charges brought by the Council and those raised before Pilate were significant but Senior wisely noted that while there was "historical logic in Luke's account", his recasting of Mk may be due more to theology than to history, and thus sought to portray the "unjust" nature of the trial[139]. The charges, drawn from Mk, were made more explicit.

In the final portion of the trial before Pilate (23,13-25) Luke further highlighted the presentation of Jesus: "Luke skillfully edits the scene to bring to the fore major themes in his portrayal of Jesus as a prophet-martyr: Jesus' innocence from crime, yet his rejection by Israel"[140]. Luke further honed Mark's account, building on the contrasts between the declaration of innocence by Pilate and the demand by the people and their leaders for Jesus' execution, as well as their urging the release of the imprisoned Barabbas and the condemnation of Jesus. Like Van der Kwaak for the earlier portion of chapter 23, Senior also observed Luke's political apologetic was at work in portraying Jesus (and ultimately the Christians) as non-threatening toward Rome[141]. The theme was noted by both Van der Kwaak and Senior as a common thread running through Lk-Acts[142]. In Senior's view, Lukan redaction of the Markan account stripped away extraneous material to focus the reader's attention on the tense encounter between Pilate and the Jewish people and their leaders[143].

Senior assessed the scholarly consensus on the MA of 22,62 / Mt 26,75c as having been interpolated into Lk from Mt[144]. The reverse was the case in the MA 22,64 / Mt 26,68 where it was "more probable" that Mt was harmonized with Lk[145]. Senior did not treat the MA in his more popularized study of the Matthean account of the passion[146]. He showed well – and convincingly – how the Lukan passion narrative could have been a redaction of Mk.

Senior (1989), taking note of the "considerable debate about the historical plausibility" of the Herod scene, contrasted Marshall on the one hand with Neyrey on the other[147]. The silence of Jesus may have been inspired by Mk[148]. The

---

138. SENIOR, *The Passion of Jesus in the Gospel of Luke*, p. 105.

139. *Ibid.*, p. 107.

140. *Ibid.*, p. 116.

141. *Ibid.*, p. 117. Cf. VAN DER KWAAK, *Het Proces*, p. 163. Cf. p. 141.

142. SENIOR, *The Passion of Jesus in the Gospel of Luke*, p. 117, n. 26. Cf. VAN DER KWAAK, *Het Proces*, p. 162-163.

143. SENIOR, *The Passion of Jesus in the Gospel of Luke*, p. 118.

144. *Ibid.*, p. 208, n. 4.

145. *Ibid.*, p. 189. He entertained the slim possibility that the phrase was found in the redactor's copy of Mk, but considered it unlikely "because of the weakness of the manuscript tradition" (p. 189, n. 3).

146. SENIOR, *The Passion of Jesus in the Gospel of Matthew*, Wilmington, DE, 1985.

147. *The Passion of Jesus in the Gospel of Luke*, p. 112.

mockery of Jesus by Herod and his soldiers took the place of the one in Mk. Senior was not entirely convinced by the suggestions that the dazzling apparel was that of candidates for public office or that Luke used the scene to fulfill the requirement of Dt 19,15[149].

J. Edgar Bruns, noting Senior's resolve not to wrestle in depth with the historical matters wrote: "Since he is not writing a full-scale commentary, S. eschews exploration of 'the important historical questions that lie beneath the Passion account', but what he produces is a solid evocation of Lucan theology as it finds its consummate expression in that account"[150]. Regarding historical questions and the issue of sources J.B. Green determined "it is clear that Senior is committed to Marcan priority and to the creative hand of Luke where the Lucan narrative departs from the Marcan"[151].

Frans NEIRYNCK (1973) has argued indefatigably that Mk formed the basis of the passion narrative in Lk, rather than a Proto-Lukan or even parallel account of the passion. "Il me semble plutôt que l'évangile de Marc n'est pas abandonné en *Lc.*, XXII,14 (ou 15), mais qu'il continue de guider l'évangéliste jusqu'en XXIV, 12. Je le sais, je ne puis me contenter d'exprimer cette opinion: elle est contestée et doit donc devenir un programme d'études ultérieures"[152]. He sought to show how the elements proper to Luke, the Semitisms and the MAs of Mt-Lk against Mk, plus the transpositions were all aspects of the evangelist's redactional activity[153]. The idea that Q constituted a Gospel, as Burkitt proposed, was roundly rejected by Neirynck (1976) who asserted that Q contained no passion narrative[154].

A detailed analysis of T. Schramm's dissertation on the Markan material in Lk provided Neirynck with the forum to examine these elements[155]. Focusing on

---

148. *Ibid.*, p. 114, n. 16.

149. *Ibid.*, n. 19, and p. 114-115, n. 21.

150. *CBQ* 53 (1991) 149.

151. *CRBR*, Vol. 4, 1991, Atlanta, GA, 229-230. He esteemed this as a "model for harvesting the fruits of contemporary scholarship in a positive and pastorally-sensitive way for the church" (p. 230).

152. NEIRYNCK, *La matière marcienne*, p. 199 (= *Evangelica*, 79).

153. *Ibid.* (= 82). Neirynck called attention to Fitzmyer's similarity of views on these subjects, with only one regret, that the American Jesuit did not recognize the significance of the καὶ ἐγένετο construction for the structure of Lk. Raymond Collins, former NT professor at Leuven, rejected the idea that the special Lukan material resulted from Lukan redaction for two reasons: the material was not homogeneous and Luke was usually faithful to his sources as evidenced by his use of Mark and Q. Collins's rejection of Lukan redaction to account for the additional material was particularly strong: "The assumption that the L material derives from Luke's own creativity is clearly unwarranted" (*Introduction*, p. 135). Collins also expressed sympathy for Taylor's contention that there was a pre-Markan passion narrative in written form.

154. NEIRYNCK, *Q*, in *IDBS*, 1976, 716.

155. T. SCHRAMM, *Der Markus-Stoff bei Lukas*, 1971. Though A. Gaboury was more confident of the "redaction-critical approach" of Schramm than "all the harmonizing efforts" of Conzelmann and other scholars aligned with him (*CBQ* 34 [1972] 540-541), other reviewers were

certain elements found only in Luke, whereas Schramm, for example, attempted to assign the term σατανᾶς (22,3) to pre-Lukan vocabulary, Neirynck urged caution: "On ne peut pas réduire le vocabulaire du rédacteur aux mots dits caractéristiques et exclure de l'activité rédactionnelle un certain réemploi du vocabulaire des sources"[156]. G. Schneider concurred with Neirynck's conclusion that Schramm had not offered any valid criteria by which to judge[157]. John Drury was equally skeptical of Schramm (and Taylor) and very appreciative of the methodology followed in Neirynck's essay[158].

The occurrences of so-called Semitisms, in Neirynck's view, were signs of Lukan redaction[159]. He articulated an important principle to help discern the presence of such redaction: "L'étude du style lucanien doit se référer plutôt à des textes où Luc rédige plus librement et où l'influence des sources semble exclue: *Act.*, XVI-XXVIII, et plus spécialement les sections 'nous' et les discours"[160]. This was particularly useful to us since the trials of Paul are found in Acts 25-26. The introductions, especially, can be said to have been freely redacted by Luke and thus were important for determining how Luke recast material[161].

Two MAs of Mt and Lk were found within the section of our investigation: 22,62.64[162]. Neirynck rejected Schramm's assessment of a distinction between

not so impressed. G.N. Stanton declared: "Schramm's case is not convincing" indicating that most of the material which Schramm contended derived from non-Markan traditions was rather insignificant (*TLond* 76 [1973] 36-37). J.D. Dubois suggested that Schramm's method had too narrowly defined and thus reduced the amount of Lukan redaction (*ETR* 49 [1974] 430-432).

156. NEIRYNCK, *La matière marcienne*, p. 169 (= *Evangelica*, 49).

157. *BZ* 19 (1975) 120.

158. *JTS* 25 (1974) 166: "The recent appearance of Tim Schramm's Der Markus Stoff bei Lukas and Vincent Taylor's The Passion Narrative of Luke seemed to lead us back into laborious and unverifiable speculations about vanished sources. The writers of the essays in this book (particularly the last six which are the most precise and important) insist on the priority of studying what exists before what may have existed". Of Neirynck's contribution, Drury wrote: "With the essay by the editor we enter the most striking part of the collection: six painstaking studies of confined areas which bring to light much of Luke's character by the use of sensible literary methods. As a side-benefit they loosen the hold of several hypotheses" (p. 168). Neirynck's methodology was termed "fresh".

159. NEIRYNCK, *La matière marcienne*, p. 179 (= *Evangelica*, p. 59). Cf. p. 190 (= *Evangelica*, p. 70): "C'est sans doute la Bible grecque qui lui a prêté le modèle et il n'y a pas besoin de sources écrites dans un grec hébraïsant pour expliquer un usage artistique qui est des plus rédactionnels en *Lc.*"

160. *Ibid.*, p. 179 (= *Evangelica*, 59).

161. *Ibid.*, p. 180, 182 (= *Evangelica*, 60, 62).

162. Neirynck treated the second MA in detail in ΤΙΣ ΕΣΤΙΝ, 5-47 (= *Evangelica II*, 1991, 95-138). The first MA was treated briefly in the same article. See p. 18-19, where he proposed that 22,62 was "a copyist's insertion" (p. 19). The positions of various scholars on both MAs were recounted in F. NEIRYNCK, in collaboration with T. HANSEN and F. VAN SEGBROECK, *The Minor Agreements of Matthew and Luke against Mark with a Cumulative List*, p. 179, 182. Cf. E. SIMONS, *Hat der dritte Evangelist den kanonischen Matthäus benutzt?*, Bonn, 1880, p. 105. Eduard SIMONS, in a solution accepted by Holtzmann (cf. *Die Disposition*, 1883, see below),

significant and insignificant MAs[163]. He further demurred by preferring a literary-critical solution such as Luke's dependence upon Mt, a position adopted by friends and foes of Q alike, rather than "l'idée très vague de traditions parallèles à Marc"[164]. The criterion of few Markan words in 22,63-65, often hailed as an indication of a special source by adherents of such a view, in Neirynck's opinion (1987) "may point to significant editorial reworking of Mark's text"[165]. Based on Lukan redactional tendencies, the parallelism of the second half of 22,64 with Mk, and the authenticity afforded by textual criticism, he concluded "the most probable origin of τίς ἐστιν ὁ παίσας σε is Lukan redaction of Mk 14,65"[166]. Since the phrase was original to Luke, the possibility must be considered that the Mt was assimilated to it[167]. While he concluded that the phrase τίς ἐστιν ὁ παίσας σε; was most probably due to Luke's redaction of Mk

posited the view that Luke knew and used Mt in addition to Mk and Q. The Matthean Gospel served as a *Nebenquelle* for Lk which in Simons's opinion explained better than other proposed solutions such as "common source, oral tradition, accidental editorial coincidence", the similarity between Lk and Mt, as well as their differences from Mk (F. NEIRYNCK, *The Minor Agreements of Matthew and Luke against Mark*, p. 15, 16; see SIMONS, p. 107, 108). It offered "the first specific study of the minor agreements" (NEIRYNCK, *The Minor Agreements of Matthew and Luke against Mark*, p. 15. See also T.A. FRIEDRICHSEN, *The Matthew – Luke Agreements Against Mark*, Vol. 1, p. 179, n. 249; Vol. 2, p. 312). The influence of the Matthean Gospel was both limited in degree and interspersed rather than continuous (SIMONS, p. 105: "denn wir haben gesehn, dass die Matthäischen Einwirkungen keine ununterbrochene Kette darstellen"). It was in the passion and resurrection narratives that the Lukan dependence upon Mt was clearest. The Matthean influence was further evidenced by examining Luke's redaction of Mk, which included "stilistischen oder lexikalischen Nüancirungen, in Auslassungen oder kleinen Zuthaten" (p. 107). Luke had memorized much of the Matthean Gospel and freely redacted it (p. 108).

In the case of Peter's denials (22,54-62) Simons stated that the source options were either an abbreviation of an *Urmarkus* or Luke's use of Mt (p. 98. For material pertaining to Lk 22,54-23,25 see p. 97-100). Notice was taken of the placement of the denials before the mockery. Matthew sought to supplement the Markan προφήτευσον with the MA τίς ἐστιν ὁ παίσας σε in Mt 26,68. Once again, Luke adopted Matthew's phrase. A further proof seemed to be that Luke, in imitation of Mt, supplied λέγοντες in place of Mk's καὶ λέγουσι.

Matthean influence was seen in 22,66 where Simons claimed Luke adopted Matthew's term συνήχθησαν (Mt 26,57) (this was a preferred Matthean term, drawn from Ps 2 and used to designate the gathering of Jesus' enemies) as opposed to Mark's συνέρχονται (Mk 14,53).

163. NEIRYNCK, *La materière marcienne*, p. 193 (= *Evangelica*, 73).

164. *Ibid.*, p. 194 (= *Evangelica*, 74).

165. NEIRYNCK, ΤΙΣ ΕΣΤΙΝ, p. 17 (= *Evangelica II*, 107). He correctly observed that the "second half of Lk 22,64 is clearly in parallel with Mark..." (p. 23 = *Evangelica II*, 113).

166. *Ibid.*, p. 27 (= *Evangelica II*, 117). Cf. p. 31 (= *Evangelica II*, 121). One of the charges often leveled against Taylor and those who relied upon a statistical methodological approach was that they underestimated the Markan influence. Neirynck offered a corrective in pointing to the fact that Taylor, followed by Ernst and Fitzmyer, overlooked four other words in 22,63-65 which were shared in common with Mk (p. 17 = *Evangelica II*, 107).

167. *Ibid.*, p. 47 (= *Evangelica II*, 137).

14,65, the presence of the phrase in "Mt 26,68 would then be the exceptional case where an assimilation of Matthew to Luke has pervaded all textual witnesses"[168].

In a note appended to the article as published in the collection *Evangelica II* (1991), Neirynck took note of recent studies which gave attention to the MA of 22,64 / Mt 26,68[169]. C.M. Tuckett changed his position and no longer defended a shorter reading of Mk, swayed by Neirynck's article. In assessing Green's study, Neirynck pointed out that he based his argument on a shorter reading of Mk 14,65, precisely where Tuckett emended his point of view. Neirynck also raised questions about Green's conclusion, in that he determined that 22,64 and Mt 26,68 were "'ultimately dependent upon a common source', without examining the context in Mt"[170].

Albert VANHOYE (1992) credited Neirynck's studies on these two MAs as having solved the difficulties associated with them: "L'hypothèse du Prof. F. Neirynck trouve donc là un appui très ferme"[171]. By means of an "analogous hypothesis", and examining 22,60-65, with particular emphasis on v. 64, in the light of Luke's redactional concern for Jesus as prophet and for prophecy, Vanhoye, followed the line of his 1967 study in which he affirmed that in the passion narrative, Luke redacted Mk. Vanhoye took exception to Schneider's conclusion (1969) that the phrase in v. 64 was original to Mt, but agreed that Luke's approach in this section was paranetic[172]. For Vanhoye even the change in order with the denials attested to this "personal-paranetic" approach which Luke adopted in his Gospel[173]. Like Catchpole and others, Vanhoye called attention to the potential difficulty posed by αὐτόν (v. 63) where it would seem to refer to Peter rather than Jesus, but offered no further explanation. Vanhoye wrote very convincingly how the changes over against Mk, most radically in 22,66-71,

---

168. ΤΙΣ ΕΣΤΙΝ, p. 47; see p. 27 (= *Evangelica II*, 117).
169. NEIRYNCK, ΤΙΣ ΕΣΤΙΝ, in *Evangelica II*, 138.
170. *Ibid.*, in *Evangelica II*, p. 138 (additional note).
171. A. VANHOYE, *L'intérêt de Luc pour la prophétie en Lc 1,76; 4,16-30 et 22,60-65*, in FS Neirynck, Vol. 2, 1548. M.D. Goulder was not so convinced of Neirynck's solution: "There is in addition the notorious MA of five words, τίς ἐστιν ὁ παίσας σε;, which both Matthew and Luke add to Mk. 14:65 προφήτευσον (παίειν being a hapax in both Gospels). Here Neirynck devotes an entire article to the desperate argument that *all* the MSS of Matthew have been corrupted by assimilation to Luke: that is, that *no* MS of Matthew written before Luke became well-known has left its trace on our tradition. I am constantly surprised how many scholars (including textual scholars) are unaware that the standard solution to the synoptic problem rests on this sandy foundation" (*NT* 35 [1993] 201-202). But compare the view of Tuckett who argued "such a theory is thus easy to ridicule but is not inherently impossible" (*Synoptic Problem*, in *ABD* 6, p. 267).
172. VANHOYE, *L'intérêt de Luc*, p. 1544, 1545. The agreement was not total since they arrived at their conclusions by different means. For the theme of prophets and prophecy in Lk, see also GEORGE, *Le sens*, p. 207 (= *Études*, 1978, 185-212): "Luc porte un intérêt particulier aux prophètes de l'Ancien Testament". Cf. GEORGE, *Israël dans l'œuvre de Luc*, in *RB* 75 (1968) p. 483 (= *Études*, 1978, 87-125).
173. VANHOYE, *L'intérêt de Luc*, p. 1543-1544.

stemmed from Luke's redactional concerns and interests. One of these was the relationship between various people, particularly between Jesus and his disciples.

In a 1992 retrospective essay Neirynck examined the development of literary-critical methodologies, where he again gave particular attention to the MA of 22,64 (/ Mt 26,68)[174]. Of this he wrote: "The debate is not closed, but I see a growing number of scholars for whom an exceptional instance of conjectural reading is no longer methodologically unacceptable"[175]. The scholars to whom he referred were B. Aland and A. Vanhoye[176].

The publication of a 1994 Oxford dissertation by M.S. Goodacre focusing on M.D. Goulder provided Neirynck with yet another opportunity to revisit the issue of the MAs[177]. Goodacre rejected the solution of conjectural emendation, to which Neirynck responded that the author had merely defined conjectural emendation and not offered a "justification of its rejection in the case of Mt 26,68"[178]. He repeated his 1992 statement, once more referring to B. Aland, Vanhoye, Tuckett and adding a recent reference to Légasse[179].

The transposition of pericopes enabled Peter to witness to the fact that Jesus indeed was a prophet (cf. 22,34), though the mockery cast doubt on Jesus' ability to prophesy. Peter's presence, in effect, confirmed Jesus' prophetic role, despite his silence. Not only was Peter's faith in Jesus affirmed, but Luke's readers were invited to share in that faith as well[180]. Luke's redactional treatment of Jesus as prophet was confirmed by Vanhoye at several points in the section 22,54-71 showing how this theme provided the thread of continuity throughout this section[181].

---

174. *Literary Criticism: Old and New*, in C. FOCANT (ed.), *The Synoptic Gospels. Source Criticism and the New Literary Criticism* (BETL, 110), Leuven, 1992, 11-38, p. 18.

175. *Ibid.*

176. *Ibid.*, n. 33: B. ALAND, *Das Zeugnis der frühen Papyri für den Text der Evangelien diskutiert am Matthäusevangelium*, in FS Neirynck, Vol. 1, 326-335, esp. p. 326, and VANHOYE, *L'intérêt*, p. 1544-1547. On the theoretical discussion about conjectural emendation, see C.M. TUCKETT, *Reading the New Testament. Methods of Interpretation*, London, 1987, p. 34.

177. NEIRYNCK, *Goulder and the Minor Agreements*, in *ETL* 73 (1997) 84-93. M.S. GOODACRE, *Goulder and the Gospels. An Examination of a New Paradigm* (JSNT SS, 133), Sheffield, 1996. Diss. Oxford, 1994 (dir. J. MUDDIMAN).

178. NEIRYNCK, *Goulder*, p. 92.

179. *Ibid.*, n. 25. See above n. 176. He added C.M. TUCKETT, *The Minor Agreements and Textual Criticism*, in G. STRECKER (ed.), *Minor Agreements*, 1993, p. 135-138, and his *Q and the History of Early Christianity*, Edinburgh, 1996, p. 17, n. 41; 24, n. 59; and S. LÉGASSE, *Le procès*, t. 2, p. 205-206.

180. *Ibid.*, p. 1546.

181. *Ibid.*, p. 1547. Vanhoye demonstrated how Luke portrayed Jesus as a prophet throughout the denials, mockery and Sanhedrin trial by calling attention to the following elements: In v. 61 Peter recalled the prophetic words of Jesus. Later, Jesus' prophetic word was fulfilled and the guards who mocked Jesus demanded that he prophesy (v. 64). Though silent here, Jesus prophesied eloquently in the presence of the Sanhedrin (v. 69) and identified himself as the Son of God (v. 70), so that the Sanhedrin found no use for any other testimony, because they had

In Neirynck's view because the order of Mk and Lk were basically the same, it was reasonable to assume that Mk served as the foundation for Lk[182]. J.C. Hawkins had early on discerned such divergence in the order of the pericopes between the two Gospels, but did not posit a special source, for which he was chastised by Streeter[183]. Many authors based a decision in favor of a special source upon the argument from order. Neirynck treated this aspect of the question in several articles[184]. His contention was that the order of the Gospels must be considered in light of the redaction-critical tendencies of the individual evangelists[185]. "More especially in the study of the Passion narrative, Luke's dislike of the transposition of sections, not of sentences, was employed as a principle of exegesis. It seems to me that it may have withdrawn attention from the potentialities of the Lucan redaction ..."[186]. In examining the phenomenon of order in Lk 6 and 8 and in an earlier section of Lk 22, Neirynck showed how Luke sometimes rearranged Markan material for literary or theological, that is christological or ecclesiastical reasons.

Paul WALASKAY authored a study (1975) on the Lukan account of the trial and death of Jesus[187]. He referred to earlier works by Cullmann, Winter, Blinzler[188], Cohn and Brandon[189]. The manner in which Luke used written or

what they needed "from his lips" (v. 71). By opting for the shorter reading, Vanhoye illustrated well how this fit with Luke's retelling of the Markan story, but viewed through the lens of prophecy. He earlier noted how much more evident than Mark's was Luke's interest in prophecy (p. 1529).

182. NEIRYNCK, *La matière marcienne*, p. 159 (= *Evangelica*, 39).

183. STREETER, *FG*, 1924, p. 202: "The conclusion to which these facts point Sir John himself hesitates to draw". Cf. NEIRYNCK, *La matière marcienne*, p. 195 (= *Evangelica*, 75).

184. NEIRYNCK, *La matière marcienne*, p. 198-199 (= 78-79). NEIRYNCK, *Les transpositions dans l'évangile de Luc et l'acolouthie marcienne*, in *ETL* as recorded in NEIRYNCK, *La matière marcienne*, p. 198, n. 173. NEIRYNCK, *The Argument from Order and St. Luke's Transpositions*, in *ETL* 49 (1973) 784-815 (= ID., in collaboration with T. HANSEN and F. VAN SEGBROECK, *The Minor Agreements of Matthew and Luke against Mark with a Cumulative List* [BETL, 37], Leuven, 1974, 291-322 = *Evangelica*, 737-768). He recently treated the subject in *Synoptic Problem*, in *NJBC*, Pt. 2, 1990, p. 589-590.

185. Cf. NEIRYNCK, *Argument*, p. 794 (= *Minor Agreements*, 301 = *Evangelica*, 747).

186. *Ibid.*, p. 814 (= *Minor Agreements*, 321 = *Evangelica*, 767).

187. P. WALASKAY, *The Trial and Death of Jesus in the Gospel of Luke*, in *JBL* 94 (1975) 81-93. The study concentrated on "four sections of the trial narrative which vividly bring out the Lucan perspective: the Sanhedrin hearing, the Roman trial, Jesus before Herod, and finally the mocking, crucifixion, and ultimate verdict" (p. 82).

188. A later critique of Blinzler was that he and others neglected to consider the relationship between the high priest and Rome. "The high priest was an appointee of Rome and his loyalty was expected and received; in Jesus' time, the high priest and his party did form the backbone of the conservative element which remained loyal to the Roman government" (p. [85]-86, n. 14).

189. *Ibid.*, p. 81. He did not list their individual works at this point. Within the essay the author relied on the Lukan commentaries of Manson, Klostermann, Lampe, Easton, Godet, Caird, Findlay, Plummer and Creed in addition to various studies of Flender, Taylor, Sherwin-White,

oral sources betrayed his "peculiar perspective" which was clearly "pro-Roman, anti-Sanhedrin".

Regarding the Sanhedrin hearing Walaskay argued Luke was simply redacting Mk which reflected his conviction that Jesus "did not receive a proper trial before the Sanhedrin"[190]. Luke was credited with dividing the Markan question in Mk 14,61 into two separate questions. The differences between Lk and Mk were intended to not only highlight the responsibility of the Jews[191], but to contrast Jewish and Roman justice. In a note Walaskay drew attention to Taylor's posthumous study of the passion narrative, complimenting O. Evans "for an outstanding job of preparing this book for publication", which included recounting more recent arguments favoring the Proto-Lk theory. Walaskay found his own position similar to Taylor's on the matter of "Luke adjusting his sources to fit his perspective" in several instances[192]. Luke's charges clarified what Mark had only vaguely referred to. Rather than accusing Jesus for a religious infraction, the charge took a decidely political turn.

Luke once more followed Mk in the response of Jesus in 23,3b of the Roman trial. Walaskay took issue with the view that Luke's presentation of Pilate offered a pro-Roman apologia on behalf of the church[193]. Rather, Luke's reconstruction of Pilate's trial had been "given to the church to help it better appreciate the person of the prefect and the 'fairness' – even though Luke presents a rather distorted view of Roman fairness – of the imperial judicial system"[194]. Pilate's declarations of Jesus' innocence were a sign "to Luke's church that Roman magistrates are just in their judgments" but that "the plan of God must not be overcome even by Roman law"[195]. Recently, Légasse offered the critique on Walaskay's explanation of the reconciliation between Pilate and Herod that "cette explication est hautement aventueuse"[196].

In 1983 Walaskay published a book treating the Lukan political perspective[197]. The third chapter appears to be a revision of his 1975 article, though surprisingly he made no reference to that fact[198]. His goal to advance the

---

Blinzler, Winter, Conzelmann, Dibelius and Cadbury, among others.

190. *Ibid.*, p. 82; see also p. 83 (= *'And So'*, 1983, p. 38): "While Mark attempts to reconstruct a legitimate Sanhedrin trial, Luke sets out to destroy any semblance of legitimacy".

191. *Ibid.*, p. 83. See also p. 86 (= *'And So'*, 41): "Luke stands at the beginning of a long line of Christian writers who consciously praise the Romans at the expense of the Jews".

192. *Ibid.*, p. 83, n. 8 (= *'And So'*, p. 87, n. 2, slightly revised). Cf. TAYLOR, *Passion Narrative* (1972), esp. p. 82-84, 86-89.

193. WALASKAY, *Trial*, p. 85 (= *'And So'*, 40).

194. *Ibid.*, p. 85 (= *'And So'*, 41; see also p. 86-87 = *'And So'*, 41).

195. *Ibid.*, p. 87 (= *'And So'*, 42).

196. LÉGASSE, *Le procès*, t. 2, p. 376, n. 78.

197. WALASKAY, *'And So We Came to Rome'. The Political Perspective of St Luke* (SNTS MS, 49), Cambridge, 1983.

198. There was no admission of this fact in the preface and the title was absent from the section of his bibliography containing periodical articles (p. 111-113). The chapter was substantially the same in the sections with which we are concerned.

idea that Luke was attempting to promote the Roman empire to the Church rather than vice versa was inspired by Acts 17,6. "According to this perspective, the Christian church and the Roman empire need not fear or suspect each other, for God stands behind both institutions giving to each the power and the authority to carry out his will"[199]. Walaskay generally stood by his earlier conclusions concerning Luke's redaction of Mk in the Sanhedrin hearing and the Roman trial as well as the composition of the Herod pericope. He seemed to have tempered his view that Paul's trial served as the model for that of Jesus. In his essay he maintained, "*it may well be* that the reverse process took place, so that Luke has styled the account in the Gospel after the lavish and full account that he has included in Acts 26 ..."[200]. That was emended to, "it *might be*" and "perhaps" was also added[201].

In a subsequent chapter treating the trial of Paul, Walaskay again raised the possibility that the "description of Paul's trial" influenced the composition of the trial of Jesus, particularly with regard to the "Herodian involvement in both trials"[202]. But the fact that the brief discussion was relegated to a note might suggest further that Walaskay was not so convinced of that theory.

Walaskay (1975) rehearsed the five theories why Pilate sent Jesus to Herod[203]. Godet proposed that Pilate wanted to pass off an unwanted case[204]. Walaskay dismissed this view since Herod offered very little assistance. As to the view of Sherwin-White and Hoehner that Pilate was seeking to placate Herod for a massacre, which was plausible, Walaskay rejected it since no information was given about the event and it did not appear that Pilate was afraid of Herod. As regards Caird's and Findlay's suggestion that Luke possessed some special sources, Walaskay was unconvinced since Luke omitted "the most well-attested story about the tetrarch, the beheading of John the Baptist"[205]. Walaskay repudiated Mommsen's contention that Herod possessed the power to try Jesus because of a law of *forum domicilii*. Since it was unlikely that Jesus would have been accorded the right given under Octavian to be tried in his own native land or free city, and even more unlikely that Herod would have been able to retain the broad powers extended to his father for extradition, Walaskay eliminated this as a possibility.

Walaskay endorsed the view of Dibelius and Cadbury that Luke composed the account based on Ps 2,1-2[206]. But Walaskay added further a point taken up later

---

199. *Ibid.*, p. ix-x.

200. *Trial*, 1975, p. 89.

201. *'And So'*, p. 43 [emphasis added]. Cf. *Trial*, p. 89.

202. *'And So'*, p. 100, n. 37. He invited comparison with CADBURY, *Making*, 1927, p. 310, and J. MUNCK, *The Acts of the Apostles*, Garden City, NY, 1967, lxxvii-lxxviii.

203. *Trial*, in *JBL* 94 (1975) 87-90.

204. *Ibid.*, p. 87.

205. *Ibid.*, p. 88.

206. WALASKAY, *Trial*, p. 88, n. 23. Cf. DIBELIUS, *From Tradition* (1935), p. 199, and *Herodes und Pilatus* (1915). Cf. further CADBURY, *Making*, 1927, p. 231.

by Matera, that the Herod story was fashioned on the account in Acts 26[207]. Because of the obvious contrast, that Jesus was silent though Paul offered his apologia, this did not seem to be the case. But Walaskay was correct to note that the mockery contained in the Herod scene was taken from Mk. The recasting of the story highlighted the innocence of Pilate and Rome while portraying Herod and the Jewish leaders in a very negative light. Herod linked the Roman empire with the Jewish leadership, the Sanhedrin.

But Walaskay took issue with Dibelius's interpretation of Ps 2. Because Herod Agrippa, who had been appointed king for the tetrarchy of Philip, had sought the help of Herod Antipas in Palestine, Walaskay contended this presented problems[208]. "This brings into question the theory that Herod Antipas and Pilate are the 'king and ruler' of Luke's exegesis of Psalm 2. Luke is certainly aware that Herod is no king; in 9:7 he corrects the title given to Herod by Mark (6:14), and in Acts 12:1 he rightly refers to 'Herod (Agrippa) the king'"[209]. Verse 23,12 was interpreted to mean that both Pilate and Herod had fallen from the favor of the emperor, Pilate because of his mistreatment of Samaritans and Herod on account of conspiring with Sejanus and the Parthian king Artabanus, resulting in their being friends, rather than friends to Caesar[210].

Michael D. GOULDER (1977-78) argued "the minor agreements in fact provide the most important test of the 4ST [four source theory]"[211]. Following his study of various MAs including 22,62.64, he announced his conclusion: "I do not see how we are to avoid the conclusion that Luke knew Matthew: and that conclusion entails the end of Q"[212].

---

207. WALASKAY, *Trial*, p. 89: "But with regard to the episode of the accused before the house of Herod, it may well be that the reverse process took place, so that Luke has styled the account in the Gospel after the lavish and full account that he has included in Acts 26, where Paul gives his last, grand apology before Herod Agrippa, Festus, Bernice, and all the great men of Caesarea". See also MATERA, *Luke 23,1-25*, ²1989, p. 545, n. 31. Kurz also subscribed to this view (*CBQ* 40 [1978] 633).

208. WALASKAY, *Trial*, p. 89: "Now one of the first acts of Tiberius' successor, Gaius, was to name Aristobulus' prodigal son, Herod Agrippa, as king over the tetrarchy of Philip. Herod Agrippa then journeyed to Palestine to solicit the aid of his brother-in-law Herod Antipas (the Herod of Jesus' trial)".

209. *Ibid.*, p. 89, n. 28.

210. *Ibid.*, p. 89, 90.

211. M.D. GOULDER, *On Putting Q to the Test*, in *NTS* 24 (1977-78) 218-234. T.A. Friedrichsen who closely analyzed the phenomenon of MAs observed Goulder was a student of A. Farrer (*The Matthew-Luke Agreements Against Mark. A Survey of Recent Studies: 1974-1989*, in F. NEIRYNCK [ed.], *L'Évangile de Luc – The Gospel of Luke* [BETL, 32], Leuven, ²1989, p. 335-391, p. 366); see also p. 380, n. 182.

212. GOULDER, *On Putting*, p. 234. He continued: "The evidence from the agreements shows that Luke knew Matthew, and that Q is therefore no longer a valid hypothesis".

Goulder (1989) authored a two-volume commentary on Lk which disclosed that he shared a similarity of methodology with Gundry[213]. Goulder eschewed the interaction with other commentators, such as Schürmann, Marshall and Fitzmyer, choosing rather to focus on his text and his own interpretation of it[214]. Not only that, he endorsed the idea that Luke knew Mt which explained, among other things, the MA in 22,64 / Mt 26,68 diff Mk 14,65[215]. Goulder also asserted that copyists had a tendency to use Mt as the model to which the other conformed, and thus the need for Q was eliminated. He was strongly opposed to the idea of a special source which he termed a "soft line solution". Here he referred to Léon-Dufour and Schramm, but he was even more critical of Boismard's theory which he believed to be "an extreme alternative"[216]. Thus, he leaned in the direction of simplicity for the solution of the synoptic problem. He further distinguished himself from Gundry and Morgenthaler who, though accepting that Luke knew Mt, also endorsed the existence of Q. It must be said that Goulder was very attentive to Luke's use of Mk.

While not denying the possibility that Luke may have obtained some of this special material from other oral or written traditions, Goulder was clear that some of the special material may stem from Luke himself[217]. The consensus of the various studies of special Lukan vocabulary indicated that most of it derived from Luke's redaction of Mk[218]. A lesser amount was supplied by Luke's redaction of "Q/Mt". Goulder quoted Hawkins that there was no vocabulary "characteristic of any *source* (whether Logian, Marcan or specially Lukan)". Further, Goulder negatively assessed Rehkopf's list and Jeremias's too neat division between tradition and redaction. The mention of Joanna (8,3) was taken from Luke's *Sondergut*, though the information about Mary Magdalene and other women had been transposed from Mk 15,40f. to this place in Lk.

Goulder offered in Chapter 3 his critique of Taylor, Schürmann and Rehkopf and thus rejected the idea of an additional source in the Lukan passion narrative[219]. Goulder detected Markan influence at the following points in the

213. GOULDER, *Luke: A New Paradigm* (JSNT SS, 20), 2 vols., Sheffield, 1989 (esp. Vol. 1, p. 72; Vol. 2, p. 719-720, 747-762).

214. *Ibid.*, Preface.

215. *Ibid.*, p. 7. For Goulder's reaction to Neirynck's discussion of this MA, see p. 8-9. Neirynck responded further that Goulder misstated his position (*The Minor Agreements and the Two-Source Theory*, in F. VAN SEGBROECK [ed.], *Evangelica II*, 1991, 3-42, esp. p. 27-28 = *Die Minor Agreements in den synoptischen Evangelien*, 1993, 25-63, esp. p. 49-50; Neirynck added: "The section on Mt 26,68 / Lk 22,64 is a later insertion in the text of Goulder's Chapter 1: 'A House Built on Sand', a revised version of his essay in A.E. HARVEY [ed.], *Alternative Approaches to the New Testament*, London, 1985, p. 1-24" [NEIRYNCK, p. 28, n. 143 = p. 49, n. 143]).

216. GOULDER, *Luke*, p. 10.

217. *Ibid.*, p. 79.

218. *Ibid.*, p. 80. See Goulder's list of Lukan vocabulary, Vol. 2, p. 800-809.

219. *Ibid.*, p. 719.

Lukan text: 22,54 (συλλαβεῖν from Mk 14,48), παιδίσκη (22,56 / Mk 14,67 plus the "form of the sentence"), πρὸς τὸ φῶς (22,56 / Mk 14,54), ἰδών (22,58 / Mk 14,69 ἰδοῦσα), ἀληθείας, καὶ γὰρ Γαλιλαῖος (22,59 / Mk 14,70 ἀληθῶς ... καὶ γὰρ Γαλιλαῖος εἶ); "Man, I do not know what you are saying" (22,60 / Mk 14,68, but revised). The words of 22,61f. were basically the same as in Mk 14,72, having only replaced τὸ ῥῆμα with the phrase τοῦ ῥήματος τοῦ κυρίου[220]. The MA (v. 62) was ascribed to Luke on the basis of the very Lukan vocabulary of ὁ κύριος and στραφείς. Luke also revised the Markan mockery scene with more specific indications and Goulder offered good rebuttal to those who maintain this story derived from L[221]. But even here some Matthean influence was detected by Goulder.

Further Markan influence was perceived at 22,66 (Mk 15,1f.), though Luke changed the Sanhedrin to refer to the council chambers (cf. Acts 4,15). The parallelism in 22,68 Goulder believed to stem from Mk 14,61 just as μαρτυρία (22,71) derived from Mk 14,59 and ἐγώ εἰμι (22,71) came from Mk 14,62. Lk 23,3 was "a virtual transcription" of Mk 15,2[222]. The crowds at 23,5 were taken from Mk 15,8. Luke took from Mk also the idea of the persistence of the religious leaders (Mk 15,11.14b), as well as the term ἀνασείειν (23,5 / Mk 15,11). Shouting was found in both Mk and Lk (23,18 Ἀνέκραγον / Mk 15,13 πάλιν ἔκραξαν). The phrase "release for them Barabbas" (Mk 15,11b) was improved by Luke in 23,18. The references to the insurrection and murder were also drawn from Mk by Luke, who adopted πάλιν (23,20 from Mk), though this was not his general practice.

Other aspects of Lk were similar to Mk, for example, the timing of the mockery. Goulder rightly looked for connection in Acts as in the case of the demand for Jesus' execution (23,18; Acts 21,36; 22,22). Luke's redaction involved improving the portrayal of Peter, so that he will not appear as being afraid of a serving girl, of telescoping Markan material (the two remarks of the girl), and in toning down the "overevehement Markan wording" in Peter's denial (22,60 / Mk 14,71)[223]. Further Luke changed Mk through omissions, such as the deleted story of the mockery by the Roman soldiers (Mk 15,16-20) but shifted the elements to the story of Herod[224]. In Goulder's view Luke's recasting of Mk can sometimes be "rather forceful manipulation"[225].

There is much in Goulder's commentary to recommend it. But Goulder also considered Mt an additional source. In Luke's composition of the account of Peter's denial based on Mk and embellished with Mt, Lk and Mt agreed twice within eleven verses[226]. The ὁ δὲ Πέτρος ἠκολούθει ... μακρόθεν (22,54 / Mt

220. *Ibid.*, p. 749. Goulder had λόγου in place of ῥήματος.
221. *Ibid.*, p. 752.
222. *Ibid.*, p. 756.
223. *Ibid.*, p. 749.
224. *Ibid.*, p. 756.
225. *Ibid.*
226. *Ibid.*, p. 747.

26,58) reflected Matthean influence for Goulder, but Gundry did not mention it. While Gundry believed that ἐκάθητο (22,55 / Mt 26,58) was a replacement for the Markan periphrastic ἦν συγκαθήμενος, Goulder claimed Luke employed Mt's ἐκάθητο[227]. Like Gundry, Goulder detected Matthean influence in the elimination of the term ἐκ δευτέρου (22,60 / Mt 26,74). While it can only be assumed that Gundry held that the MA in v. 62 resulted from Matthean influence, Goulder was quite explicit[228]. Goulder further asserted the MA 22,64 / Mt 26,68 stemmed from Luke's use of Mt (contra Tuckett and Neirynck) because of similar word order for seven words (only one of which occurred in Mk) and the limited use of παίειν in Lk-Acts[229]. Goulder offered helpful insight in resolving the difficulty of the αὐτόν in 22,63. Luke intermittently failed to make clear his subject in a transition (9,10 referring to Herod; 23,27, Simon; 23,49 the centurion)[230]. Is it not significant that in the instances Goulder cited, Luke was dealing in the first case with Herod and in the other, two instances in the passion narrative? Gundry maintained that in one case Luke combined Mt and Mk. Goulder also claimed this to be the case in 22,66 (Mk 15,1f. and Mt 27,1f. with Mt 26,57)[231]. Further Matthean influence was ascribed to "elders of the people" (πρεσβυτέριον 22,66 / Mt 27,1 πρεσβύτεροι τοῦ λαοῦ), συνήχθησαν (22,66 / Mt 26,57), and ἀπήγαγον (22,66 / Mt 26,57 and Mk 14,53) reflected Matthean as well as Markan (so also at 22,70f.). Lk 22,67 reflected once more the Matthean influence (Mt 26,63) though Luke placed the words εἰπὸν ἡμῖν at the end of the sentence.

Luke's purported revision of 22,69 from Mt was quite radical. Luke omitted "you will see", changed ἀπ' ἄρτι (Mt 26,64) to ἀπὸ τοῦ νῦν as Gundry also proposed, retained the Matthean order of καθήμενος ἐκ δεξιῶν (22,69 / Mt 26,64) as Gundry likewise maintained, and substituted τοῦ θεοῦ for τῆς δυνάμεως[232].

Matthew was made responsible for σὺ ... ὁ υἱὸς τοῦ θεοῦ (22,70 / Mt 26,63). But Luke combined the Markan and Matthean responses and added ὑμεῖς λέγετε ὅτι ἐγώ εἰμι. Further probable influence was seen in ἤγαγον αὐτόν (23,1 / Mt 27,1 αὐτὸν ἀπήγαγον). In 23,1-5 it was very clear that Goulder supported Lukan redaction of Mk, so also in 23,18-23 with no reference to any Matthean influence at all. However some similarity between Mt and Lk was detected at 23,25 (/ Mt 27,26 ἀπέλυσεν ... τὸν (B.) ... τὸν δὲ Ἰησοῦν παρέδωκεν) and although Goulder did not expressly state his position, we can assume here that Luke was following Mt[233].

227. GUNDRY, Matthew, p. 541. Cf. GOULDER, Luke, Vol. 2, p. 747. However, Goulder claimed the augmented form at 18,35 was derived from Mk. In addition, later Goulder invited comparison of the term with Mk's συγκαθήμενος (Vol. 2, p. 751).
228. GOULDER, Luke, p. 750. Cf. GUNDRY, Matthew, p. 551.
229. GOULDER, Luke, p. 750. Cf. Vol. 1, p. 6-9.
230. Ibid., p. 752.
231. Ibid., p. 753.
232. Ibid., p. 754.
233. Ibid., p. 761.

The transposition in 22,54-71 resulted from Luke's collapsing the two Sanhedrin meetings, eliminating their formal judicial character and portraying the Jewish authorities "in the worst possible light"[234]. Luke himself was responsible for introducing certain material including the third accusation of the denial story[235]. The omission of the trial arose from two reasons: Luke assembled the denial material to transpire in conjunction with the dawn and Luke's redactional tendency in dealing with Jewish leaders to present their proceedings as folly[236]. This was not such a significant lacuna at this point in the Gospel, for Goulder rightly pointed out that many of the details were transferred to the story of Stephen (Acts 6,11-14).

Goulder (1989) rejected the Herod scene as historical for two reasons: its absence from Mk and the unlikelihood that Pilate would have transferred Jesus to Herod[237]. But Luke did not simply create the scene *ex nihilo*. Certain linguistic evidence led Goulder to surmise that Luke was drawing on Mt. Because Lk 23,9 and Mt 27,12 had οὐδὲν ἀπεκρίνατο where no Markan parallel existed, and whereas Mk has οὐδὲν ἀπεκρίθη (Mk 15,5), Goulder believed that Mt served as the source. Goulder maintained his view was further reinforced by the appearance of λίαν in 23,8 / Mt 27,14. Although it appeared four times in Mk, Luke changed it in each instance. Also because Matthew employed the term ἡγούμενος (23,9a / Mt 27,11), this too suggested to Goulder Luke's adaptation of Mt. While Luke began by using Mk's account as the basis for 23,1-15, he then shifted to use Mt's account of the trial before the prince.

The parallel elements included the interrogation by the prince (Mt 27,11 / 23,9a), Jesus' silence (Mt 27,12 / 23,9b), the accusations by the Jewish leaders (Mt 27,12 [elders] / 23,10 [scribes]), the prince's soldiers (Mt 27,27) were shifted with the mockery (Mt 27,31 / 23,11) and the mention of the vesture (Mt 27,28f. / 23,11). Because Luke understood that the scene was over and the account of Pilate resumed, he began to conclude his episode (23,13). Luke deduced from Mt 27,14 that a cordial relationship now existed between Herod and Pilate, which was reflected in 23,12[238].

Goulder aligned himself with Grundmann and against Dibelius, Bultmann, and Creed, holding that the story provided a second witness to the innocence of Jesus. The pericope's origin in Ps 2 was rejected since the Herod story did not speak of a conspiracy. Goulder believed Luke drew the story from Mt, though the story did not appear in Mt.

---

234. *Ibid.*, p. 748.
235. *Ibid.*, p. 749.
236. *Ibid.*, p. 753.
237. *Ibid.*, p. 757.
238. *Ibid.*, p. 758-759. HOEHNER, *Herod Antipas*, p. 227, also envisioned the possibility that the Herod trial was based upon a Matthean tradition.

The Reception of Goulder's Commentary

Frederick Danker penned reviews of Goulder's work in two periodicals. In the first he pointed out that Goulder was dissatisfied "with research based principally on word counts and concordance study"[239]. Further, Danker indicated that Goulder rejected the idea that the special Lukan material was in written form, and should rather be ascribed to Luke's creativity[240]. In Danker's view, Goulder's commentary offered "disquieting evidence" which will shake the self possessed and complacent advocates of the two-source theory who hold both that Q and a special Lukan source existed[241].

In his slightly later and more expanded review Danker observed Goulder's new paradigm basically abolished any semblance of L; Lukan creativity then became responsible for such material[242]. He commented that Goulder's attempt to dismiss the idea of a special source or sources for Lk resulted from the fact that "Luke frequently sacrifices poetic quality in Matthew and comes up with clumsy expressions, while at the same time displaying varying degrees of ignorance about agriculture and business"[243]. He also took exception to Goulder's categorization of Luke as a writer of poor quality.

Danker concurred that word counts were a less effective means of determining dependence than this type of reasoning. But Danker ultimately challenged Goulder's procedure. "Indeed, without Luke's creativity and Matthew's poetic genius Goulder would have no case for the elimination of L and Q. But once the door is ajar for romance, scientific exegesis must exit, and endless possibilities triumph over historical probabilities. One must therefore wonder whether Goulder's endeavor to map the creative processes of the right side of Matthew's and Luke's brains more adequately meets the demands of the scientific inquiry than the simpler solution represented, e.g. by the four-source hypothesis and variations thereof"[244].

According to Robert O'Toole, of the two "novel" conclusions which Goulder introduced, the elimination of Q and the elimination of the *Sondergut* in favor of Luke's creativity, O'Toole found the second to be the more radical[245]. While O'Toole was not convinced by Goulder's arguments dismissing Q in particular, nor of his arguments in general, he was nonetheless favorably impressed with Goulder's method of determining Lukan redaction. "G. does provide many helpful insights into Luke's vocabulary, style, characteristics, and background, and the vast amount of data that he gathers and organizes in defense of his theses is truly

239. *CurrTMiss* 17 (1990) 230.
240. *Ibid.*, p. 231.
241. *Ibid.*
242. *JBL* 110 (1991) 163.
243. *Ibid.*
244. *Ibid.*, p. 164.
245. *CBQ* 53 (1991) 326.

impressive"[246]. But O'Toole further critiqued Goulder's attempt to refute the special source(s) of Luke on the ground that it was difficult to distinguish what stemmed from Luke and what from the source, since Luke so thoroughly "dominates his material". The "possibility of conjecture" sometimes then was reduced to nothing more than "guesswork"[247]. I. Howard Marshall likened the work to Gundry's and welcomed it as a fresh study which would call for reaction from Goulder's opponents to refute his source theory and counter arguments[248].

Though John Nolland did not consider Goulder's attempt successful, he complimented him for "regularly acute" observations, which included honing in on the weakness of the traditional source theories[249]. But in the end, Goulder fell prey to what he railed against, "of treating a non-proof of the opposite as establishing his own case"[250]. While Nolland evaluated Goulder as unsuccessful, nevertheless, the work was "valuable". John Fenton called attention to the fact that Goulder was continuing in the line of A.M. Farrer, but like Danker, O'Toole and Nolland, Fenton did not find the work convincing[251].

F. Neirynck highlighted Goulder's thesis about the calendrical theory that the section 22,54-65 would be read at 3 a.m., 22,66–23,12 at 6 a.m. and 23,13-32 at 9 a.m. as part of an all day liturgy on passover[252]. The more significant aspect of Goulder's new paradigm, in Neirynck's opinion, was the list of Lukan words. Though lacking a comparison to similar lists compiled by other scholars, Neirynck acknowledged 383 expressions which "can be considered a welcome extension of Hawkins' list"[253].

F. Scott Spencer queried "whether the fascinating connections Goulder makes between Luke and Matthew and the OT owe more to Goulder's lively imagination than to Luke's"[254]. Rather than viewing Mt as one of the sources referred to in the Lukan Prologue, Spencer preferred to see "independent traditions". On the positive side, Goulder did "raise some legitimate questions" about source and redaction criticism. Spencer voted in favor of the synchronic method of interpretation which valued the final product over an investigation of the process of how the Gospels came to be.

F. Gerald Downing rejected Goulder's attempt at a solution, firmly convinced of the correctness of the Two-Document hypothesis[255]. The practice of conflating

---

246. *Ibid.*, p. 325, 326.
247. *Ibid.*, p. 326.
248. *ExpT* 101 (1989-90) 311, 312.
249. *ScotJT* 43 (1990) 271-272.
250. *Ibid.*, p. 271.
251. *TLond* 93 (1990) 68.
252. *ETL* 67 (1991) 434.
253. *Ibid.*, p. 436.
254. *WestTJ* 53 (1991) 365.
255. *A Paradigm Perplex: Luke, Matthew and Mark*, in *NTS* 38 (1992) 15-36. Although chiefly directed as a negative critique of Goulder, Downing also included Boismard and those whose solution tended toward complexity in sources and compositional technique. See also

"two parallel accounts of the same event would be very uncommon"[256]. Regarding the anointing, both Downing and Goulder agreed that Luke could have redacted it and transposed it to the position it held in Lk (7,36-50)[257]. In the passion narrative, Luke's method would have been much freer[258]. Downing's characterization of Goulder's assumption of Luke alternating between numerous written scrolls and use of his memory was almost comical. Much of Downing's argument came from the writing style in use in late antiquity. The educational program of this period would have taught the student to "paraphrase, précis, expand and simply omit"[259]. "When Lucian talks about writing history, there is no instruction on splicing sources, let alone unravelling them first. Livy, Polybius, Dionysius, Josephus, Plutarch and the rest just go ahead and write, on the basis of a single prior text in front of them, paraphrasing, précising, expanding, omitting, while relying otherwise for the most part only on unchecked memories of other sources and even of the one in front of them"[260]. He also noted why changes would be incorporated: "The criteria for change, for what counts as improvement, are narrative coherence, plausibility, interest, clarity, religious piety and propriety, and informal 'political' apologetic"[261]. Downing castigated Luke for attempting to harmonize his account with the other Synoptics, when in fact, Downing astutely observed, the resulting Lk was quite different from the other two. He was not always opposed to Goulder's findings[262].

Downing also ascribed to Luke the likelihood of freely reshaping and even creating material, such as speeches. He understood order as referred to in the Prologue (1,3) to mean "logical rather than factually chronological"[263].

DOWNING, *Compositional Conventions and the Synoptic Problem*, in *JBL* 107 (1988) 69-85. For Goulder's response to Downing's critique see GOULDER, *Luke's Compositional Options*, in *NTS* 39 (1993) 150-152, esp. p. 150, where Goulder alleged "these criticisms are difficult to follow, and in some places appear to be self-contradictory".

256. DOWNING, *A Paradigm Perplex*, p. 17.

257. *Ibid.*

258. *Ibid.*, p. 18. "In those places where close visual attention to a single source seems discernible, the result will often be a paraphrase rather than word-for-word quotation. Thus Luke's freer renderings (especially the Passion narrative) would not be at all unexpected. Indeed, we might rather be surprised at Luke's so often including so much of Matthew's wording as exactly as on this hypothesis he does". Stressing the freedom with which Luke revised Mk, Downing wrote: "He has all the liberty he requires to allow him to achieve any theological interpretation or narrative impact that appeals to him" (p. 31).

259. *Ibid.*, p. 22.

260. *Ibid.*

261. *Ibid.*

262. *Ibid.*, p. 23: "[Luke] might on a few occasions have produced the results we find, as I have already allowed, and even for at least some of the reasons Dr Goulder allows". For elements which could well have influenced Luke's writing, see the list p. 23-24.

263. *Ibid.*, p. 26.

MAs were considered possible by means of the paraphrasing, but this seemed highly unlikely to me[264]. If, as Goulder suggested, Luke was working from the other Synoptics, then such "scant reconciliation" was unusual. Thus, based on conventional writing practice of the period and reference to secular writers ultimately Downing rejected Goulder's solution for not being as simple as he claimed. Downing also suggested, jokingly, that Goulder had read the mind of Luke[265].

At the 1991 Göttingen Symposium on the MAs, Goulder argued that although in 22,64 Luke was redacting Mk, "five words identical" with Mt indicate Luke's knowledge of that Gospel[266]. While Neirynck offered, in his opinion, "the most persuasive defense of the standard position"[267], Goulder remained unconvinced. He considered it unlikely that a copyist of Mt would have misunderstood the text in the same way as Luke and that there would be no surviving copies. Goulder asserted that "it is nearly agreed that if Luke wrote 22,62 he must have taken it from Matthew"[268]. The verse was consistent with Luke's portrayal of Peter throughout the Gospel. Goulder judged Tuckett's arguments that v. 62 was best omitted as "not strong"[269].

Neirynck (1997) reacted to a work by M.S. Goodacre which analyzed, in part, Goulder's positions on the MAs[270]. Goodacre described the MA at Mk 14,65 (Lk 22,64 / Mt 26,68) as Goulder's "key MA"[271]. After Neirynck laid out Goodacre's evaluation of Goulder's arguments, and Goodacre's rejection of the solution of conjectural emendation, he underscored that Goodacre had only defined conjectural emendation, but did not provide a "justification of its rejection in the case of Mt 26,68"[272]. Thus, he reasserted this solution and noted the "growing number of scholars for whom an exceptional instance of conjectural reading is no longer methodologically unacceptable"[273].

---

264. *Ibid.*, p. 29.

265. *Ibid.*, p. 35.

266. GOULDER, *Luke's Knowledge of Matthew*, in G. STRECKER (ed.), *Minor Agreements: Symposium Göttingen* (GTA, 50), Göttingen, 1993, 153-154. He treated the MAs in 22,62.64 on p. 153-156.

267. NEIRYNCK, ΤΙΣ ΕΣΤΙΝ (1987).

268. *Ibid.*, p. 155.

269. Ibid., p. 156. Cf. C.M. TUCKETT, *On the Relationship between Matthew and Luke*, in *NTS* 30 (1984) 130-142.

270. *Goulder and the Minor Agreements*, in *ETL* 73 (1997) 84-93, which involved an analysis of M.S. GOODACRE, *Goulder and the Gospels. An Examination of a New Paradigm* (JSNT SS, 133), Sheffield, 1996, esp. p. 89-130: "The Minor Agreements and Characteristic Language". Diss. Oxford, 1994 (dir. J. MUDDIMAN).

271. GOODACRE, *Examination*, p. 101-107.

272. NEIRYNCK, *Goulder*, p. 92.

273. *Ibid.* He referred to his article *Literary Criticism*, citing the support of B. ALAND, *Das Zeugnis der frühen Papyri für den Text der Evangelien diskutiert am Matthäusevangelium*, in FS NEIRYNCK, Vol. 1, 1992, p. 326-335, esp. 326, and VANHOYE, *L'intérêt, ibid.*, p. 1529-1548, esp. 1544-1548.

One of the most recent proponents of the idea that Luke knew and used Mt was Barbara SHELLARD (1995). She signaled her agreement with Goulder, among others. But she also indicated that Luke had "independent knowledge of some of the material shared by Matthew", a position she stated was contrary to Goulder[274].

She dedicated a section to Jesus' appearance before the Jewish authorities (Lk 22,54-71; 23,6-12; Jn 18,12-28). Observing that the "denial sequence" differed in Lk from the other Gospels, she added: "Some features of this sequence are characteristically Lukan, such as the presumably reproachful glance Jesus directs at Peter in 22:61, which provokes the disciple's immediate remorse. The whole scene is thus more pathetic and provides a more direct illustration of Luke's theme of repentance"[275]. She argued 22,59 "contains echoes" of Mk 14,70 and Jn 18,26[276]. Luke was also credited with "condensing the two trials into one", as were reported in the other Synoptics[277].

Though Evans argued that Luke was condensing and freely redacting Mk 14,55-64, Shellard insisted this approach "ignores the closer parallel between Luke 22:67-71 and John 10:24-25,36"[278]. At least at one point she maintained that Luke combined Mk and Jn. She noted Luke postponed the reference to false witnesses and the threat against the Temple to the trial of Stephen in Acts[279].

Drawing on Taylor and H. Klein she evaluated the Herod story, commenting the "account reflects [Luke's] own interests"[280]. Using Taylor's statistics she asserted there were 15 characteristically Lukan terms and concluded "there is little to suggest the use of a source here"[281]. She insisted, however, that there was "some literary relationship" between Lk and Jn[282].

---

274. B. SHELLARD, *The Relationship of Luke and John: A Fresh Look at an Old Problem*, in *JTS* 46 (1995) 71-98, p. 71, n. 1. Her solution to the relationship question was that Luke used Jn.

275. *Ibid.*, p. 87.

276. *Ibid.*, p. 88.

277. *Ibid.*, p. 89.

278. *Ibid.* Cf. C.F. EVANS, *St. Luke*, 1990, p. 833.

279. SHELLARD, *Relationship*, p. 84. See further p. 89, where she repeated this assertion and noted similarities with Paul's situation in Acts 23,4.

280. *Ibid.*, p. 90. See TAYLOR, *Passion Narrative*, p. 87, and H. KLEIN, *ZNW* 67, p. 367f.

281. SHELLARD, *Relationship*, p. 90.

282. *Ibid.*, p. 91.

Others who adhered to the idea that Luke employed Matthew included Gregory
MURRAY (1985)[283], Bernard ORCHARD (1988)[284], Harold RILEY (1993)[285],
D.B. PEABODY (1992-95)[286], and possibly Jon WEATHERLY (1994)[287].

283. Murray held what he considered to be the probable view that Mark used Mt and Lk,
combining and correcting them and adding material "on Peter's evidence" (*Saint Peter's Denials*,
in *DownR* 103 [1985] 297). The prediction of the denial also gave the impression Mark conflated
the other Synoptics since Mk contained both "today, this night" (cf. Mt 26,34 this night; Lk
23,34 today).

284. Orchard suggested Paul commanded Luke to compose a new Gospel "from original
sources", though using Mt as a model (*The Formation of the Synoptic Gospels*, in *DownR* 106
[1988] 10). Omitting what would have been of no interest to the Gentiles for whom he was
writing, Luke during a two year sojourn in Jerusalem, inquired of a great number of original
witnesses information about the life and times of Jesus (p. 10). Though written before Mk, Lk
was not published until after it (p. 15).

285. An advocate of the Griesbach theory, Riley argued that while Luke used Mt in many
parts of his Gospel, in the passion "Luke shows an independence from Matthew" (*Preface to
Luke*, Macon, GA, 1993, p. 35, 4). He also rejected Streeter's proposal of Proto-Lk (p. 14).

286. A group of scholars, proponents of the Two-Gospel hypothesis, have been collaborating
in an analysis of the narrative outline and composition of Lk (L. COPE, D.L. DUNGAN, W.R.
FARMER, A.J. MCNICOL, D.B. PEABODY, and P.L. SHULER, *Narrative Outline of the
Composition of Luke according to the Two-Gospel Hypothesis*, in *SBL 1992 Seminar Papers* (Lk
1,1-7,10), 82-120; *SBL 1993 Seminar Papers* (7,11-9,50), 303-333; *SBL 1994 Seminar Papers*
(9,51-19,27), 526-573). In a 1995 contribution Peabody examined 22,66b-71 and 23,1,25. He
contended that in the Sanhedrin scene Luke followed Mt's order arguing that Luke split Mt 26,57-
75, placing them in two different locales (*SBL 1995 Seminar Papers* [19,28-24,53], 636-687, p.
673 = A.J. MCNICOL, D.L. DUNGAN and D.B. PEABODY [eds.], *Beyond the Q Impasse – Luke's
Use of Matthew. A Demonstration by the Research Team of the International Institute for Gospel
Studies*, Valley Forge, PA, 1996, esp. p. 245-317). As with many Markan priorists, Peabody
viewed the Lukan account as removing the blame from the Romans and placing it, even as he
intensified it, upon the Jewish authorities. In 22,66 Matthean influence was credited with the
reference to day (Mt 27,1), and echoes reflected in ἀπήγαγον (Mt 26,57) and συνέδριον (Mt
26,59). However, the phrase καὶ ὡς was deemed Lukan (See J.G.F. COLLISON, *Linguistic Usages
in the Gospel of Luke*. Diss. Southern Methodist U., Dallas, TX, 1977 [dir. W.R. FARMER], p.
117), and the "use of καὶ ἐγένετο is a classic Lukan Septuagintism" (PEABODY, p. 674 =
MCNICOL, p. 296; cf. COLLISON, *Linguistic*, p. 42-43). The analysis of 22,67a focused on the
omission of the early portion of Matthew's account of this scene, including reference to false
witnesses and the comment about the destruction of the Temple. Peabody claimed Luke was
responsible for separating the question in Mt 26,63b into two questions. Lk 22,69 was drawn
from Mt 26,64, but in this case Luke "completely de-eschatologizes Matthew's quotation of Dan
7:7-13" (PEABODY, p. 674 = MCNICOL, p. 296). Luke's substitution of ἀπὸ τοῦ νῦν for ἀπ᾽
ἄρτι was also seen as confirming Luke's use of Mt, but also improving the style. In 22,70-71
Luke was seen as taking material from Mt 26,63b.64a and combining it, indicating that the
changes reflected "Luke's missionary agenda in the wider Gentile missionary world" (PEABODY,
p. 675; cf. MCNICOL, p. 297).

For the section 23,1-25 Luke improved Matthew's order in which he "creates a dramatic series
of sharply etched trial scenes" (PEABODY, p. 675 = MCNICOL, p. 298). For 23,1-3 Luke
combined material from Mt 27,2.11-14. The omission of the Matthean account of Judas' death
(Mt 27,3-10) was explained by Luke's intention to recount it in Acts 1,16-20. Characteristic

Returning to our treatment of Luke's redaction of Mk, Robert J. KARRIS has been
more concerned to investigate the *Sitz im Leben* of the Lukan writings than to delve
deeply into source criticism[288]. His Lukan commentary (1977) offered little in the

Lukan vocabulary or construction included ἀνιστᾶν (23,1) and [ἅ]πας τὸ πλῆθος (PEABODY, p.
675 = MCNICOL, p. 298-299). In composing 23,2-3 Luke modified Mt 27,11-12. The charges
in 23,2 were seen as Lukan composition. 23,3a was based upon Mt 27,11a. A similarity between
Lk and Acts was detected in 23,2 when compared with Acts 24,2. For 23,4-5 Luke recast Mt
27,12-14 because he may have found Matthew's version "dramatically deficient" and Pilate's
reaction in Mt "too wishy-washy and ambiguous" (PEABODY, p. 676 = MCNICOL, p. 299). An
echo of the language in 23,5 was found in Acts 10,37. The "formulation" of the triple
declarations of Jesus' innocence (23,4.14.22) "may be Luke's own creation". For the Barabbas
episode, in 23,18-19 Luke abbreviated Mt 27,17-26, in 23,20-23 he modified Mt 27,21-23, and
in 23,24-25 he summarized Mt 27,24-26 (PEABODY, p. 676-677 = MCNICOL, p. 300-301).
     The Herod story (23,6-12) was judged to be "probably a Lukan composition" (PEABODY, p.
676 = MCNICOL, p. 300). Herod's desire to see Jesus was viewed as an echo of 9,7-9; 13,31-32.
The friendship of Herod and Pilate, stemming from their agreements on the innocence of Jesus,
was a "subsidiary theme". 23,13-16 was regarded as the "focal point of the pericope" as Pilate
reaffirmed his judgment. Despite the assertion that, "The language of this vignette is filled with
Lukan linguistic characteristics", Peabody cited only a few. Among them were πρός with a verb
of saying, the possible Lukan phrase παιδεύσας οὖν αὐτὸν ἀπολύσω (23,16.22b) and the term
παιδεύειν, which "occurs only in Lk among the canonical gospels".
     287. In a published version of his 1991 Aberdeen dissertation Weatherly suspended "a final
judgment on the Synoptic question", though he entertained the possibility that "Luke used
Matthew or had traditions parallel to Mark at several points" (*Jewish Responsibility for the Death
of Jesus in Luke-Acts* [JSNT SS, 106], Sheffield, 1994, p. 53, 51-52). He concluded his
introductory treatment of Luke's sources in the following manner: "All in all, these assumptions
demand that the text of the Gospel of Luke be interpreted with caution in regard to sources which
must always remain hypothetical and with attention to the wider scope of the entire narrative" (p.
54).
     Observing that 22,54 was "clearer than in the parallels" (p. 60), Weatherly attributed this to
the possibility of Lukan editing. With regard to the sources for the mockery and Sanhedrin trial
he asserted: "Luke's use of sources in his account of the mocking (22.63-65) and the Sanhedrin
trial (22.66-71) is notoriously difficult to ascertain (See also his comment, p. 63). His
transposition of the mocking scene, elimination of witnessing of separation of the high priests'
questions may be his own redaction or part of a non-Markan (or non-Matthean) source" (p. 60).
However, a little later he seemed to favor the idea of special Lukan sources (p. 61). An
explanation of the omission of the witnesses and sentencing at the hearing, like that for the
mockery and Sanhedrin trial, was likewise "difficult to assess". Although he maintained that
22,67b-68 was "easier to assess", he did not offer an opinion as to whether these elements
stemmed from tradition, redaction or a combination of both (p. 62).
     Moving to Lk 23, Weatherly maintained the same ambigiuity suggesting that 23,1 could either
be Lukan redaction of Mk 15,1 or it could have derived from a special Lukan source (p. 63).
Although he briefly treated aspects of the Herod pericope, he was not concerned with questions
of sources (p. 95-96), nor of the relationship of this passage to Acts 4,25-28 (p. 85, 92-93, 95,
n. 1).
     288. See for example, *The Lukan Sitz im Leben. Methodology and Prospects*, in *SBL 1976
Seminar Papers*, 219-234; *Poor and Rich. The Lukan Sitz im Leben*, in C.H. TALBERT (ed.),
Perspectives on Luke-Acts, 1978, 112-125; *Missionary Communities: A New Paradigm for the*

way of a comment on sources[289], though he suggested that Lk was "an account which will supplement Mark's Gospel"[290]. In *What Are They Saying about Luke and Acts?* (1979), although he wrote about the Prologue, he offered no assessment of how exegetes and theologians were treating the source question[291]. He favored the idea that in Lk-Acts Jesus's death was portrayed as that of a martyr[292]. Though he examined the Lukan account of the death of Jesus in several articles, he focused more on the theology[293].

Approaching the Lukan passion, and specifically Lk 23, as literature (1985) Karris called attention to Luke's presentation of Jesus as God's rejected prophet[294]. "In the context of Luke 23 and within that chapter itself there are a number of references to Jesus as prophet"[295]. Not only that but Luke wove this thematic through the earlier portion of the Gospel (4,18.24; 7,16; 9,22-23; 9,43b-45; 18,31-34; 13,33-34)[296]. He did not offer a detailed exegesis of Lk 23 nor did he engage in a discussion of historicity or sources[297]. Yet, for the question of sources in this section of the Gospel he referred the reader to Taylor's *The Passion Narrative of St Luke*[298].

In a 1986 essay Karris sought to highlight Luke's perspective of Jesus' death which involved a reversal of his view on the portrayal as a martyrdom[299]. His

---

Study of Luke-Acts, in *CBQ* 41 (1979) 80-97; *Windows and Mirrors. Literary Criticism and Luke's Sitz im Leben*, in *SBL 1979 Seminar Papers*, 47-58.

289. *Invitation to Luke. A Commentary on the Gospel of Luke with Complete Text of The Jerusalem Bible*, Garden City, NY, 1977, p. 21: "[Luke] used the sources of Christian tradition available to him – Mark's Gospel, collections of Jesus' sayings common to his Gospel and Matthew's, and his own church's tradition to answer the faith questions of his community".

290. *Ibid.*, p. 25. On Luke's redaction of 22,54-62, see p. 254. It was not explicit whether he favored the idea of Luke's redaction of Mk or an independent source (or sources) for 22,63-65.66-71 (p. 254-255); 23,1-25 (p. 256-259).

291. *What Are They Saying about Luke and Acts? A Theology of the Faithful God*, New York, 1979, p. 33-34.

292. *Ibid.*, p. 44.

293. An example of this is, *Luke's Soteriology of With-ness*, in *CurrTMiss* 12 (1985) 346-352.

294. *Luke: Artist and Theologian, Luke's Passion Account as Literature* (Theological Inquiries), New York, 1985, p. 18-20, 93-94.

295. *Ibid.*, p. 18. These references included 19,45-46; 22,64; 23,28-30; 23,34; 23,43; 24,19-20 (p. 18-19).

296. *Ibid.*, p. 18. On 13,33-34 see also p. 79.

297. *Ibid.*, p. 80, 81.

298. *Luke: Artist and Theologian*, p. 81, n. 9; also p. 117.

299. *Luke 23:47 and the Lukan View of Jesus' Death*, in *JBL* 105 (1986) 65-74, p. 65 (= D.D. SYLVA [ed.], *Reimaging*, 1990, 68-78, p. 68): "Luke's view of Jesus' death has a bad press. There has been a tendency to evaluate Luke's presentation by an explicit or implicit comparison with Mark and Paul". In the same volume edited by Sylva there appeared an article by E. Richard in which he examined the passion and death of Jesus in Acts. He viewed this material as having been subjected to heavy Lukan redaction (*Jesus' Passion and Death in Acts*, p. 125-152, 204-210, p. 138). He also endorsed what he considered to be the scholarly consensus that Jesus' death is regarded as a martyrdom (p. 133). Further, Richards saw Acts 4,27-28 as

change in position centered on a critique of Dibelius[300], and he now insisted the Lukan Jesus was not a martyr[301]. His view leaned more in the direction of Vanhoye suggesting the death of Jesus offered a model for his followers[302].

Karris (1990) referred only to Mk in briefly treating the question of sources in 19,28-24,54. He considered the Lukan account of Jesus' final days to be a redaction of Mk in which Luke recalled themes which he developed thoughout his Gospel[303]. Paraenesis dictated Luke's transposition of the Markan arrangement and christology helped to refashion the source material. The questioning by two men in the denials was perhaps in line with the requirement of Dt 19,15. Jesus as prophet and the able use of irony were also influential. The fact that no charge of blasphemy was made against Jesus permitted the understanding that the religious authorities blasphemed Jesus who is the Son of God. Karris was emphatic that Luke and not another source was responsible for the differences between Mk and Lk. These included: a morning trial, omission of reference to the false witnesses, no accusation against Jesus claiming to destroy the Temple, though readers were referred to Acts 6,12-14, and the Sanhedrin, rather than the high priest, carry out the proceedings. Karris did not go into detail explaining Luke's reasons for such revision. He noted how the trial in Acts followed the pattern of Jesus', which he predicted. Karris also followed Neyrey in several of his positions, particularly on the material dealing with the trial.

Karris (1977) offered few clues in his *Invitation to Luke* commentary as to what he believed to be the source for the Herod scene[304]. The Prologue indicated Luke intended to supplement Mk[305]. Karris also saw in the dual witness of Pilate and Herod the OT requirement of Dt 19,15[306]. In his later work, *Luke: Artist and Theologian* (1985), he likewise bypassed discussing the source issue, referring the reader instead to Taylor, *The Passion Narrative of St. Luke*[307]. Like Drury,

---

"composed of a citation of Ps.2:1-2 and a midrashic application of the text to the Christ-event" (p.144).

300. Cf. DIBELIUS, *From Tradition*, [n.d.], p. 201.

301. KARRIS, *Luke 23:47*, p. 68 (= SYLVA, *Reimaging*, 1990, p. 71).

302. *Ibid.*, p. 70 (= 73): "The martyr parallels may have taken hold in the analysis of Luke 22-23 because they allow the reader to grasp more easily, as a whole, the paraenetic and paradigmatic thrust of these chapters".

303. KARRIS, *The Gospel according to Luke*, in *NJBC*, 1990, p. 676. However, in the Lukan account of Jesus' ministry, Luke was said to have employed Mk, Q and L. J.M. DAWSEY, *What's in a Name? Characterization in Luke*, in *BTB* 16 (1986), 143-147, to whom Karris referred in his commentary, was also of the opinion that Luke rewrote the Markan trial scene for 22,67f. (p. 147).

304. KARRIS, *Invitation*, 1977.

305. *Ibid.*, p. 25.

306. *Ibid.*, p. 258.

307. *Luke: Artist and Theologian*, p. 81, n. 9. Willem Cornelis VAN UNNIK (1973) regarded the trial before Herod as an artistic element which underscored the dramatic heightening of entire trial (*Éléments artistiques de Luc*, in F. NEIRYNCK [ed.], *L'Évangile de Luc*, 1973, p. 137 = ²1989, 47). Unfortunately, Van Unnik did not concern himself with the historical value of this

Karris regarded 23,12 as the focal point with its highlight of reconciliation[308]. The motif of silence was not ascribed to Mk, but rather to the influence of Is 53,7 and to Luke's portrayal of Jesus as the righteous just one who trusted the Father completely. Following the reasoning of P. Joüon, Karris proposed the idea that the dazzling apparel was not royal clothing, but "the white garment (*toga candida*) which a candidate for office wore"[309]. The dazzling apparel may either signify purity or the clothing of a political candidate. Jesus' "candidacy" referred to the possibility that he might be "elected" to be freed rather than Barabbas. Such an interpretation was unconvincing[310].

In his commentary in the *NJBC* (1990) Karris did not treat the source question in detail either, suggesting as before that the silence motif stemmed from Is 53,7[311]. The dazzling clothing Karris understood to be white, symbolizing the purity of Jesus as well as signifying the garment worn by candidates for public office. Adopting the stance of Soards, the friendship between Pilate and Herod was seen as revealing the power of Jesus to reconcile.

Karlheinz MÜLLER (1979) advocated the view that Luke composed 23,6-12, which Müller described as a "kleine literarische Schöpfung"[312]. Although the pre-Lukan tradition provided no information of such an encounter between Jesus and Herod (23,6-12.15), nevertheless Luke attached great value to this scene.

Müller was convinced that there were points in the trial and indeed in the larger passion narrative which were "eindeutig" dependent upon Mk (22,67.69.71; 23,3.22a)[313]. Luke's conception of the trial was such that he worked to put into order the events drawn from Mk 14,60.61; 15,4.5[314]. The motif of Jesus' silence was also indicative of Markan dependence[315]. Worthy of note was Müller's conception that Luke transferred Peter's denial from the Markan position where it appeared in the context of the trial so that in the Lukan version Peter's denials were not likened to the false witnesses[316].

---

and other Lukan artistic elements: "L'origine et la valeur historique de ces données au sens où nous les comprenons, ne doit pas nous retenir en ce moment. Il nous suffit de constater que la structure lucanienne du récit de la passion est très dramatique" (p. 138).

308. KARRIS, *Luke: Artist and Theologian*, p. 85.

309. *Ibid.*, p. 87. Cf. JOÜON, *Luc 23,11*.

310. Karris then moved from the significance of clothing to stating that Jesus exercised kingly power in 23,42-43. Nevertheless, he already stated that to be stripped of one's clothing was to be stripped of one's identity (cf. *Luke: Artist and Theologian*, p. 86).

311. KARRIS, *Gospel*, in *NJBC*, 1990, p. 718. Karris listed Luke's sources as Mk, Q and L ("his special materials") (p. 676). Further, he suggested: "In his account of Jesus' last days Luke redacts Mark and recapitulates many of the themes he has been developing in his Gospel".

312. K. MÜLLER, *Jesus vor Herodes*, in G. DAUTZENBERG, H. MERKLEIN, and K. MÜLLER (eds.), *Zur Geschichte des Urchristentums* (QD, 87), Freiburg, 1979, p. 141.

313. *Ibid.*, p. 113, n. 14.

314. *Ibid.*, p. 123.

315. *Ibid.* Note further p. 126, 127.

316. *Ibid.*, p. 112.

Following his analysis of the Lukan vocabulary in the Herod episode, Müller concluded the Lukan style was present not only in the beginning and end of the scene, but throughout, which linked this story with other parts of Lk as well as Acts[317]. A case in point was the use of the title of "tetrarch" for Herod. In Mk 6,14 Herod was referred to only as "king" with no additional information concerning his territorial jurisdiction[318]. Luke, on the other hand, already in 3,1 clarified that Herod was "tetrarch over Galilee". Subsequent references throughout the Gospel (3,19; 8,3; 9,7; 13,31; 23,7ff.) help the reader to understand who this Herod is before whom Jesus must stand trial[319]. This enables the reader to comprehend the reason for Herod's presence in Jerusalem at this time.

It was Müller's opinion that 23,6-7 were viewed "sicher als redaktionelle Bildung des Lukas"[320]. The same was to be said for 23,8. In 23,8b, Herod's longstanding desire to see Jesus was finally fulfilled which pointed to Luke's "kompositorischen Perspektivplan"[321]. Similarly, 23,9 was credited to Luke's redactional work[322]. It was probable that Mk 15,4 (and 5) served as a model for 23,9b[323]. Lukan redaction was also responsible for linking 23,10 to other places in the Gospel such as 22,66 where chief priests and scribes were also mentioned, and changes in 23,10 from the Markan vocabulary and style can be easily ascribed to Luke's customary usage, but especially the tendency of his presentation[324].

Although 23,6-10 were nothing more than Lukan redaction, 23,11.12 may be perceived, at first glance, as yielding new information. But Müller again concluded that 23,11 was "im Ganzen ein Produkt der lukanischen Redaktion"[325]. Comparing the use of the term "dazzling apparel" in Acts (10,30) as well as other places in the NT, Müller decided the term was used in a positive sense and thus it should be understood as a sign that Herod, too, believed Jesus to be innocent[326]. Luke lacked sufficient room to include another mockery of Jesus by the entire Roman cohort (Mk 15,16), so omitted Mk 15,16-20, the omission of which reflected his apologetic interests toward Rome. Due to the common use of the term ἐμπαίζειν in 23,11 and Mk 15,20a, but especially since the differences between the two accounts can be easily explained by the circumstances, Müller reached the "unausweichlich" conclusion that 23,11 was the result of Lukan redaction[327].

317. *Ibid.*, p. 116.
318. *Ibid.*, p. 117. Mt 14,1 contained the change from the Markan "king" to "tetrarch" but like Mk, Mt was silent on the matter of the territory Herod governed.
319. *Ibid.*, p. 118-119.
320. *Ibid.*, p. 119.
321. *Ibid.*, p. 120.
322. *Ibid.*, p. 123.
323. *Ibid.*, p. 131.
324. *Ibid.*, p. 127-128. See p. 131.
325. *Ibid.*, p. 137.
326. *Ibid.*, p. 135.
327. *Ibid.*, p. 137.

Lk 23,12 and especially 23,12a, according to the suggestion of Dibelius, was dependent upon the LXX[328]. But whereas Acts 4,27 focused on the alliance between the conspiring leaders, Lk 23,11f. highlighted their animosity toward one another. At the same time, Müller rightly contended that the similarity of the trials of Jesus and Paul was no accident. Acts 26,30f. detailed the situation already begun in 23,11f., which signaled "die Eröffnung einer Lebensmöglichkeit für das Christentum innerhalb des römischen Imperiums"[329]. The responsibility of the Jews for the death of Jesus was not to be charged collectively to the Jews, as 23,27-31 and Acts 13,27f. made clear. More than any other verse 23,12 reflected the current situation out of which Luke was writing[330].

Erwin BUCK (1980), in a particularly convincing and lucid treatment, made an eloquent case for the view that the Herod pericope, though a "repetitious and seemingly obscure story" functioned primarily paradigmatically and parenetically to encourage Christian disciples in the face of Jewish opposition, and only secondarily on an apologetical level[331]. The source question was not the primary concern of the article[332]. Like Corbin, Buck detected Luke was drawing parallels between events pertaining to Jesus and those of the early Church. In a vein similar to Hoehner[333], but in contrast to K.L. Schmidt, Buck observed the story was "tightly connected within the literary composition of the Gospel as a whole"[334]. With reference to Dibelius, Buck contended "an old source" was responsible for the midrash on Ps 2 as found in Acts 4,24ff.[335]. The obvious connection between

328. *Ibid.*, p. 138.
329. *Ibid.*, p. 140.
330. *Ibid.*, p. 141.
331. E. BUCK, *The Function of the Pericope "Jesus Before Herod" in the Passion Narrative of Luke*, in W. HAUBECK and M. BACHMANN (eds.), *Wort in der Zeit*, FS K.H. RENGSTORF, Leiden, 1980, p. 178. See p. 172-173: "Clearly, then, the 'trial' before Herod, too, is portrayed by Luke as a paradigm for the experience of the young church". Despite this view, it is clear that Buck oscillates on what serves as the primary function of the story. "In other words, the function of the Herod pericope in Luke's over-all construction is primarily *paradigmatic*" (p. 176). Yet, Buck's view that the story functioned apologetically only secondarily was tempered in the conclusion: "While it cannot be denied that the entire Passion Narrative (and not only that of Luke) is permeated by apologetic concerns, this essay has attempted to demonstrate that in Luke *this apologetic motif is accompanied by a very pronounced paradigmatic-parenetic orientation*, and that this is so also with respect to the Herod pericope" (p. 178) [emphasis added].
332. *Ibid.*, p. 166, n. 4: "The source-critical question is particularly difficult to settle ... In this essay source-critical questions have been touched upon only where they seemed particularly pertinent to the discussion". At one point Buck suggested that at least part of the Herod pericope stemmed "from a source" (p. 168).
333. Cf. HOEHNER, *Herod Antipas*, p. 227.
334. BUCK, *Function*, p. 166. Cf. K.L. SCHMIDT, *Der Rahmen*, p. 307.
335. BUCK, *Function*, p. 167; cf. p. 174, 175. He based this judgment upon the mention of Jerusalem and "the primitive παῖς θεοῦ Christology" (p. 167, n. 10). He accused Dibelius of "somewhat one-sidedly" interpreting Luke's purpose as exonerating Pilate while incriminating the Jews (p. 170).

Acts 4,24f. and 23,12 stemmed "most likely" from Luke himself, or at least betrayed heavy redaction by him[336]. In keeping with the other Synoptic accounts, the Lukan version portrayed Jesus as having been twice mistreated. However, in contrast to the other accounts, Luke presented the perpetrators as Jewish, rather than Roman soldiers[337]. What was more, in the Lukan account the beatings resulted not from a previous decision, but were totally unwarranted[338]. Claiming that "hortatory concerns" were threaded throughout the passion narrative (22,24-30.31-34.39.54-71; 23,27-32)[339], the Herod pericope was thought to serve the same purpose.

Buck was further convinced of the correctness of this view in light of the parallels between Lk and Acts. Jesus (22,66-71) as well as Peter and John stood before the Sanhedrin (Acts 4,1,ff.), so too Jesus appeared before Herod (23,6-12) just as Peter stood before another Herod (Acts 12,1ff.).

Buck also reduced the apparent differences between Lk and the accounts of Mk and Mt. Jesus was silent in response to accusations from the Jews and not totally silent in Pilate's presence. "We have the following situation, then: all the references to any silence on the part of Jesus during his trial either before Pilate or before the Sanhedrin, have specific reference to the opposition emanating from Judaism. In this respect Luke does not seem to differ from the other Synoptics. We appear to be face to face not with a Lucan peculiarity but with an early Christian consensus: in response to the Jewish charges, Jesus prefers to remain silent. In this regard Luke is unique among the Synoptics only in so far as he expresses this consensus with unusual vigor in his Herod pericope: before Herod Jesus says *absolutely nothing*!"[340].

In comments on Jesus' prediction of the coming persecution of the Church (21,12-19), Buck stated Luke "may well" have been dependent upon a Palestinian source[341]. Yet, the changes were such that, in my opinion, the Herod pericope, in light of redaction probably made on Mk 13,9f., these were part of Luke's redaction and elaboration of Markan material. "In his version of the prediction of the coming persecution of the church (Mk. 13:9f.) Luke embeds a seemingly insignificant little detail. When Mark states (Mk. 13:9b): ἐπὶ ἡγεμόνας δὲ καὶ

336. *Ibid.* Cf. F. SCHÜTZ, *Der leidende Christus: Die angefochtene Gemeinde und das Christuskerygma der lukanischen Schriften* (BWANT, 89), Stuttgart, 1969, p. 128ff.

337. BUCK, *Function*, p. 169; cf. n. 19: "That apologetic concerns [in the two mockings] are there, cannot be denied. Luke goes out of his way to make it clear that Jesus was not beaten by Pilate's soldiers. He omits the φραγελλώσας of Mk at the conclusion of the trial before Pilate and, with complete consistency, in Lk. 21:12 passes over the δαρήσεσθε of Mk. 13:9". It was apparent here, as well as other points in the essay, that Buck was endebted to Schneider.

338. *Ibid.*

339. *Ibid.*, p. 171-173. Buck considered the denials of Peter, which he defined as 22,54-71, to be based upon the Markan account (p. 172).

340. *Ibid.*, p. 176.

341. *Ibid.*, p. 177, n. 46. He also indicated the phrase referring to kings and governors may also have derived from a Palestinian source (p. 177, n. 47).

βασιλεῖς ἀχθήσεσθε ἕνεκεν ἐμοῦ ... Lk. 21:12b chooses to list the two main authorities in the inverse sequence: ἐπὶ βασιλεῖς καὶ ἡγεμόνας ἕνεκεν τοῦ ὀνόματός μου). Now we can see an interesting connection between this phraseology and that of Acts 4,27 where, as a midrash to Ps 2 the experience of the church is interpreted in analogy to the trials of Jesus before Herod and Pilate, in that order"[342]. Not only did that change promote the idea that Luke was consciously drawing connections between Jesus and the early Church, but gave evidence that Mk was forefront in Luke's mind even in the composition of the Herod episode.

Though Buck was reluctant to entirely dismiss the possibility that Luke had access to some (Palestinian) source for certain elements of Lk related to persecutions[343], as well as for the prayer for boldness of the Christian community, following the release of Peter and John from the Sanhedrin[344], it was clear the story served well the apologetic and paradigmatic-parenetic motifs from which Luke's readers would have benefitted.

Franz Georg UNTERGASSMAIR (1980) viewed the Herod story (23,6-12) as focusing on the theme of as a dramatic unfolding[345]. He was unconvinced of Taylor's supposition of a non-Markan source because "die Beweis dafür fehlen"[346]. It was not clear what exactly the Lukan redactor contributed to the scene. In relating the various mockery scenes, Untergassmair argued Luke remained true to Mk. "Im Prinzip bleibt Lk darin seiner Mk-Vorlage treu"[347]. In his article, *Thesen Sinndeutung des Todes Jesu in der lukanischen Passionsgeschichte*, also published in 1980, Untergassmair clearly affirmed his preference for seeing the changes in 23,26-49 as Lukan redaction of the Markan *Vorlage*[348].

In the FS for J. Ernst (1996) Untergassmair contributed an essay on the Herod pericope (23,6-12) in which he concluded that the pericope finds its origin in Lukan redaction, to the exclusion of other explanations such as a tradition variant of Mk 15,16-20 or a pre-Lukan Herod story[349]. The article contained four parts: 1) *Zur Problematik*, 2) *Der lukanische Sprachgebrauch*, 3) *Die Perikope im Kontext von Evangelium und Apostelgeschichte*, and 4) *Schlussfolgerungen*.

---

342. *Ibid.*, p. 177. Mt 10,18a has the same order as Mk 13,9b.

343. *Ibid.*, p. 177, nn. 46, 47.

344. *Ibid.*, p. 167, n. 10; cf. p. 177.

345. *Kreuzweg und Kreuzigung Jesu* (PTS, 10), Paderborn, 1980, p. 66-67. Habil. 1977 (dir. J. ERNST). He also referred to 23,6-12 as a mockery scene (p. 182, n. 32).

346. *Ibid.*, p. 67, n. 271.

347. *Ibid.*, p. 180.

348. *TGl* 70 (1980) 180-193, p. 182. This article represented, in abbreviated form, the essence of the conclusion to his Habilitationschrift, *Kreuzweg* (*Thesen*, p. 180, n. 1).

349. *Zur Problematik der lukanischen Passionsgeschichte. Jesus vor Herodes (23,6-12)*, in K. BACKHAUS and F.G. UNTERGASSMAIR (eds.), *Schrift und Tradition*. FS J. ERNST, Paderborn, 1996, 273-292.

The problematic of the passion narrative is closely connected to that of the entire two-volume Lukan work. He briefly recalled eight German studies on individual sections in Lk 22,7–23,49, including his own[350]. Adherents of the Proto-Lk hypothesis placed great emphasis on word statistics which, Untergassmair pointed out, "lassen oft kein sicheres Urteil zu"[351]. He also observed the shift in methodology which had a dual effect: "a) eine Rückkehr zur 'Protolukashypothese' (ist) ausgeschlossen und b) nach wie vor (interessieren) in der heutigen Lk-Forschung die Fragen nach der lukanischen Redaktion mit ihren theologischen und soteriologischen Aussagen"[352]. But he warned that whatever the methodology, philological and historical knowledge ought not be neglected. A review of literature by G. Schneider on Lk-Acts in the previous years highlighted the fact that the passion had been treated only marginally[353]. Untergassmair believed Luke served a double role: "Für Lk gilt, dass er Historiker und Theologe sein wollte und war. Als Historiker respektiert er die Tatsachen, die zwar mit dem Heil nicht identisch sind, in denen sich aber das Heil offenbart, was Inhalt seiner Theologie ist, und so verwirklicht er sein Programm gemäss Lk 1,1-4, seinem Vorwort"[354]. The Prologue remains "der beste Schlüssel" for understanding the Lukan project. In addition, Lukan vocabulary usage and "innerlukanische Verankerung" are important instruments of interpretation[355]. Untergamssmair rightly examined the Herod Pericope in light of both Lk and Acts and noted the parallels between the trials of Jesus and Paul. He also detected Markan influence in the mockery scenes (23,11.26)[356]. This article serves as a useful state of the question concerning not only the source question of Lk 23,6-12, but also the theological themes which it contains.

Richard T. FRANCE (1980) considered 22,67 to correspond to the second part of the answer in Mk 14,62 and 22,70 to relate to the first part of Mk 14,62[357]. Luke more freely formulated the dialogue because he was reluctant to use the clear affirmations since those will result only in a dead end[358]. In light of the omission of the phrase "coming on the clouds of heaven", France noted Jeremias considered

---

350. *Ibid.*, p. 274-275. These included Schürmann (1980, 1955, 1953), Rehkopf (1959), Kuhn (1952-53), Lescow (1967), Schneider (1969), Hofrichter (1988-89), Müller (1979) on the Herod pericope, to which he added Soards (1985) and Tyson (1959), and Untergassmair (1980).

351. UNTERGASSMAIR, *Zur Problematik*, p. 275.

352. *Ibid.*, p. 277.

353. *Ibid.*, p. 276-277; cf. G. SCHNEIDER, *Literatur zum lukanischen Doppelwerk. Neuerscheinungen 1990/91*, in *TRev* 88 (1992) 1-18.

354. UNTERGASSMAIR, *Zur Problematik*, p. 278.

355. *Ibid.*, p. 279.

356. *Ibid.*, p. 287: "In jedem Fall ist davon auszugehen, dass Mk 15,16-20 für sämtliche Verspottungsszenen bei Lukas die Basis bildet".

357. R.T. FRANCE, *Jésus devant Caïphe*, tr. G. BRAY and D. SCHELL, in *Hokhma* 15 (1980) 23.

358. *Ibid.*, p. 27.

the Lukan account more original. If that was the case, then Mark went beyond the word of Jesus and supplied an additional concept[359]. France regarded the differences between the Gospels to stem from varying theological perspectives[360]. Thus, while France never explicitly stated his position, it seemed that he rejected the idea of a special source.

Manuel CHICO CANO (1980) prepared a dissertation at Münster treating the trial of Jesus in 23,1-25[361]. He concluded that Luke essentially based his account upon that of Mk 15,1-15 and enriched it with new elements[362]. Although he entertained the views that Luke employed an independent source[363] or that Luke combined *Sondergut* with Mk[364], he rightly argued that only through a thorough literary- and redaction-critical investigation could a determination be made whether Luke employed an independent passion tradition or whether the differences can be explained by Luke's dependence upon, and redaction of Mk. The assumption of "einer Sonderquelle", Chico Cano ultimately reasoned, was "unnötig"[365].

He divided this section of the passion narrative into the following parts: 23,1-5.6-12.13-25. This last portion was further subdivided into vv. 13-16.18-23.24-25. Chico Cano concluded that 23,1-5 was a redaction of Mk[366]. In vv. 13-16 where the redactional work of Luke was clearly recognizable, Luke inserted these verses into Mk[367]. Luke carefully redacted Mk in 18-23[368]. Chico Cano denied there was a special tradition reflected in 23,24-25[369]. Luke's political-apologetic tendency helped to shaped the account.

---

359. *Ibid.*, p. 30.

360. *Ibid.*, p. 34-35.

361. M. CHICO CANO, *Der Prozess Jesu. Eine literarkritische und redaktionsgeschichtliche Untersuchung zu Lk 23,1-25.* Diss. Münster, 1980 (dir. K. KERTELGE).

362. *Ibid.*, p. 225.

363. *Ibid.*, p. 3, n. 4. He listed as proponents SCHÜRMANN, *Der Abendmahlsbericht*, 1957; K.G. KUHN, *Jesus in Gethsemane*, 1952/53; REHKOPF, *Die lukanische Sonderquelle*, 1959; J. JEREMIAS, *Die Abendmahlsworte Jesu*, 1963; SCHNEIDER, *Verleugnung*, 1969; CATCHPOLE, *Trial*, 1971; and TAYLOR, *Passion*, 1972.

364. CHICO CANO, p. 3, n. 5. Supporters included DIBELIUS, *Formgeschichte*, p. 200, 204; SCHMIDT, *Rahmen*, p. 303; FINEGAN, *Überlieferung*, p. 31; GROBEL, *Formgeschichte*, p. 104; SCHICK, *Formgeschichte*, p. 40; to which he added: "seit 1958 auch BULTMANN Geschichte, Ergänzungsheft 42".

365. CHICO CANO, p. 226: "Die luk Besonderheiten machen die Quellenfrage sehr schwer und problematisch. Trotzdem sind der Sprachgebrauch und Stil in diesen Stellen so deutlich lukanisch, dass die Annahme einer Sonderquelle für das luk Sondergut unnötig ist. Vielmehr lässt sich das Sondergut als luk Redaktionsarbeit an seiner Mk-Vorlage mit sicherheit erklären". In the introduction he insisted: "Hypothesen über Sonderquellen in der luk Passionsgeschichte, in denen die Redaktionstätigkeit des Evangelisten und sein Interesse an den theologischen Motiven unberücksichtigt bleiben, sind kaum überzeugen" (p. 4).

366. *Ibid.*, p. 30. See also p. 112.

367. *Ibid.*, p. 58.

368. *Ibid.*, p. 72. "Diese [vv. 18-23] ist eine Überarbeitung und Kürzung von Mk 15,6-15". See also p. 149-150. V. 17 was omitted on textual grounds (p. 59-60).

369. *Ibid.*, p. 77. See also p. 155.

The Herod pericope was defined frequently as 23,6-12, though twice as 23,8-12, and once as 23,5-12[370]. The purpose of the story was clearly to present another witness for the innocence of Jesus[371]. Chico Cano reviewed the various source-critical positions namely, that the pericope stemmed from: a written source[372]; a special or Proto-Lukan source which was combined with Mk[373]; an oral tradition independent of a continuous source[374]; or Luke himself[375]. Chico Cano surmised that the account was a Lukan composition in which Luke combined oral tradition with material he redacted from Mk[376]. He criticized Finegan who "geht zu weit" in arguing that the Herod pericope was formed from various Markan materials[377]. Luke was prompted to pass over the mockery by the Roman soldiers (Mk 15,16-20) because of his political apologetic[378]. Chico Cano regarded 23,11 as "ein Ersatz" for that Markan passage[379].

Regrettably this dissertation did not draw the attention it deserved. The detailed analysis and sage conclusions merited consideration, not only of the Herod pericope, but for all of Lk 23,1-25.

Frank MATERA (1986) set forth his view of the source question for the Lukan passion narrative declaring that Mk was Luke's primary source and that the majority of differences between Lk and Mk can be accounted for by Luke's redactional activity, utilizing "special traditions not employed by or known to Mark"[380]. The differences were characterized as absence of some Markan

---

370. *Ibid.*, p. 13, 16, 31, 45, 46, 48, 50, 64, 78, 133, 114, 140, where he cited the passage as 23,6-12. On p. 207, 210, he referred to it as 23,8-12. He also mentioned the passage as 23,5-12 (p. 225). See his discussion of the Herod scene, p. 31-50. On the relation of Acts 4,27 to the Herod scene in the Gospel, see p. 46-47.

371. *Ibid.*, p. 31.

372. *Ibid.*, p. 45, n. 100, where he indicated that this idea was strongly supported by the English and listed TYSON, *Lucan Version*, p. 252; *Jesus and Herod*, 239-246; WINTER, *Trial*, p. 136ff.; BRANDON, *Trial*, p. 119ff.; TAYLOR, *Passion*, p. 84-89. He also referred readers to GRUNDMANN, *Lukas*, p. 421 and SCHNEIDER, *Passion*, p. 91.

373. See GASTON, *No Stone*, p. 244ff.

374. CHICO CANO, p. 46, n. 103, where he cited HAUCK, *Lukas*, p. 278, and HAHN, *Prozess*, p. 35, n. 17.

375. CHICO CANO, p. 46. See DIBELIUS, *Herodes*, p. 113ff.

376. CHICO CANO, p. 49.

377. *Ibid.*, n. 112. Cf. FINEGAN, *Überlieferung*, p. 27-29.

378. CHICO CANO, p. 77.

379. *Ibid.*, p. 37, n. 72. See further the discussion of 23,11 (p. 40-43, 120-124). His position, as well as the language of his statement, was very reminiscent of the position of SCHNEIDER, *Lukas*, p. 475.

380. F.J. MATERA, *Passion Narratives and Gospel Theologies. Interpreting the Synoptics Through Their Passion Stories* (Theological Inquiries), New York - Mahwah, NJ, 1986, p. 155. Previously Matera discussed the question of sources citing Lk 23,44-48 as "an excellent test case" of whether Luke redacted Mk or employed a special passion source, concluding that the differences could be adequately explained by Lukan redaction (*The Death of Jesus according to Luke: A Question of Sources*, in *CBQ* 47 [1985] 470). He nonetheless conceded that Luke "may

material[381], addition of material not found in Mk[382], and a different order[383]. Matera rejected the idea Luke would have created events *ex nihilo*. As we turn to his treatment of 22,54–23,25[384] we will be attentive to his views on the Markan material, the difference in order, MAs and, of course, the Herod pericope.

Matera considered that Luke probably had access to "some other traditions" for the denial, mockery and Sanhedrin trial, though it was not necessary to posit a non-Markan passion account[385]. Although the Lukan order of the account of Peter's denials differed from that of Mk, "Luke's account is similar to Mark's", other significant differences notwithstanding[386]. The change in order permitted a contrast between Jesus and Peter and separated Peter from the subsequent mistreatment of Jesus[387]. The mockery (22,63-65) highlighted Jesus' prophetic

have drawn from individual traditions not known to Mark", though Mk formed the basis of his account (p. 472, n. 11).

Matera wrote as his dissertation a redaction criticism of the Markan passion narrative (Mk 15) in order to "demonstrate a unity between composition and theology" (p. 5) (*The Kingship of Jesus. Composition and Theology in Mark 15* [SBL DS, 66], Chico, CA, 1982. Diss. Union Theol. Sem., Richmond, VA, 1981 [dir. P. ACHTEMEIER]). Not much was devoted to a comparision with Lk, but there was an exception which has a bearing on our discussion. He remarked it was "questionable" whether Luke used Mk for his mockery scene, referring only to Taylor (p. 22; see TAYLOR, *Passion*, p. 89). He noted, however, that the mockery took place at Herod's trial (23,11). Highlighting various differences between Mk and Lk he concluded it was probable that Lk had not used Mk. What was noteworthy was that Luke "placed the mockery in a new setting". In the same chapter he discussed another mockery (22,63-65) in relation to Mk 14,65, noting once again the difference in order in Lk. Lukan dependence was held to be "difficult to say". While contact between the two accounts could be signaled by περικαλύψαντες, προφήτευσον (22,64), the use of another tradition could be indicated by ἐνέπαιζον αὐτῷ δέροντες (22,63), the latter view again inspired only by Taylor (MATERA, *Kingship*, p. 32; see TAYLOR, *Passion*, p. 80). Consider Matera's view on order: "In either case, it is important for us that Luke has placed the mockery in a new position causing us to suspect the free-floating character of the material"). Luke placed the third mockery (Mk 15,35-36) at 23,36 (MATERA, *Kingship*, p. 29).

In *Passion*, a more popular treatment, in the sections dealing with the Markan account of the passion, he did not make the same comparison with Lk as he had in the dissertation (*Passion*, p. 7-79). When commenting on 22,63-65 he referred not to Taylor, but to Schneider, *Verleugnung*, though he mentioned Taylor in his overview to Lukan theology (MATERA, *Passion*, p. 153, n. 6).

381. MATERA, *Passion*, p. 152. Mk 14,3-9.33-34.38b-42.50-52.55-61a.61;15,4-5.16-20a.29-30.34-35.44-45.

382. *Ibid.*, p. 152-153. Lk 22,15-16.24-30.31-34.35-38.43-44;23,6-12.13-16.27-31.39-43.

383. *Ibid.*, p. 153. Lukan pericopes reflecting an order different from Mk were: Lk 22,21-23.33-34.54-62.63-65.66-71.

384. *Ibid.*, p. 170-179.

385. *Ibid.*, p. 170.

386. *Ibid.*, p. 171.

387. Although he stated most commentators believed that Mk was Luke's only source for the denial, he did not clearly indicate his own position (p. 171). The new arrangement also permitted a "greater unity" between the Sanhedrin trial and the trial before Pilate (p. 174-175).

role, coming just after the fulfillment of his prediction that Peter would fail. Other prophecies of Jesus must also then be taken seriously[388]. Matera did not treat either of the MAs.

In his discussion of Jesus before the Sanhedrin, which he suggested was better described as a preliminary hearing, Matera noted that though there was no reference to Jesus' remark about the destruction of the Temple as found in Mk 14,57-59, a similar detail was found in Acts 6,12-14[389]. Also, some similarity was noted between 22,69 and Acts 7,56. The titles Messiah and Son of God were equivalent terms for Luke.

For the section Jesus before Pilate and Herod (23,1-25), a difference in setting was observed between Lk and Mk, but Matera left open the issue of source(s)[390]. Because there was no recounting of the mockery by the Roman soldiers as in Mk 15,16-20, it appeared that the Jews led Jesus to the crucifixion. The omission of certain details, such as Jesus being bound (cf. Mk 15,1), was due to Luke's "sensitivity to Jesus' dignity which he heightens throughout the passion"[391]. He adopted the position there was one charge specified in a dual manner. Mention was also made of the triple declaration of innocence, the first of which was 23,4. It was this theme which was emphasized when Jesus again stood before Pilate (23,14-15.22)[392]. The fact that Luke's account of Barabbas was the shortest of the four Gospels was due once more to Luke's sensitivity to Jesus' dignity. No formal condemnation was recorded but Jesus was delivered up to the will of the Jews which was part of God's plan (24,26).

Matera adopted the position that the Lukan account served the apologia that Jesus and his preaching posed no threat to the Romans[393]. Four themes found within the Lukan passion were highlighted: 1) the destiny of Jesus; 2) a model for discipleship; 3) the rejection of Jesus the Prophet; and 4) the death of God's royal

---

388. *Ibid.*, p. 172; see also p. 174.

389. *Ibid.*, p. 172-173. Reference to the Temple may have been omitted since it "still has a role to play" in Acts and Luke "avoids any impression that Jesus spoke against the Temple" thereby focusing more directly on the messianic issue (p. 173).

Alert to the parallels as well as the differences between the Gospel and Acts, as for example, he compared the death of Jesus with that of Stephen (Acts 7) and the portrayal of Jesus as a prophet (p. 151). For the discussion on the Jesus and Stephen parallels see p. 172-173, 174, 219. On Jesus as a prophet, see p. 206. The relationship of the two was found on p. 212. Matera viewed another similarity between the two Lukan works as the theme of recollection of the words of the Lord. A major difference was the presentation of Herod and Pilate (p. 177-178). See below.

390. *Ibid.*, p. 175: "There is a great deal of debate concerning Luke's source or sources. Several authors are convinced that he is working with a non-Marcan passion account, while others argue that they can explain the entire scene in light of Luke's editorial activity. Whatever the answer, it is evident that his account has a slightly different emphasis from that found in Mark".

391. *Ibid.*, p. 176.

392. In Acts 3,17 the people of Israel were said to have acted out of ignorance.

393. *Ibid.*, p. 177.

Son[394]. Changes then can be understood as reflecting Luke's christology and theology.

In the first of two later articles (1989) Matera focused on the Sanhedrin trial (22,66-71)[395] by means of a comparison of the Markan and Lukan accounts, a treatment of Luke's theological concerns[396], and the relation of history and theology within Luke's account. He claimed that while many scholars adopted a redactional solution to the problematic differences between Mk and Lk[397] it was necessary to situate it in the "context of Luke-Acts"[398]. The difference in order again served as a starting point and Luke's version was characterized as a simplification of the Markan account. Matera's position underwent a shift as he modified his 1986 position that Luke employed other traditions. The variations were now explained simply in terms of Luke's redaction of Mk[399].

The new order resulting from "Luke's redactional purpose"[400], provided a more "orderly account", was both more plausible and more dramatic, and allowed Luke to join the Sanhedrin trial and the proceedings before Pilate and Herod (23,1-25) enabling him "to develop a single trial"[401]. The timing of the morning trial was occasioned by the transposition of material and "seems more plausible than Mark's account". Descriptions of trials in Acts may also have influenced the change[402]. The charge of Jesus being a messianic pretender resulted in Lk from the portrayal of Jesus successfully teaching in the Temple[403]. This was in contrast to Mk where Jesus threatened to destroy the Temple. Luke revised Mk to avoid such an impression.

---

394. Asserting that Dibelius had not gone far enough in viewing Jesus in the Lukan passion as a martyr, it was argued he must have been regarded as "more than a martyr" since he was presented as a prophet and "God's royal Son" (p. 151-152; see also p. 190). Cf. DIBELIUS, *From Tradition*, p. 201.

395. *Luke 22,66-71. Jesus before the* ΠΡΕΣΒΥΤΕΡΙΟΝ, in *ETL* 65 (1989) 43-59 (= NEIRYNCK [ed.], *L'Évangile de Luc – The Gospel of Luke*, ²1989, 517-533).

396. These were: the arrangement of Luke's material, the morning trial, the Messianic charge, the Temple charge, the christological titles, the testimony of Jesus and the judgment of condemnation. Among the scholars whom he treated were Blinzler, Catchpole, Winter, Bailey, Lémonon, Sherwin-White, Benoit, Sloyan, Neyrey, Neirynck, Soards, Schneider, Marshall and Fitzmyer.

397. Perry and Taylor were named as supporters of the special source theory, while those who sought a redactional solution comprised Neyrey (1985), Neirynck (1987), Soards (1987), Schneider (1988), and Radl (1988).

398. *Ibid.*, p. 520. Neyrey was cited as an exception who attended to this (p. 519, n. 13).

399. *Ibid.*, p. 532: "Luke has composed his account employing Mark as his primary, and probably his sole, source in such a way as to present an 'orderly account'. And indeed, the Evangelist has succeeded!"

400. *Ibid.*, p. 522.

401. *Ibid.*, p. 523.

402. *Ibid.*, p. 524: "It would appear that Luke viewed a night trial as something improbable and irregular, and hence not even his polemic against the Jewish leaders allowed him to follow Mark at this point".

403. This argument was supported by references to 20,2 and Acts 3,11-4,22; 5,12-21.

Matera further proposed that Luke rearranged the Markan christological titles in order to place the title "Son of God" in "a more dramatic position" which had the effect of emphasizing it rather than "Christ"[404]. The absence of a condemnation was a deliberate omission of Luke since it would have been "premature" at this point in the narrative and because the crowds and the people had not yet participated in formally rejecting Jesus. R.E. Brown critiqued Matera's study stating "he does not seem to recognize that he has not proved the right to jump from Mark as the primary source of Luke to Mark as the *sole* source"[405].

This line of reasoning on the source question and Lukan redaction of Mk for 23,1-25 was resumed in a second article, *Luke 23,1-25. Jesus before Pilate, Herod, and Israel* (1989)[406], in which he appeared even more insistent on the view that Mk was Luke's only source[407]. He offered three reasons why the material was a rewriting of Mk rather than drawn from a non-Markan source or L or combination of all three: "(1) to prepare for the role of people in the condemnation of Jesus, (2) to emphasize the innocence of Jesus, and (3) to explain that the real reason the Jews opposed Jesus was that he taught the people in his capacity as Israel's royal Messiah"[408].

Luke fashioned his account to portray all of Israel, the leaders and people alike, as responsible for the death of Jesus. Omission of some Markan material was explained as resulting from Luke's desire to temper or remove those details "which heighten the humiliation of Jesus"[409]. Other omitted Markan material, such as Mk 15,3-5, was transferred to the Herod story. Matera believed the Lukan presentation of Jesus was influenced by the evangelist's knowledge of the life of Paul, particularly in the matter of the innocence motif[410]. Matera took the position that the charge that Jesus was a king had been subordinated to that of misleading the people. The results were summarized as 23,1 constituting a revision of Mk's introduction to Jesus before Pilate, the charge (23,2) was introduced by

404. *Ibid.*, p. 529.

405. BROWN, *Death*, p. 485, n. 2. Cf. MATERA, *Luke 22,66-71*, p. 58 (= NEIRYNCK [ed.], *L'Évangile de Luc – The Gospel of Luke* [BETL, 32], Leuven, 517-533, p. 532). Brown cited as an example Matera's treatment of 22,67, preferring instead the "more careful" treatment of SOARDS, *Passion*, p. 103-104.

406. MATERA, *Luke 23,1-25. Jesus before Pilate, Herod, and Israel*, in F. NEIRYNCK (ed.), *L'Évangile de Luc – The Gospel of Luke*, ²1989, 535-551. This portion of the Gospel was treated in three sections: 23,1-5.6-12.13-25. In addition to scholars considered in the first article, he also consulted Taylor, Ernst, Boismard, Gaston, Hoehner, Dibelius and Walaskay.

407. Dropping the nuance that marked his position on sources for 22,66-71, Matera now wrote: "All the differences between Luke and Mark in Luke 23,1-25 should be attributed to Luke's redactional activity" (p. 535). See also his statement in the article's conclusion (p. 550). The source-critical positions of Schneider, Fitzmyer, Ernst, Boismard, Taylor and Marshall were first considered.

408. *Ibid.*, p. 537-538.

409. *Ibid.*, p. 538.

410. *Ibid.*, p. 540. Note the disclaimer about the manner and extent of Luke's familiarity with Paul (n. 16).

Luke "to prepare for Pilate's question", Mk 15,3-4 was omitted as unnecessary here (though transferred to a later place in Lk), and 23,4-5 were Lukan composition. The accusation that Jesus misled the people by his teaching was emphasized over the charge of Jesus as "King of the Jews" as in Mk[411].

The section 23,13-16[412] was seen as a Lukan composition serving as a transition and highlighting the responsibility of the people while 23,18-19 was an abbreviation of Mk 15,6-11a in order to concentrate on the "guilt of the people". Lk 23,20 drew from and added to Mk 15,12 while 23,21 reflected verbal changes over against Mk 15,13. Luke's revision was evident in 23,22[413] as was his expansion of Mk 15,14b in 23,23[414]. In 23,24 Luke once again edited Mk and 23,25 followed from that. "The entire scene is composed in order to emphasize the responsibility of the priests, rulers and people"[415].

Regarding the structure in this section of the passion narrative, Matera insisted there was "*one* trial scene with four panels", thereby arguing against Neyrey's contention that there were four trials[416]. The material was divided in the following way: Jesus before the Sanhedrin (22,66-71); Jesus before Pilate (23,1-7); Jesus before Herod (23,8-12); Jesus before Israel (23,13-25). The teaching of Jesus was emphasized while the political charge receded into the background. Two of the overarching influences in Luke's redaction of this material were his own experience of the Jews and his understanding of the teaching and trial of Paul. Rejected was the view that Lk may be more historically reliable not only because of the "polemic against the Jews", but also because Luke relied on Mk as his primary source. What was most significant, perhaps, was that Matera abandoned his earlier idea that Luke had access to traditions unknown to and unused by Mk[417].

Matera's article on the Sanhedrin trial consciously attempted to employ a proper and necessary methodological consideration by situating the interpretation of the passage "within the context of Luke-Acts"[418]. This involved comparison of terminology, the timing of trials, the apostle's preaching in the Temple in Acts compared to Jesus' teaching in the Gospel, the concepts of witnesses and

---

411. *Ibid.*, p. 541.

412. He contended 23,13 "controls the entire unit" (p. 548). For the purpose of examination, Matera divided the verses following v. 12 into two sub-sections: material having no parallel in Mark (vv. 13-16) and that which had a Markan parallel (vv. 18-25) but added the qualification that the material in Mk 15,6-11a, consisting of the introduction to the Barabbas incident, was lacking (p. 547).

413. Note the similarity of phrasing with Acts 13,28.

414. The term αἰτούμενοι was also in Acts 3,14.

415. *Ibid.*, p. 549.

416. *Ibid.*, p. 551. See also p. 523. Luke reworked Mk "in order to present an extended trial composed of four scenes ..." (p. 535). Cf. NEYREY, *Passion*, p. 69, 80, 98.

417. MATERA, *Luke 23,1-25*, p. 550: "This study has argued that in the composition of 23,1-25, Luke is not dependent upon other sources or traditions in addition to Mark's Gospel". See above.

418. *Ibid.*, p. 520.

622 CHAPTER TEN

testimony, and the theme of responsibility for Jesus' death. His article on 23,1-25 continued in a similar vein, focusing on shared vocabulary, the role of all Israel in the condemnation of Jesus, the similarity of charges made against Jesus and some early Christians (23,5 / Acts 17,6-7), the innocence motif, and the negative reaction of the Jewish leaders to the teaching of the apostles.

Commenting on the pericope Jesus before Herod (23,6-12) Matera (1986) observed that 23,9-10 bore a certain resemblance to Mk 15,3-4 in the silence of Jesus and the accusations of the religious leadership, but he did not directly address the source question[419]. Following a review of material in Lk concerning the Herods which prepared for this scene in Lk 23, it was noted that Herod was disappointed with meeting Jesus. Matera interpreted the "bright apparel" as reflecting "Jesus' true dignity" and as a form of mockery[420]. He followed Fitzmyer in believing that the episode demonstrated the reconciling power of Jesus[421]. The story also testified to the innocence of Jesus which was compared with Paul's situation recounted in Acts 26,30-32. He contrasted the Herod episode in the Gospel with Acts 4,25-31 and recognized the tension between them, for in the latter the rulers were presented "in a more negative light"[422]. He resolved this dilemma simply by stating that all the events fell within the providence of God.

In his 1989 article on 23,1-25 Matera held to the view that Luke employed no sources other than Mk in the composition of 23,6-12[423]. What would constitute a major disagreement between Matera on the one hand, and Schneider and Radl on the other, involved Matera's assumption that Paul's trial in Acts inspired the Herod episode[424]. He concluded that the transitional verses 23,6-7[425] were due to Lukan editorializing. Lk 23,8 completed the theme found in 9,9 and 13,31[426].

419. *Passion*, p. 177. But consider his comments on sources in his overview to Lk: "... I am in agreement with those authors who view Luke as a more creative writer. This is not to say that he created events where there were none. By calling Luke creative I mean that he edits and arranges his traditions in a manner which expresses his theological convictions" (p. 154). At the same time Matera allowed for certain special traditions unavailable to Mk (p. 155).
420. *Passion*, p. 177-178. The verbal connection with Acts 10,30 was indicated.
421. *Ibid.*, p. 178, n. 33. See FITZMYER, *Luke*, p. 1480.
422. MATERA, *Passion*, p. 178. As to the origin of the passage in Acts, he said only: "In its prayer for boldness the Church, in the light of Psalm 2, remembers Jesus' appearance before Pilate and Herod".
423. MATERA, *Luke 23,1-23*, ²1989, p. 535-551. On p. 535, n. 3, Matera stated that although he considered vv. 1-7 to comprise the scene before Pilate, for the purpose of comparison with other authors he adopted the more customary division of the first pericope constituting only 23,1-5. Thus the material is separated in the following manner: 23,1-7.8-12.13-25.
424. See his qualification: "I am not implying that Luke was a witness to the events of Paul's trial, or that the description in Acts is historically accurate. I am simply making the point that it is more probable that Luke was better acquainted with the events of Paul's trial than Jesus'" (*Luke 23,1-25*, p. 540, n. 16).
425. Lk 23,6 has a parallel in Acts 23,34. The verb ἀνέπεμψεν (23,7) was also found in 23,11.15.
426. Herod's hostility toward Jesus was foreshadowed in 13,31.

Markan influence (Mk 15,3-5) was detected in 23,9-10, while 23,11 was an abbreviation of Mk 15,16-20[427]. Noting the opposing proposals of Dibelius who argued "Luke developed the episode on the basis of Acts 4,24-28" and Fitzmyer who contended the scene was probably a "Lucan conflation of disparate elements of tradition which come to him from 'L'", Matera presented the weaknesses of Dibelius's position, similar to critiques already adopted by Schneider and Radl[428].

Matera raised three objections against the position of Dibelius who maintained that Acts 4,24-28, which in turn was inspired by Ps 2, gave rise to the Herod episode in the Gospel[429]. First, the Herod reference in Acts varied greatly from the account in the passion[430]. There was no conspiracy between Herod and Pilate to find Jesus guilty. On the contrary, they declared Jesus was innocent. Second, in the passion it was not the Gentiles but the people of Israel who were responsible for Jesus' crucifixion. Third, a number of tensions existed not only between this scene in Acts and the passion account in the Gospel, but also internally within Acts.

Matera discussed this third objection by saying this scene and the rest of Acts clashed because of discrepancies in the presentation of Pilate[431]. What is more,

427. *Luke 23,1-25*, p. 545. Concerning Luke's redaction of Mk 15,16-20 for 23,11 he contended: first, Luke wished to give the impression that Pilate handed Jesus over to the Jews and thus eliminated the role of the Roman soldiers. Secondly, the mockery of Jesus as "King of the Jews" was unnecessary because Jesus stood in Herod's court. The political charge was from the perspective of the Romans. The details of the crown and scepter faded away because Jesus was not mocked as a king. Since the royalty motif was subdued, the purple robe was eliminated in favor of the "gorgeous apparel" (p. 544). This vestiture of Jesus parallels that of the angel who visited Cornelius (Acts 10,30). Matera argued further that because Luke did not describe Jesus in a manner similar to Herod in Acts 12,21 that was another indication that Luke did not wish to suggest here that Jesus was condemned as "king of the Jews" (n. 29). No mention was made of 23,12, which was unusual since he briefly treated it in *Passion* (p. 178).

428. *Luke 23,1-25*, p. 541-542. Like Radl, Matera had a special interest in showing parallels with material from Acts, e.g. in his treatment of 23,6 (p. 543).

429. *Ibid.*, p. 542. He referred to the position as advanced in the article of DIBELIUS, *Herodes und Pilatus*. Cf. in the same volume as Matera, G. BOUWMAN, *Le "premier livre" (Acts., I,1) et le date des Actes des Apôtres*, p. 564: "C'est surtout la concordance de *Lc.* XXIII, 12 avec le midrash du *Ps.* II dans *Acts.*, IV,27 qui saute aux yeux", with reference to Dibelius's article (n. 74). Schneider made no reference in *Das Verfahren* (1988) to this particular suggestion, but RADL, *Sonderüberlieferungen*, 1988 (esp. p. 137-138), as we have seen, discussed it.

430. MATERA, *Luke 23,1-25*, p. 542. Cf. RADL, *Sonderüberlieferungen*, 1988, p. 137, n. 21, where he stated that whether and how far Luke was dependent upon a tradition in Acts 4,27f. need not be decided at this point. He proposed that with regard to the inherent tensions in the Lukan passion account, one can think of the taking over of a tradition. Luke was able to write Acts 4,27f. This was possible not only because Pilate became an accomplice, but above all because Ps 2 already spoke of the position of the ruler against the Lord and his anointed. The influence of this christologically significant psalm was seen in that all of the people to a person shared in the judgment of Jesus, that various individuals attested to his innocence and also because the chiastic structure reflected exactly what took place in Acts 4,27 (p. 137-138).

431. MATERA, *Luke 23,1-25*, p. 542. Acts 3,13 and 13,28 contained favorable descriptions

this scene varied from the Lukan view of the passion in other parts of Acts in which the people of Israel and their leaders were presented as being "primarily responsible for Jesus' death"[432]. Because of these inherent contradictions Matera proposed as a better solution that Acts 25,13-26,32 inspired the Herod scene[433].

Matera suggested, therefore, that the trial of Paul before Agrippa and Festus (Acts 25,13-26,32) served as the source of the Herod story, rather than resulting from a fulfillment of Ps 2 as reflected in Acts 4,24-28[434]. This extended passage in Acts described the following events. Given that Festus was leery of the Jewish charges against Paul and finding no infraction deserving of death, he submitted the case to King Agrippa for his consideration. A verdict of innocence was ultimately rendered by Festus, Agrippa and Bernice (26,30-32). Matera suggested the parallel should not be pressed too far, because there was nothing in the passion account to compare with the defense speech by Paul (26,2-23)[435].

Matera, however, granted the difficulty of determining just exactly from whence this material derived. Thus, his goal was only to show that there were reasonable grounds for assuming that Luke developed the Herod episode "in accord with his redactional purpose" and not from his special material[436].

While acknowledging that the Gospel was composed before Acts, Matera's position rested upon the postulate that "what is written first, however, does not necessarily serve as the inspiration for what is composed later"[437]. Rather, because the details of Paul's trials "were surely fresher in Luke's mind and he undoubtedly had better access to information surrounding them than he did to the trial of Jesus", Matera was lead to the conviction that events in the life of Paul inspired the recounting of those in the life of Jesus[438]. Wishing to establish a parallel between Jesus and Paul, Luke supposed that Jesus appeared before a

of Pilate.

432. *Ibid.* While Acts 4,24-28 indicated Herod, Pilate, the Gentiles and the people of Israel were equally responsible, such a presentation contradicted the portrayal as found in Acts 2,23.36; 3,14-15; 4,10; 5,30; 7,52; 10,29; 13,27-29, where Luke presented "the people of Israel and their leaders as those who are primarily responsible for Jesus' death" (p. 542).

433. *Ibid.*, p. 545. Matera credited WALASKAY, *'And So'*, 1983, p. 43, with the idea. Matera noted that S.G. WILSON made a similar observation in *The Jews and the Death of Jesus in Acts*, in P. RICHARDSON and D. GRANSKOU (eds.), *Anti-Judaism in Early Christianity*. Vol. 1. *Paul and the Gospels*, 1986, p. 155-164 (MATERA, *Luke 23,1-25*, p. 545, n. 31).

434. MATERA, *Luke 23,1-25*, p. 545.

435. *Ibid.*

436. *Ibid.*, p. 542-543.

437. *Ibid.*, p. 546. See WILSON, *Jews*, who wrote: "It might be thought natural to assume that Luke's understanding of Jesus has affected his description of the trials of Stephen and Paul. But might not the reverse also be true? Could it be that some elements of the trial of Paul, for example, have spilled over into the trial of Jesus – especially the theme of Jewish culpability, since it is the Jews who are consistently portrayed as the opponents of Paul in Acts?" (quoted in MATERA, *Luke 23,1-25*, p. 545, n. 31).

438. MATERA, *Luke 23,1-25*, p. 546.

Herodian and a Roman governor because Paul had[439]. Schneider already dismissed such a possibility saying that the account in Acts was also a Lukan composition[440].

The innocence motif, suggested Matera, was likewise developed by Luke "from his understanding of Paul's life"[441]. Though Schneider and Radl would disagree with Matera on this point, all hold that the purpose of the Herod scene was to officially witness, together with Pilate, to the guiltlessness of Jesus[442]. Matera asserted that the threefold pattern of the declaration of Jesus' innocence was due to Lukan redaction and not to a non-Markan source[443]. Schneider more

---

439. Here one must weigh the value of Matera's suggestion against that of Schneider in light of Luke's introduction that the information he received came to him from those who were "eyewitnesses and ministers of the word" (1,2) and given Luke's propensity for OT fulfillment.

440. SCHNEIDER, Das Verfahren, 1988, p. 128.

441. MATERA, Luke 23,1-25, p. 540. SCHNEIDER, Das Verfahren, did not address this theme. However, in his commentary, Lukas, 1977, ²1984, p. 473, he wrote: "Die Unschuldsbezeugung des römischen Beamten, die im weiteren Zusammenhang dreimal begegnet (VV 4.14f.22), hat apologetische Funktion". This statement was quoted almost verbatim from Die Passion Jesu, 1973, p. 92-93. In the commentary Schneider substituted the words "im weiteren" for "in unserem".

442. MATERA, Luke 23,1-25, p. 546. He also maintained this scene was important in establishing "the responsibility of the Jews for [Jesus'] death" (p. 545). Cf. SCHNEIDER, Das Verfahren, 1988, p. 128: "Die theologische Hauptabsicht des Lukas ist es, mit der Herodesszene einen zweiten prominenten Zeugen für die Schuldlosigkeit Jesu zu benennen" (see also p. 126). Note his position already in Die Passion Jesu, 1973, p. 94. RADL, Sonderüberlieferungen, 1988, p. 136. "Vor allem aber ist es hier, wie Lk 23,15 entnommen werden kann, das Signal dafür, dass Herodes Jesus für unschuldig hält". See further RADL, Das Lukas-Evangelium, 1988, p. 126: "Dass der jüdische König mit dem Fall Jesu befasst wird (23,6-12), dient der Bestätigung des Eindrucks von der politischen Harmlosigkeit Jesu, steht also im Dienst der Wahrheitsfindung, zeigt das Bemühen des römischen Beamten um die Klärung des Sachverhalts (vgl. Apg 22,24.30; 23,28f.; 25,26f.) So kommt es auch zu keiner Verurteilung, sondern Pilatus 'überlässt' Jesus den ihn bedrängenden Juden (23,25)".

443. MATERA, Luke 23,1-25, p. 540. G. SCHNEIDER in Die Passion Jesu, 1973, called attention to the three occurrences of testimony of innocence by the Roman officials (p. 92-93, 94, 103). He observed it was important for the Lukan presentation that Pilate already in v. 4 positively acknowledged the guiltlessness of Jesus. Later he stated that v. 22b.c referred to Mk 15,14. Both statements were repeated verbatim, with the exception noted above in n. 846, in Das Evangelium, 1977, ²1984, p. 473, 477. Since he contended 23,13-16 should be considered a Lukan formation in its entirety, he wrote that for the evangelist the scene in vv. 13-16 served as the third statement of Jesus' innocence by Pilate (Das Evangelium, 1977, ²1984, p. 476; cf. Die Passion Jesu, 1973, p. 93). In Das Verfahren (1988), Schneider also treated the issue of Luke's threefold declaration of Jesus' innocence: "Statt der Verwunderung des Pilatus über Jesu Schweigen (Mk 15,5) lässt Lukas den Statthalter eine erste Unschuldserklärung zugunsten Jesu abgeben (Lk 23,4). Nach der Herodesszene folgt eine zweite Erklärung über die Schuldlosigkeit Jesu (23,14f.). Mit der Bemerkung, Pilatus habe Jesus freilassen wollen (23,16), leitet Lukas zur Barabbasszene über.

Ohne von der herkömmlichen Übung einer Gefangenen-Freilassung zum Festtag zu berichten (vgl. Mk 15,6) erzählt Lukas, dass die Juden den Tod Jesu forderten und im Gegenzug die

explicitly declared that 22b.c referred to Mk 15,4. Radl referred to Lukan redaction in stating that the purpose of 23,13-16 was to provide an apologia for Jesus, "die Lukas selbst als Zweck der Handlung in 23,15 benennt"[444].

However, a further disagreement exists on the issue of the source of the Herod scene. Unlike Schneider, Matera made no allowance for the possibility of a legendary note[445]. "All the differences between Luke and Mark in Luke 23,1-25 should be attributed to Luke's redactional activity"[446].

All three scholars agree that the Herod scene was inspired by some Markan material. Verse 23,9 was based upon Mk 15,5 and 23,10 derived from Mk 15,3. The motif of silence "is better kept for the Herod scene" because of Herod's ambivalence toward Jesus[447].

Matera is more emphatic than either Schneider or Radl in his assertion that v. 11 was derived from Mk[448]. He claimed the mockery (v. 11) was the result of Luke rewriting and abbreviating his Markan source, Mk 15,16-20 and Matera sought to offer reasons for such redaction. First, Luke wished to give the impression that Pilate handed Jesus over to the Jews and thus eliminated the role of the Roman soldiers. Secondly, the mockery of Jesus as "King of the Jews" was unnecessary because Jesus stood in Herod's court. The political charge was from the perspective of the Romans[449]. The details of the crown and scepter faded away because Jesus was not mocked as a king. Since the royalty motif was subdued, the purple robe was eliminated in favor of the "gorgeous apparel"[450]. Matera would agree that Luke composed the scene not only from selected Markan

---

Freilassung des politischen Mordgesellen Barabbas verlangten (23,18f). Pilatus fragt die Judenschaft 'zum dritten Mal: Was hat er denn Böses getan? Ich fand an ihm nichts, was den Tod verdiente' (23,22)" (SCHNEIDER, *Das Verfahren*, 1988, p. 120).

RADL, *Das Lukas-Evangelium*, 1988, p. 126, wrote: "In keinem anderen Evangelium beteuert Pilatus, der die Haltlosigkeit der politischen Anklage (23,2) sofort erkennt, die Schuldlosigkeit Jesu so intensiv wie hier (23,4.14.15.22), plädiert er so oft für Jesu Freilassung (23,16.20.22) ... Diese Erklärungen der politischen Schuldlosigkeit Jesu hat Lukas im Lauf des Evangeliums schon vorbereitet, wenn auch nicht immer bewusst (vgl. im einzelnen Conzelmann, Mitte 129-131)".

444. RADL, *Sonderüberlieferungen*, p. 139-140.

445. MATERA, *Luke 23,1-25*, p. 547: "But if one is convinced that Luke is responsible for the Herod episode, as I have argued above, there is little need to appeal to another source at this point".

446. *Ibid.*, p. 535. RADL, *Sonderüberlieferungen*, p. 135, n. 15, conceded the difficulty in resolving such an issue.

447. MATERA, *Luke 23,1-25*, p. 544.

448. *Ibid.*, p. 544-545. Cf. SCHNEIDER, *Das Verfahren*, 1988, p. 127, and RADL, *Sonderüberlieferungen*, p. 136.

449. MATERA, *Luke 23,1-25*, p. 544-545.

450. *Ibid*, p. 544. The gorgeous apparel of Jesus paralleled that of the angel who visited Cornelius (Acts 10,30). Matera argued further that because Luke did not describe Jesus in a manner similar to Herod in Acts 12,21 was another indication Luke did not wish to suggest here that Jesus was condemned as "king of the Jews" (n. 29).

material, but also from previous portions of Lk[451]. He made no comment on the meaning of v. 12 as Schneider and Radl had done[452].

All three scholars treated parallels between the Gospel and Acts. In examining the similarities between 23,6-12 and Acts 25,1-26,32, Radl stated this extended passage shed light upon the Lukan interests behind Lk 23,6-12(16)[453], but did not refer to the possibility that Acts inspired it. Schneider, though, remained unconvinced of the proposal that Acts 25,13-26,32 gave rise to the Herod scene in Lk[454].

Matera gave much more weight to v. 13 than Schneider by declaring this verse "controls the entire unit"[455]. He argued this was "the clearest indication of Lukan editorial activity" because here the people were first mentioned explicitly in the trial narrative and from this point onward, the people, in union with their rulers, figured noticeably in Jesus' condemnation[456].

451. *Ibid.*, p. 545. In his treatment of 23,8 Matera also showed where this verse had been prepared for by 9,9 and the aspects of curiosity and animosity were threaded through the Gospel at 9,9 and at 13,31 (p. 543). See SCHNEIDER, *Das Verfahren*, 1988, p. 127, n. 82, on 9,7-9 as well as 13,31, and RADL, *Sonderüberlieferungen*, p. 135-136, who called attention to 3,1.19; 8,3; 9,7-9 and 13,31.

452. Notwithstanding, in a previous work Matera wrote: "The result of this strange incident is that Herod and Pilate become friends. This is Luke's way of suggesting that the power of Jesus is such that even during his passion he reconciles enemies" (MATERA, *Passion Narratives*, 1986, p. 178). Matera referred in his footnote to FITZMYER, *Luke*, p. 1480.

453. RADL, *Sonderüberlieferungen*, p. 139. "Natürlich ist diese Erzählung nicht nur von einem einzigen Motiv geprägt. So hat sie sich paränetische, paradigmatische und auch christologische Bedeutung. Aber das vorherrschende Kennzeichen und darum wohl auch das Motiv für diese Komposition ist doch die in ihr liegende Apologie für Jesus, die Lukas selbst als zweck der Handlung in 23,15 benennt. Dass die dortige Unschuldserklärung aber nicht nur im Sinn einer Verteidigung Jesu gemeint ist, zeigt eben die Parallele bei Paulus. Hier bietet Lukas, freier und breiter entfaltet als im engen Rahmen der Passionsgeschichte Jesu, in erster Linie politische Apologetik für die Christen. In beiden Fällen zieht er den sachkundigen Repräsentanten des Judentums als zweiten Zeugen für die Unschuld und damit die Loyolität der Angeklagten hinzu" (p. 139-140).

454. SCHNEIDER, *Das Verfahren*, 1988, p. 128: "Im Blick auf den Prozess des Paulus, von dem die Apostelgeschichte berichtet, kann man die Parallelen hervorheben, die darin bestehen, dass auch er vor dem Synedrium, vor dem römischen Statthalter und vor einem herodianischen König steht. Hat Lukas gar die Begegnung Jesu mit Herodes deshalb erzählt, weil er in seiner Überlieferung die Szene 'Paulus vor Agrippa' (Apg 26) vorfand? Doch wird man für Apg 25,13 – 26,32 gleichfalls sagen müssen, 'dass der ganze Abschnitt eine freie Komposition des Lukas ist'". Here Schneider was quoting RADL, *Paulus und Jesus*, p. 197. According to Radl's later book, *Das Lukas-Evangelium*, 1988, p. 27, the "man of the world" type of presentation in Acts 25,13-26,32 would seem to indicate that above all the people Luke was addressing were the educated classes, the high and mighty. Radl discussed this extended passage not in a possible relationship to the trial of Jesus, but in the context of the issue of wealth.

455. MATERA, *Luke 23,1-25*, p. 548. Radl considered only 23,6-12 in his treatment (*Sonderüberlieferungen*, p. 134-140).

456. MATERA, *Luke 23,1-25*, p. 548. SCHNEIDER, *Die Passion*, 1973, p. 93, noted the people were now included: "Pilatus ruft die Synedristen, dazu nun auch das Volk, zusammen und möchte

Israel and its leaders were summoned together at this point in the narrative in order for Pilate to communicate the judgment of innocence which he and Herod decided[457]. The role the Jewish people played in the condemnation of Jesus was highlighted much more by Matera than by Schneider[458]. However, he argued, as Schneider had done, that 23,13-16 was due to Lukan redaction on account of the way in which the material was integrated into the immediate context[459].

Concerning the issue of separating tradition and redaction Matera declared: "In part, one's judgment about these verses (13-16) is dependent upon one's evaluation of the Herod episode since these verses are so closely linked to it. If one thinks that the Herod episode derives from special Lucan material, one might also be inclined to include these verses as part of that material. But if one is convinced that Luke is responsible for the Herod episode, as I have argued above, there is little need to appeal to another source at this point"[460]. Radl expressed a similar opinion: "Ob man diesen Befund auf eine Quelle neben dem Markus-Evangelium zurückführen muss, hängt davon ab, wieviel an redaktioneller Arbeit dem Evangelisten zugetraut werden kann. Ein Blick auf seine Apostelgeschichte fürht zu einem sehr zuversichtlichen Urteil. Abgesehen von solchen grundsätzlichen Erwägungen lässt sich zeigen: Lukas kann mit Hilfe vorhandener Bausteine sowohl Einzelverse als auch ganze Perikopen componieren. Das ist zu 23,2 ebenso schon nachgewiesen worden (Schneider, Anklage) wie zu 23,6-12 (Müller, Jesus vor Herodes; Soards, Tradition)"[461].

In summary, Matera ascribed 23,9-10 to Mk 15,3-5 and 23,11 was credited as an abbreviation of Mk 15,16-20 while 23,6-7.8(?).13-16 were attributed to Lukan redaction[462]. No specific mention was made of the origin of 23,12.

What function does the Herod scene serve according to Matera? "Luke's primary concerns throughout the narrative are to establish the innocence of Jesus and the responsibility of the Jews for his death"[463]. What is more, it serves as

sie zum Einlenken bewegen". Cf. *Lukas*, 1977, ²1984, p. 477, where he emphasized "und das Volk" by setting the phrase off in quotation marks.

457. MATERA, *Luke 23,1-25*, p. 548: "Verse 13, therefore, portrays an assembly of Israel summoned by Pilate so that he can declare Jesus innocent and release him".

458. *Ibid.*, p. 537-538. "For Luke it is not simply the religious leaders who are responsible for Jesus' death; it is the whole people of Israel as well" (p. 538).

459. *Ibid.*, p. 548. This language was very similar to that of Schneider who spoke of the embeddedness of these verses. Cf. Recently Schneider stated: "Die Auffassung, Lukas habe für die Herodesszene eine Quelle besessen, wird sich schwerlich behaupten können. Gegen sie spricht einerseits die deutlich redaktionelle Einbettung der Szene (23,5-7.13-16), andererseits der wenig zusammenhängende und eher aufzählende Duktus der Szene selbst (23,8f.10.11.12)" (*Das Verfahren*, 1988, p. 127).

460. MATERA, *Luke 23,1-25*, p. 547.

461. RADL, *Das Lukas-Evangelium*, p. 33.

462. Regarding 23,8 Matera said only that it was "intended to complete the theme introduced by Luke 9,9" (*Luke 23,1-25*, p. 543; see also p. 545).

463. MATERA, *Luke 23,1-25*, p. 545.

a transition to the Barabbas story[464]. These conclusions are wholly consistent with Schneider[465]. Radl, as we have noted, saw the passage not only as witnessing to the innocence of Jesus[466], but as providing a "politische Apologetik für die Christen"[467].

The collective result of Luke's redactional activity, according to Matera, was that the innocence of Jesus was highlighted while the guilt and the participation of the people, along with their priests and rulers, were compounded. All three scholars agreed that a fundamental purpose was to provide a prominent witness to the innocence of Jesus. However, over and above Schneider, Radl saw paranetic, paradigmatic and christological goals, while Matera directed attention to the question of culpability.

Matera (1990), though noting a certain relationship between Acts 4,27-28 and Lk 23,6-12, decided that because of the dissimilarity in the presentation of Pilate, Luke was drawing on another tradition for the material in Acts[468].

Matera (1991) recently reaffirmed his position that Luke used only Mk without recourse to any other historical information[469]. In a remark apparently directed to Neyrey, Matera held that in the Lukan account there was only one trial, with four scenes[470]. He concluded that Pilate and the chief priests were "primarily responsible for the death of Jesus", rather than the historical peoples of Israel and Rome[471].

Matera[472] provided an illuminating contrast because of certain nuances, as well as proposals which were distinct from those of Schneider and Radl concerning the origin and inspiration of particular passages. This was not to deny, however, that they held much in common.

---

464. *Ibid.*, p. 547. "First, in vv. 13-16 Luke has created a transition between the Herod episode and the Barabbas scene". Concerning a view like Matera's, Schneider earlier wrote: "Somit muss zum Verständnis der eigentlichen Barabbasszene des dritten Evangelisten die 'Überleitung' der Verse 13-16 herangezogen werden" (*Die Passion Jesu*, 1973, p. 102; see also *Lukas*, 1977, ²1984, p. 476).

465. SCHNEIDER, *Das Verfahren*, 1988, p. 128. Not only did the scene acknowledge a second prominent witness to the innocence of Jesus, but it served as "der politischen Entlastung Jesu durch Pilatus" (p. 129). See *Lukas*, 1977, ²1984, p. 474.

466. RADL, *Sonderüberlieferungen*, p. 135, 137, 139-140.

467. *Ibid.*, p. 140.

468. MATERA, *Responsibility for the Death of Jesus According to the Acts of the Apostles*, in *JSNT* 39 (1990) 82. See also p. 92, n. 18. In the essay Matera built on the work of J.T. SANDERS, *The Jews in Luke-Acts* (1987), agreeing with its conclusion.

469. MATERA, *The Trial of Jesus. Problems and Proposals*, in *Interpr* 45 (1991) 9.

470. *Ibid.*, p. 10.

471. *Ibid.*, p. 15-16.

472. MATERA, *Luke 23,1-25*, p. 535-551.

Matera on Lk 23,2.5

Matera shared with Schneider and Radl the conviction that Luke used Mk as his source in revising this portion of the passion narrative and in constructing Ch 23. Regarding the scene before Pilate (23,1-5) he announced his view, "... that Luke is not drawing upon another source in addition to Mark at this point but is rewriting his Markan source ..."[473]. Both Schneider and Matera acknowledged that Luke had more fittingly arranged the material from his Markan *Vorlage*[474].

Both Matera and Radl accepted the conclusions reached in Schneider's 1984 article concerning the charge against Jesus that for 23,2 Luke was not drawing upon "a non-Markan (literary) source"[475]. In line with both German exegetes, Matera considered that the verse was composed under the influence of earlier portions of Lk[476].

In contrast to Schneider who mentioned it only in passing, but like Radl, Matera examined a parallel to the charge against Jesus found in Acts 17,6-7. This charge, lodged against Jason and some of the brethren, was similar to 23,2. Further, the charge against Paul (Acts 24,5) was the same as the charge against Jesus. Therefore, Matera concluded "Luke is not drawing upon another source, but employing a motif which he develops in Acts as well: Christians, like their founder, are falsely accused of disturbing society by their teaching"[477].

Matera perceived the charges in a somewhat different light than Schneider as evidenced by the following: "In effect, the charge of Mark's Gospel, that Jesus was condemned as the 'King of the Jews', is subordinated to the charge that Jesus misleads the people by his teaching"[478]. Both agreed Mk inspired the charge. It would seem, however, that for Matera, the charge of king did not originate from the offense of disturbing the people, as Schneider repeatedly argued. In support of his contention, Matera observed that the title "king of the Jews", which played a prominent role in the Markan account (15,2.12.18), was used only once in the Lukan trial account[479]. Disagreement seemed to exist, then, between Matera, who saw the charge of king being subordinated to the primary accusation of misleading

---

473. *Ibid.*, p. 537.

474. *Ibid.*, p. 536. See SCHNEIDER, *Das Verfahren*, p. 121 (= *Jesusüberlieferung*, 286).

475. MATERA, *Luke 23,1-25*, p. 539. Cf. RADL, *Sonderüberlierungen*, p. 133.

476. MATERA, *Luke 23,1-25*, p. 539. Cf. SCHNEIDER, *Das Verfahren*, p. 122 (= *Jesusüberlieferung*, 287), and RADL, *Sonderüberlieferungen*, p. 133. Cf. also WALASKAY, *Trial*, p. 84, n. 9.

477. MATERA, *Luke 23,1-25*, p. 539.

478. *Ibid.*, p. 541. The primary focus of 23,1-7 was the charge against Jesus (p. 551). Matera did not refer to a new and alternate interpretation that Schneider entertained in *Das Verfahren*, p. 122 (= *Jesusüberlieferung*, 287), which proposed the converse: both charges of perverting the nation and advocating the imperial tax boycott could be thought of as deriving from the claim to be king.

479. MATERA, *Luke 23,1-25*, p. 541, n. 17.

the people while Schneider viewed the royal claim as a concretization of the accusation of perverting the people.

The charge against Jesus was nuanced in a slightly different manner by Matera. He emphasized the motif and the centrality of Jesus' teaching activity more than Schneider. Jewish opposition to Jesus results because he "taught the people in his capacity as Israel's royal Messiah"[480]. Matera indicated Luke presented Jesus as teaching throughout the Gospel[481]. Jesus' teaching activity was the means by which the Jews construed that he was misleading the people.

Matera suggested the differences between Lk 23,1-25 and its Markan *Vorlage*, Mk 15,1-15, can be explained on one level by Luke's redactional goal of preparing for the role of the people in the condemnation of Jesus. This aspect, too, Matera emphasized in contrast to Schneider. But they agreed it was important to the evangelist that the highest Roman office publicly declare Jesus innocent and that this should be attributed to Lukan redaction[482].

Because Matera earlier allowed for the influence of other traditions, rather than simply the Markan *Vorlage*, his position was similar to Schneider's, who contended Luke constructed the passion narrative by filling in Mk with traditions[483]. Although Matera wrote initially of Mk as Luke's only source[484], at various subsequent points he referred to other influences, such as events in Paul's life[485].

Matera argued Luke had no source for 23,1-25 other than Mk and that Luke reworked his source "in order to present an extended trial composed of four scenes ..."[486]. Matera referred to Schneider's position that Lk 23,13-25 was "eine lukanische Bildung"[487]. Concerning the assertion that there was only one trial, Matera's position was closer that of Schneider than that of Neyrey[488].

---

480. *Ibid.*, p. 537-538.

481. *Ibid.*, p. 540. Lk 4,15.31; 5,3.17; 20,1; 21,37. In his effort to draw parallels between the Gospel and Acts as well as between Jesus and his followers, Matera showed that this teaching motif was Lukan, and also described how the disciples encountered the same kind of reactions.

482. *Ibid.*, p. 541. "... Luke has introduced the material of 23,4-5, his own work, in order to focus upon the innocence of Jesus ...". Cf. SCHNEIDER, *Das Verfahren*, p. 126 (= *Jesusüberlieferung*, 291).

483. E.g. SCHNEIDER, *Lukas*, p. 436.

484. MATERA, *Luke 23,1-25*, p. 535.

485. *Ibid.*, p. 545-546. For example, Matera suggested Paul's life was the inspiration not only for the innocence motif, but also for the details that Jesus appeared before an Herodian and a Roman governor.

486. *Ibid.*, p. 535. Cf. SCHNEIDER, *Das Verfahren*, p. 119, nn. 44 and 45 (= *Jesusüberlieferung*, p. 284, n. 44 and 45).

487. MATERA, *Luke 23,1-25*, p. 546. He referred to the position as espoused in SCHNEIDER, *Das Evangelium*, p. 476: "Das Sondergut-Stück 23,13-16 mit der zweiten Unschuldserklärung des Pilatus für Jesus (V 14c; vgl. V 4) nimmt sowohl auf die Anklage der Synedristen (V 14a.b; vgl. VV 2.5) als auch auf die Herodesszene (V 15; vgl. V 11) Bezug. Es dürfte insgesamt eine lukanische Bildung sein, nicht zuletzt auch deswegen, weil es zur Barabbasszene (23,18-25) überliefert".

488. MATERA, *Luke 23,1-25*, p. 535. See SCHNEIDER, *Das Verfahren*, p. 119 (=

Sitz im Leben

Schneider addressed the tension between Christians and Jews in the first century in his reference to the Jewish Jesus polemic[489]. Matera drew attention to this dimension as well. Although Luke considered the relationship between Christians of his day and ancient Israel to be one of unity, his writings, indeed his account of the trial of Jesus, reflected a powerful aversion to his Jewish contemporaries[490]. Radl preferred to focus on the political apologetic rather than on the growing tensions between the Jewish and Christian communities[491].

Luke: Historian or Theologian?

The perceptions of Schneider and Radl varied on the manner in which Luke was seen to have recorded his account. Luke was envisioned by Schneider as working to reconstruct and plausibly narrate events in the role of a historian. But he clearly adhered to theological goals in so doing[492]. Radl, on the other hand, argued that in the three places which were investigated, Lk 22,67f.; 23,2 and 23,6-12, the evangelist did not offer "mehr oder bessere historische Information als Markus"[493]. Rather, it was because Luke wrote his account as a theologian that it took this shape[494]. From the overall comparison it became apparent that the agreements which united these two scholars were far greater than the differences which separated them. Both agreed that it was Luke's theology that guided and shaped his composition. And where do the views of Matera stand in relation to Schneider and Radl?

The final sentence of the article summed up Matera's view on whether Luke was writing as theologian or historian. "Because Luke's version of the trial

Jesusüberlieferung, 284). Cf. NEYREY, *Passion*, p. 69.

489. SCHNEIDER, *Das Verfahren*, p. 124-125 (= *Jesusüberlieferung*, p. 289-290). "Und es ist ausserdem festzuhalten: Nicht die markinische Passionsdarstellung erweckt den Eindruck, Jesus sei als Volksverführer angeklagt und verurteilt worden, sondern die jüdische Jesuspolemik gegen Ende des 1. Jahrhunderts sowie die Spiegelung dieser Polemik (oder sollte man lieber sagen: Apologetik?) in den nach-mk Evangelienschriften" (p. 125 = *Jesusüberlieferung*, 290).

490. MATERA, *Luke 23,1-25*, p. 551. His argument continued: "More specifically, I propose that Luke writes his version of the trial of Jesus with the trial of Paul in mind. Just as the Jews viewed Paul as a false teacher and brought him to trial, so they saw Jesus as a false teacher and brought him to trial".

491. RADL, *Sonderüberlieferungen*, p. 140.

492. SCHNEIDER, *Das Verfahren*, p. 129 (= *Jesusüberlieferung*, 294), was of the opinion that Luke, writing as an historian, with perhaps at times a legendary note, was guided by his theological goals.

493. RADL, *Sonderüberlieferungen*, p. 147.

494. *Ibid*. It is worth noting that in his 1975 dissertation, RADL, *Paulus*, p. 201, penned the following: "Dass Lukas Historiker ist, 'schliesst nicht aus, dass er auch einmal eine ganze Szene erfindet ...'", drawing upon the view of E. HAENCHEN, *Die Apostelgeschichte* (MeyerK III[15]), Göttingen, [6]1968, p. 366, n. 3.

represents such a powerful polemic against the Jews, and because Luke is dependent upon Mark as his primary source, Luke's account of Jesus' trial, as orderly as it is, is not a good place to begin a historical investigation of the events surrounding Jesus' death"[495]. Material included in Lk but lacking in Mk did not necessarily signal historical details derived from some other source. Rather, they were due to Luke's free editorial reworking of Mk[496]. This was not to suggest, however, that Markan elements which were reworked by Luke were necessarily unreliable. Indeed, they may reflect historical fact[497].

Do each of the three scholars envision Luke writing in a slightly different way? Schneider argued that Luke, writing as a historian and employing juridical terminology, was guided by theological goals. On this issue Radl and Matera shared more common ground because they perceived Luke as writing as a theologian. All would agree that the Lukan account reflected not only his theology, but also the milieu of later first century Christianity.

Luke Timothy JOHNSON (1986) accepted the statement of the Prologue that Luke possessed oral and written sources in composing his Gospel. The written sources included "Mark, materials from Q, and other distinctive materials designated L"[498]. Discovering where Luke employed a source was particularly difficult in the Gospel and even more so in Acts because of the evangelist's ability to engage a "variety of styles"[499]. As to the question of order in the Gospel, Luke followed Mark's arrangement more closely than Matthew. Johnson was especially attentive to the relationship between Lk and Acts since Acts "both continues the story of the Gospel and fulfills or confirms it", and provided "the first and authoritative interpretation" of Lk[500].

In the passion narrative Johnson observed Luke's modification of Mk through deletions, additions and the rearrangement of pericopes[501]. "The evangelist also transposed material from Lk to Acts. The christology of the passion was seen in light of the *sophos* of Hellenistic moral ideals, whose self control, freedom from fear, and courage are a model to his followers"[502]. The innocence of Jesus enunciated by Pilate (23,4.14.22) was reinforced by Herod (23,15).

495. MATERA, *Luke 23,1-25*, p. 551.

496. *Ibid.*, p. 550: "If the results of this literary investigation are correct, it means that Luke did not have access to other historical details about the trial of Jesus apart from Mark's Gospel. More specifically, the charge against Jesus (23,2), the role of Herod (23,6-12), the role of the people of Israel (23,13), and the explicit identification of Barabbas as a murderer (23,19) are due to Luke's redactional activity; they do not represent independent historical facts".

497. *Ibid.* Whether or not these elements corresponded to historical fact, Matera asserted, would require a prior literary investigation of the Markan account.

498. L.T. JOHNSON, *The Writings of the New Testament*, Philadelphia, PA, 1986, p. 200.

499. *Ibid.*, p. 201.

500. *Ibid.*, p. 207.

501. *Ibid.*, p. 219.

502. *Ibid.*, p. (219-)220.

Johnson continued to set forth his ideas on Lukan sources, redaction and related issues in a Lukan commentary (1991) and an article on Lk-Acts (1992). He maintained the Prologue indicated Luke had access to written and oral sources, including eyewitnesses (who may have been responsible for the Herod material in 8,3; 23,6-12; Acts 12,2-23, as well as the "we sections" in Acts), though he also relied on "his own careful research"[503]. Mk, which Luke used "extensively", and Q were regarded as main sources. Luke revised Mk for stylistic improvement, clarification, and out of concern for "consecutiveness". However, Johnson conceded that determining the sources was difficult due to Luke's variety of compositional styles. One of Johnson's major concerns was to show the relationship between Lk and Acts[504].

Much of the shaping of the special material, Johnson contended, "may be due to Luke himself"[505]. This was also true of the section concerning the Sanhedrin trial. Besides Mk and possibly other unspecified traditions, Johnson argued Luke's "own imaginative grasp of Jesus' significance" helped fashion the account[506]. The evangelist patterned his language after that of the LXX, giving it a more ancient flavor in order to emphasize its claim to antiquity. Johnson also alerted readers to Luke's use of parallelism as a narrative device, as in the trial of Stephen (Acts 6,8-15) which "echoes that of Jesus in Luke 22:66-71". The connection between the two was "unmistakable" in Acts 7,56 (cf. Lk 22,69)[507]. Paul's "passion" (Acts 21,1-14) was also seen to have some similarity with that of Jesus.

Johnson was clear that "attempts to locate a separate written Lukan source for the passion have not proven successful"[508]. He highlighted a number of omissions throughout 22,54–23,25 which sometimes were counted as evidence of a special passion source. Instead Johnson saw the omissions as indicative of Luke's lean redactional tendency[509]. Even the reference to the passage of about an hour (22,59), which some believed pointed to a special source, only testified to Luke's

---

503. *The Gospel of Luke* (Sacra Pagina, 3), Collegeville, MN, 1991, p. 28. Johnson was especially influenced by the commentaries of Danker, Talbert, Marshall and Fitzmyer, the last being described as the "most complete and best commentary now available" among the contemporary English language commentaries (p. xi). In Johnson's article on Lk-Acts in the *ABD* he affirmed that the Prologue demonstrated Luke was dependent upon oral and written sources and that Mk was one of the latter (*Book of Luke-Acts*, in Vol. 4, 1992, p. 404, 405, 406).

504. *Luke*, p. 1. See for example, comments on 23,1.2 (p. 364). Note further his position that Acts served as a commentary on the Gospel, a view drawn from Van Unnik (*Book*, p. 405, 411, 412).

505. JOHNSON, *Luke*, p. 3-4.

506. *Ibid.*, p. 361-362.

507. *Ibid.*, p. 14. See also p. 359-360, and JOHNSON, *Book*, p. 409-410. The parallelism yielded a connectedness between main characters and united the narrative.

508. *Ibid.*, p. 334.

509. JOHNSON, *Luke*, p. 359. The cumulative effect of the transposition of some material, omission of other material was significant. "The result of these alterations is a notably spare hearing, scarcely a 'trial'". See also p. 357.

"much closer attention to temporal relationships"[510]. Luke was credited with separating the two titles in 22,67 "with the result that the charge against him by the leaders in 23:2 appears especially deceptive"[511].

The order of the material within Lk was an important factor. Mk and other similar attempts "lacked a convincing sort of order"[512]. Luke's rewriting of Mk was done with a view to consecutiveness, to make various connections more explicit, to highlight certain events, or to permit a "quick transition" to subsequent portions of the Gospel[513]. Examples included the transposition of Peter's denials and the mockery (22,54-62.63-65). The denial was relocated to treat the apostles more gently and to portray Jesus as a prophet. The shifting in position of the mockery permitted the fulfillment of the prediction that the religious leadership opposed God's will and God's prophet[514]. Johnson credited the evangelist with identifying Jesus as ὁ κύριος, which was sometimes claimed as indicative of a special source[515].

For the mockery Luke transformed the characters to portray those who arrested Jesus as also being the ones who abuse him. By omitting mention of spitting (ἐμπτύειν Mk 14,65 / Mt 26,67) and substituting "beating" (δέροντες) Luke reprised the abuse of God's messengers in 20,10-11.

Even the variations in the Lukan account of the Sanhedrin trial, which Johnson admitted were radically different from Mark's version, were attributed to Luke. Of all the changes the omissions were the most notable. At times Luke's redaction may be minimal, as in the case of 22,69, but the result was "a startlingly different meaning"[516]. The response of Jesus in 22,70 reflected Septuagintal influence. It was the resurrection, not the parousia that helped Luke shape his account, especially in 22,69-70.

The purview of Ch 23 highlighted the responsibility of the Jewish authorities for the death of Jesus. But Luke also respectful of tradition, included the detail that the people too were involved, information which was also conveyed in Acts 3,13-14.17. Here again Johnson was alert to the various similarities with Acts[517]. On the question of the *ius gladii* he argued the prefects enjoyed a certain freedom in its application. While Johnson did not give any clear indication of his opinion on the origin of 23,3, he stated there was basic agreement in all four Gospels which

510. *Ibid.*, p. 357.

511. *Ibid.*, p. 359.

512. *Ibid.*, p. 30. See also JOHNSON, *Book*, p. 405, 408. The effect of Luke's approach provided a "coherent and interconnected story" which "has a persuasive force".

513. See for example JOHNSON, *Luke*, p. 30, 362, 364.

514. *Ibid.*, p. 357, 358, 362. Johnson perceptively observed Luke recounted all of the material relating to Peter consecutively rather than interspersing it as found in the other Gospels (p. 357).

515. *Ibid.*, p. 358. Note the remarks on 22,61.65. See also the comment on 7,13 (p. 118).

516. *Ibid.*, p. 359. Johnson detected the link with Acts 7,55-56 where Stephen saw the Son of Man.

517. *Ibid.*, p. 364-365. See comments on 23,1.2.4.7.

"probably reflects some nucleus of historical fact". Once more the prophecy spoken by Jesus was being fulfilled. The silence of Jesus was also regarded as having historical basis, but understood in light of the Suffering Servant (Is 53,7). Attentive to his Hellenistic readers, Luke shaped his portrayal of Jesus' passion after the manner of a *sophos*.

The description of Barabbas as a murderer was reprised in Acts 3,14. The omission of the mockery (Mk 15,16-20) gave the impression the Jews led Jesus to be crucified.

Though Johnson recognized the MA in 22,62, noting a similarity with LXX Is 22,4; 33,7; Ezek. 27,30, he did not attempt an explanation. He passed over the MA in 22,64 without comment[518].

The Lukan redaction of the Markan material has several results. Such a portrayal highlighted the responsibility of the Jewish leaders for the death of Jesus. A dimension of Luke's style involved providing links with previous material such that 23,1 recalled 22,47, 23,8 pointed back to 9,9; 23,10 and 23,14 rehearsed 23,2, while 23,11 harkened back to 18,9 which was linked with material in Acts as well[519]. Sometimes Luke apparently wished to soften the "political overtones", as in the case of referring only generally to Barabbas. In a lean presentation of Jesus before the Sanhedrin, Pilate and Herod, as well as the crucifixion, Luke recapped the "major themes". The first theme, that of Jesus' innocence, became increasingly more general. Not only was Jesus innocent of the charges raised by the Jews, but he was not guilty of misleading the people. Further, he had not done anything worthy of death. The declarations of Jesus' innocence served a dual purpose: they provided the Christian apologetic toward Rome and portrayed Jesus as the suffering righteous one. The second major theme treated responsibility for Jesus' death. Though it fell on the shoulders of the Jewish leadership, the involvement of the populace, stemming from a tradition, was also clearly stated[520]. Luke shaped his presentation in such a way that Jesus was characterized as a sage and a prophet.

While attentive to the new literary criticism, Johnson did not neglect source or redaction criticism. Though not excluding the possibility Luke might have had access to some sources other than Mk, Johnson showed well how the various changes reflected Lukan theology and redactional technique[521].

Johnson (1991) claimed eyewitnesses may have provided the Herod story (23,6-12)[522]. The evangelist was very faithful to his source at this point in the

518. *Ibid.*, p. 358.
519. *Ibid.*, p. 364, 365, 366, 370.
520. *Ibid.*, p. 374. See also his comments, p. 364, 370.
521. See the review of Johnson's commentary by J.M. HARRINGTON, in *LouvSt* 18 (1993) 181-183.
522. *Ibid.*, p. 6. Johnson also defined the passage as 23,7-12 (p. 131). Though he was not explicit as to the source, he intimated it might be Joanna or her husband (8,3) or Manaen (Acts 13,1). In an earlier contribution Johnson commented Luke "significantly ... adds to his Markan source" which included a "separate hearing before Herod (23:6-12)" (*Writings*, 1986, p. 219).

Gospel. The transfer from Pilate to Herod was effected as a means of avoidance by Pilate. Johnson revived an idea also proposed by J. Weiss that the ἡμᾶς (23,15) reflected the royal plural. The robe served as a parody of kingship. The friendship between the two political figures (23,12) reflected Luke's knowledge of the concept of friendship in the Hellenistic world. Johnson compared Jesus' trial before Herod with trials of philosophers as found in Hellenistic literature, and the martyrdom confrontations of Moses, Daniel and the Maccabeans and a rabbi in the Bar Kochba revolt. Johnson maintained the Gospel presentation was "disappointing" in contrast. Jesus' silence had a historical basis. In this story Jesus was portrayed not only in the light of the Isaian Suffering Servant (cf. Acts 8,32-35), but as a Greek sage.

In Johnson's article in the *ABD* (1992), which appeared shortly after the commentary, he drew attention to the difficulty of determining Lukan sources, which was made more problematic because of: 1) the common Hellenistic practice of rewriting sources, and 2) Luke's ability to compose using various styles[523]. As Johnson maintained in his commentary, he continued to argue that Luke's story sought to demonstrate that God's promises were fulfilled. Luke's literary work was both a theodicy and an apologia.

Assuming the Markan basis for the passion narrative without mention of any specific additional sources, Johnson argued that through deletions, transpositions and additions Luke offered a presentation in which Jesus was portrayed as a *sophos* and the involvement of the people was reduced[524]. The purpose of the double literary work was to convince Luke's Gentile readers "that God's fidelity to his promise should give them confidence in their commitment to him"[525].

In the same *ABD* (1992) George W.E. NICKELSBURG offered his views on the passion narratives[526]. He nuanced his position by suggesting the majority of changes in the Lukan passion narrative over against Mk can be explained by Lukan redaction, thereby making the theory of a special source "unnecessary"[527]. The more prominent christology in this section of Lk was Jesus as "the Chosen One, the Christ", an idea found both in the Gospel and Acts. Jesus was depicted by Luke as "a model of patient and selfless suffering" worthy of imitation by his disciples, a relationship that underwent a change since Luke eliminated much of the negative portrayal of Jesus' followers. The christology had a paradigmatic quality.

Nickelsburg was attentive to the numerous parallels between the Gospel and Acts. This was true of confrontations between Jesus and his followers on the one hand, and the Jewish authorities on the other, and was especially the case with Stephen (Acts 6-7). Much of the material deleted from the account of the

---

He proposed that the information concerning Herod "perhaps" came from oral reports of eyewitnesses (p. 200).

523. *Book*, p. 406.

524. *Ibid.*, p. 414. Johnson was influenced by American Lukan scholars including W. Kurz, J. Neyrey, R. Karris and J. Kodell.

525. *Ibid.*, p. 418.

526. *Passion Narratives*, in *ABD* 5, p. 172-177 (esp. p. 174-175).

527. *Ibid.*, p. 174-175.

Sanhedrin trial in the Gospel was found in the Stephen material in Acts[528]. Nickelsburg also adopted the idea that the charge set forth in 23,2 was anticipated in 20,20-26. He did not address the source question for the Herod story but asserted that this episode helped to emphasize Pilate's declaration of Jesus' innocence[529].

K. SCHUBERT (1984) included G. Schneider, C. Colpe and Jacob Kremer "among advocates of the priority of the Lukan passion-narrative"[530]. On the other hand, additional scholars who confirmed the Markan basis of Lk included William BAIRD (1971)[531], Günther BORNKAMM (1971)[532], Franz ZEHRER (1972)[533], Marinus

528. *Ibid.*, p. 175.
529. *Ibid.*
530. K. SCHUBERT, *Biblical Criticism Criticised: With Reference to the Markan Report of Jesus's Examination before the Sanhedrin [Mk 14:55-64; 15:2-5; Lk 22:66-71]*, in E. BAMMEL and C.F.D. MOULE, (eds.), *Jesus and the Politics of His Day*, Cambridge, 1984, 385-402, esp. p. 389, 391-392. See G. SCHNEIDER, *Jesus vor dem Synedrium*; C. COLPE, *Der Begriff "Menschensohn" und die Methode der Erforschung messianischer Prototypen*, in *Kairos* 13 (1971) 1-17, esp. p. 13; J. KREMER, *'Verurteilt as "König der Juden" – verkündigt as "Herr und Christus"'*, in *BLit* 45 (1972) 23-32, esp. p. 29.
531. *The Gospel according to Luke*, in C.M. LAYMON (ed.), *The Interpreter's One-Volume Commentary on the Bible*, Nashville, TN, 1971, 672-706. See also BAIRD, *The Acts of the Apostles* in *Ibid.*, p. 729-767. Baird regarded Mk as Luke's basic source for material and structure. The special material was assigned to "a source (or sources)" though in his introduction he omitted mention of the passion narrative within the material he assigned to this source (*Luke*, p. 673). The doubling of names, which J. Weiss claimed stemmed from Luke's special Jewish-Christian source, was seen by Baird as reflecting Septuagintal influence as was the parallelism of various illustrations, which possibly reflected the Deuteronomic requirement of two witnesses (Dt 19,15). This could account for the parallel trials before Pilate and Herod. Luke's theological conviction of witness was strong, a duty which he fulfilled in his writings. Concerning the order, Baird observed that Luke "mainly follows Mark", and the differences may be chiefly geographical, rather than sequential.
The Lukan account of the denials "is slightly different from Mark's" and the passing of one hour increased the climatic suspense (p. 703). The MA in 22,62 was possibly assimilated from Mt 26,75. Baird contended the account of the Sanhedrin trial was drawn from the special (L) source, but recast with help from Mk 14,53-65. Arguing that Luke's trial (22,66-68) was more theological than historical, yet he also stated "Luke's version of the hearing conforms more closely to Jewish legal process". The recasting found in 22,69-71 was to have the Jewish leadership shoulder the responsibility for deciding about Jesus' identity.
L was also the main source for 23,1-5. In 23,18-23 once more, however, Luke used Mk as his source and employing irony (23,24-25) showed how the innocent one was condemned while a murderer was set free.
Baird was not so convinced as others that Herod would have been in Jerusalem for the feast. The mystery of the silence motif was compared with Is 53,7 (p. 703). Baird viewed the mockery here as a substitute for the Markan version (Mk 15,16-20) and it suited Luke's pro-Roman apologetic. The dazzling apparel was described using the same term Josephus used for the raiment of Solomon. The absence of the account from the other Gospels raises doubts about its historicity. It was improbable that Pilate would have made recourse to a political ruler of inferior standing

DE JONGE (1975)[534], Herman HENDRICKX (1977)[535], Michael WILCOCK

and thus Baird sided with Dibelius that it was inspired by Ps 2,2, and its purpose clarified in Acts 4,25-28 (p. 703). See also BAIRD, *Acts*, 1971, p. 733-734. In his commentary on Acts Baird added that the purpose of Paul's trial before Agrippa (Acts 25,13–26,32) was "to present a parallel to Luke 23:6-12 and to fulfill the prophecy of 9:15" (*Acts*, p. 762). The influence of Dt 19,15 was visible once again (*Gospel*, p. 704).

532. *Bibel: das Neue Testament. Eine Einführung in seine Schriften im Rahmen der Geschichte des Urchristentums*, Stuttgart, 1971 (= *The New Testament. A Guide to Its Writings*, tr. R.H. FULLER and I. FULLER, Philadelphia, PA, 1973, p. 29). The pagination refers to the ET. Bornkamm held to the basic Two-Source theory, claiming that the numerous attempts to gather the special material into coherent, unified sources had "not led to any generally accepted result". Cf. p. 27, concerning his defense of the Two-Source theory. He took the position that the oral tradition remained fluid even as the written tradition became determined. In an apparent rejection of the views of Bertram who considered the passion to have been heavily influenced by the community, Bornkamm resolutely argued that the passion narrative showed no "perceptible influence of the passion kerygma" (p. 47). He believed that variations in order were required by the needs of the composition, but also resulted from Luke's intention to combine other traditions with the Markan material (p. 26).

533. *Jesus, der "Herr" in der Passion*, in *TPQ* 120 (1972) 203-210, p. 203. Zehrer observed the term κύριος was found far more frequently in the Lukan passion narrative (22,33.38.49.61) than in Mt (26,22). It did not occur at all in the passion accounts of Mk or Jn. In contrast to the Markan account which stressed the human elements of the passion of Jesus, Luke emphasized the majestic details especially in the Sanhedrin trial, so that in the Lukan portrayal Jesus was presented as superhuman ("übermenschlicher") and thus majestic (p. 209). The post-Easter faith, displayed in "einem stufenweisen Crescendo bereits in den Leidensgeschichte nach Mk, Mt und Lk", presented Jesus as the exalted Lord who has been invested with divine power (p. 210).

In an article published one year later, Zehrer, recalling the claim by E. Nestle that there was a stronger influence of the OT in the passion narratives than in the other parts of the Gospels, noted, for example, the relation of the silence of the Isaian Servant of God (Is 53,5) and the silence of Jesus before the Sanhedrin, Pilate and Herod (ZEHRER, *Sinn und Problematik der Schriftverwendung in der Passion*, in *TPQ* 121 [1973] 18-25, p. 18). Likewise, the mockery of Jesus by the Jews, Herod and the Roman soldiers recalled the OT scenes of the suffering just ones. Partly because Luke's use of the OT in his account differed from the other two Synoptics the speculation of a non-Markan source had been raised (p. 21). Luke abbreviated Ps 110 in 22,69 whereas Mk 14,62 and Mt 26,64 had the same wording. Following the arguments of R. Schnackenburg and A.M. Ramsey, Zehrer seemed to endorse the view Luke had access to sources more numerous than in other parts of his Gospel, in addition to Mk, which he opted occasionally not to use (p. 20-21, n. 12). Cf. A.M. RAMSEY, *The Narratives of the Passion*, in *StEv* 2 (= TU 87), 1964, p. 127-130, and R. SCHNACKENBURG, *Das Johannesevangelium* (HTHKNT, 4/1), 1965, 20-22. In a recent contribution Schnackenburg, who served as Schneider's dissertation director, affirmed that Luke drew on Mk, the Logia source as well as sources unknown to us which stemmed from "einzelnen mündlichen Überlieferungen". Luke then shaped his account of Jesus in accord with historical reality (*Die Person Jesu Christi im Spiegel der vier Evangelien* [HTKNT Suppl 4], Freiburg, 1993, p. 153).

534. *The Use of* ὁ χριστός *in the Passion Narratives*, in J. DUPONT (ed.), *Jésus aux origines de la christologie* (BETL, 40), Leuven, 1975, ²1989, p. 184. De Jonge adopted the view that Luke narrated the account of Peter's denials in 22,54-65 in a unified fashion as opposed to Mk. After rehearsing several differences, de Jonge noted how the second answer in Lk corresponded to the reply given to the high priest (p. 185). He also called attention to the fact that while the

theme of blasphemy did not occur in Lk as in Mk, the term can still be found in 22,65. Christology was seen to be a guiding influence as de Jonge wrote: "Luke obviously is at pains to emphasize that Jesus will begin to exercise his royal authority ἀπὸ τοῦ νῦν as XXII, 69 has made clear" (p. 186). Luke's redactional skill permitted him to insert the trial before Pilate and other events into the narrative "in a more organical way" than Mk.

As the same time that de Jonge's article originally appeared, J. Duncan M. DERRETT published another in which he specifically noted that 22,67-68 "received very little attention", except for Schneider (J.D.M. DERRETT, *Midrash in the New Testament: The Origin of Luke XXII 67-68*, in *ST* 29 [1975] 147-156, p. 147 = *StNT*, Vol. 2, 1978, p. 184-193, p. 184). Derrett's thesis was "my own view supports St. Luke in a particular understanding of Mark, viz., that Jesus consciously played out the scriptural role he understood himself to have assumed: thus the words belonged to him, and were truthfully believed to have belonged to him, whether he actually uttered them or not" (*Ibid.*). Derrett contended Luke had no separate source for this material, and the "widely held" view of an independent source "may be losing ground" (p. 149 = 186). Derrett cited the various views of Bultmann, Finegan and Bertram, among those who argued Luke possessed no independent source in this section or that if he did he did not employ it in this portion of the Gospel, and that Grundmann "gently doubts Luke's special source" (n. 8). Schneider, Perry, Taylor, Tyson, Benoit and Catchpole were listed among the supporters of a special source (n. 9). Derrett considered it "notable" that Rehkopf had not treated 22,67-68 (p. 150, n. 12 = *StNT*, p. 187, n. 12; cf. REHKOPF, *Die lukanische Sonderquelle*). Derrett's reasoning that if Luke were simply adding to Mark's account of silence, E.P. Sanders would have studied them in his work *Tendencies of the Synoptic Tradition*, seemed quite presumptuous. Influenced by the figure of the Isaian Suffering Servant (Is 41,26-28 and 53,12), Luke asserted Jesus was himself that person and that Mark's account directed his christological formation along these lines (DERRETT, *Midrash*, p. 154 = 191). Later he wrote: "Thus, if I am right, Jesus asserts, in answer to the question whether he is the Christ, that he is the Servant come to judge, the Son of Man, and, letting the ambivalent terminology remain apparently on their lips (not his), the Son of God" (p. 155 = 192).

535. *Passion Narratives*, London, 1977, ²1984, p. 5 (esp. p. 52-61, 79-89, 146-149). Hendrickx approached the passion narratives from the perspective of redaction criticism and contended that Luke's particular focus in redacting Mk in the passion narrative was the power of Jesus' death to effect conversions. "There is no evidence that any of the evangelists knew of a generally accepted, pre-Marcan formulation of the passion narrative. Apparently much of the material found in these chapters existed independently, and was combined for the first time by Mark. Matthew and Luke then recast that passion narrative in conformity with their own theological perspectives" (p. 2). Luke's redaction of the Markan passion was further shaped by the model of the martyr, the insistence on the innocence of Jesus, his care for the poor, and the motif of prayer (p. 146-149).

Hendrickx generally offered a feasible explanation of why an account had been changed by Luke over against Mk. He noted the change of order in the Lukan account and suggested that the arrest, at a later point in Lk, was situated in light of the prohibition against additional resistance (22,51).

The MA of v. 62 was ascribed as possibly conforming the Lukan account to the Matthean (p. 56). He made no reference at the appropriate place to the MA in v. 64 / Mt 26,68 (cf. p. 41, 57). Hendrickx made an interesting case for distinguishing between Peter's denial of Jesus as knowing him and denying him as Messiah. Though interesting, that interpretation rested on too fine a line and thus should be rejected (p. 56).

Hendrickx noted the difference of order in Mk and Lk concerning the mockery suggesting that Luke may have wanted to join more closely the proceedings of the Sanhedrin with those of Pilate.

But Hendrickx himself was not entirely convinced of that explanation (p. 57). The account possibly was written as a fulfillment of Is 50,6.

Lukan dependence upon Mk was very clear in the Sanhedrin trial at 22,67a.69.71, but differed in the presentation of the christology and eschatology (p. 61). Omissions were credited to Luke's revision of Mk, as in the case of deleting ὄψεσθε (Mk 14,62), since presumably Luke believed the Sanhedrin would not see the parousia or exalted Christ.

The accounts of Mk and Lk (Lk 23,1-25) were basically the same, the latter being a clarification of the former. The addition of the Herod story was what significantly distinguished the two. Hendrickx pointed up the similarities with Acts and asserted the charges reflected Luke's interest in emphasizing the political detail (p. 79. See Acts 17,7; 24,2-5; 25,7-8 compared with Lk 23,2.5). The political nature of the charges was highlighted only to be revealed as false. Mk 15,1b served as the basis for 23,1. The foundation for the third accusation was Mk 11,9. Mk 15,2 served as the basis for Lk 23,3. While Mk 15,14 did not provide the basis of Lk 23,4 Hendrickx showed the clear relation to Acts 16,35-39; 18,12-15; 19,31-41; 24,22-23; 25,18.25-26; 26,31-32, where Paul was consistently found innocent of the charges brought against him. A summary statement was provided by 23,5.

The purpose of 23,13-16 was to connect what preceded and followed. But the omission of Mk 15,16-20 prompted Luke's explanation of Barabbas' identity (p. 86). Hendrickx likened the phrase "away with this man" (23,18) to Is 53,8. While Mk 15,7 may have grounded 23,19, material was added to it. Luke doubled the crowd's appeal in Mk for Jesus' crucifixion (Mk 15,13), which was also mentioned in the corresponding place in Lk for the first time (p. 87). Agreement was found also between 23,22 and Mk 15,14. Luke extrapolated at 23,23 on Mk 15,13-15. Verse 23,25 shared the phrase "delivered up" in common with Mk.

While Luke's apologetic placed greater responsibility upon the shoulders of the Jews, it was situated within "a serious call to conversion" (p. 89). Dependence upon Mk, Markan influence or changes based upon the Markan source were indicated by Hendrickx in the following: 22,54.(Mk 14,54) 55(cf. Mk 14,54.66).56(Mk 14,67).57.58(Mk 14,69).59.60.61.63.67a.69(Mk 14,62).71(Mk 14,63); 23,2.3.18.20(Mk 15,12b).21(Mk 15,13).22(Mk 15,14).23(Mk 15,13-15).25(Mk 15,15). Probable Markan influence was seen at 22,66; 23,1 (Mk 15,1). Possible Markan influence was considered for 23,19 (Mk 15,7). Editorial contribution and OT influence explain 22,65. Hendrickx has done well to show how Luke's presentation could have been based upon Mk, shaped by the OT, but also reflected the evangelist's own abilities as shown by connections to Acts.

Hendrickx observed that, concerning the Herod pericope, the "vocabulary and style are typically Lucan" (p. 81). He regarded Acts 4,25-27 as a traditional unit which Luke included in his work. Hendrickx offered a qualified endorsement of Dibelius's view, though cautioning that "this explanation is not without difficulties". But in his discussion of 23,10-11 he confessed his belief that Luke had some bit of tradition which contained reference to Herod's involvement in the trial, including the mockery and the vesture in the robe (p. 83). Cf. p. 84, where he stated "Luke must have known a tradition which attributed to Herod a negative role in the trial of Jesus". Hendrickx suggested the white robe indicated a positive verdict. Contrary to scholars such as Goulder, Hendrickx considered the οὐδὲν ἀπεκρίνατο as indicative of Luke's dependence upon Mk (p. 83).

Two possible explanations were offered by Hendrickx for the reconciliation of Pilate and Herod. One was based on Prov 15,28 LXX, where Pilate and Herod joined forces against a common threat, the Jewish leaders. The second was that both rulers were deposed at about the same time, suggesting that both fell from favor of Caesar.

Robert Wild's most serious criticism of the work was that Hendrickx failed to include the Johannine passion (Jn 18–19) which reduced the book's "overall usefulness" (*CBQ* 40 [1978]

(1979)[536], Walter SCHMITHALS (1980)[537], David TIEDE (1980)[538], Brian BECK

275). But he offered the greatest praise for Hendrickx's ability to show OT influence on the pericopes and called the work a "positive achievement".

536. *The Savior of the World. The Message of Luke's Gospel*, Downers Grove, IL, 1979, p. 25; see also p. 195. Wilcock viewed Lk as comprising eyewitness testimony and a large amount of Mk. The details from Mk could be verified by the still living witnesses of the Twelve apostles.

537. *Das Evangelium nach Lukas* (ZBKNT 3/1), Zürich, 1980, p. 9. Schmithals argued that in addition to Mk, Luke used Q which contained pre-Easter traditions, but lacked passion and Easter narratives and was devoid of christology and ecclesiology. He did not know oral tradition. Schmithals considered Luke's effort to be a criticism of the work of his predecessors (p. 18). Writing on the Prologue, Schmithals argued: "Viele haben schon vor ihm einen entsprechenden Bericht versucht. Dabei denkt Lukas an die Verfasser seiner Quellen: das Markusevangelium, die Spruchquelle, die Vorlage(n) seine Sondergutes, die der Apostelgeschichte zugrundeliegenden schriftlichen Überlieferungen". There was no other source for the account of Peter's denial than Mk (Mk 14,53-54.66-72) (p. 216). Jesus was viewed as a martyr (p. 217). As for the MA in v. 62 Schmithals declared: "Er könnte deshalb aus Mat. 26,75b erst sekundär bei Lukas eingedrungen sein" (p. 217). The change in the order of the mockery (22,63-65) over against Mk was noted, thereby giving it a different sense.

The shift in the timing of the Sanhedrin trial (22,66-23,1) was credited to Luke since Mark's account was improbable (p. 218). In 23,2-25 Luke composed according to his apologetical tendency (p. 219). This section was divided into the trial before Pilate (23,2-7); the trial before Herod (23,8-12); and the decision of Pilate (23,13-25). The section 23,13-25 was based upon Mk 15,6-15 (p. 222). The omission of the mockery by the Roman soldiers (Mk 15,16-20a) was explained by the fact that in Luke's account Pilate rendered no guilty verdict and no judgment (p. 222; see also p. 221). Schmithals made frequent comparisons with Acts.

There was a connection between the trial before Herod (23,8-12) "mit dem Weissagungsbeweis nach Ps. 2,1" (p. 220; see also p. 221). Luke was believed to have followed a corresponding tradition. The purpose of this story was to provide another official witness to the innocence of Jesus as confirmed by 23,15. The similarity with the innocence of Paul in Acts 25,23–26,32 was also highlighted. Schmithals also cited the Jewish legal requirement of two witnesses (p. 221). The story reflected thorough Lukan style.

The silence motif (23,9) rested upon Is 53,7, but given the fact that Luke borrowed from Mk 15,4f. in 23,3, it seemed that Schmithals was willing to credit Markan influence. Jesus' silence was not directed against the charges, but in reaction to Herod's curiosity. Luke depicted a brief mockery scene to underscore that Herod did not take the charges of the Jewish religious leaders seriously, and so made light of Jesus' claim. The "dazzling apparel" mocks Jesus' status as king of the Jews. The clothing was understood to be either white or purple. Interpreting the friendship of Herod and Pilate as "ein deutliches Signal der Unschuld Jesu", Schmithals believed this portrayal corresponded to that found in the Scriptures (Ps 2,1) and that Jesus was no political liability.

Schmithals (1985) supported the view that Luke did not have an independent account of the passion in addition to the Mk (*Einleitung*, p. 332). The supporters of the special source were faulted for not sufficiently crediting Luke for redactional material. They underestimated the extent of Luke's influence as an evangelist and author (p. 331). When the supporters of the special source take into consideration Luke's redactional contributions their arguments lack any force and the special Lukan material crumbles into individual pieces. Schmithals conceived of the Lukan passion narrative as a political apologetic which also cast Jesus in the light of a martyr to be imitated (p. 356). Cf. p. 353, where Schmithals contended Luke did not put forward the sin-atoning meaning of Jesus' death, but rather presented it as fulfilling Scripture and proving the continuity between Israel and the ministry of Jesus.

538. *Prophecy and History in Luke-Acts*, Philadelphia, PA, 1980, p. 103. Tiede suggested that the speeches of Peter and Paul to Israel in Acts provided the best commentary on the Lukan passion narrative. What was more, the genre seemed to reflect Greek tragedy and particularly that of "the tragic historians of the Greco-Roman era". He also favored the view that the Lukan passion account was shaped by a "pro-Roman apology" that cast the Jews in a negative light. But this was a part of Luke's effort to understand Jesus' life, ministry and death "*within* the framework of the scriptural prophecies to Israel". God's purpose directed all the action as the events unfolded.

Tiede's comments on source criticism are worth noting. "Again, since Luke can be shown to have used Mark's Gospel as a literary source and since Acts offers an extensive interpretation of Paul's ministry and preaching that can be compared with Paul's own letters, any responsible historical treatment of Luke-Acts must involve careful assessments of Luke's appropriation and alteration of his sources and discriminating judgments concerning Luke's presentation of Paul and his theology. Yet employing Mark as a control for interpreting Luke has not only obscured the complexity of Luke's relations to his sources; it has also tended to impose a very peculiar Markan standard for what constitutes a 'gospel' on the Lucan literature" (p. 12). He continued: "To be sure, interpreting Luke as a redaction of Mark has demonstrated that Luke's eschatology, Christology, and pneumatology are significantly different from Mark's or Paul's, but the method must be criticized for having prejudged Luke-Acts on the basis of criteria that were abstracted from other early Christian books whose historical occasion and literary genre also differed sharply from Luke's" (p. 12-13). Tiede maintained Luke drew upon numerous sources, including "a broad range of Jewish Scriptural sources and traditions, along with Mark and other possible literary collections (e.g., Q) and Christian traditions" (p. 13).

While Tiede attempted to diminish the role of Pilate and Herod in the trial, referring to them as "only plot functionaries", they remain significant nonetheless because of the perspective offered by Ps 2 in Acts 4,25-28 and this proved that Luke considered both leaders as culpable (p. 109). Yet, the story bore historical plausibility. Pilate sent Jesus to Herod "for further public spectacle and denunciation" by the people and their religious leaders. "... the thought that Pilate was only baiting the Jews to evoke further denunciation of Jesus is both historically credible and conceivable within the irony of Luke's account" (p. 113).

In a Lukan commentary designed for laity, students and clergy Tiede (1988) adopted the Two-Source theory, though he considered it possible that Luke may have used Proto-Lk. However, he observed "efforts to reconstruct such sources and stages of the development of the narrative have not proved convincing or especially helpful" (*Luke* [Augsburg Commentary on the NT], Minneapolis, MN, 1988, p. 26; also p. 35 on 1,1). While Tiede believed that Luke was familiar with "other traditions beyond Mark's account" for the passion narrative he added it was "not necessary to reconstruct additional literary accounts of the passion story to understand Luke's version". Tiede clearly stated that Mk formed the basis of Lk in the passion narrative as both its "literary framework and source" (p. 374; see further p. 395). He did not address the MAs in 22,62.64. He concluded that the denial (22,54-62) and mockery (22,63-65) were based on Mk. For the Sanhedrin trial (22,66-71) Tiede seemed to indicate that Luke drew on Mk as well as a non-Markan source. He claimed, in addition, "much of the detail in this scene had been transmitted in oral recitations and preaching" (p. 399). A non-Markan source was considered possible for 23,1-16, though the scenes in these verses were deemed "thoroughly Lukan" (p. 403). While he did not directly address the source question for 23,13-25, he compared some of these verses with Mk.

Addressing the source question for the Herod pericope (23,6-12) he noted that "the whole scene [23,1-16] may well be read as Luke's amplification of Peter's sermon on Psalm 2 in Acts 4:23-

$(1981)^{539}$, possibly Violaine MONSARRAT $(1982)^{540}$ and Josephine Massyngberde FORD $(1984)^{541}$. Other scholars who favored the view that Luke

31" as he also recalled the suggestion that some scholars believed Luke "created the episode" (p. 403; see also p. 407, with mention of Acts 4,26-30). Tiede rejected the proposal that Herod was a second witness to the innocence of Jesus since he rendered no verdict (p. 407). He seemed to indicate there were similarities with the trial of Paul in Acts 25-26.

In an essay published the same year as the commentary (1988) Tiede commented that whatever traditions source critics believed reflected earlier Jewish stages in the development of the Gospel were now Lukan compositions (*'Glory to thy People Israel': Luke-Acts and the Jews*, in J. NEUSNER, E.S. FRERICHS, P. BORGEN, and R. HORSLEY [eds.], *The Social World of Formative Christianity and Judaism*, FS H.C. KEE, Philadelphia, PA, 1988). See p. 329: "Remarkably, many of the very materials the source critics had been so eager to assign to earlier 'Jewish' stages of the tradition have emerged again as fundamental to Luke's literary project. The coherence and significance of the speeches of Acts and the infancy narratives are particularly telling cases. Through whatever traditions or sources these stories and their declarations may have been conveyed to the author, they are now Lukan compositions, and those who speak within these passages are reliable narrators". He recently affirmed (1991) Luke based his account on Mk (*Contending with God: The Death of Jesus and the Trial of Israel in Luke-Acts*, in B.A. PEARSON [ed.], *The Future of Early Christianity: Essays in Honor of H. Koester*, Minneapolis, MN, 1991, p. 303). This is not to say that Luke was not influenced by other literary genres. "Among the Hellenistic histories, Luke's narrative imitates and draws on literary and theological traditions that are particular to Israel's past" (p. 302). What distinguished the Lukan account was that it was presented as a theodicy which did not attempt to explain Jesus' death in terms of expiation (p. 301, 308). Tiede maintained: "In Luke, Jesus' identity and mission are clear, and he dies knowingly obedient to God's will ... But Luke is not merely a revision of Mark, and more is at stake than a displacement of Mark's theology of the cross" (p. 303). Recall that L.T. Johnson also viewed the Lukan passion as a theodicy (*Luke*, p. 10; *ABD* 4, 1992, p. 408).

539. *'Imitatio Christi' and the Lucan Passion Narrative*, in W. HORBURY and B. McNEIL (eds.), *Suffering and Martyrdom in the New Testament*, FS G.M. STYLER, Cambridge, 1981, p. 34, n. 14. Beck worked from an understanding that Luke based his depiction of Jesus' passion upon that of Mk though he inserted other traditions. He adopted Dibelius's view that the Lukan passion was a martyrdom, presented for others to imitate. Like Danker, Beck saw the possible influence of the Book of Wisdom (p. 44, 47; cf. DANKER, *Jesus*, 1972, p. 233 (= 365). More recently (1989), he contended that evidence was against Proto-Lk (BECK, *Christian Character in the Gospel of Luke*, London, p. 3, n. 3).

540. *Le récit de la Passion: un enseignement pour le disciple fidèle Luc 22-23*, in *FoiVie* 81 (1982) 40. Monsarrat indicated several differences in the Lukan account though it followed the same "schema" as the other Synoptics. The Jesus depicted in Lk was fashioned to provide a model for Christians to emulate. The evangelist related how the disciples abandoned Jesus, who was designated "Lord" (22,31.33.38.49.61.62)(p. 42). At v. 61 the evangelist portrayed Jesus as faithful to Peter in Monsarrat's view. Monsarrat also showed connections between the two Lukan works and what place chapters 22-23 had in the whole Lukan corpus. Although Monsarrat did not expressly say so, the author gave the definite impression that Luke redacted Mk, rather than relied on a separate one.

541. Ford was open to the possibility that Luke employed a special source, but she was able to see how Lk could be a redaction of Mk (*My Enemy is My Guest. Jesus and Violence in Luke*, Maryknoll, NY, 1984 [esp. p. 108-135, 147-149] p. 108: "Luke may have possessed a special source for his passion, but even if he used Mark, he has radically redacted his material to bring

redacted Mk included Charles H. GIBLIN (1985)[542], Eugene LAVERDIERE (1986)[543], Robert O'TOOLE (1984)[544], and Jack T. SANDERS (1987)[545]. Philip

out the unique characteristics of his theology"). Ford also subscribed to the idea that Luke depicted Jesus as the ideal martyr (p. 118). While noting the variation in order of the denials, she did not offer an opinion on whether the cause was source or redaction, but said the new position allowed Peter to distance himself from Jesus, deny that he himself was a revolutionary and thus should escape death (p. 122). Further v. 61 would not have been possible without the new setting. She wrote: "The differences in Luke's account of Peter's denial may be accounted for in that Luke wished to portray Peter in a better light because Jesus' prayer for his protection against Satan must not be ineffectual (Luke 22:31-34)" (p. 122. For an earlier and quite similar point of view, see F. RIENECKER, *Das Evangelium des Lukas* [Wuppertaler Studienbibel], Wuppertal, 1959, [6]1976, p. 513. The strength of Jesus was contrasted with the weak disciple).

Variations in the mockery stemmed from Luke's view that the Romans did not possess any incriminating evidence of Jesus' supposed criminal activity. She referred to the positions of Taylor and Catchpole in suggesting that the recasting of the mockery had to do with replacing political overtones with messianic ones.

The contrast between Jewish and Roman justice was highlighted by Luke's shaping of the Sanhedrin trial. Ford asserted Luke was here following his source, but did not specify whether she was thinking of Mk or a special source. Luke's presentation focused on the political dimension while denying the formality of the trial and the evangelist further altered the account by additions and omissions. In this section Ford relied heavily on Blinzler, Walaskay and Sherwin-White.

The account 23,17-25 differed significantly from the other Synoptics. Luke articulated that Barabbas was imprisoned for political reasons (v. 19) and repeated this information (v. 24) (FORD, *My Enemy*, p. 127). The Lukan theology of the passion was described in the following manner: "The total picture in Luke is that of a nonviolent, innocent man condemned to a revolutionary's death and the release of a man whom all recognized to be guilty of sedition and murder" (p. 127). In a subsequent work (1987) Ford assumed Markan priority and also examined 22,56-71 (*Bonded with the Immortal. A Pastoral Introduction to the New Testament*, Wilmington, DE, p. 273, 277-280).

Ford (1984) seemed to have thought of the Herod pericope as historical since it was feasible that Herod was in Jerusalem for the feast (FORD, *My Enemy*, p. 127). She referred to Sherwin-White for part of her analysis. She understood the dazzling apparel as a white robe, to be a further mockery of a "revolutionary candidate". The scene was paralleled with that of Simon bar Giora from Josephus' *Jewish Wars*. Additionally, Ford noted two differences over against Mt/Mk. First, the chastisement occurred prior to the death sentence and secondly, the means of chastising Jesus was not as harsh and usually intended only as a warning (p. 128).

542. *The Destruction of Jerusalem according to Luke's Gospel* (AnBib, 107), Rome, 1985, noted that at 22,54 Luke began subsequent scenes with a form of the verb ἀπάγειν (22,54.66; 23,1.26) to reach conclusion at 23,33 with ὅτε ἦλθον where Luke altered the Markan phrase (p. 93-94). That Luke was redacting Mk in the Sanhedrin scene was clear from indications such as Giblin's reference to Luke omitting the Markan phrase ἐρχόμενον μετὰ τῶν νεφελῶν τοῦ οὐρανοῦ and replacing it with a reference to ascension (p. 31, n. 9; see p. 44-45, n. 58, for Giblin's assessment of Gaston's arguments regarding Proto-Lk).

543. LaVerdiere approached the question from a redaction-critical perspective in asserting that each of the evangelists freed "the traditions from earlier settings and formulations, oral or written" in order to fit them to their pastoral circumstances (*The Passion-Resurrection of Jesus according to St. Luke*, in ChSt 25 [1986] 35-50, p. 35). It was clear that Luke was dependent upon Mk as his primary source: "Luke used many of the elements in Mark's story, but he

presented them in an entirely different way" (p. 47).

In his commentary (1980), though he did not devote any attention to the source question, LaVerdiere noted the parallels between the trials of Jesus and Paul, the point of both being the innocence of the accused. While some scholars pointed to Joanna (8,3) as the possible source of information, if the scene were historical, LaVerdiere conceived of the reference to the women in 8,3 as preparatory for their role in the passion, and also as indicative of the role of women in the early church (Acts 17,4) (*Luke*, p. 112).

544. *The Unity of Luke's Theology. An Analysis of Luke-Acts* (Good News Studies, 9), Wilmington, DE, 1984, p. 11, 86. O'Toole stated that one of his presuppositions was Luke's use of Mk and Q. In an extensive investigation of the parallels between Jesus (23,1-25) and Paul (Acts 25–26), he rendered a decision in favor of Luke's redaction of Mk for 23,1-25. For O'Toole, the parallels indicated that Jesus continued to work through his disciples and that certain demands will be made upon them, since they were imbued with the same qualities as Jesus. Finding some of the Markan material unacceptably positioned (Mk 14,60-61a; 15,3-5.16-20a), Luke transferred it in such a way as to have it refer to Herod and his soldiers, though O'Toole did not entirely exclude the possibility that some "earlier tradition" may underlie it (p. 70). For an extensive comparison of the passion of Jesus and the suffering of the disciples, see p. 82-86. Note the similarity of viewpoint concerning the question of historicity with that of Boismard. The silence motif was likened to Is 53,7 rather than ascribed to Markan influence. Although the possibility existed that the Herod episode rested upon an historical basis, O'Toole found the possibility that the story was a Lukan creation an appealing one. He further observed that the Herodian scenes in both Lk and Acts could be omitted without disturbing the flow of the narrative (p. 71).

In a 1993 article O'Toole reaffirmed his support of the Two-Source theory which, in his opinion, "still best explains the Synoptic problem" (*Reflections on Luke's Treatment of the Jews in Luke-Acts*, in *Bib* 74 [1993] 529-555, p. 530). Although in *Reflections*, O'Toole passed over the section 23,1-5, in an earlier essay he treated at least 23,2 in the context of clear parallels between Jesus and Moses (*The Parallels Between Jesus and Moses*, in *BTB* 20 [1990] 24). The charge of the Jewish leaders against Jesus of perverting the people was closely paralleled with a charge by Pharaoh against Moses and Aaron (Ex 5,4 LXX) perverting his people from their work (cf. 1 Kgs 18,17). O'Toole referred to D. SCHMIDT, *Luke's 'Innocent' Jesus: A Scriptural Apologetic*, in R.J. CASSIDY and P.J. SHARPER (eds.), *Political Issues*, 1983, p. 119. In what will be important for our exegesis of the Herod pericope (see below), O'Toole saw clear Luke parallels between Jesus and Moses in the Transfiguration account (9,28-36) in Jesus' Moses-like journey (9,51: exodus) to Jerusalem and a probable parallel in Lk 13,31-33 in the reference to Jesus casting out demons and performing cures, reminiscent of Moses (cf. Acts 7,22; Lk 24,19; Acts, 7,26). "All prophets suffer, but this characteristic of prophets constitutes an extensive basis for the Lukan parallel between Jesus and Moses. As prophets, both are misunderstood, denied and rejected. While they can address an audience 'as a perverse and crooked generation,' they themselves are accused of perverting the people and disrupting service or taxes due the king" (p. 28). Keeping in mind that Luke carefully prepared for the succeeding parts of the Gospel in the initial portions, these parallels should not be neglected when we examine the Herod pericope. Though he did not treat the denials of Peter, he cited the position of Ascough that there was a similarity between the repentance of Peter and those Jewish people who repented and became part of the Christian community (O'TOOLE, *Reflections*, p. 539, n. 18. See ASCOUGH, *Rejection*). In the account of the mockery (22,63-65) he highlighted the differences between Lk and the other Synoptics. No reference was made to the MA in v. 64. Like Van der Kwaak he insisted that the focus of the Sanhedrin trial (22,66-71) was christological as indicated by the two questions. O'Toole contended that this episode clarified why the Jewish authorities were still held accountable in part for the death of Jesus. In 23,13-25 he was more concerned with the question of Jewish culpability than with the source question, although he pointed out the difference between Mk and Lk in the demand of the people for Barabbas' release (O'TOOLE, *Unity*, p. 539). This section clearly stood as part of Luke's apologia toward Rome in presenting the officials in a more positive light toward Christians (p. 539; see also p. 531, 553). Luke's omission of Mk 15,16-20a was seen as part of this strategy. The omission was also due to Luke's not wishing to present Jesus as the victim of such harsh treatment. O'Toole further maintained Luke followed Mk in Mk 15,16.25.39.44-45. (In addition see his comment, p. 553). O'Toole properly referred to related material in other parts of the Gospel and Acts. Luke's readers were identified as "Gentile Christians very strongly influenced by the LXX".

O'Toole (1993) asserted 23,6-12 was a Lukan composition (O'TOOLE, *Reflections*, p. 551-552). Not only did the passage serve as "an extended parallel" between the passion of Jesus and that of Paul, but it allowed Luke to employ Markan material (Mk 14,60-61a; 15,3-5.16-20a), though in reference to Herod rather than to Pilate. Thirdly, it formed part of the theme of Jesus' innocence.

545. *The Jews in Luke-Acts*, London, 1987, p. 16 (esp. p. 220-226). Sanders wrote from the standpoint that Luke redacted Mk's account which held the Jewish religious leaders and their security force responsible for the crucifixion. Allowing for the possibility that there might have been other sources, Sanders was of the firm conviction that the finished product was decidedly Lukan. "Even if this version of the crucifixion could be shown to have derived from some source, still the choice to use this version and not Mark's was Luke's choice" (*Ibid.*). That concession notwithstanding, the depiction of the trial and crucifixion coincided with the manner in which the evangelist presented the Jewish people in Lk-Acts. It was the evangelist rather than some source who so configured the story. So radical was Luke's revision that Sanders claimed the evangelist "distorted the passion narrative tradition".

Luke, being confused about matters Palestinian, mistakenly understood the Sanhedrin to refer to a place rather than a group of leaders. Regarding the omission of the charge of blasphemy Sanders viewed this as an attempt on the part of the evangelist not to confuse the situation, since immediately following political charges were brought against Jesus.

Sanders credited Luke with transposing the mockery (22,63-65) though the reasoning was not so evident. The most plausible explanation for Sanders was to link more closely the intervention of the Sanhedrin and Pilate's trial. The Markan and Lukan accounts are similar in detail.

The omission of Markan material in 22,66-71 permitted attention to be focused on the political charges and to show that the charges were false. Luke's substitution of τὸ πλῆθος (23,1) for ὅλον τὸ συνέδριον (Mk 15,1) allowed for the introduction of the people into the conspiracy. It was quite likely that the charges reflect those which the Jews raised against Christians in the Diaspora and Sanders noted the similarities with Paul's case in Acts. The evangelist's purpose sought to show that the accusations were unfounded. In the brief recounting of Jesus with Pilate (23,1-5) Sanders argued Luke had not omitted Markan material. Rather he added to it. Although Sanders did not write directly of Lukan redaction of Mk in 23,13-25, he contended that Luke was attempting to bring his portrayal of the Jews into line with what will be found in the initial speeches in Acts accusing the Jews of killing Jesus.

Sanders gave consideration in an article (1988) to the role of the Jewish people in the passion narrative (*The Jewish People in Luke-Acts*, in J.B. TYSON [ed.], *Luke-Acts and the Jewish People*, Minneapolis, MN, 1988, 51-75). They were portrayed as favorably disposed toward Jesus before Ch 23, they then aligned themselves with the religious leaders calling for the death of Jesus, but returned to their earlier disposition. Sanders believed Luke intended to have the people share the blame, though ensuring that the lion's share of the responsibility would be credited to the religious authorities (p. 69). The image that emerged from Sanders's reading was a kind of

Francis ESLER (1987) observed the differences between Mk and Lk at Lk 23,1-5.13-25, but declined to enter into the source debate considering it "unnecessary" for his purpose[546].

In a 1984 dissertation presented at Union Theological Seminary (NY) under the direction of R.E. Brown, Marion L. SOARDS focused on the special material in Lk 22[547]. He distinguished his work from previous investigations because "the work moves away from earlier studies that focused primarily on word-statistical analysis and deals with the lines of thought that run through Luke 22, relating this chapter to the Gospel according to Luke as a whole"[548]. That method was not ignored, but was not primary as in other studies. He rejected the view that Luke employed a continuous non-Markan source, refashioning the Markan Passion in light of his christology, eschatology, and ecclesiology[549]. Soards noted that the commentary by Fitzmyer and a study by Matera appeared after his dissertation, but he was

schizophrenia. Though in the passion narrative they were for a time conspirators, still they must be presented in such a way that in Acts 1-5 they can be converted. "By giving the people such a strange role in the passion, Luke has prepared the way for both necessities in Acts, that of the success of the gospel among 'the Jews' and that of their rejection of the gospel. If Luke had constructed his script so that the people entered completely the mode of rejection at the end of the Gospel, then the narrative of the Acts would be anticlimactic, but if they expressed no hostility to the purposes of God during the passion narrative, then the absolute reality expressed in the sayings and speeches from the Nazareth episode and on would not be correct. So Luke gave to the Jewish people the ambiguous role in the passion narrative already described" (p. 73-74). Sanders commented that the people acted similarly in Acts.

Sanders (1987) focused on the inconsistent presentation of Herod who longed to see Jesus (23,8) but then vigorously interrogated him (23,9) (*The Jews in Luke-Acts*, p. 224; cf. p. 13-14). See further Sanders's discussion on p. 342, n. 70, where he commented that Fitzmyer disagreed with Dibelius's proposal while coming to "no definite conclusion" himself. The additional inconsistency between Herod's earlier desire to kill Jesus and later finding him innocent, was attributed to "revisionist historical writing" (p. 342, n. 70). The point of the story is that political authorities always "find Jesus and the Christians innocent" (p. 225).

546. *Community and Gospel in Luke-Acts. The Social and Political Motivations of Lucan Theology* (SNTS MS, 57), Cambridge, 1987, p. 202. Diss. Oxford, 1984 (dir. R. MORGAN). And yet his conclusion about the political dimension of the Gospel might lead one to conclude that Esler favored redaction over special source, especially when he wrote: "Legitimating Christianity to them [the Roman members of Luke's congregation] inevitably involved providing a reassurance that faith in Jesus Christ was not incompatible with allegiance to Rome" (p. 217). This perspective seemed further confirmed by the following statement: "From the discussion in this chapter, one may conclude that the way Luke has handled the relationship between Rome and Christianity has been motivated and influenced by the pressures upon the Roman members of his community generated by their continuing allegiance to the state they served. In responding to these pressures, Luke reshaped Gospel traditions in the service of a particular community at a particular point in its history" (p. 219). This sounds very much like redaction criticism.

547. M.L. SOARDS, *The Passion According to Luke. The Special Material of Luke 22* (JSNT SS, 14), Sheffield, 1987. Diss. Union Theol. Sem. 1984 (dir. R.E. BROWN).

548. *Ibid.*, p. 7.

549. See especially p. 116-113.

"encouraged" by the frequent similar conclusions which he and Fitzmyer reached independently[550]. Part of the task which Soards set for himself was to define what was meant by special material, which he interpreted to be additional material.

Soards critiqued Taylor's approach for three reasons: 1) Markan elements may not provide an adequate picture of the manner in which Luke used Mk. Taylor's method ignored motifs and themes in choosing to focus merely on the vocabulary; 2) the method was reductionistic, permitting only an either/or dichotomy. No room was left for any other alternative; and 3) it reflected a peculiar understanding of the evangelist's compositional technique which flowed from the statistical method[551].

Soards consciously chose to restrict the literature he would review, which included the other Gospels, the Dead Sea Scrolls, the Pauline corpus, Philo, Josephus and the apocryphal GP. He rightly observed that a study of the Lukan passion narrative must necessarily be conducted in the light of the whole of Lk-Acts.

For the "material entirely without parallel in Mark", Soards assigned: 22,39a-b.40b.48a-b.49a-b.51a-e.52b.53c-d.61a.64d-65.66a-68b.70a-d.Other material that was roughly parallel included: 22,45a.c.55a-60d.61b-62b.63a-64c[552]. In his second category "material representing an agreement of Luke with Matthew or John against Mark" he detected: 22,42a-d.48a-b.51a-c.60d.62a-b.64d.67a-e. There was similarity between Lk and Jn in the striking of the sword before Jesus' arrest (22,49a-50b)[553]. The third group of material was defined as that "forming a story sequence different from that of Mark": 22,54a.56a-62b(except 61a).63a-64c.67a-71c. Other differences included the transposition of two significant units of material. Differences in story line and position in Gospel were noted for 56a-62b at 57b and 60b as well as 67a-71c at 69 and 70b. Verses 39a-b and 40b were said to be of a "complicated nature"[554]. Soards moved next to "material with a low level of verbal correspondence between Luke and Mark" in which he employed a statistical method as Taylor had done. Ignoring the non-parallel material, Soards concluded that section (22,39-71) was marked by a noticeable homogeneity and a "remarkably consistent" amount of verbal agreement[555]. Finally, he examined the "so-called telltale Lukan language" for which he found Hawkins, Easton, Cadbury, and Rehkopf "especially helpful"[556]. He divided the terms into preferred Lukan terms and those indicative of Luke's ideas and interests. This latter list was grouped into five segments: 1) Jesus in authority; 2) the plan of God; 3)

550. *Ibid.*, p. 8. But he referred to Fitzmyer's commentary in his work since the dissertation was published three years after its completion (e.g. p. 16).
551. *Ibid.*, p. 18.
552. *Ibid.*, p. 70.
553. *Ibid.*, p. 83.
554. *Ibid.*, p. 85.
555. *Ibid.*, p. 89.
556. *Ibid.*, p. 152, n. 93; cf. p. 89.

eschatology; 4) prayer; and 5) information about the disciples[557]. As a general conclusion Soards indicated there was no part of 22,39-71 which was lacking in vocabulary "that is characteristic of the evangelist".

Concerning the origin of special material in 22,54-71, Soards reached the following conclusions: Only v. 61a was a pure Lukan composition while v. 62a-b stemmed from oral tradition. The rest was a combination of materials drawn from oral tradition, Mk, and Luke's creativity. For the mockery, while v. 64d was believed to be from oral tradition, the remainder was Lukan redaction of Mk: vv. 63a-64c were based on Mk 14,65 and v. 65 relied upon Mk 14,55-61a. Soards rightly concluded the mockery (22,63-65) was a Lukan redaction based on Mk 14,65[558].

In the Sanhedrin trial v. 67a-e was a Lukan redaction of Mk 14,61 which was based on oral tradition likewise found in Jn 10,24-26 and v. 68a-b was a pure Lukan composition. But for the rest, Luke was redacting Markan material: v. 66a-d (Mk 14,53 and possibly Mk 15,1); v. 69 (Mk 14,62); v. 70a-b (Mk 14,61); 70c-d (Mk 14,62; 15,2); and v. 71a-c (Mk 14,63b-64a)[559].

The special material extended throughout the Gospel and was listed as: 22,3a.15a-16c.19a-20c.24a-b.27a-32d.35a-38d.39b.40b.42a-d.48a-49b.51a-e.52b.53c-d.61a.62a-b.64d.66a-68b. Soards denied that it constituted any kind of continuous source but reflected "independent units" and thus Soards saw himself attacking one of the central tenets of the Proto-Lukan theory[560].

In determining the origin of the MA in 22,62 / Mt 26,75 Soards sided with those who attributed it to oral tradition. The unlikelihood that independent redaction by both Luke and Matthew accounted for the similarity prompted his decision[561]. Soards reached the same conclusion for 22,64 / Mt 26,68[562].

Soards assigned the transpositions to the evangelist and noted they served the following purpose: "Luke's arrangement of the scenes reinforces the image of Jesus' determination. When Jesus stands before the Assembly (66a-71c) he has already witnessed Peter's denying him three times (54a-62b), and he has already suffered the indignity of injurious, mocking treatment from his captors (63a-65). Despite being abandoned and abused, Jesus is not intimidated as he faces the

557. *Ibid.*, p. 95.
558. *Ibid.*, p. 102.
559. *Ibid.*, p. 105-106.
560. *Ibid.*, p. 119-120.
561. *Ibid.*, p. 101-102.
562. *Ibid.*, p. 102: "Therefore, it seems justified to conclude that Luke and Matthew had access to the same oral tradition in Greek. We may infer that in retelling the incident of Jesus' mockery, after the challenge to Jesus to prophesy was narrated, early Christians made clear *what* Jesus was dared to say. Luke and Matthew had heard this clarification of the command to prophesy and independently added *tis estin ho paisas se* to their versions of the story". The decision favoring oral tradition also applied to σὺ λέγεις in 23,3 / Mk 15,2 / Mt 27,11 (p. 104).

Assembly"[563]. Such an arrangement allowed the portrayal of Jesus as prophet to become more clearly perceptible.

There was a discernable order within the account of the Sanhedrin trial as well which reflected logic and intention. Luke, using Mk as his "basic source" embellished it with material drawn from oral tradition as well as details he himself composed. The idea that Luke used only written sources Soards regarded as "artificially restrictive". Changes in Luke over against Mk were ascribed to the evangelist's "theological motives". Indeed, Soards suggested Luke redacted Mk "in order to alter subtly the image of Jesus and the impact of his passion"[564]. Overall, Luke intended to assure his readers, as he indicated in the Prologue, that Jesus was the Christ and that Christianity was willed by God.

Reception of Soards's Dissertation

Brian G. Powley criticized the study for not taking the unified nature of Luke-Acts into greater consideration[565]. Without being specific, he offered his judgment: "This monograph falls short of being a significant contribution to the literature of redaction criticism".

Joel Green noted that while many other studies of the Lukan passion in recent decades centered on compositional and literary matters, Soards focused on source-critical questions[566]. Green praised Soards for concentrating on that issue "in such detail" and for placing "the whole discussion on a somewhat broader base" and for pointing out the weaknesses of Taylor's methodology. Green believed the current scholarly consensus favored redaction over special written sources to account for the differences between Lk and Mk. But Green found Soards's recourse to the oral tradition solution "particularly distressing methodology" and faulted the study for relying on presuppositions which Soards had not examined. Green also took issue with Soards over the non-Markan material that had been inserted rather than integrated. Such an understanding of the evangelist's compositional technique would explain why the special material did not form a continuous narrative.

For Martin Rese the strengths of the investigation lay in Soards's methodology and conclusions[567]. Although Soards did not often enter into debate with the positions of other scholars, it was evident that he was coversant with a great deal of secondary literature. The weaknesses included Soards's use of the term "Lukan Sondergut" more broadly than was generally the case, and employing a quantitative methodology similar to Taylor. Rese's overall assessment, like that of Powley, was

---

563. *Ibid.*, p. 107.
564. *Ibid.*, p. 123.
565. *ExpT* 99 (1987-88) 215.
566. *JBL* 108 (1989) 154.
567. *TLZ* 115 (1990) 197-198.

that Soards's was not a significant contribution to the study of the Lukan passion narrative[568].

Steven M. Sheeley was favorable toward the work and credited Soards with two valuable contributions: a methodology that considered the themes in the entire narrative and "a good example" for redaction criticism[569]. The drawback was that, as a dissertation, in scope as in its conclusions, it was limited.

Frederick Danker took a much more positive view of the work[570]. Citing as Soards's "distinctive contribution" his decision to highlight the thought and content of the narrative in conjunction with his criteria, Danker also praised him for distancing himself from word analysis after the fashion of Taylor. Although Danker noted some (unspecified) minor methodological disagreements, he considered the book a "solid platform" for advancing understanding of the Gospel.

In a later study (1990) Soards focused attention on the mockery (22,63-65), claiming as he had in his dissertation that Luke relied on oral sources[571]. He echoed his critique of the use of "word statistics and stylistic matters" declaring they were "weak criteria"[572]. He denied that the mockery accounts found in Mk and Lk were "matching", though 23,63a-64c was like that recounted in Mk 14,65. His final conclusion was that 22,63-65 was a redaction of Mk 14,65 with the following exceptions: 23,64d stemmed from oral tradition and 23,65 was Luke's summation of the Markan material in Mk 14,55-61a[573]. The difference in order was viewed as bringing the narrative in line with 9,22[574].

Soards highlighted the MA in 22,64 / Mt 26,68 and called the "best" explanation that which attributed to Luke and Matthew knowledge of the same non-Markan oral tradition[575]. The phrase was appended independently by both evangelists. Like Baird, Matera, Binz, Heil, Karris and Stein, Soards alluded to the irony found in this section of the Gospel[576].

In a recent essay (1991) Soards described his thesis on the place of oral tradition in the formation of Gospel literature in the following manner: "First, I shall make the case that oral PN traditions existed prior to the composition of the

---

568. *Ibid.*, p. 198.

569. *RExp* 85 (1988) 353.

570. *CBQ* 53 (1991) 150-151.

571. M.L. SOARDS, *A Literary Analysis of the Origin and Purpose of Luke's Account of the Mockery of Jesus*, in E. RICHARD (ed.), *New Views on Luke and Acts*, Collegeville, MN, 1990, 86-93; notes, 174-177. See his *Passion*, p. 84-85, 96, 102, 103, 106, 118, 120.

572. SOARDS, *Literary*, p. 86.

573. *Ibid.*, p. 91.

574. *Ibid.* Soards was attentive to the importance of the phenomenon of order as signaled by his reference to NEIRYNCK, *The Argument from Order* (SOARDS, *Literary*, p. 174, n. 1).

575. SOARDS, *Literary*, p. 89. He also entertained, but ultimately rejected, the possibility that one evangelist was familiar with an oral and the other a written tradition (p. 90).

576. *Ibid.*, p. 91. See BAIRD, *Gospel*, 1971, p. 704; MATERA, *Passion*, p. 178; S.J. BINZ, *The Passion*, p. 84; J.P. HEIL, *Reader-Response and the Irony of Jesus before the Sanhedrin in Luke 22:66-71*, and *Reader-Response and the Irony of the Trial of Jesus in Luke 23:1-25*; KARRIS, *Gospel*, p. 717; STEIN, *Luke*, p. 582.

canonical Gospels. Secondly, I shall show that oral tradition influenced the evangelists as they wrote their accounts. And thirdly, I shall argue that oral PN traditions persisted long after the composition of the canonical Gospels and that these traditions continued to influence the minds of later Christian authors as they reflected on the Passion of Christ"[577]. His focus was on the events in the garden of Gethsemane. Soards contrasted the position in his dissertation concerning the special source with that of Green as indicative of the polarity in recent studies, adding that "this important interpretative issue may never be settled finally"[578].

Soards (1985) investigated the Herod pericope in which he concluded the story was a Lukan composition comprised of materials derived from tradition, from Mk and from Luke's own hand[579]. Materials ascribed to tradition were vv. 9a.12b and possibly 7b and 11c[580]. Mk was responsible for vv. 9b.11a.b and possibly 9a. Lukan free composition contributed vv. 8c.d.e, 10 and maybe 9a gleaned from previous parts of the Gospel. In order to situate the narrative in its place and to provide a cohesive narrative Luke composed vv. 6a.b, 7a, 8a.b, 12a and possibly 7b, 9a, and 11c. It was clear that v. 9a pertained to each of the compositional elements and formed the "basis of the entire pericope"[581].

Soards's insights into the statistical methodology are well worth noting. "For at least three reasons the criteria of language and style are used only in a supplementary fashion for this work. First, there is almost universal agreement

---

577. SOARDS, *Oral Tradition Before, In, and Outside the Canonical Passion Narratives*, in H. WANSBROUGH (ed.), *Jesus and the Oral Gospel Tradition* (JSNT SS, 64), Sheffield, 1991, 335. In a note Soards expressed gratitude to R.E. Brown for 75 typescript pages of his forthcoming book, *The Death of the Messiah* (Soards, *Oral Tradition*, p. 337, n. 2). Soards was influenced by Brown's methodology for isolating probable oral tradition influence. In an 1978 Oxford dissertation which was not published until 1993, Loveday ALEXANDER also argued for a greater role for oral tradition as a Lukan source (*The Preface to Luke's Gospel. Literary Convention and Social Context in Luke 1.1-4 and Acts 1.1*, Diss. Oxford, 1978 (dir. D. NINEHAM), Cambridge, 1993, p. 208-209). Dissatisfied with Cadbury's proposal that Luke revised Mk to stylistically improve it, Alexander believed "that the triumph of literacy over orality in the ancient world has been overestimated" (ALEXANDER, p. 209; cf. H.J. CADBURY, *The Making of Luke-Acts*, 1927, p. 137-139). What was more, "even after material of this sort is written down, its period of fluidity is not at an end" (p. 209). Alexander also pointed out that one's position on the synoptic problem would influence one's interpretation of the Preface (p. 207).

578. SOARDS, *Oral*, p. 336, n. 3.

579. SOARDS, *Tradition*, 1985, 344-364.

580. *Ibid.*, p. 358.

581. *Ibid.*, p. 359. Among those scholars who considered the story as derived from a source, Soards included: Perry, Tyson, Grundmann, Winter, Rengstorf, Hoehner and Ellis. Those who attributed the account to free Lukan composition were: Baur, Dibelius, Bultmann, Klostermann, Creed, Finegan, Beare, Leaney, Sloyan, H. Klein, H. Hendrickx and K. Müller. Finally, those who regarded the episode as a Lukan composition resting upon a "basic tradition" were Dodd, Taylor, Ernst, Schneider, as well as Pesch and R. Kratz (p. 346). Soards earlier added in a note that both Ernst and Schneider adduced "a historical basis for this story is possible but not probable" (p. 345, n. 9).

among those who have carefully studied the linguistic issues of 23,6-12 that the pericope is peculiarly Lukan. Second, language and style are weak criteria because of the questionable results they can produce when employed as a primary method. Third, in the present state of biblical studies those doing strictly linguistic criticism have argued one another into a stalemate. Therefore, this study works primarily with the content and thought of Luke 23,6-12, bringing in linguistic matters only to support points made on other grounds. This analysis works from the assumption that the text of the Gospel is to be attributed to the hand of the author unless demonstrated otherwise"[582].

Since the silence of Jesus attracted much attention, it is well to note Soards believed that "since Luke almost certainly employed Mark in the composition of his Gospel, it is not necessary to go beyond Mark 14,60-61 and 15,4-5 for striking parallels"[583]. Though Luke's purpose in recounting the vesting of Jesus in dazzling apparel escapes scholars, Soards decided that this probably derived from Mk[584].

Soards also evaluated three minor[585] and five major reasons[586] why Luke would have included this account in his passion narrative. He reasoned that the primary purpose of its inclusion was to underscore the innocence of Jesus, and that a "secondary motif" of the reconciliation of Pilate and Herod was also at work here[587].

In the same year (1985) Soards published another article in which he examined the silence of Jesus in the Herod episode[588]. He rehearsed four types of interpretations previously proposed[589]. Departing slightly from Marshall and

---

582. *Ibid.*, p. 347-348.

583. *Ibid.*, p. 352.

584. *Ibid.*, p. 355-356.

585. *Ibid.*, p. 360. These were: 1) Luke obtained "a relatively insignificant tradition" (Meyer); 2) the scene anticipated the preaching of the apostles in Acts (Danker); 3) it highlighted the reconciling effect of the passion of Jesus (Talbert and Schweizer). Each of these was rejected by Soards in course.

586. *Ibid.*, p. 360-362. The first reason, that Rome was presented in a more positive light, was dismissed since: 1) the Jewish leaders appeared the same here as in other parts of Lk; 2) it was not clear whether Herod was presented as a Jew or a Roman; 3) Rome was not seen in a better light since Pilate ultimately yielded to the demands of the Jews. The second reason, that the Herod episode highlighted the innocence of Jesus, was convincing. The requirement of Dt 19,15 for a second witness, the third proposed purpose of the story, was rejected since it was not clear that Luke was composing out of this purview. Fourthly, that Herod was contrasted with Jesus, though true, was too general, and thus cannot be the reason Luke included it. Finally, focusing on the dissimilarity of Lk 23,6-12 and Ps 2, Soards repudiated Dibelius's suggestion that the Gospel pericope fulfilled Ps 2.

587. *Ibid.*, p. 363.

588. SOARDS, *The Silence of Jesus Before Herod: An Interpretative Suggestion*, in *AusBR* 33 (1985) 41-45.

589. *Ibid.*, p. 41. The four interpretations were: 1) theological, espoused by Manson and Schweizer; 2) Jesus fulfilled the role of the Suffering Servant in Is 53,7, a view championed by Marshall and Sloyan; 3) the silence connoted divinity, as understood by Grundmann and Danker;

Sloyan on the issue of the Isaian background of the silence, Soards contended that Isaian elements were woven through the Gospel and did not impose an Isaian framework from without[590]. Drawing upon Josephus, Soards argued the silence was a sign of nobility. Both the Isaian influence and the nobility such as depicted by Josephus of the wife of Herod the Great, served in complementarity to portray "Jesus' refusal to speak as an indication of the noble character manifested by Jesus as he does God's will"[591].

In his dissertation (1987) Soards advocated the view that Luke composed the Herod pericope using two pieces of information not contained in Mk: first, that Herod took part in Jesus' trial and secondly, that Herod and Pilate were at odds[592]. There were, however, at least three and possibly four elements which Soards attributed to Mk in contrast to Taylor[593]. The twofold purpose of the story was to emphasize Jesus' innocence and to indicate that "Jesus' involvement in events brings about something good". Soards noted the portrayals, particularly of Herod in the Gospel and Acts, suggested "a basic historical remembrance of Herod's participation in the trial of Jesus that was put to different uses in different places"[594]. As regards 23,11 Soards commented that "loose parallels" of the mockery and vesting in dazzling apparel were found in Mk 15,16-20.

Christopher Francis EVANS (1990) suggested that while the term "many" in the Prologue (1,1) was more than a literary convention, Luke did not imply "whether he had read or used them"[595]. Evans supported the view that Luke and Matthew both independently redacted Mk. The order Luke followed was that of Mk. Further, Evans rejected the Proto-Lk hypothesis, particularly where the Q material was said to have been inserted into a single continuous written document[596]. Evans reacted against Easton, while agreeing there was a common style and

---

and 4) the "form-critical" view, that the silence provided a model for Christians to imitate, as suggested by Dibelius and Buck.

590. *Ibid.*, p. 42.

591. *Ibid.*, p. 43. Cf. Josephus, *Antiquities*, 15.7.6 para. 234-235.

592. SOARDS, *Passion*, p. 130, n. 18. He gave the background of his article, *Tradition*, 1985, 344-364, which began as a paper, *Luke's Account of Jesus before Herod Antipas*, presented to the CBA in 1983.

593. SOARDS, *Passion*, p. 18. These included Jesus' silence (23,9b), the mockery (23,11a) and Jesus' vesture (23,11b). Soards speculated the act of the questioning of Jesus, albeit by Herod (23,9a), may also have stemmed from Mk.

594. *Ibid.*, p. 131, n. 36.

595. C.F. EVANS, *Saint Luke* (TPI NTC), London, 1990, p. 15 (esp. p. 15-29, 122-123, 765-770, 822-859). This series originally appeared as the Pelican commentaries. As such, this commentary was the successor to that of Caird. Evans suggested the term "many" referred to one or possibly two, and that "...'many', was an established rhetorical cliché for catching the attention at the beginning of a speech (cf. A.24²), and had spread to other forms of expression (cf. Heb. 1¹), including prefaces" (p. 123).

596. *Ibid.*, p. 27. See also p. 20-21.

vocabulary in some of the L material, it cannot account for all of it[597]. It stemmed possibly from a number of sources, though there may have been some collections of material also available.

Evans astutely remarked that Luke's redactional tendencies can only be ascertained in those sections where Luke was clearly dependent upon Mk. Thus, in studying the passion, recourse must always be made to other sections of the Gospel. Luke's method was "not a mechanical transcription"[598]. Gospel tradition, the LXX and Greco-Roman civilization all helped Luke to shape his account. Furthermore, the martyr influence may also be at work here.

The passion account was further shaped by an apologetic which portrayed Rome as having found Christians not a political threat, and at the same time cast blame toward the Jews. Evans divided the pertinent material in our section into three groups: 1) "comparatively self-contained and detachable from the context" (23,6-12); 2) Markan (possibly 22,54-62); and 3) Markan and non-Markan (24,54.63-71; 23,1-5.13-25)[599].

Departing from a majority of scholars, Evans insisted the purpose of Peter's denial was "not obvious", but certainly would not have served to deter Christians from apostasy as a warning against such behavior nor did it explain 12,9 Peter's confessions of faith (9,20; Acts 2,36). For Evans the story devolved to a comparison of the strength of Jesus as opposed to the weakness of the disciples. Evans followed Taylor's judgment, predicated on verbal similarity, that the section was based upon Mk, rather than Perry's who believed the "time intervals" suggested a non-Markan source[600]. Evans implied the order allowed the account of Peter to be related as a whole rather than divided as found in Mk, but did not directly address the issue of transposition here.

According to Evans, the mockery (vv. 63-65) was borrowed from Mk[601]. He called attention to "the awkward connection" involving αὐτόν but did not explain why that was indicative of dependence upon Mk. At v. 66 a similar awkwardness was found in referring to those who led Jesus away. Septuagintal influence of Is 50,6 was also detected here. The term used here of mocking (ἐμπαίζειν) was to be found in Herod's trial (23,11) as well.

While the MA in v. 62 could be considered to be Luke's adaptation of the Matthean phrasing, Evans considered it more likely that the Latin MSS were

---

597. *Ibid.*, p. 27.

598. *Ibid.*, p. 31.

599. *Ibid.*, p. 769. But he clarified his position at the end of the section of 23,1-25: "In view of [Luke's apologetic], and of the high literary quality of vv. 1-25, there is no necessity to postulate a non-Markan passion narrative as the source of Luke's extended account of Pilate's sessions. It could be explicable as his own development, on the basis of Mark and the story about Herod, of the theme of the innocence of Jesus" (p. 859).

600. *Ibid.*, p. 823. The expression "after an interval of about an hour" Evans understood to be "the narrator's art" (p. 826).

601. *Ibid.*, p. 828. But cf. p. 823, where Evans was more hesitant in assigning the mockery to Mk 14,65.

correct and that it was a result of the work of copyists assimilating Lk to Mt[602]. The account of the denial would thus end with the gaze of Jesus and the recollection of Peter. But it seems to us that this fit well with Luke's theme of contrition which gave some physical sign of inner disposition (7,38; 23,48). For the MA in v. 64, Luke was trying to "make sense" of the Markan account. Thus Evans seemed to suggest that it resulted from Luke's redaction of Mk. He stated there was little evidence for Streeter's view that the phrase was original to Lk, except that there was no reference to blindfolding in Mt[603].

The Sanhedrin trial (22,66-71), in Evans's opinion, was possibly the "crucial section" not only of the passion account, but of the whole Gospel. The accounts in the four Gospels were minimal because the tradition "had been weak here from the first"[604]. In light of Mk, Luke possibly was forced to compress his material. The question of a special source was answered negatively by Evans who saw v. 69 as containing Markan "traces". He argued against Easton that Luke would have weakened v. 69 by the passive "shall be seated", but Evans was convinced that was what Luke would have done because of similarities with Acts. This section was revamped in light of Lukan christology. Since a formal condemnation was not reported, Luke may have intimated that such action was beyond the power of the Sanhedrin.

While the account of Stephen may suggest otherwise, the tendency which surfaced here was the persecution of Christians by the Jews thus shifting blame to them for the death of Jesus. Evans took issue with Sherwin-White's position that the Sanhedrin would have approached Pilate when he finished his work for the day. Evans believed our sources for Pilate were not adequate to make such a determination[605].

The decision of what was Markan or non-Markan was not as clearly set forth in Evans's treatment as in Schneider's. We attempted to discern his positions based on what Evans wrote. Definite Markan material/dependence: 22,55.56.59.62.63-65.71; 23,2.3.4.18.19.[13-25]. Probable Markan material: vv. 54.66.67-70. Possible Markan material: 23,1. Stemmed from evangelist: 22,61.

Omissions, such as the release of a prisoner for the Paschal feast, were explained by Luke's judgment. In the case of the Paschal custom, Evans held that Luke considered such a custom improbable[606].

C.F. Evans referred to the "semi-independent story of Herod, which highlights the innocence of Jesus"[607]. He was not completely satisfied that Acts 4,25-30 presupposed it, since the two accounts offered varying perspectives. He seemed to favor the view that the scene was not historical, referring to C. Guignebert, M.

---

602. *Ibid.*, p. 828.
603. *Ibid.*, p. 829.
604. *Ibid.*, p. 831.
605. *Ibid.*, p. 844.
606. *Ibid.*, p. 856.
607. *Ibid.*, p. 843.

Goguel and J.M. Creed[608]. He noted further the parallel in Acts 23,34. Observing that Dibelius's explanation arose because of a lack of "an adequate historical explanation", Evans concluded: "In whatever form Luke knew this tradition, he has written it up in order to show the isolation and responsibility of the Jews in Jerusalem in their demand for Jesus' death in the face of the judgements of both the Roman governor and the Jewish ruler"[609]. Evans detected that the episode "appears to have been constructed out of borrowed materials". These were all compared with Mk: Herod's long standing desire to see Jesus (Mk 6,14; cf. 9,9) the questioning by Herod, the silence of Jesus and the accusations of the Jewish leadership (Mk 14,55-63; 15,3-5), and a mockery by soldiers (Mk 15,16-20). Evans considered 23,9-11 to be the central part of the story and likened several elements to those found in Mk. These were: that Herod questioned Jesus (Mk 15,4), Jesus' silence (Mk 15,5), and the vesture (Mk 15,17). Evans contended that 23,12 was obviously from Luke's own hand, which was also credited with transferring the mockery to Herod and his soldiers[610].

I.H. Marshall complimented Evans for a fair and balanced treatment of various issues in the introduction, so much so, that often Evans cannot make up his mind[611]. While Marshall accused Evans of not giving sufficient evidence of his idea of the structure of Lk as a whole, surely Evans's reference to Mk serving as the basis must address that concern[612].

Robert H. STEIN (1987) advocated Markan priority as part of the solution to the synoptic problem[613]. In citing the Proto-Lk theories as proposed by Feine and Streeter Stein maintained it had better textual support than Proto-Mt, while referring readers to Kümmel for critics of the Proto-Lk hypothesis[614]. Stein argued that in 23,18-21 Luke used Mk as his source though the evangelist omitted reference to any explanation of the amnesty custom.

While the argument from order could not by itself solve the synoptic problem, Stein insisted that Lachmann's insights "argue strongly" for the theory of Markan priority[615]. Kümmel was cited as one who was convinced by such argumentation.

---

608. *Ibid.*, p. 849, n. s. Cf. C. GUIGNEBERT, *Jesus*, London; New York, 1935, p. 467; GOGUEL, *The Life of Jesus,* London; New York, 1933, p. 515; CREED, *Gospel*, p. 280.

609. C.F. EVANS, *St. Luke*, p. 851.

610. *Ibid.*, p. 853.

611. *JTS* 42 (1991) 215-218, p. 216.

612. *Ibid.*, p. 217.

613. *The Synoptic Problem. An Introduction*, Grand Rapids, MI, 1987, p. 88. He reached this conclusion because of the "cumulative weight" of seven arguments. Among the various sources at the evangelist's disposal Stein listed written sources and "an even more extensive oral tradition" (p. 126; see further p. 137-138).

614. *Ibid.*, p. 131. Stein erroneously listed Feine's contribution as 1881 when it should read 1891.

615. *Ibid.*, p. 70. See also p. 87.

Stein took up the issue of the MAs and noted 22,64 / Mt 26,68 though he did not offer a particular solution for this case[616]. This phenomenon did not completely unhinge Markan priority as some opponents would contend. While arguing that Matthew and Luke did not know each other's works[617], Stein held there was no one simple explanation. There were, in fact, different solutions. These included independent redaction of Mk, especially concerning omissions, overlapping of particular sources, textual corruption and overlapping traditions[618].

In a 1992 study of the MAs, Stein identified them as the central crux in resolving the synoptic problem from the perspective of the Two- (or Four-) Source theory[619]. Following a review of eight commonly proposed solutions he announced his preference for "the use of overlapping traditions, either oral and/or written", which he judged to be probable[620]. Citing 23,3 / Mt 27,11 / Mk 15,2 / Jn 18,33.37, as also 23,18 / Mt 27,21 against Mk 15,11-12, in addition to 22,70 / Mt 26,64, Stein suggested the similarities were due to "overlapping traditions of the trial of Jesus"[621]. Differences may signal Luke's use of a special source, according to Stein[622]. In the matter of the cock crow (22,60 / Mt 26,70 against Mk 14,72) he identified with Soards's solution that oral influence was responsible for the single cock crow[623].

---

616. *Ibid.*, p. 123. In general remarks preceding the example Stein eliminated coincidental editorial changes to Mk as a solution in this case. He did not address the MA in 22,62.

617. *Ibid.*, p. 103, 123, 127. Stein credited the similarity of Jesus' response in 22,67-70 / Mt 26,63b-64 to oral tradition (p. 126-127).

618. *Ibid.*, p. 124, 125, 126.

619. *The Matthew-Luke Agreements Against Mark: Insight from John*, in *CBQ* 54 (1992) 482. Stein complimented Neirynck's "superb study" of the MAs.

620. *Ibid.*, p. 483-485. They were: 1) coincidental modifications of Mark's grammar; 2) coincidental omissions of Markan material; 3) coincidental modifications of Mark's difficult passages; 4) the common use of a different Mk; 5) preferred textual variants which agreed with Mt and Lk; 6) harmonization by later scribes who sought to make Lk agree with Mt; 7) coincidental changes made by Matthew and Luke; 8) the use of overlapping traditions, either oral and/or written, which Matthew and Luke chose to follow over Mk. See also p. 494.

621. *Ibid.*, p. 488. Also mentioned was the similarity in 22,60 / Mt 26,74 / Mk 14,72 / Jn 18,27, as well as similarities found in the parallels of 22,54-71; 23,1; 23,25 (p. 489). Still later he identified the agreement of 23,18 and Jn 18,40 against Mt and Mk, though he observed Mk had an earlier description of the identity of Barabbas (Mk 15,7) (p. 493). In addition see p. 499. Stein also related the rejection of Jesus over against Barabbas in the Gospel with the rejection of Jesus in Acts by the people (Acts 3,13-15) (p. 500). For Stein's mention of probable dependence of 22,70 and Mt 26,64 upon "a common overlapping tradition", see p. 501.

Already in 1978 Stein focused on 22,70 / Mk 14,62 / Mt 26,64 proposing that the Lukan and Matthean versions "represent more accurately the actual historical situation in pointing out that Jesus did not like the particular form of the question put to him by Caiaphas". It was Stein's position that "Matthew and Luke preserve more carefully the original words spoken" (*The Method and Message of Jesus' Teachings*, Grand Rapids, MI, 1978, p. 124).

622. STEIN, *Matthew-Luke*, p. 498, n. 51. Stein called attention to SPITTA, *Die synoptische Grundschrift*.

623. STEIN, *Matthew-Luke*, p. 498, n. 50. See SOARDS, *Passion*, p. 37, 78.

In his full scale commentary on Lk (1992) Stein continued defending Markan priority and arguing against Luke's use of Mt[624]. Luke used various written and oral sources though it was unclear whether Q and L were written[625]. The term πολλοί (1,3) should be taken to mean "others" rather than giving some specific numerical value. The date of Lk was set between 70-90 AD while the place of composition was uncertain, although it was intended for a Gentile audience. Certain Markan material (Mk 6,45-8,26) was omitted because it did not serve Luke's purposes, or sometimes because it was assumed that the readers understood the background as in the case of the Passover amnesty (23,18-20)[626].

Stein maintained "Luke tends to follow the Markan outline quite closely"[627], all the while allowing for changes such as omissions, additions[628] and rearrangement. The order Luke followed was logical rather than chronological[629]. The new location of Peter's denial was explained as part of Luke's effort to link Jesus' earlier instructions to the disciples with the subsequent evidence of their failures. By doing so, Luke eliminated the "various changes in scene" as found in the other Synoptics[630].

In the discussion of the passion narrative, which he defined as 22,1-23,56, Stein called attention to the special source theory and Proto-Lk in particular. He

---

624. *Luke* (NAC, 24), Nashville, TN, 1992, p. 25, n. 14. See also p. (28)-29, n. 17. Stein referred the reader to his earlier work, *The Synoptic Problem*. He offered an important caveat that he was not concerned in the commentary to explain how the Gospel came to be or to reconstruct the historical events (p. 57). He dialogued with other Lukan scholars such as Benoit, Blinzler, Catchpole, Conzelmann, Ellis, C.F. Evans, Fitzmyer, Nolland, Tannehill, Talbert and Winter.

625. See also STEIN, *Difficult Passages in the New Testament. Interpreting Puzzling Texts in the Gospels and Epistles*, Grand Rapids, MI, 1990, p. 30-31, 176. He also took up discussion of sources and order in his 1983 analysis of the Prologue (*Luke 1:1-4 and* Traditionsgeschichte, in *JETS* 26 [1983] 421-430 = *Luke 1:1-4 and Tradition Criticism*, in ID., *Gospels and Tradition. Studies on Redaction Criticism of the Synoptic Gospels*, Grand Rapids, MI, 1991, 35-47). Stein insisted one cannot determine the number to which πολλοί referred but "it functioned as a TOPOS and that we should therefore beware of placing too great an emphasis on this word" (*Luke 1:1-4*, 1991, p. 37). In his treatment Stein cited CADBURY, *Commentary*, I.I. DU PLESSIS, *Once More. The Purpose of Luke's Prologue (Lk 1 1-4)*, in *NT* 16 (1974) 259-271, R.J. DILLON, *Previewing*, and J. BAUER, ΠΟΛΛΑΙ. *Luk 1,1*, in *NT* 4 (1960) 263-266. Stein understood the term καθεξῆς (1,3) to mean "'organized' or 'logical'" though in other parts of the two-volume Lukan work the term can also mean a geographical or temporal sequence (STEIN, *Luke 1:1-4*, 1991, p. 44).

626. See STEIN, *Luke*, p. 567, n. 67, for a list of Luke's omissions in the account of the Sanhedrin hearing.

627. *Ibid.*, p. 29.

628. *Ibid.*, p. 533, n. 1. Stein enumerated the following as additions to the Lukan passion account: 22,15-17.24-32.35-38;23,2.4-16.27-32.39b-43. One of Luke's tendencies present in his redaction was the effort "to eliminate or minimize violence in his sources", such as the omission of reference to the crowning with thorns (cf. Mk 15,16-20) (p. 579).

629. *Ibid.*, p. 563, 564. See also his discussion on 1,3 (p. 65). For a chronological reconstruction of events, see p. 568. Luke's attempt to provide an orderly account was recognized even at 23,5 (p. 575).

630. The reordering by Luke allowed for continuity within the narrative (p. 574).

argued "there are a number of difficulties with the proto-Luke hypothesis" but he did not engage in a detailed refutation. It appeared Stein does not defend the special source theory since he discussed the difficulties of the theory in the text, while confining the supporting evidence to a footnote[631]. He was more direct later in his commentary. "Whether this material came from a non-Markan passion narrative such as L or Proto-Luke is much debated but impossible to demonstrate"[632]. What was most significant for Stein was that the Lukan passion narrative demonstrated a narrative unity.

The MA in 22,62 was ascribed to "traditional material" which both Luke and Matthew opted to use in place of Mk[633]. The MA in 22,64 stemmed from the possibility that Luke and Matthew included "a well-known part of the passion tradition that Mark omitted"[634].

In the exegetical section of the denial (22,54-62) Stein did not concern himself with Lukan redaction of Mk with the exception of two omissions. The first was Luke's omitting Peter's denial of Jesus as recounted in Mk 14,70. The second was the deletion of reference to Peter's cursing and swearing (Mk 14,71). Both in the denial and in the mockery Stein highlighted the christology in which Jesus was portrayed as a prophet both here and earlier in the Gospel. The troublesome αὐτόν (22,63) was explained by claiming that the readers were so familiar with the passion account that the proper name "Jesus" was unnecessary at that point[635].

Christology was seen as the central element in the Lukan version of the Sanhedrin trial, which was only about half as long as the Markan. Luke combined the two Markan accounts (Mk 14,53-65; Mk 15,1) in order to achieve this effect[636]. The omission of the witnesses and the Temple saying (Mk 14,55-60) served this end. Luke possibly omitted ὄψεσθε to avoid the impression that Jesus' prophecy had not been fulfilled[637]. Stein immediately referred to the reference to this in the Stephen story (Acts 7,54). The omission of ἐρχόμενον μετὰ τῶν νεφελῶν τοῦ οὐρανοῦ (cf. Mk 14,62) and the addition of τοῦ θεοῦ (22,69) also reflected Luke's editorial activity.

631. *Ibid.*, p. 30, n. 19. These arguments included the general difference between the Markan and Lukan accounts, including additions which did not seem to stem from L and distinct vocabulary.

632. *Ibid.*, p. 533-534. In contrast to Kelber, Stein held that the similarities in the passion among the four Gospels can be explained by "an early passion narrative" (p. 534). Cf. KELBER (ed.), *Passion*, 1976, 153-159.

633. STEIN, *Luke*, p. 565.

634. *Ibid.*, p. 566. Although his article on the MAs in the *CBQ* appeared to have been published prior to the commentary, surprisingly Stein did not refer the reader to the pertinent sections of that article which dealt with these two MAs (*Matthew-Luke*, 1992).

635. *Luke*, p. 566.

636. *Ibid.*, p. 567, 572. See also his comment on 22,66 (p. 569). For the matter of the omission of the witness testimony see further the commentary on 22,71 where he observed this redaction emphasized Jesus' testimony (p. 571).

637. The fulfillment of prophecy theme was treated on p. 576.

Stein was attentive to the relationship between the Gospel and Acts. The role of Jewish leaders was interwoven throughout, as were the themes of Jesus' innocence, in addition to his rejection by Israel[638]. The parallel of the trials of Jesus and Paul were also noted[639]. Certain vocabulary, such as διαστρέφοντα (23,2), was common to Acts (Acts 13,8.10; 20,30). The point of the Gospel, according to Stein, was to provide an apologia for Rome that Jesus and his followers posed no threat. Like Johnson and Heil, Stein detected the presence of irony in the account, especially in 23,18-25[640].

Stein (1992) accepted the Herod account (23,6-12) as historical[641]. Joanna and Manaen were named as likely informants for details concerning Herod[642]. The story served the purpose of confirming the innocence of Jesus[643]. The portrayal of the people's involvement in the trial was suggested as possibly reflecting Luke's loyalty to the tradition, left unspecified by Stein.

Dibelius's position was rejected for three reasons: 1) Ps 2,1-2 "seems too vague" to have given rise to the Herod episode; 2) the absence of direct reference to the Ps in the account; and 3) since Herod was historically prominent, the account was easily verifiable. Nevertheless, the reason for the transfer of Jesus to Herod remained "unclear". In contrast to Mk 14,61 Luke sought to demonstrate that Jesus, rather than the political authorities, was in charge.

Jesus' silence in Herod's presence was regarded by Stein as a fulfillment of Is 53,7 rather than as a redactional detail arising from it. Allowing for the possibility that the text of 23,11 indicated that Herod dressed himself in the robe, in light of Mk 15,17-20 however, Stein took this to mean that Herod mocked Jesus' kingship by vesting him in the elegant robe *contra* Fitzmyer[644]. Like Soards, Stein viewed the reconciliation of Herod and Pilate as resulting from the passion of Jesus.

Others who treated aspects of Luke's redaction of Mk during this period included Fred B. CRADDOCK (1988)[645], Jean-Luc VESCO (1988)[646], Peter HOFRICHTER

---

638. *Ibid.*, p. 572; see also p. 56. In addition to these references, Stein subsequently discussed the theme of Jesus' innocence and the responsibility of the Jewish authorities (p. 576, 583).

639. *Ibid.*, p. 573. Triple charges were lodged against Paul as well (p. 574).

640. *Ibid.*, p. 582.

641. *Ibid.*, p. 577. He directed readers to HOEHNER, *Herod Antipas*.

642. STEIN, *Luke* p. 577. See further his comment on 8,3 (p. 241). He also pointed to references to Herod in Lk and Acts (p. 241, n. 185).

643. *Ibid.*, p. 577, 579, 580.

644. *Ibid.*, p. 578, n. 95. Cf. FITZMYER, *Luke*, p. 1482.

645. He regarded it as "highly likely" that 1,2 referred to oral sources, conceding that it was extremely difficult to make such a determination (*Luke*, in J.L. MAYS, [ed.], *Harper's Bible Commentary*, San Francisco, CA - Cambridge, 1988, p. 1011). The special material, designated as L, could be oral or written, but it was clear Mk "provides the basic structure for Luke" (p. 1012). Luke was credited with placing the account of Peter's denial before the Sanhedrin trial (p. 1041). In his extended commentary (1990) Craddock stated more directly that the sources alluded

(1988-89)[647], Stephen BINZ (1989)[648], Frank CONNOLLY-WEINERT (1989)[649],

to in 1,1-2 were considered to be both written and oral (*Luke* [Interpretation], Louisville, KY, 1990, p. 5). The material unique to Lk was still thought to have been drawn in large part from oral sources. The written sources were identified as Q and Mk, the latter providing the structure of Lk despite the rather sizable omission of Markan material (p. 17).

Craddock (1990) maintained that Luke's sources were "multiple", consisting of both oral and written (*Ibid.* The L material was generally attributed to oral sources. In his earlier commentary, Craddock was likewise circumspect in assigning a particular source for this episode. In both commentaries he asserted Ps 2,2 was fulfilled which was related to Acts 4,25-28 and 23,13-16 was seen as a Lukan summary of the trial (*Luke*, in J.L. MAYS [ed.], *Harper's*, 1988, p. 1041; see also *Luke*, 1990, p. 270). While not explicitly naming Joanna as the source of 23,6-16, Craddock noted that her husband served in Herod's government (CRADDOCK, *Luke*, 1990, p. 107). Though the apologetic toward Rome was discerned in the address to Theophilus as well as in the favorable treatment Paul received as recounted in Acts (p. 267), Craddock took exception to the view that Pilate's responsibility was lessened. Craddock also believed that the Jewish leaders accompanied Jesus in his transfer to Herod as well as in his return to Pilate. Stating that "Ps 2:2 is fulfilled" by the turn of events, Craddock did not necessarily imply that this influenced the writing of the account. Verses 13-16 were attributed to redaction, since this material summarized "Luke's position on the trial of Jesus" (p. 270).

646. He supported the Two-Source theory, which he described as "l'hypothèse la plus couramment admise" (J.-L. VESCO, *Jérusalem et son prophète*, Paris, 1988, p. 11). There was relatively great probability, according to scientific exegesis, that Luke employed these two sources. In addition, he recalled the hypothesis that a third source contained the material proper to Lk. He cautioned that this explanation did not account for everything, including partial or intermediary successive redactions (p. 11-12). Vesco viewed Luke not as simply an editor or compiler, but as an historian and theologian-catechist. His redaction included improving poor Greek, omitting details or episodes which were of no interest for his theological preoccupations or were not in accord with his chronological, theological and literary order, and to provide transitions by inserting summary verses. As regards the passion, Luke followed the same sequence of episodes as Mk and Mt though he added more new elements which stressed his own theology (p. 101). See also his discussion of 22,54-23,12, (p. 102-103). Vesco referred readers to BENOIT, *Passion*, 1966, and VANHOYE, *Structure*, 1967 (p. 129).

647. *Das dreifache Verfahren über Jesus als Gottessohn, König und Mensch. Zur Redaktionsgeschichte der Prozesstradition*, in *Kairos* 30-31 (1988-89) 69-81. In a unique interpretation Hofrichter suggested that the trial of Jesus took place in a three stage sequence. The Sanhedrin, with theological competence, examined Jesus as Son of God (22,66-71). Luke focused attention on this dimension by placing the question about his relationship to God (22,70f.) in a key position. Pilate, on the other hand, and Herod in the case of Lk, whose competence was political, was concerned with Jesus as king (23,1-4.5-12). Finally, the multitude was concerned for an innocent fellow human being (23,13-18) (p. 70). The use of the term ἄνθρωπον in 23,14 was seen as an intentional Lukan correction of Mk. Note the error in identifying 22,1-4.5-12 and 22,13-18 when they are found in chapter 23 (p. 73). The Markan material of Jesus before the crowd was significantly revised by Luke. This structure, Hofrichter insisted, was especially evident in Lk and resulted from a redaction- critical investigation of the Lukan passion over against Mk. Hofrichter subscribed to the view that Luke was concerned to present Pilate in a favorable light and the Jews in a more negative one. All of Luke's efforts were directed to clarifying the Markan *Vorlage* and making explicit this threefold christology.

Hofrichter considered there was little chance that the Herod pericope came from a special tradition (p. 74). He referred readers to the commentaries of Schneider and Ernst. But he did not clearly state his position whether it was a free Lukan composition or drawn from elements of Mk. The inclusion of the story put Herod on an even keel with Pilate and portrayed him as part of the "kosmichen Herrschaft".

648. *The Passion and Resurrection Narratives of Jesus. A Commentary*, Collegeville, MN, 1989 (esp. p. 71, 81-86). Binz assigned Mk as Luke's "principal source", though the differences, including omissions and additions, were accounted for by Luke's knowledge of other traditions. Differences in order were ascribed not only to these additional traditions, but the evangelist's desire "creatively to highlight his own unique themes" (p. 71). Binz adopted the view of the unity of Lk-Acts and therefore counseled interpreting passages from the Gospel in light of Acts. He further subscribed to the idea that the Lukan passion portrayed Jesus as a martyr.

The change in the order of the pericope of Peter's denial allowed Luke to "contrast the reaction of Jesus to that of Peter" (p. 81). In the mockery the evangelist presented Jesus as a prophet, as was done "throughout the Gospel". The meeting of the Sanhedrin did not appear to be a trial, in Binz's opinion. In this passage (22,66-71) Jesus was portrayed as Messiah, Son of Man and Son of God. Similarity with Jesus' response was found in Jer 38,15. Luke revised Mark's understanding to show the passion and resurrection gave rise to Jesus' "enthronement in glory" (p. 82-83). This presentation was connected with Stephen in Act 7,56. For 23,13-25 Binz spoke in terms similar to those of Matera in describing these events as the "trial of Israel" (p. 85).

Binz did not address the source question but defined the passage as 23,6-12 (p. 83-84). The addition of this story highlighted the innocence of Jesus. The agreement between the political figures on Jesus was also remarked to be the same with Paul in Acts (Acts 22,30f.; 25). The reconciliation of the two leaders was regarded as irony. Oblique reference was made to Ps 2, showing a certain continuity with 21,12. Jesus was presented as a model to be imitated.

649. *Assessing Omissions as Redaction: Luke's Handling of the Charge against Jesus as Detractor of the Temple*, in M.P. HOGAN and P.J. KOBELSKI (eds.), *To Touch the Text*, FS J.A. FITZMYER, New York, 1989, p. 360, n. 5. In an engaging and insightful treatment, Connolly-Weinert held the view that Lukan redactional activity was evident in 22,54–23,1 as well as in 22,14-38 and 23,32-49. He concentrated on the omission of Mk 14,57-58 from Lk 22,66-71 and sought to explain the evangelist's rationale for doing so. The omission of the charge was intentional for four reasons: 1) the material was missing twice in two different contexts (22,66-71; 23,33-43); 2) similarity with the Stephen story (Acts 6,13-14) and Mk 14,57-58a indicating Luke was cognizant of such a tradition; 3) only a particular section was missing while the majority of the Markan material was retained; and 4) the pericope betrayed other aspects of redaction. Like Stanton, Connolly-Weinert detected a juxtaposition of Jesus with other individuals.

"Five main redactional concerns" were entertained. The omission permitted a positive regard for the Temple while focusing the opposition to Jesus on the Jewish leadership. The person of Jesus and attention to his prophetic word take center stage, so the words were omitted to eliminate any distraction. The omission drew attention to the present rather than to eschatological events. Luke could be keen to drop Markan apocalyptic elements. In the evangelist's effort to emphasize the innocence of Jesus, even as he was victimized by the proceedings, the charge was left aside. Though each of these were plausible, Connolly-Weinert opted for the first explanation, which highlighted the tension between Jesus and the religious authorities (p. 363). Luke's use of omission as a tool of redaction was not a matter the evangelist would have taken lightly. Such a change served to portray Jesus as the victim of an official and organized scheme, though he himself was innocent. Luke cast Jesus in the light of a royal messiah who acted out of religious and prophetic roles. By redacting in this manner both the Temple and the people Israel can be treated as themes in a positive light. Jesus had been effective in his ministry within the Temple (19,47), so Luke recast this account which allowed that impression to stand. Though this article focused primarily on only one aspect of Luke's reworking of the Markan account of the Sanhedrin

Mark Allan POWELL (1989)[650], William KURZ (1990)[651], John T. CARROLL (1990)[652], Neil J. MCELENEY (1990)[653], Wolfgang SCHENK (1990)[654], Craig

hearing, the author briefly summarized that Markan material omitted from the account of the hearing, included Mk 14,57-58.55b-56.59-61a. The movement of Mk 15,1 was considered a transposition as it substituted for Mk 14,55a. Connolly-Weinert considered the transposition of the mockery (22,63-65) to be the redactional work of the evangelist which resulted in the subsequent narrative in an emphasis on the prophet Jesus as well as his prophetic message (p. 563, n. 14).

650. *What Are They Saying about Luke?*, New York - Mahwah, NJ, 1989, p. 36 (esp. p. 35-38). In a popular presentation of the state of the question on various aspects of Lukan scholarship, Powell noted numerous studies had been devoted to defining the form and extent of a special source in the passion narrative. He cited Perry (1920) and Taylor (1972) as examples, with the conclusion that "in general, the results of such studies have cancelled each other out without providing a clear solution" (p. 36). The works of Soards and Matera were briefly discussed with the latter's efforts in *Passion Narratives* (1986) being described as "less meticulous" than Soard's dissertation. The assessment should have considered the differing genre of the works. Powell nonetheless reasoned that the differences between Lk and Mk reflected the evangelist's theology. But this view was issued with caution: "Most scholars are interested in Luke's use of sources because of the light this throws on understanding the evangelist as a theologian ... Lately, however, a lack of scholarly consensus concerning the validity of the Two-Source Hypothesis has limited the acceptance of this approach. Although the majority of scholars continue to work with the established model (as the remainder of this book will show), they do so with the frustrating awareness that their results will be regarded by some as tenuous" (p. 40). It was this dilemma which caused the current shift to literary criticism.

651. *Narrative Models for Imitation in Luke-Acts*, in D.L. BALCH (ed.), *Greeks, Romans, and Christians*, FS A. MALHERBE, Minneapolis, MN, 1990, 186. Kurz noted the similarity between the account of the death of Jesus (Lk 23) and Stephen (Acts 7), describing them as "paradigmatic portrayals". He seemed to indicate that the Lukan account was not only a redaction of the Markan: "The Lukan redactional themes all go in the direction of portraying Jesus as a model of how to die, as Plato had presented Socrates" (p. 186), but it also relied on other unspecified sources (p. 187).

In a more recent contribution (1993) Kurz moved in the direction of narrative criticism (*Reading Luke-Acts. Dynamics of Biblical Narrative*, Louisville, KY). He revealed the motivation for his shift: "As is true of many practitioners of narrative biblical criticism, my initial interest was partially fed by pastoral and theological concerns about the need to 'put Humpty Dumpty back together again' after the disintegrating and alienating effects of some historical criticism of the Bible" (p. ix). Crediting the "Lukan narrator" with drawing the accounts of Peter's denials together "without interruption" unlike the narrators in Mt and Mk, he also noted the Lukan account of the morning trial may be more historically accurate (p. 63). For his discussion of the passion narrative Kurz relied on Fitzmyer, *Luke*, and Neyrey, *Passion*, both of whom approached the passion from the perspective of redaction criticism. Kurz also cited Tannehill, Talbert and Aletti who subscribed to new literary-critical methodology. The reference to the false witnesses, as in Mk, was found later in the account of Stephen's trial in Acts. There was no need for them in Lk because of the way the narrative was arranged. Kurz recognized the innocence of Jesus as "a major motif of the Lukan passion account" (KURZ, *Reading*, p. 65). This served as part of Luke's apologetic toward Rome (p. 11).

652. *Luke's Crucifixion Scene*, in D.D. SYLVA (ed.), *Reimaging the Death of the Lukan Jesus* (BBB, 73), Frankfurt, 1990, p. 114. Carroll credited Luke with transposing the denials to their present position, the purpose being that "the narrative illustrates Jesus' prophetic prowess before

it is made the object of scorn (v. 64)". He described Luke as painting a picture of Jesus who was a victim of injustice and whose innocence was further underscored through repetition of the people's choice of the release of the murderer (Lk 23,19.25; Acts 3,14) (p. 117; cf. J.M. FORD, *My Enemy*, p. 128, who previously noted this element, though without detecting its presence in Acts). Contrary to the article by Karris in the same volume, Carroll regarded Luke's depiction of Jesus' death as a martyrdom which provided an example confirmed in the story of Stephen (Acts 7) (cf. KARRIS, *Luke 23:47*).

For the MA in 22,64 Carroll appeared to adopt the view that both Matthew and Luke independently added the phrase. "Like Matthew (26:68), Luke adds to the imperative ("Prophesy!") the question, 'Who is it that struck you?' This expansion makes clear that Jesus' alleged prophetic perception is the object of ridicule. Curiously, Matthew's mockers address Jesus as 'Christ' when challenging him to play the prophet" (CARROLL, *Luke's*, p. 198, n. 33).

Carroll and J.B. GREEN (1995) clearly affirmed that Luke drew upon Mk (J.T. CARROLL and J.B. GREEN with R.E. VAN VOORST, J. MARCUS, D. SENIOR, *The Death of Jesus in Early Christianity*, Peabody, MA, 1995, p. 60-81, esp. p. 60, n. 1). Their approach was that Luke's account of the passion was a combination of tradition and redaction, though their intention was not to delve into questions of source criticism: "Our concern in this chapter is not to reconstruct the prehistory of Luke's narrative. Rather, granting that Luke tapped available tradition and with considerable literary and theological artistry fashioned it into the narrative we now read, our aim is to explore in that narrative the web of meanings spun for Luke's readers as they ponder the death of one who is Lord, Messiah, and Savior"(p. 62). In a brief nod to source-critical studies they cited MATERA, *Death* (1985), SOARDS, *Passion* (1987) and GREEN, *Death* (1988) (n. 8).

They noted the change in order of the denial (CARROLL and GREEN, *Death*, p. 61). The Lukan account of the denial, in their opinion, "lacks the dramatic intensification present in both Mark and Matthew" (p. 75, n. 50). Concerning 22,61-62, see p. 77. Luke was credited with delaying the Sanhedrin trial until morning. The omission of the Markan account of the mockery (Mk 15,16-20a) was observed, "a comparable mocking scene" (22,63-65) had been included in Lk.

Similarity between the account of Paul in Acts and Jesus in the Gospel was maintained by the motif of innocence (p. 72, n. 43, where readers were directed to J.T. CARROLL, *Luke's Apology for Paul*, in *SBL 1988 Seminar Papers*, 106-118; see also CARROLL and GREEN, p. 73, [79]-80, n. 58). Although mention was made of Acts 4,26-30, there was no discussion of the relationship with Lk 23 (CARROLL and GREEN, *Death*, p. 78). Jesus-Stephen parallels were also noted, but the omissions of a temple charge and false witnesses were of particular significance. "Especially since these two features disrupt a pattern of symmetry between the passion of Jesus and that of Stephen, one suspects that the move to deflect these serious charges from Jesus to Stephen is no accident. The result is a clearer picture of an innocent Jesus, wrongfully accused and condemned, not clouded by somewhat ambiguous details" (p. 81).

The Herod pericope added not only the mockery theme but the affirmation of Jesus' innocence (p. 61). While the passage was twice delineated as 23,6-12, later in a discussion of 13,31 and the Herod story in the passion it was defined as 23,7-12 (p. 42, n. 7 and p. 61; cf. p. 68, n. 30). The first reference was in the context of a comparison between the Matthean and Lukan accounts. See further p. 73, for brief comments concerning the Herod pericope.

653. *Peter's Denials – How Many? To Whom?*, in *CBQ* 52 (1990) 467. McEleney astutely observed that "older commentators – generally anxious to safeguard the historicity of NT events – made great efforts to reconcile these divergent details and to harmonize Peter's many denials into 'three'". While noting that Bultmann argued Luke had access to a separate account from Mk for the denials (p. 468, n. 2), McEleney quite rightly asserted that Luke and Matthew used Mk and their changes over against that Gospel betrayed "their respective editorial techniques" (p. 468). McEleney attributed the changes in Lk to what he termed Luke's "staging technique". This

EVANS (1990)[655], Robert HERRON (1991)[656], John S. KLOPPENBORG (1992)[657],

involved: "(1) clearing the stage of its actors or subject to prepare the way for another scene, and (2) dividing and protracting the material into successive scenes or stages" (p. 469). To substantiate his view McEleney offered the scene where Mary departed from the home of Zechariah (1,39-56) before relating events of the birth of John the Baptist (1,57-59). Similarly, Luke "moves up" the rejection of Jesus at Nazareth before concentrating on Jesus' advance to Capernaum. In like manner, the shift occurred from the denials in the courtyard to the appearance of Jesus before the Sanhedrin and Pilate (p. 469). The method of dividing into separate stages, was found not only in the Gospel (Lk 24, in the Ascension, for example), but also in Acts (Acts 2, the sending of the Holy Spirit), according to McEleney (p. 469-470). In applying this to the denials, he claimed "Luke *separates* the bystanders into two men" (p. 471). He also took issue with Fitzmyer, among others, who claimed there were two male witnesses which fulfilled the prescription of Dt 19,15, arguing that too much was made of this perspective. McEleney queried: "Would Luke emphasize forensic elements in the case of Peter while making little of them in the case of Jesus?" (p. 471, n. 5). McEleney's conclusion was clear: no need existed for positing a special source: "In the present explanation, there is no need to appeal to special sources of information for these evangelists [i.e. Luke and Matthew]. Their own editorial techniques of doubling and staging supply adequate reason for their divergences from Mark's account of Peter's denials" (p. 472). While even Taylor and other adherents admitted this episode was dependent upon Mk, McEleney's article is important for helping us to better understand Luke's redactional method.

654. Contrary to Schneider (who argued for a special source in the trial and mockery) and Taylor (who maintained there was a continuous special source), Schenk asserted the Lukan passion was a revision of that found in Mk (*Leidensgeschichte Jesu*, in TRE 20, 1990, p. 717). The evangelist was credited with transposing the material so that the sequence was denial, mockery, and trial. Omissions included the anointing, the flight of the disciples and the mockery by the soldiers. Additions by Luke included the charges (23,3.5) and the Herod pericope (23,6-15) which served to highlight the innocence of Jesus. Schenk maintained Luke created the words of Jesus in 22,67f. Schenk indicated that Herod story intensified the theme of Jesus' innocence (p. 718). It, as well as the parallel of Paul's experience before a Herodian king, served to testify to their political harmlessness.

Schenk rightly noted the parallels between the passion of Jesus and of Paul as found in Acts. For the arrest: Acts 21,30 / Lk 22,54; the demand for death: Acts 21,36; 22,22 / Lk 23,18; rejection by the Sanhedrin: Acts 22,30-23,10 / Lk 22,66-71; encounter with the Roman authority: Acts 24 / Lk 23,1-6 followed by an appearance before a Herodian king: Acts 25,22–26,32 / Lk 23,6-16. (So also John J. KILGALLEN [1993] who drew attention to the parallels between the trials and treatment of Paul with that of Jesus, the point of both stories being that Paul and Jesus were innocent and that Christianity was not a threat the Roman government (*Persecution in the Acts of the Apostles*, in G. O'COLLINS and G. MARCONI [eds.], *Luca-Atti: Studi in onore di P. Emilio Rasco nel suo 70o compleanno*, Assisi, 1991 = *Luke and Acts*, tr. M. O'CONNELL, FS E. RASCO, New York, 1993, p. 159).

655. *Luke* (NIBC), Peabody, MA, 1990, p. 3-4 (esp. p. 325-336). Evans strangely passed over reference to the special Lukan material after announcing he subscribed to the views of Markan priority and Q. Throughout he relied heavily upon Fitzmyer for various interpretations. In his discussion of Peter's denials (22,54-62), although Evans did not exclude the possibility that the evangelist had access to other sources which "may" have contributed some elements, still other details were due to the evangelists. The reference to Peter's cursing and swearing may have been Luke's attempt to polish Peter's coarse behavior (22,60. cf. Mk 14,71 / Mt 26,74), while substituting a man for the female servant in the second denial would have been done with a view

to fulfilling the requirements of Dt 19,15 (p. 328).

Other than 23,4-16, the material of Jesus' trial was based upon Mk 14,55-15,15. The account of the mockery (22,63-65) was said to parallel the account in Mk. The difference in order was noted but not specifically ascribed to Luke. The demand that Jesus prophesy was ironical, highlighting that Jesus had already indeed done that for Peter. Evans noted the lack of reference to the claim to destroy the Temple, but only referred the reader to Acts 6,13-14 without any explanation. The charges in 23,1-5 were recast from religious to political ones, but Evans offered no reason why that should be so. The assignment of blame for the death of Jesus to the Jewish authorities was situated within Luke's theology that they resisted the design of God, but it also agreed with Luke's pro-Roman apologetic.

Evans did not specifically treat the source question for the Herod pericope, but argued the transfer was the result of Pilate's effort to divest himself of a problem (p. 332-333). The attestation of Herod and Pilate for the innocence of Jesus was considered in the light of Dt 19,15.

656. Writing in a recent dissertation, Herron considered both Lk and Mt as "reinterpretations" of Mk. Luke's choice not to duplicate Mk's order in Peter's denials was motivated by the desire to narrate Peter's story in a continuous, uninterrupted fashion (*Mark's Account of Peter's Denial of Jesus. A History of Its Interpretation*, Lanham, MD - London, 1991, p. 14. Diss. Rice, Houston, TX, [n.d.] [dir. N.C. NIELSEN, Jr.]).

657. He affirmed that Luke redacted Mk while suggesting that Plato's *Phaedo* may have influenced him (*Exitus clari viri: The Death of Jesus in Luke*, in *TJT* 8 [1992] 106-120). The possibility remained Luke read the *Phaedo* according to Kloppenborg (p. 115, 120, n. 43). Noting that the majority of scholars argued that Luke used Mk as his only written source, Kloppenborg pointed out Green's recent effort to uncover a written pre-Lukan source (p. 118, n. 16). "It should be expected that Luke would also tailor the passion narrative to the sensibilities of his audience, especially since the subject -the execution of Jesus by crucifixion on an essentially political charge – was so sensitive a matter" (p. 106-107). The death of Jesus was presented in a way that was in accord with portrayals of other notable personalities.

Lukan redaction, prompted by various apologetic interests, attempted to show that Jesus was the victim "of the concerted efforts of the priestly elite". Consequently, in recounting the trial apologetics replaced historical accuracy (p. 117, n. 9: "Luke's depiction of the politics of the trial should not be confused with the actual issues at stake in the trial of the historical Jesus. Luke's is an apologetic enterprise, designed to remove any suspicion that Christians were subversive").

Alert to the Lukan omissions of Markan material, Kloppenborg cleverly demonstrated that the evangelist's deletion of the reference to the amnesty custom resulted in the request of the priests appearing "both willful and baseless".

Luke also presented the disciples in a more favorable light than Mk and allowed Jesus to be portrayed as compassionate toward them (p. 108, 113-115). Jesus was one whose life was worthy of imitation by his disciple friends. Luke was said to be responsible for the transposition of the Markan material about the mockery (Mk 15,16-20) deleting the detail of physical abuse in the process (p. 117, n. 7).

Kloppenborg credited Luke with including the Herod pericope (23,6-12) "to remove suspicion from Jesus" but carefully avoided the source dilemma (p. 107). Herod was portrayed throughout the Gospel as not disposed toward prophets. "But this characterization only throws into sharper relief the fact that one so ill-disposed to prophets could not find or invent a reason to have Jesus executed" (p. 107) Kloppenborg did not deny Tannehill's contention that the previous references to Herod presented him as interested in Jesus' miracles and contemptuously rejecting Jesus, but these were secondary to finding no fault deserving death in Jesus (p. 117, n. 6; TANNEHILL, *The Narrative Unity of Luke-Acts*. Vol. 1. *The Gospel according to Luke*, 1986, p. 196-97).

Terrence PRENDERGAST (1992)[658], Jane SCHABERG (1992)[659], Richard AS-
COUGH (1993)[660]. Joseph PLEVNIK (1991) concentrated on 22,69 concluding Luke
had redacted Mk[661]. More recently C.M. TUCKETT (1995) investigated the Son

In a recent study on the historical Jesus Kloppenborg (1996) denied that Q contained a passion
narrative, though he insisted that those who framed Q would have been aware of Jesus' death
(KLOPPENBORG, *The Sayings Gospel Q and the Quest of the Historical Jesus*, in *HTR* 89 [1996]
307-344, p. 331). The Sayings Gospel simply reflected a different understanding and articulation:
"...for Q the 'passion narrative' has not yet become privatized as Jesus' passion" (p. 331). See
p. 332: "Q shows that the development of a passion narrative was *not* inevitable and encourages
one to look for multiple origins of early Christian attempts to render plausible and meaningful the
facts of persecution and death".

658. *Trial of Jesus*, in *ABD* 6, New York, 1992, 660-663. Prendergast drew attention to the
differences between the Gospel accounts. Notice was taken that Matera argued that Luke
employed only Mk in the Sanhedrin trial (p. 660; cf. MATERA, *Luke 22:66-71*, 1989).
Prendergast was also influenced by Neyrey at various points in his essay (See NEYREY, *Passion*,
1985). The striking similarities between the trial and death of Jesus and the death of Stephen (Acts
6,11-7,60) were emphasized. Likewise, the trials of Peter, Paul and Stephen in Acts were seen
as continuations of the trial of Jesus. The passion narrative was viewed as parenesis in providing
a model for the disciples to follow (PRENDERGAST, *Trial*, p. 662).

The historicity of the "referral of Jesus to the tetrarch Herod for an opinion" (23,6-12) has
been questioned by scholars since the account reflected the "interests and formulations" of the
evangelist. However, Prendergast opined that Joanna was possibly the source of the information
(p. 662). The omission of the mockery of Jesus by the Roman soldiers was noted and "instead"
of that story, Luke recounted the mockery in 23,11. This story was part of a series which referred
to Herod (cf. 3,1.19; 9,7.9; 13,31) (p. 662).

659. She adopted the view that, in addition to Mk and Q, Luke employed the special material
L which was comprised of both oral and written sources (*Luke*, in Carol A. NEWSOM and Sharon
H. RINGE [eds.], *The Women's Bible Commentary*, London - Louisville, KY, 1992, p. 276).
Since her primary interest was material featuring women Schaberg did not treat the section of the
passion narrative with which we are concerned. Although she examined 8,1-3, she made no
mention of Joanna as a possible source of information regarding Herod. Schaberg noted a pro-
Roman, anti-Jewish thread running through the Gospel and Acts which she believed was an
"historically innacurate and unjust depiction" of the Jews for the purpose of portraying the
Christians as politically harmless (p. 277).

660. *Rejection and Repentance: Peter and the People in Luke's Passion Narrative*, in *Bib* 74
(1993) 349-365, esp. p. 352, n. 10: "The two-source hypothesis will be assumed throughout this
paper and the question of sources other than Mark for Luke's account will not be addressed". In
a study of Peter and the people in Luke-Acts, although not concerned with source criticism
beyond Luke's use of Mk, Ascough observed at several points that Luke omitted Markan
material. These included the omission of the Markan mockery (Mk 15,15-20), the reference to
the passover amnesty, and the detail about the chief priests inciting the people (Mk 15,11) (p.
352, 355). While Ascough noted the change in order of the Lukan mockery where it preceded
the Sanhedrin trial in Lk, nothing was said as to the reason for such a variation. Ascough made
continual reference to similarities between the Gospel and Acts. The refashioning of the account
of the passion was motivated by Luke's intention to portray the Jewish religious leaders as
principally responsible for Jesus' death (p. 365; see also p. 352-353). Ascough highlighted the
"common use of triads in Luke's gospel" as exemplified in three temptations, three passion
predictions, and three trials (Sanhedrin, Pilate and Herod) (p. 357).

661. *Son of Man Seated at the Right Hand of God: Luke 22,69 in Lucan Christology*, in *Bib*

of Man saying in 22,69, endorsing the view that it was a redaction of Mk 14,62, though he seemed to be unaware of the essay by Plevnik[662]. Kalervo SALO (1991) also treated some issues related to the Lukan passion[663]. Wolfgang REINBOLD

72 (1991) 331-347. Plevnik examined the particular meaning of 22,69 within the context of 22,66-71 concluding the reference to Jesus sitting at the right hand of God was linked to a Son of God christology. While Plevnik characterized the scholarly consensus that this scene stemmed from a special source, "some dependence here on Mark is generally conceded, especially for v. 69" (p. 332). He contrasted Fitzmyer's position with that of Schneider. He went beyond this finding to declare that "all the changes in Luke 22,69 can be understood as Luke's redaction of Mark" (p. 338). Plevnik explained the omission of ὄψεσθε (14,62) by Luke's desire to downplay the theme of vindication "without denying the parousia of the Son of Man" (p. 338). The τοῦ θεοῦ was added to clarify, but Plevnik did not mention why the clarification was needed or for whom it was intended. The second question, and he indicated Luke separated the Markan question into two parts, thus stated what the council inferred from what Jesus said. By means of these changes, Luke made it more explicit than Mk that the condemnation of Jesus resulted from his claim to be the Son of God, which was the implication of the reference to sitting at God's right hand.

Plevnik further noted that exegetes often detected that an element of the story of Stephen (Acts 7,56) was patterned on that of Jesus. Luke's perspective at this point in Acts served to comment on the response of the council in 22,69-71 that they rejected Jesus' claim as Son of Man (p. 340). It was not so much a difference of christology between Mk and Lk, but how that christology was played out. Mark referred to Jesus as Son of God initially in his work and again at the end. Luke portrayed Jesus as Son of God throughout. "But the sitting on God's right hand, which became manifest at Jesus' ascension, is seen as God's glorification of his Son in the sight of the disciples" (p. 346; cf. Acts 1,11). Once again, an element in Acts confirmed some detail in the Gospel which ultimately was Lukan redaction of Markan material.

Another scholar, in the line of Plevnik, who regarded 22,69 as a Lukan redaction of Mk was A.W. ZWIEP, *The Ascension of the Messiah in Lukan Christology* (NTSuppl, 87), Leiden - New York - Cologne, 1997, p. 147-149; also p. 16. Diss. Durham 1996 (dir. J.D.G. DUNN). Zwiep mentioned Plevnik's article in a note (p. (147)-148, n. 3). H.D. BUCKWALTER, in a more detailed treatment, concluded that Luke sought to clarify Mk 14,61b-62 in Lk 22,69 (*The Character and Purpose of Luke's Christology* [SNTS MS 89], Cambridge, 1996. Diss. Aberdeen [dir. I.H. MARSHALL]).

Gerald O'COLLINS (1993) also recognized the similarities of Acts 7,56 and 22,69, the purpose being "to link this first Christian martyrdom with the death of Jesus" (*Luke on the Easter Appearances*, in G. O'COLLINS and G. MARCONI [eds.], *Luca-Atti*, 1991 = *Luke and Acts*, 1993, p. 165).

662. *The Lukan Son of Man*, in ID. (ed.), *Luke's Literary Achievement: Collected Essays* (JSNTS, 116), Sheffield, 1995, 198-217, esp. p. 199, 201, 208, 211-214.

663. A redaction-critical investigation of Luke's perspective on the law involved Salo's analysis of Jesus in Jerusalem (19,45–24,53) (*Luke's Treatment of the Law. A Redaction-Critical Investigation* [AASF DHL, 57], Helsinki, 1991). See his brief discussion of the synoptic problem (p. 23-24). Noting that "the majority of scholars" favored the view that Luke employed special source material in 22,66-67, Salo added the "differences between these two Gospels are not so great that the result is self-evident" (p. 159-160). Source analysis studies to which he referred included Green ("the most profound discussion of the source question at this point"), in addition to Rengstorf, Tyson, Schneider, Catchpole, Taylor, Ernst and Fitzmyer. Winter was said to have offered "the most extraordinary theory" (p. 160, n. 5). Luke intentionally omitted Mk 14,55-61a.64b which apparently was later used in Acts 6,8-15 (p. 160, n. 4). As in the account of the

(1992/93)[664], Sharon RINGE (1995)[665], Mark STRAUSS (1995)[666] and R.A.

Sanhedrin hearing following TYSON, *Lukan Version*, 254-256, Salo adopted the view this was "a preliminary hearing rather than a normal court session" (*Luke's Treatment*, p. 160, n. 7), so also in 23,1-5, he believed the evangelist was combining Mk with other special Lukan source material.

664. *Der älteste Bericht über den Tod Jesu. Literarische Analyse und historische Kritik der Passionsdarstellungen der Evangelien* (BZNW, 69), Göttingen, 1993. Diss. Göttingen, 1992/93 (dir. H. STEGEMANN). Reinbold concluded: "Die Hypothese einer besonderen lukanischen Passionsquelle PB^{Lk} ist nicht notwendig" (p. 72). The passion narrative was defined as 22,1–24,12. Acknowledging that the question of a special source for Luke's passion narrative was longstanding, supporters were identified as Taylor, Jeremias, Schürmann, Rehkopf, Winter and Green (whose methodology was likened to that of Taylor in explaining Markan passages as insertions within the Lukan passion narrative) while the opponents consisted of Lietzmann, Bultmann, Dibelius, Creed, Conzelmann, Kümmel, Vielhauer and Fitzmyer. Notice was made that there was greater support for the special source theory in England than in Germany.

Regarding literature newly published between the time he ended his work in 1992 and the publication of the dissertation in 1993 he stated: "Die seitdem erschienene Literatur habe ich eingearbeitet, soweit es mir nötig erschien" (Vorwort). Following an introduction the chapter entitled *Das Problem einer besonderen lukanischen Passionsquelle* contained the following sections: "Klärung der Beweislast und der Fragestellung, Das Verhältnis des Markusstoffes im lukanischen Passionsbericht zu Mk, Das Sondergut in der lukanischen Passionsdarstellung, Warum redigiert Lukas das Markusevangelium in seiner Passionsdarstellung überdurchschnittlich stark?, Das Sonderproblem des Verhältnisses zwischen lukanischem und johanneischem Passionsbericht and finally, Ergebnis".

The most important arguments in favor were characterized as: 1) the relatively high amount of *Sondergut* in the passion, 2) relatively low Lk-Mk verbal agreement, and 3) Lk-Jn agreements against Mk. In contrast there was no need to assume a special source since the differences between Lk and Mk as well as the presence of the *Sondergut* could be explained by other means. As regards Luke's use of Mk, Reinbold wrote: "wir *sicher* wissen, dass Lukas das Markusevangelium nicht nur benutzt, sondern (sehr wahrscheinlich) sogar zur Grundlage seine Evangeliums gemacht hat" (p. 50).

Three assertions were uncontested: 1) Luke more radically changed Mk in the passion narrative than he usually did, 2) Luke introduced *Sondergut* in his account of the passion, and 3) there were clear agreements between Lk and Jn. The percentages of verbal similarity discovered by Taylor between the Markan material in the Lukan passion and Mk "zwar prinzipiell korrekt sind" (p. 52; see p. 52(-53) n. 9). His conclusion: "Die wörtlichen Übereinstimmungen des Markusstoffes im lukanischen Passionsbericht mit Mk sind erkennbar geringer als in – *cum grano salis* – vergleichbaren Partien des Lk-Evangeliums" (p. 54).

Various passages, including 22,63-65.66-71; 23,6-16, were studied as possibly of non-Markan origin (p. 54-55). The other passages were 22,15-18.19c-20.21-23.24-30.31-34.35-38;23,27-31.35-37.39-43.56. It was clear from this, then, 22,54-62 and 23,1-5.18-25 were thought to have been from Mk. Frequent reasons for considering 22,63-65 as non-Markan were "sehr vage" agreements with Mk 14,65, the difference in order and the MA in 22,64 / Mt 26,68 (p. 59). Reinbold responded to each, beginning with the last. He did not believe that the MA should be used as an argument favoring a special Lukan source. The change in order was necessitated to fill out the night and to save time in the morning between the trial and crucifixion. Noting that Luke abbreviated the mockery and did not include the mockery by the Roman soldiers (Mk 15,16-20), he also here demonstrated a tendency for "Abschwächung". The language was very Lukan and therefore Reinbold concluded: "Lk 22,63-65 lässt sich gut als lukanische Komposition auf der Basis von Mk 14,65 interpretieren" (p. 60).

Summing up his results for the Sanhedrin trial, he declared: "Der Abschnitt Lk 22,66-71 lässt sich gut als lukanische Redaktion von Mk 14,55-64 interpretieren" (p. 61). The changes were due to redaction in light of Lukan eschatology and christology. Material in v.67a.69-71 corresponded to Mk 14,61.62b.63b. The transfer of the trial to the morning recalled Mk 15,1 and reflected Luke's typical "historisierenden Darstellungeweise".

He was more confident of his analysis of the Herod pericope (23,6-16): "lässt sich sehr gut als freie lukansiche Komposition interpretieren" (p. 62). Even supporters of the special source theory admitted the language and style of the passage was Lukan. Taking his cue from Conzelmann, he viewed the story as furthering Luke's "apologetische Tendenz" (p. 62, n. 64. CONZELMANN, *Die Mitte*, p. 79, n. 2).

In closing, Reinbold offered five reasons why Luke revised Mk in the passion more than he customarily did in other parts of the Gospel (REINBOLD, *Der älteste Breicht*, p. 66-67). Luke sought to round off Mk employing transpositions, expansion and corrections. Some specific threads of Lk run together. Within the Markan material were sometimes found Lukan cross references (23,2.4f.). Rather than a passive role as in Mk, the Lukan Jesus demonstrated his sovereignty. Luke minimized the role of the Romans and portrayed the disciples in a better light. "Die markinische Passionsgeschichte weist eine Reihe formaler und inhaltlicher Spezifika auf, die sowohl den Schriftsteller als auch den Historiker und den Theologen Lukas zu einer ungewöhnlich starken Überarbeitung seiner Vorlage nötigen. Vielleicht kann man sogar mit Marion L. SOARDS so weit gehen zu sagen, dass Lukas 'wrote his Gospel, rewriting Mark, in order to alter subtly the image of Jesus and the impact of his Passion' (Passion 123)" (REINBOLD, *Der älteste Bericht*, p. 67; see also "Ergebnis", p. 71-72).

In addition consider B. KOLLMANN, *Ursprung und Gestalten der frühchristlichen Mahlfeier* (GTA, 43), Göttingen, 1990. Diss. Göttingen, 1988/89 (dir. H. STEGEMANN), who concluded there was no special tradition in Lk 22,15-18. Rather, the evangelist redactionally shaped the verses based upon Mk 14,25 (p. 164).

665. *Luke* (WeBC), Louisville, KY, 1995. Few full scale Lukan commentaries have been written by women. Ringe made no reference in her own commentary to Schaberg's which she helped to edit (cf. J. SCHABERG, *Luke*, 1992; see above). Recently, Ringe authored one intended for the laity. In a brief general discussion of sources she noted that Markan priority was the position held by the majority of scholars. In addition to Mk and Q, which could have been written or oral, Luke used special material "which probably includes stories about and teachings of Jesus that had circulated in the author's community (but apparently not in those of the other Gospel writers) as well as the author's own comments and editorial work", though without specifying the material or citing any examples (RINGE, *Luke*, p. 17).

In introducing the passion narrative Ringe took account of the debate surrounding sources but opted only to focus on the "final form" of Luke's account, though her intention was to pay "special attention" to Luke's differences as over against Mk. "If Luke had Mark's Gospel as a basis for his new Gospel, it is probable that he also knew Mark's passion narrative (or at least a version of it very similar to the one now in that Gospel, allowing the probability that later editors might have altered a few details (p. 255-256). The differences between Luke's passion account and Mark's have led to a debate among scholars about whether Luke has as one of his sources a different passion narrative, which he interwove with Mark's, or whether he simply incorporated isolated details he had found and then edited the results in order to emphasize his own theological interpretation of the passion and its aftermath. The evidence can be read both ways, and scholars are divided about their conclusions.

The approach I have followed in this book is to focus on Luke's final form of the narrative, paying special attention to points he appears to emphasize. One way to identify such emphases is to take particular note of points at which Luke's narrative differs from Mark's, since it is at those points that he has most clearly chosen either to follow his other source (if he had one) or to adapt Mark's narrative himself". The section 22,54–23,25 was termed "The Judicial Process" (p. 267).

The transfer of Jesus from Pilate to Herod was effected because of a "jurisdictional technicality" (p. 271). Although Ringe insisted "there is no way to judge the historical accuracy of Luke's account" of Jesus before Herod (23,6-12), she added it "seems a bit far fetched as a historical report" (p. 271, 272). It was consistent with Luke's efforts to exonerate Rome and provided a second "Roman witness to Jesus' innocence" (p. 272). She noted previous references in the Gospel to Herod (9,7-9; 13,31) and alluded to Ps 2,2 in discussing 23,12 without referring to Acts 4,25-27.

666. *The Davidic Messiah in Luke-Acts. The Promise and its Fulfillment in Lukan Christology* (JSNT SS, 110), Sheffield, 1995, p. 32. In a study of the Davidic-Messiah in Luke-Acts, presented as a 1992 Aberdeen thesis, Strauss asserted the two-sources theory had "weathered the storm" from opponents and therefore he assumed within his work Markan priority and the independent use of a common source by Matthew and Luke. Strauss's methodology was to examine sources in such cases as they can be determined with some certainty. Where this was not possible, he shifted to more of a literary analysis (p. 33).

Relying heavily upon Green and in comparison with Soards, Strauss argued that in addition to Mk, Luke employed "additional source material". "The question of sources in Luke's passion is a difficult one owing to the significant differences from Mark. While the idea that Luke's passion was a part of a Proto-Luke has not found widespread support, it seems certain that Luke has made use of additional source material in compiling his account. While this should caution against placing too much emphasis on alterations from Mark, it must be added that Luke almost certainly has Mark's passion account available to him and so consciously chose to depart from it – either through his own redaction or by following another source or sources. To arrive at Luke's purpose, therefore, alterations from Mark should be weighed together with clear signs of Lukan redaction, the general thrust of Luke's narrative development and the theological perspective expressed elsewhere in Luke-Acts" (p. 318). In referring to Proto-Luke, Strauss cited TAYLOR, *Passion Narrative* (1972) (n. 1). See J.B. GREEN, *Death*, 1988, and M. SOARDS, *Passion*, (1987). Lukan redaction "serves to emphasize Jesus' royal status", a theme which "continues in the passion narrative" (STRAUSS, *Davidic Messiah*, p. 318).

Although he entertained the possibilities of redaction or a special source in his treatment of the Sanhedrin trial (22,66-71) Strauss seemed to favor Lukan redaction of Mk (p. 319). While the omission of reference to false witnesses could be for the sake of condensing the account, it was "more likely" that the change was made to emphasize the messianic identity of Jesus. Luke was credited with separating Mk 14,61 into two questions (22,67.70) (p. 320). The omission of καὶ ἐρχόμενον μετὰ τῶν νεφελῶν τοῦ οὐρανοῦ more likely was intended "to stress Jesus' *present* reign at God's right hand", though Conzelmann's proposal that it represented part of the theme of the delay of the parousia, was also possible. Strauss was emphatic that Luke was not employing a special source in this case and "the best explanation is that his redaction is meant to stress Jesus' exaltation-enthronement as messianic Lord and Son of God, and his present heavenly reign" (p. 320). Strauss also saw evidence of Lukan redaction in the Roman trial (23,2-3).

Concerning elements in the Herod pericope, Strauss found that a "servant allusion" in the theme of Jesus' innocence in his trial and crucifixion was supported by Jesus' silence in 23,9. "Though Luke abbreviates the opening of the Jewish trial and so omits the reference to Jesus' silence at Mk 14.60-61, he retains the reference in Lk. 23.9 (cf. Mk 15.5)" (p. 332). Luke omitted the Markan mention of the purple robe and crown of thorns (Mk 15,17) "but records similar abuse before Herod (Lk. 23.11) and in the mocking of the soldiers at the cross (Lk.

CULPEPPER (1995)[667] examined various aspects of Luke's redaction of Mk, while his student Steven SHEELEY (1992) focused on narrative asides in Lk-Acts[668].

23.37)" (p. [318-]319, n. 4). Herod's declaration (23,15) was a confirmation of Pilate's assessment that Jesus was not guilty (p. 330; see also p. 322-323). His comments directed against a "purely literary approach" are well-taken. "Yet a complete rejection of source and redaction analysis may also produce skewed results" (p. 32).

667. *The Gospel of Luke: Introduction, Commentary and Reflections*, in *New Interpreter's Bible*, Vol. 9, Nashville, TN, 1995, p. 3-490, p. 7. Luke employed a combination of Mk and L in 18,15-24,11 according to Culpepper. Although he stated there was not much evidence for a second source in the passion narrative, he did not entirely exclude it. "For the entry into Jerusalem, Jesus' ministry in the Temple, and the passion narrative, Luke again follows Mark, expanding and inserting material from one or more other sources. Scholars have often suggested that Luke drew from a second passion narrative in addition to Mark, but the evidence for a second passion narrative is thin and can be accounted for by appeal to oral tradition and Lukan redaction" (p. 8). But later in his discussion of Luke's sources he hedges by adding that in addition to Mk, Q and L, Luke employed "possibly a passion narrative" (p. 40). He indicated that the mention of Herod in 8,3 prepared for 9,7-9.

For his discussion of the passion narrative proper, he seemed to rely on the commentaries of Fitzmyer and Nolland. In an appropriate shift he titled 22,63-65, "Jesus is challenged to prophesy" (p. 12). See also his discussion of Jesus as a prophet entitled, "Prophet-One Greater than the Prophets" (p. 15-17). He described five scenes in 23,1-25: Pilate's first declaration of innocence (23,1-5); Jesus before Herod (23,6-12); Jesus' second declaration (23,13-16); Pilate's third declaration (23,18-22); Pilate's capitulation to the crowd (23,23-25) (p. 12-13, 445). Although Culpepper referred briefly to the MA in 22,62 / Mt 26,75, he passed over the MA 22,64 / Mt 26,68 in silence (p. 437; cf. p. 440-441).

It would appear he accepted the Herod pericope as historical (p. 446-447). Commenting on 23,12 he saw this as a reconciliation.

668. S.M. SHEELEY, *Narrative Asides in Luke-Acts* (JSOT SS 72), Sheffield, 1992. Diss. Southern Baptist Theological Seminary, Louisville, KY, 1987 (dir. R.A. CULPEPPER). Culpepper used Shelley's dissertation in his commentary on Lk (*The Gospel of Luke*, in *NIB*, Vol. 9, 1995, p. 33). See Shelley's articles: *Narrative Asides and Narrative Authority in Luke-Acts*, in *BTB* 18 (1988) 102-107, and *The Narrator in the Gospels: Developing a Model*, in *PerspRelSt* 16 (1989) 213-223. In his dissertation and first article, parts of which were drawn from the dissertation, he gave attention to 23,12. In the former work he quoted Fitzmyer's observation on 23,12 that 'This is one more of Luke's inconsequential explicative notes, which he likes to add to his story' (SHELLEY, *Narrative Asides* [1992], p. 26; cf. FITZMYER, p. 1482). He classified the type as general information (SHELLEY, *Narrative Asides* (1992), p. 98). Shelley recalled four possible interpretations of the verse, suggesting simply that "all of these explanations may be valid" (p. 114). In his 1987 article he commented on 23,12: "Only one aside in Luke provides information of general interest to the reader. ... This passage is remarkable for its lack of evident connection with its context, but the fact that the narrator is able to impart such information to the reader bolsters the picture of the narrator as one who knows even more than what is necessary for the telling of the story" (p. 104).

Two additional verses in the Herod pericope are categorized as asides containing "material necessary to understand the story": 23,18-19 (1992, p. 98; also p. 187). These verses serve the purpose of identifying characters, in this case Barabbas, and refer to the "narrator's knowledge of events outside the story" (p. 152; also p. 166, 187; see further *Narrative Asides* (1987), p. 103).

Others, such as Philip VAN LINDEN (1986)[669], had no interest in the matter of sources.

Raymond COLLINS (1983), in his treatment of Luke's additional sources, negatively evaluated Streeter's solution on the grounds that "his arguments lacked cogency except for the extent to which they pointed to a Lucan (L) *Sondergut*"[670]. F.J. MOLONEY (1986) rejected Proto-Lk, though without offering any argumentation[671]. Opposition to Proto-Lk was also signaled by the general consensus described by J.L. HOULDEN (1990)[672] as well as the demise of Proto-Lk as recounted by J. DRURY (1990)[673]. Further, C.M. TUCKETT (1992), reviewed the theory indicating the likelihood that Luke used a separate account of

---

669. Van Linden did not treat the source question in his work (*The Gospel of Luke and Acts* [Message of Biblical Spirituality, 10], Wilmington, DE, 1986).

670. *Introduction to the New Testament*, Garden City, NY, 1983 (esp. p. 126-139), p. 133.

671. *The Living Voice of the Gospel. The Gospels Today*, New York - Mahwah, NJ, 1986, p. 86, n. 19. With particular regard to the passion narrative, citing Streeter (1924) as the scholar who "first argued" the Proto-Lk theory, and Taylor (1972) who continued it, Moloney stated: "I am still presupposing a Marcan source". He referred readers to Fitzmyer (1981), p. 89-91, 104-105.

672. J.L. HOULDEN, *Passion Narratives*, in *DBI*, 1990, 515-517, p. 517: "Luke's narrative shows far more divergence from Mark than does Matthew, so much so that many scholars have held that he had an independent passion narrative, into which he incorporated elements of the Marcan story. (This was part of a wider theory of the composition of Luke, that of Proto-Luke, first put forward by B.H. Streeter; see his *The Four Gospels*, 1924.) Plausible as this seems, perhaps especially in the light of Luke's clearly distinct account of the Last Supper, it is now generally held that much of his special and extra material is his own composition, expressing his own theological and religious ideas. Certainly, it is not hard to demonstrate the close conformity of Luke's passion narrative with the rest of Luke-Acts, as a comparison with the story of Stephen's passion in Acts 6-7 quickly shows (the disciple suffers after the manner of his Lord)".

673. J. DRURY, *Luke, Gospel of*, in *DBI*, 1990, 410-414, p. 412: "... for the sources to be convincingly present, incongruity with the rest of the book is required. Such a source was posited by Streeter ([*The Four Gospels*], ch. 8) and Vincent Taylor (*Behind the Third Gospel*, 1926), who called it 'Proto-Luke' (seen as a union of Luke's own matter and his Q material) and held that it was Luke's primary document. He had it before Mark's Gospel came his way. It was earlier than any of the Gospels and so, by implication, highly dependable as a source for Jesus' life. J.M. Creed's still unsurpassed commentary on *The Gospel According to St Luke* (1930) quietly tilted the weight of interpretation to the other end of the scale, presenting Luke's creativity as explaining the material which Streeter and Taylor attributed to Proto-Luke. The passion narrative was the decisive field. Here Creed succeeded, in fine detail and with strong economy of argument, in making out a convincing case for his theory, that 'Luke has himself freely rewritten, rearranged and enlarged St Mark. He may sometimes present independent traditions, but the continuous thread of his narrative appears to be based upon Mark' (p. 262)". Drury resumed his assessment later in the article: "The growing emphasis on Luke's creativity has had its effect on the source-critical orthodoxy which hitherto held the field. It allows for increased freedom in Luke's use of Mark, such as Creed had pioneered in his commentary. So while Luke's use of Mark remains as a survivor of that old orthodoxy, the necessity to posit Proto-Luke has gone" (DRURY, *Luke, Gospel of*, p. 413).

the passion in addition to Mk based on verbal dissimilarity and differences in order, adding that "while the theory of an independent passion narrative clearly fits a proto-Luke theory, it in no way demands it"[674]. Observing that the theory had not attracted much support beyond England, Tuckett declared that the "whole proto-Luke theory remains rather doubtful"[675] and despite the best efforts of Streeter and Taylor, "it cannot guarantee the historical reliability of Luke's gospel"[676]. D. LÜHRMANN (1995) also rejected Proto-Lk as a solution to the synoptic problem[677] M.D. GOULDER (1996) remarked: "In Britain, Proto-Luke died with B.H. Streeter ..."[678].

674. *Synoptic Problem*, in *ABD* 6, 263-270, esp. p. 269.

675. *Ibid.*

676. *Ibid.*, p. 270.

677. D. LÜHRMANN, *Q: Sayings of Jesus or Logia*, in R.A. PIPER (ed.), *The Gospel Behind the Gospels: Current Studies on Q* (NTSupp 75), Leiden, 1995, p. 97.

678. *Is Q a Juggernaut?*, in *JBL* 115 (1996) 667-681, p. 668, n. 11.

CHAPTER ELEVEN

THE RISE OF A NEW LITERARY CRITICISM

A noticeable shift took place in recent decades, especially in Lukan studies, away from source criticism, with increased attention being given to new literary-critical methods[1]. In this section we will examine proponents of this manner of investigation.

Louis MARIN (1971), a professor of aesthetics and history of philosophy, applied structural analysis in his study of the accounts of the passion, which he considered to be four variants of the same text[2]. He directed some attention to the Sanhedrin trial but was not concerned with Markan material or questions of source criticism as such[3]. A more recent attempt to interpret Lk through Semiotics was made by Agnès GUERET (1987)[4].

Jean DELORME (1981) prescinded from examining 22,54–23,25 from a redaction-critical standpoint, choosing instead to focus on the Lukan text alone[5]. Although he made this disclaimer, he noted nonetheless that Luke rejected as historically improbable that there would have been a nocturnal Sanhedrin session as in Mk[6]. Supporters of Lukan redaction of the Markan *Vorlage* exaggerated the similarity of the two accounts of the trial before Pilate by pointing to the sequence of the interrogation followed by the accusation, according to Delorme[7]. He considered their perspectives to be different, an argument which could also be used in favor of redaction.

According to Delorme, although the charges in Lk followed the questioning as in Mk, it was too superficial and the perspective of the accounts was too different to permit the suggestion that the Herod scene was based on Mk[8]. Regarding the motif of silence, Delorme interpreted this as an auditory sign which

---

1. On the distinction between the old and new literary criticism, see NEIRYNCK, *Literary Criticism*, p. 12-13.

2. *Sémiotique de la Passion. Topiques et figures* (BSR), Paris, 1971 (= *Semiotik der Passionsgeschichte*, tr. S. VIRGILS, Munich, 1976 = *The Semiotics of the Passion Narrative. Topics and Figures* [PTMS, 25], tr. A.M. JOHNSON, Pittsburgh, PA, 1980).

3. *Sémiotique*, p. 168.

4. *La mise en discours. Recherches sémiotiques à propos de l'Évangile de Luc*, Paris, 1987, p. 258-265. Diss. U. Paris - Nanterre (dir. P. GEOLTRAIN). She did not include Marin in her bibliography.

5. *Le procès de Jésus ou la parole risquée (Lc 22,54-23,25)*, in *RSR* 69 (1981) 123. This edition was a memorial to A. George and the direction for the article was suggested by George's interest in structural analysis dating to the period after 1970. Further inspiration was drawn from linguistics and semiotics (p. 129, n. 11).

6. *Ibid.*, p. 125.

7. *Ibid.*, p. 139, n. 30.

8. *Ibid.*

Jesus refused to give[9]. No indication of the color of the dazzling apparel was suggested, which would also seem to indicate that Delorme rejected the possibility of Markan influence. Ultimately Delorme referred the reader to Hoehner[10].

Robert TANNEHILL (1986) taking up the literary-critical model, rejected "elaborate arguments to distinguish tradition from Lukan redaction of that tradition"[11]. He espoused the Two-Source theory of Mk and Q, but indicated this supposition did not affect his interpretation. Such a source-critical study would divert him from his main purpose.

In his discussion of Peter's denials Tannehill noted the omission of Peter's swearing such as was found in Mk 14,71. The Lukan account had a much more dramatic flare and contrasted the "failure in faithfulness" with the "boldness in witnessing" (Acts 4-5). Tannehill was alert to the similarities between the Lukan presentation of Jesus in his passion and that of Stephen (22,69: 23,34.46 and Acts 7,55-60)[12]. No reference was made to the MAs in 22,62.64.

For Tannehill it was "God's purpose which unifies the narrative"[13]. Further Luke was sensitive to maintain the "continuity between the earlier controversies with the scribes and Pharisees and the charges against Jesus at his trial by making the effect of his teaching an important part of those charges"[14].

Tannehill (1986) uncovered important connections between the Herod scene (23,6-12) and previous material in the Gospel, especially in the passion predictions. The story underscored that Jesus was rejected by both religious and political leaders. Herod was not the only additional witness to Pilate's insistence on Jesus' innocence, the good thief and the centurion (23,41.47) witnessed too[15]. According to Tannehill, the passion story was reprised in Acts 4,25-28 which was possibly anticipated by 23,12. He took exception to the interpretation of Drury and Karris that Jesus' death resulted in the new found friendship. Then, in an apparent reversal of his understanding, Tannehill claimed that Acts 4,27 became the basis for interpreting 23,12[16].

In Tannehill's second volume which dealt with the Acts of the Apostles (1990) he stated that Acts 4,27 recalled the trial of Jesus before another Herod[17]. Lk 23,13-16 constituted part of the story which highlighted the shift of the role of the

9. *Ibid.*, p. 140, n. 31.

10. *Ibid.*, p. 141, n. 33. Cf. HOEHNER, *Herod Antipas*, 1972, Ch. 9.

11. TANNEHILL, *The Narrative Unity of Luke-Acts. A Literary Interpretation*. Vol. 1. *The Gospel according to Luke*, Philadelphia, PA, 1986, p. 6, n. 3.

12. *Ibid.*, p. 272. He indicated other connections between the Gospel and Acts (p. 26, 193, 245).

13. *Ibid.*, p. 2.

14. *Ibid.*, p. 195.

15. *Ibid.*, p. 197.

16. *Ibid.*, n. 43.

17. TANNEHILL, *Acts*, p. 152.

people in Jesus' trial[18]. The parallels between the trials of Jesus and Paul were also noted[19]. These included: ἀνακρίνας (Lk 23,14 / Acts 28,18 ἀνακίναντες); "nothing worthy of death" (Lk 23,15 / Acts 28,18 "no reason for death"); "release" (Lk 23,16 / Lk 23,20 "wishing to release"; Acts 28,18 "they were wanting to release me"); and the objection by the religious leaders and people (Lk 23,18 / Acts 28,19)[20]. The "echoes" of Jesus' trial within Paul's underscored the portrayal of Paul as a faithful disciple.

Tannehill (1996) explained his recent commentary on Lk resulted from "new methods and interests"[21]. Although he mentioned that the majority of scholars support the view that Luke used Mk and Q, he stated that his approach was not primarily that of redaction criticism[22].

Roland MEYNET (1988), using rhetorical analysis, set out to help the reader visualize the narrative, breaking it into separate passages and sequences of passages[23]. As such it was opposed to the redaction-critical method. Referring to rhetorical analysis he wrote: "Elles est radicalement autre: telle que mise en oeuvre ici, elle s'intéresse exclusivement à létat actuel du texte sane tenir aucun compte de l'histoire de sa formation. Elle refuse de même la comparaison synoptique"[24].

Meynet offered a reprise of his earlier commentary in his 1990 book on Lk which contained revisions and corrections. His method was termed rhetorical analysis and thus was situated within the new literary criticism[25]. Following the Prologue, Meynet divided Lk into four parts: 1) 1,5-4,13; 2) 4,14-9,50; 3) 9,51-21,38; and 4) 21,38-24,53[26]. One is reminded very much of the approach of M. Corbin[27]. Meynet avoided the issue of source criticism and even redaction criticism in his examination of the structure of Lk. Nevertheless, he considered that

18. *Ibid.* p. 60; cf. p. 84.

19. *Ibid.*, p. 345-346.

20. *Ibid*, p. (345-)346 n. 3. Here Tannehill appeared to be dependent upon RADL, *Paulus*, p. 252-265.

21. *Luke* (ANTC), Nashville, TN, 1996, p. 15.

22. *Ibid.*, p. 19-20. "Since I am focusing on Luke in its final form, I will give little attention to hypothetical earlier forms of the Jesus tradition that may have been adapted for use in Luke" (p. 19). For his discussion of 22,54-23,25, see p. 326-338.

23. *L'Évangile selon saint Luc*, 2 vols. Vol. 1. *Planches*; Vol. 2. *Commentaire*, Paris, 1988; Diss. Provence, 1986 (dir. J. MOLINO). Meynet cited the rather recent development of rhetorical analysis and credited James Muilenburg with coining the term at an SBL meeting in 1968 (Vol. 2, p. 7).

24. *Ibid.*, Vol. 2, p. 8.

25. *Avez-vous lu saint Luc? Guide pour la rencontre*, Paris, 1990 (esp. p. 104-111, 263). See p. 9, for a discussion of rhetorical analysis which focused on the structure or architecture of the text. Should not the title of the section dealing with 23,6-12 read "L'INTERROGATOIRE PAR HÉRODE instead of PAR PILATE" (p. 107)?

26. *Ibid.*, p. 11. See also page 281, where the section to which we have devoted attention (22,54-23,25) was designated as one of four sub-sections in the final part of Lk.

27. *Jésus devant Hérode: Lecture de Luc 23,6-12*, in *Christus* 25 (1978) 190-197.

the verdict of the Sanhedrin (22,71) lay at the heart of this section[28]. Rather than looking at the text itself, it appeared that he imposed his own structure upon Lk.

In his introduction to a more recent study of the Synoptic accounts of the passion in which he briefly treated Benoit, Boismard, Vanhoye and Blinzler, Meynet (1993) signaled his adoption of Vanhoye's methodology which studied the organization of the small literary units or pericopes in order to determine "l'orientation particulière" of each Gospel[29]. The sequence containing 22,54-23,25 was made up of seven passages: 22,54-62.63-65.66-70; 23,1-5.6-12.13-25[30]. In Meynet's view the judgment of Jesus (22,71) stood as the central focus of this entire section[31].

What distinguished the narrative approach of Jean-Noël ALETTI (1989) from others in the new literary critics studying the passion narrative, was that Aletti occasionally compared Lk with Mk and Mt, though like other literary critics he focused primarily on Lk itself[32]. He devoted a chapter to the trials before Pilate and Herod[33].

John Paul HEIL (1989) examined the concept of irony in an article on the Lukan Sanhedrin trial in which he employed the Reader-Response methodology[34]. He called attention to previous controversies between Jesus and the Jewish leaders in Lk[35]. Heil pointed out connections between 20,41-44 and 22,67 which was seen as the "continuation" of the earlier material, especially in the identification of Jesus as "Christ"[36]. This was an important observation in light of the charges brought against Jesus in Lk 23 which were related to 20,20-21. Heil also highlighted the use of the title "Son of Man" in 9,22.44; 17,24-25; 18,31-33; 22,69[37]. The title "Son of God" in 22,70 reprised what had previously been communicated about Jesus in 1,32.35; 3,22.38; 4,3.9.41; 8,28; 9,35; 10,22[38]. The indication of a prophetic utterance was often signaled by the use of the phrase "from his mouth" or simply the word "mouth". The use of the phrase in 22,71 was a culmination of

28. MEYNET, *Avez-vous lu saint Luc?*, p. 110.

29. *Passion de notre Seigneur Jésus Christ selon les évangiles synoptiques* (Lire la Bible, 99), Paris, 1993, p. 7-11. See VANHOYE, *La Passion*, 1981, p. 11-12.

30. See especially MEYNET, *Passion*, 1993, p. 143-164. In n. 1 he remarked that his analysis of the first sequence of the passion (22,1-53) according to Luke was very different from that which he presented in his earlier work, *L'Évangile selon saint Luc* (1988) (p. 63).

31. *La Passion*, p. 143, 158, 159, 161.

32. *L'art de raconter Jésus Christ*, Paris, 1989; (= *L'arte de raccontare Gesù Cristo*, tr. L. SEMBRANO, Brescia, 1991). For a positive appraisal of his work, see BOVON, *Studies in Luke-Acts*, in *HTR* 85 (1992), p. 196, 184.

33. ALETTI, *L'art*, Chapter VII, p. 155-176.

34. *Reader-Response and the Irony of Jesus before the Sanhedrin in Lk 22:66-71*, in *CBQ* 51 (1989) 271-284. The works of Tannehill, Marshall and Fitzmyer were major influences upon Heil.

35. *Ibid.*, p. 274-275.

36. *Ibid.*, p. 277, n. 20.

37. *Ibid.*, p. 280.

38. *Ibid.*, p. 281.

previous occurrences in 1,64 and 4,22 which were linked with prophecy in 22,64; 1,67 and 4,17[39]. Heil noted similar connections between "mouth" and prophecy in Acts 1,16; 3,18.21; 4,25[40]. Though he did not treat the question of the relation of Lk to Mk his observations advance our understanding of Lukan redaction. As was earlier noted, Luke often used previous portions of his Gospel in later sections. Heil's research on 22,66-71 appears to strongly confirm this assertion.

Continuing to employ the Reader-Response methodology, Heil (1991) traced the role which irony played in a further section of Lk (23,1-25)[41]. One wonders whether such an investigation suffers from too much influence of a Johannine literary technique[42]. The author pointed out connections between this and earlier portions of the Gospel. In Herod's expressing the desire to see some sign from Jesus (23,8), Heil regarded the tetrarch as identifying with the evil generation who sought a sign (11,29-30)[43]. The mockery by Herod fulfilled the earlier passion predictions. Heil's was another example of the literary-critical methodology which paid no attention to the source question. Yet, his conclusion is worth pondering: "Through the experience of the dramatic irony in the scene of the trial of Jesus in Luke 23,1-25 Luke's audience is required to hold together in indissoluble tension the paradoxical tragedy of Israel's responsibility for the death of the innocent Jesus with the tragic paradox that Jesus *must* suffer and die to accomplish God's salvific plan"[44].

Heil (1991) interpreted the dazzling apparel (23,11) on two levels[45]. While "on the surface" the clothing served to ridicule Jesus, "on the deeper level" it called attention to Jesus' "future exaltation and glory as Son of Man". Astutely Heil made the connection to the transfiguration account where the disciples not only witness "his glory" (9,32), but the transformation of his clothing (9,29). The confirmation of such an interpretation was found in Acts 10,30. Concerning 23,12 Heil understood the verse to portray the irony that two enemies unite for the roles they have in the demise of Jesus. Acts 4,26-28 confirmed this Lukan verse which, in turn, fulfilled the divine plan of Ps 2,1-2[46]. But Heil took exception to Soards's

---

39. *Ibid.*, p. 283. The use of the identical phrase "from his mouth" was also found in 11,52-53 which Heil termed "particularly illuminating" (p. 282).

40. *Ibid.*, p. 283, n. 36.

41. *Reader-Response and the Irony of the Trial of Jesus in Luke 23:1-25*, in *SEsp* 43 (1991) 175-186. Luke's use of irony in this section of the Gospel (23,25) was earlier detected and discussed by MCLACHLAN, *St. Luke*, 1920, p. 157-158.

42. HEIL, *Reader-Response and the Irony of the Trial of Jesus in Luke 23:1-25*, p. 176, nn. 4, 6. Many of the scholars Heil cited deal with irony and treated the matter in Jn. He relied heavily upon the commentaries of Marshall, Fitzmyer, and Tannehill and none of his references were earlier than 1969.

43. *Ibid.*, p. 182.

44. *Ibid.*, p. 185.

45. *Ibid.*, p. 182.

46. *Ibid.*, p. 183.

interpretation that something good came about as a result of the events leading to Jesus imminent death[47].

Bruce MALINA and Jerome NEYREY (1991) used a social science approach applying it to parts of the Lukan trial narrative[48]. The essay treated labeling and deviance theory.

Prompted by scholarly works investigating the possible roots of anti-Semitism in the NT, in his most recent book (1992) Joseph TYSON embraced more and more the new literary criticism, especially Reader-Response[49]. From his study he concluded "the implied reader is similar to those characters in Luke-Acts who are termed Godfearers, i.e., Gentiles who are attracted to Judaism but not fully committed to it"[50].

Tyson continued to argue that source criticism was an exercise in futility[51]. Nevertheless, he admitted "there are almost certainly sources behind both Luke and Acts"[52].

An examination of Tyson's index of biblical references revealed that he had little interest in comparing the Lukan account with that of Mk. Yet, he astutely observed the charge against Stephen (Acts 6,14) was basically the same as that made against Jesus in Mk 14,58. But the Lukan trial narratives did not contain either the Markan or Matthean form of the saying[53].

Certain aspects of Tyson's proposed methodology may be useful if adapted to the search for sources. He maintained the absence of references to Israel, or aspects of Jewish life and thought reflected in "words, phrases and concepts" was problematic and suggested that scholars "should be sensitive to a significant number of clues that in context suggest something about Jewish religious life. Such clues would include technical terms that refer to Jewish religious institutions,

---

47. *Ibid.*, n. 30; cf. SOARDS, *Tradition*, 1985, p. 363.

48. B.J. MALINA and J.H. NEYREY, *Conflict in Luke-Acts: Labeling and Deviance Theory*, in J.H. NEYREY (ed.), *The Social World of Luke-Acts*, Peabody, MA, 1991, 97-122. Note the pagination was incorrectly listed in W.E. MILLS, *The Gospel of Luke* (BBR, 3), Lewiston, NY - Queenston, Ontario - Lampeter, 1994, p. 194.

49. *Images of Judaism in Luke-Acts*, Columbia, SC, 1992 (esp. p. 79-99).

50. *Ibid.*, p. vii.

51. *Ibid.*, p. 15. Offering an outline of the major sections of the Gospel, Tyson stated: "In creating such devices, we should avoid putting our own stamps upon them by supplying supposed theological themes or concepts to describe the various sections. Nor should we, in the case of the Gospel of Luke, draw up an outline in terms of an alleged source of Luke, be it Mark, or Q, or Matthew. Although comparisons between Luke and the other two Synoptic Gospels may be of interest and value, the state of our knowledge about the use of sources by Luke is such that we cannot make defensible and meaningful observations on the basis of a supposed source theory". And he added: "The source problems for Acts are even more serious". See further on p. 16. Tyson cited TALBERT, *Shifting Sands*, p. 393 = J. MAYS (ed.), *Interpreting*, 1981, 231-246, in support of his view questioning the appropriateness of making Lukan redactional-critical observations on the basis of Mk.

52. TYSON, *Images*, p. 16.

53. *Ibid.*, p. 128, n. 26.

groups, and observances, names of Jewish persons and Hebrew worthies of the past, references to the Hebrew Scriptures and to acts of individual and social piety"[54].

In Tyson's opinion Jesus' appearance before the Sanhedrin (22,66-71) was simply a hearing and not a formal trial[55]. Though he eschewed the source question he credited Luke with fashioning the charges with greater care and emphasizing Pilate's judgment of innocence.

Mikeal PARSONS and Richard PERVO (1993) addressed the methodological shift away from source criticism and the implications for the study of the Gospel together with Acts: "The post-redaction-critical shift from emphasis on the manipulation of sources to concentration on the text as a self-sufficient literary product has established Luke and Acts as major controls upon one another, rather than Luke as primarily a revision of Mark and Acts as a document to be viewed (for better or worse) in the light of the Pauline corpus"[56]. In the Gospel account of the passion Jesus was portrayed as a model and the narratives of Acts also recalled the passion[57]. Parsons and Pervo argued that Luke had different intentions for each volume of his two-volume work[58].

In a study of Jesus' opponents in Lk 23, whom W. WEREN and V. DE HAAS (1995) identified as Pilate, Herod and the people, the authors employed "new theories on characterization" in an attempt to discover responsibility for the death of Jesus[59]. They referred to the previous research of F. Matera, J.P. Heil, F.F. Bruce, J. Darr, M.L. Soards and R.S. Ascough in the section of the Gospel with which we are concerned[60]. No attempt was made to reckon with the question of sources though they refer to Joanna and Manaen in relation to the Herod pericope[61].

---

54. *Ibid.*, p. 14.

55. *Ibid.*, p. 79; see also p. 86.

56. *Rethinking the Unity of Luke and Acts*, Minneapolis, MN, 1993, p. 20-21. The authors devoted a few sentences to "The Problem of Sources" recalling Nigel Turner's comment that the "final editor" imposed his style upon whatever sources he used (p. 79). See TURNER, *Style*, in *MHT* 4, 1976, p. 57.

57. PARSONS and PERVO, *Rethinking*, p. 38. See the comment in n. 75.

58. *Ibid.*, p. 40.

59. W. WEREN and V. DE HAAS, *Oog in oog met personages uit Lucas. 2. Jezus en zijn tegenspelers in Lc. 23*, in *TT* 35 (1995) 236-251, p. 251. See the first installment: 1. *Jezus en zijn volgelingen in Lc. 22-24*, in *TT* 35 (1995) 125-147. Note Weren's article also on 22,66-23,25 (*Gedragen door teksten*, in J. JANS (ed.), *Bewogen theologie. Theologie in beweging*, Tilburg, 1996, 12-23). For a critique of Weren's methdology, see M. RESE, *"Intertextualität" – Ein Beispiel für Sinn und Unsinn "neuer" Methoden*, in C.M. TUCKETT (ed.), *Scriptures*, 1997, 431-439.

60. MATERA, *Luke 23,1-25*, 1989; HEIL, *Reader-Response*, 1989; BRUCE, *Herod Antipas*, 1959; DARR, *On Character Building*, 1992; SOARDS, *Silence*, 1985; ASCOUGH, *Rejection*, 1993.

61. WEREN and DE HAAS, *Jezus en zijn tegenspelers in Lc. 23*, p. 240: "Door deze namen in zijn verhaal te vlechten, suggereert Lucas dat hij kan beschikken over informanten die uitstekend op de hoogte zijn".

For 22,66-71 the authors proposed this was only an investigation or preparation, but 23,1-25 contained juridical terms apparently suggesting the evangelist was concerned in this episode "met een echt proces"[62]. The focus of the juridical trial was on the identity of Jesus.

Weren and De Haas drew upon the work of Darr to suggest that the conflict between Jesus and Herod was styled after the fashion of the prophet's confrontation with a king as found in the OT or the philosopher's encounter with the emperor in contemporary Hellenistic literature[63]. The authors conceded the difficulty of interpreting the significance of the sending of Jesus back to Pilate by Herod. Further, the splendid garment presented problems. The ordeal with Pilate demonstrated Jesus was innocent and the encounter with Herod portrayed Jesus as a royal figure who indeed had power.

Acts 4,25-28 painted a different picture than 23,6-12[64]. Weren and De Haas pointed to "intertekstuele relaties" between the accounts in the Gospel and Ps 2 which were used in Acts[65].

R.L. BRAWLEY (1995) examined the Lukan passion from a new literary perspective that involved applying the concept of carnival[66]. In his discussion of the mockery (22,63-64) he noted echoes of Is 50,6 LXX[67]. He observed the relationship between 18,32-33 and 22,64[68]. He also detected a correspondence between the judgment of innocence in Is 53,8 and Jesus' innocence in Lk 23. He briefly treated 22,67-69.70 and 23,18-25.

In his treatment of the HP, Brawley noted the similarity of the silence of the suffering servant (Is 53,7) with Jesus' silence before Herod (23,9). Concerning the mockery in 23,11 he remarked: "The carnivalesque is all the more explicit in the mockery of Herod and his soldiers – they dress Jesus in an exquisite robe – carnival king (23:11)"[69]. He explicitly referred to a work of P. Wendland who

---

62. *Ibid.*, p. 236.

63. *Ibid.*, p. 239-240.

64. *Ibid.*, p. 244.

65. Various similarities were highlighted concerning the leaders (23,13 – Ps 2,2); the messiah (22,67; 23,2 – Ps 2,2); king (23,2.3 – Ps 2,6); son of God (22,70 – Ps 2,7); and a mockery (23,11 – Ps 2,4), and in other verses in Lk 23 beyond the scope of our study.

66. *Resistance to the Carnivalization of Jesus: Scripture in the Lucan Passion Narrative*, in *Semeia* 69/70 (1995) 33-60, p. 34 (= *Text to Text Pours Forth Speech: Voices of Scripture in Luke-Acts* [Indiana Studies in Biblical Literature], Bloomington, IN, 1995 [revised], 42-60, p. 43): "Carnival is a representation of established values so absurd as to undermine established values. It creates an inverted world alongside the norm, inside out, top to bottom. The inverted world comes to expression particularly in mockery and the grotesque body. The corresponding literary idiom is the carnivalesque, and the process of transposing the phenomena of carnival into the language of literature is the carnivalization of literature".

67. *Ibid.*, p. 44 (= 51).

68. *Ibid.*: "When those who mock Jesus demand that he prophesy (22:64), they make an ironic analeptic reference to 18:32-33 where he had already prophesied precisely what his mockers are doing. Unwittingly, they are themselves fulfilling prophecy".

69. *Ibid.*, p. 45 (= 53).

"thought that the account of Jesus before Herod preserved a reminiscence of the Saturnalia but dismissed it as unhistorical"[70].

P. DOBLE (1996) considered the "literary and theological implications" of the Sanhedrin trial (22,66-71), but discussed it "on the basis of Luke-Acts itself"[71]. While in his dissertation he argued that "Markan priority seemed to make more sense than an alternative solution", he followed another methodology for the published version[72].

Attention continued to be given to the problems surrounding the composition of the Lukan passion narrative, as well as its theology. While scholars such as Brown attempted to explain differences through appeal to oral tradition, Fitzmyer considered the possibility of both oral and written traditions. Matera, on the other hand, maintained that Luke probably redacted Mk as his only source.
Newer methodologies, which eschewed the source question, became popular in certain circles.

A Synthesis of the Evidence for Lukan Redaction
I. The Source Question

Facing the difficult question of how Luke, approximately forty years after the events of the passion, may have had access to new and reliable information derived from sources, generally unavailable to the other evangelists, those scholars who regard the changes in Lk to reflect the redactional work and tendencies of the evangelist respond to issues raised by the proponents of the special source, in the following ways:

Change in order (transpositions): Luke rearranged the order to bring related material together; to simplify the Markan presentation; to provide a narrative logic.

Change of vocabulary: generally to improve the Markan style or to give preference to Atticisms or classical style. While advocates of the special source maintained one can distinguish between Luke and LQ, opponents disagree, stating Luke adeptly mimics sources and interweaves materials so intricately, that such discernment was beyond hope. The Jewish flavor of Lk was no greater than that of Mk and Mt and was accounted for by Septuagintal influence or simply by the nature of the events recounted.

Much disparity can be attributed to the difference between the times in which the Gospels were written.

Some changes may be due to homiletic or catechetical influence.

---

70. *Ibid.*, p. 35, n. 8 (= 44, n. 7); cf. P. WENDLAND, *Jesus als Saturnalien-Köning*, in *Hermes: Zeitschrift für classische Philologie* (1899) 33.

71. *The Paradox of Salvation. Luke's Theology of the Cross* (SNTS 87), Cambridge - New York - Melbourne, 1996, p. 202-205; regarding sources, p. 3, 11-12. Diss. Leeds, 1992 (dir. J.K. ELLIOTT).

72. *Ibid.*, p. 12, n. 14.

Omissions of Markan material, in some cases, were caused by carelessness in editing, an unfortunate result of Luke's zealous attempt to abbreviate Mk.

Omissions were likewise explained by Luke's misunderstanding of some events or ideas.

Luke omitted rather than included material similar to that already recorded.

Consideration of the needs and sensibilities of his Gentile readers also guided Luke's redactional decisions to omit certain material.

Luke chose not to include some Markan material in order to retain the traditional length of a book common to that historical period.

Out of apologetical interests, Luke revised the Markan presentation of the authorities, improving the image of the Romans, while increasing the responsibility and guilt attributed to the Jews for the passion and death of Jesus.

Additional material, such as Herod's trial (23,6-16), resulted from Luke's employment of traditional motifs borrowed from Ps 2 and applied to events in the passion. Luke formed the account in view of his apologetical interests. Since not much was known of the process of the legal proceedings, elements of Pilate's trial were imposed upon that of Herod. Both underscored the innocence of Jesus. The range of opinion extended to seeing this special material as a fiction created by Luke, to a composition comprising Markan elements and other traditional themes, to a recasting of the Markan Pilate episode where Jesus was declared innocent by a Jewish authority.

It is unnecessary to posit two such similar documents as Mk and the special source.

The proof that Luke knew the Markan trial was shown by the shifting of elements to the trial of Stephen (Acts 6,10-14).

Luke did not relate the passion narrative by assembling building blocks of materials from various sources, but so crafted Mk as to address the changing needs and the circumstances of his time and place. Luke was indeed a creative and original writer.

Such are the two schools of thought: is the Lukan version historically reliable, and thus perhaps more valuable than Mk? Or was it historically compromised by certain changes, or amended in accord with a view to the most probable historical course of events, further shaped by the conditions of the times and the needs of the community for which Luke wrote? The question is not whether Luke used Mk as one of his sources. The question, rather, is to what extent and in what manner has he done so.

II. Conclusions concerning the Phenomenon of Order
The Original Order

Proponents of a special source attributed to it the variations in the Lukan order vis-à-vis the Markan. Although it was occasionally conceded that the change may result from Luke's literary and redactional plan, the order as it stood in Lk was considered the more original. Such a sequence of events was considered the more historically probable since it stemmed from a written source which found its origin in the early disciples of Jesus. The reason most often given in support of this view was that Luke generally did not disturb the order of his sources. Another explanation contended since Jesus was arrested in the middle of the night, there was a period of waiting until the Sanhedrin could assemble on the following morning.

Results of Lukan Redaction of Mk

Luke's revision was an attempt to portray a more precise chronological order than Mk was able to provide. Luke resolved to relate the story in a unified, simpler fashion. Wernle counted seven Lukan transpositions, while Hawkins numbered them at twelve. In effect, Luke was seen as better organizing the Markan material. He gathered together elements that were materially related, as in the case of Peter's denial. This was the reason most often invoked for the transposition. Further, with a view to his intended Gentile readership, Luke rearranged the material to appeal to the Greek sense of rational order. Other scholars intimated that when Luke received information that lacked any temporal indications, he simply inserted the material in its most probable context. Some few scholars, while advocating Lukan redaction, left open the possibility that a special source was responsible for the changes.

Oral Influence or Harmonization

Infrequently, a minority suggested that the changes resulted from oral influence. Equally rare was the attempt, not to explain the differences, but simply to harmonize them.

III. Conclusion concerning αὐτόν

While the majority of scholars surveyed consider the pronominal confusion to have resulted from the transposition of the denial, mockery and Sanhedrin trial, at least one scholar viewed earlier occurrences as evidence that an insertion was made into a more original text.

IV. Conclusion concerning the MAs

Though several explanations were proposed as solution for the MAs, the one that most often recurred was that they result from Matthean influence. Matthean material was inserted into Lk, a likely reason being that copyists assimilated the texts. In recent years there has been increasing openness on the part of scholars for an exceptional solution of conjectural emendation in the case of the MA in 22,64 / Mt 26,68.

V. Conclusion concerning the Sanhedrin Trial and Judgment

Proponents of the special source maintained Luke was unaware of a preliminary trial on the same night as the arrest. Those who advocate the view of Lukan redaction of the Markan material maintained Luke consistently endeavored to simplify Mk and eliminated what was unclear to him, namely, the second Sanhedrin session. Through transposing, adapting and interpreting Mark's nocturnal trial, Luke offered a trial at break of day. A mediating position suggested that both oral (eyewitness testimony) and written sources accounted for Luke's independence at this point in his Gospel. Others attempted to resolve the difference simply by harmonizing all aspects of the trial. Whatever the various conclusions concerning the number of trials, there was general consensus on the part of scholars from both sides, that the Sanhedrin returned no formal judgment, owing to a lack of juridical power in capital criminal cases at the time of Roman occupation.

Part III

THE CONUNDRUM OF THE HEROD PERICOPE:
SOURCE-CRITICAL THEORIES AND AN EXEGESIS

CHAPTER TWELVE

SOURCE-CRITICAL THEORIES ON THE HEROD PERICOPE

Source criticism of the Herod pericope can be assigned to nine different categories. Some of these contain variations within them. In addition, an important aspect of the study of this passage is to consider its relationship to the apocryphal writing known as the Gospel of Peter (GP).

Despite a renewed and intensified debate, especially in the past two decades, over the relation of the canonical Gospels to the GP in general and the Herod episode in particular, the majority of scholars still held fast to the view that the GP was a later composition, relying in part on the canonical Gospels.

Additional material, such as Herod's trial (23,6-16), resulted from Luke's employment of traditional motifs borrowed from Ps 2 applied to events in the passion of Jesus. Luke formed the account in view of his apologetical interests. Since not much was known of the process of the legal proceedings, elements of Pilate's trial were imposed upon that of Herod, both of which underscored the innocence of Jesus. The range of opinion extended from seeing this special material as a fiction created by Luke, to a composition comprising Markan elements and other traditional themes to a recasting of the Markan Pilate episode where Jesus was declared innocent by a Jewish authority.

I. Continuous Source or Tradition[1]
P. Feine (1892), J. Weiss (1892), B. Weiss ([9]1901; 1907; 1908), G.H. Müller (1908), B.S. Easton (1910, 1926), B.H. Streeter (1911, 1924), W. Haupt (1913), W.W. Holdsworth (1913), A.M. Perry (1920), V. Taylor (1926), *G.W. Wade (1934)*[2], C.C. Torrey (1936), J.A. Findlay (1937), K.H. Rengstorf (1937, [10]1965), T.W. Manson (1938), E. Hirsch (1.6, 1941), J. De Zwaan (1941), W.L. Knox (1953), R. Koh (1953), L. Cerfaux (1957), C.C. Martindale (1957?), É. Trocmé (1957/1963/1971/1983), W. Grundmann (1963), E. Ruckstuhl (1963/1965; 5, 1986), A.F.J. Klijn (1965/1967), W. Barclay (1966), H. Hoehner (1968/1972/1992), L. Gaston (1970), G.H.P. Thompson (1972), F. Bovon (1974/1993), L. Morris (1974), J. Ernst (1977), R. Cassidy (1978), J. Jeremias (1980), J.B. Green (1985/1988), P. Richardson (1987/1996), E. Schweizer (1989/1991)

II. Separate Sources or Traditions
F. Farrar (2a, 1884, 1891)[3], *H. Burton (2a, 1896)*[4], T. Zahn (2, 1899), A. Wright (2a,

---

1. Names appearing in italics are those generally not previously treated in the book or I have provided additional information specific to the Herod pericope in this section.
2. According to Wade, L was reponsible for 23,2.4-16.22(partial v. 22) (*The Documents of the New Testament*, London, 1934, p. 316-318).
3. Though Farrar wrote next to nothing about the source question for Lk, in referring to Herod's trial, he proposed Luke seemed to have access to "special information about Herod's court" (*The Gospel according to St. Luke*, Cambridge Greek Testament for Schools and Colleges, Cambridge, 1891, p. 341 = *The Gospel according to St. Luke*, The Cambridge Bible for Schools and Colleges, 1884, p. 384). See also his comment on 8,3: "Manaen at Antioch was perhaps the

692 CHAPTER TWELVE

1900), L.J.M. Bebb (2a, 1901), A. Plummer (2a or d, 1901), W. Soltau (2a + 6b.d, 1901),
C. Weizsäcker (2, ²1901), *A. Deissmann (2a, 1903)*[5], *P. Girodon (2, 1903)*[6], A. Wright
(2a?, 1903), V. Rose (2a, 1904), *G. Salmon (2a, 1907)*[7], J.M.S. Baljon (2a, 1908), A.W.
Verrall (2a, 1909), *P. Batiffol (2a, 1910)*[8], F. Dibelius (2a, 1911), *A. Garvie (2a, 1911)*[9],
M. Meinertz (2a, 1912)[10], F. Spitta (2, 1912), *W.F. Burnside (2a, 1913)*[11], *R. Eaton (2a,
1916)*[12], J. Moffatt (2, 1918), *S.C. Carpenter (2a, 1919)*[13], *H. McLachlan (2a, 1920)*[14],

source of St Luke's special knowledge about the Herodian family" (1903, p. 212). These two
commentaries were authored by Farrar. The first was *The Gospel according to St. Luke*
(Cambridge Greek Testament for Schools and Colleges), Cambridge, 1884. The other, *The
Gospel according to St. Luke* (The Cambridge Bible for Schools and Colleges), Cambridge, 1891,
contained the ET of Dr. Scrivener's *Cambridge Paragraph Bible* and included minor changes in
spelling. Other than the biblical text, the notes are essentially the same.

4. Burton focused little on the source question except to say Luke was primarily influenced
by Paul and may have had some association with individuals in contact with Herod (*The Gospel
according to St. Luke*, New York, 1896, p. 4, 7). Chuza and Manaen were regarded as the
sources.

5. Deissmann, in commenting on the figure of Manaen (Acts 13,1) as a source of information
pertaining to Herod and his court, took issue with the customary interpretation of the term
σύντροφος (*Bibelstudien. Beiträge, zumeist aus den Papyri und Inschriften zur Geschichte der
Sprache des Schriftums Urchristentums*, Marburg, 1895, ᴿ1977, p. 178-181 = *Bible Studies*, tr.
A. GRIEVE, Edinburgh, ²1903, p. 310-312). The work also contained a papyrological evidence
of the term συνέχω (22,63) (ET, p. 160), as well as parallels in Philo, Josephus and Plutarch for
the term ἀναπέμπω (23,7; Acts 25,21) (ET, p. 229). Deissmann favored *companion in education*
to *foster brother*. Such an understanding enhanced the honor, not only for Manaen, but for the
Church at Antioch as well.

6. Girodon argued in favor of oral tradition for providing the Herod story (23,7-12), which
had contact with the Herodian court and believed the tradition to be historical (*Commentaire
critique et moral sur l'Évangile selon saint Luc*, Paris, 1903, p. 21, 517).

7. Though the account of Herod's trial was lacking in the other Synoptics, Salmon was
unwilling to dismiss it as unhistorical. Joanna, the wife of Herod's steward (8,3; 24,10) was seen
as the likely source of information (*The Human Element in the Gospels*, p. 513).

8. Batiffol held the opinion that Luke had access to special information regarding Herod.
Joanna was placed in Jerusalem during the events of the passion (24,10) (*Orpheus*, 1910 =
Credibility, 1912, p. 144-145).

9. In Garvie's commentary the position of Lukan dependence upon Mk was clearly espoused
(*The Gospel according to St. Luke* [Westminster NT], New York, 1911, p. 14-16). All of the
passages from 22,54–23,26, with the exception of the Herod episode (23,7-12), stemmed from
Mk, basically in the form we now possess (cf. p. 17). Garvie maintained even though in 23,13-25
there was verbal disagreement between Lk and the other Synoptics, still they all agreed in
substance (p. 354). Luke had access to and made use of a special source which contained both
narratives and teachings but he thoroughly worked over the material. Joanna was named as the
possible source for the Herod story (p. 23; cf. p. 12, 14).

10. Meinertz credited Manaean (Acts 13,1) as the source not only for Herod's trial of Jesus,
but also for the information in 13,31ff. (*Das Lukasevangelium*, in *Biblische Zietfragen* 3³, 2,
Münster, 1912, p. 17).

11. Burnside named Joanna as the possible informant for material concerning Herod, though
Luke himself may have had contact with the Herodian household (*The Gospel According to St.
Luke*, Cambridge, 1913, p. 250).

12. Eaton appeared to accept 23,5-12 (the Herod material) as historical, suggesting that Pilate

A.T. Robertson (2a, 1920)[15], *L. Ragg (2a, 1922)*[16], H. Balmforth (2a, 1930), *C. Lavergne (2a, 1932)*[17], M. Goguel (2b + 6b, 1933), L. Soubigou (2a, 1933), J. Chapman (1937), J. Vosté (2a, 1937), H.D.A. Major (2, 6b?, 1938), *C. Raeymaekers (2a, 1939)*[18], *W. Hillmann (2a, 1941)*[19], M. Albertz (2a, 1947), A. Metzinger (2a, 1948), T. Henshaw (2a, 1952), R. Ginns (2c, 1953), V.E. Harlow (2a, 1953, [R]1954), *A. Hastings (2, 1958)*[20], J.

sent Jesus to Herod either to unburden himself or to compliment Herod (*The Gospel according to Saint Luke with Introduction, Text and Notes*, London, 1916, p. 190). In his discussion of 8,3 Chuza was mentioned as having heard details about Jesus from John the Baptist and others, but Manean was regarded as Luke's source of information about the Herodian family (p. 62-63). However, Joanna was singled out as the possible source of information about this account (p. 191). Eaton interpreted the elegant robe as mocking the garment worn by Jews who had been exonerated of capital crimes. It was a sign to Pilate that Herod regarded Jesus as an innocent fool.

13. According to Carpenter Manaen and Joanna were seen as likely sources of information about Herod (*Christianity*, London, 1919, p. 147).

14. McLachlan, noting that the Herod trial "has frequently been treated as purely fictitious" had, in other sections of his work, stated his belief that Manaen was Luke's source of valuable information (*St. Luke*, p. 27; see also p. 96, 218). As an example of those who believed that the Herod story was fictitious McLachlan quoted from an article by Robinson Smith that the account of Herod's trial was "a very patchwork of appropriations from other incidents" (*St. Luke*, p. 27; see R. SMITH, *Fresh Light on the Synoptic Problem. Matthew a Lucan Source*, in *HJ* 10 [1911-12] 622). He rejected Verrall's arguments on the textual emendations on the grounds they were not convincing but concluded with mention of Burkitt's assertion that the account was historical.

15. Robertson contended Joanna the wife of Chuza might have been Luke's informant, not only about the Herod trial, but concerning Pilate's trial as well (*Luke the Historian in Light of Research*, Edinburgh - New York, 1920; Grand Rapids, MI, [R]1977, p. 75). He included numerous other oral sources including James, Manaen, Philip and his daughters from whom Luke might have obtained valuable and reliable information.

16. Following Burkitt, Ragg accepted the Herod episode (23,8-12) as historical coming either from Manaen or Joanna or even both (*St Luke with Introduction and Notes*, WC, London, 1922, p. 293; cf. p. xxi, li, 353). But in reaction to Harnack, Ragg contended it was impossible to determine how much special material stemmed from Philip and his daughters (p. xxi).

17. Oral tradition, particularly interviews with Joanna and Manaen, appeared to account for the Herod story in the view of Lavergne (*Évangile selon saint Luc*, EB, Paris, 1932, p. 10). Regarding Joanna see also his comments on 8,3 and 24,10 (p. 100, 258). The Herod pericope (23,6-16) was treated on p. 248-250. He was a frequent collaborator with Lagrange whose 1921 commentary greatly influenced this work (p. 12).

18. Raeymaekers considered Joanna the probable candidate for special information about Herod (*Het Evangelie van Lucas*, Turnhout, 1939, p. XX, 148; [2]1949, p. XXIV, 153).

19. Hillmann dismissed Dibelius's proposal as "eine reine und unbeweisbare Vermutung" favoring instead the view that Luke obtained information from two people named in his writings (Joanna in 8,3; Manaen in Acts 13,1) (*Aufbau und Deutung der synoptischen Leidensberichte*, Freiburg, 1941, p. 186, n. 29; esp. p. 172-256). He cited Meinertz who also accepted the historicity of the scene because of oral sources (cf. MEINERTZ, *Das Lukasevangelium*, p. 17). However, Hillmann's interpretation took on a more symbolic value when he stated 23,1-7.8-12.13-25 presented Christianity in relation to the Romans and the Jews (HILLMANN, *Aufbau*, p. 254-255). Bovon described Hillmann as "a forerunner of the disciples of the *Redaktionsgeschichtliche Schule*" (*Chroniques du côté de chez Luc*, in *RTP* 115, 1983, 175-189 = *Chronicles in Lucan Studies*, in *Luke the Theologian*, 1987, 409-418, p. 409).

20. Hastings accepted 23,4-12 as historical, a view he felt was further confirmed by Acts

Blinzler (2a, 1959, 1960), J.B. Tyson (L + Mk, 1959 or 2a, 1960), J. Schmid (2c, ⁴1960), X. Léon-Dufour (5, 1960), H.C. Snape (2, 1960), É. Osty (2a, 1961), J.L. Price (2a, 1961/1971), R. Devreesse (2b, 1962), G.B. Caird (2a, 1963), W. Barclay (2, 1966/1975), *F.F. Bruce (2a, 1966)*[21], E.E. Ellis (2a, 1966), *H. Melinsky (2a, 1966)*[22], *F. Rienecker (2a, 1966)*[23], C. Stuhlmueller (2a, 1968), *H. Troadec (2, 1968)*[24], R. Summers (2, 1972), C.H. Talbert (2, 1974), *W. Wilkinson (2, 1975)*[25], H. Hendrickx (2, 1977, ²1985), *S.*

4,23-28 (*Prophet and Witness in Jerusalem*, London, 1958, p. 44-45; esp. p. 42-49). In a slight variation, Hastings argued as "highly probable" that while the story originated with Joanna, it came to Luke through Manaen (p. 49). The suggestion the story stemmed from Joanna was adopted from STREETER, *On the Trial*, p. 48, n. 1. Hastings regarded the following material which dealt with Herod as forming a unity: 3,1; 8,3; 9,7-9; 13,1-3.31-33; 23,4-12 (p. 45, 48). Lk 3,19-20 has a Markan parallel in Mk 6,17ff.). In Hastings's opinion the apostles would have known little about what happened during the Herod trial, thus explaining the story's omission from the other Gospels. But some of the material in Lk dealing with Herod came from Mk, namely 9,7-9 which was a parallel of Mk 3,19-20 (HASTINGS, *Prophet*, p. 45, 48). Finally, the slaughter of the Jews (13,1-3) could explain the enmity between the two leaders (23,12), Pilate's reason for passing the case to Herod resulted from Pilate acknowledging Herod's jurisdiction in the matter, as well as his desire to get out of a "difficult case" and to cause ill feelings between Herod and the priests (p. 46).

21. Bruce seemed to accept the historicity of the account (23,6-12) (*Herod Antipas, Tetrarch of Galilee and Peraea*, in *ALUOS* 5 [1963-1965], Leiden, 1966, 6-23; esp. p. 15-17). In a more recent treatment he suggested 23,7 indicated Herod could have been resident in Jerusalem "temporarily" (*Render to Caesar*, in BAMMEL and MOULE, eds., *Jesus and the Politics of His Day*, Cambridge - London - New York, 1984, p. 250). Luke was described as "accurate" for referring to Herod as the tetrarch, rather than king as Mk and Mt did. Luke had "independent and fuller information about the Herod family" (p. 10; cf. p. 13). Joanna was mentioned as a possible source of that news, as was Manaen who was considered the more likely candidate. (Bruce did not take a position on the meaning of the term σύντροφος). He noted the episode was recounted in the Gospel and referred to in Acts 4,27. Although aware of Sherwin-White's position, Bruce conjectured Jesus was transferred to Herod out of courtesy, though he might have possessed special extradition rights. Bruce assumed the hostility between the two leaders arose from the episode recounted in Lk 13,1-5. He argued Pilate's declaration of Jesus' innocence was re-inforced by Herod's findings, but there was no reference in the text to support such a claim.

22. Melinsky haltingly suggested Joanna may have been the source of the Herod episode and seemed to have regarded it as historical (*Luke*, p. 101-102).

23. Rienecker held the view that Lukan redaction included the addition of the *Sondergut* story about Herod, which may rest upon tradition stemming from Manaen (*Das Evangelium des Lukas* [Wuppertaler Studienbibel, 4], Wuppertal, ²1966, p. 521). Cf. p. 4, where Rienecker designated Manaen as the possible source of information about Jesus' relationship with Herod, especially 23,7-12.

24. Troadec contended that in addition to Mk and Q, one could not exclude the possibilty that Luke had access to traditions from that area where John exercised a ministry (*Évangile selon saint Luc*, Tours, 1968, p. 15). For the Herod scene as for Acts 4,27, Luke utilized an independent source (p. 208). The transfer from Pilate to Herod was effected out of politeness, but also in order for Pilate to obtain much needed advice.

25. Wilkinson proposed that Luke collected his special material during his two year sojourn in Caesarea (*Good News In Luke*, Glasgow, p. 10, 11). Furthermore, Luke knew and used Mk

Kealy (2c, 1979)[26], E. Schweizer (2a, 1982), *W. Sydnor (2c, 1982)*[27], *J. Kodell (2c?, 1983)*[28], R.B. Larson (2, 1983), *J.T. Nielsen (2a, 1983)*[29], P. Rolland (2a, 1984), *L. Sabourin (2, 1984)*[30], F.B. Craddock (2a? + 6, 1988, 1990), L.T. Johnson (2a + 6, 1991), R.H. Stein (1992), D.L. Bock (2a, 1994, 1996)

(p. 144). The Herod story possibly stemmed from Joanna (p. 146). Wilkinson noted the mockeries were carried out by Jewish soldiers (22,65; 23,11) which squared with Luke's apologetic directed toward Gentiles showing that Christianity was a world religion (p. 146-147; cf. p. 11). Luke employed a written Aramaic *Grundlage* "in every part of the Gospel". Thus, Lk exhibited traits of being a translation (p. lix; cf. WELLHAUSEN, *Das Evangelium Lucae*, p. 11. See also WELLHAUSEN, *Einleitung*, p. 79).

26. Kealy noted the commonality between Lk and Mk was "undeniable" (*Luke's Gospel Today*, Denville, NJ, p. 70-71). Author's name, John (p. 3) = Sean (p. 4). Of the similarities with Mt, three explanations were possible: a common source, that Mt depended upon Lk was unlikely, and that if Luke used Mt, his methodology varied from his use of Mk. The special material, including the Herod pericope, was believed to have derived from many sources, both oral and written, including the OT, as well as oral traditions supplied by Manaen and Joanna, who were singled out as possible informants (p. 73). Kealy qualified this later by suggesting that Luke "possibly" possessed special sources for information about Herod (p. 428). He rejected Dibelius's suggestion, noting the difference of depictions in the Gospel and Acts (p. 428). In Kealy's opinion, the scene reflected a Semitic style as well as similarity to Philo, who also mentioned Pilate and Herod. Like Vanhoye, Kealy viewed the Lukan portrayal of Herod as indicative of those who were "not seeking to really see Jesus" (p. 429). The silence motif was likened to Is 53,7 and Mk 14,61. The robe, white and reminiscent of that used by Jewish kings, was also compared to the robe of Solomon as described by Josephus.

27. Sydnor maintained Luke relied upon Mk, Q, and L which was comprised of "oral and written materials and traditions" containing miscellaneous information lacking any reference to chronology (*Jesus according to Luke*, New York, p. 4).

28. Kodell affirmed that Luke employed Mk as a source, but he left rather indistinct his assessment of the source question for the Herod pericope, stating only with reference to the whole Gospel that Luke used "other written and oral sources" in addition to Mk (*The Gospel according to Luke*, Collegeville Bible Commentary, 3, Collegeville, MN, 1983, p. 7 = *Luke*, in D. BERGANT and R.J. KARRIS, [eds.], *The Collegeville Bible Commentary*, Collegeville, MN, 1989, p. 936). The context revealed Luke was following the Markan structure, though Luke made additions to highlight the innocence of Jesus. The reconciliation between Pilate and Herod was "later seen as the fulfillment of prophecy (Ps 2:1-2; Acts 4:25-28)", thus seemingly pointing to acceptance of Dibelius's point of view for at least this detail (p. 110 = 976, 977).

29. Nielsen queried whether Luke may have obtained the information about Herod's trial from Joanna, and thus most likely regarded it as historical (*Het Evangelie naar Lucas* [PNT, 3], 2 vols., Nijkerk, Vol. 2, p. 220, esp. p. 220-222; see also his comment on 8,3 in Vol. 1, p. 237).

30. Sabourin reaffirmed his belief in Markan priority despite the recent tempest (*The Gospel according to St Luke*, Bombay, p. v = *L'évangile de Luc*, Rome, 1985). He rightly rejected Goulder's contention that Luke knew Mt (p. 12). The term "many" may simply refer to others, and did not *de facto* indicate a large number (p. 46). Sabourin favored the historical basis of the Herod scene, with Manaen being the possible informant. In Sabourin's view, Hoehner defended the historicity (p. 380). But in discussing Jesus' silence it was suggested not only was this historical, but that just as in Is 53,7 and Ps 39,10, Jesus underwent his suffering with dignity. Although Sabourin acknowledged certain similarities between the mockeries by Pilate's and Herod's soldiers he dismissed any dependence, saying the accounts "were probably unconnected literarily and historically".

III. UNSPECIFIED SOURCES INDEPENDENT OF MK
H.J. Holtzmann (1863), C. Weizsäcker, (1864, ²1901), *K. Bornhäuser (1929; 1921)*[31], B.
Reicke (1963)[32], G. Schneider (1973; 1977, ²1984?), J. Delorme (1981), P.-G. Müller
(1984/²1986)

IV. UNSPECIFIED SOURCE(S) IN CONJUNCTION WITH MK
H.J. Holtzmann (1886/1892), A. Wautier d'Aygalliers (1920), *B. Rigaux (1970)*[33], W.
Schmithals (1980)

V. HISTORICAL ACCOUNT WITH NO REFERENCE TO NATURE AND EXTENT OF SOURCE
A.B. Bruce (1897/²1907), J. Hawkins (1903), *A. Merx (1905)*[34], F.C. Burkitt (1907), A.

31. Bornhäuser appeared to accept the episode as historical, though he did not advance any
information concerning the exact nature of the source (*Die Beteiligung des Herodes am Prozesse
Jesu*, in *NKZ* 40 [1929] 714-718). "Es ist aber eine recht ernst zu nehmende Frage, ob Lukas
innherhalb des Evangeliums den Text selbständig formuliert hat, oder ihn bereits formuliert
vorfindet und einfach übernimmt. Im letzteren Falle wäre zu sagen, dass man an das
palästinensische Griechisch nicht die strengen Anforderungen stellen darf, wie an das klassische"
(716). See also his *Zeiten und Stunden in der Leidensgeschichte und Auferstehungsgeschichte*
[BFCT, 26/4], Gütersloh, 1921, esp. p. 35. To the argument that the other Gospels were silent
on Herod's supposed participation in the process, Bornhäuser responded that Luke, more than the
other evangelists, had an intense interest in Herod. In agreement with Dibelius, though without
referring to him, Bornhäuser contended that there was "einem bestimmten Zusammenhang"
between Lk 23,6ff. and Acts 4,27 (*Die Beteiligung*, p. 715). Acts related "ausdrücklich" what
Lk 23 narrated "näher" (p. 718).
    For the vesting, Bornhäuser adopted Luther's translation that Herod vested Jesus in a white
garment, while taking exception to the "rationalistiche Exegese" which saw in the vesture a sign
of Jesus' innocence (p. 718). Bornhäuser maintained Herod enrobed Jesus in his own
"Staatsgewand", which Jesus continued to wear when Herod personally returned Jesus to Pilate.
This personal accompaniment not only allowed the friendship between the two leaders to develop,
but was a testimony of respect (p. 717). However, such collaboration did not diminish in any way
Pilate's guilt. If anything, Herod was shown to be just as guilty and just as responsible as Pilate
for the crucifixion of Jesus (p. 718).
    32. Reicke contended Luke had numerous traditions from which to draw (*Lukasevangeliet*,
Stockholm, 1962 = *The Gospel of Luke*, tr. R. Mackenzie, Richmond, VA, 1963, p. 11). From
these he took the Herod trial (23,6-16) which contained a noticeable "Jewish Christian style and
Palestinian orientation" (p. 31). "It is clear that Luke has included this material without
Hellenizing it to suit the stylistic ideal which he expressed in the prologue. The simplest
explanation is that he had a special reverence for these traditions, and included them in
unamended form, since these traditions were Jewish Christian and went back to the early church
in which Luke, because of his conception of redemptive history, had a vigorous interest".
    33. Rigaux argued that in the passion Luke employed certain sources, just as in the special
material he made use of "sources diverses" (*Témoignage de l'évangile de Luc*, Paris, p. 22).
Concerning Joanna's name in 8,3 Rigaux said only the women's names "ont été conservés avec
vénération dans l'Église" (p. 178). According to Rigaux only a small minority of scholars rejected
Markan dependence (p. 61). And although Luke appeared quite independent of Mk in the passion,
this in no way suggested Luke did not use Mk (p. 69). Rigaux rejected Proto-Lk in favor of
Lukan dependence upon Mk with the addition of material from Q (p. 76).
    34. For material in 23,1-7, the charge of urging the people to refuse to pay taxes to Caesar

Harnack (1911), M.-J. Lagrange (1921), E. Meyer (1924), C.J.G. Montefiore (1927), C. *Gore (1928)*[35], W. Manson (1930), P. Dausch (1932), P. Benoit (1940, 1966), T. *Innitzer (1948)*[36], *A.M. Hunter (1950)*[37], N. Geldenhuys (5 or 2c?, 1951), W. Arndt (1956), J.-S. Javet (1957), M. Black (1959), E.M. Dalmau (1963?), *H.H. Hobbs (1966)*[38], A. Stöger (1966), *F. Stagg (1967)*[39], E. Dąbrowski (1968), I.H. Marshall (1970a, 1978), L. Morris (1974, [2]1988), D. Tiede (1980?), *G. Lohfink (1981)*[40], J.M. Ford (1984), J.A. Fitzmyer (5 or 2c.d, 1985), *L. Foster (1986?)*[41], *G. Gander (1986)*[42], B.G. McGing (1986; 3,

was clearly a lie in light of Lk 20,25, according to Merx (*Die Evangelien des Markus und Lukas*, p. 480). The reason for the transfer of Jesus arose from Pilate's sole interest in the political ramifications, whereas matters of heresy were subject to the jurisdiction of the Sanhedrin. Herod, who was present for Passover being a political official and a Jew, was able to investigate both the political and religious dimensions of the charges (p. 481-482).

Merx considered the authenticity of 23,10-12 in depth for three reasons: 1) the contradiction that the high priest and scribes led Jesus to Herod and were present again when Jesus returned from Herod; 2) the accurate presentation of the mockery involved the Jews and not the Roman soldiers for the Centurion would not have allowed such misbehavior. Luke transferred v. 36 to an earlier point near the crucifixion; and 3) the threefold form of v. 15 suggested that 23,10-12 were inserted as a unit (p. 484-485). Merx concluded: "Wir haben bisher in Cap XXIII die Tendenz zur Änderung in Vs. 2, 5, 6 syr. und den Einschub Vs. 10-12 allgemein ausser Syrsin, so wie die Überarbeitung von Vs. 15, die wegen des Einschubs vorgenommen ist, kennen gelernt, aber auch den in der verschiedensten Weise geprüften Syrsin als ursprünglich schätzen gelernt, wir werden ihm daher bei der vergleichenden Betrachtung der Darstellung des Prozesses zu folgen nicht umhin können" (p. 487).

35. *The Gospel According to St. Luke*, London - New York, p. 237; cf. p. 208.

36. Innitzer accepted the Herod episode as historical on the grounds that Herod came to Jerusalem for Passover (*Kommentar*, [4]1948, p. 202). Pilate remanded Jesus to him since he was tetrarch of Galilee. But Pilate also gained some time in delaying a painful duty. Further, he sought to improve their relationship by extending a courtesy to Herod.

37. Hunter agreed with Streeter that Pilate's sending Jesus to Herod "is good history" (*The Work*, p. 119; see STREETER, *On the Trial*, p. 229-231.

38. Hobbs claimed the Lukan Prologue referred to both oral and written witnesses (*An Exposition of the Gospel of Luke*, Grand Rapids, MI, p. 18; esp. p. 18-20, 326-328). Although he made no clear claim concerning the Herod episode, it seemed likely that Hobbs accepted it as historical, insofar as he regarded the transfer of Jesus to be the result of a legal loophole, when Pilate discovered that Jesus was under Herod's jurisdiction (p. 326). The theological import of the passage, in light of the last verse, was that Jesus reconciles enemies (p. 328).

39. Stagg's position was very similar to that of Hobbs, interpreting the Prologue to mean both oral and written sources (*Studies in Luke's Gospel* 4, Nashville, TN, p. 5; esp. p. 132-134). Stagg, too, seemed to accept the historicity of the account, because Herod would have been in Jerusalem for Passover. The purpose of the transfer was twofold: to "flatter" Herod and to allow Pilate to rid himself of a difficult situation. The pressure of the Sanhedrin was also taken into consideration (p. 133).

40. Lohfink accepted the historicity of the Herod story despite its absence from the other Gospels (*Der letzte Tag Jesu*, Freiburg = *The Last Day of Jesus*, tr. S. ATTANASIO, Notre Dame, IN, 1984, p. 44). This conclusion recommended itself since in previous parts of the Gospel and Acts, Luke provided significant information about Herod.

41. Foster appeared to accept the Herod episode as historical (*Luke*, Cincinnati, OH, p. 277; cf. p. 269). He dismissed the Two-Source theory contending that neither this nor two other source

1991), *E.H. Kiehl (1990)*[43], *F. Millar (1990)*[44], *D.C. Braund (1992)*[45], D.L. Bock
(1994), R.A. Culpepper (1995), A.J. Saldarini (1997?)

VI. LUKAN COMPOSITION: A) Based on traditional materials, B) Lukan redaction of Mk,
C) Arising from Ps 2, D) influenced by Paul's experience recounted in Acts, E) Using other
materials (Derrett)
P. Wernle (1899), A. Jülicher (1904), J. Wellhausen (1904), F. Nicolardot (6a.d, 1908),
V.H. Stanton (1909), M. Dibelius (1915), R.W. Husband (1916?), A. Loisy (1, 1908; 6b,
1924/1936), E. Klostermann (6c, 1919), R. Bultmann (6c, 1921), J.M. Creed (6c, 1930),
H. Lietzmann (6c, 1931), M. Goguel (6a, 1932; 4, 1933), *C. Guignebert (6a.b, 1933)*[46],

theories "can be confidently established" (p. 332).
    42. Gander regarded the Herod scene as historically authentic (*L'Évangile pour les étrangers
du monde. Commentaire de l'Évangile selon Luc*, Lausanne, p. 983). What was more, he
specified the time and place as Friday between 7 and 7:30 a.m. in the palace of the Hasmoneans.
Conversely, its absence from the other Gospels "ne signifie pas ipso facto l'inauthenticité". He
further explained: "Si les autres évangelistes ne la relatent point, c'est que cela charge le judaïsme
et qu'ils sont judéochrétiens".
    43. Kiehl accepted the account as historical (*The Passion of Our Lord*, Grand Rapids, MI,
p. 107). As for the reason for the transfer, he listed Sherwin-White's proposal that the extradition
rights of Herod the Great may have been inherited by Antipas, and another view that Pilate was
courting Herod's favor. But Kiehl took no position on the matter.
    44. Millar reasoned that the Herod pericope (23,5-12) was authentic because it was probable
that Herod was in Jerusalem (*Reflections on the Trial of Jesus*, in P.R. DAVIES and R.T. WHITE,
eds., *A Tribute to Geza Vermes. Essays on Jewish and Christian Literature and History* [JSOT
SS, 100], FS G. VERMES, Sheffield, p. 355-381). This account in Lk and its reiteration in Acts
4,24-28 indicated to Millar Luke exercised great liberty in using available sources, though earlier
in the article he stated he took no position on the question of sources. His final argument, that
"its inauthenticity cannot be demonstrated", was a bit of circular reasoning. The lack of proof for
one position does not automatically prove the case for another (p. 368-369).
    45. Apparently accepting the Herod story (23,6-12) as historical, Braund proposed that since
Herod Antipas "was ruler of Jesus' home province of Galilee, [he] was given an opportunity to
question and ridicule Jesus during his trial before Pilate" (*Herod Antipas*, in *ABD* 3, p. 160; see
also his article, *Four Notes on the Herods*, in *Classical Quarterly* 33 [1983] 239-242). Verse 23,7
was cited in reference to Herod's attendance at religious feasts in Jerusalem.
    46. One of the clearest and most articulate early proponents of the Herod pericope as a Lukan
composition was Guignebert, who considered it "a piece of pure hagiography" (*Jésus*, Coll.
l'Évolution de l'Humanité, 29, Paris = *Jesus*, tr. S.H. HOOKE, London, 1935, p. 467). Its
historicity was doubted on the grounds it was highly unlikely that Pilate would have renounced
his power in such a manner. Further, the law required the crime be tried by the official of the
area where the action took place. Finally, such a transfer would have seriously undermined
Pilate's power. The similarity of the Herod scene and Acts 4,27 was credited to the fact that they
"probably" stemmed from the same author.
    Guignebert took account of the similarities of the Herod episode with the GP and Mk.
Concerning the apocryphal gospel, he asserted a legend detailing Herod's involvement was the
cause which eventually cast the entire burden of responsibility upon Herod (p. 467-468). The
Herod story was similar to the Sanhedrin account and worked to achieve the same end. "This is
proved by the fact that Luke omits the trial: Herod represents for him the Jewish authorities as
did the Sanhedrin for Mark. It may have been fear of flatly contradicting the Marcan account that

J. Finegan (6b.c, 1934), F. Hauck (6c? or 2, 1934), *E. Bickermann (6c, 1935)*[47], R. *Morgenthaler (1949)*[48], S. McL. Gilmour (2, 1948; 6b.c, 1952), W. Bundy (1955?), A. Leaney (6 or 2a, 1958), P. Winter (post editorial, 1955; 6 or post Lucan redactor, 1961/²1974), Γ. Beare (1962), G.W.H. Lampe (5 or 6c, 1962), J.A. Bailey (1965), *G. Rau (6a, 1965)*[49], E.J. Tinsley (1965), E. Haenchen (1966?), *J. Dupont (6c?, 1967/1979/1984)*[50], S.F. Brandon (6 or 6c or 2a, 1968), *T. Holtz (6a.c, 1968)*[51], J.

restrained him from going as far as the *Gospel of Peter*" (p. 468).

47. Bickermann appraised the unanimous opinion of critics that the Herod scene was "une pure invention" arising from Ps 2 (*Utilitas crucis. Observations sur les récits du procès de Jésus dans les Évangiles canoniques*, in *RHR* 112 [1935] 204 = *Studies in Jewish and Christian History*, pt. 3, Lein, 1986, p. 108). Loisy was cited as a minority, opposing view that the episode derived from a written, though inauthentic source. Bickermann contended that because Jesus was born in Bethlehem he was not a subject of Herod. Bickermann regarded Herod as a delegate of Pilate in this case (p. 206 = 110). The parallel with Paul before Felix (Acts 23–24) was also noted. The scene revealed nothing as part of a provincial procedure except that it displayed Pilate's deference toward Herod (23,12) (p. 208 = 111).

48. Morgenthaler, in an analysis of Luke's double sections, such as two mistreatments (22,63-65 and 23,11) as well as two judges (23,1-25), viewed the dual mockeries at least, as indicative of Luke's compositional technique (*Die lukanische Geschichtsschreibung al Zeugnis* [AbhTANT, 14-15], 2 vols. Vol 1: *Gehalt*. Vol. 2. *Gestalt*, Zürich, 1949, Diss. Bern, 1945 [dir. D.W. MICHAELIS], Vol. 1, p. 98; see further p. 116). See also p. 133, where Luke was credited with the "grössere architektonische Einheiten". Later, Morgenthaler seemed to back away from this statement, when in his discussion of Dt 19,15 he claimed the two part architectonic structure "ist nichts anderes als der formale Ausdruck des einmütigen Willens der ganzen ersten Christenheit und nicht zuletzt des Lk. selber, der Umwelt Zeugnis abzulegen von den Ereignissen um Jesus von Nazareth" (Vol. 2, p. 8). Morgenthaler rightly pointed to parallels between Jesus and Paul in Acts. While his suggestion that Herod's imprisonment of John the Baptist (3,20) could parallel Herod's trial of Jesus (23,6-12) in some manner, Morgenthaler was more than stretching the idea when he attempted to press similarities between John the Baptist's advice to soldiers (3,14) and the mistreatment of Jesus by Herod and his coterie (Vol. 1, p. 167).

Morgenthaler saw yet another parallel, though distinct in presentation, in the Jerusalem scene: "Pilatus und Herodes werden Freunde durch die gemeinsame Schuld an der Verurteilung des unschuldigen Christus. 23,1-25" and "Pilatus und Herodes haben sich gemeinsam gegen den Christus erhoben. Acts 4,27" (Vol. 1, p. 181).

49. Rau conjectured that Luke may have had individual traditions in addition to Mk, but did not have a continuous independent source (*Das Volk in der Passionsgeschichte des Lukas. Eine Konjektur zu Lk 23,13*, in *ZNW* 56 [1965] 50). R.S. Ascough dismissed Rau's suggestion due to lack of "manuscript support" (*Rejection*, in *Bib* 74 [1993] 354). Rau supported the view that the Lukan passion narrative revealed the tendency to place the responsibility of the death of Jesus on the Jews while exonerating Pilate and the Romans (RAU, *Das Volk*, p. 42). To explain the changes in the people, who were at times portrayed as sympathetic to Jesus, at other times direly opposed, Rau observed recourse was sometimes made to a special passion source. But the intrusion of the people and the intensification of the motif of the people, in contrast to the leaders, argued against such a supposition (p. 47). The Pilate scene constituted for Rau the middle point, not some "erratischer Block" for it revealed that Jesus was viewed by the people as a powerful prophet (p. 49-50). The leaders were thus made responsible for Jesus' crucifixion and death. Transpositions, as well as omissions, can be accounted for by the Lukan motif of the people in relation to the theme of the guilt for the death of Jesus.

50. Dupont noted that Luke alone alluded to 23,6-16 by means of Acts 4,25-27 (*Études sur*

Reumann (6 or 1, 1968)[52], *J. Riedl (6b, 1968)*[53], K.H. Rengstorf (6a, [14]1969), H. Van

les Actes des Apôtres [LD, 45], Paris, 1967, p. 297, n. 41). The prayer in Acts was cited as an example of primitive christological exegesis in seeing the persecution of Jesus in Ps 2 (p. 320). Later (1979), Dupont recognized similarities of early Christian interpretation with that found at Qumran (*The Salvation of the Gentiles. Essays on the Acts of the Apostles*, tr. J.R. KEATING, New York, 1979, p. 119, 120). He maintained (1984) that the apostles saw a reflection of Jesus' persecution in Ps 2, but not their own. As regards the source, he lightly touched on the matter in suggesting that Acts 4,25.27.30 were based upon a tradition which reflected early Christian theology containing an echo of the christology of the Servant of God (*Nouvelles études sur les Actes des Apôtres* [LD, 118], Paris, 1984, p. 94).

51. Holtz sided with Dibelius that Ps 2,1f. helped to shape the development and form of the christological meaning of the scene (*Untersuchungen über die alttestamentlichen Zitate bei Lukas*, in TU 104, Berlin, p. 52). Luke employed it later in Acts 4,25f. Agreeing with Haenchen that although the meaning may have derived from early Christian tradition, Holtz asserted that the form stemmed from Luke himself.

52. Reumann conjectured that the Herod material in Lk derived either from Luke's own hand or from the L source, but noted that the Herod episode was compatible with the thematic also contained in Acts that Christianity was not politically threatening (*Jesus in the Church's Gospels: Modern Scholarship and the Earliest Sources*, Philadelphia, PA, p. 73). He further pointed out parallels with Pilate. "A final decision [of source of origin] depends in part on how one evaluates the L source and whether one thinks there was enough time during the early morning hours to accomodate the hearing before Antipas" (p. 74).

The transfer of Jesus to Herod was prompted by Pilate's twofold purpose of showing kindness to Herod by helping him to fulfill a longstanding desire and for Pilate to divest himself of a bothersome problem. But Reumann credited Herod with being sufficiently astute "not to do Pilate's 'hatchet work'".

Reumann did not consider the perspective in the Gospel inconsistent with that found in Acts 4,25-28. On the contrary, the mockery by the Herodian soldiers (23,11) fell in line with the fulfillment of Ps 2 in Acts (p. 73). He contended, moreover, that 23,11 was a substitution for the second mockery by the Roman soldiers (p. 343). Sherwin-White earlier adopted this same view. Cf. A.N. SHERWIN-WHITE, *The Trial of Christ*, in D.E. NINEHAM (ed.), *Historicity and Chronology in the New Testament* (Theological Collections, 6), London, 1965, p. 114. This essay was a resumé of his book, *Society and Roman Law in the New Testament* (p. 97, n. 1).

53. Riedl maintained Luke substantially followed the Markan *Vorlage* and that Luke formed the account of Pilate's trial as "einer zusammenhängenden Erzählung", into which Herod's trial was inserted (*Die evangelische Leidensgeschichte und ihre theologische Aussage*, in BLtg 41 [1968] 102; cf. p. 76). Verse 23,13 served as a new introduction. By omitting the Markan mockery scene, Luke allowed the perception that the Jews led Jesus to the crucifixion (23,26a). Describing the piece as a unified Lukan composition, Riedl observed how Luke changed from the Markan report in three areas: 1) Pilate was portrayed as a defender of Jesus' innocence; 2) Pilate allowed the Jews to carry out the execution; and 3) Pilate was exonerated while the Jews were further implicated. The moment of the blaming of the Jews was more subtle. The scene, while offering nothing concrete other than the introduction (23,6-8) and the conclusion (23,12), consisted in three known motifs, presumably understood from Mk: 1) Jesus' silence; 2) the accusations of the Jewish religious leadership; and 3) the mockery by Herod and his soldiers. Adopting the view that this scene fulfilled the requirement of Dt 19,15, Riedl explained the function as providing a second witness to the innocence of Jesus who was not a political threat (p. 103, n. 243). Riedl, obviously swayed by Dibelius as well as by Grundmann's concept of martyrdom, held that the enemies (for Herod, cf. Lk 13,31 and Acts 4,27) became witnesses to

der Kwaak (6a.b.c., 1969), W.R. Wilson (6, "probably", 1970), W. Baird (6c, 1971), M.-É. Boismard (6b, 1972; with A. Lamouille: 3, 8, 1990), F.W. Danker (6a.b, 1972/1988), V. Taylor (6a, 1972), A. Denaux (6c, 1973)[54], J. Drury (6b.c.e, 1973; 6c, 1976)[55], G.S. Sloyan (1973), D. Dormeyer (6b, 1974)[56], C.H. Talbert (6d, 1974), A.J. Mattill (6a[oral].d + 2a, 1975)[57], W. Radl (6c, 1975; 6, 1988), P. Walaskay (6a.b.d, 1975), H. Klein (6a.b.c, 1976), R. Pesch (6b?, 1977/R. Pesch and R. Kratz (9, 1980), G. Schneider (6a.b.c, 1977-1988), A. Büchele (6b, 1978)[58], W. Kurz (6d, 1978), K. Müller (6b, 1979),

Jesus' innocence.

54. Denaux seemed to favor the view, along the lines of Dibelius, that the Herod episode was "une composition rédactionnelle" (L'hypocrisie des pharisiens et le dessein de Dieu. Analyse de Lc., XIII, 31-33, in F. NEIRYNCK, ed., L'Évangile de Luc [BETL, 32], Gembloux, p. 264, n. 57 = ²1989, p. 174, n. 57). Following Conzelmann and Ellis, Denaux regarded the primary purpose of the account as providing an additional witness to the innocence of Jesus.

55. In his commentary Drury subscribed to the view that Luke used both Mk and Mt (The Gospel of Luke, J.B. Phillips NT Commentaries, New York, 1973, p. 12, n. 1). The "many" referred to in the Prologue indicated "Luke did not have direct access to the facts". Drury detected a type of concentric pattern as Corbin (1978), and considered the section 23,1-25 a free composition of Luke, guided by Mk. An argument against the historicity of the Herod scene was its absence from the other Gospels (p. 206). Further, since the portrayal of Pilate did not square with the other Gospels, Drury was of the opinion that the section was inspired by Ps 2, Mk 15,16ff. (transferring the mockery to Herod's soldiers), and Eph 2,11-18 which emphasized the reconciliation of Jew and Gentile. The attribution of responsibility to the Jews reflected Luke's sentiment that "the Christ came to his own and they rejected him".

In his later work, Tradition and Design in Luke's Gospel, Drury maintained the story was a composite involving reminiscences from Mk as well as Luke's own observations about Herod (1976, p. 16-17; see also p. 95). Drury observed that the Herod scene (23,8-12) was composed from elements taken from Mk combined with some of Luke's own contributions, the purpose being to show that Gentiles and Jews were reconciled through Christ. "The passage brings to mind that curious addition which Luke made to Mark's passion narrative, the trial before Herod at Luke 23,8-12. Source-wise it consists of jumbled reminiscences of Mark's trials before the Sanhedrin and before Pilate, and of the mockery by Pilate's soldiers (Lk 23,9-11), sandwiched between Luke's observations that Herod had long wished to see Jesus and that having seen him 'Herod and Pilate became friends with each other that very day: for before they were at enmity between themselves'. Judicially the incident is inconclusive and from the point of view of narrative it is a detour. Its thrust and point is in the last sentence. The Jewish ruler is reconciled to the gentile on the very day of the shedding of Christ's blood" (p. 16-17).

56. Dormeyer considered Luke as having redacted Mk in the Herod pericope. He regarded 23,9.10 as a redactional adaptation of Mk 15,2-5 (Die Passion Jesu als Verhaltensmodell. Literarische und theologische Analyse der Traditions- und Redaktionsgeschichte der Markuspassion [NTAbh, 11], Münster, 1974, p. 178. Diss. Münster, 1972 [dir. J. GNILKA]).

57. Mattill accepted the Herod pericope as a story composed by Luke (The Jesus-Paul Parallels and the Purpose of Luke-Acts: H.H. Evans Reconsidered, in NT 17 [1975] 39-40). The evangelist was quite familiar with Paul's experience of the trial before Herod and the parallels between Jesus and Paul were numerous here. The evangelist was also cognizant that the community understood Ps 2,1-2 as referring to Herod and Pilate (pace Dibelius). Yet, Mattill also supported the view that Luke had access to oral sources (p. 40).

58. Büchele regarded the Herod story, part of the Lukan Sondergut (so also 23,2.4.5 (Der Tod Jesu, p. 32, n. 54). Cf. p. 29, n. 26, where he maintained no special Lukan source need be postulated for vv. 4.5, as building on motifs drawn from Mk, though placed in new contexts (p.

E. Buck (6a.b.c, 1980), M. Chico Cano (6a.b, 1980), F.G. Untergassmair (6b, 1980; 1996), B.E. Beck (6a.b, 1981), *O.C. Edwards (6b?, 1981)*[59], J.-P. Lémonon (6a.b, 1981), *J.D.M. Derrett (6e, 1982)*[60], E. Schweizer (6a oral, 1982), *A. Weiser (6a 1982-83)*[61], D.J. Moo (6a + 2, 1983), R.F. O'Toole (2 or 3 or 6b, 1984; 6, 1993), *J. Neyrey (6b.c, 1985)*[62], M.L. Soards (6a.b, 1985, 1987), W. Schmithals (1985 not specifically about

32; cf. p. 36, n. 80). These Markan motifs included the silence motif (Mk 15,3f.), the mockery scene (Mk 15,16-20a), and the charges by the Sanhedrin and the high priests (p. 32, n. 56; see further on the silence motif, p. 64). Elements of redaction typical of Luke included the doubling of sentences, scenes and sections (p. 37, n. 93; cf. MORGENTHALER, *Die lukanische Geschichts- schreibung*, 1949). Among these were doubled sentences (23,4.14.15.22), and double sections of judges (23,1-23; 23,6-12) and the mistreatment (22,63-65; 23,11). Büchele raised the possibility that, out of concern for Rome, Luke redacted the mockery by the Roman soldiers to a mistreatment by Jewish soldiers (p. 39, n. 107).

Büchele dismissed the source question as unimportant for his thematic treatment, opting instead to examine the story as it currently exists in Lk (p. 33, n. 60; cf. p. 29, n. 26). Nevertheless, his considered opinion on the use of word statistics to determine sources was that they do not as a rule lead to "eine ausreichende Sicherheit" (p. 29, n. 26). Büchele referred readers who were interested in the source question to NEIRYNCK, *The Argument from Order and St. Luke's Transpositions*, as well as HAENCHEN, *Historie und Verkündigung bei Markus und Lukas*, in G. BRAUMANN (ed.), *Das Lukas-Evangelium. Die redaktionsgeschichtliche und kompositions- geschichtliche Forschung* (WdF, 280), Darmstadt, 1974, 287-316, who reached similar conclusions. The purpose of the pericope was threefold: 1) to show that Jesus was not a political threat, 2) that he was innocent, and 3) that he was the suffering just one (BÜCHELE, *Der Tod Jesu*, p. 33). I am grateful he made a copy of his book available to me.

59. Edwards rejected Dibelius's suggestion that the scene arose from Ps 2 for two reasons: the rulers did not plot against Jesus and Luke offered no evidence that he was thinking of this passage (*Luke's Story of Jesus*, Philadelphia, PA, p. 90-91). Neither was Edwards impressed by the proposal that the pericope satisfied the requirement for the "testimony of three witnesses", presumably a reference to the requirement of Dt 19,15. Luke's intention, in his view, appeared to be transferring the mockery from the Roman to the Jewish soldiers.

60. Derrett found some similarities between the Daniel-haggadah and the trial of Jesus before Herod (*Daniel*, in *DownR* 100, 1982, 62-68; esp. p. 66-67 = *StNT* 4, 132-138). Herod consulted Jesus and Derrett saw in this the same term describing the consultation of an oracle. Both Jesus and Daniel were vigorously accused (Dan 6,5 LXX; cf. Lk 23,10), both maintained silence during their trials. Fitzmyer was right in easily dismissing this suggestion in a few lines (FITZMYER, *Luke*, p. 1480). See also BROWN, *Death*, p. 771, who also was not impressed by Derrett's argumentation and cited Fitzmyer's rejection.

61. Weiser stated that concerning 23,6-12: "Luke probably composed this scene on the basis of a historical reminiscence. In the communal prayer in Acts 4:27 ('Herod and Pontius Pilate') Luke redactionally refers again to this scene (*contra* Dibelius). Luke emphasizes his own agenda by having Pilate three times attest Jesus' innocence and in that way defend both Jesus and Christians before the Roman state (Luke 23:4, 14f. 22)" (Πιλᾶτος, in *EWNT* 3, cols. 205-207 = p. 87).

62. Neyrey proposed the idea that within the one trial of Jesus, there were four separate trials, one of which was the trial before Herod (*Passion*, p. 69). Neyrey regarded the source question as "the most important issue connected with Jesus' trial before Herod" (p. 77). Neyrey's sentiments in this matter were clarified in a note referring to the Sanhedrin trial: "Even if the history could be perfectly reconstructed and the nagging question of sources resolved, one important area of scholarship would remain: Luke's interpretation of the trial, his redaction of the

Herod), L. Gaston (6b.d, 1986), F.J. Matera (6b, 1986; 6b.d, 1989; 9, 1990; 6b, 1991), R.C. Tannehill (6a, 1986), J.B. Tyson (6c, 1986; 10, 1992), *C.V. Manus (6a.b, 1987)*[63], J. Kremer (6b?, 1988), R. Pesch (6b, 1988), G. Schneider (6a.b, 1988), *W. Wiefel (6b, 1988)*[64], D. Senior (6b, 1989), C.F. Evans (6b, 1990), J.L. Houlden (6, general special

sources, and the meaning of this trial in Luke-Acts" (p. 201, n. 1). Rather than deriving from a special source, Neyrey contended the scene was a Lukan composition, applauding the convincing efforts of Finegan. "In short, all of the materials in Lk 23:6-12 may be found either in the Markan source to the passion narrative (Mk 15:3-5,16-20), in Lukan redactional additions to Mark's text (Lk 9:9 to Mk 6:14-16), or in Scriptural prophecies which are fulfilled (Acts 4:25-26). There is no need to demand a special source for 23:6-12" (p. 79). Finally, Neyrey treated what he considered to be the threefold function of the Herod episode. Not only did the scene establish another witness to the innocence of Jesus and provide a model for later Christians to imitate, but "Luke presents one more instance of Israel rejecting God's prophet" (p. 80).

63. Manus believed there were "over nine Schools of thought" regarding the meaning and role of 23,6-12 in Lk (*The Universalism of Luke and the Motif of Reconciliation in Luke 23:6-12*, in *AfTJ* 16 [1987] 124). The story: resulted from a variety of sources (H.A.W. Meyer); represented "later apostolic preaching" in Acts (Danker); reflected the theme of reconciling animosity (Talbert, Schweizer), a view to which Manus subscribed; reflected the "anti-Jewish/pro-Roman apologetic" (C.F. Baur, Rengstorf, Ernst, Ellis, Corbin); emphasized the innocence of Jesus (Bruce); fulfilled the requirement of Deuteronomic law for a second witness (Leaney, Karris, Marshall, Talbert); contrasted Jesus and Herod (A. George); the Herod account was a Lukan composition based on Acts 4,1-22 "to find its fulfillment in a Royal song of the Psalter" (Marshall, Talbert); served the purpose literarily to underscore Jesus' innocence (Soards). In this confusing section, Manus combined source criticism with a discussion of the function of the pericope. One wonders, for example, why the views of Bruce and Soards were separated if both suggested the innocence of Jesus was the focus of the story? Further, although the study was not specifically anthropological or a social science interpretation, Manus used the experience of African culture to attempt to explain first century middle Eastern culture at the juncture of two civilizations: "As traditional rulers in most communities in Africa can identify, caution or exculpate persons suspected to be criminals in their areas; so perhaps, did Pilate expect Herod to have done in the case of Jesus of Nazareth" (p. 126).

Manus followed Soards in viewing 23,8c.d as being based on material from the earlier section of Lk, especially 9,7-9. The motif of the silence was ascribed to the Synoptic tradition, specifically derived from Mk 14,60-61, and Manus argued that Jesus silenced the authorities. Manus raised the question whether the silence could be a part of the secrecy motif of Mk (p. 133-134, n. 31). Verse 10 reprised material from previous sections of Lk. Verse 11 was seen as a redaction of Mk 15,16-20 (p. 134, n. 34). Verse 12 was regarded as "a distinctively Lukan composition" and Manus rejected Soards's view that it reflected material taken from tradition (p. 127; cf. SOARDS, *Tradition*, 1985, p. 357).

Manus concluded the source-critical section in the following words: "Luke 23:6-12 is in many respects a Lucan composition based on rudimentary traditions and bits of the Markan story. But a lot more derives from Luke's own ingenuity and artistry. In any event, Luke appropriates and re-works ideas from the Markan Passion Narrative. But he vivifies the account in this particular pericope in such a manner that he creates an eloquent symbolism that responds to his mission theology and notion of the universal significance of the death of Christ. The technique of re-utilization of parts of material from his Gospel goes a long way to mark this passage as one that is purposefully designed to address itself to Gentile interests" (MANUS, *Universalism*, p. 128).

64. Wiefel saw that Luke was building not only on the Markan basis (Mk 6,14-16), but on an earlier portion of his own Gospel as well (9,7-9) (*Das Evangelium nach Lukas* [THKNT, 3],

material, 1990), *C.K. Barrett (6?, 1992; 2a and 6, 1994)*[65], F. Neirynck (1993), D.B. Peabody (probably, 1995), *J.S. Sibinga (6?, 1997)*[66]

VII. THE HEROD PERICOPE WAS INSPIRED BY MATTHEW'S GOSPEL
H. Hoehner (1972), M.D. Goulder (1988)

VIII. NON-HISTORICAL WITHOUT FURTHER INFORMATION
P. Wendland (1898)[67], W.R. Wilson (1960), *H. Cohn (1967, 1971)*[68], S.H. Ringe (1995?)

Berlin, p. 389). Though acknowledging Dibelius's assessment, Wiefel noticed that both B. Weiss and G. Schneider argued that Herod's trial was possible (p. 390, n. 4). He dismissed the possibility that the account could go back directly to Joanna, though without explaining his position. The purpose of the pericope, which was much more important to Wiefel than the source or historicity questions, was to provide additional witnesses to the innocence of Jesus. The dazzling apparel was a form of mockery directed to Jesus' claim as Messiah. Wiefel gave the impression that at 23,16 Luke substituted παιδεύειν for the Markan φραγελλοῦν (Mk 15,15).

65. Barrett followed van Unnik, in a qualified sense, in viewing Acts as a confirmation of the Gospel (*The Third Gospel as a Preface to Acts? Some Reflections*, in FS Neirynck, Vol. 2, p. 1451-1466; cf. W.C. VAN UNNIK, *The 'Book of Acts' the Confirmation of the Gospel*, in *NT* 4 [1960] 26-59). Almost as an afterthought Luke decided to write his second volume to show how Christianity's growth validated what the evangelist wrote in his first volume. But he also suggested in another sense the Gospel served as a preface for Acts. He considered these two assertions "correct" and "complimentary" (BARRETT, *Third Gospel*, p. 1462). Noting that the collaboration of Pilate and Herod was referred to in both the Gospel and Acts (23,6-12; Acts 4,27), what distinguished the texts was that in Acts the cooperation of these political leaders was presented as fulfillment of Scripture. Barrett seemed to suggest that the Herod pericope in the Gospel was a Lukan composition: "it is reasonable to think that in the gospel Luke was preparing narrative material that could be used in the later book" (p. 1461). Barrett described his methodology: "In dealing with this question the first step is to read through the gospel asking at every point whether what we read seems intended in some way to point forward to, or prepare for, some constituent of Acts" (p. 1453). Barrett apparently attached some importance to the Herod story since it was among the select material from the Gospel that was referred to in Acts: "Apart from the crucifixion and resurrection, hardly anything of the gospel story is recalled – hardly more than the baptism preached by John and the agreement between Herod and Pilate (Acts 4,27)" (p. 1462).

In his commentary on Acts (1994) Barrett conjectured in his discussion of Acts 4,27 that because "Luke shows some hints of access to the Herod family (Lk. 8.3; Acts 13,1), [...] it may be that he had heard a story about Herod and Pilate which reflection finally led him to connect with Ps. 2" (*A Critical and Exegetical Commentary on The Acts of the Apostles* [ICC], Vol. 1, Edinburgh, p. 247).

66. J.S. SIBINGA, *The Making of Luke 23:26-56. An Analysis of the Composition Technique in Luke's Crucifixion Narrative*, in *RB* 104 (1997) 378-404, esp. p. 392.

67. Noting that Mk 15,16-20 was missing from Lk, Wendland considered Lk 23,11 to be "nur ein Nachklang" of the Markan account and therefore unhistorical (*Jesus als Saturnalien-Koenig*, in *Hermes* 33 [1898] 175-179, 175, n. 1 and 179).

68. Cohn denied the historicity of the Herod episode because of timing (*Trial*, p. 181). Paul MAIER (1990) complained of revisionist histories such as Cohn's, *Trial*, which claimed that the Jewish religious leaders were on Jesus' side, rather than opposed to him (*Who Killed Jesus?*, in *ChrTod* 34 [1990] 17-18). Maier's thesis was that "logic and extrabiblical sources, then, offer a

IX. UNDETERMINED: PROVIDED NO INFORMATION ON SOURCE OF HEROD PERICOPE

F.W. Farrar (1891), *J. Schniewind (1914)*[69], *F.X. Pölzl and C.C. Martindale (1919)*[70], K.L. Schmidt (1919), G. Bertram (1922), A. Schlatter (1931, other editions), *P. Joüon (1936)*[71], L. Fendt ([2]1937), *A. Merk (1940)*[72], J. Blinzler (1947), *W. v. Loewenich*

better solution to the tangled problem of the prosecution on Good Friday, one that does no violence to the New Testament sources or to historical fact" (p. 19). The extrabiblical sources to which Maier referred were Josephus, Eusebius, Polycarp and Justin.

69. Concerning the Herod pericope, Schniewind (1930) posed more questions than he answered, though he stated that the manner in which the common (oral) tradition gave rise to Lk and Jn was a complicated one (*Die Parallelperikopen bei Lukas und Johannes*, Leipzig, 1914; Hildesheim, [2]1958: unchanged photocopy of the first edition, p. 75; Darmstadt, [3]1970).

70. Although Pölzl and Martindale did not address the source question there were several noteworthy observations. The term ἀνέπεμψεν (23,7) was thought to refer, not to a higher authority, but to a higher geographical location (F.X. PÖLZL, *The Passion and Glory of Christ. A Commentary on the Events from the Last Supper to the Ascension*, tr. A.M. BUCHANAN, rev. and ed. C.C. MARTINDALE, New York, p. 169). The authors took great latitude in presupposing what transpired between Herod and Jesus. The silence of Jesus (23,9) was interpreted as Jesus' "condemnation" of Herod, while the dazzling apparel (23,11) was regarded as Herod's retaliation for the silence. The clothing was a mockery against Jesus' royal claim. It was not clear whether the raiment may have been white priestly vestments or the white toga of Roman government candidates. Whatever the case, it clearly was a sign of Jesus' "innocence and royal dignity" (p. 170). The basis for the enmity between Pilate and Herod (23,12) was found in 13,1 where Pilate had ordered the massacre of worshipping Jews.

71. Drawing upon comparisons of the Peshitto and Vulgate, Joüon (1936) argued the Lukan text contained many difficulties for translators, but opted for a translation of ἐσθῆτα λαμπράν in 23,11 as "d'un vêtement d'un blanc éclatant" (*Luc 23,11:* ἐσθῆτα λαμπράν, in *RSR* 26 [1936] 80). The verb περιβάλλειν normally accompanied the term ἱμάτιον which was found in Acts 12,8 (p. 80). The term was also found in Jn 19,2 and Rev 19,13. Contrary to Verrall, Joüon did not believe the term referred solely to the tunic. The deliberate choice of the term by Luke had a symbolic meaning. The proper translation of λαμπρός as rendered by the Vulgate in numerous places, was *candidus* (p. 81-82. Cf. Acts 10,30; Jas 2,2; Rev 15,6; 19,8). Although in 23,11 the Vulgate rendered the term *albus*, Joüon maintained that *candidus* would have been a better choice of terms. Drawing on S. Krauss, Joüon pointed out that distinctions were made in the Talmudic period, not only between colored and white clothing, but that the white garments reflected multiple symbolic meanings (p. 82, n. 7, and 84; cf. S. KRAUSS, *Talmudische Archäologie* I, Leipzig, 1910, p. 145. They could variously portray distinguished social class, joy and purity. In contradistinction to Verrall, Joüon argued it was quite evident that the "dazzling apparel" signified innocence, even noting that Josephus had written of presenting accused persons before the Sanhedrin in black or dark clothing (JOÜON, *Luc 23,11*, p. 84-85, n. 16). Vesting Jesus in the "dazzling apparel" served as part of the preparation of returning Jesus to Pilate. While not denying the symbolism of the vesture, could the reference not have recalled the Transfiguration, reminding the readers that what the apostles experienced with Jesus on the mount and what he predicted, was now coming about? Not only would such an interpretation bode well with Luke's penchant for setting the stage earlier in the Gospel for later events, but it shows Jesus' word being fulfilled. It might also recall the words of Jesus in 7,25-26 about John the Baptist preparing the way for Jesus.

72. For the material proper to Lk, such as 23,2-15, Merk was noncommittal whether it came from written sources, although he entertained the possibility that it may have come from a single source. This was only one option among multiple sources and oral tradition (*Introductionis in S.*

(1947)[73], *E.V. Rieu (1952)*[74], *H. Conzelmann (1953/1957/1961)*[75], *S. Sandmel (1957)*[76], H.J. Cadbury (1958), J. Dillersberger (1958), H. Gollwitzer (1958), *H. van Vliet (1958)*[77], *W.R.F. Browning (1960)*[78], A. Barr (1963), *G. Voss (1965)*[79], W.G. Kümmel (1964,

Scripturae Libros Compendium, Paris, [12]1940, p. 673). Merk regarded the Nazareth pericope (4,16-30) as having come from a source other than Mk (p. 672).

73. von Loewenich contended Luke portrayed Herod as "eines Mannes von griechischer Bildung", as having an interest in things religious (*Der Mensch im Lichte der Passionsgeschichte*, Stuttgart, p. 19-20). The presentation was compared with Herod Agrippa and Paul in Acts 26. Earlier in the Gospel (9,9) Luke made it clear Jesus was only "eine interessante religiöse Erscheinung" for Herod. This religious interestedness, which lacked seriousness and personal responsibility, was a caricature of faith.

74. Rieu maintained the special material in Lk and Mt derived from "the Evangelists' own industry in drawing on yet other written sources, on the oral tradition, or on the memories of individuals" (*The Four Gospels. A New Translation from the Greek*, Penguin Classics, London, p. xviii).

75. *Die Mitte*, p. 72, n. 1 (= 86, n. 2): "Die Traditionsgeschichte der Szene ist umstritten. Ob sie von Lc geschaffen (*Dibelius* ZNW 1915) oder vorgefunden ist (*Bultmann* S. 294), ist kontrovers. Deutlich ist der Zusammenhang mit den anderen Herodesszenen, die stark redigiert sind".

76. The Lukan addition of Pilate's sending Jesus to Herod, Sandmel noted, contained mention of the royal apparel. Whereas in the other Synoptics the Roman soldiers dressed Jesus in this garment, in Lk it was Herod's soldiers (*A Jewish Understanding of the New Testament*, Cincinnati, OH, 1957 p. 188 = 1974 [Augmented edition]. Cf. S. SANDMEL, *Herod*, Philadelphia, PA, 1967. In this work Sandmel referred only to Herod Antipas in Lk 13,32).

Sandmel (1962) later argued the absence of a pericope like Lk 23,6-12 in the other Gospels "suggests strongly that this passage is legendary" (*Herod*, in *IDB* 2, 1962, 585-594, p. 593. In another article appearing in the *IDB* on the trial of Jesus, Pierson Parker noted only: "[Pilate] sends Jesus to Herod Antipas (23:6-13), who is visiting Jerusalem, but who has no juridiction here" (*Trial of Jesus*, in *IDB* 4, 1962, 697-698, p. 698). It was observed that Acts 4,25-26 referred back to this story (*Herod*, in *IDB* 2, p. 593). By recalling that Creed maintained the mockery by the Roman soldiers (Mk 15,16-17) was perhaps transferred to this setting Sandmel seemed to advocate that the passage was part of Luke's apologetic. Sandmel also pointed out that the role of Herod was intensified in GP.

77. Van Vliet, following Morgenthaler, deemed that Luke was writing his two-volume work as a witness "and therefore took care to give twofold or threefold evidence" (*No Single Testimony. A Study on the Adoption of the Law of Deut. 19:15 par. into the New Testament* [Studia Theologica Rheno-Traiectina, 4], Utrecht, p. 3. Cf. MORGENTHALER, *Die lukanische Geschichtsschreibung als Zeugnis*). Van Vliet accused Morgenthaler of "overstraining his point" (p. 3). Although Van Vliet did not address the trial of Jesus directly, he made the following observation: "All this means that in cases of crime or punishable offence against the law and still less in capital cases the testimony of one was not sufficient to make a valid complaint. Two or three witnesses were necessary to sustain a charge" (VAN VLIET, *No Single Testimony*, p. 65).

78. With regard to the Herod episode, Browning maintained that while Luke probably envisioned it as a fulfillment of Ps 2,2, this did not suggest he created the story. Browning appeared to equate the mockery by Herod's cohort with that of the Roman soldiers reported in the other two Synoptics (*The Gospel according to Saint Luke*, Torch Bible Commentaries, London, p. 162-163).

79. Voss, speaking of the anti-Jewish tendency in the Lukan account of the passion, used the connection of Acts 4,27 with Ps 2, to understand 23,12 (*Die Christologie der lukanischen*

1973), W. Harrington (1967), *M. Tolbert (1967)*[80], A. Vanhoye (1967, 1981), A.F. Page (1968, but serves Luke's theological interests), *W.P. Farmer (1969)*[81], W.C. van Unnik (1973), E. Delebecque (1976), *M. Corbin (1978)*[82], R.J. Karris (1977), A. George (1978),

Schriften in Grundzügen, Studia Neotestamentica, 2, Paris, p. 126, 127). Noting the use of the term ἐσθῆτι λαμπρᾷ also in Acts 10,30, he dismissed the view that it referred to the purple cloak mentioned in Mk 15,17. The "sinngemässe" parallel was 15,22 where the father insisted that the prodigal son be vested in a στολὴ πρώτη. However, Voss pointed to the similarities between Herod and Pilate who mocked Jesus, wished to let him go, but handed him over nonetheless (p. 127). As a result of the proceedings, Jesus was revealed "als den Meister, den Königlich-Grossen, den Unschuldigen" (p. 128).

80. Tolbert did not treat the source question but saw the Herod scene as setting the stage so the responsibility for the death sentence would rest squarely on the shoulders of Jesus' Jewish opponents (*Leading Ideas of the Gospel of Luke*, in *RE* 64, 446 = *Die Hauptinteressen des Evangelisten Lukas*, tr. H. STEGEMANN, in G. BRAUMANN, ed., *Das Lukas-Evangelium. Die redaktions- und kompositionsgeschichtliche Forschung*, WdF, 280, Darmstadt, 1974, p. 346).

81. Farmer, in the section 23,6-16, assigned a few words in the following manner: οὐδέν (23,9) reflected complete verbatim agreement between the three Synoptics (*Synopticon. The Verbal Agreement between the Greek Texts of Matthew, Mark and Luke Contextually Exhibited*, Cambridge, (esp. p. xi and 222). The term ἀπεκρίνατο (23,9) was complete verbatim agreement between Mt and Lk. In addition, οἱ ἀρχιερεῖς and αὐτοῦ (23,10) represented not only complete verbatim agreement between Mk and Lk, but significant though incomplete agreement between Mt and Lk. Finally, the word κατηγοροῦντες exhibited not only significant but incomplete agreement between Mt and Lk, as well as significant though incomplete agreement between Mt and Mk.

82. Although Corbin did not clearly articulate his position of authorship, he maintained the Herod pericope derived from a single source (*Jésus devant Hérode: Lecture de Luc 23,6-12*, in *Christus* 25 [1978] 193). He arrived at this conclusion based on his perception of the concentric symmetry of the passage and correspondences between the verses (p. 192-193). Unfortunately, he did not offer any additional information concerning the origin or extent of such a supposed source. For a number of reasons, reading between the lines, it would seem Corbin understood the Herod pericope as a theological construct of the evangelist. While the shuffling of Jesus back and forth between Herod and Pilate "demeure incompréhensible au niveau d'une *simple* interprétation historique" (p. 192), Corbin tended toward a more theological understanding which regarded this reconciliation as symbolic of the end of the enmity between the Jews and Gentiles resulting from Jesus' death. While one cannot agree that this pericope formed the "l'épisode central de la Passion" (p. 190), Corbin's observation that the Herod episode was framed by two other parts of the trial (23,1-5.13-23), which in turn, were framed by two other episodes ascribing responsibility for the death of Jesus to the leaders of the Jews (22,66-71; 23,24-25), is worthy of further consideration.

Corbin's reliance on Dibelius's interpretation of Ps 2,1-2 was apparent. Corbin not only saw the passion of Jesus mirrored in the persecutions of the church, but the figures of the Herod, Pilate, Israel and the Gentiles were understood in the use of the psalm in Acts 4,24-28 (p. 194). What was more, the enthronement of Jesus was particularly emphasized and the connection was made clear in the use of Ps 2 (albeit v. 7), in the baptism of Jesus (3,22) and in Paul's preaching to the Jews in Antioch where the text refers specifically to the resurrection (Acts 13,33) (p. 194-195; cf. DIBELIUS, *Herodes und Pilatus*, p. 124-125). By employing Ps 2 in both the Gospel and Acts, the evangelist portrayed the ancient Scriptures as having been definitively fulfilled.

Though Corbin has done much to highlight the form and themes in the Herod pericope by drawing attention to the careful structuring of the episodes with clear echoes from the Gospel

E.A. LaVerdiere (1980), *P. Bossuyt and J. Radermakers (1981)*[83], F. Bovon (1981), *D. Juel (1983)*[84], *R. Obach and A. Kirk (1985)*[85], R. Tannehill (1986), *R.L. Brawley (1987)*[86], P.F. Esler (1987), D. Gooding (1987), *P. Parker (1987)*[87], J. Sanders (1987), *P. Hofrichter (1988-1989)*[88], F. Bovon (1989), J. Nolland (1989), S. Binz (1989), C.A. Evans (1990), P. Maier (1990), W. Schenk (1990), T.R. Schreiner (1990), J.P. Heil (1991),

found in Acts, the emphasis of certain theological ideas which were endemic to Luke (reversal, reconciliation, seeing the experiences of Jesus reflected in the life of the church), and the fulfillment from prophecy, Corbin's investigation would seem to support more the case for redaction in this section of the passion narrative.

83. Bossuyt and Radermakers affirmed Luke was dependent upon Mk, but it was difficult to decide whether in its present form or in an earlier edition (*Jésus Parole de la Grâce selon saint Luc*. Vol. 2. *Lecture continue*, Brussels, p. 17). Luke was very respectful of the sources he used. The section 23,1-25 was "habilement construit" (p. 491). The authors did not take a stand on the source question, but referred to Corbin's concentric symmetry and point to the Lukan theological issues as reconciliation between Jew and Greek and the mockery, which was a kind of acknowledgement of divine royalty (p. 493).

84. Juel, although he endorsed Markan priority, noted that source criticism was only one methodology among many and that to focus solely on sources "may detract from the finished product" (*Luke-Acts. The Promise of History*, Atlanta, GA, p. 5). Although Juel was indecisive as to the historicity of the pericope, he viewed Acts 4,25-26 as offering an explanation for it (p. 52, 53). "Whatever historical basis there may or may not be for the tale, the little episode fits like a piece in a puzzle. It was anticipated, predestined, necessary" (p. 53).

85. Obach and Kirk spoke only generally about Luke's special tradition, but considered the inclusion of the Herod story as providing "a secular ruler's testimony regarding the innocence of Jesus" (*A Commmentary on the Gospel of Luke*, New York, p. 12, 241).

86. Brawley connected the prophetic fulfillment of Ps 2,1-2 in Acts 4,23-28 with the Lukan account of the passion (*Luke-Acts and the Jews. Conflict, Apology, and Conciliation* [SBL MS, 33], Atlanta, GA, p. 146). The evangelist forced a fit by not following the strict parallelism of the Psalm. In place of Gentiles in v. 1, Luke wrote so that "peoples" referred instead to Israelites.

87. Parker noted that a common position was that Acts 4,24-31 recalled 23,7-12 (*Herod Antipas and the Death of Jesus*, in E.P. SANDERS, *Jesus, the Gospels, and the Church. Essays in Honor of William R. Farmer*, Macon, GA, 197-208; esp. p. 197. See C.S.C. WILLIAMS, *A Commentary on the Acts of the Apostles*, New York, 1957, p. 86, and F.F. BRUCE, *The Acts of the Apostles*, Chicago, IL - Grand Rapids, MI, 1952, p. 127-128). He argued "specifically, (1) Jesus' death was determined *in advance* by Herod Antipas, Pilate and the Jerusalem Sanhedrin acting *in concert*; (2) this three-way alliance was *instigated by Herod Antipas* (PARKER, *Herod Antipas*, p. 198)". Parker plausibly explained why Herod would have been interested in seeing Jesus. Perceiving him as *"John the Baptist redivivus"*, and understanding that Jesus had been at work in Galilee, Herod was eager to dispose of him (p. 206). Parker suggested Luke was responsible for having Herod vest Jesus in the dazzling garment to emphasize Herod's participation in the events and to indicate that Herod felt that Jesus was "a political rival". Parker was not certain of the origin of the animosity between the two rulers, though he rehearsed two of the most oft-repeated suggestions (p. 207). The reasons offered were the events of 13,1 and the positioning of shields in the former palace of Herod's father.

88. *Das dreifache Verfahren*, 1988-89, p. 73-74. He rejected a *Sondertradition* as the source. Cf. Schneider (1977), p. 473f., and J. Ernst (1977), p. 624f. The passage was delineated as 23,5-12. See above for a discussion of other aspects of Hofrichter's position.

J.A. Darr (1992)[89], J.S. Kloppenborg (1992), G.W.E. Nickelsburg (1992), J.B. Tyson (1992), W.S. Kurz (1993), M.D. Hooker (1994)

No Information or Unclear Opinion
J.O.F. Murray (1893), H. McLachlan (1920), E. Klostermann (1921), K.L. Schmidt (1944), F. Amiot (1952), V. Harlow (1953), W. Schneemelcher (1987), M.P. McHugh (1990), P. Pilhofer (1990), J.K. Elliott (1991), F. Bovon (1995)

89. Darr adopted the new literary-critical approach and thus was unconcerned with the source question (*On Character Building. The Reader and the Rhetoric of Characterization in Luke-Acts*, Louisville, KY). In fact, Darr seemed piqued by redaction criticism and similar methodologies: "Atomistic methodologies have largely shielded critics from perceiving the overarching predator/prey imagery in this passage. For an exception, see Verrall (1908/09:353)" (p. 192, n. 16). Such a venue notwithstanding, he identified the story in line with a martyr's account (p. 162-163). He gave a great deal of attention to the Herod pericope (23,6-12) which he viewed as a confrontation between Jesus and Herod. This episode dramatically contrasted the self-control and boldness of each character (p. 78-79). He was also aware of the connections between this account and previous ones in the Gospel (9,7-9; 13,31-35).

The silence of Jesus was linked to that of Is 53 as was made clear by an earlier reference (22,37; see Is 53,7). Darr understood the silence to indicate for Greco-Roman readers "strong self-control" (p. 165). He followed Hoehner's interpretation that the transfer of Jesus from Pilate to Herod was effected by Pilate's desire to rid himself of a difficult situation (p. 166; see Hoehner, *Why did Pilate*, p. 88). The friendship resulted (23,12) because Herod imitated Pilate and supported his verdict of innocence. Concerning the relation of 23,6-12 to Acts 4,23-31 Darr confirmed Dibelius's view that 23,12 joined the Gospel account with Acts 4,27 (Darr, *On Character Building*, p. 195, n. 22). It was at this point that Darr observed that much of the redactional study of the passage in Acts concluded that it was a Lukan composition (p. 195, n. 2). Darr listed Holtz (1968), p. 53, Rese (1969), p. 94-97, and Schneider, *Die Apostelgeschichte* (1980), p. 354-355. Note the objection raised p. 195, n. 23. He minimized the difference in the portrayals of Herod and Pilate in the Gospel over against Acts. But continuity was seen in Paul's trials in Acts, which followed the pattern established in the Gospel (Darr, *On Character Building*, p. 168).

CHAPTER THIRTEEN

AN EXEGESIS OF LK 23,6-16: JESUS BEFORE HEROD

Introduction

It has now become obvious that Lk 23,6-16 is one of the most studied and often debated sections of the Lukan passion narrative. There have been several significant studies on the Lukan composition of this passage[1]. Yet even these have yielded a variety of source-critical proposals as our survey demonstrated. They include the suggestions that Jesus' trial before Herod composed by Luke was: a) based upon traditional materials, either oral or written, b) a redaction of elements borrowed from Mk, c) inspired by Ps 2, d) influenced by Paul's experience as recounted in Acts, or e) created freely by Luke himself. In some instances, it was proposed that the pericope came to be from a mixture of some of these various elements. Further, there is no general agreement on the extent of the passage, though it is more frequently defined as either 23,6-12 or 23,6-16[2].

A general consensus seems to exist that the pericope was intended by Luke to provide another witness to the innocence of Jesus. But as regards the function of the pericope there is also a broad spectrum of ideas. These include: an apologetic that Christianity is not a political threat to Rome; a paradigm, providing a model for Christian disciples to follow; a reconciliation between enemies; or another instance of Israel rejecting God's prophet. A final disputed question revolves around the relationship of 23,6-16 to Acts 4,25-27.

1. F. NICOLARDOT, *Les procédés*, 1908; M. DIBELIUS, *Herodes*, 1915; J. FINEGAN, *Die Ueberlieferung*, 1934; H. VAN DER KWAAK, *Het Proces*, 1969; M.-É. BOISMARD, *Synopse*, 1972; W. RADL, *Paulus*, 1975; *Sonderüberlieferung*, 1988; *Das Lukas-Evangelium*, 1988; P.W. WALASKAY, *Trial*, 1975; K. MÜLLER, *Jesus*, 1979; E. BUCK, *Function*, 1980; J. FITZMYER, *Luke*, 1981/1985; J. NEYREY, *Passion*, 1985; M. SOARDS, *Silence*, 1985; *Tradition*, 1985; *Herod*, 1986; J.A. DARR, *Glorified*, 1987; C.V. MANUS, *Universalism*, 1987; G. SCHNEIDER, *Das Verfahren*, 1988; M.D. GOULDER, *Luke*, 1989; F.J. MATERA, *Luke 23,1-25*, 1989; R.E. BROWN, *Death*, 1994; S. LÉGASSE, *Le procès*, 1994/95, F.G. UNTERGASSMAIR, *Zur Problematik*, 1996. Valuable studies of Lukan vocabulary and style include RADL, *Paulus*, esp. p. 396-435; FITZMYER, *Luke* (1981), esp. p. 107-127; and GOULDER, *Luke*, esp. p. 800-809. A particularly useful tool is the article by NEIRYNCK, *Le texte des Actes des Apôtres et les caractéristiques stylistiques lucaniennes* (M.É. BOISMARD – A. LAMOUILLE.), in *ETL* 61 (1985), 304-339, esp. p. 317-330 (= *Evangelica II*, 1991, 243-278, esp. p. 256-269), which contained a list of parallel words in Lk-Acts assembled by Boismard and Lamouille. Neirynck also referred to the works of PLUMMER, *Luke*, 1896, ³1900 (p. xli-xlvii: *Characteristics, Style, and Language*), HAWKINS, *Horae Synopticae*, 1898, ²1909; T. VOGEL, *Zur Characteristik*, ²1899; HARNACK, *Lukas der Arzt* and *Sprüche und Reden Jesu*; CADBURY, *Style of Luke. 2. The Treatment of Sources in the Gospel*; MORGENTHALER, *Statistik*; and J. JEREMIAS, *Die Sprache*. The inclusion of words does not always signify a judgment on Neirynck's part. See further the additional note (*Evangelica II*, p. 278). Finally see BOISMARD, *En quête*, p. 123-124.

2. Also 4-15; 5-16; 7-15; 8-12.

Reasons Advanced for Lukan Redaction

Having rehearsed various attempted solutions, we assembled the numerous reasons which have been advanced throughout our survey in support of the view that Lk 23,6-12.(13-16) is Lukan redaction rather than tradition. These include: 1) the story is found only in Lk[3]; 2) similarly, "it is remotely unlikely that the account is historical, since it is not in Mark, and the substance of the story is found in Mk 15,4f., 16f."[4]; 3) it fits well in its context[5]; 4) the passage contains Markan material omitted in parallel places in Lk, specifically details about the death of John the Baptist (Mk 6,17-29)[6], and other information found in Mk: the silence of Jesus (Mk 15,3f.), the mockery (Mk 15,16-20a), and the charges raised by the religious authorities (Mk 15,3)[7]; 5) both the style and vocabulary are Lukan[8]; 6)

3. DRURY, *The Gospel of Luke*, 1973, p. 206: "If the trial before Herod were historical it would surely figure in the other gospels". Cf. DRURY, *Tradition*, 1976, p. 16-17.

4. GOULDER, *Luke*, Vol. 2, p. 757. So also BROWN, p. 760: "Granted the unified Lukan structure of chap. 23, this can be looked on as an isolated episode only by comparison with the Marcan outline, from which it is absent. (That absence is significant because much of what precedes and follows in Luke's trial account is present in Mark)".

5. SCHNEIDER, *Das Verfahren*, p. 127 (= 292); also p. 119 (= 284). K. MÜLLER, *Jesus*, p. 116: "Einschlägig ist zunächst die Beobachtung, dass Lk 23,6f nahtlos an den vorausgehenden V.5 anschliesst"; CHICO CANO, p. 31: "Die Herodesperikope bildet eine zusammenhängende Sinneinheit im Prozess Jesu"; see also p. 225: "Der Prozess Jesu vor Pilatus (Lk 23,1-25) geh ört zum ersten Abschnitt des K. 23 und bildet eine formale und inhaltliche Einheit"; BUCK, p. 166, n. 5: "Not only is the Herod pericope in its present shape tightly connected within the literary composition of the Gospel as a whole ..."; DARR, *Glorified*, p. 283: "The reference to Galilee in these verses [6-7] not only seamlessly binds the present narrative together in a plausible cause and effect relationship ..., but also tied the passion of Jesus to his Galilean ministry". And later: "The pericope 'Jesus before Herod' is well integrated into its narrower context (Luke 23:1-25)" (p. 304). See further BROWN, p. 757, 760-761; BÜCHELE, *Der Tod*, p. 25; SOARDS, *Tradition*, 1985, p. 344, n. 1. Even HOEHNER, *Herod Antipas*, p. 226-227, who advocated a special source, spoke of the obvious unity of this section.

6. DENAUX, *L'hypocrisie*, p. 264, n. 57; BÜCHELE, p. 33, n. 57, 58, 59.

7. BÜCHELE, p. 32, n. 56; see BOISMARD, *En quête*, p. 126-127, who assigned οὐδὲν ἀπεκρίνατο (Lk 23,9) to the Mk/Mt tradition.

8. BOISMARD, t. 2, 1972, p. 418, and *En quête*, p. 124; TAYLOR, *Passion*, p. 87; BÜCHELE, p. 32: "Es finden sich darin typisch lk Vocabular und lk Wendungen"; HENDRICKX, *Passion Narratives*, 1990, p. 81; K. MÜLLER, *Jesus*, p. 114-116; SOARDS, *Tradition*, 1985, p. 347; BROWN, p. 761; LÉGASSE, t. 1, p. 107. On the other hand, a few scholars such as Green deny this: "It is alleged that the language and style of the pericope is Lukan" (*Death*, p. 80-81, p. 80). Also: "In any case, the vocabulary of the pericope does not turn out to be *peculiarly* Lukan after all". His ultimate judgment on the authorship of the pericope: "*Luke's redactional hand* is therefore evident in this pericope, but there is insufficient basis here for insisting that the whole is a *Lukan creation*" (p. 81). However, the view that the style and vocabulary was basically Lukan was endorsed even by those who held there was a special continuous source or a form of Proto-Lk (TAYLOR, *Passion*, p. 80. BOISMARD, *Synopse*, t. 2, 1972, p. 418: "Le caractère 'lucanien' de toute la scène est indéniable" and "une composition entièrement lucanienne"). Cf. Fitzmyer who treated what he considered to be Lukan redactional elements (*Luke*, p. 1479).

the episode emphasizes the Lukan theme of innocence, theology, and apologetics (e.g. to excuse Pilate and assign greater responsibility to the Jews); 7) there are similarities with Paul's trials in Acts[9]; 8) there is no clear reason why Pilate sent Jesus to Herod[10]; 9) there was insufficient time for Herod's trial to take place[11]; and 10) the episode seems to lack purpose or significance[12].

In his commentary on the passion narratives R. Brown reached the following conclusion: "In my judgment we must settle for a Lucan author of 23:6-12 who is neither a simple recorder of historical fact nor totally a creative, imaginative novelist. He transmits early tradition about Herod Antipas – tradition that had a historical nucleus but had already developed beyond simple history by the time it reached Luke. By weaving this tradition and other items into the narrative of 23:6-12, Luke not only made an important theological statement about Jesus' innocence and the healing power of his passion; he also contributed to the further development of the picture of Herodian involvement"[13]. Brown proposed that

9. RADL, *Paulus*, p. 196-202; *Das Lukas-Evangelium*, p. 125-128; WALASKAY, *Trial*, p. 88-89; O'TOOLE, *Parallels Between Jesus and His Disciples in Luke-Acts: A Further Study*, in *BZ* 27 (1983) 195-212, esp. p. 207-209; *Unity*, p. 67-71, 82-86; NEYREY, *Passion*, p. 89-107; MATERA, *Luke 23,1-25*, p. 545; see also comments by MORGENTHALER, *Die lukanische Geschichtsschreibung*, T. 1, p. 179; T. 2, p. 18-19, and UNTERGASSMAIR, *Kreuzweg*, p. 74-75.

10. SCHNEIDER, *Das Verfahren*, p. 127 (= 292); cf. A.N. SHERWIN-WHITE, *Roman Society*, p. 31, n. 3; HOEHNER, *Why Did Pilate*, 1970, p. 88-90; SOARDS, *Tradition*, 1985, p. 344. Walaskay highlighted the difficulty presented by this aspect of the pericope. "In all our sources of Palestine during the lifetime of Jesus, this narrative gives us the only instance of direct dealings between the prefect and the tetrarch, though they both held long, contemporary reigns. Because of this it has been very difficult to do much more than speculate about why Pilate sent Jesus to Herod or why they became friends after Jesus appeared before the tetrarch" (*Trial*, p. 87).

11. GILMOUR, *Gospel*, in *IB* 8, 1952, p. 398; BEARE, *Earliest*, 1962, p. 235; REUMANN, *Jesus*, 1968, p. 74.

12. BRANDON, 1968, p. 121; PESCH, 1977, p. 409; FITZMYER, p. 1480: "In the Lucan passion narrative this scene is actually a minor one. It has no significance for the understanding of Jesus' person or fate". Nevertheless, Fitzmyer observed: "The upshot is that, though one cannot be apodictic about the matter, the evidence does not all point toward Lucan fabrication. The appearance of Jesus before Herod could be just as historical as the Lucan depiction of the morning session of the Sanhedrin interrogation" (*Luke*, p. 1479). In contrast to Fitzmyer, Brown was more generous in his evaluation (*Death*, p. 786, n. 49). Gaston, too, questioned the value of the story: "It is difficult to understand how the story functions in the total narrative which is seemingly not advanced at all by this digression" (*Anti-Judaism*, p. 147). Consider also Drury who regarded the story as "judicially pointless in its outcome, but theologically and morally effective in the reconciliation effected between two enemies" (*Tradition*, p. 112). Cf. BUCK, p. 166: "... it is evident that at its present place in the Gospel of Luke the pericope plays a vital role".

13. BROWN, p. 785-786. See also p. 778-779. In his opinion this was confirmed by "so many echoes in the NT and added echoes in Ignatius and *GPet* ..." (p. 785). He organized his presentation in three parts: translation, comment (verse by verse), and analysis which contained two subsections: the formation of the story and its historicity.

Luke employed "the early Antipas tradition" to which he added material drawn from Mk, a schema like that found in the trial of Paul (Acts 25,13–26,32) and sayings concerning Herod, especially from an earlier portion of Lk (13,31-33)[14].

It is important to note that Brown nuanced his understanding of the Antipas tradition. "When I wrote above of an early tradition about a Herodian role in the death of Jesus or a lethal Herodian opposition to Jesus, I was deliberately using a broadly phrased description. I think this same tradition may show up in Mark as Herodians seeking to kill Jesus; in Matt's infancy narrative as Herod (the Great) trying to kill Jesus at Bethlehem; in Luke-Acts as Herod (Antipas) wanting to kill Jesus and taking part in his trial, and perhaps even as Herod (Agrippa I) putting Jesus' leading follower(s) to death"[15]. Brown contended the evangelist "working from Marcan guidelines [...] adapted that Herod tradition, preserving only part of the hostility and using it for a different effect"[16]. Thus "23,6-12(14-15) is scarcely a direct historical account"[17]. We concur that it is hardly a direct historical account. Rather than depending on some Antipas tradition beyond Mk, we propose that the Antipas material in Mk as well as other Markan traditions formed the core of Luke's account, supplemented by earlier material in his own Gospel, so that he crafted the episode, employing his own style and preferred terms, and often casting it in Septuagintal language, in line with his redactional purposes.

It is sometimes argued that although the language of a passage may be Lukan, this does not necessarily indicate redaction; only that Luke has retold the events in his own words[18]. This evidence considered alone could lead one to that conclusion. But when coupled with other telltale signs of Lukan redaction such as use of Markan materials, including vocabulary and motifs, omitted in parallel Lukan contexts, the reader is led to other conclusions.

In our analysis of the Herod pericope we will examine the following distinct elements: 1) Markan material; 2) Luke's method of preparing 23,6-16 through earlier Lukan pericopes; 3) their later development in Acts; and 4) Lukan redaction.

---

14. *Ibid.*, p. 782: "The story we encounter in Luke 23:6-12 is not simply a Lucan adaptation of the Ps 2 and Acts 4 interpretation but another Lucan variation of the early Antipas tradition, fleshed out by three addenda: (a) material from Mark about the questioning of Jesus during the trial (in Mark by Pilate), about the silence of Jesus before the questioner, and about the mockery of Jesus; (b) a schema of the Roman governor inviting a Herodian prince to examine a Jewish prisoner accused by the leaders of his own people – a schema similar to that in the account of Festus inviting Agrippa II to examine Paul in Acts 25:13–26:32; (c) sayings pertinent to Herod preserved especially in Luke 13:31-33". Earlier Brown, commenting on whether the silence motif was drawn from Mk, queried: "Luke reported neither of those two Marcan silences [Mk 14,61; 15,5]; has he chosen to move the theme to here?" (p. 772).

15. *Ibid.*, p. 785.

16. *Ibid.*, p. 783.

17. *Ibid.* On the historical background of the reign of Herod Antipas see HOEHNER, *Herod Antipas*, p. 83-109; FITZMYER, p. 1481, n. on 23,7; BROWN, p. 763.

18. For example, D.L. BOCK, *Proclamation*, p. 204.

Though Luke sometimes omitted Markan material in parallel places, he nonetheless utilized such vocabulary and motifs, and in the case of the Herod story, especially from the story of the death of the Baptist (Mk 6,14-29). He drew on Markan material from Pilate's trial of Jesus (the motif of silence: Mk 15,5 / Lk 23,9), editing the many accusations (Mk 15,3), focusing instead on the intensity of the accusers (23,10), and borrowed themes from the Markan account of the mockery by the Roman soldiers (Mk 15,16-20, particularly the vesting). Elaborating on these themes in Acts, Luke continued to portray Jesus as the prophet whom God confirmed by signs though he was rejected in Jerusalem[19]. We must also be alert to Luke's redaction of a brief but significant phrase concerning Herod (12,1 diff. Mk 8,15).

The Use of the Markan Baptist Material: Mk 6,14-29 and Lk 23,6-16

What must not be neglected is the significant Lukan omission of Markan material namely Mk 6,17-29 (Herod's ordering the death of John the Baptist). The parallels between the death of the Baptist (Mk 6,17-29) and the death of Jesus (Mk 15,1-46) have sometimes been noted[20]. We shall be alert to similarities between Mk 6,17-29 and 23,6-16. Schürmann remarked: "Mk 6,17-29 hat Luk gelesen und ausgelassen"[21]. How did Luke utilize the material in Mk concerning John the Baptist and Herod? Our research has been guided by the working hypothesis that Luke employed vocabulary from Markan passages he chose to omit, which would also apply in this case.

It is necessary for us to consider possible reasons which prompted Luke to omit the Markan account of Herod ordering the execution of John the Baptist (cf. Mk 6,17-29)[22]. F.H. Woods suggested it was because it would be "of little

---

19. Hastings observed: "A word about St Luke's fondness for duality. It is found all through the structure of his writing, pre-eminently in the relation of Gospel and Acts – two parts of a single whole. They are united by a multitude of common themes, by their internal parallelism and continuity of plot [...] There are several other examples of dual structure, and in each case the first part is preparatory for the second, in which it finds its achievement. Thus there is the parallelism between the birth of John and that of Jesus; and there is the Galilean ministry, followed by the journey to Jerusalem. In the Acts there is the section centring on Peter and the section centring on Paul. An awareness of this device is useful for understanding the more important matters and relating individual parts to the complete literary scheme" (*Prophet*, p. 11-12).

20. R.A. GUELICH, *Mark 1-8:26* (WBC 34A), Dallas, TX, 1989, p. 328; see also C. WOLFF, *Zur Bedeutung Johannes des Täufers im Markusevangelium*, in *TLZ* 102 (1977) 857-865; J. GNILKA, *Das Martyrium Johannes des Täufer (Mk 6,17-29)*, in FS SCHMID, 1973, 78-92, esp. p. 80-81; J. ERNST, *Das Evangelium nach Markus* (RNT), 1981, p. 186.

21. H. SCHÜRMANN, *Das Lukasevangelium. T. 1*, p. 508.

22. See R.L. WEBB, *John the Baptizer and Prophet. A Socio-Historical Study* (JSNT SS, 62), Sheffield, 1991, p. 60-61, which offered a helpful overview of the 28 pericopes containing Baptist material in Lk-Acts.

importance to St. Luke's Gentile readers"[23]. Marshall proposed Luke "presupposed a fuller knowledge on the part of his readers, no doubt derived from current traditions"[24]. Hoehner mustered five different reasons to account for the omission[25]. R.A. Guelich observed this was "Mark's only story without any reference to Jesus"[26]. Perhaps Luke omitted it to allow more space for stories of Jesus. Other explanations exist[27]. The significant omission by Luke of Mk's

23. F.H. WOODS, *Origin*, p. 73.

24. MARSHALL, *Luke*, p. 149.

25. HOEHNER, *Herod Antipas*, p. 112-113: "One reason for Luke's omission of the story may have been that he has already included a great deal about the Baptist, as for example his birth narrative. Secondly, since Luke had concluded the content of John's preaching near the beginning of his Gospel culminating in the Baptist's imprisonment (3:19-20), it would be unnatural for him to follow Mark in mentioning it again here. This is not the only example of an incident omitted by Luke because he had already included a similar story before having seen Mark. Thirdly, having finished with John in 3:19-20, Luke may not have wanted to mix up the Baptist and Jesus stories. Fourthly, it may be that he thought it less important, either because it did not appeal to him, or because he thought it unsuitable for his special purpose. Fifthly, in every case Luke's interest in Herod Antipas was in relationship to Jesus, and since this pericope shows no direct relationship to Jesus this may explain its omission". In addition, see W. WINK, *John the Baptist in the Gospel Tradition* (SNTS MS, 7), Cambridge, p. 28, 46, 50, 55. For a brief treatment see also his article *John the Baptist*, in *IDBS*, p. 487-488, esp. p. 488. Walaskay used the omission of the account of the beheading of John the Baptist to counter the view that Luke had special access to information from the Herod household. "If Luke was so well informed about the affairs of Herod, then why did he neglect the most well-attested story about the tetrarch, the beheading of John the Baptist?" (*Trial*, p. 88).

26. GUELICH, *Mark 1-8:26*, p. 328.

27. CADBURY, *Style*, p. 94: "Similar shielding of his hero is perhaps shown by Luke in his omission of the account of John the Baptist's death, Mark 6,21-29 (although it is implied in Luke 9,7.9.19); and some would add, in the omission from Acts of the martyrdom of Peter and Paul. In view of the *mortes persecutorum* in Acts 1,18.19; 12,23, it cannot be said that Luke avoids violent death scenes for artistic reasons, or out of sensitiveness". See A. HASTINGS, *Prophet*, p. 42-43: "While the first two gospels treat of the Baptist's martyrdom as something of importance and interest in itself, St Luke is only concerned with it as throwing light on the relationship between Herod and Jesus, with which the first two evangelists were not concerned. This fits in with Luke's whole treatment of St John. He starts with a detailed account of the Precursor's birth and preaching; then suddenly after 3:20 John fades out of the picture. ... Luke's treatment of St Peter in Acts is worth comparing".

E. Bammel affirmed Luke's abbreviation of a portion previous to this section: "Mark vi. 14-16 is shortened by Luke (ix. 7-9) but preserved in essence. We find a certain loosening of the connection between John and Jesus in v. 9; but this is a literary device that enables the author to look ahead to the Herodean scene in the trial of Jesus.

It is due to the same intention to shorten the account that the story of John's death, which may have been at the disposal of Luke in two forms, was mentioned only in one summarizing sentence (iii. 19f.)" (*The Baptist in Early Christian Tradition*, in *NTS* 17-18 [1972] 95-128, p. 107).

Denaux pointed out Luke omitted other Markan material "où Jean le Baptiste est identifié implicitement avec le prophète Élie" (*L'hypocrisie*, p. 283 = ²1989, p. 193). These were Mk 1,6; 9,9-13. According to Denaux Luke saw that Jesus, much more than John, was comparable to Elijah. He believed the omission by Luke of Mk 15,35 where Jesus called out to God was

account of Herod's ordering the death of John the Baptist, plus the inclusion of vocabulary and themes from that section of Mk, support the view that Luke used this Markan passage to compose the Herod pericope in his passion narrative.

The Use of the Markan Mockery Material: Mk 15,16-20 and Lk 23,6-16

One of the weaknesses of previous studies is that the only Markan vocabulary evaluated, if at all, was that of Mk 15, without examining vocabulary and motifs that Luke may have drawn from other parts of Mk[28]. We should pay close attention to a working hypothesis articulated by Brown that "we must take into account Luke's habit of drawing upon the vocabulary of other Marcan passages that he has omitted"[29]. If this is the case, and we believe it is, the story of the mockery by the Roman soldiers (Mk 15,16-20 om. Lk) has been put to good use

---

confirmation of this interpretation. See also SCHÜRMANN, *Das Lukasevangelium*, T. 1, p. 508, and DARR, *Glorified*, p. 228, n. 43, 233-234, 237.

D.A.S. Ravens proposed that Luke "left the detailed account of John's death because it would not only obscure the structure of the section but also that, for Luke, there was only one prophet whose death was important (13,33)" (*Luke 9,7-62 and the Prophetic Role of Jesus*, in *NTS* 36 [1990] 119-129, p. 122).

J.P. Meier affirmed the likelihood of Mk as Luke's only source for the Baptist's arrest. "The mention in passing of John's arrest in Luke 3:19-20 is most probably based solely on Mark 1:14 + 6:17-29. Luke proceeds to omit Mark 6:17-29, preserving only a reference to John's beheading as Antipas puzzles over Jesus in Luke 9:9. [...] There is no reason to suppose that Luke knew anything about John's imprisonment and execution beyond what Mark's Gospel told him" (*A Marginal Jew. Rethinking the Historical Jesus*. Vol. 2. *Mentor, Message, and Miracles* [ABRL], New York, 1994, p. 227, n. 243). See also GNILKA, *Das Martyrium*, 78-92, esp. p. 89-90. In addition, see the discussion of Mk 6,14-29 in J. ERNST, *Johannes der Täufer. Interpretation – Geschichte – Wirkungsgeschichte* (BZNW, 53), Berlin - New York, 1989, esp. p. 25-30, who observed: "Johannes erleidet wie Jesus das Prophetenschicksal: wegen seines mutigen Zeugnisses (3,19f.) wird er von Herodes, der in der lukanischen Passionserzählung neben Pilatus as Repräsentant der bösen Welt (23,6-12) erscheint, ins Gefängnis geworfen und getotet. Lukas hat zwar nicht wie Markus ein ausführliche täuferische Leidensgeschiche, aber das Matryrium klingt doch in der Bemerkung des Herodes: 'Johannes habe ich selbst enthaupten lassen' (9,9) unüberhörbar an. ... Der Täufer ist für Lukas der Prototyp Jesu, angefangenbei der Ankündigung der Geburt bis hin zum gewaltsamen Tode" (p. 111).

28. Two notable exceptions were F. HAHN, *Der Prozess Jesu nach dem Johannesevangelium* (EKK NT Vorarbeiten, Heft 2), Neunkirchen - Vluyn, 1970, p. 35, n. 17, who regrettably, did not treat the matter in detail, and W.J. Bennett who wondered whether the Herod story stemmed from the Markan reference to the Herodians (Mk 3,6). "Could it be that Mark's reference to the Herodians has been the inspiration for this story?" (*The Herodians in Mark's Gospel*, in *NT* 17 [1975] 9-14, p. 13, n. 19). Referring to the account as "Jesus' audience before Herod", he was not sure whether the episode derived "solely from Luke's special traditions or is due to Luke's own imagination".

29. BROWN, *Death*, p. 581. Hawkins gave the example of Mk 6,20 (ἠπόρει) in comparing Lk 9,7 (διηπόρει) stating: "Lk does not give the part of the narrative in which Mk uses ἠπόρει" (*Horae Synopticae*, 1899, p. 59; ²1909, p. 74). See further BÜCHELE, p. 31, n. 43.

in Lk 23,6-12. We now examine Lukan passages that prepare for the Herod story (23,6-16) to discern Luke's redactional hand.

Preparatory Lukan Passages Concerning Herod

Our position is that Luke carefully prepared for the scene through earlier episodes (primarily 9,7-9 / Mk 6,14-16 and 13,31-33)[30]. The only reference in Lk to the Baptist's death is 9,9. Luke offered a summary statement (3,19 diff. Mk 6,17) περὶ πάντων ὧν ἐποίησεν πονηρῶν ὁ Ἡρῴδης. The brief reference to the Baptist's death at this part of Lk is the occasion when "Luke *thematically* separates John's ministry from that of Jesus (which began at his baptism)"[31]. Brown declared that Luke reduced the Markan account "to two one-verse notices (3:20; 9:9)"[32]. As we have seen in our survey, one sign of Lukan redaction is the abbreviation of source material. It would appear Luke reduced the Baptist account and used some of the Markan vocabulary and themes in other parts of his Gospel.

Hastings recognized the connection of 9,7-9 not only with the Baptist material of Mk 6,14-16, but also with Herod's reaction in Lk 23,8: "The source of our first passage 9:7-9 is clearly the parallel passage in Mark 6:14-16. But what is significant in the Lucan version is the last line (no parallel in Mark): 'And he was eager to see him.' This obviously links us with 23:8. 'Herod was overjoyed at seeing Jesus; for a long time he had been eager to have sight of him'"[33]. He

---

30. BROWN, p. 769-770, also highlighted 3,19-20; 9,7-9; and 13,31-33 as relevant to a discussion of 23,6-16. Légasse commented: "L'interrogation d'Herode et son effort pour voir Jésus relèvent d'une addition de Luc à Mc 6,14-16" (*Le procès*, t. 2, p. 372, n. 48). Note the following related observation: "At a later time when Jesus had gained some notoriety, which included having crowds follow him and sending his disciples out on a preaching mission, he looked like John to Antipas (MK 6:14-16) and Antipas became intent on arresting and killing him (LK 13:31-33). But Jesus left his territory and frustrated this intention. This analogy between Jesus' movement and John's is confirmed by Josephus [*Ant*. 18, 118] in that he also attibutes Antipas' attention to John to the fact that he was leading a mass movement that was seen by Antipas as a political threat" (P. HOLLENBACH, *Social Aspects of John the Baptizer's Preaching Mission in the Context of Palestinian Judaism*, in *ANRW* II.19.1, Berlin - New York, 1979, 850-875, p. 863). To a lesser extent we should also bear in mind the Transfiguration (9,28-36). Shortly before the Transfiguration Luke reported Herod's confusion about Jesus' identity and his desire to see him (9,7-9).

31. WEBB, *John the Baptizer*, p. 64. So also DARR, *Glorified*, p. 235. Note his interesting suggestion that Luke's treatment of 3,18-20 was fashioned on the model of the "ubiquitous prophet-versus-king confrontation of the Septuagint" (p. 232; see further p. 182-197). This has a bearing on 23,6-16. "Herod's interaction with Jesus continues the prophet versus king pattern evoked by the relationship between John and the Tetrarch" (p. 316).

32. BROWN, *Death*, p. 764.

33. HASTINGS, *Prophet*, p. 45. So also SCHÜRMANN, *Lukasevangelium*, T. 1, p. 505, and WEBB, *John the Baptizer*, p. 61, 66. Consider SCHÜRMANN, *Das Lukasevangelium*, T. 1, p. 509: F. NEIRYNCK, *La matière marcienne*, in ID., *L'Évangile de Luc*, p. 168, n. 47 (= ²1989, p. 78, n. 47 = *Evangelica*, 1982, p. 48, n. 47). So also FITZMYER, p. 756; MARSHALL, *Luke*, p. 149: "The paragraph [3,18-20] is Luke's own composition, strongly Lucan in language, and probably

further noted that Herod's attitude toward Jesus was basically the same as that of Herod toward the Baptist (Mk 6,20). Prior to this passage (9,7-9) Luke has already been setting the stage by focusing on Jesus' identity[34]. It was necessary for Luke to refashion Mark's presentation of Herod here in light of 23,8-11[35]. As in the Herod trial, Luke's redaction led him to generalizations. In this case Luke referred more generally to τὰ γινόμενα πάντα (9,7) in place of Mark's reference to the miracles of Jesus (Mk 6,14)[36]. Verbal reminiscences from Mk 6,17-29 in 9,7-9 include: ἠπόρει (Mk 6,20) – διηπόρει (9,7); ἀκούσας αὐτοῦ πολλά – περὶ οὗ ἀκούω ποιαῦτα (9,9b); καὶ ἡδέως αὐτοῦ ἤκουεν – καὶ ἐζήτει ἰδεῖν αὐτόν (9,9c)[37].

In a discussion of "Phrases of Mark Misunderstood or Transferred by Luke" Cadbury observed: "In Mark 6,15, Herod is told by some that Jesus is a prophet like one of the prophets; Luke (9,8) understands this to mean that one of the ancient prophets is risen, an idea parallel to the other suggestions, that he is John the Baptist risen from the dead, or that Elias has appeared.

It is possible that Luke makes the same change in 9,19, for there he suggests again ὅτι προφήτης τις τῶν ἀρχαίων ἀνέστη (cf. Mk 8,28, ὅτι εἷς τῶν προφητῶν). Matthew also apparently understands this phrase of Mark to apply to dead prophets, and here this may even be the view of Mark. But that Mark did not feel that a new prophet was impossible, that the line was finally extinct, is clear from Mark 6,15 just quoted"[38].

Mk 6,16 indicated that Herod believed that John the Baptist had been raised from the dead. Luke did not report this since he did not directly recount the death of the Baptist. However, at Lk 9,7 the possibility of the raising of the Baptist was posed by others[39].

resting on Mk. 6:14-29 which Luke otherwise passes over". Cadbury commented: "In Mark 6,14 and Luke 9,7 it is implied that John the Baptist is dead, though neither Gospel has thus far mentioned his death. Mark at once explains the reference by narrating (6,17-29) the circumstances of John's death (note γάρ, vs. 17) but Luke nowhere directly relates it" (Style, p. 102). See also Gundry, Mark, p. 317: "and given Herod's regarding Jesus merely as a curiosity in Luke 23:8-12 (whose tradition has probably led to redaction of Mark 6:14-16 in Luke 9:9 ...)".

34. SCHÜRMANN, Lukasevangelium, T. 1, p. 505-506: "Die eigentliche redaktionelle Bestimmung der Einlage ist aber eine andere: Schon seit 7,16.19f.49; 8,25.28 ist die Frage lebendig: 'Wer ist dieser?' Sie wird nun hier erneut und betonter (diff Mk!) vom Landesherrn Jesus (vgl. 23,6) gestellt".

35. Ibid., p. 508: "Den angsterfüllten Herodes von Mk 6,16 konnte Luk im Hinblick auf 23,8-11 nicht brauchen". Note further Schürmann's evaluations of the Lk-Mk relationship. "Die luk Mk-Differenzen sind alle so sehr aus der luk Intention zu erklären, dass neben der Mk-Vorlage keine luk Sondertradition nachweisbar ist und auch nicht auf eine vom Mk-Text abweichende Mk-Vorlage geschlossen werden muss. [...] Mk 6,17-29 hat Luk gelesen und ausgelassen".

36. So FITZMYER, p. 757.

37. I am indebted to F. NEIRYNCK, La matière marcienne, p. 168, n. 47 (= ²1989, p. 78, n. 47 = Evangelica, p. 48, n. 47), for these comparisons.

38. CADBURY, Style, p. 97.

39. HAWKINS, Horae Synopticae, 1899, p. 56, 59; ²1909, p. 71, 74, and CADBURY, Style,

Luke also transposed material concerning the Baptist. As detected by Cadbury: "The account of the imprisonment of John the Baptist, which occurs in Mark 6,17-29, is found in Luke, greatly abbreviated, after the account of John's preaching (Luke 3,19-20)"[40]. The reason for this is explained as "clearly the desire to conclude at once a subject when it has been introduced. Thus Luke anticipates the actual imprisonment of John the Baptist by inserting it immediately after the account of John's teaching"[41].

Of particular importance is the omission of the Markan phrase τῆς ζύμης 'Ηρῴδου (Mk 8,15 diff. Lk 12,1) which Luke understood to mean hypocrisy (ὑπόκρισις). He sought to eliminate any insinuation that Herod's testimony was unreliable[42].

One should not overlook the Lukan account of the Transfiguration (9,28-36) in relation to this pericope[43]. The context is important since it follows the first passion prediction (9,22 / Mk 8,31). The connection between the Transfiguration and passion has been noted. "Zweck der himmlischen Erscheinung wird die Leidensansage; damit ist bewiesen, dass das Leiden göttlicher Bestimmung entspricht. ... Das ganze Geschehen hat so einen typologischen Sinn im Blick auf die Ereignisse in Jerusalem"[44].

---

p. 100.

40. CADBURY, Style, p. 77.

41. This was also the motivation for the transposition of material concerning Peter since Luke treated the denials before the Sanhedrin trial (22,54-62 cf. Mk 14,54.66-72).

42. Cf. HOEHNER, Herod Antipas, p. 211, who dismissed the difference as unimportant.

43. J.P. Meier argued Luke had no other source for the Transfiguration than Mk (Marginal, Vol. 2, p. [971]-972, n. 9). Cf. Barbara E. REID, The Transfiguration: A Source- and Redaction-Critical Study of Luke 9:28-38 (CahRB 32), Paris, 1993. Diss. Catholic U., Washington, D.C., 1988 (dir. J.P. MEIER), who maintained Luke employed a non-Markan source in addition to Mk for the Transfiguration. Although her study has been favorably received by I.H. Marshall (JTS 45 [1994] 662-664), J. Taylor (RB 101 [1994] 623-624, esp. p. 624: "This confident and convincing study of Luke's account of the Transfiguration has several important implications") and W.R. Stegner (JBL 114 [1995] 526-527), Meier was "ultimately not convinced by the carefully argued thesis" of Reid. Previously R.H. STEIN, The Transfiguration (Mark 9:2-8) A Misplaced Resurrection-Account?, in JBL 95 (1976) 79-96, esp. p. 95, n. 76, remarked that TAYLOR, Behind, p. 89; BLINZLER, Die neutestamentlichen Berichte über die Verklärung Jesu, Münster, 1937, 42-44, 57-62; and R.H. FULLER, The Foundations of New Testament Christology, New York, 1965, p. 172, supported the view that Luke employed a special tradition for his account of the Transfiguration. But see NEIRYNCK, La matière marcienne, in L'Évangile de Luc, p. 173-174 (= ²1989, p. 83-84 = Evangelica, p. 53-54), for an examination of the Markan material of the Lukan Transfiguration account.

44. CONZELMANN, Die Mitte, p. 46 = 57, p. 47 = 59. Catchpole also recognized the connection between the Transfiguration and the passion: "Firstly, the redactional μετὰ τοὺς λόγους τούτους, Lk 9.28, connects the event, even more closely than the Markan account had done, with the sayings about Jesus' way of suffering, Lk 9.23-27. Secondly, the change from ἀγαπητός, Mk 9.7, to ἐκλελεγμένος, Lk 9.35, cf. 23.35, makes more explicit the allusion to Is 42.1, cf. Is 49.2. The occurrence of the latter word in only the two places, at the Transfiguration and at the passion is itself important as part of the scheme connecting the two

There is, in addition, the preparatory passage in 13,31-33[45]. Denaux raised the possibility that 13,31 was a Lukan use of the motif in Mk 6,19 that Herod desired to kill the Baptist. Luke employed it in referring to Jesus[46]. Luke's redaction in 13,31-35 sought to emphasize the prophetic end of Jesus[47]. In 23,8 reference was made to Herod's desire to see some σημεῖον, which Jesus referred to broadly in 13,32: ἰδοὺ ἐκβάλλω δαιμόνια καὶ ἰάσεις[48]. This also built on the material of 9,9.

Moreover, 20,1-26, a dispute over the authority of Jesus compared to that of the Baptist, pits Jesus against the chief priests, scribes and elders; the controversy concerning payment of taxes to Caesar, will be important to consider. The term ἐξουσία (23,7) also occurs at 20,2.8. Again this discussion included reference to John the Baptist. Note further "the chief priests and scribes" (20,1.19 [different order]; cf. 23,10 / Mk 15,3) and their response of silence (20,26).

We should look next at Jesus' prophecy (21,12) that his disciples will be delivered up to the synagogues (chief priests and scribes) and prisons (John the Baptist in the Gospel and the apostles in Acts). This is connected with 12,11-12 (cf. Mk 13,11) and basically repeats what is contained there. Luke added καὶ τὰς ἀρχὰς καὶ τὰς ἐξουσίας (12,11) to Mk 13,11 which may simply be a variation of vocabulary for kings and governors[49]. Mk 6,25.26.27 referred to Herod as king (cf. Mk 6,23 kingdom). Brown also focused on the relation between 21,12 and the Herod pericope[50]. Note again the use of the term ἐξουσία (23,7; 12,11; 22,53;

---

theologically" (CATCHPOLE, *The Trial of Jesus*, 1971, p. 181). Consider the remark of D.A.S. Ravens: "The transfiguration is itself prophetic of later events, the passion, the ascension, and in its eschatological character, but, more immediately, it serves to show that the prophet Jesus who is about to set out for Jerusalem and the Son of Man who will come in glory and judgement, and of whom Jesus speaks so often, are ultimately the same" (*Luke 9,7-62*, p. 126).

45. See DENAUX, *L'hypocrisie*, p. 265-268 (= [2]1989, p. 175-178). Cf. R. SCHNACKENBURG, *Lk 13,31-33. Eine Studie zur lukanischen Redaktion und Theologie*, in C. BUSSMANN and W. RADL (eds.), *Der Treue Gottes Trauen*, FS G. SCHNEIDER, Freiburg - Basel - Vienna, 1991, 229-241. Ernst highlighted the comparsion of Mk 6,14-16 and Lk 13,31-33: "Bedenkenswert ist der Vergleich mit der barschen Kritik Jesu an Antipas (der Fuchs), die im Zussamenhang mit der Furcht des Landesherrn vor der 'Volksbewegung' (Mk 6,14-16) und der Tötungsabsicht (Lk 13,31-33) gesehen werden muss" (*Johannes der Täufer*, p. 315).

46. DENAUX, *L'hypocrisie*, p. 265 (= 175). He concluded that 13,31-33 was the redactional work of Luke based on the judgment that there was not a single non-Lukan word in the pericope and because the passage contained several themes germane to Luke's theological perspective which were well integrated into the passage (p. 284 = 194). For an evaluation of Denaux's theory, see FITZMYER, p. 1028. Darr disagreed with various aspects of Denaux's argument (*Glorified*, p. 259-260).

47. DENAUX, *L'hypocrisie*, p. 265, n. 60 (= 175, n. 60).

48. NEIRYNCK, *La matière marcienne*, p. 168, n. 47 (= [2]1989, p. 78, n. 47 = *Evangelica*, p. 48, n. 47), recommended Denaux's article (p. 265-268) for its examination of the contacts between 13,31 and Mk 6.

49. Also noted by BUCK, p. 177.

50. BROWN, *Death*, p. 764: "In Luke 21:12 [Jesus] warns his followers that they would be led 'before kings and governors for the sake of my name.' It is not surprising, then, to find Jesus

Acts 26.12.18). Having highlighted various similarities of vocabulary and themes between previous parts of Lk with 23,6-16, we now undertake an exegesis of the pericope.

Verse by Verse Exegesis of 23,6-16

Verse 6

Πιλᾶτος δὲ ἀκούσας ἐπηρώτησεν εἰ ὁ ἄνθρωπος Γαλιλαῖός ἐστιν.

"When Pilate heard this, he asked whether the man was a Galilean".

Although in Mk reference to Pilate is found only in chapter 15[51], mention of Pilate together with Herod already occurs in Lk 3,1, the latter identified as τετρααρχοῦντος τῆς Γαλιλαίας (not in Mk); 3,19 Ἡρῴδης ὁ τετραάρχης (diff. Mk 6,17 Ἡρῴδης); 9,7 Ἡρῴδης ὁ τετραάρχης (diff. Mk 6,14 ὁ βασιλεὺς Ἡρῴδης)[52]; see also Acts 13,1 (Ἡρῴδου τοῦ τετραάρχου). Lk 3,1-2, it has been said, is "wohl redaktionelle Bildung des Luk"[53]. Other scholars observed the similarity of these verses with the beginning of the prophetic books of Hos 1,1 and Jer 1,1[54]. The reference to Herod in 3,1 is also preparatory for the account about John the Baptist (3,19-20). Pilate is named in 23,1 (=Mk 15,1).3 (= Mk 15,2).20 (= Mk 15,12).24 (= Mk 15,15).52 (= Mk 15,43) and 23,4.6.11.12.13; elsewhere; 13,1; Acts 3,13; 4,27; 13,28[55]. Taking into consideration Luke's predilection for preparing later passages by means of earlier ones, by placing the names in close proximity (cf. 3,1) he is already anticipating 23,6-16. The only other reference to Pilate in Lk outside chapter 23 is in connection with Galileans who are referred to three times (13,1.2bis), mention also being made of Jerusalem in the context (13,4)[56]. This passage is frequently used to explain the animosity between Pilate and Herod (23,12).

himself led before a king as well as a Roman governor".

51. Mk 15,1.2.4.8.[9: he].12.14.15.43.44.

52. Other references to Herod Antipas were 3,19; 8,3; 9,7.9; 23,7-15 (FITZMYER, p. 457). See SCHNEIDER, *Lukas*, p. 83-84. Darr noted that the figure of Herod provided a continuity in Lk-Acts which extended from 3,1 to Acts 13,1 (*Glorified*, p. 314). This, in contrast to Mk and Mt which contained references to Herod primarily in the encounter with John the Baptist (p. 314, n. 176, and 315, n. 178). On the designation of Herod Antipas as king in Mk, see P. DSCHULNIGG, *Sprache, Redaktion und Intention des Markus-Evangeliums. Eigentümlichkeiten der Sprache des Markus-Evangeliums und ihre Bedeutung für die Redaktionskritik* (SBB, 11), Stuttgart, 1984. Diss. Luzern, 1983-84 (dir. E. RUCKSTUHL and W. KIRCHSCHLÄGER), p. 222-223.

53. SCHÜRMANN, *Das Lukasevangelium*, T. 1, p. 153.

54. GRUNDMANN, *Lukas*, ²1963, p. 101. So also MARSHALL, *Luke*, p. 149.

55. FITZMYER, p. 456.

56. All of the other references to Pilate were found in Lk 23,1.3.4.6.11.12.13.20.24.52.On the use of the term Galileans compare Acts 5,37.

The aorist participle ἀκούσας + δέ is found in Mk 6,16 (diff. 9,9), with
reference to Herod who had beheaded the Baptist, just as in 23,6⁵⁷. ἀκούσας +
δέ is an element of Lukan style⁵⁸. Luke employed the phrase ἤκουσεν δέ in 9,7,
which is one of the verses which sets the stage for Jesus' encounter with Herod.
It occurs thirteen times in Acts, six of those in chapters 1–15 and seven in chapters
16–28. In the Acts account of Paul and the Roman Tribune the phrase ἀκούσας +
δέ appears (Acts 22,26). In the following chapter the phrase occurs again this time
relating a plot against Paul's life (Acts 23,16).

ἐπερωτάω occurred 56 times in the NT, of which 25 were in Mk, 17 in Lk
and 2 in Acts⁵⁹. The term ἐπερωτάω is a preferred Markan term. Luke borrowed
from Mk 6 times (8,30 aorist ἐπηρώτησεν δὲ αὐτόν / Mk 5,9 imperfect καὶ
ἐπηρώτα αὐτόν; 9,18 / Mk 8,27; 18,18 / Mk 10,17; 20,27 / Mk 12,18; 20,40
present infinitive / Mk 12,34; 21,7 / Mk 13,3) and changed the form in every
instance⁶⁰. In 5 cases he substituted the aorist for the imperfect and in one case
he used the present infinitive in place of the aorist (20,40)⁶¹. Although
ἐπηρώτησεν is used in Mk 15,2 in Pilate's interrogation of Jesus, the Lukan
parallel (Lk 23,3) contains the simple form ἠρώτησεν. The compound form occurs
again in Mk 15,4, though there is no direct parallel in Lk. It seems reasonable to
assume that he transferred it to 23,9, exactly as in Mk 15,4.

One scholar argued that Luke preferred the simple form (ἐρωτάω) to the
compound (ἐπερωτάω) on the basis of 9,45 (Mk 9,32); 20,3 (Mk 11,29); 23,3
(Mk 15,2)⁶². But a comparison of his numerical computations of Mk, Lk, and
Acts shows there is not such a significant difference. Indeed, in Lk-Acts there is
almost a balance between use of both forms⁶³. It is important to note that

57. Note the repetition of the motif in Mk 6,14.16 (NEIRYNCK, *Duality*, ²1988, p. 98). See
G. SCHNEIDER, ἀκούω, in *EWNT* 1, col. 126-131, esp. col. 128 (= p. 52-54, esp. p. 53). See
23,8 below. See further Boismard and Lamouille in NEIRYNCK, *Le texte*, p. 317 (= 256). The
term was employed in the LXX. See for example *GELS(TP)*, p. 7-8, and *GELS*, p. 16. Mark also
used the aorist participle in Mk 2,17; 10,47; 12,28.

58. RADL, *Paulus*, p. 398, Boismard and Lamouille in NEIRYNCK, *Le texte*, p. 256,
BOISMARD, *En quête*, p. 124 (cf. ἀκούσας δέ 7,9; 14,15; 18,22; Acts 7,12; 8,14; 14,14; 18,26;
22,26; 23,16), and GOULDER, *Luke*, p. 800.

59. *NTV*, p. 27; see also BÜCHELE, p. 32, n. 55.

60. *NTV*, p. 250; cf. W. SCHENK, ἐπερωτάω, in *EWNT* 2, cols. 52-53 (= p. 21): "Luke (17
occurrences + Acts 5:27; 23:34) takes it over from Mark 7 times and in 8:9 [/ Mk 4,10]
exchanges the Markan simple form for the compound", though he did not specify where the term
occurred. CADBURY, *Style*, p. 167, cited 8,9 / Mk 4,10, where Luke preferred the compound.
See further Boismard and Lamouille in NEIRYNCK, *Le texte*, p. 322 (= 261), and BOISMARD, *En
quête*, p. 124.

61. See CADBURY, *Style*, p. 160, where he indicated the imperfect was "frequently corrected
by Luke to the aorist". Cadbury's list was basically the same with the exception that 20,40 was
not listed while Lk 9,20 / Mk 8,29 is.

62. CADBURY, *Style*, p. 167.

63. Cadbury maintained that Luke preferred the simple form over the compound: 8,9 / Mk
4,10; 9,45 / Mk 9,32; 20,3 / Mk 11,29; 23,3 / Mk 15,2. However, the statistics he offered in

ἐπερωτάω, which appeared in v. 7, is repeated in v. 9. Luke appears to have borrowed the imperfect ἐπηρώτα (Mk 15,4) for the Herod pericope (23,9). It was previously used in the conflict story concerning payment of taxes to Caesar (20,21 ἐπηρώτησαν; diff. Mk 12,14) which forms part of the background for the charges against Jesus (23,3) and in the mockery (22,64: ἐπηρώτων + τίς ἐστιν ὁ παίσας σε; diff. Mk 14,65[64]). Note also the ἐπηρώτησαν δὲ αὐτόν in 21,7, in lieu of ἐπηρώτα αὐτόν in the parallel Mk 13,3. When Jesus queried the disciples who people thought he was, with one response being John the Baptist, both Mark and Luke used ἐπερωτάω (Mk 8,27-28 ἐπηρώτα / Lk 9,18-19 ἐπηρώτησεν). The phrase ἐπερωτάω + δέ was found in Lk 3,14 (special material) where John was responding to various questions put forward by tax collectors and soldiers (στρατευόμενοι)[65].

It was also employed in what has been described as "the parallel passage, Acts 23,34"[66], where Paul was asked (ἐπερωτήσας) his province of origin by the governor. The other occurrence in Acts (Acts 5,27) is in the context of the arrest of the apostles who are questioned by the high priest in the presence of the Sanhedrin. The compound form in the NT is "more frequent than the simple form ..., as was the case already in the LXX", where it is found approximately 85 times in the LXX[67]. Thus, this term is very significant for our argument.

The indirect interrogative εἰ is used frequently in classical Greek[68]. In Mk 15,44 Pilate asked whether Jesus was already dead (ἐπηρώτησεν αὐτὸν εἰ πάλαι

---

support of his statement suggest Luke used the simple only three instances more than the compound. The simple ἐρωτάω occurred 15 times in Lk and 7 in Acts while there were 17 instances of the compound in Lk and 2 in Acts (*Style*, p. 167). And at least in one case Luke replaced the Markan καὶ ἐπηρώτα with εἶπεν δέ (Mk 8,29 / 9,20) (p. 160). In a comparison of simple and compound, the tally was: Mk: 3/25; Lk: 15/17; Acts 7/2. The total in Lk-Acts of 22 simple versus 19 compound did not seem to convey such a strong preference in favor of the simple form.

64. See NEIRYNCK, *Luke 14,1-6. Lukan Composition and Q Saying*, in C. BUSSMANN and W. RADL (eds.), *Der Treue Gottes*, FS G. SCHNEIDER, 1991, 243-263, p. 248 (= *Evangelica II*, 1991, 183-203; 203-204: Additional Note; p. 189).

65. See below on 23,11.

66. GOULDER, *Luke*, Vol. 2, p. 759.

67. SCHENK, ἐπερωτάω, in *EWNT* 2, cols. 52-53 (= p. 21); cf. *GELS*, p. 167, which indicated the term is found 75 times in the LXX. See further *GELS(TP)*, p. 87, which listed the following examples: LXX Ps 40,9; Ec 3,11.13.22; 9,1.12; Is 14,16; 17,7; 22,25; 32,2; Jer 9,12; 11,3; 17,5; 20,15.16; Ez 18,5.

68. F.C. CONYBEARE and St. George STOCK, *Grammar of Septuagint Greek. With Selected Readings from the Septuagint According to the Text of Swete*, Boston, MA, 1905; Peabody, MA, 1988, p. 89. See also M. ZERWICK, *Biblical Greek. Illustrated by Examples*, tr. J. SMITH, adapted from the fourth Latin ed., Rome, 1963, p. 137, § 402. ἐπηρώτησεν αὐτὸν εἰ πάλαι ἀπέθανεν. See further Lk 6,7 / Mk 3,2 which contain the indirect interrogative. A.T. ROBERTSON, *A Grammar of the Greek New Testament in the Light of Historical Research*, New York, ²1915; ³1919, ⁴1923, p. 916: "The use of εἰ in a question is elliptical. It is really a condition with the conclusion not expressed or it is an indirect question (cf. Mk 15:44; Lu. 23:6; Ph. 3:12). It is used in the N.T., as in the LXX quite often (Gen. 17:17, etc.)".

ἀπέθανεν / Mk 15,44-45 no par.)[69]. In 23,6 we have ἐπηρώτησεν ... εἰ exactly as in Mk 15,44[70]. Again, our working hypothesis applies. Indicating that Lk 23,6 was "bordering on the indirect question" and thus may be a direct question, Nigel Turner believed that other instances of the interrogative use of εἰ could be definitively ascribed to Luke. "This undoubted Semitism appears only in Biblical Greek. Doubtless it originated in the translated books of the LXX, rendering *'im*, and thence passed into the free Biblical Greek of 2 Maccabees, the Clementine Homilies, the Gospel of Thomas, and the Testament of Abraham. This idiom is Luke's own, not from sources, plain evidence that he is writing free Semitic Greek"[71].

It has been suggested the term ὁ ἄνθρωπος is Lukan vocabulary[72] and "was no doubt derogatory"[73]. Notice the confession of the centurion (Mk 15,39 / Lk 23,47) to which Luke added οὗτος δίκαιος, repeating a phrase found in Lk 2,25 used to describe Simeon[74]. Perhaps Luke reiterated this phrase, applying it to Jesus in the passion narrative to help recall the prophecy uttered by Simeon, and signaling the fulfillment.

The use of the phrase τῷ ἀνθρώπῳ τούτῳ (23,4) should also be considered. Mark used τὸν ἄνθρωπον τοῦτον in Peter's third denial, though Luke omitted it (Mk 14,71 / diff. 22,60). However, it becomes part of Pilate's first declaration of Jesus' innocence (23,4) and occurs twice in 23,14[75].

---

69. See also *NTV*, p. 238, which indicated the εἰ in 6,7 depended upon Mk 3,2. Marshall invited comparison with 6,7, which is taken over from Mk 3,2 (*Luke*, p. 855). See also Mk 10,2 and Mk 15,44: ἐπηώτων αὐτὸν εἰ (diff 16,18). Lukan redaction of Mk was clearly demonstrated in another passage when Luke added ἐπερωτῶ ὑμᾶς εἰ (6,9 / Mk 3,4). On 6,9 see NEIRYNCK, *Luke 14,1-6*, p. 248 (= 189): "'Επερωτῶ ὑμας εἰ is indeed added by Luke ...". See FITZMYER, p. 611: "This Lucan addition ...".; JOHNSON, *Luke*, p. 102. Markan commentaries such as NINEHAM, *Mark*, p. 435, and HOOKER, *Mark*, p. 381, called attention to the omission of Mk 15,44-45 by Luke and Matthew. Consider also TAYLOR, *Mark*, ²1966, p. 600. See further Boismard and Lamouille in NEIRYNCK, *Le texte*, p. 320 (= 259).

70. See comments on εἰ (23,6) in NEIRYNCK, *Luke 14,1-6*, in FS G. SCHNEIDER, p. 248 (= 189); cf. GOULDER, *Luke*, p. 759.

71. *MHT* 4, p. 54. In addition, consult G. LÜDEMANN, εἰ, in *EWNT* 1, cols. 931-933 (= p. 384-385). Consider, however, CHICO CANO, p. 33: "diese Konstruktion [εἰ introducing an indirect question] (ist) nicht sehr beliebt bei Lukas". Radl identified εἰ as Lukan in introducing direction questions (*Paulus*, p. 407).

72. GOULDER, *Luke*, p. 801.

73. MARSHALL, *Luke*, p. 855. See also Mk 14,21 diff. Lk 22,22.

74. Marshall considered to be a redaction of Mk though Fitzmyer did not (MARSHALL, *Luke*, p. 876; FITZMYER, p. 1520). SCHNEIDER, *Lukas*, p. 487: "Das Bekenntnis ist lukanische Neufassung von Mk 15,39", citing G.D. KILPATRICK, *Theme*, in support of such a view. Consider Boismard and Lamouille in NEIRYNCK, *Le texte*, p. 318 (= 257). Mark employed ὁ ἄνθρωπος earlier in his Gospel, though Luke elected not to borrow it (Mk 2,27 diff. Lk 6,5).

75. Consider LÉGASSE, t. 2, p. 211, n. 22. See also Lk 4,4 in a quotation from Dt. PLUMMER claimed: "The reply is a pointed refutation, however, of the special suggestion to Himself, ὁ ἄνθρωπος having direct reference to υἱὸς τ. θεοῦ" (*St. Luke*, ⁵1922, p. 110). The use in Lk 14,30 was found in material having no Markan parallel. See *GELS*, p. 37, concerning LXX Lv

Γαλιλαῖος has been categorized among the Lukan vocabulary of the pericope[76]. The designation is applied to Peter (22,59 / Mk 14,70 hapax) and later to Jesus (23,6)[77]. Previously the term was used in 13,1.2bis, which some scholars conjectured was the basis of the enmity between Pilate and Herod. In addition, the term occurs three times in Acts (1,11; 2,7; 5,37).

In the Markan passion narrative (Mk 15,41) the evangelist, referring to the women from Galilee who witnessed the crucifixion, stated they had followed Jesus and ministered to him (cf. Lk 8,1-3 where there is also mention of Herod Antipas, and Lk 23,49)[78]. In the burial scene Luke again referred to the women who had followed Jesus from Galilee (23,55).

In contrast to Mk 1,9, Luke omitted the indication that Jesus came ἀπὸ Ναζαρὲτ τῆς Γαλιλαίας (diff. 3,21), but the point is made clear in 2,39 and hinted at in 1,26 and 2,4. For Γαλιλαία see the reference in Mk 6,21 (τῆς Γαλιλαίας), omitted by Luke, which is part of the description of Herod's birthday banquet for Herodias prior to the death of the Baptist[79].

The reference to Galilee in 23,6 links the episode to 23,5 which reported that Jesus "stirs up the people, teaching throughout all Judea, from Galilee even to this place". It has been observed that the "mention of Galilee is often taken by scholars to be part of Luke's portrait of the Jewish leaders' propaganda against Jesus, because Galilee was considered a hotbed of revolutionary activity"[80]. The

---

27,28; Jer 17,16.19; Is 17,11. See comments below on 23,14.

76. CADBURY, Style, p. 4; BOISMARD, Synopse, t. 2, p. 418. See further Boismard and Lamouille in NEIRYNCK, Le texte, p. 319 (= 258). GOULDER, Luke, p. 801.

77. As noted by FITZMYER, p. 1006. See BROWN, p. 763, who highlighted the Lukan theme of the shift "from a ministry in Galilee to a denouement in Jerusalem" over and above the Galilean identities of Jesus and his disciples.

78. So also TAYLOR, St. Mark, p. 598; HOOKER, Saint Mark, p. 379; GUNDRY, Mark, p. 951-952. Consider CONZELMANN, Theology, p. 47: "The appearance of the Galilean women assigns the passage to the first epoch of Jesus' ministry. The mention of them of course points forward to the Passion, but that is not all, for they also have a function as 'witnesses from Galilee' similar to that of the disciples, as we see from the part they play later". In this regard we need also consider the role of the women at 23,49 and 24,10, the latter being drawn from Mk 15,40-41. He continued: "The motif of the Galilean women is of course connected with Mark xv,40. The fact that the names vary no doubt indicates a subsidiary tradition, but not necessarily a new 'source' in the specific sense". See also p. 51, 86.

79. Cf. Mk 6,17-29; Mt 14,3-12 omitted this detail that Herod was entertaining the leading men of Galilee. The term Galilee was found 13 times in Lk, 4 of which have been taken over from Mk (4,14 / Mk 1,14; 4,31 / Mk 1,28; 23,49 / Mk 15,41; 24,6 / Mk 16,7) with an additional three cases in Acts (Acts 9,31; 10,37; 13,31) (See CONZELMANN, Die Mitte, p. 18-48 = 27-60), and M. VÖLKEL, Γαλιλαία, ας, Γαλιλαῖος, in EWNT 1, cols. 559-562 (= p. 233-234).

80. SOARDS, Tradition (1985), p. 348, n. 16. He marshalled the following list in support of such a "standard" interpretation of 23,5: J. SCHMID, Lukas, ²1951, 256; D. MILLER, St. Luke, London, 1959, p. 161; A. STÖGER, Saint Luke, 1969, 220; RENGSTORF, Lukas, ¹³1969, 262; DANKER, Jesus, 1972, 232; ERNST, Lukas, 623; HENDRICKX, Narratives, 92; SCHWEIZER, Lukas, 234 (= 351); TALBERT, Reading, 216.

summary reference in 23,5 expressly links the beginning of Jesus' ministry in Galilee (4,14), a theme Luke will repeat in Acts 10,37[81].

Fundamental for 23,6-16 is the detail in 3,1 that Herod is the tetrarch of Galilee and immediately preceeds mention of John (3,2). Luke established early in his Gospel that Jesus drew his witnesses from among those in Galilee. In 8,1-3 Luke wrote of the Galilean women who had followed Jesus, one of whom was married to a man who served in Herod's court (cf. 23,49). Although Galilee is not specifically mentioned in 9,7-9 it serves a definite redactional purpose: "The reason why Herod wishes to 'see' Jesus is a pragmatic one: Luke needs this motif in view of the part which Herod plays later in the departure of Jesus from Galilee and in the Passion"[82]. Mention of Galilee emphasizes that Jesus ministered in the territories of both Pilate and Herod. "The journey to Galilee, of which Mark xiv, 28 and xvi, 7 speak, is replaced by a prophecy spoken in Galilee concerning what will take place in Jerusalem, and in particular by the predictions of the Passion"[83]. The reference to Galilee in 23,5 provides the link between the Herod trial and that of Pilate.

Concerning the parallels between the Gospel and Acts the identical phrases ἀρξάμενος ἀπὸ τῆς Γαλιλαίας (23,5; cf. 24,47 ἀρξάμενοι ἀπὸ Ἰερουσαλήμ[84]) and ἀρξάμενος ἀπὸ τῆς Γαλιλαίας (Acts 10,37) should be noted[85]. Galilee is significant for it is the region where Jesus began his ministry[86]. In Acts Peter

81. É. SAMAIN, La notion de APXH dans l'œuvre lucanienne, in F. NEIRYNCK (ed.), L'Évangile de Luc, 299-328, p. 307, see also p. 304-305, 325 (= 217, 214-215, 235); J. DELOBEL, La rédaction de Lc., IV,14-16a et le "Bericht vom Anfang", in Ibid., p. 203-223, 212, n. 34 (= 122, n. 34); J. DUPONT, Les discours de Pierre dans les Actes et le chapitre XXIV de l'évangile de Luc, in Ibid., p. 329-374, 336 (= 246).

82. CONZELMANN, Theology, p. 51. On the role of Galilee in Lk, see p. 27-60.

83. Ibid., p. 93.

84. J. JEREMIAS, Die Sprache, p. 322: "ἀρξάμενοι ἀπό: → 23,5 Red S. 301 sub καθ' ὅλης". Consult further p. 301: "ἀρξάμενος mit Nennung des Ausgangspunktes (ἀπό) ist lukanisch (Mt 20,8; Lk 23,5; 24,27.47 / Apg 1,22; 8,35; 10,37)".

85. See F.F. BRUCE, The Acts of the Apostles. The Greek Text with Introduction and Commentary, Grand Rapids, MI - Leicester, ³1990, p. 262: "'Beginning from Galilee' characterizes Jesus' ministry as 'beginning from Jerusalem' (Lk. 24:47) characterizes that of the apostles (with an allusion, perhaps, to Isa. 2:3 par. Mic 4:2, where the word of the Lord goes forth from Jerusalem)". Consider the opinion of C.K. Barrett who recounted that, "Moulton goes on to cite the view of Blass that ἀρξάμενος ἀπὸ τῆς Γαλιλαίας is interpolated from Lk. 23.5" (Critical, Vol. 1, 1994; cf. MHT 1, 1908, p. 240). See further H. CONZELMANN, Die Apostelgeschichte, Tübingen, ²1972 (= Acts of the Apostles, tr. J. LIMBURG, A.T. KRAABEL and D.H. JUEL, Philadelphia, PA, 1987, p. 83).

86. As Conzelmann remarked, "Mit der ersten Nennung von Galiläa setzt das eigentliche Problem unserer Untersuchung ein. Dabei werden sich Geographie und Komposition als stark ineinander verflochten zeigen" (Die Mitte, p. 20 = 29). In the Lukan perspective Jesus never extended his ministry beyond Galilee and Judea except for Gadara (p. 31, 43). See further E. LOHMEYER, Galiläa und Jerusalem (FRLANT, 52), Göttingen, 1936, p. 36f., as well as M. VÖLKEL, Der Anfang Jesu in Galiläa. Bemerkungen zum Gebrauch und zur Funktion Galiläas in den lukanischen Schriften, in ZNW 64 (1973) 222-232. See J. WEISS, Lukas, ⁸1892, p. 640, and

praises Jesus' whole ministry while in 23,5 the opponents condemn it[87]. "Jetzt zeigt sich der Sinn der ersten Phase des Wirkens Jesus: in ihr werden die späteren 'Zeugen' gesammelt. Es ist kein Zufall, wenn sie als 'Galiläer' bezeichnet werden. Damit wird vor allem ihre spätere Stellung in Jerusalem charakterisiert"[88]. Thus, Lukan redaction of Mk is confirmed by the theme of Galilee.

Verse 7

καὶ ἐπιγνοὺς ὅτι ἐκ τῆς ἐξουσίας Ἡρῴδου ἐστὶν ἀνέπεμψεν αὐτὸν πρὸς Ἡρῴδην, ὄντα καὶ αὐτὸν ἐν Ἱεροσολύμοις ἐν ταύταις ταῖς ἡμέραις.

"And when he learned that he belonged to Herod's jurisdiction, he sent him over to Herod, who was himself in Jerusalem at that time".

καὶ ἐπιγνοὺς ὅτι. The compound ἐπιγινώσκειν reflects the Hellenistic preference for stronger forms[89]. Mark employed ἐπιγινώσκειν 4 times: Mk 2,8; 5,30 ἐπιγνούς (diff. Lk 8,46 ἔγνων); 6,33 ἐπέγνωσαν (Lk 9,11 γνόντες).54 ἐπιγνόντες (om. Lk), as opposed to 7 in Lk and 13 in Acts[90]. The term ἐπιγινώσκειν ὅτι is a feature of Lukan style[91]. ἐπιγνούς is especially well attested in Acts[92]. For the phrase καὶ ἐπιγνούς it is probable that Luke was inspired by καὶ γνούς in Mk 15,45[93]. Another case taken over from Mk is 5,22 + ὅτι / Mk 2,8[94]. It is also the same form as found in 23,7, which is followed

BROWN, p. 742-743, 762, 766.

87. As noted by Brown, p. 743, 769. He continued: "Some have thought that by mentioning Galilee these opponents are playing on the memory of Judas the Galilean (Acts 5:37), who came from Galilee to stir up revolt against the Romans in AD 6. In the Lucan narrative, however, 'Galilee' stirs up the possibility of sending Jesus to Herod (Antipas) the tetrarch of Galilee (Luke 3:1) and asking that ruler to conduct a preliminary investigation". So also p. 763: "The Galilee motif brings on the scene Herod, called by Luke 'the tetrarch' of Galilee (3:1; 9:7)".

88. CONZELMANN, *Die Mitte*, p. 28 (= 38). Consider also: "'Galiläa' hat für Lukas nicht *als Landschaft* grundsätzliche Bedeutung ..." (p. 31 = 41).

89. M. ZERWICK, *An Analysis of the Greek New Testament*, Vol. 1, p. 275. See also his *Biblical Greek*, p. 162, §484. Brown referred to this latter reference, suggesting that "Koine Greek often prefers verbs compounded with prepositions over simple forms, without any implication of special significance" (*Death*, p. 764). As for the use of the term in LXX, *GELS*, p. 168. There are 44 uses in the NT (NTV, p. 47).

90. *NTV*, p. 47.

91. CADBURY, *Style*, p. 89; Boismard considered the phrase "ayant appris que ... il était" to be Lukan, since it appears once in Lk and twice in Acts (*Synopse*, t. 2, p. 418); RADL, *Paulus*, p. 410; GOULDER, *Luke*, p. 804; BROWN, *Death*, p. 761, and UNTERGASSMAIR, *Zur Problematik*, p. 280. See further Boismard and Lamouille in NEIRYNCK, *Le texte*, p. 322 (= 261).

92. CHICO CANO, *Der Prozess Jesu*, p. 34, n. 57, who cited 13 uses in Acts and 7 in Lk.

93. Mark also related that Pilate perceived (ἐγίνωσκεν) that the Jewish authorities had handed Jesus over to him out of envy (Mk 15,10).

94. For a discussion of ἐπιγνούς in Mk 2,8 see NEIRYNCK, *Mt 12,25a / Lc 11,17a et la rédaction des évangiles*, in *ETL* 62 (1986) 122-133, p. 124 (= *Evangelica II*, 481-492, p. 483). It also occurred in some of the prophetic literature of the LXX. See *GELS(TP)*, p. 89-90, and *GELS*, p. 168.

immediately by ὅτι. There are several instances where Mark has γινώσκω + ὅτι: Mk 12,12 (/ Lk 20,19); 13,28(Lk 21,30).29(Lk 21,31); 15,10 (om. Lk).

Both in the Gospel and in Acts the word has the meaning of "to learn" (7,37 + ὅτι; 23,7; Acts 9,30; 12,14 "recognize"; 19,34; 22,24.29; 23,28; 24,8.11; 28,1). Its use in Acts 22,29 is important since ἐπιγνοὺς ὅτι occurs in the account of Paul before the Roman Tribune as 23,7. The aorist infinitive of the compound is employed in Acts 23,28 in the governor Felix's letter concerning Paul[95]. The term can be used in a technical and legal sense meaning "to ascertain" (Acts 23,28; 24,8.11 + ὅτι and 22,24)[96]. On formulations similar to the phrase ἐπιγνοὺς ὅτι ... 'Ηρῴδου ἐστίν compare Acts 19,34 (ἐπιγνόντες δὲ ὅτι 'Ιουδαιος ἐστιν); 22,29 (ἐπιγνοὺς ὅτι 'Ρωμαῖός ἐστιν)[97]. The term is especially frequent in the LXX, having been used 145 times[98].

ἐκ τῆς ἐξουσίας 'Ηρῴδου ἐστὶν. The term ἐξουσία both in 4,6 and 23,7 has been understood to refer to the "territorial domain (of Herod)"[99]. The relation between the use of the term in 22,53 and Acts 26,18 must also be considered as referring to the domain of Satan[100]. The word can be translated as "(sphere of) power"[101]. ἐξουσία is considered to be Lukan[102]. In 7 cases Luke borrowed from Mk[103]. Lukan redaction used the term to refer to human authorities and government officials in 12,11 as a substitute for Mk 13,9 in a discussion of handing a person over for trial. The use of the term in 20,20 must also be related: τῇ ἐξουσίᾳ τοῦ ἡγεμόνος has the connotation of ruling or official power. Its use in 20,20 in addition to the Markan material (Mk 12,13-17) is significant since the context in the Markan account is a conspiracy of some Pharisees together with some Herodians against Jesus. Verses 6-7a "appear to be a redactional clamp composed by Luke to bind the Herod scene to the preceding material in 23,1-5"[104]. The term is employed in a similar fashion in the LXX at 2 Kgs 20,13 and Ps 113,2.

---

95. See W. HACKENBERG, ἐπιγινώσκω, in *EWNT* 2, cols. 61-62, esp. col. 62 (= p. 24-25, esp. p. 24). *BAGD* added a usage found in 1 Mac 6,17 (p. 291).

96. *BAGD*, p. 291. So also in 2 Mac 14,9.

97. GOULDER, *Luke*, p. 759.

98. *GELS*, p. 168.

99. I. BROER, ἐξουσία, in *EWNT* 2, cols. 23-29, esp. col. 27 (= p. 9-12, esp. p. 11). So also *BAGD*, p. 278. See further FITZMYER, p. 1481, and BROWN, *Death*, p. 762. Taylor included it among Luke's "distinctive words and phrases" (*Passion*, p. 87). See *GELS*, p. 162, which noted the use in LXX Dn 3,2.

100. So BROER, p. 11, and *BAGD*, p. 278, concerning 22,53 alone. Brown also considered this theme applicable to 23,7: "Thus Lucan readers might well think that there is a Satanic threat when Jesus is sent into Herod's *exousia*" (*Death*, p. 765).

101. BROWN, *Death*, p. 760.

102. K. MÜLLER, *Jesus*, p. 114, and UNTERGASSMAIR, *Zur Problematik*, p. 280.

103. 4,32 / Mk 1,22; 4,36 / Mk 1,27 [both of these represent differing forms in the Lukan accounts]; 5, 24 / Mk 2,10; 9,1 / Mk 6,7; 20,2[ab] / Mk 11,28[ab]; 20,8 / Mk 11,33.

104. SOARDS, *Tradition*, 1985, p. 348. For his subdivision of verses, see p. 347, 358-359.

Beginning at 3,1 and through the Herod material in 9,7-9 and 13,31-35 Luke sets the stage for the events detailed in Herod's trial. Ambivalence marks Herod's attitudes towards Jesus as described in these two pericopes. In the first, Herod is perplexed and desires to see Jesus (9,7.9b)[105]. In the second Jesus is warned that Herod is seeking to kill him (13,31). Luke sometimes is thought to have drawn on different traditions and is accused of being inconsistent in his portrayal[106]. In this way, the suspense can be heightened since in the trial scene it is not known how Herod might react to Jesus[107]. Seven of the eight references to Herod Antipas in Mk are found in the account of the beheading of John (Mk 6,14-29)[108].

Frequently it is claimed that ἀνέπεμψεν was employed in a technical sense to indicate that someone is sent to a higher authority (23,7; Acts 25,21)[109], though

105. CADBURY, *Style*, p. 98: "While the influence of Mark on Luke, outside the parallel passages, is slight and cannot be estimated as a whole, a few instances may be mentioned here in which an unusual expression in Luke may have been suggested by reminiscence of its occurrence in a neighboring context in Mark. This explanation has a higher degree of plausibility in proportion to the infrequency of the word or phrase and to the proximity of the passage in Mark. Luke 9, 7 διηπόρει. Herod's perplexity about Jesus (nowhere else in Luke); cf. ἠπόρει of Herod's perplexity about John, Mark 6,20 (אBL; nowhere else in Mark), a passage that immediately follows the one Luke is using, but which Luke omits, having already summarized it in Luke 3,19,20".

106. These approaches also apply to the differences between 23,6-12 and Acts 4,25-27.

107. Luke was more exact than Mark in reporting that Herod was a tetrarch rather than a king (3,1; cf. Mk 6,14), a detail which was also reflected in numismatic evidence (J.A. OVERMAN, *Recent Advances in the Archaeology of the Galilee in the Roman Period*, in *Currents in Research: Biblical Studies* 1 [1993] 35-57, esp. p. 43: "The coins of Herod Antipas usually bear the title 'Herod Tetrarch', and a number of Antipas's coins carry the name Tiberius, which is the first mention of the city that would for a time rival or displace Sepphoris as the queen city of the Galilee". See also PLUMMER, *Luke*, ⁵1922, p. 83: "His coins have the title tetrarch, and, like those of his father, bear no image"). According to Hastings Herod Antipas was referred to 4 times in Mt, 10 times in Mk (a total which includes two references to Herodians) and 13 in Lk (*Prophet*, p. 42). Mk 6.14.16.17.18.20.21.22; 8,15. The other Markan references were to the Herodians: Mk 3,6; 12,13. Hastings's total of 13 refers to Lk-Acts: 1,5; 3,1.19bis; 8,3; 9,7.9;13,31; 23,7.8.11.12.15; Acts 4,27; 12,1.6.11.19.21; 13,1; 23,35. Brown, on the other hand, offered a total of 13 in the Gospel and 2 in Acts (*Death*, p. 764). Hastings maintained that all provided "new and interesting information" concerning Herod except Lk 3,1; 8,3; 3,19-20 (*Prophet*, p. 43, n. 1).

108. BROWN, p. 764. The other reference is Mk 8,15.

109. So *BAGD*, p. 59, with reference to HOEHNER, *Why Did Pilate*, 1970, 84-90, who in turn referred to A. STEINWENTER, *Il processo di Gesù*, in *Jus* 3 (1952) 471-490, esp. p. 486-487. See also SPICQ, *NLNT* 3, 1982, 40-43, esp. p. 42 (= *TLNT* 1, p. 108-109). Brown regarded the use of the term in Acts 25,21 as having this meaning (*Death*, p. 765). Cf. BLINZLER, *Prozess*, p. 287, n. 11. So also JEREMIAS, *Die Sprache*, p. 301. Of a total of 5 occurrences 3 were found in Lk, 1 in Acts and the other in Phlm 11. Cf. GREEN, *Death*, p. 81: "Little can be decided from the use of ἀναπέμπω". The use in Acts 25,21 was also noted by J. WEISS, *Lukas*, ⁸1892, p. 640. B. Weiss subscribed to the view that it meant simply to send back in 23,11. But in 23,7 as in Acts 25,21 it conveyed the meaning of transfer to a higher power (*Lukas*, ⁹1901, p. 661). On ἀναπέμπω as "found almost entirely in Luke/Acts", see TAYLOR, *Passion*, p. 87. See also

sometimes it is argued that its use in 23,11.15 only suggests to "send back"[110]. This term has been identified as Lukan redaction[111]. It has been observed that "during the Hellenistic period, this compound verb ... often has the same meaning of the simple form"[112]. Rather than higher authorities, the term might have the connotation of "competent" authorities[113]. It appears that the term in 23,7b means only "to send"[114]. Phlm 12, the only use of the term outside the Lukan corpus, would appear to confirm the idea that the word could be used to mean simply "to send". It seems preferable to believe that Luke drew on technical terminology only to give the scene a more realistic sense[115]. Further, Luke shows a preference for compounds which is perhaps also evidence of Septuagintal influence[116].

ὄντα. Mk contained a form of ὤν in two sentences referring to location. Both are genitive absolutes. In Mk 14,3 we read that Jesus was in Bethany (ὄντος αὐτοῦ ἐν Βηθανίᾳ diff. Lk 7,36). In the account of Peter's denial we find a similar construction: ὄντος τοῦ Πέτρου κάτω ἐν τῇ αὐλῇ (Mk 14,66 om. Lk)[117].

Similar to the phrasing in 23,7 (ὄντα ... ἐν Ἱεροσολύμοις) is the expression in 24,6: ὤν ἐν τῇ Γαλιλαίᾳ. See also Acts 11,22 (οὔσης ἐν Ἱερουσαλήμ) in addition to 7,2; 16,3; 24,10.

SCHNEIDER, *Die Apostelgeschichte*, T. 2, p. 364, n. 22. Consider LÉGASSE, t. 2, p. 371, n. 45, who noted that only in Acts 25,21 would it have had this particular nuance.

110. PLUMMER, *Luke*, p. 522; *BAGD*, p. 59.

111. PLUMMER, *Luke*, p. lix, in a list of "expressions not found in the other Gospels and more frequent in S. Luke's Writings than in all the rest of N.T."; VOGEL, *Zur Charakteristik*; BOISMARD, *Synopse*, t. 2, p. 418, who also listed 3 occurrences in Lk and 1 in Acts. He did not specifically list the use in 23,11; FITZMYER, p. 1479, where he distinguished the term in 23,7.11 from 23,15; and JEREMIAS, *Die Sprache*, p. 301. See K. MÜLLER, *Jesus*, p. 114, Boismard and Lamouille in NEIRYNCK, *Le texte*, p. 318 (= 257), BOISMARD, *En quête*, p. 124, and UNTERGASSMAIR, *Zur Problematik*, p. 280, so also at 23,11, p. 281.

112. SPICQ, *TLNT*, p. 107.

113. *Ibid*., p. 108-109. For his comment on the use of the term in Acts 25,21, see p. 110.

114. So also SOARDS, *Tradition*, 1985, p. 349, n. 17. He judged that v. 7b was Lukan composition: "While v. 7b seems related to tradition, it is probably best to understand this line as Luke's composition to meet that need" (p. 350; see further p. 359).

115. So also BROWN, p. 765: "Perhaps the best solution is to avoid either extreme (whereby it would mean either simply 'to send' or legally 'to remand' a prisoner) and to recognize that Luke uses it to enhance the legal atmosphere".

116. See A.T. ROBERTSON, *Grammar*, ²1915, ³1919, ⁴1923, p. 561, who observed in a section on different prepositions following verbs that compounds of ἀνά were followed by a variety of prepositions including πρός and stated "as a rule πρός refers to personal relations". He concluded this section: "Delicate shades of meaning will be found in all these prepositions without undue refinement. See Conybeare and Stock, p. 88, for different prepositions with verbs in the LXX" (²1915, ³1919, ⁴1923, p. 562; cf. CONYBEARE and STOCK, *Grammar*, 1905; 1988, p. 87-88: "The great use made of prepositions after verbs is one of the main characteristics of Biblical Greek. It is partly a feature of later Greek generally, but to a still greater extent it is due to the influence of Hebrew").

117. On local expressions in Mk, see NEIRYNCK, *Duality*, p. 50-53.

καὶ αὐτός is counted among Lukan phraseology[118]. This expression reflects Septuagintal usage[119], though it is also found in Mk (Mk 6,47; 15,43[120]). The phrase is considered a "Septuagintism favored by Luke"[121].

It has often been observed that Lk contains two different forms of "Jerusalem"[122]. Note the references to Ἰερουσαλήμ in 13,33.34bis. This is seen as a Lukanism[123]. Ἰερουσαλήμ is a word characteristic of Luke[124]. Mention of Jerusalem is significant in light of the role that the city plays in Lk (9,31.51.53; 13,22; 17,11; 18,31; 19,28) but especially arising from the conviction that "it cannot be that the prophet should die away from Jerusalem" (13,33). Jerusalem continues to play a important role in Acts[125].

ἐν ταύταις ταῖς ἡμέραις. The temporal ἐν occurred more frequently in Lk than in the other Gospels[126]. There are six occurrences of ταύταις in Lk-Acts[127]. This phrase

118. BOISMARD, Synopse, t. 2, p. 418, GOULDER, Luke, p. 801.

119. NEIRYNCK, La matière marcienne, p. 189, n. 160 (= ²1989, p. 99, n. 160 = Evangelica, 69, n. 160). FITZMYER, p. 120-121.

120. B. WEISS, Lukas, ⁹1901, p. 661, cited Mk 15,43.

121. BROWN, Death, p. 761. See also K. MÜLLER, Jesus, p. 114, and UNTERGASSMAIR, Zur Problematik, p. 280.

122. See for example LÉGASSE, t. 2, p. 371, n. 47. Some scholars believe this is indicative of a special source. Jeremias regarded the form here as stemming from tradition (Die Sprache, p. 301).

123. NEIRYNCK, La matière marcienne, in L'Évangile de Luc, p. 183, n. 127 (= ²1989, p. 93, n. 127 = Evangelica, 63, n. 127). GOULDER, Luke, p. 805. See T. SCHRAMM, Markus-Stoff, p. 41, n. 1, who agreed with CADBURY, Four Features, p. 87f. and Style, as well as BAGD, p. 373: "No certain conclusions can be drawn concerning the use of the two forms of the name". See L. HARTMAN, Ἰεροσόλυμα, Ἰερουσαλήμ, in EWNT 2, cols. 432-439 (= p. 176-178), and especially the valuable bibliography.

124. HAWKINS, Horae Synopticae, 1899, p. 16; ²1909, p. 19. Although it did not occur in Mk, it was found twice in Mt 23,37. Of a total of 27 instances in Lk, 14 were in material peculiar to Lk, 8 in common parts and a further 5 in Lk 1-2. Acts contained a total of 36 times, 22 of those being in Acts 1-12, 14 in Acts 13-28 and an additional 3 in the "We" sections. The alternate form can be classified as follows: Mt 11, Mk 10, Lk 4, Paul 3, Jn 12. In the 1909 edition Hawkins observed that Ἰερουσαλήμ "always in LXX, except Tob, Macc (and I Esdr A)" (p. 19, n. m). Brown, taking note of various explanations, rejects the suggestion of a special source for the term in 23,7 (Death, p. 761-762). The phrase ἐν Ἰεροσολύμοις was identified by Boismard as Lukan (BOISMARD, Synopse, t. 2, p. 418, and En quête, p. 124). See further Boismard and Lamouille in NEIRYNCK, Le texte, p. 323 (= 262).

125. SABBE, Le récit, p. 94 (= Studia, p. 94): "Dans l'évangile de Lc., et dans les Actes, Jérusalem se trouve au centre, étant l'achèvement de la vie de Jésus et le point de départ de la predication évangélique". See, for example, Acts 10,39.

126. JEREMIAS, Die Sprache, p. 15. See also p. 301: "Zur Vorliebe der Redaktion für das temporale ἐν → 1,5 Trad". Radl included ἡμέρα in his list of Lukan vocabulary (Paulus, p. 412).

127. BROWN, Death, p. 761. He commented further that, "there is nothing implausible about Herod Antipas being in Jerusalem for the Passover, even if one suspects that like his father, Herod the Great, he may have come not primarily from piety, but from the political importance of a correct religious gesture" (p. 765). On the question of why Pilate would have sent Jesus to

is classified among those characteristic of Luke since it is found only in Lk-Acts[128]. It also reflects Septuagintal influence[129].

The phrase should also be compared with ἐν ἐκείναις ταῖς ἡμέραις (Mk 1,9), omitted by Luke in the parallel passage (3,21) as part of the description of Jesus' baptism by John[130]. It appears that Luke was drawn to include a similar phrase

---

Herod, see p. 766. Another reason Brown proposed for the transfer was that Herod "would be highly competent in detecting insurrectionists". He insisted that the encounter of Jesus and Herod was an *anakrisis*, a "delegated investigation, rather than a formal ceding of jurisdiction" due to the parallel with Acts 25,23-27 (p. 766-767). Additionally, it would have been an "ingenious diplomatic way to neutralize the tetrarch and prevent further trouble" (p. 767).

128. HAWKINS, *Horae Synopticae*, 1899, p. 15, 32; ²1909, p. 18, 40. Of a total of 4 occurrences in Lk, 1 was found in Lk 1-2 (1,39), 2 in the special material (23,7; 24,18), and 1 in the common parts (6,12). In Acts the phrase occurred 3 times (Acts 1,15; 6,1; 11,27) only in Acts 1-12. Hawkins added that the phrase ἐν ταῖς ἡμέραις ἐκείναις "is more usual" so Mt 3, Mk 4, Lk 5, Acts 3, Rev 1. In the 1909 edition he added the following explanation: "but of these 16 only 7 are in narrative". They were Mt 3,1; Mk 1,9; 8,1; Lk 2,1; 4,2; 9,36; Acts 9,37 (p. 40). Mk 1,9 contained not only a reference to Galilee, but it was in the context of the story of Jesus being baptized by John. See also BOISMARD, *Synopse*, t. 2, p. 418; CHICO CANO, p. 34; TAYLOR, *Passion*, p. 87; BÜCHELE, p. 32, n. 55; JEREMIAS, *Die Sprache*, p. 301 (who called attention to the similarity between 23,7 and Acts 11,27); and FITZMYER, p. 110, 362, 1479; GOULDER, *Luke*, p. 804; UNTERGASSMAIR, *Zur Problematik*, p. 280. Consider LÉGASSE, t. 2, p. 371, n. 46. See further Boismard and Lamouille in NEIRYNCK, *Le texte*, p. 322 (= 261), and BOISMARD, *En quête*, p. 124.

129. In the comment on 4,2 Fitzmyer not only indicated this phrase was frequently used by Luke, but that Acts 2,18 demonstrated "its LXX origin" (*Luke*, p. 514). In redacting Mk 2,20 for 5,35 Luke made Mark's expression plural (p. 599). See *GELS*, p. 198, with the example from 2 Chr 24,18: "ἐν τῇ ἡμέρᾳ ταύτῃ *in that day* corr?". In his analysis of the phrase in Acts 1,15 Barrett remarked: "The expression is one of several Septuagintalisms in the verse ..." (*Acts*, 1994, p. 95). So also CONZELMANN, *Die Apostelgeschichte*, 1963, p. 23; ²1972, p. 28 (= *Acts*, 1987, p. 10): "Der ganze Abschnitt ist von seiner biblizistischen Sprache durchzogen: 'in diesen Tagen'"; and E. HAENCHEN, *Die Apostelgeschichte*, ¹⁴1965, p. 123-124 (= *Acts*, 1971, p. 159): "Nearly every turn of phrase in this sentence can be traced back to the Septuagint, which means that it sounded to Luke's readers like the beginning of a biblical story". In a note he added: "The LXX expression 'in these (those) days' occurs in Luke 1.39, 2.1, 4.6, 6.12, 9,36, 21.23 and 23.7; Acts 1.15, 2.18, 7.14, 9.37 and 11.27" (n. 1 = *Die Apostelgeschichte*, p. 123, n. 1).

130. See FITZMYER, p. 479. The omission of Jesus' baptism "by John" was necessitated in the Lukan version because of the description of John's imprisonment immediately preceding. Consider Taylor's comment on the Markan phrase: "The vague expression of time ἐν ἐκείναις ταῖς ἡμέραις, found also in viii.I, xiii.17,24, appears to be editorial" (*The Gospel According to Saint Mark*, ²1966, p. 159; see also p. 517). Luke did not recount the feeding of the four thousand (Mk 8,1-10), though he copied the phrase exactly as it appears in Mk 13,17 (/ 21,23). The phrase was omitted in the case of Mk 13,24 (diff 21,25). Hooker identified this Markan expression as "Old Testament phraseology (e.g. Judg. 19.1; 1 Sam. 28.1)" (M. HOOKER, *Mark*, p. 45). See also NEIRYNCK, *Duality*, p. 95, 180. The account of the Transfiguration contains the phrase ἐν ἐκείναις ταῖς ἡμέραις (9,36) and should be compared with ἐν ταύταις ταῖς ἡμέραις (23,7). See further SABBE, *La rédaction*, p. 92, 93 (= *Studia*, p. 92, 93).

because of its Septuagintal background. Consider the construction of ᾿Εν αὐτῇ τῇ ὥρα (13,31). Lk 23,7c is "probably Lukan composition"[131].

Verse 8

ὁ δὲ ῾Ηρῴδης ἰδὼν τὸν ᾿Ιησοῦν ἐχάρη λίαν, ἦν γὰρ ἐξ ἱκανῶν χρόνων θέλων ἰδεῖν αὐτὸν διὰ τὸ ἀκούειν περὶ αὐτοῦ καὶ ἤλπιζέν τι σημεῖον ἰδεῖν ὑπ᾿ αὐτοῦ γινόμενον.

"And when Herod saw Jesus, he was very glad, for he had long desired to see him, because he had heard about him, and he was hoping to see some sign done by him".

"There is an overuse of the particle δέ in this scene (7 in 7 verses; 548 times in Luke; 558 times in Acts)"[132]. Luke already used the term once in 23,6. In what sense can it be said that one occurrence per verse constitutes an overuse? δέ has been counted among Lukan vocabulary[133].

ἰδών. This term recalls Herod's wish earlier in Lk, καὶ ἐζήτει ἰδεῖν αὐτόν (9,9) where the themes of seeing and hearing Jesus are likewise linked[134]. ἰδών/-

131. SOARDS, *Tradition*, 1985, p. 350.

132. BROWN, *Death*, p. 768. This data was previously noted in SOARDS, *The Silence of Jesus Before Herod*, in *ABR* 33 (1985) 41-45, p. 42. Neirynck provided a slightly different calculation than Brown. Of a total of 1199 occurrences in the Synoptics, there are 163 instances in Mk and 542 in Lk. Lk borrowed from Mk 72 times (*NTV*, p. 229). Note the use of this particle in the earlier Lukan material concerning Herod's confusion about the identity of John and Jesus (Mk 6,15bis / Lk 9,8bis; Mk 6,12 / Lk 9,9). There are several occurrences in Acts when Paul appeared before Herod Agrippa: Acts 26,1.15bis.24.25.28.29.32.

133. RADL, *Paulus*, p. 404.

134. See NEIRYNCK, *La matière marcienne*, p. 168, n. 47 (= ²1989, p. 78, n. 47 = *Evangelica*, 48, n. 47), recommended that for the reminiscences of Mk 6,17-29 in Lk 9,7-9, one consult SCHÜRMANN, *Lukasevangelium*, p. 508-509, who argued, based on verbal similarities, "Dass diese Übereinstimmungen nicht zufällig sind, beweist die Benutzung von Mk 6,17-29 in Lk 3,19f, denn hier verraten keinerlei unluk Spracheigentümlichkeiteneine luk Vorlage" (p. 509). On the contacts between Mk 6 and Lk 13,31, see DENAUX, *L'hypocrisie*, 245-285, esp. p. 265-268 (= ²1989, 155-195, esp. p. 175-178). It should be noted that ἐζήτει (9,9) was also found in the Markan passion (Mk 14,11 / 22,6). Neirynck called attention to the relationship between seeing and hearing. "J. Roloff further developed this view. In his opinion, the order of 'things they saw (first) and heard' (Lk 7, 22; Acts 4,20) is applicable only to the acts of Jesus, and the inversion of the words in Acts 8,6 (they heard and saw) indicates subordination of the miraculous activity to the preaching. The miracle has no missionary purpose – 9,35 and 9,42 notwithstanding. Sometimes it provides a mere occasion for preaching" (*The Miracle Stories in the Acts of the Apostles. An Introduction*, in *BETL* 48 [1979] p. 203-204 = *Evangelica*, 869-870; cf. J. ROLOFF, *Das Kerygma und der irdische Jesus. Historische Motive in den Jesus-Erzählungen der Evangelien*, Göttingen, 1970). The reference in Acts 4,20 occurred shortly before Acts 4,27 where Herod and Pilate were mentioned together in a conspiracy against Jesus. See further REID, p. 140: "Although the process of faith is circumvented in Herod, he is anxious not only to hear of Jesus but to see him as well (9:9; 23:8)". See also KARRIS, *Luke: Artist and Theologian*, p. 87-88, who focused solely on seeing, and DARR, *Glorified*, p. 287-291, 319.

ὄντες δέ has been counted among the list of Lukan characteristics[135]. When the messengers of John the Baptist ask Jesus about his identity he responds: πορευθέντες ἀπαγγείλατε Ἰωάννῃ ἃ εἴδετε καὶ ἠκούσατε (7,22). In the Transfiguration the themes of listening and seeing are also found in this context (9,35-36 / Mt 17,5). In this regard consider 10,23-24 (Q; diff. Mt 13,16-17)[136]. While in the Transfiguration the order is hearing then seeing, the order is reversed in the Herod pericope[137].

ἐχάρη λίαν. χαίρω, having the meaning of greeting, has been listed among the characteristic words of Luke[138]. The term is typical of Lukan style. Here the term means "rejoice" rather than "greet"[139]. χαίρειν is indicative of Lukan vocabulary[140]. There are 87 instances of χαίρω in the LXX and 74 in the NT, of which 19 are found in Lk-Acts[141]. Consider Mk 14,11, describing the reaction

135. RADL, *Paulus*, p. 407; Boismard and Lamouille in NEIRYNCK, *Le texte*, p. 323 (= 262); GOULDER, *Luke*, p. 805. See also JEREMIAS, *Die Sprache*, p. 86: "dass Lukas [schreibt] die Wendung gern".

136. For the Markan phrase καὶ ἡδέως αὐτοῦ ἤκουεν (Mk 6, 20) compare καὶ ἐζήτει ἰδεῖν αὐτόν (9,9b). Luke, showing an aversion for the term, omitted ἡδέως (Mk 12,37b) in his redaction of Mk in another passage (20,45). Shortly before the Transfiguration Jesus addressed the disciples with the words drawn from the prophecy in Is 6,9: ὑμῖν δέδοται γνῶναι τὰ μυστήρια τῆς βασιλείας τοῦ θεοῦ, τοῖς δὲ λοιποῖς ἐν παραβολαῖς, ἵνα βλέποντες μὴ βλέπωσιν καὶ ἀκούοντες μὴ συνιῶσιν (8,10; cf. Mk 4,12). See FITZMYER, p. 709: "Luke has certainly not fashioned his form of this saying on anything resembling the LXX (contrast Matt 13,13-15, where the LXX is actually quoted). His starting point is clearly Mark 4:12. He makes the ptcs. *blepontes* and *akouontes*, which in the LXX and Mark are the equivalent of the intensifying Hebrew infin. absol. into good Greek circumstantial ptcs., with concessive force".

137. Luke's freedom of rearrangement in redaction is highlighted when we consider Neirynck's recollection of Conzelmann's caution "against overemphasis on that order of the two verbs [seeing first, then hearing] because of the inversion in [Acts] 8,6 and the more general Lucan use of verbs of seeing" (*Miracle Stories*, p. 203, n. 191 = *Evangelica*, 1982, p. 869, n. 191; see CONZELMANN, *Die Mitte*, p. 165-167 = 190-193).

138. HAWKINS, *Horae Synopticae*, 1899, p. 20, 39; ²1909, p. 23, 49. The term χαίρω occurred 3 times in Mt (Mt 2,10; 5,12; 18,13), 1 in Mk (Mk 14,11). Of a total of 11 in Lk 1 was found in Lk 1-2 (1,14), 6 in special material (10,20bis; 13,17 [incorrectly printed as 13,7 in the 1899 edition]; 15,32; 19,6; 23,8) and 4 in common parts (6,23 Q, used in relationship with prophets; 15,5Q; 19,37; 22,5). A further 5 were employed in Acts (Acts 5,41; 8,39; 11,23; 13,48; 15,31): 3 in Acts 1-12 and 2 in Acts 13-28. FITZMYER, p. 111. "Rejoicing can be the reaction to 'seeing' [19,37; 23,8] and to hearing" [Acts 13,48] (K. BERGER, χαίρω, in *EWNT* 3, cols. 1079-1083, esp. col. 1082 = p. 451-452, esp. p. 452; cf. *BAGD*, p. 873: "The reason or obj. is expressed by a ptc."). See also BÜCHELE, p. 32, n. 55. Taylor, too, counted this as an example of Luke's characteristic language (*Passion*, p. 87).

139. BOISMARD, *Synopse*, t. 2, p. 418; BROWN, p. 768. For the use of the term in some parts of the LXX see *GELS(TP)*, p. 248.

140. K. MÜLLER, *Jesus*, p. 114, GOULDER, *Luke*, p. 809, and UNTERGASSMAIR, *Zur Problematik*, p. 280.

141. *GELS*, p. 512, and *NTV*, p. 189. Rehkopf listed χαίρειν among his special pre-Lukan vocabulary, additionally noting that it occurred in the passion (*Die lukanische Sonderquelle*, p. 106, # 77).

of the chief priests to Judas' betrayal: οἱ δὲ ἀκούσοντες ἐχάρησαν / καὶ ἐχάρησαν (22,5). Both the Markan account of the Baptist's death and the Lukan Herod pericope contain references to the tetrarch's emotional reaction. "[Herod] was very glad (ἐχάρη λίαν), for he had long desired to see him, because he had heard about him" (23,8) / "[Herod] heard him gladly (ἡδέως)" (Mk 6,20)[142]. The transfer of the positive reception from the Baptist to Jesus could account for the detail in 23,8. Mk 12,37 (ἤκουσεν αὐτοῦ ἡδέως diff. Lk 20,45) possibly influenced Luke.

Also in Mk 6,20 Herod was portrayed as πολλὰ ἠπόρει ("he was very much perplexed"), while in 9,7 Herod διηπόρει ("was perplexed")[143]. διαπορέω occurs only here in Lk in addition to three times in Acts (2,12; 5,24; 10,17). Thus it is Lukan vocabulary[144]. Mk 6,26 recounted that the king (Herod) was περίλυπος ("exceedingly sorry"). Luke would not want to portray Herod in such a sympathetic fashion[145].

In each of the Markan cases of the term λίαν (Mk 1,35; 6,51[146]; 9,3 Transfiguration[147]; 16,2) Luke either altered or omitted it[148]. Since this adverb

---

142. GUELICH, *Mark 1-8:26*, p. 327, proposed evidence of Markan redaction: "... the πολλά in 6,23, the comment, ἡδέως αὐτοῦ ἤκουσεν (6:20, cf. 12:37), ... may reflect an occasional thumbprint". ἡδέως is found only 5 times in the NT. Of the occurrence in the Synoptics, only in Mk (2x). Dschulnigg noted that the phrase ἡδέως ἀκούειν occurs in Mk 6,20; 12,37 adding: "Als sprachliche Variationsmöglichkeiten vgl. z.B (für ἡδέως ἀσμένως (Apg 21,17), ... oder auch für den ganzen Ausdruck Umschreibungen mit χαίρω oder ἥδομαι + Partizip." (*Sprache*, p. 156). In examining the use of the phrase in Mk 12,37 and comparing it with the Lukan parallel (20,45) it is clear that Luke omitted it, favoring instead simply ἀκούοντος.

143. For the use of ἀπορέω (Mk 6,20) compare Lk 24,4 (ἀπορεῖσθαι) (diff Mk 16,5) and Acts 25,20 (ἀπορούμενος) as part of Felix's explanation of Paul's case to Herod Agrippa and Bernice. Luke's use of the middle voice corresponds with the practice in classical Greek (TAYLOR, *Mark*, ²1966, p. 313).

While John was described as a righteous man (Mk 6,20 ἄνδρα δίκαιον καὶ ἅγιον), Jesus was called δίκαιος at 23,47. Consider also Acts 3,14 where Jesus was described as τὸν ἅγιον καὶ δίκαιον.

144. Boismard and Lamouille in NEIRYNCK, *Le texte*, p. 320 (= 259), noted also in PLUMMER, *Luke*, 1896, ³1900; HAWKINS, *Horae Synopticae*, and VOGEL, *Zur Charakteristik*, ²1899.

145. Mark employed περίλυπος at Mk 14,34 (om. Lk 22,40). Luke wrote περίλυπος in the account of the rich ruler (18,23 diff Mk λυπούμενος).

146. Luke omitted the account of Jesus walking on the water (Mk 6,45-52), which included the term at Mk 6,51. The term also occurred in the LXX.

147. Here the term was used in connection with the description of Jesus' garment (λευκὰ λίαν = "intensely white", RSV). It could easily have been transferred to the Lukan account of Herod's trial because of the connection with the clothing in 23,11.

148. GOULDER, *Luke*, Vol. 2, p. 758. Mark employed the term to describe the degree of an emotional response of the disciples (Mk 6,51): λίαν [ἐκ περισσοῦ] ἐν ἑαυτοῖς ἐξίσταντο. On Luke's redaction of λίαν in Mk, cf. REID, p. 58, n. 122. Jeremias regarded it as stemming from tradition (*Die Sprache*, p. 302). Marshall argued Luke had not borrowed the term from Mk (*Luke*, p. 855).

was also found in the LXX Luke could have taken it either from there or from Mk[149]. Once more Luke employed Markan vocabulary from those Markan parallel passages where he elected to omit it. We concur that v. 8a.b "seem to be further pieces of Lukan composition"[150].

ἦν γὰρ ἐξ ἱκανῶν χρόνων θέλων τον 'Ιησοῦν. The terms ἤθελεν (Mk 6,19) and γάρ (Mk 6,17.18.20) which occurred in the Baptist pericope were omitted by Luke. The use of γάρ is indicative of Markan style[151]. The word γάρ also was found in the scene of Peter's denials (22,59 / Mk 14,70)[152]. Further, Luke included it in the account of the Sanhedrin trial (22,71). As regards Lukan vocabulary patterns, γάρ was found three times in the brief Herod trial pericope (vv. 8.12.15).

ἐξ ἱκανῶν χρόνων. In the Markan account of Peter's denial there is the temporal use of ἐκ (Mk 14,72: ἐκ δευτέρου). For the sense of duration see Mk 9,21 and Mk 10,20 / Lk 18,21 (ἐκ νεότητος, so also in Acts 26,4 in Paul's defense before Agrippa[153]). Further, ἐκ νεότητος was found in the LXX[154].

In Acts there were phrases such as ἐξ ἐτῶν ὀκτώ (Acts 9,33); ἐκ γενεῶν (Acts 15,21). What is more important for our consideration is the phrase used in Paul's trial in his defense before Felix: ἐκ πολλῶν ἐτῶν (Acts 24,10). The expression ἐξ ἱκανῶν χρόνων corresponded to Lukan vocabulary and style[155].

Luke employed ἱκανός in 3,16 in a different way from Mk 1,7 when John the Baptist compared himself with Jesus. This word is part of a group "occurring upwards of four times in Luke's Gospel, which [does] not occur there *twice as*

149. See *BAGD*, p. 472, and *GELS*, p. 281. It was employed 12 times in the NT (*NTV*, p. 134).

150. SOARDS, *Tradition*, p. 351.

151. According to R.H. Gundry. Commenting on the use of the term in the Baptist story (Mk 6,14.17) he stated: "Editorial γάρ-clauses characterize Mark (and here γάρ, 'for' is best taken as governing all the intervening clauses [vv 14b-15], just as γάρ in v 17 makes the whole of the story concerning John's beheading an explanation of Herod's adopting the identification of Jesus with John" (*Mark. A Commentary on His Apology for the Cross*, Grand Rapids, MI, 1993, p. 314). He further noted a link between the story of the death of the Baptist and the Transfiguration (Mk 9,6): "The structure of the present γάρ-clause – predicate adjective + γάρ + a form of γίνομαι, 'become' – matches the structure of an apparently editorial statement in 9:6" (p. 314).

152. See CADBURY, *Style*, p. 165, on the phrase καὶ γάρ which appears not only in 22,59, but also in 1,66; 6,32.33a.b.34; 7,8; 11,4; 22,37, a use which he declared to be Lukan, as had Harnack (*Sayings*, p. 62, 65). On γάρ in LXX see, *GELS*, p. 86.

153. G. LÜDEMANN, ἐκ (ἐξ), in *EWNT* 1, cols. 977-980, esp. col. 978 (= p. 402-403, esp. p. 403). See A.T. ROBERTSON, *Grammar*, ²1915, ³1919, ⁴1923, p. 597: "With expressions of time ἐκ gives the point of departure, like ἐκ νεότητος (Mk. 10:20), ... ἐξ ἱκανῶν (Lu. 23:8), ... ἐκ πολλῶν ἐτῶν (Ac. 24,10)".

154. Ps 70,5 and in 1 Mac 2,66.

155. RADL, *Paulus*, p. 413; JEREMIAS, *Die Sprache*, p. 301; CHICO CANO, *Der Prozess Jesu*, p. 36; Boismard and Lamouille in NEIRYNCK, *Le texte*, p. 323 (= 262) under ἱκανός (temporal); GOULDER, *Luke*, p. 805. See 8,27; 20,9; Acts 8,11; 9,23.43; 14,3; 20,11. Consider CADBURY, *Style*, p. 196.

often as in Matthew and Mark together, but which are found *in Luke and Acts together four times as often as in Matthew and Mark together*[156]. Luke employed the adjective more frequently than Mt and Mk, a use which was attributed to redaction and termed "exzessive" (Lk 9x; Acts 18x) in comparision to the other Synoptics[157]. Significant support exists for the view that this term is indicative of Lukan redaction[158]. The word was found in Acts 12,12; 14,21 and 19,19[159]. The term was frequently employed in Hellenistic literature as well as in the LXX[160].

χρόνος is yet another term found frequently in Lk-Acts and has been identified as Lukan vocabulary[161]. In the Lukan parallel to Mk 2,19 Luke omitted the term (5,34)[162]. Luke also omitted the term in his account of Jesus healing a boy possessed by a spirit (9,42 diff. Mk 9,21)[163].

156. HAWKINS, *Horae Synopticae*, ²1909, p. 27, 187. See FITZMYER, p. 112, and BÜCHELE, p. 32, n. 55. According to Hawkins, the term occurred 3 times each in Mt and Mk. Of the 9 total occurrences in Lk, none were found in chapters 1-2, 4 times in other peculiar parts and 5 times in the common parts. Of the 18 total instances in Acts, 6 were located in chapters 1-12, 12 in chapters 13-2? and 4 in the 'We'- sections. His note specified: "Used of time Lk 3, Acts 8 (including 'We'- sections 3), Paul 1 (?), only" (p. 27). In a related use, see Acts 19,26 (ἱκανὸν ὄχλον). But consider Haenchen's observation on Luke's use of ἱκανός: "We may indeed point to certain words, expressions, turns of phrase, for which Luke appears to have a special liking. But here we must ask ourselves to what extent Luke thereby distinguishes himself from contemporary writers of similar cultural background. For example, he likes to use ἱκανός in the sense of 'great' or 'much.' The word can be seen gradually acquiring this sense in the later books of LXX - μέγας and πολύς are so hackneyed! What is 'Lucan,' therefore, is probably only the frequency of his use of the word" (E. HAENCHEN, *Die Apostelgeschichte*, ¹⁴1965, p. 69 = *The Acts of the Apostles. A Commentary*, tr. B. NOBLE, G. SHINN, H. ANDERSON, R. MCL. WILSON, Philadelphia, PA, 1971 p. 77; see also p. 303, n. 3: "... is a favourite word of Luke's"); K. MÜLLER, *Jesus*, p. 115, n. 27, indicated this information was derived from HAENCHEN, *Apostelgeschichte*, ⁶1968, p. 69, but the edition appeared to have been incorrectly stated. It should read ¹⁵1968). In a note Brown stipulated that in 23,9 "Luke reflects the later LXX books that tend to substitute *hikanos* for *megas* and *polys*" (*Death*, p. 768, n. 10).

157. K. MÜLLER, *Jesus*, p. 115.

158. RADL, *Paulus*, p. 413; JEREMIAS, *Die Sprache*, p. 301, 302 ("lk Vorzugswort"); FITZMYER, p. 1479, 112; Boismard and Lamouille in NEIRYNCK, *Le texte*, p. 323 (= 262); GOULDER, *Luke*, p. 805; BROWN, *Death*, p. 768; LÉGASSE, *Le procès*, t. 2, p. 372, n. 50; UNTERGASSMAIR, *Zur Problematik*, p. 280.

159. BARRETT, *Acts*, 1994, p. 583, on Acts 12,12: "ἱκανοί ... the word is Lucan"; and his comment on Acts 14,21: "... is a favourite Lucan word" (p. 685).

160. P. TRUMMER, ἱκανός, in *EWNT* 2, cols. 452-453, esp. col. 452 (= p. 184-185, esp. p. 184). See *GELS*, p. 213, which referred to Hab 2,13, and reported 46 instances in the LXX.

161. Boismard and Lamouille, in NEIRYNCK, *Le texte*, p. 330 (= 269), χρόνοι; GOULDER, *Luke*, p. 809.

162. Marshall insisted: "Luke omits Mk. 2:19b, as does Matthew, no doubt because it seemed redundant, and goes straight on to the period of contrast" (*Luke*, p. 225).

163. Fitzmyer affirmed that Luke followed Mk but "omits all the secondary description in Mark 9:20c-25a" (*Luke*, p. 806).

The combination of terms was found only in Lk-Acts[164]. We found a phrase similar to 23,8 in 8,27: χρόνῳ ἱκανῷ, cf. Mk 5,2; Acts 8,11: ἱκανῷ χρόνῳ[165]; Acts 14,3: ἱκανὸν ... χρόνον[166]; Acts 27,9: Ἰκανοῦ δὲ χρόνου, the only difference being that in 23,8 the phrase was plural[167]. Note the plural form and that it is among those words which "occur at least six times in Luke and Acts taken together while not occurring at all in Matthew or Mark"[168]. On the Lukan use of ἱκανός see 20,9: χρόνους ἱκανούς (cf. Mk 12,10); 23,9: λόγοις ἱκανοῖς (below). In 8,32 Luke substituted ἱκανῶν for μεγάλη (Mk 5,11)[169]. Luke showed a preference for connecting the terms χρόνος ἱκανός in the singular as well as the plural[170]. The expression is representative of Lukan vocabulary and style[171]. Consider also Acts 20,11; 27.9[172]. The terms were also found in the LXX[173].

θέλων ἰδεῖν αὐτὸν[174]. This recalled 9,9: ἐζήτει ἰδεῖν αὐτόν. In 8,20 ἰδεῖν

164. H. HÜBNER, χρόνος, in *EWNT* 3, cols. 1170-1173, esp. col. 1170 (= p. 488-489, esp. p. 488).

165. BARRETT, *Acts*, p. 408.

166. See HAENCHEN, *Die Apostelgeschichte*, p. 361, n. 8 (= *Acts*, p. 420, n. 5), SCHNEIDER, *Die Apostelgeschichte*, T. 2, p. 151, n. 17, and BARRETT, *Acts*, p. 670: "... a Lucan expression".

167. See HAENCHEN, *Die Apostelgeschichte*, p. 624 (= *Acts*, p. 699): "ἱκανός here and v. 9: a favorite Lucan word". See further Boismard and Lamouille in NEIRYNCK, *Le texte*, p. 329 (= 268).

168. HAWKINS, *Horae Synopticae*, ²1909, p. 28-29, 51. See also TAYLOR, *Passion*, p. 87, FITZMYER, p. 112, BÜCHELE, p. 32, n. 55, as well as GREEN, *Death*, p. 81, "one should lean towards regarding it as redactional here".

169. CADBURY, *Style*, p. 196. This term was considered by Taylor to be characteristic of Luke's vocabulary (*Passion*, p. 87). B. WEISS, *Lukas*, ⁹1901, p. 661, invited comparision with πολλοῖς γὰρ χρόνοις in 8,29 (cf. Mk 5,4.5 πολλάκις, παντὸς νυκτὸς καὶ ἡμέρας). The term πολλάκις also occurred in Mk 9,22 (diff 9,42 where Luke omitted some details).

170. K. MÜLLER, *Jesus*, p. 115.

171. BOISMARD, *Synopse*, t. 2, p. 418. On ἱκανός, see also Boismard and Lamouille in NEIRYNCK, *Le texte*, p. 262. RADL, *Paulus*, p. 413. JEREMIAS, *Die Sprache*, p. 64, 301. See also SPICQ, *NLNT* 3, 345-350, esp. p. 347, n. 2 (= *TLNT* 2, p. 219, n. 14).

172. SPICQ, *TLNT* 2, p. 219, n. 14.

173. See 2 Mac 7,5; 8,25.

174. On this phrase as an example of the progressive imperfect, see A.T. ROBERTSON, *Grammar*, ²1915, ³1919, ⁴1923, p. 884: "Sometimes the imperfect looks backward or forward, as the case may be. ... This idea is, however, often expressed by μέλλω, but without the backward look also. Cf. Lu. 9:31; 10,1". The citation of 9,31 is from the Transfiguration account. Karris treated the thematic of faith as seeing: "The final theme to occupy our attention in Luke 23:6-12 is seeing. It occurs thrice in 23:8 ... Perhaps the best single text to use as a sample of the theme of seeing is found in Acts 26:17-18 where Paul talks about his commission from the Lord Jesus ... To see is to see deeply, to see with the eyes of faith, to be converted and to walk in the light. Herod is not able to see who Jesus is. He wants a miracle from Jesus, but receives none" (*Luke: Artist and Theologian*, p. 87; on 23,8 see also KARRIS, *Luke 24:13-35*, in *Interpr* 41 [1987] 57-61, esp. p. 60). Reid also emphasized the link between seeing and faith: "From the very opening of the Gospel (1:2), Luke stresses the importance of the testimony of eyewitnesses, setting the tone for a theme of seeing that leads to faith and then to proclamation of the word. ... Some, like Herod, in 9:9; 23:8, or Simon the Pharisee in 7:39, or the crowd in

θέλοντές σε (Mk 3,32: ζητοῦσίν σε) Luke made a substitution for Markan terminology[175]. Luke employed θέλει (13,31) when writing of Herod's desire to kill Jesus. In the special material of the story of Zacchaeus we find: ἐζήτει ἰδεῖν τον Ἰησοῦν (19,3)[176]. The aorist infinitive ἰδειν was typical of Lukan vocabulary[177].

ἦν ... θέλων. The periphrastic construction was frequent in the Markan passion[178]. ἦν + ptc. θέλων gives evidence of Lukan redaction[179]. This example in 23,8 was "more likely a Septuagintism than the product of direct Hebrew/Aramaic influence (which might point to a source)"[180]. It has been observed that "die periphrastische Konstruktion einer solchen Zwischenbemerkung einen sicheren Hinweis auf Lukas [gibt]", which is "durch und durch lukanisch"[181]. Luke employed the periphrastic imperfect which required the pluperfect in English[182]. Seven of the Lukan cases were taken over from Mk:

19:7, see but do not come to faith" (*Transfiguration*, p. 131).

175. Also noted by LÉGASSE, *Le procès*, t. 2, p. 372, n. 51. On θέλων, see also 23,20. The phrase in 10,24 (Q) is also relevant here: πολλοὶ προφῆται καὶ βασιλεῖς ἠθέλησαν ἰδεῖν ἃ ὑμεῖς βλέπετε καὶ οὐκ εἶδαν.

176. See also ζητῆσαι in 19,10.

177. UNTERGASSMAIR, *Zur Problematik*, p. 280.

178. NEIRYNCK, *L'évangile de Marc (II). À propos de R. Pesch, Das Markusevangelium, 2. Teil*, in *ETL* 55 (1979) 1-42, p. 21 (= *Evangelica II*, 520-561, p. 540). Cf. Chico Cano, who argued Luke generally avoided the periphrastic construction, especially where he followed Mk (*Der Prozess Jesu*, p. 36).

179. RADL, *Paulus*, p. 431: "Sie [periphrastic conjugation] ist bei Lukas besonders beliebt und begenet bei ihm ...", and he specifically mentioned 23,8; FITZMYER, *Luke*, p. 1479, 122-123; BROWN, *Death*, p. 768. See also NEIRYNCK, *Minor Agreements*, p. 242.

180. *Ibid.*, p. 122-123. Moulton offered these reflections: "Restricting our survey to the periphrastic imperf. we notice that this is fairly frequent in the LXX (see Conybeare and Stock, Selections, p. 69)" (*MHT* 2, 1919, ²1929, p. 451. See CONYBEARE and STOCK, p. 70: "In the N.T. these analytic tenses are even commoner than in the LXX"). Among the imperfect are Acts 10,30; 11,5; 12,5; 21,3; 16,12; 1,13. Further, Lk 4,44 was listed and readers are invited to compare this example with 23,8 (p. 71). He listed among other instances those cases in the NT where we find the imperfect of εἰμί with the present participle. Focusing on the examples in Mk and Lk-Acts (Mk 1,12; 2,6.18; 4,38; 5,5.11; 9,4; 10,22.32 (bis); 14,4.40.49.54; 15,40.43. In Lk: 1,10.21.22; 2,33.51; 4,20.31.38.44; 5,1.16(bis).29; 6,12; 8,40; 9,53; 11,14; 13,10.11(bis); 14,1; 15,1; 19,47; 21,37; 23,8.53; 24,13.32. In Acts: 1,10.13.14; 2,2.5.42; 8,1.13.28; 9,9.28; 10,24.30; 11,5; 12,5.6.20; 14,7; 16,9.12; 18,7; 21,3; 22,19.20), he concluded: "The most important results from an analysis of this data are Mt's almost complete avoidance of this locution when following Mark's narrative, Luke' rejection of it in every instance where a Marcan parallel allows comparison, and yet the freedom with which it occurs in the Lucan writings. It is so often introduced by Luke when absent from the Marcan source that one hesitates to suggest its frequency in cc. 1,2, in 'Proto-Luke,' and in Ac 1-12 as evidence of fidelity to Aramaic originals. (Lagrange, S. Luc, p. cv, observes that most of the examples in the Gospel accord with Greek usage.)" (*MHT* 2, p. 452). On θέλω, see *GELS*, p. 203.

181. K. MÜLLER, *Jesus*, p. 114-115. He was speaking of the phrase from ἦν ... αὐτοῦ. Quoted by UNTERGASSMAIR, *Zur Problematik*, p. 280.

182. ZERWICK, *Analysis*, Vol. 1, p. 275. Jeremias viewed this as a preferred Lukan form

5,12 (Mk 1,40); 5,13 (Mk 1,41); 9,23 (Mk 8,34); 9,24 [γάρ] (Mk 8,35); 18,41 (Mk 10,51); 20,46 (Mk 12,38); 22,9 (Mk 14,36). The phrase θέλω ἵνα occurred in the Markan Baptist account (Mk 6,25)[183]. The combined use with an infinitive is possibly redactional[184].

The phrase ἦν ... θέλων could also recall Herodias' attitude toward the Baptist (ἤθελεν αὐτὸν ἀποκτεναι Mk 6,19) which might have served as the inspiration for Herod's desire for the death of Jesus: 'Ηρῴδης θέλει σε ἀποκτεῖναι (Lk 13,31)[185]. The term θέλω was used 4 times in the account of the Baptist's death (Mk 6,19.22.25.26). The word also occurred when Pilate asked the crowd whether they wanted Jesus or Barabbas released (Mk 15,9.12). In addition, it was employed at the end of the Markan account of the Transfiguration: ἐποίησαν αὐτῷ ὅσα ἤθελον (Mk 9,13), a prophecy fulfilled.

διὰ τὸ ἀκούειν περὶ αὐτοῦ. There were several instances of διὰ τό + inf. throughout the Gospel (2,4; 6,48; 8,6; 9,7; 11,8; 19,11) and also in Acts (Acts 4,2[186]; 8,11; 12,20; 18,2.3; 27,4.9; 28,18)[187]. Its use in 9,7 (διὰ τὸ λέγεσθαι) should be emphasized since it occurred there in one of the preparatory Herod pericopes. "Luke substitutes an elegant διὰ τό with infinitive phrase for Mark's

---

(Die Sprache, p. 301). See K. Müller's comment, drawing on Haenchen, that the periphrastic construction in the incidental remark was a certain indication of Lukan style (Jesus, p. 114-115, n. 23; HAENCHEN, Die Apostlegeschichte, ⁶1968, p. 116, n. 7). ZERWICK, Biblical Greek, p. 125-126: "The use of the periphrastic construction has in the NT a distribution which gives more than a half of the total number of occurrences to the writings of Luke alone. When the comparison is restricted to the periphrasis of the imperfect alone, Luke still is far ahead other writers: his gospel has about 30 examples and the Acts about 24, of which 17 are found in the earlier or Palestinian section of the book, and only 7 in the rest of it (chapters 13-38) (MOULTON). This seems to suggest that this Aramaizing use is to be attributed rather to Luke's sources than to his own ways of expressing himself, but against this we have HOWARD'S observation (p. 451) that though this construction is very frequent in the sections proper to Luke, he avoids it where he finds it in Mark, while on the other hand using it even in passages paralleled by Mark, where Mark does not use it". See also REID, p. 66, n. 191.

183. DSCHULNIGG, Sprache, p. 161. The phrase also was found at Mk 9,30; 10,35. The one instance of it in Lk 6,31 is Q material.

184. Ibid. p. 161. "Zu sprachlichen Variationsmöglichkeiten vgl. z.B. die Parallelen zu Mk 6,25 und 10,35 bei Mt 14,8; 20,20 oder auch eine mögliche Umschreibung mit folgendem Infinitiv".

185. See HOEHNER, Herod Antipas, p. 158-162 (The problem of change in persons: Who desired to kill John), and DENAUX, L'hypocrisie, p. 265 (= ²1989, p. 175). In the Markan passion we also find the phrase ἐζήτουν ... ἀποκτείνωσιν (Mk 14,1).

186. HAENCHEN, Die Apostelgeschichte, ¹⁴1965, p. 174 (= Acts, p. 215), who referred readers to BD, §402,1.

187. A.J. HESS, διά, in EWNT 1, cols. 712-713, esp. col. 713 (= p. 296-297, esp. p. 297): "With inf. and subj. acc. indicates (more frequently than in classical) cause". Jeremias declared: "Zur Vorliebe des Lukas für präpositionalen substantivierten Infinitive →1,8f. Red S. 29 sub B 2b, speziell zu διὰ τό mit Inf. → 2,4 Red S. 79" (Die Sprache, p. 302). See further SOARDS, Tradition, p. 351, n. 23.

impersonal plural ἔλεγον ..."[188]. The formulation of διά + the accusative of the articular infinitive is typical of Luke's style[189]. In 23,8 the construction can be explained as "pres. inf. w. force of imperfect"[190]. Although διά was used in Mk 6,14.17.26, it was found in Mk 5,4 in the same sense as Lk 23,8. Both Mk 6,26 and 23,8 were used to indicate Herod's reason or purpose. The formulation διὰ τό + inf. was also employed in Mk 4,5.6. Luke avoided repetition by using the phrase only once in his parallel (8,6).

ἀκούω was found four times in the Markan account of the Baptist's death (Mk 6,14.16.20a.b). It means "hear" in Mk 6,14.16 and "listen" in Mk 6,20b. Luke could easily have fashioned this part of 23,8 using Mk 6,14-16 as the basis since those verses are concerned with Herod hearing about Jesus' reputation[191]. Note also the following cases in Acts: ἀκουσόμεθά σου περὶ τούτου (Acts 17,32); ἤκουσεν αὐτοῦ περὶ τῆς εἰς Χριστὸν 'Ιησοῦν πίστεως (Acts 24,24 Paul's trial before Felix and Priscilla). It can also be used as a technical legal term, as in the case of Acts 25,22[192]. In the pericope of the woman with the hemorrhage (Mk 5,25-34 / Lk 8,43-48) we found the phrase ἀκούσασα περὶ τοῦ 'Ιησοῦ (Mk 5,27; om. Lk) in connection with discussion about the garment of Jesus[193]. A similar phrase occurred in Mk 7,25 within a passage Luke elected not to include. Further, περί was also found in the Lukan reference to Herod (3,19) in the context of John's imprisonment. Consider 5,15 (ἀκούειν) ὁ λόγος περὶ αὐτοῦ; 7,3 ἀκούσας δὲ περὶ τοῦ 'Ιησοῦ; the very important preparatory passage of 9,9: τίς δέ ἐστιν οὗτος περὶ οὗ ἀκούω τοιαῦτα. This statement of Herod bears an uncanny resemblance to 16,2: τί τοῦτο ἀκούω περὶ σοῦ; Note also the phrase in Acts 11,22 (ἠκούσθη ... περὶ αὐτῶν)[194] which preceded the mention that Barnabas

188. MARSHALL, Luke, p. 356.

189. BOISMARD, Synopse, t. 2, p. 418, though he only listed 15 instances; JEREMIAS, Die Sprache, p. 79, and LÉGASSE, Le procès, t. 2, p. 372, n. 49, who called attention to Jeremias's position; FITZMYER, p. 1479; Boismard and Lamouille in NEIRYNCK, Le texte, p. 320 (= 259); GOULDER, Luke, p. 802; BROWN, p. 768; K. MÜLLER, Jesus, p. 115, and CHICO CANO, p. 36, who both cited BD, §402,1, which in the ET indicated this phrase "used to denote cause is frequent in Lk". Marshall stated that διὰ τό was "Lucan" in 2,4, but he neglected to recall that comment for this verse (Luke, p. 105). Concerning διά, see GELS, p. 101.

190. ZERWICK, Analysis, Vol. 1, p. 275.

191. See GUELICH, Mark 1-8:26, p. 325-329. There is reference to "listen" (9,35 / Mk 9,7; cf. 23,6.8) and "seeing" (9,32.36) in the Transfiguration account.

192. G. SCHNEIDER, ἀκούω, in EWNT 1, cols. 126-131, esp. col. 126 (= p. 52-54, esp. p. 52).

193. See also the story of the Syrophoenician woman (Mk 7,25; omitted by Luke): ἀκούσασα γυνὴ περὶ αὐτοῦ.

194. See SCHNEIDER, Die Apostelgeschichte, T. 2, p. 90, n. 30: "Das passivische ἠκούσθη begegnet im NT nur noch Mk 2,1 und Joh 9,32 (jeweils mit folgendem ὅτι)". On the Septuagintal influence in a passage in Acts containing the passive form see the comments on Acts 11,22 by HAENCHEN, Acts, p. 366: "(cf. Isa. 5.9 LXX [ἠκούσθη γὰρ εἰς τὰ ὦτα κυρίου]) - Luke remains true to the biblical way of speaking", and BRUCE, Acts, ³1990, p. 273: "Of its use here after ἠκούσθη, C.C. Torrey says, 'No Greek writer would ever have perpetrated this - unless he had

rejoiced (ἐχάρη) just as was used to describe Herod's reaction in 23,8. Further, Acts 11,22-23 reports what was heard and seen. On the link of hearing and seeing the following should be observed: Lk 8,18; 10,23; Acts 2,33; 8,6[195]; 28,26[196]. The phrase ἀκούειν – περί + gen. has also been counted among the Lukan characteristics of Lk-Acts[197]. V. 8c.d was the result of Lukan composition[198].

καὶ ἤλπιζέν τι σημεῖον ἰδεῖν. The term ἐλπίζω occurred three times in Lk (6,34; 23,8; 24,21) and twice in Acts (24,26 Paul's appearance before Felix[199]; 26,7 Paul's speech to Agrippa)[200]. Three times in 23,8 Luke employed the verb ἰδεῖν pointing to Herod's intense desire to see Jesus and some sign performed by

wished to create the impression that he was using a Semitic 'source' [...]', or unless (we may add) he were writing deliberately in a septuagintal style" (Cf. C.C. TORREY, *Composition and Date of Acts* [HTS, 1], Cambridge, MA, 1916, p. 36).

195. BARRETT, *Acts*, p. 403: "Luke describes a process in which attention precedes faith. The hearers were impressed as they listened to Philip's words [...] and also as they witnessed [...] the signs that he performed".

196. See NEIRYNCK, *The Eschatological Discourse,* in D.L. DUNGAN (ed.), *The Interrelations of the Gospels: A Symposium Led by M.-É. Boismard – W.R. Farmer – F. Neirynck, Jerusalem 1984* (BETL, 95), Leuven, 1990, 108-124, p. 111 (= *Evangelica II*, 493-510, p. 496), who in commenting on Q passages remarked: "The association of seeing and hearing may be Lukan (because of its occurrences in Acts), but it is not a Lukan exclusivity". Just prior to that he observed that "the inversion in Lk 7:22 (εἴδετε καὶ ἠκούσατε [diff Mt 11,4]) is probably due to Luke ...".

197. Boismard and Lamouille in NEIRYNCK, *Le texte*, p. 317 (= 256); GOULDER, *Luke*, p. 800 (ἀκούειν-περί), 807 (περί + gen.). See JEREMIAS, *Die Sprache*, p. 255, and RADL, *Paulus*, p. 398.

198. SOARDS, *Tradition*, 1985, p. 351: "Given this connection, v. 8c and d is probably best related to the earlier verses in the ministry section of the Gospel and is, therefore, from Luke's pen".

199. See SCHNEIDER, *Die Apostelgeschichte*, T. 2, p. 352, n. 21. On the use in the LXX see *GELS*, p. 145.

200. H.E. Dana and J.R. Mantey cited 23,8 as an example of the progressive imperfect. "The imperfect may contemplate the process as having gone on in past time up to the time denoted by the context, but without any necessary inference as to whether or not the process has been completed" (*A Manual Grammar of the Greek New Testament*, New York, 1927, 1957, ᴿ1994, p. 187; see also p. 188). See further SPICQ, *NLNT* 3, 259-272, esp. p. 259 (= *TLNT* 1, 480-492, esp. p. 480). The following should be noted concerning the publication of Spicq's word studies: "In 1978 the original two volumes of Ceslas Spicq's *Notes de lexicographie néo-testamentaire* were published by Editions Universitaires de Fribourg, Switzerland (in the series Orbis Biblicus et Orientalis) and by Vandenhoeck & Ruprecht of Göttingen. These were followed four years later by a third volume, incorporating both newer material on some of the words covered in the original two volumes and also a large number of new entries. In 1991, Editions Universitaires collaborated with Cerf (Paris) in a single-volume reissue of the three-volume set. The reissue had a new title (*Lexique théologique du Nouveau Testament*) and merged the articles of the third volume into alphabetical order with the first two volumes but was otherwise unchanged" (Translator's Preface, in C. SPICQ, *TLNT* 1, tr. and ed. J.D. ERNEST, Peabody, MA, 1994, p. ix).

him²⁰¹. The term is Lukan, while the construction of ἐλπίζω with the infinitive is indicative of Luke²⁰².

τι is a distinctive Lukan term²⁰³ and an indication of Lukan style and vocabulary²⁰⁴. For similar construction, see for example τι ὕδωρ (Acts 8,36). The term was also used at the end of Acts (28,3 τι πλῆθος), the latter word having been identified as preferred Lukan vocabulary²⁰⁵.

σημεῖον. In Mk 8,11 the Pharisees were described as ζητοῦντες παρ᾽ αὐτοῦ σημεῖον. The Lukan parallel in 11,16 related σημεῖον ... ἐζήτουν παρ᾽ αὐτοῦ (diff. Mk 3,22-23)²⁰⁶. Even prior to his encounter with Herod (23,8) Jesus rejected the demand to perform a sign. Such insistence reflected the lack of faith on the part of "this generation" (Mk 8,12). According to 11,29 no other sign will be given except the sign of Jonah (/ Mt 12,39; 16,4; diff. Mk 8,12). Here also the idea of desire / seeking was coupled with a sign²⁰⁷. The term was found in the eschatological discourse of Lk 21,2.11.25. In this regard attention should be paid to 21,27 which is similar to 22,69²⁰⁸.

Acts 2,22 [τέρασι καὶ σημείοις] attested that God worked signs through Jesus²⁰⁹. The term σημεῖον "refers to miracles confirming the claim of a savior or prophet sent by God; they are meant to awaken faith (Exod 4:1-9) and are

201. BÜCHELE, p. 31, n. 39.

202. BOISMARD, *Synopse*, t. 2, p. 418. He cited 3x in Lk and 2x in Acts. Boismard and Lamouille in NEIRYNCK, *Le texte*, p. 321 (= 260). In addition see JEREMIAS, *Die Sprache*, p. 145, and GOULDER, *Luke*, p. 803.

203. TAYLOR, *Passion*, p. 87; NOLLAND, *Luke 18:35-24:53*, p. 1123.

204. JEREMIAS, *Die Sprache*, p. 302. See also p. 15, to which LÉGASSE, *Le procès*, t. 2, p. 372, n. 52, called attention. GOULDER, *Luke*, p. 809. According to his calculations there were 21 in Mt, 33 in Mk, 78 in Lk and 112 in Acts. See further NOLLAND, *Luke 18:35-24:53*, p. 1123; UNTERGASSMAIR, *Zur Problematik*, p. 280. Consider the remark of A. Horstmann: "τις occurs in all NT writings, with particularly high frequency in the two Lukan works (80 times in Luke, 115 in Acts)..." (A. HORSTMANN, τις, τι, in *EWNT* 3, cols. 866-869, col. 867 (= 362-363, p. 362).

205. J. ZMIJEWSKI, πλῆθος, ους, τό, in *EWNT* 3, cols. 245-249, col. 245 (= 103-105, p. 103): "Of the 31 unmistakable occurrences in the NT, 24 are in Luke-Acts (8 in the Gospel, 16 in Acts). This is thus one of Luke's 'preferred words' (Schneider, Die Apostelgeschichte, 1980, Vol. 1, p. 381, n. 23)".

206. In Mk the term ζητέω was also used to describe the effort to kill Jesus (Mk 11,18; 14,1) or to seek testimony against him (Mk 14,55).

207. NOLLAND, *Luke 18:35-24:53*, p. 1123, argued that 23,8 "is likely to have been inspired by these texts" viz. 11,16.29. See also K. MÜLLER, *Jesus*, p. 121, 122. Brown added 4,9-12 as an example of diabolic testing and 4,23-24 which exemplified a lack of faith as other aspects of demands for a sign (*Death*, p. 770).

208. Acts 2,19 speaks of Pentecost being accompanied by eschatological signs.

209. God also worked signs and wonders through the apostles (Acts 2,43; 5,12) as well as Stephen (Acts 6,8) and Philip (Acts 8,6.13) and Paul and Barnabas (Acts 14,3; 15,12). "Τέρατα καὶ σημεῖα (usually in the reverse order) is a common LXX phrase" (BARRETT, *Acts*, p. 141, and 167; see also BRUCE, *Acts*, ³1990, p. 132: "The collocation of these two words is common in the LXX and NT"; see also p. 123).

demanded or prompted rather than requested"[210]. The elaboration in Acts helped
to clarify the idea that the signs comprised an essential part of the portrayal of
Jesus as a prophet. "The revelatory and instrumental character of these signs is
grounded in the idea of mission, oriented toward Moses, and designed for
continuity: Moses 'performed wonders and signs in Egypt and at the Red Sea, and
in the wilderness,' thus point to a coming prophet equal to himself (7:36f.):
Because God is to empower and send this prophet (Deut 18:15), God is also the
source of the signs that legitimize Jesus"[211].

ὑπ' αὐτοῦ γινόμενον. Mark used the phrase ὑπ' αὐτοῦ (Mk 1,5; cf. Lk 3,7
Q) in the account of the baptisms by John. It was also found in the story of the
Gerasene demoniac (Mk 5,1-20) while Mk 5,4-5 was omitted in the Lukan parallel
(cf. Lk 8,27-28)[212]. Luke employed the phrase in his abbreviated account of
Herod's imprisonment of John (3,19). The expression was also found in special
Lukan material: where Jesus healed a crippled woman on the sabbath (13,7) and
concerning the invitation to the marriage feast (14,8). The phrase "sign done by
him" is possibly an echo of 9,9[213]. This phrase is Lukan[214].

What is particularly significant for our consideration is that the phrase was
also employed in the plural in Paul's trial before the chief priests and Sanhedrin
(Acts 23,10 ὑπ' αὐτῶν). In that same section of Acts, the phrase in the plural
occurs again in Acts 23,27 in a message sent to the governor Felix[215]. Luke also
employed the passive voice in Acts 4,16 (γὰρ γνωστὸν σημεῖον γέγονεν δι'
αὐτῶν)[216].

γινόμενον. The word was used in 9,7 (γινόμενα) in a reference to "all that
was done" by Jesus. "Le participe ginomenon renvoie à ta ginomena en 9,7"[217].
The phraseology is Lukan[218]. The phrase ἴδητε ταῦτα γινόμενα occurs in Mk
13,29 and its Lukan parallel at 13,21. Note the similarity with ἰδεῖν ὑπ' αὐτοῦ
γινόμενον (23,8). Luke employed comparable formulations of σημεῖον ... ὑπ'
αὐτοῦ γινόμενον in Acts 2,43; 4,16[219]. "v. 8e is best understood as Lukan
composition"[220].

210. O. BETZ, σημεῖον, in EWNT 3, cols. 569-575, esp. col. 571 (= 238-241, esp. p. 239).
211. Ibid., col. 573 (= p. 240).
212. See above on v. 8 about the use of διά.
213. BROWN, Death, p. 768.
214. BOISMARD, Synopse, t. 2, p. 418, who stated it was found twice in both Lk and Acts.
215. For the use in the singular as in 23,8 see also Acts 2,24.
216. Consider also Acts 4,22: ὃν γεγόνει τὸ σημεῖον.
217. LÉGASSE, Le procès, t. 2, p. 372, n. 53.
218. MARSHALL, Luke, p. 855-856; cf. Acts 2,43; 4,16.22.30; 5,12; 8,13; 14,3. See RADL,
Paulus, p. 402-404.
219. GOULDER, Luke, Vol. 2, p. 759, who erroneously cited Acts 2,46; 4,13. See
SCHNEIDER, Die Apostelgeschichte, T. 1, p. 350, n. 75.
220. SOARDS, Tradition, 1985, p. 352.

Verse 9

ἐπηρώτα δὲ αὐτὸν ἐν λόγοις ἱκανοῖς, αὐτὸς δὲ οὐδὲν ἀπεκρίνατο αὐτῷ.
"So he questioned him at some length; but he made no answer".

"The verse is generally seen (probably correctly) as a recasting of Mark 15:4-5 (and cf. 14:60-61), for which Luke had no place in his account of the trial before Pilate"[221]. It has been suggested that the silence of Jesus may be understood against the background of Is 53,7, but that such behavior also reveals Jesus' noble character[222]. Drawing on the account of Jesus before the Sanhedrin (Mk 14,61) which rests upon the prophecy of Is 53,7, as well as the silence of Jesus in response to some of the questioning of Pilate (Mk 15,5), for both of which Luke has no parallel, he now employed the motif in the Herod trial. Luke quoted Is 53,7 in Acts 8,32-33[223]. Thus, Luke's method was similar to that used in 22,69 where he displaced the reference to the coming of the Son of Man (Mk 14,62) to Acts 7,46 in the speech of Stephen. The silence of Jesus provided a remarkable contrast with the talkative Herod (v. 9) and the vehement accusations of the chief priests and scribes (v. 10)[224].

The theme of Jesus' silence was present in the Markan account of Jesus before the Sanhedrin (Mk 14,60.61) as well as before Pilate (Mk 15,4.5)[225]. Many scholars have recognized a similarity between 23,9 (οὐδὲν ἀπεκρίνατο) and Mk 14,61 (οὐκ ἀπεκρίνατο οὐδέν; ἐσιώπα καὶ οὐκ ἀπεκρίνατο οὐδέν)[226] as well

221. J. NOLLAND, *Luke 18:35-24:53*, p. 1123.
222. SOARDS, *The Silence of Jesus*, in *ABR* 33 (1985) 41-45. See his review of four kinds of interpretations of the silence (p. 41). His understanding of the nobility was influenced by a description of Mariamme, wife of Herod the Great, as contained in Josephus, *Ant.* 15.7.6, para. 234-235 (p. 43).
223. JOHNSON, *Luke*, p. 367. See also HAENCHEN, *Die Apostelgeschichte*, [14]1965, p. 261 (= *Acts*, p. 311), on Acts 8,32: "The quotation from Isaiah 53 LXX begins in the middle of verse 7 and ends in the middle of verse 8", and BRUCE, *Acts*, [3]1990, p. 227: "From Isa. 53:7ff., LXX". On the phrase οὕτως οὐκ ἀνοίγει τὸ στόμα αὐτοῦ he commented: "Cf. the passion narratives Mk. 14:61; 15:5; Lk. 23:9; Jn. 19:9".
224. SOARDS, *Silence*, p. 43. See also BROWN, p. 771-772: "To all this Jesus answers nothing – in startling contrast to Herod's verbosity". LÉGASSE, *Le procès*, t. 2, p. 372, n. 54: "*En logois hikanois* (voir ici n. 50) forme un contraste avec *ouden apekrinato autôi*, l'abondance des paroles d'Hérode s'opposant au silence total de Jésus".
225. Chico Cano argued that the silence motif in L was probably due to Markan influence (*Der Prozess Jesu*, p. 38). Also noted by B. WEISS, *Lukas*, [9]1901, p. 661: "obwohl an Mk 14,61. 15,5 errinernd, sehr begreiflich ist".
226. See W. RADL, σιωπάω in *EWNT* 3, col. 591 (= p. 247): "Jesus' Passion is the most important context in which σιωπάω appears". The term also occurred in Mk 3,4 (the Pharisees are silent in response to Jesus' question; diff Lk 6,9 the phrase is omitted); Mk 4,39 (Jesus commanded the sea to be still; diff Lk 8,24 the words of the command were omitted); Mk 9,34 (the disciples were silenced by Jesus' question; diff 9,46 omitted); Mk 10,48 (bystanders commanded Bartimaeus to be silent; diff Lk 18,39 σιγήσῃ). Luke used σιωπάω in the special material of 1,20 and 19,40 as well as in Acts 18,9, where the Lord in the context of reassurance commanded Paul not to be silent.

as Mk 15,5 (οὐκέτι οὐδὲν ἀπεκρίθη), though this latter example less directly[227]. Luke was probably influenced in 23,9 by the Markan tradition[228]. Luke did not relate the silence of Jesus either in his encounter with the Sanhedrin (22,66-71) or with Pilate (23,1-5)[229].

ἐπηρώτα δέ. For both terms, see the previous discussion on 23,6. The term δέ was employed in the Markan account of the death of the Baptist (Mk 6,24) where it had the copulative sense as in Lk 23,8[230]. The use of ἐπηρώτα here is a verbal reminiscence of Mk[231].

It might be objected that in 23,9a there was no dialogue as in the meeting of Jesus with Pilate in which case this would hardly have been inspired by the Markan narrative even if it be granted that the detail of Jesus' silence (23,9b) stemmed from Mk 15,5. Yet even this omission or abbreviation of dialogue would be consistent with Lukan redaction[232]. "While this line [v. 9a] is certainly related to the tradition of Herod's involvement in Jesus' trial and is consistent with other scenes in that trial, the lack of specificity and the colorful description suggest that the line probably comes from Luke's pen"[233].

Darr did not envision the possibility that the silence motif was derived from Mk, though he considered the influence of Is 53,7 (*Glorified*, p. 292-296). In addition, the Greco-Roman reader would have recognized Jesus' "courageous self-control [αὐτάρκεια] in the face of death" (p. 295). Darr later added Jesus demonstrated not only αὐτάρκεια, but also παρρησία (courage, boldness) in the trial narrative as well as in 13,31-35 (p. 301; also p. 317, 318). The theme of boldness in a context which mentioned Herod will also be found in Acts 4,23-31. Shortly before that there was mention of ἃ εἴδαμεν καὶ ἠκούσαμεν (Acts 4,20), another motif we found in 23,6-12. On the relationship of the Jesus-Paul parallels, Darr pointed to a bibliography but did not attempt to answer such questions as whether Paul's trial shaped that of Jesus (p. 312, n. 173; cf. p. 8 n. 14). He argued further that the depiction of Herod in Acts 4,25-28 was not so different from that found in Jesus' trial and he rejected the criticism that there was a lack of continuity between the accounts. For a differing perspective, see MATERA, *Luke 23,1-25*, p. 542. Darr focused on the similarity between 23,6-12 and Acts 4,23-31 in asserting: "However, the similarities are clearly intentional and meaningful. The lesson is clear: if one chooses to be a true witness – one who sees, hears, responds, and tells – then one will inevitably encounter a 'Herod'" (*Glorified*, p. 312).

227. Note also the similarity of Mk 14,60 (οὐκ ἀποκίνη οὐδέν) and Mk 15,4 (οὐκ ἀποκίνη οὐδέν).

228. BROWN, p. 772. A further explanation was that since Jesus had already responded to Herod (13,32) no further response was required (p. 772, 773).

229. We should also recall that Paul spoke to Herod Agrippa II in Acts.

230. SOARDS, *Silence*, p. 42, also noted this use which was supported by *LSJ*, p. 371, and H.W. SMYTH, *Greek Grammar*, Cambridge, 1920, para. 2836. The term was used as an adversative in Mk 6,15a.b.16 describing the occasion when Herod learned of various opinions concerning Jesus. See further the discussion in LÉGASSE, *Le procès*, t. 2, p. 373, n. 57.

231. CHICO CANO, *Der Prozess Jesu*, p. 37, no. 73, who referred to SCHÜRMANN, *Traditionsgeschichte*, p. 111-125.

232. CADBURY, *Style*, p. 79-80. Consider: Mk 1,44 / 5,14; Mk 4,30 / 8,24; Mk 5,8 / 8,29; Mk 5,28 / 8,44; Mk 9,33 / 9,47; Mk 15,12 / 23,20; Mk 15,14 / 23,23. Even Mark used the means of recounting in summary fashion (Mk 6,30).

233. SOARDS, *Tradition*, 1985, p. 353.

ἐν λόγοις ἱκανοῖς. Luke employed ἐν in an instrumental sense[234]. λόγος has also been identified as a Lukan term[235]. Concerning ἱκανοῖς see also above on v. 8[236], but note Luke's penchant for repeating terms he used only shortly before[237]. This description served to heighten the contrast with the silence of Jesus. ἱκανός was employed differently in Mk 15,15 so its use in Acts 20,11 has more the sense of a very long time[238]. The term occurred in special material in 22,38.51 signifying sufficiency. Both πολλά (Mk 15,3) and ποσά, which Mark used interchangably, could have suggested to Luke a lengthy interrogation process. In Mk 9,21 the phrase πόσος χρόνος was used. Though Luke omitted all of Mk 9,21-24 (cf. Lk 9,42), we established above that ἐξ ἱκανῶν χρόνων (20,9; 23,9; Acts 8,11; 27,9) was used by Luke in much the same way. He could have simply supplanted πόσος with ἱκανός[239]. He would have read it in the Markan account of Pilate's questioning (Mk 15,4)[240]. In Acts 15,32 the phrase διὰ λόγου πολλοῦ occurs. As we noted, Luke used διά in 23,8[241].

Luke's use of ἱκανός as a substitute for μέγας and πολύς reflected a similar practice in the more recent books of the LXX[242]. This practice corresponds to Septuagintal usage[243], and is a clear sign of Lukan vocabulary[244].

αὐτὸς δὲ οὐδὲν ἀπεκρίνατο αὐτῷ. The αὐτὸς δέ here and in 4,30 has been viewed as "christologisch"[245]. It has also been judged to be Lukan redaction[246].

---

234. See ZERWICK, Biblical Greek, p. 40, § 119.

235. RADL, Paulus, p. 416. See SCHNEIDER, Verleugnung, p. 93.

236. GELS(TP), p. 114. The term ἱκανός is found in the LXX Prophets in Ob 5; Na 2,13; Hb 2,13; Zc 7,3. See SPICQ, NLNT 3, 345-350, p. 346 (= TLNT 3, 217-222, p. 218). See further CADBURY, Style, p. 196.

237. HAENCHEN, Die Apostelgeschichte, [14]1965, p. 71 (= Acts, p. 79): "Like the rest of us [Luke] has the habit of soon repeating a word when he has used it". Haenchen offered examples in n. 3: Acts 19,35.36 καταστέλλω; 19,38.40 ἐγκαλέω; 20,1.2 παρακαλέσας; 9,13.32.41 ἅγιοι; 13,46.48 ζωὴ αἰώνιος; 15,32.41 ἐπιστηρίζω; 5,29.32 πειθαρχέω; 2,42.46 προσκαρτεροῦντες. He drew upon T. VOGEL, Zur Charakteristik, [2]1899, p. 17, for the last five examples. According to Haenchen, Luke was also known to vary his expressions in different portions of his work. "Hence certain words and expressions occur in one part of his writings and others in another part" (Die Apostelgeschichte, p. 71 = 79).

238. SPICQ, TLNT 2, p. 219, n. 14. Luke also employed it in Acts 20,8 to refer to many lights and in Acts 20,37 in regard to abundant tears (p. 218, n. 11). See also 2 Mac 7,5; 8,25. In addition, consider the comment in SCHNEIDER, Die Apostelgeschichte, T. 2, p. 287, n. 34. On its use in the LXX see GELS(TP), p. 114.

239. See Acts 20,8: λαμπάδες ἱκαναί.

240. Luke replaced μεγάλη (Mk 5,11) with ἱκανῶν in the parallel at Lk 8,32.

241. See also Acts 20,2.

242. K. MÜLLER, Jesus, p. 115.

243. UNTERGASSMAIR, Zur Problematik, p. 280.

244. BOISMARD, Synopse, t. 2, p. 418; Boismard and Lamouille in NEIRYNCK, Le texte, p. 323 (= 262); GOULDER, Luke, p. 805.

245. J. JEREMIAS, Die Sprache, p. 128, 302.

246. BOISMARD, Synopse, t. 2, p. 418, and FITZMYER, p. 1479, 120.

This phrase constituted a "literary touch"[247]. Luke omitted this phrase in the parallel place (Mk 14,60.61; diff 22,66-67), chosing instead to redact it from Pilate's interrogation in Mk 15,4-5[248]. "His [Jesus'] silence, usually described by a negative with ἀποκρίνομαι (Mark 14:61; 15:5 par. Matt 27:[12]14; Luke 23:9) ... allows him to appear in the role of the suffering righteous person (cf. Isa 53:7; Pss 37:14-16; 38:9f. LXX)"[249].

ἀπεκρίνατο αὐτῷ. Luke used "ἀποκριθείς with a verb of saying quite as often as the other Evangelists"[250]. Mark employed the middle aorist ἀπεκρίνατο more than any other NT writer[251]. ἀποκρίνομαι has also been listed among Lukan vocabulary[252]. Notice the use of the first middle aorist ἀπεκρίνατο οὐδέν in 23,9 (Mk 14,61) as well as the use of ἀπεκρίνατο in the pericope about John the Baptist responding to those who were questioning him (3,16 = Mk 1,7-8)[253]. The word ἀπεκρίνατο was found in 3,16 where the Baptist responded to those who were asking how they should live, which included soldiers (στρατευόμενοι 3,14) who have been identified as non-Romans in the employ of Herod Antipas[254]. In connection with Paul note Acts 25,4(ἀπεκρίθη).16(ἀπεκρίθην). The term was also used in the LXX[255].

247. BROWN, Death, p. 768.
248. ZERWICK, Biblical Greek, p. 74, § 229: "Just as the active took the place of the middle in the future of active verbs, so too the middle loses ground, but in favor of the passive, in 'deponent' verbs. The commonest example of this in the NT is the aorist ἀπεκρίθη (195 times) instead of ἀπεκρίνατο, which is found only four times in the synoptic gospels, οὐδὲν ἀπεκρίνατο being said of Jesus three times in non-parallel passages (Mt 27,12; Mk 14,61; Lk 23,9), to which must be added 3,16; Jo 5,17; Acts 3,12; nor is the middle form found elsewhere in the NT. This seems to confirm Moulton-Milligan's observation that the form ἀποκρίνασθαι was an especially 'solemn' one in Hellenistic usage". See BÜCHELE, p. 31, n. 42. Jeremias judged ἀπεκρίνατο to be traditional (Die Sprache, p. 302).
249. RADL, σιωπάω, in EWNT 3, col. 591 (= p. 247).
250. CADBURY, Style, p. 170. Luke borrowed the term from Mk in 8 places: 8,21 / Mk 3,33; 9,20 / Mk 8,29; 9,41 / Mk 9,19; 20,3 / diff Mk 11,29; 20,7 / Mk 11,33; 10,27 / Mk 12,39; 20,39 / Mk 12,34; 22,3 / Mk 15,2. It should be noted that 9,20 / Mk 8,29 followed mention of John the Baptist. 20,3 / diff Mk 11,29 preceded mention of John in 20,4.6 / Mk 11,30.32.
251. K. MÜLLER, Jesus, p. 123.
252. RADL, Paulus, p. 400-401, and BOISMARD, En quête, p. 124.
253. The form was also used in Acts 3,12. The only other occurrences were Jn 5,17.19. See HAWKINS, Horae Synopticae, 1899, p. 61; ²1909, p. 76, where he observed "in LXX it is proportionally still rarer, being used on four or five times" (p. 76-[77], n. 1), and CADBURY, Style, p. 101. Cadbury further insisted: "In Luke also Jesus' own persistent silence is not so prominent" (Style, p. 94). On οὐδέν see also GELS(TP), p. 178. See LXX 40,23; 4 Mac 8,27; cf. LXX Is 36,21.
254. MARSHALL, Luke, p. 143; FITZMYER, Luke, p. 470; See BDF § 413. Cf. CREED, p. 53. For its use in the LXX, see GELS, p. 446. Note other verbal similarities between 3,10-14, a passage also unique to Lk, and 23,6-16: ἐπηρωτάω (3,10.14); πρὸς αὐτός (3,12.13); repeated use of δέ (3,10.11.12.13.14); οὖν (3,10); ὁ δέ (3,13; 23,8); τελῶναι (3,12) and θέλων (23,8); compare the phrases εἶπαν πρὸς αὐτόν (3,12) and εἶπεν πρὸς αὐτούς ... εἶπεν αὐτοῖς (3,13) with εἶπεν πρὸς αὐτούς (23,14) and ἐπηρώτων δὲ αὐτόν (3,14) with ἐπηρώτα δὲ αὐτόν (23,9).
255. GELS, p. 51; GELS(TP), p. 25. Exactly as in Ex 19,19. Cf. LXX 1 Kg 28,6; 3 Kg

"αὐτός, intensive, is a favorite word with Luke, especially the nominative in the expressions καὶ αὐτός, αὐτὸς δέ, which are often used in recasting prefaces of sections from Mark, and elsewhere"[256]. (See above on v. 7). In 8,54 Luke borrowed the phrase from Mk 5,40[257]. 23,9b reflects Lukan redaction[258].

Our judgment for v. 9 is that this is probably Lukan redaction of Markan material, which is confirmed both by verbal similarity and by the theme of silence.

Verse 10

εἱστήκεισαν δὲ οἱ ἀρχιερεῖς καὶ οἱ γραμματεῖς εὐτόνως κατηγοροῦντες αὐτοῦ.

"The chief priests and the scribes stood by, vehemently accusing him".

"If v 9 is from Mark, so will v 10 be (Mark 15:3)"[259]. The phrase εἱστήκεισαν δέ also appeared in 23,49 (diff. Mk) describing all the acquaintances and the women from Galilee watching the crucified Jesus from a distance. In Mk 15,35 we read παρεστηκότων ἀκούσαντες, omitted in Luke, as was also the case of Luke's omission of ὁ παρεστηκώς to describe the centurion observing Jesus' dying breath (Mk 15,39), and the omission of παρεστῶσιν, παρεστῶτες in the account of Peter's denials (22,58.59 diff. Mk 14,69.70). In 24,2 Luke has ἐπέστησαν αὐταῖς (cf. Mk 16,5; see also Acts 1,10; 10,30). On the construction ἐιστήκει(-σαν) with participle, in addition to this verse, see 23,35(the third mockery).49 (cf. Mk 15,40)[260]. Observe that the same form of the verb was used in Acts 9,7 in reference to companions of Paul[261]. The verb "may have an adversative thrust", while noting that Acts 25,7 describes Paul's Jewish enemies as περιέστησαν[262]. The word was found often in the LXX and it was likely Luke drew it from there[263].

οἱ ἀρχιερεῖς καὶ οἱ γραμματεῖς. The high priesthood of Annas and Caiaphas was first mentioned in 3,2 following the reference to Pilate and Herod in the context of a discussion regarding John the Baptist. The double mention of high

18,21; Is. 36,21.

256. CADBURY, *Style*, p. 193. Also p. 150: "The use of αὐτὸς δέ and καὶ αὐτός is especially frequent in Luke".

257. In addition see for example 11,17 (/ Mk 3,23) and 18,39 (diff Mk 10,48).

258. SOARDS, *Tradition*, 1985, p. 353: "It is reasonable to conclude that Luke brings to this scene the motif of silence which he dropped from his version of the earlier scenes. And so, v. 9b may be attributed to Luke's editorial activity".

259. J. NOLLAND, *Luke 18:35-24:53*, p. 1124.

260. Pointed out by NEIRYNCK, *Minor Agreements*, p. 242.

261. In Mk 14,60 there was reference to the high priest standing (ἀναστάς) and asking (ἐπηρώτησεν), just as in Mk 14,61 there was the phrase ὁ ἀρχιερεὺς ἐπηρώτα.

262. BROWN, *Death*, p. 771.

263. E.g. Gen. 18,2; Ex 20,21; 24,10; 33,8; Num 16,27; Dt 5,5; 10,10; Jo 4,10; 2 Kgs 17,17; 3 Kgs 13,28; Is 6,2; Ez 1,21; 10,9.17; Zch 2,3; 3,1.4.5.6. See further *SV*, p. 147, and *GELS(TP)*, p. 115.

priests and scribes was found in Mk 11,18 (/ 19,47)²⁶⁴.27 + πρεσβύτεροι (/ 20,1)²⁶⁵ as well as in Mk 14,1 (/ 22,2)²⁶⁶.43 + τῶν πρεσβυτέρων (diff 22,47). The combination of religious leaders is found in the passion prediction (9,22 = Mk 8,31). The chief priests and scribes (20,1) played a major role in the dispute over Jesus' authority (20,1-8). Later, in 20,19 (diff. Mk) they were referred to again, though in reverse order²⁶⁷. In 22,2 (= Mk 14,1) as in 19,47 (= Mk 11,18), οἱ ἀρχιερεῖς καὶ οἱ γραμματεῖς were seeking the death of Jesus. The religious leaders were last mentioned together in 22,66²⁶⁸. "If Mark provides the major element of the Passion story and the secondary elements are dependent on the Marcan frame, then it is not surprising that the Marcan term γραμματεύς is used throughout the Lucan Passion, at xxiii. 10 as well as at xxii. 2, 66"²⁶⁹. Unlike Mk 15,1 where the "elders of the people" were listed as a separate group, for Luke οἱ πρεσβύτεροι is a comprehensive term comprising the chief priests and scribes. This phrase, which occurred 6 times in Lk though not at all in Acts, has been assigned to Luke²⁷⁰. Such a grouping betrays Lukan redaction²⁷¹. The use of the phrase "high priests and the scribes" is indicative of Lukan dependence upon Mk²⁷².

εὐτόνως is found only in 23,10 and Acts 18,28²⁷³. For that reason the term

264. This Markan verse also contains a form of the word ζητέω as in 9,9 and expressed sentiments very similar to the intention of Herod described in Lk 13,31. Taylor argued 23,6-16 "has nothing characteristic of Mark except οἱ γραμματεῖς in verse 10". Despite granting that, he concluded "we cannot claim that Luke of himself never uses it (cf. xxii.66)" (Passion, p. 87). On γραμματεῖς in the LXX see also GELS, p. 92-93.

265. Note the use of the term ἐξουσία in Mk 11,28.29.33 in the context of a discussion about the authority of the Baptist and Jesus. Although different from the use in 23,7, it should still be considered.

266. The term ἐζήτουν and the intention to kill Jesus should also be noted.

267. A similar reversal of order took place in 21,12 βασιλεῖς καὶ ἡγεμόνας / Mk 13,9 ἡγεμόνων καὶ βασιλέων. Haenchen's comments on this aspect of Lukan style are useful. He suggested three reasons why Luke inverted word order, a common practice in Hellenistic literature. These included "specific difficulties of formulation", "considerations of rhythm", as well as "to bring what is being stressed into the emphatic positions, i.e. the beginning and the end" (Acts, p. 78, 79 = Die Apostelgeschichte, ¹⁴1965, p. 70, 71). It is this third case which explains the great number of Luke's changes in word order.

268. Also noted by Brown (p. 771). See a related discussion in DSCHULNIGG, Sprache, p. 102-103, esp. p. 103.

269. G.D. KILPATRICK, Scribes, Lawyers, and Lucan Origins, in JTS 1 (1950) 56-60, p. 58 (= Principles, 246).

270. BOISMARD, Synopse, t. 2, p. 418.

271. UNTERGASSMAIR, Zur Problematik, p. 281.

272. CHICO CANO, Der Prozess Jesu, p. 39.

273. So also BROWN, p. 768; JEREMIAS, Die Sprache, p. 302; SCHNEIDER, Die Apostelgeschichte, T. 2, p. 262, n. 28; LÉGASSE, Le procès, t. 2, p. 373, n. 58, who cited Lc 18,28 [sic]. The use of the term in Acts followed a reference to John the Baptist (Acts 18,25). It is also found in LXX Jos 6,7 (T. GILBRANT [ed.], The New Testament Greek-English Dictionary Vol. 2, Springfield, MO, 1990, p. 653). B. WEISS, Lukas, ⁹1901, p. 661, cited Jos

is judged to be Lukan²⁷⁴. This Lukan adverb is a possible substitute for the Markan πολλά²⁷⁵. Luke already clarified Mark's imprecise reference to the many charges (πολλά, πόσα Mk 15,3.4) by specifying that there was a primary charge further designated in two examples (διαστρέφοντα τὸ ἔθνος 23,2; cf. ἀποστρέφοντα τὸν λαόν, 23,14)²⁷⁶. In contrast to Mk Luke focused on the vigor with which the Jewish leaders were arguing their case. The use of this term can be likened to ἐπίχυον in 23,5 (hapax). This served to strengthen 23,2²⁷⁷. On Septuagintal use recourse can be made to related terms in 2 Mac 12,23; 4 Mac 7,10.

κατηγοροῦντες αὐτοῦ. The term κατηγορέω occurred in Lk 4 times and in Acts 9 times and has been categorized as Lukan vocabulary²⁷⁸. The infinitive κατηγορεῖν with the object αὐτοῦ occured only in Lk 6,7; 23,2; Acts 24,2²⁷⁹. Luke borrowed this juridical technical term²⁸⁰ twice from Mk, though, he modified the word in both cases: εὕρωσιν κατηγορεῖν αὐτοῦ (6,7 / κατηγορήσωσιν αὐτοῦ Mk 3,2). The second instance was 23,2 (Ἤρξαντο δὲ κατηγορεῖν), borrowed from Mk 15,3 (κατηγόρουν). Statistics indicate that ἤρξαντο was a preferred Markan term²⁸¹. κατηγορέω is repeated in Mk 15,4.

Of the occurrences in Acts all refer to Paul and are concentrated in the following sections: his trial before the Sanhedrin (22,30), the governor Felix (24,2.8.13.19), Festus (25,5.11), Herod Agrippa (26,16) and as part of Paul's

6,8 and 2 Mac 12,23; cf. J. WEISS, *Lukas*, ⁸1892, p. 640, 2 Mac 18,23 (sic). See also *SV*, p. 131, which listed Jos 6,8; Lk 23,10 and Acts 18,28. Note further *GELS*, p. 190.

274. K. MÜLLER, *Jesus*, p. 115; see also p. 131; BOISMARD, *Synopse*, t. 2, p. 418; Boismard and Lamouille in NEIRYNCK, *Le texte*, p. 322 (= 261); UNTERGASSMAIR, *Zur Problematik*, p. 281. Although Brown suggested the adverb "may have the connotation 'at full pitch'", he made no mention that the word was Lukan or that it also appeared in Acts 18,28 (*Death*, p. 771). CHICO CANO, p. 40, argued Luke used the term to attain a stronger emphasis of the sentence.

275. DSCHULNIGG, *Sprache*, p. 107. On the Markan usage, see also NEIRYNCK, *The Redactional Text of Mark*, in *ETL* 57 (1981) 144-162, esp. p. 149, n. 17 (= *Evangelica*, 618-636, esp. p. 623, n. 17).

276. K. MÜLLER, *Jesus*, p. 131: "Davon ist zudem der ersatz von πολλά (Mk 15,3b) durch εὐτόνως (Lk 23,10b) betroffen: an allen Stellen, wo der dritte Evangelist bei Markus den als Adverb gebrauchten Akkusativ Neutrum Plural πολλά las, strich er ihn entweder oder er tauschte ihn gegen eine andere Formulierung aus". He cited Mk 1,45; 3,12; 5,10.23.38.43; 9,26 cf. 15,3 (n. 63). See NOLLAND, *Luke 18:35-24:53*, p. 1124, who accepted Müller's argument.

277. H. BALZ, ἐπισχύω, in *EWNT* 2, col. 102 (= p. 41).

278. SCHNEIDER, *Political Charge*, p. 409 (= 179); Boismard and Lamouille in NEIRYNCK, *Le texte*, p. 324 (= 263); *NTV*, p. 51. The term is also found in LXX 1 Mac 7,6.25; 2 Mac 4,47; 10.13.21; 4 Mac 9,14. See *GELS*, p. 249.

279. I am indebted to SCHNEIDER, *Political Charge*, p. 409 (= 179), for this information.

280. H. BALZ, κατηγορέω, in *EWNT* 2, col. 672 (= p. 272). Concerning the construction ἑστήκεισαν ... κατηγοροῦντες, Jeremias stated: "Finite Formen von ἔστηκα/εἰτήκειν + Part.coniunct. finden sich im Doppelwerk häufiger als im übrigen NT" (*Die Sprache*, p. 302).

281. SCHNEIDER, *Political Charge*, p. 409 (= 179).

recollection of the events (28,19)[282]. 23,10 is due to Luke, building as he does, upon previous material in his Gospel[283]. In the LXX see 1 Mac 7,25.

Verse 11

ἐξουθενήσας δὲ αὐτὸν [καὶ] ὁ Ἡρῴδης σὺν τοῖς στρατεύμασιν αὐτοῦ καὶ ἐμπαίξας περιβαλὼν ἐσθῆτα λαμπρὰν ἀνέπεμψεν αὐτὸν τῷ Πιλάτῳ.

"And Herod with his soldiers treated him with contempt and mocked him; then, arraying him in gorgeous apparel, he sent him back to Pilate".

"The scene of Mk 15,16-20a is omitted by Luke, or, more correctly, it has been transferred on the one hand to the Herod episode (Lk 23,11a ἐξουθενήσας δὲ αὐτὸν ὁ Ἡρῴδης σὺν τοῖς στρατεύμασιν αὐτοῦ καὶ ἐμπαίξας περιβαλὼν ἐσθῆτα λαμπρὰν ...) and on the other into the mocking of the soldiers after the crucifixion: Lk 23,36 ..."[284].

ἐξουθενήσας δὲ αὐτόν. Mark used ἐξουδενηθῇ in Mk 9,12[285], concerning the Son of Man, a passage omitted by Luke[286]. In the Gospels ἐξουθενέω is found only in Lk 18,9 and 23,11[287]. It occurred also in Acts 4,11, drawn from a quote of Ps 118,22, where it has the meaning of rejection[288]. This use should be compared with Mk 12,10 (/ Lk 20,17 / Mt 21,42) which also quoted Ps 118,22. The term employed in all three Synoptic accounts is ἀπεδοκίμασαν, which is what is found in the LXX Ps 117,22. Luke's subsitution of the term in Acts could serve to strengthen the connection with the mockery in the passion narrative. His

282. It is worth noting that the present infinitive occurred twice in Lk and three times in Acts. See SCHNEIDER, *Die Apostelgeschichte*, T. 1, p. 320, n. 19.

283. SOARDS, *Tradition*, 1985, p. 355: "The consistency between 23,10 and other parts of the Gospel suggests that here Luke draws upon ideas found in the earlier portions of his Gospel to compose this part of the scene".

284. NEIRYNCK, ΤΙΣ ΕΣΤΙΝ, p. 22 (= *Evangelica II*, 112).

285. ἐξουθενωθῇ. *HR*, Vol. 1, p. 500, treated the terms together. See further *MHT* 2, p. 111, 408. Brown observed the use of the term in Mk 9,12 (*Death*, p. 773). In the LXX the term ἐξουθενοῦσι is found in Am 6,1 (*GELS[TP]*, p. 85). Consider also LXX Jer 6,14.

286. Mt 17,12b omitted the Markan ἐξουδενηθῇ. Cf. Mk 6,14-15 and Herod's confusion about Jesus: whether he was the resurrected John the Baptist or Elijah.

287. J. Weiss attributed the use in 18,9 to LQ (*Lukas*, ⁸1892, p. 640). The term ἐξουθενήσας in both instances was designated by Jeremias as redaction (*Die Sprache*, p. 302). On Septuagintal use note *GELS*, p. 162, which mentions 8 instances. There are 11 occurrences in the NT (*NTV*, p. 42).

288. See *MIBNTG*, 1953, ²1959, ⁸1979, p. 37, which stated that while many verbs with the meaning of caring for or despising take the genitive, ἐξουθενεῖν in 23,11 took an accusative. See further the comment in *MHT* 2, p. 72. Consider G. SCHNEIDER, *Die Apostelgeschichte*, T. 1, p. 348: Acts 4,11 did not rest on the text of the LXX "sondern auf einer selbständige Übersetzung von Ps 118,22".

preference for the participial form as a grammatical signal of his redaction has been noted[289]. It also occurs in the LXX (Pss 64,8; 118,22)[290].

It was widely noted that Luke omitted the Markan account of the mockery by the Roman soldiers (Mk 15,16-20; cf. 23,11.36). Succinctly, Luke abbreviated the material, as he had previously done in the pericope concerned with the Baptist (3,19-20 / Mk 6,17-29), and used it in 23,11. The shift is reasonably explained by the apology directed toward Rome. It is probably also due, in part, to Luke's desire to soften the report of the mistreatment of Jesus. No contempt for Jesus was expressed in v. 11a by calling attention to the presence of αὐτόν[291].

[καὶ] ὁ Ἡρῴδης σὺν. Herod clearly joined in the abuse of Jesus. σύν "has the Lucan sense 'and'"[292]. This term can be classified among the elements of Lukan redaction[293]. Luke substituted σύν for μετά in 8,38 (Mk 5,18); 8,51 (5,37); cf. 22,14 (Mk 14,17); 22,56 (Mk 14,67)[294]. Notice should also be made of the phrase in the Lukan Transfiguration (9,32): Πέτρος καὶ οἱ σὺν αὐτῷ[295]. Further, in the Lukan account of the calling of the first disciples we read: αὐτὸν (Peter) καὶ πάντας τοὺς σὺν αὐτῷ (5,9).

In addition, he employed σύν in his account of Paul's appearance before Agrippa and Bernice (Acts 25,23) and shortly thereafter in Paul's recounting his conversion to Agrippa (Acts 26,13 με ... καὶ τοὺς σὺν ἐμοὶ πορευομένους). The presence of στρατιώτης in Acts 28,16 is of particular interest since σύν was used in reference to the soldier guarding Paul.

289. RADL, Paulus, p. 434.

290. GELS, p. 162, which indicates the term is found 8 times in the LXX.

291. Death, p. 773-774, 775, against VERRALL, Christ, p. 340-344 (= 366-370).

292. FITZMYER, p. 1482. See further ROBERTSON, Grammar, ²1915, ³1919, ⁴1923, p. 628, who commented "καί rather than σύν might have occurred" in Acts 14,5 and Lk 23,11. In addition, BÜCHELE, p. 32, n. 55, noted the frequency of the term in Lk-Acts including it among the typical Lukan vocabulary and expressions. So also TAYLOR, Passion, p. 87, and JEREMIAS, Die Sprache, p. 302: "Lukas hat eine ausgesprochene Vorliebe für diese Präposition" (see also p. 63). BROWN, p. 773, provided statistics and noted how the addition allowed Herod's soldiers to become involved. See further W. ELLIGER, σύν, in EWNT 3, cols. 697-699, esp. col. 697 (= p. 291-292, esp. p. 291). The word also appears in the LXX in the prophetic literature (GELS[TP], p. 221-222).

293. CADBURY, Style, p. 203; RADL, Paulus, p. 427; K. MÜLLER, Jesus, p. 115; J. JEREMIAS, Die Sprache, p. 63; FITZMYER, p. 1479; Boismard and Lamouille in NEIRYNCK, Le texte, p. 328 (= 267); GOULDER, Luke, p. 808; UNTERGASSMAIR, Zur Problematik, p. 281. See also LÉGASSE, Le procès, t. 2, p. 374, n. 63.

294. CADBURY, Style, p. 203. The reverse was the case in 6,4 τοῖς μετ᾽ αὐτοῦ (Mk 2,26 καὶ τοῖς σὺν αὐτῷ οὖσιν); 9,30 (Mk 9,4); 20,1 σύν τοις πρεσβυτέροις (Mk 11,27 καὶ οἱ πρεσβύτεροι). See also Acts 14,5; 15,22; 16,32 (FITZMYER, p. 1482).

295. See REID, who observed that Luke adopted the term from Mk (23,32 / Mk 15,27), but "in other instances where σύν occurs in Mark (Mark 2:26 [diff Lk 6,4 μετ᾽ αὐτοῦ]; 4:10 [diff Lk 8,9]; 8:34 [om]; 15:32 [diff 23,39]) Luke eliminates or alters it in his corresponding passages" (Transfiguration, p. 65, n. 186).

τοῖς στρατεύμασιν αὐτοῦ. στράτευμα does not occur in Mk. Mk 15,16 (hapax) referred to στρατιῶται as those who carry out the mockery. Further, Luke used that term in 23,36, the third of the mockeries he related (cf. 22,63; 23,11)[296]. Mocking Jesus as the "King of the Jews" recalled the question of Pilate (23,3)[297]. In 23,11 Herod takes part in the mockery with his soldiers. There is mention of military personnel in the account of the death of the Baptist (Mk 6,21.27), using different terms. Mk 6,27 speaks of a soldier of the guard (σπεκουλάτορα) who was dispatched by Herod to give the orders for the beheading[298]. This was the "kind of soldier who formed the body-guard of princes, one of whose duties was to put criminals to death"[299]. Commenting on 23,11 it had been proposed: "It was one of these perhaps that [Herod] had sent to behead John in the prison (Mk. vi.27; Mt xiv.10)"[300]. Given Luke's propensity for avoiding Latin loanwwords, it is not surprising that a different term is used at 23,11.

στρατιώτης, the term used in Mk 15,16 is employed 13 times in Acts (10,7; 12,4.6.18; 21,32bis.35; 23,23.31; 27,31.32.42; 28,16)[301]. The word occurred 6 times in the LXX, all in the Maccabean literature. Finally, it was used three times in GP 8,30-32[302].

What is also significant for our investigation is that στρατευόμενοι questioned John the Baptist (3,14)[303]. "These were not Roman soldiers, since there were no

296. DANKER, *Jesus*, 1972, p. 238 (= 376): "Soldiers now enter the act. Mark had introduced them earlier in his narrative (15:16-20). Luke reserves the recital of their mockery for this moment, since their horseplay related to Jesus as a royal figure". The sentence which follows in the 1972 edition was revised in the second edition: "Also, divorced from the praetorium (Mark 15:16), their mockery would not reflect so strongly on the Roman military. In a situation like this one could expect something of the sort". Consider MARSHALL, *Luke*, p. 869; UNTERGASSMAIR, *Kreuzweg*, 58-59, with attention to 58, n. 228; FITZMYER, p. 1505; so also in 7,8 (/ Mt 8,9 Q).

297. BÜCHELE, p. 48, 84; TIEDE, *Luke*, p. 419.

298. SCHÜRMANN, *Das Lukasevangelium, T. 1, Kap. 1,1–9,50*, 1969, p. 508-509. See SPICQ, πράκτωρ, σπεκουλάτωρ, in *NLNT* 2, 730-737, esp. p. 735-737 [= 1991, 1286-1293, esp. 1291-1293] = *TLNT* 3, p. 152-159, esp. p. 157-159. He noted the term was "unknown in the LXX" and that they were "called upon to perform quite varied services", including the function of "bodyguards" (*NLNT* 2, p. 736 [= 1991, 1292] = *TLNT* 3, 158), concluding: "So we must classify the *spekoulatōr* of Mark 6:27, a biblical hapax, as one of the Latinisms of the Second Gospel" (*NLNT* 2, p. 737 [= 1991, 1293] = *TLNT* 3, 159). See also TAYLOR, *St. Mark*, ²1966, p. 316-317.

299. H.K. MOULTON, *The Analytical Greek Lexicon Revised*, London, 1977; Grand Rapids, MI, 1978, p. 372. Consider the bibliography of BALZ, σπεκουλάτωρ, in *EWNT* 3, col. 629 (= p. 263).

300. PLUMMER, *Luke*, p. 523, adding: "It was fitting that the prince who murdered the Baptist should mock the Christ".

301. The term is located in the account of Peter's deliverance from prison where there is also a mention of Herod (Acts 12,6; cf. 12,1: "Herod the king"). Perhaps more importantly, it is used frequently in Acts in connection with Paul (21,32bis.35; 23,23.31; 27,31.32.42; 28,16).

302. See the text of GP in NEIRYNCK, *Apocryphal Gospels*, p. 173 (= 765).

303. O. BAUERNFEIND, στρατεύομαι, in *TWNT* 7, 701-713, p. 709 (= *TDNT* 7, 701-713,

legions stationed in Palestine in this time, nor auxiliaries from other provinces. They should be understood as Jewish men enlisted in the service of Herod Antipas, of whose troops Josephus gives testimony (Ant. 18,5,1 § 113)"³⁰⁴. The term also occurred in Acts 23,10 στράτευμα.27 σὺν τῷ στρατεύματι, where it signified "a smaller detachment of soldiers"³⁰⁵.

καὶ ἐμπαίξας. In the NT the term is found only in the Synoptics (22,63; 23,11.36; cf. Mk 15,20.31; see also Mk 14,29; Lk 18,32 / Mk 10,34)³⁰⁶. Mark used it initially in the third passion prediction (Mk 10,34 ἐμπαίξουσιν) which Luke adopted using a different form (18,32 ἐμπαιχθήσεται)³⁰⁷. Luke redacted the Markan passion prediction by adding three passives, including ἐμπαιχθήσεται, to remove the ambiguity created by Mark who has "two series of verbs, in the same form, all connected with καί and with no subject expressed"³⁰⁸. More than that, while the Markan Jesus indicated that he would be handed over to the Gentiles who will mistreat him, Luke separated this and by using the passive did not necessarily implicate the Gentiles in the mockery. This allowed others, namely the Jews, to be understood as mistreating Jesus. In 23,11 he apparently was drawing upon Mk

---

p. 709): "Lk. 3:14 mentions στρατευόμενοι among John's audience without saying whether they were Gentile or Jewish troops". Consider also Cadbury's insight: "In characteristic fashion also Luke specifies the different classes of people who came to John the Baptist and received appropriate answers, Luke 3,10-14, οἵ ὄχλοι ... τελῶναι ... στρατευόμενοι" (Style, p. 120). In addition see B. KENMAN, Luke's Exoneration of John the Baptist, in JTS 44 (1993) 595-598, esp. p. 597-598.

304. FITZMYER, p. 470. See also his comment on 23,11: "probably bodyguards or retinue" (p. 1482). For a similar intepretation of soldiers in 3,14 see PLUMMER, Luke, p. 92; MARSHALL, Luke, p. 143. However, Walaskay observed: "We might also add that a study of Lucan military vocabulary reveals only that Luke does not clearly define which soldiers report to Jews and which are under the imperium" (Trial, p. 92). For a similar view see CREED, Luke, p. 53.

305. BAGD, p. 770. See SCHNEIDER, Die Apostelgeschichte, T. 2, p. 333, n. 50; LÉGASSE, Le procès, t. 2, p. 374, n. 62. LAKE and CADBURY, in FOAKES JACKSON and LAKE (eds.), Beginnings, Pt. 1, Vol. 4, p. 290: "a detachment of soldiers on duty". The term is found in the LXX as well. See GELS, p. 441.

306. F.G. UNTERGASSMAIR, ἐμπαίζω, in EWNT 1, cols. 1085-1087, esp. col. 1085 (= p. 444-445, esp. p. 445). CADBURY, Style, p. 185, observed that the term was frequent in the LXX. See for example Hab 1,10 (GELS[TP], p. 76) as well as Ex 10,2; Pr 23,35; Zac 12,3; Is 33,4; Jer 10,15; Ez 22,5. (BAGD, p. 255; GELS, p. 146, listed Gen 39,14; Ex 10,2; Is 33,4; Zach 12,3). Its use in the NT is as follows: 5 Mt, 3 Mk, 5 Lk (NTV, p. 45, 246). See SABBE, The Trial of Jesus Before Pilate in John and Its Relation to the Synoptic Gospels, in A. DENAUX (ed.), John and the Synoptics (BETL, 101), Leuven, 1992, p. 355, n. 27 (= Studia, p. 482, n. 27); cf. JEREMIAS, Die Sprache, p. 302, who believed ἐμπαίξας stemmed from tradition. See also 14,29.

307. On the use of the passive form, see also LXX 2 Mac 7,10. In the Lukan special material the term can also be found in 14,29. See NEIRYNCK, ΤΙΣ ΕΣΤΙΝ, p. 21-22 (= 111-112): "The verbs ἐμπτύω and ἐμπαίζω are closely connected in the third prediction of the passion, Mk 10,34 ... par. Lk 18,32". Cf. NEIRYNCK, Note on a Test Case. A Response to W.R. Farmer, in ETL 67 (1991) 73-81, esp. 79-80 (= Evangelica II, 49-58, esp. 56-57).

308. NEIRYNCK, Note, 1991, p. 80 (= p. 57).

15,20a in the mockery by the Roman soldiers which he omitted. Mark utilized the word again in his account of the crucifixion when Jesus was mocked by the chief priests and scribes (Mk 15,31). In the Lukan parallel (23,35) Luke substituted ἐκμυκτηρίζω from the LXX[309]. The word ἐμπαίζω is found in the LXX[310].

The mockery by Herod and his soldiers is the second of three mockeries[311]. In the first (22,63 ἐνέπαιζον), Jesus was mocked and taunted to prophesy by those who were restraining him. In the third mockery (23,36) the soldiers present at the crucifixion abused Jesus and mocked him as king of the Jews. The individual actions detailed by Mark were included by Luke in his use of ἐμπαίζω [312]. These served as a fulfillment of the prophecy made in the passion prediction. Luke freely redacted the Markan account of the passion in the case of 23,11a as he had done in 23,9b[313]. This also involved omitting the Markan mockery by the Roman soldiers[314]. Since Jesus is presented in all the Synoptic accounts of the mockery as a prophet (22,63-65 / Mk 14,65 / Mt 26,67-68)[315], the reminiscence of this portrayal will not be lost in the subsequent Lukan account of yet another mockery.

περιβαλὼν ἐσθῆτα λαμπράν. Mark employed περιβεβλημένος in the account of the young man who fled naked during the arrest of Jesus (Mk 14,51). He was wrapped in a linen cloth. Luke omitted this story. Our working hypothesis is that Luke drew on vocabulary from Markan passages he elected to omit. The second instance is found in the account of the resurrection (Mk 16,5 περιβεβλημένον

309. On the four uses in LXX see *GELS*, p. 138. The term is found in 16,14 as well as 23,35. The former is found in material which is unique to Lk and detailed the reaction of the Pharisees to a parable told by Jesus. Marshall claimed the word was Lukan, while Fitzmyer held that, "an OT expression is used here" (MARSHALL, *Luke*, p. 625; cf. FITZMYER, *Luke*, p. 1113). Shortly after the use of the term in 16,14 was a reference to John the Baptist and the statement that everyone enters the kingdom of God violently (16,16 / Mt 11,12-13 Q). See further W. STENGER, βιάζομαι, in *EWNT* 1, cols. 518-521, esp. cols. 519-520 (= p. 216-217, esp. p. 216).

310. *GELS*, p. 146, which reports 29 instances.

311. Also noted in BROWN, p. 773.

312. UNTERGASSMAIR, ἐμπαίζω, in *EWNT* 1, col. 1086 (= p. 445). In Luke's third passion prediction (18,32-33), as in the Markan source (Mk 10,33) there is mention of spitting. In the mockery by the Roman soldiers, they spit upon Jesus (Mk 15,19). We should not be surprised that many of the actions detailed in the Markan account are not specified in Luke's version of the mockery by Herod and his soldiers. Cadbury acknowledged that Luke tended toward generalization. Sometimes the generalization was in addition to some specific information Luke drew from Mk, as in 3,19 (/ Mk 6,18) where Luke added that Herod did other evil things besides marrying Herodias (*Style*, p. 115). At other times Luke omitted "details of all sorts", such as the "dress and food of John the Baptist" (3,1-6 / Mk 1,6). See Cadbury's comment on the omission of Mk 15,16-20 (*Style*, p. 102). Hastings insisted "it is also true that St Luke speaks less of Jesus' sufferings than Matthew or Mark, and he toned down their picture of the Passion, concentrating more on the glory" (*Prophet*, p. 59). See also SABBE, in A. DENAUX (ed.), *John and the Synoptics*, 1992, esp. p. 355-356 (= *Trial*, in ID., *Studia*, esp. p. 482).

313. SOARDS, *Tradition*, 1985, p. 354.

314. *Ibid.*, p. 355.

315. In material unique to Lk, see also 7,16 where Jesus was identified as a great prophet in response to the raising of the widow's son at Nain.

στολὴν λευκήν; note the περί-prefix) where a young man dressed in a white robe announced to the women that Jesus was risen[316]. Luke did not adopt the Markan language. Instead his account described the clothing as ἐν ἐσθῆτι ἀστραπτούσῃ[317]. In these two cases Luke refrained from using color to describe the clothing of Jesus and angels. It appears that celestial beings are depicted better by using adjectives like brilliant and dazzling to suggest clothing "of beauty and heavenly dignity"[318].

In 12,27 περιεβάλετο (/ Mt 6,29 Q) Jesus taught the disciples not to be anxious about earthly things. Shortly prior to that Jesus was teaching that they should not be anxious if they are brought before authorities (12,11 ἐξουσίας)[319]. In Acts 12,8 Peter was instructed by an angel: περιβαλοῦ τὸ ἱμάτιόν σου καὶ ἀκολούθει μοι. In addition, περιβάλλειν is found often in the LXX[320].

In redacting Mk 9,3 (τὰ ἱμάτια αὐτοῦ) Luke changed it slightly employing ἱματισμός[321]. There followed a reference to ὁ ἱματισμὸς αὐτοῦ (9,29). The term was used to describe Jesus at the Transfiguration (9,31.32; cf. 24,26) and the pericope emphasized what the disciples saw (9,32.36). Note that Luke already used ὁ ἱματισμός in describing John the Baptist in contrast to οἱ ἐν ἱματισμῷ ἐνδόξῳ

316. See NEIRYNCK, La fuite du jeune homme en Mc 14,51-52, in ETL 55 (1979) 43-66, esp. p. 48, 60 (= Evangelica, 215-238, esp. p. 220, 232). The other use of the term is found at Mk 16,5 (/ 24,4), describing a young man sitting in the tomb of Jesus. Luke's account of the women at the tomb varies in some details. There are two men, rather than one as in Mk. Luke did not employ περιβεβλημένον στολὴν λευκήν, but wrote: ἐν ἐσθῆτι ἀστραπτούσῃ. See further NEIRYNCK, Duality, p. 84. It should also be noted that the term occurred in GP 55. Cf. GP 7. See Brown's discussion of various interpretations of the term including those of Bornhäuser, Blinzler, Hoehner and K. Müller (Death, p. 774, n. 21).
317. Cf. the Transfiguration account (9,29 / Mk 9,3).
318. SENIOR, The Passion of Jesus in the Gospel of Luke, p. 114.
319. See also 19,43, with the enemies surrounding.
320. GELS, p. 367. There are 23 instances in the NT (NTV, p. 57). In 1 Mac 10,64-66 we find several similar terms and motifs – accusers, himself, invested in purple, friends, governor, Jerusalem and gladness. See also LXX Zch 3,5 where the term was also used to refer to the act of clothing someone (GELS[TP], p. 189). Note further LXX Gen 28,20; 1 Kg 28,8; 3 Kg 1,1; 11,29; Ps 44,9; 108,19; Is 4,1; 59,17. See also LXX Jon 3,6.8 and Hag 1,6 for the use of the middle voice.
321. GELS, p. 214, and is used 32 times. NTV, p. 102, indicates the term occurs 5 times in the NT which includes 3 in Lk-Acts.

found in royal courts (7,25 Q)[322]. Goulder invited comparison of ἔνδοξος with the Lukan δόξα[323].

In Mark's account of the Roman soldiers mocking Jesus (Mk 15,16-20) it was recounted that ἐνδιδύσκουσιν αὐτὸν πορφύραν (Mk 15,17)[324]. The only other use of ἐνδιδύσκω was in Lukan special material (16,19): ἐνδιδύσκετο πορφύραν καὶ βύσσον.

ἐσθῆτα λαμπράν. Outside of Lk-Acts (24,4; Acts 10,30; 12,21)[325] the term ἐσθής is found only in Jas (2,2bis.3)[326]. This has been judged to be Lukan vocabulary[327]. In Acts the term was used of angels and kings. It does not seem likely that Luke was attempting to convey the idea that 23,11 might be suggesting that Antipas clothed Jesus in his own garment since Acts 12,21 showed that Luke employed a specific reference to royal clothing[328]. The term ἐσθής was used four times in LXX (e.g. 2 Macc 8,35; 11,8) and 8 times in the NT[329].

λαμπρῶς is an adverb peculiar to Lk which is not found in the LXX[330].

322. Diff Mt 11,8 ἐν μαλακοῖς ἠμφιεσμένον. The term ἱματισμός is also found in Acts 20,33 in an address of Paul to the elders at Ephesus. For a differing interpretation see the discussion on clothing in Lk in KARRIS, Luke: Artist and Theologian, p. 85-87, 99. Reid reported: "It is clear from Luke 7:25, where both ἱματίοις and ἱματισμός appear, that Luke regards the two nouns as interchangeable. Luke uses ἱμάτιον more frequently than ἱματισμός. In 9:29 Luke has replaced Mark's ἱμάτια with ἱματισμός perhaps as an improvement in elegance or exactness of expression" (Transfiguration, p. 57).
The term ἔνδοξος is found in the Gospels only in Lk 7,25 and 13,17 and was explained by Marshall as "probably Lucan" (Luke, p. 294). The theme of seeing (7,24 [θεάσασθαι].25[ἰδεῖν]) and hearing (7,29[ἀκούσας]) is present here as in 23,6-12.
323. GOULDER, Luke, p. 395. δόξα occurred 166 times in the NT including: Mk 3; Lk 13; Acts 4.
324. Even Matthew did not retain the Markan purple but instead described the garment as scarlet or crimson (Mt 27,28 κόκκινος). See D. SENIOR, Passion Narrative, p. 265-266.
325. See the related terms in Acts 1,10 (ἐσθήσεσι λευκαῖς) and Acts 12,21 (ἐσθὴς βασιλική). Note W. RADL, ἱμάτιον, EWNT 2, cols. 458-460, esp. cols. 458-459 (= p. 186-188, esp. p. 187): "Luke (Luke 23:11; 24:4; Acts 1:10; 10:30; 12:21) uses ἐσθής of esp. striking clothing (Wilckens 690)". See U. WILCKENS, TWNT 7, 687-692 (= TDNT 7, p. 687-691); G. SCHNEIDER, ἐσθής, in EWNT 2, col. 146 (= p. 58), who called attention to the use of the clothing as intended to ridicule Jesus; REID, p. 113-114. On Acts 10,30 see BARRETT, Acts, p. 518, and HAENCHEN, Die Apostelgeschichte, [14]1965, p. 296 (= Acts, p. 351), who remarked that "the angel coming to the rescue of the Jews in II Macc. 11.8 appears ἐν λευκῇ ἐσθῆτι".
326. Jas 2,2 has the phrase ἐσθῆτι λαμπρᾷ just as Jas 2,3 has τὴν ἐσθῆτα τὴν λαμπράν. Luke preferred ἐσθής, according to Jeremias, as suggested by 23,11; 24,4 and Acts 1,10; 10,30; 12,21 (Die Sprache, p. 302). Brown pointed out that it never occurred in another Gospel and that it twice referred to angelic clothing (24,4; Acts 10,30) (Death, p. 774).
327. BOISMARD, Synopse, t. 2, p. 418; Boismard and Lamouille in NEIRYNCK, Le texte, p. 322 (= Evangelica II, p. 261); JEREMIAS, Die Sprache, p. 217.
328. So also K. MÜLLER, Jesus, p. 135, and REID, p. 115, n. 74. See further, SCHNEIDER, Die Apostelgeschichte, T. 2, p. 108. n. 80.
329. GELS, p. 182, which cited 1 Ez 8,68.70; 2 Mac 8,35; 11,8. On the NT usage, see NTV, p. 102.
330. HAWKINS, Horae Synopticae, 1899, p. 166; [2]1909, p. 202. See further SPICQ, NLNT

Writing of the Transfiguration scene Cadbury observed: "Instead of making the language of his source stronger, Luke sometimes omits or tones down emphatic words" and proceeded to cite Lk 9,29 (λευκός) as a redaction of Mk 9,3 (λευκὰ λίαν, οἷα γναφεὺς ἐπὶ τῆς γῆς οὐ δύναται οὕτως λευκᾶναι)³³¹.

A related adjective λαμπρός which was found in the LXX has the meaning of bright or brilliant³³². The noun form λαμπρότης was found at Acts 26,13 ("brighter than the sun", or "the sun, shining"), used in Paul's description of the light that preceded his conversion. The interpretation of the term in 23,11 as "loud outfit" is unsatisfactory³³³. There is a tendency among scholars to interpret the gorgeous apparel in light of Mark's "purple cloak"³³⁴. We would argue that Luke intended neither to convey the idea of purple, suggesting royalty³³⁵, nor of white as suggested by the *toga candida*³³⁶. The account of the death of Herod Agrippa I (Acts 12,20-23, especially v. 21) is valuable for comparison with 23,11-12. There is some similarity on the thematic level since it concerned enmity between Herod and the people of Tyre and Sidon and a subsequent attempt at reconciliation. Some similarity of vocabulary between Lk-Acts also exists (τακτῇ δὲ ἡμέρᾳ ὁ ῾Ηρῴδης ... πρὸς αὐτούς). But this comparison is also valuable because of the contrast it provides with 23,11: ἐνδυσάμενος ἐσθῆτα βασιλικήν. It is highly unlikely that Luke wished to convey the idea of royal clothing in 23,11 since he has a phrase for it in Acts 12,21³³⁷.

The term ἐνδύω occurred three times in Mk: Mk 1,6 containing a description of John the Baptist which was omitted by Luke; Mk 6,9 diff 9,3; Mk 15,20 the mockery by the Roman soldiers omitted by Luke. In addition to Acts 12,21 the term is found in Lk in 8,27 (diff. Mk 5,2; 12,22 / Mt 6,25 Q); and 15,22; 24,49, both of which are unique to Lk. The word is also employed in the LXX³³⁸.

Had Luke intended the idea of *toga candida*, or indeed of some other white garment, he possessed the necessary vocabulary in the Transfiguration account

1, p. 460-465, esp. p. 460 = *TLNT* 2, 364-368, esp. p. 365, and the discussion in LÉGASSE, *Le procès*, t. 2, p. 375, n. 72.

331. CADBURY, *Style*, p. 118. Jesus' clothing becomes dazzling white (9,29; see also 9,32: "they saw his glory"; cf. 23,11) (M. SABBE, *La rédaction du récit de la Transfiguration*, in *RechBib* 6 [1962] 65-100, esp. p. 66, n. 2 = *Studia*, 65-104, esp. p. 66, n. 2). This is a *hapax legomenon* in the NT. It was further noted that a similar term was found in LXX Dan 10,6).

332. See *GELS*, p. 276, which indicated there were 7 instances in LXX. There are 9 in the NT (*NTV*, p. 131). See further *TLNT* 2, p. 364-368, p. 365.

333. SOARDS, *Tradition*, 1985, p. 355, n. 35. See also SCHNEIDER, *Die Apostelgeschichte*, T. 2, p. 74, n. 134.

334. FITZMYER, p. 1482; DARR, *Glorified*, p. 297. See also Matera's comments in *Luke 23,1-25*, p. 544-545.

335. See CREED, *Luke*, p. 282.

336. See JOÜON, *Luc 23,11*; KARRIS, *Luke: Artist and Theologian*, p. 86-87.

337. See also HAENCHEN, *Die Apostelgeschichte*, ¹⁴1965, p. 330, n. 1 (= *Acts*, p. 386, n. 5), who commented that according to Josephus Herod's raiment was "made entirely of silver"; so also BRUCE, *Acts*, London, 1951, p. 250.

338. *GELS*, p. 151. The term (or ἐνδύνω) occurs 27 times in the NT (*NTV*, p. 44).

(9,29 hapax / Mk 9,3) or in Acts 1,10. Likewise, the requisite vocabulary was available in the account of the women at the tomb. Although Mark wrote of a young man "dressed in a white robe" (περιβεβλημένον στολὴν λευκήν) Luke changed it to ἐν ἐσθῆτι ἀστραπτούσῃ (24,4)[339]. The language of ἀστραπή is found in the great theophany of LXX Ex 19,16[340]. λαμπράν has been rated as redaction since, "Lukas eine Vorliebe für die Derivate des Stammes λαμπ-hat"[341]. Some have concluded that ultimately the clothing signified Jesus' innocence[342].

The encounter between Jesus and Herod was reminiscent of "confrontation between John and the Tetrarch much earlier in the narrative (3:19-20)"[343]. The garment and Jesus' prophetic identity have been linked: "Herod and his court obviously intend it as mockery for this mute and defenseless 'prophet' who stands debased before them"[344]. Verse 11b, like v. 11a should be ascribed to Luke's free redaction of the Markan passion[345].

ἀνέπεμψεν αὐτὸν τῷ Πιλάτῳ. The term ἀνέπεμψεν was used once again here as in v. 7, and this is seen as Lukan redaction[346]. The use of ἀνέπεμψεν in 23,7.11 is regarded as an inclusion[347]. Although it should be thought of as having a juridical technical sense, Luke was not using it strictly as sending to a higher authority. His preference for compounds is evident here[348].

---

339. On ἀστράπτω in LXX see *GELS*, p. 67-68. For NT references see also Lk 17,24 and 24,4.

340. See J. ZMIJEWSKI, ἀστραπή, in *EWNT* 1, cols. 420-422, esp. col. 422 (= p. 174-175, esp. p. 175); cf. Pss 18,14; 50,3.

341. *Die Sprache*, p. 80; see also p. 302. See the various forms in: (17,24; Acts 12,7); (Acts 20,8); (23,11; Acts 10,30); (16,19); (Acts 26,13); (2,9; Acts 26,13).

342. DARR, *Glorified*, p. 298: "The implication is that the *esthēta lampran* is intended as a message to Pilate". So also p. 300: "In essence, it was a dramatic and sardonic way of indicating to Pilate that Herod had found nothing worthy of death in Jesus". He rightly rejected Verrall's proposal that the gesture was a positive one (*Glorified*, p. 297; cf. VERRALL, *Christ*, p. 343-344 = 369-370). Darr compared 23,11 with Mk 15,17.20 but did not offer a detailed analysis of the vocabulary (*Glorified*, p. 297, 298).

343. DARR, *Glorified*, p. 301.

344. *The Passion of Jesus in the Gospel of Luke*, p. 114.

345. SOARDS, *Tradition*, 1985, p. 355.

346. Boismard and Lamouille in NEIRYNCK, *Le texte*, p. 318 (= 257); K. MÜLLER, *Jesus*, p. 115. See the comment on 23,7, as well as SPICQ, *NLNT* 3, 40-43, esp. p. 42, n. 2 (= *TLNT* 1, p. 107-110, esp. p. 109, n. 11). It is worth noting that in the Markan account of the Baptist's death we have the phrase γὰρ ὁ Ἡρῴδης ἀποστείλας (Mk 6,17) as well as ἀποστείλας ὁ βασιλεὺς σπεκουλάτορα (Mk 6,27). These could have served as inspiration for Luke's composition of the Herod pericope in ch. 23.

347. BROWN, *Death*, p. 774. See also 23,15: Ἡρῴδης, ἀνέπεμψεν γάρ.

348. CADBURY, *Style*, p. 166: "Luke's changes in Mark indicate the same preference for compound verbs that is revealed both by a comparison of the passages derived from Q and by the general ratio of simple to compound verbs". J. Weiss believed this to mean "einfach: zurücksenden" (*Lukas*, ⁸1892, p. 640).

Some scholars such as Marshall reject the possibility that Luke employed Mk 15,16-20[349]. Cadbury maintained: "The omission of Mark 15,16-20, describing the maltreatment of Jesus by the soldiers (Matt. 27,27, the soldiers of the governor), leaves unfulfilled the prediction in Luke 18,32ff. which is derived from Mark 10,34. Note especially in Luke 18,32f. ἐμπτυσθήσεται and μαστιγώσαντες and the fulfillment of prophecy in φραγελλώσας, ἐνέπτυον (Mark 15,15,19, but not in Luke). Further, the omission of στρατιῶται (Mark 15,16) gives a vague or mistaken idea of the subject of the verbs that follow in Luke 23, e.g., vs. 26, ἀπήγαγον, vs. 33, ἐσταύρωσαν, vs. 34, διαμεριζόμενοι ἔβαλον, until in vs. 36 the στρατιῶται are brought in as though they had been mentioned before"[350].

We respond to each of Cadbury's objections in the order in which he presented them. In redacting the third Markan passion prediction (18,32 / Mk 10,34) Luke more clearly established an allusion to LXX Is 50,6 (αἰσχύνης ἐμπτυσμάτων) by the parallelism ὑβρισθήσεται καὶ ἐμπτυσθήσεται. Further, in the first of the mockeries (22,63) Luke omitted the Markan ἐμπτύω in favor of ἐμπαίζω as characterizing the variety of actions[351]. This may also be the case in the second mockery (23,11). Such a process could be compared to Luke particularizing the charge of perverting the nation (23,2b) in two further complaints (prohibiting the tribute and claiming to be a king). However, in the subsequent references (23,5.14), he used only the overarching term (or synonyms). Cannot this be compared to 18,32 so that though Luke referred to the general term of abuse in the third passion prediction (ἐμπαιχθήσεται), repeating it in 22,63; 23,11, he omitted mention of the detail of spitting (22,63-65 diff Mk 14,65; 23,11 diff Mk 15,16)?

It is likely that Luke opted not to employ the Markan μαστιγώσαντες, which can mean to chastise[352], choosing to supplant it with παιδεύσας (23,16), a term found in the LXX. Cadbury himself pointed out Luke's tendency to tone down descriptions of acts of violence toward Jesus. Thus, it is not necessarily the case that Luke left unfulfilled the prediction in 18,32f., but wrote of it more generally. Note that Paul questioned the centurion whether he, a Roman citizen, should be whipped though he had not been condemned (Acts 22,25). In this case Luke used

---

349. MARSHALL, *Luke*, p. 857: "The whole scene is recorded with the minimum of detail, and it is hardly likely that Luke has abbreviated the more colourful description in Mk 15:17-20". Is is not possible that if Luke substituted the summary in 3,19-20 for Mk 6,17-29, that he also offered 23,11 in place of Mk 15,16-20?

350. *Style*, p. 102.

351. NEIRYNCK, ΤΙΣ ΕΣΤΙΝ, p. 22 (= 112). It should also be noted that Matthew omitted Mark's ἐμπτύσουσιν (Mt 20,19 diff Mk 10,34) in the third passion prediction. Possible explanations range from the omission was not clear (McNEILE, *Matthew*, p. 286); it was "otiose after the ridiculing" (GUNDRY, *Matthew*, ²1994, p. 401); it was prompted by literary reasons, providing a series of three actions: mock, scourge, crucify (W.D. DAVIES and D.C. ALLISON, *Matthew*, Vol. 3, Edinburgh, p. 81, n. 9). Cf. NEIRYNCK, ΤΙΣ ΕΣΤΙΝ, p. 31 (= 121).

352. *BAGD*, p. 495; H. BALZ, μαστιγόω, in *EWNT* 2, cols. 973-974, col. 974 (= 395-396, p. 395).

μαστίζω which is not as strong as μαστιγόω³⁵³. Again here Luke chose vocabulary which muted the description of the force of the action.

That Luke did not employ the Markan Latinism φραγελλώσας (Mk 15,15) can be easily explained that in other instances he made similar substitutions (20,22 Καίσαρι φόρον diff Mk 12,14 κῆνσον Καίσαρι)³⁵⁴ and is indicative of the fact that he generally avoided them³⁵⁵. Given this tendency we should expect that he would not write φραγελλώσας 23,16.

As for the confusion which could arise from the "vague or mistaken idea of the subject of the verbs in Luke 23", this too could be Luke's intention, due in part to his Gentile audience and in light of his Roman apologetic. The lack of precision concerning the subject of the actions could imply that the involvement of the Jews continued in leading Jesus away (23,26), crucifying him (23,33) and casting lots to divide his garments (23,34). Perhaps this reflects the historical situation or the increasing tension between the Jewish and Christian communities at the time Luke was writing. It would also deflect responsibility from the Romans.

The differences must certainly be reckoned with. Pilate takes no part in the mockery by the Roman soldiers as recounted in Mk. In Lk Herod, together with soldiers, mocked Jesus. This involvement recalls 13,31 relating Herod's intention to do harm to Jesus. Herod's declaration of innocence is all the stronger when affirmed by one who was his opponent³⁵⁶.

If, as we contend, Luke is casting Jesus in the role of a prophet (9,8-9; 13,33; 22,63-65) can we expect there is something of that theme also present as the drama unfolds here and conversely not so much emphasis on Jesus as a king? Is it possible that Luke borrowed and adapted Mark's pattern of three's, as in the case not only of the mockeries (22,63; 23,11.36; cf. 14,29; 18,32 / Mk 15,20.29.31; cf. Mk 10,34), but also in the declarations of innocence (23,4.14.22)³⁵⁷?

The Markan version of the mockery involved clothing Jesus in a purple cloak, a crown of thorns, a salutation, striking the head of Jesus with a reed, spitting upon him and kneeling down in homage before him. Lk contained no mention of these actions. We have already noted Luke's tendency to generalize, which included eliminating various Markan details. The use of the term "mockery" could also be part of this redactional propensity. As Cadbury observed: "Violent or

---

353. Spicq, μαστιγόω, in *TLNT* 2, 453-456, p. 455, n. 13.

354. The relationship of 20,22 to the charge raised against Jesus in 23,3 is obvious.

355. Cadbury, *Making*, ²1958, p. 89, n. 15, 126, 180. See below additional comments on 23,16.

356. So also Matera, *Luke 23,1-25*, p. 545: "The witness of Herod is especially powerful since he is otherwise portrayed as one who has recently sought to kill Jesus. If even Jesus' enemies acknowledge his innocence, how innocent must he be!".

357. See also Neirynck, *Duality in Mark. Contributions to the Study of the Markan Redaction* (BETL, 31), Leuven, 1972, ²1988, p. 110-112, 242-243. D. Senior, *The Passion of Jesus in the Gospel of Luke*, p. 145, commented that some interpreters understood the Roman officer to be a third witness, along with Pilate and Herod, to the innocence of Jesus.

impatient or disrespectful conduct either to Jesus or in his presence is elsewhere avoided by Luke"³⁵⁸.

In Mk the soldiers dress Jesus in a purple cloak, a sign of royalty. It has been queried whether it is historically correct that the soldiers would have had access to such a garment³⁵⁹. Luke eliminates this detail since he seeks to emphasize Jesus' identity as a prophet. Jesus is presented frequently as "the king of the Jews" in Mk, either directly or by means of charges (Mk 15,2.9.12.18.26.32[the king of Israel]). Conversely, Luke utilized it only in 23,2.3.32, downplaying the aspect of royalty³⁶⁰. This can adequately explain the absence of the reference to the purple cloak and crown of thorns.

While the soldiers in Mk are understood to be Roman, in Lk they are Jewish. Though Mk offered the detail that the mockery occurred in the praetorium Luke mentioned no location. Although there are differences between the accounts, we should again pay close attention to the working hypothesis that Luke utilized vocabulary from Markan passages he chose to omit. The term for soldiers (στρατιῶται Mk 15,16) is found in 23,36³⁶¹. The second example constitutes the third of three mockeries in Lk. Not only has Luke employed the Markan term for soldiers, but also the word ἐνέπαιξαν, exactly as found in Mk 15,20. Just as Jesus was silent in Pilate's interrogation (Mk 15,5) as well as during the mockery by the Roman soldiers, so in the Herod pericope he offered no resistance and did not speak in his own defense. It would seem that Luke, in omitting the Markan scene of the mockery by the Roman soldiers, has displaced it to this point in his Gospel.

Let us examine the wording of Mk 15,16-20 as found in Lk 23,6-16 and other places in Lk-Acts.

Mk 15,16: οἱ δέ (cf. 23,8 ὁ δέ); ἀπήγαγον αὐτόν (23,26; cf. 23,1 ἤγαγον αὐτόν diff. Mk 15,1 ἀπήνεγκαν; ἔσω (cf. Acts 5,23); τῆς αὐλῆς (cf. 22,55 / Mk 14,54); ὅ ... ἐστιν (cf. 23,6 ὁ ... ἐστιν); πραιτώριον (cf. Acts 23,35 πραιτωρίῳ τοῦ 'Ηρῴδου); συγκαλοῦσιν (cf. 23,13 συγκαλεσάμενος and Acts 5,21; 10,24; 28,17); σπεῖραν (cf. Acts 10,1 σπείρης; 21,31; 27.1)

Mk 15,17: ἐνδιδύσκουσιν ... πορφύραν (cf. 16,19 ἐνεδιδύσκετο πορφύραν; 23,11 περιβαλὼν ἐσθῆτα λαμπράν; 8,27; 12,22; 15,22; Acts 12,21)

---

358. CADBURY, *Style*, p. 93. As examples of this style he continued: "Even the trial and crucifixion scenes are softened by Luke. He omits not only the whole incident of the mockery (Mark 15,16-20), but a number of details: the spitting on Jesus (Mark 14,65, cf. Luke 22,63-65), the beating with rods by the ὑπηρέται (*ibid.*), the binding of Jesus (Mark 15,1 δήσαντες), and the scourging with the *flagellum* (15,15)" (p. 94). This was also possible in the omission of the account of the Baptist's death (Mk 6,21-29). See also N. TURNER, *MHT* 4, p. 58: "Luke tends to remove some of Mark's more vivid details".

359. SENIOR, *The Passion Narrative According to Matthew*, p. 265.

360. So MATERA, *Luke 23,1-25*, p. 544.

361. Also a Q passage in 7,8.

Mk 15,18: ἤρξαντο (cf. 23,2 ἤρξαντο); ἀσπάζεσθαι (cf. Acts 25,13 ἀσπασάμενοι); χαῖρε (cf. 23,8 ἐχάρη); βασιλεῦ τῶν Ἰουδαίων (cf. 23,3 = Mk 15,2 βασιλεὺς τῶν Ἰουδαίων.37.38)

Mk 15,19: ἔτυπτον (cf. 12,45 Q; 18,13 ἔτυπτεν; 23,48 τύπτοντες; Acts 18,17; 21,32; 23,2.3bis); τὴν κεφαλήν (cf. Acts 18,6 τὴν κεφαλήν); καλάμῳ (cf. 7,24 Q); καὶ ἐνέπτυον αὐτῷ (cf. 18,32 καὶ ἐμπτυσθήσεται); τιθέντες τὰ γόνατα (cf. 5,8 προσέπεσεν τοῖς γόνασιν; 22,41 θεὶς τὰ γόνατα diff. Mk 14,35; Acts 7,60; 9,40; 20,36; 21,5); προσεκύνουν αὐτῷ (cf. 4,7 Q; see also 8,28 προσέπεσεν αὐτῷ diff. Mk 5,6 προσεκύνησεν αὐτῷ; Acts 7,43; 8,27; 10,25; 24,11)

Mk 15,20: καὶ ὅτε (cf. 23,33 καὶ ὅτε diff. Mk 15,22); ἐνέπαιξαν αὐτῷ (cf. 23,11 ἐμπαίξας ... αὐτόν); ἐξέδυσαν αὐτὸν τὴν πορφύραν (see Mk 15,17 above; cf. 8,28 οὐκ ἐνεδύσατο ἱμάτιον diff. Mk 5,2.3); ἐξάγουσιν αὐτόν (cf. 24,50 Ἐξήγαγεν; Acts 5,19; 7,36.40; 12,17; 13,17; 16,37.39; 21,38); σταυρώσωσιν αὐτόν (cf. 23,21.23.33; 24,7 diff. Mk 16,7; Acts 2,36; 4,10).

The theme of mockeries also confirms Lukan redaction of Markan material. Luke demonstrated an interest in the mockeries endured by Jesus. While Mark reported the mistreatment of Jesus following the Sanhedrin trial (Mk 14,65) and by the soldiers in preparation for the crucifixion (Mk 15,16-20), Luke related three mockeries. The first (22,63-65) emphasized Jesus' identity as a prophet and followed upon Peter's denial of Jesus, an action which confirmed Jesus' prophetic insight (22,31-34). While Luke elected to omit the Markan account of the mockery by the soldiers following the trial before Pilate, probably in light of the Roman apologetic, the Herod episode (23,11) served the same purpose. The third mockery (23,35-38), which detailed the rulers of the people scoffing at Jesus and the soldiers offering him vinegar as they challenged him to save himself, operates with the same sort of irony as the first mockery[362]. God's prophets are mocked and rejected.

Verse 12

ἐγένοντο δὲ φίλοι ὅ τε Ἡρῴδης καὶ ὁ Πιλᾶτος ἐν αὐτῇ τῇ ἡμέρᾳ μετ' ἀλλήλων· προϋπῆρχον γὰρ ἐν ἔχθρᾳ ὄντες πρὸς αὐτούς.

"And Herod and Pilate became friends with each other that very day, for before this they had been at enmity with each other".

It has been remarked: "V. 12 ist eine erläuternde Zwischenbemerkung, wie Lukas sie liebt"[363]. Similarly, the entire verse has been counted as Lukan redaction,

---

362. D. SENIOR, *The Passion of Jesus in the Gospel of Luke*, p. 131: "In this scene Luke has two sets of mockers hurl their challenges at Jesus, the rulers and the soldiers. The scene is punctuated with another sort of mockery, the placing of a placard on the cross. The words of mockery help accentuate the issues at stake in Jesus' death: his identity as Messiah, his ability to save others, and, foundational to everything, his relationship with God".

363. *Die Sprache*, p. 302. On Walaskay's creative, though unconvincing theory about the origin of the "friendship" between Pilate and Herod, see his article, *Trial*, p. 89-90.

with the suggestion this was the "sort of inconsequential explicative note that Luke likes to add"³⁶⁴.

ἐγένοντο δὲ φίλοι. Mark used ἐγένοντο in his Transfiguration account (Mk 9,6), the only time this form occurred in his Gospel. Luke omitted it in his redaction of the Transfiguration (9,34). Our working hypothesis that Luke employed Markan vocabulary which he earlier omitted seems once again confirmed. He employed it in the account of the Galileans whose blood Pilate mingled with their sacrifices (13,4 ἐγένοντο). As previously noted, this incident was frequently cited as the reason Pilate sent Jesus to Herod: in an effort to make amends. The phrase ἐγένοντο δὲ has been judged to be "eine luk Vorzugswendung" which was very frequently used in the LXX³⁶⁵.

δέ. "These two verses [vv. 11-12] continue the frequent Lucan use of de ['But'] at the beginning of each"³⁶⁶.

φίλος has been counted among the Lukan vocabulary³⁶⁷. In 7,34 Q (/ Mt 11,19) the term was used in a comparison of John the Baptist and the Son of Man. In the Q material of 12,4 (diff Mt 10,28) the Lukan version included reference to friends. The use in 23,12 could perhaps be read in light of 21,16 where Jesus prophesied that παραδοθήσεσθε δὲ καὶ ὑπὸ γονέων καὶ ἀδελφῶν καὶ συγγενῶν καὶ φίλων, καὶ θανατώσουσιν ἐξ ὑμῶν³⁶⁸. Over against his source Mk 13,12, Luke added friends. This is the last mention of friends prior to 23,12. Luke was preparing not only for the Herod story, but the accounts in Acts detailing the conspiracy of Herod and Pilate (Acts 4,26-27) and the deaths of Stephen (Acts 7,54-60) and James (Acts 12,1-2)³⁶⁹. The reference to friendship denotes equality³⁷⁰. Explicit mention of friends is found in Acts 10,24; 19,31; 27,3. φίλος is found in the LXX³⁷¹.

364. *Luke*, p. 1479.

365. CHICO CANO, *Der Prozess Jesu*, p. 43. He invited comparison with 1,8; 2,1; 3,21; 5,1; 6,7.12; 9,37; 11,27 as well as other places.

366. BROWN, p. 773.

367. BOISMARD, *Synopse*, t. 2, p. 418; Boismard and Lamouille in NEIRYNCK, *Le texte*, p. 330 (= 269); Müller observed Luke had a special liking for the word (*Jesus*, p. 140); CHICO CANO, p. 44; GOULDER, *Luke*, p. 809; LÉGASSE, *Le procès*, t. 2, p. 377, n. 79; UNTERGASSMAIR, *Zur Problematik*, p. 288. The word occurred in 7,6.34; 11,5bis.6.8.; 12,4; 14,10.12; 15,6.9.29; 16,9; 21,16; 23,12; Acts 10,24; 19,31; 27,3. Also noted by BROWN, p. 774-775. J. Weiss attributed 15 unspecified instances in Lk to LQ (*Lukas*, ⁸1892, p. 640). B. WEISS, *Lukas*, ⁹1901, p. 661, called attention to the use of the term in 16,9. The term is also found in the LXX as in Mi 7,5 (*MGEL*, p. 244). See SPICQ, *TLNT* 3, φίλος τοῦ Καίσαρος, p. 458-461.

368. References to friends are found in Lukan special material in 15,6 (τοὺς φίλους καὶ τοὺς γείτονας).9 (τὰς φίλας καὶ γείτονας).29 (τῶν φίλων).

369. See FITZMYER, p. 1340. Darr considered various possibilities to explain the friendship, reasoning that "all of them are highly conjectural" (*Glorified*, p. 302-303, p. 303; on rejecting Dibelius's solution, see p. 302, n. 162).

370. JOHNSON, *Luke*, p. 366. For a unique explanation for the origin of the enmity see PLUMMER, *Luke*, p. 523.

371. *GELS*, p. 504, where it was said to occur 187. In addition, it is found 29 times in the

ὅ τε ʽΗρῴδης καὶ ὁ Πιλᾶτος. The chief actors were mentioned together again as in 3,1, though in reverse order and without their titles of office, and prepare for what followed in Acts 4,26-27[372]. τέ has often been judged to be Lukan[373]. The position of τέ was capable of being an indication of Lukan redaction[374]. It has been noted that "by far the most frequent usage of τέ in the NT (not counting Acts) is in combination with καί"[375]. The phrase ὅ τε ... καί is evidence of Lukan style[376]. In reference to 23,12 the coordination of conjunctions "expands φίλοι"[377]. A similar construction, whereby two names are joined, is found in 2,16: τήν τε Μαριὰμ καὶ τὸν ʼΙωσήφ[378]. The construction is also found in Acts "at least 40 times" and "almost exclusively connects information about persons or places"[379]. The τε καί phrase in 22,66 should also not be overlooked (cf. Acts 1,1.8.13; 26,3 [Paul's defense before Agrippa])[380]. In the account in Acts of the

NT (*NTV*, p. 185).

372. BÜCHELE, p. 32, n. 55, included τέ among his list of typical Lukan expressions. Concerning the reference to the friendship of Pilate and Herod in 23,12 as a preparation for Acts 4,27, see also DARR, *Glorified*, p. 304: "In short, Luke 23:12 prepares the reader for the linking of Herod and Pilate at Acts 4:27 and also provides the sounding board for the intra-textual echoes evoked by Paul's trial (Acts 25-26) before both a Herodian prince and a Roman governor who are on friendly terms" (see also p. 305).

373. RADL, *Paulus*, p. 428; BOISMARD, *Synopse*, t. 2, p. 418; Boismard and Lamouille in NEIRYNCK, *Le texte*, p. 329 (= 268); TAYLOR, *Passion*, p. 87; FITZMYER, p. 111 (cf. HAWKINS, *Horae Synopticae*, ²1909, p. 22); GOULDER, *Luke*, p. 808; UNTERGASSMAIR, *Zur Problematik*, p. 281. See also K. MÜLLER, *Jesus*, p. 115. Note the use in 22,66 and Acts 13,1, and JEREMIAS, *Die Sprache*, p. 302: "τε ... καί: Lukas bevorzugt die enklitische Partikel τέ → 2,16 Red. S. 85. Zu der Kombination τέ ... καί (50mal in der Apg) → ebd. sub b". BROWN, p. 774: "A 'both ... and' function is played by *te* (almost 150 times in Luke-Acts, compared to 0 in Mark, 3 in Matt, 3 in John), and placing it after the definite article that accompanies *Hērōdēs* is quite Lucan".

374. K. MÜLLER, *Jesus*, p. 115: "Schon die Stellung des korrelativen τέ hinter dem Artikel vor Herodes vermag auf eine Sprachgebärde des Lukas aufmerksam zu machen". Also noted by BROWN, p. 774. For a similar word order see 2,16. MARSHALL, *Luke*, p. 113, commented that "this is a common connective particle in Lk.-Acts". K. Müller (*Jesus*, p. 115) called attention to the treatment of τέ in BDR, p. 374, §444.5,6. There it was also noted that τέ is a preferred term in Acts (§443, p. 372; so also K.-H. PRIDIK, τέ in *EWNT* 3, cols. 812-815 (= 339-340, esp. 339). Note further the use of τέ in 22,66 and particularly in 21,11 where it occurred twice in the verse prior to Jesus' prophecy that his disciples will be delivered up to kings and governors (21,12).

The particle also occurred several times in the account of Paul's trial in Acts 25,2.16.23.24; 26,3.4.10(bis).11.14.16.20(bis).22(bis).23.30.Construction such as we had in 23,12 is also found in Acts 26,30 where τέ follows the article.

375. PRIDIK, τέ, in *EWNT* 3, esp. col. 813 (= p. 339). See also MARSHALL, *Luke*, p. 113, who remarked that "normally it follows the noun to which it refers".

376. CHICO CANO, *Der Prozess Jesu*, p. 44.

377. *Ibid.* Consider BD, p. 230, §444, who maintained this formula "provides a closer connection than simple καί".

378. See JEREMIAS, *Die Sprache*, p. 85.

379. *Ibid.*

380. *BDF*, p. 230, §444: "Τε καί which is not infrequent in classical without an intervening

trials of Paul we find instances in 25,2 and 26,11.20.23.30³⁸¹. τε and the construction τε ... καί are found in the LXX³⁸².

ἐν αὐτῇ τῇ ἡμέρᾳ. The phrase ἐν ἐκείναις ταῖς ἡμέραις occurs in Mark's description of Jesus coming to John for baptism (Mk 1,9; om. Lk 3,21; also Mk 4,35 ἐν ἐκείνῃ τῇ ἡμέρᾳ diff Lk 8,22; Mk 8,1 om. Lk; Mk 13,17 / Lk 21,23; Mk 13,24 diff Lk 21,25; Mk 14,25 ἕως τῆς ἡμέρας ἐκείνης diff Lk 22,18). The word ἡμέρας occurred in Mk 6,21 speaking of the event which occasioned the death of John the Baptist.

We find ἐν αὐτῇ τῇ ἡμέρᾳ also in 24,13³⁸³. The word αὐτῇ was included a statistical table of Lukan vocabulary³⁸⁴. This phrase has been classified as a probable Septuagintism and singled out as evidence of Lukan redaction³⁸⁵. It has been categorized with the typical Lukan vocabulary and expressions³⁸⁶ and identified as redaction³⁸⁷. The substitution of αὐτός for ἐκεῖνος is considered to be a clear sign of Luke's hand³⁸⁸. The phrase occurs only in Lk-Acts³⁸⁹.

μετ᾽ ἀλλήλων. In three instances Luke substituted ἀλλήλων for what he found in Mk³⁹⁰. Mark's favorite expression was πρὸς ἀλλήλους (Mk 4,41 / 8,25; Mk 8,16 om. in Lk; Mk 9,34 diff. Lk; Mk 15,31 diff Lk 23,35; cf. Mk 9,50)³⁹¹. The most important instance for our consideration is the phrase in the

word is also common in the NT". See also SCHNEIDER, Verleugnung, p. 108.

381. On Acts 26,30 F.F. Bruce remarked, "this gathering in pairs is purely stylistic" (Acts, 1951, p. 450). Bruce also noted that the connective τέ was used in Acts 13,1 referring to Manaen and Herod (p. 253). Attention should also be given to the similar τε ... τε construction. "The correlative use τε ... τε (as distinct from the usual τε ... καί) is found only once in the NT, and that in the mouth of Paul before Agrippa, Acts 26,16, i.e. in highly rhetorical style" (ZERWICK, Biblical Greek, p. 157). BGD, p. 807, mentions that τε is used 9 times in Lk and about 150 times in Acts, which represents the most frequent use in the NT. Consider the use in the account of Paul's defense before Agrippa (Acts 26,10f.). Excluding Acts, τε and καί are generally used in combination in the NT (PRIDIK, EWNT 3, col. 813 = p. 339).

382. GELS, p. 470, e.g. Gen. 2,25.

383. Also noted by BROWN, p. 774. GREEN, Death, p. 80, termed the phrase "undoubtedly Lukan". For the similar phrase ἐν αὐτῇ τῇ ὥρᾳ see: 10,21; 12,12; 13,31; 20,19; 24,33; Acts 16,18; 22,13; cf. 7,21; 13,1; Acts 16,33. Cf. J. WEISS, Lukas, ⁸1892, p. 640, who attributed the use of this phrase in 24,13 to LQ. See LXX Lv 23,28.29.30; cf. LXX Lv 23,14; Nu 6,11; 9,6.

384. BOISMARD, Synopse, t. 2, p. 418. See also GOULDER, Luke, p. 804.

385. FITZMYER, p. 117-118, 1479. Brown concurred with Fitzmyer observing further that "this type of phrase occurs in Luke-Acts 11 times but not in the other Gospels" (Death, p. 774). JEREMIAS, Die Sprache, p. 98, 302, regarded this as redaction. See further ROBERTSON, Grammar, ²1915, ³1919, ⁴1923, p. 686, who also detected a similarity with 2,38.

386. BÜCHELE, p. 32, n. 55.

387. JEREMIAS, Die Sprache, p. 302-303: "ἐν αὐτῇ ἡμέρᾳ· αὐτὸς ὁ/αὐτὴ ἡ/αὐτὸ τό mit Substantiv der Zeit im NT nur im Doppelwerk → 2,38 Red S. 98". See further, Boismard and Lamouille in NEIRYNCK, Le texte, p. 319 (= 258).

388. K. MÜLLER, Jesus, p. 115-116, and UNTERGASSMAIR, Zur Problematik, p. 281.

389. CHICO CANO, Der Prozess Jesu, p. 44.

390. 4,36 ἀλλήλους / Mk 1,27 ἑαυτούς; 6,11 διελάλουν πρὸς ἀλλήλους / Mk 3,6 συμβούλιον ἐδίδουν; 20,14 ἀλλήλους / Mk 12,7 ἑαυτούς.

391. See also Lk 2,15; 4,26; 6,11; 8,25; 20,14; 24,14.17.32; Acts 4,15; 26,31 (Paul's trial

Markan account of a mockery of Jesus on the cross by the chief priests (Mk 15,31). πρὸς ἀλλήλους was used in 6,11 (diff Mk 3,6) in the context of a conspiracy by the scribes and Pharisees in plotting the demise of Jesus. In 7,32 ἀλλήλοις (Q; diff Mt 11,16 ἑτέροις) preceded mention of John the Baptist. In the parable of the vineyard and the tenants πρὸς ἀλλήλους (20,14 diff Mk 12,7 πρὸς ἑαυτούς) was used to refer to a conspiracy to kill the beloved son of the vineyard owner. In 20,5 Luke copied πρὸς ἑαυτούς from Mk 11,31. One scholar, commenting on 20,14 declared, "ἀλλήλους is better than ἑαυτούς"[392]. μετ' ἀλλήλων is a possible verbal variation of the Markan πρὸς ἑαυτούς[393]. "Das klassische reziproke Pronomen ἀλλήλων ist von Lukas gern gebraucht"[394].

ἀλλήλων is found 8 times in Acts[395]. It occurs in the account of Paul's appeal to Agrippa where the king, the governor and Bernice speak with one another (Acts 26,31). The term is also found in LXX[396].

προϋπῆρχον. The only other place in the NT this term is found is Acts 8,9. It was also employed in the LXX[397]. This word is identified as Lukan[398]. "[S]ome verbs came to express adverbial ideas; they were used as main verbs, but the main verbal idea was transferred to an inf. or ptc."[399]. The following examples were cited: "For beforehand προλαμβάνω c. inf. Mk 14[8], προϋπάρχω c. ptc. Lk 23,[12]"[400]. Luke used γάρ in 23,8.12.15[401].

before Herod Agrippa); 28,4.25.

392. MARSHALL, Luke, p. 730.

393. DSCHULNIGG, Sprache, p. 101-102. Cf. Boismard and Lamouille in NEIRYNCK, Le texte, p. 324 (= 263).

394. CHICO CANO, Der Prozess Jesu, p. 44. RADL, Paulus, p. 398, and GOULDER, Luke, p. 800, also include it in their lists of Lukan vocabulary.

395. NTV, p. 75. Acts 4,15; 7,26; 15,39; 19,38; 21,6; 26,31; 28,4.25.

396. GELS, p. 20. See also LXX Am 4,3 (MGEL, p. 9). In addition there is the use in Is 34,15.

397. See BDF, p. 213, § 414, 1; JEREMIAS, Die Sprache, p. 82, 303. See also MHT 3, p. 159, where it was noted that the term is also found in Josephus; see further p. 227; ZERWICK, Biblical Greek, § 360, n. 3. ROBERTSON, Grammar, ²1915, ³1919, ⁴1923, p. 888, 1102-1103, 1121. The participle was employed with ὑπάρχω (Acts 8,16) as with προϋπάρχω (Lk 23,12). On προϋπάρχω as "found almost entirely in Luke/Acts", see TAYLOR, Passion, p. 87. K. MÜLLER, who also observed the term only occured in Lk-Acts in these two places, stated that despite the infrequent use of the term, the evangelist favored both the prefix προ as well as the verb ὑπάρχειν (Jesus, p. 116, n. 31). BROWN called attention to the similarity of the construction προϋπάρχειν with a participle between 23,12 and Acts 8,9 (Death, p. 775). The single use of the term in the LXX is Job 42,17b. See GELS, p. 407.

398. BOISMARD, Synopse, t. 2, p. 418; Boismard and Lamouille in NEIRYNCK, Le texte, p. 328 (= 267); MARSHALL, Luke, p. 857; JEREMIAS, Die Sprache, p. 303; UNTERGASSMAIR, Zur Problematik, p. 281.

399. MHT 3, p. 226.

400. Ibid., p. 227. It is interesting to note that the term προλαμβάνω occurs in the anointing at Bethany (Mk 14,8) which Luke omitted in the parallel place (cf. Lk 7,36-50). However, there is one instance of the term as a variant reading in special Lukan material (19,4 προλαβών). See further H. BALZ, προλαμβάνω, in EWNT 3, col. 380-381 (= p. 158).

γὰρ ἐν ἔχϑρᾳ ὄντες πρὸς αὐτούς. On γάρ see the discussion above on 23,8. Note that the term is used again in 23,15.

Earlier in the Gospel, in the prophecy of Zechariah, the related term ἐχϑρός is mentioned (1,71.74). Upon drawing near to Jerusalem Jesus prophesied that enemies would "surround you, and hem you in on every side" (19,43). ἔχϑρα is found in the LXX[402]. On the use of ἐν with an emotional state compare Acts 22,17[403].

ὄντες. See comment above on ὄντα (23,7). The use in 23,12 is remarkable since it was combined with ὑπάρχειν[404]. Again Luke is fond of the periphrastic construction and also used repetition of vocabulary in this brief pericope. The following examples from Acts may have some bearing: ὄντες αὐτῷ φίλοι (Acts 19,31) and ὄντες πρὸς ἀλλήλους ἀπελύοντο (Acts 28,25).

πρὸς αὐτούς. The phrase expressed a reciprocal meaning and is found both in Mk and Lk[405]. πρός + accusative rather than the dative is Lukan[406]. It has also been noted that amicable disposition (1 Th 5,14) as well as hostile was frequently indicated by use of πρός[407].

Though one scholar maintained 23,12a derived from Lukan composition, while 23,12b "seems to be from tradition"[408], an analysis of the vocabulary in 23,12 led another to the conclusion: "that the verse is, if not Luke's own creation, at least heavily redacted by him, has been made plausible by the vocabulary statistics of Schütz"[409]. Yet another determined: "V. 12 entspricht demnach deutlich luk Sprachgebrauch und Stil"[410].

---

401. ZERWICK, Biblical Greek, p. 159, §473b. See also PRIDIK, γάρ in EWNT 1, cols. 571-573 (= p. 238-239).

402. GELS, p. 193. Gen 3,15; Num 35,20.22; Prov 6,35; 10,18; 15,17; 25,10; 26,26; Is 63,10; Jer 9,8; Ez 35,5.11; Mic 2,8. On the use of the term in a sampling of the LXX, see MGEL, p. 100.

403. GOULDER, Luke, p. 759.

404. ZERWICK, Biblical Greek, p. 125, n. 3.

405. BDF, p. 35, § 64 (1), p. 150, § 287. See Mk 6,48.51; 9,14.16; 12,4.6.12 in addition to Lk 2,18.20.49; 3,13; 4,21.23.43; 5,22.31.34.36; 6,3.9; 8,21.22; 9,3.13; 10,2; 11,5; 12,15.16; 13,23; 14,5.7.25; 15,3; 16,30; 18,31; 19,31.33; 20,3.19.23.25.41; 22,15.70; 23,14.22; 24,17.25.44. See also MIBNTG, p. 119; MHT 2, p. 180; MHT 4, p. 53; ROBERTSON, Grammar, [2]1915, [3]1919, [4]1923, p. 289, 690. On πρός with the accusative as typical of Luke, see TAYLOR, Passion, p. 87. Jeremias counted this among the traditional elements of the pericope (Die Sprache, p. 303). He also pointed to the πρὸς ἑαυτούς in 22,23. But this is to neglect πρὸς αὐτούς in Mk 9,10 (Transfiguration preceding mention of Elijah in v. 11; cf. Lk 9,36); 11,21 (discussion about John the Baptist / Lk 20,5: Jeremias did not treat this material since he concluded it stemmed from a Markan block! See Die Sprache, p. 282); 16,3 (diff Lk 24,1-2: material omitted by Luke); see also Mk 1,27; 10,26; 12,7; 14,4).

406. CADBURY, Style, p. 203; TAYLOR, Passion, p. 87; RADL, Paulus, p. 425.

407. ROBERTSON, Grammar, [2]1915, [3]1919, [4]1923, p. 625. For a cogent explanation of the hostility between Pilate and Herod, see HASTINGS, Prophet, p. 46-47.

408. SOARDS, Tradition, 1985, p. 357.

409. BUCK, Function, p. 167. See F. SCHÜTZ, Der leidenden Christus, 128ff.

410. CHICO CANO, Der Prozess Jesu, p. 44.

V. 12 has been characterized as "one more of Luke's inconsequential explicative notes"[411]. Because of a lack of historical evidence, neither the attitude of hostility nor friendship was implausible. Rather, v. 12 is a reflection of "Luke's theology of the passion as forgiveness and healing"[412].

Commenting on vv. 13-16 it has been stated: "De même, les vv. 13-16 - où le v. 14 ne fait que reprendre le thème du v. 2a et où le v. 16 pourrait n'être qu'un dédoublement du v. 22c, qui lui est absolument identique - semblent un ajout destiné à renouer le fil du récit primitif, interrompu par l'insertion de la comparution de Jésus devant Hérode (le cas du v. 14b, qui contient la seconde déclaration d'innocence de Jésus par Pilate et qui a donc son parallèle dans Jn, envisagé plus loin). En résumé, on peut considérer tout le bloc des vv. 5-16 comme une addition à la source suivie par Lc"[413]. Some of these verses echoed earlier verses and this unit reconnected the thread of the narrative which was interrupted by the Herod pericope. Rather than deriving from some other source, our investigation will show that there is a significant amount of Lukan and Markan vocabulary present in these verses[414]. These facts, combined with Luke's method of preparing the later material in his Gospel by means of earlier passages strongly suggests Luke composed these verses.

Verse 13

Πιλᾶτος δὲ συγκαλεσάμενος τοὺς ἀρχιερεῖς καὶ τοὺς ἄρχοντας καὶ τὸν λαόν

"Pilate than called together the chief priests and the rulers and the people,"

The phrase Πιλᾶτος δέ is also found in 23,6. It has been proposed that this phrase began the new scene in 23,6 just as it introduced a new scene in 23,13[415]. Compare Mk 15,4.9.12.14.15.44 (ὁ δὲ Πιλᾶτος) with 23,3.4.20. Lk 23,8 contains the phrase ὁ δὲ Ἡρῴδης.

συγκαλεῖν is found in the Markan account of the mockery by the soldiers (Mk 15,16 συγκαλοῦσιν hapax in Mk)[416]. It was also employed in Lk 9,1; 15,6.9; Acts 5,21; 10,24; 28,17[417]. Its use in 9,1 occurred in a pericope immediately

411. BROWN, *Death*, p. 777. See FITZMYER, p. 1482.

412. BROWN, *Death*, p. 778; also p. 281, 786.

413. BOISMARD, *Synopse*, t. 2, p. 412. He repeated the assertion in section 1b. The section 23,5-16 as a whole was considered to be "la comparution de Jésus devant Hérode" which was inserted by "l'ultime Rédacteur lucanien" (*Synopse*, t. 2, p. 417: on the final Lukan redactor see also p. 44-46. esp. p. 45 §1c). See also Fitzmyer, who argued that 23,13-16 is "a logical sequel to vv. 6-12 and difficult to separate from them" (*Luke*, p. 1484).

414. Boismard did not lay out "le tableau statistique" for vv. 13-16 as he had done for vv. 6-12 (p. 418).

415. BÜCHELE, *Der Tod*, p. 33, n. 64.

416. Noted also by BROWN, *Death*, p. 789, and MATERA, *Luke 23,1-25*, p. 548. See further GREEN, *Death*, p. 83. Consider 23,33 diff Mk 15,22.

417. It was used in the active voice in Mk 15,16 and Lk 15,6.9 but was employed in the

preceding another which treated of Herod (9,7-9). Lk 9,1 was derived from Mk 6,7 (προσκαλεῖται[418]) though Luke substituted a different participle[419]. This Markan passage containing Mk 6,7 is just prior to the account of Herod's encounter with John the Baptist which ended with his death. συνκαλεῖν has been identified as a preferred Lukan term[420]. We previously noted that Luke favored words with the συν- prefix[421]. In Acts 5,21 the high priest called together τὸ συνέδριον. The chief priests figured prominently in Paul's trial (Acts 25,2.15; 26,10) and paralleled the experience of Jesus. The simple form (καλούμενος) has been included among the characteristic Lukan terms[422]. Lk 23,13 has been assessed as "largely Lukan" on the basis of συγκαλεσάμενος, τοὺς ἄρχοντας and τὸν λαόν[423]. συγκαλεῖν occurs 13 times in the LXX[424].

τοὺς ἀρχιερεῖς καὶ τοὺς ἄρχοντας καὶ τὸν λαόν. This combination of groups is unique in Lk[425]. It symbolizes "the whole of Israel"[426]. "Except for the

middle voice in the other instances (G. SCHNEIDER, συγκαλέω, in *EWNT* 3, col. 676 = p. 282). See also MARSHALL, *Luke*, who argued the use of the active for the middle in 15,6 was "pre-Lucan" (p. 602; see p. 351). See further B. WEISS, *Lukas*, ⁹1901, p. 662. See *MHT* 3, p. 55.

418. Of the 29 occurrences in the NT 6 were found in Mt, 9 in Mk, 4 in Lk, 9 in Acts and 1 in Jas (H. BALZ, προσκαλέομαι, in *EWNT* 3, 414-415, esp. col. 414 = p. 172). In comparing Mk and Lk we found: Mk 3,13 diff Lk 6,13; Mk 3,23 diff Lk 11,17; Mk 6,7 diff Lk 9,1; Mk 7,14 diff Lk; Mk 8,1 diff Lk; Mk 8,34 diff Lk 9,23; Mk 10,42 diff Lk 22,24-25; Mk 12,43 diff Lk 21,3; Mk 15,44 diff Lk 23,52. Consider Plummer's comment on 9,1: "All three mention this summons or invitation on the part of Jesus. Mt. and Mk. describe it by their usual προσκαλεῖσθαι, for which Lk. has συνκαλεῖσθαι, which he more commonly uses in his Gospel (ix.1, xv.6,9, xxiii,13), while in the Acts he generally uses προσκαλεῖσθαι (ii.39, v.40, vi.2, xiii.2, etc.)." (*St. Luke*, 1896, p. 239). Guelich stated "Mark frequently used the participial form of προσκαλεῖται to introduce a pronouncement by Jesus or to set a new scene (e.g. 3:23; 7:14; 8:1, 34; 10:42; 12:43)" (*Mark 1-8:26* [WBC 34A], Dallas, TX, 1989, p. 321). Mark employed the present indicative form only in Mk 6,7; 3,14.

Swete maintained προσκαλεῖται "implies authority" (*The Gospel According to Mark. The Greek Text with Introduction, Notes and Indices*, London, 1898, ³1909; Grand Rapids, MI, 1951 [reprint of 1909 "with slight changes"], p. 115).

419. FITZMYER, *Luke*, p. 753.

420. TAYLOR, *Passion Narrative*, p. 87; RADL, *Paulus*, p. 426; FITZMYER, *Luke*, p. 1077: "a favorite of Luke's". See also GOULDER, *Luke*, p. 761, 808; Boismard and Lamouille in NEIRYNCK, *Le texte*, p. 328 (= 267), with reference to HAWKINS, *Horae Synopticae*, 1899, p. 19 (= ²1909, p. 22), and JEREMIAS, *Die Sprache*, p. 246. Cf. PERRY, *Sources*, p. 114, who counted συνκαλέω among the vocabulary of the J document.

421. See for example J. JEREMIAS, *Die Sprache*, p. 246: "Lukas hat eine ausgesprochene Vorliebe für Verbkomposita mit συν-". He attributed the term in 15,6.9, as well as 23,13 to redaction (p. 246, 247, 303).

422. HAWKINS, *Horae Synopticae*, 1899, p. 17, 34; ²1909, p. 19, 42.

423. NOLLAND, *Luke 18:35-24:53*, p. 1126.

424. *GELS*, p. 444. Consider further LXX Zch 3,10 (*MGEL*, p. 219). The participial form is exactly as in LXX 2 Mac 15,31. Other uses of the term are found in LXX Ex 7,11; Jos 9,22; 10,24; 22,1; 23,2; 24,1.

425. It is interesting to note, however, that Mark wrote in terms of a tripartite group of chief priests, elders and scribes (Mk 15,1). See also Mk 8,31 (/ Lk 9,22); 11,27 (/ Lk 20,1); 14,43

reference to Abiathar in Mark 2:26 (1 Sam 21:7) ἀρχιερεύς occurs in the Gospels and Acts only in connection with the trial of Jesus and the persecution of the early Church ..."[427]. The combination οἱ ἀρχιερεῖς καὶ οἱ πρεσβύτεροι καὶ οἱ γραμματεῖς is found in Mk 14,53 (cf. Mk 15,1). The reference to the chief priests in 23,13 harkened back to 22,66 who gathered together (συνήχθη) at that time as part of the Sanhedrin trial. It also recalled their vehement accusations against Jesus in the presence of Herod (23,10). The high priesthood of Annas and Caiaphas[428] was mentioned shortly after the initial reference in the Gospel to Herod (3,1) and in conjunction with the preaching of John the Baptist (3,2). Jesus the prophet foretold his rejection by the chief priests, among others, shortly before the Transfiguration (9,22 / Mk 8,31; see also 18,31 / Mk 10,33; cf. 9,44 / Mk 9,31)[429]. In 19,47 (/ Mk 11,18) the conspiracy of οἱ δὲ ἀρχιερεῖς καὶ οἱ γραμματεῖς ... καὶ οἱ πρῶτοι τοῦ λαοῦ against Jesus was related. Observe the tripartite grouping of the conspirators[430]. Note, in contrast, that the people were presented in a favorable light listening intently to Jesus (19,48; cf. Mk 11,18). The efforts of the scribes and chief priests came to the fore again in 20,19 (cf. Mk 12,12), recalling the exact situation as portrayed in 20,1[431]. Their reluctance to act was due to their fear of the people (τοῦ λαοῦ)[432]. All this is consistent with Luke's tendency of preparing for later material by means of earlier passages. Finally, the two disciples on the way to Emmaus will recount for the risen Jesus how the high priests and scribes delivered Jesus up to crucifixion (24,20) which shows that the prophecy of Jesus, the prophet and Christ of God, was fulfilled. Note how earlier in the passion Luke referred to three segments of the Jewish population, two of which will figure prominently in 23,13: οἱ ἀρχιερεῖς καὶ γραμματεῖς ... τὸν λαόν (22,2). The difference between these two verses may not be so significant when we consider the following: "In the Passion narrative of Mark 14f. the scribes are regularly associated with high priests and/or elders and understood as members of the Sanhedrin (so also Acts 4:5; 6:12) while outside the

(cf. Lk 22,47).53 (cf. Lk 22,54 [Sanhedrin trial]).

426. MATERA, *Luke 23,1-25*, p. 543. See BROWN, *Death*, p. 790.

427. U. KELLERMANN, ἀρχιερεύς, in *EWNT* 1, 394-397, esp. col. 395 (= p. 164-165, p. 164). On priests, see further FITZMYER, *Luke*, p. 780.

428. Cf. Acts 4,6.

429. See the previous discussion about Jesus' identity which centered around the popular conception that Jesus was one of the prophets. Peter confessed that Jesus was the Christ of God (9,18-20 / Mk 8,27-30). References in Lk to high priests are: 3,2; 9,22; 19,47; 20,1.19; 22,2.4.50.52.54.66;23,4.10.13; 24,20. In Acts they are: 4,6.23; 5,17.21.24.27; 7,1; 9,1.14.21; 19,14; 22,5.30; 23,2.4.5.14; 24,1; 25,2.15; 26,10.12.

430. See also 20,1 and consider its Markan parallel (Mk 11,27) where there is mention of the chief priests, scribes and elders (cf. Mk 14,53; 15,1 with an order which varied from Mk 11,27).

431. The only difference between 20,1 and 20,19 was the change in order between scribes and chief priests.

432. Consider Mk 11,18 where the chief priests and scribes were said to fear Jesus.

Passion narrative this combination is not predominant (cf. also Acts 23:9)"[433]. This could simply reflect Luke's desire for some variation since the term was used in 23,10. In 23,13 ἄρχοντας "must refer to the elders, chief priests, and Scribes of 22:66"[434].

The almost identical phrase, though missing reference to the people (τοὺς ἀρχιερεῖς καὶ τοὺς ἄρχοντας), occurred in 24,20[435]. The phrase is counted among Lukan vocabulary[436].

The καὶ … καί construction "most often emphasizes the additional and the special character of the combination"[437]. On δὲ … καὶ … καί, as we have here, see also Acts 26,29 where Paul spoke in the presence of Agrippa.

τοὺς ἄρχοντας. There is a "wide range" of personnel included in the term but its use here indicates "members of the Sanhedrin"[438]. The word has been judged to be Lukan[439]. The term recurred in 23,35; 24,20; Acts 3,17; 4,5[τοὺς ἄρχοντας καὶ τοὺς πρεσβυτέρους καὶ τοὺς γραμματεῖς][440].8[441]; 13,27; 14,5. The word is also found in LXX[442].

Already in 22,66 there was reference to the elders of the people, which included the chief priests and the scribes. "'[T]he people' in Luke 23:13 is surely not significantly different from 'the crowds' in 23:4-5 who were insistent on accusing Jesus before Pilate"[443]. There was no distinction between the two terms

---

433. G. BAUMBACH, γραμματεύς, in *EWNT* 1, 624-627, esp. cols. 624-625 (= p. 259-260, esp. p. 260).

434. FITZMYER, *Luke*, p. 1484. See also JOHNSON, *Luke*, p. 359, 370. Of the occurrence of the term in LXX, see *GELS*, p. 65.

435. So also FITZMYER, *Luke*, p. 1564.

436. TAYLOR, *Passion*, p. 87; GOULDER, *Luke*, p. 761, 801.

437. PRIDIK, καί, in *EWNT* 2, cols. 557-560, esp. col. 560 (= p. 227-228, p. 228). See also *BAGD*, p. 393.

438. BROWN, *Death*, p. 790. See CADBURY, *Style*, p. 120, n. 2. Concerning leaders, consult the comment on 14,1 in FITZMYER, *Luke*, p. 1040. See NEIRYNCK, *Jesus and the Sabbath*, in DUPONT, *Jesus aux origines*, p. 227-270 (= *Evangelica*, 637-680); SCHNEIDER, *Lukas*, p. 476.

439. HAWKINS, *Horae Synopticae*, 1899, p. 14, 30; ²1909, p. 16, 36; RADL, *Paulus*, p. 401; GREEN, *Death*, p. 83; GOULDER, *Luke*, p. 801.

440. See HAENCHEN, *Die Apostelgeschichte*, ¹⁴1965, p. 174-175 (= *Acts*, p. 215-216; CONZELMANN, *Acts*, p. 32); BRUCE, *Acts*, ³1990, p. 149. Cf. Mk 14,53 and Mk 15,1.

441. BARRETT, *Acts*, p. 226: "ἄρχοντες τοῦ λαοῦ takes up v. 5 (and 3.17), though the combination does not occur elsewhere in the NT".

442. *GELS*, p. 65. There are 37 instances in the NT (*NTV*, p. 80).

443. BROWN, *Death*, p. 790-791. See also p. (790)-791, n. 4. In addition, consider KODELL, *Luke's Use of Laos, 'People' Especially in the Jerusalem Narrative*, in *CBQ* 31 (1969) 327-343. Note further TYSON, *Death*, p. 32, 35; and MATERA, *Luke 23,1-25*, p. 548: "The clearest indication of Lucan editorial activity, however, comes in v. 13 which controls the entire unit. In this verse Pilate assembles the whole of Israel: Πιλᾶτος δὲ συγκαλεσάμενος τοὺς ἀρχιερεῖς καὶ τοὺς ἄρχοντας καὶ τὸν λαόν. The verse is striking because this is the first explicit mention of the people in the trial narrative, and from this point forward they as well as their rulers, play a prominent role in the condemnation of Jesus. The presence of the people, however, is not completely unexpected. Above, I noted that in 23,1 Luke employs the purposely vague expression

and Luke's desire to vary his vocabulary accounts for the difference. λαός "has
more of a formal collective sense"[444]. Numerous scholars are also of the opinion
that λαός was Lukan[445]. The frequency of use in Lk confirmed that it was a
preferred term and served as a synonym of ὄχλος[446]. The word is found only 3x
in Mk: Mk 7,6 (diff Lk)[447]; Mk 11,32 v.l. (/ Lk 20,6)[448]; Mk 14,2 / 22,2.

It has been said that "Luke has consciously and intentionally inserted λαός into
his double work"[449]. The word is found frequently in the LXX[450]. "*Laos* is the
Septuagintal word for God's people and the frequency with which Luke uses it
from now [18,43] to the end of the Gospel is striking (it will appear nineteen
times), and it is often used in contrast to the leaders of Jerusalem (esp. from
19:47-48 on). Mark never uses 'all the people', Matthew has it only once (27:25),
and John only once (8:2)"[451]. The use of the term in 23,13 set the stage for Acts
3,11. "In Acts 3:11, the entire λαός can appropriately be charged with
responsibility for the death of Jesus and called to repentance, in keeping with Luke
23:13"[452]. The word recurred in 23,14.

τὸ πλῆθος αὐτῶν and in 23,4 he has Pilate respond to the priests and τοὺς ὄχλους. The
appearance of the people at this juncture has been well prepared for and accords with Luke's view
in Acts which makes the people responsible for handing over, denying, crucifying, and killing
Jesus (Acts 2,23.36; 3,13-15; 10,39)". Matera's view that 23,13 "controls the entire unit", seems
somewhat excessive.

444. D. SENIOR, *The Passion of Jesus in the Gospel of Luke*, p. 116, n. 25. See Boismard
and Lamouille in NEIRYNCK, *Le texte*, p. 326 (= 265).

445. HAWKINS, *Horae Synopticae*, 1899, p. 17; ²1909, p. 20; TAYLOR, *Passion*, p. 87;
GREEN, *Death*, p. 83. He counted it among "Luke's characteristic vocabulary"; RADL, *Paulus*,
p. 416; Boismard and Lamouille in NEIRYNCK, *Le texte*, p. 324 (= 263), cites HAWKINS, *Horae
Synopticae*, 1899, p. 17 (= ²1909, p. 20), MORGENTHALER, *Statistik*, p. 51, and JEREMIAS, *Die
Sprache*, p. 30. See further GOULDER, *Luke*, p. 761, 806.

446. CADBURY, *Style*, p. 189. He cited 23,5 and Mk 15,11 as an example. See BROWN,
Death, p. 791, n. 4, and BÜCHELE, *Der Tod*, p. 34, n. 66.

447. TAYLOR, *St. Mark*, ²1966, p. 337, on Mk 7,6: "As might be expected in a quotation,
the vocabulary includes words not common in Mk: λαός xiv.2 ...".

448. MARSHALL, *Luke*, p. 725: "the people (λαός, diff. Mk. ὄχλος, has a theological
nuance)"; cf. FRANKEMÖLLE, λαός, col. 839 (= p. 340): "The sense of the word that has no
theological significance is found in the sg. twice in Mark (11:32; 14:2)"; JOHNSON, *Luke*, p. 304.

449. FRANKEMÖLLE, λαός, in *EWNT* 2, 837-848, esp. col. 843 (= p. 339-344, p. 341).

450. *Ibid.*, col. 840 (= p. 340): "In passages, however, where the λαός is contrasted to the
leading circles, which reject Jesus (Luke 23:2, 23:5; Acts 6:12, 10:41; 13:15), or where λαός
is integrated into the front which rejects Jesus (Luke 23:15), what is decisive is not only the usage
of the LXX ..., but also the Lukan conception, which is based on the LXX ...". See also *GELS*,
p. 277.

451. FITZMYER, *Luke*, p. 1217.

452. FRANKEMÖLLE, λαός, col. 843 (= p. 342).

Verse 14

εἶπεν πρὸς αὐτούς· προσηνέγκατέ μοι τὸν ἄνθρωπον τοῦτον ὡς ἀποστρέφοντα τὸν λαόν, καὶ ἰδοὺ ἐγὼ ἐνώπιον ὑμῶν ἀνακρίνας οὐθὲν εὗρον ἐν τῷ ἀνθρώπῳ τούτῳ αἴτιον ὧν κατηγορεῖτε κατ᾽ αὐτοῦ.

"and said to them, 'You brought me this man as one who was perverting the people; and after examining him before you, behold, I did not find this man guilty of any of your charges against him'";

"In 23:14 we find much Lucan vocabulary"[453]. Luke attempted to highlight Pilate's efforts to release Jesus[454].

εἶπεν πρὸς αὐτούς. "εἶπεν is by far the commonest word for introducing sayings or speeches in dialogue ..."[455]. Luke preferred πρός with the accusative rather than a dative, as for example 23,22 (diff Mk 12,14)[456]. "La construction εἶπεν πρός est incontestablement une caractéristique de la rédaction lucanienne ..."[457]. The construction πρός plus the accusative is a Lukan trait[458], as is this construction with a verb of saying[459]. In 23,4 there occurred εἶπεν πρός. See

___

453. BROWN, *Death*, p. 791, among which are included: εἶπεν πρός, καὶ ἰδού, ἐνώπιον, and ἀποστρέφοντα. The parallels between the ἀνακρίνας of Jesus in Lk and Paul in Acts are also noted. Boismard argued that owing to the three affirmations of Jesus' innocence (23,4.14.22 / Jn 18,38b; 19,4.6) as well as Pilate's explicit desire to release Jesus (23,20 / Jn 19,12) the literary contact between Lk and Jn "est donc certain" (*Synopse*, t. 2, 1972, p. 411; see also p. 412, 413, 417). He claimed further this common source was "un proto-Lc" (p. 412). While the relationship of the Synoptics to Jn is an important issue, it is beyond the scope of this essay. On this particular topic see further A. DENAUX (ed.), *John and the Synoptics*, 1992, especially F. NEIRYNCK, *John and the Synoptics*, p. 3-61, and D.M. SMITH, *John Among the Gospels. The Relationship in Twentieth-Century Research*, Minneapolis, MN, 1992.
Boismard offered a hypothesis of how the Lukan redactor composed this section. "Rappelons-nous ici que Lc, comme Jn, contient *trois* affirmations par Pilate de l'innocence de Jésus (vv. 4.14.22 de Lc; Jn 18,38b; 19,4.6), mais que l'une de ces affirmations (v. 14) se trouve maintenant dans une section (vv. 13-16) ajoutée par le Rédacteur lucanien. Une hypothèse se présente alors: pour composer cette section additionnelle, le Rédacteur lucanien n'aurait-il pas transposé au v. 14 la seconde déclaration d'innocence de Jésus, qui primitivement se trouvait au v. 20? Ce v. 20 redeviendrait normal, sous cette forme: 'De nouveau Pilate leur addressa la parole, voulant relâcher Jésus: Voici, noi, ayant instruit l'affaire devant vous, je n'ai trouvé en cet homme aucun motif (de condamnation)'" (*Synopse*, t. 2, p. 413).
454. H.F.D. SPARKS, *The Partiality of Luke for 'Three'*, in *JTS* 37 (1936) 141-145, p. 143: "Similarly, the three denials of Peter in Mark and the three attempts of Pilate to persuade the people that Jesus should be released are by Luke made far more explicit".
455. CADBURY, *Style*, p. 169.
456. *Ibid.*, p. 203.
457. NEIRYNCK, *Luc 24,36-43. Un récit lucanien*, in *À cause de l'évangile. Mélanges offerts au R.P. Jacques Dupont* (LD, 123), Paris, 1985, 655-680 (= *Evangelica II*, 205-226, p. 216).
458. TAYLOR, *Passion*, p. 87.
459. GOULDER, *Luke*, p. 761, 808, and NOLLAND, *Luke 18:35-24:53*, p. 1127; cf. GREEN, *Death*, p. 83 ("probably Lukan").

also 20,19[460] [describing the conspiratorial efforts of the scribes and chief priests]; 23,22; 24,17.25[461]. Cf. Mk 12,12 (πρὸς αὐτοὺς ... εἶπεν). In addition it appears frequently in Acts[462].

The term προσφέρω occurred three times in Mk, two of which were parallel in Lk (Mk 1,44 / 5,14; Mk 10,13 / Lk 18,15)[463]. Attention should also be given to Mk 15,1 ἀπήνεγκαν (hapax), that stems from the same root, which may have influenced Luke here[464]. Though some argued that the term in 23,14 was not Lukan[465], others conjectured that it "may be Lukan"[466]. Luke employed προσφέροντες in the third of his mockeries (23,36). Note that both in that verse and in 23,14 we have the same construction: προσφέρειν with the accusative object and dative of person[467]. This was also the case in 18,15 (/ Mk 10,13). The term use of προσφέρω in Acts 7,42 was derived from LXX Amos 5,25-27[468]. We should keep in mind εἰσφέρωσιν in 12,11 (diff Mk 13,11 ἄγωσιν) about the disciples being brought before the synagogues, rulers and authorities[469]. προσφέρω is found 161 times in the LXX[470].

The phrase "this man" occurred twice in 23,14[471]. The term is Lukan[472]. The use of "this man" or "the man" in 23,4.6.14bis, is never found in the Markan or Matthean parallels[473]. The Markan account of Peter's denial contained the phrase τὸν ἄνθρωπον τοῦτον (Mk 14,71[474]) which Luke elected not to borrow

---

460. Boismard and Lamouille in NEIRYNCK, *Le texte*, p. 321 (= 260).

461. See also 24,44 which contained the phrase εἶπεν δὲ πρὸς αὐτούς.

462. Acts 1,7; 2,29.37; 4,19; 5,35; 7,3; 8,20; 9,10.15; 10,21; 12,8; 12,15; 15,7.36; 18,6; 19,2; 22,8.10.21.25; 23,3; 28,21.

463. In another case, whereas Mk had προσενέγκαι αὐτῷ διὰ τὸν ὄχλον (Mk 2,4), Luke has substituted εἰσενέγκωσιν αὐτὸν διὰ τὸν αὐτόν (Lk 5,19; see also 5,18). Of the 47 occurrences in the NT, 15 were in Mt, 3 in Mk, 4 in Lk, and 3 in Acts [Acts 7,42; 8,18; 21,26]. On the other hand, Lk-Acts accounted for 5 instances of εἰσφέρω. On the selected use of the term in LXX Am 5,25, see *MGEL*, p. 204-205. There are other instances in the LXX, as for example Nu 7,2 προσήνεγκαν οἱ ἄρχοντες.

464. Luke employed ἀποφέρω at 16,22 and Acts 19,12.

465. JEREMIAS, *Die Sprache*, p. 303.

466. GREEN, *Death*, p. 83 (= Ch 3, p. 104).

467. As discussed by UNTERGASSMAIR, *Kreuzweg*, p. 59.

468. GREEN, *Death*, p. 83. In addition the term appears in Acts 8,18; 21,26. On Septuagintal use consult *GELS*, p. 406, which listed 161 instances compared with 47 in the NT (*NTV*, p. 62).

469. Of the 8 instances of this term in the NT, 4 occur in Lk and 1 in Acts.

470. *GELS*, p. 406.

471. See also Acts 4,16 (plural); 5,28.35(plural).38(plural); 6,13; 22,26; 23,9; 26,31.32; 28,4.

472. HARNACK, *Lukas der Arzt*, 1906, p. 36 (= *Luke the Physician*, 1908, p. 50-51); Boismard and Lamouille in NEIRYNCK, *Le texte*, p. 318 (= 257); GOULDER, *Luke*, p. 761, 801.

473. BOISMARD, *Synopse*, t. 2, p. 413. He also commented that the Lukanisms in 23,2-5.13-25 were abundant (p. 413-414).

474. PESCH, *Das Markus-Evangelium*, 1977, p. 451: "distanziert formuliert". Gundry commenting on Mk 14,71 proposed: "... and distantly, perhaps disparagingly, he calls Jesus τὸν ἄνθρωπον τοῦτον, 'this man,' a far cry both from Jesus' synchronous confession of himself as

(22,60). A similar expression was found in the centurion's confession of Jesus' innocence in Mk 15,39 which was was taken up by Luke in 23,47 (οὗτος ὁ ἄνθρωπος / ὁ ἄνθρωπος οὗτος)[475]. "[T]he usage may reflect legal terminology"[476]. In 23,18 the crowds referred to Jesus simply as τοῦτον. This emphatic has been recognized as a sign of Lukan redaction[477]. There is resemblance between 23,14 and Acts 26,31.32[478]. In Acts 5,28 is also found the phrase τοῦ ἀνθρώπου τούτο[479].

ὡς ἀποστρέφοντα τὸν λαόν. ὡς occurs 504 times in the NT. Of those 22 are found in Mk, 51 in Lk and 63 in Acts[480]. It has been identified as Lukan vocabulary[481]. It is a conjunction which introduces the "characteristic of something that is of particular importance in the context", in this case "an imagined or asserted characteristic (Luke 23,14; Acts 3,12; 23,15.20; 27,30)"[482]. On several occasions Luke substituted ὡς for a variety of Markan terms (3,4 / Mk 1,2; [6,4] / Mk 2,26; 20,37 / Mk 12,26; 22,27 / Mk 10,45; 22,66 / Mk 15,1; 23,55 / Mk 15,47[483]. The use of the particle ὡς with the present participle is also found in 16,1; 22,27 diff Mk 10,45; Acts 23,15.20; 27,30[484]. "[T]he addition of ὡς ... will express subjective motive" as in Lk 16,1; 23,14; Acts 3,12; 28,19[485].

'the Christ, the Son of the Blessed One' (vv 61-62) and from Peter's own, earlier confession of Jesus as 'the Christ' (8:29; against M. Ruhland [*Markuspassion* 10], who sees no relation between the contents of Peter's denials and Jesus' confession" (*Mark*, p. 890; M. RUHLAND, *Die Markuspassion aus der Sicht der Verleugnung*, Eilsbrunn, 1987).

475. TAYLOR, *St. Mark*, ²1966, p. 597: "... but it is perhaps probable that Luke's version ... (xxiii.47) is more primitive. Cf. Easton, 353. Plummer, *St. Lk*, 539, thinks there is not much difference in the two expressions". See further UNTERGASSMAIR, *Kreuzweg*, p. 91, n. 410, who observed the phrase is less frequent in the other Gospels.

476. MARSHALL, *Luke*, p. 858.

477. JEREMIAS, *Die Sprache*, p. 303. See also p. 212, where he stated there were 8 uses in Lk and 10 in Acts. See further T. HOLTZ, οὗτος, αὕτη, τοῦτο, in *EWNT* 2, cols. 1341-1343 (= p. 548-549).

478. As also noted by F.F. BRUCE, *Acts*, 1951, p. 450; ³1990, p. 506-507.

479. Bruce maintained this usage was in keeping with the directive given in Acts 4,17 to avoid the name of Jesus (*Acts*, 1951, p. 142).

480. *NTV*, p. 193.

481. Boismard and Lamouille in NEIRYNCK, *Le texte*, p. 330 (= 269).

482. G. SCHNEIDER, ὡς, in *EWNT* 3, cols. 1216-1217 (= 508-509). See also *BADG*, p. 897-899, p. 898: "a quality that exists only in someone's imagination or is based solely on someone's statement". R.T. Robertson and W.H. Davis called attention to this element: "The participle does not state the cause or reason, but only implies it. ... Often in such cases the participle is added to make plain the alleged reason which may or may not be the true one" exemplified by 16,1; 23,14; Acts 2,2 (*RD*, 1931, 1933, §429).

483. *NTV*, p. 422.

484. *BDF* § 425 (3); *BAGD*, p. 423, 898. See also Acts 3,12. Compare also the use of the term ἀποστρέφειν in Acts 3,26; 20,30 *v.l.* (cf. Lk 23,2 διαστρέφειν, where it has the same sense as 23,14; FITZMYER, *Luke*, p. 1484; MARSHALL, *Luke*, p. 858, 859). Comparison should also be made of the phrase ἐν τῷ ἀποστρέφειν with ἐν τῷ τὴν χεῖρά (Acts 4,30) in the passage which referred to Pilate and Herod (BRUCE, *Acts*, p. 115). See further *MGEL*, p. 255-256.

485. *MHT* 3, p. 158. See also ROBERTSON, *Grammar*, p. 966: "But ὡς occurs with the

The term ἀποστρέφω did not occur in Mk, though it occurred in the NT⁴⁸⁶. ἀνασείει τὸν λαόν (23,5) can be compared with ἀνέσεισαν τὸν ὄχλον (Mk 15,11), and ἀνασείω is not found elsewhere in the NT⁴⁸⁷. There are only two instances in the Lukan corpus, once in Lk (23,14) and once in Acts (3,26)⁴⁸⁸. In 23,2 Luke employed διαστρέφω which was also found in 9,41; Acts 13,8.10; 20,30⁴⁸⁹. ἀποστρέφω can be considered a variant for διαστρέφω⁴⁹⁰. The two terms were used in the same sense⁴⁹¹. Whereas in 23,2 τὸ ἔθνος was the object of the subversion, in 23,14 it is τὸν λαόν. This verse can been seen as a condensation of the three charges (23,2) into one⁴⁹². However, one can argue that here "Pilate sums up the main charge of 23:2b, repeated in v. 5 and explained in 23cd"⁴⁹³.

In addition, ἀποστρέφω appears in the LXX, as does διαστρέφω⁴⁹⁴. The expression "this man" is found in LXX Jer 33,11 (κρίσις θανάτου τῷ ἀνθρώπῳ τούτῳ).16 (τῷ ἀνθρώπῳ τούτῳ κρίσις θανάτου), as well as LXX Jer 45,4 (ὁ ἄνθρωπος οὗτος)⁴⁹⁵. ἀποστρέφω appeared shortly before Jer 33,11 in LXX Jer 33,3. Consider also LXX Jer 39,40 where it referred to turning away from God. A verse dealing with the rejection of the message of the prophets is found in LXX Jer 42,15, where God invited the people to turn back from all their evil ways.

participle to give the alleged reason, which may be the real one or mere assumption. ... Cf. Lu. 16,1; Ac. 2:2. But in Lu. 23:14, ὡς ... λαόν, Pilate does not believe the charges against Jesus to be true". Further: "Pilate makes a similar use of ὡς ... λαόν in Lu. 23:14. He declines by the use of ὡς to accept the correctness of the charge of the Sanhedrin against Jesus". Similar usage was indicated for Acts 23,15.20; 27,30 (p. 1141).

486. *GELS*, p. 38. The only other places in the Gospels it occurred were Mt 5,42; 26,52. There are 9 uses in the NT (*NTV*, p. 36).

487. CADBURY, *Style*, p. 99. See BROWN, *Death*, p. 791.

488. J. WEISS, *Lukas*, ⁸1892, p. 641, noted ἀποστρέφειν in Acts 3,26.

489. Consult Boismard and Lamouille in NEIRYNCK, *Le texte*, p. 320 (= 259), who included this in stylistic characteristics of Acts and Lk, citing in addition PLUMMER, *St. Luke*, p. lix, and JEREMIAS, *Die Sprache*, p. 300. See BOISMARD, *Synopse*, t. 2, p. 414.

490. BROWN, *Death*, p. 791.

491. FITZMYER, *Luke*, p. 1484. The adjectival form in 9,41 is considered by Fitzmyer to be a Lukan addition (*Luke*, p. 809). Marshall believed the term was "reminiscent of Dt. 32:5,20" (*Luke*, p. 391), in which case we are considering Septuagintal influence. In commenting on Acts 13,10 Haenchen remarked that almost the entire verse is found in the LXX resulting from a combination of Prov. 10,9 and Hosea 14,10 (*Die Apostelgeschichte*, ¹⁴1965, p. 343, n. 3 = *Acts*, p. 400, n. 3).

492. PLUMMER, *St. Luke*, ⁵1922, p. 524.

493. FITZMYER, *Luke*, p. 1484. In partial agreement, Matera maintained this phrase "recalls διαστρέφοντα τὸ ἔθνος (v. 2)" (*Luke 23,1-25*, p. 547). See also SCHNEIDER, *Political Charge*, p. 408 (= 178), who observed that for Luke the charges can be viewed together in 23,2b.5.14.

494. *MGEL*, p. 26-27, and *GELS*, p. 56; 110.

495. Cf. LXX Jer 22,30: τὸν ἄνδρα τοῦτον. ἄνθρωπος is frequent in the LXX and occurs 550 times in the NT (*GELS*, p. 37). *NTV*, p. 77, listed 550 instances in the NT and indicated that was a corrected number of statistics found in Aland's Wortstatistik published in Vol. 2 of *Völlstandige Konkordanz* (1978) (*NTV*, p. 7).

καὶ ἰδού. Though καὶ ἰδού does not appear in Mk, the evangelist employed ἰδού 7 times. Of those Luke borrowed from Mk twice. Mark employed the word twice in the Gethsemane scene (Mk 14,41.42), a passage which Luke omitted.

καὶ ἰδού, frequent in Lk, is a Septuagintism "since it is found abundantly in the LXX"[496]. "La formule καὶ ἰδού, qui dans la LXX est la traduction de l'expression hébraïque wᵉhinnêh, peut être considérée comme lucanienne. Il nous semble que, même dans les 29 cas d'usage absolu, on ne peut nier la possibilité d'un emploi lucanien"[497]. This phrase constitutes a Lukan characteristic[498]. καὶ ἰδού was also employed in 23,15.

ἐγω ἐνώπιον ὑμῶν ἀνακρίνας. The ἐγώ was added for emphasis. It served to contrast v. 15[499].

The term ἐνώπιον is not found in Mk where the preference is ἔμπροσθεν. Whereas Mk employed ἔμπροσθεν in the Transfiguration account, Luke omitted it (Mk 9,2 / Lk 9,29). Consider also 5,25 ἐνώπιον αὐτῶν preceded by an aorist participle / Mk 2,12 ἔμπροσθεν πάντων; 8,47 diff Mk 5,33; Acts 19,9; 27,35. ἐνώπιον is characteristic of Lukan vocabulary[500]. For ἐνώπιον ὑμῶν consider Acts 4,10[501]. ἐνώπιον is a "Septuagintal equivalent of a preposition, used some

496. FITZMYER, *Luke*, p. 121, believed the phrase originated in Q. See also *BDF*, p. 3, §4[2], and NEIRYNCK, *La matière marcienne*, p. 54, 69, 71, 72, 73 (= *Evangelica*, p. 174, 189, 191, 192, 193). The phrase is found in: 1,20.31.36; 2,25; 5,12.18; 7,12.37; 8,41; 9,30.38.(39); 10,25; 11,31.32.41; 13,11.30; 14,2; 19,2; 23,14.15.50; 24,4.13.49 as well as Acts 5,28; 10,30 (together with ἐσθῆτι λαμπρᾷ); 27,24. See also RADL, *Paulus*, p. 413. See further REID, p. 59: "This abundant use of introductory καὶ ἰδού in every type of Lucan material is most readily explained as coming from the hand of Luke. ... As is the case with other Septuagintisms in Luke, καὶ ἰδού in 9:30 was probably a touch from Luke's pen and reveals nothing about his source" (n. 126). In addition, consult NEIRYNCK, *La matière marcienne*, p. 181 (= ²1989, 91 = *Evangelica*, 61), and *Les accords mineurs et la rédaction des évangiles. L'épisode du paralytique*, in *ETL* 50 (1974) 215-230, esp. p. 225, n. 34 (= *Evangelica*, 781-796, esp. p. 791, n. 34). Jeremias pointed out that the phrase καὶ ἰδοὺ ἀνήρ occurs in the NT only in Lk-Acts (*Die Sprache*, p. 135). See NEIRYNCK, *La matière marcienne*, Note additionnelle, in *Evangelica*, p. 82 (= ²1989, 304), for related information. In addition consult *MGEL*, p. 113. On ἰδού, see *GELS*, p. 212.

497. DENAUX, *L'hypocrisie*, p. 269 (= 1989, p. 179).

498. Boismard and Lamouille in NEIRYNCK, *Le texte*, p. 323 (= 262); NOLLAND, *Luke 18:35-24:53*, p. 1127. See BROWN, *Death*, p. 791, who referred to FITZMYER, *Luke*, p. 121.

499. B. WEISS, *Lukas*, ⁹1901, p. 663. For the phrase καὶ ἰδοὺ ἐγώ, exactly as in 23,14, consider 23,49. See FITZMYER, *Luke*, p. 1584, and B. METZGER, *Textual*, p. 188-189.

500. HAWKINS, *Horae Synopticae*, 1899, p. 15; ²1909, p. 18; TAYLOR, *Passion*, p. 87; RADL, *Paulus*, p. 409; Boismard and Lamouille in NEIRYNCK, *Le texte*, p. 321 (= 260); GOULDER, *Luke*, p. 761, 803; NOLLAND, *Luke 18:35-24:53*, p. 1127. Cf. GREEN, *Death*, p. 83 ("may also be Lukan").

501. For examples of the singular compare 13,26; 15,18.21. Contrast also ἐνώπιον αὐτῶν (24,11.43). B. Weiss pointed out that the term occurred previously in 8,47 (*Lukas*, ⁹1901, p. 662).

35 times in Luke-Acts, once in the other Gospels"[502]. There are approximately 540 instances in the LXX[503].

The term ἀνακρίνω is found in Lk-Acts, but not in the other Gospels[504]. This word can be counted among the list of Lukan stylistic characteristics[505]. Concerning ἀνακρίνας it has been remarked: "In its forensic sense of a judicial investigation the word is peculiar to Lk. in N.T. (Acts iv.9, xii.19, xxiv.8; xxviii.18)"[506]. The word is found 6 times in LXX[507].

οὐθὲν εὗρον. The findings of Pilate (and Herod v. 15 οὐδέν) were contrasted with the those of the Jewish priests, leaders and people[508]. The guilty residents of Jerusalem are juxtaposed with the innocent just one (23,4.14f.22.41.47)[509]. In regard to οὐθέν, we may point back to ἐξουθενήσας (23,11)[510], a term which may be compared with 18,9 and Acts 4,11[511]. On Jesus' innocence see the

---

502. BROWN, *Death*, p. 791. See also FITZMYER, *Luke*, p. 114, and H.A.A. KENNEDY, *Sources of New Testament Greek or The Influence of the Septuagint on the Vocabulary of the New Testament*, Edinburgh, 1895, p. 155, who called attention to the use of the word in the LXX. *MGEL*, p. 81, cited evidence from the LXX prophetic literature concerning its use.

503. H. KRÄMER, ἐνώπιον, in *EWNT* 1, cols. 1130-1131, esp. col. 1130 (= p. 462). See also *GELS*, p. 156, and *MGEL*, p. 81.

504. Lk 23,14; Acts 4,9; 12,19; 17,11; 24,8; 28,18. The noun is found in Acts 25,26. See also GREEN, *Death*, p. 83: "In the NT, only in Luke-Acts is ἀνακρίνω used with its forensic nuance of juridical investigation". Nolland argued it is "likely to be Lukan" (*Luke 18:35-24:53*, p. 1127). It is infrequent in the LXX but occurred in 1 Kg 20,12. See *GELS*, p. 29.

505. RADL, *Paulus*, p. 399; Boismard and Lamouille in NEIRYNCK, *Le texte*, p. 318 (= 257) drew attention also to Jeremias who designated it as a preferred Lukan term (*Die Sprache*, p. 303).

506. PLUMMER, *St. Luke*, ⁵1922, p. 524. He downplayed the idea that the term suggested a preliminary investigation. This was confirmed by Haenchen: "In Attic Greek ἀνακρίνομαι is indeed used of a preliminary enquiry, but Acts 12.9, 24.8 and 28.18 show that in Luke's work it means 'to be put on trial'" (*Acts*, 1971, p. 216, n. 6; see also p. 653, 722 (= *Die Apostelgeschichte*, ¹⁴1965, p. 175, n. 6); see also p. 581, 644-645). See further J. WEISS, *Lukas*, ⁸1892, p. 641; BRUCE, *Acts*, 1951, p. 121; ³1990, p. 151: "ἀνοκρινόμεθα] In Attic Gk., this verb is used of a preliminary inquiry; in Hellenistic Gk, of any legal questioning (cf. 12:19; 24:8; 25:26; 28:18)"; and GOULDER, *Luke*, p. 761.

507. *GELS*, p. 29. E.g. 1 Kings 20,12. It is found 16 times in the NT (*NTV*, p. 31).

508. PLUMMER, *St. Luke*, ⁵1922, p. 524: "Pilate's οὐθὲν εὗρον is in direct contradiction to their εὗραμεν (ver. 2)".

509. F.G. UNTERGASSMAIR, *Der Spruch vom "grünen und dürren Holz"* (*Lk 23,31*), in *SNTU/A* 16 (1991) 55-87, p. 56; cf. G. SCHNEIDER, *Lukas*, Bd. 2, p. 481. Regarding the context, Untergassmair remarked that Luke possessed no other written source for Lk 23,26-32 besides Mk 15,20b.21. He also contended Luke drew on the vocabulary of the LXX in discussing Jerusalem: "Es darf davon ausgegangen werden, dass die Worte über und gegen Jerusalem im Neuen Testament aus dem atl. Reservoir ähnlicher Wrote zum Teil angereichert wurden und vor allem ein atl. Sprachgewand (LXX) übergestülpt bekamen" (UNTERGASSMAIR, *Der Spruch*, p. 82).

510. ZERWICK, *Analysis*, Vol. 1, p. 276. οὐθέν occurred 5 times in the NT, including Acts 15,9 (P.-G. MÜLLER, οὐδείς, in *EWNT* 2, cols. 1323-1325, col. 1323, 1324 (= p. 541-542, p. 541).

511. MARSHALL, *Luke*, p. 856, who also pointed out Jesus' prophecy in Mk 9,12.

similar constructions in Lk 23,4.14.22. Comparison should also be made with the parallel in Paul's experience as described in Acts 13,28[512]; 23,9; 25,25; 26,31[513]; 28,18[514]. On the Pharisees and scribes observing Jesus in order to gather evidence to incriminate him see 6,7 (diff Mk 3,2).

The word εὑρίσκω is a preferred Lukan term[515] and was used forensically[516]. It was employed in the Markan account of the Sanhedrin trial (Mk 14,55) describing the attempt to obtain testimony against Jesus, information which Luke elected to omit[517]. However, another form of εὑρίσκω was used at 23,2 where the whole company, referring to those mentioned previously in the account of the Sanhedrin trial, brought Jesus Pilate. In addition, Luke borrowed εὗρον from Mk 14,16 in his account of the preparation for the Passover at the beginning of the passion narrative (22,13). The term recurred in 23,23 and the phrase ἐν τῷ ἀνθρώπῳ τούτῳ appeared exactly as in 23,4[518]. εὑρίσκω occurs 613 times in the LXX[519].

αἴτιον ὧν κατηγορεῖτε. The term αἴτιος is found only in the Lukan corpus (23,4.14.22; Acts 19,40)[520]. αἴτιος can be included among the characteristic language of Lk-Acts[521]. The use in the Gospel can be distinguished from that of Acts[522]. αἴτιον in 23,4.14.22 and αἰτία in Acts 13,28; 28,18 et passim is

512. BRUCE, Acts, 1951, p. 267-268; ³1990, p. 308; BARRETT, Acts, p. 640.

513. BRUCE, Acts, 1951, p. 450; ³1990, p. 506-507: "Here and in v. 32 Luke emphasizes the official agreement on Paul's innocence of the crimes alleged against him; cf. Antipas and Pilate's agreement on Jesus' innocence in Lk. 23:14f.".

514. See MATERA, Luke 23,1-25, p. 540. Boismard also highlighted similarities of the Gospel with Acts 13,28; 24,8; 25,18; and 28,18 (Synopse, t. 2, p. 414). On Acts 28,18 Conzelmann remarked: "A summary, in Lukan language" (Acts, 1987, p. 227).

515. RADL, Paulus, p. 411; GOULDER, Luke, p. 804.

516. H. PEDERSEN, εὑρίσκω, in EWNT 2, cols. 206-212, esp. col. 211 (= p. 82-84, p. 84); SCHNEIDER, Political Charge, p. 410 (= 180).

517. See also Mk 14,37 / 22,45. Commenting on Mk 1,37 Taylor wrote: "καὶ εὗρον αὐτὸν λέγουσιν is so characteristically Markan" (St. Mark, ²1966, p. 183).

518. On Septuagintal occurrences see GELS, p. 189.

519. GELS, p. 189.

520. So also PLUMMER, St. Luke, ⁵1922, p. 521: "αἴτιον = αἰτία is peculiar to Lk., and is always combined with a negative: vv. 14, 22; Acts xix.40". See HAWKINS, Horae Synopticae, 1899, p. 167; ²1909, p. 203. Boismard distinguished between αἰτία in Jn and Acts but αἴτιον in Lk (Synopse, t. 2, p. 414). In the LXX see 1 Kg 22,22. Consult GELS, p. 13, which listed Gen 4,13; 1 Erz 2,17; 1 Mac 9,10 for αἰτία, and 1 Sm 22,22; 2 Mac 4,47; 13,4; 4 Mac 1,11 for αἴτιον.

521. Boismard and Lamouille in NEIRYNCK, Le texte, p. 317 (= 256). He referred to PLUMMER, Luke, 1896, ³1901; HAWKINS, Horae Synopticae, 1899, p. 167 and ²1909, p. 175; VOGEL, Zur Charakteristik, ²1899, p. 61; and JEREMIAS, Die Sprache, p. 300(-301). See also RADL, Paulus, p. 397.

522. MHT 2, p. 341: "... adjectival abstracts in -ιον expressing a state or attribute. The change in relation to verbal action may account partly for the two meanings of αἴτιον in Ac. 19:40 (= cause) and in Luke 23:4.14.22 (= crime)".

evidence of Luke's "tendency to slight variation"[523]. The word was found in the
triple declaration of Jesus' innocence. Mk contained αἰτίας in the crucifixion (Mk
15,26 diff. Lk 23,38)[524]. It is likely this Mark term inspired Luke. Since he
described the charges against Jesus in other terms (23,2.5), the statement became
an affirmation in the Lukan view rather than a charge or criminal offense[525]. This
apologetic was paralleled in Paul's experience (Acts 25,18.27; 28,18)[526]. οὐδὲν
αἴτιον has been assigned to Lukan vocabulary[527]. The term αἴτιος occurs 8 times
in LXX[528]. The phrase οὐθὲν ... αἴτιον appears to be Lukan redaction[529].

ὧν κατηγορεῖτε. "ὧν is abbreviated from τούτων ὧν"[530]. See Acts 24,8;
25,11[531].

---

523. H.J. CADBURY, *Four Features of Lucan Style*, in L.E. KECK, and J.L. MARTYN (eds.),
Studies in Luke Acts. FS P. SCHUBERT, Nashville, TN, 1966; London, 1968; Philadelphia, PA,
1980, 87-102, p. 94. See further BARRETT, *Acts*, p. 640: "αἰτία is frequently found in forensic
speech; αἰτία θανάτου is *causa capitalis* (BA 50[W. BAUER, *Griechisch-Deutsches Wörterbuch
zu den Schriften des Neuen Testament und der frühchristlichen Literatur*, K. ALAND and B.
ALAND (eds.), Berlin - NY, ⁶1988, p. 50]), a capital charge; what could not be found was the
evidence to prove it". Concerning the use of αἰτία, there are 21 instances in the LXX (*GELS*,
p. 13) and 20 in the NT (*NTV*, p. 73).

524. Note the use of αἰτία in 8,47. Marshall identified the use of διά with αἰτία as being
Lukan citing its additional use in Acts 10,21; 22,24; 28,18 (*Luke*, p. 346). See further
CONZELMANN, *Die Mitte*, 117-124 (= 137-144); RADL, *Paulus*, 252-265, 325-345; RADL, αἰτία,
in *EWNT* 1, cols. 104-105, esp. col. 104 (= p. 43-44).

525. So also RADL, αἰτία, *EWNT* 1, cols. 104-105, col. 104 (= p. 44): "... it is surely
intentional that in his version of the inscription over the cross Luke (23:38; Mark and Matthew
present it differently) does not speak of an αἰτία".

526. MATERA, *Luke 23,1-25*, p. 548, detected the similarity between 23,13 and Paul's
experience detailed in Acts 28,18.

527. GOULDER, *Luke*, p. 761, 800. Swete pointed out that αἰτία was also found in Acts
13,28; 25,18 (*The Gospel According to St. Mark*, 1898, ²1902, 1908 ("reprinted with slight
changes").

528. *GELS*, p. 13, in comparison with 5 times in the NT (*NTV*, p. 73). On the use in LXX,
see for example 1 Kg 22,22 and 2 Mac 13,4.

529. JEREMIAS, *Die Sprache*, p. 303.

530. MARSHALL, *Luke*, p. 859. See also Robertson remarked on this phenomenon. "*Verbs
of Accusing and Condemning*. Blass observed that the old Greek usage of the genitive of the thing
has well-nigh vanished in the N.T. ... However, in the case of κατηγορέω we do find ὧν in Lu.
23:14 and Acts 25:11 but in each instance the genitive seems to be due to attraction to the case
of the suppressed antecedent τούτων. Cf. Ac. 24:13 for περί. Still the point is not absolutely
certain and ὧν could be due to κατηγορέω. ... Cf. also Mk 15:3 where we have the genitive and
accusative, κατηγόρουν αὐτοῦ πολλά" (*A Grammar of the Greek New Testament in the Light of
Historical Research*, ⁴1934, p. 511; also p. 720). Consider also GUNDRY, *Mark*, p. 933: "... for
κατηγόρουν, 'were accusing,' already has an object of the person in the genitive αὐτοῦ, 'him,'
so that πολλά would have to be an accusative of general reference, 'concerning many things,'
if it were not an adverbial accusative of degree. But nowhere else in the NT does κατηγορέω take
an accusative of general reference".

531. H.A.W. MEYER, *Handbuch über die Apostelgeschichte* (KEK), (ed. H.H. WENDT),
Göttingen, ⁵1880, p. 492. Cf. H.A.W. MEYER, *Handbook to the Acts of the Apostles*, tr. P.J.

The word κατηγορέω was previously used in 23,2. κατηγορέω is counted among the Lukan stylistic characteristics[532]. It was found in Mk 15,3.4 in the context of the charges and accusations of the chief priests[533], and is also used in the LXX[534]. The term is more frequent in Lk-Acts (Lk 6,7; 11,54 v.l.; 23,2.10.14; Acts 22,30; 24,2.8.13.19; 25,5.11.16; 28,18).

κατ' αὐτοῦ. It occurred in Mk 3,6 referring to the conspiracy of the Pharisees and Herodians against Jesus. κατά plus the genitive is used in a hostile sense as, for example, in Mk 9,40 (/ 9,50)[535]. The Markan Sanhedrin account (Mk 14,56.57) contained two examples of this expression. κατ' αὐτοῦ is a hapax in Lk. In Acts this phrase was employed in the account of Paul's trial (Acts 25,3.15.[both with αἰτούμενοι]27[with αἰτίας])[536].

Verse 15

ἀλλ' οὐδὲ Ἡρῴδης, ἀνέπεμψεν γὰρ αὐτὸν πρὸς ἡμᾶς, καὶ ἰδοὺ οὐδὲν ἄξιον θανάτου ἐστὶν πεπραγμένον αὐτῷ·
"neither did Herod, for he sent him back to us. Behold, nothing deserving of death has been done by him";

This verse is key to interpreting the Herod episode[537]. What is the relation of v.

GLOAG and W.P. DICKSON, New York - London, 1883, p. 456 (= [4]1869, *Handbuch*).

532. Boismard and Lamouille in NEIRYNCK, *Le texte*, p. 324 (= 263).

533. It also appeared earlier in Mk (Mk 3,2) in the account of Jesus healing a man with a withered hand in the context of a Sabbath controversy. There it was the Pharisees and the Herodians who conspired against him (Mk 3,6).

534. *GELS*, p. 249, where it was reported that the term surfaced 6 times in the LXX. It was employed 23 times in the NT (*NTV*, p. 51).

535. W. KÖHLER, κατά, in *EWNT* 2, 624-627, col. 625 (= p. 253-254, esp. p. 254). See also B. WEISS, *Lukas*, [9]1901, p. 663. See further ROBERTSON, *Grammar*, [4]1934, p. 560: "A similar rarity as to repetition exists in the case of κατά, but we note κατηγορεῖτε κατ' αὐτοῦ (Lu. 23:14)".

536. Also Acts 14,2; 19,16 (plural); 21,28. Of the hostile sense of κατά alone see Acts 24,1; 25,2, both concerning Paul. Compare the use of the term + genitive in the local sense in Lk 4,14; 23,5. See further *BAGD*, p. 405, § β, and *BDF*, § 225: "Κατά with genitive is far less strongly attested; it most often means 'against someone' (in a hostile sense). It does not appear often in a local sense: ... 'throughout' (only in Lk, Acts and always with ὅλος) ...".

537. CONZELMANN, *Die Mitte*, p. 72, n. 1 (= 86, n. 2): "Den Sinn der Herodesszene spricht V. 15 aus. Herodes stellt durch einen symbolischen Akt die politische Harmlosigkeit Jesu fest. Er und Pilatus arbeiten sich in die Hände - daher V. 12. Das erhoffte Schauspiel kann Herodes jetzt sowenig zu 'sehen' bekommen als früher". Notice his elaboration of Herod's attestation of Jesus' innocence: "Er nimmt also eine gewisse Mittelstellung ein (sofern er auf der anderen Seite die Unschuld bestätigt - darauf kommt dem Lukas viel an)" (p. 72 = 87). Note also the view of NOLLAND, *Luke 18:35-24:53*, p. 1127: "πεπαγμένον, 'has been done,' and καὶ ἰδού (lit. 'And behold') are the only clearly Lukan contributions to this verse, but the question must be raised whether Luke has formulated the verse to bind his narrative scenes more closely together. This is the more likely because its presence makes for a fourfold affirmation by Pilate of Jesus' innocence (though this one, indirectly, is Herod's statement and is probably intended by Luke to

15 to the rest of the pericope? "The Herod scene also is tied to its narrower context at 23:15, where Pilate mentions that Herod too found Jesus innocent"[538]. Though studies which attempted to assign a color to the splendid garment must be rejected, nonetheless from the context it signified innocence since Herod offered no verbal report[539]. Further, the significance of the dual witness of Herod and Pilate was not persuasive because of the Jewish law requiring two witnesses (Dt 19,15), "but because of their status. The facts that Herod has been ill-disposed toward Jesus (9:7-9; 13:31-33), that Jesus had not responded to him to win his favor, and that Herod had treated him with contempt and mockery make Herod's refusal to condemn him all the more impressive"[540].

ἀλλ᾽ οὐδέ is also found in Acts 19,2[541]. It has been argued unconvincingly that this phrase should be rendered: "But not so Herod"[542]. In Mk 13,32 Mark employed οὐδέ to indicate that not even the angels knew the time of coming of the

establish a parallel between Pilate and Herod as witnesses to Jesus' innocence [cf. Schneider, 'Verfahren' 128]".

Some similarity with 19,34 might be observed where "Luke does not hesitate to repeat (dramatically) the proleptically provided answer. It enhances his picture of Jesus drawing near to his destiny" (FITZMYER, p. 1250). In much the same way, Luke did not hesitate to allow Pilate to voice Herod's finding through indirect discourse. This had already been proleptically asserted in the predictions such as 17,25; 18,32. Compare, too, the reference to garments (19,35) and the report that the people of Jerusalem praise God for the "mighty works they had seen" (19,37), a reaction far different from that of Herod. In 19,35 Luke substituted ἐπιρίπτω, a term found in LXX 2 Sam 20,21 and 1 Kg 19,19, for Mark's ἐπίβαλλω.

Attention should be paid to Luke's use of indirect discourse. For example, while Mark was content simply to state that the people who witnessed the exorcism of the Gerasene demoniac "told what had happened" (Mk 5,16), Luke redacted the passage to make clear what had transpired. The witnesses "told them how he who had been possessed with demons was healed" (8,36). The use of indirect discourse is also found in the Lukan resurrection account (24,6-7), making this a recollection of "what was said by Jesus in Galilee. This rephrasing preserves an association of the risen Christ with 'Galilee,' but only by way of recollection" (FITZMYER, p. 1545). It also emphasized Jesus' prophetic role as well as the prophecy/fulfillment motif (JOHNSON, Luke, p. 388).

538. DARR, Glorified, p. 281. So BROWN, Death, p. 775: "In 23:14-15 Pilate will interpret Herod's sending Jesus back as a sign of Jesus' innocence".

539. BROWN, Death, p. 776-777.

540. Ibid., p. 777.

541. See ROBERTSON, Grammar, 1914, ⁴1923, p. 1186: "In Ac. 19:2, ἀλλ᾽ οὐδ᾽, the thought answers the preceding question and is probably adversative, as is possible in 1 Cor. 3:3. The ἀλλά at any rate is negative like the οὐδέ. So as to ἀλλ᾽ οὐδὲ Ἡρῴδης (Lu. 23:15)". See BD, p. 233, § 448. Both Plummer and Creed took this phrase to mean "no, nor yet Herod" (PLUMMER, Luke, ⁵1922, p. 524, and CREED, Luke, p. 282-283). DARR, Glorified, p. 299, translated it as "neither did Herod". Jeremias regarded this phrase as traditional (Die Sprache, p. 303). In LXX Job 32,21 we find the phrase ἀλλὰ μὴν οὐδέ which included an intensifying particle. On ἀλλά along in the LXX, see GELS, p. 19-20.

542. HARLOW, Destroyer, p. 236. His interpretation was followed by F.C. GRANT, Review in ATR 19 (1937) 146. Cf. B. WEISS, Lukas, ⁹1901, p. 663: "Dass οὐδέ ausdrücklich besage: auch nicht einmal Herod".

Son of Man⁵⁴³. Luke omitted this in his parallel (cf. Lk 21,33). ἀλλά is a stronger adversative than δέ and he included οὐδέ to strengthen that even more, much as was found in 18,13 (cf. Acts 7,5)⁵⁴⁴. It appears he used this for rhetorical intensification to emphasize that not only did Pilate find Jesus innocent, but not even Herod, who sought to bring him harm (13,31), found him guilty⁵⁴⁵.

ἀνέπεμψεν γὰρ αὐτὸν πρὸς ἡμᾶς. The term ἀνέπεμψεν, exactly as in 23,7.11 would seem to be redaction⁵⁴⁶. See comments above on 23,7.11.

The word γάρ is frequent in the NT⁵⁴⁷ and there is reason to identify it as Lukan vocabulary⁵⁴⁸. See the discussion at 23,8.12. It was used in Mk 15,14 where Pilate inquired of the crowd which had been incited by the chief priests, what evil Jesus had done.

πρὸς ἡμᾶς, though used differently in Mk 6,3, was omitted by Lk (cf. Lk 4,22)⁵⁴⁹. πρὸς + the accusative is Lukan⁵⁵⁰.

καὶ ἰδού. See above on 23,14.

οὐδὲν ἄξιον θανάτου. Mark related the account of Jesus before the Sanhedrin (Mk 14,53-65) declaring that no testimony was presented that would result in a verdict of death (Mk 14,55). Luke omitted this in his description (cf. 22,66-71). The Markan account of Jesus before Pilate did not make it explicit that Jesus had done nothing deserving of death (Mk 15,14)⁵⁵¹. Luke repeated this phrase with only a slight variation and added yet a third attestation of Jesus' innocence by Pilate (Lk 23,22: τί γὰρ κακὸν ἐποίησεν οὗτος; οὐδὲν αἴτιον θανάτου εὗρον ἐν αὐτῷ; cf. Lk 23,4.14)⁵⁵². In the Markan account it was rather the high priest, together with the chief priests, elders and scribes who condemned Jesus as deserving death (Mk 14,64: οἱ δὲ πάντες κατέκρινον αὐτὸν ἔνοχον εἶναι θανάτου)⁵⁵³. But Luke did not include this judgment in 22,71⁵⁵⁴. Already in

543. Cf. Mk 12,10.
544. H. BALZ, οὐδέ, in *EWNT* 2, col. 1322 (= p. 541); also *BAGD*, p. 591; RADL, *Paulus*, p. 398.
545. See DARR, *Glorified*, p. 300: "Even Jesus' enemy, the notorious Herod, agrees with Pilate that the accused is not guilty". So also MATERA, *Luke 23,1-25*, p. 545: "The witness of Herod is especially powerful since he is otherwise portrayed as one who has recently sought to kill Jesus. If even Jesus' enemies acknowledge his innocence, how innocent must he be!".
546. JEREMIAS, *Die Sprache*, p. 303; cf. GREEN, *Death*, p. 83.
547. Total in the NT: 1041. Of these: Mt 124; Mk 66; Lk 97; Acts 80.
548. RADL, *Paulus*, p. 402. In addition, it occurred 1529 times in the LXX (*GELS*, p. 86).
549. Cf. 7,20: Ἰωάννης ὁ βαπτιστὴς ἀπέστειλεν ἡμᾶς πρὸς σὲ λέγων.
550. CADBURY, *Style*, p. 203; TAYLOR, *Passion*, p. 87; RADL, *Paulus*, p. 425. It is also found in the special Lukan material, in the parable of the rich man and Lazarus (16,26), and a Q text (12,41).
551. So also the findings of the chief priests and the whole council (Mk 14,55).
552. See UNTERGASSMAIR, *Kreuzweg*, p. 74, n. 317, who compared Acts 26,31 with Lk 23,22 as well as Acts 23,29; 26,20.
553. Already the third passion prediction included the information that Jesus would be condemned to death (Mk 10,33). Luke elected not to borrow this detail (Lk 18,31). On the anarthrous use of θάνατος, see ROBERTSON, *Grammar*, ⁴1923, p. 794.
554. It should be noted that in the parallel to the third Markan passion prediction (Mk 10,33)

Mk 14,55 (εἰς τὸ θανατῶσαι αὐτόν) a conspiracy was announced seeking a way to kill Jesus. Since the phrase οὐδὲν ἄξιον θανάτου was unique to Lk-Acts it is likely redaction[555]. On Luke's use of θάνατος consider also Jesus' prediction of Peter's denial: μετὰ σοῦ ... εἰς θάνατον πορεύεσθαι (22,33) as opposed to Mk 14,31: συναποθανεῖν σοι.

A parallel with 23,15 exists in Paul's trial before Festus (Acts 25,11: ἄξιον θανάτου πέπραχά τι[556]; cf. Acts 13,28) where Paul insisted on his own innocence[557]. This was underscored in Acts 25,25 where Festus declared Paul was not guilty: ἐγὼ δὲ κατελαβόμην μηδὲν ἄξιον αὐτὸν θανάτου πεπραχέναι[558]. This served as a reprise of Paul's appearance before and judgment by the governor Felix (Acts 23,29: μηδὲν δὲ ἄξιον θανάτου ἢ δεσμῶν ἔχοντα ἔγκλημα). Festus then presented Paul's case to Herod Agrippa (Acts 25,18)[559]. Acts 25,16 speaks of the opportunity the accused had to make a defense (ἀπολογία) against the charge[560]. Similar phrases are also found in Acts 25,25; 26,31; 28,18[561].

"In Luke 23:15 and most of the occurrences in Acts the word [ἄξιος] is used in a negative sense to denote the appropriateness of captial punishment for a particular crime"[562]. In special Lukan material one of the thieves crucified with Jesus made a similar confession (Lk 23,41: ἄξια γὰρ ὧν ἐπράξαμεν ἀπολαμβάνομεν· οὗτος δὲ οὐδὲν ἄτοπον ἔπραξεν; cf. Mk 15,32b)[563]. The first occurrence of the term in Lk is 3,8 (Q), in the context of the preaching of John the

Luke omitted the phrase κατακρινοῦσιν αὐτὸν θανάτῳ (cf. 18,31-32).

555. JEREMIAS, *Die Sprache*, p. 303.
556. BRUCE, *Acts*, 1951, p. 432; ³1990, p. 488: "Even after the εἰ the negative οὐδέν is preferred to μηδέν as denoting greater absoluteness: 'nothing at all'". See οὐδέν which occurs in Acts 25,10.
557. So also B. WEISS, *Lukas*, ⁹1901, p. 663. See further SCHNEIDER, *Die Apostelgeschichte*, T. 2, p. 359, n. 35.
558. MARSHALL, *Luke*, p. 859.
559. See HAENCHEN, *Die Apostelgeschichte*, ¹⁴1965, p. 576, 603 (= *Acts*, p. 648, 677). See further, W. BIEDER, θάνατος in *EWNT* 2, col. 319-328, esp. cols. 324-326 (= p. 129-133, esp. p. 131-132).
560. See U. KELLERMANN, ἀπολογία, in *EWNT* 1, cols. 329-330 (= p. 137). See Lk 12,11 Q; cf. Mt 10,19 and 21,14 (cf. Mk 13,11).
561. Consider MATERA, *Luke 23,1-25*, p. 540.
562. P. TRUMMER, ἄξιος, in *EWNT* 1, cols. 271-272 (= p. 113). He asserted the term was "very rare in the LXX" but "frequent in the papyri".
563. MARSHALL, *Luke*, p. 872, recognized the presence of Lukan redaction in 23,41 though he insisted: "This last statement may be Lucan in wording, but the Jewish sentiment expressed in the first part makes it unlikely that the whole saying is due to Luke". UNTERGASSMAIR, *Kreuzweg*, p. 74-76, esp. p. 74, took heed of the "auffallender wörtlicher Übereinstimmung" of 23,41 with 23,15 as well as Acts 25,11.25; 26,31. Brown maintained it was "not impossible to think of the scene [23,40-43] as a Lucan theological creation", but he seemed to favor the idea that Luke developed the account from some aspect of "independent tradition" (*Death*, p. 1001). He doubted Luke took the episode from a source (p. 1002). He further observed that the pattern "in answer ... said" was Lukan and reflected LXX usage (p. 1002, n. 51).

Baptist. Synonymous expressions occurred in various parts of Acts, particularly employing the term ἄτοπος, which also is found in the LXX[564]. ἄξιος is a Lukan term[565], which is also found 41 times in the LXX[566].

ἐστὶν πεπραγμένον αὐτῷ. πράσσειν is considered to be typically Lukan[567]. The construction εἶναι + perfect participle, as found here and in 1,7, is considered by some to be redaction[568]. The periphrastic perfect indicating extensive use signifies a completed act[569]. What is of particular importance was that Luke showed a preference for it[570]. In the first instance in the Gospel the term was used in a pericope concerning the Baptist. The context of its use in 19,23 was a discussion at the Last Supper as to which of the disciples would betray Jesus. The penitent thief at the crucifixion contrasts the wrongdoing of the two thieves with the innocence of Jesus (23,41). The aorist form of the term is found twice in the account of the two thieves.

In Acts 3,17 Peter addressed the people of Israel and declared that they acted out of ignorance, as did their rulers (οἱ ἄρχοντες) in crucifying Jesus[571]. In the description of the uproar in Thessalonica (Acts 17,7) the accusation was made against Paul and other Christians that "they are all acting against the decrees of Caesar, saying that there is another king, Jesus". That is reminiscent of the charges raised in Lk 23,2.3.

"[T]he verb πράσσω occurs 39 times in the NT, half in the Lukan literature (6 in Lk, 13 in Acts)"[572]. Its use is similar to that in secular Greek and in the

---

564. UNTERGASSMAIR, *Kreuzweg*, p. 76. See for example *GELS*, p. 70, and *MGEL*, p. 21.

565. VOGEL, *Zur Charakteristik*, p. 65: θανάτου ἄξιον (αἴτιον, αἰτία); RADL, *Paulus*, p. 400; Boismard and Lamouille in NEIRYNCK, *Le texte*, p. 318 (= 257).

566. *GELS*, p. 43.

567. TAYLOR, *Passion*, p. 87; RADL, *Paulus*, p. 425; JEREMIAS, *Die Sprache*, p. 289; Boismard and Lamouille in NEIRYNCK, *Le texte*, p. 327 (= 266).

568. JEREMIAS, *Die Sprache*, p. 303, 24. He cited 8 examples where Luke introduced this construction in material taken over from Mk (5,17 / Mk 2,2; 5,18 / Mk 2,3; 9,32 / Mk 9,4; 9,34 / Mk 9,32; 18,34 / Mk 10,34; 20,6 / Mk 11,32; 23,51 / Mk 15,43; 23,55 / Mk 15,47) (p. 24, n. 40).

569. ROBERTSON, *Grammar*, ⁴1923, p. 903.

570. ROBERTSON and DAVIS, *New Short Grammar*, p. 381, § 461 (a): "This idiom [the periphrastic conjugation] is common, rather more so in the vernacular than in the literary Attic, and in the New Testament an increase due also to the influence of the LXX and the Aramaic fondness for the idiom. Luke, in particular, is fond of it". In addition to 23,12 mention is made of 13,10.11. See further the discussion the instrumental case. Other instances of the instrumental case included 7,38 and Acts 12,2 (p. 241, § 346 (f)). Jeremias also identified εἶναι + perfect participle construction as redaction. In addition he cited 1,7 (*Die Sprache*, p. 303; see also p. 24).

571. See SCHNEIDER, *Die Apostelgeschichte*, T. 1, p. 322, n. 73.

572. G. SCHNEIDER, πράσσω, in *EWNT* 3, cols. 349-351, esp. col. 349 (= p. 145-146, esp. p. 145). The term πράσσω occurred 6 times in Lk (3,13[deals with John the Baptist]; 19,23; 22,23; 23,15.41bis) and 13 times in Acts (Acts 3,17; 5,35; 15,29; 16,28; 17,7; 19,19.36; 25,11.25; 26,9.20.26.31). See TAYLOR, *Passion*, p. 87, and GREEN, *Death*, p. 83: "Πράσσω, ... is probably Lukan ... On the other hand, its use in the Third Gospel does not point unambiguously to Lukan redaction". Consider further UNTERGASSMAIR, *Kreuzweg*, p. 75.

LXX since God was never the subject and it referred only to human actions[573]. In Lk the term is found in the Baptist's instructions to tax collectors (3,13) immediately prior to his advice to the soldiers. It was used in the Lukan account of the Lord's supper in reference to the betrayal (22,23). πράσσω was one of the elements in this verse whose "whole construction is clearly Lucan"[574].

The largest concentration of πράσσω occurs in the description of Paul's activities in Acts 25-26. The language of Acts 25,11(πέπραχά)[575].25; 26,31 is especially reminiscent of 23,15. This phrase in Acts 25,11 could be possibly translated as "in his case"[576]. The combination of ἄξια and πράσσοντας is found in Acts 26,20. The exact form as in 23,15 is found in Acts in the account of Paul's appeal to Herod Agrippa (Acts 26,26). As in Lk where Jesus' innocence was attested by two rulers, so in Acts Paul's innocence was affirmed by two political figures, initially a governor, then a king (Acts 25,11; 26,31).

It will also be recalled that Herod originally did what he could to protect the Baptist (Mk 6,20). Later, he ordered the death of that prophet. The parallel with Jesus, while not exact, shows that Herod was protective in rendering a decision of innocence, though he ultimately did nothing to prevent the execution. Similarities of what transpired after the deaths of the Baptist and Jesus should not be overlooked[577].

Verse 16

παιδεύσας οὖν αὐτὸν ἀπολύσω.

"I will therefore chastise him and release him".

Luke probably had Mk 15,15 in mind in composing v.16[578]. This statement in its entirety was repeated in 23,22[579]. Mk 15,15 reported that Pilate had Jesus

---

573. 1 Mac 10,35: οὐχ ἕξει ἐξουσίαν οὐδεὶς πράσσειν. See also 2 Mac 6,22: ἵνα τοῦτο πράξας ἀπολυθῇ θανάτου. Note further, *GELS*, p. 392. The term appeared 39 times in the NT (*NTV*, p. 163).

574. MARSHALL, *Luke*, p. 810.

575. *Ibid.*, p. 859.

576. *MIBNTG*, p. 204, and *MHT* 3, p. 240. On the infrequent use of the dative of agent see *MHT* 3, p. 240. Note this unusual form was also found in GP 11: τοῖς ἀγαπωμένοις. See also *BDF*, p. 102, § 191; *MHT* 2, p. 459; ROBERTSON, *Grammar*, ⁴1923, p. 534, 542; DANA and MANTEY, *Manual*, p. 161; ZERWICK, *Biblical Greek*, p. 21, § 59. J.A. BROOKS and C.L. WINBERY, *Syntax of New Testament Greek*, Washington, D.C., 1979, p. 45, called attention to this instance of the instrumental of agency as an example of the substantive without a preposition. A.T. ROBERTSON and W.H. DAVIS, *A New Short Grammar of the Greek Testament for Students Familiar with the Elements of Greek*, New York, 1931, p. 245, § 347 (g), insist "it cannot be clearly determined whether we have dative of personal agent or the instrumental case in Lu. 23:15". But cf. p. 241, § 346 (f), where it was identified as the instrumental case.

577. Mk 6,29; 15,45-46; Lk 23,53.

578. See B. WEISS, *Lukas*, ⁹1901, p. 663, though Nolland interpreted v. 16 as reflecting a "pre-Lukan character" in view of Jn 19,1 (*Luke 18:35-24:53*, p. 1127).

579. As also noted by GOULDER, *Luke*, p. 761, and NOLLAND, *Luke 18:35-24:53*, p. 1127.

scourged (φραγελλώσας)⁵⁸⁰. Consider the use of μαστιγώσουσιν in the third passion prediction (Mk 10,34 / Lk 18,33).

Among the gospels παιδεύω is found only in Lk (23,16.22). It also occurred twice in Acts: 7,22; 22,3, though with a different sense⁵⁸¹. It has been argued that because of the scarce use "there is little basis for attributing the word to Luke"⁵⁸². However, that scarcity has lead others to conclude the word is one of the Lukan stylistic characteristics in Lk-Acts⁵⁸³.

παιδεύω is also used frequently in the LXX⁵⁸⁴, especially in 3 Kgdms 12,11.14 (= 1 Kgs); 2 Chr 10,11.14⁵⁸⁵. It is employed in the LXX prophetic literature with the meaning "to teach [a] lesson by way of punishment, to discipline"⁵⁸⁶. Several reasons could have prompted Luke's redactional change. If, as we believe, Luke wished to portray Jesus as a prophet, what better way than to draw on vocabulary from the prophetic writings. There is merit to the proposal that the term was a linguistic reminiscence of LXX Is 53,5 (παιδεία)⁵⁸⁷. Recall that Luke referred to Is 53,7 in Acts 8,32-35, confirming that Luke had the verse in mind⁵⁸⁸. If Luke was intent on portraying Jesus as the prophet of God, then Luke may have looked to the prophetic literature. The possibility of Lukan redaction of Mk is a reasonable consideration⁵⁸⁹. Also since Luke made great efforts to cast Jesus in the role of a teacher, he continued to include irony in his material where Pilate will now attempt to discipline/teach Jesus⁵⁹⁰.

---

580. See H. BALZ, φραγελλόω, in *EWNT* 3, col. 1047 (= p. 437): "φραγελλώσας; Luke 23,25 weakens this".

581. MARSHALL, *Luke*, p. 859. Also G. SCHNEIDER, παιδεύω, in *EWNT* 3, cols. 7-8, esp. col. 8 (= p. 3-4, esp. p. 4, §2). See in addition GREEN, *Death*, p. 83-84.

582. GREEN, *Death*, p. 83-84. On the basis of Jn 19,1-12 he argued the idea of a scourging as a compromise was pre-Lukan. What is more, "the remaining terminology of this verse offers no help for pointing to Luke's possible source(s)" (p. 84).

583. Boismard and Lamouille in NEIRYNCK, *Le texte*, p. 326 (= 265). See also WALASKAY, *And So*, p. 44.

584. H.A.A. KENNEDY, *Sources*, p. 155. See also *GELS*, p. 346, which listed 88 instances. There are 13 uses in the NT (*NTV*, p. 153).

585. *BAGD*, p. 603-604, p. 604; MARSHALL, *Luke*, p. 859; G. SCHNEIDER, παιδεύω, in *TDNT* 3, p. 3-4, p. 4; FITZMYER, *Luke*, p. 1485. See also JOHNSON, *Luke*, p. 370, who referred to 1 Kg 12,11.14 but then 2 Chr 14,12 [sic: not listed in *HR*, p. 1047]; BROWN, *Death*, p. 792-793. See further *BDF* §5.1b.

586. *MGEL*, p. 181.

587. STUHLMUELLER, *Luke*, p. 161; cf. MARSHALL, *Luke*, p. 859.

588. See above. JOHNSON, *Luke*, p. 367.

589. MARSHALL, *Luke*, p. 859: "The word may indicate a less severe punishment than φραγελλόω, which is used in Mk. 15:15 of the scourging which was a preliminary to the crucifixion; here an alternative to crucifixion is in mind ...".

590. Would Luke have ironically intended to suggest that Pilate could educate Jesus who had been "teaching throughout all Judea, from Galilee even to this place" (23,5)? On the redactional focus of Luke on Jesus' teaching see MATERA, *Luke 23,1-25*, p. 540, 551.

Thirdly, the change could have been made in light of the Roman apologetic[591]. It has been observed that 23,16.22 "is a substitution for Mark 15:15"[592]. Luke could have substituted παιδεύω for a Latinism[593]. In addition, this could reflect an effort to reduce the violence directed toward Jesus[594]. When this is read in conjunction with 23,25, that view may be strengthened[595]. 23,16 can be compared with Acts 16,22-28; 22,24, in which case this would serve as another Paul and Jesus parallel[596]. Luke's apologetic toward Rome likely influenced his redaction here.

οὖν. The last use of the term prior to 23,16 was in the Sanhedrin account (22,70)[597]. Though infrequent in Mk it is found in Mk 15,12 when Pilate addressed the crowds as to whom they wished to be released[598]. Its use here highlighted Pilate's conclusion reached as a result of the proceedings and his consultation from Herod. The term is found 61 times in Acts, of which 9 of those were found in Acts 25–26, the account of Paul's trial (Acts 25,1.4.5.11.17.23; 26,4.9.22)[599]. οὖν has been identified as characteristic of Lk-Acts

591. Consider BROWN, *Death*, p. 793: "Luke knew Mark's account where Jesus is flogged by the Romans; he softens that to an offer by Pilate (seemingly not carried out) of whipping".

592. SCHNEIDER, παιδεύω, in *EWNT* 3, col. 8 (= p. 4): "In light of the fact that Luke 23:16, 22 is a substitution for Mark 15:15 (par. Matt 27:26 φραγελλώσας), it is doubtful that Luke intended with the phrase παιδεύσας οὖν αὐτὸν ἀπολύσω (Luke 23:16, 22) to express an actual and intentional 'flogging' of Jesus (cf. παιδεύω in Acts). Luke does, in any case, avoid any report of 'discipline' administered to Jesus".

593. CADBURY, *Style*, 1920, p. 157; *Making*, ²1958, p. 89, n. 15: "perhaps *flagellum* (φραγελλόω)" (see also p. 126).

594. CADBURY, *Style*, p. 94: "... omissions ... which are usually explained as due to Luke's reverence for the person of Jesus". Cf. BLINZLER, *Trial*, 1959, 225f. Hendrickx suggested Luke may be using the term "as a euphemism for the brutal scourging", though he was aware that some believed it reflected a light whipping as in Acts 16,22-24; 22,24 (*Passion*, p. 85-86). Cf. GOULDER, *Luke*, p. 761, who insisted that though Lk reflected "nicer Greek ... the meaning [compared with Mk] is equally nasty".

595. H. BALZ, φραγελλόω, in *EWNT* 3, cols. 1046-1047 (= p. 437): "According to Mark 15:15 par. Matt 27:26 Pilate had Jesus *scourged* before the crucifixion (φραγελλώσας; Luke weakens this)".

596. SHERWIN-WHITE, *Roman Society*, p. 27f; ELLIS, *The Gospel of Luke*, 1974 (rev. ed.), p. 264, who made reference to Sherwin-White; DANKER, *Jesus*, 1972, p. 234 (= 1988, p. 368); HENDRICKX, *Passion*, 1984 (rev. ed), p. 85-86. See also M. GREENBERG, *Scourging*, in *IDB* 4, p. 245-246, esp. p 245. Brown distinguished between three degrees of Roman scourging which pertained either to correction or capital punishment (*John XIII-XXI*, p. 874; see also the discussions in BEASLEY-MURRAY, *John*, p. 335, and SENIOR, *The Passion of Jesus in the Gospel of John*, p. 84, n. 14).

597. While there are a total of 96 instances in Lk (33) and Acts (63), there are only 6 occurrences in Mk. H. BALZ, οὖν, in *EWNT* 2, cols. 1326-1327, esp. col. 1326 (= p. 542-543, esp. p. 543). See 11,13 (/ Mt 7,11 Q).

598. It was also found in Mk 10,9 suggesting inference though there is no Lukan parallel.

599. *NTV*, p. 151; see also Acts 8,25.

vocabulary⁶⁰⁰. The word is found in the Q text of 3,7 (diff Mt 3,7) in material dealing with John the Baptist⁶⁰¹. The term occurs 260 times in the LXX⁶⁰².

αὐτὸν ἀπολύσω. This phrase pertains to the release of prisoners. ἀπολύω occurs in Mk 15,6.9[ἀπολύσω, though here it is an aorist subjunctive].11.15. Mk refers to Pilate's custom of releasing of a prisoner during the Passover feast (Mk 15,6), unattested outside the Gospels⁶⁰³. It is probable that Luke redacted Mk 15,6 since a practice associated with a Jewish religious feast would have had little meaning for a Gentile audience. Again, the Roman apologetic may also be at work here. Luke employed the term 14 times each in the Gospel and Acts⁶⁰⁴. The imperative form in 23,18 corresponded to the same in Mk 15,11⁶⁰⁵. It appeared already in 22,68⁶⁰⁶. It was found subsequently in 23,18.20.22.25⁶⁰⁷; Acts 3,13⁶⁰⁸; 5,40⁶⁰⁹; 16,35.36; 26,32⁶¹⁰; 28,18. There is also some similarity with Acts 26,32 (ἀπολελύσθαι). Note the use of ἀπολύσω in Acts 19,40 which also contained the word αἴτιον. The term appears 35 times in the LXX⁶¹¹.

It would seem that v. 16 together with v. 22 formed a sort of inclusio around the Barabbas scene⁶¹². The function of 23,13-16 was to provide a transition from the trial before Herod⁶¹³.

600. RADL, *Paulus*, p. 421.

601. οὖν was also found in another Q text 19,12; cf. Mt 25,14.

602. *GELS*, p. 342.

603. FITZMYER, *Luke*, p. 1485-1486.

604. *NTV*, p. 35. Mark used it 12 times.

605. JEREMIAS, *Die Sprache*, p. 303. Regarding Septuagintal use consider *GELS*, p. 53.

606. B. WEISS, *Lukas*, ⁹1901, p. 663.

607. G. SCHNEIDER, ἀπολύω, in *EWNT* 1, cols. 336-337 (= p. 140). Could Luke have been intending an ironical use to suggest "let die" as was the case in 2,29?

608. See BRUCE, *Acts*, 1951, p. 108; ³1990, p. 140: "Cf. Lk. 23:16,22, παιδεύσας οὖν αὐτὸν ἀπολύσω". BARRETT, *Acts*, p. 195: "κρίναντος ἐκαίνου ἀπολύειν. More strongly than Matthew or Mark, Luke emphasises Pilate's reluctance to condemn and execute Jesus; see Lk. 23.4,14,15,20,22".

609. Compare the δείραντες (Act 5,40) and δέροντες (22,63).

610. See HAENCHEN, *Die Apostelgeschichte*, ¹⁴1965, p. 616 (= *Acts*, 1971, p. 690): "This imaginary acquittal is the highest recognition of Paul and his innocence (and hence that of Christianity!) which is possible in these circumstances". See Bl-Debr, ¹¹1963, §358, 1 Supplement.

611. *GELS*, p. 53. See, for example, 2 Mac 4,47; 12,25; 4 Mac 8,2; 12,8. *NTV*, p. 35, indicates there are 65 instances in the NT.

612. MATERA, *Luke 23,1-25*, p. 548.

613. CREED, *Luke*, p. 282; SCHNEIDER, *Die Passion*, p. 93; *Lukas*, p. 476: "... weil es zur Barabbasszene (23,18-25) überleitet"; MATERA, *Luke 23,1-25*, p. 547; JOHNSON, *Luke*, p. 373; BROWN, *Death*, p. 789. Büchele wrote that these verses "dient der Vorbereitung der Barabas-Szene" (*Der Tod*, p. 36). Cf. MARSHALL, *Luke*, p. 858, suggested then rejected the idea: "Vs. 13-16 are closely linked with the preceding scene and could be regarded as its conclusion". This view was followed by GREEN, *Death*, p. 82.

Luke's Method of Composition

It has been our contention that Mk continued to guide Luke in the redaction of his Gospel through 24,12. Even in this relatively brief Herod story (23,6-16) there is a fair amount of Markan vocabulary and repetition of various vocabulary[614], which itself is a sign of Lukan redaction.

We have seen there is clear evidence of Markan vocabulary, constructions, themes and motifs in these verses. We have witnessed that there is much vocabulary in common with portions of the Mk which Luke elected to omit. Further, there were many examples of vocabulary and construction characteristic of Lukan style. Such indications of style have been confirmed by corresponding or parallel passages in Acts. Occasionally it appears that Luke drew on vocabulary from Q. Finally, Luke modeled much of his narrative style and choice of vocabulary upon the LXX, the influence of which is evident throughout the pericope.

Drawing on elements found in Mk, Luke incorporated material chiefly from Mark's account of the Baptist's death (Mk 6,14-29) and of the mockery by the Roman soldiers (Mk 15,16-20), modified in Lk wholly in line with the evangelist's compositonal method in the first case and out of regard for the apology toward Rome in the second. Likewise, themes and descriptions of events in Lk were found in Acts. By incorporating omitted Markan material, which included pericopes as well as portions of individual verses, and interweaving the Herod trial with the language of the LXX, which was "very appropriate for a solemn and dignified style"[615], Luke crafted an account which served his Gospel well.

There remains to discuss the brief but significant omission (καὶ τῆς ζύμης Ἡρῴδου Mk 8,15[616]) and subsequent addition (ἥτις ἐστὶν ὑπόκρισις) Luke made in 12,1b. T.J. Keegan noted both Matthew and Luke "spell out the meaning of the metaphor of leaven"[617]. He linked the Markan phrase about the leaven of Herod with the death of the Baptist[618]. Neirynck argued convincingly for Markan

614. Repeated terms include: Πιλᾶτος (23,6.11.12), δέ (23,6.8.9.10.11.12), ἀκούειν (23,6.8), ἐπερωτάω (23,6.9), πρός (23,7.12.15), Ἡρῴδης (23,7bis.8.11.12.15), ἀναπέμπω (23,7.11.15), ὄντα/ὄντες (23,7.12), ἐν (23,7bis.9.12bis), ἐν ταύταις ταῖς ἡμέραις (23,7.12 ἐν αὐτῇ τῇ ἡμέρᾳ), ἰδεῖν (23,8bis), ἱκανός (23,8.9), γάρ (23.8.12.15), οὐδέν (23,9.15); τὸν ἄνθρωπον τοῦτον (23,14bis).

615. *BDF*, p. 3, §4[2].

616. NEIRYNCK, *Duality*, p. 84, 103 and 109, pointed out that this verse contained a double imperative, a synonymous expression and a double group of persons, all characteristic features of Markan style.

617. T.J. KEEGAN, *The Parable of the Sower and Mark's Jewish Leaders*, in *CBQ* 56 (1994) 501-518, esp. p. 513. The evangelists understood it differently. Matthew interpreted it as teaching while Luke viewed it as hypocrisy (n. 69).

618. *Ibid.*, p. 516: "In a similar fashion one can see that when Jesus warns about the leaven of Herod he is warning about the response illustrated by the third type of seed, the seed that fell among thorns, a response prefigured by Herod in the execution of John the Baptist and fulfilled

influence on Luke in 12,1b (Mk 8,15 / Mt 16,6)[619]. In reaction to Fitzmyer he showed that 12,1b was Lukan redaction based on four arguments: 1) a high percentage of words in this brief saying in common with Mk[620]; 2) a similar Lukan substitution of imperatives at 20,46; 3) typical Lukan phraseology (προσέχετε ἑαυτοῖς) in Lk and Acts; and 4) similar Lukan uses of Mk in framing other Q sections[621].

by the crowds and the chief priests. He is warning the disciples not to be swept up by earthly concerns into a course of action that will result in the choking of the word, the death of Jesus". Cf. HOOKER, *Mark*, 1991, p. 194-195, esp. p. 195: "The leaven of which the disciples are to beware, however, was perhaps understood by Mark as the *cause* of this hostility and of Herod's treatment of John – namely, the refusal to recognize and accept the truth"; W.J. HARRINGTON, *Mark* (NTM, 4), Wilmington, DE, 1979, p. 114. JOHNSON, *Luke*, p. 194, commented that Luke transferred the saying in 12,1 "from its narrative context in Mark 8:15". In his opinion, Luke's purpose at this point was to "focus exclusively on the Pharisees". Taylor suggested that 12,1 might stem from L (*St. Mark*, ²1966, p. 365), as did Fitzmyer (p. 953; see his bibliography for 12,1, p. 955). For a differing view consult DRURY, *Tradition*, p. 83, 100, who believed Luke was editing Mt (Mt 16,6).

Fitzmyer observed that προσέχετε was both a Lukanism (17,3; 20,46; 21,34; Acts 5,35; 20,28) and a Septuagintism (Gen 24,6; Ex 10,28; 34,12; Dt 4,9) (p. 954). Hypocrisy (ὑπόκρισις) in the form of an abstract noun, occurred only here in Lk, but related verses included 6,42; 12,56; 13,15. The term is found only once in the LXX, at 2 Mac 6,25 (p. 955). See further SPICQ, ὑποκρίνομαι, in *NLNT* 3, 650-657, esp. p. 652 (= 1991, p. 1546-1553, esp. p. 1548 = *TLNT* 3, p. 406-413, esp. p. 408), and H. GIESEN, ὑπόκρισις, in *EWNT* 3, cols. 963-965 (= p. 403).

Meier attempted to establish a link between Mk 6,14-16 and Mk 8,14-21: "(3) More to the point, the redactional nature of Mark 6:14-16 is seen from the fact that it brackets the so-called 'bread-section' in Mark (from 6:32-44 to 8:14-21), where almost every pericope has some reference to bread. The bread section culminates in the story of Peter's confession of faith near Caesarea Philippi, in which the enumeration of theories about Jesus' true identity (6:14-16) is repeated in 8:28. (4) Even in the redactional statement of Mark 6:14, the reference to miraculous powers means that *because* the Baptist has been *raised from the dead, therefore* miraculous powers are at work in Jesus. In other words, it is not the Baptist *qua* Baptist who is the source of the miracles, but rather the Baptist *qua* raised from the dead by supernatural power who is the source of supernatural power in the one called Jesus" (*Marginal*, Vol. 2, p. 226, n. 241). As the disciples in Mk 8,14-21 suffered from a lack of understanding and hardness of heart, so too did Herod in 23,6-12.

619. *The Minor Agreements and Q*, in R.A. PIPER (ed.) *The Gospel Behind the Gospels. Current Studies on Q*, Leiden -New York - Cologne, 1995, 49-72, esp. p. 60-61. See T.A. FRIEDRICHSEN, *Mt-Lk Agreements Against Mk 4,30-32*, in FS Neirynck, Vol. 2, p. 663, n. 69. In the same volume see references to 12,1 in R.C. TANNEHILL, *The Lukan Discourse on Invitations (Luke 14,7-24)*, p. 1603-1616, esp. p. 1606 (with an additional mention of TANNEHILL, *Narrative Unity of Luke-Acts* 1 [n. 3] 254-257), and R.A. PIPER, *Social Background and Thematic Structure in Luke 16*, p. 1637-1662, esp. p. 1646.

620. The common words were ἀπὸ τῆς ζύμης τῶν φαρισαίων; cf. FITZMYER, p. 953.

621. NEIRYNCK, *The Minor Agreements and Q*, p. 60. He observed some recent commentaries assigned 12,1b to Q. These included DAVIES and ALLISON, *Matthew II* (1991) 589; GNILKA, *Matthäusevangelium II* (1988) 43; and WIEFEL, *Lukas* (1988) 232 (p. 60, n. 60). Already in 1978 Marshall argued it stemmed from Q (*Luke*, p. 510, 511), as Neirynck also pointed out. Notice should also be taken of Gundry's position: "But whether Luke 12:1 derives

Yet another reference to hypocrisy occurred in the Markan version of paying tribute to Caesar (Mk 12,13-17 / 20,20-26) where "some of the Pharisees and some of the Herodians" (Mk 12,13) collaborated seeking to entrap Jesus. Luke had only "they" (20,20). Whereas Mark mentioned the hypocrisy of Jesus' opponents (Mk 12,15), in the parallel place (20,23) Luke omitted mention of ὑπόκρισιν referring instead to their πανουργία. He moved the reference to their hypocritical behavior (ὑποκρινομένους) to 20,20[622]. We contend all these redactional changes were done in order to present Herod as a credible witness to the innocence of Jesus in 23,6-16.

Two omissions of Markan material referring to the Herodians (6,11 / Mk 3,6; 20,20 / Mk 12,13 / Mt 22,16) also have bearing on this matter and seem to confirm Luke's intention to present Herod in 23,6-16, as well as those associated with him, as not intending Jesus any harm. Whereas in Mk 3,6 Mark wrote of οἱ φαρισαῖοι ... μετὰ τῶν Ἡρῳδιανῶν, Luke amended the text so that it referred to οἱ γραμματεῖς καὶ οἱ φαρισαῖοι (6,7). In the Lukan parallel (6,11) Luke employed simply αὐτοὶ δέ[623].

---

from Q or L, or even Mark, the saying may have been detached from a narrative context as easily as a narrative context fabricated for it" (*Mark*, p. 411).

Other instances where Luke used Mk to frame Q sections included: 11:16,29 (Mk 8,11); 11,37-38 (cf. Mk 7,1.5); 12,1 (cf. Mk 8,14-15), "all from the great omission and all referring to the Pharisees" (p. 61).

622. F.W. YOUNG, *Hypocrisy*, in *IDB* 2, p. 668-669, esp. p. 669, who continued: "The only passage in the NT which clearly retains the original Greek meaning is the verb form used in Luke 20:20, where the scribes and high priests send spies who 'pretended to be sincere' (ὑποκρινομένους). In view of the Gentile background of the author of Luke, this is not surprising. With this one exception the occurrences of 'hypocrisy' and 'hypocrite' in the NT must be understood against the background of the peculiar development of meaning in Jewish thought and the OT". See NEIRYNCK, *Mt 12,25a / Lc 11,17a*, p. 123 (= 482).

623. FITZMYER, p. 605, called attention to the omission by Luke and observed "Luke mollifies the plans made by the Pharisees with the Herodians, who seek in Mark (3:6) to 'destroy him'" (p. 611). So also JOHNSON, *Luke*, p. 102. Marshall expressed a similar view: "The closing verse [6,11] is completely rewritten by Luke. In Mk. the Pharisees plot with the otherwise almost completely unknown Herodians to destroy Jesus. Luke omits mention of the Herodians (cf. 20:20 diff. Mk. 12:13), although later he mentions Herod's own threats against Jesus (13:31), and he leaves the reaction of the Pharisees much more vague" (*Luke*, p. 236). Schmithals regarded the omission as being in line with Luke's "apologetischen Tendenz" (*Lukas*, p. 76). Gundry argued in favor of the historicity of the Herodian involvement in a plot to kill Jesus against the view of W.J. BENNETT, *The Herodians of Mark's Gospel*, in *NT* 17 (1975) 9-14, insisting "it does not seem that anyone has added v 6 purely in anticipation of 11:18; 12:12; 14:1, or that Mark brings in the Herodians to set up a kind of parallel between Herod Antipas's execution of John the Baptist (6:21-29) and the Herodians' joining with the Phraisees to plot Jesus' death". The absence of mention of the Herodians in the passion narrative was seen by Gundry as a confirmation of the historicity since "why would anyone falsely implicate them in a plot against Jesus' life when they will play no role in the actual taking of it?" (*Mark*, p. 156). See further NEIRYNCK, *Argument from Order*, in *ETL* 49 (1973) 810 (= *Evangelica*, p. 763), SCHNEIDER, *Lukas*, 1977, ²1984, p. 144, and MEIER, *Marginal*, Vol. 2, p. 497, n. 193, 626, 730(-731), n. 15.

In the second instance (20,20 / Mk 12,13) Luke replaced Mark's τινας τῶν φαρισαίων καὶ τῶν ᾽Ηρῳδιανῶν with a general reference which harkened back to 20,1: οἱ ἀρχιερεῖς καὶ οἱ γραμματεῖς σὺν τοῖς πρεσβυτέροις[624]. The exact identity of the Herodians is unclear[625].

Luke typically prepared later passages by means of earlier ones. This applies not only within the Gospel but may also be said to prepare for material within Acts. Thus references to Herod (3,1; 9,7-9; 13,31-33) prepare the reader for the encounter between Jesus and the tetrarch.

The christology of the passage, more implicitly than explicitly, suggests that Jesus is God's prophet[626]. As we noted Hastings, Darr and Senior interpreted the

624. Schneider commented that 20,20-26 was a redaction of Mk though B. WEISS, *Quellen*, 1907, p. 212-214, assumed Luke drew on a special source (*Lukas*, 1977, ²1984, p. 401). He insisted the change was implemented "um die Verfänglichkeit der Anfrage für Jesus zu unterstreichen" (p. (401-)402). Marshall suggested other reasons for the omission: "Luke has dropped the description of the deputation as being composed of Pharisees and Herodians possibly because the latter group were no longer significant, or because an association of the two groups seemed unlikely to him" (*Luke*, p. 734). Fitzmyer remarked: "Luke, however, has composed his own introductory verse (v. 20), eliminating all mention of the Pharisees and the Herodians (cf. Mark 12:13) and making more explicit reference to Roman political jurisdiction and the prefect's authority" (*Luke*, p. 1289). The unspecified reference "they", as also in v. 19, was understood by Fitzmyer to refer back the "Scribes and chief priests" (p. 1294; so also MARSHALL, *Luke*, p. 733). See further CONZELMANN, *Die Mitte*, p. 65, 119 (= 78, 139); he stressed links between 20,20ff. and 23,2 on p. 71, 119, 163 (= 85, 140, 188). Consider also NEIRYNCK, *Paul and Sayings of Jesus*, in A. VANHOYE (ed.), *L'Apôtre Paul. Personnalité, style et conception du ministère* (BETL, 73) Leuven, 1986, 265-321, p. 291 (= *Evangelica II*, 1991, 511-568, p. 537). With regard to Mk 12,13 Gundry insisted: "Their [Herodians] presence in Jerusalem makes good sense for Passover season, but especially good sense if Herod Antipas has come (so Luke 23:7)" (*Mark*, 1993, p. 696; see also p. 154).

625. Nineham argued: "It is not certain who these were. The usual view is that they were friends and political supporters of Herod Antipas, rather than a religious sect, and that they joined forces with Pharisees against Jesus because of the danger of political unrest inherent in his movement: cf., however, B.W. Bacon, *The Gospel of Mark*, p. 74ff., who thinks the term is an anachronism here and refers to the religious group which gathered around Agrippa in St. Mark's own day" (*St. Mark*, 1963, p. 111; see also p. 316). Sandmel noted the omission of the term in Lk was intentional redaction of his Markan source (*Herodians*, in *IDB* 2, 1962, p. 594-595, p. 595; see also his bibliography, p. 595). J.L. McKenzie held "it is more probable that they were those who favored the house of Herod i.e., they supported the Herodian rule and the Roman rule upon which it rested" (*Herodians*, in ID., *Dictionary of the Bible*, New York, 1965, 356-357, p. 357). Taylor subscribed to the view that this group consisted of "friends and supporters of Herod Antipas" (*St. Mark*, ²1966; Grand Rapids, MI, ᴿ1981, p. 224; consult his suggestions for further reading. See too p. 478. HOOKER, *Mark*, 1991, p. 108, 280, also considered them to be supporters of Herod Antipas). GUNDRY, *Mark*, 1993, p. 152, 154, 156, 692, 693, 696, likewise contended it probable that this was their identity. G. Vermes understood the Herodians to refer to the "native aristocracy" of Galilee who served as "administrators of the 204 cities and villages of Upper and lower Galilee and of the Valley" (*Jesus the Jew. A Historian's Reading of the Gospels*, London, 1973; Philadelphia, PA, 1981, p. 45).

626. There are no titles used of Jesus in this brief passage. His name occurred only in 23,8.

portrayal of Jesus as prophet in the Herod pericope[627]. Although Pilate sought to obtain information concerning the accusation that Jesus was a king (23,2.3), the interrogation of Herod (23,9) did not make this explicit. The thread of Jesus as prophet theme (9,8[628]; 13,33) was taken up again when the two disciples on the way to Emmaus announced Jesus "was a prophet mighty in deed and word before God and all the people" (24,19) who was delivered over to death. A connection between early Christian prophets and Herod Tetrarch was made in Acts 13,1 with the mention of Manaen.

Other than the reference to him as ὁ ἄνθρωπος Γαλιλαῖος (23,6), he was generally referred to simply using the pronoun (23,7.8bis.9.10.11ter.15bis).

627. In line with this, Hastings wrote: "But did Herod then avoid his share of responsibility for Jesus' martyrdom? Hardly. The day of the Crucifixion was the day he became friends with Pontius Pilate. Like the latter, he was one of the princes, one of the kings of the earth, who conspired together against the Lord and His Christ that day in Jerusalem. And this is very much part of Luke's theme. Pilate too, no doubt, had his good points, but that does not excuse him from being part of that Jerusalem which was 'still murdering the prophets, and stoning the messengers that are sent to thee' (13:34). They were both part of the generation that 'will be answerable for all the blood of prophets that has been shed since the beginning of the world' (11:50). And this because Jesus was himself a prophet, *the* prophet, and 'there is no room for a prophet to meet his death, except at Jerusalem' (13:33) But at Jerusalem it was fitting that Herod of Galilee, murderer of the last and greatest of the Old Testament prophets, should be present to join with Pilate and the chief priests in doing to death Jesus the Galilean".

He continued: "Thus Luke's series of passages form a unity; the early ones explain the later, and the whole gives us a theme running through the Gospel. This theme in its turn links up with the much bigger and more important one of Jesus as a prophet, the heir of the Old Testament prophets, and destined as such to meet his death in Jerusalem where all the murderers of the prophets came together to destroy him" (HASTINGS, p. 48; see also DENAUX, *L'hypocrisie*, p. 282-284 = [2]1989, 192-194). DARR, *Glorified*, p. 316: "Herod's interaction with Jesus continues the prophet versus king pattern evoked by the relationship between John and the Tetrarch. Jesus is the prophet par excellence who combines the roles of Elijah, Herod and Jeremiah while surpassing them in importance". The inclusion of Herod in this list of prophets seems very odd however. See further, SENIOR, *The Passion of Jesus in the Gospel of Luke*, p. 114.

On the Lukan theme of Jesus as a prophet see P.F. FEILER, *Jesus the Prophet: The Lucan Portrayal of Jesus as the Prophet Like Moses*, Diss. Princeton Theol. Sem., 1986 (dir. D.R. ADAMS), esp. p. 238-244; RADL, *Das Lukas-Evangelium*, p. 74, 81-83; J.M. SCHUBERT, *The Image of Jesus as Prophet Like Moses in Luke-Acts as Advanced by Luke's Reinterpretation of Deuteronomy 18:15,18 in Acts 3:22 and 7:37*, Diss. Fordham, 1992 (dir. C.H. GIBLIN); A. VANHOYE, *L'intérêt*, p. 1529-1548. See further J.D. KINGSBURY, *Jesus as the "Prophetic Messiah" in Luke's Gospel*, in A.J. MALHERBE and W.A. MEEKS (eds.), *The Future of Christology. Essays in Honor of Leander E. Keck*, Minneapolis, MN, 1993, 29-42, who nuanced the discussion by claiming that prophet was not a christological title in Lk though the evangelist cast Jesus in the role of the prophetic messiah (p. 31, n. 11; see also p. 41-42).

628. VANHOYE, *L'intérêt*, p. 1529-1548. CADBURY, *Style*, p. 97, called attention to the identification of Jesus as a prophet in response to Herod's inquiry (Mk 6,15). "... Luke (9,8) understands this to mean that one of the ancient prophets is risen, an idea parallel to the other suggestions, that he is John the Baptist risen from the dead, or that Elias has appeared". More recently, see also J.B. GREEN, *The Theology of the Gospel of Luke*, Cambridge, 1995, p. 61-62.

Purpose of the Episode

Our previous survey revealed it is frequently held that the purpose of Lk 23,6-16 was to emphasize the innocence of Jesus, a view which I consider to be correct. Some suggested further that a secondary purpose of the story is to: 1) show that Jews and Gentiles were reconciled through Christ[629]; 2) make an important theological statement about "the healing power of his passion"[630]; 3) highlight the reconciliation of Pilate and Herod[631]. I do not find these suggestions convincing. Enemies were indeed reconciled, but not to God or Christ. Rather, I would propose that 23,6-16 set the stage for the conspiracy as described in Acts 4,25-28.

In light of my investigation I further believe that the Herod story confirmed what was lacking or at least was only very weakly conveyed in Mk[632]. Luke sought to strengthen this conviction that "nothing deserving of death has been done by him" (23,15). Further, as Jesus was presented as a prophet throughout Lk, a theme already found in Mk (Mk 6,4; 6,15 referring to the Baptist; 8,28), the encounter between Jesus and Herod is yet one more instance of the fulfillment of prophecy (13,33; 21,12 / Mk 13,9)[633]. Thirdly, parallels exist between the passion of Jesus and the experience of the early Christians, especially Paul, as recounted in Acts, and therefore these events prepare for the second volume of Luke's work[634]. These experiences served a parenetic function for those who chose to follow Jesus (9,23 / Mk 8,34).

Relationship to Acts 4 and GP

This aspect of the debate has in recent years experienced a resurgence of attention as our historical survey demonstrated. Buck expressed the conviction that "an intended connection between Acts 4:27 and Lk. 23:12 may also be taken for granted"[635]. Through the latter part of our study we consistently attempted to examine the relationship between Lk and Mk as well as Lk and Acts in order to determine whether particular material was derived from tradition or redaction. This

---

629. DRURY, *Tradition*, p. 17.

630. BROWN, *Death*, p. 785-786.

631. SOARDS, *Tradition*, 1985, p. 363.

632. Recall the discussion of various proposed purposes for the Herod story in SOARDS, *Tradition*, 1985, p. 360-363.

633. See NEYREY, *Passion*, p. 84-88.

634. On the parallelism, consider the comment of D.T.N. Parry: "The involvement of (a) Herod in action against Jesus is a distinctive part of Luke's narrative (9.9; 13.31-32; 23.6-12; Acts 4.27), and a Herod becomes involved in action against Paul (25.13-26.32) as well as here against James and Peter. The same kind of vascillating attitude of Herod that we find in the Gospel (hostility to the Baptist and Jesus, but then concurrence with Pilate in Jesus' innocence) is found in Acts, between the action against James and Peter, and Agrippa II's verdict on Paul" (*Release of the Captives - Reflections on Acts 12*, in C.M. TUCKETT [ed.], *Luke's*, 1995, 156-164, p. 159).

635. BUCK, *Function*, p. 167.

important methodological control is no less necessary in a comparison of material concerning Pilate, Herod and Jesus, especially in Lk 23,6-16 and Acts 4,25-27[636]. Brown discussed this topic in the context of one of three proposed solutions to the question of the source of the Herod story[637]. Dibelius's article, suggesting that Luke created 23,6-12 on the basis of Acts 4,24-28, has been extremely influential, though frequently disputed[638].

Brown, arguing that "Dibelius's line of thought can be challenged on several scores"[639], listed numerous objections: "The interpretation of the psalm in Acts involves ingenious stretching to fit the facts of the passion. To understand 'the peoples' of the psalm to refer to 'the people [pl.!] of Israel' is extraordinary. Elsewhere Luke refers to Herod Antipas as a tetrarch, never in the Gospel as a king; he does not refer to Pilate as an *archōn*. If there were not already a tradition of Herod's involvement against Jesus, how could reading the psalm suggest such interpretations? As for Justin, if his interpretation is not dependent on Luke (even through oral memory), he could be dependent on the same type of tradition about Herod that Luke drew from"[640]. These were not Brown's only counter-arguments. He further called attention to the dissimilarity of presentations of Herod's role in Acts 4,24-28 and Lk 23,6-15[641]. Despite the differences Brown added in a note: "While the approaches to Herod's role in Luke 23 and Acts 4 are different, one should not treat them as contradictory"[642].

636. For a useful bibliography on Acts 4,23-31, see HAENCHEN, *Die Apostelgeschichte*, [14]1965, p. 183-184 (= *Acts*, p. 225).

637. *Death*, p. 779-783.

638. *Herodes*, 1915, 113-126 (= *BG* 1, 278-292).

639. *Death*, p. 780.

640. *Ibid.*

641. *Ibid.*: "In Acts 4 Herod and Pontius Pilate are gathered together against Jesus, as are the peoples of Israel. In Luke 23:14-15 both Herod and Pilate find Jesus not guilty, and in Luke 23:27,35 the 'people' are not particularly hostile". A final objection, that early Christian literature, such as Ignatius in his letter to the Smyrnaeans or GP, does not draw on Ps 2, is also advanced (p. 781). But consider BARRETT, *Acts*, p. 246, commenting on Acts 4,25: "οἱ ἄρχοντες recalls, and was no doubt intended to recall 4.5, as well as Lk. 23.13,35; 24.20".

642. *Death*, p. 781, n. 35. Other scholars likewise noted certain discrepancies or inconsistencies between the two passages. So already HOEHNER, *Herod Antipas*, p. 228-230, esp. p. 229; GREEN, *Death*, p. 81; and MARSHALL, *Luke*, p. 855. MATERA, *Luke 23,1-25*, p. 542, for example, noted three differences between the accounts: "First, the Herod episode, as presented in Acts, is significantly different from the passion account. In the Passion, Herod and Pilate do not conspire against Jesus but find him innocent. Second, in the Passion, it is the people of Israel, not the Gentiles, who bring Jesus to crucifixion. Third, not only is this episode of Acts in tension with the Passion at this point, it is also in tension with Luke's view of the Passion in the rest of Acts where he presents Pilate in a favorable light (3,13; 13,28) and the people of Israel and their leaders as those who are primarily responsible for Jesus' death (2,23.36; 3,14-15; 4,10; 5,30; 7,52; 10,29; 13,27-29)". Matera concluded Luke was inspired in the composition of 23,6-12 by Paul's trial before Herod Agrippa and Festus (Acts 25,13–26,32) reasoning that "the trials of Paul before Felix, Festus and Agrippa were surely fresher in Luke's mind, and he undoubtedly had better access to information surrounding them than he did to the trial of Jesus" (p. 545, 546).

Hoehner offered three counter-arguments in support of the view that Acts 4 did not serve as the source of 23,6-12[643]. First, drawing on M. Black, he observed that the account in Acts "assumes an acquaintance with the story of Luke 23:5ff"[644]. Secondly, Sparks and Wilcox focused on the Semitic flavor of the passage in Acts as well as "several close Septuagint parallels"[645]. Finally, the

On the issue of whether Paul's life may have influenced the account of Jesus, Brown maintained initially that it is hard to know which way the influence went (*Death*, p. 74-75). In a note he wrote: "It is not impossible that a similar significant detail may have been present in early Christian tradition both about Jesus and about Stephen or Paul; but such a coincidence would hardly explain all the parallels" (p. 75, n. 89; see also p. 401, n. 3). However, later Brown affirmed this as his own position (p. 756: "Within Luke-Acts the influence most likely came from Paul's trial to Jesus' trial, rather than vice versa"). He draws on S.G. WILSON, *The Jews*, p. 162-164. Examples include 23,2 apparently influenced by Acts 24,5-6; likewise 23,6-7.11b-12 by Acts 25,13ff. (p. 782, n. 40). Consider p. 738: "Luke may have had a source for the trial of Paul; certainly he had popular knowledge of how Roman gubernatorial trials were conducted; and he is following that pattern for both Jesus and Paul". In the matter of the relation of 23,6-12 to Acts 4,24-28 Fitzmyer's pragmatic approach deserves consideration: "Why is Acts 4:27-28 not merely a reflection of Luke 23:6-12, the normal expectation in the second volume of any author's work? That there may be an allusion to Ps 2:1-2 is acceptable; but does that allusion certainly explain the genesis of the story? Its details? The allusion is at best vague" (p. 1479; so also MARSHALL, *Luke*, p. 855).

It is interesting to recall that while J. Weiss noted the allusion made to 23,1-12 in Acts 4,27, that comment was deleted by B. Weiss in the revision (J. WEISS, *Lukas*, [8]1892, p. 638; cf. B. WEISS, *Lukas*, [9]1901, p. 659). Other scholars, such as Taylor, do not examine the relationship between the two passages (cf. *Passion*, p. 87).

Notice should be taken of the perspective of Conzelmann: "The cooperation of Herod [...] and Pilate [...] is illustrated by Luke 23:6-12 [...]. However, the general tone here is different from that of Luke's passion narrative. There Pilate is exonerated in a apologetic manner whereas here, in line with Luke's fundamental view of salvation history, Pilate's guilt is stressed" (*Acts*, 1987, p. 35). Consider once again the view of BARRETT, *Acts*, p. 247: "It is Luke only (Lk. 23.12) who describes the reconciliation of Herod and Pilate at the time of the crucifixion; there must be some connection between Luke's account of the reconciliation and his use here of Ps. 2.1f. It is not however easy to say what the connection is. Did Luke know of the reconciliation, and invoke Ps. 2 to show that it had been determined by God? Did he know the Psalm as a Messianic prophecy and invent the incident to show that it had been fulfilled? The incident in the gospel is not there brought into connection with the Psalm and it would be unwise therefore to say that Luke invented it in order to demonstrate a fulfilment which he does not trouble to mention. On the other hand there is no other evidence for a quarrel and its resolution. Luke shows some hints of access to the Herod family (Lk. 8.3; Acts 13.1), and it may be that he had heard a story about Herod and Pilate which reflection finally led him to connect with Ps. 2".

643. Rather than Acts 4,25-26 giving rise to 23,6-12 Hoehner argued, "the reverse is more likely to be the case" (*Herod Antipas*, p. 228).

644. *Ibid.* M. BLACK, *Arrest*, p. 24.

645. HOEHNER, *Herod Antipas*, p. 228-229. H.F.D. SPARKS, *The Semitisms of Acts*, in *JTS* (1950) 16-28, esp. p. 24; M. WILCOX, *The Semitisms of Acts*, Oxford, 1965, p. 70, affirmed Sparks's finding arguing that the prayer contained 6 Lukanisms. These included: "ἐν τῷ with infin., μετὰ παρρησίας, ἅγιον, τε, ἡ βουλή (of God's will), τὸν λόγον σου (i.e. God's word, or the gospel)".

disparity between the accounts can be explained by the efforts of the early Church to "see as much as possible of the Messianic Psalm 2 as fulfilled in Christ"[646].

Michael Dömer (1978) proposed five reasons in favor of Lukan composition in Acts 4,25-26[647]. Schneider (1980) included Dömer among his resources, and came to a very similar conclusion[648]. Darrell L. Bock (1987), however, responded to Dömer, favoring a view which was articulated, though not endorsed by Stählin: "that Luke formed the account from traditional material is the best solution to the question of traditional origin or compositional creation"[649]. Bock's argumentation, which in two instances was based in part upon appeal to contemporary situations of prayer and news reporting, rather than the text, is particularly weak.

If, as we believe, Acts 4,24-28 did not give rise to Lk 23,6-16 (since each gives evidence that they were freely composed by Luke drawing on other materials), what is the relationship between the two? If 23,6-16 makes much more explicit the innocence of Jesus over against the Markan account, what is the purpose of Acts 4,24-28?

The apparent contradiction between the portrayal of Pilate and Herod in Lk 23 as opposed to Acts 4 could possibly be explained that though the two political leaders were "for" Jesus in declaring his innocence, still they did nothing to prevent the crucifixion. In this sense, then, the early Church could have understood them to be against Jesus. This collusion in the Gospel set the stage for Acts 4,25-28. In light of the newfound friendship of Herod and Pilate (23,12), the readers of Acts could understand that the two leaders were gathered together against Jesus. Matera offered an insightful explanation. "The data suggest that the material of Acts 4,24-28 comes from a tradition somewhat at odds with Luke's overall view of the Passion, and that it is not the origin of the Herod episode found in the Gospel. This is not improbable when we recall that Luke's primary purpose at this point in Acts is to describe the community's prayer for boldness, not to retell the passion account"[650]. The fact that the passage in Acts appears "somewhat at

---

646. HOEHNER, *Herod Antipas*, p. 229.

647. M. DÖMER, *Das Heil Gottes. Studien zur Theologie des lukanischen Doppelwerkes* (BBB, 50), Köln - Bonn, 63-66. Diss. Bonn, 1977/78 (dir. H. ZIMMERMANN). Those who maintain that Acts 4,24-30 "keineswegs [wiedergeben] etwa ein traditionelles urchristliches Gemeindegebet" included O. BAUERNFEIND, *Die Apostelgeschichte* (THK, 5), Leipzig, 1939, p. 78f., and H. SCHÜTZ, *Entstehung und Bedeutung des urchristlichen Gemeindegebets*, Diss. Heidelberg, 1925, 149-157.

648. SCHNEIDER, *Die Apostelgeschichte*, T. 1, p. 355: "Der 'Knick', den der heutige Text ausweist, ist am ehesten darauf zurückzuführen, dass *Lukas* mit 4,25-28 ein christologisches Testimonium aufgriff und es in ein Gemeindegebet einfügte, das er *im ganzen* nach dem Vorbild von Jes 37,16-20 LXX schuf". See DÖMER, *Das Heil*, p. 65-66.

649. D.L. BOCK, *Proclamation*, p. 204-205, esp. p. 205. See G. STÄHLIN, *Die Apostelgeschichte* (NTD, 5), Göttingen, 1936, 1962, p. 78. Bock gave the impression Stählin adopted the view of tradition, but in a note admitted that Stählin "states but does not support this opinion" (*Proclamation*, p. 205; cf. p. 362, n. 162).

650. *Luke 23,1-25*, p. 542.

odds" with that of 23,6-16 should not surprise us as Luke included varying attitudes of Herod regarding Jesus. We have seen in the Gospel that Luke employed portrayals of Herod that were at odds with one another. In 9,7-9 Herod was described simply as perplexed and desirous of seeing Jesus. The attitude in 13,31 differed significantly where Herod was reported to be seeking to kill Jesus. Is it not also possible then, that Luke will employ differing portrayals, not only within the Gospel, but also between Lk and Acts?

We would further suggest that a connection with Acts 4 quoting Ps 2, indeed a preparation for it as we have seen was typical of Luke's redactional hand, was found in Lk 24,44. This prepared the reader for the Christian community's prayer for boldness in Acts 4,25-27. Such an interpretation is confirmed by examining 24,27 which spoke only of "Moses and all the prophets"[651]. In 24,44 "the psalms" were added[652]. The portrayal of Jesus as prophet continued in Acts both preceding and following the reference to Herod in Acts 4,27 (Acts 3,22-24; 7,37).

Buck proposed that "before Peter can be a confessing disciple, so it seems, he needs a demonstration by his master. After he has witnessed the confession of Jesus before the Sanhedrin and Herod, he, too, can face the Sanhedrin (Acts 4:1ff.) and Herod (Acts 12:1ff.) with boldness"[653]. Both 23,6-16 and Acts 4,24-28 contained the fulfillment of prophecy motif.

In an appendix which follows, we extensively examine the relationship of 23,6-16 to GP and took note of the increased interest scholars have shown in the apocryphal gospels in general and GP in particular. Because of the evidence of vocabulary and events from all four canonical Gospels and the increasing hostility toward Judaism displayed in GP we would agree with the majority of scholars that GP was dependent upon the canonical Gospels.

Luke expertly inserted the Herod pericope into the Markan framework. By making use of Markan material, ranging from certain terminology or phrases to sizeable pericopes which he omitted in parallel places in his own Gospel, and drawing on the style and vocabulary of the LXX, Luke fashioned an account to highlight the innocence of Jesus. Further, 23,6-16 reinforced the view of Jesus as a prophet whose prophecy in 13,31-33 and 21,12 (/ Mk 13,9) was fulfilled. Finally, it prepared the reader for the accounts in Acts, building upon earlier material in Lk, in which the disciples and early Christians experience much opposition, abuse and sometimes support for their innocence similar to the example of Jesus.

---

651. See also Acts 3,18.
652. In Acts 1,20 Luke wrote of the fulfillment of the book of Psalms in light of Judas' death.
653. BUCK, p. 172; see further p. 174-175, 177.

Conclusion

The results of our exegesis of Lk 23,6-16 may be succinctly summarized as follows:

1) Although a variety of source- and redaction-critical solutions have been advanced, our analysis has shown that Luke composed the Herod pericope using Markan materials he omitted in parallel places namely Mk 3,6; 6,14-29; 15,16-20. This has been demonstrated by the presence of Markan vocabulary, constructions and themes. No appeal to a special source such as Proto-Lk need be made. Indeed Mk has continued to guide Luke in the passion narrative.

2) Our working hypothesis, that Luke employed Markan materials he elected to omit in parallel places, may now be regarded as a principle.

3) Luke composed this passage by building on previous Herodian material in his own Gospel, especially Lk 3,1; 9,7-9; 13,31-33, and the material in Lk, particularly 23,6-16, serves as a basis for related material in Acts.

4) Lk 23,13-16 is closely related to vv. 6-12 providing a transition to the material which follows.

5) The strong presence of Lukan language, and the omission of the Latinism (23,16), a practice consistent with Luke's redactional style, also support Lukan authorship of the Herod story.

6) The significant redaction of 12,1, which in turn was based upon Mk, helps to confirm Luke's redactional interests contained in the Herod pericope.

7) The Lukan vocabulary of 23,6-16 appears extensively throughout the trial of Paul (Acts 25–26) and serves not only to link the events, but emphasizes the parallels between Jesus and his disciples. Further it accentuates the unity of Lk-Acts.

8) While a few scholars have argued that accounts in Acts served to inspire stories in Lk, the opposite seems to be the case, as we have noted for Acts 4,24-28.

9) Our study reaffirms the widely held interpretation that the purpose of this brief pericope is to witness to the innocence of Jesus. Luke's description of the ἐσθῆτα λαμπράν, without reference to a color, seems to have been intended to highlight Jesus' divinity.

10) A majority of scholars advocate the view that the author of GP employed at least some of the canonical Gospels as sources. There is sufficient reason to believe

that the author had access to a written copy of Lk and that the influence was not inverse.

CONCLUDING OBSERVATIONS AND IMPLICATIONS FOR FURTHER STUDY

Our historical survey serves to fill the lacuna indicated by M. Rese that not much is known about late 19th Century and early 20th Century solutions to the synoptic problem. Frequently, cursory reviews of the history of the debate surrounding Lukan sources highlighted the British, American and German contributions. One result of our research has been to recognize there has been significant French support for the idea of the evangelist's use of a special source or sources[654].

Several scholars, including M. Dibelius, H. Schürmann, G. Schneider, A. Vööbus, A. Büchele and M.L. Soards, have expressed reservations about a purely statistical method of determining Lukan vocabulary in an effort to discern redactional characteristics of Luke. Another select group of scholars proposed that events in the life of Paul have likely influenced the composition of the account of Jesus' trial. At an early point Acts was proposed as having shaped the Gospel account. Such a view, held by Nicolardot and Goguel, related to Acts 26, was adopted by Chase, Williams, Koh, Walaskay, Matera, and Kurz[655].

H.G. RUSSELL (1955) sought to determine whether Lk or Acts was written first[656]. His research yielded the outcome that as of that time, only three people proposed the idea that Acts was written before Lk. These were F.H. Chase, C.S.C. Williams and R. Koh[657]. Following this period G. BOUWMAN (1968) also

---

654. Such French scholars included P. Girodon, A. Wautier d'Aygalliers, X. Léon-Dufour, A. Jaubert, É. Trocmé, F. Bovon, P. Benoit and M.-É. Boismard.

655. Marshall, *Acts and the 'Former Treatise'*, in B.W. WINTER and A.D. CLARKE (eds.), *The Book of Acts in its first Century Setting. 1. The Book of Acts in Its Ancient Literary Setting*, Grand Rapids, MI - Carlisle, 1993, 163-182, p. 166, who argued that the "more realistic possibility is that Luke wrote the Gospel first without any thought of a sequel, and then wrote Acts *much later*" He cited G. SCHNEIDER, *Die Apostlegeschichte*, Vol. 1, 1980, 76-82. He also commented on Talbert's remark that "Acts has the logical priority in the Lucan scheme" (C.H. TALBERT, *The Redaction Critical Quest for Luke the Theologian*, in *Jesus and Man's Hope*, Vol. 1, 1970, 171-222, p. 202 = *Perspectives* 11). Marshall continued: "[Talbert] argues that Luke's purpose was to present the theme of sucession and show how the life of Jesus was lived out in the lives of his successors. On this view Acts was part of Luke's scheme right from the beginning, and it should not be thought of as in any way an afterthought to the Gospel" (MARSHALL, *Acts*, p. 166, n. 13).

656. H.G. RUSSELL, *Which was Written First, Luke or Acts?*, in *HTR* 3 (1955) 167-174, esp. p. 174: "My intention in discussing the possibility of Acts' priority to Luke has not been to prove its probability, but rather by offering it as a possibility to question the validity of the alternative and traditional view".

657. F.H. CHASE, *The Gospels in the Light of Historical Criticism*, in H.B. SWETE (ed.), *Cambridge Theological Essays*, London, 1905, 373-419, esp. 380-381; WILLIAMS, *Review of W.L. Knox, Acts of the Apostles, 1948*, in *JTS* 49 (1948) 201-204; KOH, *Writings*, 1953, p. 23-35.

advocated this position[658]. These are but a few of the aspects which have been covered in our study which is based on the conviction that at this point in the debate we can move forward only by looking back, taking stock of the diverse approaches employed by scholars and focusing on the relationship of Lk to Mk without neglecting the relation of Acts to the Markan story.

Finally, it is no small matter that Schneider, who devoted his scholarly career to research on Lk-Acts, and Brown, who published a magisterial study of the passion narratives, have changed their original positions and no longer subscribe to the view that Luke employed a special continuous source in the account of the passion. Schürmann backed away from the theory of a continuous source after reading Rese. Ernst, too, has rejected the view of a special continous source in the Lukan passion narrative. Green also seems to be backing away from a continuous source proposal. Indeed, our study confirms that Mk has continued to guide Luke in the passion narrative.

---

658. Bouwman's paper, originally in Dutch, was translated and subsequently published (*Le "premier livre" (Act., I,1) et la date des Actes des Apôtres*, in NEIRYNCK (ed.), *L'Évangile de Luc*, ²1989, p. 553-569. See *De Derde Nachtwake. De Wordingsgeschiedenis van het evangelie van Lukas*, 1968, Lannoo - Tielt - Den Haag, p. 75-81 (= *Das dritte Evangelium. Einübung in die formgeschichtliche Methode*, Düsseldorf, 1968).

Part IV

BIBLIOGRAPHY, APPENDICES AND INDEXES

ABBREVIATIONS

Journals, Series, Festschriften and Reference Tools

AASF DHL	*Annales Academiae Scientiarum Fennicae. Dissertationes Humanarum Litterarum* (Helsinki)
AB	*Anchor Bible* (Garden City NY)
ABD	D.N. FREEDMAN (ed.), *Anchor Bible Dictionary*, 6 vols., 1992
ABRL	The Anchor Bible Reference Library (New York)
AfTJ	*African Theological Journal* (Arusha Tanzania)
AGJU	*Arbeiten zur Geschichte des antiken Judentums und des Urchristentums* (Leiden)
AJT	*American Journal of Theology* (Chicago IL)
ALBO	*Analecta Lovaniensia et Biblica Orientalia* (Leuven)
ALUOS	*Annual of the Leeds University Oriental Society* (Leeds)
AmiCl	*Ami du clergé* (Langres)
AnBib	*Analecta Biblica* (Rome)
AnBoll	*Analecta Bollandiana* (Brussels)
ANQ	*Andover Newton Quarterly* (Newton Center MA)
ANRW	A. TEMPORINI - W. HAASE (eds.), *Aufstieg und Niedergang der römischen Welt*
ANTC	Abingdon New Testament Commentaries (Nashville TN)
AssSeign	*Assemblées du Seigneur* (Brugge - Paris)
ASTI	*Annual of the Swedish Theological Institute* (Leiden)
ATANT	*Abhandlungen zur Theologie des Alten und Neuen Testaments* (Zürich)
ATLA	*American Theological Library Association* (Evanston IL)
ATR	*Anglican Theological Review* (Evanston IL)
AusBR	*Australian Biblical Review* (Melbourne)
B-A	W. BAUER - K. ALAND, *Griechisch-deutsches Wörterbuch*, [6]1988
BA	*Biblical Archeologist* (Atlanta, GA)
BAC	*Biblioteca de autores cristianos* (Madrid)
BAGD	W. BAUER - W.F. ARNDT - F.W. GINGRICH - F.W. DANKER, *A Greek-English Lexicon*, [2]1979
BAR	*Biblical Archaeology Review* (Des Moines IA)
BBB	*Bonner biblische Beiträge* (Bonn)
BBR	*Bibliographies for Biblical Research* (Lewiston, NY - Queenston Ontario - Lampter Wales)
BDF	F. BLASS - A. DEBRUNNER - R. FUNK, *A Greek Grammar of the NT*, 1961
BDR	F. BLASS - A. DEBRUNNER - F. REHKOPF, *Grammatik des neutestamentlichen Griechisch*, [17]1990
BECNT	M. SILVA (ed.), *Baker Exegetical Commentary on the NT* (Grand Rapids MI)
Beginnings	F.J. FOAKES JACKSON - K. LAKE (eds.), The Beginnings of Christianity (1920-1933)
BETL	*Bibliotheca Ephemeridum Theologicarum Lovaniensium* (Leuven)
BEvTh	*Beiträge zur evangelischen Theologie* (Munich)
BFCT	*Beiträge zur Förderung christlicher Theologie* (Gütersloh)
BG	M. DIBELIUS, *Botschaft und Geschichte*, Vol. 1, 1953

BHTh	*Beiträge zur historischen Theologie* (Tübingen)
Bib	*Biblica* (Rome)
BibLeb	*Bibel und Leben* (Düsseldorf)
BIS	*Biblical Interpretation Series* (Leiden - New York - Cologne)
BJRL	*Bulletin of the John Rylands University Library of Manchester* (Manchester)
BK	*Bibel und Kirche* (Stuttgart)
BLtg	*Bibel und Liturgie* (Klosterneuburg)
BNTC	*Black's New Testament Commentaries* (London - Peabody MA)
BR	*Biblical Research* (Chicago IL)
BS	*Bibliotheca Sacra* (Dallas TX)
BSNA	*Biblical Scholarship in North America* (Missoula MT - Chico CA)
BSR	*Bibliothèque de sciences religieuses* (Paris)
BSt	*Biblische Studien* (BSt[F] Freiburg or Neukirchen)
BTB	*Biblical Theology Bulletin* (Jamaica NY)
BThS	*Biblisch-theologische Studien* (Neukirchen-Vluyn)
BTrans	*Bible Translator* (London)
BWANT	*Beiträge zur Wissenschaft vom Alten und Neuen Testament* (Stuttgart)
BZ	*Biblische Zeitschrift* (Paderborn)
BZAW	*Beihefte zur Zeitschrift für alttestamentliche Wissenschaft* (Berlin)
BZNW	*Beihefte zur Zeitschrift für neutestamentliche Wissenschaft* (Berlin)
BZSF	*Biblische Zeit- und Streitfragen des Glaubens, der Weltanschauung und Bibelforschung* (Berlin - Lichterfelde)
CBC	D. BERGANT - R.J. KARRIS, *The Collegeville Bible Commentary*, 1989
CBQ	*Catholic Biblical Quarterly* (Washington DC)
CCHS	B. ORCHARD - E.F. SUTTCLIFFE - R.C. FULLER - R. RUSSELL (eds.), *A Catholic Commentary on Holy Scripture*, 1953
CE	*Cahiers Évangile* (Paris)
CECNT	*Meyer's Critical and Exegetical Commentary of the New Testament* (KEK) (Göttingen) → KEK
CH	*Church History* (Indiolantic FL)
ChSt	*Chicago Studies* (Mundelein IL)
ChrTod	*Christianity Today* (Carol Stream IL)
CivCatt	*Civiltà Cattolica* (Rome)
CNam	*Collationes Namurcenses* (Namur)
CNI	*Christian News from Israel* (Jerusalem)
CNT	*Commentaire du Nouveau Testament* (Geneva)
CoBRA	*Collectanea Biblica et Religiosa Antiqua* (Brussels)
CQR	*Church Quarterly Review* (London)
CRBR	*Critical Review of Books in Religion* (Atlanta GA)
CritR	*Critical Review of Theological and Philosophical Literature* (Edinburgh)
CSS	Cursus Scripturae Sacrae
CTL	*Crown Theological Library* (London)
CurrTMiss	*Currents in Theology and Mission* (Chicago IL)
DAC	J. HASTINGS (ed.), *Dictionary of the Apostolic Church*, 1915
DB	F. VIGOUROUX (ed.), *Dictionnaire de la Bible*, 5 vols., 1895-1912
DBDL	J. HASTINGS - J.A. SELBIE - A.B. DAVIDSON - S.R. DRIVER - H.B. SWETE (eds.), *Dictionary of the Bible Dealing with its Language*, 1909; 1963, ^{2}1965 (eds. F.C. GRANT and H.H. ROWLEY)

DBE	J. HASTINGS (ed.), *A Dictionary of the Bible*, Extra Vol., 1904
DBI	R.J. COGGINS - J.L. HOULDEN (eds.), *A Dictionary of Biblical Interpretation*, 1990
DBS	*Supplément au Dictionnaire de la Bible*
DCG	J. HASTINGS - J.A. SELBIE - A.B. DAVIDSON - S.R. DRIVER - H.B. SWETE (eds.), *A Dictionary of Christ and the Gospels*, 1906-1908
DJG	J.B. GREEN - S. MCKNIGHT - I.H. MARSHALL (eds.), *Dictionary of Jesus and the Gospels*, 1992
DownR	*Downside Review* (Bath)
DTC	A. VACANT - E. MANGENOT (eds.), *Dictionnaire de theologie catholique*, 1899-1972
EB	*Études bibliques* (Paris)
EB(C)	*Encyclopedia Biblica* (T.K. Cheyne), 1899-1903; 1914
EBD	A.C. MEYERS (ed.), *The Eerdmans Bible Dictionary*, 1987
EdF	*Erträge der Forschung* (Darmstadt)
EDNT	*Exegetical Dictionary of the New Testament*, 1990-1993 → EWNT
ÉglT	*Église et théologie* (Ottawa)
EHS	*Europäische Hochschulschriften* (Frankfurt - Bern)
EKK	*Evangelisch-katholischer Kommentar* (Zürich - Einsiedeln - Cologne - Neukirchen-Vluyn)
EKL	E. FAHLBUSCH (ed.), *Evangelisches Kirchenlexikon*, 1985
ErfTSt	*Erfurter theologische Studien* (Leipzig)
EstBib	*Estudios biblicos* (Madrid)
EstFranc	*Estudios Franciscanos* (Barcelona)
ETL	*Ephemerides Theologicae Lovanienses* (Leuven)
ETR	*Études théologiques et religieuses* (Montpellier)
EvQ	*Evangelical Quarterly* (London)
EvTh	*Evangelische Theologie* (Munich)
EWNT	H. BALZ - G. SCHNEIDER, *Exegetisches Wörterbuch zum Neuen Testament*, 1980-1983 → EDNT
ExpT	*Expository Times* (Edinburgh)
ExT	P. BENOIT, *Exégèse et Théologie*, 1961 → JG
FG	B.H. STREETER, *The Four Gospels*, 1924
FoiVie	*Foi et vie* (Paris)
Forum	*Forum* (Sonoma CA)
FRLANT	*Forschungen zur Religion und Literatur des Alten und Neuen Testaments* (Göttingen)
FS Fitzmyer	M.P. HOGAN - P.J. KOBELSKI (eds.), *To Touch the Text*, 1989
FS Lindars	D.A. CARSON - H.G.M. WILLIAMSON (eds.), *It is Written*, 1988
FS Malherbe	D.L. BALCH (ed.), *Greeks, Romans, and Christians*, 1990
FS Michel	O. BETZ - M. HENGEL - P. SCHMIDT (eds.), *Abraham unser Vater*, 1963
FS Mussner	P-G. MÜLLER - W. STENGER (eds.), *Kontinuität und Einheit*, 1981
FS Neirynck	F. VAN SEGBROECK - C.M. TUCKETT - G. VAN BELLE - J. VERHEYDEN (eds.), *The Four Gospels 1992*, 1992
FS Schmid	P. HOFFMANN, N. Brox and W. Pesch (eds.), *Orientierung*, 1973
FS Schmidt	G. KRETSCHMAR - B. LOHSE (eds.), *Ecclesia*, 1961
FS Schubert	L.E. KECK - J.L. MARTYN (eds.), *Studies*, 1966, 1968, 1980
FS Stählin	O. BÖCHER - K. HAACKER (eds.), *Verborum Veritas*, 1970

810 ABBREVIATIONS

FS Vögtle	R. Pesch (ed.), *Jesus*, 1975
FTG	M. Dibelius, *From Tradition to Gospel*, 1965
FTS	*Frankfurter theologische Studien* (Frankfurt)
GELS	J. Lust - E. Eynikel - K. Hauspie with the collaboration of G. Chamberlin, *A Greek-English Lexicon of the Septuagint*, 2 vols., 1992-1996
GELS(TP)	T. Muraoka, *A Greek-English Lexicon of the Septuagint (Twelve Prophets)*, 1993
Greg	*Gregorianum* (Rome)
GrNT	*Grundrisse zum Neuen Testament* (Göttingen)
GST	R. Bultmann, *Die Geschichte der synoptischen Tradition*, 1921
HeythJ	*Heythrop Journal* (London)
HJ	*Hibbert Journal* (London)
HNT	*Handbuch zum Neuen Testament*
HR	E. Hatch - H.A. Redpath. *Concordance*, 2 vols. 1897; Supplement, 1906
HST	R. Bultmann, *History of the Synoptic Tradition*, 1921 → GST
HTKNT	*Herders theologischer Kommentar zum Neuen Testament* (Freiburg i.Br.)
HTKNT Supp	*Herders theologischer Kommentar zum Neuen Testament Supplementband* (Freiburg i.Br.)
HTR	*Harvard Theological Review* (Cambridge MA)
HTS	*Harvard Theological Studies* (Cambridge MA)
IB	G.A. Buttrick (ed.), *The Interpreter's Bible*, 1951-1957
IBNTG	C.F.D. Moule, *An Idiom Book of New Testament Greek*, 1953, ^{2}1959, ^{R}1979
IBS	*Irish Biblical Studies* (Belfast)
ICC	*International Critical Commentary* (Edinburgh)
IDB	*Interpreter's Dictionary of the Bible*
IDBS	*Interpreter's Dictionary of the Bible Supplement*
Interpr	*Interpretation* (Richmond VA)
ISBE	G.W. Bromiley (ed.), *The International Standard Bible Encyclopedia*, 1979-1988
IVP NTCS	G.R. Osborne (ed.), *The InterVarsity Press NT Commentary Series*, Downers Grove, IL - Leicester
JAAR	*Journal of the American Academy of Religion* (Boston MA)
JATL	*Journal für auserlesene theologische Literatur* (Nürnberg)
JBC	R.E. Brown - J.A. Fitzmyer - R.E. Murphy (eds.), *The Jerome Biblical Commentary*, 1968
JBL	*Journal of Biblical Literature* (Atlanta GA)
JBR	*Journal of Bible and Religion* (Boston MA)
JDT	*Jahrbücher für deutsche Theologie* (Gotha)
JEH	*Journal of Ecclesiastical History* (London)
JETS	*Journal of the Evangelical Theological Society* (Jackson MS)
JG	P. Benoit, *Jesus and the Gospel*, Vol. 1, 1973 → ET
JJS	*Journal of Jewish Studies* (Oxford)
JN	J.B. Green - M.M. Turner (eds.), *Jesus of Nazareth*, 1994
JPTh	*Jahrbücher für protestantische Theologie* (Lepzig - Freiburg - Braunschweig)
JR	*Journal of Religion* (Chicago IL)

JSNT	*Journal for the Study of the New Testament* (Sheffield)
JSNT SS	*Journal for the Study of the New Testament. Supplement Series* (Sheffield)
JSOT SS	*Journal for the Study of the Old Testament. Supplement Series* (Sheffield)
JT	D. WENHAM, *The Jesus Tradition*, 1984
JTS	*Journal of Theological Studies* (Oxford)
KEK	*Meyer's Kritisch-exegetischer Kommentar über das Neue Testament* (Göttingen); → CECNT
KNT	*Kommentar zum Neuen Testament* (Leipzig)
LBS	*Library of Biblical Studies* (New York)
LD	*Lectio Divina* (Paris)
LDC	*Lectio Divina Commentaires* (Paris)
LingBib	*Linguistica Biblica* (Bonn)
LouvSt	*Louvain Studies* (Leuven)
LSJ	H.G. LIDDELL - R. SCOTT, *A Greek-English Lexicon*, 2 vols., 1843; ^{9}1897; ed. H.S. JONES and R. MCKENZIE, 1925-40; ^{9}1940
LTK	J. HÖFER - K. RAHNER (eds.), *Lexikon für Theologie und Kirche*, ^{2}1957-1968
MHT 1	J.H. MOULTON, *Grammar. 1. Prolegomena*, 1906, ^{3}1978
MHT 2	J.H. MOULTON - W.F. HOWARD, *Grammar. 2. Accidence*, 1919, ^{2}1929
MHT 3	N. TURNER, *Grammar. 3. Syntax*, 1963
MHT 4	N. TURNER, *Grammar. 4. Style*, 1976
MMJ	H.D.A. MAJOR - T.W. MANSON - C.J. WRIGHT (eds.), *The Mission and Message of Jesus*, 1938
Month	*The Month* (London)
MThS	*Münchener theologische Studien* (Munich)
MTS	*Marburger theologische Studien* (Marburg)
MüTZ	*Münchener Theologische Zeitschrift* (Munich)
NABPR BS	*National Association of Baptist Professors of Religion Bibliographic Series* (Chicago IL)
NAC	*The New American Commentary* (Nashville TN)
NBC	D. GUTHRIE - J.A. MOTYER (eds.), *The New Bible Commentary*, ^{3}1970
NCC	R.C. FULLER - L. JOHNSTON - C. KEARNS (eds.), *New Catholic Commentary*, 1969
NCE	*New Catholic Encyclopedia* (Washington DC), 1967
NCHS	C. GORE - H.L. GOUDGE - A. GUILLAUME (eds.), *A New Commentary on Holy Scripture*, 1928
NedTT	*Nederlands theologisch tijdschrift* (Wageningen NL)
NIB	L. KECK et al. (eds.), *The New Interpreter's Bible*, 12 vols., Nashville, TN, 1994-
NIBC	*New International Bible Commentaries* (Peabody MA)
NICNT	*New International Commentary on the New Testament* (Grand Rapids MI - Cambridge)
NIGTC	*New International Greek Testament Commentary* (Exeter - Grand Rapids MI)
NJBC	R.E. BROWN - J.A. FITZMYER - R.E. MURPHY (eds.), *The New Jerome Biblical Commentary*, 1990
NJDTh	*Neue Jahrbücher für deutsche Theologie* (Bonn)
NKZ	*Neue Kirchliche Zeitschrift* (Erlangen)

NLNT	C. Spicq, *Notes*, 3 vols., 1978, 1982 (= *Lexique théologique*, 1991, 3 vols. in 1 vol.) → TLNT
NRT	*Nouvelle revue théologique* (Tournai)
NT	*Novum Testamentum* (Leiden)
NTAbh	*Neutestamentliche Abhandlungen* (Münster)
NTC	*New Testament Commentaries*
NTD	*Das Neues Testament Deutsch* (Göttingen)
NTI	W. Kümmel, *Introduction to the New Testament*, 1975 → *Einleitung in das Neue Testament*, [17]1973
NTM	*New Testament Message* (Wilmington DE)
NTS	*New Testament Studies* (Cambridge)
NTSuppl	*Supplements to Novum Testamentum* (Leiden)
NTV	F. Neirynck - F. Van Segbroeck, *New Testament Vocabulary*, 1984
OBO	*Orbis Biblicus et Orientalis* (Fribourg)
OCB	B.M. Metzger - M.D. Coogan (eds.), *The Oxford Companion to the Bible*, 1993
ÖTNT	*Ökumenischer Taschenbuchkommentar zum Neuen Testament* (Gütersloh - Würzburg)
PBSB	Petite bibliothèque des sciences bibliques Nouveau Testament (Paris)
PCB	M. Black - H.H. Rowley (eds.). *Peake's Commentary on the Bible*, 1962
PerspRelSt	*Perspectives in Religious Studies* (Danville VA)
PerspRelSt SS	*Perspectives in Religious Studies Special Series* (Danville VA)
PNT	*De Prediking van het Nieuwe Testament* (Nijkerk)
PrincSemB	*Princeton Seminary Bulletin* (Princeton NJ)
PrTMS	*Princeton Theological Monograph Series* (Allison Park PA)
PTMS	*Pittsburgh Theological Monograph Series* (Pittsburgh PA)
PTS	*Paderborner theologische Studien* (Paderborn)
QD	*Quaestiones Disputatae* (Freiburg i.Br.)
RAp	*Revue apologétique* (Paris)
RB	*Revue biblique* (Jerusalem - Paris)
RD	A.T. Robinson and W.H. Davis, *New Short Grammar*, 1931; [10]1977
RE	A. Hauck (ed.), *Realencyklopädie*, 24 vols., [3]1896-1913
RechBib	*Recherches bibliques* (Paris)
RevÉtudGrec	*Revue des études grecques* (Paris)
RevSR	*Revue des sciences religieuses* (Strasbourg)
RExp	*Review and Expositor* (Louisville KY)
RGG	F.M. Schiele - L. Zscharnack (eds.), *Die Religion in Geschichte und Gegenwart*, 5 vols., 1909-1913; [2]1927-1932 (ed. H. Gunkel); [3]1957-65 (ed. K. Galling)
RHPR	*Revue d'histoire et de philosophie religieuses* (Strasbourg)
RHR	*Revue de l'histoire des religions* (Paris)
RNT	*Regensburger Neues Testament* (Regensburg)
RSR	*Recherches de science religieuse* (Paris)
RThom	*Revue thomiste* (Bruges)
RTP	*Revue de théologie et de philosophie* (Lausanne)
RTQR	*Revue de theologie et des questions religieuses* (Montauban)
SANT	*Studien zum Alten und Neuen Testaments* (Munich)
SB	*Sources bibliques* (Paris)

SBA	*Stuttgarter Biblische Aufsatzbände - Neues Testament* (Stuttgart)
SBL MS	*Society of Biblical Literature. Monograph Series*
SBT	*Studies in Biblical Theology* (London)
SC	*Sources chrétiennes* (Paris)
ScC	*Scuola cattolica. Revista di scienze religiose* (Milan)
ScEc	*Sciences ecclésiastiques* (Montréal)
ScotJT	*Scottish Journal of Theology* (Edinburgh)
ScriptB	*Scripture Bulletin* (Twickenham England)
SecCent	*Second Century* (Abilene TX)
SEsp	*Science et esprit* (Montréal)
SNT	*Die Schriften des Neuen Testaments neu übersetzt und für die Gegenwart erklärt*
SNTA	*Studiorum Novi Testamenti Auxilia* (Leuven)
SNTS MS	*Studiorum Novi Testamenti Societas. Monograph Series* (Cambridge)
SNTU	*Studien zum Neuen Testament und seiner Umwelt* (Linz)
SPAW	*Sitzungsberichte der Preussischen Akademie der Wissenschaften*
SPB	*Studia Post-Biblica* (Leiden)
SPNT	*Studies on Personalities of the New Testament* (Columbia, SC)
SSP	W. SANDAY (ed.), *Oxford Studies in the Synoptic Problem*, 1911
ST	*Studia Theologica* (Lund)
STBNT	*Studia Theologiae Biblicae Novi Testamenti* (Rome)
StEv	*Studia Evangelica* (Berlin)
StNT	J.M.D. DERRETT, *Studies in the New Testament*, 5 vols., 1977-1986
StPat	*Studia Patristica*
STS Supp	*Strassburger theologische Studien Supplement* (Freiburg)
SUNT	*Studien zur Umwelt des Neuen Testaments* (Göttingen)
SV	F. REHKOPF, *Septuaginta-Vokabular*, 1989
SWJTh	*Southwest Journal of Theology* (Seminary Hill TX)
TBei	*Theologische Beiträge* (Wuppertal)
TDNT	G. KITTEL - G. FRIEDRICH (eds.), *Theological Dictionary of the New Testament*, 1964-1976 → TWNT
TGl	*Theologie und Glaube* (Paderborn)
THKNT	*Theologischer Handkommentar zum Neuen Testament* (Berlin)
ThL	*Theologische Lehrbücher* (Leipzig)
ThZS	*Theologische Zeitschrift aus der Schweiz* (Zürich)
TJ	*Theologischer Jahresbericht* (Braunschweig - London - New York - Paris)
TJT	*Toronto Journal of Theology* (Toronto)
TLNT	C. SPICQ, *Theological Lexicon*, 3 vols., 1994 → NLNT
TLond	*Theology* (London)
TLZ	*Theologische Literaturzeitung* (Leipzig)
TNTC	*Tyndale New Testament Commentaries* (London)
TPI NTC	*Trinity Press International New Testament Commentary* (London)
TPQ	*Theologisch-praktische Quartalschrift* (Linz)
TQ	*Theologische Quartalschrift* (Munich)
TR	*Theologische Rundschau* (Tübingen)
TRE	*Theologische Realenzyklopädie* (Berlin)
TRev	*Theologische Revue* (Münster)
TrU	H. SCHÜRMANN, *Traditionsgeschichtliche Untersuchungen*, 1968

TS	*Theological Studies* (Washington DC)
TSK	*Theologische Studien und Kritiken* (Hamburg)
TT	*Tijdschrift voor Theologie* (Nijmegen)
TTZ	*Trierer Theologische Zeitschrift* (Trier)
TU	*Texte und Untersuchungen* (Berlin)
TWNT	G. KITTEL - G. FRIEDRICH (eds.), *Theologisches Wörterbuch zum Neuen Testament*, 1933-1979 → TDNT
TZ	*Theologische Zeitschrift* (Basel)
VC	*Vigiliae Christianae* (Leiden)
VD	*Verbum Domini* (Rome)
VGTB	*Van Gorcum's theologische bibliotheek* (Assen NL)
VieI	*La vie intellectuelle* (Paris)
VKAB	*Verhandelingen van de Koninklijke Academie voor Wetenschappen, Letteren en Schone Kunsten van België. Klasse der Letteren* (Brussels)
VKGNT	K. ALAND (ed.), *Völlstandige Konkordanz*, 3 vols., 1975-1983
VoxT	*Vox Theologica* (Assen NL)
VS	Verbum Salutis (Paris)
WBC	*Word Biblical Commentary* (Waco TX)
WC	*Westminster Commentaries* (London)
WdF	*Wege der Forschung* (Darmstadt)
WeBC	*Westminster Bible Companion* (Louisville KY)
WestTJ	*Westminster Theological Journal* (Philadelphia PA)
WUNT	*Wissenschaftliche Untersuchungen zum Neuen Testament* (Tübingen)
ZBKNT	*Zürcher Bibelkommentare zum Neuen Testament* (Zürich)
ZKT	*Zeitschrift für katholische Theologie* (Vienna)
ZNW	*Zeitschrift für die neutestamentliche Wissenschaft und die Kunde der älteren Kirche* (Berlin)
ZRGG	*Zeitschrift für Religions- und Geistesgeschichte* (Cologne)
ZSRG.R	*Zeitschrift der Savigny-Stiftung für Rechtsgeschichte. Romanistische Ablteilung* (Weimar)
ZTK	*Zeitschrift für Theologie und Kirche* (Tübingen)
ZWB	*Zürcher Werkkommentare zur Bibel* (Zürich)
ZWT	*Zeitschrift für wissenschaftliche Theologie* (Frankfurt)

Other Abbreviations

adj.	adjective	n.d.	no date
Aufl.	Auflage	NAB	New American Bible
Bd.	Band	NEB	New English Bible
CBA	Catholic Biblical Association	NIV	New International Version
		no., #	number
ch.	chapter	NRSV	New Revised Standard Version
col., cols.	Column, columns		
diff.	differ	ns, NS	new series
diss.	dissertation	NT	New Testament
ed(s).	editor(s), edition(s)	OT	Old Testament
esp.	especially	par., pars.	parallel, parallels
ET	English translation	pt.	part
et al.	et alii, and others	repr., R	reprint
FS	Festschrift	RSV	Revised Standard Version
FT	French translation	rev.	revised, revision
gen.	genitive	SBL	Society of Biblical Literature
GP	the Gospel of Peter		
grad.	graduate	SNTS	Studiorum Novi Testamenti Societas
GS	Grundschrift		
GT	German translation	t.	tome
Habil.	Habilitationsschrift	T.	Teil
Hochsch.	Hochschule	Theol.	Theology, theological
Id.	Idem	tr.	translated by
KULeuven	Katholieke Universiteit Leuven	U.	University
		vgl.	German equivalent for cf. (confer); compare
Lit(s).	literature(s)		
LXX	Septuagint	*v.l.*	*varia lectio*; alternative reading
MA(s)	minor agreement(s)		
MS(S)	manuscript(s)	vol., vols.	volume, volumes
n., nn.	note, notes		

BIBLIOGRAPHY

Works preceded by an asterisk in the margin indicate studies of special interest for Lk 22–23 (trials and Herod). Those prefaced by a small "p" highlight specific titles on the Gospel of Peter.

ABBOTT, E.A. *The Corrections of Mark Adopted by Matthew and Luke* (Diatessarica, 2), London, 1901.

ABRAHAMS, I. *Studies in Pharisaism and the Gospels* (Second Series), Cambridge, 1924.

ADENEY, W.F. *St. Luke*, London, 1910.

* AICHER, G. *Der Prozess Jesu*, Bonn - Cologne, 1929; Amsterdam, ᴿ1963.

ALAND, B. Das Zeugnis der frühen Papyri für den Text der Evangelien diskutiert am Matthäusevangelium. — FS NEIRYNCK, Vol. 1, 1992, 326-335.

ALAND, K., M. BLACK, B.M. METZGER and A. WIKGREN in cooperation with the Institute for New Testament Textual Research, *The Greek New Testament*, Münster - New York - London - Edinburgh - Amsterdam - Stuttgart, 1966; [+C.M. MARTINI], ²1968; ³1975; corrected, 1983; Fourth Rev. Ed., eds. B. ALAND, K. ALAND, J. KARAVIDOPOULOS, C.M. MARTINI, and B.M. METZGER, Stuttgart, 1993.

ALAND, K. *Synopsis Quattuor Evangeliorum. Locis parallelis evangeliorum apocryphorum et patrum adhibitis*, Stuttgart, 1963; ⁸1973; ⁹1976; ¹²1982; ¹³1985; = *Synopsis of the Four Gospels. Greek-English Edition of the Synopsis Quattuor Evangeliorum: loci parallelis evangeliorum apocryphorum et patrum adhibitis*, [Stuttgart], 1976, ⁴˒⁵1980/1982, ¹³1985.

— *Vollständige Konkordanz zum griechischen Neuen Testament unter Zugrundelegung aller modernen kritischen Textausgaben und des Textus Receptus*, 3 vols., Berlin, 1975-1983 (= VKGNT).

ALBERTZ, M. *Die synoptischen Streitgespräche. Ein Beitrag zur Formengeschichte des Urchristentums*, Berlin, 1921.

— *Die Botschaft des Neuen Testamentes*. 2 vols. Vol. 1/1-2. *Die Entstehung der Botschaft*, Zürich, 1947.

ALETTI, J.-N. *L'art de raconter Jésus Christ*, Paris, 1989; = *L'arte di raccontare Gesù Cristo. La scrittura narrativa del vangelo di Luca* (Biblioteca biblica, 7), tr. L. SEMBRANO, Brescia - Queriniana, 1991.

ALEXANDER, L. *The Preface to Luke's Gospel. Literary Convention and Social Context in Luke 1.1-4 and Acts 1.1* (SNTS MS 78), Cambridge, 1993. Diss. Oxford, 1978 (dir. D. NINEHAM).

ALLEN, W.C. Did St. Matthew and St. Luke Use the Logia? — *ExpT 11* (1899-1900) 424-426.

— *A Critical and Exegetical Commentary on the Gospel According to St. Matthew*, Edinburgh, 1907, ²1907, ³1912.

— The Aramaic Background of the Gospels. — *SSP*, 1911, 287-312.

— and L.W. GRENSTED. *Introduction to the Books of the New Testament*, Edinburgh, 1913, ²1918, ³1929.

ALLIOLI, J.F., L.C. GRATZ and D. HANEBERG, *Handbuch der biblischen Alterthumskunde*, Landshut, 1844.

p   AMANN, E. Évangiles apocryphes. — *DTC* 5, Paris, 1913, 1624-1640.

p   — Apocryphes du Nouveau Testament, L'Évangile de Pierre ou selon Pierre. — *DBS* 1, 1928, 476-477.

p   AMIOT, F. *La Bible apocryphe. Évangiles apocryphes*, Paris, 1952.

ANONYMOUS. Review of R.W. HUSBAND, Prosecution, 1916. — *BS* 74 (1917) 169.

— Review of A.M. PERRY, Sources, 1920. — *BS* 77 (1920) 238-239.

— Review of B.H. STREETER, The Four Gospels, 1924. — *ExpT* 36 (1924-25) 386-388.

— Review of R.H. CROMPTON, Synoptic Problem, 1928. — *ExpT* 40 (1928-29) 258.

— Review of H. BALMFORTH, Gospel, 1930. — *ExpT* 41 (1929-30) 546.

p   — Gospel of Peter. — *EBD*, 1987, 820-821.

ARNDT, W. *The Gospel according to St. Luke* (Bible Commentary), St. Louis, MO, 1956, R1981, R1986.

*   ASCOUGH, R.S. Rejection and Repentance: Peter and the People in Luke's Passion Narrative. — *Bib* 74 (1993) 349-365.

BACKHAUS, K. and F.G. UNTERGASSMAIR (eds.), *Schrift und Tradition*. FS J. ERNST, Paderborn, 1996.

BACON, B.W. *An Introduction to the New Testament*, New York - London, 1900; R1902, R1905, R1907, R1924.

— *The Beginnings of the Gospel Story. A Historico-Critical Inquiry into the Sources and Structure of the Gospel According to Mark, with Expository Notes Upon the Text, for English Readers*, New Haven, CT - London, 1909.

— *The Making of the New Testament*, London - New York - Toronto, n.d.

— The 'Order' of the Lukan 'Interpolations'. — *JBL* 34 (1915) 166-179; 37 (1917) 112-139; 38 (1918) 20-53.

— A Turning Point in Synoptic Criticism. — *HTR* 1 (1917) 48-69.

— More Philological Criticism of Acts. — *AJT* 22 (1918) 1-23.

— *Is Mark a Roman Gospel?* (HTS, 7), Cambridge, MA, 1919.

— La date et l'origine de l'évangile selon Marc. — *RHPR* 3 (1923) 268-285.

— Jesus and the Law. — *JBL* 47 (1928) 203-231.

— *The Story of Jesus and the Beginnings of the Church*, London, 1928.

— *Studies in Matthew*, London, 1930.

BAILEY, J.A. *The Traditions Common to the Gospels of Luke and John* (NTSuppl, 7), Leiden, 1963.

BAIRD, W. The Gospel according to Luke. — C.M LAYMON (ed.), *Interpreter's*, 1971, 672-706.

— The Acts of the Apostles. — *Ibid.*, 729-767.

— *History of New Testament Research. 1. From Deism to Tübingen*, Minneapolis, MN, 1992.

*   BAJSIĆ, A. Pilatus, Jesus und Barrabas. — *Bib* 48 (1967) 7-28.

BALCH, D.L. (ed.), *Greeks, Romans, and Christians*. FS A. MALHERBE, Minneapolis, MN, 1990 (= FS Malherbe).

p   BALJON, J.M.S. Het Evangelie van Petrus. — *Theologische Studiën* 12 (1894) 1-34.

— *Commentaar op het Evangelie van Lukas*, Utrecht, 1908.

BALMFORTH, H. *The Gospel according to St. Luke in the Revised Version with Introduction and Commentary* (The Clarendon Bible), Oxford, 1930, R1958.

BALZ, H., G. SCHNEIDER, *Exegetisches Wörterbuch zum Neuen Testament*, 3 vols., Stuttgart, 1980, 1981, 1983 (= EWNT);

= *Exegetical Dictionary of the New Testament*, 3 vols., Grand Rapids, MI, 1990, 1991, 1993 (= EDNT).

— ἀναπέμπω, in *EWNT* 1, col. 208; = *EDNT* 1, 87.

— ἐπισχύω, in *EWNT* 2, col. 102; = *EDNT* 2, 41.

BAMMEL, E. Erwägungen zur Eschatologie Jesu. — *Studia Evangelica* 3 (TU 88), Berlin, 1964, 3-32.
— Das Ende von Q. — FS STÄHLIN, 1970, 39-50.
* — (ed.), *The Trial of Jesus. Cambridge Studies in Honour of C.F.D. Moule* (SBT, 2/13), London, 1970.
— The Baptist in the Early Christian Tradition. — *NTS* 18 (1971-72) 95-128.
— and C.F.D. MOULE (eds.), *Jesus and the Politics of His Day*, tr. D.R. CATCHPOLE, Cambridge - London - New York, 1984.
BARCLAY, W. *The First Three Gospels*, London - Philadelphia, PA, [1966]; *Introduction to the First Three Gospels. A Revised Edition of The First Three Gospels*, Philadelphia, PA, ²1975.
BARKER, G.W., W. LANE and J.R. MICHAELS. *The New Testament Speaks*, New York, 1969.
p   BARNES, W.E. The Newly-Found Gospel in Relation to the Four. — *ExpT* 5 (1893-94) 61-64.
* BARR, A. The Use and Disposal of the Marcan Source in Luke's Passion Narrative. — *ExpT* 55 (1943-44) 227-231.
— *A Diagram of Synoptic Relationships*, Edinburgh, 1963.
BARRELL, E.V. and K.G. BARRELL, *St. Luke's Gospel. An Introductory Study*, London, 1982.
BARRETT, C.K. *Luke the Historian in Recent Study* (Facet Book BS, 24), Philadelphia, PA, 1960, ²1968.
— Luke/Acts. — FS LINDARS, 1988, 231-244.
— The Third Gospel as a Preface to Acts? Some Reflections. — FS NEIRYNCK, Vol. 2, 1992, 1451-1466.
— *A Critical and Exegetical Commentary on the Acts of the Apostles* (ICC), Vol. 1, Edinburgh, 1994.
BARTLET, J.V. The Sources of St. Luke's Gospel. — *SSP*, 1911, 313-363.
* BARTON, G.A. On the Trial of Jesus Before the Sanhedrin. — *JBL* 41 (1922) 205-211.
BARTSCH, H.-W. *Wachet aber zu jeder Zeit! Entwurf einer Auslegung des Lukasevangelium*, Hamburg, 1963.
BATIFFOL, P. Comment s'est formé le Nouveau Testament. À propos des Bampton Lectures de 1893. — *RB* 3 (1894) 375-386.
— *Six leçons sur les Évangiles*, Paris, 1897.
— *Orpheus et l'Évangile*, Paris, 1910;
    = *The Credibility of the Gospel*, tr. G.C.H. POLLEN, London, 1912.
BAUCKHAM, R.J. The Study of the Gospel Traditions Outside the Canonical Gospels: Problems and Prospects. — *JT*, 1984, 369-403.
p   — A Bibliography on Recent Works on Gospel Traditions Outside the Canonical Gospels. — *Ibid.*, 405-419.
p   — Gospels (Apocryphal). — *DJG*, 1992, 286-291.
BAUER, J.B. ΠΟΛΛΟΙ. Luk 1,1. — *NT* 4 (1960) 263-266;
    = *Scholia*, 1972, 75-78.
— *Scholia Biblica et Patristica*, Graz, 1972.
p   BAUER, W. Petrusevangelium. — *RGG* 4, Tübingen, ²1930, 1116.
— *A Greek-English Lexicon of the New Testament*, tr. and adapted W.F. ARNDT and F.W. GINGRICH, 2nd ed. rev. and augmented by F.W. GINGRICH and F.W. DANKER from BAUER'S 5th ed., Chicago, IL, 1957, 1979 (= BAGD).

— *Griechisch-deutsches Wörterbuch zu den Schriften des Neuen Testaments und der frühchristlichen Literatur*, ed. K. and B. ALAND, Berlin - New York, ⁶1988 ("völlig neu bearbeitete Auflage") (= B-A).

BAUERNFEIND, O. *Die Apostelgeschichte* (THK, 5), Leipzig, 1939.

— στρατεύομαι. — *TWNT* 7, 701-713; = *TDNT* 7, 701-713.

BAUMAN, E.W. *The Life and Teaching of Jesus*, Philadelphia, PA, 1960.

— *An Introduction to the New Testament*, Phildelphia, PA, 1961.

BAUMAN, M. and M.I. KLAUBER (eds.), *Historians of the Christian Tradition*, Nashville, TN, 1996. → S. MCKNIGHT

BAUMBACH, G. γραμματεύς. — *EWNT* 1, 624-627 (= *EDNT* 1, 259-260).

BEARE, F.W. *The Earliest Records of Jesus*, Oxford - New York, 1962.

BEASLEY-MURRAY, G.R. *John* (WBC, 36), Waco, TX, 1987.

* BEAUCHAMP, P. Narrativité biblique du récit de la passion. — *RSR* 73 (1985) 39-59.

BEBB, L.J.M. Gospel of Luke. — *DBDL* 3, New York, 1901, 162-173.

* BECK, B.E. 'Imitatio Christi' and the Lucan Passion Narrative. — W. HORBURY and B. MCNEIL (eds.), *Suffering*, 1981, 28-47.

— *Christian Character in the Gospel of Luke*, London, 1989.

p BELL, H.I. and T.C. SKEAT, *Fragments of An Unknown Gospel and Other Early Christian Papyri*, London, 1935.

BELLINZONI, A.J. (ed.), *The Two-Source Hypothesis. A Critical Appraisal*, Macon, GA, 1985.

BELSER, J. *Einleitung in das Neue Testament*, Freiburg, 1901, ²1905.

p — Das Petrusevangelium. — *Ibid.*, ²1905, 809-814.

* — *Geschichte des Leidens und Sterbens, der Auferstehung und Himmelfahrt des Herrn nach den vier Evangelien ausgelegt*, Freiburg, 1903; Freiburg - St. Louis, MO, ²1913; = *History of the Passion. Death and Glorification of Our Saviour, Jesus Christ*, tr. F.A. MARKS, ed. A. PREUSS, St. Louis, MO - London, 1929.

p BENNETT, E.N. The Gospel According to Peter. — *The Classical Review* 7 (1893) 40-42.

BENNETT, W.J. The Herodians of Mark's Gospel. — *NT* 17 (1975) 9-14.

* BENOIT, P. Le procès de Jésus. — *VieI* 2 (1940) 200-213; 3 (1940) 371-378; 4 (1940) 54-64;
= *BET*, Vol. 1, 265-289;
= The Trial of Jesus. — ID., *Jesus and the Gospel*, Vol. 1, tr. B. WEATHERHEAD, New York, 1973, 123-146.

* — Jésus devant le sanhédrin. — *Angelicum* 20 (1943) 143-165;
= *BET*, Vol. 1, 290-311;
= Jesus Before the Sanhedrin. — ID., *Jesus and the Gospel*, Vol. 1, New York, 1973, 147-166.

— Review of J. BLINZLER, Der Prozess Jesu, 1951. — *RB* 60 (1953) 452-453(454);
= Le procès de Jésus selon J. Blinzler et P. Démann. — *BET*, Vol. 1, 312-314.

— Review of H. SCHÜRMANN, Der Paschamahlbericht, 1953. — *RB* 61 (1954) 284-287.

— Review of H. SCHÜRMANN, Der Einsetzungsbericht, 1955. — *RB* 63 (1956) 460-461.

— *Exégèse et Théologie*, 3 vols., Paris, 1961-1968;
= *Exegese und Theologie: gesammelte Aufsätze*, Düsseldorf, 1965;
Jesus and the Gospel, 2 vols., tr. B. WEATHERHEAD, New York, 1973-1974 (1973) (= BJG);
= *Exégèse et Théologie*, Vol. 1 (= BET);
Exegesis y teologia, Vol. 1, tr. D.E. REQUENA, Madrid, 1974.

— Review of P. WINTER, On the Trial, 1961. — *RB* 68 (1961) 593-599;

= *Le procès de Jésus selon Paul Winter*. — *BET*, Vol. 3, Paris, 1965, 243-250.
* —— Les outrages à Jésus prophète (Mc xiv 65 par.). — W.C. VAN UNNIK (ed.), *Neotestamentica et Patristica*, 1962, 92-110;
= *BET*, Vol. 3, Paris, 1968, 251-269.
* —— *Passion et Résurrection du Seigneur*, Paris, 1966;
= *The Passion and Resurrection of Jesus Christ*, tr. B. WEATHERHEAD, New York, 1969.
—— and M.-É. BOISMARD, *Synopse des quatre évangiles en français*, Vol. 1: *Textes*, Paris, 1965; Vol. 2: *Commentaire par M.-É. Boismard avec la collaboration de A. Lamouille et P. Sandevoir*, Paris, 1972.
—— Review of G. SCHNEIDER, Verleugnung, 1969. — *RB* 78 (1971) 135-137.
BERGANT, D. and R.J. KARRIS, *The Collegeville Bible Commentary*, Collegeville, MN, 1989 (= CBC).
BERKELBACH VAN DER SPRENKEL, S.F.H.K. *Het Evangelie van Lucas*, 's Gravenhage, 1964.
BERNARD, J.H. *A Critical and Exegetical Commentary on the Gospel According to St. John* (ICC), 2 vols., Edinburgh - New York, 1928.
* BERTRAM, G. *Die Leidensgeschichte Jesu und der Christuskult*, Göttingen, 1922.
BEST, E. Review of V. TAYLOR, Passion Narrative, 1972. — *ScotJT* 25 (1972) 474- 475.
BETHUNE-BAKER, J.F. Review of B.S. EASTON, The Gospel before the Gospels, 1928. — *JTS* 30 (1928-29) 99.
BETZ, O., M. HENGEL and P. SCHMIDT (eds.), *Abraham unser Vater*. FS O. MICHEL, Leiden, 1963 (= FS Michel).
* BETZ, O. Probleme des Prozesses Jesu. — *ANRW* II.25.1 (1982) 565-647.
BÉVENOT, H. Alte und neue lukanische Quellen. — *TQ* 110 (1929) 428-447.
BEYSCHLAG, K. *Die verborgene Überlieferung von Christus*, Munich, 1969.
* BICKERMAN, E. Utilitas crucis. Observations sur les récits du procès de Jésus dans les Évangiles canoniques. — *RHR* 112 (1935) 169-241;
= *Studies in Jewish and Christian History*, Pt. 3, 82-138.
—— *Studies in Jewish and Christian History*, Pt. 3 (AGJU, 9), Leiden, 1986.
BIEDER, W. θάνατος. — *EWNT* 2, col. 319-328 (= *EDNT* 2, 129-133).
BIHLER, J. *Die Stephanusgeschichte im Zusammenhang der Apostelgeschichte* (MTS, 1/16), Munich, 1963.
* BINZ, S.J. *The Passion and Resurrection Narratives of Jesus. A Commentary*, Collegeville, MN, 1989.
BISHOP, E.F.F. Local Colour in Proto-Luke. — *ExpT* 45 (1933-34) 151-156.
BIVIN, D. A New Solution to the Synoptic Problem. — *Jerusalem Perspective* 4 (1991) 3-5.
BLACK, C.C. Review of J.D. CROSSAN, The Cross that Spoke, 1988. — *JR* 69 (1989) 398-399.
* BLACK, M. *The Arrest and Trial of Jesus and the Date of the Last Supper*. — A.J.B. HIGGINS (ed.), *New Testament Essays*, Manchester, 1959, 19-33.
—— and H.H. ROWLEY (eds.), *Peake's Commentary on the Bible*, London, 1962, [R]1964 (= PCB).
—— (ed.), *Studies in the Gospels and Epistles*, Manchester - Philadelphia, PA, 1962.
BLAIR, J. Review of E. LINNEMANN, Historical Criticism, 1990. — *Grace Theological Journal* 11 (1990) 246-248.
BLANCHARD, M. *Luke. An Introduction and Commentary*, Madras, 1969.
BLASS, F. *Evangelium secundum Lucam*, Leipzig, 1897.

— and DEBRUNNER, A. *Grammatik des neutestamentlichen Griechisch*, Göttingen, 1896 (F. Blass), ⁴1913 (rev. by A. DEBRUNNER); F. REHKOPF, ¹⁴1975, ¹⁶1984, ¹⁷1990 (= BDR);
= *A Greek Grammar of the New Testament and Other Early Christian Literature*, tr. and ed. R.W. FUNK, Chicago, IL, 1961 (= BDF).

BLEEK, F. *Synoptische Erklärung der drei ersten Evangelien* (ed. H.J. HOLTZMANN), Leipzig, 1862.

* BLEVINS, J.L. The Passion Narrative. — *RExp* 64 (1967) 513-522.

BLINZLER, J. *Die neutestamentlichen Berichte über die Verklärung Jesu*, Münster, 1937.

— *Herodes Antipas und Jesus Christus* (Bibelwissenschaftliche Reihe, 2), Stuttgart, 1947.

* — *Der Prozess Jesu*, Regensburg, 1951, ²1955, ³1960, ⁴1969;
= *The Trial of Jesus*, tr. I. and F. MCHUGH from ²1955 rev. and enlarged German ed., Westminster, MD, 1959;
= *Le procès de Jésus*, tr. G. DAUBIÉ, Tours, 1962.

* — Herodes und der Tod Jesu. — *Klerusblatt* 37 (1957) 118-121.

* — Passionsgeschehen und Passionsbericht des Lukasevangeliums. — *BK* 24 (1969) 1-4.

— Review of H. VAN DER KWAAK, Het Proces van Jezus, 1969. — *TR* 66 (1970) 382-386.

* — The Trial of Jesus in the Light of History. — *Judaism* 20 (1971) 49-55.

BLOMBERG, C. → D. WENHAM

BOCK, D.L. *Proclamation from Prophecy and Pattern. Lucan Old Testament Christology* (JSNT SS, 12), Sheffield, 1987. Diss. Aberdeen, 1982 (dir. I.H. MARSHALL).

* — The Son of Man Seated at God's Right Hand and the Debate over Jesus' 'Blasphemy'. — *JN*, 1994, 181-191.

— Gospel of Luke. — *DJG*, 1992, 495-510.

— *Luke* (IVP NTCS), Downers Grove, IL - Leicester, 1994.

— *Luke 1:1-9:50* (BECNT), Vol. 1, Grand Rapids, MI, 1994; Vol. 2. *Luke 9:51-24:53* (BECNT), Grand Rapids, MI, 1995.

— *Luke. The NIV Application Commentary*, Grand Rapids, MI, 1996.

BÖCHER, O. and K. HAACKER (eds.), *Verborum Veritas*. FS G. STÄHLIN, Wuppertal, 1970 (= FS Stählin).

BOERS, H. Review of V. TAYLOR, Passion Narrative, 1972. — *Interpr* 27 (1973) 112-114.

BOISMARD, M.-É. Review of H. SCHÜRMANN, Jesu Abschiedsrede, 1957. — RB 66 (1959) 140-141.

— → BENOIT, 1965.

— Review of É. TROCMÉ, La formation, 1963. — *RB* 72 (1965) 451-452.

— and A. LAMOUILLE, avec la collaboration de G. ROCHAIS. *L'évangile de Jean. Commentaire* (Synopse des quatre évangiles en français, 3), Paris, 1977.

— and A. LAMOUILLE, *Les Actes des Deux Apôtres. 1. Introduction-Textes. 2. Le sens des récits. 3. Analyses littéraires* (EB, 12, 13, 14), Paris, 1990.

— *L'évangile de l'enfance (Luc 1-2) selon le proto-Luc* (EB 35), Paris, 1997.

* — *En quête du Proto-Luc* (EB 37), Paris, 1997.

BOLES, H.L. *A Commentary on the Gospel according to Luke* (NT Commentaries, 3), Nashville, TN, 1974.

* BORNHÄUSER, K. *Zeiten und Stunden in der Leidensgeschichte und Auferstehungsgeschichte* (BFCT, 26/4), Gütersloh, 1921.

* — Die Beteiligung des Herodes am Prozesse Jesu. — *NKZ* 40 (1929) 714-718.

BORNKAMM, G. *Bibel: das Neue Testament. Eine Einführung in seine Schriften im Rahmen der Geschichte des Urchristentums*, Stuttgart, 1971;

= *The New Testament. A Guide to Its Writings*, tr. R.H. and I. FULLER, Philadelphia, PA, 1973.

BOUSSET, W. Der Gebrauch des Kyriostitels als Kriterium für die Quellenscheidung in der ersten Hälfte der Apostelgeschichte. — *ZNW* 15 (1914) 141-162.

BOSSUYT, P. and J. RADERMAKERS, *Jésus parole de la grâce selon saint Luc.* Vol. 2. *Lecture continue*, Brussels, 1981.

BOUTTIER, M. Review of P. BENOIT and M.-É. BOISMARD, Synopse, 1972. — *ETR* 47 (1972) 459.

BOUWMAN, G. *De Derde Nachtwake. De wordingsgeschiedenis van het derde evangelie* (Theologische monografieën. Woord en beleving, 2/7), Tielt, n.d. [1968];
= *Das Dritte Evangelium. Einübung in die formgeschichtliche Methode*, Düsseldorf, 1968.

— *Le "premier livre" (Actes., I,1) et la date des Actes des Apôtres.* — F. NEIRYNCK (ed.), *L'évangile de Luc - The Gospel of Luke*, ²1989, 553-565.

BOVER, J.M. Review of M.-J. LAGRANGE, Évangile selon saint Luc, 1921. — *Bib* 3 (1922) 353-358.

* BOVON, F. *Les derniers jours de Jésus. Textes et événements*, Neuchâtel - Paris - Brussels - Montréal, 1974.

— Le Dieu de Luc. — J. DELORME and J. DUPLACY (eds.), *La parole de grâce. Études lucaniennes à la memoire d' Augustin George*, Paris, 1981 (= RSR 69 (1981) 279-300);
= *New Testament Traditions*, 1995, 66-80.

— Chroniques du côté de chez Luc, in *RTP* 115 (1983) 175-189;
= Chronicles in Lucan Studies. — *Luke the Theologian*, 1987, 409-418.

— Le privilège pascal de Marie-Madeleine. — *NTS* 30 (1984) 50-62;
= *New Testament Traditions*, 1995, 147-157.

— *Luc le théologien. Vingt-cinq ans de recherches (1950-1975)*, Neuchâtel - Paris, 1978;
= *Luke the Theologian. Thirty-three Years of Research (1950-1983)*, tr. K. MCKINNEY, Allison Park, PA, 1987.

— *Évangiles de Luc et Actes des Apôtres.* — J. AUNEAU et al., *Évangiles synoptiques et Actes des Apôtres* (Petite bibliothèque des sciences bibliques. Nouveau Testament, 4), Paris, 1981, 195 -279.

— *Das Evangelium nach Lukas. 1. Teilband. Lk 1,1-9,50* (EKK 3/1), Zürich, 1989;
= *L'Évangile selon saint Luc (1,1-9,50)* (CNT, 3A), Geneva, 1991.

—, 1991 → H. KOESTER

— *Révélations et écritures. Nouveau Testament et littérature apocryphe chrétienne* (Le monde de la bible, 26), Geneva, 1993.

— Studies in Luke-Acts: Retrospect and Prospect. — *HTR* 85 (1992) 175-196;
= Études lucaniennes. Rétrospective et prospective. — *RTP* 125 (1993) 113-135.

* — Le récit lucanien de la passion dans l'évangile de Luc. — C. FOCANT (ed.), *The Synoptic Gospels. Source Criticism and the New Literary Criticism* (BETL, 110), Leuven, 1993, 393-423.

— *New Testament Traditions and Apocryphal Narratives* (PTMS, 36), tr. J. HAAPISEVA-HUNTER, Allison Park, PA, 1995.

BOWEN, C.R. Review of M. GOGUEL, Introduction aux Évangiles synoptiques. 1. Introduction au Nouveau Testament, 1923. — *JR* 4 (1924) 102-103.

* BOYD, W.J.P. Peter's Denials - Mark 14:68, Luke 22:57. — *ExpT* 67 (1955-56) 341.

BRADLEY, D.G. Review of H. SCHÜRMANN, Der Einsetzungsbericht, 1955. — *JBL* 75 (1956) 69-70.

* BRANDON, S.F.G. *The Trial of Jesus of Nazareth*, London - New York, 1968;
= *Het proces tegen Jezus van Nazareth*, tr. C.E. VAN AMERONGEN-VAN STRATEN, Amsterdam, 1969.

* BRANDT, W. *Die evangelische Geschichte und der Ursprung des Christentums auf Grund einer Kritik der Berichte über das Leiden und die Auferstehung Jesu*, Leipzig, 1893.

BRANTON, J.R. Review of A. LOISY, Origins, 1950. — *JBR* 19 (1951) 156- 157.

BRATCHER, R.G. *A Translator's Guide to the Gospel of Luke*, London - New York - Stuttgart, 1982.

BRAUMANN, G. (ed.), *Das Lukas-Evangelium. Die redaktions- und kompositionsgeschichtliche Forschung* (WdF, 280), Darmstadt, 1974.

BRAUND, D.C. Four Notes on the Herods. — *Classical Quarterly* 33 (1983) 239-242.

* — Herod Antipas, in *ABD* 3, 1992, 160.

BRAWLEY, R.L. *Luke-Acts and the Jews. Conflict, Apology, and Conciliation* (SBL MS, 33), Atlanta, GA, 1987.

— Resistance to the Carnivalization of Jesus: Scripture in the Lucan Passion Narrative. — *Semeia* 69/70 (1995) 33-60;
= *Text to Text Pours Forth Speech: Voices of Scripture in Luke-Acts* (Indiana Studies in Biblical Literature), Bloomington, IN, 1995 (revised).

BRIGGS, R.C. *Interpreting the Gospels. An Introduction to Methods and Issues in the Study of the Synoptic Gospels*, Nashville, TN, 1969.

BRINKMAN, F.J. Review of H. VAN DER KWAAK, Het Proces van Jezus, 1969. — *VoxT* 40 (1970) 201-203.

BROADHEAD, E.K. *Prophet, Son, Messiah. Narrative Form and Function in Mark 14-16* (JSNT SS, 97), Sheffield, 1994. Diss. Zürich (dir. H. WEDER).

BRODIE, T.L. A New Temple and a New Law. The Unity and Chronicler-based Nature of Luke 1:1 -4:22a. — *JSNT* 5 (1979) 21-45.

— Luke 7,36-50 as an Internalization of 2 Kings 4,1-37: A Study in Luke's Use of Rhetorical Imitation. — *Bib* 64 (1983) 457-485.

— The Accusing and Stoning of Naboth (1 Kgs 21:8-13) as One Component of the Stephen Text (Acts 6:9-14; 7:58a). — *CBQ* 45 (1983) 417-432.

— Towards Unravelling the Rhetorical Imitation of Sources in Acts: 2 Kgs 5 as One Component of Acts 8:9-40. — *Bib* 67 (1986) 41-67.

— Towards Unravelling Luke's Use of the Old Testament: Luke 7,11-17 as an Imitation of 1 Kings 17:17-24. — *NTS* 32 (1986) 247-267.

— The Departure for Jerusalem (Luke 9,51-56) as a Rhetorical Imitation of Elijah's Departure for the Jordan (2 Kgs 1,1-2,6). — *Bib* 70 (1989) 96-109.

— Luke 9:57-62: A Systematic Adaption of the Divine Challenge of Elijah (1 Kings 19). — *SBL 1989 Seminar Papers*, 237-245.

— A Century of Proto-Luke (1891-1991): Towards Giving New Life to an Old Theory, unpublished paper, 1991 SBL Meeting, Kansas City, KS.

— *The Quest for the Origin of John's Gospel. A Source-Oriented Approach*, New York - Oxford, 1993.

— Reopening the Quest for Proto-Luke. The Systematic Use of Judges 6–12 in Luke 16:1–18:8. — *The Journal of Higher Criticism* 2 (1995) 68-101.

— Intertextuality and Its Use in Tracing Q and Proto-Luke. — C.M. TUCKETT (ed.), *Scriptures*, 1997, 469-477.

BROMILEY, G.W. (ed.), *The International Standard Bible Encyclopedia*, 4 vols., Grand Rapids, MI, 1979-88 (= ISBE).

BRONSEN, J. *Verlaat het Vaderhuis*, Amersfoort, 1986.

BROOK, R. Review of V.H. STANTON, The Gospels as Historical Documents. Pt. 2, 1909. — *JTS* 13 (1911-12) 115-119.

BROOKE, A.E. Review of C.G. MONTEFIORE, The Synoptic Gospels, 1927. — *JTS* 29 (1927-28) 47- 48.

BROOKS, J.A. and C.L. WINBERY, *Syntax of New Testament Greek*, Washington, D.C., 1979.

BROWN, R.E., J.A. FITZMYER and R.E. MURPHY (eds.), *The Jerome Biblical Commentary*, Englewoods Cliffs, NJ, 1968 (= JBC); *The New Jerome Biblical Commentary*, Englewood Cliffs, NJ, 1990 (= NJBC).

p   — Apocrypha; Dead Sea Scrolls; Other Jewish Literature. — *JBC*, 1968, 535-560; *NJBC*, 1990, 1055-1082.

— *The Gospel According to John (xiii-xxi)* (AB 29A), Garden City, NY, 1970.

— The Relation of 'the Secret Gospel of Mark' to the Fourth Gospel. — *CBQ* 36 (1974) 466-485.

*   — The Passion according to Luke. — *Worship* 60 (1986) 2-9.

p   — The Gospel of Peter and Canonical Gospel Priority. — *NTS* 33 (1987) 321-343.

— and T.A. COLLINS, Church Pronouncements. — *NJBC*, 1990, 1166-1174.

*   — *The Death of the Messiah. From Gethsemane to the Grave. A Commentary on the Passion Narratives in the Four Gospels* (ABRL), 2 vols., New York, 1994.

— *An Introduction to New Testament Christology*, New York - Mahwah, NJ, 1994.

— *An Introduction the New Testament* (ABRL), New York - London - Toronto, 1997.

BROWN, S. Review of J. ERNST, Das Evangelium nach Lukas, 1977. — *JBL* 98 (1979) 149-151.

BROWNING, W.R.F. *The Gospel according to Saint Luke* (Torch Bible Commentaries), London, 1960, ⁶1981.

BRUCE, A.B. *The Synoptic Gospels* (The Expositor's Greek Testament, 1), London, 1897, ²1907.

BRUCE, F.F. *Are the New Testament Documents Reliable?*, London - Grand Rapids, MI, 1943, ⁴1954.

— *The Acts of the Apostles. The Greek Text with Introduction and Commentary*, London, 1951; Chicago, IL - Grand Rapids, MI, 1952; Grand Rapids, MI - Leicester, ³1990.

— Herod Antipas, Tetrarch of Galilee and Peraea. — *ALUOS* 5 (1963-65), Leiden, 1966, 6-23.

— *Jesus and Christian Origins Outside the New Testament*, London - Grand Rapids, MI, 1974.

— Review of É. TROCMÉ, Formation, 1975. — *EvQ* 48 (1976) 117-118.

— *Render to Caesar*. — E. BAMMEL and C.F.D. MOULE, *Jesus*, 1984, 249-263.

BRUNS, J.E. Review of D. SENIOR, The Passion of Jesus in the Gospel of Luke, 1989. — *CBQ* 53 (1991) 149-150.

*   BUCK, E. The Function of the Pericope "Jesus Before Herod" in the Passion Narrative of Luke. — W. HAUBECK and M. BACHMANN (eds.), *Wort in der Zeit*, 1980, 165-178.

BUCKLEY, E.R. *An Introduction to the Synoptic Problem*, London, 1912.

BUCKWALTER, H.D. *The Character and Purpose of Luke's Christology* (SNTS MS 89), Cambridge - New York - Melbourne, 1996. Diss. Aberdeen (dir. I.H. MARSHALL).

*   BÜCHELE, A. *Der Tod Jesu im Lukasevangelium. Eine redaktionsgeschichtliche Untersuchung zu Lk 23* (FTS, 26), Frankfurt, 1978. Diss., Frankfurt, 1977 (dir. F. LENTZEN-DEIS).

*   BÜCHSEL, F. Die Blutgerichtsbarkeit des Synedrions. — *ZNW* 30 (1931) 202-210.

BÜSCHING, A.F. *Die vier Evangelisten mit ihren eigenen Worten zusammengesetzt*, Vol. 1, Hamburg, 1766, 96ff.

BULTMANN, R. *Die Geschichte der synoptischen Tradition*, Göttingen, 1921, ²1931, ³1957, ⁴1958, ⁵1961, ⁶1964, ⁷1967, ⁸1970, ⁹1979 (= GST);
— = *History of the Synoptic Tradition*, tr. J. MARSH, Oxford, 1963; New York, 1968; repr. Peabody, MA, 1993 (= HST).
— *Ergänzungsheft*, Göttingen, 1958, ²1962, ³1966 (eds. G. THEISSEN and P. VIELHAUER), ⁴1971, ⁵1979.

BUNDY, W.E. *Jesus and the First Three Gospels. An Introduction to the Synoptic Tradition*, Cambridge, MA, 1955.

* BURKILL, T.A. The Competence of the Sanhedrin. — *VC* 10 (1956) 80-96.
* — The Trial of Jesus. — *VC* 12 (1958) 1-18.
* — The Condemnation of Jesus: A Critique of Sherwin-White's Thesis. — *NT* 12 (1970) 321-342.

BURKITT, F.C. *The Gospel History and Its Transmission*, Edinburgh, 1906, ²1907, ³1911.
— The Lost Source of Our Savior's Sayings [Review of A. HARNACK, Sprüche und Reden Jesu]. — *JTS* 8 (1907) 454-459.
— Review of B. BACON, Beginnings, 1909. — *JTS* 10 (1908-09) 604-607.
— *The Earliest Sources for the Life of Jesus*, London, 1910, ²1922.
— Review of A.M. PERRY, Sources, 1920. — *JTS* 22 (1920-21) 69- 70.
— The Use of Mark in the Gospel According to Luke. — F.J. FOAKES JACKSON and K. LAKE, *Beginnings*, 1/2, 1922; ᴿ1979, 106-120.
— Commentary on the Preface of Luke, Appendix B. — *Ibid.*, 489-510.
— Vestigia Christi according to Luke, Appendix B. — *Ibid.*, 485-487.
— Review of B.H. STREETER, The Four Gospels, 1924. — *JTS* 26 (1924-25) 278-294.

BURNSIDE, W.F. *The Gospel According to St. Luke*, Cambridge, 1913.

BURTON, E.D. *Some Principles of Literary Criticism and their Application to the Synoptic Problem* (The Decennial Publications printed from Vol. V), Chicago, IL, 1904.
— Some Phases of the Synoptic Problem. — *JBL* 31 (1912) 95-113.
— and E.J. GOODSPEED, *A Harmony of the Synoptic Gospels*, Chicago, IL, 1917.

BURTON, H. *The Gospel according to St. Luke*, New York, 1896.

BUSE, I. St. John and the Marcan Passion Narrative. — *NTS* 4 (1957-58) 215-219.
* — St. John and the Passion Narratives of St. Matthew and St. Luke. — *NTS* 7 (1960-61) 65-76.

BUSSMANN, C. and W. RADL (eds.), *Der Treue Gottes trauen. Beiträge zum Werk des Lukas*. FS G. SCHNEIDER, Freiburg - Basel - Vienna, 1991.

BUSSMANN, W. *Synoptische Studien*, 3 vols. 1. *Zu der Geschichtsquelle*, 1925; 2. *Zur Redenquelle*, 1929; 3. *Zu den Sonderquelle*, Halle, 1931.

BUTIN, J.D. *L'Évangile selon Luc commenté par les Pères*, Paris, 1987.

BUTLER, B.C. St Luke's Debt to St Matthew. — *HTR* 32 (1939) 237-308.
— *The Originality of St. Matthew. A Critique of the Two-Document Hypothesis*, Cambridge, 1951.
— The Synoptic Problem. — B. ORCHARD et al. (eds.), *CCHS*, 1953, 760-764.
— The Synoptic Problem. — R.C. FULLER et al. (eds.), *NCC*, 1969, 815-821;
— = A.J. BELLINZONI, 1985, 97-118.

BUTTRICK, G.A. et al. (eds.), *The Interpreter's Bible*, New York - Nashville, TN, 1951-57 (= IB).
—, T.S. KEPLER and J. KNOX (eds.), *The Interpreter's Dictionary of the Bible*, 4 vols., Nashville, TN, 1962 (= IDB).

CADBURY, H.J. *The Style and Literary Method of Luke* (HTS, 6), Pt. 1. *The Diction of Luke and Acts*, 1-72; Pt. 2. *The Treatment of Sources in the Gospel*, 73-205, Cambridge, MA, 1920; New York, ᴿ1969.
— Luke - Translator or Author? — *AJT* 24 (1920) 436-455.
— Review of H. MCLACHLAN, St. Luke, the Man and His Work, 1920. — *JR* 1 (1921) 328-329.
— Commentary on the Preface of Luke, Appendix C. — *Beginnings*, 1/2, 1922; ᴿ1979, 489-510.
— *The Making of Luke-Acts*, London, 1927, ²1958, ᴿ1961.
— Review of J.M. CREED, The Gospel according to St. Luke, 1930. — *JR* 11 (1931) 283-286.
— Four Features of Lucan Style. — FS SCHUBERT, 1966, repr. 1968, 1980, 87-102.
CAIRD, G.B. *The Gospel of St Luke* (The Pelican Gospel Commentaries), Harmondsworth - New York, 1963, ᴿ1968.
— Review of V. TAYLOR, Passion Narrative, 1972. — *ExpT* 83 (1971-72) 379.
* CAMBE, M. Les récits de la passion en relation avec différents textes du IIᵉ siècle. — *FoiVie* 81 (1982) 12-24.
CAMBIER, J. *Historicité des évangiles synoptiques et Formgeschichte*. — J. HEUSCHEN (ed.), *La formation des évangiles. Problème synoptique et Formgeschichte*, Brugge, 1957, 195-212.
CAMERON, R. *Sayings Traditions in the Apocryphon of James* (HTS, 34), Philadelphia, PA, 1984. Diss. Harvard, 1983 (dir. H. KOESTER).
p — (ed.), *The Other Gospels: Non-Canonical Gospel Texts*, Philadelphia, PA, 1982.
— Review of J.D. CROSSAN, Four Other Gospels, 1985. — *JBL* 106 (1987) 558-560.
p — (ed.), *The Apocryphal Jesus and Christian Origins* (= Semeia, 49), Atlanta, GA, 1990.
* CARLSON, R.P. The Role of the Jewish People in Luke's Passion Theology. — *SBL 1991 Seminar Papers*, 82-102.
CARPENTER, J.E. *The First Three Gospels*, London, 1890, ⁴1906.
CARPENTER, S.C. *Christianity According to S. Luke*, London, 1919.
CARRINGTON, P. *The Primitive Christian Calendar*, Vol. 1, Cambridge, 1952.
— *According to Mark. A Running Commentary on the Oldest Gospel*, London, 1960.
CARROLL, J.T. Luke's Apology for Paul. — *SBL 1988 Seminar Papers*, 106-118.
* — Luke's Crucifixion Scene. — D.D. SYLVA (ed.), *Reimaging the Death of the Lukan Jesus* (BBB, 73), Frankfurt, 1990, 108-124 (notes: 194-203).
* — and J.B. GREEN with R.E. VAN VOORST, J. MARCUS and D. SENIOR, *The Death of Jesus in Early Christianity*, Peabody, MA, 1995.
CARSON, D.A., R.T. FRANCE, J.A. MOTYER and G.J. WENHAM (eds.), *New Bible Commentary. 21st Century Edition*, Leicester - Downers Grove, IL, 1953, ²1954, ³1970, ⁴1994 (completely revised).
— and H.G.M. WILLIAMSON (eds.), *It is Written: Scripture Citing Scripture*. FS B. Lindars, Cambridge, 1988 (= FS Lindars).
CARTLEDGE, S.A. *A Conservative Introduction to the New Testament*, Grand Rapids, MI, 1938.
CARTLIDGE, D.R. and D.L. DUNGAN, *Sourcebook of Texts for the Comparative Study of the Gospels: Literature of the Hellenistic and Roman Period Illuminating the Milieu and Character of the Gospels* (Sources for Biblical Study, 1), Missoula, MT, 1971;

= *Documents for the Study of the Gospels*, Philadelphia, PA, 1980; Revised and enlarged ed., 1993.

CARY, G. *The Synoptic Gospels*, New York, 1900.

p CASSELS, W.R. *The Gospel according to Peter. A Study*, London - New York, 1894.

CASSIDY, R.J. *The Social and Political Stance of Jesus in Luke's Gospel*. Diss. Graduate Theological Union, 1976 (dir. E.C. HOBBS).

— *Jesus, Politics, and Society. A Study of Luke's Gospel*, Maryknoll, NY, 1978.

— and P.J. SCHARPER (eds.), *Political Issues in Luke-Acts*, Maryknoll, NY, 1983.

— Luke's Audience, the Chief Priests, and the Motive for Jesus' Death. — R.J. CASSIDY and P.J. SCHARPER (eds.), *Political*, 1983, 146-167.

* CATCHPOLE, D.R. The Problem of the Historicity of the Sanhedrin Trial. — E. BAMMEL, *Trial*, 1970, 47-65.

* — The Answer of Jesus to Caiaphas (Matt. xxvi. 64). — *NTS* 17 (1970-71) 213-226.

* — *The Trial of Jesus: A Study in the Gospels and Jewish Historiography from 1770 to the Present Day* (SPB, 18), Leiden, 1971. Diss. Cambridge, 1968 (dir. E. BAMMEL).

* — Trial of Jesus. — *IDBS*, 1976, 917-919.

— *The Quest for Q*, Edinburgh, 1993.

CERFAUX, L. À propos des sources du troisième évangile: proto-Luc ou proto-Matthieu. — *ETL* 12 (1935) 5-27;
= *Recueil Lucien Cerfaux* (BETL, 6-7), Gembloux, 1954, 389-414;
= *Recueil Lucien Cerfaux*, t. 3, 1962 (BETL, 71), Leuven, 1985 (nouvelle édition revue et complétée).

— and J. CAMBIER, Luc. — *DBS* 5, 1957, 545-594.

— En marge de la question synoptique. — J. HEUSCHEN (ed.). *Les formation*, 1957, 24-33;
= *Recueil Lucien Cerfaux*, t. 3 (BETL, 18), Gembloux, 1962, 99-110; repr. (BETL, 71) 1985.

CEROKE, C. Review of V. TAYLOR, Passion Narrative, 1972. — *CBQ* 35 (1973) 558- 559.

CEULEMANS, F. *Commentarius in Evangelium secundum Matthæum*, Mechelen, 1898, ²1900, ³1928.

— *Commentarius in Evangelium secundum Lucam*, Mechelen, 1899.

— *Commentarius in Evangelium secundum Marcum*, Mechelen, 1899.

* CHANCE, J.B. The Jewish People and the Death of Jesus in Luke-Acts: Some Implications of an Inconsistent Narrative Role. — *SBL 1991 Seminar Papers*, 50-81.

CHAPMAN, J. *Matthew, Mark and Luke. A Study in the Order and Interrelation of the Synoptic Gospels*, ed. J.M.T. BARTON, London, 1937.

p CHAPUIS, P. L'Évangile et l'Apocalypse de Pierre I. — *RTP* 26 (1893) 338-355.

p CHARLESWORTH, J.H. (ed.), *The New Testament Apocrypha and Pseudepigrapha: A Guide to Publications, with Excurses on Apocalypses* (ATLA Bibliography Series, 17) Metuchen, NJ -London, 1987.

p — Research on the New Testament Apocrypha and Pseudepigrapha. — *ANRW* II.25.5 (1988) 3919- 3968.

p — and C.A. EVANS, *Jesus in the Agrapha and Apocryphal Gospels*. — B. CHILTON and C.A. EVANS (eds.), *Studying*, 1994, 479-533.

CHASE, F.H. Peter (Simon). — *DBDL* 3, Edinburgh, 1900, 756-779.

— The Gospels in the Light of Historical Criticism. — H.B. SWETE (ed.), *Cambridge Theological Essays*, 1905, 373-419.

CHEYNE, T.K. and BLACK, J.S. (eds.), *Encyclopedia Biblica. A Critical Dictionary of the Literary, Political and Religious History, the Archaeology, Geography and Natural*

History of the Bible, 4 vols., London, 1899-1903; in one vol. 1903; new ed. with corrections, 1914.

* CHICO CANO, M.C. *Der Prozess Jesu. Eine literarkritische und redaktionsgeschichtliche Untersuchung zu Lk 23,1-25*. Diss. Munster, 1980 (dir. K. KERTELGE).

CHILTON, B. and C.A. EVANS (eds.), *Studying the Historical Jesus. Evaluation of the State of Current Research*, Leiden, 1994.

CLARKE, W.K.L. *New Testament Problems*, London, 1929.

— Reviews in *TLond*: 13 (1926) 46-49: V. TAYLOR, Behind, 1926;

= *New Testament Problems*, 66-70; 19 (1929) 60: R.H. CROMPTON, Synoptic Problem, 1928; 21 (1930) 54- 55: W. BUSSMANN, Synoptische Studien, Vols. 1 and 2, 1925/1929; 24 (1932) 300: W. BUSSMANN, Synoptische Studien, Vol. 3, 1931.

CLOGG, F.B. *An Introduction to the New Testament*, London, 1937, ³1948, ᴿ1959.

COGGINS, R.J. and J.L. HOULDEN (eds.), *A Dictionary of Biblical Interpretation*, London - Philadelphia, PA, 1990 (= DBI).

COHEN, D. Einige Bemerkungen zum Prozess Jesu bei den Synoptikern II. — *ZSRG.R* 102 (1985) 445-452.

* COHN, H. *The Trial and Death of Jesus*, New York, 1967, ᴿ1971.

COLLINS, A. YARBRO, Review of W. SCHNEEMELCHER (ed.), New Testament Apocrypha Vol. 1, 1991. — *CBQ* 55 (1993) 180-182.

COLLINS, R.F. *Introduction to the New Testament*, Garden City, NY, 1983.

COLLISON, J.G.F. *Linguistic Usages in the Gospel of Luke*. Diss. SMU, Dallas, TX, 1977 (dir. W.R. FARMER).

COLPE, C. ὁ υἱὸς τοῦ ἀνθρώπου. — *TWNT* 8, cols. 403-481; = *TDNT* 8, 400-477.

— Der Begriff "Menschensohn" und die Methode Erforschung messianischer Prototypen. — *Kairos* 13 (1971) 1-17.

* CONNOLLY-WEINERT, F. Assessing Omissions as Redaction: Luke's Handling of the Charge against Jesus as Detractor of the Temple. — FS FITZMYER, 1989, 358-368.

CONZELMANN, H. Zur Lukasanalyse. — *ZTK* 49 (1952) 16-33.

— *Die Mitte der Zeit. Studien zur Theologie des Lukas*, Tübingen, 1953, ²1957, ³1960, ⁴1962, ⁵1964; = *The Theology of St. Luke*, tr. G. BUSWELL, New York, 1961 (= ²1957).

— *Die Apostelgeschichte* (HNT, 7), Tübingen, 1963, ²1972;

= *Acts of the Apostles*, tr. J. LIMBURG, A.T. KRAABEL and D.H. JUEL, Philadelphia, PA, 1987.

* — Historie und Theologie in den synoptische Passionsberichten. — F. VIERING (ed.), *Zur Bedeutung des Todes Jesu: Exegetische Beiträge*, Gütersloh, 1967, 35-53; *Theologie als Schriftauslegung. Aufsätze zum Neuen Testament* (BEvT, 65), Munich, 1974, 74-90; History and Theology in the Passion Narratives of the Synoptic Gospels. — *Interpr* 24 (1970) 178-197.

— and A. LINDEMANN, *Arbeitsbuch zum Neuen Testament* (UTB, 52), Tübingen, 1975, ²1976, ³1977, ⁴1979, ⁵1980, ⁶1982 (esp. 260-266: *Das Lukasevangelium*), ⁸1985, ⁹1988 (esp. 285-293: *Das Lukasevangelium*);

= *Interpreting the New Testament. An Introduction to the Principles and Methods of New Testament Exegesis*, tr. S.S. SCHATZMANN, Peabody, MA, 1988 (esp. 229-236: Gospel of Luke) (= ⁸1985).

— Literaturbericht zu den synoptischen Evangelien. — *TR* 43 (1978) 3-51, 321-327.

COOGAN, M.D. → B.M. METZGER, 1993

COOPER, T. → J. NAVONE, 1986

COPE, L. Review of R.H. GUNDRY, Matthew, 1982. — *ATR* 65 (1983) 218-220.

* —, D.L. DUNGAN, W.R. FARMER, A.J. MCNICOL, D.B. PEABODY and P.L. SHULER, Narrative Outline of the Composition of Luke According to the Two-Gospel Hypothesis. — *SBL 1995 Seminar Papers*, 636-687;
  = A.J. MCNICOL, D.L. DUNGAN and D.B. PEABODY (eds.), *Beyond the Q Impasse - Luke's Use of Matthew. A Demonstration by the Research Team of the International Institute for Gospel Studies*, Valley Forge, PA, 1996.
— Review of H. SCHÜRMANN, Der Paschamahlbericht, 1953. — *ETL* 31 (1955) 132-133.
* CORBIN, M. Jésus devant Hérode: lecture de Luc 23,6-12. — *Christus* 25 (1978) 190-197.
CORBISHLEY, T. Review of H. HOEHNER, Herod Antipas, 1972. — *HeythJ* 14 (1973) 208-210.
CORNELY, R. *Compendium Introductionis in S. Scripturas*, Paris, 1889, ²1891, ³1896, ⁴1900, ⁵1905, ⁶1909, ⁷1911, ⁸1914 (eds. R. CORNELY and M. HAGEN).
— *Historica et Critica Introductio in U.T. Libros Sacros*, Vol. 3. *Introductio Specialis in Singulos Novi Testamenti Libros*, Paris, 1886, ²1897, ᴿ1925.
— *Introductionis in S. Scripturae Libros Compendium*, ed. A. MERK, Paris, ⁹1927, ¹⁰1929, ¹²1940.
* COUSIN, H. *Le prophète assassiné. Histoire des textes évangéliques de la Passion*, Paris, 1976.
— *L'Évangile de Luc. Commentaire pastoral*, Paris - Outremont - Quebec, 1993.
CRADDOCK, F.B. Luke. — J.L. MAYS (ed.), *Harper's Bible Commentary*, 1988, 1010-1043.
— *Luke* (Interpretation), Louisville, KY, 1990.
CREED, J.M. Review of B.S. EASTON, The Gospel according to St. Luke, 1926. — *JTS* 28 (1926-27) 420-421.
— Review of H.J. CADBURY, The Making of Luke-Acts, 1927. — *JTS* 29 (1927-28) 433-435.
— *The Gospel according to St. Luke*, London, 1930; London - New York, ᴿ1965.
— Some Outstanding New Testament Problems: 2. L and the Structure of the Lucan Gospel. — *ExpT* 46 (1934-35) 101-107.
* — The Supposed 'Proto-Luke' Narrative of the Trial before Pilate: A Rejoinder. — *ExpT* 46 (1934- 35) 378-379.
CRIBBS, F.L., A Study of the Contacts that Exist between St. Luke and St. John. — *SBL 1973 Seminar Papers*, 1-93.
— The Agreements that Exist between John and Acts. — C.H. TALBERT (ed.), *Perspectives*, 1978, 40-61.
CROMPTON, R.H. *The Synoptic Problem and a New Solution*, Edinburgh, 1928.
p CROOK, W.M. The Gospel and Apocalypse of St. Peter. — *The Review of the Churches* 3 (1892) 162-165.
p CROSSAN, J.D. *Four Other Gospels. Shadows on the Contours of Canon*, Minneapolis, MN, 1985.
*p — The Cross that Spoke. The Earliest Narrative of the Passion and Resurrection. — *Forum* 4 (1987) 3-22.
*p — *The Cross that Spoke. The Origins of the Passion Narrative*, San Francisco, CA, 1988.
p — Thoughts on Two Extracanonical Gospels. — R. CAMERON (ed.), *The Apocryphal Jesus* (= Semeia, 49), 1990, 155-168 (esp. 155-161: response to A.J. Dewey).
p CULLMANN, O. Petrusevangelium. — *RGG* 5, Tübingen, ³1961, 260.
CULPEPPER, R.A. The Gospel of Luke: Introduction, Commentary and Reflections. — *NIB*, Vol. 9, 1995, 3-490.

* DABROWSKI, E. The Trial of Christ in Recent Research. — *StEv* 4/1 (Berlin) 1968, 21-27.

DAHL, N.A. Die Passionsgeschichte bei Matthäus. — *NTS* 2 (1955-56) 17-32;
= M. LIMBECK (ed.), *Redaktion*, 1981, 205-225;
= The Passion Narrative in Matthew. — N.A. DAHL, *Jesus in the Memory of the Early Church*, Minneapolis, MN, 1976 37-51;
= G. STANTON (ed.), *The Interpretation of Matthew*, 1983, 42-55; [2]1995, 53-67.

DALMAN, G. *Die Worte Jesu*, Leipzig, 1930.

DANA, H.E. and J.R. MANTEY, *A Manual Grammar of the Greek New Testament*, New York, 1927, 1957, [R]1994.

* DANBY, H. *The Bearing of the Rabbinical Criminal Code on the Jewish Trial Narratives in the Gospels, with a Translation of the Mishnah and Tosefta of the Tractate Sanhedrin*, B.D. Thesis, Oxford, 1919.

* — The Bearing of the Rabbinical Criminal Code on the Jewish Trial Narratives in the Gospels. — *JTS* 21 (1919-20) 51-76.

DANIELS, J.B. *The Egerton Gospel: Its Place in Early Christianity*. Diss. Claremont, 1990 (dir. J.M. ROBINSON).

DANKER, F.W. *Jesus and the New Age*, St. Louis, MO, 1972; completely revised and expanded, Philadelphia, PA, [2]1988.

— Reviews: M.D. GOULDER, Luke: A New Paradigm, 1989. — *CurrTMiss* 17 (1990) 230-231; *JBL* 110 (1991) 162-164.

— Review of M.L. SOARDS, The Passion according to Luke, 1987. — *CBQ* 53 (1991) 150-151.

* DARR, J.A. *"Glorified in the Presence of Kings". A Literary-Critical Study of Herod the Tetrarch in Luke-Acts*. Diss. Vanderbilt, 1987 (dir. M.A. TOLBERT).

— *On Character Building. The Reader and the Rhetoric of Characterization in Luke-Acts*, Louisville, KY, 1992.

* DAUBE, D. "For They Know Not What They Do, Lk. 23:24". — *StPat*, 7 (TU, 79), 1961, 240-254.

DAUER, A. *Die Passionsgeschichte im Johannesevangelium. Eine traditionsgeschichtliche und theologische Untersuchung zu Joh 18,1-19,20* (SANT, 30), Munich, 1972. Diss. Würzburg, 1968/69 (dir. R. SCHNACKENBURG).

— Review of T.A. MOHR, Markus- und Johannespassion, 1982. — *TRev* 81 (1985) 18-22.

* — Spuren der (synoptischen) Synedriumsverhandlung im 4. Evangelium. Das Verhältnis zu den Synoptikern. — A. DENAUX (ed.), *John and the Synoptics*, 307-339.

DAUSCH, P. *Die synoptische Frage*, Münster, 1914.

— *Die drei älteren Evangelien* (Die Heilige Schrift des Neuen Testament, 2), Bonn, [4]1932.

DAUTZENBERG, G. → J. SCHREINER

—, H. MERKLEIN and K. MÜLLER (eds.), *Zur Geschichte des Urchristentums* (QD, 7), Freiburg, 1979.

DAVIDSON, F., assisted by A.M. STIBBS and E.F. KEVAN, *The New Bible Commentary*, London, 1953; Grand Rapids, MI, [2]1954; London - Grand Rapids, MI, [3]1970 completely revised (eds.: D. GUTHRIE, J.A. MOTYER, A.M. STIBBS and D.J. WISEMAN), *The New Bible Commentary Revised* (eds.: D.A. CARSON, R.T. FRANCE, J.A. MOTYER and G.J. WENHAM), Leicester - Downers Grove, IL, [4]1994 (completely revised).

DAVIDSON, R. → A.R.C. LEANEY

DAVIES, W.D. *Invitation to the New Testament*, New York, 1966.

— and D.C. ALLISON, *The Gospel according to Saint Matthew* (ICC), 3 Vols., Edinburgh, 1988-1997.

DAWSEY, J.M. What's in a Name? Characterization in Luke. — *BTB* 16 (1986) 143-147.

DEAN, J. *The Synoptic Gospels* (Westminster NT), Vol. 1, Pt. 3: *The Gospel according to St. Luke*, London, 1935.

DE HAAS, V. → WEREN, W.

DEISSMANN, A. *Bibelstudien. Beiträge zumeist aus den Papyri und Inschriften zur Geschichte der Sprache des Schrifttums und der Religion des hellenistischen Judentums und des Urchristentums*, Marburg, 1895; Hildesheim - New York, ᴿ1977.

— *Neue Bibelstudien. Sprachgeschichtliche Beiträge, zumeist aus den Papyri und Inschriften, zur Erklärung des Neuen Testaments*, Marburg, 1897;
= *Bible Studies*, tr. A. GRIEVE, Edinburgh, 1901, ²1903.

— D. Bernhard Weiss. — *Theologische Blätter* 6 (1927), 241-251.

* DE JONGE, M. The Use of ὁ χριστός in the Passion Narratives. — J. DUPONT (ed.), *Jésus aux origines de la christologie* (BETL, 40), Leuven, 1975, ²1989) 169-192;
= *Jewish Eschatology*, 1991, 63-86.

— (ed.), *L'évangile de Jean. Sources, rédaction, théologie* (BETL, 44), Leuven, 1977, ²1987.

— *Jewish Eschatology, Early Christian Christology and the Testament of the Twelve Patriarchs. Collected Essays* (NTSuppl, 63), Leiden, 1991.

DEL AGUA, A. Review of J. ERNST, Das Evangelium nach Lukas, 1977. — *EstBib* 36 (1977) 303-304.

DE LA POTTERIE, I. (ed.), *De Jésus aux Évangiles. Tradition et rédaction dans les Évangiles synoptiques* (BETL, 25), Gembloux, 1967.

* DELBRÜCK, R. Antiquarisches zu den Verspottungen Jesu. — *ZNW* 41 (1942) 124-145.

DELEBEQUE, E. *Évangile de Luc. Texte traduit et annoté* (Études anciennes de l'Association G. Budé), Paris, 1976.

DELOBEL, J. La rédaction de Lc., IV,14-16a et le "Bericht vom Anfang". — F. NEIRYNCK (ed.), *L'évangile de Luc*, 1973, 203-223 (= ²1989, 113-133).

DELORME, J. Le procès de Jésus ou la parole risquée (Lc 22,54-23,25). — *RSR* 69 (1981) 123-146.

DENAUX, A. L'hypocrisie des Pharisiens et le dessein de Dieu. Analyse de Lc., XIII, 31-33. — F. NEIRYNCK (ed.), *L'Évangile de Luc*, 1973, 245-285; ²1989, 155-195 (316-323: note additionnelle).

— (ed.), *John and the Synoptics* (BETL, 101), Leuven, 1992.

p DENKER, J. *Die theologiegeschichtliche Stellung des Petrusevangeliums. Ein Beitrag zur Frühgeschichte des Doketismus* (EHS, 23/36), Frankfurt, 1975.

DERRETT, J.D.M. Midrash in the New Testament: The Origin of Luke XXII 67-68. — *ST* 29 (1975) 147-156;
= *StNT*, Vol. 2, 1978, 184-93.

— *Studies in the New Testament*, 6 vols., Leiden, 1977-95 (= StNT).

— Daniel and Salvation-History. — *DownR* 100 (1982) 62-68;
= *StNT*, Vol. 4, 1986, 132-138.

p DE SANTOS OTERO, A. *Los Evangelios Apocrifos. Colección de textos griegos y latinos, versión crítica, estudios introductorias y comentarios* (BAC, 148), Madrid, 1956, ²1963, ³1975, ⁶1988.

p — Pedro, Evangelio de. — *Enciclopedia de la Biblia* 5, Barcelona, 1965, ²1969, 979.

DESCAMPS, A. *Les justes et la justice dans les évangiles et le christianisme primitif hormis la doctrine proprement paulinienne* (UCL, 2/43), Louvain, 1950.

DE SOLAGES, B. *Synopse grecque des évangiles*, Leiden - Toulouse, 1959.

DEVREESSE, R. *Les évangiles et l'évangile*, Paris, 1962.

p   DEWEY, A.J. "Time to Murder and Create": Visions and Revisions in the Gospel of Peter.
— CAMERON, R. (ed.), *Apocryphal Jesus*, 1990, 101-107.

p   — The Gospel of Peter: Translation, Introduction and Notes. — R.J. MILLER (ed.),
Complete Gospels, 1992, 393-401.

DE ZWAAN, J. *Het Evangelie van Lucas*, Groningen, 1917, ²1922.

— *Inleiding tot het Nieuwe Testament*, Haarlem, 3 vols. 1. *Evangeliën en Handelingen*,
1941, ²1948.

DIBELIUS, F. Die Herkunft der Sonderstücke des Lukasevangeliums. — *ZNW* 12 (1911)
325-343.

*   DIBELIUS, M. Herodes und Pilatus. — *ZNW* 16 (1915) 113-126;
= ID., in *Botschaft und Geschichte. Gesammelte Aufsätze* (ed. G. BORNKAMM), Vol.
1, Tübingen, 1953, 278-292.

— Die alttestamentlichen Motive in der Leidensgeschichte des Petrus- und
Johannesevangeliums. — *BZAW* 33 (1918) 125-150;
= *Botschaft und Geschichte*, Vol. 1, (ed. G. BORNKAMM), Tübingen, 1953, 221-247.

— *Die Formgeschichte des Evangeliums*, Tübingen, 1919, ²1933;
= *FTG*, New York, 1965 (= ²1933).

— Review of V. TAYLOR, Behind, 1926. — *TLZ* 52 (1927) 146-148.

*   — Das historische Problem der Leidensgeschichte. — *ZNW* 30 (1931) 193-201.

— *Geschichte der urchristlichen Literatur*. 1. *Evangelien und Apokalypsen*. 2.
Apostolisches und Nachapostolisches (Sammlung Göschen Nr. 934.935), Berlin -
Leipzig, 1926; Munich, ᴿ1975; = *A Fresh Approach to the New Testament and Early
Christian Literature*, London, 1936, ᴿ1937.

— Die Apostelgeschichte als Geschichtsquelle. — *Forschungen und Fortschritte* 21/23
Jahrgang 67-69, Berlin, 1947, 91-95;
= ID. and H. GREEVEN (ed.), *Aufsätze zur Apostelgeschichte* (FRLANT, 60; "Neue
Folge", 42), Göttingen, 1951, ⁴1961 ("durchgesehene"), 91-95.
= The Acts of the Apostles as an Historical Source. — *Studies in the Acts of the
Apostles*, tr. M. LING, London, 1956, 102-108.

DIDIER, M. (ed.), *L'évangile selon Matthieu. Rédaction et théologie* (BETL, 29),
Gembloux, 1971.

DIEFENBACH, M. *Die Komposition des Lukasevangeliums unter Berücksichtigung antiker
Rhetorikelemente* (FTS, 43), Frankfurt, 1993.

DIETRICH, W. *Das Petrusbild der lukanischen Schriften* (BWANT, 94), Stuttgart, 1972.
Diss. Münster, 1970 (dir. K.H. RENGSTORF).

DIEZ MACHO, A. and S. BARTINA (eds.), *Enciclopedia de la Biblia*, Barcelona, 1965,
²1969.

DILLERSBERGER, J. *Lukas. Das Evangelium des heiligen Lukas in theologischer und
heilsgeschichtlicher Schau*, Salzburg, Vol. 1, 3, 4 (3rd ed.), Vol. 2 (= 4th ed.), 1947;
= *The Gospel of Saint Luke*, tr. from the third German ed., Westminster, MD, 1958.

DILLON, R.J. Previewing Luke's Project from His Prologue (Luke 1:1-4). — *CBQ* 43
(1981) 205-227.

DINWOODIE, C. Review of A.Q. MORTON and G.H.C. MACGREGOR, Structure, 1964. —
ScotJT 18 (1965) 212-218.

DIRKSEN, A. Review of K.H. SCHELKLE, Die Passion Jesu, 1949. — *CBQ* 14 (1952) 406-
408.

DOBLE, P. Luke 23.47 - The Problem of DIKAIOS. — *BTrans* 44 (1993) 320-330.

— *The Paradox of Salvation. Luke's Theology of the Cross* (SNTS 87), Cambridge - New York - Melbourne, 1996. Diss. Leeds, 1992 (dir. J.K. ELLIOTT).

DODD, C.H. *The Parables of the Kingdom*, London, 1935; 1936 (Revised Ed.); London - Glasgow - New York, 1961 (Revised Ed.).

— A New Gospel. — *BJRL* 20 (1936) 56-92;
= ID., *New Testament Studies*, Manchester, 1953, 12-52.

DÖMER, M. *Das Heil Gottes. Studien zur Theologie des lukanischen Doppelwerkes* (BBB, 50), Köln - Bonn, 1978. Diss. Bonn, 1977/78 (dir. H. ZIMMERMANN).

DONAHUE, J.R. From Passion Traditions to Passion Narrative. — W.H. KELBER (ed.), *Passion*, 1976, 1-20.

*   — Passion Narrative. — *IDBS*, 1976, 643-645.

— Review of É. TROCMÉ, Formation, 1975. — *Interpr* 31 (1977) 202(-204).

DONLON, S.E. Review of J. CHAPMAN, The Four Gospels, 1944. — *TS* 5 (1944) 392-395.

DORMEYER, D. *Die Passion Jesu als Verhaltensmodell. Literarische und theologische Analyse der Traditions- und Redaktionsgeschichte der Markuspassion* (NTAbhNF, 11), Münster, 1974. Diss. Münster, 1972 (dir. J. GNILKA).

DOWNING, F.G. Compositional Conventions and the Synoptic Problem. — *JBL* 107 (1988) 69-85.

— A Paradigm Perplex: Luke, Matthew and Mark. — *NTS* 38 (1992) 15-36.

DRIVER, S.R., T.K. CHEYNE, and W. SANDAY (eds.), *Studia Biblica et Ecclesiastica. Essays Chiefly in Biblical and Patristic Criticism by Members of the University of Oxford*, Vol. 2, Oxford, 1890.

DROGE, A. and J. TABOR, *A Noble Death. Suicide and Martyrdom among Christians and Jews in Antiquity*, Edinburgh, 1992.

DRURY, J. *Luke* (J.B. Phillips Commentaries, Fontana Book), London, 1973;
= *The Gospel of Luke* (J.B. Phillips NT Commentaries), New York, 1973.

— Review of V. TAYLOR, Passion Narrative, 1972. — *JTS* 24 (1973) 541-543.

— Review of F. NEIRYNCK (ed.), L'Évangile de Luc, 1973. — *JTS* 25 (1974) 165-170.

— *Tradition and Design in Luke's Gospel*, London, 1976; Atlanta, GA, 1977.

— Luke, Gospel of. — *DBI*, 1990, 410-414.

DSCHULNIGG, P. *Sprache, Redaktion und Intention des Markus-Evangeliums. Eigentümlichkeiten der Sprache des Markus-Evangeliums und ihre Bedeutung für die Redaktionskritik* (SBB, 11), Stuttgart, 1984, ²1986. Diss. Lucerne, 1983/84 (dirs. E. RUCKSTUHL - W. KIRCHSCHLÄGER).

DUBOIS, J.D. Review of T. SCHRAMM, Der Markus-Stoff bei Lukas, 1971. — *ETR* 49 (1974) 430- 432.

DULING, D.C. Review of J.D. CROSSAN, Four Other Gospels, 1985. — *JAAR* 55 (1987) 142-144.

DUNCAN, G.S. Review of V. TAYLOR, Behind, 1926. — *The Review of the Churches* 3 (1926) 438- 439.

DUNCAN, T.S. Review of B.S. EASTON, The Gospel according to St. Luke, 1926. — *BS* 83 (1926) 366-368.

DUNGAN, D.L. (ed.), *The Interrelations of the Gospels. A Symposium Led by M.-É. Boismard - W.R. Farmer - F. Neirynck, Jerusalem 1984* (BETL, 95), Leuven, 1990.

DUNNET, W.C. → M.C. TENNEY

DU PLESSIS, I.I. Once More: The Purpose of Luke's Prologue (Lk 1,1-4). — *NT* 16 (1974) 259-271.

DUPONT, J. *Études sur les Actes des Apôtres* (LD, 45), Paris, 1967;

= *The Salvation of the Gentiles. Essays on the Acts of the Apostles*, tr. J.R. KEATING, New York, 1979.

— L'interprétation des psaumes dans les Actes des Apôtres. — ID., *Études*, 1967, 283-307;

= Messianic Interpretation of the Psalms in the Acts of the Apostles. — ID., *Salvation*, 1979, 103-128.

— *Nouvelles études sur les Actes des Apôtres* (LD, 118), Paris, 1984.

— Les discours de Pierre dans les Actes et le chapitre XXIV de l'évangile de Luc. — F. NEIRYNCK, (ed.), *L'évangile de Luc*, 1973, 329-374 (= ²1989, 239-284);

= *Nouvelles études*, 1984, 58-111.

— (ed.), *Jésus aux origines de la christologie* (BETL, 40), Gembloux - Leuven, 1975; Leuven, ²1989.

DURKEN, D. (ed.), *Sin, Salvation, and the Spirit*, Collegeville, MN, 1979.

EASTON, B.S. Linguistic Evidence for the Lucan Source L. — *JBL* 28-29 (1909-10) 139-180.

— The Special Source of the Third Gospel. — *JBL* 30 (1911) 78-103.

*   — The Trial of Jesus. — *AJT* 19 (1915) 430-452.

— *The Gospel According to St. Luke. A Critical and Exegetical Commentary*, Edinburgh - New York, 1926.

— *The Gospel Before the Gospels*, London - New York, 1928.

— Reviews in *ATR*: 13 (1931) 87-89: J.M. CREED, The Gospel according to St. Luke, 1930; 13 (1931) 89-90: W. MANSON, The Gospel of Luke, 1930; 13 (1931) 90: H. BALMFORTH, The Gospel according to Saint Luke, 1930; 13 (1931) 80-81: W. BUSSMANN, Synoptische Studien, Vols. 1-2, 1929; 14 (1931) 74-75: Vol. 3, 1931; 14 (1932) 195: R. BULTMANN, Die Geschichte der synoptischen Tradition, 1931; 15 (1933) 246-249: F.C. GRANT, Growth, 1933.

EATON, R. *The Gospel according to Saint Luke with Introduction, Text and Notes*, London, 1916.

EDWARDS, O.C. *Luke's Story of Jesus*, Philadelphia, PA, 1981.

EDWARDS, W.R. Review of É. TROCMÉ, Formation, 1975. — *PerspRelSt* 4 (1977) 294-295, 298.

p   EHRHARD, A. *Die altchristliche Litteratur und ihre Erforschung von 1884-1900*. 1. Abteilung: *Die vornicänische Litteratur* [STS Supp, 1], Freiburg, 1900 [127-135: *Das Petrusevangelium*]).

EHRLICH, E.L. Review of D.R. CATCHPOLE, The Trial of Jesus, 1971. — *Freiburger Rundbrief* 23 (1971) 109-110.

ELLIGER, W. σύν. — *EWNT* 3, cols. 697-699; = *EDNT* 3, 291-292.

p   ELLIOTT, J.K. The Apocryphal Gospels. — *ExpT* 103 (1991-92) 8-15.

— Review of H. KOESTER, Ancient Christian Gospels, 1990. — *NT* 34 (1992) 207-208.

p   — *The Apocryphal New Testament. A Collection of Apocryphal Christian Literature in an English Translation*; Revised and newly translated ed. of *Apocryphal New Testament*, tr. by M.R. JAMES, 1924; Oxford - New York, 1993, 150-158.

p   — *The Apocryphal Jesus. Legends of the Early Church*, Oxford, 1996.

ELLIS, E.E. *The Gospel of Luke* (The Century Bible. New Ed.), London, 1966, ²1974; Greenwood, SC, ᴿ1977.

— La composition de Luc 9 et les sources de sa christologie. — J. DUPONT (ed.), *Jésus aux origines de le christologie* (BETL, 40), Gembloux, 1975, 193-200:

= The Composition of Luke 9 and the Sources of Christology. — G.W. HAWTHORNE (ed.), *Current Issues*, 1975, 121-127.

— *Gospel Criticism. A Perspective on the State of the Art.* — P. STUHLMACHER (ed.), *Das Evangelium*, 1983, 27-84;
  = *The Gospel*, 1991, 26-52.

— Gospel according to Luke. — *ISBE* 3, 1986, 180-186.

— Review of J.B. GREEN, The Death of Jesus, 1988. — *SWJTh* 32 (1989) 60.

ELWELL, W.A. (ed.), *Evangelical Commentary on the Bible*, Grand Rapids, MI, 1978.

ENSLIN, M.S. *Christian Beginnings*, New York, 1938.

p   — Peter, Gospel of. — *IDB* 3, 1962, 766-767.

— Review of V. TAYLOR, Passion Narrative, 1972. — *Religion in Life* 42 (1973) 275-277.

EPP, E.J. and G.W. MACRAE (eds.), *The New Testament and its Modern Interpreters*, Philadelphia, PA, 1989.

ERDMAN, C.R. *The Gospel of Luke. An Exposition*, Philadelphia, PA, 1921, 1949, 1966.

ERNST, J. *Das Evangelium nach Lukas* (RNT, 3), Regensburg, ⁵1977 ("völlig neu bearbeitete"), ⁶1993.

— *Das Evangelium nach Markus* (RNT, 2), Regensburg, 1981.

— *Johannes der Täufer. Interpretation - Geschichte - Wirkungsgeschichte* (BZNW, 53), Berlin - New York, 1989.

ESLER, P.F. *Community and Gospel in Luke-Acts. The Social and Political Motivations of Lucan Theology* (SNTS MS, 57), Cambridge, 1987.

EVANS, C.A. *Luke* (NIBC), Peabody, MA, 1990.

p   — *Noncanonical Writings and New Testament Interpretation*, Peabody, MA, 1992.

— and D.A. HAGNER (eds.), *Anti-Semitism and Early Christianity. Issues of Polemic and Faith*, Minneapolis, MN, 1993.

— Review of W. REBELL, Neutestamentliche Apokryphen, 1992. — *CRBR* 6 (1993) 280-282.

EVANS, C.F. Review of V. TAYLOR, Passion Narrative, 1972. — *TLond* 76 (1973) 35-36.

— *Saint Luke* (TPI NTC), London - Philadelphia, PA, 1990.

EVANS, O.E. Synoptic Criticism Since Streeter. — *ExpT* 72 (1960-61) 295-299.

EYNIKEL, E. → J. LUST

FAHLBUSCH, E. et al. (eds.), *Evangelisches Kirchenlexicon. Internationale theologische Enzyklopädie*, 3 vols., Göttingen, 1985 (= EKL).

FARMER, W.R. *The Synoptic Problem. A Critical Analysis*, New York, 1964; Dillsboro, NC, ᴿ1976.

— *Synopticon*, Cambridge, 1969.

— (ed.), *New Synoptic Studies. The Cambridge Gospel Conference and Beyond*, Macon, GA, 1983.

FARRAR, F.W. *The Gospel According to St. Luke* (Cambridge Greek Testament for Schools and Colleges), Cambridge, 1884, ᴿ1912;
  = *The Gospel According to St. Luke* (The Cambridge Bible for Schools and Colleges), Cambridge, 1891.

FARRER, A. *A Study in Mark*, Westminster, 1951.

*   FEIGEL, F.K. *Der Einfluss des Weissagungsbeweises und anderer Motive auf die Leidensgeschichte. Ein Beitrag zur Evangelienkritik*, Tübingen, 1910.

FEILER, P.F. *Jesus the Prophet: The Lucan Portrayal of Jesus as the Prophet Like Moses.* Diss. Princeton Theol. Sem., 1986 (dir. D.R. ADAMS).

FEINE, P. Ueber das gegenseitige Verhältniss der Texte der Bergpredigt bei Matthäus und bei Lukas. — *JPTh* 11 (1885) 1-85.

— Zur synoptischen Frage. — *JPTh* 12 (1886) 462-528; *II*: 13 (1887) 39-102; *III*: 14 (1888) 275-313; 388-422; *IV*: 14 (1888) 504-549.

— Die alte Quelle in der ersten Hälfte der Apostelgeschichte. — *JPTh* 16 (1890) 84-133.

— *Eine vorkanonische Ueberlieferung des Lukas in Evangelium und Apostelgeschichte. Eine Untersuchung*, Gotha, 1891.

— *Theologie des Neuen Testaments*, Leipzig, 1910, ²1912, ⁵1931, ⁸1950.

— *Einleitung in das Neue Testament*, Leipzig, 1913.

— *Die Religion des Neuen Testaments*, Leipzig, 1921.

FELDMEIER, R. Review of J.B. GREEN, The Death of Jesus, 1988. — *TLZ* 114 (1989) 891-893.

FENDT, L. *Der Christus der Gemeinde. Eine Einführung in das Evangelium nach Lukas*, Berlin, 1937.

FENTON, J. Review of M.D. GOULDER, Luke: A New Paradigm, 1989. — *TLond* 93 (1990) 67-68.

FERGUSON, E. (ed.) *Encyclopedia of Early Christianity*, Chicago - London, 1990; 2 Vols, New York - London, ²1997.

FIEBIG, P. Review of A. SCHLATTER, Das Evangelium des Lukas, 1931. — TLZ 57 (1932) cols. 293- 295.

p FILLION, L. Pierre (Écrits apocryphes de saint). — *DB* 5, 1912, 413-415.

FILSON, F.V. *Origins of the Gospels*, New York, 1938.

p FINDLAY, A.F. Gospels (Apocryphal). — *DBDL* 1, 1906, Edinburgh, 677-678.

FINDLAY, J.A. *The Acts of the Apostles*, London, 1934, ⁴1952.

— *The Gospel according to St. Luke*, London, 1937.

* FINEGAN, J. *Die Überlieferung der Leidens- und Auferstehungsgeschichte Jesu*, Giessen, 1934.

FITZMYER, J.A. The Priority of Mark and the "Q" Source in Luke. — D.G. BUTTRICK (ed.), *Jesus*, 1970, 131-170;
   = *To Advance*, 1981, 3-40 (in revised form);
   = A.J. BELLINZONI, 1985, 37-52.

— Review of J. ERNST, Das Evangelium nach Lukas, 1977. — *TS* 40 (1979) 349-351.

— *The Gospel According to Luke. Introduction Translation and Notes*. 1. *I-IX*; 2. *X-XXIV* (AB, 28/28A), Garden City, NY, 1981/1985.

— *To Advance the Gospel: New Testament Studies*, New York, 1981.

— The Gospel According to Luke. — *OCB*, 1993, 469-474.

FLENDER, H. *Heil und Geschichte in der Theologie des Lukas*, Munich, 1965. Diss. Erlangen, 1964 (dir. G. FRIEDRICH);
   = *St. Luke: Theologian of Redemptive History*, tr. R.H. and I. FULLER, Philadelphia, PA, 1967.

FLESSEMANN VAN LEER, E. Die Interpretation der Passionsgeschichte vom AT aus. — F. VIERING (ed.), *Zur Bedeutung des Todes Jesu*, Gütersloh, 1968, 79-96.

FLUSSER, D. *Jesus in Selbstzeugnissen und Bilddokumenten* (Rohwohlts Monographien, 580), Hamburg, 1968;
   = *Jesus*, tr. R. WALLS, New York, 1969.

— Der Gekreuzigte und die Juden. — *Jahresbericht* 1975-76, Lucerne Theological Faculty and Catechetical Institute;
   = The Crucified One and the Jews, tr. Y. BEARNE. — *Immanuel* 7 (1977) 25-37.

— Mishle Jeshu Vehameshalim Basifrut Chazal. — ID., *Yahadut Umekorot Hanatzrut*, Tel Aviv, 1979, 28-49.

* — *The Last Days of Jesus in Jerusalem. A Current Study of the Easter Week*, Tel Aviv, 1980;
  = *Die letzten Tage Jesu in Jerusalem*, tr. H. ZECHNER, Stuttgart, 1982.

* — At the Right Hand of the Power. — *Immanuel* 14 (1982) 42-46.

— Die synoptische Frage und die Gleichnisse Jesus. — ID., *Die rabbinischen Gleichnisse und der Gleichniserzähler Jesus*, Bern, 1981, 193-233.

— "Sie wissen nicht, was sie tun". — FS MUSSNER, 1981, 393-410.

— What Was the Original Meaning of Ecce Homo? — *Immanuel* 19 (1985) 29-30.

* — "Who is it that Struck You?" — *Immanuel* 20 (1986) 27-32;
  = *Judaism and the Origins of Christianity*, Jerusalem, 1988, 604-609.

—, et al., Tributes to Robert L. Lindsey. — *Jerusalem Perspectives* 49 (1995) 24-26.

FOAKES JACKSON, F.J. Professor C.C. Torrey on the Acts. — *HTR* 10 (1917) 352-361.

— and K. LAKE (eds.), *The Beginnings of Christianity: The Acts of the Apostles*, 5 vols., London, 1920-1933; repr. Grand Rapids, MI, 1979 (= Beginnings).

FOCANT, C. (ed.), The Synoptic Gospels. Source Criticism and the New Literary Criticism (BETL, 110), Leuven, 1993.

— The Synoptic Gospels. Source Criticism and the New Literary Criticism. Colloquium Biblicum Lovaniense XLI (1992). — *ETL* 68 (1992) 494-499.

FORD, J.M. 'Crucify him, crucify him', and the Temple Scroll. — *ExpT* 87 (1975-76) 275-278.

— *My Enemy is My Guest. Jesus and Violence in Luke*, Maryknoll, NY, 1984.

* — *Bonded with the Immortal. A Pastoral Introduction to the New Testament*, Wilmington, DE, 1987.

FOSTER, L. *Luke*, Cincinnati, OH, 1986.

* FOULON-PIGANIOL, C.L. Le rôle du peuple dans le procès de Jésus: Une hypothèse juridique et théologique.— *NRT* 98 (1976) 627-637.

FOURNIER, W.J. The Third Gospel: A Hidden Source. — *ExpT* 46 (1934-35) 428.

* FRANCE, R.T. Jésus devant Caïphe (tr. G. BRAY and Dorothée SCHELL). — *Hokhma* 15 (1980) 20- 35.

— Reading the Gospels. — D.A. CARSON et al. (eds.), *NBC*, [4]1994, 896-903.

FRANKLIN, E. Review of J.L. NOLLAND, Luke 1-9:20, 1990. — *JTS* 42 (1991) 218-222.

FRANZMAN, M.H. *The Word of the Lord Grows*, St. Louis, MO, 1961.

FREEDMAN, D.N. (ed.), *The Anchor Bible Dictionary*, 6 vols., New York, 1992 (= ABD).

FRICKE, W. *Standrechtlich gekreuzigt. Person und Prozess des Jesus aus Galiläa*, Buchschlag bei Frankfurt, 1986;
  = *The Court-Martial of Jesus. A Christian Defends the Jews against the Charge of Deicide*, tr. S. ATTANASIO, NY, 1990.

— *Der Fall Jesus. Eine juristische Beweisführung*, Hamburg, 1995.

FRIEDRICHSEN, T.A. *The Matthew - Luke Agreements against Mark. A Survey of Recent Studies*. — F. NEIRYNCK, *L'évangile de Luc - The Gospel of Luke* (BETL, 32), Leuven, [2]1989, 335-391.

— *The Matthew - Luke Agreements Against Mark 1974-1991*, Vol. 1, unpublished Diss., KULeuven, 1992 (dir. F. NEIRYNCK).

— Mt-Lk Agreements Against Mk 4,30-32. — FS NEIRYNCK, Vol. 1, 1992, 649-676.

p FUCHS, A. *Das Petrusevangelium* (SNTU, B2,1), Linz, 1978 (esp. 81-115: Bibliography).

FULLER, R.C., L. JOHNSTON and C. KEARNS (eds.), *A New Catholic Commentary on Holy Scripture*, London - Nashville, TN - New York, 1969 (= NCC).

FULLER, R.H. *The New Testament in Current Study*, New York, 1962.
— *The Foundations of New Testament Christology*, New York, 1965.
— *A Critical Introduction to the New Testament*, London, 1966.
p FUNK, R.W. and R.W. HOOVER (eds.), *The Five Gospels: the Search for the Authentic Words of Jesus*, New York, 1993.
FUNK, X. Fragmente des Evangeliums und der Apokalypse des Petrus. — *TQ* 75 (1893) 255-288.

GABOURY, A. *La structure des évangiles synoptiques* (NTSuppl, 22), Leiden, 1970.
— Review of T. SCHRAMM, Der Markus-Stoff bei Lukas, 1971. — *CBQ* 34 (1972) 540-541.
GÄCHTER, P., *Summa Introductionis in Novum Testamentum*, Leipzig, 1938.
— Review of H. SCHÜRMANN, Der Paschamahlbericht, 1953. — *ZKT* 73 (1953) 483-484.
GALLAGHER, E.V. Review of H. KOESTER, Ancient Christian Gospels, 1990. — *CBQ* 54 (1992) 159- 161.
GALOT, J. Review of G. SCHNEIDER, Verleugnung, 1969. — *Greg* 51 (1970) 771.
GANDER, G. *L'Évangile pour les étrangers du monde. Commentaire de l'Évangile selon Luc*, Lausanne, 1986.
GARCÍA PÉREZ, J.M. El relato del Buen Ladrón (Lc 23,39-43). — *EstBib* 44 (1986) 263-304.
p GARDNER-SMITH, P. The Gospel of Peter. — *JTS* 27 (1925-26) 255-271.
p — The Date of the Gospel of Peter. — *JTS* 27 (1925-26) 401-407.
— *The Narratives of the Resurrection. A Critical Study*, London, 1926.
* GARLAND, D.E. *One Hundred Years of Study on the Passion Narratives* (NABPR BS, 3), Macon, GA, 1989.
GARVIE, A. *The Gospel according to St. Luke* (Westminster NT), New York, 1911.
GAST, F. Synoptic Problem. — *JBC*, 1968, 1-6.
GASTON, L. Sondergut und Markusstoff in Lk. 21. — *TZ* 16 (1960) 161-172.
— *No Stone on Another. Studies in the Significance of the Fall of Jerusalem in the Synoptic Gospels* (NTSuppl, 23) Leiden, 1970.
— *Horae Synopticae Electronicae. Word Statistics of the Synoptic Gospels*, Missoula, MT, 1973.
— Review of V. TAYLOR, Passion Narrative, 1972. — *JBL* 93 (1973) 455-456.
* — Anti-Judaism and the Passion Narrative in Luke and Acts. — P. RICHARDSON and D. GRANSKOU (eds.), *Anti-Judaism*, 1986, 127-153.
GELDENHUYS, N. *Commentary on the Gospel of Luke* (NIC NT), London - Edinburgh, 1950; Grand Rapids, MI, 1951, ᴿ1956.
GEORGE, A. La royauté de Jésus selon l'évangile de Luc. — *ScEc* 14 (1962) 57-69; = *Études*, 1978, 257-282.
— *L'annonce du salut de Dieu. Lecture de l'évangile de Luc*, Paris, 1963.
— Jésus fils de Dieu dans l'évangile selon Saint Luc. — *RB* 72 (1965) 185-209; = *Études*, 1978, 215-236.
— Tradition et rédaction chez Luc. La construction du troisième Évangile. — I. DE LA POTTERIE (ed.), *De Jésus aux Évangiles*, 1967, 100-129; = La construction du troisième Évangile. — *Études*, 1978, 15-41.
— Israël dans l'œuvre de Luc. — *RB* 75 (1968) 481-525; = *Études*, 1978, 87-125.
— Le sens de la mort de Jésus pour Luc. — *RB* 80 (1973) 186-217; = *Études*, 1978, 185-212.

— Pour lire l'évangile selon saint Luc. — *Cahiers évangiles* 5 (1973) 1-70;
  = *Lettura del vangelo di Luca*, Assisi, 1975;
  = *El evangelio según san Lucas* (Cuadernos Biblicos, 3), Estella, 1976; [8]1987.
— *Études sur l'œuvre de Luc* (SB), Paris, 1978.

p GERO, S. Apocryphal Gospels: A Survey of Textual and Literary Problems. — *ANRW* II.25.5 (1988) 3969-3996.

GEWALT, D. Das "Petrusbild" der lukanischen Schriften als Problem eine ganzheitlichen Exegese. — *LingBib* 34 (1975) 1-22.

GIBLIN, C.H. *The Destruction of Jerusalem according to Luke's Gospel* (AnBib, 107), Rome, 1985.

GIESEN, H. ὑπόκρισις. — *EWNT* 3, cols. 963-965; = *EDNT* 3, 403.

GILBRANT, T. (ed.), *The New Testament Greek-English Dictionary*, 6 vols., Springfield, MO, 1990- 91.

GILES, K. "L" Tradition. — *DJG*, 1992, 431-432.

GILMOUR, S.McL. A Critical Re-Examination of Proto-Luke. — *JBL* 67 (1948) 143-152.
— The Gospel according to St. *Luke* (IB, 8), New York, 1952, 3-434.

GINNS, R. The Gospel of Jesus Christ according to St. Luke. — *CCHS*, 1953, 935-970.

GIRODON, P. *Commentaire critique et moral sur l'Évangile selon saint Luc*, Paris, 1903.

GLASSWELL, M.E. Review of É. TROCMÉ, Formation, 1975. — *JTS* 28 (1977) 146-149.
— Francis Crawford Burkitt. — *TRE* 7 (1981) 424-428.

GNILKA, J. Das Martyrium Johannes des Täufer (Mk 6,17-29). — FS SCHMID, 1973, 78-92.
— *Das Matthäusevangelium*. I T. *Kommentar zu Kap. 1,1-13,58*. II. T. *Kommentar zu Kap. 14,1- 28,20 und Einleitungsfragen* (HTKNT 1/1-2) Freiburg, 1986/1988.

GODET, F. *Commentaire sur l'évangile saint Luc*, Neuchâtel, 1871, [3]1888/1889, [4]1969;
  = *A Commentary on the Gospel of St. Luke*, tr. E. SHALDERS and M. CUSIN, Edinburgh, [3]1894 (= [2]1872, Paris);
  = *Kommentar zu dem Evangelium des Lukas*, tr. F.R. WUNDERLICH and K. WUNDERLICH, [2]1890 from the third French ed., [3]1888/1889; Giessen, 1986; (= Hannover, [2]1890).

GOGUEL, M. *L'Évangile de Marc et ses rapports avec ceux de Matthieu et de Luc*, Paris, 1909.

* — Juifs et romains dans l'histoire de la passion. — *RHR* 62 (1910) 165-182; 295-322.
— *Les sources du récit johannique de la Passion*, Paris, 1910.
— *Introduction au Nouveau Testament*. 1. *Les évangiles synoptiques*, Paris, 1923.

* — À propos du procès de Jésus. — *ZNW* 31 (1932) 289-301.

* — Did Peter Deny His Lord? A Conjecture. — *HTR* 25 (1932) 1-27.
— Jésus et les origines de l'universalisme chrétien. — *RHPR* 12 (1932) 193-211.
— *Jésus et les origines du christianisme*, Vol. 1, Paris, 1932;
  = *Jesus and the Origins of Christianity*, 2 vols., New York, 1933, [R]1960.
— Luke and Mark: with a discussion of Streeter's Theory. — *HTR* 26 (1933) 1-55.
— *La Vie de Jésus*, Paris, 1932;
  = *The Life of Jesus*, tr. O. WYON, New York, 1933, [R]1945.
  = *Das Leben Jesu*, tr. R. BINSWANGER, Zurich - Leipzig, 1934.

GOLLWITZER, H. *Die Freude Gottes: Einführung in das Lukasevangelium* (Studienreihe der Jungen Gemeinde, 27-29), 3 vols. in 1, Berlin-Dahlem, 1940-41; Munich, [2]1952; Gelnhausen, 1979.

= *La Joie de Dieu*, tr. E. DE ROBERT and A. LOCOCQUE and J. CARRÈRE, Neuchâtel - Paris, 1958. FT, 1958, combined *Die Freude Gottes* with *Jesu Tod und Auferstehung nach dem Bericht des Lukas*.

* — *Jesu Tod und Auferstehung nach dem Bericht des Lukas* (Theologische Existenz heute, 77), Berlin, 1941; (Kaiser - Traktate, 44), Munich, ²1951, ³1953, ²1979;
= *The Dying and Living Lord*, tr. O. WYON, London - Philadelphia, PA, 1960.

GOODACRE, M.S. *Goulder and the Gospels. An Examination of a New Paradigm* (JSNT SS, 133), Sheffield, 1996. Diss. Oxford, 1994 (dir. J. MUDDIMAN).

GOODING, D. *According to Luke. A New Exposition of the Third Gospel*, Grand Rapids, MI, 1987.

GOODSPEED, E.J. *New Solutions of New Testament Problems*, Chicago, IL, 1907.

— *An Introduction to the New Testament*, Chicago, IL, 1937.

— *New Chapters in New Testament Study*, New York, 1937.

GORE, C. The Gospel according to St. Luke. — *NCHS*, 1928, 207-239; repr. with correction of some misprints 1929, 1951.

—, H.L. GOUDGE and A. GUILLAUME (eds.), *A New Commentary on Holy Scripture*, London - New York, 1928 (= NCHS).

Gospel of Luke. — P. FAIRBAIRN (ed.), *The Teachers' and Students' Bible Encyclopedia*, Toledo, OH, 1902, 127-133.

GOULDER, M.D., On Putting Q to the Test. — *NTS* 24 (1977-78) 218-234.

— A House Built on Sand. — A.E. HARVEY (ed.), *Alternative Approaches to the New Testament*, London, 1985, 1-24.

— *Luke: A New Paradigm* (JSNT SS, 20), 2 vols., Sheffield, 1989.

— Luke's Compositional Options [Reply to F.G. DOWNING]. — *NTS* 39 (1993) 150-152.

— Luke's Knowledge of Matthew. — G. STRECKER (ed.), *Minor Agreements*, 1993, 143-162.

— Review of F. NEIRYNCK, Evangelica II, 1991. — *NT* 35 (1993) 199- 202.

— Is Q a Juggernaut? — *JBL* 115 (1996) 667-681.

GOURGUES, M. Les psaumes et Jésus, Jésus et les psaumes. — *CE* 25 (1978) 1-64.

— Jésus devant sa passion et sa mort. — *CE* 30 (1979) 1-64.

GRÄSSER, E. *Das Problem der Parusieverzögerung in den synoptischen Evangelien und in der Apostelgeschichte* (BZNW, 22), Berlin, 1957.

GRANT, F.C. A New Testament Bibliography for 1914 to 1917 Inclusive. — *ATR* 1 (1918) 58-91.

— Review of A. WAUTIER D'AYGALLIERS, Les sources, 1920. — *ATR* 5 (1922) 137-139.

— *The Growth of the Gospels*, Cincinnati, OH, 1933.

— Review of E.B. REDLICH, Student's Introduction, 1936. — *ATR* 18 (1936) 187.

— Review of K. GROBEL, Formgeschichte, 1937. — *ATR* 19 (1937) 214-216.

— Review of V.E. HARLOW, Jesus' Jerusalem Expedition, 1936. — *ATR* 19 (1937) 144-146.

GRANT, R.M. and D.N. FREEDMAN. *The Secret Sayings of Jesus according to the Gospel of Thomas*, London - New York, 1960;
= *Apocrypha N.T. Evangelium Thomae. Geheime Worte Jesu: das Thomas Evangelium*, tr. J.B. BAUER, Frankfurt, 1960.

— *A Historical Introduction to the New Testament*, New York, 1963.

— *Heresy and Criticism. The Search for Authenticity in Early Christian Literature*, Louisville, KY, 1993.

GRAYSTON, K.J. Review of J.B. GREEN, The Death of Jesus, 1988. — *JTS* 41 (1990) 182-183.

GREEN, J.B. Review of É. TROCMÉ, The Passion as Liturgy, 1983. — *EvQ* 56 (1984) 185-188.

p ⸺ The Gospel of Peter: Source for a Pre-Canonical Passion Narrative? — *ZNW* 78 (1987) 292-301.

* ⸺ *The Death of Jesus. Tradition and Interpretation in the Passion Narrative* (WUNT, 2/33), Tübingen, 1988. Diss. Aberdeen, 1985 (dir. I.H. MARSHALL).

⸺ Review of M.L. SOARDS, The Passion According to Luke, 1987. — *JBL* 108 (1989) 154-156.

* ⸺ The Death of Jesus, God's Servant. — D.D. SYLVA (ed.), *Reimaging*, 1990, 1-22, 170-173.

⸺ Review of J.D. CROSSAN, The Cross that Spoke, 1988. — *JBL* 109 (1990) 356-358.

⸺ Review of D.P. SENIOR, The Passion of Jesus in the Gospel of Luke, 1989. — *CRBR* 4 (1991), Atlanta, GA, 229-230.

⸺, S. MCKNIGHT and I.H. MARSHALL (eds.), *Dictionary of Jesus and the Gospels*, Downers Grove, IL - Leicester, 1992 (= DJG).

* ⸺ Passion Narrative. — *DJG*, 1992, 601-604.

⸺ The Death of Jesus and the Rending of the Temple Veil (Luke 23:44-49): A Window into Luke's Understanding of Jesus and the Temple. — *SBL 1991 Seminar Papers*, 543-557;

⸺ and M.C. MCKEEVER, *Luke-Acts and New Testament Historiography*, Grand Rapids, MI, 1994.

⸺ The Demise of the Temple as 'Culture Center' in Luke-Acts: An Exploration of the Rending of the Temple Veil (Luke 23.44-49). — *RB* 101 (1994) 495-515.

⸺ and M.M. TURNER (eds.), *Jesus of Nazareth: Lord and Christ. Essays on the Historical Jesus and New Testament Christology*, Grand Rapids, MI - Carlisle, UK, 1994 (= JN).

⸺ *The Theology of the Gospel of Luke*, Cambridge, 1995.

⸺ Review of R.E. BROWN, The Death of the Messiah, 1994. — *Interp* 50 (1996) 187-189.

⸺ *The Gospel of Luke* (NICNT), Grand Rapids, MI - Cambridge, 1997.

⸺ The Death of Jesus and the Ways of God. Jesus and the Gospels on Messianic Status and Shameful Suffering. — *Interp* 52 (1998) 24-35.

GREENBERG, M. Scourging. — *IDB* 4, 245-246.

GREGORY, C.R. *Einleitung in das Neue Testament*, Leipzig, 1909.

GREIJDANUS, S. *Het Evangelie naar Lucas opnieuw uit de grondtekst vertaald en verklaard* (Korte verklaring der Heilige Schrift), 2 vols., Kampen, 1941, ²1955, ³1972.

GRENSTED, L.W. → W.C. ALLEN

GRIEVE, A.J. Luke. — A.S. PEAKE and A.J. GRIEVE (eds.), *Commentary*, 1920, 724-742.

GROBEL, K. *Formgeschichte und synoptische Quellenanalyse* (FRLANT, 53), Göttingen, 1937.

GRUNDMANN, W. *Das Evangelium nach Lukas* (THKNT, 3), Berlin, 1961, ²1963, ⁴1966, ⁶1971.

⸺ Review of G. SCHNEIDER, Verleugnung, 1969. — *TLZ* 96 (1971) 905-908.

GUELICH, R.A. *Mark 1-8:26* (WBC, 34A), Dallas, TX, 1989.

GUEURET, A. *La mise en discours. Recherches sémiotiques à propos de l'Évangile de Luc*, Paris, 1987, 258-265. Diss. Paris - Nanterre (dir. P. GEOLTRAIN).

GUIGNEBERT, Ch. *Jésus* (L'Évolution de l'Humanité, 29), Paris, 1933;
= *Jesus*, tr. S.H. HOOKE, London, 1935.

GUNDRY, R.H. *The Use of the Old Testament in St. Matthew's Gospel. With Special reference to the Messianic Hope* (NTSuppl, 18), Leiden, 1967.

—— *Matthew. A Commentary on His Literary and Theological Art*, Grand Rapids, MI, 1982, ²1994.

—— *Mark. A Commentary on His Apology for the Cross*, Grand Rapids, MI, 1993.

—— Matthean Foreign Bodies in Agreements of Luke with Matthew against Mark Evidence that Luke Used Matthew. — FS NEIRYNCK, Vol. 2, 1992, 1467-1495.

GUNKEL, H. (ed.), *Die Religion in Geschichte und Gegenwart: Handwörterbuch für Theologie und Religionswissenschaft*, 6 vols., Tübingen, ²1927-32; K. GALLING (ed.), 7 vols., ³1957-65.

GUTHRIE, D. *New Testament Introduction. The Gospels and Acts*, London, 1962-65; *New Testament Introduction*, Downers Grove, IL, ⁴1990.

—— → F. DAVIDSON

GUY, H.A. Did Luke Use Matthew? — *ExpT* 83 (1971-72) 245-247.

—— *The Gospel of Luke*, London, 1982 (= 1972).

HACKENBERG, W. ἐπιγινώσκω. — *EWNT* 2, cols. 61-62; = *EDNT* 2, 24-25.

HAENCHEN, E. *Der Weg Jesu. Eine Erklärung des Markus-Evangeliums und der kanonischen Parallelen* (Sammlung Töpelmann, 2/6), Berlin, 1966, ²1968.

—— *Die Apostelgeschichte* (KEK, 3), Göttingen, ⁶1968; (= Meyer's, 3¹⁵).

—— Historie und Verkündigung bei Markus und Lukas. — G. BRAUMANN (ed.), *Das Lukas-Evangelium*, 1974, 287-316.

HAHN, F. *Der Prozess Jesu nach dem Johannesevangelium* (EKK NT Vorarbeiten, Heft 2), Zurich - Einsiedeln - Cologne - Neukirchen-Vluyn, 1970.

HAHN, G.L. *Das Evangelium des Lucas erklärt*, 2 vols, Breslau, 1892/1894.

p HALL, I. The Newly Discovered Apocryphal Gospel of Peter. — *The Biblical World* 1 (1893) 88-98.

HANSON, R.P.C. Further Evidence for Indications of the Johannine Chronology of the Passion to be Found in the Synoptic Evangelists. — *ExpT* 53 (1941-42) 178-180.

—— Does δίκαιος in Luke XXIII 47 Explode the Proto-Luke Hypothesis? — *Hermathena* 55 (1942) 74-78.

HARDWICK, J.C. Burnett Hillman Streeter (1875-1937). — *ExpT* 49 (1937-38) 249-254.

HARLOW, V.E. *Jesus the Man. An Historical Study*, Oklahoma City, OK, 1924.

—— *Jesus' Jerusalem Expedition*, Oklahoma City, OK, 1936.

* —— *The Destroyer of Jesus. The Story of Herod Antipas Tetrarch of Galilee*, Oklahoma City, OK, 1953, ᴿ1954.

p HARNACK, A. *Bruchstücke des Evangeliums und der Apokalypse des Petrus*, Leipzig, ²1893.

—— *Lukas der Arzt. Der Verfasser des dritten Evangeliums und der Apostelgeschichte* (Beiträge zur Einleitung in das Neue Testament, 1), Leipzig, 1906; = *Luke the Physician* (CTL, NT Studies, 1), tr. J.R. WILKINSON, London, 1907.

—— *Sprüche und Reden Jesu. Die Zweite Quelle des Matthäus und Lukas* (Beiträge zur Einleitung in das Neue Testament, 2), Leipzig, 1907; = *The Sayings of Jesus* (CTL, NT Studies, 2) tr. J.R. WILKINSON, London, 1908.

—— *Neue Untersuchungen zur Apostelgeschichte und zur Abfassungszeit der synoptischen Evangelien* (Beiträge zur Einleitung in das Neue Testament, 4), Leipzig, 1911; = *Date of the Acts and the Synoptic Gospels* (CTL, NT Studies, 4), tr. J.R. WILKINSON, London, 1911.

HARRINGTON, J.M. Review of L.T. JOHNSON, The Gospel of Luke, 1991. — *LouvSt* 18 (1993) 181- 183.

— Review of R.E. BROWN, The Death of the Messiah, 1994. — *LouvSt* 21 (1996) 87-90.

HARRINGTON, W. *Key to the Bible*. 3. *Record of the Fulfillment. The New Testament*, Chicago, IL, 1966; rev. and updated Canfield, OH, 1975.

— *The Gospel according to St. Luke*, Westminster, MD, 1967.

— *Mark* (NTM, 4), Wilmington, DE, 1979.

p HARRIS, J.R. *A Popular Account of the Newly-Recovered Gospel of Peter*, London, 1893.

p — The Structure of the Gospel of Peter. — *The Contemporary Review* 64 (1893) 212-236.

HARRIS, S.L. *The New Testament. A Student's Introduction*, Mountain View, CA - London - Toronto, 1988, ²1995.

HARRISON, E.F. *Introduction to the New Testament*, Grand Rapids, MI, 1964, ²1971.

HARRISVILLE, R.A. *Benjamin Wisner Bacon. Pioneer in American Biblical Criticism* (BSNA, 2), Missoula, MT, 1976.

HARVEY, A.E. (ed.), *Alternative Approaches to the New Testament*, London, 1985.

HASTINGS, A. *Prophet and Witness in Jerusalem. A Study of the Teaching of Saint Luke*, London, 1958.

HASTINGS, J. - J. SELBIE - A.B. DAVIDSON - S.R. DRIVER - H.B. SWETE (eds.), *A Dictionary of Christ and the Gospels*, New York, 1901 (= DCG).

— (ed.), *A Dictionary of the Bible Dealing with its Language, Literature and Contents*, Edinburgh - New York, 1898-1902 (= DBDL); Extra Vol., 1904 (= DBE).

— and J.A. SELBIE (eds.), *Dictionary of the Bible*, Edinburgh, 1909; 1963, ²1965 (eds. F.C. GRANT and H.H. ROWLEY).

— (ed.), *Dictionary of the Apostolic Church*, Edinburgh - New York, 1915 (= DAC).

HATCH, E. and H.A. REDPATH, *A Concordance to the Septuagint and the Other Greek Versions of the Old Testament* (Including the Apocryphal Books), 2 vols., Oxford, 1897; Supplement, 1906 (= HR).

HAUBECK, W. and M. BACHMANN (eds.), *Wort in der Zeit. Neutestamentliche Studien*. FS K.H. RENGSTORF, Leiden, 1980 (= FS RENGSTORF).

HAUCK, A. (ed.), *Realencyklopädie für protestantische Theologie und Kirche*, 24 vols., Leipzig, ³1896-1913 (= RE).

HAUCK, F. *Das Evangelium des Lukas*, Leipzig, 1934.

HAUGG, D. *Judas Iskarioth in den neutestamentlichen Berichten*, Freiburg, 1930.

HAUPT, W. *Worte Jesu und Gemeindeüberlieferung*, Leipzig, 1913.

HAUSPIE, K. → J. LUST

HAWKINS, J.C. *Horae Synopticae. Contributions to the Study of the Synoptic Problem*, Oxford, 1899, ²1909, ᴿ1968.

— Three Limitations to St. Luke's Use of St. Mark's Gospel. 1. The Disuse of the Marcan Source in St. Luke ix.51-xviii.14, 28-59 (= *ExpT* 14 (1902-1903) 18-23, 90-93, 137-140); 2.The Great Omission by St. Luke of the Matter contained in St. Mark vi.45-viii.26, 60-74; 3. St. Luke's Passion-Narrative Considered with Reference to the Synoptic Problem, 75-94 (= *ExpT* 15 (1903-04) 122-126, 273-276). — W. SANDAY (ed.), *SSP*, 1911.

HAWTHORNE, G.F. and O. BETZ (eds.), *Tradition and Interpretation in the New Testament*. FS E.E. ELLIS, Grand Rapids, MI - Tübingen, 1987.

HAWTHORNE, G.W. (ed.), *Current Issues in Biblical and Patristic Interpretation*. FS M.C. TENNEY, Grand Rapids, MI, 1975.

p HEAD, P.M. On the Christology of the Gospel of Peter. — *VC* 46 (1992) 209-224.

p HEADLAM, A.C. The Akhmîm Fragments. — *The Classical Review* 7 (1893) 458-463.

— *The Life and Teaching of Jesus the Christ*, London, 1923, ²1927.

HEANEY, J.J. Modernism. — W.J. MCDONALD et al. (eds.), *NCE* 9, 1967, 991-995.

844   BIBLIOGRAPHY

— Oath Against Modernism. — *Ibid.*, 995-996.
HEARD, R. *An Introduction to the New Testament*, London - New York, 1950.
HEEN, E. Review of J.D. CROSSAN, The Cross that Spoke, 1988. — *Harvard Divinity Bulletin* 20 (1990) 16.
* HEIL, J.P. Reader-Response and the Irony of Jesus before the Sanhedrin in Luke 22:66-71. — *CBQ* 51 (1989) 271-284.
* — Reader-Response and the Irony of the Trial of Jesus in Luke 23:1-25. — *SE* 43 (1991) 175-186.
HEININGER, B. *Metaphorik, Erzählstruktur und szenisch-dramatische Gestaltung in den Sondergutgleichnissen bei Lukas* (NTA NF 24), Münster, 1991. Diss. Würzburg (dirs. H.-H.-J. KLAUCK / K. MÜLLER).
HEITMÜLLER, W. Die Quellenfrage in der Apostelgeschichte (1886-1898) I. — *TR* 2 (1899) 47-59.
HELMBOLD, H. *Vorsynoptische Evangelien*, Stuttgart, 1953.
* HENDRICKX, H. *The Passion Narratives. Studies in the Synoptic Gospels*, Manila, 1977, ²1984 (rev. ed.); Makati, Philippines, 1990.
p HENNECKE, E. and W. SCHNEEMELCHER (eds.), *Neutestamentliche Apokryphen*. 1. *Evangelien*, Tübingen, ³1959, 118-124; ⁶1990;
    = *New Testament Apocrypha*, I. *Gospels and Related Writings*, tr. R. McL. WILSON, Philadelphia, PA, 1963, 179-187; rev. ed., Cambridge - Louisville, KY, 1991.
HENSHAW, T. *New Testament Literature in the Light of Modern Scholarship*, London, 1952, ²1957.
HERBERMANN, C.G. (ed.), *The Catholic Encyclopedia*, 15 vols., New York, 1907.
HERBST, W. *Das Evangelium des Lukas übsersetzt und ausgelegt* (Bibelhilfe für die Gemeinde. Neutestamentliche Reihe, 3), Berlin, 1957.
* HERRANZ MARCO, M. Un problema de crítica histórica en el relato de la Pasión: la liberación de Barrabás. — *EstBib* 30 (1971) 137-160.
* — El proceso ante el Sanhedrín y el Ministerio Público de Jesús. — *EstBib* 34 (1975) 83-111.
HERRON, R.W. *Mark's Account of Peter's Denial of Jesus. A History of Its Interpretation*, Lanham, MD - London, 1991. Diss. Rice, Houston, TX, [n.d.] (dir. N.C. NIELSEN, Jr.).
p HERVIEUX, J. *Ce que l'évangile ne dit pas*, Paris, 1958;
    = *The New Testament Apocrypha*, New York, 1960;
    = *What Are Apocryphal Gospels?*, London, 1960.
HESS, A.J. διά. — *EWNT* 1, cols. 712-713 (= *EDNT* 1, 296-297).
HEUSCHEN, J. (ed.), *La formation des évangiles* (Recherches Bibliques, 2), Brugge, 1957.
— La formation des évangiles. — *Ibid.*, 11-23.
HIGGINS, A.J.B. (ed.), *New Testament Essays*, Manchester, 1959.
— *Jesus and the Son of Man*, London, 1964.
— *The Son of Man in the Teaching of Jesus* (SNTS MS, 39), Cambridge, 1980.
p HILGENFELD, A. Das Petrus-Evangelium über Leiden und Auferstehung Jesu. — *ZWT* 36/1 (1893) 439-454; 36/2 (1893) 220-267.
* HILL, D. Jesus Before the Sanhedrin: On What Charge? — *IBS* 7 (1985) 174-186.
* HILLMANN, W. *Aufbau und Deutung der synoptischen Leidensberichte*, Freiburg, 1941.
HIRSCH, E. *Frühgeschichte des Evangeliums. 2. Die Vorlagen des Lukas und das Sondergut des Matthäus*, Tübingen, 1941.

HOBART, W.K. *The Medical Language of St. Luke: A Proof from Internal Evidence that "The Gospel according to St. Luke" and "The Acts of the Apostles" Were Written by the Same Person, and that Writer was a Medical Man*, Dublin, 1882; Grand Rapids, MI, ᴿ1954.

HOBBS, H.H. *An Exposition of the Gospel of Luke*, Grand Rapids, MI, 1966.

HÖFER, J. and K. RAHNER (eds.), *Lexikon für Theologie und Kirche*, 14 vols. Freiburg, ²1957-68 (= LTK).

* HOEHNER, H.W. Why Did Pilate Hand Jesus over to Antipas? — E. BAMMEL (ed.), *The Trial of Jesus*, 1970, 84-90.

* — *Herod Antipas* (SNTS MS, 17), Cambridge, 1972. Diss. Cambridge, 1968 (dir. E. BAMMEL); Grand Rapids, MI, 1980.

* — Herodian Dynasty. — *DJG*, 1992, 317-326.

* — Pontius Pilate. — *Ibid.*, 615-617.

* — Herodian Dynasty. — *OCB*, 1993, 280-284.

HÖPFL, H., B. GUT and A. METZINGER (eds.), *Introductio Specialis in Novum Testamentum*, Rome, 1938, ⁵1948, ᴿ1956.

HOFFMAN, R.-A. *Das Marcusevangelium und seine Quellen*, Königsberg, 1904.

HOFFMANN, P., N. BROX and W. PESCH (eds.), *Orientierung an Jesus. Zur Theologie der Synoptiker. Für Josef Schmid*, Freiburg - Basel - Vienna, 1973 (= FS Schmid).

* HOFRICHTER, P. Das dreifache Verfahren über Jesus als Gottessohn, König und Mensch. Zur Redaktionsgeschichte der Prozesstradition. — *Kairos* 30-31 (1988-89) 69-81.

HOGAN, M.P. and P.J. KOBELSKI (eds.), *To Touch the Text*, FS J.A. FITZMYER, New York, 1989 (= FS Fitzmyer).

HOLDEN, L. Review of É. TROCMÉ, Formation, 1975. — *Modern Churchman* 19 (1976) 172-173.

HOLDSWORTH, W.W. *Gospel Origins. A Study in the Synoptic Problem*, New York, 1913.

HOLLENBACH, P. Social Aspects of John the Baptizer's Preaching Mission in the Context of Palestinian Judaism. — *ANRW* II.19.1 (1979) 850-875.

HOLTZ, T. *Untersuchungen über die alttestamentlichen Zitate bei Lukas* (TU, 104), Berlin, 1968.

HOLTZMANN, H.J. *Die synoptischen Evangelien. Ihr Ursprung und geschichtlicher Charakter*, Leipzig, 1863.

— Lucas und Josephus. — *ZWT* 16 (1873) 85-93.

— Noch einmal Lucas und Josephus. — *ZWT* 20 (1877) 535-549.

— Anzeigen: K.F. Nösgen, Lukas und Josephus. — *ZWT* 23 (1880) 121-125.

— Die Disposition des dritten Evangeliums. — *ZWT* 26 (1883) 257-267.

— *Lehrbuch der historisch-kritischen Einleitung in das Neue Testament*, Freiburg i.Br., 1885, ²1886, ³1892.

— *Die Synoptiker - Die Apostelgeschichte* (Hand-Commentar zum Neuen Testament, 1), Tübingen, 1889, ²1892, ³1901, 18-21, 301-424.

— Literatur zum Neuen Testament. IV: Evangelienfrage. — *TJ* 12 (1892) 117-120.

— *Lehrbuch der neutestamentlichen Theologie*, Freiburg, 1897: 1, 438-463: *Lucas*; ²1911: 1, 515-539.

— *Das messianische Bewusstsein Jesu. Ein Beitrag zur Leben-Jesu Forschung*, Tübingen, 1907.

HOLTZMANN, O. *Das Neue Testament nach dem Stuttgarter griechischen Text übersetzt und erklärt. 1. Die Synoptischen Evangelien. Apostelgeschichte*, Giessen, 1926.

HOLZMEISTER, U. Die Passionsliteratur der letzten sechs Jahre (1909-1914). Eine Übersicht über die Behandlung der Hauptfragen aus dem Leiden Christi. — *ZKT* 39 (1915) 318-367.
— Zur Frage der Blutgerichtsbarkeit des Synedriums. — *Bib* 19 (1938) 43-59; 151-174.
HOOKER, M.D. *Jesus and the Servant*, London, 1959.
— *Studying the New Testament*, London, 1979; Minneapolis, MN, 1982.
— *The Gospel According to Saint Mark* (BNTC), London - Peabody, MA, 1991.
* — *Not Ashamed of the Gospel. New Testament Interpretations of the Death of Christ*, Carlisle, UK, 1994 - Grand Rapids, MI, 1995.
* HORBURY, W. The Passion Narratives and Historical Criticism. — *TLond* 75 (1972) 58-71.
— and MCNEIL, B. (eds.), *Suffering and Martyrdom in the New Testament*. FS G.M. STYLER, Cambridge, 1981.
* HORSLEY, R.A. The Death of Jesus. — B. CHILTON and C.A. EVANS (eds.), *Studying*, 1994, 394- 422.
— Review of H. HOEHNER, Herod Antipas, 1972. — *ExpT* 84 (1972-73) 24-25.
HORSTMANN, A. τις, τι. — *EWNT* 3, cols. 866-869; = *EDNT* 3, 362-363.
* HORVATH, T. Why Was Jesus Brought to Pilate? — *NT* 11 (1969) 174-184.
HOSKYNS, E.C. Review of J.M. CREED, The Gospel according to St. Luke, 1930. — *TLond* 22 (1931) 352-354.
— Review of H. BALMFORTH, The Gospel according to Saint Luke, 1930. — *TLond* 22 (1931) 350- 351.
— and N. DAVEY. *The Riddle of the New Testament*, London, 1931, ²1936, ³1947.
HOSTETLER, M.S. *The Place of B.H. Streeter in the Study of the Synoptic Problem*. Diss. Hartford Seminary Foundation, Hartford, CT, 1952 (dir. G. JOHNSTON).
HOULDEN, J.L. Review of A.Q. MORTON and G.H.C. MACGREGOR, Structure, 1964. — *JTS* 17 (1966) 140-143.
— Review of É. TROCMÉ, The Passion as Liturgy, 1983. — *ExpT* 94 (1982-83) 277-278.
— Review of J.D. CROSSAN, Four Other Gospels, 1985. — *ExpT* 97 (1984-85) 87-88.
* — Passion Narratives. — *OCB*, 1990, 515-517.
HOWARD, W.F. The Language of the New Testament. — T.W. MANSON (ed.), *Companion*, 1939, 22-30.
— *The London Quarterly and Holborn Review*, Jan. 1952, 11.
HUBY, J. Review of B.H. STREETER, The Four Gospels, 1924. — *RSR* 17 (1927) 165-167.
— Review of H.J. CADBURY, The Making of Luke-Acts, 1927. — *RSR* 19 (1929) 187-188.
— L'évangile selon saint Luc. — A. ROBERT and A. TRICOT (eds.), *Initiation biblique*, Tournai, 1939; Paris - Tournai - Rome - New York, ²1948, ³1954 ("refondue"), 221-225; Tournai,1957-59, 231-257;
= ID., The Gospel according to Saint Luke. ID. (eds.). *Guide to the Bible*, Vol. 1, tr. from the third French ed. E.P. ARBEZ and M.R.P. MCGUIRE, Westminister, MD, 1951-55; Paris -New York, ²1960 (= ³1954), 402-408.
HÜBNER, H. χρόνος. — *EWNT* 3, cols. 1170-1173; = *EDNT* 3, 488-489.
HULL, W.E. A Structural Analysis of the Gospel of Luke. — *RExp* 64 (1967) 421-425.
HUNKIN, J.W. The Composition of the Third Gospel with Special Reference to Canon Streeter's Theory of Proto-Luke. — *JTS* 28 (1926-27) 250-262.
— *The New Testament. A Conspectus*, London, 1950.
HUNTER, A.M. *Introducing the New Testament*, Philadelphia, PA, 1945, ²1957, ³1972.
— *The Work and Words of Jesus*, Philadelphia, PA, 1950; Revised ed., 1973.
— *Interpreting the New Testament 1900-1950*, Philadelphia, PA, 1951.

— *The New Testament for Today*, Atlanta, GA, 1975.

HURD, J.C. *A Bibliography of New Testament Bibliographies*, New York, 1966.

HUSBAND, R.W. *The Prosecution of Jesus*, Princeton, NJ, 1916.

— The Pardoning of Prisoners by Pilate. — *AJT* 21 (1917) 110-116.

HUTTON, D.D. *The Resurrection of the Holy Ones (Mt 27:51b-53): A Study of the Theology of the Matthean Passion Narrative*. Diss. Harvard, 1970 (dir. H. KOESTER).

HYLKEMA, T.O. and D.A. WUITE VAN MASSIJK, *Het heilig Evangelie naar de beschrijving van Lucas*, Haarlem, 1947.

IBER, G. *Neuere Literatur zur Formgeschichte*. — M. DIBELIUS, *Die Formgeschichte des Evangeliums* (ed. G. BORNKAMM), Tübingen, ³1959, 302-312.

* INNITZER, T. *Kommentar zur Leidens- und Verklärungsgeschichte Jesu Christi*, Vienna, ⁴1948.

IRMSCHER, J. Σὺ λέγεις (Mk. 15,2 - Mt. 27,11 - Lk. 23,3). — *Studii Clasice* 2 (1960) 151-158.

IVERACH, J. Review of F. SPITTA, Die synoptische Grundschrift, 1912. — *ExpT* 24 (1912-13) 162.

JACKSON, H.L. The Present State of the Synoptic Problem. — H.B. SWETE (ed.), *Essays*, 1909, 421- 460.

— Review of W. SANDAY (ed.), SSP, 1911. — *JTS* 13 (1911-12) 112.

JACKSON, S.M. (ed.), *New Schaff-Herzog Encyclopedia of Religious Knowledge*, New York - London, 1910.

JACKSON CASE, S. Review of B.H. STREETER, The Four Gospels, 1925. — *JR* 5 (1925) 428-431.

JACOBSON, A.J. Review of J.D. CROSSAN, Four Other Gospels, 1984. — *BTB* 16 (1986) 123.

JACQUEMET, G. (ed.), *Catholicisme. Hier, Aujourd'hui, Demain*, 7 vols., Paris, 1948.

JACQUES, X. Review of G. SCHNEIDER, Verleugnung, 1969. — *NRT* 93 (1971) 681-682.

— Review of P. BENOIT and M.-É. BOISMARD, Synopse, 1972. — *NRT* 94 (1972) 806-807.

— Reviews of M.G. MARA, L'Évangile de Pierre, 1973. — *NRT* 96 (1974) 531-532; *Civiltà Cattolica* 126/2 (1975) 307-308.

p JAMES, M.R. Apocrypha. — *EB(C)* 1, 1899, 1914, 249-261.

p — *The Apocryphal New Testament*, Oxford, 1924, ᴿ1955. → cf. ELLIOTT.

JANS, J. (ed.), *Bewogen theologie: Theologie in beweging*, Tilburg, 1996. → W. WEREN

JAUBERT, A. *Le date de la Cène. Calendrier biblique et liturgie chrétienne* (EB), Paris, 1957;

= *The Date of the Last Supper*, tr. I. RAFFERTY, New York, 1965.

* — Les séances du sanhédrin et les récits de la passion. — *RHR* 166 (1964) 143-169; 167 (1965) 1-33.

— Review of É. TROCMÉ, Jésus de Nazareth, 1971. — *RHR* 185 (1974) 213-214.

JAVET, J.-S. *L'Évangile de la grâce. Commentaire sur l'Évangile selon saint Luc*, Geneva - Paris, 1957.

JELLICOE, S. (ed.), *Studies in the Septuagint: Origins, Recensions, and Interpretations. Selected Essays with a Prolegomenon* (LBS), New York, 1974.

JEREMIAS, J. *Die Abendmahlsworte Jesus*, Göttingen, 1935, ²1949, ³1960, ⁴1967; = *The Eucharistic Words of Jesus*, tr. A. EHRHARDT, New York, 1955 (= ²1949); tr. N. PERRIN, London, 1966 (= ³1960); Philadelphia, PA, 1977 (= ⁴1967).

— Untersuchungen zum Quellenproblem der Apostelgeschichte. — *ZNW* 36 (1937) 205-221.

— *Die Gleichnisse Jesu* (AThANT, 11), Zürich, 1947; Göttingen - Zürich, [2]1952; Göttingen, [3]1954; [4]1956; [5]1958; [6]1962.

* — Zur Geschichtlichkeit des Verhörs Jesu vor dem Hohen Rat. — *ZNW* 43 (1952) 145-150;

= *Abba*, 139-144.

— Review of H. SCHÜRMANN, Der Paschamahlbericht, 1953. — *TZ* 10 (1954) 140-143; ID., Der Einsetzungsbericht, 1955; ID., Jesu Abschiedsrede, 1957. — *TZ* 15 (1959) 64-66.

— Perikopen-Umstellungen bei Lukas? — *NTS* 4 (1957-58) 115-119;

= *Abba*, 93-97.

— *Abba: Studien zur neutestamentlichen Theologie und Zeitgeschichte*, Göttingen, 1966.

— *Neutestamentliche Theologie 1*, Gütersloh, 1971, [2]1973;

= *New Testament Theology 1*, tr. J. BOWDEN, London, 1971.

— *Die Sprache des Lukasevangeliums. Redaktion und Tradition im Nicht-Markusstoff des dritten Evangeliums* (KEK), Göttingen, 1980.

JEREMIAS, J.J. *Das Evangelium nach Markus. Versuch einer urchristlichen Erklärung für die Gegenwart*, Chemnitz - Leipzig, 1928.

— *Das Evangelium nach Lukas, eine urchristliche Erklärung für die Gegenwart*, Chemnitz - Leipzig, 1930.

— *Der apostolische Ursprung der vier Evangelien. Mit einer kurzgefassten Einleitung in die neueste Geschichte der Schallanalyse*, Leipzig, 1932.

Jesus and Man's Hope (Pittsburgh Festival for the Gospels), Vol. 1, Pittsburgh, PA, 1970 (= *Perspective* 11).

p JOHNSON, B.A. *Empty Tomb Tradition in the Gospel of Peter Related to Mt 28,1-7*. Diss. Harvard, 1965 (dir. H. KOESTER).

p — The Gospel of Peter: Between Apocalypse and Romance. — E.A. LIVINGSTONE (ed.), *StPat* (16,2; TU, 129), Berlin, 1985, 170-174.

JOHNSON, L.T., *The Writings of the New Testament. An Interpretation*, Philadelphia, PA, 1986.

— *The Gospel of Luke* (Sacra Pagina, 3), Collegeville, MN, 1991.

— Book of Luke-Acts. — *ABD* 4, 1992, 403-420.

— Review of R.E. BROWN, The Death of the Messiah, 1994. — *Commonweal* (May 20, 1994) 25-27.

— *The Real Jesus. The Misguided Quest for the Historical Jesus and the Truth of the Traditional Gospels*, San Francisco, CA, 1996.

JOHNSON, S.E. Review of F. FILSON, Origins, 1938. — *ATR* 21 (1939) 53-54.

JOHNSON, S.L. Review of H. HOEHNER, Herod Antipas, 1972. — *BS* 129 (1972) 255-257.

JONES, D.L. Luke's Unique Interest in Historical Chronology. — *SBL 1989 Seminar Papers*, 378-387.

JONES, M. *The New Testament in the Twentieth Century*, London, 1914, [2]1924, [3]1934.

— *The Four Gospels. Their Literary and their Special Characteristics*, London, 1921.

JOÜON, P. *L'Évangile de Notre-Seigneur Jésus-Christ. Traduction et commentaire du texte original grec compte tenu du substrat sémitique* (VS, 5), Paris, 1930.

* — Luc 23,11: esthēta lampran. — *RSR* 26 (1936) 80-85.

JUEL, D. *Luke-Acts. The Promise of History*, Atlanta, GA, 1983.

JÜLICHER, A. *Einleitung in das Neue Testament*, Tübingen, [1,2]1894, [3,4]1901, [5,6]1906, [7]1931;

= *An Introduction to the New Testament*, tr. J. PENROSE WARD, London, 1904.

JÜNGST, J. *Die Quellen der Apostelgeschichte*, Gotha, 1895.

JUSTER, J. *Les Juifs dans L'Empire Romain*, Vol. 2, New York, 1914.

KARRIS, R.J. *The Lukan Sitz im Leben. Methodology and Prospects.* — *SBL 1976 Seminar Papers*, 219-234.

— *Invitation to Luke*, Garden City, NY, 1977.

— Poor and Rich. The Lukan Sitz im Leben. — C.H. TALBERT (ed.), *Perspectives*, 1978, 112-125.

— Missionary Communities: A New Paradigm for the Study of Luke-Acts. — *CBQ* 41 (1979) 80-97.

— Windows and Mirrors. Literary Criticism and Luke's Sitz im Leben. — *SBL 1979 Seminar Papers*, 47-58.

— *Luke: Artist and Theologian* (Theological Inquiries), New York, 1985.

* — Luke 23:47 and the Lukan View of Jesus' Death. — *JBL* 105 (1986) 65-74; = D.D. SYLVA (ed.), *Reimaging*, 1990, 68-78, 187-189.

— Luke 24:13-35. — *Interpr* 41 (1987) 57-61.

— The Gospel according to Luke. — *NJBC*, 1990, 675-721.

* KASTNER, K. *Jesus vor Pilatus. Ein Beitrag zur Leidensgeschichte des Herrn*, Münster, 1912.

KEALY, J.P. *Luke's Gospel Today*, Denville, NJ, 1979.

KEATHLEY, N.H. (ed.), *With Steadfast Purpose. Essays on Acts in Honor of Henry Jackson Flanders, Jr.*, Waco, TX, 1990.

— The Temple in Luke and Acts: Implications for the Synoptic Problem and Proto-Luke. — *Ibid.*, 77-105.

KECK, L.E. and J.L. MARTYN (eds.), *Studies in Luke-Acts*, FS P. SCHUBERT, Nashville, TN, 1966; London, 1968; Philadelphia, PA, 1980 (= FS Schubert).

— et al. (eds.), *The New Interpreter's Bible*, 12 vols., Nashville, TN, 1994- (= NIB).

KEE, H.C. *Jesus in History*, New York, 1970, ²1977.

—, E.M. MEYERS, J. ROGERSON and A.J. SALDARINI, *The Cambridge Companion to the Bible*, Cambridge - New York - Melbourne, 1997.

— The Formation of the Christian Community. — *Ibid.*, 441-583.

KEEGAN, T.J. The Parable of the Sower and Mark's Jewish Leaders. — *CBQ* 56 (1994) 501-518.

KELBER, W.H. (ed.), *The Passion in Mark. Studies on Mark 14-16*, Philadelphia, PA, 1976.

KELLERMANN, U. ἀρχιερεύς. — *EWNT* 1, 394-397 (= *EDNT* 1, 164-165).

KEMPTHORNE, R. The Marcan Text of Jesus' Answer to the High Priest (Mark XIV 62). — *NT* 19 (1977) 197-208.

KENMAN, B. *Luke's Exoneration of John the Baptist.* — *JTS* 44 (1993) 595-598.

KENNARD, J.S. Syrian Coin Hoards and the Tribute Question. — *ATR* 27 (1945) 248-252.

KENNEDY, H.A.A. *Sources of New Testament Greek or The Influence of the Septuagint on the Vocabulary of the New Testament*, Edinburgh, 1895.

— Review of B. WEISS, Die Evangelien des Markus und Lukas, ⁹1901. — *ExpT* 13 (1901-02) 544-545.

* KERTELGE, K. (ed.), *Der Prozess gegen Jesus. Historische Rückfrage und theologische Deutung* (QD, 112), Freiburg, 1988.

KEULERS, J. *De Evangeliën van Marcus en Lucas* (De boeken van het Nieuwe Testament, 2), Roermond - Maaseik, 1936, 117-367; ²1951, 102-299.

* KIDDLE, M. The Passion Narrative in St Luke's Gospel. — *JTS* 36 (1935) 267-280.

KIECKERS, E. *Die Stellung des Verbs im Griechischen und in den verwandten Sprachen* (Untersuchungen zur indogermanischer Sprach- und Kulturwissenschaft, 2), Strassburg, 1911.

KIEHL, E.H. *The Passion of Our Lord*, Grand Rapids, MI, 1990.

KILGALLEN, J.J. Persecution in the Acts of the Apostles. — G. O'COLLINS and G. MARCONI (eds.), *Luke and Acts*, 1993, 143-160.

—— Review of L.T. JOHNSON, The Gospel of Luke, 1991. — *Bib* 74 (1993) 287-290.

* KILPATRICK, G.D. A Theme of the Lucan Passion Story and Luke xxiii. 47. — *JTS* 43 (1942) 34-36; = *Principles*, 1990, 327-329.

* —— Scribes, Lawyers, and Lucan Origins. — *JTS* 1 (1950) 56-60; = *Principles*, 245-249.

* —— *The Trial of Jesus* (Sixth Lecture of Dr. Williams's Library), Oxford, 1953.

—— The Gentiles and the Strata of Luke. — O. BÖCHER and K. HAACKER (eds.), *Verborum Veritas*, 1970, 83-88; = *Principles*, 1990, 313-318.

—— *The Principles and Practice of New Testament Textual Criticism* (BETL, 96), ed. J.K. ELLIOTT, Leuven, 1990.

KINGSBURY, J.D. Jesus as the "Prophetic Messiah" in Luke's Gospel. — A.J. MALHERBE and W.A. MEEKS (eds.), *Future*, 1993, 29-42.

p   KIRK, A. Examining Priorities: Another Look at the Gospel of Peter's Relationship to the New Testament Gospels. — *NTS* 40 (1994) 572-595.

KITTEL, G. and G. FRIEDRICH (ed.), *Theologisches Wörterbuch zum Neuen Testament*, Stuttgart, 1933-79 (= TWNT); = *Theological Dictionary of the New Testament*, Grand Rapids, MI, 1964-1976, ᴿ1977 (= TDNT).

* KLEIN, G. Die Verleugnung des Petrus. — *ZTK* 58 (1961) 285-328; = *Rekonstruktion und Interpretation. Gesammelte Aufsätze zum Neuen Testament* (BEvTh, 50), Munich, 1969, 49-98; *Nachtrag*, 90-98.

* KLEIN, H. Die lukanisch-johanneische Passionstradition. — *ZNW* 67 (1976) 155-186; = M. LIMBECK (ed.), *Redaktion*, 1981, 366-403.

—— *Barmherzigkeit gegenüber den Elenden und Geächteten. Studien zur Botschaft des lukanischen Sonderguts* (BThS 10), Neukirchen - Vluyn, 1987.

KLIJN, A.F.J. *De wordingsgeschiedenis van het Nieuwe Testament*, Utrecht-Antwerp, 1965; = *An Introduction to the New Testament*, tr. M. VAN DER VATHORST-SMIT, Leiden, 1967.

—— Review of H. VAN DER KWAAK, Het Proces van Jezus, 1969. — *NedTT* 24 (1969) 60-61.

* KLOPPENBORG, J.S. Exitus clari viri: The Death of Jesus in Luke. — *TJT* 8 (1992) 106-120.

—— Review of E. LINNEMANN, Is There A Synoptic Problem?, 1992. — *CRBR* 6 (1993) 262-264.

—— The Sayings Gospel Q and the Quest of the Historical Jesus. — *HTR* 89 (1996) 307-344.

KLOSTERMANN, E. *Die Evangelien. 1. Die Synoptiker* (HNT, 2), Tübingen, 1919 (359-612: *Lukas*); *Das Lukasevangelium* (HNT, 5), ²1929, ³1975 ("3. Auflage, unveranderter Nachdruck der zweiten Aufl.").

p   —— *Apocrypha I: Reste des Petrusevangeliums, der Petrusapokalypse und des Kerygma Petri* (Kleine Texte), Bonn, ²1921.

KNABENBAUER, J. *Commentarius in quatuor S. Evangelica Domini Nostri Jesu Christi. 3. Evangelium secundum Lucam* (CSS, 3/3), Paris, 1896, ²1905, 1926.

KNOX, J. *Marcion and the New Testament*, Chicago, IL, 1942; New York, 1980.

KNOX, W.L. *Acts of the Apostles*, Cambridge, 1948.
— *The Sources of the Synoptic Gospels*. 1. *The Gospel of Mark*; 2. *St. Luke and St. Matthew* (ed. H. CHADWICK), Cambridge, 1953/1957.
KOCH, K. *Das Buch der Bücher. Die Entstehungsgeschichte der Bibel*, Berlin, 1963;
= *The Book of Books. The Growth of the Bible*, tr. M. KOHL, Philadelphia, PA, 1968.
* KODELL, J. Luke's Use of *Laos*, 'People' especially in the Jerusalem Narrative (Lk 19,28-24,53). — *CBQ* 31 (1969) 327-343.
* — Luke's Theology of the Death of Jesus. — D. DURKEN (ed.), *Sin*, 1979, 221-230.
— *The Gospel according to Luke* (CBC, 3), Collegeville, MN, 1983;
= *Luke*. — *CBC*, 1989, 936-980.
KÖHLER, W. κατά. — *EWNT* 2, 624-627 (= *EDNT* 2, 253-254).
p KOESTER, H. Apocryphal and Canonical Gospels. — *HTR* 73 (1980) 105-130.
— *Introduction to the New Testament*, 2 vols., Philadelphia, PA, 1982.
p — Überlieferung und Geschichte der frühchristlichen Evangelienliteratur. — *ANRW* II.25.2 (1984) 1463-1542.
p — *Ancient Christian Gospels*, London - Philadelphia, PA, 1990.
— and F. BOVON, *Genèse de l'écriture chrétienne* (Mémoires Premières), Turnhout, 1991.
— Written Gospels or Oral Traditions. — *JBL* 113 (1994) 293-297.
KÖSTLIN, K.R. *Die Ursprung und die Composition der synoptischen Evangelien*, Stuttgart, 1853.
KOH, R. *The Writings of St. Luke. Brief Notes on the Material Peculiar to the Writings of St. Luke and on the Possibility of the Acts of the Apostles being Composed Before the Third Gospel*, Hong Kong, 1953.
KOLLMANN, B. *Ursprung und Gestalten der frühchristlichen Mahlfeier* (GTA, 43), Göttingen, 1990. Diss. Göttingen, 1988-89 (dir. H. STEGEMANN).
KRÄMER, H. ἐνώπιον. — *EWNT* 1, cols. 1130-1131 (= *EDNT* 1, 462).
KRATZ, R. → R. PESCH, 1977
KRAUSS, S. *Talmudische Archäologie*, 3 vols., Leipzig, 1910-12.
KREMER, J. Review of G. SCHNEIDER, *Verleugnung*, 1969. — *TPQ* 119 (1971) 176-177.
* — Verurteilt als "König der Juden" - verkundigt als "Herr und Christus". — *BLit* 45 (1972) 23-32.
— (ed.), *Les Actes des Apôtres. Traditions, rédaction, théologie* (BETL, 48), Gembloux - Leuven, 1979.
— *Lukasevangelium* (Neue Echter Bibel, 3), Würzburg, 1988.
— "Dieser ist der Sohn Gottes" (Apg 9,20). Bibeltheologische Erwägungen zur Bedeutung von "Sohn Gottes" im lukanischen Doppelwerk, in C. BUSSMANN and W. RADL (eds.), *Die Treue Gottes*, 1991, 137-158;
= *Die Bibel*, 1995, 59-83.
— *Die Bibel beim Wort genommen. Beiträge zu Exegese und Theologie des Neuen Testaments* (eds. R. KÜHSCHELM and M. STOWASSER), Freiburg - Basel - Vienna, 1995.
KRETSCHMAR, G. and E. LOHSE (eds.), *Ecclesia und Res Publica*, FS K.D. SCHMIDT, Göttingen, 1961 (= FS Schmidt).
KÜHNER, R. *Ausführliche Grammatik der griechischen Sprache*, 4 vols., Third edition by F. BLASS and B. GERTH, Hannover - Leipzig, 1890-1904.
KÜMMEL, W.G. *Einleitung in das Neue Testament* [¹²1963], Heidelberg, ¹⁷1973, XIX-548 (92- 120: *Das Lukasevangelium*), ¹⁹1978; ²¹1983;

    = *Introduction to the New Testament*, tr. A.J. MATTILL, [14]1965; tr. H.C. KEE, [[17]1963], Nashville, TN 1975, [5]1984 (122-151, 174: *The Gospel of Luke*).

— *Das Neue Testament. Geschichte der Erforschung seiner Probleme*, Freiburg, 1970; = *The New Testament, The History of the Investigation of Its Problems*, tr. S.MCL. GILMOUR - H.C. KEE, Nashville, TN, 1972.

— Lukas in der Anklage der heutigen Theologie. — *ZNW* 63 (1972) 149-165; = G. BAUMANN (ed.), 1974, 416-436; = *Heilsgeschehen und Geschichte*, 1978, 87-100; = Luc en accusation dans la théologie contemporaine, tr. T. SNOY. — F. NEIRYNCK (ed.), *L'Évangile de Luc*, 1974, 93-109; [2]1989, 3-19, 295; = Current Theological Accusations against Luke, tr. W.C. ROBINSON, Jr. — *ANQ* 16 (1975) 131-145.

— *Heilsgeschehen und Geschichte*. Bd. 2. *Gesammelte Aufsätze 1965-1977* (MTS, 16). Ed. E. GRÄSSER - O. MERK, Marburg, 1978.

*   — Jesusforschung seit 1965: Pt. 6. Der Prozess und der Kreuzestod Jesu. — *TR* 45 (1980) 293-337; = *Dreissig Jahre*, 1985, 375-419.

*   — *Dreissig Jahre Jesusforschung (1950-1980)* (BBB, 60), Königstein/Ts Bonn, 1985.

KUHN, K.G. Jesus in Gethsemane. — *EvTh* 12 (1952-53) 260-285; = M. LIMBECK (ed.). *Redaktion*, 1981, 81-111.

— (ed.), *Sifre zu Numeri* (Rabbinische Texte 2/2), Stuttgart, 1959.

p   KUNZE, J. *Das neu aufgefundene Bruchstück des sog. Petrusevangelium übersetzt und beurteilt*, Leipzig, 1893; = Das Petrusevangelium. — *NJDTh* 2 (1893) 583-604; 3 (1894) 58-104.

KURZ, W.S. Review of J. ERNST, Das Evangelium nach Lukas, 1977. — *CBQ* 40 (1978) 631-633.

— Narrative Models for Imitation in Luke-Acts. — D.L. BALCH (ed.), *Greeks*, 1990, 171-189.

— *Reading Luke-Acts. Dynamics of Biblical Narrative*, Louisville, KY, 1993.

La Bible. Traduction française sur les textes originaux par É. OSTY avec la collaboration de J. TRINQUET; introductions et notes d'É. OSTY et de J. TRINQUET, [Paris], 1973.

LAGRANGE, M.-J. Les sources du troisième Évangile. — *RB* 4 (1895) 5-22; 5 (1896) 5-38.

— Mélanges. — *RB* 3 (1906) 561-574.

— *Évangile selon saint Luc*, Paris, 1921, [2]1926 (plus Addenda, 623-625), [3]1927 (corrected), [8]1948.

— Reviews in *RB*: 11 (1902) 632-633: P.C. SENSE, Critical, 1901; *13* (1904) 612-614: V. ROSE, Évangile selon S. Luc, 1904; 31 (1922) 286-292: R. BULTMANN, Die Geschichte der synoptischen Tradition, 1921; 32 (1923) 442-445: G. BERTRAM, Die Leidensgeschichte Jesu, 1922; 34 (1925) 454-458: B.H. STREETER, FG, 1924; 36 (1927) 123-124: B.S. EASTON, The Gospel according to St. Luke, 1926; 36 (1927) 120-123: V. TAYLOR, Behind, 1926.

LAKE, K. Review of W.F. BURNSIDE, The Gospel according to Luke, 1913. — *HTR* 8 (1915) 557- 559.

— The Problem of Christian Origins. — *HTR* 15 (1922) 97-114.

— *An Introduction to the New Testament*, London, 1938.

— → F.J. FOAKES JACKSON

LAMBRECHT, J. *Marcus Interpretator*, Brugge - Utrecht, 1969.

LAMOUILLE, A. Review of P. BENOIT and M.-É. BOISMARD, Synopse, 1972. — *RThom* 73 (1973) 273-278.

LAMPE, G.W.H. Luke. — *PCB*, 1962, ᴿ1964, 820-843.

LARFELD, W. *Die neutestamentlichen Evangelien nach ihrer Eigenart und Abhängigkeit*, Gütersloh, 1925.

LARSON, B. *Luke* (The Communicator's Commentary, 3), Waco, TX, 1983.

LATIMER JACKSON, H. Review of F. NICOLARDOT, Les procédés, 1908. — *JTS* 10 (1908-09) 607-609.

— Review of W. SANDAY (ed.), SSP, 1911. — *JTS* 13 (1911-12) 105-114.

LATTEY, C. Introduction to the Gospel according to St. Luke. — ID. and J. KEATING (eds.), *The Synoptic Gospels*, Vol. 1 (Westminster NT), London, 1935, ²1938, xiii-xxiv.

LAVERDIERE, E.A. Review of H. HOEHNER, Herod Antipas, 1972. — *CBQ* 35 (1973) 155-158.

— *Luke* (NTM, 5), Wilmington, DE, 1980.

* — The Passion-Resurrection of Jesus according to St. Luke. — *ChSt* 25 (1986) 35-50.

LAVERGNE, C. *Évangile selon saint Luc* (EB), Paris, 1932.

LAYMON, C.M. (ed.), *The Interpreter's One-Volume Commentary on the Bible*, Nashville, TN, 1971.

LEANEY, A.R.C. *The Sources of the Gospel according to St. Luke*, unpublished B.D. thesis, Oxford, 1952.

— *A Commentary on the Gospel according to St. Luke* (BNTC), London, 1958, ²1966.

— and R. DAVIDSON. *Biblical Criticism* (The Pelican Guide to Modern Theology, 3), Harmondsworth, England - Baltimore - Victoria, Australia, 1970.

— *The New Testament*, London, 1972.

— Review of V. TAYLOR, Passion Narrative, 1972. — *ATR* 55 (1973) 511-513.

* LÉGASSE, S. Jésus devant le Sanhédrin. Recherche sur les traditions évangeliques. — *RTL* 5 (1974) 170-197.

— L'apologétique à l'égard de Rome dans le procès de Paul, Actes 21,27-26,32. — *RSR* 69 (1981) 249-255;
= J. DELORME and J. DUPLACY (eds.), *La parole de la grâce. Études lucaniennes à la mémoire d'A. George*, Paris: Recherches de science religieuse, 1981;
= *RSR* 69 (1981) 248-256.

— *Stephanos. Histoire et discours d'Étienne dans le Actes des Apôtres* (LD, 147), Paris, 1992.

* — *Le procès de Jésus. L'histoire* (LD, 156), Paris, 1994;
= *The Trial of Jesus*, tr. J. BOWDEN, London, 1997.

* — *Le procès de Jésus. La passion dans les quatre évangiles* (LDC, 3), Paris, 1995.

LEHMANN, M. *Synoptische Quellenanalyse und die Frage nach dem historischen Jesus* (BNZW, 38), Berlin, 1970.

p LEJAY, P. L'évangile de Pierre. — *RevÉtudGrecq* 6 (1893) 59-84; 267-270.

LEMME, L. *Das Jakobsevangelium* (BZSF 13/11-12), Berlin - Lichterfelde, 1920.

LÉMONON, J.-P. *Pilate et le gouvernement de la Judée. Textes et monuments* (EB), Paris, 1981.

LÉON-DUFOUR, X. Review of L. VAGANAY, Le problème synoptique, 1954. — *RSR* 42 (1954) 557-572.

— Review of P. PARKER, The Gospel before Mark, 1953. — *RSR* 42 (1954) 572-576.

— Review of W.L KNOX, Sources, Vol. 1, 1953. — *RSR* 42 (1954) 581-584.

— *Les évangiles synoptiques*. — A. ROBERT and A. FEUILLET (eds.), *Introduction à la Bible*, Tournai, 1959, 144-334;

= *The Synoptic Gospels*. — A. ROBERT and A. FEUILLET (eds.), *Introduction to the New Testament*, tr. P.W. SKEHAN, et al., New York, 1965, 140-324;

= X. LÉON-DUFOUR and C. PERROT, *L'annonce de l'Évangile* (Introduction à la Bible. Le Nouveau Testament, 2; eds. A. GEORGE and P. GRELOT), Paris, 1976.

*   — Passion. — *DBS* 6, 1960, 1419-1492.

— *Les évangiles et l'histoire de Jesus*, Paris, 1963;

= *The Gospels and the Jesus of History*, tr. and ed. J. MCHUGH, New York, 1968.

L'EPLATTENIER, C. *Lecture de l'Évangile de Luc*, Paris, 1982.

LESCOW, T. Jesus in Gethsemane. — *EvTh* 26 (1966) 141-159.

— Jesus in Gethsemane bei Lukas und im Hebraerbrief. — *ZNW* 58 (1967) 215-237.

p   LICHTENBERGER, H. Apocryphen. — *Evangelisches Kirchenlexikon* 1, Göttingen, 1985, 207-211 (= EKL).

LIDDELL, H.G and R. SCOTT, *A Greek-English Lexicon*, Oxford, 1843, [8]1897; new ed. H.S. JONES and R. MCKENZIE, 2 vols., Oxford, 1925-1940 (= LSJ).

*   LIETZMANN, H. Der Prozess Jesu. — *SPAW, phil.-hist. Klass.* 14 (1931) Berlin, 1934, 313-322;

= *Kleine Schriften II, Studien zum Neuen Testament*, ed. K. ALAND, Berlin, 1958, 251-263.

*   — Bemerkungen zum Prozess Jesu. I. — *ZNW* 30 (1931) 211-215; II. — *ZNW* 31 (1932) 78-84;

= *Kleine Schriften II, Studien zum Neuen Testament*, ed. K. ALAND, Berlin, 1958, 264-268; 269-276.

LIGHTFOOT, J.B. *Biblical Essays*, London, 1893.

LIGHTFOOT, R.H. *History and Interpretation in the Gospels* (Bampton Lectures), New York, 1934.

— *Locality and Doctrine in the Gospels*, London, 1938.

— Form Criticism and Gospel Study. — *ExpT* 53 (1941-42) 51-54.

— *The Gospel Message of St Mark*, Oxford, 1950: Form Criticism and the Study of the Gospels, 98-105.

*   LIMBECK, M. (ed.), *Redaktion und Theologie des Passionsberichtes nach den Synoptikern* (WdF 481), Darmstadt, 1981.

LINDARS, B. *New Testament Apologetic*, Philadelphia, PA, 1961.

LINDESKOG, G. *Die Jesusfrage im neuzeitlichen Judentum. Ein Beitrag zur Geschichte der Leben- Jesu-Forschung*, Uppsala, 1938; "mit Nachtrag", Darmstadt, [R]1973.

— Der Prozess Jesu im jüdisch-christlichen Religionsgespräch. — FS MICHEL, 1963, 325-336.

— Review of D.R. CATCHPOLE, The Trial of Jesus, 1971. — *ZRGG* 25 (1973) 189-192.

LINDSEY, R.L. A Modified Two-Document Theory of the Synoptic Dependence and Interdependence. — *NT* 6 (1963) 239-263.

— *A Hebrew Translation of the Gospel of Mark. Greek-Hebrew Diglot with English Introduction*, Jerusalem, 1969, [2]1973.

— A New Approach on the Synoptic Gospels. — *CNI* 22 (1971) 56-63.

— *A Comparative Concordance of the Synoptics Gospels*, 3 vols., Jerusalem, 1985.

— A New Approach to the Synoptic Gospels. — *Mishkan* 17-18 (1992-93) 87-106.

— Unlocking the Synoptic Problem. Four Keys for Better Understanding Jesus. — *Jerusalem Perspective* 49 (1995) 1-17, 38.

*   LINNEMANN, E. Die Verleugnung des Petrus. — *ZTK* 63 (1966) 1-32.

* — *Studien zur Passionsgeschichte* (FRLANT, 102), Göttingen, 1970.

— *Wissenschaft oder Meinung? Anfragen und Alternativen*, Neuhausen, 1986;
= *Historical Criticism of the Bible: Methodology or Ideology*, tr. R.W. YARBOROUGH, Grand Rapids, MI, 1990.

— *Gibt es ein synoptisches Problem?*, Neuhausen, 1992;
= *Is There a Synoptic Problem? Rethinking the Literary Dependence of the First Three Gospels*, tr. R.W. YARBOROUGH, Grand Rapids, MI, 1992.

* LIPPERT, G. *Pilatus als Richter. Eine Untersuchung über seine richterliche Verantwortlichkeit an der Hand der den Evangelien entnommenen amtlichen Aufzeichnung des Verfahrens gegen Jesus*, Vienna, 1923.

LOCKTON, W. The Origin of the Gospels. — *CQR* 94 (1922) 216-239.

— *The Resurrection and the Virgin Birth*, London, 1924.

— *The Three Traditions in the Gospels*, London, 1926.

— *Certain Alleged Gospel Sources*, London, 1927.

p LODS, A. *L'évangile et l'apocalypse de Pierre*, Paris, 1893.

* LOHFINK, G. *Der letzte Tag Jesu*, Freiburg, 1981;
= *The Last Day of Jesus*, tr. S. ATTANASIO, Notre Dame, IN, 1984.

LOHMEYER, E. *Galiläa und Jerusalem* (FRLANT, 52), Göttingen, 1936.

LOHSE, E. Lukas als Theologe der Heilsgeschichte. — *EvTh* 14 (1954) 256-275.

* — *Der Prozess Jesu Christi*. — FS SCHMIDT, 1961, 24-39.

— συνέδριον. — *TWNT* 7, 858-869; = *TDNT* 7, 1971, 860-871.

* — *Die Geschichte de Leidens und Sterbens Jesu Christi*, Gütersloh, 1964;
= *History of the Suffering and Death of Jesus Christ*, tr. M.O. DIETRICH, Philadelphia, PA, 1967.

LOISY, A. Chronique. — *L'enseignement biblique* 2 (mars-avril, 1893) 17-64.

p — Livres apocryphes. L'évangile et l'apocalypse de Pierre. — *L'enseignement biblique* (1893) 48-61; 90-93.

— *Les évangiles synoptiques*, Paris, Vol. 1, 1907; Vol. 2, 1908.

— *Les livres du Nouveau Testament traduits du grec en français avec introduction général et notices*, Paris, 1922.

— *L'Évangile selon Luc*, Paris, 1924.

— *Les origines du Nouveau Testament*, Paris, 1936;
= *The Origins of the New Testament*, tr. L.P. JACKS, London, [1950]; New Hyde Park, NY, 1962.

LONGSTAFF, T.R.W. and P.A. THOMAS, *The Synoptic Problem. A Bibliography 1716-1988* (New Gospel Studies, 4), Macon, GA, 1988.

LOWE, M. The Demise of Arguments from Order for Markan Priority. — *NT* 24 (1982) 27-36.

— From the Parable of the Vineyard to a Pre-Synoptic Source. — *NTS* 28 (1982) 257-263.

— and D. FLUSSER. Evidence Corroborating a Modified Proto-Matthean Synoptic Theory. — *NTS* 29 (1983) 25-47.

p LUCAS, H. The New Apocrypha. — *Month* 77 (1893) 1-15.

LUCK, U. *Kerygma und Tradition in der Hermeneutik Adolf Schlatters* (AFLN-W, 45), Cologne - Opland, 1955.

LÜDEMANN, G. εἰ. — *EWNT* 1, cols. 931-933; = *EDNT* 1, 384-385.

— ἐκ (ἐξ). — *EWNT* 1, cols. 977-980; = *EDNT* 1, 402-403.

p LÜHRMANN, D. POx 2949: EvPt 3-5 in einer Handschrift des 2./3. Jahrhunderts. — *ZNW* 72 (1981) 216-226.

— Q: Sayings of Jesus or Logia. — R.A. PIPER (ed.), *Gospel*, 1995, 97-116.

LUMMIS, E.W. *How Luke was Written: Considerations Affecting the Two-Document Theory with Special Reference to the Phenomena of Order in the Non-Marcan Matter Common to Matthew and Luke*, Cambridge, 1915.

— A Case Against 'Q'. — *HJ* 24 (1925-26) 755-765.

LUOMANEN, P. (ed.), *Luke-Acts: Scandinavian Perspectives* (Publications of the Finnish Exegetical Society, 54), Helsinki - Göttingen, 1991.

LUST, J. - E. EYNIKEL - K. HAUSPIE with the collaboration of G. CHAMBERLIN, *A Greek-English Lexicon of the Septuagint*, 2 vols., Stuttgart, 1992-1996 (= GELS)

LUZ, U. Review of V. TAYLOR, Passion Narrative, 1972. — *TZ* 30 (1974) 239-240.

LYON, D.G. and G.F. MOORE (eds.), *Studies in the History of Religions, Presented to Crawford Howell Toy*, New York, 1912.

p MAAS, A.J. The Lately Recovered Apocryphal Gospel According to Peter. — *American Catholic Quarterly Review* 18 (1893) 313-328.

p MCCANT, J.W. *The Gospel of Peter: The Docetic Question Re-examined*. Diss. Emory, Atlanta, GA, 1976 (dir. L.E. KECK).

p — The Gospel of Peter. Docetism Reconsidered. — *NTS* 30 (1984) 258-273.

MCCOOL, F.J. Synoptic Problem. — W.J. MCDONALD (ed.), *NCE* 13, 1967, 886-891.

MCDONALD, W.J. (ed.), *New Catholic Encyclopdeia*, 15 vols., Washington, D.C., 1967.

* MCELENEY, N.J. Peter's Denials - How Many? To Whom? — *CBQ* 52 (1990) 467-472.

* MCGING, B.C. The Governorship of Pontius Pilate: Messiahs and Sources. — A.D.H. MAYES (ed.), *Proceedings of the Irish Biblical Association* 10 (1986) 55-71.

* — Pontius Pilate and the Sources. — *CBQ* 53 (1991) 416-438.

p MCHUGH, M.P. Gospel of Peter. — E. FERGUSON (ed.) *Encyclopedia*, 1990, 383; ²1997, Vol. 2, 476-477.

MCINTYRE, D.M. The Building of the Third Gospel. — *EvQ* 1 (1929) 130-146.

— *Some Notes on the Gospels*, (ed. F.F. BRUCE), London, 1944.

MCKENZIE, J.L. Review of H. SCHÜRMANN, Der Paschamahlbericht, 1953. — *CBQ* 16 (1954) 262- 263; ID., Der Einsetzungesbericht, 1955. — *CBQ* 17 (1955) 528-529.

— *Dictionary of the Bible*, New York - London - Milwaukee, WI, 1965.

MCKNIGHT, S. and M.C. WILLIAMS, Luke. — M. BAUMAN and M.I. KLAUBER (eds.), *Historians*, 1996, 39-57.

MCLACHLAN, H. *St. Luke. Evangelist and Historian*, London, 1912.

— *St. Luke. The Man and His Work*, Manchester, 1920.

MCLANGHLIN, G. *Commentary on the Gospel according to St. Luke*, Chicago, 1912.

MCLOUGHLIN, S. Les accords mineurs Mt-Lc contre Mc et le problème synoptique. Vers la théorie des deux sources. — *ETL* 43 (1967) 17-40;

    = I. DE LA POTTERIE (ed.), *De Jésus aux Évangiles. Tradition et rédaction dans les Évangiles synoptiques* (BETL, 25), Gembloux, 1967, 17-40.

MCNEIL, B. Review of É. TROCMÉ, The Passion as Liturgy, 1983. — *HeythJ* 27 (1986) 186-187.

MCNEILE, A.H. *An Introduction to the Study of the New Testament*, Oxford, 1927, ²1953 (revised by C.S.C. WILLIAMS).

— *The Gospel According to St. Matthew. The Greek Text with Introduction, Notes, and Indices*, London - Melbourne - Toronto - New York, 1915.

p MACPHERSON, J. The Gospel of Peter. A Criticism and Exposition. — *ExpT* 5 (1893-94) 556-561.

MADER, J. *Die heiligen vier Evangelien und die Apostelgeschichte*, Einsiedeln, 1911.

MAIER, J. Review of H. VAN DER KWAAK, Het Proces van Jezus, 1969. — *Bib* 51 (1970) 280-283.

MAIER, P.L. Who Killed Jesus? — *ChrTod* 34 (1990) 16-19.

MAJOR, H.D.A., T.W. MANSON and C.J. WRIGHT (eds.), *The Mission and Message of Jesus*, New York, 1938 (= MMJ).

MALHERBE, A.J. and W.A. MEEKS (eds.), *The Future of Christology*. FS KECK, Minneapolis, MN, 1993.

MANGAN, E.A. Review of D.W. RIDDLE, The Gospels, 1939. — *CBQ* 2 (1940) 188-189.

MANGENOT, E. Luc (Évangile de Saint). — *DB* 4, Paris, 1908.

— *Les évangiles synoptiques*, Paris, 1911.

MANRODT, M. Review of R.H. CROMPTON, Synoptic Problem, 1928. — *BS* 86 (1929) 349-351.

MANSON, T.W. The Life of Jesus: A Survey of the Available Material. (3) The Work of St. Luke. — *BJRL* 28 (1924) 382-403;
= ID., The Work of St. Luke. — M. BLACK (ed.), *Studies*, 1962, 46-67.

— *The Sayings of Jesus*. — MMJ, 1938, 301-544.

— (ed.), *A Companion to the Bible*, Edinburgh - New York, 1939.

— The New Testament and Other Christian Writings of the New Testament Period. — ID. (ed.), *Companion*, 1939, 97-129.

— The Cleansing of the Temple. — *BJRL* 33 (1951) 271-282.

— *The Sayings of Jesus*, London, 1954.

MANSON, W. *The Gospel of Luke* (The Moffatt NT Commentary), London - New York, 1930.

MANTEY, J.R. → H.E. DANA

* MANUS, C.V. The Universalism of Luke and the Motif of Reconciliation in Luke 23:6-12. — *AfTJ* 16 (1987) 121-135.

p MARA, M.G., *L'Évangile de Pierre* (SC, 201), Paris, 1973.

MARCHAL, L. *Evangile selon saint Luc* (La Sainte Bible, 10), Paris, 1935; ²1950.

MARIN, L. *Sémiotique de la Passion. Topiques et figures* (BSR), Paris, 1971;
= *Semiotik der Passionsgeschichte*, tr. S. VIRGILS, Munich, 1976;
= *The Semiotics of the Passion Narrative. Topics and Figures* (PTMS, 25), tr. A.M. JOHNSON, Pittsburgh, PA, 1980.

MARSHALL, I.H. Luke. — D. GUTHRIE and J.A. MOTYER (eds.), *The New Bible Commentary Revised*, ³1970 (completely revised), 887-925; D.A. CARSON, R.T. FRANCE, J.A. MOTYER and G.J. WENHAM (eds.), Leicester - Downers Grove, IL, ⁴1994 (completely revised), 978-1020 (= NBC).

— *Luke: Historian and Theologian*, Exeter, 1970; ³1989.

— *The Gospel of Luke. A Commentary on the Greek Text* (NIGTC, 3), Exeter - Grand Rapids, MI, 1978.

— Review of M.D. GOULDER, Luke: A New Paradigm, 1989. — *ExpT* 101 (1989-90) 311-312.

— Review of C.F. EVANS, Saint Luke, 1990. — *JTS* 42 (1991) 215-218.

— Acts and the 'Former Treatise'. — B.W. WINTER and A.D. CLARKE (eds.), *The Book of Acts*, 1993, 163-182.

— Review of B.E. REID, The Transfiguration, 1993. — *JTS* 45 (1994) 662-664.

MARTINDALE, C.C. *The Gospel According to St. Luke. With an Introduction and Commentary* (Stonyhurst Scripture Manuals), Westminster, MD, 1957.

p MARTINEAU, J. The Gospel of Peter. — *The Nineteenth Century* 33 (1893) 905-926; 34 (1893) 633- 656.

MARTINEZ DALMAU, E. *A Study on the Synoptic Gospels. A New Solution to an Old Problem. The Dependence of the Greek Gospels of St. Matthew and St. Luke upon the Gospel of St. Mark*, New York, 1963.

MARXSEN, W. *Einleitung in das Neue Testament. Eine Einführung in das Neue Testament*, Gütersloh, 1963, ³1964, ⁴1978;
    = *Introduction to the New Testament. An Approach to its Problems*, tr. G. BUSWELL, Philadelphia, PA, 1968.

MASSAUX, É. *Influence de l'Évangile de saint Matthieu sur la littérature chrétienne avant saint Irénée* Louvain - Gembloux, 1950; (BETL, 75), Leuven, 1986;
    = *The Influence of the Gospel of Saint Matthew on Christian Literature before Saint Irenaeus*, tr. N.J. BELVAL and S. HECHT; ed. A.J. BELLINZONI (New Gospel Studies, 5/1-3), Macon, GA, 1990-93.

*   MASSON, C. Le reniement de Pierre. — *RHPR* 37 (1957) 24-35.

MATERA, F.J. *The Kingship of Jesus. Composition and Theology in Mark 15* (SBL DS, 66), Chico, CA, 1982. Diss. Union Theol. Sem., Richmond, VA, 1981 (dir. P. ACHTEMEIER).

*   — The Death of Jesus according to Luke. A Question of Sources. — *CBQ* 47 (1985) 469-485.

*   — *Passion Narratives and Gospel Theologies. Interpreting the Synoptics through their Passion Stories* (Theological Inquiries), New York, 1986.

*   — Luke 22,66-71. Jesus Before the ΠΡΕΣΒΥΤΕΡΙΟΝ. — *ETL* 65 (1989) 43-59;
    = NEIRYNCK, F. (ed.), *L'Évangile de Luc - The Gospel of Luke*, ²1989, 517-533.

*   — Luke 23,1-25. Jesus Before Pilate, Herod and Israel. — *Ibid.*, ²1989, 535-551.

— Review of J.D. CROSSAN, The Cross that Spoke, 1988. — *Worship* 63 (1989) 269-270.

— Responsibility for the Death of Jesus According to the Acts of the Apostles. — *JSNT* 39 (1990) 77- 93.

— Review of J.B. GREEN, The Death of Jesus, 1988. — *Interpr* 44 (1990) 206-207.

*   — The Trial of Jesus. Problems and Proposals. — *Interpr* 45 (1991) 5-16.

MATTILL, A.J. The Jesus-Paul Parallels and the Purpose of Luke-Acts: H.H. Evans Reconsidered. — *NT* 17 (1975) 15-46.

MAURER, C. Knecht Gottes und Sohn Gottes im Passionsbericht des Markusevangeliums. — *ZTK* 50 (1953) 1-38.

p   — Petrusevangelium. — E. HENNECKE and W. SCHNEEMELCHER (eds.), *Neutestamentliche Apokryphen*. 1. *Evangelien*, ³1959, 118-124; ⁶1990;
    = The Gospel of Peter. — E. HENNECKE and W. SCHNEEMELCHER (eds.), *New Testament Apocrypha*, I. *Gospels and Related Writings*, 1963; 1973, 179-187; 1991, 216-227.

p   — W. SCHNEEMELCHER, Petrusevangelium. — ID. (ed.), *Neutestamentliche Apokryphen in deutscher Übersetzung*, Tübingen, 1987, 180-188.

MAYER, R. Review of D.R. CATCHPOLE, The Trial of Jesus, 1971. — *TZ* 29 (1973) 439-440.

*   MAYO, C.H. St Peter's Token of the Cock Crow. — *JTS* 22 (1921) 367-370.

MAYS, J. (ed.), *Interpreting the Gospels*, Philadelphia, PA, 1981.

MAYS, J.L. (ed.), *Harper's Bible Commentary*, San Francisco, CA - Cambridge, 1988.

MEALAND, D.L. Review of R.H. GUNDRY, Matthew, 1982. — *JAAR* 52 (1984) 255-257.

MEGIVERN, J.J. (ed.) *Bible Interpretation* (Official Catholic Teachings), Wilmington, NC, 1978.

MEIER, J.P. Review of R.H. GUNDRY, Matthew, 1982. — *JBL* 103 (1984) 475-477.

— Review of J.D. CROSSAN, The Cross that Spoke, 1988. — *Horizons* 16 (1989) 378-379.

— *A Marginal Jew. Rethinking the Historical Jesus* (ABRL). 1. *The Roots of the Problem and the Person*; 2. *Mentor, Message, and Miracles*, New York - London, 1991, 1994.

MEINERTZ, M. Das Lukasevangelium. — *Biblische Zeitfragen* 3³, 2, Münster, 1912, 3-46.

— *Einleitung in das Neue Testament*, Paderborn, 1933.

MELINSKY, H. *Luke* (The Modern Reader's Guide to the Gospels), London, 1966.

MERK, A. *Introductionis in S. Scripturae Libros Compendium*, Paris, ⁹1927, ¹²1940.

* MERKEL, H. Peter's Curse. — E. BAMMEL (ed.), *Trial*, 1970, 66-77.

MERX, A. *Die Evangelien des Markus und Lukas nach syrischen im Sinaikloster gefundenen Palimpsesthandschrift*, Berlin, 1905.

METZGER, B.M. *The New Testament: Its Background, Growth and Content*, Nashville, TN, 1965.

— *A Textual Commentary on the Greek New Testament*, London - New York, 1971.

— *The Canon of the New Testament. Its Origin, Development, and Significance*, Oxford, 1987;
= *Der Kanon des Neuen Testaments. Entstehung, Entwicklung, Bedeutung*, tr. Hans-M. RÖTTGERS, Düsseldorf, 1993.

— and M.D. COOGAN (eds.), *The Oxford Companion to the Bible*, New York - Oxford, 1993 (= OCB).

p MEYBOOM, H.U. *Oud-Christelijke Geschriften in Nederlandsche Vertaling*, Leiden, 1907.

MEYER, E. *Ursprung und Anfänge des Christentums*, 3 vols., 1921-23; Vol. 1, Stuttgart, 1921; Darmstadt, ᴿ1962.

MEYER, H.A.W. *Kritisch Exegetischer Handbuch über die Evangelien des Markus und Lukas* (KEK, 1/2), Göttingen, 1832, ²1846, ³1855, ⁴1857, ⁵1867, 193-518.

— *Handbuch über die Apostelgeschichte* (KEK), Göttingen, 1835, ²1854, ³1861, ⁴1869, ⁵1880 (ed. H.H. WENDT);
Handbook to the Acts of the Apostles, tr. P.J. GLOAG and W.P. DICKSON, New York - London, 1883 (= ⁴1869).

MEYERS, A.C. (ed.), *The Eerdmans Bible Dictionary*, Grand Rapids, MI, 1987 (= EBD).

MEYERS, E.M. → H.C. KEE

MEYNET, R. *L'Évangile selon saint Luc*, 2 vols. 1. *Planches*. 2. *Commentaire*, Paris, 1988.

— *Avez-vous lu saint Luc? Guide pour la rencontre*, Paris, 1990.

— *Passion de notre Seigneur Jésus-Christ* (Lire la Bible, 99), Paris, 1993.

MICHAELIS, W. *Einleitung in das Neue Testament*, Bern, 1946, ³1961.

MICHIELS, R. *Binnen het jaar. Het lijden en de dood van Jesus* (Cahiers voor levensverdieping, 45), Averbode, 1983.

* — Het Passieverhaal volgens Lucas. — *Collationes* 14 (1984) 191-210.

MICHL, J. Evangelien. — *LTK* 3, Freiburg, 1959, 1217-1233.

MILLAR, F. Review of H. HOEHNER, Herod Antipas, 1972. — *JJS* 24 (1973) 93-94.

* — Reflections on the Trial of Jesus. — P.R. DAVIES and R.T. WHITE (eds.), *A Tribute to Geza Vermes. Essays on Jewish and Christian Literature and History* (JSOT SS, 100), Sheffield, 1990, 355-381.

MILLER, D.G. *St. Luke* (The Layman's Bible Commentaries, 18), London, 1959.

* MILLER, D.L. EMΠAIZEIN Playing the Mock Game (Lk 22:63-64). — *JBL* 90 (1971) 309-313.

MILLER, R.J. (ed.), *The Complete Gospels: Annotated Scholar's Version*, Sonoma, CA, 1992.

MILLIGAN, G. The Literary Character of the New Testament Writings -- The Gospels and Acts. — ID., *The New Testament Documents*, 1913, 129-168.
— *The New Testament Documents. Their Origin and Early History*, London, 1913.
MILLS, W.E. *An Index of Reviews of New Testament Books Between 1900-1950* (PerspRelSt SS, 2), Danville, Va, 1977.
—(ed.), *Mercer Dictionary of the Bible*, Macon, GA, 1990.
— *The Gospel of Mark* (BBR, 2), Lewiston, NY - Queenston, Ontario - Lampeter, 1994.
— *The Gospel of Luke* (BBR, 3), Lewiston, NY - Queenston, Ontario - Lampeter, 1994.
MINEAR, P.S. Review of É. TROCMÉ, Jesus as Seen, 1975. — *Religious Studies* 10 (1974) 358-359.
p   MIRECKI, P.A. Gospel of Peter. — *ABD* 5, 278-281.
MITTON, C.L. Vincent Taylor: New Testament Scholar. — V. TAYLOR, *New Testament Essays*, London, 1970, 5-30.
MOFFATT, J. *An Introduction to the Literature of the New Testament*, Edinburgh, 1911, ²1912, ³1918 (repr. 1920, 1927, 1933, 1949).
p   — Gospels (Uncanonical). The Gospel of Peter. — *DAC*, 1915, 496-498.
— Review of B.H. STREETER, The Four Gospels, 1924. — *HJ* 23 (1925) 562-564.
MOHR, T.A. *Markus- und Johannespassion. Redaktions- und traditionsgeschichtliche Untersuchung der Markinischen und Johanneischen Passionstradition* (ATANT, 70), Basel, 1982. Diss. Basel, 1980 (dir. H. BALTENSWEILER).
MOLONEY, F.J. *The Living Voice of the Gospel. The Gospels Today*, New York - Mahwah, NJ, 1986.
*   MONSARRAT, V. Le récit de la Passion: un enseignement pour le disciple fidèle Luc 22-23. — *FoiVie* 81 (1982) 40-47.
MONTEFIORE, C.G. *The Synoptic Gospels*, London, 2 vols., 1909. Vol. 2. *Gospel of Luke*, 844- 1099; New York, ²1927, 1968, Vol. 2, 360-646. Revised and partly rewritten. — *Library of Biblical Studies*, ed. H. ORLINSKY. Vol. 1 states ²1927; 1968.
MONTEFIORE, H. Does 'L' Hold Water? — *JTS* 12 (1961) 59-60.
MOO, D.J. *The Old Testament in the Gospel Passion Narratives*, Sheffield, 1983. Diss. St. Andrews, 1979 (dir. M. BLACK).
*   MORELL BALADRÓN, F. El Relato de la Pasión según San Lucas. De Streeter a Brown: 70 años de investigación de la composición de Lc 22–23. — *EstBib* 54 (1996) 79-114; 225-260.
MORGAN, G.C. *The Gospel according to Luke*, London, 1932; repr. 1976.
MORGAN, R. Which Was the Fourth Gospel? The Order of the Gospels and the Unity of Scripture. — *JSNT* 54 (1994) 3-28.
MORGENTHALER, R. *Die lukanische Geschichtsschreibung als Zeugnis* (ATANT, 14-15), 2 vols., Zürich, 1949. Diss. Ev. Theol. Faculty, Bern, 1945 (dir. D.W. MICHAELIS).
— *Statistik des neutestamentlichen Wortschatzes*, Zürich - Frankfurt, 1958.
— *Statistische Synopse*, Zürich - Stuttgart, 1971.
MORRIS, L. *Luke* (Tyndale NTC, 3), Leicester - Grand Rapids, MI, 1974, ²1986, rev. ed. 1988.
MORTON, A.Q. and G.H.C. MACGREGOR, *The Structure of Luke and Acts*, London, 1964.
MOTYER, J.A. → F. DAVIDSON
MOULE, C.F.D. *An Idiom Book of New Testament Greek*, Cambridge, 1953, ²1959, ʀ1979 (= MIBNTG).
— Review of H. SCHÜRMANN, Der Paschamahlbericht, 1953. — *JTS* 5 (1954) 88-89; ID., Der Einsetzungsbericht, 1955. — *JTS* 7 (1956) 112-113; ID., Jesu Abschiedsrede, 1957. — *JTS* 9 (1958) 360-362.

— *The Birth of the New Testament*, London, 1962; San Francisco, CA, ³1982 (completely new and revised).

— Review of G. SCHNEIDER, Verleugnung, 1969. — *JTS* 22 (1971) 194-197.

— G.M. Styler and the Cambridge New Testament Seminar. — W. HORBURY and B. MCNEIL (eds.), *Suffering*, 1981, xi-xxi.

MOULTON, J.H. Review of P. FEINE, Eine vorkanonische Überlieferung, 1891. — *CritR* 2 (1892) 368- 375.

p   — The 'Gospel of Peter' and the Four. — *ExpT* 4 (1892-93) 299-300.

— *A Grammar of New Testament Greek*. 1. *Prolegomena*, Edinburgh, 1906, ³1978 (= MHT 1).

— The Gospel According to Paul. — *The Expositor*, Eighth Series 2 (1911) 16-28.

— and G. MILLIGAN, *The Vocabulary of the Greek Testament. Illustrated from the Papyri and Other Non-Literary Sources*, London, 1914-29.

— and W.F. HOWARD, *A Grammar of New Testament Greek*. 2. *Accidence and Word-Formation with an Appendix on Semitisms in the New Testament*, Edinburgh, 1919, ²1929 (= MHT 2).

— → N. TURNER (MHT 3 and 4).

MÜLLER, G.H. *Zur Synopse. Untersuchung über die Arbeitsweise des Lk und Mt und ihre Quellen, namentlich die Spruchquelle, im Anschluss an eine Synopse Mk-Lk-Mt*, Göttingen, 1908.

*   MÜLLER, K. Jesus vor Herodes. — G. DAUTZENBERG, H. MERKLEIN and K. MÜLLER (eds.), *Zur Geschichte*, 1979, 111-141.

*   — Möglichkeit und Vollzug jüdischer Kapitalgerichtsbarkeit im Prozess gegen Jesus von Nazaret. — and K. KERTELGE (ed.), *Der Prozess gegen Jesus*, 1988, 41-83.

MÜLLER, P.-G. Conzelmann und die Folgen. — *BK* 4 (1973) 138-142.

— and W. STENGER (eds.). *Kontinuität und Einheit*, FS F. MUSSNER, Freiburg, 1981 (= FS Mussner).

— *Lukas-Evangelium* (SKK, 3), Stuttgart, 1984, ²1986.

MUNCK, J. *The Acts of the Apostles* (AB), Garden City, NY, 1967.

MURAOKA, T. *A Greek-English Lexicon of the Septuagint (Twelve Prophets)*, Louvain, 1993 (= MGEL).

MURPHY-O'CONNOR, J. Review of P. BENOIT and M.-É. BOISMARD, Synopse, 1972. — *RB* 79 (1973) 431-435.

MURRAY, G. Saint Peter's Denials. — *DownR* 103 (1985) 296-298.

p   MURRAY, J.O.F. Evangelium secundem Petrum. — *Expositor* 7 (1893) 50-61.

MUSSNER, F. Review of K. KERTELGE (ed.), Der Prozess gegen Jesus, 1988. — *TRev* 84 (1988) 353- 360.

NARBOROUGH, F.D.V. The Synoptic Problem. — *NCHS*, 1928, 33-42.

NAVONE, J. and T. COOPER, *The Story of the Passion*, Rome, 1986.

NEBE, G. *Prophetische Züge im Bilde Jesu bei Lukas* (BWANT, 127), Stuttgart, 1989.

NEILL, S. and T. WRIGHT, *The Interpretation of the New Testament 1861-1961* [1st ed.: S. NEILL, 1861-1961, London, 1964], Oxford - New York, ²1988.

NEIRYNCK, F. La rédaction matthéenne et la structure du premier évangile. — *ETL* 43 (1967) 41-73; = I. DE LA POTTERIE (ed.), *De Jésus aux évangiles*, 1967, 41-73; = *Evangelica*, 1982, 3-35.

— Hawkins's Additional Notes to His "Horae Synopticae". — *ETL* 46 (1970) 78-111; = *ALBO* 5,2, Leiden, 1970.

862   BIBLIOGRAPHY

— The Gospel of Matthew and Literary Criticism. A Critical Analysis of A. Gaboury's Hypothesis. — M. DIDIER (ed.), *L'évangile selon Matthieu*, 1971, 37-69; = *Evangelica*, 1982, 691-723.
— Duplicate Expressions in the Gospel of Mark. — *ETL* 48 (1972) 150-209; = *Evangelica*, 1982, 83-142.
— The Argument from Order and St. Luke's Transpositions. — *ETL* 49 (1973) 784-815; = *The Minor Agreements* (BETL, 37), 1974, 291-322; = *Evangelica*, 1982, 737-768.
— (ed.), *L'Évangile de Luc. Problèmes littéraires et théologiques* (BETL, 32), 1973; = *L'Évangile de Luc - The Gospel of Luke* (BETL, 32), Revised and enlarged edition, Leuven, ²1989.
— La matière marcienne dans l'évangile de Luc. — ID. (ed.), *L'Évangile de Luc* (BETL, 32), 1973, 157-201; = ²1989, 67-111; = *Evangelica*, 1982, 37-81.
— Minor Agreements Matthew-Luke in the Transfiguration Story. — P. HOFFMANN, N. BROX and W. PESCH (eds.), *Orientierung*, 1973, 253-266; = *Evangelica*, 1982, 797-809.
— Les accords mineurs et la rédaction des évangiles. L'épisode du paralytique. - *ETL* 50 (1974) 215- 230; = *Evangelica*, 1982, 781-796.
— in collaboration with T. HANSEN and F. VAN SEGBROECK, *The Minor Agreements of Matthew and Luke against Mark with a Cumulative List* (BETL, 37), Leuven, 1974.
— Q. — *IDBS*, 1976, 715-716.
— Synoptic Problem. — *Ibid.*, 845-848; = A.J. BELLINZONI (ed.), 1985, 85-93.
— John and the Synoptics. — M. DE JONGE (ed.), *L'évangile de Jean*, 1977, ²1987, 73-106; = *Evangelica*, 1982, 365-398.
— The Symbol Q (= Quelle). — *ETL* 54 (1978) 119-125; = *Evangelica*, 1982, 683-689.
— La fuite du jeune homme en Mc 14,51-52. — *ETL* 55 (1979) 43-66; = *Evangelica*, 1982, 215-238.
— The Miracle Stories in the Acts of the Apostles. — J. KREMER (ed.), *Les Actes des Apôtres*, 1982, 835-879; = 1979, 169-213 (= *Evangelica*)
— L'évangile de Marc (II). À propos de R. Pesch, Das Markusevangelium. 2. T. — *ETL* 55 (1979) 1-42; = *Evangelica*, 1982, 520-561.
— The Redactional Text of Mark. — *ETL* 57 (1981) 144-162; = *Evangelica*, 1982, 618-636.
— *Evangelica. Gospel Studies - Études d'évangile. Collected Essays* (BETL, 60), ed. F. VAN SEGBROECK, Leuven, 1982; [= *Evangelica*].
— The Griesbach Hypothesis: The Phenomenon of Order. — *ETL* 58 (1982) 111-122; = *Evangelica II*, 1991, 281-292.
— and F. VAN SEGBROECK, *New Testament Vocabulary* (BETL, 65), Leuven, 1984 (= NTV).
— Le texte des Actes des Apôtres et les caractéristiques stylistiques lucaniennes, 1985, 304-339; = *Evangelica II*, 1991, 243-278.

—— Luc 24,36-43. Un récit lucanien. — À cause de l'évangile. Mélanges offerts au R.P. Jacques Dupont (LD, 123), Paris, 1985, 655-680;
= Evangelica II, 205-226.

—— Mt 12,25a / Lc 11,17a et la rédaction des évangiles, in ETL 62 (1986) 122-133;
= Evangelica II, 481-492.

—— Paul and Sayings of Jesus. — A. VANHOYE (ed.), L'Apôtre Paul, 1986, 265-321;
= Evangelica II, 1991, 511-568.

* —— ΤΙΣ ΕΣΤΙΝ Ο ΠΑΙΣΑΣ ΣΕ Mt 26,68/Lk 22,64 (diff. Mk 14,65). — ETL 63 (1987) 5-47;
= Evangelica II, 1991, 95-137.

p —— The Apocryphal Gospels and the Gospel of Mark. — J.-M. SEVRIN (ed.), The New Testament, 1989, 123-175;
= Evangelica II, 1991, 715-767.

—— ΚΑΙ ΕΛΕΓΟΝ en Mc 6,14, in ETL 65 (1989) 110-118;
= Evangelica II, 330-338.

—— Mark and His Commentators: Mk 1,1-8,26 [R.A. Guelich, D. Lührmann]. — ETL 65 (1989) 381 -389;
= Evangelica II, 1991, 347-355.

—— and T.A. FRIEDRICHSEN, Note on 9,22. A Response to M.D. Goulder. — ETL 65 (1989) 390-394;
= F. NEIRYNCK (ed.), L'Évangile de Luc - The Gospel of Luke, 1989, 393-398;
= Evangelica II, 1991, 43-48.

—— The Two-Source Hypothesis: Introduction. — D.L. DUNGAN (ed.), The Interrelations of the Gospels: A Symposium Led by M.-É. Boismard, W.R. Farmer, F. Neirynck, Jerusalem, 1984 (BETL, 95), Leuven, 1990, 3-22.

—— The Eschatological Discourse. — D.L. DUNGAN (ed.), Interrelations, 108-124;
= Evangelica II, 493-510.

—— Synoptic Problem. — NJBC, 1990, 587-595.

—— Evangelica II: 1982-1991. Collected Essays (BETL, 99), ed. F. VAN SEGBROECK, Leuven, 1991.

—— Luke 14,1-6: Lukan Composition and Q Saying. — C. BUSSMANN and W. RADL (eds.), Der Treue Gottes trauen, 1991, 243-263;
= Evangelica II, 1991, 183-203 (203-204: Additional note).

—— The Minor Agreements and Proto-Mark. A Response to H. Koester. — ETL 67 (1991) 82-94;
= Evangelica II 1991, 59-73.

—— The Minor Agreements and the Two-Source Theory. — ID., Evangelica II, 1991, 3-41;
= G. STRECKER (ed.), Minor Agreements, 1993, 25-64.

—— The Minor Agreements in a Horizontal-line Synopsis (SNTA, 15), Leuven, 1991.

—— Note on a Test Case. A Response to W.R. Farmer. — ETL 67 (1991) 73-81;
= Evangelica II, 1991, 49-58.

——, J. VERHEYDEN, F. VAN SEGBROECK, G. VAN OYEN and R. CORSTJENS. The Gospel of Mark. A Cumulative Bibliography (BETL, 102) Leuven, 1992.

—— John and the Synoptics: 1975-1990. — A. DENAUX (ed.), John and the Synoptics, 1992, 3-61.

—— Literary Criticism: Old and New. — C. FOCANT (ed.), The Synoptic Gospels, 1992, 11-38.

p —— The Historical Jesus. Reflections on an Inventory. — ETL 70 (1994) 221-234.

*   —   Gospel Issues in the Passion Narratives. Critical Note on a New Commentary. — *ETL*
          70 (1994) 406-416.
      —   The Minor Agreements and Q. — R.A. PIPER (ed.), *Gospel*, 1995, 49-72.
      —   Goulder and the Minor Agreements. — *ETL* 73 (1997) 84-93.
      —   Note on the Argument(s) from Order. — *ETL* 73 (1997) 383-392.
      —   Reviews in *ETL*: 48 (1972) 570-573: G. SCHNEIDER, Verleugnung, 1969; 54 (1978)
          191-193: J. ERNST, Das Evangelium nach Lukas, 1977; G. SCHNEIDER, Das
          Evangelium nach Lukas, 1977; 55 (1979) 405-409: X. LÉON-DUFOUR, Les évangiles
          synoptiques, 1976 (= *Evangelica I*, 1982, 724-728); 56 (1980) 174-176: I.H.
          MARSHALL, The Gospel of Luke, 1978; 58 (1982) 391-396: J.A. FITZMYER, The
          Gospel according to Luke (I-IX), 1981; 59 (1983) 146-147: E. SCHWEIZER, Das
          Evangelium nach Lukas übersetzt und erklärt, 1982; 149: R.A. HARRISVILLE,
          Benjamin Wisner Bacon, Missoula, MT, 1976; 60 (1984) 403-404: P. ROLLAND, Les
          premiers évangiles, 1984; 61 (1985) 393-395: P. DSCHULNIGG, Sprache, Redaktion,
          und Intention des Markus-Evangeliums, 1984; 63 (1987) 408-410: R. GUNDRY,
          Matthew, 1982; 66 (1990) 417: A. DE SANTOS OTERO, Los Evangelios Apócrifos,
          ⁶1988; 67 (1991) 426-429: F. BOVON, L'Évangile selon saint Luc/Das Evangelium
          nach Lukas. I, 1989/1991; 434-436: M.D. GOULDER, Luke: A New Paradigm, 1989;
          69 (1993) 419-421: B. ALAND et al. (eds.), The Greek New Testament. Fourth
          Revised ed., 1993; 428-429: G. STRECKER (ed.), Minor Agreements, 1993; 70 (1994)
          160-162: R.W. FUNK and R.W. HOOVER (eds.), The Five Gospels, 1993; 164-167:
          D. CATCHPOLE, The Quest for Q, 1993; 171-174: H. SCHÜRMANN, Das
          Lukasevangelium, 2/1, 1994; 177-178: C.A. EVANS, Non-canonical Writings and New
          Testament Interpretation, 1992; 458-459: S. LÉGASSE, Le procès de Jésus, 1994; 73
          (1997) 450-452: M.-É. BOISMARD, L'évangile de l'enfance (Luc 1-2), 1997; 452-455:
          En quête du proto-Luc, 1997.
NEUER, W. *Adolf Schlatter. Ein Leben für Theologie und Kirche*, Stuttgart, 1995.
NEUSNER, J. Review of H. HOEHNER, Herod Antipas, 1972. — *Interpr* 27 (1973) 106.
—, E. FRERICHS and C. FLESCHER-MCCRACKEN (eds.), *To See Ourselves as Others See
          Us: Christians, Jews, "Others" in Late Antiquity*, Chico, CA, 1985.
—, E.S. FRERICHS, P. BORGEN and R. HORSLEY (eds.), *The Social World of Formative
          Christianity and Judaism*. FS H.C. KEE, Philadelphia, PA, 1988.
NEVILLE, D.J. *Arguments from Order in Synoptic Source Criticism. A History of Critique*
          (New Gospel Studies, 7), Macon, GA, 1994.
NEWSOM, C.A. and S.H. RINGE (eds.), *The Women's Bible Commentary*, London -
          Louisville, KY, 1992.
*   NEYREY, J. *The Passion according to Luke* (Theological Inquiries), New York, 1985.
*   NICKELSBURG, G.W.E. Passion Narratives. — *ABD* 5, 1992, 172-177.
     NICKLE, K.F. *The Synoptic Gospels: An Introduction*, Atlanta, GA, 1980.
*   NICOLARDOT, F. *Les procédés de rédaction des trois premiers évangélistes*, Paris, 1908.
     NIELSEN, J.T. *Het Evangelie naar Lucas* (PNT, 3), 2 vols., Nijkerk. 1. 1979; 2. 1983.
     NINEHAM, D.E. *St. Mark* (The Pelican Gospel Commentaries), Harmondsworth -
          Baltimore, MD, 1963; New York, 1968; = Philadelphia, PA, ᴿ1978.
     —   (ed.). *Historicity and Chronology in the New Testament* (Theological Collections, 6),
          London, 1965, 97-116.
     —   Review of É. TROCMÉ, Jesus as Seen, 1975. — *JTS* 25 (1974) 160-162.
     —   Review of É. TROCMÉ, Formation, 1975. — *TLond* 79 (1976) 173-174.
     —   Review of É. TROCMÉ, The Passion as Liturgy, 1983. — *TLond* 87 (1984) 226-228.

NOBER, P. Review of H. SCHÜRMANN, Der Paschamahlbericht, 1953. — *Bib* 36 (1955) 532-533.

NOËL, F. *De compositie van het Lucasevangelie in zijn relatie tot Marcus. Het probleem van de "grote weglating"* (VKAB, 150), Brussels, 1994. Leuven, 1992 (F. NEIRYNCK).

NÖSGEN, K.F. *Die Evangelien nach Matthäus, Markus und Lukas*, Munich, ²1897.

NOLLAND, J. *Luke 1-9:20*; Vol. 2. *Luke 9:21-18:34*; Vol. 3. *Luke 18:35-24:53* (WBC, 35 A-B-C), Dallas, TX, 1989, 1990, 1993.

— Review of M.D. GOULDER, Luke: A New Paradigm, 1989. — *ScotJT* 43 (1990) 269-272.

OBACH, R.E. and A. KIRK. *A Commentary on the Gospel of Luke*, New York, 1985.

O'COLLINS, G. and G. MARCONI (eds.), *Luca-Atti: Studi in onore di P. Emilio Rasco nel suo 70o compleanno*, Assisi, 1991;
= *Luke and Acts*, tr. M. O'CONNELL. FS E. RASCO, New York, 1993.

O'COLLINS, G. Luke on the Closing of the Easter Appearances. — *Ibid.*, 1993, 161-166.

OLMSTEAD, A.T. *Jesus in the Light of History*, New York, 1942.

* O'NEILL, J.C. The Silence of Jesus. — *NTS* 15 (1968-69) 153-167.

* — The Charge of Blasphemy at Jesus' Trial before the Sanhedrin. — E. BAMMEL (ed.), *Trial*, 1970, 72-77.

— The Synoptic Problem. — *NTS* 21 (1974-75) 273-285.

OPIE, I. and P. *Children's Games in Street and Playground*, Oxford, 1969.

ORCHARD, J.B. The Solution of the Synoptic Problem. — *Scripture Bulletin* 18 (1987) 2-14.

—, E.F. SUTCLIFFE, R.C. FULLER and R. RUSSELL (eds.), *A Catholic Commentary on Holy Scripture*, London - New York, 1953 (= CCHS).

— The Formation of the Synoptic Gospels. — *DownR* 106 (1988) 1-16.

ORR, J. *Neglected Factors in the Study of the Early Progress of Christianity*, London, 1899.

OSTY, É. *L'Evangile selon saint Luc* (La Sainte Bible traduite en français sous la direction de l'École Biblique de Jérusalem), Paris, 1948, ³1961.

* — Les points de contact entre le récit de la passion dans saint Luc et dans saint Jean. — *Mélanges Jules Lebreton, Vol. 1*. — *RSR* 39 (1951) 146-154.

O'TOOLE, R.F. Parallels Between Jesus and His Disciples in Luke-Acts: A Further Study. - *BZ* 27 (1983) 195-212.

— *The Unity of Luke's Theology. An Analysis of Luke-Acts* (Good News Studies, 9), Wilmington, DE, 1984.

— The Parallels Between Jesus and Moses. — *BTB* 20 (1990) 22-29.

— Review of M.D. GOULDER, Luke: A New Paradigm, 1989. — *CBQ* 53 (1991) 325-326.

— Reflections on Luke's Treatment of the Jews in Luke-Acts. — *Bib* 74 (1993) 529-555.

OVERBECK, F. *Kurze Erklärung der Apostelgeschichte*; = *Kürzgefasstes exegetisches Handbuch zum NT I,4⁴* W.M.L. DE WETTE, Leipzig, 1870.

OVERMAN, J.A. Recent Advances in the Archaeology of the Galilee in the Roman Period. — *Currents in Research: Biblical Studies* 1 (1993) 35-57.

* PAGE, A.F. *Proto-Luke Reconsidered: A Study of the Literary Method and Theology in the Gospel of Luke*. Diss. Duke, Durham, NC, 1968 (dir. D.M. SMITH).

PARKER, P. A Proto-Lukan Basis for the Gospel according to the Hebrews. — *JBL* 59 (1940) 471-478.

— *The Gospel Before Mark*, Chicago, IL, 1953.

* — Trial of Jesus. — *IDB* 4, 1962, 697-698.

— The 'Former Treatise' and the Date of Acts. — *JBL* 84 (1965) 52-58.

— A Second Look at *The Gospel Before Mark*. — *JBL* 100 (1981) 389-413.

— The Posteriority of Mark. — W.R. FARMER (ed.), *New Synoptic Studies*, 1983, 67-142.

* — Herod Antipas and the Death of Jesus. — E.P. SANDERS (ed.), *Jesus*, 1987, 197-208.

PARRY, D.T.N. Release of the Captives - Reflections on Acts 12. — C.M. TUCKETT (ed.), *Luke's*, 1995, 156-164.

PARSONS, M.C. and R.I. PERVO. *Rethinking the Unity of Luke and Acts*, Minneapolis, MN, 1993.

PATTON, C.S. *Sources of the Synoptic Gospels* (Univ. of Michigan Studies Humanistic Series, 5), London, 1915.

* PAULUS, Ch. Einige Bemerkungen zum Prozess Jesu bei den Synoptikern I. — *ZSRG.R* 102 (1985) 437-445.

PEAKE, A.S. and A.J. GRIEVE (eds.), *A Commentary on the Bible*, London, 1920.

— Review of V. TAYLOR, Behind, 1926. — *The Holborn Review* July (1926) 368-370.

PEARSON, B.A. (ed.), *The Future of Early Christianity: Essays in Honor of H. Koester*, Minneapolis, MN, 1991.

PEDERSEN, H. εὑρίσκω. — *EWNT* 2, cols. 206-212 (= *EDNT* 2, 82-84).

PERKINS, P. Review of J.D. CROSSAN, Four Other Gospels, 1985. — *Interpr* 40 (1986) 316.

— *Peter. Apostle for the Whole Church* (SPNT), Columbia, SC, 1994.

— Review of R.E. BROWN, The Death of the Messiah, 1994. — *America* 170 (1994) 19, 21.

p PERLER, O. L'Évangile de Pierre et Méliton de Sardes. — *RB* 71 (1964) 584-590.

* PERRY, A.M. *The Sources of Luke's Passion-Narrative* (Historical and Linguistic Studies in Literature Related to the NT, 2/4,2), Chicago, IL, 1920. Diss. Chicago, 1918 (dir. E.D. BURTON).

— Jesus in Jerusalem. A Note on Chronology. — *JBL* 43 (1924) 15-21.

— "Proto-Luke" and the "Chicago Theory" of the Synoptic Problem. — *JBL* 47 (1928) 91-116.

— A Judaeo-Christian Source in Luke. — *JBL* 49 (1930) 181-194.

* — Some Outstanding New Testament Problems. V. Luke's Disputed Passion Source. — *ExpT* 46 (1934-35) 256-260.

— The Growth of the Gospels. — *IB* 7, Nashville, TN, 1951, 60-74.

PESCH, R. Der Christ als Nachahmer Christi. — *BK* 24 (1969) 10-11.

— *Jesus und der Menschensohn*. FS A. VÖGTLE, Freiburg, 1975 (= FS Vögtle).

— *Das Markusevangelium* (HTKNT, 2,1-2), Freiburg, 1977, ³1980.

* — and R. KRATZ. *So liest man synoptisch*. 7. *Passionsgeschichte*, T. 2, Frankfurt, 1980.

* — *Der Prozess Jesu geht weiter*, Freiburg, 1988;
  = *The Trial of Jesus Continues*, tr. D.G. WAGNER, Allison Park, PA, 1996.

PETERSEN, N. Review of G. SCHNEIDER, Verleugnung, 1969. — *JBL* 89 (1970) 496-497.

PETRIE, C.S. The Proto-Luke Hypothesis. — *ExpT* 54 (1942-43) 172-177.

* — The Proto-Luke Hypothesis: Observations on Dr. Vincent Taylor's Rejoinder. — *ExpT* 55 (1943- 44) 52-53.

PETZKE, G. *Das Sondergut des Evangeliums nach Lukas* (Zürcher Werkkommentare zur Bibel), Zürich, 1990.

PFEIFFER, C.F. and E.F. HARRISON (eds.), *The Wycliffe Bible Commentary*, Chicago, IL, 1962.

PFLEIDERER, O. *Das Urchristentum: seine Schriften und Lehren in geschichtlichem Zusammenhang*, 2 vols. Berlin, 1902;
= *Primitive Christianity. Its Writings and Teachings in their Historical Connections* (Theological Translation Library), 4 vols., New York, 1906-1911.

PIEPIÓRKA, B. Review of G. SCHNEIDER, Verleugnung, 1969. — *ZKT* 93 (1971) 225-226.

PIERSON, B.A. Review of G.N. STANTON, Jesus, 1974. — *Interpr* 30 (1976) 330-331.

p PILHOFER, P. Justin und das Petrusevangelium. — *ZNW* 81 (1990) 60-78.

PIPER, R.A. Social Background and Thematic Structure in Luke 16. — FS NEIRYNCK, Vol. 2, 1992, 1637-1662.

— (ed.), *The Gospel Behind the Gospels. Current Studies on Q* (NTSupp, 75), Leiden - New York - Cologne, 1995.

PIROT, L., A. ROBERT and H. CAZELLES (eds.), *Supplément au Dictionnaire de la Bible*, 10 vols., Paris, 1928-85.

PITTNER, B. *Studien zum lukanischen Sondergut. Sprachliche, theologische und formkritische Untersuchungen zu Sonderguttexten in Lk 5-19* (ErfTSt 18), Leipzig, 1991. Diss. 1987-88 (dir. H. SCHÜRMANN and K.-P. MÄRZ).

* PLEVNIK, J. Son of Man Seated at the Right Hand of God: Luke 22,69 in Lucan Christology. — *Bib* 72 (1991) 331-347.

PLUMMER, A. *A Critical and Exegetical Commentary on the Gospel according to S. Luke*, Edinburgh, 1896, ²1898, ³1900, ⁴1901 (repr. 1905, 1906, 1908), ⁵1922 (repr. 1969).

PÖLZL, F.X. *Kommentar zum Evangelium des heiligen Lukas mit Ausschluss der Leidensgeschichte* (Kurzgefasster Kommentar zu den vier heiligen Evangelien, 2/2), T. INNITZER (ed.), Graz, ²1912.

— *Kurzgefasster Kommentar zur Leidens- und Verklärungsgeschichte Jesu Christi* (Kurzgefasster Kommentar zu den vier heiligen Evangelien, 4), Graz, ²1913.

— *The Passion and Glory of Christ. A Commentary on the Events from the Last Supper to the Ascension*, tr. A.M. BUCHANAN, rev. and ed. C.C. MARTINDALE, New York, 1919.

PONTIFICAL BIBLICAL COMMISSION, *De auctore, de tempore compositionis et de historica veritate Evangeliorum sec. Marcum et sec. Lucam, die 26 Junii 1912*;
= *On the Author, Time of Composition and Historical Truths of the Gospels According to St.*
Mark, and St. Luke, 242-245) and *De quaestione synoptica sive de mutuis relationibus inter tria priora Evangelia, eodem die 26 Junni 1912*; (= *On the Synoptic Question or the Mutual Relations Between the First Three Gospels*, 245-246). — J.J. MEGIVERN (ed.). *Bible Interpretation*, 1978.

PORTER, L.E. The Gospel of Luke. — F.F. BRUCE, H.L. ELLISON and G.C.D. HOWLEY (eds.), *A Bible Commentary for Today Based on the RSV*, London, 1979; *The International Bible Commentary*, Basingstoke - Grand Rapids, MI, 1986 (Rev. ed. with the NIV; ed. F.F. BRUCE), 1182-1228.

POWELL, M.A. *What Are They Saying about Luke?*, New York - Mahwah, NJ, 1989.

— The Religious Leaders in Luke: A Literary-Critical Study. — *JBL* 109 (1990) 93-110.

POWLEY, B.G. Review of M.L. SOARDS, The Passion According to Luke, 1987. — *ExpT* 99 (1987- 88) 215.

* PRENDERGAST, T. Trial of Jesus. — *ABD* 6, 1992, 660-663.

* PRETE, B. *La passione e la morte di Gesu nel racconto di Luca* (Studii biblici, 112/115), 2 Vols., Brescia, 1996/97.

PREUSCHEN, E. *Die Apostelgeschichte* (HNT, 4/1), Tübingen, 1912.

PRICE, J.L. The Gospel According to Luke. — *Interpr* 7 (1953) 195-212.
— *Interpreting the New Testament*, New York, 1961, ²1971.
PRICE, S.G. The Authorship of Luke-Acts. — *ExpT* 55 (1943-44) 194.
PRIDIK, K.-H. καί. — *EWNT* 2, cols. 557-560; = *EDNT* 2, 227-228.
— τέ. — *EWNT* 3, col. 812-815; = *EDNT* 3, 339-340.

QUASTEN, J. *Patrology*. 1. *The Beginnings of Patristic Literature*, Utrecht, 1950.
QUESNELL, Q. Review of É. TROCMÉ, La Formation, 1963. — *Bib* 46 (1965) 237-238.

RACKHAM, R.B. *Acts of the Apostles* (Westminster), London, 1901, ²1904, ³1906.
RADL, W. *Paulus und Jesus im lukanischen Doppelwerk* (EHS, 23/49), Bern - Frankfurt, 1975. Diss. Ruhr, Bochum, 1974 (dir. G. SCHNEIDER).
— σιωπάω — *EWNT* 3, 1982-83, col. 591 = *EDNT* 3, 1993, 247.
— *Das Lukas-Evangelium* (EdF, 261), Darmstadt, 1988.
* — *Sonderüberlieferungen bei Lukas? Traditionsgeschichtliche Fragen zu Lk 22,67f; 23,2 und 23,6- 12.* — K. KERTELGE (ed.), *Der Prozess*, 1988, 131-147.
— → C. BUSSMANN
— Review of J. ERNST, Das Evangelium nach Lukas, 1993. — *TRev* 93 (1997) col. 214.
RAEYMAEKERS, C. *Het Evangelie van Lucas*, Turnhout, 1939, ²1949.
RAGG, L. *St Luke with Introduction and Notes* (Westminster Commentaries), London, 1922.
RAHLFS, A. (ed.). *Septuaginta. Id est Vetus Testamentum graece iuxta LXX interpretes*, Stuttgart, 1935.
RAHNER, K. → J. HÖFER
RAMSEY, A.M. The Narratives of the Passion. — F.L. CROSS (ed.), *StEv* 2/1, TU 87 (1964) 122-134; = *Contemporary Studies in Theology* 1, London, 1962.
* RAU, G. Das Volk in der Passionsgeschichte des Lukas. Eine Konjektur zu Lk 23,13. — *ZNW* 56 (1965) 41-51.
REDLICH, E.B. *The Student's Introduction to the Synoptic Gospels*, London, 1936.
— *Form Criticism. Its Value and Limitations*, London, 1939, ᴿ1948.
REHKOPF, F. *Die lukanische Sonderquelle. Ihr Umfang und Sprachgebrauch* (WUNT, 5), Tübingen, 1959. Diss. Göttingen, 1956 (dir. J. JEREMIAS).
— *Septuaginta-Vocabular*, Göttingen, 1989.
REICKE, B. *Lukasevangeliet*, Stockholm, 1962;
= *The Gospel of Luke*, tr. R. MACKENZIE, Richmond, VA, 1963.
— *The Roots of the Synoptic Gospels*, Philadelphia, PA, 1986.
— The History of the Synoptic Discussion. — D.L. DUNGAN (ed.), *Interrelations*, 1990, 291-316.
REID, B.E. *The Transfiguration: A Source- and Redaction-Critical Study of Luke 9:28-38* (CahRB, 32), Paris, 1993. Diss. Catholic U., Washington, D.C., 1988 (dir. J.P. MEIER).
p REID, G.J. Apocrypha. — C.G. HERBERMANN (ed.), *The Catholic Encyclopedia*, 1907, Vol. 1, 601- 615.
REILLY, W.S. Saint Luke. — *CBQ* 1 (1939) 314-324.
* REINBOLD, W. *Der älteste Bericht über den Tod Jesu. Literarische Analyse und historische Kritik der Passionsdarstellungen der Evangelien* (BZNW, 69), Berlin - New York, 1994. Diss. Göttingen, 1992/93 (dir. H. STEGEMANN).
RENGSTORF, K.H. *Das Evangelium nach Lukas* (NTD, 3), Göttingen, 1937, ⁸1958, ¹⁰1965, ¹¹1966, ¹⁴1969, ¹⁵1974.

RESCH, A. *Agrapha. Ausserkanonische Evangelienfragmente* (TU 5/4), Leipzig, 1889, ²1906.

— *Ausserkanonische Paralleltexte zu den Evangelien*, Leipzig, 1893-97; *II. Matthaeus und Markus* (TU 10/2), Leipzig, 1894, 34-48.

* RESE, M. *Die "Stunde" Jesu in Jerusalem (Lukas 22,1-53). Eine Untersuchung zur literarischen und theologischen Eigenart des lukanischen Passionsberichts*, unpublished theol. Habil. Münster, 1971.

— Das Lukas-Evangelium. Ein Forschungsbericht. — *ANRW* II.25.3 (1984) 2258-2328.

— Review of M.L. SOARDS, The Passion according to Luke, 1987. — *TLZ* 115 (1990) 196-198.

— Review of G. PETZKE, Das Sondergut, 1990. — *TLZ* 116 (1991) 669- 671.

— "Intertextualität" - Ein Beispiel für Sinn und Unsinn "neuer" Methode. — C.M. TUCKETT (ed.), *Scriptures*, 1997, 431-439.

REUMANN, J. *Jesus in the Church's Gospels: Modern Scholarship and the Earliest Sources*, Philadelphia, PA, 1968.

REUSS, E. *Geschichte der Heiligen Schriften Neuen Testaments*, Halle, 1842; Braunschweig, ²1853, ³1860, ⁴1864, ⁵1874, ⁶1887.

REUSS, R. *La Bible. 1. Histoire évangélique. Synopse des trois premiers évangiles*, Paris, 1876.

RICHARD, E. (ed.), *New Views on Luke and Acts*, Collegeville, MN, 1990.

— Jesus' Passion and Death in Acts. — D.D. SYLVA (ed.), *Reimaging*, 1990, 125-152, 204-210.

RICHARDSON, A. *The Gospels in the Making*, London, 1938.

RICHARDSON, P. Review of D.R. CATCHPOLE, The Trial of Jesus, 1971. — *JBL* 91 (1972) 264-266.

— and GRANSKOU, D. (eds.), *Anti-Judaism in Early Christianity. 1. Paul and the Gospels* (Studies in Christianity and Judaism, 2), Waterloo, Ontario, 1986.

— Gospel Traditions in the Church in Corinth (with Apologies to B.H. Streeter). — G.F. HAWTHORNE and O. BETZ (eds.), *Tradition*, 1987, 301-318.

— *Herod. King of the Jews and Friend of the Romans*, Columbia, SC, 1996.

RIDDLE, D.W. Review of B.W. BACON, Story, 1927. — *JR* 7 (1927) 469-472.

— The Aramaic Gospels and the Synoptic Problem. — *JBL* 54 (1935) 121-138.

— *The Gospels, Their Origin and Growth*, Chicago, IL, 1939.

RIEDL, J. Die evangelische Leidensgeschichte und ihre theologische Aussage. — *BLtg* 41 (1968) 70- 111.

RIENECKER, F. *Das Evangelium des Lukas* (Wuppertaler Studienbibel, 4), Wuppertal, 1959, ²1966, ⁶1976.

RIESNER, R. *Jesus als Lehrer. Eine Untersuchung zum Ursprung der Evangelien-Überlieferung* (WUNT, II/7), Tübingen, 1981. Diss. Tübingen, 1980 (dir. O. BETZ).

— Prägung und Herkunft der lukanischen Sonderüberlieferung. — *TBei* 24 (1993) 228-248.

RIEU, E.V. *The Four Gospels. A New Translation from the Greek* (Penguin Classics), London, 1952.

RIEZLER, R. *Das Evangelium unseres Herrn Jesus Christus nach Lukas*, Brixen, 1900.

RIGAUX, B. *Témoignage de l'évangile de Luc*, Paris, 1970.

RIGGS, J.S. Introduction. — B. WEISS, *A Commentary on the New Testament. 1. Matthew - Mark*, tr.

G. SCHODDE and E. WILSON, New York, 1906.

RINGE, S.H. *Luke* (WeBC), Louisville, KY, 1995.

ROBBINS, V.K. Review of É. TROCMÉ, Formation, 1975. — *ATR* 60 (1978) 100-102.

ROBERT, A. and A. TRICOT (eds.), *Initiation biblique*, Tournai, 1939; Paris - Tournai - Rome - New York, ²1948, ³1954 ("refondue"); Tournai, 1957-59;
   = *Guide to the Bible*, Vol. 1, tr. E.P. ARBEZ and M.R.P. MCGUIRE, Westminister, MD, 1951-55; Paris - New York, ²1960 ("revised and enlarged" = ³1954).

ROBERTSON, A.T. Review of J. MOFFATT, Introduction, 1911. — *RExp* 9 (1912) 259-260.

—— *A Grammar of the Greek New Testament in the Light of Historical Research*, London - NY, 1914; ⁴1923; ⁵1931, NY.

—— *Luke the Historian in Light of Research*, Edinburgh - New York, 1920; Grand Rapids, MI, ᴿ1977.

—— Review of V. TAYLOR, Behind, 1926. — *RExp* 23 (1926) 496.

—— Review of B.S. EASTON, The Gospel according to St. Luke, 1926. — *RExp* 24 (1927) 85-86.

—— Review of H.J. CADBURY, The Making of Luke-Acts, 1927. — *RExp* 25 (1928) 105-106.

—— Review of R.H. CROMPTON, Synoptic Problem, 1928. — *RExp* 26 (1929) 228.

—— and W.H. DAVIS. *A New Short Grammar of the Greek New Testament*, New York, 1931; Grand Rapids, MI, ¹⁰1977 (= RD).

p   ROBINSON, J.A. The Gospel according to Peter. A Lecture on the Newly Recovered Fragment. — ID. and M.R. JAMES (eds.), *The Gospel According to Peter and the Revelation of Peter*, London, ²1892.

p   —— Gospel of Peter. — A. MENZIES (ed.), *Ante-Nicene Christian Library* 9, Edinburgh, 1897;
   = Grand Rapids, MI, repr. of fifth edition, *Original Supplement to the American Edition*, Vol. 10, 1980, 7-8.

p   —— Introduction. — *Excluded Books of the New Testament*, tr. J.B. LIGHTFOOT, M.R. JAMES and H.B. SWETE, et. al., London - New York, 1927, vii-xxiii.

ROBINSON, J.A.T. The Most Primitive Christology of All. — *JTS* 7 (1956) 177-189;
   = *Twelve New Testament Studies* (SBT, 34), London, 1962, 139-153.

—— *Redating the New Testament*, London - Philadelphia, PA, 1976;
   = *Wenn entstand das Neue Testament?*, Wuppertal, 1986.;
   = *Re-dater le Nouveau Testament* (Bible et Vie Chrétienne: Référence), tr. Marie de Mérode, Paris, 1987.

ROBINSON, W.C. *Der Weg des Herrn*, Hamburg, 1964.

RODD, C.S. Review of É. TROCMÉ, Formation, 1975. — *ExpT* 87 (1975-76) 248.

p   RODRÍGUEZ RUIZ, M. El Evangelio de Pedro. ¿Un Desafío a los Evangelios Canónicos? — *EstBib* 46 (1988) 497-526.

ROGERSON, J. → H.C. KEE

ROHRBACH, P. *Der Schluss des Markusevangeliums, der vier evangelien Kanon und die kleinasiastischen Presbyter*, Berlin, 1894.

ROLLAND, P. *Les premiers évangiles. Un nouveau regard sur le problème synoptique* (LD, 116), Paris, 1984.

ROLOFF, J. *Das Kerygma und der irdische Jesus. Historische Motive in den Jesus-Erzählungen der Evangelien*, Göttingen, 1970.

RONEN, Y. [= RONNING, H.] Mark 7,1-23 - "Traditions of the Elders". — *Immanuel* 12 (1981) 44-54.

RONNING, H. [= RONEN, Y.] Why I am a Member of the Jerusalem School. — *Mishkan* 17-18 (1992-93) 82-86.

ROPES, J.H. An Observation on the Style of St. Luke. — *Harvard Studies in Classical Philology* 12 (1901) 299-305.
— Review of M. JONES, New Testament, 1914. — *HTR* 8 (1915) 415- 417.
— *The Apostolic Age in the Light of Modern Criticism*, New York, 1921.
— *The Synoptic Gospels*, Cambridge, MA, 1934.
ROSE, V. *Études sur les Évangiles*, Paris, 1902;
   = *Studies on the Gospels*, tr. R. FRASER, London - New York - Bombay, 1903.
— *Évangile selon S. Luc*, Paris, 1904.
ROSENBLATT, M.-E. *Paul the Accused. His Portrait in the Acts of the Apostles*, Collegeville, MN, 1995.
ROUILLER, G. *Évangile selon St. Luc*, Freibourg (Swisse), 1980;
   = *Il vangelo secondo Luca. Testi e teologia.* Tr. by U. CAVALIERI (Bibbia per tutti), Assisi, 1983.
ROWLINGSON, D.T. *Introduction to New Testament Study*, New York, 1956.
— Synoptic Problem. — *IDB* 4, 1962, 491-495.
* RUCKSTUHL, E. *Die Chronologie des Letzten Mahles und des Leidens Jesu* (Biblische Beiträge, 4), Einsiedeln, 1963;
   = *Chronology of the Last Days of Jesus. A Critical Study*, tr. V.J. DRAPELA, New York, 1965.
* — Chronologie der Leidensgeschichte. — *SNTU* 10 (1985) 27-61; 11 (1986) 97-129;
   = *Jesus*, 1988, 101-139; 141-184.
— *Jesus im Horizont der Evangelien* (SBA 3), Stuttgart, 1988.
RUDBERG, G. Die Verhöhnung Jesu vor dem Hohenpriester. — *ZNW* 24 (1925) 307-309.
RUHLAND, M. *Die Markuspassion aus der Sicht der Verleugnung*, Eilsbrunn, 1987.
RUSSELL, H.G. Which Was Written First, Luke or Acts? — *HTR* 48 (1955) 167-174.
p RUTHERFORD, A. *Introduction to the Gospel of Peter* and *Synoptical Table.* — A. MENZIES (ed.), *Ante-Nicene Christian Library*, Grand Rapids, MI, repr. of fifth ed., *Original Supplement to The American Edition*, Vol. 10, 1980, 3-5, 10-31.
RYAN, M.R. (ed.). *Contemporary New Testament Studies*, Collegeville, MN, 1965.

SABBE, M. La rédaction du récit de la Transfiguration. — *RechBib* 6 (1962) 65-100;
   = *Studia Neotestamentica*, 1991, 65-104.
— *Studia Neotestamentica. Collected Essays* (BETL, 98), Leuven, 1991.
* — The Trial of Jesus Before Pilate in John and Its Relation to the Synoptic Gospels. — ID., *Studia Neotestamentica*, 467-513;
   = A. DENAUX (ed.), *John and the Synoptics*, 1992, 341-385.
SABOURIN, L. The Synoptic Problem: Old and New Approaches. — *BTB* 3 (1973) 306-315.
— *The Gospel according to St Luke*, Bombay, 1985;
   = *L'évangile de Luc. Introduction et commentaire*, Rome, 1985.
SAHLIN, H. *Der Messias und das Gottesvolk. Studien zur protolukanischen Theologie*, Uppsala, 1945.
SALDARINI, A.J. Jewish Responses to Greco-Roman Culture. — H.C. KEE, et al., *The Cambridge Companion*, 1997, 288-240. → H.C. KEE
SALMON, G. *The Human Element in the Gospels. A Commentary on the Synoptic Narratives*, ed. N.J.D. WHITE, London, 1907.
SALO, K. *Luke's Treatment of the Law. A Redaction-Critical Investigation* (AASF DHL, 57), Helsinki, 1991. Diss. Helsinki, 1991 (dir. L. AEJMELAEUS).
SAMAIN, E. La notion de ΑΡΧΗ dans l'œuvre lucanienne.— in F. NEIRYNCK (ed.), *L'Évangile de Luc*, 1973, 299-328 (= ²1989, 209-238).

SANDAY, W. *Inspiration. Eight Lectures on the Early History and Origin of the Doctrine of Biblical Inspiration* (Bampton Lectures, 1893), London - New York, 1893, 1901.

— A Plea for the Logia. — *ExpT* 11 (1899-1900) 471-473.

— Jesus Christ. — *DBDL*, 1901, 603-653.

— Professor Burkitt on the Gospel History. — *ExpT* 18 (1906-07) 249-255.

— *The Life of Christ in Recent Research*, Oxford, 1907.

— The Bearing of Criticism upon the Gospel History. — *ExpT* 20 (1908-09) 103-114.

— (ed.), *Studies in the Synoptic Problem by Members of the University of Oxford*, Oxford, 1911 (= SSP).

— Introductory. — *Ibid.*, vii-xxvii.

SANDERS, E.P. The Argument from Order and the Relationship between Matthew and Luke. — *NTS* 15 (1968-69) 249-261.

— Review of P. BENOIT and M.-É. BOISMARD, Synopse, 1972. — *JBL* 94 (1975) 128-132.

— (ed.), *Jesus, the Gospels, and the Church: Essays in Honor of William R. Farmer*, Macon, GA, 1987.

SANDERS, J.T. *The Jews in Luke-Acts*, London - Philadelphia, PA, 1987.

— The Jewish People in Luke-Acts. — J.B. TYSON (ed.), *Luke-Acts*, 1988, 51-75.

SANDMEL, S. *A Jewish Understanding of the New Testament*, Cincinnati, OH, 1957; New York, 1974.

*   — Herod (Family). — *IDB* 2, 1962, 585-594.

*   — Herodians. — *Ibid.*, 594-595.

*   — *Herod*, Philadelphia, PA, 1967.

— Review of H. HOEHNER, Herod Antipas, 1972. — *CBQ* 35 (1973) 91-92.

— *Anti-Semitism in the New Testament*, Philadelphia, PA, 1978.

SAWYER, R.D. Was Peter the Companion of Cleopas on Easter Afternoon? — *ExpT* 61 (1949-50) 91- 93.

SCHABERG, J. Luke. — C.A. NEWSOM and S.H. RINGE (eds.), *Women's Bible Commentary*, 1992, 275-292.

SCHÄFER, J. *Das heilige Evangelium nach Lukas übersetzt und erklärt*, Steyl, 1923.

SCHÄFER, K.Th. *Grundriss der Einleitung in das Neue Testament*, Bonn, 1938, ²1952.

p   SCHAEFFER, S.E. *The "Gospel of Peter", the Canonical Gospels and Oral Tradition*. Diss. Union Theol. Sem., New York, 1991 (dir. R.E. BROWN).

p   — The Guard at the Tomb (Gos. Pet. 8:28-11:49 and Matt 27:62-66; 28:2-4,11-16): A Case of Intertextuality? — *SBL 1991 Seminar Papers*, 499-507.

SCHALIT, A. Kritische Randbemerkungen zu Paul Winters "On the Trial of Jesus". — H. KOSMALA, et. al. (eds.), *ASTI* 2 (1963), 86-102.

SCHANZ, P. *Commentar über das Evangelium des heiligen Lucas*, Tübingen, 1883, ²1926 (with Addenda, 623-625); ³1927 (corrected).

*   SCHELKLE, K.H. *Die Passion in der Verkündigung des Neuen Testaments*, Heidelberg, 1949.

— Review of H. SCHÜRMANN, Der Paschamahlbericht, 1953. — *TQ* 133 (1953) 253; Der Einsetzungsbericht, 1955. — *TQ* 135 (1955) 345.

— *Das Neue Testament. Seine literarische und theologische Geschichte*, Kevelaer, 1963, ³1966.

*   SCHENK, W. Leidensgeschichte Jesu. — *TRE* 20, 1990, 714-721.

SCHENKE, L. Review of G. SCHNEIDER, Verleugnung, 1969. — *TTZ* 80 (1971) 381-382.

SCHICK, E. *Formgeschichte und Synoptikerexegese* (NTAbh, 18/2,3), Münster, 1940.

SCHIELE, F.M. and L. ZSCHARNACK (eds.), *Die Religion in Geschichte und Gegenwart. Handwörterbuch für Theologie und Religionswissenschaft*, 5 vols., Tübingen, 1909-1913; ²1927-1932 (ed. H. GUNKEL); ³1957-65 (ed. K. GALLING) (= RGG)

* SCHILLE, G. Das Leiden des Herrn. — *ZTK* 52 (1955) 161-205.

SCHLATTER, A. *Einleitung in die Bibel*, Stuttgart, 1889; ²1894; ³1901; ⁴1923; ⁵1933.

— *Erläuterungen zum Neuen Testament*, Stuttgart, 1908, ⁴1928.

— *Die Theologie des Neuen Testaments und die Dogmatic*, Gütersloh, 1909-10.

— *Theologie des Neuen Testaments*, 2 Bd., Stuttgart, 1909-10.

— *Das Evangelium des Lukas aus seinen Quellen erklärt*, Stuttgart, 1931; ᴿ1960, ᴿ1975.

— *Die Evangelien nach Markus und Lukas* (Erläuterungen zum Neuen Testament, 2), Stuttgart, 1910, ²1916, 1947, ²1961, 1987, 156-409; ³1975.

SCHLEIERMACHER, F. *Über die Schriften des Lukas. Ein kritischer Versuch*, Berlin, 1817;
= *Sämmtliche Werke*, Vol. 1, 2, Berlin, 1836, 1ff.;
= *A Critical Essay on the Gospel of St. Luke*, tr. C. THRILWALL, London, 1825;
= *With Essays, Emendations and Other Apparatus* by T.N. TICE, Macon, GA, 1993.

SCHMID, J. *Matthäus und Lukas. Eine Untersuchung des Verhältnisses ihrer Evangelien* (BSt, 23/2-4), Freiburg, 1930.

— *Das Evangelium nach Lukas* (RNT, 3), Regensburg, 1940, ²1951, ⁴1960.

— Review of H. SCHÜRMANN, Der Einsetzungsbericht, 1955. — *MüTZ* 7 (1956) 159-160.

SCHMIDT, D. Luke's 'Innocent' Jesus: A Scriptural Apologetic. — R.J. CASSIDY and P.J. SHARPER (eds.), *Political*, 1983, 111-121.

p SCHMIDT, D.H. *The Peter Writings: Their Redactors and Their Relationships*. Diss. Northwestern, Evanston, IL, 1972 (dir. A. SUNDBERG).

SCHMIDT, K.L. *Der Rahmen der Geschichte Jesu*, Berlin - Darmstadt, 1919, ²1964, ᴿ1969.

p — *Kanonische und apokryphe Evangelien und Apostelgeschichten* (ATANT, 5), Basel, 1944, 37-78.

SCHMIDT, T.E. Mark 15.16-32: The Crucifixion Narrative and the Roman Triumphal Procession. — *NTS* 41 (1995) 1-18.

SCHMITHALS, W. *Das Evangelium nach Lukas* (ZBKNT 3,1), Zürich, 1980.

— *Einleitung in die drei ersten Evangelien*, Berlin, 1985.

SCHNACKENBURG, R. *Das Johannesevangelium* (HTKNT, 4/1), Freiburg, 1965.

— Lk 13,31-33. Eine Studie zur lukanischen Redaktion und Theologie. — C. BUSSMANN and W. RADL (eds.), *Der Treue Gottes*, 1991, 229-241.

— *Die Person Jesu Christi im Spiegel der vier Evangelien* (HTKNT Suppl 4), Freiburg - Basel - Vienna, 1993.

p SCHNEEMELCHER, W. (ed.), *Neutestamentliche Apokryphen in deutscher Übersetzung*, Bd. 1. *Evangelien*, Tübingen, ³1959 ("vollig neubearbeitete Auflage");
= *New Testament Apocrypha*. 1. *Gospels and Related Writings*, Rev. ed., tr. W. McL. WILSON from the German ⁶1990, Cambridge - Louisville, KY, 1991.

* SCHNEIDER, G. *Verleugnung, Verspottung und Verhör Jesu nach Lukas 22,54-71. Studien zur lukanischen Darstellung der Passion* (SANT, 22), Munich, 1969. Habil., Würzburg, 1967/68 (R. SCHNACKENBURG).

* — Gab es eine vorsynoptische Szene "Jesus vor dem Synedrium"? — *NT* 12 (1970) 22-39;
= *Jesusüberlieferung* (revised), 1992, 258-275.

* — Jesus vor dem Synedrium. — *BibLeb* 11 (1970) 1-15;
= *Lukas, Theologe*, 1985, 158-172.

* — Das Problem einer vorkanonischen Passionserzahlung. — *BZ* 16 (1972) 222-244;
= *Jesusüberlieferung*, 1992, 213-235.

— Die Verhaftung Jesu. Traditionsgeschichte von Mk 14,43-52. — *ZNW* 63 (1972) 188-
    209;
    = *Jesusüberlieferung*, 1992, 236-257.
* — *Die Passion Jesu nach den drei älteren Evangelien*, Munich, 1973.
— "Der Menschensohn" in der lukanischen Christologie. — FS VÖGTLE, 1975, 267-282;
    = *Lukas, Theologe*, 1985, 98-113.
— *Das Evangelium nach Lukas* (ÖTNT, 3/1-2), Gütersloh, 1977, ²1984.
— (ed.) *EWNT*, 3 vols., 1978-1983; = *EDNT*, 3 vols. 1990-1993 → H. BALZ.
— *Die Apostelgeschichte* (HTKNT, 5/1-2), Freiburg, 1980-82.
— ἐσθής. — *EWNT* 2, col. 146; = *EDNT* 2, 58.
— πράσσω. — *EWNT* 3, cols. 349-351; = *EDNT* 3, 145-146.
* — The Political Charge against Jesus (Luke 23:2). — E. BAMMEL and C.F.D. MOULE
    (eds.), *Jesus*, 1984, 403-414;
    = Die politische Anklage gegen Jesus (23,2). — *Lukas, Theologe*, 1985, 173-183.
— *Lukas, Theologe der Heilsgeschichte: Aufsätze zum lukanischen Doppelwerk* (BBB, 59),
    Bonn, 1985.
* — Das Verfahren gegen Jesus in der Sicht des dritten Evangeliums (Lk 22,54-23,25).
    Redaktionskritik und historisch Rückfrage. — K. KERTELGE (ed.), *Der Prozess*, 1988,
    111-130;
    = *Jesusüberlieferung*, 1992 (revised), 276-295 (see also *Literatur - Nachträge*, 375-
    378).
— Neuere Literatur zum dritten Evangelium (1987-1989). — *TRev* 86 (1990) 353-360.
— *Jesusüberlieferung und Christologie. Neutestamentliche Aufsätze 1970-1990* (NTSuppl,
    67), Leiden, 1992.
— Literatur zum lukanischen Doppelwerk. Neuerscheinungen 1990/91. — *TRev* 88 (1992)
    1-18.
— Reviews in *BZ*: 16 (1972) 272-274: D.R. CATCHPOLE, The Trial of Jesus, 1971; 17
    (1973) 114-115: T. SCHRAMM, Der Markus-Stoff bei Lukas, 1971; 18 (1974) 110-111:
    É. TROCMÉ, Jésus de Nazareth, 1971; 19 (1975) 119-121: F. NEIRYNCK, L'évangile
    de Luc, 1973; 24 (1980) 285-287: I.H. MARSHALL, The Gospel of Luke, 1978; 24
    (1980) 289-290: A. BÜCHELE, Der Tod Jesu, 1978.
— Reviews in *TRev*: 69 (1973) 285-286: V. TAYLOR, Passion Narrative, 1972; 76 (1980)
    375-376: A. GEORGE, Études, 1978; 77 (1981) 20-22: J. JEREMIAS, Die Sprache,
    1980.
SCHNIEWIND, J.D. *Die Parallelperikopen bei Lukas und Johannes*, Leipzig, 1914;
    Hildesheim, ᴿ1958; Darmstadt, ᴿ1970.
— *Evangelion. Ursprung und erste Gestalt des Begriffs Evangelium*, Gütersloh, 1931;
    Darmstadt, ᴿ1970.
SCHRAMM, T. *Der Markus-Stoff bei Lukas. Eine literarische und redaktionsgeschichtliche
    Untersuchung* (SNTS MS, 14), Cambridge, 1971. Diss. Hamburg, 1966 (dir. C.-H.
    HUNZINGER).
SCHRECK, C.J. *The Nazareth Pericope: Luke 4,16-30 in Recent Study*. — NEIRYNCK, F.
    (ed.), *L'évangile de Luc - The Gospel of Luke*, ²1989, 399-471.
— *Luke 4,16-30: The Nazareth Pericope in Modern Exegesis: A History of Interpretation*.
    Diss. Leuven, 1990 (dir. F. NEIRYNCK).
SCHREIBER, J. *Die Markuspassion. Wege zur Erforschung der Leidensgeschichte Jesu*,
    Hamburg, 1969.
— Das Schweigen Jesu. — K. WEGENAST (ed.), *Theologie*, 1969, 79-87.

SCHREINER, J. and G. DAUTZENBERG (eds.), *Gestalt und Anspruch des Neuen Testament*, Würzburg, 1969.

SCHREINER, T.R. Luke. — W.A. ELWELL (ed.), *Evangelical Commentary*, 1978, 799-839.

SCHUBERT, J.M. *The Image of Jesus as Prophet Like Moses in Luke-Acts as Advanced by Luke's Reinterpretation of Deuteronomy 18:15,18 in Acts 3:22 and 7:37.* Diss. Fordham, 1992 (dir. C.H. GIBLIN).

SCHUBERT, K. Kritik der Bibelkritik. Dargestellt an Hand des Markusberichtes vom Verhör Jesu vor dem Synedrium. — *Wort und Wahrheit* 27 (1972) 421-434.

* — Biblical Criticism Criticised: With Reference to the Markan Report of Jesus's Examination before the Sanhedrin [Mk 14:55-64; 15:2-5; Lk 22:66-71]. — E. BAMMEL and C.F.D. MOULE (eds.), *Jesus*, tr. W. HORBURY, 1984, 385-402.

SCHÜRER, E. *Lehrbuch der neutestamentlichen Zeitgeschichte*, Leipzig, 1874;
= *Geschichte des jüdischen Volkes im Zeitalter Jesus Christi*, Leipzig, ^{2}1886, ^{3,4}1901-09;
= *A History of the Jewish People in the Time of Jesus Christ*, Vol. 1, Second Division, tr. S. TAYLOR and P. CHRISTIE, New York, 1891;
A revised English version, *The History of the Jewish People in the Age of Jesus Christ (175 B.C.- A.D. 135)*, Vol. 2, G. VERMES, F. MILLAR and M. BLACK (eds.), Edinburgh, 1979; E. SCHÜRER with G. VERMES, New English Version Revised, Edinburgh, 1986.

SCHÜRMANN, H. Die Dubletten im Lukasevangelium. Ein Beitrag zur Verdeutlichung des lukanischen Redaktionsverfahrens. — *ZKT* 75 (1953) 338-345;
= TrU, 272-278.

* — *Der Paschamahlbericht Lk 22,(7-14) 15-18. I. Teil. Einer quellenkritischen Untersuchung des lukanischen Abendmahlsberichtes Lk 22,7-38* (NTAbh, 19,5), Münster, 1953, ^{2}1968, ^{3}1980; *Der Einsetzungsbericht Lk 22,19-20. II. Teil. Einer quellenkritischen Untersuchung des lukanischen Abendmahlsberichtes Lk 22,7-38* (NTAbh, 20,4), Münster, 1955, ^{2}1970, ^{3}1986; *Jesu Abschiedsrede Lk 22,21-38. III. Teil. Einer quellenkritischen Untersuchung des lukanischen Abendmahlsberichtes Lk 22,7-38* (NTAbh, 20,5), Münster, 1957, ^{2}1977. Diss. Münster, 1950 (dir. M. MEINERTZ).

— Die Dublettenvermeidungen im Lukasevangelium. — *ZKT* 76 (1954) 83-93;
= TrU, 279-289.

* — Protolukanische Spracheigentümlichkeiten? Zu Fr. Rehkopf, Die lukanische Sonderquelle. Ihr Umfang und Sprachgebrauch. — *BZ* 5 (1961) 266-286;
= TrU, 209-227.

— *Traditionsgeschichtliche Untersuchungen zu den synoptischen Evangelien*, Düsseldorf, 1968 (= TrU).

— *Das Lukasevangelium.* T. 1. *Kap. 1,1-9,50* (HTKNT, 3), Freiburg, 1969, ^{2}1982; Vol. 2/1, Freiburg - Basel - Vienna, 1994.

* SCHÜTZ, F. *Der leidende Christus: Die angefochtene Gemeinde und das Christuskerygma der lukanischen Schriften* (BWANT, 89), Stuttgart, 1969.

SCHÜTZ, H. *Entstehung und Bedeutung des urchristlichen Gemeindegebets.* Diss. Heidelberg, 1925.

SCHWEITZER, A. *Von Reimarus zu Wrede. Eine Geschichte der Leben-Jesu-Forschung*, Tübingen, 1906;
= *The Quest for the Historical Jesus. A Critical Study of Its Progress from Reimarus to Wrede*, tr. W. MONTGOMERY, London, 1910.

SCHWEIZER, E. Eine hebraisierende Sonderquelle des Lukas. — *TZ* 6 (1950) 161-185.

— Review of H. SCHÜRMANN, Der Paschamahlbericht, 1953. — *TLZ* 80 (1955) 156-157; ID., Der Einsetzungsbericht, 1955. — *TLZ* 81 (1956) 217-219; ID., Jesu Abschiedsrede, 1957. — *TLZ* 83 (1958) 190.

— *Das Evangelium nach Markus übersetzt und erklärt* (NTD, 1), Göttingen, [11(1)]1967; [12(2)]1967; [13(3)]1969; [14(4)]1973; [15(5)]1979; [17(7)]1989;
= *The Good News According to Mark*, tr. D.H. MADVIG, Atlanta, GA - London, 1970.

— *Das Evangelium nach Lukas übersetzt und erklärt* (NTD, 3), Göttingen, 1982;
= *The Good News According to Luke*, tr. D.E. GREEN, Atlanta, GA, 1984.

— Zur Frage der Quellenbenutzung durch Lukas. I. Sprachliche und sachliche Beobachtungen. II. Analyse lukanischer Perikopen. — ID. (ed.), *Neues Testament und Christologie im Werden. Aufsätze*, Göttingen, 1982, 33-85.

SCOBIE, C.H.H. Apocryphal New Testament. — *DBDL*, 1963, [2]1965, 41-45.

— *John the Baptist*, Philadelphia, PA, 1964.

SCOTT, E.F. and B.S. EASTON (eds.), *An Outline of Christianity. TheStory of Our Civilization*, New York, 1926.

— Review of B.S. EASTON, The Gospel according to St. Luke, 1926. — *JR* 6 (1926) 425-427.

— Review of H.J. CADBURY, The Making of Luke-Acts, 1927. — *JR* 8 (1928) 285-287.

— *The Literature of the New Testament*, New York, 1932.

— Review of F.C. GRANT, Growth, 1933. — *JR* 13 (1933) 326-327.

SELAND, T. *Establishment Violence in Philo and Luke. A Study of Non-Conformity to the Torah and Jewish Vigilante Reactions* (BIS, 15), Leiden - New York - Cologne, 1995.

SELWYN, E.G. Editorial, The Earliest Gospel? — *TLond* 14 (1927) 121-123.

SEMERIA, G.B. La question synoptique. — *RB* 1 (1892) 520-559.

p   — L'évangile de Pierre. — *RB* 3 (1894) 522-560.

SENIOR, D. *The Passion Narrative according to Matthew. A Redactional Study* (BETL, 39), Leuven, 1975, [2]1982. Diss. Leuven, 1972 (dir. F. NEIRYNCK).

— *The Passion of Jesus in the Gospel of Mark*, Wilmington, DE, 1984.

— *The Passion of Jesus in the Gospel of Matthew*, Wilmington, DE, 1985.

*   — *The Passion of Jesus in the Gospel of Luke*, Wilmington, DE, 1989.

— *The Passion of Jesus in the Gospel of John*, Collegeville, MN - Herefordshire, 1991.

— Review of J.B. GREEN, The Death of Jesus, 1988. — *CBQ* 53 (1991) 327-329.

— Review of R.E. BROWN, The Death of the Messiah, 1994. — *CBQ* 57 (1995) 797-800.

— Review of W. REINBOLD, Der älteste Bericht, 1994. — *JBL* 115 (1996) 138-141.

SENSE, P.C. *A Critical and Historical Enquiry into the Origin of the Third Gospel*, London - Oxford, 1901.

p   SETZER, C.J. *Jewish Responses to Early Christians. History and Polemics, 30-150 C.E.*, Minneapolis, MN, 1994. Diss. Columbia U., 1990 (dir. R.E. BROWN).

SEVRIN, J.-M. (ed.), *The New Testament in Early Christianity* (BETL, 86), Leuven, 1989.

SHEELEY, S.M., Narrative Asides and Narrative Authority in Luke-Acts. — *BTB* 18 (1988) 102-107.

— Review of M.L. SOARDS, The Passion According to Luke, 1987. — *RExp* 85 (1988) 352-353.

— The Narrator in the Gospels: Developing a Model. — *PerspRelSt* 16 (1989) 213-223.

— *Narrative Asides in Luke-Acts*, Sheffield, 1992. Diss. Southern Baptist Theological Seminary, Louisville, KY, 1987 (dir. R.A. CULPEPPER).

SHELLARD, B. The Relationship of Luke and John: A Fresh Look at an Old Problem. — *JTS* 46 (1995) 71-98.

*   SHERWIN-WHITE, A.N. *Roman Society and Roman Law in the New Testament*, Oxford, 1963.
*   — The Trial of Christ. — D.E. NINEHAM (ed.), *Historicity and Chronology*, 1965, 97-116.
        SIBINGA, J.S. The Making of Luke 23:26-56. An Analysis of the Composition Technique in Luke's Crucifixion Narrative. — *RB* 104 (1997) 378-404.
        SIEGMANN, E.F. Review of H. SCHÜRMANN, Jesu Abschiedsrede, 1957. — *CBQ* 20 (1958) 576-577.
        SIEVERS, E. *Textaufbau der griechishen Evangelien* (Klanglich untersucht. 41, Bd. d. Abh. d. Sächs. Akad. d. Wiss.), Leipzig, 1931.
        SIMONS, E. *Hat der dritte Evangelist den kanonischen Matthäus benutzt?*, Bonn, 1880.
        SLOYAN, G.S. The Gospel According to Luke. — *Worship* 33 (1959) 633-641;
        = M.R. RYAN (ed.), *Contemporary*, 1965, 185-191.
*   — *Jesus on Trial. The Development of the Passion Narratives and Their Historical and Ecumenical Implications*, Philadelphia, PA, 1973.
        — *The Crucifixion of Jesus. History, Myth, Faith*, Minneapolis, MN, 1995.
        SMALLWOOD, E.M. *The Jews Under Roman Rule*, Leiden, 1976.
        SMITH, B.D.T. Review of V. TAYLOR, Formation, 1933. — *JTS* 34 (1933) 275-278.
        — Review of F.C. GRANT, Growth, 1933. — *JTS* 34 (1933) 278-280.
        SMITH, D.M. The Problem of John and the Synoptics in Light of the Relation Between Apocryphal and Canonical Gospels. — A. DENAUX (ed.), *John and the Synoptics*, 1992, 147-162.
        — *John Among the Gospels. The Relationship in Twentieth-Century Research*, Minneapolis, MN, 1992.
        SMITH, R. Fresh Light on the Synoptic Problem. Matthew a Lucan Source. — *HJ* 10 (1911-12) 615- 625.
        SMITH, R.F. Inspiration and Inerrancy. — R.E. BROWN et al. (eds.), *JBC*, 1968, 499-514.
        SMYTH, H.W., *Greek Grammar*, Cambridge, 1920.
        SNAPE, H.C. The Composition of the Lukan Writings: a Re-Assessment. — *HTR* 53 (1960) 27-46.
*   SOARDS, M.L. The Silence of Jesus Before Herod: An Interpretative Suggestion. — *AusBR* 33 (1985) 41-45.
*   — Tradition, Composition, and Theology in Luke's Account of Jesus before Herod Antipas. — *Bib* 66 (1985) 344-364.
*   — Herod Antipas' Hearing in Lk 23:8. — *BTrans* 37 (1986) 146-147.
*   — A Literary Analysis of the Origin and Purpose of Luke's Account of the Mockery of Jesus. — *BZ* 31 (1987) 110-116;
        = E. RICHARD (ed.), *New Views*, 1990, 86-93.
*   — *The Passion According to Luke. The Special Material of Luke 22* (JSNT SS, 14), Sheffield, 1987. Diss. Union Theol. Sem., New York, 1984 (dir. R.E. BROWN).
ⵜ   — Tradition, Composition and Theology in Jesus' Speech to the "Daughters of Jerusalem" (Luke 23,26-32). — *Bib* 68 (1987) 221-244.
*p   — Oral Tradition Before, In, and Outside the Canonical Passion Narratives. — H. WANSBROUGH (ed.), *Jesus*, 1991, 334-350.
        — The Speeches in Acts in Relation to Other Pertinent Ancient Literature. — *ETL* 70 (1994) 65-90.
        SOLTAU, W. *Eine Lücke der Synoptischenforschung*, Leipzig, 1899.
        — Die Entstehung des ersten Evangeliums. — *ZNW* 1 (1900) 219-248.
        — *Unsere Evangelien. Ihre Quellen und ihr Quellenwert*, Leipzig, 1901.

— Die Anordnung der Logia in Lukas 15-18. — *ZNW* 10 (1909) 230-238.

SOROF, M. *Die Entstehung der Apostelgeschichte*, Berlin, 1890.

SOUBIGOU, L. *Sous le charme de l'Évangile selon saint Luc*, Paris, 1933.

SPARKS, H.F.D. The Partiality of Luke for 'Three'. — *JTS* 37 (1936) 141-145.

— The Semitisms of St. Luke's Gospel. — *JTS* 44 (1943) 129-138;
    = S. JELLICOE (ed.), *Studies*, 1974, 497-506.

— The Semitisms of Acts. — *JTS* 1 (1950) 16-28.

— *The Formation of the New Testament*, London, 1952.

— St. Luke's Transpositions. — *NTS* 3 (1956-57) 219-223.

— Luke (Gospel) and Acts. — *DBDL*, ²1965, 596-601.

— Review of P. BENOIT and M.-É. BOISMARD, Synopse, 1972. — *JTS* 75 (1974) 485-
    486.

SPENCER, F.S. Review of M.D. GOULDER, Luke: A New Paradigm, 1989. — *WestTJ* 53
    (1991) 363- 365.

SPICQ, C. *Notes de lexicographie néo-testamentaire* (OBO 22/1-3), Fribourg, 1978, 1982
    (= NLNT) (= *Lexique théologique du Nouveau Testament*, Paris, 1991, 3 vols. in 1
    vol.);
    = *Theological Lexicon of the New Testament*, 3 vols., tr. and ed. J.D. ERNEST,
    Peabody, MA, 1994 (= TLNT).

SPITTA, F. *Die Apostelgeschichte, ihre Quellen und deren geschichtlicher Wert*, Halle,
    1891.

— *Streitfragen der Geschichte Jesus*, Göttingen, 1907.

— *Die synoptische Grundschrift in ihrer Überlieferung durch das Lukasevangelium*,
    Leipzig, 1912.

STAAB, K. *Das Evangelium nach Markus und Lukas* (Echter Bibel), Würzburg, 1956.

STÄHLIN, G., *Die Apostelgeschichte* (NTD, 5), Göttingen, 1936, 1962.

STAGG, F. *Studies in Luke's Gospel*, Nashville, TN, 1967.

STANTON, G.N. Review of T. SCHRAMM, Der Markus-Stoff bei Lukas, 1971. — *TLond* 76
    (1973) 36- 37.

— *Jesus of Nazareth in New Testament Preaching* (SNTS MS, 27), Cambridge, 1974.

— (ed.), *The Interpretation of Matthew* (Issues in Religion and Theology, 3), London -
    Philadelphia, PA, 1983, 42-55; ²1995, 53-67.

— Aspects of Early Christian-Jewish Polemic and Apologetic. — *NTS* 31 (1985) 377-392.

— *The Gospels and Jesus*, Oxford, 1989.

STANTON, V.H. The 'Gospel of Peter': Its Early History and Character Considered in
    Relation to the History of the Recognition in the Church of the Canonical Gospels. —
    JTS 2 (1900-01) 1-25.

— *The Gospels as Historical Documents. 2. The Synoptic Gospels*, Cambridge, 1909.

STATHER HUNT, B.P.W. *Primitive Gospel Sources*, New York, 1951.

STAUDINGER, J. Testis "primarius" Evangelii sec. Lucam. — *VD* 33 (1955) 65-77;129-142.

— *Die Bergpredigt*, Vienna, 1957.

STEGNER, W.R. Lucan Priority in the Feeding of the Five Thousand. — *BR* 21 (1976) 19-
    28.

— The Priority of Luke: An Exposition of Robert Lindsey's Solution to the Synoptic
    Problem. — *BR* 27 (1982) 26-38.

— Review of B. REID, The Transfiguration, 1993. — *JBL* 114 (1995) 526-527.

STEIN, R.H. Is the Transfiguration (Mark 9:2-8) a Misplaced Resurrection-Account? — *JBL*
    95 (1976) 79-96.

— *The Method and Message of Jesus' Teachings*, Philadelphia, PA, 1978.

— *The Synoptic Problem. An Introduction*, Grand Rapids, MI, 1987.

— *Difficult Passages in the New Testament: Interpreting Puzzling Texts in the Gospels and Epistles*, Grand Rapids, MI, 1990;
= *Difficult Passages in the Gospels*, Grand Rapids, MI, 1984; *Difficult Sayings in the Gospels: Jesus' Use of Overstatement and Hyperbole*, Grand Rapids, MI, 1985.

— *Gospels and Tradition. Studies on Redaction Criticism of the Synoptic Gospels*, Grand Rapids, MI, 1991.

— The Matthew-Luke Agreements Against Mark: Insight from John. — *CBQ* 54 (1992) 482-502.

— *Luke* (NAC, 24), Nashville, TN, 1992.

STEINMUELLER, J.E. and K. SULLIVAN (eds.), *Catholic Biblical Encyclopedia. New Testament*, New York, 1950.

* STEINWENTER, A. Il processo di Gesù. — *Jus* 3 (1952) 471-490.

STENGER, W. βιάζομαι — *EWNT* 1, cols. 518-521; = *EDNT* 1, 216-217.

STEPHENSON, T. Fresh Light on the Synoptic Problem. — *JTS* 33 (1923) 250-255.

p STILLMAN, M.K. The Gospel of Peter. A Case for Oral-Only Dependency? — *ETL* 73 (1997) 114-120.

— Footprints of Oral Transmission in the Canonical Passion Narratives. — *ETL* 73 (1997) 393-400.

* STÖGER, A. Eigenart und Botschaft der lukanischen Passionsgeschichte. — *BK* 24 (1969) 4-8.

— *Das Evangelium nach Lukas* (Geistliche Schriftlesung 3/2), Düsseldorf, 1964/1966;
= *The Gospel according to St. Luke* (NT for Spiritual Reading), 2 vols., New York, 1969.

STONEHOUSE, N.B. *The Witness of Luke to Christ*, London - Grand Rapids, MI, 1951.

— Review of H. CONZELMANN, The Theology of St. Luke, 1960. — *WTJ* 24 (1961) 65-70.

— *Origins of the Synoptic Gospels. Some Basic Questions*, Grand Rapids, MI, 1963; London, 1964.

STRACK, H.L. and P. BILLERBECK, *Das Evangelium nach Markus, Lukas und Johannes und die Apostelgeschichte erläutert aus Talmud und Midrasch* (Kommentar zum Neuen Testament aus Talmud und Midrasch, 2), Munich, 1924, ⁴1965.

STRAUSS, M.L. *The Davidic Messiah in Luke-Acts. The Promise and its Fulfillment in Lukan Christology* (JSNT SS, 110), Sheffield, 1995.

STRECKER, G. (ed.), *Minor Agreements: Symposium Göttingen 1991* (GTA, 50), Göttingen, 1993.

* STREETER, B.H. On the Trial of Our Lord before Herod: A Suggestion. — W. SANDAY (ed.), SSP, 1911, 229-231.

— The Synoptic Problem. — A.S. PEAKE and A.J GRIEVE (eds.), *Commentary*, 1920, 672-680.

— Fresh Light on the Synoptic Problem. — *HJ* 20 (1921-22) 103-112.

— *The Four Gospels*, London, 1924, 1930 (4th imprint rev.), ᴿ1964.

— Sources of the Gospels. — E.F. SCOTT and B.S. EASTON (eds.), *An Outline*, 1926, 349-359.

— *The Primitive Church Studied with Special Reference to the Origins of the Christian Ministry*, London - New York, 1929.

— Die Ur-Lukas Hypothese. — *TSK* 102 (1930) 332-340.

— Modern Criticism and the Synoptic Gospels. — *Modern Churchman* 24 (1934) 435-451.

STROBEL, A. Review of H. VAN DER KWAAK, Het Proces van Jezus, 1969. — *TLZ* 95 (1970) 665- 667.
— *Die Stunde der Wahrheit* (WUNT, 21), Tübingen, 1980.
p STÜLCKEN, A. Petrusevangelium. — E. HENNECKE (ed.), *Neutestamentliche Apokryphen*, 1904, 27-32.
STUHLMACHER, P. Warum musste Jesus sterben? — *TBei* 16 (1985) 273-285.
— (ed.), *Das Evangelium und die Evangelien* (WUNT, 2/28), Tübingen, 1983, 27-84; = *The Gospel and the Gospels*, tr. J. VRIEND, Grand Rapids, MI, 1991.
STUHLMUELLER, C. The Gospel according to Luke. — *JBC*, 1968, 115-164.
STYLER, G.M. The Priority of Mark. Excursus 4. — C.F.D. MOULE, *Birth*, 1962, 223-232; ³1982, 285-316;
= A.J. BELLINZONI (ed.), 1985, 63-75 (= 1962).
— Synoptic Problem. — *OCB*, 1993, 724-727.
SUMMERS, R. *Commentary on Luke*, Waco, TX, 1972.
SURKAU, H.W. *Martyrien in jüdischer und frühchristlicher Zeit*, Göttingen, 1938.
SWAIN, L. Review of É. TROCMÉ, Formation, 1975. — *Month* 237 (1976) 248-249.
SWEETLAND, D.M. Review of R.H. GUNDRY, Matthew, 1982. — *CBQ* 46 (1984) 160-162.
p SWETE, H.B. Εὐαγγέλιον κατὰ Πέτρον: *The Akhmîm Fragment of the Apocryphal Gospel of Peter*, London, 1891, ²1893.
p — *The Apocryphal Gospel of Peter. The Greek Text of the Newly-Discovered Fragment. With Some Corrections from the MS*, London, 1892 (without the corrections), ²1893.
— (ed.), *Cambridge Theological Essays*, London, 1905.
— (ed.), *Essays on Some Biblical Questions of the Day by Members of the University of Cambridge*, London, 1909.
SYDNOR, W. *Jesus according to Luke*, New York, 1982.
* SYLVA, D.D. (ed.), *Reimaging the Death of the Lukan Jesus* (BBB, 73), Frankfurt a.M., 1990.

TALBERT, C.H. *Luke and the Gnostics*, Nashville, TN, 1966.
— The Lukan Presentation of Jesus' Ministry in Galilee. — *RExp* 64 (1967) 485-497.
— The Redaction Critical Quest for Luke the Theologian. — *Perspective* 11 (1970) 171- 222;
= D.G. MILLER (ed.), *Jesus*, 1970, 171-222.
— An Anti-Gnostic Tendency in Lucan Christology, in *NTS* 14 (1968) 259-271; = Die antidoketische Frontstellung der lukanischen Christologie. — G. BRAUMANN (ed.), *Das Lukas-Evangelium*, 1974, 354-377.
— and E.V. MCKNIGHT, Can the Griesbach Hypothesis Be Falsified? — *JBL* 91 (1972) 338-368.
— *Literary Patterns, Theological Themes, and the Genre of Luke-Acts* (SBL MS, 20), Missoula, MT, 1974.
— Shifting Sands: The Recent Study of the Gospel of Luke. — *Interpr* 30 (1976) 381 - 395;
= J. MAYS (ed.), *Interpreting*, 1981, 231-246.
— (ed.), *Perspectives on Luke-Acts* (PerspRelSt SS, 5), Danville, VA - Edinburgh, 1978.
— *Reading Luke. A Literary and Theological Commentary on the Third Gospel*, New York, 1982.
— Martyrdom in Luke-Acts and the Lukan Social Ethic. — R.J. CASSIDY (ed.), *Political*, 1983, 99- 110.

— (ed.), *Luke-Acts. New Perspectives from the Society of Biblical Literature Seminar*, New York, 1984.

— Promise and Fulfillment in Lucan Theology. — ID. (ed.), *Luke-Acts*, 1984, 91-103.

— Luke-Acts. — E.J. EPP and G.W. MACRAE (eds.), *New Testament*, 1989, 297-320.

— Gospel of Luke. — W.E. MILLS (ed.), *Mercer Dictionary of the Bible*, Macon, GA, 1990, 529-531.

TANNEHILL, R.C. *The Narrative Unity of Luke-Acts. A Literary Interpretation*. 1. *The Gospel according to Luke*, Philadelphia, PA, 1986; 2. *The Acts of the Apostles*, Minneapolis, MN, 1990.

— The Lukan Discourse on Invitations (Luke 14,7-24). — *TFG 1992* = *FS Neirynck*, 1603-1616.

— *Luke* (ANTC), Nashville, TN, 1996.

TANNER, E.S. Review of H. SCHÜRMANN, Der Paschamahlbericht, 1953. — *JBL* 73 (1954) 177-178.

p   TASKER, J.G. Apocryphal Gospels. — *DBE*, 1904, 420-438.

TAYLOR, J. Review of B.E. REID, The Transfiguration. — *RB* 101 (1994) 623-624.

TAYLOR, V. Proto-Luke. — *ExpT* 33 (1921-22) 250-252.

— The Value of the Proto-Luke Hypothesis. — *ExpT* 36 (1924-25) 476-477.

— *Behind the Third Gospel. A Study of the Proto-Luke Hypothesis*, Oxford, 1926.

— The Four Document Hypothesis. — *London Quarterly Review* 146 (1926) 48-62.

— The First Draft of Luke's Gospel. — *TLond* 14 (1927) 131-164;
= *The First Draft of Luke's Gospel*, London, 1927.

— The Proto-Luke Hypothesis. A Reply to Dr. W.K. Lowther Clarke's Queries. — *TLond* 14 (1927) 72-76.

— Is the Proto-Luke Hypothesis Sound? — *JTS* 29 (1928-29) 147-155.

— The Synoptic Gospels and Some Recent British Criticism. — *JR* 8 (1928) 225-246.

— *The Gospels. A Short Introduction*, London, 1930, ²1933, ³1935, ⁴1938 (enlarged), ⁵1945, ⁶1948, ⁷1952, ⁸1956, ⁹1960.

— *The Formation of the Gospel Tradition*, New York, 1933, ²1935, ᴿ1968, 44-62: *The Passion-Narratives*; 191-201: *The Proto-Luke Hypothesis and Some Recent Criticism*.

— Professor J.M. Creed and the Proto-Luke Hypothesis. — *ExpT* 46 (1934-35) 236-238.

— After Fifty Years. I. The Gospel and the Gospels. — *ExpT* 50 (1938-39) 8-12.

— The Proto-Luke Hypothesis. A Rejoinder. — *ExpT* 54 (1942-43) 219-222.

— The Passion Sayings. — *ExpT* 54 (1942-43) 249-250.

— The Life and Ministry of Jesus. — G.A. BUTTRICK et al. (eds.), *IB* 7, 1951, 114-144. Cf. *The Life and Ministry of Jesus*, London, 1954, a revision and enlargement of the 1951 article.

— *The Gospel According to St. Mark*, London, 1952, ²1966; Grand Rapids, MI, ᴿ1981 does not contain section L, "Recent Markan Studies", 667-671.

— *The Names of Jesus*, London, 1953, ᴿ1962.

— Important Hypotheses Reconsidered. 1. The Proto-Luke Hypothesis. — *ExpT* 67 (1955-56) 12-16.

— *Jesus and His Sacrifice. A Study of the Passion-Sayings in the Gospels*, London, 1955.

*   — Sources of the Lukan Passion Narrative [P. Winter]. — *ExpT* 68 (1956-57) 95.

— Milestones in Books. — *ExpT* 70 (1955-59) 231-233;
= ID., *New Testament Essays*, 1970, 31-35.

— Modern Issues in Biblical Studies. Methods of Gospel Criticism. — *ExpT* 71 (1959-60) 68-72.

— Theologians of Our Time. Heinz Schürmann. — *ExpT* 74 (1962-63) 77-81.

*   — Theologians of Our Time. Friedrich Rehkopf. — *ExpT* 74 (1962-63) 262-266.
*   — Rehkopf's List of Words and Phrases Illustrative of Pre-Lukan Speech Usage. — *JTS* 15 (1964) 59-62.
      — Gospel of Luke. — *IDB* 3, 1962, 180-188.
      — New Testament Essays, London, 1970.
*   — The Passion Narrative of St Luke. A Critical and Historical Investigation (SNTS MS, 19), ed. O.E. EVANS, Cambridge, 1972.
TELFORD, W.R. Review of J.D. CROSSAN, Four Other Gospels, 1985. — *TLond* 89 (1986) 402-404.
TEMPORINI, A. and W. HAASE (eds.), *Aufstieg und Niedergang der römischen Welt. Geschichte und Kultur Roms im Spiegel der neueren Forschung. II. Prinzipat.* Vol. 25/1-5: Religion (vorkonstantinisches Christentum: Leben und Umwelt Jesu: Neues Testament [Kanonische Schriften und Apokryphen]), Berlin - New York, 1982 (25/1); 1984 (25/2); 1985 (25/3); 1987 (25/4); 1988 (25/5-6) (= ANRW).
TENNEY, M.C. *The New Testament. An Historical and Analytical Survey*, Grand Rapids, MI, 1953; *New Testament Survey*, Grand Rapids, MI, ²1961, ᴿ1985 (rev. by W.C. DUNNET).
      — The Gospel according to Luke. — C.F. PFEIFFER and E.F. HARRISON (eds.), *Wycliffe*, 1962, 1027- 1070.
THOMPSON, G.H.P. *The Gospel According to Luke* (The New Clarendon Bible), Oxford, 1972.
TIEDE, D.L. *Prophecy and History in Luke-Acts*, Philadelphia, PA, 1980.
      — 'Glory to thy People Israel': Luke-Acts and the Jews. — J. NEUSNER et al. (eds.), *Social World*, 1988, 327-341.
      — Luke (Augsburg Commentary on the NT), Minneapolis, MN, 1988.
*   — Contending with God: The Death of Jesus and the Trial of Israel in Luke-Acts. — B.A. PEARSON (ed.), *Future*, 1991, 301-308.
      — "Fighting Against God": Luke's Interpretation of Jewish Rejection of the Messiah Jesus. — C.A. EVANS and D.A. HAGNER (eds.), *Anti-Semitism*, 1993, 102-112.
TINSLEY, E.J. *The Gospel according to Luke* (The Cambridge Bible Commentary. NEB), Cambridge, 1965.
TITIUS, A. *Das Verhältnis der Herrenworte im Marcusevangelium zu den Logia des Matthäus*, Göttingen, 1897.
TÖDT, H.E. *Der Menschensohn in der synoptischen Überlieferung*, 1959, Gütersloh, ²1963; = *The Son of Man in the Synoptic Tradition*, tr. D.M. BARTON, Philadelphia, PA, 1965.
TOLBERT, M. Leading Ideas of the Gospel of Luke. — *RExp* 64 (1967) 441-451; = *Die Hauptinteressen des Evangelisten Lukas*, tr. H. STEGEMANN. — G. BRAUMANN (ed.), *Das Lukas-Evangelium*, 1974, 337-353.
TORREY, C.C. The Translations Made from the Original Aramaic Gospels. — D.G. LYON and G.F. MOORE (eds.), *Studies*, 1912, 270-317.
      — The Composition and Date of Acts (HTS, 1), Cambridge, MA, 1916.
      — Facts and Fancy in Theories Concerning Acts. — *AJT* 23 (1919) 61-86; 189-212.
      — The Four Gospels. A New Translation, London - New York, 1933 (= ²1947; same pagination with a new introduction, v-xv).
      — Our Translated Gospels. Some of the Evidence, London, n.d. [1936].
p   TREAT, J.C. The Two Manuscript Witnesses to the Gospel of Peter. — *SBL 1990 Seminar Papers*, 391-399.

TRICOT, A. La question synoptique. — A. ROBERT and A. TRICOT (eds.), *Initiation biblique*, Paris - Tournai - Rome - New York, 1939, ²1948, 319-334; ³1954 ("refondue"), 356-374;
= The Synoptic Question. — A. ROBERT and A. TRICOT (eds.), *Guide to the Bible*, Westminster, MD, 1951; London, ²1960, tr. E.P. ARBEZ and M.R.P. MCGUIRE, Vol. 1, 563-583 (= ³1954).

TROADEC, H. *Évangile selon saint Luc*, Tours, 1968.

TROCMÉ, É. *Le "Livre des Actes" et l'histoire*, Paris, 1957.

— *La Formation de l'Évangile selon Marc* (Études d'histoire et de philosophie religieuses, 57), Paris, 1963;
= *The Formation of the Gospel according to Mark*, tr. P. GAUGHAN, Philadelphia, PA, 1975.

— *Jésus de Nazareth vu par les témoins de sa vie*, Neuchâtel (Switzerland), 1971;
= *Jesus as Seen by His Contemporaries*, tr. R.A. WILSON, London - Philadelphia, PA, 1973.

— Review of G.N. STANTON, Jesus, 1974. — *TLond* 78 (1975) 555-557.

* — *The Passion as Liturgy. A Study in the Origin of the Passion Narratives in the Four Gospels*, London, 1983 (esp. 27-37: The Passion Narrative in Luke).

— The Jews as Seen by Paul and Luke. — J. NEUSNER et al. (eds.), *To See Ourselves*, 1985, 145-162.

TRUMMER, P. ἄξιος. — *EWNT* 1, cols. 271-272; = *EDNT* 1, 113.

— ἱκανός. — *EWNT* 2, cols. 452-453; = *EDNT* 2, 184-185.

TUCKETT, C.M. On the Relationship Between Matthew and Luke. — *NTS* 30 (1984) 130-142.

— (ed.), *Synoptic Studies. The Ampleforth Conferences of 1982 and 1983* (JSNT SS, 7), Sheffield, 1984.

— Arguments from Order. Definition and Evaluation. — *Ibid.*, 197-219.

— *Reading the New Testament. Methods of Interpretation*, London, 1987.

— Synoptic Problem. — *ABD* 6, 1992, 263-270.

— The Minor Agreements and Textual Criticism. — G. STRECKER (ed.), *Minor Agreements*, 1993, 119-142.

— (ed.), *Luke's Literary Achievement. Collected Essays* (JSNTS, 116), Sheffield, 1995.

— The Lukan Son of Man. — ID., *Luke's*, 1995, 198-217.

— *Q and the History of Early Christianity*, Edinburgh, 1996.

— (ed.), *The Scriptures in the Gospels* (BETL, 131), Leuven, 1997.

p TURNER, C.H. The Gospel of Peter. — *JTS* 14 (1913-14) 161-195.

TURNER, H.E.W. The Chronological Framework of the Ministry. — D.E. NINEHAM (ed.), Historicity, 1965, 59-74.

* TYSON, J.B. The Lukan Version of the Trial of Jesus. — *NT* 3 (1959) 249-258.

* — Jesus and Herod Antipas. — *JBL* 79 (1960) 239-246.

— *A Study of Early Christianity*, New York - London, 1973;
cf. *The New Testament and Early Christianity*, New York - London, 1984 ("expanded and reorganized").

— Source Criticism of the Gospel of Luke. — C.H. TALBERT (ed.), *Perspectives*, 1978, 24-39.

— The Jewish Public in Luke-Acts. — *NTS* 30 (1984) 574-585.

— The Two-Source Hypothesis. A Critical Appraisal. — A.J. BELLINZONI (ed.), 1985, 437-452.

* — *The Death of Jesus in Luke-Acts*, Columbia, SC, 1986.

— (ed.), *Luke-Acts and the Jewish People*, Minneapolis, MN, 1988.
— *Images of Judaism in Luke-Acts*, Columbia, SC, 1992.

ÜBELACKER, W. Das Verhältnis von Lk/Apg zum Markusevangelium. — P. LUOMANEN (ed.), *Luke- Acts*, 1991, 157-194.

* UNTERGASSMAIR, F.G. *Kreuzweg und Kreuzigung Jesu. Ein Beitrag zur lukanischen Redaktionsgeschichte und zur Frage nach der lukanischen "Kreuztheologie"* (PTS, 10), Paderborn, 1980. Diss. Paderborn, 1977 (dir. J. ERNST).

* — Thesen Sinndeutung des Todes Jesu in der lukanischen Passionsgeschichte. — *TGl* 70 (1980) 180- 193.

* — Der Spruch vom "grünen und dürren Holz" (Lk 23,31). — *SNTU* 16 (1991) 55-87.

* — Zur Problematik der lukanischen Passionsgeschichte. Jesus vor Herodes (23,6-12). — FS Ernst, 1996, 273-292. → K. BACKHAUS

VACANT, A. and E. MANGENOT (eds.), *Dictionnaire de theologie catholique*, 15 vols. plus Index in 28 vols., Paris, 1899-1972 (= DTC).

p VAGANAY, L. *L'Évangile de Pierre* (EB), Paris, 1930.
— Review of A. SCHLATTER, Das Evangelium des Lukas, 1931. — *RevSR* 12 (1932) 605-607.

p — Apocryphes du Nouveau Testament. — G. JACQUEMET (ed.), *Catholicisme*, 1948, Vol. 1, cols. 699-704.
— *Le problème synoptique. Une hypothèse de travail*, Tournai, 1954.

VALENSIN, A and J. HUBY. *Évangile selon saint Luc* (VS, 3), Paris, ¹⁻¹¹1927; ²¹1929; ⁴¹1952.

VAN ANDEL, J. *Het evangelie naar de beschrijving van Lukas aan de gemeente toegelicht*, Leiden - Amsterdam, 1902; Kampen, ²1932.

VAN CAMPENHAUSEN, H. *Die Entstehung der christlichen Bibel* (BHT, 39), Tübingen, 1968;
= *La formation de la Bible chretienne* (Le monde de la bible), tr. D. APPIA and M. DOMINCÉ, Neuchâtel, 1971;
= *The Formation of the Christian Bible*, tr. J.A. BAKER, Philadelphia, PA, 1972, ᴿ1977.

VAN DEN ENDE, E. Review of G. SCHNEIDER, Verleugnung, 1969. — *TT* 10 (1970) 454-455.

VAN DER LOOS, A. *Jezus Messias-Koning. Een speciaal onderzoek naar de vraag of Jezus van Nazaret politieke bedoelingen heeft nagestraefd*, Assen, 1942. Diss. Utrecht.

* VAN DER KWAAK, H. *Het Proces van Jezus* (VGTB, 42), Assen, 1969.

p VAN DE SANDE BAKHUYZEN, W.H. *Het fragment van het evangelie van Petrus*, in *Verslagen en mededeel. d. Koninkl. Akad. van Wetensch. Afd. Letterkunde*, III R., IX D., 1893, 329-358.

p — Evangeliën buiten het Nieuwe Testament. — H.U. MEYBOOM, *Oud-Christelijke Geschriften*, 1907, (esp. 52-74: Evangelie van Petrus).

* VANHOYE, A. *Structure et théologie des récits de la passion dans les évangiles synoptiques.* — *NRT* 89 (1967) 135-163;
= *Structure and Theology of the Accounts of the Passion in the Synoptic Gospels*, tr. C.H. GIBLIN (The Bible Today Supplementary Studies, 1), Collegeville, MN, 1967.
= *Struktur und Theologie der Passionsberichte in den synoptischen Evangelien*, tr. G. MEYER. — M. LIMBECK (ed.), *Redaktion*, 1981, 226-261.

* — Les récits de la Passion dans les évangiles synoptiques. — *AssSeign* (II) 5 (1969), 77-86;
= A. VANHOYE, I. DE LA POTTERIE and C. DUQUOC (eds.). *La passion*, 1981, 11-63.

— I. DE LA POTTERIE and C. DUQUOC (eds.). *La passion selon les quatre Évangiles* (Lire la Bible, 55), Paris, 1981.

— (ed.), *L'Apôtre Paul. Personnalité, style et conception du ministère* (BETL, 73) Leuven, 1986.

* — L'intérêt de Luc pour la prophétie en Lc 1,76; 4,16-30 et 22,60-65. — FS NEIRYNCK, Vol. 2, 1992, 1529-1548.

VAN LINDEN, P. *The Gospel of Luke and Acts* (Message of Biblical Spirituality, 10), Wilmington, DE, 1986.

p   VAN MANEN, W.C. Het Evangelie van Petrus. — *Theologisch Tijdschrift* 27 (1893) 317-333; 379-432; 517-572.

VAN OYEN, G. *De studie van de Marcusredactie in de twintigste eeuw. Met een bijdrage tot de verklaring de broodwonderen* (SNTA, 18; VKAB, 147), Brussels, 1993. Diss. Leuven, 1993 (dir. F. NEIRYNCK).

VAN SEGBROECK, F. and G. SELONG. *Bibliografie Evangeliecommentaren - Bibliography: Gospel Commentaries* (SNTA, 9). Ed. F. NEIRYNCK, Leuven, 1972.

— *The Gospel of Luke. A Cumulative Bibliography 1973-1988* (BETL, 88), Leuven, 1989; (CoBRA, 2), Brussels, 1989.

—, C.M. TUCKETT, G. VAN BELLE and J. VERHEYDEN (eds.), *The Four Gospels 1992*. FS F. NEIRYNCK (BETL, 100), 3 vols., Leuven, 1992 (= FS NEIRYNCK).

* VAN UNNIK, W.C. Jesu Verhöhnung vor dem Synedrium (Mc 14,65 par.). — *ZNW* 29 (1930) 310- 311.

— (ed.), *Neotestamentica et Patristica* (NTSuppl, 6). FS O. CULLMANN, Leiden, 1962.

— *Sparsa Collecta. The Collected Essays of W.C. van Unnik* (NTSuppl, 29-31), Pt. 1, Leiden, 1973.

— The 'Book of Acts' - The Confirmation of the Gospel. — *NT* 4 (1960) 26-59.

— *Éléments artistiques de Luc.* — F. NEIRYNCK (ed.), *L'Évangile de Luc* (BETL, 32), Gembloux, 1973, 129-140; = ²1989, 39-50.

VAN VLIET, H. *No Single Testimony. A Study on the Adoption of the Law of Deut. 19:15 par. into the New Testament* (Studia Theologica Rheno-Traiectina, 4), Utrecht, 1958.

p   VAN VOORST, R.E. Extracanonical Passion Narratives. — J.T. CARROLL and J.B. GREEN, *Death*, 1995, 148-161.

p   VERHEYDEN, J.P. Gardner-Smith and the "Turn of the Tide". — A. DENAUX (ed.), *John and the Synoptics*, 1992, 423-452.

VERMES, G. *Jesus the Jew. A Historian's Reading of the Gospels*, London, 1973; Philadelphia, PA, ᴿ1981.

* VERRALL, A.W. Christ before Herod. — *JTS* 10 (1908-09) 321-353;
= ID., *Bacchants of Euripides and Other Essays*, London, 1910, 335-390.

VESCO, J.-L., *Jérusalem et son prophète*, Paris, 1988.

* VIA, E.J. According to Luke, Who Put Jesus to Death? — R.J. CASSIDY and P.J. SCHARPER (eds.), *Political*, 1983, 122-145.

VIDLER, A.R. Review of E.B. REDLICH, Student's Introduction, 1936. — *TLond* 32 (1936) 376.

p   VIELHAUER, P. *Geschichte der urchristlichen Literatur. Einleitung in das Neue Testament, die Apokryphen und die Apostolischen Väter*, Berlin - New York, 1975, 641-648.

VIERING, F. (ed.). *Zur Bedeutung des Todes Jesu*, Gütersloh, 1968.

VIGOUROUX, F. (ed.), *Dictionnaire de la Bible*, 5 vols., Paris, 1895-1912 (= DB).

—, M. BACUEZ and A. BRASSAC (eds.), *Manuel Biblique*. 3. *Nouveau Testament*, Paris, ¹³1910;

= A. BRASSAC, *The Student's Handbook to the Study of the New Testament*, tr. J. WEIDENHAN from the 13th French ed., London, 1913.

VÖLKEL, M. *Der Anfang Jesu in Galiläa. Bemerkungen zum Gebrauch und zur Funktion Galiläas in den lukanischen Schriften.* — *ZNW* 64 (1973) 222-232.

VÖÖBUS, A. *The Prelude to the Lukan Passion Narrative: Tradition-, Redaction-, Cult-, Motif-Historical and Source-Critical Studies*, Stockholm, 1968.

VOGEL, P.J.S. Über die Entstehung der drei ersten Evangelien. — *JATL* 1 (1804) 1ff.

VOGEL, T. *Zur Charakteristik des Lukas nach Sprache und Stil*, Leipzig, 1897, ²1899.

VOGELS, W. Review of J.D. CROSSAN, Four Other Gospels, 1985. — *ÉglT* 17 (1986) 237-238.

VON HANEBERG, D.B. *Die religïosen Altertümer der Bibel*, Munich, ²1869. Revision of J.F. ALLIOLI, L.C. GRATZ and D. HANEBERG, *Handbuch der biblischen Alterthumskunde*, 2 vols. Vol. 1. *Politische, häusliche und religïose Alterthumer der Hebräer*, Landshut, 1844.

VON LOEWENICH, W. *Der Mensch im Lichte der Passionsgeschichte*, Stuttgart, 1947.

p   VON SCHUBERT, H. *Die Composition des pseudopetrinischen Evangelien-Fragments* (mit einer synoptischen Tabelle als Ergänzungheft), Berlin, 1893.

p   VON SODEN, H. *Das Petrusevangelium und die canonischen Evangelien.* — *ZTK* 3 (1893) 52-92.

VOSS, G. *Die Christologie der lukanischen Schriften in Grundzügen* (Studia Neotestamentica, 2), Paris, 1965.

VOSTÉ, J.-M. *De Synopticorum mutua relatione et dependentia*, Rome, 1928.

— *De Passione et Morte Iesu Christi* (STBNT, 3), Rome, 1937.

p   WABNITZ, H. Les fragments de l'évangile et l'apocalypse de Pierre. — *RTQR* 2 (1893) 280-294; 353-370; 474-487.

WADE, G.W. *New Testament History*, London, 1922 (148-207: The Synoptic Gospels; 194-207: Luke).

— *The Documents of the New Testament*, London, 1934.

p   WAITZ, H. Apokryphen des Neuen Testament, Das Petrusevangelium. — *RE* 23, Leipzig, ³1913, 86- 87.

*   WALASKAY, P.W. The Trial and Death of Jesus in the Gospel of Luke. — *JBL* 94 (1975) 81-93.

*   — *'And So We Came to Rome': The Political Perspectives of St Luke* (SNTS MS, 49), Cambridge, 1983.

WANSBROUGH, H. Review of É. TROCMÉ, Formation, 1975. — *ScriptB* 6 (1975) 40.

— (ed.), *Jesus and the Oral Gospel Tradition* (JSNT SS 64), Sheffield, 1991.

*   WATSON, A. *The Trial of Jesus*, Athen, GA - London, 1995.

*   WAUTIER D'AYGALLIERS, A. *Les sources du récit de la passion chez Luc*, Alençon, 1920.

WEATHERLY, J.A. *Jewish Responsibility for the Death of Jesus in Luke-Acts* (JSNT SS, 106), Sheffield, 1994.

WEGENAST, K. (ed.), *Theologie und Unterricht*, Gütersloh, 1969.

WEISER, A. Πιλᾶτος. — *EWNT* 3, cols. 205-207; = *EDNT* 3, p 87.

WEISS, B. Zur Entstehungsgeschichte der drei synoptischen Evangelien. — *TSK* 1 (1861) 29-100.

— Die Redestücke des apostolischen Matthäus. Mit besonderer Berücksichtigung von "Dr. Holtzmann, Die synoptischen Evangelien". — *JDT* 9 (1864) 49-140.

— Die Erzahlungsstücke des apostolischen Matthäus. — *JDT* 10 (1865) 319-376.

— *Das Marcusevangelium und seine synoptischen Parallelen*, Berlin, 1872.

— *Das Matthäusevangelium und seine Lucas-Parallelen*, Halle, 1876.

— *Die Evangelien des Markus und Lukas* (KEK, 1/2), Göttingen, ^{6}1878, 235-608; ^{7}1885, ^{8}1892 (*Lk* = J. WEISS), 270-666; ^{9}1901, 250-694.

— *Das Leben Jesu*, 2 vols. Berlin, 1882;
= *The Life of Christ*, 3 vols., Edinburgh, 1883.

— *Das Matthäus-Evangelium* (KEK, 1/1), Göttingen, ^{7}1883, ^{8}1890, ^{9}1898, ^{10}1910.

— *Lehrbuch der Einleitung in das Neue Testament*, Berlin, 1886, ^{2}1889, ^{3}1897.

— *Die Apostelgeschichte. Textkritische Untersuchungen und Textherstellung* (TU 9/3,4), Leipzig, 1893.

—*Das Neue Testament*, Leipzig, 2 vols., 1904;
= *A Commentary on the NT*, 4 vols., Vol. 1: *Matthew - Mark*; 2: *Luke-The Acts*; 3: *Romans - Colossians*; 4: *Thessalonians - Revelation*, tr. G. SCHODDE and E. WILSON, New York - London, 1906.

— *Die Quellen des Lukasevangeliums*, Stuttgart - Berlin, 1907.

— *Die Quellen der synoptischen Überlieferung* (TU, 32/3), Leipzig, 1908 (97-198: Aufstellung der Lukasquelle).

WEISS, J. Die Parabelrede bei Markus. — *TSK* 64 (1891) 289-321.

— *Die Evangelien des Markus und Lukas* (KEK), ^{8}1892, 270-666.

— *Die Predigt Jesu vom Reiche Gottes*, Göttingen, 1892, ^{2}1900; ^{3}1964 (ed. F. HAHN);
= *Jesus' Proclamation of the Kingdom of God*, tr. R.H. HIERS and D.L. Holland, Philadelphia, PA, 1971; Chico, CA, ^{2}1985.

— Review of P. FEINE, Eine vorkanonische Überlieferung, 1891. — *TLZ* 11 (1892) 273-276.

— *Das älteste Evangelium*, Göttingen, 1903.

— Synoptische Fragen. — *TR* 6 (1903) 199-211.

— *Die drei älteren Evangelien* (SNT), Göttingen, 1906, ^{2}1907, ^{3}1917 (eds. W. BOUSSET - W. HEITMÜLLER), 392-511, ^{4}1929.

— *Synoptische Tafeln zu den drei älteren Evangelien mit Untersuchung der Quellen in vierfachem Farbendruck*, Göttingen, 1913.

— *Das Urchristentum*, Göttingen, 1917;
= *The History of Primitive Christianity*, Vol. 1, tr. F. GRANT, New York, 1937.

WEISS, K. Review of D.R. CATCHPOLE, The Trial of Jesus, 1971. — *TLZ* 97 (1972) 443-444.

WEISSE, C.H. *Die evangelische Geschichte kritisch und philosophisch bearbeitet*, Leipzig, 1838.

WEIZSÄCKER, C. *Untersuchungen über die evangelische Geschichte, ihre Quellen und den Gang ihrer Entwicklung*, Leipzig - Tübingen, 1864, ^{2}1901.

— *Das apostolische Zeitalter der christlichen Kirche*, Freiburg i.Br., 1886-1889; Tübingen, 1886, ^{2}1892 ("neubearb."), ^{3}1902;
= *The Apostolic Age of the Christian Church*, tr. J. MILLAR, from the 2nd and rev. ed., London - New York, 1894-1899, ^{3}1907.

WELCH, J.W. *A Biblical Law Bibliography* (Toronto Studies in Theology, 51), Lewiston, NY, 1990, 135-137.

WELLHAUSEN, J. *Das Evangelium Lucae*, Berlin, 1904;
= *Evangelienkommentare*, ed. M. HENGEL, Berlin - New York, 1987, 459-600.

— *Einleitung in die drei ersten Evangelien*, Berlin, 1905; ^{2}1911 (= *Evangelienkommentare*).

WENDLAND, P. Jesus als Saturnalien-König. — *Hermes: Zeitschrift für classische Philologie* 33 (1899) 175-179.

— *Die urchristlichen Literaturformen* (HNT 1/3), Tübingen, [2,3]1912.

WENDLING, E. *Urmarkus*, Tübingen, 1905.

— *Die Entstehung des Markus-Evangeliums*, Tübingen, 1908.

WENHAM, D. *The Jesus Tradition Outside the Gospels* (Gospel Perspectives, 5), Sheffield, 1984 (= JT).

— and C. BLOMBERG (eds.), *The Miracles of Jesus* (Gospel Perspectives, 6), Sheffield, 1986.

WENDT, H.H. → H.A.W. MEYER

* WEREN, W. and V. DE HAAS, Oog in oog met personages uit Lucas. 1. Jesus en zijn volgelingen in Lc. 22-24. — *TT* 35 (1995) 125-147; 2. Jesus en zijn tegenspelers in Lc. 23. — *TT* 35 (1995) 236-251.

* — Gedragen door teksten [Lk 22,66–23,25]. — J. JANS (ed.), *Bewogen theologie. Theologie in beweging*, 1996, 12-23.

WERNLE, P. *Die synoptische Frage*, Freiburg, 1899.

— Altchristliche Apologetik im Neuen Testament. — *ZNW* 1 (1900) 42-65.

— *Die Quellen des Lebens Jesu*, Halle, 1904, [2]1905; Tübingen, [2]1906; = *The Sources of our Knowledge of the Life of Jesus*, tr. E. LUMMIS, London, 1907.

WEST, W.P. A Primitive Version of Luke in the Composition of Matthew. — *NTS* 14 (1967-68) 75- 95.

WHITE, J.T. *St. Luke's Gospel* (White's Grammar School Texts), New York, 1927.

WICKES, D.R. *The Sources of Luke's Perean Section* (Historical and Linguistic Studies, Second Series - Vl. 2, Pt. 2), Chicago, IL, 1912. Diss. Chicago, 1912 (dir. E.D. BURTON).

WIEFEL, W. *Das Evangelium nach Lukas* (THKNT, 3), Berlin, 1988.

WIKENHAUSER, A. *Einleitung in das Neue Testament*, Freiburg, 1953, [5]1963, [6]1973 ed. J. SCHMID ("völlig neu bearbeitete Auflage"); = *New Testament Introduction*, tr. J. CUNNINGHAM, New York, 1963.

WIKGREN, A. Wellhausen on the Synoptic Gospels: A Centenary Appraisal. — *JBR* 12 (1944) 174- 180.

WILCKENS, U. ἱμάτιον. — *TWNT* 7, 687-692 (= *TDNT* 7, 687-691).

WILCOX, M. *The Semitisms of Acts*, Oxford, 1965.

— *The Savior of the World. The Message of Luke's Gospel*, Downers Grove, IL, 1979.

WILD, R.A. Review of H. HENDRICKX, Passion Narratives, 1977. — *CBQ* 40 (1978) 275-276.

WILKINSON, J. Review of H. HOEHNER, Herod Antipas, 1972. — *ATR* 54 (1972) 363-365.

WILKINSON, W. *Good News In Luke*, Glasgow, 1975.

WILLIAMS, C.S.C. Review of W.L. KNOX, Acts, 1948. — *JTS* 49 (1948) 201-204.

— The Date of Luke-Acts. — *ExpT* 64 (1952-53) 283-284.

— → A.H. MCNEILE, *An Introduction*, [2]1953.

— *A Commentary on the Acts of the Apostles*, New York, 1957.

p WILSON, R.McL. Apokryphen II. Petrusevangelium. — *TRE* 3 (1978) 331-332.

WILSON, S.G. The Jews and the Death of Jesus in Acts. — P. RICHARDSON and D. GRANSKOU (eds.), *Anti-Judaism*, 1986, 155-164.

WILSON, W.R. *The Execution of Jesus. A Judicial, Literary and Historical Investigation*, New York, 1970. *The Trial of Jesus: A Judicial, Literary and Historical Study*. Diss. Duke, Durham, NC, 1960 (dir. K.W. CLARK).

WINBERY, C.L. → J.A. BROOKS

WINK, W. *John the Baptist in the Gospel Tradition* (SNTS MS 7), Cambridge, MA, 1968. Diss. Union, New York.

— Review of P. BENOIT and M.-É. BOISMARD, Synopse, 1972. — *CBQ* 35 (1973) 223-225.

WINTER, B.W. and A.D. CLARKE (eds.), *The Book of Acts in Its First Century Setting*, Grand Rapids, MI - Carlisle, UK, 1993.

WINTER, P. Review of H. SCHÜRMANN, Der Paschamahlbericht, 1953. — *NTS* 2 (1955-56) 207-209; ID., Der Einsetzungesbericht, 1955; ID., Jesu Abschiedsrede, 1957. — *NTS* 4 (1957-58) 223-227.

* — The Treatment of His Sources by the Third Evangelist in Lk XXI-XXIV. — *ST* 8 (1954-55) 138-172.

* — Luke XXII.66b-71. — *ST* 9 (1955-56) 112-115.

— On Luke and Lucan Sources: A Reply to the Reverend N. Turner. — *ZNW* 47 (1956) 217-242.

* — *On the Trial of Jesus* (Studia Judaica, 1), 1961, Second edition revised and enlarged by T.A. BURKILL and G. VERMES, Berlin, ²1974.

WITTICHEN, C. Zur Marcusfrage. — *JPTh* 7 (1881) 366-375.

— Zur Frage nach den Quellen des Lucas-evangeliums. — *JPTh* 7 (1881) 713-720.

WOLFF, C. Zur Bedeutung Johannes des Täufers im Markusevangelium. — *TLZ* 102 (1977) 857-865.

WOOD, H.G. Review of V. TAYLOR, Behind, 1926. — *The Friend* 66 (1926) 671-672.

WOODS, F.H. The Origin and Mutual Relation of the Synoptic Gospels. — S.R. DRIVER et al. (eds.), *Studia*, 1890, 59-104.

WRIGHT, A. *A Synopsis of the Gospels in Greek*, London, 1896, ²1903, ³1906.

— *Some New Testament Problems*, London, 1898.

— *The Composition of the Four Gospels*, London, 1900.

— *The Gospel according to S. Luke in Greek. After the Westcott and Hort Text*, London, 1900.

— The Gospel According to Luke. — *DCG*, Vol. 2, 1908, 84-91.

WRIGHT, C.J. Incidents Recorded in St. Luke's Gospel, But not in St. Mark's or St. Matthew's Gospel: Text and Commentary. — H.D.A. MAJOR et al. (eds.), MMJ, 1938, 259-297.

p WRIGHT, D.F. Apocryphal Gospels: The 'Unknown Gospel' (Pap. Egerton 2) and the Gospel of Peter. — D. WENHAM (ed.), *Jesus Tradition*, 1984, 207-232.

p — Apologetic and Apocalyptic: The Miraculous in the Gospel of Peter. — D. WENHAM and C. BLOMBERG (eds.), *Miracles*, 1986, 401-418.

p — Papyrus Egerton 2 (the *Unknown* Gospel) - Part of the *Gospel of Peter*? — *SecCent* 5 (1985-86) 129-150.

— Review of J.D. CROSSAN, Four Other Gospels, 1985. — *Themelios* 12 (1987) 56-60.

WRIGHT, N.T. Jesus, Israel and the Cross. — *SBL 1985 Seminar Papers*, 75-95.

p YAMAUCHI, E. Agrapha and Apocryphal Gospels. — *ISBE* 1, 1979, 69-71; 181-188.

YOUNG, B.H. *Jesus and His Jewish Parables. Rediscovering the Roots of Jesus' Teaching* (Theological Inquiries), New York, 1989.

YOUNG, F.W. Hypocrisy. — *IDB* 2, 668-669.

ZAHN, T. *Geschichte des neutestamentlichen Kanons*, Erlangen - Leipzig, 3 vols. Vol. 2/2, 1892; Hildesheim - New York, ᴿ1975.

p   — Das Evangelium des Petrus. — *NKZ* 4 (1893) 143-218; repr. *Das Evangelium des Petrus*, Erlangen, 1893.

— *Einleitung in das Neue Testament*, Leipzig, Bd. 2, 1897-99, ²1900; *Introduction to the New Testament*, tr. M.W. JACOBUS et al. from the third German ed., 3 vols., Edinburgh, 1909 (esp. Vol. 3, 1-173: The Writings of St. Luke).

— *Das Evangelium des Lucas* (Kommentar zum Neuen Testament, 3), Leipzig, ¹·²1913, ³·⁴1920; Wuppertal, ᴿ1988.

ZEHRER, F. *Einführung in die synoptischen Evangelien*, Klosterneuburg bei Wien, 1959.

— Jesus, der "Herr" in der Passion. — *TPQ* 120 (1972) 203-210.

— Sinn und Problematik der Schriftverwendung in der Passion. — *TPQ* 121 (1973) 18-25.

ZEITLIN, S. *Who Crucified Jesus?*, New York, 1942, ²1947, ³1955, ⁴1964, ⁵1976.

ZELLER, E. *Die Apostelgeschichte nach ihrem Inhalt und Ursprung kritisch untersucht*, Stuttgart, 1854.

ZERWICK, M. *Untersuchungen zum Markus-Stil. Ein Beitrag zur stilistischen Durcharbeitung des Neuen Testaments* (Scripta Pontificii Instituti Biblici), Rome, 1937.

— *Biblical Greek. Illustrated by Examples*, tr. J. SMITH, adapted from the fourth Latin ed., Rome, 1963.

ZIENER, G. Die synoptische Frage. — J. SCHREINER and G. DAUTZENBERG (eds.), *Gestalt*, 1969, 173-185.

ZMIJEWSKI, J. ἀστραπή. — *EWNT* 1, cols. 420-422 (= *EDNT* 1, 174-175).

— πλῆθος, ους, τό. — *EWNT* 3, cols. 245-249 (= *EDNT* 3, 103-105).

ZWIEP, A.W. *The Ascension of the Messiah in Lukan Christology* (NTSuppl, 87), Leiden - New York - Cologne, 1997. Diss. Durham, 1996 (dir. J.D.G. DUNN).

SPECIAL LQ VOCABULARY AND CONSTRUCTIONS
ACCORDING TO J. WEISS[1]

J. Weiss was the first to firmly develop the LQ source emphasizing both vocabulary and style[2]. In an effort at reconstruction, he attempted to isolate the vocabulary and types of expressions coming from LQ, which extended through the Gospel as well as Acts[3]. The list is presented in three parts: the first part details the LQ material J. Weiss ascribed to Markan sections. The words are cited as they are found in the text; the second part records the terms as they occur in the order of the Gospel; the third is an alphabetical listing.

I. References to LQ in the Markan Sections

3,1-6: 4 ἐν βίβλῳ, 5 πληρωθήσεται; 3,18-20: 20 προσέθηκεν; 3,21-38: 23 ὡσεί?; 4,1-13: 5 βασιλείας, 9 ἐντεῦθεν, 13 πειρασμόν. "Q or A?"; 4,14-15: "Mk + Q"; 4,31-44: 38 συνεχομένη, 39 ἐπιστάς; 5,12-16: 12 πεσὼν ἐπὶ πρόσωπον; 5,17-26: 19 ἔμπροσθεν; 5,27-39: [33] ὁμοίως; 6,1-11: 6 σαββάτῳ; 6,12-19: [15] καλούμενον, 17 ἐπὶ τόπου πεδινοῦ;
8,11-15: 11 ὁ λόγος τοῦ θεοῦ; 8,16-18: 16 εἰσπορευόμενοι; 8,19-21: 19 παρεγένετο "häufig in LQ, Zusatz des Lk"; 8,40-56: 41 πόδας, 49 σκύλλε, 52 ἐκόπτοντο, 55 πνεῦμα; 9,7-9: 8 ἐφάνη, 9 περὶ οὗ ἀκούω; 9,10-17: [10] καλουμένην, [εἰς τόπον ἔρημον], 12 ἡ δὲ ἡμέρα ἤρξατο, κλίνειν?, πορευθέντες, καταλύσωσιν, ὧδε, 13 πορευθέντες, ἀγοράσωμεν?, 14 ὡσεί, 15 ἐποίησαν οὕτως. A + LQ; 9,18-27: 18 ὄχλοι, 20 χριστόν, 23 καθ᾽ ἡμέραν?, 27 [sic] ὧδε. Stems from source of A; 9,28-36: 28 ὡσεί, 29 ὁ ἱματισμός, ἐξαστράπτων, 31 ἤμελλεν?, πληροῦν, Ἰερουσαλήμ, 32 βεβαρημένοι, διαγρηγορήσαντες (Luke or LQ?), 33 ἐπιστάτα, ὧδε, 35 ἐκλελεγμένος, 36 εὑρέθη, μόνος, [καὶ αὐτοί]; 9,37-43: 37 τῇ ἑξῆς, 38 ἐβόησεν, ἐπιβλέψαι, μονογενής, 41 ὧδε, 42 ἀπέδωκεν; 9,44-45: 44 θέσθε ὑμεῖς εἰς τὰ ὦτα ὑμῶν, παραδίδοσθαι εἰς χεῖρας ἀνθρώπων, 45 παρακεκαλυμμένον; 9,46-50: 46 τίς, 47 ἐπιλαβόμενος; Theme: the small and the lowly are close to God's heart (9,46-48);
18,15-30: 15 βρέφη, 16 προσεκαλέσατο, 18 ἄρχων, 21 ἐφύλαξα, 22 διάδος, 24 εἰσπορεύονται; 18,31-43: [31] τελεσθήσεται, 34 συνῆκαν, κεκρυμμένον, [34] καὶ αὐτοί, 35 ἐπαιτῶν, 36 διαπορευομένου, ἐπυνθάνετο, 37 παρέρχεται, 38 ἐβόησεν, 40 σταθείς;

---

1. See the discussion of J. Weiss's contribution, p. 13-23.
2. Feine's list was much less extensive (*Eine vorkanonische Überlieferung*, p. 247-252). While the majority of vocabulary was taken from the body of the commentary, the siglum † refers to "specifische Ausdrücke der Rede" that J. Weiss insisted were drawn from the Jewish-Christian source from which the material unique to Lk derived (LQ) (*Lukas*, [8]1892, p. [386-]387, n. 3). A list of words containing the prefix διά-, for which he argued LQ showed a predilection, are contained in a note (p. 399. n. 1).
3. Throughout his discussion, J. Weiss listed vocabulary which he attributed to LQ. Typographical errors are corrected in our list as indicated by the exponential letter [c]. To mention only a few, in referring to ἀτενίζω, Weiss cited Lk 4,26 instead of 4,20. Similarly, he specified 23,38 for στραφείς, when in fact it occurs in 23,28. These and other cases are noted in the alphabetical list.

20,1-8: 1 ἐπέστησαν, ἀρχιερεῖς; 20,27-38: 34 υἱοὶ τοῦ αἰῶνος τούτου, 36 ἀναστάσεως υἱοί, 37 ὡς. "nach A" (36-38 + LQ); 20,41-47: 42 ἐν βίβλῳ; 21,1-4: 4 τὸν βίον. A?; 22,7-13: 8 πορευθέντες, ἑτοιμάσατε, 9 ἑτοιμάσωμεν, 11 κατάλυμα, 12 ἑτοιμάσατε, 13 ἡτοίμασαν. "Die Mahlbereitung, im Wesentlichen wie bei Mk 14,12-16 erzählt" (p. 615).

How is it possible for Weiss to account for the presence of LQ vocabulary in L, Q and Markan sections? The pattern becomes obvious through the analysis. The LQ vocabulary was drawn from L and Q. Secondly, a redaction of LQ was added to Q which later underwent revision by Luke. Finally, there was Lukan redaction of A which was influenced by the tradition and reworking of LQ. Weiss was aware of these various distinctions though the words and phrases are simply referred to by the designation LQ. The LQ word was attributed to more than one level.

For Weiss LQ was a combined document and there were instances where he differentiated among L, LQ and Q[4]. The phrase βασιλεία τοῦ θεοῦ Weiss held as definitely stemming from Q[5]. For some words, such as ὄχλοι, Weiss was not able to determine whether Q or LQ was the source[6]. In other cases, LQ appeared to have added material to Q[7]. Pertaining to ὅπως, Weiss claimed five cases for LQ (2,35; 7,3; 16,26.28; [24,20]), but assigned one to Q (10,2)[8]. Even in material which was unique to Lk, Weiss found that certain vocabulary also appeared in Q[9]. Weiss differentiated between δακτύλῳ θεοῦ (11,20 LQ) and τῶν δακτύλων (11,46 Q)[10]. Yet another example was the verb μισεῖν though 6,27 and 16,13 were from Q, 1,71; 6,22; 14,26 were ascribed to LQ[11]. Weiss even was able to separate LQ material (2,7) from *Urmarkus* (22,11) in the case of καταλῦσαι[12]. He assigned a phrase such as ἐπ᾽ ἀληθείας both to LQ (4,25; 22,59) and to A (20,21). In one case he recognized two different forms (Q and L) of the same parable[13].

4. *Ibid.*, p. 643. Consider his treatment of the forms of the term προσφωνέω. Luke was responsible for 6,13, Q for 7,32 and LQ for 13,12.

5. *Ibid.*, p. 388.

6. *Ibid.*, p. 435.

7. *Ibid.*, p. 467. As for example 14,28ff. and 17,7ff.

8. *Ibid.*, p. 478, n. 1. A similar situation existed for the term χαίρω. Two instances were due to Q (6,23; 15,5), while approximately 10 others were from LQ (p. 572). See additional examples (p. 574, n. 2 and 587, n. 1).

9. *Ibid.*, p. 523. A form of the term σαροῦν was found both in 11,25 (Q) and 15,9 (L).

10. *Ibid.*, p. 545. He made a similar distinction for ἡλικία: 2,52 was from LQ and 12,25 was from Q (p. 571). The parallel from 12,25 was Mt 6,27.

11. *Ibid.*, p. 574, n. 2. In 6,27 was found μισοῦσιν and in 16,13 was μισήσει. The supposed LQ passages contained μισούντων, μισήσωσιν (6,22), and μισεῖ (14,26).

The same situation applied in the case of προστίθημι: 12,25 (προσθεῖναι), 12,31 (προστεθήσεται) derived from Q while 3,20 (προσέθηκεν); 17,5 (πρόσθες); 19,11 (προσθεὶς) stemmed from LQ.

12. *Ibid.*, p. 572. Cf. p. 579, n. 2. See further where Weiss stated that the LQ material of 21,20-28 appeared to be a second revision of Q material (p. 606).

13. *Ibid.*, p. 513, n. 3: "Lk 14,11 stand jedenfalls in Q (Mt 23,12), ob aber auch die Parabel? In manchen Zügen ist sie parallel dem Appendix an die Hochzeitsparabel Mt 22,11ff. (die Besichtigung der Gäste durch den Wirth, die Anmassung des Gastes), so dass man an zwei verschiedene Gestaltungen derselben Parabel (eine in Q und eine in L) denken könnte".

The next list of the LQ vocabulary indicates the words and phrases in the form and order in which they appear in Lk. In addition, after the vocabulary for the respective pericopes, stylistic and thematic elements indicative of LQ are recorded.

II. LQ sections

1,5-2,52: 1,5 ἱερεύς, 6 ἐντολαῖς, 7 καθότι, 9 κατὰ τὸ ἔθος 10 πλῆθος, προσευχόμενον, τῇ ὥρᾳ τοῦ θυμιάματος, 15 ἐνώπιον [τοῦ] κυρίου, πλησθήσεται, κοιλίας, 17 καὶ αὐτός (possibly), προελεύσεται, καρδίας, ἑτοιμάσαι, 20 ἀνθ᾽ ὧν, πληρωθήσονται, 22 ὀπτασίαν, καὶ αὐτός ("ohne Betonung"; common in LQ), διανεύων, διέμενεν, 23 ὡς, ἐπλήσθησαν, 25 οὕτως ... πεποίηκεν, 29 διελογίζετο, 30 χάριν, 32 ὑψίστου, 33 βασιλεύσει, βασιλείας, 35 ὑψίστου, 36 συγγενίς, καλουμένη, 39 ἀναστᾶσα, τὴν ὀρεινήν, 41 ὡς, ἐσκίρτησεν, βρέφος, κοιλία, ἐπλήσθη, 42 κοιλίας, 44 ὡς, εἰς τὰ ὦτά μου, ἐσκίρτησεν, βρέφος, κοιλία, 47 ἠγαλλίασεν, 48 ἐπέβλεψεν, ἀπὸ τοῦ νῦν, 50 φοβουμένοις, 51 διεσκόρπισεν, 52 καθεῖλεν, καὶ ὕψωσεν ταπεινούς, 53 ἐνέπλησεν, ἀγαθῶν, ἐξαπέστειλεν, 54 ἀντελάβετο, παιδός, μνησθῆναι, 56 ὡς, 57 ἐπλήσθη, 58 συγγενεῖς, ἐμεγάλυνεν κύριος τὸ ἔλεος αὐτοῦ μετ᾽, συνέχαιρον, 60 οὐχί, ἀλλά, 61 καλεῖται τῷ ὀνόματι, 62 τὸ τί, 64 τὸ στόμα, 65 τῇ ὀρεινῇ, διελαλεῖτο, 66 ἔθεντο ... ἐν τῇ καρδίᾳ, χεὶρ κυρίου, 67 ἐπλήσθη, 68 ἐπεσκέψατο, λύτρωσιν, 69 παιδός, 70 διὰ στόματος, 71 ἐχθρῶν, μισούντων, ἐκ χειρὸς πάντων τῶν μισούντων, 72 ποιῆσαι ἔλεος μετά, μνησθῆναι, 74 ἐκ χειρὸς ἐχθρῶν, 75 τῆς ζωῆς v.l., 76 ὑψίστου, ἑτοιμάσαι, 77 γνῶσιν, 78 ἐπισκέψεται, 79 καθημένοις, εἰς ὁδὸν εἰρήνης, 80 ἀναδείξεως

2,6 ἐπλήσθησαν, 7 τόπος, καταλύματι, 8 χώρᾳ, 9 ἐπέστη, 11 χριστός, 12 βρέφος, κείμενον, 13 πλῆθος, αἰνούντων, 14 εἰρήνη, ἀνθρώποις εὐδοκίας, 15 ὡς, 16 σπεύσαντες, βρέφος...κείμενον, 20 δοξάζοντες, αἰνοῦντες, 21 ἐπλήσθησαν, πρὸ τοῦ συλλημφθῆναι, κοιλίᾳ, 22 ἐπλήσθησαν, 25 Ἰερουσαλήμ, παράκλησιν, 26 ἰδεῖν, χριστόν, 28 ἐδέξατο, 29 ἐν εἰρήνῃ, 30 ὀφθαλμοί, 31 ἡτοίμασας, 34 κεῖται ἀντιλεγόμενον, 35 ὅπως, καρδιῶν, 37 χήρα, λατρεύουσα, 38 αὐτῇ τῇ ὥρᾳ, ἐπιστᾶσα, λύτρωσιν, Ἰερουσαλήμ, 39 ὡς, ἐτέλεσαν, 40 πληρούμενον, χάρις, 41 Ἰερουσαλήμ, 42 κατὰ τὸ ἔθος, 43 Ἰερουσαλήμ, 44 συγγενεῦσιν, τοῖς γνωστοῖς, 45 Ἰερουσαλήμ, 46 ἐν μέσῳ, 48 ἐποίησας...οὕτως, ὀδυνώμενοι, 50 καὶ αὐτοί, συνῆκαν, 52 ἡλικίᾳ, χάριτι
Style: often used the imperfect rather than the aorist (2,3).
Particular settings reflect the LQ source: encounters with priests (1,5); going to the temple to pray (1,10; 2,37).
Themes: a concern for the relationship of children to mothers (chapter 1f.); various people's claims to salvation (1,7); the LQ author's expectation of the illustrious restoration of the Davidic kingdom (1,32); the coming to term of a certain period of time when something should happen (1,57; 2,6.21.22); the reversal of situations concerning possessions (1,53); the completion or supplementation of certain things (1,78); the small and the lowly are close to God's heart (1,57ff.); the messianic reign being described as "the house of his/one's father" signifying the people Israel (1,33.69).

3,7-17: 7 ἔλεγεν οὖν, 8 ἄρξησθε, ἐν ἑαυτοῖς, 11 ὁμοίως, ποιείτω but lacking the οὕτως, 13 πλέον παρὰ τὸ διατεταγμένον, 14 διασείσητε, συκοφαντήσητε, 15 διαλογιζομένων
Themes: sharing and giving, though the vocabulary varies (3,11); contemptuous and righteous behavior (3,12f.).

4,16-30: 16 ἀνέστη, 17 ἐπεδόθη, τόπον, 20 ἀποδούς, ἀτενίζοντες, 21 ἤρξατο, πεπλήρωται, ἐντοῖς ὡσὶν ὑμῶν, 22 ἐκ τοῦ στόματος αὐτοῦ, ἔλεγον, υἱὸς Ἰωσήφ, 23 εἰς meaning ἐν, ὧδε, 25 ἐπ᾽ ἀληθείας, χῆραι, ἐπὶ ἔτη τρία καὶ μῆνας ἕξ, ὡς, ἐγένετο, 26 ἐπέμφθη, χήραν, 28 ἐπλήσθησαν, 29 ἀναστάντες, ᾠκοδόμητο, ὥστε. "L"
Style: frequent use of the imperfect rather than the aorist (4,22.30).

5,1-11: 1 ἐπικεῖσθαι, καὶ αὐτός, 3 ἕν, ἠρώτησεν, ὀλίγον, 4 ὡς, ἐπαύσατο, 5 ἐπιστάτα, 6 πλῆθος, διερρήσσετο, 7 ἔπλησαν, 8 ἁμαρτωλός, 10 ὁμοίως, ἀπὸ τοῦ νῦν. LQ

6,20-49: 20 ἐπάρας τοὺς ὀφθαλμούς, ἔλεγεν, πτωχοί, 22 μισήσωσιν, 23 σκιρτήσατε, κατὰ τὰ αὐτά, ἐποίουν, 24 παράκλησιν, 25 ἐμπεπλησμένοι, κλαύσετε, 26 κατὰ τὰ αὐτά, ἐποίουν, 27 ἐχθρούς, μισοῦσιν, ποιεῖτε, 29 τύπτοντι, πάρεχε, αἴροντος, κωλύσῃς, 30 ἀπαίτει, 31 ποιεῖτε, ὁμοίως, 32 χάρις ἐστίν, ἁμαρτωλοί, 34 ἀπολάβωσιν, 35 ὑψίστου, 36 γίνεσθε, οἰκτίρμονες, οἰκτίρμων, 38 κόλπον, ἀντιμετρηθήσεται, 39 ἐμπεσοῦνται, 45 τὸ στόμα αὐτοῦ, 47 πᾶς ὁ ἐρχόμενος, ὑποδείξω, τίνι, 48 ἔσκαψεν, ἔθηκεν θεμέλιον, οὐκ ἴσχυσεν, οἰκοδομῆσθαι, 49 οἰκοδομήσαντι
Style: frequent use of the imperfect rather than the aorist (6,20).
Themes: sharing and giving, though the vocabulary varied (6,27.30.36.38); how God treats the ungrateful (6,34-35); how to conduct oneself (6,36).

7,1-10: 1 ἐπλήρωσεν, 2 ἤμελλεν, ἔντιμος, 3 ἐρωτῶν, ὅπως, διασώσῃ, 4 παραγενόμενοι, ἄξιος, παρέξῃ, 5 ἔθνος, ᾠκοδόμησεν, 6 ἤδη, μακραν, ἀπέχοντος, ἔπεμψεν, φίλους, σκύλλου, εἰσέλθῃς, 7 παῖς, 9 στραφείς, 10 οἱ πεμφθέντες

7,11-17: 11 ἑξῆς, καλουμένην, 12 ὡς, δὲ ἤγγισεν, μονογενής, καὶ αὐτή, χήρα, 13 ἐσπλαγχνίσθη, [13] ὁ κύριος, 14 βαστάζοντες, νεανίσκος, 15 ἀνεκάθισεν, ἔδωκεν, 16 ἐδόξαζον, προφήτης, ἐπεσκέψατο
Theme: the completion or supplementation of certain things (7,16).

7,18-23: 18 προσκαλεσάμενος, 19 ἔπεμψεν, πρὸς τὸν κύριον, 20 παραγενόμενοι, 21 ἐκείνῃ τῇ ὥρᾳ, 22 πορευθέντες

7,24-35: 24 ἀγγέλων, ἤρξατο, 25 ἱματισμῷ, ἐνδόξῳ, 29 ἐδικαίωσαν, τὸ βάπτισμα, 30 οἱ νομικοί, τὴν βουλὴν τοῦ θεοῦ, ἠθέτησαν, 31 ὁμοιώσω, 34 πίνων, [34] ἁμαρτωλῶν, 35 ἡ σοφία

7,36-50: 36 ἠρώτα, εἰσελθών, 37 καὶ ἰδού, ἁμαρτωλός, 38 ὀπίσω, ἤρξατο, βρέχειν πόδας, 39 ἰδών, ἐν ἑαυτῷ, προφήτης, τίς ... ἥτις, ἁμαρτωλός, 40 ἔχω ... εἰπεῖν, [40] ἔφη, 41 χρεοφειλέται, δανιστῇ, ὤφειλεν, 42 μὴ ἐχόντων, ἀποδοῦναι, ἐχαρίσατο, 43 ἐχαρίσατο, ὑπολαμβάνω, εἰπεν... ὀρθῶς, ἔκρινας, 44 στραφείς, εἰσῆλθον, ἔβρεξεν, [44] ἔφη, 45 φίλημα, αὕτη δὲ ἀφ᾽ ἧς, εἰσῆλθον, διέλιπεν, 47 ὀλίγον, 49 ἤρξαντο, συνανακείμενοι, ἐν ἑαυτοῖς, 50 σέσωκεν, εἰς εἰρήνην
Style: frequent use of the imperfect rather than the aorist (7,36).
Particular settings reflected the LQ source: dining in the home of Pharisees who had not made a decision about Jesus (7,36).

8,1-3: 2 καλουμένη, 3 διηκόνουν

8,4-8: 5 κατεπατήθη, πετεινά, 7 ἐν μέσῳ

9,51-62: 51 ἐστήρισεν, Ἰερουσαλήμ, 52 ἀγγέλους, πορευθέντες, ὥστε *v.l.*, ἐτοιμάσαι, 53 Ἰερουσαλήμ, 55 στραφείς, 56 ἑτέραν, 58 πετεινά, κατασκηνώσεις, οὐκ ἔχει ποῦ, 59 ἕτερον, 60 νεκρούς, διάγγελλε, 61 ἕτερος, ἀποτάξασθαι, εἰς, 62 ἄροτρον, βλέπων εἰς τὰ ὀπίσω, εὔθετος
Theme: an interest in the Samaritans (9,51ff.).

10,1-16: 1 μετὰ δὲ ταῦτα, ἀνέδειξεν, ὁ κύριος, τόπον, ἤμελλεν, 2 ἐκβάλῃ, τοῦ κυρίου τοῦ θερισμοῦ, 4 βαστάζετε, βαλλάντιον, 5 εἰρήνη, 6 εἰρήνης, εἰρήνη, 8 παρατιθέμενα, 9 ἤγγικεν, 10 εἰς τὰς πλατείας, 11 κολληθέντα, ἤγγικεν, 12 ἐν τῇ ἡμέρᾳ ἐκείνῃ, 16 ἀθετῶν, ἀθετεῖ
Style: the change from relative to demonstrative sentences (10,8); the loose construction of relative sentences (10,12).

10,17-20: 18 ἐθεώρουν, τὸν σατανᾶν, ἀστραπήν, 19 ἐξουσίαν τοῦ πατεῖν, ἐπάνω, ὄφεων, σκορπίων
Style: frequent use of the imperfect rather than the aorist (10,18).

10,21-24: 21 ἐν αὐτῇ τῇ ὥρᾳ, ἠγαλλιάσατο, ἀπέκρυψας, 22 τίς ἐστιν, 23 στραφείς, ὀφθαλμοί

10,25-37: 25 νομικός, 28 ὀρθῶς ἀπεκρίθης, 29 δικαιῶσαι, 30 ὑπολαβών, ἄνθρωπός τις, Ἰερουσαλήμ, ἐπιθέντες, 31 ἱερεύς, ἀντιπαρῆλθεν, 32 ὁμοίως, γενόμενος κατὰ τὸν τόπον, 33 ἐσπλαγχνίσθη, 34 τραύματα, ἐπιβιβάσας, πανδοχεῖον, ἐπεμελήθη, 35 ἐπὶ τὴν αὔριον, ἐκβαλών, προσδαπανήσῃς, ἐπανέρχεσθαι, ἀποδώσω, 36 ἐμπεσόντος, 37 ὁ ποιήσας τὸ ἔλεος μετ', ποίει ὁμοίως
Style: transitional questions (10,29).
Particular settings reflected the LQ source: encounters with priests (10,31).
Theme: an interest in the Samaritans (10,33ff.).

10,38-42: 38 ὑπεδέξατο, 39 καλουμένη, ἣ καί, πόδας τοῦ κυρίου, ἤκουεν τὸν λόγον, 40 διακονίαν, ἐπιστᾶσα, διακονεῖν, εἰπὲ ... συναντιλάβηται, 41 Μάρθα Μάρθα, 42 ὀλίγων *v.l.*, ἐξελέξατο, ἀφαιρεθήσεται

11,1-13: 1 ἐν τόπῳ τινὶ προσευχόμενον, ὡς, ἐπαύσατο, 3 καθ' ἡμέραν, 4 ὀφείλοντι, πειρασμόν, 5 τίς ἐξ ὑμῶν ἕξει, φίλον, φίλε, 6 ἐπειδή, φίλος, παρεγένετο, οὐκ ἔχω, παραθήσω, 7 πάρεχε, ἤδη, εἰς, 8 ἀναστάς, χρῄζει, 11 αἰτήσει, ὄφιν, ἐπιδώσει, 12 ἐπιδώσει, σκορπίον

11,14-26: 17 διαμερισθεῖσα, πίπτει, 18 διεμερίσθη, 20 δακτύλῳ θεοῦ, 21 ἐν εἰρήνῃ, 22 ἐπελθών, αἴρει, ἐπεποίθει, διαδίδωσιν, 24 ἀνάπαυσιν
Theme: apocalyptic terrors (11,22).

11,27-28: 27 ἐπάρασά τις φωνήν, βαστάσασα, μαστοί, 28 φυλάσσοντες, λόγον τοῦ θεοῦ
Theme: a concern for the relationship of children to mothers (11,27f.).

11,29-36: 31 ὧδε, 32 ὧδε, 33 εἰσπορευόμενοι, 36 μῆτι - ἀστραπῇ
Theme: a particular eschatology which assumed that the resurrection of the just will happen at the same time as the general resurrection (11,31).

11,37-54: 37 ἐρωτᾷ, ὅπως, ἀριστήσῃ, ἀνέπεσεν, 38 ἰδὼν ἐθαύμασεν, πρῶτον, πρὸ τοῦ, ἀρίστου, 39 ὁ κύριος, 40 ἄφρονες, 41 ἐλεημοσύνην, 42 παρέρχεσθε, 44 ἐπάνω, 45 τις τῶν νομικῶν, 46 νομικοῖς, καὶ αὐτοί, 47 οἰκοδομεῖτε, 48 μάρτυρες, αὐτοί, οἰκοδομεῖτε, 49 ἡ σοφία τοῦ θεοῦ, 51 ἀπολομένου, ναί, 52 νομικοῖς, ἤρατε, γνώσεως, ἐκωλύσατε, 54 ἐκ τοῦ στόματος αὐτοῦ
Style: transitional questions (11,45). This verse was not a question however.
Particular settings reflected the LQ source: dining in the home of Pharisees who had not made a decision about Jesus (11,37).

12,1-12: 1 καταπατεῖν, ἤρξατο, προσέχετε ἑαυτοῖς, 3 ἀνθ᾽ ὧν, 4 φίλοις, μετὰ ταῦτα, μὴ ἐχόντων, περισσότερόν τι, 5 ὑποδείξω, τίνα, ἀποκτεῖναι ἔχοντα ἐξουσίαν, ναί, φοβήθητε, 6 πωλοῦνται, 8 ἀγγέλων, 9 ἀγγέλων, 11 τὰς ἀρχάς, μήτι, 12 τῇ ὥρᾳ

12,13-21: 13 εἰπὲ ... μερίσασθαι, 15 ἡ ζωή, 16 ἀνθρώπου τινὸς πλουσίου, ἡ χώρα, 17 διελογίζετο, ἐν ἑαυτῷ, τί ποιήσω, οὐκ ἔχω ποῦ, συνάξω, 18 καθελῶ, οἰκοδομήσω, συνάξω, ἀγαθά, 19 ἀγαθά, κείμενα, ἀναπαύου, πίε, εὐφραίνου, 20 ἄφρων, ἀπαιτοῦσιν, ἡτοίμασας
Style: transitional questions (12,13). This was not a question but an imperative directed to Jesus. Characters in the parables often asked and then answered their own questions (12,17). Theme: the treatment of the godless (12,20).

12,22-34: 24 κατανοήσατε, 26 ἐλάχιστον, 27 κατανοήσατε, 30 χρῄζετε (LQ from Q), 31 προστεθήσεται, 32 δοῦναι, τὴν βασιλείαν, 33 πωλήσατε, δότε ἐλεημοσύνην, βαλλάντια

12,35-48: 35 περιεζωσμέναι, 37 ἐλθών, περιζώσεται, παρελθών, διακονήσει, 39 ποίᾳ ὥρᾳ, 40 γίνεσθε, δοκεῖτε, 41 κύριε, πρὸς ἡμᾶς, 42 ὁ κύριος, οἰκονόμος, ὁ φρόνιμος, 43 ποιοῦντα οὕτως, 45 ἄρξηται, [45] τύπτειν, παῖδας, 46 ὁ κύριος τοῦ δούλου, 47 γνούς, ἑτοιμάσας, δαρήσεται, 48 ἄξια, δαρήσεται, ὀλίγας, περισσότερον, αἰτήσουσιν
Style: transitional questions (12,41).
Themes: sharing and giving, though the vocabulary varied (12,33); how to conduct oneself (12,40).

12,49-53: 49 βαλεῖν, εἰ, ἤδη, 50 βάπτισμα, ἔχω βαπτισθῆναι, συνέχομαι, τελεσθῇ, 51 δοκεῖτε, εἰρήνην, παρεγενόμην, δοῦναι ἐν, οὐχί, λέγω ὑμῖν, ἀλλ᾽, 52 ἀπὸ τοῦ νῦν, διαμεμερισμένοι, 53 διαμερισθήσονται
Theme: reference to the division between parents and children over Christianity (12,52ff.).

12,54-59: 54 ἔρχεται, 56 τὸ πρόσωπον, δοκιμάζειν, 57 κρίνετε, 58 ὡς, ἄρχοντα, [58] ἀντιδίκου, 59 ἀποδῷς

13,1-9: 1 ἐν αὐτῷ τῷ καιρῷ, 2 δοκεῖτε, ἁμαρτωλοί, παρὰ πάντας, 3 οὐχί, λέγω ὑμῖν, ἀλλ᾽, μετανοῆτε, ἀπολεῖσθε, 4 ἐφ᾽ οὓς ἔπεσεν, δοκεῖτε, ὀφειλέται, ἐγένοντο, Ἰερουσαλήμ, 5 μετανοῆτε, ἀπολεῖσθε, 6 εἶχέν τις, πεφυτευμένην, 7 τρία ἔτη ἀφ᾽ οὗ, 8 ἕως ὅτου, σκάψω, κόπρια
Style: the change from relative to demonstrative sentences (13,4).
Theme: how to conduct oneself (13,2.4).

13,10-17: 11 ἀνακύψαι, 12 προσεφώνησεν, 13 ἐπέθηκεν, ἐδόξαζεν, 14 ἐν αὐταῖς, ἐρχόμενοι, τοῦ σαββάτου, 15 ὁ κύριος, 16 θυγατέρα ᾿Αβραάμ, ὁ σατανᾶς, 17 ἀντικείμενοι, ἐνδόξοις

13,18-21: 18 ἔλεγεν οὖν, ὁμοία ἐστίν, ὁμοιώσω, 19 πετεινά, κατεσκήνωσεν

13,22-30: 22 διεπορεύετο, [᾿Ιερουσαλήμ], 24 οὐκ ἰσχύσουσιν, 25 ἀφ᾿ οὗ ἄν, ἄρξησθε, 26 ἄρξεσθε, 27 ἀδικίας, 28 ὁ κλαυθμός
Theme: the messianic meal (13,29).

13,31-35: 31 ἐν αὐτῇ τῇ ὥρᾳ, τινες Φαρισαῖοι, πορεύου, ἐντεῦθεν, 32 πορευθέντες, τελειοῦμαι, 33 οὐκ ἐνδέχεται, προφήτην, ἀπολέσθαι
Theme: the messianic reign being described as "the house of his/one's father" signifying the people Israel (13,35).

14,1-14: 1 τινος τῶν ἀρχόντων τῶν Φαρισαίων, σαββάτῳ, καὶ αὐτοί, 2 ἔμπροσθεν, 3 νομικούς, τῷ σάββατῳ, 4 ἡσύχασαν, ἐπιλαβόμενος, 5 τίνος ὑμων, τοῦ σαββάτου, [5] πεσεῖται, 6 οὐκ ἴσχυσαν, ἀνταποκριθῆναι, πρὸς ταῦτα, 7 ἐξελέγοντο, 8 ἐντιμότερος, 9 τόπον, ἄρξῃ, 10 πορευθείς, ἀνάπεσε, τόπον, συνανακειμένων, 11 ὁ ταπεινῶν ἑαυτὸν ὑψωθήσεται, 12 ἄριστον, δεῖπνον, φώνει, φίλους, συγγενεῖς, γείτονας, καὶ αὐτοί, ἀνταπόδομα, 14 οὐκ ἔχουσιν, ἀνταποδοῦναι, ἀνταποδοθήσεται
Particular settings reflected the LQ source: dining in the home of Pharisees who had not made a decision about Jesus (14,1).
Theme: a particular eschatology which assumed that the resurrection of the just will happen at the same time as the general resurrection (14,14).

14,15-24: 15 συνανακειμένων, 16 ἄνθρωπός τις, δεῖπνον, 17 δείπνου, ἤδη, ἕτοιμα, 18 ἤρξαντο, ὁ πρῶτος, ἀγρόν, ἠγόρασα, ἐξελθών, ἐρωτῶ, 19 ἕτερος, ἠγόρασα, δοκιμάσαι, ἐρωτῶ, 21 παραγενόμενος, ὀργισθείς, ταχέως, εἰς τὰς πλατείας καὶ ῥύμας τῆς πόλεως, ὧδε, 22 τόπος, 23 ἀνάγκασον, γεμισθῇ, 24 δείπνου
Style: asides ("Zwischenbemerkungen") (14,15).

14,25-35: 25 στραφείς, 26 τις ἔρχεται, μισεῖ, 27 βαστάζει, ὀπίσω, 28 οἰκοδομῆσαι, πρῶτον, καθίσας, δαπάνην, 29 θεμέλιον, μὴ ἰσχύοντος, ἐκτελέσαι, θεωροῦντες, ἄρξωνται, ἐμπαίζειν, 30 οἰκοδομεῖν, οὐκ ἴσχυσεν, 31 πρῶτον, ἐρχομένῳ, 32 πόρρω, πρεσβείαν, ἀποστείλας, ἐρωτᾷ, πρὸς εἰρήνην, 33 ἀποτάσσεται, 35 κοπρίαν - εὔθετον

15,1-10: 1 δὲ ... ἐγγίζοντες, ἁμαρτωλοί, 2 διεγόγγυζον, ἁμαρτωλούς, 4b ἀπολέσας, ἀπολωλός, 5 ἐπιτίθησιν, 6 φίλους, γείτονας, συγχάρητε, ἀπολωλός, 7 ἁμαρτωλῷ, μετανοοῦντι, 8 ἐπιμελῶς, ἕως οὗ, 9 φίλας, γείτονας, συγχάρητε, 10 ἁμαρτωλῷ μετανοοῦντι
Theme: stories filled with anti-Pharisaic sentiment (15,2).

15,11-32: 11 ἄνθρωπός τις εἶχεν, 12 τὸν βίον, 13 συναγαγών, ὁ νεώτερος, χώραν μακράν, διεσκόρπισεν, 14 δαπανήσαντος, ἐγένετο, κατὰ τὴν χώραν, ἤρξατο, ὑστερεῖσθαι, 15 πορευθεὶς ἐκολλήθη, ἑνί, πολιτῶν, ἔπεμψεν, εἰς τοὺς ἀγρούς, 16 ἐπεθύμει, γεμίσαι v.l., [16] κοιλία v.l., 17 ὧδε, [17] ἔφη, 18 ἀναστάς, ἐνώπιόν σου, 19 ἄξιος, 20 ἀναστάς, μακράν, ἀπέχοντος, ἐσπλαγχνίσθη, 22 δότε ... εἰς, 23 εὐφρανθῶμεν, 24 ἀπολωλώς, εὐφραίνεσθαι, 25 ἐν ἀγρῷ, ὡς, ἐρχόμενος, ἤγγισεν, 26 προσκαλεσάμενος, ἕνα, παίδων, ἐπυνθάνετο, 27 ἀπέλαβεν, 28 ὠργίσθη, 29 ἐντολήν, παρῆλθον, φίλων, εὐφρανθῶ, 32 εὐφρανθῆναι, νεκρός

16,1-13: 1 ἄνθρωπός τις ἦν, πλούσιος, οἰκονόμον, διεβλήθη, διασκορπίζων, 2 φωνήσας, ἀκούω περὶ σοῦ, ἀπόδος, 3 τί ποιήσω, ὁ κύριός μου, ἀφαιρεῖται, σκάπτειν, οὐκ ἰσχύω, ἐπαιτεῖν, 4 τί, 5 προσκαλεσάμενος, χρεοφειλετῶν, τοῦ κυρίου ἑαυτοῦ, τῷ πρώτῳ, 6 δέξαι, καθίσας, ταχέως, 7 ὀφείλεις, δέξαι, 8 ὁ κύριος, ἀδικίας, φρονίμως, ἐποίησεν, υἱοὶ τοῦ αἰῶνος τούτου, υἱοὺς τοῦ φωτός, 9 φίλους, ἀδικίας, ἵνα ὅταν ἐκλίπῃ, δέξωνται, 10 ἐλαχίστῳ
Style: characters in the parables often asked and then answered their own questions (16,3.4); the use of the title ὁ κύριος (16,8).

16,14-31: 15 ἐστε οἱ δικαιοῦντες ἑαυτούς, καρδίας, 17 παρελθεῖν, 19 εὐφραινόμενος, καθ᾽ ἡμέραν, λαμπρῶς, 20 ἐβέβλητο, 21 ἐπιθυμῶν, ἐρχόμενοι, 22 ἀγγέλων, κόλπον, 23 ἐπάρας τοὺς ὀφθαλμούς, ἀπὸ μακρόθεν, κόλποις, 24 ἐλέησόν με, ὀδυνῶμαι, 25 μνήσθητι, ἀπέλαβες, ἐν τῇ ζωῇ, ὧδε, παρακαλεῖται, ὀδυνᾶσαι, 26 ἐστήρικται, ὅπως, διαβῆναι, διαπερῶσιν, 28 ὅπως, διαμαρτύρηται, καὶ αὐτοί, τόπον, 30 εἶπεν· οὐχί, πάτερ Ἀβραάμ, ἀλλ᾽, μετανοήσουσιν
Themes: a view that equated πτωχοί with ἁμαρτωλοί. This viewpoint contended that the poor have been chosen by God, even if they are sinners, rather than the rich and righteous (16,15); a concept of paradise and Hades (16,23); the messianic reign being described as "the house of his/one's father" signifying the people Israel (16,27); reference to Moses and the prophets (16,29); the special meaning of the term to "rise from the dead" (16,31).

17,1-10: 1 ἀνένδεκτόν ἐστιν, 2 λυσιτελεῖ, 3 προσέχετε ἑαυτοῖς, μετανοήσῃ, 5 τῷ κυρίῳ, πρόσθες, 6 ὁ κύριος, φυτεύθητι, 7 τίς δὲ ἐξ ὑμῶν, ἀροτριῶντα, ἐκ τοῦ ἀγροῦ, παρελθών, ἀνάπεσε, 8 ἑτοίμασον, τί, δειπνήσω, περιζωσάμενος, διακόνει, πίω, μετὰ ταῦτα, 9 ἔχει χάριν, διαταχθέντα, [οὐ δοκῶ] v.l., 10 ὃ ὠφείλομεν

17,11-19: 13 καὶ αὐτοί, ἦραν φωνήν, ἐπιστάτα, ἐλέησον, 14 πορευθέντες, ἱερεῦσιν, 15 δοξάζων, 16 ἔπεσεν ἐπὶ πρόσωπον, πόδας, εὐχαριστῶν, 18 εὐρέθησαν, 19 ἀναστάς, σέσωκεν
Particular settings reflect the LQ source: encounters with priests (17,14).
Themes: how God treats the ungrateful (17,11-19); an interest in the Samaritans (17,16).

17,20-37: 21 ὧδε, 22 ὅτε, ἐπιθυμήσετε, ἰδεῖν, 23 ὧδε, 24 ἀστραπὴ ἀστράπτουσα, 28 ἠγόραζον, ἐπώλουν, ἐφύτευον, ᾠκοδόμουν, 29 ἔβρεξεν, 30 κατὰ τὰ αὐτά, 31 ἐν ἐκείνῃ τῇ ἡμέρᾳ, εἰς τὰ ὀπίσω
Style: the loose construction of relative sentences (17,31).

18,1-8: 1 πρὸς τὸ δεῖν, 2 κριτής, φοβούμενος, ἐντρεπόμενος, 3 χήρα, ἐκδίκησον ἀντιδίκου, 4 ἐπὶ χρόνον, μετὰ δὲ ταῦτα, ἐν ἑαυτῷ, φοβοῦμαι, ἐντρέπομαι, 5 παρέχειν, χήραν, ἐκδικήσω, ἐρχομένη, 6 ὁ κύριος, τί, κριτής, ἀδικίας, 7 ἐκδίκησιν, ἐκλεκτῶν, βοώντων, 8 ἐκδίκησιν
Style: use of the title ὁ κύριος (18,6).

18,9-14: 9 πεποιθότας ἐφ᾽ ἑαυτοῖς ὅτι εἰσὶν δίκαιοι, ἐξουθενοῦντας, 10 προσεύξασθαι, 11 σταθείς, πρὸς ἑαυτόν, εὐχαριστῶ, 12 τοῦ σαββάτου, 13 μακρόθεν οὐδὲ τοὺς

ὀφθαλμοὺς ἐπᾶραι, ἔτυπτεν τὸ στῆθος, ἁμαρτωλῷ, 14 δεδικαιωμένος, ὁ ὑψῶν ἑαυτὸν ταπεινωθήσεται, ὁ δὲ ταπεινῶν ἑαυτὸν ὑψωθήσεται
Particular settings reflected the LQ source: going to the temple to pray (18,10).
Themes: stories filled with anti-Pharisaic sentiment (18,9); contemptuous and righteous behavior (18,9-14).

19,1-10: 2 καὶ ἰδού, ὀνόματι καλούμενος, καὶ αὐτός, 3 τίς ἐστιν, ἡλικίᾳ, 4 ἔμπροσθεν, ἤμελλεν, 5 ὡς, ἦλθεν ἐπὶ τὸν τόπον, σπεύσας, μεῖναι, 6 ὑπεδέξατο, χαίρων, 7 διεγόγγυζον, ἁμαρτωλῷ, εἰσῆλθεν, καταλῦσαι, 8 σταθείς, τὸν κύριον, ἐσυκοφάντησα, ἀποδίδωμι, 9 καθότι - υἱὸς Ἀβραάμ, 10 ἀπολωλός
Themes: various people's claims to salvation (19,1-9); contemptuous and righteous behavior (19,8).

19,11-27: 11 προσθείς, ἐγγὺς εἶναι Ἰερουσαλήμ, δοκεῖν, μέλλει, 12 χώραν μακράν, 14 πολῖται, ἐμίσουν, ἀπέστειλαν, πρεσβείαν, ὀπίσω, βασιλεῦσαι, ἐφ᾿, 15 ἐπανελθεῖν, βασιλείαν, φωνηθῆναι, διεπραγματεύσαντο, 16 παρεγένετο, ὁ πρῶτος, 17 ἐλαχίστῳ, ἐπάνω, 21 ἐφοβούμην, 22 ἐκ τοῦ στόματός σου, 24 ἄρατε, [27] ὧδε
Theme: how to conduct oneself (19,17).

19,28-48: 28 ἔμπροσθεν?, 29 ὡς, ἤγγισεν, καλούμενον, 35 ἐπεβίβασαν, 37 τὸ πλῆθος, χαίροντες, αἰνεῖν, [37?] ἤδη, 40 [ὅτι], 41 ὡς, ἤγγισεν, ἔκλαυσεν ἐπ᾿ αὐτήν, 42 εἰ, ἔγνως, πρὸς εἰρήνην, ἐκρύβη, ὀφθαλμῶν, [43] συνέξουσιν, 44 ἀνθ᾿ ὧν, ἔγνως, ἐπισκοπῆς, (ἀγορ.); 47 καθ᾿ ἡμέραν, 48 τί
Theme: stories filled with anti-Pharisaic sentiment (19,37).

20,9-19: 10 ἐξαπέστειλαν, δείραντες, 11 προσέθετο, πέμψαι, δείραντες, ἐξαπέστειλαν, 12 προσέθετο, πέμψαι, τραυματίσαντες, 13 ὁ κύριος τοῦ ἀμπελῶνος, πέμψω, ἐντραπήσονται, 18 πεσὼν ἐπ᾿, 19 αὐτῇ τῇ ὥρᾳ, πρὸς αὐτούς?
Style: characters in the parables often asked and then answered their own questions ("Selbstgespräch") (20,13); the use of asides ("Zwischenbemerkung") (20,16).
20,20-26: 20 δικαίους - ἀρχῇ, 21 ὀρθῶς λέγεις, 23 κατανοήσας, 26 οὐκ ἴσχυσαν

21,5-38: 9 πτοηθῆτε, 12 τὰς χεῖρας αὐτῶν, [πρὸ τοῦ], 16 συγγενῶν, [16?] φίλων, [18] ἀπόληται, 20 δὲ ... ἤγγικεν, 21 φευγέτωσαν, ἐν μέσῳ, χώραις, 22 ἐκδικήσεως, πλησθῆναι, 23 λαῷ τούτῳ, 24 μαχαίρης, πληρωθῶσιν, 25 ἀπορίᾳ, [25] ἀντιποκρ, 26 ἐπερχομένων, 28 ἀνακύψατε, ἐπάρατε τὰς κεφαλάς, ἐγγίζει, ἀπολύτρωσις, 34 προσέχετε ἑαυτοῖς, βαρηθῶσιν, καρδίαι, ἐπιστῇ, ἡ ἡμέρα ἐκείνη, 35 ἐπεισελεύσεται, καθημένους, ἐπὶ πρόσωπον, 36 ἐκφυγεῖν, 37 ὄρος τὸ καλούμενον Ἐλαιῶν. LQ + A
Style: the loose construction of relative sentences (21,34).
Themes: reference to the division between parents and children over Christianity (21,16); a time of battle, when Christians were fleeing (21,21); apocalyptic terrors (21,26.35).

22,1-6: 1 ἤγγιζεν δέ, 3 σατανᾶς

22,14-20: 14 ἡ ὥρα, ἀνέπεσεν, 15 ἐπεθύμησα, πρὸ τοῦ με παθεῖν, 16 πληρωθῇ, 17 δεξάμενος, εὐχαριστήσας, διαμερίσατε, 18 ἀπὸ τοῦ νῦν, ἕως οὗ, 19 λαβών, 20 δειπνῆσαι
Themes: the messianic meal (22,18); the meaning of Jesus' death (22,19a) as "einfache göttliche Notwendigkeit" (p. 622; so also "die göttliche Willensbestimmung" (p. 620).

22,21-23: 21 ἡ χεὶρ τοῦ παραδιδόντος, 23 καὶ αὐτοί, συζητεῖν, μέλλων. "nach LQ"
Theme: the meaning of Jesus' death (22,22) as "einfache göttliche Notwendigkeit" (p. 622).

22,24-27: 24 τὸ τίς, 26 ὁ νεώτερος, 27 ἐν μέσῳ. LQ or A

22,28-30: 28 διαμεμενηκότες, πειρασμοῖς, 29 διατίθεμαι, διέθετο, βασιλείαν, 30 ἔσθητε. "nach LQ"
Theme: the messianic meal (22,30).

22,31-34: 31 [ὁ κύριος], Σίμων Σίμων, ὁ σατανᾶς, 32 ἵνα μὴ ἐκλίπῃ, στήρισον. "wohl aus LQ"
Theme: Jesus' prayer for Peter's faith (22,32; cf. 17,6).

22,35-38: 35 ὑστερήσατε, 36 βαλλάντιον, πωλησάτω, ἀγορασάτω, μάχαιραν, 37 τελεσθῆναι, 38 ὧδε "Die Rede vom Schwerdt, dem Luk. eigenthümlich, aber unzweifelhaft ihrer Grundlage nach aus Q herrührend (Ws. Mt-Ev., 395), jedoch durch die Hand von LQ hindurchgegangen".
Theme: a time of battle, when Christians were fleeing (22,36).

22,39-53: 39 κατὰ τὸ ἔθος, 40 γενόμενος δὲ ἐπὶ τοῦ τόπου, 41 ὡσεί, 44 ὡσεί, 47 προήρχετο, 48 φιλήματι, 52 παραγενομένους, 53 καθ᾽ ἡμέραν, τὰς χεῖρας, ὑμῶν ἡ ὥρα. "... die Annahme einer anderen Quelle (ist) fast unabweislich. So 7. Aufl. Aber auch schon die Erzählung von Wege nach dem Oelberg ist ganz von Mk unabhängig".
Style: the direct question with εἰ (22,49).

22,54-71: 55 μέσος but other versions have ἐν μέσῳ, 56 παιδίσκη, ἀτενίσασα, 59 διαστάσης, ἐπ᾽ ἀληθείας, 61 στραφείς, ὁ κύριος, 63 οἱ συνέχοντες, ἐνέπαιζον, δέροντες, 65 βλασφημοῦντες, 66 ὡς, 69 ἀπὸ τοῦ νῦν, 71 ἀπὸ τοῦ στόματος αυτοῦ. "So könnte Lk mit seinem Bericht, der auch im Uebrigen von Mt Mk unabhängig ist, doch die ursprüngliche Darstellung haben".

23,1-12: 1 τὸ πλῆθος, 2 ἔθνος, κωλύοντα, 5 ὧδε, 8 ἀκούειν περὶ αὐτοῦ, 11 ἐξουθενήσας, ἐμπαίξας, ἐσθῆτα, λαμπράν, 12 ἐν αὐτῇ τῇ ἡμέρᾳ. "Pilatus und Herodes, zeigt nur in v. 3 mit A Verwandtschaft, sonst dem Lk ganz eigenthümlich, aus LQ".

23,13-25: 13 ἄρχοντας, 15 ἄξιον, 19 βληθείς v.l. βεβλημένος, 20 προσεφώνησεν, 23 ἐπέκειντο, 25 βεβλημένον. "'sachlich = Mk 15,6-15, aber in der Darstellung fast ganz abweichend.' 7. Aufl. V. 13-16 ist zunächst ganz selbständig".

23,26-32: 26 ὡς, ἐπέθηκαν αὐτῷ, 27 πλῆθος, ἐκόπτοντο, 28 στραφείς, ἐφ᾽ ἑαυτὰς κλαίετε, 29 κοιλίαι, μαστοί, 30 ἄρχονται, πέσετε. "... bis auf V. 26 dem Lk ganz eigenthümlich, aus LQ".
Themes: a concern for the relationship of children to mothers (23,28); the treatment of the godless (23,31).

23,33-38: 33 καλούμενον, 34 ὁ δὲ Ἰησοῦς ἔλεγεν· πάτερ, ἄφες αὐτοῖς, οὐ γὰρ οἴδασιν τί ποιοῦσιν. διαμεριζόμενοι δὲ τὰ ἱμάτια αὐτοῦ ἔβαλον κλήρους, 35 ἄρχοντες, ὁ ἐκλεκτός, 36 ἐνέπαιξαν. "von Lk in einer von Mk 15,22-32 ganz unabhängigen Form erzählt".

23,39-43: 39 ἐβλασφήμει, 40 φοβῇ σὺ τὸν θεόν, 41 ἄξια, ἀπολαμβάνομεν, 42 μνήσθητι, βασιλείαν, 43 παραδείσῳ. "... eine dem Lk eigenthümliche Erzählung".
Theme: a concept of paradise and Hades (23,43).

23,44-56: 44 ὡσεί, 46 εἰς χεῖρας, πνεῦμα, 47 ἐδόξαζεν, ὄντως, 48 τύπτοντες τὰ στήθη, 49 οἱ γνωστοί, 54 σάββατον, 56 σάββατον, ἡσύχασαν. "entspricht der Darstellung Mk 15,33-47, ist aber doch wohl von ihr unabhängig".

24,1-12: [3] τοῦ κυρίου, 4 ἀπορεῖσθαι, ἐν ἐπέστησαν (the simple form in [4]), ἀστραπτούσῃ, 6 ὧδε, μνήσθητε, 7 παραδοθῆναι εἰς χεῖρας, ἁμαρτωλῶν, 8 ἐμνήσθησαν, 11 ἐφάνησαν, ὡσεί. "wohl nicht 'frei nach Mk 16,1-8', sondern nach LQ".

24,13-35: 13 ἐν αὐτῇ τῇ ἡμέρᾳ, ἀπέχουσαν, 14 καὶ αὐτοί, 15 συζητεῖν, 16 ὀφθαλμοί, 17 ἀντιβάλλετε, 19 προφήτης, 20 ἄρχοντες, [20] ὅπως, 21 μέλλων, λυτρούσθαι, 23 καὶ ὀπτασίαν, 27 ἀρξάμενος ἀπὸ Μωϋσέως ἐν πᾶσι τοῖς προφήταις διηρμήνευσεν (LQ variant), 28 πορρώτερον, 29 μεῖνον, κέκλικεν ἤδη ἡ ἡμέρα, 30 ἐπεδίδου, 31 διηνοίχθησαν, ὀφθαλμοί, 32 διήνοιγεν, 33 αὐτῇ τῇ ὥρᾳ, 34 ὄντως, ὁ κύριος, 35 καὶ αὐτοί. "dem Lk eigenthümlich und ohne Zweifel aus LQ".

24,36-49: 36 ἐν μέσῳ, 37 πτοηθέντες, ἐδόκουν, 42 ἐπέδωκαν, 44 πληρωθῆναι, 45 διήνοιξεν, συνιέναι, 48 μάρτυρες. "dem Lk eigenthümlich nach einer an Joh 20,19-23 erinnernden Ueberlieferung".
Style: later verses recall previous ones (24,45 hearkens back to 24,32).

24,50-53: 50 ἐπάρας τὰς χεῖρας, 51 διέστη, 52 καὶ αὐτοί, 53 αἰνοῦντες v.l. "Lk folgt eben hier einer anderen Tradition".

The special LQ vocabulary are listed below in alphabetical order. Preceding some of the words will be found the letters A, B, C and D. These refer to the classification of B. Weiss's L vocabulary as rendered by B.S. Easton, who used it in an attempt to prove the literary unity of a written L source[14]. The four divisions are: A especially characteristic

---

14. B.S. EASTON, *Linguistic Evidence for the Lucan Source L*, in *JBL* 29 (1910) 139-180 (esp. p. 145-167); *The Special Source of the Third Gospel*, in *JBL* 30 (1911) 78-103. In the first article Easton relied on the following works of B. Weiss to assemble his list: *Lukas* (⁹1901), *Die Quellen des Lukasevangeliums* (1907) and *Die Quellen der synoptischen Ueberlieferung* (1908) (*Linguistic Evidence*, p. 139). Furthermore, Easton added some terms which were not found as L in the works of Weiss. These are: ἁμαρτωλός A1, ἄρχω A5, ἐγένετο ἐν τῷ followed by the infinitive A7, καὶ αὐτός A11, ἀμήν B4, ἀνακλίνω B5, δόξα B20, ἐλεέω B22, ἔμπροσθεν B25, εὐφραίνω B30, θαυμάζω ἐπί B33, πίμπλημι in the temporal sense B42, and συγγενεύς and cognates B49.

Words from Easton's list marked with an asterisk invite comparison but they are not identical to terms in the list of J. Weiss (e.g. A1* for ἁμαρτωλός). Though we found no definite reference in J. Weiss that he identified A10 εὐλογέω as LQ vocabulary (cf. p. 314), we mention it here because B. Weiss (1908, p. 113) and Easton (1910, p. 147) both identified this term as stemming from L. On the issue of vocabulary, comparison should also be made with B.S. EASTON, *The Gospel According to St. Luke*, Edinburgh - New York, 1926, p. xxiv-xxvii, which drew upon his two *JBL* articles (p. xxiv).

of L; B probably characteristic of L; C cited by Weiss as characteristic of L, and possibly corroborative; D classed by Weiss as characteristic of L on insufficient (?) evidence. The number following the letter is that assigned to the word in Easton's list in each section.

III. Alphabetical List

	ἀγαθός	1,53 LQ; 12,18.19 LQ
	ἀγαλλιᾶν	10,21 LQ; cf. 1,47
B1	ἄγγελος	9,52 LQ; 16,22 LQ; cf. 7,24
	ἀγοράζειν	9,13 LQ?; 14,18.19 LQ; 17,28 LQ; [19,45] LQ; 22,36 LQ
	ἀγρός	14,18 LQ; 15,25 LQ; cf. 15,15; 17,7
	ἀδικία	16,8.9 LQ; 18,6 LQ; cf. 13,27
	ἀθετεῖν	7,30 LQ; 10,16 LQ
B3	αἰνεῖν	2,13.20 LQ; 24,53 LQ v.l.; cf. 19,37; also Acts 2,47; 3,8.9
	αἴρειν	6,29 LQ; 6,30 LQ; 11,22 LQ; 19,24 LQ; cf. 11,52
C72	αἴρειν φωνήν	11,27 LQ; cf. 17,13; see also Acts 2,14; 4,24
	αἰτεῖν τινά τι	11,11 LQ; cf. 12,48
	ἀκούειν τι περί τινος	16,2ᶜ LQ; 23,8 LQ; cf. 9,9
	ἀκούειν τὸν λόγον	an LQ expression meaning faith; cf. 10,39
†A1*	ἁμαρτωλός	5,8 LQ; 6,32 LQ; [7,34] LQ; 7,37.39 LQ; 13,2 LQ; 15,1.2.7.10 LQ; 18,13 LQ; 19,7 LQ; but 5,30.32 and 24,7 are from Mk (p. 386-387, n. 3); yet later (p. 502) Weiss assigned 24,7 to LQ
	ἀναγκάζειν	14,23ᶜ LQ
C1	ἀναδεικνύναι	10,1 LQ
C1	ἀνάδειξις	1,80 LQ
	ἀνακαθίζειν	7,15 LQ; see Acts 9,40
B6	ἀνακύπτειν	21,28 LQ; cf. 13,11
	ἀναπαύειν	12,19 LQ; cf. 11,24
A2	ἀναπίπτειν	11,37 LQ; 14,10 LQ; 17,7 LQ; 22,14 LQ
†	ἀντί-	LQ showed a preference for words with this prefix.
†C2	ἀνθ᾽ ὧν	1,20 LQ; 12,3 LQ; 19,44 LQ; see also Acts 12,23
	ἄνθρωπος εὐδοκίας	2,14 a genitive standing for an adj.? p. 331.
	ἄνθρωπός τις	10,30 LQ and 15,11 LQ, "ohne jede Einleitung" (p. 459); 12,16 LQ; 14,16 LQ; 16,1 LQ
	ἄνθρωπός τις πλούσιος	12,16 LQ; cf. 16,1
	ἀνιστάναι	1,39 LQ: 4,16.29 LQ; 15,18.20 LQ; 17,19 LQ; cf. 11,8
†	ἀνταποδιδόναι, ἀνταπόδομα	14,12.14 LQ; [21,15] LQ; 24,17 LQ; but cf. 14,6 LQ
†	ἀνταποκρίνεσθαι	14,6 LQ
†	ἀντειπεῖν	21,15 Luke?
†	ἀντιβάλλειν	24,17 was not specifically designated as LQ
†	ἀντίδικος	[12,58 LQ]; 18,3 LQ
†	ἀντικαλεῖν	14,12 but not marked as LQ
†B7	ἀντικείμενοι	13,17 LQ; but 21,15?
	ἀντιλαμβάνειν	1,54 LQ; cf. 10,40: συναντιλαμβάνειν

†	ἀντιλέγειν	2,34 LQ; but 20,27 Lk?
†	ἀντιμετρεῖν	6,38[15]
†	ἀντιπαρελθεῖν	10,31 LQ
	ἄξιος	7,4 LQ; 12,48ᶜ LQ; 15,19 LQ; 23,15.41 LQ
†	ἀπαιτεῖν	6,30 LQ; 12,20 LQ
B8	ἀπέχειν	7,6 LQ; 24,13 LQ; cf. 15,20
A3	ἀπὸ τοῦ νῦν	1,48 LQ; 5,10 LQ; 12,52 LQ; 22,18.69 LQ; see Acts 18,6
	ἀποδιδόναι	4,20 LQ; 7,42 LQ; [9,42] LQ; cf. 10,35; 12,59 LQ; 16,2 LQ; 19,8 LQ; but 20,25 is from Mk
†A4	ἀπολαμβάνειν	6,34 LQ; 15,27 LQ; 16,25 LQ; 18,30 LQ; 23,41 LQ
	ἀπολλύναι	11,51 LQ; 13,3.5.33 LQ; 15,4b.6.24 LQ; 19,10 LQ; 21,18 LQ
	ἀπορεῖσθαι	the simple form in [24,4] is LQ; but 9,7 διαπορεῖν was Luke
B9	ἀπορία	21,25 LQ; cf. 24,4; see also Acts 25,20
	ἀποτάσσειν	9,61 LQ; cf. 14,33
B11	ἄριστον	14,12 LQ; cf. 11,37
C5	ἄροτρον	9,62 LQ; 17,7 LQ
	ἀρχαί	20,20 LQ?; cf. 12,11
A5	ἄρχεσθαι	3,8 LQ; 4,21 LQ; 7,24.38.49 LQ; 12,1.45 LQ; 13,25.26 LQ; 14,9.18.29 LQ; 15,14 LQ; cf. 23,30
C6	ἄρχων	12,58 LQ; 14,1 LQ; 23,13.35 LQ; 24,20ᶜ LQ; cf. 18,18
	ἀστράπτειν	10,18 LQ; 11,36 LQ; 17,24 LQ; 24,4 LQ; cf. 9,29; see also Acts 9,3; 22,6
	ἀτενίζειν	4,20ᶜ LQ; cf. 22,56
	αὐτῇ τῇ ὥρᾳ	and similar expressions 2,38 LQ; 7,21 with ἐν LQ; 10,21 with ἐν LQ; 13,31 with ἐν LQ; 20,19 with ἐν LQ; 24,33 LQ; cf. 12,12
	αὐτοί	13,4 possibly reflected the emphasized form contained in LQ
	αὐτός	"ohne Betonung"; common in LQ; so 1,22
	ἀπό	reference to past time 7,45 LQ; 13,25 LQ; cf. 13,7
B12	ἀφαιρεῖσθαι	10,42 LQ; cf. 16,3
	ἄφρων	11,40 LQ; 12,20 LQ
	βαλλάντιον	10,4 LQ; cf. 12,33; 22,35 LQ
	βάλλειν	23,19 LQ; 23,25 LQ; cf. 16,20
	βάπτισμα	7,29 LQ; cf. 12,50
	βαρεῖν	21,34 LQ; cf. 9,32
	βασιλεία	1,33 LQ; 4,5 LQ; 22,29 LQ; 23,42 LQ; cf. 19,15
B13	βασιλεύειν	ἐπί τινα 1,33 LQ; cf. 19,14
	βαστάζειν	10,4 LQ; 11,27 LQ; 14,27 LQ; cf. 7,14; but 22,10 is A

15. Note the list of words using the prefix ἀντι-, all mentioned with reference to this term in 6,30, p. (386-)387, n. 3.

	βίβλος	20,42 LQ; also in Acts 1,20; 7,42; but 3,4 "lukanische Citationsformel"
	βίος	21,4 LQ; cf. 15,12; but 8,43 is Luke
	βλασφημεῖν	23,39ᶜ LQ; cf. 22,65
	βοᾶν	[9,38] LQ; 18,7 LQ; but 18,38 Luke?
	βρέφος	1,41.44 LQ; 2,12.16 LQ; cf. 18,15; also in Acts 7,19
	βρέχειν	7,38 LQ; 7,44 LQ; cf. 17,29; see also Jas 5,17
B2	γείτων	15,6.9 LQ; cf. 14,12
	γεμίζειν	14,23 LQ; 15,16 LQ v.l.
A6 A7* B14	γίνεσθαι	4,25 LQ; 6,36 LQ; 12,40 LQ; cf. 13,4; 15,14
	γινώσκειν	19,42.44 LQ; cf. 12,47
B15	γνῶσις	1,77 LQ; cf. 11,52; 12,47.48
B15	γνωστοί	2,44 LQ; cf. 23,49
	δάκτυλος	11,20 LQ
	δανειστής	7,41 LQ
	δαπανᾶν	15,14 LQ; cf. προσ- 10,35; δαπάνη 14,28
	δειπνεῖν	14,12.16.17.24 LQ; 22,20 LQ; cf. 17,8
	δείρειν	12,47.48 LQ; 20,10.11 LQ; cf. 22,63; see also Acts 5,40; 16,37; 22,19
	δέχεσθαι	2,28 LQ; 16,6.7.9 LQ; cf. 22,17
	διά-	LQ had a predilection for compounds with this prefix[16]
	διαβαίνειν	16,26 LQ
	διαβάλλειν	16,1ᶜ LQ
	διαγγέλλειν	9,60 LQ
B16	διαγογγύζειν	15,2 LQ; 19,7 LQ
	διαγρηγορεῖν	9,32 Lk or LQ?
	διαδιδόναι	11,22 LQ; but 18,22 was Luke
B18	διακονεῖν	8,3 LQ; 10,40 LQ; 12,37 LQ; 17,8 LQ
	διαλαλεῖν	1,65 LQ, but 6,11 was Luke
	διαλείπειν	7,45 LQ
	διαλογίζεσθαι	1,29 LQ; 3,15 LQ; cf. 12,17
	διαμαρτυρεῖν	16,28 LQ
	διαμένειν	1,22 LQ; 22,28 LQ
	διαμερίζειν	11,17.18 LQ; 12,52.53 LQ; 22,17 LQ; while 23,34 from Mk?
	διανεύειν	1,22 not specifically designated as LQ
	διανοίγειν	24,31.32.45 LQ
	διανυκτερεύειν	6,12 Luke
	διαπερᾶν	16,26 LQ
	διαπορεῖν	[24,4] LQ; 9,7 Luke
	διαπορεύεσθαι	13,22 LQ; but 6,1; 18,36 and Acts 16,4 were due to Luke
	διαπραγματεύεσθαι	19,15 LQ

16. See p. 399, n. 1; cf. διασώσῃ 7,3, and διακονεῖν 8,3, which were not mentioned in the note, but cited in the text ad loc.

	διαρρήσσειν	5,6 LQ; but 8,29 was Luke
	διασείειν	3,14 LQ
	διασκορπίζειν	1,51 LQ; 16,1 LQ; cf. διεσκόρτισεν 15,13, p. 524, n. 1
C10	διατάσσειν	3,13 LQ; cf. 17,9; but Weiss ascribed 8,55 to Luke
	διατίθεσθαι...βασιλείαν	22,29 LQ; cf. 12,32
	διασῴζειν	7,3; also in Acts 5 times
	διδόναι	7,15 LQ; 12,51 LQ; cf. 9,42; 15,22
	διδόναι εἰς	12,51 LQ; cf. 15,22
B23	διδόναι ἐλεημοσύνην	12,33 LQ
C11	διϊστάναι	24,51 LQ; cf. 22,59; see Acts 27,28
	δίκαιος	16,15 LQ; 18,9 LQ; cf. 20,20
	δικαιοῦν	18,14 LQ; 7,29 LQ; 16,15 LQ; cf. 10,29: LQ or Lk?, p. 459: "in anderem Sinne"
B19	δοκεῖν	12,40.51 LQ; 13,2.4 LQ; 17,9 LQ, v.l.; 19,11 LQ; 24,37 LQ
	δοκιμάζειν	12,56 LQ; 14,19 LQ
	δοξάζειν	2,20 LQ; 7,16ᶜ LQ; 13,13 LQ; 23,47 LQ; but 5.25.26 are Luke
	ἑαυτοῦ	7,39.49 LQ; 12,17 LQ; cf. 3,8
A8	ἐγγίζειν	7,12 LQ; 10,9.11 LQ; 12,33 LQ; 15,1.25 LQ 19,41 LQ; 21,20.28; cf. 22,1 and 22,47; the following are Lk?: 18,35.40; 19,29.37; 21,8¹⁷
	ἐγγὺς Ἰερουσαλήμ	Acts 1,12 LQ; cf. 19,11
	ἔθνος	23,2 LQ; cf. 7,5
	εἰ	"mit Ind. d. Aor. = utinam" 19,42 LQ; cf. 12,49
	εἰπέ	with Inf. 10,40 LQ; cf. 12,13
C14	εἰρήνη	Q and LQ: 1,79; 2,14.29; 7,50; 10,5.6; 12,51; 14,32; 19,42; cf. 11,21
	εἰς	1,44 LQ; 4,23 LQ meaning ἐν; 9,61 LQ; 11,7 LQ
	εἰς	5,3 LQ; 15,15 LQ; 15,26 LQ; cf. 11,46
	εἰσέρχεσθαι	7,6.36.44.45 LQ; cf. 19,7; also in Acts 1,13.21; 11,3 etc.
	εἰσπορεύεσθαι	11,33 LQ; cf. 18,24; but the present form in 8,16 was Luke
	ἐκβάλλειν	10,2.35 LQ; cf. 12,49
	ἐκδικεῖν	18,3.5 LQ
C15	ἐκδίκησις	18,8a LQ; cf. 21,22
	ἐκλέγεσθαι	10,42 LQ; cf. 14,7
B21	ἐκλείπειν	16,9 LQ; 22,32 LQ
	ἐκλεκτός	23,35 LQ; cf. 9,35; 18,7
	ἐκφεύγειν	cf. 22,36
	ἐλάχιστος	16,10 LQ; 19,17 LQ; cf. 12,26

---

17. At one point J. Weiss assigned with certainty 11 occurrences of ἐγγίζω to LQ (p. 631) without enumerating them, but compare his previous list (p. 614). In his discussion of the use of the term in 24,28 he cited also 18,35; 19,29 which would lead one to conclude that, in his view, the use of the term in ch 24 was possibly from Luke (p. 658).

B22* ἐλεεῖν   16,24 LQ; 17,13 LQ; cf. 18,38.39?
      ἔλεος   see ποιεῖν
B23   ἐλεημοσύνη   12,33 LQ; cf. 11,41
      ἐλθών   11,7 LQ [sic]; but he may have been comparing the
                                uses of aorist participles, e.g. 11,7; cf. 12,37
B24   ἐμπαίζειν   14,29 LQ; 23,11.36 LQ; but 18,32?
†C17 ἐμπιμπλάναι   1,53 LQ; cf. 6,25
      ἐμπίπτειν   10,36 LQ; [14,5 LQ]; cf. 6,39
B25* ἔμπροσθεν   14,2 LQ; 19,28 LQ?; cf. 5,19; 19,4
      ἐν αὐταῖς   13,14 LQ
      ἐν αὐτῇ τῇ ἡμέρᾳ   24,13 LQ; cf. 23,12
      ἐν τῇ ἡμέρᾳ ἐκείνῃ   10,12 LQ; 17,31 LQ; cf. 21,34
      ἐν αὐτῇ τῇ ὥρᾳ   13,31 LQ; see αὐτῇ τῇ ὥρᾳ
      ἐν αὐτῷ τῷ καιρῷ   13,1 LQ; cf. 13,31 LQ
      ἐν ἑαυτῷ   18,4 LQ; cf. 18,11
      ἐν μέσῳ   2,46 LQ; 21,21 LQ; 22,27.55 LQ; 24,36 LQ; cf.
                                8,7

      ἐνδέχεσθαι   13,33 LQ; cf. 17,1
      ἔνδοξος   7,25 LQ; 13,17 LQ
      ἐντεῦθεν   13,31 LQ; but at 4,9 was an addition of Luke (p.
                                362). However, later Weiss claimed it reflected LQ
                                (p. 509)
C18   ἔντιμος   7,2 LQ; 14,8 LQ
      ἐντολή   1,6 LQ; cf. 15,29
      ἐντρέπεσθαι   18,2.4 LQ; cf. 20,13
      ἐνώπιον   1,15 LQ; 16,15 LQ; cf. 15,18
      ἐξαποστέλλειν   1,53 LQ; 20,10.11 LQ?
      ἐξέρχεσθαι   11,7 LQ [sic]; cf. 14,18
      ἐξῆς   7,11 LQ; cf. 9,37; three times in Acts
C19   ἐξουθενεῖν   18,9 LQ; 23,11 LQ; also Acts 4,11
B27* ἐξουσία τοῦ πατεῖν   10,19 LQ - authority with the inf.; cf. 12,5
      ἐπ᾽ ἀληθείας   4,25 LQ; cf. 22,59; but 20,21 was from A[18]
B28   ἐπαίρειν   6,20 LQ; 11,27 LQ; 16,23 LQ; 18,13 LQ; 21,28
                                LQ; 24,50 LQ
      ἐπαιτεῖν   16,3 LQ; cf. 18,35
C20   ἐπανέρχεσθαι   10,35 LQ; 19,15 LQ
      ἐπάνω   10,19 LQ; 11,44 LQ; cf. 19,17; but 4,39 was Luke
      ἐπειδή   11,6 LQ
      ἐπέρχεσθαι   21,26 LQ; 21,35 LQ; cf. 11,22; but 1,35 was Luke
      ἐπί   5,12; 17,16 LQ
      ἐπί   with the accusative of time 4,25 LQ; 10,35 LQ; cf.
                                18,4; often in Acts
      ἐπὶ γῆς   2,14 and the striking position of the phrase; see also
                                7,17 LQ; cf. Acts 26,13?

18. *Ibid.*, p. 635. Whereas Weiss asserted in his discussion of 22,59 that the phrase in 20,21
derived from A, he did not previously indicate that at 20,21. Instead he simply stated that both
4,25 and 22,59 came from LQ (cf. p. 591).

	ἐπιβιβάζειν	10,34 LQ; 19,35 LQ
	ἐπιβλέπειν	1,48 LQ; cf. 9,38
	ἐπιδιδόναι	4,17 LQ; 11,11.12 LQ; 24,30.42 LQ
	ἐπιθυμεῖν	15,16 LQ; 16,21 LQ; 22,15 LQ; cf. 17,22
	ἐπικεῖσθαι	5,1 LQ; 23,23 LQ
	ἐπιλαβεῖν	14,4 LQ; cf. 9,47
	ἐπιμελεῖσθαι	15,8 LQ; cf. 10,34
B29	ἐπισκέπτεσθαι	1,68.78 LQ; 7,16 LQ; cf. 19,44; see also Acts 15,14
	ἐπιστάτης	5,5 LQ; 9,49 LQ; 17,13 LQ; but 8,24.45 were Luke
C21	ἐπιστρέφειν	17,31 LQ; Mk 13,16; cf. 9,62
	ἐπιτιθέναι	10,30 LQ; 13,13 LQ; 15,5 LQ; cf. 23,26
	ἔρχεσθαι	12,54 LQ; 13,14 LQ; 15,25 LQ; 16,21 LQ; 18,5 LQ; cf. 14,31
	ἐρχόμενος	6,47 LQ; 14,26 LQ
C24	ἐρωτᾶν	5,3 LQ; 7,3.36 LQ; 11,37 LQ; 14,18.19 LQ; cf. 14,32
	ἐσθής	23,11 LQ; cf. 24,4; see also Acts 1,10; 10,30; 12,21
	ἕτεροι	9,56.59.61 LQ; cf. 14,19
A9	ἑτοιμάζειν	1,17.76 LQ; 2,31 LQ; 9,52 LQ; 12,20.47 LQ; 14,17 LQ; 22,9.12.13 LQ; cf. 17,8
D6	ἐφιστάναι	2,9.38 LQ; 4,39 LQ; 10,40 LQ; 20,1 LQ; 21,34 LQ; 24,4 LQ; see also Acts 12,7; 17,5
	εὔθετος	9,62 LQ; cf. 14,35
	εὑρίσκειν	9,36 LQ?; cf. 17,18
B30*	εὐφραίνεσθαι	12,19 LQ; 15,23ff.ᶜ LQ; 15,24 LQ; 15,29 LQ; 15,32 LQ; 16,19 LQ
	εὐχαριστεῖν	18,11 LQ; 22,17 LQ; cf. 17,16
	ἔχειν	with negation 7,42 LQ; 14,14 LQ; cf. 7,40
	ἔχειν	with the inf. 7,40.42 LQ; 12,4.50 LQ; 14,14 LQ; cf. 12,5
	ἔχειν	7,42 LQ; 9,58 LQ; 12,4.17 LQ; "not having" as also an expression of embarrassment; cf. 11,6
B31/C40	ἐχθροί, μισοῦντες	1,71 LQ; the terms stood in parallel in LQ; cf. 6,27
	ἕως	15,8 LQ; 22,18 LQ; cf. 13,8
	ζωή	1,75 LQ *v.l.*; 12,15 LQ; cf. 16,25
	ἤ	in a comparison 17,2 LQ; cf. 15,7
	ἤδη	11,7 LQ; 12,49 LQ; 14,17 LQ; [19,37?] LQ; cf. 7,6
C26	ἡλικία	2,52 LQ; 19,3 LQ
	ἡμέρᾳ ἐκείνῃ	10,12 LQ; 21,34 LQ cf. 17,31
	ἡσυχάζειν	23,56 LQ; so 14,4
†C27	θεμέλιον τιθέναι	6,48 LQ - cf. p. 519
	θεμέλιος	14,29 LQ
	θεωρεῖν	10,18 LQ; cf. 14,29
	θυγάτηρ Ἀβραάμ	13,16 LQ
	ἰδεῖν	2,26 LQ; cf. 17,22; also Acts 2,31

	ἱερεῖς	1,5 LQ; 10,31 LQ; 17,14 LQ; cf. 20,1; also Acts 4,1; 6,7
B34	Ἰερουσαλήμ	the Hebrew form 2,25.38.41.43.45 LQ; [9,31] LQ; 9,51.53 LQ; 13,4.22 LQ; etc. in LQ; so 10,30
	ἱματισμός	7,25 LQ; 9,29 LQ?; but also Acts 20,33
	ἵνα ὅταν ἐκλίπῃ	16,9 LQ; cf. 22,32
	ἱστάναι	13,39 [sic] LQ; cf. 22,30[19]
	καθ᾽ ἡμέραν	9,23 LQ?; 11,3 LQ; 16,19 LQ; 19,47 LQ; cf. 22,53
	καθαιρεῖν	1,52 LQ; cf. 12,18
	καθῆσθαι	1,79 LQ; cf. 21,35
	καθίζειν	14,28 LQ; cf. 16,6
	καθότι	19,9 LQ; cf. 1,7; Acts 2,24
	καί	5,2 LQ; 7,12 LQ; cf. 10,39
	καὶ αὐτοί	often in LQ: 2,50 LQ; [9,36] LQ; 11,46 LQ; 14,1.12 LQ; 16,28 LQ; 17,13 LQ; [18,34] LQ; 22,23 LQ; 24,14.35.52 LQ
A11*	καὶ αὐτός	1,17 possibly LQ; 1,22 LQ; 5,1 LQ; 19,2 LQ continued the Hebrew style
	καὶ ἰδού	7,37 LQ; cf. 19,2
	καὶ ὀπτασίαν	1,22 LQ; cf. 24,23; see also Acts 26,19
C32	καλεῖν/καλεῖσθαι ὀνόματι	1,61 LQ; cf. 19,2
C45	καλεῖσθαι	1,36 LQ; [6,15] LQ; 7,11 LQ; 8,2 LQ; [9,10 LQ]; 10,39 19,2.29 LQ; 21,37 LQ; 23,33 LQ; but 6,15 was Luke; the term occurred often in Acts
	καλούμενος	1,61; 19,1 LQ
	καρδία	1,17 LQ; 2,35 LQ; 16,15 LQ; cf. 21,34
	κατά	with the accusative of place 15,14 LQ; cf. 10,32 γινέσθαι; 10,35
	κατὰ τὰ αὐτά	6,23.26 LQ; cf. 17,30
A12	κατὰ τὸ ἔθος	1,9 LQ; 2,42 LQ; cf. 22,39
	καταλύειν	2,7 LQ; 19,7.12 LQ; 22,11 appeared initially as LQ, then A? and finally definitely A
	κατανοεῖν	12,24.27 LQ; cf. 20,23; also Acts 7,31.32; 11,6; 27,39; but Lk 6,41 was Q
	καταπατεῖν	12,1 LQ; cf. 8,5
	κατασκηνοῦν	13,19 LQ; cf. 9,58
	κεῖσθαι	2,12.16.34 LQ; cf. 12,19
B36	κλαίειν	19,41 LQ; 23,28 LQ
	κλαυθμός	13,28 LQ; cf. 6,25
	κλίνειν	9,12 LQ?; 24,29 LQ
C33	κοιλία	1,15.41.42.44 LQ; 2,21 LQ; 11,27 LQ; 15,16 LQ v.l. N[25]; "especially" 23,29 LQ[20]

19. J. WEISS, *Lukas*, [8]1892, p. 623. Chapter 13 extends only to verse 35. There is a reference at 13,25, but it is difficult to determine whether this was the verse Weiss intended.

20. *Ibid.*, p. 473, n. 2; cf. p. 525, where only 11,27 and 23,29 were mentioned in the context of 15,16.

	κολλᾶσθαι	15,15 LQ; cf. 10,11; also in Acts 5,13; 8,29; 9,26; 10,28; 17,34
C34	κόλπος	16,22.23 LQ; cf. 6,38
	κόπτειν	23,27 LQ; cf. 8,52
	κόπριον	13,8 LQ; cf. 14,35
	κρίνειν	7,43 LQ; 12,57 LQ
	κριτής	18,2.6 LQ
C36	κρύπτειν	10,21 LQ; 19,42 LQ; cf. 18,34
A13	κύριος	frequent LQ designation for Jesus: [7,13ᶜ]; 10,1.39; 11,39; 12,42; 13,15; 16,8; 17,5.6; 18,6; 19,8; 22,31.61; 24,3.34; but the term at 19,31 was from A. He also cited usage in Acts 1,21; 2,47; 4,33; 5,14; 8,16.22.24.25.26.39; 9,1.10.11.13.15.17 and so on[21]
	κύριος	with the genitive 10,2 LQ; 12,46 LQ; 16,3.5 LQ; 16,8 without the genitive LQ; cf. 20,13
	κύριος	πρός 20,19 LQ; cf. 12,41
	κωλύειν	6,29 LQ; 23,2 LQ; cf. 11,52
	λαμβάνειν	22,19 LQ
	λαμπρός	23,11 LQ; cf. 16,19; also Acts 10,30;26,13 and Jas 2,2.3
	λαὸς οὗτος	21,23 LQ; the term was used in opposition to "the chosen ones" 18,7
	λέγειν	3,7 LQ; 4,22 LQ; 6,20 LQ
	λέγειν οὖν	3,7 LQ; 10,2 LQ; cf. 13,18
	λόγος θεοῦ	5,1; 11,28 LQ; cf. 8,11
A14	λύτρωσις	1,68 LQ; 2,38 LQ; cf. 21,28; 24,21; see also Acts 7,35
	μακράν	7,6 LQ; 15,20 LQ; 19,12 LQ
	μακρόθεν	18,13 LQ; cf. 16,23
	μάρτυς	24,48 LQ; cf. 11,48
	Μάρθα Μάρθα	10,41ᶜ LQ; cf. 22,31; see Acts 9,4
	μαστοί	23,29 LQ; cf. 11,27
	μάχαιρα	21,24 LQ; cf. 22,36
C41	μέλλειν	7,2; 9,31? LQ; 10,1 LQ; 19,4.11 LQ; 22,23 LQ; 24,21 LQ
B38	μιμνήσκεσθαι	1,54.72 LQ; 23,42 LQ; 24,6.8 LQ; cf. 16,25
	μένειν	24,29 LQ; cf. 19,5
	μετὰ ταῦτα	10,1 LQ; 12,4 LQ; 17,8 LQ; 18,4 LQ; but 5,27 was Luke
	μετανοεῖν	13,3.5 LQ; 15,7.10 LQ; 16,30 LQ; cf. 17,3
	μήτι	11,36 LQ; 12,4 LQ; cf. 12,11; but 8,51 was Luke
	μισεῖν	1,71 LQ; 6,22 LQ; 14,26 LQ; cf. 19,14; but 6,27 and 16,13 were from Q
	μονογενής	7,12 LQ; cf. 9,38; but 8,42 Luke

---

21. *Ibid.*, p. 651. See also p. 401, n. 1. At Lk 24,3 Weiss noted that the phrase τοῦ κυρίου Ἰησοῦ which was found in some versions, stemmed from LQ.

	ναί	12,5 LQ; cf. 11,51
	νεανίσκος	7,14 LQ; see Acts 5,10
	νεκρός	15,32 LQ; cf. 9,60
	νεώτερος	15,12.13 LQ; 22,26 LQ; Acts 5,6
	νομικός	7,30; 10,25; 11,45.46.52; 14,3 all LQ; but never in Acts
	ὀδυνᾶσθαι	2,48 LQ; 16,24.25 LQ; see Acts 20,38
	οἰκοδομεῖν	4,29 LQ; 6,48.49 LQ; 7,5 LQ; 11,47.48 LQ; 12,18 LQ; 14,28 LQ; 14,30 LQ; 17,28 LQ
	οἰκονόμος	12,42 LQ; cf. 16,1
	οἰκτείρειν	6,36 LQ; earlier it was possibly LQ - p. 394, 561
	ὀλίγος	5,3 LQ; 7,47 LQ; 10,42 LQ, v.l. N[25]; cf. 12,48
	ὅμοιος / ὁμοιοῦν	13,18 LQ; note the parallelism between the words in the verse; cf. 7,31[22]
†B39	ὁμοίως	3,11 LQ; 5,10 LQ; [5,33: besides 5,33 the term was found 10 times in LQ] LQ; 6,31 LQ; 10,32 LQ
	ὄντως	24,34 LQ; cf. 23,47
C77	ὀπίσω	7,38 LQ; 9,62 LQ; 14,27 LQ; 17,31 LQ; cf. 19,14
	ὅπως	besides 10,2 Q only from LQ: 2,35 LQ; 7,3 LQ; 16,26.28 LQ; [24,20] LQ; cf. 11,37
	ὁρᾶν	7,39 LQ; cf. 11,38
	ὀργίζεσθαι	14,21 LQ; cf. 15,28
	ὀρεινός	1,39.65 LQ
	ὀρθῶς	7,43 LQ; 10,28 LQ; cf. 20,21
C45	ὄρος τὸ καλούμενον	Ἐλαιῶν 21,37 LQ
	ὅστις	approximately 13 of the 17 occurrences in Lk came from LQ, but were not specified initially; cf. 12,1; in a later reference he listed 1,20 LQ; 2,4.10 LQ; 7,37.39 LQ; 8,3 LQ; 15,7 LQ
	ὅτε	17,22 LQ, but was not found at 23,44 in N[26]; is it possible that Weiss intended 23,33?; cf. 19,40
	ὀφείλειν	7,41 LQ; 11,4 LQ; 16,7 LQ; cf. 13,4 and 17,10
	ὀφθαλμοί	2,30 LQ; 10,23 LQ; 24,16.31 LQ; cf. 19,42; also Acts 26,18
	ὄφις, σκορπίος	10,19 LQ; 11,11.12 LQ; the same connection of words was observed
	οὐκ ἔχειν ποῦ	9,58 LQ; cf. 12,17
†	οὐκ ἰσχύειν	6,48 LQ; 13,24 LQ; 14,6 LQ; 14,29 LQ; 14,30 LQ; 16,3 LQ; cf. 20,26; but 8,43 was Luke
B40	οὖς	1,44 LQ; 9,44 LQ; cf. 4,21; also Acts 11,22
A15	οὐχί, ἀλλά	emphatic negation 1,60 LQ; 12,51 LQ; 16,30 LQ; cf. 13,3
	ὄχλοι	9 (10) times from Q or LQ out of total of 15 in Lk; cf. 9,18
	παῖς	1,54.69 LQ; 7,7 LQ; 15,26 LQ; 22,56 LQ; but see 12,45

22. *Ibid.*, p. 408.

	πανδοχεύς	10,34 LQ
A16	παρά	with the acc. meaning "more than" 3,13 LQ; cf. 13,2
	παραδιδόναι	1,71.74 LQ; 21,12 LQ; 22,21.53 LQ; 23,46 LQ; 24,7 LQ; cf. 9,44
C47	παραγίνεσθαι	7,4.20 LQ; 11,6 LQ; 12,51 LQ; 14,21 LQ; 19,16 LQ; 22,52 LQ; but 8,19 is Luke
	παράδεισος	23,43 LQ
	παρακαλύπτειν	9,45 LQ
†	παράκλησις	2,25 LQ; 6,24 LQ; 16,25 LQ
	παρατιθέναι	10,8; The term was from Q and LQ respectively; cf. 11,6
C49	παρέρχεσθαι	11,42 LQ; 12,37 LQ; 15,29 LQ; 16,17 LQ; 17,7 LQ; cf. 18,37
†	παρέχειν	6,29 LQ; 7,4 LQ; 11,7 LQ; 18,5 LQ
†	πᾶς ὁ ἐρχόμενος	14,26 but not labeled as LQ[23]
	παύειν	5,4 LQ; cf. 11,1
	πείθειν	11,22 LQ; 18,9 LQ
	πειρασμός	4,13 LQ; 11,4 LQ; 22,28 LQ; but 8,13 was Luke
C50	πέμπειν	4,26 LQ; 7,6.10.19 LQ; 15,15 LQ; 20,11.12.13 LQ; cf. 16,24
B41	περιζωννύναι	12,35.37 LQ; 17,8 LQ; cf. 12,35
	περισσός	12,48 LQ; cf. 12,4
	πετεινόν	9,58 LQ; 13,19ᶜ LQ; cf. 8,5
	πίνειν	7,34 LQ; 17,8 LQ; cf. 12,19
	πίπτειν	17,16 LQ; but 5,12 was Luke
	πίπτειν ἐπί	13,4 LQ; 20,18 LQ; 23,30 LQ; cf. 11,17
	πλατεῖα	14,21 LQ; cf. 10,10; but 13,26 was Luke
C52	πλῆθος	1,10 LQ; 2,13 LQ; 5,6 LQ; 19,37 LQ; 23,1.27 LQ; but 6,17 and 8,37 were from Luke
	πληροῦν	1,20 LQ; 2,40 LQ; 3,5 in a citation LQ; 4,21 LQ; 7,1 LQ; 9,31 LQ - though at an earlier point in the commentary listed as 9,31 LQ?; 21,22.24 LQ; 22,16 LQ; 24,44 LQ; cf. 2,40
	πλησθῆναι	1,15.23.41.57.67 LQ; 2,6.21.22 LQ; 4,28 LQ; 5,7 LQ; cf. 21,22; but 5,26 and 6,11 were Luke
	πνεῦμα	23,46 LQ; cf. 8,55; Acts 7,59
C53	ποιεῖν	1,25 LQ; 2,48 LQ; 3,11 LQ; 6,23.26.27.31 LQ; 10,37 LQ; 12,43 LQ; 16,8 LQ; cf. 9,15
A17	ποιεῖν τὸ ἔλεος μετά	1,58.72 LQ; cf. 10,37
C54	πολῖται	15,15 LQ; 19,14 LQ; Acts 21,39
	πορεύεσθαι	7,22 LQ; 9,12.13.52 LQ; 13,32 LQ; 14,10 LQ; 15,15 LQ; 17,14 LQ; 22,8 LQ; and never in Mk
B43	πορρώτερον	24,28 LQ; cf. 14,32

23. *Ibid.*, p. 386-387, n. 3. At the end of the list Weiss wrote: "fast alles in LQ". He was contrasting this phrase with εἴ τις ἔρχεται (14,26).

912 APPENDIX I

	πούς	7,38 LQ; 8,41 LQ; 10,39 LQ; 17,16 LQ; cf. 8,35; an additional 7 times in Acts
C55	πρεσβεία	14,32 LQ; cf. 19,14
	πρὸ τοῦ	2,21 LQ; [21,12] LQ; 22,15 LQ; cf. 11,38
	πρὸ τοῦ	with infinitive 2,21 LQ; cf. 22,15; also Acts 23,15
C9*	προσδαπανᾶν	10,35 LQ; 15,14 LQ simple form; 14,28 LQ; but Weiss assigned Mk 5,26 to Deutero-Markus
	προέρχεσθαι	1,17 LQ; cf. 22,47; also in Acts 12,10; 20,5.13
	πρὸς εἰρήνην	14,32ᶜ LQ; 19,42 LQ
	πρὸς ταῦτα	14,32 LQ; 18,1 LQ; 19,42 LQ; 20,19 LQ?; cf. 14,6
	πρὸς τὸν κύριον	7,19 LQ
	προσεύχεσθαι	1,10 LQ; 2,37 LQ; cf. 18,10; see also Acts 3,1; but 19,46 was from Mk
C58	προσέχειν ἑαυτοῖς	12,1 LQ; 17,3 LQ; 21,34 LQ; but προσέχειν without the ἑαυτοῖς was from A; cf. 20,46
	προστιθέναι	3,20 LQ; 12,31 LQ, but later Weiss assigned 12,31 to Q [p. 550, 587, n. 1]; 17,5 LQ; 19,11 LQ; cf. 20,12; 12,25 was also assigned to Q; also προστίθεσθαι in Acts 12,3
	προσφωνεῖν	13,12 LQ; cf. 23,20; but 6,13 was from Luke and 7,32 was from Q; see also Acts 21,40 and 22,2
	πρόσωπον	12,56 LQ; 17,16 LQ; 21,35 LQ; but 5,12 was Luke; see also Acts 17,26
	προφήτης	Jesus as prophet 7,16.39 LQ; 13,33 LQ; 24,19 LQ; see also Acts 3,22; 7,37; 7,52f.ᶜ
	προσκαλεῖσθαι	7,18ᶜ LQ; 15,26 LQ; 16,5 LQ; cf. 18,16
	πρῶτον	14,28.31 LQ; cf. 11,38
	πρῶτος	16,5 LQ; 19,16 LQ; cf. 14,18
	πτοεῖσθαι	24,37 LQ; cf. 21,9
	πτωχός	6,20 LQ; cf. 2,24
	πυνθάνεσθαι	15,26 LQ; cf. 18,36
	πωλεῖν	12,6 LQ; 12,33 LQ; cf. 17,28
B32*	σάββατον	6,6 LQ; 14,1.3.5 LQ; 18,12 LQ; 23,54.56 LQ; the singular form due to LQ; cf. 13,14.15
	σατανᾶς	13,16 LQ; 22,3.31 LQ; cf. 10,18; the idea of Satan as the opponent was unique to LQ
†	σκάπτειν	6,48 LQ; 13,8 LQ; 16,3 LQ; 13,8 and 16,3 were listed on p. 386-387, n. 3 without the specific LQ designation, but on p. 398 with it
†B46	σκιρτᾶν	1,41.44 LQ; cf. 6,23
	σκύλλεσθαι	7,6 LQ; cf. 8,49
	σοφία	11,49 LQ; cf. 7,35
C60	σπεύδειν	2,16 LQ; cf. 19,5
B47	σπλαγχνίζεσθαι	7,13 LQ; 10,33 LQ; 15,20 LQ
	στῆθος	23,48 LQ; cf. 18,13
	στῆναι	18,11 LQ; 19,8 LQ; cf. 18,40; also Acts 2,14; 5,20; 11,13; 17,22; 25,18; 27,21
B48	στηρίζειν	9,51 LQ; 22,32 LQ; cf. 16,26

	στόμα	1,64.70 LQ; 4,22 LQ; 6,45 LQ; 11,54ᶜ LQ; 19,22 LQ; 22,71 LQ; 21,15?
A18	στρέφειν / στραφείς	7,9.44 LQ; 9,55 LQ; 10,23 LQ; 14,25 LQ; 22,61 LQ; 23,28 LQ
B2	συγγενής	1,36.58 LQ; 2,44 LQ; 14,12 LQ; cf. 21,16; also Acts 10,24
	συγχαίρειν	1,58 LQ; 15,6.9 LQ
	συζητεῖν	22,23 LQ; cf. 24,15; see also Acts 6,9; 9,19
C63	συκοφαντεῖν	3,14 LQ; cf. 19,8
	συνάγειν	12,17.18 LQ; 15,13 LQ
	συνανακεῖσθαι	7,49 LQ; 14,10.15 LQ
	συνέχεσθαι	12,50 LQ; [19,43] LQ; cf. 4,38; 22,63; also Acts 28,8
	συνιέναι	2,50 LQ; 24,45 LQ; cf. 18,34; see also Acts 7,25; but 8,10 was Luke
	σώζειν	7,50 LQ; cf. 17,19
	ταπεινοῦν / ταπεινός	14,11 LQ; 18,14 LQ; cf. 1,52
	ταχέως	16,6 LQ; cf. 14,21
	τέκνον	19,44ᶜ LQ; cf. 23,28²⁴
C78	τελεῖν	2,39 LQ; 12,50 LQ; [18,31] LQ; 22,37 LQ
	τελειοῦν	13,32 LQ; cf. 14,29
	τί	1,62 LQ; 22,24 LQ; cf. 19,48
	τί ποιεῖν	16,3 LQ; cf. 12,17
B51	τίθεσθαι...ἐν τῇ καρδίᾳ	1,66 LQ; cf. 9,44
	τις τῶν ἀρχόντων τῶν Φαρισαίων	14,1 LQ; cf. 13,31 LQ
	τίς	6,47 LQ; 7,39 LQ; 9,46 LQ; 10,22 LQ; 16,4 LQ; 17,8 LQ; 18,6 LQ; 19,3 LQ; cf. 12,5
	τις	frequent in LQ
	τίς ἐξ ὑμῶν	11,5 LQ; 17,7 LQ; cf. 14,5
	τίς...ἕξει	11,5 LQ; 15,11 LQ; cf. 13,6
	τις ἔρχεται	14,26 LQ
	τίς ἐστιν	7,39 LQ; 10,22 LQ; cf. 19,3; but 4,34 was from Luke
C65	τόπος	2,7 LQ; 4,17 LQ; [6,17 LQ; 9,10 LQ]; 10,1.32 LQ; 14,9.10.22 LQ; 16,28 LQ; 19,5 LQ; cf. 11,1
B52	τόπος	without the demonstrative pronoun 10,32, LQ; 19,5 LQ; 22,40 LQ; cf. 10,1
	τόπος	an undetermined location 10,32 LQ; 11,1 LQ; 19,5 LQ; cf. 22,40
	τραῦμα / τραυματίζειν	10,34 LQ; cf. 20,12; see also Acts 19,16ᶜ
†	τύπτειν	[12,45 LQ]; 18,13 LQ; 23,48 LQ; cf. 6,29; but v.l. 22,64 was from Mk
C66	τύπτειν τὰ στήθη	18,13 LQ; 23,48 LQ
	υἱός	with a genitive 4,22 LQ; 16,8 LQ; 20,34.36 LQ
	υἱὸς 'Αβραάμ	19,9 LQ

24. *Ibid.*, p. 644. Weiss made reference to 19,49, but no such verse exists. Lk 19,44 contains the term τέκνα. Lk 23,28 contains a reference to ἐφ' ἑαυτὰς κλαίετε καὶ ἐπὶ τὰ τέκνα ὑμῶν.

	ὑποδεικνύναι	12,5 LQ; cf. 6,47
C67	ὑποδέχεσθαι	10,38 LQ; 19,6 LQ; also Acts 17,7 and Jas 2,25
C68	ὑπολαμβάνειν	7,43 LQ; cf. 10,30: "hier anders gebraucht"
	ὑστερεῖν	15,14 LQ; 22,35 LQ
	or ὑστερεῖσθαι	15,14 LQ; 22,35 LQ
	ὕψιστος	1,32.76 LQ; 6,35 LQ; cf. 1,35; but 8,28 was not assigned to any source
	φαίνεσθαι	24,11 LQ; cf. 9,8
	φάναι	7,40.44 LQ; cf. 15,17: the form from LQ stands in place of εἶπεν in 15,17 in other versions
	φεύγειν	21,21 LQ; cf. 22,36
	φίλημα	7,45 LQ; cf. 22,48
	φίλοι	7,6 LQ; 14,12 LQ; 15,6.29 LQ; 16,9; [21,16?] LQ; 15 occurrences in Lk from LQ
	φίλοι...γείτονες	14,12 LQ; 15,6.9 LQ
	φοβεῖσθαι	1,50 LQ; 12,5 LQ; 18,2.4 LQ; 19,21 LQ; 23,40 LQ; also in Acts 10,2.22.35; 13,16.26
	φρόνιμος	12,42 LQ; cf. 16,8
	φυλάσσειν	11,28 LQ; cf. 18,21; see Acts 7,53
	φυτεύειν	13,6 LQ; 17,6 LQ; cf. 17,28; 20,9?
	φωνεῖν τινα	14,12 LQ; 16,2 LQ; cf. 19,15
	χαίρειν	approximately 10 unspecified times in LQ; cf. 19,6.37; two other instances from Q
	χαρίζεσθαι	7,42.43 LQ, but in Acts it was from Luke; cf. 7,21
†C73	χάρις	1,30 LQ; 2,40.52 LQ; 17,9 LQ; cf. 6,32; see also Acts
C80	χείρ	1,66.71.74 LQ; 22,21 LQ
	χήρα	2,37 LQ; 4,25.26 LQ; 7,12 LQ; cf. 18,3.5; also in Acts. 6,1; 9,39.41 and Jas 1,27
	χρεοφειλέτης	7,41 LQ; 16,5 LQ
	χρῄζειν	12,30 LQ from Q; cf. 11,8
	χριστός	2,11.26 LQ; cf. 9,20
	χώρα	2,8 LQ; 12,16 LQ; cf. 21,21
C74	χώρα μακρά	15,13 LQ; 19,12 LQ
	ὧδε	4,23 LQ; 9,27.33.41 LQ; 11,31.32 LQ; 14,21 LQ; 15,17 LQ; 16,25 LQ; 17,21.23 LQ; [19,27] LQ; 22,38 LQ; 23,5 LQ; 24,6 LQ LQ; cf. 9,12
C75	ὥρα	1,10 LQ; 10,21 LQ; 12,39 LQ; 22,14.53 LQ; cf. 12,12
	ὥρα τοῦ θυμιάματος	1,10 LQ; cf. 22,14
	ὡς	in the temporal sense 1,23.41.44 LQ; 2,15.39 LQ; 4,25 LQ; 5,4 LQ; 7,12 LQ; 11,1 LQ; 12,58 LQ; 15,25 LQ; 19,5.29 LQ; 20,37 LQ; 22,66 LQ; 23,26 LQ; cf. 19,41

	ὡσεί	1,56? later without the question mark; 3,22?; 3,23?; 9,14 LQ? 9,28 LQ later with a question mark; 22,41.44.59 LQ; 23,44 LQ; 24,11 LQ[25]
B53	ὥστε	4,29 LQ; 9,52 LQ - *v.l.*; cf. 20,20

---

25. *Ibid.*, p. 635 should be compared with the list on p. 433.

APPENDIX II

THEORIES OF LUKAN PRIORITY

William LOCKTON (1922) took issue with the belief of Jackson and Lake that a solution for the synoptic problem had been found and with Moffatt's assumption of Markan priority[1]. The MAs posed a significant obstacle especially for the latter. For Lockton Lk represented the primitive Gospel derived from oral tradition, as suggested by the Prologue. Peter and John were singled out as primary sources in general and perhaps Joanna and Manaen for information about Herod[2]. The formation of Lk was dated around 48 AD, though Lockton conceded that some parts of it had possibly previously been set down in writing. The place was not so clearly defined, but the return journey to Antioch was proposed[3].

Lockton referred to the reception of his theory of Lukan priority in the preface to *The Three Traditions in the Gospels* (1926): "By all but a few critics his earlier work was well received, but several, in spite of the statement to the contrary in the preface of the former book, seemed to think that the theory of the priority of Luke would be useless for the explanation of the gospels as a whole, though for special reasons it might seem to give more or less satisfactory results when applied to the Resurrection narratives"[4]. Here it was noted that 22,61 could only have come from Peter[5]. In addition to the Johannine tradition, there was the tradition belonging to Peter and James which descended from a common, primitive Gospel and thus were two strains of one source[6]. Lockton noted the similarity between Acts 6,12-14 and Mk concerning the accusation made against Jesus and Stephen with regard to the Temple. Likewise, Lockton recognized that a certain similarity existed between the Markan portrayal of Jesus before Pilate with that of Jesus before Herod in Lk. The latter was simply explained as the refusal to indulge Herod's curiosity, while the former was more puzzling. Lockton thus concluded that Mark had mistakenly taken the Lukan material and inserted it into the account of Pilate's trial[7]. Peter and John did not abandon Jesus and so Lockton deduced that they were the sources for information concerning the trials.

1. LOCKTON, *The Origin of the Gospels*, in *CQR* 94 (1922) 216-219, p. 216, 217.

2. *Ibid.*, p. 226.

3. *Ibid.*, p. 236. Acts was composed fourteen or more years after the writing of the Gospel. Mk, like Lk, was also written at Antioch at about the same time (49 AD), but Mt, produced at Corinth, was assigned a date of "50 or 51" (p. 233, 234). Mark redacted Lk in the light of oral tradition for the purpose of highlighting the Petrine perspective.

Lockton continued to employ the principles outlined in this article in his application of the theory for the Resurrection Narrative and account of the Virgin Birth in *The Resurrection and the Virgin Birth* (1924). Both the article and the book had their origins in papers presented to the Winchester Clerical Association (p. vi).

4. LOCKTON, *The Three Traditions of the Gospels*, London, 1926, p. v. Note the summary of Lockton's position (p. 304-306). See especially his discussion of Mark's redaction of Lk for the events in the palace of the high priest, the denials of Peter and the mocking (p. 183-273). A review in the *CQR* called this work: "A book of extraordinary originality and of real learning" (*Certain Alleged Gospel Sources*, p. [ii]).

5. LOCKTON, *Three Traditions*, p. 49.

6. *Ibid.*, p. 75. The tradition derived from James was superior to that ascribed to Peter and John, though the latter two sometimes offered a more primitive form of an account (p. 306).

7. *Ibid.*, p. 205.

Markan redaction of Lk involved occasional simple additions of vocabulary or the conflation of material as in the case of the two questions asked of Jesus (22,67.70) combined into one (Mk 14,61). Lockton credited Luke with the placing of the mockery prior to the Sanhedrin trial[8]. The influence of Deutero-Isaiah on the Lukan account of the mockery was also highlighted. The Matthean account was regarded as a combination of material from the other two Synoptics. The MA in 22,64 was due to the fact that Mark omitted the phrase, rendering the command to prophesy "meaningless". In what follows, however, Lockton offered contradictory evidence: he had just indicated that Mark had omitted the phrase τίς ἐστιν ὁ παίσας σε;, not more than a few lines later he added: "The statement that they 'covered' His face is also omitted, the question, 'Who is he that struck thee?' added to Mark's account from Luke being thus deprived of meaning"[9].

It was also Mark who shifted the Sanhedrin trial to nighttime offering "a doublet of the first part of Luke's account". All of this was done to fulfill Talmudic requirements. Luke's account squared with the Talmud in referring to the legal body as the Sanhedrin. Once more the Markan redactional technique may be described as a compilation, this time involving Lk and the Talmud. In this particular segment of the Gospel Mark incorporated material from the Johannine tradition.

For the account of Peter's denials Mark was predominantly dependent upon the Petrine tradition as mediated through Lk, though his version also agreed in minor details with the Johannine account[10]. Because of the variations in the order of the denials, Lockton ascribed this feature to the tradition of James. The Markan method was thus one of alternating between two accounts, the Petrine for the first denial and the Jacobean for the remainder with which details from John were intermixed. The intermingling of the Johannine and Jacobean traditions may have already taken place prior to the composition of the account of the denials.

Lockton perceived similarity between the mockery by soldiers as recounted in Mk with that of Herodian soldiers in Lk. However, Mark was not dependent upon Lk at this point, rather he was drawing upon Jn. Mark must have been aware of the event but opted to omit it, though Lockton did not suggest why[11]. The "prophecy" that Pilate wished to have Jesus scourged, while reported in Lk, was only carried out in the other Synoptics.

In a comparison of the account of the death of Jesus in the Gospel and that of Stephen in Acts, Lockton surmised that they were due either to Luke or to his source[12]. The Acts account was judged to be earlier and "the primitive gospel tradition" was consequently adapted to it. The author was thought to be extremely conversant with the LXX as well as contemporary Jewish literature using the *Testaments of the Twelve Patriarchs* as a model.

Lk, derived essentially from the traditions descending from Peter and James, was composed of large blocks of these materials. Mk, on the other hand, reflects a composite of a much broader range of smaller units of authentic source material, which have been so redacted, particularly in the passion, that they provided a different account from Lk and Jn.

---

8. *Ibid.*, p. 219.

9. *Ibid.*, p. 220-221.

10. *Ibid.*, p. 232.

11. *Ibid.*, p. 254: "Though the story of the mocking before Herod is omitted from Mark, yet other material from the Petrine tradition preserved in Luke is conflated with John in the compilation of the account of the second gospel".

12. *Ibid.*, p. 299.

Lockton continued to advance his theory in *Certain Alleged Gospel Sources* (1927) in response to criticisms leveled against his earlier book[13]. Critics faulted him for not dealing more directly with Streeter, so in this study he engaged not only Streeter's *The Four Gospels*, but Taylor's *Behind the Third Gospel*, as evidence for the Proto-Lk theory which Lockton found "unconvincing". A chief complaint of Lockton's was that neither Streeter nor Taylor seriously considered alternative hypotheses. Taylor's statistical method was criticized on the grounds that the evidence was not that dramatic in favor of Lukan dependence on Mk since Lockton believed that an almost equally salient case could be made for Mark's dependence upon Lk. The debate was noteworthy since, as was noted earlier, Lockton was a teacher of mathematics. Furthermore, Lockton attacked Taylor's second line of defense that the omission of the Markan material left a rather complete Gospel intact. In a fashion anticipating Creed's cutting remark, Lockton found Proto-Lk minus the Markan material "in some places no better than a collection of unrelated fragments, which it is difficult to believe can have formed the complete text of a source"[14].

Lockton focused in one section on the mockery (22,63-65), an account to which Streeter and Taylor had given considerable attention[15]. While Streeter argued that the Markan and Lukan accounts were independent, Lockton once more asserted that for this scene Mark had combined Lk and Jn recasting it with material from Isaiah. The position of the mockery after the Sanhedrin trial in Mk was attributed to Mark's equating the Johannine account of Annas's interrogation of Jesus with the trial in Lk. While Streeter maintained that the final sentence in Lk (22,65) was without parallel in Mk (Mk 14,64) Lockton disagreed once more, suggesting that Mark's redactional method had simply reinterpreted and rephrased the Lukan material.

Directing attention to Mark's purported conflation of the two Lukan answers of Jesus in the Lukan account of the Sanhedrin trial (22,67.70), Lockton rejected Taylor's contention that this was due to Proto-Lk. Easton's comment in *The Gospel According to St. Luke* that the Markan account could have been derived from "L" appealed to Lockton who had criticized Taylor and Streeter for not envisioning alternative solutions[16].

Lockton devoted one, albeit short, chapter to the MAs[17]. Streeter was chided for underestimating the amount of MAs due in part to relying on the lists of Hawkins and Abbott. Lockton dispensed with Q and accounted for the MA's by Matthew's dependence upon the other two Synoptics.

Lockton viewed his work as a critique not only of the Proto-Lk hypothesis, but also of Markan priority and Q. He considered the Prologue (1,1-4) as indicating two lines of tradition, written and oral; the latter would continue to remain fluid while the former became fixed. Surprisingly, Lockton did not explicitly refer at this point to the three traditions he outlined in *The Three Traditions in the Gospels*. The idea of a "Jerusalem source" was rejected as unnecessary.

It would be easy to pass over Lockton's name. Yet, Taylor considered him one of the respected opponents of the Proto-Lk theory: "The supporters of the hypothesis have set out

---

13. LOCKTON, *Certain Alleged Gospel Sources*, London, 1927, p. v. V. Taylor cited Lockton and this work in *The Gospels. A Short Introduction*, London, [8]1956, [9]1960, p. 41, n. 3, among other scholars, who had pointed up difficulties with the theory.

14. LOCKTON, *Certain Alleged Gospel Sources*, p. 4.

15. *Ibid.*, p. 31-35.

16. *Ibid.*, p. 43-44.

17. *Ibid.*, p. 49-56.

in great detail the arguments upon which it rests, but their opponents, with the honorable exceptions of W. Lockton and J.M. Creed, content themselves with vague expressions of dissent"[18]. Still, Lockton was often overlooked precisely because of his alternative proposal of Lukan priority.

Robert Lisle LINDSEY (1963) described his position as advocating "a more radical form of the *Urmarkus* theory in which Luke, followed by Mark and Matthew used a Proto-Narrative in conjunction with Q"[19]. Lindsey was correct in proceeding on the assumption that "it would obviously be preferable to diminish rather than enlarge the number of sources, if this is possible"[20]. He proposed that this would solve not only the problem of the MAs, but also those associated with "Proto-Luke, or the special Lucan source of the 'Passion narrative'"[21].

While translating the Gospels into modern Hebrew, Lindsey (1969) continued developing the idea of Lukan priority. Seeing a reference in A.H. McNeile's *An Introduction to the Study of the New Testament* to W. Lockton's 1922 article in *CQR*: "Mark was formed out of Luke the earliest Gospel, and Matthew out of both Luke and Mark", Lindsey believed this confirmed his research[22].

David Flusser, writing in the Foreword to *A Hebrew Translation of the Gospel of Mark*, though enthused by Lindsey's idea, recognized it had not recommended itself to the scholarly community. What the proposal had in common with major theories was two major sources and interdependence among the Synoptics. One criticism of Synoptic studies put forward by Flusser was that so much of the research on the trial concentrated on Mt and Mk to the neglect of Lk. Winter's proposal was intriguing to Flusser if only to highlight that in Lk one finds neither the mention of condemnation nor the charge of blasphemy[23]. Mark rewrote the Lukan account in order to startle the readers.

18. V. TAYLOR, *After Fifty Years. I. The Gospel and the Gospels*, in *ExpT* 50 (1938-39) 8. Cf. PAGE, *Proto-Luke Reconsidered*, 1968, p. 15, n. 1.

19. R.L. LINDSEY, *A Modified Two-Document Theory of the Synoptic Dependence and Interdependence*, in *NT* 6 (1963) 241. See p. 251: "The revision begins in Luke; Mark redacts PN and Luke; Matthew uses Mark but often reverts to the wording of the undertexts". † 1995. Cf. D. FLUSSER, et al., *Tributes to Robert L. Lindsey*, in *Jerusalem Perspectives* 49 (1995) 24-26.

20. LINDSEY, *Modified*, p. 242.

21. *Ibid.*, p. 262.

22. LINDSEY, *A Hebrew Translation of the Gospel of Mark. Greek-Hebrew Diglot with English Introduction*, Jerusalem, 1969, p. 32. See also R.L. LINDSEY, *A Comparative Concordance of the Synoptics Gospels* 1, Jerusalem, 1985 (esp. p. vii-xviii [pagination supplied]). Cf. A.H. McNEILE, *An Introduction*, 1953, p. 64. See also W. LOCKTON, *The Origin of the Gospels*, in *CQR* 94 (1922) 216-239; *The Resurrection and the Virgin Birth*, London, 1924; *The Three Traditions in the Gospels*, London, 1926, in which he argued that the Synoptic Gospels were based upon traditions stemming from Peter, James and John; *Certain Alleged Gospel Sources. A Study of Q, Proto-Luke and M*, London, 1927. Brief attention was given to the theory by F. NEIRYNCK, *The Minor Agreements*, p. 43, n. 141, and T.A. FRIEDRICHSEN, *The Matthew-Luke Agreements against Mark. A Survey of Recent Studies: 1974-1989*, in F. NEIRYNCK (ed.), *L'Évangile de Luc - The Gospel of Luke*, ²1989, p. 343-345. See J. SCHMID, 1930, p. 181, n. 2.

23. D. FLUSSER, *Foreword*, in LINDSEY, *A Hebrew Translation*, p. 6, 7. See T.A. FRIEDRICHSEN, *The Matthew-Luke Agreements Against Mark 1974-1989*, p. 344, and *The Matthew-Luke Agreements Against Mark 1974-1991*, Vol. 1, p. 134-136.

Both Flusser and Lindsey had originally maintained Markan priority, but were convinced later that they were dealing with an Ur-Gospel. The source to which Lk went back was termed PN (Proto-Narrative) and "was indeed a highly literal Greek translation of a Semitic original"[24].

Lindsey concisely explained his theory that Luke employed the Proto-Narrative and Q. Mark, in turn, used the Proto-Narrative and Lk and possibly recollected a few lines from Q. Matthew, finally, drew on Mk, the Proto-Narrative and Q[25].

Attention was also given to the MAs which Lindsey believed showed that Luke was dependent upon a non-Markan text. Lockton, as an earlier advocate of Lukan priority, also stressed the importance of the MAs, setting their number minimally at six hundred, while Abbott, upon whom Streeter relied, counted only 230[26]. Lindsey differed from Lockton who supposed that Matthew used Mk and Lk.

Reactions to reviews of the first edition prompted several changes in the second edition (1973). These included minor corrections, both typographical as well as statistical, in addition to a few updates of subsequent research[27]. An index was also added. On a more significant level, the diagrams were redrawn since they had originally been done in a manner used to indicate dependency other than Lindsey had intended it. The "stemma" as he called them, had caused confusion in at least one case[28]. He also took the opportunity to extrapolate on his theory: "The order of interdependence is Luke - Mark - Matthew: The writers Matthew and Luke are independent but each one knows one or more parallel texts and this includes a common text which roughly parallels the Gospel of Mark. Luke used a version of this text which is verbally *like* but also very *unlike* the text of Mark and the same basic text was known by Matthew who combined phrases from it and from Mark in composing his own Gospel. Both Matthew and Luke know versions of at least one other common text which can perhaps be roughly described as a sayings source and which serves as the main source for the non-Markan common pericopae of Matthew and Luke. The first text appears to be a narrative of the life of Jesus, seems to have descended from an original document which was composed in Hebrew, and is best preserved by Luke"[29]. This original document, translated then into Greek, served as source for all the Gospels. It was further suggested that Luke may not only have known the Proto-Narrative, but also the Greek GS which served as its source. This finally sounds very much like Ur-Markus and canonical Mk. The use of the term GS recalls Spitta's theory, yet no mention was made of it. An editor at some point, to prepare the Q material for combination with the Proto-Narrative, "re-narrativized" the sayings material. The process took place in four stages: the creation of the Hebrew original followed by Greek translations. The GS became divided into Q and the Proto-Narrative which were later recombined in our extant Lukan and Matthean Gospels[30]. Although Lindsey believed that "many reviewers" were sympathetic toward his

24. LINDSEY, *A Hebrew Translation*, p. 16.

25. *Ibid.*, p. 44-45.

26. *Ibid.*, p. 42. Cf. LOCKTON, *Certain Alleged Gospel Sources*, 1927, where the number of the agreements was placed at approximately 750.

27. LINDSEY, *A Hebrew Translation*, [2]1973, p. VIII-XVI. He also included a brief bibliography of his works and those of Flusser which explained or applied his theory, the most useful perhaps being Lindsey's *A New Approach to the Synoptic Gospels*, in *CNI* 22 (1971) 56-63 (p. VI).

28. LINDSEY, *A Hebrew Translation*, [2]1973, p. XVI.

29. *Ibid.*, p. XVII.

30. *Ibid.*, p. XIX.

proposal, he also noted that no scholar had tested his theory, save some of his students in his annual seminar. That was the situation when William R. Stegner, a participant in one of the seminars, applied the theory in his study of the feeding of the Five Thousand[31].

In the second edition of *A Hebrew Translation of the Gospel of Mark*, a portion of the Sanhedrin trial (22,67-70) was cited as an example which reflected "the accepted rabbinic procedure in debate: the one asked a question is allowed to ask a question in return". Lindsey took the addition of τῆς δυνάμεως (22,69) to be a Jewish circumlocution and Flusser and Lindsey equated the titles Son of God and Messiah. Instead of Luke transferring the reference to the Son of Man to Acts, it was Mk which contained "verbal echoes from Acts".

Lindsey hoped that the publication of the second edition would provide the necessary impetus for other scholars to test the theory. This, it would appear, has not succeeded to any significant degree. Those who adopted the theory include D. FLUSSER[32], M. LOWE[33], Y. RONEN = Halvor RONNING (IDEM)[34], B.H. YOUNG[35], and D. BIVIN[36].

---

31. W.R. STEGNER, *Lucan Priority in the Feeding of the Five Thousand*, in *BR* 21 (1976) 19-28. In an attempt to advance the cause of the Lukan priority theory, the author published another study: *The Priority of Luke: An Exposition of Robert Lindsey's Solution to the Synoptic Problem*, in *BR* 27 (1982) 26-38.

32. See below.

33. M. LOWE, *The Demise of Arguments from Order for Markan Priority*, in *NT* 24 (1982) 27-36; *From the Parable of the Vineyard to a Pre-Synoptic Source*, in *NTS* 28 (1982) 257-263; M. LOWE and D. FLUSSER, *Evidence Corroborating a Modified Proto-Matthean Synoptic Theory*, in *NTS* 29 (1983) 25-47. In the first article Lowe contended that Markan priority suffered in the opposition to the Griesbachian theory by arguments from order. Logic and statistics were employed to support Lowe's position. In his study of the parable of the vineyard, Lowe suggested that Proto-Mt served as the possible source for Mk, Lk and the Gospel of Thomas; he regarded Lindsey and Boismard as lending support to such a view, though he was quick to add that they did not interpret their findings as a Proto-Mt hypothesis (p. 261). Lowe summed up his theory: "The scheme sketched above supposes only a Proto-Matthew employed by Mark and Luke, whose gospels were respectively sources for the M-revisions [Markan influenced] and AJ-revisions [anti-Jewish] in the extant Matthew. If one further assumes that Mark knew and employed Luke (rather than the converse), the result is a variation of the Griesbach hypothesis in which the Proto-Matthew takes the place of Matthew. In this sense, much of the evidence adduced in favor of the Griesbach hypothesis will also support the theory outlined above" (*From the Parable*, p. 263, n. 23).

34. Y. RONEN, *Mark 7,1-23 -"Traditions of the Elders"*, in *Immanuel* 12 (1981) 44-54. Ronen referred to Lindsey and Flusser as "the 'Jerusalem School' of synoptic interpretation" (p. 44). This section of Mk was chosen to test the Lukan priority theory and to examine Markan redaction in light of it "because of the great number of 'innovations'".

H. RONNING, *Why I am a Member of the Jerusalem School*, in *Mishkan* 17-18 (1992-1993) 82-86. In 1962 Ronning regarded Lindsey's proposal of Lukan priority as "an interesting theory". But he changed his mind. "Over the years I have come to trust its reliability from my own observation" (p. 82).

35. B.H. YOUNG, *Jesus and His Jewish Parables. Rediscovering the Roots of Jesus' Teaching* (Theological Inquiries), New York, 1989 (esp. p. 144-146 and Figure III, p. 151). Young, a former student of Flusser at Hebrew U., reacted against the view that Luke redacted Mk: "Has the importance of Luke been minimized? The Lucan form of the tradition merits serious consideration, and one should avoid the danger of always treating Luke as a freehanded reworked

In a later article (1971) Lindsey wrote that his view rested on two observations: that a significant portion of the Synoptic Gospels derived from a Hebrew document which had been translated into Greek and, in an attack on form criticism, denied that the stories about Jesus and his sayings had circulated independently prior to being written down[37]. Differences in order were accounted for by Mark's occasional disuse of Luke's order. Matthew, though familiar with another order from his second source, generally followed the Markan order. One argument Lindsey put forward concerning Markan dependence on Luke was his attempt to explain the absence of some forty occurrences of "and immediately" parallel Markan and Lukan passages while Luke used it in one non-parallel passage[38]. This is easily explained by Luke's desire to improve the Markan style and to avoid monotonous repetition. Further changes by Mark resulted from his drawing on Acts and Pauline works and thus inserting "odd expressions". Changes made by Mark were done "for no reason more serious than the 'love of change'".

Lindsey offered harsh criticism for Markan priority and form criticism. The former, the "first error of all modern New Testament research" prevents investigation of the Semitic origin of the Synoptics while the latter "brought intelligent Gospel criticism to a halt"[39]. Markan priorists were credited with recognizing the importance of variations in order among pericopes. The form critics were accused of denying the historicity of the Gospels: "This means that our Gospels cannot be trusted as real history of the life of Jesus and his disciples: they are just late collections of unhistorical material, the only elements in them which may go back to Jesus himself being a few of the sayings ascribed to him, but even these are stamped with the 'faith' of the Later Church and we cannot easily restore their original meaning"[40]. Lindsey concentrated his attack on K.L. Schmidt whose fundamental error was focusing on the framework instead of on the "radical word dissonance". The MAs point to the value of the Proto-Narrative which contained theology, eschatology and christology.

version of Mark's Gospel" (p. 134). He noted the change of order for the denial and mockery (22,56-62) (p. 134, 150, 155, n. 20). Cf. T.A. FRIEDRICHSEN, *The Matthew-Luke Agreements Against Mark 1974-1991*, Vol. 1, 1992, p. 134, n. 70.

Without elaborating, Young commented that Lindsey and Flusser were not in total agreement on how the Gospels developed, referring readers to FLUSSER, *Die synoptische Frage und die Gleichnisse Jesus*, in ID., *Die rabbinischen Gleichnisse und der Gleichniserzähler Jesus*, Bern, 1981, 193-233, and FLUSSER, *Mishle Jeshu Vehameshalim Basifrut Chazal*, in ID., *Yahadut Umekorot Hanatzrut*, Tel Aviv, 1979, 28-49.

36. D. BIVIN, *A New Solution to the Synoptic Problem*, in *Jerusalem Perspective* 4 (1991) 3-5. David Bivin identified himself as one of Lindsey's first students in Jerusalem (p. 3). The article offered a brief summary of Lindsey's position, claiming an undetermined "number of scholars in Israel" have adopted his theory. The focus of these scholars was upon the work of M.H. Segal, a Hebrew U. professor who believed that people at the time of Jesus wrote and spoke Hebrew as their primary language (p. 5).

37. LINDSEY, *A New Approach*, in *CNI* 22 (1971) 56-63. He referred to VAGANAY, *Le probleme synoptique*, 1964, for a discussion of the basic form of the Markan priority position.

38. LINDSEY, *A New Approach*, p. 58.

39. *Ibid.*, p. 59. Lindsey cited R.C. BRIGGS, *Interpreting the Gospels. An Introduction to Methods and Issues in the Study of the Synoptic Gospels*, Nashville, TN, 1969, 74-76, for a useful analysis of form criticism.

40. LINDSEY, *A New Approach*, p. 59.

In the introduction of his synoptic concordance (1985) Lindsey viewed the idea of a Proto-Mk as a "blind alley"[41]. Characterizing the Proto-Lk theory espoused by Streeter and Taylor as a "serious modification of the Markan hypothesis", as well as an "afterthought" by Markan priorists, Lindsey penned: "The arguments of those who hold the Proto-Luke hypothesis include the analysis of the parallels to Mark and Matthew in the last three chapters of Luke's Gospel and from this analysis it is maintained that Luke's differences in story and detail from those in Mark are much too severe to allow for the theory that Luke has borrowed from Mark. None of these scholars seem to have considered that it just might be Mark who has vigorously rewritten the Lukan materials where it suited him and that his revision seriously affected Matthew. Such a view would allow for the superior texts of Luke and account for the difficulties in Matthew where he is opposite Mark"[42]. Lindsey pointed to the importance of the passion narrative for the Proto-Lukan theory. He admitted that his theory required further proof. He was more explicit about the sources Mark used besides Lk which he mentioned in his 1971 article. In addition to Acts, Mark favored use of 1 and 2 Thessalonians, 1 and 2 Corinthians, Romans and Colossians, the Epistle of James and a few other writings. Mark was described as "a kind of targumic rewriter of Luke (and perhaps the Basic Source ...)". But Lindsey offered no rationale why Mark should have done so.

The MAs were indicative of the Basic Source in Lindsey's opinion. Streeter was the only scholar cited in this discussion. In light of the contributions of F. Neirynck who adheres to Markan priority one must also take issue with the following assertion by Lindsey: "Nevertheless, it is to the credit of the Matthean-Lukan priorists that they have noted the value of the Matthew-Luke agreements (of all kinds) against Mark"[43].

The Lukan priority theory generally does not make its way into the main stream of the scholarly literature. That is why E.E. Ellis's reference in an article on Lk is all the more striking[44].

According to Lindsey, Lk was written first and was used by Mark, whose Gospel in turn was used by Matthew who did not use Lk. His theory postulated two non-canonical documents that were unknown to the Synoptists (a Hebrew biography of Jesus, and a literal

---

41. LINDSEY, *Foreword*, in ID. (ed.), *Comparative Greek Concordance*, Vol. 1, 1985, p. [vii]. Lindsey now favored the term "basic source" in lieu of "proto-narrative" (p. 6, 7, 8). Cf. B. YOUNG, *Review: R.L. LINDSEY, A Comparative Greek Concordance, 1985*, in *Immanuel* 20 (1986) 38-44. Young called attention in his review to the problem that the introductory pages were lacking pagination faulting the printers for the mistake. He calculated dos Santos's preface as being p. v, and Lindsey's foreword as beginning on p. vii (p. 44). In a perusal of book reviews for the period 1986-1988, Young's was only one of two which we found of Lindsey's concordance. Consider Young's analysis that scholars have bypassed this unique approach: "Unfortunately, the majority of New Testament scholars have not acquainted themselves with Lindsey's approach, as outlined in his previous book and in several articles, which is surely worthy of serious consideration" (p. 44). Apparently, the scholars believe otherwise. See further F. NEIRYNCK, *Review*, in *ETL* 63 (1987) 375-383.

42. *Ibid.*, p. [xvi].

43. *Ibid.*, p. [xiii]. See F. NEIRYNCK, *The Minor Agreements of Matthew and Luke against Mark with a Cumulative List*, 1974.

44. E.E. ELLIS, *Gospel according to Luke*, in *ISBE* 3, p. 184. See also the brief mention of T.R. SCHREINER, *Luke*, in W.A. ELWELL (ed.), *Evangelical Commentary on the Bible*, Grand Rapids, MI, 1989, 799-839, p. 802.

Greek translation of the original), and two other non-canonical sources known to one or more of the Synoptists.

While the basic premise remained the same, Lindsey (1992-93) further refined his terms[45]. Beginning in 1969 with the sources of the Synoptic Gospels consisting of the Proto-Narrative (PN) and Q, these were revised and expanded in the second edition ([2]1973) to include a Hebrew Saga, Greek *Grundschrift*, Sayings Excerpt - Q, and a Narrative Digest - PN and a Q revision[46]. In the most recent article he wrote of the anthology ("sometimes labeled Q") which was used interchangably with the term "Reorganized Scroll"[47]. This is followed by the "First Reconstruction" which was "a shorter and more chronological version"[48]. Attempting to provide an historical outline of the development of the various writings, Lindsey suggested a Hebrew Life of Jesus was composed about 36-37 AD, followed by the Greek translation of the Life of Jesus in 41-42 AD which was necessitated by Christian diaspora. The Anthology or Reorganized Scroll was composed in 43-44 AD but led to part of the Greek life being taken out of context. Thus a reconstruction of the original Anthology was called for (55-56 AD) in order to offer a chronological arrangement. Lk, written in 58-60 AD, comprised the Anthology and the First Reconstruction. The passion narrative would have been contained in this latter document. Mk, dating to 65-66 AD, made use not only of Lk but also Acts, some Pauline and deutero-Pauline letters and the letter of James. Finally, Mt (68-69 AD) enlisted Mk and the Anthology as sources[49].

The order of the pericopes, verbal disparity between the Gospels and the MAs were all cited as elements in the solution. Those who advocated Lukan redaction of Mk would concur. Lindsey saw the basic source of the Synoptic Gospels as essentially a biography and of high historical value[50].

Reference continued to be made to Lockton as having independently arrived at a similar conclusion[51]. Once again Lindsey castigated K.L. Schmidt and the form critics, rejecting the idea that portions of the Gospel had independently circulated prior to being committed to writing. There was very little interaction with works of the wider scholarly community and what there was, was not recent. In describing Markan priority as "the first error of all modern New Testament research", Lindsey sounded very much like Spitta[52].

45. LINDSEY, *A New Approach*, in *Mishkan* 17-18 (1992-93) 87-106.

46. LINDSEY, *A Hebrew Translation*, 1969, p. 44; [2]1973, p. XVIII.

47. LINDSEY, *A New Approach*, in *Mishkan* 17-18 (1992-93) 88. Later the Anthology was explained as having "separated many of the more narrative parts of the earlier stories from the teachings of Jesus on this or that occasion and from His supplementary parables given on the same occasion" (p. 94). Lindsey previously stated: "The Anthology is a revision made by dividing the story units of the Greek translation into (1) narrative incidents, (2) Jesus' discourses, and (3) his parables" (p. 88).

48. *Ibid.*, p. 94. See also p. 88, where he defined it as "a short compilation of excerpts from the Anthology".

49. *Ibid.*, p. 102.

50. *Ibid.*, p. 105, 106.

51. *Ibid.*, p. 96. The material dealing with Lockton was authored by D. Bivin which has been inserted into Lindsey's article.

52. *Ibid.*, p. 99. See SPITTA, *Die synoptische Grundschrift*, p. V. Note that like Spitta Lindsey also used the term *"Grundschrift"*.

David FLUSSER (1968) has been the other major contemporary proponent of Lukan priority. In his work *Jesus in Selbstzeugnissen und Bilddokumenten* he combined redaction-criticism with Lindsey's solution[53]. He affirmed his adoption of Lindsey's view in 1971[54].

Flusser assumed that Luke best preserved the "original report" concerning Jesus, that Mark revised the Lukan material, and that Matthew depended upon Mk[55]. In some cases Luke and Mark possessed the same material, but Mark dealt with his material "according to his taste and inclination"[56].

Flusser argued that the possibility existed that Luke omitted the reference to the false witnesses and words about the Temple, using them later in the Stephen story in Acts, in order to avoid repetition[57]. If such were the case, Flusser reasoned that the intercession of Jesus was not original to the Gospel, but had been inserted into the Gospel by someone copying the intercession of Stephen. In a note, Flusser explained Lindsey's preferred solution and that Lk was the first Gospel[58]. Mark found the elements of the false witnesses and Temple words in Lk, and Matthew in turn followed Mk.

In Flusser's introduction to the German edition of the treatment of the final days of Jesus (1980), he noted that Lindsey had further developed his hypothesis, but his later results were not that much different from those Flusser presented in this book[59]. Flusser discussed the generally accepted scholarly position of the Two-Source theory[60]. In contrast, he introduced Lindsey's idea that a large part of the contents of the Synoptics had been directly translated from a Semitic language, possibly Hebrew[61] and that Mark employed an existing manuscript of Lk[62]. Flusser noted that the Markan Gospel used by Matthew and Luke was not the same as our Mk, but a forerunner which was designated as "Story" (S). Our Mk is a thorough revision of "S" for which the redactor also drew upon Lk[63]. Flusser regarded Lindsey's method as "sehr wichtig" for a study of Jesus' trial and his final sojourn in Jerusalem. Thus, Lk can be regarded as the decisive source for the trial of Jesus[64].

---

53. FLUSSER, *Jesus in Selbstzeugnissen* (Rohwohlts Monographien, 580), Reibeck bei Hamburg, 1968, p. 11 (= *Jesus*, tr. R. WALLS, New York, 1969); *Foreword*, in LINDSEY, *A Hebrew Translation*, ²1973; *At the Right Hand of the Power*, in *Immanuel* 14 (1982) 42-46; *The Last Days of Jesus in Jerusalem. A Current Study of the Easter Week*, Tel Aviv, 1980 (= *Die letzten Tage Jesu in Jerusalem*, tr. H. ZECHNER, Stuttgart, 1986); *"Who is it that Struck You?"*, in *Immanuel* 20 (1986) 27-32 (= *Judaism and the Origins of Christianity*, Jerusalem, 1988, 604-609).

54. FLUSSER, *A Literary Approach to the Trial of Jesus*, in *Judaism* 20 (1971) 32-42, p. 32.

55. FLUSSER, *Der Gekreuzigte und die Juden*, in *Jahresbericht* 1975-76, Lucerne Theological Faculty and Catechetical Institute (= *The Crucified One and the Jews*, tr. Y. BEARNE, in *Immanuel* 7 [1977] 25-26). See D. FLUSSER, *Jesus*, p. 10ff. He treated 23,26-49 in this article.

56. FLUSSER, *Crucified*, p. 36.

57. FLUSSER, *"Sie wissen nicht, was sie tun"*, in P.-G. MÜLLER and W. STENGER (eds.), *Kontinuität und Einheit*, FS F. MUSSNER, Freiburg, 1981, p. 400.

58. *Ibid.*, p. 400, n. 13.

59. FLUSSER, *Last Days*, 1980 (= *Die letzten Tage*, 1982, p. 14). Pages are from the German edition.

60. *Ibid.*, (= p. 16; see also p. 23).

61. *Ibid.*, (p. 22). These comments were made in the overall presentation which incorporated Lindsey's ideas, p. 16-27.

62. *Ibid.*, (p. 24).

63. *Ibid.*, (p. 26).

64. *Ibid.*, p. 27; cf. p. 93-94.

In the article in which David Flusser and Malcolm Lowe collaborated (1983), the authors acknowledged their debt to Lindsey: "His indispensable contribution ... has passed largely unnoticed or unappreciated, perhaps because he worked then under the double disadvantage of being both an outsider and a pioneer"[65]. They conceived of Proto-Mt as a predominantly Hebrew written source. While Luke was "very faithful" to recording this source, especially as regards the dominical sayings, he was rather free in the transposition of material and in constructing frameworks for the sayings[66]. Given Luke's faithfulness in rendering the original source, Lowe and Flusser explained the nomenclature. "It may be asked why the common source should be called a 'Proto-Matthew' rather than a 'Proto-Luke', since Luke's Gospel often preserves its wording more faithfully. The answer is that the extant Matthew is closer to the source both in its overall *structure* and in generally preserving the original *context* of given sayings and episodes; in these respects Luke's Gospel shows some remarkable deviations, presumably as a result of his aim of καθεξῆς γράψαι (Lk. 1.3)"[67].

In a later article (1986) which focused on the MA phrase "who is it that struck you?" (22,64), he attempted to prove that Luke's account was historically valuable providing the correct order of events[68]. Flusser was dependent upon Taylor at several points, including the assertion that Luke accurately presented the facts. Though Matthew was dependent upon Mk, he also knew the original account, but had "forgotten" to mention that Jesus had been blindfolded[69]. Luke offered the sensible version of the sequence of events while Mark, who was later followed by Matthew, presented a peculiar and confusing account. Lk was not explicitly said to be the source for the other two Synoptics, but the reader is given that impression. Further, because Luke sensed that the account of the mistreatment found in the source was "cursory", he added 22,65. Flusser rejected as "highly improbable" the view that there had been a nocturnal Sanhedrin trial. Mark redacted his source to compensate for the lack of events during the night after the arrest, but it was his "bad conscience" that prompted him to add καὶ οἱ ὑπηρέται ῥαπίσμασιν αὐτὸν ἔλαβον (Mk 14,65b)[70].

Flusser regarded the events of the mockery as part of a game. His interest in this line of research was spurred by a novel about events taking place in a twentieth century German prison, that were found to have occurred in a Polish prison as well[71]. The *Sitz im Leben* of the game was thought to be prisons. However, as confirmation of his view he cited a work which noted that British children played this game at Christmastime[72]. The authors held that Jesus' guards would have been familiar with this game that pre-dated Jesus. Flusser based his judgment, in part, upon the idea that the Hebrew term for "prophesy"

65. M. LOWE and D. FLUSSER, *Evidence*, in *NTS* 29 (1983) 27.

66. *Ibid.*, p. 26.

67. *Ibid.*, p. 40, n. 3.

68. FLUSSER, *Who is it that Struck You?*, in *Immanuel* 20 (1986) 27-32 (= *Judaism and the Origins of Christianity*, p. 604-609). This brief study was "a companion-piece" of another Flusser article, *What Was the Original Meaning of Ecce Homo?*, in *Immanuel* 19 (1985) 29-30.

69. *Ibid.*, p. 29, n. 4. See also p. 27, n. 2.

70. *Ibid.*, p. 29.

71. *Ibid.*, p. 30.

72. *Ibid.*, p. 31. See I. OPIE and P. OPIE, *Children's Games in Street and Playground*, Oxford, 1969, p. 292-294. Surprisingly, Flusser made no mention of the article D.L. MILLER, ΕΜΠΑΙΖΕΙΝ: *Playing the Mock Game (Luke 22,63-64)*, 1971. Cf. F. NEIRYNCK, ΤΙΣ ΕΣΤΙΝ, in *ETL* 63 (1987) 5-47, esp. p. 21-22.

could mean "to guess". The conclusion was that Luke had more accurately reported what was contained in the original account.

Flusser (1968) accepted the Herod story as historical citing Acts 4,25-28 as proof[73]. The account in Acts reflected the customary interpretation as found in the Essene commentary. Flusser also noted that the account was the same as that found in the apocryphal GP and the Jewish-Christian text by Pinès.

Flusser and Lindsey (1980 = 1986) appear to suggest that Luke found the Herod story in his source, which also accounted for the lack of material found in Mk, because Luke was a careful historian "der sich am getreusten an die Urquelle hält"[74].

Walter SCHMITHALS (1985) observed that the theory of Lukan priority has played a relatively small role in the attempt to solve the synoptic problem[75]. For a long time there were no champions of the theory until Lindsey, Ronen and Stegner in the recent period[76]. Schmithals noted that a Lukan priority theory had been advanced as far back as 1766 by Anton Friedrich Büsching who maintained that Luke did not possess any apostolic writings, but only reports which descended from the apostles[77]. In his concept, Matthew used Lk. Another form of the theory was proposed by P.J.S. Vogel (1804) who argued that Mk was prior to Mt. Matthew clearly preferred Mk to Lk because he believed Mk was based upon details from Peter[78]. One of the chief stumbling blocks confronting the theory, according to Schmithals, is the reference in the Lukan prologue to the "many" (1,1).

Timothy A. FRIEDRICHSEN (1992) more recently traced developments in the theories of Flusser and Stegner[79]. K.F. Nickle correctly observed: "No one seems to be inclined to tackle the monumental problems involved in proposing the priority of Luke"[80].

---

73. FLUSSER, *Jesus in Selbstzeugnissen*, p. 141, n. 222. See also p. 124 (= *Jesus*, 1969).

74. FLUSSER, *The Last Days*, 1980 (= p. 116-117).

75. W. SCHMITHALS, *Einleitung in die drei ersten Evangelien*, Berlin, 1985 (esp. p. 137-138). In the recent period Schmithals, Neirynck, Ellis and Sloyan have each referred to Lindsey's position. As Schmithals noted Lindsey was obviously not the first to suggest something of this sort. Rowing against the tide of consensus, the author of the article in *The Teachers' and Students' Bible Encyclopedia* (1902) asserted that Luke wrote independently of both Mk and Mt (*Gospel of Luke*, in P. FAIRBAIRN [ed.], *The Teachers' and Students' Bible Encyclopedia*, Toledo, OH, 1902, p. 129). Listing Büsching, Evanson and Vogel as proponents of the view that, of the Gospels, Luke's was written first, the author reasoned that the Lukan Prologue hinted that Luke was unaware of any extant authoritative Gospel, proposing further that they may not have been in existence at that time. What is more, the Prologue insinuated that those accounts of the life of Christ with which he was familiar were in one way or another defective. Luke's sources included Paul, apostles, Mary or her relatives, in addition to documentary sources of an unexplained nature (p. 131).

76. SCHMITHALS, *Einleitung*, p. 137. He referred to LINDSEY, *A New Approach*, 1971.

77. SCHMITHALS, *Einleitung*, p. 137, 138. Cf. A.F. BÜSCHING, *Die vier Evangelisten mit ihren eigen Worten zusammengestzt*, Vol. 1, Hamburg, 1766, p. 96ff.

78. *Ibid.*, p. 138. See P.J.S. VOGEL, *Über die Entstehung der drei ersten Evangelien*, in *JATL* 1 (1804) 1ff.

79. T.A. FRIEDRICHSEN, *The Matthew-Luke Agreements Against Mark. A Survey of Recent Studies: 1974-1989*, in F. NEIRYNCK (ed.), *L'Evangile de Luc*, ²1989, p. 344-345, and *The Matthew-Luke Agreements Against Mark 1974-1991*, Vol. 1, 1992, p. 135, 136, n. 78.

80. K.F. NICKLE, *The Synoptic Gospels: An Introduction*, Atlanta, GA, 1980, p. 189, n. 21.

Lindsey's proposal could offer an explanation for the reference to πολλοί in the Prologue in suggesting the existence of "digest scrolls". However, one must question the methodology which assumes a Hebrew original simply because particular texts can easily be translated into that language. Lindsey claimed what he was doing was illustrating rather than proving Lukan priority[81].

I am indebted to T.A. Friedrichsen for this reference.

81. Notice should be taken of an opposing position which suggested that Lk was the last canonical Gospel to be composed. See R. MORGAN, *Which Was the Fourth Gospel? The Order of the Gospels and the Unity of Scripture*, in *JNTS* 54 (1994) 3-28, esp. p. 7-8, 28.

THE RELATION OF THE HEROD PERICOPE
TO THE GOSPEL OF PETER

The debate concerning the date and relation of the apocryphal gospels to the canonical Gospels is not new, though in recent decades it has experienced renewed interest[1]. In this section we will first treat those who claim independence of GP from the canonical Gospels followed by those who argue against such a view. Finally, we will present scholars who offered either no position or an unclear position.

The Gospel of Peter prior to or contemporaneous with the Canonical Gospels

J.H. MOULTON (1892) argued GP was "really independent of our *written* Gospels, except, perhaps, St. Mark". In dating GP, he proposed it was composed at a time when Lk "was yet unknown in most churches"[2]. E.N. BENNETT (1893) questioned Headlam's assertion that GP used the canonical Gospels[3]. He remained unconvinced that such was the case. "If the trial before Herod is taken from St. Luke why are the details so varied? No certain

---

1. See F. NEIRYNCK, *The Apocryphal Gospels and the Gospel of Mark*, in J. SEVRIN (ed.), *The New Testament in Early Christianity* (BETL, 86), Leuven, 1989, p. 130 (= *Evangelica* II, p. 722): "The debate about the apocryphal Gospels is not new. The question of independence of or dependence upon the canonical Gospels has been raised after the publication of each of them, the Gospel of Peter in 1892 ...".
   Scholars have attempted to make the numbering system of the GP verses uniform. Swete's system employed chapter numbers for 12 chapters and renumbered each line of text on every page beginning with 1. There are on some pages as few as two lines or as many as 13. As R.E. Brown pointed out: "It is now normal to use *both* systems of reference simultaneously, e.g. v. 14, which ends chap. 4 (= 4:14), is followed by v. 15 opening chap. 5 (= 5:15)" (*Death*, p. 1317, n. 3). Neirynck, on the other hand, recently appealed to American colleagues to "abandon the double reference system and simply use the Harnack division" (*Historical*, p. 226, n. 32). His use of the double system in the Appendix (text of GP) was meant to be a key for readers who use the other system (*Apocryphal*, p. 171-175; cf. *Evangelica II* (= 1983), p. 733, n. 103).
   Albert EHRHARD (1900) authored a useful section on GP which detailed a number of early works written about the apocryphal gospel (*Die altchristliche Litteratur und ihre Erforschung von 1884-1900*. 1. Abteilung: *Die vornicänische Litteratur* [STS Supp, 1], Freiburg, 1900 [127-135: *Das Petrusevangelium*]). The list of works cited was grouped according to the nationality of the author. Although a useful survey, one can only surmise that he believed that the author of GP employed the Synoptics (p. 135: "Über den ursprünglichen Umfang des Petrusevangeliums lassen sich natürlich nur Hypothesen aufstellen. Sicher ist jedoch, dass es die Anlage unserer Synoptiker hatte". The combined use of the bibliographies of Ehrhard, Vaganay, Mara and Fuchs would provide a substantial basis upon which to work. More substantial bibliographies than Brown (1994) can be found in Vaganay, Mara, and Fuchs.
2. J.H. MOULTON, *The "Gospel of Peter" and the Four*, in ExpT 4 (1892-93) 299-300, p. 300.
3. E.N. BENNETT, *The Gospel according to Peter*, in *The Classical Review* 7 (1893) 40-42, esp. p. 40. He was reacting to Headlam's Oxford address which was published in the *Guardian* on Dec. 7th. Unfortunately, Bennett did not provide more precise information. See below, n. 189.

inferences can be drawn from the occurrence of a common word like παρέκυψαν or the employment of καθίζω in an active sense"[4].

The position of Walter Richard CASSELS (1894) can best be summed up in the following statement: "[GP] is not a compilation from our Gospels, but presents unmistakable signs of being an independent composition, and consequently a most interesting representation of Christian thought during the period when our Synoptic Gospels were likewise giving definite shape to the same traditions"[5]. He reacted to the argument that the dependence of GP upon the canonical Gospels can be proven on the basis of the similarity of a few words[6]. The Herod pericope was defined as 23,6-15 and he indicated there was "curious agreement with the spirit of Peter's account when he represents Pilate (xxiii. 6-7)"[7]. Cassels claimed GP 2 agreed with 23,11 and he also believed he detected a similarity between 23,12 and GP, though he was cautious in his second assertion. He concluded the Herod account in GP was "a much more probable account, and perhaps an earlier tradition" than the Pilate tradition[8]. The more refined character of the Synoptic Gospels was explained by their circulation, which GP lacked. The latter testified to the "fluidity of the early reports" and represented a "primitive and less crystallised form of the Christian tradition"[9].

Still there were other early proponents, much fewer in number, who believed GP was antecedent to and independent of the canonical Gospels. Those who subscribed to this position were A. HILGENFELD[10], K. MANCHOT[11], W.C. VAN MANEN[12] and W.H. VAN

---

4. BENNETT, *Gospel*, p. 41. Reflecting on the transmission of the early material he continued: "All that we can safely infer from the fragment is that it made use of certain διηγήσεις, written or oral, which contained some facts recorded and others unrecorded by the four canonical gospels. But if such extraordinary corruption and variety of narrative could exist in Christian communities by 125 A.D. what may have happened 40 years before?".

5. [W.R. CASSELS], *The Gospel according to Peter. A Study*, by the author of "Supernatural Religion", London - New York, 1894, p. 107. In addition, consult p. 47 and 109. He was reluctant to assign even an approximate date to GP (p. 42). This must be considered the most serious lacuna since the dating of the fragment would have direct bearing on the discussion of its relationship to the Synoptic Gospels.

6. *Ibid.*, p. 52. He referred to this in a discussion of Lk 23,50-51.

7. *Ibid.*, p. 48.

8. *Ibid.*, p. 108.

9. *Ibid.*, p. 133.

10. A. HILGENFELD, *Das Petrus-Evangelium über Leiden und Auferstehung Jesu*, in *ZWT* 36/1 (1893) 439-454; 2: 36/2 (1893) 220-267. The guilt for the death of Jesus was ascribed to Herod and the Jews (36/1, p. 445). Hilgenfeld attended to similarities between GP and 23,6-12: "Herodes erscheint hier wohl, wie Luc, 23,6-12, gleichfalls als in Jerusalem anwesend, aber als der eigentliche Urheber der endgültigen Verurteilung Jesu, welche er ja geradezu anordnet (V. 2) und leitet (V. 4.5). Seine Anrede an den 'Bruder Pilatus' (V. 5) lässt auch wenigstens nichts mehr davon durchblicken, dass Beide früher Feinde gewesen wären (Luc. 23,12)" (p. 445-446). Then directing his attention to the mockery he declares: "Höchst eigentümlich erzählt V. 6-9 die Verspottung und Misshandlung Jesu, welche Mt. 26,67.68 Mc 14,65 von jüdischer Seite nach der jüdischen Verurteilung, Mt. 27,27f. Mc. 15,16f. von den römischen Soldaten nach der römischen Verurteilung, bei dem paulinischen Lucas 22,63f. von jüdischer Seite an dem noch nicht einmal verurteilten Jesus, dann 23,12 von Soldaten des jüdischen Fürsten Herodes gleichfalls an dem noch nicht verurteilten Jesus geschieht" (p. 446-447).

In the second article after referring to Harnack, Lods and Zahn, Hilgenfeld once again considered the relation of GP and 23,6-12, declaring: "Herodes erscheint hier ganz anders

DE SANDE BAKHUYZEN[13]. Later A. WAUTIER d'AYGALLIERS (1920) stated his belief that GP was familiar with a tradition analogous to that of the Herod pericope and perhaps was even the same[14]. The apocryphal account was composed nonetheless of original details. At the same time, A.J. GRIEVE proposed that Luke may have obtained the story from "some very early form of the Gospel of Peter and used it as emphasising the innocence of Jesus, the goodwill of Pilate, and the insults of the Jewish (rather than the Roman) ruler and his guard"[15].

beteiligt an der Verurteilung Jesu, als in dem Lucas-Evg. und in der Apostelgeschichte (4,23), wo Herodes und Pontius Pilatus mit Heiden und Völkern Israels die Tötung Jesu ausführen" (36/2, p. 244; see also p. 250). On the relation of GP to Lk, although Harnack maintained it was probable that the author of GP had known Lk, Lods left the matter undecided. Hilgenfeld added: "Unsereiner kan die vielen Vorgänger des Lucas (1,1), welche nicht sofort spurlos verschwunden sein werden, nicht vergessen" (36/2, p. 254-255). His final conclusion was: "aus allem erhellt, dass das PE. auf keinen Fall eine klägliche Compilation aus den kanonischen Evangelien ist, sondern noch dem frischen Flusse der Evangelienbildung angehört" (36/2, p. 266-267). He dated it as early as approximately 97 AD.

11. K. MANCHOT, *Die neuen Petrus-Fragmente*, in *Protestantische Kirchenzeitung* 40/6 (1893) 126-143; 7: 160-166; 8: 176-183; 9: 201-213. He contended "dass das neugefundene Petrusevangelium unseren heutigen Evangelien ähnlich aus verschiedenen Quellen zusammengearbeitet ist, dürfte mit vorstehendem erwiesen sein" (40/8, p. 179). See VAGANAY, p. 22.

12. W.C. VAN MANEN, *Het Evangelie van Petrus*, in *Theologisch Tijdschrift* 27 (1893) 317-333; 379-432; 517-572 (esp. p. 547-549). This first installment of the article contained a useful bibliography. In the third installment Van Manen believed the author of GP knew and used one or more of the older non-canonical gospels (p. 547). "Deze slotsom luidt: de tekst van Petrus is niet geboren uit navolging van één of meer der in het N.T. geplaatste Evangeliën" (p. 549). In his view GP was entirely independent of the canonical Gospels. See also the bibliography, p. 567-568. Cf. VAGANAY, p. 22.

13. W.H. VAN DE SANDE BAKHUYZEN, *Evangeliën buiten het Nieuwe Testament*, in H.U. MEYBOOM, *Oud-Christelijke Geschriften in Nederlandsche Vertaling*, Leiden, 1907, 52-74: *Evangelie van Petrus*, p. 67-68: "Wanneer wij ons fragment met de kanonieke evangeliën vergelijken, rijst de vraag of de schrijver deze gekend en gebruikt heeft. Deze vraag is niet zo gemakkelijk te beantwoorden". See p. 69-70, on similarities with Lk. He continues: "Vatten wij nu dit alles samen, dan vinden wij geen grond voor de bewering dat Petrus onze evangeliën nageschreven heeft, en, richten wij het oog op zijne voorstelling van de hemelvaart (onmiddellijk na de opstanding) en van de eerste verschijning van Jezus, die geheel alleen staat en als ouder dan die onzer evangeliën mag worden beschouwd, vgl. 1 Cor. 15:5, dan komen wij tot de slotsom dat hij, evenals de vier evangelisten vrij en zelfstandig gebruik heeft gemaakt van mondelinge en schriftelijke overleveringen die wij niet meer bezitten, dat er in de dagen toen hij schreef nog geen vorm van verhalen vaststond, en dat hij op dezelfde wijze te werk is gegaan als b.v. Lucas na diens vele voorgangers". On the question of the date, p. 72-73: "De tijd, waarin het evangelie geschreven is, laat zich niet nauwkeurig bepalen, maar uit het feit dat het omstreeks 200 n. C. als een echt evangelie werd gebruikt, mogen wij afleiden dat het niet later dan in de helft der 2ᵉ eeuw is opgesteld. Het kan natuurlijk ouder zijn". See an earlier work by the author: *Het fragment van het evangelie van Petrus, in Verslagen en mededeel. d. Koninkl. Akad. van Wetensch. Afd. Letterkunde*, III R., IX D., 1893, 329-358.

14. A. WAUTIER d'AYGALLIERS, *Les sources*, 1920, p. 201, n. 1.

15. A.J. GRIEVE, *Luke*, in A.S. PEAKE and A.J. GRIEVE (eds.), *A Commentary on the Bible*, London, 1920, 724-742, p. 741. He defined the passage as 23,6-16.

P. GARDNER-SMITH (1925-26) responded to Robinson, James and Swete and in two articles argued, based on the differences between the Lukan account and that found in GP, that both authors were dependent upon an early circulating tradition that Herod was involved in Jesus' trial[16]. While James and Robinson dated GP around 150 AD, Gardner-Smith proposed a date of sixty years earlier, or possibly between 80 and 110 AD, that is to say around the time of the composition of Mt and Lk[17].

Writing in a 1965 Harvard dissertation under H. Koester, Benjamin Arlen JOHNSON challenged the prevailing view that GP was dependent upon the canonical Gospels[18]. He noted that Harnack championed the view that GP is "early and independent", while Zahn advocated its dependence upon the canonical Gospels[19]. Research on GP "has been at a virtual standstill since 1930" when Vaganay published his study in support of Zahn's thesis[20]. Johnson proposed Antioch in Syria as the most likely place of origin, dating it between 70 and 130 AD with the years 90-100 AD as a possibility[21].

In a later article (1985) he conceived of the distinction between canonical and non-canonical biblical literature as indicative of a "shift from narrative to reflective style", the former representing "significant history" and the latter "banal history"[22]. While concurring with Mara that the author of GP lacked familiarity with the events of the first half of the first century, and agreeing with Mara and Beyschlag that GP is "fundamentally a secondary work"[23], in contrast to both, Johnson contended that GP was an independent gospel.

---

16. P. GARDNER-SMITH, *The Gospel of Peter*, in *JTS* 27 (1925-26) 262-263: "Once more we must insist that the gospels are not romances created out of nothing by the evangelists; the gospels are collections of current traditions, and if Luke met a tradition that Herod was concerned in the trial of Jesus, it is not inconceivable that 'Peter' met it too. He may have learnt it in a different form, and he may have elaborated it in accordance with his own views, but learn it he did, and not necessarily or even probably from the third gospel". See also *The Date of the Gospel of Peter*, in *JTS* 27 (1925-1926) 401-407. Cf. J. VERHEYDEN, *P. Gardner-Smith and the "Turn of the Tide"*, in A. DENAUX (ed.), *John and the Synoptics* (BETL, 101), Leuven, 1992, 423-452, p. 434-435.

17. GARDNER-SMITH, *Date*, p. 407.

18. B.A. JOHNSON, *Empty Tomb Tradition in the Gospel of Peter related to Mt 28,1-7*. Diss. Harvard, 1965 (dir. H. KOESTER). He focused on the account of the women and the guards at the tomb, concluding that for the first story GP was not dependent upon the canonical Gospels and that in the second case, GP was not dependent upon Mt. F. NEIRYNCK, *Apocryphal*, p. 132 (= *Evangelica II*, 724) observed: "Benjamin A. Johnson's dissertation on the Gospel of Peter was written at Harvard with the purpose of applying Koester's method of studying the sayings material in the Gospel of Thomas to the narrative tradition and the passion material outside the canonical gospels (1965)".

19. JOHNSON, *Empty*, p. 3. However, Johnson noted that Harnack revised his position of the likelihood that GP was dependent upon Mk for the story of the women at the tomb for the second edition of *Bruchstücke* (n. 9).

20. *Ibid.*, p. 4.

21. *Ibid.*, p. 124, 127.

22. JOHNSON, *The Gospel of Peter: Between Apocalypse and Romance*, in E.A. LIVINGSTONE (ed.), *Studia Patristica*, 16,2 (TU, 129), Berlin, 1985, p. 170. He did not treat the Herod episode specifically, but used examples of the guard at the tomb and the mourning of the women.

23. *Ibid.*, p. 172. Cf. M.G. MARA, *L'Évangile de Pierre*, and K. BEYSCHLAG, *Die verborgene Überlieferung von Christus*, Munich, 1969.

Differences of the second century non-canonical gospels from the canonical ones were prompted by the influence of the still-fluid oral tradition[24].

Jürgen DENKER (1975) thought it more probable that Lk and the author of GP had access to the same tradition regarding Herod's involvement in Jesus' trial[25]. Following Dibelius and Lindars, Denker claimed the Herod episode contributed nothing to the flow of the account in Lk, but he believed that the tradition developed out of Ps 2 in Luke's customary manner of stylizing and reshaping material[26]. The figure of Herod was employed in the same fashion as Pilate. Herod played a role in proving the innocence of Jesus. But the Petrine account preserved an older version of the tradition, in accord with Acts 4,25-27, though in contradiction to the Lukan presentation in the passion narrative.

Taking note of the dating by Vaganay and Denker, B.M. METZGER (1987) dated the GP "about in the middle of the second century (or even earlier)" and argued that while the author of the apocryphal Gospel was familiar with the four canonical Gospels, the GP "seems, in general, to have taken only limited notice of them"[27]. He recounted that in the

---

24. JOHNSON, *The Gospel of Peter*, p. 173.

25. J. DENKER, *Die theologiegeschichtliche Stellung des Petrusevangelium. Ein Beitrag zur Frühgeschichte des Doketismus* (EHS, 23/36), Frankfurt/M, 1975, p. 48.

26. *Ibid.*, p. 151, n. 100. Cf. B. LINDARS, *New Testament Apologetic*, Philadelphia, PA, 1961, p. 143: "On the other hand the citation of Ps. 2.1f. in the prayer of Acts 4.24-30, in spite of the archaic δέσποτα and τὸν ἅγιον παῖδά σου, is probably due to Luke's own composition. The 'plot' of the psalm has been fitted to the events of the Passion in a way that appears to be dependent on Luke's own Passion narrative". He refers to J.A.T. Robinson who had earlier written: "In iv.27 we do indeed have ἔχρισας (referring to an undefined moment prior to the Passion) used as though in explanation of the phrase τοῦ χριστοῦ αὐτοῦ quoted from Ps. ii.2. But, though this prayer (iv.24-30) incorporates primitive phraseology, it bears many of the marks of being a later, Lukan construction. Like the Nunc Dimittis (Luke ii.29-32), it opens with the rare address δέσποτα, which seems to reflect the Church's liturgical use ... Again, 'thy holy servant Jesus', repeated in vv. 27 and 30, has a liturgical ring, and *in liturgical contexts* – but only in these – παῖς continued to be used long after it may be regarded as a mark of primitive material ... Peculiarly Lukan features, apart from stylistic traits like μετὰ παρρησίας λαλεῖν τὸν λόγον (v. 29, cp. the Lukan narrative of v. 31), are (a) the association of Herod with Pilate in the death of Jesus (found only in Luke xxiii.6-12) and (b) the combination of the people of Israel with the 'peoples' of the Gentiles, forced out of an Old Testament quotation (cp. again Luke ii.31f.; also Acts xxvi.17 and 23). In light of this, it looks as if ἔχρισας is another piece Luke's theology (cp. Luke iv.18) introduced to explain and justify his quotation. Taken all in all, it would be extremely hazardous to regard this prayer as pre-Lukan or to accept it as evidence for the use of χριστός in the apostolic preaching, especially when it is applied to Jesus prior to the Passion". Cf. J.A.T. ROBINSON, *The Most Primitive Christology of All*, in *JTS* 7 (1956) 177-189, p. 179 (= *Twelve New Testament Studies* [SBT, 34], London, 1962, 139-153, p. 141-142). In a note Robinson observed that H.F.D. Sparks came to the same conclusion that the prayer (Acts 4,23-31) was not pre-Lukan (*The Semitisms of Acts*, in *JTS* 1 [1950] 24): "Did St. Luke translate into LXX language and edit an Aramaic source? Did he edit and more thoroughly septuagintalize a Greek source? Or did he hear in general terms by words of mouth what had happened on this occasion, and then write his own account of it, including a typical apostolic prayer cast in an appropriately biblical mould? I prefer the last of these alternatives", to which he added in a note, "The occurrence of the Lucanisms μετὰ παρρησίας and τὸν λόγον σου within the prayer is an additional point in favour of St. Luke as its author" (n. 7).

27. *The Canon of the New Testament. Its Origin, Development, and Significance*, Oxford,

view of Denker, the GP resulted from a compilation of material from the OT, especially Isaiah and Psalms. He noted Crossan's perspective and called attention to Brown's rebuttal[28].

Helmut KOESTER (1980) challenged the existing assumption that GP was a "secondary compilation on the basis of the canonical gospels"[29]. Instead, following Denker, he believed it to be the result of various scriptural references. He proposed the view that GP along with other apocryphal gospels "are perhaps at least as old and as valuable for the earliest developments of the traditions about Jesus"[30]. David R. CARTLIDGE and David L. DUNGAN (1980), former students of Koester, while suggesting that GP "could be based on traditions going back to the first century", indicated that it appeared that GP employed the canonical Gospels, though they left open the possibility that it reflected independent traditions[31]. Their judgment concerning the use of the canonical Gospels was based in part on the evidence of an increase of "militant anti-Semitism". In the revised and enlarged edition (1994) they significantly revamped their postion on the relationship of GP to the canonical Gospels and retranslated the text[32]. Influenced by Crossan and Cameron they now maintained "there appear to be traditions underlying the Gospel of Peter that go back to the first century and that are independent of and as old as those of the New Testament's Gospels"[33]. They continued to espouse the view that GP also employed material from the canonical Gospels.

In Koester's extended treatment (1990) he expressed doubt that there was some connection between Lk and GP. "... there is little in Luke to indicate that he was acquainted with the particular tradition of scriptural interpretation that was used by the other canonical

---

1987, p. 172 (= *Der Kanon des Neuen Testaments. Entstehung, Entwicklung, Bedeutung*, tr. Hans-M. RÖTTGERS, Düsseldorf, 1993, p. 169).

28. *Ibid.*, p. 172, n. 19 (= p. 169-170, n. 19); cf. CROSSAN, *Four Other Gospels* (1985), and Brown's 1986 SNTS presidential address published in *NTS* 33 (1987) 321-343.

29. H. KOESTER, *Apocryphal and Canonical Gospels*, in *HTR* 73 (1980) 126. See also his *Introduction to the New Testament*, 2 vols., Philadelphia, PA, 1982 (esp. Vol. 1, p. 48-49, 162-163).

30. *Ibid.*, p. 130. Cf. DENKER, *Die theologiegeschichtliche Stellung*.

31. D.R. CARTLIDGE and D.L. DUNGAN, *Documents for the Study of the Gospels*, Philadelphia, PA, 1980, p. 83: "It is clearly a part of a larger document, perhaps originally resembling one of the canonical Gospels, from which it seems to have drawn many phrases and scenes, intermixing new (or older) material with what has been taken over". They continued: "It may also be that the author of the Gospel of Peter had traditions independent of the canonical Gospels which underlie the work as we have it". This second sentence was not part of their original introduction in *Sourcebook of Texts for the Comparative Study of the Gospels: Literature of the Hellenistic and Roman Period Illuminating the Milieu and Character of the Gospels* (Sources for Biblical Study, 1), Missoula, MT, 1972, p. 157. The earlier work was dedicated to Koester.

32. D.R. CARTLIDGE and D.L. DUNGAN, *Documents for the Study of the Gospels*, Minneapolis, MN, 1994 (Revised and Enlarged Ed.), 76-79. In the preface they stated: "We have also reworked our translation of the Gospel of Peter, recast the introduction to the volume, and attempted to correct several of the sins of commission and omission that we made in the earlier edition" (p. xii). Footnotes have been added. In the 1994 edition they indicated they were using Mara's Greek text as the basis for their translation (p. 76, n. 2).

33. *Ibid.*, p. 76. See J.D. CROSSAN, *The Cross*, 1988, and R. CAMERON, *The Other Gospels*, p. 77.

Gospels and by the *Gospel of Peter*"[34]. Without specifying whether he was speaking of the Herod pericope, Koester maintained that at least some of the special Lukan material was inserted into the framework of the Markan narrative by Luke[35]. Koester favored the view that Luke, rather than depending upon a single source, had access to and made use of both written and oral sources. But J.K. Elliott recognized the extremism of Koester's view on the value of the apocryphal gospels and urged caution[36].

In yet another essay Koester (1991) stated that until recent times the nearly universal judgment of specialists was that GP was based upon the canonical Gospels[37]. But he contended, as he had in 1980, that Denker's work showed, "d'un manière très convaincante", that GP was based upon various scriptural references.

Ron CAMERON (1982) wrote on the heels of Koester's first contribution that GP was not only independent of the canonical Gospels, but might have been prior to them, serving as a source for them[38]. Because the author of GP employed a method of using scriptural

---

34. H. KOESTER, *Ancient Christian Gospels. Their History and Development*, Philadelphia, PA, 1990, p. 227, n. 1.

35. *Ibid.*, p. 336. In Koester's most recent statement on the role of oral tradition as well as the place of non-canonical writings, including GP, in early Christian tradition, he suggested the "ritual celebration of the memorial meal" as the context where the passion narrative "could be written down in order to be read rather than simply told" (*Written Gospels or Oral Tradition*, in *JBL* 113 [1994] 293-297, p. 294; see also p. 297: "the passion narrative was known because it was embedded into the Christian liturgy"). He contrasted his approach with that of "Edouard Massaux's monumental *Influence de l'Évangile de saint Matthieu sur la littérature chrétienne avant saint Irénée* ... whose presupposition is that the beginning of the tradition of sayings is written gospels, and especially the canonical Gospels" (KOESTER, *Written*, p. 293, 297; cf. E. MASSAUX, *Influence* [Universitas Catolica Lovaniensis. Dissertationes ad Gradus Magistri in Facultate Theologica vel in Facultate Iuris Canonici consequendum conscriptae. Series 2, T. 42], Louvain, 1950; [BETL, 75], Leuven, 1986 with Supplement: Bibliographie 1950-1985 by B. DEHANDSCHUTTER = *The Influence of the Gospel of Matthew on Christian Literature before Irenaeus*, tr. N.J. BELVAL and Suzanne HECHT; ed. A.J. BELLINZONI [New Gospel Studies, 5/1-3], Macon, GA, 1990-1993). In concluding remarks, Koester asserted: "Today, however, we know that the history of the written gospels is more complex; their texts were not stable during the first hundred years of their transmission; there were more written sources for these canonical gospels; and the evidence for apocryphal writings has gained more and more weight" (KOESTER, *Written*, p. 297).

36. J.K. ELLIOTT, Review in *NT* 34 (1992) 208: "Gospels like Coptic Thomas and Peter are seen by Koester, and argued as such by some of his pupils, as works that are independent of the synoptic tradition. Frans Neirynck and R.E. Brown among others have occasionally provided helpful antidotes to some of the more extreme manifestations of this viewpoint. We should perhaps not be too over-influenced by Koester's persuasive style in accepting the independence of the so-called apocryphal sayings and gospels from the New Testament Gospels to quite the degree that he does". See below, n. 385.

David F. WRIGHT had earlier analyzed the positions of Denker and Koester observing, "Denker and Koester are right to stress the OT undergirding of much of the *EvP*, but wrong to deny the parallel undergirding of the canonical gospels. More sensitive and accurate is Mara's assessment of the work" (*Apocryphal Gospels*, 1985, p. 227).

37. H. KOESTER and F. BOVON, *Genèse de l'écriture chrétienne* (Mémoires Premières), Turnhout, 1991, p. 92.

38. R. CAMERON (ed.), *The Other Gospels: Non-Canonical Gospel Texts*, Philadelphia, PA,

references, Cameron inferred from this that the "Gospel of Peter shows no knowledge of the special material distinctive to each of the four gospels now in the New Testament"[39]. In my opinion, this type of reasoning would reflect only the most mechanical understanding of redaction and excludes the possibility that the author of GP might have more creatively redacted his sources, including Lk, in light of the circumstances in which he was writing. Dating of the composition of GP falls somewhere in the period of 50 AD, with the latest possibility being "in the second half of the second century"[40]. But he suggested the probability that GP dated in the second half of the first century[41].

Charles Hedrick penned two general, but favorable reviews of Cameron's book, complimenting the introductions to the individual Gospels where "every sentence is tightly packed with essential information"[42]. Similarly, Thomas Best extolled the background surveys[43]. But these reviewers were in a minority. In contrast, Stevan Davies critiqued the introductions for contributing nothing to the scholarly exchange, and offering little more than a summary of information already found in Hennecke-Schneemelcher[44]. B.D. Ehrman, S.G. Hall and R. McL. Wilson each specifically took Cameron to task for presenting his own views as if they represented the scholarly consensus, or at least failing to indicate that the dating of GP and the possibility of its supposed influence on the four Gospels were the subject of ongoing and intense debate[45]. E. Yamauchi, while not referring specifically to GP, wrote that Cameron's view on the relationship of the apocryphal to the canonical Gospels "is decidedly optimistic and in many cases one-sided"[46].

M.L. SOARDS (1985) sided with Denker's interpretation that GP developed independently from the tradition contained in the canonical Gospels[47]. Subsequently,

---

1982, p. 78. His book, *Sayings Traditions in the Apocryphon of James* (HTS, 34), Philadelphia, PA, 1984. Diss. Harvard, 1983 (dir. H. KOESTER), was a slightly revised version of his doctoral dissertation.

39. *The Other Gospels*, p. 77.

40. *Ibid.*

41. *Ibid.*, p. 78.

42. *Biblical Archaeologist* 46 (1983) 190; *BAR* 10 (1984) 14-17. Reviews: BEST, T.L., *Encounter* 45 (1984) 181; DAVIES, S.L., *CBQ* 46 (1984) 343-344; EHRMAN, B.D., *PrincSemB* 4 (1983) 208; HALL, S.G., *JEH* 35 (1984) 600; HEDRICK, C.W., *BA* 46 (1983) 190 and *BAR* 10 (1984) 14-17; WILSON, R.McL., *ScotJT* 38 (1985) 120-122; YAMAUCHI, E., *SecCent* 5 (1985-86) 49-51.

43. *Encounter* 45 (1984) 181.

44. *CBQ* 46 (1984) 343, 344.

45. B.D. EHRMAN, in *PrincSemB* 4 (1983) 208. Ehrman further faulted the "selected" bibliography since it provided little or no clue to literature in which the gospels were analyzed for their historical, literary or theological significance. In a prudent caveat Ehrman stated: "In the mind of this reviewer, such judgments are better reserved for the scholarly debate than presented matter-of-factly to the general reading public as though they represent assured critical results." S.G. HALL in *JEH* 35 (1984) 600. R. McL. WILSON, in *ScotJT* 38 (1985) 121: "The suggestion that [GP] may have served as a source for the canonical gospels is most unlikely".

46. E. YAMAUCHI, Review in *SecCent* 5 (1985-86) 50. He also referred readers to two of his articles: *Agrapha* and *Apocryphal Gospels*, in *ISBE* 1, 1979, p. 69-71, and 181-188. In his article on the apocryphal gospels, he asserted: "The Gospel of Peter makes use of the four canonical Gospels (p. 183)".

47. SOARDS, *Tradition*, 1985, p. 358-359, n. 41.

Soards, whose views were often similar to those of Brown, referred to GP as a way of showing the influence of oral tradition in the passion narratives of the Gospels[48]. He remained, however, uncommitted as to the relation of the Synoptic Gospels and GP. "But, whatever theory of Synoptic interrelatedness one holds, clearly there is additional material incorporated into the PN by the subsequent evangelists; and, in turn, whatever, if any, the relationship of the Fourth Gospel and the *Gospel of Peter* to the Synoptics, the authors of those Gospels also offer a wealth of additional PN material"[49]. The addition of new material, including both details and scenes, was characteristic of later writings. He pointed out that the problem posed was to "determine whether the additions are creations of the authors or reflections of oral traditions" as well as to identify the "antiquity of the tradition"[50].

Writing in the introduction to the section on GP in the fifth edition of *Neutestamentliche Apockryphen* ([5]1987) W. SCHNEEMELCHER broke with the conclusions of his two predecessors and maintained it was very difficult to offer "ein präzises Urteil" about the relationship of GP to the canonical Gospels and of the dating of GP itself[51].

Stephen GERO (1988) accepted Denker's dissertation as having proved that GP was independent of the written canonical Gospels, as he likewise suggested that Mara's study "rightly discards the arbitrary opposition of canonical verity and apocryphal forgery which vitiates the magisterial study of Léon Vaganay"[52]. While not all apocryphal gospels were of equal value, Gero sought to elevate GP and similar works to the level of the canonical Gospels "which have early attestation and which clearly reflect pre-synoptic traditions"[53].

John Dominic CROSSAN (1985) called attention to the split "well established by 1893" between Harnack who argued for independence and Zahn who maintained the opposite point of view[54]. Though he noted Lk shared two episodes with GP, Jesus before Herod and the

---

48. SOARDS, *Oral Tradition*, 334-350, p. 337.

49. *Ibid.*, p. 340. See further a reference to GP on p. 347.

50. *Ibid.*, p. 349-350.

51. C. MAURER and W. SCHNEEMELCHER, *Petrusevangelium*, in W. SCHNEEMELCHER (ed.), *Neutestamentliche Apokryphen*, [5]1987, 180-188 (*Einleitung*, 180-185), p. 183; [6]1990 (= ET, 1991, p. 219). See also p. 184-185; [6]1990 (= ET, Rev. ed, 1991, p. 221). Schneemelcher traced the history of the question referring to Dibelius, Vielhauer, Mara, Denker and Köster. Although Köster's explanation of the development of the tradition is "möglich", Schneemelcher also commented that it was "kaum beweisbar". In a review of the ET of the sixth edition ([6]1990), Adela Yarbro Collins noted that Schneemelcher ([6]1990 = [5]1987) provided a new introduction to the section on GP and Maurer had slightly revised his translation of the text of GP (*CBQ* 55 [1993] 181). In his preface to the sixth German edition Schneemelcher remarked that "the present sixth edition is a corrected reprint of the fifth edition, in which printing errors have been removed; at one point some supplementary material has been introduced".

52. S. GERO, *Apocryphal Gospels: A Survey of Textual and Literary Problems*, in *ANRW* 2.25.5 (1988) 3985. Implicitly, Gero may be suggesting, as Brown had done, that some influence may have been oral.

53. *Ibid.*, p. 3995.

54. J.D. CROSSAN, *Four Other Gospels. Shadows on the Contours of Canon*, Minneapolis, MN, 1985, p. 133, where he added: "Harnack argued for independence, except for the possible use of Mark especially in the *Women and Youth* incident". But see below, n. 68. Reviews: WRIGHT, D.F. *Themelios* 12 (1987) 56-60.; J.L. HOULDEN, *ExpT* 97 (1984-85) 87-88; W. VOGELS, *ÉglT* 17 (1986) 237-238; R. CAMERON, *JBL* 106 (1987) 558-560; D. DULING, *JAAR* 55 (1987) 142-144; P. PERKINS, *Interpr* 40 (1986) 316; W.R. TELFORD, *TLond* 89 (1986) 402-

good thief, he chose to focus on the second, concluding that Luke was dependent on GP[55]. He acknowledged that "a reverse dependency is possible but much less likely"[56]. Koester's insight regarding the contrast between apocryphal and canonical Gospels was also recalled: "The canonical gospels, on the other hand, show an increasing historicizing interest, add martyrological features, and want more precisely to demonstrate, in apologetic fashion, the correspondence between prophecy and fulfillment"[57].

J.L. Houlden, though denying that one must "accept all Crossan's suggestions of the traditio-historical story", nevertheless contended that the "basic material" of the passion account in GP "may well precede any of the canonical parallels"[58]. Walter Vogels, though offering no opinion on the specific relation of the two Herod accounts stated: "It can no longer be said that these extracanonical texts are imitations or reworkings of the canonical Gospels. The relation of the one to the other and of these 'other gospels' to the canonical gospels is complex and different in each case"[59]. R. Cameron considered Crossan's theory "original" and "worthy of further serious study"[60].

Dennis Duling responded to Crossan's theory that the apocryphal GP was formed from the inclusion of an ancient account of the passion and resurrection plus three episodes used by all four canonical Gospels. He wondered: "would the similar intertwining of canonical verses in Tatian's *Diatessaron* suggest the view that *Peter* is secondary"?[61]. Pheme Perkins urged caution in proposing that "one might be less confident in assigning textual relationships and developments in some cases than Crossan is"[62].

W.R. Telford, while impressed by many aspects of Crossan's *Four Other Gospels*, remained unconvinced by his "source-critical conjectures on dependency"[63]. Instead of the canonical Gospels relying on the apocryphal gospels, he believed the process "in most cases" was reversed[64]. Though Arland Jacobson was not persuaded by Crossan's arguments, nonetheless, he seemed to maintain that the non-canonical gospels were not as unreliable as previously thought[65].

In reaction against Crossan's treatise that the Gospel of Thomas, Egerton 2, Secret Mark and GP were more original than the canonical Gospels, Brown argued (1987) that GP was dependent upon Lk[66]. He observed that GP more nearly approximated the tradition found in Acts 4,25-27 where Herod was understood to be a king. In Luke's passion

404; A.J. JACOBSON, *BTB* 16 (1986) 123.

   55. *Ibid.*, p. 142-143; cf. p. 137.
   56. *Ibid.*, p. 143.
   57. *Ibid.*, p. 138. Cf. H. KOESTER, *Apocryphal*, p. 127-128.
   58. *ExpT* 97 (1984-85) 88.
   59. *ÉglT* 17 (1986) 238.
   60. *JBL* 106 (1987) 559.
   61. *JAAR* 55 (1987) 144.
   62. *Interpr* 40 (1986) 316.
   63. *TLond* 89 (1986) 404.
   64. *Ibid.*, p. 403.
   65. *BTB* 16 (1986) 123: "The assumption that only the canonical gospels are reliable, that all the noncanonical ones are late and derivative, is becoming increasingly untenable".
   66. R.E. BROWN, *The Gospel of Peter and Canonical Gospel Priority*, in *NTS* 33 (1987) 337. See also p. 323. Brown suggested the idea of orality in his treatment of "Scriptural memory" which was inspired by M. DIBELIUS, *Die alltestamentliche Motive* (1918 = 1953). See also the critique of Crossan's theory by F. NEIRYNCK, *Apocryphal*, 1989 (= *Evangelica II*).

narrative Herod was presented as a tetrarch. Further, Brown rejected Denker's support of Dibelius that the Herod described in the passion narrative of the Lk was derived from Acts 4. The Herod described in the Lukan passion was more similar to the Herod depicted in Acts 26,30-31. "Christian tradition has different images of the Herodian kings"[67].

In an 1987 article which anticipated the publication of his book, *The Cross that Spoke*, a year later, Crossan mentioned that Harnack opted for independence of GP from the canonical Gospels in *Bruchstücke*[68]. Though many critics judged GP as a later presentation of anti-Jewish, pro-Roman sentiments, Crossan argued that the process was more involved than might be suspected. Like Denker and Koester, Crossan made a case for showing how the "passion of Jesus in the Cross Gospel" alluded to the Hebrew Scriptures, citing Ps 2,1 as the basis for the authorities mentioned in GP 1[69].

Again in his book (1988), Crossan offered a brief history of the debate on dependence or independence[70]. Noting the haste with which Harnack's lectures were published, the criticism was made that they were "so vague as to be frequently infuriating". It was further critiqued for its lack of clarity on the nature of the source. In a sympathetic tone Crossan added: "It is possible that precisely what Harnack sensed was the ambiguous relationship of the *Gospel of Peter* to the intracanonical tradition"[71]. But the task Crossan set out for himself and other scholars who advocated the position of independence "is to do a much better job than Harnack in detailing the relationship between the *Gospel of Peter* and the intracanonical tradition and in explaining how that relationship fits into the development of Passion and Resurrection tradition"[72].

Crossan articulated the view that the *Cross Gospel* perspective presumed that Herod was responsible for the proceedings, while Pilate was placed in that position in the intracanonical tradition[73]. But the development of the Herod pericope was rather complex. In writing about 23,12, Crossan surmised, "That was indeed a vicious circle since, for me, Herod Antipas in the original *Cross Gospel* at *Gospel of Peter* 1:1-2 lead to his mention in Luke 23:6-12 and thus back to the mention of 'friend' in the redactional scene preparation at *Gospel of Peter* 2:3-5a"[74].

---

67. BROWN, *The Gospel of Peter*, p. 343, n. 61. Cf. DENKER, *Die theologiegeschichtliche Stellung*.

68. J.D. CROSSAN, *The Cross that Spoke. The Earliest Narrative of the Passion and Resurrection*, in *Forum* 4 (1987) 3-22, p. 5. Cf. HARNACK, *Bruchstücke*, ²1893, p. 32: "Ich habe oben bemerkt, unser Evangelium scheine auf den kanonischen Evangelien zu fussen und also jünger wie diese zu sein". But a final decision was difficult to render: "Um ein sicheres Urtheil zu gewinnen, reichen sie m.E. nicht aus. Immerhin mag die nicht wahrscheinliche Annahme offen bleiben, dass der Verfasser unser Lukas-Evangelium gekannt, es v. 1-5 höchst frei ausgeführt und v. 13 corrigirt hat". P.A. Mirecki also noted this: "Adolf von Harnack proposed, as early as his lectures of November 3 and 10, 1892, that *Gos. Pet.* might preserve some independent traditions, but his discussion is too vague to be anything more than suggestive (1893: 32-37, 47)" (*Gospel of Peter*, in *ABD* 5, 278-281, p. 280; see below).

69. CROSSAN, *The Cross that Spoke*, in *Forum* 4 (1987) 3-22, p. 20.

70. CROSSAN, *The Cross that Spoke. The Origins of the Passion Narrative*, San Francisco, CA, 1988, 13-15.

71. *Ibid.*, p. 14.

72. *Ibid.*, p. 15.

73. *Ibid.*, p. 103.

74. *Ibid.*, p. 104.

Reception of Crossan's Theory

This work of Crossan also attracted wide attention. D.F. Wright (1987) devoted a review article to an evaluation of Crossan's *Four Other Gospels*, in which he suggested there was a "growing tendency" among American scholars to regard non-canonical gospels as independent of the canonical[75]. Crossan was chided for not considering the "possible implications" of POx. 2949 as it diverged from the Akhmîm fragment[76]. Wright, suspicious of Crossan's "questionable interpretation within the gospel tradition" in comparing Mt 27,62-66 and GP 28-33, contended Crossan "offers virtually no evidence for regarding *GP* as the original"[77]. Although Crossan attempted to distinguish various levels of composition, Wright queried whether there should not be some variation in the matter of vocabulary and style, lamenting "this is another issue Crossan does not tackle"[78].

In a highly critical and often acerbic assessment, John Meier argued: "In the end, Crossan's baroque construct is less convincing than the view that GP is a second-century pastiche of traditions from the canonical Gospels recycled through the imagination of popular piety, with a hilarious disregard for historical probabilities"[79]. Meier (1991) later treated Crossan's book, complimenting it as "perhaps the most impressive full-scale attempt to establish" the view that some of the apocryphal gospels were as old or older than the canonical Gospels[80]. However, he favored the work of Vaganay and McCant over that of Crossan "who has to spin a complicated and sometimes self-contradictory web as he assigns documents questionably early dates or unlikely lines of dependence"[81]. With language reminiscent of his earlier review of the book, Meier described GP as a "pastiche" of traditional material drawn from the canonical Gospels dating from the second century.

In a similar vein, Frank Matera was "skeptical and unconvinced" by Crossan's theory and argumentation[82]. He challenged, among other things, the contention that the theory of the *Cross Gospel* "is as good a hypothesis as is the existence of Q". Furthermore, the methodology was "highly subjective" and one was prevented of speaking of the genre of such a gospel if one cannot produce such a text. With the assistance of Matera's insights, one sees here similarities with arguments of those who hold the Proto-Lk theory.

---

75. WRIGHT, *Four Other Gospels [by J.D. Crossan]: Review Article*, in *Themelios* 12 (1987) 56-60, p. 56. See below, for additional contributions by Wright. Also, see below the critiques offered by R.E. Brown and F. Neirynck. Reviews: J.P. MEIER, *Horizons* 16 (1989) 378-379; F.J. MATERA, *Worship* 63 (1989) 269-270; C.C. BLACK, *JR* 69 (1989) 398-399; J.B. GREEN, *JBL* 109 (1990) 356-358; E. HEEN, *Harvard Divinity Bulletin* 20 (1990) 16.

76. *Ibid.*, p. 59. The reader was referred to Wright's 1985 article, p. 222-225.

77. WRIGHT, *Four*, p. 59.

78. *Ibid.*, p. 60. This point was not lost on R.E. Brown who observed that Wright made the "interesting objection" to Crossan "that the Cross Gospel and the insertions and redactions seem to share the same vocabulary and style" (*Death*, p. 1332, n. 24).

79. *Horizons* 16 (1989) 378. Meier was extremely critical of Crossan's "bold thesis" which involved a "complicated and sometimes self-contradictory web" of tradition history.

80. J.P. MEIER, *A Marginal Jew*, Vol. 1, p. 116. A later comment also pointed to the centrality of Crossan's work in the discussion, calling it "perhaps the best-argued case for a large piece of pre-Synoptic tradition in an apocryphal gospel" (p. 118).

81. *Ibid.*, p. 116-117.

82. *Worship* 63 (1989) 270.

C. Clifton Black, though intrigued by Crossan's theory, wondered whether it would attract "an appreciable consensus of scholarly opinion"[83]. But more to the point of the passion narratives themselves, he posed questions which touched on some of Crossan's assumptions: "First, was the chasm between historical event and evangelical proclamation as gaping as Crossan believes? Did the early Christians quarry their passion narratives out of biblical prophecy, or did their remembrance of at least some actual occurrences direct them in the selection of biblical modes, congenial with their interpretation of that experience (as appears to have happened at Qumran)?"[84].

Nor was Joel Green convinced by Crossan's elaborate theory[85]. But it was Crossan's theory of an early passion tradition for which Green believed the book will best be remembered. He faulted the study for three major reasons. Crossan "presupposes the creative agency of the OT in a passion tradition practically devoid of historical memory"[86]. Furthermore, he relied too heavily on unsubstantiated late and non-canonical writings to corroborate earlier writings. Finally, Crossan believed that whatever was not found in the canonical Gospels and was supposed to have been borrowed from GP, was due to the redactional creativity of the evangelists. Green argued that if, as Crossan supposed, varying traditions were available to the authors of the canonical Gospels, why could it not also be the case for the authors of the apocryphal writings?[87].

While Erik Heen asserted that Crossan's book served as a resource for the study of the passion narrative, brings the passion narrative back to the center of scholarly discussion and "builds an impressive case for his thesis", still, Heen regarded the severe limiting of the historicity contained in the passion narrative as also reducing it "to an interesting exercise in textual hermeneutics"[88]. J.H. Charlesworth contended that with regard to the relation of the apocryphal to the canonical Gospels, "the most sensational claims are now made by J.D. Crossan"[89]. In his recent treatment of noncanonical writings Craig A. EVANS (1993) queried whether the apocryphal gospels having parallels with the canonical Gospels could reflect "more primitive tradition"[90]. Although he did not answer the question directly he pointed to Crossan as an example of a contemporary scholar who endorsed this view. It is somewhat surprising, then, when in listing parallels between L material and pseudepigraphal gospels that Evans omitted any reference to the Herod story and GP[91]. It should be added that Crossan's presentation on the question of the relation of GP to the canonical Gospels was also misleading. To state that "there were always proponents on both sides of the arguments" does not clarify the majority position favors dependence of GP on the canonical Gospels[92]. If anything Crossan left the reader with the impression that the sides were

83. *JR* 69 (1989) 399.

84. *Ibid.*, p. 398.

85. *JBL* 109 (1990) 358.

86. *Ibid.*, p. 357.

87. *Ibid.*, p. 358.

88. *Harvard Divinity Bulletin* 20 (1990) 16.

89. J.H. CHARLESWORTH, *Research on the New Testament Apocrypha and Pseudepigrapha*, in *ANRW* 2.25.5 (1988) 3935.

90. C.A. EVANS, *Noncanonical Writings and New Testament Interpretation*, Peabody, MA, 1993, p. 153.

91. *Ibid.*, p. 223.

92. CROSSAN, *The Cross*, 1988, p. 14. References to those arguing for independence was rather scant as he referred only to Gardner-Smith, Denker, and Koester in addition to two

equally balanced. In a recent essay co-authored by Charlesworth and Evans (1994) an analysis of Crossan's 1985 "provocative conclusion" was undertaken[93]. They reasoned: "Does not the evidence suggest that the *Gospel of Peter* is little more than a blend of details from the four intracanonical Gospels, especially from Matthew, that has been embellished with pious imagination, apologetic concerns, and a touch of anti-Semitism? It is difficult to conclude that this material, no matter how deftly pruned and reconstructed, could possibly constitute the primitive substratum of tradition on which the passion narratives of the New Testament Gospels are dependent"[94].

Jay Curry TREAT (1990) called into question Crossan's method of dating GP by referring to POx 2949[95]. While he concurred that the Oxyrynchus fragment was "a very early witness to a passion tradition about Joseph, Pilate and Herod found in the Akhmîm excerpt of the Gospel of Peter", still the differences between the two reflected the continuing development of GP tradition[96]. Consequently, Treat urged caution in their use to attempt to date GP.

Harold HOEHNER (1992) opposed the suggestion that the Herod story originated with GP since it offered "no real parallel" with the Lukan account[97]. Secondly, Herod was not held to be as responsible in the Lukan version as he was in GP.

While noting that a majority of scholars propounded the view that GP was dependent upon the canonical Gospels, George W.E. NICKELSBURG, Jr. (1992) claimed that some elements, such as the story of the guard at the tomb, were primitive. In his opinion, Crossan erred in assigning too much to primitive tradition[98]. Thus Nickelsburg represented a mediating position. GP shared with the four Gospels the tendency to lessen Pilate's responsibility while increasing it for the Jewish leaders. D. Moody SMITH also advocated the independence of GP[99].

Harvard dissertations which Koester directed, B.A. JOHNSON, *Empty Tomb Tradition* (1965), and D.D. HUTTON, *The Resurrection of the Holy Ones (Mt 27:51b-53): A Study of the Theology of the Matthean Passion Narrative* (1970). In his discussion within the summary to Ch. 3 of contact with tradition, Hutton claimed: "That we are dealing here with genuine tradition and not merely editorial embellishment is evident from the presence of the number of non-Matthean expressions and individual parallels in other early Christian literature, notably the canonical Gospels, Acts, and the Gospel of Peter" (p. 93).

93. J.H. CHARLESWORTH and C.A. EVANS, *Jesus in the Agrapha and Apocryphal Gospels*, in B. CHILTON and C.A. EVANS (eds.), *Studying the Historical Jesus. Evaluations of the State of Current Research*, Leiden - New York - Cologne, 1994, 479-533, p. 504-514.

94. *Ibid.*, p. 511-512. Note the following relative to the wider question of sources: "Just as Matthew and Luke, who are dependent upon Mark, follow the evangelist's account of the passion right up to the discovery of the empty tomb (Mark 16:1-8), then go their separate ways because there is no more Mark to follow, so the *Gospel of Peter* follows Mark (and the other two Synoptics)" (p. 513). Part of the evidence was the mistaken perception "that 'Herod the king' exercised authority in Jerusalem (1.2)" (p. 506).

95. J.C. TREAT, *The Two Manuscript Witnesses to the Gospel of Peter*, in *SBL 1990 Seminar Papers*, p. 398.

96. *Ibid.*

97. H. HOEHNER, *Herodian Dynasty*, in *DJG*, 1992, p. 324.

98. G.W.E. NICKELSBURG, *Passion Narratives*, in *ABD* 5, p. 176-177. "Even if the *Gospel of Peter* is not completely independent of the canonical gospels, it seems to contain pre-Markan material" (p. 177; see also p. 172).

99. D.M. SMITH, *The Problem of John and the Synoptics in Light of the Relation Between*

Concerning the possible relation to GP, F. BOVON (1993) raised more questions than he answered[100]. Acts 4,27-28 and GP 1-5 attested that Herod took part in the trial of Jesus. In some parts GP appeared more ancient than Lk[101]. Ultimately, Bovon concluded that the matter of GP remains enigmatic[102]. In another work (1993) Bovon asserted that GP was difficult to situate and to date[103].

Arthur J. DEWEY (1990) offered a critical evaluation of Crossan's "intriguing insights", applying genre elements from stories of persecution and vindication as suggested by G.W. Nickelsburg, Jr.[104]. Though Dewey saw much of value in Crossan's works[105], he nonetheless sought to offer "an alternative construction to the history" of GP[106]. Notice was taken of the impasse on the question of the relation of GP to the canonical Gospels which arose in 1893 as a result of the research of Harnack and Zahn as well as Crossan's efforts to circumvent it. It will be remembered that he proposed that GP was both independent of and dependent upon the canonical Gospels. He further delineated three compositional levels, each containing three units. Dewey advanced the idea of four layers

---

Apocryphal and Canonical Gospels, in A. DENAUX (ed.), *John and the Synoptics* (BETL, 101), Leuven, 1992, 147-162, p. 161: "The apparent unconcern with which John differs from the synoptics is matched by the account of Jesus' passion that we find in the Gospel of Peter. In fact, in tone and content Peter's account is, if anything, more remote from, or independent of, the synoptics (or the canonical gospels including John). I am not convinced that the author of the Gospel of Peter had access to more primitive, as well as independent, tradition in composing his passion narrative, although it seems to me quite possible that like John he knew a primitive account of Jesus' appearance to disciples beside the Sea of Galilee". As to dating he asserted: "Certainly most – if perhaps not all – the apocryphal gospels were written at a time when the now canonical gospels had come into existence and were circulating" (p. 155). Smith's essay treated Gardner-Smith's article (p. 147-148, 152-153, though no reference was made to the article of VERHEYDEN, *P. Gardner-Smith*) as well as the more recent contributions by Koester and Crossan (p. 148-151). The "more specific criticisms" of Brown and Neirynck against Crossan, however, were likewise considered (p. 150). Cf. BROWN, *The Gospel of Peter*, and NEIRYNCK, *Apocryphal*.

100. F. BOVON, *Le récit*, p. 417.

101. *Ibid.*, p. 418. Bovon maintained this was the case in the GP parallel with 23,39-43.

102. *Ibid.*, p. 420.

103. *Révélations et écritures. Nouveau Testament et littérature apocryphe chrétienne* (Le monde de la bible, 26), Geneva, 1993, p. 221.

104. A.J. DEWEY, *"Time to Murder and Create": Visions and Revisions in the Gospel of Peter*, in *Semeia* 49 (1990) 101-127. See G.W. NICKELSBURG, Jr., *The Genre and Function of the Markan Passion Narrative*, in *HTR* 73 (1980) 153-184.

105. DEWEY, *Time*, p. 103: "First of all, it must be observed that Crossan's work represents a major redactional advance. He has read the text closely and sensitively and has introduced a new vantage point concerning the possible compositional levels of *Gos. Pet.* Moreover, he has brought the literary insight of intertextuality to bear upon the long-standing dilemma regarding the relationship of *Gos. Pet.* to the canonical gospels. It must further be noted that he does not merely observe literary inconsistencies without recognizing the need to place them within the larger issue of the compositional history of the gospel". For additional positive assessments of Crossan's work see p. 104, 108, 115, 116, 117.

106. *Ibid.*, p. 101. R.E. Brown included Dewey in his list of scholars who believe GP was "composed on the basis of independent tradition" (*Death*, p. 1332, n. 22). F. Neirynck observed that "Dewey's reaction to Crossan's 'provocative' and 'intriguing insight' shows obvious similarities with Koester's position" (*Apocryphal*, in *Evangelica II*, Additional Notes, p. 770).

of material, believing it was possible to detect a level prior to the first layer described by Crossan[107]. This would be achieved by a "closer redactional inspection of the entire document".

With respect to a redactional analysis of material concerning Herod, though Crossan was correct in viewing GP 1.2; 3.4 as preparation for 23-24, Dewey contrasted GP 1.2 with 4 observing that Herod and Pilate were not in the same place in 4. This led him to conclude "that 2.3-4 may well represent not simply a redactional preparation which Crossan rightly suggested, but also a fragment of an independent tradition of which *P. Oxy.* 2949 is a variant"[108].

Part of Dewey's disagreement with Crossan centered on the latter's failure to "deal formally with the verses which he patterns into narrative units", as in the case of GP 25-49[109]. While Crossan held that the empty tomb story in GP 50-57 was dependent upon Mk 16,1-8 Dewey was fascinated but "not thoroughly convinced"[110]. He preferred a solution that pre-Markan and pre-Petrine traditions existed and the respective authors used them independently[111]. Further, while Crossan argued that GP 58-60 was dependent upon Jn 21,7-8, Dewey was "not at all convinced about the dependency".

The formation of GP was thought to have occurred in four layers: 1) the original layer which contained the story of the vindicated just one[112]; 2) the secondary layer, involving the epiphany story[113]; 3) the tertiary layer comprising fragments and redactional elements[114]; and 4) the final redaction layer[115]. In Dewey's opinion the final redaction of GP took place at about the time of Mk. Not only did this apocryphal gospel contain "some of the earliest gospel material", but it was possible that it also "holds within it the generic seeds of the subsequent passion narratives". At the original layer what was found was not a "sheer historical report", but "an imaginative attempt to discern the Wisdom of God". Reponding to Dewey, Crossan reasserted his position that the passion account

107. For Dewey's comments on methodology see *Time*, p. 103-104. On what he called the primary compositional layer prior to Crossan's first layer, see p. 108-109.
108. DEWEY, *Time*, p. 106. In addition, he suggested that GP 2,3-4 and 6,23-24 were originally unified material which he named the "Joseph Fragment". GP 2,5a.b, the earlier part which contained Herod's reference to Pilate as "brother" was also considered a redactional addition. GP 2,3-4; 6,23b.24 and GP 1,1-2 were assigned by Dewey to the tertiary level which contained fragments and redactional elements (p. 104; see further the appendix, p. 124).
109. *Ibid.*, p. 116.
110. *Ibid.*, p. 121.
111. *Ibid.* Concerning the pre-Markan tradition, see also p. 114.
112. *Ibid.*, p. 124. Verses attributed to this stage were GP 2,5c-5,15a; 5,16-6,21; 8,28b. This "meager" material was "derived from speculation upon the prophets, psalms, and, possibly, the ancient political ideology of Israel" (p. 123).
113. *Ibid.*, p. 124. This stage included GP 8,28a; 8,29b-9,37; 10,39b; 10,40; 11,45 and "may well have come during the early stages of missionary advancement by the Jesus movement".
114. *Ibid.* This segment consisting of GP 2,3-4; 6,23b-24 (Joseph fragment); 10,41-42 (Cross fragment); 1,1-2; 2,5a.b; 5,15b; 6,22-23a; 8,29a; 10,38-39a.c; 10,43; 11,46-49, emphasized specific individuals as well as the guilt of the leaders of the people.
115. *Ibid.* The following verses, derived from the period after the fall of Jerusalem, were ascribed to this level: GP 7,25; 7,26-27; 11,44; 12,50-13,57; 14,58-60. This material reflected the distinction between Christian disciples and "the Jews".

together with the epiphany formed the first layer and that vindication by miracle rather than by martyrdom was the controling model[116].

Subsequently, Dewey (1992) provided a new translation of GP, as well as notes and an introduction where he highlighted the longstanding debate surrounding the relationship of GP to the canonical Gospels[117]. Though there was agreement on the origin being "a Syrian petrine tradition", scholarly judgments concerning the extracanonical gospels must be re-evaluated. "The most important result established by this research is that the original stage of Peter may well be the earliest passion story in the gospel tradition and, as such, may contain the seeds of subsequent passion narratives"[118]. Dating the foundational level of GP around "the middle of the first century"[119] Dewey insisted the "basic assumptions about the historical development of early Christian literature" must be reconsidered. In commenting on GP 3 he focused on the difference between the canonical Gospels and GP where in the latter Herod was in charge of Jesus' trial, at least until GP 5. Another difference was suggested in GP 6 where "the people are in control of the fate of Jesus"[120].

In a brief article in *ABD* (1992), Paul A. MIRECKI argued that "an earlier form of [GP] probably served as one of the major sources for the canonical gospels", which had circulated "in the mid-1st century"[121]. Although he indicated that the debate continues over the literary relations, he gave no indication of what the majority position was. He suggested that the scholars who supported literary dependence of GP on the canonical Gospels followed the "generally more conservative, and perhaps less critical approach of an earlier generation"[122]. Supporters of dependence included Robinson (1892) and Vaganay (1930) while advocates of independent traditions were Gardner-Smith (1925-26), Denker (1975), "most notably" Koester (1980, 1982) and Crossan (1988). Crossan should be considered the starting point for any future discussion on GP in Mirecki's opinion.

More recently Robert VAN VOORST (1995) observed how the scholarly consensus developed shortly after the discovery of GP that it "was a popularizing and docetic adaptation of the canonical Gospels, especially Matthew", and how interest in the apocryphal gospel has been renewed in recent years, particularly in regard to the debate as to whether GP was a source for the canonical Gospels[123]. "The most controverted - and controversial - issue in current scholarship on the *Gospel of Peter* is its place in early Christian tradition"[124]. Highlighting the works of Koester and Crossan, Van Voorst was critical of them, comparing their studies with those of Green, Brown and S. Schaeffer, who

---

116. J.D. CROSSAN, *Thoughts on Two Extracanonical Gospels*, in *Semeia* 49 (1990) 155-168 (esp. p. 155-161: response to A.J. Dewey).

117. A.J. DEWEY, *Gospel of Peter*, in R.J. MILLER (ed.), *The Complete Gospels: Annotated Scholar's Version*, Sonoma, CA, 1992, 393-401, p. 393.

118. *Ibid.*, p. 394. See a similar assertion made in the introduction to the entire book (p. 5).

119. Cf. p. 6, where the date of the first edition of GP was listed as "probably 50-100 C.E.".

120. *Ibid.*, p. 396.

121. *Peter, Gospel of*, in *ABD* 5, p. 278-281, p. 278; on the date of "the mid-1st century", see also p. 280. The works of Mara and McCant are missing from his bibliography.

122. *Ibid.*, p. 279-280.

123. R.E. VAN VOORST, *Extracanonical Passion Narratives*, in J.T. CARROLL and J.B. GREEN with R.E. VAN VOORST, J. MARCUS and D. SENIOR, *The Death of Jesus in Early Christianity*, Peabody, MA, 1995, 148-161, p. 149. In n. 4, Van Voorst listed significant literature on GP.

124. *Ibid.*, p. 152.

held opposing views[125]. J.T. Carroll and J.B. Green bypassed the debate merely calling attention to the opposing views espoused by Crossan and Green[126].

Luke Timothy Johnson challenged Crossan's methodology in his book, *The Real Jesus* (1996)[127]. While he credited Crossan with demonstrating "consistent commitment to certain methodological procedures", and complimented him as a "gifted writer", one of the weaknesses of his approach was that "he never enters into debate with those who do *not* share such views. The position, in other words, is presumed, not proved"[128]. This pertained to Crossan's "bias against canonical materials in favor of apocryphal ones"[129]. It was precisely on the basis of his source theories where Crossan's treatment of the death of Jesus was "flawed most"[130].

The Canonical Gospels as the Sources for the Apocryphal Gospel of Peter

Adolph HARNACK (1892, ²1893) originally contended the relationship between Lk and GP could not be definitively decided[131]. In his treatment of the Herod material he was open to the possibility of some influence: "Um ein sicheres Urtheil zu gewinnen, reichen sie m.E. nicht aus. Immerhin mag die nicht wahrscheinliche Annahme offen bleiben, dass der Verfasser unser Lucas-Evangelium gekannt, es v. 1-5 höchst frei ausgeführt und v. 13 corrigirt hat"[132]. A short time later (1894) Harnack concluded it was "wahrscheinlich" that the canonical Gospels lay at the base of GP[133].

---

125. *Ibid.*: "Those who advocate such a source-critical position [as Koester and Crossan that GP was a source for the canonical Gospels] must do a much more careful job of establishing their hypothesis and defending it against criticism. For example, Crossan's major statement of his hypothesis, *The Cross that Spoke*, features no sustained, detailed display of his source-critical efforts. He asserts his hypothesis and explains it, but the documentation is missing. Until those who promote such a source hypothesis for the *Gospel of Peter* match the source-critical scope, detail, and precision of those who oppose it (e.g. Green, Brown, Schaeffer), this fascinating hypothesis will continue to hold a minority position".

126. J.T. CARROLL and J.B. GREEN, *Death of Jesus*, 1995, p. 183: "Whatever earlier traditions may underlie the *Gospel of Peter*, this extracanonical passion narrative in its present form may be dated to the mid-second century C.E.". See also n. 2.

127. L.T. JOHNSON, *The Real Jesus. The Misguided Quest for the Historical Jesus and the Truth of the Traditional Gospels*, San Francisco, CA, 1996, esp. p. 44-50.

128. *Ibid.*, p. 47.

129. *Ibid.*

130. *Ibid.*, p. 47-48: "He spends an inordinate amount of effort trying to demonstrate the dependence of all the passion accounts on an early edition of the apocryphal *Gospel of Peter*. The reader begins to suspect that such textual prestidigitation must stem from a commitment to consider *any* source outside the canon as more reliable than a source inside the canon, and that something more than a desire for sober historical reconstruction is at work".

131. A. HARNACK, *Bruchstücke des Evangeliums und der Apokalypse des Petrus*, in *Sitzungsberichte der K. Pr. Akademie der Wissenschaften*, Berlin, 1892; second edition in *TU* 9/2 (1893), 98 p. Harnack observed: "Ob unser Verfasser den Lucas gekannt hat oder nur lucanische Quellen, lässt sich m. E. nicht sicher entscheiden" (p. 79).

132. *Ibid.*, p. 34. See also p. 12-13.

133. *TLZ* 19 (1894) 17: "Das Problem, welches das PE stellt, ist m.E. durch die Mittel nicht lösbar, die der Verf. [Schubert] aufgeboten hat. Doch verkenne ich nicht dass wir seiner gründlichen Arbeit eine sehr bedeutende Förderung verdanken: er hat es wahrscheinlich gemacht,

Joseph Armitage ROBINSON (1892) was sure that the author of GP was acquainted with the canonical Gospels. While it is possible that the author could have used some other gospel, no proof exists for such a position[134]. In a later work (1927) Robinson noted the tendency of the author of GP to accuse the Jews and excuse the Romans[135]. He dated the work "as early as the year 150". The author of the apocryphal gospel was familiar with and employed the four canonical Gospels, though without intending to plagiarize. H.J. HOLTZMANN (1892) also believed that GP presumed knowledge especially of Mt and Mk[136].

Henry Barclay SWETE (1892), in publishing the GP fragment "added punctuation and made some obvious corrections" as well as offered some "tentative conjectures"[137]. Suggesting that a comparison of GP with the canonical Gospels would be very interesting, he refrained since his intention was only to provide a text "for immediate use". An analysis of the contents would follow a short time later. After establishing there was a great deal of material in GP not found in the canonical Gospels (1893) he reasoned: "Thus notwithstanding the large amount of new matter which it contains, there is nothing in this portion of the Petrine Gospel which compels us to assume the use of historical sources other than the canonical Gospels"[138]. In a comparison of the canonical Gospels with GP Swete noted, among other things, that three points in the GP were found in Lk alone. These were

---

dass unsere kanonischen Evv. hinter dem PE liegen, auch das Joh.-Ev. (f. die Ausführungen zu v. 24)". This was taken from a review of *H. VON SCHUBERT, Die Composition des pseudopetrinischen Evangelien-fragments, Berlin, 1893; Das Petrus Evangelium, Berlin, 1893 (= The Gospel of St. Peter. Synoptical Tables with Translation and Critical Apparatus*, tr. J. MACPHERSON, Edinburgh, 1893).

134. J.A. ROBINSON, *The Gospel according to Peter. A Lecture on the Newly Recovered Fragment*, in ID. and M.R. JAMES (eds.), *The Gospel According to Peter and the Revelation of Peter*, London, ²1892, p. 32-33. See his translation of GP in A. MENZIES (ed.), *Ante-Nicene Christian Library* 9, Edinburgh, 1897 = Grand Rapids, MI, reprint of fifth edition, *Original Supplement to the American Edition*, Vol. 10, 1980, p. 7-8. Andrew Rutherford penned the introduction (p. 3-5), arranged the Synoptical Table (p. 10-31) and argued: "The accompanying Synoptical Table shows where the Petrine narrative agrees with and where it varies from those supplied by the canonical Gospels. Of that part of the Passion history which it narrates, it gives an account which follows the main lines of the canonical tradition, but with important variations in detail" (p. 4). Concerning the date he recalled that Harnack situated it in the first quarter of the second century while Robinson and others proposed a later date. In his table GP 1 was compared not only with 23,7 concerning Herod but also with 22,66 and Acts 4,27 about the judges. GP 5 was compared with 23,12 where Herod referred to Pilate as brother (p. 10-11).

135. J.A. ROBINSON, *Introduction*, in *Excluded Books of the New Testament*, tr. J.B. LIGHTFOOT, M.R. JAMES, H.B. SWETE, et al., New York, 1927, p. xiv.

136. H.J. HOLTZMANN, *Literatur zum Neuen Testament. IV: Evangelienfrage*, in *TJ* 12 (1892) 117-120, p. 120: "Letztere, zumal Matthäus und Marcus, gehören zu den Voraussetzungen unseres Apokryphs". Note that FUCHS, *Das Petrusevangelium*, misdated the entry as 1893.

137. H.B. SWETE, *The Apocryphal Gospel of Peter. The Greek Text of the Newly Discovered Fragment*, London - New York, 1892, p. [5].

138. H.B. SWETE, ΕΥΑΓΓΕΛΙΟΝ ΚΑΤΑ ΠΕΤΡΟΝ. *The Akhmîm Fragment of the Apocryphal Gospel of St Peter. Edited with an Introduction, Notes and Indices*, London - New York, 1893, p. xv. The work was composed of an introduction, followed by the Greek text with notes, a translation and finally indices. The translation was republished in *Excluded Books of the New Testament*, London - New York, 1927, p. 109-117.

Herod's role in Jesus' trial, the acknowledgement of Jesus' innocence by one of the malefactors, and the spectators being seized with remorse. The verbal comparison did not yield such strong results as was the case with Mt and Mk, but the vocabulary between GP and Lk "are sufficiently close to create a strong presumption in favour of its use"[139]. He concluded: "Our investigation has thus far established a strong probability that in one form or another the canonical Gospels were known to the Petrine writer; a probability which approaches to a certainty in the case of the Second Gospel, possibly also of the First and of the Third, and which even in the case of the Fourth Gospel is sufficient to justify assent"[140].

GP was regarded as "a free harmony of the canonical Gospels" which the author treated in a rather conservative manner[141]. Western Syria was suggested as the place of origin with a date of approximately 165 AD[142].

In the section containing the text and notes Swete linked GP 2 with Lk 23,7 as well as Petrine recollections of the words of Ps 2,2 and the comment in Acts 4,27. In the treatment of GP 5[143] consisting of the use of ἀδελφέ, Swete referred to Lk 23,12 where Pilate and Herod were described as φίλοι. The similarity of the term περιβάλλω in GP 7 and Lk 23,11 was also highlighted[144].

Isaac HALL (1893) likewise endorsed the view that the author of GP knew and used the canonical Gospels[145]. There was much in common between his point of view and that of J.A. Robinson. Without specifically mentioning the Herod perciope, Hall observed that "there occur – and these may be seen noted in the margin of Robinson's text – expressions taken from or certainly suggested by each one of the four canonical Gospels, where the particular Gospel that is the source has no parallel in either of the other three"[146]. Hall made only one specific reference to Herod in that he appeared more powerful than Pilate[147].

J. Rendel HARRIS (1893) maintained: "Equally striking are the coincidences with the synoptic Gospels. The material is very freely handled, and the writer makes all sorts of fantastic combinations; but he leaves enough of the language in agreement with the originals

139. SWETE, ΕΥΑΓΓΕΛΙΟΝ, p. xix.

140. *Ibid.*, p. xx. This text was quoted by Headlam. See above. Consider also Swete, p. xlv: "The Akhmîm fragment presupposes a knowledge and use of the Four Gospels, and of a text of the Gospels which is already marked by a characteristic interpolation".

141. *Ibid.*, p. xxxvi: "He is unwilling to go far beyond the lines of the canonical narrative. He is prepared to shift, transpose, reset his materials, but not to invent important sayings for which there is no authority in the canonical tradition".

142. *Ibid.*, p. xliv, xlv. He believed it was written no later than 170 AD with the earliest possible date of composition being placed at the mid second century.

143. SWETE, ΕΥΑΓΓΕΛΙΟΝ, p. 2, line 9.

144. *Ibid.*, p. 4, line 3. However, he treated this in his comment on line 2.

145. I. HALL, *The Newly Discovered Apocryphal Gospel of Peter*, in *The Biblical World* 1 (1893) 88-98. In conclusion he stated: "that it [GP] gives clear testimony throughout to the existence and undoubted acceptance of the four Gospels, and possibly of other portions of the New Testament" (p. 98). This article was presented at the SBL meeting in New York on Dec. 29, 1892.

146. *Ibid.*, p. 93. Hall believed the author of GP either used the four canonical Gospels or a harmony thereof.

147. *Ibid.*, p. 96.

to make identification of its sources comparatively easy"[148]. In an article that same year he ascribed to the view that the author of GP employed material from the canonical Gospels[149]. He reacted strongly to what he considered the attempt to legitimize GP claiming this reflected a "vain desire to lower the dignity of the Canonical Gospels"[150]. Harris objected to an article by James MARTINEAU, who in a reply claimed that he had misunderstood his position[151].

H. VON SODEN (1893) rejected that there were any literary connections between Lk and GP[152]. Of the Herod story, he wrote: "Die Beteiligung des Herodes an der gerichtlichen Untersuchung über Jesus, wobei Herodes und Pilatus einander näher rücken. Hier vertritt Lc deutlich ein früheres Stadium der Ueberlieferung, sofern die Betheiligung des Herodes eine ganz episodische ist. Dagegen scheint schon Act 4,27 die Ueberlieferung weiter entwickelt in der Richtung auf Ev. Pt. hin"[153].

The view that the author of GP was familiar with the canonical Gospels, at least Mt and Lk, was also endorsed by W.E. BARNES (1893)[154]. GP sought to clarify what was

148. J.R. HARRIS, *A Popular Account of the Newly-Recovered Gospel of St. Peter*, London, 1893, p. 68. Later he added: "Probably enough has been said to show the use of the four canonical Gospels, and the only question is whether the daring Docetist who concocted the book had access to other sources of information than these" (p. 72).

149. HARRIS, *The Structure of the Gospel of Peter*, in *The Contemporary Review* 64 (1893) 212-236. While not objecting to assigning to GP a date of 130 AD, Harris continued: "but whatever may be the date finally assigned to the fragment, it certainly presupposes earlier gospels which have been made the subject of an extended study side by side with the Old Testament, and it will be very difficult to prove that these are any other than our primitive authorities, the Canonical four" (p. 236; see also p. 212).

150. *Ibid.*, p. 227.

151. J. MARTINEAU, *The Gospel of Peter*, in *The Nineteenth Century* 33 (1893) 905-926; 34 (1893) 633-656; p. 921: "That it affects the problems of the origin and relations of our Synoptical gospels, and of the authorship of the fourth, cannot be doubted; but *how* it affects them it is too soon to say ... It even appears premature to some of us to say, with Harnack, that it is based chiefly upon our first gospel". He suggested an approximate date of 130 AD. Harris objected to the first article: "To draw attention to certain features in the literary structure of the 'Gospel of Peter,' which stamp it indelibly as an artificial and late product, belonging to a lower period than any of the canonical Gospels" (*Structure*, p. 232). Martineau responded in the second article citing where both Harris and he basically agree and where they differed, as summed up by the latter: "(1) that the literary features of the fragment offer no objection to a date as early as A.D. 130; (2) that its Docetism is compatible with that date; (3) that its contents presuppose earlier gospels – presumably, our Synoptists; inferentially the fourth" (34, 1893, p. 633). Unlike Harris (*Structure*, p. 236), Martineau saw no dependence of GP upon Jn (p. 634). See VAGANAY, p. 19-20.

152. H. VON SODEN, *Das Petrusevangelium und die canonischen Evangelien*, in *ZTK* 3 (1893) 52-92, p. 67: "Die drei anderen canonischen Evangelien sind ihm unbekannt. Zwischen Lc und Pt sind gar keine literarischen Beziehungen vorhanden. Auch die mündlichen Ueberlieferungen, aus denen beide schöpfen, berühren sich nur in einzelnen nebensächlichen Punkten".

153. *Ibid.*, p. 82. See also p. 85.

154. W.E. BARNES, *The Newly-Found Gospel in Relation to the Four*, in *ExpT* 5 (1893-94) 61-64, p. 61. Indication of the use of the canonical Gospels by GP was indirect. "When we say that Petrine Fragment contains evidence to the Canonical Gospels, we do not mean that it contains quotations acknowledged or even unacknowledged from our Gospels, nor that is servilely copies

lacking in the Synoptics. "The Synoptists say a little vaguely that Pilate delivered or betrayed (the same word is used in describing the betrayal of Judas) Jesus to be crucified; Pilate is passive rather than active. Who then gave the actual order for the crucifixion? The Fragment satisfies the doubt: 'Herod the king commandeth the Lord to be taken, saying, Whatever I commanded you to do to Him, do ye it'"[155].

In the same volume of *ExpT* as the article by Barnes there appeared another by John MACPHERSON (1894) who likewise maintained the author of GP had known the canonical Gospels[156]. The portrayal of Herod was characterized as "unhistorical" as was the shifting of the silence of Jesus from the trial before Herod (23,9) till the crucifixion as found in GP[157]. The compositional method of the author of GP was described in the following way: "It is the work of one who had before him our four Gospels, which he knew to be generally accepted as authoritative. From these, therefore, he drew his materials, giving, however, free play to his imagination in grouping, explaining, and amplifying the statement of facts thus obtained"[158]. H. WABNITZ (1893) also adhered to the view that there were a number of similarities between GP and the canonical Gospels[159] as did W.M. CROOK (1893)[160].

them; we mean that it presupposes them, and so shapes its narrative as to recognize theirs, both generally and in detail" (p. 61-62).

155. *Ibid.*, p. 62.

156. J. MACPHERSON, *The Gospel of Peter*, in *ExpT* 5 (1893-94) 556-561. Harnack and von Soden were listed as supporters of the view of an early date for GP, with Robinson, Swete, Harris, Zahn and Schubert cited as those who regarded the canonical Gospels among the sources for GP (p. 557).

157. *Ibid.*, p. 558.

158. *Ibid.*, p. 560. GP was described as "an early free paraphrase of the evangelical narrative" (p. 561).

159. H. WABNITZ, *Les fragments de l'évangile et l'apocalypse de Pierre*, in *RTQR* 2 (1893) 280-294; 353-370 (on the Herod pericope see esp. p. 356-360); 474-487, p. 287: "La lecture attentive du fragment que nous avons traduit aussi littéralement que possible, et sans égard pour des exigences de style qui peuvent être subordonnées à celles de l'exactitude scientifique, peut convaincre, au premier abord, que des ressemblances nombreuses existent entre ce récit de la passion et de la résurrection de Jésus et ceux de nos Évangiles canoniques". On the relationship of GP to Lk in the Herod pericope: "Quant au fait, sous-entendu, que Pilate abandonne son siège judiciaire à Hérode, cette divergence s'explique, jusqu'à un certain point, par le fait que dans Luc (XXIII,6-7) Pilate renvoie Jésus devant le tétrarque de Galilée, comme seul compétent pour juger et condamner un sujet galiléen. L'Évangile de Pierre a visiblement tenu compte de ce récit de Luc, et c'est là aussi un des motifs qui l'ont amené à nous montrer dans *le roi* Hérode le remplaçant de Pilate au tribunal de prétoire et le juge suprême qui ordonne le supplice de Jésus (v. 2)".

160. W.M. CROOK, *The Gospel and Apocalypse of St. Peter*, in *The Review of the Churches* 3 (1892) 162-165. Though his position was not explicit, consider the following: "[Robinson] has printed in the margin of his text references to all the four Gospels, where the writer of this apocryphal book has used an expression *peculiar* to one of the four writers. From an analysis of these marginal references, we find that he uses such expressions of St. Matthew six times, of St. Mark five, of St. Luke nine, and of St. John eleven, besides other references. This is a strong argument to prove that the Gospel of St. John had at least equal acceptance with the Synoptics when this Gospel was written". As to date he proposed "nearer to the beginning than to the middle of the second century" (p. 165).

Writing *Geschichte des neutestamentlichen Kanons* (1892), Theodor ZAHN examined information concerning GP provided by Origen, Eusebius and Serapion[161]. He conjectured that its composition coincided with the development of the Docetic community in Antioch around 160 AD. Agreeing with Serapion, the Docetics were not considered the authors of the work, but heirs and successors of the originator of GP. The date of composition could possibly have been 120 AD. Zahn wrote: "Etwa 40 Jahre alt mochte es damals sein"[162].

Shortly thereafter in *Das Evangelium des Petrus* (1893) he noted how quickly the publication of GP drew the attention of Harnack, Robinson and James. This apocryphal gospel was more significant and more defined in comparison to others[163]. In comparing GP with the canonical Gospels he detected four major differences[164]. Specifically, with regard to the Herod material in GP, it was noted that Herod was inaccurately referred to as king. A similar inaccuracy was found in Mk 6,14.22-26 and Mt 14,9. Within the entire presentation, in all the essential elements, the author relied on a tradition reproduced by the four canonical Gospels, calling it "eine tendenziöse Umdichtung"[165]. In Zahn's estimation the author of GP had no other sources than the canonical Gospels[166]. The dependence

---

161. T. ZAHN, *Geschichte des neutestamentlichen Kanons*, Erlangen - Leipzig, Vol. 2/2, 1892; Hildesheim - New York, [R]1975, p. 742-751. See also Vol. 1, Leipzig, 1888, p. 177-179.

162. *Ibid.*, p. 751.

163. *Das Evangelium des Petrus*, in *NKZ* 4 (1893) 143-180; 181-218, p. 144 (= *Das Evangelium des Petrus. Das kürzlich gefundene Fragment seines Textes aufs neue herausgegeben, übersetzt und untersucht*, Erlangen - Leipzig, 1893, p. 1-2). The work was divided into six sections: 1) Einleitung, p. 143-148 (= 1-6); 2) Text und Übersetzung, p. 149-157 (= 7-15); 3) Geist und Art des Buchs, p. 158-180 (= 16-38); 4) Die Quellen des Evangeliums "nach Petrus", p. 181-199 (= 38-56); 5) Einfluss des Petrusevangeliums auf die kirchliche Litteratur, p. 200-213 (= 57-70); and 6) Ursprung des Petrusevangeliums, p. 213-218 (= 70-75). In the book form Zahn also included "Zusätze", p. 76-80, and "Nachtrag", p. [81]. In *Das Evangelium des Lukas augelegt* (Kommentar zum Neuen Testament, 3), Leipzig - Erlangen, [1,2]1913, p. 697, n. 99; [3,4]1920, p. 696, n. 99, he referred to the "geschichtswidrige Darstellung des Petrusevangelium" and recommended that the reader see his 1893 work on the subject.

164. *Das Evangelium des Petrus*, p. 158 (= 16): "1) durch die Art, wie der Evangelist sich selbst einführt, 2) durch die Sprache, 3) durch eine eigentümliche Vorstellung von dem Verhältniss der bei der Passion Christi zusammenwirkenden irdischen Machthaber, 4) durch eine Ansicht von der Person und der Natur des Herrn, welche sowohl seinem Tod als seiner Auferstehung eine ganz andere Bedeutung gibt, als sie nach der hierin wie in den anderen hervorgehobenen Punkten gegenüber dem PE einhelligen Darstellung der vier Evangelisten diesen Ereignissen zukommt".

165. *Ibid.*, p. 169 (= 27).

166. *Ibid.*, p. 190 (= 47): "Die einzigen Quellen, aus welchen das PE seinen Stoff schöpfte, sind unsere 4 Evv. und zwar diese in einem Text, welcher zu seiner Entwickelung schon einige Zeit seit der Entstehung dieser Evv. nötig gehabt hat. Darin liegt die grosse Bedeutung des PE". At this point Zahn was reacting against HARNACK, *Bruchstücke* (1892), p. 34, 35. The author of GP was particularly ignorant of Jesus' historical situation. "Dieser arme 'Petrus' wusste ja nichts, als was er aus unseren Evv. gelernt hatte, und er wusste nichts von den geschichtlichen Verhältnissen, unter welchen Jesus gelebt hatte" (p. 191 = 48). Zahn continued to insist the author had no other sources: "Anderweitige Quellen und Überlieferungen besass er nicht und er war ehrlich genug, sich auch nicht den Schein zu geben, als ob er solche besisse, oder als ob er selbst ein Augenzeuge der evangelischen Geschichte wäre. So blieb ihm nicht übrig, als aus dem aufs schärfste von ihm kritisierten kirchlichen Evangelientext, insbesondere aus dem lukanischen,

upon Mk was also certain[167]. He was convinced that the author of GP knew of Herod's role in the passion of Jesus through Lk 23,4-16[168]. In composing he drew not only on our canonical Gospels, but also on "seine Phantasie und vorgefasste Ideen". As for the date, it was hardly earlier than 130 AD and "mit annähernder Sicherheit" Zahn maintained that GP had been written around the middle of the second century in or around Antioch[169].

Hans VON SCHUBERT (1893) assessed the two possibilities of composition for GP: it was either a production analogous to the canonical Gospels or it was a later second compilation with set tendencies[170]. Those advocating the first position were Harnack, von Soden and Manchot, while Robinson, Harris, Zahn and Kunze defended the second. In his study of GP 1-2, it was noted that only Lk contained information about Herod's involvement in the trial of Jesus (23,6-16)[171]. The opening scene apparently was a combination of details from the canonical Gospels. In a discussion of Herod's address of Pilate as brother, reference was made to 23,12 which helped to clarify the GP material[172]. The scene of derision (GP 6-9) was a combination of borrowed traits including 22,63-65 as well as the Lukan Herod scene[173].

In treating the relation of GP to the canonical Gospels, von Schubert recalled Harnack's warning that we were dealing with only a short fragment of this apocryphal gospel[174]. That caution notwithstanding, he was insistent there was a correspondence with

sein neues Ev. herzustellen".

167. *Ibid.*, p. 195 (= 52).

168. *Ibid.*, p. 198 (= 55).

169. *Ibid.*, p. 214, 215 (= 71, 72). See also p. 218 (= 75). A date of approximately the middle of the second century, and then "um 150" was also assigned in his *Einleitung* (Vol. 2, 1899, p. 94, 447). See the discussion about Rohrbach, following Harnack, that the author of GP used the lost original ending of Mk for his own (p. 237; cf. HARNACK, *Bruchstücke*, ²1893, p. 33, and P. ROHRBACH, *Der Schluss des Markusevangeliums, der Vier Evangelien Kanon und die kleinasiatischen Presbyter*, Berlin, 1894, p. 27-33). According to Vaganay, Zahn was one of the rare critics who dated GP back at 140-145 AD without relying on the testimony of Justin (*L'Évangile de Pierre*, p. 162, n. 2).

170. H. VON SCHUBERT, *Die Composition des pseudopetrinischen Evangelienfragments (mit einer synoptischen Tabelle als Ergänzungsheft)*, Berlin, 1893, p. VI. See also his *Das Petrusevangelium. Synoptische Tabelle nebst Übersetzung und kritischem Apparat*, Berlin, 1893 (= *The Gospel of St. Peter. Synoptical Tables with Translation and Critical Apparatus*, tr. J. MACPHERSON, Edinburgh, 1893). See the review by A. HARNACK, in *TLZ* 19 (1894) 9-18.

171. *Die Composition*, p. 1, 12. See also p. 2, and the extended discussion regarding Herod which reflected the tendency to excuse Pilate and place the guilt upon the Jews (p. 4-5).

172. *Ibid.*, p. 8: "Das hier im PE. Sinnlose bekommt von hier aus Sinn".

173. *Ibid.*, p. 13: "Das PE. erscheint auf den ersten Blick wieder wie eine abgekürzte Combination aus der synoptischen und johanneischen Relation mit besonderer Benutzung der lucanischen Herodesepisode, so dass die drei verschiedenen kanonischen Berichte hier wiedergefunden werden können und eine frühere Verspottungsscene unwahrscheinlich ist (ähnlich wie in Johannes)". See VAGANAY, p. 77. Von Schubert's conclusion for this section is worth noting: "Auch dieser Absatz v. 6-9 kann nur den Eindruck verstärken, dass unsere kanonischen Ev. bekannt sind und die Abweichungen Folgen des abkürzenden Verfahrens und Consequenzen von Veränderungen und namentlich einzelner Rollenverschiebungen sind, die ihrerseits in bestimmter Tendenz ihre Veranlassung haben" (*Die Composition*, p. 20; see further, p. 165).

174. *Ibid.*, p. 157.

our four Gospels in the choice and composition of the GP material as a whole[175]. Even though the author of GP showed a preference for Mk and Mt, there were a surprising number of connections with Lk[176]. He concluded thus: "Summiert man das, so überwiegt die Wahrscheinlichkeit, dass nicht nur die lucanische Sondertradition, sondern von Lucas auch die Partien bekannt sind, in denen er mit den andern parallel erzählt, nur in Einzelheiten abweichend, also eine andere Version bietend. Das PE. kennt und benutzt dieselbe Geschichte bereits in ihren Verzweigungen, so wie sie uns vorliegen"[177]. As to the date and place of composition, Schubert proposed that GP stemmed from Syria in the middle of the second century[178].

   G.B. SEMERIA (1894) concluded it was probable that the author of GP had known Lk[179]. Without minimizing or dismissing "la différence profonde" between the two accounts, he stated that the accounts of Herod's involvement in Jesus' trial contained significant elements in common. Paul WERNLE (1899), too, argued that GP was based upon Lk[180].

   Judging that GP presumed knowledge of the four canonical Gospels, H. STOCKS (1902) claimed that it was influenced in its form by various Jewish literature[181]. A. STÜLCKEN (1904), in his article in Hennecke's *Neutestamentliche Apokryphen*, detected a literary, verbal and material relationship between GP and the four canonical Gospels and judged it to be a free reworking of them which did not extend our knowledge of the life of Jesus[182].

---

175. *Ibid.*, p. 158: "Die Auswahl und Composition des Stoffes im Ganzen entspricht dem Material, das unsere vier Evangelien bieten. Die Leidensgeschichte erzählen die Synoptiker mit Joh. parallel bis zur Bestattung, das PE hat hier gleichmässig Berührung mit dem Mc.-Mtth.-Stoff wie dem specifischen Lc.-Stoff und dem johanneischen Material".
176. *Ibid.*, p. 164. He recapitulated his position on the relation of GP to Lk on p. 164-166. There was a reference on p. 1-2, to 23,1-16.
177. *Ibid.*, p. 166. Von Schubert was of the opinion that the apocryphal Acts of Pilate also served as a source for GP. See especially, p. 168-190.
178. *Ibid.*, p. 195: "Ich möchte glauben, dass es in Syrien bald nach der Mitte des 2. Jahrh. entstanden und hier in den Gebrauch der Doketen übergegangen ist".
179. G.B. SEMERIA, *L'évangile de Pierre*, in *RB* 3 (1894) 522-560 (esp. p. 541, 547, 550). He cited Robinson, Harris, Funck [sic], Schürer, Duchesne, Loisy, Lejay and Chiappelli as following Harnack that GP was familiar with and had employed the canonical Gospels. But Harnack's position had undergone development. Although he initially (1892) maintained the position that GP knew and used the canonical Gospels, his position later shifted in the opposite direction only to return to his original point of view in 1894 (p. 541-542). Adolphe Lods argued that GP was familiar with some of the canonical Gospels, though not Lk, while Reinach supported the view that GP was prior to the canonical Gospels.
180. P. WERNLE, *Die synoptische Frage*, 1899, p. 95.
181. H. STOCKS, *Zum Petrusevangelium*, in *NKZ* 13 (1902) 276-314; 14 (1903) 511-542. Stocks's conclusion to the first section ran thus: "Das Petrusevangelium setzt unsere heutigen kanonischen Evangelien voraus, hat aber schon mit der Ausmalung von deren Berichten nach Art des jüdischen Midrasch begonnen und aus den jüdischen Midraschim u. a. jüdischer Litteratur neue Vorstellungen übernommen" (1902, p. 314). With regard to the Herod story, see p. 284-285. See also: "Dass die Quelle Pseudopetri die vier Evangelien gebildet haben, scheint uns, zuletzt durch von Schuberts Untersuchungen, sichergestellt und jetzt auch von solchen, die früher daran zweifelten, zugegeben – mehr oder weniger ausdrucklich" (1902, p. 282).
182. A. STÜLCKEN, *Petrusevangelium*, in E. HENNECKE (ed.), *Neutestamentliche Apokryphen*, Tübingen, 1904, 27-32, p. 28, 29; ²1924, p. 59-63.

In the third edition of the work (^{3}1959), Stülcken's article was replaced by one authored by C. MAURER, but the conclusion remained the same[183]: GP developed materials found in the four Gospels. He argued more specifically that Lk served as the source for the detail of Herod's involvement in Jesus' trial. Direct or indirect influence of the four canonical Gospels upon GP was, according to V.H. STANTON (1900), the most reasonable explanation for the similarity of events and verbal expressions[184]. In contrast to the other Gospels GP "betrays gross ignorance of the actual historical relations of Herod and the rulers of Jerusalem, and the position of both under the Roman government"[185]. The extent of the author's creative contribution cannot be ascertained. In the opinion of C.H. TURNER (1914)[186] the author of GP not only knew, but used the four canonical Gospels in composing his own[187]. The Herod episode in GP found its genesis in Lk.

Other early proponents who affirmed GP's dependence upon the canonical Gospels were: F.X. FUNK[188], A.C. HEADLAM[189], A. LODS[190], A. LOISY[191], P. LEJAY[192],

---

183. C. MAURER, *Petrusevangelium*, in [E. HENNECKE] and W. SCHNEEMELCHER (ed.), *Neutestamentliche Apokryphen in deutscher Übersetzung*. I. *Evangelien*, Tübingen, ^{3}1959, 118-124, p. 118 (= *The Gospel of Peter*, in E. HENNECKE and W. SCHNEEMELCHER [eds.], *New Testament Apocrypha* I. *Gospels and Related Writings*, tr. R. MCL. WILSON, Philadelphia, PA, 1963, 179-187, p. 180).

184. V.H. STANTON, *The 'Gospel of Peter': Its Early History and Character Considered in Relation to the History of the Recognition in the Church of the Canonical Gospels*, in *JTS* 2 (1900-01) 21-22. "The writer, though he knew of Four Gospels, yielded to the desire which has been felt in different generations, as for example by writers of lives of Christ in our own, to tell the story afresh. He might consider himself the more justified in doing so because he had often heard it orally given, and had delivered it himself, in a form in which matter derived from the Gospels had been more or less transformed, and other elements had been introduced through the working of fancy under the influence of circumstances and tendencies of the time" (p. 25).

185. *Ibid.*, p. 11.

186. C.H. TURNER, *The Gospel of Peter*, in *JTS* 14 (1913-14) 167.

187. *Ibid.*, p. 187.

188. F.X. FUNK, *Fragmente des Evangeliums und der Apokalypse des Petrus*, in *TQ* 75 (1893) 255-288. Mentioning the solutions of Lods, Harnack and Robinson for the issue of the relationship and dependence of GP, he concluded: "Demgemäss legt sich zunächst der Gedanke einer Bekanntschaft mit allen nahe. Nur ist die Benützung der einzelnen Evangelien eine verschiedene, bei den zwei letzten sehr freie" (p. 263). As to date he claimed "das Petrusevangelium wird zuerst um das J. 200 erwähnt" (p. 257; see also pp 262, 263). See VAGANAY, p. 27. (All such references in this section are to *L'Évangile de Pierre*).

189. A.C. HEADLAM, *The Akhmîm Fragments*, in *The Classical Review* 7 (1893) 458-463, p. 460: "... it is an apocryphal document dating from some period in the second century, and hardly later than the year 170". But see also p. 462, where he suggested it may be as early as 130. In considering both the date and the relation of GP to the canonical Gospels, he credited Zahn with "by far the best examination [...] and no one who reads that carefully ... can doubt that however late be the latest portion of the Four Canonical Gospels, this document is later". But it was Swete to whom Headlam appealed in seeking to answer the dilemma about the relationship, believing that the reader "will feel that the author is justified in his conclusion" (p. 461). Then he quoted Swete at length: "Our investigation has thus far established a strong probability in one form or another the Canonical Gospels were known to the Petrine writer; a probability which approaches to a certainty in the case of the Second Gospel, possibly also of the First and of the Third, and which even in the case of the Fourth Gospel is sufficient to justify assent" (SWETE,

H. Lucas[193], A.J. Maas[194], J. MacPherson[195], J. Kunze[196], J.M.S. Baljon[197],

The Akhmîm Fragment, 1893, p. xx).

190. A. Lods, *L'évangile et l'apocalypse de Pierre*, Paris, 1893 (esp. p. 63-74). See Lods's bibliography in his preface, p. 3-5. "Je serais, en somme, porté à croire que l'auteur a utilisé au moins les deux premiers de nos évangiles, peut-être le troisième, qu'il a ignoré le quatrième. Cette appréciation peut se discuter: une chose est certaine, c'est que le nouveau document n'est pas un amplification des quatre évangiles, à la façon des ouvrages apocryphes de date récente, il est, à plusieurs reprises, en contradiction avec les textes canoniques"(p. 72-73). Lods assigned the origin to Rhossus (p. 74). See Vaganay, p. 21.

191. A. Loisy, *Livres apocryphes. L'évangile et l'apocalypse de Pierre*, in *L'enseignement biblique* (1893) 48-61; 90-93, p. 93: "Il est à peu près certain qu'il a connu et employé nos quatre Évangiles. Il a pu connaître aussi par exemple quelqu'un des évangiles non canoniques mentionnés dans le prologue de saint Luc. Seulement, au lieu de contrôler ses documents par la tradition apostolique, il les a exploités avec son imagination et peut-être au point de vue d'une théologie particulière". See further p. 54, regarding the relation of GP and the canonical Gospels and Loisy's comment on the Herod pericope (23,6-12): "Dès le début du fragment, on reconnaît le parti pris d'enlever à Pilate la responsabilité de la mort de Jésus pour la transporter tout entière sur Hérode: pure invention, greffée sur la donnée de saint Luc touchant la présence d'Hérode à Jérusalem et son rôle dans l'histoire de la passion (*Luc* XXIII,6-12). Cependant pour affirmer avec certitude la dépendance de l'apocryphe à l'égard du troisième Évangile, il faudrait savoir comment l'auteur introduisait la participation d'Hérode à la condamnation de Jésus". See also *Les livres du Nouveau Testament traduits du grec en français avec introduction général et notices*, Paris, 1922, 702-709.

192. P. Lejay, *L'évangile de Pierre*, in *RevÉtudGrecq* 6 (1893) 59-84; 267-270. In this article Lejay interacted with Harnack noting his shift in position. See also his reference to St. Luc (p. 62) and the date (p. 83). "L'évangile de Pierre marque donc nettement sur ce point un progrès dans l'evolution du christianisme si on le compare aux évangiles canoniques. Ceux-ci sont inintelligibles pour qui ne connaît la Judée du Ier siècle; ils ont en même temps mille liens avec le passé. Cette considération seule devrait suffire pour placer le nouveau document après les anciens" (p. 71-72). He continued: "Voilà la conclusion à laquelle on aboutit quand on compare les textes. L'évangile de Pierre n'est pas un document mais une œuvre littéraire fruit de la dextérité et du talent poétique d'un inconnu. Cet auteur, possédant suffisamment les écritures canoniques, s'est essayé à reproduire les scènes peintes par les maîtres …" (p. 75).

193. H. Lucas, *The New Apocrypha*, in *Month* 77 (1893) 1-15, p. 2: "For the most part, the narrative is nothing but a more or less clumsy patchwork made up of shreds from our four canonical Gospels, a patchwork, however, in which the order of events is jumbled up in a somewhat bewildering fashion". He dated GP at between 150-175 AD (p. 11).

194. A.J. Maas, *The Lately Recovered Apocryphal Gospel According to Peter*, in *The American Catholic Quarterly Review* 18 (1893) 313-328, p. 323, listed references in the four canonical Gospels where the author of GP used them, including Lk 23,7. He dated the work "about the middle of the second century" (p. 328).

195. J. MacPherson, *The Gospel of Peter. A Criticism and Exposition*, in *ExpT* 5 (1893-94) 556-561, p. 557: "This is certainly the question of primary importance in connexion with this gospel fragment: Is it part of a work which is analogous to and practically contemporary with our Gospels, or is it a later production making use of these as its chief or only sources? The latter view has been maintained with abundant learning by our own English scholars, Robinson, Swete, and Rendel Harris, as well as of the great German historian of the Canon, Theodor Zahn, and also by von Schubert of Kiel, who has investigated the subject with most laborious care and most competent scholarship. The former view is advocated by Harnack in the second edition of his

956   APPENDIX III

A. RESCH[198], and P. BATIFFOL[199]. Interest in GP continued to inspired studies of varying

work ...".

In writing of "variations, amplifications or so-called additions" (p. 557) MacPherson stated: "Herod is made prominent as king, by implication the King of the Jews, so that his acts are theirs; and the people are the executioners of his will, as in our Gospels the soldiers are the executioners of the commands of Pilate. If again, with Völter, we regard verses 3-5 (Joseph's obtaining permission to take and bury the body from Herod through Pilate's mediation) as an interpolation, and there is much to commend such a supposition, we find a later redactor doing with Peter what we are fancying Peter may have done with Matthew's narrative. In any case, the unhistorical representation of Herod as King of the Jews, with a jurisdiction even in Jerusalem superior to that of Pilate, is of itself sufficient to make the authorship of our Gospel impossible even in the early years of the second century. Of a very similar kind is the divergences in regard to the silence of Jesus which the canonical Gospels report in connexion with His trial before Herod (Luke xxiii.9) and Pilate (Matt.xxvii.14; Mark xv.3,5; John xix.9) ..." (p. 558).

And in his conclusion: "It is the work of one who had before him our four Gospels, which he knew to be generally accepted as authoritative. From these, therefore, he drew his materials, giving, however, free play to his imagination in grouping, explaining, and amplifying the statement of facts thus obtained. Some peculiarities of personal taste and feeling are probably enough to account for the legendary additions and corresponding modifications of facts and arrangements by which his work is differentiated from the canonical Gospels. Though extremely interesting as a specimen of an early free paraphrase of the evangelical narrative, it furnishes no additional detail such as we might expect from sources from which the selection known to us in the four Gospels was made" (p. 560-561).

196. J. KUNZE, *Das Petrusevangelium*, in *NJDTh* 2 (1893) 583-604; 3 (1894) 58-104. See his bibliography (1893), p. 584-586. The following was taken from (1894) 104: "Sieht man auf der einen Seite in PE. den Beweis, dass der evangelische Geschichtsstoff noch im Flusse war und unsere kanonischen Evangelien jedes besonderen Ansehens entbehrten, so wird man, wenn unsre Auffassung die richtige ist, das mit Energie geltend machen dürfen, was Zahn S. 75 am Schlusse seiner Abhandlung sagt: 'Die geschichtliche Bedeutung des PE. steht vor allem darin, dass es die um 150 (oder bald nachher, der Verf.) bereits fest begründete Alleinherrschaft der 4 kanonischen Evv. aufs neue beweist.' ... Andrerseits beweisen jene Ereignisse in Rhossus, dass allerdings eine gewisse Freiheit der Bewegung noch herrschte ...". See also his *Das neu aufgefundene Bruchstück des sogen. Petrusevangeliums übersetzt und beurteilt*, Leipzig, 1893. VAGANAY, p. 27, placed him in line with Zahn.

197. J.M.S. BALJON, *Het Evangelie van Petrus*, in *Theologische Studiën* 12 (1894) 1-34, p. 24: "Een tweede punt van gewicht is de verhouding van ons evanglie tot de canonieke evangeliën. Er is merkwaardige overeenkomst, maar ook groot verschil. De meeste overeenkomst vinden wij met Mattheüs en Markus, minder met Lukas en zeer weinig met Johannes". (See reference on p. 25 to Lk 23,7, GP and compare Acts 4,27). He continued: "Mijn resultaat is, dat ik wel geneigd ben, bekendheid van Petrus met Mt. en Mk, aan te nemen, maar dat onzeker is, of Petrus ook Lk. en Joh. gebruikt heeft". See VAGANAY, p. 22-23.

198. A. RESCH, *Aussercanonische Paralleltexte zu den Evangelien. II. Matthaeus und Markus* 1894 (TU 10/2), p. 34-48, p. 47: "Alles in Allem stand das doketische Petrusevangelium tief unter den canonischen Evangelien und verdankte diesen das Beste, was es bieten konnte ...". See VAGANAY, p. 21.

199. P. BATIFFOL, *Six leçons sur les Évangiles*, Paris, 1897, esp. p. 30-33, p. 31: the second century saw the beginning of "une série de faux évangiles, imités des premiers" and he fixed the date between 100 and 130 AD. In addition: "que l'auteur s'est servi pour l'écrire des données que lui fournissaient nos trois premiers évangiles et sans doute aussi l'évangile de saint Jean".

lengths favoring the perspective of dependence upon canonical Gospels, including the works of F.H. CHASE[200], J. BELSER[201], V. ROSE[202] J.G. TASKER[203], A.F. FINDLAY[204], G.J. REID[205], L. FILLION[206], P. WENDLAND[207] E. AMANN[208], H. WAITZ[209], M.

200. F.H. CHASE, *Peter (Simon)*, in J. HASTINGS (ed.), *A Dictionary of the Bible*, Vol. 3, Edinburgh, 1900, 756-779, p. 776: Referred to Harnack that "in the fragment the four Gospels are not placed on the same level ... And, further, the text of the Gospel had already had a history before it was used by the author of the Petrine *Gospel*; indeed there is strong reason to think that he used a harmony of the Gospels". Following Swete and Zahn he suggested that the date of GP "can hardly be much before 150".

201. J. BELSER, *Einleitung in das Neue Testament*, Freiburg, 1901, [2]1905, 809-814: *Das Petrusevangelium*, p. 810: "Nach diesem Fragment muss als ausgemacht gelten, dass der Verfasser des Petrusevangeliums unsere vier kanonischen Evangelien alle benutzt". Still later (p. 812): "Auch mir erscheint es völlig unbegreiflich, wie man die Abhängigkeit des Verfassers von unsern kanonischen Evangelien oder wenigstens jene vom Johannesevangelium ernstlich in Zweifel ziehen mag".

202. V. ROSE, *Études sur les Évangiles*, Paris, 1902 (= *Studies on the Gospels*, tr. R. FRASER, London - New York - Bombay, 1903, p. 36): "Another conclusion, and more worthy of serious attention, is to be drawn from the Gospel of Peter. In the judgment of all, it contains quotations from our four gospels".

203. J.G. TASKER, *Apocryphal Gospels*, in J. HASTINGS (ed.), *A Dictionary of the Bible Dealing with its Language, Literature and Contents*, Extra Vol., Edinburgh - New York, 1904, 420-438, p. 427: "A careful study of the contents of this Gospel reveals many close resemblances to, and some striking divergences from, the canonical Gospels". He referred to Harnack, Zahn and Swete concluding: "From the nature of the case absolute proof is not attainable, but the solution of this complex problem, to which the investigations of many scholars point, is that the Petrine Gospel is later than the canonical Gospels; that its author was acquainted with them; that his sources are treated with great freedom, many of the changes being due to his recasting of the Gospel history in the form of a personal narrative; and that possibly he had access to other sources, which may have included, as Harnack rightly says, some good traditions".

204. A.F. FINDLAY, *Gospels (Apocryphal)*, in J. HASTINGS and J.A. SELBIE (eds.), *DCG*, Vol. 1, 1906, Edinburgh, p. 677-678, p. 678: "The Gospel is of the Synoptic type. It has close linguistic and material relations with the Synoptics, although there are many deviations in order and detail. There is a considerable probability that the author knew and made use of *all* our canonical Gospels, which he treated with great freedom, embellishing the narrative in the interest of his own point of view, and making additions of a legendary and highly miraculous character. That he had an independent tradition at he command is possible, and even probable (? ancient *Acts of Pilate*); but whether that be so or not, his Gospel adds nothing to our knowledge of the life of Christ". Dated at the middle of the second century, it originated "almost certainly" in Syria.

205. *Apocrypha*, in C.G. HERBERMANN (ed.), *The Catholic Encyclopedia*, New York, 1907, Vol. 1, 601-615, p. 608: "[GP] betrays a dependence, in some instances literal, on the four inspired Gospels, and is therefore a valuable additional testimony to their early acceptance. While the apocryphon has many points of contact with the genuine Gospels, it diverges curiously from them in details, and bears evidence of having treated them with much freedom".

206. L. FILLION, *Pierre (Écrits apocryphes de saint)*, in *DB* 5, Paris, 1912, 413-415, p. 413: "L'auteur fait successivement des emprunts aux quatre Évangiles canoniques". Unsure about the date, he asserted it certainly existed before the end of the second century (p. 414).

207. *Die urchristlichen Literaturformen* (HNT 1/3), Tübingen, [2,3]1912, p. 296: "Das Petrusevangelium hat keine andere Quellen als unsere kanonischen Evangelien gehabt; nirgends

Rhodes JAMES[210] and J. MOFFATT[211]. M. DIBELIUS (1918) maintained that the material concerning Herod reflected a late formation because of the Jewish polemic, and the author of GP certainly was dependent upon the Synoptics[212]. The form in which the account eventually made its way to GP cannot be determined with certainty. But the tradition was still fluid where it concerned the use of the OT.

Léon VAGANAY (1930), in his classic exposition[213], saw scholarly opinion divided into two

haben wir einen Grund, unabhängige Traditionen zu suchen. Der Autor hat mit einem gewissen Raffinement sich die Varianten der Evangelien zusammengesucht, aber er hat aus der Kompilation nicht eine Evangelienharmonie, sondern ein Evangelium geschaffen, das Neues and Eigenes geben will; dieser Anspruch, Besseres geben zu wollen, kommt schon darin zum Ausdruck, dass Petrus berichtet. Abhängigkeit von der Tradition und völlig freie novellistische Bearbeitung in der Art der Griechen stehen in seltsamem Kontrast".

208. E. AMANN, *Évangiles apocryphes*, in *DTC* 5, Paris, 1913, 1624-1640, p. 1630. There was no doubt the author of GP used a canonical tradition in amplifying. However, the critics were not in agreement which Gospels were used. He referred to Swete and Harnack. As to the date: "La date reste encore indécise". In a later contribution, *Apocryphes du Nouveau Testament, L'Évangile de Pierre ou selon Pierre*, in *DBS* 1, Paris, 1928, 476-477, p. 476, at one point writes: "Ici le texte rejoint sensiblement celui des évangiles canoniques". As to the date: "à placer avant 150 la date de composition. Mais, à coup sûr, elle est postérieure à l'époque où les quatre évangiles canoniques étaient en circulation, car il semble bien, quoi qu'en dise Harnack, que le rédacteur a connu le tétramorphe, dont il dépend" (p. 477).

209. H. WAITZ, *Apokryphen des Neuen Testament, Das Petrusevangeliums*, in *RE* 23, Leipzig, ³1913, 86-87, p. 86: "...so zeigt doch ein eingehender Vergleich mit den kanonischen Evangelien, dass das PE diese (auch Jo) durchweg voraussetzt. Mag der Verfasser im einzelnen ältere Traditionen benutzt haben ... so stellt sich sein Evangelium als Ganzes als eine mehr oder weniger freie Bearbeitung der evangelischen Geschichte dar, wie sie im NT vorliegt". *RE* eventually became *TRE*. See below the contribution by R.McL. WILSON.

210. M.R. JAMES, *Apocrypha*, in *EB(C)* 1, London, 1899, 1914, 249-261, p. 258 (= a one volume by same title 1914, with the correction of some typographical errors): "The conclusions upon which critics seem agreed at this moment are: [...] that [GP] shows a knowledge of all four canonical Gospels". In a later contribution (1924) James shared the late dating of around 150 AD with Robinson. He was not convinced that Justin made use of the apocryphal passion gospel (*The Apocryphal New Testament*, Oxford, 1924, p. 90). He further concurred with Robinson that the author employed the four canonical Gospels, casting the Jews in a negative light while portraying Pilate more positively.

211. J. MOFFATT, *Gospels (Uncanonical). The Gospel of Peter*, in J. HASTINGS (ed.), *DAC*, Edinburgh - New York, 1915, 496-498, p. 497, dated GP sometime "within the first quarter of the second century". He continued: "The dependence on Mark and even Matthew is, we think, to be granted. The coincidences between 'Peter' and Luke and John [...] are not quite so clear. There is room still for the hypothesis that 'Peter' represents a popular, early type of the inferior narratives which Luke desired to supercede". The matter of dependence upon Lk and Jn must be considered in light of extant oral traditions which could account for them instead.

212. M. DIBELIUS, *Die alttestamentlichen Motive in der Leidensgeschichte des Petrus- und Johannes-Evangelium*, in *BZAW* 33 (1918) 125-150 (= ID. [ed. G. BORNKAMM], *BG*, Vol. 1, 1953, 221-247, p. 243. See further p. 239.

213. L. VAGANAY, *L'Évangile de Pierre* (EB), Paris, 1930. Reviews: ALLO, E.B., *RB* 40 (1931) 435-442; AMANN, E., *RevSR* 11 (1931) 88-96; ANONYMOUS, *EstFranc* 44 (1932) 444-445; CHARUE, A., *CNam* 25 (1931) 332-333; COPPENS, J., *ETL* 8 (1931) 456-458; DE AMBROGGI,

rival schools and defined them as those following either Harnack or Zahn, the latter being described as "un chef autorisé" against Harnack[214]. Zahn was followed by the majority of critics. His position was summarized in Vaganay's words: "Le fragment découvert ne renferme, en effet, aucune tradition de valeur pour l'historien de la vie de Jésus"[215]. Disunified language, an incoherent exposition, plus tendentious remnants of the canonical Gospels contributed to this judgment. Vaganay criticized "ces systèmes fermés" of both scholars for attempting to justify preconceived ideas and thus he attempted to remedy the situation: "Peut-être y a-t-il place ... pour un examen moins incomplet et pour une interprétation plus dégagée des influences d'école"[216]. His study was particularly useful because of the valuable bibliography and the chapter which surveyed the opinions of modern critics[217].

Under the heading of "ressemblances légères", Vaganay referred to the role of Herod in Jesus' trial comparing GP 1-5 with Lk 23,6-12[218]. Individual texts which reflected some similarity were highlighted (GP 4 = Lk 23,7 and GP 5 = Lk 23,12). Despite the similarities, the role of Herod was different in the two accounts. Although the connections between GP and Mt were more numerous than those between GP and Lk and certain divergences were notorious, he insisted that "elles n'empêchent pas de croire que le pseudo-Pierre ait connu l'évangile de Luc"[219].

In discussing the historical witness of GP he devoted some pages to an examination of GP and the story of Herod in 23,6-16[220]. Citing Loisy's earlier opinion that Luke found the Herod story in an unknown gospel[221], he described this hypothesis as "une gageure". GP contained information not found in Lk[222]. GP 4 was seen to be "une déformation" of Lk 23,6-7. In a very free redaction the author of GP borrowed from Lk. Vaganay's

---

ScuolC 59 (1931) 308-309; DEVREESSE, P., RSPT 20 (1931) 559-561; DRAGUET, R., RHE 27 (1931) 854-856; GÄCHTER, P., ZKT 56 (1932) 620-621; GOGUEL, M., RHPR 11 (1931) 225-228; JAMES, M.R., JTS 32 (1930-31) 296-269; LEBRETON, RSR 21 (1931) 607-608; MEINERTZ, M., TRev 31 (1932) 236; PETERS, P., AnBoll 49 (1931) 419-420; PIEPER, K., TGl 24 (1932) 770-771; VENARD, L., RAp 55 (1932) 97-100; VITTI, A., Bib 12 (1931) 247-248.

214. VAGANAY, L'Évangile de Pierre, p. 23. Vaganay, who relied heavily on Schubert's study, praised his analysis though tempering it with a critique: "Il convient toutefois de signaler tout spécialement un autre critique, von Schubert, qui soumit l'Évangile de Pierre à une enquête détaillée, à coup sûr la plus minutieuse de celles qui ont vu le jour". Though adding, "L'analyse de von Schubert est souvent plus méticuleuse que pénétrante" (p. 27; see also p. 204, in his commentary on GP 2).

215. Ibid. Vaganay referred frequently to ZAHN, Geschichte des neutestamentlichen Kanons on matters pertaining to vocabulary and various theories (VAGANAY, p. 1, n. 1, 2, n. 3, 3, n. 1, 11, 14, 23; other references to Zahn were found on p. 78, 79).

216. Ibid., p. 32.

217. A weakness of the survey was that Vaganay did not cite the pages of the works to which he was referring. See the bibliography, p. IX-XXIII, and the chapter on the modern critics, p. 13-32.

218. Ibid., p. 54. See the entire section on the relation of GP to Lk, p. 54-59.

219. Ibid., p. 58-59.

220. Ibid., p. 129-131.

221. Ibid., p. 129, n. 1. Cf. LOISY, Évangiles synoptiques, Vol. 2, p. 634-640. Vaganay called attention to an apparent change in Loisy's point of view in L'Évangile de Luc, p. 58-59.

222. VAGANAY, L'Évangile de Pierre, p. 130: "De toute évidence, le discours d'Hérode (v. 5), inconnu de Luc, est un replâtrage mal fait".

considered opinion was: "il n'est pas besoin d'imaginer d'autre source que nos
évangiles"[223].

He insisted in his commentary on GP 1-2 that material from the canonical Gospels had
been completely transposed[224]. The author of GP demonstrated "une superbe indifférence"
in recounting the historical events. "Inutile de supposer que le rédacteur aurait eu en main
une source écrite où Hérode était protagoniste et présidait à la condamnation de Jésus. Les
seules données du troisième évangile devaient suffire à un écrivain qui ne craint pas de
broder sur un thème initial (cf. vv. 7, 13-14, 18, 39-44), qui malmène volontiers les textes
qu'il utilise (cf. vv. 28-34, 45-49, 50-57), et qui est dominé par des préoccupations d'ordre
apologétique. Toute la mise en scène de notre auteur: les Juifs seuls coupables et Pilate sans
reproche, dénote uniquement, en dehors de l'emploi des évangiles canoniques, une certaine
puissance d'imagination mise au service de la polémique courante"[225]. GP 4 reflected "un
libre remaniement" of the Herod story in Lk 23,6-16 and especially 23,7. The response of
Herod (GP 5) was likened to Lk 23,54; Mk 15,15; Mt 27,26; Lk 23,25 and Jn 19,16a[226].
GP 7 also reflected similarity with Lk 23,11 in the use of the term περιβάλλω[227]. Herod's
address to Pilate using the title "brother" was indubitably a reminiscence of 23,12.

Writing in the preface, Lagrange made it clear that by including Vaganay's work in
the EB series he was not classifying GP as one of the canonical Gospels. He praised
Vaganay who "a réalisé excellemment, avec toute l'ampleur et la précision désirable, sans
perdre jamais de vue l'objet propre de son enquête"[228]. The use of the comparative
method as well as internal criticism earned further accolades. The dependence of GP upon
the canonical Gospels also drew Lagrange's attention: "Les éléments les plus nets et de
bonne qualité historique sont empruntés aux évangiles"[229].

Vaganay continued to support the view that the author of GP employed the canonical
Gospels. In a brief encyclopedia entry (1948) he stated: " L'ouvrage dépend à coup sûr des
quatre évangiles canoniques"[230].

Reception of Vaganay's Work

M.R. James described the book as the "most extensive" ever written on GP[231]. He

223. *Ibid.*, p. 131. In n. 1, he referred to the position of M. GOGUEL, *Juifs et romains dans
l'histoire de la passion* (Suite), in *RHR* 62 (1910) 295-322, p. 304-305, that GP 5 derived from
"une tradition indépendante".

224. VAGANAY, *L'Évangile de Pierre*, p. 198.

225. *Ibid.*, p. 200. See also p. 203: "Et, à la base de cette invention, il n'y a sans doute
qu'une combinaison arbitraire des données de *Mt*. XXVII, 24 avec celles de *Lc*. XXIII,6-12".
Discussing the orders of Herod (GP 2) Vaganay observed "la tradition antérieure (cf. Act., IV,26-
27)" combined Herod and Pilate as providential instruments of the death of Jesus using the words
of Ps 2 (p. 204; see also p. 205).

226. *Ibid.*, p. 213.

227. *Ibid.*, p. 224, 225.

228. Préface, p. VII.

229. *Ibid.*, p. VIII. He added the following appreciative note about the comparative method.
"On voit de là, pour les évangiles canoniques, le bénéfice de cette comparaison. L'Évangile de
Pierre n'est ni canonique, ni biblique, mais fait mieux comprendre et goûter les vrais évangiles".

230. *Apocryphes du Nouveau Testament*, in G. JACQUEMET (ed.), *Catholicisme. Hier,
Aujourd'hui, Demain*, Paris, Vol. 1, 1948, cols. 699-704, 700.

231. *JTS* 32 (1930-31) 296-299, p. 296, adding: "It is really an admirable piece of work, and

highlighted that for Vaganay "the influence of oral teaching has been strong". As to Vaganay's date of 120 AD, he regarded it as "full early"[232]. Generally, he was in agreement with Vaganay's position[233]. In summation: "We are left with a very clear idea of all aspects of the fragment: a thoroughly secondary production which never had a great vogue. I, of course, am still of opinion that the Akhmim MS preserves for us *two* fragments of the Gospel – the Passion and the Apocalyptic piece ..."[234]. E.B. Allo, in an extended review in *RB* of Vaganay's "excellent" book, which was based on "une très vaste érudition", observed that Loisy considered GP a source of Lk because of the role Herod played in the Passion in GP[235].

M. Goguel also commented on the "solide érudition", but was more critical, claiming the book was very good, not perfect[236]. He wondered whether Vaganay had downplayed the value of GP too much, signaled by referring to the author as "faussaire", just as Harnack had exaggerated its value[237]. He regretted that Vaganay did not more carefully examine the composition of GP. He considered it possible that if GP had sources, some of them may have reflected an earlier stage of the tradition[238]. Vaganay's conclusions on the relation of GP to the canonical gospels "ne sont guère nouvelles"[239]. Finally, Goguel took issue with Vaganay's dating[240].

More positively, J. Lebreton considered Vaganay's conclusions "très judicieuses", and regarded the study as "un excellent instrument de travail"[241], while J. Coppens complimented it as "un modèle accompli d'un ouvrage de critique littéraire et historique"[242].

W. BAUER (1930) in *RGG* also maintained that GP had known the canonical Gospels and that it developed between 130-180 AD[243]. In the third edition of *RGG* Oscar CULLMANN (1961) viewed the GP as certainly having developed sometime around the middle of the second century in Syria employing all four canonical Gospels[244]. H.I. BELL and T.C. SKEAT (1935) called attention to the majority position that GP employed the Synoptics,

---

deserves to hold the field for many years to come". This was a judgment shared by P. Gächter: "V.s Buch wird jedenfalls für die Beurteilung des Petrusevangelium auf Jahre hinaus massgebend bleiben" (*ZKT* 56 [1932] 620-621, p. 621).

232. *Ibid.*

233. *Ibid.*, p. 298-299. See his disagreement as to the interpretation of Origen's evidence.

234. *Ibid.*, p. 299.

235. *RB* 40 (1931) 435-442, p. 442, 436.

236. *RHPT* 11 (1931) 225-228, p. 225.

237. *Ibid.*, p. 226.

238. *Ibid.*, p. 227, as he continued: "M. Vaganay a peut-être été trop dominé par l'idée *a priori* que l'Évangile de Pierre est un document sans aucune valeur historique positive pour avoir aperçu toute l'importance et toute la signification du problème de composition".

239. *Ibid.*

240. *Ibid.*, p. 228: "Au point de vue de la date de composition, M. Vaganay ne s'écarte pas sensiblement des conclusions généralement admises".

241. *RSR* 21 (1931) 607-608, p. 608.

242. *ETL* 8 (1931) 456-458, p. 458.

243. W. BAUER, *Petrusevangelium*, in *RGG* 4, Tübingen, ²1930, 1116.

244. O. CULLMANN, *Petrusevangelium*, in *RGG* 5, Tübingen, ³1961, 260: "Der Darstellung des P.s liegen als Quelle alle 4 kanonischen Evangelien zugrunde".

"though he handled very freely the material they offered"[245]. Further this apocryphal work did not enjoy a wide circulation[246]. In the view of C.H. DODD (1936) "the Gospel according to Peter, so far as it is preserved, contains a Passion-narrative which depends on all four canonical Gospels, and probably not only independent tradition"[247].

Aurelio DE SANTOS OTERO (1956), though conceding the difficulty in assigning a date for GP, conjectured 150 AD[248]. Detecting heavy apologetical interests which helped to shape the account, such as eliminating Pilate's responsibility in Jesus' death, while increasing that of Herod and the Jews, GP showed "dependencia manifesta" upon the canonical Gospels[249]. Such was also the opinion of J. HERVIEUX (1958)[250] and J. MICHL (1959)[251]. M.S. ENSLIN (1962) considered dependence of GP upon the canonical Gospels as "unmistakable", suggesting that the "most probable date is the third decade of the second

245. H.I. BELL and T.C. SKEAT, *Fragments of An Unknown Gospel and Other Early Christian Papyri*, London, 1935, p. 31.

246. As to the date they wrote: "The composition of [GP] has indeed by some critics been put back as early as the end of the first century, but seems on the whole unlikely. M.R. James (*The Apocryphal New Testament*, Oxford, 1924, p. 90) thinks it 'not safe to date the book much earlier than A.D. 150'; Vaganay (p. 163) inclines to a date shortly after A.D. 120. In either case it is at least unexpected to find it circulating in Middle Egypt by the middle of the century".

247. C.H. DODD, *A New Gospel*, in *BJRL* 20 (1936) 56-92, p. 87 (= ID., *New Testament Studies*, Manchester, 1953, 12-52, p. 46). In the original essay it was noted this was "an elaboration of the lectures delivered in the John Rylands Library on the 13th of November, 1935" (p. 56). He acknowledged in *New Testament Studies* that this article along with several others "are reprinted virtually in their original form. I have corrected misprints, made some slight verbal changes, and omitted a few sentences which not longer seemed pertinent. But I have made no attempt to bring them up to date" (p. v-vi).

248. A. DE SANTOS OTERO, *Los Evangelios Apocrifos*, Madrid, 1956, p. 400 (esp. p. 68-72; 398-417); ²1963 (esp. p. 64-67; 375-393); ³1975 (esp. p. 64-67; 375-393); ⁶1988 (p. 60-63 and 369-387, esp. p. 371). See F. NEIRYNCK, Review in *ETL* 66 (1990) 417, where he called this a classic work, though noting that the bibliography of the sixth edition ends at 1974.

249. DE SANTOS OTERO, p. 400; (= ⁶1988, p. 371): "Sin embargo, la composición de los evangelios canónicos, de los que arguye dependencia manifesta, y el testimonio de Serapión, obispo de Antioquía (190-211), son dos buenos jalones entre los que hay que situar necesariamente la composición". A later entry is not so clear on the question of dependence: "El fragemento ... describe las últimas escenas de la Pasión, ofreciendo rasgos comunes con los canónicos, a lost que añade notas curiosas ..." (*Pedro, Evangelio de*, in *Enciclopedia de la Biblia* 5, Barcelona, 1965, ²1969, 979). The date was approximately 150 AD while the place of composition was probably Syria.

250. J. HERVIEUX, *Ce que l'Évangile ne dit pas*, Paris, 1958, p. 126 (= *What Are Apocryphal Gospels?*, London, 1960 = *The New Testament Apocrypha*, tr. W. HIBBERD, New York, 1960, p. 153): "The apocryphal literature set out to refashion the Gospel narrative in its own way so as to provide a version revised and corrected according to partisan views". So also p. 154: "It is simply a radical recasting of the Gospel narratives". On the role of Herod in the trial and the anti-Jewish polemic, see *Ce que*, p. 127-132 (= 155, 162). The GP was treated in *Ce que*, p. 126-133 (= p. 153-162).

251. J. MICHL, *Evangelien*, in *LTK* 3, 1959, 1217-1233, p. 1228: "das abhängig v. den kanon. Evv., aber phantast. ausgeschmückt das Leiden u. die Auferstehung Jesu erzählt, wobei alle Schuld am Tod Jesu dem Herodes u. den Juden aufgebürdet wird". It developed in Syria, presumably in the second century.

century"[252]. Charles H.H. SCOBIE (1963) observed that "it is particularly interesting as indicating how canonical material could be elaborated and changed in the interests of the Docetic heresy"[253]. A probable date of the mid second century was estimated.

Proposing that GP was composed around 150 AD and drew upon all four canonical Gospels, Raymond BROWN (1968) also noted that "although at first some scholars argued that GPet contained real historical knowledge not preserved in the canonical Gospels, today most look upon it as an imaginative misdrash on gospel materials"[254]. In his revision of the article (1990), while noting that many scholars regarded GP as "an imaginative pastiche dependent on all four Gospels", Brown also rehearsed the view of scholars such as Harnack, Gardner-Smith and Koester who advocated the independence of GP from the canonical Gospels[255]. He further recalled the position of Crossan that GP provided the basis for the passion narratives in the canonical Gospels. Brown emended his earlier position: "Perhaps *Gos. Pet.* represents popular, fluid developments of early traditions free from the control of the apostolic kerygma (e.g. Herod's role against Jesus). These imaginatively expanded accounts may have been written down and combined with stories remembered from past hearing or reading of canonical Gospels"[256].

So significant is the GP that Brown (1994) devoted a first appendix of his commentary on the passion narratives to it[257]. In effect, all the references in *Death*, plus the appendix, would certainly have constituted a commentary on GP though such was not his intention. This section contained the following four major sections: a literal translation of GP; a discussion of the sequence and contents of GP[258]; aspects of the theology of GP[259]; and date and place of composition. A working bibliography was included. He contended that the author of the second century GP contained "echoes" of the canonical Gospels as well as traditions known to the evangelists, though at a more developed level[260]. It was

252. M.S. ENSLIN, *Peter, Gospel of*, in *IDB* 3, 1962, 766-767, p. 766.

253. C.H.H. SCOBIE, *Apocryphal New Testament*, in J. HASTINGS (ed.), *Dictionary of the Bible*, (eds. F.C. GRANT and H.H. ROWLEY), Edinburgh, 1963, ²1965, 41-45 (esp. p. 43-44), p. 43.

254. R.E. BROWN, *Apocrypha; Dead Sea Scrolls; Other Jewish Literature*, in *JBC*, Englewood Cliffs, NJ, 1968, 535-560, p. 546.

255. R.E. BROWN, *Apocrypha; Dead Sea Scrolls; Other Jewish Literature*, in *NJBC*, Englewood Cliffs, NJ, 1990, 1055-1082, p. 1067-1068.

256. *Ibid.*, p. 1068.

257. BROWN, *Death*, Appendix I, p. 1317-1349. On Brown's earlier critique of Crossan, cf. above, n. 66.

258. The subsections included a sequence table comparing the GP with the canonical Gospels, a comparison of their contents, and an overall proposal about their contents.

259. He rehearsed the debate about Docetism as well as other aspects of the theology of the apocryphal gospel.

260. BROWN, *Death*, p. 781, where he also announced his opposition to the "extravagant" theory of Crossan (n. 36; see also p. 1321: "I see little to recommend the compositional theory of D. Crossan"). Apparently, the author of GP would only know Mk secondarily: "There is no column for Mark because the basic Marcan sequence is the same as Matt's, and the *GPet* has no scene peculiar to Mark" (p. 1322). Brown was most influenced by Swete, Vaganay, Beyschlag and Mara. He supplied his own translation of Mara's Greek text, "with one significant change", *para[alē]mphthēnai* in 1,2, which Neirynck printed at the end of *Aprocryphal*, p. 171-175 (p. 1318, n. 6, 7 = *Evangelica II*, p. 763-767). He stated the majority opinion was that the GP was dependent upon the canonical Gospels, a view supported by Beyschlag, Burkitt, Dodd, Finegan,

"incredible" that the canonical evangelists drew on GP because of sequence, which in this regard, more closely resembled Mt than Lk[261]. There were three principal objections to the originality of GP. If the canonical Gospels had employed GP, why was the vocabulary and word order not adopted? Secondly, why were there such glaring omissions of GP material. Thirdly, why do not Mt, Lk and Jn agree on the non-Markan GP material and never agree with GP against Mk in what they added[262]. Frequently the author of GP heard Mt in worship and he had spoken with people familiar with Lk and Jn. A date of composition was proposed of between 100-150 AD in an area around Antioch, though probably in one of the smaller towns of Syria like Rhossos[263]. GP supposedly came into existence as a popular production, being read publicly in small Syrian towns and consequently was given a status alongside the canonical Gospels[264]. Brown dismissed the perspective of D. Crossan[265]. Specifically with regard to the Herod pericope (23,6-12.15) he accepted the "surface likelihood" that it was the same Herod being discussed in this episode, Acts 4,25-28 and GP, though it was possible GP contained confused memories and thus did not differentiate between the various Herods[266].

While Brown considered GP a second-century writing, based on the view of "the likelihood ... that the author used echoes from the canonical Gospels of Matt, Luke, and John", Neirynck took issue with his omission of Mk[267]. Brown's comments on the relationship of GP to the canonical Gospels in the appendix on GP "are more reserved" than in the rest of the commentary[268]. While "Brown emphasizes orality and distant memory" Neirynck argued for literary dependence. He generally agreed with Brown's refutation of Crossan's theory of the Cross Gospel[269].

In 1989 Neirynck argued that "the new look at the passion-resurrection story in the Gospel of Peter [has] serious consequences for the interpretation of the Gospel of Mark"[270]. This was important since this essay contained a study of the dependence of GP 50-57 upon Mk 16 concerning the women at the tomb[271]. More recently, in reaction to

Harris, M.R. James, Lührmann, Mara, Maurer, Meier, Moffatt, J.A. Robinson, Swete, Turner, Vaganay, Wright and Zahn while those opposed included Cameron, Crossan, Denker, A.J. Dewey, Gardner-Smith, Harnack, Hilgenfeld, Koester, Moulton, Völter, von Soden and Walter (BROWN, *Death*, p. 1332, n. 21, 22).

261. See BROWN, *Death*, p. 1330: "When these differences are added to the failure of *GPet* to follow unique patterns in the Lucan sequence, it is clear that in content and sequence *GPet's* relationship to Luke is more distant than *GPet's* relationship to Matt.".

262. *Ibid.*, p. 1332-1333. There were major differences between Lk and GP despite the following three items shared by both: Herod's role in Jesus' trial, the friendly relations between Herod and Pilate and that Jesus was given to the Jews and only later to the Romans (p. 1330). On other comparisions between Lk and GP see p. 856.

263. *Ibid.*, p. 1342-1345. A. Lods also suggested this town as place of origin (cf. above n. 190).

264. *Ibid.*, p. 1347.

265. *Ibid.*, p. 1321; see also p. 1322, n. 9, p. 1325, n. 10, p. 1328, n. 16, and p. 1333, n. 27.

266. *Ibid.*, p. 1330, n. 19.

267. *Ibid.*, p. 1342. Cf. F. NEIRYNCK, *Historical Jesus*, p. 226-229.

268. NEIRYNCK, *Historical Jesus*, p. 229.

269. *Ibid.* But see also n. 50.

270. NEIRYNCK, *Apocryphal Gospels*, 1989, p. 132 (= *Evangelica II*, p. 724).

271. For a similar view, see J.W. MCCANT, *The Gospel of Peter*, 1976, p. 70, 113-114. See

Brown's repeated assessment that the GP "draws on the canonical Gospels", he remarked: "Only the Gospel of Mark is left out of the picture, without good reason"[272]. Neirynck responded in turn to each of Brown's reservations[273]. Regarding Brown's claim that Neirynck "had to make" changes in the sequence of the Markan verses to highlight the parallelism with GP he insisted such modifications were "minimal"[274]. Secondly, the "good deal of difference in internal sequence and word order" observed by Brown was regarded by Neirynck as insignificant in some cases or could reflect a proper understanding of the Markan text in others[275]. Thirdly, where Brown challenges dependence based upon the amount of shared vocabulary, Neirynck argued that the "configuration of the words is more important than their total number"[276]. As for Brown's specific challenge of the term νεανίσκος Neirynck effectively used an earlier article of Brown's to show dependence upon Mk in the apocryphal tradition[277].

Use of all the canonical Gospels as sources by the author of GP does not *de facto* require that he would have used all parts of each of the Gospels[278]. Therefore, GP 50-57 may indeed be the most "Markan" section of the apocryphal gospel. Also Brown postulated the view that Mk and Mt were so similar that it was virtually impossible to distinguish them[279]. That being the case, then Brown must accept that the author of GP was dependent upon Mk as well.

Change in the arrangement of the material or of words does not exclude the possibility that the author of GP was dependent upon Mk, or indeed any of the other canonical Gospels. As Brown himself noted regarding Matthean and Lukan redaction of Mk: "In the canonical Gospel PNs, we have an example of Matt working conservatively and Luke working more freely with the Marcan outline and of each adding material ..."[280]. The author of GP could likewise have treated his canonical sources in a very free manner.

below.

272. NEIRYNCK, *Historical Jesus*, p. 229. Cf. BROWN, *Death*, p. 1327-1328. Even among those who argued GP was based on an independent tradition, there were some who argued that the author of GP knew Mk, as Brown himself observed (*Death*, p. 1332, n. 22). Others, like J.H. MOULTON, *The 'Gospel of Peter' and the Four*, in *ExpT* 4 (1892-93) also expressed doubt whether the author of GP employed Mk. That view could be contrasted with H.J. HOLTZMANN, *Literatur zum Neuen Testament. IV: Evangelienfrage*, in *TJ* 12 (1892) 117-120, who insisted that GP was especially dependent upon Mt and Mk. Cf. above n. 136.

273. *Ibid.*, p. 227-229.

274. NEIRYNCK, *Historical Jesus*, p. 227. Brown made no special case for Mk in the matter of comparing its sequence with that of GP arguing that Mk's was the same as Mt's (BROWN, *Death*, p. 1322).

275. BROWN, *Death*, p. 1328. Cf. NEIRYNCK, *Historical Jesus*, p. 228.

276. *Ibid.*

277. NEIRYNCK, *Historical Jesus*, p. 228. Cf. BROWN, *The Relation of "the Secret Gospel of Mark" to the Fourth Gospel*, in *CBQ* 36 (1974) 466-485, p. 484, 469, 476, n. 23.

278. Consider McCant's view that "GP used four stories which were unique to their authors – Matthew's guard story, Mark's empty tomb story, John's Galilean resurrection story and Luke's Pilate-Herod scene" (*The Gospel of Peter*, p. 113-114).

279. BROWN, *Death*, p. 57: "In discussing Synoptic interdependence [...], I explained my acceptance of the thesis that Matt knew Mark's PN and followed it so closely that many times there is no major difference in what they narrate". See NEIRYNCK, *Gospels Issues in the Passion Narratives. Critical Note on a New Commentary*, in *ETL* 70 (1994) 406-416, esp. p. 415.

280. BROWN, *Death*, p. 1325.

Swete, upon whom Brown depended for some of his comparisons between GP and the canonical Gospels, did not find that there was such strong verbal similarity between GP on the one hand and Mt and Mk on the other. Swete contended nonetheless that it was "a probability which approaches to a certainty in the case of the Second Gospel" that the author of GP knew Mk[281].

Further, scholars such as H. Schürmann, A. Vööbus and Brown's student M.L. Soards expressed reservations about a purely statistical method of determining Lukan vocabulary in an effort to discern redactional elements of Luke. That same caution should be applied to a study of this nature.

Brown again addressed the issue of the relationship of GP to the canonical Gospel in his NT Introduction (1997), stating that the majority of scholars supported the view that GP was dependent upon the canonical Gospels[282]. His comments frequently involved rejecting the position of Crossan[283].

Susan E. SCHAEFFER, in a 1991 Union Theological Seminary (NY) dissertation directed by R.E. Brown[284], focused on three questions, two of which have been central to our survey: the date of GP and the issue of the relationship of GP to the canonical Gospels, which Harnack termed "das wichtigste Problem"[285]. Her intention was to challenge a "longstanding conviction that the *GosPet* was developed from a dependence on the written text of the canonical gospels"[286]. Her view was that the term "dependence" must be interpreted more broadly concluding that the relationship "is best explained as dependence through oral transmission"[287]. As to the date, she argued for the second quarter of the second century, the place of composition being Western Syria[288]. While it was possible that the author of GP had heard the canonical Gospels, perhaps numerous times[289], it was quite probable that the author "knew that there were written gospels"[290].

281. SWETE, ΕΥΑΓΓΕΛΙΟΝ, p. xx. Cf. BROWN, *Death*, p. 1325, n. 11, where he referred to SWETE, ΕΥΑΓΓΕΛΙΟΝ, p. xvi-xx.

282. *Introduction*, p. 112.

283. See, for example, p. 822, 829, 836.

284. Susan E. SCHAEFFER, *The "Gospel of Peter", the Canonical Gospels, and Oral Tradition*, Diss. Union Theol. Sem., 1991 (dir. R.E. BROWN). Following an introduction (ch 1), the work was divided into two main parts: part one treated the unity and date of GP and part two, entitled the same as the dissertation, investigated the relationship between GP, the canonical Gospels and oral tradition. A chapter summarizing results and conclusions rounded out the study. In taking stock of earlier works she wrote that von Schubert's five gospel parallels, "while not altogether satisfying, have been an invaluable aid" (p. 120).

285. Cf. HARNACK, *Bruchstücke*, ²1893, p. V.

286. SCHAEFFER, *Gospel*, Abstract, p. 1.

287. Cf. p. 119, n. 14: "Brown, 'Priority' 335, recently suggested that the *GosPet* was related to the canonical gospels through 'oral dependence'". So also, p. 240: "I proposed that the relationship between the *GosPet* and the canonical gospels was best explained as a link through oral traditions, a suggestion that was made in some prior studies but never fully explored". LODS (*L'évangile*, p. 79) and more hesitantly BENNETT (*Gospel*, p. 41) were regarded as precursors in considering oral tradition as a solution (p. 151-152). She relied on the works of J. Vansina, W. Ong and D. Buchan in her treatment of orality (see for example, p. 179, 183, 184). The passion account of GP was also influenced by the LXX (p. 185).

288. SCHAEFFER, *Gospel*, Abstract, p. 2; p. 112-113, 241. See also p. 4-5.

289. *Ibid.*, p. 155. So also p. 160.

290. *Ibid.*, p. 184. See also p. 159: "If oral tradition is involved in the origin of *GosPet*, the

She cited the "radical proposal" of H. Koester, B.A. Johnson, J.M. Robinson, and J.D. Crossan that GP was not only "an early and independent source for the canonical traditions" but that it must be studied alongside the four Gospels[291]. In her second chapter she examined Koester's triple criteria for establishing priority. She dismissed the first criterion, more frequent Scripture citations, since that can be easily reversed. Rather than being indicative of an early text, it may reflect "a conscious effort ... to match scripture to plot developments", much as was the case with later apologists[292].

A second criterion proposed by Koester to indicate priority was one scriptural passage per scene. This was in contrast to the canonical Gospels wherein it may be spread over several scenes. In support Koester offered two examples. As regards the first, Is 50,6 in the mockery scenes, Schaeffer judged this "problematic" since it occurred at a fragmentary portion of GP and therefore was inconclusive[293]. The second example, the offering of a drink was "also arguable". In Schaeffer's opinion, simplification of a narrative may be redaction and not "an earlier stratum of the tradition"[294]. The third criterion, purity of form, was examined using the texts of GP 28-49 and Mt 27,62-66; 28,2-4.11-15. Because this involved such detailed argumentation, we shall only mention that she rejected this criterion as well "based on close readings of the two texts". Unpersuaded she argued that Mk and not GP was the earliest passion narrative[295].

Schaeffer, in contradistinction to Crossan, believed that GP was "a unified composition". She disputed his position on the basis of MS, grammatical (also called linguistic), and compositional evidence which she treated in her third chapter. The MS evidence involved, in part, a comparison of the Akhmîm fragment with POx 2949[296]. Building on this, "late vocabulary, the possibility of a late liturgical form and the employment of Atticist features ... are compelling pieces of linguistic evidence that point to composition no earlier than the second century"[297]. Finally, she insisted GP 3-5a was not a redactional insertion. Rather, it was "an integral, even an essential, piece of the

document we are studying is the record of oral tradition in *written* form".

291. *Ibid.*, p. 12. Koester was credited with having "started the current debate on the *GosPet*" with his 1980 article (p. 13). The positions of Koester, Johnson and Crossan were evaluated in chapters 2 and 3.

292. *Ibid.*, p. 22. See p. 23: "Instead of using explicit citations, the *GosPet* weaves scriptural allusions through the passion narrative". Following a case study of GP 3,5b-9 and Mk 15,15b-19, she concluded: "In terms of Koester's own criterion of scriptural use, the *GosPet* must represent a stage of the tradition that is later than Mark ... In the *GosPet*, the evangelist uses a different and more subtle technique – weaving scriptural allusions into the narrative fabric through selected vocabulary links" (p. 27-28).

293. *Ibid.*, p. 28, 29.

294. *Ibid.*, p. 30. Perceptively she noted Koester, Denker and Crossan all relied on Johnson's 1965 dissertation, *Empty Tomb* (p. 34-35).

295. SCHAEFFER, *Gospel*, p. 77: "Thus far in our study, we have not found sufficient evidence to support claims that the *GosPet* deserves to replace Mark as the earliest passion narrative".

296. Reference was made to LÜHRMANN, *POx 2949*, and NEIRYNCK, *Apocryphal*, p. 143 (p. 82, n. 9 and 84, n. 12).

297. SCHAEFFER, *Gospel*, p. 93.

GosPet and also a composition by none other than the person who wrote the entire gospel"[298].

The Herod material in GP did not occupy a central place in her study, but she touched on it in several places[299]. Reference to Herod was included among those elements in GP which were unique to Lk[300]. Schaeffer was very aware that the account in GP was quite different from that found in Lk for she acknowledged that "while the canonical gospels report the Pilate tradition with differing dramatic, apologetic, and evangelistic developments, surely their report that Jesus was crucified by Pilate's order is faithful to the tradition in a way that the *GosPet* is not when it has Pilate subservient to Herod who has Jesus crucified"[301]. In her most extended treatment of the Herod material she indicated that GP 1 may have meant that Pilate departed the scene (so Beyschlag), but Pilate would never have yielded to Herod[302]. The similarity between GP 4 and Lk 23,7 was detected, though Luke, unlike the author of GP, "clearly observes the sense of place". While oral tradition could account for the resemblance, the author of GP was evidently confused[303].

298. *Ibid.*, p. 100.

299. *Ibid.*, p. 121: "The passages chosen are those most often cited in arguments for literary dependence". These were GP 24 (p. 121-125); 50-57 (p. 125-135); 30 (p. 164-170); 53 (p. 170-179). In light of this one must question her assertion that "with the exception of Crossan's 1988 book, the present work is the first full-length study of the entire *GosPet* to appear in English since 1893" (p. 10).

Occasional references to the Herod account in Lk (and GP) were found on p. 6, 82. GP 2 and 5 were included among verses using direct discourse (p. 200). Lk 23,7.11 were mentioned in the context of a discussion of the Geographical *Loci* of the Canonical Passion Narratives, where she also added: "The change from the oral to the written medium, as well as redactional changes, have undoubtedly obscured in our texts some of the references to the places where each episode occurred, but the basic structure of the narrative around these *loci* can still be seen" (p. 218; on 23,11 see also p. 250).

300. *Ibid.*, p. 180-181. Though some features are common with Lk she continues, "the material is handled very differently, which suggests a more distant recollection of Luke or possibly a knowledge only of common tradition".

301. *Ibid.*, p. 192, n. 17.

302. *Ibid.*, p. 220. Cf. BEYSCHLAG, *Petrusevangelium*, p. 33. She was impressed by Beyschlag's conception and distinction of the use of oral and written sources: "Above all one must imagine the 'use' of written 'sources' in our case is not altogether strong. Besides, Luther, as everyone knows, when he began to translate it, knew the New Testament better in his head than on paper. And so also is to be understood the agreed procedure in the early period of Christianity. An echo, a parallel, indeed, a whole piece of the New Testament that in similar form returns in an apocryphal gospel must by no means have been unconditionally copied from a written 'Vorlage' lying along side [it]. Far more obvious is above all the assumption of a memory-like reproduction or combination from oral tradition whereby it is naturally not impossible that at the author's disposal were written sources whose contents he had in his head" [ET by Schaeffer] (p. 152-153; cf. BEYSCHLAG, p. 51-52).

303. She extrapolated: "The geographical and temporal distance of oral narrators from the historical places, persons, and events can easily account for many of the changes in the *GosPet*. If in the process of oral transmission a loss of place was coupled with an unclear knowledge of who Pilate was and where he governed, of who Herod was and the limits of his authority, this ignorance could have abetted the cause of storytellers with polemical and apologetical interests. A vaguely conceived Pilate, no longer bound to a historical memory, could have, first, yielded

Though the work was well written one must nonetheless question her concept of redaction for being too narrowly conceived[304]. She granted, correctly in my estimation, that one must also take into consideration "such common features as plot, theme, episodes, and setting", and not merely verbal similarity or dissimilarity[305]. Though she was right in stating that "opinion [on literary dependence/independence] has remained divided for almost a century", there was a clear majority favoring literary dependence, which she duly noted[306]. D.L. BOCK (1996) was also influenced by Brown who noted "an elaborate version" of Herod's trial appeared in GP saying that this work "attests to an independent tradition"[307].

Utilizing Schaeffer's unpublished annotated bibliography on GP, Claudia SETZER (1994), whose 1990 Columbia University dissertation Brown also directed[308], rejected literary dependence "in either direction" and suggested Brown's position was a "useful working hypothesis". However, she cautioned that "the reader should know that the relationship of the Gospels and *Gos. Pet.* is highly disputed"[309]. She noted that while the majority of GP was "material shared with the Gospels, the sequence and character of the material are confused"[310]. She dated the final redaction of GP at "around 110-150"[311].

responsibility for Jesus' death to a Jewish leader and then later confessed Jesus to be 'the Son of God' (*GosPet* 11:46)" (SCHAEFFER, *Gospel*, p. 220-221).

304. "Yet, does the method of comparing minute textual samples, some as small as a single word, provide sufficient evidence to conclude that the *GosPet* is a wholly derivative work? When larger blocks of texts, such as full sentences are compared, the argument for literary dependence are revealed as weak and unconvincing, because the amount of sustained verbal agreement between the *GosPet* and the canonical gospels is actually quite limited" (p. 119-120).

305. *Ibid.*, p. 157. J.W. McCant was judged as correctly having seen this: "Thus, McCant's decision about the *GosPet*'s dependence based on its common themes and structures was on the right track" (n. 19).

306. *Ibid.*, p. 6-7, 13. She continued to treat a number of these issues in a subsequent publication: *The Guard at the Tomb (Gos. Pet. 8:28-11:49 and Matt 27:62-66; 28:2-4,11-16): A Case of Intertextuality?*, in *SBL 1991 Seminar Papers*, 499-507, p. 507: "Elsewhere, I have developed a view of the *GosPet* as a product of oral tradition that is 'dependent' on the canonical gospels". She referred here to her study, *The Gospel of Peter*, esp. chapters V and VI (n. 33).

307. BOCK, *Luke 9:51-24:53* (BECNT, 3b), 1996, p. 1817. See BROWN, *Death*, p. 781.

308. C.J. SETZER, *Jewish Responses to Early Christians. History and Polemics (30-150 C.E.)*, Minneapolis, MN, 1994 (= Diss. Columbia U., 1990 [dir. R.E. BROWN]). Cf. S. SCHAEFFER, *An Annotated Bibliography on the Gospel of Peter*. Unpublished manuscript, May 1987 (SETZER, p. 240). Also in the line of Brown and Schaeffer advocating only oral dependence of GP upon the canonical Gospels is M.K. STILLMAN, *The Gospel of Peter. A Case for Oral-Only Dependency*, in *ETL* 73 (1997) 114-120.

309. SETZER, p. 116. At the end of the chapter she argued: "For the purposes of this study, I have already discounted *Gos. Pet.* as direct testimony to events surrounding the Passion and placed it in the milieu of second-century Jewish-Christian polemic. *Gos. Pet.* testifies to traditions about the Jews and their treatment of Jesus's followers that are generally found in the canonical Gospels as well, but paints them with bolder, simpler strokes. ... The fact that [GP] uses traditional material but reworks it in such a way that it always implicates the Jews cannot be accidental" (p. 124).

310. *Ibid.*, p. 117.

311. *Ibid.*, p. 116. She indicated that both Lk and GP mentioned Herod's involvement with Jesus (p. 214 n. 4).

Karlmann BEYSCHLAG (1969) was of the opinion that "kann es heute kaum zweifelhaft sein (kann), dass dem Evangelisten mindestens die ersten drei Evangelien (Matt, Mark, Luk) sicher bekannt waren"[312]. Taking note of the increased role Herod played in contrast with Pilate who became "eine Nebenfigur"[313], he highlighted the lack of knowledge the author of GP betrayed in describing Herod as king[314]. As to date, he spoke generally of the second century[315].

In a 1972 Northwestern University dissertation D.H. SCHMIDT observed that the GP fragment bears a "strong resemblance to the canonical gospels"[316]. He recalled that scholarship was divided into two camps concerning the origin. The first, proposing that GP may be older than the Synoptics, was endorsed by Harnack (1893), Hilgenfeld (1893), Cassels (1894), and Gardner-Smith (1926). Zahn (1893), Swete (1893), and Semeria (1894) supported the second. He was of the opinion that the Lukan Herod story (23,6-12) may have inspired GP 3, adding: "But again there is no attempt to be faithful to Luke, if that was his source"[317]. On the overall relationship between Lk and GP he concluded: "Thus the lack of clear parallels between Peter and Luke and the distorted forms of the few parallels which do appear suggest that the writer of the Gospel of Peter might have known Luke or oral traditions which the writer of Luke used but was not quoting Luke *per se*. Rather reminiscences from Lukan tradition possibly helped faintly in forming some of his polemic, but Luke was not a major source for the writer of the Gospel of Peter"[318]. He reiterated that the author of GP may have only known oral traditions which were later incorporated into Lk[319]. As to the date, a possible clue is the link between the gospel and apostolic authority, "a good indication that the Gospel of Peter represents a time after that of the synoptics"[320].

312. K. BEYSCHLAG, *Das Petrusevangelium*, in ID., *Die verborgene Überlieferung von Christus* (Siebenstern-Taschenbuch, 136), Munich - Hamburg, 1969, 27-64, p. 52. He extended dependence to Jn as well: "Vielmehr ist der Verfasser, soweit sich das wissenschaftlich überhaupt feststellen lässt, durchweg von allen vier kanonischen Evangelien – und darüber hinaus von keinen fünften – abhängig, die er als bekannte Sammlung bereits deutlich voraussetzt und darum auch mehr oder minder phantasievoll kombiniert" (p. 62; see also p. 64).

313. *Ibid.*, p. 33-34. See further p. 49.

314. *Ibid.*, p. 44-45.

315. *Ibid.*, p. 50. See also p. 32.

316. D.H. SCHMIDT, *The Peter Writings: Their Redactors and Their Relationships*. Diss. Northwestern, Evanston, IL, 1972 (dir. A. SUNDBERG), esp. p. 136-160, p. 136. See his bibliography, p. 216-219.

317. *Ibid.*, p. 145. See p. 150-151, where he wrote of synoptic material which was transformed by GP. Noting that Herod, not Pilate, was involved wih the trial he contrasted GP 2 with Mk 15,15 and par. without mentioning Lk 23,6-12. He also stipulated that the author of GP "may not have known Luke" (p. 151).

318. *Ibid.*, p. 146.

319. *Ibid.*, p. 158. As regards the other Gospels, Schmidt maintained that the author of GP knew Mt and probably knew Mk. He was familiar with oral traditions which subsequently were taken up into Jn.

320. *Ibid.*, p. 156. See also his discussion of early authors who refer to GP, wherein he asserted that the "knowledge of the Gospel of Peter is primarily limited to Syria and its environs in the second and third century" (p. 180-184, p. 184).

Maria Grazia MARA (1973) observed the contested views on the relation of GP to the canonical Gospels, stating that "il semblait que Vaganay avait prononcé, définitivement, le denier mot sur ce texte si discuté"[321]. Although she was very appreciative of his work[322], she took strong exception to some aspects of it. She believed that Vaganay's reaction was inspired, in part, by an unconscious fear that questions related to the GP would be "dangereuses pour l'autorité des Évangiles canoniques"[323]. He presupposed the historical truth of the canonical Gospels, which he believed were free from theological re-elaboration and thus objective. Mara maintained, in contrast, that the canonical Gospels were themselves dependent upon an interpretation of the facts. Vaganay did not pursue his study objectively because of his predisposition to regard GP in a negative light. This was evidenced, for example, by referring to the author of GP as "faussaire". Such an attitude, according to Mara, was his "préoccupation constante" and was particularly obvious in the chapter on the literary problem[324]. Mara called attention to the fact that while Vaganay made an observation about the poverty of the vocabulary and style of GP, he nonetheless proposed "une liste très substantielle" of elements of the literary elegance which it contained[325]. Further, she reacted against Vaganay's repeated reference to GP by the term "faussaire", stating it was a misnomer[326]. In addition, as to passages which Vaganay designated as non-historical, Mara asserted "nous refusons de présupposer que la non-historicité dépende de la discordance avec le récit évangélique"[327].

She regarded the following four issues as the problems posed by GP: 1) its relationship to the canonical Gospels; 2) the date and place of redaction; 3) the docetic or gnostic elements; and 4) the passion in what many consider to be a popular or heterodox presentation[328]. She did not offer a detailed study of the first problem. Instead, she referred readers to Vaganay who had already done this "de façon magistrale". The particular theological thought of GP, that the responsibility of the judgment of Jesus rested with the Jews, "nous permet de mieux comprendre les rapports entre Ev.P. et les Évangiles canoniques"[329]. The differences can be accounted for, not by ignorance, but by this theological perspective.

321. M.G. MARA, *Évangile de Pierre. Introduction, texte critique, traduction, commentaire et index* (SC, 201), Paris, 1973, p. 16. Cf. above on Vaganay. This particular issue was "le problème devenu fondamental" (p. 17). She included Harnack, Cassels, Reinach, Soden, Hilgenfeld, Völter, Manchot and Van Manen as advocating the view that GP was earlier than the canonical Gospels (p. 17-18). Her work was comprised of an *avant-propos*, bibliography, introduction, preface, text and translation (in which she used the double reference system of Robinson and Harnack), commentary, and conclusion. This was followed by three indices: the first containing Greek words, a second relating affinities between GP and Scripture, and finally, a third consisting of authors and ancient texts.

322. GP was "amplement exposé" in Vaganay's work, which was further characterized as a "vaste travail, plein d'érudition", and an "analyse attentive".

323. *Ibid.*, p. 24-31, p. 25.

324. *Ibid.*, p. 26. Cf. VAGANAY, *L'Évangile*, p. 141-147.

325. *Ibid.*, p. 28.

326. *Ibid.*, p. 29.

327. *Ibid.*, p. 30.

328. MARA, *Évangile*, p. 34.

329. *Ibid.*, p. 72-73.

As for specific connections between GP and Lk, several brief references were found in the section containing the text and translation[330]. Treating several verses of the apocryphal gospel together briefly (GP 3, 4, 5), she pointed to similarities ("renvois ... à l'Évangile de Luc") with Lk 23,11; 22,7; 23,6-12; 23,54[331]. In her index of affinities between GP and the Scriptures in the Scriptural order she listed the following: 23,6-16 (= GP 4); 23,9 (= GP 10); 23,11 (= GP 2); 23,11-12 (GP 3, 4, 5); 23,13-23 (= GP 46); 23,16 (= GP 9)[332]. It is also important to note that she understood the vesture in 23,11 as "un vêtement blanc éclatant"[333].

In offering her conclusions about the relationship of GP with the canonical Gospels, she acknowledged that the author of the apocryphal gospel was deficient in certain aspects of his understanding[334]. However, "il est mesuré et avisé dans la réélaboration théologique des données évangéliques. Non seulement il connaît les Évangiles canoniques, l'Apocalypse, l'Ancien Testament et d'autres textes de la littérature apocalyptique, mais il y puise librement, avec l'intention précise de situer la passion, la mort et la gloire du Κύριος à la lumière de ce qu'avait annoncé l'Ancien Testament"[335]. She believed that the author of GP followed the Synoptics in recounting the episodes, but derived theology from Jn and Rev. As for the date, she signaled her preference for a date in the first half of the second century[336]. Observing that scholars generally favored Syria, though Völter had suggested Egypt, Mara indicated her choice as Asia Minor. F.F. BRUCE (1974) entertained the possibility that GP "may draw in part from separate traditions" but was convinced that the author was familiar with the canonical Gospels[337].

Reception of Mara's Work

Noting that Vaganay may have edited GP "most throughly", B.M. Metzger compared Mara's work saying it was "convenient and up-to-date" and that her commentary was "balanced"[338]. P.-M. Bogaert hailed the study as "concis, clair et bien informé", and "précis"[339]. N. Walter emphasized the differences between Mara and Vaganay, while

---

330. *Ibid.*, p. 41, n. 2 (reference to Vaganay and the connection of GP 2 and Ps 2,2); p. 42, n. 3 (GP 4: "Rappel possible, mais très altéré, de Lc 23,6-16".); and p. 43, n. 4 (GP 5 concerning 'Αδελφὲ Πειλᾶτε, listing Lk 23,12; Ps 2,1-2, and Acts 4,27; see also p. 80). However, no reference was made on p. 44, n. 3, about a possible similarity between GP 7 and περιβάλλω with Lk 23,11; but cf. p. 94.

331. *Ibid.*, p. 80.

332. *Ibid.*, p. 228. Following this she offered the material in the order found in GP: GP 2 (= 23,11); GP 4-5 (= 23,6-16); GP 5a (23,12); GP 9b (= 23,16); GP 10b (= 23,9) and GP 46 (= 23,13-23) (p. 233-234).

333. *Ibid.*, p. 94.

334. *Ibid.*, p. 213: "l'auteur du fragment est inexpérimenté et gauche quand il touche à l'histoire de la Palestine en général, et à ce qui concerne les institutions juives et le milieu de vie du Κύριος en particulier".

335. MARA, p. 213.

336. *Ibid.*, p. 215.

337. *Jesus and Christian Origins Outside the New Testament*, Grand Rapids, MI, 1974, p. 88 (esp. p. 88-93).

338. *CH* 43 (1974) 529-530, p. 530.

339. *RBén* 84 (1974) 231.

noting that Mara had built upon the work of Vaganay[340]. He also drew attention to Mara's critique that Vaganay continually referred to the author of GP as "faussaire". C. Kannengiesser, too, stressed that Mara's analysis was prompted by a reaction against Vaganay[341]. E. Trocmé pointed to Mara's desire to correct Vaganay's theses[342]. Y.-M. Duval situated Mara in the line of O. Perler[343].

Writing in a 1976 Emory U. dissertation Jerry W. McCANT argued that "GP used four stories which were unique to their authors – Matthew's guard story, Mark's empty tomb story, John's Galilean resurrection story and Luke's Pilate – Herod scene"[344]. Concerning the Lukan material, the difficulty of establishing a probable relationship between 23,1-16, described as the "Pilate-Herod trial scene", and GP 1-5 was acknowledged[345]. C.H. Turner and J.A. Robinson, on the one hand, were contrasted with P. Gardner-Smith on the other[346]. Further, the positions of M. Dibelius and R. Bultmann were highlighted to show the lack of scholarly consensus on the tradition history of the Lukan passage. The function of the account was to "prove the innocence of Jesus" while secondarily it served to exonerate Pilate and convict the Jews[347]. As to the source of the Luke account, McCant wrote: "Since the theme of the Pilate-Herod trial is consonant with Lk's understanding of the death of the Lord elsewhere and the vocabulary is Lucan, there is little reason to suppose that this pericope came from anyone other than Luke"[348]. The author of GP blended "canonical materials" and altered the Luke account of the Pilate-Herod trial scene[349]. The absence of the Markan mockery by the Roman soldiers in Lk was noted, though it was replaced by the mockery by Herod and his soldiers, a mockery even more hostile in GP[350]. The position of J. Denker on the independence of GP from Lk was cited, the conclusion based on a lack of verbal similarities and the difference in presentation of Jesus' death. In Lk he suffered a martyr's death, while the GP reflected no interest in such

340. *TLZ* 100 (1975) 270-272, col. 270. Reviews of M.G. MARA: BOGAERT, P.-M., *RBén* 84 (1974) 231; CROUZEL, H., *BullLitEccl* 76 (1975) 69; DUVAL, Y.M., *Esprit et Vie* 84 (1974) 192; JACQUES, X., *NRT* 96 (1974) 531-532 and *Civiltà Cattolica* 126/2 (1975) 307-308; KANNENGIESSER, C., *RSR* 64 (1976) 312; LAUZIÈRE, M.É., *RThom* 74 (1974) 483; METZGER, B.M., *CH* 43 (1974) 529-530; ORBE, A. *Greg* 56 (1975) 576-577; SMULDERS, P., *Bijdragen* 36 (1975) 95; TROCMÉ, É., *RHPR* 54 (1974) 428; WALTER, N., *TLZ* 100 (1975) 270-272.

341. *Esprit et Vie* 64 (1976) 312.

342. *RHPR* 54 (1974) 428.

343. *Esprit et Vie* 84 (1974) 192; cf. Perler (1964).

344. J.W. McCANT, *The Gospel of Peter: The Docetic Question Re-examined*, Diss. Emory, Atlanta, GA, 1976 (dir. L.E. KECK), p. 35-115: *The Relationship to Canonical Literature*; p. 78-90: *GP and its Relationship to Luke*, p. 113-114. See Susan E. Schaeffer's discussion of this dissertation (*The 'Gospel of Peter'*, p. 149-150). Here she evaluated that "McCant offers a sound critique of Johnson's thesis". See also p. 157, n. 19.

345. *Ibid.*, p. 78.

346. Cf. C.H. TURNER, *The Gospel of Peter*, in *JTS* 14 (1913-14) 166; J.A. ROBINSON, *The Gospel According to Peter*, p. 16-17; P. GARDNER-SMITH, *The Gospel of Peter*, in *JTS* 27 (1925-26) 263.

347. McCANT, p. 82; cf. p. 81.

348. *Ibid.*, p. 81. In support of this contention he referred to LEANEY (1958) and GILMOUR (1951). HAWKINS, *Horae Synopticae*, p. 15ff., was also mentioned (n. 108).

349. McCANT, *Gospel of Peter*, p. 85, 86.

350. *Ibid.*, p. 88; see also p. 83.

a portrayal. Though Denker was correct, in his estimation, in arguing there was too low a verbal agreement to claim dependence of GP on Lk, the development of similar themes left open the possibility that GP knew Luke's version of the story and indeed Luke's Gospel. McCant believed Denker was possibly correct that Ps 2,1-2 was the source for the Pilate – Herod trial in GP[351]. The inconsistency of Denker's argumentation was emphasized in McCant's remark: "It is strange that Denker would reject dependence of GP on Luke because of a lack of verbal similarity, but posits dependence on Ps 2 where the verbal similarity is nil"[352]. In a subsequent article (1984) McCant regarded the four canonical Gospels as GP's "primary sources"[353].

Dieter LÜHRMAN (1981) contended Denker erred in seeing an independent tradition in various details of GP[354]. Instead, he favored K. Müller's study which "erweist" that Lk 23,6-12 was a redactional work[355]. Lührman observed that the designation "king" for Herod occurs in Mk 6,14, but that the term "tetrarch", which was historically more accurate, was found in Mt 14,1 and Lk 3,1.19; 9,7[356].

J. CAMBE (1982) viewed the second century accounts of the passion, among which he included GP, as continuing, developing and imitating the canonical Gospels[357]. But he did not eliminate the possibility that the tradition found in GP was more ancient than that found in the four Gospels[358]. Though É. TROCMÉ (1983) was not speaking specifically of the Herod story, the apocryphal Gospels, including the GP, were considered later than the canonical Gospels and thus would not have served as possible sources, a position he had already taken in 1957[359].

351. *Ibid.*, p. 90.
352. *Ibid.*, p. 90. n. 126.
353. MCCANT, *The Gospel of Peter. Docetism Reconsidered*, in *NTS* 30 (1984) 258-273, p. 267.
354. D. LÜHRMAN, *POx 2949: EvPt 3-5 in einer Handschrift des 2./3. Jahrhunderts*, in *ZNW* 72 (1981) 216-226, p. 222. Lührman singled out Gardner-Smith as Denker's precursor in supporting both an independent tradition as well as an early date for GP (p. 228, n. 28). F. NEIRYNCK supported Lührmann's conclusions: "His identification of Fr.(1), lines 5-8, with GP 3 is quite convincing" (*Apocryphal*, p. 141-142 = *Evangelica II*, p. 733-734). See also J.C. TREAT, *The Two Manuscript Witnesses to the Gospel of Peter*, in *SBL 1990 Seminar Papers*, p. 393, n. 10, 395, n. 14, 397, n. 17, who was dependent upon Lührman at several points.
355. LÜHRMANN, *POx 2949*, p. 221, n. 19. Cf. above, K. MÜLLER, *Jesus*.
356. LÜHRMANN, *POx 2949*, p. 221, n. 20.
357. J. CAMBE, *Les récits de la Passion en relation avec différents textes du Iᵉ siècle*, in *FoiVie* 81 (1982) 12-24, p. 12. According to Cambe GP probably stemmed from Syrian Christians around 140 A.D (p. 13). For a treatment of the silence of Jesus before Herod see p. 22, 24.
358. *Ibid.*, p. 13: "Cet Ev. de P. semble s'inspirer d'une manière si étroite des quatre évangiles qu'on a pu soutenir qu'il en constituait une relecture ou une 'harmonie'. Disons plus prudemment qu'il puise avec une remarquable liberté dans les courants traditionnels qui s'expriment dans les synoptiques et dans l'Ev. de Jean. Il n'est pas exclu qu'il atteste plusieurs données sous une forme plus archaïque que celle qu'elles revêtent dans les quatre évangiles".
359. TROCMÉ, *The Passion as Liturgy*, p. 3. See his *Le "Livre des Actes"*, 1957, p. 43. Trocmé dated the GP at 150 AD and cited C. MAURER in E. HENNECKE, *Neutestamentliche Apokryphen*, Vol. 1, Tübingen, ³1959, p. 118f. (= *New Testament Apocrypha*, in R. McL. WILSON (ed.), ²1973, Vol. 1, p. 180), quoted in *The Passion as Liturgy*, p. 95, n. 3.

David F. WRIGHT (1984), in a test case of Koester's theory as presented in his 1980 article, was critical not only of his method, but of his findings. While Koester appealed to external evidence in an attempt to show that early Christian writers did not distinguish between canonical and apocryphal gospels, Wright countered that since all of the MSS to which Koester referred originated in Egypt "where Christianity is known to have had a particularly strong heterodox character for much of the second century, their evidence can scarcely be held to be representative"[360]. This being said, Wright indicated the frequent difficulty of establishing "with certainty" if the canonical Gospels had been employed by early Christian writers. He further critiqued Koester for a lack of precision evidenced by the former's initial restriction to "'use' of the gospels" which later was extended to "'knowledge' of gospels". Similarly, he challenged the accuracy, and therefore the usefulness, of Koester's table.

Addressing GP more specifically, Wright acknowledged that Koester had correctly assessed the "almost universal" scholarly judgment that GP was a secondary compilation based on the canonical Gospels, which was the view held by Mara, "the most recent editor" of the GP text[361]. He tested Koester's theory on GP 3-5, a passage that Koester himself did not treat. This section emphasized the responsibility of the Jews for the death of Jesus which Wright considered to be the "central apologetic motif" in GP. Though the secondary character of GP was easier to prove than its dependence on the canonical Gospels, he asserted that Koester and Denker were correct that the "OT undergirding" existed in much of GP[362]. Their error was rejecting the "parallel undergirding of the canonical gospels"[363]. Wright favored Mara's "more sensitive and accurate" judgment[364].

Wright (1985-86) observed that while a majority of scholars opted for "substantial dependence" of GP upon "all or most" of the canonical Gospels, some entertained the possibility of "influence from oral tradition"[365]. He called attention to Swete's perception of the manner in which the author of GP may have proceeded[366].

---

360. D.F. WRIGHT, *Apocryphal Gospels: The 'Unknown Gospel' (Pap. Egerton 2) and the Gospel of Peter*, in D. WENHAM (ed.), *The Jesus Tradition Outside the Gospels* (Gospel Perspectives, 5), Sheffield, 1984, p. 208. Cf. H. KOESTER, *Apocryphal and Canonical Gospels*, in *HTR* 73 (1980) 105-130.

361. WRIGHT, *Apocryphal*, p. 221. Cf. KOESTER, *Apocryphal*, p. 126, and MARA, *Évangile*, p. 214. In a note, Wright stated that "Koester does not mention this edition" (p. 231, n. 58).

362. WRIGHT, *Apocryphal*, p. 227; see also p. 221, 225.

363. *Ibid.*, p. 227.

364. *Ibid.* Cf. MARA, *Évangile*, p. 31-32.

365. *Papyrus Egerton 2 (the Unknown Gospel) - Part of the Gospel of Peter?*, in *SecCent* 5 (1985-86) 129-150, p. 134, 135.

366. *Ibid.*, p. 135-136: "H.B. Swete's invaluable tabulation of the details of *EvP*'s relationship to the canonical Gospels leads him to the conclusion that if its author is no mere compiler or harmonist, his harmonizing tendency is nevertheless well established. Indeed, so intermeshed is his text with that of the Gospels, in Swete's view, as to create a strong presumption that he used a pre Tatianic gospel harmony, even if he also knew one or more single Gospels. Even if such a view has not found much support, it illustrates the kind of judgment scholars have been led to in seeking to identify *EvP*'s preculilarly close, yet selective affinities with the canonical Gospels". Cf. SWETE, *The Akhmîm Fragment*, 1893, p. xvii, xxv. For a discussion of Wright's overall view see J.B. DANIELS, *The Egerton Gospel: Its Place in Early Christianity*, Diss. Claremont, 1990 (dir. J.M. ROBINSON), p. 239-242.

In a subsequent essay (1986), although Wright did not directly address the relation of GP to the canonical Gospels, he referred to an earlier article when he stated, "I have elsewhere tested Koester's theory against one section of *EvP* and found it wanting"[367]. Koester, whom he termed a "modern counterpart" to Harnack, and Crossan were highlighted for their views on the independence of GP. Wright was convinced there was a definite relationship between GP and the canonical Gospels, though he distinguished levels of redactional freedom by the author of GP[368].

J.H. CHARLESWORTH (1988) pointed out "scholars' predeliction for the priority of the intracanonical gospels", a view he himself had supported for a twenty year period[369]. While it appeared he continued to endorse this stance, he proposed a methodological shift which would require the study of the apocryphal passion accounts alongside those of the canonical Gospels[370].

367. D.F. WRIGHT, *Apologetic and Apocalyptic: The Miraculous in the Gospel of Peter*, in D. WENHAM and C. BLOMBERG (eds.), *The Miracles of Jesus* (Gospel Perspectives, 6), Sheffield, 1986, 401-418, p. 401. On his assessment of Koester's position see WRIGHT, *Apocryphal Gospels*, p. 222-225. Explaining the indirect relevance of his essay for the question of independence or dependence he wrote: "The aim of this paper is to assess the prevalence of miracles in *EvP*, and to characterize the nature of any special interest in miracles that *EvP* may display. It may thereby contribute to the reassessment of the significance of the extra-canonical, including post-canonical, gospel traditions for which Richard Bauckham pled in his epilogue to the previous volume of *Gospel Perspectives*" (*Apologetic*, p. 402; see also p. 409; cf. R. BAUCKHAM, *The Study of Gospel Traditions Outside the Canonical Gospels: Problems and Prospects*, in D. WENHAM, *The Jesus Tradition*, 1984, 369-403, p. 401).

368. WRIGHT, *Apologetic*, p. 414: "But as we have seen, a distinction probably has to be drawn between those parts of *EvP* where the author remains firmly in contact with the canonical gospel tradition (whether he had access to it in the form of our actual Gospels or not), and those where he seems considerably freer of the control of his tradition. The latter comprise the core of his resurrection narrative, including 9:34-10:42. In the passion story and the last part of the resurrection account (12:50-14:60, and probably 11:43-49 also), despite numerous modifications of various kinds, the shape of the canonical tradition remains clearly recognizable". See also p. 415.

369. J.H. CHARLESWORTH, *Research on the New Testament Apocrypha and Pseudepigrapha*, in *ANRW* II.25.5 (1988), p. 3934, 3935. Cf. ID., *The New Testament Apocrypha and Pseudepigrapha: A Guide to Publications, with Excursuses on Apocalypses* (ATLA Bibliography Series, 17), Metuchen, NJ - London, 1987 (esp. p. 95).

370. *Research*, p. 3939-3940.

Still others contributed to the ongoing debate, including P. VIELHAUER[371], R. MCL. WILSON[372], E.M. YAMAUCHI[373], H. LICHTENBERGER[374], as well as the author of the entry on GP in *The Eerdmans Bible Dictionary*[375] and R.J. BAUCKHAM[376].

Joel GREEN (1987) surveyed the controversy surrounding the "possible existence and shape of a pre-canonical passion narrative"[377]. He questioned the assumption, such as that held by Koester, that the passion story arose from a reflection on the OT[378]. Further, Koester's observation that elements stemming from an individual biblical passage were found solely in one scene in the apocryphal gospel, was not so significant. In the final analysis, Green concluded GP was dependent upon the canonical Gospels and resolved:

---

371. *Geschichte der urchristlichen Literatur. Einleitung in das Neue Testament, die Apokryphen und die Apostolischen Väter*, Berlin - New York, 1975, 641-648, p. 645: "Auch sonst erweist sich das PetrEv als junges Werk (Vielhauer's note reads: "Hierzu ausführlich: Vaganay, 43-82"). Es setzt die vier 'kanonischen' Evangelien (noch nicht den Kanon der vier Evangelien) voraus und benutzt sie". Specifically regarding Lk: "Im lukanischen Sondergut haben zwei wichtige Züge ihre Analogien: das Auftreten des Herodes Antipas im Prozess Jesu und seine Freundschaft mit Pilatus (1-5)".

372. *Apokryphen II. Petrusevangelium*, in *TRE* 3 (1978) 331-332, p. 331: "die Verwendung von Material aus den kanonischen Evangelien und andere Faktoren zeigen, dass das Petrusevangelium ein verhältnismässig junges Werk ist (Vielhauer 645)". See further p. 331: "Das Petrusevangelium verwendet die vier kanonischen Evangelien, and nach Swete (XV) gibt es keinen zwingenden Grund für die Annahme anderer historischer Quellen".

373. *Aprocryphal Gospels*, in *ISBE* 1, 1979, 181-188, p. 183: "The Gospel of Peter makes use of the four canonical Gospels". Concerning the date he suggested it was "composed early in the 2nd cent., probably in Syria".

374. *Apocryphen. Nt.liche A.*, in E. FAHLBUSCH et al. (eds.), *Evangelisches Kirchenlexicon (EKL). Internationale theologische Enzyklopädie*, Vol. 1, Göttingen, 1985, 207-211, p. 208: "Das EvPetr. setzt die vier kanonischen Evangelien voraus, will aber keine Harmonie schaffen, sondern eine neue Darstellung bieten". He also maintained that GP certainly developed in the second half of the second century in Syria (p. 208).

375. *Gospel of Peter*, in A.C. MEYERS (ed.) *The Eerdmans Bible Dictionary*, Grand Rapids, MI, 1987, p. 820-821, p. 821: "The writer of this account seems to have drawn from all four canonical Gospels". The author dates it around 150 AD.

376. *Gospels (Apocryphal)*, in *DJG*, 1992, 286-291 (esp. p. 287-288), p. 288, noted that the relationship of GP to the canonical Gospels was disputed and took note of Crossan's proposal, dismissing it. What was needed was "a more plausible view". Bauckham believed that the author of GP "drew primarily on Mark's Gospel and on Matthew's special source, independently of Matthew's Gospel". The latter was given priority and was supplemented by Mk. In an earlier essay (1984) Bauckham declared: "I do not deny that the Gospel of Peter shows some signs of dependence on the canonical Gospels, but I think it can also be shown to have had independent access to something like Matthew's special source" (*The Study of the Gospel Traditions Outside the Canonical Gospels: Problems and Prospects*, in D. WENHAM (ed.), *The Jesus Tradition Outside the Gospels* [Gospel Perspectives, 5], Sheffield, 1984, 369-403, p. 401, n. 41; see also p. 380). Note in the same volume by the same author: *A Bibliography on Recent Works on Gospel Traditions Outside the Canonical Gospels*, p. 405-419, esp. p. 411.

377. *The Gospel of Peter: Source for a Pre-Canonical Passion Narrative?*, in *ZNW* 78 (1987) 292-301, p. 292.

378. Cf. H. KOESTER, *Apocryphal*, 126-130, and *Introduction to the New Testament*, 2 vols., Philadelphia, PA, 1982 (esp. Vol. 1, p. 48-49, 162-163).

"The Gospel of Peter, therefore, cannot be employed as a separate, independent witness to a prototypical passion narrative"[379].

Miguel Rodríguez RUIZ (1988) concluded there was *"gran probabilidad"* that the canonical Gospels formed the basis of GP[380]. In the discussion of the similarities between Lk and GP, he was somewhat tentative about the dependence of the apocryphal gospel upon Lk, but suggested nonetheless that the Herod pericope demonstrated how the author of the apocryphal gospel "changes the function" of the figures in the story[381].

F. NEIRYNCK (1989) noted the difference between Koester's line arguing for the independence of GP and the canonical Gospels as contrasted with "the alignment of Louvain" which included Vaganay, Coppens and Massaux[382]. He declared the "new look at the passion-resurrection story in the Gospel of Peter [has] serious consequences for the interpretation of the Gospel of Mark"[383]. In an appended note to the republication of his study of the apocryphal gospels and Mk (1991), he updated his bibliography for the subject and analyzed the current debate, especially the reactions by Koester and Dewey to Crossan[384]. Notice was taken of Koester's influence upon Crossan[385], who had even maintained that Mark knew of Herod's involvement in Jesus' crucifixion because of the Cross Gospel[386]. In a more recent contribution (1993) Neirynck acknowledged "a certain relationship" between various Lukan passages, including 23,6-12, and those found in GP, but argued that it was the apocryphal gospel which was dependent upon Lk[387].

---

379. GREEN, *Gospel of Peter*, p. 301. Also writing in 1987 was P. PARKER who did not offer a position on the question of priority. He said only that in GP Jesus was not condemned by Herod, commenting "that author evidently did not know the legal situation" (*Herod Antipas*, p. 207, n. 34).

380. *El Evangelio de Pedro. ¿Un Desafío a los Evangelios Canónicos?*, in *EstBib* 46 (1988) 497.

381. *Ibid.*, p. 511-512. "En el relato fragmentario de EvPe, Pilato no aparece implicado en el proceso de Jesús. Por tanto, en caso de que este relato dependa de Lc, tenemos ahí un ejemplo típico de cómo el autor del EvPe manipula sus fuentes, cambiando las funciones de sus personajes" (p. 512).

382. *Apocryphal*, 123-175 (esp. p. 130-132; 140-157) = *Evangelica II*, Leuven, 1991, 715-772 (esp. p. 722-724; 732-749). References are to: L. VAGANAY, *L'Évangile de Pierre*, J. COPPENS, Review: *L. VAGANAY, L'évangile de Pierre, 1930*, in ETL 8 (1931) 456-458, and É. MASSAUX, *Influence de l'Évangile de saint Matthieu sur la littérature chrétienne avant saint Irénée*, Louvain - Gembloux, 1950; (BETL, 75), Leuven, 1986 (esp. p. 358-388).

383. F. NEIRYNCK, *Apocryphal*, p. 132 = *Evangelica II*, p. 724.

384. *Ibid.*, 1991, p. 769-770 DEWEY believed that GP 1-2, which treated Herod, was redactional (*"Time"*, in *Semeia* 49 [1990] 101-107).

385. NEIRYNCK, *Apocryphal*, p. 126 (= p. 718): "The influence of H. Koester is undeniable. Crossan himself presents his book as a partial answer to Koester's challenge to the scholarly world to 'write the literary history of the gospels in early Christianity considering all gospel materials which are available'".

386. *Ibid.*, p. 749: "The influence of the Cross Gospel also extends far beyond the passion narrative. The mention of the Herodians (3,6; 12,13) and of Herod (8,15) 'is simply because Mark knows the *Cross Gospel* account in which Herod is in charge of Jesus' crucifixion'".

387. *Literary Criticism: Old and New*, in C. FOCANT (ed.), *The Synoptic Gospels*, p. 26. See his earlier statement concerning the relationship of POxy 2949 and GP where "emphasis on the responsibility of Herod is one of the characteristics of the Gospel of Peter" (*Apocryphal*, p. 142 = *Evangelica II*, 734).

In 1994 he once more took up Crossan's theory that GP, containing the *Cross Gospel*, was the source of the passion and resurrection narratives of the canonical Gospels[388]. Though Neirynck agreed with Crossan that Matthew and Luke employed our text of Mk[389] and stated that "Crossan rightly emphasizes the Johannine background of the material added to Mk 16"[390], they differed on more points of discussion[391]. Crossan maintained that all four canonical Gospels shared the same source in the passion and resurrection narratives which was found in GP[392]. GP 1-2, the verses dealing with Herod, were considered part of the original stratum or the *Cross Gospel*[393].

Also allowing for the possible influence of oral tradition was P.M. HEAD (1992) who concluded that "GP is a redaction of the canonical material"[394]. Originally, James Keith ELLIOTT (1991) took notice of Crossan's suggestion that GP was a source for the canonical Gospels and Brown's rejoinder[395]. "The gospel is certainly early – although not as early as Crossan argued". But Elliott was not any more specific than that. He later (1993) endorsed the view that the differences between GP and the canonical Gospels "may be due to the influence of oral traditions"[396], though the scholarly concensus was that GP was "secondary to and dependent on the accounts of the passion in the canonical Gospels"[397]. Brown and Neirynck have convincingly defended against Crossan's claims. More recently (1996) Elliott maintained it was "likely" that GP was a second century composition arguing "it seems clear that the writer of the Gospel of Peter has drawn on these New Testament accounts [of the four canonical Gospels] for his version of Jesus' Passion"[398]. Alan KIRK (1994) advocating the priority of the canonical gospels and the dependence of GP upon them, rejected Brown's proposal of oral tradition in favor of literary dependence[399].

---

388. *The Historical Jesus. Reflections on an Inventory*, in *ETL* 70 (1994) 221-234.

389. *Ibid.*, p. 225. See F. NEIRYNCK, *The Minor Agreements and Proto-Mark. A Response to H. Koester*, in *ETL* 67 (1991) 82-94 (= *Evangelica*, 59-73).

390. *Historical Jesus*, p. 226, quoting from *Evangelica II*, p. 736, 737.

391. Crossan assigned a "relatively late date" to Mk. *The Gospel of Mark that was composed in the early seventies contained the SG fragments (Secret Gospel of Mark)*. Canonical Mk as we know it "is a later expurgated version of that first gospel" (p. 224). By assigning Jn 2,1 and 4,54 to the redaction of the final author, Crossan eliminated from the miracle collection "the two Cana miracles which are the classic starting point of all Signs Source hypotheses" (p. 225).

392. *Ibid.*, p. 225. Cf. CROSSAN, *The Historical Jesus. The Life of a Mediterranean Jewish Peasant*, San Francisco, CA, 1991, p. 429.

393. NEIRYNCK, *Historical Jesus*, p. 227. Cf. CROSSAN, *The Cross that Spoke* [Uncorrected Proof], p. 16, 409.

394. P.M. HEAD, *On the Christology of the Gospel of Peter*, in *VC* 46 (1992) 209-224, p. 218.

395. J.K. ELLIOTT, *The Apocryphal Gospels*, in *ExpT* 103 (1991) 8-15 (esp. p. 12-13), p. 12.

396. J.K. ELLIOTT, *The Apocryphal New Testament. A Collection of Apocryphal Christian Literature in an English Translation*; Revised and newly translated ed. of *Apocryphal New Testament*, tr. by M.R. JAMES, 1924; Oxford - New York, 1993, 150-158, p. 150.

397. *Ibid.*, p. 151.

398. J.K. ELLIOTT, *The Apocryphal Jesus. Legends of the Early Church*, Oxford, 1996, p. 66, 67.

399. A. KIRK, *Examining Priorities: Another Look at the Gospel of Peter's Relationship to the New Testament Gospels*, in *NTS* 40 (1994) 572-595, p. 594: "We have argued for the priority of the four gospels now found in the New Testament over the *Gospel of Peter* and for the dependence of the *Gospel of Peter's* narrative upon the narratives of these four gospels".

Influenced by the work of P. Vielhauer, Walter REBELL (1992) maintained "nun ist aber unser Fragment des Petrusevangelium keineswegs *durch und durch* ein sekundäres Werk, den kanonischen Evangelien an Alter und Authentizität des Berichteten eindeutig unterlegen"[400]. The work of Dibelius convinced him that GP also contained ancient elements, though he insisted that the author of GP used the canonical Gospels. Rebell was skeptical, however, of the recent efforts of Koester and Crossan[401]. He concluded that a precise judgment remained difficult. As to the time and place of origin a date of the middle of the second century in Syria was proposed.

H.C. KEE (1997) clearly asserted that not only was GP based on the canonical Gospels, but that the Lukan pericope of Jesus before Herod (23,6-12) "has been considerably expanded" in GP[402]. Concerning the date of composition he claimed that "the author is obviously writing at a time and in a culture in which first-century Palestinian Jewish practices are not accurately known"[403].

Others who wrote on GP provided no information on the question or their position was unclear[404]. While there did not seem to be any evidence that the debate will soon wane,

Following a brief historical survey which included J.A. Robinson, Harnack, Zahn, Gardner-Smith, Vaganay, Johnson, Crossan, Koester, R.E. Brown and Neirynck, Kirk stated that his position was distinguished from Brown in that GP's use of the canonical Gospels "presupposes the texts of the New Testament gospels" rather than "memories of the four gospels" (p. 574; cf. R.E. BROWN, *The Gospel of Peter*, 333-338, p. 335). Frequent reference was made to Mara in footnotes (KIRK, *Examining*, p. 577, n. 20; 580, n. 29; 581, nn. 31, 32; 583, n. 35; 591, n. 55). Kirk did not specifically treat the Herod material in GP.

400. W. REBELL, *Neutestamentliche Apokryphen und Apostolische Väter*, Munich, 1992, 92-99, esp. p. 95; so also p. 96. Cf. P. VIELHAUER, *Geschichte der urchristlichen Literatur*, p. 645, 646. The "knappe, aber instruktive" introductions to GP by Maurer and Schneemelcher were recommended as were the "umfangreiche" commentaries of Vaganay and Mara (REBELL, *Neutestamentliche Apokryphen*, p. 99).

401. REBELL, *Neutestamentliche Apokryphen*, p. 96. References were made to BROWN, *The Gospel of Peter*, on p. 96, n. 9, and 98. Cf. DIBELIUS, *Die alttestamentlichen Motive*, p. 242, 243; KOESTER, *Überlieferung und Geschichte*, and *Einführung in das Neue Testament*; CROSSAN, *Four Other Gospels*.

402. *The Formation of the Christian Community*, in H.C. KEE, et al., *The Cambridge Companion*, 1997, p. 561-562.

403. *Ibid.*, p. 562.

404. J.O.F. MURRAY, *Evangelium secundem Petrum*, in *Expositor* 7 (1893) 50-61. It is unclear what his position was. H. MCLACHLAN viewed the account of Herod in GP as reflecting a "later stage in the legend", though it will be remembered that he viewed Manaen as the source for the account in Lk. He dated the apocryphal gospel around 110-130 A.D. (*St. Luke*, 1920, p. 29). E. KLOSTERMANN, *Apocrypha I. Reste des Petrusevangeliums, der Petrusapokalypse und des Kerygma Petri* (Kleine Texte für Vorlesungen und Übungen), Bonn, ²1921; Berlin, 1933 "unveränderter Neudruk" contains only the text but no commentary. K.L. SCHMIDT, *Kanonische und apokryphe Evangelien und Apostelgeschichten* (ATANT, 5), Basel (1944) 37-78. It is unclear what his position was. V. HARLOW, *Destroyer*, 1953, p. 178. He did not directly address the source question, but argued that though the GP account was different from that contained in Lk, it did not contradict it. While Catholics had rejected the apocryphal account on grounds of Docetism, Harlow noted support from "several authentic references". He included Eusebius, History 2,5,1; Acts 4,27; Ignatius, Smyrnaeans 1,5. To these he added the first few verses of the

the majority position of dependence of the GP upon the canonical Gospels, to which I also subscribe, seems firmly defended.

THE RELATION OF THE HEROD PERICOPE TO THE GOSPEL OF PETER

GP PRIOR TO OR CONTEMPORANEOUS WITH CANONICAL GOSPELS

J.H. Moulton (1892), E.N. Bennett (?1893), H. Hilgenfeld (1893), K. Manchot, W.C. van Manen, H. von Soden (except for the trial of Herod, where Luke obviously possessed an earlier stage of the tradition), W.R. Cassels (1894), W.H. van de Sande Bakhuyzen (1907), A.J. Grieve (1920), A. Wautier d'Aygalliers (1920), P. Gardner-Smith (1925-26), B.A. Johnson (1965, 1985), D.D. Hutton (1970), J. Denker (1975), H. Koester (1980, 1982, 1990, 1994), R. Cameron (1982), J.D. Crossan (1985, 1987, 1988), J.L. Houlden (qualified, 1985), M.L. Soards (1985; 1991), S. Gero (1988), A.J. Dewey (1990, 1992), P.A. Mirecki (1992, "probably"), G.W.E. Nickelsburg (?1992), D. Moody Smith, C.A. Evans (?1993), R.E. Brown (1994), D.L. Bock (1996)

GP DEPENDENT UPON THE CANONICAL GOSPELS

J.A. Robinson (²1892; 1927), H.J. Holtzmann (1892), A. Harnack (1892, ²1893; 1894: "wahrscheinlich"), H.B. Swete (1892, 1893), T. Zahn (1892, 1893), W.M. Crook (1893), F.X. Funk, I.H. Hall, J.R. Harris, A.C. Headlam, J. Kunze, A. Lods, A. Loisy, P. Lejay, H. Lucas, A.J. Maas, J. Martineau, H. von Schubert, H. Wabnitz, W.E. Barnes (1893-94), J. MacPherson, J.M.S. Baljon (1894), A. Resch, G.B. Semeria ("probable"), P. Batiffol (1897), A. Rutherford (?), M.R. James (1899, 1924), P. Wernle (1899), F.H. Chase (1900), A. Ehrhard, V.H. Stanton (1900-01), V. Rose (1902), H. Stocks, A. Stülcken (1904), J.G. Tasker, J. Belser (1905), A.F. Findlay (1906), G.J. Reid (1907) L. Fillion (1912), P. Wendland (1912), H. Waitz (1913), C.H. Turner (1913-14), M. Dibelius (1918), J. Moffatt, E. Amann (1928. cf. 1913), L. Vaganay, W. Bauer (1930), H.I. Bell and T.C. Skeat (1935), C.H. Dodd (1936), J. Quasten (1950), A. de Santos Otero (1956; ?1969), É.

account of GP. R.M. GRANT and D.N. FREEDMAN, *The Secret Sayings of Jesus according to the Gospel of Thomas*, London, 1960, p. 37-43, p. 43 = Garden City, NY, 1960, p. 40-47, p. 46: "First, they provide us with materials with which to compare the canonical gospels, even though in nearly every instance the comparison proves that the canonical gospels are more original". They also insisted that "in many respects it is like the four canonical gospels" (p. 41 = p. 45 = *Apocrypha N.T. Evangelium Thomae. Geheime Worte Jesu: das Thomas Evangelium*, tr. J.B. BAUER, Frankfurt, 1960 = *Het Thomas-Evangelie. Vertaling en toelichting*, tr. J. MOOY, Utrecht - Antwerp, 1962, p. 44). M.P. MCHUGH identified GP as a second century apocryphal NT writing, but noted that "scholarly opinion on the date of the composition ... is divided" (*Gospel of Peter*, in E. FERGUSON [ed.], *Encyclopedia of Early Christianity*, Chicago - London, 1990, p. 383; New York - London, ²1997, Vol. 2, 476-477, p. 476. P. PILHOFER, *Justin und das Petrusevangelium*, in ZNW 81 [1990] 60-78 (esp. p. 61-62). Though he referred to the continuing debate concerning the question of the relation of GP to the canonical Gospels, he sidestepped the issue without indicating his preference. As regards the date he wrote: "Die Entstehung des Petrusevangeliums ist daher m. E. spätestens um 130 anzusetzen" (p. 78). F. BOVON observed GP "is difficult to situate and to date. Probably written in the beginning of the second century, it must be the work of marginal Christians of docetic leanings" (*Le privilège pascal de Marie-Madeleine*, in NTS 30 [1984] 50-62 = *Mary Magdalene's Paschal Privilege*, in ID., *New Testament Traditions and Apocryphal Narratives* [PTMS, 36], Allison Park, PA, 1995, 147-157, esp. p. 150-151). He referred to Mara in an endnote (p. 231, n. 25).

Trocmé (1957, 1983), J. Hervieux (1958), Chr. Maurer (1959), R.M. Grant and D.N. Freedman (1960/1962), J. Michl, O. Cullmann (1961), M.S. Enslin (1962), O. Perler (?1964), C.H.H. Scobie (1965), R.E. Brown (1968; 1987; 1997), K. Beyschlag (1969), D.R. Cartlidge and D.L. Dungan (1972, though possible that this reflected independent traditions; 1980), M.G. Mara, (1973), F.F. Bruce (1974), P. Vielhauer (1975), J.W. McCant (1976, 1984), R. McL. Wilson (1978, 1985), E.M. Yamauchi (1979, ?1985, 1986), D. Lührman (1981), J. Cambe (qualified, 1982), B.D. Ehrmann (?1983), R.J. Bauckham (1984, 1992), H. Lichtenberger (1985), W.R. Telford (1986), Anonymous in *ISBE* (1987), B.M. Metzger (?1987), J.B. Green, J.H. Charlesworth (1988; with C.A. Evans, 1994), W. Radl (1988), M.R. Ruiz (1988), J.P. Meier (1989), S.E. Schaeffer (1991), F. Neirynck, J.K. Elliott (?; 1996), H.W. Hoehner, P.M. Head, W. Rebell (1992), A. Kirk (1994), H.C. Kee (1997), M.K. Stillman

INDEX OF AUTHORS

NEW TESTAMENT
TOOLS AND STUDIES

edited by

BRUCE M. METZGER, PH.D., D.D., L.H.D., D. THEOL., D. LITT.

and

BART D. EHRMAN, PH.D.

VOL. XI *Studien zum Neutestamentlichen Briefformular,* von Franz Schnider und Werner Stenger. 1987. ISBN 90 04 08414 2

VOL. XII *Strukturale Beobachtungen zum Neuen Testament,* von Werner Stenger. 1990. ISBN 90 04 90113 0

VOL. XIII *Life of Jesus Research: An Annotated Bibliography,* by Craig A. Evans. 1989. ISBN 90 04 09180 7

VOL. XIV *A Key to the Peshitta Gospels;* vol. I: *ʾĀlaph-Dalath,* by Terry C. Falla. 1991. ISBN 90 04 09354 0

VOL. XV *Text and Interpretation: New Approaches in the Criticism of the New Testament,* edited by P. J. Hartin and J. H. Petzer. 1991. ISBN 90 04 09401 6

VOL. XVI *An Index to Periodical Literature on the Apostle Paul,* by Watson E. Mills. 1993. ISBN 90 04 09674 4

VOL. XVII *The Gospel of John as Literature: An Anthology of Twentieth-Century Perspectives,* edited by Mark W. G. Stibbe. 1993. ISBN 90 04 09848 8

VOL. XVIII *Nag Hammadi Texts and the Bible: A Synopsis and Index,* edited by Craig A. Evans, Robert L. Webb and Richard A. Wiebe. 1993. ISBN 90 04 09902 6

VOL. XIX *Studying the Historical Jesus: Evaluations of the State of Current Research,* edited by Bruce Chilton and Craig A. Evans. 1998 (second impression). ISBN 90 04 11142 5

VOL. XX *The New Testament in Greek*, IV. *The Gospel According to St. John*, edited by the American and British Committees of the International Greek New Testament Project. Volume One: *The Papyri*, edited by W. J. Elliott and D. C. Parker. 1995. ISBN 90 04 09940 9

VOL. XXI *Comparative Edition of the Syriac Gospels: Aligning the Sinaiticus, Curetonianus, Peshîttâ and Harklean Versions*, by George A. Kiraz; 4 volumes. Vol. 1: Matthew; Vol. 2: Mark; Vol. 3: Luke; Vol. 4: John. 1996. ISBN 90 04 10419 4 (set)

VOL. XXII *Codex Bezae*. Studies from the Lunel Colloquium, June 1994, edited by D. C. Parker and C.-B. Amphoux. 1996.
ISBN 90 04 10393 7

VOL. XXIII *Bibliography of Literature on First Peter*, by Anthony Casurella. 1996. ISBN 90 04 10488 7

VOL. XXIV *Life of Jesus Research: An Annotated Bibliography*, by Craig A. Evans. Revised edition. 1996. ISBN 90 04 10282 5

VOL. XXV *Handbook to Exegesis of the New Testament*, edited by Stanley E. Porter. 1997. ISBN 90 04 09921 2

VOL. XXVI *An Annotated Bibliography of 1 and 2 Thessalonians*, by Jeffrey A.D. Weima and Stanley E. Porter. 1998. ISBN 90 04 10740 1

VOL. XXVII *Index to Periodical Literature on Christ and the Gospels*, by Watson E. Mills. 1998. ISBN 90 04 10098 9

VOL. XXVIII Volume One: *Authenticating the Words of Jesus*, edited by Bruce Chilton and Craig A. Evans. 1999. ISBN 90 04 11301 0

VOL. XXVIII Volume Two: *Authenticating the Activities of Jesus*, edited by Bruce Chilton and Craig A. Evans. 1999. ISBN 90 04 11302 9 Set ISBN 90 04 11141 7

VOL. XXIX *A Key to the Peshitta Gospels;* vol. II, by Terry C. Falla. 2000. ISBN 90 04 11148 4 *In preparation*

VOL. XXX *The Lukan Passion Narrative. The Markan Material in Luke 22,54 – 23,25. A Historical Survey: 1891-1997*, by Jay M. Harrington. 2000. ISBN 90 04 11590 0

Carnegie Mellon 1900–2000
A Centennial History

Carnegie Mellon 1900–2000
A Centennial History

By Edwin Fenton

Carnegie Mellon University Press
Pittsburgh 2000

To the five distinguished presidents whom
I have known, admired, worked beside,
and—like all faculty members—
criticized now and then during my 46 years
at Carnegie Tech / Mellon:

✾

Jake Warner

✾

Guy Stever

✾

Dick Cyert

✾

Robert Mehrabian

✾

Jerry Cohon

Library of Congress Catalog Card Number 99–74774
ISBN 0–88748–323–2 Pbk.
Printed and bound in the United States of America
10 9 8 7 6 5 4 3 2 1

Contents

Preface

I have written this book primarily for Carnegie Mellon University's alumni, faculty, staff, students, prospective students and their families, and many friends. It covers the entire history of Carnegie Mellon University since its founding as the Carnegie Technical Schools in 1900. Previous books by Arthur Wilson Tarbell, Glen U. Cleeton, Austin Wright and Ludwig F. Schaefer covered one or two of the administrations of Carnegie Mellon's first seven presidents. They are now out of print and, perhaps, too detailed for the alumni, students, faculty, staff members and friends of the University for whom the present volume is intended. The centennial of the founding of the Carnegie Technical Schools in 1900 provides an appropriate moment to publish this brief, generously illustrated account.

Too few people, even among the faculty and staff, are aware of the remarkable history of Carnegie Mellon. I have been unable to find students who even recall the names by which the University has been known: the Carnegie Technical Schools (CTS), the Carnegie Institute of Technology (CIT), Carnegie University and Carnegie-Mellon University—both with and without a hyphen. Everyone knows that steel-maker Andrew Carnegie's money and philanthropic beliefs founded the school, but only a few people know about the vital role that our "second founders," members of the extended Mellon family, have played in its history. Only a handful of people claim to have read all of the University's four previous histories.

Steven Calvert, at the time the Director of Alumni Relations, first suggested to me that the University needed a one-volume history written primarily for alumni and students. Over time after Calvert left Carnegie Mellon, the scope of the volume changed until it became part of the University's centennial celebration with an expanded audience. From the beginning, Calvert and I had envisaged a book with voluminous illustrations and intriguing first-person commentary from alumni, faculty and staff. Dan and Libby Boyarski, who designed the book, have woven these strands together.

Rather than write a chronological history, I decided to write chapters about Andrew Carnegie and the Mellons and the administrations of each of the University's eight presidents and to intersperse them with "snapshots" of the school at twenty-year intervals in and around 1908, 1928, 1948, 1968 and 1988. The final chapter presents a picture of the University today and speculates about its future. The snapshots provide dramatic evidence of the rapid changes characteristic of an institution that transformed itself from a trade and technical school offering two-year certificates and three-year diplomas into a research university where more than half the graduates each year receive master's or doctor's degrees.

In a strenuous endeavor to control the page limit, I omitted many important developments in the University's history. Then during the last months of preparation for publication, I cut a total of 30 pages from the text. If you cannot find your name in the book, I can assure you that it rests in the scraps of paper on the editorial cutting room floor. Please forgive me.

I cannot thank everyone who has contributed to this volume. Eight under-graduates wrote papers about the early history of the University for a seminar taught by Ed Schatz and me. They are Maureen Bartek, Matt Cline, Mike Leonard, Christa Sherwood, Ed Slavishak, Scott Styfco, Jason Togyer, Randall Woyicki and Steve Woyicki. More than 200 alumni sent paragraphs containing reminiscences of their lives as students. I was able to include fewer than half of them in the text. Dozens of individuals have contributed their ideas and insights in other ways. Among those who read and commented on parts of the manuscript are Susan Ambrose, Benno Bernt, Al Brannick, Richard Buchanan, Steve Calvert, Robyn Choi, Paul Christiano, Jared Cohon, Maureen Cohon, Doug Cooper, Mark Coticchia, Ann Curran, Margaret Cyert, Bill Elliott, John Fetkovich, Kyle Fisher Morabito, Eric Johnson, Angel Jordan, Don Hale, Marcie Mastracci, Robert Mehrabian, Erwin Steinberg and Paul Tellers.

I owe particular debts of gratitude to four remarkable archivists—Martin Aurand, Jennifer Aronson, Sharon Maclean and Gabrielle Michalek—who cheerfully responded to my repeated requests for documents or photographs; to Edmund Delaney, Bruce Gerson and Ann Curran who provided information and photos from their publications; to Ken Andreyo and Bill Redic who artfully photographed Carnegie Mellon throughout many years; to Kevin Lamb and Jeffrey Bolton who supplied reams of data from their well-kept files; to Ria David who made sense of scattered data found in dusty archival files; to Lil Draskovich and Marcie Mastracci who tolerated my invasion of their office space with good humor and helping hands; to Ann Curran, Don Hale and Kyle Fisher Morabito whose editorial skills contributed to both the readability and the content of the book; to Cynthia Lamb whose fine eye detected proofing gaffes that the rest of us missed; and, of course, to my wife, Barbara, who sustained me in so many ways as I groused, complained and occasionally sulked my way through this project from conception to publication. Finally, Libby and Dan Boyarski's design turned a somewhat conventional history into a visually appealing account of a remarkable institution. For any mistakes or omissions that have survived this scrutiny, I am, of course, wholly responsible.

Edwin Fenton

Pittsburgh, Pennsylvania
January 2000

MILLIONS MORE FOR CAUSE OF EDUCATION

Mr. Andrew Carnegie Makes Formal Announcement
of His Latest and Greatest Gift for Pittsburg—
A Magnificent Technical School.

STARTS WITH ENDOWMENT OF $1,000,000 IN GOLD BONDS

Introduction

Carnegie Mellon University: an educational stripling

During the past century, Carnegie Mellon University has come a greater distance at a faster rate than any other American university. The pace of change has accelerated steadily since the end of World War II and dramatically during the last 30 years. The Carnegie Technical Schools (CTS) came into existence, at least on paper, in 1900 when founder Andrew Carnegie promised to endow a technical and trade school with $1 million if the city fathers of Pittsburgh would provide a site. Carnegie wanted the school to educate young men and women, particularly working young men and women from Pittsburgh. A century later, Carnegie Mellon is an internationally renowned research university drawing faculty and students from throughout the world. Its impact on society is far greater than its small size would suggest.

It's not your typical university. Carnegie Mellon has no law school, no medical school, no departments of sociology, anthropology or geology—or many others, for that matter—and no big-time athletic teams or insoluble parking problems. Carnegie Mellon never felt that it should imitate other schools. Instead of developing a department for each discipline, the University organized schools, centers, institutes and consortia whose members cross disciplinary lines. New centers sprout like crocuses in the spring and, if they cannot succeed, disappear with equal speed.

Almost all of Carnegie Mellon's academic and housing units are concentrated on a 101-acre central campus adjacent to a large public park, the Carnegie museums and a middle-class neighborhood. Not a typical setting for an urban university. In the fall of 1999, the University enrolled 5,138 undergraduate, 2,122 master's and 1,051 doctoral students. Not a typical distribution for a research university. Large numbers of its full-time 560 tenure-stream faculty, 78 research faculty, 83 lecturers and 533 full- and part-time special faculty engage in research and educational efforts that cross departmental—even college—lines. Not a typical practice. The Andrew computer system enables the 10,000 or so computers on campus to communicate with each other through the first wireless network established in a university. Not a typical electronic environment.

Carnegie Mellon has intriguing traditions: buggy races in which muscular "pushers" propel sophisticated student-built buggies driven by tiny women students

Carnegie Mellon University Colleges & Departments

Carnegie Institute of Technology (CIT)
Chemical
Civil & Environmental
Electrical & Computer
Engineering & Public Policy
Materials Science
Mechanical

College of Fine Arts (CFA)
Architecture
Art
Design
Drama
Music

College of Humanities & Social Sciences (H&SS)
Economics
English
History
Modern Languages
Philosophy
Psychology
Social & Decision Sciences
Statistics

Mellon College of Science (MCS)
Biology
Chemistry
Mathematics
Physics

School of Computer Science (SCS)

Graduate School of Industrial Administration (GSIA)

H. John Heinz III School of Public Policy and Management

through a hilly course; a purportedly 76-year-old fence (the occasional bug-infested rail or post has been replaced) that serves as a non-electronic bulletin board as students paint messages on it nightly; an annual student-written and directed show (one, *Godspell,* became a hit on Broadway); and an annual mobot race featuring student-made robots that steer themselves through a curved, uneven course. Scottish traditions and names persist on campus: Skibo after Carnegie's castle in Scotland, *The Tartan* newspaper, *The Thistle* yearbook, Scotch 'n' Soda theater group, The Kiltie Band and a bagpipe band. Not to mention the only bagpipe major in the world. Hearing them practice is not as frightening as it may seem.

A leading research university

Carnegie Mellon now ranks among the nation's premier national research universities. It achieved this rank despite an impressive number of handicaps. Compared to its peers, it is strikingly young. It will be only 100 years old in the year 2000. Of the 25 best of the nation's 228 national public and private universities listed in *U.S. News and World Report* in 1999, Carnegie Mellon was the youngest. It is an educational stripling.

Carnegie Mellon is also underendowed. Its endowment per student ranks near the bottom of a list of peer institutions which it uses as benchmarks. The youth of Carnegie Mellon and its small size contribute to its small endowment. It has fewer graduates who have inherited or made the large fortunes on which development drives depend for most of their funds. Of its 50,000 active alumni, 31,000 have graduated since 1970.

Rather than cover entire fields, Carnegie Mellon focuses its resources on areas where it has comparative advantages. For example, the 24 tenure-stream faculty in Carnegie Mellon's renowned Psychology Department concentrate their efforts in four of the nine major psychological areas: cognitive, cognitive neuroscience, developmental and social psychology. The Department's output is small, publishing only 210 papers during the period 1990-1994, between one half and one fourth as many as large departments. The Institute for Scientific Information, however, ranked the Department as the leading producer of high impact papers in the nation. Its papers were cited an average of 8.52 times each, more frequently than the papers of any other psychology department. It's the quality of the faculty and their research that counts, not the number of faculty or research papers.

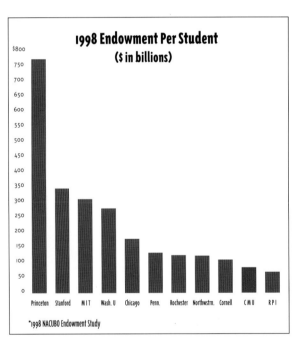

1998 Endowment Per Student
($ in billions)

*1998 NACUBO Endowment Study

On the other hand, small size has yielded significant benefits. Carnegie Mellon is flexible. Its administrators can make decisions quickly. The University can move resources into new fields to take advantage of the latest breakthroughs. Because departments are small, faculty can get to know colleagues from other departments or colleges more easily than they can in larger institutions. And they can and do collaborate: in drama and computer science, in robotics and biology, in business and psychology.

From a humble trade school

This book traces the development of Carnegie Mellon University since its founding as the Carnegie Technical Schools in 1900. Unimpressed by liberal arts institutions, Andrew Carnegie founded a set of four technical and trade schools offering two-year certificates and three-year diplomas to workers from Pittsburgh and its neighboring towns. The Carnegie Technical Schools included the School of Science and Technology, the School of Fine and Applied Arts, the School for Apprentices and Journeymen and Margaret Morrison Carnegie School for Women. The institution began to offer four-year degrees in 1912 when it changed its name to the Carnegie Institute of Technology.

Both research projects and graduate work grew slowly until after World War II. Then within a decade, the already outstanding engineering, fine arts and women's colleges were joined by four new ventures: the Graduate School of Industrial Administration, research in nuclear physics focused on a new synchro-cyclotron, the development of one of the nation's first programs in computing and the invention of a new field of research in artificial intelligence. In 1967 Carnegie Tech merged with the Mellon Institute, a research organization specializing in chemistry, to form Carnegie Mellon University. Within a few years, Carnegie Mellon embraced six colleges and schools. The School of Computer Science became a seventh independent school in 1988.

Distinguished presidents have led Carnegie's development. Five of them have been engineers; one, a distinguished scientist; another, a humanist; and the eighth, an expert in organizational theory and management. They have served for unusually long terms: two for seven years, three for 15 years, and two for 18, an average tenure of 14 years. The first president, Arthur Arton Hamerschlag, began to shape the Carnegie Technical Schools in 1903 when he was only 31 years old. The other presidents assumed office between the ages of 49 and 53. Because of their long tenures, each man left his stamp on the institution.

Support from Andrew Carnegie and the Mellon family

Carnegie Mellon's founder Andrew Carnegie and the Mellon family also left their marks on the University. Carnegie himself and the Carnegie Corporation that he endowed made 50 grants and gifts to the school, largely during its early incarnations as the Carnegie Technical Schools and Carnegie Institute of Technology. Carnegie financed construction of the seven distinguished original campus buildings designed by Henry

WHEN CARNEGIE HAD NO SITE

NO PLACE IN SIGHT, FOR A SITE.

A cartoon from *The Pittsburgh Press,* September 24, 1902. Pittsburgh did not provide a site for the schools until 1903.

November 15, 1900.

Hon. Wm. J. Diehl,

If the City of Pittsburg will furnish a site, which I
hope will be of ample size for future extensions, I will be delight-
ed to ~~furnish~~ *provide* the money for a ~~Technical~~ School ~~of the first class,~~ *such a*
~~suitable in size for Pittsburg to begin with.~~ *taking* Care ~~would be~~ *erected*
~~taken~~ *provide room* to ~~arrange~~ for ~~future~~ additions to the buildings to meet the
certain ~~increase~~ *growth* of Pittsburg.

I would ~~also~~ endow it with $1,000,000 five per cent.gold
bonds, ~~giving it~~ *yielding* a revenue of $50,000 per year.

Right:
The letter of transmittal from Carnegie to Pittsburgh's mayor corrected in Carnegie's own handwriting.

Below:
The original Mellon Institute and today's Carnegie Mellon Research Institute

Hornbostel. Translated into today's buying power, his gifts total more than $400 million. After World War II, 200 separate gifts, grants and bequests from members of the extended Mellon family and their foundations have made major contributions to the University's seven colleges, the Carnegie Mellon Research Institute, building programs,

scholarship funds and other activities. These gifts amount to almost $600 million in today's dollars. As a result of such support, Carnegie Mellon grew into a university and expanded its name, with considerable persuasion, to embrace its second great 20th century supporter: the Mellon family.

The present campus bears little relationship to the grounds and buildings of 1908 when the Charter Class graduated. The Carnegie Technical Schools began with 32 scrub-covered acres next to Schenley Park. By 1908, two buildings, Industries Hall (now Porter) and the Margaret Morrison building were almost complete and construction on Engineering Hall (now Doherty) was under-way. Muddy paths connected one building with another, piles of rubble dotted the campus, landscaping was only a dream, and the campus lacked dormitories, a student center, athletic facilities, cafeterias and other amenities that grace the modern campus.

By 1999, a distinguished, landscaped campus had grown to 101 acres featuring more than 50 major buildings. Plans or construction were underway for several structures that will complete elaborate campus plans made in 1984. In addition, Carnegie Mellon has a number of research and administrative buildings located off campus. By its centennial in the year 2000, Carnegie Mellon will have one of the most distinguished urban university campuses in the nation.

Both faculty and students change

The institution's faculty has undergone dramatic transformations. When the first class graduated in 1908, the full-time faculty consisted of 101 members, only 14 with graduate degrees; indeed 43 had no college degrees. Ninety years later in 1998, the tenure-stream faculty had grown to 593, 98 percent with terminal degrees. In addition, the University staff included 78 research scientists, 80 lecturers, 642 special faculty—largely postdoctoral fellows and visiting or adjunct faculty—and 16 part-time special faculty. Carnegie Mellon's faculty has changed far more radically during these 90 years than the faculties of peer institutions.

Research began slowly and until after World War II was carried on in laboratories by men and women who were not tenure-stream faculty. Increasingly after 1945, Carnegie faculty began to undertake research in their departments and in the 50 or so centers, institutes and consortia that mark the present University. In 1950 the research budget was $1 million; in 1997 sponsored research contracts totaled $166 million. Cross-disciplinary efforts continue to characterize Carnegie Mellon's research projects. These efforts often take place at the boundaries of disciplines such as biology and chemistry where expertise from both disciplines is essential to the solution of problems.

The student body has been equally transformed. In 1908, 720 day and 879 night students enrolled in programs that could earn them a two-year certificate or a three-year diploma. Many of the day students were not high school graduates, and most of the night school students had only elementary school educations. Ninety percent of the students came from Pennsylvania and most of the remainder from nearby states. Men outnumbered women by five to one; women could not enroll in the School of Science and Technology or the School for Apprentices and Journeymen. Almost every student was a descendant of northern or western European immigrants; minorities were conspicuous for their almost complete absence. An additional 20 students—nine of them Canadian—came from seven foreign countries. In the three decades between 1905 and 1935, the yearly registration of night students exceeded the day school registration by 20,000.

Ninety years later, Carnegie Mellon enrolled 5,138 undergraduate and 3,074 graduate students in 177 different programs leading to bachelor's, master's or doctor's degrees. The University and its students invented some of the academic degrees to take advantage of Carnegie Mellon's strengths. The University's students rank among the nation's most able. Carnegie Mellon competes for students with the nation's elite "high-select" universities. In 1998 one third of Carnegie Mellon's students were women, enrolled in all seven of its colleges and schools. The 1999 student body includes students from 50 states as well as 1,785 international students from 90 countries. They rank among the most talented students in their nations—and in the University. Twenty-one percent of the student body are members of minority groups, that is, Asian, Hispanic, African-American and Native American.

1998-99 SAT Average*
*(Average of 25th & 75th)

Harvard (MA)	1490
Massachusetts Institute of Technology	1480
Princeton (NJ)	1450
Stanford (CA)	1450
Brown (RI)	1395
Columbia (NY)	1390
University of Pennsylvania	1390
Johns Hopkins (MD)	1385
Carnegie Mellon University (PA)	1370
Northwestern University (IL)	1370
Case Western (OH)	1355
Cornell University (NY)	1355
University of California (Berkeley)	1340
Washington University (MO)	1335
New York University	1315
University of Virginia	1310
University of Rochester (NY)	1305
Rensselaer Polytechnic Institute (NY)	1265
Penn State (PA)	1206

*U.S. News and World Report Ranking

An early women's dorm and today's coed Resnik residence hall

Student life in 1999 bears little resemblance to student life nine decades ago. In 1908 almost all students commuted to campus. The Carnegie Technical Schools had no dormitories, although it did rent two houses near the campus for out-of-town students. The rest commuted either from their homes or from boarding houses in the city. Almost all of the night students lived at home and either walked to school or arrived by streetcar. The lives of these students outside of classes focused on their families and neighborhood social and religious groups. Only a few full-time day students became involved in student life on campus.

In 1999, only a handful of Carnegie Mellon's students commuted from their homes while 58 percent of the students, including all freshmen, lived in on-campus dormitories, fraternity houses or sorority houses. The University offers a rich student life.

Students can join one or more of 175 officially recognized student organizations that reflect the wide-ranging interests of a diverse student body. The Office of Student Affairs sponsors a wide variety of programs to nurture students and to develop their physical and mental health and their intellectual, social, cultural and religious lives.

In 1908 the major contribution of the Carnegie Technical Schools to the community came from the lives of its graduates and of the tens of thousands of students who took a few courses, mainly in the night school, to increase their skills. Even in the early years, faculty frequently spoke at meetings of local organizations and at professional conferences.

Today Carnegie Mellon serves the community in a host of ways: by the contributions of its graduates to engineering, the sciences, management and the arts and humanities; by transferring its discoveries to the wider society through start-up companies, licensing agreements and consulting; by spurring economic development in southwestern Pennsylvania and beyond; by tutoring and mentoring programs conducted in local schools by students and faculty; and by curriculum projects to develop learning materials for schools and colleges.

An early electrical engineering laboratory, and the "clean room" in today's University

How and why did this remarkable set of transformations take place? No single factor accounts for them. Distinguished leadership helped. So did the University's values and traditions. But where did they come from? Why was Carnegie Mellon able to develop traditions such as innovation, interdisciplinary activities, problem solving and dedication to work? This book attempts to answer these questions. It contains chapters about founder Andrew Carnegie and the Mellon family and the achievements of each presidential administration. It also provides "snapshots" of the institution at 20-year intervals beginning in 1908 when the first class—58 survivors from an entering class of 120—graduated from the Carnegie Technical Schools. These snapshots capture the dramatic changes taking place over a two-decade period as well as the ongoing development of longstanding traditions and values. A remarkable story, as amazing as the life of the Scottish immigrant who started the process.

Carnegie Mellon's vision and mission

Our vision

Carnegie Mellon will be a leader among educational institutions by building on its traditions of innovation, problem solving and interdisciplinary collaboration to meet the changing needs of society.

Our mission

To create and disseminate knowledge and art through research and artistic expression, teaching and learning; and to transfer intellectual products to society.

To serve our students by teaching them problem-solving, leadership and teamwork skills and the value of commitment to quality, ethical behavior, society and respect for one another.

To pursue the advantages provided by a diverse community open to the exchange of ideas, where discovery, artistic creativity, and personal and professional development can flourish.

Carnegie Mellon in 1999

Pronouncing "Carnegie"

An indignant letter comes to the editor, signed merely "Inquisitive." It runs thus: "I had a telephone call on Sunday from an old friend I had not heard from in more than thirty years. He had just been listening to a NBC program and he was riled once again, as he has been for years, with the New York pronunciation of 'Carnegie.' He said he had it from his grandfather, who had it from Andrew Carnegie himself, and his own father also had it from friends in Scotland, that the pronunciation was 'Car-négie not 'Car´ne-gie.'

In reply we can only say, "Yes, a thousand times yes!" The correct pronunciation is definitely "Car-négie," with accent on the second syllable. It is surprising, with a name that is internationally known, that the incorrect form is so frequently used away from Pittsburgh, although here in the home locality of the steel man and philanthropist the accent is generally placed as it should be.

—*Carnegie Alumnus*, December 1947

"It is really astonishing how many of the world's foremost men have begun as manual laborers. The greatest of all, Shakespeare, was a woolcarder; Burns, a plowman; Columbus, a sailor; Hannibal, a blacksmith; Lincoln, a rail-splitter; Grant, a tanner. I know of no better foundation from which to ascend than manual labor in youth."

Andrew Carnegie

I.

Founder Andrew Carnegie
To die rich is to die disgraced

On November 15, 1900 the trustees of Pittsburgh's Carnegie Institute honored their patron Andrew Carnegie with a banquet. Carnegie had founded the Carnegie Library in 1890 and provided additional funds to support a music hall, museum, lecture hall and art gallery in the Oakland section of Pittsburgh in 1895. The Board of Trustees, all Pittsburghers, governed this complex known as the Carnegie Institute. At the banquet Carnegie read a letter he had prepared offering to give $1 million in 5 percent gold bonds to found a technical institute to serve Pittsburgh and its workers. Carnegie had observed the growth of technical schools in Boston; Worcester, Massachusetts; Philadelphia; Brooklyn and Chicago. Two technical schools in Great Britain, the Keighly Institute and the Halifax Institute, had also impressed him when he visited them. In these schools, more than half of the students worked during the day and pursued their studies at night, as Carnegie himself had done.

Carnegie respected people who worked with their hands. His grandfather, whose name he bore, had written an essay entitled "Handication versus Headication" in which he pointed to the role which manual labor had played in the lives of many famous and successful men. In his letter setting up the technical schools, Carnegie echoed his grandfather's sentiments:

> It is really astonishing how many of the world's foremost men have begun as manual laborers. The greatest of all, Shakespeare, was a woolcarder; Burns, a plowman; Columbus, a sailor; Hannibal, a blacksmith; Lincoln, a rail-splitter; Grant, a tanner. I know of no better foundation from which to ascend than manual labor in youth. We have two notable examples of this in our own community whose fame is world-wide: George Westinghouse was a mechanic; Professor Brashear, a millwright.
> —Dean Arthur Wilson Tarbell in *The Story of Carnegie Tech: Being a History of Carnegie Institute of Technology from 1900-1935.*

Carnegie might have added that he himself began his working days as a bobbin boy in a textile mill in Slabtown, Pennsylvania, now on Pittsburgh's North Side. The school he proposed to found would serve young men and women, the sons and daughters of mill workers, trained in "handication."

In his speech and in the letter to the trustees of the Carnegie Institute, Carnegie declared that a first class technical school would develop latent talent throughout the Pittsburgh area. If the City of Pittsburgh would furnish a site for such a school, he would provide the funds. He asked the trustees of the Carnegie Institute to take charge of the development of the school and its endowment, an arrangement that continued until 1959 when Carnegie Institute of Technology established an independent board of trustees. The letter ended with the phrase "My heart is in the work," words which became emblazoned in the official seal of Carnegie's school.

Carnegie formed by his family and Dunfermline

Andrew Carnegie was born in Dunfermline, Scotland, 14 miles north of Edinburgh, on November 25, 1835. His father, William, wove linen on hand looms. His mother, Margaret, an enterprising woman who set a standard for Andrew to imitate, was the driving force in the family. The family lived in one room in a cottage down the hill from the high street where his mother's sister, who had married a merchant, lived. When his brother Tom was born, Andrew, then eight, began grammar school in Dunfermline. He spent four years in school, but much of his education came at the feet of his uncles, George Lauder and Will Morrison, who filled the boy's head with tales of Scottish heroes and introduced him to Shakespeare's plays, the poetry of Robert Burns and the achievements of famous American statesmen, intellectuals and inventors.

Dunfermline's workers were among Scotland's most radical, and Andy's father and his uncle, Will Morrison, were leaders among them. They helped to found a branch of the Chartists, an organization striving for universal suffrage for men, the secret ballot, annual elections to parliament, equal electoral districts, the removal of property qualifications for parliament and pay for the members of parliament. Young Andy embraced the principles of the Charter. Throughout his life he argued that political inequality accounted for many of the shortcomings of his homeland. On the other hand, he thought that equal political status, on which economic progress depended, accounted for the rise of the United States to prominence in the world. These ideas emerged clearly in his book *Triumphant Democracy*, published in 1886.

Ironically the sort of technological innovations that Carnegie later fostered in the steel industry drove his father out of Scotland. The advent of steam looms undermined the economic position of hand weavers. Soon they had landed on the technological scrap heap, and at 43, Will Carnegie was ill-equipped to learn a new trade. When

Above:
The Carnegie Cottage in Dunfermline, Scotland

Below:
Andrew and his brother Tom as boys in Pittsburgh

Opposite page:
Andrew's mother, Margaret Morrison Carnegie

Carnegie Quirk
He gave Princeton University a lake instead of money in order to keep the young men's minds on crew and away from football, which he disliked.

hard times forced him to sell his hand looms to make ends meet, Margaret Carnegie sewed shoes in their little cottage to put food on the table. Ten years younger than her husband and with children to feed, she determined in 1847 to follow some of her fellow villagers and her two younger sisters to America. To raise money for the journey, she sold the family's household goods and borrowed 20 pounds from a friend. Landing in New York in 1848 after a seven-week voyage in an old whaling schooner, they were met by family friends and then began a three-week trip to Pittsburgh via the Hudson River to Albany; the Erie Canal, Mohawk River and Lake Erie to Buffalo and Cleveland; the Ohio Canal to Akron and Beaver Falls, Pennsylvania; and finally upstream on the Ohio River to Pittsburgh. Margaret's sister Annie Aitken welcomed them and provided free lodging on Rebecca Street in Slabtown, now on Pittsburgh's North Side, until the family could get started in the new land. Andy was 13 years old.

The early years in Dunfermline planted the seeds of two often conflicting characteristics in young Carnegie. On the one hand, he embraced the idealism of his forbearers, an idealism that led him to trumpet the virtues of American democracy and even support trade unionism in principle. On the other, it fostered a keen competitive streak and a driving determination to get to the top, characteristics he saw so vividly in the mother he idolized throughout her life.

Only Andy and his mother fared well in the new land. For a few years, Margaret Morrison Carnegie sewed shoes as she had done in Scotland until Andrew made enough money to support her. Will Carnegie worked for a short period in a mill and then drifted back to his hand loom, selling his products as an itinerant peddler. He died in 1855. Andrew's younger brother Tom tagged along after his brother who gave him various positions in his far-flung enterprises. He died in 1886 after a checkered career marked by frequent bouts of drinking. Andrew succumbed to neither despair nor alcohol.

From bobbin boy to railroad superintendent

Within 11 years of his arrival in the United States, Andrew Carnegie was superintendent of the Western Division of the Pennsylvania Railroad and on his way to becoming a very rich and remarkably well-educated young man. His first job as a bobbin boy in a textile mill owned by a Scot brought him wages of $1.20 a week, which seemed a small fortune to a poor immigrant boy. He soon left this position for a better paying mill job with Dunfermline expatriate John Hay. Hay occasionally took him out of the factory to work in the office. Taking this opportunity as a challenge, Carnegie decided to study double-entry bookkeeping in night school. Across the Allegheny River he trudged in the middle of winter, night after night after a 12-hour working day. And on Saturday afternoons, he visited the library of Colonel James Anderson who permitted working boys to borrow books from his 400-volume library. Carnegie was 14 years old.

In the spring of 1849, he became a telegraph messenger. His Uncle Hogan played checkers with David Brooks who ran the O'Reilly telegraph office. One evening O'Reilly asked Hogan to recommend a boy for a job as a messenger. Andrew got the job the next morning, happily liberated from the coal hole and oil vat where he worked at the textile mill. "I felt that my foot was on the ladder and that I was bound to climb," he

At age seventeen, Carnegie earned $1.20 a week.

Carnegie Prepares for His Future

At the age of seventeen he was already exhibiting most of the qualities which would carry him to wealth and power. In addition to working so hard and believing in his own destiny, he had enough charisma to persuade others to follow him. He made the right friends; he admired strength and despised weakness. He was loyal, kind, and independent in his dealings with most people, although he showed streaks of guile and obsequiousness now and again. He was physically durable and mentally acute; he had a retentive memory and an uncanny instinct for opportunity. The years in the telegraph office put these qualities through a basic training in business, adding acquired techniques to inherent talent. The railroad presented an unprecedented challenge; he assaulted it with the same restless ambition he had always shown.
—*Harold C. Livesay, Andrew Carnegie and the Rise of Big Business, 1975*

wrote in his *Autobiography* many years later. As always, he threw himself energetically into his new job. He quickly learned his way around the city, memorized the names and occupations of Pittsburgh's rising industrialists so that he could greet them by name and figured out the business and personal relationships among them. Soon he knew as much as anyone in the city about Pittsburgh's business people. More importantly, he had learned how business was conducted in a booming American city.

Within the year, he had learned on his own to operate the telegraph key. O'Reilly rewarded him with a raise from $2.50 to $3.00 a week and with an opportunity to work part time as an operator. In 1851 he became a full-time telegrapher. Soon afterward he taught himself to take messages by ear, by interpreting the sound of the key without waiting for the hard copy. He exploited every opportunity to get ahead and to educate himself. Many of his opportunities had come about at the hands of Scots who were looking out for the fortunes of immigrant boys from Scotland. Few other boys, however, responded with the energy, diligence and high intelligence that Carnegie exhibited. These qualities soon bore fruit.

In 1852 Carnegie's friend and mentor Tom Scott became the superintendent of the Western Division of the Pennsylvania Railroad. Impressed by the young Carnegie, he offered him a job as his personal telegrapher and secretary. Andy jumped at the chance. He was 17. He embarked on a series of apprenticeships that would soon turn him into one of the most successful men in the nation.

From railroad superintendent to steel magnate: "I'm rich; I'm rich."

During the following three decades, Carnegie had careers as a railroad superintendent, an entrepreneur with investments in several companies that he organized, largely with borrowed money, a bond salesman who reaped commissions of two and one-half percent on $30 million worth of bonds sold in Europe, a speculator in Pennsylvania's newly opened oil industry and a highly successful manager of the largest steel company the world had ever known. By 1863 he was able to proclaim to a friend, "I'm rich; I'm rich" when he realized that he had an annual income of more than $48,000 (about $850,000 in today's dollars). He was 28 years old. He was to become the richest man in the world.

During this whirlwind of activity, Carnegie learned or developed most of the techniques that made American industry the most productive in the world. His early experiences as a bookkeeper and a railroad superintendent taught him to examine costs in detail and to drive them down relentlessly until they were far lower than any that his competitors could match. In the steel industry he bought or built whole new mills with the latest equipment so that he could keep ahead of his rivals. Unlike most of them, he scrapped relatively new machinery when improvements came to his attention, lowering costs in the long run by doing so. He also pioneered in vertical integration, owning or controlling all stages of manufacture and sale from raw materials to the final products. He could do so only by producing in huge amounts that drove down per-unit prices.

Finally, he pioneered new management techniques. He encouraged his subordinates by giving successful men a share in his business and forcing others out ruthlessly. Among the first industrialists to hire scientists, he brought in a chemist to analyze raw materials, another move which enabled him to make substantial cost reductions. He described the steel business in the following words:

The Homestead Steel Works
owned by Andrew Carnegie

*The eighth wonder of the world is this: two pounds of iron-stone purchased on
the shores of Lake Superior and transported to Pittsburgh; two pounds of coal
mined in Connellsville and brought to Pittsburgh; one-half pound of limestone mined east of the Alleghenies and brought to Pittsburgh; a little manga-
nese ore mined in Virginia and brought to Pittsburgh; and these four-and-
a-half pounds of material manufactured into one pound of solid steel and sold
for one cent. That's all that need be said about the steel business.*
—Harold C. Livesay in *Andrew Carnegie and the Rise of Big Business*

His triumphs helped to convince him that energetic, enterprising people could climb the
ladder to success and that he should help them to educate themselves by founding free
public libraries and institutions such as the Carnegie Technical Schools.

Carnegie's ambivalent attitude about labor

During his entire career in the steel industry, Carnegie held ambivalent attitudes
toward labor. In two articles published in *The Forum* in 1886, he argued that the refusal
of American business to recognize unions led to strife and bitterness. He also condemned
the use of strikebreakers, arguing that the sight of a scab trying to take a worker's job
almost inevitably resulted in violence. Instead of hiring scabs, Carnegie proclaimed, industries should shut down during strikes and await the results. He followed this policy to
the letter during a strike at the Edgar Thompson Works, a steel mill in nearby Braddock,
in 1888. He finally won the strike after a five-month battle during which he again proclaimed that Andrew Carnegie would not use strikebreakers to take away a man's job.
He even tried to institute the eight-hour day. During the late 19th century, steel workers
labored seven days a week, 12 hours a day—24 consecutive hours when day and night
shifts changed on weekends. Every other week, workers had a full 24 hours free. During
the 1880s, spurred by Captain William Jones, superintendent of his Edgar Thompson

Carnegie Quirk
He allocated funds for the acquisition
of the most complete dinosaur skeleton found
in Wyoming. The Carnegie Institute's Natural
History Museum in Pittsburgh cast
reconstructions of the Diplodocus Carnegiei,
and sent them to museums
all over the world.

Works, Carnegie agreed to experiment with the eight-hour day, hoping that his competitors would follow suit. When they failed to do so after two years, his mills returned to 12-hour shifts following a bitter strike. On the other hand, Carnegie thirsted for profits and frequently cut wages, particularly during recessions, to increase profit margins. The rights of workers and Carnegie's cost cutting tendencies met head on.

These conflicting attitudes came to a head in the notorious Homestead Strike of 1892. Two issues were at stake. Carnegie and partner Henry Clay Frick wanted to reduce wages on the grounds that the price they were receiving for steel had been cut. They also wanted to eliminate union representation in the mill. Carnegie left Frick, an ardent foe of unions, in charge while he went off for his annual vacation to Scotland, knowing full well what was likely to ensue. The worst happened. Frick floated 300 Pinkerton detectives down the Monongahela River on barges, expecting them to take over the mill in preparation for the arrival of strikebreakers. The workers assaulted them from the shore in a day-long battle. The Pinkertons surrendered. The workers ran them through a gauntlet as they left the barges, killing four and injuring most of the remainder. Then the governor sent 8,000 troops to occupy the plant, and the strike was eventually broken. During this bitter strife, Carnegie remained incommunicado in Scotland. Workers everywhere and much of the press denounced him, contrasting what he had written in his books and articles with what had happened at Homestead. In later years, Carnegie called Homestead the greatest mistake of his career.

Steel tycoon Carnegie in his great double role. As the tightfisted employer he reduced wages so that he might play philanthropist and give away money for libraries.

Private life and public philanthropy

Andrew Carnegie's life was not all business. Far from it. In 1867 he moved his residence from Pittsburgh to a hotel suite in New York City. There he began a careful self-assessment and decided that he was displeased with part of what he discovered. Anxious to improve himself, he began to travel widely, particularly to England. In both New York and England, he met the leading intellectuals of the day—Herbert Spencer, Henry Ward Beecher and Matthew Arnold among others—and began to spend his free hours among them. Spencer's Social Darwinism—that survival of the fittest explained success and failure in economic life as well as in the natural world—helped him to rationalize his business practices and put his egalitarian tendencies to flight. His interests in art, literature and music blossomed amid his new acquaintances. He entertained them in the mansion he had built for himself on New York's East 91st Street.

By 1868 he was worth $400,000 and had an annual income of $50,000. He was 33 years old. Successful, rich, and respected, he wrote *Triumphant Democracy* in which he praised American political institutions and the economic opportunities they fostered and outlined the major ideas about what rich people should do with their money: give it away in an effort to improve society.

This idea received full treatment in a famous essay entitled "Wealth" which he published in 1889 in the *North American Review*. Commonly known as "The Gospel of

20

Wealth," this essay contained perhaps the most famous sentence that he ever wrote: "To die rich is to die disgraced." Pointing to his own rise from poverty through night school and self-education, he argued that rich people should endow universities, libraries, schools and similar institutions through which talented young men and women could find ways to rise to the top. After all, he was a classic example of what self-education could achieve. And he kept his word, giving away more than $400 million (perhaps $7 billion in today's purchasing power) before his death in 1919.

In 1880 when he was 45 years old, he met and fell in love with 23-year-old Louise Whitfield, who at five foot six inches, stood three inches taller than her suitor. Their engagement was off and on. His mother's opposition to his marriage delayed the nuptials until 1887, some months after his mother died. The marriage was a happy one; Louise supported his resolve to give away his fortune. After 1898, they lived part of the time in Skibo Castle which Carnegie purchased in Scotland and renovated lovingly over the years. Its 7,500 acres featured a golf course, a trout stream, a lake, tennis courts and all the amenities of a baronial estate. By all accounts, he was living a happy and productive personal life.

Carnegie Quirk
He spent five to six months of each year at Skibo Castle, his Scottish estate, enjoying his private golf course, fish hatchery, heated saltwater pool and yacht.

Carnegie's home on East 91st Street in New York City

Dec. '68
St. Nicholas Hotel, N.York

Thirty three and an income of 50,000 $ per annum. By this time two years I can arrange all my business as to secure at least 50,000 per annum. Beyond this never earn— make no effort to increase fortune, but spend the surplus each year for benevelent {sic} purposes. Cast aside business forever except for others.

Settle in Oxford & get a thorough education making the acquaintance of literary men—this will take three years active work— pay especial attention to speaking in public.

Settle then in London & purchase a controlling interest in some newspaper or live review & give the general management of it attention, taking a part in public matters especially those connected with education & improvement of the poorer classes.

Man must have an idol—The amassing of wealth is one of the worst species of idolitary {sic}. No idol more debasing than the worship of money. Whatever I engage in I must push inordinately therefore should I be careful to choose that life which will be the most elevating in its character. To continue much longer over whelmed by business cares and with most of my thoughts wholly upon the way to make more money in the shortest time, must degrade me beyond hope of permanent recovery.

I will resign business at Thirty five, but during the ensuing two years, I wish to spend the afternoons in securing instruction, and in reading systematically.

"THE" THISTLE

In 1881 he and his mother Margaret Morrison Carnegie had made a triumphant return to Dunfermline, keeping a promise he had made to her when he was still a boy. The two Carnegies assembled a party to make the trip. Andrew wanted to take Louise Whitfield with them and sent his mother to negotiate with Louise's mother. Instead of welcoming Louise as a member of the party, Margaret Morrison Carnegie told Louise's mother that if she were the mother, no daughter of hers would be permitted to go. Then she invited Louise to a dinner party at which all the other guests talked excitedly about the upcoming trip. No wonder that Louise Carnegie later in life called her mother-in-law the most unpleasant person she had ever known. Carnegie left Louise behind. He had already given a swimming pool to Dunfermline and was to give it a library a few years later. He and his mother rode in triumph through the town in a coach-and-four. His mother rode atop the coach that stopped before her sister's house on the high street while townsmen cheered and held up signs proclaiming, "Welcome Carnegie; Generous Son."

In the midst of this hectic life, Carnegie found time to leave an extensive literary legacy. Without the aid of a ghostwriter, he produced eight books including two accounts of his travels, a biography of James Watt, his autobiography and four books about economics and politics. He also wrote 70 magazine articles, publishing them in the most prestigious journals of the day. Twenty-five of his speeches reached print in pamphlet form. In addition, he wrote hundreds of personal and business letters. His style was interesting and straightforward. He wrote with a stub pencil on a pad that he held on his knees. No other industrialist of the age even approached Carnegie in the volume or quality of his writings.

His public life was no less successful. Most of his vast fortune came from the sale of the Carnegie Steel works to J. P. Morgan and his allies who turned it into the United States Steel Corporation. No one else could compete with Carnegie's efficient mills. His firm, however, lacked facilities to make finished steel products. When rivals threatened to build basic steel mills in order to control their supplies of steel, Carnegie countered them, ordering his lieutenants to make plans immediately to build plants making finished products such as rods, wire, nails and tubes. This move sent his competitors into panic since they knew that Carnegie could produce at far lower costs than theirs. Eventually as the key figure in a conglomerate, J. P. Morgan offered Carnegie $400 million for his companies, an offer which Carnegie accepted. It was 1900. Carnegie, 65 years old, was the richest man in the world.

Left:
The triumphant return to Dunfermline

Below:
Two cartoonists' views of Carnegie

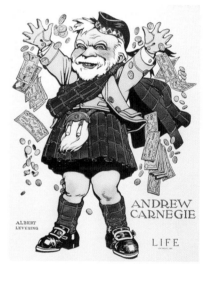

ALBERT LEVERING

ANDREW CARNEGIE

LIFE

Carnegie Quirk
He established the Simple Spelling Board in 1903, proposing such words as "wisht," "believt" and "wer" to promote worldwide communication and eventual peace.

During his long lifetime—he died in 1919 at the age of 84—he built almost 3,000 libraries at a cost of $60 million which were used by 25 million people in 1925. He gave organs to about 4,100 churches. He founded trusts for the universities of Scotland, New York City's Carnegie Hall, Carnegie Institutes in Pittsburgh and Washington and the Carnegie Endowment to which he left $125 million. He also became a leader in the movement for world peace and provided funds to build the Peace Palace at The Hague, Netherlands. By his own standards, he did not die disgraced. He had given away the world's largest fortune before he died.

What would he make of his technical schools now?

And, of course, he established the Carnegie Technical Schools which later became Carnegie Institute of Technology and later still, Carnegie Mellon University.

Skibo Castle, Carnegie's estate in Scotland

Despite the fact that Carnegie Tech was the only institution of higher learning to bear his name, he seemed somewhat indifferent to it. Four of his five visits to the campus coincided with meetings at the Carnegie Institute that he attended. When he visited Pittsburgh in 1914 to unveil a statue of Scottish poet Robert Burns, he spent the following two days with students at Tech. He responded cheerfully to notes from the student body and opened his purse frequently when Tech's first director, Arthur Arton Hamerschlag, appealed for funds for new buildings or the endowment.

Compared to other interests, such as libraries or world peace, Tech received little attention from its founder except for financial support. Even with this support, Carnegie Tech was underendowed compared to other universities, such as Stanford or the University of Chicago, also founded by rich philanthropists. On the other hand, despite the fact that Carnegie Tech failed to meet the requirements that he had set up, he insisted that the school should be included on the roll of institutions whose teachers were eligible for retirement allowances from the Carnegie Foundation for the Advancement of Teaching.

The modern reader should see Carnegie's generous financial contributions in contemporary perspective. The buying power of his gifts to the Carnegie Technical Schools and to Carnegie Tech amounted to about $400 million in today's dollars. He contributed $215 million from his personal funds in the period 1900-1913. The school used this money to erect 20 buildings and to establish Tech's original endowment fund. After 1913, an additional $180 million came to Tech and Carnegie Mellon from the Carnegie Corporation. With the exception of $8 million ($62,560,000 today) added to the endowment in 1946, most of this money supported projects proposed by faculty who wrote winning grant proposals in competition with faculty from other universities.

It is interesting to speculate about how Carnegie would judge his school if he could spend time on the campus today. He was an optimist, particularly about a project in which he had a direct interest. Given his upbeat focus, Andrew Carnegie viewing Carnegie Mellon would no doubt experience the following reactions:

- He would glory in the success story—a trade school that graduated its first three-year class in 1908 and became an internationally renowned research university in less than a century.

- He would recognize and admire the nimbleness of the institution, its ability to build programs, scrap them when the times began to change and build anew, just as he ran his steel mills.

- He would support the tradition of hard, disciplined work that has always characterized its administrators, faculty, staff, students and alumni.

- He would love the scientists and engineers who first made Carnegie Tech famous, the sorts of people he had hired to run his mills and rewarded with partnerships.

- He would feel equal affection for the fine artists, humanists and social scientists who have contributed to the intellectual and cultural life he embraced.

- He would respond with equal fervor to the managers trained in the Graduate School of Industrial Administration and the Heinz School to conduct industry and public affairs using modernized versions of his management techniques.

- He would find intriguing the University's computer scientists and the revolution in research and education they have fostered, seeing in late 20th century electronics promises of a technological revolution which may have a greater societal impact than his own late 19th century achievements.

- He would dote on the Scottish traditions which still remain: the Kiltie Band, The Pipe Band, *The Tartan* newspaper, *The Thistle* yearbook, the Skibo Coffeehouse and the football fight songs.

- He would love the students—all of them—but have a special place in his heart for the men and women from the early days who poured by the thousands into night school classes after long working days in mills and offices, and for the men and women now studying in evening programs to earn master's degrees in the Heinz School and the Graduate School of Industrial Administration.

- He would take great pride in the alumni, men and women, now 51,000 in number, who have made their mark on virtually every segment of American life.

- He would spend hours in the laboratories where he would find "handication" linked to "headication" in the sort of educational environment he advocated.

- And he would boast about the contributions Carnegie Mellon has made by transferring knowledge and skills to the wider society.

  His heart would still be in the work.

Andrew Carnegie is "Laird" of Skibo Castle.

Carnegie Quirk
He discouraged the practice of naming libraries after himself, asking instead that the entrance to to each library be inscribed with the words, "Let there be light."

2.

Arthur Arton Hamerschlag 1903–1922
He laid a firm foundation

Both Arthur Arton Hamerschlag and the Carnegie Technical Schools seem unlikely precursors of a modern internationally renowned research university. Hamerschlag, 31 years old when he became director of the Carnegie Technical Schools, never attended college. The Carnegie Technical Schools offered two- and three-year degrees mainly to the sons and daughters of Pittsburgh working people. Most of the students attended night courses in practical trades such as carpentry or sewing. Still, Hamerschlag and his colleagues laid a firm foundation on which their successors could construct a dramatically different institution.

Hamerschlag was born in New York City, November 22, 1872, the son of William and Francesca Hamerschlag. Some of his biographers, however, report that he was born in Sweetwater, Nebraska. Family tradition explains this anomaly. Thinking correctly that the authorities would not bother to check birth records from a small Midwestern town, he lied about both his age and his birthplace when he applied for a job remodeling an electric plant on a Cuban sugar plantation. He was a precocious 16-year-old at the time. He got the job and for several years did fieldwork in Cuba, Mexico and the United States.

His father, a chemist, was born in Austria in 1843 and emigrated to the United States at the outbreak of the Civil War. According to oral traditions in his family, his parents were Jews, but both Hamerschlag and his mother converted to the Episcopal Church. Little is known from written records about young Hamerschlag's childhood and education except that he attended the Hebrew Technical Institute from 1886 to 1889. He graduated from its three-year course, specializing in electricity. Beyond this schooling, the first president of what would become Carnegie Mellon University had no formal education. Several honorary doctorates entitled him to be called "Doctor" Hamerschlag to the confusion of generations of casual readers.

Above:
The Pittsburgh Mayor, welcoming troops home in 1919, awarded this service medal to President Hamerschlag.

Opposite page:
Andrew Carnegie and President Hamerschlag greet students. Mrs. Hamerschlag signaled the start of building operations by sinking a spade on April 3, 1905.

1900

• Andrew Carnegie founds a technical school; "My heart is in the work."

1903

- Pittsburgh provides a site for the school.
- Hamerschlag becomes director of Carnegie Technical Schools.

1906

- *The Tartan* and *The Thistle* begin publication.

Settling down in New York City, he began a career as an electrical and mechanical engineer. In his spare time, he did research on cathode rays and induction coils which won him a medal of excellence from the American Institute in 1898. In the meantime, St. George's Trade School hired Hamerschlag to teach mechanical drawing. Within a year, he became superintendent of the school. In 1897 he became consulting engineer for the New York Trade School where he reorganized much of the curriculum and gave courses in electricity. He also served as a consultant to four other trade schools in the New York area. This work brought him to the attention of Andrew Carnegie.

William H. Frew, chairman of the Board of Trustees of the Carnegie Institute and Andrew Carnegie's Pittsburgh lawyer, had appointed a committee on Technical Schools to plan Carnegie's new educational venture. Frew, who is commemorated in Frew Street at the southern edge of campus, invited Hamerschlag to serve on a subcommittee of three to make recommendations about the school. The 1903 preliminary plan they submitted specifically maintains that the school should not aspire to be a college or university.

The original plans for the institution described a trade school to help young working people learn skills that would lead to advancement in their fields. These plans did not envision an institution offering bachelor's degrees, and certainly not graduate work. Yet Hamerschlag himself presided over a rapidly growing and changing institution that offered both undergraduate and graduate degrees and sponsored major research projects before the end of his administration in 1922.

Hamerschlag so impressed his two colleagues on the planning committee that they recommended him to Andrew Carnegie as the school's ideal director, a title changed to president in 1919. Hamerschlag was 31 years of age when he received this offer in 1903 and embarked on his life's work. In response to criticism of technical education, he wrote a letter to Andrew Carnegie in 1907 stating the philosophy that guided him as an educator. He began the letter by defining three words: Technical, Educated, and Mechanic.

While Andrew Carnegie's philanthropy made the Carnegie Technical Schools possible, Arthur Arton Hamerschlag's vision and energy brought it to life. Before Hamerschlag was appointed, the trustees had decided that the Carnegie Technical Schools would be organized into four units, each with its own faculty and buildings, and all under a central administration. They were: the School of Science and Technology; the School of Fine and Applied Arts; the School for Apprentices and Journeymen; and Margaret Morrison Carnegie School for Women. Rather than compete with the Western University of Pennsylvania, now the University of Pittsburgh, all four focused their efforts on practical, vocational training leading to three-year diplomas or two-year certificates, not bachelor's degrees. With these vague plans, $2 million in 5 percent gold bonds (in 1901 Carnegie added another $1 million to his original grant), 32 acres of overgrown hills and valleys contributed by the city of Pittsburgh and the support of the trustees who also oversaw Carnegie Institute, Hamerschlag began work.

Technical
Educated
Mechanic

Hamerschlag, Carnegie and Henry Hornbostel, the architectural genius who designed the original campus, were master builders. Since Hornbostel maintained his offices in New York, day-to-day supervision of the building projects in Pittsburgh often fell to Hamerschlag who may have devoted half his time to campus construction. In this endeavor Hamerschlag focused on coordinating the buildings with the academic program and persuading Carnegie to continue to provide funds for 20 buildings and for the endowment that kept the growing educational programs afloat.

Hamerschlag oversaw the hiring of three faculties. The first, 19 men strong, became the nucleus of the Carnegie Technical Schools. In addition to engineers, scientists and architects, it soon included carpenters, bricklayers, secretaries and home economists. Some lacked college credentials. Hamerschlag's second faculty consisted of men and women with advanced degrees who taught the daytime classes, particularly after 1912 when the newly-named Carnegie Institute of Technology began to offer four-year programs leading to bachelor's degrees. The third faculty consisted of adjuncts who instructed in the night classes that enrolled more than half of the students throughout the Hamerschlag regime.

A flexible and nimble innovator, Hamerschlag developed a technical and trade school catering primarily to local men and women who, typically, had not finished high school. His background in New York provided abundant experience for this task. By 1910, it had become clear that the Carnegie Technical Schools had to change if they were to succeed. Local unions required graduates of the apprenticeship programs to serve four-year apprenticeships even after they had won two-year certificates. Subsequently, the full-time enrollment of apprentices fell off dramatically, forcing Hamerschlag to rethink the role of the new institution he headed. In addition, students, attracted from far and wide by Carnegie's name, found that their three-year diplomas failed to qualify them for the jobs they sought. Finally, many prospective faculty refused to join an institution that offered only three-year diplomas. So Hamerschlag led the way in developing four- and five-year programs leading to bachelor's and master's degrees. In 1912, the Carnegie Technical Schools became the Carnegie Institute of Technology in recognition of this dramatic change. The two-year trade courses in Margaret Morrison declined rapidly after Carnegie Tech began to focus on college-level programs. Many of the trade courses in the School for Apprentices and Journeymen, however, continued to function for decades.

Under Hamerschlag, Carnegie Tech developed rapidly in numerous directions without a coherent overall plan. Tech soon competed with local colleges, a development that the original plans forbade. When opportunities such as the establishment of a School for Life Insurance Salesmanship developed, Hamerschlag jumped at the chance, despite the anomalous presence of such an institution in a school of technology. Turning the campus over to the government to train troops during World War I completely disrupted the ongoing academic program. These projects required money, money that could well have been used for projects that focused on Tech's strengths. Hamerschlag's administrative style stands in sharp contrast to the disciplined planning that characterized the careers of most of his successors, particularly Robert E. Doherty.

Arthur and Elizabeth Hamerschlag

Technical, Educated and Mechanic

Technical, meaning applied principles of science; Educated, the ability to use the knowledge acquired; and Mechanic, skill of an individual in industrial processes. Therefore, technically educated mechanics can be produced either in schools or in the industries because technical training may be self-acquired or obtained through instruction. When this training is shop or self-acquired, it is a slow crude process and is at best incomplete in fundamental essentials. . . . . This training is called experience which means familiarity with, rather than exact understanding of underlying causes.
—Hamerschlag to Carnegie, December 18, 1907

1908

- The Charter Class of 1905 graduates 58 students.

1912

- Carnegie Technical Schools become Carnegie Institute of Technology with the power to grant degrees.

Students attending a lecture in the College of Industries (now Porter 100) in 1906

The Hamerschlag administration saw dramatic changes in the student body. The first class in the School of Science and Technology that met in October 1905 in Industries Hall 104 (now Porter Hall 100) consisted of 120 men, all but a handful from the Pittsburgh area. The tuition in the day school was $20 a year (about $360 in today's dollars) for Pittsburgh residents and $30 for others; six hours study a week in evening school cost $5 for Pittsburghers and $7 for others. In 1906, 607 evening students enrolled. By 1910 total enrollment had increased to 2,224, and by the end of Hamerschlag's administration in 1922, to about 5,000.

To Hamerschlag and his staff, Tech's dramatic growth presented a series of challenges such as entrance requirements, housing, curricula, record keeping, recreation and student affairs. Some of these challenges remained for his successor to meet.

Hamerschlag's administration also saw the beginnings of a distinguished research tradition at Carnegie Tech, something that the original plans for the school had not envisioned. In 1916, Carnegie Institute of Technology founded the Division of Applied Psychology which fostered six bureaus focused on human engineering. They developed psychological tests to perfect rating scales for placing the right person in the right job. Soon, the school affiliated with 30 firms, each contributing $1,000 annually. Tech's applied psychological research made a substantial contribution to national defense during World War I by developing the tests and rating scales used to place more than two million enlisted men and 150,000 officers into the ranks of the armed forces.

Tech develops ties to the community

Hamerschlag's administration began to develop close ties to the Pittsburgh community, initiating a tradition that continues to this day. Even before the Carnegie Technical Schools opened, faculty and guest speakers gave lectures at eight centers in the city to civic groups numbering 19,000. Like the presidents who followed him, Hamerschlag participated as a leader in a host of civic and governmental bodies. During the first World War, he became a dollar-a-year man to assist General Goethals in the

Quartermaster General's Department. The major contribution to the community, however, lay in the students from the evening school who studied at Carnegie Tech. Workers from more than 1,000 firms attended evening school classes in a typical year, a major contribution to the economy of the Pittsburgh area.

Hamerschlag made concerted efforts to cooperate with Pittsburgh industry. Carnegie had founded the Carnegie Technical Schools to educate and train Pittsburgh's workers, not to offer four-year college degrees. This focus on the Pittsburgh area continued after a new charter in 1912 changed the name to the Carnegie Institute of Technology. Its charter specified that the new corporation was "formed to administer the trust created by Andrew Carnegie for the benefit of the people of Pittsburgh, Pennsylvania." Hamerschlag asked a committee to find out what business executives needed in their work force. The committee got nowhere because executives refused to take the time to talk to committee members. A study in 1919 revealed that only 70 percent of the graduates of the School of Applied Industries between 1908 and 1919 found jobs in the Pittsburgh area. The figures for the School of Applied Science—41 percent—and the School of Applied Arts—28 percent—were even lower. These findings disturbed both Hamerschlag and trustees of the Carnegie Institute. Why was Carnegie Tech, an institution that sent almost half of its graduates to jobs out of the city, controlled by a board of trustees composed entirely of Pittsburghers, particularly when leading local industrialists refused to talk about this situation?

During World War I, the Tech campus became a military encampment. Thirteen days before the United States declared war on Germany, the trustees placed the services and equipment of Tech at the disposal of the government. Within four days, a thousand Tech students were taking part in voluntary daily drills on campus.

Panoramic view of the Carnegie Technical Schools campus, circa 1915

Hamerschlag Lectures Men on the Evils of Flirting

Flirting at Carnegie Tech School is causing worry among the faculty and yesterday Director Hamerschlag gave a lecture to male students on the evils of goo-goo eyes and other forms of flirtation. While it had some effect, it was not heeded by all. The buildings in which the cooking school and domestic sciences branches are taught is within convenient flirting distance of the industrial rooms, and as a result of gestures several students have been strolling through the park with companions of the opposite sex.
—The Carnegie Tartan Anniversary Issue, November 25, 1930

1914

- The first master's degree is conferred.
- The *Carnegie Alumnus* is published.

Above:
Carnegie Tech during World War I

Below:
1918 World War I course buttons given to faculty for their work in war training

1918

- Tech resembles a military encampment.
- The Langley Laboratory, later to become Skibo, opens.

1921

- The Carnegie Corporation increases Tech's endowment and promises $8 million in 1946.

In November 1917 the first contingent of draftees arrived for training. Altogether 8,000 soldiers studied and lived on campus and in nearby buildings in the city. They specialized in 17 army classifications, including auto mechanics, band musicians, electricians, pattern makers, propeller makers and truck drivers. To meet these new demands, Tech erected the Langley Aeronautical Laboratory, a "temporary" building that lasted until the 1960s as Skibo, the student center. Additional men's dormitories sprang up along Woodlawn Avenue (later Margaret Morrison Street). Across the campus, soldiers dug mock trenches, and engineers made a level drill field and parade ground out of the Cut, the deep valley that once divided the present campus.

In its early years, Carnegie Tech faced serious financial problems. Andrew Carnegie originally wished to establish a tuition-free school, but agreed to permit low fees at first. The share of instructional and operating costs from tuition had been only 7 percent in 1906. To help meet expenses, the trustees raised tuition time after time: to $50 in 1908, $75 in 1918, $135 in 1920 and $200 in 1922. By 1927 during President Thomas S. Baker's administration, tuition had reached $300, yielding about the same amount as income from endowment. Endowment income had decreased slowly because the yield from fixed income investments had fallen as interest rates declined. According to officials at the Carnegie Corporation, Hamerschlag always spent money freely, arguing that nothing was too good for Carnegie Tech.

The death of Andrew Carnegie in 1919 brought about an evaluation of Carnegie Tech and the role that its president should play. Hamerschlag and Carnegie had a warm personal relationship that both treasured. Personal appeals from Hamerschlag to Carnegie for funds usually met a welcome response. The last direct gift from Carnegie, $1.5 million for buildings and $2.15 million for the endowment, came in 1913. After that, the Carnegie Corporation, which Carnegie had endowed with $125 million, took over, giving small annual appropriations to cover deficits.

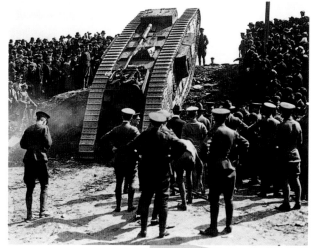

Carnegie Tech exceeds early expectations

      To decide what to do in response to repeated requests for money, the Carnegie Corporation, in January 1921, appointed a Survey Commission composed of distinguished educators. This Commission reported in June. In addition to high praise for Tech and a recital of its many virtues, the commissioners advanced 20 suggestions for change and improvement. The Corporation then advanced $400,000 to build a gymnasium and $7,640,000 as an addition to the endowment. It further approved a grant of $8 million to be paid in 1946 on the condition that Tech raise $4 million in the meantime. In other words, Carnegie Tech could no longer rely on generous gifts from its founder's fortune.

      This situation distressed Hamerschlag. The Commission made a number of recommendations, seven of them involving Tech's relationships—or in some instances lack of relationships—to the University of Pittsburgh. Some of them seemed to undermine much of what Hamerschlag had accomplished, and others implied substantial changes in administrative practices. A hectic schedule and occasional bitter battles among faculty over policies had brought Hamerschlag to the verge of a nervous breakdown, but his ensuing resignation had deeper causes. The financial situation troubled him. Since he was not a member of the Board of Trustees of the Carnegie Institute, he felt excluded from participation in discussions of the needs of the schools. He also saw control of policy making slipping from his hands and from the hands of Pittsburghers to a committee of outsiders appointed by the Carnegie Corporation in New York. After taking a vacation from January to June 1922, he returned to announce his resignation.

      In his retirement, he again took up his practice as an engineer and consultant. He died in New York City in 1927 leaving behind him as his heritage in Pittsburgh an educational institution which grew under his leadership in less than two decades from a small vocational school to a thriving institute of technology. What a distinguished career, particularly for a man with a three-year degree from a trade school!

The 1905 Charter Class of the Carnegie Institute of Technology began with 120 men, graduating 58, and the 1908 Charter Class of the Women's College began with 70 women, graduating 43.

3.

Snapshot 1905–1908
Bringing together the pieces of plaid

The faculty, students and relatives of the graduating class of the Carnegie Technical Schools joined in celebration in the Music Hall of the Carnegie Institute in June 1908. They heard an address by Robert S. Woodward, president of the Carnegie Institution in Washington. Then the surviving 58 of the original 120 members of the Charter Class of 1905 marched across the stage to receive their diplomas from the hands of the school's smiling director, Arthur Arton Hamerschlag. They had enrolled in the School of Science and Technology or the School of Fine and Applied Arts in 1905. Their three-year diplomas were in six fields: architectural practice (four), chemical engineering practice (two), metallurgical engineering practice (eight), civil engineering practice (seven), electrical engineering practice (23) and mechanical engineering practice (14). Selections by the Glee Club preceded and followed the diploma ceremony. The happy graduates, all white men, sent their patron Andrew Carnegie a telegram of thanks and congratulation. He responded: "Great news. Delighted. Thanks to the class. Carnegie."

What was campus life like in that first graduation year—1907-08—for administrators, faculty and students? And how was the campus itself?

FROM THE FOUNDER

March 30, 1906

Dear Editor

. . . . No scholars ever made a more promising start. None was ever besieged, I think, by so many more students than could be taken. Mr. Hamerschlag has proved the right man in the right place, and his earnest assistants no less so. As for the eight hundred students— their behavior, assiduity and anxiety to learn, I am informed, was never surpassed. We have made a great start! Where it is all to end, we cannot predict; but I for one believe that Pittsburgh is to rank in the world as one of the chief centers of technical education. The Founder is very proud of his latest gift to the city and the people to whom he still remains a grateful debtor.

ANDREW CARNEGIE
The Thistle, 1906

Hamerschlag maintained the Carnegie connection

Andrew Carnegie established Pittsburgh's Carnegie Library in 1890, the accompanying museum, music hall and art gallery that made up the Carnegie Institute in 1895, and the Carnegie Technical Schools in 1900. He gave all three units to serve the people of Pittsburgh. Logically he placed them under the same Board of Trustees. This arrangement haunted Carnegie Tech for more than a half century. In 1908 the board consisted of 36 members, all worthy men of affairs from Pittsburgh and the surrounding area. Nine of them formed a subcommittee with special responsibility for the schools.

A ravine cut through the center of the original campus in 1908. The land was filled but the name "the Cut" continues to this day. The two original buildings and campus property are shown below.

What an inefficient way to oversee an educational institution, Hamerschlag must have thought. He did not belong to the Board of Trustees or the subcommittee for the schools. He could only make recommendations to a committee that reported to a board whose members discussed the schools at secondhand and then made decisions. Given this situation, Hamerschlag soon learned that personal access to Carnegie provided a shortcut to his patron's ample pocketbook. Back and forth to New York City he went by train

to lay the case for additional support to his benefactor. Usually he returned with good news to the delight of his executive staff.

Imagine an executive staff for an educational institution consisting of a registrar, secretary, cashier, accountant, engineer, two engineering assistants, and officers in charge of stenographic forces and of records. No vice presidents. No deans. No student life officials. No counselors. Of course, many colleges and universities lacked student life officials, deans and counselors in 1908. The staff reflected Hamerschlag's priorities: getting the buildings up and classes underway. Moreover, only four of the nine officials held bachelor's degrees. The other five had no college degrees and, as seen, Hamerschlag himself never attended college. Academic prominence carried little weight in choosing administrators at the Carnegie Technical Schools, nor had it counted for much in the trade schools where Hamerschlag cut his administrative eye teeth.

No place to take a Sunday stroll

No one in his right mind would have taken a stroll for pleasure around the campus of the Carnegie Technical Schools in 1908. It was a mess. It consisted of a plot of 32 acres next to Schenley Park purchased by the City of Pittsburgh from its political boss, Christopher Magee, for $350,000. The plot began in the middle of Boundary Street across the railroad tracks in the center of Junction Hollow, reached the present campus near the site of Scaife Hall, extended up Frew Street past the present library, up present Margaret Morrison Street to about where Donner Hall is, and then back across the present campus beyond the present Forbes Avenue end of the Fine Arts Building, all the way back to Boundary Street. The land along Frew Street, the site Hornbostel chose for his first building, Industries Hall (now Porter), sloped gently.

The hillside on the original campus

During 1908 the campus resembled one vast construction site. Work on the exterior of Industries Hall was completed in 1906, but the reverberations from saws and hammers inside the building plagued faculty and students alike for several years. The Margaret Morrison building, begun in 1907, was even less complete, although students attended classes there. An article in *The Carnegie Tartan*, February 27, 1907, described with delight the equipment soon to be installed in the Margaret Morrison building:

On the fourth floor in the west wing is the large lunch room, also the model apartment containing living room, dining room, two bedrooms, bathroom, butler's pantry and kitchen where the economy, beautifying and care of the home will be taught. In the east wing is the gymnasium with large dressing room, lockers and bathroom with six showers and two tubs.

Construction began on Engineering Hall (now Doherty) in 1908. Muddy paths connected one building to another. Landscaping was virtually nonexistent. The buildings and grounds of the Carnegie Technical Schools gave little evidence that they would eventually grow into one of the nation's most distinctive urban campuses. Not a happy choice for a leisurely Sunday stroll with one's sweetheart.

The rest of the land between the campus and Forbes Street, still in private hands, was all hills and valleys; about 140 feet separated its high and low points. Until 1917, a ravine or "cut" extending from the present site of the tennis courts to the deep ravine on the Forbes Street side of Wean Hall marked the edge of campus. Hornbostel had planned to build a bridge across the valley, but instead the ravine was filled in by 1917 after Tech acquired the land that separated the campus from Forbes Street. About one million cubic feet of earth from a nearby hill filled the Cut. In 1908 making one's way from Forbes Street to the existing campus across what is now a level lawn (the Cut) would have meant a scramble down one side of a steep, brush-covered slope and another scramble up the other side. No wonder that students got off their streetcars before the Carnegie Library and then walked across the bridge spanning Junction Hollow to arrive at Industries Hall via Frew Street.

Imagine This. . .

Eighty-five years ago, in the eighteen fifties, there was an unpromising range of land, three miles from the confluence of the Allegheny and Monongahela Rivers, that was given over to the raising of garden truck for the people of Pittsburgh. It was then known as the Chadwick Farm. It was treeless; it was none too fertile ground that ran mainly to cabbages; and it was all either sharp hillside or deep ravine, with scarcely a level square rod of ground in the whole area of thirty-two acres. At one end of the gulch was a quarry of Morgantown sandstone, and at the other end a small pond, principally mud, while along the bottom a sorry-looking creek managed to worm its way westward to the Monongahela. By no flight of fancy could one have then stood at this location and imagined its ever becoming an attractive college campus. It did, nevertheless.
—Dean Arthur Wilson Tarbell in *The Story of Carnegie Tech 1900-1935*

Hornbostel of the "wind-blown scarf" school shapes campus

More than anyone else, Henry Hornbostel turned this unpromising beginning into a distinguished campus. In 1903, the trustees of the Carnegie Institute announced a competition for an architect to design the Carnegie Technical Schools. The New York firm of Palmer and Hornbostel won the competition, received a $1,000 prize and began work. The first building, a portion of Industries Hall, opened for limited use by late 1905, when the entire student body, 120 in all, met together on October 16 in Industries Hall 104, now Porter 100.

Henry Hornbostel had worked for a number of architectural firms in New York City before and after completing his training at Columbia University in 1891. Between 1893 and 1897, he studied at the École des Beaux Arts in Paris, the Mecca of 19th century architects. The beaux arts style imposed order and symmetry around open spaces and vistas on a group of buildings at the same time that it employed a series of levels and a variety of adornments drawn from the classical and romantic periods to serve as decorative elements. Hornbostel became an acknowledged master of the beaux arts style.

He was also a colorful character, a legend among architects and students. Architectural historian David Henderson called him an architect ". . .in the romantic tradition of the wind-blown scarf." He had an elegant Vandyke beard and always wore a bright, plaid bow tie. He often appeared on campus with a monkey perched on his shoulder. He christened the drafting room used by night students the "atelier (studio) Hornbostel"; irreverent students called it his "shanty." At his suggestion, architectural students began to carry canes until peers from other departments claimed that the canes were evidence of what they had always suspected—that architects needed visible means of support. In 1911 he proposed that Carnegie Tech hold an annual masquerade ball. The result was the Beaux Arts Ball that promoted unlimited revelry for more than seven decades until it ran afoul of a Student Senate investigation, only to be revived under more stringent rules in 1990.

Hornbostel's winning design featured a large mall on the same location as the one still connecting the Fine Arts building to Hamerschlag Hall (then Machinery Hall). On either side of this mall Hornbostel planned two long buildings with a number of wings to admit light from windows on three sides, an important matter considering

Pittsburgh's dark winters. The upper end of the mall ended in a large turreted building on the location of the present Fine Arts Building. The terrace in front of that building extended northward onto what is now the Cut and ended in a pavilion which, in turn, led into a small quadrangle surrounded by more winged buildings. Plans for the lower end of the mall included a small, cruciform structure with a small power plant and smokestack behind it on the crest of Junction Hollow.

Never attracted to liberal arts colleges, Andrew Carnegie wanted to endow an institution to educate men and women for careers in Pittsburgh's industries. To associate technology with the humanities and fine arts, however, he wanted to link the Carnegie Technical Schools with the library, museum and music hall he had founded. They had been under construction since 1890 across Junction Hollow. Hornbostel's long mall ended at the other side of Junction Hollow from the Carnegie Institute and pointed directly to it, particularly after 1912 when the school mounted the bow of the USS Pennsylvania, a loan from the government, on a concrete pedestal on the Junction Hollow end of Machinery Hall. Symbolically, it suggested that students should explore the library, music hall and galleries across the hollow. Lacking provisions for a library, Tech scattered its meagre collection of books and periodicals in a number of buildings, including a World War I canteen called The Hut, until 1961 when Hunt Library was built.

Opposite page:
Hornbostel's original campus plan

Below:
Hornbostel designed but never erected this building reaching down into Junction Hollow on the present site of Roberts Hall (behind Hamerschlag Hall).

The 1907 faculty of the School of Applied Science

Far from a diverse faculty

The best educated members of the faculty taught in the School of Applied Science. Forty-two out of its 50 faculty members had at least one college degree, seven of them Ph.D.s. The 43 men and women without college degrees clustered in the School for Apprentices and Journeymen (20 of 28) and Margaret Morrison (11 of 16). Six members of the faculty were listed as professors, one as an associate professor, six as assistant professors and the remainder as instructors, lecturers, mechanicians, acting instructors, substitute instructors and assistants. Two members of the administration were women. One woman taught chemistry in the School of Applied Science. The faculty of Margaret Morrison consisted of nine women and seven men. The entire faculty included no African-Americans, Hispanics or Asians and, if names accurately reveal ancestry, no descendants of southern or eastern Europeans. At least one staff member, Hunter Johnson, was African-American. His photo appeared at the end of an article about the 1911 football team in the 1912 *Thistle*. A diverse faculty and staff were decades away.

Imagine "A Day in the Life of" the 1908 faculty. It would often include a day and a night. Most daytime faculty conducted classes 20 hours a week during the daylight hours. Many of them also taught in the night school for extra hourly pay. The periods between classes gave no respite. Since students had no other meeting places, they spent much of their time between classes in classrooms or labs where they could at least keep warm and read under satisfactory lights. Many faculty offices were in their shops. They had no research assistants or teaching assistants to help them. They ate their lunches and sometimes their dinners in a roughly furnished room on the main floor of Industries Hall. Going home for lunch or dinner before the days of automobiles involved streetcars or long walks in Pittsburgh's gloomy weather made darker by clouds of smoke from Pittsburgh's mills, now no longer owned by Andrew Carnegie.

"A day in the life of" many of the night school teachers may have been even more hectic. Adjunct faculty—carpenters, bricklayers, sign painters, secretaries and seamstresses, for example—worked from eight to ten hours at their jobs. Then they walked or hopped streetcars for the trip to the campus and another session at their trade, this time in a role as an instructor, a role for which many of them were unprepared. Only a few of their students had more than an elementary school education, so instruction was largely hands-on. Many faculty members were finding their way in academia for the first time. Even grading presented a problem:

I wonder if you remember how simple our first plan was: just four grades— 1, 2, 3, and 4; though we soon found it desirable to grade some men "in between" by adding a plus sign or a minus."
—George H. Fellows, "Memories of Carnegie," *The Carnegie Alumnus,* May 1924

The Tartan

VOL. 1, No. 32   PITTSBURG, PA., WEDNESDAY, JUNE 19, 1907   PRICE FIVE CENTS

TERRIBLE OUTRAGE!
STARTLING DISCLOSURES MADE PUBLIC FOR THE FIRST TIME REGARDING THE FACULTY BASE BALL TEAM

[SPECIAL TO THE TARTAN]

PITTSBURG, PA., JUNE 18—On the eve of the greatest athletic contest ever held by the Carnegie Technical Schools comes the announcement that the Faculty is confident of winning the championship over the Junior class. This rumor seems to be well founded for it has been discovered that the man who is to hold down the slab was once a premier artist in this line somewhere up the state; the left fielder has been known to knock the ball over Flagstaff hill during a practice game and first baseman Dosey can step to the pitcher's box in three steps. Dr. Sill, having lost his beard since the last game, has no difficulty in following the progress of the speediest ball. Prof. Keller has spent many sleepless nights figuring out the exact angle necessary for a safe hit. Mr. Reed is going to give the fellows one more chance. Mr. Lightcap is a new player but it is rumored that State College made a great effort to retain him. Every one ought to attend and observe for himself these wonderful doings.

To go into details would be wasting space. Suffice it to say that the Juniors are about as blue as the proverbial indigo over their impending defeat. The result of the last Faculty game does not seem to have any brightening effect.

JUNE 18 (6:45 P. M.)—The result of the findings of the board of advisors has been given out. The line up is as follows:

Pitcher..............Mr. Leete
Catcher...............Dr. Sill
1st Base.............Mr. Dosey
2nd Base.........Prof. Crabtree
3rd Base...........Prof. Keller
Shortstop.............Mr. Reed
Left Field............Mr. Pfouts
Middle Field.......Mr. Lightcap
Right Field...........Mr. Field
Official Kicker....Mr. McIntosh
Substitutes—Dr. Hokansen; Mr. Mamatey, Dr. Knox.
Chief of Publicity..Mr. Hamilt[

The WUP Football Game

George Fellows, a member of the first Carnegie Technical Schools faculty, wrote some years later about a football game between the school and WUP (Western University of Pennsylvania, later Pitt), as it was derisively called on the Tech side of the Hollow:

The game was played over in Allegheny at the old Exhibition Grounds, and there must have been a crowd of several hundred spectators. Our Faculty went in a body, the whole twenty-four of them. . . (Fellows did not report the score.)
—George H. Fellows, "Memories of Carnegie," *The Carnegie Alumnus,* November 1923

Faculty/student relationships were friendly and supportive:

The intimate relationship that exists between the Faculty and student body of the Carnegie Technical Schools has few if any counterparts. The democratic, ever ready to help spirit of the professors and instructors is appreciated by all; more fully perhaps by those who have been subjected to the old-style straight-laced system under which the professor is looked upon as a Deity by the students. . . . There are a few men in school, however, who require that old-style method previously spoken of as a preliminary training. . . . They would then doubtless learn the importance of showing the Faculty members the proper amount of respect. It would be possible to realize then that even though a professor or instructor has given them individual instruction and incidentally told a good story that there would be no provocation to address the teacher with "Say Cap't" or call him simply by his last name.
—*The Tartan,* February 27, 1907

Top:
Pennant from the early days of the Carnegie Technical Schools, circa 1908

Bottom:
Watch fob

1907-08 Student Enrollment

School	Day	Night	Total
Applied Science	305	164	469
Apprentices & Journeymen	160	462	622
Applied Design	34	79	113
Margaret Morrison	221	174	395
Special Classes, Day & Evening			236
Total	**720**	**879**	**1,835**

Above:
Two of the first buildings: Industries Hall and Administration Hall

The handful of architecture students soon bonded with Henry Hornbostel:

We became so prosperous that by Christmas we were given the "Shanty" as our permanent quarters. This move was so agreeable to us that we celebrated the event by holding a 'shindig' which we very frequently look back upon with the most pleasant recollections. Hardly an evening passed that we did not have music by some members who had lung power to spare or an impromptu vaudeville show. On Tuesday evenings Mr. Hornbostel would add variety to our entertainment by giving us illustrated talks and by telling us funny stories which would make our lower jaws drop very listlessly and cause our eyes to pop out of our heads.
—The Thistle, 1908

Nothing in the records indicates that these faculty conducted research or creative activities. A branch of a United States Government Laboratory was scheduled to begin work when Machinery Hall was finished in 1909, still a year away. The United Paint Manufacturers of America had erected a fence on campus to test its paints, but company scientists carried on this work. In addition, engineers and scientists from steel companies carried on investigations in the school's laboratories, but faculty were not involved. Henry Hornbostel was an exception. A professor of architectural practice in the School of Applied Design, he planned and supervised the construction of all major buildings on the school's burgeoning campus.

Students came from grammar schools and prep schools

How did students in the Charter Class of 1908 endure the Carnegie Technical Schools? Many of the faculty were new to teaching. There were no student life personnel, such as deans of men or deans of women. The curriculum was in flux. The campus had only two buildings, Industries Hall (now Porter) and Margaret Morrison, and neither was finished nor fully equipped. The school boasted no on-campus dormitories, no satisfactory dining halls, no student union, no meeting rooms, no men's gymnasium and only a rough, temporary, gravel-littered athletic field. Many classes during the first couple of years had no textbooks, and students were expected to "absorb" knowledge from lectures. Today's students would throw up their hands and leave. Or sue for return of tuition.

A flurry of publicity surrounding the new institution and its low tuition rates attracted these students. The full-time day students in most of the courses sought three-year diplomas. It took five years to earn a similar diploma in the evening school. Most night students and a minority of those in the day school enrolled for certificates requiring two years of study. Many of these latter students took only a class or two to learn new techniques in their trades. The drop-out rate, particularly in night classes in the School of Applied Science, was alarmingly high by modern standards.

In 1907-08, the Carnegie Technical Schools served a local clientele. Ninety percent of the student body came from Pennsylvania and another 5 percent from three nearby states. Nine of the 20 foreign students were Canadian citizens; the remainder came from six countries. A student's chances of making friends from anywhere except Pennsylvania and the surrounding states were very slim.

Distinctly different students with widely varying backgrounds and aspirations filled the ranks of the three-year diploma and two-year certificate programs. The three-year diploma students attended the Schools of Applied Science, Applied Design and Margaret Morrison. The two-year certificate students enrolled in the School for Apprentices and Journeymen and Margaret Morrison mainly, but not exclusively, in the evening. On the whole, the diploma students came from middle-class families and had graduated from high school, some of them from private schools such as Kiski and Worcester Academies. Most of their families supported them so that they could attend school full time without working. They entered school in their late teens like typical college students, and they wanted a typical college experience. The men among them aspired to careers in engineering or architecture; the women hoped to become housewives but also to prepare themselves for careers.

Two-year certificate students, on the other hand, came mainly from working class families and, indeed, in most cases already had jobs and families of their own. Very few among them had graduated from high school; most, in fact had only a grammar school education and had entered the work force at an early age. The journeymen among them sought to prepare themselves for supervisory positions in their trades, jobs such as foremen. The apprentices were beginners aspiring to become journeymen. Most Margaret Morrison students in certificate programs already worked and wanted new skills to advance—to become executive secretaries or dietitians, for example. After long days on the job and a full diet of night courses, they had little time or energy to devote to the type of shenanigans that occupied the attention of many day students.

Above:
Margaret Morrison Hall

Below:
1906-07 Carnegie Technical Schools course catalogue

School of Applied Science

Entrance Requirements

Applicants for admission must be at least sixteen years of age and have a natural aptitude for a technical and scientific career. A satisfactory examination must be passed in the first three subjects mentioned below and in one of the subjects included under the heading "Optional."

1 MATHEMATICS

Arithmetic; Algebra, through Quadratics; Plane Geometry, five books

2 ENGLISH

Spelling; Grammar; Composition. Ability to express thought in clear, concise and accurate English

3 SCIENCE

Elementary Physics, dealing with simple laws and phenomena of nature

4 OPTIONAL

   a General Chemistry
   b Mechanical Drawing
   c Shop Practice

Owing to the limited number of students that can be accommodated in the Night School of Applied Science for the year of 1906-1907, it is desirable that all applicants take the entrance examinations in October.

Tuition Fee

For residents of the City of Pittsburgh . . . $5.00 per year
For all others . . . . 7.00 "

The entire tuition fee for the year must be paid in advance. A breakage fee of $3.00 must be deposited by every student at the beginning of each school year. The unused portion will be returned at the end of the year.

Every student should provide himself with a set of drawing instruments. These instruments, as well as all necessary text books and other supplies, can be obtained from the Schools at cost.

Calendar

Examinations for entrance to the Night School of Applied Science will be held at the School building, October 1 and 2, 1906. Classes will begin October 15, 1906. Sessions will be held on Monday, Wednesday, and Friday evenings from 7:30 to 9:30. There will be no sessions of the School on legal holidays. There will be two weeks' vacation at Christmas and a week's recess at E... The school year will end May 17, 1907

The covers of the first three *Thistles,* the yearbook of the Carnegie Technical Schools

Admission standards varied among the first Carnegie schools

Admission standards varied from one school to another. The School of Applied Science and the School of Applied Design demanded the most of applicants. They had to pass examinations in algebra through quadratics, plane geometry, English, and either physics or chemistry, and receive an exemplary rating on a personal interview. From the beginning, the School of Applied Science selected the best students from numerous applicants. No local college offered concentrations in technical subjects like those at the Carnegie Technical Schools. Some 1,723 students applied for membership in the Charter Class. The faculty interviewed 600 and enrolled 120. Admission may have been less formal than the school's catalogue specified:

It is quite true that there were certain "examinations" and nominally "entrance requirements." But you were admitted. . . virtually on a "high sign" from the Director . . . . So at the first gathering in Room 104, you met Director Hamerschlag; he shook you by the hand, looked at you, smiled at you, asked you some question, or said something to you. . .and then admitted you. Perhaps you did not stay very long, but you were a member of the charter class during those first few months at least, and that is something you will never forget.

—George H. Fellows, "Memories of Carnegie," *The Carnegie Alumnus,* February 1924

Diploma students in Margaret Morrison were also mainly high school graduates. The few who were not demonstrated their competence on examinations in English, mathematics and "general information."

Faculty referred students who failed to meet the standards for the three-year diploma programs to the night preparatory courses, the School for Apprentices and Journeymen or the Margaret Morrison certificate courses. Journeymen applicants in both the day and night schools had to be at least 20 years old, had served an apprenticeship in a trade and had some experience as a journeyman. They took courses in properties of materials, mathematics, English, drawing, principles of mechanics, and shop practice in order to prepare themselves for supervisory positions.

Admission standards for apprentices were far less demanding: 16 years of age, at least a grammar school education, letters of recommendation from employers or teachers and an interview. The faculty designed practical courses for beginners in the trades. They spent two thirds of instructional time in shops and the remaining third divided among lectures, mechanical drawing and shop practice. Certificate candidates in Margaret Morrison also spent most of their time in shops and laboratories where they practiced cooking, sewing or secretarial skills. Candidates for certificates as journeymen, apprentices, secretaries or home economists clearly had lower aspirations than diploma candidates.

Of the 1,924 students, 1,604 were men and 320, all in Margaret Morrison, were women, a five to one ratio. If names are an accurate indicator, students in the diploma programs were almost exclusively of northern and western European extraction: English, Scots, Irish, Welsh and Germans. Perhaps 10 percent of the certificate students were descendants of southern and eastern Europeans. Stories in *The Pittsburgh Press* named three "Negro" students who had attended Margaret Morrison and a man who studied sanitary equipment and construction; no Asian names appear on the rolls. Names also indicate a mix of Protestant, Catholics and a few Jewish students. The great mass of men from southern and eastern Europe who labored in Carnegie's

mills are conspicuously absent in 1907-08 from the schools Carnegie's fortune created. As in the faculty, diversity in the student body lay decades ahead.

Science and Design colleges demanded the most of students

Like admission standards, courses of study were most demanding in the School of Applied Science and in the School of Applied Design. All students in Applied Science took the same first-year curriculum: English, economics, mathematics, physics, chemistry, drawing, and shop practice. Students who completed this year enrolled in one of six majors corresponding to modern fields of engineering: chemical practice, metallurgical practice, civil practice, electrical practice, mechanical practice or mining practice. There were no science options. The School of Applied Design accepted only architectural students in 1907-08 and offered three-year courses of study. Day and night students took the same courses and attained the same degree of proficiency, although night students required at least five years to earn a diploma. The 13 required courses in the School of Applied Design included architectural, design and drawing courses, mathematics, science, engineering, English and economics.

Margaret Morrison had a similar set of requirements but far different goals, as the 1908 Course Catalogue made clear:

The courses of instruction offered in this school are planned to develop womanly attributes and give a foundation on which to build a career in distinctly feminine fields. Its emphasis is primarily laid upon the home, which is esteemed the important and logical sphere for educated women.

This conception of women's role appeared in a different form carved onto the inside of the portico before the Margaret Morrison Carnegie Building, where it remains to this day.

A Balanced Sentence

Jokes From Early Thistles

In Bookkeeping Class:
Mr. Wood: Miss A., your cash is out of balance by thirteen cents.
Miss A.: Oh, I don't mind a little thing like that.

❦

Plebe #1 to Plebe #2, who was writing at a terrific rate: I say, what are you in such a hurry for?
Plebe #2: I want to get this proof written before my fountain pen runs dry.

❦

Miss Boal: Do you like codfish balls, Miss Dymsai?
Miss Dymsai: I can't say, I never attended any.

Margaret Morrison Carnegie School

Bookkeeping
& Office Work
Cooking
Millinery
Stenography
Sewing

Maggie Murphs to Organize Basketball

It is understood that within a very short time the girls of the Margaret Morrison Carnegie School for Women intend organizing a basketball team. As they put it, they intend to make it superior to any other girls team in the country. They say this may sound like boasting, yet considering that many of the girls have played before, they have no hesitation in saying that they will fulfill their purpose. As one girl puts it:

We do not intend to maltreat or kill any person in our scrimmages (at least not willfully), but we do intend to put into the game all of the enthusiasm and vim necessary to carry off honors.

The Tartan, October 31, 1906

This inscription has an intriguing history. Hornbostel had asked the Building Committee to provide a suitable inscription for the portico. The first two —"The Margaret Morrison Carnegie School for Women" and "To train Women for the Home • The Margaret Morrison School for Women was founded by Andrew Carnegie in Memory of his Mother"—failed to meet with approval. The final version, now in the Carnegie Mellon archives, is written on stationery of the Duquesne Club, the exclusive refuge of Pittsburgh's business elite. Perhaps the all-male committee members at the time met over lunch while they wrote their version of an appropriate role for educated women. An architectural historian saw a somewhat different meaning in the portico:

I would be remiss if I did not point out that the symbolic center of the women's side of the campus is this oval contained within the arms of a pavilion, while the male campus has as its organizational center visual climax the ornate smokestack [on Machinery Hall.]
—Rives Trau Taylor, *The American College and Its Architecture: An Institutional Perspective,* diss., Massachusetts Institute of Technology, 1988.

The first-year courses required of all Margaret Morrison candidates included English, history, accounts, personal hygiene, principles of science and economics, social ethics, sewing, drawing and principles of cookery and preparation of food. During the second and third years, students specialized in a secretarial course, household arts and institutional management, technical dressmaking, costume design, applied design, or architectural and interior decoration.

Students enrolled in two-year certificate courses for journeymen in the School for Apprentices and Journeymen received instruction to supplement what they had

Duquesne Club
Pittsburgh

To make and inspire the home;
To lessen suffering and increase happiness;
To aid mankind in its upward struggles;
To ennoble and adorn life's work, however humble:-
These are woman's high prerogatives.

already learned as apprentices and to prepare them for more advanced positions in their trades. They chose among three options: mechanical draftsmen, machinery trades (machine work, pattern making, backsmithing and forging, and moulding and foundry work) and building trades (plumbing, bricklaying, sheet metal and cornice work, and electrical wiring). Students enrolled as apprentices in the evening school could prepare for the four machinery trades and six building trades, including house painting and sign painting that were not offered to journeymen. The certificate program in Margaret Morrison offered two-year courses in stenography, cooking, sewing, millinery, or bookkeeping and office work.

Social Ethics & Tech Beer

Evidently some members of the general public had misconceptions about the Margaret Morrison curriculum. Ruth Henderson, class of 1910, reported the following incident in *The Carnegie Tartan* of March 11, 1908. On her way home from school she had encountered a lady and engaged her in conversation about a course she was taking in social ethics. Asked to explain what these words meant she began by reciting:

. . .the well-learned definition 'Social Ethics means morals—that is, relating to right and wrong in character.' Scarcely had I said the words when she returned indignantly 'It would be a little better for Pittsburgh if more of this subject were published instead of so many advertisements for Tech Beer.' Before I could assure her that our beloved Tech School had nothing to do with this advertisement, she continued. 'And I suppose you learn all the fine points of brewing Tech beer in your cooking lessons.' Finally, I convinced the lady of her terrible mistake and I left her.

Cars were a luxury in the early 1900s. Many students paid a token to ride the streetcar to school, arriving on campus at the corner of Forbes and Dithridge Streets.

Day and night students seldom crossed paths

Carnegie Technical Schools students lived in different worlds depending on whether they studied in the evening or during the day. Virtually all night students lived at home where families, religious institutions, neighborhoods and social groups provided for their social, cultural, emotional and spiritual needs. They arrived on campus by streetcar after a long day's work, getting off at the corner of Forbes and Dithridge Streets across Forbes from the Carnegie Institute. They made their way across the Junction Hollow bridge and up Frew Street to the campus. School to them meant a few advanced classes in their occupation, usually taught by a master craftsman, along with friendly exchanges in classrooms, shops and laboratories where they spent their time before, between and after classes.

Campus life seldom involved night students. *The Tartan* carried stories about events in the night school, but few of these events featured apprentices or journeymen. A small minority of night students took part in sports, occasionally challenging the day students to a game of baseball or basketball. Every year night student organizations sponsored "smokers," banquets at which hearty good fellowship and speeches

by faculty or visitors took place amid clouds of smoke from the pipes and cigars of these all-male assemblies. Students also met their faculty informally in classrooms and laboratories. Now and then, one or two night students won a position on one of the intercollegiate athletic teams, happy exceptions to the general rule. Night students seemed to see themselves as second-class citizens, or at least this article in *The Tartan*, May 27, 1908, implied as much:

The day students as a body do not realize the importance of the night departments, but will perhaps have some idea of the great number of students attending. Carnegie Tech [Carnegie Technical Schools students began to use the terms "Carnegie Tech" and "Tech" well before the name changed to the Carnegie Institute of Technology in 1912] is leading the colleges of the country in the introduction of night courses, especially in the applied science division. Any student who has sufficient backbone to attend his classes four or five nights in the week after working hard all day, is sure to be well acquainted with hardship and, consequently, though the amount of learning he obtains will not equal that to be had in the day courses the self denial he must practice will stand him in good stead for the balance. Very few night students are fortunate enough to take in all the activities, with the notable exceptions of the glee and mandolin clubs. . .

Many night students fell by the wayside. The night class studying for diplomas from the School of Industries that enrolled in 1906 numbered 140. It took five years to obtain a degree. By 1909, only 39 remained enrolled. The 1909 edition of *The Thistle* contained an explanation by class historian Harry F. Gump:

During the first two years a number of students had to give up. In most instances, their withdrawal was involuntary, and was imperative by reason of employment being lessened; others who still held positions were

School of Applied Science

Chemistry
  Industrial Chemistry
  Electro-Chemistry

Civil
  Structural Design
  Railroad Construction
  Municipal Engineering

Electricity
  Generation & Transmission
  Electrical Apparatus Design

Mechanics
  Machine Design
  Prime Movers
  Furnace & Mill Machinery

Metallurgy
  Iron & Steel Manufacture
  Non-ferrous Metallurgy

Mining
  Mine & Quarries Location
    & Operation
  Smelting & Refining

LECTURE ROOM IN PHYSICS.
— SCHOOL OF APPLIED SCIENCE —

SCIENCE

School of Applied Design

Architectural Design
Bricklaying
Building Construction
Descriptive Geometry
English
Economics
Electrical Wiring
Freehand Drawing
Graphical Statics
History of Architecture
History of Ornament
Masonry
Mathematics
Physics
Plumbing
Shades & Shadows,
Perspective

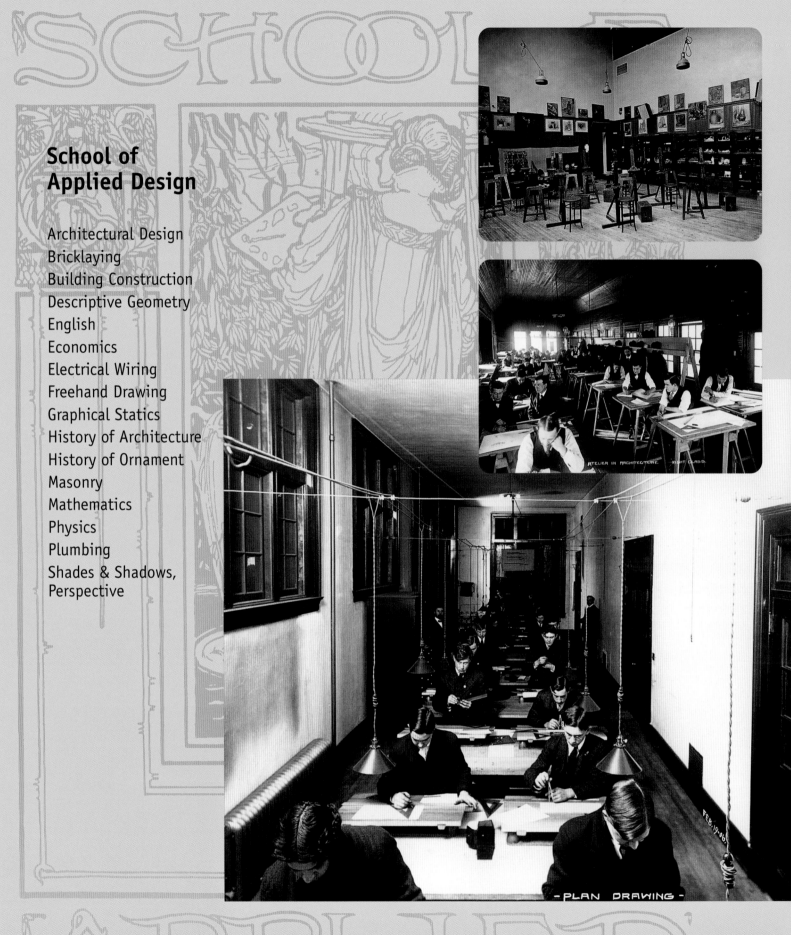

often unable to regularly attend; and still others were not able, physically, to carry on their work. The class now contains the students who will probably graduate— barring circumstances over which they have no reasonable control.

Gump was an optimistic prophet. Only 11 members of the class graduated in 1911.

Today's Student Affairs officers identify seven fields of responsibility of their offices: intellectual/artistic development, occupational preparation, physical welfare, and social, cultural, emotional and spiritual development. The Carnegie Technical Schools provided for only two of these: intellectual/artistic development and occupational preparation. The President's Report for the year 1907-08 put physical welfare in these terms:

The problem of physical well-being and recreation in a city institution is one fraught with many difficulties; and where the land belonging to the school is inadequate, it seems wise, temporarily, to cooperate with student initiative to provide those facilities which are imperatively needed and will undoubtedly assist in the creation of that comradeship and student life so dear to the hearts of our boys and girls.

Like night students, most day students walked to school or commuted from their homes or from boarding houses. They soon discovered a small tobacco shop kept by an English couple, the Morrises, at Forbes and Dithridge Streets. Their store soon became the school's unofficial hangout. The Morrises even provided a shelf on which first-year students, called Plebes, could leave their civilian headgear in order to don the "dinks" that upperclassmen required all Plebes to wear. This store served Tech students for 30 years until the city widened Forbes Street, forcing the Morrises into retirement.

Since the schools had no dormitories on campus, the administration rented two houses on Woodlawn Avenue (now Margaret Morrison Street) for a score or so of male students and provided food service and safe water for them. This makeshift arrangement failed to meet student needs. Most out-of-town male students stayed in boarding houses, many of them along nearby Mawhinney Street. The schools provided no dormitories for the small number of women students who did not commute. Instead the administration circulated a list of approved boarding houses and another list of residences where one or more students could rent rooms.

The administration provided little else, and in the absence of central leadership, the students and faculty took over. They moved so quickly that Hamerschlag was forced to appoint a board to supervise athletics in 1906. Its members included four faculty officers, 11 undergraduates and the student managers from the major sports teams—football, baseball, basketball, hockey and track. In the 1906-07 academic year, Hamerschlag appointed a board of student activities, again with both faculty and students, to supervise student organizations such as the newspaper, yearbook, glee club, orchestra, mandolin and White Friars Dramatic clubs. After 1909, this board controlled a new $5 student activity fee.

Every freshman was required to own a freshman hat (dink). Freshmen in civilian clothes were required to wear the dink on campus. Freshmen wearing uniforms were required to carry dinks with them.

Churee, Charaw, Haw! Ha! Ha!
Moom-a-rang, Bang-a-tang! Sis Boom! Bah!!!
Eat 'em up! Beat 'em up! Chase 'em up a tree!!!
Nineteen Eleven of Car-neg-ie!!!
The Thistle, 1908

Above:
Some night students picked up the rah-rah spirits of their daytime peers. Plebes of the night class of 1911 gathered together to serenade the day students with this cheer.

Tartan editor paid school fees with advertising revenues

In the absence of initiative from the administration, the students organized themselves. In September 1906, Fred Foster, who was the class president, manager of the White Friars Dramatic Troupe, a member of both the Crucible Club and Sigma Tau and who was soon to become the captain of the football team, appointed himself the editor and owner of a school newspaper which he called *The Carnegie Tartan.* With the assistance of a few friends, he produced an issue a week for two years until he graduated in 1908. During the first year, an annual subscription cost a dollar and each copy cost five cents. The school took over this publication in 1908-09 and distributed it free of charge. In the meantime, Foster and a friend or two earned enough money from advertisements and sales to help pay their expenses.

Foster's many roles may account for the heavy emphasis on football and on school spirit that characterized early editions of the newspaper. Except for an excellent hockey team, Tech's sports teams were consistent losers, despite the fact that they sometimes played against secondary schools. Foster usually claimed that defeats were really moral victories, and he sometimes omitted the scores when Tech's teams lost. On the more serious side, his newspapers carried long articles about technical subjects that provided both useful information and filled up space in a publication that had a shortage of reporters.

In addition to Foster, a number of students from the School of Applied Science led the way. Clearly these students wanted typical collegiate experiences. They elected class officers after the first meeting of the class in October 1905. By the end of the academic year in June 1906, they had published a yearbook, given a glee club concert in the Carnegie Music Hall, formed a local fraternity, held a class banquet, played their first interscholastic baseball game, held their first track meet, selected a tartan for the school's colors and designed a Scottish cap that the next year's Plebes would be required to wear on campus. In March 1906, they greeted the arrival of Margaret Morrison "girls" (as they were called in those politically incorrect days) with such enthusiasm that the administration designated an exclusive campus entrance for the use of female students and erected a partition in the lunchroom to segregate the sexes.

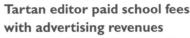

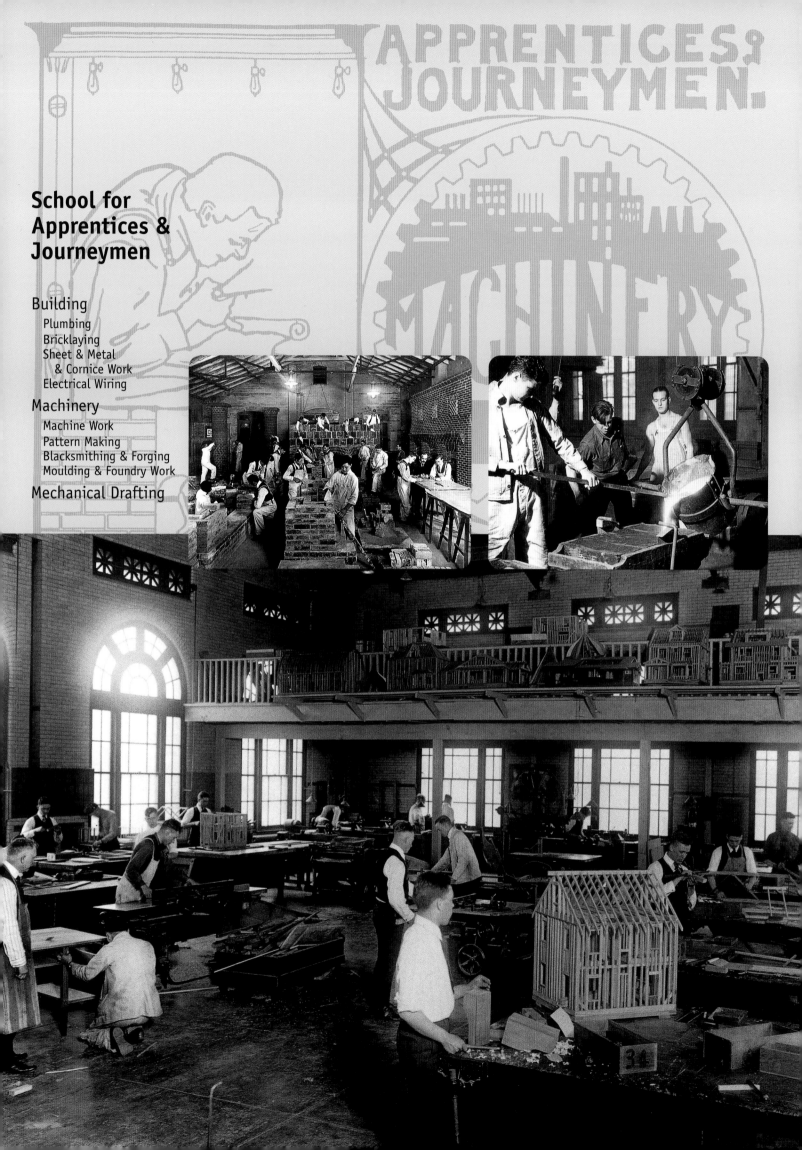

School for Apprentices & Journeymen

Building
Plumbing
Bricklaying
Sheet & Metal
 & Cornice Work
Electrical Wiring

Machinery
Machine Work
Pattern Making
Blacksmithing & Forging
Moulding & Foundry Work

Mechanical Drafting

APPRENTICES,
JOURNEYMEN.

MACHINERY

Above:
1914 words of advice to freshmen

Below:
1908 rules for freshman Plebes

Keeping the Plebes in their place

Hazing the incoming Plebes—a standard ritual in all acceptable colleges at the time—began in the fall of 1906. Hostilities between Plebes and juniors (the Charter Class simply omitted sophomore standing in a school offering three-year diplomas) broke out on the first day of school in September when Plebes saw a flag flying from an electric light pole on the campus. In giant letters it bore the insignia '08. The Plebes attempts to tear it down failed when a member of the junior class who had stationed himself part of the way up the pole used his feet to beat back his attackers. Later that day, an organized interclass competition featuring a tug of war was won by the juniors who tied the end of their rope to a pole. Subsequently, the juniors published the following scholarly proclamation in the October 31, 1906 *Tartan*:

PROCLAMATION

When in the course of college events it becomes necessary for the welfare of the school and of the Plebes themselves, that they be taught their places in relation to the JUNIOR CLASS and the institution, we said JUNIOR CLASS do proclaim and announce these rules to be followed and obeyed strictly by said Plebes:

1. The operation of drawing in and blowing out of tobacco smoke by said Plebes shall not under any circumstances be permitted in the buildings.
2. Said Plebes shall not loiter on the front steps of Industries [now Porter Hall] or on the pavement immediately in front of them.
3. Said Plebes shall not ascend aforesaid steps and enter by [the] upper aperture as this is to be kept HOLY and used only by the faculty and CLASS OF 1908.
4. Said Plebes shall not wear plaid in any form 'till after Easter.
5. Said Plebes shall not wear any insignia, numerals, letters or pins of any other schools.
6. Said Plebes shall not pour hot metal upon themselves as the odor of burning flesh is disagreeable to the JUNIORS.

Above rules decreed and approved by CLASS OF 1908.

The feuds between classes increased in intensity throughout the years. *The Tartan*, on February 6, 1907, carried the following account of a snowball fight involving students from the class of 1908:

The Snowball Fight

No one knows exactly how it started but all who took part in the battle of last Friday know how much fun was gotten out of it. It appears that at about 12:15 some Juniors started to initiate the Plebes into the mysteries of some nice fresh winter apples, and their application to the reduction of a swelled head. At first the Plebes were slightly out-numbered, but they fought stubbornly for a quarter of an hour until the rest of the class arrived in the recitation rooms. But the sight of their classmates being worsted was too much for the latter, and they flung lessons to the winds and sailed in. . . . The Juniors lacked a leader but stubbornly contested every foot of street from the main entrance to the architects' "Shanty". . . . This is the kind of spirit that ought to prevail in a school and it is understood that the faculty like to see such evidence of class spirit when they do not occur too often.

As seniors, the Charter Class of "Naught Eight" commented on the spirit of the incoming Plebes:

First among our duties as Seniors was that of refereeing the athletic contests between the Juniors and Plebes. The Plebes who then seemed to be a spiritless bunch stood around and watched the Juniors perform. When the Plebe president was led around the field, his arms tied behind him, they viewed the performance with astonishment and permitted it. Imagine that spirit in Naught Eight!
—The Thistle, *1908*

Class presidents often found themselves kidnapped and confined by their enemies on the evening of the class banquet. Class teams competed in baseball and basketball. Class identification presented serious problems in the Carnegie Technical Schools. Students entering in a particular year, 1906 for example, might graduate with a two-year certificate in 1908, a three-year diploma from the day school in 1909, or after five years of study in the night school in 1911. Two of these three groups could not identify with the zealots from the School of Applied Science who dominated social life and incorporated the graduating year of all entering students into their own.

The 1908 Plebe Initiation

An eventful day was the 21st of September, 1908. All the Plebes ducked across the Schenley Bridge with haunted looks as though it was St. Peter, instead of the fatherly Sophs, looking for them. This feeling was increased by large posters, headed with a skull and crossbones, one of which was handed to each Plebe as he entered the building. It stated that the Plebes should show respect for the old age and infirmities of the upperclassmen. Order was soon brought out of chaos by the first class meeting, when we were addressed by several of the upper classes. Coldren and Buhl of the Juniors gave some fatherly advice and dwelt upon the great love they had for the "lambs." Buhl gently broke the news that we were invited to a little tête-à-tête on the Schenley Oval on Thursday. There were to be three separate contests: a tug of war, a push ball game, and a flag rush. . .
—*The Thistle*, 1909

Plebe Initiation, circa 1914-1919
1   The "Prisoners of War"
2   Barrel Tilting Contest (Sophs v.s. Plebes)
3   Plebes throwing their shoes in a pile
4   Tug of war (Sophs v.s. Plebes)
5   The "Grand Scramble"

Left:
Men reserved a dance with a special girl by signing her dance card.

Center:
The senior household girls entertain their mothers.

Right:
The Plumbers Smoker in 1913

Housekeeping in the "House"

One of the most important events of the year was when the Senior Household Arts girls began housekeeping in "The House." The girls in the other classes will never forget the pleasant times they had there, especially when the reception was given to the "mothers." . . . There was great rejoicing when the Household Arts girls took charge of the lunchroom. "Feasts" became things of the past and the hungry mob contented itself with dainty noontime lunches. It is appalling when one considers how expensive it is when one purchases food containing the proper number of calories.

—*The Thistle*, 1909

Teas for women; smokers for men

Students also identified themselves by their school and within schools by their departments. Each school held banquets and dances in nearby hotels and restaurants; the Park Schenley Hotel, now the Pitt student union in Oakland, was a favorite. Some classes and departments fielded athletic teams. All departments held functions of one sort or another: teas and dances for the Margaret Morrison women, and smokers for sturdy men who met in a banquet room to be entertained by singing, enlightened by speeches from the faculty and surrounded by smoke. Students and faculty had established five technical organizations by 1907-08: the Civil Engineering Society, Crucible Club, Inventor's Society, Electrical Society and Tech Aeronautical Club.

Athletic facilities were lacking

The Carnegie Technical Schools suffered from poor or nonexistent athletic facilities. Faculty volunteered as coaches. Outdoor practices took place on a bumpy, gravel-cluttered level space at the upper end of Industries Hall (now Porter). The football team played all but one of its games away; the one home game took place in a natural oval in Schenley Park. The school rented a nearby gymnasium for basketball practice and occasional home games and rented the ice rink at the Duquesne Gardens for hockey. No wonder so many teams suffered so many defeats. Even under these trying circumstances, an occasional victory over rivals such as WUP (the Western University of Pennsylvania, now Pitt) produced joyous celebrations on campus, as they did later in the heyday of Tech football during the 1920s and 1930s. In a campaign to improve athletic facilities, students voted to assess themselves in order to accumulate money for an athletic field. By May 1908 the Tech Bowl had been built in a hollow parallel to Woodlawn Avenue and behind Margaret Morrison, approximately on the site of today's Gesling Stadium. Contractors made the stands from used lumber to save money, but *The Tartan* rejoiced in this substantial improvement to athletic facilities. Students continued to petition Director Hamerschlag to ask Andrew Carnegie for funds to build a gymnasium, money that did not arrive until the early 1920s after Carnegie's death.

In retrospect

The 1908 grandparent of what is now Carnegie Mellon University had little in common with its grandchild. Its goals reflected the mores of its contemporary society, goals with their roots sunk deeply into the soil of past social and economic trends rather than the aspirations of a new world already in the making. It consisted of a collection of trade and technical schools offering only two-year certificates and three-year diplomas—no bachelor's, master's and doctor's degrees. Ninety percent of its students came from the Pittsburgh area, and more than half of them studied part time in night classes. More than 99 percent of them were white descendants of northern and western Europeans. Forty percent of its faculty—like its director—had no college degrees, and were, like its students, descendants of northern and western Europeans. Only one or two faculty involved themselves in research projects or creative activities. The campus consisted of 32 acres and three still-unfinished buildings. Small tuition payments supplemented generous grants from founder Andrew Carnegie, who provided all the funds for buildings and most of the money for annual budgets. Since it did not yet have alumni, it made little impact on the society around it. How could it be further removed from the dynamic research university it was to become in 90 years? Today's students and faculty, beamed down onto the 1908 campus, would hardly recognize at first glance the grandparent of their distinguished research university.

Given time, however, these faculty and students would recognize their kinship with many aspects of the Carnegie Technical Schools. Some are easy to recognize: *The Tartan, The Thistle,* budding fraternities, technical societies, musical organizations, athletic teams, a dramatics society and three buildings, now lovingly restored. Beneath these surface features lie far more vital ties. First, as they do today, faculty and students in the Carnegie Technical Schools worked very hard, beginning a tradition of dedication to their work that has always characterized the institution. Second, they attempted a new educational innovation, an attempt to provide excellent technical education for men and women

of limited educational backgrounds. Third, the entrepreneurial spirit of the student population and the way in which they organized themselves and their lives, strikes a responsive chord among today's administrators, faculty, researchers and students. Finally, by educating so many western Pennsylvania residents, the Carnegie Technical Schools were about to make substantial contributions to the wider Pittsburgh community, a tradition of responsibility to the society that has grown apace in many ways, particularly since the end of World War II. Not a bad legacy for an institutional grandparent to leave.

The Locomotive Yell

C-a-r-n-e-g-i-e
(Slowly)

C-a-r-n-e-g-i-e
(Medium)

C-a-r-n-e-g-i-e
(Fast)

Ray! Ray! Ray! Tech!!!

The Tech Bowl was located approximately on the site of today's Gesling Stadium.

4.

Thomas Stockham Baker 1922–1935
He removed muddy paths and
fostered research and graduate study

When Thomas Stockham Baker became president of Carnegie Institute of Technology in 1922, the school was suffering from a severe case of growing pains. In many ways, his background and personality prepared him to cope with the legacy of the Hamerschlag years but not to break new ground in engineering education. Born in Aberdeen, Maryland, in 1871 to parents from well-established families, Baker attended public schools and Johns Hopkins University in Baltimore. He studied the following year at the University of Leipzig in Germany, returning to Johns Hopkins to receive a Ph.D. degree in 1895. He taught German at Johns Hopkins and lectured there for a decade on modern German literature. At the same time, he was music critic for *The Baltimore Sun*. In 1900 he joined the faculty of the Jacob Tome Institute, a preparatory school for boys in Port Deposit, Maryland, and became its director in 1909. In 1919, he moved to Pittsburgh to serve as secretary, a job equivalent to vice president, of Carnegie Tech. When Hamerschlag resigned in 1922, the trustees appointed Baker president at the age of 51.

A bachelor who lived in the Pittsburgh Athletic Association, Baker gave himself unsparingly to the work of the institution, spending evening after evening talking about Tech to audiences all over the Pittsburgh area. In several lecture tours abroad (he spoke both French and German fluently), he discussed American education, the American character and European affairs before a wide range of audiences. Simultaneously, he strove to understand and lead a technical institution with an evening school whose poorly educated students were workers in local industry studying to win better jobs by furthering their technical education.

Under Baker's leadership, the barren and haphazard campus that Hamerschlag left behind changed markedly. Throughout the Hamerschlag years, constant building projects had kept the campus in turmoil as steam shovels began to fill in the Cut, workmen erected 20 buildings and piles of building materials littered the campus. With the exception of the gymnasium, no major building projects marked the Baker years. Instead, crews directed by a landscape architect seeded lawns and planted trees, and workmen replaced the muddy paths that had connected one building to another with

Above:
President Baker

Opposite page top:
The Forbes Street entrance to
Carnegie Institute of Technology

Opposite page bottom:
An early picture of President
Baker (left) with Mr. & Mrs. H.K.
Kirkpatrick. Professor Kirkpatrick
served on the faculty from
1920 to 1959.

1922

- Baker becomes president.
- The first Kiltie band is formed.
- Bob Schmertz writes "Fight for the Glory of Carnegie."

concrete walks. Tech also erected two flagpoles, the Senior Fence (by the class of 1923), an open-air theater on the present site of Posner Hall, a stone shelter for students using streetcars at the Forbes Street end of the Cut and a grove of young sycamore trees in memory of those who died in World War I. Tech mounted the bronze bow ornament from the cruiser USS Pennsylvania on a pedestal behind Hamerschlag Hall facing the Carnegie Institute.

Hamerschlag had focused his attention on the physical plant and the educational program. Baker focused on spiritual, cultural and character-building efforts. Even before he became president, he had added a baccalaureate service and a musical program to graduation exercises. Soon after his inauguration, he began voluntary, nonsectarian chapel services led by clergy from the surrounding area. He provided a variety of support for the YMCA and YWCA organizations that had reached the campus between 1916 and 1918. In the academic programs, Baker increased significantly the amount of English required, laying the groundwork for the social relations program of the Doherty administration.

Throughout his years both before and after joining Tech, Baker wrote and lectured widely. He published two scholarly books about German literature when he was in his twenties; a long stream of articles and speeches followed during his years as president. They cover a wide range of American and European subjects with no particular focus. Not a single article about engineering education appears in his collected papers in the Carnegie Mellon archives. His lifelong interest in German and French affairs growing out of his scholarly training in those fields guided his pen far more than the education of Tech's students.

Tech mounted the bronze bow ornament from the cruiser USS Pennsylvania on a pedestal behind Hamerschlag Hall facing the Carnegie Institute.

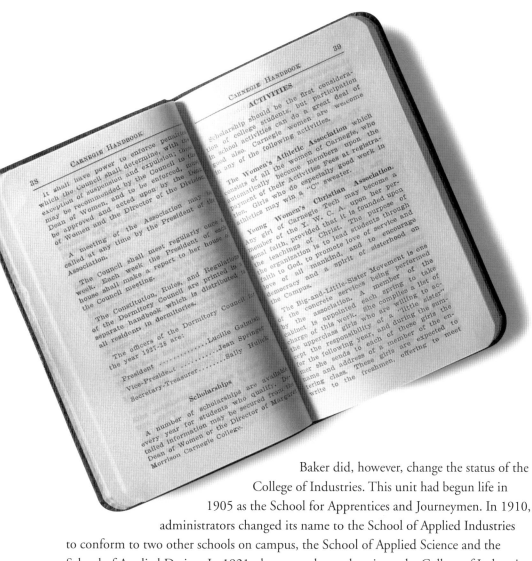

The 1927-28 *Carnegie Institute of Technology Handbook* outlined guidelines and services for the Tech students.

1923

- The first senior fence is erected.

1924

- The Bureau of Metallurgical Research is established.

Baker did, however, change the status of the College of Industries. This unit had begun life in 1905 as the School for Apprentices and Journeymen. In 1910, administrators changed its name to the School of Applied Industries to conform to two other schools on campus, the School of Applied Science and the School of Applied Design. In 1921, the name changed again to the College of Industries and the curriculum lengthened to four years so that graduates could earn a bachelor of science degree and its members play on intercollegiate athletic teams. In 1923, the freshman class of the College of Industries merged with the freshman class in the College of Engineering. Finally, in 1934 Carnegie Institute of Technology phased out the College of Industries, and its programs merged with those in the College of Engineering. In 1930, Tech added the Library School, located in a wing of the Carnegie Institute, but offering a graduate degree through Carnegie Tech.

Through most of the Baker years, Margaret Morrison Carnegie College and the Drama and Architecture Departments of the College of Fine Arts prospered and grew in reputation. The February 1928 *Carnegie Alumnus* described the Margaret Morrison programs:

Margaret Morrison as a Technical College

The nature of its admission requirements indicates that Margaret Morrison is not merely a private school but a school with collegiate standing, for applicants must take college preparatory courses in high school or preparatory school before entrance. The Margaret Morrison Carnegie College offers major work in seven fields as follows: General Science, Household Economics, Costume Economics, Secretarial Studies Regular Course, Secretarial Studies English Minor, Social Work, and Library Work. Those who have entered the fields of science, home economics and social work have received the greatest success in the way of remuneration, with secretarial work following closely.

1926

- Tech defeats Pitt and Notre Dame in football.
- Tech hosts first International Coal Conference.

1927

- Tech adopts College Board examinations.

In a letter to alumni written in July 1927, Baker praised the impact of the Drama Department on American theater:

> *A notable achievement in the development of the little theater movement has been the remarkable growth of the Play House in Cleveland under the direction of Frederick McConnell, a graduate of the Drama Department. With a company consisting chiefly of former students of the drama department, he has received such enthusiastic support from the people of Cleveland that a new theater has been built for his organization. It opened this spring with great success.*

Right:
The Little Theater in the Fine Arts Building

Below:
An exciting moment in the 1924 production of *The Blue Bandana*

The Carnegie Tartan echoed his sentiments in the October 25, 1927 edition:

> *Many actors of fame who appear in Pittsburgh from time to time have shown a keen interest in the Drama Department. Such prominent men as Otis Skinner and K. H. Southern have visited the school and have been favorably impressed. . . . The curriculum of the Drama Department is considered the most difficult on Tech's campus. It is now being recognized by the general public and by theatrical managers that these students are both thoroughly and practically trained in both acting and stage technique.*

Building on some halting beginnings under his predecessor, Baker instituted a number of programs of community service. Several thousand students from about 1,000 firms studied in the evening school, but this major contribution to the economic and social life of the community was largely unrecognized. Baker invited executives from firms whose employees studied at Tech to visit campus and see what was going on. As a result, some companies appointed "company deans" to coordinate the studies of their employees. Partly because of this effort, night school enrollment increased from 1,693 in 1921-22 to 4,829 at its peak in 1929-30, when it was almost double the day school enrollment. In addition, Baker instituted a program of free public lectures by famous visitors—including Nobel Prize winners Albert Einstein and Niels Bohr—aimed at college-educated executives employed at local industries. Finally, Tech became host to many conventions of national societies of scientists, engineers, printers and dramatists.

Tech served the community in many other ways. Plays at The Little Theater were open free-of-charge to the public and attracted thousands of Pittsburghers every year. In 1930, Margaret Morrison began a nurses' training course to meet a need for instructors in nurses' training schools. Tech held an open house every year and attracted visitors from the schools and the community to campus.

Research begins in metals, coal, physics and chemistry

Baker's administration also played a major role in the development of research at Carnegie Tech. Building on the success of the Division of Applied Psychology, Hamerschlag had founded six bureaus with similar aims. They included, for example, the Research Bureau for Retail Training and the School of Life Insurance Salesmanship. Baker closed these bureaus, arguing that they did not build on Tech's technological strengths and turned research at Tech in new directions.

In 1923 the Baker administration founded the Metallurgical Advisory Board that opened a metals laboratory in 1924 to organize research into the application of physics and chemistry to the production of metals. The metallurgists, physicists and chemists who collaborated in this laboratory represent the first major interdisciplinary research effort at Carnegie Tech, a foretaste of what was to become a Carnegie Mellon trademark. A number of major companies, the Carnegie Corporation and Carnegie Tech sponsored fellowships to support this research effort, again a feature of today's research programs.

Among President Baker's major research innovations were international conferences on bituminous coal in 1926, 1928 and 1931. These conferences represent Tech's first significant impact beyond the borders of the United States, but the internationalization of the institution was not sustained during the years that followed. Baker made several trips to Europe to advertise these conferences and to recruit speakers. Five thousand delegates presented credentials for these three meetings, meetings which produced seven volumes of proceedings and marked Carnegie Tech as a leading player in this industry, so vital to western Pennsylvania. As a result of the bituminous coal conferences, Tech founded the Carnegie Coal Research Laboratory, supported by the Buhl Foundation and a number of America's largest industries. This development established research partnerships between Tech and many American corporations, partnerships that have increased steadily over the years. By the end of Baker's administration, the laboratory had a staff of 28 investigators.

1929

• Night school enrolls twice as many students as day school.

Discoveries Brought to Light at International Coal Conference

The "City of Smoke" is a fitting setting for the Second International Coal Conference. Pittsburgh lives on coal and should therefore be more interested in the coal conference than most of her sister cities.

The conference was opened yesterday with an address of welcome by President Baker. In the course of the next few days it is expected that many scientific investigations and discoveries made in the past two years, will be brought to light. . . .

. . . .One of the most outstanding matters to be considered is the liquefaction of coal to be used as fuel oil. The process originated in Germany and seems at present to be of great interest to the Standard Oil Company.
—*The Carnegie Tartan,*
November 2, 1928

In 1943 Otto Stern won the Nobel Prize in Physics.

In 1933, President Baker made a trip to Europe to recruit refugee scientists from Germany for the Tech faculty. As a result, three distinguished men, Ernst Berl of the University of Darmstadt, and Otto Stern and Immanuel Estermann from the University of Hamburg, moved to Tech to lead research in applied chemistry and molecular physics. Berl and Stern received the title of "research professor," a designation that temporarily discontinued when they retired in 1945. In 1943 Stern won the Nobel Prize in physics, an event that brought worldwide attention to him and to Carnegie Tech. Tech built new laboratories for each of these scholars. During the Baker years none of the staff members of the laboratories received faculty appointments.

The formation of these four research laboratories resulted in a marked increase in graduate instruction. Four architecture students received the first master of arts degrees in 1914. The school awarded its first master of science degrees in 1914, and its first earned doctorate in 1920. By 1925, the school had registered 25 students for graduate work; by the end of Baker's administration in 1935, that number had increased to 151, many of them teaching fellows or assistants in the coal or metal research laboratories. In all, 13 departments offered graduate work in 1935. In addition, during the decade 1925-1935, about 1,000 graduates of engineering colleges who were not degree candidates took graduate courses at Carnegie Tech in the night school. To coordinate graduate programs, Baker appointed a permanent secretary of graduate instruction in 1933. These developments erected a solid foundation for graduate work, a foundation on which the Doherty and Warner administrations could build.

Legendary victories over Pitt and Notre Dame

Football thrived during Baker's administration. Students had demanded winning teams from the very beginning of the Carnegie Technical Schools in 1906. Then in 1914 Tech hired Walter P. Steffen, a judge who was a former star at the University of Chicago, to coach the team. He commuted from Chicago to attend to his coaching duties. By the 1920s Tech's football fortunes reached their apex. The Tartans defeated Pitt four times and Notre Dame twice during the 1920s and won once from each school in the succeeding decade.

Caught up in the excitement, Baker permitted an alumni group to supervise Tech's football fortunes. The alumni recruited students, rented Forbes Field or the Pitt stadium for home games and built up a substantial debt in the process. Students, alumni and football fans everywhere, however, praised tiny Tech to the skies, particularly in 1928 when only a loss in the last game of the year prevented Tech from winning the national championship. It remained for President Doherty to bring football under control after 1938 when the last of the players recruited during the Baker years took Tech to the Sugar Bowl.

1930
- The Coal Research Laboratory opens.
- Spring Carnival begins.

1933
- Baker recruits three scientists from Germany.

Baker's achievements

In 1927 the trustees raised tuition to $300 a year. No further raises occurred during the Baker administration. During the Depression that began in 1929, the rate of return on the endowment, which was invested in fixed income securities, diminished steadily. The budget remained in the black throughout the Baker years, and the administration even maintained substantial reserves. A host of upcoming problems—higher salaries, more equipment, research expenditures, faculty retirement plans, etc.—foreshadowed financial troubles ahead. So did the requirement that Tech raise $4 million by 1946 in order to qualify for the two-to-one Carnegie Corporation grant of $8 million. Both Baker and the trustees failed to face this situation squarely.

President Baker suffered throughout his tenure at Tech from poor health. He took several extended leaves from his duties at Tech while he recuperated. In 1934 his health began to wane more rapidly. An ocean voyage failed to revive him. The chairman of the Committee on the Institute of Technology of the Carnegie Institute's Board of Trustees, John L. Porter, carried on Tech's administrative work for two years. During most of the years between 1930 and 1935, Tech seemed to drift with the tide, and the tide was flowing out. Baker finally resigned in September 1935. The Board of Trustees appointed him president emeritus and invited him to join the board. He died in 1939 leaving his estate to support the Baker Professorship in the English Department.

Fewer new developments took place under Baker than under any of the institution's other presidents. Hamerschlag had presided over an institution in constant change as one innovation succeeded another in rapid fire succession. Baker slowed the pace, giving the institution time to breathe. Even during the Depression years, he kept Tech out of debt and, indeed, left substantial reserves for his successor to draw upon. Neither Baker nor his colleagues faced a host of problems looming on the academic horizon. They remained for Baker's successor, Robert E. Doherty.

Under Baker's administration, Tech still made significant progress in several directions, directions that reflected Baker's training and personality. Baker brought a new dignity to campus life. He led a movement to beautify the campus and another to enrich student life. His administrative reforms closed or consolidated several educational units. He helped to found four new research institutes, fostering and enlarging programs of graduate education. Finally, under his leadership Tech had formed new bonds both with industry and with Pittsburgh's citizenry. Despite the fact that Doherty succeeded Baker in the midst of the nation's worst depression, he found firm foundations on which to build.

1935

- One hundred fifty-one students register for graduate work.
- Baker retires, leaving his estate to Tech.

President Baker led a movement to beautify the Tech campus.

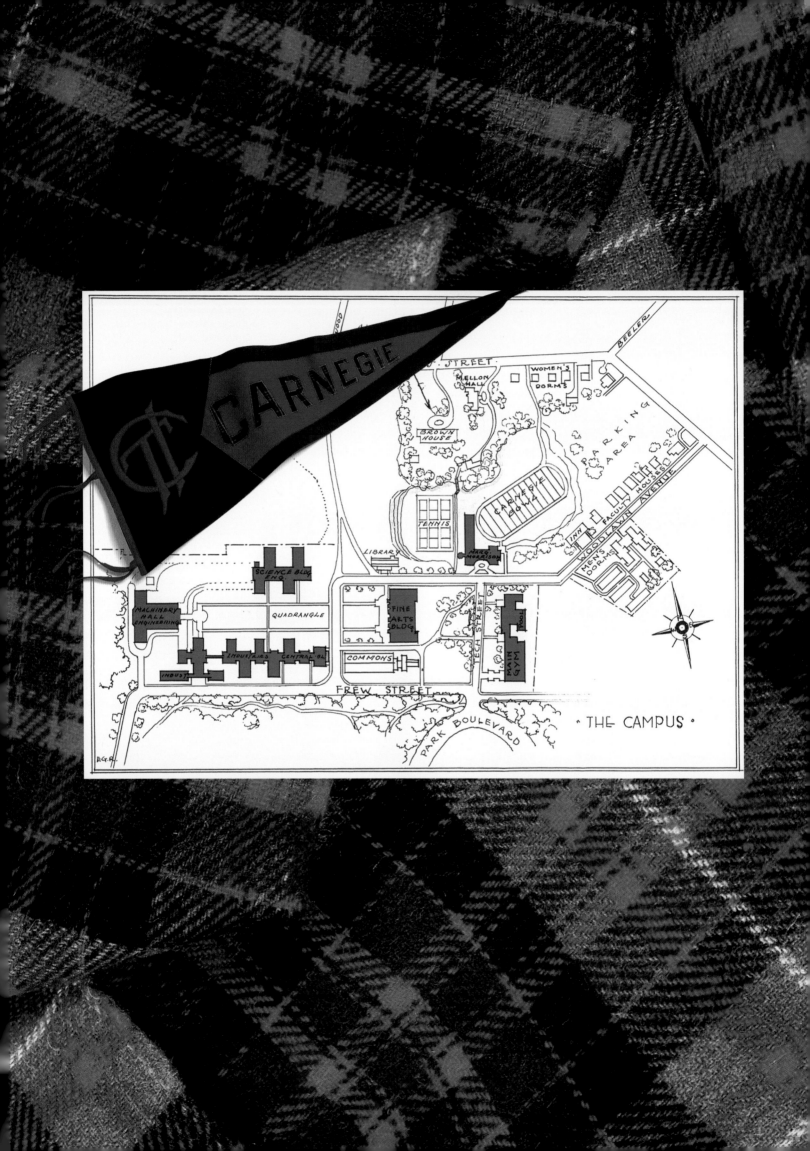

5.

Snapshot 1927–1929
A trade school transforms itself and its students

The commencement exercises of the Carnegie Institute of Technology in 1928 took place in nearby Carnegie Music Hall, site of the first ceremony in 1908. Walter Lippman, a nationally known columnist from *The New York World,* delivered the address. Though the sites of the two ceremonies were the same, the graduating classes of 1908 and 1928 differed dramatically and illustrate the fundamental changes taking place in the institution.

In contrast to the all-male class of 1908, 156 of the graduates (27 percent) in 1928 were women, 102 from Margaret Morrison and 54 from Fine Arts; women were still not admitted to the remaining two colleges: Engineering and Industries. Surviving records do not indicate that any graduates were African-American, Asian or Hispanic. Only a handful of names reveal ancestry from southern or eastern Europe.

The graduating class of 1928 portrays an institution in transition. Tech still offered two-year certificates and three-year diplomas in fields such as heating and ventilating, plumbing, coal mining and technical dressmaking, although it had become an institute of technology in 1912 able to offer bachelor's, master's and doctor's degrees. The College of Fine Arts

offered bachelor of arts degrees while both Margaret Morrison and Engineering offered a bachelor of science. In the engineering college, two students received bachelor degrees in chemistry, two in physics, two in mathematics and the remainder in seven engineering disciplines: chemical, civil, commercial, electrical, mechanical, mining and metallurgy. Twenty-eight undergraduates accepted commissions as second lieutenants in the Officer Reserve Corps. Tech had begun to offer programs leading to a master's degree in chemistry and in four engineering departments. They totaled only 3 percent of the graduates. Although a few students had previously earned a doctorate, none completed doctoral work in 1928.

Carnegie Tech reorganizes

The Carnegie Technical Schools had transformed themselves in the 20 years between 1908 and 1928. The four schools of 1908 had become four colleges: the Colleges of Engineering, Industries, Fine Arts and Margaret Morrison. In addition, Tech included a Division of General Studies with departments of English, History, Mathematics, Modern Languages, and Psychology and Education. Other programs included Printing, Industrial

Changing Commencement Statistics	1908	1928
Number of Graduates	58	382
Number of Different Degrees	6	46
Pre-Collegiate	58	52
Two-Year Certificates	0	44
Three-Year Diplomas	58	8
Bachelor's Level	0	319
Bachelor of Science	0	226
Bachelor of Architecture	0	12
Bachelor of Arts	0	76
Professional Degrees	0	5
Master's Level	0	11
Master of Science	0	11

Students celebrated the laying of the cornerstone for the School of Applied Design with a pageant on April 25, 1912.

Education, an Evening School, Summer School, ROTC program, Bureau of Metallurgical Research, Library School and Bureau of Recommendations (placement office). The transition from the Carnegie Technical Schools to Carnegie Mellon University had begun.

By 1928 the trustees committee on the Institute of Technology consisted of 11 members of the Board of Trustees of the Carnegie Institute and five "special" members who did not belong to that board. In 1928, two of these "special" members were Tech alumni. The president of the Carnegie Institute still had executive responsibility for Tech, and the Institute kept Tech's official books. The authority of President Baker was vitally limited; he was not a member of the board of the Institute and, although he attended meetings of the committee that supervised Tech, his role was limited to making recommendations. This unusual situation distressed both President Baker and the Tech faculty. Why should Tech, an educational institution with a growing national reputation, be a department of an institution whose mandate was to focus its attention solely on the Pittsburgh region?

Unlike Tech's relationship to the Carnegie Institute, the composition of its administration reflected major changes in the institution during the 20 years after 1908. The engineer and his two assistants had disappeared from the administrative rolls. New additions included directors in charge of academic affairs in each of the four colleges and for part-time, summer and special students. Newcomers also included a dean of men and a dean of women. All these officials had college degrees including three with Ph.D.s and one with a master's degree. Instead of focusing on building a campus as it did in 1908, the administration of Carnegie Tech 20 years later strove to improve academic standards and nurture student life.

Architect Henry Hornbostel shapes the campus

Perhaps the most dramatic change between 1908 and 1928 was in the campus and its buildings; at least, that development was the most obvious one. Hornbostel's original plan had undergone a number of significant changes and modifications during these two decades. Hornbostel had increased the size and reduced the number of wings on the buildings facing the central mall, designed a building for the School of Applied Design (later the College of Fine Arts), replaced the untidy courtyard with the Margaret Morrison Carnegie College building and designed Machinery Hall to include the power plant and enclose the smokestack in a tower. He completed the buildings in the following order: Industries, 1906; Margaret Morrison, 1907; Engineering Hall, 1908; the main building of the School of Applied Design, 1912; Machinery Hall, 1913; Administration Hall, 1914; the Applied Design wings, 1916; and the Gymnasium, 1923.

By 1928, Hornbostel's genius could be appreciated by contrasting his treatment of the building for the School of Applied Design, now the College of Fine Arts, with his work in Industries Hall and Administration Halls, now Porter/Baker Halls. Each of these buildings had a clear public function as part of an overall

campus plan, one defining one end of the mall and the other defining one of its sides. Both utilized the buff-colored brick, polychrome terra cotta and low, overhanging tile roofs which became Hornbostel trademarks. But each had characteristics in its private space—that is, the interior of the building—that differentiated one from the other and spoke clearly of its educational functions.

The Applied Design building became the only building in any university designed to house five fine arts departments: Architecture, Art, Design, Drama and Music. Hornbostel placed sculpture studios in the basement; a theater, music hall, gallery and drama classrooms on the first floor; music rooms on the mezzanine; drafting spaces for architecture and design on the second floor; art studios on the third; and tiny spaces, flooded with natural light from skylights, used as studios by both faculty and advanced students, in the attic. Throughout the building, Hornbostel surrounded the students with references to great artistic works of western culture. Some of them strike casual observers as mere decorations —columns which have no structural function, for example. But they functioned in another way—as examples to students of great art through the ages.

Inside the doorway Hornbostel presented a great entrance hall built with gray limestone walls and a vaulted roof

adorned with frescoes by J.M. Hewlett— "a celestial atlas of art history," one historian called it. The gray Tennessee marble floor contains a floor plan of St. Peter's Basilica done in green Vermont marble. (St. Peter's itself has plans of several cathedrals inset into the main aisle of the nave.) Up a flight of marble stairs and across the corridor, the entrance to the dean's offices reproduces a plaster cast of the entrance to the City Hall in Toulon, France. At either end of the vaulted transverse corridor, Hornbostel placed raised landings screened by columns in the style of Louis XVI. Plans for the Parthenon, Chartres Cathedral and the Temple of Edfu in Egypt appear in marble on the floors of this transverse hallway. The entire building, which presents a variety of vistas and points of view, both classical and romantic, is a setting designed to inspire budding young artists.

The Niches

Hornbostel planned elaborate sculptural treatments for five semicircular niches in the front of the building, but only one was brought near to completion. An Italian craftsman named Archille Giammartini executed it for $50,000, but Carnegie refused to pay for the remaining niches when he saw the size of the bill.

Above left:
The newly completed Applied Design Building

Above right:
The only completed niche

Below:
A drawing/painting class, circa 1920

Applied Design Building
(Now the Fine Arts Building)

1912

This page clockwise from top left:

Main Hall looking toward front door

Entrance to the Dean's Office

Transept of Main Hall

Drawing class, circa 1923

Administration Hall
(Now Baker Hall)

1914

This page clockwise from top right:

Main circular stairway

Machine shop, Apprentices
& Journeymen

Main entrance to building

Main hallway arch

The interiors of Industries and Administration Halls stand in intriguing contrast to the Applied Design (now Fine Arts) Building. Just inside the entrance to Administration Hall (now Baker) stands the main staircase, a structure that reveals the engineer in Hornbostel, who had worked on four New York City bridges. The circular stairway, designed so that the treads on the curved corners are approximately equal in width to those along the straight walls, avoids the tiny corner wedges typical of circular stairways. The entire staircase is self-supporting; it has no beams, only steel reinforcing. Instead of beams, Hornbostel used the curving tile underfaces as structural elements held rigid at the wall and stiffened at the outer edge by the balustrade. What a fitting entrance to a building that was the home of building craftsmen and engineers for many decades!

Just beyond the staircase begins a one-eighth mile corridor which connects Administration and Industries Halls (Baker and Porter) and slopes for most of its length at a 4.25 percent grade. Since the land on which these two halls were built sloped downward toward Junction Hollow, Hornbostel was forced either to

place stairs at intervals or to slope the corridor. He chose the latter plan so that machinery could be moved from one wing to another without going up and down stairways. This arrangement has often been compared to an assembly line, an apt analogy for Industries Hall. According to an apocryphal story, Carnegie ordered the architects to build the hallway on a slant so that the buildings could be converted to a factory if the school failed. No evidence in the printed record supports this story, although generations of students and alumni stubbornly believe it.

On either side of the central hallway lie a series of wings similar to those in Hornbostel's first campus plan. Originally empty spaces, they have been adapted over the years to a wide variety of uses, and additional ones have been built as the need arose and funding became available. Hornbostel placed functional, exposed angular iron supports over the vaulted entrances to these wings and around the brick columns of the staircases. He fashioned the light fixtures along these corridors, the interior window frames, and many interior doors from copper. He also made the handrails on the stairways from metal pipes, later a common practice in

Above:
The official 1927-28 *Carnegie Institute of Technology Handbook* fit easily into the palm of a student's hand.

Right:
Administration Hall, now Baker Hall

many buildings. Different grades of factory-made brick provide color accents, and the ceiling resembles a gently curved segment of a barrel vault. In 1928, hundreds of craftsmen and engineers studied in these halls built from the bricks, mortar and metal they were learning to use in their classes.

The dominating vertical element among Hornbostel's buildings is Machinery Hall (now Hamerschlag). For decades, it served as the symbol of Carnegie Tech, and a suitable symbol it was. Hornbostel began with an interesting problem. In 1906, he had built a small power plant to generate steam and electricity. Its tall chimney near the edge of Junction Hollow dwarfed the plant. In 1911, the school asked Hornbostel to design a building incorporating these structures that would also house the Departments of Mechanical and Electrical Engineering. Moreover, the original power plant lay on a much lower level than the mall stretching before it toward the new Fine Arts Building.

To cope with these problems, Hornbostel placed the first floor of Machinery Hall below the level of, and set back from, the mall. To get to the entrance of the building, which is on the second floor, Hornbostel built an ascending staircase forming a bridge from the mall over a driveway. The staircase ascends to a semicircular niche which houses the main doorway. At the rear of the building high above Junction Hollow, Hornbostel designed the tower, combining both classical and romantic elements, that disguised the smokestack. On either side of the tower, Hornbostel built the wings still clearly visible from across the Junction Hollow Bridge. By 1928, the original Hornbostel quadrangle was almost complete, awaiting only two buildings on either end of Engineering Hall, Wean Hall at the Junction Hollow extremity, and Doherty Hall facing Fine Arts.

Left:
Machinery Hall, now Hamerschlag Hall

Below:
Underground tunnels connected the buildings, carrying steam, hot water, electricity and telephone lines.

As he worked on plans for Machinery Hall, Hornbostel developed sketches for a building that would extend from the campus into the Junction Hollow valley. This building never reached fruition, but the George A. Roberts Engineering Hall occupies this same site, a symbolic link of the present distinguished campus planners to their equally distinguished predecessor. Hornbostel tied his buildings together with underground tunnels, about eight feet tall and six feet wide, that carried lines for steam, hot water, electricity, telephones and now computer lines. In addition to their indispensable utilitarian functions, they became the stuff of stories and legends, many of which may have grown in the telling.

By 1928 additional Hornbostel buildings dotted the campus. During World War I, Carnegie Tech had become a military encampment. Eight thousand soldiers and sailors lived on campus at the peak of wartime activity in 1918. To cope with this influx, the government erected 16 temporary structures. Two of them lasted for many student generations. The Langley

Right:
The Carnegie Inn

Left:
The Hut, Tech's Library

Laboratory of Aeronautics, designed by Hornbostel, rose in 23 days on the present site of Hunt Library. By 1928 it had become the main campus cafeteria and was variously known as "The Beanery" or "Skibo" after Andrew Carnegie's Scottish castle. At times, it also served as a gymnasium, lecture hall, automobile shop, art studio, arsenal for the ROTC, storage quarters, registration room, dance floor and studio theater.

Another "temporary" building began as a YMCA canteen, a clubhouse for soldiers. Tech moved it to the campus in 1920 and placed it on the Cut at the Margaret Morrison end of the Senior Fence to serve as a library. Always known to students as "The Hut," it served as a library until World War II when it was once again used as a canteen for service personnel on campus.

While Hornbostel's major building projects held center stage, the campus expanded in other ways. Carnegie Tech began to acquire land adjacent to its original campus and, in some cases, also acquired the houses on this land, 17 of them in all. The two most notable were Mellon Hall, the home of Andrew W. Mellon on a hill along Forbes Avenue, and Forbes Hall on the site of the present Warner Hall. Carnegie Institute of Technology refurbished each to house

women students. The school also built a football practice field, the Tech Bowl, and a small athletic field house, designed by Hornbostel, on Margaret Morrison Street on the site of the present Donner Hall. In 1924 after the Gym was built, this building was remodeled to become the Carnegie Inn, a once beloved building with ivy-covered walls, wrought iron ornamentation and casement windows. Inside were two dining halls and a basement grill with a large stone fireplace that helped to establish an atmosphere of ease and good fellowship.

Tech had seven rather crude men's dormitories in 1928. Between 1915 and 1918, the school had built its first men's dormitories designed by Hornbostel and named in tribute to Tech graduates killed in World War I: McGill and Boss Halls in 1915; Henderson, Miller and Engelbrecht in 1917; and Scobell and Welch in 1918, the latter two helping to house the soldiers arriving on campus in large numbers for training. The school built all of these buildings, located across Margaret Morrison Street from the main campus, as cheaply as possible to house out-of-town students who were enrolling in the school in increasing numbers.

Students from 1928 remember another building, Skibo Inn, with particular fondness. It began in 1916 as a lean-to across Margaret Morrison Street from the Carnegie Inn when two enterprising architecture students figured that their fellow students must be as hungry as they were. When these men joined the army in 1917, a co-ed (as women students were called in those days) from Painting and Design took over. When business boomed, she called on her father for help. He added to the building, hired a student or two, and developed a campus fixture regaled in song and story.

More qualified faculty continue to work long hours

The faculty had also changed dramatically. It now numbered 205, double the size of the 1907-08 faculty. Faculty who lacked college degrees clustered in the College of Industries where they taught shop courses; many had been members of the original faculty of the Carnegie Technical Schools. Seven new hires in the fall of 1927 had graduated from Carnegie Tech with bachelor's degrees. In addition to regular faculty, 70 "outside men" and 20 daytime undergraduate students—undergraduates functioning as instructors or teaching assistants—taught in the night school.

Faculty teaching loads remained high, but significantly lower than the 20 plus hours typical for faculty in 1908. Full professors taught from nine to 12 hours weekly and all others, from 12 to 18 hours. Faculty could earn additional income if they taught night courses, for which they were paid by the hour. One hundred and forty of the full faculty of 205 did so, bringing their total teaching loads to between 14 and 21 hours.

Reports about faculty research are curiously varied. In his Annual Report for 1928, President Baker failed to mention research by the general faculty. *The Faculty Bulletin* presented a different picture. Its biweekly, mimeographed reports listed 29 books, creative works or research papers, 14 articles in more popular publications, 29 speeches before academic conferences and 77 talks to community groups by faculty mainly from the Division of General Studies, the College of Fine Arts and the College of Engineering. Evidently faculty gave higher priorities than their administrators to research and communication with the general public. Not a single report of a research grant to a faculty member appears in any Tech publication in 1928.

Faculty conditions improved slowly but steadily. In 1914, faculty became eligible for non-contributory pensions through the Carnegie Institute for the Advancement of Teaching. Andrew Carnegie himself had asked to have Tech included in this program even though it failed to meet one of the established criteria for membership: a majority of faculty with doctor's degrees. Beginning in 1920 a general faculty organization began to meet to discuss matters of faculty welfare such as insurance, housing and a faculty club. Subsequently, Tech provided term life insurance for its faculty and offered them opportunities to purchase additional policies.

Educational Levels of Faculty

	1907-08	1927-28
Ph.D.	9	18
Masters	2	45
Bachelors	45	90
No college degree	43	36
Private study	0	14
M.D.	2	0
Unknown	0	2
Total	**101**	**205**

The administration also set aside a room for faculty dining in the Carnegie Inn when it was renovated for faculty and student use after the new gymnasium was completed in 1924. No faculty club appeared until 1933. Then the school moved Hornbostel's shanty to a site near the Fine Arts Building to serve as a faculty club. Tech publications provided no information about faculty salaries, but the willingness of two thirds of the faculty to teach in the night school for hourly wages provides mute testimony to inadequate salary levels.

In addition to heavy teaching loads and low salaries, faculty in 1928 lacked many of the rights and privileges that today's faculty enjoy. All teachers were on one-year appointments. No one had tenure. There were no written criteria for re-appointment and promotion. Deans simply recommended faculty for promotion and, if the president agreed, the deed was done. Neither senior faculty nor trustees played a role in these decisions. Finally, Tech had no agreed-upon retirement provisions. Under these conditions, faculty were at the mercy of their administrators.

Tech students remain largely local

During the 20 years after 1908, student life also changed dramatically. By 1928, veteran professors formed the core of the faculty. In addition, Tech recruited new and better educated teachers as the faculty doubled in size. The campus had five classroom buildings, a gymnasium, two dining halls, an athletic field, four student hangouts, seven men's dormitories, 14 women's dorms all in houses near the campus that Tech bought and refurbished, 19 fraternity houses scattered around the Oakland/Squirrel Hill, area and an enlarged and beautified campus with a formal entrance on Forbes Street, paved

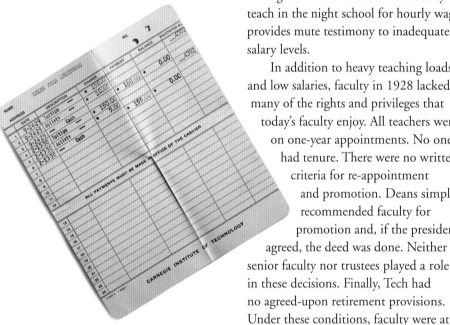

1929-30 Carnegie Institute of Technology record of tuition payments

walks and landscaped grounds. Today's students could stroll across this campus and recognize its most important features.

Enrollment that had totaled 1,835 in 1908 increased almost fourfold during the next 20 years. Tuition was still a bargain, although by 1928 the trustees had increased tuition for incoming students to $300.

Carnegie Tech still served a predominantly local and regional population. Sixty-nine percent of the day students in 1928 were Pennsylvanians, mainly from Pittsburgh and Allegheny County, down from 90 percent in 1908. Two thirds of the day students and 94 percent of night students were male. All of the women students studied in Margaret Morrison and Fine Arts. Day students came from 42 states in addition to Pennsylvania, with the largest numbers from the central and northeast regions; an additional 31 students came from 17 foreign countries. Day students ranged in age from 16 to 32 and averaged 21.5 years old. They belonged to 37 religious groups, more than three-fourths Protestant, 15 percent Roman Catholic, 7 percent Jewish and a tiny scattering of adherents to the Russian, Greek and Serbian Orthodox faiths. A few children and grandchildren of immigrants from southern and eastern Europe had become Tech students. Few of them enrolled in the College of Science, but, if names provide an accurate measure, as many as 10 percent attended the night sessions of the School for Apprentices and Journeymen.

Students in the College of Engineering encountered a serious curricular problem. From the beginning the Carnegie Technical Schools required engineering students to enroll in a number of shop courses— wiring for electrical engineers and foundry work for civil engineers, for example. Then, as knowledge of technology grew during the first years of the century, faculty began to add one course after another in their specialties to the curriculum. By 1928 many engineering students faced a daunting array of required technical courses that crowded out study in the sciences, humanities and social sciences. Engineering reformers denounced this trend, arguing that engineering schools were training technologists rather than educating engineers who could solve problems and understand their societal implications. During the Depression that began in 1929, this situation became even more pressing. As industries closed, engineers trained in narrow specialties failed to find employment outside their fields. President Baker and his staff did not face the problems inherent in this situation.

Night and summer school students remained almost exclusively local, that is from Pittsburgh and western Pennsylvania. Night school students were both younger and older, ranging in age from 16 to 56 and averaging 23.2 years. The 210 high school students who attended Saturday morning classes in architecture, music, painting and decoration, and sculpture all lived in the Pittsburgh region, mainly in the city itself. Some of these Saturday classes for high school students still attracted hundreds of teenagers in the summer of 1999.

If the differences between the day and night school populations had changed at all since 1908, they had increased. Higher tuition which strained family budgets had kept many working class students from attending school except at night. Day students focused their attention on typical collegiate activities: their studies, football, fraternities, clubs and activities such as Campus Week. Since tuition for part-time study in the night school was less than full-time tuition in the day school and jobs demanding new skills were plentiful, the night school's enrollment increased

steadily. Night students who worked all day and attended class from two to five evenings a week had neither the time nor the money to play with their daytime classmates. Occasionally, however, they got together.

Admission standards changed for day school students in the fall of 1927. In previous years, Tech had admitted any graduate of a Pittsburgh high school who had maintained a C average. Tech required students from outside Pittsburgh to take entrance examinations, but the admissions office noticed that scores on exams taken at some high schools where proctoring was questionable were consistently higher than scores of students who took their exams at Tech. As a consequence, Tech changed to admission based partly on the new testing program organized by the College Entrance Examination Board, the now ubiquitous Scholastic Aptitude Tests.

Enrollment in Carnegie Institute of Technology 1927-28

	Day	Night	Total
College of Engineering	572	856	1428
College of Industries	384	2,460	2844
College of Fine Arts	662	514	1176
Margaret Morrison Carnegie College	519	0	519
Freshmen, Engineering & Industry	346	0	346
Part time	456	0	456
Summer	665	0	665
Total	**3604**	**3830**	**7434**

ENGLISH I Assignment, First Semester, 1928-29

Copy these sentences, correcting all mistakes of spelling, diction grammar and rhetoric.

1. Want to buy a jack-knife and cigar cutter if you have the two articles in stock. Send me also, like you always do, some kind of shaving soap for my bro. the M.D.

2. This examination isn't easy, but they were harder in chemistry. Thinking of each seperate correction which as to be made is harder than to write them down.

3. Coming into the room her large brown eyes were seen, and you noticed her pretty white teeth.

4. The Carnegie Institute of Technology is different than the University of Pittsburgh, it was founded in 1905 by Andrew Carnegie, one of the most benevolent of humans.

5. One should save their money for those kind of parties one could afford to have about once every fourty days.

6. The professor has so much temperament. Anyone might of thought he was an artist.

7. Having taken our seats, the proctor began passing out the blue books, like they always do at the examinations in February.

Student life complements academic activity

Student life for night students changed little between 1908 and 1928. Since almost all night students commuted from their homes to campus, most of them ignored much of campus life. Many commuters, however, began to arrive by automobiles instead of streetcars, provoking a parking crisis that, in the absence of sufficient parking lots, was worse than today's endemic problem. In October 1928 a new page devoted to the night school and called "The Carnegie Plaid" began to appear in *The Carnegie Tartan.* The Plaid announced that a *CIT Night Student Handbook* had just been published and carried stories about upcoming smokers, meetings of a new Night Students' Council, and a column of commentary.

nautical and automobile engineering kept pace with student demand in these two new professions. Stories about class reunions always reported a number of successful graduates enjoying outstanding careers.

Interest in students' physical welfare can serve as an example of changed administrative attitudes. By 1928, Tech had developed a well-established health service located in the gymnasium. By 1928 all freshmen and sophomores took required physical education courses three times weekly. An extensive intramural program matched teams from fraternities and men's dormitories in several sports: soccer, touch football, speedball and cross county in the fall; basketball, volleyball and handball in the winter; and baseball, track and tennis in the spring. Women's teams competed in field hockey, bowling, archery, volleyball and softball, and participated in both gymnastics and folk dancing. Finally, Tech fielded interscholastic teams in men's football, track, basketball, tennis and rifle. Women competed with other schools only in rifle, a sport in which they won national honors.

Left:
In 1928 women competed nationally only in rifle. The 1937 Women's Rifle Team is pictured here.

Right:
Medal from a 1928 track meet

Student life for day students changed radically during the two decades after 1908. The faculty's emphasis on intellectual and occupational development, already clear in 1908, increased. Both the faculty and the administration joined with students to organize honorary fraternities and clubs for chemical, civil, mechanical, industrial, metallurgical, mining and electrical engineers, printers, coal miners, social workers, women scientists, costume economists, household economists, secretaries, architects, musicians, journalists and ROTC members. New majors in aero-

In 1908, Tech had built an athletic field, the Tech Bowl, located in a hollow parallel to Woodlawn Avenue (now Margaret Morrison Street) and still in use in 1928. Although its crude stands were built with used lumber and football players complained that its surface changed from concrete in dry weather to a mud puddle in the rain, at least the team could practice there. Tech's gymnasium was far more satisfactory. The gym had basketball and volleyball courts, a large swimming pool, handball courts and offices for Tech's Health Services. The pool was open for recreational swimming for men three days a week and for women on two. Men and women swimming together? Shocking!

Religious, cultural and social events increase

The YMCA dominated religious and spiritual organizations. Brought by then Secretary Baker to the campus in 1921, it received funding from Student Council. The school provided a meeting room in the administration building. The YMCA offered Bible study classes and promoted weekly chapel meetings that Tech had organized beginning in 1922. Local clergymen conducted these services. St. Paul's Cathedral (Roman Catholic) and nine local Protestant churches advertised their services in the 1928 *Handbook.* No mention of the YWCA appeared in the *Handbook;* only the ad for St. Paul's Cathedral mentioned the Newman Club, a college organization for Roman Catholic students; not even a brief notice advertised services for Tech's 168 Jewish students.

Carnegie Tech and the Pittsburgh area provided a host of cultural opportunities to students in 1928. Neither the Drama nor the Music Departments charged entrance fees for plays and concerts. Nor did the neighboring Carnegie Institute charge to attend exhibitions of paintings and sculpture, some of which attracted internationally famous artists. Each year Tech presented scores of lectures by faculty and visiting scholars alike. *The Carnegie Tartan* kept students well informed about upcoming cultural events that they could partake of in abundance.

By 1928 the Drama Department had established a glowing national reputation.

Above:
The 1928 production of
Oh Imogene

It began in 1914 as one of the five departments of the School of Applied Design. Andrew Carnegie agreed to provide funds to erect a building and support a school that would offer baccalaureate degrees, house all the arts in a single building, be co-educational and develop a firm foundation in crafts, including theater crafts. Concerned about Carnegie's reaction to including in the building a theater to prepare actors and produce plays, Hornbostel labeled the Little Theater a Dramatic Laboratory on his blueprints. When Hornbostel later led Carnegie onto the stage to face a cheering audience of students, he remarked, "So that's the dramatic laboratory," waving toward the finest little theater of the time as he did so.

Hornbostel, the consulting dean of the school, and Russell Hewlett, its director, invited Thomas Ward Stevens to become the Drama Department's first head. He faced a difficult challenge—to create where no precedents existed a fully accredited college course leading to a baccalaureate degree that included both scientific and cultural studies in addition to theatrical work. Some of the nation's leading actors, playwrights and critics—including Otis Skinner who visited in 1928 —cheered the effort. The two principles upon which the Department was founded were soon in place. First, every student

received a thorough grounding in every aspect of theater: costumes, stage design, lighting, dramatic literature, voice, movement, etc. Second, every student must have direct experience as an actor on the stage. These principles remain in force today. As they did in 1928, they help to explain why drama graduates, in addition to distinguished careers on the stage, in film and television, formed equally notable careers in community theater and academia.

By 1928, students had four major hangouts in and around campus on which to focus their informal social life. The Morrises' tobacco shop, now with snacks and sundries, on Forbes; Skibo on Woodlawn Avenue; The Beanery, a cafeteria in the old Langley Aeronautical Building; and the Carnegie Inn, formerly the Field House across Woodlawn Avenue from Skibo. Old grads remember all of these places as the sites of perpetual bridge games played with cards sticky with grease from hamburgers and french fries. Many a romance began in these storied hangouts, some of the few places on campus shared by men and women.

Dormitories and fraternity houses provided another focus for social life. The seven Hill Dorms along Woodlawn Avenue housed male students, while 11 dorms, located in renovated houses, mainly along Forbes Street and Woodlawn

Above right:
The Alpha Tau Omega fraternity house

Below:
Tech men gathered on dormitory steps.

Avenue, catered to women who were closely supervised by housemothers. About a third of the daytime male students lived in 19 fraternity houses scattered in residential neighborhoods around Oakland and Squirrel Hill. They provoked a constant series of complaints about noise and—even during this prohibition period—about alcohol from local residents. None of the four women's sororities had houses. No Tech publication censured fraternities and sororities for discriminating against Jews, African-Americans and, less vigorously, Catholics, common practice on most campuses during this period.

About one third of male daytime students belonged to fraternities in 1928. Fraternity members dominated student life: student government offices, athletic teams, intramural sports, publications, Campus Week, the buggy races—almost everything. In 1912, Theta Xi had chartered a local fraternity, the Kappa Gamma Club, the first national fraternity to be recognized on campus. By 1928 the number of national fraternities had increased to 19 and commandeered 40 pages to describe themselves in *The Thistle,* Tech's yearbook. When established fraternities discriminated against them, Jews and Catholics established fraternities of their own. An Interfraternity Council loosely supervised rushing, pledging, initiation and the recognition of new organizations as well as acting as a liaison with the administration.

A long contest for control between the fraternities and the administration broke out in 1925. Spring Carnival, rushing and Hell Week lay at the heart of the controversy. Fraternities had sponsored an annual Migratory Dance during which participants moved from one fraternity house to another throughout a long and noisy evening of music, dancing, drinking and general gaiety. The issue came to a head in 1928.

In the past, fraternities had begun to rush students as soon as school opened and to involve freshmen in a constant round of parties and receptions, many of them generously supplied with illegal alcoholic drinks. Then came Hell Week when the brothers put their pledges through an endless round of high jinks and petty tasks, often dangerous to life and limb, both on and off campus. In addition, as soon as pledges were installed, they abandoned campus housing to move into frat houses, producing a serious financial problem for the housing office.

The administration appointed a Special Committee on the Conservation of Freshmen (an intriguing choice of words) to investigate these practices. Rushing had traditionally taken place during the first few weeks of the academic year. Many incoming freshmen spent their nights on a round of fraternity visits where they were feted and wooed. Then during Hell Week pledges did nothing except what their future brothers demanded. Alarmed at the high freshman failure rate, the administration ordered the fraternities to conduct rush after mid-semester exams of the first semester instead of at the beginning. This experiment took place in 1927 to the dismay of fraternity membership. In a letter to the Executive Board, the Inter-fraternity Council complained that the academic standing of upperclassmen had suffered though this new arrangement and that fraternities had spent far too much

time and money as they wooed new members. In response, the Executive Board pointed out that freshman grade point averages had improved substantially and that the scholarship of only half of the fraternities had suffered. Upper-class members, the board added, had been given two years to plan for the new arrangement and should have been able to control their expenditures. The board held firm. Financial problems for fraternities became acute after 1929 when the Depression reduced fraternity membership from 500 to 350. By the 1940s only 12 fraternities remained.

Campus Weaker—"What kind of lipstick is that?"
Campus Weakest—"Kissproof!"
Campus Weaker—"Well, take it off. We've got work to do!"

Fraternity paddle probably used on pledges' bottoms during Hell Week

The 1927-28 *Student Handbook,* a 101 page pamphlet small enough to fit into a man's inside jacket pocket, listed a wide variety of social and professional organizations. They included the Men's Glee Club, Women's Glee Club, Kiltie Band, C Club for men who had won an athletic letter, Citmas Club composed of members of the Masonic Order, Western Association for students from western states, Sine Nomine Club for men chosen for trustworthiness and good character, Non-Degree Association for students in non-degree programs, Technon Club for students interested in the discussion of Christian principles, Inter-Collegiate Cosmopolitan Club composed of both foreign and American students from Tech and Pitt, clubs for printers, coal miners and societies of chemical, civil, mechanical, industrial, metallurgical, mining and electrical engineers. This array of clubs offered a rich choice of social organizations for most students.

Petty Exclusiveness

The recent action of the Interfraternity Council of excluding dormitory men from the migratory dance, on the surface of things, is the most flagrant display of would-be exclusiveness that has occurred in Carnegie's fraternal history. It is true that the migratory is, strictly speaking, a fraternity affair, but it has come to be a part of Campus Week and it should remain such. Everyone who is eligible to attend Campus Week affairs should likewise be eligible for the migratory. Dormitory men have rarely if ever been the responsible parties for any undesirable happenings at the migratory. If there were any such unfortunate affairs, they were almost invariably caused by fraternity men of the Rah-Rah variety.
—*The Carnegie Tartan,* April 24, 1928

Top:
1929 dance card

Bottom:
Girls from the Forbes Street
dormitories, 1929

Clubs directed women toward expected roles

Most of the women's clubs had different goals. Margaret Morrison's dean banished women's social sororities from campus in 1918, arguing that they were undemocratic and kept the non-sorority girl from participating in the full range of campus activities. Clubs for women included a philanthropic organization The Guild, the Social Workers, Costume Economics, Household Economics, Secretarial and Science Clubs and the YWCA. Dean Mary Bidwell Breed organized a women's honorary society, Mortar Board, and encouraged women to become involved in charitable endeavors, reflecting a role women were expected to assume once they graduated and became housewives.

Margaret Morrison deans carefully supervised the morals of their students in 1928. They took *in loco parentis* seriously. Housemothers in women's dormitories scrupulously enforced curfews and forbade men to enter the dorms. Dean Breed, alarmed that "undesirable women" had been seen on campus when soldiers were there during World War I, had asked President Hamerschlag to forbid soldiers to trespass on Margaret Morrison grounds in order to make certain that no man in uniform made inappropriate advances to female students. Imagine the reactions of housemothers and deans if they could return to today's campus with its co-ed dorms, unrestricted dress and general belief in the equality of the sexes.

The social calendar

The Student Handbook also provided a social calendar for the academic year. It listed one reception, one smoker, a concert, Campus Week, a "Gambol of the Guilds" and 14 dances. The handbook also sternly advised freshmen to observe all the regulations for entering students published in the handbook and described Freshman Week, a compulsory session held before the beginning of classes to help incoming students adjust to college life.

Juniors and seniors complained in *The Carnegie Tartan* that sophomores failed to enforce these regulations to the letter and bewailed the lack of school spirit indicated by such irresponsible behavior. Sophomores pointed out in response that the freshman class included a large number of very big football players; they hesitated to accost these particular freshmen for infractions such as forgetting to wear a dink, missing an assembly, speaking to a member of the opposite sex or failing to say "hello." Freshman hazing was on its way out.

By 1927 a baker's dozen of student activities had become established on campus. In 1920 Alumni Secretary Gilmore L. Tilbrook conceived the idea of Campus Week, a three-day homecoming celebration in May designed to attract alumni to campus. Before 1920, students, led by Margaret Morrison girls, had celebrated May Day.

Surprising what the Maggie Murphs of 1918 would do. For May Day we needed 40 barrel hoops which we located on Carson Street on the South Side. Two of us set out to get them. It had to be a streetcar job—what else? We chose off hours in the morning to go, but had to take three different trolleys to Tech. The conductors were all amazing—they just laughed and gave us the rear platforms and a bit of assistance. When we got off at Margaret Morrison Street there was plenty of help—and hoop rolling too. How times have changed!
—Florence Bechtel Whitwell, MM'18

Tilbrook asked students to plan a new type of entertainment for 1920 and, with a wave of an energetic, youthful student wand, they transformed Campus Week into an undergraduate event that soon got so out of hand that faculty began to call it Campus Month.

The faculty and administration cracked down after the 1928 Campus Week. Celebrations began with a Migratory Dance during which students "migrated" from one fraternity house to another on Wednesday night. The Campus Week program listed a "vodvil" show, men's and women's athletic events, men's and women's sweepstakes, an ROTC review, a Campus Week student show, a carnival, a cabaret dance, a Queen's Coronation ceremony and ball, and a variety of banquets and lunches. Planning and preparations for these events consumed weeks of labor during which academics suffered severely. Senior final examinations came two weeks later, often with disastrous results. In dismay, the faculty decided to cancel Campus Week entirely in 1929. It emerged again in 1930 as a two-day celebration eventually called Spring Carnival.

Maggie Murphs recall:
Dean of Women, Mary Watson Green issued two directives to all women students:
1) Girls are not to wear bifurcate garments (slacks, shorts, culottes etc.) on campus, and
2) Carnegie Tech women are not to sing that popular song "All of Me, Why Not Take All of Me?"
—Silvia Sconza Schmidt, A'34

When we were freshmen in 1927, Margaret Morrison maintained a Milk Bar in the basement. The names of all underweight (skinny, slender?) MMCC freshmen girls were put on the bulletin board Milk List; we were required to drink a glass of milk each morning at a designated time. So we paid for the milk and we drank it. What a laugh for students of today!
—Gertrude Novak Kemper, MM'32

In my day all the freshmen had to wear dinks. As if they couldn't tell we were new on campus! And tea dances in the afternoons so that girls and boys could meet one another. And housemothers—a shoulder to cry on when the first semester grades came out, and you got your first D ever. Well, we did grow up and survive; on graduation day we donned our caps and gowns proudly and after graduation looked forward to our first job. With me it was off to Joseph Horne Co. with high expectations.
—Doris P. McCleery, MM'28

Top:
Attendants of the Campus Week Queen, circa 1924

Bottom:
1928 Campus Week program

**Tech footballers down both Pitt
and Notre Dame—twice each**

In 1928 Tech defeated both Pitt and Notre Dame in football. The Notre Dame story begins in 1926. Knute Rockne, legendary coach of the Irish, preferred to scout the Army/Navy game in Chicago rather than accompany his team to Pittsburgh to play Tech. To the surprise of the entire nation, Tech won the game by a score of 19 to 0. The campus—indeed all of Pittsburgh—celebrated boisterously as the Kiltie Band paraded through the streets of Oakland, touching off an extended celebration. The Irish team returned home licking its wounds and vowing to exact vengeance when Tech appeared at South Bend two years later. In the meantime, Tech senior tackle and student body president Lloyd (Bulldog) Yoder, (A'27) won All-American honors in the spring.

The victory over Notre Dame attracted an influx of big, talented, freshman football players to campus in the fall of 1927. Alumni had launched a recruiting drive and provided scholarship funds.

No one defeated the Plebes in 1927. By 1928 under the leadership of its distinguished coach Wally Steffen, Tech was ready to compete for the national championship, led by Howard Harpster, its slight (six foot, 150 pound) senior quarterback, and seven sophomore starters fresh from their undefeated Plebe season. After three warm-up victories over small schools, Tech defeated four of the 1920s perennial football powers: Washington and Jefferson (19-0), Pitt (6-0), Georgetown (13-0), and Notre Dame (27-7) on successive Saturdays.

Above left:
Howard Harpster (A'30), All-American quarterback, played on the Tartan team that defeated Notre Dame in 1926 and 1928.

Above right:
Irene Tedrow (A'29) and friends wear men's cheerleader coats backwards.

Right:
Carnegie Tech beat Notre Dame in football to the surprise of the entire nation.

The nation's newspapers heralded the victory over the Irish. As it always did, Notre Dame had started its second string, expecting Tech to collapse when the first team trotted menacingly onto the field. Instead Tech scored two touchdowns in eight minutes against the first-stringers—the second and third touchdowns scored against the powerful Notre Dame team all year—and ended the game in the fourth quarter when Howard Harpster added two drop kicks for field goals. The victory at Notre Dame marked the first loss the Irish suffered at home in 23 years. But the drive for an undefeated season, a Rose Bowl bid, and a national championship fell when a battered and bruised Tech 11 lost to an inspired New York University team in the final game of the year. Harpster's election to the All-American team provided only a little solace.

In other interscholastic sports, Tech's men had a mixed record in 1928, posting winning seasons in rifle matches (24-3), cross country (4-0), and tennis (5-2) while losing in basketball (3-13), track (0-4), and swimming (1-6). Its only women's inter-scholastic team, rifle, had a distinguished record of 19 wins and two losses and captured third place in the nation in the National Rifle Association's Intercollegiate match. Despite this impressive record, Tech's athletic board refused to award these women athletes their varsity letters, even though members of the men's rifle team had won them. During the 1930s, Tech's women's rifle team won the national championship three times. Tech's success in rifle competition developed from coaching by ROTC officers and the presence of an indoor rifle range in the basement of Margaret Morrison, providing year-round practice facilities for Tech teams.

Sweepstakes, or buggy, began in 1920 as a major feature of Campus Week. Students designed the early buggies for pageantry rather than competition.

Originally each team included a driver and a single pusher. They changed positions halfway through the race at a "pit stop" where they switched rear wheels in order to demonstrate their mechanical ability. To speed up the race, organizers abandoned the pit stop in 1921. By 1928 the competition included judging the buggies for design and engineering and eliminating the humorous entries of early years, and the race had assumed many of its present features: preliminary heats that reduced the finals to a manageable number, a fifth pusher, and the present course up Tech Street, through Schenley Park and up Frew Street. In 1929, independent organizations, that is non-fraternities, were invited to compete.

Women's sweepstakes pitted representatives of women's dormitories against each other. *The Carnegie Tartan* described in detail the secrecy in which these contestants and their supporters made costumes in the Margaret Morrison sewing labs for the race. The course ran through the campus. Each contestant, suitably attired, sat astride a kiddie car, propelling it with her feet. Today tiny women students lying face down inside drive the buggies for both the men's and women's sweepstakes.

Tech girls sit astride kiddie cars in 1924.

CAMPUS WEEK

This page counterclockwise
from top right:
Campus Week buggy, 1925
Campus Week entrance, 1925
Coronation ceremonies, 1925
The Burial of the Plebe
Regulations, circa 1920

Our Fifth Anniversary

No one knew five years ago just how the Campus Week idea would finally develop. It was only an idea—one based on a need which had been felt for a long time by both students and those in charge of alumni affairs—a need to establish a closer bond between alumni and their Alma Mater, the students and the faculty. There was no precedent which could be followed. Other colleges have reunions, but something new and unique was wanted, something distinctly "Carnegie." The original committee performed a great deal of planning and preparing for the first Campus Week celebration. This celebration had to be a success or little hope could be held out for its repetition as an annual affair.
—*The Carnegie Alumnus*, June 1924

Re: Campus Week

In his letter of December 7, 1928, A.W. Tarbell, Chairman, Committee on Student Activities of the Executive Board informed John C. Stauffer, President, Day Student Council CIT, that Campus Week was to be discontinued.

. . . . The teaching staff of the institution, through the General Faculty, at its meeting on May 15, 1928, went formally on record as opposed to the continuation of Campus Week. For several years there had been an increasing dissatisfaction over the interference with the scholastic schedule and work caused by this occasion. Apart from the two and a half days in which all classes were suspended, the work of the entire institution had been slighted to a considerable extent in advance of the event, and an excessive number of absences occurred for several days prior to the event, while preparations were being made. In addition there had been a noticeable drop in concentration for a week afterwards. Because Campus Week took place one week prior to the final examinations taken by seniors, and less than two weeks prior to the examinations for all other students, some departments found it useless to attempt any new work after Campus Week and were compelled to devote the time to reviewing. . . .

This page counterclockwise from top right:

Kappa Sigma buggy, circa 1920

Campus Week float, circa 1920

Geisha Girls, 1923

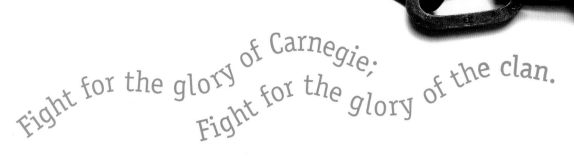

Fight for the glory of Carnegie; Fight for the glory of the clan.

Above:
From 1908 until World War II,
a new link was welded to the
Class Chain for each entering class.

Opposite page top:
Pin securing a Kiltie's sash

Opposite page bottom:
The Kiltie Band parades (no date)

The Fence, the Chain, & the Kiltie Band

Tech students in 1928 inherited the Senior Fence from the class of 1923. In 1922, the Student Senate appropriated $75 for materials and $60 for labor to construct the fence in front of what is now Doherty Hall. A locust tree contributed six stout posts about 12 inches in diameter, connected over the fence's 49 foot length by eight-inch-square fir beams. The student construction crew carved their names on the fence and assorted other carvings appeared from time to time, but by 1928 no one had painted it entirely. Seniors claimed the fence as private property. In a letter to the *Carnegie Alumnus,* Hugh Sprinkle (E'23) told students and alumni alike that the fence should be "kept as a reminder of the greatness that is the senior and of the vast gulf lying between him and the underclassmen." Seniors forbade all underclassmen to sit on the fence and found intriguing ways to punish any who did. Tech men and Maggie Murph women often met there, particularly when springtime fostered romantic liaisons.

The entering class in 1928 also inherited the Class Chain. In 1915, John S. Taylor, the head instructor in the forge shop, dressed as Vulcan, welded a short chain composed of one link for each class beginning in 1908. In an imposing ceremony, he forged a new link for the entering class. By 1927-28 the custom was well established. Freshmen gathered to see a new link forged, and seniors rallied around to see their graduating year stamped onto their link. This tradition ended during World War II when the forge shop was dismantled. The chain, now in the University Archives, awaits some imaginative students or alumni to forge new links to Carnegie Mellon's storied past.

This ceremony took place during Campus Week at the Qualification Day exercises. Two events in addition to the ceremonies with the chain took place. First, the presidents of honorary societies called the names of seniors who had been voted to membership, a coveted honor among talented students. The second ceremony was less academic, but far more fun. Freshmen who had suffered throughout the year from the indignities of hazing threw their freshman handbooks into a coffin, bore it through the campus, and buried it, symbolizing that they were now full citizens of Carnegie Tech.

Dear Old Tech

Tune: "Dear Old Moonlight"

8

Words by
JACK CAMERON, '15
HOWARD CORNWALL, '17

in the bounds of Schen-ley, 'Mid
the field of glo-ry, We

By 1928 the Kiltie Band had a 20-year history. It began in 1908 when seven students got together to make some noise at football games on four cornets, two alto horns and a bass horn. By 1911 a full marching band had become a recognized student activity supported by the student activity fee. Then in 1920 drum major Luther J. Morris (I'23) spent his own money to dress himself in kilts and a giant bearskin headgear to the delight of students and alumni alike. Within two years, the student senate had raised $3,000 to purchase outfits for the entire band. In all its regalia, it appeared at the 1922 Notre Dame game held at Forbes Field near the Tech campus. By 1928 the bandmaster faced a difficult annual problem: how to keep clean, polished and together more then 50 uniforms each with 11 pieces—kilt, tunic, plaid, sporran, hose tops, garters, spats, belt, Glengarry, belt buckle and plaid buckle. His struggle was worth the effort when the Tech band marched triumphantly through Oakland in the fall of 1928 to celebrate victories over both Pitt and Notre Dame.

Down the streets of Oakland they marched playing "Dear Old Tech" and "Fight for the Glory of Carnegie." John A. Cameron (E'15) wrote the chorus of "Dear Old Tech" during a trip to West Virginia with the Glee and Mandolin Clubs and set them to the tune of "Dear Old Moonlight." Howard L. Cornwall (I'17) helped him with the verses, and the full song was introduced to the campus at the home concert of the Carnegie Musical Clubs in 1915. Sophomores required every entering freshman in 1927 to learn the words to both the verses and the chorus.

They also learned the stirring football fight song, "Fight for the Glory of Carnegie." It originated in the old Building Bureau in 1922 when Henry Hornbostel and his draftsmen were

designing the new gymnasium. Four of the draftsmen, all graduates of the class of 1921, broke the tension by picking out tunes on a washtub and three tin whistles. Out of this cacophony emerged an idea for a song. Robert W. Schmertz (A'21) did the band arrangement, and Edward F. "Sully" Sullivan directed its first presentation at half time of the football game with Geneva College in the Tech Bowl. By 1928 the heart of every loyal Tech student and alumnus beat proudly when the band struck up the tune, and the words floated with the breeze across the football field and down the streets of Oakland.

Freshmen in 1927 were also required to learn the words of the "Alma Mater." They had been written by Charles Jay Taylor, a painting and design professor, in 1913, and set to the tune of the Austrian national anthem. No one then or now pretends to understand some of the lyrics: "Gypsy tide and toiling shore" is perhaps the densest example. Mysterious or not, freshmen in 1927 learned all three verses of the "Alma Mater" during freshman week without complaint, at least in the hearing of upperclassmen.

Dear Old Tech

Within the bounds of Schenley,
Mid flower, bush, and tree,
Stands Carnegie, Stands Carnegie.
It towers tall and stately—
No others can I see
Than Carnegie, than Carnegie
Loyal sons with hearts so true and tender
Vie with one another to defend her,
Honor Truth and Friendship
All unite to be
Our Carnegie—Our Carnegie!

Chorus
Dear Old Tech—Carnegie Tech;
It's the best of all the schools I ever knew.
Dear Old Tech—Carnegie Tech:
Where every single fellow is true blue,
and the girls too.
When I go a strolling out thru Schenley
Tech's the only place that takes my eye,
And when I'm far away from Pittsburgh,
I'll remember you Tech till I die.

THE FENCE

The President's Daughter

It used to be the custom of upper-classmen, mainly sophomores, to lurk at the Senior Fence and think up things for freshmen to do. One after-noon I was going to cross the Cut on my way home. The assembled sophomores "suggested" that I carry the books of a female student that was coming across the Cut from Fine Arts. These sophomores knew her; I didn't. During our walk across the Cut, I learned that she was Vera Doherty, the daughter of CIT's President.

—Joe Cameron, E' 41

Students rub the nose of this 1928 bas relief of President Hamerschlag for good luck.

Newcomers learned these songs during Freshman Week. For five days before the start of classes, entering freshmen in 1927 met together on campus to prepare themselves for college life, get settled and acquainted, and complete requirements for entrance and registration. All freshmen took part in song and cheer practices under the watchful eyes of upperclassmen, ever alert for a slacker or scoffer. They also learned about how to behave in contests with the sophomores scheduled for the beginning days of school. On a more serious note, freshman week illustrates a new interest in student welfare, a by-product of the work of Tech's deans of men and women. No longer would incoming students be left to seek their own ways.

In the fall of 1928, Tech unveiled a bas relief of President Arthur A. Hamer-schlag in the entryway to Administration Hall (now Baker Hall). It soon became a student icon. Some anonymous, quaking student rubbed Hamerschlag's nose before a particularly difficult exam. Naturally, he aced it. Elated by this story of easy success, students began to fall in line to pass their fingers over Hamerschlag's bronze nostrils. To this day the nose of the bas relief shines brightly amid the dull bronze of the rest of the sculpture. According to believers, rubbing the nose inevitably produces high grades. Students who have rubbed and failed anyway are clearly skeptics, advocates argue. True believers in Hamerschlag magic succeed;

the insincere and skeptical justifiably fail. No one knows how to test this fragment of student lore. Credit 1928 students for this intriguing campus custom.

Student government organizations supervised most of these activities. In 1928 a single Student Council run by an annually elected Student Senate and class officers managed matters requiring joint action of the entire student body. The council allocated the student activities fee of $15 and decided what organizations received funds. For many years they gave two thirds of the money to support athletics, particularly the football team. An Evening Student Council performed similar functions for night students. Although Tech's Executive Board held veto rights over Student Council decisions, the board had never exercised that right by 1928.

Sadly—at least according to the editors of Form, a new 1928 publication of fine arts students—no Beaux Arts Ball was held in 1928. The ball had become an annual event in the Fine Arts college starting in 1914. Each ball committee chose a theme—the Bacchanalian Revel, the Court of Charlemagne, the Slavonic Ball, and the Norse Ball, etc. Each year the ball became more and more elaborate. The committee decorated the entire Fine Arts Building, made elaborate costumes in keeping with the year's theme, imported big-name bands, provided elaborate refreshments and even sponsored a post-ball dance open to the entire campus on the night after the ball in order to defray expenses, expenses that increased steadily as revelers damaged the Fine Arts Building. The curse of bigness inevitably meant higher ticket prices and larger deficits. The huge deficit produced by the 1927 ball, Revels of the Russians, was the final straw. The ball was canceled in 1928 and not revived until 1933.

Alumni continue tradition

By 1928 Tech's alumni, although concentrated in western Pennsylvania, had spread throughout the nation. Alumni organizations for the various colleges had been established beginning with the Charter Class of 1908 and brought together into a General Alumni Association in 1912, reorganized as the Carnegie Alumni Federation in 1919. In order to support itself, the association charged dues of $3 per year. After 1914, paid-up members began to receive copies of a new publication, the *The C.I.T. Alumnus.* By 1928 men's and a few women's clans had sprung up in almost 30 cities from New York to Los Angeles. The alumni secretary visited most of them in 1928, encouraging them to contribute to the drive to raise the $4 million needed to match the 1946 grant from the Carnegie Corporation. By 1928, the Alumni Federation had a page in each issue of *The Carnegie Tartan.* It carried general news about Tech and accounts of the activities of Carnegie Clans.

Members of the Alumni Association placed the first of a series of bronze plates in the floor at the entrance to Administration Hall (Baker Hall) at Homecoming in October 1928. Members of the Charter Class of 1908 had gathered for their 20th class reunion to be feted at a lunch with President Baker and a banquet and dance at the Webster Hall Hotel. On Saturday morning, members of the Charter Class cemented a plate, four times as large as the others, into place along with smaller plates, each the size of a floor tile, for every succeeding class. The Alumni Federation intended to have each class install a plate when reunions were held. The tradition ended temporarily in 1973, but it was revived in 1989 following the recommendation of alumnus Dan Corbett (HS'86). Each year at homecoming alumni install a new tile, a welcome tie to Carnegie Mellon's distinguished past.

In retrospect

By 1928 the Carnegie Institute of Technology was abandoning its trade school roots. It had become an institute of technology that included a College of Fine Arts with a rapidly growing national reputation. In addition to two-year certificates and three-year diplomas, it awarded both bachelor's and master's degrees at the 1928 commencement to students in its three colleges. Thirty-one percent of its students came from outside Pennsylvania, although more than half of its students—almost all Pittsburghers—continued to attend school in the evening and were not degree candidates. A number of viable student traditions had begun to flourish. Both the student body and the faculty were markedly homogeneous, although less so than they had been two decades previously. A significant number of faculty had become involved in research projects or creative activities. Interdisciplinary research characterized many of these efforts. A remarkable football team had spread Carnegie Tech's name over the nation's sport pages. An Alumni Federation had begun to function in major cities. The campus boasted six handsome, major buildings and a score or so of less imposing structures. Cut loose from its moorings in Andrew Carnegie and the Carnegie Corporation to which he left most of his fortune, the institution stood on its own feet, although its trustees still focused their attention on the Carnegie Institute, for which they were also responsible. Beamed down in 1928, contemporary students and faculty members might dimly recognize the shadowy ancestor of today's University.

Bronze plates in the floor at the entrance to Administration Hall (now Baker Hall)

CARNEGIE CORPORATION
OF NEW YORK
522 FIFTH AVENUE
NEW YORK
18, N.Y.

OFFICE OF THE PRESIDENT

Mr. William Frew
    Chairman of the Board
Carnegie Institute of Technology
Pittsburgh 13, Penna.

Dear Mr. Frew

al gran   condition-
five yea   on twenty-
met the   Technology
and scien   to youth
grant was   upon which this

and his fac   congratulations to Dr. Doherty
what has already been done and confidence
in still gr   er achievements to come, I transmit this check
for $8,000,000.

    This gift for endowment is of a kind which
Carnegie Corporation made often in the past but which has now
been displaced by other patterns of giving. Fortunately, the
Pittsburgh community by subscribing $4,000,000 has not only met
the conditions attached to this grant but has given promise of
continuing support that will guarantee the preeminence which
Carnegie Tech deserves.

                           Sincerely yours

                           Devereux C. Josephs

6.

Robert E. Doherty 1936–1950
He laid the foundations for a new Carnegie Tech and for Carnegie Mellon University

Carnegie Tech was in the doldrums when Robert E. Doherty became its third president in March 1936 in the midst of the great Depression. What an inauspicious moment! Three years later, World War II (1939-1945) broke out. In these troubled times, Tech faced one financial crisis after another. Doherty brought with him a superb preparation for leadership: a clear vision of what technical education ought to be, a firm commitment to promote both graduate education and research and a marked administrative ability. To meet his goals, he was forced to raise money and to reform the entire institution. His life had been a continuous preparation to achieve these ambitious goals.

Robert Doherty learned mostly on the job

Robert Doherty grew up in Clay City, a rural community in Illinois, in a family that included seven siblings. For many years, Clay City had neither electricity nor a telegraph office, and the first electric lights in the community intrigued Doherty enough to suggest a career. By the time he entered high school, he had built his own successful telegraph instrument. In his spare time he began to hang around the Baltimore and Ohio station to learn telegraphy. After graduating from high school he took a job as a telegrapher with the B&O for a salary of $45 a month for a 12-hour night shift. Andrew Carnegie, who learned telegraphy as an unpaid apprentice after a 12-hour workday, would have approved.

Since the Clay City schools left him unprepared for college, Doherty used his earnings as a telegrapher to finance a year in a prep school and then at the age of 21 entered the University of Illinois as a freshman, aiming for a degree in electrical engineering. During that freshman year, he was inspired by a lecture by Charles Steinmetz, the electrical genius from the General Electric Company in Schenectady. Upon graduation he joined the GE staff. On a memorable Saturday, he screwed up his courage and called on Steinmetz at his home. The two men liked each other immediately and began to meet every Saturday.

Opposite page:
The $8,000,000 check from Carnegie Corporation was given to President Doherty by Devereus C. Josephs in September 1946.

1936

- Doherty becomes president.
- The Alumni Federation is organized.

95

Steinmetz had emigrated from Germany in 1889 to escape persecution for his activities as a socialist and became a leader of progressive engineers soon after he went to work at GE's new laboratories in 1892. Committed to a view of the engineer as a societal reformer, he became the most prominent member of a group of progressive engineering reformers called the Technical Alliance. By 1921 the Alliance had dissolved and its members turned to less expansive plans more in keeping with American mores.

As a good mentor should, Steinmetz helped his protégé learn how to define problems and identify the principles that could be applied to solve them. Impressed by Doherty's keen, curious mind, Steinmetz made him his assistant in 1918, a position in which he served until Steinmetz's death in 1923. For the next eight years, Doherty was a full-time consulting engineer with GE. In his new position, he came in contact with hundreds of young engineers, an experience that convinced him that colleges and universities failed to help students learn problem-solving techniques. To help young engineers at GE learn problem solving, he organized an "Advanced Course in Engineering" given one full morning each week. Herein lies one seed of the Carnegie Plan. While involved in these activities, Doherty earned an M.S. from Union College. He never earned a Ph.D. degree.

Doherty's commitment to society also developed during his years at General Electric. He served for a year as mayor of the village of Scotia where he lived and for three additional years as a school board member. In addition, he led a boy scout troop for many years. This involvement in society prepared him to play a vital role with Richard K. Mellon in the development of the Pittsburgh Renaissance.

When the depression began to take a serious toll on GE's engineers, Doherty accepted an offer to become head of the Department of Electrical Engineering at Yale. Two years later, he was appointed Dean of Engineering and set out to develop the kind of analytical engineering education he had pioneered at GE. He organized two courses in electrical engineering. The first focused on problem solving in order to develop a student's creative, analytical powers. The second, taught by a professor of history, required each student to research and present a full-scale investigation of a humanistic or social problem. He failed, however, in an attempt to develop an "industrial engineering" program at Yale, an effort that predisposed him to support the concepts underlying Tech's School of Industrial Administration. Then in 1936 when Doherty was 51, Carnegie Tech gave him an opportunity to guide an entire educational institution toward the fulfillment of his vision by becoming its third president. His career had fully prepared him for his new responsibilities.

Both Hamerschlag and Baker had widespread experience in secondary schools. That experience weighed heavily in their appointments and conditioned their policies. Doherty had no background in either trade or preparatory schools. Instead he had worked in industry and been a dean at Yale, so he saw Carnegie Tech in a different light from his predecessors. Wisely, rather than impose on Tech a ready-made program for reform, he spent much of his first 15 months on campus finding out what Tech was like, developing and publicizing his plans, and taking a few steps to implement them.

1937

• Doherty launches the Carnegie Plan of Professional Education.

Doherty demonstrates his ability as a planner and leader

Most of the seeds of today's Carnegie Mellon University—an internationally renowned research institution—were sown during the Doherty administration. In 1936, with the exception of several engineering departments, the Drama and Architecture Departments, research in four laboratories, and a football team, Tech's reputation extended only a few miles beyond the three rivers that defined Pittsburgh's landscape. Doherty set the institution, particularly its engineering departments, on paths that steadily led it to its present excellent reputation. He began by making a careful study of the institution, developing plans to reform it, and publicizing these plans in his Annual Reports for 1936 and 1937. The 1937 report outlined his plans succinctly:

1938

• Tech loses to Texas Christian in the Sugar Bowl.

Robert E. Doherty Named New President

In spite of published rumors to the contrary there won't be any drastic upheavals in the educational policies of Carnegie when Robert E. Doherty succeeds Dr. Thomas S. Baker as president of the institution. Mr. Doherty looks forward to his new duties "with excitement."

In an interview with your *Tartan* correspondent, the new president made himself definite that, "Matters of policy will be reviewed with the faculty." He deplored any uncompromising attitude between faculty and administration and added, "It is a fundamental fallacy, in my opinion, to assume that the basic interests of the faculty and Institute are antagonistic to each other."

Mr. Doherty, 51, partly bald, and possessing a quiet manner has been connected with educational work since 1931. In 1932 he was appointed Dean of the Engineering School of Yale University. "I'm a little green as a professor," he confesses.

Dean Doherty intends to have the best possible program at Tech. There will be no sacrificing the interests of undergraduates to those of research or graduate study.

—*The Tartan*, March 3, 1936

DOHERTY'S PLANS FOR CARNEGIE TECH

The fundamental thoughts which inform our educational policy are clearly defined objectives for every program and improved quality in all we do. These settle certain other questions of policy and of the budget. They mean that with present resources.... we should stick to the three general fields now represented by our Colleges, eliminate those courses and activities not pointed directly toward the objectives set by the Colleges, improve those that remain, and add new ones and new facilities required in the reconstructed plan. They mean restricting enrollment to a point where our facilities are adequate to our purposes, thus to about 2,000 undergraduates in the three Colleges. They mean placing our faculty in. . . . the position of having reasonably adequate time for rest, recreation, and self improvement, a feeling of reasonable financial security, freedom of intellectual pursuit, and a greater voice in the councils of the institution.

There must be less stress; a reduction must be made in the intensity of scheduled work.... (S)tudents must have less (sic) scheduled hours per day. This is to be accomplished by (1) a reduction of the total schedule, (2) Saturday morning classes, (3) one six-weeks summer session for engineering students.... We must also reduce the load on the instructors. We want smaller numbers in classes and fewer classes per instructor, and this means both restricted enrollment and an increase in the number of instructors.

There are two other noteworthy aspects of general policy. One relates to the place of scientific research. The three programs—undergraduate, graduate, and research —are essential components of a balanced plan of higher learning.... The other relates to the future development of the campus. We should work out a plan that would assure to us ultimately a campus of simple dignity and beauty and the most efficient use of our limited space.... The general educational policy stated above has especial significance in the College of Engineering.

1940

• Nine fraternities agree to move into housing on campus.

1942

• Enrollment drops as U.S. enters World War II.

Most of the plans Doherty advanced came to fruition during his years as president, a tribute to his analytical powers and to his administrative skills. Insufficient finances stood in the way, however. The Baker administration had developed substantial reserves, but hard times clearly lay ahead. Despite an increase in endowment under Baker of $1.7 million, diminished return on investments had reduced annual income from the endowment by $50,000 since 1922. Faculty salaries had been maintained throughout the Baker administration, but in 1937 the faculty petitioned its new president for across-the-board faculty raises. Engineering deans pointedly asked for expanded budgets for equipment and new facilities. In addition, less than one tenth of the $4 million required to obtain the two-for-one matching grant of $8 million from the Carnegie Corporation had been raised during the Baker years. Finally, Doherty had ambitious plans for projects in undergraduate education, new graduate programs and increased research.

The trustees had promised Doherty to raise money themselves so that he could concentrate on reforming the institution. He soon learned what every university president knows: presidents must become fundraisers. Almost immediately, Doherty, the trustees, the faculty and the alumni began an organized fund drive, the first in the institution's history. In 1940, the fund passed the $1 million mark and reached $2 million in 1944. Two years later on July 1, 1946, Tech reported that it had raised $4,060,000. More than $1 million came in substantial grants to support endowed professorships from the Maurice and Laura Falk Foundation, Buhl Foundation, Alcoa, Westinghouse Electric Corporation, American Radiator & Standard Sanitary Company and trustee George Tallman Ladd. The $8 million check from the Carnegie Corporation set off a relieved round of rejoicing on campus.

The Board of Trustees of the Carnegie Institute promised to raise money for Carnegie Tech so that Doherty could concentrate on running the institution. Doherty soon realized that he would have to take the lead.

98

Of the total $12 million fund, $3.5 million was spent to renovate and remodel Tech's older buildings, erect an addition to Engineering and Science Hall, now known as Doherty Hall, acquire Morewood Gardens, an apartment building that became a women's dormitory, and purchase land near the central campus. Despite these expenditures, Tech's endowment increased from $17 million to $31 million during the Doherty years.

Carnegie Tech acquired and renovated Morewood Gardens, an apartment building, creating a women's dormitory.

Grants support research in nuclear physics

During the Doherty administration, Tech began to receive significant amounts of money from the federal government. Throughout World War II, faculty members took part in widespread research efforts both on and off campus. The most notable was work on the atomic bomb headed by Professors John C. Warner (Chemistry) and Frederick Seitz (Physics). Six Carnegie Tech men witnessed the first explosion of the atomic bomb at Alamogordo, New Mexico. In addition, Tech scientists and engineers received funds to support 14 separate research projects in a variety of technical and scientific fields. After the war, the federal government played an increasing role in the financial affairs of Carnegie Tech, a role that continues today.

After World War II, the federal government supported establishment of Tech's nuclear research facilities. In 1946, Frederick Seitz, head of the Department of Physics, began to plan for a program in nuclear physics. He hired a number of physicists who had experience in nuclear physics on the Manhattan Project and in several nuclear laboratories. They included John G. Fox, Roger B. Sutton, Martyn H. Foss and Edward C. Creutz. The Buhl Foundation contributed $300,000 and Carnegie Mellon $250,000 to this effort. The remaining $2 million came from the Atomic Energy Commission and the Office of Naval Research, the first major peacetime grants to Tech from the federal government. Among the sites considered was the Carnegie Tech football field, a suggestion that upset much of the faculty and student body. Then the Westinghouse

Electric Corporation offered to give Tech the 63 acre site of its KDKA transmitter in
Saxonburg, Pennsylvania. On the 50th anniversary (1996) of the start of nuclear physics
at Carnegie Tech, Creutz described in a letter to John G. Fetkovich some of the
problems that the new project faced early in its life:

> *In a few months we were well into the conceptual design of our 300 MeV*
> *cyclotron when Powell in England announced that the meson related to*
> *nuclear structure was the pi meson, which he had just discovered in cosmic*
> *rays, and which was about 50 percent heavier than the mu meson. This*
> *meant that our planned proton energy was too low by at least 100 MeV.*
> *We estimated that our 1000 ton magnet design was 500 tons too small to*
> *produce such energetic protons. The extra steel we needed would cost*
> *$100,000. Undaunted, or only slightly daunted, we called Urner Liddel,*
> *head of the DNR (Department of Naval Research) programs, and told him*
> *the news. Could we please have $100,000 more? He said, "I'll call you*
> *back in two hours." He did, and we had the extra funds.*

Getting the parts of the synchro-cyclotron to Pittsburgh, however, presented
serious problems. The equipment included two metal coils each of which weighed about
96 tons. When Tech sought final papers to permit it to haul the coils by truck from the
New York Shipyard where they were made to Saxonburg, Pennsylvania, the Keystone
State highway authorities said no. Finally, the coils were shipped by boat from New York
to New Orleans and then by barge up the Mississippi, Ohio and Allegheny Rivers to
Kittanning, Pennsylvania. The entire affair, particularly the last 13 miles by road from
Kittanning to Saxonburg at the rate of three-miles-an-hour, produced nationwide
publicity. The facility did not become fully operative, however, until late 1950, several
months after Doherty's death.

1943

- Otto Stern wins Nobel Prize.
- ASTP brings GIs to campus.

Left:
WWII barracks served as temporary housing for married veterans.

Right:
GI, Vance E. Senecal (E'47, '48, '51) combines home life with college study in 1947.

Enrollment booms with the GI Bill

The student body and student life underwent fundamental changes between 1936 and 1950. Full-time day enrollment increased by a third while evening numbers decreased from 4,308 to 1,465. Scholarship money to support these students more than tripled. In addition, the Westinghouse Electric Corporation established Westinghouse Fellowships which paid full tuition for four years for 10 students chosen in a national competition. Within four years, 40 Westinghouse Fellows were studying engineering at Tech. Doherty also had a marked impact on student life. He established a Division of Student Personnel to coordinate all non-academic services to students. He also met regularly with a Student Advisory Committee that studied student problems and informed him about them. In addition, Tech purchased land north of Forbes Street and established a fraternity area by purchasing a dozen houses, bringing fraternity life under the supervision of the administration. Finally, it turned the Schiller residence at the corner of Forbes and Beeler Streets into a combined student union and alumni headquarters.

World War II temporarily produced radical changes in the student body. For a time most engineering students had been deferred from the draft because their services would become vital to national defense. When this policy changed in 1943, enrollment declined to the low 600s in 1944 and 1945. During the war, Carnegie Tech filled the enrollment gap with three Army Specialized Training Programs. At its peak more than 1,900 military personnel were enrolled in programs on campus. Then in 1946-47 with the end of the war and the advent of the GI Bill that paid tuition and stipends to veterans, enrollment boomed to 3,200. Many veterans lived in temporary barracks located at the corner of Forbes and Margaret Morrison Streets. By 1950 the bulge in enrollment produced by the veterans had ended.

GI into Student

Former servicemen now constitute approximately 80 percent of the male student population at Carnegie. In addition to entering freshmen and students previously enrolled, Carnegie has admitted a group of transfer students and graduates of other colleges with advanced standing who are likewise enrolled under the GI Bill of Rights. These veterans, consciously or unconsciously, determine the nature of the student body in general, and it is interesting to observe how they have succeeded in making the adjustment from military to civilian life. The problems of the married veterans and those who have been disabled are familiar to all, and Carnegie knows them well, but an examination shows that as a student the veteran is making good use of the opportunities afforded him on campus.
—Carnegie Alumnus, September 1947

1944

- Wartime research projects are underway.

Above right:
The bust of W. L. Mellon found in lobby of the GSIA building

Below:
An architect's drawing of the School of Industrial Administration building

In his 1937 report, Doherty stressed the importance of increased graduate study as one of the three major foci of his forthcoming administration. Led by a newly appointed Dean of Graduate Studies, John C. Warner, the number of graduate students increased during his administration from 45 to 369, and the graduate degrees granted increased from 27 to 192. Engineering and science students earned more than 75 percent of these degrees. The remainder, earned in the College of Fine Arts and Margaret Morrison, went primarily to night and summer students, many of whom were teachers working for master's degrees who paid their own way. The deans of these two colleges showed relatively little interest in promoting graduate work, particularly at the doctoral level.

During World War II Doherty began to play an active role in the community and to establish mutually supportive relationships with the Mellon family, which would become one of Tech's great benefactors. Except for Andrew Mellon's gift of his home on Forbes Street to Tech in 1921, the Mellons had not supported the school. Andrew Mellon, a close friend of Henry Clay Frick and by then Carnegie's enemy, devoted his time and money to the University of Pittsburgh and Mellon Institute. In 1943, in cooperation with Andrew Mellon's nephew, Richard King Mellon, Doherty helped to organize the Allegheny Conference on Community Development, one of the major organizations responsible for the Pittsburgh Renaissance. Doherty served as its chairman for three years. Chapter 8 documents the key role that the Mellon family played in the University's development since this early contact.

During the late 1940s Doherty responded to another member of the Mellon family, William Larimer Mellon. W. L., as he was known, approached the president with a proposal to found a School of Industrial Administration to prepare undergraduate and master's students to become managers. Mellon had become dissatisfied with the caliber of managers he had been able to hire at Gulf Oil, where he was chairman. This initiative led to a grant of $6 million to found a School of Industrial Administration, the origin of the Graduate School of Industrial Administration (GSIA) that began to flourish during Warner's years as president.

Doherty began to provide the conditions under which faculty members could improve their teaching and focus more of their efforts on research. He increased average faculty salaries from their 1936 levels of $2,200 for instructors and $4,700 for full professors to $3,200 and $7,200, respectively, by 1950. To provide time for them to work, Doherty reduced the teaching load. In 1936, it was 9-12 hours for full professors and 12-18 hours for all other ranks. In addition, many faculty added evening courses to their loads, a practice that in some instances increased classroom time to between 14 and 21 hours weekly. By 1950 the standard teaching load had been reduced to nine hours per week for full professors and 12 for all others. Doherty demanded that faculty do research. To support them, research expenditures increased fivefold.

Illustrations featured in a piece produced by the Public Relations Department of the Carnegie Institute of Technology March 1950.

Doherty initiates the Carnegie Plan

Immediately upon his arrival on campus, Doherty began to implement the curriculum reforms that eventually became known as the Carnegie Plan of Professional Education. Its goal was to develop in students the character and ability needed to help them think independently about all aspects of their responsibilities—as engineers, in public life and as citizens. Around him he gathered a distinguished teaching faculty led after 1945 by Elliott Dunlap Smith, a Yale faculty member who became Tech's first provost.

To achieve his goals, Doherty divided the curriculum into two stems: the scientific and the humanistic-social. The scientific stem would teach problem solving by laying a foundation in fundamental scientific courses. In 1940 Engineering and Science required all freshmen to enroll in a common set of courses. The humanistic-social stem would give students social knowledge through a course each semester culminating in a senior-year course involving a social-technical project, such as slum clearance, that involved both stems of the program. Doherty argued that this curriculum should educate students to *become* engineers, not to train them to *be* engineers.

Formulas will not open every door. . .

. . .but a Carnegie man learns to make his keys.

Doherty and Smith recruited interested faculty members, particularly in Science, Engineering and Humanities and Social Studies, the three areas most involved in the Carnegie Plan. The new courses in science, technology and the humanistic and social studies disciplines focused on problem solving and on providing students with the underlying scientific, mathematical and engineering principles essential to help them learn how to solve problems. To provide more time to study these new courses and to enjoy recreation, Doherty ended all classes at 4:30, began Saturday classes, and eliminated shop courses, replacing them with a voluntary six-week summer session in shop work for engineers. Engineering and Science students were required to take about one fourth of their courses in humanistic and social studies. These courses— English, History, Economics and so forth—employed the same problem solving focus that characterized the engineering curriculum. Doherty characterized this emphasis as "liberal/professional education," a term that caught on and lasted for decades.

Faculty members wrote papers about this new educational focus, outlining what they did and why and how they did it. By the 1940s, the Carnegie Plan had become big news. Visitors poured in to find out what the fuss was all about as national publications, such as *Time* described the Carnegie Plan in glowing terms. A genuine educational revolution was underway. By 1942 it had reached Tech's College of Fine Arts where a new general education course each year—Thought and Expression, The Arts and Civilization, Individual and Social Psychology, and electives in one of these fields—became requirements.

Doherty's administration reorganized and modernized administrative practices. Doherty set up a conference committee of the General Faculty to develop administrative

1945
• Six Tech faculty and graduate students see first atomic bomb explode.

The Great Goal Posts Caper

Contrary to stories in the newspapers, no watchman was slugged during the stealing of the goal posts on Sunday night. Nevertheless the nine men who went over the top for Tech had to show some ingenuity before the night was over. These men, together with various others, left Tech about midnight Sunday and went over to the stadium. They put the goal posts on the rumble seat of Costello's car and with the grounds-ends dragging on the street, rolled back to Scobell Hall. After about 25 fellows had gathered on the lawn, they sang, "Dear Old Tech" and gave an "Institute" that should have waked everybody. An effigy, consisting of one stuffed pillowcase, several cardboard boxes, and an old towel was hung from the goal post and decorated with the Tech-Pitt score.

Meanwhile more fellows were joining in the fun. They gathered paper, wood, and broken furniture for a bonfire in the street. The police arrived, however, and "suggested" that the boys move the woodpile to the bare space to the right of Scobell Hall. When the press photographers arrived, everyone forgot the fire long enough to take pictures. But they suddenly remembered it when when two fire trucks rumbled up. A stream of water made short work of the blaze.

Last Tuesday night about thirty ill-advised Pitt men tried to steal the goal posts in front of Scobell Hall. When the men to whose rooms the guywires led heard the wires creak, they looked out and raised the alarm. The men of Scobell came down the stairway like firemen down a pole, and in a surprisingly short time, men from all five dorms and even the boarding houses were congregated about the scarcely damaged trophy and were pursuing the vandals toward the Cut. The few captives were immediately dragged into the Scobell Hall clubroom.

The method of punishment was most unusual. Scissors were produced and the culprits' hair was cut off close to the head. Pitt retaliated by snatching Wes Dorsheimer of Scobell. A large group took him to the Pitt campus where a humiliating P was clipped into his hair. A great deal of the rest of the night was spent in alarms and excursions. The girls from Cedar said they would have had the goal posts put in front of their dorm if they had known how many Pitt men it would bring in.
—*The Dorm Bagpiper*, Nov. 9 and 16, 1938

Pitty Kitty!

On a magical fall afternoon in 1938 we beat Pitt 20 to 10. On Monday, a motorcade formed on Forbes in front of the fraternity houses and proceeded down the street to the Pitt campus. We drove around the Cathedral of Learning singing, "The Old Pitt Panther ain't what it used to be," and then headed downtown via Bigelow Boulevard.
—Ruth Martsolf Cover, A'39

104

policy in faculty affairs. During his first year as President, he took the initiative to found a new Alumni Federation with a permanent Executive Secretary and a staff, using institutional funds to support this office. Subsequently, the number of alumni clubs—Carnegie Clans—increased from five in 1936 to 35 in 1950 and contributed almost $400,000 to the two-for-one gift from the Carnegie Corporation.

On two occasions, Doherty appointed a committee to develop a long-range campus plan. The committees developed models, put them on display and described them in the *Carnegie Alumnus*. War conditions and construction costs, however, stood in the way, and the plans were stillborn. At least they called attention to the need for a coherent campus plan, a need that planners recognized when they began to build today's campus during the 1980s. These plans included a library building, a crying need. During Doherty's administration, library holdings increased from 23,000 to 91,000 volumes, but in 1950 they were scattered across the campus in five buildings.

Doherty de-emphasizes football

Tech's attempts to remain a national football power continued into Doherty's administration. Tech continued to play big-time opponents and as a result, failed to have a winning season between 1931-1937. Then despite a loss to Notre Dame in 1938, Tech established an 8 to 1 record, including a 20 to 10 victory over Pitt, and won the Lambert Trophy, emblematic of supremacy in eastern football. Tech students held uproarious celebrations of their victory over Pitt.

Chosen to play in the Sugar Bowl, Tech lost to Texas Christian, led by a future Hall of Fame quarterback Davey O'Brien, by a score of 15 to 7. "The experience was disappointing," said President Doherty, "not because we lost the game but because of the devastating effect of the episode upon scholarship, and it has consequently been determined that we will not play any more post-season games." Both the students and the alumni, however, reveled in both the winning season and the Bowl game.

Doherty saw the situation differently. During the 1930s Tech's intercollegiate athletics had been run by an independent Athletic Council which had built up a substantial financial deficit. So, even knowing what the reaction would be, Doherty abolished the Athletic Council and set up an Athletic Board, bringing intercollegiate athletics under the control of the administration. To cope with the deficit, Doherty ordered the board to stop renting Forbes Field or Pitt Stadium for games, drop big-time opponents and terminate athletic scholarships. The resulting decline in Tech's athletic fortunes prompted some of Tech's students to hang their president in effigy, but Doherty stood his ground, commenting, "I think that some of you have come to the wrong school."

1946

- Carnegie Corporation grants $8 million when Tech raises $4 million in matching funds.

Left page from top to bottom:

November 5, 1938 Carnegie Tech v.s. Pitt Football program

The victory drive around the Cathedral of Learning after beating Pitt 20 to 10

Tech students steal the Pitt goal posts.

Above left:
Protesting Tech students hang President Doherty in effigy.

Above right:
Ad from 1948 *Scottie*

1948

- Flood of GI students abates.
- Morewood Gardens opens.

Doherty as he saw his accomplishments and as others saw him

Doherty summarized the achievements of his administration in a review written in 1950. The list of achievements is most impressive. In retrospect, however, what the report omits reveals as much as its contents. The report mentions neither the College of Fine Arts nor Margaret Morrison, although a number of significant developments had taken place there, particularly in Fine Arts. By 1950, for example, any theater professional could name a number of Tech graduates in each of the following categories: actors, producers and directors, designers and technicians, writers, and community or educational theater operations.

The establishment of the Graduate School of Industrial Administration, however, received several laudatory paragraphs. Clearly, Doherty saw Carnegie Tech primarily as an engineering and science institution with a promising new business school, not as the comprehensive university it was to become 16 years after his presidency ended.

Doherty had an intriguing private side that few of his colleagues knew. Tasso Katselas (A'50) remembers an encounter with his president when Katselas was a student:

> A group of architecture students decided to invite Frank Lloyd Wright to speak to the school and the general public. In order to raise funds for his honorarium, we sold tickets for the lecture to be held in the Little Theater in the Fine Arts Building. On the day of the lecture, we were called in to face an angry president. He informed us that we had violated school policy by selling tickets to a performance in the Little Theater. The event had to be called off, he said. Startled by this admonition, I vividly recall swallowing, looking innocently at the president, and proclaiming that the tickets were for the potato chips and lemonade reception. I noticed a twinkle in the president's eyes. The performance went on. No tickets were collected, and the potato chips and lemonade were consumed.

Lucille Orr Crooks (MM'43) had heard many complaints about Doherty's opposition to big-time football and his advocacy of the unpopular social relations program:

> My perception of him changed completely, though, in my junior year when I became a member of his Student Conference Committee. To the surprise of all of us, we found him friendly and caring, an attentive listener genuinely interested in what we young students had to say. . . . And then I really got to know him when I had the good fortune to work as a secretary in his office in 1944-45. He was every secretary's dream: pleasant, reasonable, considerate, never condescending, though he was leagues ahead of us in intellect. Expecting the best of us, he treated us as his colleagues in the exciting enterprise of education.

Mrs. Doherty also had a warm, human side. The Dohertys' daughter, Vera, attended Carnegie Tech and belonged to a sorority. Virginia Wright Schatz (A'43) remembers her and her mother fondly:

Vera Doherty's sorority sisters (of which I was one) were often invited to the Dohertys for dinner or sleep-overs. Mrs Doherty even found me housing when I returned to campus after serving in the Red Cross during World War II. Vera and her mother (in hat and gloves) drove me around to investigate housing ads. Passing a house on Fifth Avenue, Mrs. Doherty said, "Mrs. Anderson lives there all by herself. You just knock on the door and tell her you need someplace to live. Don't tell her I sent you because she is a very proud lady." Well, I did. She called the Y to check on me and then gave me two rooms on the third floor where I lived happily for two years before Ed (Edward Schatz, long a distinguished faculty member at Carnegie Tech/Mellon) and I were married. It turned out that Mrs. Anderson was the widow of Carnegie Tech's first doctor and a long-time friend of Mrs. Doherty. I never told Mrs. Anderson how it happened that I turned up at her door.

President Doherty retired in June 1950 to be succeeded by John Christian Warner, Dean of Graduate Studies. Doherty died suddenly a few months later at his home in Scotia, New York. His successors built upon the foundation he laid. The years between 1945 and 1950 prepared the ground for the golden age of Carnegie Tech. Doherty left behind him a student body in which full-time undergraduates and new cohorts of graduate students outnumbered part-time night students, a revitalized faculty whose members focused their energies on both teaching and research, a dramatic new curriculum, a reorganized administrative structure, a new school soon to become one of the premier business schools in the country, a fresh commitment to serve the wider community, an endowment that had almost doubled, quadrupled library holdings, new relationships with funding agencies such as corporations, foundations and the federal government, and a successor—John Christian Warner—fully prepared to take Tech to new heights of achievement.

1949

• W. L. Mellon founds GSIA with grant of $6 million.

1950

• Nuclear Research Center established at Saxonburg, Pennsylvania.

President Doherty was an accomplished painter. He won first prize at an exhibition of Pittsburgh's Associated Artists with this self-portrait.

1. Administration Hall
2. College of Industries
3. Machinery Hall
4. Engineering Hall
5. The Hut
6. College of Fine Arts
7. Margaret Morrison Carnegie College
8. Gymnasium
9. Commons
10. Carnegie Inn
11. Dormitories for Men
12. Margaret Morrison Street Group
13. Mellon Hall
13. Forbes Hall
12, 13, 14. Dormitories for Women

A CAMPUS GUIDE
for the
CARNEGIE INSTITUTE
OF TECHNOLOGY.

CARNEGIE INSTITUTE OF TECHNOLOGY
PLAN FOR EXPANDED CAMPUS
Alfred Morton Githens and Francis Keally, Architects

1 Administration Building
2 Library
3 Auditorium
4 Theater

5 Student Activities Buildi
(Carnegie

7.

Snapshot 1947–1949
Tech discards its trade school origins

On June 27, 1948, 725 students received their diplomas at Carnegie Tech's 50th commencement at Soldiers and Sailors Memorial Hall in Oakland, the largest facility nearby. For the first time, the swirl of bagpipes accompanied the graduates, faculty, and honored guests to the platform. The composition of the graduating class had changed significantly since 1928 and even more dramatically since the Charter Class of 1908.

The 725 degrees were the largest number granted to date by Carnegie Tech. Women received 206 degrees (27 percent), all but two in Margaret Morrison and Fine Arts, and night students received 29 (4 percent), all in engineering and science. Thirteen percent of the graduates received master's or doctor's degrees, up from 3 percent two decades previously. The graduates included 500 Pennsylvanians, 67 percent of the total, along with students from 36 other states and 10 foreign countries.

As it had in 1928, the composition of the graduating class portrayed an institution in transition from a trade school to a modern university. Between 1928 and 1948, Tech had merged the College of Industries with the College of Engineering and Science and begun a library school in

cooperation with the nearby Carnegie Library. Tech no longer granted either two-year certificates or three-year diplomas, both of which had still been offered in 1928. The number of master's degrees had more than quadrupled and, in addition, 14 delighted, new doctors of science received the newly designed Carnegie Mellon doctor's hood in 1948. Changes were evident throughout the institution. In the Carnegie Tech of 1948, the outlines of a modern research university had begun to emerge.

The Carnegie Institute loosens its hold on Tech

Between 1928 and 1948, Tech had developed a new relationship with the Carnegie Institute and its trustees. President Doherty had made this new arrangement a priority. After several years of study, the bylaws of Carnegie Tech had been thoroughly revised in 1939. These revisions separated Carnegie Institute of Technology completely from the Carnegie Institute except that the Board of Trustees of the Institute also served as the Board of Trustees for Tech. Tech's president became its chief executive officer, and a separate controller became responsible for Tech's financial accounts.

Changing Commencement Statistics

	1908	1928	1948
Number of Graduates	58	382	725
Number of Different Degrees	6	46	42
Pre-Collegiate	**58**	**52**	**0**
2-Year Certificates	0	44	0
3-Year Diplomas	58	8	0
Bachelor's Level	**0**	**319**	**633**
Bachelor of Science	0	226	528
Bachelor of Architecture	0	12	7
Bachelor of Arts	0	76	0
Bachelor of Fine Arts	0	0	98
Professional Degrees	0	5	0
Master's Level	**0**	**11**	**65**
Master of Science	0	11	56
Master of Social Work	0	0	9
Terminal Degrees	**0**	**0**	**27**
Master of Fine Arts	0	0	13
Doctor of Science	0	0	14

The 1942-43 *Carnegie Handbook* included a map of the campus and a plan of an extended campus, none of which had been built by 1949.

109

1947 brochure for students entering Carnegie Tech

At the same time, Tech's president became a member of the Board of Trustees of the Carnegie Institute.

A subcommittee of the Institute's board was still responsible for the operation of Carnegie Tech. In 1948 it had 16 members including five "special members" who were not members of the main board of the Institute. Four of them were Tech alumni. By 1948, however, Tech had begun to develop a national reputation in both research and education. Despite devoted service on the part of some trustees, Tech's growth was hindered by a board composed mainly of Pittsburghers with responsibilities both for Tech and for its mother institution across Junction Hollow. The year 1948, however, marked a key development in Tech's relationships to its trustees. Tech graduate Walter J. Blenko (E'21) became chairman of Tech's Executive Committee, the first alumnus to hold this important position. Roy A. Hunt, who later made vital financial contributions to Tech, served under him on the board, and both William Larimer Mellon and Richard K. Mellon belonged to the Board of Trustees of the Carnegie Institute, a position from which they could constantly stay informed about affairs at Carnegie Tech.

Tech was now organized into three colleges, each headed by a director: The College of Engineering and Science, the College of Fine Arts and Margaret Morrison Carnegie College. The College of Industries had merged with engineering in 1934. Tech also included a Division of Humanistic and Social Studies that offered no degrees. A small Library School, coal, metals, physics and chemistry research laboratories, a Division of Student Personnel and Welfare, a Division of Physical Welfare and a Reserve Officers Training Corps completed the administrative structure. Except for the four research labs, Tech had no institutions parallel to the

dozens of centers, institutes and consortia that are the focus of much of modern Carnegie Mellon's interdisciplinary research and educational efforts.

Tech had no development office in 1948. President Doherty himself, with the support of the trustees, the alumni and a few distinguished faculty had raised $3.6 million between 1936 and 1946. A gift of $6 million from William Larimer Mellon in 1949, negotiated mainly by President Doherty, provided funds for the Graduate School of Industrial Administration. Doherty and faculty from Engineering and Science obtained funds from the federal government, foundations and industry to supplement Carnegie Institute of Technology funds allocated for the synchrocyclotron project.

With the end of the financial bonanza created by the GI Bill of Rights and with inflation eating into income, Carnegie Tech needed the independence that would enable it to control its own finances and organize ongoing development efforts. Income from tuition already exceeded endowment income by 2.5 to 1. The list of gifts, grants and bequests for the fiscal year 1947-48 also reveals Tech's inadequate financial resources. Its endowment of $31 million, invested almost exclusively in fixed income securities, returned only 3.66 percent. Gifts, grants and bequests to current operating funds totaled $870,529, all of it to Engineering and Science, and 70 percent of this total to Metallurgical Engineering and Physics alone.

Faculty members move the Carnegie Plan forward

In 1948 the faculty numbered 276 full-time and 101 part-time members. Of the full-time faculty, 62 were women, 38 in Margaret Morrison, 11 in Fine Arts, eight in the Division of Humanities and Social Sciences, three in the Library School, a dean of women, and a women's physician.

New hires to the faculty present an intriguing mixture. Of the 64 new faculty members, only seven held Ph.D. or M.F.A. degrees, 32 had earned master's degrees, 20 had no degrees beyond the bachelor's level, three (all in Fine Arts) had studied privately and two had no college degrees. Of the 64, 16 had degrees from Carnegie Tech. Only three incoming faculty members, two in music and one in foreign languages, had been educated abroad. Of the 96 graduate students who served as teaching assistants, 37 had undergraduate degrees from Carnegie Tech. Three teaching assistants had studied abroad, two in Canada and one in Italy. Like its undergraduates, many of Carnegie Tech's incoming faculty members and graduate students were local products.

Four fifths of the 101 part-time faculty were instructors, many of them members of the Pittsburgh Symphony Orchestra who taught in the Department of Music. Two additional categories of personnel, each indicating a new school priority, joined the faculty as researchers between 1928 and 1948. Fourteen individuals served as research assistants to the faculty in the Departments of Physics and Chemistry. In addition, 44 individuals, many of them women, had research appointments in the Coal and Metals Research Laboratories. Finally, Engineering and Science offered a number of teaching assistantships for graduate students who conducted laboratory classes, but not recitation sessions of lecture courses. A 14-member library staff, 27 individuals in Student Services, including housing and 139 non-academic staff members, such as secretaries, supported these teachers and researchers. Almost all members of the support staffs were women, some of them serving two masters:

During the 1930s each department in what was then the College of Engineering and Science had only one secretary, and some departments had only half a secretary. Chemistry and Printing Management departments were two of the latter, and I worked half-time for each one.
—Janet McVicar Fugassi, MM'38

1946-47 Sources of Income

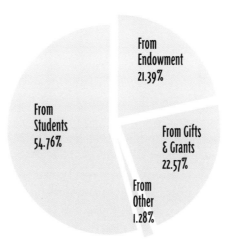

From Endowment 21.39%

From Students 54.76%

From Gifts & Grants 22.57%

From Other 1.28%

A rise in the Consumer Price Index that far exceeded raises in Tech's salary and wage scales caused faculty income to decline in purchasing power between 1928 and 1948. One of Doherty's goals —reasonable financial security—had not been accomplished by 1948. His successor, John C. Warner, inherited this unpleasant problem. The faculty in 1948 had, however, benefited from other reforms that Doherty had instituted: a greater voice in the councils of the Institute, increased freedom of intellectual pursuits and reduced teaching loads. A 30-page booklet, "Policies and Procedures: A Handbook for the Information of Members of the Faculty," first published in 1944, spelled out these new conditions.

In March 1936 the General Faculty had agreed to present President Baker's

No Longer on Easy Street

War and economic conditions have played havoc with our 1921 rosy dream. The school has more than 3500 students; return on invested funds has shrunk until it is hard to get 3% with safety; income other than tuition is less than in 1921; the cost of administration, instruction and operation has risen to almost $2,500,000; and the Carnegie Corporation says we are "on our own" now. Carnegie Institute of Technology is no longer on "Easy Street." To keep out of the red and balance a budget of close to $3,000,000 for the coming year, the tuition has been "jacked-up" until it is almost a rich man's school.
—1947 Letter from Albert C. May, Chairman, Alumni Fund Campaign Committee

successor with a proposal to form a faculty committee to express faculty sentiments on salaries, instructional facilities and the failure of the Board of Trustees to consult with the faculty on the selection of a new president. No faculty members belonged to the committee that chose Robert Doherty as Tech's third president, and the faculty had learned about the identity of their new president through a newspaper article. Doherty sought faculty advice and appointed a six-member Conference Committee that began to meet in January 1937. By the end of the year, the Committee reported to the general faculty that the administration had taken action on many of its suggestions: parking, access to buildings, dates for notifying faculty about their appointments and teaching loads. In subsequent years, the Committee initiated action on a host of issues raised by the faculty: relationships between department heads and faculty, tuition remission for faculty spouses, improvements in faculty dining facilities, the need for greater publicity about the scholarly activities of faculty, making faculty participation in retirement plans compulsory, and clarifying policies with reference to retirement age. By 1948 the Conference Committee provided a vital way for faculty to participate in Tech's governance. Tech was on its way to becoming a community of scholars rather than a hierarchically structured institution in which initiative and decisions always traveled from the top down.

By 1948 a new tenure and appointment policy had been in place for a decade. Rather than yearly appointments, the custom before 1938, professors and associate professors appointed for a second term received indefinite tenure, and stated terms were established for other faculty appointments. Faculty with tenure were assured of the academic freedom essential to both scholarship and teaching in post-secondary institutions. New tenure procedures also gave tenured department members a strong voice in tenure decisions. Appointment by fiat of administrative officers had become a thing of the past, another indication that Tech was no longer a trade school.

An informal group that called itself "The Young Turks" provides further evidence that Tech was in the midst of fundamental changes. Most of them were recent faculty appointees, having studied in leading doctoral programs such as those at Massachusetts Institute of Technology or Yale. They had in common an enthusiastic response to President Doherty's emphasis upon research, an emphasis that some of their older colleagues and a number of department heads only tolerated or quietly opposed. They rejoiced when President Doherty appointed one of their leading members, Jake Warner, Dean of Graduate Studies in the College of Engineering and Science. In 1950 Warner became Tech's fourth president.

The Forty-Fifth Annual Report of the President lists 10 pages of publications and artistic productions for the academic year 1947-48. Thirty-six percent of Tech's faculty either published a book or an article, gave a creative performance or participated in an exhibition during 1947-48. Moreover, the administration highlighted this faculty productivity by giving it a prominent place in the President's Annual Report. Seven faculty members in Engineering and Science with distinguished research records had been awarded endowed chairs by 1948. The message was becoming clear: Carnegie Tech's administrators expected faculty to exercise their analytical and creative talents by contributing to knowledge in their fields. This new attitude represents a dramatic change that took place in the two decades between 1928 and 1948.

By 1948 Carnegie Tech's faculty included a number of men and women

Alumni Recall Favorite Faculty

Can anyone forget the professors who made a significant difference in one's life? Although amusing events from my college days still bring a chuckle, most of my undergraduate memories are woven around the very distinctive personalities of three teachers. . . .They are Webster Aitken, piano professor, who showed me another way to think about music; Henny Rosenstrauch, professor of eurhythmics, who showed me a new way of experiencing and eventually teaching music; and Astere (Austie) Claeyssens, an English teacher whose humanity, intellect, energy, enthusiasm and zest for life combined to give new meaning to the art of teaching. These three great teachers helped to shape my career, and, indeed, my life.
—Annabelle Sachs Joseph, A'53

After Morewood Gardens opened, Forbes Hall, long a women's dormitory, became the faculty club.

Professor Charles Leopold Willibald Trinks, a Westphalian by birth was head of Mechanical Engineering for many years. He knew all of his students by name and always addressed them as Mister. Few students knew that after graduation he had his assistant cut out the pictures of each ME graduate from The Thistle, paste them on 4 by 6 cards and copy pertinent information onto them. He included an evaluation of each student by each of his professors. When a graduate called, he had only to pop open his file with hundreds of names in alphabetical order to find a thumbnail sketch of the man who was calling.
—William L. McGaw, Jr. E'39

Daytime physics classes during the late 1920s were always very small. Only five physics majors graduated in 1930 at a time when CIT had 12 physics faculty. One of the pleasant features of being a physics major was the annual dinner party for faculty and students provided by Professor Harry S. Hower, the department head. He always took us to a very good place, such as the University Club, which was an unusual treat for some of us less affluent students.
—Samuel F. Lybarger, E'30

I'll always remember fondly a wonderful curmudgeon named John Neely who taught calculus. He had a dent about the size of a half-dollar right in the middle of his forehead, the result of having been hit by a line drive when he was a pitcher for the Washington Senators. That collision ended his baseball career, but it certainly didn't ruin his brain. He taught me calculus during my first semester as a student. What a great teacher! He made me think, he stretched my brain in new directions, and he aroused my curiosity about mathematics as he showed me its beauty as well as its usefulness. He also threw chalk with deadly accuracy at anybody who dared doze off in his 8:30 calculus class.
—Hugh D. Young, E'52

Faculty Club Opens

An Open House will be held in the new Faculty Club (4916 Forbes Street) on Wednesday, October 20, 1948, between four and six P.M. All members of the Faculty and Administration are cordially invited to attend.

The committee appointed by the Executive Committee of the General Faculty has reported that the annual dues will have to be in the neighborhood of the following figures.

Professors...................................$40
Associate Professors...............30
Assistant Professors................20
Instructors.............................15
—Faculty Bulletin, October 20, 1948

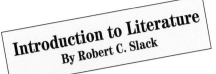

Introduction to Literature
By Robert C. Slack

The Education of Professional
Students for Citizenship
By Elliot Dunlap Smith

The Educational Task
By Robert E. Doherty

The Use of Problems and
Substances to Make
Education Professional
By Richard Teare, Jr.

Technological Education
at Carnegie
By D.W. Verplank

Publications, Creative Works and Exhibitions 1947-48

	Number	Authors
Engineering & Science	43	37
Metals Research Lab	12	10
Coal Research Lab	12	12
College of Fine Arts	10	7
Margaret Morrison	2	4
Humanities & Social Studies	41	29
Administration	1	1
Total	**121**	**100**

with established national scholarly reputations. Among others, they included Otto Stern, Edward C. Creutz and Frederick Seitz in Physics; Ernest Berl and John C. Warner, Chemistry; Robert F. Mehl, director, Metals Research Laboratory, Metallurgy; B. Richard Teare, Electrical Engineering; Warren L. McCabe, Chemical Engineering; Dennistoun W. Ver Planck, Mechanical Engineering; Richard J. Duffin and J. L. Synge, Mathematics; George Leland Bach and William W. Miller, Economics; Max Schoen and B. von Haller Gilmer, Psychology; Gladys Schmitt, English; Nikolai Lopatnikoff, Frederick Dorian and H. Talbott Pearson, Music; Hans Vetter and John Knox Shear, Architecture; Henry Boettcher and Lawrence Carra, Drama; Robert L. Lepper (A'27) and Samuel Rosenberg, Painting and Design; and H. H. Lowry, director of the Coal Research Laboratory.

Many faculty members, particularly in engineering, science and the humanities and social studies, focused much of their attention in 1948 on the development of the Carnegie Plan. When Doherty arrived at Tech in 1936, he found a curriculum badly out of date and a small group of faculty ready to join a reform movement. Carnegie Tech had inherited an array of shop courses from the curriculum of the Carnegie Technical Schools.

Doherty found a few preliminary reforms already underway. The faculty in Engineering and Science had developed educational plans early in the 1930s in preparation for a visit by an accreditation team. The faculty had specified the need for basic courses in physics, chemistry, mathematics and mechanics and had begun to incorporate them. In 1933 the Educational Senate had voted to require more humanities courses for engineers. This preliminary work prepared the faculty to undertake more far-reaching reforms when Doherty assumed leadership.

The reforms in both the science and the humanistic and social studies stems involved faculty from across departmental lines. Engineers from all departments met to identify the content of courses in science and mathematics. Faculty from all but one engineering department agreed to teach a course in the humanistic and socials studies stem. Faculty in history who taught the freshman course also taught sophomore economics in order to bring continuity to a sequence of courses.

By 1948 the Carnegie Plan had won a national reputation, and Tech faculty were deeply involved in its development and implementation. During World War II many of the older faculty retired, and Doherty replaced them with his vigorous young recruits. In 1945 Elliott Dunlap Smith had become provost and the major figure behind the social relations program. Smith initiated many schemes to get the faculty involved. They included informal weekly discussion groups that met at the homes of interested faculty, committees to develop new courses, seminars on teaching methods led by department heads and monthly sessions attended by all involved faculty focusing on teaching and effective educational methods. By 1948 the reforms of the Carnegie Plan had reached the College of Fine Arts where Gladys Schmitt taught Thought and Expression to freshmen, and Norman Dawes and Balcomb Greene taught Arts and Civilization to sophomores.

At a meeting of the Council of the Division of Humanistic and Social Studies in the spring of 1948, psychology professor B. von Haller Gilmer suggested a name for the new educational program: The Carnegie Plan. The name stuck. Faculty, who had been writing accounts of their educational activities, presented papers in 1948 at the "Inter-Professions Conference on Education for Professional Responsibility" hosted by Carnegie Tech

Both educational journals and the popular press described the Carnegie Plan in dozens of articles.

and supported by the Carnegie Corporation. At this meeting top-level administrators from across the country listened to Tech faculty report on their activities and discussed their applicability to other institutions. As a result, Tech faculty played hosts to dozens of visitors from other campuses and, in turn, visited other campuses in order to disseminate the ideas behind Tech's educational programs. Along with Doherty and Smith, they wrote a series of educational papers that analyzed the Carnegie Plan in detail.

Planning documents for recent strategic planning meetings at Carnegie Mellon have identified seven key values and traditions that permeate the University's culture: leadership, innovation, transcending disciplinary boundaries, responsibility to society, learning, dedication to work, and commitment to quality. More than any other single event in the first half-century of its history, the

development and dissemination of the Carnegie Plan, and the plan itself, speak to the origins of these values and traditions.

Another educational innovation in 1948 was the use of a Faculty Rating Sheet prepared by a Student/Faculty Liaison Committee of the College of Engineering and Science. Students from Electrical and Mechanical Engineering had originally designed and tested an instrument in fall 1947. It included a series of questions designed to help faculty identify the strengths and weaknesses of their teaching. Each instructor distributed and collected his own rating sheets. Faculty volunteered to use the revised rating instrument in many courses at the end of the spring 1948 semester. It is the direct ancestor of the Faculty Course Evaluation now used throughout Carnegie Mellon. The administration now requires faculty to evaluate their teaching and publishes the results both in print and electronically.

Night school enrollment falls while graduate enrollment increases

By the fall of 1947, Tech's enrollment had begun to drop from its postwar peak. Day classes, evening classes and summer classes had totaled 6,033 in 1946-47; 5,999 students enrolled in September 1947. "As far as I'm concerned, the rush is over," wrote Carnegie Institute of Technology's Director Webster Jones as he announced that the summer sessions instituted to speed graduation for veterans were ended.

"And the whole wonderful idea came to me during a home-management lecture at Margaret Morrison."

In addition to numbers, the most significant changes in the student population between 1928 and 1948 were in the decrease in night students and the increase in graduate enrollment. The number of evening students decreased by two-thirds; graduate enrollment, on the other hand, shot up by 16 times. The changes in both the evening and the graduate enrollment reflected President Doherty's priorities.

Women students were concentrated in Margaret Morrison, where they outnumbered men by 606 to 12. In Fine Arts men outnumbered them by 514 to 255. Engineering and Science, which had admitted women for the first time during World War II, presented a radically different picture. Of 2,489 students

enrolled full time in September 1947, only 16 were women, and 13 of the 16 studied in the sciences rather than engineering. The war years, when millions of women had worked in factories and served in the armed forces, had begun to change the image of women in the work force, but science, and particularly engineering, as careers for women remained almost immune to societal trends. "The Women's Song" printed in the 1948 *Student Handbook* bears testimony to the vitality of conservative traditions. It suggests a life of service.

Carnegie Tech no longer recorded the religious preferences of its students, nor did it continue to record their race or ethnic background. In 1948 Tech eliminated questions about race on its admission forms and modified its admission policies "to avoid possible criticisms concerning discrimination. . .on the basis of race, national descent, and religion." Graduates who were on campus during the postwar years, however, recall seeing only a handful of African-Americans or Hispanics and no native Americans, and this small number were concentrated in Margaret Morrison and Fine Arts. With the exception of international students, men and women of Asian descent were also conspicuous by their absence. The number of descendants of southern and eastern Europeans, however, was increasing, judging by their names, admittedly an imprecise measure. The GI Bill that paid both tuition and a stipend for veterans had opened the door to higher education for millions of the descendants of recent immigrants, and hundreds of them passed through Tech's imposing portals on Forbes Street. Almost all students who were not veterans paid their own way ($600 in Engineering and Science and the College of Fine Arts and $500 in Margaret Morrison) or were supported by scholarship money. Only 39 students received

Life in Margaret Morrison Carnegie College

Margaret Morrison gave its students a subtle push toward a career of some sort. There were women models in the college and also a sense that one had to earn a living just in case one did not capture an engineer. I know three women from my era (1943-1947) who long ago achieved professional status in the job market: a home ec major who became a manager at Heinz, a secretarial major who became an editor at the Pittsburgh Post-Gazette, and a dietitian who became director of all of Kaufmann's dining services. So despite the message over the entrance to the building, the college tried to do for women what engineering did for men.
—Lois Shoop Fowler, MM'47

People took campus politics seriously in my day. Bill Thunhurst and Tom Riley, for example, distributed leaflets from the air in the 1946 Campus Queen campaign. Both men had been in the Air Force during the war. To highlight Ann Sweeney's campaign, they decided to drop leaflets on the campus. Errant breezes carried the first drop to Forbes and Murray. Wetting fingers to test wind direction, they made a second run about over Pitt Stadium. This time the leaflets hit the campus. Sweeney won, of course.
—Celeste Silberstein Behrend, MM'49

Senior Home Ec majors were required to live in the Home Management House on Margaret Morrison Street for five weeks during their senior year. Five girls assumed the jobs generally found in a family home: hostess (wife, mother, "lady of the house"), cook, housekeeper, marketing and meal planning. The jobs rotated weekly. Each student occupied a single bedroom in the three-story, brick-and-stucco house. Each year students gave a dinner for their parents. They were very proud to eat a meal planned, cooked, and served by their daughters.
—Maxine Shermer Slesinger, MM'38

I'll never forget the 1940 Maggie Murph Freshman Initiation. We were attired in PJs, galoshes and bathing caps and had cold cream smeared on our faces. They set us to work scrubbing the rotunda with toothbrushes. Then we had to go up to the Fence on our knees. The final embarrassment took place when some upper class "friends" took our pictures.
—Virginia Bruce Walker, MM'44

Now and then the guys used to organize panty raids on the girls dorms. Mrs. Patty, our housemother and a very genteel lady, was concerned that fraternity men would get into her dorm. We coeds responded by pouring buckets of water from the second floor windows on the men gathered at the door.
—Ruth Lauffer Cost, MM'39

We all wanted to live in Whitfield Hall, the brick women's dorm which stood on a knoll high above Forbes Avenue. To get to it, we either walked through the gate in the wrought iron fence and then strolled up the long, curving driveway or climbed the 106 stairs from the backyard to the campus. Inside, a baby grand piano and a huge fireplace with a carved oak mantel graced the living room. My roommate and I had a large marble bathroom to ourselves. The shower stall had circular water pipes that sprayed us from head to foot. What luxury! Originally Whitfield House was the old Brown mansion which Carnegie Institute of Technology acquired in 1932. Hence, the luxury.
—Virginia Wade Schalles, MM'41

Whitfield Hall

1947-48 Student Enrollment

	Grad	Sr	Jr	Soph	Fresh	Spec	Night	Total
Engineering & Science	276	463	626	525	586	13	891	3380
Fine Arts	11	140	192	177	219	30	373	1142
Margaret Morrison	52	121	122	148	152	22	48	665
H&SS	0	0	0	0	114	0	0	114
Library School	25	0	0	0	0	2	0	27
Summer 1947*	0	0	0	0	0	0	87	87
Total	**364**	**724**	**940**	**850**	**1071**	**67**	**1399**	**5415**

*The total 1947 Summer enrollment was 1,272 but more than half of these students were counted during the academic year.

1947-48 Graduate Student Statistics

Enrollment

Engineering & Science	276
Margaret Morrison	52
Library School	25
Fine Arts	11
Total	**364**

loans totaling $19,430 in 1947-48. Today hundreds of individuals graduate with outstanding loans that far exceed the total of student loans 50 years ago.

Surprisingly, the percentage of Pennsylvania students, mainly from Pittsburgh and Allegheny County, enrolled at Carnegie Tech increased from 69 percent in 1928 to 74 percent two decades later. Day students came from 33 additional states, mainly in the Northeast. The 59 international students, up from 26 in 1928, came from 17 countries with Canada (14) and India (12) leading the way. Echoing administration sentiments the *Carnegie Alumnus* appealed for

". . .increased alumni interest and activity at points distant from Pittsburgh" in order to encourage students from across the nation to take advantage of the "exceptional educational opportunities" that Carnegie Tech offered. Night school and summer high school student programs continued to attract an almost exclusively local population.

Tech's three colleges selected incoming students by different standards. Engineering and Science required the College Board Examinations or Pre-Engineering Inventories together with school records and evidence about personality and character. Fine Arts students submitted high school records and scores on College Board or other academic entrance examinations and underwent rigorous departmental technical tests to measure their ability to learn in their chosen fields. Margaret Morrison students did not have to take College Boards. The college based admission on high school records and other pertinent information.

The student population provides an image of Carnegie Tech during the 1947-48 academic year. It was mainly an engineering school; of the full-time day students, about 60 percent enrolled in Engineering and Science. The criteria for admission in E&S were higher than those in Fine Arts or Margaret Morrison. Tech was overwhelmingly an undergraduate school: only 6 percent of its students studied in graduate programs. It was a regional institution: 74 percent of its students came from Pennsylvania. Its population did not reflect American society: about 85 percent of its students were male, about 80 percent of them veterans, and more than 99 percent of all the students were white and mainly of northern or western European descent. What a contrast with the student population 50 years later in 1997-98!

The campus changes little physically

By 1948 two beloved buildings, Skibo on Margaret Morrison Street and The Hut, the World War I canteen that had served as Tech's library, had been torn down. Food service moved to the old Langley Aeronautical building which was renamed Skibo and library holdings were scattered to every classroom building, with the main holdings on the third floor of Administration Hall. A number of temporary structures that had not existed in 1928 had also appeared on campus.

Like hundreds of other educational institutions, Carnegie Tech had acquired buildings from the armed forces at the end of World War II and moved them to the campus. They included three wooden classroom buildings named Web, Newton, and Jones Halls after Webster Newton Jones, the Dean of Engineering. They also included four barracks that provided housing for students at the corner of Forbes and Margaret Morrison Streets. Under the terms of the Lanham Act, the government furnished and erected the buildings after the College prepared the site and provided utilities. Finally, a few Quonset huts provided faculty housing. An incoming faculty member, Richard M. Cyert, with his wife, Margaret, and their first child moved into one of them in the

fall of 1948. He was to become Carnegie Mellon's sixth president in 1972. Students in crowded housing may have been luckier, however, than their peers who entered in the fall of 1946. *The Carnegie Tartan,* October 8, 1946, reported:

The housing shortage on the campus of Carnegie Tech has been greatly alleviated by the timely aid given by the local churches. The Church of the Redeemer, Hugh Clark, Rector, provided living quarters for 100 students during the registration period. . . . A loan of 200 beds, mattresses and blankets to the churches was very generously agreed to by the American Red Cross.

At the end of the 1940s, the school planned two new buildings: an addition to Engineering Hall (now Doherty Hall) that faced the Fine Arts Building and a building to house the Graduate School of Industrial Administration at the corner of Tech and Frew Streets. Unfortunately, President Doherty, who helped to raise funds for these structures, died before their completion.

Top:
This corner of Tech's new library space in Administration Hall spoke clearly to the need for a library building.

Center:
Tech students listen to WCIT.

Bottom:
Skibo is torn down.

Station WCIT

A wired radio or carrier current system which has been dubbed "WCIT" was inaugurated at Carnegie Institute of Technology last evening (Monday) from seven to eight o'clock with a special program featuring greetings from the officers of administration, music and news of interest to students who were listening in on their radios in the dormitories and elsewhere on the Carnegie campus.

The apparatus, together with the necessary microphones, turntables, and control equipment has been installed in a small studio with separate control brooth, in the College of Fine Arts. The studio is part of the facilities of the Drama Department. This project was carried out by the students with the advice of Prof. E.M. Williams of the Department of Electrical Engineering which lent the transmitter and other necessary components of the system for this purpose.
—*Carnegie Alumnus,* December 1946

Bud Yorkin

Yorkin studied engineering at Tech but after World War II returned to college, having made some career decisions. "I didn't know what I wanted to do, but had a hint that somewhere in the entertainment industry would be interesting for me."

Throughout the 1950s and 1960s he wrote, produced and directed many beloved and honored television shows including "The Tennessee Ernie Ford Show" and "The George Gobel Show." He then went on to do comedy/variety specials for Danny Kaye, Henry Fonda, Duke Ellington, Bobby Darin, Dick Cavett, Don Rickles and Carol Channing. A highlight of his career was the 1958 special "An Evening with Fred Astaire." In the 1960s Yorkin teamed up with Norman Lear and by the 1970s was creating and producing series such as "All in the Family," "Maude," "Sanford and Son," "Good Times" and "Diff'rent Strokes."
—*Carnegie Mellon Magazine,* Summer 1992.

No Time for Dating

The long nights we spent in the theater played havoc with our private lives. With classes in the morning, rehearsals in the afternoon, and performances or crew in the evenings, 'dramats' had no time for dating in the conventional sense. Rather they learned about one another in the shared labor of achieving a barely imaginable goal— a fully professional stage production.
—Nancy Brink Cheffey, A'49

A scene from the 1949 Scotch 'n' Soda production *Molecule Man* in which veterans played prominent roles.

Veterans raise the standards on campus

Student life in 1948 reflected seven divisions in the student body: veterans and non-veterans, day and night students, commuters and non-commuters, graduates and undergraduates, students in the three colleges, Greek and non-Greek, and male and female. Of the seven, only the presence of veterans had added a new kind of diversity to student life.

Most of the veterans were in a hurry. The majority were in their early 20s and eager to get on with their lives. They carried extra academic loads and attended school year-round in order to graduate in two or three calendar years. By the fall of 1947, about 90 percent of the Carnegie Tech students whose education had been interrupted by the war had returned to campus and finished their education. Other veterans were in their 30s or 40s and came to college for the first time with the support of the GI Bill. Faculty rejoiced when they saw these serious, hard-working students arrayed before them. The veterans raised academic standards, sometimes to the dismay of typical 18-year-old high school graduates in their classes. They won academic honors; at the May 1947 commencement, 26 veterans

graduated with honors, and the honor roll for the spring 1947 semester contained 483 names, most of them veterans. They refused to abide by the rules governing the behavior of freshmen and ignored the handful of upperclassmen who tried to enforce them. In turn, according to a story in *The Carnegie Tartan* of September 22, 1948, veterans refused to enforce freshman regulations to the dismay of some of *Tartan's* reporters. Thus ended freshman hazing, a practice that President Doherty —and many students—had found juvenile and reprehensible but had been unable to stamp out completely until the veterans came along.

Many of the veterans plunged into extracurricular life enthusiastically. A nucleus of half-a-dozen veterans, former members of Scotch 'n' Soda, staged *Rock 'n' Riot,* a musical comedy in the Carnegie Music Hall. A group of management engineering students, largely veterans, organized a student chapter of The Society for the Advancement of Management. Veterans organized the publication of a literary magazine, *Cano,* and made up its major contributors. A veteran revived and managed the Men's Glee Club that had been dissolved during the war. Older, more mature, and better

able to manage their time, veterans who wanted to do so could maintain high academic standards and participate widely in co-curricular activities at the same time.

One of the four World War II barracks erected at the corner of Forbes and Margaret Morrison Streets housed 24 married veterans and their children. Dozens of other married vets found housing in the city. Their lives centered around their families, their studies, social occasions with other married students and Pittsburgh's varied recreational activities. An editorial in *The Carnegie Tartan*, no doubt written by a non-veteran, chided them and other veterans for failing to join student organizations and take part in some student activities. The 1948 and 1949 graduating classes marked the waning of the wave of veterans which had engulfed the campus beginning in 1945-46.

The lives of day and night students differ

The 3,290 day students and 1,380 evening students in 1948 lived in different worlds. As they did in both 1908 and 1928, evening students commuted to campus after working all day in Pittsburgh's mills, factories, offices and shops. Their lives outside of work and school focused on families, neighborhood

Veterans & Their Female Classmates Recall

During World War II the science and engineering majors were rushed through on an accelerated academic calendar. My occasional heavy academic loads (90 units during one trimester) were mellowed by participation in the symphony and the Kiltie Band. Although the war had a sobering effect on all of us, my undergraduate days at Carnegie Tech were among the happiest and most fulfilling of my life.
—George E. Pake, E'45

In 1946 I returned to Schenley Park as a combat veteran to complete my interrupted CIT education. Light-hearted college days and undergraduate didoes had been set aside—the new look was dominated by crowded classes, young wives, babies, year-round classes and an intensity of educational purpose that surprised and challenged the faculty. The vets were ambitious, energetic, hard-driving and most of all, impatient. We changed Carnegie Tech irreversibly and in the process set the stage for today's world-class university. What a difference a war makes!
—Robert A. Charpie, E'48

In 1946 I transferred from another university to Carnegie Tech to study civil engineering. What a change! The students, many of them veterans, were serious, talented and eager to get on with their lives. I went through a period of shock as I began to recognize the intensity of the work load and the expectations of the faculty. After a period of adjustment, I joined in the work and learned to appreciate the faculty, especially the head of Civil Engineering, Dr. Ted Mavis.
—Robert B. Pease, E'49

We returning veterans took over the campus after World War II. I returned to CIT in 1946 supported, like all the vets, by the G.I. Bill. Like most of us, I remained on campus through the summer of 1947 rather than take a summer break. By the end of the next academic year, many of us had only a few courses to go to earn our degrees, so we stayed through the following summer and graduated in October 1948. On the alumni rolls, we are included in the class of 1949.
—Frank R. Boyd, E'49

Hot Dog! And Hooray! World War II was over! It was September 1945, and the campus would be full of returning G.I. Joes. Under the G.I. Bill of Rights, all veterans had the right to study higher education with the support of Uncle Sam. The admissions office was inundated; the girls were delighted.
—Diana Kutchukian Thomasian, MM'49

The first drawing class of the year which used a nude model always created a stir. My section in Painting and Design in 1947 consisted of 11 young women directly out of high school, 10 male veterans between 25 and 35 years old, and one lonely male directly out of high school. The first day the nude female model posed for our class, I kept my head turned toward the model, not looking left or right at the older male students. Immediately one of the veterans nudged me on the elbow and said "Kitty is built exactly like my fiancée"—an unforgettable embarrassing moment.
—Janice Seiner Colker, A'51

Life as a Commuter

Girls who commuted to Carnegie Tech used to bring brown bag lunches and eat them in the rec hall on the fourth floor of Maggie Murph. They discussed their classes and sometimes finished their regular Friday English themes. Most of these girls were able to attend Carnegie Tech during the depression because they earned partial scholarships in high school. They commuted by trolley using round, brass tokens with a diamond cut in the middle. Some rode the Pennsylvania Railroad and walked up Morewood Avenue from the Shadyside station near the J. A. Williams warehouse.
—Louise Wunderlich Manka, MM'37

Commuters, the largest group of students at Tech for many years, had no place to meet at Homecoming. The CITcom (CIT Commuters) Clan obtained permission to hold the CHOP (CITcom Homecoming Open House) party at the gym for the '47 Homecoming, partly based on pledged backing of expenses from CITcom GIs. The KDKA staff orchestra provided the music, and CITcom sweated out meeting expenses for this event which was not well advertised. Admission charges and 25 cent Coca Colas covered expenses. It was a ball and a first for ex-commuters.
—William J. Ward, E'48

Commuting by street car to CIT really tested one's commitment to education. I caught the #15 Bellevue car from our home in West View about 7 a.m. The route took me through Bellevue, along California Avenue, through the narrow streets of the North Side, and across the Sixth Street Bridge into downtown. I would get off at Sixth and Penn and hurry over to Forbes to transfer to one of the cars which ran up Forbes to Tech. I got off at Morewood and hiked across the Cut and down the quadrangle to the Civil Engineering Department in Porter Hall, arriving in the nick of time for my 8:30 a.m. class. I reversed the trip in the evening, leaving campus after my 4:30 p.m. lab and arriving at home a little after 6 p.m. Fare was a token, three for a quarter. Who could forget three hours a day, 15 hours a week, 240 hours a semester, 480 hours a year, 1,920 hours in four years—on streetcars?
—James H. McCartney, E'54

and community social and religious organizations. A small number became involved in organizations and events at Tech. The night school contributed a page to each issue of *The Carnegie Tartan.* It carried stories about night school events such as smokers. A few night school students took part in intramural athletics. On the whole, however, night school students had no time to devote to making booths or competing with buggies in events such as Spring Carnival. Few of them were degree candidates. The director of the Night School commented that many of the courses served the community by providing a way for students to improve on or acquire specific skills. The distinguished handful that managed to earn a degree after at least nine years of study, many of them descendants of southern and eastern European immigrants, always received an enthusiastic hand at graduation exercises.

Commuters often felt left out of campus activities. They took no part in residence life programs nor could they participate fully in fraternity life that focused on men living in fraternity houses. In order to find a place in the community, they formed the CITcom Clan, an organization that held meetings, ran candidates for office, organized social events, and fielded a few athletic teams. In 1948 commuters did not erect a booth at Spring Carnival or enter a buggy in the sweepstakes, although they did sponsor a CITcom Hop at homecoming for present and past commuters.

Students lead very different lives

Nor did graduate and undergraduate students share common lives. Most doctoral students forged close professional and often personal ties with faculty with whom they studied. Single graduate students lived in graduate dorms or in apartments in the community, so they took no part in undergraduate resident life programs. Many of them had teaching assistant assignments, putting them in roles as teachers of undergraduates. Often married and sometimes parents, graduate students focused much of their out-of-class time on their families or friends who shared their lifestyle. They watched buggy races and took their children to the midway at Spring Carnival, but at these events most of them were spectators rather than full participants.

Undergraduate students in the three colleges also lived somewhat different lives. More than half of Carnegie Tech's students enrolled in Engineering and Science, giving them a numerical advantage in elections. Hence, they dominated the leadership in student organizations such as the Student Senate. Many engineering and science students saw little that they had in common with the dramats and artists from fine arts, and they attended plays and concerts less frequently than fine arts students. Students identified themselves as dramats or double Es. The Maggie Murphs were an exception.

Carnegie Tech treated men and women differently. They paid different tuitions. Deans of Women still enforced dress codes, refused to let men enter women's dorms, and enforced curfew hours for women. Tech had no sorority houses, although by 1948 it recognized seven national sororities. Although women were permitted to enroll in Engineering and Science, few chose to subject themselves to an all-male faculty, classes in which they would often be the

only woman and social events such as smokers. Women's organizations featured social service activities in the wider community, providing outreach from the campus to the city.

Finally, members of fraternities and, to a lesser degree sororities, lived different lives from non-Greeks. Fraternity members consistently won student elections; in January 1948, the president and vice president of the commuters organization, the CITcom Clan, complained in a letter to *The Carnegie Tartan* that for the first time in history, Carnegie Tech had an all-fraternity student council. Each fraternity member had been given a list of candidates to vote for, and fraternity officers got out the vote, effectively shutting out non-fraternity members from elective office. Fraternities forbade dormitories to participate in the Migratory Dance, a feature of Spring Carnival in which participants migrated from one fraternity house to another throughout a long evening. Fraternities dominated the events of Spring Carnival, particularly the buggy races in which they had the advantage of strong support from house alumni. Finally, of course, most fraternity members lived in fraternity houses where they built powerful friendships, many of which lasted for a lifetime.

Andy Warhol

When classes at Carnegie Tech began in 1945, Andy joined 60 freshmen in painting and design. Most were young women. At 5'9" and 135 lbs., Andy was easy to overlook; he was a mild-mannered, soft-spoken, naive introvert.

When Andy left for New York City, he left behind a network of friends and his shy boyish personality. In the ensuing years, he evolved into the public's image of him—never quite accurate—a flamboyant publicity-seeker wanting the center of attention. Warhol catapulted to the very apex of Pop Art and culture through his many masterpieces made in Manhattan.
—*Carnegie Mellon Magazine,* Summer 1994

Philip Pearlstein

Pearlstein's study at Carnegie Tech began in 1942 before the U.S. entered World War II. He returned to campus in 1946 with thousands of ex-soldiers on the GI Bill.

There are good reasons why Philip Pearlstein (A'49) is an American master. His quiet nudes are world famous. Besides his paintings of more than 40 years, Pearlstein's fame rests on helping to turn art from the tired abstract expressionism of the late 1950s to a new realism. He has profoundly influenced younger artists.
—*Carnegie Mellon Magazine,* Winter 1995

Above:
Student Andy Warhola, the only male member of the Modern Dance Club in 1947

1949 SPRING CARNIVAL

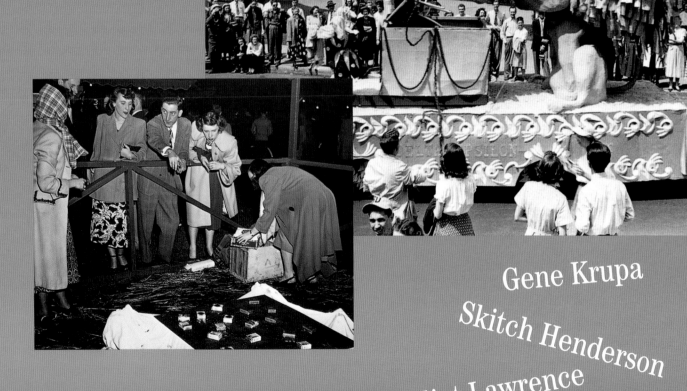

Gene Krupa

Skitch Henderson

Elliot Lawrence

Woody Herman

SPRING CARNIVAL
1947–49

Kappa Sigs, Delts Sweep Contests

Spring Carnival weekend, "Winsome Will" Hawkins' (the Carnival chair) gift of good times, is over. After a prelude of four performances of Scotch 'n' Soda and an overture of a few hours of Midway on Thursday night, the big event overcame uncertain weather to become an almost unqualified success.

It was a particularly good holiday for the men of Delta Tau Delta and Kappa Sigma, the athletic Delts winning the Sweepstakes speed cup and the canoe tilt, and the artistic Kappa Sigs winning both the float parade and the Sweepstakes design trophies. Alpha Epsilon Phi produced the winning Varsity Variety skit.

Queen June Castner and her court of seven presided as the honoraries called activities, men and women and scholars assorted to their ranks and Vernon Neubert was named "Most Promising Senior Engineer" by Theta Tau. Skitch Henderson and Elliot Lawrence were as good as promised on Friday and Saturday nights (their bands played for dances in the gym).

The Midway glowed brilliantly as the social and even the honorary organizations were out in force to spray the Cut with barkers cries, raucous music, and the sweetish smells of very mixed confections and refreshments. The unexpectedly great financial success scored by many of the organizational booths provided an exhilarating finale which will make the 1948 Spring Carnival long remembered.

—*The Carnegie Tartan,* May 18, 1948

The administration improves student life

By 1948 the administration had made significant progress in providing for six of the seven responsibilities that today's student affairs officials have identified. Clearly, intellectual/artistic development and occupational preparation were in good hands, as they had been since 1908. Required physical training for underclassmen, an improved medical facility in the gym, and voluntary intramural sports had an impact on physical welfare. About half of the men on campus in 1948 participated in intramural sports. *The Carnegie Tartan* and the *Student Handbook* advertised a wealth of cultural activities, although many students failed to take advantage of them—many, but not all. Philip Morrison (S'36) tells about his first encounter with Albert Einstein:

Albert Einstein, we physics types heard with delight, would speak at the Carnegie Institute shortly after Christmas, 1934. The event became such a public draw that students could not get tickets. I knew, however, that Tech drama students used the hall for plays, and I persuaded a friend to show me the ropes. Two hours before the speech was scheduled, we found our way into the theater and clambered high up behind the stage into the flies, all but against the ceiling. I lay down at the edge of the open framework to peer at the stage 50 feet below me. Far below I could see the Einstein head of hair, but little more of him, and I could only hear the soft murmuring of his voice without being able to catch a word. I crawled down when the applause ended, no wiser about relativity but happily content. Twenty years later I was able to tell Professor Einstein this very same story of his early renown in America.

—Philip Morrison, S'36

The YMCA, YWCA and local churches, synagogues and temples pro-

Above and Below Right:
Tech bought the old Schiller Mansion in 1938 to serve as a student union and alumni headquarters.

Below Left:
Two 1948 articles from *The Carnegie Tartan*.

Two Bands Play At Hop

Both Jazz and Sweet Music Are Featured

The Scotch Hop introduces two orchestras at the first all school dance of the semester on Saturday, March 6. Lee Barrett and his thirteen piece orchestra will play sweetly and slowly in the gym, while Walt Harper and his nine piece orchestra will play jazz and be-bop in Thistle Hall. The ____ is sponsored by the ____ men's sophomor____ the Cwens, wo____ honorary.

Walt Harper's ja____ provide music for li____ ure and fast dancing. ____ will play for slow da____ romantic mood.

Music will last from ____ until 1:00 a. m. with no ____ sions, and dress is ir____ Tickets may be obtained ____ 11:30 a. m. to 1:30 p. m. in ____ or from any Scimitar or Cwe____ $2.50 per couple.

Glee Clubs Give Concert

A combined concert of the Men's and Women's Glee clubs was presented on April 27 during the Chapel hour in the little Theatre.

The Women's Glee club, directed by Miss Carolyn Kennedy, sang "Ave Maria" by Kodaly, and the "Czech Dance Song." These selections were followed by "Children of the Moon" and Sigmund Romberg's "Will You Remember" sung by the women's sextet. Estelle Berenfield, student director of the girl's group, conducted the "Italian Street Song." Their final selection was "Let All My ____ Music." ____ resulted in com-

vided opportunities for spiritual development. An innovation in housing—upper-class students living in Morewood Gardens on freshman floors—introduced the system of resident advisers (RAs), now a feature of all residence life. Deans of men and women supervised these activities and sponsored many of them. Today's students could recognize the forerunners of many programs now featured on campus in the campus scene a half-century ago.

Hanging out in 1948

Two of the beloved hangouts of earlier years had disappeared by 1948. The Morrises' store at Forbes and Dithridge had fallen prey to wider streets, and Skibo, the shack at the corner of Margaret Morrison Street had been torn down in 1945. Gretchen Goldsmith Lankford (MM'43) talks about Skibo:

I used to hang out at the old Skibo, the hut on the bend of what is now Margaret Morrison Street. Charlie Fortier, the owner, presided over it. Do you remember the hours spent playing bridge in the booths? The cards were all greasy from lunches of hamburgers and french fries. Many a romance began over Cokes and potato chips between classes. Lots of commuters made Skibo their social center, the place where they felt part of campus life during the 1930s and 1940s.

An enlarged cafeteria renamed Skibo occupied most of the old Langley Aeronautical building, and a refurbished Carnegie Inn still offered a grille and rooms in which students could meet. Students could also buy refreshments at the Black Cat Lounge in the gymnasium, located near Thistle Hall, the site of on-campus dances. By 1948 the Student Union had also become a fixture on campus. Tech had bought the old Schiller Mansion at 5075 Forbes Street in 1938 and renovated it to serve as both a Student Union and an Alumni Headquarters. For resident students, the dormitories provided

lounges and meeting places. Fraternity houses remained the focus of social life but for a far smaller percentage of male students than in 1928. To bring the fraternities under control, the administration had purchased a dozen houses near campus and slowly moved fraternities into them. Off campus, in addition to dances and banquets in hotels, alumni have particularly fond memories of a number of local bars. A story by Arnie Christenson (E'48) in the *Scottie,* March 1946, Tech's humor magazine, described "The Greeks":

In the past few days, in order to write such a story, I have been carrying on a program of extensive research. I have discovered that the main reason that the C.I.T. students frequent the Craig and Forbes Emporium is to carry on practical experiments for their hydraulics (the study of the flow of liquids) class. . . . Monday and Friday seem to be the big Greek nights. Since Tuesday is a comparatively light day on almost everybody's schedule, and because of the fact that most of the frats have their meetings on Monday evenings, "the Greeks" is usually hoarded (sic) with Greeks on Monday nights. On some Friday nights, it seems that the whole Tech campus has broken loose. If one happens to be strolling in the near vicinity on a Friday evening, he will hear every Tech song that has been written. . . .

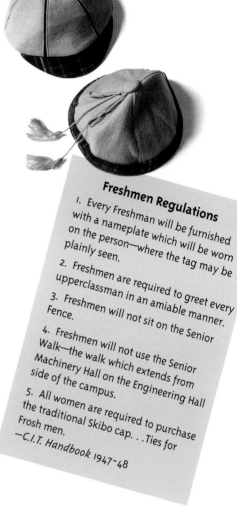

Freshmen Regulations

1. Every Freshman will be furnished with a nameplate which will be worn on the person—where the tag may be plainly seen.

2. Freshmen are required to greet every upperclassman in an amiable manner.

3. Freshmen will not sit on the Senior Fence.

4. Freshmen will not use the Senior Walk—the walk which extends from Machinery Hall on the Engineering Hall side of the campus.

5. All women are required to purchase the traditional Skibo cap. . .Ties for Frosh men.
—*C.I.T. Handbook 1947-48*

Above:
Freshman dinks worn in 1949

Below:
Tech guys and gals, post-WWII

The Greeks is now undergoing an extensive remodeling. . .to make it suitable for dancing once again. The reason for the discontinuation of dancing during the war was the levying of a Federal Cabaret Tax in the early days of the conflict. The tax law will run out soon enabling the University Grill (that is its official name) to allow dancing without raising its prices unreasonably.

Dramats hung out around the corner of Craig Street at The Little Greeks:

Down in Oakland on Forbes Street was the raucous rah-rah college hangout for beer and song called "The Greeks." We dramats called it "The Big Greeks" because around the corner was an inconspicuous little "gin mill" with a bar and eight or nine tables along the opposite wall. We called it "The Little Greeks." This was the province exclusively of the dramats. It was a quiet neighborhood tavern, convenient for casual talk and discussion of things theatrical. A beer or two would be nursed, but the proprietor never minded, understanding that we were students with limited resources.
—A. Starke Drischell, A'50

A full page describing off-campus hangouts appeared in the *Carnegie Tech Puppet* in January 1927. Here are two entries:

We were up at Khans in Squirrel Hill the other night. There are always some of the fraternity boys up there. The beer and pretzels go over big, and the meals are great. It is about the most collegiate spot around campus, and they cater to students in a big way.

Personally, we have a weakness for sepia entertainment. And that is why we recommend the Harlem Casino, Center Avenue. Lew Mercor MCs the show which is red, hot and dark. "Harlem on Parade" is the name of the show. There is always lots of stuff bordering on the risqué. Leroy Bradley plays for dancing. Prices are reasonable, with a cover charge of 50 cents per person.

One tradition flourishing in 1928 had disappeared 20 years later. When the forge shop was dismantled during the war, no facilities were available to forge a link to the class chain, and it was relegated to the archives. The most noticeable change, however, occurred in the role that football played on campus. After Doherty de-emphasized football in 1939, Tech had losing records through 1943. Then football was canceled during 1944 and 1945, returning to campus with smaller schools as opponents at the end of the war in 1946, the nadir of football at Carnegie Mellon. According to Hans Lange (E'52) and Pete Cruget (E'48):

Intercollegiate sports returned haltingly to Carnegie Tech after World War II. Football. . .had been canceled for two years. Then servicemen and coaches began to return to campus in 1946 to begin building a program, but without support from President Doherty. Football players who missed Saturday classes to take part in a game received a failing mark for the day. The team failed to score a touchdown during the 1946 season. In 1947, we scored but won no games. Finally, in the last game of the 1948 season, freshman John Luchok ran down a muddy field at Grove City for a game winning touchdown. A huge celebration took place on Monday, with no one attending classes, and Carnegie Tech football started its upward climb. Eddie Baker came in as head coach, and Jake Warner became president. Football and academics were united, and from then on, winning seasons prevailed.

128

In addition to the traditional *Carnegie Tartan* and *Thistle*, students published three magazines, *Cano, The Carnegie Technical,* and *Scottie,* during the 1947-48 academic year. *Cano* was a literary magazine featuring the best student writing and an occasional article by a faculty member. The *Scottie* was a humor magazine with articles submitted by Tech students and humor culled from a variety of sources. *The Carnegie Technical* was the voice of students in the College of Engineering and Science. It began in 1935 as a publication of undergraduates and appeared six times yearly until its demise in 1971. Undergraduates, graduate students, faculty and alumni contributed to its pages during its long and distinguished history. The title page of the December 1948 issue carried the following description of the contents of this typical issue:

All the articles of this issue were contributed by members of the local chapter of Tau Beta Pi. In order to fulfill their pledge requirements the Tau Beta Pi pledges are required to submit an essay on the social phase of engineering education. In "Educat-

ing the Engineer" the winning essay of the present pledge class, Millard Brown proposes two separate engineering curricula: one to serve as preparation for "professional" engineering, the other for "practical" engineering. The feature article of the issue deals with electroencephalography or, for the uninitiated, the study of "brain waves." The author, John Grace, explains the design of the apparatus used and its applications in medical diagnosis. One very versatile tool of the research physicist, the mass spectrometer, is discussed in an article by Robert Siegel. Although primarily a research instrument, the mass spectrometer is now being applied industrially to such diverse problems as the analysis of petroleum products and the detection of leaks in vacuum systems. The role of structural vibrations in bridge failure is explained in an article by Vernon Neubert, and in the final article Graham Renberg explains the advantages of liquid over vapor phase catalytic processes.

Over its life span, hundreds of Carnegie Tech students, alumni and faculty contributed to *The Carnegie Technical.* Widely distributed, it won a deserved reputation as one of the best publications of its kind. Scores of its contributors went on to distinguished careers in engineering.

Preparations for homecoming in October 1948 occupied much of the

"He edits the SCOTTIE!"

Humor from an Early "Scottie"

"The human brain is wonderful. It starts right in working in the morning, and doesn't stop until you are called on in class."

"All this stuff you read in college magazines is a bunch of hooey. I'm a college girl, and I haven't smoked, necked or drunk beer yet."
"How long yuh been in college?"
"I just registered."

"George Washington is said to have been fond of wine and women. We find at least six colleges named after him."

"But, darling, why aren't you wearing my fraternity pin?"
"All the fellows say it rips their coats."
—*The Scottie,* December 1947

Above:
A spread from a 1949 *Scottie*

Left:
This November 1948 *Cano* cover was designed by Andy Warhol while a student at Carnegie Tech.

student body for a month. The Student Council took over homecoming planning in an attempt to involve the entire student body rather than only members of fraternities and sororities. The administration agreed to cancel Saturday classes. Festivities began on Friday evening, October 15, with a pep rally held in the Tartan Bowl and a parade led by the Kiltie Band, followed by a dance in the gym featuring Walt Harper and his orchestra. This dance provided an opportunity for dormitory and commuter students and non-fraternity alumni to celebrate together. Most fraternity members and alumni attended fraternity open houses. On Saturday morning freshman and sophomore men competed in a greased pole contest, won by freshman Joseph Winkelman, and the freshman queen, Nancy Davis, was crowned. In the afternoon, the Kiltie Band led a parade down Forbes Street to Forbes Field, the site of the football game with Franklin and Marshall. In the evening, Gene Krupa's band played for an all-school dance in the gym during which Kappa Sigma accepted its Homecoming cup for its display, an animated farmer who milked a cow and proclaimed, "I'm pulling for Tech."

By 1948 Spring Carnival had become a fixture on campus. After a year's absence when the faculty abolished Campus Week for 1929, Carnival took over under more restrictive rules than Campus Week had enforced. Scotch 'n' Soda, a club that wrote and produced student-written musicals, performed four times during Carnival. The Scotch 'n' Soda club had been founded by three students in the Drama Department in 1938 and had produced a show each year until a four-year gap during World War II. In the fall of 1947, returning members of the club produced a Spring Carnival revue called "Take It From Here." By 1948 the club,

led by senior drama student, David Crantz, had fully revived and enrolled 200 members. They produced *Lady's At Work,* an original musical in two acts held in the Carnegie Music Hall and featuring a cast of 80, 27 songs and "New Look" costumes.

To the delight of the College of Fine Arts, students and faculty alike reveled in a Beaux Arts ball in 1948.

The alumni

Between 1928 and 1948 the Alumni Federation came under the purview of Tech's administration. Originally independent, it included only dues-paying alumni. Many graduates never joined or dropped out during the depression. By 1936 President Doherty had intervened, giving the Alumni Federation a new executive secretary, new quarters and a plan of operation that included financial support from Tech. Henceforth, all alumni were automatically members of the Federation. A new Alumni Council consisting of one representative from each Carnegie Clan was created. In return, the Federation established a plan for voluntary contributions to an Alumni Fund to be disbursed by a committee of the Federation and the administration.

In 1948, 24 Carnegie Clans functioned in 21 cities. Three cities, Pittsburgh and Philadelphia, Pennsylvania, and

Youngstown, Ohio had two clans each, one for men and one for women. Each clan established its own meeting schedule ranging from monthly to biannually. The alumni secretary tried to visit every clan every year, and administration and faculty often addressed clan meetings. The Federation tried valiantly to persuade members to attend Homecoming at which the Pittsburgh Clan held a reception, a number of classes held reunion dinners and a business meeting of the Federation elected new officers.

Albert C. May, the founder of the Alumni Fund and its 1947-48 chairman, reported to the alumni through an article in the *Carnegie Alumnus*. Contributions to the Alumni Fund, he revealed, had reached $21,016.36 in 1947-48, or $4,956.57 more than in the previous year. While cheering this improvement, May pointed out that only 7 percent of Tech's alumni had contributed to the Fund while 26 percent of all alumni nationally had given to their alma maters. "We must regard as a challenge the fact that so many of our alumni turn a deaf ear to the very obvious needs of our school. There must be some way to rekindle their interest and arouse them to a desire to help those who follow them as students," he wrote. The Alumni Fund Board allocated $5,540 from its 1948 revenues to support activities under the Carnegie Plan. Most of the remaining fund went to endowment, largely to endowed scholarships. Carnegie Tech's failure to bond graduates to the institution continued for several more decades.

In retrospect

By 1948 Carnegie Tech had abandoned almost all of its trade school origins. Unlike his two predecessors who came from pre-collegiate schools, Tech's president Robert Doherty came from a background in industry with a stint at Yale University. Tech offered no two-year certificates or three-year diplomas at its 1948 commencement. Instead, 605 undergraduates and 78 graduate students, including 14 candidates for the doctor of science degree, earned their degrees from Tech's three colleges. Day school students now substantially outnumbered those in the night school, and the graduate student population had reached a new peak. Both undergraduate and graduate students still came predominately from Pennsylvania and were still overwhelmingly white. The Carnegie Plan had revolutionized undergraduate education in engineering and science and brought a national reputation to Tech's educational endeavors. With their hours in the classrooms reduced, the faculty's increasingly talented members turned part of their attention to research and creative activities. Four research laboratories also marked Carnegie Tech's emergence as a research institution, a development that attracted excellent graduate students. Administrative reforms brought both the Alumni Association and the athletic activities under the control of the administration and brought an abrupt halt to big-time football. A development drive had netted $4 million, producing a two-for-one matching grant from the Carnegie Corporation, a grant signifying that Tech must look elsewhere in the future for its funding. The outlines of a research university with a distinguished undergraduate program now seemed clear.

Beaux Arts Ball Poem

Bennard B. Perlman (A'49) co-publicity chairman for the [Beaux Arts] ball, sent copies of a somewhat inaccurate and inelegant poem he wrote to several national publications. Here are the first and last verses:

We artists here at C.I.T.
are having soon our yearly spree
and thought that we should tell you all
about our annual beaux arts ball.
The Pittsburgh papers already know
of this our greatest beaux arts show
but we would like to count on you
as being represented too.

To which Associate Editor Herbert J. Brean of *Life Magazine* replied:

Thanks for your letter on the
beaux arts ball
it sounds like a LIFE-like
kind of brawl
It was a fine brawl,
but LIFE did not attend.

Opposite Page:
The 1949 Beaux Arts Ball

Left:
Plaid numbers from 1949

131

Thomas Mellon
1813-1908

James Ross Mellon
1846-1934

Andrew William Mellon
1855-1937

Richard Beatty Mellon
1858-1933

William Larimer Mellon
1868-1949

Paul Mellon
1907-1999

Richard King Mellon
1899-1970

8.

The Mellon Family
Carnegie Tech finds a new benefactor

The weather was clearing in Pittsburgh on April 28, 1921 when newly appointed Secretary of the Treasury Andrew W. Mellon rose to speak at the Founder's Day celebration of the Carnegie Institute, Andrew Carnegie's museum and library complex. Mellon was clearly the most respected member of President Warren G. Harding's cabinet and, perhaps, Pittsburgh's favorite son. One of the richest men in America, he had substantial investments in banking, steel, coal, oil, petrochemicals, railroads, aluminum and numerous other industries.

Carnegie Tech particularly looked forward to this visit. Andrew Carnegie's death in 1919 had left the school without its benefactor, and the Carnegie Corporation, which controlled Carnegie's estate, felt that Pittsburgh had seen enough of Carnegie's money for a while. Both the Carnegie Institute and the Carnegie Institute of Technology, which it controlled through a shared board of directors, faced financial difficulties. Tech in particular hoped that Mellon might become its new benefactor. After all, his mansion on Forbes Street was only about 100 yards away from Margaret Morrison Carnegie College, and rumor had it that Mellon would make a major announcement at Founder's Day.

No announcement was forthcoming. Later in the day, a reporter learned that the major announcement concerned a new group of federal office buildings in Washington, D.C. Rather than support the Carnegie Institute and Carnegie Tech, Mellon had decided to concentrate his local philanthropy on developing the Mellon Institute of Industrial Research in Oakland. Later in 1921, however, he presented his Forbes Street home to Tech, the first significant contribution to the school from anyone except Carnegie himself. The home served as a dormitory, first for women undergraduates and later for men graduate students, for more than 30 years.

Who could have predicted that the school to whose needs Andrew W. Mellon did not respond in 1921 would one day bear his family's name? Fortunately for Carnegie Mellon, Pittsburgh's most important family later became the University's most valued and generous friend. Fifty-six family members and nine family foundations have given Carnegie Mellon more than 200 grants, gifts and bequests totaling in today's buying

A Happy Homecoming

Six days from today, sixty years ago, I was born about sixty feet above Skibo Hall. It was not because my mother was in a balloon, but because our house stood on a hill which has only recently been bulldozed away. So, in a sense, this is a happy homecoming to me, and I have to say that I am pleased and proud to claim that I was born on (or perhaps I should say "airborn, above") the campus of Carnegie Tech.

—Paul Mellon in a commencement address at Carnegie Tech in 1967

Mellon Hall, a women's dormitory from 1921–1960, was the former home of Andrew W. Mellon. It stood on the site of the University Center.

133

power about $583 million. In addition, Carnegie Mellon has received many generous gifts from corporations that the Mellons helped to found—Mellon Bank, Alcoa and Gulf Oil, for example. Mellon family gifts have played a major role in the development of each of Carnegie Mellon's seven colleges and schools, its building campaigns, its administration and the Carnegie Mellon Research Institute.

From Poverty Point to Common Pleas Court

During the early 19th century, hard times drove Scotch-Irish commoners by the thousands from the north of Ireland. Andrew Mellon, his wife Rebecca and son Thomas,

who was five years old, joined the exodus in 1818, the last members of a large family to emigrate. America held far more promise for a prosperous future than 23 acres of farmland in County Tyrone. After an arduous voyage across the Atlantic in a sailing ship, the Mellons settled on a farm in the tiny town of Poverty Point near present-day Murrysville in Westmoreland County, Pennsylvania.

Farm life did not appeal to Andrew's son, Thomas. At the age of 10, he walked by himself to Pittsburgh—more than nine miles away—intrigued by the bustle and excitement of a growing city on its way to becoming an industrial giant. At the age of 14, Thomas found the book that changed his life: the *Autobiography of Benjamin Franklin.* "It delighted me with a wider view of life and inspired me with new ambition," Mellon later wrote in his autobiography. "For so poor and friendless a boy [as I] to be able to become a merchant or a professional man had before seemed an impossibility; but here was Franklin, poorer than myself, who by industry, thrift, and frugality had become learned and wise, and elevated to wealth and fame." For the first time, Thomas told his mother that he wanted to become a doctor, lawyer or preacher. To placate him, his father sent him to a boarding school in nearby Greensburg. Still hopeful, his father offered to buy him a nearby farm when his son was 17. Thomas spurned the offer. After a few preparatory courses at a local academy, he enrolled in the Western University of Pennsylvania, the ancestor of the University of Pittsburgh.

Thomas

After graduating and considering what profession to enter, Thomas Mellon began to work as a judge's law clerk. After a year-and-a-half while he taught Latin at his alma mater to support himself, he passed the bar examination and became a lawyer in 1839 at the age of 24. He prospered so rapidly through investments in mortgages and real estate that he was able to purchase an expensive home in Pittsburgh's exclusive East End and persuade his parents to move in with him. He was worth $12,000 (a small fortune in those days) when he

married Sarah Jane Negley, a member of one of Pittsburgh's leading families, in 1843. They had eight children: Thomas Alexander, James Ross, Sarah Emma, Annie, Samuel, Andrew William, Richard Beatty and George Negley.

Practicing law soon lost its luster for Thomas Mellon, and he began to look for new challenges. In 1859 he won the Republican nomination for a seat on the Allegheny County Common Pleas Court and, in a day when Republican candidates in Pittsburgh were virtually assured of success at the polls, he became Judge Mellon, a title he proudly continued to use throughout his life. At the same time, he began to invest quietly in a number of Pittsburgh industries. Soon he met Andrew Carnegie, another poor immigrant from the British Isles, and watched in astonishment as his new acquaintance quickly made his fortune. Instead of standing for reelection in 1869, Mellon resigned from the bench and on January 1, 1870 opened a new bank, T. Mellon and Sons, at 145 Smithfield Street on the site now occupied by the Henry W. Oliver Building in downtown Pittsburgh. In the post-Civil War period, a lender could get 12 percent for his money, and Thomas Mellon's fortunes increased steadily. Soon his son Andrew William (A. W.) Mellon became his right-hand man.

Andrew had begun his career in business at age nine by selling vegetables raised on his father's farm. The Judge thought that men valued what they had to work for. Slight in build and with a gentle personality, A.W. contrasted sharply with his forceful, robust father. He learned quickly at his father's knee as he became increasingly involved in the Judge's everyday business. A.W. sometimes spent days at a time at the courthouse listening at the bench as his father heard cases. "The Judge talked to his son not as to a little boy but as to one with a mature intellect, and thereby challenged the youngster to think as a man," wrote Andrew's nephew, William Larimer Mellon in *Judge Mellon's Sons.* "I sometimes think that this companionship shortened A.W.'s boyhood. . . . [As] a boy, he was less addicted to play than other boys, and, later on, than other men."

At 13 A.W. was sent to the Western University of Pennsylvania, even though the Judge felt that his own education there had been somewhat dubious. Midway through his sophomore year, his father's bank opened, and he soon found himself serving an apprenticeship in the office. The strain of maintaining both an academic and a professional life, however, began to take its toll. Concerned for his son's health, the Judge advised him to leave school at age 17, and Andrew eagerly assented. As a sort of nongraduation present, Judge Mellon set up A. W. and his younger brother Richard Beatty (R. B.) in the construction supply business by purchasing a lumberyard for them near the present town of Carnegie, Pennsylvania. R. B. left school to join this enterprise, although he was only 14 years old. Within a few years, the boys had built the company into a thriving business and sold it at a tidy profit to a cross-town rival. They were well on their way to becoming the most famous of Thomas and Sarah Mellon's children. Then, in 1874, Andrew became a full-time employee of the bank.

Left:
Thomas Mellon's first bank, T. Mellon and Sons

Bottom:
Thomas Mellon's second bank building (the original Mellon Bank) at 514 Smithfield Street

A.W.

R. B.

"My brother and I" becomes a Mellon mantra

Richard Beatty and Andrew W. Mellon were as opposite, but just as closely connected, as night and day. A. W. had a quiet wit and a reserved demeanor. R. B. was robust and high-spirited with a quick temper and a ready laugh, and he delighted in horseplay and off-color stories. A. W. was cautious, and his conservative nature provided a check on his brother's impetuousness. Their complementary traits helped them to develop into an excellent team. For many years, they maintained adjoining offices separated only by a swinging door so that they could wander into and out of each other's offices throughout the day. They purchased identical numbers of shares of stock in most ventures and were partners in almost everything. Both of them began to use the phrase "My brother and I" to the amusement of Pittsburgh's leading citizens.

In 1882, Thomas Mellon turned T. Mellon and Sons over to his son Andrew, who, five years later, gave half of it to his brother Richard Beatty. W. L. Mellon printed a copy of the transaction in his book *Judge Mellon's Sons*:

> *Pittsburgh, January 5, 1882*
> *Proposition to son Andrew for services past and future. He to have the entire profits of the bank from January 1, 1881, including my salary, the books to be readjusted accordingly, from 1st January instant. He to have entire net profits of bank and pay me an annual salary of two thousand dollars as its attorney and fifteen hundred per annum rent for the banking room; and I to allow him forty-five hundred per annum for attending to my private affairs and estate—selling lots, collecting rents, etc., as done heretofore. This arrangement to last till suspended by another or annulled by either party.*
> *Thomas Mellon*

T. Mellon and Sons, however, was a private bank. Assisted by his brother R. B. and by Andrew's close friend, the coal and coke magnate, Henry Clay Frick, A. W. organized the Federal Trust Company which eventually became the Union Trust. T. Mellon and Sons joined the Federal Reserve System in 1902 and changed its name to Mellon National Bank. Through Union Trust, Mellon Bank and a galaxy of smaller, satellite banks, the Mellons financed, underwrote and insured Pittsburgh's role in America's industrialization. Thomas Mellon proudly watched his sons' careers from the sidelines until his death in 1908 at the age of 95.

Aluminum and "the scratch heard 'round the world"

A. W. soon turned the bank in a new direction: he became a venture capitalist and a genuine financial genius. He and his brother explained their business philosophy in the following words:

> *Find a man who can run a business and needs capital to start or expand.*
> *Furnish the capital and take shares in the business, leaving the other man to run it except when it is in trouble. When the business has grown sufficiently to pay back the money, take the money and find another man running a business and in need of money and give it to him, on the same basis.*
> —Charles J. V. Murphy, "The Mellons of Pittsburgh," *Fortune Magazine,* October 1967.

"My brother and I"

R. B.'s son, Richard King Mellon, evidently applied these maxims to education. He found four Carnegie Tech/Mellon presidents, Robert E. Doherty, John C. Warner, H. Guyford Stever and Richard M. Cyert, funneled money to them, and kept out of their way as they turned a small regional technical school into an international research university.

Taking a cue from New York bankers, A. W. began to support new, promising enterprises, taking shares of stock in return for financial support. Hence, when three young men, Arthur Vining Davis, Captain Alfred E. Hunt (whose son Roy later provided the funds for Carnegie Mellon's Hunt Library) and George Clapp arrived on the bank's doorstep, they met with a welcome response. They showed A. W. a shining piece of aluminum, the first he had ever seen.

In debt to another bank, they asked Mellon for $4,000. A week later, he offered them a $25,000 line of credit in order to provide sufficient working capital for their firm, the Pittsburgh Reduction Company, to manufacture and market the metal. Although the company's factory on Smallman Street in downtown Pittsburgh had been running to capacity, the business had failed financially. Soon the Mellons purchased a major block of the company's stock and engineered the company's move to Niagara Falls where electricity was less expensive. By the 1920s the Mellons owned 35 percent of the company, by then known as the Aluminum Company of America, or Alcoa, which later was to become a major supporter of Carnegie Mellon.

The outcome of this visit was echoed in 1895 when Edward Acheson arrived in Pittsburgh with a strange lump of a synthetic abrasive in his pocket. In what became known in the Carborundum Company's lore as "the scratch heard 'round the world," Acheson used the stone to inscribe a deep groove in a paperweight he picked up from Mellon's desk. The Mellon brothers were impressed. In return for a one-sixteenth interest in the company, the Mellons took $50,000 of a $75,000 bond issue. The money provided funds to move the company near cheap electricity at Niagara Falls. The Mellons steadily increased their holdings in Carborundum stock.

A. W. and R. B. soon held large interests in a myriad of companies including Koppers, a chemical company, The Monongahela Street Railway Company, Pittsburgh Coal, Westinghouse Electric and Westinghouse Air Brake, McClintic-Marshall, an engineering firm, the Standard Steel (RR) Car Company and a score of public utilities. By the time he died, A. W. owned substantial holdings in about 300 companies. The most successful and well-known of the Mellon brothers' firms, however, was guided and shaped by their nephew, William Larimer (W. L.) Mellon, who was only a few years younger than his uncles and who felt closer to them than to his own father, James Ross Mellon.

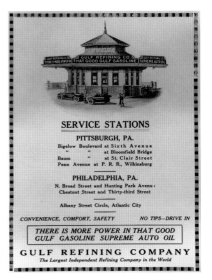

W. L.

The Mellon brothers had intriguing private lives. Both belonged to the Duquesne Club where they lunched daily with a small group of close friends in a third-floor dining room. In that intimate company, A. W.'s shyness disappeared. His jovial side also appeared at home where he slid down banisters, went sled riding, played cards and blindman's buff and read aloud to his two children. R. B. purchased 20 square miles of mountains and valleys east of Pittsburgh and turned them into the Rolling Rock Farms and Rolling Rock Club. Soon dozens of his friends had houses near the club where they rode to the hounds, hunted, fished and generally enjoyed themselves. Rolling Rock to the Mellons was like Skibo to Andrew Carnegie.

Mellon oil money builds Tech's business school

The Mellons had invested in speculative drillings in West Texas, drillings that paid off when Colonel James M. Guffey struck oil at Spindletop, near Beaumont, Texas in 1901. The Mellons loaned $4 million to Guffey, and for a time, his company rode a wave of gushers to success. Some of the wells seemed to have gone dry, however, and on an investigative visit to Texas in 1902, W. L. discovered that Guffey was expanding his company far faster than he could repay his debts. Installed as executive vice president, W. L. dismissed several of the colonel's incompetent old cronies and began to reposition the company. In serious financial trouble, Guffey sold block after block of his stock to the Mellons until they finally bought out the company and a subsidiary, the Gulf Refining Company, for $3 million. They were reorganized into the Gulf Oil Company in 1907. W. L. Mellon used part of the fortune he amassed in this venture to found the Graduate School of Industrial Administration at Carnegie Tech.

Above right:
An early ad for Gulf Refining
Service stations

Below:
The first Mellon Institute
resided in a frame building on
the University of Pittsburgh's
campus.

"The Chemistry of Commerce"

During the summer of 1909, Andrew Mellon invited Professor Robert Kennedy Duncan from the University of Kansas to visit him in Pittsburgh in order to discuss Duncan's book, *The Chemistry of Commerce.* Before moving to Kansas, Duncan, a Canadian, had been head of the Department of Chemistry at Washington & Jefferson College where his research had solved several problems for local companies. Convinced that academics failed to share their ideas with the public, he began to write articles about science for general interest publications. In short order, he consolidated his writings into three books, including *The Chemistry of Commerce,* in which he called for a greater partnership between science and industry.

This idea fascinated both A. W. and R. B. Mellon. They invited Duncan to come to the University of Pittsburgh, promising to help him build an institute of industrial research there. Pitt would provide Duncan with a laboratory and administer the institute in exchange for services as a faculty member. Corporate donors would pay research costs. Duncan accepted. The first Mellon Institute and School of Specific Industries resided in a one-story frame building on the Pitt campus. To Duncan's delight, it rapidly outgrew its makeshift quarters, and the Mellon brothers agreed to finance the construction of a building Duncan had planned. Sadly, he died before that building was completed.

Duncan's institute, however, survived; indeed, it thrived. By 1920, 83 scientists conducted $300,000 worth of research each year on projects that included a smog abatement program for Pittsburgh, the invention of the gas mask, a pneumonia serum, a rainbow of paints, dyes, and varnishes, and a series of discoveries that led to the creation of the petrochemical industry. Mellon Institute also spawned a host of similar research centers at other universities and spurred several companies to launch their own research departments.

In 1928 the Mellon Institute separated from the University of Pittsburgh and was incorporated as the Mellon Institute of Industrial Research. At the time, the institute employed 135 fellows supported by fellowships from 65 companies. Clearly another building was needed. The Mellons bought land for this new building at the corner of Fifth Avenue and Bellefield Street near the Pitt campus.

A third generation of Mellons supports Carnegie Tech

The significant connections between the Mellons and Carnegie Tech developed after World War II with Judge Mellon's grandsons, not with his sons. Both A. W. and R. B. Mellon occupied themselves with other matters during the 1920s and 1930s. Between 1921 and 1933, Andrew W. Mellon served as Secretary of the Treasury during the Harding, Coolidge and Hoover administrations and then as Ambassador to the Court of St. James. His brother took control of the family's far-flung business enterprises from his offices in Pittsburgh. A. W. returned to Pittsburgh in March 1933, three weeks after Franklin D. Roosevelt was inaugurated, in time to cope with the bank holiday that closed all the banks while examiners certified their safety. Both Mellon Bank and the Union Trust withstood the storm. Not one Mellon bank failed. R. B. Mellon stood in the lobby of one of the banks as his tellers stacked currency at their windows for all to see.

Left:
The Mellon Institute quickly outgrew its makeshift quarters, and the Mellon brothers agreed to finance the construction of a new building.

Above:
The columns for the Mellon Institute were created at an Indiana quarry, transported to Pittsburgh by train, and from the rail yard in East Liberty to the Oakland site by truck.

Building the Mellon Institute

During the six years between 1931 and 1937, all of Pittsburgh watched as the Mellon Institute rose next to Pitt's Cathedral of Learning. Architects Janssen and Cocken modeled its proportions after the Parthenon and its architectural details after the Temple of Athena on the Acropolis and the Temple of Sardis in Asia Minor. Since the plans called for a building of 6.5 million cubic feet (432,700 square feet of floor space), much of it had to be placed underground in order to adhere to the dimensions of the Parthenon. The architects first built a model of the building and then erected a full-scale model of a pier and two columns in a cornfield in Fox Chapel. Finally, they erected two fully equipped laboratories in order to find answers to questions about layout, plumbing, wiring and lighting.

The building is shaped like a trapezoid. Some 306 feet long in front, 227 feet at the rear and 334 feet on each side. Three of its nine stories are underground. The most striking feature of the building's exterior is the colonnades. The limestone columns were cut at a newly opened quarry in Indiana that yielded a particularly white limestone. Workers wrapped each column in layers of burlap that were kept wet for 14 months while the stone cured. Stonecutters then turned them on a lathe to their finished weight of 60 tons each. These columns are monoliths, that is, smooth, one-piece shafts unbroken by horizontal lines. They were shipped to Pittsburgh by railroad, one to a flatcar, and trucked from the rail yard in East Liberty on special trucks with attached trailers. They are the largest monoliths ever erected anywhere.

The plans called for the monoliths to stand vertically on their bases. A gantry crane lifted each column into place. Workmen took two hours to erect each column and cement it into place with a special limestone mortar. In total, the columns with their bases and capitals weighed 4,432 tons. Each of the capitals, also lifted by gantry crane, weighed 6.5 tons and measured 5.5 by 7.5 feet. Some experts contend that the stonework, the world's largest colonnade consisting of monoliths, ranks among the world's finest.

Left:
The columns arrive at the site and one by one are lifted by a crane and set into place.

Below:
The completed Mellon Institute contained the world's largest colonnade.

Clearly, however, the era of the Mellon brothers was coming to a close. In 1933, A. W. was 78; R. B. was 75 and had only a few months to live. A. W. died four years later in 1937. In the midst of the depression, both of them, particularly R. B., had been involved in the construction of the Mellon Institute, an activity that consumed their interest, time and money. It was time for the next generation to take the reins of the Mellons' far-flung interests.

Andrew Mellon, who married a 21-year-old British woman when he was 45, had been divorced and had two children, Paul and Ailsa. Paul attended Choate, Yale and Cambridge. He was a brilliant student and became an excellent speaker and writer, a distinguished patron of the arts, an accomplished horseman and a public-minded citizen. Upon completing his formal education, he joined Mellon Bank to please his father, but he disliked banking, particularly the endless meetings. He began to realize his true potential when he moved to a 200-acre farm, the nucleus of his 4,000 acre Virginia estate, leaving the world of finance to become a philanthropist, a patron of the arts, a trustee of Mellon Institute and the administrator of his father's estate. For many years, he was a trustee of three Mellon foundations and chairman of the Andrew W. Mellon Educational and Charitable Trust. Almost half of the disbursements from this fund in its early years went to support his father's favorite project, the National Gallery in Washington, D.C. It was also a frequent and generous supporter of many Carnegie Tech/ Carnegie Mellon projects.

R. B. also had two children, Richard King and Sarah Cordelia Mellon. Sarah married Alan Scaife, head of the Scaife Company, the oldest manufacturing company west of the Alleghenies. During the 1960s, the Sarah Mellon Scaife Foundation and Scaife family interests built both Tech's Scaife Hall of Engineering and Tech's administration building, Warner Hall. Unlike his cousin Paul, R. K. took an active interest in banking and learned the business from the ground up. His first task upon his father's death would be to settle the $37 million state and federal tax bill presented to the family. R. B. had given away most of his holdings while he was still alive, leaving an estate of only $200 million.

The General leads a Renaissance

R. K.

During World War II, both Paul and Richard King Mellon served as officers in the army. R. K. emerged as a general, a title he used throughout his life. After the war, he and his wife Constance returned to a gloomy and depressing Pittsburgh. Their apartment in the William Penn Hotel overlooked a dreary scene. Forty percent of the downtown buildings were empty, the business district was crisscrossed by railroad tracks, and drivers used their headlights at high noon to cut through the smog and smoke. Neither Constance nor R. K. Mellon wanted to live in Pittsburgh's smog, but unlike some of his predecessors, the General was loyal to his hometown. When he had been 16, his father had taken him to New York where he saw the mansions of three men who had made their fortunes in coal, coke and steel in Pittsburgh: Andrew Carnegie, Henry Clay Frick and Charles Schwab. In addition, his cousins, Paul and Ailsa, also spent little time in

Fifth Avenue at 11 o'clock in the morning of November 5, 1945— before smoke control took effect

142

their hometown. Rather than live in the city, however, R. K. made his home at Rolling Rock Farms in Ligonier, 50 miles from Pittsburgh, and commuted by automobile each day to his downtown offices.

Mellon had been appointed president of the Pittsburgh Regional Planning Association, and in 1943, he had formed the Allegheny Conference on Community Development, whose first chairman was Carnegie Tech's president, Robert E. Doherty. R. K. Mellon, Doherty, Edward Weidlein of the Mellon Institute and Willard E. Hotchkiss, Carnegie Institute of Technology's dean of humanistic and social studies, directed a group of committees studying the city's problems. With plans in hand, the General decided that the time for action had arrived when the war ended.

In partnership with Pittsburgh's Democratic mayor, David L. Lawrence, the Mellon group envisioned a "Golden Triangle" on the 23 acres of vacant warehouses and slums at the confluence of the Allegheny and Monongahela Rivers. Bulldozers soon cleared the area and the new Gateway Center office buildings and Point State Park rose on the site. Alcoa built a gleaming new office building—of aluminum, of course—while U.S. Steel and Mellon Bank erected a 41-story steel skyscraper near the William Penn Hotel. Over the pleas of some business leaders who seemed to believe that soot was good for the lungs, Lawrence enforced the city's smog abatement ordinances. All this activity marked the beginning of the Pittsburgh Renaissance. Today, in the shadow of the Alcoa and Mellon Bank buildings, sits a little oasis, a welcome destination for weary office workers. Its name is Mellon Square—a fitting tribute to the General who marshaled his forces to eliminate urban blight.

Equitable Life's Gateway Center, Pittsburgh's first redevelopment project

The Mellons discover Carnegie Tech

Mellon family members, as well as officials from the companies and foundations in which the Mellons had major interests, had had intermittent relationships with Carnegie Tech. For example, in 1921 Andrew W. Mellon gave Tech his mansion on Forbes Street. Mellons or their employees served on the board of the Carnegie Institute during the years before 1967 when that board also controlled Carnegie Tech. Roy Hunt, CEO of Alcoa, served for many years on the subcommittee of the Carnegie Institute's Board of Trustees that held responsibility for Carnegie Tech. Richard K. Mellon joined this subcommittee in 1940. Occasionally a Mellon, including Cordelia Mellon Scaife May and Richard King Mellon, enrolled or was tutored at Tech, although no family member received a degree there before World War II. During the 1940s, the A. W. Mellon Educational and Charitable Trust gave at least six small grants to Tech's scholarship funds. Then came the alliance in the Allegheny Conference on Community Development between R. K. Mellon and Robert Doherty. After the war, a number of projects drew the Mellons and Tech together.

William Larimer Mellon took the first step. As chairman of the board of Gulf Oil, he had been unable to recruit qualified executives to work for the company. Those with practical knowledge of industry lacked requisite academic and scientific backgrounds; newcomers with business school backgrounds lacked experience in the real world. No current university program solved this problem. Tech's Carnegie Plan, however, seemed to fit Mellon's aspirations. It combined problem solving with a humanistic and social component that could be adapted to a business school.

The initiative came from W. L., who took the idea for a new type of business school education to Tech's president Robert Doherty, who had seen similar problems years before when he worked for General Electric. Later, as Yale's dean of engineering, he had tried without success to institute an industrial administration program. As a result of the discussions between W. L. and Doherty, the William L. and May T. Mellon Foundation granted Tech $5 million in endowment and a $1 million building fund to found a School of Industrial Administration. Both Mellon and Doherty had in mind a school that would educate undergraduates and master's students. "The objective of the school," Doherty said, "is to assure a thorough understanding of the economic system in which the student lives and business operates." Doherty, however, chose as the first dean George Leland Bach, who had come to Carnegie Tech in 1947 at age 30 as head of the Department of Economics with a promise that he could start a small doctoral program. When William Larimer Mellon died in 1949 and Doherty died in 1950, Bach had a clear field to develop his long-anticipated doctoral program. During the Warner administration in the 1950s and 1960s, money from two Mellon foundations and four family members supported other major initiatives at Carnegie Tech. Then Carnegie Tech became a university, again through the vision and initiative of another member of the Mellon family.

Mellon Institute and Carnegie Tech merge

Despite Judge Mellon's observations about the value of higher education, his descendants had always been disposed to help out his, and A.W.'s, alma mater, the University of Pittsburgh. Their support for Pitt came as much from a genuine concern about education as from their vested interest that was closely tied to Pitt—Mellon Institute. During the early 1920s, however, Pitt was heavily in debt and suffering from poor morale. Its newly appointed Chancellor, John Bowman, began a search for someone to help him turn the institution around. After he won R. B.'s support, A.W.'s initial resistance ebbed. The Mellon brothers paid off Pitt's debts and purchased 14 acres of land in Oakland on which the Cathedral of Learning would be built.

This grand building, however, did nothing to improve the relationships between Mellon Institute and Pitt. Compared to similar institutions, Mellon Institute made two major strategic decisions which would plague it. First, it committed itself to long-range projects that industries were unwilling to finance, rejecting problems that might be solved in a few months or a year. Secondly, it did little to establish and maintain ties to the federal government, the source of major funding in the post-World War II years.

Paul

In addition, Mellon Institute was deeply rooted in the sciences of the early part of the century. Mellon Institute's landmark home on Fifth Avenue (the city changed the name from Fifth Street to Fifth Avenue in 1957) had been designed, after all, as the most advanced set of chemistry laboratories in the world, and the Institute was having trouble embracing physics and electronics. A comprehensive study by a commission headed by Karl Compton of Massachusetts Institute of Technology pointed to these and other shortcomings. Despite some groundbreaking work in radiation and atomic energy, including the construction of its $4 million Bushy Run facility in 1959, Mellon Institute was looking decidedly old-fashioned.

Paul Mellon decided to strengthen Mellon Institute's work in pure science by transferring $10 million from the A.W. Mellon Educational and Charitable Trust into an endowment for basic research. R. K. Mellon and Sarah Mellon Scaife contributed another $5 million. A new research director, Paul Flory, was appointed. This new emphasis, however, was never a good fit. A schism soon developed between the applied research and pure research teams at Mellon Institute. By the mid-1950s the monetary value of research at Carnegie Tech had surpassed the value of the research at Mellon Institute, and the gap between the two widened steadily.

Facing this situation squarely, Paul Mellon proposed a merger between the two institutions. The negotiations at first were top secret; one meeting was even held in Cleveland. Still word leaked out, and institute staffers cried foul. Even R. K. Mellon resisted the idea temporarily, and Pitt Chancellor Edward Litchfield, in the midst of an ambitious development plan of his own, opposed the idea vigorously. By 1966, however, Litchfield had died in a small plane accident and the situation at Mellon Institute was becoming increasingly critical. After another round of negotiations, the Tech Board of Trustees approved a merger plan on April 17, 1967. Paul Mellon's initiative and fortitude had created Carnegie Mellon University.

In what some observers saw as a wedding present, R. K. Mellon offered the new university $10 million to found a School of Urban and Public Affairs. Like other cities, Pittsburgh needed good public administrators if the Pittsburgh Renaissance was going to succeed. Carnegie Mellon's president, H. Guyford Stever, accepted this generous offer with delight. William W. Cooper, one of the founders of the Graduate School of Industrial Administration, became the new school's first dean, and after a few rocky years, the School of Urban and Public Affairs was launched on a distinguished career. In 1992, it became the repository for the papers of Senator John Heinz, a Republican and a member of the famous Heinz family from Pittsburgh, who had been killed in an airplane crash in 1991, and the school was renamed the H. John Heinz III School of Public Policy and Management. How appropriate! The founders of the three family fortunes supporting Carnegie Mellon and the Heinz School—Andrew Carnegie, Thomas Mellon and H. J. Heinz—had been friends when they were still vigorous young men.

Although the Institute had been designed with the most advanced set of chemistry laboratories in the world, Mellon Institute was looking decidedly old-fashioned in 1959.

The Creation of SUPA
(Excerpts from the Letter)

December 30, 1968

Dr. H. Guyford Stever
President
Carnegie-Mellon University
Pittsburgh, Pennsylvania 15213

Dear Dr. Stever:

Recognizing some time ago that Carnegie-Mellon University had some unique qualities in certain areas which placed the University in the field of urban education, the Trustees listened with interest to your proposal to create a new School of Urban and Public Affairs at Carnegie-Mellon University.

It is the hope of the Trustees that this School which has been formed under the leadership of Dr. William W. Cooper will become a nationally prominent contributor of men and ideas to the field of urban affairs with a particular interest and emphasis on Pittsburgh and Western Pennsylvania problems. We see a great opportunity for this School to provide assistance to the city, the state and the nation in the massive effort which is needed to educate, train and motivate managers in the field of urban affairs. . . .

Sincerely yours,
Joseph D. Hughes
Richard King Mellon Charitable Trusts
Administrative Trustee

Mellon gifts continued to support Carnegie Mellon enterprises throughout the Cyert, Mehrabian and Cohon administrations. Among the most important gifts was a contingency fund contributed by the R. K. Mellon Foundation between 1973 and 1984. Totaling $12 million, it allowed Carnegie Mellon's president, Richard M. Cyert, to initiate and support new endeavors. These initiatives often resulted in the development of new centers able to win funding from the government, private foundations or individuals. In this way, Mellon seed money produced abundant fruit.

The Mellon family and Carnegie Mellon

Gifts from members of the Mellon family, their foundations, and the companies they founded have shaped Carnegie Mellon University since World War II more than any other single factor. Carnegie Mellon's records list more than 200 separate grants from family members and their foundations. In 1996 purchasing power, they total more than $583 million. These gifts have been so influential for three major reasons. First, they have had an impact on all of Carnegie Mellon's seven colleges and schools, the Carnegie Mellon Research Institute and the central administration. Second, they have supported virtually every aspect of the life of the University: the endowment, research, building programs, student scholarships, educational experiments, student life and projects that connect the University to the community. Third, they have provided the basic funding that enabled schools such as the Graduate School of Industrial Administration, the School of Urban and Public Affairs and the School of Computer Science to establish reputations that helped them gain support from the government, corporations and private foundations. In addition, a number of companies founded by the Mellons, such as Mellon Bank, Alcoa, Gulf Oil, Carborundum and Koppers, have been substantial contributors to the University.

The contributions of the Mellon family take on added meaning when they are viewed in terms of 1999 buying power. In today's money, the $1 million allocated for the business school building in 1949 would fall short of building and equipping a single modern lecture hall. The following table translates the contributions of the Mellon family into 1999 dollars in order to present them in a meaningful perspective for the contemporary reader.

Contributions of the extended Mellon family to Carnegie Mellon

- Buildings, equipment and endowment valued at $292.7 million to the Mellon Institute and the Mellon College of Science, transforming Carnegie Institute of Technology into Carnegie Mellon University in 1967

- Twenty gifts totaling $55 million to the Graduate School of Industrial Administration

- Six gifts totaling $47 million to the School for Urban and Public Affairs, now the H. John Heinz III School of Public Policy and Management

- Five gifts totaling $26 million to the Department (later School) of Computer Science

- Five gifts totaling $6.3 million to the Carnegie Mellon Research Institute

- Two gifts totaling $314,000 to Margaret Morrison Carnegie College

- Twelve gifts totaling $12.4 million to the College of Humanities and Social Sciences

- Twenty gifts totaling $35 million to the College of Fine Arts

- Seven gifts totaling $3.3 million to the Carnegie Institute of Technology, Carnegie Mellon's engineering college

- In addition to the original Graduate School of Industrial Administration building grant of $1 million, 55 gifts totaling $22.8 million to building campaigns

- Ten gifts totaling $24.8 million to Presidential Discretionary Funds

- Thirty unrestricted gifts totaling $31.3 million

- Forty gifts totaling $14.2 million to various projects such as lecture series, scholarship funds, and outreach to the community

- Three gifts to the Mellon College of Science totaling $12.2 million

- One gift of $30,000 to the library

This relationship has been mutually beneficial. The Graduate School of Industrial Administration developed the type of business leaders that W. L. Mellon desired and the business community needed. The School of Urban and Public Affairs, now The Heinz School, has trained leaders for the public sector, just as General Mellon hoped it would. The University has contributed in innumerable ways to the Pittsburgh Renaissance, a movement set in motion by R. K. Mellon, as well as to the more recent Regional Economic Development effort in southwestern Pennsylvania. The colleges of Fine Arts and of Humanities and Social Sciences have enriched the community's cultural and social life in directions that reflect major interests of Paul Mellon and other family members. Scaife Hall has contributed to the development of engineering and manufacturing as so many Scaife enterprises had done in the past. The Carnegie Mellon Research Institute has adapted and advanced the pioneering work of the Mellon Institute to a new technological era. Dozens of Mellon family grants to Carnegie Mellon have fostered growth in education and culture in the wider community, as have many Mellon grants to other institutions. Warner Hall provided a home for the University's administrators while generous unrestricted grants provided funds for the endowment as well as for innovative projects. Can any other university boast of such an outstanding partnership with five generations of a single family, the Mellons?

Thoughts in a Mellon Patch

If Grandpa Thomas with his plough
Could only see us Mellons now
(Especially those who misbehave!)
He'd turn abruptly in his grave.

A Puritan who had the gift
Of soberness and work and thrift,
He'd scarce believe we'd be such fools
To sun ourselves at swimming pools.

And ride around in fancy cars
Smoke cigarettes and big cigars,
Drink alcohol like mother's milk,
and dress ourselves in brightest silk.

And he might think our clothes outrageous,
our miniskirts, like mumps contagious,
Our rock and roll too loud to bear,
Too wild our boys with maxi-hair.

But other days bring other ways,
And while each child and grandchild pays
The Piper (each great-grandchild too),
Such revolutions are not new.

Each generation has its rules
And Mellons never have been fools.
Some have thrived, a few have failed,
But hardly any have been jailed.

Though some of us are fond of horses,
And some have scandals and divorces,
And some like fishing, some like art,
Our paths are never far apart.

We mind our business, love our friends,
Grow old, collect our dividends,
Nor do we shrink from healthy toil,
(Though sometimes it is eased with oil!)

Each generation has to face
Its triumphs or its faults with grace.
Each, as it labors or relaxes,
Itself is faced with Death and Taxes.

So though he was a stern old Judge,
I'm sure he wouldn't now begrudge
Our foibles and extravaganzas,
(Or even these poor foolish stanzas!)

Perhaps he'd smile from up above
With ancient grand-paternal love
To see us dance and dine and wine,
All Mellons on his fruitful vine.
—Paul Mellon H'67

9.

John Christian Warner 1950–1965
He led Carnegie Tech during its golden years

John Christian Warner, "Jake" to everyone who knew him well, was born in Goshen, Indiana, on May 28, 1897. His father, a farmer, died when Jake was eight; his mother, who had been a schoolteacher before her marriage, was left with four sons to rear. Warner's education began in a one-room schoolhouse in Goshen. In 1915 he entered Indiana University where his outstanding academic record won him election to both Phi Beta Kappa and Sigma Xi, a science honorary.

Short and stocky, Jake Warner was well-rounded in both senses of the word. While an undergraduate, he played violin in the symphony orchestra, won a letter in wrestling and played halfback on the football team. Commenting on Jake's intelligence and lifestyle, a classmate once remarked that, "Jake could pass anything at Indiana except the Delta Gamma House." Louise L. Hamer, who lived in that house, became his bride in 1925. He earned a bachelor of arts degree in 1919, a master of arts in 1920 and a Ph.D. in 1923, all at Indiana.

While studying for his doctorate, he served as an instructor in chemistry for several years. Then he worked for two years as a research chemist for three Indiana companies before coming to Carnegie Tech as an instructor in 1926. He was soon a leader among the "Young Turks," junior faculty who pressed for a stronger research program and more graduate work. He rose to the rank of professor, became head of the Department of Chemistry in 1938, dean of graduate studies in 1945, vice president and president-elect in 1949 and president in 1950 when he was 53 years old.

Warner's background provided superb preparation for his career as president. His undergraduate years familiarized him with the interplay of academic and co-curricular activities at a modern university. His interdisciplinary training prepared him to foster interdisciplinary projects at Tech. His years on the faculty gave him firsthand experience with faculty culture, the Carnegie Plan and programs in the fine arts. His career as a researcher within a department rather than a research institute prepared him to develop a fresh research agenda. Finally, as Dean of Graduate Studies and President-elect, he came to know directly the financial and administrative challenges he was soon to face as he sought to make Carnegie Tech into what he called "a center of learning."

Above:
John Warner received the Pittsburgh Award in 1945.

Opposite page top:
President Doherty and President-elect Warner celebrate Tech's first football win after 25 losses.

Opposite page bottom:
Warner and trustees examine a campus plan.

1950

- John Christian Warner becomes Tech's fourth president.
- The first alumni awards are given as part of his inauguration ceremony.

He was a distinguished researcher and author. His bibliography lists 87 publications, about two-thirds on scientific and technical subjects and the remaining on education in colleges and secondary schools. During World War II he headed government research on the purification and metallurgy of plutonium for the Manhattan Project that developed the atomic bomb. With a half dozen other Tech faculty and graduate students, he witnessed the explosion of the first atomic bomb at Alamogordo, New Mexico. Fourteen colleges and universities presented him with honorary degrees.

Warner's personality and work habits also suited him for leadership. He was thoughtful, friendly and concerned, a smart scientist who loved Carnegie Tech and its people. He was also frank and direct so that his subordinates knew exactly where they stood, admirable qualities in a leader. He could leave his work at the office. He turned out excellent meals on the family's outdoor grill and enjoyed golf with his wife and friends until a wartime work schedule followed by his administration at Tech pushed his golf clubs into the closet.

Warner faces a host of problems

Warner faced a host of problems which he discussed at length with Doherty during the year before he became president. Carnegie Institute of Technology still had only three functioning colleges: Engineering and Science, Fine Arts and Margaret Morrison. Engineering and Science enrolled more students than the other two combined and also dominated graduate instruction. In addition, Tech had a division of Humanities and Social Studies which granted no degrees although its faculty taught about 30 percent of the total class enrollments. Tech also included a small Library School, a Department of Social Work, a program in printing management and a new Graduate School of Industrial Administration (GSIA). Except for GSIA—and even GSIA within a few years—all of them needed additional resources if they were to succeed. Warner took a step toward solving this problem by phasing out the Department of Social Work, the Library School and the program in printing management.

Carnegie Tech had no development office to raise money and no independent board of trustees to provide leadership. Its endowment of $31 million invested mainly in fixed income securities provided just over $1 million in annual income. Atop all these problems lay an impending faculty crisis focusing on inadequate salaries and fringe benefits. Knowing about all these problems, Warner nevertheless saw his role clearly when he became president. In his inaugural address, he said: "For the near future, it is my opinion that Carnegie Tech needs no reorientation and it needs no new educational philosophy. We need a period for consolidating our gains and for bringing our plans to fruition."

Warner moved simultaneously on many fronts. Perhaps the most important for Tech's future was the establishment of an independent board of trustees. Tech's board was still under the control of the trustees of the Carnegie Institute. While the Institute was well served by local trustees, Carnegie Tech needed a board drawn from across the nation in order to meet its growing mission. After protracted legal negotiations, the Court of Common Pleas decreed in 1959 that the two institutions could establish separate boards. This decision laid the groundwork for remarkable growth both during the remainder of the Warner years and under his successors. Among the members of the new board were Charles E. Wilson (E'09), an alumnus and at the time Secretary of Defense, Benjamin F. Fairless, Gwilym A. Price, John P. Toche and Sidney A. Swensrud who were soon to head Tech's new development drive.

Warner appointed committees, the forerunners of strategic planning groups, to examine Tech's financial standing and to make plans for a development drive. The committees developed three reports submitted in 1952, 1954 and 1955. They reviewed Tech's growth from the beginning of the Carnegie Technical Schools and developed a plan for the future. The report compared Tech's status and its endowment with a number of its sister independent institutions. Of the 34, Tech's endowment per student ranked 22nd, ahead of distinguished institutions such as Stanford, Washington University, Western Reserve, Case and Cornell. In the order in which endowment was increasing, however, Tech ranked 25th with the five distinguished institutions that trailed Tech in endowment-per-student all increasing at a faster rate. Warner read the handwriting on the wall. Tech must increase its endowment if it intended to increase in quality or even hold its place among peer independent colleges and universities. His summary of the proposed development program outlined in the 1955 report reads:

> *A careful analysis of Carnegie's present resources and a realistic appraisal of these with the resources of first-rate educational institutions of similar kinds has led to the conclusion that Carnegie should undertake a development program to obtain additional annual income of $1,052,000 and capital funds for new construction of $12,950,000. If the additional annual income is capitalized at 4%, endowment for this purpose should be increased by approximately $25,000,000. Thus the total development program should provide new funds in the amount of $38,000,000 to $40,000,000.*

1952

- The Graduate School of Industrial Administration building is completed.

1956

- Tech's first computer, an IBM 650, arrives on campus.
- Tech recruits Alan J. Perlis to establish the Computation Center.

Finally an Independent Board!

In a Winter 1987 article in *Carnegie Mellon Magazine*, Warner reminisced about the way in which an independent board had come to fruition. Not having trustees in cities outside Pittsburgh handicapped Tech officials when they called to tell Tech's story:

This led us to raise the question in an executive committee meeting about the feasibility of changing Tech's trustees setup so that we would have a board completely separated from Carnegie Institute and national in character. We were reminded by several trustees who were attorneys that legal opinion on this possibility had been sought on two occasions in the past, and each time the opinion had been given that the change could not be made. [Benjamin] Fairless then remarked, "In our corporation when we think something should be done and that it is the right thing to do, we ask our lawyers to tell us how we can do it." Within a week, our lawyers told us how we could do it.

Above:
Carnegie Tech's first independent Board of Trustees

Opposite page:
"Jake" Warner and family

151

1959

- Tech establishes an independent Board of Trustees.

The trustees could soon count on the work of Tech's first development office. Warner established the office in 1957, appointing H. Russell Bintzer as Tech's first Vice President for Development and Public Relations. Plans for a major development drive were already underway when Bintzer assumed office and an official announcement of a drive to raise $24,350,000 (not the $40,000,000 that the 1955 report suggested) over 10 years was made. By the end of Warner's administration, $26 million had been raised toward a revised goal of $28 million. This dramatic performance, along with steady increases in tuition from $600 per year ($480 in Margaret Morrison) to $1,700 in 1959-60 helped to alleviate some of Tech's difficult financial problems.

Bintzer was largely responsible for a number of innovations that had a lasting effect on both the administration and on academic life. He took administrative responsibility for the supervision of the India Steel Training and Educational Program supported by the Ford Foundation. It brought 600 graduate Indian engineers to Carnegie Tech over a five-year period to study steel making so that they could take charge of the newly nationalized steel industry in India. Tech had become an international player, at least for a few years. Bintzer and his colleagues set up a full system for organizing development campaigns, the residue of which remains at Carnegie Mellon. He reorganized the public relations, alumni affairs and placement offices and hired new directors for each.

New buildings rise on the campus

The influx of funds from the development drive supported Tech's second era of new construction. The Warner era saw four major buildings, six housing developments, a number of renovations on campus and the addition to the central campus of five contiguous properties. This building program gave Tech a little room in which to grow. Thanks to a generous gift in 1964 from Mrs. Alan M. Scaife, a new administration building named in Warner's honor supplemented the construction program when it was erected in 1966, soon after Warner's retirement.

Above right:
Warner Hall, fondly dubbed the flashcube

Right:
The Hunt Library

152

Contemporary campus planners bewail the appearance of the five major buildings erected during and immediately after the Warner years: Donner Hall, an aluminum and glass residence hall; Hunt Library; Scaife Hall, housing engineering offices and classrooms; Skibo, the student center; and Warner Hall, the administration building that students promptly dubbed "the flashcube." None of them fits comfortably with either the original Hornbostel buildings or the new construction begun during the middle 1980s. The 1960s buildings were the product of a school of architecture, popular at the time, that paid scant attention to the way in which new buildings fit into an overall plan. Hunt Library, for example, sends a jarring note to the campus' public face even though it solved for many years one of Tech's major problems—lack of library facilities.

The development drive and new investment policies also had a dramatic effect on both endowment and income. By 1965 the endowment had increased to $74 million, partly through capital gains of $12 million on securities. Income from endowment doubled between 1950 and 1965 from $1 million to $2 million. A $5 million grant to the endowment from the A. W. Mellon Educational and Charitable Trust supported four Andrew Mellon Professorships in architecture, drama, music and painting, design and sculpture in the College of Fine Arts, as well as visiting professors and salary increases. Jake Warner, who had played the violin in his college symphony orchestra, was delighted.

Computing comes to Carnegie Tech

New funding also supported the development of the Computation Center, the origin of Carnegie Mellon's leadership in computing. After several years of planning, the University established the Computation Center in 1956 as a joint project of the Graduate School of Industrial Administration and the departments of Psychology, Electrical Engineering and Mathematics. Alan J. Perlis (S'42),

a remarkably talented and energetic scientist from Purdue, became the head of the new Center where he worked closely with Herbert A. Simon, Allen Newell (IA'57) and a number of other innovative faculty members and graduate students. Simon and Newell directed most of their energy to research on artificial intelligence (AI). According to Edward Feigenbaum (E'56, IA'60) one of his distinguished students, Simon told his class one day that, "Over Christmas, Allen Newell and I created a thinking machine." The Center's first year budget, when it had a staff of four, was $53,000. By the end of the Warner years, the Computation Center had brought in many millions of dollars in

Top:
The Alan M. Scaife Hall of Engineering

Center:
The dormitory, Donner Hall

Bottom:
Skibo, the new student center

153

grants and had become one of the most distinguished institutions of its kind in the nation both in research and in education.

In 1958 the Computation Center began to offer a course in programming for freshmen, the first such course in the nation. Thus Carnegie Tech pioneered in offering computer science to undergraduates, a practice now universal in universities. In 1960 half of the engineering and science freshman class

elected computing courses, and by the end of the Warner years, several departments were offering options in computing. At Tech computing became an integral part of both research and education throughout the institution rather than an isolated department with relatively little impact ouside its own boundaries. By the end of the Warner administration, Carnegie Tech's programs in computing were consistently rated with those at

Massachusetts Institute of Technology and Stanford as the best in the nation. A year after Warner's retirement, the Computation Center became the Department of Computer and Information Science with the support of a $5 million grant from Richard King Mellon.

Robert E. Doherty had concentrated his attention on revolutionizing undergraduate education. Under Warner, the Carnegie Plan continued to improve education in Engineering and Science, Humanities and Social Studies and the business school, and to make somewhat halting inroads in both Fine Arts and Margaret Morrison. A 1972 grant from the Carnegie Corporation sponsored awards for outstanding teachers, awards that were continued later with the William H. Ryan (E'24) and Frances S. Ryan Teaching Awards. The reputation of the Carnegie Plan, led by Elliott Dunlap Smith, continued to attract visitors to campus and to encourage similar reforms in post-secondary education throughout the nation.

With undergraduate education well in hand, Warner focused attention on the reorganization of research and graduate studies, the remaining two of Doherty's tripartite goals. Graduate enrollment increased by 92 percent, and the number of doctors' degrees granted by 144 percent, during his administration. By 1965 Tech ranked ninth nationally—fourth among private institutions—in the production of engineering doctorates and was in the top quarter in doctorates in the physical sciences and mathematics. To encourage research throughout the faculty, Warner incorporated three engineering and scientific laboratories into college departments. The establishment of the office of Dean of Research in 1961 coordinated faculty research efforts. Sponsored research increased from $1 million in 1949-50 to $19.5 million a decade later, and the number of faculty publications, exhibitions and performances increased from 182 to 665.

The business school blossoms

The Graduate School of Industrial Administration blossomed during the Warner years. Both of the originators of the School of Industrial Administration, William Larimer Mellon and Robert E. Doherty, died in 1950. This left the ground open for the first dean, George Leland Bach, to fashion the school after his own interests. Bach began with a clean slate. He had been brought to Carnegie Tech in 1946 as head of the Department of Economics with a promise that he could begin a doctoral program. Within a short time, he hired 15 economists most of whom, like Bach, had widespread experience in government positions during World War II. Then he was made Dean of the School of Industrial Administration. Since the school was new, he had no entrenched faculty or institutional restraints to overcome. Bach rejected the approach to business education represented by Harvard's Case Study method. Instead he argued that business education should be based on theories of individual and collective human behavior based on social science research expressed quantitatively.

He soon recruited a remarkable faculty which included Herbert A. Simon, William W. Cooper, James March and Charles Holt. Shortly, Franco Modigliani, Richard M. Cyert, Allen Newell (IA'57), and a number of additional distinguished scholars joined the group. Within a short time, the school was renamed the Graduate School of Industrial Administration and was organized around four programs— a Ph.D., a two-year master's degree, an undergraduate program and a Program for Executives—all of which broke new grounds. Within a few years, the business school regularly ranked among the top three or four in the country and won substantial financial support from the Ford Foundation and other funding sources. Business students frequently won the Ford Foundation's awards for the best business school doctoral dissertations.

GSIA fostered interdisciplinary research projects. Instead of setting up watertight departments, the school appointed faculty from a number of disciplines to its general faculty and encouraged them to work together. To encourage interdisciplinary ties, the dean scattered the offices of faculty from the same discipline throughout the GSIA building rather than cluster all economists or all organizational theorists in the same area. Warner, who himself had backgrounds in several disciplines, encouraged interdisciplinary research particularly after 1959 when Tech received a grant of $400,000 from the Carnegie Corporation to promote and develop new interdisciplinary programs in areas such as systems and communications sciences, information processing, applied materials sciences, applied space sciences and nuclear science and engineering. This interdisciplinary emphasis has become a hallmark of much of Carnegie Mellon's research.

Opposite page top:
Professors Simon and Newell playing chess

Opposite page center:
Jake Warner viewing one of the earliest computers at Tech

This page:
The Nuclear Research Center at Saxonburg

Research reports soon began to flow steadily

The Saxonburg cyclotron and a cyclotron at the University of Chicago had the highest energy pion beams in the world in the early 1950s. At Saxonburg Julius Ashkin and collaborators measured the scattering of pions from hydrogen and discovered a resonance that proved to be the most excited state of the proton. . . . Sergio DeBenedetti and his collaborators measured the X-rays from these exotic atoms for a whole series of nuclei. These spectra provide a beautiful example of atomic physics in a new domain and also provide important information on the pion-nucleus interaction.
—*Interactions Newsletter of the Department of Physics*, 1997

1960

- Skibo, the student union, Hamerschlag House and a new football stadium are opened.

Carnegie Tech had built a synchro-cyclotron during the last years of the Doherty administration. Tech faculty utilized this facility in nearby Saxonburg extensively throughout the Warner years. In addition to the synchro-cyclotron itself, the Saxonburg site soon included dormitories, a cafeteria, athletic facilities and many of the amenities of a satellite college campus. Gradually, however, Tech physicists began to utilize more powerful machines at national accelerator laboratories, and the Saxonburg facility was finally closed in the early 1970s.

Fine Arts expands graduate offerings while Margaret Morrison struggles

Throughout the Warner years, the College of Fine Arts continued to provide excellent undergraduate education and to increase its offerings at the graduate level. An independent Department of Graphic Arts established in 1960 brought the college to its present alignment of five departments, now called schools: Architecture, Art, Design, Drama and Music. Each of the fine arts departments continued to attract highly talented students aiming for professional careers in their field. Both Drama and Architecture had well-established national reputations with Music and Painting, Design and Sculpture not far behind. Nine members of the Art Deparment were chosen as Man of the Year by the Arts and Crafts Center of Pittsburgh, a tribute to their artistic talent and their service to the community. During the Warner years, the Music Department granted master of fine arts degrees to 91 students, while Drama granted 76 master's and three doctorates. All of the fine arts departments, however, suffered from inadequate budgets, cramped quarters and a general feeling that Carnegie Tech was neglecting them.

In contrast to the rest of Carnegie Tech, Margaret Morrison Carnegie College suffered from an increasing number of problems during the Warner years. Competition from less expensive public-supported colleges reduced the applicant pool for home economics, business studies and teaching. In some years, half of Margaret Morrison's graduates became public school teachers. Few members of the Margaret Morrison faculty carried on research, a growing anomaly during Tech's golden years, and, in addition, tenured faculty were nearing retirement age. Several studies by the administration revealed these problems and resulted in phasing out several programs, such as a degree in social work.

Fine Arts Alumni Remember Their Teachers

Henry Boettcher's way of introducing freshmen to the Drama School amazed us. Our first gathering in 1955 met in the Experimental Theater that was part of Skibo. All of the freshmen gathered with the faculty seated in random order. Henry went to the front of the stage and said something like, "Dear me, I forgot my class list, so I will have to call roll as you are seated." He then proceeded to go through the room and name everyone. I can never forget the impact of that event, since it implied the personal approach that was so much a part of training at Carnegie.
—Peter E. Sargent, A'59

As Herb Olds' students, we used to sneak out of Morewood Gardens after 11:00 o'clock to finish his assignments. Down we went to the basement where we escaped through the fire exit. . . . Off we went across campus to the window of the sculpture studio in the basement of CFA. Through the window, across the radiator, and down to the floor we went, and then up the stairs to the Loge where we set to work. When we heard security guards coming, we circled through the faculty studios and down the stairs, cut through the architectural studios, and went back up the other stairs—and back to work. Herb Olds often told me the next day that I looked tired and should get more sleep. He didn't know about my sneaky ways, the result of his intense drawing assignments. He challenged us to work to the limit of our skills; we were willing to break the rules to meet his standards.
—Helen E. Webster, A'69

Bes Kimberly taught us in so many ways. I went to her a week before the end of my senior year to tell her, that, having been assistant designer for a show celebrating the 100th anniversary of the Presbyterian Church in the United States, I didn't think I could possibly finish the large batch of tracings I had yet to do for her costume history class. I remember her sitting at her desk and telling me, "I think you can solve that, Bob." With not a smidgen of judgmental attitude, she very properly left me with the problem. I thought about it and spent every waking non-class hour in the CFA library, lowered my tracing standards a tad, and finished all the tracings. It was a good lesson for me to learn. But Bes taught the lesson with such grace that I respected the fact that she had not lowered her standards or the standards of the department a bit. She knew that I was trying to get around a difficult situation and assisted me by not giving in.
—Robert W. Wolff, A'60

Everyone in the Department of Music during the years in which Oleta Benn was on the faculty has his or her favorite story of an encounter with her. I remember walking into the class with a terribly stylish "pixie" haircut and receiving "that look." She then put me in my place by saying, "Natalie, that is cheap and common and vulgar." There was never need to guess where she stood on important issues.
—Natalie Laird Ozeas, A'60

This page top:
Drama instructor Henry Boettcher with students

This page bottom:
Oleta Benn

Opposite page:
Drawing instructor Herb Olds with student

1961

- **The Hunt Library opens.**
- **A grant from William H. and Frances S. Ryan establishes an award for meritorious teaching.**

Warner Describes Tech's Athletic Policies

Warner described his athletic policies in a 1961 article in *Monsanto Magazine*:

Admission standards are the same for all students. . . . Athletically gifted students receive no concessions when it comes to qualification for remaining in school or for graduation. . . . The proportion of students engaged in athletics—those who have been aided by scholarships based on genuine need—should be close to the proportion of all male students receiving deserved help. Their level of grades should also be similar. . . . We haven't yet found any satisfactory reason for an educational institution to provide an athletic "show" on a commercial scale for a high proportion of the general public.

A Rousing Tune

A lone bagpiper used to practice in Schenley Park in the late '50s, no doubt driven from his dorm by roommates who could not stand the screech. One fall afternoon in the middle of a cross country race, I was trudging up the long hill from the bottom of Panther Hollow, wondering if I would make it to the top and mentally giving up the idea of trying to pass the Slippery Rock runner just ahead of me. Suddenly, in the woods above us, the lone bagpiper burst forth with a rousing tune! A combination of surprise and (perhaps) Carnegie Tech Scots loyalty quickly got my adrenaline flowing, and the rival runner was left in the dust. I never did actually see the lone piper, but to this day I remember his music and its effect.
—Richard D. (Dick) Hamilton, E'59

Warner, however, was determined to make Margaret Morrison successful. He started by asking the board to approve an L-shaped addition to the College's single wing. The addition, which was ready in the fall of 1960, included new laboratories for foods and nutrition and clothing and textiles, two of the programs in Home Economics, new space for the Children's School, in which many Home Economics students had practice teaching experiences and new office space.

There were other attempts to strengthen the College's programs. The Department of Secretarial Studies became the Department of Business Studies, and the Department of General Science was phased out in favor of a new Department of Biology, for which new laboratories were provided and new faculty brought in. Required general education courses in the humanities and social studies were integrated so that Margaret Morrison students took them jointly with students from Engineering and Science. With support from Mrs. Alan M. Scaife, the College also began a modest research program. Applications to the College continued to drop, however, as did enrollment, and it became difficult to attract qualified faculty to replace retiring faculty.

Efforts in high schools and among African-Americans

A number of grants reopened relationships between Tech and the public schools. Between 1951 and 1965, projects in eight departments brought high school teachers and students to campus in an effort to bring scholarship in the schools up to date. One of these projects, led by professors Edwin Fenton and Robert Slack, resulted in the development of advanced placement courses that still function in 20 Allegheny County schools. During the later years of the Warner administration, the United States Office of Education supported study centers to devise and test curricular materials for secondary schools in English, social studies and the fine arts. These three projects, all of which extended into the Stever administration, played major roles in the national curriculum reform efforts of the so-called Education Decade.

Two projects focused attention on the education of African-American students. In 1964 the History Department began the Cooperative Program in History that brought faculty from predominately black colleges to study at Carnegie Tech and participate in the development of curricular materials in history for their schools. It was led by history professors David H. Fowler and Ludwig F. Schaefer. During the Warner years, Tech also founded the School College Orientation Program in Pittsburgh (SCOPP). It was the brainchild of deans Richard M. Cyert, Erwin R. Steinberg and John R. Coleman. SCOPP brought minority students to campus for summer study to prepare them for college work. SCOPP served as a prototype for the national program called Upward Bound. The descendant of the SCOPP program, now called the Carnegie Mellon Action Program (CMAP), continues to provide vital services to minority students at Carnegie Mellon. The Cooperative Program in History and SCOPP represent the first significant efforts at Tech to take responsibility for the education of minority students.

Recognizing that none of this progress would be possible without a distinguished faculty, Warner took a number of steps to improve faculty salaries and fringe benefits. Average salaries more than doubled. New employment policies supported paid faculty leaves, strengthened retirement income, assisted faculty in financing the education of their children and improved life insurance and health insurance coverage.

Jake Warner, who had played halfback on his college team and whose son Tom (IM'54) was a Tech team captain, also set new policies for intercollegiate athletics. Tech had won its first game after 25 consecutive losses while Warner was president-elect. During his administration, Tech's football teams played schools that adhered to similar athletic policies. Led for most of his administration by a distinguished coach, Eddie Baker, Tech's football teams compiled a gratifying 61-53-3 record. The athletic policies that Jake Warner initiated are still in effect at Carnegie Mellon, now a member of the University Athletic Association, a league of nine urban research universities in which Carnegie Mellon more than holds its own in both men's and women's sports.

President Warner retires

In 1964 Warner appointed a vice president for academic affairs and a vice president for research. He argued that these positions would make the presidency more attractive to his successor. In a review of his administration written in 1965, he praised the work of his predecessor, gave credit to the faculty and trustees for much of Tech's progress and listed a host of developments. This report, well-organized, well-developed, clearly written, personally modest and comprehensive describes the golden age of Carnegie Tech. It also characterizes both Jake Warner and his administration. He then addressed student concerns: the relationship between research and education, the growth of graduate programs under his administration, educational facilities and a score of others. Never patronizing, he addressed students as interested members of the community entitled to know what their outgoing president thought of the school whose faculty he had joined as an instructor in 1926.

Richard M. Cyert described Warner's impact on Tech in an issue of *Carnegie Mellon Magazine,* Summer 1989, shortly after Warner died at the age of 92, leaving much of his estate to the school to which he had devoted his life.

Jake's imprint on the school really came from the kind of leadership he gave. He was a no-nonsense fellow. He didn't waste time on flattery. He was very blunt so you knew exactly where you stood. It was a refreshing and healthy way to run the institution. He was hard-working, and he and his wife devoted themselves to the school. They made the whole University more of a family. . . . Warner stood for a high quality of scholarship. We recognized him as a distinguished scholar and scientist, and this was stimulating for us. He became a good model. I believe that the foundations for what the university has attained in the past 10 years were really laid during Jake's administration.

1965

- The Mellon College of Science founds the Computer Science Department.

CARNEGIE UNIVERSITY PLANNED

EXTRA | carnegie tech **TARTAN** | EXTRA

Special ★ ★ ★ ★ Edition   September 14, 1966

NEW UNIVERSITY PROPOSAL
LINKS CIT-MELLON INSTITUTE

New Programs Planned ... ld embrace | 1949. One of the country's | duties similar to those which
Endowm... ... | outstanding schools of ad- | they now hold. Senior re-
... | ministration it ... | ...llows would become ... of

10.

Horton Guyford Stever 1965–1972
He oversaw the birth of Carnegie Mellon University

Finding a worthy successor to Jake Warner proved to be no easy task. He had served Tech for almost four decades and was approaching the compulsory retirement age of 68. Three search committees had been unable to settle upon a candidate. Finally, Warner agreed to remain an additional year, shrewdly insisting that Tech appoint two vice presidents, one for academic affairs, Edward R. Schatz (E'43, '49), and one for research, Charles Law McCabe, during the transition year. In the meantime, a search committee looked for a youngish individual from outside Tech with a combination of academic and personal qualities that only a genius with the values of a saint and the constitution of an Olympic athlete could meet.

The committee finally settled on H. Guyford Stever, the 49-year-old head of the Departments of Mechanical Engineering and Naval Architecture and Marine Engineering at Massachusetts Institute of Technology. In his years at MIT, Stever had built a reputation as an aeronautical expert, a consultant to the government, particularly as chief scientist for the United States Air Force, and as an active consultant to the aerospace industry. Born in Corning, New York in 1916 he had earned a B.A. from Colgate and a Ph.D. in physics from California Institute of Technology. He had married Louise Ridley in 1946, and the couple had four children, two of whom were still in elementary school when Stever came to Tech. Rather than live in the president's house on busy Morewood Avenue, the Stevers moved into the the former Henry Hillman residence on Devon Road overlooking the campus. Stever's background included the experience in pure and applied science, government service and academic administration that the trustees favored.

Stever was personable, open and optimistic. As an administrator, he believed strongly in the value of consensus in the decision-making process, a belief that sometimes stood in the way of decisive action. Because he saw his mission as consolidating gains and continuing projects already underway, he kept Warner's management team, particularly Vice President Edward R. Schatz, in place throughout his administration. He consistently delegated broad powers to staff members, particularly when he was in Washington or on consulting contracts for industry.

1965

- Horton Guy Stever becomes Carnegie Tech's fifth president.

Opposite page (left to right): Aiken Fisher, Chairman of Carnegie Tech's Board of Trustees; Paul Mellon, for Mellon Institute; and Guy Stever announce plans for Carnegie University.

1966

- **The new administration building, Warner Hall, opens.**

Trustees work out a merger and form a new university

Just over a year after his inauguration, Stever announced that Carnegie Tech had become Carnegie University. Negotiations for a merger with Mellon Institute had been going on since 1960. They were finalized in discussions among trustees of both institutions, led by Paul Mellon for Mellon Institute and Aiken Fisher, his counterpart at Tech. Neither faculty at Tech nor staff members at Mellon took part in these preliminary negotiations, and both groups resented this omission. By the 1960s Mellon Institute's emphasis on chemistry made it ill-suited to an era emphasizing electronics and physics. A merger with Carnegie Institute of Technology seemed a natural development.

At first the merger was called Carnegie University. A few months later the Mellons agreed to add their name to the new institution, and it became Carnegie-Mellon University. Carnegie-Mellon's charter appears with a hyphen (see logotype below), and the University seal has a hyphen in it. The hyphen still appears on University legal documents. In 1985 when Carnegie Mellon adopted a new logo—the tilted square—University Relations began to drop the hyphen from its publications, a custom that quickly caught on.

The merger added the Mellon Institute of Research to Tech's roster, increased by half the size of Carnegie Tech's endowment and added a number of distinguished chemists and biologists to its faculty. Although a decade passed before all the kinks in the merger were worked out, it was immediately clear that a new university with enormous promise had been created. Eventually the Mellon Institute became the Carnegie Mellon Research Institute, now located in an industrial park beside the Monongahela River.

Going for a Touchdown   —By Hungerford

Carnegie -Mellon University

During the next few years, Carnegie Mellon phased out one college, founded two new ones, and divided another. Margaret Morrison Carnegie College had been losing enrollment steadily for many years. Between 1955 and 1965, majors in home economics declined by about half and in business studies by two-thirds while they grew steadily in both the sciences and humanities and social sciences. Moreover, most of the Margaret Morrison tenured faculty were reaching retirement age. In 1968 a Visiting Committee issued a report that suggested that the four major programs in the College should be closed. The Faculty Senate voted to approve this plan, noting that only 41 freshmen enrolled in 1969.

162

Finally, in November 1969 the Board of Trustees approved a recommendation of President Stever to phase out the College. No new students were to be admitted and the College would be closed in 1973 when the freshman class of 1969 graduated. This decision alienated many Margaret Morrison Carnegie College graduates (5,355 women held degrees from Margaret Morrison), but given enrollment figures and the economic climate, the new University had no realistic alternative.

Many Margaret Morrison students enrolled in the New College, later to become the College of Humanities and Social Sciences (H&SS). Clearly a major university had to include both undergraduate and graduate studies in the humanities and social sciences. A committee of senior faculty appointed by Margaret Morrison's dean, Erwin Steinberg, developed a plan for the ambitious New College in 1967. It featured departments of English, History, Modern Languages and Psychology. A rigid core curriculum to be supplemented by seminars and cultural events, such as concerts and plays, dominated study during the first year. In September 1969, 124 men and women of the class of 1973 opened the New College.

Students wanted to do their own thing

These enthusiastic students entered the New College with unrealistic notions of what to expect. They looked for a cooperative venture in which faculty and students together would shape their educational program. Moreover, they belonged to a generation rapidly becoming accustomed to demand major roles in public issues such as civil rights and the conduct of the war in Vietnam. Almost immediately they were in revolt, objecting to required courses, a rigid curriculum, the quality of the teaching and grading procedures. Eager to do their own thing, they organized a mass meeting in Skibo to air their complaints and urge reforms. They challenged almost every principle on which the New College had been founded. Largely as a result of demands from students and disaffected younger faculty members, the administration and senior faculty yielded on a number of issues during the second semester of the academic year and met to discuss the College in a goals' committee consisting of faculty and students in the fall of 1970.

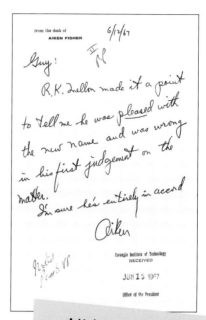

A University is Created

The bright children of two proud Pittsburgh families joined hands in Oakland this weekend and promptly gave the City a 200-million-dollar wedding gift called Carnegie-Mellon University.

United were: Carnegie Institute of Technology, founded in 1900 by Andrew Carnegie to train skilled persons for industry. . .and. . . Mellon Institute, founded in 1913 by Andrew W. Mellon and Richard B. Mellon to conduct industrial research.

Emerging from the marriage is one of the nation's great private universities, committed to teaching and research in science and technology, the elevation of the fine arts, the improvement of business management and a liberal education in the humanities and social sciences.

—The Pittsburgh Press, July 2, 1967

Protesting students expressed their opinions about the merger of Carnegie and Mellon.

163

1967

- Carnegie Tech and the Mellon Institute join to form Carnegie-Mellon University.

1968

- Students protest the war in Vietnam.
- $10 million from General and Mrs. R. K. Mellon funds the School for Urban and Public Affairs.
- The University launches the Fund for Distinction.

After several years of self-examination and reform, the College, now called the College of Humanities and Social Sciences (H&SS), settled down. Both History and English began to offer master's degrees for teachers who wanted further study in a subject area in a program supported by the Ford Foundation. Building on the new master's degree and the work in history and English curriculum development centers, the Carnegie Foundation in 1967 granted Tech $1 million to found the Carnegie Education Center. The Center invented a new degree called the doctor of arts and organized D.A. programs in history, English, mathematics, fine arts and science. Candidates enrolled in courses for two years and then developed and tried curriculum materials for their dissertations. The program's directors recruited large numbers of both African-American and women students in Tech's first successful effort to increase the number of under-represented graduate students. The D.A. rapidly spread to several dozen other institutions, but it was eventually phased out at Carnegie Mellon when the faculty embraced more conventional Ph.D. programs and government support for curriculum projects diminished.

The Mellons support additional colleges

The remaining new College was the School of Urban and Public Affairs (SUPA), like the Graduate School of Industrial Administration (GSIA), begun through the initiative of a member of the Mellon family. On December 30, 1968 President Stever received a proposal from the Richard King Mellon Foundation to start a new graduate school supported by an endowment eventually totaling $10 million. The offer also included $1 million to add to the endowment of GSIA. Stever set up a university-wide committee that developed preliminary plans, drafted by Professor Otto Davis, for the new venture. They focused on a quantitatively oriented, problem-solving program in public policy much like the ground-breaking quantitative programs in GSIA.

SUPA's first dean, William W. Cooper, a management scientist, transferred from GSIA where he had had a distinguished career. He and Associate Dean Otto Davis took advantage of several opportunities that a fresh start offered. SUPA wanted to deal with urban problems in the public sector, problems that spanned traditional departmental lines. Since no institutional restraints existed in a new school, they could appoint faculty to the school rather than to existing departments. The small size of the school also provided an advantage.

Housed at first in the Margaret Morrison building, SUPA quickly began to forge a distinguished record. Cooper and his staff realized that preparing managers for modern urban areas implied programs to recruit and nurture African-American students. Like the directors of the doctor of arts program, they made special efforts to recruit both African-American and women students, an emphasis that still continues. To prepare some of these students for demanding quantitative work, SUPA organized an eight-week program in quantitative skills paid for by the school in the summer before their graduate work commenced. And in order to focus on problem-solving techniques, every student was required to take at least one project course in which a group of students studied and made recommendations for the solution of a real-life urban problem. By 1999, 2,250 men and women held graduate degrees from the school. Today's descendant of SUPA is the H. John Heinz III School of Public Policy and Management.

In addition to phasing out one college and beginning two new ones, the Stever years witnessed the division of the College of Engineering and Science into the Mellon College of Science and the Carnegie Institute of Technology, the present name for the engineering school. This division took place in 1970 when the departments of Mathematics, Physics, Chemistry, the Biological Sciences and Computer Science became the Mellon College of Science. Carnegie Institute of Technology retained all of the engineering departments and added Engineering and Public Affairs, later renamed Engineering and Public Policy, a distinguished effort to infuse public policy and management considerations into the engineering profession.

Computing initiatives expand

During the Stever administration, Carnegie Tech made dramatic advances in computing. Alan Perlis (S'42), the first head of CIT's Computation Center, once said that, "Getting involved with a computer is like having a cannibal as a valet." The demands for computing power were indeed voracious and gobbled up every available cubic foot of space and every last dollar. Each new piece of hardware cost an impressive number

of dollars, most of them supplied by grants from government agencies. A grant from the National Institutes of Health to the Psychology Department supported pioneering study in the simulation of human thinking. In the fall of 1964 the Advanced Research Projects Agency (ARPA) of the Department of Defense awarded a contract of $3 million to Carnegie Tech to establish a Center for the Study of Information Processing. Spurred by these grants, Tech established in 1965 an autonomous Computer Science Department underwritten the following year by a $5 million grant from the Richard King Mellon Foundation. Tech's work in artificial intelligence and in the design of sophisticated programming languages subsequently attracted further large grants from both the government and private foundations, laying the groundwork for a host of advances in computing both for research and for education. Today's School of Computer Science (established in 1988), the Robotics Institute, the Software Engineering Institute, the Andrew Network, numerous start-up companies and a growing educational revolution grew out of these developments.

1969

- The University begins to run an increasing deficit.

New UNIVAC Added to Computer Facilities

Carnegie Tech computation facilities have taken a giant leap forward with the purchase of a computer system able to execute more than 1,000,000 instructions per second.

The system, a UNIVAC 1108 from Sperry Rand's UNIVAC Division, cost $1,860,000. David H. Nickerson, director of Tech's Computation Center, said the new system will give Tech more than $6,000,000 worth of functioning computer equipment, making it one of the most complete facilities in the country.

UNIVAC 1108 was purchased through $1,000,000 provided in a $5,000,000 grant from Lt. Gen. Richard K. Mellon and charitable trusts created by him with the remainder from Tech funds. The Mellon grant was made in 1965 to establish Tech's department of computer and information sciences.
—Carnegie Alumni News, May 1967

Lowering the UNIVAC 1108 into Scaife Hall through a hole in the roof

1970

- The College of Engineering & Science divides into the Carnegie Institute of Technology (engineering) and the Mellon College of Science.

1971

- Wean Hall is completed.
- Astronaut Edgar Mitchell (IM'52) takes the Carnegie Mellon flag on a lunar visit.

Computing's Birth Pangs

Like other students, I used to spend long nights in Science Hall trying to get my computer program to run. In Engineering and Public Affairs in the early 1970s you punched your program on cards, lined up to read it through the card reader, and waited anxiously for your output. The chuck-chuck-chucking of the printer brought a crowd of students scurrying to the long, inclined air-blown printer ramp. A friend of mine left the long line of students behind him at the card reader aghast when he took a portion of his program and shuffled it like a deck of cards prior to entering it. They didn't know, of course, that it was a data file for a sequence of random numbers.
—Mitchell Small, E'75

A possibly apocryphal story was part of the folklore when I arrived, and went along the following lines: A senior engineer with Bendix, Dave Evans, knew Alan Perlis and knew that Carnegie Mellon was searching for a new computer to replace the 650. He therefore met Al at a Joint Computer Conference in Boston, took him out to dinner, and made his sales pitch. He described the features of this new computer to Al. After much back-and-forth about features, representations, etc., Al finally said, "This sounds like a fine machine. We'll buy one," at which point Dave replied, "That's great. We'll build one!"
—Joseph M. Newcomer, S'75

In search of a cheap place to live, one student, in collaboration with a couple of others, built a loft apartment. The drop ceiling in a seventh-floor office in Wean Hall was removed, and a floor was constructed. An opening was left in one side for access and the ceiling tile was replaced. Access was by climbing a ladder and pushing aside the ceiling tile. Equipped with a sleeping bag, battery-powered lamp and radio, it was a quite comfortable apartment. Laundry and shower facilities in the gym were readily accessible through the steam tunnels. A huge segment of the CS department knew about the loft; I visited it when Eric gave a "house tour" to some CS faculty members.
—Joseph M. Newcomer, S'75

Top:
Wean Hall

Bottom:
Students with one of the first computers on campus

All this notable growth—new colleges, new programs, and an increasing student body—placed new demands on the University's aging buildings. A few major building projects marked the Stever years. Thanks primarily to the generosity of Mrs. Alan M. Scaife, a new administration building, Warner Hall, rose along Forbes Avenue. Science Hall, renamed Wean Hall, filled in the space at the end of the mall and provided quarters for most departments in the Mellon College of Science. A new wing on Mudge House and four new fraternity buildings helped to relieve the housing crunch. Despite this building program, space remained Carnegie Mellon's most scarce commodity.

Top:
A sketch for one of the four new fraternity buildings

Bottom left:
A new wing was added to Mudge House to help relieve the housing crunch.

Bottom right:
A lounge in Mudge House

Protest comes to campus

Student protest movements marked campus life during the Stever years. Chapter 11 examines some of them in detail. They were less violent than their counterparts at Columbia, Berkeley or Wisconsin. Neither students nor faculty members were killed or injured nor were buildings destroyed or damaged. Protesters did, however, temporarily close down construction of Wean Hall in support of the Black Construction Coalition. A few students, aided and abetted by off-campus elements, disrupted a speech by South Carolina's Republican Senator Strom Thurmond by pelting him with

marshmallows. When the national press picked up the story, it seemed that Carnegie Mellon had at last joined the big-time protesters. After the National Guard shot four students at Kent State University in 1970, a few students occupied Warner Hall overnight and threw papers from the ROTC out of its offices in Margaret Morrison. Other students quietly put them back. Finally the editors of *The Thistle* released an issue that offended a large part of the student body and many supporters. Two members of the Mellon family were so angered by attacks on "King Mellon" that they resigned from the Board of Trustees.

Jeers and Marshmallows

C-MU students may go on record as the first ones ever to throw marshmallows at a U.S. Senator. The target of a handful of vociferous antagonists in the audience in the Skibo Ballroom was the Republican Senator from South Carolina, Strom Thurmond, who spoke here on Tuesday, January 20. The Senator survived the barrage and later said, "I've never seen anything like it."

The first speaker on the schedule of the Activities Board of distinguished lecturers, the Senator spoke to an audience which was determined to hear him despite frequent interruptions by persistent detractors. Senator Thurmond spoke on topics ranging from electoral reforms to welfare and did not fail to demonstrate why he is called "the perfect conservative" by Americans for Constitutional Action.

—*The Tartan*, January 23, 1970

Through these episodes, President Stever walked a fine line, defending the right of students and faculty members to free speech while he attempted to explain his stand to the students who did not share the views of the protesters. He argued that the University as an institution should take moral stands but avoid political positions. As an individual, he publicly took a number of political positions, for example, joining other college presidents in a letter asking President Richard M. Nixon to speed withdrawal from Vietnam. Protesters were not mollified. Some unfortunate, off-hand remarks at a mass meeting also irritated many members of the faculty as well as activists among the student body. In the long run, Stever pleased almost no one who had strong views on either side of many issues.

In retrospect, Stever and his two major administrative officers, Edward Schatz and Robert Kibbee, formed a triumvirate that kept the lid on a potentially explosive situation. They refused to censure student publications, even when they contained offensive material. They never called in police to restrain students, a move that would almost certainly have led to violence as it did on many campuses. They issued clear and sensible statements about the rights of students and the responsibilities of university administrators. Indicted by a few alienated students, faculty, staff, alumni and trustees, they have seldom received credit for steering a steady course through troubled waters.

Amid these student troubles, Carnegie Mellon was fast approaching a financial crisis. In 1968 the trustees approved the kick-off of a campaign called the Fund for Distinction with a goal of $140 million, $55 million of which was to be raised during the first three years. These funds were needed to support a new effort in the biological sciences, improvements in engineering education, a new School of Urban and Public Affairs, a new computer building, faculty development and a number of similar ambitious projects. By January 1969, $15 million had been received and an additional $8 million subscribed. Then it slowed down. By the time that President Stever left the campus in February 1972, only $37.2 million had been raised. Despite income from the new development campaign, inflation, increased salaries and fringe benefits, reduced enrollment, $8 million taken from the endowment to complete Science (Wean) Hall, unforeseen expenses for the Computation Center, and many other factors, the surplus built up in previous years had been exhausted and the budget had fallen seriously into the red. Alarmed, the Board of Trustees demanded that the administration defer maintenance and make drastic cuts in expenditures.

In the midst of this impending crisis, on November 17, 1971 President Nixon announced that he had nominated Guyford Stever to become director of the National Science Foundation. This job greatly appealed to Stever. He had a long record of public service in various governmental positions which he had enjoyed. He submitted his resignation to the board effective February 1, 1972.

Stever reorganized the institution during the seven years of his administration. It became a university instead of an Institute of Technology. It acquired a distinguished research arm in the Mellon Institute. Margaret Morrison Carnegie College for Women disappeared. New colleges and schools—the College of Humanities and Social Sciences, Mellon College of Science, Carnegie Institute of Technology and the School of Urban and Public Affairs—took their places beside the College of Fine Arts and the flourishing Graduate School of Industrial Administration. New initiatives in computing brought challenging intellectual developments in both research and teaching. These years were also marked by three major building projects and an increase in endowment from $55 to $112 million. Along with some serious financial problems, Stever's successor, Richard M. Cyert, inherited rich potential.

An Open Letter to All Members of the CMU Campus Community

. . . During the past year, Carnegie-Mellon has been engaged in a widespread discussion to attempt to understand these changes and to develop mechanisms to enhance excellence in our students' educational experience. Some of these discussions have been both productive and enjoyable. We believe that we have made progress but that we must continue in this effort. We should note, also, that there have been peaceful demonstrations during the past year which were responsibly carried out by students concerned about the University or some social cause. As expressions of free speech entirely proper in a university community, they followed the guidelines in the *Carnegie Student Handbook*:

CMU recognizes the right and privilege of all students to exercise the constitutional guarantees of free assembly and expression. As a university sincerely espousing the philosophy of academic freedom, CMU urges and supports its students' desires and efforts to pursue these rights.

In instances where students wish to use these rights through protest or demonstration, the rights and privileges of others must be considered. Thus,

1. The protest or demonstration must be of an orderly nature so that no acts of violence shall occur and the normal orderly operation of the University will not be impeded.

2. The protest or demonstration shall not infringe upon the rights or privileges of students not in sympathy with it. Thus, all students are assured that the ideas or desires of others shall not be inflicted upon them and that they will be allowed to exercise the right of free choice.

3. Finally, the freedom to demonstrate on the campus shall be limited to members of the campus community only.

—*Office of the President,* September 5, 1969

1972

- Students pelt Senator Strom Thurmond with marshmallows and trash ROTC headquarters.
- President Stever resigns to become the director of the National Science Foundation.

II.

Snapshot 1967–1970
A new university with growing pains

Carnegie Mellon's 71st commencement exercises were held on June 3, 1968 on the Mall in front of the College of Fine Arts. The size of the graduating class had outgrown the capacity of any building on or near the campus. Hornbostel's terrace before the Fine Arts Building, where the major dignitaries sat, had been renovated for the ceremony. The faculty, students and their parents, friends and relatives sat on chairs placed on the Fine Arts lawn. Pipers led the academic parade amid brilliant sunshine. Gerard Piel, the president and publisher of *Scientific American,* delivered the commencement address. Candidates for doctor of philosophy degrees then received their hoods. Diploma ceremonies in nine different locations followed the procession. The number of bachelor and master degree candidates had grown far too large to present diplomas to them individually while their parents, relatives and friends sat in the hot sun.

The composition of the graduating class again highlights dramatic changes in the institution. Graduates came from all 50 states and the District of Columbia. Thirty-three percent of the graduates were women, up from 27 percent in 1948. The number of bachelor of science

Changing Commencement Statistics 1908-1968

	1908	1928	1948	1968
Number of Graduates	58	382	725	1112
Number of Different Degrees	6	46	42	82
Pre-Collegiate	**58**	**52**	**0**	**0**
2-Year Certificates	0	44	0	0
3-Year Diplomas	58	8	0	0
Bachelor's Level	**0**	**319**	**633**	**681**
Bachelor of Science	0	226	528	435
Bachelor of Architecture	0	12	7	31
Bachelor of Arts	0	76	0	85
Bachelor of Fine Arts	0	0	98	130
Professional Degrees	0	5	0	0
Master's Level	**0**	**11**	**65**	**294**
Master of Science	0	11	56	243
Master of Social Work	0	0	9	0
Master of Arts	0	0	0	43
Master of Architecture	0	0	0	8
Terminal Degrees	**0**	**0**	**27**	**137**
Master of Fine Arts	0	0	13	25
Doctor of Science	0	0	14	0
Doctor of Philosophy	0	0	0	111
Doctor of Arts	0	0	0	1

Opposite top:
1962 aerial view of the campus

Opposite center:
Students protest on the Cut.

Opposite bottom:
1967 Commencement

degrees had diminished by 93, but the master of arts candidates had increased more than fourfold. Forty percent of the graduates received master's or doctor's degrees, up from 3 percent in 1928 and 13 percent in 1948. Carnegie Mellon was clearly expanding programs in graduate work and research as two of its major missions.

The graduating class had begun to represent the reorganized Carnegie Mellon. Graduates came from five colleges: the Carnegie Institute of Technology, the College of Fine Arts, Margaret Morrison Carnegie College, the Graduate School of Industrial Administration and the newly formed College of Humanities and Social Sciences. Fifty-five percent of the graduates were enrolled in the Carnegie Institute of Technology which still included the sciences and mathematics.

Temporary Financial Security
Again in 1967-68 the financial outcome of the year was satisfactory, with expenditures and income applicable to the budget in balance. . . . [S]uch a result is reason for satisfaction. It should be noted that this balanced operation could not have been possible without a large volume of voluntary support. In 1967-68 this support, for the third time in the past eleven years, exceeded $8 million.
—President Stever's 1967-68 Annual Report

The trustees and President Stever begin to organize a university

At last Carnegie Mellon had its own Board of Trustees independent from the trustees of the Carnegie Institute. Its 55 members met three times a year to conduct University business. Walter Blenko (E'21) chaired the executive committee of the board as he had through the Warner administration. Fifty-three of its members were white males, 44 of them businessmen. There were two women members, Anna Loomis McCandless, a 72-year-old member of the class of 1919, and Mrs. Clifford S. Heinz, a director of the H. J. Heinz Company, but no African-Americans, Hispanics, Asians or citizens of other countries. Twenty-one trustees held degrees from Carnegie Tech. In a February 1969 article in *The Tartan,* President Stever defended the composition of the board and declared that he had no reason to change it.

Throughout the Stever administration (1965-72) Edward R. Schatz (E'43, '49) was Vice President for Academic Affairs, a position from which he and Robert J. Kibbee acted as spokespersons for the University when Stever was out of town in Washington or consulting. Robert Kibbee held a new position as Vice President for Administration and Planning. Two other vice presidents were responsible for business affairs and development and public relations. Deans headed each of the five colleges. Midway through 1968, George K. Brown resigned as Dean of Student Affairs and was replaced by Earle R. Swank, a professor of English. Stever appointed Charles V. Williams Dean of Men, the first African-American person to hold an administrative position in the entire history of the institution. These officials helped to guide the University through the troubled waters of the late 1960s and early 1970s.

$55 MILLION CAMPAIGN ANNOUNCED

Financial clouds appear on the horizon

In his Annual Report, President Stever summarized the University's financial situation. After listing the sources of support, Stever added that $656,000 accumulated from past gifts had been applied to the budget. In other words, the University had used past surpluses to keep the budget in balance, a practice that boded ill for the future since past surpluses would soon disappear. In fact, they were exhausted by the end of the 1970-71 fiscal year. Total expenses in 1967-68 had increased by 18 percent over the previous year with prospects of similar increases in sight. Sponsored research ($14.4 million) and gifts and grants ($5.3 million) were keeping the University afloat. The market value of the endowment had increased about $4 million to $117 million during the academic year, returning $3.4 million to the budget.

At their fall 1968 meeting, the trustees had approved plans for a 10-year development campaign to be called the Fund for Distinction. By the end of the year, gifts and subscriptions had reached more than $23 million, including $10 million from General and Mrs. Richard King Mellon as an endowment for the new School of Urban and Public Affairs (SUPA). The immediate future of the new University would depend heavily on whether the campaign could reach the goal of $53 million set for the first three years of a campaign whose 10-year total was $140 million. Support from the Mellons would be essential.

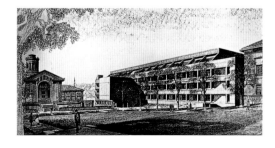

173

1968 Percentage of Degrees Earned & Academic Rank of Faculty

	MMCC	CIT	H&SS	CFA	GSIA
Total, Full Time	24	231	124	81	29
Percentage of Degrees					
Doctors or MFA Degrees	50%	95%	64%	31%	87%
Masters	50%	4%	31%	20%	3%
Bachelors	0%	1%	4%	34%	7%
Others	0%	0%	1%	13%	3%
Percentage of Academic Rank					
Professors	18%	45%	23%	26%	48%
Associate Professors	34%	17%	20%	48%	17%
Assistant Professors	30%	34%	32%	20%	28%
Instructors	1%	0%	21%	6%	0%
Lecturers	11%	5%	3%	0%	7%

Colleges show diversity in faculty, activities

In his annual report, Dean Erwin Steinberg made a revealing comment about the status of the new University: "If it weren't that letterheads and other such forms read 'Carnegie-Mellon University,' I wouldn't be much aware of the change." The annual reports of the four 1967-68 academic deans confirm this judgment and reveal widely disparate interests and priorities inherited from the past. Dean Norman Rice of the College of Fine Arts discussed the place of the artist in society in order to raise a fundamental question: "What is the real reason for our existence—not as an entertainment center, but as a college of the arts?" Reporting for Margaret Morrison Carnegie College and the newly formed College of Humanities and Social Sciences, Dean Steinberg outlined the strengths and weaknesses of the two Colleges and the newly formed Education Center, pleaded for additional support, and concluded with an extensive list of faculty activities, honors and publications. Dean Richard M. Cyert of GSIA devoted 26 pages of his 33-page report to an impressive list of faculty activities, research interests and publications. Dean William W. Mullins of the Carnegie Institute of Technology submitted the longest report in which he discussed grants, students, curriculum, physical plant, changes in the administration, and new programs and appended a 35-page list of faculty publications. Clearly the deans and the colleges they represented faced different problems and had divergent aspirations for their administrative units.

The composition of the faculty in the colleges also points to their diversity. Overwhelmingly, the faculty in both CIT and GSIA held doctor's degrees, an indication of their research orientation. Similarly, about half of these faculty members were full professors, an indication of their standing in the University. Look at Margaret Morrison in contrast. Fifty percent of its faculty held doctor's degrees, but only 18 percent had won promotion to full professor. In Fine Arts, about one third of the faculty held doctor's or master's of fine arts degrees, not unusual in a college where creative activities and teaching take precedence over research. H&SS was still different. It had recently been proclaimed a college after having been a service division for decades. Less than a fourth of its faculty held full professorships despite the fact that 64 percent of them held doctor's degrees.

The Annual Report of research listed 387 publications in CIT; 144 in Mellon Institute; 58 in GSIA; three in Margaret Morrison; 31 in the Department of Psychology, which was administered by GSIA; eight in the Department of Statistics, administered jointly by GSIA and CIT; eight scholarly articles, 14 book reviews and 31 books and articles about curriculum or teaching in H&SS; and six scholarly articles and 209 exhibitions, performances, addresses, recitals and other creative activities by members of the CFA faculty.

Faculty reorganizes, asserts its role in decision making

Since the beginning of the Doherty administration, a faculty committee had brought faculty issues to the attention of the administration. Disturbed because the faculty had no part in the decision to become a university, the faculty asserted its right to have a more significant role in decision making. With the approval of the administration, the faculty developed a new constitution early in 1968 and approved it by a 10-1 vote. The constitution established an elected campus-wide organization to represent the entire faculty. It was to meet seven times each year and be led by an Executive Committee that met monthly between full faculty meetings. The constitution gave the Faculty Senate significant powers:

The Senate is empowered to consider any and all issues relevant to the interest of the University and to make known its views and recommendations either to the Faculty or to the President. . . . The Faculty have a responsibility for initiating, considering, and making recommendations on questions of educational policy and problems arising therefrom, whether concerning current operations of the University or long-range

policy (admissions policy, proposals for new degrees, establishment of educational and research units, the size of the University, auxiliary cultural agencies and questions concerning the status and privileges of the Faculty).

Four distinguished faculty members chaired the Faculty Senate through 1968 and the troubled years that followed: Sergio DeBenedetti, James S. Langer (S'55), Akram Midani and Daniel P. Resnick. The Senate organized five Councils or permanent committees: Educational Policy, Research Policy and Services, Faculty Affairs, Student Affairs and Campus Planning. After February 1969 they operated from the Senate's new offices in Baker Hall 150-52.

The minutes of the Executive Committee and of the full Faculty Senate reveal the vital functions that the new organization played. Among the issues it raised were student housing, the functions of the discipline committee, the need to recruit more black faculty, the role of the ROTC on campus, ways to improve communication with students, policies about disruptive student behavior and sit-ins, ways to improve the quality of teaching, the status of the Biology Department and a Center for Sponsored Research, the state of the library and, of course, the student disturbances accompanying the urban riots and the war in Vietnam. The faculty had become a participating partner in setting University policy.

Some reforms happened quickly. The Senate distributed cards to all faculty members and asked them to post their office hours on their office doors. Senators began a series of student-faculty luncheons to explore issues that students raised. The Senate inserted notices about forthcoming events in *The Tartan* in order to publicize lectures and other events in which students might be interested. On the whole, students ignored these over-

Faculty Overtures

Faculty Chairman Sergio DeBenedetti appealed to students to respond to faculty overtures in a letter to *The Tartan* dated December 11, 1968:

The poor faculty have tried all possible things in order to overcome this lack of personal contact with students' frustration. We have posted office hours and no one comes to see us; we have organized public lectures and very few students ever come to listen to us; we have held open meetings on the question of student participation in the affairs of the Faculty Councils, and only a few students came to testify.

What is wrong with us? Nobody loves us—or do we suffer from halitosis? Now. . .we propose a program of free lunches which will be offered to any group of students who want to talk with the faculty. . . . President Stever has already allocated some money for this purpose. Thanks, Guy.

WAR REQUIEM
by
Benjamin Britten

Performed by Carnegie-Mellon Department of Music

On Recital Hall   Sunday at 1:00

WRCT Radio · 900

tures. Changing an entrenched student culture required far more than opportunities to meet with faculty members.

The Faculty Senate and the faculty in general played vital roles in the disturbances that rocked the campus between 1968 and 1971. Not that Carnegie Mellon was a hotbed of agitation. When a handful of students and some outsiders occupied Warner Hall during the night of May 4-5, 1970, James Langer, Chair of the Senate, joined Dean Earle Swank in a successful nightlong effort to persuade them to leave the building unharmed by the time the staff returned in the morning. On May 6, Langer, Deans Cyert and Mullins and a number of faculty joined students in a march on the downtown Federal Building to protest the war in Vietnam and the tragic events at Kent State University in which four students were killed. The new Faculty Senate gave faculty members a forum from which they helped both the administration and the students to avoid the tragic violence that marked so many disturbances on other campuses.

Enrollment changes between the 1947-48 and 1967-68 academic years

The surge in enrollment following World War II had abated by 1948 when it still totaled 5,999. Then enrollment fell during the 1950s and recovered slowly during the 1960s reaching a total of 6,865 in the fall of 1967. The accompanying table shows the full-time, fall 1967 enrollment in the day school. Total enrollment also included part-time evening, Saturday, and summer school students. Students came from 48 states, 54 percent from Pennsylvania. One hundred ninety-four students came from 47 foreign countries. As in 1947, CIT had more than half of the total full-time enrollment. Carnegie Mellon remained a regional university focusing heavily on engineering and science.

Graduate enrollment showed the most dramatic increases since 1948. In 1967-68 CIT enrolled 972 graduate students, 620 in engineering, 295 in science and mathematics, 49 in computer science, and eight in statistics. H&SS enrolled 112 in history, 69 in English and three in psychology. The history and English students studied for a master of arts or doctor of arts degree intended primarily for students preparing for careers as teachers and curriculum developers. Thirty-eight of the 45 Margaret Morrison graduate students were enrolled in home economics education. Four departments in the College of Fine Arts enrolled graduate students: 17 in architecture, 33 in drama, 32 in music, and nine in painting and sculpture. GSIA had 151 graduate students and psychology, administered by GSIA, 28. The dramatic changes in the 20 years since 1947-48 were to become even more noticeable by 1987-88.

1967-68 Carnegie Mellon Student Enrollment

	Fresh	Soph	Junior	Senior	Grad	Spec	Total
CIT	483	373	346	320	972	5	2,499
CFA	243	206	203	174	91	9	926
MMCC/H&SS	156	181	190	149	231	5	912
GSIA	0	0	0	0	151	0	151
Admin.& Mgt. Science	14	41	49	34	0	0	138
Psychology	0	0	0	0	28	0	28
Total	896	801	788	677	1,473	19	4,654

Like the faculty, students assert themselves peacefully

People who lived through 1968-70 remember the triphammer effect one tragedy after another had on our lives: the murders of Reverend Dr. Martin Luther King, Jr. and Robert F. Kennedy, the war in Vietnam and the protests against it, riots and looting in dozens of cities, the Soviet occupation of Czechoslovakia, the riots in Chicago during the Democratic National Convention, and the death of four students at Kent State University. These events affected students at the new Carnegie Mellon University. Compared to Columbia, Berkeley, Harvard or Wisconsin, Carnegie Mellon was distinctly peaceful. No students were killed, no faculty members injured, no buildings destroyed, no police called in. Still the national climate of the period influenced the mood of the campus.

The new mood appeared in numerous guises. Demonstrations drew the most attention. Students occupied Warner Hall for a night, temporarily shut down construction of the new science building, threw documents through the windows of the ROTC offices, threw marshmallows at Senator Strom Thurmond when he spoke on campus, and staged several protest meetings and demonstrations. Relatively small numbers of students, as well as a sprinkling of outsiders, took part in these demonstrations and protests, none of which resulted in violence. A carefully developed administration policy accounts in part for the peaceful nature of protests at Carnegie Mellon. Not a single student was arrested on campus during what Professor Herbert A. Simon called "the student troubles" nor were city police called in. Instead administrators and faculty members turned out to reason with protesters or even to lead demonstrations when it looked as if violence might erupt. Three cheers for common sense.

The University met many of these demands in cooperative efforts with students and faculty. The Student Senate played a key role in most of these new ventures.

Graduate students also began to assert themselves. They organized a Graduate Affairs Organizing Committee in March 1968 primarily in response to a presidential executive order ending graduate students' deferment from the draft except for those in the health professions. The new committee appeared before the Faculty Senate's Academic Affairs Committee, and it took steps to request continued deferment for graduate students who served as teaching or research assistants or had full-time scholarships. In the fall of 1969, graduate students were elected to the Student Senate for the first time. In addition, a handful of graduate students took a leadership role in campus protests and demonstrations.

Carnegie Mellon Students Demanded To:

- Require teaching evaluations by students through a comprehensive faculty course evaluation system
- Include students on committees that considered faculty reappointment, promotion and tenure decisions
- Revise the academic year calendar to extend summer vacations, provide for a reading period and make several other changes
- Ban the ROTC from campus, or at least, remove its academic status
- Lower the prices charged for meals in Skibo
- Contribute money from Student Senate funds for a new organization, The Fringe, that enrolled students from all colleges who were not involved in other social organizations, so that they could build a buggy and erect a booth at Spring Carnival
- Organize co-educational dormitories
- Develop and distribute a pamphlet about birth control
- Restrict outsiders, particularly "flower children" from local high schools, from attending functions in Skibo
- Renovate the men's dormitories, many of which were old and decaying
- Sponsor a "Free University" open to everyone and taught by volunteers, many from Carnegie-Mellon and Pitt faculties
- Organize tutoring programs for under-represented students
- Support NEED, the Negro Education Emergency Drive, through contributing funds, soliciting funds in the community, and supporting the Martin Luther King Scholarship Fund
- Abolish or seriously modify the parietal rules, particularly those that distinguished between men and women students
- Add student members to the Faculty Senate to turn it into a university senate

Students presented demands to the administration. One demand was to require teacher evaluations.

THE QUESTIONNAIRE

```
(a) Mid-term grade                          1   2   3   4   5   6   7
(b) Per cent class discussion               A   B   C   D   R   F   N/A
(c) Hours of study per week                10% 20% 30% 50% 70% 90% N/A
(d) Is the amount of work required          1   2   3   5   7   9   11
    Much too much work 1  2  3  4  5  appropriate for the credit received?
(e) Is this one of your required courses?   1(YES) 2(NO)    Almost no work required
    THE FOLLOWING 3 QUESTIONS REFER TO THE COURSE READINGS
(f) Informative   1  2  3  4  5  N/A Useless
(g) Interesting   1  2  3  4  5  N/A Boring
(h) Up to date    1  2  3  4  5  N/A Not current enough for the course

(i) Number of major projects  1  2  3  4  5  6  N/A
(j) Number of exams (3 quizzes = 1 exam)  1  2  3  4  5  6  N/A
(k) Do you feel that the exams were a fair test of your knowledge?
    Exams covered material well  1  2  3  4  5  N/A Exams were irrelevant

(l) Teacher's competence with the material
    Highly competent  1  2  3  4  5  Gives misinformation
(m) Teacher's presentation of the course material
    Stimulating ans exciting 1  2  3  4  5  Puts you to sleep
(n) Teacher's ability to communicate with the class
    Organized & easy to understand  1  2  3  4  5  Unclear & hard to follow
(o) How is the course fulfilling your needs?(Consider your immediate as
    well as your future goals.)
    Meaningful, relevent  1  2  3  4  5  Worthless
(p) Overall evaluation:
    (1) Delightful class, never wanted to cut.
    (2) Good professor, good books, classes usually worth going to.
    (3) Typical lecture & discussion routine. Not generally exciting
        or inspirational.
    (4) Dull book, dull class, almost every one sleeps or cuts and
        probably should.
    (5) Unless required, don't bother to register for this one, as classes
        don't come any worse.
```

The University focuses on the status of black Americans

The administration, faculty and students suddenly awoke to the plight of black Americans near the end of the 1960s. What few black students had attended Carnegie Tech before the 1960s were "lone travelers," that is isolated individuals in a lily-white student population. One graduate claims that she was the only black student during her years on campus, 1934-38. Tech graduated only three black Ph.D.s and one GSIA master's student during the entire decade of the 1960s. As seen, neither the Cooperative Project in History that brought black professors from the South to study and develop curriculum materials during the summer, nor the School College Orientation Program in Pittsburgh (SCOPP) offering summer and Saturday classes for black Pittsburgh high school students, contributed significantly to Tech's student population. Nor did either program receive financial support from the University after soft money grants ran out.

By 1968 the University had already made its stand on discrimination clear. In a strongly worded statement in September 1967 the administration wrote:

Carnegie-Mellon will not permit any student or other organization to operate on campus which either by affiliation with a national organization or by its own constitution, by-laws or established selection procedure or practice, discriminates against racial, ethnic or religious groups in the selection of its members.

Then in 1968 the administration, faculty and students actively began recruiting black students, helping to prepare them for college and supporting them when they arrived on campus.

The assassination of the Reverend Martin Luther King Jr. touched off a flurry of activity following a memorial service held on April 5. Members of the Faculty Senate's Academic Affairs Committee set up the Martin Luther King, Jr. Scholarship Fund that raised $19,000 in donations from faculty, staff and students. The money went to NEED, the Negro Education Emergency Drive to support black students on campus. In the fall of 1968, Carnegie Mellon started CMAP, the Carnegie Mellon Action Project that brought a carefully selected group of black students to campus and provided them with financial, academic and psychological support. Other programs beginning in 1968-70 included tutoring projects for elementary and secondary school students, a for-credit course to prepare students for their tutoring duties and Project 2001 in which fourth-year architecture students helped residents of Center Street renovate housing and clean up nearby streets.

By far the most important and long-lasting program was CMAP, whose leaders aimed to have students graduate from, rather than merely attend, Carnegie Mellon. The University supported CMAP by providing space and financial aid for students, but it failed to provide operating funds and new quarters until the Mehrabian administration beginning in 1990. CMAP officials solicited funds from businesses and foundations. Its original focus on Humanities and Social Sciences shifted in 1969 to engineering since most businesses were more willing to funnel money into programs that would provide future employees. By 1976 Carnegie Mellon was the third largest producer of minority engineers in the country.

Financial pressures soon undermined CMAP, however. In the mid-1970s, 60 percent of scholarship aid went to only 3 percent of the student body, largely to minorities. When financial aid began to include more loans than outright grants, prospective students began to accept more generous offers from competing schools. Throughout the decade after 1974,

Martin Luther King Scholarship Fund Established to Help Needy Negro Scholars

Upward Bound Aims To Break Cycle

C-MU Projects Serve Ghetto

Need Results Stated: Vote for Integration

Carnegie Mellon graduated an average of 32 African-Americans per year, 40 percent of them in engineering. Despite the services of counselors and tutors in CMAP, the attrition rate for African-American students remained high, as it did in most select universities.

In addition to CMAP, a number of additional programs to support African-Americans began in the 1968-70 period. They included tutoring programs in elementary and secondary schools, a for-credit course to prepare tutors, a Saturday evening coffee house and a project to help inner-city residents renovate their neighborhoods. None of these programs lasted more than a few years.

The incident that focused the most attention on the role of blacks in American society took place while the University was erecting Science (now Wean) Hall in 1969. Following several disturbances in Pittsburgh, Mayor Joseph Barr requested a moratorium on construction sites that employed few minority workers. Building trades craft unions had no or very few black members. Carnegie Mellon halted construction on Science Hall for three days

In 1968 Carnegie Mellon started the CMAP program that brought a group of black students to campus and provided them with financial, academic and psychological support.

179

STOP
SUPPORTING BIGOTRY
RALLY & MARCH 9:20 A.M.
MONDAY ON THE CUT TO HALT
CONSTRUCTION ON OUR CAMPUS
cmu friends of black construction coalition

and equal employment opportunities in them, urged the President and the Attorney General to sue the crafts unions, requested federal agencies to undertake a compliance review of Carnegie Mellon's construction projects and instructed the University's attorneys to renegotiate existing contracts in order to provide equal employment opportunity on work sites and develop new contract standards for all future contracts.

The memorandum failed to persuade the protesters. At 11:30 A.M. on Tuesday, students and a few faculty members threw up a human barricade at the entrance to the Science Hall construction site. Construction workers wielding hammers and crowbars appeared to threaten the protesters. An Emergency Committee previously organized by the University warned the protesters that they would be disciplined if they did not disband. The workers returned to their jobs, and the protesters dispersed, having made their point. Personnel from Security and Student Affairs, particularly Dean Earle Swank, had handled the situation skillfully. No one was injured, and the issue of discrimination against blacks had risen to the top of the University's agenda.

and then opened the site again. Members of the faculty and the student body protested. Hearing that some students and faculty members planned to prevent trucks from entering the construction site on Monday, September 22, Stever called a one-day moratorium for September 22 during which he met with faculty and students to define the University's position.

The mass meeting in the gym attracted about 200 people on Monday and added to the tension. Appeals for harmony and peaceful solutions fell on deaf ears, particularly after Stever, describing a luncheon he had had with black students, used a phrase he always regretted—that he found them to be "really human beings." A series of meetings took place during the afternoon. That evening Stever issued a memorandum approved by his Policy Advisory Committee and the Executive Committee of the Board of Trustees. It stated that the University as a community supported the demands for equal membership in construction unions

Activists control both *The Tartan* and *The Thistle*

Beginning in the late 1960s activists won editorial control of *The Tartan*. Students volunteered to staff the newspaper and then elected their own editor from among the volunteers. Increasingly the staff fell under the control of activists, particularly after 1969. Full-page articles termed "Broadsides" began to appear. They were signed articles of opinion critical of University policy and the role of the government in American society, particularly the war in Vietnam and race relations. A second series entitled "The Poverty of Student Life," a phrase lifted from the French revolutionary student leader, Daniel Cohn-Bendit, followed. A few letters of protest began to appear from students who objected both to editorial policy and to coverage, but the editors stuck to their guns.

In 1970, Professor Herbert Simon's patience ran out. Charging that *The Tartan* had fallen under control of student Maoists and becoming increasingly annoyed at student incivility, he wrote a letter to the October 8, 1970 *Tartan* in which he urged the University to end its subsidy. The editors printed the letter and responded with outrage, a sentiment shared by the president of the Student Senate. Several faculty members, particularly professors Thomas Kerr and Robert Lepper (A'27), joined in on the students' side, arguing that the principle Simon advanced would prevent the University from supporting any publication or speaker. In response, Simon offered to provide a series of letters containing some alternative views about the University, the society, and how to change them. Eight provocative columns followed under the heading "Simon Says." They ended early in 1971 partly because some students complained that they had no space in the paper to express their own views.

Broadside

The views expressed in Broadside are not necessarily those held by *The Tartan*, Carnegie-Mellon University, or the student body in either published or unofficial statements. The authors are solely responsible for the material presented in Broadside.

1984 is almost tomorrow

And in the United States, you get the feeling that it might be today.

Brutality, clubbings and smashed skulls are now the reply to dissent and questioning.

On the verge of destruction of man's right to dissent, stand the forces of the honorable Mayor of Chicago, and those who seek to abolish the honest interaction of men among themselves.

On the verge of the annihilation of all life, stand those who would empower man with weapons, beyond man's ability to control.

On the verge of a society that operates with malice and violence, stand the hate-mongers, the assassins, and the apathetic.

Law and order built on the shattered hopes of another man will not yield justice for any man.

Peace, be it in our neighborhood or the world, can be our heritage, for there will be no heritage if we fail to achieve peace.

Today is 1968
Inaction Today, Tomorrow, 1984

Bertram Robert Cottine
Gerald A. Glaser
Karen Lee Norbut
Mary Ellen Boosy

The Tartan, October 2, 1968

Interested in Pigeons?

I took an undergraduate course in cognitive psychology because the legendary Professor Herbert Simon, a Nobel Laureate, was teaching it. I didn't have the faintest idea what cognitive psychology was about. On the first day of class, Herb began describing in scintillating detail Skinner's work on training pigeons to do remarkable things. I was fascinated, and like Pavlov's dog, salivating at the prospect of dreaming up ways to make pigeons do even more impressive things. After about an hour, Herb paused, looked intently at us, and said something like, "This is all very interesting if you are interested in pigeons." Incidentally, Herb's course was the first occasion I had to do a research paper, and look what it did to me!

—Daniel Nagin, IM'71, IA'71, HNZ'76

SIMON SAYS

Genuine reform, alas, is a tougher matter (but it can be fun). It starts with trying to clarify goals, and forces us to think hard about what we want those goals to be. It doesn't, of course, neglect concrete action—what we have to do is reach our goals. And it doesn't neglect power—for power is the whatever-it-is that enables us to take the needed action.

WE HELD RALLIES ON THE CUT...

AND NOTHING HAPPENED...

PRESIDENT STEVER TRIES A LITTLE EXTEMPORANEOUS SPEAKING ...

"I HAD LUNCH WITH SOME BLACK STUDENTS YESTERDAY AND I FOUND OUT THEY'RE REALLY HUMAN BEINGS"

Illustrations from the controversial 1970 *Thistle*

The 1970 *Thistle,* the University yearbook, caused an even greater stir. Its editors were also elected from members of its volunteer staff. In midsummer, *The Thistle's* publisher sent page proofs to the administration, fearing that some of the material it contained might have been libelous. Although President Stever found the publication to be "in bad taste, unrepresentative of campus life and scurrilous," he refused to either approve or disapprove the publication on the grounds that the University did not censor student publications. The Student Senate, on being asked to review the publication, directed the publisher to print it, basing its decision on the principle of freedom of the press. This selection from the Foreword of the yearbook reflects its tone and the motives of its editors:

> There are people who aren't going to like this yearbook. . . . It has been said that students are niggers. We are inclined to agree and have changed the name of the yearbook accordingly. Now every student can have a slice of the watermelon, The Carnegie Melon. . . . The Melon attempts to provide the reader with the variety of specific experiences that many students have encountered during their four, or more, year stay here. . . . When you open this book, then (providing the binding holds up) you may be reminded of the follies of yourselves or your friends, be they due to activism or inactivism. At any rate, we are sure that this is a book that you will keep and cherish, since we doubt that there will be an organization to send it back to.

Instead of striking out at the editors, the administration wisely made Student Government, the sponsor of the yearbook, a corporate entity as a way to avoid liability for student publications in the future. It also drafted a statement on the Goals, Rights and Responsibilities of Carnegie Mellon University and printed the statement in both the student and faculty handbooks. In the meantime, the yearbook, along with demonstrations about alleged activities of major corporations, such as Gulf Oil and U.S. Steel, with particularly damning comments about the Mellon family, aroused the ire of many Carnegie Mellon supporters who thought that the administration should have been more active in suppressing student activists. Support for the Fund for Distinction diminished, and both Richard K. Mellon and Richard M. Scaife resigned from the Board of Trustees.

In the meantime, life went on

Of course it did. As in 1948, the 3,140 undergraduate day students, 777 part-time evening students and 1,361 day and evening graduate students lived in different worlds. The composition of the evening school population, however, had changed significantly since 1948. In 1968 they were all degree candidates, about a third of them seeking graduate degrees. Their lives outside of classes revolved, as they had in 1948, around jobs, families, neighborhoods and social and religious groups, leaving little time or inclination to erect booths or push buggies at Spring Carnival. Instead they watched buggy races or smiled proudly as their children rode the merry-go-round at Spring Carnival. Similarly, the handful of commuters who could not participate in residence life programs or live in fraternity houses were cut off from much of campus life.

Graduate students continued to form personal ties with the faculty with whom they studied. Single graduate students lived in a few graduate dormitories or in apartments in the city, so they took part only occasionally in undergraduate activities. Many graduate students served as teaching assistants, putting them in roles as instructors of undergraduates. Often married and sometimes with children, they tended to focus what out-of-class time they had on their families and friends.

As they had in 1948, Greeks and non-Greeks led different lives. The 1968 *Student Handbook* listed 12 social fraternities and seven sororities, accompanying these lists with the following comment:

It should be noted that a large part of the social activities on the campus are provided by and supported by the fraternities. Social functions are an intrinsic part of the fraternal calendar. In their efforts to develop the social graces, the art of good living, and the qualities of courtesy and kindness,

Do As The Gods Do.... **GO GREEK!** Sponsored By Panhellenic Council

GO GREEK

Fraternity Rush Opens Friday With House Tours

A Phi O Smoker Invitation to Service

Sororities Pledge 54 in Formal Rush

Fraternities Conduct Live-In Sit-In

Forever 19 in My Memory

Co-ed housing came to Welch Hall in the fall of 1969. Rather than a hotbed of sexual liberation as some worry-warts predicted, Welch Hall turned out to be just people of both sexes living in the same dorm—and leaving me with my most vivid memories of C-MU: a now 40-something woman who is forever 19 in my memory; a friend who has grown to middle age with me; Betsy with a hot water bottle on her stomach; poker games; watching the Vietnam draft lottery with my roommate and his girlfriend—no, he wasn't, and, yes, she still is. I proposed to my wife in Welch Hall.

—Charles J. Vukotich, Jr., S'71

Opposite page top:
Cartoon from *The Tartan,*
February 12, 1969

Opposite page bottom:
Freshman Camp

fraternities hope to provide a well-balanced and refreshing social program. Good manners, good taste, and good companionship are a part of the social training experienced by each fraternity member.

In a letter to the February 12, 1968 *Tartan,* an officer of the Council of Fraternity Presidents presented a somewhat different view of fraternity life when he invited freshman students to participate in rush week:

For those of us who are a part of the fraternity system, fraternity life is many things. It is working together with your brothers to get the rough calculus assignment done. It's playing your best or cheering until your voice gives out at an intramural game. It's eating, sleeping, studying, laughing, discussing and living with the greatest bunch of friends one will ever have. It's getting together and raising money for a worthy cause. It's building a Homecoming booth, singing at Greek Sing, and pushing a buggy during Spring Carnival. To me, fraternity life is all of these things, and much more. You really can't define fraternity; it's more a way of life.

Stories about fraternity and sorority rush appeared every year in *The Tartan.* In addition to all-Greek activities such as Greek Sing, Greek organizations dominated the buggy races, booths at Spring Carnival, elections to school-wide offices, intramural athletics and parties throughout the year. Occasionally non-Greeks challenged this domination. In 1968 a

group calling itself the Fringe appealed to the Student Senate for funds so that its members could erect a booth and build a buggy. Fringe still exists as an independent organization.

Men and "girls," as the official *Residence Hall Handbook* termed them, still lived under different rules. For example, the University established no curfew hours in the men's dormitories, but specified hours for women. Similarly, men had no housekeeping standards, while regulations for women required them, among other things, to make their beds before leaving the building and to prepare their rooms for a weekly inspection necessary because, "Cleanliness is essential in maintaining standards for health and thorough cleaning of your room at least once a week is expected."

The rules were changing, however. In 1968, the administration granted sophomore women who had their parents' written permission freedom from the curfew rules. Freshman women petitioned for the same privilege in the fall of 1968, pointing to the fact that freshman men had no such restrictions. In December 1968 the Executive Board issued new parietal rules opening the men's and women's lounges and the first floors and basements of fraternity houses until 1:30 A.M. on Friday and Saturday. Restrictions on freshman women's curfew rules were lifted in 1969.

MDC: A PLAN FOR COED LIVING

Men's Dormitory Council feels that the students at this school **want, need,** and are **ready** for co-educational dormitories. . . . We feel that a coeducational dormitory will go a long way toward bringing both the colleges and the sexes closer together. The proximity of the opposite sex will stimulate and provide an opportunity for social interaction among **all** dorm residents. The women will act as a catalyst for the men and there will be an overall increase in communications. . . .

The Tartan, February 12, 1969

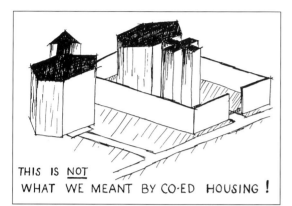

THIS IS <u>NOT</u> WHAT WE MEANT BY CO-ED HOUSING !

In the meantime, student agitation for coed dorms had been gathering steam in both the Men's Dormitory Council and the Association of Women Students. In April 1969 Dean Swank announced that an experiment in coed housing for sophomores, juniors and seniors would be tried in the fall in one dormitory, Welch Hall. Men and women were to be housed on the same floors in one- or two-room suites with semi-private baths. The experiment enrolled 54 students—33 men and 21 women—maintaining the typical Carnegie Mellon male-female ratio. A coed housing committee consisting of seven students chose the participants. An immediate success, coed housing rapidly spread to other dormitories.

Only a minority of student activists directed their energies to protest meetings, capturing control of *The Tartan* and *The Thistle*, or attending classes in the Free University. Some freshmen began the year with a three-day orientation in September 1968 at Camp Lutherlyn about 40 miles north of Pittsburgh and the entire class participated in the orientation activities that followed on campus. Rain marred the three-day Freshman Camp, driving the campers indoors for most of the time. In addition to concerts and dances, the freshmen heard a speech in which Professor Thomas Kerr distinguished between the rights of students and the rights of the faculty. The freshmen gave him an ovation.

The campers returned to campus to begin a formal orientation program with classmates who had passed up the voluntary freshman camp. They met the deans of their respective colleges as well as the deans of men and women, attended religious services if they chose to do so, took psychological tests, heard lectures from professors, met fraternity and sorority representatives and attended more dances and concerts. Some of these events required coat and tie. The new University was attending to incoming students' needs as they made the transition from secondary school to college.

Then the whole student body went to classes—some, as usual, intermittently—did their homework, wrote papers and took examinations. They helped alumni return to campus for homecoming in the fall; celebrated Spring Carnival, Scotch 'n' Soda, and the Ugly Man on Campus contest; played both intramural and intercollegiate sports; complained about food, Skibo, housing, and their professors; lived for the first time in a coed dormitory; and shrugged collective shoulders at announcements of grants for research or a campaign to raise $55 million for the Fund for Distinction.

Boys Being Boys

During the winter of 1968-69 some of the guys on the second floor of Donner Hall decided to convert one of the shower stalls into a swimming pool. They got a piece of plywood and some plastic sheeting, placed a barrier across the door of the shower, plugged up the drain with some old socks, and turned on the shower. The water rose to waist height, and the guys were having a good time in the impromptu indoor pool until, without warning, the plywood gave way. A wall of water half-a-foot deep swept down the second floor hallway, eddying into the rooms and carrying objects out like a miniature tsunami. The wave found its way to the stairs in the center of the building and cascaded into the basement in a spectacular waterfall. Fortunately, damage was light—and the floors never looked cleaner.

—Charles Laing, E'72

And Girls Being Girls

The Morewood Gardens water battle started on a hot spring Sunday when everyone was washing cars. Well, it got a little out of hand, and soon water balloons were dropping from dorm windows. A bucket of water hit a poor, unsuspecting visiting parent. Students coming back from the library were soaked down by hoses, balloons, and buckets of water. When students started to hose down oncoming cars, one poor convertible owner, soaked to the skin, called in the police. Well, as the guys were loaded into the cars, they escaped and ran out the other side. It was like a Laurel and Hardy show right before your eyes.

—Barrie Dinkins Simpson, MM'68

Right:
The Scotch 'n' Soda production, *Pippin Pippin,* dropped one *Pippin* from its title when it played on Broadway.

MADAME MADAME!

The *Student Handbook* called the Oakland sector of Pittsburgh ". . .a unique island of culture, education, science, and entertainment surrounded by industrial Greater Pittsburgh." Carnegie Mellon students could exploit this rich social and cultural environment as well as participate in campus events. Students could attend Drama Department plays without charge. The Pittsburgh Symphony performed in the nearby Syria Mosque and numerous musical performances took place in the Carnegie Music Hall just across the bridge from campus. The biennial Pittsburgh International exhibition attracted artists from all over the world to exhibit in the galleries of the Carnegie Institute.

The *Student Handbook* also listed 23 student clubs, 16 departmental societies, 12 academic honorary societies, six class honoraries and 15 religious organizations, including Protestant, Catholic, Jewish, Eastern Orthodox, Unitarian and Christian Scientist. Unlike most universities, Carnegie Mellon had no chapel, so religious groups utilized their own churches and temples or occasionally held meetings in classrooms.

In 1968, for the first time in history, Scotch 'n' Soda produced two shows, one in the fall and the other in April. The fall show, *For Heaven's Sake,* produced on four previous occasions, was a musical satire on the church and some of the problems of the late 1960s. The spring show, *MADAME, MADAME,* gave five performances in the Skibo Ballroom during Spring Carnival. *The Tartan* outlined the plot of the musical which was directed by Sam Platt (A'70) and written by Mark Pirolo (A'70) with costumes by Arnold Levine:

Although it lacks the controversy of a Hair, MADAME, MADAME *isn't without its share of theatrical sex. The show centers around a certain "establishment" on the left bank in Paris during Napoleon's reign. The owner of the establishment, La Madame, played by Beth Powell had accumulated great wealth as a result of her chain of "establishments" throughout Europe. But her wealth can't give her the respectability a title of nobility would. She attempts to solve this problem by marrying Baron Munchausen, an extravagant eccentric traveler who has spent his life spending large sums of money on far-fetched expeditions. In Paris to raise money for more of his trips, the Baron meets an old friend, La Madame. The match seems perfect for both—money for the baron, a title for the Madame. . .*

Scotch 'n' Soda captured the hearts and minds of some participants more than any other experience they had on campus.

The Ugliest Man on Campus contest, as it had in the past, aroused spirited competition for this dubious honor. The sponsors encouraged ballot box stuffing since each vote cost a penny and Campus Chest received the proceeds to distribute to worthy charities. Delta Tau Delta collected $361 of the total of $735 raised by the UMOC contest for its nominee. In 1969, each candidate assumed a pseudonym, among them The Great Horny Owl, Dr. O. R. Gasm, and Loose Bruce. The winner, H. Guyford Buhle, sponsored by Delta Tau Delta, received the Ugly Mug at the Spring Carnival dance while Chi Omega's Great Horny Owl took a newly conceived Baby Ugly Mug. Alpha Phi Omega, which sponsored the contest, donated the proceeds, $653.17, to the Negro Education Emergency Drive.

Spring Carnival 1969 included amusement rides; booths erected by fraternities, sororities and a few dormitories; the sight and sound of carnival callers hawking their booths; strings of lights; and the odor of cotton candy, hot dogs, coke and popcorn that filled the air to the delight of students, faculty members and their children. On Saturday, a group of alumni defeated the varsity football team by the score of 14 to 8. Beta Theta Pi won both the buggy design contest and the buggy race. Only fraternities won a race including the consolation and preliminary events.

Spring Carnival 1969

The 1969 Spring Carnival featured the conventional events:

Friday, May 2

9:00 AM	Buggy Derby
11:30 AM	Picnic
1:00 PM	Call Day
2:30 PM	Egg Toss & Sorority Relays
8:30 PM	The Iron Butterfly, A Concert in Carnegie Music Hall
12:00 Noon – 9:00 PM	Midway open

Saturday, May 3

10:00 AM	Buggy Derby Finals & Consolation Heats
1:00 PM	Deep Purple, A Concert in the Gym
2:15 PM	Plank Joust on Kappa Sigma Lawn
9:00 PM	Dance on Skibo Patio
12:00 Midnight	Awards Presentation
12:00 Noon – 8:00 PM	Midway open

Qualifications for UMOC

Anyone possessing the following three qualifications is eligible to enter UMOC: he must be a male; he must be a C-MU student; and he must be ugly. To preserve some degree of competition, faculty members have been declared ineligible. . . . If you can't seem to find an ugly member in your organization, why not look in the mirror? Then talk one of your friends into running before he realizes that you would make the best choice.
—*The Tartan,* March 13, 1968

The 1968 Beaux Arts Ball

There were two memorable costumes. As Batman, Miggs Borrows entered the hall at midnight leaping from the balcony above the dean's office. He was tethered to a wire and flew from there to the stage built over the front entrance. Someone from Painting and Design came as a "Pile of Shit." He made a great papier-mâché mound, which he painted brown, and spent the entire evening inside with his girlfriend and a bottle of scotch. But best of all, he had made a beautiful fly with translucent wings. He attached this fly to a supple wire so that the fly hovered over the mound all night long.

—William D. (Doug) Cooper, A'70

Hinsdale Day

In the '60s a somewhat pixilated collection of fine arts students founded Hinsdale Day in honor of the urinals in the Fine Arts Building. Each urinal bore the Hinsdale logo and date of patent, November 10th, 1910, in bold blue letters about chest height. The conspirators posted handwritten signs proclaiming Hinsdale Day, the 10th of November, and provoking widespread bewilderment, particularly among women students who lacked access to the urinals. By the late '60s, enthusiastic celebrants installed a keg of beer in a urinal, surrounding it with ice and providing input where only output had heretofore reigned supreme.

—A composite of contributions from: Christopher E. Lozos, A'66, Mark Mentzer, A'73 and William D. (Doug) Cooper, A'70

Delights and dismays of daily life

In an article entitled "It's A Live-In" in the September 13, 1968 *Tartan*, Dave Kamons (E'69) gave sage advice to his fellow students:

Life in the Mellon patch can be laughs if it is taken for what it's worth. . . . Naturally every guy's first thought is of the girls in Morewood Fortress. Finding a girl requires. . . ingenuity. The Orientation Committee provides the initial push with the Freshman Mixer. Failing there (guys do outnumber co-eds by about 3 to 1) a guy can turn to dorm mixers, dances at Pitt where there are some 7,000 women, nursing schools and two girls' colleges. The man with real guts may even pick a phone number at random from the C-Book and take his chances. . . . The girls have it easy. All they have to do is sit back and wait for the phone to ring.

Privacy on a date is the number one premium. Donner and Morewood lounges are comfortable in an institutional way but they are fishbowls. The obvious solution is Schenley Park. . . . The most popular feature of curfew time is the traditional Super-Kiss. Starting time is shortly after the five-minute warning rings. You must see this in person to appreciate it; no description can do it justice.

Boys would be boys, however. Floor counselors and security personnel settled most rule violations quietly, but they referred a few to the Men's Dormitory Court. Records for the 1968-1969 year reveal the following charges: four for having female visitors in a room, two for making too much noise, two for altering tokens for the laundry machines, two for drinking alcoholic beverages, and one each for possessing a weapon (a bayonet) in the dorm, damage to private property, damage to a dormitory wall and setting off firecrackers.

Alumni reorganize

In July, 1963 Robert G. McCurdy became executive secretary of the Alumni Association, an organization with 27,000 members. McCurdy rapidly took control. In 1964 the alumni office began to issue clan charters and to charter new clans. It replaced the *Carnegie Alumnus* with a tabloid size journal called the *Alumni News* and increased the number of forums and other meetings it sponsored around the country. By 1968 a new era in alumni relations was well underway.

The Association attempted to organize Carnegie Tech's alumni—10,000 of them within 50 miles of Pittsburgh—into 34 active, chartered clans, five of them from geographic districts around Pittsburgh. Two other clans, architects and musicians, represented disciplines. One clan, Pittsburgh women, consisted of graduates of Margaret Morrison and another, Pittsburgh businessmen, included graduates from Tech's colleges engaged in business downtown. The remaining 25 clans were concentrated in the Northeast, although there were three in southern California and three in Florida.

By 1967 the number of Carnegie Tech alumni had risen to 28,000. Of this number, about half had never given money to Carnegie Tech. The managers of the Alumni Fund Campaign planned a thorough solicitation program for the coming year, including four mailings and telephone and personal solicitations for alumni who had given generously in past years. They set a goal of $360,000, $13,000 more than had been raised in 1966-67.

Twenty-eight percent of the alumni gave to the fund, four times the percentage in 1948. They contributed $531,114, exceeding their goal by more than $170,000. In future years, solicitation became a regular feature of annual alumni fund drives.

In retrospect

By 1968 no trace of the trade school origins of the Carnegie Technical Schools remained. The days when graduates had won two-year certificates or three-year diplomas had ended long ago. In fact, 40 percent of the 1968 graduates were master's or doctor's students, up from 3 percent in 1928 and 13 percent in 1948. Incoming students were more talented than they had been in the past although they remained predominately regional and almost exclusively white. By 1968 a distinguished Graduate School of Industrial Administration, almost two decades old, had won national prominence. In 1967, the merger with Mellon Institute had added a distinguished set of researchers to the institution as well as an increased endowment of $60 million and the extensive facilities of the Mellon Institute building on Fifth Avenue. Although Margaret Morrison and the night school were fading, Carnegie Mellon had announced the formation of a College of Humanities and Social Sciences and a School of Urban and Public Affairs. Research in engineering, science, management and the Mellon Institute was thriving, as were the creative activities of faculty in the College of Fine Arts. A new development drive was well underway with the blessings of Carnegie Mellon's new patrons, the Mellon family. The faculty had won new roles in University government. Alumni had begun to rally round.

Shadows were soon to cloud this rosy picture, however. The student troubles, soon to become more prominent, focused attention away from academic affairs and angered some of the new University's strongest supporters just as the development drive was gathering steam. Financial problems loomed on the horizon as inflation outpaced income and reserves reached the vanishing point. A New

College, scheduled to open in the fall of 1969 as a part of Humanities and Social Sciences, soon faced a student revolt, provoking years of soul searching and experimentation. Carnegie Mellon had had a painful birth. Once the delivery pains subsided, however, the childhood and adolescence of the new University resulted by 1988 in a robust early adulthood. In the two decades after 1968 Carnegie Mellon became one of the great success stories of American education in the twentieth century, a tale for which President Richard M. Cyert's distinguished leadership provided the story line.

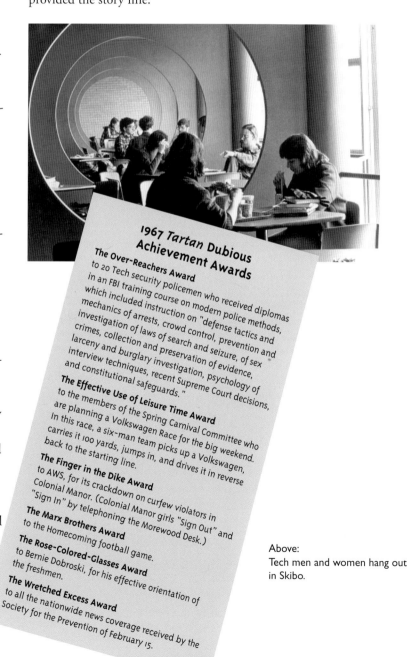

Thanks to TGIF

We lived all week for TGIF in Skibo every Friday from 4:30 to 6:30 during the 1960s. Everyone came—nerds, druggies, one bizarre physics student who wore shorts through the whole winter, the guy who lived in the steam tunnels, high school kids (like me), regular folks from all over the campus—everyone. Did we dance! Billy Price had the best band. TGIF was every week's social event for the whole student body and a host of hangers-on. It kept us all sane during an insane decade.

—Rebecca (Fenton) Knobil

1967 Tartan Dubious Achievement Awards

The Over-Reachers Award
to 20 Tech security policemen who received diplomas in an FBI training course on modern police methods, which included instruction on "defense tactics and mechanics of arrests, crowd control, prevention and investigation of laws of search and seizure, of sex crimes, collection and preservation of evidence, larceny and burglary investigation, psychology of interview techniques, recent Supreme Court decisions, and constitutional safeguards."

The Effective Use of Leisure Time Award
to the members of the Spring Carnival Committee who are planning a Volkswagen Race for the big weekend. In this race, a six-man team picks up a Volkswagen, carries it 100 yards, jumps in, and drives it in reverse back to the starting line.

The Finger in the Dike Award
to AWS, for its crackdown on curfew violators in Colonial Manor. (Colonial Manor girls "Sign Out" and "Sign In" by telephoning the Morewood Desk.)

The Marx Brothers Award
to the Homecoming football game.

The Rose-Colored-Glasses Award
to Bernie Dobroski, for his effective orientation of the freshmen.

The Wretched Excess Award
to all the nationwide news coverage received by the Society for the Prevention of February 15.

Above:
Tech men and women hang out in Skibo.

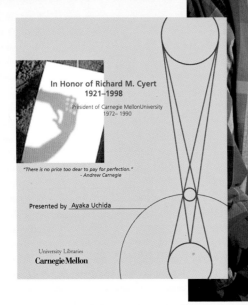

12.

Richard Michael Cyert 1972–1990
He turned Carnegie Mellon into a research university

If Robert E. Doherty sowed the seeds of the modern research university that Carnegie Tech was to become, Richard M. Cyert harvested the crops. Not that the intervening administrations stood still. Without major developments in both the Warner and Stever administrations, Cyert would have been unable to make such dramatic progress on so many different fronts. Nevertheless, the Cyert administration marks the full emergence of a modern research university from what began as a trade school offering a three-year diploma or a two-year certificate.

Dick Cyert was born in Winona, Minnesota, in 1921, the eldest of three children. His parents were both orphans sent from New York to be reared in Minnesota. His father became a successful salesman during the 1920s when Cyert was a child, but like many other Americans, the Cyerts fell upon hard times during the depression. By the time Cyert entered high school in Minneapolis, he was delivering newspapers to help pay the rent and put food on the family's table. This experience helped to shape his life and his attitude toward money. Playing baseball on his high school team engendered a lifetime devotion to the sport.

A precocious student, he entered the University of Minnesota in 1939, lived at home rather than in a dormitory and took a job as a library page for 25 cents an hour to help to pay expenses. Although he was enrolled in the business school and majored in accounting, he spent much of his time studying economics, applied mathematics and statistics. When the United States entered World War II, Cyert, who had enrolled in an ROTC program in college, became a naval officer, serving in the Pacific theater. His landing craft put armor ashore in the Marshall Islands, and when the Japanese sank his vessel, he survived by swimming ashore. Discharged in 1946, he went back to Minnesota, met and married Margaret Shadick, an intelligent, attractive and personable home economics major at the University of Minnesota. That fall he went off to study for his doctorate at Columbia University supported, like millions of other veterans, by the G.I. Bill. Finishing his course work in 1948 at the age of 27, he accepted a job as an instructor at Carnegie Tech. With Margaret and their first child, Lynn, he moved into a three-room apartment in one end of a Quonset hut on campus.

1972

- Richard Michael Cyert becomes Carnegie Mellon's sixth president.
- The Andrew Carnegie Society is organized.

Opposite page:
President Cyert circled by bookplates designed by Carnegie Mellon students in his memory

Above:
Cyert with Stever: the new president takes over.

Cyert expected to stay at Tech for only two or three years while he finished work on his dissertation. Inspired by two of his ex-professors, George Stigler at Minnesota and Arthur Burns at Columbia, he expected to move on to a major research university. Tech, however, began to offer both opportunities for research and brilliant colleagues. When the School of Business Administration opened in 1950 with Lee Bach as dean, Cyert, by then an assistant professor, was on a faculty that included Herbert A. Simon, William Cooper, Franco Modigliani and a number of other distinguished scholars. James March, a political scientist, joined this faculty in 1953. They constituted a "hot group," a handful of brilliant, energetic scholars who broke through conventional academic boundaries. Ten years later, Cyert and March published *A Behavioral Theory of the Firm,* a book that established both of their scholarly reputations. It focused on what large organizations implied for social behavior, stress in the workplace, new forms of decision making, increased bureaucracy and the handling of huge amounts of data. The Institute for Scientific Information later named this volume as a *Citation Classic.*

> ### The Management Game
>
> I acted as President for our firm for the Management Game. We had a retired Chairman of Republic Steel as our game firm chairman. This was great, but he refused to treat it as a game. He'd call meetings at 11:00 p.m. and insist on a breakfast meeting. If I said I had a class, I'd get a lecture on the role of the CEO, so I learned to play the game of CEO. I began to refer to my marketing class as a customer meeting and to finance class as a meeting with bankers. This technique even affected grading which was handled by a "Compensation Committee" with him as Chair. I had to justify our team's bonus, including my own—all good preparation for my current job [as CEO of Xerox].
> —Paul A. Allaire, IA '66

The Graduate School of Industrial Administration (GSIA) became the most innovative and intriguing business school in the nation during the 1950s. Compared to other business schools, GSIA was more scholarly, more data based and more attuned to organizational structure. Its doctoral program attracted brilliant students who consistently won prizes for their dissertations. Between 1965 and 1970 six business schools chose new deans who had either taught or studied at Carnegie Tech. When Tech's first computer arrived and was installed in a room at GSIA, pioneering GSIA faculty members, led by Simon, and including Dick Cyert, began to simulate corporate and organizational problems on the machine. In 1959 they began to develop the Carnegie Tech Management Game in which teams of students competed with each other to solve mock industrial management problems on the computer. Within years, it became famous as a new teaching device.

In 1960 Cyert was named full professor and in 1962, when Lee Bach resigned, Dean of GSIA. Cyert loved being dean, loved to run things. As dean, he continued to write scholarly papers and to carry on a full scholarly life, a practice he continued after he became president. All told, he authored or co-authored 12 books and more than 100 articles in a variety of fields including economics, behavioral science, management and statistics. While Lee Bach had kept a balance between research and management, Cyert pushed the faculty toward the research end of the spectrum, building outstanding faculties in both economics and operations research.

Cyert becomes president

When Guyford Stever resigned in 1971, the trustees chose Richard M. Cyert from among five distinguished final candidates as president of what had become Carnegie Mellon University. He was fully prepared to assume his new responsibilities. He had an insider's grasp of management techniques and a flair for leadership, and he was open, analytical, logical and, when he needed to be, tough.

Rather than move into Carnegie Mellon's huge president's home on Devon Road, Cyert and Margaret stayed in their comparatively modest ranch-style house in Fox Chapel, a suburb of Pittsburgh. Later the Cyerts moved into a larger home of their own in the same neighborhood. Cyert's offices on the top floor of Warner Hall were undistinguished. He kept an additional office where be could hide out when he had an empty hour or two on his calendar. For many years, he took piano lessons from Harry Franklin, a professor of music. To the delight of the athletes, he often showed up at varsity football and basketball games, sometimes accompanied by his aging father. He also spent many afternoons, often with his family or his colleague, Jim March, cheering the Pirates at Three Rivers Stadium.

Throughout his career at Carnegie Mellon, Margaret Cyert praised her husband's talents as she shared the demands of his office and reared their three daughters. She was present at hundreds of meetings, entertained with grace and charm and even established "Margaret's Muffins"—free coffee and food on the steps of Doherty Hall during examination periods. She also forged a career of her own, winning her master's degree in child development from the University of Pittsburgh, participating in civic organizations and working closely with many area organizations interested in early childhood education.

Both of the Cyerts had long supported the work of the Carnegie Mellon Child Care Center, an organization that in recent years has committed itself to adopting the principles of the schools of Reggio Emilia, Italy to the United States. In April 1998 the school dedicated its new $1.5 million quarters and changed its name to the Margaret Shadick Cyert Center for Early Education and Program for Collaborative Learning, a tribute to Margaret's long services to the Pittsburgh community and to the contributions, both financial and personal, of both the Cyerts to the school.

Dick Cyert and his wife, Margaret, relaxing at home

Richard Cyert's Inauguration

At Cyert's inauguration in March 1973, the Reverend David A. Johnson, minister of the First Unitarian Church in Pittsburgh, delivered the following insightful invocation:

Lord of this resplendent earth,
We know this is a hard time to become a college president.
We gather, nonetheless, to bless this man on his way,
Knowing that he shall require
The wisdom of Solomon and the patience of Job,
The resourcefulness of Horatio Alger,
The endurance of Methuselah,
The loving openness of St. Francis,
And the tenacity of Winston Churchill,
The creative intellect of Einstein,
And the strength and stick-to-it-iveness of epoxy resin.
Sustain this good and courageous man
In the days and years ahead,
And surely it would not be too much to hope
For a few friends with the wealth of Croesus
And the generosity of Andrew Carnegie.
Bless this man, our friend, and the cause
Of excellence, education and truth
To which he and this university are dedicated.
Amen

The Cook Called in Sick

My first campus work-study job was as a receptionist/typist/director's assistant at the Child Care Center. When the cook called in sick, I learned (very quickly) how to make lunch for forty-five children.
—Mary Ann Ulishney, MM '78

Carnegie Mellon faces eight major problems in 1972

With a stroke of the pen in 1967 an excellent regional technical school had become a university. In 1972 it was still a mixture of strengths and weaknesses. Some schools and some departments of Carnegie Mellon had achieved national prominence. The engineering school consistently ranked among the top 10 nationally. GSIA, now two decades old, had successfully challenged the entrenched business schools, such as Harvard, Stanford and Chicago, for national leadership. An even younger department, Computer Science, competed with Massachusetts Institute of Technology, Stanford and Berkeley for first place in this promising new field. The Drama Department in the College of Fine Arts ranked among the nation's best. So did Psychology, soon to become part of the College of Humanities and Social Sciences (H&SS). Before the new University could attain overall excellence, however, it had to solve eight major problems while it sustained progress in its outstanding programs.

• The School of Urban and Public Affairs (SUPA) existed only on paper. It had an excellent dean in William Cooper and a small but distinguished faculty, but neither its education nor its research agenda was yet in place. Its enrollment was well below target levels. Inflation was eating into the endowment, forcing the school either to increase income by recruiting more students or to seek outside funding. The central administration had no spare dollars to support this infant school.

• The College of Humanities and Social Sciences (H&SS) had four departments, History, English, Modern Languages and Psychology, only one of which had a Ph.D. program. Both English and History had thriving master of arts and doctor of arts programs designed primarily for teachers and prospective teachers at the college and high school levels. They and the curriculum projects on which they were built were supported generously by grants from the government and private foundations, but involved only a minority of the members of each department. Since resources were scarce, new ventures would have to be developed without increases from the University's Education and General Operating (E&GO) budget.

Tradition demanded that only senior dramats could write their names backstage in the Kresge Theater. Holly Hunter, later an Oscar winner, broke this tradition.

• Three departments in the Mellon College of Science (MCS) needed help. Some of the luster in the Physics Department had tarnished when the University decommissioned the synchro-cyclotron in 1965. Chemistry faced the difficult problem of assimilating 21 new tenured faculty members from the Mellon Institute into a department that had 16 members before the merger. Finally, the Department of Biological Sciences had no sharp focus and no significant research efforts.

• The College of Fine Arts (CFA) crowded more than 1,000 students into a building built for 300 students in 1916. The commitment to build a new Drama building freeing space for other departments in Fine Arts was shaky because a funding drive had come up short and the building could only be erected by tapping endowment funds. Government grants for research that were destined to play such a dominant role in the development of other Carnegie Mellon colleges and schools never became available in the fine arts.

• Recruiting a larger, able, diverse student body was becoming more difficult. Carnegie Mellon was still a regional university. Enrollment had reached a low point since the end of World War II in both engineering and science. With the end of the baby boom, the number of high school graduates would decline annually for many years to come. This decline in the college-age population would increase competition for a smaller number of able students and prevent Carnegie Mellon from raising tuition faster than its peer institutions.

• An aging physical plant would soon need attention. Roofs were leaking, and the handsome Hornbostel buildings were hidden beneath a layer of smoke and grime. Classrooms looked very much as they had when the buildings were erected. Facilities for student life—Skibo, the gym, the athletic fields and many of the residence halls— cried out for attention. Additional research space was at a premium. On the whole, the campus presented a dingy and somewhat neglected appearance unattractive to both students and prospective students.

• Carnegie Mellon had only a modest presence in the wider Pittsburgh community. It had been a university for only five years, years during which it had focused its attention on getting its new house in order in the midst of student protests and financial stringencies. Yet, if the new University was to reach its full potential, it would have to make positive contributions to Pittsburgh and the surrounding counties.

• Carnegie Mellon's financial situation complicated all of these problems. Cyert inherited a three-year deficit totaling about $3 million and a projected deficit of $1.4 million. The Fund for Distinction had been allowed to lapse quietly, far short of its goal. The size of the endowment was increasing more slowly than endowments at peer universities. Finally, student protests over the war in Vietnam and racial issues had alienated some of Carnegie Mellon's generous financial supporters.

President Cyert maintained an open-door policy

Dick Cyert lived to compete. Always impatient to get to where he was going, he occasionally got speeding tickets as he drove from his home in Fox Chapel to the University. Rather than hug the baseline in tennis matches, he charged the net. He kept himself in excellent physical shape by lifting weights, jogging and walking up six flights of steps to reach his office on the top floor of Warner Hall. And he worked very hard— 12-hour days were routine—keeping up a flow of scholarly research at the same time that he presided over a rapidly growing University where each day brought unexpected new challenges, challenges that he usually saw as opportunities.

Cyert kept an open office. He believed that a successful manager had to pay personal attention to details, and he gathered information both indirectly from his administrative staff and directly from members of the community. In addition to his administrative staff, he saw individual faculty and staff members, as well as students, and listened carefully to what they had to say.

Literally dozens of faculty and staff members credit Cyert with giving them a start or a boost at a significant turning point in their careers. He had a constitutional aversion to discouraging anyone. Many visitors left his office believing that the president had promised to support whatever they had proposed only to learn later that funding was unavailable. On the other hand, his colleagues soon learned that they could disagree with him, that he valued colleagues who had minds of their own. He even appointed joint provosts so that he could bounce ideas off both of them instead of relying on a

Pass The Dressing, Please

As a magazine publisher, I often tell the uninitiated that I eat meals for a living. Each time that I say, "Pass the dressing, please," I think fondly of Dick Cyert. He didn't use salad dressing. Consequently, at dinners he hosted for honors students, none of the honorees ever imbibed the oil and vinegar either. At my first dinner, I succumbed to a bland salad. At the second, I skipped the salad. At my third dinner, I contemplated allowing my grades to drop to avoid this tortuous meal. Then, against considerable inertia, I blurted out a request for dressing. The immense relief I felt when the University's President poured dressing on my salad taught me one of CMU's most valuable lessons—the value of challenging the status quo.
—Linda A. Dickerson, HS'81

Airport Commitments

We used to talk about airport commitments. People would run into Dick at the airport and he promised them something and then they would show up wanting to collect. It was my job in the early days. . .to explain that airport commitments were not binding.
—Provost Richard Van Horn

195

1987-88 Average Faculty Salaries*
(Adjusted for Regional Cost of Living)

Institution	Professor	Associate	Assistant
Stanford	$71.0	$50.2	$39.7
U of CA (B)	68.5	42.2	35.9
Yale	67.7	40.8	32.4
MIT	66.6	48.2	37.8
U of PA	64.3	46.3	38.3
Carnegie Mellon	63.4	42.8	37.8
NW	61.0	41.0	37.0
Cornell	59.6	42.3	35.5
U of MI	59.1	44.5	36.8
RPI	59.0	42.8	36.4
Wash U	55.3	38.8	32.1
Purdue	55.1	38.8	32.3
Lehigh	53.8	39.2	32.8
U of WI	52.1	38.2	33.7

* IPEDS/AAUP Survey

single opinion. He frequently talked over issues with a small group of close advisers and then made a decision. He was an activist with an impatient, optimistic, entrepreneurial spirit. He knew that occasional failure was the price one paid for trying fresh approaches, but he also knew that great achievements required great risks. On more than one occasion when he recognized that he had gone too fast or too far, he retreated briefly while he mended fences with disgruntled colleagues.

To achieve his goals, Cyert relied on strategic planning principles focusing on areas in which the University had a comparative advantage over peer institutions and on problem solving, both of which drew upon well-entrenched Carnegie Tech traditions. He focused strategic planning efforts on triennial meetings that brought administrators and faculty together for several days in order to discuss departmental and college plans and seek areas where Carnegie Mellon had comparative advantage. By comparative advantage he meant a way in which an administrative unit could utilize its resources in personnel or equipment to put it on the cutting edge of research or education; that is, that it could do a specified task better than its rivals. Problem solving served as a means to evaluate whether or not comparative advantage had indeed been achieved and exploited. It also served as a major curriculum focus throughout the University.

Carnegie Mellon has always had appointed department heads, not elected department chairs. Cyert believed that department heads were the most important members of the administration. They hired incoming faculty members and set standards for achievement. He met with them four times yearly so that they could listen to and learn from each other while they were reporting on and assessing their own work. Only department heads and Cyert himself participated regularly in these meetings. In this way, Cyert was able to maintain close relationships with department heads and become acquainted firsthand with departmental problems.

To keep administrators on their toes, he established a system of periodic evaluations. First, he asked the faculty to evaluate him near the end of his first term as president. The committee polled the faculty and submitted a report that in retrospect understated Cyert's achievements by a wide margin. Cyert, nevertheless, found this process so valuable that he set up five-year evaluations of all major administrators, including department heads. The second and third evaluations of Cyert's stewardship also mixed praise with pointed suggestions for change. This system, still in full force at Carnegie Mellon, effectively controls the amount of dead or decaying wood in key positions.

Cyert established an intriguing method of setting overall salary levels. There have never been set salary ranges for all faculty at the same rank at Carnegie Mellon. This policy means that a relatively new associate professor in computer science may make far more money than a veteran full professor in one of the arts or humanities. Cyert thought that the market should set salaries and that Carnegie Mellon's should be among the highest in order to attract top-flight professors. Hence, he asked each department head to write to the 10 or so schools with which the department competed for faculty, asking them for the range of salary paid for each rank. Then he reported the rankings but not the actual dollar amounts to the faculty both in meetings and in writing. When a Carnegie Mellon department fell near the bottom of its list, he appropriated additional funds to the department to bring it up to standard.

196

Cyert had a remarkable talent for spotting up-and-coming young people with administrative talent, giving them responsibilities and nurturing their growth. Many of them were in their late 20s or their 30s when Cyert first hired them. They include Richard Van Horn, formerly Vice President for Business Affairs who later became President first of the University of Houston and then of the University of Oklahoma; Patrick J. Keating, formerly Vice President for Business Affairs and now Chief Finance Officer, Knowledge University; Frederick A. Rogers (HNZ'74), Keating's predecessor as Vice President for Business and now Senior Vice President and Chief Financial Officer, Cornell University; four of Carnegie Mellon's present key administrators, William F. Elliott, Vice President for Enrollment; Michael C. Murphy (HNZ'86), Dean of Student Affairs; Jeffrey W. Bolton, Vice President for Business and Planning; and Michael A. Steidel (S'78), Director of Admission.

Sometimes these appointments reached beyond the administration. When Chuck Klausing resigned as football coach, Cyert promptly appointed the 28-year-old Rich Lackner (HS'79), who had been an assistant to Klausing, to the head coaching job. Cyert personally persuaded a large number of talented scholars to join the Carnegie Mellon faculty, including several statisticians who soon brought nationwide prestige to the department. His guiding hand appeared throughout the University.

The President's Report Card

The Report from the 1987 Commission to Evaluate the President summarized faculty judgment about Cyert's leadership:

> *President Cyert's vision in seeing opportunities and his delineation of a clear educational strategy have enabled the University to concentrate resources and exploit many areas of comparative advantage. His enthusiasm and ability to obtain support for initiatives within and outside the University has been indispensable. Many of the successes in the current capital campaign are also due to his direct influence on prospective donors. The president recognized early on that it was important to strengthen the ties with industry; the Robotics Institute and other more recent research institutes, created with substantial funding from business, are examples of the success of this policy. A truly professional job was done—involving as a major component many political contacts—in bringing the Software Engineering Institute to Carnegie Mellon.*

> *The president's performance was equally impressive in helping to gain for Pittsburgh the new Pittsburgh Supercomputing Center, which is a very useful collaboration of Carnegie Mellon, the University of Pittsburgh and Westinghouse. The hoped-for development of the former J&L site [Jones and Laughlin steel mills along the Monongahela River] is another example of the usefulness of the president's talent in dealing with government in the interests of the University and in helping to improve the economic conditions of Pittsburgh. The news magazine* Insight *recently recognized these contributions by naming him, rather than an industrialist, a businessman or a politician, as a prime mover in the rejuvenation of the city.*

President Endorses Evaluations

It is difficult for trustees who are not in academic life to know how to evaluate a president properly. There is a tendency to utilize the same methods for evaluation as in business. Thus, the president who balances the budget is viewed as a good president. I do not want, in any sense, to demean the importance of this aspect of the presidency, but for a great university like this one, that criterion is insufficient. The president must be judged on the basis of quality improvements in the university. To understand that part of the job, it is necessary to utilize faculty members who are on the inside and can make a better judgment of the quality of the president's leadership.
—*Carnegie Mellon Magazine,* Spring 1988

1973

- Carnegie Mellon's budget is back in the black.

197

In 1986 a major fund-raising campaign was launched at a gala celebration called Carnegie Salutes Carnegie.

Taking the vital first steps

In his inaugural address Cyert stressed two major goals. First, he wanted to balance the budget by reducing expenditures, increasing efficiency and finding new sources of revenue. Second, he aimed to improve both education and research efforts in a drive to achieve excellence and establish a national reputation. That he attained both of these goals simultaneously speaks clearly to his skill as an administrator based on his intimate knowledge of management techniques and organizational theory.

Cyert moved swiftly to cope with the immediate financial crisis. He fired 40 nonacademic employees, including 10 administrators, cut unessential campus services, separated the capital and operating budgets and halted planning for a new dramatic arts practice theater. Rather than ask deans how much money they needed for their colleges, he gave each dean a budget and insisted that they live within it, allowing them at the same time to allocate their budgets as they wished. Merit raises replaced across-the-board faculty salary increases. To the delight of the trustees, the University ended the fiscal year with a $150,000 surplus instead of a $1.4 million deficit.

Within a few years, the budget was under control. The Andrew Carnegie Society, organized in 1972 to recognize donors who gave at least $1,000 a year, produced almost $5 million in its first four years. Alumni giving kept pace and reached a then record $3.1 million in 1976. Tuition and fees rose annually from $2,500 in 1972 to $13,080 in 1990 when it still trailed tuition charged in peer universities. As seen, the ill-fated Fund for Distinction had been allowed to lapse quietly in 1973, having reached 80 percent of its $55 million goal. Then in 1976 the Board of Trustees announced a three-year $100 million fund-raising campaign named Investments in Progress. The campaign eventually netted $103 million in gifts and pledges. In 1986 a second major fund-raising campaign was launched at a gala celebration called Carnegie Salutes Carnegie that attracted 5,000 participants to the Civic Arena. By the end of Cyert's administration, its $200 million goal in gifts and pledges had been reached.

At the same time, Cyert took steps to increase income from the endowment. He removed endowment funds from the Trust Department of Mellon Bank and placed them in the hands of competing investment managers whose results could be compared and monitored. The new policy quickly brought results. Altogether the endowment which stood at $102 million in 1972 rose to $291 million at the end of the Cyert administration. In comparison to peer institutions, however, Carnegie Mellon's endowment was growing far too slowly.

A new federal law allowed tax-exempt institutions to borrow money from the state at tax-exempt rates and then to invest it at taxable rates. With this law in mind, President Cyert and his staff played a major role in persuading Pennsylvania Governor Richard L. Thornburgh's administration to change the state policy for financing college and university building projects. The difference in the two rates, often 2 percent or more, added substantially to the University's budget.

Cyert on Building Programs

In his inaugural address in March 1973 Cyert had made his position clear in the light of the financial crisis that the University was facing at the time:

Some people associate a quality education with fine, new buildings. Yet every new building increases the operating budget for maintenance and service, and the University may end up with fewer funds for its educational and general operating budget than it had before the new building was built. Thus, from the financial point of view it is far better for a university to make do with present space rather than get into the construction business.

1976

- **The Investments in Progress development drive begins.**

198

Without overhead on government-funded research projects, however, Carnegie Mellon's finances would have been a disaster area. Overhead included business expenses not chargeable to a particular project—that is, energy costs, administrative expenses, equipment, the library and so forth. The University's overhead rate negotiated with the government ranged from 37 to 70 percent during the Cyert years and was 55 percent in 1982-83. This meant that a grant for a $1 million project contributed $645,000 directly to the project and $345,000 to the overall University budget. Because of overhead payments, the University often found itself able to transfer millions of dollars annually from its E&GO budget to its capital budget where it could be used for new and renovated buildings and other capital projects. In 1989, for example, research overhead amounted to 24 percent of the E&GO budget of the University while the endowment contributed only 9 percent. If government funding diminished or the overhead rate fell, however, the budget would come under significant restraints, a problem that continues to haunt Carnegie Mellon's financial officials today.

Fostering an electronic revolution

With the budget problem coming under control, Cyert set out to redesign Carnegie Mellon University. Perhaps the most vital developments took place in the role of computing on the campus. The story involves the efforts of hundreds of faculty and staff members before, during and after the Cyert years, but Cyert's sponsorship of computing initiatives and his willingness to take risks and grasp opportunities played a leading role in the development of what may be the most computing intensive environment of any university.

Computer Science was indeed fortunate to win the favor of DARPA, the Defense Advanced Research Project Agency. For many years, DARPA gave a block grant to Carnegie Mellon's computer scientists and permitted them to decide how best to use the money. This research funding freed many faculty members from responsibility to write grant proposals and gave the faculty as a unit an opportunity to decide what directions research should take. It also gave Carnegie Mellon a head start on the Internet; Carnegie Mellon was one of the original sites that formed an electronic network to connect sites to each other. This network was the precursor of the modern Internet. A $5 million grant from R. K. Mellon in 1966, a year after Computer Science became an independent department, further advanced overall funding. Four faculty members, Edward R. Schatz (E'43), Herbert A. Simon, Allen Newell (IA'57), and Alan J. Perlis (S'42) negotiated the grant.

As president, Cyert was able to exploit opportunities to press Carnegie Mellon's comparative advantage in strategic planning. In addition, vendors eager to get a foothold on its ground floor gave the University impressive gifts of hardware amounting in some years to $4 million. President Cyert rejoiced in this freshet of money. It played a key role throughout the University because the government grants added millions of dollars annually in overhead to the overall University budget, money that could be used for any purpose. So could presidential discretionary funds eventually totaling about $12 million from the R. K. Mellon Foundation. Mellon funds enabled Cyert to support new initiatives outside of the regular budget process.

Andrew Carnegie Society

Date	Members	Total
72-73	138	$1,300,000
73-74	151	700,000
74-75	181	700,000
75-76	207	2,200,000
76-77	234	1,300,000
77-78	260	2,100,000
78-79	295	1,200,000
79-80	323	2,000,000
80-81	350	1,600,000
81-82	378	4,700,000
82-83	443	2,500,000
83-84	475	3,600,000
84-85	478	13,900,000
85-86	542	2,600,000
86-87	604	5,000,000
87-88	655	5,900,000
88-89	701	5,500,000
89-90	793	5,600,000
90-91	810	7,000,000
91-92	826	5,400,000
92-93	850	7,000,000
93-94	1066	6,700,000
94-95	960	10,900,000
95-96	804	9,100,000
96-97	1119	10,100,000
97-98	1013	17,300,000
98-99	1139	13,000,000

1978

- **The Robotics Institute opens.**
- **Professor Herb Simon receives the Nobel Prize.**

Above:
Robot used in the cleanup after the Three Mile Island disaster

Below:
President Cyert with François Mitterrand when he presented the Legion of Honor medal to Raj Reddy on March 27, 1984.

Cyert encouraged the development in computing in numerous ways. The Robotics Institute, now the largest academic research center of its kind in the world, serves as an example. Allen Newell had suggested a major effort in robotics to President Cyert early in the 1970s. Cyert saw robotics as a possible solution to domestic manufacturing problems, an opportunity to challenge Japanese dominance in the field. He asked Professor Raj Reddy, a specialist in artificial intelligence who had joined the Computer Science Department to work with Simon and Newell, to undertake a study. These three men formed the nucleus of another "hot group" that included a number of faculty colleagues and a host of talented graduate students. In 1978 Reddy suggested to Cyert

that the time had come to get into robotics in a major way. Cyert agreed quickly and Reddy became the head of a new Robotics Institute. Westinghouse contributed $1 million annually to provide financial resources for the new Institute, and Alcoa contributed another $500,000. Angel Jordan, then Dean of Carnegie Institute of Technology and a co-founder of the Institute along with Daniel Berg, then Dean of Mellon College of Science, marshaled the support of engineering department heads and recruited the first faculty members and students to work under Reddy. Within a few months, the Institute was launched, another example of the speed with which a small university such as Carnegie Mellon can move when it has leadership like Cyert's.

Like typical Carnegie Mellon projects, the Robotics Institute drew on the talents of personnel from many departments in addition to Computer Science. The Field Robotics Center is a good example. Its director, William L. "Red" Whittaker (E'75),

began his career at Carnegie Mellon as a graduate student in civil engineering and then as a member of the Civil Engineering Department. Focused on his research and the pursuit of grants to support it, his productivity in publications of refereed papers indicated that he would not be granted tenure when his case came up for review in a few years. Hence, President Cyert encouraged Reddy and Jordan to appoint him to a position as senior research scientist, roughly the equivalent of a full professor but not on the tenure track. Cyert had found a way to foster a diversity of talents under the academic umbrella. In 1983 the Field Robotics Center was created with Whittaker as director, working with his close colleague Lawrence G. "Larry" Cartwright (E'76, '87) and a team of researchers and students, another "hot group." In 1984 they developed the robots that cleaned up the nuclear waste after the Three Mile Island disaster. Whittaker also served as a consultant to the Soviet Union after the

Students Comment on the Electronic Revolution

We students couldn't believe that the University would change the name of Science Hall to Wean Hall—just like that. We wondered if it would change the name of a college or department if someone gave enough money. That year as part of Greek Sing, Pi Lambda Phi sang "It's Still Science Hall to Me" to the tune of Billy Joel's "It's Still Rock and Roll to Me." My fellow students agreed that we would someday get together and make a large contribution to CMU in the name of Mr. Science.
—Amy Levinson Gilligan, IM'85

Like many other students, I dreaded the mastery exam in Computer Science. It was the most feared moment of my years at CMU. When we arrived on campus as freshmen, upper class students warned us in chorus, "Wait till you have to take the MASTERY." Some of my most memorable experiences at CMU are the all-nighters I pulled finishing Pascal programs. With the exception of Commencement, my happiest day in college was when I passed that damn, dreaded test.
—Lisa Lightner, IM'89

What a drag it was—queuing up to register for classes. We used to sit on the floor outside designated rooms in Baker Hall and wait, wait, wait. When I arrived at CMU, I thought that everyone would sit down at a computer terminal, enter the classes he or she wanted, add the units, and sign a card. Then reality dawned. CMU used its vaunted computer system for other purposes. I remember standing in a line through four lunch hours to sign up for a class only to be told on the fifth day that the class was filled.
—Marjorie Palcsey, E'90

In 1983 the Computation Center announced that, "the PCs are now ready for use." At that time, we had only eight brand new IBM PCs available for the entire campus to use. You might also remember the situation a few years before that. Many of us were still using DEC writers connected to mainframe computers as our exclusive computing environment. In addition, laser printers were just coming on the scene. Finally, people thought that FORTRAN was the "language of choice" for engineers and we still taught it.
—Jim Garrett, E'82,'83,'86

A weird collection of animals used to live in Wean Hall, despite regulations against pets. Bill Chiles' dog, Colby, wandered the 3200 corridor where Bill had his office. Colby was a friendly little guy who could easily be mistaken for a dust mop. Barak Pearlmutter kept a ball python, Sid, in his office in Doherty for a while. The snake liked to curl up under the monitor of his work station. Barak used to send out announcements when he was about to feed it a rat so we could come watch.
—Dave Touretzky, CS'84

Excitement in the Air!

The campus seemed charged with electricity that fall day in 1978 when Herbert Simon was awarded the Nobel Prize in Economics. The entire day is still vivid to me. I recall especially Francis McMichael's beaming pride in the accomplishment of his faculty colleague. He spent a significant part of our fluid mechanics class that day describing Professor Simon's work for us.
—David Dzombak, E'80

1981

• College-level teaching awards are established.

Chernobyl disaster. In 1987, Whittaker and his colleague Todd Simonds co-founded their own robotics company, RedZone, that develops robots for the nuclear power and hazardous waste industries. By the end of the Cyert administration, the Robotics Institute had an annual budget of about $12 million coming from contracts with private firms and the government. In 1988 it employed 35 full-time research faculty, 50 engineers and programmers and about 45 graduate assistants, many of them doing research for their doctoral dissertations.

The Software Engineering Institute (SEI) provides another example of administrative cooperation and leadership. It came to Pittsburgh in 1984 when Carnegie Mellon, in alliance with the University of Pittsburgh and Westinghouse, won a hotly contested competition for a contract awarded by the Department of Defense. Provost Angel Jordan (E'59), along with the then head of Computer Science, Nico Habermann, played a major role in the development of the proposal and in the contract negotiations leading to the establishment of the SEI at Carnegie Mellon. The first five-year contract for $103 million was renewed in 1989 for an additional $156 million over five more years. The major mission of the SEI is technology transfer, to move software development into practical application. One of its major programs involved the development of a master's program in software engineering.

This page:
The Software Engineering Institute (SEI) came to Pittsburgh in 1984 when Carnegie Mellon, together with the University of Pittsburgh and Westinghouse, won a contract awarded by the Department of Defense.

Opposite page:
The University Computation Center was built in 1983 to house computing services. A pair of pink flamingos perched on the roof during the tenure of James Gosling, IBM employee and system designer who is credited with creating Java.

1983

- **The University Teaching Center is established.**
- **IBM and Carnegie Mellon establish the Information Technology Center.**

Throughout its history during the Cyert years, the role of the SEI provoked opposition from some faculty members, students and local citizens. They raised questions about sponsorship of the SEI by the Department of Defense which might lead to classified research. Cyert mobilized responses to these criticisms. He assured the community that Carnegie Mellon continued to ban classified research, and he and Jordan pointed to the long-run effects that research at SEI might have on the local economy.

The remaining major computing initiative fostered by the Cyert administration was the Andrew Network. Herbert A. Simon was an early and enthusiastic proponent of making facilities for computation available to everyone on the campus to see what would happen if a university saturated its faculty, staff and student body with sophisticated computing facilities. Computation involves communicating and processing information electronically and includes word processing, electronic mail, interactive graphics, the Internet, and desktop publishing, among other things. In the early 1980s, most computing took place on time-sharing mainframe computers. With time sharing, users get access through remote terminals with no computing power of their own to a single, powerful computer in a central location. By 1980 about 3,800 Carnegie Mellon students and faculty members had become active users of the five mainframe computers on campus, making reliance on mainframes inadequate.

The provost, Richard Van Horn, strove to make computing available to everyone. The answer lay in personal computers, or so Van Horn, Simon, Newell and Reddy told Dick Cyert. Naturally these ambitious plans upset some traditional faculty members. To reassure them, Cyert in 1981 appointed a Task Force on the Future of Computing chaired by Allen Newell. The members of the task force produced an extensive report arguing that computers would be valuable tools for a variety of educational and administrative purposes such as computing grades, text editing, information display in classrooms, simulations and problem solving in data-rich disciplines such as statistics. To bring this dream into reality, however, an expensive electronic local area network had to be developed.

Cyert and Van Horn approached IBM with a proposal to become partners in a networking effort in the fall of 1981. In return for its investment of upwards of $35 million, IBM received entry into the most sophisticated university computing environment in the nation as well as ownership of the networking technology that would be developed. The agreement produced the Andrew Network (after Andrew Mellon and Andrew Carnegie), a distributed personal computer network that made

personal computers and work stations available over a network with 11,000 outlets located in every classroom, office, laboratory or dormitory room in the entire University. The network connects powerful PCs and work stations to central storage facilities called servers. Instead of a central mainframe computer, the network is made up of about 10,000 personal computers each of which has its own processor. Thousands of printers in offices and computer clusters connect to these machines. To house computing services, the University erected the University Computation Center in 1983, a glass-enclosed structure along Forbes Avenue, which became Richard M. Cyert Hall in 1993.

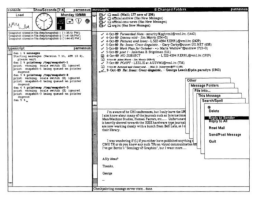

Top:
An original Andrew screen

Bottom:
A National Science Foundation grant brought the CRAY X-MP/48 to Pittsburgh for sophisticated high-speed computing.

The first of its kind in the world, the Andrew System catapulted Carnegie Mellon into the forefront of efforts in academic computing just as the Carnegie Plan had established Tech's reputation in education four decades previously. Visitors came from throughout the nation and from abroad to see what the fuss was all about. The national publicity associated with the project and the announcement that Carnegie Mellon had allegedly required all incoming students to have a personal computer branded the University in the eyes of many observers as "Computer U." Without the Andrew System, the widespread revolution in educational computing now underway on the campus could never have begun. The foresight of Richard Cyert and his colleagues, and their willingness to take a risk on an unproved project paid big dividends.

In the middle 1980s, Carnegie Mellon joined the University of Pittsburgh and Westinghouse to develop a proposal for a supercomputing center. Professor Michael J. Levine of the Department of Physics led the way for Carnegie Mellon. This tripartite initiative, strongly supported by President Cyert, Provost Angel G. Jordan (E'59), and Robert F. Sekerka, Dean of Mellon College of Science, won one of five supercomputing grants from the National Science Foundation (NSF). The grant brought a new CRAY X-MP/48 machine to Pittsburgh where it was used for sophisticated, high-speed computing by scientists from throughout the nation. Once again, strategic planning and faculty initiative paid big dividends.

Giant Humming Machines

Giant humming machines with thousands of cable connections fill the stark windowless room. Thick steel bars are placed beneath the floor to support the 11,900-lb. massive computer. The machine's innards, consisting of millions of tiny wires intertwined like a messy unraveled ball of yarn hang loose. The temperature of the room is normal, but there is a moist, cool sensation as air filters through from the refrigeration pipes waiting to be hooked up to the powerful computer.

The Cray people as they are called, move quietly and efficiently rolling in 16 man-sized disk drives that behave like overgrown floppy discs when operating. The Cray men roll in the parts over heavy metal sheets to avoid crushing the floor. Walking into this room filled with oversized, overstuffed machines is not unlike an Alice-in-Wonderland experience. But this is not a scene from the futuristic sequel to Land of the Giants; nor is it the future of the world as envisioned by Tom Thumb. It is the home of one of the most sophisticated and powerful machines in the world.
—*Carnegie Mellon Magazine*, Fall 1986

By the late 1980s Computer Science played such a large role in the University that it clearly deserved independent status. Outside financial support reached almost $40 million in 1988, most of it from the federal government. Only about 10 percent of the department's budget came from the University's E&GO budget; 90 percent came from grants. By 1988 the department had grown to 65 full-time members with a support staff of about 100 and a graduate school population of 165. After reporting to several open faculty meetings, the administration finally established the School of Computer Science in December 1988.

1984

- The SEI is established at Carnegie Mellon.
- Planning for a new master plan for the campus begins.

ДИЗАЙН США

Colleges and schools forge ahead

Each of Carnegie Mellon's other six colleges and schools made dramatic progress during the Cyert years. All of them benefited from the leadership of Cyert and his senior administrators, and from the growing reputation of the University as a whole. In order to shake things up, he brought in new vice presidents, deans and department heads in a search for "real doers." Although all the colleges and schools benefited in both research and education from the computerization of the University, differences in disciplines, availability of funding and national priorities helped to determine progress in each of the University's divisions.

At the beginning of the Cyert years, the profession of engineering was in decline. In the late 1960s, the administration had reduced the engineering budget and decreased faculty size. Government support of graduate fellowships, which had supported about 100 students annually through the National Defense Education Act, practically disappeared. By 1973 engineering enrollment had declined to 774 undergraduate and 389 graduate students. It then grew steadily through the early 1980s when it began to stabilize, although the proportion of under-represented minorities, including women, rose steadily.

In 1976, Carnegie Institute of Technology consisted of departments in five of the six original engineering fields represented in the first commencement of the Carnegie Technical Schools: Chemical, Civil, Electrical, Mechanical and Metallurgical Engineering. In that year the college added a sixth department, Engineering and Public Policy, an ambitious and wholly successful attempt to build bridges connecting the engineering professions, the social sciences in Humanities and Social Sciences and the public policy emphases of the School of Urban and Public Affairs. Programs in biomedical engineering, manufacturing and nuclear engineering, along with a shifting array of centers and institutes, brought faculty members and researchers together from a number of departments both within CIT and in other colleges and schools.

Led by two energetic and talented deans through most of the Cyert years—Herbert Toor and Angel Jordan—the Carnegie Institute of Technology remained among the nation's top 10 engineering schools. Its most distinguished department, Electrical Engineering, renamed itself Electrical and Computer Engineering (ECE) in 1983 in recognition of its international reputation in computer hardware and computer-aided design. Despite its relatively small size, ECE was widely recognized as one of the top four similar departments in the nation, along with Massachusetts Institute of Technology, Stanford and Berkeley. The department spawned three research centers in the early 1980s, laying the background for winning a National Science Foundation grant in 1985 to establish the Engineering Design Research Center (EDRC). The EDRC was the first nationally awarded research center at Carnegie Mellon organized specifically to perform interdisciplinary research involving key faculty members and students from other departments and to form partnerships with industry for the strategic development of new technologies. When the National Science Foundation decided in 1997 not to renew contracts for engineering research centers, the EDRC changed its name to the Institute for Complex Engineered Systems and obtained financial support from private industry and the Commonwealth of Pennsylvania.

In 1989 Georgette Demes, Administrative Director of the EDRC, Professors Joseph Bally and Dan Droz of Design, and a Pittsburgher Gerald Proctor presented a seminar on interdisciplinary design collaboration in Moscow. The exhibition title in Cyrillic letters translates as "Design USA."

Interdisciplinary collaboration on a wearable computer project at EDRC with students and researchers from electrical computer engineering, software engineering, industrial design, computer science and mechanical engineering

1985

- The NSF establishes the Engineering Design Research Center.
- Carnegie Mellon purchases five US Bureau of Mines buildings to renovate for SUPA and Robotics.

1986

- Judith Resnik is killed in the Challenger disaster.
- The Carnegie Salutes Carnegie campaign is launched in Pittsburgh's Civic Arena.

In 1990 CIT won another NSF competition, this time to establish the Data Storage Systems Center (DSSC) making Carnegie Mellon the only university in the nation with two NSF sponsored engineering research centers. The DSSC grew out of the pioneering work of the Magnetics Technology Center founded in 1952 with funding from five government departments and nine industrial partners. Eight full-time core faculty from four departments, led by professor Mark Kryder of Electrical and Computer Engineering, and supported by 15 additional affiliated faculty, worked in the center whose major goal was to build a world-class research program in magnetic and magneto-optic recording technology. The DSSC grew into the largest academic research center of its kind in the United States and is now housed in the George A. Roberts Engineering Hall, opened in 1997. Carnegie Mellon's pioneering work in interdisciplinary research, a tradition that began in the Metals Research Laboratory during the 1920s, has paid off handsomely throughout the engineering disciplines.

The Mellon College of Science underwent dramatic changes during the Cyert years. During a period in the early 1970s national enrollment in the sciences declined markedly, as it had also done in engineering. Then both graduate and undergraduate enrollment began to rise steadily, reaching a stable state during the early 1980s. Enrollment at Carnegie Mellon followed these trends, except in Computer Science. That department, however, had no undergraduate program, so each of the remaining departments—Physics, Chemistry, the Biological Sciences and particularly Mathematics—opened a computer science track within its undergraduate curriculum, tracks which attracted ever-higher proportions of undergraduate students interested in computing. Increased enrollment in mathematics stretched that department to the breaking point.

Chemistry and the Biological Sciences faced opposite problems. After the establishment of Carnegie Mellon University in 1967, the Chemistry Department added 21 Mellon Institute chemists to its 16-member department. Digesting this huge influx took decades. Some chemists had joined Mellon Institute specifically because they did not want to teach in a university. Friction arose between some of them and the Carnegie Mellon faculty. Gradually the research and graduate study in chemistry were transferred to the Mellon Institute building several blocks from the main campus separating the faculty geographically from the rest of the University and from undergraduate chemistry classes, still held in obsolete teaching laboratories on the central campus. The department revived during the 1980s when the administration committed funds to hire new faculty, renovate graduate chemistry laboratories and develop new programs at the interface of chemistry and biology.

Instead of too many faculty members, the Department of Biological Sciences had too few. The department had been transferred from Margaret Morrison Carnegie College to the College of Engineering and Science in 1964, but its traditional program failed to attract many students. By 1970 most faculty members were part-time employees. In 1971, however, the department was reorganized by combining biochemists and biophysicists with new hires to form a department of 12 members. Then in 1977, President Cyert, having solved short-term financial problems, committed major resources in an attempt to shape a distinguished program in molecular and cellular biology, genetics, biochemistry and biophysics. The department added new faculty and installed new laboratories for them, led by Dr. Chien Ho, a biophysicist recruited from the University of Pittsburgh. Grants from the National Science Foundation and the National Institutes of Health laid the foundation for research leading to national leadership in genetic engineering. Both undergraduate and graduate enrollment increased steadily until it reached a par with chemistry by the end of the Cyert years.

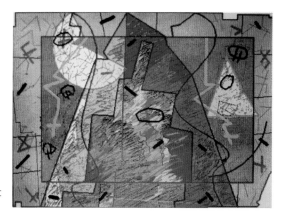

Palo Duro #10, computer-generated art by Professor Harry Holland, 1988

Carnegie Mellon's other original school, the College of Fine Arts, fared less well. Fine Arts could never tap the deep government pockets that supplied funds so lavishly to engineering, science and computer science. For years, one administration after another had met CFA's requests for more space with inadequate responses. One proposal after another to relieve overcrowding with a new drama building failed when funding drives fell short. In one of his first moves as president, Dick Cyert, unwilling to further increase an already threatening deficit, scrapped tentative plans for a drama building, using the money that had been contributed to renovate existing facilities.

Under Dean Akram Midani, who took office on the same day that Cyert became president, the college moved steadily to require its students to take more courses out of their departments and to open the college to undergraduates from the remainder of the University. Midani also encouraged both faculty members and students to break away from the insularity of the campus. He urged the fine arts departments to take advantage of Carnegie Mellon's computing environment. The Architecture Department, for example, organized the nation's first computer-aided design studio in the field. In 1985 these scattered efforts coalesced in a new Center for Art and Technology, supported by generous grants from the R. K. Mellon Foundation and other private donors.

The College of Humanities and Social Sciences transformed itself during the Cyert years. When John Patrick "Pat" Crecine (IM'61, IA'63, '66) took over as dean in 1976, the College consisted of four departments: English, History, Modern Languages and Psychology. By 1990 History and English had begun to phase out the doctor of arts program designed for college and secondary school teachers in favor of Ph.D. degrees and sharply focused research programs. Psychology eventually took firm root in H&SS and won a national reputation in cognitive psychology where its work was widely recognized as world class. In addition, the College had added three new departments by 1990: Statistics, Social and Decision Sciences and Philosophy.

Pat Crecine guided most of this development. He focused attention on two major thrusts: the development of a core curriculum for the entire College and the attainment of national stature in sharply focused areas of research in each department where Carnegie Mellon had a comparative advantage. The core curriculum project occupied the energy of key faculty members in weekly meetings taking place during 1976-77, its formative years. The goal was to develop a relevant curriculum in which structured pieces fit with and built upon each other in a unique way befitting a liberal/professional education. All five interdisciplinary course clusters emphasized problem solving and focused on an important facet of liberal/professional education. In 1980, Ted Fiske, the education editor of the *New York Times,* declared that the core was ". . .perhaps the most creative general education program of any American university."

Making it Through

Do you remember how bewildered you felt for several days after you arrived on campus? I do. For the first time, I was away from family and friends and had been unable to join any of the packs of students I saw chattering together as they crossed the Cut. Then a group of students I met at dinner invited me to join them to climb through a sculpture erected on the Cut. On the grass at the corner of the Fine Arts parking lot stood a twisted, pretzel-like metal form open on each end and made from welded aluminum. In I went to join perhaps a dozen others shouting and laughing and inching their way. When we emerged, I felt that even though my life had changed, there was adventure ahead and that, somehow, I would make it through all right.
—Roy D. McKelvey, A'79

1987

- The Andrew network linking all computers on campus is launched.
- Carnegie Mellon University Press, founded by English professor Gerald Costanzo, published Rita Dove's *Thomas and Beulah*, which won the 1987 Pulitzer Prize for poetry.

1988

- The School of Computer Science is established.
- Mellon Institute is renamed Carnegie Mellon Research Institute.
- The Robert E. Doherty Prize for Educational Leadership is established.

The research agenda in each department focused on one or two special areas of inquiry: rhetoric in English, social history in History, cognitive processes in Psychology, the Bayesian approach to statistics, logic and computation in Philosophy and decision making in the Social and Decision Sciences. Various rating surveys have placed the programs in cognitive psychology, statistics and rhetoric among the top 10 in the nation, a remarkable achievement for such a young college.

The College of Humanities and Social Sciences reveals the power of strategic planning and comparative advantage. Forced to rely on his present budget, Dean Crecine squeezed personnel and funds from the History and English Departments to support new ventures in other disciplines. Grants from foundations contributed additional money, and so did tuition income from a rapidly increasing undergraduate population. Crecine founded a Department of Social Sciences in 1976 with a nucleus of four faculty members. The development of a major in information systems within this department resulted in a flood of students. In 1985 with the appointment of Robyn Dawes as department head, it adopted a new name, Social and Decision Sciences. Statistics, a favorite of Cyert who had a keen scholarly interest in the field and warm personal rela- tions with several Carnegie Mellon statisticians, began as a free-floating department unattached to a college, and reluctantly joined H&SS in 1984. Finally, the philosophers broke away from the History Department to stand on their own feet in 1985. A distin- guished new college offering excellent undergraduate education and nationally ranked research programs had been developed in less than two decades.

The Graduate School of Industrial Administration had a different history. When Richard Cyert left his deanship to become president of Carnegie Mellon, GSIA was at the height of its reputation and influence. Ranking surveys consistently placed it among the top three or four business schools in the country. Under Cyert's successor as dean, Arnold R. Weber, the management style became more bureaucratic and less hands-on. The "hot group" that had built its original reputation had dissolved. The school grew, and the number of specialists in a field increased so much that they could interact with each other rather than with scholars from other disciplines. Although each of the school's four major programs continued to thrive, GSIA dropped in the rankings until it was only 13th nationally at the end of the Cyert administration in 1990. However, architects had designed a much-needed addition to double the office and classroom space of GSIA and most of the money for the new building had been raised. The future indeed seemed bright.

During the first years of the 1970s, the future of the School for Urban and Public Affairs seemed threatened. When William Cooper resigned as dean in 1975, Cyert persuaded Otto Davis to take his place. As a condition of accepting the deanship, he received a commitment from the president that SUPA would remain independent of GSIA and control income from its own endowment, tuition and research funds. For a few years, recruiting students presented serious problems. Then Associate Dean Norman Johnson, an African-American recruited from the Carnegie Mellon Action Program, took over the recruiting function and organized the Quantitative Skills Summer Institute for incoming students unprepared to cope with SUPA's quantitative orientation. The target class of 60 entering students was reached in 1980, and a steady-state total student population of 165 Master of Science students in residence in 1985. By the end of the Cyert administration, the master's class contained more than 40 percent women and almost 25 percent African-Americans. As early as 1976, the *Chronicle of Higher Education* proclaimed SUPA as a national leader in the public policy area.

Davis fostered a mid-career master's degree for working professionals led by Harry Faulk, a distinguished retired public school superintendent. By 1984, 80 part-time students were enrolled in programs designed to strengthen their managerial skills. When Carnegie Mellon purchased the Bureau of Mines complex, SUPA moved into its refurbished main building, named Hamburg Hall after a generous trustee. Outside funding supported five new centers, each headed by a SUPA faculty member. The 1988 Middle States evaluation heaped praise on SUPA. Despite its growing pains, it had made a remarkable record in a short span of two decades.

In 1990, much of the research throughout the University took place in 54 centers, institutes, consortia, groups, coalitions and laboratories rather than in traditional departments, many of them organized around small "hot groups." They were supported by grants and contracts from both government and private sources totaling about $120 million. With only a few exceptions, these institutions drew their members from several departments and schools. Carnegie Mellon's long tradition of interdisciplinary research had played a key role in the development of a modern research university.

Recruiting a national student body

Enrollment at Carnegie Mellon rose from 4,285 in 1972-73 when Cyert became president to 7,090 in 1989-90, largely because enrollment in the graduate programs roughly doubled during the Cyert years. Geographic diversity increased at equal speed. Instead of 40 percent from outside Pennsylvania in 1970, 70 percent of Carnegie Mellon's students came from other states 18 years later. The enrollment of under-represented minorities rose more slowly. Women made up 30 percent of the student body. The University also enrolled 174 African-American and almost 900 students from 51 foreign countries.

More than anyone else, William F. Elliott was responsible for this excellent showing. He had come to Carnegie Mellon in 1970 as Associate Director of Admissions and became Director of Admissions in 1972. Together Cyert and Elliot developed a plan to move Carnegie Mellon from a regional to a national recruitment base. They faced a fundamental demographic fact: there would be 15 percent fewer high

In addition to a professional library and stacks of papers, Bill Elliott's office houses his extensive collection of Carnegie Mellon memorabilia.

ONLY **3** MORE
SLEEPING BAG
WEEKENDS

THE SPRING SLEEPING BAG CAMPAIGN IS
FOR ADMITTED STUDENTS OF ALL MAJORS.
WE NEED YOUR HELP TO MAKE THIS A
SUCCESS SO, HOST A BAGGER
BEFORE SUPPLIES RUN OUT.

YOUR NAME_____ MAJOR_____
DORM & ROOM_____
BOX #_____ PHONE #_____

___ I'D LOVE TO HOST___ BAGGERS JAN. 31.
___ I'D LOVE TO GIVE A TOUR JAN. 31(2-5pm)

___ I'D LOVE TO HOST___ BAGGERS APRIL 10-11
___ I'D LOVE TO GIVE A TOUR APRIL 10-11(2-5pm)

___ I'D LOVE TO HOST___ BAGGERS APRIL 25-26
___ I'D LOVE TO GIVE A TOUR APRIL 25-26(2-5pm)
PLEASE RETURN TO WARNER HALL, RM/01 —
x2082.

school graduates in 1985 than in 1978, and the number of graduates would continue to decrease yearly for some years after that. Elliott developed a national marketing plan that brought Carnegie Mellon to the attention of parents as well as guidance counselors. To inform parents directly, Elliott and his colleagues invited prospective students and their parents to visit campus where they could obtain firsthand knowledge of what Carnegie Mellon had to offer. The staff also sponsored sleeping bag weekends during which prospective students brought their own sleeping bags to campus and lived in the residence halls while they toured the campus and sampled university life.

Carnegie Mellon had, and still has, a need-blind admissions policy. The University admits students without knowing how much financial aid they need and then finds a combination of scholarships, grants, loans and work-study jobs to meet their financial requirements. This policy keeps faith with Andrew Carnegie's desire to create a school for working class boys and girls. It also puts a major strain on the budget. On campus, Elliott and the Student Affairs group developed programs to make student life more appealing. A survey about the quality of life on campus found many areas to complain about, most of which remained for Cyert's successor to face. Cyert had already begun a program to improve undergraduate teaching.

Improving teachers and teaching

President Cyert contended that excellent teaching and excellent research went hand in hand. Early in his administration he offered financial support for faculty members to undertake curriculum renovations. The $150,000 fund was administered by Herbert A. Simon, Allen Newell and Cyert himself. By 1985 a university core program in both writing and computing had been developed, and additions to the core were in planning stages. Most curriculum reform, however, took place in individual colleges or departments rather than through a central initiative.

To improve teaching, Cyert expanded the annual university-wide Ryan Teaching Award, begun in 1961 from funds given by William F. Ryan (E'24) and his wife, Frances, to annual awards in each of the seven colleges, and in 1989 he established the Robert E. Doherty Prize to honor sustained contributions to education. A firm believer in evaluation, Cyert required all instructors to administer a Faculty Course Evaluation at the end of each semester, and he published the results each year naming each teacher and reporting the score their students gave them on a number of variables. In 1982 he established the University Teaching Center (now the Eberly Center for Teaching Excellence) to seek ways to improve undergraduate education. Directed by Edwin Fenton, the center established nine programs including faculty luncheon seminars, personal consultations, providing opportunities to view one's teaching on videotape and incoming faculty seminars.

The Center also organized programs to prepare graduate students who served as teaching assistants. At the request of President Cyert, the Center organized the English as a Second Language Center, now the Intercultural Education Center. It evaluated the ability of international students to communicate in English and organized programs to bring up to standard any teaching assistant whose English would hinder learning in the classroom. Graduate students whose first language was not English could not enter the classroom as teaching assistants until they had passed language proficiency tests.

Designing the new Carnegie Mellon campus

By the middle of the 1980s, Carnegie Mellon faced a facilities crisis. The student center was far too small, deteriorating rapidly and located on a prime building site. The football stadium was poorly sited and obsolete. Parking presented a crisis. The main campus needed a physical plant building, residence halls, dining areas, a Fine Arts Center, engineering facilities, an addition to GSIA, updated classrooms, a computation center, renovations to some of Hornbostel's treasured buildings, and renewed attention to open spaces and landscaping. Away from the central campus, the University would soon need space for the Software Engineering Institute, the Carnegie Mellon Research Institute, and Robotics. All this work might cost $250 million, a daunting figure. Yet almost all of it was accomplished in a little more than a decade under the Cyert, Robert Mehrabian and Jared L. Cohon administrations. Cyert resisted demands for new buildings for more than a decade.

Hornbostel's original mall surrounded by five of his distinguished buildings remained at the heart of the campus. Wean and Doherty Halls had filled in the open side. In addition, the Hunt Library, well-sited but out-of-keeping with Hornbostel's Beaux Arts structures, had been added to this space. Buildings on the remainder of the central campus, however, had no consistent relationship to an overall plan, presenting to architects a problem they call "campus fill-in"—seeking patterns in already existing buildings and filling in or clearing spaces around them to bring order and a sense of community to the campus. Solving this problem required a master plan—and a lot of money.

In 1984, Carnegie Mellon contracted with CRS/Sirrine, a Houston architectural firm, to develop a master plan for the campus. At a trustee meeting, Theodore D. Nierenberg (E'44) argued that this plan was too modest and failed to solve pressing problems such as the need for additional parking, residence halls, and dining areas. Early in 1987, Carnegie Mellon announced a competition to respond to a revised version of the CRS/Sirrine Master Plan for the first $100 million of new facilities. The winning

Winners of the Robert E. Doherty Prize for Educational Leadership

1987 Edwin Fenton
History

M. Granger Morgan
Engineering & Public Policy

1988 Tung Au
Civil Engineering

Erwin Steinberg
English

1989 Lawrence Carra
Drama

1990 Joel A. Tarr
History

1991 Indira Nair
Engineering & Public Policy

1993 Elizabeth Jones
Biological Sciences

1994 Peter Stearns
History

1995 Steve Fenves
Civil & Environ. Engineering

1996 Hugh Young (S'52, '53, '59, A'72)
Physics

1997 Susan Ambrose (HS'86)
Eberly Center & History

1998 Angel Jordan (E'59)
Robotics Institute

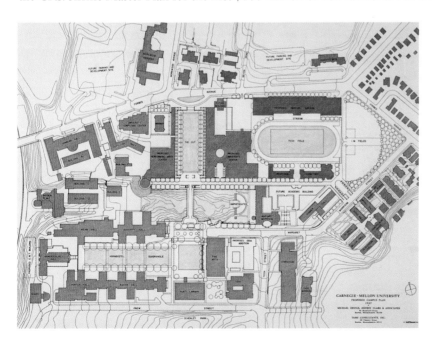

The Boston firm of Dennis, Clark and Associates won the 1987 competition to revise the 1984 Master Plan for Carnegie Mellon University.

design, submitted by the Boston firm of Dennis, Clark and Associates, picked up themes from several previous plans. The campus would be organized around three quadrangles: the original Hornbostel mall; the Cut, the central focus of campus spaces and campus life; and an athletic quadrangle on the east end of the campus.

The heart of the scheme focused on the Cut bracketed by two colonnaded buildings. One was a wholly new University Center designed to fill the space occupied by Skibo, which would be torn down, and its parking area. The other colonnade, part of a Center for the Arts, would define the opposite side of the Cut and conceal Warner Hall's modernist architecture. The buildings planned to flank the Cut incorporated the form and materials of the Hornbostel buildings. On the Forbes Avenue end of the colonnades the architects planned to develop a new campus entrance. While this planning was taking place, the University built a new physical plant building to house construction and maintenance units that had been scattered all over the campus.

The $35.5 million East Campus Project, begun in 1987, forms a third quadrangle. It is bounded on the east by intramural fields at the corner of Forbes Avenue and Margaret Morrison Street. A parking garage for 600 cars marks its boundary on Forbes Avenue. On the campus side of that garage, architects placed stands overlooking the football field and running track. Their synthetic surfaces and excellent lighting make them available for recreation far into the evening hours. On the other side of the field stand two matching dormitory buildings housing 360 students, as well as a dining area. One building is named for Judith Resnik (E'70), an astronaut killed in the 1986 space shuttle Challenger disaster. The basement holds dressing rooms for athletic events and weight and training rooms.

President Cyert had to be persuaded to launch the East Campus Project. He always thought that programs should take precedence over buildings. The money was to come from state loans that would increase the University's indebtedness, although rents and fees would repay most of the loan over 30 years. It took three visits by a trio of vice presidents—Frederick A. Rogers (HNZ'74), Patrick J. Keating and William F. Elliott—to convince him to sign the contract for the project. But sign he did, launching the development of today's refurbished campus.

Throughout most of the 1980s, the University renovated many of its older buildings. The main Bureau of Mines building received an $8 million makeover and became the new home of the School for Urban and Public Affairs, later the H. John Heinz III School of Public Policy and Management. A second Bureau of Mines building, now named Smith Hall, became the home of The Robotics Institute. Extensive renovations in Baker and Porter Halls provided room for research in engineering, and renovations in Margaret Morrison relieved some of the pressure for space in the College of Fine Arts. To the delight of everyone, the exteriors of the Hornbostel buildings were all cleaned, restoring them to their original luster.

Cyert set up an Educational Facilities Committee consisting of staff and a faculty member from each college and allocated $300,000 annually to renovate classrooms. Within a decade, every lecture hall and classroom building on the campus had been

completely renovated and equipped with
carpets, new furniture, window treatments,
chalkboards and overhead projectors. Many
rooms also received permanently installed
projectors for film, video and computers.
Landscape crews beautified the grounds with
flowers, shrubs and trees. Although space was
still at a premium, facilities were vastly better
than they had been in 1972 and plans for
the University Center, a new drama building,
an addition to GSIA, an electronic technology
building and the Carnegie Mellon Research
Institute were on the drawing boards with
some of the money for each already in hand.

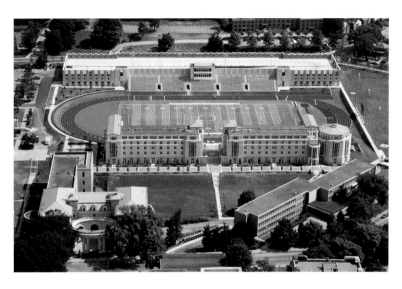

Aerial view of the completed
East Campus project

     Soon after the release of the 1987 master plan, a design review committee was
established to ensure that new buildings and renovations fit into the culture and fabric of
the campus. The committee, led by Vice President Patrick J. Keating who had been
overseeing the entire building program, developed a list of 10 principles to guide future
campus developments. They focused on building design, open space, future building
sites, the impact of the campus on the environment and the impact of the campus on its
neighbors. These principles have been used to guide the development of a new master
plan focusing on the west campus area, soon to be the site of both new buildings and
extensive renovations of facilities acquired in the purchase of the Bureau of Mines
property.

Dick Cyert and the University he loved

     At a faculty and staff meeting in Skibo in January 1989, Cyert announced that
the next academic year would be his last. "My heart tells me to stay on and on," he said,
"but my mind tells me that the time has come to leave." His voice was choked with so
much emotion that he could barely get the words out. The crowd gave him a standing
ovation. In 1990 he left the presidency to assume a series of appointments in his original
Carnegie Tech home, the Graduate School of Industrial Administration where he became
the Richard M. and Margaret S. Cyert Professor of Economics and Management. From
1990 to 1992 he headed the Carnegie Bosch Institute endowed by Germany's Bosch
Institute to study and improve international management. Despite a courageous six-year
bout with cancer, he maintained an active intellectual life until he finally succumbed to
cancer in October 1998.

     Early in October 1998 Chriss Swaney, the University Relations officer in GSIA,
decided that a quiet and joyful celebration of Cyert's 50 years of service to the University
was in order. Margaret Cyert helped her to identify a number of people with close personal relationships to her husband to attend. In addition to Carnegie Mellon colleagues,
they included Cyert's driver, his barber of 40 years, two of his secretaries, and a neighbor
and her children. Cyert was upstairs in bed, but fully clothed. As he had always done,
Cyert asked each colleague about how things were going at the University he loved.

Richard Cyert Remembered

One thing that made all this possible was Dick's leadership style. He did not equate a lively and productive organization with a neat one. Strict lines of command and communication were not for him. He talked with, and listened to, anyone and everyone on campus, often to the dismay of his deans and vice presidents who thought that everything should go through "channels." He understood how to pay for vigor at a reasonable cost in chaos. In this way, his earlier study of organizational decision making stood him in good stead, for he had learned the difference between real organizations and those drawn as charts on paper.
—Herbert A. Simon, Richard King Mellon University Professor of Computer Science and Psychology, Carnegie Mellon University

I first met Dr. Cyert in the spring of 1995 when I was putting together a group of investors to help purchase the Pirates. Dr. Cyert sat on the board for the previous ownership group and was very instrumental in giving me direction on how to maneuver through the very diverse political and corporate channels throughout the city. Without Dr. Cyert's support and introduction to many influential people throughout the city, our purchase of the Pittsburgh Pirates might not have happened. But because of his persistence and dedication, the team that he loved will be in the city that he loved for many, many years.
—Kevin McClatchy, CEO and Managing General Partner, Pittsburgh Pirates

Richard Cyert was an extraordinary leader. His vision for Carnegie Mellon drove all of us far beyond our individual goals toward a new level of excellence for the whole University. He gave department heads the elbow room to make changes and to move their units forward. He allowed us to take risks and encouraged us to strive for quality. Watching him give 200 percent all the time inspired us to do the same. His leadership shines for me as brightly today as ever before.
—Marilyn Taft Thomas, Director of Graduate Studies, School of Music, Carnegie Mellon University

During my years in the public service, both as a member of City Council and now as mayor, I have been impressed with the significant contributions of Dr. Cyert to the social, cultural, civic and academic well-being of our community. On those occasions when it was my good fortune to meet with Dr. Cyert, the sincerity and determination with which he approached his responsibilities were always evident. He is an extraordinary man. The Pittsburgh region owes him much—not only for his dynamic leadership in the field of academia—but as a positive influence in the Pittsburgh area's ongoing progress.
—Sophie Masloff, Mayor of Pittsburgh

[Dick Cyert] provided me with the opportunity to, as he put it, "compete in the major leagues" of academia. And he did this with a personal courage that I've come to appreciate and admire more and more over time. In 1963 in his first year as Dean of the Graduate School of Industrial Administration, Dick invited me to a job interview at the AEA (American Economics Association) winter meeting on the strength of a recommendation by Bill Starbuck, who was then only a graduate student. Several weeks later, Dick offered me a job based on that interview alone: no visit to GSIA, no job talk, just his own evaluation. And a year later, he hired Nancy Schwartz, my co-author for the next 17 years, in the same way. Each of Dick's junior hires in 1963 have gone on to chaired professorships and one, Bob Lucas, was awarded the Nobel Prize.
—Morton I. Kamien, Joseph and Carole Levy Distinguished Professor of Entrepreneurship, Northwestern University

While we have many good memories of working and living with Dick and Margaret around the GSIA between 1951 and 1965, we were perhaps closest in two experiences off the job: a campaign of protest, leading eventually to our families' resigning, when our suburban swim club banned an oriental guest, and discussions over strategy and neighbors' reactions as we each became involved in initiatives to help blacks buy or rent houses in the Fox Chapel Area. Dick never hesitated, even though in those years such actions could alienate business support that a GSIA dean and soon a presidential candidate needed.
—William R. Dill, IA'53

President Cyert's influence went beyond Carnegie Mellon to the City of Pittsburgh.

Then he made his way downstairs to the dining room, his arms draped around the shoulders of two old friends. They seated him in a chair facing the patio where Swaney had assembled the Carnegie Mellon Pipe Band. They played five numbers, the swirl of bagpipes echoing through the rooms where so many members of the Carnegie Mellon community had been entertained. "I will remember this for the rest of my life," Cyert said. And after a moment, "Of course, you know my life now is very short." Then he was carried back upstairs in a chair. He died 11 days later.

On November 9, friends and admirers from throughout the country packed McConomy Auditorium in the University Center to celebrate the life and memory of this remarkable man. His daughter Martha and seven former colleagues remembered their friend in words that spoke to his remarkable personal and professional qualities. Remembrances printed in the memorial brochure echoed these themes.

The legacy

By 1990, when President Cyert retired, Carnegie Mellon had become established as a national research university. The four areas of excellence in 1972—Carnegie Institute of Technology, Computer Science, the Graduate School of Industrial Administration, and individual departments such as Drama and Psychology, were all thriving. The eight problems facing Cyert in 1972 had been solved or were on their way to solution. The School of Urban and Public Affairs, firmly established as an independent school in its own building, had blossomed into one of the leading institutions of its type in the country. Humanities and Social Sciences had grown from four to eight departments, each of which had established a national reputation in the area in which it chose to focus its efforts. Biological Sciences had become a major department with research projects that brought its faculty into collaborative projects with colleagues from several other departments. Chemistry had at last assimilated most of the faculty from the merger

with the Mellon Institute. The Fine Arts College had a thriving program in collaboration with computer science. Both undergraduate and graduate students came from throughout the nation and from an increasing number of foreign countries. A beginning had been made on the development of an outstanding undergraduate program. An aging physical plant had been renovated and cleaned and several new buildings erected. Moreover, a campus master plan was firmly in place. Finally, the worst of the financial crises were well in the past. Cyert's successor, Robert Mehrabian, inherited a thriving research university whose strengths extended through every college and school and whose reputation as a center of both education and research had become worldwide.

> ## Richard Cyert on Leadership
>
> Leadership requires the manager to take initiative, to be articulate, and to be convincing. Leadership is taking action, not reacting.
>
> ❧
>
> An innovative organization requires a team effort. The desire to be innovative must be pervasive.
>
> ❧
>
> I want to see Carnegie Mellon revolutionize the way education is carried on.
>
> ❧
>
> I want to see us continually breaking new ground, because it's really the only way in which higher education can improve itself.
>
> ❧
>
> I don't think you can manage without getting into the details.

13.

Snapshot 1987–1989
A success story with many loose ends

P arents, relatives and friends of the graduates were delighted to see a huge, colorful tent erected on the Cut, the site of graduation exercises in 1988. In addition to shelter from either sun or rain, the tent added a festive touch to the ceremony. The graduates, grouped by colleges, were massed before the platform erected for Carnegie Mellon's dignitaries, administration, and speakers. Pipers and faculty marshal, Professor Hugh Young (S'52, '53, '59, A'72), led the academic procession through thousands of spectators gathered to honor the graduating class.

As it had in 1968, the composition of the graduating class reflected a rapidly changing university. Since 1968 the number of graduates had increased from 1,112 to 1,798 and the number of different degrees from 82 to 140. The most dramatic percentage changes took place at the graduate level. The master's degree candidates more than doubled—from 294 to 596—and the Ph.D. candidates increased by a third—from 111 to 145.

The composition of the graduating class reflected many of the changes that had taken place during the Cyert years. For example, 150 of the master's candidates came from the new School of Urban and Public Affairs (SUPA), and 185

Changing Commencement Statistics 1908-1988

	1908	1928	1948	1968	1988
Number of Graduates	58	382	725	1112	1798
Number of Different Degrees	6	46	42	82	140
Pre-Collegiate	**58**	**52**	**0**	**0**	**0**
2-Year Certificates	0	44	0	0	0
3-Year Diplomas	58	8	0	0	0
Bachelor's Level	**0**	**319**	**633**	**681**	**1015**
Bachelor of Science	0	226	528	435	741
Bachelor of Architecture	0	12	7	31	60
Bachelor of Arts	0	76	0	85	69
Bachelor of Fine Arts	0	0	98	130	145
Professional Degrees	0	5	0	0	0
Master's Level	**0**	**11**	**65**	**294**	**596**
Master of Science	0	11	56	243	542
Master of Social Work	0	0	9	0	0
Master of Arts	0	0	0	43	23
Master of Architecture	0	0	0	8	19
Master of Engineering	0	0	0	0	12
Terminal Degrees	**0**	**0**	**27**	**137**	**187**
Master of Fine Arts	0	0	13	25	36
Doctor of Science	0	0	14	0	0
Doctor of Philosophy	0	0	0	111	145
Doctor of Arts	0	0	0	1	6

Carnegie Mellon's 1988
Commencement Ceremonies

others from the Graduate School of Industrial Administration (GSIA). Humanities and Social Sciences (H&SS) awarded more Master's and Bachelor's of Science than of Arts, a reflection of new departments, as well as new emphases in traditional humanities departments. Finally, the spread of Ph.D. candidates throughout the University—most of Fine Arts excepted—indicated clearly that the University's research orientation had become institution-wide.

The graduates hailed from every state and Puerto Rico, every continent except Antarctica and 57 foreign countries with India (32), Taiwan (17), Korea (17), the People's Republic of China (13) and Japan (10) leading the way. A total of 25 graduates were western European citizens. The graduates' names, particularly among the master's and doctor's candidates, read like a meeting of the United Nations. To many parents and relatives, the degrees won by their loved ones seemed unusual, to say the least: Logic and Computation, Information and Decision Systems, Biomedical Engineering and many others. To all but the scientifically and technologically sophisticated among them, the titles of dissertations read much like foreign languages. The entire ceremony, the variety of students, their fields of study and thousands of spectators gathered under a huge tent would no doubt bewilder a member of the first graduating class— 58 white men from the Pittsburgh area— if one could be resurrected and invited to join his new fellow alumni.

The administration grows

During the Warner administration, the Board of Trustees had separated completely from the Carnegie Institute. Gradually the composition of the board had changed. In 1968 the board had 55 members including 44 businessmen, two women and no African-Americans. By 1988, the board's 65 members included two African-Americans, five women and eight members whose major professional background was neither business nor industry. The composition of the major administrative offices of the University had also begun to change. There were no African-Americans in major administrative positions, but one dean, Elizabeth Bailey of GSIA, was a woman and two key administrators, the provost, Angel Jordan (E'59), and the director of the Robotics Institute, Raj Reddy, had international backgrounds. The eight vice presidents and the remainder of the 25 senior administrators were all white males. Significant diversity within both the Board of Trustees and the major administrative offices lagged behind the increasing diversity of the student body.

In addition to the eight vice presidents, the administration focused on the provost to whom the seven deans and the directors of the Mellon Institute, the Robotics Institute and the Software Engineering Institute reported. In turn, the department heads reported to their respective deans. Key administrative officers and a representative from the faculty constituted the resource, capital and space allocation boards that approved the budgets of the main subdivisions of the University. The deans' council set general university policy through two special bodies, the University Research Council and the University Educational Council, each headed by a dean. Each college also had a council to set policies and receive suggestions from faculty and administrators. The Faculty Senate represented the faculty organization while the Staff Council spoke for staff members. Finally, the student government organization brought student opinion to the attention of the administration and allocated student activity funds among the various student organizations. In addition to this formal organization, President Cyert's open door maintained informal lines of communication with administrators, faculty, staff and students.

The financial clouds darkening the skies over Carnegie Mellon in 1968 had dissipated in 20 years. Cyert had balanced the budget during each of his years in office—and the overall budget had increased almost sixfold. For the fiscal year 1988, the educational and general operating budget of the University totaled $103 million. More than half of the University's income came from tuition and fees, almost a fourth from research overhead and only 9 percent from the endowment as the accompanying pie chart shows. Research overhead helped to cover the large capital budget—16 percent of total expenditures—that constituted the University's second largest expenditure. The budget was balanced but its reliance on research overhead posed a potential threat and no provisions had been made to repay an unfunded debt of about $50 million.

The sponsored research budget totaled $111 million compared to $14.4 million in 1968. This dramatic eightfold increase testifies to Carnegie Mellon's new research orientation. It was, however, distributed unevenly through the University's colleges, school and institutes. Computer Science ($33.5 million), the Carnegie Institute of Technology (CIT) ($21.6 million), and the Software Engineering Institute ($19.3 million) accounted for about 75 percent of the total. Most of this money came from grants from the federal government.

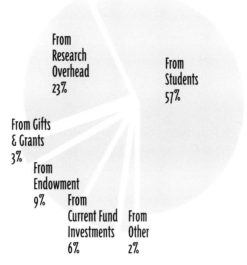

Fiscal Year 1988 Sources of Income

From Students 57%
From Research Overhead 23%
From Gifts & Grants 3%
From Endowment 9%
From Current Fund Investments 6%
From Other 2%

On the other hand, GSIA ($953,000), SUPA ($474,000) and the College of Fine Arts (CFA) ($334,000), lacking grants from the federal government totaled just over $1.5 million.

The endowment had grown between 1968 and 1988—from $77 million to $265 million. After 1975 both the equities and the bond funds in the endowment had been shifted from the Trust Department of Mellon Bank to special investment managers who could be monitored. Still, the universities, such as Stanford, Case Western and Washington in St. Louis that had smaller endowments than Carnegie Tech in 1948, had leaped ahead twenty years later. Catching up presented serious problems. Carnegie Mellon's $200 million five-year capital campaign launched in 1985 included only $33 million for the endowment.

For the 1988-89 academic year, undergraduate tuition was $12,000, up from $11,100 in 1987-88. Graduate tuition ranged from $12,000 to $13,566. Tuition had been rising steadily through the 1980s, but it still trailed costs in peer institutions. Carnegie Mellon continued its need-blind admission policy; that is,

Carnegie Mellon's new "tilted square logo," designed by the New York design firm, Siegel (Alan P. Siegel, A'70) and Gale, was introduced in 1986.

it admitted the freshman class without considering the financial needs of individual students. Sixty-two percent of the undergraduate student body had financial needs in 1988. These needs were met by $15 million in scholarship aid, half from the University's Education and General Operating budget (E&GO), and almost $9 million in the form of loans. Undergraduate financial aid constituted 7 percent of the University's total overall budget. Still hundreds of undergraduates each year carried thousands of dollars in debt away with them as they clutched their hard-won diplomas.

The establishment of a separate School of Computer Science (SCS) in 1988 brought the total of schools and colleges to seven. Three of them, Fine Arts, the Carnegie Institute of Technology and the Mellon College of Science, traced their ancestry to two of the four original Carnegie Technical Schools. Humanities and Social Sciences had grown out of the old Social Relations Department. The remaining three schools, the Graduate School of Industrial Administration, the School of Urban and Public Affairs and the School of Computer Science, had all been formed without direct antecedents in the first 50 years of Carnegie Mellon's existence. The 53 centers, institutes, programs, groups and laboratories scattered throughout the

University, like GSIA, SUPA and SCS, were also products of the period since World War II. This formidable structure, laid out in organizational charts to make lines of responsibility clear, would amaze a 1908 graduate.

The central campus contained 53 buildings, 25 academic and administrative structures and 28 residence halls. Dedication ceremonies were held for the Software Engineering Institute's building in December 1987. Early in 1988, the School of Urban and Public Affairs left the Margaret Morrison building for its newly furnished quarters in Hamburg Hall. Several months later, occupants began moving into the new Physical Plant building. These moves freed space in both the Margaret Morrison building and Porter Hall, touching off a typical battle among space-strapped departments for additional classroom, laboratory and office space. During the summer of 1987 the University broke ground for the East Campus Project, the first part of the new campus plan. It encompassed two residence halls, a football stadium and athletic field, a parking garage and intramural fields. Our resurrected student from 1908, a year when the roar and bang of new construction echoed over the campus, might have felt right at home amid the clamor and bustle of all these construction projects.

Right:
The Physical Plant Building

Opposite page:
One of the trailers temporarily increasing space for GSIA

Seven colleges and schools report similar activities

In 1968 the deans of Carnegie Mellon's colleges and schools reported widely varying activities and prospects for the future. One college, Margaret Morrison, seemed too weak to survive, SUPA was suffering from birth pangs, and H&SS had yet to establish a firm direction for itself. Fine Arts, H&SS and the Mellon College of Science (MCS) had one or more departments with severe problems. Two decades later the deans of the schools described more parallel institutions. Each dean commented on substantial improvements in physical plant, the addition of distinguished scholars to the faculty, excellent students, extensive reforms in curriculum and instruction and widespread research activities. Each college and school identified particularly notable programs and equally impressive achievements of individual faculty members. Even allowing for rose-colored glasses, the reports portray a vigorous, dynamic university in which no college or school stood out as an academic basket case, although a few departments were clearly in trouble. The differences between the 1968 and the 1988 deans' reports capture the development of a major university from a scattered group of schools and colleges of widely differing quality and with contrasting orientations.

In 1988, for example, the new School of Computer Science stood in sharp contrast to Margaret Morrison Carnegie College which it had replaced on the ros-

ter of the University. Its faculty was filled with distinguished scholars whose research had won international recognition. Ninety percent of its budget came from research contracts. It was inundated with applicants for admission. Its influence extended throughout the University. Rating surveys consistently placed it among the top four schools of its kind in the nation: Carnegie Mellon, MIT, Stanford and Berkeley. In typical fashion, Carnegie Mellon had phased out one college where it had no comparative advantage and fostered another whose cutting edge research helped to pull an entire university along with it to greater achievements.

The faculty and staff

In the fall of 1988, Carnegie Mellon employed 2,679 persons. They included 527 members of the full-time tenure-stream faculty, 247 full- and part-time special faculty and 564 researchers. The full-time tenure-stream faculty was composed of 290 tenured members, 232 additional tenure-stream members and five instructors. Eighty-five percent of the faculty held Ph.D. degrees, more than half of them from 10 of the nation's best universities (Carnegie Mellon, MIT, Stanford, Berkeley, Harvard, Michigan, Yale, California Institute of Technology, Minnesota and Cornell). The highest percentage of tenured faculty came from MCS and CIT, both with more than 60 percent, while the smallest percentage, 40 and under, were in Fine Arts, the University's oldest college, and SUPA, one of its newest. Faculty salaries for 1987-88 averaged $63,400 for professors, $42,800 for associate professors and $37,800 for assistant professors. Eighty-six percent of the regular faculty were males and 14 percent females; 3 percent of the faculty were Asian, 1 percent black and 1 percent Hispanic; 69 percent of the faculty were between 30 and 50 years of age and only 11 percent were over 60. The faculty were better educated and better paid than they were in 1968 but, like the administration, they remained overwhelmingly white males despite vigorous attempts to hire more women and more members of minority groups.

No university office has a copy of the booklet listing faculty publications for 1987-88. The nearest year—1984-85—lists a total of 1,343 books and articles published by the faculty. Almost every tenure-stream faculty member published something during the academic year, and many of those who did not were in the College of Fine Arts where performances, exhibitions and other creative endeavors not listed in the booklet occupied faculty members' attention. The sheer quantity of research speaks clearly to the status of Carnegie Mellon as a major research university.

The faculty played increasing roles in the life of the University. The 71-page *Faculty Handbook* described faculty rights and responsibilities in great detail and listed an impressive roster of faculty benefits including health insurance, tuition waivers, retirement plans, disability and survivor benefits, accident insurance, a home purchase plan and child-care fee remissions. These benefits had been growing steadily for a half-century during which time the faculty had consistently lobbied the administration on behalf of the faculty and staff. The *Handbook* also listed 15 University policies including several that grew out of the student disturbances of the late 1960s: Statement Concerning Controversial Speakers, University Policy on Free Speech and Assembly and Separation of Individual's and Institution's Interests.

The role of the faculty in evaluating the work of the president and setting criteria for a new presidential appointment indicate the faculty's increasing influence in major University decisions. Fourteen of

the 18 members of the Commission to Evaluate the President in 1987 were distinguished members of the faculty, two from each college and school, chaired by University Professor Dana S. Scott, of the Computer Science Department. The members of the Commission interviewed faculty, staff, trustees and a few students; identified a set of creative tensions, such as liberal education vs. professional education, that marked University culture; highlighted the achievements of the administration during the five years since the previous evaluation; and assessed the position of the University on a wide range of issues. This document laid the background for a second paper discussing the search for a new president to succeed Dick Cyert. These two documents involving virtually every decision maker and many important faculty members helped to set the agenda for the decade to follow. In 1936 the faculty had learned about Carnegie Tech's new president through an article in a newspaper. In 1990 they played a vital role defining what the new president should do and how he should do it.

FOCUS, the voice of the Faculty Senate, responded to many requests from the faculty to publish an account of the University's funding sources. Provost Angel Jordan released for publication a complete list of all 250 contracts and grants held by University personnel. The accompanying table lists the largest of these 250 contracts and grants. All but one of them came from the federal government. They went to 10 departments and involved 24 principal investigators, several of whom were involved in more than one grant. Most of the grants extended over several years, typically from three to five, although the grant from the Department of Energy to the Physics Department extended from 1950 to 1989. The March/April 1989 issue of *FOCUS* revealed that Carnegie Mellon ($41.5 million) was third

Carnegie Mellon University's Largest Contracts and Grants 1981-1991

Title	Award	Source	Department	Dates	Principal Investigator
Software Engineering Institute	$103,068,144	Department of Air Force	Software Engineering Institute	12/18/84– 12/17/89	L. Druffel
Basic Energy Sciences/ High Energy Physics	40,917,654	Department of Energy	Physics	9/01/50– 12/31/89	R. Kraemer
Pittsburgh Center for Advanced Computing	36,000,000	NSF/MPC	Pittsburgh Super- computing Center	2/01/86– 9/30/90	M. Levine R. Roskies
Strategic Computing	28,683,191	Department of Navy	Computer Science	2/02/87– 2/28/90	H. Kung
Information Processing Research	18,101,764	Department of Navy	Computer Science	7/15/87– 7/14/90	S. Fahlman A. Newell A. Spector
Learning, Teaching & Discovery in Artificial Intelligence & Psychology	11,575,053	Department of Navy	Psychology	9/15/86– 9/14/91	H. Simon
Speech Recognition Research	7,298,664	Department of Navy	Computer Science	12/27/84– 3/12/89	R. Reddy
The Carnegie Mellon Engineering Design Center	6,711,550	NSF	Engineering Design Research Center	5/01/86– 4/30/89	A. Westerberg
Proposal for Acquiring Additional WARP Machines, Related Support, and Fault-Tolerance 2-Dimensional Systolic Array Architectures	5,939,781	Department of Army	Computer Science	8/15/86– 4/15/89	H. Kung
Foundations for Program Derivation	5,053,009	Department of Navy	Computer Science	6/15/84– 9/30/91	W. Scherlis D. Scott
Research & Development of a Road-following Vision System	3,985,425	Department of Army	Robotics Institute	1/15/85– 1/14/89	T. Kanade C. Thorpe
Autonomous Planetary Rover	3,000,000	NASA	Robotics Institute	10/01/87– 9/30/89	W. Whittaker T. Kanade T. Mitchell
Autonomous Mobile Robot	2,720,175	Department of Navy	Robotics Institute	7/01/81– 5/30/89	H. Moravec
Parallel Algorithms for Computer Vision	2,548,680	Department of Army	Robotics Institute	1/15/81– 4/1/89	T. Kanade J. Web
Experimental Medium Energy Physics	2,100,000	Department of Energy	Physics	12/01/86– 11/30/89	P. Barnes
Development of an Integrated ALV System	2,050,733	Department of Army	Robotics Institute	7/01/86– 12/31/89	C. Thorpe W. Whittaker
Research on Constraint-Directed Planning: Opt. 1-Strategic Planning	2,046,948	Department of Air Force	Robotics Institute	11/30/87– 11/29/90	M. Fox
Spectroscopy Program	1,925,000	Lucille P. Markey Charitable Trust	Biological Sciences	8/01/85– 8/31/90	C. Ho
Research in Distributed Tactical Decision Making: Decentralized Resource Management in Tactical Computer Executives	1,899,652	Department of Navy	Statistics	8/01/84– 9/30/91	J. Lehoczky
Experimental Research in Electronic Submission (EXPRES)	1,833,850	NSF	Information Technology Center	10/1/86– 1/31/89	J. Morris

223

in the nation that year in receiving support from the Department of Defense, trailing MIT ($407 million) and Johns Hopkins ($355 million). Support from the Department of Defense had grown steadily from 17 percent of total research funding in 1975 to 44 percent in 1989.

In 1971 the Faculty Senate had created *FOCUS,* a news and opinion publication whose purpose was to build a better sense of community. Its editor was Professor David Demarest of the Department of English. Articles in *FOCUS* kept faculty and staff informed and examined University policy from wide-ranging points of view often hostile to the administration. Its pages kept administrators on their toes and often stirred up controversy within the faculty and between faculty members and administrators.

On June 22-24 about 100 faculty and administrators participated in a retreat at Wheeling, West Virginia's Oglebay Park. They discussed two general issues: Relationships and Tensions between Faculty and Administrators and The Campus Environment. According to an article in the September 1988 *FOCUS,* the faculty members involved called the meeting an excellent idea.

The faculty played vital roles in setting and carrying out University policy in both education and research. Virtually every faculty member designed his or her own course, and many of them worked cooperatively with department or college colleagues to develop overall educational programs. The newly formed University Education Council, chaired by Dean Stephen Fienberg, focused on five issues in 1988-89: continued work on a university-wide core program, creating a university-wide honor program, coordinating teaching awards and recognition, reviewing the Faculty

Course Evaluation (FCE) system and linking the results of the FCEs to a program of sustained research on educational excellence and innovation. By 1988 the University Teaching Center founded in 1982 conducted a dozen programs to improve teaching, including videotaping faculty members in the classroom, consulting about course and syllabus development, conducting faculty and faculty/student luncheon seminars and organizing a seminar each fall for incoming faculty members. Over several years, almost half of the faculty participated in one or more of these programs. Finally, hundreds of faculty were involved in the development and use of the Andrew system, the world's first university-wide computer network.

Through the Faculty Senate, participation in dozens of University committees and voices such as *FOCUS,* the faculty made itself heard in an organizational setting that focused clearly on Richard Cyert's strong administrative leadership.

Enrollment changes, 1967-68 to 1987-88

Full-time enrollment at Carnegie Mellon increased from 4,654 in 1967-68 to 5,749 two decades later. The accompanying table (above right) shows the fall, 1987 full-time enrollment: an additional 957 students studied part time, bringing the total enrollment to 6,706. The student population had grown by about 1,100 during the two decades after 1967, reflecting clear University policy—to grow slowly and only in areas where the University had comparative advantages. This overall numerical change disguises more important changes underway, however.

Carnegie Mellon students came from all 50 states and 43 foreign countries. The international student population had grown from 194 to 639, a more than threefold increase. The largest delegations of international students came from India

1987-88 Carnegie Mellon Full-Time Student Enrollment

	Undergraduate	Graduate	Total
CIT	1238	493	1731
CFA	878	87	965
H&SS	985	119	1104
IM	241	0	241
MCS	779	193	972
CS	0	161	161
GSIA	0	413	413
SUPA	12	146	158
Non-Degree	4	0	4
Total	**4137**	**1612**	**5749**

(117), the People's Republic of China (89), Taiwan (51), South Korea (45), Canada (37) and Japan (37). A total of 97 came from 13 western European countries. Of the total full- and part-time students, men outnumbered women by more than two to one. Undergraduate minority population remained low: 196 in 1986-87 of whom 102 were African-American, 85 Asian, five Hispanic and four Native American. The number of minority students increased more than threefold to 658 by 1991-1992. Scores on the Scholastic Aptitude Test had been rising steadily through the 1980s. Freshmen in 1987 averaged 1,222 on their SATs compared to a national average of 906. Carnegie Mellon was now competing for excellent students with the nation's high-select universities.

Investigating the quality of student life

The war in Vietnam, racial troubles and general student unrest dominated much of campus life during the 1967-69 period. The 1968 yearbook, *The Thistle*, described both incidents on campus and in the nation at large in some detail. Not that students were passive twenty years later. A minority of the student body still agitated

for change in both national affairs and campus problems. Students continued to be involved, as they had in 1968, in constructive attempts to improve campus life. In March 1989, for example, black students from Spirit temporarily occupied the office of Brad Walter, the Dean of Student Affairs, to complain about the treatment of black students on campus by Carnegie Mellon security forces. Both *The Tartan* that carried this story and an alternative student newspaper, the *Student Union,* frequently took the administration to task over a host of issues.

From one viewpoint, student morale reached a low point at the end of the 1980s. Dave Maloney, Assistant Vice President for Development, recommended that the University cancel the senior banquet after three years when two dozen incidents of rude, drunken or vulgar behavior disrupted the program. A few months later a survey based on 48 student interviews concluded that the quality of student life at Carnegie Mellon was very low and that students thought that the administration's focus on research and return on investment was largely responsible for students' negative attitudes. Clearly something had to be done.

The something began as the Quality of Life Task Force composed of 70 administrators, faculty members and students. They were divided into four subcommittees each headed by an administrator. In order to gather information about the quality of student life—the focus of one of

Pugwash

Student Pugwash, a recently formed CMU organization working its way toward winning funding from Student Senate, may have a funny name, but its purpose is anything but humorous.

"The textbook definition is that it's 'an international organization of graduate and undergraduate students that promotes discussion on ethical issues in science and technology,'" says Pugwash chair Tony Bradshaw, a MechE/EPP junior. "Basically we bring in speakers and have discussions on issues the group—and possibly the times—considers important."

Pugwash is an international organization originally conceived by Albert Einstein and Bertrand Russell after the development of the atomic bomb.

The impetus for a Pugwash chapter at CMU came about two years ago from EPP's Indira Nair, who was "concerned that students—particularly in engineering and the sciences—do not seriously consider the social ramifications of their present and future work."
—*FOCUS,* December 1988

Weaned on Chinese Food

At noon on the first floor of Wean Hall, near the elevators, people line up to buy Chinese food that is vended in styrofoam boxes from cardboard cartons. The entrepreneur is Debbie Lee, owner and manager of Squirrel Hill's Dragon Palace Chinese Restaurant—and now proprietor of an Asian food delivery service to the CMU community.

According to Lee, it all started three years ago when a student called and asked for a delivery. "The same student called again and again, so one day we brought a few extra dinners to see if anyone would want them, and they all sold."

Before long Lee posted a menu on the fourth floor and the number of orders multiplied. Today the delivery service has grown into a popular and successful operation. "Sometimes when we arrive there is already a line of people waiting for us. We often sell 50 lunches." Lee says smiling.
—*FOCUS,* October 1988

the committees—the University commissioned a survey of student attitudes. After meeting for several months, the task force made five recommendations to the Board of Trustees at a trustees' meeting at The Greenbrier in West Virginia. Some of the students who attended the Greenbrier meeting greeted the proceedings skeptically, but the administration quickly began to take steps to carry out some of the specific recommendations of the report. Then the students made themselves heard about a major thrust of the report—the need for a University Center.

In his State of the University speech in 1989, President Cyert had fended off criticism that the University Center project had been postponed indefinitely. In response the Student Senate collected more than 2,000 signatures on a petition to President Cyert. The petition and a letter to Cyert had been drafted by a group of student leaders assembled by student government president Andy Robitshek (IM'89). After listing the inadequacies of Skibo and the need for a variety of new facilities—office space for student organizations, adequate dining facilities, more meeting rooms, better book stores, informal meeting places, etc.—the Senate expressed student sentiment in a petition printed in *The Tartan* on April 11, 1989: "We the Student Senate of Carnegie Mellon, as a student voice, demand that the University Center be placed at the top of the priority list of both the current administration and the one to follow." The student body spoke with a single voice, perhaps an unprecedented unanimity. Both the administration and the Board of Trustees heard that voice clearly. The November 24, 1989 *Tartan* proclaimed in an exultant headline: "Trustees: It's a go, Carnegie Mellon commits to a $41 million University Center."

The student body failed to use its voice, however, in the controversy over the place of the Software Engineering Institute in the University. Immediately after the contract for the SEI was announced in 1984, an alliance of Pittsburgh citizens formed the River City Campaign to protest the work of Pittsburgh organizations that campaign members believed contributed to the arms race and to the nation's first-strike capability. Members began to demonstrate every Saturday at the construction site on Fifth Avenue and to pass out leaflets on campus. At the dedication ceremony in December 1988, about 100 protestors carried banners, blocked traffic and shouted slogans. Although several Carnegie Mellon faculty and staff took part in these demonstrations, students were conspicuous by their absence. There was no nationwide clamor; the issues seemed abstract and distant; students' lives were not directly involved. And times had changed.

Student Survey Sampler

Results of the Carnegie Mellon University Student Survey conducted in September are still being analyzed. A few sample questions and answers follow.

Most students cheat on exams, labs, papers, or homework assignments during their college career.
Strongly Disagree 1   2   3   4   5   6   7 Strongly Agree
7%   16%   8%   14%   18%   18%   20%

Drinking alcohol is a common way for students to relax.
Strongly Disagree 1   2   3   4   5   6   7 Strongly Agree
1%   4%   5%   9%   22%   32%   27%

Students at CMU hardly ever seem to study.
Strongly Disagree 1   2   3   4   5   6   7 Strongly Agree
58%   27%   7%   5%   1%   1%   1%

Students are so cutthroat about grades that they rarely help each other understand and learn difficult material.
Strongly Disagree 1   2   3   4   5   6   7 Strongly Agree
16%   28%   23%   9%   16%   8%   1%

There is a strong feeling of belonging here.
Strongly Disagree 1   2   3   4   5   6   7 Strongly Agree
13%   20%   22%   17%   18%   8%   2%

Students feel the faculty are interested in them.
Strongly Disagree 1   2   3   4   5   6   7 Strongly Agree
9%   12%   25%   19%   23%   9%   3%

Students tend not to compete with each other.
Strongly Disagree 1   2   3   4   5   6   7 Strongly Agree
28%   28%   24%   7%   8%   5%   1%

Students are generally satisfied with their education.
Strongly Disagree 1   2   3   4   5   6   7 Strongly Agree
3%   7%   18%   14%   27%   24%   8%

Students feel the university administration is inflexible.
Strongly Disagree 1   2   3   4   5   6   7
3%   7%   10%   17%   23%   23%   17%

There are plenty of nice places to socialize on campus.
Strongly Disagree 1   2   3   4   5   6   7
21%   24%   18%   11%   11%   12%   3%

Students have a voice in how the university is run.
Strongly Disagree 1   2   3   4   5   6   7
17%   27%   25%   18%   11%   3%   0%

Students believe faculty care more about research than about teaching.
Strongly Disagree 1   2   3   4   5   6   7
3%   3%   15%   21%   21%   22%   15%

Most students have a strong sense of loyalty to CMU.
Strongly Disagree 1   2   3   4   5   6   7
14%   19%   17%   19%   17%   10%   4%

Students work hard to get top grades.
Strongly Disagree 1   2   3   4   5   6   7
0%   2%   2%   4%   19%   39%

...ud to tell people that I attend CMU.
1   2   3   4   5   6   7
2%   4%   7%   18%   30%

Another side to student life

The Thistle, the University yearbook for 1989, presented quite a different view of student life, and the student newspaper, *The Tartan,* sometimes echoed many of its themes. *The Thistle* began with photos of freshman camp. All smiling faces. Then came "moving in." Smiling faces and mounds of baggage. The section on Academics gave four pages to each college and school. Both faculty and students smiled constantly. Fourteen pages documented life in Pittsburgh, clearly one of the world's cleanest and most exciting cities according to this account. Seventeen pages about life in residence halls carried the same message. The editors devoted 15 pages to an "art gallery," artistic photos taken by staff members. The long section on activities included shots of students rowing, fencing, dancing, rappelling, listening, speaking, singing, eating, voting, politicking, juggling, soldiering, ping-ponging and drawing—and not a sad face. Photos of 10 athletic teams show fit men and women competing successfully with their peers. The reader must search carefully through the long section devoted to photographs of graduating seniors to find a face without smile. Clearly someone was having a good time.

Parents help students move into their residence halls.

During 1987-89, the pages of *The Tartan* mixed sharp criticism of the administration with stories about the variety of activities students were enjoying. The paper usually listed topics and locations of lectures, the titles of films shown four nights each week in Doherty Hall 2210, a directory of religious organizations, a full page devoted to what was going on in town, announcements of such events as Newfest, a musical concert on the Cut, and, of course, glowing accounts of Carnival, Sweepstakes, Greek Sing and Scotch 'n' Soda.

These seemingly irreconcilable viewpoints were both accurate. Many students enjoyed themselves thoroughly at Carnegie Mellon, at least part of the time. At the same time, they felt stressed out in Carnegie Mellon's competitive atmosphere and voiced their complaints vigorously.

The First Double Winner

The Tartan editorial board has traditionally awarded thistles to members of the Carnegie Mellon community whose achievements or actions deserve special merit or recognition, and thorns to those whose achievements or actions. . .well, whose achievements or actions don't deserve much of anything, except to be forgotten.

Our first thistle goes to the Quality of Life Committee. The Committee was able to identify serious problems and propose viable solutions. Unfortunately that's where it ended, so quality of life becomes our first double winner.
—*The Tartan,* April 26, 1988

Clangs, rings, guitars that sing: NewFest on the Cut

Senior Banquet Cancelled

Another year, another $17,000

Focal Point: A new group that focuses on Asians

CMU doesn't foster teamwork

CMU Women's Center to open in Margaret Morrison Plaza

Cyert offers words of welcome & encouragement

Carnegie Mellon Dining Services doesn't meet students' needs

Fraternities must change with times

Sing Helps Big Brother Program

Trayin'

One of the few remaining *legal* traditions open to today's Carnegie Mellon student is traying.

Traying involves "borrowing" a tray from one of the University Dining Services establishments, waiting for a heavy snowfall, and finally riding the tray down the nearest hill.

Flagstaff is traditionally The Hill. There are essentially two different runs on Flagstaff.

From the top of the hill, the run to the right of the basketball court is the slower and longer run of the two. On the left side of the basketball court, the other run is much faster and a little shorter. The left side is the more exciting of the two.

—*The Tartan*, February 21, 1989

In 1988, most of the complaints focused on the lack of progress toward starting the University Center project. It promised to solve many of the problems on which students focused attention and it provided a legitimate, specific target. The other major complaint—that the University was obsessed with research and the bottom line—grew out of the publicity generated by the millions of dollars pouring into Carnegie Mellon to support research. Many students did not know all the facts: that research money could not be used for buildings, that research overhead was responsible for much of the capital improvement that had taken place on campus and that Carnegie Mellon's slim endowment would not support the enormous hit that the University Center would deliver. Money for new buildings was hard to come by. The problem, along with many other student complaints about the quality of life, was left in 1990 for Cyert's successor, Robert Mehrabian, to solve.

Many of the factors that caused students to live different types of lives in the early days of Carnegie Tech had disap-

peared or had been substantially reduced by 1988. Most graduate students, of course, still formed close ties with their faculty mentors and often served as teaching assistants, roles seldom occupied by undergraduates. Most of the night students were now professional people studying in SUPA or GSIA for master's degrees instead of working people taking a few courses or working toward a bachelor's diploma. Only a few veterans of Vietnam rather than the flood of GIs from World War II were on campus. The University treated men and women much more equally than they had in previous student generations. For example, the same residence life rules applied to both men and women, and co-ed dorms were widespread. Even some of the differences between the lives of Greeks and Independents had been reduced.

Greek life

Throughout the three years beginning in 1987, Greek organizations played an increasing role on the Carnegie Mellon campus. Their numbers had been rising steadily. In 1983 only about 10 percent of Carnegie Mellon students belonged to fraternities and sororities. By 1988, however, about a third of the undergraduate student population had joined. This increase was part of a national trend. By 1988 up to 70 percent of undergraduates on some campuses had pledged Greek organizations. Three aspects of Greek life rose to the surface at Carnegie Mellon during these years.

228

Carnegie Mellon's 22 fraternities and sororities consistently pointed to their charitable work. It took many forms and supported a variety of organizations. For example, in 1987 and 1988 the annual Greek Sings involving all the Greek organizations raised a total of $8,400 to establish a campus chapter of Big Brothers and Sisters of Greater Pittsburgh. In 1987 Pi Lambda Phi fraternity raised over $1,700 for United Cerebral Palsy of Pittsburgh in the First Annual Jolly Laddies Steel City Shootout, a flag football championship involving Pi Lambda Phi chapters from nine colleges and universities. And in their annual pole-sit in 1988, three sororities, Theta Xi, Delta Delta Delta and Kappa Alpha Theta, raised money for charity, supplementing the pole-sit with a pie-in-the-face event.

Fraternities and sororities devoted far more of their time and attention to social life, however, and social life took a number of forms. Many of the fund-raisers—Greek Sing is perhaps the best example—delighted participants and audiences as well. Fraternity parties attracted the most attention and provoked the most criticism. But Greek members emphasized the powerful bonds that developed among brothers or sisters through Greek Sing, participating in buggy or building a booth for Spring Carnival as well as raising money for charity. The bonds formed in fraternities and sororities often lasted through a lifetime as alumni returned to campus for homecoming or Spring Carnival. Greek alumni are among the University's most generous financial supporters.

Complaints about fraternities focused on drinking. There were other complaints, of course. A couple of fraternities sent their members to urinate on the houses of rivals, sometimes touching off pitched battles that in a few cases sent students to hospitals. Faculty, honoring a long Carnegie Mellon tradition, continued to com-

plain that building a buggy or practicing for Greek Sing had replaced books as the focus of students' lives. Domination of the Interfraternity Council by the fraternities prompted the sororities to withdraw from the organization because it focused so much on fraternities that the sororities were excluded from having their needs addressed. And the excesses of Rush Week always brought mounds of complaints to administrative offices.

Drinking became a public issue in November 1987 when 35 state police, Liquor Control officials and Pittsburgh police raided parties at Pi Kappa Alpha and Delta Tau Delta, one of eleven raids at universities throughout the state. About 150 students were arrested, loaded into rented buses and arraigned before a judge. A total of 127 students were convicted of underage drinking, possession of alcohol, disorderly conduct or selling alcohol to minors or selling alcohol without a license. The raid had been planned over several weeks when undercover agents had infiltrated fraternity parties across the state to gather evidence. The Carnegie Mellon raid took place while one of the fraternities involved was conducting a fund-raiser for charity by charging two dollars for admission and donating the beer.

The University called a press conference to discuss the raid. President Cyert pointed out that Carnegie Mellon supported state liquor laws and forbade underage drinking; then he condemned the

Above:
Greeks gather outside their house.

Opposite page left:
Greek Sing

Opposite page right:
Pole-sitting for charity

Above:
An invitation from the Asian Student Association to join in celebrating the year of the snake

Below:
Gloria Hill, Director of Carnegie Mellon Action Project (CMAP), with celebrating Spirit buggy team

Liquor Control Board and the State Police for harassing students and violating their rights. Complaints, he said, should be handled by the University and not by state agencies. In subsequent weeks, the administration restricted advertising for fraternity parties and warned that both individuals and their fraternities would be fined if anyone was caught drinking outside the houses.

Independent life

Two-thirds of Carnegie Mellon students, however, remained Independents in 1988; that is, they did not join Greek organizations. They found ways in which to receive some of the benefits of Greek life outside formal fraternity or sorority bounds. If they wished, they could get a Greek friend to put them on a fraternity guest list for a particular event without assuming the obligations that fraternity life involved. One group of Independents with a strong group identity named themselves "Eta Pi" and strolled around campus in their Eta Pi t-shirts. Eta Pi was a roundabout way to generate a sense of belonging that many Independents lacked. Organizations such as Pioneers, Carnegie Involvement Association (CIA), Fringe

and Spirit enabled their members to become involved in Sweepstakes and Spring Carnival and to receive funds from student activities fees to support their efforts. Membership in Alpha Phi Omega (A Phi O), a national service organization, provided opportunities for a group of friends to associate and do things together. Both men and women members of A Phi O served the community through projects like working with scout troops and publishing the campus phone directory.

Non-Greeks had innumerable ways to spend their evenings. The University Housing Office offered a variety of social programming in residence halls. Activities Board sponsored films in Doherty Hall and charged only a dollar for admission. Each week *The Tartan* published a calendar of events for the upcoming week, a rich tapestry that included movies, lectures, exhibits, workshops, concerts and so forth. In 1985, the University had opened Scotland Yard, a non-alcoholic pub developed and managed by students in Skibo. In addition to non-alcoholic mixed drinks, finger-food, sandwiches and desserts, Scotland Yard offered a wide variety of entertainment—singers, bands, comedians or movies on the wide-screen TV. Students could easily bury themselves in all these co-curricular activities. Some did. Some of them left school as a result.

Excerpts from the 1987-88 *Student Handbook*

Alcohol in Public Areas

Alcoholic beverages are not permitted in public areas. The legal use of alcoholic beverages must not violate any rights of another resident. Unlawful drugs are not permitted and are subject to state and federal laws.

Controversial Speakers

When as they will, speakers from within or from outside the campus challenge the moral, spiritual, economic, or political consensus of the community, people are uneasy, disturbed, and at times outraged. In times of crisis, this is particularly true. But freedom of thought and freedom of expression cannot be influenced by circumstances. They exist only if they are inviolable. They are not matters of convenience but of necessity. This is a part of the price of freedom.

Demonstrations

The University recognizes the right and privilege of all students to exercise the constitutional guarantees of free assembly and expression. As a university sincerely espousing the philosophy of academic freedom, the University urges and supports its students' desires and efforts to pursue these rights.

Pets

Dogs, cats, and other pets are not permitted in any University buildings including dormitories and fraternities under any circumstances. Specifically, pets are prohibited from being in offices, class-rooms, hallways, and other areas at all times.

Privacy on computers

On shared computer systems every user is assigned an ID. Nobody else should use an ID without explicit permission from the owner. All files belong to somebody. They should be assumed to be private and confidential unless the owner has explicitly made them available to others. Messages sent to other users should always identify the sender. Network traffic should be considered private. Obscenities should not be sent by computer. Records relating to the use of computing and information resources are confidential.

Privacy in Rooms

All residents have the right to determine the private activity which takes place in their assigned rooms. Members of the floor also have the right to determine community standards of the floor. Roommates have equal voices in determining the private activities of the room, but one roommate's rights must not infringe upon the others.

Sexual Harassment Policy

Sexual harassment is prohibited by the University. Any faculty member, staff employee or student found to have violated the University's policy against sexual harassment will be subject to immediate and appropriate disciplinary action, including possible suspension, termination or expulsion.

Smoking

Smoking is prohibited in certain campus areas because of safety hazards. In addition, an instructor may prohibit smoking in classrooms.

Steam Tunnels

Because of the danger to all who enter them, the steam tunnels are locked and anyone found in the tunnels will be subject to serious disciplinary action. The Security Office is responsible for keeping the tunnels locked and apprehending anyone trespassing.

Student Activity Fees

By action of the Board of Trustees, a required Student Activities Fee of $30.00 per semester (in addition to tuition) is charged to all undergraduate students and graduate students who enroll for 19 units or more. No student enrolled at Carnegie Mellon may on the basis of race, color, sex, creed, age, handicap, or national origin be barred access to an activity, program, facility or service, publication or enterprise provided by such fees. No use made of the fees described above may be intended to violate or circumvent the policies of the University or the law of the land. All Carnegie Mellon students shall have access without hindrance to the functions and services provided by the fee.

King of the Hill

Affectionately referred to by its residents as the King of the Hill, the all-male Hamerschlag House has a reputation as the wildest dorm on campus.

Some CMU females share the opinion of Freshman Shizuka Otake, who states: "That place is scary. I wouldn't go in there without an armed police escort, and even then only if my life depended on it. The guys who live there are a little warped sometimes."

'Schlag residents dislike this sort of bad press: one resident protested, "All we're trying to do is have a good time. And more often than not, we succeed." He continued to describe some of the goings-on in 'Schlag, such as the great apocalyptic waterfight: "Well, it started out as just a waterfight— you know, water pistols, water balloons, that sort of thing. Then three of us decided to take one of those really big trash cans and fill it with water. . . . We won." Do Hamerschlag residents do this sort of thing often? "Of course, man. This sort of thing happens all the time."

—*The Thistle,* 1988

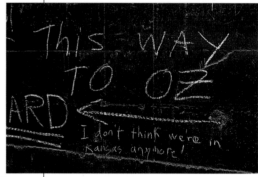

A few graffiti scrawled on the walls of the steam tunnels still guide the visitor to its secret delights.

Athletics

Carnegie Mellon had become a member of the Presidents' Athletic Conference (PAC) in 1972. In addition to Carnegie Mellon, the conference included John Carroll University and five colleges: Bethany, Grove City, Hiram, Thiel and Washington and Jefferson. The Tartans had established an outstanding record in this conference, winning 29 conference titles including eight in men's cross-country, seven in track and field and six in football. The men's cross-country team celebrated its 100th consecutive dual-meet win. Among additional outstanding athletic achievements of Tartan teams in 1988-89, was fourth place in the nation in ultimate frisbee, first place in Division III cross-country, first place with PAC women's basketball and first place in crew in the Bucknell Invitational meet. Carnegie Mellon had just begun to compete in crew. *Carnegie Mellon Magazine* headlined the

event, "Rowing the Sport of Perfectionists." Then in 1987, Carnegie Mellon became a founding member of the University Athletic Association (UAA), a conference sometimes called the Ivy League of Division III. In addition to Carnegie Mellon, its members include Brandeis, Case Western Reserve, Chicago, Emory, Johns Hopkins, NYU, Rochester, and Washington University in St. Louis, all private urban research universities with excellent academic standing. The UAA provided competition among athletes who faced similar academic pressures to those at Carnegie Mellon and enabled Carnegie Mellon students to travel to cities such as Chicago, New York and Atlanta. During its first year of UAA play in 1990, Carnegie Mellon's football team was undefeated and won the conference championship. Not a bad start.

Three traditional celebrations

Like the fraternities, the Beaux Arts Ball fell victim to alcohol in 1988. It had flowed freely at the 1985 ball, a notorious success that had attracted 1,300 participants and resulted in about $40,000 in damages to the College of Fine Arts building. The 1988 organizing committee chose a theme, Extremes, and scheduled the ball for March 11, 1989. CFA Dean Akram Midani refused to sanction the ball unless the committee agreed to prohibit alcohol. When the committee took no action, Dean of Student Affairs Braden Walter canceled the ball citing poor management of alcohol and drugs as his reason. The next day, about 60 students picketed Warner Hall chanting, "Where's our funding?" and "Dick has our ball." The Student Senate took up the issue, passing a resolution condemning cancellation and stating that ". . .we view it [the cancellation] as an insult to the character and sensibilities of the students in the College of Fine Arts." Later in February, the committee made tentative plans for an off-campus ball at Metropol. When only 14 tickets were sold, however, the committee canceled the ball.

Over the spring and summer, Michael Murphy (HNZ'86) replaced Brad Walter as Dean of Student Affairs and Lowry Burgess succeeded Akram Midani as Dean of CFA. During the fall of 1989, both students and the administration agreed on a plan for a ball that outlined rules and regulations and banished alcohol. Tickets for Risorgimento (Rebirth) went on sale to fine arts students, faculty, alumni and their guests and the Beaux Arts Ball, minus drugs and alcohol, once again filled the Fine Arts Building with revelry on the night of February 10, 1990. A *Tartan* staff writer reported the event with tongue in cheek:

Thirteen people were trampled to death last Saturday night at the Beaux Arts

Ball during Dean Lowry Burgess' "Let the Ball prosper" speech. Paramedics described the scene as "grim" and "yucky" and commented that many of the bodies were "squished-up real bad." An investigation into the matter is underway.

Okay, okay—it's a lie. Nobody got trampled, several giddy couples were observed getting "squished-up" in rooms on the upper floors, but they weren't in need of the paramedics. No bodies thrown from the fourth floor, no naked LSD fiends jumping through glass doors, no gunfights, nothing. What a disappointment!

Shhh! Don't Tell. . .

The Beaux Arts Ball: An event so notorious for its flagrant hedonism, debauchery, and outright narcotic-induced lunacy that to quote a friend, "Caligula would have blushed." The unwritten rule for past balls was, "Booze on the first floor, drugs on the second floor, sex on the third floor, and. . ." I forget what was on the fourth floor, but let's say for argument's sake it was more sex. Anyway people would drop like flies at these previous balls, usually due to the drugs and alcohol, but occasionally because of the exhausting sexual athletics. Injuries and overdoses were everywhere. And to add to the cacophony, the word "organization" had the same impact as, say, the word "sober." Acts were rescheduled, cancelled, stoned or ignored and security was just lax enough to allow for about $40,000 worth of damage, last ball alone (This figure varies from $15,000 to $50,000.)

—*The Tartan,* February 13, 1990

buggy!

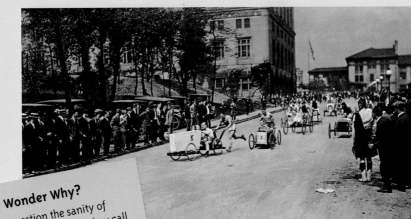

Wonder Why?

You may question the sanity of Carnegie Mellon students. They call this fun? Getting up hours before the crack of dawn on weekends, staying awake late at night for push practice? They must've left their brains logged into that new Andrew system. But look around the course again. You'll see mechanics who have learned more in three months of buggy-ing than they have in the engineering courses. And those push teams that have come together through physical training and now work in coordination with one another. And in the Chute, the guy waving the florescent flag is contributing to the overall success of his organization with little or no recognition because he's part of the team. But best of all, you'll see something that most people say doesn't exist at Carnegie Mellon: Enthusiasm and School Spirit. The EE is handing off the buggy (driven by an art major) to someone from H&SS. Everywhere, students have put away their books, logged off their terminals, and are simply relaxing and having a good time, joining the alumni in experiencing what college is really all about. And all of a sudden, you don't remember why you questioned buggy in the first place.
—*The Buggy Book, 1988*

soap-box buggy

buggy 1. The event which is Buggy; collective name for the annually-run Sweepstakes. 2. The sport which is Buggy; the year-round sport of preparation and training for Sweepstakes.

buggy course The series of roads on which the buggies travel during the race. There is only one such course in the United States.

the Chute The area of the free roll with the tightest turn, in which buggies travel their fastest. The Chute is lined with bales of hay to protect the buggy and driver in the event of a crash.

driver The student who rides inside a buggy and steers it around the course. Drivers are short, lightweight and usually female.

exchange 1. The act of passing a buggy from one pusher to another pusher. 2. One of three neutral zones in which buggies can be passed.

free roll 1. The portion of time during a buggy's run when it is not being pushed. 2. The section of the buggy course between Hills 2 and 3, in which the buggy is not pushed.

pizza men The people who get the most irritated by the closing of streets during push practice. These people can be very dangerous to the flaggers who halt traffic.

the Plug A fireplug on Frew Street past the Porter Hall windows. The ultimate gauge of a buggy's speed in the free roll. "Wow, they made the Plug."

push team The group of five pushers who push a single buggy around the course. There are three push team categories: men's, women's, and alumni.

roll 1. To run a buggy in Sweepstakes or practice. ("Are the buggies rolling today?") 2. To roll past. ("That buggy rolled seven windows.")

windows The main guage of a buggy's performance in the free roll. Next to the base of Hill 3 lies Porter Hall, which has nine windows facing the street. The more windows a buggy can roll, the higher its speed and the better its performance.

The Buggy Book, 1988

1920
The first Interfraternity Sweepstakes Race is held as part of the first alumni celebration, a springtime Campus Week.

1923
Buggy rules change to include a permanent driver and four pushers along the course.

1928
Independent organizations, other than fraternities, enter Buggy for the first time.

1930-50
Early buggies are designed using the old Indy 500 car as a model. In the 30s aluminum is used to build buggies and the 60-pound minimum weight rule is abandoned.

1946
After World War II, the soap-box derby model with four wheels becomes common. Most drivers ride in crouched sitting positions.

amusing buggy

modern buggy

the buggy course

from the 1989 *Buggy Book*

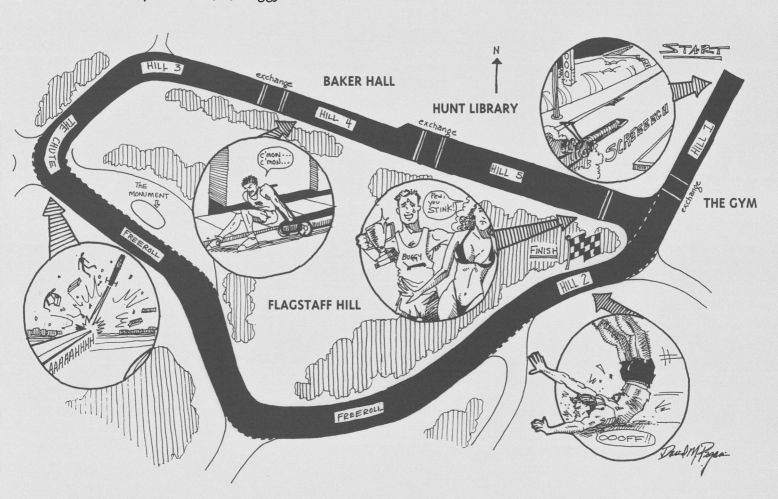

1951
Brakes are required.

1953
Alpha Tau Omega's (ATO) Golden Goose brings about a radical change in buggy design. The driver lies prone, face forward in a buggy built low to the ground.

1981
Women's heats are run for the first time.

1989
The Carnegie Involvement Association (CIA) is the first independent buggy organization to win Sweepstakes.

2000
Buggy continues into the next century.

A year earlier in 1987 Spring Carnival had its share of troubles. When petty thefts took place and a number of fights broke out, the authorities closed the Midway early Friday evening. The committee installed new security measures for the 1988 carnival to head off a recurrence.

The theme, Fairy Tales, provided inspiration for the fraternities, sororities, and independents who built booths. The customary variety of events tumbled one upon another through three days, April 14-16. There were movies, dances, athletic events, bands in concert, the UMOC contest, performances of Scotch 'n' Soda, fireworks, award ceremonies, Sweepstakes and— of course—the Midway with its booths and rides. The Midway's 32 booths filled the two Skibo parking lots. In addition to fraternities and sororities, a number of organizations erected booths. They included athletic teams; the army ROTC; independents such as Pioneers, Fringe, CIA and Spirit; the Computer Club and the campus radio station. Spring Carnival had evolved into an all-university event— no more exclusive migratory dances.

Sweepstakes typified the new age of Carnegie Mellon. Fifty-three buggies from 19 organizations entered Sweepstakes. An independent, Pioneers, won the design competition. Spirit, another independent with a notable group of pushers, won the race. In 1989 both Spirit's men and women came in first. Women, who had raced their own buggies for ten years, entered 21 buggies. Kappa Alpha Theta won. Tiny women students drove all of the men's buggies as well. The days of kiddee cars for women and buggies for men seemed ridiculous to modern students, men and women alike.

Carnegie Mellon's Soapers

The men of Beta are enjoying the most popular daytime soap opera in the house, *Days of Our Lives.*

At three o'clock across campus at Donner Hall, ten viewers—half men, half women—are scattered around the lounge in groups of twos and threes watching *General Hospital.* The atmosphere is more formal than at Beta— perhaps fewer people know each other. But enthusiasm is evident in people's comments to each other.

Soapers are everywhere at Carnegie Mellon. In a recent survey, *FOCUS* asked 125 random students if they currently follow a soap. Thirty-eight percent said they do. The 48 self-confessed soapers included fine arters, jocks, hackers, engineers, and even graduate students.

Most of the students surveyed either love or hate soaps. Basically, those who hate them say soaps are stupid; those who love them say the people who hate them just don't understand.

—FOCUS, November 1987

Alumni increase and prosper

At the end of 1987, Carnegie Mellon boasted 46,071 alumni. The whereabouts of 3,712 of them was unknown. Well over half of the remainder were concentrated in 10 states—13,818— more than one fourth of all Carnegie Mellon alumni, in Pennsylvania alone. Surprisingly, California had the third largest number of alumni (3,671). Florida was in sixth place (1,595) and Texas in eleventh (996). More than 1,200 alumni lived in foreign countries. These alumni were organized into Carnegie Clans in 33 cities. Pittsburgh still had separate men's and women's clans. Several new "special interest" clans had emerged since 1986 including SUPA alumni, SUPA black alumni and New York GSIA alumni that took their places beside the West Coast and New York drama clans. The Clans were served by an alumni office under Dave Maloney. Three times a year they received copies of *Carnegie Mellon Magazine* containing articles about the University and its alumni.

Lewis Sternberg (E'52) became head of the Alumni Association in 1987. He worked with Director of Alumni Relations Dave Maloney and with an alumni board drawn from alumni clans throughout the nation. In the summer of 1986, the board organized more than 4,500 personal interviews by students with alumni in the Pittsburgh and New York areas and continued the interviews in 22 additional cities in 1987. One topic that turned up frequently through these interviews was the lack of networking opportunities—the West Coast and New York Drama clans excepted—among Carnegie Mellon graduates. Both the alumni organization and the Office of Career Services and Placement began to organize networking efforts as a result. In 1988-89, 30 percent of the alumni contributed to the alumni fund, a total of just over $8 million.

Homecoming in 1988 attracted alumni, their families and friends to campus from October 20 to 22. The celebration was arranged by the Student Alumni Relations Council, a group that had been organized to establish and improve relationships between students and alumni. The program offered something for everyone including dinners, a 5K race, tricycle races, highlander games on the Cut, concerts, a parade of alumni before the football game and a dance cruise on the Gateway Clipper.

In retrospect

In 1988 Carnegie Mellon was a national research university competing for students and faculty with elite institutions that were both older and richer. The transition from an excellent regional institute of technology to a national university focusing on excellent research and education had taken place under the leadership of Richard M. Cyert. The decision to do a few things and do them well had paid off handsomely. In many ways, the University was thriving. Its faculty across colleges and schools had attended the nation's best universities and were doing outstanding research. Publications growing out from this research helped to place Carnegie Mellon among the country's elite institutions. Its students increased steadily in quality. Except for a few departments, its programs were rated highly by national

accreditation bodies. Architects had drafted a campus plan and the first part of that plan, the East Campus Project, was well underway.

There were problems, however, among them an unfunded debt of about $50 million; a small endowment that was growing less rapidly than that of peer schools; student dissatisfaction, particularly over the lack of adequate student facilities; an undergraduate education program that required attention; and a need for a number of new buildings and the funds to finance them. Carnegie Mellon's history during the Cyert years accounts for most of these problems. They were the products of success, of the process that turned a good regional institute of technology into a national research university.

Distinguished Alumni

As of 1988, 18 Carnegie Mellon alumni were presidents of other universities and 39 were deans; 66 were chairman of the board, 18 were chief executive officers and 2,704 were presidents or vice presidents of various businesses nationwide.
—*Carnegie Mellon Ninety-first Commencement,* The Cut, May 15, 1988

Drama Alumni

The Carnegie Mellon Drama Department is the oldest in the nation. Founded in 1914, it boasts such alumni as Rene Auberjonois, William Ball, Shari Belafonte-Harper, Steven Bochco, Barbara Bosson, Ted Danson, Barbara Feldon, Robert Foxworth, Frank Gorshin, Charles Haid, Mariette Hartley, Holly Hunter, Arthur Kennedy, Jack Klugman, Judith Light, Nancy Marchand, Kim Miyori, George Peppard, George Romero, Polly Rowles, Sada Thompson, Blair Underwood and Bruce Weitz.
—*Carnegie Mellon Ninety-first Commencement,* The Cut, May 15, 1988

14.

Robert Mehrabian 1990–1997
He wove loose ends and new projects into whole cloth

Robert Mehrabian (H'97) inherited a thriving national research university when he became president in 1990. The University had been transformed during President Cyert's administration. By 1990 Carnegie Mellon competed with many of the nation's best universities for faculty, students and reputation. Its fame as a research center had reached national stature in all its colleges and schools. That success, however, had helped to produce a group of serious problems that remained for Cyert's successor to solve.

Richard Cyert had faced eight diverse problems when he became president in 1972. He had solved most of them and made a start on solving others. Still other issues had remained near the bottom of Cyert's very crowded agenda. They included relationships between the University and its trustees, the undergraduate program, campus buildings and a number of vital financial and administrative issues. The 1987 report of the Commission to Evaluate the President, while heaping praise on Cyert's leadership, added that the rapid changes he had fostered had created strains and stretched University resources. Carnegie Mellon needed someone who could identify its problems and solve them one by one.

A man in a perpetual fix-it mode

The trustees finally chose Robert Mehrabian from a candidate pool that began with 500 nominees. Robert Mehrabian was born of Armenian parents in Tehran, Iran in 1941. His father owned a factory that fabricated aluminum, perhaps the origin of Mehrabian's interest in metallurgy. He spent the first 17 years of his life in Tehran in a small Christian community surrounded by Muslims. In school he learned to speak and read Armenian, English and Persian, play soccer and box. He spent his senior year of high school at New Hampshire's Phillips Exeter Academy where he thrived in science and mathematics courses taught on a college level—and on the soccer team.

Mehrabian entered the Massachusetts Institute of Technology in 1960 earning a bachelor of science degree in 1964 and a Ph.D. in 1968, both in materials science and engineering. He also captained both the freshman and varsity soccer teams and

Opposite page:
Carnegie Mellon President Robert Mehrabian leads the groundbreaking ceremony for the Purnell Center for the Arts.

1990

• President Robert Mehrabian is inaugurated.

239

played a mean game of tennis. At Carnegie Mellon he practiced with both the men's and women's soccer teams until he tore an anterior cruciate ligament and hobbled around campus in a cast for several months. After graduation he stayed at MIT, first as a research assistant and then as assistant professor and associate professor. Like many other Carnegie Mellon presidents, he had personal experiences in the arts. At MIT he taught classes in casting and glass blowing for people interested in both the sciences and the arts. In 1975 he became a professor of metallurgy and mechanical engineering at the University of Illinois, Urbana-Champaign. In 1977 he met Victoria George, a teacher at a small private school, when he was at a conference in California. After they married she moved with him to Illinois and then to Gaithersburg, Maryland where Mehrabian had become Chief of Metallurgy and, subsequently, Director of the Center for Materials Science at the National Institute of Standards and Technology. An accomplished horsewoman, Victoria took her horses with her.

In 1983 Mehrabian became Dean of Engineering at the Santa Barbara campus of the University of California. He and Victoria lived on a small ranch where she could keep and break horses and he could play on the tennis court. He arrived with fresh ideas of what he wanted to get done and a time frame in which to do it. Methodically, he built a new engineering complex, began seven multidisciplinary research centers, established a new Materials Department and recruited 65 new faculty in less than seven years. In 1990 *U.S. News and World Report* ranked the engineering school at Santa Barbara as the number one up-and-coming college of engineering in the United States. Mehrabian brought his ability developed at Santa Barbara to sort through piles of data, ask the right questions and zero in on the right answers with him to Carnegie Mellon.

By this stage in his career he had become an internationally recognized materials scientist. Atop his duties as dean at Santa Barbara, he carried on major funded research projects working with a group of about 20 graduate students and colleagues. He had written more than 140 technical papers and edited six books, become a participant in a start-up company and was the holder of eight United States and more than 40 foreign patents. His research earned him membership in the National Academy of Engineering as well as other academic awards, speaking engagements and membership in numerous commissions, civic organizations and committees that gave him national exposure.

His name rose to the top of a pile of about 500 candidates for Carnegie Mellon's presidency. Both a trustee committee and a faculty committee headed the search with the faculty committee doing most of the spadework over a 15-month period. Only three names survived to the final round from which Robert Mehrabian was chosen.

1991

- East Campus Project is completed.
- A system of advisory boards is established.

Mehrabian had the qualities that the faculty and trustee search committees desired. He was a distinguished scholar with an established national reputation. He had widespread experience as a teacher, researcher, government official and innovative academic administrator. He had served on the faculties of three diverse departments of engineering, and as a dean of engineering he had transformed an undistinguished engineering school into a national leader in only seven years. The faculty met him and his wife, Victoria, at a meeting in a jammed Skibo ballroom on April 5, 1990. How the process had changed from the days when faculty members found out about President Doherty's appointment through an article in the newspaper. After living for a year in rented quarters, the Mehrabians bought a small estate with a large home, a pasture, a riding trail and a stable in nearby Butler County.

Robert A. Charpie (S'48, '49, '50), chair of the Carnegie Mellon Board of Trustees, had also headed the trustee search committee. Soon after Mehrabian arrived on campus, he, Charpie and Herbert A. Simon met to draft a statement about the role of the trustees in the governance of the University and to identify problems on which to focus. A meeting with the Executive Committee of the Board of Trustees produced a longer list of problem areas. In June 1991 the trustees met with Mehrabian and his top administrative staff at a retreat to focus on the challenges confronting the University and to establish guidelines for meeting them. The major goals and problems they identified were:

☮ A need to increase meaningful trustee involvement in the University

☮ A need for a coherent vision, mission and strategic plan

☮ An undergraduate program that had not received emphasis commensurate with the University's graduate and research programs

☮ An entering student body whose quality was at the low end of leading universities

☮ A high student attrition rate

☮ Some academic departments that had not received significant attention or resources, such as Chemistry, Design and Modern Languages

☮ A lack of space to accommodate the major growth in the 1980s in research and personnel

☮ Unchecked deficit spending in the administration and some academic units and no systematic fiscal analysis or decision making

☮ A need to evolve the administrative structure to meet the challenges of a complex and modern research university

☮ An unfunded debt of $49.9 million

☮ A downgraded credit rating as a result of substantial borrowing in the 1980s

☮ A need for maintenance and renovation of campus buildings

☮ A poorly run physical plant operation that was managed by an outside firm at a cost of $900,000

1992

- The NSF establishes a Center for Light Microscope Imaging and Biotechnology.
- The Technology Transfer Office is established.
- SUPA is renamed H. John Heinz III School of Public Policy and Management.

Jack Klugman's Keynote Address

Jack Klugman's (A'48) keynote address at Carnegie Mellon's 98th commencement was part Oscar Madison, part Quincy and "all from the heart," said the Pittsburgh Post Gazette. The following is an excerpt from that talk.

Thank you, Dr. Mehrabian, for your introduction. When I get an introduction like that I always wish there were two more people here, my mother and my father. My father because he would have enjoyed it and my mother because she would have believed it.
—Carnegie Mellon News, June, 1, 1995

○ A large number of unfunded building projects

○ Plans for the University's building at the Pittsburgh Technology Center stalled by potential site contamination and a requirement to match a $16 million state grant

In seven years, President Mehrabian and his staff solved many of these problems and made admirable progress toward the remainder as well as several others not on the original list, particularly increasing the endowment. One of his closest colleagues once claimed that Mehrabian was in a "perpetual fix-it mode," a mode that suited his task as he set out to solve this long list of problems.

Mehrabian set high standards both for himself and for those who worked with him. Like his predecessor, Dick Cyert, he paid little attention to clocks and calendars and, again like Cyert, could keep a dozen organizational balls in the air without dropping one. Colleagues soon learned to appreciate his thirst for data on which to base decisions and his devotion to benchmarking, that is, to comparing trends or institutions at Carnegie Mellon with those elsewhere. And he always did his homework; his detailed knowledge about individual budgets often astounded administrative colleagues. Tightly organized, he kept folders in which he classified different aspects of his job—campus mail, external correspondence and so forth. Because he hated a cluttered desk, he quickly responded to correspondence and returned papers from staff and colleagues sprinkled with handwritten comments.

Mehrabian conducted the business of the University through the administrators he appointed. Rather than see individual members of the faculty, he preferred to have them work through their deans or vice presidents. He rarely met with a faculty member unless the provost or the person's dean was present. He held weekly meetings with his closest advisers and formed the more inclusive President's Council that met every month. This administrative style functioned well, but it offended some faculty and staff members who were accustomed to having direct contact with the man in the president's chair.

Within a few years, Mehrabian had assembled a fresh administrative team. He retained key members of Cyert's staff, such as Vice Presidents Edward R. Schatz (E'43, '49), William Elliott, Don Hale and Patrick J. Keating, but appointed a new Provost, Paul P. Christiano (E'64, '65, '68), a new Vice President for Development, Eric Johnson, and within a few years, new deans for all seven colleges and schools. He also set out to develop new relationships with the trustees.

Early in 1990, the chair of the Board of Trustees appointed a Committee on Trustee Governance to recommend improvements in trustee organization and functions. The full board met to consider the report of the committee and to act upon it. As a result, the board reorganized its committee structure and streamlined the agenda for trustee meetings. In addition, the board agreed to set up advisory boards, each headed by trustees, to pay periodic visits to every department and major administrative unit in order to oversee operations and make recommendations for change. Oral and written reports from advisory board chairs were designed to keep all board members fully informed about all parts of the University.

Defining the University and its culture

Mehrabian and the trustees agreed in 1990 that the University needed coherent vision and mission statements and a strategic plan to carry them out. Mehrabian asked each college, department and administrative unit to submit a written vision and mission statement. At the same time, he developed and widely publicized a university-wide statement that brought a measure of coherence to the exercise.

The University's Vision

Carnegie Mellon will lead educational institutions by building on its traditions of innovation and of transcending disciplinary boundaries to meet the changing needs of society.

The University's Mission

To create and disseminate knowledge and art through research and artistic expression, teaching and learning, and transfer to society.

To serve our students by teaching them leadership and problem-solving skills, and our values of quality, ethical behavior, responsibility to society and commitment to our work.

To pursue the advantages provided by a diverse community open to the exchange of ideas, where discovery, artistic creativity, and personal and professional development can flourish.

The University's Values and Traditions

Leadership. *We lead through innovation and excellence; we establish new directions by talent and example, influencing the behavior of other institutions.*

Innovation. *We identify challenges and opportunities presented by evolving human needs, new research methods and technologies, and promptly assemble the talent and resources needed to exploit them. Our innovative capability is one of the foundations upon which our leadership capacity is built.*

Transcending disciplinary boundaries. *We transcend traditional boundaries to exploit our comparative advantages.*

Responsibility to society. *We serve society through transfer of technology, continuing educational programs, public service and enrichment of the community through the arts.*

Learning. *We build on our heritage of the Carnegie Plan to become a leading institution that combines first-rate research with outstanding undergraduate education through our focus on learning and problem solving.*

Dedication to our work. *Our students, staff and faculty are committed to our heritage, as reflected by Andrew Carnegie and emblazoned on our seal: "MY HEART IS IN THE WORK."*

Commitment to quality. *We focus our energies on understanding the needs of the communities we serve while applying principles of self-evaluation, benchmarking and continuous improvement to fulfill their needs.*

1993

- A two-day strategic planning meeting is held.
- Posner Hall is dedicated.

Developing a coherent strategic plan for the University occupied the attention and energies of hundreds of administrators, faculty members and staff. Throughout the Mehrabian administration, the University maintained an almost constant process of self-study. Three rounds of advisory board visits brought members of every educational, research and administrative unit together to focus on what they were doing. Each academic, research and administrative unit developed its own specific mission statement and strategic plan. Although departmental plans varied, most of them included a mission statement, a statement of goals and objectives, assessments of undergraduate and graduate education and plans for research and for the future. Each college compiled a document containing a short overview, statements about its vision, mission and goals and strategies, and an assessment of its resources. Participants discussed these plans in two-day meetings held in July 1993 and July 1997, the latter shortly after President Jared L. Cohon arrived on campus.

This program of self-study had several major characteristics. It was continuous rather than intermittent. It got things done so that people were encouraged to work harder. It involved hundreds of individuals from throughout the University who worked together on common problems. It helped individuals isolated in their own units to see wider University issues. It encouraged each unit in the University to identify its own strengths and weaknesses. It helped to focus the attention of the entire community on major projects—undergraduate education, new facilites and cross-disciplinary research efforts, for example. And it strengthened the reputation of the University as a well-run institution.

Improving education, research and administration through advisory boards

Visiting committees, another name for advisory boards, have functioned for many years at American universities. In 1961, President Warner began a visiting committee program at Carnegie Tech. This system never functioned well. Some departments failed to organize committees. In other cases, committee members became discouraged because no one followed up on their recommendations. After 1972-73, the use of visiting committees faded rapidly despite an occasional plea from President Cyert to organize them throughout the University. Visiting committees, where they existed, were set up and scheduled by individual departments as they wished. In short, an effective system did not exist.

President Mehrabian asked physicist John Fetkovich (S'53, '56, '59), who had been chair of both the Faculty Senate and of the Presidential Search Committee, to undertake the organization of a new system to be called advisory boards. Mehrabian wanted a comprehensive, required system that would operate throughout the institution. Fetkovich began by surveying the existing visiting committee structure and soon learned that it functioned in only a few departments. He recommended that Carnegie Mellon should organize 33 visiting committees, each with 10 to 15 members. Each committee should have a trustee as chair and two or three trustee members supported by three to five alumni and a number of outsiders chosen from distinguished members of the profession. Each committee was to meet every other year typically for one-and-a-half to two days.

244

After studying documents prepared by the department, meeting with faculty, administrators and students, and having private sessions with key administrators, the committee members would prepare a report for the administration and the trustees. Two years later, the advisory board would meet again to assess progress toward the goals it had identified and set new ones. Some faculty members groused about these plans, perhaps not realizing that the advisory boards could be powerful allies.

This system paid handsome dividends. It focused on two of Mehrabian's major goals: to increase meaningful trustee involvement in the University and to help him and the departments to bring themselves to, or keep themselves at, the level of the best departments in the country. The Design Department can serve as an example. Design was one of three departments that had some serious problems, such as inadequate facilities and poor faculty morale.

An advisory board helps to remake the Design Department

During the Mehrabian years, an advisory board visited the Design Department three times, in 1991, 1993 and 1996. Trustee Hans N. Lange (IM'64) chaired all three boards with the help of three other trustees, each of whom served once. Four members chosen from other universities and the design industry remained on the board for all three meetings; two additional members served twice and several others only once. This membership pattern permitted the board to assess changes between one meeting and the next at the same time that it provided fresh viewpoints. Each board filed a substantial written report. The department chair then responded to this report in writing a year or so after a visit in order to indicate what had happened as a result of the board's recommendations.

The first board found a host of problems that made it clear to both the president and the trustees that conditions were worse than previously thought. They included inadequate facilities, an out-of-date curriculum, lack of a shared vision among the faculty, inadequate leadership, insufficient relationships with other departments and some faculty problems among tenured staff, junior members and adjuncts. Acting Head Steve Stadelmeier wrote, "Some of the observations and criticisms were hard to hear, but needed to be said. I thank you for the cod liver oil. . . ." He and his colleagues set to work. As a direct result of the 1991 meeting, President Mehrabian granted the department $240,000 for a new departmental computing cluster, a shot in the arm that seemed to energize the entire department. Within a year, Design had organized a search for a new department head, begun to work with Design and Construction to solve the worst of the facilities problems, taken initial steps to establish links with other University units, particularly the Engineering Design Research Center, and implemented the first year of a new four-year curriculum.

The 1993 report of the board praised both the progress that had been made and the work of the new department head, Richard Buchanan. One of his first activities had been to write an educational philosophy for the department. The board noted that students were far more positive about the department, that the faculty was working hard, that the new curriculum represented a significant change for the better, and that collaboration had begun both with other departments and with a number of outside companies.

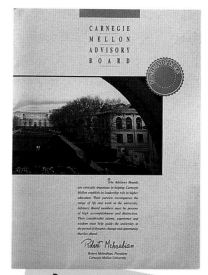

From the Report of the Third Design Advisory Board

The advisory board was delighted at the performance the department showed at all levels of operation. The undergraduate program is well articulated, the academic staff is capable and highly motivated, graduate and undergraduate students feel very positive about the institution and about their work, and the students' work is significantly better than what was seen at the last advisory board meeting. While there are areas for improvement, which are discussed in the present report, the board wishes to make clear that the Department of Design stands today in a very strong position in its field, and that there are many indications that this position may be further strengthened in the immediate future.
—1996

245

PittsburghNet

Above and right:
The first graduate students in the Design Department designed a Web site, *PittsburghNet,* for the city of Pittsburgh.

Below:
Graduate students met with Mayor Murphy to present their ideas.

It also noted a number of remaining weaknesses. Buchanan's reply in 1994 told the board members about periodic department meetings and two all-day retreats held to discuss the board's reports and to take action on its recommendations. He replied to each of the recommendations advanced by the board and outlined recent developments in the department, including a brief description of two new graduate programs.

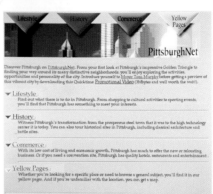

In addition to increasing trustee involvement in the University and bringing an academic department up to standard, the work of the Design Department's advisory board had an impact on three additional goals identified by Mehrabian and the trustees. It resulted in a clear mission statement and strategic plan for the department. It fostered the development of a fresh undergraduate curriculum in the department and the development of new graduate programs. Finally, it helped to recruit better students who were far more satisfied with their educational experiences at the University. Advisory boards in other departments had similar positive impacts.

The Task Forces

- Admission
- Career Center
- Computing and Undergraduate Education
- Core Curriculum Committee of the College of Humanities & Social Sciences
- Cultural Diversity
- English as a Second Language
- Language Across the University
- Learning Skills
- Learning Support Services
- Library
- Metacurriculum Research Opportunities for Undergraduates
- Teaching and the Teaching Center
- Undergraduate Advising and Academic Support Services
- Undergraduate Education at Carnegie Mellon University: Statement of Mission
- Writing in the Disciplines

Revitalizing undergraduate education

An effort to revitalize undergraduate education, relatively neglected compared to graduate work and research during the Cyert years, also touched several goals: focusing attention on undergraduates, improving the quality of the incoming student body and reducing the high student attrition rate. At an August 1990 trustee retreat, a 26-member undergraduate education breakout group consisting of 13 trustees, assisted by deans, faculty and administrators identified the problems and listed more than a score of recommendations. They were implemented throughout the Mehrabian administration.

Mehrabian wanted to know that someone woke up every morning concerned with the quality of the undergraduate experience. He found that someone in Dr. Erwin Steinberg, Baker Professor of English and a former dean of both Margaret Morrison Carnegie College and the College of Humanities and Social Sciences, and appointed him to a new position as Vice Provost for Education. Steinberg organized 16 faculty/staff task forces, each responsible for an area of undergraduate education or student life. Typically each task force had 10 members, so in total, about 160 members of the faculty and staff participated in this endeavor. The chairs included a vice president, two deans, two associate deans, two department heads and eight distinguished professors.

The work of the task forces quickly brought results reported periodically as key action items divided into two groups: accomplishments and opportunities. The 1996 report listed 120 accomplishments and an additional 80 opportunities to be explored in the future. Among the more specific accomplishments were revised undergraduate curricula in six colleges, expansion of the international student orientation, establishment of a university advising award, doubling of tutoring services provided by Learning Support Services, establishment of an Undergraduate Research Initiative with a director and central office space, expansion of merit-based aid for students resulting in support to middle-income families and creation of a fellowship program in the Center for Innovation in Learning to assist faculty in developing innovative educational projects.

The work of the task force on teaching and the teaching center can serve as an example. Its membership included eight full-time faculty from seven departments and three staff members, including Susan A. Ambrose (HS'86), Director of the University Teaching Center. The members of the task force divided themselves into several groups in order to gather data and conduct interviews with faculty, staff and students. Their report included a number of recommendations that resulted in significant progress under Steinberg and his successors, Professors Ed Ko and Indira Nair, including:

- ⚙ Moving the center from crowded quarters in out-of-the-way Smith Hall to a suite of offices and meeting rooms in Warner Hall, the administration building at the center of the campus

- ⚙ Adding a second full-time professional to the staff

- ⚙ Establishing an endowment for the center through a grant of $2.5 million from the Eberly Family Charitable Trust, and renaming the center the Eberly Center for Teaching Excellence

- ⚙ Continuing successful center programs, including massive time commitment to one-on-one faculty consultations that include classroom observations, critiques of videotapes of instructors at work and consultation about syllabi and other teaching instruments

- ⚙ Focusing more attention on teaching competency in promotion and tenure procedures

- ⚙ Expanding programs for teaching assistants that included a "future faculty program" in which Carnegie Mellon graduate students learn to teach and leave the University with a document describing their training and abilities, writing and distributing two pamphlets, "Best Practices for Teaching First-Year Undergraduates" and "Collected Wisdom: Strategies and Resources for TAs (Teaching Assistants)" and hiring a part-time coordinator of TA development

- ⚙ Hiring a part-time staff member responsible for efforts to improve writing across the curriculum

- ⚙ Obtaining a five-year grant from the National Science Foundation setting up a summer program to introduce new Ph.D. engineering graduates from across the country to sound teaching practices

Eberly Trust Gives $2.5 Million to Expand Teaching Center

The Eberly Family Charitable Trust of Uniontown, Pa., has awarded Carnegie Mellon $2.5 million to establish the Eberly Center for Teaching Excellence at the University.

The grant will enable Carnegie Mellon to expand the activities of its University Teaching Center (UTC), a program founded in 1982 to help faculty and graduate students enhance their teaching skills.

"The expanded programs this gift makes possible will allow us to make greater contributions to the quality of teaching on our campus and to share our resources with neighboring schools," President Mehrabian said.
—*Carnegie Mellon News*, March 8, 1996

Susan Ambrose (HS'86), Director of the University Teaching Center, counsels faculty members Joan Dobkin (left) and Beatrice DeAngelis (right).

Undergraduate Advising Award Winners

1991 Robert P. Kail
Dean's Office, CIT

1992 Eric W. Grotzinger
Biological Sciences

Mark Stehlik
Computer Science

1993 Indira Nair
Engineering and Public Policy

1994 Joseph E. Devine (HS'84)
Dean's Office, H&SS

1995 Kenneth Kotovsky
Psychology

1996 Claudia A. Kirkpatrick (HS'82)
Undergraduate Industrial Management Program

1997 Amy L. Kennedy (S'90)
Biological Sciences

1998 Gloria P. Hill
Director CMAP

The overall effort to improve undergraduate education succeeded for several reasons. The administration supported it strongly in both word and deed. It was data based; that is, the task forces began by gathering information from written records and interviews. It involved a high proportion of faculty and staff members responsible for undergraduate education. Distinguished members of the faculty and administration led the effort. Their reports quickly led to action so that members of the task forces and the community in general realized that something important was happening. It was sustained over many years. Finally, its recommendations affected many activities throughout the University, including the work of such units as the Counseling Center and the Career Center.

The undergraduate education initiative achieved notable success. For example, scores on faculty course evaluations increased from 3.82 to 4.01 and on instructor evaluations from 3.98 to 4.12. Spurred by the work of the University First-Year Council, the drop-out rate between the freshman and sophomore years decreased from 15.5 percent to 9.8 percent, narrowing the gap between Carnegie Mellon and its peer schools. The number of applicants for the freshman class more than doubled from 6,100 to 13,000 between 1990 and 1996, and the quality of the freshman class as indicated by college board examinations increased steadily. The work of the undergraduate education initiative continues in the Cohon administration under the leadership of Vice Provost for Education Indira Nair.

A campus renewed

Completing the building program begun during the Cyert years became a top priority of the Mehrabian administration. Cyert seldom focused his attention on bricks and mortar until the middle 1980s, but the success of Carnegie Mellon during his administration thrust new buildings to the top of his successor's agenda. In the fall of 1991, Mehrabian presided over the dedication of Gesling Stadium, the last piece of the East Campus project that included a parking garage, intramural playing fields, a new football stadium, two new residence halls and a dining facility. Then the administration forged ahead on a building program costing more than $180 million that increased total campus space by about 27 percent. It included:

Posner Hall, a 660,000-square-foot addition to the Graduate School of Industrial Administration completed in 1993, doubled the space available to the business school. Its hallways are lined with classrooms, offices, lecture halls and computer clusters. Posner Hall's brickwork, overhanging eaves and ornamental striping echo features of Hornbostel's original buildings. This three-story building, attached to the original GSIA structure, is capable of supporting an additional story, now under construction. The building is named for Henry Posner, Sr. who dropped out of Carnegie Tech in 1912 when he ran out of money. His son, Henry Posner, Jr., an emeritus life trustee of Carnegie Mellon and his wife, Helen, gave the largest single-family contribution to the new building. Rachel Mellon Walton, daughter of GSIA's founder, William L. Mellon, and a score of other Mellon family members who had contributed to the building, took part in the dedication ceremony.

The Pittsburgh Technology Center, on the site of the old Jones and Laughlin steel mill on the Monongahela River, was completed in 1994. The Carnegie Mellon Research Institute relocated to this building from the Mellon Institute building on Fifth Avenue, freeing about 38,000 square feet of space for Mellon College of Science. Mehrabian also led an effort that persuaded Union Switch and Signal to build a $20 million building on the site, fulfilling Carnegie Mellon's obligation to match a state grant of $16 million that paid for its building.

Above:
Posner Hall, the addition to the Graduate School of Industrial Administration

Center:
The Pittsburgh Technology Center on the site of the old Jones and Laughlin Steel Mill

Below:
The NASA Robotics Engineering Consortium in Lawrenceville

In 1995, Carnegie Mellon opened a center for the NASA Robotics Engineering Consortium in an old building in the Lawrenceville section of Pittsburgh. A grant of $6.5 million from the Commonwealth of Pennsylvania funded its purchase and renovation. The consortium develops robots for farming, hazardous environments and planetary exploration.

The University Center, the key to improving life on the campus, was dedicated in August 1996. This $47 million building stands on the site of Skibo Hall, razed to make room for the University Center. Provost Paul Christiano (E'64, '65, '68) called it "the campus family room." It brings together the entire community—students, faculty, staff, alumni, parents and visitors. It features extensive fitness facilities including lap and diving pools; basketball, handball and squash courts; an aerobics room; a ballroom that can be divided into three smaller areas; an auditorium; meeting rooms; a variety of dining areas; offices for all student organizations; an alumni meeting room; an interdenominational chapel; a small gallery and both book and art stores.

The University Center

The Cooper Mural

The Cooper mural occupies the UC rotunda with the Kirr Commons at its heart, the "central orienting space in the building." The artwork is a way of orienting viewers in space, time and memories as well.

Doug Cooper (A'70) began his mural off-site in his Greenfield studio. Using vine charcoal, he drew the mammoth mural, working on 24-foot-wide sections.

The mural's west wall recreates the view of campus and the city looking toward the west showing the campus in the present and the future. The east wall shows campus around 1965, and the north wall follows a roughly receding time line beginning with Pittsburgh today and moving to Pittsburgh, circa 1904 when Carnegie's intention of founding a technical school began to materialize.
—*Carnegie Mellon Magazine*, Summer 1997

The Mannino Tiles

Tiles created by Joseph Mannino (right), Associate Professor of Art, and Erika Bonner, the daughter of University Center architect Michael Dennis, decorate the building's loggia. Mannino's sculptures (two inches thick, 10 inches wide and 32 inches long), which represent the arms and hands of students, faculty and staff, are placed high along the outside wall of the walkway and can be seen from the Cut. Bonner's color ceramic tiles (five-inch squares), which line the inside of the loggia, are open to self-inter-pretation, although some have titles that reflect actual experiences.
—*Carnegie Mellon News*, September 20, 1996

The George A. Roberts Engineering Hall at the base of Hamerschlag Hall was dedicated in May 1997 and completed in the spring of 1998. Roberts Hall solved a space problem that had haunted the College of Engineering for more than a decade. Named for the major donor, trustee George A. Roberts (E'39), it contains 42,000 square feet of

laboratory, office and conference room space. The Data Storage Systems Center and NSF-funded Engineering Research Center led by Mark N. Kryder promptly occupied half the space in the new building. Its laboratories support experimental research in electronic and magnetic materials and are used by faculty from three engineering departments. The circular Henry E. Singleton Room on the top floor provides space for large workshops, seminars and receptions. Atop the entire structure sits a replica of the prow of the USS Pennsylvania. The original prow, loaned to Carnegie Tech by the U.S. Navy in 1912 and mounted where Roberts Hall now stands, was returned to the Navy.

The Intelligent Workplace or "office of the future," completed in December 1997, is a laboratory for office environments and innovations for the School of Architecture. It covers 7,000 square feet on the rooftop of Margaret Morrison Carnegie Hall and provides a technologically advanced setting for research and demonstrations in heating, ventilation and cooling, and interior and telecommunications components such as flexible workspaces and electronic hookups.

The Purnell Center for the Arts, completed in the spring of 2000, occupies the space across the Cut from the University Center. This 99,600-square-foot building provides performance space for the School of Drama, housing a theater, television studio, educational and rehearsal spaces, faculty offices and support areas, such as scenery and costume shops. The attached Regina Gouger Miller Gallery will serve the Schools of Art, Architecture and Design. The facade of this building mirrors the University Center and provides definition to the Cut, the main north-south campus quadrangle. Space freed when the Drama School moved fully into the new building provides for better fa-

cilities for the Schools of Architecture, Design, Music and the College of Humanities and Social Sciences.

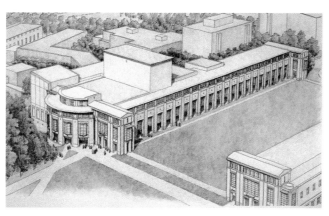

Top:
John L. Anderson (left), Dean of Carnegie Institute of Technology, attired for the inauguration of the George A. Roberts Engineering Hall (right)

Center:
The Intelligent Workplace, a laboratory for office environments on the roof of Margaret Morrison Carnegie Hall

Bottom:
Architect's rendering of the Purnell Center for the Arts

The Fine Arts Niches

A New Face for Fine Arts

After 80 years, the five niches on the front of the College of Fine Arts are completed. They are a visual feast as interesting and entertaining as Indiana limestone, a computer and the hand of man can make them.

Begun in 1912 at a cost of $50,000, the niche project came to a halt after about two thirds of the work on the Renaissance niche and part of the entrance niche were finished. The three other niches remained untouched.

For years the niches yawned their incompleteness to the world. And only by the insistence of the late Vernor S. Purnell (A'26), a well-known Pittsburgh interior designer, were the huge blocks of stone anchored to the building's steel frame brought to life.
—*Carnegie Mellon Magazine,* Winter 1993

In addition to these new buildings, major renovations took place in four of Hornbostel's structures. Stone carvers led by Nicholas Fairplay filled the five niches at the front of the Fine Arts Building with statuary—a visual feast, the *Carnegie Mellon Magazine* called it—representing five schools of architecture: Greek, Roman, Medieval, Renaissance and World. Masons also restored the terrace before the building to its original dimensions, providing a fitting setting for the stone-carved masterpieces in the niches. Architects restored the crumbling portico of Margaret Morrison Carnegie Hall and renovated the exterior of Hamerschlag Hall which, like Margaret Morrison, was beginning to crumble. Finally, the University began a series of renovations on the Gymnasium to bring its facilities for varsity athletics up-to-date.

The University also acquired five properties to accommodate growth in research, educational and academic support services. After years of protracted negotiations, Carnegie Mellon acquired the Naval Reserve Building between Cyert and Hamburg Halls and used it as a student center while the University Center was under construction. In addition, it bought an office and warehouse facility remote from campus and two office buildings on the border of the campus.

President Mehrabian deserves much of the credit for this impressive building program, perhaps the most far-reaching contemporary effort of any private university in the nation. Building on campus plans already in place when he became president, he pushed trustees, staff, and faculty members to find funding, organized the funding effort and personally raised substantial sums, particularly for the Purnell Center. As a result of the careful planning of the Cyert administration and the dedication and hard work of Mehrabian, Carnegie Mellon now has one of the most distinguished central campuses of any urban university in the nation.

The building program has had an impact on several of the problems identified by the trustees in 1990. They include building the Pittsburgh Technology Center, raising most of the money to fund the unfunded buildings begun by the Cyert administration, providing additional space to accommodate both research and education and perhaps even reducing the attrition rate by providing facilities for both student recreation and education.

Research finds new foci during the 1990s

During the 1980s sponsored research from all sources roughly tripled from $37 million to $128 million. From 1990 to 1997, however, research funds increased only 24 percent from $128 million to $166 million. As a result, income from indirect costs rose slowly through most of the decade. In addition, while increases in research funds outpaced inflation during the 1980s, they fell behind inflation in 1990 and 1991. Increases in total sponsored research revenue diminished in constant dollars in the period 1989-92 and then rose slowly through the end of the decade. These reductions in both direct and indirect revenue from sponsored research grants delivered sharp blows to the University's budget.

Reductions in federal research funding account for most of the failure to maintain the increased pace in research growth achieved during the 1980s. In that decade,

Robert Foxworth (A'65), Jean Stapleton, Mariette Hartley (A'65) and Rene Auberjonois (A'62) sing and dance at a Beverly Hills event to raise funds for the Purnell Center.

1994

- Carnegie Mellon acquires Naval Reserve Building.
- The Center for Innovation in Learning is established.

Above right:
SarMapper, a real-time inter-active tool, is useful to ecologists, geologists and the military.

Above left:
Vuman 3, a wearable computer, replaces the need for a cumbersome maintenance manual.

the University began to receive large annual grants to support the Software Engineering Institute, the Data Systems Storage Center, the Engineering Design Research Center and a number of projects in computing. The government began to cut or eliminate some of these grants during the 1990s. In addition, a long investigation of projects supported by the Department of Defense, although they cleared Carnegie Mellon of any wrongdoing, resulted in a diminished overhead rate, cutting the income on indirect costs. In light of these developments, the ability of the administration to balance the overall budget, reduce the percentage of income taken from the endowment and sustain an impressive number of initiatives is quite remarkable.

A number of new research initiatives marked the Mehrabian years. The National Science Foundation supported a project in green design, an interdisciplinary effort to improve product design in environmentally friendly ways. The R. K. Mellon Foundation contributed $6 million to fund a joint project with the University of Pittsburgh to study the neural basis of cognition. The National Air and Space Administration contributed $2.5 million to establish a robotics engineering consortium to commercialize mobile robotics technology. Carnegie Mellon became a partner in a $51 million effort to develop a national multimedia database for doctors. The Heinz School received $12.2 million to create the National Consortium on Violence Research. A number of grants beginning in 1994 supported a new Human-Computer Interaction Institute that works on a half-dozen projects including wearable computers and the use of computing to teach algebra and geometry in schools. Dozens of additional grants supported research in all seven Carnegie Mellon colleges and schools. A dedicated, energetic faculty combined with Carnegie Mellon's interdisciplinary centers and institutes deserve much of the credit for finding new research projects and adapting older ones to an era when the federal government reduced funding.

Investigation Ends; No Charges Filed

Carnegie Mellon officials have been notified that the U.S. Department of Justice civil investigation into Defense Department contracts, sub-contracts and grants at the university has been officially closed and no charges will be filed.

The civil and criminal investigation into Carnegie Mellon's government-funded research began in October 1993. Criminal aspects of the investigation were dropped in January 1996. No payments or settlements were made.

"We are extremely pleased that the Justice Department investigation has been concluded," President Mehrabian said. "Throughout the more than three years of this inquiry, the university has cooperated fully with the investigators, commiting the resources necessary to provide all the documentation they requested."
—*Carnegie Mellon News,*
January 31, 1997

NASA Grants $500,000 to Design a Mobile Robot to Inspect Tiles on Space Shuttles

Heinz School to Receive $12.2 Million to Create "National Consortium on Violence Research"

NIMH Awards $2.2 Million to Psychology for a Project Entitled "Toward a Model of Normal and Disordered Cognition"

"Green Design" Responds to Concerns About Environme[n]

Robotics Institute Receives Grant from NASA to Establish a Robotics Engineering Consortium

Improving the financial picture

Beginning as soon as he arrived on the campus, Mehrabian began to tighten the management of the University's financial resources. At his urging, the Board of Trustees implemented a plan to pay off Carnegie Mellon's unfunded debt of about $50 million. The trustees agreed to set aside $1.7 million annually in order to meet payments on debt accumulated under the Cyert administration. By the end of Mehrabian's administration, the unfunded debt had been reduced to $29.8 million, and its full liquidation was clearly in sight. As a result, the University's long-term bond rating was upgraded from A+ to AA-.

Sponsored Research, 1990-1997 ($ in thousands)

	Federal Direct	Federal Indirect	Non-Federal Direct	Non-Federal Indirect	Total
1990-91	74,117	19,705	24,627	9,380	127,829
1991-92	79,317	23,104	24,978	9,505	136,904
1992-93	85,889	27,849	23,349	9,640	146,727
1993-94	93,352	27,086	21,501	8,770	150,709
1994-95	91,134	25,146	26,208	9,490	151,978
1995-96	100,356	25,151	29,394	10,028	164,929
1996-97	100,911	27,386	28,796	8,750	165,843

Each year Mehrabian balanced both operating and capital budgets without reducing staff or cutting academic programs. In addition, the University set out to reduce administrative costs in order to allocate additional resources to academic programs. During his administration, administrative and facilities costs dropped from 10.7 to 8.4 percent of the annual budget. Teams of staff members led re-engineering programs to improve the ways in which the University purchased goods and services, registered and enrolled students and managed its financial system. Reforms in the purchasing system, the health care program, and stepped-up energy management saved the University more than $25 million during the seven years of the Mehrabian administration. Finally, the

University took control of the physical plant operation that had been managed by an outside firm at considerable expense. These reforms had an impact on four of the goals identified by the trustees in 1990.

In November 1997, only months after Mehrabian left office, Carnegie Mellon announced a major development campaign with a goal

of $350 million. About half of this sum is earmarked for endowment to support professorships, undergraduate financial aid, fellowships and programmatic support. The "quiet" phase of the campaign had begun in 1994 and had raised $240 million in gifts and pledges by the time the University announced the public side of the campaign. Some of this money had gone to support endowed professorships. In 1990, Carnegie Mellon had 42 endowed chairs; 53 new chairs, two of them named in Mehrabian's honor, were added during the Mehrabian years. Their holders are distinguished professors in all seven Carnegie Mellon schools and colleges. Gifts to the University, a thriving stock market and excellent work by the trustee committee that oversaw investments increased Carnegie Mellon's endowment from $229 to $608 million during the Mehrabian years. Despite this dramatic increase, Carnegie Mellon's per-student endowment fell further behind the per-student endowment of its peer schools as the chart on page eight indicates. The end of the campaign will coincide with Carnegie Mellon's centennial in the year 2000.

Left:
Vice President Eric C. Johnson exhibits his "vanity" license plate advertising the 1997 major development campaign.

Right:
President Mehrabian with Teresa Heinz and Master of Arts Management student, Sharon Coggan (HNZ'92)

1995

- Carnegie Mellon Research Institute moves into a new building at the Pittsburgh Technology Center.
- Carnegie Mellon inaugurates a chapter of Phi Beta Kappa.
- A university-wide staff award program is established.

Build It and They Will Come!

In 1994, Michael "Fuzzy" Mauldin, a Carnegie Mellon professor, announced a new Internet technology that evolved into the World Wide Web portal site known as Lycos. Working closely with the [CMU] Technology Transfer Office and its director, Mark Coticchia, Mauldin was able to create a company around the technology and took a leave of absence to get it off the ground.

"I was the business guy and he was the technology guy," recalls Coticchia. He and Mauldin flew all over the country making deals and securing partnerships for Lycos. Yet when all was said and done and the company was formed, its headquarters ended up in the more Internet-savvy city of Boston, not Pittsburgh. After all his hard work, was Coticchia disappointed? He says no. After all, both the university and Mauldin each received a 10 percent stake in the company, which amounts to about $10.2 million based on a Sept. 29 stock price of $34. And some 90 technology jobs (out of a total 460) remain in Pittsburgh as part of Lycos' operations. "There was a clause in the licensing agreement that a significant part of the business will remain in southwestern Pennsylvania," says Coticchia.

—*TECHcapital*, November/December 1988

Developing technology transfer

Formal technology transfer programs had been a major activity at some American research universities since the early 1980s. Research and development projects supported by the federal government had produced a number of technologies that held promise for commercial development. The passage of the 1980 Bayh-Dole Act gave universities the right to accept ownership of intellectual properties generated with federal funds and to license them to businesses or support spin-off companies. Many universities, led by Stanford and MIT where technology transfer was already well entrenched, quickly began formal technology transfer programs. Carnegie Mellon lagged behind until 1992. Carnegie Mellon had fostered about 20 spin-off companies by that year in contrast to many hundreds—perhaps thousands—from Stanford and MIT.

During a Carnegie Mellon trustee meeting in October 1992, Benno Bernt, (IA'54), a trustee and chair of the advisory board for Computer Science, pointed to a need for a technology transfer office. President Mehrabian then asked Bernt to assess the potential opportunities in technology transfer and recommend a program. Upon receiving a report, Mehrabian asked Bernt to organize a program and become its director, an invitation he accepted. Faculty interest in the potential commercialization of Carnegie Mellon ideas, however, ranged from low to cautious to hostile largely because few Carnegie Mellon faculty had experienced much personal success from technology transfer and because everyone had heard horror stories of administrative delays associated with previous transfer efforts.

Bernt and his associate, Mark E. Coticchia, carefully studied transfer activities at other institutions that could serve as benchmarks. As a result, they were able to establish a Carnegie Mellon model that drew from the best of others' practices but still suited the particular culture of this University. The results after five years exceeded all expectations. Instead of breaking even financially in five years—the original projection—total income from transferred technologies reached $50 million. Income from technology transfer, particularly the sale of Lycos stock, has provided the $20 million needed to build new facilities for Computer Science now nearing completion on the west campus.

The success of technology transfer illustrates several attributes of the Mehrabian administration. The impetus came from the work of the advisory board for the School of Computer Science. Bernt and his associates used successful programs at other universities as benchmarks and then developed an office that fit comfortably into Carnegie Mellon's culture. The University carefully developed an intellectual property policy over a three-year period in which faculty from throughout the University played vital roles. Finally, technology transfer has begun to make substantial contributions to the economy of western Pennsylvania through licensing agreements and start-up companies.

Reaching out to the community

In addition to technology transfer, Carnegie Mellon reached out to serve the wider western Pennsylvania community during the Mehrabian administration in at least three ways. In 1990, Mehrabian and Provost Paul Christano (E'64, '65, '68) asked Edwin Fenton to organize a Center for University Outreach. Fenton found a surprising amount of activity throughout the campus. He was able to identify some 25 projects that con-

nected the University to local public and independent schools. They included five tutoring, mentoring and role modeling programs that each year involved up to 500 Carnegie Mellon students, faculty and staff members who tutored individuals and small groups of students. Most of these students were underachievers, many from minority groups. The projects also included 14 enrichment programs for K-12 students involving personnel from all seven Carnegie Mellon colleges. Finally, the University sponsored five major in-service programs for teachers. To support these programs, the University raised about $2 million in grants each year and contributed $150,000 annually in cash and $1 million in in-kind contributions.

Left:
Pittsburgh area teachers toured the Robotics Institute where they met a robot named Jeeves.

Above:
A brochure summarizing partnerships between Carnegie Mellon University and Elementary and Secondary Schools in Pennsylvania

Below:
Pittsburgh's senior citizens participated in the Academy for Lifelong Learning (ALL).

Instead of focusing on school students, the Academy for Lifelong Learning (ALL) has tapped the learning aspirations of alumni and other Pittsburgh senior citizens. The brainchild of former alumni director Steven Calvert, ALL modeled itself after similar organizations at other colleges and universities. Its members, largely well-educated retired persons, organize a wide variety of courses and study groups led by ALL members, Carnegie Mellon and Pitt faculty and staff and members of the community. ALL has become so popular that it has been forced recently to close its membership at 720.

ALL has provided a vital service to Pittsburgh's senior citizens and to Carnegie Mellon. Many members enroll in several courses or study groups at the same time. Excursions, lectures and occasional social events supplement the array of courses. The organization elects its own officers and sets its own agenda. The entire administration has welcomed ALL and fostered its growth. Carnegie Mellon's students see these white-haired people strolling on the campus as they move from class to class, a visual symbol of the importance of lifelong learning. In addition, through word of mouth of its members, ALL arguably has become one of the University's best public relations vehicles.

Carnegie Mellon also played a vital role in promoting the economic development of southwestern Pennsylvania. Late in 1992 the Allegheny Conference on Community Development asked President Mehrabian to undertake a study of civic organizations that contribute to economic development in Pittsburgh and southwestern Pennsylvania. Mehrabian and his colleagues decided that the role of civic organizations missed the heart of the problem. Instead, they identified a different issue: leaders in business, labor, education, government, foundations and civic organizations lacked a shared vision of where the local economy should be going.

Alumni Jack Daniels, A'26 and Richard Hawley Cutting, A'26

Mehrabian proposed a two-part benchmarking study focusing on the region's past and present economic structure and an assessment of what other regions were doing to revitalize their economies. A committee of leaders from the public and private sectors first produced a white paper published in November 1993 detailing what they had learned about both the Pittsburgh area and the regions that had been benchmarked. It was written at Carnegie Mellon by Professor Richard Florida of the Heinz School and Robert E. Gleeson (HS'80, '97) and supported by a grant from 12 foundations and four corporations and pro bono efforts from Carnegie Mellon. The study painted a gloomy picture that emphasized the seriousness of the decline in the area's economy.

A year later, the Regional Economic Revitalization Initiative, an organization created by Carnegie Mellon's Center for Economic Development, produced a second study entitled "The Greater Pittsburgh Region: Working Together to Compete Globally." Eighteen companies and foundations contributed funds to support the project, and 126 leaders from the area participated in its deliberations. Six work groups, each headed by one or two distinguished members of the community, developed recommendations designed to provide 100,000 new jobs by the year 2000, the number needed to keep pace with the projected national average rate of growth.

The initiative succeeded in providing a vision of the area's economic future and a set of recommendations about how to achieve specific goals. It could not, of course, provide the resources needed to achieve those goals. As a University, Carnegie Mellon played an appropriate role in this entire project. Led by President Mehrabian, it responded to an invitation from community leaders to undertake an important study. It then provided the organization and the intellectual leadership to get the project underway and to carry it to its conclusion.

Courting the alumni

Many Carnegie Mellon alumni have expressed mixed feelings about their alma mater. They praise the education that prepared them for successful careers. At the same time, they argue that the faculty paid too much attention to research rather than education, that the quality of life on the campus left much to be desired and that they suffered from Carnegie Mellon's stressful lifestyle. President Mehrabian sponsored a number of efforts to court alumni and bring them closer to the University.

During his first year in office, he spoke at meetings of every Carnegie Clan. He increased the budget of the *Carnegie Mellon Magazine,* a publication that is sent quarterly to alumni. In 1991, Mehrabian invited all alumni who had graduated during Hamerschlag's administration to attend homecoming. Twenty-three men and women, most of them in their nineties, came to be honored by the University. In succeeding years, Mehrabian invited alumni from the Baker, Doherty, Warner and Stever years to homecoming celebrations, and a total of 700 accepted the invitation. The University Relations staff presented a slide show each year to celebrate the major events of the era, and each person signed a plaque honoring the occasion. The five plaques are now displayed in the President's Dining Room in the University Center.

Spreading the word

Except for gossip, news in even a small university such as Carnegie Mellon often travels slowly and fails to reach everyone. In October 1988 near the end of the Cyert administration, Vice President for University Relations Don Hale began to publish *The 8-1/2 x 11 News,* a weekly newsletter printed on both sides of a single page of typing paper. It contained short news items collected by staff from University Relations and made available all over campus both in hard copy and electronically on the news bulletin board. Mehrabian added funds to support this publication. *The 8-1/2 x 11 News* serves a vital function and continues to serve the University in its 12th year.

President Mehrabian soon learned that faculty and staff often failed to receive information he had given to administrative staff despite both the *News* and the electronic bulletin board. In November 1993, the first issue of an eight-page *Carnegie Mellon News* reached faculty, staff, students, trustees and emeriti faculty. At first a monthly, it soon became bi-weekly during the academic year. Its pages are filled with news about faculty, staff and students and University events in general.

To keep residents of the neighborhoods around Carnegie Mellon informed about University affairs, Mehrabian and Hale began the *Good Neighbors* newsletter. Published three times yearly, it is mailed to the homes of local residents. In emphasizes stories about events that may have an impact on the lives of the University's neighbors—construction projects, the dates of Spring Carnival, outreach projects to local schools and so forth. As a result, relations between the University and local residents have steadily improved.

Finally, President Mehrabian began to publish a periodic *Letter from the President* of Carnegie Mellon University in the fall of 1992. Through this four-page newsletter, he strove "to keep valued friends and supporters well-informed about the University" and to open a dialogue with its readers.

1996

- **The Robotics Institute Building opens in Lawrenceville.**
- **Seven Strategic Planning Task Forces are formed.**

The Carnegie Mellon Web site, originally created in 1994, was updated in 1997.

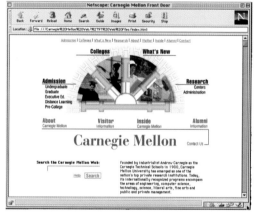

Carnegie Mellon communications included: *Carnegie Mellon Magazine, Carnegie Mellon News, The 8-1/2 x 11 News,* the *Good Neighbors* newsletter, and *Letter from the President.*

Nothing left to fix?

On March 15, 1996, Robert Mehrabian announced his decision to retire as president of the University. His wife's father had died, and she had returned to California to be near her mother. In addition, Mehrabian could see that most of the goals he had set for himself had been accomplished. During the following 15 months while the search for a successor took place, Mehrabian continued to work at his accustomed energetic pace as he attempted to bring closure to many of the programs he had initiated. After April 15, 1997 when the University announced the election of Jared L. Cohon as Carnegie Mellon's eighth president, Mehrabian devoted much of his time to making sure that the transition to a new administration went smoothly. And it did. Cohon found an excellent administrative team in place, a carefully crafted strategic plan and a University widely acknowledged as among the nation's best. Shortly after his retirement from Carnegie Mellon, Mehrabian received an offer that he accepted to oversee the aerospace business of Allegheny Teledyne. Early in 1999, the company announced plans to spin off four of its businesses into a new corporation with Robert Mehrabian as its chief operating officer.

President Mehrabian could leave Carnegie Mellon with pride in his achievements. He began his administration with a list of 15 goals (see p. 241) and he had accomplished all of them. The new buildings that graced the campus were the most visible signs of his work, but accomplishing the other goals he had set for himself, though less striking to the eye, may prove to be more important.

President Mehrabian's achievements

- The trustees had become more deeply involved in the University primarily through their leadership of the advisory boards.

- The University and each of its divisions had developed clear missions and visions to be implemented by carefully crafted strategic plans.

- The undergraduate program had been revitalized and an administrative structure devised to maintain progress.

- The quality of the entering student body had increased.

- The high student attrition rate, particularly between the freshman and sophomore years, had been reduced.

- The three academic units most in need of attention had all been reorganized and revitalized.

- Additional space had been provided through the building program.

- ⊛ The deficit inherited from the Cyert administration had been reduced and would soon disappear.

- ⊛ The administrative structure had been reorganized, resulting in savings of millions of dollars yearly.

- ⊛ The University's credit rating had risen from A+ to AA-.

- ⊛ Major renovations, particularly in Margaret Morrison, Hamerschlag Hall, the Gymnasium and the Fine Arts Building, had reversed deterioration that had begun to threaten the physical plant.

- ⊛ The University had taken over the physical plant operation from an outside firm, making it more responsive to University wishes and saving money in the process.

- ⊛ Most of the money for the unfunded building projects, particularly the University Center, Posner Hall, Roberts Hall, the Intelligent Workplace and The Purnell Center, had been raised.

- ⊛ A building to house the Carnegie Mellon Research Institute had been built in an industrial park along the Monongahela River.

The achievements of the Mehrabian administration reached far beyond the original goals that he, Herb Simon and Robert Charpie had compiled in 1990. In addition, the University had mounted a $350 million development drive and raised about two thirds of the money in gifts and pledges by the time Mehrabian left campus. A new Technology Transfer Office had been set up and achieved remarkable results. The University had led in the development of a plan to revitalize the economy of southwestern Pennsylvania. Carnegie Mellon faculty, staff and students had played increasing roles in the wider community, particularly in area schools. The remarkable research record of the Cyert administration had been maintained—even broadened. Relationships with alumni had improved. A remarkable record in seven years.

1997

- A development drive is launched.
- Jared L. Cohon is elected Carnegie Mellon's eighth president.

Opposite page:
In May 1995 Carnegie Mellon organized the Schenley Golf Operating Corporation to manage a city-owned nine-hole golf course contiguous with the Carnegie Mellon campus. Shown at the opening of the renovated course are Lawrence Gumberg, whose company manages the course; Schenley Park Director of Golf Rick Hanus; President Mehrabian; Mayor Murphy; and City Councilmen Bob O'Connor and Alan Hertzberg.

This page:
President Mehrabian, a long-standing supporter of people with disabilities, with Carnegie Mellon trustee Linda Dickerson (HS'81) at a meeting of the Three Rivers Center for Independent Living.

*I think the important thing is that
Dr. Cohon can pick up the momentum.
He is very good with people.*

—President Robert Mehrabian

15.

Jared Leigh Cohon 1997–
He leads an excellent university toward new achievements

Parents, relatives and friends of the graduates gathered in Gesling Stadium on the Carnegie Mellon campus on May 17, 1998 to participate in the University's one-hundred-and-first commencement. The stadium was the seventh commencement site since the first graduation exercise took place in the Carnegie Music Hall in 1908. Additional commencement exercises at the end of summer and in mid-winter, particularly during World War II, account for 101 commencements in 90 years.

Former Presidents Cyert and Mehrabian welcome President Cohon and his wife, Maureen.

A canopy covered the platform built on the dormitory side of the field where dignitaries and commencement officials were seated. The graduates sat on chairs in the center of the field facing the platform. The University's pipe band provided dramatic accompaniment as trustees, dignitaries and faculty, wearing colorful academic hoods from dozens of distinguished universities, marched to their seats. Guests sat on either side of the graduates or on seats in the stadium. Few of these students or their guests—or of the faculty and trustees for that matter—were aware of the dramatic changes in the composition of graduation classes during Carnegie Mellon's history.

Graduates came from all 50 states, Puerto Rico and the District of Columbia. Among the graduates were 652 women, 30 percent of the class, enrolled in all seven of Carnegie Mellon's colleges and schools. The graduates also included 506 international students from 88 countries—almost a fourth of the total—and 241 Asian-Americans, 54 Hispanics and 27 African-Americans. The composition of this graduating class testified to the steadily increasing gender, racial, ethnic and geographic diversity of the entire student body. The statistics also speak to the increasing importance of graduate students and research at Carnegie Mellon. The number of degrees awarded to undergraduate students had increased by only 148 since 1988, but graduate degrees increased by 416. Graduate students in 1998 received more than half of the diplomas—1,199 to 1,163. All segments of Carnegie Mellon had clearly become parts of a national research university with a considerable international presence—and a distinguished university at that.

1997

- Members of the Robotics Institute received Newell Medals for Research Excellence for work on the Nomad, Navlab and Heli projects.
- Carnegie Mellon astrophysicists installed a powerful new telescope at the South Pole.
- Carnegie Mellon received $5.9 million in equipment and service from Intel Corporation.
- The NSF awarded $700,000 to Carnegie Mellon's Studio for Creative Inquiry for its Tracking the Human Brain Project.
- Students in the Graduate School of Industrial Administration were required this fall to use a laptop computer in all classes.
- The College of Humanities & Social Sciences introduced freshman seminars led by faculty in small group settings.
- Students in the fall 1997 freshman class were the most accomplished ever admitted to the University.
- Jared Cohon was inaugurated as Carnegie Mellon's eighth president on November 10.
- Dana Scott, Hillman University Professor of Computer Science, Mathematical Logic and Philosophy, was awarded the prestigious Rolf Schock Prize in Logic and Philosophy.

Changing Commencement Statistics 1908-1998

	1908	1928	1948	1968	1988	1998
Number of Graduates	58	382	725	1112	1798	2427
Number of Different Degrees	6	46	42	82	140	177
Pre-Collegiate	**58**	**52**	**0**	**0**	**0**	**0**
2-Year Certificates	0	44	0	0	0	0
3-Year Diplomas	58	8	0	0	0	0
Bachelor's Level	**0**	**319**	**633**	**681**	**1015**	**1222**
Bachelor of Science	0	226	528	435	741	916
Bachelor of Architecture	0	12	7	31	60	42
Bachelor of Arts	0	76	0	85	69	80
Bachelor of Fine Arts	0	0	98	130	145	171
Bachelor of Humanities & Arts	0	0	0	0	0	13
Professional Degrees	0	5	0	0	0	0
Master's Level	**0**	**11**	**65**	**294**	**596**	**971**
Master of Science	0	11	56	243	542	686
Master of Social Work	0	0	9	0	0	0
Master of Arts	0	0	0	43	23	27
Master of Architecture	0	0	0	8	19	0
Master of Engineering	0	0	0	0	12	0
Master of Arts Management	0	0	0	0	0	18
Master of Building Science	0	0	0	0	0	2
Master of Chemical Engineering	0	0	0	0	0	8
Master of Design	0	0	0	0	0	6
Master of Human-Computer Int.	0	0	0	0	0	15
Master of Information Systems	0	0	0	0	0	28
Master of Music	0	0	0	0	0	24
Master of Philosophy	0	0	0	0	0	2
Master of Public Management	0	0	0	0	0	117
Master of Sustainable Develop.	0	0	0	0	0	3
Master of Software Engineering	0	0	0	0	0	35
Terminal Degrees	**0**	**0**	**27**	**137**	**187**	**234**
Master of Fine Arts	0	0	13	25	36	31
Doctor of Science	0	0	14	0	0	0
Doctor of Philosophy	0	0	0	111	145	203
Doctor of Arts	0	0	0	1	6	0

Carnegie Mellon's eighth president

In 1998 the administration was headed by Carnegie Mellon's eighth president, Jared L. Cohon, who had succeeded Robert Mehrabian on July 1, 1997. President Cohon had spent more than 25 years at private research universities, having held a variety of faculty and administrative positions. Immediately before coming to Carnegie Mellon, he had been Dean of the School of Forestry and Environmental Studies at Yale. Previously he had served for 19 years at Johns Hopkins University where he became Associate Dean of Engineering and then Vice Provost for Research.

Jared and Maureen Cohon with their daughter, Hallie

Cohon was born in Cleveland, Ohio, the son of Delbert Samuel and Ruth Sylvia Kaplan Cohon. Cohon's father, a graduate of Western Reserve University, with a B.S. in accounting and an LL.B. from the law school, moved his family to an eastern suburb, Beachwood, when Jared was nine years old. Cohon had a busy high school schedule. He played offensive guard and tackle on the football team, took lessons from the principal percussionist in the Cleveland Symphony Orchestra and was a drummer in a percussion ensemble that competed successfully in a statewide competition. He also visited Pittsburgh frequently during the 1950s where he visited his mother's brother, Sidney Kaplan, the principal french horn player in the Pittsburgh Symphony.

He had already met his future wife, Maureen Nathanson, while they were both in second grade. When her family moved to Beachwood, the two childhood friends began dating in their senior year. After high school, Cohon enrolled in the University of Pennsylvania while Maureen entered Cleveland State University. They married after their sophomore years when he was 19 years old and she was 20. Maureen had received her associate degree in business administration and worked first in Philadelphia and then in Boston while Cohon won his master's and Ph.D. degrees. After their daughter, Hallie, was born in 1971, Maureen finished her B.A. in sociology at the University of Baltimore and won her J.D. there in 1981. She then practiced law first in Baltimore and then in Connecticut while Cohon served on the faculties of Johns Hopkins and Yale.

Cohon received his undergraduate degree in civil engineering from the University of Pennsylvania in 1969 and his master's and doctor's degrees, also in civil engineering, from MIT. He remembers the distance that separated Penn's president from assertive students during the campus troubles of the late 1960s, a lesson he took to heart. As president he is determined to stay in touch with students and learn what makes them tick, and he has made a good start. He and Maureen turn up annually to serve more than 1,000 students at the Almost Midnight Breakfast served to undergraduates between 10:00 P.M. and midnight on an evening during exam week, an event that harks back to Margaret Cyert's Maggie's Muffins. They also host informal breakfasts and dinners with randomly selected groups of students as well as brunches for faculty and their spouses at the new president's home.

President Cohon on the Future of Oakland

Oakland is an exciting place to be, but it could be a whole lot more. For Pittsburgh to reclaim its place as an economic engine among America's leading cities, Oakland must become the center around which our region's new technology economy revolves.

The small start-up companies hunkered down along Craig Street represent the first steps in the development of a robust technology-oriented economy in our region. But in order for our vision for the future to take flight we need to follow up these first steps with a game plan, a design for growth and development of Oakland.

We must provide the resources, the facilities and the infrastructure that will foster successful technology-oriented businesses. State, county and city officials need to work with the leaders of Oakland's institutions and its community leaders to build consensus on a blueprint for the future, one that is focused on making Oakland ground zero for the new Pittsburgh economy.
—*Pittsburgh Post Gazette*
December 26, 1999

President Cohon jams with the Boilermaker Jazz Band at the annual staff picnic, May 20, 1998.

Cohon had widespread experience as an investigator in funded projects, a consultant, adviser or committee member of dozens of organizations and the author or coauthor of more than 90 books, conference proceedings, technical reports and articles in refereed journals. His research and teaching have centered on the development of systems analysis techniques and their application to environmental problems especially river basin planning, water quality management, the siting of energy facilities and nuclear waste planning. As vice provost at Johns Hopkins he led that university's efforts in technology transfer and high-technology business efforts in the Baltimore area.

In the midst of his scholarly and administrative activity, he found time to play the drums in a graduate student/faculty band at Johns Hopkins. He was appointed in January 1997 as chair of the Nuclear Waste Technical Review Board by President Bill Clinton, another recreational musician. Clearly he is well prepared to lead a university with an excellent research faculty and a swinging student body. He and his wife now live in Carnegie Mellon's recently purchased president's home on Northumberland Street within walking distance of the action in both research laboratories and the University Center. The home also serves as the site for numerous University functions.

Cohon was the unanimous choice of several search committees. Their members had gathered about 600 names of candidates from other universities, industry, government, non-profit firms and within the University itself and carefully assessed them for several months before selecting Cohon. In announcing the trustees' choice Thomas A. McConomy (E'55), Chairman of the Board, expressed an opinion seemingly echoed by everyone who met Cohon:

> *There is no better way our search for the eighth president of Carnegie Mellon could have succeeded than in bringing Jared Cohon to our university. His proven abilities as a scholar, teacher and administrator make him a superb choice. But his personal qualities are what truly distinguish him. We expect much of him, but I have every confidence that he will fulfill our expectations. I look forward to having Dr. Cohon take the lead in guiding Carnegie Mellon into its second century.*

Cohon was equally elated:

> *It was all I could do to contain myself when Tom McConomy called to tell me that he wanted to fly to New Haven to talk to me about Carnegie Mellon. He didn't say "to offer you the presidency," but why else would the Chair of the Board of Trustees travel all that way. Right? When he finally did offer the job over dinner with Maureen and me, I was elated, proud and amazed. It was, and is, an enormous honor.*

And take the lead he did. Within a few months, he had visited every department in the University to talk to faculty members and learn their concerns. He has had periodic meetings with two student groups: the Black Students' Advisory Committee and the President's Student Advisory Committee, and has met with individual students during a weekly hour reserved for student appointments. During the past 30 months, he has spoken to members of most of the alumni association's Carnegie Clans. Finally, he has visited leading donors to the University; individuals, foundations and corporations.

Participants in all these groups commented on his remarkable ability to remember a person's name and associate it with whatever he or she had said in the midst of a meeting. At a strategic planning meeting in January 1998 he was able to call every one of the 100 or so participants by their first names, a remarkable achievement for a man who had been on campus for little more than six months. His ability to remember ideas and to synthesize them in summary statements demonstrates his unusually marked listening skills as well as his ability to make sense of what he hears.

Cohon inherited an excellent administrative team that had been engaged in strategic planning meetings initiated by President Mehrabian in anticipation of an evaluation by the Middle States Association of Colleges and Schools. Each department and each college had contributed to the plan that was brought together in an impressive document examining every aspect of Carnegie Mellon. Cohon embraced the plan, the planning process and the men and women who had been involved in its creation. He saw no need for radical changes in direction and no dead wood to cut away. Lucky man.

Today's Carnegie Mellon

President Cohon inherited a small, thriving, national research university. The preliminary report of a 10-person evaluation team representing the Middle States Association of Colleges and Schools began its report with the following summary paragraph:

Carnegie Mellon is a research- and technology-based university that has, in just 30 years, created an important niche for itself among American research universities. It has developed from a regional institute of technology drawing most of its students from Western Pennsylvania into a national university with several excellent graduate and professional programs, strong research centers and institutes, and a competitive student body drawn from the United States and abroad. Though smaller and more narrowly focused than other "Tier 1" research universities, [CMU] now compares favorably with some of those institutions in quality of faculty, students, and graduate and professional programs. It has achieved this status by leveraging its strengths in interdisciplinary research, by increasing its federal research grants and contracts, by taking full advantage of the revolutions in computer and communications technology, by focusing on problem solving, and by providing strong incentives for faculty entrepreneuralism [sic]. The University has had assertive administrative leadership and a cohesive decision-making process, and has thereby overcome the handicaps of a relatively small endowment, a short history as a university, and consequent limitations such as a small library and a modest infrastructure. The Trustees, administration, faculty and staff are to be congratulated on this record of achievement.

1998

- Carnegie Mellon and RedZone Robotics, a Carnegie Mellon spin-off company, teamed up to develop a teleoperated mobile robot to inspect and assess structural damage to the Chernobyl nuclear station in the Ukraine.

- Carnegie Mellon was one of 15 universities to pilot an electronic mentoring program for women students in engineering and science.

- The Electrical and Computer Engineering Department received an Innovative Program Award from the National Electrical Engineering Department Heads Association.

- The University received $11 million from the R. K. Mellon Foundation to build new state-of-the-art science laboratories.

- Researchers at the Robotics Institute created an autonomous mobile robot tour guide for the Dinosaur Hall at Pittsburgh's Carnegie Museum of Natural History.

- John Pople and Walter Kohn, former Carnegie Mellon faculty, were awarded Nobel Prizes in Chemistry.

- Robert Page, Director of Choral Studies at Carnegie Mellon, received the Pennsylvania Artist of the Year award.

- The University formed Carnegie Learning, Inc. to commericalize its software-based cognitive algebra and geometry tutors.

- The Robert Bosch GmBH Company pledged $2 million to add a third floor to GSIA's Posner Hall.

- Four Mellon College of Science students won prestigious Goldwater Scholarships.

1999

- The University installed the largest wireless computing network in the world.

- Carnegie Mellon researchers in medical robotics formed a partnership with Johns Hopkins University and MIT in a new NSF Engineering Research Center in Computer-Integrated Surgical Systems and Technology.

- GSIA offered the nation's first degree program in electronic commerce.

- Rich Lackner (HS'79) became the winningest football coach in Carnegie Mellon's history on September 12 when the Tartans defeated Case Western Reserve University, 14-7.

- The women's cross country team won the NCAA Division III Mid-east Conference Regional Championship in the fall, and the men's team finished second in the championship meet.

- About 37 percent of computer science freshmen in the fall semester were women, compared to 20 percent in 1998.

- The University joined the Community College of Allegheny County to introduce the Minority Transfer Scholarship to enable African-American students to transfer from CCAC to Carnegie Mellon.

- Professors John R. Anderson and Stephen Fienberg were elected to the National Academy of Sciences.

- An outbreak of Beetles drew national media attention. Each of five faculty of the School of Design bought new Volkswagen Beetles in five different colors.

- The total number of print volumes in Carnegie Mellon's library neared one million.

Carnegie Mellon now competes for students and faculty with many of the nation's first-tier universities. In order to provide perspective on the University, Carnegie Mellon had identified 10 similar private institutions with which to make comparisons. The middle states evaluation team referred in their report to these institutions. They are Princeton, MIT, Stanford, Chicago, the University of Pennsylvania, Northwestern, Cornell, Washington University (St. Louis), Rochester and Rensselaer Polytechnic Institute (RPI). Intriguing data emerged from these studies:

- Carnegie Mellon was the youngest of the 11 schools.

- Only RPI had a lower endowment per student than Carnegie Mellon. The endowment of four schools (Chicago, Washington, MIT and Stanford) exceeded Carnegie Mellon's from two to four times. Princeton's was 10 times as large.

- Carnegie Mellon was exactly in the middle—sixth place among 11 schools—in combined math and verbal scores of entering students on the Scholastic Aptitude Tests.

- Carnegie Mellon was also in sixth place on the percentage of alumni giving to their alma mater.

- Nine of the schools—all but Northwestern—charged higher tuition than Carnegie Mellon.

- Carnegie Mellon was slightly less selective in admission than the average of the peer schools. Six of the schools—all but Washington, Rochester, Chicago and RPI—admitted a smaller percentage of student applicants.

- Only RPI had lower retention and graduation rates than Carnegie Mellon.

Comparisons with a pool of private, high-select universities provide additional data:

- More students in the comparative schools had parents who had college degrees and parents with larger incomes than Carnegie Mellon students, perhaps evidence that Carnegie Mellon continues to reach out to the working-class people the Carnegie Technical Schools were designed to serve.

- Students in the comparative schools scored somewhat higher on measures of self-concept, including drive to success, leadership ability and expectation of having a satisfactory time in college.

What to make of these data? Carnegie Mellon now ranks among the top tier of national universities in the United States. It competes for faculty and students with much larger, older and richer institutions such as Princeton, MIT, Stanford and the University of Pennsylvania. Its students are excellent, but they come from somewhat less prosperous and less well-educated families and have somewhat lower opinions of themselves and of their prospects than students in peer schools. These attitudes may stem partly from the fact that Carnegie Mellon is not the first choice of some of its students. Like modern students everywhere, they applied to several universities and colleges and some of them entered Carnegie Mellon when their first choice rejected them. Such is the price of entering the big leagues as an academic expansion team.

President Cohon found many departments and schools at Carnegie Mellon rated by outside experts as among the best in the nation. In 1999, *U.S. News and World Report* rated Carnegie Mellon's undergraduate programs as the twenty-fifth best among the nation's 228 national public and private universities that offer a full range of undergraduate majors and master's and doctor's degrees. *The Gourman Report: A Rating of Undergraduate Programs in American and International Universities* ranked 23 of Carnegie Mellon's undergraduate programs among the nation's top 25 in each category.

Many graduate programs also won high rankings from *U.S. News and World Report.* The School of Computer Science was third behind Stanford and MIT. Carnegie Institute of Technology was rated eighth among all national engineering graduate schools. The Heinz School ranked eighth among schools of public affairs and GSIA was ranked eighteenth. Recent evaluations of individual graduate programs rather than entire schools have rated highly many Carnegie Mellon departments or areas of concentration. For example, the 1998 study by *U.S. News and World Report* listed 31 of Carnegie Mellon's graduate programs among the nation's best. It included programs in each of Carnegie Mellon's seven colleges and schools.

Cohon found an excellent administrative staff in place. It is small, flexible and unburdened with bureaucratic hurdles that hamper decision making. Observers often comment on the speed with which Carnegie Mellon can respond to a new opportunity or a new challenge. Carnegie Mellon's vice presidents, provost, deans, department heads and division heads provide part of the answer. So does the relatively small size of the University.

Except for a comparatively inadequate, although steadily rising, endowment—it reached $804 million in December 1999—Cohon found Carnegie Mellon's finances in excellent shape. The budget had been balanced each year for decades. The expenses of managing the University had been reduced year after year, yielding annual savings as large as $10 million. Thanks to recent reforms, long-term debt had been funded. Even though federal government assistance had been declining, research funds had almost held their own in steady-state dollars. Faculty salaries competed with those of peer institutions; in 1999, in fact, the salaries of full professors based on cost of living ranked fifth among the nation's 81 major research universities. Tuition remained slightly below what most of Carnegie Mellon's peer institutions charged. To continue to balance the budget, however, the Board of Trustees raised tuition by 11.3 percent to $24,600 for the fall of 2000.

Outsiders comment on how unusual the faculty has become. Although its median age is increasing, it is still younger than most faculties and less tenured. Because institutional funds are scarce, faculty members must scramble for outside support for research and innovative educational projects. Hence, the faculty attracts feisty, entrepreneurial types who can thrive in this demanding culture. Instead of immersing themselves in their departments or schools, many faculty members do much of their research in centers, institutes or consortia where they interact with faculty from other parts of the University and with personnel on research contracts. Without exception, every department and school boasts members with distinguished national reputations in their fields. The University takes pride in the number of its rising stars that other schools, private firms and research institutions try to woo away with offers of endowed chairs or outstanding research opportunities. Such is the price of quality.

Cohon also found a student body that was steadily increasing in quality. Since 1990, the number of applicants for admission had more than doubled from about 6,000 to more than 14,000. As a consequence, the University was able to reduce the percentage of applicants it admitted in order to meet its freshman enrollment goal of 1,280. Enrollment pressure was particularly acute in several departments and schools. In 1998, for example, the Drama School received 792 applicants for a class of 52; 2,364 applicants flooded the School of Computer Science for a class of 130. Lights burn late into the night as admission personnel winnow through applications arriving by surface mail or electronically in order to choose a distinguished and diverse freshman class. Carnegie Mellon plays in the academic big leagues. As recently as 1983, Penn State and Pitt headed Carnegie Mellon's list of admittance overlap institutions, that is, schools that both admitted the same students. The 1998 list is very different, as the chart above left indicates.

Students who enroll at Carnegie Mellon expect both first-class education and first-class facilities—and they are difficult to please. They compare Carnegie Mellon to the other universities they have visited and to which they have applied. Carnegie Mellon lacks the athletic reputations of Penn State or Michigan. It lacks the prestige and the long histories and traditions of Ivy League schools such as Harvard, Brown or Princeton. In many instances—the Drama School, for example—Carnegie Mellon used to lack the facilities of competitors such as Stanford, Harvard, Yale or Northwestern. The new Purnell Center for the Arts has now corrected this deficiency. Until Gesling Stadium and the University Center were completed and the renovations in the Gymnasium begun, Carnegie Mellon lacked the athletic and recreational facilities of most of its rivals. Yet applications increased and students seem happier.

A vigorous attempt to improve student life during the past decade or so has produced excellent dividends. New buildings and renovated dormitories and classrooms have contributed. A renewed emphasis on undergraduate education and advising has made another contribution. Specific attention to the freshman year has reduced the drop-out rate for freshmen from 15 to 8.2 percent, not much above the 5 percent of schools in the University's comparison group. The Office of the Dean of Student Affairs has worked a small revolution in residence life, student government and student affairs generally. Students report a high level of satisfaction with recreational activities, counseling and learning services. The campus now boasts dozens of areas, both indoors and out, where students can meet informally. University officials listened to what students told them in the 1988 Quality of Life survey.

When President Cohon took over, he could see earth-moving equipment digging the foundation for the last building on the central campus project, the Purnell Center for the Arts. That building and several others are now complete. Even with the completion of the building program, every dean pressed the administration for additional space. Work is almost (February 2000) complete on a new $20 million computer science facility, Newell-Simon Hall, incorporating two of the old Bureau of Mines buildings. It was funded by income from technology transfers, particularly sales of stock in Lycos, a search engine for the Internet developed primarily by a Carnegie Mellon faculty member, Michael Mauldin. Construction is underway on a new wing to Baker Hall to serve the needs of H&SS. The steel skeleton for an additional floor atop Posner Hall is disappearing behind the floor's brick walls. Most of the required funds to catch up on deferred maintenance are in budgets planned for the next decade. Housing services, for example, completed 50 projects during the summer of 1999 toward its 10-year, $55 million renovation plan.

This page above:
Philosophy Professor Teddy Seidenfeld leads a freshman seminar, kept small to encourage participation and student-faculty interaction.

This page below:
Newell-Simon Hall

Opposite page:
Applications for admission to Carnegie Mellon steadily increase.

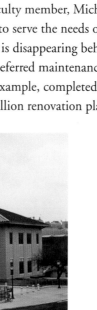

PURNELL CENTER FOR THE ARTS

State-of-The-Art-Everything

The Purnell Center houses state-of-the-art performance and educational facilities, including a 450-seat theater, a 140-seat "black box" studio theater, a three-camera soundstage, four design studios, a scene shop, a costume shop, dance and movement studios, faculty offices and a multitude of classrooms.

The Philip Chosky Theatre has state-of-the-art capabilities for sound, lighting and staging. . . .The theater. . . contains a motorized orchestra pit, acoustical panels that move to create different audio experiences and a complete audio recording and editing system.

The Purnell Center is named for the late Vernor S. Purnell (A'26) who made the lead gift of $7 million toward the project.

The theater has been named the Philip Chosky Theater in honor of Philip Chosky (E'48), a 1996 recipient of the Andrew Carnegie Philanthropic Award.
—*Carnegie Mellon News,*
August 30, 1999

A new master planning effort has begun. It focuses on the north and west parts of the campus, campus beautification and ways to better connect off-campus sites to the core campus. A 22-member master plan steering committee representing a variety of university constituencies guides the development of the plan, working closely with a master planning consulting firm, Ayers/Saint/Gross, University Architect Paul Tellers and Director of Planning Services Kevin Lamb. The committee has held town meetings and solicited comments through an online survey. A comprehensive plan should be ready during the spring of 2000.

President Cohon also found the administration and faculty in the midst of a strategic planning endeavor that had begun in 1996. Organized into task forces, about 100 members of the community examined the present state of Carnegie Mellon and looked a decade ahead. Each department, college and administrative division drew up strategic plans and met in conferences to refine and justify them. As a result, the University presented the Middle States Association of Colleges and Schools with a carefully prepared document covering every aspect of the institution. In the process, the strategic planning groups made some educated guesses about the future. A shorter publication entitled *Carnegie Mellon: Goals and Strategies* summarized its findings.

A vision of Carnegie Mellon's future

The Competitive Positioning Task Force composed of 14 individuals from the administration, student body and faculty of all seven schools and colleges met during 1996 and 1997 to discuss the future of the University and suggest directions in which it could move in the coming decade. The first step was to assess the past and present position of Carnegie Mellon among other institutions of higher education in the United States. However, instead of employing detailed statistical measures which tend to blur the diverse educational philosophies of different types of institutions, the task force employed two contrasting elements of vision that could serve to characterize the wide range of colleges and universities in the United States. What is the relative emphasis given to theory and practice among Carnegie Mellon's competitors? What is the relative emphasis given to developing the whole person as a leader in society or to preparing an individual to meet the expectations of a discipline or profession? The diagram on page 274 displays the task force's view of the relationships among many types of institutions and selected individual institutions. It also shows the changing vision and competitive position of Carnegie Mellon from its early days as the Carnegie Technical Schools to the Carnegie Institute of Technology to its present form as Carnegie Mellon University.

This diagram provoked intense discussion—as diagrams always do at Carnegie Mellon—but it also helped to focus attention on the strategic issues that face the University community. What path to the future would be most appropriate for Carnegie Mellon? Should it seek to emulate the Ivy League schools and the University of Chicago or should it move deliberately in another direction, perhaps more in keeping with its original genius?

Scotty's Corner

Staff Council dedicated "Scotty's Corner," a parklet built into the hillside adjacent to Doherty Hall, to university staff on a sunny and bright October 12.

The parklet was constructed this past spring by students in Larry Cartwright's (E'76, '87) Civil and Environmental Engineering senior design class. The idea for an outdoor space to honor staff was initiated by Staff Council's Rewards and Recognition. . . . "Scotty's" is an acronym for Staff Council's Outdoor Tribute to You, Staff.
—*Carnegie Mellon News*, November 1, 1999

Carnegie Mellon Campus Plan Planning Principles

1. Promote meaningful discourse about space and facilities
2. Promote campus green space
3. Plan outdoor campus space with definition
4. Preserve future building sites for most appropriate use
5. Maintain circulation patterns that provide orientation, a sense of place
6. Capitalize on the architectural heritage of the University
7. Design buildings with regard to their environmental impact
8. Adhere to universal design in all campus improvements
9. Design with regard to the neighborhoods of Squirrel Hill and Oakland
10. Maintain the highest technical and functional standards for human need and comfort

Ayers/Saint/Gross Architects and Planners, December 1999

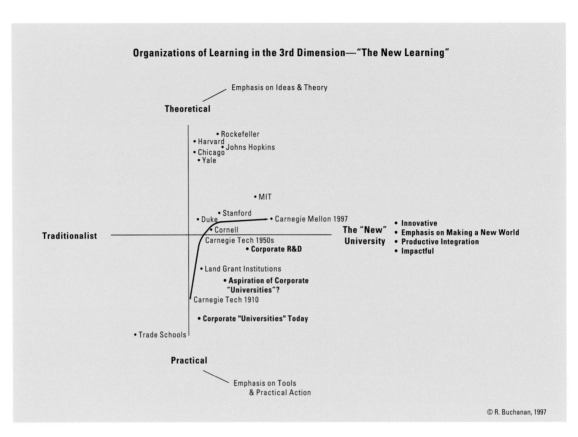

Organizations of Learning in the 3rd Dimension—"The New Learning"

Emphasis on Ideas & Theory

Theoretical

• Rockefeller
• Harvard
• Johns Hopkins
• Chicago
• Yale

• MIT

• Stanford
• Duke
• Carnegie Mellon 1997
• Cornell
Carnegie Tech 1950s
  • **Corporate R&D**

Traditionalist

The "New" University
• **Innovative**
• **Emphasis on Making a New World**
• **Productive Integration**
• **Impactful**

• Land Grant Institutions
  • **Aspiration of Corporate "Universities"?**
Carnegie Tech 1910

  • **Corporate "Universities" Today**

• Trade Schools

Practical

Emphasis on Tools & Practical Action

© R. Buchanan, 1997

Back to the Roots

About 50 students in Steve Lee's "Materials and Assembly" architectural studio got a lesson from master mason Sergio Lazzaris on February 18, 1998. Lazzaris of the International Masonry Institute, demonstrated proper techniques for constructing a brick wall. Lee says these types of hands-on demonstrations allow students to become familiar with materials they use in drawings.
—*Carnegie Mellon News,*
February 27, 1998

In assessing options for the University, the task force performed one further service: it tried to put words to the intense feeling of many in the University community that Carnegie Mellon is different from other institutions of higher education in a fundamental way. The first step was recognition that theory and practice at Carnegie Mellon are always in a delicate balance, with neither side taking a dominant position. This reflects the character of research at the University—never far from practical application but never afraid to speculate about fundamental problems that may overturn current practice. The second step was recognition that liberal professional education, expressed in the Carnegie Plan, offered a new balance between development of the whole person and preparing leaders for impact on society through professional excellence. This reflects the character of education at a university that struggles for a balance between breadth and depth of the educational experience.

These two features of the culture of Carnegie Mellon offer one way to account for the dramatic transformation of the institution between 1905 and 2000. However, they are not sufficient to explain the University's position today. As the above diagram suggests, Carnegie Mellon may be viewed among a cluster of distinguished universities that include Stanford, Cornell and Duke. Yet, something more is needed to explain why a comparison with such institutions seems inadequate to the spirit of innovation that characterizes Carnegie Mellon.

To capture this, the task force turned once again to the history of the University, to its early development of the fine arts and, subsequently, to its special emphasis on "making" in all of the forms of human production, including the fine arts, engineering,

274

computer science, public policy, business administration and the creation of entirely new disciplines. Such matters have small place among traditional universities. But at Carnegie Mellon, where the first thinking machine—the Logic Theorist—was created in 1955 by Allen Newell (IA'57), Herbert Simon, and J. C. (Cliff) Shaw, "making" is another area of expertise that is balanced with thinking and doing.

With this in mind, the task force returned to its initial diagram and suggested revision that would compare the relative emphasis that universities place on making and human production. The diagram below shows a third axis, a line between traditional institutions that merely study what human beings have produced and a new kind of university in which students and faculty work together to design and realize in concrete form the products of human imagination.

Members of the task force suggested that the competitive position of Carnegie Mellon would be found along that third axis, in the direction of a new type of university that prizes a balance among theory, practice and making. In fact, they argued that Carnegie Mellon had already moved farther along that line than perhaps any other university in the United States. Should Carnegie Mellon elevate its niche position in the next century, moving into the mainstream of institutions of higher education with a new vision of education that combines the three distinguishing features that have characterized its history? Or, should it abandon the effort and use its current success to return to the group of traditional distinguished universities?

A New Breed of Explorer

Nomad, a four-wheeled machine built by Carnegie Mellon University's Robotics Institute in Pittsburgh, is in Antarctica to see if it can discover something without human assistance.

The machine is designed to search rock-strewn areas of ice that are known to harbor meteorites and pick out the objects that fell from space from ordinary rocks and stones. Nomad's builders believe that the robot has enough intelligence to sort out information from its sensors and choose the rocks composed of extraterrestrial material, a job normally done by humans experienced in meteorite detection. They hope Nomad will discover at least one meteorite on its own.
—*The New York Times*, January 18, 2000

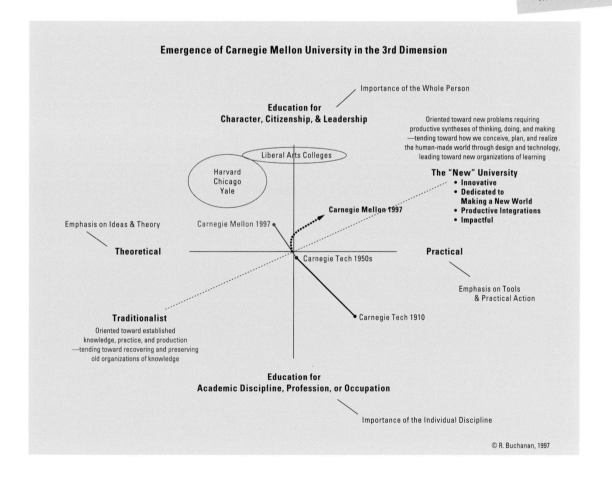

© R. Buchanan, 1997

275

Carnegie Mellon cannot, however, expect to challenge the positions of the major traditional universities with their national name recognition, entrenched departments and colleges, imposing array of professional schools and huge financial and capital resources. How many billions—no, tens of billions—of dollars would be required to turn Carnegie Mellon into a university with the physical plants and the widespread educational and research programs of institutions such as Harvard, Stanford, Yale or Chicago? Carnegie Mellon is a niche player, a small but distinguished research university that specializes in a discrete number of areas. Carnegie Mellon can become a better traditional university, but it cannot—and does not wish to—compete across the board with comprehensive universities in the top tier—the Harvards and Stanfords of the educational world.

This conclusion suggests that Carnegie Mellon should pursue a different course toward developing a new type of university, a university that is innovative, dedicated to making things, focused on having an impact on society and filled with people able to integrate diverse disciplines in order to solve problems, particularly problems that overlap traditional academic specialties. The dotted line pointing to the right in the preceding diagram suggests that the University has already made a head start in this direction. The events described in this volume testify that it has. Striving to become a model of a new university would permit Carnegie Mellon to exploit its comparative advantages in computing, engineering, management and the fine arts.

Rising from the Ashes

With the collaboration of engineers from CIT and artists from The Studio for Creative Inquiry, a whole new work of art is rising from the ashes of a Pittsburgh slag heap. And no, it's not mere artistic comment. It's a real working urban/suburban community being developed right now on the Monongahela shores. The project is being watched eagerly around the country as a potential new formula for urban redevelopment in the next century.
—*Carnegie Mellon Centennial Campaign Brochure*, May 1997

Into the Microcosm of Life

Today, an interdisciplinary team of Carnegie Mellon researchers is once again helping scientists delve deeper into the microcosm of life. This time the tool is the standing wave fluorescence microscope.

Created at our Center for Light Microscope Imaging and Biotechnology, the standing wave fluorescence microscope allows scientists to visualize structures much smaller than any seen before—as small as a single molecule of protein.
—*Carnegie Mellon Centennial Campaign Brochure*, May 1997

Every Carnegie Mellon department has developed a written strategic plan covering the decade ahead. Departments and administrative units have identified their strengths and weaknesses and made cases for the additional resources they need to meet their goals. These blueprints for the future provoke two reactions from many readers. On the one hand, every department and division has ambitious plans and energetic leaders to pursue them. That's a tribute to the University. On the other hand, everyone demands more resources—more space, more endowed chairs, more laboratories, more staff. That's a problem for the University. Where are these resources to come from? Not that this situation is new. Carnegie Mellon's strategic plans have exhibited the same characteristics since the beginning of the Cyert years.

President Cohon found a major development drive well underway when he assumed office. Begun by President Mehrabian, the drive had raised $228 million toward a final total of $350 million during its quiet phase. The goals include endowed professorships, scholarship aid, support for building projects and money for discretionary funds. The University announced the public phase of the drive in the fall of 1997. By March 2000 the total had reached $337 million, on schedule to meet its goal on November 15, 2000, the centennial anniversary of Andrew Carnegie's offer to fund the Carnegie Technical Schools. Both the immediate future of Carnegie Mellon and its ability to compete with its peer universities during the coming decade depend on the success of this drive and drives to come among trustees, alumni, foundations, corporations and friends of Carnegie Mellon.

In the meantime, the University has pressed ahead with plans for projects identified by the strategic planning process. During the 1999-2000 academic year, the strategic planning group settled on four major priorities: broadening and enriching educational programs across campus; increasing diversity in all parts of the University; pursuing promising interdisciplinary research and education programs in areas of leadership; and leveraging Carnegie Mellon's global impact to support the economic, social and cultural success of Pittsburgh and southwestern Pennsylvania. In August, President Cohon and Provost Christiano (E'64, '65, '68) earmarked $5 million to support initial planning efforts. With all constituencies firmly aboard, four groups working on the four major initiatives and substantial sums of money already in place, the results of this intensive planning process are already evident throughout Carnegie Mellon.

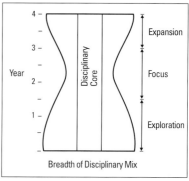

Undergraduate Education Process

New educational programs are being developed under the leadership of Indira Nair, Vice Provost for Education. The committee looks at the undergraduate experience as a sort of hourglass with broad proportions at the top and bottom and a narrow, cylindrical section in the middle. Nair calls the three sections exploration, focus and expansion. The University has provided seed money to create more interdisciplinary and community-based courses, undergraduate research opportunities and programs aimed at expanding personal and professional development. New opportunities for internships in the community and opportunities to work with community groups are underway. For example, a course called "Computer Science in the Community" which sends Carnegie Mellon students out to community groups to assist them with the development of their computer programs is being expanded. The "Open Mind Mondays" series features lectures and seminars designed to bring the University together as an intellectual community. Finally, the Division of Student Affairs led by Dean Michael Murphy (HNZ'86) has been expanding several programs aimed at students' personal development such as "Dimensions," a workshop series aimed at helping students meet their academic and personal goals; "Soup 'n' Substance," informal noontime presentations by interesting faculty and staff; and the "Last Lecture Series," a program that asks faculty members to deliver a lecture as if it were their last.

Carnegie Mellon today is far more diverse than it has ever been. Of the 16 new members of the Board of Trustees appointed during the Cohon administration, four are women and three are people of color. Carnegie Mellon now has 78 full-time, tenure-track minority faculty members—53 Asians, 13 African-Americans and 12 Hispanics. About 350 staff members, 12 percent of the total staff, are of African-American, Asian or Hispanic descent. Minorities work in 48 percent of the University's 166 departments and women in 93 percent. The fall 1999 freshman class of 1,300 included 361 Asians, 60

Left:
Vice Provost for Education
Indira Nair

Right:
Senior Matthew M. McHenry worked with members of the Hazelwood Senior Center to set up a computer lab in a course called "Computer Science in the Community."

277

Hispanics and 43 African-American students. President Cohon has asked faculty and staff search committees to seek minority personnel among their candidate pools. He personally chairs a Diversity Advisory Council which will seek to identify new initiatives, increase awareness of diversity issues and monitor University progress. The committee will work with the 17-page report prepared by the members of the task force on diversity. Clearly the University is launching a significant, coherent attempt to deal with an issue which it has faced since its inception.

Much of Carnegie Mellon's success as a research university has been grounded in interdisciplinary research. A third major initiative involves selected areas in which Carnegie Mellon can leverage its comparative advantages primarily in interdisciplinary efforts—biotechnology and health policy, environmental research and education, information and communication technology, and fine arts and humanities.

A committee of deans, department heads and faculty led by Vice Provost for Research Duane Adams controls $1 million in seed money to start new interdisciplinary initiatives. They expect to focus on medical imaging, cell and tissue engineering, biomedical and health engineering, medical robotics and cognitive neuroscience. They have begun to implement green practices in the University and have taken steps to integrate these practices into teaching and research. Plans are in place to organize an Office of Technology Enhanced Education pulling together efforts from a number of existing resources, including the new wireless Andrew computing network. Other projected efforts include a digital library project and a new Center for Entertainment Technology.

The fourth major initiative focuses on the University's global impact, particularly its impact on the Pittsburgh district. Part of this effort involves technology transfer. In fiscal 1998 alone, the University and its faculty inventors realized more than $30 million as a result of 34 patent applications, 15 licensing agreements and the development of five local companies. The Heinz School's Donald F. Smith (HNZ'94) now chairs a committee that will work to coordinate the many activities at the University that affect economic development. Another committee coordinates the outreach and enrichment opportunities the University sponsors for adults, teachers and school students.

Each of these initiatives builds upon longstanding Carnegie Mellon traditions that have played a role in University affairs during most of the past century, particularly since the end of World War II. The Carnegie Plan began the University's focus on educational quality. Increasing diversity has been a major goal of the Cyert, Mehrabian and Cohon administrations and has now become a major institutional priority. Interdisciplinary research got its start in the Warner years and picked up speed in every succeeding administration. President Doherty began the University's significant impact on the local community when he became the colleague of General Mellon to revitalize Pittsburgh after World War II. His successors followed in his footsteps, particularly Robert Mehrabian, who led an effort to revitalize the economy of the Pittsburgh region in the 1990s.

The quality of student life revisited

Student morale at Carnegie Mellon seemed to have reached its nadir near the end of the 1980s. A survey revealed that, while students were proud to tell others that they attended Carnegie Mellon and were generally well satisfied with their education, they complained about many aspects of University life. Among them were inadequate student facilities, a perceived lack of contact with faculty involved in research, intense academic pressure resulting in stress, an inflexible administration that had failed to respond to demands for a university center, the absence of nice places on campus to hang out and intense competition for grades.

Partly in response to this situation, the University established The Quality of Life Task Force to investigate student and faculty complaints and make plans for reform. The major recommendations of this task force appear on page 226. During the 12 years since this report was filed, Carnegie Mellon has reacted vigorously to improve the quality of student life in many dimensions. The University Center provided offices for student organizations, meeting rooms, informal lounges where students can hang out, a wide variety of food and snacks, a chapel, fitness facilities and an auditorium with a superb sound system. The administration has become more responsive to student opinion and includes students on its major task forces and committees. Major improvements have been made in student housing. Expanded student advising, a larger number of small seminars, expanded services for graduate students and Student Undergraduate Research Grants have strengthened the ties between students, faculty and staff, and helped to reduce stress. The campus is now sprinkled with lounges, parklets, outdoor benches, coffee shops and food carts.

On the following pages, a collection of photographs and quotations from students speak to these reforms. They describe a new Carnegie Mellon in which the quality of student life and educational experience are on a par with the research endeavors that made the University famous during the Cyert years.

2000-2001 Student Housing

Dorms	Occ. Max.	F	M	Coed
Amberson	62			♀♂
Boss	72		♂	
Cathedral Mansions	207			♀♂
Doherty	152			♀♂
Donner	253	♀	♂	
Fairfax	112			♀♂
Hamerschlag	168		♂	
Henderson	40			♀♂
Margaret Morrison	112			♀♂
Marybelle	36			♀♂
McGill	72		♂	
Morewood A&B	224			♀♂
Morewood C&D	243	♀		♀♂
Morewood E	234	♀	♂	
Mudge	311			♀♂
Resnik	151			♀♂
Roselawn	60			♀♂
Scobell	85		♂	
Shirley	41			♀♂
Webster	94			♀♂
Welch	54			♀♂
West Wing	147			♀♂
Woodlawn	30			♀♂

Special Interest Houses

ARCC (Awareness of Roots of Chinese Culture), Forbes House, Hong Kong Student Association, International House, Men's Soccer House, Sigma Phi Epsilon, Spirit House and Tech House.

Greek Life

There are 12 fraternity and five sorority houses on campus.

In 1999, approximately 3500 undergraduates lived in on-campus housing, about 70 percent of the total undergraduates.

Students Honor Great Traditions. . .

High jinks still enliven dorm life.
As I entered my freshman dorm, I recalled the words that my tour guide had used to describe living in the all-male, all-freshman Hamerschlag House to which I had been sentenced. "It's a love-hate relationship," he said. Throughout that year, I learned that my resident assistant was crazy in a good way—he once tried to bleach his hair but only succeeded in turning it orange. That year I also discovered the real staples of life in a residence hall: pool, foosball, Ping-Pong, Adam Sandler movies, networked computer games and hallway soccer (look out for the lights!). My original anxieties have now been replaced by happy memories from the testosterone-laden hallways I now refer to as Schlag.
—David P. Trost, E 2002
(High jinks: see pp. 54-55, 104, 185, 188)

Students still find food in imaginative ways.
My roommate and I had attended a number of information sessions and club meetings when a flashbulb went off in our heads. We could live comfortably on free food if we planned carefully. We poured over the long list of campus events scheduled daily at the University. Then we became the feasting nomads of Carnegie Mellon, dining without expense for a good four weeks. Along the way we made a number of new acquaintances, took part in some intriguing discussions, learned how cosmopolitan and diverse a university we had joined and discovered how to use an institution's organizations to fill our stomachs.
—Paul G. Jacobs, IM 2000
(Eating: see pp. 74-75, 225)

Spring Carnival still rivals academics.
Working on a booth comes to mind when I think of Spring Carnival. For most students, Carnival means going to the Midway, seeing its sights and playing its games. To me, Carnival implies all of that— and also Booth. Booth means power tools, paint brushes and working with duct tape. It means pulling all-nighters, skipping classes and last minute panic. It is band aids, exhaustion and sweat, but it is also a great time spent with friends. Sure it's a lot of work; what at Carnegie Mellon isn't? But I wouldn't have missed it for the world.
—Stephen A. Zdancewic, CS'96
(Spring Carnival: see pp. 85-87, 123-125, 187, 236)

Above:
The Kiltie Band still thrills the crowd.
(Kiltie Band: see pp. 8, 81, 89, 130)

Below:
Students still paint the fence.
(The Fence: see pp. 8, 60, 90-91)

Young grads still reminisce.
Little snippets of people and events define my experience at Carnegie Mellon: a warm Spring Carnival followed by four rainy and snowy ones, reading on the hill between Morewood Gardens and Mudge House, enduring endless construction projects, learning how to use email, the feeling of accomplishment when I've done well in class, spending time with my friends at fraternity parties, just walking in Schenley Park. I attended Carnegie Mellon for five years, and I can honestly say I did more than I ever thought I would and regret far less than I imagined.
—Stacey W. Jenkins, HS 2000
(Grads reminisce: see pp. 83, 106-109, 117, 121-122, 154, 157, 158, 207, 258)

Football games still rouse the faithful.
A Division III school, Carnegie Mellon boasts few sporting enthusiasts, but the 1998 homecoming game showed a different side of Carnegie Mellon. A noisy crowd filled Gesling Stadium for the game. Both the Kiltie Band and Spirit of Skibo members ran down to the track to help the cheerleaders rouse the crowd. Seven male members of Spirit of Skibo painted their bodies in school colors and each had painted a letter on his chest to spell TARTANS. Plaid Power towels waving, the crowd looked more like professional football fans than students and alumni from a university known for its academic standards.
—April M. DuPont, HS 2000
(Football: see pp. 56, 64, 84-85, 232)

Above:
The Tartan still brings the news.
(The Tartan: see pp. 52, 180-181, 227)

Right:
Students still enjoy "cheap flicks."
(Films: see pp. 79, 227, 230)

The Beaux Arts Ball still produces fond memories.
I attended the Beaux Arts Ball as a sophomore with my then boyfriend and now husband, Nathan Hauser. At a store in the Strip we rented matching costumes: clown suits, makeup, big red wigs and silly red noses. Nathan's nose had a blinking red light inside. At the ball, as we enjoyed the bands, enjoyed the food and checked out the other costumes, we saw parts of CFA I didn't know even existed. When I got tired of my nose sliding off my face, I gave it to my friend, Suri Siddharth (A'95). Three years later, wearing that same nose, he toasted Nathan and me at our wedding. The nose now rests in our china closet as a prized memory of a magical night— and an even more magical wedding.
—Christa Sherwood Hauser, BHA'97, IA'99
(Beaux Arts Ball: see pp. 92, 131, 233)

Students still thrive off-campus.
I live on Wilkins Avenue. Every day I walk up Beeler Street from the campus to get to Wilkins. These are the streets we end up living on—we who can't take dorm food and crave kitchens, who want to paint the walls and get a kitten or plant flowers in a window box. Every weekend I watch the street come off its feet—house parties with DJs spinning records in dark basements— three or four on a nice weekend. Some of these houses are legendary—5503, with two basements and two DJs, or that two-story house full of design students. Last semester they called their party "Heaven and Hell." It was historic. This school has a thousand cultures, a thousand lives that extend way beyond the edge of the campus, and for that I am grateful.
—Anne E. Ray, HS 2000
(Off-campus life: see pp. 54-55, 104, 185, 188)

shakespeare in love
the mummy
notting hill
tarzan
entrapment
big daddy
the corruptor
austin powers 2
the haunting
american pie
mystery men
blair witch project
the thomas crown affair

fallFILMS99

Students still hang out off-campus.
We loved the Panther Hollow Inn and Ritter's Diner. Known to the student body as PHI, Panther Hollow Inn, just a few yards away from campus on Forbes Avenue, was a popular Thursday night watering hole to hang out with friends and throw back a few suds. Although PHI had only a dozen tables, it was always packed to capacity with the Thursday Carnegie Mellon crowd. Ritter's was (still is) an all-night diner on Baum Boulevard that we'd frequent to cap off a long night of hard work or to fill our hunger for grease after an evening at PHI. Ritter's was as interesting for its eclectic assortment of nighttime characters as it was for food.
—Stephen K. Woyicki, IM'96
(Hangouts: see pp. 75, 80, 127-128)

Buggy still welds individuals into teams.
I joined buggy as a mechanic. If I'm going to get up early on weekends, I thought, I want to be rewarded with donuts, not running up hills. Being a mechanic provided opportunities to apply some of my classroom knowledge to the design and building of a buggy. I quickly learned that buggy had even more to offer. I found a whole new circle of friends, and together we worked as a team. Occasional parties and other social events helped to create a feeling of belonging among team members. Aside from the people and the work, I enjoyed taking part in a tradition that is truly unique.
—Vince A. Giarnella, E 2001
(Buggy: see pp. 85, 187, 234-235, 236)

. . . And Cope with a New World

New degree programs develop.

I am a graduate of a new degree program leading to a Bachelor of Humanities and Arts. As its name implies, it is an interdisciplinary degree spanning two colleges, a typical Carnegie Mellon innovation. What a great learning experience to work on the cutting edge of research in several disciplines and to see them brought together in a new synthesis. The degree program began about seven years ago when a group of students began to design their own unique academic careers. Because the program is new, I have been asked over and over again: "What is a BHA degree?" Answering that question helped me to define my work and choose the courses that would contribute to it and emphasized the responsibility to share my insights with others. Many Carnegie Mellon students face my situation when they are challenged to describe their unusual interdisciplinary degree programs.

—Jessica Phillips-Silver, BHA 2000, S 2001

Seven colleges promote academic diversity.

When I tell someone that my major is Spanish with a minor in Chinese, I often get a strange look as if to say "You're a Spanish major at Carnegie Mellon University!" I usually explain that, although Carnegie Mellon is most renowned for computer science, engineering and drama, the University also excels in the arts, management and humanities. You don't find that sort of balance in most universities that rank highly in technical fields. Carnegie Mellon's academic diversity brings an interesting array of students to campus and lets us build a unique mix of friends. I can't think of an environment that could provide a better perspective than one gains from other students at Carnegie Mellon.

—Season C. Dietrich, HS 2001

Computer gaming takes hold.

At a college campus where computers almost outnumber students, it is not surprising that one of the most popular pastimes is computer gaming. My first trip into the land of gaming was in Donner One West. The game of choice on this floor is "Counter Strike." As on many floors of the dorms at Carnegie Mellon, the guys on the floor log onto the network and play against each other on a regular basis. These days most of them usually keep the sessions to a half-hour in length, but when they first discovered the joys of networked games, that was not the case. We didn't care about work; all we cared about was doing this. "The best part is that you don't play by yourself. You play with your friends," José Lee said.

—Elizabeth Dodson, HS 2003 in *The Tartan*, October 25, 1999

Top:
Students use a wireless laptop to check their email.

Bottom:
Both undergraduate and graduate students worked on the robot Dante II which descended into Alaska's Mt. Spur Volcano.

Above:
New labs are filled with powerful networks of computers where students perform experiments using computational modeling—a new tool of scientific investigation.

The challenge of interdisciplinary courses

Last spring I took a course called Building Virtual Worlds. I've talked about the class so much that I'm even beginning to annoy myself. I can't help it; BVW was the best class I have ever taken. Randy Pausch, the instructor and a professor in the Entertainment Technology Center, designed a fully interdisciplinary course. He brought computer scientists and engineers together with visual artists and drama students in order to create immersive, virtual reality environments. In addition, the course introduced us to a wide variety of people and taught us to work together. Every person had something important and unique to contribute toward completing our projects.
—Joseph W. Hocking, S 2001

Top right & bottom right:
Since 1990, 1,392 students have received Small Undergraduate Research Grants (SURG) of up to $500 each. One grant supported the research of undergraduate Cindi L. Dennis (S 2000), pictured with Sara Majetich in Majetich's physics lab. Another grant helped to support Peninah Goldman's (A'98) interactive multimedia exhibit, "One of Six Million—Holocaust through Interaction."

Center:
"Spiderman World," a virtual reality environment created in an interdisciplinary class called Building Virtual Worlds, and a headset and glove used to enter a virtual world.

SURG grants sponsor valuable undergraduate research.

I joined Dr. Sara Majetich's Buckyball Research Project during my first semester at Carnegie Mellon. Through my Small Undergraduate Research Grant (SURG) project, I learned how research evolves and identified exactly what area of physics I wanted to pursue. The interaction with both undergraduate and graduate students produced lively, challenging lab discussions. Sara has made it easy to ask questions and she has been instrumental in encouraging me to apply for other SURG grants, internships and scholarships that have greatly broadened my background and experience.
—Cindi L. Dennis, S 2000,
Rhodes Scholar 2000

First experiences with email

Like many freshmen, I was unfamiliar with email. After a difficult week, I wrote a sad email letter to my father. With tears in my eyes, I clicked "send" only to realize that I had mistakenly sent it to the Associate Dean of the College, Eric Grotzinger, a man I had met only once during the first week of school. Panicky, I asked a cluster mate how to retrieve the message. He smiled and said, "Send another that says "Oops, don't read that." I did. The Dean didn't follow my instructions. Instead, he responded like a father, asking if I was all right and expressing his concern.
—Elizabeth A. Nadolny, S 2000

Left:
Seventeen student-built mobots (MObile roBOTS) entered the 1999 Spring Carnival competition. They traversed a curved white line on the pavement outside Wean and Doherty Halls.

In retrospect

More than most universities, Carnegie Mellon is a work in process. Always has been. Consider the distance traveled and the rapidity of change over the past century:

⚙ In 1908 the Carnegie Technical Schools had a single financial supporter, Andrew Carnegie. Today (January 2000) Carnegie Mellon has thousands of backers: alumni; national, state and local governments; public and private foundations; corporations and other businesses; and friends of the University.

⚙ In 1908 the Carnegie Technical Schools were governed by a committee of eight Pittsburgh-area businessmen selected from among the trustees of the Carnegie Institute. Today Carnegie Mellon's trustees number 67 men and women from throughout the nation and from many backgrounds, both personal and professional.

⚙ In 1908 the four trade schools that comprised the Carnegie Technical Schools offered three-year diplomas and two-year certificates. Today Carnegie Mellon has seven colleges and schools offering 177 different bachelor's, master's and doctor's degrees.

⚙ The 1908 faculty had 101 members and included 43 who held no college degree. Today's faculty includes 593 tenure-stream members, 98 percent of whom hold terminal degrees whose work is supplemented by more than 800 research scientists, lecturers and full-time special faculty, almost all of whom hold terminal degrees.

⚙ The student body in 1908 was an all-white, predominantly male group, 90 percent of whom came from the Pittsburgh area and studied mainly in the night school. Today's highly selective undergraduate and graduate students are drawn from all ethnic and racial groups from across the nation and from more than 80 foreign countries.

⚙ The campus in 1908 contained 32 scrub-covered acres of hills and valleys in which muddy paths connected incomplete buildings. Today's Carnegie Mellon has a handsome 101-acre campus with more than 50 major buildings sited among green spaces and landscaped grounds.

⚙ Tech's educational tradition began with poorly prepared instructors teaching many below-average students. Today Carnegie Mellon has made an institutional-wide commitment to further improve learning, teaching and advising for its highly selective student body.

⚙ Carnegie Tech's research tradition grew intermittently and slowly until the 1950s when the pace of change accelerated. Today all of Carnegie Mellon's schools and colleges, many of its departments or graduate programs within departments and the personnel in its 50 centers, institutes and consortia involve almost all members of its faculty and staff in significant research or creative efforts.

⚙ In 1908 the Carnegie Technical Schools could not claim to be a peer of any college or university. Today, it ranks among the nation's finest universities.

What a remarkable success story—and the best is yet to come.

All is well, since all grows better.

ANDREW CARNEGIE

Carnegie Mellon Class Codes

Codes

A	College of Fine Arts
AM	Administration and Management Science
BHA	Humanities and Arts
CS	School of Computer Science
E	Carnegie Institute of Technology (engineering)
H	Honorary doctorate
HA	Honorary alumnus (a)
HNZ	H. John Heinz III School of Public Policy and Management
HS	College of Humanities and Social Sciences
I	Industries
IA	Graduate School of Industrial Administration
IM	Industrial Management
INI	Information Networking Institute
L	Library School
MI	Mellon Institute, Honorary Alumnus (a)
MM	Margaret Morrison Carnegie College
PE	Program for Executives
PM	Printing Management
S	Mellon College of Science
*	Attended

Commonly Used Acronyms

Codes

CFA	College of Fine Arts
CIT	Carnegie Institute of Technology
CTS	Carnegie Technical Schools
E&GO	Education and General Operating Budget
GSIA	Graduate School of Industrial Administration
H&SS	College of Humanities and Social Sciences
MCS	Mellon College of Science
MIT	Massachusetts Institute of Technology
NSF	National Science Foundation
SCS	School of Computer Science

Credits

Pages

Front cover:
Top photo: Carnegie Mellon University Archives
Bottom photo: Ken Andreyo
Back cover:
Painting of Andrew Carnegie (detail): Andy Warhol, 1981, Carnegie Museum of Art
Top photo: Carnegie Mellon University Archives
Bottom photos: Ken Andreyo
Illustration of author: Mark Mentzer
Title page photo: Ken Andreyo

1 *Photo:* Ken Andreyo

6-237 *Unless otherwise noted, all photos, artwork & artifacts are by courtesy of:* Carnegie Mellon University Archives Hunt Library Carnegie Mellon University Pittsburgh, PA 15213
All photos of artifacts: Ken Andreyo

9 *Cartoon: Pittsburgh Press,* September 24, 1902

10 *Bottom photo:* Ken Andreyo

11 *Bottom photo:* Ken Andreyo

12 *Bottom photo:* Ken Andreyo

13 *Illustration:* Jim Trusilo for Carnegie Mellon Admissions

19 *Etching:* Steel Industry Heritage Corporation, coordinator of the Rivers of Steel National Heritage Area

20 *Illustration: The Saturday Globe,* New York, July 9, 1892

24 *Bottom photo:* Carnegie Library of Pittsburgh

41 *Bottom artifact:* W. Elliot Collection

48 *Photo:* Carnegie Library of Pittsburgh

52 *Center artifact:* W. Elliot Collection

60 *Photo:* Ken Andreyo

70 *Main hall photo:* Ken Andreyo
Transept photo: Scott Goldsmith

71 *Stairway photo:* Scott Goldsmith *Entrance, & hallway photos:* Ken Andreyo

73 *Center & bottom photos:* Ken Andreyo

76 *Artifact:* W. Elliot Collection

78 *Bottom artifact:* W. Elliot Collection

82 *Top artifact:* W. Elliot Collection

89 *Artifact:* W. Elliot Collection

94 *Logo:* General Electric Company

104 *Artifact:* W. Elliot Collection
Illustration: Ruth Martsolf Cover

108 *Artifacts:* W. Elliot Collection

110 *Artifact:* W. Elliot Collection

127 *Artifacts:* W. Elliot Collection

Pages

129 *Top artifact:* W. Elliot Collection

131 *Artifact:* W. Elliot Collection

132 *Mellon photos:*
Thomas: Richard K. Mellon and Sons
James: Richard K. Mellon and Sons
Andrew: Richard K. Mellon and Sons
Richard B: Richard K. Mellon and Sons
William: Graduate School of Industrial Administration (GSIA), Carnegie Mellon University
Richard K: Richard K. Mellon and Sons
Paul: Yousuf Karsh

134-135 Richard K. Mellon and Sons

137 *Top photo:* Alcoa Archives
Bottom photo: Carnegie Library of Pittsburgh

138 *Top photo:* Carnegie Library of Pittsburgh

142 *Photo:* Carnegie Library of Pittsburgh

143 *Photo:* Carnegie Library of Pittsburgh

162 *Cartoon:* Hungerford for the *Pittsburgh Post Gazette,* July 16, 1966

168 *Top photo:* Jerome N. Siskind, E'72

190 *Center photo:* Tom Barr
Bookplate designs clockwise from top left:
Keywon Chung
Hillary Greenbaum
Maria Manautou
Anna Main
Awaka Uchida
Julie Hick

192 *Bottom photo:* Ron Appelbe for *Business Week,* December 5, 1970

193 *Photo:* Tom Barr

194 *Photo:* Michael Haritan

195 *Photo:* unknown

198 *Photo:* Ken Andreyo

200 *Top photo:* The Robotics Institute, Carnegie Mellon University
Bottom photo: Stan Franzos

201 *Photo:* Harold Corsini

202 *Cartoon:* Rob Rogers for the *Pittsburgh Press,* 1984
Photo: Glenn Brooks

203 *Drawing:* Deeter, Ritchey and Sippel Associates
Photo: Bill Redic

204 *Interface design:* Information Technology Center (ITC) researchers
Photo: Ken Andreyo

205 *Photo:* Jeff Macklin

207 *Computer generated art:* Harry C. Holland

209 *Bottom photo:* Ken Andreyo

211 *Drawing:* Michael Dennis, Jeffery Clark and Associates

Index

[Note: references to photos and illustrations containing information not covered in the text are italicized.]

Colophon

The text of this book was set in
Adobe Garamond Roman and Italic
with Gill Sans Bold subheads.
Sidebars were set in Triplex Roman and Italic.
A myriad of other typefaces was used
to illustrate the variety of rich traditions
found at Carnegie Mellon.

❋

The book is the result of a thoroughly enjoyable
collaboration among author, designers,
archivists, proofreaders and a printer.
We learned a lot from each other
as we sometimes laughed and sometimes fretted
our way through this project.

❋

The book was printed by Broudy Printing Inc.
in Pittsburgh, Pennsylvania.
We are especially thankful for the painstaking
care and attention to detail in the
production of the book
by Brian Herman of Broudy.
He took a collection of photographs of
differing quality from a variety of sources
and worked wonders.
Thank you also to Justin Cina (A 2001)
for helping to track down photo credits and
tie up many loose ends.

Libby & Dan Boyarski
Book Design